Teacher's Wraparound Edition

★

United States Government

DEMOCRACY IN ACTION

Richard C. Remy

*Associate Director of the Mershon Center for Research and Education
at The Ohio State University*

★

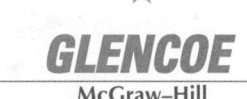

McGraw–Hill

New York, New York   Columbus, Ohio   Mission Hills, California   Peoria, Illinois

ABOUT THE AUTHOR

Richard C. Remy, Ph.D., is Associate Director of the Mershon Center for Research and Education at The Ohio State University, where he also holds appointments as a Mershon Senior Faculty in political science and as Associate Professor in the College of Education. He received his Ph.D. in political science from Northwestern University, has taught in the Chicago public schools, and has served as a consultant to numerous school systems, state departments of education, and federal government agencies. His books include: *Teaching About International Conflict and Peace, Approaches to World Studies, Teaching About National Security, American government and National Security, Civics for Americans, Lessons and the Constitution,* and *Citizenship Decision Making.* Dr. Remy is co-directing projects to develop new civic education programs with the Polish Ministry of National Education and with the Lithuanian Ministry of Culture and Education. He serves as consultant on civic education to the United States Information Agency and the National Endowment for Democracy. He also serves on national advisory boards for such organizations as the American Bar Association and the ERIC Clearinghouse for Social Studies/Social Science Education.

Glencoe/McGraw-Hill

A Division of The **McGraw·Hill** Companies

Send all inquiries to:
Glencoe/McGraw-Hill, 936 Eastwind Drive, Westerville, Ohio 43081-3374

ISBN 0-02-822061-7 (Student Edition) ISBN 0-02-822062-5 (Teacher's Wraparound Edition)

Printed in the United States of America
1 2 3 4 5 6 7 8 9 10 11 12 VH/LP 02 01 00 99 98 97

Cover: United States Capitol, Washington, D.C.
Photo: Robert Llewellyn

CONTENTS

Teacher's Wraparound Edition

CONTENTS

Student Edition

Alternative Presentation Methods

United States Government: Democracy in Action is a comprehensive text that is suitable for a full-year course. Because some government courses are taught for only one semester, the following outlines suggest five one-semester courses, each with a different emphasis.

— OUTLINE 1 —

Emphasizes the foundations and structure of government (17 chapters)

Unit	1	Foundations of American Government
		Chapters 1, 2, 3, 4
Unit	4	The Legislative Branch
		Chapters 13, 14, 15
Unit	5	The Executive Branch
		Chapters 16, 17, 18
Unit	6	The Judicial Branch
		Chapters 19, 20
Unit	8	State Government
		Chapters 24, 25
Unit	9	Local Government
		Chapters 26, 27
Unit	10	Comparative Government and Economic Systems
		Chapter 28

— OUTLINE 2 —

Emphasizes political processes and public policy (19 chapters)

Unit	1	Foundations of American Government
		Chapters 1, 2, 3
Unit	2	Citizenship and Civil Liberties
		Chapters 6, 7
Unit	3	Influencing Government
		Chapters 8, 9, 10, 11
Unit	4	The Legislative Branch
		Chapters 13, 14, 15
Unit	5	The Executive Branch
		Chapter 17
Unit	7	Public Policies and Services
		Chapters 21, 22, 23
Unit	8	State Government
		Chapter 25
Unit	9	Local Government
		Chapters 26, 27

— OUTLINE 3 —

Emphasizes citizenship and civic participation (19 chapters)

Unit	1	Foundations of American Government
		Chapters 1, 2, 3
Unit	2	Citizenship and Civil Liberties
		Chapters 5, 6, 7
Unit	3	Influencing Government
		Chapters 8, 9, 10, 11, 12
Unit	4	The Legislative Branch
		Chapter 15
Unit	5	The Executive Branch
		Chapters 16, 17
Unit	7	Public Policies and Services
		Chapters 21, 23
Unit	8	State Government
		Chapter 25
Unit	9	Local Government
		Chapters 26, 27

— OUTLINE 4 —

Emphasizes law education and civil rights (19 chapters)

Unit	1	Foundations of American Government
		Chapters 1, 2, 3, 4
Unit	2	Citizenship and Civil Liberties
		Chapters 5, 6, 7
Unit	4	The Legislative Branch
		Chapters 13, 14, 15
Unit	5	The Executive Branch
		Chapters 17, 18
Unit	6	The Judicial Branch
		Chapters 19, 20
Unit	7	Public Policies and Services
		Chapters 21, 23
Unit	8	State Government
		Chapters 24, 25
Unit	10	Comparative Government and Economic Systems
		Chapter 28

— OUTLINE 5 —

Emphasizes comparative governments and international relations (17 chapters)

Unit	1	Foundations of American Government
		Chapters 1, 2, 4
Unit	2	Citizenship and Civil Liberties
		Chapters 5, 6, 7
Unit	4	The Legislative Branch
		Chapters 14, 15
Unit	5	The Executive Branch
		Chapters 16, 17, 18
Unit	7	Public Policies and Services
		Chapters 21, 22, 23
Unit	10	Comparative Government and Economic Systems
		Chapters 28, 29, 30

Themes In Government

Interwoven throughout the sections and chapters of this text are 15 major themes that define the structure of American government and characterize the nature of American democracy. Students need to understand and be able to recognize these themes, to develop the ability to apply these themes to their study of government, and to understand how these themes interact with one another.

Growth of Democracy
American democracy today is the product of prolonged expansion and evolution both in theory and in practice.

Federalism
The American system of spreading power between state and national governments has become a model throughout the world.

Separation of Powers
Not only is power divided between state and national governments, but national power is further spread among the three branches of government.

Checks and Balances
Closely related to separation of powers, this additional safeguard allows each branch to block the powers of the others.

Civil Liberties
A fundamental principle of American democracy is that government must respect the basic freedoms of the people.

Civil Rights
American government not only guarantees individual freedoms, it promotes equal rights and protects against discrimination.

Civic Participation
A healthy democracy is built on widespread public participation in political, economic, and social processes.

Civic Responsibility
Although a narrower duty than civic participation, this role requires Americans to serve government at the ballot box, on juries, and in offices of public trust.

Comparative Government
Comparing the American political and economic system to its counterparts in other nations provides a special perspective to the study of United States government.

Global Perspectives
As the world becomes increasingly interdependent, the actions of almost any nation have ramifications far beyond its borders.

Constitutional Interpretations
Through interpretation and amendment, the Constitution continues to meet the needs of a nation that bears little resemblance to the nation it established more than 200 years ago.

Political Processes
The forces that shape government go far beyond the actions of voters and public officials to include a wide range of mechanisms both within and outside of government.

Public Policy
Government responses to society's problems and concerns are not limited to legislative or executive action. Policy may be made and carried out in ways far removed from public influence or accountability.

Free Enterprise
This economic system, which is an inseparable element of individual rights and freedoms, is the driving force behind the resurgence of democracy throughout the world.

Cultural Pluralism
This nation's history is the sum of the diverse peoples who live within its boundaries. Recognition of these groups and their contributions to society is essential to a true understanding of American government.

SCOPE AND SEQUENCE

Chapter	1	2	3	4	5	6
Growth of Democracy		Section 1, 2, 3,4	Section 3			Section 2, 3
Federalism	Section 1, 2	Section 3	Section 2, 3	Section 1, 2, 3		
Separation of Powers			Section 1, 4			
Checks and Balances		Section 4	Section 1, 2, 4			
Civil Liberties		Section 1, 2				Section 1, 2, 3, 4
Civil Rights						
Civic Participation					Section 3	
Civic Responsibility					Section 3	
Comparative Government	Section 1, 3					
Global Perspectives	Section 4				Section 1, 2	
Constitutional Interpretations				Section 1	Section 1	Section 4
Political Processes	Section 2, 3			Section 2, 4		
Public Policy				Section 3, 4		
Free Enterprise	Section 4					
Cultural Pluralism		Section 2			Section 2	Section 1
Critical Thinking Skills	Section 1, 2, 3, 4 Page 35, 43	Section 1, 2, 3, 4 Page 65, 73	Section 1, 2, 3, 4 Page 84, 97	Section 1, 2, 3, 4	Section 1, 2, 3 Page 161, 175	Section 1, 2, 3, 4 Page 183, 199
Social Studies Skills						
Study and Writing Skills				Page 138, 145		

Themes in Government

7	8	9	10	11	12	13	14	15
	Section 1, 2		Section 3			Section 1		
		Section 3				Section 4		
							Section 1	
					Section 2, 3	Section 2, 3	Section 3	Section 1, 2, 3
Section 3								
Section 1, 2		Section 3					Section 2	
	Section 3		Section 1					
		Section 1, 2, 4			Section 3, 4			
	Section 1							
					Section 1			
Section 1, 2						Section 1		
	Section 2, 3	Section 1, 2, 4	Section 1, 2, 3	Section 1, 3	Section 2, 4	Section 2, 3, 4	Section 1, 2, 3	Section 1, 2, 3, 4
Section 3			Section 2	Section 2, 3				Section 4
					Section 1			
Section 2			Section 2	Section 1, 2		Section 2		
Section 1, 2, 3	Section 1, 2, 3 **Page 242, 253**	Section 1, 2, 3, 4	Section 1, 2, 3 **Page 294, 301**	Section 1, 2, 3	Section 1, 2, 3, 4	Section 1, 2, 3, 4 **Page 379, 387**	Section 1, 2, 3 **Page 400, 407**	Section 1, 2, 3, 4 **Page 422, 433**
		Page 274, 281		**Page 308, 319**	**Page 327, 351**			
Page 208, 221								

SCOPE AND SEQUENCE

Chapter	16	17	18	19	20	21
Growth of Democracy						
Federalism	Section 2			Section 1, 2		Section 3
Separation of Powers	Section 3			Section 2, 3		Section 1
Checks and Balances	Section 1, 3, 4	Section 1, 2	Section 1, 2, 4	Section 3		
Civil Liberties						
Civil Rights	Section 2			Section 1, 3		
Civic Participation			Section 3			
Civic Responsibility						Section 1
Comparative Government						
Global Perspectives	Section 4	Section 2, 3				
Constitutional Interpretations	Section 1, 4				Section 1, 2	
Political Processes		Section 1, 3	Section 1, 2, 3, 4		Section 2, 3	Section 2
Public Policy		Section 2, 3	Section 3		Section 1, 3	Section 1, 2, 3
Free Enterprise						
Cultural Pluralism			Section 2	Section 2		
Critical Thinking Skills	Section 1, 2, 3, 4	Section 1, 2, 3 **Page 486, 495**	Section 1, 2, 3, 4 **Page 524, 531**	Section 1, 2, 3 **Page 552, 561**	Section 1, 2, 3 **Page 574, 583**	Section 1, 2, 3 **Page 604, 611**
Social Studies Skills						
Study and Writing Skills	**Page 449, 471**					

Themes in Government

22	23	24	25	26	27	28	29	30
Section 1, 5				Section 2		Section 1		
	Section 2, 3, 4, 5	Section 1, 4	Section 2, 3, 4	Section 1, 3	Section 2, 3			
Section 3					Section 1, 3			
Section 3, 4								
						Section 4		
			Section 2					
	Section 3							
				Section 1, 2				
					Section 1, 3	Section 1, 2 3, 5	Section 2, 3	
Section 1, 4, 5							Section 2, 3	Section 1, 2, 3
	Section 1, 4	Section 3	Section 3					
Section 2, 4		Section 1, 2, 3, 4				Section 2, 3, 4, 5		
Section 1, 2, 3, 5	Section 5	Section 2	Section 1, 4	Section 3			Section 1	Section 1, 3
	Section 1, 2		Section 1		Section 2		Section 1, 2, 3	Section 2
	Section 1		Section 1	Section 2				Section 2
Section 1, 2, 3, 4, 5	Section 1, 2, 3, 4, 5 Page 653, 673	Section 1, 2, 3, 4 Page 690, 713	Section 1, 2, 3, 4 Page 733, 741	Section 1, 2, 3 Page 758, 771	Section 1, 2, 3 Page 787, 795	Section 1, 2, 3, 4, 5 Page 824, 831	Section 1, 2, 3	Section 1, 2, 3 Page 872, 879
Page 622, 639								
							Page 840, 855	

Teacher's Classroom Resources

Reading Comprehension

Reading Comprehension activity sheets help students organize their study of the text and enhance their understanding of what they read.

Guided Reading Activities

Guided Reading Activities for each section of the chapter help students master information as they read.

Name _____ Class _____ Date _____

CHAPTER

8

SECTION 2

| Guided Reading |

PARTY ORGANIZATIONS AND FUNCTIONS

After reading Section 2, you should be able to summarize the characteristics of political party organization and identify the functions that political parties fulfill.

Directions As you read Section 2, answer the questions below.

1. Name three categories of political party workers.

_____ _____ _____

2. Why is the political party system of the United States considered decentralized?

_____

_____

3. Name the three basic local units of a political party, from geographically smallest to largest.

a. _____ b. _____ c. _____

4. What three functions does the state central committee of a political party serve?

a. _____

b. _____

c. _____

5. What are the two parts of the national party organization, who heads it, and what are this person's main duties?

_____

_____

_____

_____

_____

6. Define *patronage* and tell why it is an important political tool.

_____

_____

7. Name at least two general functions of political parties.

_____

_____

_____

_____

_____

Name _____ **Class** _____ **Date** _____

CHAPTER

2 Limited English Proficiency Activity

THE CREATION OF THE FEDERAL GOVERNMENT

Directions Fill in the blanks in the chart below that traces the development of the American government from colonial times to the writing of the Constitution. Text page numbers are given as a guide to help you.

I Government In the Colonies
1600s–1700s (pages 49-50)

1. Give two examples of written constitutions in colonial America.
   a. _____
   b. _____
2. Name the first legislature in America.
   _____
3. Separation of Powers
   Colonial powers were divided between
   the _____ and the governor.

War of Independence 1775-1781

II Declaration of Independence 1776
(pages 55-56)

1. Written by: _____
   _____
2. Purposes:
   a. _____
   _____
   b. _____
   _____
3. Parts of the document:
   a. _____
   b. _____
   c. _____

Limited English Proficiency Activities for each chapter meet the special learning needs of students with English language difficulties.

III A New Government Plan 1777-1787
(pages 61-63)

Articles of Confederation

1. It was a *League of Friendship*, not a ___
   _____
2. Weaknesses of the Articles:
   a. _____
   b. _____
   c. _____
   d. _____
   e. _____
   f. _____
   g. _____

A Stronger Government 1787

IV The Writing of the Constitution 1787
(pages 66-70)

1. Written in what year? _____
2. Went into effect in what year? _____
3. Key Agreements:
   a. Divide power among _____,
   _____, and
   _____ branches.
   b. Create a _____
   government.
4. The first 10 Amendments are called the
   _____

Reteaching

Reteaching activities provide students with comprehensive reinforcement of chapter information and government study skills.

Reteaching Activities help students focus on key concepts and themes in each chapter.

= Reteaching Activities =

CHAPTER

21   Reteaching

TAXING AND SPENDING

The Budget and Accounting Act of 1921 gave the President the responsibility for preparing a national budget. The President, therefore, must make major decisions about national budget priorities.

Directions Imagine that you are the President of the United States and that it is time to prepare the yearly budget to send to Congress. First, of course, you must budget for uncontrollables, and then you must provide for other major expenditures. In column A, below, list the uncontrollables in the federal budget. Then, in column B, list the other major budget items.

A. Uncontrollables	B. Other Budget Items
_____	_____
_____	_____
_____	_____
_____	_____

To balance the budget, you decide that taxes will have to be raised. Define each of the following kinds of taxes, then write a paragraph on the lines below explaining which taxes you would raise and why.

1. corporate income taxes _____

2. customs duties _____

3. estate taxes _____

4. excise taxes _____

5. individual income taxes _____

6. social insurance taxes _____

_____

_____

_____

_____

_____

_____

Skill Reinforcement

CHAPTER 6

CRITICAL THINKING SKILLS: SYNTHESIZING INFORMATION

Learning to combine information from several sources is a valuable skill in helping you to evaluate evidence. Information from one source often amplifies or clarifies information from another source. To synthesize information, first examine each source separately. Then decide if the information in each source is comparable. When you find sources with comparable information, you can combine that information and formulate new conclusions or hypotheses. Then you can state those conclusions or hypotheses in your own words.

Directions Study the line graphs below. Then answer the questions that follow.

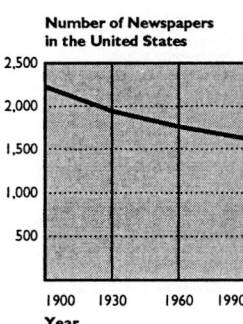

Number of Newspapers in the United States

United States Newspaper Circulation (in millions)

United States Population (in millions)

1. What information in the graphs is comparable?

_____

2. How has the total number of daily newspapers changed since the beginning of the century?

_____

3. How many daily newspapers did the United States have in 1930?

_____

4. Has newspaper circulation kept pace with the growth of the population?

_____

5. Write a sentence that expresses a synthesis of the information presented in the graphs.

_____

_____

_____

Copyright © by the Glencoe Division of Macmillan/McGraw-Hill School Publishing Company

Skill Reinforcement Activities for each chapter help students master the critical thinking, social studies, and study and writing skills presented throughout the text.

Extension and Enrichment

Extension and Enrichment activities provide a wide variety of materials to motivate and challenge students while building skills and expanding understanding.

Primary and Secondary Source Readings

Name   Class   Date

CHAPTER

2   *Primary Source Reading*

EXAMINING THE SOURCES

Directions Read the excerpts below and answer the questions that follow.

The Separatist Argument

Tom Paine's pamphlets so powerfully outlined the wrongs of England that George Washington confided, "A few more of such flaming arguments . . . will not leave numbers at a loss to decide upon the propriety of a separation." Here, in an excerpt from the pamphlet *Common Sense*, published in 1776, Paine continues to attack the effects of George III's colonial policies, referring to them as a "negative."

. . . The powers of governing still remaining in the hands of the king, he will have a negative over the whole legislation of this continent. And as he has shown himself such an inveterate enemy to liberty, and discovered such a thirst for arbitrary power, is he, or is he not, a proper person to say to these colonies, "You shall make no laws but what I please!" And is there any inhabitant of America so ignorant as not to know that according to what is called the *present constitution*, this continent can make no laws but what the king gives leave to? And is there any man so unwise as not to see that (considering what

we shall go backward, or be perpetually quarreling, or ridiculously petitioning. We are already greater than the king wishes us to be, and will he not hereafter endeavor to make us less? To bring the matter to one point: Is the power who is jealous of our prosperity a proper power to govern us? Whoever says "No" to this question is an *independent*, for independency means no more than this— whether we shall make our own laws, or, whether the king, the greatest enemy which this continent has or can have, shall tell us "There shall be no laws but such as I like."

But the king, you will say, has a negative . . . the people there can make no . . . his consent. In point of right . . . der, it is something very ridicu- . . . outh of twenty-one (which has . . . ed) shall say to several millions . . . der and wiser than himself, I for- . . . at act of yours to be law.

. . . mmon Sense, Boston, 1776.

. . . es Inglis. In a direct . . . Inglis argued that . . . ed to what he termed

. . . have been accustomed to a simi- . . . government. But Britons never . . . he extremes, either of monarchy . . . hism. Some of their kings have . . . potism, but always failed.

STATES GOVERNMENT: DEMOCRACY IN ACTION   **10**

Name   Class   Date

Repeated efforts have been made toward democracy, and they equally failed. Once, indeed, republicanism triumphed over the constitution; the despotism of one person ensued; both were finally expelled. [Inglis now refers to the rule of Oliver Cromwell, whose Puritan troops overthrew the monarchy. Cromwell was, in turn, overthrown for his strict policies, and the Stuart kings were restored.] . . . If we may judge of future events by past transactions, in similar circumstances, this would most probably be the case of America were a republican form of government adopted in our present ferment. After much blood was shed, those confusions would terminate in the despotism of some one successful adventurer; and should the Americans be so fortunate as to emancipate themselves from that thralldom [slavery], per-

haps the whole would end in a limited monarchy, after shedding as much more blood. Limited monarchy is the form of government which is most favorable to liberty, which is best adapted to the genius and temper of Britons; although here and there among us a crackbrained zealot for democracy or absolute monarchy may be sometimes found.

Besides the unsuitableness of the republican form to the genius of the people, America is too extensive for it. That form may do well enough for a single city or small territory, but would be utterly improper for such a continent as this. America is too unwieldy for the feeble, dilatory administration of democracy.

—Charles Inglis, *The True Interest of America Impartially Stated in Certain Strictures on a Pamphlet Intitled Common Sense*, 2nd edition. Philadelphia, 1776.

Recalling Facts and Ideas

1. **Define** *independence* in Paine's own words.

_____

2. **Name** the pamphlet to which *The True Interest of America* is a response.

_____

Exploring Themes

3. **Civil Liberties** Why does Inglis argue that democracy would decrease liberties?

_____

4. **Growth of Democracy** Paine thinks that it is "ridiculous" to give a monarch the right to rule. What major principle of American government is reflected in this criticism?

_____
_____

Critical Thinking

5. **Understanding Cause and Effect** Inglis says that America is too big for a democracy. What did he overlook that Paine saw clearly? What unifying forces offset geography?

_____
_____
_____
_____
_____

Primary and Secondary Source Readings for each chapter provide insights into government by policymakers and expert observers, and ask students to analyze and apply this information.

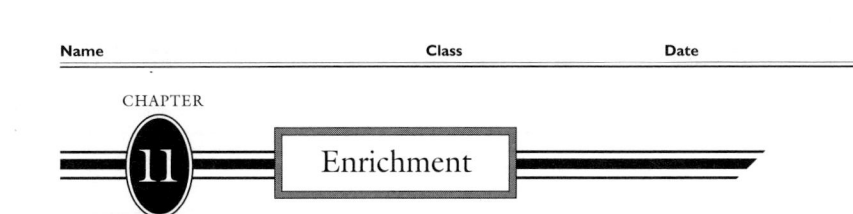

Enrichment Activities

Name _____ Class _____ Date _____

CHAPTER
11

| Enrichment |

> **Enrichment Activities**
> for every chapter expand government themes and concepts, motivate students, and help build thinking skills.

...NION

...n August 1990, Iraqi troops invaded Kuwait, disrupting the supply of crude oil ...sian Gulf. While United States citizens were aware of their dependency on Gulf ...pparently not willing to take risks to reduce that dependency.

...ad the poll, conducted August 17–22, 1990, by the *Los Angeles Times*. Then answer ...elow.

Poll	
Question	Do you favor drilling to support less dependence on Arab oil supplies, or oppose drilling in order to protect the scenic beauty of California, and of the environment?
Results	57% oppose drilling 37% favor drilling 6% not sure
Sample	1,586 registered voters in California
Method	telephone interview
Margin of error	plus or minus 3%

1. What is the universe of this poll?

_____

2. Given the margin of error in the poll, what is the range of Californians who oppose drilling? Who favor drilling?

_____

3. Did the pollsters use a standard method of gathering information?

_____

4. Do you think the poll question was asked in such a way as to get non-biased results? Explain your answer.

_____

5. Reword the question to cover offshore drilling in all United States coastal areas.

_____

6. If you were in Congress, about to vote on whether or not to allow offshore drilling in all coastal states, how might this poll affect your decision?

_____

ENRICHMENT ACTIVITIES   UNITED STATES GOVERNMENT: DEMOCRACY IN ACTION   **11**

Copyright © by the Glencoe Division of Macmillan/McGraw-Hill School Publishing Company

Extension and Enrichment

Cooperative Learning Activities

Name	Class	Date

CHAPTER

22 · Cooperative Learning Activity

FOREIGN POLICY AND NATIONAL DEFENSE

Connection to Chapter As you read in Chapter 22 (pages 612–639), the foreign policy of the United States since 1945 has been concerned with checking the spread of communism. Many of the major events in our history during the post-World War II years were part of this global struggle. Like battles in a war, some of these events were victories, and others not. Only now can historians begin to assess the importance of each event in the overall pattern.

Group Research Directions Using the chapter and library resources, pick one of the events that was part of the cold war. Describe the event and assess its effect and importance on United States foreign policy. Mention the actions of the President, Congress, and other officials who took part in the decision-making process.

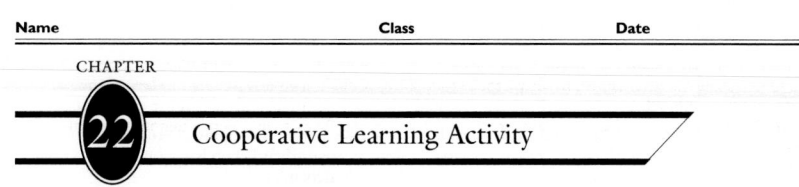

Truman Doctrine	Formation of NATO	Marshall Plan
Collapse of the Soviet Union	The Cold War	Arms Race
Detente	Vietnam War	Korean War

Cooperative Group Process

1. **Decision Making** Use the diagram above to assign each group member one of the events or policies that were part of United States foreign policy in the cold war.

Work Research the topics you selected to find out how United States goals olicy or event, what part United States foreign-policy makers played in it, cts the policy or event had on the cold war.

ng/Decision Making Researchers share information with the group. The s how to present its findings to the class. Possibilities include a panel a bulletin board, or a game such as Cold War Trivia.

Questions

agree on the assignment of tasks?

mber share information?

mber contribute ideas at meetings?

listen carefully to each other's contributions and give helpful criticisms?

22 UNITED STATES GOVERNMENT: DEMOCRACY IN ACTION   COOPERATIVE LEARNING ACTIVITIES

Cooperative Learning Activities for each chapter reinforce learning and build management and interpersonal skills by requiring students to work together to acquire, organize, and present information.

Name   Class   Date

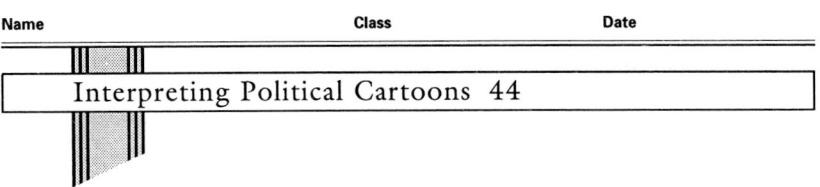

Interpreting Political Cartoons 44

CONFUSION IN THE SOVIET UNION

As the dust cleared from the coup in Moscow, it was evident that Soviet President Mikhail Gorbachev would have to make room at the top for Russian President Boris Yeltsin. The new liberal path to reform seemed to be lead by Yeltsin, who had gained immense popularity during the hours of the coup, when leadership was needed and Gorbachev was held captive by the perpetrators of the coup. Yeltsin now seemed to be a man with a stronger plan for liberal reform, and Gorbachev would have to move quickly to regain the confidence of the people. Gorbachev resigned as General Secretary of the Communist party and began negotiating with Yeltsin as to what to do next.

The cartoon below shows a bewildered Gorbachev answering the reporter's question by saying that he had only gone to get a "Big Mac and Fries."

Directions Study the cartoon, then answer the questions that follow.

© 1990 Dan Foote, *The Dallas Times Herald,* reprinted with permission of the *Dallas Morning News.*

Analyzing the Cartoon

1. What is the significance of the American symbol of McDonald's?

   _____

   _____

2. Why is the reporter implying that Mr. Gorbachev had said he was "stepping down and breaking ties"

   _____

   _____

Critical Thinking

3. **Making Comparisons** Compare the Gorbachev of this cartoon to the Gorbachev of the previous cartoon. Why is each cartoon humorous?

   _____

> **Interpreting Political Cartoons** activities enrich and motivate by providing 55 visual activities that challenge students with provocative perspectives on key issues.

Extension and Enrichment

Supreme Court Case Studies

the education and mental development of Negro children and to deprive them of some of the benefits they would receive in a racially integrated school system."

Agreeing with this statement, Warren concluded, "Whatever may have been the extent of psychological knowledge at the time of *Plessy* v. *Ferguson*, this finding is amply supported by modern authority. Any language in *Plessy* v. *Ferguson* contrary to this finding is rejected."

On this basis the Court concluded "that in the field of public education the doctrine of 'separate but equal' has no place. Separate educational facilities are inherently unequal. Therefore we hold that the plaintiffs and others similarly situated for whom the actions have been brought are, by reason of the segregation complained of, deprived of the equal protection of the law guaranteed by the Fourteenth Amendment. This disposition makes unnecessary any discussion whether such segregation also violates the due process clause of the Fourteenth Amendment."

Analyzing the Case

1. How does the *Brown* case differ from *Sweatt* v. *Painter*?

_____

_____

_____

2. What was the question raised by both *Plessy* and *Brown*?

_____

_____

_____

3. On what basis did the Court reach its decision in *Brown*?

_____

_____

_____

Critical Thinking

4. **Evaluating Information** How would you have interpreted the phrase "separate but equal"? Do you agree or disagree with the ruling in the *Brown* case? Explain your answer.

_____

_____

_____

_____

_____

_____

_____

_____

_____

_____

44 United States Government: Democracy in Action   Supreme Court Case Studies

---

Supreme Court Case Studies activities reinforce government themes and concepts by presenting 66 Supreme Court cases that consider fundamental constitutional questions.

Name   Class   Date

SUPREME COURT CASE 22

BROWN V. BOARD OF EDUCATION OF TOPEKA, KANSAS (1954)

Background of the Case

Brown represents a collection of cases, all decided together. The cases had one common feature: African American children had been denied admission to segregated white public schools.

These cases reached the U.S. Supreme Court by way of appeals through lower courts, all of which had ruled in accordance with the decision in *Plessy* v. *Ferguson* (1896). The Plessy case determined that separate but equal facilities did not violate the Fourteenth Amendment's guarantee of "equal protection of the law."

An earlier case, *Sweatt* v. *Painter* (1950) had held that African Americans must be admitted to the previously segregated University of Texas Law School because no separate but equal facility existed in the state. In *Brown*, however, there were findings "that the Negro and white schools involved have been equalized or were being equalized. . . ."

Constitutional Issue

The *Brown* case was an explicit reappraisal of the question in *Plessy* v. *Ferguson*. Did separate but equal public facilities violate the equal protection clause of the Fourteenth Amendment?

The Court's Decision

Chief Justice Earl Warren wrote the Court's unanimous decision.

Justice Warren began by noting that attempts to determine the precise intent of the Fourteenth Amendment's original sponsors have proved inconclusive. Even more difficult was any effort to discover its relation to the issue of public schools, as so few were in existence when the Amendment took effect.

Warren explained that the Court's method of examination, then, was to "look to the effect of segregation itself on public education" in order to determine "if segregation in public schools deprives these plaintiffs of the equal protection of the law." Warren added, "In approaching this problem, we cannot turn the clock back to 1868 when the [Fourteenth] Amendment was adopted, or even to 1896 when *Plessy* v. *Ferguson* was written. We must consider public education in the light of its full development and its present place in American life throughout the Nation. . . . Only in this way can it be determined if segregation in public schools deprives these plaintiffs of the equal protection of the law."

Warren quoted a Kansas state court ruling, which held that "segregation with the sanction of law, therefore, has a tendency to retard the educational and mental development of Negro children and to deprive them of some of the benefits they would receive in a racially integrated school system." Likewise, the U. S. Supreme Court concluded that segregation of African American schoolchildren "generates a feeling of inferiority as to their status in the community that may affect their hearts and minds in a way unlikely ever to be undone."

Recognizing further the huge psychological impact of segregation, Warren quoted the finding of a lower court with which he agreed (even though that court did rule against the plaintiffs). That lower court stated the finding based on psychological authority that, "Segregation of white and colored children in public schools has a detrimental effect upon the colored children. The impact is greater when it has the sanction of the law; for the policy of separating the races is usually interpreted as denoting the inferiority of the Negro group. A sense of inferiority affects the motivation of a child to learn. Segregation with the sanction of law, therefore, has the tendency to [retard]

Supreme Court Case Studies   United States Government: Democracy in Action **43**

Copyright © by the Glencoe Division of Macmillan/McGraw-Hill School Publishing Company

T20

Name   **Class**   **Date**

THE PRESIDENT'S CABINET SIMULATION

Student Activity

Directions In this simulation activity, you and your classmates are cabinet secretaries and cabinet secretaries' staff members. It is your job to advise the President on the hypothetical situation outlined below.

Scenario

In an attempt to recover from the devasting Persian Gulf War, Iraq has proposed to sell large quantities of oil to the United States at favorable prices in return for a series of agreements. Included would be

- A trade agreement to ship surplus grain to Iraq. Iraq's agriculture was devastated by the war, and many people face starvation.
- A military agreement to allow Iraq to rebuild some of its military installations, for defensive purposes only.
- A guarantee of Kurdish autonomy in the north of the country.

Additional Factors

- Gasoline prices in the United States have been rising dramatically, and economic experts warn of the possibility of gas shortages in the near future.
- American farmers are faced with serious surpluses. Grain prices in the United States have plummeted as a result.
- United States intelligence reports indicate that Iran may be massing its forces along the border with Iraq.
- Officials of other Middle Eastern nations have warned United States officials that any deal with Iraq would jeopardize Middle Eastern peace initiatives.
- There is a sizable segment of public opinion in the United States that wants nothing to do with Iraq; there is an equally large number of people who are appalled at the suffering that the war inflicted on innocent Iraqis and Kurds.

Follow your teacher's instructions for preparing advice to give the President.

UNIT

5   PARTICIPATING IN GOVERNMENT

Teacher Notes

Purpose To understand how the executive branch examines issues and advises the President. By acting the parts of cabinet members and their staffs, students will gain a greater appreciation of the many issues involved in making policy decisions and how the interest of one federal department may differ from those of others.

Background

Because of the complexity of domestic and world issues, no chief executive can formulate policy without weighing the advice of cabinet members and advisers. Every course of action has both advantages and disadvantages and these must be carefully examined in order to arrive at a sound policy.

Organizing the Activity

Ask students to name critical decisions the President has had to make lately. Then ask them to speculate about which advisers the President called upon as he formulated his decisions. Explain that in this simulation students will have the chance to advise the President about a major policy issue. They will need some background on executive branch departments and the role of the cabinet in advising the President (Chapters 16–18, pages 442–529).

Pacing

Day 1 For this scenario, you can serve as the President, or choose a student to play that role. The President then appoints four cabinet secretaries: Secretary of State, Secretary of Defense, Secretary of Agriculture, and Secretary of Energy. Assign other students to be staff members for each secretary. Then pass out the President's Cabinet Simulation handout.

Day 2 Secretaries and their staffs meet to discuss the scenario described on the handout and identify issues that affect the responsibilities of their department. Each secretary assigns staff members to investigate specific implications.

Days 3–5 Staff members investigate issues, using library and other resources, and prepare a report for the secretary.

Day 6 Staff members report their findings to their secretary. Each group then discusses its findings and prepares recommendations the secretary can give to the President.

Day 7 Hold a cabinet meeting in front of class at which each secretary presents his or her department's recommendations. The President is encouraged to challenge secretaries to defend their recommendations and propose alternative actions.

Day 8 The President announces his or her decision. Hold a class discussion to evaluate the decision-making process.

PARTICIPATING IN GOVERNMENT   UNITED STATES

Name   **Class**   **Date**

CHAPTER

16   PARTICIPATING IN GOVERNMENT

EXPRESSING YOUR OPINION

Directions A 1983 federal report, *A Nation at Risk*, prompted a nationwide debate about the state of education in the United States. What is your opinion? Use the information below, then list your own thoughts, in preparation to write a letter to the editor of your local paper expressing your opinion about education in the United States.

Findings

- "Secondary school curricula have been homogenized, diluted, and diffused to the point that the curricula no longer have a central purpose. In effect, we have a cafeteria-style curriculum in which the appetizers and desserts can easily be mistaken for the main courses."
- "The amount of homework for high school seniors has decreased (two-thirds report less than 1 hour a night) and grades have risen as average student achievement has been declining."
- "In many other industrialized nations, courses in mathematics (other than arithmetic or general mathematics), biology, chemistry, physics, and geography start in grade 6 and are required of all students. The time spent on these subjects, based on class hours, is about three times that spent by even the most science-oriented United States students, i.e., those who select 4 years of science and mathematics in secondary school."
- England and other industrialized countries, it is not unusual for academic high school students to spend 8 hours a day at school, 220 days per year. In the United States, by contrast, the typical school day lasts 6 hours and the school year is 180 days."

Recommendations

...recommend that State and local high school graduation requirements be strengthened and that, at a minimum, all students seeking a diploma be required to lay the foundations in the Five New Basics by taking the following curriculum during their 4 years of high school: (a) 4 years of English; (b) 3 years of mathematics; (c) 3 years of science; (d) 3 years of social studies; and (e) one-half year of computer science. For the college-bound, 2 years of foreign language in high school are strongly recommended in addition to those taken earlier.

We recommend that schools, colleges, and universities adopt more rigorous and measur-able standards, and higher expectations, for academic performance and student conduct, and that 4-year colleges and universities raise their requirements for admission. This will help students do their best educationally with challenging materials in an environment that supports learning and authentic accomplishment.

We recommend that significantly more time be devoted to learning the New Basics. This will require more effective use of the existing school days, a longer school day, or a lengthened school year.

—The National Commission on Excellence in Education, *A Nation at Risk: The Importance for Educational Reform*, April, 1983

Write your opinion on a separate sheet of paper.

Participating in Government activities for every unit and chapter bring students into direct touch with government through simulations and citizenship activities.

Evaluation

Evaluation materials help you measure the progress of your students through a large selection of testing and assessment resources.

Section Quizzes and Performance Assessment

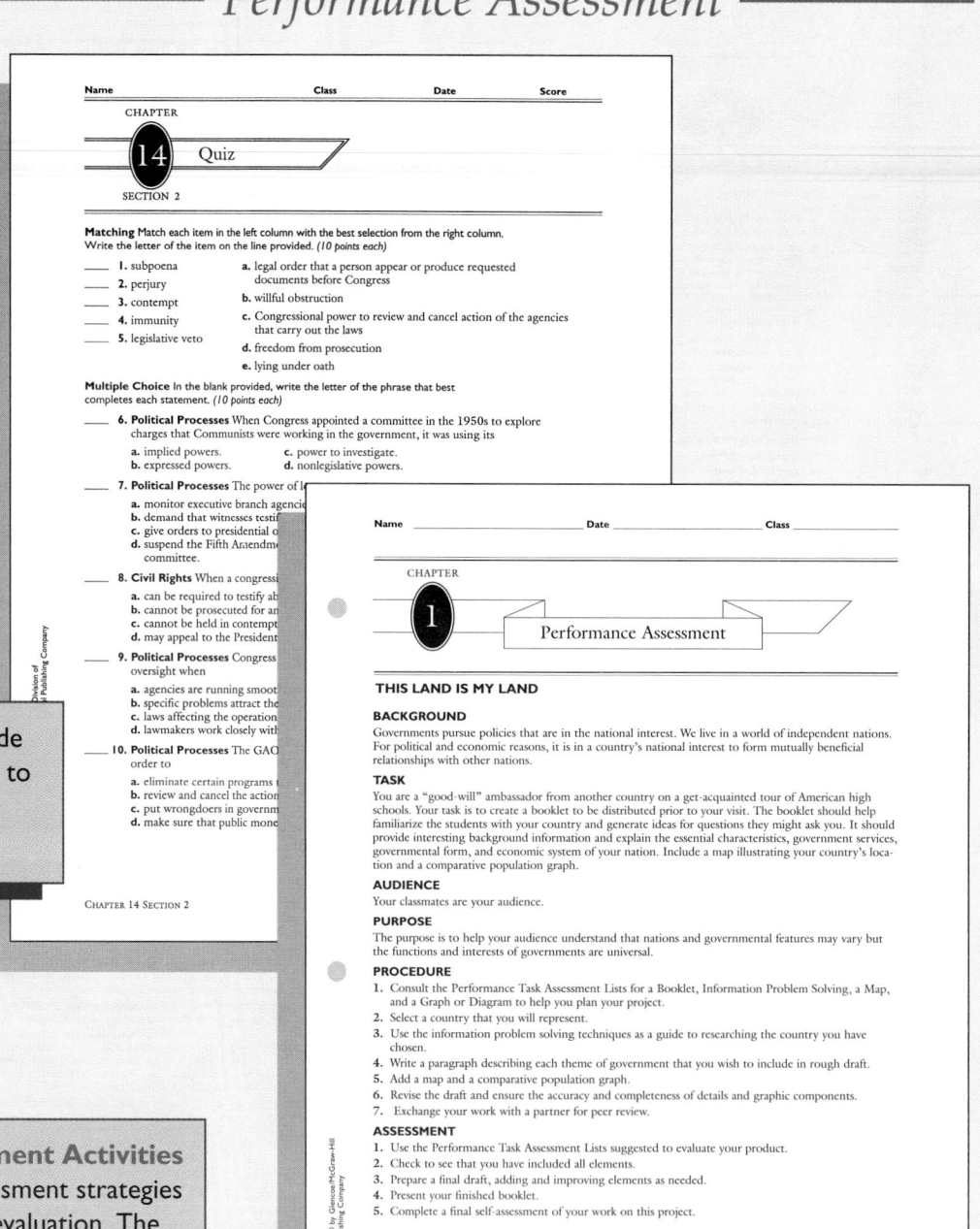

Section Quizzes provide a quick and effective way to check understanding and monitor daily progress.

Performance Assessment Activities provide alternative assessment strategies for greater flexibility in evaluation. The booklet also contains classroom assessment lists and scoring rubrics.

Tests and Testmaker Software

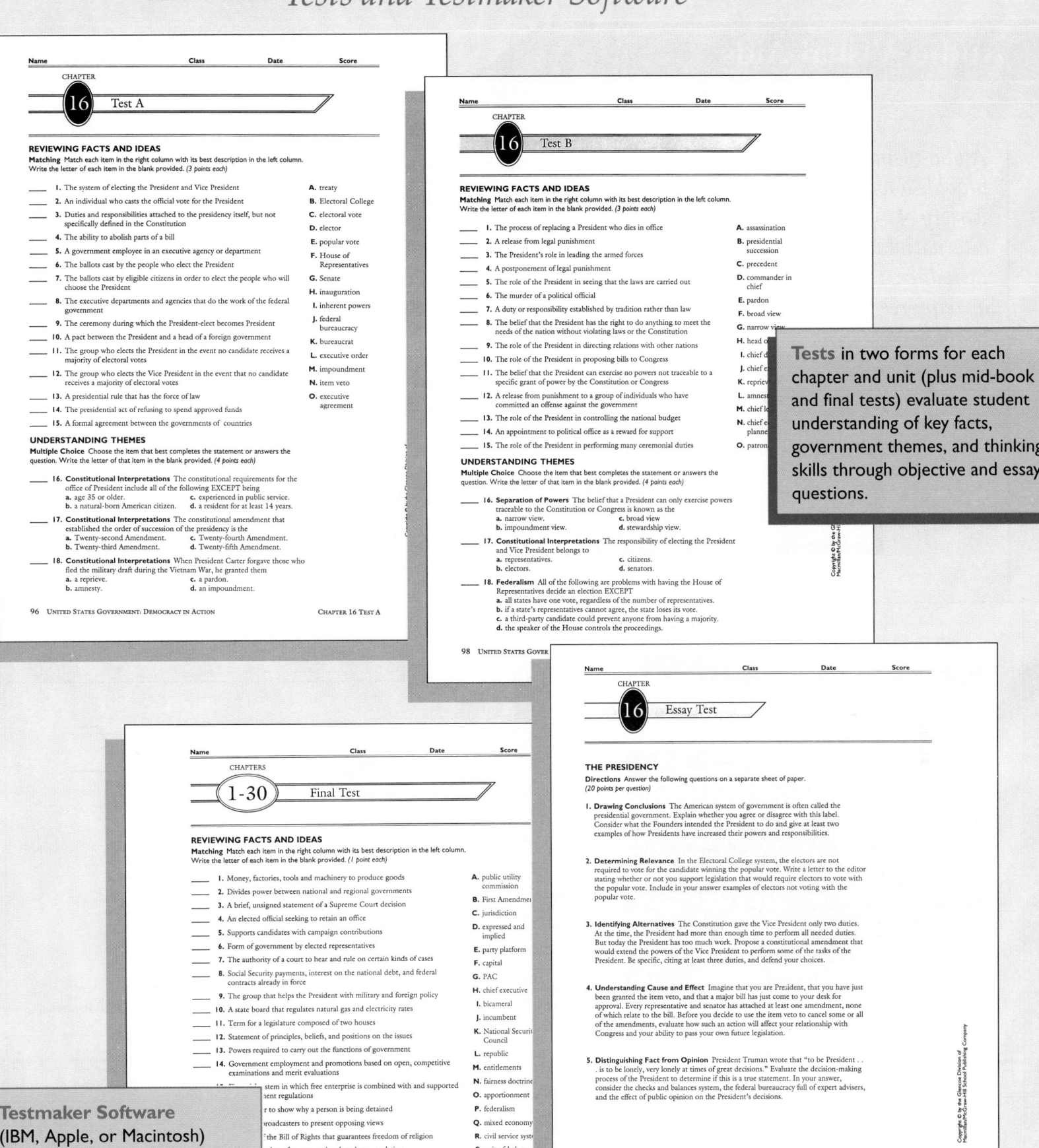

Name   **Class**   **Date**   **Score**

CHAPTER 16 — Test A

REVIEWING FACTS AND IDEAS

Matching Match each item in the right column with its best description in the left column. Write the letter of each item in the blank provided. *(3 points each)*

____ 1. The system of electing the President and Vice President
____ 2. An individual who casts the official vote for the President
____ 3. Duties and responsibilities attached to the presidency itself, but not specifically defined in the Constitution
____ 4. The ability to abolish parts of a bill
____ 5. A government employee in an executive agency or department
____ 6. The ballots cast by the people who elect the President
____ 7. The ballots cast by eligible citizens in order to elect the people who will choose the President
____ 8. The executive departments and agencies that do the work of the federal government
____ 9. The ceremony during which the President-elect becomes President
____ 10. A pact between the President and a head of a foreign government
____ 11. The group who elects the President in the event no candidate receives a majority of electoral votes
____ 12. The group who elects the Vice President in the event that no candidate receives a majority of electoral votes
____ 13. A presidential rule that has the force of law
____ 14. The presidential act of refusing to spend approved funds
____ 15. A formal agreement between the governments of countries

A. treaty
B. Electoral College
C. electoral vote
D. elector
E. popular vote
F. House of Representatives
G. Senate
H. inauguration
I. inherent powers
J. federal bureaucracy
K. bureaucrat
L. executive order
M. impoundment
N. item veto
O. executive agreement

UNDERSTANDING THEMES

Multiple Choice Choose the item that best completes the statement or answers the question. Write the letter of that item in the blank provided. *(4 points each)*

____ 16. **Constitutional Interpretations** The constitutional requirements for the office of President include all of the following EXCEPT being
a. age 35 or older.
b. a natural-born American citizen.
c. experienced in public service.
d. a resident for at least 14 years.

____ 17. **Constitutional Interpretations** The constitutional amendment that established the order of succession of the presidency is the
a. Twenty-second Amendment.
b. Twenty-third Amendment.
c. Twenty-fourth Amendment.
d. Twenty-fifth Amendment.

____ 18. **Constitutional Interpretations** When President Carter forgave those who fled the military draft during the Vietnam War, he granted them
a. a reprieve.
b. amnesty.
c. a pardon.
d. an impoundment.

96   UNITED STATES GOVERNMENT: DEMOCRACY IN ACTION   CHAPTER 16 TEST A

Name   **Class**   **Date**   **Score**

CHAPTER 16 — Test B

REVIEWING FACTS AND IDEAS

Matching Match each item in the right column with its best description in the left column. Write the letter of each item in the blank provided. *(3 points each)*

____ 1. The process of replacing a President who dies in office
____ 2. A release from legal punishment
____ 3. The President's role in leading the armed forces
____ 4. A postponement of legal punishment
____ 5. The role of the President in seeing that the laws are carried out
____ 6. The murder of a political official
____ 7. A duty or responsibility established by tradition rather than law
____ 8. The belief that the President has the right to do anything to meet the needs of the nation without violating laws or the Constitution
____ 9. The role of the President in directing relations with other nations
____ 10. The role of the President in proposing bills to Congress
____ 11. The belief that the President can exercise no powers not traceable to a specific grant of power by the Constitution or Congress
____ 12. A release from punishment to a group of individuals who have committed an offense against the government
____ 13. The role of the President in controlling the national budget
____ 14. An appointment to political office as a reward for support
____ 15. The role of the President in performing many ceremonial duties

A. assassination
B. presidential succession
C. precedent
D. commander in chief
E. pardon
F. broad view
G. narrow view
H. head o
I. chief d
J. chief e
K. reprie
L. amnes
M. chief l
N. chief e plann
O. patron

UNDERSTANDING THEMES

Multiple Choice Choose the item that best completes the statement or answers the question. Write the letter of that item in the blank provided. *(4 points each)*

____ 16. **Separation of Powers** The belief that a President can only exercise powers traceable to the Constitution or Congress is known as the
a. narrow view.
b. impoundment view.
c. broad view.
d. stewardship view.

____ 17. **Constitutional Interpretations** The responsibility of electing the President and Vice President belongs to
a. representatives.
b. electors.
c. citizens.
d. senators.

____ 18. **Federalism** All of the following are problems with having the House of Representatives decide an election EXCEPT
a. all states have one vote, regardless of the number of representatives.
b. if a state's representatives cannot agree, the state loses its vote.
c. a third-party candidate could prevent anyone from having a majority.
d. the speaker of the House controls the proceedings.

98   UNITED STATES GOVER

Tests in two forms for each chapter and unit (plus mid-book and final tests) evaluate student understanding of key facts, government themes, and thinking skills through objective and essay questions.

Name   **Class**   **Date**   **Score**

CHAPTERS 1-30 — Final Test

REVIEWING FACTS AND IDEAS

Matching Match each item in the right column with its best description in the left column. Write the letter of each item in the blank provided. *(1 point each)*

____ 1. Money, factories, tools and machinery to produce goods
____ 2. Divides power between national and regional governments
____ 3. A brief, unsigned statement of a Supreme Court decision
____ 4. An elected official seeking to retain an office
____ 5. Supports candidates with campaign contributions
____ 6. Form of government by elected representatives
____ 7. The authority of a court to hear and rule on certain kinds of cases
____ 8. Social Security payments, interest on the national debt, and federal contracts already in force
____ 9. The group that helps the President with military and foreign policy
____ 10. A state board that regulates natural gas and electricity rates
____ 11. Term for a legislature composed of two houses
____ 12. Statement of principles, beliefs, and positions on the issues
____ 13. Powers required to carry out the functions of government
____ 14. Government employment and promotions based on open, competitive examinations and merit evaluations

A. public utility commission
B. First Amendment
C. jurisdiction
D. expressed and implied
E. party platform
F. capital
G. PAC
H. chief executive
I. incumbent
J. bicameral
K. National Security Council
L. republic
M. entitlements
N. fairness doctrine
O. apportionment
P. federalism
Q. mixed economy
R. civil service syste
S. writ of *habeas corpus*
T. *per curiam* opinion

____ ____ system in which free enterprise is combined with and supported ____ ent regulations
____ ____ r to show why a person is being detained
____ roadcasters to present opposing views
____ the Bill of Rights that guarantees freedom of religion
____ mber of representatives based on population
____ the President in seeing that legislation passed by Congress is

G THEMES

____ ose the item that best completes the statement or answers the ____ er of that item in the blank provided. *(2 points each)*

Democracy "The United States intends to be an independent ____ f-governing nation" is the essential message of the
a. Declaration of Independence.
c. United States Constitution.
b. Articles of Confederation.
d. Bill of Rights.

FINAL TEST   UNITED STATES GOVERNMENT: DEMOCRACY IN ACTION   195

Name   **Class**   **Date**   **Score**

CHAPTER 16 — Essay Test

THE PRESIDENCY

Directions Answer the following questions on a separate sheet of paper. *(20 points per question)*

1. **Drawing Conclusions** The American system of government is often called the presidential government. Explain whether you agree or disagree with this label. Consider what the Founders intended the President to do and give at least two examples of how Presidents have increased their powers and responsibilities.

2. **Determining Relevance** In the Electoral College system, the electors are not required to vote for the candidate winning the popular vote. Write a letter to the editor stating whether or not you support legislation that would require electors to vote with the popular vote. Include in your answer examples of electors not voting with the popular vote.

3. **Identifying Alternatives** The Constitution gave the Vice President only two duties. At the time, the President had more than enough time to perform all needed duties. But today the President has too much work. Propose a constitutional amendment that would extend the powers of the Vice President to perform some of the tasks of the President. Be specific, citing at least three duties, and defend your choices.

4. **Understanding Cause and Effect** Imagine that you are President, that you have just been granted the item veto, and that a major bill has just come to your desk for approval. Every representative and senator has attached at least one amendment, none of which relate to the bill. Before you decide to use the item veto to cancel some or all of the amendments, evaluate how such an action will affect your relationship with Congress and your ability to pass your own future legislation.

5. **Distinguishing Fact from Opinion** President Truman wrote that "to be President . . . is to be lonely, very lonely at times of great decisions." Evaluate the decision-making process of the President to determine if this is a true statement. In your answer, consider the checks and balances system, the federal bureaucracy full of expert advisers, and the effect of public opinion on the President's decisions.

100   UNITED STATES GOVERNMENT: DEMOCRACY IN ACTION   CHAPTER 16 ESSAY TEST

Testmaker Software (IBM, Apple, or Macintosh) offers a bank of more than 3,000 questions, and provides the flexibility to edit existing questions and add new ones.

T23

Audio-Visual Aids

Audio-visual aids provide a wide variety of alternatives to introduce, teach, or reinforce lessons.

Unit Digest Transparencies

Unit Digest Transparencies with their supporting strategies, activities, and tests provide the means to introduce or review units quickly and effectively, or to teach units in a short period of time.

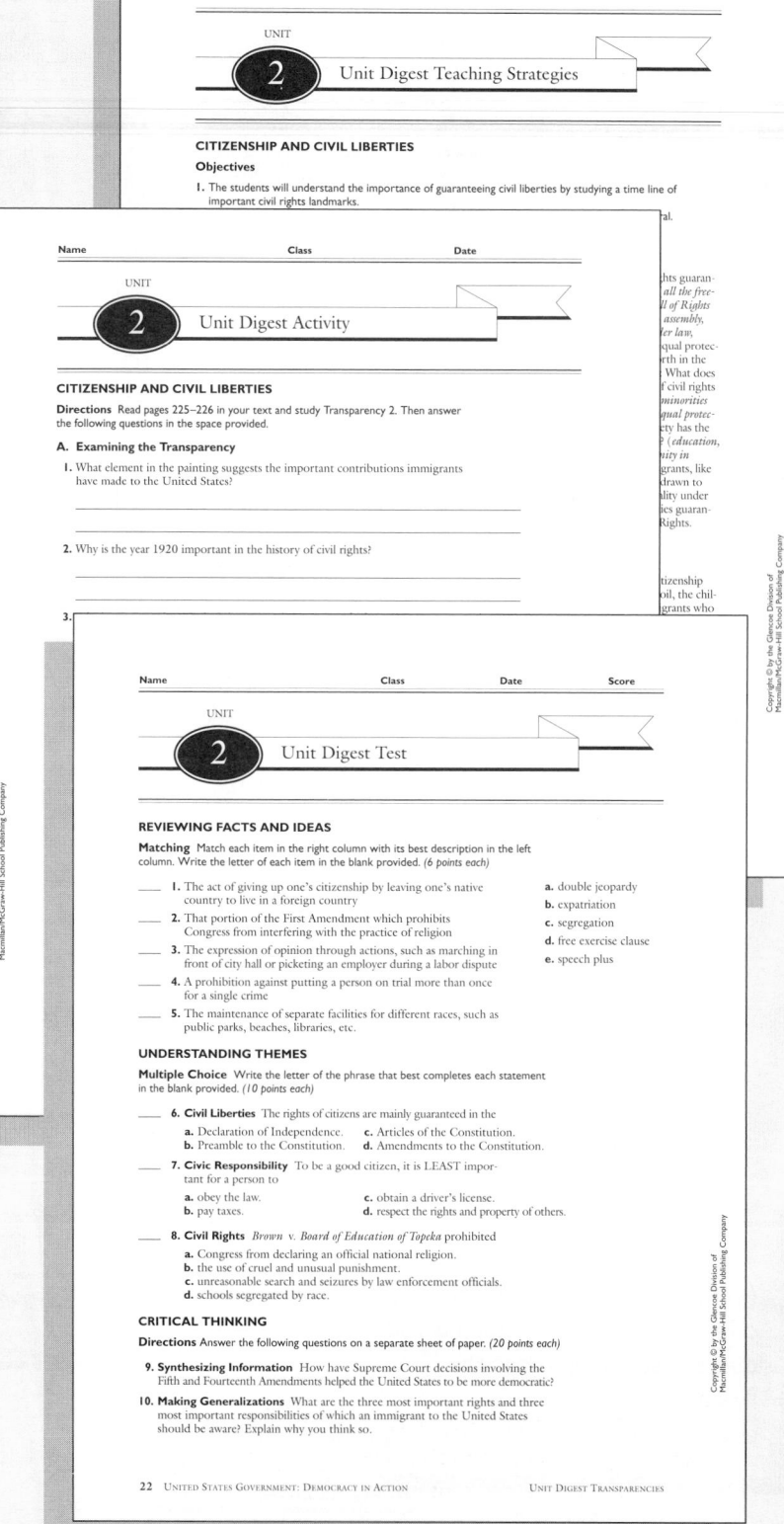

UNIT
2 Unit Digest Teaching Strategies

CITIZENSHIP AND CIVIL LIBERTIES
Objectives

1. The students will understand the importance of guaranteeing civil liberties by studying a time line of important civil rights landmarks.

Name _____ Class _____ Date _____

UNIT
2 Unit Digest Activity

CITIZENSHIP AND CIVIL LIBERTIES

Directions Read pages 225–226 in your text and study Transparency 2. Then answer the following questions in the space provided.

A. Examining the Transparency

1. What element in the painting suggests the important contributions immigrants have made to the United States?

2. Why is the year 1920 important in the history of civil rights?

3.

Name _____ Class _____ Date _____ Score _____

UNIT
2 Unit Digest Test

REVIEWING FACTS AND IDEAS

Matching Match each item in the right column with its best description in the left column. Write the letter of each item in the blank provided. *(6 points each)*

_____ **1.** The act of giving up one's citizenship by leaving one's native country to live in a foreign country

_____ **2.** That portion of the First Amendment which prohibits Congress from interfering with the practice of religion

_____ **3.** The expression of opinion through actions, such as marching in front of city hall or picketing an employer during a labor dispute

_____ **4.** A prohibition against putting a person on trial more than once for a single crime

_____ **5.** The maintenance of separate facilities for different races, such as public parks, beaches, libraries, etc.

a. double jeopardy
b. expatriation
c. segregation
d. free exercise clause
e. speech plus

UNDERSTANDING THEMES

Multiple Choice Write the letter of the phrase that best completes each statement in the blank provided. *(10 points each)*

_____ **6. Civil Liberties** The rights of citizens are mainly guaranteed in the
a. Declaration of Independence.   **c.** Articles of the Constitution.
b. Preamble to the Constitution.   **d.** Amendments to the Constitution.

_____ **7. Civic Responsibility** To be a good citizen, it is LEAST important for a person to
a. obey the law.   **c.** obtain a driver's license.
b. pay taxes.   **d.** respect the rights and property of others.

_____ **8. Civil Rights** *Brown v. Board of Education of Topeka* prohibited
a. Congress from declaring an official national religion.
b. the use of cruel and unusual punishment.
c. unreasonable search and seizures by law enforcement officials.
d. schools segregated by race.

CRITICAL THINKING

Directions Answer the following questions on a separate sheet of paper. *(20 points each)*

9. Synthesizing Information How have Supreme Court decisions involving the Fifth and Fourteenth Amendments helped the United States to be more democratic?

10. Making Generalizations What are the three most important rights and three most important responsibilities of which an immigrant to the United States should be aware? Explain why you think so.

22 UNITED STATES GOVERNMENT: DEMOCRACY IN ACTION   UNIT DIGEST TRANSPARENCIES

UNIT
2 Unit Digest Transparency

Citizenship and Civil Liberties

Einstein and Other Immigrants, a section of a mural painted by Ben Shahn, 1938–39

1800	1850		1900	1950
	1848 Seneca Falls Declaration	1863 Abraham Lincoln signs the Emancipation Proclamation	1870 Fifteenth Amendment ratified	1920 Nineteenth Amendment ratified	1964 Congress passes the Civil Rights Act

UNITED STATES GOVERNMENT: DEMOCRACY IN ACTION

Spanish Unit Digest Transparencies

Page 1 (top left)

Ciudadanía y libertades civiles

Einstein y otros inmigrantes, una sección de un mural pintado por Ben Shahn, 1938–39

1800	1850	1900	1950
1848 Seneca Falls— Declaración	**1863** Abraham Lincoln firma la Proclamación de la Emancipación	**1870** Ratificación de la Enmienda XV	**1920** Ratificación de la Enmienda XIX	**1964** El Congreso aprueba el Acto de los Derechos Civiles

---

Page 2 (top right)

CIUDADANIA Y LIBERTADES CIVILES

Capítulo 5
La ciudadanía en los Estados Unidos
Un ciudadano es un miembro de una sociedad política—una nación. Como tal, un ciudadano de los Estados Unidos tiene ciertos derechos, deberes y responsabilidades. La Constitución garantiza los derechos básicos en la Declaración de Derechos—en las primeras diez (10) enmiendas—y en varias enmiendas adicionales. Entre los deberes del ciudadano se encuentra la obediencia a la ley, pagar los impuestos, y ser leal al gobierno norteamericano y sus principios básicos. Como participantes en el gobierno, los ciudadanos tienen la responsabilidad de mantenerse informados, votar, respetar los derechos y propiedades de los demás, y respetar opiniones y modos de vida diferentes.

Los ciudadanos pueden ejercer sus derechos y privilegios de ciudadanía también de otras maneras. Por ejemplo, apoyando las iniciativas de una asociación de votantes en particular, para influir sobre la legislación, o discutir diversas cuestiones con un legislador o un miembro del aparato gubernamental. Otras formas en que los ciudadanos pueden participar son escribir cartas a los periódicos, firmar o hacer circular una petición sobre un asunto que le interese personalmente, o ejerciendo su derecho a disentir de una manera legal y ordenada. El continuo ejercicio de estos principios es el único modo de asegurar el vigor y vitalidad de los mismos.

Casi todas las personas nacidas en los Estados Unidos son automáticamente ciudadanos norteamericanos. También los inmigrantes pueden convertirse en ciudadanos siguiendo el proceso de naturalización (o nacionalización). Desde 1820, fecha en que el gobierno de los Estados Unidos comenzó a registrar estadísticas sobre inmigración, han llegado a los Estados Unidos más de cincuenta y siete (57) millones de inmigrantes. Llegados de todos los rincones del mundo, estos inmigrantes han contribuido enormemente a enriquecer la vida norteamericana.

Solamente el gobierno puede conceder la ciudadanía y quitarla. El gobierno americano pierda su ciuda...

tres modos: (1) **expatriación,** o renuncia a su ciudadanía para dejar su país de origen y vivir en otro país; (2) castigo por un crimen de carácter grave; (3) **desnaturalización,** o la pérdida de ciudadanía por fraude o engaño durante el proceso de naturalización.

Capítulo 6
La Primera Enmienda y la libertad de expresión
La Primera Enmienda garantiza la libertad de religión en dos cláusulas. En la primera, conocida como **"establishment clause"** (cláusula de fundación), afirma que "el Congreso no redactará ninguna ley relativa a la fundación de una religión". La segunda cláusula, denominada **"free exercise clause"** (cláusula del libre ejercicio), establece que el Congreso no puede prohibir el libre ejercicio de la religión. A lo largo del tiempo, el Congreso ha publicado varias resoluciones refinando estas dos cláusulas.

La Primera Enmienda garantiza también la libertad de palabra y la libertad de prensa, así como la libertad de asociación con fines pacíficos. La Corte Suprema ha distinguido tres clases generales de discurso. La expresión verbal de pensamiento y opinión ante una audiencia, o **discurso puro** (pure speech), es la forma habitual de expresión hablada. Si a la expresión hablada le acompañan acciones como pueden ser marchas de protesta o manifestaciones, se le llama **discurso acompañado** (speech plus). Debido a que el discurso acompañado incluye acciones, el gobierno puede aplicar restricciones que no se aplican al discurso puro. El tercer tipo de discurso, el **discurso simbólico** (symbolic speech) consiste en que acciones y símbolos toman el lugar de las palabras para expresar opiniones. Por ejemplo, durante la guerra del Vietnam, los manifestantes llevaban puestas bandas negras en el brazo para ex-

---

Page 3 (bottom left)

CIUDADANIA Y LIBERTADES CIVILES

Instrucciones: Lea las páginas 225–226 del libro de texto y observe la diapositiva 2. Después conteste en el espacio en blanco las siguientes preguntas.

A. Comentario de la diapositiva

1. ¿Qué elemento de la pintura sugiere las importantes contribuciones de los inmigrantes a los Estados Unidos?

2. ¿Por qué el año 1919 es importante para la historia de los derechos civiles?

3. ¿Qué sucesos del esquema cronológico documentan el progreso de la igualdad ante la ley de los americanos de raza africana?

B. Estudio de la unidad

Repaso de los conceptos

1. **Enumere** tres tipos de discurso amparados por la primera enmienda.

2. **Cite** tres maneras en que los ciudadanos de los Estados Unidos pueden perder su ciudadanía.

Profundización en los temas

3. **Derechos civiles** ¿Cuál fue el significado del dictamen del caso *Brown v. Consejo de Educación de Topeka?*

Reflexión crítica

4. **Expresemos los problemas con claridad** Considerando avances de los últimos cuarenta años para acabar con la discriminación y hacia la igualdad de oportunidades de minorías y mujeres, ¿cree usted que aún son necesarios los programas de acción afirmativa?

Page 4 (bottom right)

HECHOS E IDEAS CLAVES

Emparejar Empareje cada uno de los términos en la columna a la derecha con la mejor descripción que aparezca en la columna a la izquierda. Escriba la letra de cada término en el espacio indicado. *(6 puntos cada uno)*

_____ 1. La acción de renunciar a la ciudadanía propia al dejar el país de origen y trasladarse a un país extranjero

_____ 2. La parte de la Primera Enmienda que le prohíbe al Congreso interferir en la religión

_____ 3. La expresión de opiniones mediante acciones tales como protestar ante el ayuntamiento o piquetear un negocio

_____ 4. Prohibición de enjuiciar a una persona más de una vez por un sólo delito

_____ 5. La provisión de facilidades separadas para distintas razas, como por ejemplo, parques, balnearios, bibliotecas públicas, etcétera

a. doble peligro
b. expatriación
c. segregación
d. cláusula de libre ejercicio
e. discurso acompañado

TEMAS CLAVES

Selección múltiple Escriba en el espacio indicado la letra de la frase que mejor complete cada oración. *(10 puntos cada uno)*

_____ 6. **Libertades civiles** Los derechos de los ciudadanos están garantizados principalmente en
a. la Declaración de Independencia
b. el Preámbulo a la Constitución
c. los Artículos de la Constitución
d. las Enmiendas a la Constitución

_____ 7. **Responsabilidades cívicas** Para ser un buen ciudadano, lo menos importante es
a. obedecer las leyes
b. pagar los impuestos
c. obtener una licencia de manejar
d. respetar los derechos y las propiedades de los demás

_____ 8. **Derechos civiles** El caso de la Corte Suprema llamado Brown vs la Junta de Educación de Topeka prohibió
a. que el Congreso declarara una religión oficial nacional
b. el uso de condenas crueles y poco habituales
c. el registro y la incautación desmedidas por parte de oficiales
d. escuelas separadas para blancos y negros

REFLEXION CRITICA

Direcciones Conteste las preguntas que siguen a continuación en una hoja de papel aparte. *(20 puntos cada uno)*

9. **Síntesis de información** ¿De qué manera han contribuido los dictámenes de la Corte Suprema concernientes a la Quinta y Decimocuarta Enmiendas al fortalecimiento de la democracia?

10. **Generalizaciones** ¿Cuáles son los tres derechos y las tres responsabilidades más importantes de los que debe de estar al tanto un inmigrante en los Estados Unidos? Explique porqué.

Spanish Unit Digest Transparencies, Activities, and Tests include unit digests in Spanish and an English/Spanish glossary to help Spanish-speaking students master the key content of each unit.

Audio-Visual Aids

Government Themes Transparencies

Government Themes Teaching Strategies 15
Checks and Balances

ENTIAL APPROVAL

_ve_
will view a photograph representing the presidential power to approve or veto laws and
clusions based upon it.

RE NOTES

ment of theme material, use Theme Trans-
5 and have students complete Theme
5.

is made law when approved by the Presi-
may sign it in a ceremony involving
porting the bill or most likely to benefit
The President may have had little to do
bill, but such ceremonies often take place
President and his advisers feel that they
e occasion to gain publicity or some
advantage.
President's power to check Congress is
le at times when the Chief Executive
o veto a bill. Although in theory this
be balanced by Congress's own power
le a veto with a two-thirds vote in both
practice vetoes are seldom overturned.
f the more than 2,470 vetoes Presidents
since 1789, only 104 have been overrid-
e Congress. No veto was overturned by
until the term of John Tyler (1841–45).
Andrew Johnson, highly unpopular with
can Congress, saw only 15 of his vetoes
n. Harry S Truman, who vetoed 250
rebuffed by Congress only 12 times.
ocket veto is a variation of the veto
the President can allow a bill to die by
o act on it if Congress has adjourned
days of the time the President receives
an astonishing 40 percent of all vetoes

Although the power to propose legislation is
not actually a checking power, it does help to balance the power of the executive and legislative
branches. This power has grown over the years as
Congress, faced with increasingly technical issues
and soaring budgets, has come to rely on the
President more and more for leadership in legislative matters.
By contrast, conflict between the executive
and judicial branches is much less often observed.
As early as 1867 the Supreme Court rejected a
suit in which a state tried to prevent President
Andrew Johnson from enforcing Reconstruction
statutes (_Mississippi v. Johnson_). In its opinion, the
court cited "general principles that forbid judicial
interference with the exercise of Executive discretion." The President may, however, find his executive orders subject to review by the Supreme
Court. A notorious and recent case of this was
United States v. Nixon (1974), when the Court
disagreed with then President Richard Nixon's
claim that his definition of executive privilege was
not subject to judicial review.

Activity

Supply students with a newspaper account of a bill
recently vetoed by the President. (_If necessary,
choose a law that was approved by the President, but
for the sake of the exercise have students consider it
vetoed._) Divide the class into two groups and have
them prepare to debate the pros and cons of the
President's action. When they are ready, conduct
ress
resi-
cluded,
y can

Government Themes Activity 15
Checks and Balances

PRESIDENTIAL APPROVAL

About the Photograph
The picture shows President George Bush in a ceremonial signing of legislation. Supporters or beneficiaries of the new law are often invited to participate in such ceremonies.

Responding to the Transparency

1. What power in the checks and balances system is represented by this ceremonial signing?

_____

2. Who can you infer is the beneficiary of the legislation President Bush is signing into law?

_____

3. In what ways may the legislative and judicial branches be concerned with a bill signed by
the President?

_____

4. Some laws are the result of executive activity. How do Presidents affect the lawmaking
process not only at the signing stage, but in the legislative stage

_____

Going Beyond the Transparency

5. Many Presidents have requested item veto power, the pow
proposed law, especially a budget law. Imagine you are a
vention called to consider such an amendment. Take a po
ment and write a short speech on a separate sheet of pap
of the amendment on the system of checks and balances.
main ideas.

Government Themes Transparency 15
Checks and Balances

Presidential Approval

esident Bush signs a bill dealing with access for handicapped citizens.

**Government Themes
Transparencies** provide more than
60 engaging images with strategies and
activities that help students visualize,
understand, and apply the key themes
and concepts of American government.
Each transparency is correlated to
appropriate chapters in the text.

Chapter Transparencies

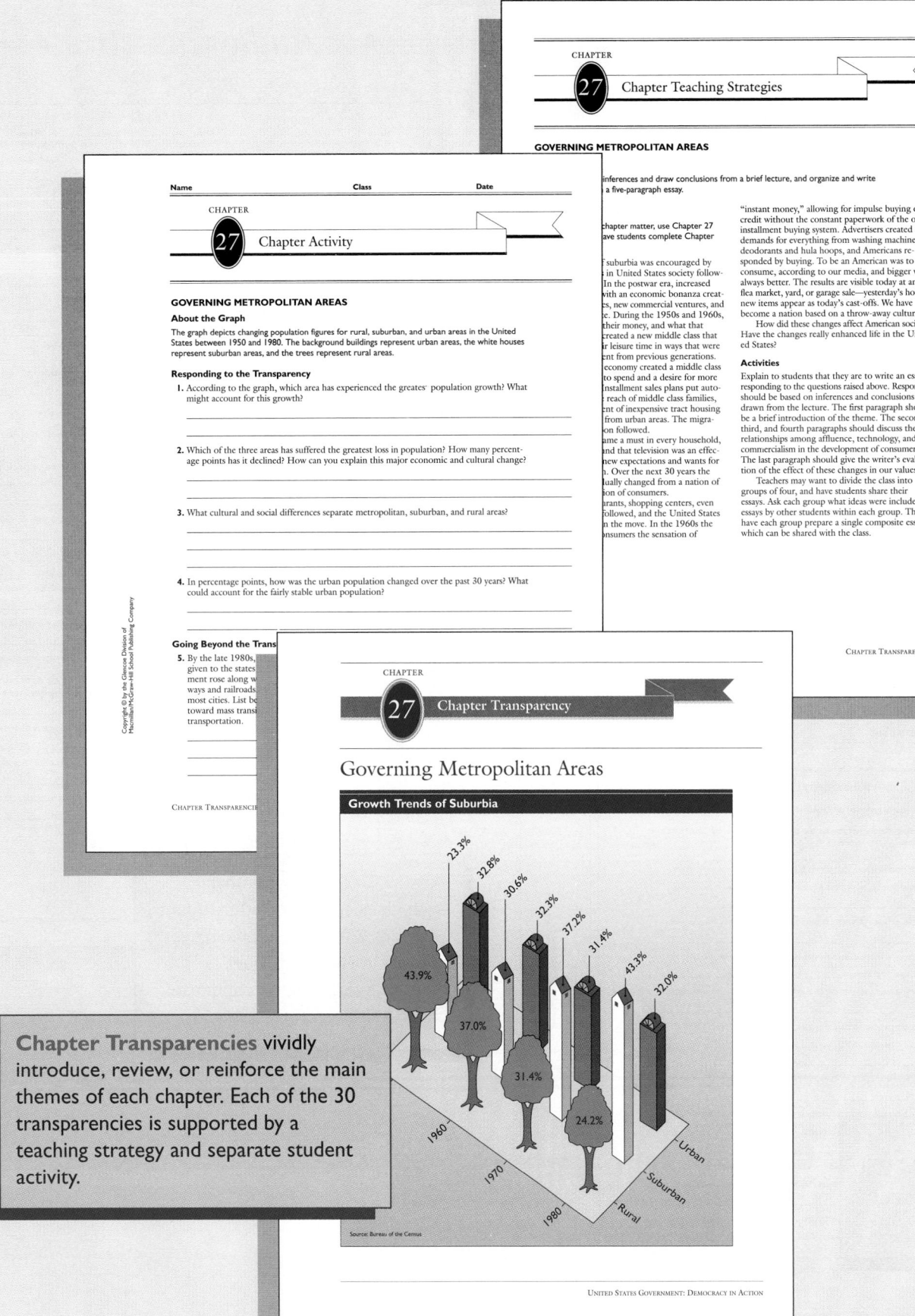

CHAPTER

27 Chapter Teaching Strategies

GOVERNING METROPOLITAN AREAS

...inferences and draw conclusions from a brief lecture, and organize and write... a five-paragraph essay.

...chapter matter, use Chapter 27 ...ave students complete Chapter

...suburbia was encouraged by ...n United States society follow- ...In the postwar era, increased ...with an economic bonanza creat- ...es, new commercial ventures, and ...e. During the 1950s and 1960s, ...their money, and what that ...created a new middle class that ...ir leisure time in ways that were ...ent from previous generations. ...economy created a middle class ...to spend and a desire for more ...installment sales plans put auto- ...reach of middle class families, ...ent of inexpensive tract housing ...from urban areas. The migra- ...ion followed. ...ame a must in every household, ...and that television was an effec- ...new expectations and wants for ...h. Over the next 30 years the ...ually changed from a nation of ...ion of consumers. ...rants, shopping centers, even ...followed, and the United States ...n the move. In the 1960s the ...onsumers the sensation of

"instant money," allowing for impulse buying on credit without the constant paperwork of the older installment buying system. Advertisers created new demands for everything from washing machines to deodorants and hula hoops, and Americans responded by buying. To be an American was to consume, according to our media, and bigger was always better. The results are visible today at any flea market, yard, or garage sale—yesterday's hottest new items appear as today's cast-offs. We have become a nation based on a throw-away culture.

How did these changes affect American society? Have the changes really enhanced life in the United States?

Activities

Explain to students that they are to write an essay responding to the questions raised above. Responses should be based on inferences and conclusions drawn from the lecture. The first paragraph should be a brief introduction of the theme. The second, third, and fourth paragraphs should discuss the relationships among affluence, technology, and commercialism in the development of consumerism. The last paragraph should give the writer's evaluation of the effect of these changes in our values.

Teachers may want to divide the class into groups of four, and have students share their essays. Ask each group what ideas were included in essays by other students within each group. Then have each group prepare a single composite essay which can be shared with the class.

CHAPTER TRANSPARENCIES

Name   **Class**   **Date**

CHAPTER

27 Chapter Activity

GOVERNING METROPOLITAN AREAS

About the Graph

The graph depicts changing population figures for rural, suburban, and urban areas in the United States between 1950 and 1980. The background buildings represent urban areas, the white houses represent suburban areas, and the trees represent rural areas.

Responding to the Transparency

1. According to the graph, which area has experienced the greatest population growth? What might account for this growth?

2. Which of the three areas has suffered the greatest loss in population? How many percentage points has it declined? How can you explain this major economic and cultural change?

3. What cultural and social differences separate metropolitan, suburban, and rural areas?

4. In percentage points, how was the urban population changed over the past 30 years? What could account for the fairly stable urban population?

Going Beyond the Trans...

5. By the late 1980s, ... given to the states ... ment rose along w... ways and railroads... most cities. List b... toward mass transi... transportation.

CHAPTER TRANSPARENCIES

CHAPTER

27 Chapter Transparency

Governing Metropolitan Areas

Growth Trends of Suburbia

23.3%
32.8%
30.6%
32.3%
37.2%
31.4%
43.3%
32.0%

43.9%
37.0%
31.4%
24.2%

1960
1970
1980

Urban
Suburban
Rural

Source: Bureau of the Census

UNITED STATES GOVERNMENT: DEMOCRACY IN ACTION

Chapter Transparencies vividly introduce, review, or reinforce the main themes of each chapter. Each of the 30 transparencies is supported by a teaching strategy and separate student activity.

Audio-Visual Aids

Audio Cassettes

CHAPTER 6

Audio Cassette Test

CHAPTER 6

Audio Cassette Activity

PROTECTING BASIC FREEDOMS

Directions: After listening to the cassette tape for Chapter 6, complete the following items.

Read each statement below. Check (✔) those that are correct. Underline the incorrect section of the others and write in the correct information after the sentence.

1. ____ The Constitution upholds the separation of church and state, neither forcing people to nor preventing them from practicing religion, as long as such worship does not interfere with the law.

2. ____ The law requires that people salute the flag even if doing so violates religious principles.

3. ____ Most forms of free speech are protected as long as they don't involve marching or demonstrating.

4. ____ Free speech can be restricted if a "clear and present danger" to national security is involved.

5. ____ Slander involves written words and libel involves spoken words that damage a person's name, character, or reputation.

6. ____ Freedom of peaceable assembly is subject to limits, just as freedom of speech is.

7. ____ The term "heckler's veto" has to do with public pressure against freedom of religion for members of some churches.

8. ____ The "press" includes magazines, radio, and telephone communication as well as newspapers.

9. ____ A term that means government censorship of information before it is published or broadcast is *sedition*.

10. ____ Shield laws give reporters some protection against having to reveal confidential information or sources in court.

UNITED STATES GOVERNMENT: DEMOCRACY IN ACTION   11

Audio Cassettes summarize each chapter and include student activities and tests, providing yet another means to review, reteach, reinforce, or condense chapter content.

Spanish Audio Cassettes

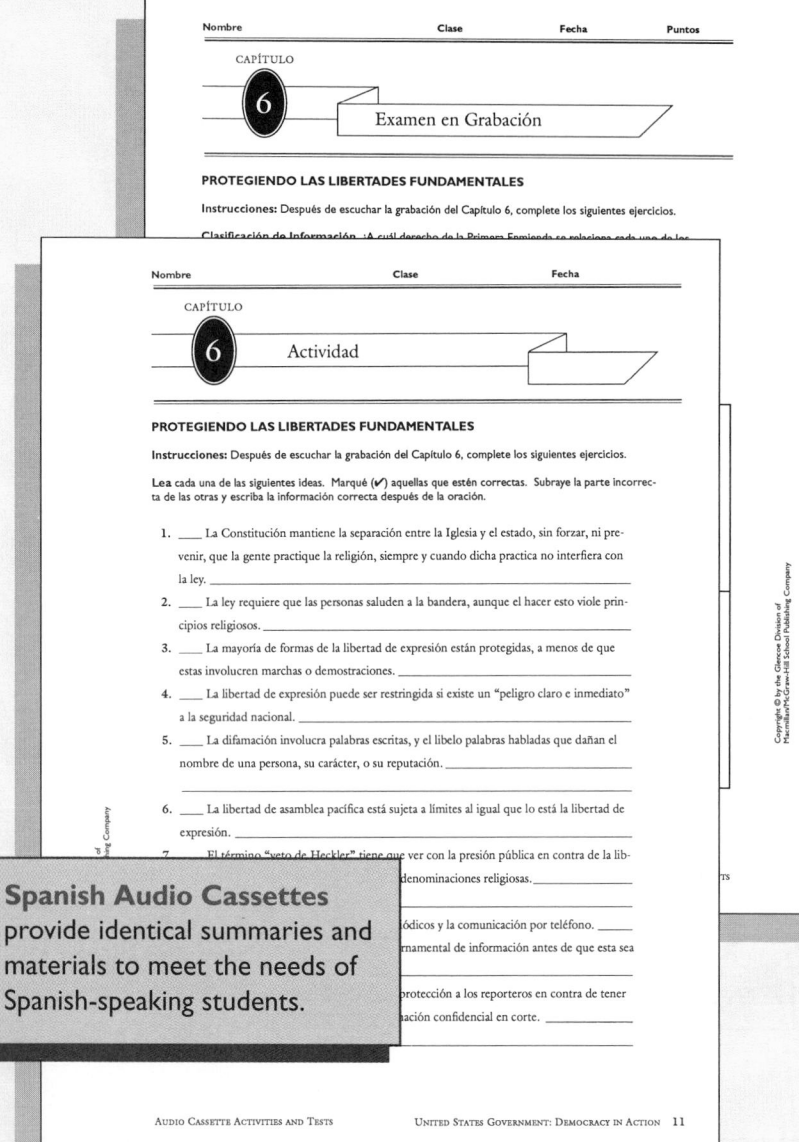

CAPÍTULO 6

Examen en Grabación

PROTEGIENDO LAS LIBERTADES FUNDAMENTALES

Instrucciones: Después de escuchar la grabación del Capítulo 6, complete los siguientes ejercicios.

Clasificación de Información: ¿A cuál derecho de la Primera Enmienda se relaciona cada uno de los

CAPÍTULO 6

Actividad

PROTEGIENDO LAS LIBERTADES FUNDAMENTALES

Instrucciones: Después de escuchar la grabación del Capítulo 6, complete los siguientes ejercicios.

Lea cada una de las siguientes ideas. Marqué (✔) aquellas que estén correctas. Subraye la parte incorrecta de las otras y escriba la información correcta después de la oración.

1. ____ La Constitución mantiene la separación entre la Iglesia y el estado, sin forzar, ni prevenir, que la gente practique la religión, siempre y cuando dicha practica no interfiera con la ley.

2. ____ La ley requiere que las personas saluden a la bandera, aunque el hacer esto viole principios religiosos. ____

3. ____ La mayoría de formas de la libertad de expresión están protegidas, a menos de que estas involucren marchas o demostraciones. ____

4. ____ La libertad de expresión puede ser restringida si existe un "peligro claro e inmediato" a la seguridad nacional. ____

5. ____ La difamación involucra palabras escritas, y el libelo palabras habladas que dañan el nombre de una persona, su carácter, o su reputación. ____

6. ____ La libertad de asamblea pacífica está sujeta a límites al igual que lo está la libertad de expresión. ____

7. ____ El término "veto de Heckler" tiene que ver con la presión pública en contra de la libertad denominaciones religiosas. ____

____ódicos y la comunicación por teléfono. ____

____rnamental de información antes de que esta sea

____protección a los reporteros en contra de tener

____ación confidencial en corte. ____

Spanish Audio Cassettes provide identical summaries and materials to meet the needs of Spanish-speaking students.

Reproducible Lesson Plans

Grade _____	Class(es) _____	Date(s) _____	M Tu W Th F
Teacher's Name _____		Date _____	

CHAPTER

1

Lesson Plan

SECTION 1

GOVERNMENT AND OUR LIVES

Local Objectives	TWE – Teacher's Wraparound Edition TCR – Teacher's Classroom Resources
	Objectives ___ **Identify** the essential features of a state. ___ **Distinguish** between the unitary system and the federal system of government.
	Focus ___ Chapter Opener, TWE pp. 16,17 ___ Focus, TWE, p. 18 ___ Background, TWE, p. 19 ___ *Guided Reading*, TCR, p. 1 ___ Audio Cassette, chapter 1, section 1

	Teach
	■ Guided Practice
	   ___ Activities, TWE, pp. 19-20
	   ___ Special Needs Strategy, TWE, p. 21
	   ___ Lesson Plan, TWE, pp. 16-23
	   ___ Study Guides pp. 19, 20
	   ___ Cooperative Learning, TWE, p. 20
	   ___ *Chapter 1 Transparency* material, TCR
	■ Independent Practice
	   ___ Activities, TWE, pp. 20-21
	   ___ Critical Thinking Activity, TWE, p. 22
	   ___ *Guided Reading*, TCR, p. 1

	Assess ___ Assess, TWE, p. 22 ___ Section Quiz, TCR, p. 1 ___ Testmaker

	Close
	___ Close, TWE, p. 23
	■ Reteaching
	   ___ *Skill Reinforcement,* TCR, p. 1
	■ Enrichment
	   ___ Global Connection, TWE, p. 22
	   ___ The Living Constitution
	   ___ SAT Practice Tests

1   UNITED STATES GOVERNMENT: DEMOCRACY IN ACTION

REPRODUCIBLE LESSON PLANS

Reproducible Lesson Plans let you spend less time planning and more time teaching.

Interactive Videos

Social Studies Videos provide primary-source footage of the major political campaigns and speeches on the great issues of the United States in the twentieth century.

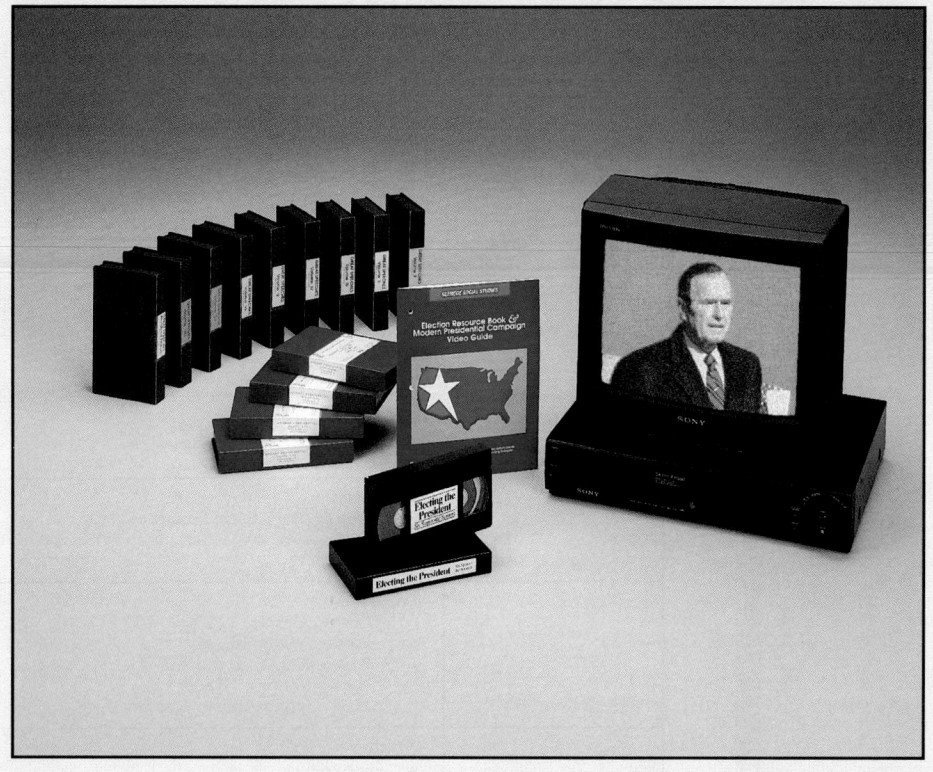

Focus on Government: an Interactive Laser Videodisc Program contains electronic field trips as well as segments designed to help students make connections with past learning, shots of students speaking out on relevant topics, and lecture launchers. This three-hour series is also available in videotape format.

United States Government

DEMOCRACY IN ACTION

PRESIDENTIAL ELECTION EDITION

United States Government

DEMOCRACY IN ACTION

Richard C. Remy

*Associate Director of the Mershon Center for Research and Education
at The Ohio State University*

GLENCOE

McGraw-Hill

New York, New York   Columbus, Ohio   Mission Hills, California   Peoria, Illinois

ABOUT THE AUTHOR

Richard C. Remy, Ph.D., is Associate Director of the Mershon Center for Research and Education at The Ohio State University, where he also holds appointments as a Mershon Senior Faculty in political science and as Associate Professor in the College of Education. He received his Ph.D. in political science from Northwestern University, has taught in the Chicago public schools, and has served as a consultant to numerous school systems, state departments of education, and federal government agencies. His books include: *Teaching About International Conflict and Peace, Approaches to World Studies, Teaching About National Security, American Government and National Security, Civics for Americans, Lessons on the Constitution,* and *Citizenship Decision Making.* Dr. Remy is co-directing projects to develop new civic education programs with the Polish Ministry of National Education and with the Lithuanian Ministry of Culture and Education. He serves as consultant on civic education to the United States Information Agency and the National Endowment for Democracy. He also serves on national advisory boards for such organizations as the American Bar Association and the ERIC Clearinghouse for Social Studies/Social Science Education.

ACADEMIC CONSULTANTS

Robert L. Lineberry
Professor of Political Science
University of Houston

Thad L. Beyle
Professor of
Political Science
University of North Carolina
at Chapel Hill

Leon Hurwitz
Professor of Political Science
Cleveland State University

Susan Welch
College of the Liberal Arts
Penn State University

Linda P. Brady
John M. Olin Distinguished
Professor of National
Security Studies
Department of Social Sciences
United States Military Academy

Mary Hepburn
Vinson Institute of Government
University of Georgia

CONTRIBUTING WRITERS

The European Union
Nigel Armstrong
Foreign Service Officer, Retired
Department of State

The President's Cabinet
John Wolfe
American Historical Association

Voter's Handbook
Denny Schillings
President-Elect, National
Council for the Social Studies

The Press Gallery
Donald A. Ritchie
Associate Historian of the United
States Senate Historical Office

Glencoe/McGraw-Hill

A Division of The McGraw-Hill Companies

Send all inquiries to:
Glencoe/McGraw-Hill, 936 Eastwind Drive, Westerville, OH 43081-3374

ISBN 0-02-822061-7 (Student Edition)   ISBN 0-02-822062-5 (Teacher's Wraparound Edition)
Printed in the United States of America.

1 2 3 4 5 6 7 8 9 10 11 12 VH 02 01 00 99 98 97

The Responsibilities of Freedom

Dear Student,

You are becoming a student of government during what is probably the greatest expansion of freedom in human history. People the world over want democracy because they believe it is the form of government that will give them the greatest chance to be free and to develop their talents to the fullest extent possible.

During the last decade in nations around the globe such as Poland, Czechoslovakia, Hungary, Argentina, Chile, and Kenya, millions of people have struggled, and many have died, to gain what Americans take for granted—the right to govern themselves.

Yet for millions around the world, the struggle is just beginning. They are learning that along with their new rights as citizens come responsibilities. These include the duty to protect the rights of others as well as their own rights; to respect the law and yet be willing to criticize government; to act not only for their own good but also for the good of the community. If citizens do not meet such responsibilities, democracy and the freedom it brings can be easily lost.

My goal in writing this book is to help you develop the knowledge, skills, and ideals you need to protect your own freedom; to keep democracy alive in the United States. In the pages that follow you will find information to help you better understand how the machinery of representative government works and why it sometimes does not work. You will have the chance to develop skills for making sound judgments about public policy and for taking part in politics. And you will read about key principles of democracy such as majority rule with minority rights, free elections, and individual liberty. These core civic ideas and principles of government are what unite us as Americans, no matter what our ethnic heritage.

In the last several years, I have had the chance to help educators and political leaders who overthrew the Communist regime in Poland develop educational programs on democracy for Polish students and teachers. Working with these brave people has reminded me just how fragile democracy can be and how hard citizens everywhere must work to protect it.

The Polish political philosopher Leszek Kolakowski echoed our own Founding Fathers when he said, "Freedom is never assured. It is always to be defended." Defending freedom is the responsibility of competent citizens; it is your responsibility.

Richard C. Remy
Political Scientist and Educator

Contents

Special Features

IMAGES
· OF ·
GOVERNMENT

GLOBAL CONNECTION

Interdependence

Comparing Governments

Issues

Focus on Freedom

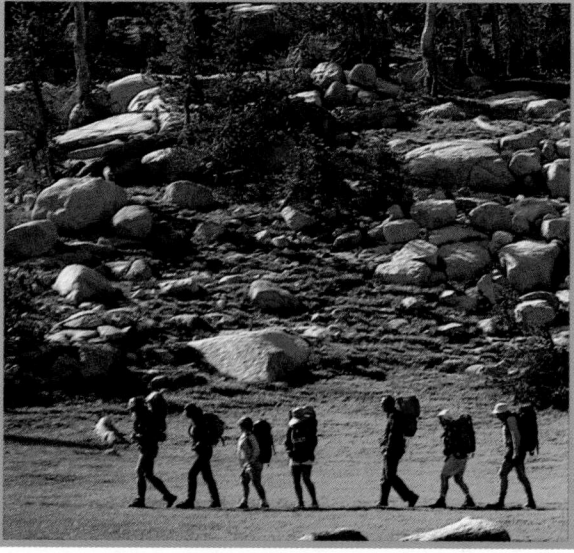

PARTICIPATING IN GOVERNMENT

GOVERNMENT STUDY SKILLS

Critical Thinking Skills

Study and Writing Skills

Social Studies Skills

★ PERSONAL PERSPECTIVES ★

CHARTS AND GRAPHS

DIAGRAPHICS

MAPS

Text Organization

As citizens in a democratic society, it is everyone's responsibility to take part in government. Only through active citizen participation can a democracy survive. *United States Government: Democracy in Action* has been designed to help you learn the functions and organization of our government, your responsibilities in our democratic system, and especially how you can participate to protect our democracy.

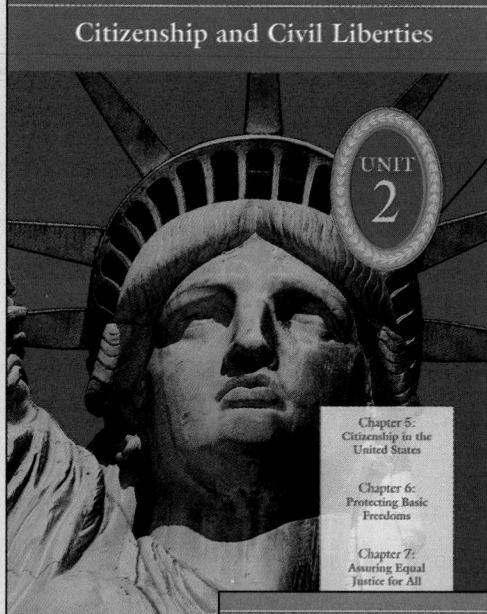

The Unit Opener includes a dynamic full-page photograph and a list of chapters in the unit.

The Chapter Opener includes a Chapter Preview. The preview begins with a brief overview of what you are about to study. The preview also includes a list of objectives as well as a list of the themes and critical thinking skills the chapter emphasizes.

The author, Richard C. Remy, a noted political scientist, has achieved these goals in a variety of ways. First, the text is divided into 10 units, 30 chapters, and 110 sections. Each section is suitable for one day of study as you learn more about United States government. Next, the author has included hundreds of visuals—photographs, fine art, maps, charts, and graphs—to emphasize certain key themes and principles of government. Finally, the author has included a number of special high-interest features to help you understand various elements of government.

Each chapter is divided into three to five sections. Primary-source quotes, photographs, fine art, maps, charts, and graphs work with the narrative to make government come alive.

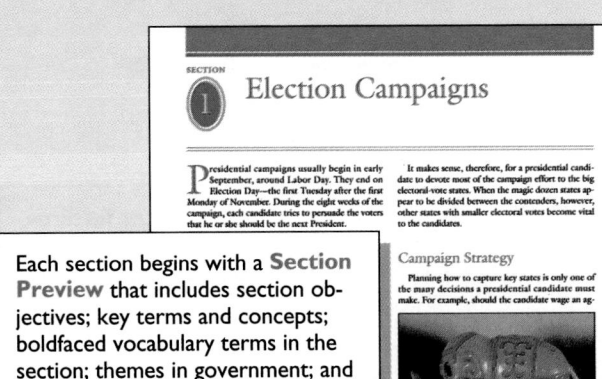

Each section begins with a **Section Preview** that includes section objectives; key terms and concepts; boldfaced vocabulary terms in the section; themes in government; and critical thinking skills.

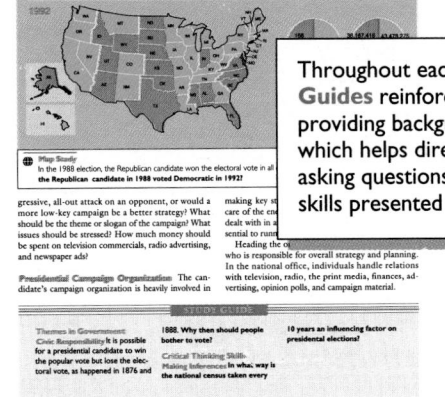

Throughout each section, **Study Guides** reinforce themes and skills by providing background information which helps direct your reading by asking questions about the themes and skills presented in the Section Preview.

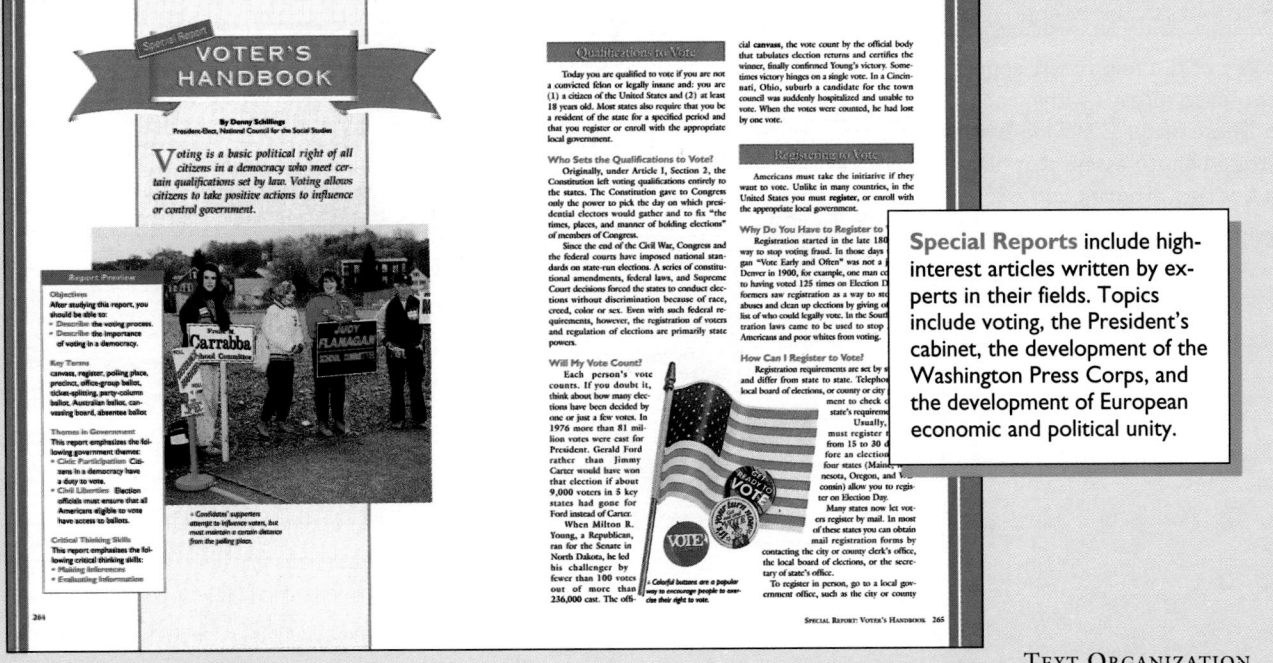

Special Reports include high-interest articles written by experts in their fields. Topics include voting, the President's cabinet, the development of the Washington Press Corps, and the development of European economic and political unity.

Special Features

United States Government: Democracy in Action includes a variety of special features, each designed to enhance your understanding of our democratic system.

Unit Features

Point/Counterpoint features, located at the beginning of each unit, use primary sources to illustrate the debate on certain key constitutional issues.

Images of Government appear as two-page spreads within each unit. These features include lavishly illustrated photo essays that highlight both government and art.

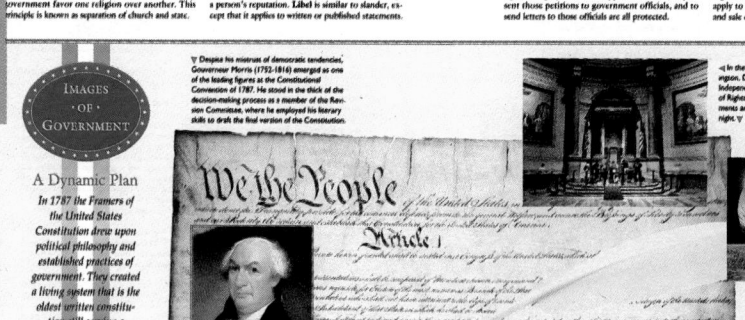

Multicultural Heritage features include 10 full-page analyses focusing on the rich and diverse cultural backgrounds that have contributed so greatly to our nation's heritage.

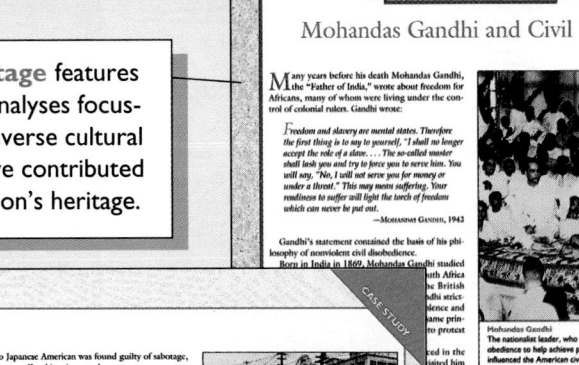

Case Studies appear at the end of each unit. These 10 in-depth studies show the evolution of important constitutional issues. These features will help you see that our Constitution is indeed a vibrant, living document—able to adapt to the changes of a technological society.

Chapter Features

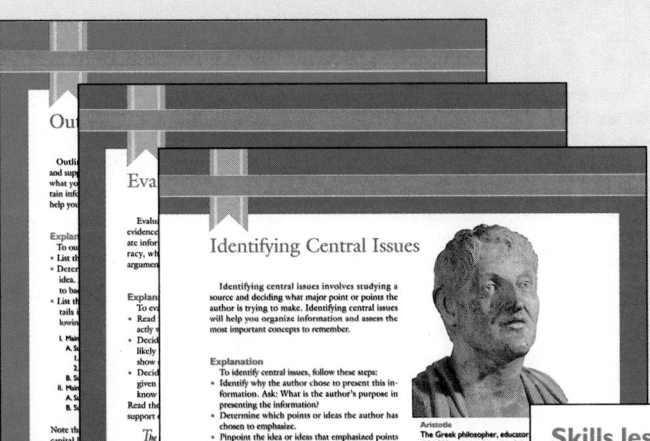

Skills lessons are divided into three strands: Social Studies Skills, Study and Writing Skills, and Critical Thinking Skills. These lessons are designed to help you sharpen your critical thinking, social studies, and reading and writing skills. To reinforce your understanding of each chapter's skill, the Chapter Review provides a follow-up activity.

Focus on Freedom includes a series of 30 key documents that make up part of our rich constitutional heritage.

Personal Perspectives include excerpts of addresses from 30 people from all walks of life. Each address concentrates on the personal aspects of government.

Participating in Government features consist of articles detailing exactly how you can make an impact on our government and what role you can play in preserving our heritage.

Global Connection contains brief discussions linking developments in the United States to world development.

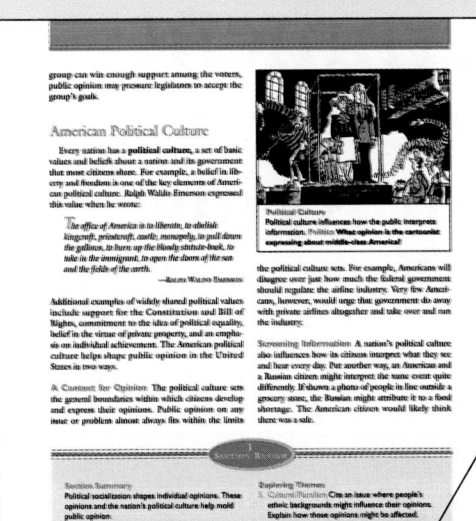

At the end of each section, the **Section Review** provides a Section Summary; a list of questions that cover the key ideas presented in the section under the head Checking for Understanding. Categories under this head include Recalling Facts, Exploring Themes, and Critical Thinking Skills.

At the chapter level, there is a two-page **Chapter Review** that helps you review and synthesize the major facts and concepts in the chapter. In addition, the Linking Past and Present and Investigating Further portions of the Chapter Review help you extend what you have learned in the narrative.

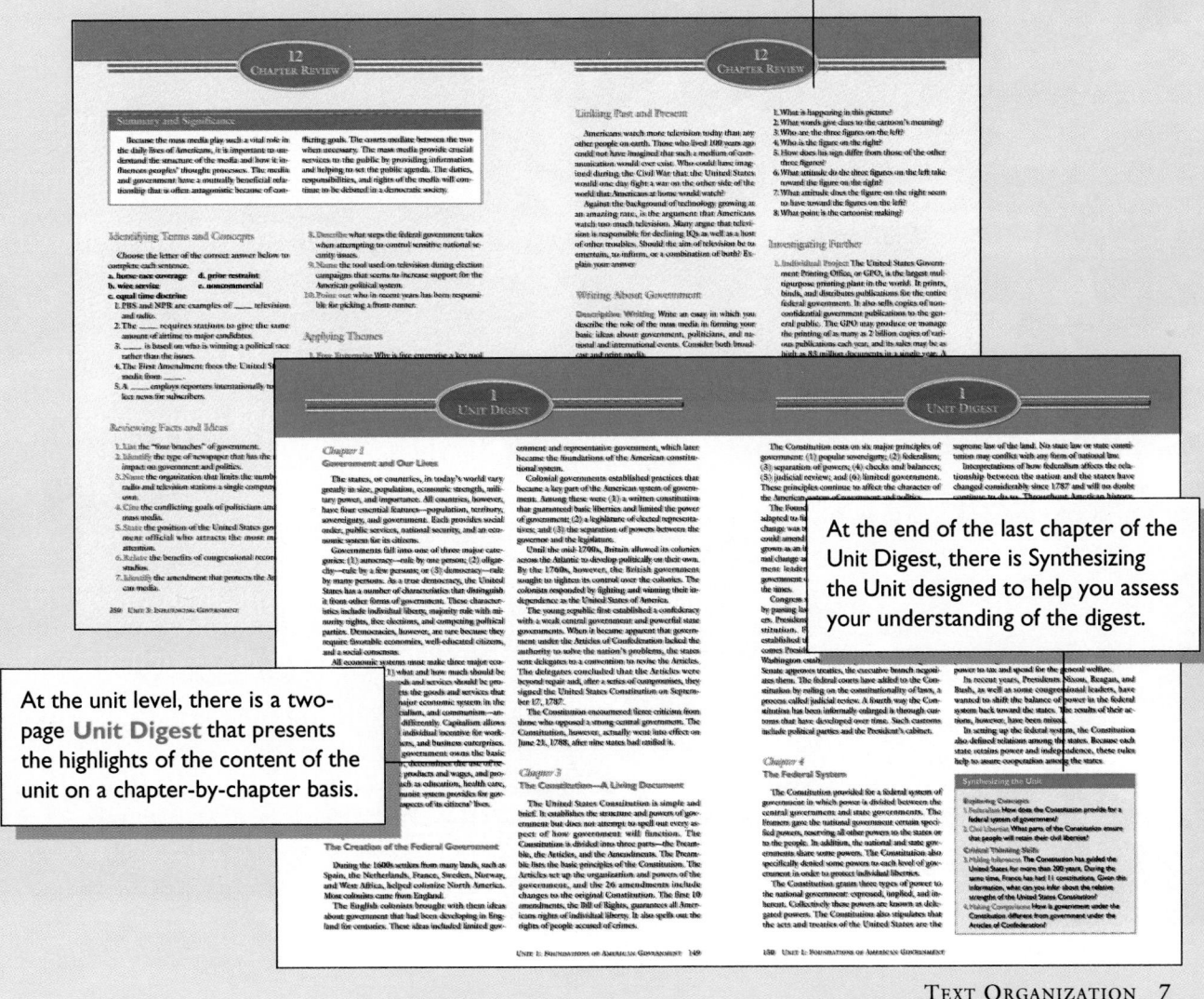

At the unit level, there is a two-page **Unit Digest** that presents the highlights of the content of the unit on a chapter-by-chapter basis.

At the end of the last chapter of the Unit Digest, there is Synthesizing the Unit designed to help you assess your understanding of the digest.

Themes in Government
AND
Critical Thinking Skills

U nited States Government: Democracy in Action emphasizes 15 key themes of government. These themes are designed to help you better understand our democratic institutions and see how the United States Constitution has allowed our government to operate for more than 200 years. These themes also will help you understand the impact that our system of government has had on governments throughout the world. The textbook also emphasizes 20 critical thinking skills designed to help you analyze the information presented.

8

Themes in Government

Each section preview and study guide emphasizes the important government themes in that section. Section and chapter reviews reinforce these themes by asking you to interpret important information. These themes include:

Growth of Democracy

Our democratic system is constantly developing and expanding. This important theme will help you understand how the United States Constitution has helped the government develop to include equal rights and participation for all groups of Americans.

Federalism

The Founders wrote the Constitution shortly after the United States had won independence from Britain. Recently freed from British tyranny, the Americans feared establishing an all-powerful central government. As a result, the Founders set up a government in which the central government shared power with the states—a system known as federalism. Although the central government is supreme under this system, the states retain many powers.

Separation of Powers

To prevent any one part of the central government from seizing total power, the Founders adopted the principle of separation of powers. Under this system, power is divided among three branches of government—legislative, executive, and judicial.

Checks and Balances

Closely related to the theme of separation of powers, the theme of checks and balances outlines specific procedures that each branch may take in order to check the powers of the other branches.

Civil Liberties

The United States has a long history of personal freedoms, unparalleled in the history of the world. *United States Government: Democracy in Action* describes these liberties and shows how they relate to you as Americans.

Civil Rights

As citizens, all Americans are entitled to equal rights. The theme of civil rights explains how the United States government safeguards these rights.

Civic Participation

For a democratic system to survive, its citizens must take an active role in government, a concept known as civic participation. The author emphasizes this important theme throughout the narrative. In addition, Dr. Remy has included a special feature in each chapter highlighting exactly how you can participate in government and describing how your participation does indeed have an impact on government.

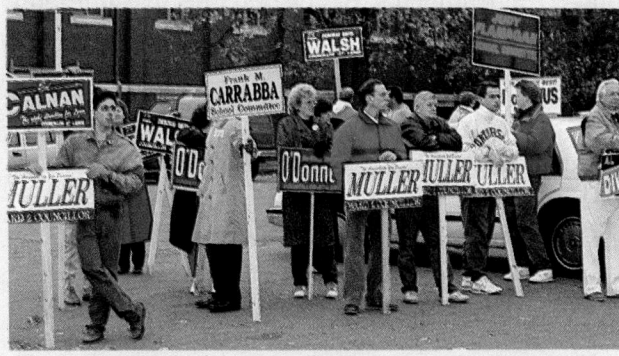

Civic Responsibility

The theme of civic responsibility is closely related to the theme of civic participation. As Americans, you have certain duties, or responsibilities, to fulfill. These duties include voting and knowing about laws and government. The author analyzes these responsibilities throughout the narrative.

Comparative Government

Any study of government would be incomplete without comparisons between the United States and other governments of the world. This textbook includes a special unit devoted to these comparisons. In addition, the narrative includes references to developments in other parts of the world throughout the textbook as well as special features detailing global developments.

9

Global Perspectives

We live in an interdependent world in which actions in one nation often have profound effects on developments in other nations. The theme of global perspectives examines this interdependence and emphasizes it in today's world.

Constitutional Interpretations

The Founders believed that the United States Constitution should outline the framework of the new American government. They realized that the government would undoubtedly have to deal with unforeseen changes. As a result, they wrote the Constitution in language vague enough to give the government the flexibility to deal with these changes.

After almost two centuries, the Constitution, with only 27 amendments, has proved effective at leading the nation through these changes. The theme of constitutional interpretations analyzes how the Constitution has remained a flexible, living document.

Political Processes

The procedures for governing the nation on a daily basis are known as political processes. The author emphasizes this important theme by detailing the organization and workings of the government throughout the textbook. Understanding these underlying principles will help you better understand the operations of the government today.

Public Policy

The course of action a government takes in response to some political issue or problem is called public policy. Throughout the textbook the author emphasizes the development of this important theme, often comparing it to policy during earlier years of the Republic. This comparison reemphasizes how the Constitution has acted as a living, flexible document that has allowed government actions to meet the needs of a changing world.

Free Enterprise

Government and economics are often interrelated. The author has emphasized this point by developing the theme of free enterprise. The United States is one of the world's leading examples of a free enterprise economy. Such an economy is a system in which buyers and sellers in the marketplace make economic decisions with minimal governmental control. The free enterprise system is consistent with the strong history of rights and freedoms in the United States.

Cultural Pluralism

The United States is a nation of immigrants who have contributed elements of their own cultures to American society and government. To help you understand the contributions of many of these groups, the author often discusses them in the narrative. In addition, the feature entitled "A Multicultural Heritage" gives in-depth coverage to many of these contributions that have helped shape American life today.

Critical Thinking Skills

Each section preview, study guide, and section and chapter review includes specific critical thinking skills designed to help you gain an in-depth understanding of American government. In addition, the textbook includes lessons fully developing each of the skills.

These skills, organized under specific skills strands, include:

Clarifying Issues

Identifying Central Issues

Identifying Central Issues involves analyzing a primary or secondary source and putting the author's main idea into your own words.

Understanding Cause and Effect

To understand cause and effect you must decide why an event occurred. A cause is the action or situation that produces an event—the reason. An effect is the result or consequence of an action or a situation.

Making Generalizations

A generalization is a broad statement based on specific details and facts. To make generalizations you will need to analyze information and express your broad conclusions.

Distinguishing Fact From Opinion

To distinguish between facts, which can be proved or disproved, and opinions, which are based on peo-

10

ple's differing values and beliefs, you need first to study the information carefully. Then decide whether the information can be proved or verified. If so, it is a fact. If not, it is an opinion.

Formulating Questions

Asking questions requires that you first determine the information you need and then compose questions designed to produce this information. You need to formulate good questions in order to learn more about a particular topic.

Expressing Problems Clearly

Expressing problems clearly involves studying all the evidence in order to determine what real problems underlie the obvious effects. In addition, you need to understand the consequences of proposed solutions. As you read about specific human actions, you need to analyze these actions to assess what problem they were designed to alleviate. Such analysis will help you understand the action itself. You should ask, "What is the problem?" You should then evaluate the solution and decide what possible new problems the solution might create.

Recognizing Ideologies

An ideology is a set of beliefs that guides a person or group of people. Recognizing a particular ideology will help you understand why a person or a group of people act the way they do. If you know a group's ideology, you know many of its values and assumptions, and you can make fairly reliable predictions about its positions on many issues. Comparing the solutions people with different ideological orientations proposed will help you form your own unique political views.

Evaluating Evidence

Analyzing Information

Analyzing information involves examining a source to determine what the author is trying to say. Citizens must be able to analyze information in order to form responsible opinions.

Evaluating Information

To evaluate information you need to analyze and then decide whether the information is useful as well as valid. In so doing you should determine whether emotion or bias might have swayed the author, thus making the information suspect.

Making Inferences

Making inferences involves going beyond the evidence that is displayed to reach conclusions or new ideas that are implicit. Evidence is the information from which an inference is drawn. A citizen might conclude a candidate has no chance to be elected (the inference) from the results of a pre-election poll (the evidence). You make inferences when you use evidence to reach new ideas, discover meanings that were obscure, or project likely consequences. An inference can be no better than the evidence from which it was drawn. The ability to make inferences supported by evidence is basic to good citizenship.

Making Comparisons

To make comparisons you need to identify the similarities and differences between two or more items. Making comparisons is an important citizenship skill because it helps you choose between alternative candidates or policies.

11

Recognizing Bias

People often think that bias and prejudice are the same. Prejudice is a positive or negative opinion based on ignorance. Bias, however, is nothing more than the attitude of a writer or speaker. To recognize bias you need to determine basic facts in information being presented and decide whether the author has included details that shed a negative or positive light on the facts.

Synthesizing Information

Synthesizing information involves integrating information from two or more sources. To synthesize information you need to describe what you can learn or what new hypotheses you can make by combining information in the sources.

Checking Consistency

Checking consistency includes analyzing two or more sets of data to see whether they follow the same principles. To check consistency, you need to examine each set of data carefully and decide whether the sets are comparable.

Identifying Assumptions

Writers often assume, or take for granted, certain beliefs. You need to identify these assumptions in order to understand exactly what the author is trying to say. To identify assumptions you should read a statement carefully, determine what "missing links" are in the argument, and break down the assumptions on which the statement is based so that you can examine them critically.

Demonstrating Reasoned Judgment

Demonstrating reasoned judgment involves using your own knowledge and experience to evaluate policies or decisions. One important way in which you use this skill as a citizen is to make decisions about how to solve a problem. Often you will have to evaluate a variety of proposed solutions to a given problem. You will then need to decide which you think should be implemented and which among these should be given priority.

Drawing Conclusions

To draw conclusions you need to examine the evidence you have about a topic and use your reason to gain further insight. You also need to state two or three things that seem important about the information. Finally, you will have to decide what inferences you can reasonably make to draw a conclusion that goes beyond the facts.

Predicting Consequences

Each time a person or group chooses among alternatives, there are consequences because these choices set up a chain of results. To predict these consequences reliably you need to define the issue, gather facts and evidence directly related to the issue, and determine potential positive and negative effects of your choice.

Determining Relevance

Determining relevance includes evaluating information to determine what source or sources would be useful if you wanted to learn more about a particular topic. To determine relevance you need to identify the topic about which you wish to learn and sift through information to determine what is useful to your study.

Identifying Alternatives

When you identify alternatives, you search for possible solutions to a well-defined problem, then evaluate each solution in terms of its costs and benefits. To identify alternatives you need to define the problem, determine what particular conditions create this problem, decide what solutions might alleviate the problem, assess the effects that each possible solution might have, and conclude whether any of the proposed solutions would improve conditions.

12

Foundations of American Government

UNIT
1

Chapter 1:
Government and Our Lives

Chapter 2:
The Creation of the Federal Government

Chapter 3:
The Constitution—A Living Document

Chapter 4:
The Federal System

Introduce

Unit Objectives

After studying this unit, students should be able to:
- Describe the major categories of government and explain why governments are established.
- Analyze the political ideas and historic documents that form the foundation of the American system of government.
- Discuss the unique features of the American system of government.

Unit Overview

Unit 1 outlines the legal, historical, and philosophical foundations of the American political system.

Chapter 1 focuses on the nature of government, the forms of government in the modern world, and the relationship between government and economic systems.

Chapter 2 reviews the long heritage of American self-government.

Chapter 3 describes the United States Constitution as a relatively brief, flexible document that has survived for 200 years.

Chapter 4 explains federalism, a framework for government in which powers are divided between national and state governments.

1
UNIT DIGEST

Use the Unit Digest on pages 149–150 to introduce, review, reteach, or condense the information in this unit.

Introducing the Unit

Point out that this unit explains why governments are necessary and discusses how such concepts as *democracy, freedom, liberty,* and *federalism* became the foundation of American government.

Unit Project

Have students work cooperatively or individually to develop an illustrated handbook of the documents on which United States government is based. Suggest that students include such documents as the Magna Carta, Petition of Right, English Bill of Rights, Mayflower Compact, Fundamental Orders of Connecticut, Declaration of Independence, Articles of Confederation, and United States Constitution. Each document should be accompanied by brief historical information and an explanation of its connection to the United States system of government. Have students display their handbooks for the rest of the class to review.

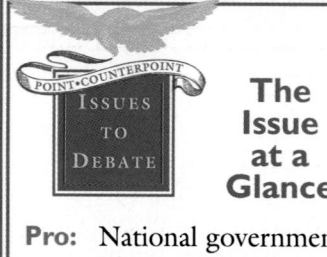

ISSUES
TO
DEBATE

The Issue at a Glance

Pro: National government represents all interests.
Con: National government cannot represent everyone.

Focus

Ask the following question: Should there be any limits on your rights and freedoms? Discuss students' answers. *(Some may contend that rights and freedoms are absolute. Others may recognize that society's needs and the rights of others limit individual freedoms.)*

Tell students that the debate centers on minority rights in a system of majority rule. Have them keep this in mind as they read the debate.

Teach

Guided Practice

Have students describe the kind of government that both Madison and Brutus wanted. *(government by the majority that protected the rights of all people)* Ask them what *minority* means in this reading. *(any group that does not side with the majority)*

Point out that Brutus and Madison each used the nation's diversity to support his arguments. How did Madison believe diversity would protect against majority tyranny? *(The majority will be combinations of minority groups.)* Why did Brutus believe that diversity would prevent government from being democratic? *(The government cannot represent all groups equally.)* Which level of government—local, state, or national—would Brutus trust the most? the least? why? *(local the most and national the least)*

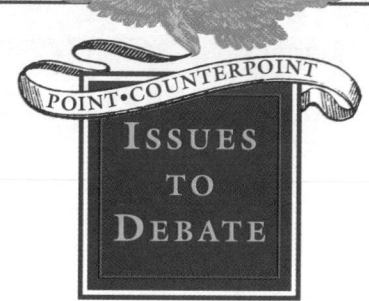

Does Our Constitution Provide for Free Government?

Written more than 200 years ago, the United States Constitution set down the basic framework for a bold new experiment in free government. The Framers of the Constitution wanted this government to be based on the will and the rights of the people living under it.

How well does the Constitution provide for this type of government? The Federalists—those who supported the Constitution, and the Anti-Federalists—those who opposed the Constitution, engaged in a classic debate on this question. Both groups wanted free government based upon majority rule, or government with the consent of the governed. They, however, had very different opinions about how a constitution could achieve such a government. In their debates the Federalists and Anti-Federalists tried to resolve two very important questions. When does majority rule interfere with the rights of minorities and become tyranny? How can a government ensure that it is meeting the needs of all citizens?

Pro

Federalist James Madison believed in majority rule, but he thought that a principal role of the Constitution was to protect minorities and individuals from the tyranny of the majority. He expressed his point of view in *The Federalist*, No.51, in February 1788.

It is of great importance in a republic not only to guard the society against the oppression of its rulers, but to guard one part of the society against the injustice of the other part. Different interests necessarily exist in differ-ent classes of citizens. If a majority be united by a common interest, the rights of the minority will be insecure. There are but two methods of providing against this evil; the one by creating a will in the community independent of the majority—that is, of the society itself; the other, by [including] in the society so many separate descriptions of citizens as will render an unjust combination of a majority of the whole very improbable, if not impracticable. The first method prevails in all governments possessing an hereditary or self-appointed authority [monarchy or dictatorship]. This, at best, is but a precarious security; because a power independent of the society may as well espouse the unjust views of the major as the rightful interests of the minor party, and may possibly be turned against both parties. The second method will be exemplified in the federal republic of the United States. Whilst all authority in it will be derived from and dependent on the society, the society itself will be broken into so many parts, interests, and classes of citizens, that the rights of individuals, or the minority, will be in little danger from interested combinations of the majority. . . . In the extended republic of the United States, and among the great variety of interests, parties, and sects which it embraces, a coalition of a majority of the whole society could seldom take place on any other principles than those of justice and the general good.

—JAMES MADISON, *THE FEDERALIST*, NO. 51, 1788

Con

The Anti-Federalists had a completely different view on the issue. Using the pen name Brutus, one Anti-Federalist (probably Robert Yates of New York) wrote "that a consolidation of this extensive continent under one government [under the Constitution

More About Issues to Debate

Supporters of the Constitution ran well-organized ratification campaigns. The Federalists recruited the best speakers to present their case. In addition, James Madison, Alexander Hamilton, and John Jay wrote a series of widely published essays arguing in favor of ratification. They used political, military, and economic arguments to point out the weaknesses of government under the Articles of Confederation. They also stressed, however, that the power of the new government would be limited by the checks and balances of the Constitution.

The 85 essays were written primarily for New York state, since the Federalists believed the support of this large state was necessary for the new govof 1787] . . . cannot succeed, without a sacrifice of your liberties." He concluded that the Constitution did not emphasize liberty and could never provide for a free government. In October 1787, he wrote:

In every free government, the people must give their assent to the laws by which they are governed. This is the true criterion between a free government and an arbitrary one. The former are ruled by the will of the whole [the people], expressed in any manner they may agree upon; the latter by the will of one, or a few. If the people are to give their assent to the laws, by persons chosen and appointed by them, the manner of the choice and the number chosen must be such, as to possess, be disposed, and consequently qualified to declare the sentiments of the people; for if they do not know, or are not disposed to speak the sentiments of the people, the people do not govern, but the sovereignty is in a few. Now, in a large extended country, it is impossible to have a representation, possessing the sentiments, and of integrity, to declare the minds of the people. . . .
—BRUTUS, 1787

One month later, in November 1787, Brutus wrote:

In . . . a good constitution . . . the power is committed to [representatives with] the same feelings . . . and . . . the same objects as the people [have] . . . who transfer to them their authority. There is no possible way to effect this but by an equal, full and fair representation. . . . For without this it cannot be a free government; let the administration of it be good or ill, it still will be a government, not according to the will of the people, but according to the will of a few. . . .

A farther objection against the feebleness of the representation [in the Constitution of 1787] is that it will not possess the confidence of the people. . . . If then this government [Constitution of 1787] should not derive support from the good will of the people, it must be executed by force, or not executed at all; either case would lead to the total destruction of liberty.
—BRUTUS, 1787

The Debate Continues

The debate over how well the Constitution and the United States government protect the liberties of Americans continues today. Supporters point out that this government offers more protections against injustice than any other government in the world. For example, Americans accused of crimes are guar-

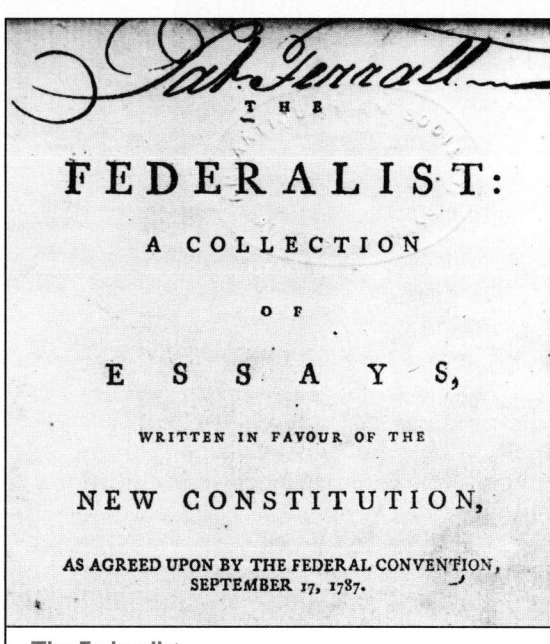

The Federalist
Published in 1787-88, *The Federalist*, a series of essays by Alexander Hamilton, James Madison, and John Jay, exerted a strong influence in the drive to ratify the proposed United States Constitution.

anteed free trials, and many laws protect citizens from discrimination based on race, age, sex, or disability. Critics suggest that the national government has grown so large that it can no longer be concerned with the rights of individuals and minorities.

Examining the Issue

Recalling Facts

1. Identify Madison's attitude toward majority rule.
2. Explain why Brutus opposed the Constitution.

Critical Thinking Skills

3. Identifying Central Issues Why did Madison favor the Constitution?
4. Evaluating Information Why did Brutus think that the United States could not have a free government under the Constitution?

Investigating Further

Find information on the government of the People's Republic of China. Would Brutus or Madison have classified this government as a free government? Why or why not?

Independent Practice

Ask students to identify and copy the sentence in each argument that best summarizes the author's position on the ability of government under the Constitution to protect minority rights. Then have them restate each sentence in their own words. (Madison: *In the extended republic of the United States . . . coalition of the majority of the whole society could seldom take place on any other principles than those of justice and the general good;* Brutus: *Now, in a large extended country, it is impossible . . . to declare the minds of the people.*)

Assess

Have students complete **Examining the Issue**.

Answers

1. He supported it, but not at a cost of minority rights.
2. It could not succeed unless government deprived some people of rights.
3. The federal republic it created protected society against government, and elements in society against one another.
4. There were so many groups in such a large nation that not all would be represented in government.

Close

Ask if conflict between majority rule and minority rights is present today. Ask students to cite examples.

ernment to succeed. Before the vote, Hamilton intimidated upstate New Yorkers by threatening the secession of New York City if the state did not join the new nation. The New York convention ratified the Constitution, but only by a three–vote margin.

Close votes were recorded in other states as well. The Massachusetts ratifying convention adopted

the Constitution by a vote of 187–168; the vote in Virginia was 89–79. The support of these three powerful and populous states, however, was assured.

Chapter Organizer

Objectives	Special Feature Pages	Supplemental Materials
Section 1 The State as the Basic Political Unit *pp. 18–23* 1. Identify the essential features of a state. 2. Distinguish between the unitary system of government and the federal system of government.	Point/Counterpoint: Does Our Constitution Provide for Free Government? pp. 14–15 Global Connection: Interdependence: Multinational Corporations p. 22	Guided Reading Activities Reproducible Lesson Plans Section 1 Quiz Testmaker Chapter Transparencies 1 The Living Constitution SAT Practice Tests
Section 2 How Governments Serve the State *pp. 24–29* 1. Name ways that governments serve the state. 2. Describe the differences between constitutions and constitutional governments.	Focus on Freedom: The English Bill of Rights p. 28	Guided Reading Activities Reproducible Lesson Plans Primary and Secondary Source Readings 1 Section 2 Quiz Testmaker The Living Constitution SAT Practice Tests Writer's Guidebook
Section 3 Different Forms of Government *pp. 30–35* 1. Compare democracy with other forms of government. 2. Explain the relationship between democracy and free enterprise. 3. Understand the dilemma of minority rights in a democracy.	Participating in Government: Student Government p. 31 Critical Thinking Skills: Identifying Central Issues p. 35	Guided Reading Activities Reproducible Lesson Plans Participating in Government 1 Supreme Court Case Studies 17 Section 3 Quiz Skill Reinforcement Activity 1 Testmaker SAT Practice Tests Writer's Guidebook
Section 4 Government and Economic Systems *pp. 36–41* 1. Contrast capitalism, socialism, and communism. 2. Identify the basic economic decisions that confront every society.	Personal Perspectives: Violeta Barrios De Chamorro on Democracy in Nicaragua p. 41	Guided Reading Activities Reproducible Lesson Plans Reteaching Activities 1 Enrichment Activities 1 Section 4 Quiz Chapter 1 Tests Testmaker Limited English Proficiency Activities 1 Audio Cassettes (English and Spanish) SAT Practice Tests Writer's Guidebook

If time does not permit teaching this chapter, assign the Chapter 1 summary in the Unit 1 Digest on pages 149–150.

Key To Ability Levels

Teaching strategies have been coded for varying learning styles and abilities.

L1   Level 1 activities are **basic** activities and should be within the ability range of all students.

L2   Level 2 activities are **average** activities and should be within the ability range of the average to above-average student.

L3   Level 3 activities are **challenging** activities designed for the ability range of above-average students.

LEP   These activities should be within the ability range of **Limited English Proficiency** students.

Multicultural Activities

The United States has often been called a "nation of nations" because of the ethnic and racial diversity of its population. This diversity has not always been considered a blessing. In 1912 Theodore Roosevelt had this to say about the nation's rising tide of immigrants: "The one absolutely certain way of bringing this nation to ruin, of preventing all possibility of its continuing to be a nation . . . would be to permit it to become a tangle of squabbling nationalities . . . each preserving its separate nationality." Review with the class the difference between a state and a nation. Discuss the ways in which such groups as African Americans, Mexican Americans, Native Americans, or Asian Americans resemble nations. Then ask: What has kept the American state from becoming a "tangle of squabbling nationalities" as Theodore Roosevelt feared?

On August 10, 1988, President Ronald Reagan signed into law a bill which gave $20,000 tax-free in reparations to the 60,000 Japanese Americans still alive who had been interned in relocation camps during World War II. A leader in the fight for this bill was Senator Daniel Inouye of Hawaii. He led the drive in 1980 to establish a Commission on Wartime Relocation and Internment of Civilians and worked for its passage for the next 8 years. Interested students might investigate the history of Japanese American internment and the role played by Senator Inouye and his colleague Senator Spark Matsunaga, also of Hawaii, in the passage of this legislation.

Chapter Resources

Readings for the Student

Carter, Gwendolyn M. and John H. Herz. *Government and Politics in the Twentieth Century.* Praeger, 1972.

Hofstadter, Richard. *The American Political Tradition and the Men Who Made It.* Vintage, 1991.

Paine, Thomas. *Common Sense and Other Political Writings.* Bobbs-Merrill, 1953.

Rodee, Carlton C., et. al. *Introduction to Political Science.* McGraw-Hill, 1983.

Readings for the Teacher

Bahmueller, Charles F., ed. *Civitas: A Framework for Civic Education.* Center for Civic Education/National Council for the Social Studies, 1991.

Barry, Christopher J. *Human Nature.* Humanities Press International, 1986.

Falcone, Vincent J. *Great Thinkers, Great Ideas: An Introduction to Western Thought.* North River Press, 1988.

Grimes, Alan P. and Robert Horwitz. *Modern Political Ideologies.* Oxford University Press, 1959.

Tocqueville, Alexis de. *Democracy in America.* Knopf, 1945.

Wetterau, Bruce. *CQ's Desk Reference on American Government,* Congressional Quarterly, 1994.

Multimedia

Videocassettes and Films

American Enterprise Series: Government. Phillips Petroleum Company. (film, 29 minutes)

Colonial America in the 1760s: American History. Social Studies School Service. (v/c, 17 minutes)

Man and the State—Machiavelli on Political Power. BFA Educational Media. (film, 28 minutes)

Software

American Government I. Intellectual Software. (Apple, IBM disk; Apple disk with management facility also available; part of a 5-part set). Students complete a tutorial program focusing on key concepts of American democracy, the American political system, and the Constitution.

The CIA World Factbook. Qanta Press Educational Products Information Exchange Institute, database of U.S. government's almanac of facts and figures for 249 countries. Macintosh 512E, 512K 3.5" disk drive CD-ROM drive.

The United States Constitution: Our Guarantee of Liberty. Thoroughbred Educational Software (SCM Software Systems). (Apple IIe with extended 80-column card [128K], 1 disk drive, color monitor; Apple IIc 128K, color monitor). Students complete a tutorial program covering the Constitution and Preamble, Articles I-VII, and the Bill of Rights.

Introduce

Chapter Overview

Chapter 1 focuses on the nature of government, the forms of government in the modern world, and the relationship between government and economic systems.

Section One clarifies the terms *state, nation,* and *nation-state;* explores the four essential features of a state—population, territory, sovereignty, government—and highlights the features that influence government in the world today.

Section Two explains how government serves the state by maintaining social order, providing public services, national security and common defense, and controlling the economic system.

Section Three explains the major types of government and describes the characteristics of democracy and the special environment necessary for its growth.

Section Four describes the relationship of government and economic systems and compares the characteristics of capitalism, socialism, and communism.

Chapter 1 Themes

Have students read Themes in Government on page 17. Have them indicate the word in each description that they think applies to the United States. Have volunteers present their choices and explain why they selected some words but not others.

Government and Our Lives

CHAPTER

1

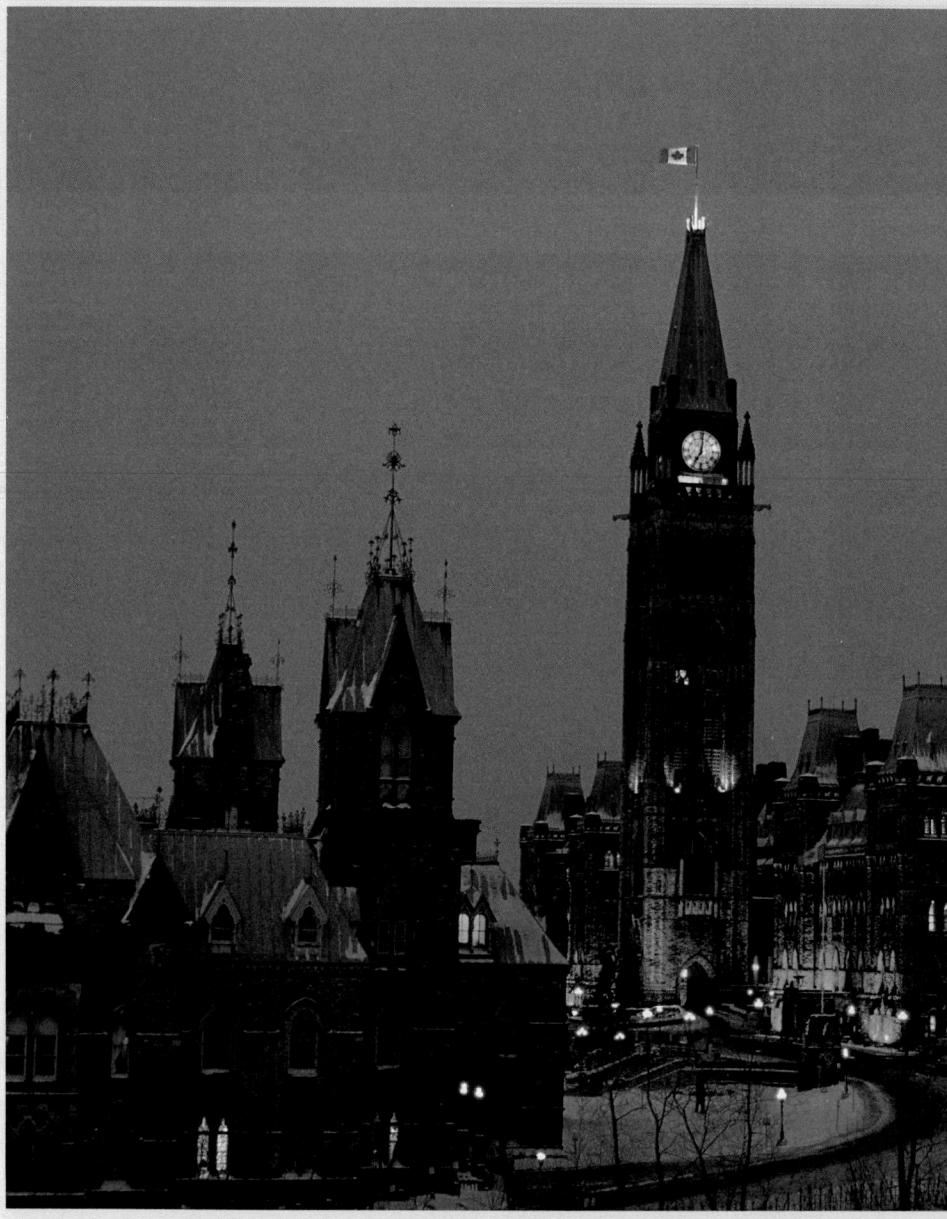

Like the United States, Canada, with its national governing body housed in Parliament in Ottawa, has a federal system of government that divides power between national and state or provincial levels.

16   UNIT 1: FOUNDATIONS OF AMERICAN GOVERNMENT

About the Chapter Opener

Teaching With Illustrations Have students read the caption and examine the photograph on pages 16 and 17. Then ask the following questions: What building in the United States has the same function as the Parliament in Ottawa? *(the Capitol in Washington, D.C., where the United States governing body meets)* Why do you think governments build such impressive structures to house their governing bodies? *(Answers will vary. Students might suggest they reflect the importance of government.)* How does the photo reflect the chapter title, "Government and Our Lives"? *(Answers will vary. Students might suggest that the photo shows some public services that reflect a function of government.)*

Chapter Preview

Overview

The functions of government are to provide social order, security, public services, and economic systems.

Objectives

After studying this chapter, you should be able to:

1. **Describe** the essential characteristics of a state.
2. **Explain** the services that governments provide.
3. **Identify** the main features of a constitutional government.
4. **Compare** capitalism, socialism, and communism.

Themes in Government

This chapter emphasizes the following government themes:

- **Federalism** A federal system of government divides power between the central government and state or provincial governments. Sections 1 and 2.
- **Comparative Government** Governments of the world include autocracies, oligarchies, and democracies. Sections 1 and 3.
- **Political Processes** Constitutions provide outlines for the powers of governments. Section 2.
- **Free Enterprise** Under capitalism people make their own economic choices. Sections 3 and 4.
- **Global Perspectives** The three major economic systems of the world are capitalism, socialism, and communism. Section 4.

Critical Thinking Skills

This chapter emphasizes the following critical thinking skills:

- Making Comparisons
- Understanding Cause and Effect
- Drawing Conclusions
- Predicting Consequences
- Distinguishing Fact From Opinion
- Recognizing Ideologies
- Making Inferences

CHAPTER 1: GOVERNMENT AND OUR LIVES 17

Introducing the Chapter

To preview the chapter, have students leaf through the chapter, noting section heads and subheads, pictures, captions, special features, and charts. Then ask: Why do we have governments? How would our lives be different if there were no governments at all? Write students' answers on the chalkboard.

Chapter Project

Organize the class into four groups. Assign each group one of the four sections in this chapter. Each member of the four groups is to find a newspaper or magazine article that pertains to their assigned section's topic. They should read the article, paste it on a sheet of paper, and write three questions with answers that pertain to the article.

After students complete the assignment, have each group meet to review its collection of articles. Have the group select the article they think best relates to the section topic and present it to the class at the close of chapter study.

Linking Past and Present
Nationalism brings both unity and dissension to world history. Slavic groups wanting their own nation-states caused political unrest in eastern Europe in the 1800s. After World War I, several Slavic peoples were united to form Yugoslavia. In the 1990s, however, nationalism undermined this state, as Croats, Serbs, and other Slavic groups fought among themselves over sovereignty.

Setting the Scene Democracy today has been influenced by the history of Greek city-states, which were established in ancient Greece by 700 B.C. In the city-states all citizens had the right to vote on government policies, hold political office, and serve on a jury. However, women and slaves were not allowed any political rights. Athens became the most successful democracy of ancient Greece. Male citizens had the right to serve permanently in an assembly and every year citizens selected a council of 500 men. This council conducted the daily affairs of business, and issues were voted on by lot.

Focus

Bell Ringer

While attendance is being taken, ask students to read the first two paragraphs of Section 1 to find out what symbol reminded George Alger that he is a citizen of a state.

Motivating Activity

Discuss students' Bell Ringer answers. Ask students to list other reminders that they live in a state. *(money, military service, taxes, laws, and so on)* Then ask students to imagine that each state in the United States is a separate country. How might their lives be different if that were the case? *(Avoid discussion of differing customs and focus on the effects of individual sovereignty.)*

Vocabulary Precheck

Write the vocabulary terms for this section on the chalkboard. Ask students to use those that they know in sentences. **LEP**

CONNECTIONS

Global Perspectives
Throughout history, people have conducted censuses. The Chinese conducted a census as early as 3000 B.C. for tax purposes. In ancient Rome, census takers prepared lists of people and property for purposes of taxation and military service.

The State as the Basic Political Unit

George Alger stepped off the plane in Rome and headed for customs along with his fellow passengers. Suddenly Alger had a sinking feeling in his stomach. His passport, legal proof of his United States citizenship, was not in his coat pocket! He knew that countries require newcomers to prove their citizenship before crossing their borders, and frantically searched his belongings for the precious document. Where was the passport? Was it back home? Had he left it on the plane? At this point it did not really matter. George knew that without his passport he probably could not enter Italy.

Alger's problem illustrates that the basic political unit in the world today is the country. The terms *country* and *state* have basically the same meaning. **State** precisely identifies a political community that occupies a definite territory and has an organized government with the power to make and enforce laws without approval from any higher authority. The name *United States* was first used in 1776 when the thirteen British colonies became states after declaring their independence. At that time each state thought of itself as independent. Even though the states later joined together as one nation under the Constitution, the term *state* has always been used to describe the main political units within the United States.

The more than 160 states, or countries, in today's world vary greatly in size, population, economic strength, military power, and importance. The Republic of Nauru, an island in the Pacific Ocean, for example, is one of the smallest states, with an area of only 8.2 square miles (21 square kilometers). The People's Republic of China, on the other hand, is one of the largest states. More than 1.13 billion people live in an area of nearly 4 million square miles (9.5 million square kilometers).

The term *nation* is often used to describe states like Italy or the United States. Strictly speaking, a **nation** is any sizable group of people who are united by common bonds of race, language, custom, tradition, and, sometimes, religion. Usually the territorial boundaries of modern states and those of nations are the same. For example, the territory of both the nation of France and the state of France coincide. The term *nation-state* is often used to describe such a country.

Not all groups that consider themselves to be nations have their own states. Eastern Canada, for example, includes many French-speaking Catholics who prefer to follow French culture and traditions rather than those of the English-speaking non-Catholic majority of Canada. Some of these people want to break away from Canada and establish their own state. On the other hand, in Africa the populations of some national groups are divided among several African states, a result of artificial borders set up when these states were European colonies. The popular use of the term *nation* fits the standard definition of state. For this reason this text will use the terms *state* and *nation* interchangeably.

Essential Features of the State

The states that make up today's political world share four essential features: population, territory, sovereignty, and government.

SECTION PREVIEW

Objectives
After studying this section, you should be able to:
- Identify the essential features of a state.
- Distinguish between the unitary system and the federal system of government.

Key Terms and Concepts
state, nation, nation-state, consensus, sovereignty, government, unitary system, federal system, developed nation, developing nation

Themes in Government
- Federalism
- Comparative Government

Critical Thinking Skills
- Making Comparisons
- Understanding Cause and Effect

Classroom Resources for Section 1

- Guided Reading Activities
- Reproducible Lesson Plans
- Section 1 Quiz
- Testmaker

- Chapter Transparencies 1
- The Living Constitution
- SAT Practice Tests

United States Acquisitions

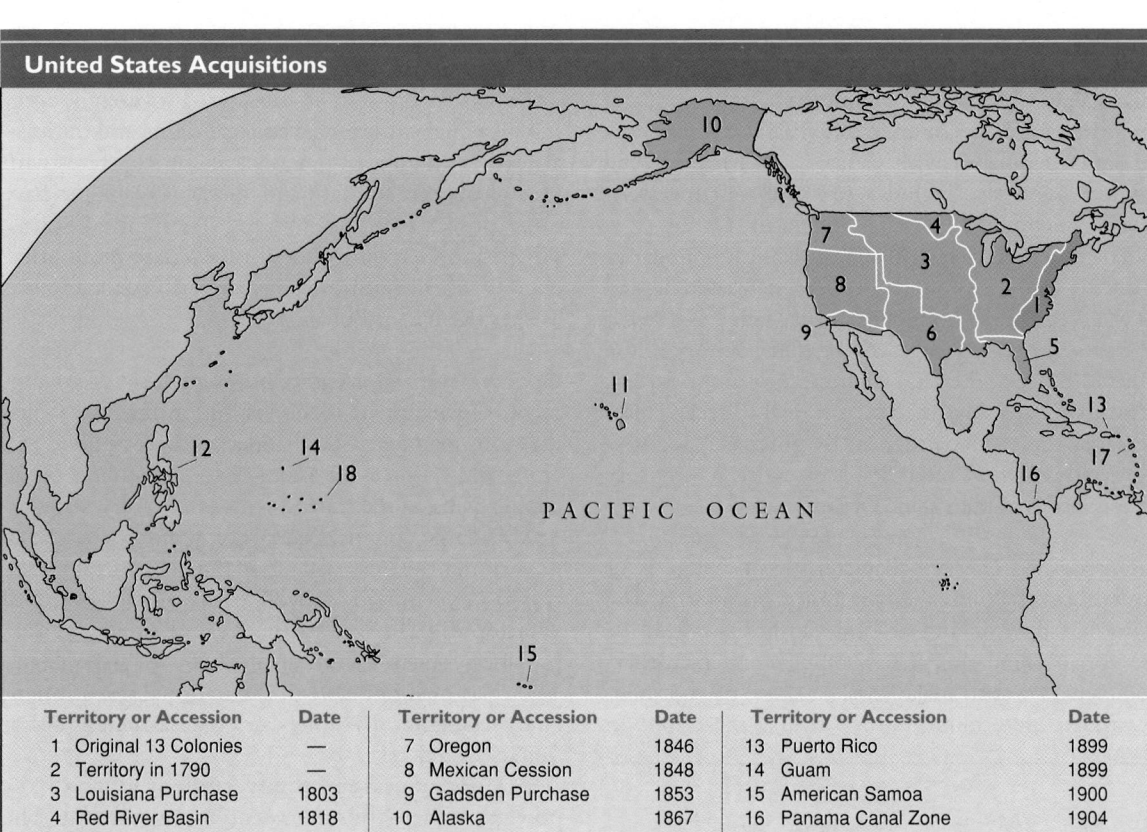

Territory or Accession	Date	Territory or Accession	Date	Territory or Accession	Date
1 Original 13 Colonies	—	7 Oregon	1846	13 Puerto Rico	1899
2 Territory in 1790	—	8 Mexican Cession	1848	14 Guam	1899
3 Louisiana Purchase	1803	9 Gadsden Purchase	1853	15 American Samoa	1900
4 Red River Basin	1818	10 Alaska	1867	16 Panama Canal Zone	1904
5 Florida	1819	11 Hawaii	1898	17 Virgin Islands	1917
6 Texas	1845	12 Philippines	1898	18 Trust Territory of Pacific Islands	1947

Map Study
The Treaty of Paris established the original boundaries of the United States. The Philippines were granted independence in 1946, and by treaty Panama will gain control of the Panama Canal in 2000. **By what three means did the United States acquire its many territories?**

Population The most obvious essential for a state is people. The nature of its population has a direct effect on the stability and political organization of the state. States where the population shares a general political and social **consensus**, or agreement about basic beliefs, have the most stable governments. For example, most Americans share basic beliefs about the value of democratic government.

Another way that population affects the political organization of a state is its mobility. The American population is not only growing, but it is also very mobile. About 18 percent of all Americans change residences each year. A major shift in population has been from the North and East to the South and West. As a result, political power is shifting. Some southern and western states gained representatives in Congress based on the 1990 census, while some states in the North and East lost representation. Some of the population has moved from inner cities to suburban areas, with a similar resulting shift in political power.

STUDY GUIDE

Themes in Government
Comparative Government Explain why many people in eastern Canada want to form their own state.

Critical Thinking Skills
Understanding Cause and Effect How has the shift in population from the northern and eastern regions of the United States affected political power in those areas?

Background

The earliest territorial-based political entities were small bands of people. Later, Egypt and Sumer marked the beginning of civilizations whose people lived in independent cities and city-states. The idea of large states and nation-states developed slowly, however. In some areas such as the Middle East and Far East, long-lasting empires were established. In others, small feudal states, or kingdoms, persisted even into relatively recent times. The first large entities resembling nation-states in the Western world developed in Spain, England, Holland, and France between 1250 and 1500.

Teach

Guided Practice

L1 Developing Vocabulary
Have students locate the terms *state*, *nation*, and *nation-state* in the text and ask someone to read the definition of each word. Write the definitions on the chalkboard and review the characteristics of a state, nation, and nation-state. Have students write sentences using the terms. Ask volunteers to read their sentences. **LEP**

L2 Concept Mapping Develop a concept map that depicts the four essential features of a state. Write the word *state* on the chalkboard and box it. Draw four vertical lines extending downward and ask volunteers to name each of the four features of a state. (*population, territory, sovereignty, government*) Place each feature under one of the vertical lines and box it. Ask students to explain how each feature affects the stability and political organization of a state.

Map Study Answer
By purchase, treaty, and war

STUDY GUIDE

Theme Answer
Many of the people in eastern Canada are French Canadians who want to follow their own traditions rather than those of the English-speaking majority who dominate the government.

Critical Thinking Answer
North and East have lost congressional representation resulting from the shift in population determined by the 1990 census.

L3 Economics Have students work in pairs to list advantages and disadvantages of multinational corporations. Ask several pairs to present their lists and have the remaining students add to the list the pairs create. *(advantages: promotes economic efficiency; prevents war by promoting economic interdependence; disadvantages: concerned with profits not people; produce unfair competition and labor-saving devices that cause unemployment to rise; promote governments that safeguard their interests)*

Independent Practice

L1 Media Have students use magazines or newspapers to find evidence of the four essential features of the state. Students should look for photographs or illustrations to describe population, territory, sovereignty, and government. Below each illustration have students write a sentence describing the nature and quality of the evidence they find.

LEP

Caption Answer
weak industrial base, starvation, disease, and political turmoil

---

STUDY GUIDE

Theme Answer
unitary system gives all key powers to central government; federal system divides power between national, state, and local governments.

Critical Thinking Answer
developed: more educated population, more advanced technology, more resources or access to resources, politically stable; *developing:* not as educated, poor health and living conditions, political instability

---

Territory A state has established boundaries. The total area of the United States is 3,618,770 square miles (9,363,123 square kilometers). Its continental boundaries are the Atlantic and Pacific Oceans and recognized borders with Canada and Mexico. The United States also includes Alaska in northwestern North America and Hawaii in the Pacific Ocean.

The exact location or shape of political boundaries is often a source of conflict between states and has led to wars. Territorial boundaries may change as a result of war, negotiations, or purchase. The territory of the United States, like that of some other states, has grown considerably since the original thirteen states declared their independence. By purchase, negotiation, and war the United States extended its territory to the shores of the Pacific Ocean.

Sovereignty The key characteristic of a state is its **sovereignty**. Political sovereignty means that the state has supreme and absolute authority within its territorial boundaries. It has complete independence, complete power to make laws, to shape foreign policy, and to determine its own course of action. In theory, at least, no state has the right to interfere with the internal affairs of another sovereign state.

Because every state is considered sovereign, every state is equal with respect to legal rights and duties—at least in theory. In practice, of course, states with great economic strength and military capabilities have more power than other states. The United States, Japan, and Germany, therefore, exercise more influence in world politics today than do such states as Turkey, Kenya, or Bolivia.

Government Every state has some form of government. **Government** is the institution through which the state maintains social order, provides public services, and enforces decisions that are binding on all people living in the state.

Most large countries have several different levels of government. These usually include a central or national government, as well as the governments of smaller divisions within the country, such as provinces, states, counties, cities, towns, and villages. The relationship between the national government and the smaller divisions can be described as either unitary or federal.

A **unitary system** of government gives all key powers to the national or central government. The central government creates state, provincial, or other local governments and gives them very limited sovereignty. Great Britain, Italy, and France are examples of unitary government.

A **federal system** of government divides the powers of government between the national government and state or provincial governments. Each level of government has sovereignty in some areas. The United States has a federal system. Other countries with federal systems include Canada, Switzerland, Mexico, Australia, and India.

Growing Pains
In developing countries, the disparities between rich and poor are often apparent. **Economics What obstacles do emerging countries face?**

States in the Twentieth Century

Several features influence the conduct and policies of national governments in the world today. These

---

STUDY GUIDE

Themes in Government
Comparative Government What are the similarities and the differences between a unitary system of government and a federal system?

Critical Thinking Skills
Understanding Cause and Effect What, do you think, are the main factors that cause certain nations to become developed nations?

What do you think are the main factors that cause nations to remain developing nations?

Cooperative Learning Activity

Organize students into Home Teams of three members each. Have Home Teams number off 1, 2, 3. Assign all students with the same number one of the three characteristics of the modern state system that affect the policies of national governments: major inequalities among states, growing interdependence among states, non-state international groups. Ask each group member to find recent magazine or newspaper articles on his or her characteristic. Then have all like-numbered students from each group form an Expert Team, whose task is to summarize the articles on their characteristic. Students should share the findings of their Expert Team with their Home Team.

features help explain the setting in which American government operates.

Major Inequalities Among States Citizens of France can expect to live to the average age of 78 years. However, life expectancy in Bangladesh, a country in Southeast Asia that borders India, is only about 54 years. The world today is full of such contrasts because great inequalities among countries mark the modern state system.

The United States and about 20 other states, such as Japan, Canada, Australia, and France, are **developed nations**. Developed nations have large industries and advanced technology that provide a more comfortable way of life than developing nations do. **Developing nations** are only beginning to develop industrially. More than 100 developing nations have average per capita, or per person, incomes that are a fraction of that of industrialized nations. In the poorest countries, starvation, disease, and political turmoil are a way of life. Many states of Africa south of the Sahara and of Southeast Asia are developing nations. Between these two levels of nations are many newly developed states like Mexico. This group includes states in Eastern Europe, the Middle East, and South America.

Growing Interdependence Among States Although each state is sovereign, it must exist in a world of many nations. Nations today are in constant contact with one another, and they are becoming more and more interdependent.

Interdependence means that nations must interact or depend on one another, especially economically and politically. The countries of North America—Canada, Mexico, and the United States—are developing greater economic, social, and political ties. In 1993 the United States signed the North American Free Trade Agreement that would link North America in a far-reaching trade partnership. Ultimately the agreement, known as NAFTA, would phase out all tariffs on goods produced and sold between the United States, Canada, and Mexico. President Clinton, lobbying hard for the agreement said:

This debate about NAFTA is a debate about whether we will embrace change and create jobs of tomorrow, or try to resist those changes, hoping we can preserve the economic structure of yesterday.
—PRESIDENT BILL CLINTON, 1993

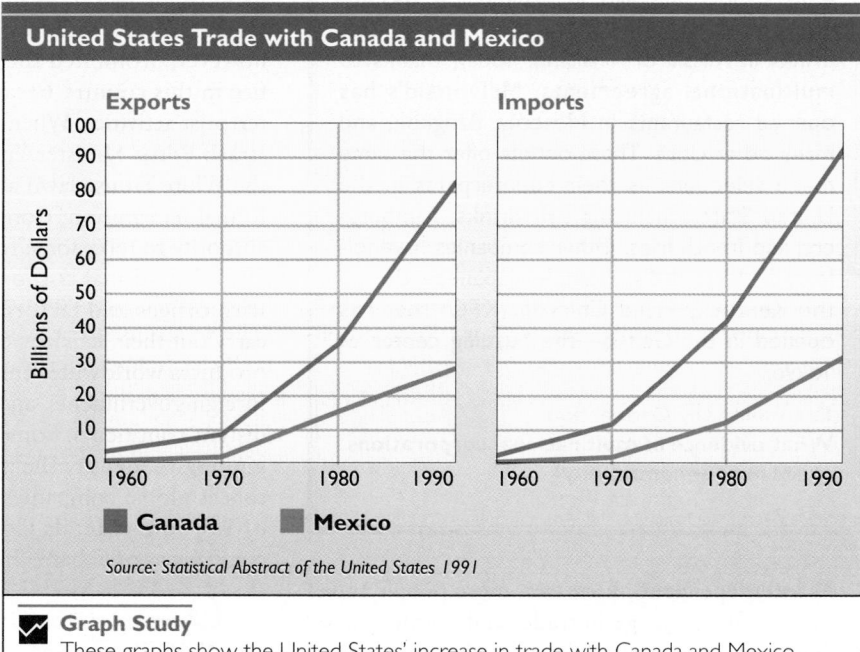

United States Trade with Canada and Mexico

Exports / Imports

Billions of Dollars

■ **Canada** ■ **Mexico**

Source: Statistical Abstract of the United States 1991

☑ Graph Study
These graphs show the United States' increase in trade with Canada and Mexico. **What aspects indicate that there is growing interdependence between the United States and its neighbors?**

Interdependence affects the developing states. Many of the developing states have become very dependent on the developed ones for economic aid, medical supplies, financial investment, assistance to cope with natural disasters, and military aid.

Growing interdependence means that events in one nation affect events throughout the world. In 1990, for example, President Bush sent troops to Saudi Arabia after Iraq invaded neighboring Kuwait. The United States relied on the Middle Eastern states for an important part of its oil supply. As war threatened to break out in the region, people feared that there would be an oil shortage in the United States. As a result, oil prices increased. When the United States and its allies defeated Iraq in the Persian Gulf War in 1991, oil prices dropped to prewar levels.

CHAPTER 1: GOVERNMENT AND OUR LIVES   21

Chapter 1, Section 1
Lesson Plan, pages 18–23

L2 Research Have students do research to create a chart on the standard of living in the United States, Japan, and Mexico. Students should gather statistics such as population density, per capita GNP, literacy rate, life expectancy, infant mortality rate, and access to safe water. One source for this information is *The Statesman's Yearbook.*

L3 Classifying On the chalkboard list horizontally the four essential features of the state: *population, territory, sovereignty,* and *government.* Then list the following political entities on the chalkboard: Singapore, Japan, Navajo Nation, New Mexico, Lithuania, Palestine, Scotland, Colombia, Cuba. Have students research each political entity and determine which ones are states and then list the essential features of statehood lacking in each of the remaining entities.

Graph Study Answer
Imports and exports with both nations are steadily increasing.

━━ CONNECTIONS ━━

Economics
The leading trade partners with the United States in 1992 were Canada, Japan, and Mexico. Canada became the leading trade partner in 1991. In 1992 the largest foreign investors in the United States were the United Kingdom, Japan, and the Netherlands.

Special Needs Strategy

Study Strategy Students with a variety of special learning needs have difficulties understanding how texts are organized. They can understand the text better if they are familiar with the textbook's guides. Have them look through the table of contents and identify the major sections of the book, the sub-sections, and any listed special features such as maps, indices, glossaries, and timelines. Be sure they understand the use of each of these features in general, and specifically those features that will be important to help them learn the material in this chapter.

GLOBAL CONNECTION

In the early 1990s, of the 600 restaurants that McDonald's opened each year, 240 were overseas. About 25 percent of its 11,000 restaurants were outside the United States, but contributed 33 percent of McDonald's sales.
Examining the Connection
Answer: *Students should name local companies that are multinational corporations.*

STUDY GUIDE

Theme Answer
States that give corporations greater flexibility would likely experience greater economic growth.

Critical Thinking Answer
1960: relatively little with either; 1990: trade with both up sharply but more with Canada, imports rising faster than exports with each

---

Assess

Check for Understanding

Have students complete Section 1 Review on page 23.

Meeting Objectives

Each section objective is tested by the Section Review questions that follow it in parentheses.
• Identify the essential features of a state. (2, 6)
• Distinguish between the unitary system of government and the federal system of government. (3, 5)

GLOBAL CONNECTION

Interdependence

Multinational Corporations Multinational corporations that span the globe have revolutionized lifestyles in every corner of the world. Only a short time ago, for example, it was impossible to buy American hamburgers or soft drinks in Russia or Thailand. Today, thanks to multinational agreements, McDonald's has opened restaurants in Moscow, Bangkok, and many other cities. These outlets offer the same menu selections as their counterparts in the United States, including soft drinks, hamburgers, and french fries. Other companies have followed McDonald's example. Japanese throng the Kentucky Fried Chicken (KFC) that has opened in the Gensia—the bustling center of Tokyo.

Examining the Connection
What evidence of multinational corporations exists in your community?

As interdependence increases, more people travel between states, engage in trade, and communicate with one another. United States trade figures illustrate this growing interdependence. In 1970 United States exports of goods and services were more than $62 billion, while imports were nearly $60 billion. By 1990 United States yearly exports climbed to more than $630 billion and imports passed the $666 billion mark. An increase in international communications more than matched this huge increase in trade. Fiber optic telephone cable enabled Americans to exceed a tenfold increase in overseas telephone contacts between 1977 and the early 1990s. Satellite television has connected people of every continent.

Non-State International Groups Today's world also contains some groups that are not states but that play an important role in international politics. These non-state groups fall into three categories: (1) political movements such as national liberation organizations; (2) multinational corporations; and (3) international organizations. Non-state groups play major roles in international affairs because they impact policies and decisions of the diverse states of the world.

The Palestine Liberation Organization (PLO) is a national liberation organization that maintains diplomatic relations with many states. The United States, however, prohibited the PLO from operating an office in this country because PLO agents engaged in terrorist activities. When PLO leader Yasir Arafat and Israeli Prime Minister Yitzhak Rabin shook hands on the White House lawn after signing an agreement of formal recognition, Congress gave President Clinton authority to relax some restrictions on the PLO.

Multinational corporations are huge companies with offices and factories in many countries. They carry out their activities on a global scale, selling their products worldwide, entering into agreements with foreign governments, and developing the resources of distant continents. Some business executives are beginning to identify the major international competitors as global companies. Richard Holder, President of Reynolds Metals Company identified a global company as one that

Operates as a worldwide, integrated system in which all operations, wherever they may be, are interdependent in terms of operations and strategies. Every decision . . . is considered in the light of a world-wide system.
—RICHARD HOLDER, speech to the Utility Purchasing Management Group, Chicago, Illinois, October 2, 1989

General Motors, American Telephone and Telegraph, Unilever, Nabisco, British Petroleum, Royal Dutch Shell, Mitsubishi, and Sony are examples of such global corporations.

STUDY GUIDE

Themes in Government
Federalism Multinational corporations that are headquartered in the United States receive their corporate charters from individual states. Some states permit a more flexible corporate structure. **How would this fact affect economic growth?**

Critical Thinking Skills
Making Comparisons Using the graph on page 21, compare international trade between the United States and Canada and between the United States and Mexico in 1960 and 1990.

Critical Thinking Activity

Understanding Cause and Effect Have students write a speech to present before the United Nations. Ask them to assume that they are an ambassador from a developing country. Have students explain in their speeches the positive and negative effects that global interdependence has had on the people in their nation. Some effects may involve multinational corporations, trade agreements, economic aid, international communications, and changes in culture and living standards.

These organizations have attained worldwide economic importance. For example, the largest 500 multinational corporations control as much as 80 percent of the world's productive capacity and affect the employment of more than 20 percent of the world's entire labor force. In one year General Motors had total annual sales that exceeded the economic output of 130 of the world's independent political states. Multinational corporations control an estimated 55 percent of the manufacturing in Canada. In recent years multinational corporations based in Western Europe and Japan have increased their holdings greatly in United States industry.

Because multinational corporations are so large, their decisions about such matters as where to open and close plants can greatly influence the economy and political stability of many states. Such corporations may become directly involved in the internal politics of a state. For example, in the early 1970s the International Telephone and Telegraph Company (ITT) was accused of promoting a violent revolution in Chile. At the time Salvador Allende, who had been popularly elected, headed the government of Chile. Rumors indicated that the International Telephone and Telegraph Company helped foment a revolution after Allende and the socialist government seized ITT's operations in Chile.

Finally, the modern world includes many international organizations. These groups range from the United Nations (UN) to more specialized organizations such as the International Sugar Council and the Universal Postal Union. These organizations undertake a wide variety of tasks, often to serve the needs

Customers on All Continents
Today's multinational corporations conduct business around the corner and around the world.
Economics How can global companies affect foreign governments?

of member states. The World Meteorological Organization, for example, facilitates the exchange of weather information among states. In summary, while states remain the basic political units in the modern world, other important groups affect the health and well-being of the international community.

Caption Answer
Their decisions on where to invest and open or close factories can influence a nation's economic well-being.

Evaluate

📁 Section 1 Quiz

🔲 Testmaker

Reteach

🔷 Display transparency 1 from the *Chapter Transparencies* in the Teacher's Classroom Resources and use the accompanying teaching strategy and student activity to reteach the essential features of a state.

Enrich

Have students research a multinational corporation to investigate the location of the headquarters, the numbers and locations of offices and factories, and the total annual sales. A source for this is *Everybody's Business: A Field Guide to the 400 Leading Companies in America* by Milton Moskowitz.

Close

Ask students how the following non-state international groups might affect international politics: IBM, Red Cross, Amnesty International, Greenpeace, OPEC.

---

1 — SECTION REVIEW

Section Summary
A state is a basic political unit whose government has sovereignty over the people living within its territorial boundaries.

Checking For Understanding
Recalling Facts
1. Define state, nation, nation-state, consensus, sovereignty, government, unitary system, federal system, developed nation, developing nation.
2. Name the four essential features of a state.
3. Explain sovereignty in a unitary system of government.
4. Describe three non-state groups that play important roles in international politics.

Exploring Themes
5. Federalism How is political sovereignty shared in a federal system of government?
6. Comparative Government What are some essential features of a state that are not features of national liberation organizations or multinational corporations?

Critical Thinking Skills
7. Making Comparisons How may the large difference in life expectancies in Bangladesh and France reflect living conditions in those countries?
8. Understanding Cause and Effect What trends have led to the great increase in the number of multinational corporations in recent years?

Section 1 Review Answers

1. Definitions of terms appear on pages indicated: **state,** 18; **nation,** 18; **nation-state,** 18; **consensus,** 19; **sovereignty,** 20; **government,** 20; **unitary system,** 20; **federal system,** 20; **developed nation,** 21; **developing nation,** 21
2. population, territory, sovereignty, government
3. Central government has nearly unlimited sovereignty;

state and local governments have only the powers granted by central government.
4. political movements, multinational corporations, and international organizations
5. Central government has sovereignty in some matters; state and local governments share sovereignty in other areas.
6. National liberation organizations have no recognizable national boundaries; multinational corporations have lands

scattered inside boundaries of other states and limited sovereignty over employees.
7. Answers should indicate that the quality of life in Bangladesh is poorer than in France.
8. mergers and consolidations, increased world trade, locating where labor costs less, growing competitiveness of Western European and Japanese companies

Focus

Bell Ringer

While attendance is being taken, have students write an answer to the following question:

What do you think is the purpose of government? *(maintain order, provide services and security, provide and control economic system)*

Motivating Activity

Discuss students' Bell Ringer answers and make a class list on the chalkboard. Then ask students how they acquired their ideas about the purpose of government. *(family, school, media)* Tell students they will learn about the purposes of government and the relationship of politics and government in this section.

Vocabulary Precheck

Call on students to read aloud the definitions of the terms and concepts from the Glossary. Then have volunteers use each term in a sentence. **LEP**

Chart Study Answer
Local governments affect people most directly via police, fire departments, and schools.

CONNECTIONS

Health
U.S. Government regulation extends even to hamburgers. Buns must contain certain nutrients and patties must be less than 30 percent fat.

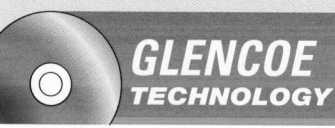

GLENCOE TECHNOLOGY

Focus on Government
Video 2
**Lecture Launcher:
Government and Our Lives**
Running Time: 3:43
Videodisc 1, Chap. 2
VHS Tape 1, Begins 5:04

SECTION 2
How Governments Serve the State

Without some form of government, no state or other large group of people could exist for very long. When the United States broke away from Great Britain, each state provided a government for its citizens. The Articles of Confederation failed to provide the essential government powers for a large nation and had to be replaced with the Constitution. Today, the United States has more than 83,000 governments at several different levels—local, state, and national. What purposes do these governments serve? What is the relationship between government and politics? What role do constitutions play in government?

The Purposes of Government

Governments serve several major purposes for the state: (1) to maintain social order; (2) to provide public services; (3) to provide for national security and a common defense; and (4) to provide for and control the economic system. In carrying out these tasks, governments must make decisions that are binding on all citizens of the state. Government has the authority to require all individuals to obey these decisions and the power to punish those who do not obey them.

Maintaining Social Order A question that has challenged historians and philosophers for centuries is: How did government originate? One significant theory about the origin of government is the social contract. Thomas Hobbes and John Locke in England and Jean Jacques Rousseau in France developed this idea in the seventeenth and eighteenth centuries.

Number of Government Units, by Type	
US Government	1
State Governments	50
Local Governments	86,692
County	3,043
Municipal	19,296
Township and town	16,666
School district	14,566
Special district	33,121
Total	**86,743**

Source: Statistical Abstract of the United States, 1993

✓ **Chart Study**
The federal system has many levels of government.
By which level are most citizens affected?

The theory says that the government began when people united and gave the state the power to provide safety and order. John Locke, writing in *Two Treatises of Government* in 1690, explained:

> *M*en being, as has been said, by Nature, all free, equal and independent, no one can be put out of this Estate, and subjected to the Political Power of another, without his own Consent. The only way whereby any one divests himself of his Natural Liberty, and puts on the bonds of Civil Society is by agreeing with other Men to joyn and unite into a Community. . . .
>
> —John Locke, *Two Treatises of Government*, 1690

SECTION PREVIEW

Objectives
After studying this section, you should be able to:
- Name ways that governments serve the state.
- Describe the differences be-

tween constitutions and constitutional governments.

Key Terms and Concepts
politics, constitution, constitutional law

Themes in Government
- Political Processes
- Federalism

Critical Thinking Skills
- Drawing Conclusions
- Predicting Consequences

24 Unit 1: Foundations Of American Government

Classroom Resources for Section 2

📁 Guided Reading Activities
📁 Reproducible Lesson Plans
📁 Primary and Secondary Source Readings 1
📁 Section 2 Quiz

✦ Testmaker
The Living Constitution
SAT Practice Tests
Writer's Guidebook

beings—needing the companionship of other people. People need government to maintain social order because they have not yet discovered a way to live in groups without conflict. Two people may argue over the boundary line between their properties. Members of a community may disagree about what is best for the group. In any group, some members may try to take unfair advantage of others. Conflict seems to be an inescapable part of group life. Governments provide ways of resolving conflicts among group members, helping to maintain social order.

Governments have the power to make and enforce laws. Governments can require people to do things they might not do voluntarily, such as pay taxes or serve in the army. Governments also provide structures such as courts to help people resolve disagreements in an orderly manner. Without government, civilized life would not be possible. An effective government allows citizens to plan for the future, get an education, raise a family, and live orderly lives.

Providing Public Services Abraham Lincoln said:

> *The legitimate object of government is to do for a community of people whatever they need to have done but cannot do at all, or cannot so well do for themselves in their separate and individual capacities. But in all that people can individually do for themselves, government ought not to interfere.*
> —ABRAHAM LINCOLN, 1854

Lincoln meant that one of the important purposes of government is to provide essential services that make community life possible and promote the general welfare. Governments undertake projects, such as building sewer systems, that individuals could not or would not do on their own. Governments build and operate dams, roads and expressways, mass transit systems, public parks, and many other facilities.

Governments also provide an essential service by making and enforcing laws that promote public

On the Public Health Watch
Some foods are subject to inspection by both state and federal agencies. **Economics** **In what ways do federal public health agencies affect your life?**

health and safety. Government inspectors check meat and fresh produce to prevent the sale of spoiled food. Members of a city fire department check buildings for fire hazards. State legislators pass laws that require people to pass a driving test.

Providing National Security A third task of government is to protect the people against the threat of attack by other states or from internal subversion. Protecting its national security is a major concern of each sovereign state. In today's world of nuclear weapons, spy satellites, international terrorists, and huge armies, the job of providing for the defense and security of the state is a complex task.

Guided Practice

L1 **Outlining** Write the incomplete outline of Section 2 below on the chalkboard.

How Governments Serve States
  1. Purposes
    A.
    B.
    C.
    D.
  2. Relationship Between Government/Politics
    A.
    B.
  3. Constitutions and Government
    A.
    B.
    C.

Have students complete the outline by paraphrasing the section subheadings and using them as major entries. Have volunteers write their outlines on the chalkboard. Make any necessary changes. **LEP**

Caption Answer
They help to ensure that, for example, the medicines are effective and that food is healthful.

Background

The Aztec Indians of Mexico and Central America developed a strong central government. An emperor headed the government, army, and religion. Clan leaders helped the emperor collect taxes, keep the peace, and prepare the army for war. The Inca civilization of South America also was led by a powerful emperor whose duties included expanding the empire, enforcing religious customs, and providing for the well-being of everyone in the empire. Most Inca men had to work on government projects, serve in the army, or work in mines. Inca women had to make cloth to give to the government.

a common defense are high—almost $300 billion each year. This represents about one-fourth of all expenditures by the national government. Because of relaxed tensions with the former Soviet Union, the United States began to marginally reduce its defense budget in 1991.

In addition to protecting the nation from attack, government handles the state's normal relations with other nations. The United States Constitution gives our national government a monopoly over our nation's dealings with foreign countries. Thus, for example, our national government has the exclusive power to make treaties with other nations. Some state governments in the United States maintain informal relations with foreign governments for trade and cultural purposes. The national government, however, has the power to limit these arrangements.

Making Economic Decisions Governments pass the laws that provide and control the economic environments for the nation. This function could be as limited as simply providing a national currency, or it could be as extensive as controlling every individual's economic decisions.

Governments also may make choices that distribute benefits and public services among citizens. For example, the government can make payments to farmers who raise certain crops or allow tax advantages to certain industries. The government's decision to build a veterans' hospital in a certain town benefits some of the people and not others.

Finally, governments make decisions that define a people's goals and the methods used to attain them. Governments usually try to stimulate economic growth and stability through controlling inflation, encouraging trade, and regulating the development of natural resources.

Politics and Government

The effort to control or influence the conduct and policies of government is called **politics**. One of the issues that concerned the Framers of the United States Constitution was the possibility that political

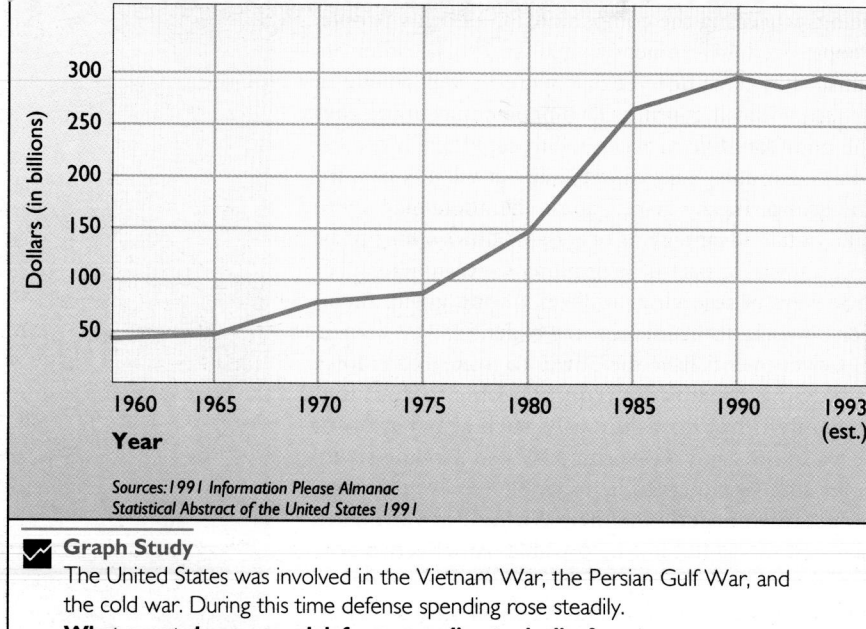

Dollars (in billions)

300
250
200
150
100
50

1960 1965 1970 1975 1980 1985 1990 1993 (est.)
Year

Sources: 1991 Information Please Almanac
Statistical Abstract of the United States 1991

Graph Study
The United States was involved in the Vietnam War, the Persian Gulf War, and the cold war. During this time defense spending rose steadily.
What events have caused defense spending to decline?

STUDY GUIDE

Themes in Government
Federalism Because the national and state governments derive their powers from the Constitution, each state is able to make many of its own decisions within broad areas. **Why does the national government have the power to limit informal relations between states and foreign governments?**

Critical Thinking Skills
Predicting Consequences Providing for national security is the responsibility of the central government in the United States. **How might immediate and large-scale cuts in defense spending have a negative effect on the nation's economy?**

struggles would hinder the launching of the new government. James Madison explained his concerns in *The Federalist*:

Among the numerous advantages promised by a well-constructed Union. . .[is] its tendency to break and control the violence of faction. . . . By a faction, I understand a number of citizens . . . who are united and actuated [moved] by some common impulse of passion, or of interest, adverse to the rights of other citizens, or to the permanent and aggregate interests of the community. . . .

—JAMES MADISON, *THE FEDERALIST*, No. 10, 1787

The Constitution did not prevent the development of politics because politics and government are closely related. A major political struggle developed over the ratification of the Constitution itself.

People are taking part in politics when they join a citizens' group protesting higher taxes or when they meet with the mayor to ask the city to repave the streets in their neighborhood. Legislators are acting politically when they vote to have government buildings constructed in the districts they represent.

Seeking Government Benefits Politics arises because people realize that government has the potential to influence their lives in many ways. Different people make different demands on government. Construction workers may want government to support the building of new highways to create jobs. Conservationists may want the government to spend its money on mass transit and public parks instead. Still other people, who favor lower taxes, may want neither the new highways nor more public parks.

In a large, diverse nation like the United States, there is a continual struggle over what benefits and services government should provide, how much they should cost, and who should pay for them. Politics, as one political scientist put it, is the struggle over who gets what, how, when, and why. Through politics, individuals and groups seek to maximize the benefits they get from government while they try to reduce

Making Their Voice Heard
Special interest groups often take to the streets to voice their opinions. **Politics In what ways can demonstrations affect the political process?**

the costs of these benefits. Through politics, people also seek to use government to turn their values and beliefs into public policy. One group, for example, tries to influence government to ban smoking in public places. Other people pressure government not to restrict smoking in any way.

Importance of Politics Through politics, conflicts in society are managed. As people seek rewards and benefits, politics provides a peaceful way for them to compete with one other. Some people equate politics with bribery or corruption. This misuse of politics should not obscure the value of a political system. The outcomes of politics—the struggle to control government—affect such key matters as the quality of air and water, economic conditions, peace and war, and the extent of citizens' rights and freedoms.

Constitutions and Government

A **constitution** is a plan that provides the rules for government. A constitution serves several major purposes. (1) It sets out ideals that the people bound by the constitution believe in and share. (2) It establishes the basic structure of government and defines the

STUDY GUIDE

Themes in Government
Political Processes People with similar opinions on an issue sometimes form special-interest groups to influence government. These groups support candidates and legislation that agree with their political agenda. **What other actions do you think an interest group could take to influence the political process?**

Critical Thinking Skills
Predicting Consequences What do you think might happen if the United States Congress decided to ignore the political pressures of all citizen's groups?

CHAPTER 1: GOVERNMENT AND OUR LIVES   27

Independent Practice

L1 Journalism Pair students and tell them their task is to prepare a booklet designed to explain the four purposes of government to a sixth-grade class. Students should write each purpose at the top of a separate sheet of paper, provide several examples of each purpose, and add illustrations from newspapers and magazines that picture the purpose. **LEP**

L2 Mathematics Have students select and investigate a particular benefit the federal government supplies—national defense, environmental protection, agricultural aid to farmers, and so on. Ask students to research the costs of the benefits over the last ten-year period. Have them prepare a line graph using the figures they find and make several generalizations based on this information.

Caption Answer
They affect legislative and funding processes and voting.

STUDY GUIDE

Theme Answer
stage marches or other events to make people aware of issues, sponsor letter-writing campaigns, talk to legislators and encourage others to do the same

Critical Thinking Answer
Interest groups would be frustrated and determined to defeat members of Congress that ignored their input. These groups would support challengers rather than incumbents in elections.

Special Needs Strategy

Study Strategy Many students with learning disabilities have trouble using an index. The variety of type styles, abbreviations, and arrangement of information by both categories and names are sometimes difficult for these students to use effectively.

Walk students through the index showing them how to locate names, terms, illustrations, maps, and other features. Provide practice activities by asking students to look for various topics in this section in the index.

Focus on Freedom

Ask students how the English Bill of Rights guarded against absolute rule. (*The ruler would be subject to laws; the ruler could not pass laws, impose taxes, or maintain armies without consent of Parliament.*)

Answers

1. raised taxes without consent of Parliament
2. excessive bail required, excessive fines imposed, and illegal and cruel punishments inflicted
3. that quartering soldiers in time of peace was illegal, excessive bail could not be required, nor excessive fines imposed, nor cruel or unusual punishments inflicted

Assess

Check for Understanding

Have students complete Section 2 Review on page 29.

Meeting Objectives

Each section objective is tested by the Section Review questions that follow it in parentheses.
• Name ways that governments serve the state. (2, 3, 5, 7)
• Describe the differences between constitutions and constitutional governments. (3, 4, 5, 8)

Evaluate

📁 Section 2 Quiz

⬛ Testmaker

---

government's powers and duties. (3) It provides the supreme law for the country. Constitutions provide rules that shape the actions of government and politics, much as the rules of basketball define the action in a basketball game.

Constitutions may be written or unwritten. In most modern states, constitutions are written. The United States Constitution, drawn up in 1787, is the oldest written constitution still serving a nation today. Other nations with written constitutions include France, Kenya, India, Italy, and Switzerland. Great Britain, on the other hand, has an unwritten constitution based on hundreds of years of legislative acts, court decisions, and customs.

All governments have a constitution in the sense that they have some plan for organizing and operating the government. In this sense the People's Republic of China has a constitution. The term *constitutional government*, however, has a special meaning. It refers to a government in which a constitution has authority to place clearly recognized limits on the powers of those who govern. Thus, constitutional government is *limited* government. Despite the existence of a written constitution, the People's Re-

---

Focus on Freedom

THE ENGLISH BILL OF RIGHTS

The Act of Succession of 1689, after the overthrow of King James II, is also known as the English Bill of Rights because it incorporated into law the principles of representative government and the rights of subjects.

Whereas the late King James the Second, by the assistance of divers [diverse] evil counsellors, judges and ministers employed by him, did endeavor to subvert and extirpate [destroy] the Protestant religion and the laws and liberties of this kingdom;

By assuming and exercising a power of dispensing with and suspending of laws and the execution of laws without consent of Parliament; . . .

By levying money for and to the use of the Crown by pretence of prerogative for other time and in other manner than the same was granted by Parliament;

By raising and keeping a standing army within this kingdom in time of peace without consent of Parliament, and quartering soldiers contrary to law; . . .

By violating the freedom of election of members to serve in Parliament; . . .

And excessive bail hath been required of persons committed in criminal cases to elude the benefit of the laws made for the liberty of the subjects;

And excessive fines have been imposed; And illegal and cruel punishments inflicted; . . .

All which are utterly and directly contrary to the known laws and statutes and freedom of this realm; . . .

And thereupon the said Lords Spiritual and Temporal and Commons . . . declare . . .

That the pretended power of dispensing with laws or the execution of laws by regal authority, as it hath been assumed and exercised of late, is illegal; . . .

That levying money for or to the use of the Crown by pretence or prerogative, without grant of Parliament, for longer time, or in other manner than the same is or shall be granted, is illegal;

That it is the right of subjects to petition the king, and all commitments and prosecutions for such petitioning are illegal . . .

That excessive bail ought not to be required, nor excessive fines imposed, nor cruel and unusual punishments inflicted.

—From An Act declaring the Rights and Liberties of the Subject, and settling the Succession of the Crown, 1689

Examining the Document

Reviewing Facts
1. Explain the principle of "levying money" or raising taxes that James violated.
2. Describe how people accused of crimes had been deprived of fair treatment.

Critical Thinking Skills
3. Making Comparisons What principles of the English Bill of Rights became a part of the American Bill of Rights?

Critical Thinking Activity

Recognizing Ideologies Read the following two statements to the class: The two-party political system in the United States has outlived its usefulness. The two-party political system helps keep the government of the United States strong. Ask students which statement they believe is true. Let them discuss reasons for their choices.

public of China does not have constitutional government. In that country, there are few limits on the power of the government.

Constitutions themselves are important but incomplete guides to how a country is actually governed. They are incomplete for two reasons. First, no written constitution by itself can possibly spell out all the laws, customs, and ideas that grow up around the document itself. In the United States, for example, until Franklin D. Roosevelt was elected President four times, it was custom, rather than law, that no person should be elected President more than twice. Only when the Twenty-second Amendment went into effect was a President limited by law to two elected terms.

Second, a constitution does not always reflect the actual practice of government in a country. The People's Republic of China has a written constitution filled with statements about the basic rights, freedoms, and duties of citizens. Yet, for years the Chinese government has maintained an extensive police force to spy on Chinese citizens and punish those whose ideas are not acceptable to the state. Although the government relaxed some restrictions in the late 1980s, authorities brutally crushed a pro-democracy movement in 1989.

A Statement of Goals Most constitutions contain a statement that sets forth the goals and purposes to be served by the government. This statement is usually called the preamble. The Preamble to the United States Constitution states the major goals of American government:

We the people of the United States, in Order to form a more perfect Union, establish Justice, insure domestic Tranquility, provide for the common defence, promote the general Welfare, and secure the Blessings of Liberty to ourselves and our Posterity, do ordain and establish this Constitution for the United States of America.
— PREAMBLE TO THE CONSTITUTION, 1787

A Framework for Government The main body of a constitution sets out the plan for government. In federal states, such as the United States, the constitution also describes the relationship between the national government and state and local governments. Most written constitutions also describe the procedure for amending or changing the constitution.

The main body of a constitution is usually divided into parts called sections and articles. The United States Constitution has 7 articles containing a total of 24 sections. The French constitution has 92 articles grouped under 15 titles. The Indian constitution, the longest in the world, consists of hundreds of articles.

The Highest Law Constitutions provide the supreme law for states. A constitution is usually accepted as a superior, moral binding force. It draws its authority from the people or from a special assembly chosen by the people to create the constitution. Constitutional law involves the interpretation and application of the constitution. Thus, **constitutional law** primarily concerns defining the extent and limits of government power and the rights of citizens.

---

2 SECTION REVIEW

Section Summary
Governments serve the state by maintaining social order, providing public services, providing national security, and making economic decisions.

Checking For Understanding
Recalling Facts
1. Define politics, constitution, constitutional law.
2. Identify four major purposes of government.
3. Explain "the legitimate object of government" according to Abraham Lincoln.
4. Discuss the difference between constitutional government and the government of a state that merely has a constitution.

Exploring Themes
5. Political Processes Why do people try to influence public policy?
6. Federalism Why does the United States Constitution prohibit the state governments from conducting relations with foreign nations?

Critical Thinking Skills
7. Drawing Conclusions Would it be possible to have government without politics? Explain your answer.
8. Predicting Consequences What do you think would happen in the United States if the federal government decided to punish authors whose ideas were not acceptable to the state?

Reteach

Have students work in groups of three, and, using the outline they prepared for the L1 Guided Practice activity on page 25, write summary statements for each of the three major sections on the outline.

Enrich

Have students read *The Federalist*, No. 10 from which the quote by James Madison on page 27 was excerpted. Ask students to summarize Madison's arguments.

📁 Have students complete activity 1 in the *Primary and Secondary Source Readings* in the Teacher's Classroom Resources.

Close

Have a volunteer reread Abraham Lincoln's quote on page 25 to the class. Then ask: Have popular attitudes toward government changed since Lincoln's time? Why or why not?

CONNECTIONS

Literature
Lord of the Flies by William Golding portrays young schoolboys' futile attempt to establish a democratic society on a deserted island.

Section 2 Review Answers

1. Definitions of terms appear on pages indicated: **politics,** 26; **constitution,** 27; **constitutional law,** 29
2. maintain social order, provide public services, provide for national security and a common defense, provide for and control economic system
3. to do for the people what they need done but cannot do for themselves, to provide services that individuals cannot provide on their own
4. In a constitutional government, the powers of those who govern are limited by a constitution. In some nations, even written constitutions are ignored by those who govern.
5. because they want government to respond to their needs and values
6. The Framers of the Constitution wanted foreign governments to view the United States as one nation.
7. Because people seek to influence government, it would be difficult to have government without politics. Though many Framers wanted to prevent "faction" or politics, people formed factions and interest groups even while the Constitution was being adopted.
8. Authors would take their cases to court, claiming First Amendment protection.

Different Forms of Government

Focus

Bell Ringer

Ask students to complete the sentence below while attendance is being taken:

Nothing is more fundamental to democracy than _____.

Motivating Activity

Discuss students' Bell Ringer answers and list them on the chalkboard. Through a class vote, rank students' choices. (Save the list for use in the section Close activity on page 34.) Tell students they will learn about the characteristics of democracy in this section.

Vocabulary Precheck

Call on volunteers to tell what they think each key term and concept means. Have students check the accuracy of their definitions in the Glossary. **LEP**

CONNECTIONS

History

The oldest known monarchy was in Ethiopia. Rulers claimed descent from Solomon and Sheba and ruled for about 2,000 years until the military overthrew the monarchy in 1974.

Over the centuries, people have organized their governments in many different ways. In Saudi Arabia, for example, the ruling royal family controls the government and its resources. Family members choose the king from among themselves. Thousands of miles away, in Burkina Faso in Africa, a small group of wealthy landowners and military officers governs that country. In Sweden the people elect the Riksdag, the national legislature, which in turn selects the prime minister to carry out the laws.

The United States has established a representative democratic government that has served as a model for many other countries around the world. Yet other forms of government outnumber true democracies.

Major Types of Government

Governments can be classified in many ways. The most time-honored system comes from the ideas of the ancient Greek philosopher, Aristotle. It is based on a key question: Who governs the state? Under this system of classification, all governments belong to one of three major groups: (1) **autocracy**—rule by one person; (2) **oligarchy**—rule by a few persons; or (3) **democracy**—rule by many persons.

Autocracy Any system of government in which the power and authority to rule are in the hands of a single individual is an autocracy. This is the oldest and one of the most common forms of government. His-

torically, most autocrats have maintained their positions of authority by inheritance or the ruthless use of military or police power. Several forms of autocracy exist. One is absolute or **totalitarian dictatorship**. In a totalitarian dictatorship, the ideas of a single leader or group of leaders are glorified. The government seeks to control all aspects of social and economic life. Examples of totalitarian dictatorship include Adolf Hitler's government in Nazi Germany (from 1933 to 1945), Benito Mussolini's rule in Italy (from 1922 to 1943), and Joseph Stalin's regime in the Soviet Union (from 1924 to 1953). In such dictatorships, government is not responsible to the people, and the people lack the power to limit their rulers.

Monarchy is another form of autocratic government. In a **monarchy** a king, queen, or emperor exercises the supreme powers of government. Monarchs usually inherit their positions. **Absolute monarchs** have complete and unlimited power to rule their people. The king of Saudi Arabia, for example, is such an absolute monarch. Absolute monarchs are rare today, but from the 1400s to the 1700s, kings or queens with absolute powers ruled most of Western Europe. These monarchs based their power on the idea of **divine right**. This view held that God granted those of royal birth the right to rule their people. Any challenge to or revolt against a monarch was regarded as a sin as well as treason. During the seventeenth and eighteenth centuries in Europe, the belief that the people were sovereign replaced this idea. The ruler's power came not from God but from the people.

SECTION PREVIEW

Objectives
After studying this section, you should be able to:
- Compare democracy with other forms of government.
- Explain the relationship between democracy and free enterprise.
- Understand the dilemma of minority rights in a democracy.

Key Terms and Concepts
autocracy, oligarchy, democracy, totalitarian dictatorship, monarchy, absolute monarch, divine right, constitutional monarch, direct democracy, representative democracy, republic, political party, free enterprise

Themes in Government
- Comparative Government
- Free Enterprise

Critical Thinking Skills
- Understanding Cause and Effect
- Distinguishing Fact From Opinion

---

30 UNIT 1: FOUNDATIONS OF AMERICAN GOVERNMENT

Classroom Resources for Section 3

- Guided Reading Activities
- Reproducible Lesson Plans
- Participating in Government 1
- Supreme Court Case Studies 17
- Section 3 Quiz
- Testmaker
- SAT Practice Tests
- Writer's Guidebook

PARTICIPATING IN GOVERNMENT

Student Government

In many ways, student governments resemble other levels of government. Each draws up policies and regulations that influence many aspects of citizens' lives. For example, your student council works with faculty advisers to improve your school or plan social events. They organize clean-up days and sponsor student guides who help new students or show visitors around the school. Social events include dances or pep rallies before important football or basketball games. Of course, organizing such events costs money. Because student government, unlike other levels of government, does not have the power to tax, the council sponsors fund-raising events, including bake sales and car washes, to pay for their programs.

Participating in student government by helping with campaigns, holding office, or volunteering to help out with fund-raising events or other projects will help you feel more a part of your school. It will also help you understand some of the duties of citizens. These experiences will help you see why citizens of a democracy need to participate in all levels of government if those governments are to truly represent the people.

Investigating Further

Interview a member of your student council or faculty to find out the qualifications for class officers. Then list the qualifications in a brief summary.

Today some countries, such as Great Britain, Sweden, Japan, and the Netherlands, have **constitutional monarchs.** These monarchs share governmental powers with elected legislatures or serve mainly as the ceremonial leaders of their governments.

Oligarchy An oligarchy is any system of government in which a small group holds power. The group derives its power from wealth, military power, social position, or a combination of these elements. Sometimes religion is the source of power. Today the governments of many communist countries are really oligarchies. In such countries, leaders in the Communist party and the armed forces control the government.

Both dictatorships and oligarchies sometimes claim they rule for the people. Such governments may try to give the appearance of control by the people. They might hold elections, but offer only one candidate, or control the election results in other ways. Such governments may also have some type of legislature or national assembly elected by or representing the people. These legislatures, however, only approve policies and decisions already made by the leaders. As in a dictatorship, oligarchies usually suppress all political opposition—sometimes ruthlessly.

Democracy A democracy is any system of government in which rule is by the people. The term democracy comes from the Greek *demos* (meaning "the people") and *kratia* (meaning "rule"). The ancient Greeks used the word *democracy* to mean government by the many in contrast to government by the few.

STUDY GUIDE

Themes in Government
Comparative Government What are similarities and differences between autocracy and monarchy?

Critical Thinking Skills
Understanding Cause and Effect What are likely results when government "is in the hands not of a few, but of the many" as in a democracy?

CHAPTER 1: GOVERNMENT AND OUR LIVES   31

Background

The late 1980s and early 1990s brought a tremendous move toward more democratic governments in totalitarian nations. The Solidarity movement won democratic elections for Poland. In China students held demonstrations in Tiananmen Square in May and June of 1989 demanding an end to communism. In 1989 Czechoslovakia voted to end communism in the government. The Berlin Wall came down and Germany was reunited. Free multiparty elections took place in Romania in 1990. Many Soviet republics followed the Baltic states in announcing their independence from the USSR, and in 1991 the Soviet Union formally dissolved.

PARTICIPATING IN GOVERNMENT

Discuss the following questions: What would happen if there were no student government at our school? What opportunities are there to participate in student government? What issues should student government address?

Have students complete activity 1 in *Participating in Government* in the Teacher's Classroom Resources.

Teach

Guided Practice

L1 Classifying Write the four characteristics of democracy on the chalkboard. Ask each student to give an example of one of the characteristics on a sheet of paper. Example: People can attend the church of their choice. *(individual liberty)* Collect students' papers, read selected examples, and have students identify the characteristic of democracy to which each pertains.

STUDY GUIDE

Theme Answer
Both vest authority and power in a single person. Both positions may be inherited. Autocratic rulers may rule by force, creating a police state. Today a constitutional monarch, as in Great Britain, may be a ceremonial head of state, sharing power with elected legislatures.

Critical Thinking Answer
Power is shared, by consent. People can make choices.

L2 **Expressing Opinions** Write the following statement on the chalkboard:

It makes no difference what kind of government a country has as long as the citizens are safe, well-fed, and comfortable.

Ask students if they agree or disagree with the statement and why. Briefly list their reasons on the chalkboard in *Agree* or *Disagree* columns. Have the class discuss which arguments are most persuasive.

L3 **Dramatizing** Write the following types of government on separate pieces of paper: totalitarian dictatorship, absolute monarchy, constitutional monarchy, oligarchy, direct democracy, representative democracy. Then organize the class into groups of three or four. Have each group choose one of the types to act out in dialogue. Have the class guess which one it is.

Independent Practice

L1 **Creating a Quiz** Have students work in pairs to create a quiz on the major types of government. Suggestions for types of quizzes might be the following: matching, multiple choice, or true/false.

STUDY GUIDE

Theme Answer
Democracy advocates sharing of power and government with consent of governed; also advocates freedom of choice.

Critical Thinking Answer
Fact: government for the people; power is shared. *Opinion:* Democracy is the best system; people will always elect best candidate.

Pericles, a great leader of ancient Athens, declared, "Our constitution is named a democracy because it is in the hands not of the few, but of the many."

The key idea of democracy is that the people hold sovereign power. Abraham Lincoln best captured this spirit by describing democracy as "government of the people, by the people, and for the people."

Democracy may take one of two forms. In a **direct democracy**, the people govern themselves by voting on issues individually as citizens. Direct democracy exists only in very small societies where citizens can actually meet regularly to discuss and decide key issues and problems. Direct democracy is still found in some New England town meetings and in some of the smaller states, called *cantons*, of Switzerland. No country today, however, has a government based on direct democracy.

In indirect or **representative democracy**, the people elect representatives and give them the responsibility and power to make laws and conduct government. An assembly of the people's representatives may be called a council, a legislature, a congress, or a parliament. Representative democracy is practiced in cities, states, provinces, and countries where the population is too large to meet regularly in one place.

As Benjamin Franklin was leaving the last session of the Constitutional Convention in Philadelphia in 1787, a woman approached him and asked, "What kind of government have you given us, Dr. Franklin? A republic or a monarchy?" Franklin answered, "A republic, Madam, if you can keep it." Franklin's response indicated that the Founders preferred a republic over a monarchy. In a **republic**, voters hold sovereign power. Elected representatives who are responsible to the people exercise that power.

For most Americans today, the terms *representative democracy, republic,* and *constitutional republic* mean the same thing: a system of limited government where the people are the ultimate source of governmental power. It should be understood, however, that not every democracy is a republic. Great Britain, for example, is a democracy but not a republic because it has a constitutional monarch as the head of state.

Today some nations of the world misuse the word *democracy*. Many countries call their governments "democratic" or "republic" whether they really are or not. The government of North Korea, for example, is an oligarchy, because a small number of Communist party leaders run the government. Yet these leaders call their country the Democratic People's Republic of Korea. In 1973 military leaders overthrew Chile's elected civilian government and formed a four-man council headed by Augusto Pinochet to rule the country. Pinochet became the country's president and ruled ruthlessly until democracy was restored in 1990. Nevertheless, throughout Pinochet's regime, the official name of the country remained the Republic of Chile. From 1977 until its new constitution in 1991, a military council that allowed only one political party ruled the People's Republic of the Congo.

Characteristics of Democracy

A true democratic government, as opposed to one that only uses the term *democracy* in its name, has some characteristics that distinguish it from other forms of government.

Individual Liberty No individual, of course, can be completely free to do absolutely anything he or she wants. That would result in chaos. Rather, democracy requires that all people be as free as possible to develop their own capacities. This does not mean that all people are born with equal talents or deserve an equal share of material goods. Rather, it means that they should have an equal opportunity to develop their talents to the fullest extent possible. Government in a democracy works to promote that kind of equality.

Majority Rule With Minority Rights Democracy also requires that government decisions be based on majority rule. In a democracy, people usually accept decisions made by the majority of voters in a free election. Representative democracy means that laws enacted in the legislatures represent the will of the majority

STUDY GUIDE

Themes in Government
Free Enterprise Free enterprise describes the capitalist system: private citizens, rather than the government, own most resources, factories and sales outlets. People

compete for profits in the marketplace. **How has democracy aided the growth of free enterprise?**

Critical Thinking Skills
Distinguishing Fact From Opinion **State two facts and two opinions about democracy.**

Cooperative Learning Activity

Organize students into three groups. Ask each to imagine that it has been marooned on a desert island in the Pacific and needs to set up a society and adopt rules and regulations. Assign each group a major type of government: autocracy, oligarchy, or democracy. Have the group plan how its government will distribute jobs, build shelters, and gather food. What will it do about education and health care? Will there be any police or military? Have each group present its plans for a society to the rest of the class. After the class hears each plan, have it decide which one it would like to live under.

Planting the Seeds of Democracy
Winslow Homer's *New England Country School* idealizes the nineteenth-century American public school, which was championed as the door to democracy and opportunity.
History Why is an educated public critical to democracy?

of lawmakers. Because these lawmakers are elected by the people, the laws are accepted by the people.

At the same time, the American concept of democracy includes a concern about the possible tyranny of the majority. The Constitution helps ensure that the rights of the minority will be protected.

Respect for minority rights can be difficult to maintain, especially when society is under great stress. For example, during World War II, the government imprisoned more than 100,000 Japanese Americans in relocation camps because it feared they would be disloyal. The relocation program caused severe hardships for many Japanese Americans and deprived them of their basic liberties. Even so, the program was upheld by the Supreme Court in *Korematsu* v. *United States*, 1944.

In recent years, however, this wartime action has been severely criticized as an unjustified denial of individual rights and as proof that tyranny can occur in even the most democratic societies. The constitutional mechanisms for protecting the rights of minorities did, however, survive. After the war, some of the internees used these constitutional safeguards to regain property that had been taken from them. In 1948 Congress recognized the damage done by relocation and offered small compensation payments. Finally, in 1988 Congress acknowledged the "grave injustice" of the relocation experience and offered payments of $20,000 to each internee still living.

Free Elections All genuine democracies have free and open elections. Free elections give people the chance to choose their leaders and to voice their opinions on various issues. Free elections also help ensure that public officials pay attention to the wishes of the people.

In a democracy, several characteristics mark free elections. First, everyone's vote carries the same weight—a principle often expressed in the phrase "one person, one vote." Second, all candidates have the right to express their views freely, giving voters access to competing ideas. Third, citizens are free to help candidates or support issues. Fourth, the legal requirements for voting, such as age, residence, and citizenship, are kept to a minimum. Thus, racial, ethnic, religious, or other discriminatory tests cannot be used to restrict voting. Fifth, citizens may vote freely by secret ballot, without coercion or fear of punishment for their voting decisions.

Competing Political Parties Political parties are an important element of democratic government. A **political party** is a group of individuals with broad common interests who organize to nominate candidates for office, win elections, conduct government, and determine public policy. In the United States, while any number of political parties may compete, a two-party system in which the Republicans and the Democrats have become the major political parties has developed.

Rival parties help make elections meaningful. They give voters a choice among candidates. They also help simplify and focus attention on key issues for voters. Finally, in democratic countries, the political party or parties that are out of power serve as a "loyal opposition." That is, by criticizing the policies and actions of the party in power, they can help make those in power more responsible to the people.

CHAPTER 1: GOVERNMENT AND OUR LIVES **33**

Meeting Objectives

Each section objective is tested by the Section Review questions that follow it in parentheses.

• Compare democracy with other forms of government. (2, 3, 5, 7, 8)
• Explain the relationship between democracy and free enterprise. (6, 7)
• Understand the dilemma of minority rights in a democracy. (4, 5, 8)

Evaluate

 Section 3 Quiz

Testmaker

Reteach

Ask students to describe the role citizens play in each of the three major forms of government—autocracy, oligarchy, and democracy.

Enrich

Assign case 17, *Korematsu v. United States,* in *Supreme Court Case Studies* in the Teacher's Classroom Resources.

Close

Review students' Bell Ringer answers. Ask: What additional characteristics of democracy can you add to the list? Are there any you would delete? Discuss students' reasons for additions and deletions.

The Soil of Democracy

Today relatively few nations practice democracy. One reason may be that real democracy seems to require a special environment.

A Favorable Economy Democracy seems to have a better chance in countries that do not have extremes of wealth and poverty and that have a large middle class. The opportunity to control one's economic decisions provides a base for making independent political decisions. In the United States this concept is called **free enterprise**. If people do not have the power to control their own economic lives, they will not likely be free to make political decisions.

Countries with stable, growing economies seem better able to support democratic government. In the past, autocrats who promised citizens jobs and food have toppled many democratic governments during times of severe economic depression. People who are out of work or unable to feed their families often become more concerned about security than about voting or exercising other political rights.

Widespread Education Democracy is more likely to succeed in countries with an educated public. The debate over public education in America was settled in the 1830s. For example, in 1835 Pennsylvania voted to fund public schools. Thaddeus Stevens, speaking in favor of the funding legislation, said:

If an elective republic is to endure for any great length of time, every elector must have sufficient information . . . to direct wisely the legislature, the ambassadors, and the executive of the nation. . . . [I]t is the duty of government to see that the means of information be diffused to every citizen.
—THADDEUS STEVENS, speech to the Pennsylvania State Legislature, April 1835

A Social Consensus Democracy also prospers where most people accept democratic values such as individual liberty and equality for all. Such countries are said to have a social consensus. Countries divided by disagreements about basic values may have difficulty supporting democratic governments.

History shows that conditions in the American colonies favored the growth of democracy. Most white people had an opportunity to get ahead economically. The American colonists were among the most educated people of the world at the time. The English heritage provided a general consensus of political and social values. Shortly after writing the Declaration of Independence, Thomas Jefferson remarked that Americans

Seem to have deposited the monarchial and taken up the republican government with as much ease as . . . [they] would throwing off an old and putting on a new suit of clothes.
—THOMAS JEFFERSON, 1776

3 SECTION REVIEW

Section Summary
In some forms of government the state is all powerful, while in democracy the people rule through free elections.

Checking For Understanding
Recalling Facts
1. Define autocracy, oligarchy, democracy, totalitarian dictatorship, monarchy, absolute monarch, divine right, constitutional monarch, direct democracy, representative democracy, republic, political party, free enterprise.
2. List the three classifications of government according to Aristotle.
3. Identify the origin of the term *democracy*.
4. Discuss the challenge of maintaining minority rights and majority rule.

Exploring Themes
5. Comparative Government What characteristics of democracy distinguish it from other forms of government?
6. Free Enterprise Why has free enterprise been conducive to the growth of democracy?

Critical Thinking Skills
7. Understanding Cause and Effect Many nations of the world are attempting to move toward democracy. Choose one as an example and predict its potential success based on its present internal conditions.
8. Distinguishing Fact From Opinion If you were to interview the president of the Islamic Republic of Mauritania, what questions would you ask to determine whether it is a democracy?

Section 3 Review Answers

1. Definitions of terms appear on pages indicated: **autocracy,** 30; **oligarchy,** 30; **democracy,** 30; **totalitarian dictatorship,** 30; **monarchy,** 30; **absolute monarch,** 30; **divine right,** 30; **constitutional monarch,** 31; **direct democracy,** 32; **representative democracy,** 32; **republic,** 32; **political party,** 33; **free enterprise,** 34
2. autocracy, oligarchy, democracy

3. comes from the Greek *demos*—"the people" and *kratia*—"rule"
4. While majority should rule in democracy, rights of the minority should be protected. Difficult when society is under great stress, or when majority believes that interests of the minority might be dangerous to state.
5. individual liberty, majority rule with minority rights, free elections with secret ballots, rival political parties

6. People free to make their own economic decisions are more likely to be free to make political choices.
7. The nations students choose will vary.
8. Answers may include: How many political parties are there? Do people vote by secret ballot? Do people have equal opportunity to develop talents? How are minority rights protected?

Identifying Central Issues

Identifying central issues involves studying a source and deciding what major point or points the author is trying to make. Identifying central issues will help you organize information and assess the most important concepts to remember.

Explanation

To identify central issues, follow these steps:
- Identify why the author chose to present this information. Ask: What is the author's purpose in presenting the information?
- Determine which points or ideas the author has chosen to emphasize.
- Pinpoint the idea or ideas that emphasized points support. Ask: What part of the information conveys the main idea of the selection?

Read the following excerpt from a speech that the Athenian leader Pericles made to honor soldiers who had died fighting for their city.

> *Our constitution is called a democracy because power is in the hands not of a minority but of the whole people. When it is a question of settling private disputes, everyone is equal before the law, when it is a question of putting one person before another in positions of public responsibility, what counts is not membership of a particular class, but the actual ability which the man possesses. . . .*
> *And, just as our political life is free and open, so is our day-to-day life in our relations with each other.*
> —THUCYDIDES, *THE HISTORY OF THE PELOPONNESIAN WARS*, 400S B.C.

The first step in identifying the central issue is to establish the purpose behind Pericles' speech. He wanted to take this opportunity to explain the type of government that Athens had at the time.

Pericles emphasizes equality before the law, ability rather than influence as the basis of public responsibility and freedom in private life. These points support the central issue that Athens is a democracy in which "power is in the hands not of a minority but of the whole people."

Aristotle
The Greek philosopher, educator, and scientist (384-322 B.C.) proclaimed in *Politics* that "the basis of a democratic state is liberty."

Practice

Aristotle, a philosopher from ancient Athens, recorded his ideas about government in *Politics*. Read the excerpt below and answer the following questions.

> *The basis of a democratic state is liberty; which, according to the common opinion of men, can only be enjoyed in such a state:—this they affirm to be the great end of every democracy. One principle of liberty is for all to rule and be ruled in turn . . . whence it follows that the majority must be supreme, and that whatever the majority approve must be the end and the just. Every citizen, it is said, must have equality, and therefore in a democracy the poor have more power than the rich, because there are more of them.*
> —ARISTOTLE, *POLITICS*, CA 300 B.C.

1. Why did Aristotle write the above information?
2. What points does Aristotle emphasize?
3. What is the central issue?

Additional Practice

To practice this skill, see **Reinforcing the Skill** on page 43.

Practice Answers

1. to explain his views about the relationship of liberty, democracy, and government
2. Liberty is the basis of democracy and cannot be enjoyed without democracy. In a democracy, each citizen has political equality. Some groups have greater power than others because they have greater numbers.
3. In a democracy the majority is supreme.

For additional practice, have students complete activity 1 in *Skill Reinforcement Activities* in the Teacher's Classroom Resources.

Focus

Ask students to recall how they studied for the last big test they took. Did they try to memorize every fact or did they look for the big ideas and try to understand those?

Tell students this lesson will help them learn techniques which will help them identify the central issues in material they read.

Teach

Briefly orient students to the time and place of the two excerpts. Emphasize the importance of democracy to the Athenians. As a class, read over the speech by Pericles. Ask: What is the topic of the speech? *(definition of democracy)* How does Pericles feel about his topic? *(He believes that democracy is the only way to run a government.)*

Review the steps in identifying the central issue: identifying the author's purpose, determining the points the author wanted to emphasize, and identifying the information that conveys the main idea.

Assess

Have students complete the **Practice** exercise.

Close

Discuss recent instances in which students have grappled with identifying central issues in current events. *(sample: breakup of Soviet Union)*

Focus

Government and Economic Systems

Bell Ringer

Write the headlines below on the chalkboard and ask students to note in writing what they have in common.

CONGRESS PASSES NEW
BANKING LAWS

PRESIDENT ACTS TO HEAD
OFF TRUCKERS' STRIKE

RUSSIA INCREASES AMERICAN
WHEAT IMPORTS

COURT RULES ON
IMPORT QUOTAS

Discuss students' answers. *(All deal with actions by government that relate to economic matters.)*

Motivating Activity

Have students read the first paragraph of this section. As they are reading, write the three basic economic decisions every society must make on the chalkboard: 1) what and how much should be produced, 2) how goods and services should be produced, 3) who gets the goods and services that are produced. Ask students to explain how scarcity is involved in each decision.

Vocabulary Precheck

Write the terms and concepts on the chalkboard. Ask students how each term and concept relates to economics. **LEP**

CONNECTIONS

Global Perspectives
Some rural groups in Africa, South America, and Asia have traditional economies in which economic decisions are made according to traditions and customs handed down from one generation of people to another.

Employment and wages, taxes and spending, production and distribution of products—these are concepts that relate to economics. **Economics** can be defined as the study of human efforts to satisfy seemingly unlimited wants through the use of limited resources. Resources include natural materials such as land, water, minerals, and trees. Resources also include such human factors as skills, knowledge, and physical capabilities. There are never enough resources to produce all the goods and services people could possibly want. Therefore, people in every nation must decide how these resources are to be used. Governments generally regulate this economic activity.

The Role of Economic Systems

Governments around the world provide for many kinds of economic systems. All economic systems, however, must make three major economic decisions: (1) what and how much should be produced; (2) how goods and services should be produced; and (3) who gets the goods and services that are produced. Each major type of economic system in the world—capitalism, socialism, and communism—answers these questions differently.

Capitalism

At one end of the spectrum is an economic system in which freedom of choice and individual incentive for workers, investors, consumers, and business enter-

prises is emphasized. The government assumes that society will be best served by any productive economic activity that free individuals choose. This system is usually referred to as "free enterprise" or **capitalism**. Pure capitalism has five main characteristics: (1) private ownership and control of property and economic resources; (2) free enterprise; (3) competition among businesses; (4) freedom of choice; and (5) the possibility of profits.

Origins of Capitalism No one person invented the idea of capitalism. It developed gradually from the economic and political changes in medieval and early modern Europe over hundreds of years. Two important new concepts laid the foundation for the market system that is at the heart of capitalism. First is the idea that people could work for economic gain. The other idea is that wealth should be used aggressively.

Major changes in the economic organization of Europe began with the opening of trade routes to the East in the thirteenth century. As trade increased, people began to invest money to make profits. By the eighteenth century, Europe had national states, a wealthy middle class familiar with money and markets, and a new attitude toward work and wealth. Included in this new attitude were the ideas of progress, invention, and the free market. The **free market** meant that buyers and sellers were free to make unlimited economic decisions in the marketplace.

In 1776 Adam Smith, a Scottish philosopher and economist, provided a philosophy for this new system. Smith described capitalism in his book *The Wealth of Nations*. From the writings of Smith and others came the basic idea of *laissez-faire* economics.

SECTION PREVIEW

Objectives
After studying this section, you should be able to:
- Contrast capitalism, socialism, and communism.
- Identify the basic economic decisions that confront every society.

Key Terms and Concepts
economics, capitalism, free market, *laissez-faire*, socialism, democratic socialism, bourgeoisie, proletariat, communism, command economy

Themes in Government
- Free Enterprise
- Global Perspectives

Critical Thinking Skills
- Recognizing Ideologies
- Making Inferences

---

36   UNIT 1: FOUNDATIONS OF AMERICAN GOVERNMENT

Classroom Resources for Section 4

- 📁 Guided Reading Activities
- 📁 Reproducible Lesson Plans
- 📁 Reteaching Activities 1
- 📁 Enrichment Activities 1
- 📁 Section 4 Quiz
- 📁 Chapter 1 Tests

- ✚ Testmaker
- 📁 Limited English Proficiency Activities 1
- 🎧 Audio Cassettes (English and Spanish)
- SAT Practice Tests
- Writer's Guidebook

Laissez-faire, a French term, means "to let alone." According to this philosophy, government should keep its hands off the economy. In laissez-faire economics, the government's role is strictly limited to those few actions needed to ensure free competition in the marketplace.

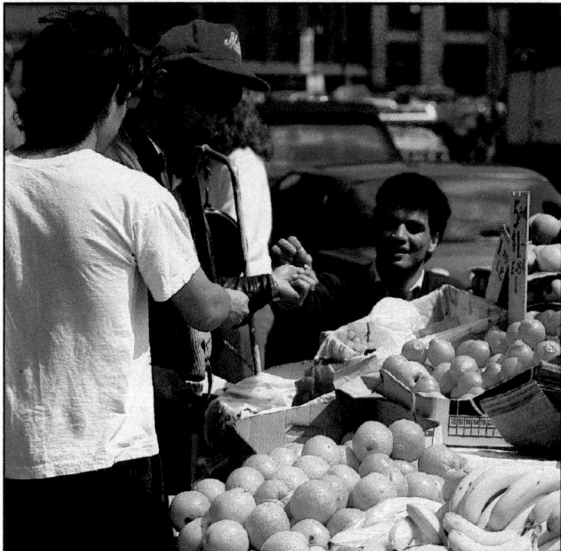

At the Base of Capitalism
In the marketplace, the buyer demands and the producer and seller supply. **Economics** **Why do governments in capitalist societies often step in to ensure competition?**

In theory, what does a free-enterprise economy mean? In a free-enterprise or pure market economy, economic decisions are made by buyers (consumers) and sellers (producers). Sellers own businesses that produce goods or services. Buyers pay for those goods and services that they believe best fit their needs. Thus, the answer to the question of what to produce is determined in the marketplace by the actions of buyers and sellers, rather than by the government.

Competition plays a key role in a free-enterprise economy. Sellers compete with one another to produce goods and services at reasonable prices. Sellers also compete for resources. At the same time, consumers compete with one another to buy what they want and need. These same consumers in their roles as workers try to sell their skills and labor for the best wages or salaries they can get.

Free Enterprise in the United States No nation in the world has a pure capitalist system. The United States, however, is a leading example of a capitalist system in which the government plays a role. For the most part, the government's main economic task has been to preserve the free market. The national government has always regulated American foreign trade, and it has always owned some property. Nevertheless, the government has tried to encourage business competition and private property ownership. Since the early 1900s, however, the national government's influence on the economy of the United States has increased in several ways.

First, as the nation's government has grown, it has become the single largest buyer of goods and services in the country. Local, state, and national governments buy more than one-fifth of all goods and services produced in the United States. These governments buy trucks, cars, gasoline and oil, office furniture, typewriters, and thousands of other items.

Second, since the early 1900s, the United States government has increasingly regulated the economy for various purposes. The Meat Inspection Act and Pure Food and Drug Act were early attempts by government to protect the consumer. Since then, many laws have been passed giving the government a role in such areas as labor-management relations, the regulation of environmental pollution, and control over many banking and investment practices.

Third, the Great Depression of the 1930s left millions of Americans without jobs. The national government set up the Social Security System, programs to aid the unemployed, and a variety of social programs. In addition, the government began to set up public corporations like the Tennessee Valley Authority that competed directly with private companies to provide services such as electricity.

=== STUDY GUIDE ===

Themes in Government
Free Enterprise **Why is there no nation in the world with a pure capitalist system?**

Critical Thinking Skills
Recognizing Ideologies **Discuss how each of the five characteristics of pure capitalism on page 36**

contributed to the development of the United States economy.

Teach

Guided Practice

L1 **Expressing Viewpoints** Have volunteers explain the differences between *communism* and *socialism*. Lead a class discussion on the reasons why the terms *socialism* and *communism* are controversial in the United States. List the reasons on the chalkboard. If students don't mention it, remind them that many people came to America because they wanted to own property and choose their own occupation. **LEP**

Caption Answer
to preserve free markets

=== STUDY GUIDE ===

Theme Answer
need for some government regulation of foreign trade to protect consumers, to control pollution, or allocate resources; government may own property or be buyer of goods and services

Critical Thinking Answer

Private ownership—by choice—and control of property and resources, enhanced by the possibility of making profits, was very tempting to Americans. They chose to compete with others to make their product better, cheaper, and faster.

Background

In a command economy the government sets the prices of goods produced. The government can set low prices for consumer goods and provide financial support for factories that lose money. Consumers can be assured of buying goods at a reasonable price when those goods are available. In the Soviet Union the government provided its citizens low-cost housing, free medical care, and free education. Today the economy of this area is changing along with its government. Factories are becoming more self-sufficient, some farmers own their land, and some people own small businesses.

L2 Making Comparisons Write the headings *Market Economy* and *Command Economy* on the chalkboard. Call on students to list ways in which market and command economies answer the three basic economic questions.

L3 Debate Organize students into three groups and assign each group one of the economic systems: capitalism, socialism, communism. Have the groups discuss and list the advantages and disadvantages of each system. Then let a spokesperson from each group propound the group's list. Have the class vote on which economic system is most advantageous.

Independent Practice

L1 Creating a Chart Have students work in pairs to make a chart that compares capitalist, communist, and socialist economic systems. Their chart should indicate the following information about each economy: who owns the means of production, who makes the economic decisions, and whether or not there is competition and a profit motive. **LEP**

Caption Answer
Socialism promised them equal shares of the benefits of industrial production.

Today the American economy and others like it are described by economists as mixed-market economies. A mixed-market economy is an economy in which free enterprise is combined with and supported by government decisions in the marketplace. Government keeps competition free and fair and protects the public interest. It respects the right to own private property and the freedom to make economic choices.

The Socialist System

Under the second type of economic system—**socialism**—the government owns the basic means of production, determines the use of resources, distributes the products and wages, and provides social services such as education, health care, and welfare. Socialism has three main goals: (1) the distribution of wealth and economic opportunity equally among people; (2) society's control through its government of all major decisions about production; and (3) public ownership of most land, of factories, and of other means of production.

The basic ideas behind modern socialism began to develop in the nineteenth century. Industrialization in Europe caused several problems. A class of low-paid workers—including women and children—lived in terrible poverty, slums grew in cities, working conditions became miserable. In reaction to these problems, some socialists rejected capitalism and favored violent revolution. Others planned and built socialist communities where laborers were supposed to share equally in the benefits of industrial production.

The socialists who believed in peaceful changes wanted to work within the democratic political system to improve economic conditions, under a system called **democratic socialism**. Under this system the people have basic human rights and have some control over government officials through free elections and multiparty systems. However, the government owns the basic means of production and makes most economic decisions.

Harsh Lives, New Hopes
Socialism attracted many people living and working in miserable urban conditions. **Economics What attracted these poor people to socialism?**

Great Britain, Tanzania, and several Scandinavian countries today operate under a form of democratic socialism. The government controls steel mills, shipyards, railroads, and airlines. It also provides services such as health and medical care.

Opponents of socialism say that it stifles individual initiative. They also claim that socialist nations' high tax rates hinder economic growth. Further, some people argue that, since socialism requires increased governmental regulation, it helps create big government and thus may lead to dictatorship.

The Communist System

Karl Marx (1818–1883), a German thinker and writer, was a socialist who advocated violent revolu-

---

Cooperative Learning Activity

Have students make a bulletin board illustrating the ongoing changes in countries that are moving toward democracy. In the center of the bulletin board have them post an outline map of the world with *countries in transition* marked in red. Around the map students can post newspaper and magazine articles and photographs about each transitional country. Have students change the articles as new reports are printed. Students might use yarn to connect each article with its transitional country.

tion. After studying the conditions of his time, he concluded that the capitalist system would collapse. He first published his ideas in 1848 in a pamphlet called *The Communist Manifesto*. He later expanded his ideas in his book called *Das Kapital* (1867). Marx believed that in industrialized nations the population is divided into capitalists, or the **bourgeoisie** (BOOR•zhwah•ZEE) who own the means of production, and workers or the **proletariat**, who work to produce the goods. Capitalists are a ruling class because they use their economic power to force their will on the workers. The workers, Marx argued, do not receive full compensation for their labor because the owners keep the profits from the goods the workers make.

Marx interpreted all human history as a class struggle between the workers and the owners of the means of production. Friedrich Engels, a close associate of Marx, wrote:

Former society, moving in class antagonisms, had need of a state, that is, an organization of the exploiting class at each period for the maintenance of external conditions of production: . . . for the forcible holding down of the exploited class in the conditions of oppression.

—FRIEDRICH ENGELS

Marx predicted that, as time passed, a smaller and smaller group of capitalists would control all means of production and, hence, all wealth. Eventually the workers would rise in violent revolution and overthrow the capitalists. The goal of this revolution was government ownership of the means of production and distribution.

Karl Marx first called his own ideas "scientific socialism." He believed that in time socialism would develop into full communism. Under **communism** one class would evolve, property would all be held in common, and there would be no need for government.

Karl Marx not only believed that economic events would finally lead to communism by means of revolution, he encouraged it:

In short, communists everywhere support every revolutionary movement against the existing social and political order of things. . . . Let the ruling class tremble at the communist revolution. The proletarians have nothing to lose but their chains. Working men of all countries, unite!

—KARL MARX, *COMMUNIST MANIFESTO*, 1848

Communism as a Command Economy The communist system is called a **command** economy because the government decides how much to produce, what to produce, and how to distribute goods and services. The state owns the land, natural resources, industry, banks, and transportation facilities. The state also controls all mass communications including newspapers, magazines, and broadcast stations.

Under communism, people have limited economic and political freedom. While the state provides security, such as jobs and medical care, people lack freedom to choose their own careers. People are free to spend their money as they wish, but their choices are limited to what the government decides to produce. Citizens have little influence on government's economic decisions with their votes, because one party chooses all the candidates.

Communism in Practice Communism did not develop in the way Marx predicted. The Soviet Union was formed from a communist revolution in 1917. As the world's leading communist country, it developed a huge, powerful government. The Communist party Secretariat, the executive branch of the party, built a staff estimated at 100,000 to 200,000. The government used a secret police (KGB) to spy on and control Soviet citizens.

Instead of eliminating social classes, communism in the Soviet Union developed a privileged class of government officials. Party officials, scientists, sports heroes, and other professionals received larger incomes and had more opportunities than the masses of workers. The anticipated changes in human nature

---

STUDY GUIDE

Themes in Government
Global Perspectives Name the major characteristics of the communist system and indicate why each did or did not work in the Soviet Union.

Critical Thinking Skills
Making Inferences What can you infer about the future of communism from the political cartoon on page 40?

Recognizing Ideologies What was the ultimate goal of true communism, according to Karl Marx?

Critical Thinking Activity

Recognizing Ideologies Discuss with students political events in Poland, Romania, Czechoslovakia, and the former USSR since 1989. Then have students reread pages 39–40. Ask students to discuss whether history has confirmed or failed to confirm the theories of Karl Marx.

L2 Expressive Writing Have students research and write about the Russian economy from the point of view of one of the following: a student from Moscow, an American businessperson, a farm worker, a foreign newspaper correspondent, or a visiting American student.

STUDY GUIDE

Theme Answer
Government ownership of property, means of production, resources, communication; did not work—no motivation for profit, pride of ownership, or entrepreneurial spirit. People had limited freedom to choose their work, housing; limited influence on government policies and leaders; people could not choose their leaders.

Critical Thinking Answers
It is threatened by the rising tide of democracy.

to eliminate class differences, private property, and government

Assess

Check for Understanding

Have students complete Section 4 Review on page 40.

CONNECTIONS

Biography
Karl Marx was a close friend of Friedrich Engels, the son of wealthy factory owners. Much of Marx's ideology about the class struggle between the proletariat and the bourgeoisie is based on his experiences at the Engels' factory. Throughout his life he depended on financial support from Engels and died a very poor man.

Meeting Objectives

Each section objective is tested by the Section Review questions that follow it in parentheses.

- Contrast capitalism, socialism, and communism. (5, 6, 7, 8)
- Identify the basic economic decisions that confront every society. (2, 4, 5, 6, 8)

Evaluate

📁 Section 4 Quiz

▣ Testmaker

Reteach

📁 Have students complete activity 1 in *Reteaching Activities* in the Teacher's Classroom Resources.

Enrich

📁 Have students complete activity 1 in *Enrichment Activities* in the Teacher's Classroom Resources.

Caption Answer
a free market where buyers and sellers have choices

Close

Ask students why the federal government and the economy are so closely related. Have them speculate about what might happen if government took no part in the economy.

---

did not occur. People remained competitive and individualistic. Religion and traditional institutions refused to die.

By the 1980s the Soviet Union's command system had failed to produce economic gains to match those of Western capitalist nations. Workers and owners in these nations found nonviolent ways to settle disagreements, and the middle class prospered. The Soviet people and those in communist Eastern European nations began to demand greater economic and political freedom. People forced communist governments to allow more private enterprise and opposing political views. The Soviet Union, Poland, and other communist nations held free elections. East Germany renounced communism and united with West Germany.

In 1949 the Communist party won control of mainland China and formed the People's Republic of China. The party dominated the government, the bureaucracy, and the army. At first it redistributed land among the peasants. Then the peasants were required to combine their farms into collectives.

The Communists brought most economic activity under state control. A plan for bringing China into the industrial age stressed development of heavy industry. In the 1970s and 1980s, however, the failure to develop significant economic gains resulted in conflicts between moderates and radicals within the Communist party.

The government chose to adopt some free market practices in the 1980s, and production increased. Many Chinese people expected that political reforms

At the Receding Shores of Communism
Around the world, communism is giving way to the capitalist way of life. **History** **What does capitalism offer people that communism does not?**

would accompany the economic reforms. In April 1989, hundreds of thousands of students filled Tiananmen Square in Beijing calling for democracy. The Chinese government responded with force, killing many people. A period of government repression followed.

Today the government encourages free enterprise in special economic zones, and allows some private business. Community-owned township and village enterprises (TVEs) account for a large portion of China's gross national product. Instead of encouraging privately owned business, the Chinese government has chosen to transform state enterprises into joint stock companies that people may invest in. Will economic growth foster a more democratic society? This is the key question in China's future.

---

4 SECTION REVIEW

Section Summary
Under capitalism buyers and sellers make economic decisions in a free market; socialism is based on government economic planning and ownership of key industries; communism gives government total control over the economic and political systems.

Checking For Understanding
Recalling Facts
1. Define economics, capitalism, free market, laissez-faire, socialism, democratic socialism, bourgeoisie, proletariat, communism, command economy.
2. Explain how economics relates to government.
3. Identify the authors of *The Wealth of Nations* and *Das Kapital*.
4. List the three functions of economic systems.

Exploring Themes
5. Free Enterprise How does a market economy determine what and how much should be produced?
6. Global Perspectives What caused the recent changes in Soviet and Eastern European economic and political systems?

Critical Thinking Skills
7. Recognizing Ideologies Describe one main similarity and one main difference between communism and democratic socialism as economic systems.
8. Making Inferences What ideas presented by Karl Marx were likely to appeal to people in nations where wealth was unevenly distributed?

Section 4 Review Answers

1. Definitions of terms appear on pages indicated: **economics,** 36; **capitalism,** 36; **free market,** 36; *laissez-faire,* 37; **socialism,** 38; **democratic socialism,** 38; *bourgeoisie,* 39; **proletariat,** 39; **communism,** 39; **command economy,** 39
2. Governments provide rules that create or maintain economic systems.
3. Adam Smith, Karl Marx

4. what and how much should be produced, how goods and services should be produced, who gets the goods and services produced
5. by the sum of the actions of buyers and sellers in the market place
6. demand for more consumer goods, greater economic and political freedom

7. Both believe in public ownership of the means of production and in government control over economic decisions. Communism taught that state would wither away; socialism permits democratic participation.
8. Workers would revolt against capitalists, property would be held in common, and one class would evolve.

P E R S O N A L P E R S P E C T I V E S

Violeta Barrios De Chamorro on Democracy in Nicaragua

In 1990 Nicaraguan President Violeta Barrios De Chamorro took office, becoming her country's first popularly elected president in more than 100 years. Before the election civil war had split the nation. When Chamorro delivered her inaugural address in Managua, she offered her fellow citizens hope for a return to democracy.

During my electoral campaign, I promised that Nicaragua was going to be a republic again. Today marks the dawn of that republic that was born from the people's vote and that was born, not from shouts and bullets, but from the deepest silence of the Nicaraguan soul. From the conscience. . . .

There is no sovereignty without freedom or justice without freedom. There cannot even be any Nicaraguan without freedom because Nicaragua's soul and reason to exist is freedom.

However, freedom also means respect—respect for the rights of others; respect for the law; respect for the property of others; respect for other peoples' feelings and opinions. Freedom will never imply a bored fatherland of puppets who think alike. Freedom is a fatherland of initiatives and pluralism with citizens who respect beliefs and opinions. . . . In the task of consolidation of democratic liberties, I demand the greatest responsibility from the men who will represent the armed branch and the police. To them and to the judges and magistrates who will impart justice, we demand that they never trample a law or a freedom under my government. . . . I am going to grant broad unconditional amnesty for all common political crimes and related crimes committed by Nicaraguan individuals as of this date. This amnesty will include persons arrested, tried, sentenced, or pending trial, and those captured and sentenced who have served their sentences, who have now been favored forever with a pardon. Let there be no torturing ever again. . . .

There cannot even be any Nicaraguan without freedom because Nicaragua's soul and reason to exist is freedom.

The new stage in our history demands that we reduce the army and reduce its budget, which is stifling the Nicaraguan people's economy.

It is the second task of my government to maximally boost economic production. . . . To further this purpose, we will also eliminate all controls and regulations that hindered and stagnated economic production and creativity. . . . The farm owner will be able to decide what he is going to produce, to whom he will sell what he has produced. . . . Businessmen will be free to choose in what activity they want to invest and what risk they want to take in their businesses. . . .

The third task of my government is to reduce social inequalities. . . . We will amend the labor laws in a democratic manner and we will guarantee all Nicaraguans an increasingly fairer salary so that together we will achieve measures of well-being that will bring greater benefits to the worker and his family. . . .

Nicaraguans, the eyes of the world are on us. . . . I am proud to be a Nicaraguan . . . and I have the solidarity of the Nicaraguans.

—VIOLETA BARRIOS DE CHAMORRO, 1990

Examining the Reading

Reviewing Facts
1. List the three major tasks Chamorro outlines for her government.
2. Describe Chamorro's plan for dealing with political prisoners.

Critical Thinking Skills
3. Identifying Central Issues How does Chamorro use freedom to unify her address?

More About Personal Perspectives

In the mid-1970s widespread protests began against the rule of Nicaraguan dictator Anastasio Somoza Debayle. By 1978 the protests had escalated into civil war, and in 1979 Somoza resigned and fled the country. A new government, headed by the leftist Sandinista National Liberation Front, introduced radical economic policies and threatened the stability of neighboring nations. New opposition developed and civil war began again. Finally, in 1989, the Sandinistas agreed to hold free elections. Newspaper publisher Violeta Barrios De Chamorro, a vocal critic of the Sandinista government, was elected President in 1990.

Focus

Have students imagine they have been elected leader of a nation recently torn by civil war. What would they say to try to unite the nation? List several students' responses on the chalkboard.

Teach

Ask: What two ways of creating a republic does Chamorro contrast? *(shouts and bullets, vote from the conscience)* What does she imply about the previous government? *(It has been guilty of trampling the law.)*

Assess

Have students complete **Examining the Reading.**

Answers

1. to consolidate liberties by reducing militarism, to broaden economic opportunities, and to reduce social inequalities
2. She will grant amnesty for political crimes and free those serving in prisons for such crimes.
3. She emphasizes the value of freedom by pointing to its meaning: respect for the rights of others, responsibility to administer the laws justly, opportunity to be creative, and promoting of social equality.

Close

Ask students to explain in their own words Chamorro's concept of freedom.

Identifying Terms and Concepts

1. state, 2. sovereignty, 3. democracy, 4. constitution, 5. autocracy, 6. republic, 7. capitalism, 8. free market, 9. communism, 10. command economy

Reviewing Facts and Ideas

1. established their sovereignty by declaring independence from Great Britain

2. federal system

3. absolute, constitutional

4. national liberation organizations, multinational corporations, international organizations

5. Through politics people try to influence government to respond to their individual needs and values.

6. Government tries to ensure free competition in the marketplace.

7. bourgeoisie, proletariat

8. Great Britain, Tanzania, and several Scandinavian countries

9. government officials

10. Government has not withered away—but has become large and powerful. Social classes—party officials, scientists, managers—took place of bourgeoisie.

Applying Themes

1. between the central government and state or provincial governments

2. Dictators have unlimited powers. Constitutional monarchs usually cannot make laws, oversee court systems, or set foreign policy.

3. Answers will vary, but the level of government contacted should be appropriate to the problem.

4. The United States was founded at the time capitalism became important in Europe. Adam Smith wrote his book in the same year that the United States declared its independence. Our economic system grew out of that of Great Britain.

5. capitalism

Summary and Significance

Because governments play such a vital role in people's lives, understanding how governments operate and why they differ is important. Governments provide the security that people need and the economic environment in which they live. Because governments have authority to respond to needs and values, people often organize politically to influence governments. This kind of participation is expected in democracies where government depends on knowledgeable participants. It is not permitted in nations in which the leaders view popular opinion as a threat to their rule.

Identifying Terms and Concepts

Insert the terms below into the following paragraph to describe the nature of government and differing political and economic systems. Each term should be used only once.

constitution, sovereignty, democracy, communism, autocracy, capitalism, state, free market, republic, command economy

Every (1) has a form of government that has (2) within its territorial boundaries. A (3) is a government of and by the people that may have a (4) that protects the rights of the people—unlike an (5) that concentrates power in the hands of one person. The United States is a (6) with elected representation. It has a mixed economy based on (7). The (8) allows buyers and sellers to make economic decisions. By contrast, under (9), the People's Republic of China and other states have operated a (10) with government planning.

Reviewing Facts and Ideas

1. **Explain** why the thirteen British colonies in America became known as "states."
2. **Describe** what system of government divides powers among different levels rather than giving all power to a central government.
3. **List** two types of monarchs ruling today.
4. **Describe** the three kinds of non-state groups that influence international politics.
5. **Define** the role politics plays in the government of a democratic nation.
6. **Define** the role of government in a laissez-faire economic system.

7. **List** the two classes into which Karl Marx divided all people in industrialized nations.
8. **Name** two countries that operate under a form of democratic socialism.
9. **Describe** who makes most economic decisions in a command economy.
10. **Explain** why communism as described by Karl Marx has never developed as he predicted.

Applying Themes

1. **Federalism** How does federalism divide the powers of government?
2. **Comparative Government** What are some powers of a totalitarian dictator that are not shared by a constitutional monarch?
3. **Political Processes** Identify one need that your community or neighborhood has that could be addressed by government. What level of government should be contacted?
4. **Free Enterprise** Given its historic origins, why was it natural for the United States to adopt the free enterprise system?
5. **Global Perspectives** Which of the following ideas do you perceive to be the most powerful force in the world today: communism, capitalism, or socialism?

Critical Thinking Skills

1. **Drawing Conclusions** Despite the efforts of some of the Framers of the Constitution to prevent the development of political groups, the United States has always had competing political

Critical Thinking Skills

1. Answers may include: a.) Government works better when it is closer to the people—more power should be given to the states. Large national problems are not easily handled at the local level—more power should be given to the national government. b.) Democracy means that the majority should have the power to make decisions for the good of all. All people have rights, whether they are in the majority or not—these rights must be preserved. c.) Government is the only institution that can be entrusted with the general welfare of all the people, so government should make the major economic decisions. Government control over economic decisions infringes on individual liberties and could threaten political freedom.

2. oligarchies—rules by a few persons whose power is derived from wealth, military power, or social

parties. These parties usually disagree over one or more of the following three issues. Write a brief statement favoring or opposing each of these issues.
a. more power to the states at the expense of the national government
b. majority rule at the expense of minority rights
c. a larger role and responsibility for government in economic decisions

2. **Making Comparisons** How do oligarchies and democracies compare?

3. **Understanding Cause and Effect** Why are so many people in the United States moving to southern and western states?

4. **Predicting Consequences** What are the likely political consequences of recent shifts in United States population?

5. **Distinguishing Fact From Opinion** State one fact and one opinion about communism.

6. **Making Inferences** What do you think would be the most difficult problem faced by government officials in a command economy?

7. **Recognizing Ideologies** What are the major features of capitalism?

Linking Past and Present

The Soviet Union and the People's Republic of China developed two different styles of communism. When those systems failed to provide the significant progress that their citizens demanded, each nation chose its own path away from state communism. How have reforms affected the people of Russia and China? Will economic changes bring increased political freedom to these countries? While these important questions will not be completely answered in the near future, they are interesting to study. Write your own observations based on what is happening in Russia and China today.

Writing About Government

Persuasive Writing Write a letter to a dictator of a small state to persuade that person to consider democratic reforms for the people. Describe the advantages of democratic government and how they might apply to the state he or she governs.

Reinforcing the Skill

Identifying Central Issues Read the following selection from a speech that Representative Shirley Chisholm gave before her fellow members of Congress in 1969. Then write a brief description detailing the central issue of the selection.

> *I* intend to vote No on every money bill that comes to the floor of this House that provides any funds for the Department of Defense. Any bill whatsoever, until the time comes when our values and priorities have been turned right side up again, until the monstrous waste and the shocking profits in the defense budget have been eliminated and our country starts to use its strength, its tremendous resources, for people and peace, not for profits and war.
>
> —SHIRLEY CHISHOLM, ADDRESS DELIVERED TO THE HOUSE OF REPRESENTATIVES, MARCH 26, 1969

Investigating Further

1. **Individual Project** Increasing interdependence among nations is illustrated by the great increases in international trade over the past few decades. Look through your own or your family's personal possessions. Where were your shoes and clothing made? your television? your sports equipment? your purse or wallet? your appliances? Did any multinational corporation manufacture any of these items?

2. **Cooperative Learning** Organize into groups of five people each. Have every person in each group locate each of the following items: a radio, a watch, a shirt, a pair of shoes, and a cup or mug. Each person should compile a list noting each item and the country that manufactured it. Bring the lists together and compare them to determine which nations are mentioned most frequently for each product. Have each group make a chart showing the various products and the number from each of the countries represented.

CHAPTER 1: GOVERNMENT AND OUR LIVES 43

6. Answers should include that determining how much and what to produce is a very difficult problem in a large nation.

7. freedom of choice; individual incentive for workers, investors, consumers, and business enterprises; possibility of profits

Linking Past and Present
Although Smith believed that free market competition would decide most economic questions, in the United States competition has been limited by business combinations and government regulation. Although Marx denied that government would be needed, in the Soviet Union the government managed the economy, which failed to produce goods to meet consumer demand.

Writing About Government
Students' letters will vary.

Reinforcing the Skill
Chisholm argues that too much of the nation's resources are going for the military.

Investigating Further
1. Answers will vary.
2. Groups' lists and charts will vary.

position; <u>democracies</u>—rule by many persons and the majority rules, but minority rights are protected

3. Students might suggest that people are seeking milder weather and better job opportunities.

4. Answers may include: Political power and influence will shift to areas that are growing faster. Cities may face more difficulty in getting help from the national government, and so on.

5. Answers will vary but may include—<u>fact:</u> Karl Marx predicted communism as an answer to economic problems under capitalism; <u>opinion:</u> Under communism, people become less competitive.

Chapter Organizer

Objectives	Special Feature Pages	Supplemental Materials
Section 1 Roots of American Government *pp. 46–50* 1. Explain the principle of limited government. 2. Identify the factors that shaped this nation's political heritage.	Focus on Freedom: The Mayflower Compact p. 48	Guided Reading Activities Reproducible Lesson Plans Section 1 Quiz Testmaker The Living Constitution SAT Practice Tests Writer's Guidebook
Section 2 American Colonies Unite *pp. 51–60* 1. Trace the events leading to the writing of the Declaration of Independence. 2. Identify the issues behind colonial protests.	Multicultural Heritage: The Iroquois Confederation p. 52 The Declaration of Independence pp. 57–60	Guided Reading Activities Reproducible Lesson Plans Primary and Secondary Source Readings 2 Section 2 Quiz Testmaker The Living Constitution SAT Practice Tests Writer's Guidebook
Section 3 The Articles of Confederation *pp. 61–65* 1. List the strengths and weaknesses of the Articles of Confederation. 2. Describe how the government was organized under the Articles of Confederation. 3. Summarize the problems the United States faced after independence.	Participating in Government: Applying for a Passport p. 63 Critical Thinking Skills: Analyzing Information p. 65	Guided Reading Activities Reproducible Lesson Plans Participating in Government 2 Section 3 Quiz Testmaker Government Themes Transparencies 5 Skill Reinforcement Activity 2 The Living Constitution SAT Practice Tests Writer's Guidebook
Section 4 The Constitutional Convention *pp. 66–71* 1. Outline the development of the Constitution from the Constitutional Convention to ratification. 2. Specify issues on which the delegates to the Constitutional Convention had to compromise.	Global Connection: Comparing Governments:Influencing Other Constitutions p. 70 Personal Perspectives: Abigail Adams on the Status of Women p. 71	Guided Reading Activities Reproducible Lesson Plans Reteaching Activities 2 Enrichment Activities 2 Section 4 Quiz Testmaker Chapter 2 Tests Chapter Transparencies 2 Audio Cassettes (English and Spanish) Limited English Proficiency Activities 2 The Living Constitution SAT Practice Tests Writer's Guidebook

If time does not permit teaching this chapter, assign the Chapter 2 summary in the Unit 1 Digest on pages 149–150.

Key To Ability Levels

Teaching strategies have been coded for varying learning styles and abilities.

L1 Level 1 activities are **basic** activities and should be within the ability range of all students.

L2 Level 2 activities are **average** activities and should be within the ability range of the average to above-average student.

L3 Level 3 activities are **challenging** activities designed for the ability range of above-average students.

LEP These activities should be within the ability range of **Limited English Proficiency** students.

Multicultural Activities

Wars, such as the American Revolution, changed forever the political institutions of Native American nations like the Cherokee. The Europeans had little patience for the work of Native American councils that talked through issues of war and trade until they reached a consensus. During wartime, the British, with whom most Native American groups sided, wanted immediate help and decision making from their Native American allies. To get this help, they negotiated directly with prominent warriors or traders, exchanging gifts for guarantees of Native American fighters. The British recognized these men as chiefs and they became politically powerful, while the council system of decision making in which all people participated lost authority. Have students research the council system of government, identifying political traditions associated with this system.

In 1987 the United States celebrated the 200th anniversary of the Constitution. During that year of celebration, Justice Thurgood Marshall, the first African American to serve on the Supreme Court, gave a speech in which he stated that he did not "find the wisdom, foresight, and sense of justice exhibited by the Framers, particularly profound. To the contrary, the government devised was defective from the start, requiring several amendments, a civil war, and momentous social transformations to attain the . . . respect for individual freedoms and human rights, we hold as fundamental today . . ." Have students suggest reasons for Marshall's perspective on the Constitution, and agree or disagree with his point of view.

Chapter Resources

Readings for the Student

Bowen, Catherine Drinker. *Miracle at Philadelphia*. Bantam, 1968.
The Federalist. Random House, 1937.
Mee, Charles, L., Jr. *The Genius of the People*. Harper & Row, 1987.
Meltzer, Milton. *American Revolutionaries: A History in Their Own Words, 1750–1800*. Thomas Y. Crowell, 1987.
Smith, Page. *A New Age Now Begins: A People's History of the American Revolution*. Penguin, 1989.

Readings for the Teacher

Becker, Carl. *The Declaration of Independence*. Knopf, 1966.
McDonald, Forrest. *We the People: The Economic Origins of the Constitution*. University of Chicago Press, 1958.
McPherson, James M. *Abraham Lincoln and the Second American Revolution*. Oxford University Press, 1991.
Weatherford, Jack. *Native Roots: How the Indians Enriched America*. Crown, 1991.
Wills, Garry. *Religion and American Politics*. Simon and Schuster, 1990.
Wood, Gordon. *The Creation of the American Republic: 1776–1787*. University of North Carolina Press, 1969.

Multimedia

Videocassettes and Films
The Constitution: The Compromise That Made a Nation. Learning Corporation of America. (film, 27 minutes)
George Mason. (*Profiles in Courage* series.) Zenger Films. (v/c, 50 minutes)
Inventing a Nation. (*Alistair Cooke's America: A Personal History of the United States series*). Time-Life Films, Inc. (v/c, 52 minutes)
To Keep Our Liberty. National Park Service. (v/c, 23 minutes)
The War for Independence: A Military History. Multi-Media. (v/c, 24 minutes)

Software
PFS: File—United States Government: (Constitutional Convention data base). Scholastic Publishing Company. (Apple IIe or IIc, at least 64K and 1 disk drive; must be used with *PFS: File, PFS: Report;* 2nd disk drive and printer recommended.) Students research and analyze issues related to the Constitutional Convention.
Revolutions: Past, Present, Future. Focus Media. (5 Apple disks, 4 TRS80 disks). Students compare American, French, and Russian Revolutions.

The Creation of the Federal Government

CHAPTER 2

Introduce

Chapter Overview

Chapter 2 reviews the long heritage of American self-government.

Section 1 explains the British political tradition which colonists brought with them when they came to America and traces the development of representative government by exploring the Magna Carta, the ideas of John Locke, and the Mayflower Compact.

Section 2 relates how the colonists united to protest British tax laws and how this unification led to the Declaration of Independence.

Section 3 explains the government established under the Articles of Confederation and how the weaknesses of the Articles led to an awareness of the need for a stronger government.

Section 4 traces the work of the Constitutional Convention, including compromises made by the delegates, and summarizes the debate over ratification of the Constitution.

Chapter 2 Themes

Make a concept map of the Themes in Government for this chapter by writing the four themes one under the other on the chalkboard. Then have volunteers read aloud the text that follows each theme. As a student reads, box the theme and draw downward arrows to connect each theme. Tell students this is a brief visual outline of the chapter's content. Have students refer to the concept map as they read the chapter.

Junius B. Stearns painted George Washington addressing the Constitutional Convention of 1787.

44   UNIT 1: FOUNDATIONS OF AMERICAN GOVERNMENT

About the Chapter Opener

Teaching With Illustrations Point out to students that the 55 delegates to the Constitutional Convention included many of the most able political leaders in the United States. Almost all the delegates had practical experience in government and had helped to write their state constitutions. Have students carefully examine the painting shown on pages 44 and 45 and ask them what thoughts or feelings the art evokes in them. You might also ask them what the painting shows about the influence of George Washington on the times. *(Answers will vary. Students might indicate that it reflects the importance of Washington in the establishment of the new United States government.)*

Chapter Preview

Overview

Before, during, and after the Revolutionary War, the American system of government went through a period of experimentation, resulting in a written Constitution.

Objectives

After studying this chapter, you should be able to:

1. **Identify** the factors that influenced colonial government.
2. **Relate** the events leading up to the Declaration of Independence.
3. **Describe** the achievements and weaknesses of the government under the Articles of Confederation.
4. **Trace** the development of the Constitution from the Constitutional Convention to ratification.

Themes in Government

This chapter emphasizes the following government themes:

- **Civil Liberties** The British laid the foundations of civil liberties that extend to all Americans today. Sections 1 and 2.
- **Growth of Democracy** The Americans revolted against Britain and formed their own government because the British were limiting American rights. Sections 1, 2, 3, and 4.
- **Federalism** The Constitution established a federal system of government. Section 3.
- **Checks and Balances** The Constitution provided for a limited government. Section 4.

Critical Thinking Skills

This chapter emphasizes the following critical thinking skills:

- Identifying Central Issues
- Drawing Conclusions
- Understanding Cause and Effect
- Expressing Problems Clearly
- Identifying Alternatives

Introducing the Chapter

Conduct a class discussion on what students already know about the creation of the federal government. Ask: How much control did colonists have over laws that governed them? (*Each colony's legislature made its own laws, but Parliament also passed laws affecting the colonists.*) After the Declaration of Independence did the former colonies consider themselves to be separate independent countries or one independent country? (*separate independent countries*) How and by whom was the Constitution written? (*through a series of compromises; largely by James Madison*)

Chapter Project

Organize students into four groups. Assign each group one of the sections in this chapter. Tell them their task is to create a timeline of events for the time span covered in their assigned section. They might provide illustrations of the events described on their portion of the timeline.

After students complete the study of the chapter, have the groups present their timelines and explain how the events on the timeline influenced the creation of the American system of government.

Linking Past and Present
Two lasting achievements of government under the Articles of Confederation were the Land Ordinance of 1785 and the Northwest Ordinance of 1787. The first established the system of townships that are still used today. The second established the system for admitting new states to the Union.

Focus on Government
Video 6
Making Connections:
Federal Hall and the U.S. Capitol
Running Time: 2:05
Videodisc 1, Chap. 6
VHS Tape 1, Begins 16:10

Setting the Scene Our system of government and politics emerged only gradually from the colonial experience that began with the settling of Jamestown. We sometimes forget that the period from the founding of Jamestown to the writing of the Constitution was nearly as long as the years from 1787 to now. Social theories and political attitudes changed over that 180 years just as they have changed during the 2 centuries we have lived under the Constitution. Thus the political ideas and events of the colonial period had a strong influence on the type of government we have today.

Focus

Bell Ringer

While attendance is being taken, ask students to write an answer to this question:

What countries revolted against communism in the late 1980s and the early 1990s?

Motivating Activity

Discuss students' Bell Ringer answers. *(Poland, East Germany, Romania, China, USSR)* Discuss with students why the people of these countries revolted against communism. *(to get out from under strict government control, to gain personal freedoms, to improve their standard of living)*

Tell students in this section they will read about similar factors that shaped America's political heritage and led to the growth of democracy.

Vocabulary Precheck

Ask students to speculate on the meaning of each term and concept. Then have them check their guesses by finding the definition in the section text. **LEP**

Caption Answer

limited government and representative government

Teach

Guided Practice

L1 **Identifying Main Ideas** Have students scan the minor headings and text under the main headings "An English Political Heritage" and "Government in the Colonies" to find the main ideas or central themes and then write these in their notebooks. Call on students to read what they consider to be the main idea under each minor heading. **LEP**

SECTION

1

Roots of American Government

Every year thousands of foreign and American tourists flock to Virginia to visit the remains of Jamestown, the first permanent English settlement in North America. Crumbling foundation stones and the ruins of the old church tower mark the site of the original Jamestown, founded in 1607. The decaying brick and mortar offer a striking contrast to the enduring principles of self-government inherited from the English colonists. This legacy of self-government enables Americans today to voice their opinions without fear of reprisal, to choose their leaders, and to take an active role in shaping the nation and communities in which they live. Modern Americans, like the colonists, believe that there are natural rights—life, liberty, and property—that governments are contracted to protect.

An English Political Heritage

During the 1600s people from many regions, such as Spain, the Netherlands, France, Sweden, Norway, and West Africa, settled in North America. Most colonists, however, came from England. It was the English who established and governed the original thirteen colonies along the Atlantic coast.

The English colonists brought with them ideas about government that had been developing in England for centuries. By the 1600s English government offered its citizens political liberties, such as trial by jury, that were largely unknown elsewhere. At the heart of the English system were two principles of government. These principles—limited government and representative government—greatly influenced the development of the United States.

Limited Government By the time the first colonists reached North America, the idea that government was not all-powerful had become an accepted part of the English system. The idea first appeared in the Magna Carta, or Great Charter, that King John signed in 1215. The Magna Carta established the principle of **limited government**, in which the power of the monarch, or government, was limited, not absolute. This document provided for protection against unjust punishment and the loss of life, liberty, and property except according to law. Under the

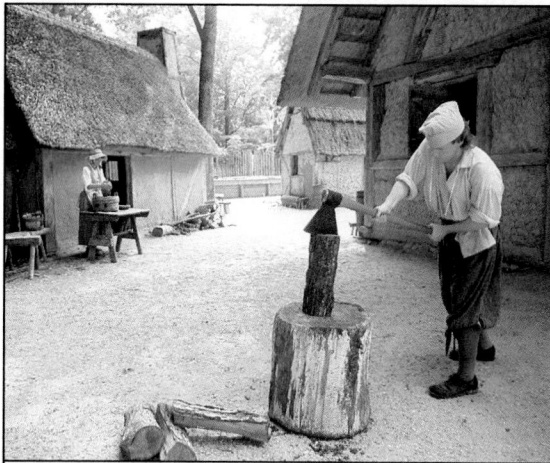

A Living Legacy
The early English colonists at Jamestown, Virginia, established the continent's first representative assembly. **History** **Which principles of British government influenced the country's early development?**

SECTION PREVIEW

Objectives
After studying this section, you should be able to:
- Explain the principle of limited government.
- Identify the factors that shaped this nation's political heritage.

Key Terms and Concepts
limited government, representative government, separation of powers

Themes in Government
- Civil Liberties
- Growth of Democracy

Critical Thinking Skills
- Identifying Central Issues
- Drawing Conclusions

46 UNIT 1: FOUNDATIONS OF AMERICAN GOVERNMENT

Classroom Resources for Section 1

- Guided Reading Activities
- Reproducible Lesson Plans
- Section 1 Quiz
- Testmaker

The Living Constitution
SAT Practice Tests
Writer's Guidebook

Magna Carta, the king agreed that certain taxes could not be levied without popular consent.

The rights in the Magna Carta originally applied only to the nobility. During the next few centuries, however, other groups won political liberties, primarily through agreements between English monarchs and the nobility and merchants. In 1689 the English Parliament, which had originated in the 1200s, passed the English Bill of Rights. This document, a landmark in the development of democratic government, was very important to the American colonists.

The English Bill of Rights set clear limits on what the ruler could and could not do. It applied to the American colonists—who were English subjects—as well as to the people in England. Incorporating elements from the Magna Carta, the key ideas of the English Bill of Rights included: (1) monarchs do not have a divine right to rule. They rule with the consent of the people's representatives in Parliament. (2) The monarch must have Parliament's consent to suspend laws, levy taxes, or maintain an army. (3) The monarch cannot interfere with parliamentary elections and debates. (4) The people have a right to petition the government and to have a fair and speedy trial by a jury of their peers. (5) The people should not be subject to cruel and unusual punishments or to excessive fines and bail.

The English colonists in North America shared a belief in these rights with the people of England. A major cause of the American Revolution was the colonists felt they were being deprived of these basic rights.

Representative Government The colonists had a firm belief in **representative government**, in which people elect delegates to make laws and conduct government. The colonists had also experienced representative government. Parliament was a representative assembly with the power to enact laws. It was made up of an upper chamber, or legislative body, and a lower chamber. The upper chamber, called the House of Lords, included members of the aristocracy. The lower chamber, called the House of Commons,

A Noble Document
In 1215 King John signed the Magna Carta, limiting the powers of the monarchy. **History Which group of people benefited from this document?**

included commoners—mostly merchants or property owners. Members of the House of Commons were elected by other property owners and merchants. In America legislatures grew directly out of this English practice of having Parliament pass laws.

The Ideas of John Locke The ideas and writings of the seventeenth-century English philosopher John Locke deeply influenced the political outlook of the American colonists. Locke spelled out his political ideas in *Two Treatises on Government*, first published in 1690. His writings were widely read and discussed in both Europe and America. Locke's ideas seemed to fit the American colonial experience. Colonial leaders such as Benjamin Franklin, Thomas Jefferson, and James Madison regarded these ideas as political truth. Locke's ideas became so influential that they have been called the "textbook of the American Revolution."

STUDY GUIDE

Themes in Government
Civil Liberties Unlike many earlier thinkers, Locke did not believe that people had a tendency to be evil. Instead, he believed that people were basically good and could

succeed based upon their abilities. **How did Locke's ideas support the principle of limited government?**

Critical Thinking Skills
Identifying Central Issues What in the backgrounds of the Ameri-

can colonists led them to expect to have representative government in the colonies?

Background

British political tradition contributed more than the principle of representative government; it also contributed a heritage of revolution. Less than 100 years before the American Revolution, the Glorious Revolution took place in England. It was a revolution initiated and controlled by conservatives. The acts of James II in trying to reestablish Catholicism

as the established religion were branded as unconstitutional and provided the reason for his overthrow. His successors, William and Mary of Orange, were chosen by Parliament which firmly established the principle of parliamentary sovereignty.

L2 Growth of Democracy
Write *Magna Carta, English Bill of Rights, limited government,* and *representative government* on the chalkboard. Ask volunteers to explain in their own words how each influenced the colonists' plan of self-government set forth in the Mayflower Compact.

L3 Interpreting Primary Sources Have students reread John Locke's quote on page 48. Then ask them to identify in the Declaration of Independence on pages 57–60 words and phrases that illustrate Locke's view of the social contract.

Caption Answer
the nobility

STUDY GUIDE

Theme Answer
He believed that people did not owe unquestioning loyalty to the ruler.

Critical Thinking Answer
A long tradition of representative government based on the Magna Carta and the rule of Parliament.

Independent Practice

L1 **Research** Have students research the settlement of Jamestown, Virginia, and the role Captain John Smith played in its establishment. Ask students to find out by whom and how the colony was governed and what eventually happened to the colony. Have them present their findings in an oral report. **LEP**

Focus on Freedom

The signers of the Mayflower Compact had very little experience in law. Most had merely been subjects of the King. The Pilgrims had to improvise according to what they thought was right under the circumstances. What action did the colonists take in the Compact? *(formed a civil body politic)* Why did they need to do this? *(because there was no governing authority in the area where they landed)*

Answers

1. for the glory of God and the advancement of the Christian faith

2. to enact, constitute, and frame laws, ordinances, acts, constitutions, and offices as was fitting for the good of the colony

3. It was the first written agreement providing for self-government drafted by the colonists.

CONNECTIONS

History

In Massachusetts colony, a law required that every town of 50 families hire a schoolmaster, and every town with 100 families hire one who could teach Greek and Latin.

Locke reasoned that all people were born free, equal, and independent. They possessed natural rights to life, liberty, and property at the time they lived in a state of nature, before governments were formed. People contracted among themselves to form governments to protect their natural rights. Locke argued that if a government failed to protect these natural rights, the people could change that government. The people had not agreed to be governed by tyrants who threatened their rights but by rulers who defended their rights.

Locke's ideas were revolutionary in an age when monarchs still claimed they had God-given absolute powers. Locke denied that people were born with an obligation to obey their rulers. Rather, in his *Second Treatise on Civil Government*, Locke insisted that:

Freedom of men under government is to have a standing rule to live by, common to every one of that society, and made by the legislative power vested in it; a liberty to follow my own will in all things, when the rule prescribes not, and not to be subject to the inconstant, uncertain, unknown, arbitrary will of another man.

—JOHN LOCKE,
Second Treatise on Civil Government, 1690

Government, then, was legitimate only as long as people continued to consent to it. Both the Declaration of Independence and the Constitution, written nearly a century after Locke, reflected Locke's revolutionary ideas.

Focus on Freedom

THE MAYFLOWER COMPACT

On November 11, 1620, after a rough journey of 65 days, the Mayflower dropped anchor in Provincetown harbor, near the tip of Cape Cod. Although the Pilgrims had pledged to set up their colony within the limits of the original grant of the Virginia Company, navigational errors led them to the New England area. With adverse winds and winter close at hand, the Pilgrims stayed where they were and set about establishing their colony. Although the Pilgrims were still English citizens, they were in a region that had no authority. The Pilgrim leaders knew, therefore, that they would have to set up some form of government. On November 11, 41 men aboard the Mayflower signed the Mayflower Compact.

In the name of God, Amen. We whose names are underwritten, the loyal subjects of our dread [revered and feared] sovereign Lord King James, by the grace of God, of Great Britain, France, and Ireland, King, Defender of the Faith, etc., having undertaken, for the glory of God, and advancement of the Christian faith, and honor of our king and country, a voyage to plant the first colony in the northern parts of Virginia, do by these presents [this document] solemnly and mutually in the presence of God, and one of another, covenant [promise] and combine ourselves together into a civil body politic [group organized for government] for our better ordering and preservation and furtherance of the ends aforesaid; and by virtue [authority] hereof, to enact, constitute, and frame such just and equal laws, ordinances [regulations], acts, constitutions, and offices from time to time, as shall be thought most meet [fitting] and convenient for the general al good of the colony unto which we promise all due submission and obedience.

In WITNESS whereof we have hereunto subscribed our names at Cape Cod, the eleventh of November, in the year of the reign of our sovereign Lord King James of England, France, and Ireland the eighteenth, and of Scotland the fifty-fourth. *Anno Domini*, 1620.

—MAYFLOWER COMPACT

Examining the Document

Reviewing Facts

1. Explain why, according to the Mayflower Compact, the Pilgrims set sail for the Americas.
2. Describe the powers the Mayflower Compact gave the Pilgrims.

Critical Thinking Skills

3. Understanding Cause and Effect Why was the Mayflower Compact an important step toward democracy?

Cooperative Learning Activity

Organize the class into four groups to research the kinds of colonial governments from 1600–1775. Assign each group one of the following colonies: Massachusetts, Connecticut, New York, Georgia. Each group should determine a) how the governors were chosen; b) the role of the governors in the colony; c) the lawmaking powers of the colonial charter; d) the kind of representative legislatures; e) the role of town councils, county courts, and committees. Have each group present its findings to the class. Discuss similarities and differences among colonial governments.

Government in the Colonies

Between 1607 and 1733, the English founded thirteen colonies along the eastern coast of North America. It was from these colonies that the present system of American government evolved. Each English colony had its own government consisting of a governor, a legislature, and a court system. Nevertheless, the British believed that all colonists owed allegiance to the monarch. For many years the colonists agreed with this philosophy.

Democracy in all the colonies grew rapidly, but it did not yet exist in its current form. Women and enslaved persons could not vote, and every colony had some type of property qualification for voting. Nine of the thirteen colonies had established an official church, and many colonists remained intolerant of religious dissent. In some of the colonies, strict religious observance was expected of citizens. In Virginia, for example, the penalty for breaking the Sabbath for the third time was death.

Despite such shortcomings, the colonial governments established practices that became a key part of the nation's system of government. Chief among these were (1) a written constitution that guaranteed basic liberties and limited the power of government; (2) a legislature of elected representatives; and (3) the separation of powers between the governor (the chief executive) and the legislature. Today the United States government embodies each of these practices.

Written Constitutions A key feature of the colonial period was government according to some type of written plan. The Mayflower Compact that the Pilgrims signed in 1620 stands as the first example of many colonial plans for self-government.

Forty-one men, representing all the Pilgrim families, drew up The Mayflower Compact in the tiny cabin of their ship, the *Mayflower.* The Pilgrim leaders realized they needed rules to govern themselves if they were to survive in the new land. Through the Mayflower Compact, they agreed to:

The Thirteen English Colonies

Massachusetts
New Hampshire
New York
Rhode Island
Connecticut
Pennsylvania
New Jersey
Delaware
Maryland
Virginia
ATLANTIC OCEAN
North Carolina
South Carolina
Georgia

New England Colonies
Middle Colonies
Southern Colonies

Map Study
There were thirteen separate English colonies. **How were their governments similar?**

*S*olemnly and mutually in the Presence of God and one of another, covenant [pledge] and combine ourselves together into a Body Politick, for our better Ordering and Preservation and Furtherance of the Ends aforesaid. . . .
—THE MAYFLOWER COMPACT, 1620

L2 Informative Writing Have students write an essay in which they explain how English political heritage affected the kinds of governments established by the colonists after 1607.

L3 Expressive Writing Ask students to assume that they are Virginia colonists. Have them write letters to their relatives in England in which they explain how American colonial government differs from and is similar to English government.

Map Study Answer
The government of each colony consisted of a governor, a legislature, and a court system.

STUDY GUIDE

Theme Answer
All had a written constitution, elected legislature, and separation of powers.

Critical Thinking Answer
All colonies had established their own constitutions and governing bodies.

CONNECTIONS

Literature
By the end of the 1600s, several colonies had at least one printing press which published broadsides, almanacs, pamphlets, and books. During this time the most widely read authors were clergymen who published sermons. One of the earliest poets was Edward Taylor, a minister from Massachusetts.

STUDY GUIDE

Themes In Government
Growth of Democracy When the thirteen colonies were founded, almost all nations had governments based upon the theory of divine right. **In what ways were colonial governments democratic?**

Critical Thinking Skills
Drawing Conclusions In the 1760s when Great Britain attempted to restrict the colonies' right to govern themselves, the king encountered strong opposition. **How had the idea of colonial self-government developed?**

Critical Thinking Activity

Drawing Conclusions John Locke, along with Jean Jacques Rousseau and James Harrington, developed the theory of the social contract to explain the relationship of people to government. Locke saw the human race as having lived in a state of nature until the civil society, a "body politic," was created through a contract or compact that established a governing authority. The government's main purpose was to protect the rights of its citizens. Ask students: How might the American colonies have influenced the ideas of John Locke?

Assess

Check for Understanding

Have students complete Section 1 Review on page 50.

Meeting Objectives

Each section objective is tested by the Section Review questions that follow it in parentheses.
- Explain the principle of limited government. (2, 3, 7)
- Identify the factors that shaped this nation's political heritage. (2, 3, 4, 5, 6, 8)

Evaluate

📁 Section 1 Quiz

🔲 Testmaker

Reteach

Have students name the practices of colonial government that became a key part of our nation's government.

Enrich

Assign students to research and write a report on the role of colonial governors during the 1600s.

Close

Ask students to explain in their own words the Section 1 Key Terms and Concepts.

The Pilgrims also agreed to choose their own leaders and to make their own laws, which they would design for their own benefit.

Beginning in 1629 new Puritan immigrants settled near Massachusetts Bay and added many towns to the original Plymouth settlement. In 1636, the colony realized a need for more comprehensive laws. It adopted the "Great Fundamentals," the first basic system of laws in the English Colonies.

In 1639 Puritans who had left the Massachusetts Bay Colony to colonize Connecticut drew up America's first formal constitution, or charter, called the Fundamental Orders of Connecticut. This document laid out a plan for government that gave the people the right to elect the governor, judges, and representatives to make laws. While it was based on the Massachusetts model, it did not restrict voting rights to church members.

Soon after, other English colonies began drawing up their own charters. These documents established a system of limited government and rule by law in each of the colonies. Several of these colonial constitutions were very democratic for their time. The Rhode Island and Connecticut charters were so democratic that they continued to serve as state constitutions even after the adoption of the United States Constitution.

Colonial Legislatures Representative assemblies also became firmly established in the colonies. The Virginia House of Burgesses, the first representative legislature in America, was established in 1619, only 12 years after the settlement of Jamestown. The newly elected lawmakers passed laws aiding farmers and curbing idleness, improper dress, and drunkenness. It was not long before other colonies set up their own legislatures. By the mid-1700s, most colonial legislatures had been operating for more than 100 years. As a result, representative government was an established tradition in America well before the colonists declared their independence from Great Britain in 1776.

The colonial legislatures dominated colonial government. The rapidly growing colonies constantly needed new laws to cope with new circumstances. For example, they had to control the distribution of land and construct public buildings and facilities such as roads, ferries, and wharves. The colonies also had to establish schools and new towns and establish civil and criminal courts.

These legislatures were examples of the consent of the governed because a large number of qualified people voted. Although there were property qualifications for voting, land was abundant and most colonists could afford property.

Separation of Powers Colonial charters divided powers of government. The governor, as the agent of the monarch, carried out the monarch's orders. The governor also enforced the laws that the colonial legislature passed. This **separation of powers** continued under the United States Constitution, which allows Congress to pass laws and gives the President the power to enforce them.

1 SECTION REVIEW

Section Summary

The principles contained in the Magna Carta and the English Bill of Rights, as well as the ideas of English philosopher John Locke, influenced the colonists as they set up their governments. The colonists established these principles in written constitutions that served even after colonies became states.

Checking for Understanding
Recalling Facts

1. Define limited government, representative government, separation of powers.
2. Name the document that established limited government in England.
3. State why John Locke believed people formed governments.

4. Identify the first written agreement providing for self-government in the colonies.

Exploring Themes

5. Civil Liberties In what specific ways is the Magna Carta, a British document, part of the American political heritage?
6. Growth of Democracy Why were the political ideas of John Locke considered revolutionary in the 1600s?

Critical Thinking Skills

7. Identifying Central Issues Why must government be limited?
8. Drawing Conclusions The right to liberty is a "natural right." What rights do you associate with liberty?

Section I Review Answers

1. Definitions of terms appear on pages indicated: **limited government,** 46; **representative government,** 47; **separation of powers,** 50
2. Magna Carta
3. to protect their natural rights
4. Mayflower Compact
5. It established the principle that the power of government is limited. It provided civil liberties and protection against taxes without consent of the citizenry. It laid the foundation for the development of constitutional government.
6. Because he denied the popular idea that people were born with an obligation to obey their rulers. Rather, he believed government was legitimate only with the consent of the people.
7. Answers should include the ideas that a government of unlimited power would be more prone to abuse that power, rulers could become tyrants, many groups would not be represented, and civil liberties/natural rights would be endangered.
8. Answers should include the rights of free speech, worship, to attend political rallies or rock concerts, to travel freely, to contract with employers, to pursue an education, to print materials.

American Colonies Unite

Interviewed years after the Revolutionary War, Captain Levi Preston of Danvers, Massachusetts, talked about why many Americans had revolted against Britain:

The old soldier was asked, "Did you take up arms against intolerable oppressions?"

He answered, "Oppressions? I didn't feel them."

"What, were you not oppressed by the Stamp Act?"

"I never saw one of those stamps. I certainly never paid a penny for one of them."

"What about the tea tax?"

"I never drank a drop of the stuff; the boys threw it all overboard."

"Then I suppose you had been reading Locke about the eternal principles of Liberty?"

"Never heard of 'em. We read only the Bible, the Catechism, Watts' Psalms and Hymns, and the Almanac."

"Well, then, what was the matter? And what did you mean in going to the fight?"

"Young man, what we meant in going for those Redcoats was this: We always had governed ourselves, and we meant to. They didn't mean we should."

—LEVI PRESTON

The old soldier's answer illustrates the fundamental cause of the Revolution. The colonists revolted because they were being deprived of their traditional rights and liberties as British citizens. Chief among these was the right to govern themselves.

The Colonies Move Toward Independence
The Mohawk chief Joseph Brant, depicted here in a Gilbert Stuart portrait, fought for the victorious British in the French and Indian War. **History What consequences did the war have on the colonists?**

American Colonies and Britain

Until the mid-1700s, Great Britain had allowed its colonies across the Atlantic to develop politically on their own. By the 1760s, however, things had begun to change dramatically as the British government sought to tighten its control over the colonies.

SECTION PREVIEW

Objectives
After studying this section, you should be able to:
- Trace the events leading to the writing of the Declaration of Independence.

- Identify the issues behind colonial protests.

Key Terms and Concepts
revenue, embargo

Themes in Government
- Civil Liberties
- Growth of Democracy

Critical Thinking Skills
- Understanding Cause and Effect
- Expressing Problems Clearly

CHAPTER 2: THE CREATION OF THE FEDERAL GOVERNMENT 51

Focus

Bell Ringer
While attendance is being taken, ask students to define *revenue* in their own words.

Motivating Activity
Discuss students' answers to the Bell Ringer. *(the money a government collects from taxes or other resources)* Then ask students to identify the types of taxes that Americans pay. *(property taxes; local, state, and federal income taxes; sales taxes on items bought in stores)*

Ask students to express the feelings people hold about taxes and discuss why taxpayers might have the feelings they do.

Then tell students this section explains how taxes helped cause the Revolutionary War and led to the writing of the Declaration of Independence.

Vocabulary Precheck
Call on a student to read aloud the definitions of *revenue* and *embargo* from the Glossary. Then have volunteers restate each definition in their own words. **LEP**

Caption Answer
They no longer depended on British protection and were expected to help repay British war debt.

CONNECTIONS

History
The Stamp Act required stamps be placed on 54 kinds of articles and documents. Duties ranged from 1 shilling on newspapers to 2 pounds for college diplomas.

Classroom Resources for Section 2

- 📁 Guided Reading Activities
- 📁 Reproducible Lesson Plans
- 📁 Primary and Secondary Source Readings 2
- 📁 Section 2 Quiz

- 💾 Testmaker
- The Living Constitution
- SAT Practice Tests
- Writer's Guidebook

Focus

Write the term *confederation* on the chalkboard and ask how a confederation differs from a nation.

Teach

Have students speculate about advantages for the member nations of participation in a confederation. *(shared resources and information, common defense, internal peace, increased security)* What evidence is there in the organization of the Iroquois Confederation of women's high status in Iroquois society? *(elected chiefs)* Why would a constitution improve the function of a confederation? *(make the organization less informal; clarify purposes, duties, and privileges of members)*

Assess

Have students complete **Examining Our Multicultural Heritage.**

Answers

1. Dekanawida and Hiawatha
2. Women leaders elected chiefs to represent them. Each nation's delegation had one vote.
3. Both provided for representative government and were loose confederations where individual governing units retained much power.

Close

Compare the structure of the Iroquois Confederation with the federal structure of American government today.

Multicultural Heritage

The Iroquois Confederation

Long before the United States had its first constitution, Native Americans in present-day New York State had crafted their own plan of government. About 1570, two Native American leaders—Dekanawida (DEK•uhn•uh•WEE•duh) and Hiawatha—urged people in their region to make peace and join together to resist invasions from other nations. Their actions led to the formation of the Iroquois Confederation of the Five Nations, which included the Mohawk, Onondaga, Oneida, Cayuga, and Seneca.

Indian legend, passed along from generation to generation, credits Hiawatha with giving the speech that laid the foundation for unity before the council of five Indian nations. Following Hiawatha's speech the leaders discussed and adopted the idea of a confederation.

A number of clans, each with its own village, made up each nation. Women leaders of each clan elected a chief to represent them at meetings of the council, the representative body of the Confederation. To ensure equality among the nations, the delegation from each nation had one vote at council meetings.

Although Native Americans in other parts of North America also created confederacies, the Iroquois Confederation was better organized and more effective. This was perhaps because they had a constitution—the first in the Americas. Though this constitution was not written down until 1850, its provisions included:

> The object of these laws is to establish peace between the numerous nations of Indians . . . for the preservation of life, property and liberty . . . And the number of chiefs in this confederation of the five Indian Nations are fifty. . . .
>
> All lords of the Five Nations Confederacy must be honest in all things. . . . It shall be a serious wrong for anyone to lead a lord into trivial affairs, for the people must ever hold their lords high in estimation out of respect to their honorable positions.
>
> When a candidate lord is to be installed he shall furnish four strings of shells (or wampum) one span in length bound together at one end. Such will constitute the evidence of his pledge to the confederate

Iroquois Wampum Belt

> lords that he will live according to the constitution of the Great Peace and exercise justice in all affairs.
> —THE CONSTITUTION OF THE IROQUOIS CONFEDERATION, TRANSCRIBED 1850

The constitution guided the Confederation for more than 200 years, ensuring peace for the member nations. During the American Revolution, however, some nations fought for the colonial cause, while others supported the British. In 1779 United States Major General John Sullivan led an expeditionary force that defeated the British supporters. The Confederation did not survive the split in loyalties or the disastrous defeat at the hands of Sullivan's forces.

Despite the ultimate defeat of the Confederation, the Native American concept of representative government influenced the course of early American democracy. The government that the Articles of Confederation established included many features similar to the characteristics of the Iroquois Confederacy.

Examining Our Multicultural Heritage

Reviewing Facts
1. Identify the founders of the Iroquois Confederation.
2. Describe the representative assembly of the Iroquois Confederation.

Critical Thinking Skills
3. Making Comparisons What features of the Articles of Confederation were similar to the constitution of the Iroquois Confederation?

More About Our Multicultural Heritage

Among the indigenous peoples of North America, the Iroquois were unique in the complexity of their political organization and military might. By the early 1600s the Iroquois Confederation had 5,500 members living in the New York area from the Hudson River north to the Saint Lawrence River. Seven of the English colonies tried to form a union similar to the Iroquois Confederation when they met in Albany, New York, in June 1754. At this meeting delegates adopted a plan calling for an elected legislature and a president-general appointed by the king. The plan failed because, fearing a loss of their powers, all seven colonial governments rejected it.

The Colonies on Their Own As British subjects, the colonists in North America owed allegiance to the monarch and the British government. As with other parts of the British empire, the colonies were supposed to serve as a source of raw materials and a market for British goods. Thus, in the eyes of the British crown, the American colonies existed for the economic benefit of Great Britain.

In practice, during the 150 years following the settling of Jamestown in 1607, the colonies in America did pretty much as they pleased. The colonies were more than 3,000 miles (5,556 kilometers) from Great Britain. Orders from the monarch took two months or more to cross the Atlantic. In addition, only the colonial legislatures were actually in a position to deal with the everyday problems facing the colonies. As a result, the colonists grew accustomed to governing themselves through their representatives.

Until the mid-1700s, the British government was generally satisfied with this arrangement. The British needed the colonists' loyalty to counter the threat of the French in Canada. The colonists remained loyal in return for a large measure of self-rule and protection from the French.

Britain Tightens Control Two events drastically changed the easy relationship between the colonies and Britain. First, the French and Indian War, fought between 1754 and 1763, threatened Britain's hold on the continent. Second, George III, who became king in 1760, had different ideas about how the colonies should be governed.

The French and Indian War started as a struggle between the French and British over lands in western Pennsylvania and Ohio. By 1756 several other European countries became involved as well. Great Britain eventually won the war in 1763 and gained complete control of what later became the eastern United States. The French were driven out.

The defeat of France in America meant the American colonists no longer depended on the British to protect them from the French. The war, however, left the British government with a large war debt that the British expected the colonies to help repay.

A Raid That Led to Rebellion
The Boston Tea Party helped spark the Revolutionary War. Economics **Why did the colonists proclaim "No taxation without representation"?**

When he took the throne, George III was determined to deal more firmly with the American colonies. The king and his ministers levied taxes on tea, sugar, glass, and paper, as well as other products. The Stamp Act of 1765 imposed the first direct tax on the colonies. It required them to pay a tax on legal documents, pamphlets, newspapers, and even dice and playing cards. Parliament also passed laws to control colonial trade in ways that benefited Great Britain but not the colonies.

STUDY GUIDE

Themes in Government
Civil Liberties The American colonists had many more rights than their French or Spanish counterparts in the Americas. This was because in part the monarchs of

Spain and France ruled by divine right. **Why did the British try to limit civil liberties in the colonies after 1763?**

Critical Thinking Skills
Understanding Cause and Effect
What factors caused the British to allow the colonists to operate with little interference between 1607 and 1763?

Teach

Guided Practice

L1 Concept Mapping Work with students to prepare a concept map showing the cause-and-effect relationship of events leading to the Declaration of Independence. As students answer each question that follows, write their answers on the chalkboard, box each answer, and connect the boxes with arrows.

Start with a box labeled *French and Indian War* and ask how the war changed the relationship between the colonists and Britain. *(Britain taxed colonists to pay for war.)* How did the colonists react? *(protests, boycotts)* How did Britain retaliate? *(Passed Coercive Acts to punish colonists.)* How did the colonists respond? *(First Continental Congress)* What did Britain do next? *(declared colonies in rebellion)* What did the colonists do? *(Declaration of Independence)*

Caption Answer
because the colonists were used to being governed by their colonial legislatures

---

STUDY GUIDE

Theme Answer
They were in debt and wanted to impose new taxes without colonial consent.

Critical Thinking Answer
distance; only colonial legislatures could deal with daily problems

---

Background

On July 5, 1775, the Second Continental Congress made one last attempt to bring a peaceful end to the crisis between the colonies and Britain. The Congress prepared the Olive Branch Petition, an appeal to the king to reconsider the consequences of British colonial policy. The petition expressed the colonists' desire for "a happy and permanent reconciliation." Radicals in the Congress, such as John and Samuel Adams and Patrick Henry, signed the petition, expecting that its rejection would bring the moderates over to their side. As they had hoped, George III refused the petition.

L2 Classifying Have students classify the methods the colonists used to resist Britain's economic policies and provide examples of each. *(boycotts: refused to buy British goods; civil disobedience: dumped British tea into Boston Harbor; organization: Stamp Act Congress and Continental Congresses; trade embargo: First Continental Congress imposed embargo prohibiting trade with Great Britain)* Ask students to provide examples of how these four techniques are still used in protests and politics today. *(Students may suggest labor strikes, boycotts of certain products, demonstrations and sit-ins, trade embargo against Iraq.)*

L3 Political Science Tell students that historians have labeled the Declaration of Independence as both a political and a philosophical statement. Have students explain this description in a short paragraph and then read their paragraphs to the class. *(political because it was a document used to justify a revolution against an unjust ruler; philosophical because it sets forth the fundamental concept of government by consent of the governed)*

Caption Answer
trade embargoes, political protests, petitions, and committees of correspondence

---

Britain's **revenue** (the money a government collects from taxes or other sources) from the colonies increased. Colonial resentment, however, grew along with the revenues. Political protests began to spread throughout the colonies. Colonists refused to buy British goods. This move led to the repeal of the Stamp Act, but the British passed other tax laws to replace it. In 1773 a group of colonists, dressed as Mohawks, dumped 342 chests of British tea into Boston Harbor. This protest against further taxes on tea became known as the Boston Tea Party.

Forging An American Identity
Alfred W. Thompson's painting depicts British soldiers plundering and burning a New England home. Harsh British measures spurred colonial resistance to British rule.
History **What were some of the ways the colonists resisted British authority?**

In retaliation, Parliament passed the Coercive Acts, which the colonists called the Intolerable Acts. One of these acts closed Boston Harbor. Another withdrew the right of the Massachusetts colony to govern itself. By the early 1770s, events clearly showed that revolution was not far off.

Colonial Unity

Before the mid-1770s, most colonists thought of themselves as British subjects. At the same time, each of the colonies developed largely on its own. Thus, most colonists also thought of themselves as Virginians or New Yorkers or Georgians. Indeed, early attempts to bring the colonies together had failed.

As early as 1754, Benjamin Franklin proposed an innovative plan for uniting the colonies—the Albany Plan of Union. The colonies rejected the plan, however, because it gave too much power to an assembly made up of representatives from all thirteen colonies.

By the 1760s the harsh new British policies spurred an American sense of community. A growing number of colonists began to think of themselves as Americans united by their hostility to British authority. At the same time, colonial leaders began to take political action against what they felt was British suppression.

In 1765 nine colonies sent delegates to a meeting in New York called the Stamp Act Congress. This was the first meeting organized by the colonies to protest King George's actions. Delegates to the Congress sent a petition to the king, arguing that only colonial legislatures could impose direct taxes such as the Stamp Tax.

By 1773 organizations called committees of correspondence were urging resistance to the British. These committees consisted of colonists who wanted to keep in touch with one another as events unfolded. Samuel Adams established the first committee in Boston. The idea spread quickly and within a few months, Massachusetts alone had more than 80 such committees. Virginia and other colonies soon joined in this network of communication.

The First Continental Congress The Intolerable Acts prompted Virginia and Massachusetts to call a general meeting of the colonies. Delegates from all the colonies except Georgia met in Philadelphia on September 5, 1774, for what was to be called the First Continental Congress. Key colonial leaders such as Patrick Henry, Samuel Adams, Richard Henry Lee, and George Washington attended.

The delegates debated what to do about the relationship with Great Britain. After two months of discussion, they imposed an **embargo**, an agreement prohibiting trade, on Britain, and agreed not to use British goods. They also proposed a meeting the following year if Britain did not change its policies.

Events then moved quickly. The British adopted stronger measures. "The New England governments

---

Cooperative Learning Activity

To consider the pre-Revolutionary period from the British point of view, organize students into groups of three or four. Have each group assume that it is a committee of Loyalists living in the American colonies. Each committee is to discuss relations between Great Britain and the colonies and to prepare a list of policy recommendations for King George III. One person from each group should take notes on the discussion and record the group's list of recommendations. As a class, compare the groups' lists to identify common solutions and innovative approaches for resolving the political crisis.

are in a state of rebellion," George III firmly announced. "Blows must decide whether they are to be subject to this country or independent."

The first blow fell early on the morning of April 19, 1775. British Redcoats clashed with colonial minutemen at Lexington and Concord in Massachusetts. This clash, later called the "shot heard 'round the world" was the first battle of the Revolutionary War.

The Second Continental Congress Within three weeks, delegates from all thirteen colonies gathered in Philadelphia for the Second Continental Congress. The Congress acted quickly, assuming the powers of a central government. It voted to organize an army and navy and to issue money to pay for the war. The delegates chose George Washington to lead the army.

The Second Continental Congress served as the acting government of the colonies throughout the war. It purchased supplies, negotiated treaties with other countries, and rallied support for the colonists' cause.

Independence

As Congress set to work, the independence movement was growing rapidly in the colonies. A brilliant pamphlet titled *Common Sense*, written by Thomas Paine, influenced many colonists. Paine, a onetime British corset-maker, called George III a "Royal Brute." He argued that monarchy was a corrupt form of government. "A government of our own is our natural right," he insisted.

Many colonists agreed with the patriot Samuel Adams. Adams asked, "Is not America already independent? Why not then declare it?"

In June 1776, more than a year after fighting had begun in the colonies, Richard Henry Lee of Virginia did just that. Lee introduced a resolution in the Continental Congress "That these United Colonies are, and of right ought to be, free and independent states."

The Declaration of Independence Congress promptly named a committee to prepare a written

"Free and Independent States"
Virginia Patriot Richard Henry Lee, painted by Charles Wilson Peale, called for the colonies to separate from Great Britain. History **Why was the Declaration of Independence revolutionary?**

declaration of independence. The committee asked Thomas Jefferson, a Virginia planter known for his writing skills, to write the draft. For the next two weeks, Jefferson worked alone on the document in the rooms he had rented from a young German bricklayer. On June 28 Jefferson asked John Adams and Benjamin Franklin to look over his draft. The two men made only minor changes.

On July 2, 1776, the Congress approved Lee's resolution. The colonies had officially broken with Great Britain. The Congress then turned its attention to Jefferson's draft. After considerable debate, a few passages were removed and some editorial changes made. On July 4 Congress approved the final draft of the Declaration of Independence. A

STUDY GUIDE

Themes In Government
Growth of Democracy In October 1774, the First Continental Congress passed the *Declaration and Resolves* that declared almost every act of Parliament since 1763

unconstitutional. **What else did the Congress do to ensure the growth of democracy in the colonies?**

Critical Thinking Skills
Expressing Problems Clearly **According to Thomas Paine, what was the major problem with British rule of the colonies?**

Special Needs Strategy

Reading Disability Students with a variety of reading and organizational difficulties may have trouble relating pictures, the captions under the pictures, and the main text. Before students read this section, have them look at the painting on page 53, read the caption, and briefly tell what the picture illustrates. After they have read the section, ask them again what the picture illustrates about the section and why the picture was included.

Independent Practice

L1 **Biography** Identify the role of the following men in the Revolutionary period: Patrick Henry, George Washington, Thomas Paine, Richard Henry Lee, Benjamin Franklin, Thomas Jefferson, John Adams. Have students select one of these men and write a brief biographical sketch to present to the class.

L2 **Expressive Writing** Have students explain in several paragraphs whether the Declaration of Independence is as important today as it was in 1776.

Caption Answer
It established the first government founded on principles of human liberty and consent of the governed.

STUDY GUIDE

Theme Answer
called for another meeting

Critical Thinking Answer
British did not allow colonial self-rule.

Assess

Check for Understanding
Have students complete Section 2 Review on page 56.

Focus on Government
Video 1
Electronic Field Trip:
Independence Hall
Running Time: 5:03
Videodisc 1, Chap. 1
VHS Tape 1, Begins 0:00

Meeting Objectives

Each section objective is tested by the Section Review questions that follow it in parentheses.

- Trace the events leading to the writing of the Declaration of Independence. (2, 3, 4, 6, 7)
- Identify the issues behind colonial protests. (2, 4, 5, 8)

Evaluate

📁 Section 2 Quiz

💻 Testmaker

Reteach

Ask students to reread the subsection "Key Parts of the Declaration" on page 56. Then ask them to explain why the Revolution happened in 1776 rather than 20 years earlier.

Enrich

📁 Have students complete activity 2 in *Primary and Secondary Source Readings* in the Teacher's Classroom Resources.

Close

Ask students to decide whether the colonists or the British were more responsible for the breakup that led to American independence and to give reasons to support their positions.

statement of the reasons for independence, the document's actual title was *The unanimous Declaration of the thirteen united States of America*.

Key Parts of the Declaration The American Declaration of Independence is one of the most famous documents in history. Jefferson drew together the ideas of thinkers such as Locke to set out the colonies' reasons for proclaiming their freedom. Indeed, the purpose of the Declaration was to justify the Revolution and put forth the principles on which the new nation was founded. Jefferson later said:

I did not consider it any part of my charge to invent new ideas, but to place before mankind the common sense of the subject in terms so plain and firm as to command their assent. . . . It was intended to be an expression of the American mind.

—THOMAS JEFFERSON

The revolutionary document stirred the hearts of the American people. No government at the time was founded on the principles of human liberty and consent of the governed. The Declaration won praise the world over and influenced the French Revolution of 1789. Over the years many nations used the Declaration as a model in justifying their efforts to gain freedom.

The Declaration has three parts. It begins with an eloquent statement of basic human rights such as equality and the "rights to life, liberty, and the pursuit of happiness." It then asserts that a just government must rest on the consent of the people.

The middle section of the Declaration contains 27 paragraphs listing specific complaints the colonists had against George III. Each item describes what the colonists regarded as a violation of their political liberties. These paragraphs were designed to justify the break with Great Britain.

The concluding paragraphs contain a statement of the colonists' determination to separate from Great Britain. The colonists' efforts to reach a peaceful solution with Great Britain had failed, leaving them no choice but to declare their freedom.

The First State Constitutions The Declaration of Independence recognized the changes that were taking place in the colonies. One of the most important of these was the transformation of the colonies into states subject to no higher authority. Thus, the states thought of themselves as "states" in the sense in which this term is used in Chapter 1.

Almost two months before the Declaration of Independence, the Second Continental Congress had instructed each of the colonies to form "such governments as shall . . . best conduce to the happiness and safety of their constituents." By 1776 eight states had adopted written constitutions. Within a few years, every former colony had a new constitution or had converted the old colonial charters into state constitutions.

Seven of the new constitutions contained a bill of rights defining the personal liberties of citizens. All recognized the people as the sole source of governmental authority. All provided for limited government.

2 SECTION REVIEW

Section Summary

The American colonists united to protest oppressive British practices, which led to the War of Independence in 1775 and the writing of the Declaration of Independence in 1776.

Checking for Understanding

Recalling Facts

1. Define revenue, embargo.
2. Name the two events that changed the relatively peaceful relationship between the colonies and Great Britain.
3. Describe the actions of the First Continental Congress.
4. Explain the purposes of the Declaration of Independence.

Exploring Themes

5. Civil Liberties What basic human rights are mentioned in the opening part of the Declaration of Independence?
6. Growth of Democracy How was the Second Continental Congress significantly different from the First Continental Congress?

Critical Thinking Skills

7. Understanding Cause and Effect At what point do you think it was too late for Great Britain and the colonies to work out a peaceful settlement? Support your answer.
8. Expressing Problems Clearly What were the central issues underlying colonial protests? Support your answer.

Section 2 Review Answers

1. Definitions of terms appear on the pages indicated: **revenue,** 54; **embargo,** 54

2. The French and Indian War threatened Britain's security on the continent, and George III came to power.

3. Delegates met and imposed an embargo on Britain and agreed not to use British goods.

4. Purposes were to justify the revolution and put forth the principles on which the new nation was founded.

5. life, liberty, and the pursuit of happiness; governments derive their power from the consent of the governed; the people have a right to abolish a destructive government.

6. The First Continental Congress took action against Britain; the Second Continental Congress became a national government—organizing an army and navy, issuing

money to pay for the war, purchasing supplies, and negotiating treaties.

7. Answers might cite the king's declaration of a rebellion, the first clashes at Lexington and Concord, the Second Continental Congress, Declaration of Independence.

8. Answers should include freedom from British control, desire of colonists to have a voice in their government and to have the rights of British citizens.

The DECLARATION of INDEPENDENCE

JULY 4, 1776

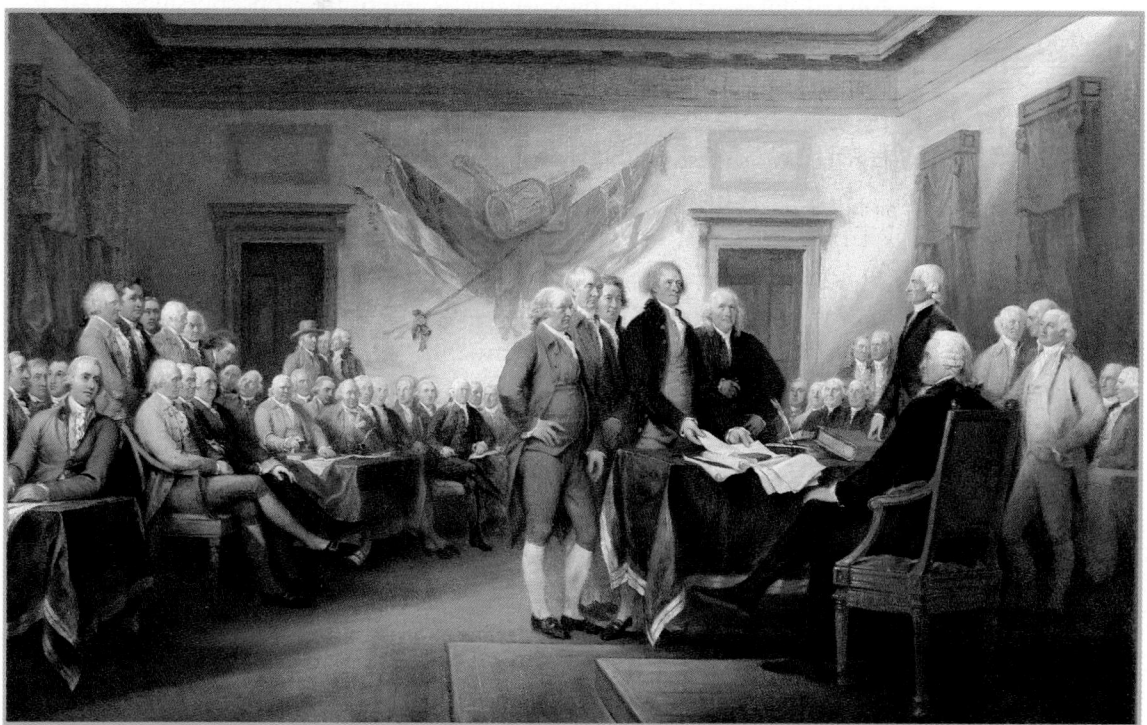

The Declaration of Independence, painted by John Trumbull

WHEN IN THE COURSE OF HUMAN EVENTS, it becomes necessary for one people to dissolve the political bonds which have connected them with another, and to assume among the powers of the earth, the separate and equal station to which the Laws of Nature and of Nature's God entitle them, a decent respect to the opinions of mankind requires that they should declare the causes which impel them to the separation.

endowed *provided*

People create governments to insure that their natural rights are protected. Governments are the servants of the people who establish them. If a government does not serve its purpose, the people have a right to abolish it. Then the people have the right and duty to create a new government that will safeguard their security.

usurpations *unjust uses of power*
evinces *shows*
despotism *unlimited power*

tyranny *absolute power*
candid *fair*
Each paragraph lists reported crimes of George III.

relinquish *give up*
inestimable *priceless*
formidable *causing dread*

Annihilation *destruction*

convulsions *violent disturbances*

Naturalization of Foreigners *process by which foreign-born persons become citizens*
In 1774 the king raised the purchase price of western lands.

WE HOLD THESE TRUTHS to be self-evident, that all men are created equal, that they are endowed by their Creator with certain unalienable Rights, that among these are Life, Liberty and the pursuit of Happiness. That to secure these rights, Governments are instituted among Men, deriving their just powers from the consent of the governed; That whenever any Form of Government becomes destructive of these ends it is the Right of the People to alter or to abolish it, and to institute new Government, laying its foundation on such principles and organizing its powers in such form, as to them shall seem most likely to effect their Safety and Happiness. Prudence, indeed, will dictate that Governments long established should not be changed for light and transient causes; and accordingly all experience hath shown, that mankind are more disposed to suffer, while evils are sufferable, than to right themselves by abolishing the forms to which they are accustomed. But when a long train of abuses and usurpations, pursuing invariably the same Objects evinces a design to reduce them under absolute Despotism, it is their right, it is their duty, to throw off such Government, and to provide new Guards for their future security.—Such has been the patient sufferance of these Colonies; and such is now the necessity which constrains them to alter their former Systems of Government. The history of the present King of Great Britain is a history of repeated injuries and usurpations, all having in direct object the establishment of an absolute Tyranny over these States. To prove this, let Facts be submitted to a candid world.

He has refused his Assent to Laws, the most wholesome and necessary for the public good.

He has forbidden his Governors to pass Laws of immediate and pressing importance, unless suspended in their operation till his Assent should be obtained; and when so suspended, he has utterly neglected to attend to them.

He has refused to pass other Laws for the accommodation of large districts of people, unless those people would relinquish the right of Representation in the Legislature, a right inestimable to them and formidable to tyrants only.

He has called together legislative bodies at places unusual, uncomfortable, and distant from the depository of their public records, for the sole purpose of fatiguing them into compliance with his measures.

He has dissolved Representative Houses repeatedly, for opposing with manly firmness his invasions on the rights of the people.

He has refused for a long time, after such dissolutions, to cause others to be elected; whereby the Legislative powers, incapable of Annihilation, have returned to the People at large for their exercise; the State remaining in the mean time exposed to all the dangers of invasions from without, and convulsions within.

He has endeavored to prevent the population of these States; for that purpose obstructing the Laws of Naturalization of Foreigners; refusing to pass others to encourage their migration hither, and raising the conditions of new Appropriations of Lands.

He has obstructed the Administration of Justice, by refusing his Assent to Laws for establishing Judiciary powers.

He has made Judges dependent on his Will alone for the tenure of their offices, and the amount and payment of their salaries.

He has erected a multitude of New Offices, and sent hither swarms of Officers to harass our people and eat out their substance.

He has kept among us in times of peace, Standing Armies, without the Consent of our legislatures.

He has affected to render the Military independent of, and superior to, the Civil power.

He has combined with others to subject us to a jurisdiction foreign to our constitutions, and unacknowledged by our laws; giving his Assent to their Acts of pretended Legislation:

For quartering large bodies of armed troops among us;

For protecting them, by a mock Trial, from punishment for any Murders which they should commit on the Inhabitants of these States;

For cutting off our Trade with all parts of the world;

For imposing Taxes on us without our Consent;

For depriving us, in many cases, of the benefits of Trial by Jury;

For transporting us beyond Seas, to be tried for pretended offenses;

For abolishing the free System of English Laws in a neighboring Province, establishing therein an Arbitrary government, and enlarging its Boundaries, so as to render it at once an example and fit instrument for introducing the same absolute rule into these Colonies;

For taking away our Charters, abolishing our most valuable Laws, and altering, fundamentally, the Forms of our Governments;

For suspending our own Legislatures, and declaring themselves invested with Power to legislate for us in all cases whatsoever.

He has abdicated Government here, by declaring us out of his Protection, and waging War against us.

He has plundered our seas, ravaged our Coasts, burned our towns, and destroyed the lives of our people.

He is at this time transporting large Armies of foreign Mercenaries to complete the works of death, desolation and tyranny, already begun with circumstances of Cruelty and perfidy scarcely paralleled in the most barbarous ages, and totally unworthy the Head of a civilized nation.

He has constrained our fellow Citizens taken Captive on the high Seas to bear Arms against their Country, to become the executioners of their friends and Brethren, or to fall themselves by their Hands.

He has excited domestic insurrections amongst us, and has endeavored to bring on the inhabitants of our frontiers the merciless Indian Savages whose known rule of warfare is an undistinguished destruction of all ages, sexes, and conditions.

In every stage of these Oppressions We have Petitioned for Redress in the most humble terms. Our repeated Petitions have been answered only by repeated injury. A Prince whose character is thus marked by every act which may define a Tyrant, is unfit to be the ruler of a free people.

Nor have We been wanting in attentions to our British brethren. We have warned them from time to time of attempts by their legislature to ex-

tenure *term*
Refers to the British troops sent to colonies after the French and Indian War

quartering *lodging*
Refers to the 1774 Quebec Act

Arbitrary *not based on law*
render *make*

abdicated *given up*

perfidy *violation of trust*

insurrections *rebellions*

Petitioned for Redress *asked formally for a correction of wrongs*

unwarrantable jurisdic-
tion *unjustified authority*

magnanimity *generous spirit*

consanguinity *originating from the same ancestor*

acquiesce in *consent to*

rectitude *rightness*

tend an unwarrantable jurisdiction over us. We have reminded them of the circumstances of our emigration and settlement here. We have appealed to their native justice and magnanimity, and we have conjured them by the ties of our common kindred to disavow these usurpations, which, would inevitably interrupt our connections and correspondence. They too have been deaf to the voice of justice and of consanguinity. We must, therefore, acquiesce in the necessity, which denounces our Separation, and hold them, as we hold the rest of mankind, Enemies in War, in Peace Friends.—

We, therefore, the Representatives of the United States of America, in General Congress, Assembled, appealing to the Supreme Judge of the world for the rectitude of our intentions, do, in the Name, and by the Authority of the good People of these Colonies, solemnly publish and declare, That these United Colonies are, and of right ought to be Free and Independent States; that they are Absolved from all Allegiance to the British Crown, and that all political connection between them and the State of Great Britain, is and ought to be totally dissolved, and that as Free and Independent States, they have full Power to levy War, conclude Peace, contract Alliances, establish Commerce, and to do all other Acts and Things which Independent States may of right do. And for the support of this Declaration, with a firm reliance on the protection of Divine Providence, we mutually pledge to each other our Lives, our Fortunes and our sacred Honor.

The signers, as representatives of the American people, declared the colonies independent from Great Britain.

Most members signed on August 2, 1776.

John Hancock,
President from Massachusetts

GEORGIA
Button Gwinnett
Lyman Hall
George Walton

NORTH CAROLINA
William Hooper
Joseph Hewes
John Penn

SOUTH CAROLINA
Edward Rutledge
Thomas Heyward, Jr.
Thomas Lynch, Jr.
Arthur Middleton

MARYLAND
Samuel Chase
William Paca
Thomas Stone
Charles Carroll of Carrollton

VIRGINIA
George Wythe

Richard Henry Lee
Thomas Jefferson
Benjamin Harrison
Thomas Nelson, Jr.
Francis Lightfoot Lee
Carter Braxton

PENNSYLVANIA
Robert Morris
Benjamin Rush
Benjamin Franklin
John Morton
George Clymer
James Smith
George Taylor
James Wilson
George Ross

DELAWARE
Caesar Rodney
George Read
Thomas McKean

NEW YORK
William Floyd
Philip Livingston
Francis Lewis

Lewis Morris

NEW JERSEY
Richard Stockton
John Witherspoon
Francis Hopkinson
John Hart
Abraham Clark

NEW HAMPSHIRE
Josiah Bartlett
William Whipple
Matthew Thornton

MASSACHUSETTS
Samuel Adams
John Adams
Robert Treat Paine
Elbridge Gerry

RHODE ISLAND
Stephen Hopkins
William Ellery

CONNECTICUT
Samuel Huntington
William Williams
Oliver Wolcott

The Articles of Confederation

When Richard Henry Lee proposed his resolution for independence in June 1776, he also proposed that a "plan for confederation" be prepared for the colonies. The Continental Congress appointed a committee to draft such a plan.

In 1777 the committee presented a plan called the Articles of Confederation. The Articles basically continued the structure and operation of government as established under the Second Continental Congress. The states wanted a confederation, or "league of friendship," among the 13 independent states rather than a strong national government. By March 1781, all 13 states had **ratified**, or approved, the Articles of Confederation and they went into effect.

Government Under the Articles

Under the Articles, the plan for the central government was simple. It included a **unicameral**, or single-chamber, Congress. It did not include an executive branch or President. Instead, a Committee of the States made up of one delegate from each state managed the government when Congress was not assembled. There was no federal court system. Instead, Congress settled disputes among states.

Each state had one vote in Congress, no matter what its size or population. Every state legislature selected its own representatives to Congress, paid them, and could recall them at any time.

Congress had only those powers expressly given to it by the Articles—mainly lawmaking. All other powers remained with the independent states. Congres-sional powers included the powers to: (1) make war and peace; (2) send and receive ambassadors; (3) enter into treaties; (4) raise and equip a navy; (5) maintain an army by requesting troops from the states; (6) appoint senior military officers; (7) fix standards of weights and measures; (8) regulate Indian affairs; (9) establish post offices; and (10) decide certain disputes among the states.

Weaknesses of the Articles

Although the Articles of Confederation gave Congress considerable power, they created a weak government. Because each state had no intention of giving up its sovereignty, the Articles had major weaknesses.

First, Congress did not have the power to levy or collect taxes. It could raise money only by borrowing or requesting money from the states. Each state had to collect taxes from its citizens and to turn the money over to the national treasury. Congress could do little, however, if a state refused to provide the money. As a result, the Confederation was almost always short of money.

Second, Congress did not have the power to regulate trade. This led to economic disputes among the various states and to difficulty in making business arrangements with other countries.

Third, Congress could not force anyone to obey the laws it passed or abide by the Articles of Confederation. Congress could only advise and request the states to comply.

SECTION PREVIEW

Objectives
After studying this section, you should be able to:
- List the strengths and weaknesses of the Articles of Confederation.
  Describe how the government was organized under the Articles of Confederation.
- Summarize the problems the United States faced after independence.

Key Terms and Concepts
ratify, unicameral, cede, ordinance

Themes in Government
- Growth of Democracy
- Federalism

Critical Thinking Skills
- Drawing Conclusions
- Expressing Problems Clearly

CHAPTER 2: THE CREATION OF THE FEDERAL GOVERNMENT 61

Focus

Bell Ringer

Write the following quotation on the chalkboard and ask: What did John Adams mean?

Our nation is not yet out of danger.

John Adams, May 1784

Discuss students' answers. (*He was addressing the need to establish a strong government.*)

Motivating Activity

Ask students to read the first two paragraphs of Section 3, "The Articles of Confederation." Then discuss why colonial leaders chose a confederation instead of a national government.

Vocabulary Precheck

Call on students to read aloud the definitions of the terms and concepts from the Glossary. Then have volunteers use each term in a sentence. **LEP**

Teach

Guided Practice

L1 Constructing a Chart Help students construct a chart showing the division of power between the states and the Congress under the Articles. Put the following headings on the chalkboard: *The States* and *The Congress*. Have students indicate on the chart the division of the following powers: make treaties (*Congress*), enforce laws (*States*), make laws (*both*), tax (*States*), regulate trade (*States*), and declare war (*Congress*). **LEP**

Classroom Resources for Section 3

- Guided Reading Activities
- Reproducible Lesson Plans
- Participating in Government 2
- Section 3 Quiz
- Testmaker

- Government Themes Transparencies 5
- The Living Constitution
- SAT Practice Tests
- Writer's Guidebook

L2 Classifying Write the three heads below on the chalkboard. Have students use the chart on page 62 to classify each weakness of the Articles under the correct heading.

1. Congress' Lack of Power and Money
   • *no power to tax*
   • *no power to regulate trade*
   • *no power to enforce laws*
2. No Central Power to Direct Policy and Settle Disputes
   • *no executive branch*
   • *no national court system*
3. Obstacles to Reaching Agreements
   • *approval of 9 states needed to enact laws*
   • *consent of all 13 states required to amend Articles*

Chart Study Answer
The nation's inability to handle security, budgets, and internal disputes made Americans realize the need for a strong central government.

STUDY GUIDE

Theme Answer
All the states would not agree.

Critical Thinking Answer
With a strong executive, one person directs all facets of policy-making.

Powers of the Congress
Articles of Confederation
Running Time :18
Side One, Chapter 4

Weaknesses of the Articles of Confederation

Weakness	Effect
Congress had no power to levy or collect taxes.	The government was always short of money.
Congress had no power to regulate interstate or foreign trade.	Economic quarrels broke out among the states. There was difficulty in arranging for trade with other countries.
Congress had no power to enforce its laws.	The government depended on the states to enforce the laws.
Approval of nine states was needed to enact laws.	It was difficult to enact laws.
Amendments to the Articles required the consent of all thirteen states.	There was no practical way to change the powers of the government.
The government had no executive branch.	There was no effective way to coordinate the work of the government.
There was no national court system.	The central government had no way of settling disputes among the states.

✓ **Chart Study**
The Articles of Confederation were only in effect for seven years. **How did their weaknesses lead to federalism?**

Fourth, laws needed the approval of 9 of the 13 states to pass. Usually, delegates from only 9 or 10 states were in Congress at any given time, making it almost impossible to pass laws. In addition, each state had only a single vote. Therefore the votes of any 5 of the smaller states could block a measure that 8 of the larger states, representing a majority of the people in the nation, supported.

Fifth, amending or changing the Articles required the consent of all states. In practice, it was impossible to get *all* the states to agree on amendments. As a result, the Articles were never amended.

Sixth, the central government did not have an executive branch. The Confederation government carried on much of its business, such as selling western lands and establishing a postal system, through congressional committees. Without an executive,

however, there was no unity in policy-making and no way to coordinate the work of the different committees.

Finally, the government had no national court system. Instead, state courts enforced and interpreted national laws. The lack of a court system made it difficult for the central government to settle disputes between the states. A legislator from North Carolina addressed the powerlessness of the Confederation in a speech to his state legislature in 1787:

The general government ought . . . to possess the means of preserving the peace and tranquility of the union. . . . The encroachments of some states, on the rights of others, and of all on those of the confederacy, are incontestible [cannot be denied] proofs of the weakness and imperfection of that system.
—WILLIAM DAVIE, 1787

STUDY GUIDE

Themes In Government
Growth of Democracy Although the Articles of Confederation had many weaknesses, they served as the first national constitution. They represented an important step in the creation of the American national government. **Why were the Articles never amended?**

Critical Thinking Skills
Drawing Conclusions How does the existence of a strong executive help a government achieve unity in policy-making?

Background

Conflicts sprang up between the United States and England over the terms of the Treaty of Paris. Congress had initially made guarantees that the states would restore confiscated Loyalist lands, but had no power to enforce this promise. Pennsylvania paid the Penn family compensation for their property, but most states failed to comply with the treaty. Although British subjects were allowed to file suit in state courts to recover their property, they found it difficult to obtain impartial hearings before American judges and juries.

PARTICIPATING IN GOVERNMENT

Applying for a Passport

A passport identifies a person as a citizen of the country that issues it. It also allows travelers privileges and lawful protection established by international treaties.

The Department of State in Washington, D.C., issues passports in the United States. Department of State officials in many major cities may also issue passports. A clerk of a federal or state court, certain judges, your local postmaster, or another postal employee may accept passport applications.

If you are planning your first trip outside the United States, you should apply for a passport several weeks in advance because processing your application may take two weeks or more.

To obtain a passport, you must appear before one of the agents listed above. You must bring a registered copy of your birth certificate or a naturalization certificate.

You will also need two identical photographs of yourself, 2 x 2 inches (5 x 5 cm), on a white background. The photographs must show a clear, full-face view, taken within the past six months.

A fee is charged for all passport applications. Passports remain valid for 5 to 10 years depending on the applicant's age.

Investigating Further

Some countries do not require passports of United States citizens. Find out where you can travel without a passport. Report your findings to the class.

Achievements

Despite its weaknesses, the Confederation accomplished much. The greatest achievement was the establishment of a fair policy for the development of the lands west of the Appalachians. The individual states **ceded**, or yielded, their claims to these territories to the central government, providing the nation with a priceless national asset that became a strong force for national unity. In addition, Congress enacted two land **ordinances**, or laws, that provided for the organization of these territories. The Northwest Ordinance of 1787, for example, established the principle that the territories owned by the government were to be developed for statehood on an equal basis with the older states.

Another important accomplishment was a peace treaty with Great Britain. Under the terms of the treaty, signed in 1783, Britain recognized American independence. Britain also greatly enlarged the nation's boundaries, granting the United States all land from the Atlantic coast to the Mississippi River and from the Great Lakes and Canada to the present-day boundary of Florida.

Congress also set up the departments of Foreign Affairs, War, Marine, and the Treasury, each under a single permanent secretary. This development set a precedent for the creation of cabinet departments under the Constitution of 1787. To encourage cooperation among the states, the Articles provided that each state give "full faith and credit" to the legal acts of the other states and treat one another's citizens

STUDY GUIDE

Themes in Government
Federalism Many nations have a federal system in which a strong central government shares power with the states.

How does a confederal system such as the one organized under the Articles of Confederation differ from a federal system?

Critical Thinking Skills
Expressing Problems Clearly
What did William Davie view as the major problem of the Articles of Confederation?

PARTICIPATING IN GOVERNMENT

Tell students passports have been in use for centuries throughout the world. However, excluding the Civil War period, foreigners traveling to the United States did not need passports until 1918. Ask students why they think passports were required at that time. *(national security following World War I)*

Have students complete activity 2 in *Participating in Government* in the Teacher's Classroom Resources.

Independent Practice

L1 Creating Political Cartoons Have students illustrate one of the weaknesses of the Articles of Confederation in a political cartoon. **LEP**

L2 Informative Writing Ask students to write an essay describing how the newly created government under the Articles of Confederation was a blend of British political heritage and the American experience.

STUDY GUIDE

Theme Answer
Confederal has a weak central government.

Critical Thinking Answer
The central government could not control the states.

Assess

Check for Understanding

Have students complete Section 3 Review on page 64.

Cooperative Learning Activity

Organize students into groups of four or five. Using one piece of paper per group, have each member take a turn writing a weakness of the Articles of Confederation. Using the same paper, have members take turns writing an example of how one of the weaknesses caused a later problem. Have each group share one weakness and example with the class. Then ask the class to determine if any information about the weaknesses of the Articles of Confederation is still missing.

Meeting Objectives

Each section objective is tested by the Section Review questions that follow it in parentheses.
- List the strengths and weaknesses of the Articles of Confederation. (6, 8)
- Describe how the government was organized under the Articles of Confederation. (2, 5, 7)
- Summarize the problems the United States faced after independence. (3, 4, 8)

Evaluate

 Section 3 Quiz

 Testmaker

Reteach

Display transparency 5 of the *Government Themes Transparencies* in the Teacher's Classroom Resources and use the accompanying teaching strategy and student activity to reteach the Articles of Confederation.

Enrich

Have students research the groups involved in conflicts over the American West in the 1780s and how the conflicts were resolved.

Close

Ask students why 1781–1787 has been called a "critical period" in American history.

---

without discrimination. Although this principle often existed in theory but not in practice, it was carried over to the Constitution.

Need for Stronger Government

Despite its achievements, the Confederation faced difficulties in dealing with problems facing the nation. The structure of the central government could not coordinate the actions of the states effectively.

Growing Problems Soon after the war, the states began to quarrel, mainly over boundary lines and tariffs. New Jersey farmers, for example, had to pay fees to sell their vegetables in New York. Some states even began to deal directly with foreign nations. Congress could do little about these matters.

Even worse, the new nation faced serious money problems. By 1787 the government owed $40 million to foreign governments and to American soldiers still unpaid after the Revolutionary War. Without money, the government could not maintain an army for defense of the states.

The states also faced growing financial troubles. By 1786 an economic depression had left many farmers and small merchants angry and in debt.

Shays's Rebellion In 1786 these economic troubles led to armed rebellion. In western Massachusetts several hundred angry farmers armed with pitchforks marched on the Springfield Arsenal to get weapons. Daniel Shays, a former captain in the Revolutionary

Army led the farmers. Unable to pay their mortgages, the farmers wanted to prevent the courts from foreclosing on mortgages and taking away their farms. To force the state to pass laws to help them, the farmers threatened to lay siege to Boston.

The Massachusetts militia put down the rebellion, but the unrest frightened American leaders. Henry Knox, later the nation's first secretary of war, echoed the growing number of Americans ready to agree to a strong national government. In a letter to George Washington, Knox wrote:

This dreadful situation has alarmed every man of principle and property in New England. [People wake] as from a dream and ask what has been the cause of our delusion. What [will] give us security against the violence of lawless men? Our government must be [strengthened], changed, or altered to secure our lives and property.

—HENRY KNOX

The Annapolis Convention In 1786 Virginia called a convention at Annapolis, Maryland, to discuss commerce. Although all states were invited, only five sent delegates. Two nationalists in attendance, Alexander Hamilton of New York and James Madison of Virginia, persuaded the other delegates to call another convention in Philadelphia in May 1787.

After some hesitation, the Confederation Congress gave its consent to hold the Philadelphia convention "for the sole and express purpose of revising the Articles of Confederation." The stage was now set for what has been called the "miracle at Philadelphia."

3 SECTION REVIEW

Section Summary
The Articles of Confederation was the first American national constitution. Despite certain positive achievements, the government under the Articles was basically weak. After serious disputes broke out between states, several leaders called for a convention to revise the articles.

Checking for Understanding
Recalling Facts
1. Define ratify, unicameral, cede, ordinance.
2. Name the document that served as the first national constitution.
3. Cite the event that led many Americans to consider creating a strong national government.

4. List four problems that the United States faced after the Revolutionary War.

Exploring Themes
5. Growth of Democracy How was the original government under the Articles of Confederation organized?
6. Federalism What were the major weaknesses of the Articles of Confederation?

Critical Thinking Skills
7. Drawing Conclusions Why did the colonists grant their states, rather than the confederation government, a great deal of power?
8. Expressing Problems Clearly What problems did Shays's Rebellion bring to light?

Section 3 Review Answers

1. Definitions of terms appear on pages indicated: **ratify,** 61; **unicameral,** 61; **cede,** 63; **ordinance,** 63
2. Articles of Confederation
3. Shays's Rebellion
4. States quarreled over boundary lines and tariffs. Confederation government did not have money to pay debts owed to foreign governments or to pay American soldiers who fought in the Revolution. Government did not have the

money to maintain an army to protect the nation. Nation was in an economic depression.
5. There was a single-chamber Congress. Instead of an executive branch, a Committee of the States made up of one delegate from each state was to manage the government when Congress was not assembled. There was no federal court system. Instead, Congress was to act as a court to settle disputes among states.
6. Congress did not have the power to tax, to regulate trade, or to require individuals or states to obey its laws.

Laws could be passed with approval of only nine of thirteen states. Amending Articles required consent of all thirteen states. Central government had no executive branch, and there was no national court system.
7. fear of centralized government, belief that government derived its power from the people and that state government was more responsive to local interests
8. Without a central government, keeping order and solving problems, such as economic ones, were difficult.

Analyzing Information

Analyzing information involves examining a source to determine what the author is trying to say. Citizens must be able to analyze information in order to form responsible opinions about what they read. They must first understand exactly what is being said.

Explanation

To analyze information, follow these steps:

- Identify the topic or topics being discussed. Ask: What is this about?
- Determine what evidence the author presents. Ask: What does each sentence or element in an illustration tell me?
- Put the author's argument into your own words.

Read the following excerpt from Thomas Paine's *Common Sense*, an essay that greatly affected public opinion about the need for a declaration of independence from Britain.

*T*he phrase parent or mother country hath been . . . adopted by the king . . . [to trick us into obedience]. Europe, and not England, is the parent country of America. This new world hath been the asylum for persecuted lovers of civil and religious liberty from every part of Europe. Hither have they fled, not from the tender embraces of a mother, but from the cruelty of a monster; and it is so far true of England, that the same tyranny which drove the first emigrants from home, pursues their descendants still.

— THOMAS PAINE, JANUARY 1776

The first step in analyzing information is to determine the author's general topic. Paine is discussing whether or not Americans owe loyalty to Britain. The next step is to determine what evidence the author presents about the issue. Paine says that (1) Americans come from all over Europe, not just from England; (2) people from many lands, including England, came to America to escape tyranny and find civil and religious liberty; and (3) Britain is now trying to impose tyranny over the American

colonists. These points tell the reader that Paine does not believe that Americans owe allegiance to Britain.

Practice

Many people agreed with Paine's eloquent arguments, and *Common Sense* created a groundswell of support for independence. In response many Loyalists—those Americans who believed they owed allegiance to the British crown—wrote pamphlets. Read the following excerpt from a pamphlet called "The True Interest of America Impartially Stated." Then answer the questions that follow.

*T*orrents of blood would be spilt, and thousands reduced to beggary and wretchedness. This melancholy contest [war] would last till one side conquered. Supposing Britain to be victorious, however high my opinion is of British Generosity, I should be exceedingly sorry to receive terms from her in the haughty tone of a conqueror. Or supposing [that she lost] . . . who can say in that case, what [Britain would do]? For my part, I should not be the least surprised if . . . she would parcel out this continent to the different European powers. Canada might be restored to France, Florida to Spain. . . .

—"THE TRUE INTEREST OF AMERICA, IMPARTIALLY STATED," 1776

1. What subject is the author addressing?
2. What are the possible consequences of a war for independence from Great Britain?
3. How would the author answer the question, Should Americans fight a war for independence against the powerful British army? What reasons might the author give?

Additional Practice

To practice this skill, see **Reinforcing the Skill** on page 73.

Focus

Distribute photocopies of a photograph and ask students to list everything they can learn from it. Discuss students' lists. Ask: What steps did you take to get information from the photograph? What questions did you ask yourself to help you understand it? Point out that a key to understanding something is the ability to analyze it.

Teach

Review the steps presented in the Explanation and the questions students can ask themselves to complete these steps. Then have them put Paine's argument into their own words. Tell them to keep both questions in mind as they rewrite Paine's argument. Select students to copy their paragraphs on the chalkboard and have the class use the steps to analyze them.

Assess

Have students complete the **Practice** exercise.

Close

Have students locate another excerpt in this chapter and write a brief analysis of it, using the steps presented.

Practice Answers

1. The subject is probable consequences of a war for independence.

2. either harsh terms following a British victory or the dismemberment of North America by European powers

3. Possible answer: No, because such a war will end in disaster. If Britain wins, we will be a conquered people; and if it loses, it may allow North America to be taken over by other European powers.

For additional practice, have students complete activity 2 in *Skill Reinforcement Activities* in the Teacher's Classroom Resources.

Focus

Bell Ringer

While attendance is being taken, ask students to define *compromise*.

Motivating Activity

Discuss students' Bell Ringer answers. *(way to settle a dispute or differences by each side giving up some of its demands)* Ask students what compromises people make in their daily lives. Discuss what would happen if people could not compromise. Point out that compromise is necessary in government since people have different views on how things should be done. Tell students in this section they will read about the compromises made by delegates to the Constitutional Convention.

Vocabulary Precheck

List the terms and concepts on the chalkboard. Have volunteers skim the section to find each term and read it in context. **LEP**

Caption Answer

for Alexander Hamilton who vigorously defended the Constitution

Teach

Guided Practice

L1 Constructing a Chart Construct a two-column chart on the chalkboard. Label one column *Compromises* and the other *Explanations*. Ask students to give five compromises made during the Constitutional Convention, and in the second column, explain the details of each. *(Compromises: form of government; representation; commerce and slave trade; presidential election; presidential term)* **LEP**

SECTION 4

The Constitutional Convention

The Constitutional Convention began its work on May 25, 1787. All the states except Rhode Island sent delegates.

The Convention Begins

The state legislatures appointed 74 delegates to the Convention, but only 55 attended. Of these, 39 took a leading role. The delegates had great practical experience in politics. Seven had served as governors of their states. Thirty-nine had served in the Confederation Congress. Many had helped write their state constitutions. Eight had signed the Declaration of Independence, and five delegates had signed the Articles of Confederation.

Several men stood out as leaders. The presence of George Washington ensured that many people would trust the Convention's work. Benjamin Franklin, world famous as a scientist and diplomat, now 81 years old, played an active role in the debates.

Two other Pennsylvanians also played key roles. James Wilson often read Franklin's speeches and did important work on the details of the Constitution. Gouverneur Morris, an eloquent speaker and writer, wrote the final draft of the Constitution.

From Virginia came James Madison, a brilliant advocate of a strong national government. His careful notes are the major source of information about the Convention's work. Madison is often called the "Father of the Constitution" because he was the author of the basic plan of government the Convention adopted.

Organization The Convention began by unanimously choosing George Washington to preside over the meetings. It also decided that each state would have

The Young Nation Celebrates
The "ship of state" makes its way down Wall Street during a celebration of the ratification of the Constitution in 1788. **History Why was the float named "Hamilton"?**

SECTION PREVIEW

Objectives
After studying this section, you should be able to:
■ Outline the development of the Constitution from the Constitutional Convention to ratification.

■ Specify issues on which the delegates to the Constitutional Convention had to compromise.

Key Terms and Concepts
interstate commerce, extralegal, anarchy

Themes in Government
■ Checks and Balances
■ Growth of Democracy

Critical Thinking Skills
■ Identifying Central Issues
■ Identifying Alternatives

66 Unit 1: Foundations of American Government

Classroom Resources for Section 4

📁 Guided Reading Activities
📁 Reproducible Lesson Plans
📁 Reteaching Activities 2
📁 Enrichment Activities 2
📁 Section 4 Quiz

➕ Testmaker
📁 Chapter 2 Tests
🎛 Chapter Transparencies 2
🎧 Audio Cassettes (English and Spanish)
📁 Limited English Proficiency Activities 2
   SAT Practice Tests

one vote on all questions. A simple majority vote of those states present would make decisions. No meetings could be held unless delegates from at least seven states were present.

The delegates decided to keep the public and press from attending the sessions. This was a key decision because it made it possible for the delegates to talk freely.

Key Agreements All the delegates agreed on many basic issues. All favored the idea of limited and representative government. They agreed that the powers of the national government should be divided among legislative, executive, and judicial branches. They all believed it was necessary to limit the power of the states to coin money or to interfere with creditors' rights. And all of them agreed that they should strengthen the national government.

The great debates and compromises of the Convention were not over these fundamental questions. Rather, they dealt with how to put these ideas into practice.

Decisions and Compromises

After the rules were adopted, the Convention opened with a surprise. It came from the Virginia delegation that presented a plan for a strong national government.

The Virginia Plan On May 29 Edmund Randolph of Virginia introduced 15 resolutions that James Madison had drafted. They came to be called the Virginia Plan. The plan proposed a government based on three principles: (1) a strong national legislature with two chambers, the lower one to be chosen by the people and the upper chamber to be chosen by the lower. The legislature would have the power to bar any state laws it found unconstitutional; (2) a strong national executive to be chosen by the national legislature; and (3) a national judiciary to be appointed by the legislature.

The introduction of the Virginia Plan was a brilliant political move on the part of the nationalists. By offering a complete plan at the very start, the nationalists set the direction and agenda for the rest of the Convention. Eventually, with a number of modifications, the Virginia Plan became the basis of the new Constitution.

The delegates debated the Virginia plan for the next two weeks. Delegates from the smaller states soon realized that the larger, more populous states would be in control of a strong national government under the Virginia Plan. The smaller states wanted a less powerful government with more independence for the states.

The New Jersey Plan On June 15 the delegates from the small states, led by William Paterson of New Jersey, made a counterproposal. The New Jersey Plan called for government based on keeping the major feature of the Articles of Confederation—a unicameral legislature, with one vote for each state. Congress, however, would be strengthened by giving it the power to impose taxes and regulate trade. A weak executive consisting of more than one person would be elected by Congress. A national judiciary with limited power would be appointed by the executive.

Paterson argued that the Convention should not deprive the smaller states of the equality they had under the Articles. Thus, his plan was designed simply to amend the Articles. The central government was to continue as a confederation of sovereign states. After some discussion the New Jersey Plan was rejected. The delegates returned to considering the Virginia Plan.

As the summer grew hotter, so did the delegates' tempers. Soon the Convention was deadlocked over the question of the representation of states in Congress. Should the states be represented on the basis of population (favored by the large-state delegations) or should they be represented equally, regardless of population (favored by the small-state delegations)? The debate was bitter, and the Convention was in danger of dissolving.

STUDY GUIDE

Themes In Government
Checks and Balances Although all delegates agreed that the new government should have executive, legislative, and judicial branches, they wanted to make certain that

no branch could become too powerful. As a result, they set up the system of checks and balances. For example, they gave the executive the power to veto acts of Congress.

Critical Thinking Skills
Identifying Central Issues Many delegates had read the latest political writings of their day. **How would such familiarity help the delegates in their work?**

Background

The Constitutional Convention disbanded in September 1787. Delegates who favored the Constitution returned home to rally support. George Washington wrote Patrick Henry: "I wish the Constitution which is offered had been made more perfect, but I sincerely believe it is the best that could be obtained at this time." Henry wrote back: "I have to lament that I cannot bring my Mind to accord with the proposed Constitution . . . . Perhaps mature Reflection may furnish me Reasons to change my present Sentiments." Henry continued to be one of the most outspoken opponents of the Constitution.

L2 Hypothesizing Ask students to hypothesize why delegates to the Convention did not debate the legal or moral aspects of slavery. Then discuss the following question: If slavery had been abolished by the Constitution, what future issues might have been avoided? What problems might such an action have caused?

Interpreting Visuals Display transparency 2 from the *Chapter Transparencies* in the Teacher's Classroom Resources and use the accompanying teaching strategy and student activity to teach the feelings and background of the Constitution's Framers.

L3 Class Debate Have teams of students simulate the Federalists/Anti-Federalists debate over the ratification of the Constitution. Have the team representing Federalists present an argument that supports an energetic, stable, and efficient national government. The team of Anti-Federalists should express their concerns about the absence of a bill of rights, too much power in the federal judiciary and executive branch, and states' rights. Have remaining students ask questions during the debate.

STUDY GUIDE

Critical Thinking Answer They would be able to draw upon the most current theories of government in their deliberations.

GLENCOE TECHNOLOGY

Focus on Government
Video 1
Electronic Field Trip:
Independence Hall
Running Time: 5:03
Videodisc 1, Chap. 1
VHS Tape 1, Begins 0:00

Independent Practice

L1 Journalism Have students convert each of the three sub-headings in Section 4 into a headline that might appear in a newspaper. The first headline might read: "Delegates Meet in Secret To Revise Articles of Confederation." Discuss student headlines.

L2 Analyzing Viewpoints Have students read and classify each of the following arguments as Federalist or Anti-Federalist. Have them explain the reason for their classification in writing.

1. Although national government needs a source of income, it may use the power to tax to squeeze the people dry. *(Anti-Federalist)*
2. A strong national government is needed to establish order. Without it, the states will go in separate directions and the people will rebel and overthrow the system. *(Federalist)*
3. Without a guarantee of individual rights, government may suppress the liberty the people so recently won. *(Anti-Federalist)*
4. Strong government is essential to the security of liberty. A weak government cannot preserve anything. *(Federalist)*

STUDY GUIDE

Theme Answer
Both would feel that their role in government was protected.

Critical Thinking Answer
It provided that at least some slaves would be counted for representation and tax purposes.

The Connecticut Compromise Finally, a special committee designed a compromise. Called the Connecticut Compromise because Roger Sherman and the delegation from that state played a key role on the committee, this plan was adopted after long debate. The compromise suggested that the legislative branch have two parts: (1) a House of Representatives, with state representation based on population. All revenue laws—concerning spending and taxes—would begin in this house; and (2) a Senate, with two members from each state. State legislatures would elect senators.

The larger states would have an advantage in the House of Representatives, where representation was to be based on population. The smaller states would be protected in the Senate, where each state had equal representation.

The Three-Fifths Compromise A second compromise settled a disagreement over how to determine how many representatives each state would have in the House. Almost one-third of the people in the southern states were enslaved African Americans. These states wanted the slaves counted the same as free people to give the South more representation.

At the same time, the southern states did not want the slaves counted at all for levying taxes. Because they did not have many slaves, the northern states took the opposite position. They wanted the slaves counted for tax purposes but not for representation.

The Three-Fifths Compromise settled this deadlock. Three-fifths of the enslaved people were to be counted for both tax purposes and for representation.

The Commerce and Slave-Trade Compromise A third compromise resolved a dispute over commerce and the slave trade itself. The northern states wanted the government to have complete power over trade with other nations. The southern states depended heavily on agricultural exports. They feared that business interests in the North might have enough votes in Congress to set up trade agreements that would hurt them. They also feared the North might interfere with the slave trade.

Again, a compromise settled the issue. The delegates decided that Congress could not ban the slave trade until 1808. At the same time, Congress was given the power to regulate both **interstate commerce**, or trade among the states, and foreign commerce. To protect the South's exports, however, Congress was forbidden to impose export taxes. As a result, the United States is one of the few nations in the world today that does not tax its exports.

The Slavery Question The word *slave* does not appear in the Constitution. Beyond the compromises just discussed, the Constitution dealt with slavery only by noting that those escaping to free states could be returned to their owners (Article IV, Section 2). At the time many of the northern states were outlawing slavery. Massachusetts had voted to end the slave trade. Delaware had forbidden importing enslaved persons. Connecticut and Rhode Island had decided that all enslaved persons brought into their states would be free. Pennsylvania had taxed slavery out of existence.

Whatever their personal beliefs about slavery, the delegates knew that the southern states would never accept the Constitution if it interfered with slavery. Thus, in order to create the badly needed new government, the Founders compromised on the slavery question. Their refusal to deal with slavery left it to later generations of Americans to resolve this great and terrible issue.

Other Compromises The delegates compromised on several other issues to complete the Constitution. The debate over how to elect the President included the election of the President directly by the people, by Congress, and by state legislatures. The present Electoral College system in which each state selects electors to choose the President, was finally agreed to as a compromise. Similarly, the President's four-year term was a compromise between those wanting a longer term and those who feared a long term.

On September 8 a Committee of Style and Arrangements began polishing the final draft. By

STUDY GUIDE

Themes in Government
Growth of Democracy The Connecticut Compromise stipulated that both houses of Congress had to pass a bill before it could become a law. **How would such a** provision ensure the support of both the large states and the small states?

Critical Thinking Skills
Identifying Alternatives Why was the Three-Fifths Compromise an acceptable alternative to both the North and the South?

Special Needs Strategy

Visual Disability Charts and time lines present special problems for students who have difficulties with visual materials and spatial organization. Using the chart on page 69, show students how the chart information is arranged. Point out the title of the chart first. Then explain that the first column gives the name of an event; the second, the date of the event; and the third, the outcome. To assess their understanding of charts, have students tell you how the chart on page 62 is organized and what it shows.

September 17 the document was ready. Thirty-nine delegates stepped forward to sign the Constitution. The aging Ben Franklin had to be helped to the table to sign. As others went up to sign, he remarked that during the long debates he had often looked at the sun painted on the back of General Washington's chair and wondered whether it was rising or setting. "But now at length I have the happiness to know," he said, "that it is a rising and not a setting sun."

Ratifying the Constitution

For the new Constitution to become law, 9 of the 13 states had to ratify it. The political debate over ratification lasted until May 29, 1790, when Rhode Island finally approved. The Constitution, however, actually went into effect on June 21, 1788, when New Hampshire became the ninth state to ratify.

The Federalists and Anti-Federalists The great debate over ratification quickly divided the United States into two groups. One group, known as the Federalists, favored the Constitution and was led by many of the Founders. Their support came mainly from merchants and others in the cities and coastal regions. The other group, called the Anti-Federalists, opposed the new Constitution. They drew support largely from the inland farmers and laborers, who feared a strong national government. The lines of support, however, were not tightly drawn, and many city and business people agreed with the opponents of the Constitution.

The Anti-Federalists criticized the Constitution for having been drafted in secrecy. They claimed the document was **extralegal**, not sanctioned by law, since the Convention had been authorized only to revise the old Articles. They further argued that the Constitution took important powers from the states.

The Anti-Federalists' strongest argument, however, was that the Constitution lacked a Bill of Rights. They warned that without a Bill of Rights, a strong national government might take away the human rights won in the Revolution. They demanded that the new Constitution clearly guarantee the people's freedoms. Patrick Henry was a strong opponent of the Constitution. He stated:

The necessity of a Bill of Rights appears to me to be greater in this government than ever it was in any government before . . . All rights not expressly and unequivocally reserved to the people are impliedly

Ratification of the Constitution

State and Date	Accept	Reject
Delaware December 7, 1787	30	0
Pennsylvania December 12, 1787	46	23
New Jersey December 18, 1787	38	0
Georgia January 2, 1788	26	0
Connecticut January 9, 1788	128	40
Massachusetts February 6, 1788	187	168
Maryland April 28, 1788	63	11
South Carolina May 23, 1788	149	73
New Hampshire June 21, 1788	57	47
Virginia June 25, 1788	89	79
New York July 26, 1788	30	27
North Carolina November 27, 1789	194	77
Rhode Island May 29, 1790	34	32

✓ **Chart Study**
Only three states unanimously ratified the Constitution. Five of the 13 states agreed to ratify by a narrow margin. **Why were these states reluctant to support the new government?**

and incidentally relinquished to rulers. . . . If you intend to reserve your unalienable rights, you must have the most express stipulation; for . . . . If the people do not think it necessary to reserve them, they will supposed to be given up.

—PATRICK HENRY, 1788

The Federalists, on the other hand, argued that without a strong national government **anarchy**, or political disorder, would triumph. They claimed that only a strong national government could protect the new nation from enemies abroad and solve the country's internal problems. They also claimed that a Bill of Rights was not needed since eight states already had such bills in their state constitutions. To gain the necessary support, however, the Federalists promised to add a Bill of Rights to the Constitution as the first order of business under a new government.

CHAPTER 2: THE CREATION OF THE FEDERAL GOVERNMENT 69

L3 Persuasive Writing Ask students to write an essay that explains the advantages of a written constitution and why a constitution provides for a stable political environment. Have students exchange essays or read them to the class.

Chart Study Answer
They feared a strong central government which took too much power from the states.

Assess

Check for Understanding
Have students complete Section 4 Review on page 70.

Meeting Objectives
Each section objective is tested by the Section Review questions that follow it in parentheses.
- Outline the development of the Constitution from the Constitutional Convention to ratification. (2, 3, 4, 5, 7)
- Specify issues on which the delegates to the Constitutional Convention had to compromise. (5, 6, 8)

Evaluate
📁 Section 4 Quiz
🖥 Testmaker

GLENCOE TECHNOLOGY

Focus on Government
Video 3
Lecture Launcher:
The Creation of the Federal Government
Running Time: 2:22
Videodisc 1, Chap. 3
VHS Tape 1, Begins 8:50

Critical Thinking Activity

Identifying Central Issues Tell students that one of the important issues facing the delegates to the Constitutional Convention was the conflict between big states and small states over representation. Heated debates surrounded the introduction of the Virginia Plan. Have students write a newspaper article on this issue in which they present arguments for both small-state and large-state positions.

Reteach

 Have students complete activity 2 in *Reteaching Activities* in the Teacher's Classroom Resources.

Enrich

Have students complete activity 2 in *Enrichment Activities* in the Teacher's Classroom Resources.

Close

Discuss what events led the Americans to create a strong national government.

GLOBAL CONNECTION

The United States Constitution is the oldest written national constitution in the world. Its great influence on other constitutions comes from the fact that its endurance is remarkable. Although the original signers provided for change in the Constitution, they did not believe that its fundamental principles should be altered. This has not always been the case in other countries. For example, Mexico has had several constitutions since its independence in 1824.

Examining the Connection: Have students share their findings.

GLOBAL CONNECTION

Comparing Governments

Influencing Other Constitutions The United States Constitution has influenced other countries in developing their plans of government. India's constitution, which went into effect in 1950, includes many parts based on the United States Constitution. The Indian bill of rights guarantees basic rights for all citizens. The Indian constitution prohibits discrimination based on race, religion, sex, or social class.

The Philippines gained independence from the United States on July 4, 1946. Despite its constitution, President Ferdinand Marcos, who ruled from 1965 to 1986, restricted freedom. Protests forced Marcos to flee the country. President Corazon Aquino pledged to restore democracy under a new constitution in 1987.

Examining the Connection
Find evidence in other constitutions that the United States Constitution influenced them.

Progress Toward Ratification With the promise of a Bill of Rights, the tide turned in favor of the Constitution. Many small states ratified quickly be-

cause they were pleased with equal representation in the new Senate. Although the Constitution went into effect when New Hampshire ratified, Virginia and New York had not approved. Without these two key states, the new government could not hope to survive. In Virginia, George Washington, James Madison, and Edmund Randolph helped swing a close vote on June 25, 1788. In New York, Alexander Hamilton argued the case for six weeks. Finally, on July 26 the Federalists in New York won by three votes.

To help win the battle in New York, Hamilton, Madison, and John Jay published more than 80 essays defending the new Constitution. Later they were collected in a book called *The Federalist*, which remains an authoritative explanation of the Constitution and the American form of government.

With ratification by Virginia and New York, the new government could get started. New York City was selected as the nation's temporary capital. George Washington was elected President and John Adams Vice President. Twenty-two senators and 59 representatives were elected, and on March 4, 1789, Congress met for the first time in Federal Hall in New York. On April 30 Washington took the oath of office as President, and the new government was under way.

To fulfill the promises made during the fight for ratification, James Madison introduced a set of amendments during the first session of Congress. Congress approved 12 amendments and the states ratified 10 of them in 1791. These first 10 Amendments later became known as the Bill of Rights.

4 SECTION REVIEW

Section Summary
After a series of compromises, the Constitutional Convention replaced the Articles of Confederation with a new Constitution. The addition of a Bill of Rights helped resolve the conflict between Federalists and Anti-Federalists.

Checking For Understanding
Recalling Facts
1. Define interstate commerce, extralegal, anarchy.
2. State the result of the Constitutional Convention held in 1787.
3. Identify the basic issues on which the delegates to the Constitutional Convention agreed.
4. Cite the authors of *The Federalist* and their purpose for writing it.

Exploring Themes
5. Checks and Balances How did the Connecticut Compromise provide fairness for both small and large states?
6. Growth of Democracy Why are compromises vital in a democracy?

Critical Thinking Skills
7. Identifying Central Issues What were the major arguments the Federalists offered in favor of the Constitution and the Anti-Federalists in opposition to the Constitution?
8. Identifying Alternatives What do you think the outcome of the Constitutional Convention might have been if the public and press had been allowed to attend the sessions?

Section 4 Review Answers

1. Definitions of terms appear on pages indicated: **interstate commerce,** 68; **extralegal,** 69; **anarchy,** 69
2. drafting and ratification of the Constitution
3. idea of limited and representative government; that the powers of the national government should be divided among legislative, executive, and judicial branches; and that a more powerful national government should be

created
4. Alexander Hamilton, James Madison, and John Jay; to defend the Constitution
5. large states: a House of Representatives, with representation based on population; small states: a Senate, with equal representation from each state
6. The principles of majority rule and minority rights might be at risk if group refused to compromise on its demands.

7. Federalists argued that a strong national government was needed to prevent anarchy, to protect the new nation from enemies abroad, and to solve the country's internal problems. Anti-Federalists argued that the Constitution was extralegal, took away important powers from states, and lacked a bill of rights.
8. The Convention could have ended with no constitution, or a very different constitution; because of public pressure, delegates would have had less freedom to debate issues, change their minds, and compromise.

P E R S O N A L P E R S P E C T I V E S

Abigail Adams on the Status of Women

Abigail Adams has often been hidden in the shadows of her husband, John, and her son, John Quincy—both of whom became Presidents of the United States. Yet father and son were quick to point out the large role Abigail played in their successful careers in government.

Abigail was a remarkable woman in her own right. Due to her husband's extensive absences as he pursued his career, Abigail shouldered responsibilities uncommon for women of her time. She ran the Adams household and farm, supervised the education of the children, managed the family's finances, and even increased their holdings.

John and Abigail had a very strong marriage, and one unusual for their time. An educated woman, Abigail wrote long letters to John, keeping him informed of political developments at home as he traveled. John considered Abigail his intellectual equal, and she served as his confidante and sounding board as the principles of the revolution

. . .you are proclaiming peace and good-will to men, emancipating all nations, you insist upon retaining an absolute power over wives

and the new nation evolved and took hold.

Abigail wrote many letters expressing her opinions on the issues of the day. Concerned with the status of women, she wrote John the following on March 31, 1776, as Congress was debating independence.

. . . I long to hear that you have declared an independency—and by the way in the new code of laws which I suppose it will be necessary for you to make I desire you would remember the ladies, and be more generous and favorable to them than your ancestors. Do not put such unlimited power into the hands of the husbands. Remember all men would be tyrants if they could. If particular care and attention is not paid to the ladies we are determined to foment a rebellion, and will not hold ourselves bound by any laws in which we have no voice, or representation.

That your sex are naturally tyrannical is a truth so thoroughly established as to admit of no dispute, but such of you as wish to be happy willingly give up the harsh title of Master for the more tender and endearing one of Friend. Why then, not put it out of the power of the

vicious and the lawless to use us with cruelty and indignity with impunity. Men of sense in all Ages abhor those customs which treat us only as the vassals of your sex. Regard us then as beings placed by providence under your protection and in imitation of the Supreme Being make use of that power only for our happiness.

—ABIGAIL ADAMS, 1776

In another letter to John, dated May 7, 1776, Abigail reinforced her position:

I cannot say that I think you are very generous to the ladies, for, whilst you are proclaiming peace and good-will to men, emancipating all nations, you insist upon retaining an absolute power over wives. But you must remember that arbitrary power is, like most other things which are very hard, very liable to be broken.

—ABIGAIL ADAMS, 1776

Examining the Reading

Reviewing Facts
1. Identify what Abigail Adams requested of her husband in the "new code of laws."
2. Cite the discrepancy Abigail Adams found in the work of the Second Continental Congress.

Critical Thinking Skills
3. Making Inferences What did Abigail Adams believe about the nature of power?

Focus

To begin discussion, ask: What might today's women demand from the United States government? Ask students to think about the status of women today as they read about Abigail Adams.

Teach

Ask: How was the Adamses' marriage unusual? Why didn't Adams seek the right to vote and hold office? *(She realized that these rights would follow educational and social equality, but not predate them.)* What can you infer about the position of women in Adams's time?

Assess

Have students complete **Examining the Reading.**

Answers

1. that he would "remember the ladies" and regard them as equals as Congress debated independence

2. that while the men were busy liberating themselves, they gave no thought to freedom for women

3. She believed that power can corrupt—"all men would be tyrants if they could"—and that it should be used judiciously. She also believed that power is arbitrary if it is assumed and not bestowed.

Close

Have students read the last sentence in Adams's letter of May 7 and paraphrase it.

More About Personal Perspectives

Abigail Adams, spouse of the second President and mother to the sixth, did not attend school. In this respect, she was not very different from most colonial women. She wrote, "Female education in the best families went no further than writing and arithmetic; in some few instances, music and dancing." Her difference lay in what she was able to do

with her minimal training. Her fight on behalf of women would have no effect on the new government, but she articulated the position that all groups have used to claim their rights—that a society founded on equality cannot exclude any of its members.

Identifying Terms and Concepts

1. ratified, 2. limited government, 3. revenue, 4. ceded, 5. representative government, 6. ordinances, 7. interstate commerce, 8. anarchy

Reviewing Facts and Ideas

1. Great Britain

2. Monarch must rule with the consent of the people's representatives; monarch must have legislature's consent to suspend laws, levy taxes, or maintain an army; monarch cannot interfere with legislative elections and debates; people have rights to petition government and to fair and speedy trials by juries of peers; people should not be subject to cruel and unusual punishments or to excessive fines and bail.

3. consent of the people

4. separation of powers between governor and legislature, legislature of elected representatives, and written constitution that guaranteed basic liberties and limited the power of the government

5. French and Indian War threatened security of Britain's hold on continent, and George III determined to deal more firmly with the colonies.

6. assumed the powers of a central government, organized an army and navy, issued money to pay for the war, named George Washington as commander of the army, purchased supplies, negotiated treaties with other countries, and rallied support for colonists' cause

7. first document to organize government on the basis of principles of human liberty and consent of governed

8. Congress had no power to levy or collect taxes, to regulate trade among the states or with foreign nations, or to force individuals or states to obey its laws or abide by the Articles.

9. establishment of a fair policy for the development of western lands; conclusion of a peace treaty

---

2 — CHAPTER REVIEW

Summary and Significance

The American system of government arose out of the English traditions of limited and representative government, as well as the ideas of philosopher John Locke. Oppressive British practices united the Americans in a common cause, resulting in the Revolutionary War and the Declaration of Independence. Despite certain achievements, the first American national constitution—the Articles of Confederation—created problems and fostered discontent because it did not provide for a strong central government. After a series of compromises, the Constitutional Convention drafted the United States Constitution. Conflict between Federalists and Anti-Federalists led to the addition of a Bill of Rights, which assured ratification. The American political tradition of compromise continues to serve the nation and its people well, enabling all to have a voice in their government. The American democracy has become a source of inspiration to people seeking freedom throughout the world·

Identifying Terms and Concepts

Write the key term that best completes each sentence.
limited government, ceded, representative government, revenue, ratified, anarchy, ordinances, interstate commerce

1. Virginia and New York _____ the Constitution only after the Federalists had strongly defended it.
2. Under the Magna Carta the king could not levy certain taxes on his subjects without their approval. This is an example of _____.
3. Britain depended heavily on the _____ it collected from the colonists.
4. Individual states provided the nation with a valuable asset when they _____ their land claims to the central government.
5. The Virginia House of Burgesses was an example of a _____.
6. Congress enacted _____ that provided for the organization of territories.
7. Congress was given the power to regulate _____, or trade among the states.
8. The Federalists believed that the lack of a strong central government would create _____.

Reviewing Facts and Ideas

1. Name the country in which many American political ideas originated.
2. Identify three key ideas found in the English Bill of Rights.

3. Relate the fundamental element that made government legitimate, according to John Locke.
4. Describe the practices established by colonial governments that became a basic part of our system of government.
5. Cite why the British government tightened its control over the colonies in the 1760s.
6. Describe the tasks of the Second Continental Congress.
7. Explain why the Declaration of Independence was a revolutionary document.
8. List three powers not given to Congress under the Articles of Confederation.
9. Specify the achievements made under the Articles of Confederation.
10. State the position of small states versus large states in the debate on the issue of representation in Congress.
11. Identify the issue the Convention delegates refused to settle in 1787.

Applying Themes

1. **Civil Liberties** Explain what was included in the English political heritage to the United States and its importance to the development of American government.
2. **Growth of Democracy** After the Revolutionary War, some Americans wanted a strong central government while others did not. Cite examples of this controversy today.

---

with Great Britain; Congress set up departments of Foreign Affairs, War, Marine, and Treasury; and provided that each state recognize the legal acts of other states and treat one another's citizens without discrimination

10. Small states favored representation on an equal basis with the large states; large states wanted representation based on population.

11. slavery

Applying Themes

1. The principles of limited government, representative government, and the ideas of philosopher John Locke were included. These ideas were brought to colonies and used when colonists created their own government.

2. Many people today fear the idea of "big government." They think government should not interfere in people's lives.

3. **Federalism** In your opinion, why was the Articles of Confederation an unworkable or unrealistic plan of government?
4. **Checks and Balances** Why did the Anti-Federalists insist on a Bill of Rights?

Critical Thinking Skills

1. **Identifying Central Issues** Colonial leaders used the British system of government as a base on which to build the new American government, even though they rebelled against the British system. How would you explain this apparent contradiction?
2. **Drawing Conclusions** Ben Franklin noted that he had often looked at the sun carved on the back of George Washington's chair, and wondered if it was rising or setting. "But now at length I have the happiness to know," he said, "that it is a rising and not a setting sun." What did he mean by this statement?
3. **Understanding Cause and Effect** What do you think was the most important reason for establishing a strong central government under the Constitution?
4. **Expressing Problems Clearly** How do you account for the contradiction between the constitutional acceptance of slavery and the ideals set forth in both the Declaration of Independence and the Constitution?
5. **Identifying Alternatives** The Constitution has been described as a "bundle of compromises." Were these compromises justifiable? Support your answer.

Linking Past and Present

The colonists used trade restrictions against the British to protest the Stamp Act and the Intolerable Acts. Since that time, nations, labor unions, consumer groups, and individuals have continued to use trade restrictions as a means to protest unpopular or unfair policies. Cite historical and present-day examples of nations or groups using these methods as a form of protest.

Writing About Government

Persuasive Writing Imagine that you are a colonial minister living in Virginia in 1765. The British have just put the Stamp Act in effect. Write a letter to George Grenville, British Minister of Finance, to protest this action.

Reinforcing the Skill

Analyzing Information Reread the second paragraph of the Declaration of Independence on page 58. Then follow the steps described in the skill lesson, Analyzing Information on page 65, to answer the following questions.
1. What is this paragraph about?
2. What four main points did Jefferson make in discussing this issue?
3. Explain how Jefferson would respond to the charge that the Declaration of Independence was an act of treason.

Investigating Further

1. **Individual Project** The Anti-Federalists agreed that the Articles of Confederation needed revision, but they argued against the strong powers of the federal government under the proposed Constitution. Political cartoons were a popular way to try to influence public opinion at the time. Suppose that you are an Anti-Federalist in 1787. Draw political cartoons depicting the American government under the Articles of Confederation and the Constitution.
2. **Cooperative Learning** Organize into groups of five to seven. Imagine that your class is aboard a space vehicle headed toward a relatively unknown planet that is capable of supporting human life. Earth is no longer inhabitable. In order to function effectively once you land on the new planet, the first task is to decide what type of government your community will have. Discuss as a group the model form of government under which you would like to live. Present your model to the class.

3. Answers may include that the Articles lacked the power of strong central government.
4. They believed a strong central government could violate individual rights unless those rights were specified.

Critical Thinking Skills

1. System itself was a good one, and colonists wanted to keep it. They rebelled against Britain because they felt these very rights were being denied to them.
2. Not until the Constitution was completed did Franklin believe it was a workable plan, and that it was the beginning of a strong nation rather than the end of a weak one.

3. Answers may include the need for a central authority to regulate business between the states and internationally, to collect taxes and enforce the law, and to settle disputes between the states.
4. Answers should include that at the time slavery was acceptable to many people and that the Founders realized Southern states would not accept the Constitution if it interfered with slavery.
5. Most students will probably agree that compromise is necessary in politics.

Linking Past and Present

Answers might include the Montgomery bus boycott; United States boycott of the 1980 Olympics; United States economic sanctions against Iraq in the 1990s; and several nations' sanctions against South Africa before 1992.

Writing About Government

Answers should include the belief that colonies were being taxed for benefit of Britain to the detriment of the colonists.

Reinforcing the Skill

1. reasons that signers considered it necessary to declare independence
2. Purpose of government is to protect people's natural rights; people have right to overthrow a government that fails to protect their rights. It would be foolish to overthrow a government unless it had become a serious threat to liberty; Great Britain had become a serious threat to American liberties.
3. British government ceased to be a legitimate government because it threatened, rather than defended the rights of Americans; Americans had not only the right, but the duty, to protect themselves from despotism.

Investigating Further

1. Cartoons will vary.
2. Groups' models will vary.

Chapter Organizer

Objectives	Special Feature Pages	Supplemental Materials
Section 1 A Plan of Government *pp. 76–79* 1. Describe the structure of the American government. 2. Identify the principles on which the Constitution is based. 3. List the parts of the Constitution.		Guided Reading Activities Reproducible Lesson Plans Primary and Secondary Source Readings 3 Section 1 Quiz Testmaker The Living Constitution SAT Practice Tests Writer's Guidebook
Section 2 Amending the Constitution *pp. 80–84* 1. Itemize the four methods of proposing and adding amendments to the Constitution. 2. Explain how the amendment process illustrates federalism.	Global Connection: Issues: Government Stability p. 82 Critical Thinking Skills: Evaluating Information p. 84	Guided Reading Activities Reproducible Lesson Plans Interpreting Political Cartoons 2 Section 2 Quiz Testmaker Skill Reinforcement Activity 3 The Living Constitution SAT Practice Tests Writer's Guidebook
Section 3 Enlarging the Constitution *pp. 85–90* 1. Identify amendments that concern individual rights. 2. Cite amendments that reflect change in society. 3. Specify amendments that affect the structure and power of government.	Images of Government: A Dynamic Plan pp. 86–87	Guided Reading Activities Reproducible Lesson Plans Enrichment Activities 3 Section 3 Quiz Testmaker Chapter Transparencies 3 The Living Constitution SAT Practice Tests
Section 4 Informal Changes in the Constitution *pp. 91–95* 1. Discuss how the Supreme Court changes the Constitution. 2. Specify ways that the President has changed the Constitution. 3. Summarize the role of Congress in constitutional change.	Focus on Freedom: *Marbury* v. *Madison* p. 92 Participating in Government: Applying for a Visa p. 93 Personal Perspectives: Nelson Rockefeller on the Constitution p. 95 The Constitution of the United States pp. 98–123	Guided Reading Activities Reproducible Lesson Plans Participating in Government 3 Reteaching Activities 3 Section 4 Quiz Chapter 3 Tests Testmaker Limited English Proficiency Activities 3 Audio Cassettes (English and Spanish) The Living Constitution SAT Practice Tests Writer's Guidebook

If time does not permit teaching this chapter, assign the Chapter 3 summary in the Unit 1 Digest on pages 149–150.

Key To Ability Levels

Teaching strategies have been coded for varying learning styles and abilities.

L1   Level 1 activities are **basic** activities and should be within the ability range of all students.

L2   Level 2 activities are **average** activities and should be within the ability range of the average to above-average student.

L3   Level 3 activities are **challenging** activities designed for the ability range of above-average students.

LEP   These activities should be within the ability range of **Limited English Proficiency** students.

Multicultural Activities

Organize students into three groups. Assign each group one of the Civil War Amendments—the Thirteenth, Fourteenth, and Fifteenth Amendments. Have groups research the origins of the amendment and why it was needed, how the Civil War contributed to its passage, how it changed the Constitution, what groups of Americans were most affected by this amendment in the late 1800s, and how it has been applied by the courts to minority rights issues today. When all groups have completed their reports, the class might discuss Thurgood Marshall's statement that "While the Union survived the Civil War, the Constitution did not. In its place arose a new, more promising basis for justice and equality, the Fourteenth Amendment." Why do students think Marshall singled out the Fourteenth as the most important of the Civil War Amendments?

One of the requirements for naturalization is that immigrants take a test that includes questions on the United States Constitution. Among these questions are: "How does an amendment become part of the Constitution?" "What is the Twentieth Amendment?" "What are the principles of the United States Constitution?" Why do students think the United States government tests new citizens on their knowledge of the Constitution? What might be some practical applications of this information in the daily life of naturalized citizens? *(in hiring or on-the-job treatment, in disputes over free speech or assembly, if accused of a crime, in identifying the rights the immigrant acquires through citizenship)*

Chapter Resources

Readings for the Student

Glasser, Ira. *Visions of Liberty: The Bill of Rights for All Americans.* Arcade, 1991.

Lindop, Edmund. *Birth of the Constitution.* Enslow, 1987.

With Liberty and Justice for All: The Story of the Bill of Rights. Center for Civic Education, 1991.

Wolf, Peter. *Constitutional Democracy.* Little, Brown, 1986.

Readings for the Teacher

Abraham, Henry J. *Freedom and the Court: Civil Rights and Liberties in the United States.* Oxford University Press, 1982.

Ackerman, Bruce. *We the People.* Harvard University Press, 1991.

Bernstein, Richard B. *Are We To Be a Nation? The Making of the Constitution.* Harvard University Press, 1987.

Kammen, Michael. *The Origins of the American Constitution: A Documentary History.* Penguin, 1986.

Keller, Clair W. and Denny L. Schillings, eds. *Teaching About the Constitution.* National Council for the Social Studies, 1987.

Mitchell, Ralph. *CQ's Guide to the U.S. Constitution.* Congressional Quarterly, 1994.

Multimedia

Videocassettes and Films

Blacks and the Constitution. WOSU-TV. (v/c, 60 minutes)

Changing the Law. Phoenix/BFA Films and Video, Inc. (film, 23 minutes)

Equal Justice Under Law 1: Marbury v. Madison. U.S. National Audiovisual Center. (v/c, 36 minutes)

Moyers: In Search of the Constitution (11-part series, recommended: *In the Beginning, Mr. Justice Blackmun, Mr. Justice Brennan, God and the Constitution, Justice Sandra Day O'Connor, For the People, Justice Lewis F. Powell*). Public Affairs Television. (7 v/cs, 60 minutes each)

Software

The Presidency Series. (Disk 1—*The Nature of the Office;* Disk 2—*Presidential Roles and Uses of Power*). Focus Media. (Apple, TRS80, Commodore 64, IBM disks). Students complete tutorial programs on the executive branch of government.

Social Studies Keyword Programs—Foundations of Government. Focus Media. (Apple, TRS80, Commodore 64, IBM disks). Students complete games to reinforce vocabulary, spelling, and word recognition focusing on the foundations of government.

The Constitution—A Living Document

Introduce

Chapter Overview

Chapter 3 describes the United States Constitution as a relatively brief, flexible document that has survived for more than 200 years.

Section 1 deals with the structure and major principles of the Constitution and details the concepts of checks and balances and separation of powers.

Section 2 describes the amendment process and the politics surrounding it.

Section 3 highlights protections in the Bill of Rights and describes amendments that reflect societal changes and affect the structure and power of government.

Section 4 presents the four methods of informally changing the Constitution that do not require changing the document itself and summarizes the roles of the Supreme Court, the President, and the Congress in constitutional change.

Chapter 3 Themes

Have students read Themes in Government on page 75. The themes in Chapter 3 create visual images. Have students select a chapter theme to illustrate. Illustrations might be in the form of diagrams or cartoons. Have volunteers present their illustrations to the class.

The festivities celebrating the Constitution, held in Washington, D.C., in 1989, reminded the nation that the document has guided the American government for two centuries.

74 UNIT 1: FOUNDATIONS OF AMERICAN GOVERNMENT

About the Chapter Opener

Teaching With Illustrations Have students read the caption and examine the photograph on pages 74 and 75. Then ask the following questions: How does this photograph reflect the idea that the Constitution is a living document? *(Answers will vary. Students might indicate that because people are cele-* *brating the two-hundredth-year anniversary of the Constitution, they most likely feel its importance in their lives today.)* How does the photograph make you feel? *(Answers will vary, but students should give reasons for their responses.)*

Chapter Preview

Overview

The United States Constitution provides a structure for self-government that has effectively met the changing needs of the nation for more than 200 years.

Objectives

After studying this chapter, you should be able to:

1. **Explain** how American government is organized under the Constitution.
2. **Describe** how the Constitution can be changed by amendment.
3. **Identify** changes that constitutional amendments have brought to the society and government of the United States.
4. **Cite** ways in which the Constitution has been changed informally.

Themes in Government

This chapter emphasizes the following government themes:

- **Separation of Powers** The Constitution divides the powers of government among the executive, judicial, and executive branches. Sections 1 and 4.
- **Checks and Balances** Each branch of government exercises some control on the others. Sections 1, 2, and 4.
- **Federalism** States play a vital role in the amendment process. Sections 2 and 3.
- **Growth of Democracy** Constitutional amendments have helped increase individual rights. Section 3.

Critical Thinking Skills

This chapter emphasizes the following critical thinking skills:

- Analyzing Information
- Identifying Central Issues
- Predicting Consequences

Introducing the Chapter

Before students begin to read the chapter, preview the chapter headings and visuals and raise the following questions: Why do you think the Constitution is called "a living document"? How can the Constitution be changed? Why did people want to add a Bill of Rights to the Constitution? Why weren't they willing to rely on the bills of rights in state constitutions?

Chapter Project

Place the following headings on a bulletin board that is divided into six parts: *Popular Sovereignty, Federalism, Separation of Powers, Checks and Balances, Judicial Review, Limited Government.* Explain that these are the six major principles of government on which the Constitution rests. Have students collect newspaper and magazine articles that relate to these principles and post them under the correct headings on the bulletin board.

Upon completion of chapter study, read one article from each bulletin-board section and have the class discuss how it relates to the principle under which it is posted.

Linking Past and Present
Since January 1789, Americans have voted every other year on persons to represent them in their national government. This has not stopped despite a civil war, two world wars, and an economic depression. The American people reaffirm in every election James Madison's belief in the people's right to choose the government we would live by.

Setting the Scene Although the republic established by the Constitution was new in the world, each of the principles underlying the Constitution had a long trial period in the colonies. Federalism, for example, seemed familiar because the colonies were used to exercising some internal powers while deferring to a higher authority which exercised other powers. So did separation of powers, because all colonial governments had an executive, a legislative, and a judiciary, each with separate functions.

Focus

Bell Ringer

While attendance is being taken, write the following question on the chalkboard:

What would happen if you tried to play a football game without rules?

Motivating Activity

Discuss students' answers to the Bell Ringer. Then ask why the Constitution might be considered a rule book for government, and why it is important that Americans understand the Constitution.

Vocabulary Precheck

Write the terms and concepts for this section on the chalkboard. Ask students to use those that they know in sentences. **LEP**

Teach

Guided Practice

L1 **Interpreting Primary Sources** Have the class read the Preamble of the Constitution. Then ask students to describe in their own words the six goals of government it lists. **LEP**

L2 **Analyzing a Chart** Have students study the chart "Major Principles of the Constitution" on page 77. Ask them to give examples of how each principle impacts on American government.

A Plan of Government

The Constitution that the Founders created more than 200 years ago still serves as the plan for American government and as the supreme law of the land. The Founders established a republic, where power is held by voting citizens and is exercised by elected representatives responsible to the people. The Constitution provides citizens with information about their rights and about what they may reasonably expect of their government. The success of this system of government depends on an informed and knowledgeable citizenry. An understanding of the Constitution is basic to comprehending the structure and operation of American government.

Structure

Compared with the constitutions of other countries, the United States Constitution is simple and brief. It establishes the structure and powers of government but does not attempt to spell out every aspect of how government will function. The Founders wisely left it to future generations to work out such operating details as the need arose. The entire Constitution contains about 7,000 words and is divided into three parts—the Preamble, the Articles, and the Amendments.

The Preamble The Preamble, or introduction, states why the Constitution was written. In the Preamble the Founders listed six goals for American government:

To form a more perfect Union, establish Justice, insure domestic Tranquility, provide for the common defence, promote the general Welfare, and secure the Blessings of Liberty.

—THE PREAMBLE

This statement indicates that the Founders wanted a government that would provide stability and order, protect citizens' liberties, and serve the people.

Seven Articles The body of the Constitution contains seven divisions called **articles**. Each article covers a general topic. For example, Articles I, II, and III create the three branches of the national government—the legislative, executive, and judicial branches. Most of the articles are, in turn, divided into sections that cover specifics about their topics.

Article I establishes the legislative branch of the national government. Section 1 of Article I creates the United States Congress. Sections 2 and 3 set forth details about the two houses of Congress—the House of Representatives and the Senate. Other sections of Article I spell out the procedures for making laws, list the types of laws Congress may pass, and specify the powers that Congress does not have.

Article II creates an executive branch to carry out laws passed by Congress. Article II, Section 1, states "The executive Power shall be vested in a President of the United States of America." Other sections detail the powers and duties of the presidency, establish qualifications for the office and procedures for electing the President, and provide for a Vice President.

SECTION PREVIEW

Objectives
After studying this section, you should be able to:
- Describe the structure of American government.
- Identify the principles on which the Constitution is based.

- List the three parts of the Constitution.

Key Terms and Concepts
article, jurisdiction, supremacy clause, amendment, popular sovereignty, federalism, separation of powers, checks and balances, veto, judicial review

Themes in Government
- Separation of Powers
- Checks and Balances

Critical Thinking Skills
- Analyzing Information
- Predicting Consequences

---

76 UNIT 1: FOUNDATIONS OF AMERICAN GOVERNMENT

Classroom Resources for Section 1

📁 Guided Reading Activities
📁 Reproducible Lesson Plans
📁 Primary and Secondary Source Readings 3
📁 Section 1 Quiz

▪ Testmaker
The Living Constitution
SAT Practice Tests
Writer's Guidebook

Article III, Section 1, establishes a Supreme Court to head the judicial branch. The section also gives the national government the power to create lower federal courts "as the Congress may from time to time ordain and establish." Section 2 outlines the **jurisdiction**, or the authority, of the Supreme Court and other federal courts to rule on certain kinds of cases. Section 3 defines treason against the United States.

Article IV explains the relationship of the states to one another and to the national government. This article requires each state to give citizens of other states the same rights as its own citizens and sets up procedures for admitting new states to the nation. The article also guarantees that the national government will protect the states against invasion or domestic violence such as riot and rebellion.

Article V spells out the ways that the Constitution can be amended, or changed. Article VI contains the **supremacy clause**, establishing that the Constitution, laws passed by Congress, and treaties of the United States "shall be the supreme Law of the Land." Finally, Article VII states that the Constitution would take effect after it was ratified by nine states.

The Amendments The third part of the Constitution consists of **amendments**, or changes. The Constitution has been amended 27 times. The amendment process provides a way this document, written more than two centuries ago, can remain responsive to the needs of a changing nation.

Major Principles

The Constitution rests on six major principles of government: (1) popular sovereignty; (2) federalism; (3) separation of powers; (4) checks and balances; (5) judicial review; and (6) limited government. These principles continue to have an impact on the character of American government and politics.

Popular Sovereignty The Constitution is based on the concept of **popular sovereignty**—rule by the

---

Major Principles of the Constitution

Popular Sovereignty
Government ruled by the people

Federalism
Governmental system in which power is divided between national and state governments

Separation of Powers
Each of the three branches of government has its own responsibilities.

Checks and Balances
Each branch holds some control over the other two branches.

Judicial Review
Courts have power to declare laws and actions of government unconstitutional.

Limited Government
The Constitution lists the powers government has and describes powers it does not have.

 Chart Study
Chief Justice John Marshall once said, "The Government of the Union is a government of the people."
To which principle was he referring?

---

people. Government in the United States is based upon the consent of the governed, and the authority for government action flows from the people.

Federalism The terms *federalism* and *the federal system* describe the basic structure of American government. These terms should not be confused with the term *federal government*, a phrase that simply refers to the national government in Washington, D.C.

The Constitution created a federal system of government in the United States. Under **federalism**, power is divided between national and state governments. Both levels—national and state—have their own agencies and officials and directly affect citizens.

STUDY GUIDE

Themes in Government
Separation of Powers All state constitutions as well as the United States Constitution include provisions for separation of powers among three branches. **Which**

articles of the Constitution set up the three branches?

Critical Thinking Skills
Analyzing Information How does the popular election of members

of the House of Representatives reflect the principle of popular sovereignty?

Critical Thinking Activity

Analyzing Information Remind students that the national government is built on the principles of separating powers among the three branches and of using the powers of each branch to check the others. The Framers, however, seemed more concerned with the powers of the legislature than with the other two branches. This might seem unusual when throughout history, the executive as dictator or divine ruler has been a dominant figure in most political systems. Ask: What evidence is there in the Constitution that its Framers considered the legislature to be more important than the executive or judicial branch? *(Article I first, more detailed than II or III)*

Chart Study Answer
popular sovereignty

L3 Checks and Balances Organize the class into three groups—executive branch, legislative branch, and judicial branch. Use the situations below and have each group determine how it could check the power of another branch.

1. The President makes an unwise appointment of a Supreme Court justice. *(Senate refuses to confirm)*
2. The Supreme Court makes several decisions that Congress determines are detrimental to public welfare. *(Congress proposes an amendment)*
3. Congress passes a law that the President opposes. *(presidential veto)*

Independent Practice

L1 Illustrating Concepts Have students find pictures of buildings, people, or actions that illustrate the concept of a "living" Constitution. Then have them write a paragraph in which they explain how their chosen illustration represents the concept.

STUDY GUIDE

Theme Answer
I, II, III

Critical Thinking Answer
The people elect officials.

 GLENCOE TECHNOLOGY

Focus on Government
Video 6
Making Connections: Federal Hall and the U.S. Capitol
Running Time: 2:05
Videodisc 1, Chap. 6
VHS Tape 1, Begins 16:10

Interpreting Source Readings Have students complete activity 3 in *Primary and Secondary Source Readings* in the Teacher's Classroom Resources.

Chart Study Answer
may rule that executive actions are unconstitutional

STUDY GUIDE

Theme Answer
propose a constitutional amendment

Critical Thinking Answer
There would be no state governments.

Assess

Check for Understanding

Have students complete Section 1 Review on page 79.

Meeting Objectives

Each section objective is tested by the Section Review questions that follow it in parentheses.
- Describe the structure of the American government. (4, 5)
- Identify the principles on which the Constitution is based. (3, 6, 7)
- List the parts of the Constitution. (2)

Evaluate

Section 1 Quiz

Testmaker

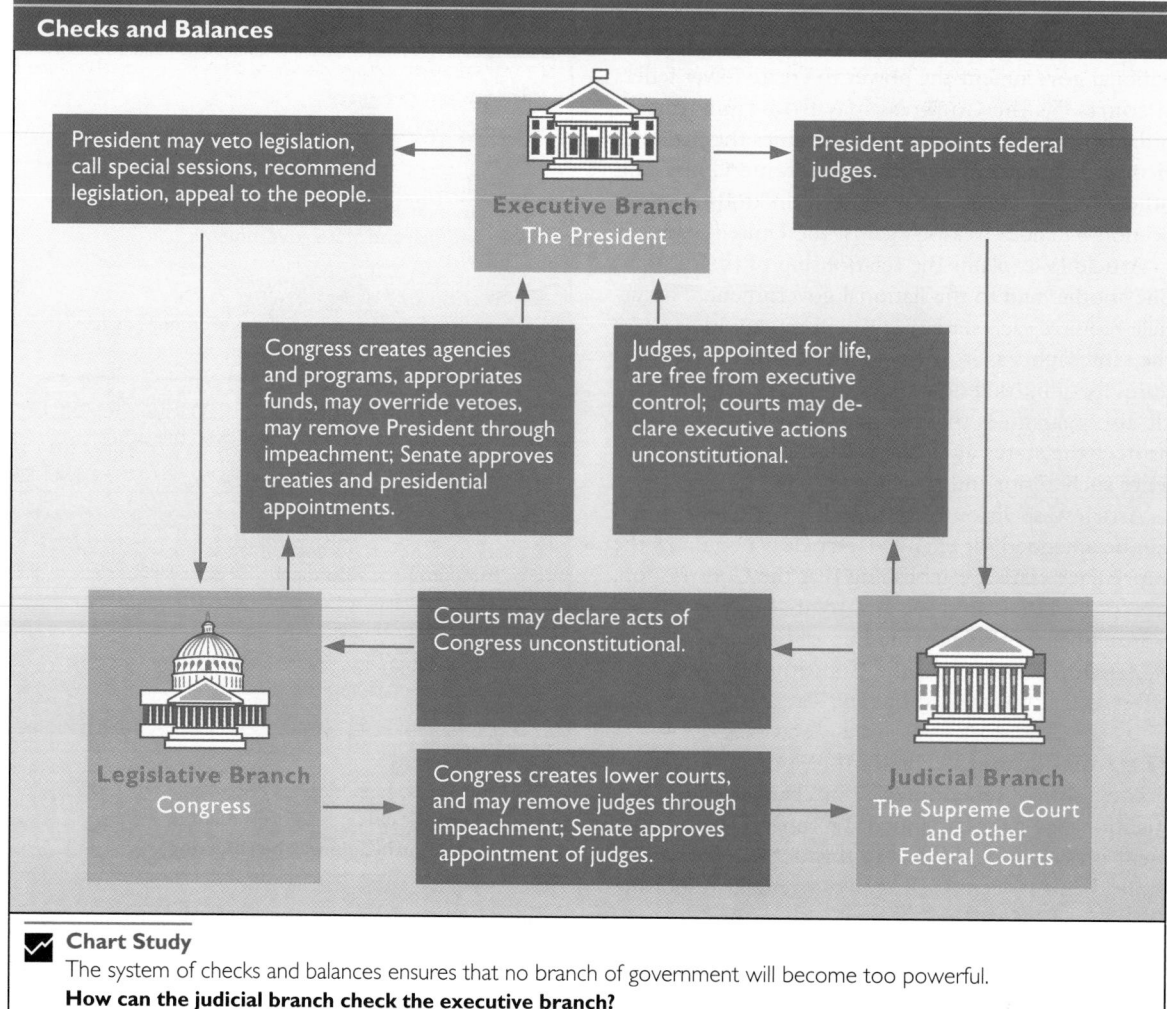

Checks and Balances

President may veto legislation, call special sessions, recommend legislation, appeal to the people.

Executive Branch
The President

President appoints federal judges.

Congress creates agencies and programs, appropriates funds, may override vetoes, may remove President through impeachment; Senate approves treaties and presidential appointments.

Judges, appointed for life, are free from executive control; courts may declare executive actions unconstitutional.

Courts may declare acts of Congress unconstitutional.

Legislative Branch
Congress

Congress creates lower courts, and may remove judges through impeachment; Senate approves appointment of judges.

Judicial Branch
The Supreme Court and other Federal Courts

☑ **Chart Study**
The system of checks and balances ensures that no branch of government will become too powerful.
How can the judicial branch check the executive branch?

Why did the Founders create such a complex system of government? Why did they choose federalism instead of a unitary form of government in which the central government has all major governing powers? In 1787, there really seemed to be no other choice. The weak union created by the Articles of Confederation had not worked, yet people remained afraid to give all power to a central government. Federalism represented a middle ground—a way to forge a union but limit central power by distributing authority between the states and the national government.

Separation of Powers The Constitution also limits the central government by dividing power among the legislative, executive, and judicial branches. Under **separation of powers,** each branch has its responsibilities, a system that the Founders hoped would prevent any branch from gaining too much power.

STUDY GUIDE

Themes in Government
Checks and Balances Since *Marbury v. Madison,* the Supreme Court has declared more than 100 acts of Congress and 1,000 state laws unconstitutional. **What can**
Congress do to reinstate a law that the Supreme Court has declared unconstitutional?

Critical Thinking Skills
Predicting Consequences How would American government be
different if the Founders had established a unitary rather than a federal system of government?

Cooperative Learning Activity

Organize students into seven groups and assign each group one of the seven articles of the United States Constitution. Ask the groups to write as many questions and answers as they can about their assigned article in a 10-minute period. Suggest to students they should divide their group's tasks by assigning each group member specific sections of the article. Collect all groups' papers and select questions to ask the entire class.

Checks and Balances To the principle of separation of powers the Founders added a system of **checks and balances**, whereby each branch of government exercises some control on the others. This system works in several ways.

Congress, for example, passes laws. The President can check Congress by rejecting—**vetoing**—its legislation. This veto power is balanced, however, by the power of Congress to override the veto by a two-thirds vote of each house.

The federal courts restrain Congress by ruling on the constitutionality of laws. This power of the judicial branch is balanced by the power of the President to appoint federal judges. This presidential power is balanced, in turn, by the Constitution's requirement that the Senate approve appointments.

Like separation of powers, the system of checks and balances was created to prevent any branch of the national government from becoming too powerful. In practice, however, checks and balances have created a system of shared powers.

Judicial Review The power of the courts to declare laws and actions of local, state, or national governments invalid if they violate the Constitution is called **judicial review**. All federal courts have this power, but the Supreme Court is the final authority on the meaning of the Constitution. Because the Constitution is the supreme law of the land, acts contrary to it must be void.

The Founders did not explicitly give such power to the judicial branch. Article III of the Constitution, however, implies that intent by stating that "the judi-cial power shall extend to all cases . . . arising under this Constitution." The Supreme Court's decision in the case of *Marbury* v. *Madison* (1803) resolved any doubts about the meaning of that clause. This case established the precedent for federal courts to rule on the acts and actions of the national government.

The principle of judicial review is particularly noteworthy. A decision of the Supreme Court can be changed only if the Court itself changes its views, if an amendment to the Constitution is passed, or if Congress revises a law the Court has declared unconstitutional.

Limited Government The principle of limited government means that the Constitution limits the powers of government. The document restricts the actions of government by specifically listing its powers and by describing powers it does not have.

The Constitution safeguards the nation against abuse of power by even its highest officials. In 1974 when President Richard Nixon resigned in the face of evidence that he had acted illegally, President Gerald Ford proclaimed:

My fellow Americans, our long national nightmare is over. Our Constitution works. Our great Republic is a government of laws and not of men. Here the people rule.

—GERALD FORD, 1974

Although the democratic principles that President Ford cited have existed for more than 200 years, the Constitution remains a flexible and dynamic basis for American government.

---

1 SECTION REVIEW

Section Summary
The 7 articles and 27 amendments of the Constitution established a structure of government based on the principles of popular sovereignty, federalism, separation of powers, checks and balances, judicial review, and limited government.

Checking for Understanding
Reviewing Facts
1. Define article, jurisdiction, supremacy clause, amendment, popular sovereignty, federalism, separation of powers, checks and balances, veto, judicial review.
2. Identify the three main parts of the Constitution.

3. Describe the underlying principles of the Constitution.

Exploring Themes
4. Separation of Powers How does the Constitution divide the powers of the federal government?
5. Checks and Balances What role do the federal courts play in checking the power of the legislative branch?

Critical Thinking Skills
6. Analyzing Information Why has the Constitution had such importance for the United States?
7. Predicting Consequences Why do you think the Founders provided that the President and Congress be elected but that federal judges be appointed?

Reteach

Ask six students to summarize briefly the six major principles of government on which the Constitution rests and write their summaries on the chalkboard. Ask remaining students to suggest improvements for the summaries and make the necessary changes.

Enrich

Have students write an essay in which they contrast American society today with the Framers' society in 1787. Have them address how today's large and culturally diverse population and global interdependence have affected the government the Framers created.

Close

Have students discuss the concept that the United States is, in John Adams's words, a "government of laws, and not of men."

CONNECTIONS

Technology
Modern technology has helped preserve the Constitution. It is scanned by electronic scanners frequently to detect any minor changes in the ink or parchment. These periodic measurements enable curators to detect if any deterioration has taken place that is invisible to the human eye.

Section I Review Answers

1. Definitions of terms appear on pages indicated: **article**, 76; **jurisdiction**, 77; **supremacy clause**, 77; **amendment**, 77; **popular sovereignty**, 77; **federalism**, 77; **separation of powers**, 78; **checks and balances**, 79; **veto**, 79; **judicial review**, 79
2. preamble, articles, amendments
3. popular sovereignty—authority to rule comes from the people; federalism—power is divided between national and state governments; separation of powers—power is limited by dividing it among branches of government; checks and balances—each branch exercises some control on the others; judicial review—courts limit acts of government that do not comply with Constitution; limited government—Constitution limits government by specifically listing its powers and by describing powers that it does not have
4. into executive, legislative, and judicial branches

5. review acts of Congress for compliance with the Constitution
6. It is both a national symbol and a basis for government. It responds through amendment or court interpretation to the changing needs of the nation.
7. Students should note value of keeping those who make or enforce laws responsive to the people and those who interpret the law and dispense justice above political considerations.

Focus

Bell Ringer

While attendance is being taken, have students turn to the Constitution and read Section 1 of the Eighteenth and Twenty-first Amendments and to note the dates of the amendments.

Motivating Activity

Have students give their Bell Ringer answers. *(establishment of prohibition [1919], repeal of prohibition [1933])* Ask if such a rapid and drastic reversal shows strength or weakness in our system of government and why.

Tell students this section describes how the Constitution can be amended and why this rarely happens.

Vocabulary Precheck

Call on students to read aloud the definitions for each term and concept from the Glossary. Then have them restate each definition in their own words. **LEP**

Teach

Guided Practice

L1 **Constructing a Chart** Work with students to construct a flow chart on the chalkboard that shows the two ways that amendments are proposed and the two ways that amendments are ratified. *(proposed: by two-thirds vote of each house of Congress, by national convention called by Congress at request of two-thirds of states; ratified: by three-fourths of state legislatures or state conventions)* Then discuss how the amendment process illustrates federalism. **LEP**

Amending the Constitution

The nation that the Founders wanted to perfect in 1787 consisted of fewer than 4 million people living in 13 agricultural states on the Atlantic coast of North America. More than two centuries later, that same Constitution provides the foundation for governing an industrial and highly technological nation of more than 250 million people in 50 states spread across the continent and beyond. The priceless heritage of the Constitution has been its ability to adapt to new conditions while preserving the basic form of American government. The words of Chief Justice John Marshall in 1819 remain true today:

> *We must never forget that it is . . . a Constitution intended to endure for ages to come, and, consequently, to be adapted to the various crises of human affairs.*
>
> —JOHN MARSHALL, 1819

The Amendment Process

The Founders created a Constitution that could be adapted to a future they could not foresee. One way they provided for change was to describe how Congress and the states could amend the Constitution. As outlined in Article V, amendments may deal with any topic except that no state can lose equal representation in the Senate without the state's consent.

Amendments may be proposed and **ratified**, or approved, in two ways. Regardless of the proposal and ratification methods used, however, the amendment process illustrates the federal system of American government. Amendments are proposed at a national level, but they are ratified on a state-by-state basis.

Proposing Amendments One method of proposing an amendment is by a two-thirds vote of each house of Congress. This is the only method that has been used to date. Dozens of resolutions asking for constitutional amendments are introduced in Congress each year. In recent years, suggestions have been made to amend the Constitution to put limits on income taxes, to limit the tenure of Supreme Court Justices to 12 years, and to give states complete control of oil deposits within their borders. None have won the necessary two-thirds vote.

The other method for proposing amendments is by a national convention called by Congress at the request of two-thirds of the states. This method has never been used, but in recent history it has almost occurred twice. In 1963 states began to **petition**, or appeal to, Congress for a convention to propose an amendment to overturn Supreme Court decisions affecting the election of state lawmakers. By 1967, 33 state legislatures, only 1 short of the required two-thirds, had voted for such a convention. The campaign failed, however, when no other states voted for the convention.

Between 1975 and 1991, 32 state legislatures petitioned Congress for a convention to propose an amendment requiring a **balanced budget**—that what the federal government spends never exceed its income. By 1995 additional states were considering the proposal, but a few states have rescinded their earlier votes.

The convention method of proposing amendments is controversial because such a convention is not required to limit itself to a specific amendment. President Jimmy Carter in the 1970s cautioned that a convention for a federal budget amendment might be "completely uncontrollable." Legal scholars warn

---

SECTION PREVIEW

Objectives
After studying this section, you should be able to:
■ Itemize the four methods of proposing and adding amendments to the Constitution.

■ Explain how the amendment process illustrates federalism.

Key Terms and Concepts
ratify, petition, balanced budget

Themes in Government
■ Checks and Balances
■ Federalism

Critical Thinking Skills
■ Identifying Central Issues
■ Predicting Consequences

80 UNIT 1: FOUNDATIONS OF AMERICAN GOVERNMENT

Classroom Resources for Section 2

📁 Guided Reading Activities
📁 Reproducible Lesson Plans
📁 Interpreting Political Cartoons 2
📁 Section 2 Quiz

💾 Testmaker
The Living Constitution
SAT Practice Tests
Writer's Guidebook

that it could propose amendments on any subject. They point out that the last Constitutional Convention, called in Philadelphia in 1787 "for the sole and express purpose of revising the Articles of Confederation," actually resulted in a new Constitution!

Ratifying Amendments When an amendment is proposed, Congress chooses one of two methods for states to approve it. One way is for legislatures in three-fourths of the states to ratify the amendment. The other is for each state to call a special ratifying convention. The amendment then becomes part of the Constitution after three-fourths of these conventions have approved it.

If a state rejects an amendment in the state legislature method, lawmakers may later reverse their decision and ratify the amendment. Suppose however, a state legislature approves an amendment and then revokes the ratification. Is this legal? This question arose over the proposed Equal Rights Amendment (ERA) designed to prohibit discrimination on the basis of sex. When 5 of the 35 state legislatures that approved the ERA later revoked their ratification, questions arose. Many constitutional scholars contended that the states' revocations were unconstitutional. The courts, however, have never resolved the issue.

Many scholars have criticized the practice of sending proposed amendments directly to state legislatures because it allows constitutional change without any input from the people. Legislators are usually elected for their positions on such state and local issues as education and taxes. Rarely are they chosen for their views on a proposed amendment.

Despite such criticisms, the other ratification method—by state ratifying conventions—has been used only once. Conventions ratified the Twenty-first Amendment, which repealed the Eighteenth Amendment that banned the sale of alcoholic beverages. Congress let each state legislature determine how the ratifying conventions would be organized and the delegates elected. Delegates in each state ran for election statewide either on a pledge to support the amendment or on a pledge to reject it. Then, at each state ratifying convention, the elected delegates voted as they had pledged to do in their election campaigns. In effect, this method gave the people a direct voice in the amending process.

Congress Sets the Rules In addition to deciding which ratification method will be used, Congress decides how much time the states will have to ratify an amendment. In modern times, Congress has set the limit at seven years.

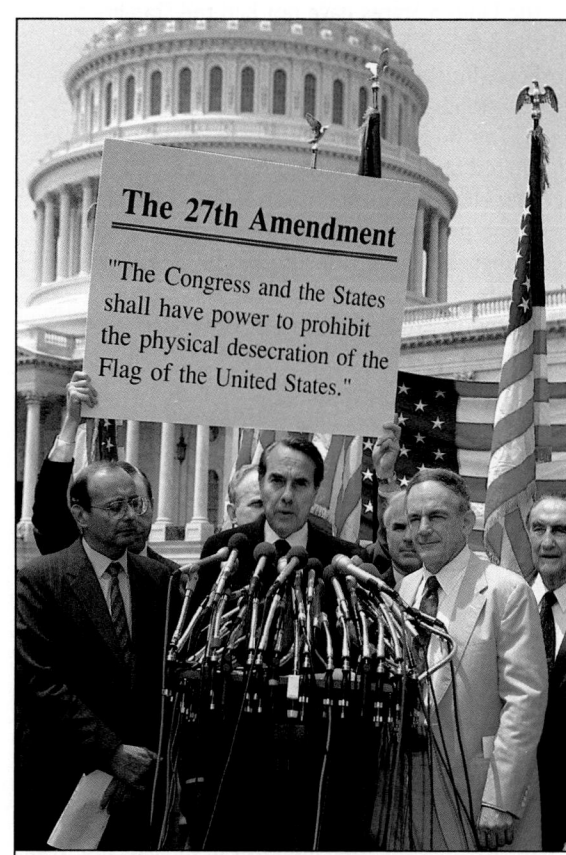

Senators Push for a New Amendment
Before the current Twenty-seventh Amendment was ratified, people debated the amendment shown here. **History What was the subject of the proposed amendment?**

Chapter 3, Section 2
Lesson Plan, pages 80–84

L2 Federalism Ask students to explain the factors that contribute to the lengthy amendment process and list them on the chalkboard. Then have students explain how these factors were reflected in the struggle over the ERA.

Independent Practice

L2 Persuasive Writing Ask students to write a paragraph defending or opposing the practice of ratifying proposed amendments by state legislatures.

Interpreting Political Cartoons Have students complete activity 2 in *Interpreting Political Cartoons* in the Teacher's Classroom Resources.

Caption Answer
to prohibit flag desecration

STUDY GUIDE

Theme Answer
No limits can be placed on the convention.

Critical Thinking Answer
allows people to vote for delegates on a specific issue

STUDY GUIDE

Themes in Government
Checks and Balances Proposing amendments allows Congress to check the power of the judicial branch. Congress may also impeach justices and change the number of courts or the number of justices on the Supreme Court. **What criticism has been raised against the convention method of proposing amendments?**

Critical Thinking Skills
Identifying Central Issues In what way is a ratifying convention more democratic than sending an amendment to state legislatures?

Special Needs Strategy

Reading Disability Students with reading difficulties often recognize fewer words than readers with few or no difficulties. One way to assess potential reading difficulties and to gauge whether the reading material is appropriate for an individual student is to count the words a student cannot recognize immediately in a defined space of text. Have students count the number of words they cannot identify quickly in the first three paragraphs of this section. More than three non-recognized words per paragraph may indicate comprehension difficulties.

Remind students that the nature of a country's population has a direct effect on the stability of its government. Point out that governments are most stable in countries where the population shares a political or social consensus about basic beliefs. Discuss with students how the United States Constitution provides ways to adjust to the changing needs of the American people.
Examining the Connection Answer: *It could not meet changing needs without amendment.*

STUDY GUIDE

Theme Answer
They would have to share representation in the Senate.

Critical Thinking Answer
pro—defend women's rights, con—destroy family life

CONNECTIONS

History
Although the Equal Rights Amendment was first proposed in 1923 by Alice Paul, the founder of the National Women's Party, there was no discussion on the amendment until 1967.

Assess

Check for Understanding
Have students complete Section 2 Review on page 83.

GLOBAL CONNECTION

Issues

Government Stability France is much older than the United States, but it has had 16 constitutions since 1789. Even nations younger than the United States have not had the stability that the United States Constitution has provided. Peru, independent since 1821, has had 13 constitutions.

The flexibility the Founders wrote into the United States Constitution has provided for the American government's stability. The amendment process and the methods of informal change allow the Constitution to meet changing needs. The system of checks and balances has provided continuity in the American government in spite of changes.

Examining the Connection
How might a more detailed Constitution have limited the flexibility of our federal government?

Congress can put the time limit either in the text of the amendment or in legislation that accompanies the amendment. Placing a time limit can alter the fate of an amendment. For example, Congress put a seven-year limit in the law accompanying the ERA. When, in the fall of 1978, it appeared that the amendment would not be ratified within this time, its supporters persuaded Congress to extend the deadline until June 1982. Because the time limit was in the law, not in the text of the amendment, the extension required a simple majority vote in the House and Senate. If the deadline had been in the amendment itself, a two-thirds vote of the House and Senate would have been needed to change the text of the amendment.

STUDY GUIDE

Themes in Government
Federalism One constitutional amendment proposed was to give the District of Columbia the status of a state and thus give its citizens full equality with the citizens of other states. **Why might the states oppose such an amendment?**

Critical Thinking Skills
Predicting Consequences What consequences did those who favored and those who opposed the Equal Rights Amendment predict if the amendment was ratified?

Politics and Amendments

Amending the Constitution is not easy. Except for the first 10 amendments—the Bill of Rights, which were quickly adopted after the Constitution was ratified—it has been formally amended only 17 times.

Barriers to Success Why have so few amendments been added to the Constitution? The amendment process is long and difficult. It often takes many years to get the large congressional majorities needed to propose an amendment and for the states to ratify it. Winning approval for an amendment may require influencing lawmakers at both the state and national levels. The process involves winning public opinion as well as building a political coalition of interest groups with national strength. The history of the proposed Equal Rights Amendment illustrates the difficulties of the amendment process.

The Equal Rights Amendment Case The earliest version of the ERA was introduced in Congress in 1923. A handful of women who had worked to win the right to vote supported the idea. Every year for the next 49 years, some form of an equal rights amendment was introduced in Congress. During most of this time, such a change in the Constitution attracted little support.

By the 1960s, however, the political climate began to change as the civil rights movement sparked new interest in women's rights. Shirley Chisholm, the first African American woman to serve in the House of Representatives, symbolized this connection. Describing her campaign, she observed:

When I decided to run for Congress, I knew I would encounter both anti-black and anti-feminist sentiments. What surprised me was the much greater virulence [strength] of sex discrimination.
—SHIRLEY CHISHOLM, 1969

By the early 1970s, an equal rights amendment had gained support from several religious, labor, and

Cooperative Learning Activity

Have the class select a topic of a proposed amendment. Then, organize the class into three groups to simulate a constitutional convention. Have Group 1 draft the wording of the amendment, Group 2 develop arguments *for* the amendment, and Group 3 develop arguments *against* it. Have Group 1 write their proposed amendment on the chalkboard and have Groups 2 and 3 debate it. Finally, have Group 1 work with the entire class to reword the amendment to satisfy objections. Then have a ratification vote.

political organizations as well as from the National Organization for Women (NOW). These groups worked hard to influence Congress to support the ERA. Finally, in 1972 both the Senate and the House approved the ERA by large margins and sent the amendment to the state legislatures. Legislatures in 22 states quickly ratified the ERA, and by the end of 1972 it looked as though the amendment would soon be added to the Constitution.

By 1973, however, strong opposition to the ERA had developed. Eventually, opponents rallied around a women's organization called STOP ERA. The opposition needed to convince only 13 states not to ratify in order to block the amendment, but ERA supporters had to win in 38 states.

As STOP ERA raised doubts about the wisdom of the amendment, public opinion began to shift, and each side worked furiously to win the support of state lawmakers. NOW called for an economic boycott of states that did not support the ERA. Some national organizations refused to hold their annual conventions in states that did not ratify the ERA. This boycott cost cities in those states millions of dollars in lost business. STOP ERA drew publicity to its cause by delivering home baked bread to lawmakers just before crucial votes, reminding them of STOP ERA's claims that the amendment would destroy family life.

By January 1977, only 35 states had ratified the amendment, and 5 states that had ratified voted to withdraw their approval. With the deadline for ratification looming near, Congress extended it to June 1982. By that date, however, ERA still did not have the necessary votes.

The long struggle over the ERA shows that formally amending the Constitution requires broad agreement at both the national and state levels. When organized opposition to a proposed amendment arises, the already long process can become even more difficult.

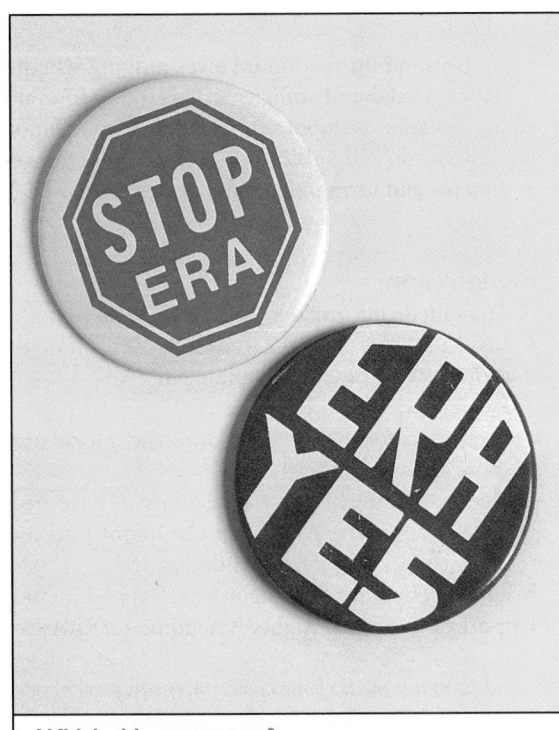

Which side are you on?
The battlelines were clearly drawn around the ERA.
Civics What group opposed the ERA?

Caption Answer
STOP ERA

Meeting Objectives

Each section objective is tested by the Section Review questions that follow it in parentheses.
- Itemize the four methods of proposing and adding amendments to the Constitution. (2, 3, 4)
- Explain how the amendment process illustrates federalism. (5, 6, 8)

Evaluate

📁 Section 2 Quiz

⬛ Testmaker

Reteach

Have students review the amendment process and indicate which route was used in the case of the ERA. Ask students at what point the amendment failed.

Enrich

Have students compare the amendment procedures in their state constitution with those in the United States Constitution.

Close

Ask students if they think that the public should be allowed to vote on amendments.

---

2 SECTION REVIEW

Section Summary
To allow the Constitution to meet future needs the Founders could not foresee, they included guidelines for changing it. This process has proven to be long, complex, and highly political.

Checking for Understanding
Recalling Facts
1. Define ratify, petition, balanced budget.
2. Cite the two ways of proposing amendments.
3. Identify the two methods of ratifying amendments.
4. Explain why the Constitution has been amended so few times.
Exploring Themes
5. Checks and Balances In what ways can the states restrain the powers of Congress in the amendment process?
6. Federalism How does the amendment process in the United States Constitution demonstrate that the United States has a federal system of government?

Critical Thinking Skills
7. Identifying Central Issues What is the connection between the civil rights movement of the 1960s and the drive for the Equal Rights Amendment in the 1970s?
8. Predicting Consequences Why do you think that Congress has established deadlines for ratifying amendments?

CHAPTER 3: THE CONSTITUTION—A LIVING DOCUMENT 83

Section 2 Review Answers

1. Definitions of terms appear on pages indicated: **ratify,** 80; **petition,** 80; **balanced budget,** 80
2. by two-thirds vote in each house of Congress or by a national convention called by Congress upon petition of two-thirds of the states
3. by three-fourths of the state legislatures or by special ratifying conventions in three-fourths of the states

4. because the amendment process is long and complicated and requires such large majorities for success at each step
5. by refusing to ratify amendments that are proposed by Congress
6. Cooperation of both state and national levels of government are necessary to amend the Constitution.

7. Answers will vary but should suggest that the success of African Americans in gaining equal rights encouraged women to press for the same.
8. Answers should recognize the potential harm of allowing controversial issues to drag on indefinitely without resolution.

Focus

Challenge the class to plan a radio ad for a product. How will they convince people to buy the product? Would listeners' ability to evaluate information in their ad influence its content?

Teach

Review the events surrounding the attempt to ratify the Equal Rights Amendment. Point out that numerous emotional appeals were made on both sides, in addition to intelligent coverage of the proposed amendment.

Have a volunteer read the excerpt from Steinem's essay; then work through the excerpt using the steps to evaluate information. Ask: What argument does Steinem make? *(that the media has done a poor job of explaining ERA)* Why does this bother Steinem? *(She feels the media has cheated the public.)* Discuss whether students need more information to form their own opinion.

Assess

Have students complete the **Practice** exercise.

Close

Ask: What are some reliable sources of information? What makes them reliable? Make sure that students understand that no one source can present all the information they need to make informed decisions.

Evaluating Information

Evaluating information involves judging whether evidence is valid and sufficient. The ability to evaluate information is important to citizens of a democracy, who must be able to assess highly charged arguments and form independent opinions.

Explanation

To evaluate information, follow these steps:
- Read the information carefully to determine exactly what argument is being made.
- Decide whether the source of the information is likely to be objective. Ask: Does the information show emotion or bias?
- Decide whether the information you have been given is adequate. Ask: What else might I need to know to make an informed decision?

Read the following statement by Gloria Steinem in support of the Equal Rights Amendment (ERA).

> *The major media have been content to present occasional interviews, debates, and contradictory reports from those who are for or against [the ERA]. . . .*
> *The audience is left confused. . . . The majority of women and men . . . support the ERA . . . but there is some evidence that 50/50 reporting has actually impeded the building of a larger majority. . . .*
> *One result of this prizefight . . . is that . . . [Americans get] the idea that women are voting against the ERA: not the two dozen or so aging white male state legislators who are actually stopping it on behalf of financial and religious interests.*
> —GLORIA STEINEM, *Ms.*, NOVEMBER 1981

The first step in evaluating information is to determine what argument is being made. Steinem argues that the news medias coverage of the ERA has confused the public. Even though the majority of Americans has always supported ERA, says Steinem, the equal time given to anti-ERA groups has caused some to doubt their own perceptions.

The second step is to assess emotion or bias. One would expect that Steinem, a strong supporter of ERA, was dismayed that it was not yet ratified.

Now evaluate the evidence. Is this description of media coverage accurate? Is the assertion that the majority of Americans supports the ERA accurate? Steinem implies that the "white male legislators" and interest groups are the only significant obstacle to the amendment. Who are the "financial and religious interests"?

Remember that no single source can give all the information you need. If an author does not back up arguments with all the evidence you need, the arguments are not necessarily invalid. It means, however, that you need to gather more information.

Practice

Read the passage below from a pamphlet and answer the questions that follow.

> *It is claimed that . . . [the ERA will guarantee women] equal pay for equal work and equal opportunities in all walks of life. . . . the ERA will give no legal rights in these areas which they do not already have. . . . [Existing] laws are not impractical in application as many ERA proponents claim. For example, if a woman is discriminated against in employment, she can file a claim with the Equal Employment Opportunity Commission. . . . It is claimed that women, as homemakers, would have greater financial security. However, under the ERA, women would lose the special concessions and protections presently afforded them by law and would actually have less financial security.*
> —FROM "ERA—LET THE AUTHORITIES SPEAK"

1. What is the author's argument?
2. Does the information include the author's emotion?
3. What three questions would you need to ask before forming an opinion about the validity of these arguments?

Additional Practice

To practice this skill, see **Reinforcing the Skill** on page 97.

Practice Answers

1. that the ERA will not give women any important rights that they do not already have and will actually take away concessions and protections that they currently enjoy

2. The author seems to be an opponent of the ERA, so the information is likely to be emotional and biased.

3. Sample questions: What evidence is there to back up the author's claim that women already have the right to equal pay for equal work? What arguments do ERA proponents make about existing laws against job discrimination? How successful have women been in filing claims with the Equal Employment Opportunity Commission? What concessions and protections would women lose as a result of ERA?

For additional practice, have students complete activity 3 in *Skill Reinforcement Activities* in the Teacher's Classroom Resources.

Enlarging the Constitution

Despite the difficulty of the amendment process, Americans put it to work almost before the ink was dry on the new Constitution. Because critics attacked the proposed Constitution for not protecting the rights of the people, the Founders promised to add a list of such rights. The First Congress quickly proposed 12 amendments for the Constitution and sent them to the states for ratification. In 1791 the states ratified 10 of the amendments, which became known as the Bill of Rights. The first proposed amendment, dealing with representation in the House, was never ratified. The second, dealing with congressional salaries, was not ratified until 1992. Both amendments indicate the difficulty of the amendment process.

The Bill of Rights

The Bill of Rights limits the powers of government. Its basic purpose is to protect two kinds of rights: rights of individual liberty, such as freedom of speech, and rights of persons accused of crimes, such as the right to trial by jury.

When the Constitution was adopted, some state constitutions had bills of rights. Thus it seemed necessary and reasonable to add similar limits to the new national government. Although the Bill of Rights originally applied only to the national government, almost all its provisions have been applied to the states through a series of Supreme Court decisions. Today the Bill of Rights protects citizens against abuses by both the national and state governments.

The First Ten Amendments

Guarantees of Basic Citizens' Rights
First Amendment: freedom of religion, speech, press, assembly, and of the right to petition the government

Protection Against Arbitrary Police and Court Action
Fourth Amendment: prohibits unreasonable searches and seizures

Fifth Amendment: requires grand jury indictment for serious crimes, bans double jeopardy, prohibits having to testify against oneself, guarantees no loss of life, liberty or property without due process of law

Sixth Amendment: guarantees right to speedy, public, impartial trial in criminal cases, with counsel and right to cross-examine witnesses

Seventh Amendment: guarantees right to jury trial in civil suits

Eighth Amendment: prohibits excessive bail or fines and cruel and unusual punishment

Protection of States' Rights and Other Rights
Ninth Amendment: rights not listed in other amendments are not necessarily denied

Tenth Amendment: powers not delegated to the national government or denied to the states are reserved to the states

Military Protection and Rights
Second Amendment: guarantees the right to organize state militias and to bear arms

Third Amendment: prohibits the quartering of soldiers in homes in peacetime

✓ **Chart Study**
The first ten amendments are also called the Bill of Rights. **What does the Ninth Amendment mean?**

Focus

Bell Ringer
While attendance is being taken, have students list the rights they think they have as residents of the United States.

Motivating Activity
Use students' Bell Ringer lists to create a list on the chalkboard. Then have students decide which rights are actually protected by the Constitution. Discuss how rights are limited, pointing out that one person's rights end where another's begin. For example, while the First Amendment protects freedom of speech, a person cannot use this freedom to damage another person's reputation. Tell students this section cites amendments that concern individual rights, reflect change in our society, and affect the structure and power of government.

Vocabulary Precheck
Write the key terms and concepts for this section on the chalkboard. Ask students to use those that they know in sentences. **LEP**

Caption Answer
that all rights not stated in the Constitution are retained by the people

---

SECTION PREVIEW

Objectives
After studying this section, you should be able to:
- Identify amendments that concern individual rights.
- Cite amendments that reflect change in society.
- Specify amendments that affect

the structure and power of government.

Key Terms and Concepts
prior restraint, slander, libel, militia, probable cause, search warrant, arrest warrant, due process of law, eminent domain, change of venue, lame duck, poll tax

Themes in Government
- Federalism
- Growth of Democracy

Critical Thinking Skills
- Analyzing Information
- Identifying Central Issues

Focus on Government
Video 4
**Lecture Launcher:
The Constitution–A Living Document**
Running Time: 2:22
Videodisc 1, Chap. 4
VHS Tape 1, Begins 11:14

CHAPTER 3: THE CONSTITUTION—A LIVING DOCUMENT 85

Classroom Resources for Section 3

📁 Guided Reading Activities
📁 Reproducible Lesson Plans
📁 Enrichment Activities 3
📁 Section 3 Quiz

✚ Testmaker
Chapter Transparencies 3
The Living Constitution
SAT Practice Tests

Teach

Guided Practice

L1 Constructing a Chart Draw a three-column chart on the chalkboard with the headings *Amendment, Purpose,* and *Example.* Beginning with the First Amendment, ask students to explain its purpose and give an example of the rights it protects. Proceed in this manner for the first 10 amendments. Then discuss why the Bill of Rights is considered part of the original Constitution and how they differ from the other amendments.

LEP

Images of Government

The Declaration of Independence, Constitution, and Bill of Rights are kept in airtight, helium-filled glass cases. Prolonged exposure to the outside atmosphere would cause damage to these documents.

Answers

1. The Framers purposely used general language in the Constitution in order to allow for the government to change as times changed.
2. In 1789 the United States Constitution was the only written constitution in the world.

The First Amendment One of the most important amendments in the Bill of Rights is the First Amendment, which states:

> *Congress shall make no law respecting an establishment of religion, or prohibiting the free exercise thereof; or abridging the freedom of speech, or of the press; or the right of the people peaceably to assemble, and to petition the Government for a redress of grievances.*
>
> —FIRST AMENDMENT, 1791

The First Amendment protects the right of Americans to worship as they please, or to have no religion if they prefer. Thus, unlike many nations, the United States does not have an official religion, nor does the government favor one religion over another. This principle is known as separation of church and state.

In addition, the First Amendment protects freedom of speech and freedom of the press. The government cannot prevent individuals from freely expressing their opinions. Citizens thus have the right to criticize government officials and decisions, and they are allowed to spread unpopular ideas.

The First Amendment protects not only individual speech, but also extends to the circulation of ideas in newspapers, books, magazines, radio, television, and, to some extent, movies. Unlike the press in some other countries, the American press is not subject to **prior restraint**—that is, government censorship of information before it is published or broadcast.

The freedoms of speech and the press are not unlimited, however. For example, laws prohibit slander and libel. **Slander** is false speech intended to damage a person's reputation. **Libel** is similar to slander, except that it applies to written or published statements.

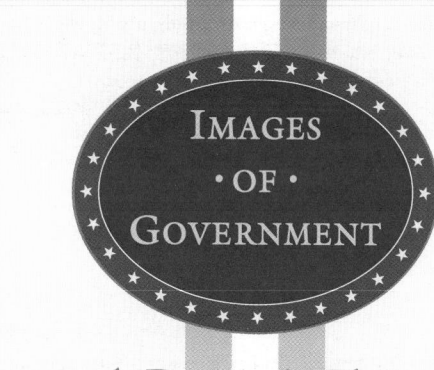

IMAGES
· OF ·
GOVERNMENT

A Dynamic Plan

In 1787 the Framers of the United States Constitution drew upon political philosophy and established practices of government. They created a living system that is the oldest written constitution still serving a nation today.

▼ Despite his mistrust of democratic tendencies, Gouverneur Morris (1752-1816) emerged as one of the leading figures at the Constitutional Convention of 1787. He stood in the thick of the decision-making process as a member of the Revision Committee, where he employed his literary skills to draft the final version of the Constitution.

86 UNIT 1: FOUNDATIONS OF AMERICAN GOVERNMENT

Background

The Fourteenth Amendment has been the basis of more Supreme Court rulings than any other part of the Constitution. Between the end of Reconstruction and the 1940s, however, the Amendment was chiefly applied to the rights of business and regulatory efforts by the states. It was no accident that this doctrine emerged just as the nation began to industrialize rapidly. But in the 1950s and 1960s, Supreme Court interpretations of the Fourteenth Amendment broadened to apply the Bill of Rights to the actions of state governments. Once again the Court adapted to societal change.

Endangering the nation's safety by giving away military secrets or calling for the violent overthrow of the government also are not protected. In addition, the courts have held that speech should be responsible. For example, no one has the right to cry "Fire!" in a crowded theater just to see what happens.

Another freedom the First Amendment protects is the right to assemble in groups and hold demonstrations. People may pass out pamphlets, hold meetings, and do other things that peaceably call attention to their beliefs. Courts have ruled, however, that the government can require a group to obtain a permit before holding meetings or demonstrations.

Finally, the First Amendment protects the right to criticize government officials and their actions. The rights to sign petitions in support of an idea, to present those petitions to government officials, and to send letters to those officials are all protected.

The Second Amendment This amendment insures citizens and the nation the right to security. It states:

> *A* well-regulated Militia being necessary to the security of a free State, the right of the people to keep and bear Arms shall not be infringed.
> —SECOND AMENDMENT, 1791

Originally, the Second Amendment was intended to prevent the national government from repeating actions that the British had taken. Before the Revolution, the British tried to take weapons away from colonial **militia**, or armed forces of citizens.

This amendment does not prevent Congress from regulating the interstate sale of weapons, nor does it apply to the states. States are free to regulate the use and sale of firearms as they see fit.

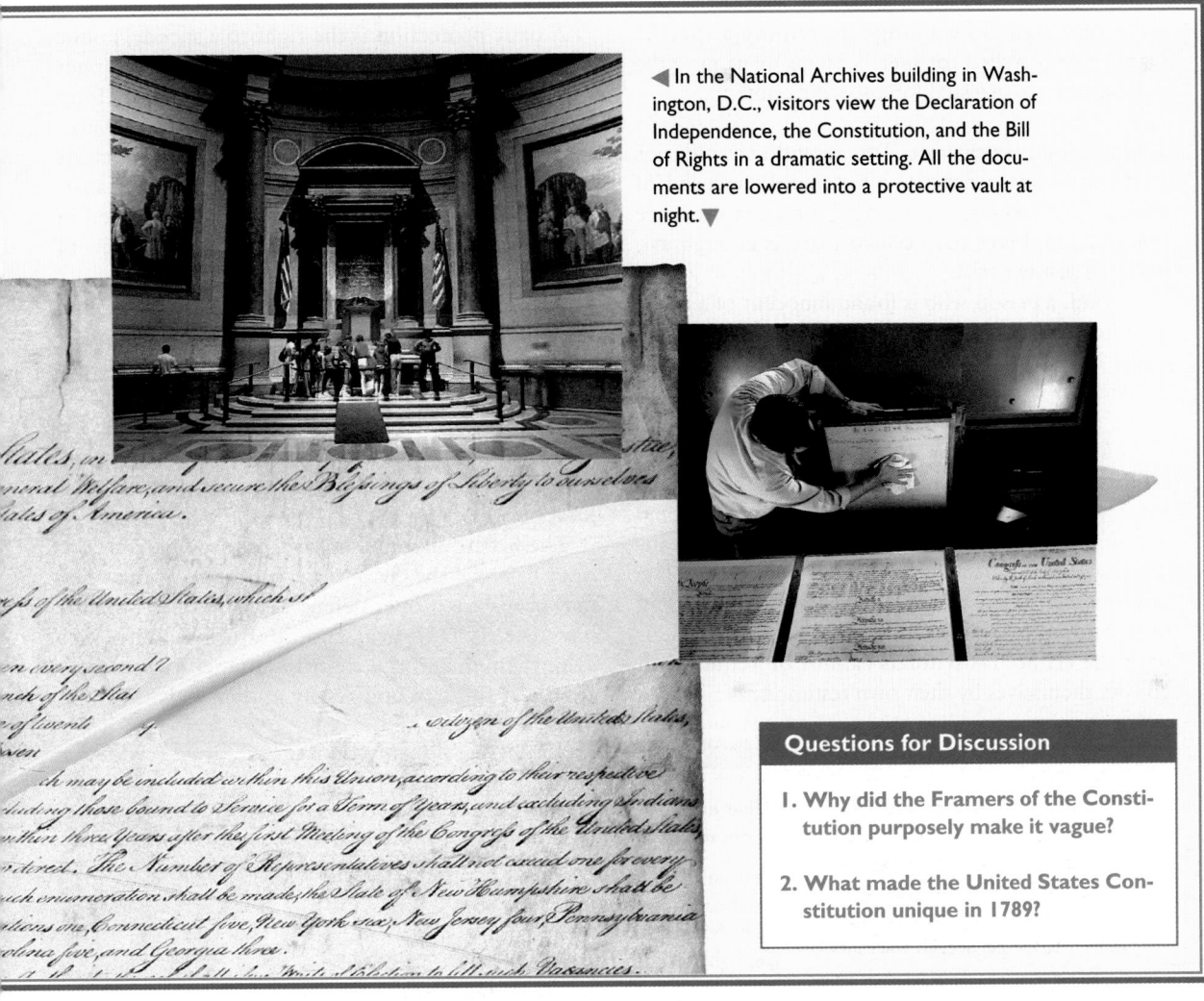

◄ In the National Archives building in Washington, D.C., visitors view the Declaration of Independence, the Constitution, and the Bill of Rights in a dramatic setting. All the documents are lowered into a protective vault at night. ▼

Questions for Discussion

1. Why did the Framers of the Constitution purposely make it vague?

2. What made the United States Constitution unique in 1789?

L2 Formulating Questions
Organize the class into two groups. Have one group study Amendments XI through XXVII in the Constitution and read the text narrative on pages 89–90. Have the second group read the same text narrative and write one question about each amendment. Have one person in each group act as leader and assign specific amendments to each group member. Close by having the question writers ask their questions of the reader group.

Interpreting Visuals Display transparency 3 from the *Chapter Transparencies* in the Teacher's Classroom Resources and use the accompanying teaching strategy and student activity to teach the purpose of the Sixteenth Amendment.

CONNECTIONS

History
The father of the Constitution, James Madison, believed that the Constitution would have to be altered as new situations arose but that this had to depend on the majority. He wrote: "If the will of the majority cannot be trusted where there are diversified and conflicting interests, it can be trusted nowhere."

GLENCOE TECHNOLOGY

Focus on Government
Video 11
**Lecture Launcher:
Assuring Equal Justice for All**
Running Time: 2:27
Videodisc 1, Chap. 11
VHS Tape 1, Begins 30:29

Cooperative Learning Activity

Organize students into five groups and assign each group the following amendments: I–V, VI–X, XI–XV, XVI–XXI, and XXII–XXVII. Ask the groups to write as many questions and answers as they can about their assigned amendments in a 10-minute period. Suggest to students they should divide their group's task by assigning each group member a specific amendment. Collect all groups' papers and select questions to ask the entire class.

Independent Practice

L1 Creating Political Cartoons Have students create a political cartoon illustrating one of the 27 amendments. The cartoon might support the passage of the amendment or point out its weaknesses. Put the cartoons together in the form of a book. **LEP**

L2 Conducting a Survey Have each student select an amendment and conduct a survey of 10 people other than his or her classmates about what that amendment means to them. Have students write a short paper on their results.

STUDY GUIDE

Theme Answer
probable cause

Critical Thinking Answer
Democracies protect the rights of *all* citizens.

CONNECTIONS

History

The Ninth and Tenth Amendments were written for the Federalists and Anti-Federalists. The Federalists did not want to state what liberties, or natural rights, people had precisely because they were "natural rights." They feared that if they spelled out the rights of the people in the Constitution, what was not included would not be considered a right. The Anti-Federalists were concerned about the loss of state power and liberty. The Tenth Amendment sustains the rights of the states.

The Third Amendment This amendment prohibits the government from forcing people to quarter—to provide shelter for—soldiers in their homes, another British practice before the Revolution. In times of war, however, Congress may require a homeowner to house soldiers but only under conditions clearly spelled out by law.

The Fourth Amendment The Fourth Amendment protects the right to privacy. It requires authorities to have a specific reason to search a premises or to seize evidence or people. Police cannot simply conduct a general search or seizure hoping to find damaging evidence or arrest someone on the chance that he or she might have committed a crime.

To be lawful, a search or arrest must be based on **probable cause**, meaning that police must have a reasonable basis to believe the person or premises is linked to a crime. A search or arrest also usually requires a **search warrant** or an **arrest warrant**. These are orders signed by a judge describing a specific place to be searched for specific items or naming the individual to be arrested for a specific crime.

The Fifth Amendment This amendment contains four important protections for people accused of crimes. First, no one can be tried for a serious crime unless a grand jury has decided there is enough evidence to justify a trial.

Second, a person who is found innocent of a crime may not be tried again for the same offense. This clause is designed to prevent continued harassment of individuals in order to convict them of a crime for which they had already been found innocent.

Third, no one may be forced to testify against himself or herself. As a result, people questioned by the police, on trial, or testifying before a congressional hearing may refuse to answer questions if their answers would connect them with a criminal act. The government must establish a person's guilt by finding independent evidence of the person's involvement with the crime. Individuals cannot be required to convict themselves by their own testimony.

Finally, the Fifth Amendment states that government may not deprive any person of life, liberty, or property without **due process of law**. This means that government must follow proper constitutional procedures in trials and in other actions it takes against individuals.

The Fifth Amendment also defines government's right of **eminent domain**—the power of government to take private property for public use such as a highway, a dam, or a park. The government must pay a fair price for the property taken and must use it in a way that benefits the public.

The Sixth Amendment This amendment protects the rights of individuals charged with federal crimes to defend themselves in a court trial. The Supreme Court, however, has ruled that these rights also apply to people charged with crimes who are subject to state courts. The Sixth Amendment gives an accused person several important rights.

A basic protection is the right to a speedy, public trial by an impartial jury. Thus, the authorities cannot purposely hold a person for an unnecessarily long time awaiting trial. This protection prevents government from silencing its critics by holding them for years without trials, as often happens under dictatorships. The requirement that trials be conducted in public assures that justice is carried out in full view of the people.

Although the amendment provides for trial by jury, an accused person may ask to be tried by a judge alone. The accused also may ask to have his or her trial moved to another community. A **change of venue**, or new trial location, is sometimes requested when unfavorable publicity indicates that the defendant cannot receive an impartial trial in the original location.

The Sixth Amendment gives accused persons the right to know the charges against them, so that they may prepare a proper defense. Accused persons also have the right to hear and question all witnesses against them and the right to compel witnesses to appear at the trial and testify in their behalf. These

---

STUDY GUIDE

Themes in Government
Federalism The Supreme Court has applied most of the rules for search and seizure to state governments. As a result, the local police must also obtain search warrants.

What evidence must police have to obtain a warrant?

Critical Thinking Skills
Analyzing Information Many non-democratic governments ignore the rights of the accused. **Why is it**

important in a democratic society for the government to follow due process of law when trying suspected criminals?

Special Needs Strategy

Reading Disability The CLOZE technique is an easy tool for assessing reading comprehension abilities related to text. Copy the first paragraph of this section and remove every sixth, seventh, or eighth word. Do not omit proper names or technical terms. Have each student fill in the blank spaces so that the passage makes sense. Example: "Despite the difficulty of the _____ (amendment) process, Americans put it to _____ (work) before the ink was _____ (dry) on the new Constitution." Poor performance may signal reading comprehension difficulties.

protections allow defendants to respond to the testimony of witnesses. In addition, accused persons have the right to be defended by a lawyer.

The Seventh Amendment The Seventh Amendment provides for the right to a jury trial to settle all disputes about property worth more than $20. When both parties in a conflict agree, however, a judge rather than a jury may settle the case.

The Eighth Amendment This amendment prohibits excessive bail—money or property that the accused deposits with the court to gain release from jail until the trial. The judge sets bail in an amount that ensures the accused will appear for trial. When the trial ends, bail is returned. If the accused does not appear, bail is forfeited.

The Eighth Amendment also prevents judges from ordering someone convicted of a crime to pay an excessive fine. Fines for serious crimes may be higher than those for less serious ones. If someone is too poor, he or she cannot be imprisoned for longer than the maximum sentence to "work off" the fine.

Finally, the Eighth Amendment bans "cruel and unusual punishment" for crimes. Like fines, these are punishments that are out of proportion to the crime committed. For example, 20 years in prison for stealing a candy bar would be cruel and unusual punishment.

The Ninth Amendment The Ninth Amendment states that all other rights not spelled out in the Constitution are "retained by the people." This amendment prevents government from claiming that the only rights people have are those listed in the Bill of Rights. The amendment protects all basic or natural rights not specifically noted in the Constitution.

The Tenth Amendment The final amendment of the Bill of Rights clarifies the nature of federalism and the relationship of government to the people. It establishes that powers not given to the national government—or denied to the states—by the Constitution belong to the states or to the people.

Other Amendments

The 27 amendments fall into 3 major groups. The first group, which includes the Bill of Rights, was added between 1791 and 1804 to put finishing touches on the original Constitution. The Eleventh and Twelfth amendments also belong to this group.

Article III, Section 1, of the Constitution gave the federal courts jurisdiction in cases arising between states, between citizens of different states, or between a state and citizens of another state. In 1793 two citizens of South Carolina sued Georgia in the Supreme Court over property confiscated during the Revolution. The Georgia legislature maintained that a sovereign state could not be summoned into federal court and ordered to defend itself. When Georgia officials refused to appear for the trial, the Supreme Court decided against the state.

Although Georgia lost the court case, it won its power struggle with the federal judiciary. The day after the Supreme Court announced its decision in *Chisholm* v. *Georgia* (1793), Congress introduced an amendment to limit the jurisdiction of the federal courts. In 1795 the Eleventh Amendment was added to the Constitution to prohibit a state from being sued in federal court by citizens of another state or of another nation.

The Twelfth Amendment, added in 1804, corrects a problem that had arisen in the method of electing the President and Vice President. This amendment provides for the Electoral College to use separate ballots in voting for President and Vice President.

Civil War Amendments The second group of amendments—Thirteen, Fourteen, and Fifteen—often are called the Civil War amendments because they grew out of that great conflict.

The Thirteenth Amendment (1865) outlawed slavery, and the Fourteenth Amendment (1868) originally was intended to protect the legal rights of the freed slaves and their descendants. Today it protects the rights of citizenship in general by prohibiting a state from depriving any person of life, liberty, or

---

STUDY GUIDE

Themes in Government
Growth of Democracy For extremely serious crimes or for people who have already been convicted of several crimes, a judge may set a very high bail for the accused.

Sometimes a judge may even decide to refuse bail for the accused. **How does granting bail help ensure the rights of the accused?**

Critical Thinking Skills
Identifying Central Issues What was the central issue in the case of *Chisholm* v. *Georgia*?

L3 Research Have students research the history of amendments that have been proposed in Congress and state legislatures such as limiting congressional terms, setting mandatory retirement ages for legislators and judges, allowing school prayer, establishing gun control, banning flag burning, or making English the official language.

STUDY GUIDE

Theme Answer
If free on bail they are better able to oversee the development of their defense.

Critical Thinking Answer
whether a state could be summoned into federal court

Assess

Check for Understanding
Have students complete Section 3 Review on page 90.

Meeting Objectives
Each section objective is tested by the Section Review questions that follow it in parentheses.
- Identify amendments that concern individual rights. (2, 4, 6, 7, 8)
- Cite amendments that reflect change in society. (3, 4, 7)
- Specify amendments that affect the structure and power of government. (5, 8)

Evaluate
📁 Section 3 Quiz
▣ Testmaker

Critical Thinking Activity

Analyzing Information Provide the following hypothetical case. Ask students to indicate which amendment, if any, is involved, the exact words referred to, and whether or not the amendment has been violated. The police think John Smith has stolen property in his house because they believe some of his friends have broken into neighborhood houses. They go to his house when his 10-year-old sister is the only person home and tell her they are checking houses in the neighborhood to find a gas leak. While there, they look around and find the stolen property in John's room, seize it, and arrest John when he returns. *(Fourth Amendment; a search or arrest must be based on probable cause.)*

Reteach

Have students work in pairs to review the list of key terms and concepts on page 85. Have one student write the definition of each term on a 3" x 5" card. The other student should write the amendment to which each term applies on the back of the card.

Enrich

Have students investigate the Civil Rights Act of 1875 which gave the federal government the power to enforce the protections of citizens' rights under the Fourteenth Amendment. Ask students to find out why this act was not enforced by the executive branch and why the Supreme Court eventually declared it unconstitutional.

Have students complete activity 3 in *Enrichment Activities* in the Teacher's Classroom Resources.

Close

Review with students which amendments have contributed to an orderly society, which have contributed to individual freedoms, and which affect the structure and power of the government. Ask: Which type of amendments might people favor in the future?

property without "due process of law." In addition, it states that all citizens have the right to equal protection of the law in all states. The Fifteenth Amendment (1870) prohibits the government from denying a person's right to vote on the basis of race.

The Later Amendments The third group of amendments all have been added in the twentieth century. They deal with a wide range of topics that reflect the pace of change in modern American society.

The Sixteenth Amendment (1913) gives Congress the power to levy individual income taxes. The Seventeenth Amendment (1913) states that the people instead of state legislatures elect United States senators.

The Eighteenth Amendment (1919) prohibited the manufacture, sale, or transportation of alcoholic beverages, concluding a crusade to abolish the use of liquor that began in the 1830s. The following year, the Nineteenth Amendment (1920) guaranteed women the right to vote. By then women had already won the right to vote in many state elections, but the amendment put their right to vote in all state and national elections on a constitutional basis.

The Twentieth Amendment (1933) set new dates for Congress to begin its term and for the inauguration of the President and Vice President. Under the original Constitution, elected officials who retired or who had been defeated remained in office for several months. For the outgoing President, this period ran from November until March. Such outgoing officials had little influence and accomplished little, and they were called **lame ducks** because they were so inactive. The amendment solved this problem by ending the terms of senators and representatives on January 3, and the term of the President on January 20 in the year following their November elections.

The Twenty-first Amendment (1933) repealed the unsuccessful Eighteenth Amendment. The Twenty-first Amendment, however, continued to ban the transport of alcohol into any state where its possession violated state law.

The Twenty-second Amendment (1951) limits Presidents to a maximum of two elected terms. It was passed largely as a reaction to Franklin D. Roosevelt's election to four terms between 1933 and 1945.

The Twenty-third Amendment (1961) allows citizens living in Washington, D.C., to vote for President and Vice President, a right previously denied residents of the nation's capital.

The Twenty-fourth Amendment (1964) prohibits **poll taxes** in national elections—taxes paid in order to vote. Some states had used such taxes to keep low-income African Americans from voting.

The Twenty-fifth Amendment (1967) established a process for the Vice President to take over leadership of the nation when a President is disabled. It also set procedures for filling a vacancy in the office of the Vice President. The Twenty-sixth Amendment (1971) lowered the voting age in all elections to 18. The Twenty-seventh Amendment (1992) made congressional pay raises effective during the term following their passage.

3
SECTION REVIEW

Section Summary
The Constitution has been amended just 27 times in more than 200 years. Most of these amendments have extended rights and liberties and limited the power of government officials.

Checking for Understanding
Reviewing Facts
1. Define prior restraint, slander, libel, militia, probable cause, search warrant, arrest warrant, due process of law, eminent domain, change of venue, lame duck, poll tax.
2. Identify the rights listed in the First Amendment.
3. State the changes brought by the three Civil War amendments.
4. Cite the twentieth-century amendments that deal with voting rights.

Exploring Themes
5. Federalism How did the Eleventh Amendment affect the relationship between national and state governments?
6. Growth of Democracy What rights do the Fourth through Eighth amendments guarantee to people accused of crimes?

Critical Thinking Skills
7. Analyzing Information How do the amendments to the Constitution show that the United States government is more democratic today than it was in 1790?
8. Identifying Central Issues Why is it important to democratic government that the rights of those accused of crimes be carefully protected? Explain your answer.

Section 3 Review Answers

1. Definitions of terms appear on pages indicated: **prior restraint,** 86; **slander,** 86; **libel,** 86; **militia,** 87; **probable cause,** 88; **search warrant,** 88; **arrest warrant,** 88; **due process of law,** 88; **eminent domain,** 88; **change of venue,** 88; **lame duck,** 90; **poll tax,** 90.
2. freedoms of religion, speech, and the press, and the rights of assembly and petition
3. slavery abolished (13), rights of citizens protected against unlawful state actions (14), denial of voting rights on basis of race prohibited (15)
4. Nineteenth extended vote to women (1920); Twenty-sixth lowered voting age to 18 (1971)
5. depriving federal courts of jurisdiction when a state is sued by residents of another state or nation
6. right to privacy (4); cannot be tried for a serious crime unless there is enough evidence for a trial, be tried twice for the same offense, be forced to testify against oneself, or be deprived of life, liberty, or property without due process of law (5); have a right to know what they are accused of, to a public trial by a jury, to hear and question all witnesses, to be defended by a lawyer (6); excessive bail, fines, and cruel and unusual punishment are prohibited (8)
7. More people have a voice in government. Through voting rights of African Americans, women, and 18-year-olds. Poll taxes banned. Senators are directly elected.
8. Answers should cite the importance of preventing authorities from using the police or judicial power to silence those who oppose the government or its policies.

Informal Changes in the Constitution

Although formal amendments have played an important role in making it a "living" document, the Constitution has kept pace with the times and has grown as an instrument of government through informal change as well. This process does not involve changes in the wording of the Constitution itself. Rather, informal changes occur as government leaders and citizens fill in the details of government on a day-to-day, year-to-year basis to suit the needs of the times.

The Constitution has been able to grow through informal changes because its language is very general. As a result, as President Franklin D. Roosevelt once observed:

It is always possible to meet extraordinary needs by changes in emphasis and arrangement without loss of essential form. That is why our constitutional system has proved itself the most superbly enduring political mechanism the modern world has produced.
—FRANKLIN D. ROOSEVELT, 1933

For example, when the Founders gave Congress the power to regulate "commerce among the several states," they made no attempt to describe exactly what that power involved. As a result, it has been Congress and the courts that have spelled out whether the power includes authority to regulate child labor or to set standards for radio and television advertising. Decisions about such issues have extended the meaning of the Constitution. It has not been necessary to amend the Constitution more than a relatively few times because most changes in the operations of government are brought about informally.

Congressional Actions

Congress shapes the meaning of the Constitution. It does so largely through the laws it enacts and the ways it uses its powers.

Changes Through Law Over the years, Congress has passed laws that have enlarged or clarified many of the Constitution's provisions. The Founders expected Congress to do this, and they gave it authority to spell out many details of the national government.

Article I, for example, gives Congress the power to "lay and collect taxes." What does this provision mean? Congress has applied the taxing authority of the Constitution and expanded its meaning by passing complex tax laws that fill many volumes.

The same is true of the executive branch that Article II of the Constitution established. Congress has greatly expanded the executive branch by creating the cabinet departments, agencies, boards, and commissions.

In Article III, the Founders created "one Supreme Court" and other courts "as the Congress may . . . establish." Congress completed the judicial branch by passing the Judiciary Act of 1789.

Over the years, Congress has changed the judicial branch many times in response to new conditions. As the nation expanded and the number of court cases increased, Congress created additional federal courts, established new rules of federal court procedure, and provided for court workers such as bailiffs and clerks.

Congressional Practices Congress has also shaped the Constitution by the way it has used its other powers. Under the Constitution, the House

---

SECTION PREVIEW

Objectives
After studying this section, you should be able to:
- Discuss how the Supreme Court changes the Constitution.
- Specify ways that the President has changed the Constitution.

- Summarize the role of Congress in constitutional change.

Key Terms and Concepts
impeach, treaty, executive agreement, judicial restraint, judicial activism

Themes in Government
- Checks and Balances
- Separation of Powers

Critical Thinking Skills
- Identifying Central Issues
- Predicting Consequences

CHAPTER 3: THE CONSTITUTION—A LIVING DOCUMENT   91

Classroom Resources for Section 4

- Guided Reading Activities
- Reproducible Lesson Plans
- Participating in Government 3
- Reteaching Activities 3
- Section 4 Quiz
- Chapter 3 Tests

- Testmaker
- Limited English Proficiency Activities 3
- Audio Cassettes (English and Spanish)
  The Living Constitution
  SAT Practice Tests
  Writer's Guidebook

Focus

Bell Ringer

Have students write the number of times the Constitution has been amended since 1787.

Motivating Activity

Discuss students' Bell Ringer answers. Remind students how difficult and time-consuming the amendment process is. Then have them brainstorm ways the Constitution can be changed without amending it.

Vocabulary Precheck

Call on students to read aloud the definitions of the terms and concepts from the Glossary. Then have volunteers use each term in a sentence. **LEP**

Teach

Guided Practice

L1 Constructing a Chart Draw a four-column chart on the chalkboard with headings that correspond to the four types of informal changes in the Constitution. Have students provide examples of each and explain what constitutional change each example brought. **LEP**

L2 Expressing Ideas Organize the class into four groups and assign each group one of the informal ways of changing the Constitution. Ask groups to plan how, using their informal process, they could require the federal government to balance the federal budget. A spokesperson from each group should present its plan to the class. Have the class discuss the viability of each group's proposal.

may **impeach**, or accuse, federal officials—including the President—while it is up to the Senate to determine the accused person's guilt or innocence. Article II states that:

> *The President, Vice-President, and all civil Officers of the United States shall be removed from Office on Impeachment for, and Conviction of, Treason, Bribery, or other high Crimes and Misdemeanors.*
> —ARTICLE II, SECTION 4

The meaning of treason and bribery is clear in the Constitution. What about "high crimes and misdemeanors"? What does the Constitution mean? It is up to Congress to decide.

Congress has investigated about 65 people on impeachment charges, including two Presidents—Andrew Johnson and Richard Nixon. Congressional

practice has established that an impeachable offense involves conduct that violates constitutional responsibilities and that implies a clear neglect of duty. Congress's use of its impeachment powers is an instance of how practice elaborates the meaning of the written Constitution.

Presidential Practices

Presidential actions have also added to the Constitution. Many of these additions affect the workings of the modern presidency.

Presidential Succession In 1841 William Henry Harrison became the first President to die in office. As provided in the Constitution, Vice President John Tyler assumed the powers of President. Did Tyler

Background

Executive agreements, one example of an informal constitutional change, have been used since Washington's day. However, their use has increased dramatically since 1940. From 1789–1939, 1,182 (an average of about 8 per year) were made. From 1940–1979, 8,628 (an average of about 221 per year) were made. From 1980–1988, 3,094 (an average of about 344 per year) were made. Presidents have kept certain executive agreements secret. To end this practice, Congress passed a law in 1950 requiring all executive agreements signed each year to be made public.

PARTICIPATING IN GOVERNMENT

Applying for a Visa

What are the requirements for travel to other countries? First, you must have a passport that the United States government issues, stating that you are a citizen. In addition, some countries require American visitors to have a visa, or document that grants permission to enter a country. Visas are not necessary for travel to Western European countries, but some Latin American nations and most countries in Africa and Asia require them.

To obtain a visa, a United States citizen must contact

the consulate of the country he or she wishes to visit. Foreign consulates are located in many major American cities as well as in Washington, D.C. Be certain to contact the consulate well in advance of your departure date because it may take several weeks for you to receive your visa.

In general, a traveler must

fill out an application stating the purpose and length of the visit and provide one or more photographs similar to those required for a passport. Some countries require proof of immunizations against certain diseases or letters of recommendation from business references or the local police department.

Investigating Further

The United States requires a visa from all foreign visitors. Find and list the six preference visa categories that the Department of State has developed.

---

actually become President or would he merely act as President until the next election?

Tyler took the presidential oath of office. Many officials opposed Tyler's interpretation of the Constitution, but no one successfully challenged him. Not until 1967, when the Twenty-fifth Amendment clarified presidential succession, was Tyler's precedent formally endorsed in the Constitution.

Foreign Affairs Modern Presidents usually conduct foreign affairs by executive agreement, instead of using the treaty process specified in the Constitution. While a **treaty** is an agreement between nations, an **executive agreement** is made directly between the President and the head of state of another country,

and does not require Senate approval. This practice has weakened the constitutional checks and balances in the conduct of foreign affairs.

Domestic Affairs The Founders thought the executive branch would be concerned mostly with carrying out laws initiated by Congress. Yet in this century Presidents have been aggressive in requesting legislation from Congress.

These presidential practices and many others have become important precedents for building the constitutional and political power of the office of the President. Today the President plays a role in American government and politics far greater than most of the delegates who wrote the Constitution ever imagined.

STUDY GUIDE

**Themes in Government
Checks and Balances** George Washington established the practice that the executive branch negotiates treaties and the Senate approves them.

Separation of Powers Executive agreements eliminate the Senate's role in foreign agreements.

**Critical Thinking Skills
Identifying Central Issues** What was the crux of *Marbury v. Madison?*

Predicting Consequences How might further expansion of presidential power affect congressional power?

Cooperative Learning Activity

Organize the class into four groups. Assign each group one of the following ways in which the Constitution may be changed informally: congressional actions, presidential practices, court decisions, and customs and usage. Then ask each group to discuss how the premise of the proposed Equal

Rights Amendment—"Equality of rights under the law shall not be denied or abridged by the United States or any state on account of sex."—might be informally added to the Constitution. Have a person from each group take notes during the discussion, and then read the notes to the class.

Explain the difference between passports and visas by pointing out that passports control who *leaves* a country and where they can travel, while visas control who *enters* a country and screen for undesirable visitors. Ask students why some countries require visas and others do not. (*More tightly controlled, undemocratic societies generally require visas.*)

Have students complete activity 3 in *Participating in Government* in the Teacher's Classroom Resources.

L3 Debate Have the class debate the President's role in informal constitutional changes. How has the President's role grown since the Constitution was written in 1787? What advantages and disadvantages are there in having a strong presidential figure?

Independent Practice

L1 Expressive Writing Have students write a paragraph explaining President Wilson's statement that, "The Supreme Court is a constitutional convention in continuous session."

Assess

Check for Understanding

Have students complete Section 4 Review on page 94.

STUDY GUIDE

Critical Thinking Answers checks and balances, equality of branches

could further limit it, or Congress could act to restrict President

Meeting Objectives

Each section objective is tested by the Section Review questions that follow it in parentheses.
- Discuss how the Supreme Court changes the Constitution. (4, 6, 8)
- Specify ways that the President has changed the Constitution. (5, 7)
- Summarize the role of Congress in constitutional change. (3, 5, 6)

Evaluate

📁 Section 4 Quiz

⬛ Testmaker

Reteach

📁 Have students complete activity 3 in *Reteaching Activities* in the Teacher's Classroom Resources.

Enrich

Have students research the types of cases in which judicial activism is most prominent.

Close

In the chapter introduction students were asked why the Constitution is called a "living document." Ask them how their answers have changed since studying this chapter.

Allow time for students to discuss and present their Chapter Projects.

Court Decisions

The third major source of informal constitutional change is the federal courts. Court decisions continually modify the Constitution. As federal courts settle cases involving constitutional questions, they interpret the meaning of the Constitution's sometimes vague words and phrases. The Supreme Court, the nation's highest court, plays a key role in this process.

Judicial Review The most important device the Court uses to interpret the Constitution is judicial review. Although the principle of judicial review is well established, people continue to disagree over how the Court should use this power. Some advocate judicial restraint; others argue for judicial activism.

The philosophy of **judicial restraint** holds that the Court should avoid taking the initiative on social and political questions. The Court should uphold acts of Congress unless the acts clearly violate a specific provision of the Constitution. In other words, people who advocate judicial restraint want the Court to leave the development of new policies to others.

The philosophy of **judicial activism**, on the other hand, holds that the Court should play an active role in shaping national policies. The Court should boldly apply the Constitution to pressing social and political questions. The Supreme Court under Chief Justice Earl Warren—from 1953 to 1969—is the best example of modern judicial activism. The Warren Court accepted cases involving many controversial issues, particularly civil rights and the rights of the accused.

Changing Court Rulings Social and political conditions of the times often affect Court interpretations of the Constitution. As times and expectations change, so may the courts' interpretation of what the Constitution means.

The Supreme Court has sometimes ruled that the Constitution means one thing and then years later reversed itself and ruled that the Constitution means something quite different. In 1896, for example, the Court ruled that separate public facilities for African Americans were constitutional so long as those facilities were equal. More than a half century later, in 1954, the Court reversed its position, denying the constitutionality of separate facilities.

Custom and Usage

A fourth way the Constitution has been informally enlarged is through customs that have developed over time. Political parties are a good example. The Constitution does not mention political parties, but they began soon after the government was organized and have been an important part of American government since then.

The amendments added to the Constitution and the changes achieved through precedent and practice have created a government that can respond to the conditions and needs of the times. Thus it becomes easier to understand why this short, simple document has continued for more than two centuries to serve as the supreme law of the land.

---

4 SECTION REVIEW

Section Summary
Informal changes resulting from the actions of each branch of the national government, and from customs developed over time, have adapted the Constitution to the needs of present-day society.

Checking for Understanding
Reviewing Facts
1. Define impeach, treaty, executive agreement, judicial restraint, judicial activism.
2. State the four sources of informal constitutional change.
3. Cite an example of how congressional action has changed the Constitution.
4. Explain how Supreme Court actions change the Constitution.

Exploring Themes
5. Checks and Balances Why have executive agreements weakened the system of checks and balances built into the Constitution?
6. Separation of Powers How could judicial activism infringe on powers given to Congress in the Constitution?

Critical Thinking Skills
7. Identifying Central Issues How have the four informal methods of amending the Constitution affected the role of the executive branch in the federal government?
8. Predicting Consequences Why do you think that the Founders intended that only the judicial branch interpret the Constitution?

Section 4 Review Answers

1. Definitions of terms appear on pages indicated: **impeach,** 92; **treaty,** 93; **executive agreement,** 93; **judicial restraint,** 94; **judicial activism,** 94
2. congressional actions, presidential practices, court decisions, custom and usage
3. expanding the meaning of its taxing authority, creating cabinet departments and other agencies in the executive branch, expanding the federal courts and changing court procedures, defining its impeachment powers
4. by changing its interpretation of what the Constitution means as new cases come before it
5. The Senate can check the President's treaty-making power by refusing to approve proposed treaties with other nations. Executive agreements are not treaties, and do not require Senate approval.
6. The Supreme Court could through its decisions force changes that otherwise would require legislation by Congress.

7. executive branch's power expanded as Congress created new executive agencies, as the President took an increasingly active role in initiating legislation, and as executive agreements supplanted the treaty-making process
8. If two or more branches interpreted the Constitution differently a crisis could arise. Since federal judges are appointed for life, they are more insulated from political pressures than elected officials.

Nelson Rockefeller on the Constitution

The United States of America celebrated its 200th birthday on July 4, 1976, with speeches, celebrations, and fireworks across the nation. At the festivities in Washington, D.C., Vice President Nelson Rockefeller spoke about the enduring principles expressed in the Declaration of Independence and the Constitution.

We Americans remain the faithful political descendants of our Founding Fathers, because we continue to agree with the ideas they immortally expressed in the Declaration and the Constitution—the belief that liberty and democracy can be a blessing to mankind if carefully structured and moderated and, if not, a curse. We Americans happily had a path marked out for us by the American Founders leading to the blessings of liberty and democracy. . . .

We . . . acknowledge our indebtedness to the principles and institutions they devised, to give witness to their success, and to renew our dedication to that compound and sober blend of liberty and democracy which is the essence of our national heritage. . . .

Liberty and democracy can be a blessing to mankind if carefully structured and moderated and, if not, a curse.

We have here tonight the assemblage of the American democratic republic, a ceremony which celebrates, which assembles all of the representative elements of our 200-year-old political system. . . .

In my constitutional capacity [Vice President] as the presiding officer of the Senate, I have the honor to represent the principle of bicameralism.

Here tonight also are governors and mayors and other local officials, representing the American principles of federalism and decentralization. And also joining in this assemblage of the republic are leaders of our private voluntary associations, representing the American principle of creative, private, voluntary action.

For all our faults and failings, we tonight, gathered with all our fellow citizens everywhere, express the principles and represent the institutions devised by our Founding Fathers—separation of powers to protect liberty and also secure competent government power; bicameralism to balance and refine the popular will; federalism and decentralization to guard against despotism and to allow the American people energetically to solve their political problems as much as possible at the local level;

and private, voluntary associations so that people themselves may freely and creatively supply their own needs without dependence upon . . . government.

Like our Founding Fathers, we do not believe in a simple centering of all power in a streamlined monolith of government; rather, we believe that liberty and democracy can only be achieved by these complex principles and institutions of the American democratic republic.

We come back here tonight to draw strength anew from our old and tested principles and institutions, so that we may go forward with orderly creativity into our third century.

—NELSON ROCKEFELLER, 1976

Examining the Reading

Reviewing Facts
1. Name the occasion for this speech by Vice President Nelson Rockefeller.
2. Explain how the people who made up the audience demonstrated the principle of federalism.

Critical Thinking Skills
3. Making Inferences Which of the six principles of American government discussed in the chapter does Rockefeller seem to support with the most enthusiasm? Cite examples from his speech to support your answer.

CHAPTER 3: THE CONSTITUTION—A LIVING DOCUMENT 95

PERSONAL PERSPECTIVES

Focus

Ask students to identify constitutional principles upon which American government is based. List their responses on the chalkboard.

Teach

Ask students to identify principles from the list on the chalkboard that the Vice President noted in his speech. Ask: Are there any constitutional principles he recognized that were left off the list?

Assess

Have students complete **Examining the Reading.**

Answers

1. the nation's bicentennial celebration in Washington, D.C., in July 1976
2. In addition to the President, members of Congress and Supreme Court justices represent national government; governors and mayors represent state and local governments.
3. Answers should focus on his enthusiasm for federalism by lauding local solutions to problems, equating decentralization and democracy, and attacking monolithic government.

Close

Ask: How might democracy be a "curse" if it is not "carefully structured and moderated"?

More About Personal Perspectives

Dissatisfied with working in his family's businesses, Nelson Rockefeller entered government in 1940 when President Roosevelt chose him to coordinate inter-American affairs. In 1944 he was named assistant secretary of state for Latin American affairs, but resigned a year later to return to private life. He reentered government in 1950 and in 1953 was named special assistant to President Eisenhower. He went on to become a four-time governor of New York, but failed in three bids for the presidency. He was appointed Vice President in 1974 when Gerald Ford became President upon the resignation of Richard Nixon.

Identifying Terms and Concepts

1. separation of powers, 2. libel, 3. eminent domain, 4. lame ducks, 5. popular sovereignty

Reviewing Facts and Ideas

1. to form a more perfect union; to establish justice; to insure domestic tranquility; to provide for the common defense; to promote the general welfare; to secure the blessings of liberty

2. popular sovereignty; federalism; separation of powers; checks and balances; judicial review; limited government

3. separation of powers

4. by listing specific powers that the national government has and describing powers that it does not have; by the guarantees in the Bill of Rights, including reserving all powers not given to the national government for the states or the people

5. proposed—by a two-thirds vote in each house of Congress or by a national convention called by request of two-thirds of the states; ratified—by the legislatures of three-fourths of the states or by special conventions in three-fourths of the states

6. prohibits government from forcing citizens to shelter soldiers in their homes

7. congressional actions, presidential practices, court decisions, custom and usage

8. political parties

Applying Themes

1. The sharing of responsibility for certain government functions has encouraged the sharing of power instead of the division of it. For example, the participation of both Congress and the President in the legislative process has resulted in the President taking much of the lead from Congress in making domestic policy.

Summary and Significance

The Constitution is a relatively brief, flexible document that has guided the operation of government in the United States for more than 200 years. It has been able to do so because it rests on principles that still receive wide support, because it can be amended, and because it can be adapted to the needs of the times. Since it went into effect, this remarkable document has been amended only 27 times.

Identifying Terms and Concepts

Choose the italicized word or phrase that best completes each of the following sentences.
1. The national government is divided into three branches according to the principle of *judicial restraint/separation of powers.*
2. Writing untrue, malicious stories about someone is classified as *libel/slander.*
3. According to the principle of *judicial review/eminent domain*, the government can force someone to sell their home to make way for a highway.
4. Officials who have not been reelected but are still in office are called *vetoes/lame ducks.*
5. *Popular sovereignty/federalism* is the principle that the people are the source of a government's power.

Reviewing Facts and Ideas

1. List the six goals of American government identified in the Preamble to the Constitution.
2. Name the six major principles of government on which the Constitution is based.
3. Identify the constitutional principle illustrated by the division of the national government into three branches.
4. Explain how the Constitution provides for limited government.
5. Describe how an amendment to the Constitution is proposed and ratified.
6. Detail what rights are protected by the Third Amendment.
7. Describe the ways in which the Constitution may be changed informally.
8. Cite an example of how custom has enlarged the Constitution.

Applying Themes

1. **Separation of Powers** How has the system of checks and balances caused the separation of powers among the three branches of government to become less distinct?
2. **Checks and Balances** Explain how the system of checks and balances established by the Constitution works and provide an example for each branch of government.
3. **Federalism** Explain how federalism accomplishes the same goal as separation of powers.
4. **Growth of Democracy** Why do the original methods of choosing the President and Senate suggest that the Founders did not have total confidence in the people?

Critical Thinking Skills

1. **Predicting Consequences** The Founders created a brief Constitution that established only a basic framework for government. What do you think might have happened if they had been more specific in describing the kind of government they believed the nation needed?
2. **Analyzing Information** Consider the many informal ways by which the Constitution can be changed. Do you think that these practices strengthen or weaken the American system of government? Explain your answer.
3. **Identifying Central Issues** Because the amendment process is very long and difficult, the Constitution has been amended only 27 times in more than 200 years. List arguments for and against the formal process for amending, or changing, the Constitution.

2. The principle is that when major power is given to one branch of government, another branch is given the means to limit that power. Examples might include: executive—makes treaties but Senate must approve; legislative—declares war but President commands military; judicial—reviews laws but President appoints judges

3. The federal system achieves the same goal as separation of powers by dividing power between state and national governments.

4. The people participated in both only indirectly. The Senate was chosen by elected state legislatures and the President by persons chosen for the Electoral College by the voters of each state.

Linking Past and Present

For nearly half the nation's history voting was the privilege of only white males age 21 and older. Although African American men got the vote in 1870, and all women in 1920, not until the Twenty-sixth Amendment was ratified in 1971 was the right to vote extended to 18-year-old citizens. Yet young people today have the lowest voting rate of any age group. What explanations can you suggest for this? How might the voting record of these citizens be improved?

Writing About Government

Expressive Writing Although only 33 amendments have been submitted to the states for approval, and just 27 ratified, more than 10,000 proposals for amendments to the Constitution have been introduced in Congress since 1789. While an amendment suggested by a private citizen has little chance of success, writing an amendment is valuable experience. Select a topic that you believe the Constitution needs to address and, using existing amendments as guides for form and language, write an amendment to the Constitution. Then write a letter to Congress proposing your amendment. In your letter cover the following points: explain what your proposed amendment will do; tell why you believe it is needed and how the nation will benefit if it is ratified; indicate what opposition you expect there to be to your amendment and why; and suggest arguments that could be used to reply to other parties' criticisms of your amendment.

Reinforcing the Skill

Evaluating Information Read the following excerpt and answer these questions:
1. How does the author think President Reagan has been inconsistent?
2. Does it seem that the author's view is colored by bias or emotion?
3. What questions would you want answered before you could decide to agree or disagree with the opinion presented in this editorial?

During his campaign, Mr. Reagan explained his position on the proposed Equal Rights Amendment to the Constitution by saying that he was for the E and the R but not for the A. . . . Doomed though it may be, ERA remains the best test of a political commitment to the principle it embodies. Like many of the President's favorite homilies [sayings], ERA is a one-liner ('Equality of rights under the law shall not be denied or abridged by the United States or by any state on account of sex.'); and while some advocates of women's rights may feel that there are better uses for their energies than fighting for its ratification, only a very quirky constitutional curmudgeon [crank] could combine outright opposition to it with a sincere belief in the civil equality of women. Mr. Reagan is not that curmudgeon. His opposition to ERA is of a piece with his deplorable record on women's rights and women's welfare.

—*NEW REPUBLIC*, OCTOBER 1981

Investigating Further

1. **Individual Project** Research one of the amendments to the Constitution and prepare a report on it. In your report provide the following information: the changes the amendment made in the Constitution; conditions in the nation at the time the amendment was proposed that seemed to make the change necessary; arguments at the time for and against the proposed amendment; and the long-term effect the amendment has had on the nation.
2. **Cooperative Learning** Organize into groups of five students each to consider the following problem: Another country has conquered the United States. The conquerors will allow the American people to retain five rights from the Bill of Rights. Imagine that your group is a committee appointed to choose the five rights from the list. The conquerors require that your group agree unanimously. Select a member of your group to record its choices and the reasons for them. Also choose a spokesperson to report your group's choices and its reasons to the class.

Answers might include apathy and ignorance about the issues and the process. Suggestions might include educating young people about government and vital issues.

Writing About Government

Answers will vary. Students should select a topic for a new amendment for the Constitution and write a letter to Congress proposing the amendment.

Reinforcing the Skill

1. The author thinks that President Reagan has been inconsistent because he claims to believe in the civil equality of women, but he opposes the Equal Rights Amendment.

2. Yes.

3. Answers will vary. Students might ask questions about President Reagan's record on women's rights and women's welfare.

Investigating Further

1. Answers will vary.
2. Answers will vary.

Critical Thinking Skills

1. Answers may suggest that as the nation and its needs changed the Constitution could have become increasingly unworkable, leading to many more amendments or a new constitution.

2. Answers will vary. Students saying "strengthen" may note that informal change is basic to the flexibility responsible for the Constitution's survival. Those saying "weaken" may point to practices that have undermined the separation of powers and other safeguards built into the document.

3. Arguments *for* could include that it prevents hasty actions and that informal changes always are possible if formal amendment is not. Arguments *against* may include that the process is too lengthy and that even if a majority favors the change, the amendment still may not be ratified.

THE CONSTITUTION
of the
UNITED STATES

ONE OF THE MOST REMARKABLE things about the United States Constitution is that it is the world's oldest written constitution. Even more remarkable is that it was the first written constitution of its kind, establishing the first government of its kind in the world. This form of government was so new and untried that for many years it was referred to as "the great experiment." That such an "experiment" has lasted for more than 200 years and has met the needs of our great nation in much the same form as when it was first adopted is a tribute to the Framers of the Constitution. It is also a tribute to the political wisdom of generations of Americans who followed them.

The Signing of the Constitution, painted by Thomas Prichard Rossiter

THE CONSTITUTION OF THE UNITED STATES

(Those parts of the Constitution that are no longer in effect are indicated in blue.)

Preamble

We, the people of the United States, in Order to form a more perfect Union, establish Justice, insure domestic Tranquility, provide for the common defence, promote the general Welfare, and secure the Blessings of Liberty to ourselves and our Posterity, do ordain and establish this Constitution for the United States of America.

Article I

SECTION 1

All legislative Powers herein granted shall be vested in a Congress of the United States, which shall consist of a Senate and House of Representatives.

SECTION 2

1. The House of Representatives shall be composed of Members chosen every second Year by the People of the several States, and the Electors in each State shall have the Qualifications requisite for Electors of the most numerous Branch of the State Legislature.

2. No Person shall be a Representative who shall not have attained to the Age of twenty-five Years, and been seven Years a Citizen of the United States, and who shall not, when elected, be an Inhabitant of that State in which he shall be chosen.

3. Representatives and direct Taxes shall be apportioned among the several states which may be included within this Union, according to their respective Numbers, which shall be determined by adding to the whole Number of free Persons, including those bound to Service for a Term of Years, and excluding Indians not taxed, three fifths of all other Persons. The actual Enumeration shall be made within three Years after the first Meeting of the Congress of the United States, and within every subsequent Term of ten Years, in such Manner as they shall by Law direct. The Number of Representatives shall not exceed one for every thirty Thousand, but each state shall have at Least one Representative; and until such enumeration shall

Preamble

The Preamble states the purpose of the Constitution and lists the six reasons for writing the Constitution. It also clearly indicates that the government is established by the consent of the governed.

Article I. Legislative Branch

Section 1. Congress

The power to make laws is given to a Congress made up of two houses. Practice has modified this clause by allowing certain federal agencies to issue regulations that have the force of laws.

SECTION 2. House of Representatives

1. Election and Term of Office. Representatives are directly elected every two years by the voters in each state who are qualified to vote for members of the larger branch of the state legislature. Several amendments have changed this. *(See the Fifteenth, Nineteenth, Twenty-fourth, and Twenty-sixth Amendments.)*

2. Qualifications. Representatives must be 25 years old, citizens of the United States for 7 years, and residents of the state they represent.

3. Division of Representatives Among the States. The number of representatives a state has is based on the population of the state. The population is determined by a census to be held every 10 years. Each state must have at least one representative. Until 1929, when Congress fixed the size of the House at 435, the number of members grew as the nation's population increased. *(See the Thirteenth, Fourteenth, and Sixteenth Amendments.)*

4. **Vacancies.** The state governor calls special elections to fill vacancies in the House of Representatives.

5. **Officers; Power of Impeachment.** The House of Representatives selects its own officers and has the power to impeach, or accuse, officers of the executive or judicial branch. *(See Article II, Section 4.)*

SECTION 3. Senate

1. **Number of Members, Term of Office, and Voting Procedure.** Each state has two senators elected for six-year terms. Each senator has one vote. The Seventeenth Amendment provides for the election of senators directly by the voters.

2. **Staggered Elections; Vacancies.** One-third of the Senate is elected every two years. Vacancies are temporarily filled by the state governor until a replacement is elected in a special election. *(See the Seventeenth Amendment.)*

3. **Qualifications.** Senators must be 30 years old, citizens of the United States for 9 years, and residents of the state they represent.

4. **President of the Senate.** The Vice President of the United States is the presiding officer of the Senate, but may vote only to break a tie.

5. **Other Officers.** The Senate selects its other officers, including a presiding officer (president pro tempore) who serves when the Vice President is absent or has become President of the United States. *(See the Twenty-fifth Amendment.)*

6. **Trials of Impeachment.** The Senate has the power to try all impeachment cases. When the President is impeached, the Chief Justice of the United States presides over the trial. Conviction requires a two-thirds vote of the senators present.

be made, the State of New Hampshire shall be entitled to chuse three; Massachusetts eight, Rhode Island and Providence Planatations one, Connecticut five, New York six, New Jersey four, Pennsylvania eight, Delaware one, Maryland six, Virginia ten, North Carolina five, South Carolina five, and Georgia three.

4. When vacancies happen in the Representation from any State, the Executive Authority thereof shall issue Writs of Election to fill such Vacancies.

5. The House of Representatives shall chuse their Speaker and other Officers; and shall have the sole Power of Impeachment.

SECTION 3

1. The Senate of the United States shall be composed of two Senators from each State, chosen by the Legislature thereof, for six Years; and each Senator shall have one Vote.

2. Immediately after they shall be assembled in Consequence of the first Election, they shall be divided as equally as may be into three Classes. The Seats of the Senators of the first Class shall be vacated at the Expiration of the second Year, of the second Class at the Expiration of the fourth Year, and of the third Class at the Expiration of the sixth Year, so that one-third may be chosen every second Year; and if Vacancies happen by Resignations, or otherwise, during the Recess of the Legislature of any State, the Executive thereof may make temporary Appointments until the next Meeting of the Legislature, which shall then fill such Vacancies.

3. No person shall be a Senator who shall not have attained to the Age of thirty Years, and been nine Years a Citizen of the United States, and who shall not, when elected, be an Inhabitant of that State in which he shall be chosen.

4. The Vice President of the United States shall be President of the Senate, but shall have no vote, unless they be equally divided.

5. The Senate shall chuse their Officers, and also a President pro tempore, in the absence of the Vice-President, or when he shall exercise the Office of the President of the United States.

6. The Senate shall have the sole Power to try all Impeachments. When sitting for that purpose,

they shall be on Oath or Affirmation. When the President of the United States is tried, the Chief Justice shall preside: And no person shall be convicted without the Concurrence of two-thirds of the Members present.

7. Judgment in Cases of Impeachment shall not extend further than to removal from Office, and disqualification to hold and enjoy any Office of Honor, Trust or Profit under the United States: but the Party convicted shall nevertheless be liable and subject to Indictment, Trial, Judgment and Punishment, according to Law.

Section 4

1. The Times, Places, and Manner of holding Elections for Senators and Representatives, shall be prescribed in each state by the Legislature thereof; but the Congress may at any time by Law make or alter such Regulations, except as to the Places of Chusing Senators.

2. The Congress shall assemble at least once in every Year, and such Meeting shall be on the first Monday in December, unless they shall by Law appoint a different Day.

Section 5

1. Each House shall be the Judge of the Elections, Returns and Qualifications of its own Members, and a Majority of each shall constitute a Quorum to do Business; but a smaller Number may adjourn from day to day, and may be authorized to compel the Attendance of absent Members, in such Manner, and under such Penalties as each House may provide.

2. Each House may determine the Rules of its Proceedings, punish its Members for disorderly Behaviour, and, with the Concurrence of two-thirds, expel a Member.

3. Each House shall keep a Journal of its Proceedings, and from time to time publish the same, excepting such Parts as may in their Judgment require Secrecy; and the Yeas and Nays of the Members of either House on any question shall, at the desire of one-fifth of those Present, be entered on the Journal.

4. Neither House, during the Session of Congress, shall, without the Consent of the other, adjourn for more than three days, nor to any other Place than that in which the two Houses shall be sitting.

7. **Penalty of Conviction.** If the Senate convicts an official in a trial of impeachment, the penalty is limited to dismissal from office and a ban from further officeholding. Convicted persons can later be tried in courts of law and sentenced if found guilty. (*See Article II, Section 4.*)

Section 4. Elections and Meetings

1. **Holding Elections.** Each state's legislature determines when, where, and how congressional elections should be held unless Congress passes election laws. Not until 1842 did Congress require that House members from each state be elected from districts rather than at large. In 1872 Congress set congressional elections in each state on the same day—the first Tuesday after the first Monday in November in even-numbered years.

2. **Meetings.** Congress must meet at least once a year. The Twentieth Amendment calls for Congress to meet on January 3 unless Congress sets a different day.

Section 5. Organization and Rules

1. **Organization.** Each house decides if its members are qualified and if they were properly elected. Both houses may refuse to seat new members. A majority of each house must be present to carry on business. Absent members can be forced to attend.

2. **Rules.** Each house sets its own rules, can punish members for disorderly behavior, and can expel a member by a two-thirds vote.

3. **Journals.** Each house must keep a journal, or official record, of its meetings, which must be published regularly. Votes of individual members on any question must be recorded in the journal if one-fifth of the members present request it.

4. **Adjournment.** Neither house may adjourn for more than three days or move to another location without the approval of the other house.

SECTION 6. Privileges and Restrictions

1. **Pay and Privileges.** Senators and Representatives are paid by the United States Treasury rather than by the states they represent. They cannot be sued or be prosecuted for anything they say on the floor of either house or in official publications. They cannot be arrested while Congress is in session, except for treason, major crimes, or breaking the peace.

2. **Restrictions.** Members of Congress may not hold any other government office while serving in Congress. Federal officers cannot serve as members of Congress.

SECTION 7. Passing Laws

1. **Revenue Bills.** All bills to raise money must begin in the House of Representatives, but the Senate can amend them.

2. **How Bills Become Laws.** Every bill passed by Congress must be sent to the President. If the President approves and signs the bill, it becomes law. If the President disapproves, or vetoes, the bill, it is returned to the house where it originated along with a written statement of the President's objections. If two-thirds of each house approves the bill after it has been vetoed, it becomes law. In voting to override a President's veto, the votes of all members of Congress must be recorded in the journals or official records. If the President does not sign or veto a bill within 10 days (excluding Sundays), it becomes law. If Congress adjourns during this 10-day period, however, the bill does not become law. This is known as a pocket veto.

President Lyndon B. Johnson signed the Civil Rights Act of 1968 into law when it was presented to him by Congress.

SECTION 6

1. The Senators and Representatives shall receive a Compensation for their Services, to be ascertained by Law, and paid out of the Treasury of the United States. They shall in all Cases, except Treason, Felony and Breach of the Peace, be privileged from Arrest during their attendance at the Session of their respective Houses, and in going to and returning from the same; and for any Speech or Debate in either House, they shall not be questioned in any other place.

2. No Senator or Representative shall, during the Time for which he was elected, be appointed to any civil Office under the Authority of the United States, which shall have been created, or the Emoluments whereof shall have been increased, during such time; and no Person holding any Office under the United States, shall be a Member of either House during his continuance in Office.

SECTION 7

1. All Bills for raising Revenue shall originate in the House of Representatives; but the Senate may propose or concur with Amendments as on other bills.

2. Every Bill which shall have passed the House of Representatives and the Senate, shall, before it become a Law, be presented to the President of the United States; If he approve he shall sign it, but if not he shall return it, with his Objections, to that House in which it shall have originated, who shall enter the Objections at large on their Journal, and proceed to reconsider it. If after such Reconsideration two-thirds of that House shall agree to pass the bill, it shall be sent, together with the objections, to the other House, by which it shall likewise be reconsidered, and if approved by two-thirds of that House, it shall become a Law. But in all such Cases the Votes of both Houses shall be determined by Yeas and Nays, and the Names of the Persons voting for and against the Bill shall be entered on the Journal of each House respectively. If any Bill shall not be returned by the President within ten Days (Sundays excepted) after it shall have been presented to him, the Same shall be a Law, in like Manner as if he had signed it, unless the Congress by their Adjournment prevent its Return, in which Case

it shall not be a Law.

3. Every Order, Resolution, or Vote to which the Concurrence of the Senate and House of Representatives may be necessary (except on a question of Adjournment) shall be presented to the President of the United States; and before the Same shall take Effect, shall be approved by him, or, being disapproved by him, shall be repassed by two-thirds of the Senate and House of Representatives, according to the Rules and Limitations prescribed in the case of a Bill.

SECTION 8

The Congress shall have the Power

1. To lay and collect Taxes, Duties, Imposts and Excises, to pay the Debts and provide for the common Defence and general Welfare of the United States; but all Duties, Imposts and Excises shall be uniform throughout the United States;

2. To borrow money on the credit of the United States;

3. To regulate Commerce with foreign Nations, and among the several States, and with the Indian Tribes;

4. To establish an uniform Rule of Naturalization, and uniform Laws on the subject of Bankruptcies throughout the United States;

5. To coin Money, regulate the Value thereof, and of foreign Coin, and fix the Standard of Weights and Measures;

6. To provide for the Punishment of counterfeiting the Securities and current Coin of the United States;

7. To establish Post Offices and post Roads;

8. To promote the Progress of Science and useful Arts, by securing for limited Times to Authors and Inventors the exclusive Right to their respective Writings and Discoveries;

9. To constitute Tribunals inferior to the Supreme Court;

10. To define and punish Piracies and Felonies committed on the high Seas, and Offenses against the Law of Nations;

11. To declare War, grant Letters of Marque and Reprisal, and make Rules concerning Captures on Land and Water;

3. **Presidential Approval or Veto.** The President must approve every action requiring the approval of both houses, except those dealing with adjournments, before it can take effect.

SECTION 8. Powers of Congress

This section describes the powers of Congress. The first 17 clauses are the expressed, or enumerated, powers. Clause 18 is the basis for the implied powers.

1. **Taxes.** Congress can levy a variety of taxes, but all taxes must be for public purposes. In addition, federal taxes must be at the same rate in every state.

2. **Borrowing.** The most common method that Congress uses to borrow is by the sale of government bonds.

3. **Commerce.** Like the taxing power, the commerce power has expanded over time and is today quite broad. Many federal regulations are based on the power of Congress over interstate commerce.

4. **Naturalization; Bankruptcy.** Naturalization is the process by which immigrants become citizens. Bankruptcy is the process by which debtors are excused from debts they cannot pay.

5. **Money; Weights and Measures.** In 1838 Congress adopted the British system of weights and measures. Attempts in the 1970s and 1980s to convert to the metric system never attracted public support. United States money, however, is based on the metric system.

6. **Counterfeiting.** Congress has made it a federal crime not only to print counterfeit money, but also to falsify United States stamps, bonds, and securities.

7. **Post Offices; Roads.** The postal service was a government monopoly since colonial times. In 1970 Congress changed it from an executive department to an independent agency. Some competition has arisen from private courier services in recent years.

8. **Copyrights; Patents.** Copyrights protect the work of writers and patents the work of inventors

9. **Courts.** To create lower federal courts

10. **Piracy.** Piracy is rare in the world today, but Congress has the power to protect American ships on the high seas, and people traveling on those ships, against other threats.

11. **Declare War.** Only Congress can declare war, but the President, as commander in chief, can commit United States forces without a formal declaration and has on more than 100 occasions. Congress limited this power, however, in the War Powers Act of 1973, stating that the President could not commit American forces to combat for more than 60 days without congressional approval.

12, 13, 14. **Armed Forces.** To raise, support, and regulate an army and navy

15. **Militias.** Militias are the volunteer armies in each state. Although under the command of state governors, they can be called to federal service by the President or Congress.

16. **Militias.** In 1916 Congress organized each state's militia into a National Guard.

17. **National Capital.** In order to avoid state interference with the national government, and to avoid interstate jealousy, the Framers provided that the nation's capital be outside any state.

18. **"Elastic Clause."** This provision is the basis for the implied powers of Congress. Any implied power, however, must be related to an expressed power.

SECTION 9. Powers Denied to the Federal Government

1. **Slaves.** "Such persons" refers to slaves. This paragraph was a compromise reached over protecting the slave trade in exchange for Congress's power over interstate commerce.

2. **Habeas Corpus.** A writ of habeas corpus is a court order that requires authorities to bring an arrested individual before a court so that a judge can decide whether the person is being held for legitimate reasons. Habeas corpus may be suspended in wartime and was during the Civil War and World War II. Courts later ruled the World War II suspension in Hawaii unconstitutional.

12. To raise and support Armies, but no Appropriation of Money to that Use shall be for a longer Term than two Years;

13. To provide and maintain a Navy;

14. To make Rules for the Government and Regulation of the land and naval forces;

15. To provide for calling forth the Militia to execute the Laws of the Union, suppress Insurrections, and repel Invasions;

16. To provide for organizing, arming, and disciplining, the Militia, and for governing such Part of them as may be employed in the Service of the United States, reserving to the States respectively, the Appointment of the Officers, and the Authority of training the Militia according to the discipline prescribed by Congress;

17. To exercise exclusive Legislation in all Cases whatsoever, over such District (not exceeding ten Miles square) as may, by Cession of particular States, and the acceptance of Congress, become the Seat of Government of the United States, and to exercise like Authority over all Places purchased by the Consent of the Legislature of the State in which the Same shall be, for the Erection of Forts, Magazines, Arsenals, dock-Yards, and other needful Buildings;—And

18. To make all Laws which shall be necessary and proper for carrying into Execution the foregoing Powers, and all other Powers vested by this Constitution in the Government of the United States, or in any Department or Officer thereof.

SECTION 9

1. The Migration or Importation of such Persons as any of the States now existing shall think proper to admit, shall not be prohibited by the Congress prior to the Year one thousand eight hundred and eight, but a tax or duty may be imposed on such importation, not exceeding ten dollars for each Person.

2. The privilege of the Writ of Habeas Corpus shall not be suspended, unless when in Cases of Rebellion or Invasion the public Safety may require it.

3. No Bill of Attainder or ex post facto Law shall be passed.

4. No capitation, or other direct, Tax shall be laid unless in Proportion to the Census or Enumeration herein before directed to be taken.

5. No Tax or Duty shall be laid on Articles exported from any State.

6. No Preference shall be given by any Regulation of Commerce or Revenue to the Ports of one State over those of another: nor shall Vessels bound to, or from, one State, be obliged to enter, clear, or pay Duties in another.

7. No Money shall be drawn from the Treasury, but in Consequence of Appropriations made by Law; and a regular Statement and Account of the Receipts and Expenditures of all public Money shall be published from time to time.

8. No Title of Nobility shall be granted by the United States: —And no Person holding any Office of Profit or Trust under them, shall, without the Consent of the Congress, accept of any present, Emolument, Office, or Title, of any kind whatever, from any King, Prince, or foreign State.

SECTION 10

1. No State shall enter into any Treaty, Alliance, or Confederation; grant Letters of Marque and Reprisal; coin Money; emit Bills of Credit; make any Thing but gold and silver Coin a Tender in Payment of Debts; pass any Bill of Attainder; ex post facto Law, or Law impairing the Obligation of Contracts, or grant any Title of Nobility.

2. No State shall, without the Consent of the Congress, lay any Imposts or Duties on Imports or Exports, except what may be absolutely necessary for executing its inspection Laws: and the net Produce of all Duties and Imposts, laid by any State on Imports and Exports, shall be for the Use of the Treasury of the United States; and all such Laws shall be subject to the Revision and Controul of the Congress.

3. No State shall, without the Consent of Congress, lay any duty of Tonnage, keep Troops, or Ships of War in time of Peace, enter into any Agreement or Compact with another State, or with a foreign Power, or engage in War, unless actually invaded, or in such imminent Danger as will not admit of delay.

3. **Bills of Attainder.** A bill of attainder is a law declaring a person or group guilty of a crime without a court trial. An ex post facto law makes an action a crime after the action has taken place.

4. **Direct Taxes.** A capitation tax is a tax on individuals. A direct tax is one paid directly to the government. Indirect taxes, such as a sales tax, are paid to another party who then pays the government. The income tax, authorized by the Sixteenth Amendment, is the exception to this paragraph.

5. **Taxing Exports.** This paragraph was part of the compromise over the slave trade.

6. **State Commerce.** Congress cannot pass laws favoring the trade and commerce of any state or region. A duty is a tax on imports.

7. **Appropriation Law.** The executive branch cannot spend money without authorization by Congress.

8. **Titles of Nobility.** This paragraph is intended to prevent establishment of a monarchy and the bribery of United States officials by another nation.

SECTION 10. Powers Denied to the States

These powers are forbidden to the states:

1. **Treaties, Coinage.** The powers listed here are either the exclusive powers of the national government, or are denied to both national and state governments. This paragraph was designed to prevent any confusion about overlapping authority between state and national governments.

2. **Taxing Imports and Exports.** Without this prohibition, Congress's power over interstate commerce would be weakened or destroyed.

3. **Duties, Armed Forces, War.** Some exceptions have developed. For example, a state may maintain a militia to protect it against internal disorders. States enter into interstate compacts, but these must be approved by Congress.

Article II. The Executive Branch

SECTION 1. President and Vice President

1. **Term of Office.** The executive power is given to the President of the United States. The President and Vice President are elected for four-year terms. (*See the Twenty-second Amendment.*)

2. **Election.** The President and Vice President are not directly elected. Instead, presidential electors from each state who form the Electoral College elect the President and the Vice President. The number of each state's electors equals the total number of its senators and representatives. No senator, representative, or any other federal officeholder can serve as an elector.

3. **Former Method of Election.** According to the original method of choosing the President and Vice President each elector voted for two candidates. The candidate with the most votes (as long as it was a majority) became President. The second-place candidate became Vice President. The Framers did not foresee the rise of political parties, so after the election of 1800 the Twelfth Amendment providing that electors cast separate ballots for President and Vice President was added.

GEORGE WASHINGTON

Because of his prestige and character, George Washington's active role in the Constitutional Convention was crucial to its ultimate success. After ratification of the Constitution in 1788, Washington became the first President in 1789.

Article II

SECTION 1

1. The executive Power shall be vested in a President of the United States of America. He shall hold his Office during the Term of four years, and, together with the Vice-President chosen for the same Term, be elected, as follows:

2. Each State shall appoint, in such Manner as the Legislature thereof may direct, a Number of Electors, equal to the whole Number of Senators and Representatives to which the State may be entitled in the Congress: but no Senator or Representative, or Person holding an Office of Trust or Profit under the United States, shall be appointed an Elector.

3. The Electors shall meet in their respective States, and vote by Ballot for two Persons, of whom one at least shall not be an Inhabitant of the same State with themselves. And they shall make a List of all the Persons voted for, and of the Number of Votes for each; which List they shall sign and certify, and transmit sealed to the Seat of the Government of the United States, directed to the President of the Senate. The President of the Senate shall, in the Presence of the Senate and House of Representatives, open all the Certificates, and the Votes shall then be counted. The Person having the greatest Number of Votes shall be the President, if such Number be a Majority of the whole Number of Electors appointed; and if there be more than one who have such Majority, and have an equal Number of Votes, then the House of Representatives shall immediately chuse by Ballot one of them for President; and if no Person have a Majority, then from the five highest on the List the said House shall in like Manner chuse the President. But in chusing the President, the Votes shall be taken by States, the Representation from each State having one Vote; a quorum for this Purpose shall consist of a Member or Members from two-thirds of the States, and a Majority of all the States shall be necessary to a Choice. In every Case, after the Choice of the President, the Person having the greatest Number of Votes of the Electors shall be the Vice President. But if there should remain two or more who have equal votes, the Senate shall chuse from them by Ballot the Vice President.

4. The Congress may determine the Time of chusing the Electors, and the Day on which they shall give their Votes; which Day shall be the same throughout the United States.

5. No person except a natural-born Citizen, or a Citizen of the United States, at the time of the Adoption of this Constitution, shall be eligible to the Office of President; neither shall any Person be eligible to that Office who shall not have attained to the Age of thirty-five years, and been fourteen Years a Resident within the United States.

6. In Case of the Removal of the President from Office, or of his Death, Resignation, or Inability to discharge the Powers and Duties of the said Office, the same shall devolve on the Vice-President, and the Congress may by Law provide for the Case of Removal, Death, Resignation or Inability, both of the President and Vice-President, declaring what Officer shall then act as President, and such Officer shall act accordingly, until the disability be removed, or a President shall be elected.

7. The President shall, at stated Times, receive for his Services, a Compensation, which shall neither be increased nor diminished during the Period for which he shall have been elected, and he shall not receive within that Period any other Emolument from the United States, or any of them.

8. Before he enter on the execution of his Office, he shall take the following Oath or Affirmation: "I do solemnly swear (or affirm) that I will faithfully execute the Office of President of the United States, and will to the best of my Ability, preserve, protect and defend the Constitution of the United States."

SECTION 2

1. The President shall be Commander in Chief of the Army and Navy of the United States, and of the Militia of the several States, when called into the actual Service of the United States; he may require the Opinion, in writing, of the principal Officer in each of the executive Departments, upon any subject relating to the Duties of their respective Offices, and he shall have Power to Grant Reprieves and Pardons for Offences against the United States, except in Cases of Impeachment.

4. Date of Elections. All electors must vote on the same day. The first Tuesday after the first Monday in November was the date Congress set for presidential elections. Electors cast their votes on the Monday after the second Wednesday in December.

5. Qualifications. The President must be a citizen of the United States by birth, at least 35 years old, and a resident of the United States for 14 years. Although not expressly stated, the qualifications for Vice President are the same.

6. Vacancies. Until the Twenty-fifth Amendment, presidential succession was based on a precedent set by John Tyler in 1841. Congress set the line of succession after Vice President in the Presidential Succession Act of 1947.

7. Salary. The President receives a salary and expenses that cannot be increased or decreased during the President's term of office. The President cannot receive any other salary from the United States government or state governments.

8. Oath of Office. Before taking office, the President must take an oath to support the Constitution and carry out the duties of the office.

SECTION 2. Powers of the President

1. Military, Cabinet, Pardons. This provision ensures civilian control of the military. The provision for written opinions from executive department heads provides the constitutional basis for the cabinet.

2. **Treaties and Appointments.** The President can make treaties and appoint ambassadors, judges, and all other officers, but these actions must be approved by the Senate. Congress can by law give the President, the courts, or cabinet officers the power to appoint lesser officials without Senate approval. In 1883 Congress created a civil service system to fill most federal jobs.

3. **Vacancies in Offices.** When the Senate is not in session, the President can temporarily appoint officials requiring Senate approval.

SECTION 3. Duties of the President

The President's formal report to Congress is the annual State of the Union Address. Recommended policies or laws are submitted in the federal budget and in special messages. The President also may call special sessions of Congress. The function of receiving ambassadors is the constitutional basis for the President's power to extend or withhold diplomatic recognition to other nations' governments.

SECTION 4. Impeachment

The President, Vice President, and all officials appointed by the President can be impeached by the House of Representatives. They are removed from office if the Senate convicts them. All presidential appointees, except for judges, also can be removed by the President.

Article III. The Judicial Branch

SECTION 1. Federal Courts

Judicial power, or the power to hear and decide cases, is given to a Supreme Court and any lower courts that Congress creates. Congress set up the nation's court system in 1789 and has added courts over the years. Federal judges hold office for life (unless impeached and convicted).

2. He shall have Power, by and with the Advice and Consent of the Senate, to make Treaties, provided two-thirds of the Senators present concur; and he shall nominate, and by and with the Advice and Consent of the Senate, shall appoint Ambassadors, other public Ministers and Consuls, Judges of the supreme Court, and all other Officers of the United States, whose Appointments are not herein otherwise provided for, and which shall be established by Law. But the Congress may by Law vest the Appointment of such inferior Officers, as they think proper, in the President alone, in the Courts of Law, or in the Heads of Departments.

3. The President shall have Power to fill up all Vacancies that may happen during the Recess of the Senate, by granting Commissions which shall expire at the End of their next Session.

SECTION 3

He shall from time to time give to Congress Information of the State of the Union, and recommend to their Consideration such Measures as he shall judge necessary and expedient; he may, on extraordinary occasions, convene both Houses, or either of them, and in Case of Disagreement between them, with respect to the Time of Adjournment, he may adjourn them to such Time as he shall think proper; he shall receive Ambassadors and other public Ministers; he shall take Care that the Laws be faithfully executed, and shall Commission all the Officers of the United States.

SECTION 4

The President, Vice-President and all civil Officers of the United States, shall be removed from Office on Impeachment for, and Conviction of, Treason, Bribery, or other high Crimes and Misdemeanors.

Article III

SECTION 1

The judicial Power of the United States, shall be vested in one supreme Court, and in such inferior Courts as the Congress may from time to time ordain and establish. The judges, both of the supreme and inferior Courts, shall hold their Offices during good Behaviour, and shall, at stated Times, receive for their Services, a Compensation, which shall not be diminished during their Continuance in Office.

Executive (when the Legislature cannot be convened) against domestic Violence.

Article V

The Congress, whenever two-thirds of both Houses shall deem it necessary, shall propose Amendments to this Constitution, or, on the Application of the Legislatures of two-thirds of the several States, shall call a Convention for proposing Amendments, which, in either Case, shall be valid to all Intents and Purposes, as part of this Constitution, when ratified by the Legislatures of three-fourths of the several States, or by Conventions in three-fourths thereof, as the one or the other Mode of Ratification may be proposed by the Congress; Provided that no Amendment which may be made prior to the Year One thousand eight hundred and eight shall in any Manner affect the first and fourth clauses in the Ninth Section of the first Article; and that no State, without its Consent, shall be deprived of its equal Suffrage in the Senate.

Article VI

1. All Debts contracted and Engagements entered into, before the Adoption of this Constitution, shall be as valid against the United States under this Constitution as under the Confederation.

2. This Constitution, and the Laws of the United States which shall be made in Pursuance thereof; and all Treaties made, or which shall be made, under the Authority of the United States, shall be the supreme Law of the Land; and the Judges in every State shall be bound thereby, any Thing in the Constitution or Laws of any State to the Contrary notwithstanding.

3. The Senators and Representatives before mentioned, and the Members of the several State Legislatures, and all executive and judicial Officers, both of the United States and of the several States, shall be bound by Oath or Affirmation to support this Constitution; but no religious Test shall ever be required as a qualification to any Office or public Trust under the United States.

Article V. The Amending Process

Proposing Amendments. Amendments may be proposed in two ways. Two-thirds of both houses of Congress may propose amendments. Or, if two-thirds of the state legislatures request it, Congress must call a convention to propose amendments.

Ratification of Amendments. Proposed amendments become part of the Constitution when approved by three-fourths of the state legislatures or by conventions in three-fourths of the states.

Prohibited Amendments. Before 1808, no amendments could prohibit the slave trade or affect the manner in which direct taxes were to be apportioned. No amendment can deprive a state of its two senators.

Article VI. National Supremacy

1. **Public Debts and Treaties.** With this provision the Framers assured other nations and this nation's creditors that the new government would honor the old government's debts and treaties.

2. **The Supreme Law.** The Constitution, federal laws, and treaties are the supreme law of the land. State judges must accept this principle despite any provisions to the contrary in state constitutions or laws. This provision is known as the supremacy clause.

3. **Oaths of Office.** All federal and state legislators, executive officers, and judges must take an oath to support the Constitution. No religious requirement shall ever be necessary to qualify for a federal office.

Article VII. Ratification of the Constitution

When the conventions of nine states ratified the Constitution, it was to go into effect among the ratifying states.

JAMES MADISON

For his active role in its development and ratification, James Madison has been called "The Father of the Constitution." In 1808 at the peak of his illustrious career, he was the fourth man elected President of the United States.

Alexander Hamilton

It took 9 months for 9 states to ratify the Constitution, thereby establishing it as the law of the land. During this pivotal period Alexander Hamilton, as one of the authors of *The Federalist*, took a leading role in persuading states to ratify.

Article VII

The Ratification of the Conventions of nine States shall be sufficient for the Establishment of this Constitution between the States so ratifying the same.

Done in Convention, by the Unanimous Consent of the States present, the Seventeenth Day of September, in the Year of our Lord one thousand seven hundred and Eighty-seven, and of the Independence of the United States of America the Twelfth. In Witness whereof We have hereunto subscribed our Names.

SIGNERS
George Washington, President and Deputy from Virginia

New Hampshire
John Langdon
Nicholas Gilman

Massachusetts
Nathaniel Gorham
Rufus King

Connecticut
William Samuel Johnson
Roger Sherman

New York
Alexander Hamilton

New Jersey
William Livingston
David Brearley
William Paterson
Jonathan Dayton

Pennsylvania
Benjamin Franklin
Thomas Mifflin
Robert Morris
George Clymer
Thomas FitzSimons
Jared Ingersoll
James Wilson
Gouverneur Morris

Delaware
George Read
Gunning Bedford, Jr.
John Dickinson
Richard Bassett
Jacob Broom

Maryland
James McHenry
Daniel of St. Thomas Jenifer
Daniel Carroll

Virginia
John Blair
James Madison, Jr.

North Carolina
William Blount
Richard Dobbs Spaight
Hugh Williamson

South Carolina
John Rutledge
Charles Cotesworth Pinckney
Charles Pinckney
Pierce Butler

Georgia
William Few
Abraham Baldwin

Attest: William Jackson, Secretary

Amendment I

Congress shall make no law respecting an establishment of religion, or prohibiting the free exercise thereof; or abridging the freedom of speech, or of the press; or the right of the people peaceably to assemble, and to petition the Government for a redress of grievances.

Amendment II

A well-regulated Militia, being necessary to the security of a free State, the right of the people to keep and bear Arms, shall not be infringed.

Amendment III

No soldier shall, in time of peace, be quartered in any house, without the consent of the Owner, nor in time of war, but in a manner to be prescribed by law.

Amendment IV

The right of the people to be secure in their persons, houses, papers, and effects, against unreasonable searches and seizures, shall not be violated, and no Warrants shall issue, but upon probable cause, supported by Oath or affirmation, and particularly describing the place to be searched, and the persons or things to be seized.

Amendment V

No person shall be held to answer for a capital, or otherwise infamous crime, unless on a presentment or indictment of a Grand Jury, except in cases arising in the land or naval forces, or in the Militia, when in actual service in time of War or public danger; nor shall any person be subject for the same offence to be twice put in jeopardy of life or limb; nor shall be compelled in any criminal case to be a witness against himself, nor be deprived of life, liberty, or property, without due process of law; nor shall private property be taken for public use, without just compensation.

Amendment VI

In all criminal prosecutions, the accused shall enjoy the right to a speedy and public trail, by an impartial jury of the State and district wherein the crime shall have been committed, which district shall have been previously ascertained by law, and to be informed of the nature and cause of the accusation; to be confronted with the witnesses against him; to have compulsory process for obtaining witnesses in

Amendments

The first 10 amendments are known as the Bill of Rights. They were proposed by the first session of Congress and were adopted in 1791. At first the guarantees limited only the national government. The Fourteenth Amendment, however, extended many to protect against actions by state governments.

Amendment 1. Freedom of Religion, Speech, Press, and Assembly

Congress may not pass any law creating an official religion or preventing people from worshiping in their own way. Congress may not limit the rights of the people to speak or write their opinions freely, to gather together in meetings, or to request the government to correct abuses.

Amendment 2. Right to Bear Arms

This right is not absolute. The national government and many state governments regulate the purchase, possession, and use of firearms.

Amendment 3. Quartering Troops

No one may be forced to keep soldiers in his or her home during peacetime, or in wartime unless requested to do so by law.

Amendment 4. Searches and Seizures

This amendment prohibits unreasonable searches and seizures. Like the Second and Third Amendments, it was intended to prevent the government from taking actions similar to British colonial practices before the Revolution. To assure that searches and seizures are reasonable, the amendment establishes proper procedures. Supreme Court interpretations of this amendment have greatly affected its provisions.

Amendment 5. Rights of Accused Persons

This amendment protects the legal rights of people in criminal proceedings. No one may be tried for a serious crime unless a grand jury finds reason to believe the accused may be guilty. A person found innocent of a crime cannot be tried a second time for the same offense (double jeopardy). People may not be forced to testify against themselves (self-incrimination). No one may be executed or deprived of his or her freedom or property without a fair hearing with all legal safeguards (due process of law). Government may not take private property for public use (eminent domain) without paying the owner a fair price.

Amendment 6. Right to a Speedy, Fair Trial

This amendment protects the procedural rights of people in criminal proceedings. People accused of a crime must be given a speedy public jury trial in the state and district where the crime occurred. The accused person must be informed of the charges against him or her and witnesses must testify in open court. The accused has the right to require witnesses in his or her favor to appear in court and is entitled to be represented by a lawyer.

Amendment 7. Civil Suits

In federal court cases where lawsuits involve more than $20, a trial by jury is guaranteed.

Amendment 8. Bail and Punishment

When a person is arrested, he or she may be released from jail on payment of a sum of money (bail) to assure that the accused will appear for trial. The amount of bail must be reasonably related to the seriousness of the crime. Bail can be, and often is, denied for those accused of the most serious crimes, such as murder, or who seem likely to flee to avoid trial. To be unconstitutional, punishments must be both cruel and unusual.

Amendment 9. Powers Reserved to the People

The rights listed in the Constitution are not the only rights retained by the people.

Amendment 10. Powers Reserved to the States

This amendment safeguards the powers of the states. Because the Fourteenth Amendment applied the Bill of Rights to the states, however, the states' powers have come under closer examination by the courts.

Amendment 11. Suits against States (Passed by Congress on March 4, 1794. Ratified on February 7, 1795.)

When a state is sued by a citizen of another state or a citizen of a foreign country, the case must be tried in a state court, not a federal court.

Amendment 12. Election of President and Vice President (Passed by Congress on December 9, 1803. Ratified on July 27, 1804.)

This amendment changed the manner in which electors vote for President and Vice President after the original system broke down in the election of 1800. It requires electors to cast separate votes for President and for Vice President. It provides that the winner need only receive a majority of the votes cast rather than the votes of the majority of electors. It reduces from the five highest to the three highest candidates from which the House must choose if no candidate has a majority of the

his favor, and to have the Assistance of Counsel for his defence.

Amendment VII

In suits at common law, where the value in controversy shall exceed twenty dollars, the right of trial by jury shall be preserved, and no fact tried by a jury, shall be otherwise reexamined in any Courts of the United States, than according to the rules of common law.

Amendment VIII

Excessive bail shall not be required, nor excessive fines imposed, nor cruel and unusual punishments inflicted.

Amendment IX

The enumeration in the Constitution, of certain rights, shall not be construed to deny or disparage others retained by the people.

Amendment X

The powers not delegated to the United States by the Constitution, nor prohibited by it to the States, are reserved to the States respectively, or to the people.

Amendment XI

The Judicial power of the United States shall not be construed to extend to any suit in law or equity, commenced or prosecuted against one of the United States by Citizens of another State, or by Citizens or Subjects of any Foreign State.

Amendment XII

The Electors shall meet in their respective States and vote by ballot for President and Vice-President, one of whom, at least, shall not be an inhabitant of the same State with themselves; they shall name in their ballots the person voted for as President, and in distinct ballots the person voted for as Vice-President, and they shall make distinct lists of all persons voted for as President, and of all persons voted for as Vice-President, and of the number of votes for each, which lists they shall sign and certify, and transmit sealed to the seat of the government of the United States, directed to the President of the Senate;—The President of the Senate shall, in the presence of the Senate and House of Representatives, open all the certificates and the votes shall then be counted;—The person having the greatest number of votes for President, shall be the President, if such number be a majority of the whole number of Electors appointed; and if no person have such majority, then from the persons having the highest numbers not exceeding three on the list of those voted for as President, the House of Representatives shall choose immediately, by ballot, the President. But in choosing the President, the votes shall be taken by states, the representation from each state having one vote; a quorum for this purpose shall consist of a member or members from two-thirds of the states, and a majority of all the states shall be necessary to a choice. And if the House of Representatives shall not choose a President whenever the right of choice shall devolve upon them, before the fourth day of March next following, then the Vice-President shall act as President, as in the case of the death or other constitutional disability of the President.—The person having the greatest number of votes as Vice-President, shall be the Vice-President, if such number be a majority of the whole number of Electors appointed, and if no person have a majority, then from the two highest numbers on the list, the Senate shall choose the Vice-President; a quorum for the purpose shall consist of two-thirds of the whole number of Senators, and a majority of the whole number shall be necessary to a choice. But no person constitutionally ineligible to the office of President shall be eligible to that of Vice-President of the United States.

Amendment XIII

SECTION 1

Neither slavery nor involuntary servitude, except as a punishment for crime whereof the party shall have been duly convicted, shall exist within the United States, or any place subject to their jurisdiction.

SECTION 2

Congress shall have power to enforce this article by appropriate legislation.

electoral votes. It also prohibits electors from voting for two candidates (President and Vice President) from their home state.

FREDERICK DOUGLASS

Frederick Douglass made a daring escape from slavery in 1838 when he was 21 years old. He went on to join the abolitionist movement and became one of its most outstanding speakers.

Amendment 13. Abolition of Slavery (Passed by Congress on January 31, 1865. Ratified on December 6, 1865.)

This amendment ended slavery in the United States and in any territory under its control. It also prohibits forcing a debtor to perform personal service. "Involuntary servitude" is allowed only as punishment for someone convicted of a crime.

Amendment 14. Rights of Citizens (Passed by Congress on June 13, 1866. Ratified on July 9, 1868.)

This amendment is among the most important parts of the Constitution. Until its adoption the Constitution did not define citizen even though it used the term in many of its provisions. The amendment has served as the basis of many Supreme Court decisions, particularly those relating to civil rights.

SECTION 1. Citizenship Defined

This section defines citizenship and extends it to African Americans. Its guarantees of due process and equal protection were intended to prevent states from denying African Americans their civil rights.

SECTION 2. Apportionment of Representatives

This section replaced the Three-Fifths Compromise of Article I, Section 2, Paragraph 3. It required that freed slaves be totally counted to determine a state's representation in the House. It also was meant to force southern states to allow African Americans to vote. If the states did not, they would have their representation reduced.

SECTION 3. Penalty for Engaging in Insurrection

This section punished the leaders of the Confederacy.

SECTION 4. Public Debt

This section promises that the debts the federal government incurred from the Civil War will be paid but that the debts of the Confederate states will not be paid, nor would any payment be made for lost or freed slaves.

Amendment XIV

SECTION 1

All persons born or naturalized in the United States, and subject to the jurisdiction thereof, are citizens of the United States and of the State wherein they reside. No State shall make or enforce any law which shall abridge the privileges or immunities of citizens of the United States; nor shall any State deprive any person of life, liberty, or property, without due process of law, nor deny to any person within its jurisdiction the equal protection of the laws.

SECTION 2

Representatives shall be apportioned among the several States according to their respective numbers, counting the whole number of persons in each State, excluding Indians not taxed. But when the right to vote at any election for the choice of electors for President and Vice-President of the United States, Representatives in Congress, the Executive and Judicial officers of a State, or the members of the Legislature thereof, is denied to any of the male inhabitants of such State, being twenty-one years of age, and citizens of the United States, or in any way abridged, except for participation in rebellion, or other crime, the basis of representation therein shall be reduced in the proportion which the number of such male citizens shall bear to the whole number of male citizens twenty-one years of age in such State.

SECTION 3

No person shall be a Senator or Representative in Congress, or elector of President or Vice-President, or hold any office, civil or military, under the United States, or under any State, who, having previously taken an oath, as a member of Congress, or as an officer of the United States, or as a member of any State legislature, or as an executive or judicial officer of any State, to support the Constitution of the United States, shall have engaged in insurrection or rebellion against the same, or given aid or comfort to the enemies thereof. But Congress may by a vote of two-thirds of each House, remove such disability.

SECTION 4

The validity of the public debt of the United States, authorized by law, including debts incurred for payment of pensions and bounties for service in suppressing insurrection or rebellion, shall not be questioned. But neither the United States nor any State shall assume or pay any debt or obligation incurred in aid of insurrection or rebellion against the United States, or any claim for the loss or emancipation of any slave; but all such debts, obligations and claims shall be held illegal and void.

SECTION 5

The Congress shall have power to enforce, by appropriate legislation, the provisions of this article.

Amendment XV

SECTION 1

The right of citizens of the United States to vote shall not be denied or abridged by the United States or by any State on account of race, color, or previous condition of servitude.

SECTION 2

The Congress shall have power to enforce this article by appropriate legislation.

Amendment XVI

The Congress shall have power to lay and collect taxes on incomes, from whatever source derived, without apportionment among the several States, and without regard to any census or enumeration.

Amendment XVII

The Senate of the United States shall be composed of two Senators from each State, elected by the people thereof, for six years; and each Senator shall have one vote. The electors in each State shall have the qualifications requisite for electors of the most numerous branch of the state legislature.

When vacancies happen in the representation of any State in the Senate, the executive authority of such State shall issue writs of election to fill such vacancies: *Provided,* That the legislature of any State may empower the executive thereof to make temporary appointments until the people fill the vacancies by election as the legislature may direct.

This amendment shall not be so construed as to affect the election or term of any Senator chosen before it becomes valid as part of the Constitution.

Amendment 15. Right to Vote (Passed by Congress on February 26, 1869. Ratified on February 3, 1870.)

This amendment replaced Section 2 of the Fourteenth Amendment by removing from the states the power to deny the right to vote based on race, color, or previous condition of servitude. Despite its provisions, many African Americans were denied the right to vote until the 1960s, when Congress took firm action to enforce its guarantees.

Amendment 16. Income Tax (Passed by Congress on July 2, 1909. Ratified on February 3, 1913.)

Congress has the power to tax individual incomes without dividing the tax among the states or according to population. This amendment provides an exception to the restrictions placed on taxation by Article I, Section 2, Paragraph 3 and Section 9, Paragraph 4.

Amendment 17. Direct Election of Senators (Passed by Congress on May 13, 1912. Ratified on April 8, 1913.)

Senators are to be directly elected by the voters of each state rather than by their state legislatures as provided by the Framers in Article I, Section 3, Paragraphs 1 and 2.

Amendment 18. Prohibition of Alcoholic Beverages (Passed by Congress on December 18, 1917. Ratified on January 16, 1919.)

The manufacture, sale, or transportation of alcoholic beverages was prohibited one year after the ratification of this amendment.

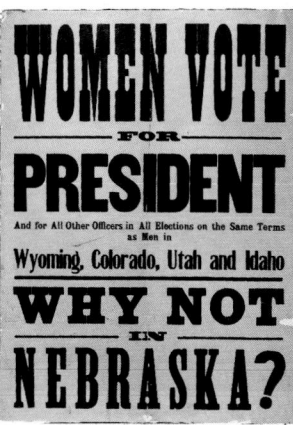

In 1869 Wyoming became the first territory to grant full voting rights to women. The Nineteenth Amendment was ratified in 1920.

Amendment 19. Woman's Suffrage (Passed by Congress on June 4, 1919. Ratified on August 18, 1920.)

Citizens of the United States cannot be prevented from voting by the United States or any state because of their sex. This amendment gave women the right to vote.

Amendment 20. "Lame-Duck" Amendment (Passed by Congress on March 2, 1932. Ratified on January 23, 1933.)

SECTION 1. Beginning of Terms of Office

The President and Vice President take office at noon on January 20; senators and representatives at noon on January 3.

SECTION 2. Beginning of Congressional Sessions

Congress must meet at least once a year beginning on noon on January 3, unless a different day is assigned.

SECTION 3. Succession of President and Vice President

If the person elected President dies before taking office, the person elected Vice President

Amendment XVIII

SECTION 1

After one year from the ratification of this article the manufacture, sale, or transportation of intoxicating liquors within, the importation thereof into, or the exportation thereof from the United States and all territory subject to the jurisdiction thereof for beverage purposes is hereby prohibited.

SECTION 2

The Congress and the several states shall have concurrent power to enforce this article by appropriate legislation.

SECTION 3

This article shall be inoperative unless it shall have been ratified as an amendment to the Constitution by the legislatures of the several States, as provided in the Constitution, within seven years from the date of the submission hereof to the states by the Congress.

Amendment XIX

The right of citizens of the United States to vote shall not be denied or abridged by the United States or by any state on account of sex.

Congress shall have power to enforce this article by appropriate legislation.

Amendment XX

SECTION 1

The terms of the President and Vice President shall end at noon on the 20th day of January, and the terms of Senators and Representatives at noon on the 3d day of January, of the years in which such terms would have ended if this article had not been ratified; and the terms of their successors shall then begin.

SECTION 2

The Congress shall assemble at least once in every year, and such meeting shall begin at noon on the 3d day of January, unless they shall by law appoint a different day.

SECTION 3

If, at the time fixed for the beginning of the term of the President, the President elect shall have died, the Vice President elect shall become President. If a

President shall not have been chosen before the time fixed for the beginning of his term, or if the President elect shall have failed to qualify, then the Vice President elect shall act as President until a President shall have qualified; and the Congress may by law provide for the case wherein neither a President elect nor a Vice President elect shall have qualified, declaring who shall then act as President, or the manner in which one who is to act shall be selected, and such person shall act accordingly until a President or Vice President shall have qualified.

SECTION 4

The Congress may by law provide for the case of the death of any of the persons from whom the House of Representatives may choose a President whenever the right of choice shall have devolved upon them, and for the case of the death of any of the persons from whom the Senate may choose a Vice President whenever the right of choice shall have devolved upon them.

SECTION 5

Sections 1 and 2 shall take effect on the 15th day of October following the ratification of this article.

SECTION 6

This article shall be inoperative unless it shall have been ratified as an amendment to the Constitution by the legislatures of three-fourths of the several states within seven years from the date of its submission.

Amendment XXI

SECTION 1

The eighteenth article of amendment to the Constitution of the United States is hereby repealed.

SECTION 2

The transportation or importation into any State, Territory, or possession of the United States for delivery or use therein of intoxicating liquors, in violation of the laws thereof, is hereby prohibited.

SECTION 3

This article shall be inoperative unless it shall have been ratified as an amendment to the Constitution by conventions in the several States, as provided in the Constitution, within seven years from the date of the submission hereof to the states by the Congress.

becomes President. If a President is not elected by January 20, or if the President-elect does not meet the qualifications for office, the Vice President-elect becomes President until a President who qualifies is elected. If neither the President-elect or the Vice President-elect meet the qualifications for office, Congress may appoint a temporary President or Vice President until someone who is qualified is elected.

SECTION 4. Filling Presidential Vacancies

Congress has the power to make a law providing what to do in case the House of Representatives must choose a President and one of the eligible candidates has died. Congress also has the power to pass a law informing the Senate of what to do in case it must choose a Vice President and one of the candidates has died. *(See Article II, Section 1, Clause 3.)*

Amendment 21. Repeal of Prohibition (Passed by Congress on February 20, 1933. Ratified on December 5, 1933.)

This amendment repeals the Eighteenth Amendment but allows states to prohibit the sale of alcoholic beverages.

Amendment 22. Limit on Presidential Terms
(Passed by Congress on March 21, 1947. Ratified
on February 27, 1951.)

No person may be elected President more than
twice. No person who completes more than two
years of another President's term may be elected
more than once.

**Amendment 23. Presidential Electors for the
District of Columbia** (Passed by Congress on
June 16, 1960. Ratified on March 29, 1961.)

The District of Columbia is given three
presidential electors. Thus residents of
Washington, D.C., have the right to vote for
President and Vice President.

Franklin D. Roosevelt's unprecedented four
consecutive terms as President concerned
many people. These people argued that no
person should serve more than two terms,
thus preventing any one President from
becoming too powerful.

Amendment XXII

SECTION 1

No person shall be elected to the office of the
President more than twice, and no person who had
held the office of President, or acted as President, for
more than two years of a term to which some other
person was elected President shall be elected to the
office of the President more than once.

But this Article shall not apply to any person
holding the office of President when this Article was
proposed by the Congress, and shall not prevent any
person who may be holding the office of President,
or acting as President, during the term within which
this Article becomes operative from holding the
office of President or acting as President during the
remainder of such term.

SECTION 2

This article shall be inoperative unless it shall have
been ratified as an amendment to the Constitution
by the legislatures of three-fourths of the several
States within seven years from the date of its
submission to the States by the Congress.

Amendment XXIII

SECTION 1

The District constituting the seat of Government
of the United States shall appoint in such manner as
the Congress may direct:

A number of electors of President and Vice
President equal to the whole number of Senators and
Representatives in Congress to which the District
would be entitled if it were a State, but in no event
more that the least populous State; they shall be in
addition to those appointed by the States, but they
shall be considered, for the purposes of the election
of President and Vice President, to be electors
appointed by a State; and they shall meet in the
District and perform such duties as provided by the
twelfth article of amendment.

SECTION 2

The Congress shall have power to enforce this
article by appropriate legislation.

Amendment XXIV

SECTION 1

The right of citizens of the United States to vote in any primary or other election for President or Vice President, for electors for President or Vice President, or for Senator or Representative in Congress, shall not be denied or abridged by the United States or any State by reason of failure to pay any poll tax or other tax.

SECTION 2

The Congress shall have power to enforce this article by appropriate legislation.

Amendment XXV

SECTION 1

In case of the removal of the President from office or his death or resignation, the Vice President shall become President.

SECTION 2

Whenever there is a vacancy in the office of the Vice President, the President shall nominate a Vice President who shall take the office upon confirmation by a majority vote of both houses of Congress.

SECTION 3

Whenever the President transmits to the President pro tempore of the Senate and the Speaker of the House of Representatives his written declaration that he is unable to discharge the powers and duties of his office, and until he transmits to them a written declaration to the contrary, such powers and duties shall be discharged by the Vice President as Acting President.

SECTION 4

Whenever the Vice President and a majority of either the principal officers of the executive departments or of such other body as Congress may by law provide, transmit to the President pro tempore of the Senate and the Speaker of the House of Representatives their written declaration that the President is unable to discharge the powers and duties of his office, the Vice President shall immediately assume the powers and duties of the office of Acting President.

Thereafter, when the President transmits to the President pro tempore of the Senate and the Speaker

Amendment 24. Abolition of Poll Tax (Passed by Congress on August 27, 1962. Ratified on January 23, 1964.)

Neither the United States nor the states may require a person to pay a poll tax to vote in federal elections.

Amendment 25. Presidential Disability and Succession (Passed by Congress on July 6, 1965. Ratified on February 10, 1967.)

Section 1. Removal, Death, or Resignation of the President
When the President dies, resigns, or is removed from office, the Vice President becomes President.

Section 2. Vice Presidential Vacancies
When the office of Vice President is vacant, the President appoints a Vice President. This appointment must be approved by a majority vote in both houses of Congress.

Section 3. Presidential Disability
When the President informs Congress of the inability to perform the duties of office, the Vice President serves as Acting President.

Section 4. Declarations of Presidential Disability
When the Vice President and a majority of the cabinet (or some other body designated by Congress) inform Congress that the President is unable to perform the duties of office, the Vice President immediately becomes Acting President.

The President shall resume presidential duties by informing Congress of the ability to take up the duties of the office. If within 4 days, the Vice President and a majority of the cabinet (or some other body designated by Congress) inform Congress that the President is still unable to perform presidential duties, Congress must decide the issue. Congress must assemble within 48 hours if it is not in session. If a two-thirds majority of both houses of Congress decides within 21 days that the President is still unable to serve, the Vice President continues as Acting President. If Congress decides the contrary, then the President resumes office.

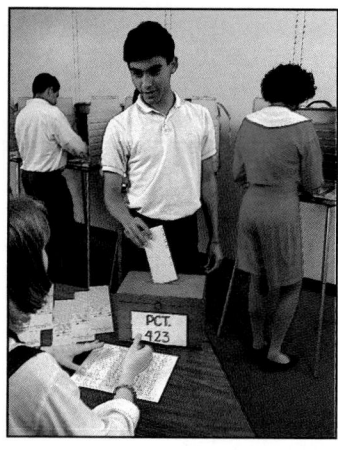

Before the ratification of the Twenty-sixth Amendment in 1971, 18-year-olds could be drafted but could not vote.

Amendment 26. Eighteen-Year-Old Vote
(Passed by Congress on March 23, 1971. Ratified on June 30, 1971.)

No one 18 years of age or older may be denied the right to vote in federal and state elections.

Amendment 27. Restraint on Congressional Salaries (Passed by Congress on September 25, 1789. Ratified on May 20, 1992.)

Any increase in the salaries of members of Congress will take effect in the subsequent session of Congress.

of the House of Representatives his written declaration that no inability exists, he shall resume the powers and duties of his office unless the Vice President and a majority of either the principal officers of the executive departments or of such other body as Congress may by law provide, transmit within four days to the President pro tempore of the Senate and the Speaker of the House of Representatives their written declaration that the President is unable to discharge the powers and duties of his office. Thereupon Congress shall decide the issue, assembling within forty-eight hours for that purpose if not in session. If the Congress within twenty-one days after receipt of the latter written declaration, or, if Congress is not in session, within twenty-one days after Congress is required to assemble, determines by two-thirds vote of both houses that the President is unable to discharge the powers and duties of his office, the Vice President shall continue to discharge the same as Acting President; otherwise, the President shall resume the power and duties of his office.

Amendment XXVI

SECTION 1

The right of citizens of the United States, who are eighteen years of age or older, to vote shall not be denied or abridged by the United States or by any State on account of age.

SECTION 2

The Congress shall have power to enforce this article by appropriate legislation.

Amendment XXVII

No law, varying the compensation for the services of Senators and Representatives, shall take effect, until an election of Representatives shall have intervened.

Amendments to the Constitution,
by Subject

Individual Rights

1 (1791)	Free expression
2 (1791)	Bearing arms
3 (1791)	No quartering of troops
4 (1791)	Searches, seizures, and warrants
5 (1791)	Criminal procedure and fair trial
6 (1791)	Criminal Procedure and fair trial
7 (1791)	Jury trials and civil suits
8 (1791)	No cruel and unusual punishment
9 (1791)	Recognition of rights not enumerated
13 (1865)	Abolition of slavery
14 (1868)	Restrictions on state interference with individual rights; equality under the law; also altered relations between states and the national government.

Political Processes

12 (1804)	Separate voting by electors for President and Vice President
15 (1870)	Removal of race as criterion for voting
17 (1913)	Popular election of United States senators
19 (1920)	Removal of gender as criterion for voting
23 (1961)	Enfranchisement of District of Columbia in voting for President and Vice President
24 (1964)	Abolition of poll tax in federal elections
26 (1971)	National voting age of 18 in all elections
27 (1992)	Restraint on congressional salaries

Nation-State Relations

10 (1791)	Powers of the state
11 (1795)	Restrictions of jurisdiction of federal courts

Operation of National Government

16 (1913)	Income Tax
20 (1933)	Shift of start of presidential term from March to January; presidential succession
22 (1951)	Two-term presidency
25 (1967)	Presidential disability and replacement of Vice President

Other

18 (1919)	Prohibition of alcoholic beverages
21 (1933)	Repeal of Eighteenth Amendment

Since the Bill of Rights (Amendments 1-10) was added in 1791, only 17 formal changes have been made in the Constitution. Most have occurred in periods of constitutional reform and have affected the manner in which officials are elected and the operation and powers of the national government.

Chapter Organizer

Objectives	Special Feature Pages	Supplemental Materials
Section 1 National and State Powers *pp. 126–129* 1. Compare the powers of the national government with those reserved to the states and the people. 2. Distinguish between the expressed, implied, inherent, reserved, and concurrent powers of government.	Global Connection: Comparing Governments: Parliamentary and Presidential Systems p. 128	Guided Reading Activities Reproducible Lesson Plans Supreme Court Case Studies 2 Primary and Secondary Source Readings 4 Section 1 Quiz Testmaker Chapter Transparencies 4 The Living Constitution SAT Practice Tests
Section 2 Changing Currents of Federalism *pp. 130–133* 1. Differentiate the nationalist and the states' rights views of federalism. 2. Identify constitutional provisions that have expanded the power of the national government.	Focus on Freedom: *The Federalist*, No. 10 p. 131	Guided Reading Activities Reproducible Lesson Plans Enrichment Activities 4 Section 2 Quiz Testmaker The Living Constitution SAT Practice Tests Writer's Guidebook
Section 3 Relations Among the States *pp. 134–138* 1. Explain how the Constitution regulates interstate relations. 2. Describe the role of interstate compacts. 3. Characterize the restrictions the national government can put on the admission of new states.	Study and Writing Skills: Writing a Paragraph p. 138	Guided Reading Activities Reproducible Lesson Plans Section 3 Quiz Testmaker Skill Reinforcment Activity 4 The Living Constitution SAT Practice Tests Writer's Guidebook
Section 4 Federalism and Political Life *pp. 139–143* 1. Explain the impact of federalism on political activity. 2. Describe how federalism has affected the making of national public policy.	Participating in Government: Recycling p. 140 Personal Perspectives: Linda Tarr-Whelan on Progressive Federalism p. 143 Case Study: The Politics of Federalism pp. 146–148 Unit 1 Digest pp. 149–150	Guided Reading Activities Reproducible Lesson Plans Participating in Government 4 Reteaching Activities 4 Section 4 Quiz Chapter 4 Tests Testmaker Audio Cassettes (English and Spanish) Limited English Proficiency Activities 4 Unit Digest Transparencies, Unit 1 Participating in Government, Unit 1 The Living Constitution SAT Practice Tests Writer's Guidebook

If time does not permit teaching this chapter, assign the Chapter 4 summary in the Unit 1 Digest on pages 149–150.

Key To Ability Levels

Teaching strategies have been coded for varying learning styles and abilities.

L1   Level 1 activities are **basic** activities and should be within the ability range of all students.

L2   Level 2 activities are **average** activities and should be within the ability range of the average to above-average student.

L3   Level 3 activities are **challenging** activities designed for the ability range of above-average students.

LEP These activities should be within the ability range of **Limited English Proficiency** students.

Multicultural Activities

During the years of the Warren Court, 1954–1969, civil rights advocates looked to the United States Supreme Court rather than to the state courts for support in upholding minority rights and ending discrimination at the state and local level. Since that time a more conservative court led by Warren Burger and William Rehnquist have practiced judicial restraint. For example, in recent decisions, the United States Supreme Court made it more difficult for women and minorities to go to court claiming job discrimination. Therefore, civil rights activists are turning to state courts and legislatures for decisions favorable to minority interests. Have students review the section "States' Rightists vs. Nationalists" on pages 130–132 and explain how these changes reflect the shifting politics of federalism.

Earlier in our nation's history, the Civil War Amendments were the primary tools for safeguarding the rights of minorities and preventing discrimination based on race. However, in recent years lawyers and judges have relied as well on the commerce clause. Two examples of the broad use of the commerce power to regulate civil rights are the 1964 cases *Heart of Atlanta Motel, Inc.* v. *United States* and *Katzenbach* v. *McClung.* In both cases owners of restaurants or motels challenged the constitutionality of the Civil Rights Act of 1964, claiming that Congress had exceeded its powers under the commerce clause in forcing them to serve African Americans. Interested students might research these cases and report on why the Court upheld Congress's actions.

Chapter Resources

Readings for the Student

Elazar, Daniel J. *American Federalism: A View from the States.* Harper & Row, 1984.

Garreau, Joel. *The Nine Nations of North America.* Houghton Mifflin, 1981.

Patterson, James T. *The New Deal and the States: Federalism in Transition.* Princeton University Press, 1969.

Rawley, James A. *Turning Points of the Civil War.* Bison, 1989.

Sanford, Terry. *Storm Over the States.* McGraw-Hill, 1967.

Wright, Deil S. *Understanding Intergovernmental Relations.* Brooks/Cole, 1982.

Readings for the Teacher

Grodzins, Morton. *The American System.* Rand McNally, 1966.

Hale, George E. and Marian Lief Palley. *The Politics of Federal Grants.* Congressional Quarterly, 1981.

Morris, Roger. *Promises of Change: The Clinton Administration and the Politics of Renewal.* Henry Holt, 1994.

Reagan, Michael D. and John Sanzone. *The New Federalism.* Oxford University Press, 1981.

Walker, David. *Towards a Functioning Federalism.* Winthrop, 1981.

Multimedia

Videocassettes and Films

Democracy and Responsibilities: Citizen Stories. Smithsonian Institution/Close Up Foundation. (v/c, 32 minutes)

Equal Justice Under Law 2: McCulloch v. Maryland. U.S. National Audiovisual Center. (v/c, 30 minutes)

The Events Which Led to the Emancipation Proclamation. Life Video. (v/c, 15 minutes)

George Washington and the Whiskey Rebellion: Testing the Constitution. Learning Corporation of America. (2 color f/s, 2 cassettes, and film, 27 minutes)

Software

Lincoln's Decisions: Simulation. Educational Activities. (Apple disk). Students play Lincoln at major decision points.

The U.S. Constitution: Nationalism and Federalism. Focus Media. (3 Apple diskettes). Students take part in the Constitutional Convention and review the ideas of Hamilton and Jefferson.

Powers of the U.S. Government. Educational Products Information Exchange Institute, Hampton Bays, New York, 11946. Macintosh Plus, 1MB, 3.5" disk drive videodisc player, color TV monitor.

The Federal System

Introduce

Chapter Overview

Chapter 4 defines and explains federalism as a framework for government in which powers are divided between national and state governments.

Section 1 compares the expressed and implied powers that the Constitution gives to the national government with those reserved to the states.

Section 2 examines the trends in federalism since 1787 explaining how the national government has gained power at the expense of the states.

Section 3 considers the rules the Constitution provides for interstate relations and the ways that states and their citizens conduct relations with each other.

Section 4 determines how federalism influences political life and public policy in the United States today.

Chapter 4 Themes

Have students read Themes in Government on page 125. Have them rewrite the statement after each theme in the form of a question. *(Example: What powers does the Constitution give to the states and to the national government?)* Tell them to note which sections will help them answer each question.

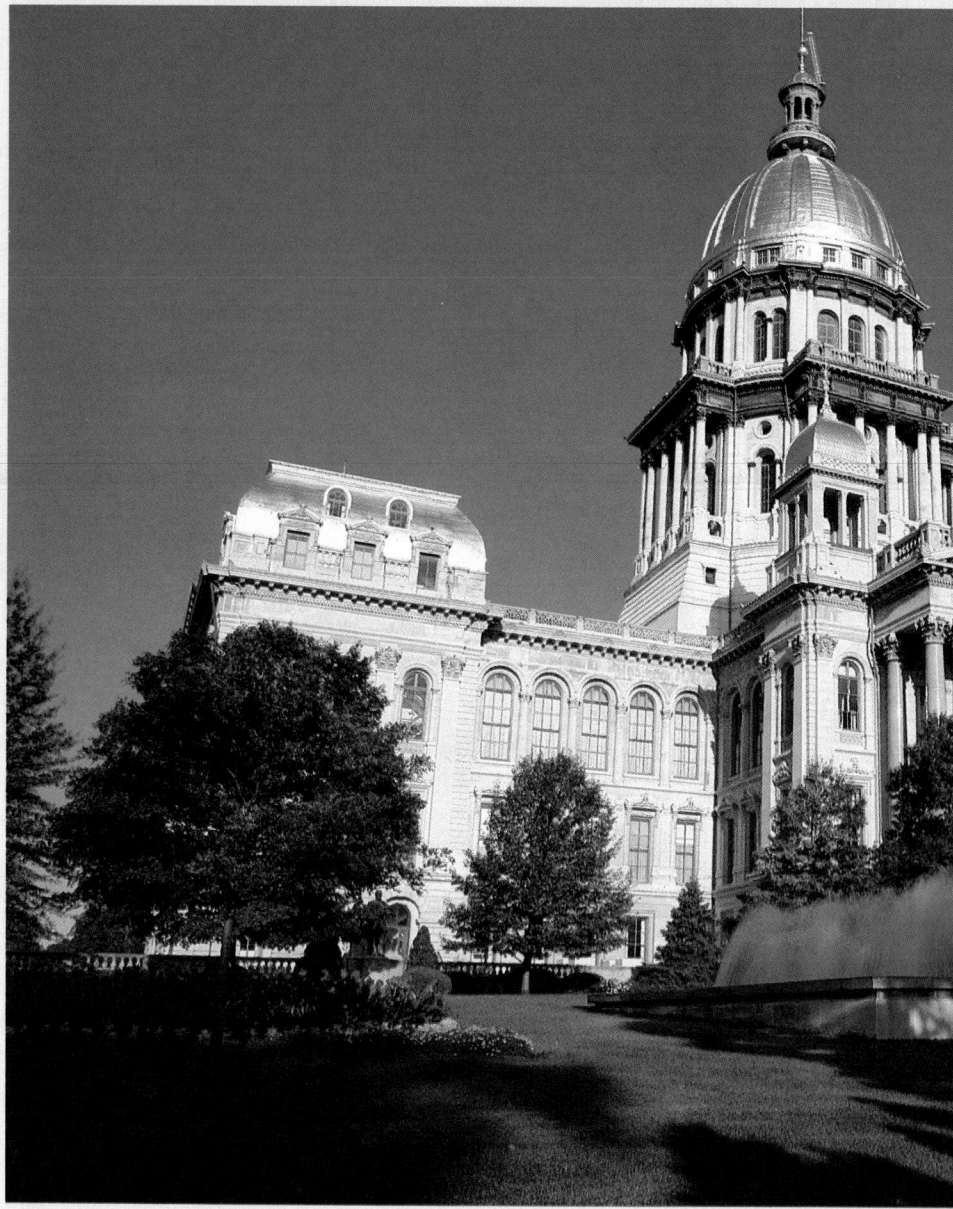

State governments, such as the Illinois legislature, housed in the state capitol in Springfield, exercise a wide range of powers reserved for them by the Constitution.

About the Chapter Opener

Teaching With Illustrations Ask students to identify the building in the photograph on pages 124 and 125. Then ask the following questions: What are some features of the architecture of the building? *(Students might point out the details of the building, such as the dome and the columns.)* How do the architectural features of this building compare with those of the United States Capitol? *(Students might indicate that both buildings feature a dome and columns.)* Is the architecture of this building appropriate for the function of the building? Why? *(Students should give reasons for their opinions.)*

Introducing the Chapter

Before beginning the chapter, review the following information. Ask: What is the definition of the term *state*? In what ways do the states of the United States meet some of the terms of that definition? In what ways do they not? How do federal and unitary systems of government differ?

Chapter Project

Have students make a notebook of articles from newspapers or magazines that illustrate the division of powers between state and national governments under the federal system. Have students identify the source and date of each article and write a sentence telling how the article relates to federalism.

Chapter Preview

Overview

Government authority in the United States is divided between the federal government and state governments.

Objectives

After studying this chapter, you should be able to:

1. **Identify** the main divisions of powers between the states and the national government.
2. **Describe** key changes in federalism from the time the Constitution was ratified.
3. **Define** the constitutional rules for relations among the states.
4. **Explain** how federalism affects politics.

Themes in Government

This chapter emphasizes the following government themes:

- **Federalism** The Constitution reserves certain powers to the states and gives others to the national government. Sections 1, 2, and 3.
- **Constitutional Interpretations** The Constitution is a flexible document that allows the national government to assume new powers. Section 1.
- **Political Processes** The federal government has grown in size and power since the Constitution was written. Sections 2 and 4.
- **Public Policy** The government can choose from many options when responding to an issue or problem. Sections 3 and 4.

Critical Thinking Skills

This chapter emphasizes the following critical thinking skills:

- Making Comparisons
- Making Inferences
- Identifying Central Issues
- Expressing Problems Clearly
- Demonstrating Reasoned Judgment
- Identifying Assumptions

CHAPTER 4: THE FEDERAL SYSTEM **125**

Linking Past and Present
Federalism in the United States has evolved from a *dual federalism* into a *cooperative federalism*. In a dual federalism, state and national governments are separate and supreme within their own spheres. Today the United States has more of a cooperative federalism in that state and national governments have mingled responsibilities and the distinctions between the governments are often blurred.

Powers of the Congress
The Federal System
Running Time 1:02
Side Two, Chapter 11

Setting the Scene Federalism has always been a controversial issue. Patrick Henry argued against ratification of the Constitution because "one government cannot reign over so extensive a country without despotism." Today many people view the growing power of the national government as a potentially dangerous force. Yet some of the former colonists worried that Shays's Rebellion posed a danger that could be dealt with only by a strong national government. Today many Americans feel that the United States faces problems that only a strong national government can solve.

Focus

Bell Ringer

While attendance is being taken, ask students to write a definition of *federalism* in their own words.

Motivating Activity

Discuss students' Bell Ringer answers and then present the following headline to students:

PRESIDENT SENDS FEDERAL TROOPS TO HELP IN MASSACHUSETTS STORM DISASTER

Tell students that federal troops are often sent to assist disaster areas in states. Ask students if they can think of other ways the federal government assists states.

Vocabulary Precheck

Write the vocabulary terms for this section on the chalkboard. Ask students to use those that they know in sentences. **LEP**

Teach

Guided Practice

L1 Interpreting Visuals Have students find pictures in this textbook that illustrate interaction between state and federal governments. Have volunteers tell which pictures they have selected and discuss. What powers are illustrated by each level of government? Can anyone find a picture showing expressed powers of the federal government? **LEP**

GLENCOE TECHNOLOGY

Focus on Government
Video 5
Lecture Launcher:
The Federal System
Running Time: 2:29
Videodisc 1, Chap. 5
VHS Tape 1, Begins 13:39

SECTION 1

National and State Powers

There are in the United States today about 3 million civilians employed by the federal government, more than 4.5 million working for state governments, and more than 11 million working for local governments. How is the enormous governmental structure that employs so many people organized? What keeps all of these governments from duplicating their functions? How do the different levels of government cooperate?

The Division of Powers

The Constitution divided government authority by giving the national government certain specified powers, reserving all other powers to the states or to the people. In addition, the national and state governments share some powers. Finally, the Constitution specifically denied some powers to each level of government.

The Constitution has preserved the basic design of federalism, or the division of government powers, over the years. The American concept of federalism, however, has changed greatly since 1787.

Federalism is not a static relationship between different levels of government. It is a dynamic concept that affects everyday decisions at all levels. An understanding of federalism must begin with the Constitution.

The Constitution grants three types of power to the national government: expressed, implied, and inherent powers. Collectively these powers are known as **delegated powers**, powers the Constitution grants or delegates to the national government.

Expressed Powers The **expressed powers** are those powers directly expressed or stated in the Constitution. Most of these powers are found in the first three articles of the Constitution. These include the power to levy and collect taxes, to coin money, to make war, to raise an army and navy, and to regulate commerce among the states. Expressed powers are also called **enumerated powers.**

Implied Powers **Implied powers** are those powers that the national government requires to carry out the powers that are expressly defined in the Constitution. While not specifically listed, implied powers spring from and depend upon the expressed powers. For example, the power to draft people into the armed forces is implied by the power to raise an army and navy.

The basis for the implied powers is the **necessary and proper clause** (Article I, Section 8). Often called the **elastic clause**, it says:

Congress shall have power . . . to make all Laws which shall be necessary and proper for carrying into Execution the Foregoing powers, and all other powers vested . . . in the Government of the United States. . . .

—ARTICLE I, SECTION 8

Implied powers have helped the national government strengthen and expand its authority to meet many problems the Founders did not foresee. Thus, Congress has used the implied powers to regulate nuclear power plants and to develop the space program.

SECTION PREVIEW

Objectives
After studying this section, you should be able to:
- Compare the powers of the national government with those reserved to the states and the people.
- Distinguish between the expressed, implied, inherent, reserved, and concurrent powers of government.

Key Terms and Concepts
delegated powers, expressed powers, enumerated powers, implied powers, necessary and proper clause, elastic clause, inherent powers, reserved powers, concurrent powers

Themes in Government
- Federalism
- Constitutional Interpretations

Critical Thinking Skills
- Making Comparisons
- Making Inferences

---

126   UNIT 1: FOUNDATIONS OF AMERICAN GOVERNMENT

Classroom Resources for Section 1

- Guided Reading Activities
- Reproducible Lesson Plans
- Supreme Court Case Studies 2
- Primary and Secondary Source Readings 4
- Section 1 Quiz
- Testmaker
- Chapter Transparencies 4
- The Living Constitution
- SAT Practice Tests

Inherent Powers **Inherent powers** are those that the national government may exercise simply because it is a government. National government must control immigration and establish diplomatic relations with other countries, even though these powers are not spelled out in the Constitution.

State Government Powers The Constitution reserves certain powers for the states. These powers belong strictly to the states and are called **reserved powers**. While the Constitution does not list these reserved powers, it grants to the states, or to the people through the Tenth Amendment, those powers "not delegated to the United States by the Constitution, nor prohibited by it to the states."

Thus the states may exercise any power not delegated to the national government, reserved to the people, or denied to them by the Constitution. As a result, states require licenses for those who practice certain professions, regulate public school systems, and establish local governments.

The Supremacy Clause What happens when states exceed their reserved powers and pass laws that conflict with national laws? Which law is supreme? Article VI, Section 2, of the Constitution clearly answers these questions. It makes the acts and treaties of the United States supreme. For this reason it is called the supremacy clause. This clause states:

This Constitution, and the Laws of the United States which shall be made in Pursuance thereof, and all treaties made . . . under the Authority of the United States, shall be the supreme Law of the Land; and the Judges in every State shall be bound thereby.
—ARTICLE VI, SECTION 2

No state law or state constitution may conflict with any form of national law. Article VI also requires that all national and state officials and judges be bound to recite an oath to support the Constitution. State officials are not permitted to use their state's reserved powers to interfere with the Constitution.

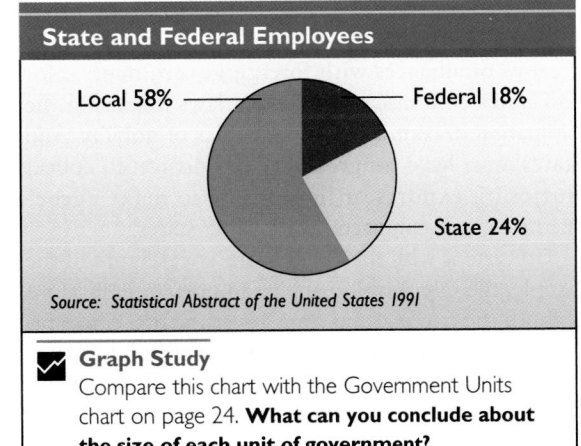

State and Federal Employees

Local 58%   Federal 18%

State 24%

Source: *Statistical Abstract of the United States 1991*

☑ **Graph Study**
Compare this chart with the Government Units chart on page 24. **What can you conclude about the size of each unit of government?**

States create local governments such as cities and counties. As such, local governments get their powers from the states. Hence, local governments are also bound by the supremacy clause—if a state is denied a certain power, so, too, are the local governments within the state.

Concurrent Powers The federal government and the states also have certain concurrent powers. **Concurrent powers** are those powers that both the national government and the states have. Each level of government exercises these powers independently. Examples of concurrent powers are the power to tax, to maintain courts and define crimes, and to appropriate private property for public use. Concurrently with the national government, the states may exercise any power that the Constitution does not reserve for the national government. Of course, state actions must not conflict with national law.

Denied Powers Finally, the Constitution specifically denies some powers to all levels of government. Article I, Section 9, enumerates those things the national government cannot do. For example, the national government cannot tax exports, and it cannot interfere with the ability of states to carry out their responsibilities.

STUDY GUIDE

Themes in Government
Federalism It is a fact that many more civilians work for local governments than for either the state or federal government. **What, in** your opinion, does this fact imply about government services?

Critical Thinking Skills
Making Inferences What kind of constitutional power did the United States government invoke when it decided to build a new United States capitol?

Chapter 4, Section 1
Lesson Plan, pages 126–129

🏴 **Interpreting Visuals** Display transparency 4 from the *Chapter Transparencies* in the Teacher's Classroom Resources and use the accompanying teaching strategy and student activity to compare the powers of the national and state governments. Then ask: Whose power is greater?

L3 **Creating a Chart** On the chalkboard write the word *Powers.* Under this head write the following heads: *Expressed, Implied, Inherent, Reserved, Concurrent.*

Ask students to contribute to the chart by first explaining each power, then indicating which powers belong to the states and which to the national government, and finally giving examples of each.

Independent Practice

📁 **Interpreting Source Readings** Have students complete activity 4 in *Primary and Secondary Source Readings* in the Teacher's Classroom Resources.

Graph Study Answer
The fewer units of government in the federal system, the larger each unit tends to be, and vice versa. For instance, local government has 58 percent of the work force, but they are divided among 83,000 units.

STUDY GUIDE

Theme Answer
that local governments provide more services than the other two levels

Critical Thinking Answer
inherent

Background

Some provisions of the Articles of Confederation were incorporated into the Constitution. Of these provisions, the "extradition," the "full faith and credit," and the "privileges and immunities" provisions were intended to reflect the sovereign nature of the states. Extradition does not exist automatically between nations, but it is often established by treaty. Likewise, "full faith and credit" is a feature of relationships among nations. The "privileges and immunities" extended to citizens of a country are often extended to citizens of other nations who are in a country.

L2 **Analyzing Media** Have students find newspaper articles that describe each of the three obligations of the national government to the states and the states' obligations to the national government. Ask students to explain the obligation each article illustrates.

STUDY GUIDE

Theme Answer
The Constitution gives Congress implied powers through the "necessary and proper" clause to carry out the expressed powers.

Critical Thinking Answer
The list of powers denied to the states is longer, but both states and national government are restricted from interfering with individual liberties.

GLOBAL CONNECTION

The British House of Lords is an aristocratic body of 1,171 members who have inherited their appointments for life or were appointed by the monarch. The House of Commons consists of 651 members who are elected from districts. Although the House of Lords has no real power, it can delay the passing of a bill. A bill rejected by the House of Lords will become a law if the House of Commons approves it a second time. Have students list three major differences between the British Parliament and the United States Congress.
Examining the Connection Answer: *advantage—stability; disadvantage—stays in power to end of term if loses support*

The next section of Article I presents a long list of powers denied to the states. No state can make treaties or alliances with foreign governments. Nor can states coin money, make any laws impairing the obligation of contracts, or grant titles of nobility. And states must have congressional permission to collect duties on exports or imports or to make agreements—called compacts—with other states.

Consistent with the belief in the sovereignty of the people, the Constitution applies important limitations to both the national and state governments. These restrictions, designed to protect individual liberties such as free speech and the rights of the accused, are set forth in Article I, Section 9, in the Bill of Rights, and in several other amendments.

Obligations to the States The Constitution obliges the national government to do three things for the states. First, the national government must guarantee each state a republican form of government. Enforcement of this guarantee has become a congressional responsibility. When Congress allows senators and representatives from a state to take their seats in Congress, it is in effect ruling that the state has a republican form of government.

The only extensive use of this guarantee came just after the Civil War. At that time, some southern states had refused to ratify the Civil War amendments granting citizenship rights to African Americans. Congress ruled that these states did not have a republican form of government. It refused to seat senators and representatives from those states until the states ratified the Civil War amendments and changed their laws to recognize African American rights.

Second, the national government must protect states from invasion and domestic violence. An attack by a foreign power on one or more states is considered an attack on the United States.

Congress has given the President authority to send federal troops to put down domestic disorders when state officials ask for help. Federal force has been used several times to help states deal with riots and internal disorders. In summer 1967 President Lyndon John-

GLOBAL CONNECTION

Comparing Governments
Parliamentary and Presidential Systems
In a parliamentary system, voters elect the members of parliament—the legislative branch of government. Parliament then chooses a prime minister, or leader of the executive branch. The prime minister chooses other members of parliament to make up a cabinet. The executives remain in office only as long as a majority in parliament supports them.

In a presidential system, voters elect the president, or chief executive, for a fixed term of office. Voters also elect members of the legislative branch. The powers of the two branches, however, are separate.

Examining the Connection
What are the advantages of electing an executive for a fixed term? What are the disadvantages?

son sent troops to Detroit to help control racial unrest and rioting. Johnson sent in the troops after Michigan's governor declared that the Detroit police and the Michigan National Guard could not cope with the widespread rioting and looting.

When national laws are being violated, federal property is threatened, or federal responsibilities are interfered with, the President may send troops without the request of local authorities—or even over local objections. In 1894, for example, President Grover Cleveland sent federal troops to Chicago to restore order during a strike of railroad workers even though the governor objected. During the strike, rioters had threatened federal property and interfered with mail delivery.

STUDY GUIDE

Themes in Government
Constitutional Interpretations
What authority does the United States Constitution provide to Congress by which it has the power to regulate nuclear power plants?

Critical Thinking Skills
Making Comparisons How do powers denied to the states by the Constitution compare with those denied to the national government by the Constitution?

Cooperative Learning Activity

Organize students into three groups to create posters with drawings or pictures from magazines and newspapers to illustrate the division of powers in the United States. Have one group illustrate the powers reserved for the national government. Have the second group illustrate the powers reserved for the state governments. Have the third group illustrate the powers shared by both governments. Students should write an explanation for each picture on the posters. Have each group choose a spokesperson to present their poster to the class.

During the 1950s and 1960s, Presidents Eisenhower and Kennedy used this power to stop state officials from blocking the integration of southern schools and universities. Eisenhower sent troops to Little Rock, Arkansas, in 1957. Kennedy used troops at the University of Mississippi in 1962 and the University of Alabama in 1963.

The national government has extended its definition of domestic violence to include natural disasters such as earthquakes, floods, hurricanes, and tornadoes. When one of these disasters strikes, the President often orders troops to aid disaster victims. The government also provides low-cost loans to help people repair damages.

Finally, the national government has the duty to respect the territorial integrity of each state. The national government cannot use territory that is part of an existing state to create a new state. To do so, the national government must have permission from the legislature of the state involved. The admission of West Virginia as a state in 1863 may be considered an exception to this rule. The western part of the state of Virginia requested admission to the Union after Virginia seceded.

Obligations of the States The states perform two important functions for the national government. State and local governments conduct and pay for elections of all national government officials, senators, representatives, and presidential electors. The

Constitution gives state legislatures the power to fix the "times, places, and manner" of election of senators and representatives (Article I, Section 4). Under the same provision, Congress has the authority to alter state election laws should it so desire.

In addition, the states play a key role in the amendment process. Under the Constitution, no amendment can be added to the Constitution unless three-fourths of the states approve it.

The Supreme Court as Umpire

Because federalism divides the powers of government, conflicts frequently arise between national and state governments. By settling such disputes, the federal court system, particularly the Supreme Court, plays a key role as an umpire for our federal system.

The question of national versus state power arose early in our nation's history. In 1819 in the landmark case of *McCulloch* v. *Maryland*, the Supreme Court ruled on a conflict between a state and national government. The state of Maryland had imposed a tax on a local branch of the Bank of the United States. The Court ruled in favor of the national government and held that in a conflict between the national government and a state government, the national government is supreme. This decision reinforced the supremacy clause of the Constitution.

---

1 SECTION REVIEW

Section Summary
The Constitution gives the national government certain specific powers and reserves other powers to the states or to the people. Under the Constitution the national government performs duties for the states, and the states, in turn, have obligations to the national government. The Supreme Court settles disputes between the states and the national government.

Checking for Understanding
Recalling Facts
1. Define delegated powers, expressed powers, enumerated powers, implied powers, necessary and proper clause, elastic clause, inherent powers, reserved powers, concurrent powers.
2. Name the part of the Constitution that is the basis for the implied powers of Congress.
3. Cite the kind of tax that the Constitution prohibits

the national government from levying on United States citizens.
4. Identify which law must yield when a state law and a national law conflict.
Exploring Themes
5. Federalism Why does the Tenth Amendment use the term *reserved* to describe the powers that belong to the people and the states?
6. Constitutional Interpretations How are disputes over the powers of the states versus the power of the national government settled?

Critical Thinking Skills
7. Making Comparisons How do the powers of the national and state governments compare?
8. Making Inferences Would it be inconsistent with federalism for the Constitution to be amended by Congress alone? Why or why not?

Assess

Check for Understanding
Have students complete Section 1 Review on page 129.

Meeting Objectives
Each section objective is tested by the Section Review questions that follow it in parentheses.
• Compare the powers of the national government with those reserved to the states and the people. (5, 6, 7, 8)
• Distinguish between the expressed, implied, inherent, reserved, and concurrent powers of government. (2, 3, 4, 5, 7)

Evaluate
📁 Section 1 Quiz
🖥 Testmaker

Reteach
Have students explain *expressed power, implied power, inherent power,* and *reserved power.*

Enrich
📁 Assign case 2 in *Supreme Court Case Studies* in the Teacher's Classroom Resources.

Close
Ask students how their government theme question has been answered by this section.

Section 1 Review Answers

1. Definitions of terms appear on pages indicated: **delegated powers,** 126; **expressed powers,** 126; **enumerated powers,** 126; **implied powers,** 126; **necessary and proper clause,** 126; **elastic clause,** 126; **inherent powers,** 127; **reserved powers,** 127; **concurrent powers,** 127
2. Article I, Section 8, the elastic clause
3. a tax on exports

4. the state law
5. People are source of all political authority; they gave some authority to the states, and the states gave authority to the national government through the United States Constitution.
6. Supreme Court usually rules in disputes between the states and the national government.

7. The federal government has only expressed, implied, and inherent powers. States have powers not delegated to national government or retained by the people.
8. Because the people through the states ratified the Constitution, the people through the states should have the power to amend it.

Focus

Bell Ringer

Ask students to decide which is more important—states' rights or national authority? Discuss students' answers.

Motivating Activity

Tell students to assume they are detectives. Ask them to find the three events which largely settled the issue of how national and state powers are related. (McCulloch *v.* Maryland, *the Civil War, and the civil rights movement*) How was the relationship resolved? *(in favor of national government)*

Vocabulary Precheck

Call on volunteers to tell what they think each key term and concept means. Have students check the accuracy of their definitions in the Glossary. **LEP**

Teach

Guided Practice

L1 Federalism Have students hold a round-table debate in which they defend either states' rights or nationalists' views on the role of the federal government in American politics.

L2 Analyzing Ideas Ask students to explain which constitutional provision that contributed to the expansion of power applies to the following actions of the national government: The Department of Education provides money for school districts to improve reading skills of migrant workers. *(power to tax and spend)* Congress passes law prohibiting restaurants from refusing to serve customers because of race. *(commerce power)* Have students explain their responses.

Changing Currents of Federalism

Early Federalists such as Alexander Hamilton, James Madison, and John Jay faced a difficult problem. They had to convince the people in the states that the new federalism of the Constitution was better than the old confederacy. While they deeply believed that the United States needed a strong central government to survive, they also knew that many people feared the centralization of power. The colonial experience with the power of British government was still fresh in people's minds.

Alexander Hamilton wrote:

The proposed Constitution, so far from implying an abolition of the State governments, makes them constituent parts of the national sovereignty, by allowing them a direct representation in the Senate, and leaves in their possession certain exclusive and very important portions of sovereign power. This fully corresponds . . . with the idea of a federal government.

—ALEXANDER HAMILTON, *THE FEDERALIST,* No. 9, NOVEMBER 23, 1787

While Hamilton's basic definition of federalism remains true, understanding the American federal system requires more than knowing the constitutional division of powers. Interpretations of how federalism affects national-state relationships have changed since 1787 and will no doubt continue to do so.

States' Rightists vs. Nationalists

Throughout American history, there have been two quite different views of how federalism should operate. One view—the **states' rights position**—favors state and local action in dealing with problems. A second view—the **nationalist position**—favors national action in dealing with these matters.

The States' Rights Position The states' rights view holds that the Constitution is a compact among the states. States' rightists argue that the states created the national government and gave it only certain limited powers. Any doubt about whether a power belongs to the national government or is reserved to the states should be settled in favor of the states. Because the national government is an agent of the states, all of its powers should be narrowly defined.

States' rights supporters believe state governments are closer to the people and better reflect their wishes than the national government. They tend to see the government in Washington, D.C., as heavy-handed and a threat to individual liberty.

At various points in United States history, the Supreme Court has accepted this view. Under Chief Justice Roger B. Taney (1836-1864), the Court often supported states' rights against powers of the national government. The same was true from 1918 to 1936, when the Court ruled new federal laws attempting to regulate child labor, industry, and agriculture in the states unconstitutional. During these times, the Court largely ignored John Marshall's principle of implied powers set out in *McCulloch* v. *Maryland*. Instead, it based its decision on the Tenth Amendment which says powers not delegated to the national government are reserved to the states or the people.

The Nationalist Position The nationalist position rejects the idea of the Constitution as merely a com-

---

SECTION PREVIEW

Objectives
After studying this section, you should be able to:
■ Differentiate the nationalist and the states' rights views of federalism.

■ Identify constitutional provisions that have expanded the power of the national government.

Key Terms and Concepts
states' rights position, nationalist position, income tax

Themes in Government
■ Federalism
■ Political Processes

Critical Thinking Skills
■ Making Comparisons
■ Identifying Central Issues

Classroom Resources for Section 2

📁 Guided Reading Activities
📁 Reproducible Lesson Plans
📁 Enrichment Activities 4
📁 Section 2 Quiz

▪ Testmaker
The Living Constitution
SAT Practice Tests
Writer's Guidebook

pact among the states. Nationalists deny that the national government is an agent of the states. They argue that it was the people, not the states, who created both the national government and the states. Therefore, the national government is not subordinate to the states.

Nationalists believe the powers expressly delegated to the national government should be expanded as necessary to carry out the people's will. They hold that the "necessary and proper" clause of the Consti-

tution means that Congress has the right to adopt any means that are convenient and useful to carry out its delegated powers. They also claim that the reserved powers of the states should not limit how the national government can use its own powers.

Nationalists believe the national government stands for all the people, while each state speaks only for part of the people. They look to the national government to take the lead in solving major social and economic problems facing the nation.

Focus on Freedom

THE FEDERALIST, NO. 10

James Madison wrote several articles supporting ratification of the Constitution for a New York newspaper. In the excerpt below Madison argues for the idea of a federal republic.

By a faction, I understand a number of citizens . . . who are united and actuated by some common impulse . . . adverse to the rights of other citizens. . . .

The inference to which we are brought is that the *causes* of faction cannot be removed and that relief is only to be sought in the means of controlling its *effects*. . . .

A republic, by which I mean a government in which the scheme of representation takes place . . . promises the cure for which we are seeking. . . .

The two great points of difference between a democracy and a republic are: first, the delegation of the government, in the latter, to a small number of citizens elected by the rest; secondly, the greater number of citizens, and greater sphere of country, over which the latter may be extended.

The effect of the first difference is . . . to refine and enlarge the public views by passing them through the medium of a chosen body of citizens, whose wisdom may best discern the true interest of their country, and whose patriotism and love of justice will be least likely to sacrifice it to temporary or partial considerations. . . .

— *The Federalist*, No. 10
James Madison

The debate over ratification aroused strong feelings. Patrick Henry challenged the Framers' use of "We the People," instead of "We the States."

And here I would make this inquiry of those worthy characters who composed a part of the late federal Convention. I am sure they were fully

impressed with the necessity of forming a great consolidated government instead of a confederation. . . . and the danger of such a government is, to my mind, very striking . . . Who authorized them to speak the language of "We, the people," instead of, "We, the states"? . . . If the states be not the agents of this compact, it must be one great, consolidated, national government of the people of all the states. . . .

If consolidation proves to be as mischievous to this country as it has been to other countries, what will the poor inhabitants of this country do? This government will . . . destroy the state governments and swallow the liberties of the people, without giving previous notice. . . .

Mr. Chairman, the necessity of a Bill of Rights appears to me to be greater in this government than ever it was in any government before. . . .

—Virginia Ratifying Convention Debate
Patrick Henry

Examining the Document

Reviewing the Facts
1. Identify the "chosen body of citizens" to which Madison refers.
2. Describe what fears caused Patrick Henry to suggest a Bill of Rights was necessary.

Critical Thinking Skills
3. Understanding Cause and Effect Why does Patrick Henry object to the use of "We the People" by the delegates to the Constitutional Convention?

Chapter 4: The Federal System   131

Focus on Freedom

The Federalist became the first analysis of modern federalism and influenced the works of other political scientists such as Great Britain's John Stuart Mill. Ask: Was Patrick Henry voicing a nationalist position or a states' rights position? *(states' rights)* Have students cite evidence to support their answers.

Answers

1. the House of Representatives
2. fears that the national government would become powerful enough to remove individual rights
3. He believes that the delegates to the convention were authorized to speak for the states, not for all the people. In using "We the people" they made the government a national contract with the people rather than one among the states.

L3 Debate Have students debate whether state-centered or nation-centered federalism is best in modern times. Students should address questions such as: Which is more effective and appropriate? What are the advantages and disadvantages of each system? Will national power continue to grow in the future? Why or why not?

GLENCOE TECHNOLOGY

Focus on Government
Video 5
Lecture Launcher:
The Federal System
Running Time: 2:29
Videodisc 1, Chap. 5
VHS Tape 1, Begins 13:39

Background

The New Deal represented a turning point in the role of the federal government. Yet, the New Deal era only began the process of bringing the federal government into the everyday lives of Americans. A great increase in national government spending came in the late 1960s and the early 1970s, when

recession and double-digit inflation significantly expanded the new entitlement programs enacted during the Johnson administration. Ronald Reagan's efforts to cut federal social programs represented the first real effort to change the direction of the New Deal since the 1930s.

Independent Practice

L1 Outlining Have students outline Section 2 using the section's main heads and subheads.

LEP

L2 Informative Writing Have students research and write a short paper comparing President Clinton's and President Reagan's approaches to federalism.

Assess

Check for Understanding

Have students complete Section 2 Review on page 133.

Meeting Objectives

Each section objective is tested by the Section Review questions that follow in parentheses.

- Differentiate the nationalist and the states' rights views of federalism. (5, 7)
- Identify constitutional provisions that have expanded the power of the national government. (2, 3, 4)

The Supreme Court established the nationalist position in 1819 in *McCulloch* v. *Maryland*, but it really gained ground in the Court during the late 1930s. At that time, the Great Depression gripped the nation. The national government under President Franklin D. Roosevelt responded by starting new social welfare and public works programs. At first, the Court ruled these programs were unconstitutional. As the Depression grew worse, however, the Court adjusted its views. It supported the expansion of the national government's powers in order to deal with the nation's terrible economic problems.

Growing National Government

A major factor shaping the development of American federalism has been the growth in the size and power of the national government. Over the years this expansion came largely at the expense of the states.

A key reason for the change is that the Constitution's flexibility has allowed the Supreme Court, Congress, and the President to stretch the government's powers to meet the needs of a modern industrial nation. The expansion of the national government's powers has been based on three major constitutional provisions: (1) the war powers; (2) the power to regulate interstate commerce; and (3) the power to tax and spend.

War Powers The national government has power to wage war. This authority has greatly expanded the federal government's power because in today's world national defense involves more than simply putting troops in the field. Such factors as the condition of the economy and the strength of the educational system can affect the nation's military capabilities.

Commerce Power The Constitution gives Congress the authority to regulate commerce. Supreme Court decisions have expanded this power.

The courts today consistently interpret the term *commerce* to mean nearly all activities concerned with the production, buying, selling, and transporting of goods. In 1964, for example, Congress passed the Civil Rights Act forbidding racial discrimination in public accommodations such as hotels and restaurants. In upholding this law the Supreme Court reasoned: (a) racial discrimination by innkeepers and restaurant owners makes it difficult for the people discriminated against to travel and thus restricts the flow of interstate commerce; (b) Congress has the power to regulate commerce; (c) therefore, Congress may pass laws against racial discrimination.

Congress has no specific constitutional authority to pass laws to promote the general welfare. Congress does, however, have authority to raise taxes and spend money for such purposes.

The Sixteenth Amendment, ratified in 1913, gave Congress the power to tax incomes. The **income tax** levied on individual earnings has become the major source of money for the national government. It has given the national government much greater financial resources than any state or local government.

Finally, Congress has used its taxing power to increase the national government's authority in two ways. First, taxes may be used to regulate businesses. For example, Congress has put such heavy taxes on certain dangerous products that it is not profitable for companies to make and sell them. Second, Congress may use taxes to influence states to adopt certain kinds of programs. Federal law allows employers to deduct from their federal taxes any state taxes they pay to support state unemployment programs. This federal tax break helped persuade all the states to set up their own unemployment insurance programs.

Federal Aid to the States

A continuing issue of federalism has been the competition between states for national government spending. Each state wants to get its fair share of national government projects because this spending affects the economies of every state.

Politics and Spending The recent population shift from the states of the Northeast and the Midwest to

132 UNIT 1: FOUNDATIONS OF AMERICAN GOVERNMENT

Critical Thinking Activity

Identifying Central Issues Tell students that the pattern of spending, taxing, and providing grants in the federal system is called *fiscal federalism*. As such, money has become the basis of the national government's relations with the states. However, many of the changes in federal aid policies during the 1980s turned responsibility for federal programs such as welfare and education over to state and local government. This involved requiring states to "match" federal funding if they wanted to retain certain programs. Identify three central issues that affect the relations between the states and the federal government in regards to "fiscal federalism."

the states of the South and the Southwest has shifted power in Washington, D.C. More federal government spending has started to go to the southern states and less to the northern states.

Direct federal aid to the states is another political issue. The national government has historically provided different types of aid to the states. In 1862 Congress passed a law giving nearly 6 million acres of public land to the states for the support of colleges. Since the 1950s, federal aid to state and local governments has increased tremendously.

State and local officials have learned that along with more federal aid comes greater federal control and red tape. This is because many federal-aid programs provide money only if the state and local governments are willing to meet conditions set by Congress.

Shifting Responsibilities In recent years, some Presidents and some congressional leaders have wanted to shift the balance of power in the federal system back toward the states. In 1969, for example, President Nixon called for a "New Federalism" that would return more authority to state and local governments.

In 1982 President Reagan called for sweeping changes in federal-aid policies. These included turning responsibility for dozens of federal programs in areas like education and welfare over to state and local governments. President Bush continued this policy, decreasing federal aid along with federal con-

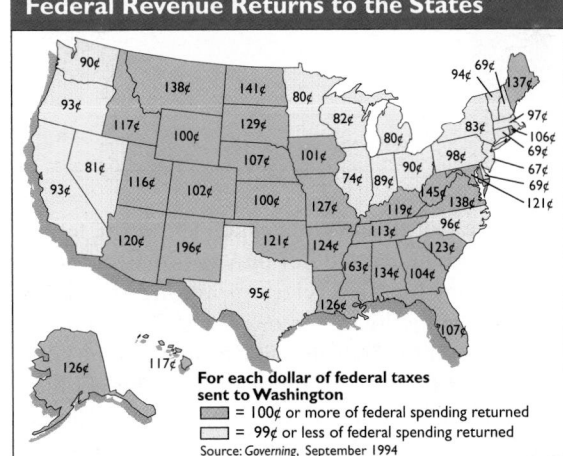

Federal Revenue Returns to the States

For each dollar of federal taxes sent to Washington
- ▨ = 100¢ or more of federal spending returned
- ☐ = 99¢ or less of federal spending returned

Source: *Governing*, September 1994

◉ Map Study
Federal revenue, collected largely from taxes in the 50 states, is distributed unevenly across the states.
How does the distribution of aid reflect a shift in political power?

trol. Between 1980 and 1990 federal grants declined dramatically—from $50 billion to $19 billion.

President Clinton has once again emphasized federal government power and responsibility. Obviously, the federal system is dynamic. The relationship between federal and state governments is affected by the policies of each administration and of Congress.

<hr/>

2 SECTION REVIEW

Section Summary
Because the national government has responded to national needs since the time of the Constitution, the national government has generally gained power at the expense of the states. Some recent Presidents have led an effort to slow the expansion of national government powers.

Checking For Understanding
Reviewing Facts
1. Define states' rights position, nationalist position, income tax.
2. Identify the clause of the Constitution that nationalists use to support their interpretation of the concept of federalism.
3. Explain the circumstances surrounding the emergence of the nationalist position now favored by the Supreme Court.

4. List three constitutional provisions that have been the basis for the tremendous growth of the national government.

Exploring Themes
5. Federalism How did the Depression of the 1930s affect the relative power of the states and national governments?
6. Political Processes Why are states in the South and Southwest gaining more influence in Washington, D.C.?

Critical Thinking Skills
7. Making Comparisons What is the major difference between the states' rights and the nationalist views of federalism?
8. Identifying Central Issues Why did Presidents Nixon, Reagan, and Bush turn over responsibility for federal programs to state and local governments?

Chapter 4, Section 2
Lesson Plan, pages 130–133

Chart Study Answer
States in the Northeast and Northcentral regions receive less aid per dollar of taxes.

Evaluate
📁 Section 2 Quiz
⬜ Testmaker

Reteach
Create a chart on the chalkboard of the three constitutional provisions leading to the growth of the national government. Have students list the government's powers under each provision and explain each.

Enrich
📁 Have students complete activity 4 in *Enrichment Activities* in the Teacher's Classroom Resources.

Have students find out more about the federal grant system: How much aid was given to state and local governments between 1980 and the present? What kind of grants are available? Encourage students to present their information in chart form.

Close

Have students read the Section Summary and explain how the relationship has changed between federal and state government.

<hr/>

Section 2 Review Answers

1. Definitions of terms appear on pages indicated: **states' rights position,** 130; **nationalist position,** 130; **income tax,** 132
2. "necessary and proper" clause
3. Supreme Court's nationalist position emerged during the Depression when new federal laws were needed to deal with the economic problems.
4. war powers, power to regulate interstate commerce, and power to tax and spend to promote the general welfare
5. The Depression presented an economic problem that the states could not solve; the national government assumed greater powers in order to address the crisis.
6. A shift of population from the North and Midwest has given these regions greater representation and thus, greater power.

7. States' rights position favors state and local action in dealing with social and economic problems. Nationalist position favors national government action in dealing with these matters.
8. These Presidents wanted to slow the expansion of federal government powers and restore power to the states and local governments.

Focus

Bell Ringer

Write the following on the chalkboard for students to answer in writing:

What happens when a person accused of a crime in one state flees to another state?

Motivating Activity

Discuss students' Bell Ringer answers and ask if they know the term that describes the process of returning a suspect to the state where the crime was committed. *(extradition)* Tell students this section explains relations among the states.

Vocabulary Precheck

Ask students to speculate on the meaning of each term and concept. Then have them check their guesses by finding the definition in the section text. **LEP**

Teach

Guided Practice

L1 Making a Flow Chart Have volunteers make a flow chart on the chalkboard that shows the basic steps in the admission of new states. **LEP**

L2 Federalism Work with students to chart on the chalkboard examples of the constitutional provisions related to interstate relations. Use the headings: *full faith and credit, privileges and immunities, extradition,* and *interstate compacts* and ask students to give examples of each.

Relations Among the States

The Constitution, in establishing the federal system, defined not only national-state relations but also relations among the states. Conflicts and jealousies among the states had been a major reason for drafting the Constitution in 1787. One way the Constitution dealt with this problem was to strengthen the national government. The second way was to set the legal ground rules for relations among the states. Because each state retains much power and independence, these rules help to assure cooperation among the states.

Interstate Relations

Article IV of the Constitution requires the states to do the following: (1) give "full faith and credit" to the laws, records, and court decisions of other states; (2) give one another's citizens all the "privileges and immunities" of its own citizens; and (3) **extradite**— that is, return to a state—criminals and fugitives who flee across state lines to escape justice.

Full Faith and Credit The Constitution states that "Full faith and credit shall be given in each state to the public acts, records, and judicial proceedings of every other state." In other words, each state must recognize the laws and legal proceedings of the other states. For example, a car registration of one state must be accepted by all the other states. This clause applies only to **civil law**, or laws relating to disputes between individuals, groups, or with the state. One state cannot enforce another state's criminal law.

The need for this kind of rule in the federal system is obvious. Without it, each state could treat all other states like foreign countries. Further, each state could become a haven for people who want to avoid their legal duties and responsibilities.

The coverage of the "full faith and credit" rule is quite broad. *Public acts* refers to civil laws passed by state legislatures. *Records* means such documents as mortgages, deeds, leases, wills, marriage licenses, car registrations, and birth certificates. The phrase *judicial proceedings* refers to the outcomes of court actions such as judgments to pay a debt.

Judicial decisions in civil matters in one state will be honored and enforced in all states. If, for example, a person in Texas loses a lawsuit requiring a specific payment, and moves to Illinois to avoid paying the money, Illinois courts will enforce the Texas decision.

Privileges and Immunities The Founders knew that when citizens traveled between states, they might be discriminated against. A citizen of Delaware, for example, might be treated as an alien in Virginia or Maryland. Therefore, the Constitution provides that "the citizens of each state shall be entitled to all privileges and immunities of citizens in several states." As interpreted by the Supreme Court, this clause means that one state may not discriminate unreasonably against citizens of another state. It must provide citizens of other states the same privileges and immunities it provides its own citizens.

The courts have never given a complete listing of "privileges and immunities." Included, however, are rights to pass through or live in any state; use the

---

SECTION PREVIEW

Objectives
After studying this section, you should be able to:
■ Explain how the Constitution regulates interstate relations.
■ Describe the role of interstate compacts.
■ Characterize the restrictions the

national government can put on the admission of new states.

Key Terms and Concepts
extradite, civil law, interstate compact, enabling act

Themes in Government
■ Federalism
■ Public Policy

Critical Thinking Skills
■ Expressing Problems Clearly
■ Demonstrating Reasoned Judgment

134 UNIT 1: FOUNDATIONS OF AMERICAN GOVERNMENT

Classroom Resources for Section 3

📁 Guided Reading Activities
📁 Reproducible Lesson Plans
📁 Section 3 Quiz
💾 Testmaker

The Living Constitution
SAT Practice Tests
Writer's Guidebook

courts; make contracts; buy, sell, and hold property; and marry.

On the other hand, states may make reasonable discriminations against nonresidents. The privileges and immunities clause does not apply to voting, serving on juries, or using certain public facilities. All states require that a person live in a state for a certain amount of time before becoming a voter or public official. States may also require individuals to establish residency before they can practice such professions as medicine, dentistry, or law.

In addition, nonresidents of a state do not have the same right to attend publicly supported institutions such as schools or to use state hospitals as do residents of the state. Nonresidents may be required to pay higher fees for hunting or fishing licenses than residents. State colleges and universities may, and usually do, charge higher tuition fees to students from other states than to resident students.

Extradition Because states are basically independent of one another, some means is needed to prevent criminals from escaping justice simply by going from one state to another. For this reason, the Constitution provides:

A person charged in any state with treason, felony, or other crime, who shall flee from justice, and be found in another State, shall, on demand of the executive authority of the State from which he fled, be delivered up, to be removed to the State having jurisdiction of the crime.
—Article IV, Section 2

This clause provides for the extradition of fugitives. Congress has made the governor of the state to which fugitives have fled responsible for returning them.

The Supreme Court has softened the meaning of the extradition provision by ruling that a governor is not required to return a fugitive to another state. Although extradition is routine in the vast majority of cases, occasionally a governor will refuse. For example, a Michigan governor once refused to return a fugitive to Arkansas because, the governor said, prison conditions in Arkansas were inhumane. Arkansas officials could do nothing about the governor's decision. In recent years Congress has acted to close the extradition loophole by making it a federal crime to flee from one state to another in order to avoid prosecution for a felony.

Interstate Compacts The Constitution requires the states to settle their differences with one another

State Colleges for State Residents
State-supported services and institutions, such as hospitals and colleges, generally require nonresidents to pay higher fees than residents. **Law** Why are states able to discriminate against nonresidents in some instances?

STUDY GUIDE

Themes in Government
Federalism **Why does the "full faith and credit" clause apply only to civil law?**

Critical Thinking Skills
Expressing Problems Clearly **What difficulties might a person have in moving from New York to**

Virginia if there were no Article IV in the Constitution?

L3 **Public Policy** Discuss the intentions of the Framers of the Constitution concerning interstate relations. Ask: Why did the Framers of the Constitution pen several constitutional clauses on interstate relations? *(to assure cooperation among the states)* What problems did they foresee? *(conflicts, jealousies, discrimination against nonresidents)* Do problems still persist between states? Give examples. *(yes; air and water pollution, water rights, acid rain)*

Independent Practice

L1 **Interpreting Visuals** Have students find pictures that illustrate interstate relations. Below each picture, have them write a sentence explaining which constitutional provision applies to the illustration. **LEP**

Caption Answer
The privileges and immunities clause does not apply to use of certain public facilities and institutions.

STUDY GUIDE

Theme Answer
One state cannot enforce another state's criminal law.

Critical Thinking Answer
States could charge for or deny a person passage, refuse to recognize a driver's license, and so on. Virginia could refuse to recognize legal documents from New York.

Special Needs Strategy

Auditory Disability Some students with auditory processing difficulties have trouble following directions and understanding the information given orally in class. To assess which students may have such problems, have students write your orally given instructions for this section in their notebooks. For students who still have problems, you might write all directions on the chalkboard or on an overhead. Keep directions as simple as possible to avoid confusion. Number the steps in your instructions when possible.

Caption Answer
Without them, each state might act as a separate nation.

L2 Geography Have students investigate states' disputes over water rights to the Colorado River. Suggest students read "The Colorado: A River Drained Dry" in *National Geographic*, June 1991, which provides an overview and dramatic visual portrayal of the issues in the disputes.

L3 Informative Writing Have students research and write a report on Puerto Rico's political status. Ask students to address the following questions: What disadvantages and advantages are there in Puerto Rico becoming a state? Do you predict Puerto Rico will become a state in the future? Why or why not?

Caption Answer
to promote harmony among the states

STUDY GUIDE

Theme Answer
It tries to get governors to return fugitives to the state from which they fled.

Critical Thinking Answer
To ensure a valid election a state must limit voting to residents.

Assess

Check for Understanding

Have students complete Section 3 Review on page 137.

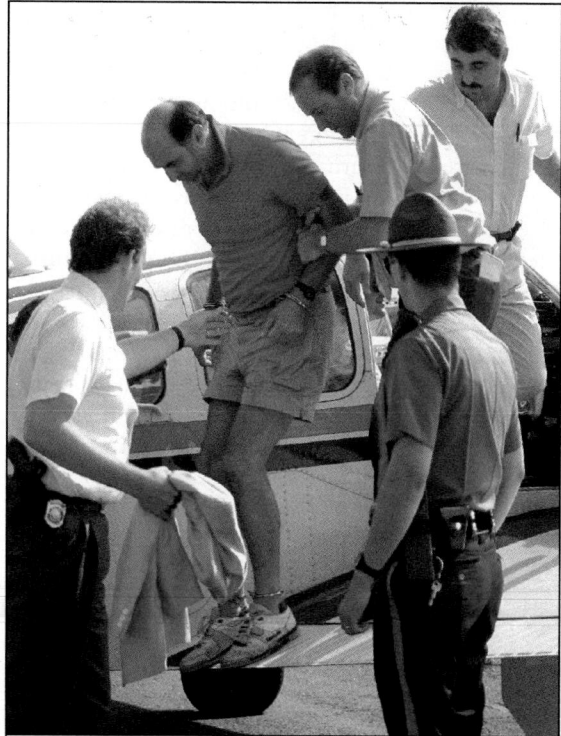

Fugitive From Justice Returned
The Constitution mandates that states cooperate in extraditing fugitives. **Law** Why does the Constitution provide rules for interstate relations?

them involved boundary disputes between states. As society has become more complex, however, the number of compacts sent to Congress has increased. Today nearly 200 compacts are in force. Many of them involve several states.

States use compacts to deal with such matters as air and water pollution, pest control, toll bridges, and transportation. New Jersey and New York helped start this trend in 1921 when they created the Port of New York Authority to develop and manage harbor facilities in the area. Many compacts today deal with the development and conservation of natural resources such as wildlife, fish, water, coal, and oil. Others deal with the transport and disposal of hazardous waste materials. Interstate compacts have become an important way for the states to deal with regional problems without resorting to national government intervention.

Lawsuits Between States Sometimes states are unable to resolve their disputes by any of the methods just described. When this happens, a lawsuit may result. Since 1789 more than 220 disputes between states have wound up in court. Suits between states are heard in the United States Supreme Court, the only court in which one state may sue another.

States bring each other to court for a variety of reasons. Cases in the West often involve water rights. Arizona, California, and Colorado have gone to the Court in disputes over water from the Colorado River. Other cases have involved sewage from one state polluting the water in another state. Still other cases are disputes over boundary lines. Arkansas and Tennessee had such a dispute as recently as 1970.

without the use of force. The principal way in which states may do this is to negotiate **interstate compacts.** Such compacts are written agreements between two or more states. The national government or foreign countries may also be part of an interstate compact.

Congress must approve interstate compacts. This requirement prevents states from threatening the Union by making alliances among themselves. Once a compact has been signed and approved by Congress, it is binding on all states signing it. Its terms are enforceable by the Supreme Court.

Interstate compacts were not very important until the twentieth century. Before 1900, only 13 compacts had received congressional approval. Most of

Admission of New States

Thirty-seven states have joined the Union since the original thirteen formed the nation. Most of these states became territories before taking steps to gain statehood. What procedures do these territories then follow to become states?

STUDY GUIDE

Themes in Government
Public Policy How does extradition attempt to get the states to cooperate in administering criminal justice?

Critical Thinking Skills
Demonstrating Reasoned Judgment Why does the

"privileges and immunities" clause not apply to voting?

Cooperative Learning Activity

Organize students into several groups. Assign each group three states to make a comparative study of public acts passed by state legislatures. Have the groups compare the following policy areas: drinking age, driver's license requirements, education, corrections, business regulations, voting requirements, and state income tax. Remind students that cultural, social, and economic characteristics influence states' policies. Within each group the students should discuss how to research and organize the information, present the information to the class, and then assign individuals to work on these tasks.

Congress Admits New States The Constitution gives Congress the power to admit new states to the Union. There are two restrictions on this power. First, as noted earlier, no state may be formed by taking territory from one or more states without the consent of the states involved and of Congress. Second, acts of admission, like all laws, are subject to presidential veto.

The procedure for admission begins when Congress passes an enabling act. An **enabling act,** when signed by the President, enables the people of the territory to prepare a constitution. Then, after the constitution has been drafted and approved by a popular vote in the area, it is submitted to Congress. If Congress is still agreeable, it passes an act admitting the state.

Conditions for Admission Congress or the President may impose certain conditions before admitting a new state, including requiring changes in the drafted constitution submitted by a territory. In 1911 President Taft vetoed the congressional resolution admitting Arizona because he objected to a section in the Arizona constitution dealing with the recall of judges. Arizona then modified the constitution, and the next year it became the forty-eighth state. When Alaska entered the union in 1959, it was prohibited from ever claiming title to any lands legally held by Native Americans or Aleuts in Alaska. Ohio was admitted in 1803 on the condition that for five years it not tax any public lands sold by the national government within its borders.

The Supreme Court has ruled that the President or Congress may impose conditions for admission of a state as they wish. Once a state is admitted, however, those conditions may be enforced only if they do not interfere with the new state's authority to manage its own internal affairs like any other state. Once Arizona was admitted as a state, it promptly amended its constitution to restore the deleted provisions about the recall of judges.

When Oklahoma was admitted in 1907, Congress forbade it to move its capital from the city of Guthrie until 1913. The Supreme Court, however, upheld the right of Oklahoma to move the capital to Oklahoma City in 1911. The Court declared that

*T*he power to locate its own seat of government, and to determine when and how it shall be changed from one place to another, and to appropriate its own public funds for that purpose, are essentially and peculiarly state powers. . . . Has Oklahoma been admitted upon an equal footing with the original states? If she has . . . [Oklahoma] may determine for her own people the proper location of the local seat of government.

—Justice Horace H. Lurton,
Coyle v. Smith, 1911

Equality of the States Once admitted to the Union, each state is equal to every other state. No state has more privileges or fewer obligations than any other. Each state is also legally separate from every other state in the Union.

---

3 SECTION REVIEW

Section Summary
The Constitution provides rules for interstate relations. These include rules governing relations between states and citizens of other states and relations among states themselves.

Checking for Understanding
Recalling Facts
1. Define extradite, civil law, interstate compact, enabling act.
2. List the three constitutional provisions that are aimed at promoting cooperation among the states.
3. Cite the conditions that may be imposed by Congress or the President on territories seeking statehood.

Exploring Themes
4. Federalism What are the goals of interstate compacts and how are they enforced?
5. Public Policy Give four examples of how states make reasonable discriminations against non-residents.

Critical Thinking Skills
6. Expressing Problems Clearly States may make interstate compacts dealing with the transportation and disposal of hazardous waste materials. What problems do you think these compacts address?
7. Demonstrating Reasoned Judgment Why does the "privileges and immunities" clause not apply to voting or serving on juries?

Meeting Objectives
Each section objective is tested by the Section Review questions that follow it in parentheses.
• Explain how the Constitution regulates interstate relations. (2, 6, 8)
• Describe the role of interstate compacts. (3, 5, 7)
• Characterize the restrictions the national government can put on the admission of new states. (4)

Evaluate
 Section 3 Quiz
 Testmaker

Reteach
Have students write a lesson summary using the section's key terms and concepts.

Enrich
Ask students to research specific interstate compacts their state has negotiated.

Close

Ask students to list ways in which this section addresses the theme *federalism.*

Section 3 Review Answers

1. Definitions of terms appear on pages indicated: **extradite,** 134; **civil law,** 134; **interstate compact,** 136; **enabling act,** 137
2. States must give "full faith and credit" to the law of other states, give citizens from every state the same privileges and immunities, and extradite fugitives who flee across state lines.
3. Congress or the President may ask for changes in the draft constitution a territory submits. Also, the Supreme Court has ruled that Congress or the President may impose other conditions as they wish.
4. States enter into compacts to settle differences and to deal with regional problems without resorting to the national government. They must be approved by Congress and are enforced by the Supreme Court.
5. States limit the practice of law to residents and require established residency for voting, holding public office, and practicing medicine, dentistry, or law; charge higher fees for hunting and fishing licenses for nonresidents, and charge higher tuition for out-of-state students.
6. States try to control transportation of hazardous waste within their borders because of the dangers involved. They also try to find safe ways to dispose of these materials. Problems arise when one state has different regulations dealing with these materials than does a nearby state.
7. Nonresidents are less likely to know the candidates or to have an interest in state's political affairs. Juries are composed of citizens who are registered to vote.

STUDY AND WRITING SKILLS

Focus

Ask students what they think are the steps to writing a good paragraph. List their answers on the chalkboard. Then have them read the first paragraph and the Explanation steps.

Teach

Have students analyze the paragraph on federalism using the steps in the Explanation. Ask: what idea explains or expands the idea of the topic sentence? *(the position switch of business groups)* What specific example supports this idea? *(auto industry)* Follow the same process for the paragraph from the Supreme Court decision. *(The first sentence is the topic sentence. Discussion of the Constitution and the nature of interstate commerce extend the idea.)*

Assess

Have students complete the **Practice** exercise.

Close

Select a paragraph from the chapter and reorder the sentences on the chalkboard. Have students rewrite the paragraph in a proper order. Have students evaluate one another's paragraphs.

Writing a Paragraph

Writing a good paragraph involves stating information clearly and arranging it in a logical order. Knowing how to write a well-organized paragraph helps you to express your ideas clearly. You can use this skill for many purposes, from writing a speech to writing the answers to the essay questions on your next test.

Explanation

To write a good paragraph, follow these steps:
• Decide on the main idea you want to express and write it in sentence form. This will be the first, or topic, sentence of the paragraph.
• Support the main idea. Include sentences that add information and explain or expand the main idea expressed in the topic sentence.
• Evaluate your paragraph. Does the topic sentence state the main idea clearly? Do the other sentences support the main idea?

Read the paragraph below. The topic sentence clearly states the main idea. *Today federalism is more complicated than simply a struggle between nationalists and supporters of states' rights.* The two sentences that follow explain the two different views.

Today federalism is more complicated than simply a struggle between nationalists and supporters of states' rights. Sometimes states' rights supporters and national government supporters switch sides, depending on which view best serves their interests at the time. For example, since 1930 most business groups have supported states' rights. These groups believe state courts and state legislatures are more likely to make decisions favorable to business than to the national government. In 1966, however, the auto industry took a nationalist position when it supported national auto safety standards. Why? The industry realized that the national standards were likely to be more moderate than the tough state regulations set by California and New York, where automakers sold nearly 20 percent of their cars.

In the mid-1930s, controversy raged over the federal government's power to regulate interstate commerce. The following excerpt is from the Supreme Court's decision invalidating the National Recovery Administration, a New Deal program that gave broad power to the federal government. Note again that the topic sentence clearly states the main idea.

It is not the province of the Court to consider the economic advantages or disadvantages of such a centralized system. It is sufficient to say that the Federal Constitution does not provide for it. Our growth and development have called for wide use of the commerce power of the federal government in its control over the expanded activities of interstate commerce, and in protecting that commerce from burdens, interferences, and conspiracies to restrain and monopolize it. But the authority of the federal government may not be pushed to such an extreme as to destroy the distinction, which the commerce clause itself establishes, between commerce "among the several States" and the internal concerns of a State. . . .

Practice

Follow the steps described above to place the sentences below in the correct order for a paragraph.
1. Reserved powers are the powers the states hold in the federal system.
2. These powers are the ones the Constitution does not give the national government.
3. The Constitution reserves power to each of the states.
4. At the same time, however, these powers are not denied to the states.

Additional Practice

To practice this skill, see **Reinforcing the Skill** on page 145.

138 UNIT 1: FOUNDATIONS OF AMERICAN GOVERNMENT

Practice Answers

Logical order version: 1, 2, 3, 4

📁 For additional practice, have students complete activity 4 in *Skill Reinforcement Activities* in the Teacher's Classroom Resources.

Federalism and Political Life

Federalism influences the practice of politics and government. It affects government policy-making, the political party system, the political activities of citizens, and the quality of life in the 50 states.

Federalism and Public Policy

A policy is a stated course of action. The high school principal says, "It is our policy that students not park in the teachers' parking lots." The local store announces, "It is our policy to prosecute all shoplifters." In each example, people are defining courses of action they take in response to problems that occur over and over again. Announcing a policy—whether on student parking or on shoplifting—means that a person or organization has decided upon a conscious, deliberate way of handling similar issues.

The course of action a government takes in response to some issue or problem is called public policy. Federalism affects public policy-making in two ways. First, it affects how and where new policies are made in the United States. Second, it introduces limits on government policy-making.

The existence of 50 states and thousands of local governments encourages experimenting with new policies and ideas. Federalism permits states and localities to serve as proving grounds where new policies can be developed and tested. Georgia, for example, was the first state to allow 18-year-olds to vote. That right has since been given to all Americans through the Twenty-sixth Amendment. In 1976 Colorado pioneered the use of sunset laws. **Sunset laws** require periodic checks of government agencies to see if they are

King Expresses His Dream
Major civil rights marches prompted the federal government to pass the Voting Rights Bill of 1965.
History How does federalism affect local policies?

still needed. Since 1976, 35 other states have passed such laws. In California local interest groups concerned with the environment were able to get the state to start new air-pollution control programs. The California laws were later used as a model and influenced Congress to pass air-pollution laws. In November

CHAPTER 4: THE FEDERAL SYSTEM 139

Focus

Bell Ringer

Ask students to answer the following question in writing:

What is the school's policy on attendance?

Motivating Activity

Discuss students' answers to the Bell Ringer question. Ask: What is the school's policy on eligibility of transfer students to play sports? What is a store's policy for returning merchandise? Point out that this section addresses policies established by national, state, and local governments which are called *public policies.*

Vocabulary Precheck

Call on students to read aloud the definitions for each term and concept from the Glossary. Then have them restate each definition in their own words. **LEP**

Teach

Guided Practice

L1 Identifying Main Ideas
Write the following on the chalkboard: *How Federalism Affects Public Policy.* Make two columns labeled *States Serve as Proving Ground* and *National Government Imposes Policy on States.* Have students give examples for each column. **LEP**

Caption Answer
National laws can override local laws.

Point out to students that corporations as well as individuals are recycling. For example, Mc-Donalds changed its bleached white carryout bags to brown ones made of recycled materials. Ask students how they could encourage corporations to participate in recycling.

Have students complete activity 4 in *Participating in Government* in the Teacher's Classroom Resources.

L2 **Analyzing Ideas** Write on the chalkboard: In what ways do citizens participating in government influence public policy? Have students share their ideas. *(support candidates that share their views, work in government jobs, work with interest groups)*

L3 **Class Debate** Have all students prepare a list of strengths and weaknesses of a federalist system. Then choose six students—three in favor of federalism, three against it—to debate this topic:

Federalism is too complicated, somewhat unwieldy, and expensive to operate in the United States. **3C, 8G**

STUDY GUIDE

Theme Answer
It has prevented one party from gaining a monopoly of power by enabling each party to win elections at some levels and locations.

Critical Thinking Answer
that the best solution often results from compromise, that rivalry is good, that without rival parties democratic government would die

---

PARTICIPATING IN GOVERNMENT

Recycling

Until recently few people thought it important to recycle their trash. Today, however, more communities are organizing recycling programs, and more people are participating. Why has recycling become essential to waste management in the United States? What are your responsibilities in participating in such programs?

Environmentalists estimate that the amount of waste from homes and businesses in the United States has more than doubled since 1960. Communities are running out of land available for solid waste sites. Incinerators, which are used to burn trash, pollute the air. In addition, the cost of these methods of waste disposal continues to rise. For these reasons, most communities have adopted recycling programs to reduce the amount of waste and save money.

Newspapers, aluminum and steel cans, plastic containers, glass, and cardboard are some materials that can be recycled. Many communities have recycling centers where residents can bring these materials. Other communities have curbside recycling programs in which recyclables are picked up in front of residents' homes.

Investigating Further

Many recycling centers depend on volunteers to help unload cars, sort materials, or bundle newspapers. Find out how you can participate in your community's program. Encourage others to join you in volunteering to help.

1976, Florida passed a **sunshine law** prohibiting public officials from holding meetings not open to the public.

Policy may also originate at the national level. Sometimes the national government will impose new policies on states in which local pressure groups have resisted change. Some of the great political struggles in the nation's history have occurred over such efforts. In the late 1950s and early 1960s, African Americans were struggling to win voting and other civil rights in many states. State and local officials were resisting these changes. Eventually, African American leaders attracted national attention and support for their cause. As a result, they were able to influence the national government to force the states to change civil rights and voting policies.

Federalism and Political Parties

Rival political parties are a key element of democratic government. Politics in America, however, is not a desperate all-or-nothing struggle for control of the national government because federalism makes victories in state and local elections possible. Each political party has a chance to win some elections somewhere in the system. In this way, federalism helps lessen the risk of one political party gaining a monopoly on political powers.

After the Civil War, in the late 1860s, the Democratic party went into a long period of decline on the national level. Yet the party survived because Democratic candidates managed to maintain control of

---

STUDY GUIDE

Themes in Government
Political Processes **How has federalism benefited the two-party system?**

Critical Thinking Skills
Identifying Assumptions **What assumptions does the following statement make: "Rival political parties are a key element of democratic government"?**

Background

American federalism represents a middle ground between a unitary system of government and separate sovereign states. It provides for greater diversity and unity. The states are often in closer touch with popular opinion and provide a counterbalance for the excessive concentration of power in the central government. Multiple levels of government make possible greater administrative flexibility in policy-making and greater participation in political parties. Many states also lead the national government in public policy issues.

many state and local offices in the southern states. With such state and local bases, a party can develop new policies and new leadership with which to challenge the majority party.

The Democratic party has controlled the White House for only 4 of the 11 presidential terms since 1953. Democratic organization at the state and local level, however, has enabled the party to win a majority in Congress during most of this period. During most of this time, the Republican party was the minority party in Congress. The national appeal of its presidential candidates, however, has put a Republican in the White House in most of the recent elections. Federalism has kept the two-party system alive and healthy.

Political Participation

Federalism also has an impact on citizens' political participation. It increases people's opportunities for political participation. It also increases the possibility that a person's participation will have some practical effect.

Many Opportunities Federalism provides for several levels of government and, consequently, for a great number of state and local government officials. For most politicians, the road to national office begins at the local level. This aspect of federalism has tended to preserve political organization from the bottom up.

American federalism gives citizens many points of access to government and opportunities for influencing public policy. Noted political scientist Martin Grodzins believes the two-party system contributes to this access:

The lack of party discipline produces an openness in the system that allows individuals, groups, and institutions (including state and local governments) to attempt to influence national policy at every step of the legislative process.
—MARTIN GRODZINS, "The Federal System," 1985

Taking Action at the Grassroots Level
Political campaigns offer people direct contact with the political process. **History Which political party has recently controlled the White House?**

Americans vote frequently for governors, state lawmakers, mayors, council members, school board members, county prosecutors, and many other state and local officials. They also vote on such local issues as whether to build a mass transit system in their city, whether to outlaw smoking in public places, or whether to increase property taxes for schools.

Citizens may also work with interest groups to influence national policies and state and local government agencies. A group of concerned neighbors may petition their county zoning board to set aside nearby land for a public playground. Members of a local labor union may work together to support their union's efforts to influence passage of a law in the state legislature. A group of business leaders may promote development of a convention center.

Increasing Chances of Success A related effect of federalism is to increase the chances that one's political participation will have some practical impact. Most people are more likely to become involved in

Independent Practice

L1 Public Policy Have students collect local newspaper articles and editorials on issues that affect the community such as air pollution, an election, zoning, taxes, and highway expansion. Have them identify the public policy issue presented. **LEP**

L2 Journalism Have students write headlines that indicate how federalism has kept the two-party system alive. (*Examples:* DEMOCRATIC MAYORS FIGHT REPUBLICAN WHITE HOUSE, BATTERED REPUBLICAN PARTY BUILDS SUPPORT IN SMALL MIDWEST TOWNS)

L3 Persuasive Writing Have students write an essay on how federalism increases the opportunities and chances for success when citizens participate in government.

Caption Answer
the Democratic party

STUDY GUIDE

Theme Answer
They influenced the national government to force states to change civil rights and voting policies.

Critical Thinking Answer
Since citizens can vote at the national, state, and local levels, if they are dissatisfied with one level of government, they can attempt to make changes at another level.

STUDY GUIDE

Themes in Government
Public Policy How have Americans used the national government to change state and local policy?

Critical Thinking Skills
Making Inferences What advantage does federalism provide a citizen who may be dissatisfied

with conditions in his or her home state or area?

CHAPTER 4: THE FEDERAL SYSTEM 141

Assess

Check for Understanding
Have students complete Section 4 Review on page 142.

Special Needs Strategy

Visual Disability Students with visual processing problems may have trouble following directions written on the chalkboard or on an overhead. They may become confused by having to transfer written information from one place to another, such as from the chalkboard or book to paper. To mediate this problem, read all written instructions to stu-

dents. Keep written instructions simple. Number the steps of a process when possible. Have a student rephrase or restate the instructions or information.

🎧 Have students listen to the chapter summary on the *Audio Cassettes* in the Teacher's Classroom Resources.

Meeting Objectives

Each section objective is tested by the Section Review questions that follow in parentheses.

- Explain the impact of federalism on political activity. (3, 4, 5, 6)
- Describe how federalism has affected the making of national public policy. (2, 4, 6, 7, 8)

Evaluate

📁 Section 4 Quiz

✚ Testmaker

Reteach

📁 Have students complete Activity 4 in *Reteaching Activities* in the Teacher's Classroom Resources.

Enrich

Have students interview a representative from the state legislature or the attorney general's office on legislation in their state that is modeled after legislation in other states. The interviewee could also talk about state laws or policy that changed as a result of national laws.

Close

Have students review the chapter themes and explain the ways in which the chapter addressed each theme.

---

political activities if they think there is a reasonable chance their efforts will bear fruit. In the federal system, there are many elected officials who represent small districts. A city council member, for example, may represent only several neighborhoods in a city. People working in the campaign of a candidate for the council need to persuade relatively few voters to elect their candidate. The increased chance for success encourages political participation.

Federalism's Professional Politicians The federal system allows ordinary citizens many avenues of access to government. Since the 1960s, however, more and more public policy has been initiated by people in government service. The great increase in federal programs beginning in the mid-1930s called for a large **bureaucracy,** or organization of government administrators, to carry out legislation. As these bureaucrats gained expertise, they increasingly offered solutions. Political writer Samuel H. Beer describes the results:

In the fields of health, housing, urban renewal, transportation, welfare, education, poverty, and energy, it has been . . . people in government service . . . acting on the basis of their specialized and technical knowledge, who first perceived the problem, conceived the program, initially urged it on president and Congress, went on to help lobby it through to enactment, and then saw to its administration.

—SAMUEL H. BEER, "FEDERALISM, NATIONALISM, AND DEMOCRACY IN AMERICA," 1986

Some have used the term *technocracy* to describe this kind of decision making based on the technical expertise of professionals.

The increase of federal programs also changed the political relationship of state and federal government officials. As mayors and other state government officials sought to take advantage of the new federal programs, they became more interested in what was happening in Washington, D.C. Many national organizations such as the United States Conference of Mayors established headquarters in the nation's capital to keep up with events and in touch with lawmakers. In time these officials acquired political influence. Generally they asked for fewer strings attached to programs and for more federal money.

Differences Among the States

Federalism contributes to real economic and political differences among the states because it permits each state considerable freedom in arranging its own internal affairs. As a result, some states do more than others to regulate business and industry, while some provide more health and welfare services to their citizens. Some states have stricter criminal laws, some have higher taxes.

Because states can create different economic and political environments, Americans have more choices in the conditions under which they want to live. This also means that when people cross a state boundary line they become members of a different political system, with its own officials, taxes, and laws.

4
SECTION REVIEW

Section Summary
Federalism permits new policies to be tested in some states or localities before they are applied nationally. Federalism also supports the two-party system and encourages participation in politics.

Checking For Understanding
Recalling Facts
1. Define sunset law, sunshine law, bureaucracy.
2. Describe two ways in which federalism influences public policy-making.
3. Explain how federalism affects the two-party system in the United States.
4. Explain why groups such as the United States Conference of Mayors have offices in Washington, D.C.

Exploring Themes
5. Political Processes How has federalism increased opportunities for political participation by American citizens?
6. Public Policy How did African Americans use national attention to change policy in state and local governments in the 1950s and 1960s?

Critical Thinking Skills
7. Identifying Assumptions "Public policy is the course of action a government takes in response to some issue or problem." What assumption about the role of government does this statement make?
8. Making Inferences How does federalism allow for political and economic diversity among the states?

Section 4 Review Answers

1. Definitions of terms appear on pages indicated: **sunset law,** 139; **sunshine law,** 140; **bureaucracy,** 142
2. It affects how and where public policies are made in the United States; it introduces limits on government policy-making.
3. By providing each party with many chances for victories in state, local, and national elections, federalism helps

lessen the risk of one political party gaining a monopoly of political powers.
4. State and local government officials seek to influence national legislation that affect them and to get more aid from the national government.
5. Federalism provides for several levels of government and many state and local officials. As a result citizens have many points of access to government and many opportunities for influencing government decision making.

6. During the 1950s and 1960s African American leaders called national attention to local areas where they saw discrimination and restriction of civil rights. National pressure caused the federal government to pass legislation that affected these areas.
7. Government does not act until an issue or problem is presented.
8. Each state has sovereignty in many areas which allows each state to adopt policies that fit its individual needs

PERSONAL
PERSPECTIVES

Linda Tarr-Whelan on Progressive Federalism

When the federal deficit seemed out of control, the national government searched for ways to trim its oversized budget. One result was cutbacks in federal aid to the states. Linda Tarr-Whelan, president and executive director for the Center for Policy Alternatives, perceived a whole new order: States lead, Washington follows.

The order of the day—"progressive federalism"—is a new set of shared relationships between Washington and the 50 state capitals. This is a recent and fundamental shift.

The players are not in Washington. They are in places like Olympia, Tallahassee, Jefferson City, Albany. . . .

Why did this change occur? Economic imperatives made it happen. As one governor said, "When unemployment hits double digits, action must be taken."

Communities were hit by wave after wave of shocks—closed plants, foreclosed farms, unemployment. The dollar skidded, the trade deficit exploded, infant mortality went up, real family incomes went down.

Nothing happened in Washington. In diplomatic terms, you'd call it a stalemate. I call it gridlock, gridlock on both ends of Pennsylvania Avenue. . . .

The problems didn't go away. Government did begin to answer. But not the federal government. The states responded—unevenly, haltingly, faster on some issues than others, hampered by the cascade of new responsibilities and the empty well of funding.

A new pattern began to emerge. Change was percolating upward. Innovative state solutions appeared for virtually every problem on the list.

No one waited for "the" national solution to be developed. In fact there was a strong disbelief that any single national program could fit for American problems. . . .

More minority representation, more women . . . now one in seven legislators . . . serve in the statehouse.

The dominant domestic policy model of the last fifty years—development of national policies by the President and/or the Congress with extensive involvement of committees, interest groups and think tanks—began to be supplanted.

New activist governors took office, and legislatures came to more closely mirror the population. More minority representation, more women . . . now one in seven

legislators . . . serve in the statehouse. . . .

National officials . . . don't want to spin their wheels. Instead, they are going where the action is. States became a place where things could happen, not where progress stopped. . . .

Perhaps most important is what this all means to our country and citizens. The new decentralized public policy is a two edged sword. What happens is the government is closer to the people, but out of the view of the public. . . .

Much of what goes on in the state capital is out of the spotlight, and the leaders are out of the limelight.

—LINDA TARR-WHELAN, AUGUST 1990

Examining the Reading

Reviewing Facts

1. State the term the author uses to describe the new relationships between Washington, D.C., and the 50 state capitals.
2. Explain why so few people realize the successful response to problems that the states have made.

Critical Thinking Skills

3. Making Comparisons How does Tarr-Whelan's attitude toward the central government compare to the attitudes of Presidents Reagan and Bush?

More About Personal Perspectives

Linda Tarr-Whelan has been President and Chief Executive Officer of the Center for Policy Alternatives since November 1985. The Center for Policy Alternatives is a 16-year-old nonprofit, nonpartisan progressive "think-tank" which focuses on innovative policies and leaders in the 50 states. Ms. Tarr-Whelan has more than 20 years of public policy experience as an advocate and government official in the areas of health care, employment, economic development, education, and women's issues.

Focus

Ask students who solves problems that arise in their school system. (*Responses will include teachers, building principals, school board, and so on.*) Ask how this process represents federalism. (*problem-solving at multiple levels*)

Teach

Ask: What shift in federalism does Tarr-Whelan identify? (*solutions flowing from state to national levels rather than the traditional reverse pattern*) What reasons does she identify for why this shift has occurred? (*The failure of the national government to solve problems has resulted in the states taking more aggressive action to solve them.*)

Assess

Have students complete **Examining the Reading.**

Answers

1. The author uses "progressive federalism."
2. There is no spotlight on what the states are doing.
3. very similar; all three agree on the inability of the national government to make national programs meet local needs.

Close

Have students discuss the statement "States are where the action is." What examples of problem-solving are ongoing in their own state?

Identifying Terms and Concepts

National government—implied powers, expressed powers, inherent powers, elastic clause; State government—reserved powers

Reviewing Facts and Ideas

1. the supremacy clause, Article VI, Section 2

2. state governments

3. when national laws are being violated, federal property is being threatened, or federal responsibilities are interfered with

4. state governments and local governments

5. in the Supreme Court

6. Alexander Hamilton

7. Supreme Court's broad interpretation of interstate commerce gave Congress this power.

8. income tax

9. to return more authority to the state and local governments

10. mortgages, deeds, leases, wills, marriage licenses, car registrations, birth certificates

11. Congress

12. House and Senate, the presidency

Applying Themes

1. Federal aid comes with greater federal control and red tape.

2. Bureaucrats have the expertise to identify problems and suggest their solutions.

3. They believe the states created the national government and gave it limited powers.

4. by passing sunshine laws

Critical Thinking Skills

1. Franklin Roosevelt supported the expansion of the national government's powers to deal with the nation's economic problems. Nixon and Reagan believed in returning power to state and local governments. They perceived that the national government had become too powerful.

4
CHAPTER REVIEW

Summary and Significance

Federalism divides power between national and state governments. The national government has expressed powers, implied powers, and inherent powers. The Constitution reserves all other powers to the states or the people. In case of conflicts between the national government and the states, the power of the national government is supreme. There are different views of how federalism should operate. One view is the states' rights position; the other view is the nationalist position. Over time, federalism has also been shaped by the increased aid given by the national government to the states. The Constitution provides for relations among the states in the "full faith and credit" clause and the "privileges and immunities" clause.

Federalism has affected public policy by encouraging states to experiment with new policies and ideas and allowing the national government to impose new policies on the states. Federalism encourages the continuation of the two-party system and increases the opportunities for people to take part in political activities.

Identifying Terms and Concepts

On a separate sheet of paper write the two headings "National Government" and "State Government." Group the five terms below under the appropriate heading.

implied powers   reserved powers
expressed powers   elastic clause
inherent powers

Reviewing Facts and Ideas

1. Name the clause of the Constitution that resolves conflicts between state law and national law.
2. Identify what governments are responsible for creating cities and counties.
3. Describe the circumstances under which a President may send troops into a state without request from local authorities.
4. Specify who pays for elections of senators, representatives, and presidential electors.
5. Explain how conflicts between national and state governments are usually settled.
6. Cite who provided Americans with a lasting definition of federalism.
7. Describe how Congress gained power to regulate farm production, child labor, wages and hours, and criminal conduct.
8. Identify the major source of income for the national government.

9. Explain what President Nixon's New Federalism was designed to do about the relative power of the state and national governments.
10. Name the kinds of state records to which the "full faith and credit" clause applies.
11. Cite the governing body that must approve interstate compacts.
12. List what national offices have been held most often by the Democrats and by the Republicans since 1953.

Applying Themes

1. Federalism State and local officials often seek aid from Washington, D.C. Why do state and local officials sometimes criticize the federal aid they have grown to depend on?
2. Political Processes Experts in government agencies initiate many national laws in such fields as health, the environment, energy, welfare, education, and business. Why do these bureaucrats today have a great influence on legislation and decision making?
3. Constitutional Interpretations On what historic basis do states' rights supporters argue that the national government is actually only an agent of the states?
4. Public Policy How have all levels of government tried to make public meetings more accessible to the public?

---

2. Answers should include that the depression Roosevelt faced called for a national government response. Better economic conditions may have provided an opportunity to ask that power be returned to the states. On the other hand, Roosevelt probably was more of a nationalist, Reagan more a states' righter, in their interpretations of the Constitution.

3. The central issue was whether in a conflict between state and national governments, the state or the national government is supreme.

4. Answers should include: When power flows to Washington, the states lose control over decision making. People tend to wait for Washington to respond to local problems. When power flows back to state and local government, lack of money and

Critical Thinking Skills

1. **Making Comparisons** Compare Presidents Nixon's and Reagan's concept of federalism with that of Franklin Roosevelt.
2. **Making Inferences** Do you think economic conditions or constitutional interpretations underlay the differences between Roosevelt's and Reagan's view of federalism? Explain your answer.
3. **Identifying Central Issues** What was the main issue in the case of *McCulloch* v. *Maryland*?
4. **Expressing Problems Clearly** What problems are caused when the flow of power and responsibility shifts from the states to Washington, D.C.? from Washington, D.C., to the states?
5. **Demonstrating Reasoned Judgment** What do you think are the main advantages and disadvantages of federalism?
6. **Identifying Assumptions** "Federalism helps lessen the risk of one political party gaining a monopoly of political powers." What assumption about the value of a two-party system does this statement make?

Linking Past and Present

In 1836 the national government distributed $35 million of surplus revenue to the states. The states used the money for a wide variety of projects from roadbuilding to paying off debts. One state even distributed the money directly to its citizens. When the national government distributes money to states today, do you believe that it should be with "no strings attached" or directed toward specific programs? Explain your answer.

Writing About Government

Narrative Writing Write a narrative paragraph that tells how a person adjusts to a move from one state to another. You may want to interview someone who has recently moved into your state. What records and licenses transfer without change? Find out the details about how a driver's license and automobile tags are changed, how voting registration is done, how enrollment in school is accomplished, and how tax levies differ.

Reinforcing the Skill

Writing a Paragraph Using the following sentences, create a well-organized paragraph about the history of the federal system.

1. Leaving civil rights up to the states, they point out, meant that segregation was legal until the 1960s, when the federal government stepped in to protect the rights of blacks.
2. Why, say advocates of uniform national laws, should the children of a poor state be condemned to a substandard education?
3. Some Americans believe that the federal system creates injustices that should not be tolerated.
4. For example, states make up their own penal codes: a crime that is punished with a 2-year jail sentence in one state may be punished with 10 years in another.
5. States are also responsible for raising most of the funds that support their school systems.
6. Some have a lot more money than others.
7. Many other injustices still exist.
8. Should it matter which side of an invisible state line a man is on when he robs a gas station?

Investigating Further

1. **Individual Project** The three Supreme Court cases *Fletcher* v. *Peck*, *Missouri* v. *Holland*, and *Heart of Atlanta Motel* v. *United States* deal with the states' relationship to the nation. Choose one case and research it to find: (a) the essential facts, (b) the central issue, and (c) the Court's decision. Write a paragraph identifying these three items.
2. **Cooperative Learning** Form a group of five or seven. Choose a Supreme Court case that deals with federalism and discuss it. Then have one person play the role of the defense attorney and one the role of the plaintiff's attorney in the case. The other students will play the roles of justices.

Allow everyone to prepare, then re-enact the case before the class. Permit each attorney an opening statement; the plaintiff's attorney speaks first. Allow time for rebuttals. The justices may ask questions at any time and the attorneys must respond. Finally, one justice gives the Court's decision.

Writing About Government

Answers should include information about registering to vote, taking a driver's test, registering an automobile, enrolling in school, and differences in tax levies.

Reinforcing the Skill

Students' sentences should be in the following order: 3, 1, 7, 4, 8, 5, 6, 2

Investigating Further

1. *Fletcher* v. *Peck* a.) In 1795 the Georgia legislature passed an act authorizing the sale of land. A new legislature annulled the sale because it found that several members of the old legislature had been promised a share in the land sales. b.) Can the legislature reverse this act? c.) No, the original act constitutes a legal contract. The state cannot constitutionally interfere with the contract. *Missouri* v. *Holland* a.) After making a treaty with Great Britain providing for a mutual effort to protect migratory birds, Congress passed the Migratory Bird Act of 1918 prohibiting the killing of certain birds. The state of Missouri, however, claimed ownership of all birds within its borders and challenged the law. b.) Did the act violate the guarantees to states in the Tenth Amendment? c.) The Court ruled that Congress had authority in pursuing terms of the treaty to pass legislation that went beyond its ordinary powers. *Heart of Atlanta Motel* v. *United States* a.) Title II of the Civil Rights Act of 1964 extended equal rights to accommodations without discrimination on the grounds of race, color, religion, or national origin. b.) The owner of the motel refused to rent rooms to African Americans and claimed the law violated his rights under the Fifth and Thirteenth amendments. c.) The Court ruled that the motel's policy was a hindrance to interstate travel and commerce and therefore subject to congressional regulation.

2. Answers will vary.

an adequate bureaucratic structure for handling problems can hinder problem solving.

5. <u>advantages:</u> Federalism provides a safeguard against central government becoming too powerful, encourages more citizen participation in government, and provides a greater variety of government responses to issues; <u>disadvantages:</u> Federalism creates confusion about who is in authority and slows government response to issues.

6. A two-party system is better than a one-party system.

Linking Past and Present

Answers will vary.

CASE STUDY

The Case at a Glance

Who: federal government, state governments, environmentalists
What: air pollution legislation
When: 1970 to the present
Where: United States
Why: fears of the effects of acid rain

Focus

Ask students who is responsible for protecting the safety of the air and of water supplies in the United States. *(local, state, and federal agencies)* Ask: What happens when the actions of these agencies conflict? In such cases, what should be done to protect clean air and water?

Explain that this case study illustrates how such conflicts are resolved.

Teach

Guided Practice

L1 **Summarizing** Summarize the sequence of events described in the case. Ask: Why was acid rain more of a problem in the East than in the West? *(The prevailing winds carry pollutants from west to east.)* What were the drawbacks of individual states passing clean air laws? *(The problems were interstate in scope and could only be worked out if a national consensus was reached.)* How was this consensus achieved? *(Environmentalists brought the issue before the public. Alarmed at the prospects of increased pollution, more people favored government*

Powers of Congress

To make all laws necessary and proper for carrying into execution . . . powers vested by this Constitution in the Government of the United States. . . .

—Article I, Section 8

Powers of the States

The powers not delegated to the United States by the Constitution, nor prohibited by it to the States, are reserved to the States respectively, or to the people.

—Tenth Amendment

The Politics of Federalism

The Case

As a noted scholar of federalism observed, "because the concerns of American politics are universal ones, there is relatively little basic conflict between the federal government and the states. . . ." Conflicts sometimes do arise, however. Recently, a conflict has arisen over acid rain—rain polluted with chemicals released into the atmosphere. Acid rain was an issue that pitted states against states, industries against industries, and ultimately, states against the national government. In 1980 relatively few Americans considered acid rain a problem. A survey taken that year, for example, indicated that only about 30 percent of the Americans questioned had even heard of acid rain. Citizens in the Northeast, however, blamed acid rain for killing forests and poisoning fish. As the director of the Center for Clean Air Policy described the problem: "How you feel about acid rain depends on where you're from."

Northeasterners' demands for action fell on deaf ears in Washington, D.C. At the time the Reagan administration was committed to a policy of less federal regulation. The administration insisted that more information on the issue be gathered. The problem that faced the northeastern states was an important outgrowth of the federal system. What could individual states, as partners in a federal system, do to solve a problem that originated in other states if the national government refused to take action?

Environmentalists decided that only a broad-based national consensus could force the federal government to take action. To build this consensus required a campaign to mobilize public opinion.

Background

The prevailing winds that blow across the United States from west to east carry with them sulfur and nitrogen oxides that produce acid rain. The northeastern states as well as many environmentalists blamed the high-sulfur coal used to fire generators in electric power plants, primarily in the Midwest and the border states. Faced with the probability of high costs and the possible loss of coal-mining jobs, the states accused of polluting fought attempts to develop strict clean-air regulations, usually denying that the problem existed. Governor Rhodes of Ohio declared the environmentalists had "latched on to acid rain as a rallying cry for a new wave of

More About the Case

The federal government passed the first antipollution law in 1899 when it outlawed dumping chemical wastes into navigable waterways. The law had little effect because it was almost never enforced. Between 1900 and 1940, air pollution became a major problem in the industrialized cities of the East and Midwest. Pollution in Pittsburgh, for example, became so rampant that, when driving during daytime, motorists had to turn on their headlights.

During the last 30 years, worldwide death rates associated with industrial pollution have increased. In the late 1970s, residents of Love Canal, a neighborhood of Niagara Falls, New York, discovered environmental hysteria." President Reagan's secretary of the interior tended to agree: "Every year there's a money-making scare. This year it's acid rain."

The Fight for Clean Air In 1970 Congress had passed the Clean Air Act designed to improve air quality. Amended in 1977, the Clean Air Act was condemned both by industry for its restrictions and by environmentalists for not doing enough to end air pollution.

To enforce the Clean Air Act and regulate the emissions of nitrogen oxide (NO_x) and sulfur dioxide (SO_2), Congress established the federal Environmental Protection Agency (EPA) in 1970. In addition, each state was required to set up a state implementation plan (SIP) to guarantee that its SO_2 and NO_x emissions would not exceed standards of the Clean Air Act. The act also gave the EPA power to ensure that no emissions from one state could "significantly interfere with the attainment and maintenance" of another state's air quality.

The Clean Air Act set standards for ambient air—air at ground level that people breathed—but not for air higher in the atmosphere. Industries and utilities considered several alternatives in light of the new standards. They could switch to more expensive low-sulfur coal mined largely in the western states, or they could buy expensive technology that would reduce SO_2 emissions. Either solution might produce undesirable effects. Jobs could be lost in the high-sulfur coal mining regions in midwestern and border states. The higher costs for coal and technology, many argued, would raise utility rates. Another solution had to be found, and it was in Canada.

In 1970 the province of Ontario ordered a copper and nickel mill to cut its SO_2 emissions. The mill responded by building a smokestack more than 1,200 feet (365 meters) tall. The air at ground level improved immensely, but the stack now belched the sulfur dioxide higher into the atmosphere where it turned into a chemical known as acid sulfate. Winds swept the acid sulfate to other areas. The idea quickly caught on with electric power plants in the United States and tall stacks sprouted across the Midwest.

The battle between the states in the Northeast and the national government began in earnest when in 1980 the EPA approved higher sulfur dioxide emissions in the Midwest. Robert Abrams, New York's at-

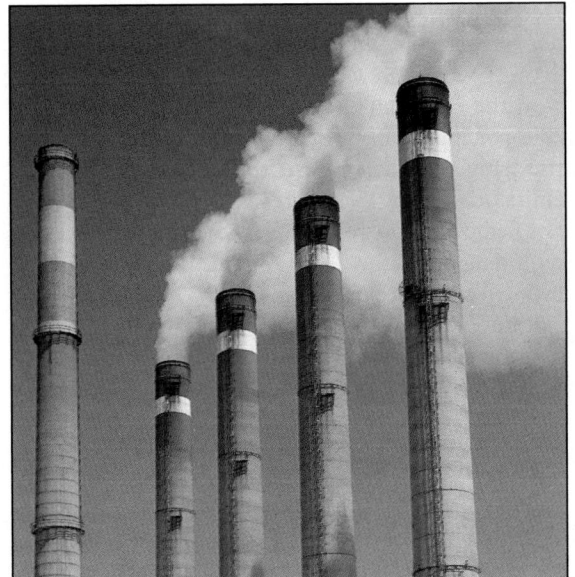

Across State Borders
Chemical emissions into the atmosphere from factories contribute to acid rain, an interstate problem that required state and federal action.

torney general, asked the EPA to cancel the increase. In accordance with the Clean Air Act, the EPA agreed to hold a hearing to settle the question.

The EPA ruled that although it was empowered to control SO_2 emissions, the agency had no jurisdiction because the Clean Air Act did not mention acid sulfate. New York switched gears. Haze became the issue.

Recently, an environmental scientist explained, "We've lived with haze so long we've come to accept it as something natural. But it's not. It's nearly all man-made." He concluded that particles of acid sulfate in the air are the main cause of haze. New York ended up arguing this point before the EPA in 1981 and 1982. Representatives for the coal industry and electric utilities argued that there was no proof that the particles originated outside New York. The companies insisted that the state should "put [its] own house in order instead of trying to cast blame elsewhere for essentially local pollution problems."

The EPA did not rush to judgment. Almost four years after the request for a hearing, New York's Robert Abrams notified the EPA that if a decision was not issued within 60 days, New York would sue. In

their homes had been built over a toxic waste dump. In Sereso, Italy, an industrial explosion released dioxin into the air, making hundreds of people severely ill. In 1984 poisonous gas released in an industrial accident in Bhopal, India, killed 2,000 people. Two years later an explosion and fire at a nuclear generating station at Chernobyl,

Ukraine, not only killed 23 people, but saturated the air with large amounts of radiation. Winds carried the radiation over much of northern Europe. These accidents created an awareness that stricter enforcement of environmental standards were needed not only in the United States but worldwide.

action.) Point out that such issues are not resolved easily; they are resolved through compromises between interest groups and legislators.

L2 Constructing a Chart Work with students to construct a chart on the chalkboard that illustrates conflict resolution in the acid rain issue. Use the following headings: *Who had the problem? Who caused the problem? How was the problem resolved?* Have students provide answers to complete the chart. (*eastern states; coal-mining states; a change in public sentiment which forced agencies, Congress, and presidential candidates to support cleaner air standards*) Then discuss how this case illustrates the principle of federalism.

L3 Panel Discussion Have six students speak on the issue of acid rain, taking the side of one of the following: a manufacturer, a legislator from a midwestern state, a legislator from an eastern state, the Canadian prime minister, an environmental scientist from California, and a coal miner from Pennsylvania.

After the role players present their points of view, ask: What do all of them have in common? (*All have to take a stance on the issue of acid rain; acid rain directly affects their livelihoods.*) How did Congress convince the midwesterners to vote for the Clean Air Act? (*Midwestern states received money for laid-off workers.*) How does this case show federalism at work?

Independent Practice

L1 Geography Provide an outline map of the United States to students and have them locate and color the areas mentioned in the case. Have students display their maps on the classroom bulletin board. **LEP**

L2 Informative Writing Have students research and write a report on clean air standards in their own community and designate who is responsible for enforcing these standards.

L3 Research Tell students that controversies similar to those over air pollution have arisen over water usage. Have students research the conflict that arose when the Chicago Metropolitan Sanitary District, in an effort to rid the Chicago River of sewage at the turn of the century, dug out the river. As a result, water from Lake Michigan rushed in. Soon, the river's sewage spread throughout the lake. States that also used Lake Michigan water were outraged. Students should find out about the conflicts that arose and what Chicago did in response. Have students draw parallels between this case and the acid rain controversy.

Assess

Have students complete **Examining the Case.**

Close

Ask: Should protection of the environment be a local, state, or federal responsibility? Why? *(Some students will recognize the value of state or local control of localized problems and the need for national control of problems with regional or larger impact.)*

December 1985, the state sued the EPA. The other northeastern states plus a number of environmentalist groups joined New York. The following year they won the case, but the EPA appealed. In 1986 the court of appeals dismissed the suit. In the meantime, the EPA denied attempts to control midwestern emissions, saying that states in the northeast "have not made a persuasive technical case that the existing requirements of the Clean Air Act are being violated by interstate transport of pollutants."

The EPA was not alone. In 1986 William M. Brown, a member of the Hudson Institute, wrote in *Fortune* magazine: "In fact, acid rain has never been conclusively shown to be the principle cause of any of the environmental problems it's accused of causing."

In 1990, after 10 years of study, the National Acid Precipitation Assessment Program reported that "the vast majority of forests in the United States and Canada are not affected by decline." Environmentalists were quick to dispute that report's conclusions.

The Public Response By the middle of the 1980s, more people favored cleaner air and an end to acid rain. Stories headlined "Acid Rain Spreads Its Deadly Sting" and "What's Killing the Sugar Maples" in national magazines fired a growing national consensus. Efforts by members of Congress from the northeastern states, however, failed to create a coalition.

Nevertheless, the mood of the country was changing. By the mid-1980s, at least half of those Americans questioned agreed that the nation's environmental laws did not go far enough. A scientist for the Environmental Defense Fund noted that 22 of the 53 Republicans in the Senate were up for reelection in 1986. He suggested that on environmental issues the senators would be:

Running toward the middle where the American public is. . . . They know there is a great deal of public support for environmental protection. I expect the next two years to be good ones for environmental legislation.

—MICHAEL OPPENHEIMER, 1985

They were not, even though Senator Max Baucus believed that: "There is now a national bipartisan consensus for tougher environmental protection."

Presidential Action Any doubt that the environment had become an important political issue was dispelled during the 1988 presidential campaign. Both candidates ran as environmentalists. Victorious, President George Bush in 1989 sent Congress a proposal for changes in the Clean Air Act that were, as one writer noted, "tougher than almost anything congressional environmentalists ever dared to offer on their own."

In autumn 1990 Congress passed amendments to the Clean Air Act that even exceeded the President's proposals. Midwestern legislators, whose states were certain to bear the heaviest costs, supported the measures because they set aside $290 million to aid workers who lost their jobs because of the amendments.

Significance

Under the American federal system, interstate rivalries and disputes can severely limit national actions when a strong national consensus has not formed on an issue. This limitation becomes particularly true when the public does not regard the dispute as a crisis.

When confronted with a problem requiring national action, states face the possibility of a stalemate in Congress and even presidential opposition. The acid rain controversy clearly illustrates the nature of our federal system.

Examining the Case

Reviewing Facts
1. Explain why some states opposed federal regulation to reduce emissions of nitrogen and sulfur oxides.
2. Describe why some states insisted that the national government needed to control acid rain.

Critical Thinking Skills
3. Demonstrating Reasoned Judgment Does the nature of the federal system encourage or discourage federal regulation of activities within different states? Why?
4. Evaluating Information Do you agree or disagree with the statement "There are issues that are beyond the capacity of the states to solve alone." Why or why not?

Examining the Case Answers

1. They wanted to avoid the high costs and the possible loss of coal-mining jobs.
2. These states argued the states in the Midwest and the West were causing the pollution.
3. Answers may vary, but students should point out that under the federal system interstate rivalries can limit national actions. In such cases the federal government needs to step in.
4. Many students will note that issues of nationwide concern often can only be resolved by the federal government. Others might stipulate that in such cases, the national government should take the opinions of the states into account.

Chapter 1
Government and Our Lives

The states, or countries, in today's world vary greatly in size, population, economic strength, military power, and importance. All countries, however, have four essential features—population, territory, sovereignty, and government. Each provides social order, public services, national security, and an economic system for its citizens.

Governments fall into one of three major categories: (1) autocracy—rule by one person; (2) oligarchy—rule by a few persons; or (3) democracy—rule by many persons. As a true democracy, the United States has a number of characteristics that distinguish it from other forms of government. These characteristics include individual liberty, majority rule with minority rights, free elections, and competing political parties. Democracies, however, are rare because they require favorable economies, well-educated citizens, and a social consensus.

All economic systems must make three major economic decisions: (1) what and how much should be produced; (2) how goods and services should be produced; and (3) who gets the goods and services that are produced. Each major economic system in the world—capitalism, socialism, and communism—answers these questions differently. Capitalism allows freedom of choice and individual incentive for workers, investors, consumers, and business enterprises. Under socialism the government owns the basic means of production, determines the use of resources, distributes the products and wages, and provides social services such as education, health care, and welfare. The communist system provides for government control of all aspects of its citizens' lives.

Chapter 2
The Creation of the Federal Government

During the 1600s settlers from many lands, such as Spain, the Netherlands, France, Sweden, Norway, and West Africa, helped colonize North America. Most colonists came from England.

The English colonists brought with them ideas about government that had been developing in England for centuries. These ideas included limited government and representative government, which later became the foundations of the American constitutional system.

Colonial governments established practices that became a key part of the American system of government. Among these were (1) a written constitution that guaranteed basic liberties and limited the power of government; (2) a legislature of elected representatives; and (3) the separation of powers between the governor and the legislature.

Until the mid-1700s, Britain allowed its colonies across the Atlantic to develop politically on their own. By the 1760s, however, the British government sought to tighten its control over the colonies. The colonists responded by fighting and winning their independence as the United States of America.

The young republic first established a confederacy with a weak central government and powerful state governments. When it became apparent that government under the Articles of Confederation lacked the authority to solve the nation's problems, the states sent delegates to a convention to revise the Articles. The delegates concluded that the Articles were beyond repair and, after a series of compromises, they signed the United States Constitution on September 17, 1787.

The Constitution encountered fierce criticism from those who opposed a strong central government. The Constitution, however, actually went into effect on June 21, 1788, after nine states had ratified it.

Chapter 3
The Constitution—A Living Document

The United States Constitution is simple and brief. It establishes the structure and powers of government but does not attempt to spell out every aspect of how government will function. The Constitution is divided into three parts—the Preamble, the Articles, and the Amendments. The Preamble lists the basic principles of the Constitution. The Articles set up the organization and powers of the government, and the 27 amendments include changes to the original Constitution. The first 10 amendments, the Bill of Rights, guarantees all Americans rights of individual liberty. It also spells out the rights of people accused of crimes.

UNIT 1: FOUNDATIONS OF AMERICAN GOVERNMENT   149

Classroom Resources for Unit I Digest

Unit Digest Transparencies, Unit 1   Participating in Government, Unit 1

Using the Unit I Digest

Use the Unit Digest to introduce, review, reteach, or condense specific chapters or the entire unit. The Unit Digest is enhanced by the corresponding transparencies and activities in the Teacher's Classroom Resources.

Focus

Write the following question on the chalkboard: Why do we have governments? Ask students to respond to the question. Write their responses on the chalkboard. For each response, ask students to discuss whether or not it is a necessary governmental function in the modern world. Cross out those functions that they think are unnecessary. Then, as students study this unit synthesis, have them consider how the American government fulfills the remaining functions.

Teach

L1 Understanding Ideas Write the following six principles of government on the chalkboard: *popular sovereignty, federalism, separation of powers, checks and balances, judicial review,* and *limited government.* Have students write a few sentences showing how each principle is reflected in the United States Constitution. Select students to read their sentences to the class. **LEP**

Interpreting Visuals Display transparency 1 from the *Unit Digest Transparencies* in the Teacher's Classroom Resources and use the accompanying teaching strategy, student activity, and student test to trace the roots of the American system of government.

that in a recent survey, the overwhelming majority of Americans
expressed support for the Bill of
Rights. However, many of those
polled did not support, and some
did not know, the individual freedoms protected by the Bill of
Rights. For example, only about
one-third of those polled said
they supported certain free-
speech and free-press rights protected by the First Amendment.
Direct students to the text of the
first 10 amendments of the Constitution on pages 113–114. For
each amendment have students
discuss the following: Should this
right be protected? Why or why
not? How would life in the United States change if it was not
protected?

Assess

Check for Understanding

Have students complete
Synthesizing the Unit.

Close

Have students review the
strengths and weaknesses of
democracy by discussing the following statement by Winston
Churchill:

". . . [I]t has been said that
democracy is the worst form of
Government except all those
other forms that have been
tried . . ."

The Constitution rests on six major principles of
government: (1) popular sovereignty; (2) federalism;
(3) separation of powers; (4) checks and balances;
(5) judicial review; and (6) limited government.
These principles continue to affect the character of
the American system of government and politics.

The Founders created a Constitution that could be
adapted to future needs. One way they provided for
change was to describe how Congress and the states
could amend the Constitution. The Constitution has
grown as an instrument of government through informal change as well. Informal changes occur as government leaders and citizens fill in the details of
government on a day-to-day basis to suit the needs of
the times.

Congress shapes the meaning of the Constitution
by passing laws and through the way it uses its powers. Presidential actions have also added to the Constitution. For example, President John Tyler
established the practice that the Vice President becomes President upon the President's death. George
Washington established the practice that although the
Senate approves treaties, the executive branch negotiates them. The federal courts have added to the Constitution by ruling on the constitutionality of laws, a
process called judicial review. A fourth way the Constitution has been informally enlarged is through customs that have developed over time. Such customs
include political parties and the President's cabinet.

Chapter 4

The Federal System

The Constitution provided for a federal system of
government in which power is divided between the
central government and state governments. The
Framers gave the national government certain specified powers, reserving all other powers to the states or
to the people. In addition, the national and state governments share some powers. The Constitution also
specifically denied some powers to each level of government in order to protect individual liberties.

The Constitution grants three types of power to
the national government: expressed, implied, and inherent. Collectively these powers are known as delegated powers. The Constitution also stipulates that
the acts and treaties of the United States are the

supreme law of the land. No state law or state constitution may conflict with any form of national law.

Interpretations of how federalism affects the relationship between the nation and the states have
changed considerably since 1787 and will no doubt
continue to do so. Throughout American history,
there have been two quite different views of how federalism should operate. One view—the states' rights
position—favors state and local action in dealing with
social and economic problems. A second view—the
nationalist position—favors national action in dealing
with these matters.

A major factor shaping the development of American federalism has been the growth in the size and
power of the national government. The Constitution's very flexibility has allowed the Supreme Court,
Congress, and the President to stretch the national
government's powers to meet the needs of a modern
industrial nation. The expansion of the national government's powers has been based on three major constitutional provisions: (1) the war powers; (2) the
power to regulate interstate commerce; and (3) the
power to tax and spend for the general welfare.

The federal system is dynamic, changing as officials
seek answers to problems. While Presidents Nixon,
Reagan, and Bush attempted to shift the balance of
power back toward the states, President Clinton has
once again emphasized the national government.

In setting up the federal system, the Constitution
also defined relations among the states. Because each
state retains power and independence, these rules
help to assure cooperation among the states.

Synthesizing the Unit

Exploring Concepts
1. Federalism **How does the Constitution provide for a
   federal system of government?**
2. Civil Liberties **What part of the Constitution ensures
   that people will retain their civil liberties?**

Critical Thinking Skills
3. Making Inferences **The Constitution has guided the
   United States for more than 200 years. During the
   same time, France has had 11 constitutions. Given this
   information, what can you infer about the relative
   strengths of the United States Constitution?**
4. Making Comparisons **How is government under the
   Constitution different from government under the
   Articles of Confederation?**

Synthesizing the Unit Answers

1. It grants supreme power to the national government but
reserves many powers to the states.
2. Bill of Rights

3. The United States Constitution is flexible and can be adjusted to reflect the times.

4. The Constitution made the central government more
powerful than the state governments.

Citizenship and Civil Liberties

Chapter 5:
Citizenship in the United States

Chapter 6:
Protecting Basic Freedoms

Chapter 7:
Assuring Equal Justice for All

Introduce

Unit Objectives

After studying this unit, students should be able to:
- Discuss the nature and rights and responsibilities of American citizenship.
- List an American citizen's basic civil liberties and review the constitutional protections provided for each.

Unit Overview

Unit 2 focuses on the nature of American citizenship and outlines the basic rights and liberties that all Americans possess.

Chapter 5 introduces students to the concept of citizenship, how it is acquired, and what it means.

Chapter 6 explains the ways in which many of our basic freedoms are protected by the First Amendment.

Chapter 7 reviews the concepts of equal rights and equal justice.

2
UNIT DIGEST

Use the Unit Digest on pages 225–226 to introduce, review, reteach, or condense the information in this unit.

Introducing the Unit

Point out that the title of this Unit is "Citizenship and Civil Liberties." Then ask students to suggest why the unit-opening illustration is appropriate for this title. *(The Statue of Liberty welcomes the "huddled masses" of all nations who yearn "to breathe free" as citizens of the United States; it is a symbol of liberty and equality for all.)*

Unit Project

Have students work in groups to develop a guide on the rights and responsibilities enjoyed by 18-year-old American students. The guide should take the form of a 4-page, illustrated pamphlet titled *Know Your Rights*. Group members should share the tasks involved in developing the pamphlet. Some might undertake research and writing, others might locate or draw illustrations, and still others might design the pamphlet. If students have access to video equipment, they might make a 5-minute tape on the same topic. Again, group members should share the work involved in producing the tape. Have groups display their pamphlets or broadcast their tapes for other government and civics classes.

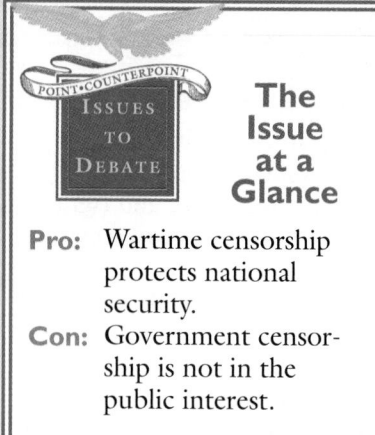

POINT·COUNTERPOINT
ISSUES
TO
DEBATE

The Issue at a Glance

Pro: Wartime censorship protects national security.

Con: Government censorship is not in the public interest.

Focus

Ask students the following: Who should have access to your student records? Have students consider such groups as teachers, parents, police, other students, college officials, news reporters, and so on. Discuss students' responses. Do they favor unlimited access? If not, what limits would they put on access to this information?

Tell students that the issue of confidentiality versus access to information is at the center of the debate in the reading.

Teach

Guided Practice

Point out that unlike access to student records, which involves confidentiality and privacy issues, access to government activities and plans during wartime raises issues related to the security of the United States. Have students cite examples of military information that, if published, could endanger national security. Ask why national security might be threatened if such information was divulged in newspapers or on the broadcast news. Ask: How did government censor the press during the Grenada invasion? the Gulf War? *(Grenada—denied them prior information, did not allow them to accompany troops; Gulf— allowed few in field, controlled movement, monitored activities)*

POINT·COUNTERPOINT

ISSUES TO DEBATE

Should Press Coverage of Wars Be Regulated?

The regulation of press coverage of wars has been a common enough practice in American history. As the Civil War raged, reports from war correspondents in the field were routinely censored. Federal troops even seized newspapers that opposed the North's war effort.

Censorship also was common during World War I and World War II. Only during the Vietnam War did reporters seemingly have a free hand to gather information. Often the information was unpleasant for the military. As a result, the debate on the press's role during wartime emerged with ardent advocates on both sides of the issue.

Pro

In fall 1983 the United States and its allies invaded the island of Grenada near the island nation of Trinidad and Tobago in the Caribbean Sea. Reporters and other members of the news media were denied prior information of the planned invasion and could not accompany the soldiers. Not all journalists agreed with those who criticized the government's treatment of the press. Syndicated columnist Ralph de Toledano argued that the press should not be told about secret military operations—in this case, the invasion of Grenada.

To brief the press before U.S. forces had made contact with the Grenadian and Cuban troops on the island would have been tantamount to announcing the imminent operation on TV evening news. . . . What was once known as the "public's right to know" has since become the "media's right to determine." In effect, the press demands that it be part of the most sensitive decision-

making process. It also claims the right to determine what is national security. If it disagrees with the President or his advisers, you may be sure that disagreement will be aired on the news pages or TV evening news. . . .

The press now argues that in not divulging information which would have jeopardized the lives of 1,000 Americans, the government violated the First Amendment. The elasticity of this logic will win the huzzas [praises] of the American Civil Liberties Union and the entrenched left, but I doubt that it will impress the American people or the families of the Americans who were caught in the vortex of violence and criminality on the island of Grenada.

—RALPH DE TOLEDANO, THE UNION LEADER,
NOVEMBER 11, 1983

When the national government decided to restrict coverage of Operation Desert Storm in 1991, the press questioned the restrictions placed on the news media. Pete Williams, assistant secretary of defense for public affairs, responded with the Defense Department's views in March 1991.

The ground rules were not intended to prevent journalists from reporting on incidents that might embarrass the military or to make military operations look sanitized. Instead, they were intended simply and solely to prevent publication of details that could jeopardize a military operation or endanger the lives of U.S. troops.
Some of the things that were not to be reported were:
• *Details of future operations;*
• *Specific information about troop strengths or locations;*
• *Specific information on missing or downed airplanes or ships while search and rescue operations were underway; and*

More About Issues to Debate

Walter Cronkite helped to shape public opinion for over 50 years. Working first as a newspaper reporter and then as a correspondent for CBS, Cronkite has chronicled many of the conflicts of the twentieth century. From 1962 to 1981, Cronkite served as managing editor of *CBS Evening News*. It was from this vantage point that Cronkite informed viewers on the conduct and direction of the Vietnam War.

The mistrust of government and the military that developed during the Vietnam conflict has never left the media. Over the last 20 years, the press has nearly always been ready to assume that government and military officials are less than truthful.

• *Information on operational weaknesses that could be used against U.S. forces. . . .*

This was, after all, an enemy that had virtually as much access to American news reporting as people had here at home. From what we've been able to learn so far, Iraqi military commanders didn't have a clue as to which coalition forces were out there, where they were, or what they were up to. They appear to have been caught totally off guard by the quick move of the 18th Airborne Corps west of Kuwait, deep into Iraq. For the sake of the operation and the lives of these troops, we could not afford to let the enemy learn that.

—PETE WILLIAMS, *THE WASHINGTON POST NATIONAL WEEKLY EDITION*, MARCH 25-31, 1991

Con

During and after the Grenada invasion, members of the press severely criticized the government's restrictions on reporters' actions. Many of these critics believed that the government had no right to curtail freedom of the press, even in times of national emergency. One critic, columnist David Broder, stressed that the press has "a clear obligation to say . . . why prior restraint or barring the press from reporting is dangerously wrong." He continued:

It is wrong because control of information gives a government control over its citizens' minds. . . . It is a power the Constitution of the United States sought to deny our government permanently by the First Amendment. . . .

The critical question is where the public comes down on the government's attempt to make itself the sole source of information about the military action in which American troops are planted on foreign soil without a declaration of war and with inevitable casualties and long-term military and diplomatic consequences.

If the American people are willing to say that in such circumstances, it is acceptable to have reporters barred (or, in the case of those already on the scene, detained and denied the right to report what they had seen), then you may be assured the precedent will be followed.

—DAVID S. BRODER, *SAN DIEGO TRIBUNE*, NOVEMBER 11, 1984

Walter Cronkite, well-known journalist and television newscaster, voiced his concern about the military's attempt to control the news coverage of Operation Desert Storm. A seasoned veteran of war reporting, Cronkite commented:

With an arrogance foreign to the democratic system, the U.S. military in Saudi Arabia is trampling on the American people's right to know. It is doing a disservice not only to the home front but also to history and its own best interest. . . .

With a rational censorship system in place, the press should be free to go where it wants when it wants, to see, hear and photograph what it believes is in the public interest. . . .

The greatest mistake of our military so far is its attempt to control coverage by assigning a few pool reporters and photographers to be taken to locations determined by the military with supervising officers monitoring all their conversations with the troops in the field. An American citizen is entitled to ask: "What are they trying to hide?"

—WALTER CRONKITE, *NEWSWEEK* FEBRUARY 25, 1991

The Debate Continues

The right of the government to control the press remains a serious question. Despite the questions raised during Operation Desert Storm, when questioned, 57 percent of the people polled believed the military should have even more control over what is reported. It appears that in the event of another military action or a "clear and present danger" to national security, the question of the First Amendment's rights will arise.

Examining the Issue

Recalling Facts

1. Name the only war in which reporters seemingly had a free hand to gather information.
2. Explain the government's ground rules for regulating press coverage of the Gulf War.

Critical Thinking Skills

3. Evaluating Information. Why does de Toledano say the press should not be told about secret operations?
4. Identifying Assumptions. What assumptions do those who defend the military's right to control the news and those who oppose the military's actions make?

Investigating Further

Use the *Readers' Guide to Periodical Literature* to locate recent articles about government censorship of secret information. After you have studied several articles, write a paragraph describing the press's current reaction to government censorship.

At the beginning of the Persian Gulf crisis, many reporters approached the issues from an antiwar perspective. Studies conducted by the Center for Media and Public Affairs showed that the press quoted antiwar advocates more often than the President. Some journalists even ostracized those of their profession who supported military intervention.

Today many media critics believe that the press, as well as the nation, needs to cleanse itself of the Vietnam mentality. They maintain that each international incident needs to be reported and discussed as objectively and independently as possible.

Tell students that some reporters contend censorship is unneeded because the media would never publish anything to harm American troops. Ask how de Toledano responds to that argument. *(Media should not decide national security because if it disagrees with government policy, it will publish the information.)* Ask why Cronkite believes that government censorship is not in its own best interests. *(People will believe government has something to hide.)*

Independent Practice

Have students write two paragraphs—one summarizing the arguments for wartime censorship of the news media and the other summarizing the arguments against such censorship.

Assess

Have students complete **Examining the Issue.**

Answers

1. Vietnam War
2. Pool reporters were permitted to move about and interview troops under military supervision. Certain items were not to be reported.
3. The media may act in its own interests, not in the best interests of the American people.
4. that media and government do not trust each other and that they do not have the same interests and goals

Close

Ask students which side they support in this debate. Ask if government censorship should extend to peacetime news that would give people ideas for criminal behavior. Have students explain consistencies or inconsistencies in their positions on these issues.

Chapter Organizer

Objectives	Special Feature Pages	Supplemental Materials
Section 1 The Basis for United States Citizenship *pp. 156–161* 1. Specify the legal bases for United States citizenship. 2. Explain how the basis of United States citizenship has changed over the years.	Point/Counterpoint: Should Press Coverage of Wars Be Regulated? pp. 152–153 Global Connection: Issues: Dual Nationality p. 158 Critical Thinking Skills: Understanding Cause and Effect p. 161	Guided Reading Activities Reproducible Lesson Plans Supreme Court Case Studies 4 Section 1 Quiz Testmaker Skill Reinforcement Activity 5 The Living Constitution SAT Practice Tests Writer's Guidebook
Section 2 A Nation of Immigrants *pp. 162–168* 1. Distinguish between immigrants and aliens. 2. Describe the five categories of aliens. 3. Summarize American immigration policy.	Images of Government: New Citizens pp. 164–165 Participating in Government: Deciding on a Job p. 166	Guided Reading Activities Reproducible Lesson Plans Participating in Government 5 Primary and Secondary Source Readings 5 Enrichment Activities 5 Section 2 Quiz Testmaker Chapter Transparencies 5 The Living Constitution SAT Practice Tests Writer's Guidebook
Section 3 Rights and Responsibilities of American Citizens *pp. 169–173* 1. Identify the constitutional rights of citizenship. 2. Describe the responsibilities of citizenship. 3. Explain the changing scope of the Bill of Rights.	Focus on Freedom: The Magna Carta p. 171 Personal Perspectives: Southeast Asians on Being a Refugee p. 173	Guided Reading Activities Reproducible Lesson Plans 19 Reteaching Activities 5 Section 3 Quiz Chapter 5 Tests Testmaker Audio Cassettes (English and Spanish) Limited English Proficiency Activities 5 SAT Practice Tests

If time does not permit teaching this chapter, assign the Chapter 5 summary in the Unit 2 Digest on pages 225–226.

Key To Ability Levels

Teaching strategies have been coded for varying learning styles and abilities.

L1   Level 1 activities are **basic** activities and should be within the ability range of all students.

L2   Level 2 activities are **average** activities and should be within the ability range of the average to above-average student.

L3   Level 3 activities are **challenging** activities designed for the ability range of above-average students.

LEP   These activities should be within the ability range of **Limited English Proficiency** students.

Multicultural Activities

Demographers predict that by the year 2050, more than one-third of all Americans will trace their origins to Africa, Asia, or Latin America. As the nonwhite and non-European population increases, many school systems will have a "majority of minorities." California's public schools will soon be the first to do so. Some educators argue that United States' schools should revise their curricula to reflect the changing population. Opponents fear that history and other disciplines will get caught up in political power struggles. Have students discuss the following: Should schools change what they teach to more accurately reflect the makeup of the population? If so, what changes would students make, who would decide what changes were made, where would these changes take place—in all schools? in majority-minority schools only? in colleges?

Write the following statement on the chalkboard: *Immigration policy reflects the changing vision our nation's leaders have of what the United States is and should be.* Have students write essays explaining this statement, focusing particularly on how immigration policy at different periods in the nation's history has reflected different views of American identity and varying attitudes toward ethnic minorities and their contributions to American life. Students might explore such questions as: Was there a time in our history when the government viewed the United States as a "white" nation? a "European" nation? a nation of immigrants?

Chapter Resources

Readings for the Student

Bode, Janet. *New Kids on the Block: Oral Histories of Immigrant Teens.* Franklin Watts, 1989.

Handlin, Oscar. *A Pictorial History of Immigration.* Crown, 1972.

Morrison, Joan, and Charlotte Fox Zabusky. *American Mosaic: The Immigrant Experience in the Words of Those Who Lived It.* New American Library, 1980.

Schreuder, Sally Abel. *How to Become a United States Citizen—A Step-by-Step Guidebook for Self Instruction.* 3rd ed. Nolo Press, 1988. (Also in Spanish)

Weisberger, Bernard. *Many People, One Nation.* Houghton Mifflin, 1987.

Readings for the Teacher

Chesterton, Gilbert K. *What I Saw in America.* Dodd, Mead, 1923.

Kessner, Thomas, and Betty Boyd Caroli. *Today's Immigrants.* Oxford University Press, 1981.

Morgan, Ted. *On Becoming an American.* Houghton Mifflin, 1978.

Multimedia

Videocassettes and Films

Citizenship: The Public Influence on Government. Close-Up Foundation. (v/c, 30 minutes)

Democracy and Responsibilities: Citizen Stories. Smithsonian Institution/Close-Up Foundation. (v/c, 32 minutes)

The Inheritance. Harold Mayer Productions. (v/c, 45 minutes)

The Young Vote—Power, Politics and Participation. Phoenix/BFA Films and Video, Inc. (film, 15 minutes)

Software

The Discussion Generator: Welcome to Ellis Island. Tom Snyder Productions. (Apple, IBM disks). Students role-play decision making involving immigrants and immigration. Disk-based management included.

Immigration: Maintaining the Open Door. Social Studies School Service. (Apple disk and backup or IBM PC/PCjr disk and backup). Students decide current immigration policies.

Social Studies Keyword Programs—Changing America. Focus Media. (Apple, TRS80, Commodore 64, IBM disks). Students complete games to reinforce vocabulary, spelling, and word recognition related to historical changes in America.

Citizenship in the United States

CHAPTER

5

Introduce

Chapter Overview

Chapter 5 introduces students to the concept of citizenship, how it is acquired, and what it means.

Section 1 explores the legal bases for citizenship in the United States, including naturalization.

Section 2 examines the immigration policies of the United States and explains the differences between immigrants and aliens.

Section 3 highlights the basic rights and responsibilities of United States citizens.

Chapter 5 Themes

Have students read Themes in Government on page 155 and note the section(s) to which each theme applies. For each theme, ask them to write one question that they think will be answered in the chapter. Collect students' questions and use them for the Close activity in the last section.

GLENCOE
TECHNOLOGY

Focus on Government
Video 9
Lecture Launcher:
Citizenship in the United States
Running Time: 2:25
Videodisc 1, Chap. 9
VHS Tape 1, Begins 25:39

In what was called the largest naturalization event in United States history, more than 10,000 joyous people were naturalized in Miami's Orange Bowl in September 1990.

154   UNIT 2: CITIZENSHIP AND CIVIL LIBERTIES

About the Chapter Opener

Teaching With Illustrations Have students read the caption and examine the photograph on pages 154 and 155. Ask them what ethnic group makes up the largest part of this gathering. *(Hispanic Americans)* Ask them to describe the feelings of the people shown in the photograph. *(Students might* *indicate pride, excitement, or joy)* Then ask students why they think people from other countries want to become United States citizens. *(Answers will vary.)* How might they feel about leaving their countries to become United States citizens?

Chapter Preview

Overview
United States citizenship is a sought-after prize that carries with it rights as well as responsibilities.

Objectives
After studying this chapter, you should be able to:
1. **Identify** the legal bases for American citizenship.
2. **Outline** the definitions for immigrants and aliens and the policies affecting these groups.
3. **Describe** the rights and responsibilities of United States citizens.

Themes in Government
This chapter emphasizes the following government themes:
- **Constitutional Interpretations** The Fourteenth Amendment outlines the basis for national citizenship. Section 1.
- **Global Perspectives** Immigrants coming to the United States must go through naturalization to become citizens. Sections 1 and 2.
- **Cultural Pluralism** The United States is a nation of immigrants. Section 2.
- **Civic Participation** Citizenship includes both rights and responsibilities. Section 3.
- **Civic Responsibility** Americans have a responsibility to ensure that constitutional rights endure. Section 3.

Critical Thinking Skills
This chapter emphasizes the following critical thinking skills:
- Synthesizing Information
- Predicting Consequences
- Making Inferences
- Identifying Alternatives

CHAPTER 5: CITIZENSHIP IN THE UNITED STATES 155

Introducing the Chapter
Ask students to define *citizenship*. Write students' ideas on the chalkboard. Come to a consensus on a definition of the term and write it on the chalkboard.

Ask students how they became citizens of the United States. *(If some students are naturalized citizens, have them briefly explain the process through which they became citizens.)*

Chapter Project
Divide the class into three groups and assign each group one of these time frames: 1880–1924, 1925–1965, 1966–present. Have the groups research and make a list of the countries from which most immigrants to the United States came. Students may need to use almanacs, historical atlases, or other sources to identify the nations.

Provide a large world map at the front of the classroom. When students have completed the chapter, have a representative from each group place one color of yarn on the map to make lines connecting the United States to those countries identified on the group's list. When the three groups have finished, ask the students to make a general statement about the information indicated on the map.

> **Linking Past and Present**
> After the 1990 census was taken, the Census Bureau estimated that 6 million legal and 2 million undocumented immigrants came to the United States during the 1980s. This total for a 10-year period is second only to the 8.8 million immigrants who arrived between 1901 and 1910.

Setting the Scene Many recent immigrants to the United States are different from those immigrants who in the past have come from poverty to find a better life in a new country. For example, citizens of India are among the most educated of the new immigrants. Many Indian scientists, physicians, and engineers who could not find jobs in their own country have found jobs in the United States. Asian Americans are the fastest growing minority in the United States. Each year more than a quarter of a million Asians immigrate to the United States. These new immigrants are above the United States average in both income and education.

Focus

Bell Ringer

Write the following on the chalkboard for students to complete while attendance is being taken:

What do you think the requirements for becoming a citizen of the United States should be?

Motivating Activity

From the students' Bell Ringer lists make a class list on the chalkboard. Then ask students which items they think are currently needed for United States citizenship. Are there any other requirements students know of that are not listed? Add those to the list.

Vocabulary Precheck

Write the key terms for this section on the chalkboard. Ask students to use those that they know in sentences. **LEP**

Caption Answer

guarantees their citizenship

Linking Past and Present
When the Supreme Court ruled on the *Dred Scott* case, slavery was a hotly debated topic. Ask: What citizenship or immigration topics are hotly debated today? Has the Supreme Court ruled on these topics? If so, how?

SECTION

1

The Basis for United States Citizenship

Citizens are members of a political society—a nation. As such, citizens of the United States have certain rights, duties, and responsibilities. The Declaration of Independence addresses these rights and responsibilities:

> *We hold these truths to be self-evident, that all men are created equal, that they are endowed by their Creator with certain unalienable Rights, that among these are Life, Liberty, and the pursuit of Happiness. . . . That to secure these rights, Governments are instituted among Men, deriving their just powers from the consent of the governed. . . .*
> —THE DECLARATION OF INDEPENDENCE

The United States government, then, draws its power from the people and exists to secure their fundamental rights and equality under the law. Duties include obeying the law, paying taxes, and being loyal to the American government and its basic principles. As participants in government, citizens have the responsibility to be informed, vote, respect the rights and property of others, and respect different opinions and ways of life. Concerned citizens must be willing to exercise both their rights and responsibilities.

National Citizenship

United States citizenship is based on legal principles, yet citizenship involves much more than law. It includes how people feel about their society, as well as their concern for fellow citizens. Good citizenship can be expressed in many ways, but it begins with one person respecting the rights of another.

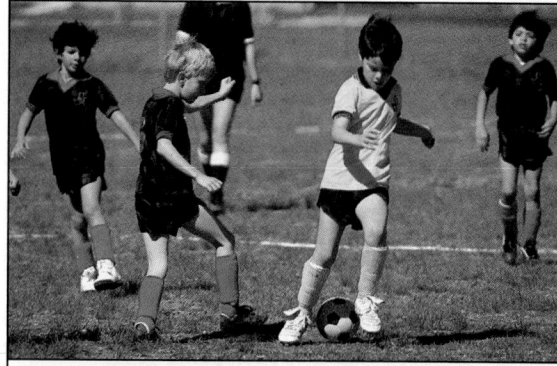

Land of Dreams
Children born of immigrant parents in the United States automatically become American citizens.
Citizenship How does the Fourteenth Amendment affect such children?

Over the years the basis of citizenship has changed significantly in the United States. Today citizenship is national, and its legal basis is described in the Constitution. This was not always so, however.

The articles of the Constitution mention citizenship only as a qualification for holding office in the federal government. The Founders assumed that the states would decide who was or was not a citizen. They also assumed that a citizen of a state was a citizen of the United States. The only exceptions were immigrants who became United States citizens through **naturalization,** the legal process by which a person is granted the rights and privileges of a citizen.

The *Dred Scott* Case The basis of state citizenship was at stake in the controversial *Dred Scott* case (1857). Dred Scott was an enslaved African American in

---

SECTION PREVIEW

Objectives
After studying this section, you should be able to:
■ Specify the legal bases for United States citizenship.
■ Explain how the basis of United

States citizenship has changed over the years.

Key Terms and Concepts
naturalization, jus soli, jus sanguinis, collective naturalization, expatriation, denaturalization

Themes in Government
■ Constitutional Interpretations
■ Global Perspectives

Critical Thinking Skills
■ Synthesizing Information
■ Predicting Consequences

Classroom Resources for Section 1

📁 Guided Reading Activities
📁 Reproducible Lesson Plans
📁 Supreme Court Case Studies 4
📁 Section 1 Quiz

💾 Testmaker
The Living Constitution
SAT Practice Test
Writer's Guidebook

Missouri, a slave state. Scott had also lived with his owner in Illinois—a free state—and the Wisconsin territory, where the Northwest Ordinance forbade slavery. Scott sued his owner's widow for his freedom, claiming that his earlier residence in a free state and a free territory made him free. A state court ruled in Scott's favor, but the Missouri Supreme Court later reversed the decision, prompting Scott's lawyers to go to the United States Supreme Court.

The Court, led by Chief Justice Roger Taney, ruled that Scott could not bring a legal suit in a federal court. Taney reasoned that African Americans, whether slaves or free, were not United States citizens at the time the Constitution was adopted. Therefore they could not claim citizenship. Only descendants of people who were state citizens at that time, or immigrants who became citizens through naturalization were United States citizens. The Court also stated that Congress could not forbid slavery in United States territories.

The Fourteenth Amendment The *Dred Scott* decision caused great outrage and protest in the North and added to the tensions that led to the Civil War. In 1868, three years after the end of the war, the Fourteenth Amendment to the Constitution put citizenship under national control.

The Fourteenth Amendment was clear and forceful about the basis of United States citizenship:

All persons born or naturalized in the United States, and subject to the jurisdiction thereof, are citizens of the United States and of the state wherein they reside. No State shall make or enforce any law which shall abridge [deprive] the privileges or immunities of citizens of the United States.

—FOURTEENTH AMENDMENT, 1868

The Fourteenth Amendment guaranteed that people of all races born in the United States and subject to its government are citizens. It also reversed the *Dred Scott* decision by making state citizenship an automatic result of national citizenship.

Citizenship by Birth

The Fourteenth Amendment set forth two of the three basic requirements for United States citizenship—birth on American soil and naturalization. The third source of citizenship is being born to a parent who is a United States citizen.

Citizenship by the "Law of the Soil" The United States follows the principle of *jus soli* (YOOS SOH•lee), a Latin phrase that means "law of the soil." Jus soli, in effect, grants citizenship to almost all people born in the United States or in American territories. Birth in the United States is the most common basis of United States citizenship. Most other countries use jus soli as a basis for citizenship as well.

Not everyone born in the United States is automatically a citizen. People born in the United States who are not subject to the jurisdiction of the United States government are not granted citizenship. For example, children of foreign diplomats are not American citizens, even though they may have been born in the United States. Similarly, a child born on a foreign ship in American territorial waters is not a United States citizen. Children born in this country to immigrant parents or to foreign parents merely passing through the country, however, are citizens of the United States.

Citizenship by Birth to an American Parent Another method of automatic citizenship is birth to an American parent or parents. This principle is called *jus sanguinis* (YOOS SAHN•gwuh•nuhs), which means the "law of blood."

The rules governing jus sanguinis can be very complicated. If an individual is born in a foreign country and both parents are United States citizens, the child is a citizen, provided one requirement is met. One of the parents must have been a legal resident of the United States or its possessions at some point in his or her life. If only one of the parents is an American citizen, however, that parent must have lived in the

---

STUDY GUIDE

Themes In Government
Constitutional Interpretations
The Constitution defined the structure of the government that presided over United States citizens but did not define citizenship itself. **If** the Constitution had defined citizenship in 1787, do you think it would have included African Americans? Why or Why not?

Critical Thinking Skills
Synthesizing Information Why might each nation define citizenship differently?

Teach

Guided Practice

L1 Analyzing Information
Read each of the following examples and ask students which source of citizenship—citizenship by the law of the soil, citizenship by birth to an American parent, or citizenship through naturalization—applies to each example. Ask students to explain their choices.

1. Natalie DiAngelo is born in the United States Virgin Islands. *(law of the soil)*
2. A former citizen of France visits the United States and wishes to stay. She goes through the process of becoming a citizen. *(naturalization)*
3. Robert Medlan is born in Switzerland. His mother and father are American citizens. *(birth to an American parent)* **LEP**

STUDY GUIDE

Theme Answer
It probably would not have, because including African Americans would have provided a basis on which they could have claimed freedom and equal rights.

Critical Thinking Answer
because such a definition is based on a nation's unique history, government, and population

---

CONNECTIONS

Biography
Shortly after the Supreme Court decision in 1857, Dred Scott was freed. Scott moved to St. Louis where he worked as a hotel porter until his death the following year.

Background

Immigrants who have become citizens have passed a test proving some knowledge of United States history and government. The following are examples of questions asked on the test: What is the supreme law of the land? How many branches are there in the United States government? Who is now President? What is the next highest office? How many senators are there in Congress? Name the senators from your state. How many representatives are there in Congress? For how many years is the President elected? For how many years does a representative and a senator serve? Studies have shown that many native-born Americans cannot answer all these questions correctly.

L2 Making a Flow Chart Draw a flow chart showing the steps in the naturalization process that immigrants must follow to become American citizens. Have students discuss the details of each step.

L3 Law Refer students to the Fourteenth Amendment excerpt on page 157. Ask students what phrase put citizenship under national control. (*All persons born . . . they reside.*) Ask how it changed the relationship between state and national citizenship. (*reversed it by making state citizenship an automatic result of national citizenship*)

GLOBAL CONNECTION

Point out to students that part of the naturalization process for citizenship in the United States involves a renunciation of loyalty to the former government. Discuss with students possible reasons for this requirement.
**Examining the Connection
Answer:** *advantages: freedom to live and work in two countries; disadvantages: may be liable for military service, taxes, and so on, in two countries*

STUDY GUIDE

Theme Answer
advantage: people from countries where English is the official language or from countries that share a common heritage with the United States; disadvantage: people from countries where English is not spoken

Critical Thinking Answer
The country would be flooded with immigrants and refugees.

GLOBAL CONNECTION

Issues

Dual Nationality A citizen born in the United States might also be a citizen of another country as well–a dual citizen.

A person can become a dual citizen by birth, by marriage, and by naturalization. A baby born to French parents in the United States would have French citizenship by jus sanguinis and American citizenship by jus soli.

In some countries a woman gains citizenship by marrying a citizen of that country. A person who marries an American citizen may become a naturalized citizen after living in this country for three years.

If a country does not require naturalized citizens to renounce their previous citizenship, they may claim dual nationality.

Examining the Connection
What might be some of the advantages and disadvantages of holding dual citizenship?

United States or an American possession for at least 10 years, 5 of which had to occur after the age of 14.

Citizenship by Naturalization

All immigrants who wish to become American citizens must go through naturalization. At the end of that process, they will have almost all the rights and privileges of a native-born citizen. The major exception is that a naturalized citizen is not eligible to serve as President or Vice President of the United States.

Congress has defined specific qualifications and procedures for naturalization. These include a residency requirement that immigrants must satisfy before they can even apply to become citizens. The Immigration and Naturalization Service, a branch of the Department of Justice, administers most of the key steps of the naturalization process.

Qualifications for Citizenship Immigrants who want to become citizens must meet five requirements. (1) Applicants must have entered the United States legally. (2) They must be of good moral character. (3) They must declare their support of the principles of American government. (4) They must prove they can read, write, and speak English. (If applicants are more than 50 years old and have lived in the United States for 20 years, they are exempt from the English-language requirement.) (5) They must show some basic knowledge of American history and government.

At the same time, draft evaders, military deserters, polygamists, anarchists, Communists, or followers of any other totalitarian system will be denied citizenship.

The Steps to Citizenship To start the naturalization process, an applicant must file a petition requesting citizenship. Anyone who is at least 18 years old and who has lived in the United States for 5 continuous years and in the state where the petition is filed for at least 3 months may apply for citizenship. If the applicant is married to a United States citizen, he or she needs only 3 years of residency before filing.

The key step in the naturalization process is an investigation and preliminary hearing that the Immigration and Naturalization Service conducts. The hearing is a test of an applicant's qualifications for citizenship, in which the individual is asked questions about his or her moral character. Two witnesses, usually close friends or people applicants know from work, are also asked about the prospective citizen's character and integrity. In addition, applicants may be asked to demonstrate their grasp of the English language.

An applicant for citizenship is also questioned about American government and history. Typical

STUDY GUIDE

Themes In Government
Global Perspectives Because of certain requirments for citizenship, such as speaking English and knowing some American history, it is more difficult for people from some nations to become citizens of the United States than for others. **What nationalities would have an advantage in these requirements? What nationalities would have the greatest disadvantage?**

Critical Thinking Skills
Predicting Consequences **What might happen if there were no procedures for becoming an American citizen?**

Cooperative Learning Activity

Remind students that people who want to become citizens of the United States must demonstrate knowledge of America's political heritage. Divide the class into several small groups. Instruct each group to develop a citizenship test of about 20 questions. Students should include questions they think every American citizen should be able to answer. After the groups have finished, have them exchange tests and see if they can answer the questions. Have students note which questions, if any, all groups' tests had in common. (You might share the information in this section's Background with the students when they complete their discussions.)

questions include: "What is the highest court in the land?" "How many states are there in the United States?" "What happens if the President dies?" Sometimes applicants are asked to identify certain American Presidents.

If an applicant makes it through this step—and most do—he or she will be asked to attend a final hearing. This hearing is usually held in a federal district court and is normally only a formality. Here the judge administers the United States oath of allegiance. The oath requires individuals to renounce loyalty to their former governments, to obey and defend the Constitution and laws of the United States, and to bear arms on behalf of the United States when required by law. The judge then issues a certificate of naturalization that declares the individual a United States citizen. Naturalized American citizens include Alexander Graham Bell, Albert Einstein, Alfred Hitchcock, Arnold Schwarzenegger, and Gloria Estefan.

New citizens receive a letter from the President, a short history of the Pledge of Allegiance, and a booklet containing important documents in American history. The new citizen also generally receives copies of pamphlets that explain how to be a good citizen.

Cuban-born Gloria Estefan Tops the Charts
Immigrants often exert a lively influence on American culture. **Sociology** In what other fields have immigrants played important roles?

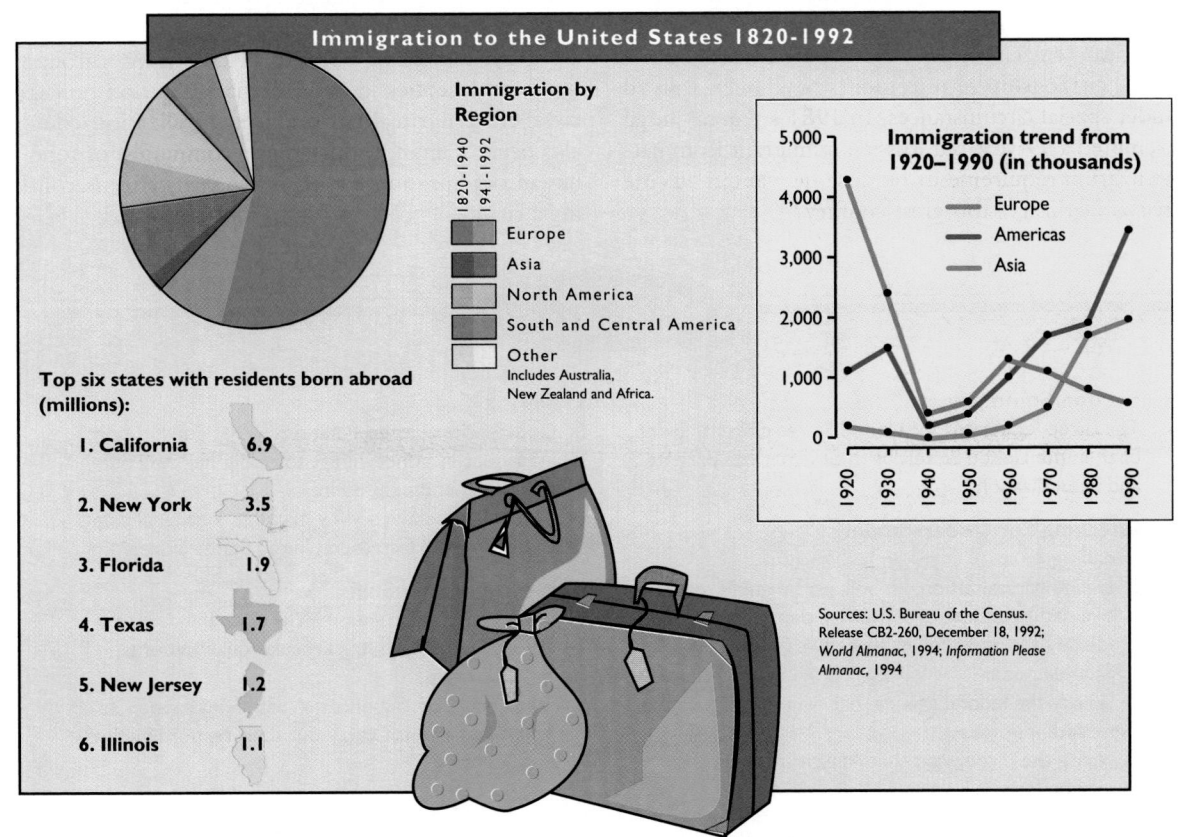

Immigration to the United States 1820-1992

Immigration by Region

1820-1940
1941-1992

- Europe
- Asia
- North America
- South and Central America
- Other
Includes Australia, New Zealand and Africa.

Top six states with residents born abroad (millions):

1. California	6.9
2. New York	3.5
3. Florida	1.9
4. Texas	1.7
5. New Jersey	1.2
6. Illinois	1.1

Immigration trend from 1920–1990 (in thousands)

- Europe
- Americas
- Asia

5,000
4,000
3,000
2,000
1,000
0

1920 1930 1940 1950 1960 1970 1980 1990

Sources: U.S. Bureau of the Census. Release CB2-260, December 18, 1992; World Almanac, 1994; Information Please Almanac, 1994

Special Needs Strategy

Reading Disability This section introduces some terms in Latin (*jus soli* and *jus sanguinis*) that may present pronunciation difficulties for all students. Students with weak reading skills may have a particularly hard time pronouncing and remembering these terms. Practice pronouncing these terms after explaining the pronunciation guides that are given in parentheses after the terms. Point out that letters often have different sounds in foreign words. The "j" in "*jus*" is pronounced as a "y," for example, and the vowel sounds are different from those in English.

Independent Practice

L1 Vocabulary Have students write the definitions for naturalization, *jus soli*, *jus sanguinis*, collective naturalization, expatriation, and denaturalization. Then have them find a sentence in the section in which the word is used. Finally, have them write original sentences using the terms. **LEP**

Analyzing Supreme Court Cases Have students complete case 4, *Dred Scott* v. *Sanford* (1857), in *Supreme Court Case Studies* in the Teacher's Classroom Resources.

L3 Interviewing Ask students to locate a naturalized citizen in their locality to interview. Students should ask the person to discuss his or her experiences in working to achieve citizenship. Have them develop their interview into a report for presentation to the class.

Caption Answer
science, education, sports, government, and many others

Assess

Check for Understanding

Have students complete Section 1 Review on page 160.

Meeting Objectives

Each section objective is tested by the Section Review questions that follow it in parentheses.
- Specify the legal bases for United States citizenship. (3, 4, 7)
- Explain how the basis of United States citizenship has changed over the years. (2, 5, 8)

Evaluate

📁 Section 1 Quiz

🔲 Testmaker

Reteach

Have students write a letter to a pen pal in another country. Students should suppose that their pen pal wishes to come to the United States and become an American citizen. Students should explain the qualifications for citizenship and the steps in the naturalization process.

Enrich

Ask students to read Edward Everett Hale's short story "The Man Without a Country," and focus on Philip Nolan's reaction to being deprived of United States citizenship. Have students write an essay describing what it would be like not to have a home country.

Close

Discuss with students in what ways feelings about citizenship might be different in people who are born citizens and in those who earn their citizenship.

Exceptions While naturalization procedures are similar for most people, some exceptions exist. One is **collective naturalization,** a process by which a whole group of people, living in the same geographic area, becomes American citizens through an act of Congress. These individuals do not have to go through the naturalization process.

Congress has used collective naturalization several times. In 1803, for example, people living in the territory gained through the Louisiana Purchase were granted American citizenship. Similarly, when Florida was purchased in 1819, and when the Republic of Texas was admitted to the Union in 1845, people living in these territories received United States citizenship. Likewise, Congress granted citizenship to all people living in Hawaii in 1900 and to the residents of Puerto Rico in 1917.

Other exceptions have occurred. For more than a century, most Native Americans were excluded from citizenship—even after their land was annexed by the United States. A few groups became citizens through treaties with the federal government, but in 1866 Congress decided that the citizenship guarantees of the Fourteenth Amendment would not apply to Native Americans. Later Congress offered citizenship to individual Indians who gave up their traditional culture. Not until 1924 did Congress make all Native Americans citizens of the United States. On the other hand, citizenship requirements have been waived under special circumstances. In 1981 a federal judge exempted a 99-year-old Russian immigrant from naturalization requirements because he wanted "to die free as a citizen of this great country."

Losing Citizenship

Only the federal government can both grant citizenship and take it away. State governments can deny a convicted criminal some of the privileges of citizenship, such as voting, but have no power to deny citizenship itself. Americans may lose their citizenship in any of three ways.

Expatriation The simplest way to lose citizenship is through **expatriation,** or giving up one's citizenship by leaving one's native country to live in a foreign country. Expatriation may be voluntary or involuntary. For example, a man or woman who marries a British citizen and establishes a home there may voluntarily give up American citizenship. A person who becomes a naturalized citizen of another country automatically loses his or her American citizenship. Involuntary expatriation would also occur in the case of a child whose parents become citizens of another country.

Punishment for a Crime A person may lose citizenship when convicted of certain federal crimes that involve extreme disloyalty. These crimes include treason, participation in a rebellion, and attempts to overthrow the government through violent means.

Denaturalization The loss of citizenship through fraud or deception during the naturalization process is called **denaturalization.** Denaturalization could also occur if an individual joins a communist or totalitarian organization less than five years after becoming a citizen.

---

1 — SECTION REVIEW

Section Summary
The three legal bases for United States citizenship are birth in the United States, birth to American parents, and naturalization.

Checking For Understanding
Recalling Facts
1. Define naturalization, jus soli, jus sanguinis, collective naturalization, expatriation, denaturalization.
2. Identify the amendment that reversed the *Dred Scott* decision.
3. Specify the federal agency that oversees the naturalization process.
4. Name the three ways that American citizenship may be lost.

Exploring Themes
5. Constitutional Interpretations What constitutional inadequacies concerning citizenship did the Fourteenth Amendment address?
6. Global Perspectives Why might an individual want to become a naturalized United States citizen?

Critical Thinking Skills
7. Synthesizing Information Why does the United States have its particular qualifications for citizenship?
8. Predicting Consequences What could happen if Americans did not carry out their responsibilities as citizens?

160 UNIT 2: CITIZENSHIP AND CIVIL LIBERTIES

Section I Review Answers

1. Definitions of terms appear on pages indicated: **naturalization,** 156; *jus soli,* 157; *jus sanguinis,* 157; **collective naturalization,** 160; **expatriation,** 160; **denaturalization,** 160
2. Fourteenth Amendment
3. Immigration and Naturalization Service, a branch of Department of Justice

4. through expatriation, punishment for a crime, denaturalization
5. basis of citizenship, position of state citizenship relative to national citizenship
6. Answers will vary, but may include more freedoms, better opportunities, escaping political or religious persecution or war.

7. Because the United States is based on self-government, it is vital that new citizens understand and support the principles of government and speak the language in order to participate.
8. Answers may include giving up their right to a voice in government, being imprisoned, eventual corruption or breakdown of the government.

Understanding Cause and Effect

Understanding cause and effect involves considering why an event occurred. A cause is the action or situation that produces an event. An effect is the result or consequence of an action or a situation. If you understand why events occur, you can make an informed decision about how to solve problems.

Explanation
To understand cause and effect, follow these steps:
• Identify two or more events or developments.
• Decide whether one event caused the other. One useful way to determine this is to look for language clues. Such words as *because, as a result of, because of, for this reason*, and *thus* often indicate a cause-and-effect relationship.
• Decide whether one event caused the other.
  For example:

The United States acquires vast, thinly settled western lands. (cause) *Abundant land becomes available to new settlers.* (effect)

Because many Californians feared that immigrants would work for lower wages, Congress passed the Chinese Exclusion Act.

The statement reflects a clear cause-and-effect relationship. The word *because* shows this relationship. Sometimes an effect produced by a cause may itself become the cause of another effect.

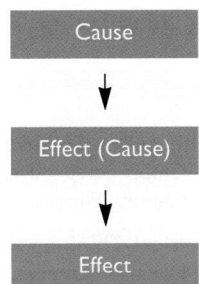

In other cases multiple causes may lead to a single effect. A single cause may also have multiple effects. For example:

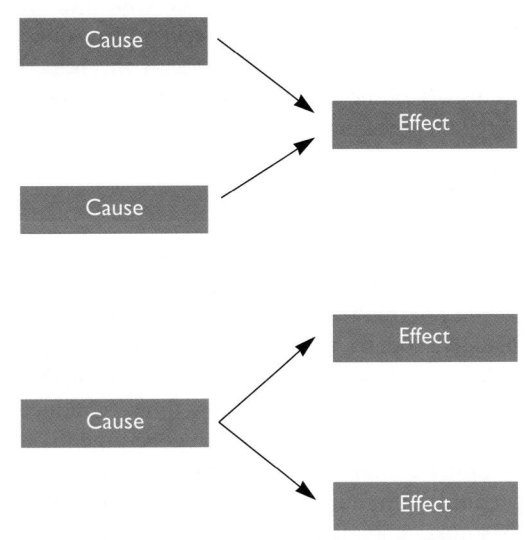

Practice
Consider the following statements. Each of these statements includes a cause and an effect. For each statement make a cause-and-effect diagram by writing the cause on the left and the effect on the right. Then connect the two parts of the statement with an arrow.
1. Because the government wanted to prevent any change in the ethnic makeup of the United States, Congress passed the Johnson Act.
2. As a result of new government policies, immigration fell sharply.
3. During World War I, German Americans were not allowed near vital war zones because of fears of sabotage.

> ### Additional Practice
> To practice this skill, see **Reinforcing the Skill** on page 175.

CHAPTER 5: CITIZENSHIP IN THE UNITED STATES 161

Focus

Ask students what happens if the school's track team is late for a meet. Discuss students' responses, reviewing with them ways events are related. Point out that one event often triggers other events, and that understanding these relationships is important to making informed decisions.

Teach

Briefly review the language clues that identify cause and effect. Stress that events are not usually one-dimensional. One event usually has multiple effects. For example, the introduction of slavery resulted in a wide range of American laws. Have students consider the reverse condition: many events can come together and create one effect. For example, the attack on Pearl Harbor was preceded by years of commercial and political rivalry between the United States and Japan. Have students explain the multiple effects that United States land acquisition had on population movement, mining, and agriculture.

Assess

Have students complete the **Practice** exercise.

Close

Have students give examples of a cause-and-effect situation that is current today.

Practice Answers

1. Because the government wanted to prevent any change in the ethnic makeup of the United States, ➝ Congress passed the Johnson Act.
2. As a result of new government policies, ➝ immigration fell sharply.
3. Because of fears of sabotage during World War I, ➝ German Americans were not allowed near vital war zones.

For additional practice, have students complete activity 5 in *Skill Reinforcement Activities* in the Teacher's Classroom Resources.

Focus

Bell Ringer

Write the following quotation from historian Oscar Handlin—reproduced on page 162—on the chalkboard:

"Once I thought to write a history of immigrants in America. Then I discovered that the immigrants *were* American history."

Ask students to write a brief explanation of what Handlin means.

Motivating Activity

Ask several volunteers to read their Bell Ringer explanations. Then ask students what they know about the immigration policies of the United States. Tell students that this section explains these policies.

Vocabulary Precheck

Call on students to read aloud the definitions of this section's key terms and concepts from the Glossary. Then have volunteers use each term or concept in a sentence. **LEP**

Caption Answer

Resident aliens permanently reside in the United States; non-resident aliens stay for a short time.

CONNECTIONS

Law

By May 1988, the deadline for amnesty under the Immigration Reform and Control Act, approximately 1.4 million illegal aliens had applied for temporary resident status. Some 71 percent of these applicants were from Mexico.

A Nation of Immigrants

Since 1820, when the United States government began recording immigration statistics, more than 57 million immigrants have come to the United States. Arriving from all corners of the world, these immigrants have made enormous contributions to American life. Oscar Handlin, a well-known American historian, put it very well: "Once I thought to write a history of the immigrants in America. Then I discovered that the immigrants *were* American history."

Immigrants and Aliens

Throughout American history immigrants have often been referred to as aliens. An **alien** is a person who lives in a country where he or she is not a citizen. Aliens may not intend to become citizens, or they may be in a country only for a short time—conducting business or working for a foreign government.

An immigrant, however, is a person who comes to a new country intending to live there permanently. Strictly speaking, immigrants are also aliens until they become naturalized citizens. Because *alien* is a legal word that seems to have unfriendly implications, many immigrants resent being called aliens. Ted Morgan, a French writer who became an American citizen, expressed the feelings of many immigrants:

I have hated that word "alien." It means foreign, distant, different in nature, adverse, whereas I wanted to be not foreign, not different, not adverse. The central aim of the immigrant is to join a society, not to be alienated from it.

—Ted Morgan

"Huddled Masses Yearning to Breathe Free"
From 1892 to 1943, millions of immigrants passed through Ellis Island, a major United States immigration station. **Law What is the difference between resident and non-resident aliens?**

United States law classifies aliens into five different categories.

Resident Aliens A **resident alien** is a person from a foreign nation who has established permanent residence in the United States. Thus, immigrants are resident aliens until they become naturalized citizens. Resident aliens may stay in the United States as long as they wish. They are not required to seek American citizenship, although most eventually do.

SECTION PREVIEW

Objectives
After studying this section, you should be able to:
- Distinguish between immigrants and aliens.
- Describe the five categories of aliens.

- Summarize American immigration policy.

Key Terms and Concepts
alien, resident alien, non-resident alien, enemy alien, illegal alien, national origins system, private law, amnesty

Themes in Government
- Global Perspectives
- Cultural Pluralism

Critical Thinking Skills
- Making Inferences
- Identifying Alternatives

162 Unit 2: Citizenship and Civil Liberties

Classroom Resources for Section 2

- Guided Reading Activities
- Reproducible Lesson Plans
- Participating in Government 5
- Primary and Secondary Source Readings 5
- Enrichment Activities 5
- Section 2 Quiz

- Testmaker
- Chapter Transparencies 5
- The Living Constitution
- SAT Practice Tests
- Writer's Guidebook

Non-Resident Aliens A **non-resident alien** is a person from a foreign country who expects to stay in the United States for a short, specified period of time. Non-resident aliens are not immigrants. A Nigerian journalist who has come to report on a presidential election and a Swiss manufacturer who has come to promote a new line of watches are examples of non-resident aliens.

Enemy Aliens An **enemy alien** is a citizen of a nation with which the United States is at war. Legally, enemy aliens living in the United States are entitled to the full protection of their life and property. During wartime, however, the public's feelings often run high, and enemy aliens have sometimes been subjected to discriminatory practices. During World War I, for example, German citizens who were living in the United States were required to register with the government and were prohibited from traveling to vital war zones. In World War II, the United States government interned more than 100,000 people of Japanese descent who lived on the West Coast, even though two-thirds were United States citizens.

Refugees People who are considered refugees from their homelands are permitted to immigrate to the United States. Recently refugees have come from El Salvador, Haiti, Eastern Europe, Afghanistan, Ethiopia, Southeast Asia, and Cuba. Under the Refugee Act of 1980, 50,000 refugees were permitted to enter the United States each year, but the number usually exceeded this figure because the President waived the limit in emergency situations. Today refugees make up at least 2 percent of the world's population. Because of their growing numbers, the United States authorized refugee admissions of more than 120,000 per year.

In 1994 poor conditions in Haiti and Cuba swelled the flow of "boat people" seeking refuge in the United States. The 1994 exodus was so overwhelming that the President ordered thousands detained while their cases were reviewed by immigration officials.

Illegal Aliens An **illegal alien** is a person who comes to the United States without a legal permit, such as a passport, visa, or entry permit. Most enter by illegally crossing United States borders, while some are foreigners who have stayed in the United States after their legal permits have expired.

The number of illegal aliens in the United States is believed to be very large. The Immigration and Naturalization Service estimates that between 2 and 3

Japanese Americans Relocated During Wartime Estelle Ishigo, wife of one of the internees, painted this view of an internment camp. **Law** **What are the rights of enemy aliens in the United States?**

million "illegals" will be in the United States during the mid-1990s.

The large number of illegal aliens in the United States has become a controversial issue in recent years. For the most part, opposition to illegal aliens centers around the charge that they are taking jobs away from people legally residing in the United States.

Aliens' Rights Aliens living in the United States enjoy most of the same rights as American citizens. The protections the Bill of Rights guarantees, such as freedom of speech and assembly, apply to aliens as well as citizens. In addition, the Supreme Court has repeatedly struck down state government attempts to limit the rights of aliens. In 1982, for example, the Supreme Court ruled that the state of Texas could not deny free public education to children of illegal aliens.

Aliens may own homes, attend public schools, carry on businesses, and use public facilities, just as citizens do. Similarly, aliens are expected to share in many of the responsibilities of American life. They are required to pay taxes, obey the law, and be loyal to the government. They cannot vote, however, and are usually exempt from military and jury duty. Unlike citizens, aliens are not guaranteed the right to travel freely in the United States. This restriction has been applied in times of war. All aliens, even those who have applied for United States citizenship, are required to notify the Immigration and Naturalization Service when they change their residence.

Background

One of the key considerations behind the amnesty proposal for illegal immigrants was practicality. Immigration and Naturalization Service officials testified that apprehending all of the illegal aliens was financially impractical. An average of 1 million illegal aliens had been deported annually between 1977 and 1981, and many of these simply returned and were not apprehended. At the same time, those illegal immigrants who remained over time were viewed by some as an underclass of people who contributed to social, political, and health problems and whose human rights were routinely violated.

Teach
Guided Practice

L1 **Making Comparisons** List on the chalkboard the five categories of aliens: *resident aliens, non-resident aliens, enemy aliens, refugees,* and *illegal aliens.* Then ask students to explain and give an example for each category.
LEP

 Interpreting Visuals Display transparency 5 from the *Chapter Transparencies* in the Teacher's Classroom Resources and use the accompanying teaching strategy and student activity to teach the rights new immigrants to the United States have.

L2 **Constructing a Chart** Work with students to construct a chart on the chalkboard of American immigration laws from 1882 to the present using *Dates of Immigration Law, Name of Law,* and *Conditions of Law* for horizontal headings. Have students suggest entries to complete the chart.

Caption Answer
They are entitled to full protection of life and property.

CONNECTIONS

Global Perspectives
Since the fall of communism and the opening of borders between East and West, immigration levels have become an issue of concern in Western Europe. A 1991 poll conducted in the 12 nations of the European Community (EC) found that more than 40 percent of the people felt there were too many immigrants.

GLENCOE
TECHNOLOGY

Focus on Government
Video 8
Electronic Field Trip:
Ellis Island
Running Time: 5:38
Videodisc 1, Chap. 8
VHS Tape 1, Begins 19:59

L3 Debate Have students debate the following point:

The rights of aliens from enemy nations should be restricted during wartime.

(*pro argument: The welfare and security of the entire country should take precedence over the welfare of a small group; con argument: All people living in the United States are entitled to the full protection of their life and property.*)

Independent Practice

L1 Mathematics Have students use library resources, particularly the *Statistical Yearbook of the Immigration and Naturalization Service,* to find the number of immigrants to the United States between 1900 and the present. Students might present their information in a line graph. In a brief paragraph, students should note and explain the trends in immigration shown on the line graph. **LEP**

L2 Research Ask students to investigate and report on the mail-in lottery established in 1991, which gave 40,000 foreigners an opportunity to live permanently in the United States. Have students report on what forces were behind the establishment of the lottery and the rules and results of the lottery.

Immigration Policy

The reasons for immigration have not changed much over the years. Every year an estimated 4 million foreigners apply to become immigrants because they see the United States as a place where they can live a better life. In the 1980s and early 1990s, Haitians came to the United States in large numbers to escape poverty and political oppression. Thousands of immigrants come from Southeast Asia, fleeing war and communist oppression. Soviet Jews have sought refuge in the United States from religious and political persecution.

The words inscribed on a plaque at the base of the Statue of Liberty continue to welcome new immigrants as they did those who have come before. The "Mother of Exiles" extends the promise of freedom and opportunity:

From her beacon-hand Glows world-wide welcome; her mild eyes command The air-bridged harbor that twin cities frame. "Keep, ancient lands, your storied pomp!" cries she With silent lips. "Give me your tired, your poor, Your huddled masses yearning to breathe free, The wretched refuse of your teeming shore. Send these, the homeless, tempest-tost to me. I lift my lamp beside the golden door!"
—EMMA LAZARUS, "THE NEW COLOSSUS," 1883

Millions of immigrants have been able to come to the United States because of the open immigration policies that have prevailed throughout much of American history.

The Constitution clearly assigns Congress the power to control immigration policy. In the years

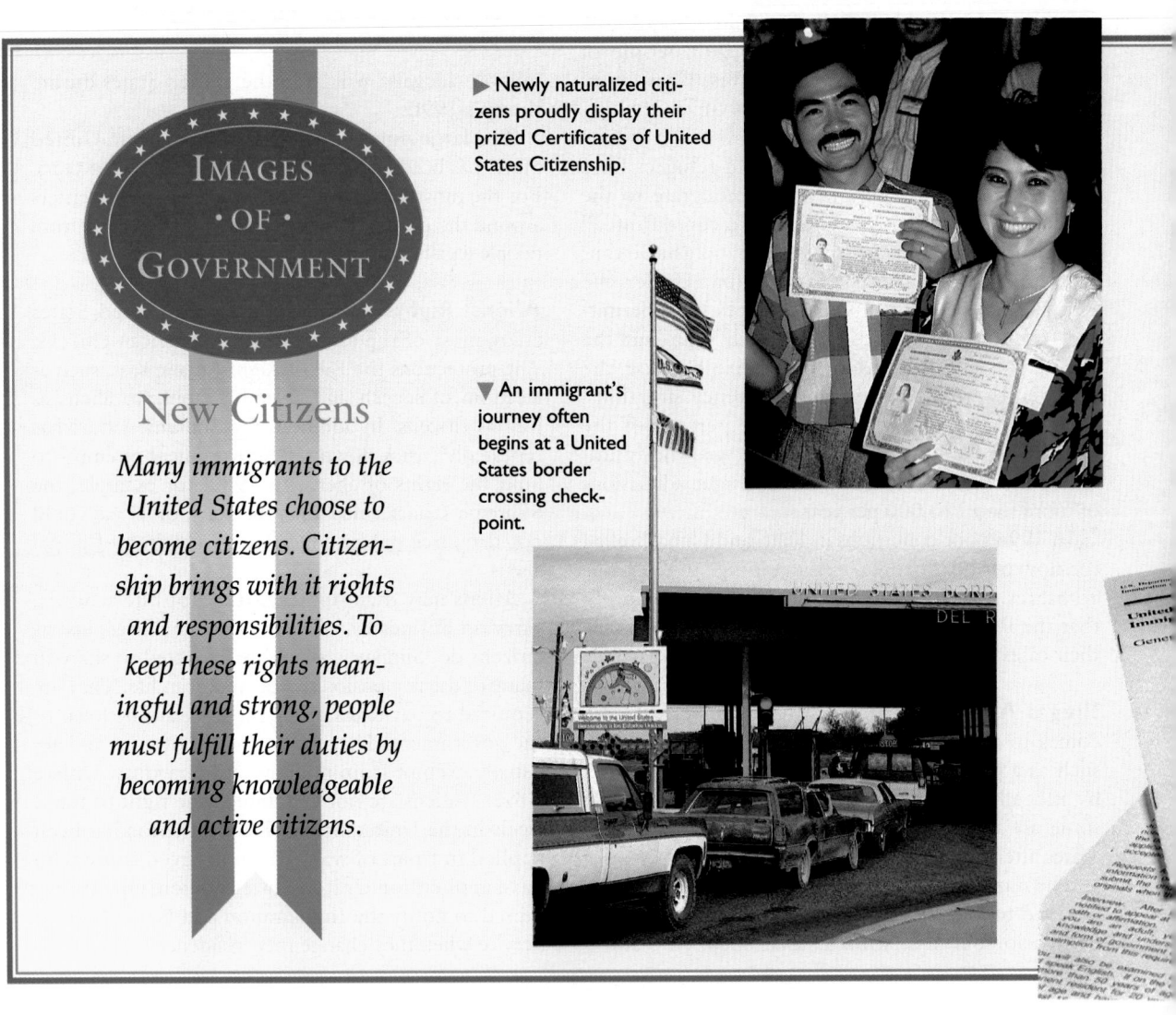

IMAGES
• OF •
GOVERNMENT

New Citizens

Many immigrants to the United States choose to become citizens. Citizenship brings with it rights and responsibilities. To keep these rights meaningful and strong, people must fulfill their duties by becoming knowledgeable and active citizens.

▶ Newly naturalized citizens proudly display their prized Certificates of United States Citizenship.

▼ An immigrant's journey often begins at a United States border crossing checkpoint.

164 UNIT 2: CITIZENSHIP AND CIVIL LIBERTIES

Cooperative Learning Activity

Organize students into small groups to research immigrant groups in their community. Have each group choose a member who will represent them at meetings. The group representatives should plan together what nationality groups they want to study, what information they want to gather, and

how information is to be presented. Students might tape first-person accounts of the immigrants' experiences, research what important immigrant groups are associated with their area, and provide cultural data on the immigrants.

before 1882, however, Congress rarely exercised this power and left immigration generally unrestricted. The reasons for American open immigration policy were varied: a spirit of generosity, based on the recognition that most United States citizens were descendants of immigrants; the availability of abundant land for new settlers; and the need for cheap labor to work the farms and factories of an expanding economy.

Since 1882, however, Congress has enacted a variety of laws that have restricted immigration. In the last 100 years, United States immigration policy has gone through distinct stages: (1) Between 1882 and 1924, Congress legislated a number of restrictions, although immigration itself remained very high. (2) Between 1924 and 1965, United States immigration policy closed the door to many immigrants and clearly favored immigrants of certain ethnic groups and

nationalities. (3) Beginning in 1965 United States immigration policy once again became more liberal, with an emphasis on kinship with relatives already living in the United States. (4) In 1990 immigration policy reflected a desire to establish a fairer policy regarding countries of origin and to encourage more professional, managerial, and skilled people to come to the United States.

1882–1924: The Growth of Restrictions In 1882 Congress passed the first major federal immigration law that barred entrance to people such as the mentally handicapped, convicts, and paupers. In that year Congress also passed the Chinese Exclusion Act that restricted the admission of Chinese laborers. At the same time, the law prevented all foreign-born Chinese from acquiring citizenship. This provision marked the first time a federal law had restricted

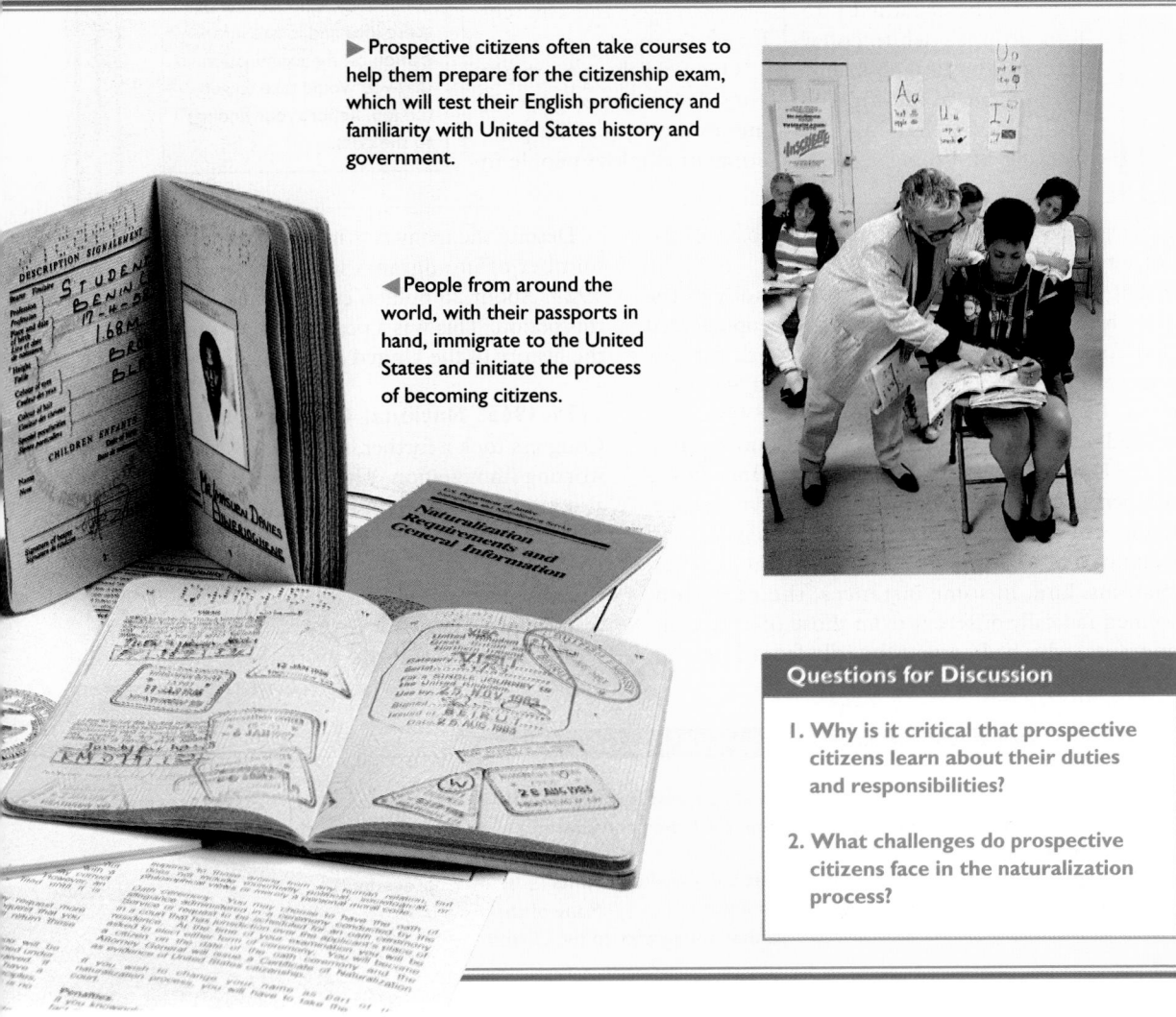

▶ Prospective citizens often take courses to help them prepare for the citizenship exam, which will test their English proficiency and familiarity with United States history and government.

◀ People from around the world, with their passports in hand, immigrate to the United States and initiate the process of becoming citizens.

Questions for Discussion

1. Why is it critical that prospective citizens learn about their duties and responsibilities?

2. What challenges do prospective citizens face in the naturalization process?

CHAPTER 5: CITIZENSHIP IN THE UNITED STATES 165

Interpreting Source Readings Have students complete activity 5 in *Primary and Secondary Source Readings* in the Teacher's Classroom Resources.

L3 Cultural Pluralism Have students investigate the status of the 600,000 war refugees from Vietnam, Cambodia, and Laos who were admitted to the United States through special legislation passed by Congress. Ask students to discover in which areas of the country these refugees now reside and what organizations worked to help them adjust to life in the United States. Suggest that students present their findings in the form of a magazine article.

Images of Government

Have students discuss how they think they would feel if they were new immigrants or if they had just become American citizens.

Answers

1. Civic participation and responsibility are essential to the continued success of our democratic system.
2. familiarize themselves with United States history and government; some must also master the English language

CONNECTIONS

History
To adjust to their new country, immigrants formed groups centered around churches, synagogues, and schools. Foreign-language newspapers served as a link among the immigrants.

Special Needs Strategy

Study Strategy Students who are inefficient readers will often profit by using a form of rapid reading called scanning to locate specific information. Tell the students you are going to demonstrate scanning to find all the dates mentioned in this section. Using your finger, model scanning by

sliding your finger rapidly down the middle of the columns of page 163. Demonstrate finding the dates 1991, 1980, 1990s, and 1982. Time students as they scan for the remaining dates in this section.

PARTICIPATING IN GOVERNMENT

Point out to students that after they have discovered a potential career choice, a good way to get a closer view of the career and what it entails is to interview someone in the particular field. Suggest that students prepare a list of questions before conducting the interview.

Have students complete activity 5 in *Participating in Government* in the Teacher's Classroom Resources.

CONNECTIONS

Language

The word *quota*, meaning specifically "the number of immigrants allowed to be admitted," is an Americanism. Before the word was used in this context, *quota* was a general word taken from the Latin *quota pars,* meaning "how large a part?"

STUDY GUIDE

Theme Answer

The Supreme Court probably considered the negative effects being taught in a foreign language would have on children, the effects of children delaying learning English, and the problems schools might face in finding teachers proficient in various foreign languages.

Critical Thinking Answer

It restricted immigration and favored immigrants from politically stable areas.

GLENCOE TECHNOLOGY

Focus on Government
Video 9
Lecture Launcher:
Citizenship in the United States
Running Time: 2:25
Videodisc 1, Chap. 9
VHS Tape 1, Begins 25:39

PARTICIPATING IN GOVERNMENT

Deciding on a Job

HELP WANTED

Deciding what you want to do after you graduate is a difficult decision. Before you can decide on a career, however, you should consider your personal goals, your abilities, and your characteristics.

Another step in choosing a career is to determine how the characteristics of different jobs suit your personal characteristics and needs. Jobs may be classified into four groups—white collar (occupations dealing mainly with people or ideas), blue collar (jobs that involve working with things), farm, and service. You also will need to find out the following kinds of information: working conditions, required skills or abilities, preparation needed, probable earnings, and chances for employment.

One field that you might consider is that of government employee. The government employs people in more than 2,000 different categories that include both white-collar and blue-collar workers. Most of these jobs require applicants to take some type of examination. Positions are then filled according to the results of the examinations.

Investigating Further

Find out what government jobs are available in your community. Choose one of these jobs and locate information on the examination that you would take to get the job. Report your findings to the class.

either immigration or citizenship on the basis of nationality or ethnic group.

The number of restrictions grew steadily in the next three decades. In the West many people feared that Asian immigrants, willing to work for low wages, would take jobs away from United States citizens. People in the rest of the country were concerned about the new kind of immigrant coming to the United States. Most of the immigrants during this period came from southern and eastern Europe, from countries such as Italy, Russia, and Poland. Their language, their appearance, their customs, and, in some instances, their religion, seemed radically different from those of earlier immigrants, who had come primarily from England, Ireland, and Germany.

Despite the many restrictions on immigration, the number of immigrants soared between 1882 and 1924. About 25 million entered the United States in this period. This was a peak period of immigration in the history of the United States.

1924–1965: National Origins Quotas In 1924 Congress took a further, more drastic step toward restricting immigration. The Immigration Act of 1924, also known as the Johnson Act, lowered the number of immigrants allowed into the country to less than 165,000 per year. This restriction represented an 80 percent decrease in annual immigration from the years before World War I.

The Johnson Act did more than limit the total number of immigrants. It also instituted a system

STUDY GUIDE

Themes in Government
Cultural Pluralism In 1974 the Supreme Court ruled in favor of bilingual education for children who cannot speak English. **What possi-**ble effects of this ruling do you think the Court considered?

Critical Thinking Skills
Making Inferences Many of the earliest immigrants to the United States were refugees fleeing persecution. **How did the Johnson Act of 1924 ignore this historical precedent?**

Critical Thinking Activity

Making Inferences Organize students into four groups and assign each group one of the following time periods: 1800 to 1882, 1882 to 1924, 1925 to 1965, and 1966 to the present. Have group members use information in this section and in American history textbooks to write a few sentences describing American immigration policy for their time period. Have group representatives read their descriptions to the rest of the class. Note the major points of each description on the chalkboard. Then have students use these points to infer the attitudes of Americans to immigrants and immigration in the four time periods.

that clearly favored immigrants from northern and western Europe. In an effort to prevent any major change in the ethnic makeup of the population of the United States, the **national origins system** established quotas for immigrants from each foreign country. The government computed these quotas by taking 2 percent of the ethnic populations of the United States in 1890 and allowing an equal number of immigrants into the country each year. This system meant that countries such as England and Ireland had high quotas because many Americans in 1890 were of English or Irish descent. On the other hand, the quotas assigned to countries such as Greece and Italy were low because there were fewer Greek or Italian Americans in 1890.

The national origins quota system continued for more than 40 years. During this period immigration dropped sharply because relatively few people in countries with large quotas were interested in coming to the United States. After World War II, however, the United States began to accept more European refugees, and immigration slowly began to increase once again.

Immigration Policy 1965-1990 When Congress passed the Immigration Reform Act of 1965, it abolished the system of national origins quotas. The 1965 law set up two categories of immigrants: (1) those who could come from countries of the Eastern Hemisphere—Europe, Asia, and Africa; and (2) those who could come from Western Hemisphere countries—Canada, Mexico, and the nations of Central and South America. Congress fixed a ceiling of 120,000 total immigrants per year from Western Hemisphere countries and 170,000 per year from the rest of the world.

The Immigration Reform Act of 1965 created a complicated system by which immigrants were selected. It established seven preference categories, giving highest preference to unmarried adult sons and daughters of United States citizens. The act gave second highest preference to husbands, wives, and unmarried children of resident aliens, and as-signed third preference to professionals such as doctors, lawyers, and scientists. The lowest preference class included refugees from communist countries, the Middle East, and people who were victims of natural disasters. The preference system originally applied only to immigrants from the Eastern Hemisphere. In 1976 amendments made the system apply to the Western Hemisphere as well.

Recent Changes in Immigration

The Immigration Reform Act of 1965 and its amendments affected origins and the number of immigrants entering the United States for 25 years. Then, in 1990 Congress passed a sweeping revision of the 1965 law. The new law was designed to once again take the countries of origin into account and to admit more highly skilled and educated immigrants.

Changes in Origin For most of United States history, the majority of immigrants came from Europe. Between 1920 and 1960, for example, 60 percent of all immigrants were Europeans. In that period only 35 percent came from the Western Hemisphere and 3 percent from Asia. The 1965 reform resulted in higher levels of immigration from Asia and Latin America than ever before. This happened because the law favored immigrants with immediate relatives in the United States. Recently arriving immigrants from Asia and Latin America naturally had many relatives in their countries of origin. By 1990, 85 percent of immigrants to the United States were coming from these 2 regions.

The Immigration Act of 1990 significantly revised United States immigration policy. It established a limit on immigrants from any single country to no more than 7 percent of the annual visas. It also established a "Transition Diversity Program" designed to open immigration to nationals from countries adversely affected by the 1965 law. Europeans, especially Irish immigrants, would benefit from these "diversity visas."

Critical Thinking Activity

Identifying Alternatives Various restrictions have been placed on immigration to the United States since the late 1800s. Since the 1920s, immigration quotas have further limited the numbers of immigrants allowed to enter the country. Have students answer the following question: Should quotas and other restrictions on immigration be eliminated? Why or why not? What other ways might immigration be controlled? *(Some students might indicate that the United States serves as a refuge for people escaping oppression. Other students might suggest that immigrants provide cheap labor and, therefore, might force down the wages of all.)*

Assess

Check for Understanding
Have students complete Section 2 Review on page 168.

Meeting Objectives
Each section objective is tested by the Section Review questions that follow it in parentheses.
- Distinguish between immigrants and aliens. (3, 4, 6)
- Describe the five categories of aliens. (2, 3, 8)
- Summarize American immigration policy. (5, 7, 8)

Evaluate
📁 Section 2 Quiz
💻 Testmaker

Reteach

Have students work in pairs to outline the text paragraphs on the "Immigration Policy of the United States."

Enrich

Have students interview the public relations officer at an embassy or consulate of a foreign nation on that nation's immigration and citizenship policies. Have students present their findings to the class.

Have students complete activity 5 in *Enrichment Activities* in the Teacher's Classroom Resources.

Close

Have students express their views on the following issues: The number of immigrants that enter the United States each year should be severely limited. Immigrants help the United States economy. Bilingual education hurts students. The United States should allow more refugees into the country.

The new law allowed immigration to climb from about 500,000 people to about 700,000 during each of the first 3 years. Then it leveled immigration to about 675,000 per year. These totals did not include refugees or people who were fleeing persecution from unjust governments in their homelands

Education and Skills The Immigration Act of 1990 encouraged immigration of workers with "extraordinary abilities." It provided 140,000 visas annually for people who had a guaranteed job when entering the United States. Of that total the new law reserved 40,000 visas for people such as managers and university professors, another 40,000 for workers with high abilities or advanced degrees, and 40,000 for skilled workers. In addition, it reserved 10,000 visas for investors who would promise to create new jobs in the United States.

Special Immigrants In addition to the immigration quotas, a category for special immigrants who can legally enter the United States exists. Congress did not limit the number of special immigrants that can enter the country each year.

Special immigrants fall into three groups. First, in addition to the President's power to admit refugees in emergency situations, Congress itself has passed special legislation to admit refugees displaced by war. Under these provisions more than 600,000 refugees from Vietnam, Cambodia, and Laos have entered the country in recent years, along with thousands more from Cuba and Central America.

Second, many special immigrants are close relatives of United States citizens. These may include a wife or husband of a United States citizen or the parent or minor child of a United States citizen.

Third, special immigrants may also enter the country through **private laws** passed by Congress. A private law is one that applies to a particular person. A private law, for example, may allow an elderly person to enter the United States. Private laws permit certain individuals to enter the United States regardless of the numerical limits on immigration.

Illegal Immigration In order to stem the tide of illegal immigrants, Congress passed the Immigration Reform and Control Act of 1986. This law also provided a way for illegal immigrants to become permanent residents and citizens and punishment for employers who hire illegal immigrants.

The major provisions of the act include: (1) Aliens who can show that they entered the United States before January 1, 1982, and have resided continuously in the country since then may apply for **amnesty.** Amnesty is a general pardon the government offers—in this case, to illegal aliens. They would first become lawful temporary residents, then after 18 months they would become permanent residents. (2) After five years of permanent residence in the United States, aliens may apply for United States citizenship. (3) Employers are forbidden to hire illegal aliens. Those who do are subject to penalties ranging from $250 to $10,000 for each illegal alien hired. For subsequent and consistent offenses, employers are subject to additional fines and even imprisonment. (4) Employers must ask applicants for documents such as passports or birth certificates to prove they are either citizens or aliens qualified to work in the United States.

---

2 SECTION REVIEW

Section Summary
The United States is a nation of immigrants. In recent years most of these immigrants have come from Latin America and Asia.

Checking For Understanding
Recalling Facts
1. Define alien, resident alien, non-resident alien, enemy alien, illegal alien, national origins system, private law, amnesty.
2. List the five categories of aliens according to United States law.
3. Identify the rights aliens do not have.
4. Describe the three categories of special immigrants.

Exploring Themes
5. Global Perspectives What role does United States immigration policy allow the nation to play in responding to international crises on a humanitarian level?
6. Cultural Pluralism What are some advantages and disadvantages of being a nation of immigrants?

Critical Thinking Skills
7. Making Inferences What changes in attitudes toward immigration does the Immigration Act of 1990 reflect?
8. Identifying Alternatives How might the United States government deal with the problem of illegal aliens?

Section 2 Review Answers

1. Definitions of terms appear on pages indicated: **alien,** 162; **resident alien,** 162; **non-resident alien,** 163; **enemy alien,** 163; **illegal alien,** 163; **national origins system,** 167; **private law,** 168; **amnesty,** 168
2. resident alien, non-resident alien, enemy alien, refugee, illegal alien
3. voting and traveling without restriction
4. refugees displaced by war, close relatives of United States citizens, immigrants who enter the country through private laws
5. Congress made special provisions for President and Congress to admit refugees in emergency situations or refugees displaced by war.
6. advantages—rich cultural heritage, community of people from all over the world; disadvantages—political strife, cultural misunderstandings and prejudice, increased demand for food and housing
7. favors skilled, educated immigrants, reflecting a desire to use immigration to the national advantage
8. Answers may include allowing more immigrants to enter United States per year, strengthening border security, increasing fines for employers who knowingly hire illegal aliens.

Rights and Responsibilities of American Citizens

B asic rights are important in American society. The belief in **human rights,** or fundamental freedoms, lies at the heart of United States citizenship and enables people to worship as they wish, speak freely, and read and write what they choose.

The Constitution guarantees the rights of United States citizens. Along with the enjoyment of these rights, however, comes a responsibility to ensure their strength and endurance. "We the people," after all, wrote the Constitution, and in many ways United States citizens remain the keepers of their own rights. Rights and responsibilities cannot be separated. As citizens, people share a common fate in the power they have to steer the course of government. Judge Learned Hand expressed this well when he said:

L iberty lies in the hearts of men and women; when it dies there, no constitution, no law, no court can save it; no constitution, no law, no court can even do much to help it.

—JUDGE LEARNED HAND

If people do not carry out their responsibilities as citizens, the whole society suffers.

Constitutional Rights

The Constitution of the United States guarantees basic rights in the Bill of Rights, the first 10 amendments, and in several additional amendments. The Framers of the Constitution believed that people had rights simply because they were people. In the words of the Declaration of Independence, people "are endowed by their Creator with certain unalienable

Union Demonstrates at Nation's Capitol
The First Amendment guarantees the right to peaceably assemble. **Citizenship What are some reasons that people participate in demonstrations?**

rights." The Constitution and the Bill of Rights inscribe into law those rights that really belong to everybody. The Bill of Rights, in particular, stands as a written guarantee that government cannot abuse the rights of individual citizens.

The language of the Bill of Rights is very important. The First Amendment begins with the words, "Congress shall make no law. . . ." Today the Bill of Rights offers individuals protection not only from congressional actions, but also from acts by state and local governments that may threaten people's basic rights.

SECTION PREVIEW

Objectives
After studying this section, you should be able to:
■ Identify the constitutional rights of citizenship.

■ Describe the responsibilities of citizenship.
■ Explain the changing scope of the Bill of Rights.

Key Terms and Concepts
human rights, nationalization

Themes in Government
■ Civic Participation
■ Civic Responsibility

Critical Thinking Skills
■ Synthesizing Information
■ Making Inferences

CHAPTER 5: CITIZENSHIP IN THE UNITED STATES 169

Classroom Resources for Section 3

📁 Guided Reading Activities
📁 Reproducible Lesson Plans
📁 Reteaching Activities 5
📁 Section 3 Quiz
📁 Chapter 5 Tests

✚ Testmaker
🎧 Audio Cassettes (English and Spanish)
📁 Limited English Proficiency Activities 5
   SAT Practice Tests

Focus

Bell Ringer

Ask students to complete the following while attendance is being taken:

List the rights guaranteed to American citizens by the Bill of Rights.

Motivating Activity

Create two columns on the chalkboard—one headed *Rights* and the other *Responsibilities.* Have students fill the column for rights from the lists they compiled for the Bell Ringer activity. Then discuss the responsibilities that accompany each right. List each responsibility next to the right.

Vocabulary Precheck

Call on volunteers to tell what they think each key term means. Have students check the accuracy of their definitions in the Glossary. **LEP**

Teach

Guided Practice

L1 Language Arts Pair students and assign each pair one of the subheads in Section 3. Have pairs discuss the information under their assigned subheads. Then ask pairs to write a sentence that expresses the main idea of their subheads. When they have completed this activity, have representatives of several pairs read their sentences aloud. **LEP**

Caption Answer

to support a candidate or issue, to protest policies or laws, or to call for better working conditions or higher wages

---

GLENCOE TECHNOLOGY

Focus on Government
Video 11
**Lecture Launcher:
Assuring Equal Justice for All**
Running Time: 2:27
Videodisc 1, Chap. 11
VHS Tape 1, Begins 30:29

L2 **Civic Participation** Point out that some people have argued that all Americans should be required to perform some type of compulsory service—not necessarily military service—for the country. Lead students in a discussion of the alternative services that people might perform.

L3 **Interpreting Primary Sources** Write on the chalkboard the following quote by Thomas Jefferson:

"If a nation expects to be ignorant and free, . . . it expects what never was and never will be."

Then ask: How does the quote relate to Bill of Rights guarantees? to students being in school? (*free speech, press, well-informed citizenry*)

Independent Practice

L1 **Art** Have students draw posters illustrating the responsibilities of being a citizen. Display completed posters in the classroom. **LEP**

Caption Answer
Many functions of democratic government depend on citizen participation.

STUDY GUIDE

Theme Answers
They can freely express their views.

Answers will vary, but should stress the relationship between rights and responsibilities.

Critical Thinking Answers
States could not deprive certain groups of their rights.

They feared the potential power of the national government.

Jury Service Is a Basic Responsibility
People from all walks of life are often required to serve on juries. **Civics** **Why is it important that citizens respond to the government's call of duty?**

The Bill of Rights was originally intended as a protection against the actions of the federal government. A process called **nationalization** extended the Bill of Rights to protect individuals from all levels of government in the United States. This change in the scope of the Bill of Rights is a fascinating example of a living Constitution. It shows how the Constitution may be adapted to accommodate changes in American society.

The Constitution drafted in Philadelphia in 1787 did not include a Bill of Rights. Because most of the state constitutions of the time contained bills of rights, the Framers believed it unnecessary to include another such list of rights in the national Constitution.

Many state leaders, however, were suspicious of the new Constitution. When the Constitution was submitted to the states for ratification, a number of states refused to approve the new Constitution unless a Bill of Rights was added. When the First Congress met in 1789, James Madison introduced a series of amendments that became the Bill of Rights in 1791. These amendments were intended to place certain limitations on the national government: to prevent it from controlling the press, restricting speech, influencing religion, and limiting other areas of personal liberty. The Bill of Rights was not intended to limit state and local governments. An important Supreme Court

case, *Barron* v. *Baltimore* (1833), upheld this view. Chief Justice John Marshall, speaking for the Court, ruled that the first 10 amendments "contain no expression indicating an intention to apply them to the state governments."

The Fourteenth Amendment As times changed, so did the Constitution. The addition of the Fourteenth Amendment in 1868 paved the way for a major expansion of the rights of American citizens. The Fourteenth Amendment not only made citizenship national, it also laid the groundwork for making citizens' rights national. The amendment states in part:

No State shall make or enforce any law which shall abridge the privileges or immunities of citizens of the United States; nor shall any State deprive any person of life, liberty, or property without due process of law. . . .

—FOURTEENTH AMENDMENT, 1868

The Supreme Court has interpreted the due process clause of the Fourteenth Amendment to apply the guarantees of the Bill of Rights to state governments. Over the years the Supreme Court has interpreted the word *liberty* in the amendment to include all freedoms the First Amendment guarantees. Thus, no state can deprive any person of freedom of speech, press, religion, or assembly because these freedoms are essential to a person's liberty.

The Supreme Court has also interpreted the words *due process* to include other protections the Bill of Rights guarantees: protection from unreasonable search and seizure; the right of the accused to have a lawyer; and protection from cruel and unusual punishment. These rights have also been applied to the states through the Fourteenth Amendment.

The Supreme Court's interpretation of the Fourteenth Amendment nationalized the Bill of Rights. In the key case of *Gitlow* v. *New York* (1925), the Supreme Court ruled that freedom of speech was a basic right and liberty that no state government could deny to any person.

STUDY GUIDE

Themes in Government
Civic Participation How does freedom of speech make it easier for citizens to participate in government?
Civic Responsibility What would

you say to a citizen who wanted to be guaranteed a jury trial but avoided jury duty?
Critical Thinking Skills
Synthesizing Information Why was the nationalization of the Bill

of Rights important to all citizens?
Making Inferences When it came time to submit the new Constitution to the states for ratification, why do you think state leaders insisted on a national Bill of Rights?

170　UNIT 2: CITIZENSHIP AND CIVIL LIBERTIES

Background

Benjamin Gitlow was indicted and convicted under New York state's Criminal Anarchy Law for distributing 16,000 copies of a pamphlet titled "Left-Wing Manifesto," which advocated the overthrow of the government by force, violence, and unlawful means. Gitlow appealed his case to the United States Supreme Court, arguing that his conviction

and three-year sentence amounted to deprivation of liberty in violation of the due process clause of the Fourteenth Amendment. The Court upheld the conviction. The most important part of the decision—that freedom of speech and of the press are fundamental rights protected by due process—was noted almost in passing!

Since the *Gitlow* case, the Supreme Court has incorporated and nationalized almost all other rights provided for in the first 10 amendments. The only exceptions are the Second, Third, and Tenth Amendments. Two judicial procedures contained in the Fifth and Seventh Amendments are also exceptions. As a result, states are not required to use a grand jury to bring formal charges for serious crimes, nor are they required to have a trial by jury in civil cases involving more than $20.

The Importance of Nationalization The nationalization of the Bill of Rights has meant that United States citizens in every part of the country have the same basic rights. On the face of it, nationalization may not seem significant because of state constitutions' bills of rights. Yet in the past, state governments have sometimes ignored individual rights. Some state governments, for example, have denied voting rights to minorities and have practiced various forms of discrimination against them. As a result of nationalization, the Bill of Rights becomes a final safeguard when personal rights are threatened.

In practice, nationalization means that citizens who believe that a state or local authority has denied them their basic rights may take their case to a federal court. If the decision of a lower federal court goes against them, they may pursue their claim all the way to the Supreme Court.

L3 Global Perspectives Have students research and write a report about the rights, duties, and responsibilities of citizenship in another country, comparing them with those in the United States.

Focus on Freedom

The Magna Carta established the principle that a monarch's rule was not above the law. Also, the ideas set forth in the Magna Carta became the basis for the rights enjoyed by all British people.

Answers

1. by common council of the kingdoms
2. lawful judgment by individual's peers or by the law of the land
3. Answers may include freedom of religion, no taxation without representation, trial by jury.

Focus on Freedom

THE MAGNA CARTA

A group of English aristocrats in 1215 forced King John of England to sign the Magna Carta, a document that granted the nobles many rights. Although the Magna Carta did not grant individual freedoms to common people, it later served as a model for American colonists who desired to guarantee their own legal and political rights.

That the English Church shall be free, and shall have her rights entire, and her liberties inviolate; . . .

2. We also have granted to all the freemen of our kingdom, for us and for our heirs forever, all the underwritten liberties, to be had and holden by them and their heirs, of us and our heirs forever. . . .

12. No scutage [tax for military purposes] nor aid shall be imposed in our kingdom, unless by the common council of our kingdom; . . .

39. No freeman shall be taken or imprisoned, or diseased, or outlawed, or banished, or in any way destroyed, nor will we pass upon him, unless by the lawful judgment of his peers, or by the law of the land.

40. We will sell to no man, we will not deny to any man, either justice or right.

41. All merchants shall have safe and secure conduct to go out of, and to come into, England, and to stay there and to pass as well by land as by water, for buying and selling by the ancient and allowed customs, without any unjust tolls, except in time of war, or when they are of any nation at war with us. . . .

42. It shall be lawful, for the time to come, for any one to go out of our kingdom and return safely and securely by land or by water, saving his allegiance to us (unless in time of war, by some short space, for the common benefit of the realm).

60. All the aforesaid customs and liberties, which we have granted to be holden in our kingdom, as much as it belongs to us, all people of our kingdom, as well clergy as laity, shall observe, as far as they are concerned, towards their dependents.

63. . . . It is also sworn, as well on our part as on the part of the barons, that all the things aforesaid shall be observed in good faith, and without evil duplicity.

Examining the Document

Reviewing Facts
1. State the only method by which taxes could be imposed in England, according to the Magna Carta.
2. Describe the provision that the Magna Carta made for those accused of crimes.

Critical Thinking Skills
3. Recognizing Ideologies What principles of the Magna Carta are reflected in the United States Bill of Rights?

CHAPTER 5: CITIZENSHIP IN THE UNITED STATES **171**

Assess

Check for Understanding

Have students complete Section 3 Review on page 172.

Meeting Objectives

Each section objective is tested by the Section Review questions that follow it in parentheses.
- Identify the constitutional rights of citizenship. (2, 5)
- Describe the responsibilities of citizenship. (4, 6, 7, 8)
- Explain the changing scope of the Bill of Rights. (2, 3)

Evaluate

📁 Section 3 Quiz

▣ Testmaker

Cooperative Learning Activity

Divide the class into three or four groups. Ask students to compile a bill of rights for high school students. For example, they might say "Students have a right to hear a variety of viewpoints on controversial subjects." Have students take turns contributing ideas by writing them on a sheet of paper and passing the paper to the other members of their group. When all the members of the group have contributed their ideas, ask one member to share the ideas with the rest of the class. Then have students compile a class list of 10 student rights and discuss the responsibilities that accompany these rights.

Reteach

Ask students to write a paragraph that defines the term *nationalization* in its political context and that explains the significance of nationalization for individual rights.

📁 Have students complete activity 5 in *Reteaching Activities* in the Teacher's Classroom Resources.

Enrich

Have students research the work of the American Civil Liberties Union (ACLU) in defending the Bill of Rights.

Close

Discuss with students the relationship between the rights and responsibilities of American citizens. Focus on possible results of the failure of American citizens to carry out their responsibilities.

Select questions about the government themes that students wrote at the beginning of the chapter and discuss them with the class.

The Responsibilities of Citizens

The ability to exercise one's rights depends on an awareness of those rights. A constitutional democracy, therefore, requires knowledgeable and active citizens.

Knowing About Rights and Laws Responsible citizens need to know about the laws that govern society. They also need to be aware of their basic legal rights. Respect for the law is crucial in modern society, but respect for the law depends on knowledge of the law.

Throughout the United States, a number of organizations help citizens learn more about their rights, laws, and government: legal aid societies, consumer protection groups, and tenants' rights organizations, to name a few. In addition, many states now require that government rules and regulations be written in everyday language so that the average person can understand them.

Citizenship Involves Participation The American ideal of citizenship has always stressed each citizen's responsibility to participate in political life. Through participation citizens help govern society and themselves and are able to fashion policies in the public interest. Through participation individuals can put aside personal concerns and learn about one another's political goals and needs. In short, participation teaches about the essentials of democracy—majority rule, individual rights, and the rule of law.

Voting The most common way a citizen participates in political life is by voting. By casting their ballots, citizens help choose leaders and help direct the course of government. Voting therefore affirms a basic principle of American political life that was inscribed in the Declaration of Independence—"the consent of the governed."

Voting is also an important way to express faith in one's political system. When a person casts a vote, he or she is joining other citizens in a common effort at self-government. Voting enables Americans to share responsibility for how their society is governed.

Many people do not vote because they believe they have little effect on political life. Others do not vote because they have little interest in any form of political life.

Voter Participation Counts There have been many close elections over the years at all levels of government. In November 1981, for example, James J. Florio and Thomas Kean squared off in an election for governor of New Jersey. When the votes were counted, the results were astonishingly close. If only one vote in each of New Jersey's election districts had been cast differently, James Florio would have been governor of New Jersey.

Ways of Participating as a Citizen Campaigning for a candidate, distributing leaflets for a political party, and working at the polls on Election Day are all important forms of participation. People can exercise the rights and privileges of citizenship in other ways as well. For example, they can support the efforts of a special interest group to influence legislation or discuss issues with a legislator or another person in government. Writing letters to the editor of a newspaper or news magazine, or exercising the right to dissent in a legal and orderly manner are other ways citizens can participate. Exercising these rights is the only way of ensuring their strength and vitality.

3 SECTION REVIEW

Section Summary
United States citizens have both rights and responsibilities.

Checking for Understanding
Recalling Facts
1. Define human rights, nationalization.
2. Describe what is meant by the nationalization of the Bill of Rights.
3. Cite the branch of government that has been primarily responsible for the nationalization of the Bill of Rights.
4. List three responsibilities of citizenship.

Exploring Themes
5. Civic Participation What role do citizens play in upholding their rights?
6. Civic Responsibility Why does a democracy require knowledgeable and active citizens?

Critical Thinking Skills
7. Synthesizing Information In your opinion, what are the most important duties and responsibilities of citizenship?
8. Making Inferences Why does society as a whole suffer if individuals do not carry out their responsibilities as citizens?

172 UNIT 2: CITIZENSHIP AND CIVIL LIBERTIES

Section 3 Review Answers

1. Definitions of terms appear on pages indicated: **human rights,** 169; **nationalization,** 170
2. It extended the protection of citizens to all levels of government.
3. judicial branch, the Supreme Court
4. knowing about laws, being aware of legal rights, and respecting the laws

5. Answers may include voicing their opinions by voting, campaigning for or protesting against an issue or candidate, taking an issue to court.
6. Answers may include to ensure the strength and endurance of citizen rights and to steer the course of government.

7. Answers should indicate voting, being informed and interested in American government and current events, informing representatives of opinions, volunteering to aid the community.
8. Answers may include that in system of self-government every individual has certain duties that ensure the strength and efficient operation of government.

PERSONAL PERSPECTIVES

Southeast Asians on Being a Refugee

The United States has accepted more than 1 million refugees from war-torn Laos, Cambodia, and Vietnam. Some refugees spent years in camps in neighboring Southeast Asian countries. Others journeyed across the open sea. The following poems and quotations reflect the thoughts of those who fled their homelands in order to save their lives.

How many boats have perished?
How many families are buried beneath those waves?
Find us.
We are lost in the open sea, looking for a shoreline to call safety.

A PRAYER FOR SAFE SHORE

The foam of the ocean surrounds everything.

We are lost in the open sea, looking for a shoreline to call safety.

We float on the deep and dark ocean like dust on a palm leaf; we wander in endless space.

Our only fear, that we do not sleep forever on the bottom of the sea.

We are without food or water and our children and women lie exhausted, crying, until they can cry no more.

No ship will stop. We float like we do not exist.

Lord Buddha, do you hear our voices? From every port we are pushed out.

Our distress signals rise and rise again.

How many boats have perished? How many families are buried beneath those waves?

Find us. We are lost in the open sea, looking for a shoreline to call safety.

—VIETNAMESE MONK, LOS ANGELES

KHMER ROUGE

It was a time of evil.

I was only thirteen when the Khmer Rouge in my country captured it. School stopped.

Work stopped and soon life stopped. To be persecuted by your own people is not real.

We never understood why all this happened.

We were to be ashamed of our books, of our schools, our teachers, our education.

Stop thinking. Stop thinking. The city is evil, the country is good.

Stop thinking. Forever I will never stop thinking about how they killed my country.

—CAMBODIAN HIGH SCHOOL STUDENT, AGE EIGHTEEN, PHILADELPHIA

The moment I raised my hand to give the oath [of allegiance], I thought of my father and I thought, what would he think about what I am doing with my life—changing my nationality? Would he say that I am renouncing my Vietnamese heritage? Would he forgive me?

—BUI VAN BINH, NATURALIZED UNITED STATES CITIZEN

Examining the Reading

Reviewing Facts
1. List the three Southeast Asian countries from which the United States has received many refugees.
2. Name the Cambodian regime responsible for persecuting Cambodians.

Critical Thinking Skills
3. Identifying Central Issues What issues might confront a refugee who becomes a naturalized United States citizen?

CHAPTER 5: CITIZENSHIP IN THE UNITED STATES 173

PERSONAL PERSPECTIVES

Focus

Have students write a brief statement on what being an American citizen means to them. Have volunteers share their statements.

Teach

Ask: How does the Vietnamese monk express his uncertainty and vulnerability? *(wandering, floating, darkness, openness, lost)* What images represent safety to boat people? *(a ship or shoreline)* What was demanded of Cambodians by their government? *(to stop thinking)* What feelings does Bui Van Binh have as he takes the oath of United States citizenship? What Vietnamese values are implied in Bui's feelings? *(reservations about loss of identity and cultural traditions)*

Assess

Have students complete **Examining the Reading.**
Answers
1. Laos, Cambodia, Vietnam
2. Khmer Rouge
3. Answers may include conflict over renouncing native citizenship, what customs and traditions to keep, how "Americanized" to become.

Close

Discuss ways students could help those from another country feel welcome in the United States.

More About Personal Perspectives

From 1976 to mid-1988, over 100,000 Vietnamese boat people were processed through Hong Kong. In 1991 many boat people were still fleeing Southeast Asia and making their way to Hong Kong. Approximately 55,000 boat people were already housed in Hong Kong's 14 detention camp dormitories awaiting opportunities for resettlement elsewhere. Since Hong Kong itself is overpopulated and land poor, it rarely assimilates Vietnamese into its society. Hong Kongers are concerned because they will face unpredictable economic struggles themselves when Hong Kong is returned to China in 1997.

Identifying Terms and Concepts

1. human rights, 2. naturalization, 3. alien, 4. resident aliens, 5. non-resident aliens, 6. illegal aliens

Reviewing Facts and Ideas

1. only as a qualification for holding office in the federal government

2. It forced the federal government to address state citizenship, the issue of slavery, and legal jurisdiction between states.

3. enter the United States legally; be of good moral character; support the principles of American government; proven ability to read, write, and speak English; demonstrate basic knowledge of American history and government

4. An immigrant enters a new country with the intention of living there permanently; intends to become a citizen. An alien is a temporary resident; does not intend to become a citizen of the country.

5. to prevent any change in the ethnic makeup of the United States population

6. Bill of Rights

7. Fourteenth Amendment

Applying Themes

1. A "living constitution" is one that continues to address the issues of the present. It is a strong foundation that is flexible enough to be applied to new problems as they arise, and open enough to further interpretation as new information is introduced.

2. That parent must have lived in the United States or an American possession for at least 10 years, 5 of which had to occur after the age of 14.

3. because these individuals, although naturalized American citizens, have their own rich heritage and ways of life to bring with them; some left their homelands in order to save their lives; they may wish to combine their

---

Summary and Significance

The three legal bases for United States citizenship are birth in the United States, birth to American parents, or naturalization. Citizens may lose their citizenship by expatriation, punishment for a crime, or denaturalization. The United States is made up of immigrants and continues to respond to the needs of immigrants and refugees. United States immigration policy has gone through many changes and remains a controversial subject. United States citizens have rights the Constitution protects, and a responsibility, through active participation, to ensure those rights for themselves and future generations. United States citizenship is of great value to those who possess it and certainly to those who seek it. It is the responsibility of all Americans to understand their rights and how the law works in order to receive the full benefits of their citizenship.

Identifying Terms and Concepts

Insert the terms below into the correct blanks in the paragraph. Use each term only once.

illegal aliens, resident aliens, naturalization, alien, human rights, non-resident aliens

People of many nations seek the (1) the Constitution guarantees through the Bill of Rights. Foreigners must go through the process of (2) to gain United States citizenship. An immigrant is a person who comes to a new country and intends to live there permanently, while an (3) may live in a country other than their own without intending to become a citizen. Immigrants are also (4) until they become naturalized citizens, but Nigerian athletes spending three weeks in the United States would be (5). People entering the United States without legal permits are referred to as (6).

Reviewing Facts and Ideas

1. **Describe** how the Constitution addressed the issue of citizenship.
2. **State** the significance of the *Dred Scott* case.
3. **List** the five qualifications for United States citizenship.
4. **Cite** the difference between an immigrant and an alien.
5. **Specify** the purpose of the national origins system that began in 1924.
6. **Name** the legal document that specifically guarantees the rights of United States citizens.

7. **Identify** the amendment that led to the nationalization of the Bill of Rights.

Applying Themes

1. **Constitutional Interpretations** What is meant by the phrase *a living Constitution*?
2. **Global Perspectives** What is required for a child to be a United States citizen if he or she is born to one American parent in a foreign country?
3. **Cultural Pluralism** Even after becoming American citizens, many former immigrants and refugees continue to hold on to their customs and traditions. Why do you suppose this is so?
4. **Civic Participation** Why are so many Americans nonvoters?
5. **Civic Responsibility** Why is voting considered a civic responsibility?

Critical Thinking Skills

1. **Synthesizing Information** How did the *Dred Scott* decision add to sectional tensions?
2. **Predicting Consequences** What might be the possible consequences if voter turnout in the United States continues to fall?
3. **Making Inferences** Why do you think so many people want to immigrate to the United States?
4. **Identifying Alternatives** Do you think native United States citizens should take an oath of allegiance? Why or why not?

---

native cultures with the culture of their new homeland.

4. Some people believe they have little effect on political life or they have no interest in political life.

5. because voting enables citizens to influence government, to choose leaders, and to show faith in the political system

Critical Thinking Skills

1. It caused great outrage in the northern states, which were free states, and added to the tensions that led to the Civil War.

2. Elections would be determined by a smaller percentage of the voting population, and we would thus have government by the minority.

3. Answers may include that people leave their countries because of war, political strife, poverty,

Linking Past and Present

George Washington once said:

The [heart] of America is open to receive not only the opulent and respectable stranger; but the oppressed and persecuted of all nations and religions; whom we shall welcome to a participation of all our rights and privileges, if by decency and propriety of conduct they appear to merit the enjoyment.

—GEORGE WASHINGTON

Cite evidence to support or refute whether most United States citizens today welcome immigrants and refugees as much as George Washington appears to have welcomed them. Be sure to support your answer with examples.

Writing About Government

Classificatory Writing Election ballots in many parts of the United States are available in languages other than English. Make a list with the following classifications: (1) other languages that could be used on election ballots in the United States, (2) areas of the United States where non-English ballots could be used. Then write a paragraph in which you use information from the two lists to give the advantages of having election ballots available in other languages.

Reinforcing the Skill

Understanding Cause and Effect Each of the following statements includes a cause-and-effect relationship. For each of the statements, decide which event caused the other. Construct a cause-and-effect chart by writing the cause on the left and the effect on the right. Show any words that indicate a cause-and-effect relationship.

1. In recent years many immigrants to the United States have entered the country because they were classified as refugees.
2. The Court ruled that African Americans were not citizens when the Constitution was adopted; therefore they could not claim citizenship.

3. Because *alien* is a legal word that seems to have unfriendly implications, many immigrants resent being called *aliens*.
4. The vast majority of immigrants came from Asia and Latin America rather than Europe due to the abolition of the national origins system.
5. As a result of open immigration policies throughout much of American history, millions of immigrants have been able to come to the United States.
6. The *Dred Scott* decision caused great outrage and protest in the North.
7. Every year an estimated 4 million foreigners apply to become immigrants because they see the United States as a place where they can live a better life.
8. There were few Greek or Italian Americans in 1890. For this reason, the national origins system established low quotas for immigrants from Greece and Italy.
9. In order to stem the tide of illegal immigrants, Congress passed the Immigration Reform and Control Act of 1986.

Investigating Further

1. **Individual Project** Make a chart with the following headings: Family, School, Peers, Media. Under the headings, give examples of how each group or organization has influenced your ideas of what you can and should do as a United States citizen. Then write one or two paragraphs describing the attitudes or values you have as a citizen.
2. **Cooperative Learning** Organize into groups of five to seven. Imagine that you have just received a new student named Ot in your class. The teacher tells you that Ot is a refugee from Laos and has a fairly good command of English. Ot has just come to the United States, and there are many things about American culture that he does not yet understand. Have each group member list two ways that the group could help him adjust to an American high school in particular and American culture in general. Then have the group combine their lists and come up with a step-by-step strategy to help Ot.

CHAPTER 5: CITIZENSHIP IN THE UNITED STATES **175**

1. because they were classified as refugees. → In recent years many immigrants to the United States have entered the country

2. The Court ruled that African Americans were not citizens when the Constitution was adopted; → therefore they could not claim citizenship.

3. Because *alien* is a legal word that seems to have unfriendly implications, → many immigrants resent being called *aliens*.

4. due to the abolition of the national origins system. → The vast majority of immigrants began to come from Asia and Latin America rather than Europe

5. As a result of open immigration policies throughout much of American history, → millions of immigrants have been able to come to the United States.

6. The *Dred Scott* decision → caused great outrage and protest in the North.

7. because they see the United States as a place where they can live a better life. → Every year an estimated 4 million foreigners apply to become immigrants

8. There were few Greek or Italian Americans in 1890. → For this reason, the national origins system established low quotas for immigrants from Greece and Italy.

9. Congress passed the Immigration Reform and Control Act of 1986. → In order to stem the tide of illegal immigrants,

Investigating Further

1. Students' charts and paragraphs will vary, but paragraphs should describe students' attitudes and values.

2. Groups' lists will vary, but should offer step-by-step strategies.

unemployment, and to reunite with family members who have previously immigrated.

4. Answers may include reference to the oath of allegiance required by naturalized citizens.

Linking Past and Present

Answers will vary, but students should cite evidence and examples in their answers.

Writing About Government

Answers should include printing election ballots in Spanish, especially for use in areas of Florida, Texas, California, and the Southwest. Paragraph answers will vary but may include as an advantage that citizens with lower English ability would be able to vote.

Chapter Organizer

Objectives	Special Feature Pages	Supplemental Materials
Section 1 Freedom of Religion *pp. 178–183* 1. Distinguish between the right to hold religious beliefs and the right to practice those beliefs. 2. Identify the tests the Supreme Court uses to determine if aid to parochial schools is constitutional. 3. Differentiate between the establishment clause and the free exercise clause.	Critical Thinking Skills: Synthesizing Information p. 183	Guided Reading Activities Reproducible Lesson Plans Supreme Court Case Studies 6, 14, 16, 18, 26, 27 Section 1 Quiz Testmaker Chapter Transparencies 6 Government Themes Transparencies 24 Skill Reinforcement Activity 6 The Living Constitution SAT Practice Tests Writer's Guidebook
Section 2 Freedom of Speech *pp. 184–188* 1. Distinguish between speech that is permitted and speech that is prohibited under the First Amendment. 2. Summarize the limits the Supreme Court puts on speech. 3. Differentiate *slander* and *libel*.	Focus on Freedom: The Emancipation Proclamation p. 186	Guided Reading Activities Reproducible Lesson Plans Supreme Court Case Studies 9, 20, 23, 37, 51, 53, 62 Section 2 Quiz Testmaker The Living Constitution SAT Practice Tests Writer's Guidebook
Section 3 Freedom of Assembly *pp. 189–192* 1. Identify the circumstances under which assemblies may be unlawful. 2. Describe the importance of the right of assembly to democracy.	Global Connection: Comparing Governments: Freedom of Religion p. 191	Guided Reading Activities Reproducible Lesson Plans Supreme Court Case Studies 13, 21, 36 Primary and Secondary Source Readings 6 Enrichment Activities 6 Section 3 Quiz Testmaker Government Themes Transparencies 21 The Living Constitution SAT Practice Tests Writer's Guidebook
Section 4 Freedom of the Press *pp. 193–197* 1. Identify the limits on freedom of the press. 2. Describe the importance of a free press to democracy. 3. Compare the freedoms of the print media and the electronic media.	Participating in Government: Volunteering in Your Community p. 195 Personal Perspectives: Helen Delich Bentley's Views on the American Flag p. 197	Guided Reading Activities Reproducible Lesson Plans 23 Participating in Government 6 Supreme Court Case Studies 11, 33, 38, 39 Reteaching Activities 6 Section 4 Quiz Chapter 6 Tests Testmaker Audio Cassettes (English and Spanish) Limited English Proficiency Activities 6

If time does not permit teaching this chapter, assign the Chapter 6 summary in the Unit 2 Digest on pages 225–226.

Key To Ability Levels

Teaching strategies have been coded for varying learning styles and abilities.

L1 Level 1 activities are **basic** activities and should be within the ability range of all students.

L2 Level 2 activities are **average** activities and should be within the ability range of the average to above-average student.

L3 Level 3 activities are **challenging** activities designed for the ability range of above-average students.

LEP These activities should be within the ability range of **Limited English Proficiency** students.

Multicultural Activities

Since the 1980s racial and ethnic tensions have flared on many college campuses. At Yale University a swastika and the words "White Power" were painted on the building housing the Afro-American Cultural Center. Nazi symbols were spray painted on the Jewish Students Union at Memphis State University. On the air waves, women, Jews, and Koreans have been objects of derision in songs by African American rap groups. Some people have called for the outlawing of racially or religiously bigoted speech, noting that prohibitions on such speech exist in Canada, Great Britain, and Germany. Have students debate this topic, examining the criteria that would be used to decide if remarks are unacceptable. Would such action lead to restraints on other kinds of speech?

When the First Amendment was added to the Constitution, the United States was a largely Protestant nation. Today Muslims, Buddhists, Jews, Hindus, Catholics, and Protestants sit side by side in school classrooms. Along with ethnic diversity has come religious diversity and controversy over the role of religion in the schools. Point out that as American society has become more diverse, schools have tried to teach more about ethnic groups, their customs, and religious beliefs. Ask: How is teaching about religion different from teaching religion in the schools? If certain schools had Asian American or Arab American majorities, should Buddhist or Muslim celebrations be official school holidays? What guidelines would students use to ensure freedom of religion is respected?

Chapter Resources

Readings for the Student

Alderman, Ellen and Caroline Kennedy. *In Our Defense: The Bill of Rights in Action.* Morrow, 1991.

Fried, Richard M. *Nightmare in Red: The McCarthy Era in Perspective.* Oxford University Press, 1990.

Hachey, Thomas E. and Ralph E. Weber, eds. *American Dissent from Thomas Jefferson to Cesar Chavez: The Rhetoric of Reform and Revolution.* Krieger, 1991.

Meltzer, Milton, ed. *The American Promise: Voices of a Changing Nation, 1945–Present.* Bantam, 1990.

Smith, George and Arlene Smith. *You Decide! Applying the Bill of Rights to Real Cases.* Midwest Publications, 1991.

Thoreau, Henry David. *On the Duty of Civil Disobedience.* Yale University Press, 1928.

Wagman, Robert J. *The First Amendment Book.* Pharos, 1991.

Readings for the Teacher

Abraham, Henry J. *Freedom and the Court: Civil Rights and Liberties in the United States.* Oxford University Press, 1982.

Downs, Donald Alexander. *Nazis in Skokie.* University of Notre Dame Press, 1985.

Lewis, Anthony. *Make No Law: The Sullivan Case and the First Amendment.* Random House, 1991.

Multimedia

Videocassettes

The Constitution: For Adults Only? Social Studies School Service. (v/c, 30 minutes)

Hollywood on Trial. Corinth. (v/c, 90 minutes)

Inherit the Wind. United Artists. (v/c, 127 minutes)

Noam Chomsky. (*Parts I & II, A World of Ideas with Bill Moyers* series.) Public Affairs Television. (v/c, 60 minutes)

Point of Order. Social Studies School Service. (v/c, 107 minutes)

Software

American Government II. Intellectual Software. (Apple, IBM disk; Apple disk with management facility also available; part two of a 5-part set). Students complete a tutorial program focusing on federalism, First Amendment rights, and other civil liberties.

The Constitutional Amendments: What They Mean to You. Thoroughbred Educational Software (SMC Software Systems). (Apple IIe with extended 80-column card [128K], 1 disk drive, color monitor, Apple IIc 128K, color monitor). Students complete a tutorial program covering the Bill of Rights and the Eleventh through the Twenty-sixth Amendments.

Protecting Basic Freedoms

Introduce

Chapter Overview

Chapter 6 introduces students to the ways in which many of our basic freedoms are protected by the First Amendment.

Section 1 identifies the issues related to freedom of religion, emphasizes the Supreme Court's role in defining separation of church and state, and interprets the establishment and free exercise clauses.

Section 2 describes the right of free speech; defines pure speech, speech plus, and symbolic speech; and explains the constitutional tests the Supreme Court uses to differentiate between speech that is permitted and speech that is prohibited under the First Amendment.

Section 3 summarizes the meaning of free assembly and explains how the right to assemble must be balanced with the need to protect the rights of others.

Section 4 describes the relationship between freedom of the press and free speech, explains the concept of prior restraint, and discusses the free press issues presented by new instruments of mass communication.

Chapter 6 Themes

Ask students about the latest fashions or musical trends. Discuss how such expression and creativity often starts with one individual—the first spiked haircut, the first rap musician, for example—and slowly spreads to other people, gaining more and more acceptance. Then ask students how this process relates to the chapter title and themes.

CHAPTER
6

At the newsstand, a wide array of publications greets Americans, whose right to publish and distribute information and opinion is guaranteed by the First Amendment.

176   UNIT 2: CITIZENSHIP AND CIVIL LIBERTIES

About the Chapter Opener

Teaching With Illustrations Have students read the caption and examine the photograph on pages 176 and 177. Ask students what basic freedoms are guaranteed by the First Amendment. *(Students might mention freedom of speech, press, assembly, and worship.)* Then ask them what basic freedom guaranteed by the First Amendment is illustrated in this photograph. *(freedom of the press)* Point out to students that when the Bill of Rights was written the term *the press* referred to printed publications such as books, newspapers, and magazines. Today the term has been extended to include other areas of communication, such as television, radio, and computer networks.

Chapter Preview

Overview

The First Amendment to the Constitution guarantees the right to express beliefs, ideas, and opinions.

Objectives

After studying this chapter, you should be able to:

1. **Identify** the issues related to the separation of church and state.
2. **Describe** the right of free speech and cite the limits on it.
3. **Summarize** the meaning of freedom of assembly and limits placed on it.
4. **Explain** the dilemmas the right to a free press presents.

Themes in Government

This chapter emphasizes the following government themes:

- **Civil Liberties** The First Amendment guarantees freedom of religion, freedom of speech, and the right to peaceably assemble. Sections 1, 2, 3, and 4.
- **Cultural Pluralism** Americans of all ethnic groups are free to practice their religion as long as these practices do not infringe on anyone else's rights. Section 1.
- **Growth of Democracy** The Supreme Court has interpreted the meaning of freedom of speech. Sections 2 and 3.
- **Constitutional Interpretations** The Supreme Court has interpreted the First Amendment to prohibit prior restraint. Section 4.

Critical Thinking Skills

This chapter emphasizes the following critical thinking skills:

- Recognizing Ideologies
- Checking Consistency
- Making Comparisons

Introducing the Chapter

Display transparency 6 from the *Chapter Transparencies* in the Teacher's Classroom Resources and use the accompanying teaching strategy and student activity to introduce the basic freedoms guaranteed by the First Amendment. Discuss ways in which students exercise these freedoms every day. Point out that Chapter 6 focuses on the ways in which basic freedoms are guaranteed to citizens and how these guarantees have evolved over the years. The chapter also discusses the dilemmas raised by these guarantees and how the individual rights of citizens are balanced against the need to protect society.

Chapter Project

Numerous court cases are presented throughout this chapter. Organize students into four groups, and assign each group one of the four sections. Have each group chart the court cases mentioned in their assigned section on a large poster board. They should include the name and date of the case, the issue involved, and the outcome. They should also illustrate the cases and the issues with various visual materials—newspaper headlines, photographs, sketches, and so on. At the end of the chapter, have groups display their posters on the bulletin board.

Linking Past and Present

In 1641 the Massachusetts Colony developed *The Body of Liberties,* a code of laws designed to govern the colony. Although not tolerant of diverse religious views, the code provided for such rights as freedom of speech and publication at town meetings. Thus, this document represents an important source of the civil liberties guaranteed in the United States today.

Setting the Scene In a democracy, an inherent conflict exists between the rights of individuals and the well-being of the larger group. For example, the right of individuals to express themselves freely sometimes conflicts with the need for an ordered and peaceful society. Our constitutional system is designed to protect individual freedoms that even a democratic government might abridge in the interests of stability and security. For two centuries the federal judiciary has mediated conflicts between individual and group rights by defining and interpreting the Constitution. Nowhere has this process been more visible than in court cases concerned with the First Amendment.

Focus

Bell Ringer

Write the following on the chalkboard for students to answer while attendance is being taken:

How is the principle of separation of church and state demonstrated in the United States today?

Motivating Activity

Discuss students' Bell Ringer answers. Ask students if they believe separation of church and state should allow religion to exist free of all government control. Continue by asking them to discuss any beliefs or practices that have aroused controversy and the possibility of government intervention. Then tell students that in this section they will learn how the Supreme Court has dealt with issues that concern freedom of religion.

Vocabulary Precheck

Write the key terms and concepts for this section on the chalkboard. Ask students to use those that they know in sentences. **LEP**

Teach

Guided Practice

L1 Concept Mapping Write *Freedom of Religion* on the chalkboard. Draw two lines extending downward from the phrase. Ask students to name the two clauses from the First Amendment that guarantee freedom of religion and add them at the end of each line. *(free exercise, establishment)* Then discuss the basic dilemmas the Supreme Court has faced in interpreting these clauses. *(government aid to religion, belief versus practice)* Ask students to find examples of each dilemma in their textbooks. **LEP**

Freedom of Religion

Writing in 1802, President Thomas Jefferson stated that the First Amendment's freedom of religion clause was designed to build "a wall of separation between Church and State." This separation makes the United States different from many countries that have a state-supported religion, as in Great Britain. In such countries, public tax money goes to support one particular form of religion. At the other extreme, some countries strongly discourage the practice of any religion.

The First Amendment guarantees freedom of religion in two clauses. The first, known as the **establishment clause,** states that "Congress shall make no law respecting an establishment of religion." The second clause, labeled the **free exercise clause,** requires that Congress not prohibit the free exercise of religion.

The First Amendment officially separates church and state. In practice, however, religion long has been part of public life in the United States. Although Article VI of the Constitution bans any religious qualification to hold public office, most government officials take their oaths of office in the name of God. Since 1864 most of the nation's coins have carried the motto "In God We Trust." The Pledge of Allegiance contains the phrase "one nation under God." Many public meetings, including daily sessions of Congress and most state legislatures, open with a prayer.

Government actually encourages religion in some ways. For example, chaplains serve with each branch of the armed forces. Most church property and contributions to religious groups are tax exempt. Thus, while the establishment clause and the free exercise clause of the First Amendment protect religion from government interference, church and state are not totally separate in the United States. Attempting to define the proper distance between the two has often resulted in continuing and sometimes heated controversy. Under the Constitution this task falls on the Supreme Court.

The Establishment Clause

Although the Supreme Court had ruled on several religious freedom cases, it did not hear one based on the establishment clause until *Everson* v. *Board of Education* (1947). The case involved a challenge to a New Jersey law allowing the state to pay for busing students to **parochial schools,** schools operated by a church or religious group. The law's critics contended that the law amounted to state support of a religion, in violation of the establishment clause. Writing the Court's decision, Justice Hugo H. Black defined the establishment clause:

> *Neither a state nor the federal government can set up a church. Neither can pass laws which aid one religion, aid all religions, or prefer one religion over another. . . .*
>
> —JUSTICE HUGO H. BLACK, 1947

The Court ruled, however, that the New Jersey law was constitutional because it benefited students rather than aided a religion directly.

SECTION PREVIEW

Objectives
After studying this section, you should be able to:
■ Distinguish between the right to hold religious beliefs and the right to practice those beliefs.
■ Identify the tests the Supreme Court uses to determine if aid to parochial schools is constitutional.
■ Differentiate between the establishment clause and the free exercise clause.

Key Terms and Concepts
establishment clause, free exercise clause, parochial school, secular, polygamy, abridge, precedent

Themes in Government
■ Civil Liberties
■ Cultural Pluralism

Critical Thinking Skills
■ Checking Consistency
■ Recognizing Ideologies

Classroom Resources for Section 1

📁 Guided Reading Activities
📁 Reproducible Lesson Plans
📁 Supreme Court Case Studies 6, 14, 16, 18, 26, 27
📁 Section 1 Quiz

🖥 Testmaker
📑 Chapter Transparencies 6
📑 Government Themes Transparencies 24
The Living Constitution
SAT Practice Tests
Writer's Guidebook

Although this 1947 decision still guides the Court, the *Everson* case illustrated uncertainty over just how high Jefferson's "wall of separation" should be. That uncertainty continues today both in the Court and among the American people. Since the *Everson* decision, the Court has ruled several more times on the establishment clause. Most of these cases have involved some aspect of religion and education.

State Aid to Parochial Schools Some of the most controversial debates over church-state relations have focused on the kinds of aid government can give church-related schools. Since the *Everson* decision, more than two-thirds of the states have given parochial schools aid ranging from driver education to free lunches for students. The Court has heard several cases arising from these programs, finding some constitutional and others not.

For example, in *Board of Education v. Allen* (1968) the Court upheld state programs to provide **secular**, or non-religious, textbooks, to parochial schools. In *Meek v. Pittinger* (1975), however, it rejected state aid for instructional materials such as films, projectors, laboratory equipment, and tape recorders. Although *Everson* permitted state-supported bus transportation to and from school, *Wolman v. Walter* (1977) banned its use for field trips.

Why are some forms of aid constitutional and others not? Since 1971 the Court has used a three-part test to decide whether such aid violates the establishment clause. To be constitutional, state aid to church schools must: (1) have a clear secular, non-religious purpose; (2) in its main effect neither advance nor inhibit religion; and (3) avoid "excessive government entanglement with religion." In *Levitt v. Committee for Public Education* (1973), for example, the Court voided a New York plan to help pay for parochial schools developing testing programs. In *Committee for Public Education v. Regan* (1980) the Court permitted New York State to pay parochial schools to administer and grade tests and report the results. The difference was that in the 1980 case the state's department of education prepared the tests. In the

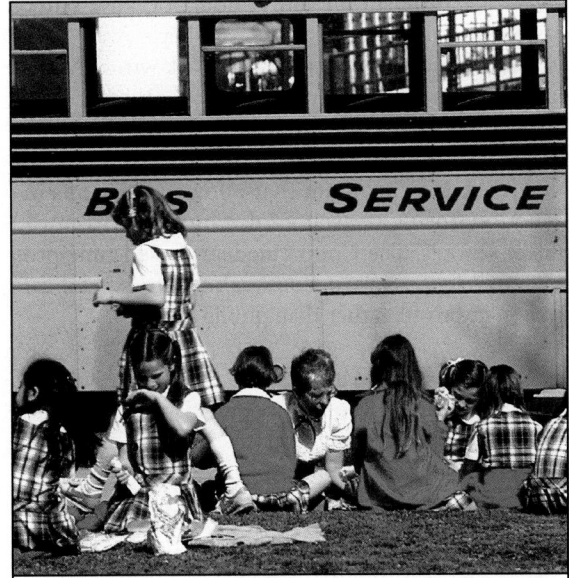
Aid to Parochial Schools
In some states, parochial schools receive governmental funding. **Law Why is the dividing line between state and church sometimes blurred?**

1973 case the tests were teacher-prepared, which the Court considered part of religious instruction.

Finally, in *Mueller v. Allen* (1983) the Court upheld a Minnesota law allowing parents to deduct tuition, textbooks, and transportation to and from school from their state income tax. Public schools charge little or nothing for these items, because taxes pay for them. Parents whose children attend parochial schools benefit from the deduction. Because the law permitted parents of all schoolchildren to take the deduction, it passed the Court's three-part test.

Released Time for Students Can public schools release students from school to attend classes in religious instruction? The Court first dealt with this question in *McCollum v. Board of Education* (1948). Champaign, Illinois, public schools had a program in which religion teachers came into the schools once a week and gave instruction to students who desired it. The Court de-

---

Chapter 6, Section 1
Lesson Plan, pages 178–183

L2 Synthesizing Information
Make three columns on the chalkboard: *State Aid to Parochial Schools, Released Time for Students,* and *School Prayer and the Bible.* For each heading, ask students to provide the key Supreme Court position on that issue. *(State Aid to Parochial Schools: must have a clear secular purpose, neither advance nor inhibit religion, and avoid excessive government entanglement with religion. Released Time for Students: constitutional if held in private rather than public facilities. School Prayer and the Bible: school-sponsored prayer and Bible reading banned in public schools. In 1990 Court allowed student prayer groups in public schools.)*

Caption Answer
because religion long has been part of public life in the United States

---

STUDY GUIDE

Critical Thinking Answer
Use of this transportation to and from school did not serve a primarily religious purpose. Its use for field trips would be an optional decision by school officials and might serve a religious purpose.

CONNECTIONS

Religion
One practical result of the freedoms guaranteed by the First Amendment is religious pluralism. The three major religions—Christianity, Islam, and Judaism—have major followings, and Buddhism is a major religion in Hawaii. In addition, there are some 650 "non-conventional" religious groups.

STUDY GUIDE

Themes in Government
Civil Liberties The First Amendment was added to the Constitution to protect civil liberties from encroachment by the national government. These are freedoms that

people inherently have, not that government provides.

Critical Thinking Skills
Checking Consistency Why did the Court allow state-supported

bus transportation for parochial schools but ban their use for field trips?

Background

While many parts of the Bill of Rights are derived from English law, the freedom of religion clause in the First Amendment is not. At the time the Bill of Rights was written, the inclusion of a statement on religious freedom was unique among the governments of the world. The fact that it was included reflects the heritage of the Quakers, Pilgrims, and other groups who came to America to escape religious persecution in England and elsewhere.

🔖 **Interpreting Visuals** Display transparency 24 from the *Government Themes Transparencies* in the Teacher's Classroom Resources and use the accompanying teaching strategy and student activity to teach about religious freedom.

Independent Practice

L1 Summarizing Main Ideas Have students summarize the main ideas in Section 1 by writing a newspaper headline for each subhead in the section.

L2 Informative Writing Have students research and describe in an essay the origins of religious freedom in the United States, such as the struggles of Roger Williams, Anne Hutchinson, and William Penn in the 1600s.

CONNECTIONS

Law

The Supreme Court decision in *Abington School District* v. *Schempp* banned the reading of the Lord's Prayer and sections from the Bible, but did not rule against teaching about religion in public schools. As the ruling noted, "Nothing we have said here indicates that . . . study of the Bible or of religion, when presented objectively as part of a secular program of education, may not be effected consistently with the First Amendment."

---

clared this program unconstitutional because school classrooms—tax-supported public facilities—were being used for religious purposes. Justice Black wrote that the program used tax-supported public schools "to aid religious groups to spread their faith."

Four years later, however, the Court accepted a New York City program that allowed religious instruction during the school day but away from the public schools. The Court ruled a released-time program of religious instruction was constitutional if carried on in private rather than public facilities.

School Prayer and the Bible Between 1962 and 1963 the Court wrote three decisions affecting prayer and Bible reading in public schools. These decisions remain highly controversial.

The school prayer issue first came to the Supreme Court from New York State. The New York Board of Regents composed a nondenominational prayer that it urged schools to use: "Almighty God, we acknowledge our dependence upon Thee, and we beg Thy blessings upon us, our parents, our teachers, and our country." In New Hyde Park, parents of 10 students challenged the prayer in court. In 1962 in *Engel* v. *Vitale*, the Court declared the Regents' prayer unconstitutional, noting the First Amendment means:

*I*n this country it is no part of the business of government to compose official prayers for any group of the American people to recite as part of a religious program carried on by government.
—JUSTICE HUGO H. BLACK, 1962

In his lone dissent from the *Engel* decision, Justice Potter Stewart wrote, "I cannot see how an 'official religion' is established by letting those who want to say a prayer say it." Stewart also argued that the New York prayer was no different from other state-approved religious expression such as referring to God in the Pledge of Allegiance.

In 1963 the Court combined a Pennsylvania case—*Abington School District* v. *Schempp*—and one from Maryland—*Murray* v. *Curlett*—for another major decision on school prayer. In these cases the Court banned school-sponsored Bible reading and recitation of the Lord's Prayer in public schools. Because tax-paid teachers conducted the activities in public buildings, the Court reasoned that these acts violated the First Amendment. The Court held that even though students could excuse themselves from the exercises, the exercises themselves constituted an establishment of religion.

In 1985, the Court struck down an Alabama law requiring teachers to observe a moment of silence for "meditation or voluntary prayer" at the start of each school day. The Court ruled that the law's reference to prayer made it an unconstitutional endorsement of religion.

Public reaction to the Court's rulings has been divided and heated. Although many people support the Court's stance, others have bitterly protested. About half the states have passed moment-of-silence laws that make no mention of prayer. Congress has considered several constitutional amendments to overturn these Court decisions, but has not yet produced the two-thirds majority needed to propose an amendment.

In 1984, however, Congress passed the Equal Access Act, allowing public high schools receiving federal funds to permit student religious groups to hold meetings in the school. The bill's sponsors made it clear that they intended to provide opportunity for student prayer groups in public schools, a position that had overwhelming support in both houses of Congress.

The Court ruled the law constitutional in 1990. The case arose from the request of students at Westside High School in Omaha, Nebraska, to form a club for Bible reading and prayer. Student organizers said that membership would be voluntary and that it would be open to students of any religion. When school officials refused to let the group meet in the school like other school clubs, the students sued. In *Westside Community Schools* v. *Mergens* (1990) the Court ruled:

*A*lthough a school may not itself lead or direct a religious club, a school that permits a student-initiated and student-led religious club to meet after school, just as it permits any other student group to do, does not convey the message of state approval or endorsement of that particular religion.
—JUSTICE SANDRA DAY O'CONNOR, 1990

Evolution and Creation Science The Supreme Court also has applied the establishment clause to classroom instruction. In *Epperson* v. *Arkansas* (1968) the justices voided an Arkansas law that banned teaching evolution in public schools. The Court ruled that "the state has no legitimate interest in protecting any or all religions from views distasteful to them."

Some state legislatures passed laws that required teaching the Bible's account of creation with evolution as an alternative point of view. In 1987, however, the Court struck down these laws. In *Edwards* v.

Cooperative Learning Activity

📁 Organize students into five groups. Assign each group one of the Supreme Court cases on religion and education (cases 14, 16, 18, 26, 27) in *Supreme Court Case Studies* in the Teacher's Classroom Resources. Ask each group to read its case and discuss the questions. Have each group come to a consensus on answers. Then have each group select a member to summarize the case and its outcome for the rest of the class.

Aguillard the Court ruled that a law requiring the teaching of creation science violated the establishment clause because its primary purpose was "to endorse a particular religious doctrine."

Other Establishment Issues Not all establishment clause issues concern education. For example, the Supreme Court has also applied the separation of church and state to Christmas displays. In *Lynch* v. *Donnelly* (1984), the Court allowed the city of Pawtucket, Rhode Island, to display a nativity scene with secular items such as a Christmas tree and a sleigh and reindeer. In *Pittsburgh* v. *ACLU* (1989), the justices upheld placing a menorah—the candelabra associated with the Jewish holiday of Hanukkah—alongside a Christmas tree at city hall. The same year, however, the Court ruled that a publicly funded nativity scene by itself violated the Constitution (*Allegheny County* v. *ACLU*).

The Court also has ruled that its ban on school prayer does not extend to government meetings. In *Marsh* v. *Chambers* (1983), the justices noted that prayers have been offered in legislatures since colonial times, and that, unlike students, legislators are not "susceptible to religious indoctrination." Therefore the establishment clause allows such prayers.

The Free Exercise Clause

In addition to banning an established church, the First Amendment forbids laws "prohibiting the free exercise of religion." But in interpreting this free exercise clause, the Supreme Court makes an important distinction between belief and practice. It has ruled that the right to hold any religious belief is absolute. What about the practice of those beliefs? What if a religion justifies using drugs?

Religious Practice May Be Limited The Supreme Court has never permitted religious freedom to justify any behavior, particularly when religious practices conflict with criminal laws. The Court first

dealt with this issue in the case of *Reynolds* v. *United States* (1879). George Reynolds, a Mormon who lived in Utah, had two wives and was convicted of **polygamy**—the practice of having more than one spouse. Reynolds's religion permitted polygamy, but federal law prohibited it. He appealed his conviction to the Supreme Court, claiming that the law **abridged**, or limited, freedom of religion. The Court, however, upheld his conviction. The *Reynolds* case established that people are not free to worship in ways that violate laws protecting the health, safety, or morals of the community.

Over the years the Supreme Court has consistently followed this principle, upholding a variety of restrictive laws. For example, in *Jacobson* v. *Massachusetts* (1905) the Court upheld compulsory vaccination laws for students even though some religions prohibit it. In *Bunn* v. *North Carolina* (1949), the Court upheld a ruling against the use of poisonous snakes in religious rites. In *Oregon* v. *Smith* (1990), the court denied unemployment benefits to a worker fired for using drugs as part of a religious ceremony.

Buddhist Worship in Massachusetts
Across the United States, people practice their right to the freedom of religion. **Civil Liberties Why is the free exercise of religion so important ?**

CHAPTER 6: PROTECTING BASIC FREEDOMS   181

STUDY GUIDE

Themes in Government
Cultural Pluralism There are many widely differing religious groups in the United States. **How did the Supreme Court's decision in Abington School District v.** *Schempp* support cultural pluralism?

Critical Thinking Skills
Recognizing Ideologies The Court ruled out laws requiring the teaching of creation science, but not the teaching of creation science itself. **Does teaching creation science in public schools serve to "endorse a particular religious doctrine"?**

📁 **Analyzing Supreme Court Cases** Assign case 6, *Reynolds* v. *United States,* from the *Supreme Court Case Studies* in the Teacher's Classroom Resources.

Caption Answer
It is a basic human right and a basic principle of our government.

STUDY GUIDE

Theme Answer
By ruling against school-sponsored religious activity, it removed the potential influence of any particular religious belief.

Critical Thinking Answer
Answers will vary but should address issues such as: Can an individual teacher present creation science objectively? If creation science is taught, is it presented as a specific religious doctrine?

Assess

Check for Understanding
Have students complete Section 1 Review on page 182.

Meeting Objectives
Each section objective is tested by the Section Review questions that follow it in parentheses.
• Distinguish between the right to hold religious beliefs and the right to practice those beliefs. (5, 6, 7, 8)
• Identify the tests the Supreme Court uses to determine if aid to parochial schools is constitutional. (3)
• Differentiate between the establishment clause and the free exercise clause. (2, 4, 7)

Special Needs Strategy

Study Strategy The ability to scan for the location of specific information will help slow readers to work more efficiently. Have the students explain the purpose of scanning (to locate specific information rapidly), and select one student to demonstrate by using a finger to track down the page. Ask students to find the paragraphs containing discussion about *Everson* v. *Board of Education, Wolman* v. *Walter,* and *Mueller* v. *Allen.* Ask students if it is easier to scan for numbers or for names.

Caption Answer
when a practice conflicts with law or public welfare

Evaluate

📁 Section 1 Quiz

⬛ Testmaker

Reteach

Have students work in pairs to make two charts, one headed *Establishment Clause,* the other *Free Exercise Clause.* Each chart should include the clause's definition, the basic issue involved, and a list of the Supreme Court cases related to it.

Enrich

Have students write a report about the issue in the 1960s involving the Navajo and their use of the hallucinogen peyote in their religious ceremonies. Students' reports should include the 1964 California Supreme Court decision in *People* v. *Woody.*

Close

Have students discuss what might happen if the First Amendment did not guarantee freedom of religion.

Amish Religious Beliefs Upheld
The Supreme Court ruled that some Amish religious practices outweighed state laws. **Civil Liberties In what instances may the free exercise of religion be limited?**

While government may limit some religious practices, the Court also has ruled that a number of other restrictions violate the free exercise clause. For example, in *Wisconsin* v. *Yoder* (1972), the Court decided that the state could not require Amish parents to send their children to school beyond the eighth grade. To do so, the Court ruled, would violate long-held Amish religious beliefs that were "intimately related to daily living" and would present "a very real threat of undermining the Amish community."

The Flag Salute Cases Two of the most remarkable free exercise cases concerned whether children could be forced to salute the American flag. The first case began in 1936 when Lillian and William Gobitis,

ages 10 and 12, were expelled from school for refusing to salute the flag. As Jehovah's Witnesses, the children and their parents believed saluting the flag violated the Christian commandment against bowing down to any graven image. In *Minersville School District* v. *Gobitis* (1940), the Court upheld the school regulation. The flag was a patriotic symbol, the Court ruled, and requiring the salute did not infringe on religious freedom.

After the *Gobitis* decision, West Virginia ordered all schools to make flag salutes part of their daily routine. When a member of Jehovah's Witnesses appealed this requirement, the Court reversed *Gobitis* and ruled such laws an unconstitutional interference with the free exercise of religion. The Court argued in *West Virginia State Board of Education* v. *Barnette* (1943) that patriotism could be achieved without forcing people to violate their religious beliefs:

> *T*o believe that patriotism will not flourish if patriotic ceremonies are voluntary and spontaneous instead of a compulsory routine is to make an unflattering estimate of the appeal of our institutions to free minds.
>
> —Justice Robert Jackson, 1943

The flag salute cases illustrate how the Supreme Court can change its interpretation of the Constitution. The Court usually follows **precedent** on decisions made on the same issue in earlier cases. As one Justice put it, however, "when convinced of former error, this Court has never felt constrained to follow precedent."

---

1 SECTION REVIEW

Section Summary
Although the First Amendment guarantees religious freedom, enforcing this right has brought government increasingly into religious issues.

Checking for Understanding
Recalling Facts
1. Define establishment clause, free exercise clause, parochial school, secular, polygamy, abridge, precedent.
2. Explain the purpose of the establishment clause.
3. List three tests the Supreme Court uses to determine if government aid to parochial education is constitutional.
4. Explain the free exercise clause.

Exploring Themes
5. Civil Liberties How did the principle the Supreme Court established in *Reynolds* v. *United States* limit the free exercise of religion?
6. Cultural Pluralism Why did the Supreme Court in *Wisconsin* v. *Yoder* permit Amish children to leave school after the eighth grade?

Critical Thinking Skills
7. Recognizing Ideologies Do you believe that prayer in public schools destroys the separation of church and state? Explain your answer.
8. Checking Consistency How well does the First Amendment protect the free exercise of religion in the United States? Explain.

Section 1 Review Answers

1. Definitions of terms appear on pages indicated: **establishment clause,** 178; **free exercise clause,** 178; **parochial school,** 178; **secular,** 179; **polygamy,** 181; **abridge,** 181; **precedent,** 182
2. to prevent government from setting up official church, aiding any religion or all religions, or preferring any religion over others

3. Aid must have secular purpose, must neither advance nor inhibit religion, must not involve government excessively with religion.
4. An individual's religious beliefs and, with limits, the right to practice those beliefs cannot be prohibited.
5. by requiring that religious practices may not violate laws that protect the community's health, safety, or public morality
6. To require Amish children to go to school beyond the

eighth grade would have violated Amish religious beliefs.
7. Answers will vary. Some may contend that if such prayers neither favor nor discriminate against specific religions, church and state separation is maintained. Others may argue that any religious activity in public schools destroys that separation.
8. Answers should note that while protection for religious belief is absolute, protection of religious practices is much more restricted.

Synthesizing Information

Synthesizing information involves integrating information from two or more sources. The ability to synthesize, or combine, information is important because information gained from one source often sheds new light upon other information. If you can synthesize information you will get more out of everything you read.

Explanation

To synthesize information, follow these steps:

• Decide whether the two sources are comparable. Ask: Can Source A give me new information or new ways of thinking about Source B?

• If you decide that the two are comparable, put into your own words what you can learn or what new hypotheses you can make.

Below are a line graph and a bar graph giving information about church and synagogue membership in the United States. The first step in synthesizing information is to examine each source separately. The line graph shows changes in church and synagogue membership between 1947 and 1988. The bar graph shows a breakdown, by age, of church membership figures from a 1988 poll.

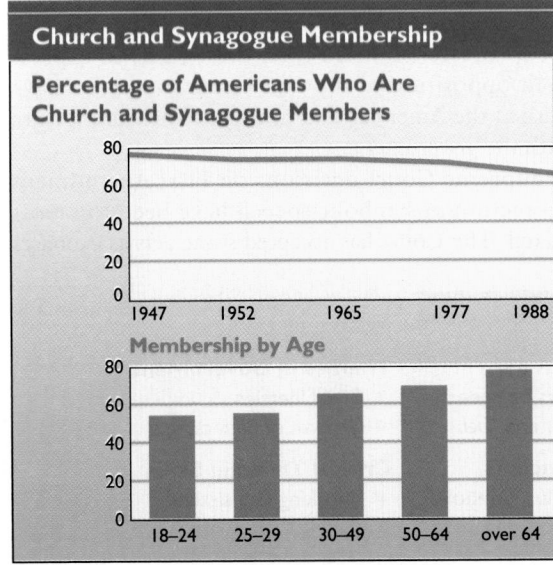

The next step is to ask whether the information given in the two sources is comparable. The answer is yes. Finally, we ask what can the bar graph tell us about the line graph? The bar graph clearly shows that age is an important factor in church membership.

Practice

Use what you have learned to examine these two sources and answer the questions that follow.

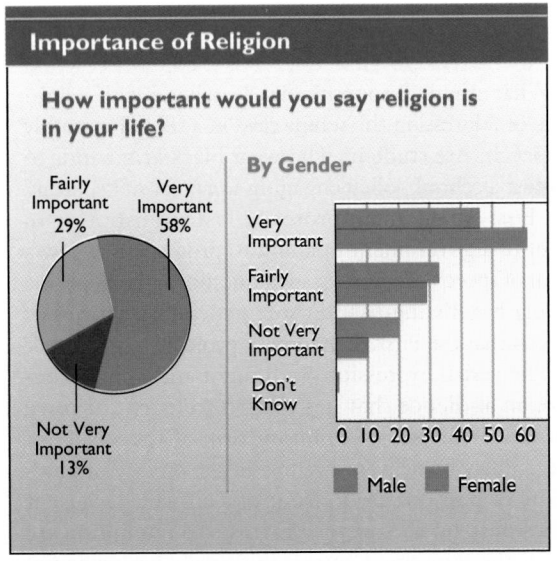

1. What percentage of women said that religion was fairly important in their lives? What percentage of men gave the same answer? What percentage of women said religion was very important to them?
2. What generalizations can you make about the relationship between gender and the importance of religion in individuals' lives?
3. Do these graphs show information that is comparable? What can each tell you about the other?

Additional Practice

To practice this skill, see **Reinforcing the Skill** on page 199.

CHAPTER 6: PROTECTING BASIC FREEDOMS 183

CRITICAL THINKING SKILLS

Focus

Tell students to suppose that they will conduct two polls: one to determine the numbers of Republicans, Democrats, and Independents in their class, and another to determine who intends to register to vote before the next national election. Ask if they could then predict about how many votes each presidential candidate will receive from their class.

Teach

Tell students that the ability to synthesize material from two or more sources is a valuable skill for understanding complex information. Review the data presented in the first two graphs. Ask what the bar graph and the line graph have in common. *(Both deal with church membership.)* Then ask: What hypothesis might you make from the bar graph to explain the trend shown in the line graph? *(Church membership is declining because fewer young people are joining to replace aging members.)*

Assess

Have students complete the **Practice** exercise.

Close

Ask how being able to synthesize information would help in writing a term paper.

Practice Answers

1. 29 percent, 33 percent, 61 percent
2. Religion plays a slightly larger role in the lives of women than of men.
3. The graphs are comparable. The pie graph provides an overall view of the general population. The bar graph shows that within that larger group, male and female responses differ widely.

For additional practice, have students complete activity 6 in *Skill Reinforcement Activities* in the Teacher's Classroom Resources.

Focus

Bell Ringer

Write the following statement on the chalkboard and, while attendance is being taken, have students write a brief paragraph reacting to it and giving reasons for their positions.

People should be able to say whatever they want.

Motivating Activity

Discuss students' Bell Ringer paragraphs. Then ask students if, and under what circumstances, they think it is acceptable to place limitations on free speech. Tell students that in this section they will learn about three types of speech and the tests the Supreme Court has used to set limits on free speech.

Vocabulary Precheck

Ask students to speculate on the meaning of this section's key terms and concepts. Then have them check their speculations by finding the definition of each term and concept in the section text. **LEP**

Teach

Guided Practice

L1 Language Arts For each subhead in Section 2, have students write statements summarizing the main ideas under the subhead. Then have them work in pairs to add to or refine the summary statements. Ask pairs to read their summaries to the class.

Chart Study Answer

to distinguish the types of speech that the First Amendment protects

---

Freedom of Speech

Democratic government requires that every person have the right to speak freely. Of course, most people agree in principle with the right of free speech. Everyone wants it for themselves, but they are sometimes tempted to deny it to others whose beliefs differ greatly from their own. The First Amendment exists to protect ideas that may be unpopular or differ from the majority. Popular ideas usually need little protection, but those who support democracy cherish diversity of opinion.

Three Types of Speech

What exactly is speech? Clearly, talking with neighbors or addressing the senior class in a school assembly is speech. Are students who wear black arm bands to protest a school policy engaging in an act of "speech" the First Amendment protects? Is demonstrating in front of a government building to protest a new law a form of speech? To answer such questions, the Supreme Court has distinguished three general categories of speech that the First Amendment protects.

The verbal expression of thought and opinion before an audience that has chosen to listen, or **pure speech**, is the most common form of speech. Pure speech may be delivered calmly in the privacy of one's home or passionately in front of a crowd. Because it relies only on the power of words to communicate ideas, the Supreme Court traditionally has provided the strongest protection of pure speech against government control.

Actions such as marching or demonstrating are **speech plus**. Because speech plus involves actions, it

---

Three Types of Speech

Pure Speech
The verbal expression of thought and opinion before an audience that has chosen to listen

Speech Plus
Actions such as marching, demonstrating, or picketing as well as words

Symbolic Speech
Using actions and symbols in place of words to express opinions

 Chart Study
Freedom of speech is protected by the First Amendment. **Why does the Court define each type?**

---

may be subject to government restrictions that do not apply to pure speech. For example, the Supreme Court has ruled that, while the First Amendment protects speech plus, the actions cannot obstruct traffic, block sidewalks, illegally trespass, or endanger public safety.

The third type of speech, **symbolic speech**, involves using actions and symbols, instead of words to express opinions. During the Vietnam War, for example, protesters burned their draft cards to express their opposition to the war. Other protesters have burned the American flag to express their displeasure with the government.

Supreme Court decisions on First Amendment protection of symbolic speech have been the most mixed. The Court has accepted some acts as exercises

---

SECTION PREVIEW

Objectives
After studying this section, you should be able to:
- Distinguish between speech that is permitted and speech that is prohibited under the First Amendment.

- Summarize the limits the Supreme Court puts on speech.
- Differentiate *slander* and *libel*.

Key Terms and Concepts
pure speech, speech plus, symbolic speech, seditious speech, defamatory speech, slander, libel

Themes in Government
- Civil Liberties
- Growth of Democracy

Critical Thinking Skills
- Checking Consistency
- Making Comparisons

184 UNIT 2: CITIZENSHIP AND CIVIL LIBERTIES

Classroom Resources for Section 2

- Guided Reading Activities
- Reproducible Lesson Plans
- Supreme Court Case Studies 9, 20, 23, 37, 51, 53, 62
- Section 2 Quiz

- Testmaker
- The Living Constitution
- SAT Practice Tests
- Writer's Guidebook

---

in free speech but rejected others. For example, in *United States* v. *O'Brien* (1968) the Court upheld the arrest of four men who burned their draft cards to protest the Vietnam War. The following year, however, the Court held that the First Amendment protected the right to wear black arm bands to high school to protest the war (*Tinker* v. *Des Moines School District*, 1969).

The Court also has reversed itself on symbolic speech issues. In 1976 the Court ruled that burning the flag was not symbolic speech (*Sutherland* v. *Illinois*). In 1989 in *Texas* v. *Johnson*, however, the justices ruled that the First Amendment protected flag burning. The Court affirmed its new position in *United States* v. *Eichman* (1990). This case declared the federal Flag Protection Act of 1989, which had been passed in response to the *Johnson* decision, unconstitutional. Such reversals clearly demonstrate the difficulty of determining the appropriate limits on freedom of speech.

Regulating Speech

Most justices have supported the idea that the rights of free speech must be balanced against the need to protect society and that some restraints on speech may exist. Congress and state legislatures, for example, have outlawed **seditious speech**—urging resistance to lawful authority or advocating the overthrow of the government. How far can government go in limiting free speech? When does speech lose the protection of the First Amendment? Different philosophies about the limits on free speech have emerged as the Supreme Court has wrestled with the issue of where to draw the line.

During this century the Court has developed three constitutional tests to establish limits on speech. These principles are not precisely defined but are general guidelines that the courts have used when deciding particular cases. They are: (1) the "clear and present danger" test; (2) the bad tendency doctrine; and (3) the preferred position doctrine.

Clear and Present Danger Test Justice Oliver Wendell Holmes developed this test in *Schenck* v. *United States* (1919). Charles Schenck was convicted of printing and distributing leaflets that urged people to obstruct the war effort during World War I. The government claimed his actions violated the Espionage Act of 1917 that made it a crime to "willfully utter, print, write, or publish any disloyal, profane, scurrilous or abusive language" about the government. Schenck argued that the First Amendment protected his actions.

The Supreme Court rejected Schenck's argument and upheld his conviction. Ordinarily the First Amendment would protect Schenck's "speech," the Court said. During wartime, however, his actions threatened the well-being of the nation:

> *The question in every case is whether the words are used in such circumstances and are of such a nature as to create a clear and present danger that they will bring about the substantive evils that Congress has a right to prevent. . . . When a nation is at war many things that might be said in time of peace . . . will not be endured [and] . . . no Court could regard them as protected by any constitutional right.*
>
> —JUSTICE OLIVER WENDELL HOLMES, 1919

Thus, when the speech in question clearly presents an immediate danger, the First Amendment does not protect it.

The Bad Tendency Doctrine Some Supreme Court justices considered the "clear and present danger" principle too lenient and moved to tighten the standard by which speech could be restricted. Several years after the *Schenck* ruling, in the case of *Gitlow* v. *New York* (1925), the Court held speech could be restricted even if it had only a tendency to lead to illegal action. This doctrine has not generally had the support of the Supreme Court itself since the 1920s. It still, however, reflects the views of many Americans. Supporters of this position acknowledge that it might occasionally lead to laws unnecessarily

📁 **Analyzing Supreme Court Cases** Have students read one of the Supreme Court cases on student free speech rights (cases 37, 51, 53) from the *Supreme Court Case Studies* in the Teacher's Classroom Resources and answer the questions that follow the selection.

Focus on Freedom

Lincoln's main goal in the Civil War was to reunite the nation. He had little interest in ending slavery if emancipation would be an obstacle to preserving the Union. As the war went on, however, he came under increasing pressure from Congress and abolition groups to add emancipation to his war goals.

Answers

1. only those slaves in areas in rebellion against the United States
2. to refrain from unnecessary violence and to work for wages
3. These whites might not have accepted their former slaves as equals.

CONNECTIONS

Law

Do laws prohibiting criminals from profiting from crime by selling their stories to the media violate the First Amendment? In *Simon & Schuster v. New York Crime Victims Board* (1991), the Supreme Court said that a 1977 New York statute did so because it "singled out speech on a particular subject for a financial burden that it places on no other speech..." This decision put the future of similar laws passed by 42 other states in doubt.

limiting speech. They believe, however, that society's need to maintain order more than balances any damages done to basic freedoms.

The Preferred Position Doctrine First developed by the Court during the 1940s, the preferred position doctrine holds that First Amendment freedoms are more fundamental than other freedoms because they provide the basis of all liberties. Thus, First Amendment freedoms hold a preferred position over

other needs. Any law limiting these freedoms should be presumed unconstitutional unless the government can show it is absolutely necessary.

Over the years, none of the three principles has been able to provide a clear guide to the great variety of free speech issues the Supreme Court considers. As a result, each position has been popular for application to certain types of cases and less so for others. The Court, however, has been fairly consistent and has generally applied the "clear and present danger"

Focus on Freedom

THE EMANCIPATION PROCLAMATION

For almost one-half of this nation's history African Americans enjoyed none of the rights, freedoms, and protections of the Bill of Rights. First brought to the American colonies in 1619, most African Americans were still enslaved when the Bill of Rights was added to the Constitution in 1791. From 1861 to 1865, a Civil War raged, in part to determine whether they should remain enslaved or be free. On January 1, 1863, President Abraham Lincoln at last proclaimed the freedom of most African Americans.

Whereas on the twenty-second day of September, A.D. 1862, a proclamation was issued by the President of the United States, containing, among other things, the following, to wit:

"That on the first day of January, A.D. 1863, all persons held as slaves within any state or designated part of a state, the people whereof shall then be in rebellion against the United States, shall be then, henceforward, and forever free; and the executive government of the United States, including the military and naval authority thereof, will recognize and maintain the freedom of such persons and will do no act or acts to repress such persons or any of them, in any efforts they may make for their actual freedom. . . ."

Now, therefore, I, Abraham Lincoln, President of the United States, by virtue of the power in me vested as Commander-in-Chief of the Army and Navy of the United States in time of actual armed rebellion against the authority and government of the United States, and as a fit and necessary war measure for suppressing said rebellion, do, on this first day of January, A.D. 1863, and in accordance with my purpose so to do . . . order and designate the states and parts of states wherein the people thereof, respectively, are this day in rebellion against the United States . . . .

And by virtue of the power and for the purpose aforesaid, I do order and declare that all per-

sons held as slaves within said designated states and parts of states are, and henceforward shall be, free; and that the executive government of the United States, including the military and naval authorities thereof, will recognize and maintain the freedom of said persons.

And I hereby enjoin upon the people so declared to be free to abstain from all violence, unless in necessary self-defense; and I recommend to them that, in all cases when allowed, they labor faithfully for reasonable wages. . . .

And upon this act, sincerely believed to be an act of justice, warranted by the Constitution upon military necessity, I invoke the considerate judgment of mankind and the gracious favor of Almighty God.

—ABRAHAM LINCOLN

Examining the Document

Reviewing Facts
1. Explain what slaves this document freed.
2. Describe what Lincoln asked of the slaves that this document freed.
Critical Thinking Skills
3. Predicting Consequences What consequences did freedom have for the former slaves and their relations with their white neighbors? Explain why.

186 UNIT 2: CITIZENSHIP AND CIVIL LIBERTIES

Critical Thinking Activity

Making Comparisons Provide the following opinions on the ruling in *Tinker* v. *Des Moines School District.* Ask students who they agree with and why. <u>Justice Abe Fortas:</u> "It can hardly be argued that either students or teachers shed their constitutional rights to freedom of speech or expression at the schoolhouse gate." <u>Justice Hugo</u> <u>Black:</u> "The record . . . shows that the armbands . . . took the students' minds off their classwork . . . . I repeat that if the time has come when pupils . . . can defy . . . orders of school officials to keep their minds on their schoolwork, it is the beginning of a new . . . era of permissiveness in this country fostered by the judiciary."

principle. Very often this principle has been used in cases dealing with seditious speech.

Sedition Laws The Espionage Act of 1917 expired at the end of World War I. Later, in the 1940s and 1950s, Congress passed three sedition laws that applied in peacetime as well as during a war. One of these, the Smith Act, made it a crime to advocate revolution. In *Dennis* v. *United States* (1951), the Court applied the "clear and present danger" test to uphold the conviction of 11 Communist party leaders under the act. In later cases, however, the Court sharply narrowed its definition of seditious speech.

In *Yates* v. *United States* (1957) the Court overturned convictions of several other Communist party members. It decided that merely expressing the opinion the government should be overthrown cannot be illegal. Thus, the Court distinguished between urging people to believe in an action and urging them to take action.

In *Brandenburg* v. *Ohio* (1969) the Court further narrowed its definition of seditious speech. When Clarence Brandenburg, a Ku Klux Klan leader, refused a police order to end a rally and cross-burning, he was arrested. The Court ruled in his favor, however, stating that advocating the use of force may not be forbidden "except where such advocacy is directed to inciting or producing imminent lawless action and is likely to produce such action." The First Amendment does not protect speech intended to advocate immediate and concrete acts of violence. People are free to speak out in support of their political objectives, however, as long as they do not use violence.

Other Speech Not Protected

In addition to seditious speech, other speech has been denied First Amendment protection. Defamatory speech and "fighting words" fall outside the First Amendment, as do some forms of student speech.

Defamatory Speech The First Amendment does not protect **defamatory speech,** or false speech that damages a person's good name, character, or reputation. Defamatory speech falls into two categories. **Slander** is spoken; **libel** is written. Thus, it is illegal to falsely make oral or written statements about someone.

The Court has restricted the definition of defamatory speech about public officials, however. In *New York Times* v. *Sullivan* (1964), the Court determined

A Justice for All Seasons
Supreme Court Justice Oliver Wendell Holmes (1841-1935) contributed greatly to constitutional law. **Civil Liberties When do society's needs outweigh the right to free speech?**

that even if a newspaper story about an Alabama police commissioner was false, it was protected speech unless the statement was made with the knowledge that it was false, or with reckless disregard of whether it was false or not.

The Court allows some defamatory speech about public officials for fear that criticism of government, a basic constitutional right, might be silenced if citizens could be sued for their statements. In recent years the justices have extended this protection to statements about public figures in general. Political candidates are included, of course, but so are professional entertainers and athletes, and even private citizens who become newsworthy. In *Hustler Magazine* v. *Falwell* (1988), for example, the Court ruled that Reverend Jerry Falwell, a televangelist, could not collect damages even for "intentional infliction of emotional distress."

"Fighting Words" In 1942 the Supreme Court ruled that words that are so insulting that they provoke immediate violence do not constitute free speech. The Court upheld a state law that prohibited any person from speaking "any offensive, derisive, or annoying word to any other person who is lawfully in any street or public place." In *Chaplinsky* v. *New Hampshire* (1942), the Court held that:

Caption Answer
when it presents a clear and immediate threat to society

Assess

Check for Understanding
Have students complete Section 2 Review on page 188.

Meeting Objectives
Each section objective is tested by the Section Review questions that follow it in parentheses.
- Distinguish between speech that is permitted and speech that is prohibited under the First Amendment. (3, 4, 6)
- Summarize the limits the Supreme Court puts on speech. (2, 7, 8)
- Differentiate *slander* and *libel*. (5)

Evaluate
 Section 2 Quiz
 Testmaker

Reteach
Using the terms in Key Terms and Concepts at the beginning of Section 2, have students write a paragraph explaining the distinction between speech that is permitted and speech that is prohibited under the First Amendment. Have several students read their paragraphs.

Focus on Government
Video 10
Lecture Launcher:
Protecting Basic Freedoms
Running Time: 2:21
Videodisc 1, Chap. 10
VHS Tape 1, Begins 28:05

Caption Answer
The Supreme Court has ruled that schools can decide what is appropriate to the school curriculum.

Enrich

Have students research the ways freedom of speech is addressed in other countries, recent issues related to this right, and the ways those issues have been resolved.

 Assign case 62, *Rust* v. *Sullivan* (1991), from the *Supreme Court Case Studies* in the Teacher's Classroom Resources.

Close

Ask students to explain why a democracy must maintain a balance between free speech and national security.

ABCNEWS INTERACTIVE™

Powers of the Supreme Court

Amendment 1 (1791)
Running Time 1:04
Side One, Chapter 8

Some Forms of Student Speech Restricted
The Supreme Court has ruled that free speech on school and college campuses, in some instances, falls outside the First Amendment. **Civil Liberties** Why are schools able to limit their students' right to free speech?

There are certain well-defined and narrowly limited classes of speech, the prevention of which has never been thought to raise any constitutional problem. These include the lewd and obscene, the profane, the libelous, and the insulting or "fighting" words— those which by their very utterance inflict injury or tend to incite an immediate breach of the peace.
—JUSTICE FRANK MURPHY, 1942

Student Speech The Court has limited student speech as well. In the 1969 *Tinker* case, the Supreme Court made it clear that students do not give up all their rights to free speech while in high school. Two Court decisions in recent years, however, have greatly narrowed students' First Amendment rights while expanding the authority of the school officials.

In *Bethel School District* v. *Fraser* (1986), the Court ruled the First Amendment does not prevent school officials from suspending students for lewd or indecent speech at school events. Even though the same speech would be constitutional outside the school building, the Court ruled in favor of school officials. The Court held that teachers and administrators can decide "what manner of speech in the classroom or in school assembly is appropriate."

Two years later, in *Hazelwood School District* v. *Kuhlmeier* (1988) the Court held that school officials have sweeping authority to regulate student speech in school-sponsored newspapers, theatrical productions, and other activities. Justice Byron White drew a distinction between "a student's personal expression," which the First Amendment protects, and speech that occurs "as part of the school curriculum."

2 SECTION REVIEW

Section Summary
The circumstances under which speech occurs may limit the right to speak freely.

Checking for Understanding
Recalling Facts
1. Define pure speech, speech plus, symbolic speech, seditious speech, defamatory speech, slander, libel.
2. Describe the three tests the Supreme Court has used to set limits on free speech.
3. Cite the types of speech the First Amendment does not protect.
4. Contrast the two types of defamatory speech.
Exploring Themes
5. Civil Liberties Do you agree that public figures should have less protection against slander and libel

than private citizens? Explain your position.
6. Growth of Democracy How have changes in Supreme Court definitions of seditious speech expanded First Amendment rights? Cite cases to support your answer.

Critical Thinking Skills
7. Checking Consistency Has the Supreme Court been consistent in defining acceptable speech in public schools and speech in settings outside school? Support your answer.
8. Making Comparisons How does freedom of speech in the United States differ in wartime and in peacetime? Refer to Supreme Court decisions in your answer.

188 UNIT 2: CITIZENSHIP AND CIVIL LIBERTIES

Section 2 Review Answers

1. Definitions of terms appear on pages indicated: **pure speech,** 184; **speech plus,** 184; **symbolic speech,** 184; **seditious speech,** 185; **defamatory speech,** 187; **slander,** 187: **libel,** 187
2. clear and present danger—speech presenting immediate danger not protected; bad tendency—speech can be restricted even if it only tends to lead to illegal action; preferred position—speech should not be limited unless

absolutely necessary
3. seditious speech, defamatory speech, and "fighting words"
4. libel—false written statement; slander—spoken untruths
5. Possible responses: agree—public officials might use laws to silence criticism; disagree: price of fame should not be one's privacy and reputation
6. *Schenck* (1919)—to be seditious, speech must present clear and immediate danger; *Yates* (1957)—allowed ex-

pressions of belief in illegal acts but not urging listeners to commit these acts; *Brandenburg* (1969)—allowed speech that encourages illegal acts as long as there is no immediate danger of lawlessness.
7. Court said student speech may be regulated by school authorities. Student speech outside school is protected.
8. Speech considered seditious during war [*Schenck* (1919) and *O'Brien*, (1968)], was protected in peacetime [*Yates* (1957) and *Brandenburg* (1969)].

SECTION 3
Freedom of Assembly

The First Amendment guarantees "the right of the people peaceably to assemble, and to petition the Government for a redress of grievances." Freedom of assembly applies not only to meetings in private homes but also to those in public places. It protects the right to make views known to public officials and others by such means as petitions, letters, lobbying, carrying signs in a parade, or marching.

Freedom of assembly is a right closely related to freedom of speech because most gatherings, no matter how large or small, involve some form of protected speech. Without this basic freedom, there would be no political parties and no interest groups to influence the actions of government.

Limits on Assembly

One of the Supreme Court's first major decisions on freedom of assembly came in 1937 in the case of *DeJonge* v. *Oregon*. Dirk DeJonge was convicted for conducting a public meeting sponsored by the Communist party. He claimed he was innocent because he had not advocated any criminal behavior but had merely discussed issues of public concern. In voting unanimously to overturn DeJonge's conviction, the Court ruled Oregon's law unconstitutional. Chief Justice Charles Evans Hughes wrote that under the First Amendment "peaceable assembly for lawful discussion cannot be made a crime."

The *DeJonge* case established two legal principles. The Court determined that the right of assembly was as important as the rights of free speech and free press. Also, the Court ruled that the due process clause of the Fourteenth Amendment protects freedom of assembly from state and local governments.

Assembly on Public Property Freedom of assembly includes the right to parade and demonstrate in public. Because these forms of assembly usually occur in parks, streets, or on sidewalks, it is very possible they could interfere with the rights of others to use the same facilities. Conflicts also arise when parades and demonstrations advocate unpopular causes.

Artists Demonstrate for Tax Equity
Special interest groups may rightfully assemble.
History Which amendment protects the right of assembly?

SECTION PREVIEW

Objectives
After studying this section, you should be able to:
- Identify the circumstances under which assemblies may be unlawful.
- Describe the importance of the right of assembly to democracy.

Key Terms and Concepts
picket, Holocaust, heckler's veto

Themes in Government
- Growth of Democracy
- Civil Liberties

Critical Thinking Skills
- Checking Consistency
- Making Comparisons

CHAPTER 6: PROTECTING BASIC FREEDOMS   189

Classroom Resources for Section 3

- 📁 Guided Reading Activities
- 📁 Reproducible Lesson Plans
- 📁 Supreme Court Case Studies 13, 21, 36
- 📁 Primary and Secondary Source Readings 6
- 📁 Enrichment Activities 6
- 📁 Section 3 Quiz
- 📘 Testmaker
- 📄 Government Themes Transparencies 21
- The Living Constitution
- SAT Practice Tests
- Writer's Guidebook

Focus

Bell Ringer
Write the following incomplete sentence on the chalkboard for students to complete:
Citizens have the right to assemble so long as. . .

Motivating Activity
Call on several students to read their completed Bell Ringer sentences. Then ask students to give examples of assemblies in their community. (*Students might indicate parades, town meetings, club activities, political rallies.*) Ask students who, if anyone, should have the right to regulate or to restrict any of these gatherings. (*Local governments require a permit for a parade or school officials might regulate club activities in schools.*)

Vocabulary Precheck
List this section's terms and concepts on the chalkboard. Have volunteers skim the section to find each term and concept and read it in context. **LEP**

CONNECTIONS

History
One of the earliest exercises of the right to petition in the United States occurred in 1836 when Congress received hundreds of petitions asking slavery to be abolished in the District of Columbia.

Caption Answer
First Amendment

Set on Freedom
The March on Washington
Running Time 1:31
Side A, Chapter 18

"I Have a Dream"/ The March on Washington
Running Time 1:42
Side B, Chapter 6

Teach

Guided Practice

L1 Making a Chart Work with students to make a chart on the chalkboard that summarizes Supreme Court decisions that have placed limits on freedom of assembly. List the following Supreme Court decisions vertically: *DeJonge* v. *Oregon, Cox* v. *New Hampshire, Cox* v. *Louisiana, Grayned* v. *City of Rockford, Lloyd Corporation* v. *Tanner*. Then ask students to provide the year and the provisions of each decision and add them to the chart. **LEP**

Interpreting Visuals Display transparency 21 from the *Government Themes Transparencies* in the Teacher's Classroom Resources and use the teaching strategy and student activity to teach about freedom of assembly.

STUDY GUIDE

Theme Answers
It upheld the right of assembly even for those who support unpopular opinions.

Assembly may interfere with the rights of other citizens to use streets and sidewalks or may arouse opposition and threaten violence.

Critical Thinking Answers
In *Grayned* the demonstration was intended to disrupt classes; in *Mosley* the city had banned all demonstrations near schools, except picketing, whether or not they disrupted classes.

Answers may vary, but should balance the rights of assembly with the potential for violence.

Demonstrations, in particular, have a high potential for violence because others, holding conflicting beliefs, often launch counterdemonstrations. The two sides sometimes engage in heated verbal, and sometimes physical, clashes. For such reasons, parades and demonstrations have always been subject to greater government regulation than exercises of pure speech and other kinds of assembly.

Limits on Parades and Demonstrations To provide for public order and safety, many states and cities require that groups wanting to parade or demonstrate first obtain a permit. The precedent for such regulation was set in *Cox* v. *New Hampshire* (1941). Cox was one of several Jehovah's Witnesses convicted of violating a law requiring a parade permit. He challenged his conviction on the grounds that the permit law restricted his rights of free speech and assembly.

The Court voted unanimously to uphold the law, ruling that the law was not designed to silence unpopular ideas. Rather, the law was intended to ensure that parades would not interfere with other citizens using the streets. In part, the decision said:

The authority of a municipality to impose regulations in order to assure the safety and convenience of the people in the use of public highways has never been regarded as inconsistent with civil liberties.
—CHIEF JUSTICE CHARLES EVANS HUGHES, 1941

Additional Limits on Public Assembly Other public facilities such as airports, libraries, courthouses, schools, and swimming pools also may be used for public demonstrations. Here again, however, the Court has set limits.

In *Adderly* v. *Florida* (1966), the Court held that demonstrators could not enter the grounds of a county jail without permission. The Court ruled that, while the jail was public property, it was not open to the public. The state has the power, the Court reasoned, "to preserve the property under its control for the use to which it is lawfully dedicated."

Other restrictions on peaceable public assembly occur when the right of assembly clashes with the rights of other people. For example, in *Cox* v. *Louisiana* (1965), the Court upheld a law that banned demonstrations and parades near courthouses if they could interfere with trials. In *Grayned* v. *City of Rockford* (1972), the justices upheld a ban on demonstrations near schools that were intended to disrupt classes.

Other Court decisions, however, require that restrictions on freedom of assembly be precisely worded and apply evenly to all groups. In *Police Department of Chicago* v. *Mosley* (1972), the Court voided a city law that banned all demonstrations near school buildings except **picketing**—patrolling an establishment to convince workers and the public not to enter it—by labor unions.

Assembly and Property Rights The right to assemble does not allow a group to convert private property to its own use, even if the property is open to the public. In *Lloyd Corporation* v. *Tanner* (1972), the Court ruled that a group protesting the Vietnam War did not have the right to gather in a shopping mall.

In recent years some right-to-life groups demonstrating outside private abortion clinics blocked the entrances. Thus far the Court appears unwilling to protect this type of assembly. In *Terry* v. *New York National Organization for Women* (1990) and *Hirsch* v. *Atlanta* (1990), the justices refused to hear appeals of bans on such demonstrations. In 1993 the Court ruled that an 1871 civil rights law could not be applied against these demonstrators. However, in *National Organization for Women, Inc., et al.* v. *Scheidler, et al.* (1994), Chief Justice William Rehnquist held that antiabortion activists might be sued under a 1970 law that was originally aimed at organized crime.

Public Assembly and Disorder

A basic principle of democracy is that people have the right to assemble regardless of the views they hold. Police and other officials, however, sometimes

---

STUDY GUIDE

Themes in Government
Growth of Democracy Why did the Court protect a meeting sponsored by the Communist party in *DeJonge* v. *Oregon?*

Civil Liberties Why is freedom of assembly subject to greater regulation than freedom of speech?

Critical Thinking Skills
Making Comparisons Why did the Court rule differently in

Mosley than in *Grayned?*
Checking Consistency Should more restrictions apply if a parade supports an unpopular cause? Support your answer.

Background

For many years the Supreme Court moved slowly in expanding the national government's protection of civil liberties. It first used the Fourteenth Amendment to guarantee First Amendment rights against interference by state governments in *United States* v. *Cruikshank* (1876). In 1883, in the Civil Rights Cases, the Court expanded on this ruling by declaring that the Fourteenth Amendment did not protect such rights from the actions of private citizens. Pointing out that the amendment declared no *state* could abridge citizens' rights, the Court declared "individual invasion of individual rights is not the subject matter of the amendment."

have difficulty protecting this principle when public assemblies threaten to result in violence and to endanger public safety.

The Nazis in Skokie In 1977 the American Nazi party, a small group patterned after Adolf Hitler's German Nazi party, announced plans to hold a rally in Skokie, Illinois, a largely Jewish suburb of Chicago. Skokie residents were outraged. Many were survivors of the **Holocaust**, the mass extermination of Jews and other groups by the Nazis during World War II. Others were relatives of the 6 million Jews killed in the Nazi death camps.

Skokie officials, citizens, and many others argued that the Nazis should not be allowed to march. They claimed that the march would cause great pain to residents and would attract a counterdemonstration.

To prevent the march, the city required the Nazis to post a $300,000 bond to get a parade permit. The Nazis claimed the high bond interfered with their freedom of speech and assembly. A federal district court ruled that no community could use parade permits to interfere with free speech and assembly.

The *Skokie* case illustrates a free speech and assembly problem some scholars have called the **heckler's veto**. The public vetoes the free speech and assembly rights of unpopular groups by claiming demonstrations will result in violence. Such claims may be effective because government officials will almost always find it easier to curb unpopular demonstrations than to take measures to prevent violence.

This dilemma leads to two related questions. Does the Constitution require the police to protect unpopular groups when their demonstrations incite violence? May the police order demonstrators to disperse in the interest of public peace and safety?

The Case of Irving Feiner In 1950, speaking on a sidewalk in Syracuse, New York, Irving Feiner attacked President Truman, the American Legion, and the mayor of Syracuse. He also urged African Americans to fight for civil rights. As Feiner spoke a crowd gathered. When the crowd grew hostile, someone called the police. When two officers arrived to investigate, an angry man in the audience told them that if they did not stop Feiner, he would. The police asked Feiner to stop speaking. When Feiner refused, the police arrested him, and he was convicted of disturbing the peace.

In the case of *Feiner v. New York* (1951) the Supreme Court upheld his conviction, ruling that the police had not acted to suppress speech but to pre-

serve public order. Chief Justice Fred M. Vinson spoke for the majority of the Court. He wrote:

It is one thing to say that the police cannot be used as an instrument for the suppression of unpopular views, and another to say that, when as here the speaker passes the bounds of argument and undertakes incitement to riot, they are powerless to prevent a breach of the peace.
—CHIEF JUSTICE FRED M. VINSON, 1951

Peaceful Demonstrations Protected The *Feiner* case still stands as a precedent that the police may disperse a demonstration in order to keep the peace. Since then, however, the Court has overturned the convictions of people whose only offense has been to demonstrate peacefully in support of unpopular causes. The case of *Gregory v. Chicago* (1969) is a good example of the Court's thinking on this matter.

Dick Gregory, an entertainer and African American activist, led a group of marchers from the city hall in downtown Chicago to the mayor's home. Calling city hall a "snake pit" and the mayor "the snake," the

Cooperative Learning Activity

Organize the class into groups of four or five and distribute three chips to each student. Each group is to discuss the dilemma that government faces when dealing with public assembly versus public disorder. When a student wishes to speak, he or she places a chip in the center of the group. All students in each group are to speak at least once. Students might focus on the Nazis in Skokie case, *Feiner v. New York*, and *Gregory v. Chicago* in their discussions.

L2 Debate Have students debate the following issue:

Demonstrations should be protected by the government.

Independent Practice

Interpreting Source Readings Have students complete activity 6 in *Primary and Secondary Source Readings* in the Teacher's Classroom Resources.

Analyzing Supreme Court Cases Have students complete cases 13, 21, and 36 on freedom of assembly in *Supreme Court Case Studies* in the Teacher's Classroom Resources.

Assess

Check for Understanding

Have students complete Section 3 Review on page 192.

Meeting Objectives

Each section objective is tested by the Section Review questions that follow it in parentheses.

- Identify the circumstances under which assemblies may be unlawful. (5, 6, 8)
- Describe the importance of the right of assembly to democracy. (2, 3, 4, 7)

Evaluate

📁 Section 3 Quiz

💠 Testmaker

Reteach

Have students work in groups of three. Assign each group one of the court cases discussed in this section. Ask each group to write a headline and the first paragraph of a news story that explains the who, what, when, where, and why of the case.

Enrich

📁 Have students complete activity 6 in *Enrichment Activities* in the Teacher's Classroom Resources.

Close

Point out to students that sometimes during demonstrations people are injured or property is destroyed. Have students discuss whether or not these actions are ever justifiable.

---

demonstrators began parading around the block demanding the ouster of the school superintendent for failing to desegregate schools. About 180 police officers were on hand to provide protection.

A crowd of 1,000 or more hostile onlookers from the all-white neighborhood gathered. They began to heckle and throw rocks and eggs at the marchers.

At 8:30 in the evening, the marchers stopped singing and chanting and paraded quietly. The crowd continued to heckle them. By 9:30 the police concluded that violence was imminent and ordered the demonstrators to disperse. When Gregory and the others refused, they were arrested. Five, including Gregory, were later convicted of disorderly conduct.

In a departure from the *Feiner* case, the Supreme Court unanimously overturned the conviction of Gregory and the marchers. The Court ruled that the demonstrators had been peaceful and had done no more than exercise their First Amendment right of assembly and petition. Neighborhood residents, not the marchers, had caused the disorders. The Court concluded that such a march, "if peaceful and orderly, falls well within the sphere of conduct protected by the First Amendment."

Protection for Labor Picketing

Workers on strike or other demonstrators often organize picket lines. For many years the Supreme Court has debated how much protection the First Amendment gives picketers. Picketing conveys a message and is therefore a form of speech and assembly. But picketing, unlike most other kinds of demonstrations, tries to persuade customers and workers not to deal with a business. Many people will not cross a picket line, depriving a business of its workers and customers.

Through much of American history, courts supported many kinds of restraints on labor picketing. Then in *Thornhill* v. *Alabama* (1940), the Supreme Court ruled that peaceful picketing was a form of free speech. It reflected the growing strength of the labor movement in American life.

In later decisions, however, the Court severely limited the position it took in *Thornhill*. In *Hughes* v. *Superior Court* (1950), the Court refused to overturn a California court's ban on picketing at a supermarket to force it to hire African American workers. The Court wrote:

> *While picketing is a mode of communication, it is inseparably something more and different. . . . The very purpose of a picket line is to exert influences, and it produces consequences, different from other modes of communication.*
>
> —JUSTICE FELIX FRANKFURTER, 1950

The Court further limited picketing in *International Brotherhood of Teamsters, Local 695* v. *Vogt*. The Court upheld a Wisconsin law that prohibited picketing a business unless there was a labor dispute. With this decision picketing unrelated to labor disputes virtually ceased to be a First Amendment right.

SECTION 3 REVIEW

Section Summary
The right to gather and demonstrate must be balanced against the rights of others whose freedoms may be abridged.

Checking for Understanding
Recalling Facts
1. Define picket, Holocaust, heckler's veto.
2. Explain why the right to assemble is important to the preservation of democracy.
3. Cite the two principles the *DeJonge* decision established.
4. List actions permitted under the right of freedom of assembly and petition.

Exploring Themes
5. Growth of Democracy Describe the dilemmas that a free society faces in setting limits on freedom of assembly.
6. Civil Liberties When may the right to assemble be limited on public and private property?

Critical Thinking Skills
7. Checking Consistency Do you think that requiring unpopular organizations, such as the Communist party and American Nazi party, to provide government with lists of their members would violate the First Amendment? Why or why not?
8. Making Comparisons If the *Feiner* case had come to the Supreme Court after its decision in the *Gregory* case, do you think the Court would have decided *Feiner* differently? Explain.

Section 3 Review Answers

1. Definitions of terms appear on pages indicated: **picket,** 190; **Holocaust,** 191; **heckler's veto,** 191
2. allows political parties and interest groups to exist as well as organized dissent against the government's policies
3. Right of assembly is of equal status with rights of free speech and free press; it is protected from state and local governments by due process clause.

4. to meet in private, to hold public meetings, to meet in public places or on private property (with permission of property owner), to parade and demonstrate to make views known
5. The rights of demonstrators may limit the rights of others and the response to some peaceful demonstrations may threaten public safety.
6. public property—when order and public safety are threatened or when proper use of facility is jeopardized; private property—when the group converts property to its

own use or when the conduct of normal operations is prevented
7. Such a requirement likely would abridge the right of assembly by inhibiting people who might otherwise join such groups or by inhibiting the activities and speech of group members.
8. Answers should include that *Gregory* established the right of peaceful demonstrations to be protected from hostile crowds instead of being curtailed and penalized.

Freedom of the Press

Freedom of the press is closely related to freedom of speech. It moves free speech one step further by allowing opinions to be written and circulated. The press is important because it is the principal way people get information. In today's world the press includes magazines, radio, and television along with newspapers because of their roles in spreading news and opinions.

Prior Restraint Forbidden

In many nations **prior restraint**—censorship of information before it is published—is a common way for government to control information and limit freedom. In the United States, however, the Supreme Court has ruled that the press may be censored in advance only in cases relating directly to national security. Two Court decisions illustrate this principle.

Near* v. *Minnesota This 1931 case concerned a Minnesota law prohibiting the publication of any "malicious, scandalous, or defamatory" newspapers or magazines. An acid-tongued editor of a Minneapolis paper had called local officials "gangsters" and "grafters." Acting under the Minnesota law, local officials obtained a court injunction to halt publication of the weekly.

By a five to four vote, the Supreme Court lifted the injunction. The Court ruled the Minnesota law unconstitutional because it involved prior restraint.

For years the *Near* case defined the Supreme Court's position on censorship. The Court stressed that a free press means freedom from government censorship.

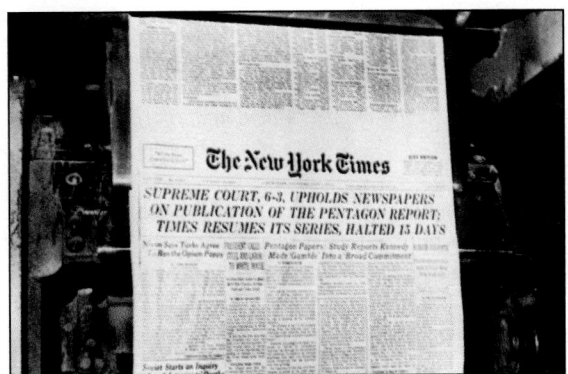

Interpreting the Bill of Rights
The Supreme Court often interprets constitutional freedoms. **History Why did the Court allow publication of the Pentagon Papers?**

The Pentagon Papers Case The Supreme Court reaffirmed its position in *New York Times Company* v. *United States* (1971)—widely known as the Pentagon Papers Case. In 1971 a Pentagon employee leaked to *The New York Times* a secret government report outlining the history of United States involvement in the Vietnam War. This report, which became known as the Pentagon Papers, contained hundreds of government documents, many of them secret cables, memos, and plans.

Realizing the Pentagon Papers showed that former government officials had lied to the American people about the war, *The New York Times* began to publish parts of the report. The government tried to stop further publication of the papers, arguing that national security would be endangered and that the documents had been stolen from the Defense Department.

SECTION PREVIEW

Objectives
After studying this section, you should be able to:
- Identify the limits on freedom of the press.
- Describe the importance of a free press to democracy.

- Compare the freedoms of the print media and the electronic media.

Key Terms and Concepts
prior restraint, sequester, gag order, shield laws, equal time doctrine

Themes in Government
- Constitutional Interpretations
- Civil Liberties

Critical Thinking Skills
- Recognizing Ideologies
- Checking Consistency

CHAPTER 6: PROTECTING BASIC FREEDOMS   193

Classroom Resources for Section 4

- Guided Reading Activities
- Reproducible Lesson Plans
- Participating in Government 6
- Supreme Court Case Studies 11, 33, 38, 39
- Reteaching Activities 6
- Section 4 Quiz

- Chapter 6 Tests
- Testmaker
- Audio Cassettes (English and Spanish)
- Limited English Proficiency Activities 6
- SAT Practice Tests

Focus

Bell Ringer

Write the following question on the chalkboard for students to consider while attendance is being taken:

Should students who publish a school newspaper be allowed to print whatever they want? Why or why not?

Motivating Activity

Discuss students' Bell Ringer answers. Then ask students to explain why freedom of the press is important to a democracy. (*It is necessary to ensure that citizens receive accurate information on issues.*)

Vocabulary Precheck

Call on students to read aloud the definitions of this section's terms and concepts from the Glossary. Then have volunteers use each term and concept in a sentence. **LEP**

Teach

Guided Practice

L1 Vocabulary Write on the chalkboard the Key Terms and Concepts listed in the Section Preview on page 193. Have students skim the section to discover the definitions of the terms and concepts. Then ask for volunteers to compose questions that use the terms and concepts in the context of this section. Have students discuss answers to these questions.

Caption Answer
because stopping publication would be prior restraint and allowing it did not threaten national security

📁 **Analyzing Supreme Court Cases** Assign case 33, *Sheppard* v. *Maxwell*, in the *Supreme Court Case Studies* in the Teacher's Classroom Resources. Discuss how this case explores the conflict between the rights of a free press and the right to due process.

L3 Debate Remind students that the government tried to stop publication of the Pentagon Papers by arguing that national security would be endangered. Have students debate the following statement:

The government should have the right to suspend freedom of the press in the interest of national security.

Independent Practice

L2 Media Tell students that, in recent years, the United States government has seriously restricted the movement of journalists in war zones—Grenada, Panama, and the Persian Gulf, for example. Ask them to take the role of a military commander or a reporter and to write a memorandum supporting or opposing this government policy.

STUDY GUIDE

Theme Answer
Justice Hugo Black believed it did, because the First Amendment prohibits government suppression of embarrassing information.

Critical Thinking Answers
Answers will vary, but should include references to Supreme Court decisions on this issue.

Answers will vary, but may include that school officials were responsible for activities that took place on school property, while the Minneapolis newspaper was privately published.

A divided Court rejected the government's claims. The Court ruled that stopping publication would be prior restraint. Writing for the majority, Justice William O. Douglas noted that "the dominant purpose of the First Amendment was to prohibit the widespread practice of governmental suppression of embarrassing information." Justice Hugo H. Black added:

> *T*he press [is] to serve the governed and not the governors. . . . The press was protected so that it could bare the secrets of government and inform the people.
> —JUSTICE HUGO H. BLACK, 1971

In later rulings, however, the Court has indicated that even where national security is not an issue protection against prior restraint is not absolute. In *Hazelwood School District* v. *Kuhlmeier* (1988), the Court allowed school officials to censor school newspapers, plays, and other "school-sponsored expressive activities" as long as their actions were reasonably related to educational concerns.

Free Press and Fair Trials

In recent years the First Amendment right of a free press and the Sixth Amendment right to a fair trial have sometimes conflicted. Does the press have the right to publish information that might influence the outcome of a trial? Can courts issue orders that limit news gathering in order to increase the chances of a fair trial? Do reporters have the right to withhold sources of information that may be important to a trial?

Pretrial and Courtroom Publicity Before and during a trial, news stories about the crime can make it difficult to secure a jury capable of fairly deciding the case. In *Sheppard* v. *Maxwell* (1966), the Supreme Court overturned the 1954 conviction of Samuel H. Sheppard, for just such reasons.

A prominent Cleveland physician, Sheppard was convicted of killing his wife. The case had attracted sensational press coverage. Pretrial news reports practically called Sheppard guilty. During the trial reporters interviewed witnesses and published information damaging to Sheppard.

The Supreme Court ruled that press coverage had interfered with Sheppard's right to a fair trial. Sheppard was later found not guilty. In the *Sheppard* decision, the Court described several measures judges might take to restrain press coverage of a trial. These included: (1) moving the trial to reduce pretrial publicity; (2) limiting the number of reporters in the courtroom; (3) placing controls on reporters' conduct in the courtroom; (4) isolating witnesses and jurors from the press; and (5) having the jury **sequestered**, or held in custody, until the trial is over.

Gag Orders Unconstitutional After the *Sheppard* case, a number of trial judges began to use gag orders to restrain the press. A **gag order** is an order by a judge barring the press from publishing certain types of information about a pending court case.

In October 1975, a man killed six members of a Nebraska family. Details of the crime were so sensational that a local judge prohibited news stories about a pretrial hearing. The gag order was challenged and eventually came to the Supreme Court as *Nebraska Press Association* v. *Stuart* (1976). The Court unanimously ruled the Nebraska gag order was prior restraint and therefore unconstitutional.

Exclusion from Court Possible In the *Nebraska* case, the press was permitted in court, even though the trial judge forbade it to report on the proceedings. In *Gannett Co., Inc.* v. *De Pasquale* (1979), the Supreme Court ruled that the public and press could be completely barred from pretrial hearings if the trial judge found a "reasonable probability" that publicity would harm the defendant's right to a fair trial. In 1980 when more than 300 trials were closed to the public, the press severely criticized the Court's decision.

STUDY GUIDE

Themes in Government
Civil Liberties In *Near* v. *Minnesota*, Chief Justice Hughes added that prior restraint might be permitted during war or when a publication incites violence or is obscene.

Constitutional Interpretations
Did the First Amendment establish an adversarial relationship between the press and the government? Explain

Critical Thinking Skills
Recognizing Ideologies Should the First Amendment protect those who publish stolen government documents? Explain your answer.
Checking Consistency Why did the court treat a Minneapolis newspaper differently than a Hazelwood school newspaper?

Background

Freedom of the press was an important issue in the American colonies. The libel trial of John Peter Zenger in 1735 set a precedent for this freedom. Zenger, the publisher of the *New York Weekly Journal,* accused a British official of corruption. As a result, Zenger was brought to trial on charges of libel. His lawyer, Andrew Hamilton, argued that Zenger was not guilty, because the accusations were true and because free speech was a basic right of English people.

PARTICIPATING IN GOVERNMENT

Volunteering in Your Community

Your community needs YOU! Every community has many programs that depend on volunteer work. Volunteering provides service to others, a sense of satisfaction for the worker, and valuable job experience as well.

Surveys indicate that more than half the teenagers in this country take part in some volunteer work each year. Consider the wide range of organizations that offer opportunities for volunteers: religious institutions, mental-health associations, scout groups, hospitals, senior centers,

libraries, environmental groups, and many more.

Some volunteer activities require only a commitment of your time. These include answering telephones, stuffing envelopes, visiting the homebound, reading to the blind, or picking up litter along roadsides. Other volunteer work makes use of

skills you already have. For example, you might tutor a school subject or coach a sport. Another category of volunteering involves some training. You might learn how to teach English as a second language, how to administer CPR, or how to coach athletes for Special Olympics.

Investigating Further

Consult your local telephone directory for a list of social service organizations. Contact one or more of the organizations to find out what opportunities exist for volunteers.

The Supreme Court ended the confusion in *Richmond Newspapers, Inc.* v. *Virginia* (1980). It ruled that trials must be open except in the most unusual circumstances. Judges can still close pretrial proceedings, however.

Protecting News Sources Many reporters argue they have the right to refuse to testify in order to protect confidential information and its source. But what if a reporter has information the defense or the government needs to prove its case? Can reporters refuse to surrender evidence? In three cases considered together in 1972, the Supreme Court said that reporters do not have such a right. The Court ruled the First Amendment does not give special privileges to news reporters. Reporters, the Court said, "like other citizens, [must] respond to relevant questions put to them in the course of a valid grand jury investigation or criminal trial." The Court added that any special exemptions must come from Congress and the states.

To date, 30 states have passed **shield laws**—laws that give reporters some means of protection against being forced to disclose confidential information or sources in state courts.

Free Press Issues

In writing the First Amendment, the Founders thought of the press as printed material—newspapers, books, and pamphlets. They could not foresee the growth of technology that has created new instruments of mass communication—and new issues regarding freedom of the press.

Radio and Television Because radio and television use public airwaves, they do not enjoy as much freedom as other press media. In order to operate, stations must obtain a three-year license from the Federal Communications Commission (FCC), a government agency that regulates their actions.

Although Congress has specifically denied the FCC the right to censor programs before they are broadcast, the FCC can require that stations observe certain standards in presenting programs. The FCC, for example, enforces an **equal time doctrine** that requires stations to provide air time to all candidates for a public office. In addition, it may punish stations that broadcast obscene or indecent language.

The growth of cable television in recent years has resulted in more First Amendment freedom for

---

Ask students what benefits there are in doing volunteer work. To help them focus on what type of volunteer work they might enjoy, have students make a list of their own interests and skills

📁 Have students complete activity 6 in *Participating in Government* in the Teacher's Classroom Resources.

📁 **Analyzing Supreme Court Cases** Have students complete one of the cases on freedom of the press (cases 11, 38, and 39) in *Supreme Court Case Studies* in the Teacher's Classroom Resources.

Assess

Check for Understanding

Have students complete Section 4 Review on page 196.

Meeting Objectives

Each section objective is tested by the Section Review questions that follow it in parentheses.
• Identify the limits on freedom of the press. (3, 4, 8)
• Describe the importance of a free press to democracy. (2)
• Compare the freedoms of the print media and the electronic media. (5, 6, 7)

Cooperative Learning Activity

Organize the class into groups of three called "Home Teams." Assign each Home Team member the number 1, 2, or 3. Have all the same-numbered students from each Home Team form an Expert Team. Assign each of the three Expert Teams one of the three main topics in Section 4—prior restraint, fair trials, and modern free press issues. Have Expert Teams create a teaching tool (chart, outline, concept map, poster) that pertains to their topic. Then have "experts" return to their Home Teams to share their teaching tools.

Caption Answer
The government felt that some information might endanger soldiers and military plans.

Evaluate

📁 Section 4 Quiz

💾 Testmaker

Reteach

📁 Have students complete activity 6 of *Reteaching Activities* in the Teacher's Classroom Resources.

Enrich

Have students investigate recent Supreme Court cases on freedom of the press and report their findings to the class.

Close

Have students discuss the following statement: The First Amendment is considered the most far-reaching of the amendments.

After the discussion, allow students time to display their Chapter Project posters, which they started at the beginning of the chapter.

---

broadcasting. The Supreme Court has ruled that cable cannot be regulated like traditional television (*Wilkinson* v. *Jones*, 1987). Other broadcasting technology—satellites and satellite dishes, for example—may raise other free press issues.

Motion Pictures In *Burstyn* v. *Wilson* (1952), the Court held that "liberty of expression by means of motion pictures is guaranteed by the First and Fourteenth amendments." The Court has also ruled, however, that movies may be treated differently than books or newspapers. Prior censorship of films may be constitutional under certain conditions, particularly when obscenity is involved (*Teitel Film Corporation* v. *Cusack*, 1968).

Obscenity The Supreme Court and most other courts have supported the principle that society has the right to protection from obscene speech, pictures, and written material. After many attempts to define obscenity, the Court finally ruled in *Miller* v. *California* (1973) that, in effect, local communities should set their own standards for obscenity.

> *It is neither realistic nor constitutionally sound to read the First Amendment as requiring that the people of Maine or Mississippi accept . . . conduct found tolerable in Las Vegas or New York City.*
> —CHIEF JUSTICE WARREN BURGER, 1973

Since the *Miller* decision, however, the Court has stepped in to overrule specific acts by local authori-

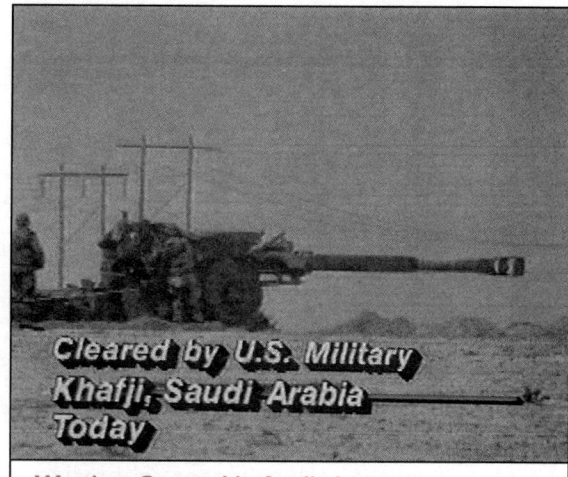

Wartime Censorship Applied
During the Gulf War, American television often broadcast government-supplied footage. **History** **Why did the government restrict reporters?**

ties, making it clear there are limits on the right of communities to censor.

Advertising Advertisers have long faced government regulation, but in the mid-1970s, the Supreme Court relaxed controls. In *Bigelow* v. *Virginia* (1975), the justices permitted newspaper advertisements for abortion clinics. Since then the Court has voided laws that ban advertising prescription prices, legal services, and medical services. Critics charge that these decisions protect advertisers' First Amendment rights at the expense of the public welfare.

SECTION 4 REVIEW

Section Summary
Printed materials and broadcast information enjoy freedom from prior censorship, but they may be limited in other ways in order to protect individual rights or the public's welfare.

Checking for Understanding
Recalling Facts
1. Define prior restraint, sequester, gag order, shield laws, equal time doctrine.
2. Summarize how a free press contributes to democracy.
3. Identify the measures a court may take to restrain press coverage in the interest of a fair trial.
4. Explain when the government may exercise prior restraint on the press.

Exploring Themes
5. Constitutional Interpretations Why do radio and television not have the same freedoms as other segments of the press?
6. Civil Liberties Why is government permitted to regulate some advertisements and not others?

Critical Thinking Skills
7. Recognizing Ideologies Some people think that television has a greater responsibility than newspapers to report events fairly. Why do you think they take this position?
8. Checking Consistency Are there any circumstances under which reporters should be required to reveal or protect their confidential information or sources? Explain your answer.

Section 4 Review Answers

1. Definitions of terms appear on pages indicated: **prior restraint,** 193; **sequester,** 194; **gag order,** 194; **shield laws,** 195; **equal time doctrine,** 195;
2. It is the principal means by which people get information they need to make informed decisions about the actions of government.
3. Courts may move or delay trial to reduce pretrial publicity, limit number of reporters in courtroom or place strict

controls on their conduct, isolate witnesses and jurors from press, and sequester jury until trial is over.
4. only in those cases relating directly to national security
5. because radio and television use public air waves to spread information
6. Both regulators and courts have consistently held that protection of public outweighs protection of First Amendment rights.
7. Answers should include the greater impact and wider

public appeal of television over newspapers. Also, brief TV reports with their powerful visual images leave a more lasting impression than extensive newspaper accounts, which can be reread for clarification.
8. Some may feel that when national security, public safety, or individual rights are jeopardized, reporters should not be shielded from mandatory disclosure. Others may argue that information that endangers someone should not be revealed.

Helen Delich Bentley's Views on the American Flag

In 1989 the Supreme Court invalidated a Texas law against flag burning on the grounds that the act was symbolic speech protected under the First Amendment. This controversial decision prompted heated public debate and aroused calls for a constitutional amendment to counter the Court's action.

Congress passed the Flag Protection Act to prohibit all forms of flag desecration for any reason, not just as an act of protest.

As Congress debated the Court's action, one of the most eloquent defenders of the flag was Representative Helen Delich Bentley of Maryland. Her congressional district includes Fort McHenry where during the War of 1812 Francis Scott Key wrote "The Star Spangled Banner." On September 7, 1989, she delivered this appeal in the House of Representatives.

Mr. Speaker, I have here the petitions containing some 10,000 signatures of Marylanders and other citizens of the United States who are asking that the Congress of the United States pass an amendment that would prevent the desecration of the flag of the United States in the future.

Mr. Speaker, we are having a vote next Tuesday, and that is not what our citizens are asking for, that particular vote. That is a vote on the law, and it is just another delay that would prevent the permanent protection of the flag of the United States...

This morning we kicked off in Baltimore and we began the proceedings honoring the 175th anniversary of the writing of the Star-Spangled Banner, that national anthem that accompanies our flag, that beautiful red, white, and blue emblem. In addition to observing the 175th anniversary of the writing of the Star-Spangled Banner by Francis Scott Key, we are also observing the 175th anniversary of the defense of North Point and of the battle of Baltimore, the defense of Fort McHenry...

That beautiful flag that flew over Fort McHenry on the morning of September 12, 1814, when Francis Scott Key who was a prisoner on a British ship offshore saw the flag still flying after the all-night bombardment... is now in the Smithsonian [museum]... We do fly replicas of that gigantic symbol of freedom over the Fort at regular intervals. This morning was one of those, and when citizens see this tremendous 15 by 30 feet, red, blue, and white symbol billowing in the wind, they will know what it has meant to the people throughout this land...

Mr. Speaker, once again I want to point out that we started in Baltimore this morning, the observance of the 175th anniversary of the Star-Spangled Banner, and we would like to see during that weeklong celebration the amendment to the Constitution passed in this very Hall.

—REPRESENTATIVE HELEN DELICH BENTLEY, SEPTEMBER 7, 1989

... when citizens see this tremendous ... red, blue, and white symbol billowing in the wind, they will know what it has meant to the people throughout this land....

Examining the Reading

Reviewing Facts
1. State what Representative Bentley is calling for in this speech to the House of Representatives.
2. Summarize Representative Bentley's views on the proposed law to protect the flag.

Critical Thinking Skills
3. Synthesizing Information Was Representative Bentley correct in her assessment of what would be necessary to protect the flag permanently? Explain why or why not.

More About Personal Perspectives

Before entering politics, Helen Delich Bentley, member of Congress from Maryland, reported for *The Baltimore Sun* for 24 years. Elected to the House in 1984, in her third attempt to defeat the long-serving incumbent, Bentley quickly earned a reputation as a stalwart and committed representative. She calls herself "the fighting lady." Political observers describe her as "fiercely protectionist, believing both in trade restrictions and in trade retaliation." She once used a sledgehammer to smash a television made by Toshiba, a Japanese company that sold vital technology to what was then the Soviet Union.

PERSONAL PERSPECTIVES

Focus

Have students discuss and list symbols that have come to stand for America on the chalkboard. Have volunteers explain what each symbol means to them.

Teach

Ask: Why is the American flag so strongly identified with the War of 1812 and the attack on Fort McHenry? What do you think motivated 10,000 Americans to sign the petition asking for a constitutional amendment to protect the flag? What "speech" do you think people who burn the flag are making? Why is such speech protected by the First Amendment?

Assess

Have students complete **Examining the Reading.**

Answers
1. an amendment to the Constitution
2. A federal law will not provide permanent protection for the flag and should be passed only in addition to an amendment to the Constitution.
3. Yes, because the Supreme Court struck down the law that Congress passed.

Close

Have students write editorials either for or against the right to burn the American flag.

Identifying Terms and Concepts

1. heckler's veto, 2. prior restraint, 3. speech plus, 4. symbolic speech, 5. libel, 6. picketing, 7. seditious speech, 8. pure speech, 9. shield law

Reviewing Facts and Ideas

1. freedom of religion, freedom of speech, freedom of assembly, freedom of the press

2. Most government officials take their oaths of office in the name of God; the nation's coins carry the motto "In God We Trust;" the Pledge of Allegiance contains the phrase "one nation under God;" daily sessions of Congress open with a prayer.

3. In this 1962 case, Supreme Court outlawed prayer in public schools.

4. <u>protected</u>—pure speech, speech plus, symbolic speech; <u>not protected</u>—seditious speech, defamatory speech, "fighting words"

5. if the statement, though false, was not made with knowledge that it was false or with reckless disregard for the truth

6. Most assemblies involve some sort of speech.

7. so that authorities can make arrangements for public's welfare, safety, and protection

8. It provided that authorities cannot block peaceful but unpopular assemblies merely because they fear violence by a hostile public.

9. Picketing involves more than just communication. Therefore, picketing unrelated to a labor dispute is not a First Amendment right.

10. Press might print or broadcast information that might influence witnesses' testimony, prejudice jurors or prospective jurors, or publish something that might otherwise influence the trial's outcome.

11. The free flow of information is basic to the success of democracy, and prior restraint is a method by which government controls information.

Summary and Significance

The First Amendment to the Constitution guarantees freedom of religion, speech, assembly, and the press. The right to express beliefs, ideas, and information is basic to democracy and necessary for its survival. Supreme Court interpretations of the First Amendment have continuously modified free expression. In general, the Court has attempted to balance the right of individual citizens to express themselves against the responsibility of government to protect society.

Identifying Terms and Concepts

From the following list, choose the term that fits each situation described below.

speech plus, shield law, pure speech, prior restraint, libel, heckler's veto, seditious speech, picketing, symbolic speech

1. Spectators threaten violence against an unpopular demonstration and, in order to keep peace, authorities break up the demonstration.
2. A government official tells a reporter she can not publish a story that might compromise national security.
3. People parade and demonstrate to call attention to their beliefs and opinions.
4. A group burns an American flag to show their objection to a government policy.
5. A newspaper publishes an untrue story that damages the reputation of a local resident.
6. Animal rights activists parade outside a store that sells furs and attempt to convince customers not to enter the establishment.
7. An individual urges a group to fight the police rather than obey a police order to disperse.
8. A person stands in front of a group and states her opinion on an issue.
9. A reporter is protected against being forced to disclose a source of information in court.

Reviewing Facts and Ideas

1. List the four freedoms the First Amendment protects.
2. Cite four examples of how religion remains part of government.
3. State the significance of *Engel* v. *Vitale*.

4. List the three categories of speech the First Amendment protects and the three kinds it does not protect.
5. Describe the circumstances under which criticism of a public official would not be defamatory speech.
6. Explain how the right to assemble is related to the right of free speech.
7. State why government may require that groups first obtain permits to parade or demonstrate.
8. Explain the significance of the Gregory case in expanding the right to assemble.
9. Summarize the Supreme Court's position on picketing.
10. Describe how freedom of the press might interfere with an individual's right to a fair trial.
11. Explain why prior restraint is forbidden in the United States.
12. Summarize the Court's position on obscenity.

Applying Themes

1. **Civil Liberties** In what ways can the rights of the press abridge the rights of the people? Cite some specific examples.
2. **Growth of Democracy** How has the Supreme Court's overall position on speech and assembly changed over the years? Cite examples to support your answer.
3. **Constitutional Interpretations** What actions has the Supreme Court taken to keep the "wall of separation" between religion and government?
4. **Cultural Pluralism** How have Supreme Court decisions protected the rights of certain minorities?

12. The Court has supported the principle that society has the right to protection from obscenity, but has allowed local communities to generally set their own standards for obscenity.

Applying Themes

1. Press coverage may deny individuals the right to a fair trial, as in the Sheppard murder case. Press reports may damage a person's reputation or invade his or her privacy as in *Hustler* magazine's treatment of Reverend Falwell.

2. Over time it generally has expanded protection of these rights. Unpopular assemblies that might provoke violence are permitted under broader circumstances, as is speech advocating resistance to authority.

3. It has prohibited many expressions of religion in public schools; has banned religious practices that

Critical Thinking Skills

1. **Recognizing Ideologies** Justice Oliver Wendell Holmes once stated, "The best test of truth is the power of thought to get itself accepted in the competition of the market." Explain this statement and whether or not you agree with it.
2. **Checking Consistency** What general principles have the courts developed to differentiate First Amendment rights in schools from personal rights outside of school settings?
3. **Making Comparisons** Compare the three tests for limiting seditious speech.

Linking Past and Present

The principle of religious freedom has always been strong in America. In 1701 the following proclamation was issued in the colony of Pennsylvania:

> *Because no people can be truly happy, though under the greatest enjoyment of civil liberties, if abridged of the freedom of their consciences as to their religious profession and worship, and Almighty God being the only Lord of conscience . . . no person . . . who shall confess and acknowledge one Almighty God . . . shall be in any case molested or prejudiced . . . nor be compelled to frequent or maintain any religious worship, place, or ministry.*
> —PENNSYLVANIA CHARTER OF PRIVILEGES, 1701

How does the religious freedom in the United States today compare with religious freedom in colonial Pennsylvania?

Writing About Government

Informative Writing Imagine that you are mayor of a small city of 35,000 people. A resident is planning a rally in a large field near the city limits to protest the government's environmental policies. Top rock groups have agreed to perform, and a crowd of 100,000 is predicted for the speeches and music. You know that heavy drug use and violence have occurred

at concerts some of these groups have given. City council has asked the mayor for information before it votes on a permit for the rally. In writing your report, summarize constitutional issues, public welfare concerns, and other matters that the council should consider in making its decision.

Reinforcing the Skill

Synthesizing Information Use what you have learned about synthesizing information to examine the chart below and answer the question that follows.

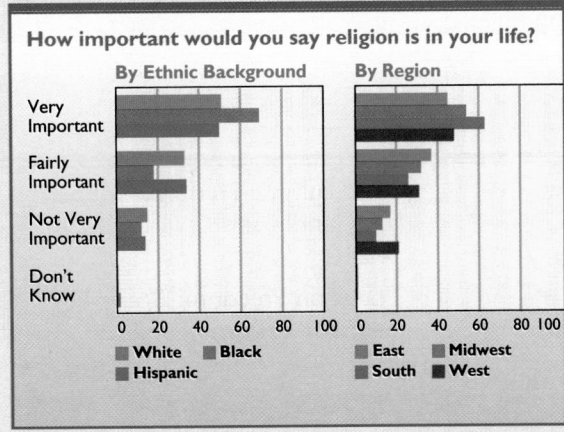

In what region do people attach the most importance to religion?

Investigating Further

1. **Individual Project** Pick one of the Supreme Court cases in the chapter that deals with a subject of particular interest to you. Using the resources of your school library and the local public library, prepare a report on the Court's opinion.
2. **Cooperative Learning** Form a group of five to seven class members and develop a questionnaire to survey other students, teachers, and members of the community about freedom of assembly and what limits, if any, they believe should be placed on this right. After the survey is completed, tabulate and analyze the results. In a short report, indicate the questions asked, the survey's results, and any conclusions that might be drawn.

violate laws protecting public safety or morality; has voided other laws that infringe on religious belief or practice; has refused to allow public funds to support religious activities.

4. Answers should suggest that these decisions protect the First Amendment rights of citizens having unpopular opinions or citizens expressing views with which others strongly disagree.

Critical Thinking Skills

1. The best ideas survive. Students agreeing may claim that in the competition of ideas the good ones will survive. Those disagreeing may argue that even a good idea could get lost among a vast variety of ideas.

Chapter Organizer

Objectives	Special Feature Pages	Supplemental Materials
Section 1 Protecting the Rights of the Accused *pp. 202–208* 1. Summarize the rights of people accused of crimes. 2. Distinguish between lawful and unreasonable searches and seizures. 3. Describe the Supreme Court's position on criminal rights.	Global Connection: Issues: Civil Rights p. 204 Study and Writing Skills: Outlining p. 208	Guided Reading Activities Reproducible Lesson Plans Supreme Court Case Studies 8, 10, 12, 15, 24, 28, 29, 32, 35, 60, 61, 63, 66 Section 1 Quiz Testmaker Skill Reinforcement Activity 7 The Living Constitution SAT Practice Tests Writer's Guidebook
Section 2 Equal Protection of the Law *pp. 209–213* 1. Explain the meaning of "equal protection." 2. Summarize the struggle for equal rights. 3. Identify the tests the Supreme Court uses to determine discrimination.	Multicultural Heritage: Mohandas Gandhi and Civil Rights p. 210 Focus on Freedom: *Brown* v. *Board of Education* p. 212	Guided Reading Activities Reproducible Lesson Plans Supreme Court Case Studies 22, 57 Primary and Secondary Source Readings 7 Section 2 Quiz Testmaker Chapter Transparencies 7 Government Themes Transparencies 22 Great Speeches, Volume I The Living Constitution SAT Practice Tests Writer's Guidebook
Section 3 New Challenges for Civil Liberties *pp. 214–219* 1. Understand the principles behind equal opportunity and affirmative action. 2. Explain legal trends concerning the right to privacy and the right to know.	Participating in Government: Contributing to Charities p. 217 Personal Perspectives: Jesse Jackson on the Need for Unity p. 219 Case Study: The Internment of Japanese Americans pp. 222–224 Unit 2 Digest pp. 225–226	Guided Reading Activities Reproducible Lesson Plans Participating in Government 7 Supreme Court Case Studies 45, 46 Interpreting Political Cartoons 3 Reteaching Activities 7 Enrichment Activities 7 Section 3 Quiz Chapter 7 Tests Testmaker Government Themes Transparencies 17, 18, 20 Audio Cassettes (English and Spanish) The Living Constitution SAT Practice Tests Writer's Guidebook Unit Digest Transparencies, Unit 2 Participating in Government, Unit 2

If time does not permit teaching this chapter, assign the Chapter 7 summary in the Unit 2 Digest on pages 225–226.

Key To Ability Levels

Teaching strategies have been coded for varying learning styles and abilities.

L1   Level 1 activities are **basic** activities and should be within the ability range of all students.

L2   Level 2 activities are **average** activities and should be within the ability range of the average to above-average student.

L3   Level 3 activities are **challenging** activities designed for the ability range of above-average students.

LEP   These activities should be within the ability range of **Limited English Proficiency** students.

Multicultural Activities

In the late 1960s, Demetrio Rodriguez organized parents in the largely Hispanic Edgewood neighborhood of San Antonio, Texas, to sue their school district over funding for Edgewood schools. Although Edgewood had the city's highest tax rate, its low property values meant it could raise only $26 per student through property taxes. Alamo Heights, a wealthier neighborhood nearby, had a lower tax rate but took in $333 per student. Rodriguez's group sued the school district claiming that Texas's school-financing law prevented their children from receiving the same education as students in wealthier districts and denied them equal protection of law. In 1973 *San Antonio Independent School District* v. *Rodriguez* went to the Supreme Court. Have students research this case and its significance for school funding.

Thurgood Marshall argued the case *Brown* v. *Board of Education of Topeka* before the Supreme Court for the NAACP. His success and his subsequent victories in 29 of the 32 major cases he brought before the Court won him the title "Mr. Civil Rights." Chief Justice Earl Warren, appointed to the Court by President Eisenhower, surprised the President with his decision in the *Brown* case. Eisenhower believed he was putting a political moderate and advocate of judicial restraint on the Court. Students can research Marshall's and Warren's accounts of this case or, to sample public reaction, look at editorials in major newspapers around the nation following the *Brown* decision.

Chapter Resources

Readings for the Student

Burnham, David. *The Rise of the Computer State.* Random House, 1983.

Hammer, Trudy J. *"Talking" a Stand Against Sexism and Sex Discrimination.* Franklin Watts, 1990.

Hentoff, Nat. *The First Freedom: The Tumultuous History of Free Speech in America.* Delacorte, 1980.

Wharton, Mandy. *Rights of Women.* Franklin Watts, 1989.

Readings for the Teacher

Bolick, Clint. *Unfinished Business: A Civil Rights Strategy for America's Third Century.* Pacific Research Institute for Public Policy, 1991.

Dees, Morris. *A Season for Justice.* Charles Scribner's Sons, 1991.

Deloria, Vine and Clifford M. Lytle. *American Indians, American Justice.* University of Texas Press, 1983.

Edsall, Thomas Byrne and Mary D. Edsall. *Chain Reaction: The Impact of Race, Rights, and Taxes on American Politics.* Norton, 1991.

Faludi, Susan. *Backlash: The Undeclared War Against American Women.* Crown, 1991.

Powledge, Fred. *Free at Last? The Civil Rights Movement and the People Who Made It.* Little, Brown, 1991.

Skolnick, Jerome H. and James Fyfe. *Above the Law: Police and the Excessive Use of Force.* The Free Press, 1994.

Multimedia

Videocassettes and Films

Assault on Affirmative Action. (*Frontline* series). Scott Craig. (v/c, 60 minutes)

Bill of Rights in Action—Women's Rights. BFA Educational Media. (film, 23 minutes)

Eyes on the Prize. Blackside, Inc. (6 v/cs, 60 minutes each)

Eyes on the Prize—Part II. Blackside, Inc. (8 v/cs, 60 minutes each)

King: Montgomery to Memphis. Martin Luther King Film Project. (v/c, 103 minutes)

Politics—The New Black Power. WETA. (v/c, 60 minutes)

The Spirit of Crazy Horse. (*Frontline* series). Michel Dubois and Kevin McKiernan. (v/c, 60 minutes)

Software

Criminal Procedure. Intellectual Software. (Apple, IBM disks). A tutorial on the various stages of criminal procedure.

Social Studies Keyword Programs—Changing America. Focus Media. (Apple, TRS80, Commodore 64, IBM disks). Games to reinforce vocabulary, spelling, and word recognition focusing on historical changes in America.

United States Constitution. (Disk 5—Amendments to the Constitution). Tutorsystems (BLS, Inc.). (Apple disk, last of a 5-part package). A tutorial covering the Bill of Rights and the Eleventh through the Twenty-sixth Amendments.

Assuring Equal Justice for All

Introduce

Chapter Overview

Chapter 7 introduces students to topics related to equal rights and equal justice.

Section 1 explains how the Constitution protects the rights of persons accused of crimes and explores searches and seizures, the right to counsel, and restrictions against self-incrimination, double jeopardy, and cruel and unusual punishment.

Section 2 discusses how the Fourteenth Amendment provides equal protection of the law to counter discrimination and traces the development of the civil rights movement.

Section 3 highlights civil liberties issues that have emerged in recent years—affirmative action, sex discrimination, the right to know, and the right to privacy.

Chapter 7 Themes

Write the following themes in government on the chalkboard:

Civil Rights
Constitutional Interpretations
Civil Liberties
Public Policy

Ask students to write these themes in their notebooks and to list the major topics in the chapter under the appropriate theme.

Set on Freedom

Freedom Rides
Running Time :22
Side A, Chapter 11

The Montgomery Bus Boycott
Running Time :43
Side A, Chapter 5

The Civil Rights Act of 1964
Running Time :29
Side A, Chapter 22

CHAPTER

7

One of the high points of the civil rights movement, the 1963 March on Washington, brought thousands together in the demand for social justice and equal opportunity.

About the Chapter Opener

Teaching With Illustrations In the 1963 March on Washington, more than 200,000 demonstrators converged on Washington, D.C. The demonstrators sang hymns and spirituals as they gathered near the Lincoln Memorial. They also heard eloquent speeches, especially from Martin Luther King, Jr., who gave his stirring "I Have a Dream" speech. The speech provided new inspiration for the civil rights movement. Have students examine the photograph on pages 200 and 201. Then ask the following question: Based on the photograph, would you consider the march effective? Why or why not?

Chapter Preview

Overview

Through its interpretations of the Constitution, the Supreme Court has assumed the responsibility of ensuring equal justice.

Objectives

After studying this chapter you should be able to:

1. Explain the constitutional guarantees that protect a person accused of a crime.
2. Describe how the Supreme Court has applied the Fourteenth Amendment to ensure equal protection of the law in cases of racial discrimination.
3. Identify the major challenges to civil liberties today.

Themes in Government

This chapter emphasizes the following government themes:

- **Civil Rights** The Constitution protects the rights of the accused and provides for equal protection under the law. Sections 1 and 2.
- **Constitutional Interpretations** The Supreme Court has issued many opinions on the rights of the accused and equal protection under the law. Sections 1 and 2.
- **Civil Liberties** Changing ideas, social conditions, and technology have combined to raise new issues for civil liberties. Section 3.
- **Public Policy** Congress has passed many laws to ensure the rights of women and make government more accessible to the public. Section 3.

Critical Thinking Skills

This chapter emphasizes the following critical thinking skills:

- Identifying Alternatives
- Making Generalizations
- Identifying Assumptions
- Expressing Problems Clearly
- Checking Consistency

CHAPTER 7: ASSURING EQUAL JUSTICE FOR ALL   201

Introducing the Chapter

Ask students to explain the meaning of the following phrase: *equal protection of the law.* Discuss with students the way this principle characterizes our system of justice. Point out that Chapter 7 explains the constitutional guarantees that protect people accused of crimes. The chapter also discusses ways that the Supreme Court has sought to apply the law equally to all people in the United States.

Chapter Project

Have students create a magazine that covers present-day examples of topics in Chapter 7. Their magazine will be called *Equal Justice for All.* Organize the class into three groups and assign each group one section in the chapter. As students read the chapter, each group should look for current newspaper or magazine articles that relate to their section's topic. Each group member should find at least one article, paste it on a sheet of paper, and write a paragraph summarizing how the article relates to their assigned section.

Linking Past and Present

"Nonviolent direct action seeks to create such a crisis and foster such a tension that a community . . . is forced to confront the issue." This description of the dynamics of protest from Martin Luther King, Jr.'s "Letter from Birmingham Jail" is still evident in current protests both here and abroad. As totalitarian governments throughout the world began to crumble in the late 1980s and early 1990s, people of diverse cultures began to turn toward democratic governments which protect personal rights and ensure equal justice for all.

Setting the Scene This chapter focuses on the constitutional protection of the civil rights of individuals. This protection guarantees fair treatment to all people under the law. At various times Supreme Court decisions in this area have reflected public opinion (such as when the Supreme Court upheld the internment of Japanese Americans during World War II) or have tried to shape public policy (as with school desegregation or affirmative action). Ultimately, the Constitution's ability to protect individual rights is dependent on both the attitudes of the justices and the American public.

Focus

Bell Ringer

Write the following on the chalkboard for students to answer in writing while attendance is being taken:

Do you think the school administration should be able to search your locker without your permission? Why or why not?

Motivating Activity

Discuss students' Bell Ringer responses. Ask students to imagine that there has been a school crime wave and many student lockers have been broken into. Some students suspect that the crimes may have been committed by a certain person in the school. However, no one is sure. Ask: Do you think the police should be able to enter and search the suspect's locker? *(without a warrant)* the suspect's home? *(only with a warrant)*

Tell students that in this section they will learn what is meant by unreasonable searches and seizures and the ways the Constitution protects those suspected of crimes.

Vocabulary Precheck

Call on students to read aloud the definitions for each term and concept from the Glossary. Then have them restate each definition in their own words. **LEP**

Caption Answer

They must have probable cause and obtain a warrant.

GLENCOE TECHNOLOGY

Focus on Government
Video 38
**Speaking Out:
Search and Seizure**
Running Time: 1:50
Videodisc 2, Chap. 38
VHS Tape 2, Begins 50:37

Protecting the Rights of the Accused

Dealing with crime and criminals poses a serious challenge to democratic political systems. On the one hand, society must protect itself against criminals. At the same time, individual rights must be preserved. Justice in a democracy means protecting the innocent from government police power as well as punishing the guilty.

To deal with this challenge, the Founders built into the Constitution and the Bill of Rights a system of justice designed to guard the rights of the accused as well as the rights of society. Laws were to be strictly interpreted, trial procedures fair and impartial, and punishments reasonable. Later, the Fourteenth Amendment further protected the rights of the accused.

Searches and Seizures

The police need evidence to accuse people of committing crimes, but getting evidence often requires searching people or their homes, cars, or offices. To protect the innocent, the Fourth Amendment guarantees "the right of people to be secure in their persons, houses, papers, and effects, against unreasonable searches and seizures." What constitutes unreasonable searches and seizures? No precise definition has been made, so the courts have dealt with Fourth Amendment issues on a case-by-case basis.

Today the police must state under oath that they have probable cause to suspect someone of committing a crime. Then they must obtain a warrant from a court official before searching for evidence or making an arrest. The warrant must describe the place to be searched and the person or things to be seized.

Before 1980, 23 states had search laws that permitted police to enter a home without a warrant if they had probable cause to believe that the occupant had committed a felony, or major crime. In *Payton* v. *New York* (1980), the Supreme Court ruled that, except in a life-threatening emergency, the Fourth Amendment forbids searching a home without a warrant.

There still are many situations in which police may conduct searches and seizures without a warrant. Police may arrest and search anyone who commits a crime in their presence or who they think is a felon. In the case of *California* v. *Greenwood* (1988), the Supreme Court upheld a warrantless search of

Police Seize Drugs
In certain instances, police may search private property for illegal drugs. **Law** How does the Fourth Amendment restrain the conduct of police?

SECTION PREVIEW

Objectives
After studying this section, you should be able to:
■ Summarize the rights of people accused of crimes.
■ Distinguish between lawful and unreasonable searches and seizures.

■ Describe the Supreme Court's position on criminal rights.

Key Terms and Concepts
exclusionary rule, counsel, self-incrimination, double jeopardy

Themes in Government
■ Civil Rights
■ Constitutional Interpretations

Critical Thinking Skills
■ Identifying Alternatives
■ Making Generalizations

Classroom Resources for Section 1

📁 Guided Reading Activities
📁 Reproducible Lesson Plans
📁 Supreme Court Case Studies 8, 10, 12, 15, 24, 28, 29, 32, 35, 60, 61, 63, 66
📁 Section 1 Quiz

➕ Testmaker
The Living Constitution
SAT Practice Tests
Writer's Guidebook

garbage outside someone's home. After police found drug paraphernalia in the suspect's trash, they obtained a warrant to search his house. The suspect was later convicted on drug charges.

Beginning in the 1980s, the Supreme Court dealt with whether certain kinds of drug tests constitute a search. In 1989 the Court held that drug tests were legal for a group of railroad employees who had refused to take the tests.

The Exclusionary Rule In the case of *Weeks* v. *United States* (1914), the Court established the **exclusionary rule,** which holds that any illegally obtained evidence—no matter how incriminating—cannot be used in a federal court. For many years, the *Weeks* decision did not apply to state courts. The landmark case of *Mapp* v. *Ohio* (1961), however, extended the protection to state courts.

Relaxing the Exclusionary Rule Since the *Mapp* decision, the Supreme Court has relaxed the exclusionary rule. In *United States* v. *Leon* (1984), the Court ruled that as long as the police act in good faith when they request a warrant, the evidence they collect may be used in court even if the warrant is defective. In the *Leon* case, for example, a judge had used the wrong form for the warrant.

That same year the Court also approved an "inevitable discovery" exception to the exclusionary rule. In *Nix* v. *Williams* (1984), the Court held that evidence obtained in violation of a defendant's rights can be used at trial. The prosecutor, however, must show that the evidence would have eventually been discovered by legal means. The *Nix* case involved a murderer whom police had tricked into leading them to the hidden body of his victim.

Fourth Amendment in High Schools Fourth Amendment protections may be limited inside high schools. In the case of *New Jersey* v. *T.L.O.* (1985), the Supreme Court ruled that school officials do not need warrants or probable cause to search students or their property. All that is needed are reasonable grounds to believe a search will uncover evidence that a student has broken school rules.

The *New Jersey* case arose when an assistant principal searched the purse of a student he suspected had been smoking tobacco in a rest room. The search turned up not only cigarettes but marijuana. The student was suspended from school and prosecuted by juvenile authorities. The Court would probably have ruled in favor of the student if a police officer had

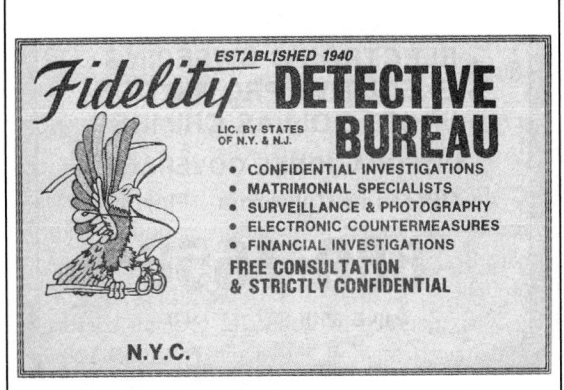

In the Pursuit of Criminals
Private detectives must be careful to operate within legal limits. **Law** **How is wiretapping a form of search and seizure?**

conducted the search, but the justices did not place the same restraints on public school officials.

Wiretapping and Electronic Eavesdropping One observer has said that in Washington, D.C., many important people assume or at least joke that their telephones are tapped. The Supreme Court considers wiretapping, eavesdropping, and other means of electronic surveillance to be search and seizure.

The Court first dealt with wiretapping in *Olmstead* v. *United States* in 1928. Federal agents had tapped individuals' telephones for four months to obtain the evidence necessary to convict them of bootlegging. The Court upheld the conviction, ruling that wiretapping did not violate the Fourth Amendment. The Court said no warrant was needed to wiretap because the agents had not actually entered anyone's home.

This precedent stood for almost 40 years. Then, in 1967, in *Katz* v. *United States*, the Court overturned the *Olmstead* decision. Charles Katz, a Los Angeles gambler, was using a public phone booth to place bets across state lines. Without a warrant, the FBI put a microphone outside the booth to gather evidence that was later used to convict Katz. In reversing Katz's conviction, the Court held that the Fourth Amendment "protects people—and not simply 'areas' " against unreasonable searches and seizures. The ruling extended Fourth Amendment protections by prohibiting wiretapping without a warrant.

Congress and Wiretaps In 1968 Congress passed the Omnibus Crime Control and Safe Streets Act. This

Teach

Guided Practice

L1 **Making Comparisons** Create a class chart on the chalkboard comparing the court cases through which the right to legal counsel evolved. Write *Case, Date,* and *Principle,* horizontally. List *Powell* v. *Alabama, Betts* v. *Brady, and Gideon* v. *Wainright* vertically. Ask students to provide answers to complete the chart. (Powell [1932]: *right to counsel only in death penalty cases;* Betts [1942]: *right to counsel in special circumstances only;* Gideon [1963]: *everyone has right to counsel)* **LEP**

Caption Answer
It invades privacy to obtain evidence.

L2 **Civil Rights** Have students participate in a panel discussion in which they explore the idea of uniform penalties for similar crimes in all states. Consider whether uniform penalties would better extend equal protection of the law. (*Some students might indicate that it is unfair that a person living in one state can be sentenced to 10 years in prison for attempted murder, while a person living in another state may get only 3 years for the same crime. Other students might point to differences in sentencing that may be related to the economic or ethnic backgrounds of the accused. Still others might indicate that having a uniform code could make it more difficult to consider the individual circumstances of each case.*)

Background

The Supreme Court under the leadership of Earl Warren made a number of historic decisions that extended the rights of persons accused of crimes, among them the *Miranda* and *Escobedo* decisions. In more recent years, with the continuing growth in crime rates, demands have been heard for a redress in the balance of criminal justice. Chief Justice Burger in his 1981 State of the Judiciary address reflected this view when he asked: "Is a society redeemed if it provides massive safeguards for accused persons . . . and yet fails to provide elementary protection of its law-abiding citizens?" The debate continues today.

Analyzing Supreme Court Cases Have students read case 24, *Mapp* v. *Ohio*, in *Supreme Court Case Studies* in the Teacher's Classroom Resources. Ask volunteers to describe the circumstances of the case, to explain its relationship to the exclusionary rule, and to indicate its effect on the exclusionary rule.

GLOBAL CONNECTION

Point out that according to Amnesty International, USA, the use of torture and political detention occur today in one-third of the world's countries. Have students investigate the treatment of political prisoners in other countries.
Examining the Connection Answer: *Students' definitions will vary.*

STUDY GUIDE

Theme Answer
protects against unreasonable searches and seizures

Critical Thinking Answer
involving law enforcement; involving parents/guardian; encouraging treatment/rehabilitation program; taking away school privileges; requiring community service, education program

Powers of the Supreme Court
Amendment 6 (1791)
Running Time 1:14
Side One, Chapter 18

GLOBAL CONNECTION

Issues

Civil Rights Governments in some countries use torture to get information or punish criminals. Brainwashing—torturing people into giving up beliefs—is often done to political prisoners.

Most democratic countries prohibit torture. Totalitarian regimes, however, routinely use it to control people. In the late 1970s, for example, the military leaders of Argentina imprisoned and tortured thousands of political opponents. Police arrested victims in the middle of the night and carted them off to prison. No one ever had a trial, and most did not survive the beatings by prison guards.

The Eighth Amendment to the United States Constitution protects citizens, including criminals from "cruel and unusual punishment."
Examining the Connection
What is your definition of "cruel and unusual punishment"?

---

law required federal, state, and local authorities to obtain a court order for most wiretaps. Then in 1978 Congress passed the Foreign Intelligence Surveillance Act, requiring a court order even for wiretapping and bugging in national security cases. These two laws virtually prohibit the government from using all electronic surveillance without a warrant.

Guarantee of Counsel

The Sixth Amendment guarantees a defendant the right "to have the assistance of counsel for his defense." The Constitution has always guaranteed the right to **counsel,** or an attorney, in federal cases. For years, however, people could be tried in state courts without a lawyer. As a result, defendants who could pay hired the best lawyers to defend them and stood a better chance of acquittal. People who could not pay had no lawyer and were often convicted because they did not understand the law.

Early Rulings on Right to Counsel The Supreme Court first dealt with the right to counsel in state courts in *Powell* v. *Alabama* (1932). Nine African American youths were convicted of assaulting two white girls in Alabama. The Court reversed the conviction, ruling that the state had to provide a lawyer in cases involving the death penalty.

Ten years later, in *Betts* v. *Brady* (1942), the Court held that states did not have to provide a lawyer in cases not involving the death penalty. The Court said appointment of counsel was "not a fundamental right, essential to a fair trial" for state defendants unless "special circumstances" such as illiteracy or mental incompetence required that they needed to have a lawyer in order to get a fair trial.

For the next 20 years, under the *Betts* rule, the Supreme Court struggled to determine when the circumstances in a case were special enough to require a lawyer. Then in 1963 Clarence Earl Gideon, a penniless drifter from Florida, won a landmark case that ended the *Betts* rule.

Gideon v. Wainwright Gideon was charged with breaking into a pool hall with the intent to commit a crime—a felony. Because he was too poor to hire a lawyer, Gideon requested the court to appoint an attorney. The request was denied. Gideon was convicted and sentenced to a five-year jail term.

While in jail, Gideon studied law books. He appealed his own case to the Supreme Court with a handwritten petition. "The question is very simple," wrote Gideon. "I requested the [Florida] court to appoint me an attorney and the court refused." In 1963, in a unanimous verdict the Court overturned *Betts* v. *Brady*. Justice Black wrote:

STUDY GUIDE

Themes in Government
Civil Rights The concept of civil rights allows each person to do whatever he or she pleases as long as the rights of other people are

not violated. **How does the Fourth Amendment protect each person's civil rights?**

Critical Thinking Skills
Identifying Alternatives What

alternatives would a school administrator have after finding illegal substances in a student's locker?

Cooperative Learning Activity

Organize the class into three groups to investigate the exclusionary rule, the right to counsel, and protection against self-incrimination. Have pairs of students in each group read cases 29 (*Escobedo* v. *Illinois*), 32 (*Miranda* v. *Arizona*), 60 (*Arizona* v. *Fulminante*), 63 (*McNeil* v. *Wisconsin*) in *Supreme Court Case Studies* in the Teacher's Classroom Resources. Each pair should summarize its case for their group and the groups should decide how the case fits the category it is investigating. Have each group appoint a spokesperson to share its findings on these cases with the class.

Those guarantees of the Bill of Rights which are fundamental safeguards of liberty immune from federal abridgment are equally protected against state invasion by the Due Process Clause of the Fourteenth Amendment. . . . Reason and reflection require us to recognize that in our adversary system of criminal justice, any person haled into court, who is too poor to hire a lawyer, cannot be assured a fair trial unless counsel is provided for him.

—Justice Hugo Black, 1963

Results of the *Gideon* Decision Gideon was released, retried with a lawyer assisting him, and acquitted. More than 1,000 other Florida prisoners and thousands more in other states who had been convicted without counsel were also set free. Because of the *Gideon* decision, no matter how poor the accused is, he or she has a right to a lawyer.

The Court has since extended the *Gideon* decision by ruling that whenever a jail sentence is a possible punishment—even for misdemeanors and petty offenses—the accused has a right to a lawyer from the time of arrest through the appeals process.

Self-incrimination

The Fifth Amendment says that no one "shall be compelled in any criminal case to be a witness against himself." The courts have interpreted this protection against **self-incrimination** to cover witnesses before congressional committees and grand juries as well as defendants in criminal cases.

This protection rests on a basic legal principle: the government bears the burden of proof. Defendants are not obliged to help the government prove they committed a crime. Nor are they obliged to testify at their own trial.

The Fifth Amendment also protects defendants against confessions extorted by force or violence. Giving people the "third degree" is unconstitutional because it forces them, in effect, to testify against

themselves. The same rule applies to state courts through the due process clause of the Fourteenth Amendment.

In the mid-1960s, the Supreme Court under Chief Justice Earl Warren handed down two decisions that expanded protection against self-incrimination and forced confessions. The cases were *Escobedo* v. *Illinois* (1964) and *Miranda* v. *Arizona* (1966).

Escobedo v. Illinois In 1960 Manuel Valtierra, Danny Escobedo's brother-in-law, was shot and killed in Chicago. The police picked up Escobedo and questioned him at length. He repeatedly asked to see his lawyer, but his requests were denied. After a long night at police headquarters, Escobedo made some incriminating statements to the police. At his trial, the prosecution used these statements to convict Escobedo of murder.

In 1964 the Court reversed Escobedo's conviction, ruling that Escobedo's Fifth Amendment right to remain silent and his Sixth Amendment right to an attorney had been violated. The Court reasoned that the presence of Escobedo's lawyer could have helped him avoid self-incrimination. A confession or other incriminating statements an accused person makes when he or she is denied access to a lawyer may not be used in a trial.

Miranda v. Arizona Two years later, the Court established strict rules for protecting suspects during police interrogations. In March 1963, Ernesto Miranda had been arrested and convicted for the rape-kidnapping of an 18-year-old woman. The victim selected Miranda from a police line-up, and the police questioned him for 2 hours. During questioning, Miranda was not told that he could remain silent or have a lawyer. Miranda confessed, was convicted, and then appealed.

In *Miranda* v. *Arizona* (1966), the Supreme Court reversed the conviction. The Court ruled that the Fifth Amendment's protection against self-incrimination requires that suspects be clearly informed of their rights before police question them. Unless they are so informed, their statements may not

STUDY GUIDE

Themes in Government
Constitutional Interpretations
Strict interpretation of the United States Constitution means that the government may exercise its powers only as stated. Loose interpre-

tation extends the power of the national government. **Has the Supreme Court favored a strict or loose view of self-incrimination in the cases discussed in this section? Give reasons for your answer.**

Critical Thinking Skills
Making Generalizations What was the Court's overall view of surveillance techniques from the 1920s to the mid-1960s?

Independent Practice

L1 **Law** Ask students to write the words police officers say when arresting suspects, as they remember them. Then have them research the exact wording that is used. **LEP**

Analyzing Supreme Court Cases Have students complete cases 8, 10, an 35 on search and seizure or cases 12, 15, and 28 on the right to counsel in *Supreme Court Case Studies* in the Teacher's Classroom Resources.

STUDY GUIDE

Theme Answer
loose; applies to congressional committees and grand juries; also applies to burden of proof on prosecution

Critical Thinking Answer
For 40+ years, wiretapping was not considered unreasonable search and seizure and did not violate Fourth Amendment; *Katz* case held that Fourth Amendment protects people and not just areas—now requires warrant.

CONNECTIONS

History
Sentencing criminals to prison is a relatively recent form of punishment. In earlier times, physical punishment was the most common way of dealing with criminals. Tormenting the body through physical pain, such as hard labor or whipping, was considered necessary to cleanse the criminal's soul of sins.

Special Needs Strategy

Study Strategy Students with reading problems often have difficulty differentiating main ideas from details. Teach these students to skim for a main idea in the first three paragraphs of this section. Read the subhead. Ask students to tell you in their own words what the paragraphs are about. Have students read the first two sentences of the first paragraph and the last two sentences of the third paragraph. Point out that main ideas are often found at the beginning and/or end of paragraphs or sections.

L2 Informative Writing Have students write an essay explaining the difference between legal and illegal uses of electronic listening devices. They should refer to Supreme Court decisions.

Map Study Answer
States exercise some power in this area.

Assess

Check for Understanding

Have students complete Section 1 Review on page 207.

Meeting Objectives

Each section objective is tested by the Section Review questions that follow it in parentheses.
• Summarize the rights of people accused of crimes. (4, 5, 7)
• Distinguish between lawful and unreasonable searches and seizures. (2, 3, 6)
• Describe the Supreme Court's position on criminal rights. (4, 8)

Evaluate

📁 Section 1 Quiz

🖥 Testmaker

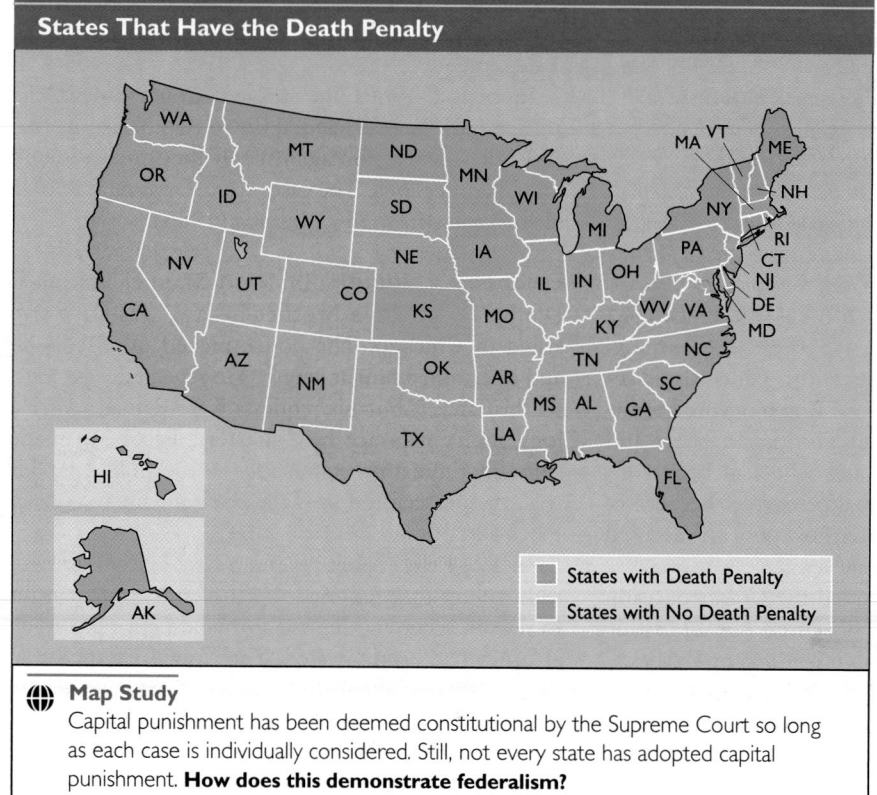

States That Have the Death Penalty

States with Death Penalty
States with No Death Penalty

🌐 **Map Study**
Capital punishment has been deemed constitutional by the Supreme Court so long as each case is individually considered. Still, not every state has adopted capital punishment. **How does this demonstrate federalism?**

be used in court. The Court set strict guidelines for police questioning of suspects. These guidelines are now known as the *Miranda* rules. The Court said:

> *Prior to any questioning, the person must be warned that he has a right to remain silent, that any statement he does make may be used as evidence against him, and that he has a right to the presence of an attorney, either retained or appointed.*
> —CHIEF JUSTICE EARL WARREN, 1966

In several cases since, the Supreme Court has qualified the *Miranda* and *Escobedo* rules. In 1975 the Court ruled that even after suspects exercise the right to remain silent about one crime, they can still be questioned about another. In *Oregon* v. *Elstad* (1985),

the Court held that if suspects confess before they are informed of their rights, the prosecution may use confessions they make later.

In the 1988 case of *Braswell* v. *the United States*, the Court narrowed the protection from self-incrimination in certain cases involving business or "white collar" crime. It ruled that employees in charge of corporate records could be forced to turn over evidence even if it might be incriminating.

In *Arizona* v. *Fulminante* (1991), the Court ruled that coerced confessions are sometimes permitted. While in prison for illegal possession of a firearm, Oreste Fulminante confessed to another prisoner that he had murdered his stepdaughter. The other inmate, who was an informant, had promised Fulminante protection from other prisoners in exchange for the confession. When the authorities were informed, Fulminante was tried and convicted. Upon appeal the Supreme Court ruled that a forced confession did not always void a conviction. In Fulminante's case, however, the Court granted a new trial because the informant had tricked him into confessing.

Double Jeopardy

The Fifth Amendment states in part that no person shall be "twice put in jeopardy of life and limb."

Critical Thinking Activity

Making Generalizations Point out to students that at times criminal cases are dismissed in court because the accused person's rights were violated. Some people argue that such technicalities protect criminals and increase the problems with crime in the society. Ask students if they agree or have them make their own generalizations about such protec-

tions for those accused of crimes. *(Some students might indicate that protecting the rights of individuals, even criminals, is extremely important in a democratic society. Other students might indicate that a minor indiscretion on the part of law enforcement officials should not result in a criminal being set free.)*

Double jeopardy means a person may not be tried twice for the same crime, thus protecting people from continual harassment. In 1989 in *United States* v. *Halper*, the Supreme Court extended this protection by ruling that a civil penalty could not be imposed on a person convicted of a crime for the same act. For example, if a person is convicted of robbing a bank (a criminal conviction), the bank cannot sue the robber for damaging the bank's property during the robbery (a civil conviction). Sometimes, however, a person may be tried more than once for the same act. In our federal system, a single act—robbing a national bank, for example—may violate both federal and state law. An accused may be tried twice: once for the federal crime and once for the state crime.

A single act may involve more than one crime. Stealing a car and then selling it involves theft and the sale of stolen goods. A person may be tried separately for each offense. When a trial jury fails to agree on a verdict, the accused may have to undergo a second trial. Double jeopardy does not apply when the government wins an appeal of a case in a higher court.

Cruel and Unusual Punishment

The Eighth Amendment forbids "cruel and unusual punishment," the only constitutional provision specifically limiting penalties in criminal cases. The Supreme Court has rarely used this provision. In *Rhodes* v. *Chapman* (1981), for example, the Court ruled that putting two prisoners in a cell built for one is not cruel and unusual punishment.

There is a great controversy, however, over the death penalty. During the 1970s the Supreme Court handed down several decisions on the constitutionality of the death penalty. In *Furman* v. *Georgia* (1972), the Court ruled that capital punishment as then administered was not constitutional. The Court found the death penalty was being imposed in apparently arbitrary ways for a wide variety of crimes and mainly on African Americans and poor people.

The *Furman* decision, however, stopped short of flatly outlawing the death penalty. Instead, it warned the states that the death penalty needed clarification. Thirty-five states responded with new death penalty laws. These laws took two approaches. North Carolina and some other states made the death penalty mandatory for certain crimes. In this way, they hoped to eliminate arbitrary decisions. In *Woodson* v. *North Carolina* (1976), however, the Court ruled mandatory death penalties unconstitutional. The Court held that such laws failed to take into consideration the specifics of a crime and any possible mitigating circumstances.

Georgia and several other states took a different approach. They established new procedures for trials and appeals designed to reduce arbitrary decisions and racial prejudice in imposing the death penalty. In *Gregg* v. *Georgia* (1976), the Court upheld the Georgia law. In the *Gregg* case, the Court ruled that under adequate guidelines the death penalty does not constitute cruel and unusual punishment. The Court stated, "Capital punishment is an expression of society's moral outrage. . . . It is an extreme sanction, suitable to the most extreme of crimes."

1
SECTION REVIEW

Section Summary
The Constitution guarantees a defendant the right to counsel and protects the accused against unreasonable searches and seizures, self-incrimination, double jeopardy, and cruel and unusual punishment.

Checking for Understanding
Recalling Facts
1. Define exclusionary rule, counsel, self-incrimination, double jeopardy.
2. Describe the procedure that police must follow in making a lawful search.
3. Identify the case in which the exclusionary rule was first applied to state courts.
4. Explain the importance of the Court's decision in *Gideon v. Wainwright*.

Exploring Themes
5. Civil Rights How does the right to counsel help guarantee a fair trial?
6. Constitutional Interpretations How has the Court differentiated between a search by a public school official and a search by the police?

Critical Thinking Skills
7. Identifying Alternatives What decisions does the accused person have to make at the time he or she hears the *Miranda* rules?
8. Making Generalizations What was the general trend of Supreme Court decisions regarding the rights of the accused in the 1960s and 1970s?

Reteach
Have students make a chart summarizing ways that the Fourth, Fifth, Sixth, and Eighth Amendments protect the rights of a person accused of a crime. The chart should include Supreme Court cases that relate to the rights guaranteed by the particular amendments.

Enrich
Have students use information in the most recent *Statistical Abstract of the United States* to develop a profile of the people currently on death row. The profile should include age, sex, level of education, marital status, and length of incarceration. Have students discuss the profiles with the class.

Have students complete case 61 (*County of Riverside* v. *McLaughlin,* 1991) or 66 (*Harmelin* v. *Michigan,* 1991) in *Supreme Court Case Studies* in the Teacher's Classroom Resources. After reading their assigned case, ask them to write a paragraph that indicates what amendment the case affects and how the Court applied the amendment to the case.

Close
Ask students if they agree or disagree with the opinion that people accused of crimes have too many legal rights.

Section 1 Review Answers

1. Definitions of terms appear on pages indicated: **exclusionary rule,** 203; **counsel,** 204; **self-incrimination,** 205; **double jeopardy,** 207
2. Police must obtain a warrant through a court by stating their probable cause to suspect the committing of a crime.
3. *Mapp* v. *Ohio*

4. Many people who had been convicted without counsel were set free. Because of this case, no matter how poor the accused is, he or she has a right to a lawyer.
5. It ensures that each person will have qualified help in preparing a defense.
6. School officials, unlike the police, do not need warrants or probable cause to search students or their property.

7. Suspects have to decide whether to say anything or to remain silent. They must decide whether to ask for an attorney to be present if they decide to talk.
8. Generally the Court expanded the rights of the accused during this period.

Focus

Write the following main ideas and subtopics in random order on the chalkboard (without Roman numerals or capital letters) and ask students to arrange them in outline form.

I. The Crime
    A. Persons Involved
    B. Nature of Crime
II. The Investigation
    A. Police Interviews
    B. Lab Reports
III. The Trial
    A. Jury Selection
    B. Opening Arguments

Discuss students' outlines. Explain that an outline helps organize information so one can see how the parts are related.

Teach

Ask: What distinguishes a main idea from a subtopic? *(Subtopics support main ideas.)* What are supporting details? *(facts that support subtopics)* What are some ways to organize main ideas or subtopics? *(samples: by time order, by importance, by parallel concepts)*

Assess

Have students complete the **Practice** exercise.

Close

Summarize ways students can use outlining in their schoolwork. Ask: What jobs might require outlining skills?

Outlining

Outlining involves highlighting the main ideas and supporting details in written material. Outlining what you have read will help you organize and retain information. Knowing how to outline will also help you write reports or essays.

Explanation

To outline a passage, follow these steps:

- List the main ideas introduced in the passage.
- Determine which subtopics support each main idea. Ask: What evidence does the author present to back up this idea?
- List the main ideas, subtopics, and supporting details in order. Your outline should have the following structure:

    I. Main idea
        A. Subtopic
            1. Supporting detail
            2. Supporting detail
        B. Subtopic
    II. Main idea
        A. Subtopic
        B. Subtopic

Note that Roman numerals identify the main ideas, capital letters show the subtopics, and Arabic numerals denote supporting details.

To outline the first part of Section 1 of this chapter, start by writing the title "Protecting the Rights of the Accused." If you use the major headings as the main ideas, your outline will look like the following outline:

Protecting the Rights of the Accused
I. Unreasonable Searches and Seizure
II. Guarantee of Counsel
III. Self-incrimination

The next step is to list the subtopics and supporting details under each main idea. A useful way to do this is to list the headings in blue type as subtopics. Then read each subtopic to find the supporting details. Your completed outline should look something like the one that follows:

Protecting the Rights of the Accused
I. Unreasonable Searches and Seizure
    A. The Exclusionary Rule
        1. *Weeks* v. *United States*
        2. *Mapp* v. *Ohio*
    B. Relaxing the Exclusionary Rule
    C. Fourth Amendment in High Schools
    D. Wiretapping and Electronic Eavesdropping
        1. *Olmstead* v. *United States*
        2. *Katz* v. *United States*
    E. Congress and Wiretaps
        1. Court Orders Required
        2. National Security Cases
II. Guarantee of Counsel
    A. Early Rulings on Right to Counsel
        1. *Powell* v. *Alabama*
        2. *Betts* v. *Brady*
    B. *Gideon* v. *Wainwright*
    C. Results of the *Gideon* Decision
III. Self-incrimination
    A. *Escobedo* v. *Illinois*
        1. Incriminating Statements
        2. Lawyers Required During Confessions
    B. *Miranda* v. *Arizona*
        1. Protects Suspects from Interrogations
        2. Must Be Informed of Rights

Practice

Follow the steps you have learned to complete the following outline of the first part of Section 2.

Equal Protection of the Law
I. The Meaning of Equal Protection
    A.
    B. Suspect Classifications
    C.
II.
    A.
        1.
        2.
    B. Impact of the *Washington* Decision
        1.
        2.
    C.

Additional Practice

To practice this skill, see **Reinforcing the Skill** on page 221.

Practice Answers

A. Rational Basis Test
C. Fundamental Rights
II. Proving Intent to Discriminate
A. Showing Intent to Discriminate
1. *Washington* case challenged a police recruiting test.
2. Though discriminatory, test upheld because no intent to discriminate.

1. Zoning ordinances prohibiting low-cost housing are constitutional.
2. Even though effect is to discriminate, no intent to do so.
C. The Struggle for Equal Rights

For additional practice, have students complete activity 7 in *Skill Reinforcement Activities* in the Teacher's Classroom Resources.

Equal Protection of the Law

The Declaration of Independence affirmed an ideal of American democracy when it stated "all men are created equal." This statement does not mean that everyone is born with the same characteristics or will remain equal. Rather, the democratic ideal of equality means all people are entitled to equal rights and treatment before the law.

Meaning of Equal Protection

The Fourteenth Amendment forbids any state to "deny to any person within its jurisdiction the equal protection of the law." The Supreme Court has ruled that the Fifth Amendment's due process clause also provides equal protection.

Generally the equal protection clause means that state and local governments cannot draw unreasonable distinctions between different groups of people. The key word is *unreasonable*. In practice, all governments must classify or draw distinctions between categories of people. For example, when a state taxes cigarettes, it taxes smokers but not nonsmokers.

When a citizen challenges a law because it violates the equal protection clause, the issue is not whether a classification can be made. The issue is whether or not the classification is reasonable. Over the years the Supreme Court has developed guidelines for considering when a state law or action might violate the equal protection clause.

The Rational Basis Test The **rational basis test** means that the Court will uphold a state law when

the state can show a good reason to justify the classification. A law prohibiting people with red hair from driving would fail the test because there is no relation between the color of a person's hair and driving safely. In *Wisconsin* v. *Mitchell* (1993), the Supreme Court upheld a state law that imposes longer prison sentences for people who commit "hate crimes," crimes motivated by prejudice. Unless special circumstances exist, the Supreme Court puts the burden of proving a law unreasonable on the people challenging the law.

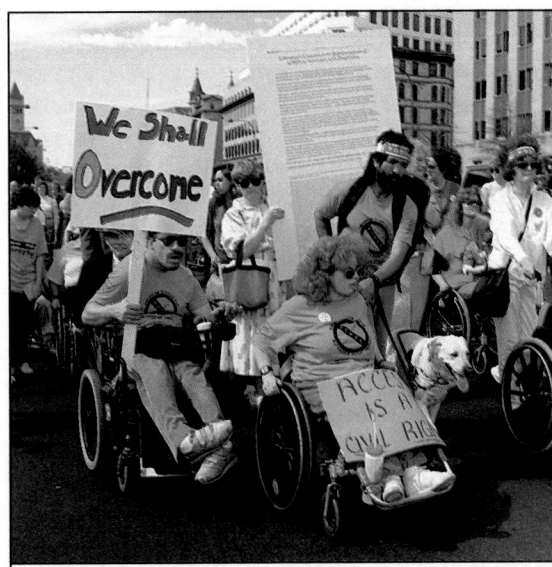

Equal Protection for Handicapped Persons
The Fourteenth Amendment reaffirms equal rights.
Civil Rights Why are some Americans continuing to demand equal treatment within the law?

SECTION PREVIEW

Objectives
After studying this section, you should be able to:
- Explain the meaning of "equal protection."
- Summarize the struggle for equal rights.
- Identify the tests the Supreme

Court uses to determine discrimination.

Key Terms and Concepts
rational basis test, suspect classification, fundamental right, discrimination, Jim Crow law, separate but equal doctrine, civil rights movement

Themes in Government
- Constitutional Interpretations
- Civil Rights

Critical Thinking Skills
- Identifying Assumptions
- Checking Consistency

Classroom Resources for Section 2

- 📁 Guided Reading Activities
- 📁 Reproducible Lesson Plans
- 📁 Supreme Court Case Studies 22, 57
- 📁 Primary and Secondary Source Readings 7
- 📁 Section 2 Quiz
- ✚ Testmaker

- 🎵 Chapter Transparencies 7
- 🎵 Government Themes Transparencies 22
- 📀 Great Speeches, Volume I
  The Living Constitution
  SAT Practice Tests
  Writer's Guidebook

Focus

Bell Ringer

Ask students to define *discrimination*.

Motivating Activity

Present the following: Imagine that you and another student are both called to the principal's office. Each of you has been truant the same number of times. The principal suspends you from school; your friend receives only a warning. Is this discrimination? *(Students may say "yes," but it is only if based on unreasonable distinction between categories of people.)*

Vocabulary Precheck

Write the terms and concepts on the chalkboard. Ask students to use those that they know in sentences. **LEP**

Caption Answer

Some groups feel they are unreasonably distinguished from other people.

Teach

Guided Practice

L1 Synthesizing Information
Ask students how each situation violates the equal protection clause and why.
1. Your state passes a law that prohibits people with long hair from attending movies that begin after 9 P.M. *(rational basis test)*
2. A student lives in an Indiana town and often travels across the Ohio line to visit friends. Indiana legislature passes a law prohibiting travel to Ohio. *(fundamental rights)*
3. Your community passes a law that says all people from Greece must stay out of the downtown area. *(suspect classification)*

Focus

Query students about their knowledge of the methods used by most civil rights activists to achieve their goals. Ask students what these methods have in common. *(All are nonviolent.)*

Teach

Have a student paraphrase Gandhi's advice to Africans. Discuss what Gandhi means by the assertion that "freedom and slavery are mental states." Point out that civil disobedience refers to refusal to obey laws considered unjust. How was Martin Luther King, Jr., influenced by Gandhi? What are some recent examples of nonviolent methods in seeking change? Why are nonviolent tactics usually more successful than violent protest in achieving reform?

Assess

Have students complete **Examining Our Multicultural Heritage.**

Answers

1. India
2. nonviolence and civil disobedience
3. because by adopting Gandhi's principle of nonviolence, he was able to help ensure the rights of African Americans

Close

Have students write an imaginary letter from Reverend King to Gandhi describing how Gandhi's concept of civil disobedience influenced King's work.

Mohandas Gandhi and Civil Rights

Many years before his death Mohandas Gandhi, the "Father of India," wrote about freedom for Africans, many of whom were living under the control of colonial rulers. Gandhi wrote:

Freedom and slavery are mental states. Therefore the first thing is to say to yourself, "I shall no longer accept the role of a slave.... The so-called master may lash you and try to force you to serve him. You will say, "No, I will not serve you for your money or under a threat." This may mean suffering. Your readiness to suffer will light the torch of freedom which can never be put out.
—MOHANDAS GANDHI, 1942

Gandhi's statement contained the basis of his philosophy of nonviolent civil disobedience.

Born in India in 1869, Mohandas Gandhi studied law as a young man. He then moved to South Africa where he began his campaign against the British rulers of the country. Frequently jailed, Gandhi strictly adhered to his basic principles of nonviolence and civil disobedience. Gandhi followed these same principles when he returned to his homeland to protest British rule there.

Gandhi's efforts had not gone unnoticed in the United States. African American ministers visited him during the 1930s to discuss their efforts to win more rights. It was during one such interview that Gandhi observed prophetically, "It may be through the Negroes that the unadulterated message of non-violence will be delivered to the world."

Gandhi's major follower in the United States was the Reverend Martin Luther King, Jr., who led the civil rights movement in the 1950s and 1960s. Often referred to as the American Gandhi, Dr. King embraced the philosophy of nonviolence. As he wrote about the civil rights movement:

I had come to see early that the Christian doctrine of love operating through the Gandhian method of nonviolence was one of the most potent weapons available to the Negro in his struggle for freedom.
—THE REVEREND MARTIN LUTHER KING, JR., 1956

Mohandas Gandhi
The nationalist leader, who practiced nonviolent disobedience to help achieve political and social change, influenced the American civil rights movement.

Dr. King led the civil rights movement until his tragic assassination in 1968. Under his leadership volunteers in the movement worked to ensure equal rights for all Americans.

Examining Our Multicultural Heritage

Reviewing Facts
1. Identify the nation that gained its independence under the leadership of Mohandas Gandhi.
2. Describe the basic principles of Gandhi's philosophy.

Critical Thinking Skills
3. Drawing Conclusions Why do you think Martin Luther King, Jr's., philosophy was important to the success of the civil rights movement?

More About Our Multicultural Heritage

Gandhi first used nonviolent tactics for protest between 1893 and 1914 when he organized Indian workers in South Africa to protest discrimination by white South Africans. In this protest he used traditional Hindu practices of meditation, fasting, and nonviolence. Reflecting his position as a spiritual as well as a political leader, Gandhi came to be called by the Indian people *Mahatma*, or Great Soul. In the fight for Indian independence, Gandhi's forms of nonviolent protest included meetings for prayer and fasting, boycotting British goods, and refusing to pay British taxes or obey British laws. Gandhi died by the violent methods he had rejected when a fanatic Hindu assassinated him in 1948.

Special circumstances arise when the Court decides that a state law involves a "suspect classification" or a "fundamental right."

Suspect Classifications When a classification is made on the basis of race or national origin, it is a **suspect classification** and "subject to strict judicial scrutiny." A law that requires African Americans but not whites to ride in the back of a bus would be a suspect classification.

When a law involves a suspect classification, the Court reverses the normal presumption of constitutionality. It is no longer enough for the state to show that the law is a reasonable way to handle a public problem. The state must show the Court that there is "some compelling public interest" to justify the law and the classifications it makes.

Fundamental Rights The third test the Court uses is that of **fundamental rights**, or rights that the Constitution explicitly guarantees. The Court gives a state law dealing with fundamental rights especially close scrutiny. The Court, for example, has ruled that the right to travel freely between the states, the right to vote, and First Amendment rights are fundamental. State laws that violate these fundamental rights are unconstitutional.

Proving Intent to Discriminate

Laws that classify people unreasonably are said to discriminate. **Discrimination** exists when individuals are treated unfairly solely because of their race, sex, ethnic group, age, physical handicap, or religion. Such discrimination is illegal, but it may be difficult to prove.

What if a law does not classify people directly, but the effect of the law is to classify people? For example, suppose a law requires that job applicants at the police department take a test. Suppose members of one group usually score better on this test than members of another group. Can discrimination be proven simply by showing that the law has a different impact on people of different races, sexes, or national origins?

Showing Intent to Discriminate In *Washington v. Davis* (1976), the Supreme Court ruled that to prove a state guilty of discrimination, one must prove that an intent to discriminate motivated the state's action. The case arose when two African Americans challenged the District of Columbia police department's requirement that all recruits pass a verbal ability test. They said the requirement was unconstitutional because more African Americans than whites failed the test.

The Court said that this result did not mean the test was unconstitutional. The crucial issue was that the test was not designed to discriminate. As the Court said in a later case, "The Fourteenth Amendment guarantees equal laws, not equal results."

Impact of the *Washington* Decision Since the *Washington* case, the Court has applied the principle of intent to discriminate to other areas. In one Illinois city, a zoning ordinance permitted only single-family homes, prohibiting low-cost housing projects. The Court ruled the ordinance constitutional, even though it effectively kept minorities from moving into the city. The reason for the decision was that the Court found no intent to discriminate against minorities.

The Struggle for Equal Rights

The Fourteenth Amendment guaranteeing equal protection was ratified in 1868, shortly after the Civil War. Yet for almost a century the courts upheld discrimination against and segregation of African Americans. Racial discrimination is treating members of a race differently simply because of race. Segregation is separation of people from the larger social group.

By the late 1800s, about half the states had adopted **Jim Crow laws**. These laws, most often in southern states, required racial segregation in such places as schools, public transportation, and hotels.

Background

Justice Harlan's opinion in the *Plessy* case (on page 212) is a good illustration of a dissenting opinion. The Kentucky-born Harlan was himself a former slaveholder. Yet in his dissent he predicted that the *Plessy* decision would prove "quite as pernicious" as the *Dred Scott* decision in 1857. A dissenting opinion, like Harlan's, argues against the majority decision in a case before the Supreme Court. Yet a dissent is not an effort to change the minds of the other justices because the Court's decision has already been made before the writing of the dissent.

ABC NEWS INTERACTIVE

Martin Luther King, Jr.
The Speech ("I Have a Dream")
Running Time 17:00
Side Two, Chapters 4-28

Focus on Freedom

A group of 93 southern members of Congress signed a "Southern Manifesto," which called the Court's ruling in the *Brown* case "a clear abuse of judicial power" and pledged to find ways to reverse the decision.

For more on the *Brown* decision, have students read case 22 in *Supreme Court Case Studies* in the Teacher's Classroom Resources.

Answers

1. The Court said education provides a child the opportunity to succeed in life; the state has chosen to provide it.
2. Segregation with the sanction of law made those children feel inferior, which affected their motivation to learn.
3. In 1896 segregation by race was more socially acceptable than it was in 1954.

Interpreting Source Readings Have students complete activity 7 in *Primary and Secondary Source Readings* in the Teacher's Classroom Resources.

Assess

Check for Understanding

Have students complete Section 2 Review on page 213.

GLENCOE TECHNOLOGY

Focus on Government
Video 11
**Lecture Launcher:
Assuring Equal Justice for All**
Running Time: 2:27
Videodisc 1, Chap. 11
VHS Tape 1, Begins 30:29

Plessy v. Ferguson The Supreme Court justified Jim Crow laws in *Plessy* v. *Ferguson* (1896). The Court said the Fourteenth Amendment allowed separate facilities for different races as long as those facilities were equal. Justice Harlan dissented:

> *I* deny that any legislative body or judicial tribunal may have regard to the race of citizens when the civil rights of those citizens are involved. . . . Our Constitution is color-blind, and neither knows nor tolerates classes among citizens. In respect of civil rights, all citizens are equal before the law.
> —JUSTICE JOHN MARSHALL HARLAN, 1896

Nevertheless, for the next 50 years the **separate but equal doctrine** was used to justify segregation in the United States. In the late 1930s and the 1940s the Supreme Court began to chip away at the doctrine in a series of decisions that have had far-reaching implications. The most important decision came in 1954 in a case involving an African American student in Topeka, Kansas.

Brown v. Board of Education of Topeka In the 1950s Topeka's schools, like schools in many other cities and towns, were racially segregated. Linda Carol Brown, an eight-year-old African American student, was denied admission to an all-white school near her home and was required to attend a distant all-black school. With the help of lawyers from the National Association for the Advancement of Colored People (NAACP), Linda's family sued the

Focus on Freedom

BROWN v. BOARD OF EDUCATION

The Fourteenth Amendment was passed to end discrimination, especially when based on race. Yet in Plessy v. Ferguson (1896), the Supreme Court denied non-whites access to certain train cars by holding that "separate but equal" facilities did not discriminate. In 1954 the Court reversed this decision in the historic case of Brown v. Board of Education. The Court ruled:

In these days, it is doubtful that any child may reasonably be expected to succeed in life if he is denied the opportunity of an education. Such an opportunity, where the state has undertaken to provide it, is a right which must be made available to all on equal terms.

We come then to the question presented: Does segregation of children in public schools solely on the basis of race, even though the physical facilities and other "tangible" factors may be equal, deprive the children of the minority group of equal educational opportunities? We believe that it does. . . .

The effect of this separation on their educational opportunities was well stated by a finding in the Kansas case by a court which nevertheless felt compelled to rule against the Negro plaintiffs:

"Segregation of white and colored children in public schools has a detrimental effect upon the colored children. The impact is greater when it has the sanction of the law; for the policy of separating the races is usually interpreted as denoting the inferiority of the Negro group. A sense of inferiority affects the motivation of a child to learn.

Segregation with the sanction of law, therefore, has a tendency to [prevent] the educational and mental development of Negro children and to deprive them of some of the benefits they would receive in a racial[ly] integrated school system."

We conclude that in the field of public education the doctrine of "separate but equal" has no place. Separate educational facilities are inherently unequal. . . .

—CHIEF JUSTICE EARL WARREN, 1954

Examining the Document

Reviewing Facts
1. Explain why the Court believed education to be a right of citizens.
2. Discuss the "detrimental effect" that the Court believed segregated education had on those who were denied the opportunity to go to an integrated school.

Critical Thinking Skills
3. Analyzing Information How were society's beliefs about race important in influencing the Supreme Court's decisions in *Plessy* v. *Ferguson* and *Brown* v. *Board of Education*?

Cooperative Learning Activity

Organize the class into four groups. Have two groups develop arguments in support of the separate but equal doctrine. These groups should give reasons people thought the doctrine was fair. Have the other two groups develop arguments against the separate but equal doctrine. Have these groups give reasons people thought the doctrine was unfair. Students should make reference to Supreme Court decisions in their arguments. Ask a representative from each group to report on the group's work to the entire class. Then conduct a class discussion to summarize the two positions stated in the reports.

Topeka Board of Education. The NAACP successfully argued that segregated schools were not and could never be equal. Therefore, such schools were unconstitutional. In 1954 the court ruled on this case and similar cases filed in Virginia, Delaware, and South Carolina. In a unanimous decision in *Brown v. Board of Education of Topeka*, the Court overruled the separate-but-equal doctrine.

The Court's decision to overturn the separate-but-equal doctrine marked the beginning of a long, difficult battle to desegregate the public schools. By early 1970 public schools across the country were no longer segregated by law.

In many areas school segregation has continued, however, largely because of housing patterns. Concentration of African Americans and other minorities in certain areas of cities has created school districts that are either largely all black or all white. Efforts to deal with this situation have involved redrawing school district boundaries, reassigning pupils, and busing students to schools out of segregated neighborhoods.

The *Brown* decision opened the gates for scores of court cases dealing with equal rights. It also established a precedent for Court decisions striking down segregation in public parks, beaches, playgrounds, libraries, golf courses, state and local prisons, transportation systems, and anywhere else the principle of segregation had been applied.

The Civil Rights Movement After the *Brown* decision, many African Americans and whites worked together to end segregation through the **civil rights movement**. Throughout the United States, but mostly in the South, African Americans deliberately and peacefully broke laws supporting racial segregation. Some held "sit-ins" at restaurant lunch counters that served only whites. When arrested for breaking segregation laws, they were almost always found guilty. They could then appeal their conviction and challenge the constitutionality of the laws themselves.

The most important leader of the civil rights movement was Dr. Martin Luther King, Jr. A Baptist minister from Atlanta, King led nonviolent protest marches and demonstrations against segregation. He understood the importance of using the courts to win equal rights. He also sought to dramatize the issue of civil rights and stir the nation's conscience.

New Civil Rights Laws Influenced by the civil rights movement, Congress began to pass major civil rights laws. These laws sought to ensure voting rights and equal job opportunities under the provisions of the Fourteenth Amendment. The Civil Rights Act of 1964 was the most comprehensive of the civil rights laws. President Lyndon Johnson said, "Passage of this bill and of the 1965 civil rights law . . . profoundly altered the politics of civil rights and the political position of Southern blacks."

Meeting Objectives

Each section objective is tested by the Section Review questions that follow it in parentheses.
- Explain the meaning of "equal protection." (4, 5, 8)
- Summarize the struggle for equal rights. (4, 6, 8)
- Identify the tests the Supreme Court uses to determine discrimination. (2, 3, 7)

Evaluate

📁 Section 2 Quiz

🖥 Testmaker

Reteach

Have students write a newspaper article that defines "equal protection" and describes three Supreme Court rulings that extend this protection.

Enrich

📁 Have students read case 57 in *Supreme Court Case Studies* in the Teacher's Classroom Resources. Ask them to write a paragraph summarizing this decision's impact on the changes brought by the *Brown* decision.

Close

Discuss why it takes such a long struggle before a minority group is able to achieve equal rights.

SECTION REVIEW 2

Section Summary
The Supreme Court has used the Fourteenth Amendment, which provides for equal protection of the law, to make major decisions on discrimination on the basis of race, sex, age, religion, and ethnic group.

Checking for Understanding
Recalling Facts
1. Define rational basis test, suspect classification, fundamental right, discrimination, Jim Crow law, separate but equal doctrine, civil rights movement.
2. List three guidelines or tests the Supreme Court uses in its judgment of cases involving equal protection under the law.
3. Describe the circumstances in which the Court requires the state to bear the burden of proof to justify a law on the basis of "some compelling public interest."

4. Explain the Court's reasoning in overturning the "separate but equal" doctrine in the *Brown* decision.
Exploring Themes
5. Constitutional Interpretations Does the equal protection clause of the Fourteenth Amendment allow the government to draw distinctions between different classes of people? Explain.
6. Civil Rights What were the far-reaching effects of the *Brown* decision?

Critical Thinking Skills
7. Identifying Assumptions What does the Supreme Court assume about a state law that is not in a suspect classification?
8. Checking Consistency Is Chief Justice Earl Warren's opinion in *Brown v. Board of Education of Topeka* consistent with Justice Harlan's dissenting opinion in *Plessy v. Ferguson*? Explain your answer.

Section 2 Review Answers

1. Definitions of terms appear on pages indicated: **rational basis test,** 209; **suspect classification,** 211; **fundamental right,** 211; **discrimination,** 211; **Jim Crow law,** 211; **separate but equal doctrine,** 212; **civil rights movement,** 213
2. rational basis test, suspect classifications, fundamental rights

3. when a law is in a suspect classification, made on the basis of race or national origin
4. The Court said that separate educational facilities are inherently unequal. Therefore, they deprive students of equal education.
5. Yes, classifications may be made if they are not unreasonable distinctions.
6. Schools redrew district boundaries, reassigned pupils, and began busing students out of segregated areas. Courts

began to hear other cases dealing with segregation in places such as public parks, beaches, libraries, and prisons.
7. The Court assumes that there was a rational basis for the law and places the burden of proof on the person attacking the law.
8. Warren and Harlan both wrote that equal protection of the laws meant that racial segregation was unconstitutional.

Focus

Bell Ringer

Write the following on the chalkboard for students to work on while attendance is being taken:

List the ways the computer has affected your life.

Motivating Activity

Discuss students' Bell Ringer lists. Then tell students that such modern technology also has created new challenges to people's civil liberties. Ask students to suggest what some of these challenges might be. *(electronic surveillance or use of computers to store information about people)* List students' responses on the chalkboard.

Tell students that among the civil rights issues presented in this section is the protection of privacy in a technologically advanced society.

Vocabulary Precheck

Ask students to speculate on the meaning of each term and concept. Then have them check their guesses by finding the terms in the text. **LEP**

Focus on Government
Video 4
Lecture Launcher:
The Constitution–A Living
Document
Running Time: 2:22
Videodisc 1, Chap. 4
VHS Tape 1, Begins 11:14

New Challenges for Civil Liberties

Changing ideas, social conditions, and technology have combined to raise new issues for civil liberties. Today, for example, the government maintains billions of computer records on individual Americans. In addition, private companies collect financial, medical, and legal information on almost everyone. Such record keeping raises important questions about the right to privacy—a right not mentioned in the Constitution. Other important issues involve affirmative action, discrimination against women, and the right to know about government actions.

Affirmative Action

Recent Supreme Court decisions and civil rights laws have clearly established that discrimination based on arbitrary factors such as race is unconstitutional. In the early 1960s, the federal government began to require employers, labor unions, and universities to adopt affirmative action programs. **Affirmative action** means that employers and other institutions must take positive steps to remedy the effects of past discrimination against minorities and women.

The *Bakke* Case The Supreme Court first ruled on affirmative action in *Regents of the University of California* v. *Bakke*, (1978). Allan Bakke claimed to have been refused admission to the University of California medical school because he was white. The medical school had set up a quota system that reserved 16 places out of 100 each year for minorities. Minority students with lower test scores than Bakke were admitted to fill the quota. Bakke sued, claiming he was a victim of reverse discrimination.

Upholding the basic idea of affirmative action by a 5-4 decision, the Court ruled that the university could consider race along with other characteristics when admitting students. The Court, however, went on to explain that a strict quota system based on race was unconstitutional and in violation of the 1964 Civil Rights Act. The Court ordered the university to admit Bakke to its medical school.

The Supreme Court has since considered many other affirmative action cases to decide whether it is proper to deny members of the majority fair treatment in order to make up for the unequal treatment of minorities in the past. Its record leaves the issue clouded because the Court has struck down as many affirmative action plans as it has upheld.

Gains for Women and Minorities In 1987 the Supreme Court favored affirmative action in a dispute involving equal protection for women. In the case of *Johnson* v. *Transportation Agency, Santa Clara County, Calif.* (1987), the Court upheld a voluntary affirmative action plan the transportation department had adopted. The plan's goal was to move women into high-ranking positions. In this case Diane Joyce and Paul Johnson had been competing for the job of road dispatcher. Johnson scored two points higher on the qualifying interview. Because of the county's affirmative action plan, however, Diane Joyce got the promotion. Johnson went to court claiming the plan violated Title VII of the 1964 Civil Rights Act.

By a vote of 6 to 3, the Court ruled against Johnson. The Court held that so long as it was carefully used, affirmative action was an appropriate remedy for past discrimination.

SECTION PREVIEW

Objectives
After studying this section, you should be able to:
■ Understand the principles behind equal opportunity and affirmative action.

■ Explain legal trends concerning the right to privacy and the right to know.

Key Terms and Concepts
affirmative action, security classification system, transcript

Themes in Government
■ Civil Liberties
■ Public Policy

Critical Thinking Skills
■ Expressing Problems Clearly
■ Checking Consistency

Classroom Resources for Section 3

📁 Guided Reading Activities
📁 Reproducible Lesson Plans
📁 Participating in Government 7
📁 Supreme Court Case Studies 45, 46
📁 Interpreting Political Cartoons 3
📁 Reteaching Activities 7

📁 Enrichment Activities 7
📁 Section 3 Quiz
📁 Chapter 7 Tests
📁 Government Themes Transparencies 17, 18, 20

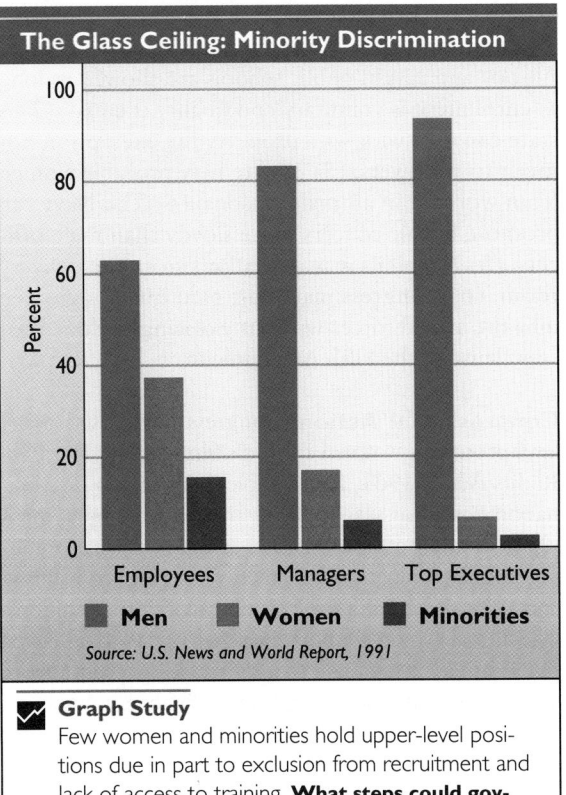

The Glass Ceiling: Minority Discrimination

Men ■ **Women** ■ **Minorities**

Source: U.S. News and World Report, 1991

✓ Graph Study
Few women and minorities hold upper-level positions due in part to exclusion from recruitment and lack of access to training. **What steps could government take to change this practice?**

Could affirmative action be used in a case that did not involve a remedy for past discrimination? In 1990 the Court answered yes by upholding a Federal Communications Commission policy of favoring women and minorities when it awards radio and television broadcast licenses. The Court agreed with the intent of the policy—to increase the number of broadcast stations owned by women and minorities.

Discrimination Against Women

Women finally won the right to vote with the Nineteenth Amendment in 1920. In recent decades new challenges to discrimination against women have been raised in such areas as jobs, housing, and credit policies. Both the Supreme Court and Congress have dealt with these challenges.

The Supreme Court's Position Because the Court treats classifications based on race and national origin as "suspect," it has examined them closely. What about classifications based on sex? Historically the Supreme Court had ruled that laws discriminating against women did not violate the equal protection clause of the Fourteenth Amendment. Many of these laws were designed to protect women from night work, overtime work, heavy lifting, and "bad elements" in society. In practice, they often discriminated against women. In the 1950s, for example, the Court said an Ohio law forbidding any woman other than the wife or daughter of a tavern owner to work as a barmaid was constitutional.

In 1971 the Supreme Court for the first time held that a state law was unconstitutional because it discriminated against women. In *Reed* v. *Reed*, the Court said a law that automatically preferred a father over a mother as executor of a son's estate violated the equal protection clause of the Fourteenth Amendment:

To give a mandatory preference to members of either sex over members of the other . . . is to make the very kind of arbitrary legislative choice forbidden by the Equal Protection Clause.
—CHIEF JUSTICE WARREN BURGER, 1971

Reasonableness Standard The *Reed* decision created a new standard for judging constitutionality in sex discrimination cases. The Supreme Court said any law that classifies people on the basis of sex, "must be reasonable, not arbitrary, and must rest on some ground of difference." That difference must serve "important governmental objectives" and be substantially related to those objectives.

The reasonableness standard is not as strict a test as the suspect classifications test used to judge racial discrimination. Since 1971, however, the Supreme Court has held that sex classifications are subject to

---

STUDY GUIDE

Themes in Government
Civil Liberties The graph above shows a form of discrimination against women. **What is the "glass ceiling"?**

Critical Thinking Skills
Expressing Problems Clearly In deciding affirmative action cases the court has tried to walk a fine line.

What are the issues involved for the Supreme Court in dealing with affirmative action cases?

CHAPTER 7: ASSURING EQUAL JUSTICE FOR ALL   215

Chapter 7, Section 3
Lesson Plan, pages 214–219

Teach

Guided Practice

L1 Making a Time Line Draw a time line on the chalkboard to chronicle the important events in protecting women against discrimination. On the left end place 1950, and on the right place the present year. Then have students discuss dates and events that should be placed on the time line.

🔖 **Interpreting Visuals** Display transparency 18 from *Government Themes Transparencies* in the Teacher's Classroom Resources. Use the accompanying teaching strategy and student activity to teach the issues involved in discrimination against women.

Graph Study Answer
by requiring affirmative action in hiring and training programs

STUDY GUIDE

Theme Answer
the invisible barrier that seems to be keeping women from top management positions; most are trapped in middle management and are receiving less compensation than male counterparts

Critical Thinking Answer
equal protection under Fourteenth Amendment; making up for past injustices to minorities while protecting majority rights

🔖 **Interpreting Visuals** Display transparency 17 from *Government Themes Transparencies* in the Teacher's Classroom Resources. Use the accompanying teaching strategy and student activity to teach about affirmative action.

Background

The Fair Credit Reporting Act provides for a consumer to learn about his or her credit rating by contacting the local credit bureau and requesting a copy of his or her credit history. A consumer who disagrees with the information in the report can notify the credit bureau in writing. The credit bureau must then investigate the complaint with the source of the disputed information. If the consumer is further dissatisfied with the result, he or she can provide a 100-word statement to be included with the credit history report.

Interpreting Visuals Display transparency 20 from *Government Themes Transparencies* in the Teacher's Classroom Resources. Use the accompanying teaching strategy and student activity to teach about privacy rights.

L3 Debate Have students debate the following issue:

Is affirmative action a good way to compensate for years of deliberate discrimination against women and minorities?

Independent Practice

L1 Economics Have some students research and graph the average salaries of male and female workers from the 1950s to the present. Have others research the percentage of women in various occupations for the same period. **LEP**

L2 Journalism Have students find a newspaper or magazine article dealing with affirmative action or discrimination based on sex, lifestyle, or ability. Have them write a paragraph that summarizes the events and identifies the legal issues raised.

Caption Answer
Colleges have established women's teams in many traditionally male sports.

STUDY GUIDE

Theme Answer
to protect women—seems to pass reasonableness standard

Critical Thinking Answer
no—decisions sometimes seem arbitrary—establishes separate but equal; in other cases, women treated equally—serving on juries, equal benefits under social security

---

very close scrutiny. In addition, in 1977 the Court said that treating women differently from men (or vice versa) is unconstitutional when based on no more than "old notions" about women and "the role-typing society has long imposed on women."

A Whole New Ball Game
Boys and girls now have an equal chance to participate in sports programs. **Law How has equal access affected college sports?**

Decisions Under Reasonableness Standard
Since the *Reed* decision courts have allowed some distinctions based on sex and overruled others. These decisions bar distinctions based on sex: (1) States cannot set different ages at which men and women become legal adults. (2) States cannot set different ages at which men and women are allowed to purchase beer. (3) States cannot exclude women from juries. (4) Employers cannot require women to take a pregnancy leave from work. (5) Girls cannot be kept off little league baseball teams. (6) Private clubs and community service groups cannot exclude women from membership. (7) Employers must pay women month-

ly retirement benefits equal to those given to men.

These decisions allow differences based on sex: (1) All-boy and all-girl public schools are allowed as long as enrollment is voluntary and quality is equal. (2) A state can give widows a property tax exemption not given to widowers. (3) A state may prohibit women from working in all-male prisons. (4) The Navy can promote female officers more slowly than male officers. (5) Hospitals may bar fathers from the delivery room. (6) Congress may draft men but not women into the armed forces without violating the due process clause of the Fifth Amendment.

Congressional Action Congress has passed many laws protecting women from discrimination. The Civil Rights Act of 1964, for example, banned job discrimination based on sex. In 1972 the Equal Employment Opportunity Act strengthened earlier laws by prohibiting sex discrimination in activities ranging from hiring and firing to promotion, pay, and working conditions. The Equal Credit Opportunity Act of 1974 outlawed discrimination against women seeking credit from banks, government agencies, and finance companies. This law also made it illegal to ask questions about a person's sex or marital status in a credit application.

In 1976 Congress acted to give women equal opportunities in education and school sports. When amending the Omnibus Education Act of 1972, Congress required all schools to give boys and girls an equal chance to participate in sports programs. Schools, however, may maintain separate teams for boys and girls, especially in contact sports.

Citizens' Right to Know

The right of citizens and the press to know what government is doing is an essential part of democracy. Citizens cannot make intelligent judgments about the government's actions unless they have adequate information. Government officials, however, are often reluctant to share information about their decisions and policies.

STUDY GUIDE

Themes in Government
Public Policy Why can a state prohibit women from working in all-male prisons?

Critical Thinking Skills
Checking Consistency Compare the seven decisions in which the Court bars distinctions based on sex to the six decisions allowing such distinctions.

Has the Supreme Court been consistent in its decisions under the reasonableness standard? Explain why or why not.

Cooperative Learning Activity

Tell students that access to information about what the government is doing is an essential part of a democracy. Organize the class into small groups. Have students in each group discuss the following: How can Americans be more aware of actions taken by government that affect their lives? Have each group select a student to report the group's progress to the class. *(A basic answer should include references to the Freedom of Information Act and the Sunshine Act.)* Then have each group select another student to work with students from other groups to compile a list of the provisions of the two acts to present to the class.

The national government's **security classification system,** operating since 1917, provides that information on government activities related to national security and foreign policy may be kept secret. Millions of government documents are classified as secret and made unavailable to the public each year.

The Freedom of Information Act In 1966 Congress passed the Freedom of Information Act requiring federal agencies to provide citizens access to public records on request. Exemptions are permitted for national defense materials, confidential personnel and financial data, and law enforcement files. People can sue the government for disclosure if they are denied access to materials.

Congress strengthened the law with several amendments in 1974. Immediately after the amendments went into effect, requests for information began flooding into the government at the rate of 12,500 per month.

The Sunshine Act Before 1976 many government meetings and hearings were held in secret. Such closed sessions made it difficult for the press, citizens' groups, lobbyists, and the public to keep an eye on government decisions. Congress, in the Sunshine Act of 1976, helped correct that situation by requiring that many meetings be opened to the public.

The law applies to about 50 federal agencies, boards, and commissions. Meetings these agencies hold must be open to the public, and at least one week's advance notice must be given. Some closed meetings are allowed, but then a **transcript,** or summary record, of the meeting must be made. People may sue to force public disclosure of the proceedings of a meeting, if necessary.

Citizens' Right to Privacy

The Internal Revenue Service and the Census Bureau are among the federal agencies that collect data about people. In addition, state bureaus and private credit bureaus also compile information. Computers make the job of storing and of sharing such information easy and routine. Do citizens have a "right to privacy"?

The Constitution and Privacy The Constitution does not mention privacy. The Supreme Court, however, interpreted the private property rights

---

PARTICIPATING IN GOVERNMENT

Contributing to Charities

By volunteering your time, you can make a valuable contribution to charities—private or public organizations working to improve social conditions—in your community. In addition to time, however, charitable organizations need money and goods. How can you help?

You might set aside a certain percentage of your earnings to donate to a religious institution or charity on a regular basis. You might donate money for a special need in your community. For example, you might purchase a ticket to a benefit

performance—a concert or play given to raise money for a particular cause.

You can also earn money for charity by participating in a walk, race, or bicycle ride and by asking people to sponsor you. Each sponsor pledges a certain amount of money for every mile (or kilometer) you complete. The money is donated to the organization that held the event.

Perhaps you have sold cookies, candy, or other items to raise money for your school or another organization. Such organizations might also sponsor a carnival, bake sale, or car wash to raise money. Clothing drives and food pantries offer opportunities for you to donate goods for the needy in your community.

Investigating Further

Find out how charities in your community raise money. Offer to participate in one of the fund-raising activities.

CHAPTER 7: ASSURING EQUAL JUSTICE FOR ALL 217

Special Needs Strategy

Study Strategy Students with many different kinds of learning problems can become overwhelmed by the amount of information in a section. Show them that this section is organized around important court decisions. Have them skim for the names of the court cases and write these in their notebooks. Then have them skim for one main idea about each case. When they have finished studying this section, have them reread their court decision list. Ask them if the list helped trigger their recall of what the section was about.

L3 **Interviewing** Have students interview local personnel directors and business owners to find out about their affirmative action programs. Students should prepare a list of questions before the interview.

📁 **Analyzing Supreme Court Cases** Have students complete cases 45 and 46 in the *Supreme Court Case Studies* in the Teacher's Classroom Resources.

PARTICIPATING IN GOVERNMENT

Remind students that many charitable organizations work to protect people who are victims of discrimination. Ask students to find what groups carry out this type of work in their communities.

📁 Have students complete activity 7 in *Participating in Government* in the Teacher's Classroom Resources.

Assess

Check for Understanding

Have students complete Section 3 Review on page 218.

Meeting Objectives

Each section objective is tested by the Section Review questions that follow it in parentheses.
- Understand the principles behind equal opportunity and affirmative action. (2, 3, 5, 8)
- Explain legal trends concerning the right to privacy and the right to know. (4, 6, 7)

Evaluate

📁 Section 3 Quiz

▪ Testmaker

Caption Answer
prevents unauthorized persons from reviewing student records

Reteach

Have students use the information under the main headings of this section to write newspaper headlines that summarize the major ideas in this section. Have students share their headlines with the class.

📁 Have students complete activity 7 in *Reteaching Activities* in the Teacher's Classroom Resources.

Enrich

Have students research the issue of discrimination against people with disabilities, including legislation that has been enacted to remedy the situation. Students might report their findings in an oral or written report.

📁 Have students complete activity 7 in *Enrichment Activities* in the Teacher's Classroom Resources.

Close

📁 Have students complete activity 3 in *Interpreting Political Cartoons* in the Teacher's Classroom Resources. Have volunteers share their answers to the activity and discuss with the class.

BENTLEY COLLEGE
UNDERGRADUATE TRANSCRIPT REQUEST FORM

Students' Right of Property Protected
Students can give written permission to release their school records. **Civics** **How does the transcript release procedure protect personal privacy?**

guaranteed in the Bill of Rights and the Fourteenth Amendment to extend to personal behavior. In cases ranging from *Pierce* v. *Society of Sisters* (1925) to *Roe* v. *Wade* (1973) the Court has recognized the right to personal privacy in many areas ranging from child rearing to abortion. The Court has also held that the right to personal privacy is limited when the state has a "compelling need" to protect society.

Legislation on Privacy In 1974 the United States Congress passed the Family Educational Rights and Privacy Act. These laws allow people to inspect information about themselves in federal agency files and challenge, correct, or amend the materials they find. The laws also protect access to files from outsiders without proper authorization.

The act also opened school files to parents and to students who are at least 18 years old. They are able to check test scores, reports of guidance counselors, and other information in the students' files. Any school that refuses to comply with the law can lose federal funding.

Sharing Credit Information For many years private credit bureaus have collected information to create reports on consumers' credit. In 1970 the Fair Credit Reporting Act was written to control the collection and distribution of information. Today, however, sophisticated computer-matching projects allow companies and the government to cross-reference data. Commercial information companies sell credit and medical details about individuals to marketing firms that use the information to sell everything from home repairs to life insurance. A growing number of lawmakers believe that the Fair Credit Reporting Act needs to be rewritten. Most agencies must keep a list of anyone who looks at a file. With few exceptions, one agency cannot transfer information about someone to another agency.

3 SECTION REVIEW

Section Summary
Two major challenges to civil liberties are how to preserve equal protection when individual rights are in conflict and how to protect individual rights in the face of technological changes.

Checking for Understanding
Recalling Facts
1. Define affirmative action, security classification system, transcript.
2. Explain the arguments for and against affirmative action.
3. Describe the importance of *Reed* v. *Reed* to the changing role of women in American society.
4. Identify the key provision of the Freedom of Information Act.

Exploring Themes
5. Civil Liberties How does the Supreme Court apply the reasonableness standard in judging discrimination against women?
6. Public Policy In what way does the Sunshine Act help citizens keep informed about public policy?

Critical Thinking Skills
7. Expressing Problems Clearly Describe the circumstances in which collecting information about citizens and consumers conflicts with the individual's right to privacy.
8. Checking Consistency Review the lists of "Decisions barring distinctions based on sex" and "Decisions allowing differences based on sex." Are there any decisions from the second list that you believe to be inconsistent with the first list? Explain your answers.

Section 3 Review Answers

1. Definitions of terms appear on pages indicated: **affirmative action,** 214; **security classification system,** 217; **transcript,** 217

2. for: Programs help to remedy the effects of past educational and employment discrimination; against: Programs may result in unfair treatment of those adversely affected by affirmative action.

3. The decision recognized sex discrimination and established reasonableness standard tests that classify people on the basis of sex.

4. requires federal agencies to provide citizens access to public records on request

5. The Court looks closely at laws that classify on the basis of sex. To be constitutional such a law "must be reasonable, not arbitrary, and must rest on some ground of difference" serving "important government objectives" and being substantially related to those objectives.

6. by requiring most meetings of federal agencies, boards, and commissions to be open to the public; transcripts of closed meetings are required

7. When government or business shares information that has been collected with other agencies, especially when it does not inform the individual, the right to privacy is jeopardized.

8. Some students may find that paying women retirement benefits equal to men, when as a group women live longer than men, is inconsistent with a state giving widows a property tax exemption not given to widowers.

Jesse Jackson on the Need for Unity

Jesse Jackson, candidate for the Democratic presidential nomination, delivered an address at the Democratic National Convention in Atlanta, Georgia, on July 20, 1988. Having won a significant number of delegates in the primary campaign, Jackson took the opportunity to challenge others who faced serious challenges to keep their hope alive.

America's not a blanket woven from one thread, one color, one cloth. When I was a child growing up in Greenville, S.C., and grandmother could not afford a blanket, she didn't complain and we did not freeze. Instead, she took pieces of old cloth—patches, wool, silk, gabardine, crockersack on the patches—barely good enough to wipe off your shoes with.

But they didn't stay that way very long. With sturdy hands and a strong cord, she sewed them together into a quilt, a thing of beauty and power and culture. . . .

What's the fundamental challenge of our day? It is to end economic violence. Plant closing[s] without notice, economic violence. Even the greedy do not profit long from greed. Economic violence. Most poor people are not lazy. They're not black. They're not brown. They're mostly white, and female and young.

But whether white, black or brown, the hungry baby's belly turned inside out is the same color. Call it pain. Call it hurt. Call it agony. Most poor people are not on welfare.

Some of them are illiterate and can't read want-ad sections. And when they can, they can't find a job that matches their address. They work hard every day, I know. I live amongst them. I'm one of them. . . .

I have a story. I wasn't always on television. Writers were not always outside my door. When I was born late one afternoon, October 8th, in Greenville, S.C., no writers asked my mother her name. . . . My mama was not supposed to make it. And I was not supposed to make it. You see, I was born to a teen-age mother who was born to a teen-age mother. . . .

Jesse Jackson is my third name. I'm adopted. When I had no name, my grandmother gave me her name. . . .

I understand, call you outcast, low down . . . you're from nobody, subclass, underclass—when you see Jesse Jackson, when my name goes in nomination, your name goes in nomination.

I was born in the slum, but the slum was not born in me. And it wasn't born in you, and you can make it. Wherever you are tonight you can make it. Hold your head high, stick your chest out. You can make it. It gets dark sometimes, but the morning comes. Don't you surrender. Suffering breeds character. Character breeds faith. In the end faith will not disappoint.

You must not surrender. You may not get there, but just know that you're qualified and you hold on and hold out. We must never surrender. America will get better and better. Keep hope alive.

—THE REVEREND JESSE JACKSON, 1988

Don't you surrender. Suffering breeds character. Character breeds faith. In the end faith will not disappoint.

Examining the Reading

Reviewing Facts

1. Identify what Jesse Jackson believes to be the fundamental challenge facing minorities and women.
2. Describe briefly the disadvantages Jackson faced as a youth.

Critical Thinking Skills

3. Evaluating Information How do you think Jackson's early experiences continue to influence his political beliefs?

Focus

Ask students to share experiences they have had in their early life that have affected their values about life today.

Teach

Ask: What metaphor does Jackson use for the racial and generic variety of America? *(his grandmother's quilt)* Jackson cites the closing of a plant without notice as an example of "economic violence." What other problems of poor people does he cite? *(illiteracy, hunger, joblessness)* What myth about the makeup of the poor population does Jackson attack? What life experiences, according to Jackson, are color-blind? *(pain, hurt, agony)*

Assess

Have students complete **Examining the Reading.**

Answers

1. economic inequality
2. born into poverty to a teen-age mother, poor and subjected to discrimination
3. He feels strong compassion for disadvantaged people and believes that America should do something about inequality.

Close

Ask students if they agree with Jackson's statement that "suffering breeds character."

More About Personal Perspectives

In addition to campaigning for the presidency in 1984 and 1988, Jesse Jackson has had a full career as a civil rights activist. He worked closely with Dr. Martin Luther King, Jr., until the latter's assassination in 1968. He later formed PUSH (People United to Serve Humanity) in Chicago, Illinois. The organization seeks to secure more African American economic power. Jackson has twice gained the release of Americans interned or imprisoned in foreign countries—in January 1984 in Syria, and later that same year in Cuba. In 1992 one of Jackson's major aims was to gain statehood for Washington, D.C.

7 CHAPTER REVIEW

1. counsel, **2.** exclusionary rule, **3.** rational basis test, **4.** Jim Crow, **5.** suspect classification, **6.** affirmative action, **7.** security classification

Reviewing Facts and Ideas

1. The warrant must describe the place to be searched and the person or things to be seized.

2. Police may arrest and search anyone who commits a crime in their presence or who they think is a felon. They may also search through trash, which is at the curb for pickup, without a warrant.

3. *Weeks* v. *United States*

4. Wiretapping is electronically listening to another person's phone calls. The Court in *Katz* v. *United States* ruled that the Fourth Amendment prohibits police wiretapping without a warrant.

5. No one "shall be compelled in any criminal case to be a witness against himself."

6. The person must be warned that he or she has a right to remain silent, any statement made may be used as evidence against the person in court, and the person has the right to the presence of an attorney.

7. right to travel freely between states, right to vote, First Amendment rights

8. Schools began to desegregate, many other cases dealing with equal rights were brought into the courts, the Supreme Court struck down segregation in public parks, beaches, playgrounds, libraries, golf courses, state and local prisons, and transportation.

Summary and Significance

The Constitution protects the rights of people accused of crimes from unreasonable searches and seizures and from illegally obtained evidence being used against them. An accused person has the right to a lawyer, and he or she cannot be forced to confess to a crime.

The Fourteenth Amendment provides for equal protection of the law. This protection applies to racial discrimination, which is prohibited if an intent to discriminate can be proven. The civil rights movement played an important role in ending segregation. Partly as a result of its efforts, laws prohibiting discrimination in employment, voting rights, and other areas were passed. Changes in society present new challenges for civil liberties including the issues of affirmative action programs, discrimination against women, access to government information, and the right to privacy.

Identifying Terms and Concepts

Match the following terms with each of the descriptions given below.

suspect classification, affirmative action, counsel, rational basis test, exclusionary rule, Jim Crow, security classification

1. an attorney
2. keeps illegally obtained evidence out of court
3. the law has a reasonable goal
4. laws that discriminated against African Americans
5. made on the basis of race or national origin
6. policy giving preference to minorities
7. how government documents are kept secret

Reviewing Facts and Ideas

1. Describe the items that must be included in a legal search warrant.
2. Describe two situations in which police may conduct a search without a warrant.
3. Identify the case that established the exclusionary rule.
4. Explain wiretapping and the Court's opinion in these cases.
5. State the key protection described in the Fifth Amendment.
6. List the three *Miranda* rules.
7. Name three fundamental rights that the Supreme Court believes should be guarded carefully.
8. Explain the short-term and long-term effects of the *Brown* decision.

Applying Themes

1. **Civil Rights** Cite a Supreme Court case showing that protection from self-incrimination does not extend to certain business crimes.
2. **Constitutional Interpretations** Why did the Court rule that wiretapping without a warrant was an illegal search and thus a violation of the Fourth Amendment?
3. **Civil Liberties** What standard does the Court use in judging laws that have classifications based on sex?
4. **Public Policy** What were the provisions of a policy adopted in 1974 by the federal government regarding access to federal agency files?

Critical Thinking Skills

1. **Identifying Alternatives** What were several possible ways that local schools could have chosen to comply with the decision in *Brown* v. *Board of Education of Topeka*?
2. **Making Generalizations** How did the *Escobedo* and *Miranda* cases extend protection against self-incrimination and forced confessions?
3. **Checking Consistency** Is the Supreme Court's decision concerning the death penalty in *Woodson* v. *North Carolina* consistent with its decision in *Gregg* v. *Georgia*? Explain your answer.
4. **Expressing Problems Clearly** Why do some criticize affirmative action programs for minorities and women as a form of reverse discrimination?

Applying Themes

1. In *Braswell* v. *United States* (1988), employees in charge of corporate records could be compelled to turn over evidence even if it might incriminate them.

2. The Court said that the Fourth Amendment protects people, and not simply areas, from search and seizure.

3. the reasonableness standard—such a law must be reasonable, not arbitrary, and must rest on some ground of difference that serves important governmental objectives

4. The law allowed people to inspect information about themselves in federal agency files and to challenge, correct, or amend materials.

5. Identifying Assumptions What did the Court indicate that it would assume regarding state actions in its decision in *Washington v. Davis* in 1976? Explain the meaning of this decision for those who in the future wished to bring charges of discrimination against a state.

Linking Past and Present

In the early 1800s Americans who wanted to get away from crowded areas could "pull up stakes" and move west. Most people lived on farms or in small communities. Yet, there was a sense of belonging to the community, and people usually knew their neighbors very well. Many people today live their lives isolated from their communities and may seldom talk with their neighbors. At the same time government and private agencies keep huge files of personal information on nearly everyone. What kind of privacy is important to you? Has the American perception of privacy changed? Explain your answers.

Writing About Government

Expressive Writing Several amendments to the Constitution have been interpreted to extend the civil rights and liberties of Americans. Choose one of the amendments referred to in Chapter 7 and write an essay expressing why you believe that it identifies an essential and fundamental principle. You may refer to cases that have been based on Supreme Court interpretations of the amendment you choose.

Reinforcing the Skill

Outlining Complete the following outline of Section 3.

New Challenges for Civil Liberties

I. Affirmative Action
   A. The *Bakke* Case
      1.
      2.
   B. Gains for Women and Minorities

   1.
   2.
II.
   A. The Supreme Court's Position
      1. Suspect Classification
      2. *Reed* v. *Reed*
   B. Reasonableness Standard
      1. Not as Strict as Suspect Classification
      2. Closely Scrutinized
   C. Decisions Under Reasonableness Standard
      1.
      2.
   D. Congressional Action
      1. Civil Rights Act of 1964
      2. Equal Employment Opportunity Act
III. Citizens' Right to Know
   A.
      1. Access to Public Records
      2. Can Sue Government for Disclosure
   B. The Sunshine Act
      1. Passed in 1976
      2.
IV. Citizens' Right to Privacy
   A.
   B. Legislation on Privacy
   C.

Investigating Further

1. **Individual Project** The Supreme Court continues to define rights by interpreting the Constitution as it applies to individual cases. Consult the *Readers' Guide to Periodical Literature* in a school or public library. Look under civil rights, right of privacy, and United States government/Supreme Court. List the kinds of magazine articles on these subjects that have appeared within the last year. What are the current issues most frequently mentioned?
2. **Cooperative Learning** Today many people want to remove sexist language from written materials. For example, policeman has become police officer; "Men Working" has become "Workers Ahead." Organize into pairs, each pair compiling a list of as many sexist terms and replacement terms as is possible in five minutes. Then make a list for the entire class.

Critical Thinking Skills
1. Local schools could reassign students, redraw district boundaries, or bus students to desegregated schools.
2. These cases overturned convictions in which confessions were made by the accused before that person had access to an attorney and before the accused was told that he or she had a right to remain silent.

3. Answers should include that in *Woodson* the Court ruled mandatory death penalties unconstitutional, while in *Gregg* it ruled that under adequate guidelines the death penalty does not constitute cruel and unusual punishment and so does not violate the Eighth Amendment.

4. Some view affirmative action programs as favoring minorities over whites and women over men.

5. The decision indicated that the Court would assume that a state was innocent of discrimination until a person could prove otherwise. It would make the task of proving discrimination more difficult.

Linking Past and Present
Answers will vary, but should include that privacy today means being able to live without interference from government or even neighbors. People do not often think about the vast files of information that government and business have compiled on them. People you will never meet have more access to personal information about you than some of your closest friends.

Writing about Government
Answers will vary.

Reinforcing the Skill
1. Claimed Reverse Discrimination
2. Quota System Unconstitutional
1. Court Upheld Affirmative Action
2. Remedy for Past Discrimination
II. Discrimination Against Women
1. Some Sex Distinctions Barred
2. Some Sex Distinctions Allowed
A. Freedom of Information Act
2. Required Open Government Meetings
A. The Constitution and Privacy
C. Sharing Credit Information

Investigating Further
1. Have students present and compare their lists.
2. Have students use the class list to write a paragraph.

CASE STUDY

The Case at a Glance

Who: Japanese Americans
What: relocation and intern-ment
When: World War II
Where: West Coast
Why: fears of invasion and sabotage

Focus

Ask students why people's rights seem to change during wartime. Have them suggest rights that may need to be con-trolled and why. *(free movement, speech, and press—for national security; production or purchase of certain products—to aid the war effort)* Tell students that rights to required legal procedures also have been limited during wartime.

Teach

Guided Practice

L1 **Civil Rights** Create a chart on the chalkboard with the fol-lowing heads: *Political Reasons, Economic Reasons, Military Rea-sons.* Have students summarize the reasons for Japanese American relocation and classify each into one of these categories. *(reasons might include: political—public pressure on officials; economic—eliminate competition for jobs and businesses; military—fear of sabo-tage and invasion)* Ask if any were good reasons to remove and in-tern Japanese Americans.

CASE STUDY

The Privilege of the Writ of Habeas Corpus shall not be suspended, unless when in Cases of Rebellion or Invasion the public Safety may require it.

—Article I, Section 9

No person [shall] . . . be deprived of life, liberty, or property, without due process of law. . . .

—Fifth Amendment

All persons born or naturalized in the United States . . . are citizens of the United States. . . . No state shall . . . deprive any person of life, liberty, or property without due process of law; nor deny to any person within its jurisdiction the equal protection of the laws.

—Fourteenth Amendment

The Internment of Japanese Americans

The Case

What one newspaper called "a stain on American history" followed Japan's attack on the United States naval base in Hawaii on Decem-ber 7, 1941. Within a few months of the attack, almost all the Japanese Americans on the West Coast had been detained in relocation centers.

The internment of Japanese Americans without formal charges, the right to counsel, or a trial raised important constitutional questions. How could the government detain citizens based on their ancestry? Could the govern-ment legally ignore the parts of the Fifth and Fourteenth amendments that guaranteed citizens the right to due process of law? The few people who opposed the internments cited the amendments in their arguments. Those who supported the internments based their arguments on "military neces-sity" and the presumed disloyalty of Japanese Americans. They also argued that the President's war powers overrode the amendments' guarantees. The question became, "What is the balance between the government's war powers and the rights of individuals during wartime?" This question would remain in the federal courts for more than two years, ultimately reaching the Supreme Court in several test cases.

Background

On Sunday morning December 7, 1941, Japan's surprise attack on Pearl Harbor severely crippled the United States Pacific fleet. The following day the United States declared war on Japan, and three days later on Germany and Italy.

Immediately, the Justice Department began to arrest enemy aliens "deemed dangerous to the public peace or safety of the United States." Within 2 months about 10 percent of the Japanese male aliens on the West Coast were in custody. An earlier State Department report summed up the government's attitude toward Japanese Americans:

> . . . *In every large city in the country and on the West Coast. These people who pass as civilians and laborers, are being drilled in military maneuvers . . . when war breaks out, the entire Japanese population will rise and com-mit sabotage.*

—DEPARTMENT OF STATE, 1934

More About the Case

President Roosevelt approved a plan to set up a Nisei regiment in February 1943. It was made up of 1,200 volunteers from the relocation camps, Hawaiian recruits of Japanese ancestry, and Nisei al-ready in the army. A second Japanese American unit was the 100th Infantry Battalion, formerly an all-Nisei Hawaiian National Guard battalion that was federalized after Pearl Harbor. Both units were trained at Camp Shelby, Mississippi.

In September 1943 the 100th Infantry Battalion took part in the invasion of Italy. During the first months of fighting, the 100th earned more than 1,000 Purple Hearts. Replacement troops came from the 442nd Regimental Combat Team sta-

No Japanese American was found guilty of sabotage, however. One historian noted:

It is sobering to recall that though the Japanese relocation . . . was justified to us on the grounds that the Japanese were potentially disloyal, the record does not disclose a single case of Japanese disloyalty or sabotage during the whole war. . . .
—HENRY STEELE COMMAGER, 1947

In the first month after the attack, people were not openly hostile to the Japanese Americans. They were "good Americans, born and educated as such" noted the *Los Angeles Times*. As fears of a Japanese invasion grew, however, sentiment shifted. In mid-January 1942, California Congressman Leland Ford demanded that "all Japanese, whether citizens or not, be placed in concentration camps."

A columnist in the *San Francisco Examiner* echoed Ford's sentiment with the words "I am for the immediate removal of every Japanese on the West Coast to a point in the interior. I don't mean a nice part of the interior either. Herd 'em up, pack 'em off and give 'em the inside room in the badlands."

The final step in the arrest and evacuation of all but a very few Japanese Americans on the West Coast came on Thursday, February 19, 1942. That day President Franklin D. Roosevelt signed Executive Order 9066. The order authorized the army to designate military areas and to exclude "any and all persons." Acting under this order, General John L. DeWitt, military commander of the West Coast region, began to evacuate Japanese Americans in the region. Soon 120,000 Japanese Americans were in relocation centers that stretched through the country from California to Arkansas. Allowed to take with them only what they could carry, the Japanese Americans lost jobs, homes, businesses and farms. Analysts later estimated that the Japanese Americans lost at least $400 million.

The Fight in Court The four important test cases regarding the rights of Japanese Americans were based on the due process clauses of the Fifth and Fourteenth amendments and the right to a writ of habeas corpus protected in Article I, Section 9. Habeas corpus is a court order determining whether or not a prisoner was lawfully arrested and detained.

Concentration Camps for Japanese
As mistrust and fear of people of Japanese descent grew in the wake of the bombing of Pearl Harbor, the federal government relocated thousands of Japanese living on the West Coast to inland camps.

Three cases involved men who had been convicted and sentenced in lower courts. Two of these challenged the curfew imposed on Japanese Americans on the West Coast. A third case questioned the forced evacuation of Japanese Americans from the West Coast. All three cases—*Yasui* v. *United States*, *Hirabayashi* v. *United States*, and *Korematsu* v. *United States*—involved native-born citizens of Japanese ancestry.

In Minori Yasui's case, the Supreme Court upheld his conviction for violating the curfew. In a similar fashion, the Court ruled that Gordon Hirabayashi also was guilty of violating the curfew, which in the Court's opinion did not violate due process. Instead, the curfew was a military necessity that reflected the government's war powers during a crisis. Although Chief Justice Stone noted that "It is jarring to me that U.S. citizens are subjected to this treatment" and that discrimination "was odious to a free people," the Court unanimously upheld Hirabayashi's conviction. The Court avoided the larger issue of confining American citizens in relocation centers.

The Supreme Court decided the third case in 1944. Fred Korematsu had decided not to report to an assembly center for evacuation from California in May 1942. Instead, he planned to move to the Midwest. Still in California at the end of May, Korematsu was arrested and convicted of ignoring the evacuation order. In a six to three decision, the Supreme Court

L2 Making Comparisons Write the four Supreme Court cases discussed in the case study on the chalkboard and ask students to summarize each one. How did the Court rule in each? What political and social factors may have overridden the legal issues in these decisions? *(racism, concern for public welfare and national security)* Ask students to find evidence of these factors by comparing the Court's decisions. *(Students may note that as invasion fears subsided, the justices' positions gradually changed.)*

L3 Synthesizing Information Refer students to the excerpts at the beginning of the case study. Ask how these guarantees applied to the relocation of Japanese Americans and to the court cases that arose from this government policy. Ask to what extent racism was a factor in relocating Japanese Americans. Point out Justice Black's opinion in the *Korematsu* case and ask if it indicated racism on the Court. *(Some students will say not, but others will note that German Americans and Italian Americans were not relocated.)*

Independent Practice

L1 Geography Have students research the sites of the relocation centers and locate them on an outline map of the United States. Ask them to write a paragraph explaining the military strategy behind the location of the camps.

tioned at Camp Shelby. In June 1944 the remaining part of the 442nd was transferred to Italy.

In October the 442nd engaged German troops fighting for control of the Vosges Mountains. It was assigned to rescue a Texas unit that found itself behind enemy lines. After intense fighting the Nisei

troops relieved the Texans, but the cost was high. The 442nd lost more than 300 men.

During the war the 442nd had the highest casualty rate in the army. It counted over 9,000 dead and wounded. At the same time men of the unit earned over 18,143 individual decorations.

L2 **Global Perspectives** Have students research and contrast the internment policies of Germany and the United States during this period. Suggest that they classify the differences and present them on a chart. (*Charts should note the different time frames of internment, different reasons for internment, different operational policies in the camps, and different fates of the internees.*)

L3 **History** Have students research government policies on civil liberties during the Civil War and World War I. Have them present their findings in a short essay.

📁 **Analyzing Supreme Court Cases** Assign case 17, *Korematsu v. United States,* from the *Supreme Court Case Studies* in the Teacher's Classroom Resources.

Assess

Have students complete **Examining the Case.**

Close

Ask if students can think of circumstances that would justify abridgement of civil liberties during wartime. Ask if the number of people affected, or their status as citizens or aliens, should make any difference.

upheld Korematsu's conviction on the grounds that the war powers provided by the Constitution also provided the President and Congress the right to order the evacuation. As Justice Black wrote, "Korematsu was not excluded from the Military Area because of hostility to him or his race. He was excluded because we are at war with the Japanese Empire. . . ."

A fourth case, that of Mitsuye Endo, was different. A native-born citizen, Miss Endo was fired from a California state job in 1942 and sent to a relocation center. Her lawyer challenged the War Relocation Board's right to detain a loyal American citizen. Ultimately the case reached the Supreme Court.

With the Allies clearly winning the war, fear of a Japanese invasion had faded. On Sunday December 17, 1944, the military commander of the Western Defense region, General Henry Platt—who had succeeded General DeWitt—revoked the exclusion order. The next day the Supreme Court ruled in *Endo* v. *United States* that Mitsuye Endo could no longer be held in custody or denied the right to return to California. Justice Murphy wrote:

> *Detention in Relocation Centers of people of Japanese ancestry regardless of loyalty is not only unauthorized by Congress or the Executive, but is another example of the unconstitutional resort to racism inherent in the entire evacuation program.... Racial discrimination of this nature bears no reasonable relation to military necessity and is utterly foreign to the ideals and traditions of the American people.*
>
> —JUSTICE FRANK MURPHY, 1944

Significance

> "Let us determine to abide by the lessons Executive Order 9066 teaches us," retired Associate Justice Tom C. Clark wrote in 1972.
>
> *First, that the mere existence of a legal right is no more protection to individual liberty than the parchment it is written on, and second, that mutual love, respect, and understanding of one another are stronger bonds than constitutions.*
>
> —JUSTICE TOM C. CLARK, 1972

Eleven years later the Commission on Wartime Relocation informed Congress that a "grave injustice, the detention of Japanese Americans, was the result of 'race' prejudice, war hysteria and a failure of political leadership."

In the four cases it reviewed, the Supreme Court ruled on narrow grounds and carefully avoided the basic constitutional question of the rights of individuals during wartime. Based on Executive Order 9066 and Public Law 503 that made it a crime to violate the military's orders, the military evacuated and detained American citizens without charges. In essence, the Court established the precedent that citizens could be interned during wartime without being charged with a crime.

The final chapter in the tragic story of the Japanese American internments came in 1988. That year Congress granted a tax-free payment of $20,000 to each of the detained Nisei—native-born Japanese Americans—who still survived. The government also officially apologized to each internee in recognition of the harm that had been done. As one of the survivors said to Peter Irons, "They did me a great wrong."

Examining the Case

Reviewing the Facts

1. Identify why the government detained Japanese American citizens.
2. Describe the effect the relocation had upon Japanese Americans during World War II.
3. Explain the basis for the Supreme Court's decisions in the cases of *Yasui* v. *United States, Hirabayashi* v. *United States,* and *Korematsu* v. *United States.*

Critical Thinking Skills

4. Distinguishing Fact from Opinion Is the following a statement of fact or opinion? "The mere existence of a legal right is no more protection to individual liberty than the parchment it is written on. . . ." Explain why you agree or disagree with the statement. How does the statement relate to the treatment of Japanese Americans during World War II?
5. Drawing Conclusions What precedent in the Japanese American cases did the Supreme Court establish regarding unpopular minorities during wartime? How might such a precedent pose a danger to democracy in the future?

Examining the Case Answers

1. The government feared they would help the Japanese war effort.
2. lost jobs, businesses, homes, and farms
3. that the government's war powers extend over citizens during a national emergency
4. Opinion; answers may vary, but students might point out that the Japanese Americans were guaranteed rights, but the government ignored the rights.
5. Unpopular minorities might be interned during wartime without being charged with a crime; other groups might lose their rights.

Chapter 5

Citizenship in the United States

A citizen of the United States has certain rights, duties, and responsibilities. The Constitution guarantees basic rights in the Bill of Rights—the first 10 amendments—and in several additional amendments. Duties include obeying the law, paying taxes, and being loyal to the American government and its basic principles. Citizens have the responsibility to be informed, vote, respect the rights and property of others, and respect different opinions and ways of life.

People can exercise the rights and privileges of citizenship in other ways as well. They can support the efforts of a special-interest group to influence legislation or discuss issues with a legislator. Writing letters to the editor, signing or circulating a petition, or exercising the right to dissent in a legal and orderly manner are other ways citizens can participate.

Almost all people born in the United States are automatically American citizens. Immigrants who go through the process of naturalization are also citizens. Since 1820, more than 57 million immigrants have come to the United States.

Only the federal government can grant citizenship and take it away. Americans can lose their citizenship in any of three ways: (1) **expatriation**, or giving up one's citizenship by leaving one's native country to live in a foreign country; (2) punishment for a serious crime; or (3) **denaturalization**, or the loss of citizenship through fraud or deception during the naturalization process.

Chapter 6

Protecting Basic Freedoms

The First Amendment guarantees freedom of religion in two clauses. The first clause, known as the **establishment clause**, states that "Congress shall make no law respecting an establishment of religion." The second clause, labeled the **free exercise clause**, requires that Congress not prohibit the free exercise of religion.

The First Amendment also guarantees freedom of speech and the press as well as freedom to peaceably assemble. The Supreme Court has distinguished three general categories of speech.

The verbal expression of thought and opinion before an audience that has chosen to listen, or **pure speech**, is the most common form of speech. Actions such as marching or demonstrating are **speech plus**. The third type of speech, **symbolic speech**, involves using actions and symbols instead of words to express opinions.

During this century the Court has developed three constitutional tests to establish limits on speech. They are (1) the "clear and present danger" test, (2) the bad tendency doctrine, and (3) the preferred position doctrine.

Freedom of the press is closely related to freedom of speech. It moves free speech one step further by allowing opinions to be written and circulated. The press is important because it is the principal way people get information. In today's world the press includes magazines, radio, television, and newspapers.

Freedom of assembly and petition involves the right to assemble with other like-minded people and discuss public issues. It applies not only to meetings in private homes but also to those in public places. It protects the right to make views known to public officials and others by such means as petitions, letters, lobbying, carrying signs in a parade, or marching.

Like freedom of the press, the right to peaceably assemble is closely related to free speech because most gatherings involve some form of protected speech. Without this basic freedom, there would be no political parties and no interest groups to influence the actions of government.

Chapter 7

Assuring Equal Justice for All

The Constitution and the Bill of Rights built a system of justice designed to guard the rights of the accused as well as the rights of society. Laws were to be strictly interpreted, trial procedures fair and impartial, and punishments reasonable.

To protect the innocent, the Fourth Amendment forbids unreasonable searches and seizures. It guarantees "the right of people to be secure in their persons, houses, papers, and effects, against unreasonable searches and seizures." Over the years the courts have interpreted what constitutes an unreasonable search and seizure.

ABCNEWS INTERACTIVE™

Martin Luther King, Jr.
Students on Racism
Running Time 2:46
Side Two, Chapter 40

Using the Unit 2 Digest

Use the Unit Digest to introduce, review, reteach, or condense specific chapters or the entire unit. The Unit Digest is enhanced by the corresponding transparencies and activities in the Teacher's Classroom Resources.

Focus

Point out that American citizenship invests people with certain rights. However, these rights are accompanied by a number of obligations. As an example, mention that most citizens over the age of 18 have the right to vote. These citizens, however, are obliged to register to vote, to become informed about issues and candidates, and to cast their votes in elections. Ask students to name as many citizenship rights as they can. List these rights on the chalkboard. Then have volunteers describe the related obligations of each listed right.

Teach

L1 Understanding Ideas Write the following terms on the chalkboard: *naturalization,* jus soli, jus sanguinis, *expatriation, denaturalization.* Have students use these terms to write a paragraph on how people become American citizens and how they can lose their citizenship. Suggest that students refer to Chapter 5 for explanations of terms not found in the Digest. Select students to read their paragraphs to the class.

GLENCOE TECHNOLOGY

Set on Freedom
The Legacy of Martin Luther King, Jr. and the Civil Rights Movement
Running Time 1:43
Side B, Chapter 12

Classroom Resources for Unit 2 Digest

Unit Digest Transparencies, Unit 2

Participating in Government, Unit 2

Assess

Check for Understanding
Have students complete **Synthesizing the Unit.**

Close

Ask students to discuss what they think is the most important basic freedom or civil liberty they possess. Make certain that they offer reasons for their selections.

The Fifth Amendment says that no one "shall be compelled in any criminal case to be a witness against himself." The courts have interpreted this protection against **self-incrimination** to cover witnesses before congressional committees and grand juries as well as defendants in criminal cases.

In *Miranda* v. *Arizona* (1966), the Supreme Court laid down strict rules for protecting suspects from police interrogations. The Court ruled that the Fifth Amendment's protection against self-incrimination requires that suspects be clearly informed of their rights before police question them.

The Fifth Amendment also states that no person shall be "twice put in jeopardy of life and limb." This prohibition against **double jeopardy** means that a person may not be tried twice for the same crime, thus protecting people from continual government harassment.

The Sixth Amendment guarantees people accused of crimes the right to **counsel,** or an attorney. The courts have ruled that this guarantee applies to state and local courts as well as federal courts. If a defendant cannot afford a lawyer, the court must provide one.

The Eighth Amendment forbids "cruel and unusual punishment," the only constitutional provision specifically limiting penalties in criminal cases. The Supreme Court has rarely found a punishment cruel and unusual. A great controversy has arisen, however, over the death penalty.

The Fifth and Fourteenth amendments forbid the national and state governments to deny anyone "equal protection of the law." Generally the equal protection clause means that government cannot draw unreasonable distinctions between different groups of people. Yet for many years the courts upheld discrimination against African Americans. Not until the late 1930s and the 1940s did the Supreme Court begin to chip away at racial discrimination in a series of decisions. The most important decision came in 1954 in *Brown* v. *Board of Education of Topeka*. This case prohibited separate public schools for African Americans and whites.

The *Brown* decision opened the gates for scores of court cases dealing with equal rights. It also gave a precedent for court decisions striking down segregation—separate facilities for different races in public parks, beaches, playgrounds, libraries, golf courses,

state and local prisons, transportation, and all other public places.

After the *Brown* decision, many blacks and whites worked together to end problems of segregation in an effort called the **civil rights movement**. The Reverend Martin Luther King, Jr., emerged as the leader of this movement.

Influenced by the civil rights movement, Congress began to pass major civil rights laws. These laws sought to ensure voting rights and equal job opportunities under the provisions of the Fourteenth Amendment.

Changing ideas, social conditions, and technology have combined to raise new issues for civil liberties. Today, for example, the government maintains billions of computer records on individual Americans. In addition, private companies collect financial, medical, and legal information on almost everyone. Such record keeping raises important questions about the right to privacy—a right not mentioned in the Constitution. Other important issues involve **affirmative action**—taking positive, legally enforceable steps to make up for past discrimination against women and minorities, and the public's right to know about government actions.

Synthesizing the Unit

Recalling Facts
1. Define expatriation, denaturalization, establishment clause, free exercise clause, pure speech, speech plus, symbolic speech, self-incrimination, double jeopardy, counsel, civil rights movement, affirmative action.
2. Explain the most common way that citizens participate in political life.

Exploring Themes
3. Civic Responsibility What are the major duties and responsibilities of American citizens?
4. Civil Rights What gains did the civil rights movement make for African Americans?

Critical Thinking Skills
5. Evaluating Information How has the Supreme Court ensured that people accused of crimes are guaranteed "due process of the law"?
6. Drawing Conclusions Why do you think the courts have assumed the role of interpreting the Bill of Rights?

Synthesizing the Unit Answers

1. Definitions of terms appear on the pages indicated: **expatriation,** 225; **denaturalization,** 225; **establishment clause,** 225; **free exercise clause,** 225; **pure speech,** 225; **speech plus,** 225; **symbolic speech,** 225; **self-incrimination,** 226; **double jeopardy,** 226; **counsel,** 226; **civil rights movement,** 226; **affirmative action,** 226
2. by exercising rights of speech and assembly

3. *duties:* obeying the law, paying taxes, being loyal to the government and its basic principles; *responsibilities:* to be informed, vote, respect the rights and property of others, respect different opinions and ways of life
4. end of segregation and passage of civil rights laws ensuring voting rights and equal opportunity under the provisions of the Fourteenth Amendment

5. by forbidding unreasonable search and seizure, informing suspects of their rights, ensuring that people are not tried twice for the same crime, providing counsel, limiting penalties, providing equal protection under the law
6. Answers will vary, but should note that it is the sole responsibility of the courts to interpret the Constitution.

Influencing Government

UNIT 3

Chapter 8
Political Parties

Chapter 9
Elections and Voting

Chapter 10
Interest Groups

Chapter 11
Public Opinion

Chapter 12
The Mass Media

Introduce

Unit Objectives

After studying this unit, students should be able to:
- Explain the functions of political parties, interest groups, and the media in the political system.
- Analyze the nature of public opinion and its impact on the political process.

Unit Overview

Unit 3 examines the ways in which citizens participate in and influence the political system.

Chapter 8 introduces students to the role of parties in the American political system.

Chapter 9 discusses voting and the ways election campaigns are organized and carried out.

Chapter 10 describes interest groups and their role in American political life.

Chapter 11 introduces students to the subject of public opinion.

Chapter 12 reviews the roles the mass media play in the political process.

3 UNIT DIGEST

Use the Unit Digest on pages 355–356 to introduce, review, reteach, or condense the information in this unit.

Introducing the Unit

Ask students how a citizen can participate in the political system. Then ask: Are you or any of your relatives members of a political party? Have you ever been involved in the work of an interest group? Have you ever taken part in a political opinion poll? Do you follow election coverage in the media? Close by noting that these are all methods of political participation discussed in Unit 3.

Unit Project

Organize students into five groups and tell them their task is to put together a scrapbook about a recent election. Assign one of the following topics to each group: 1. the office contested, main candidates, major issues, election results; 2. the role played by political parties in the election; 3. the role of interest groups in the election; 4. the results and accuracy of public opinion polls taken during the campaign; 5. media coverage of the campaign and candidates' use of the media. Suggest that group members share the work of locating and selecting information and illustrations on their topics. Have the class display the scrapbook for other government and civics classes.

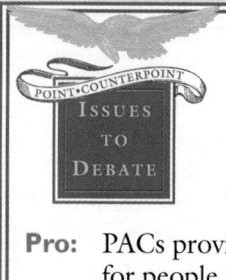

The Issue at a Glance

Pro: PACs provide a way for people to participate in the election process.

Con: PACs undermine the political process.

Focus

Write *Student Government* on the chalkboard. Ask students to list their impressions of the most recent student election campaign. Ask: Might the outcome of the election have been different if some candidates had had vastly greater resources than others?

Tell students that the issue in this reading concerns the relationship of campaign financing, elections, and the behavior of elected officials.

Teach

Guided Practice

Point out that running for a major political office is very costly, so candidates begin to raise money many months before the election. Ask students to speculate about the factors that make campaigns so expensive. *(mostly media advertising, but also large paid campaign staffs and travel expenses)* Ask: How do PACs influence the outcome of elections? *(by contributing large sums of money to certain candidates)* Why would PAC support give a candidate a big advantage over his or her opponent? *(more money for media, polling, staff, and so on)* According to critics, how has the growth of PACs changed the makeup of Congress? Why? *(Because PACs favor incumbents, their reelection rate has increased.)*

Are Political Action Committees a Good Idea?

The reelection rate of incumbent members of Congress stands at more than 90 percent. Most of these incumbents receive large campaign contributions from political action committees (PACs), organizations specifically designed to raise money for political candidates. Because the reelection rate is so high, most PACs contribute to incumbents and ignore challengers. Critics of PACs suggest that without PAC support, challengers face almost certain defeat. Defenders of the system, however, point out that it only makes sense to support those who favor their interests, as interest groups have done throughout the nation's history. Still, the question remains: Are political action committees a good idea?

Pro

For many interest groups, PACs play an important role in our system of government. Outspoken conservative spokeswoman Phyllis Schlafly, for example, believes that liberals do not like PACs because PACs tend to favor conservative candidates.

So the liberal busybodies have devised a three-point plan to outmaneuver democracy in order to advantage their candidates. (1) Get their liberal friends in the media to publish endless "news" stories, features, interviews with prominent persons, and editorials complaining about the large amounts of money donated through PACs. This is designed to have the subliminal effect of convincing people that PACs are something evil.

(2) Pass legislation severely restricting the amounts of money that PACs and political candidates may receive and spend. Label this legislation a "reform" or a

"clean campaign" bill and hope that this semantic trick will expedite passage. . . .

(3) Bring about taxpayer financing of elections to replace voluntary financing of elections through PACs. In other words, make the taxpayers pay for what the PACs are paying for now.

It's quite an exercise in campaign chicanery to try to force citizens to finance the political campaigns of candidates they don't like, while prohibiting citizens from making voluntary contributions to the political campaigns of candidates they do like. In the peculiar inverted ideology of the liberals, it is bad for American citizens to spend $100 million of their own money on candidates of their own choice, but it would be good for the Federal Government to tax you and spend a similar amount of your money to elect candidates most of whom are not of your choice.

It's quite a demonstration of the liberal dialectic to try to restrict First Amendment rights for political speech, while at the same time the entire liberal apparatus is working overtime to try to extend First Amendment rights for pornographic speech. One gets the feeling that, if PACs were promoting pornography instead of personal political views, the liberals might be supporting PACs.

In any event, it is vastly more important to the maintenance of our freedom to protect political than pornographic speech and activity. The First Amendment was written to protect political speech in order to retain our individual right to elect candidates and choose policies in a free society. PACs are simply one manifestation of your personal First Amendment right to express your political beliefs and to participate in the political process.

—PHYLLIS SCHLAFLY,
THE PHYLLIS SCHLAFLY REPORT, AUGUST 1986

More About Issues to Debate

Many manufacturing associations, corporations, unions, and interest groups create political action committees. These committees, known as PACs, collect money to support individual candidates running for office who are likely to support the organization's political agenda. Sometimes they contribute to both candidates for an office, although in differing amounts.

According to *The Almanac of American Politics 1992,* PAC contributions for the 1990 election

Those who oppose PACs often do so for different reasons. One opponent, former Senator William Proxmire from Wisconsin, said that a PAC contribution might not buy a vote, "but it may come in a speech not delivered, in a colleague not influenced . . . . It may come in hiring a key staff member who is sympathetic to the PAC."

Senator David L. Boren, a senator who refuses to accept PAC contributions, wrote:

In 1976, the Bicentennial of this country's independence, the average cost of winning a Senate seat was about $600,000. . . . If current trends continue at the same rate, 12 years from now, when this spring's high school graduates will be eligible to run for the Senate, the average cost could be $20,000,000. . . .

At the heart of the rising costs of Congressional races is special-interest money. Political Action Committees (PAC's) contributed over $49,000,000 in the 1988 election. More importantly, PAC's gave four times as often to sitting senators as they gave to challengers, allowing incumbents to outspend challengers by more than $60,000,000.

In 1982, 98 sitting members of Congress were re-elected, with over half their campaign funds coming from special-interest PAC's. In 1986, that number went up to 195! Is it any wonder that 99% of the members of the House of Representatives are re-elected . . . ?

When additional money from special interests is pumped into the system, it ends up being spent and campaign costs soar. The rising tide of special-interest money from PAC's exacerbates [worsens] the fundamental problem that there is simply too much money in our electoral system.

An alarming problem with PAC's is that these out-of-state money machines, coming from both business and labor groups, are discouraging new people with fresh ideas from getting involved in politics. With the overwhelming share of PAC contributions going to incumbents, rather than challengers, new candidates almost are forced out of running a serious campaign. . . .

A PAC does not judge a senator or Congressman on his or her over-all voting record or personal integrity the way voters and local supporters do. . . .

Instead, PAC's rate the member of Congress solely on how he or she voted on bills specifically affecting the particular financial interest groups they represent. Because Congressmen and senators receive more and more of their funds from PAC's, the narrow focus of special-interest groups makes it increasingly difficult to reach a

Does Money Talk?
The controversy surrounding PACs centers on the role special interests play in raising funds for increasingly expensive campaigns.

national consensus on important issues.
—SENATOR DAVID L. BOREN, *USA TODAY*, MAY 1990

The Debate Continues

As the debate continues to wage over and around PACs, more and more voters are discussing the possibility of campaign-funding reform. Whether or not this discussion will translate into votes on the floor of Congress remains in doubt. If Congress should consider changes in campaign funding, it will no doubt move very carefully. Few senators or representatives are likely to support changes that favor challengers over incumbents.

Examining the Issue

Critical Thinking Skills
1. Analyzing Information Why do you think some members of Congress might be opposed to any change in the present method of financing political campaigns?
2. Understanding Cause and Effect Why do many PACs support incumbents rather than challengers?

Investigating Further
Research the percentage of congressional campaign funds contributed by PACs. Write a paragraph explaining the conclusions you can draw from the information.

---

cycle made up 39 percent of the net campaign funding in federal elections, up 500 percent from 1978. Congressional PAC donations continued to rise, totaling $73.4 million in a 15-month period through March 1992. This represented a 14 percent increase over the previous 15-month period in the 1990 election cycle. Incumbents received the lion's share—about 85% of the funds donated. Democratic candidates received about two-thirds of all PAC contributions.

Point out that some reformers are calling for government campaign financing to replace the current system of private contributions. Ask whether such a reform would strengthen democracy or weaken it. *(strengthen— would create a more level playing field for elections; weaken—would deny people one way to support their candidate)*

Ask: What constitutional argument does Schlafly make in defense of PACs? *(Their activities are an extension of First Amendment free speech rights.)* How does former Senator Proxmire assess the impact of PACs on free speech? *(Elected officials may fear losing PAC support if they speak out on an issue.)*

Independent Practice

Have students write one-paragraph summaries of Schlafly's argument in support of PACs and Boren's argument opposing them.

Assess

Have students complete **Examining the Issue.**

Answers

1. PAC support is a big advantage when candidates run for reelection.

2. Incumbents have records on issues; challengers' positions are largely unproven. Also, incumbents are usually favored in elections; PAC money spent on losers is wasted.

Close

Ask students which side they support. Would abolishing PACs democratize the political process, or should interest groups be able to support candidates who favor their causes? Have students explain their opinions.

Chapter Organizer

Objectives	Special Feature Pages	Supplemental Materials
Section 1 Political Parties and Government *pp. 232–236* 1. Distinguish between one-party, two-party, and multiparty systems. 2. Explain the role of third parties in American politics. 3. Describe how the American party system developed.	Point/Counterpoint: Are Political Action Committees a Good Idea? pp. 228–229 Images of Government: Spreading the Word pp. 234–235	Guided Reading Activities Reproducible Lesson Plans Primary and Secondary Source Readings 8 Enrichment Activities 8 Section 1 Quiz Chapter Transparencies 8 Testmaker SAT Practice Tests Writer's Guidebook
Section 2 Party Organization and Functions *pp. 237–242* 1. Summarize the characteristics of political party organization. 2. Identify the functions that political parties fulfill.	Participating in Government: Working in a Political Campaign p. 239 Critical Thinking Skills: Recognizing Ideologies p. 242	Guided Reading Activities Reproducible Lesson Plans Participating in Government 8 Interpreting Political Cartoons 6 Section 2 Quiz Testmaker Skill Reinforcement Activities 8 SAT Practice Tests Writer's Guidebook
Section 3 Nominating Candidates for Office *pp. 243–251* 1. Explain the role of primary elections in selecting candidates for office. 2. Evaluate the current system for choosing presidential candidates. 3. Describe the different types of primary elections.	Global Connection: Comparing Governments: Party Systems p. 247 Focus on Freedom: Washington's Farewell Address p. 249 Personal Perspectives: Ron Brown and Clayton Yeutter on the 1992 Campaign p. 251	Guided Reading Activities Reproducible Lesson Plans Reteaching Activities 8 Section 3 Quiz Chapter 8 Tests Testmaker Government Themes Transparencies 43 Audio Cassettes (English and Spanish) Limited English Proficiency Activities 8 Great Speeches, Volume IV SAT Practice Tests Writer's Guidebook

If time does not permit teaching this chapter, assign the Chapter 8 summary in the Unit 3 Digest on pages 355–356.

Key To Ability Levels

Teaching strategies have been coded for varying learning styles and abilities.

L1   Level 1 activities are **basic** activities and should be within the ability range of all students.

L2   Level 2 activities are **average** activities and should be within the ability range of the average to above-average student.

L3   Level 3 activities are **challenging** activities designed for the ability range of above-average students.

LEP   These activities should be within the ability range of **Limited English Proficiency** students.

Multicultural Activities

The term *caucus* from the Algonquin reflects the Native American political tradition of meeting in council to discuss, persuade, educate, and make decisions. In his book *Indian Givers*, Jack Weatherford describes how the English colonists "learned from the Indians how to speak and act in group councils." Weatherford believes Americans borrowed the political institution of the caucus from the Native Americans. The caucus serves as a way of discussing issues and coming to decisions without public conflict. This, he points out, fits with the Native American tradition of resolving issues by talking through them. Students might read the chapter, "The Founding Indian Fathers," in Weatherford's book to learn what other American political traditions have Native American roots.

"Our flag is red, white, and blue, but our nation is a rainbow—red, yellow, brown, black, and white . . . ." said Jesse Jackson when he addressed the Democratic National Convention in San Francisco in 1984. Jackson hoped to become the nation's first African American presidential nominee by forging a "Rainbow Coalition" of Hispanic American, Asian American, and African American voters. However, Jackson's Rainbow Coalition failed to coalesce and his presidential bids in 1984 and 1988 failed. Have students speculate why it is difficult to create a multiethnic and multiracial voting bloc in the United States. Around what kind of issues might a multiethnic coalition be built? What qualities would the successful leader of such a coalition need?

Chapter Resources

Readings for the Student

Hoopes, Ray. *Primaries and Conventions*. Franklin Watts, 1978.
Ladd, Everett Carl. *Where Have All the Voters Gone? The Fracturing of American Political Parties*. Norton, 1978.
Lindop, Edmund and Joy Crane Thornton. *All About Democrats*. Enslow, 1985.
———. *All About Republicans*. Enslow, 1985.
O'Connor, Edwin. *The Last Hurrah*. Little, Brown, 1956.
Rakove, Milton. *Don't Make No Waves, Don't Back No Losers*. Indiana University Press, 1975.

Readings for the Teacher

Lewy, Guenter. *The Cause That Failed: Communism in American Political Life*. Oxford University Press, 1990.
Makinson, Larry and Joshua F. Goldstein. *Open Secrets, The Encyclopedia of Congressional Money and Politics*. Congressional Quarterly, 1994.
Mazmanian, Daniel A. *Third Parties in Presidential Elections*. Brookings Institution, 1974.
Ranney, Austin. *Curing the Mischiefs of Faction: Party Reform in America*. University of California Press, 1975.
Stanley, Harold W. and Richard G. Niemi. *Vital Statistics on American Politics*. Congressional Quarterly, 1990.

Multimedia

Videocassettes
The Candidate. Warners. (v/c, 111 minutes)
Running with Jesse. (*Frontline* series). Orlando Bagwell and Jeanne Jordan. (v/c, 60 minutes)

Software
American Government IV. Intellectual Software. (Apple, IBM disks; Apple disk with management facility also available; part of a 5-part set). Students complete a tutorial focusing on political parties, the presidency, and Congress.
And If Re-Elected. . . . Educational Products Information Exchange Institute, Hampton Bays, New York, 11946. IBM and PC Family and Compatibles, 640K, 5.25" disk drive, mouse, paddle, joystick, Macintosh 512E, 1MB, 3.5" disk drive.
NewsWorks—Social Studies Data Base Files. United States Government data base. Newsweek. (Apple disk; must be used with AppleWorks data-base program, Apple, Inc.). Students research and analyze data describing the election process and the party system.

Introduce

Chapter Overview

Chapter 8 introduces students to the role of political parties in the American political system.

Section 1 describes what political parties are, what they do, and what it means to be a party member. This section also discusses the development of the American two-party system and the role of third parties.

Section 2 outlines how parties are organized to carry out their various functions.

Section 3 highlights the process of nominating and electing candidates, focusing on the selection of a presidential candidate from primary elections through the national nominating convention.

Chapter 8 Themes

Write the following chapter themes on the chalkboard:

Comparative Government
Growth of Democracy
Political Processes
Civic Participation

Ask students to copy these themes into their notebooks. Then, as students read Chapter 8, have them list each major event or idea under the appropriate theme. Suggest that students compare their lists after they have completed the chapter.

Focus on Government
Video 15
Lecture Launcher:
Political Parties
Running Time: 2:27
Videodisc 1, Chap. 15
VHS Tape 1, Begins 43:15

Political Parties

CHAPTER

8

Every four years America's major political parties hold conventions where delegates from across the country select the party's nominees for President and Vice President.

About the Chapter Opener

Teaching With Illustrations Point out to students that this photograph shows the 1988 Republican National Convention, which was held in New Orleans. Then ask students to indicate how the photograph reflects the government themes of this chapter. *(Answers will vary. Students might indicate that it reflects the first theme in that it illustrates the two-party system that exists in the United States. The second theme is illustrated by the myriad of dedicated workers that a political party needs. The photograph also shows the nominating convention—the political process by which candidates are selected for President and Vice President.)*

Introducing the Chapter

Ask students to consider the following question: Why do we have political parties in the United States? Have them list as many reasons as they can for the existence of political parties. Select a number of students to read their lists to the class. Then lead students in a brief discussion on what they think is the role of political parties in American government. Draw the discussion to a close by pointing out that in Chapter 8 students will learn about the development, structure, and functions of political parties.

Chapter Project

Have students research the role of political parties in such countries as Britain, Canada, France, Germany, and Japan. Suggest that they write research papers that cover the following: type of party system, development of political parties, organization and function of parties, and how candidates are selected. Have students read their papers to the class. Use these papers as a starting point for a discussion on the differences among the world's political parties.

Linking Past and Present
While the Socialist party is one of the longest-surviving third parties, it has never garnered much support in the United States. Even at the height of its popularity—the 1912 presidential election—it won only 6 percent of the vote. However, much of its original platform has been accepted by the American people. Social security, welfare programs, workers' compensation, paid vacations, health benefits, and many other ideas first advanced by the Socialists are now part of everyday life in the United States.

Overview

The Republican and Democratic parties are part of a traditional political system that dominates American government and influences its operation and policies.

Objectives

After studying this chapter, you should be able to:

1. **Determine** ways that political parties affect the operation of government.
2. **Describe** how political parties are organized and function.
3. **Explain** how political parties select candidates for public office at all levels of government.

Themes in Government

This chapter emphasizes the following government themes:

- **Comparative Government** Political systems include one-party systems, multiparty systems, and two-party systems. Section 1.
- **Growth of Democracy** Political parties need a core of dedicated workers to succeed. Sections 1 and 2.
- **Political Processes** Nominating conventions select candidates for President and Vice President. Sections 2 and 3.
- **Civic Participation** Primary elections allow voters to participate in selecting candidates for public office. Section 3.

Critical Thinking Skills

This chapter emphasizes the following critical thinking skills:

- Making Generalizations
- Understanding Cause and Effect
- Analyzing Information

Setting the Scene Not anticipating the development of political parties, the authors of the Constitution devised the presidential election so that the candidate with the most electoral votes would become President and the runner-up would become Vice President. However, with the rise of the party system, this procedure resulted in a Federalist—John Adams—becoming President, and a Democratic-Republican—Thomas Jefferson—winning the vice presidency in the 1796 election. The Twelfth Amendment to the Constitution, ratified in 1804, prevented such a situation arising again.

Focus

Bell Ringer

Write the statement by George Washington below on the chalkboard. While attendance is being taken, have students consider what Washington meant.

"Let me . . . warn you in the most solemn manner against the baneful effects of the spirit of party . . . ."

Motivating Activity

Ask for volunteers to read aloud their Bell Ringer responses. Then lead the class in a discussion of the following questions: Based on what you know of modern-day political parties in the United States, was Washington's warning well-made? How do you think Washington would feel about political parties if he had to work with Congress today?

Encourage students to take notes during the discussion. These may prove useful in completing exercises and answering review questions later in the section.

Vocabulary Precheck

Write this section's key terms and concepts on the chalkboard. Ask students to use those that they know in sentences. **LEP**

Caption Answer

Federalists and Democratic-Republicans

SECTION 1

Political Parties and Government

People rule in a democracy, but the voice and will of the individual citizen can easily be lost in a nation as large and diverse as the United States. One way that citizens ensure that government knows their views is for them to organize into groups that wield political power. One example of such a group is the political party.

Parties and Party Systems

A **political party** is a group of people with broad common interests who organize to win elections,

. . . And May the Best Candidate Win
Since the earliest days of the Republic, political parties have used all types of paraphernalia to get their message to the voters. **History** **What were the nation's two earliest political parties?**

control government, and thereby influence government policies. Although most nations have one or more political parties, the role that parties play differs with each nation's political system.

One-Party Systems In a one-party system the party is, in effect, the government. The decisions of party leaders set government policy. In some one-party nations, political differences arise only within the party itself because the government tolerates no other opposition. In elections in such nations, only the party's candidates appear on the ballot.

One-party systems are usually found in nations with authoritarian governments. Such parties often come into power through force. For example, a revolution in 1917 brought the Communist party to power in Russia. Today Cuba, Vietnam, North Korea, and China are among the few nations that remain one-party Communist governments.

One-party systems also exist in some non-communist countries. In Iran, religious leaders dominate government, a form of government known as a **theocracy.** The Muslim clergy controls the Islamic Republican party. All major opposition parties have been outlawed or are inactive. Closer to home, Mexico is, in effect, a one-party government. As in Iran, minor party candidates may appear on the ballot. Mexico's Institutional Revolutionary party, however, has never lost a major election, and its leaders dominate Mexico's government.

Multiparty Systems In nations that allow more than one political party, the most common political

---

SECTION PREVIEW

Objectives
After studying this section, you should be able to:
- Distinguish between one-party, two-party, and multiparty systems.
- Explain the role of third parties in American politics.

- Describe how the American party system developed.

Key Terms and Concepts
political party, theocracy, ideology, coalition government, third party, single-issue party, ideological party, splinter party, single-member district, proportional representation

Themes in Government
- Comparative Government
- Growth of Democracy

Critical Thinking Skills
- Making Generalizations
- Understanding Cause and Effect

232 UNIT 3: INFLUENCING GOVERNMENT

Classroom Resources for Section 1

- Guided Reading Activities
- Reproducible Lesson Plans
- Primary and Secondary Source Readings 8
- Enrichment Activities 8
- Section 1 Quiz

- Chapter Transparencies 8
- Testmaker
- SAT Practice Tests
- Writer's Guidebook

---

system today is the multiparty system. France, for example, has 5 major parties, and Italy has 10. In such countries voters have a wide range of choices on Election Day. The parties in a multiparty system often represent widely differing **ideologies,** or basic beliefs about government.

In a multiparty system, one party rarely gets enough support to control the government. Several parties often combine forces to obtain a majority and form a **coalition government.** As might be expected when groups with different ideologies attempt to share power, coalitions often break down when disputes arise, requiring new elections. Thus many nations with multiparty systems are politically unstable.

Two-Party Systems Only about a dozen nations have systems where only two parties compete for power. Although minor parties may exist in these democracies, two major parties dominate government. In the United States, they are the Republican party and the Democratic party.

Growth of American Parties

Many of the Founders distrusted "factions," as they called groups that held differing political views, because they thought such factions were harmful to national unity. James Madison observed:

The public good is disregarded in the conflicts of rival parties, and . . . measures are too often decided, not according to the rules of justice and the rights of the minor party, but by the superior force of an interested and overbearing majority.
—JAMES MADISON, THE FEDERALIST, No. 10, 1787

In his Farewell Address of 1796, President George Washington warned against the "baneful [very harmful] effects of the spirit of party."

The Origin of Parties Even so, by the end of President Washington's second term, two political parties had arisen. The Federalists called for a strong central government. The Democratic-Republicans believed that the states should have more power than the central government.

Parties Before The Civil War After the Federalists elected John Adams President in 1796, their power quickly declined. Thomas Jefferson won the presidency under the Democratic-Republican banner in 1800 and 1804. The Democratic-Republicans dominated politics into the 1820s. Then conflicts over the major issues of the day—such as banking, tariffs, and slavery—shattered the party. By 1828, when Andrew Jackson won the presidency, the Democratic-Republicans were splitting into two parties. Jackson aligned with the group that called themselves Democrats. The other group called themselves National Republicans, or Whigs.

By the 1850s the debate over slavery had seriously divided the nation. It also created divisions within both of the young parties. The Democrats split into northern and southern factions. Many Whigs joined a new party, the Republican party that opposed the spread of slavery.

Parties After the Civil War By the time the Civil War was over, two major parties dominated the national political scene. The Republicans remained the majority party from the Civil War until well into the twentieth century. Democrats held the presidency for only 4 terms between 1860 and 1932.

Parties in the Great Depression and After In 1932 the Democratic party elected Franklin D. Roosevelt President and assumed control of Congress. For the next 50 years, Democrats remained the majority party, controlling both houses of Congress in all but 6 years. Beginning with Richard Nixon in 1968, Republicans elected 5 of the next 7 Presidents. After losing the White House to Bill Clinton in 1992, Republicans won the 1994 mid-term elections, taking both houses of Congress for the first time in 40 years. In 1995, for the first time since Truman, a Democratic

Teach

Guided Practice

L1 Understanding Ideas Display a collage of recent newspaper headlines that include words and phrases such as: *Democratic, Republican, Party Politics, Bipartisan, Voting Along Party Lines.* Discuss the relationship between these headlines and the American political system.

L2 Seeing Relationships Write the following lists of political parties and types of appeals on the chalkboard. Have students indicate what kind of appeal they think each party would make. (*1. a, 2. b, 3. c, 4. a, 5. c, 6. a, 7. b, 8. a*)

1. Libertarian
2. Prohibition
3. Democratic
4. Communist
5. Republican
6. Socialist Labor
7. Right to Life
8. States' Rights

a. bases appeal on ideology
b. bases appeal on single issue
c. designs appeal to attract wide range of supporters

Interpreting Visuals Display transparency 8 from the *Chapter Transparencies* in the Teacher's Classroom Resources and use the accompanying teaching strategy and student activity to teach about party ideologies.

STUDY GUIDE

Themes in Government
Comparative Government
The Ba'th party has been Iraq's single party since 1968.
Growth of Democracy
The Republicans won the presidency on their second try in 1860.

Critical Thinking Skills
Making Generalizations
Why does Italy form a new coalition government almost every year?

Understanding Cause and Effect
Why might the National Organization for Women want to choose and run a third-party candidate?

CHAPTER 8: POLITICAL PARTIES 233

STUDY GUIDE

Critical Thinking Answers
With 10 major parties coalitions are unstable, resulting in frequent elections.

It may be dissatisfied with the two major parties' positions on women's issues.

Background

The Republican Party, with Abraham Lincoln's victory in 1860, is the only successful third party in American history. Since 1860, only 4 third-party presidential candidates have polled more than 10 percent of the vote–Theodore Roosevelt (National Progressive) in 1912, Robert La Follette (Progressive) in 1924, George Wallace (American Independent) in 1968, and Ross Perot (United We Stand, America) in 1992. In most presidential elections since 1860, fewer than 1 out of every 20 votes was cast for a third party.

L3 Supporting a Point of View
Write the following statements on the chalkboard:

Political parties are the essence of democratic government.

Political parties are an obstacle to the efficient operation of government.

Select students to make brief presentations explaining which of the two statements they support. Ask the class to respond to these positions.

Independent Practice

L1 Chronology Have students construct an illustrated time line showing the evolution of the major American political parties from the 1790s to the present day. Have students display their time lines on the bulletin board.
LEP

Images of Government

Ask students to discuss the following question: Given recent developments in communications technology, how do you think candidates of the future will "spread the word"?

Answers

1. At that time, they were the best mass advertising vehicles available to candidates.
2. Kennedy was young and handsome, and his campaign organizers wanted to use these qualities to appeal to voters.

President had to work with a Republican Congress. In the 1990s the electorate was almost evenly divided among Democrats, Republicans and Independents.

The Role of Minor Parties

Despite the dominance of the two major parties, third parties have been part of the American political scene since the early days of the Republic. A **third party** is any party other than one of the two major parties. In any election there may be more than one party running against the major parties, yet each one of them is labeled a "third" party. Because they rarely win major elections, third parties are also called minor parties.

Third parties are formed to challenge the major parties. Although a variety of reasons motivates them, third parties all have one thing in common. They believe that neither major party is meeting certain needs. A third party runs candidates who propose to remedy this situation.

Types of Third Parties Although there may be some exceptions and overlap, minor parties generally fall into one of three categories.

The **single-issue party** focuses exclusively on one major social, economic, or moral issue. For example, in the 1840s the Liberty party and the Free Soil party formed to take stronger stands against slavery than either the Democrats or the Whigs had taken. A single-issue party generally is short-lived. The party may fade away when an issue ceases to be important, or a party with a very popular issue may become irrelevant if one of the major parties adopts the issue.

IMAGES OF GOVERNMENT

Spreading the Word

Slogans, images, and symbols play colorful roles in United States politics. Parties and movements use various means to appeal to voters. Political memorabilia often convey stories about past candidates and issues.

◄ Supporters of Abraham Lincoln proudly sported this elaborate medal during the 1860 presidential race.
▼ The "goldbug" pin from the presidential election of 1896 symbolized the Republican preference for the gold standard.

► Suffragists at the turn of the century unfurled this pennant advocating women's right to vote.

VOTES FOR WO

234 UNIT 3: INFLUENCING GOVERNMENT

Cooperative Learning Activity

Organize students into three groups and assign one of the following to each group: one-party systems, two-party systems, multiparty systems. Groups should prepare a brief illustrated report on three countries that use their assigned system. Reports should focus on the following questions: How are

government operations in these countries the same as in the United States? How are they different? Some group members might conduct research, others might write the report, and still others might provide illustrations.

Another type of third party is the **ideological party,** which focuses on overall change in society rather than on an issue. Its views are generally extreme. Ideological parties such as the Socialist Labor party and the American Communist party advocate government ownership of factories, transportation, resources, farmland, and other means of production and distribution. The Libertarian party calls for drastic reductions in government in order to increase personal freedoms.

The third type of minor party is the **splinter party,** which splits away from one of the major parties because of some disagreement. Such disputes frequently result from the failure of a popular figure to gain the major party's presidential nomination. The most notable occurrence was in 1912, when former President Theodore Roosevelt led a group out of the Republican party to form the Progressive, or Bull Moose, party. Splinter parties typically fade away with the defeat of their candidate. The Bull Moose party disappeared after Roosevelt lost in 1912, for example.

The Impact of Third Parties Minor parties have influenced the outcome of national elections. For example, Theodore Roosevelt's Bull Moose party drew so many Republican votes from President William Howard Taft in 1912 that Democratic candidate Woodrow Wilson was elected. In 1968 the American Independent party took so many votes from Democrat Hubert Humphrey that Republican candidate Richard Nixon won a narrow victory at the polls.

Third parties often have promoted ideas that were at first unpopular or hotly debated. Major parties later adopted many of their issues. For example, third parties first proposed a minimum wage for workers, the five-day work week, unemployment insurance, and health insurance.

Chapter 8, Section 1 Lesson Plan, pages 232–236

📁 **Interpreting Source Readings** Have students complete activity 8 in *Primary and Secondary Source Readings* in the Teacher's Classroom Resources.

L3 Informative Writing Have students research and write a brief report on the role Alexander Hamilton and Thomas Jefferson played in founding, respectively, the Federalist and Democratic-Republican parties. Select students to read their reports to the class.

Assess

Check for Understanding

Have students complete Section 1 Review on page 236.

Meeting Objectives

Each section objective is tested by the Section Review questions that follow it in parentheses.
- Distinguish between one-party, two-party, and multi-party systems. (2, 4, 5, 6, 7)
- Explain the role of third parties in American politics. (4)
- Describe how the American party system developed. (3, 4, 5, 8)

Evaluate

📁 Section 1 Quiz

💻 Testmaker

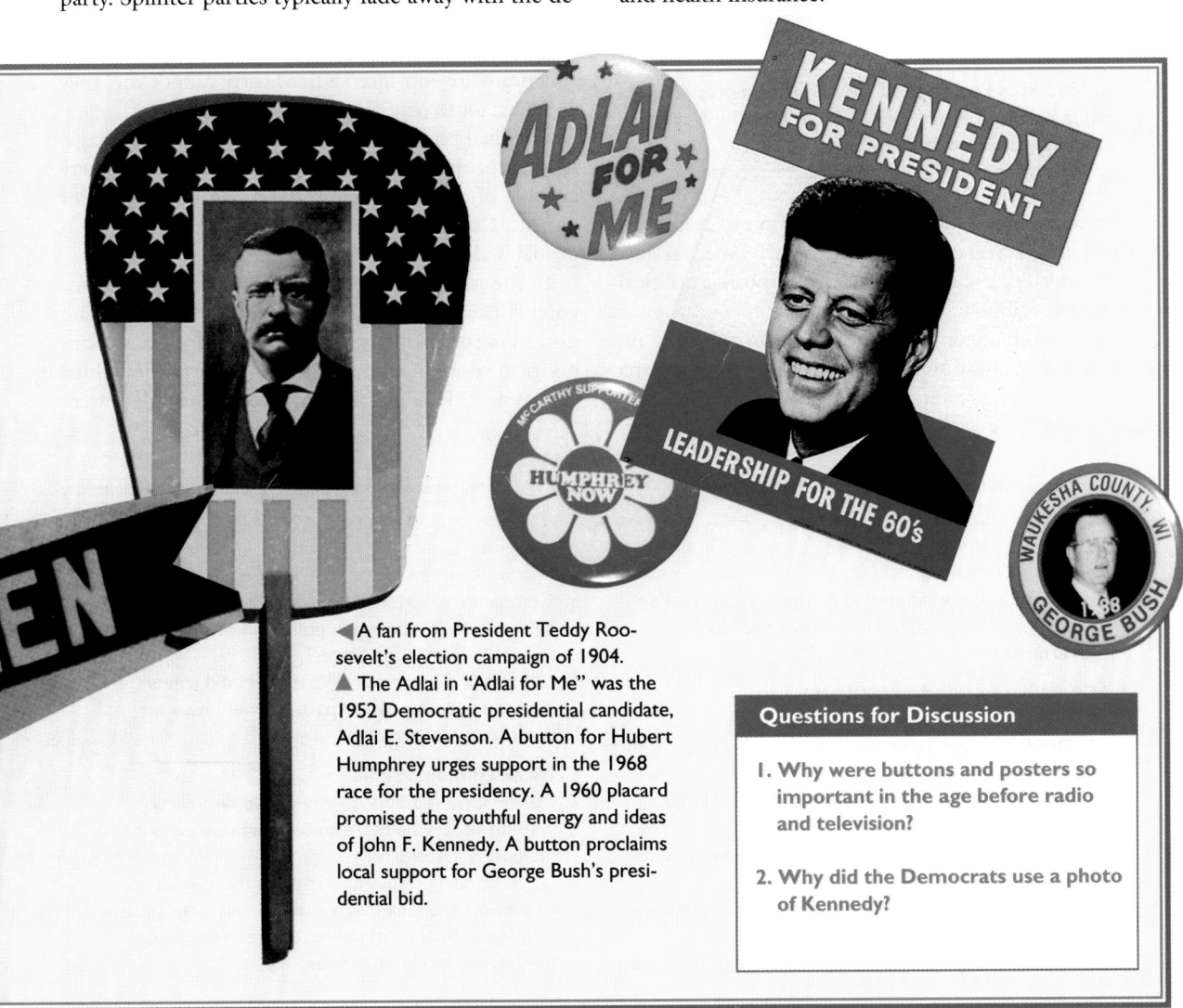

◄ A fan from President Teddy Roosevelt's election campaign of 1904.
▲ The Adlai in "Adlai for Me" was the 1952 Democratic presidential candidate, Adlai E. Stevenson. A button for Hubert Humphrey urges support in the 1968 race for the presidency. A 1960 placard promised the youthful energy and ideas of John F. Kennedy. A button proclaims local support for George Bush's presidential bid.

Questions for Discussion

1. Why were buttons and posters so important in the age before radio and television?

2. Why did the Democrats use a photo of Kennedy?

Special Needs Strategy

Learning Disability Students with some types of learning disabilities have difficulty with holistic or inductive thinking. In this section, they may have trouble understanding how the key ideas about types of political parties fit together. Based on the content of this section—which presents characteristics of party systems—have students write several sentences that explain the information contained in Images of Government on pages 234–235. Have students compare their sentences.

Caption Answer
Because most Americans believe a third party cannot win.

Reteach

Have students write in their notebooks definitions and examples of the following: *one-party system, multiparty system, two-party system.*

Enrich

Have students complete activity 8 in *Enrichment Activities* in the Teacher's Classroom Resources.

Close

Have students discuss the following question: What if the United States had no political parties?

CONNECTIONS

Law

In the case of *Norman* v. *Reed* (1992), the Supreme Court ruled that the Illinois election code's "draconian" requirements for third-party candidates to get on the ballot violated the First Amendment right of political association and, therefore, were unconstitutional. Political observers expected many state election laws would be rewritten because of this decision.

An Independent Candidate for the Presidency
In 1992 Ross Perot helped finance his own presidential campaign. **Politics Why is it hard for third-party candidates to raise money?**

Obstacles to Third Parties The party system in the United States started with only two parties. Once started, the tradition of two opposing political groups continued.

As a result, minor parties face difficulty in getting on the ballot in all 50 states. The names of Republicans and Democrats are automatically on the ballot in many states, but third-party candidates are required to obtain a large number of voter signatures in a short time.

The way in which candidates are elected to office also favors the two-party system. Almost all elected officials in the United States are selected by **single-member districts**. Under this system candidates seek a single office that represents all voters living in an area. No matter how many candidates compete, only one will win. Because most voters support a major party, the winner will almost always be a Democrat or a Republican.

By contrast, many nations use an election system based on **proportional representation**. In this system several officials are elected to represent voters in an area. Offices are filled in proportion to the votes that each party's candidates receive. Such a system encourages minor parties, whereas the American system makes their success unlikely.

A related problem is third-party finances. Political campaigns require a great deal of money. Because most Americans are convinced a third party cannot win, they are reluctant to contribute to such a campaign.

The final problem for a third party is one of image. It must project itself as being a truly national party capable of challenging and defeating the two major parties. Considering all the obstacles it faces, this is probably the most difficult challenge of all.

In the past, third parties have appealed mainly to voters in certain regions of the country or to certain groups in society. To survive, a third party must plant political roots in all parts of the country. Few third parties have demonstrated this kind of staying power.

---

1 SECTION REVIEW

Section Summary
Many parties have influenced American politics. For a number of reasons, however, only two dominate government.

Checking for Understanding
Recalling Facts
1. Define political party, theocracy, ideology, coalition government, third party, single-issue party, ideological party, splinter party, single-member district, proportional representation.
2. Describe the three types of political party systems in the world.
3. Summarize the development of the American two-party system.
4. Contrast single-issue parties and ideological parties.

Exploring Themes
5. Comparative Government What similarities and differences exist between politics in Mexico and politics in the United States?
6. Growth of Democracy What effect did James Madison believe political parties would have on democratic government?

Critical Thinking Skills
7. Making Generalizations Why would two-party systems usually be more stable than one-party or multiparty systems?
8. Understanding Cause and Effect Is there evidence to support the idea that a national crisis can cause a shift in the balance of power between two major parties? Explain your answer.

Section 1 Review Answers

1. Definitions of terms appear on pages indicated: **political party,** 232; **theocracy,** 232; **ideology,** 233; **coalition government,** 233; **third party,** 234; **single-issue party,** 234; **ideological party,** 235; **splinter party,** 235; **single-member district,** 236; **proportional representation,** 236
2. one-party—only one major party; multiparty—several major parties representing wide range of ideologies; two-party—two parties dominate government
3. Federalists and Democratic-Republicans formed from factions that developed during Washington's presidency; Federalists declined by 1820s, and Democratic-Republicans split into Democrats and Whigs; in 1850s many Whigs joined new Republican party; Republicans dominated from Civil War until Great Depression; Democrats dominated from then until 1970s; recently power divided
4. single-issue parties call for particular change, ideological parties call for sweeping changes

5. both are democracies; Mexico—one-party system, United States—two-party system
6. political conflict would be resolved in interests of majority without regard for justice, minority rights
7. one-party system—dissent could lead to unrest and instability; multiparty system—ideological differences among coalition members could destabilize government; two-party system—opposition party provides channel of dissent, party in control provides political stability.
8. Voters may blame party in power for crisis.

SECTION 2

Party Organization and Functions

In order to succeed, a political party must have a dedicated core of people who are willing to work hard for it. Both major parties employ small paid staffs in permanent party offices at county, state, and national levels. Between elections these employees carry out the day-to-day business operations of the party. At campaign time, however, political parties also use volunteers to perform a wide range of tasks. Volunteers obtain campaign contributions, publicize candidates, send out campaign literature, canvass voters, and watch at the polls on Election Day. Parties also seek the help of various professionals to win elections. These professionals include media experts to prepare television commercials, pollsters to take public opinion polls, and writers to prepare speeches for the candidates. In addition, to be successful, a party needs strong leadership and good organization at every level.

Political Party Organizations

Democrats and Republicans are organized into 50 state parties and thousands of local parties that operate independently of the national organization. Although the 3 levels generally cooperate, separate authority exists at each level. Local, state, and national parties select their own officers and raise their own funds.

Party Membership How does a voter join a political party, and what does it mean to belong? In many states citizens must declare their party preference when they register to vote or when they vote in cer-

tain kinds of elections. Joining a political party, however, is not required in the United States. A voter may declare that he or she is an **independent**, not supporting any one party.

People who belong to a political party generally do so because they support most of its ideas and candidates. Both the Republican and Democratic parties do everything they can to attract supporters. In this sense the two major parties are open parties, welcoming whoever wishes to belong and accepting whatever degree of involvement these individuals choose. Party membership involves no duties or obligations beyond voting. Members do not have to attend meetings or contribute to the party if they choose not to do so. Most people who consider themselves Democrats or Republicans do nothing more than vote for the party's candidates.

Some citizens, however, become more involved in the political process. They may support a party by contributing money or by doing volunteer work for the party or its candidates. In most states one must be a party member in order to hold an office in a party or to be its candidate for a public office. Thus party membership provides a way for citizens to increase their influence on government. The parties, in turn, depend on citizen involvement, especially at the local level, to carry out activities and accomplish goals.

Local Party Organization The basic local unit is the **precinct,** a voting district ranging in size from just a few voters to more than 1,000 voters, all of whom cast their ballots at the same polling place.

In a precinct each party has a volunteer **precinct captain** who organizes party workers to distribute in-

---

SECTION PREVIEW

Objective
After studying this section, you should be able to:
- Summarize the characteristics of political party organization.
- Identify the functions that political parties fulfill.

Key Terms and Concepts
independent, precinct, precinct captain, ward, state central committee, national convention, national committee, patronage

Themes in Government
- Growth of Democracy
- Political Processes

Critical Thinking Skills
- Analyzing Information
- Understanding Cause and Effect

CHAPTER 8: POLITICAL PARTIES **237**

Classroom Resources for Section 2

- Guided Reading Activities
- Reproducible Lesson Plans
- Participating in Government 8
- Interpreting Political Cartoons 6

- Section 2 Quiz
- Testmaker
- SAT Practice Tests
- Writer's Guidebook

Focus

Bell Ringer

While attendance is being taken, ask students to reread the definition of *political party* on page 232 and to write an answer to the following question: Based on this definition, what would you think are the functions of a political party?

Motivating Activity

Ask for volunteers to read their Bell Ringer answers. (*Responses should focus on preparing for and contesting elections and operating government.*) Then provide each student with a ballot—a piece of paper about 4 inches square. Ask students to write on their ballots the name of their favorite personality from the sports or entertainment world. Collect the ballots, then tally the results and announce the winner of the "election." Next, ask students to discuss the following: If you had the opportunity to campaign for your choice in this election, what would you have done? Steer the discussion toward such themes as joining with others of similar opinions, informing the electorate of the candidate's qualities, and so on. Close the discussion by mentioning that one focus of Section 2 is how political parties contest elections.

Vocabulary Precheck

Write the key terms and concepts for this section on the chalkboard. Ask students to explain how each term or concept relates to political party organization and functions. **LEP**

Teach

Guided Practice

L1 **Making Comparisons** Poll students by secret ballot to find their party affiliation. If students consider themselves neither Democrat nor Republican, or they do not know, suggest that they write *Independent*. Tally the results and record them, in percentage terms, on the chalkboard. Then point out that polls on political affiliation usually produce results that show voters nearly equally divided among Democrats, Republicans, and Independents. Lead a discussion comparing class results with national results. **LEP**

Chart Study Answer

The national convention which meets only every four years is outside the party structure. The national committee runs the national party's affairs and plans the convention itself.

STUDY GUIDE

Theme Answer
contacting voters by telephone, providing voters with campaign literature, organizing transportation to the polls

Critical Thinking Answer
Volunteers may have less incentive and dedication than paid workers. Students' opinions will vary.

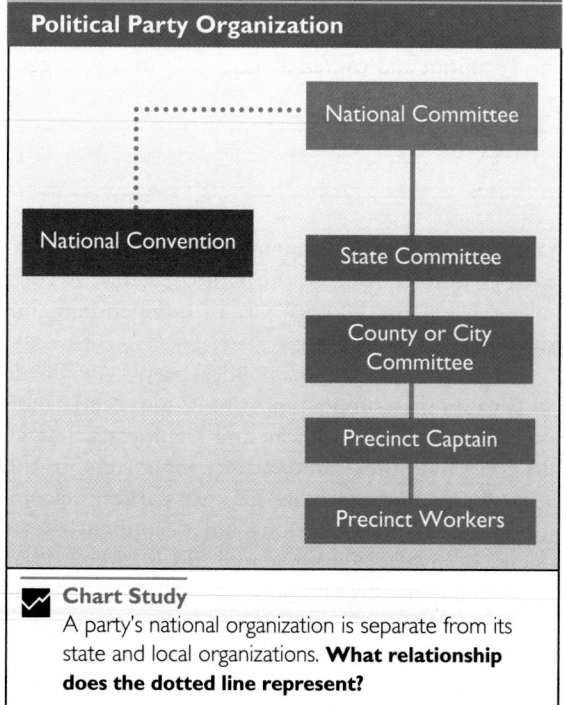

Political Party Organization

- National Committee
- National Convention
- State Committee
- County or City Committee
- Precinct Captain
- Precinct Workers

Chart Study
A party's national organization is separate from its state and local organizations. **What relationship does the dotted line represent?**

formation about the party and its candidates and to get the voters to the polls. Several adjoining precincts comprise a larger district called a **ward**. Party members in each ward select a person, also unpaid, to represent the ward at the next level of party organization—the party's county committee.

The county is the level at which the party is most united. The county committee selects a chairperson to handle the county party's daily affairs. The chairperson usually has a great deal of political power in the county. He or she is very often the key figure in determining which candidate receives the party's support. If the state's governor, for example, is from the same party, he or she may seek recommendations from the county chairperson when appointing judges and administrative officials.

At the same time, however, local parties are the weakest link in the organizational chain. One study of political parties concluded that:

The vast majority of local parties are essentially voluntary organizations. . . . They have the least influence and the fewest resources. The combination of . . . reliance on volunteers in an era when volunteers are hard to find, complex campaign finance regulations, and the general low regard in which parties are held combine to discourage the best leadership or the greatest participation.

—Xandra Kayden and Eddie Mahe, Jr.
The Party Goes On, 1985

State Party Organization In each state the most important part of a party is the **state central committee**, which usually is composed largely of representatives from the party's county organizations. The state central committee chooses the party's state chairperson. In selecting this person, however, the committee generally follows the wishes of the governor, a United States senator, or some other party leader powerful in state politics.

A main function of the state central committee is to help elect the party's candidates for state government offices. In addition, it may provide assistance to local parties and candidates and may help coordinate the activities of the local parties. Of course, it also works hard at raising money.

National Party Organization The national party organization has two main parts—the **national convention** and the national committee. The national convention is a gathering of party members and local and state party officials. It meets every four years, primarily to nominate the party's presidential and vice-presidential candidates. Beyond this function it has very little authority.

Between conventions the party's **national committee**, a large group composed mainly of representatives from the 50 state party organizations, runs the party. Some members of Congress and some state and local elected officials also may sit on the national committee, as may other selected party members.

STUDY GUIDE

Themes in Government
Growth of Democracy
Fewer and fewer registered voters bother to vote anymore. **How can a precinct captain work to overcome voter apathy?**

Critical Thinking Skills
Analyzing Information
Some people feel that local party organizations are less effective because they rely on volunteer workers rather than paid workers. **Do** you agree or disagree? Explain your answer.

---

238 Unit 3: Influencing Government

Background

A recent survey of political parties in 27 states underscored the decentralized nature of party organization. The leading state officials of both the Democratic and Republican parties said that they had little involvement in national committee affairs. National party leaders said they tended not to intervene in state party affairs unless expressly asked to do so. By and large, this "intervention" consisted of sharing research and poll results, settling rules disputes, and providing campaign instructions.

A chairperson elected by the national committee manages the daily operation of the national party. Usually the person selected is the choice of the party's presidential candidate. The national chairperson also raises money for the party, touts its achievements, and promotes national, state, and local party cooperation.

Both the Democrats and the Republicans also have independent campaign committees for Congress. These committees provide assistance to senators and representatives who are running for reelection. They also provide resources to help challengers defeat senators and representatives from the other party.

Political Party Functions

The Constitution does not provide for political parties or even mention them. Yet, political parties are an essential part of the American democratic system. Through the election process, the people select the officials who will govern them. As part of this process, political parties perform several important functions. No other body or institution in American government performs these tasks.

Recruiting Candidates Political parties seek men and women who, because of their personal qualities, background, and overall ability, seem to have a good chance of being elected. Selecting candidates for public office and presenting them to the voters for approval is the major function of political parties. It is often said that political parties are election oriented rather than issue oriented. This characteristic helps the Republicans and the Democrats maintain their status as major parties. Although members within each party share a general ideology about government and society, wide differences often exist on specific issues, even among the party's elected officials. Republicans in the Senate may refuse to support a Republican President's request for legislation, for example, and House Democrats may vote on both sides of a bill. To maintain its broad appeal, each party tries to avoid disagreements about issues and focuses on uniting behind its candidates.

Educating the Public Despite efforts to avoid division, political parties do bring important issues to public attention. Each party publishes its position on the issues of the day, such as inflation, military spending, taxes, pollution, energy, and the environment.

PARTICIPATING IN GOVERNMENT

Working in a Political Campaign

Even if you are too young to vote, you can still support the candidate of your choice and learn first-hand about the election process. Volunteer to work in a political campaign.

In any election candidates welcome the enthusiasm of young supporters. The work generally starts early in the year before the party primary. Volunteers are needed to help with the mailing effort by stuffing envelopes with campaign literature. Volunteers also attend political rallies for their candidates, and they encourage others to at-

tend. Campaign workers advertise their candidates by asking permission to display posters in store windows and by distributing bumper stickers.

As the primary or general election draws nearer, volunteers may be sent around their neighborhoods to distribute literature or talk to people about their candidate's qualifications and

stand on issues. During the last week before an election, volunteers may be asked to call people and remind them to vote. On Election Day campaign workers drive elderly or disabled voters to the polls.

Investigating Further

If you are interested in becoming involved in politics, you don't have to wait for an election year. Find out about activities sponsored by Teenage Republicans or Young Democrats of America in your community. Report your findings to the class.

Cooperative Learning Activity

Organize students into six groups and assign each group one of the six functions of political parties. Provide each group with a sheet of paper divided into two columns headed *Why?* and *Why Not?* Using the round-robin technique, have each group member write a reason why their assigned function should or should not be performed by political parties. Ask group representatives to read their reasons to the class. If any students disagree with a reason, encourage them to make a challenge.

L2 Analyzing Charts Have students study the chart on the organization of political parties on page 238. Select students to explain the chart to the rest of the class. Prompt students by asking such questions as: What levels of organization exist in the party structure? What functions does each level perform? Then lead students in a discussion of how authority operates in American political parties.

L3 Political Science Review the information on political party functions on pages 239–241. Then organize students into small groups and have them work together to think of a "real life" example of each function. Provide the following sample: nominating candidates—the Republican National Convention is held in Houston. Have groups compare their examples.

PARTICIPATING IN GOVERNMENT

Poll the class to see if any students have been involved in political campaigns. Ask those who have to share their experiences with the rest of the class.

Have students complete activity 8 in *Participating in Government* in the Teacher's Classroom Resources.

GLENCOE TECHNOLOGY

Focus on Government
Video 40
Lecture Launcher:
Taxing and Spending
Running Time: 3:44
Videodisc 3, Chap. 40
VHS Tape 3, Begins 0:00

Independent Practice

L2 Interviewing Have students interview officials of their local political parties (precinct captains, ward officials, and so on). Suggest that students focus their questions on how the local party is organized and how it relates to state and national party organizations. Select students to present their findings to the class.

Caption Answer
Campaign work enables people to get involved and support candidates and issues they believe in.

Theme Answer
Negative campaigning grabs voters' attention and appeals to emotions.

Critical Thinking Answer
to win party support at reelection time

Assess

Check for Understanding
Have students complete Section 2 Review on page 241.

Meeting Objectives
Each section objective is tested by the Section Review questions that follow it in parentheses.
• Summarize the characteristics of political party organization. (2, 3, 5, 6, 8)
• Identify the functions that political parties fulfill. (3, 4, 6, 7)

Party officials and candidates present these views in pamphlets, press conferences and speeches, and television and newspaper advertisements. These devices help citizens form opinions on controversial topics and give voters a choice between alternate approaches to important issues.

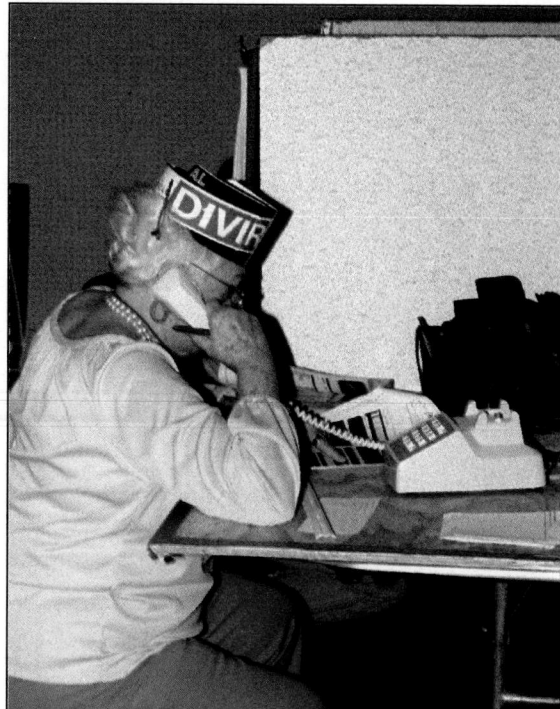

Working at the Precinct
Volunteers who help deliver the vote form the backbone of every political campaign. **History Why do people volunteer to work for political parties?**

Sometimes major party candidates feel safer attacking their opponent's views than stating their own. Important issues can become lost in a sea of personal attacks. When major party candidates fail to address key issues, a minor party candidate may force debate on these subjects. In 1992 Ross Perot brought his concern for the national debt and the nation's economic problems to the campaign agenda.

Unfortunately, many Americans are not well informed about important issues or the background of candidates. One political scientist explains it this way:

While the typical European voter may be called upon to cast two or three ballots in a four year period, many Americans are faced with a dozen or more separate elections in the space of four years.

To make a rough analogy, it would probably take an individual approximately the amount of time required for one or two college-level courses a year in order to cast a completely informed vote for all of these offices in all of these elections. Therefore, voters need shortcuts, or cues, such as partisanship [political parties], to facilitate their decision-making.
—MARTIN P. WATTENBERG, *THE DECLINE OF AMERICAN POLITICAL PARTIES, 1952-1984*

Political parties simplify elections by helping such people decide how to vote. By supporting a candidate just because he or she is a Democrat or a Republican, the voter knows generally how the candidate stands on key issues. The political party helps voters assess which candidate will be more acceptable.

Operating the Government Political parties also play a key role in running and staffing the government. Congress and the state legislatures are organized and carry on their work on the basis of party affiliation. Party leaders in the legislatures make every effort to see that their members support the party's position when considering legislation.

A party also acts as a link between a legislature and a chief executive. A chief executive works through his or her party leaders in the legislature to promote the administration's program. Frequently, however, political power is divided. One party controls the White House and the other controls one or both houses of Congress. In recent years this situation has developed between the governor and the legislature in more than half the states. This power split has reduced the ability of political parties to organize and operate government.

Themes in Government
Political Processes
Mud-slinging campaigns between political opponents are now all too common. **Why do candidates resort to negative campaigning?**

Critical Thinking Skills
Understanding Cause and Effect
Office holders and their political parties continue to work together after elections. **What long-range reason would make an already**

elected official careful to keep up a good relationship with his or her political party?

Special Needs Strategy

Learning Disability Students with conceptual or organizational learning problems may have difficulty answering question 6 in the Section Review. Have students make a chart listing issues-oriented activities (*drawing up a platform, holding press conferences, guiding legislators, staffing government* *jobs*) and election-oriented activities (*recruiting candidates, organizing party workers, attacking political opponents*). Discuss recent elections, asking students for specific examples of issues-oriented and election-oriented activities.

Dispensing Patronage Political parties also dispense **patronage,** or favors given to reward party loyalty, to their members. These favors often include jobs, contracts, and appointments to government positions. Business executives who contribute heavily to a political party, for example, may expect government to be sympathetic to their problems if that party comes to power. They may be awarded contracts to provide government with goods or services. Loyal party workers may be placed in government jobs. Although laws and court decisions have limited patronage in recent years, the practice remains a major way that parties control and reward their supporters.

The Loyal Opposition The party out of power in the legislative or executive branch assumes the role of "watchdog" over government. It observes the party in power, criticizes it, and offers its own solutions to political problems. If the opposition party does this successfully, public opinion may swing in its favor and return it to power in a future election. Concern about this possibility tends to make the party in power more sensitive to the will of the people.

Reduction of Conflict Within a complex society, conflict among many groups with differing interests is inevitable. To win an election, a political party must attract support from many different groups. To accomplish this, a party encourages groups to compromise and work together. A key outcome of this process is that parties encourage government to adopt moderate policies with mass appeal.

Parties contribute to political stability in another way, too. When one party loses control of the govern-

Transfer of Power Problems
The military forced Haiti's elected president, Jean Bertrand Aristide, from office until 1994.
History How do parties help ensure the peaceful transition of power?

ment, the transfer of power takes place peacefully. No violent revolutions occur after elections, as in some nations. In the United States, the losing party accepts the outcome of elections because its leaders know that the party in power will not attempt to silence it. The defeated party will continue to exist as the opposition party and someday will return to power.

---

2 SECTION REVIEW

Section Summary
American political parties are highly decentralized and democratic. They perform several important functions in the operation of government.

Checking for Understanding
Recalling Facts
1. Define independent, precinct, precinct captain, ward, state central committee, national convention, national committee, patronage.
2. Identify the three levels at which each major political party functions.
3. Compare the office of party chairperson at each level of party operations.

4. List six functions political parties perform.
Exploring Themes
5. Growth of Democracy Why can the Republican and Democratic parties be called open parties?
6. Political Processes Why have the two major parties become more election oriented and less issues oriented?

Critical Thinking Skills
7. Analyzing Information Why are many Americans uninformed about the issues in a campaign?
8. Understanding Cause and Effect What are the advantages and the disadvantages of decentralized organization for political parties?

Caption Answer
Losing parties know they can be an opposing voice that will not be silenced by the winning party. Also they may regain power.

Evaluate
📁 Section 2 Quiz
💻 Testmaker

Reteach
Have students work in groups of three to construct a chart showing the organization of political parties at the local, state, and national levels.

Enrich
A strong party organization, especially at the local level, can monopolize control of the government. Interested students might like to research and write a report on one such party organization, the Democratic machine in Chicago.

📁 **Interpreting Political Cartoons** Have students complete activity 6 in *Interpreting Political Cartoons* in the Teacher's Classroom Resources.

Close
Ask students to provide examples of how political parties in the United States contribute to political stability and national unity.

Section 2 Review Answers

1. Definitions of terms appear on pages indicated: **independent,** 237; **precinct,** 237; **precinct captain,** 237; **ward,** 238; **state central committee,** 238; **national convention,** 238; **national committee,** 238; **patronage,** 241
2. local or county, state, and national
3. Each is chosen by his or her party organization to manage party's day-to-day affairs. Each exercises consider-

able power, but national chairperson wields greatest power.
4. recruiting candidates, educating public, operating government, dispensing patronage, watchdog over government, reducing conflict
5. Anyone can belong simply by declaring himself or herself a member.
6. Each party seeks mass appeal and broad base of voters. Taking clear positions on issues may diminish party base.

Emphasizing common goal of electing candidates builds unity.
7. Answers should note number of elections and races confronting voters, and issues avoidance by parties and candidates.
8. Answers might include: advantages—no one person or group controls all decisions, decisions made at appropriate level; disadvantages—party organization might not run smoothly and efficiently

Focus

Ask students what government should do about unemployment. Write several responses on the chalkboard. Then have students divide the proposals into liberal and conservative responses.

Teach

Have students distinguish between liberals and conservatives. Then ask: How can you determine which a person might be? *(by comparing their views to liberal and conservative positions)* Remind students that ideologies are only general labels and that other factors may influence a person's opinion on any specific issue. For example, few people vote straight party tickets. Ask students why a supporter of one party might vote for a candidate of the opposition party? *(differences on a specific issue)* Ask if a person's ideology can ever change. *(A person's experiences may change his or her ideology.)*

Assess

Have students complete the **Practice** exercise.

Close

Ask how the ability to recognize the ideology of a political candidate helps voters make informed choices.

CRITICAL THINKING SKILLS

Recognizing Ideologies

Recognizing ideologies involves understanding the beliefs that guide a person or group. If you know a group's ideology, you know many of its values and assumptions, and you can make fairly reliable predictions about its positions on many issues.

Explanation

To decide on the ideological orientation of an author, follow these steps:

• Read the passage carefully, then try to put the author's main points into your own words.
• Compare the author's ideas to what you know of liberal and conservative ideologies.
• If you find a close fit between the ideas expressed and a particular ideology, chances are the author holds other views associated with that ideology.

An ideology is a set of beliefs about government and society. Ideologies are important in shaping parties' platforms. Ideologies also change over time. In recent decades two major ideologies have dominated American politics: liberalism and conservatism. Liberals generally support a strong role for the federal government in promoting minority rights, social reform, and efforts to regulate the economy. Conservatives generally want to limit the role of government in solving social problems.

Read the following passage:

To say "that government is best which governs least" is not to yearn for anarchy: it is to say that those laws are best that don't require a huge apparatus of surveillance and enforcement. The foolishness of Prohibition was that it pitted the law against deep-rooted ways of life. Socialism makes the same mistake on an even larger scale.
—JOSEPH SOBRAN,
NATIONAL REVIEW, DECEMBER 31, 1985

The first step in analyzing an author's ideological orientation is to restate the passage in your own words. The previous passage might be paraphrased as follows: "Laws that go against traditional ways in order to promote reform violate people's liberty."

The second step is to compare the main ideas with different ideologies. The author is concerned with preserving tradition and individual liberties and opposes social experimentation. These are conservative opinions. You can predict that the author will hold conservative views on other subjects.

Remember that such predictions can only be educated guesses. Liberal and conservative ideologies vary from time to time and from individual to individual. Many people take liberal positions on one issue and conservative positions on other issues.

Practice

Now read the following passage, and use what you have learned about ideologies to answer the questions that follow:

The welfare state is based, in the first place, upon acceptance of collective responsibility for providing all individuals with equality of opportunity. . . . Second . . . the welfare state assumes responsibility for the basic economic security of those who are unable . . . to provide such security for themselves. . . . Third, the welfare state assumes the responsibility for reducing great disparities [inequalities] in the distribution of wealth. . . . Finally, the welfare state assumes the responsibility for promoting the full employment of our manpower. . . .
—HUBERT H. HUMPHREY,
THE AMERICAN SCHOLAR, AUTUMN, 1955

1. What does the author mean by "the welfare state"? Does he approve or disapprove of it?
2. State the author's main points in your own words.
3. Do you think that the author is liberal or conservative? Explain your answer.
4. What position do you think the author would take on wage and price controls to combat inflation?

Additional Practice

To practice this skill, see **Reinforcing the Skill** on page 253.

Practice Answers

1. those functions of the federal government that relate to the social and economic welfare of citizens; approves
2. Four important functions of the federal government are to guarantee equality of opportunity, provide economic security to the unfortunate, redistribute wealth, and promote full employment and economic productivity.
3. liberal; he indicates his approval of strong federal government (able to perform the functions of the welfare state) and strong

government involvement in the economy.
4. Students should see that the liberal position would be to support government programs to promote social reform and regulate the economy.

For additional practice, have students complete activity 8 in *Skill Reinforcement Activities* in the Teacher's Classroom Resources.

Nominating Candidates for Office

The chief aim of a political party is to win elections and thereby gain control of government at the local, state, and national levels. To win elections, however, a party must first offer candidates and conduct campaigns.

How Candidates Are Selected

Individuals may seek nomination for public office in one of four ways: (1) caucus; (2) nominating convention; (3) primary election; or (4) petition. Although election laws vary greatly from state to state, all candidates reach the ballot through one or more of these methods.

Caucuses In early American history, **caucuses**—private meetings of party leaders—chose almost all candidates for office. The caucus became widely criticized as undemocratic, however, because most people had no say in selecting the candidates.

Nominating Conventions As political caucuses came under attack, the **nominating convention**, an official public meeting of a party to choose candidates for office, became popular. Under this system, local party organizations send representatives to a county nominating convention that selects candidates for county offices and chooses delegates who will go to a state nominating convention. The state convention, in turn, selects candidates for statewide office and chooses delegates who will go to the national convention.

In theory the convention system was more democratic than party caucuses because power would flow upward from the people. As the convention system developed, however, it became increasingly undemocratic. Powerful party leaders, called **bosses,** chose delegates and controlled conventions. Public reaction against the bosses led to another method of selecting candidates.

THE "BRAINS"

THAT ACHIEVED THE TAMMANY VICTORY AT THE ROCHESTER DEMOCRATIC CONVENTION.

Big Bucks Decide
In the nineteenth century, candidates were often selected by party bosses who were influenced by moneyed interests. **History** **How has the selection of candidates been made more democratic?**

SECTION PREVIEW

Objectives
After studying this section, you should be able to:
- Explain the role of primary elections in selecting candidates for office.
- Evaluate the current system for choosing presidential candidates.

- Describe the different types of primary elections.

Key Terms and Concepts
caucus, nominating convention, boss, direct primary, closed primary, open primary, plurality, runoff primary, ticket, platform, plank

Themes in Government
- Political Processes
- Civic Participation

Critical Thinking Skills
- Making Generalizations
- Analyzing Information

CHAPTER 8: POLITICAL PARTIES   243

Focus

Bell Ringer
While attendance is being taken, have students write the term that best completes this series: *caucus, primary, national nominating convention*

Motivating Activity
Discuss students' Bell Ringer responses. *(election/general election)* Then organize students into two groups, telling each group to imagine they are leading members of a political party. They must select a candidate and develop a party platform to contest an upcoming presidential election. Guide their decision-making discussions by asking the following questions: Will you select a small number of party leaders to choose a candidate? Will you poll all party members for a nomination? Will you hold a number of primary elections open to all voters to select your candidate? What issues do you think should be stressed in your platform? Have groups draw up a nominating and platform-writing plan for their party. Suggest that they compare their plans to the nominating and platform-writing methods used by the major parties.

Caption Answer
Nominating conventions and primary elections have opened up candidate selection.

CONNECTIONS

Language
The term *caucus*, which first entered the American language in the 1770s, probably derives from *caucauasu*, the Algonquin word meaning "adviser" or "counselor."

Classroom Resources for Section 3

- Guided Reading Activities
- Reproducible Lesson Plans
- Reteaching Activities 8
- Section 3 Quiz
- Chapter 8 Tests
- Testmaker

- Government Themes Transparencies 43
- Audio Cassettes (English and Spanish)
- Limited English Proficiency Activities 8
- Great Speeches, Volume IV
  SAT Practice Tests
  Writer's Guidebook

Vocabulary Precheck

List the key terms and concepts for this section on the chalkboard. Have volunteers skim the section for each term and concept and read it in context. **LEP**

Teach

Guided Practice

L1 **Vocabulary** Review for students the meaning of the following election terms: *caucus, convention, primary election, petition, general election, ballot, majority, plurality, runoff, nomination, ticket, proportional representation, platform, front-runner.* Select students at random, asking each to use one term correctly in a sentence. **LEP**

Caption Answer
to allow anyone to seek office

STUDY GUIDE

Theme Answer
A candidate must win acceptance from a wide variety of citizens, not just from a small, like-minded group of party officials.

Critical Thinking Answer
In the past, less-educated people often allowed others to make decisions on candidates for them. Today, however, better-educated people tend to want to make their own decisions.

Linking Past and Present
In 1968 just 14 states held presidential primaries. More than twice that number—38 states in all—held primaries in 1992.

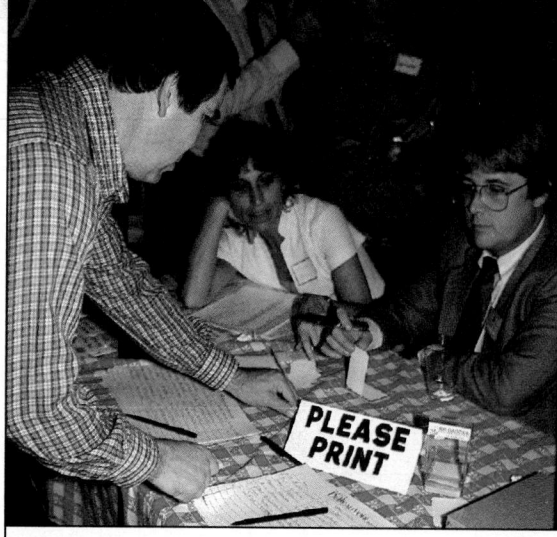

Getting on the Ballot
Some states require prospective candidates to submit petitions signed by their supporters. **Political Processes** **Why was the petition process initiated?**

In the early 1900s, primary elections began to replace nominating conventions at the state and local levels.

Primary Elections The method most commonly used today to nominate candidates is the **direct primary,** an election in which party members select people to run in the general election. Two types of primary elections are used in the United States. Most states hold a **closed primary,** where only members of a political party can vote. Thus, only Democrats pick Democratic candidates for office, and only Republicans can vote in the Republican primary. In an **open primary,** all voters may participate, even if they do not belong to the party, but they can vote in only one party's primary.

Primary elections are conducted according to state law and are held at regular polling places just as general elections are. Each state sets the date of its primary, provides the ballots and the people to supervise the election, and counts the votes. In most states a primary candidate does not need a majority of the votes to win, but only a **plurality,** or more votes than any other candidate. In a few states, however, if no candidate receives a majority, a **runoff primary** is held. The runoff is a second primary election between the two candidates who received the most votes in the first primary. The person who wins the runoff becomes the party's candidate in the general election.

In most states today, candidates for the House, Senate, governor and other state offices, and most local offices are selected in primary elections. In many states, however, party caucuses and nominating conventions continue to exist alongside primaries.

Petition Under this method a person announces his or her candidacy and files petitions a specified number of voters have signed to be placed on the ballot.

Some states require that all candidates file petitions. In a primary contest, the caucus or convention candidate has an advantage because party workers will circulate petitions. The party will also use its financial and organizational resources to back its choice. Candidates without caucus or convention support have serious obstacles to overcome. If such a candidate poses a serious threat, however, party leaders frequently are willing to make a deal. They might offer the challenger party support for another office, or appointment to a government post, to avoid a primary. Political analyst Theodore H. White once explained why:

Established leaders hate primaries for good reason; they are always, in any form, an appeal from the leaders' wishes to the people directly. Primaries suck up and waste large sums of money from contributors who might better be tapped for the November finals; the charges and countercharges of primary civil war provide the enemy party with ammunition it can later use with blast effect against whichever primary contender emerges victorious.

—Theodore H. White,
The Making of the President, 1960, 1961

STUDY GUIDE

Themes in Government
Political Processes
As the nominating process broadened, more people helped to choose candidates. **Why is a pri-** mary election better than a party caucus for selecting candidates?

Critical Thinking Skills
Making Generalizations
How might the difference between people's level of education in earlier times and today account for the methods of candidate selection then and now?

Background

The first presidential primary is held in New Hampshire, while the earliest caucuses are in Iowa. Both events usually take place in mid-February of a presidential election year. Even though these two small states represent only a handful of the votes needed to win the nomination, most presidential hopefuls actively campaign there. A good showing in the New Hampshire primary and the Iowa caucuses can give a candidate "Big Mo"—momentum—going into later primaries in the bigger states.

Presidential Nominations

The most exciting and dramatic election in American politics is the presidential election. Every 4 years, each major party gathers during July or August in a national convention. Elected or appointed delegates representing the 50 states, Guam, Puerto Rico, the Virgin Islands, American Samoa, and the District of Columbia attend the convention. Their task is to select a **ticket**—candidates for President and Vice President—that will win in the November general election. Because this ticket, if elected, can change history and affect every American's life, millions of Americans watch the televised coverage of the conventions. The drama and spectacle of a convention, however, has not always been so open to the public's view. Neither have presidential nominations always been as democratic as they are today.

The History of Presidential Nominations Before national nominating conventions, congressional caucuses chose presidential candidates. From 1800 to 1824, congressional leaders from each party met in secret and selected their party's ticket. In the presidential election of 1824, Andrew Jackson made the caucus system an issue, declaring that a small group of representatives did not speak for the nation. Although Jackson lost the election, his revolt against "King Caucus," as he called it, discredited the caucus system and led to the eventual adoption of the nominating convention.

A minor political party, the Anti-Masons, held the first national convention in 1831, an idea that the two major parties quickly copied. Since 1832 a convention of party members has chosen major party presidential candidates. To make these conventions more democratic, by 1916 almost half the states were choosing convention delegates in presidential primary elections.

For years, when citizens voted in a presidential primary, they really were choosing between groups of party members pledged to support specific candidates. The group pledged to the winning candidate became that state's delegation to the national convention.

In the 1970s, however, both major parties provided more democracy in the nomination process. For example, new party rules encouraged that women, minorities, and young people be included as convention delegates. By 1988 presidential primaries existed in 38 states and were part of the selection process for three-fourths of the delegates to the two national conventions.

Jackson Tackles "King Caucus"
In the 1824 presidential race, the caucus system was successfully attacked by Andrew Jackson, who would emerge victorious in the 1828 election. **History How have conventions become more democratic?**

Presidential Primaries Today Like other primary elections, presidential primaries operate under a wide variety of state laws. In addition, each party frequently changes its rules regarding delegate selection. Even in the same state, each party's primary may operate under different procedures. The following three generalizations, however, can be made about presidential primaries: (1) They may be a delegate selection process or a presidential preference poll, or both. (2) Either the candidate who wins the primary gets all the state's convention delegates (called "winner-take-all"), or each candidate gets delegates based on how many popular votes he or she receives in the primary. (3) Delegates selected on the basis of the popular vote may be required to support a certain candidate at the national convention, or they may be uncommitted.

Many presidential primaries were winner-take-all, but rule changes in the 1970s established proportional representation. Under this system a state's delegates must represent the candidates in proportion to the popular vote each receives in the primary.

Although proportional representation was intended to make a party's nomination process more democratic, in many states it had an unanticipated result. Combined with the other rules parties had established for state delegations, proportional representation made delegate selection almost impossibly complicated. Thus today more than half the states

Chapter 8, Section 3
Lesson Plan, pages 243–251

L2 Constructing a Flow Chart Ask students to work in small groups to construct a flow chart showing all the steps from declaring candidacy through general election that a candidate might follow in their state. Have groups compare their flow charts.

L3 Debate Have students conduct a debate on the pros and cons of the presidential primary system. Begin the debate by calling on a student who favors presidential primaries to speak for approximately one minute. Then have a student who opposes presidential primaries speak for a similar amount of time. Continue this procedure until several students have spoken for each side of the issue. Close by asking students if they favor or oppose the presidential primary system.

Caption Answer
some delegates selected by presidential primaries, greater representation of women and minorities

Interpreting Visuals Display transparency 43 from the *Government Themes Transparencies* in the Teacher's Classroom Resources and use the accompanying teaching strategy and student activity to teach about nominating conventions.

Cooperative Learning Activity

Organize students into three groups and assign one of the following to each: caucus, primary, nominating convention. Have groups develop a one-minute advertisement showing why their assigned method is the best way for a political party to select candidates for public office. Group members should divide work on the project among themselves—some might conduct research, others might write the advertisement script, and so on. Have groups perform or broadcast their advertisements for the class.

Independent Practice

L1 **Geography** Distribute outline maps of the United States that have state boundaries marked. Provide students with the following title and map key: <u>Title</u>—When States Voted in the Presidential Nominating Season. <u>Key</u>—Voting in February; Voting in March Prior to Super Tuesday; Voting on Super Tuesday; Voting After Super Tuesday. Then ask students to use different colors to mark the states according to their appropriate primary dates. Information sources include current affairs magazines or the special election edition of *Congressional Quarterly Weekly Report*. **LEP**

L2 **Illustrating Ideas** Remind students that the presidential nomination "season" runs from February, when the first caucuses and primaries are held, to July or August, the time of the national party conventions. Have students work individually or cooperatively to construct a collage showing, month by month, the major events of the most recent Democratic and Republican nomination races. Collages might include photographs, cartoons, and newspaper headlines.

Caption Answer

to increase the state's influence in choosing presidential candidates

with presidential primaries hold what have come to be called "beauty contests." They are merely preference polls in which voters indicate which candidate they would like to be the nominee. Caucuses later choose delegates.

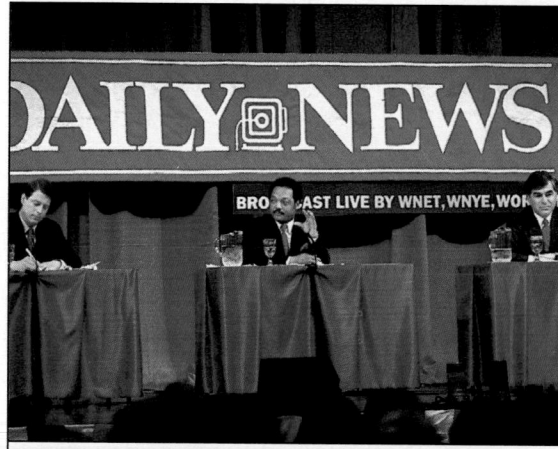

A Primary Battle of Words
Candidates for the 1988 Democratic nomination for President exchange views. **Federalism Why do states continue to experiment with primaries?**

Criticisms of Presidential Primaries While most people agree that the presidential primary system is a great improvement over the previous method of selecting convention delegates, it has its critics. A major criticism is that the primaries extend over too long a time. With the first primary held in February and the last in June, seeking a party's nomination is a very long, costly, and exhausting process. Many voters tend to lose interest during the months of campaigning.

Another criticism is that the primaries seem to make the image of the candidates more important than the issues. The news media's coverage of primary campaigns, especially television, tends to play up candidates' personalities rather than their positions on important questions. Also, relatively few people vote in primaries. Thus, the winner of a primary may not be as popular as the victory would indicate.

Candidates who win the early primaries capture the media spotlight. Often the other candidates are saddled with a "loser" image that makes it difficult for them to raise campaign contributions. Some are forced to drop out before the majority of voters in either party have the chance to pick their choice for the nominee.

Fourteen southern states joined together in 1988 to create a Democratic presidential regional primary

called "Super Tuesday." Candidates who did not fare well on this day lost hope of becoming their party's nominee. However, the "Super Tuesday" idea lost momentum in 1992 when fewer states participated.

Because primaries eliminate many opponents, they often result in one-sided convention victories for particular candidates. Some observers believe that the nominating convention itself has become simply a rubber-stamp operation. If the primary winners come to the convention with enough votes to win, they ask, why hold the nominating convention at all? Of course, it is possible that in the future, support for contenders will be more equally divided, in which case the convention will once again be an arena of real battles for the nomination.

The National Convention

From February to June, the candidates crisscross the country competing for delegate support. Meanwhile, the national committee staff is preparing for the convention.

Pre-Convention Planning Long before its convention meets, the national committee of each major party chooses the site and dates. The major parties traditionally hold their conventions in July or August, usually in a city in a politically important state—a state with a significant number of electoral votes. A party sometimes chooses a site in a state where the party's success in the election is in doubt in hopes of winning that state.

After the city and dates are chosen, the national committee tells each state party organization how many votes the state will have at the convention. In the past, states had the same number of convention votes as they had electoral votes. At recent conventions, however, the parties have used complicated formulas to determine the number of votes each state will have.

Assembling the Convention From across the country, thousands of delegates assemble in the convention city, accompanied by a mass of spectators, protesters, and news media representatives. When the delegates arrive, many are already pledged to a candidate, but others are not. All the candidates actively woo these uncommitted delegates. As rumors of political deals circulate, candidates hold news conferences, and reporters mill about in search of stories. One writer described a national convention as:

Special Needs Strategy

Language Disability Students with language organization or memory problems may have difficulty synthesizing the information on the nomination process. Have students read the text and identify the key aspects of the nomination process: *caucus, party convention, primary election, direct primary,* *closed primary, open primary, runoff primary, petition.* Then have students create a graphic organizer with *Election* at the center of a blank piece of paper. Ask students to draw lines to indicate the relationship of each of the above terms to *Election.*

*A*n American invention as native to the U.S.A. as corn pone or apple pie. . . . It has something of the gaiety of a four-ring circus, something of the sentiment of a class reunion, and something of the tub-thumping frenzy of a backwoods camp meeting.

—THEODORE H. WHITE

The delegates—in recent conventions, 2,277 Republicans, 4,162 Democrats—gather in a huge convention hall decorated with flags, pictures of famous party leaders, and banners and symbols of the party. The hall is a sea of people, ranging from the delegates on the main floor, to the spectators in the galleries, to the news reporters throughout the auditorium.

The noise and confusion subside as the party chairperson calls the opening session to order. The roll call of the states is read, and the delegates hear various welcoming speeches. The national party chairperson then asks the delegates to approve the people the national committee has selected to be temporary officers of the convention.

The evening of the opening day marks the keynote speech, an address by an important party member intended to unite the party for the coming campaign. The delegates then approve the convention's four standing committees—rules and order of business, credentials, permanent organization, and platform and resolutions—that have been at work for several weeks.

Because in recent conventions there has been little suspense about who would be either party's candidate, the only real conflict has involved committee reports. The convention spends the second and third days, or even longer, listening to these reports and to speeches about them.

The Rules Committee Each party's rules committee governs the way its convention is run. The committee proposes rules for convention procedure and sets the convention's order of business. The delegates must approve any proposed changes in the rules

GLOBAL CONNECTION

Comparing Governments

Party Systems In the United States third parties may sponsor candidates, but the winning candidate for a major elective office will most likely be either a Democrat or a Republican. Our electoral system discourages strong third parties. Only one candidate can be elected to each office on a ballot.

India, Italy, and Japan, however, are among the countries with multiparty systems. These systems generally have four or five major parties and several minor parties.

In a multiparty system, one party rarely wins the support of a majority of voters. Therefore, two or more parties form a coalition government. If the members of the coalition disagree on policies, the government fails.

Examining the Connection
Would you support a multiparty system in this country? Why or why not?

of the last convention. Although the rules committee report is usually accepted, at times real battles have developed over it. The outcome of a rules fight can be vital to a candidate for the presidential nomination. For example, at the 1980 Democratic convention, Senator Edward Kennedy was eager to capture the nomination, even though President Jimmy Carter had won a majority of the delegates in the primaries. Kennedy knew that many of the Carter delegates were not strong supporters of the President. Was there a way that he could get some of those Carter delegates to support him for the nomination?

The chance came on a vote to approve or disapprove a rule binding delegates to vote for the candi-

Major parties often ally with smaller parties to attain the parliamentary majority needed to gain control of the government. So, while small parties may only have a handful of seats in parliament, they can wield considerable power in the coalition government. **Examining the Connection Answer:** *Discuss students' opinions of the multiparty system.*

STUDY GUIDE

Critical Thinking Answer
It increased the South's influence in choosing nominees.

Linking Past and Present
The rules under which the Democratic nominating process operated in 1980 doomed Senator Edward Kennedy's attempt to win the presidential nomination. The 1992 rules would have made Kennedy's challenge much easier, for there were 772 "superdelegates"—about 18 percent of all delegates—who were not tied by their states' primary or caucus results.

STUDY GUIDE

Themes in Government
Civic Participation
Some argue that proportional representation should replace the winner-take-all electoral vote in presidential elections as well.

Critical Thinking Skills
Analyzing Information
Support for a large regional primary—"Super Tuesday"— is weak.
Why did it benefit southern states

to join in holding such a regional primary in 1988?

Critical Thinking Activity

Analyzing Information Point out to students that the process by which the major political parties select presidential candidates often has been criticized. Have students review the information on page 246. Then ask them to write a brief paragraph to answer the following: Do you think these criticisms are valid? Why or why not? What changes would you make to improve the selection process for presidential candidates? Have students compare their answers.

L3 Classificatory Writing Have students study the platforms of the two major parties for the most recent presidential election. These may be obtained from local party offices. Ask students to write an essay comparing the two platforms. Their essays should focus on such areas as taxes, civil rights, social security, welfare programs, education, and defense. Students might end their essays with an explanation of which, if either, platform would win their votes. Select students to read their essays to the class.

Caption Answer
Representation of women and minorities in state delegations improved.

CONNECTIONS

Political Processes
Although a compromise settled the credentials fight at the 1972 Democratic Convention, Chicago mayor Richard J. Daley did not actively support George McGovern in the presidential campaign because Daley suspected that McGovern's aides had played a role in the challenge to the Illinois delegation.

date who had won their state primary. If the rule was defeated, the Carter delegates would be free to support whomever they wished. Kennedy felt that many of the Carter delegates would then switch to him. When Kennedy lost this rules vote, he also lost whatever chance he had for the nomination.

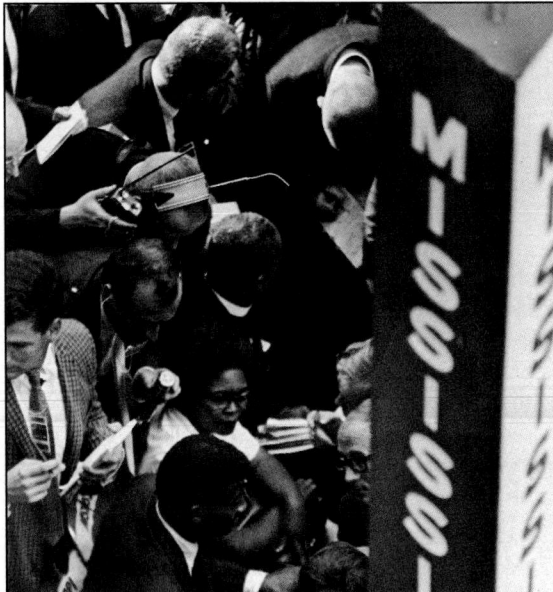

African Americans Wage Credentials Battle
The Mississippi Freedom Democratic party fought to participate in the 1964 Democratic convention. History **How did this battle affect future conventions?**

The Credentials Committee The credentials committee must approve the delegations from each state. Sometimes disputes arise over who the proper delegates are. Candidates who trail in delegate support may challenge the credentials of their opponents' delegates. Two entire rival delegations may even appear at the convention, each claiming to be a state's official delegation. It is up to the credentials committee to determine which delegates should be seated. Although the committee's decisions may be appealed on the convention floor, the delegates generally accept its report without changes.

Fights over credentials often have been livelier than rules fights at national conventions. In 1964, for example, African Americans at the Democratic convention charged that an all-white Mississippi delegation had excluded them, giving the African American citizens of Mississippi no representation at the convention. The credentials committee allowed some African Americans to be seated in the Mississippi delegation. In 1968 the same situation occurred. The committee refused to seat another all-white Mississippi delegation, and this time replaced it with an integrated rival delegation.

In 1972, a fight arose because the Illinois delegation, headed by Chicago mayor Richard J. Daley, did not comply with party rules on minority representation. Although a compromise was reached, the powerful Democratic leader and his organization did not actively support the party's candidate in the presidential campaign.

The Committee on Permanent Organization This committee selects the permanent chairperson and other permanent officials for the convention. After it reports, the delegates elect the permanent convention officials who take the day-to-day control of the convention from the temporary officials.

The Platform Committee The platform committee, as its name suggests, is assigned an important task—the writing of the party's **platform,** a statement of its principles, beliefs, and positions on vital issues. It also spells out how the party intends to deal with these issues. The party must try to adopt a platform that appeals to all factions, or divisions, at the convention—not always an easy task.

Part of the difficulty in getting platforms accepted is that individual parts of the platform, called **planks,** may divide the delegates. In 1968, for example, a pro-Vietnam War plank angered Democrats who wanted the United States to withdraw from that conflict. In 1980 the Republican platform contained a plank opposing the Equal Rights Amendment. Although this plank was controversial, it passed.

STUDY GUIDE

Themes in Government
Civic Participation
Years ago the major television networks carried the national conventions from opening to close. Due

to the lower viewer interest, they now cover only a few hours each day.

Critical Thinking
Analyzing Information
How did the credentials fight over the Mississippi delegates in the 1960s reflect what was then happening in society?

Cooperative Learning Activity

Show students one of the national convention speeches from "Great Speeches," Volume IV, *Social Studies Videos.* Then ask students to prepare a five-minute news broadcast on the speech. Some students might act as news anchors at the convention, some might act as reporters on the convention floor, others might be delegates giving their views on the speech, and still others might be "people in the street" giving their views. Have students make their broadcast for other civics and government classes.

Because the party's presidential candidate must support the platform, all contenders try to get their viewpoints into the platform. Rival candidates with opposing views often will create a fight over the platform. The danger is that a platform fight may divide the party. If the fight is bitter, as it was for Democrats in 1968, the party may become so divided that it loses the election.

Nominating the Candidates After each committee's reports are adopted, the highlight of the convention occurs. It is time to select the party's candidate for President. From the opening day, the leading contenders have been working to hold onto their delegates and to gain as many uncommitted delegates as possible.

Even if one candidate is clearly the front-runner, there still may be uncertainty over who will win. Rumors often sweep through the delegations. These rumors may say that the leading candidate does not have a majority of the delegates or that rival candidates are uniting behind closed doors to block the front-runner's nomination. Often, an air of tension hangs over the convention hall before the candidates are formally nominated. The nominating speech for each candidate sets off a demonstration, as supporters parade around the convention hall. After the nominating speeches and all the seconding speeches that follow are made, the balloting starts.

The convention chairperson now instructs the clerk to read the alphabetical roll call of the states, and the chairperson of each state delegation calls out the delegates' votes. The candidate who receives a majority of the votes becomes the party's nominee. If no candidate does, then further roll calls must be taken until one candidate wins a majority.

In recent conventions most candidates have been selected on the first ballot. In 24 conventions between 1900 and 1992, the Republican front-runner was selected on the first ballot 20 times, and the Democratic

Focus on Freedom

WASHINGTON'S FAREWELL ADDRESS

On September 17, 1796, nearing the end of his second term as President, George Washington announced that he would soon retire from public life. In the tradition of the times, Washington's Farewell Address was not delivered as a speech. Instead it was printed in a Philadelphia newspaper and later reprinted in other papers across the nation. In the speech Washington warned the American people of the dangers he believed were ahead. Among his concerns was the formation of political parties.

Let me . . . warn you in the most solemn manner against the baneful [very harmful] effects of the spirit of party. . . .

This spirit, unfortunately, is inseparable from our nature. . . . It exists under different shapes in all governments . . . and is truly their worst enemy. . . .

It serves always to distract the public councils and enfeeble the public administration. It agitates the community with ill-founded jealousies and false alarms; kindles the animosity of one part against another; foments occasionally riot and insurrection. . . .

There is an opinion that parties in free countries are useful checks upon the administration of government, and serve to keep alive the spirit of liberty. This within certain limits is probably true; and in governments of a monarchical cast patriotism may look with indulgence, if not favor, upon the spirit of party. But in those of the popular character, in governments purely elective, it is a spirit not to be encouraged. . . . There being constant danger of excess, the effort ought to be, by force of public opinion, to mitigate and assuage it. A fire not to be quenched, it demands a uniform vigilance to prevent its bursting into a flame, lest, instead of warming, it should consume.

—GEORGE WASHINGTON

Examining the Document

Reviewing Facts
1. Cite what Washington believed to be the harmful effects of political parties.
2. Describe the type of government under which political parties were acceptable to Washington.

Critical Thinking Skills
3. Making Inferences Why does Washington want to control political parties rather than abolish them?

CHAPTER 8: POLITICAL PARTIES **249**

Critical Thinking Activity

Making Generalizations Ask students to use the *Readers' Guide to Periodical Literature* to find magazine articles that review the 1996 presidential nominating process. Select a number of students to brief the class on the major points of their articles. Then ask students to write a paragraph answering the following:

Based on the information presented in these articles, what generalizations can be made about the efficiency and fairness of the presidential nominating process? What generalizations can be made about efforts to reform the process? Explain your responses.

Focus on Freedom

Tell students that the two men who contested the 1796 presidential election—Thomas Jefferson and John Adams—did not share Washington's views. Jefferson stated that if there was a clear choice between two factions, it would be dishonorable to follow a middle course. And Adams, while doubting the desirability of political parties, did not see them as a threat.

Answers

1. Partisanship distracts and weakens government, upsets and divides the people, and stirs up public unrest.
2. authoritarian forms of governments, such as monarchies
3. He believed that political partisanship could not be avoided.

Assess

Check for Understanding

Have students complete Section 3 Review on page 250.

Meeting Objectives

Each section objective is tested by the Section Review questions that follow it in parentheses.
- Explain the role of primary elections in selecting candidates for office. (2, 6, 7, 8)
- Evaluate the current system for choosing presidential candidates. (2, 3, 4, 5)
- Describe the different types of primary elections. (2, 5, 8)

Evaluate

 Section 3 Quiz

 Testmaker

Reteach

☐ Have students complete
activity 8 in *Reteaching Activities*
in the Teacher's Classroom
Resources.

Enrich

Have students interview someone who sought or who is seeking
a local political office. Suggest
that students focus their interview
questions on the procedures the
candidate had to follow to get on
the local ballot. Have students
report their findings to the rest of
the class.

Close

Have students imagine they are
writing a letter to high school
students in another country explaining how presidential candidates are selected. Discuss what
should be included in the letter.

CONNECTIONS

History

The first presidential nominee
to make an acceptance speech
was Franklin D. Roosevelt. In
a dramatic appearance before
the 1932 Democratic National Convention in Chicago he
promised "a new deal for the
American people."

Balancing the Ticket
George Bush chose Dan Quayle as his running mate at the 1988 Republican national
convention. **Politics Why is a balanced ticket important?**

tor from Massachusetts,
chose Lyndon Johnson,
an older Protestant sena-
tor from Texas, as his
running mate. In 1984,
Minnesota senator Wal-
ter F. Mondale made
New York representative
Geraldine Ferraro the
first female vice-presi-
dential candidate from
either major party.
George Bush, a 64-year-
old political moderate
from Texas, selected con-
servative Indiana senator
Dan Quayle, age 41, to
balance the Republican
ticket in 1988.

front-runner 19 times. The vice-presidential nomination, which normally takes place on the last day of the
convention, has created more suspense.

The Vice-Presidential Nomination Usually, the
party's presidential nominee selects a running mate,
and the convention automatically nominates the person chosen. Vice-presidential candidates are generally
selected to balance the ticket, meaning that he or she
has a personal, political, and geographic background
different from the presidential nominee. This balance
is designed to make the ticket appeal to as many voters as possible.

In 1960, John F. Kennedy, a young Catholic sena-

Adjournment With the nomination of the presidential and vice-presidential candidates, the convention is almost over. The presidential and vice-presidential nominees appear before the delegates and
make their acceptance speeches. These speeches intend to bring the party together, to attack the opposition party, to sound a theme for the upcoming
campaign, and to appeal to a national television audience.

The convention then adjourns. The delegates turn
homeward, emotionally and physically exhausted
from the sleepless nights and endless speeches. The
candidates set their sights on the general election.

3
SECTION REVIEW

Section Summary
Although a variety of methods has been used to
select candidates for public office, the primary election
is most common at all levels of government.

Checking for Understanding
Recalling Facts
1. Define caucus, nominating convention, boss, direct
   primary, closed primary, open primary, plurality,
   runoff primary, ticket, platform, plank.
2. Cite four ways that candidates for public office can
   get on the ballot.
3. Explain why the caucus system of choosing candidates is not democratic.
4. Summarize the criticisms of presidential primaries.

Exploring Themes
5. Political Processes Explain why proportional
   representation in presidential primaries is more
   democratic than winner-take-all.
6. Civic Participation Describe how people who have
   not been selected by their party can still become
   candidates for public office.

Critical Thinking Skills
7. Making Generalizations How might politics,
   democracy, and government in the United States
   be affected if there were no primary elections?
8. Analyzing Information Explain whether, in your
   opinion, the open primary or the closed primary is
   a better method of choosing candidates.

Section 3 Review Answers

1. Definitions of terms appear on pages indicated: **caucus,**
243; **nominating convention,** 243; **boss,** 243; **direct primary,** 244; **closed primary,** 244; **open primary,** 244; **plurality,** 244; **runoff primary,** 244; **ticket,** 245; **platform,**
248; **plank,** 248
2. caucus, nominating convention, direct primary, and
petition
3. Candidates chosen by few party leaders, not by all party

members or voters at large.
4. seeking nomination long, costly, and exhausting; candidates who make poor showing early may be forced out of
race before majority of party members make their choice;
this, and low voter turnout, may mean nominee not most
popular candidate
5. winner-take-all primary—candidate who polls most
votes takes all delegates, even though he or she may not
have been supported by majority of voters; proportional representation—candidates awarded delegates in accordance

with primary votes received
6. circulate petitions to get on ballot
7. general elections might offer many choices for each office—a candidate might be elected with only small percentage of vote; might require system of runoff elections
after general election
8. open primary—in a democracy selection of candidates
should not be left to party members alone; closed
primary—selecting candidates a party function that should
not be open to people who have no party ties

PERSONAL
PERSPECTIVES

PERSONAL PERSPECTIVES

Ron Brown and Clayton Yeutter on the 1992 Campaign

In May 1991, Democratic National Chairman Ronald H. Brown (right) spoke to a meeting of the Democratic Leadership Council called in Cleveland to map out strategy for the 1992 presidential campaign. In his address Brown touched upon many activities and problems that both major parties deal with on a daily basis.

I've always tried to be frank and clear in the past, and today will be no exception. . . . Others have tried to make this meeting about divisions in the Democratic party. I refuse to be a part of anyone's efforts to divide us. . . .

We have a lot to be proud of as Democrats, and a lot to be optimistic about. We're looking ahead to the future. . . . We're running the party like a campaign organization, not a bureaucracy. We're building a national campaign organization now. . . And last year was the test ride. . . .

We've put the old rules fights behind us; our nominating convention will be a solid opportunity to get our general election campaign underway.

We are a broad and diverse party; we draw our strength and build our policies from a breadth of backgrounds and experiences. . . . In our diversity, we cannot allow narrow caucuses or councils to speak for our party or distract us from our shared goal of winning back the White House.

We are one Democratic party. To win, we must be united. We must be willing—all of us—to come together as Democrats behind our nominee. And our nominee must rally all the members of our party. The many streams and tributaries of our party must flow together as a massive river of political power.

—RONALD H. BROWN, 1991

In June 1991, Clayton Yeutter (below), the Chairman of the Republican National Committee, addressed committee members in Houston, Texas — the site of the 1992 Republican national convention.

Texas just gets better and better the more you visit, I can tell you that. Everything is in place for a great convention and a great election for the Republican party. You all know the numbers that position us

well for significant gains in the House and Senate next year. You read the same polls I do—polls that demonstrate the trust the American people have in President Bush and [the] Republican party to solve the problems that face our country today. . . .

Ladies and gentlemen, as we sit here in George Bush's hometown, we have a lot to be proud of—[a] President who has demonstrated leadership, strength, wisdom, grace under pressure, confidence, and loyalty to his principles and beliefs. . . .

We stand for growth, for job creation, for competition, for individual freedom, for peace around the world, for leaders with the convictions to put forward dynamic ideas. . . .

—CLAYTON YEUTTER, 1991

Examining the Reading

Reviewing Facts
1. List **what Brown and Yeutter believe to be the strengths of their respective parties.**
2. Explain **what Yeutter believes the Republican party stands for.**

Critical Thinking Skills
3. Analyzing Information **Explain how, as Brown suggests, diversity could be both a strength and a weakness of a political party.**

CHAPTER 8: POLITICAL PARTIES 251

More About Personal Perspectives

In February 1989 Ron Brown became Chairman of the Democratic National Committee, the first African American to lead either major American political party. Formerly, Brown worked for the National Urban League, served as Jesse Jackson's convention manager at the 1988 Democratic convention, and as deputy chairman of the Democratic National Committee. Clayton Yeutter, former secretary of agriculture, was raised on a Nebraska farm during the Great Depression. Even as a teenager Yeutter's interest in politics soared. He received two degrees, one in law and the other a doctorate in agricultural economics.

Focus

Write *diversity, fights, united, narrow, trust, proud* on the chalkboard. Ask students which carry positive connotations and which carry negative ones. Have them note how Brown and Yeutter use these words.

Teach

Ask: What is the goal of the Democrats? *(to win back the White House)* What metaphor does Brown use to illustrate the unity and diversity of the Democrats? *(a mighty river fed by many tributaries)* According to Yeutter, what demonstrates Americans' trust in the Republicans? *(polls)* What are the Republicans proud of?

Assess

Have students complete **Examining the Reading.**

Answers

1. *Democrats:* diversity, background, experience; *Republicans:* trust of the people; confident, loyal, principled leader
2. growth, job creation, competition, individual freedom, world peace, leaders with dynamic ideas
3. Diversity strengthens a party and enables it to address the interests of a wide range of Americans. It weakens a party through internal power struggles.

Close

Have students discuss the differences between factional bickering and healthy debate.

Identifying Terms and Concepts

1. (a) ideology, (b) plank, (c) platform, (d) national convention, (e) ticket

2. (a) national convention, (b) caucus, (c) ticket, (d) bosses

Reviewing Facts and Ideas

1. Federalists/Democratic-Republicans; Democrats/National Republicans or Whigs; Democrats/ Republicans

2. single issue—narrow focus and voter appeal, generally dies when its issue loses importance (Free Soil, Liberty); ideological—broader focus and longer-lived, but its extreme positions give it narrow voter appeal (Communist, Socialist Labor, Libertarian); splinter—can focus on an issue, an ideology, and/or a person; rarely outlasts its leader (Progressive or Bull Moose, American Independent)

3. They support most of its ideas and/or candidates; they want to become more involved in political process.

4. to recruit and offer candidates for public office

5. closed primary—only party members may vote; open primary—all voters, regardless of party ties, may take part

6. congressional caucus until 1830s; national convention from 1830s to present, supplemented by primaries in some states since early 1900s

Applying Themes

1. Multiparty systems function most smoothly under proportional representation; two-party systems, for the most part, find single-member district representation efficient.

2. In a few instances, minor party candidates have influenced the outcome of elections. More often, the popularity of minor parties has influenced major parties' positions on particular issues. This

---

Summary and Significance

Although the United States is among the few nations that enjoy the democracy and stability of a two-party political system, minor parties have always played an important role in American politics. Unlike most minor parties, however, the two major parties are broad based and loosely organized. Both parties perform several political functions, the most important of which is to provide candidates for public office at the national, state, and local levels of government. Each party has attempted over the years to make the candidate selection process more democratic.

Identifying Terms and Concepts

Insert the correct terms into the sentences below. All terms will be used. Some terms will be used more than once.

bosses
ideology
plank
caucus
ticket
national convention
platform

1. A political party's _____ is expressed in each _____ of the _____ that it adopts at the _____ to select its _____.
2. Although the _____ replaced the party _____ in choosing its _____, the party's _____ continued to influence the nomination process.

Reviewing Facts and Ideas

1. Name the pairs of major parties that have existed in American history.
2. Compare the three types of third parties and name a party of each type.
3. Cite two reasons why people belong to political parties.
4. Name the main function of the two major political parties.
5. Contrast open and closed primaries.
6. Trace the changing methods used to select presidential candidates.

Applying Themes

1. Comparative Government What relationship exists between the methods of representation in democratic nations and their political-party system?
2. Growth of Democracy How has the presence of minor parties affected American politics?
3. Political Processes Why have third parties had so little success in the United States?
4. Civic Participation Identify the various ways that a person can support a political party.

Critical Thinking Skills

1. Understanding Cause and Effect The two major parties are criticized as being out of touch with the needs of many Americans. How might a successful third party affect the two major parties?
2. Making Generalizations Some critics have called for national primaries to nominate each party's presidential candidate. What would be the advantages and disadvantages of such a system?
3. Analyzing Information Explain why you agree or disagree with this statement: "Because the most important goal of a political party is to win elections and control government, third parties have failed in the American political system."

Linking Past and Present

In comparing the American political system to politics in other parts of the world, a noted historian made the following observations and conclusions:

The small ideological difference between our two political parties may be accounted for by the fact that their only disagreement is over means. Both

---

sometimes has resulted in the introduction of government policies or reforms.

3. Traditionally, minor parties have only appealed to small numbers of voters. This image as "a loser," along with a lack of national stature, makes it almost impossible for minor parties to raise money to wage winning campaigns. Further, state legislatures—controlled by the major parties—have passed laws to keep most third parties off the ballot.

4. voting for its candidates, contributing money, doing volunteer work, becoming party official

Democrats and Republicans have, on the whole, the same vision of the kind of society there ought to be in the United States. . . .

In Europe [citizens] are more [uncompromising] about politics because their politics is concerned with a more basic question: What shall be the ends of society?

In a country like Italy, for example, the political debate expresses nothing less than disagreement about the nature of "the good life" and "the good society." . . . In such a situation . . . political life is divisive. It does not express ends which all accept and seek to realize through politics. Rather it is simply another way of expressing disagreement over ends. And in a disintegrating society politics becomes a controversy over ends.

None of this is true in the United States. Here the number of people who do not accept the predominant values of our society is negligible. Politics here has therefore seldom, if ever, been . . . over ultimate values. . . .

—DANIEL J. BOORSTIN,
THE GENIUS OF AMERICAN POLITICS, 1953

Do you believe that Boorstin's views about American society, and the role that political parties play in it, are still valid? Explain your answer.

Writing About Government

Persuasive Writing Imagine you live in a colony that will soon gain independence. You have been named to a committee to plan the new independent government. The committee believes that the structure of this government will influence the development of political parties. Consider the advantages and disadvantages of one-party, two-party, and multiparty systems and write a report to the committee explaining your choice and the reasons for it.

Reinforcing the Skill

Recognizing Ideologies Read the following paragraph and use what you have learned about recognizing ideologies to answer the questions that follow.

It [our movement] is skeptical of those social programs that create vast and energetic bureaucracies to "solve social problems." . . . [It] has great respect for the power of the market to respond efficiently to economic realities while preserving the maximum degree of individual freedom. . . . [We] are well aware that traditional values and institutions do change over time, but [we] prefer that such change be gradual. . . . the individual who is abruptly "liberated" from the sovereignty of traditional values will soon find himself experiencing. . . vertigo and despair.

—IRVING KRISTOL, *NEWSWEEK,* JANUARY 19, 1976

1. **Restate** the author's main points in your own words.
2. **Match** the author's main points with aspects of conservative and liberal ideology.
3. **Describe** how you think he would respond to Hubert Humphrey's essay on the welfare state (p. 242). Which point do both essays mention? Do Kristol and Humphrey agree or disagree?

Investigating Further

1. **Individual Project** Research the history of American political parties. Choose one of these parties—either a major party or a third party—and write a brief history of it. Include a time line showing major events in the party's history.
2. **Cooperative Learning** The method by which delegates are selected to national nominating conventions depends on party rules and on the laws of each state. Organize a group to determine the process in your state. Choose a leader to coordinate the research. Divide the other members into project teams to inquire about state law and party rules and processes. Your teams should contact each party's county and state organizations and the local board of elections. Be sure to find out how many delegates your state sends to each party's national convention and how this number is determined. When all information is gathered and analyzed, present the findings to the class.

CHAPTER 8: POLITICAL PARTIES   253

Answers will vary. Some students may agree that the majority of Americans have a single set of social values. Others may suggest that in the years since Boorstin wrote this essay, society has become more fragmented, culturally diverse, and accepting of that diversity. By and large, the make-up and ideology of the major parties reflect these changes.

Writing About Government

Reports will vary.

Reinforcing the Skill

1. Typical response: I am suspicious of big government. I prefer that government not intervene in the economy, and that market forces are left to work unfettered. I believe that social change should come gradually and not be imposed by sudden reforms. I support measures to create equality of opportunity, but do not think equality of opportunity must end in equality of results.

2. The following points of the author's argument all reflect conservative ideology: opposition to large-scale social programs; concern with limiting government intervention in the economy; respect for traditional values; skepticism about reform.

3. Students should recognize that Kristol would oppose Humphrey's ideas about the responsibility of government to manage the economy and redistribute wealth. However, based on this excerpt, it appears that Kristol would agree with Humphrey's desire to ensure equality of opportunity for all Americans.

Investigating Further

1. Reports will vary.
2. Reports will vary.

Critical Thinking Skills

1. Students should recognize that the effect would be great because both the election process and the legislative process are set up around the two-party system.

2. Possible answer: <u>advantages</u>—national primary could reduce campaigning time, cut campaign costs, and force candidates to speak to national

issues; <u>disadvantages</u>—could make it more difficult for little-known candidates to make their mark, and force candidates to rely much more heavily on television to reach national electorate

3. Students should note that third parties generally are formed to bring new ideas to the people. Although they have had few candidates elected, many of their ideas have been accepted.

Chapter Organizer

Objectives	Special Feature Pages	Supplemental Materials
Section 1 Election Campaigns *pp. 256–259* 1. Explain how the electoral system influences presidential campaigns. 2. Discuss how modern campaigns are financed. 3. Evaluate the impact of the mass media on elections.		Guided Reading Activities Reproducible Lesson Plans Section 1 Quiz Testmaker Modern Presidential Campaigns, Volume II SAT Practice Tests
Section 2 Factors That Influence Voters *pp. 260–263* 1. Describe how voters' personal backgrounds influence their votes. 2. Explain the impact of issues and image on voters' choices.	Global Connection: Comparing Governments: Voter Participation p. 262	Guided Reading Activities Reproducible Lesson Plans Section 2 Quiz Testmaker Chapter Transparencies 9 SAT Practice Tests Writer's Guidebook
Special Report: Voter's Handbook *pp. 264–269* 1. Describe the voting process. 2. Describe the importance of voting in a democracy.		
Section 3 The Elimination of Voting Barriers *pp. 270–274* 1. Cite early restrictions on the right to vote in the United States. 2. Trace the process by which the right to vote was extended to women and to African Americans.	Focus on Freedom: Seneca Falls Declaration p. 271 Social Studies Skills: Interpreting an Election Map p. 274	Guided Reading Activities Reproducible Lesson Plans Enrichment Activities 9 Section 3 Quiz Testmaker Great Speeches, Volume V Skill Reinforcement Activities 9 SAT Practice Tests
Section 4 Nonvoters *pp. 275–279* 1. Outline current voting requirements. 2. Cite reasons why many American citizens do not vote.	Participating in Government: Exit Polls p. 277 Personal Perspectives: Barbara Jordan on Civic Participation p. 279	Guided Reading Activities Reproducible Lesson Plans Participating in Government 9 Interpreting Political Cartoons 8 Primary and Secondary Source Readings 9 Section 4 Quiz Chapter 9 Tests

If time does not permit teaching this chapter, assign the Chapter 9 summary in the Unit 3 Digest on pages 355–356.

Key To Ability Levels

Teaching strategies have been coded for varying learning styles and abilities.

L1   Level 1 activities are **basic** activities and should be within the ability range of all students.

L2   Level 2 activities are **average** activities and should be within the ability range of the average to above-average student.

L3   Level 3 activities are **challenging** activities designed for the ability range of above-average students.

LEP   These activities should be within the ability range of **Limited English Proficiency** students.

Multicultural Activities

Political scientists have spent thousands of hours analyzing the voting behavior of ethnic groups. In 1991 researchers conducted their first large-scale analysis of the attitudes of Hispanic voters. The 2,733 participants in the National Latino Political Survey responded to questions on such issues as racial quotas, gender equality, and government spending on social welfare. Survey results showed Puerto Ricans to be more liberal than non-Hispanic white voters, but Mexican Americans and Cuban Americans held views not statistically different from those of non-Hispanic white voters. Have students speculate on how politicians and candidates for office might use this type of information in planning campaign strategy or media presentations.

Under the Voting Rights Act and an extension of that act in 1992, localities are required to give voting help to citizens with limited English proficiency. If a county has 10,000 or more residents who are part of a language minority, it comes under the 1992 regulations. For counties with only one language minority, providing voting help has been relatively simple. Materials in two languages are available in the polling places, and a translator may even read the ballot to some voters. Counties with more than one language minority, however, face a larger challenge. Los Angeles County, for example, must give voting help in five languages other than English. Preparations for elections include sending out sample ballots in each language to all voters who request them, printing voter registration forms in each language, and distributing news releases for newspapers in non-English-speaking communities. In its first year only 3,264 people in Los Angeles County asked for bilingual voting materials. Officials expect that number to rise in succeeding elections.

Chapter Resources

Readings for the Student

Drew, Elizabeth. *Election Journal: The Political Events of 1987–1988.* Morrow, 1989.

Lindop, Edmund. *By a Single Vote: One-Vote Decisions that Changed American History.* Stackpole Books, 1987.

Meltzer, Milton. *American Politics: How It Really Works.* Morrow, 1989.

Samuels, Cynthia K. *It's A Free Country! A Young Person's Guide to Politics and Elections.* Atheneum, 1988.

White, Theodore. *The Making of the President, 1976.* Atheneum, 1977.

Readings for the Teacher

Ehrenhalt, Alan. *The United States of Ambition: Politicians, Power, and the Pursuit of Office.* Random House, 1991.

Kubiak, Greg. *The Gilded Dome: The U.S. Senate and Campaign Finance Reform.* Univ. of Oklahoma Press, 1994.

Piven, Frances Fox and Richard A. Cloward. *Why Americans Don't Vote.* Pantheon, 1989.

Simon, Roger. *Road Show: In America, Anyone Can Become President, It's One of the Risks We Take.* Farrar, Straus, Giroux, 1990.

Taylor, Paul. *See How They Run: Electing the President in an Age of Mediacracy.* Knopf, 1990.

Multimedia

Videocassettes and Films

First Vote. People for the American Way. (v/c, 12 minutes)

The Great Upset of '48. WETA. (v/c, 60 minutes)

You Are There: The Trial of Susan B. Anthony. Phoenix/BFA Films and Video, Inc. (film, 25 minutes)

The Young Vote—Power, Politics and Participation. Phoenix/BFA Films and Video, Inc. (film, 15 minutes)

Software

American Government III. Intellectual Software. (Apple, IBM disks; Apple disk with management facility also available; part of a 5-part set). A tutorial focusing on public opinion, the election process, and winning elections.

MECC Social Studies Vol. 1 (ELECT1, ELECT2, ELECT3). Minnesota Educational Computing Consortium (MECC). (Apple, TRS80 disks). Students role-play campaign strategies during campaign and elections.

Nomination. Brady (also available from Social Studies School Service). (IBM disk). Students compete against each other (or computer-based opponents) for presidential nomination. Players' success depends on the handling of press questions, their campaign financing, and their stand on recent issues.

Elections and Voting

CHAPTER

9

A presidential candidate campaigns arduously across the nation, devoting a great deal of time, energy, and money to establish an image and communicate his or her points of view.

ABC NEWS INTERACTIVE

Powers of the President

The Election Campaign
Running Time :43
Side One, Chapter 11

The Electoral College
Running Time 1:06
Side One, Chapter 14

Introduce

Chapter Overview

Chapter 9 introduces students to the way in which election campaigns are organized and carried out.

Section 1 examines the planning and financing of election campaigns.

Section 2 discusses the factors that influence a voter's choice of candidates.

Section 3 highlights the legal barriers that in the past prevented many Americans from voting.

Section 4 outlines voting requirements and examines the reasons why many Americans still do not vote.

Chapter 9 Themes

Draw students' attention to the Themes in Government section in the Chapter Preview on page 255. Have them carefully read through the explanation of each theme. Then ask them to write a paragraph that coherently and logically weaves together the four explanations. Have students compare their paragraphs.

GLENCOE TECHNOLOGY

Set on Freedom

The Voting Rights Act of 1965
Running Time 5 frames
Side A, Chapter 26

The Poor People's Campaign
Running Time :45
Side A, Chapter 42

254 UNIT 3: INFLUENCING GOVERNMENT

About the Chapter Opener

Teaching With Illustrations Have students examine the photograph on pages 254 and 255. Ask students if they have ever been involved in campaigning. Students might discuss campaigning on a school, local, state, or national level. They might discuss the kind of work involved in campaigning and their reasons for campaigning. Then ask students how the photograph reflects the Themes in Government listed on page 255. (*Students might indicate that the photograph reflects the theme of civic responsibility and the theme of political processes.*)

Chapter Preview

Overview

Voting is a privilege and a vital tool in American democracy.

Objectives

After studying this chapter, you should be able to:

1. **Explain** why election campaigns must be well planned and well financed.
2. **Describe** various factors that influence a voter's choice of candidates.
3. **Discuss** earlier restrictions on the right to vote in the United States.
4. **Identify** current voting requirements and why many American citizens do not vote.

Themes in Government

This chapter emphasizes the following government themes:

- **Civic Responsibility** Citizens in a democracy have a responsibility to take part in the electoral process. Sections 1, 2, and 4.
- **Political Processes** Political campaigns have become more publicized in recent years; nevertheless, many Americans continue to be nonvoters. Sections 1, 2, and 4.
- **Federalism** States control elections, but the federal government prohibits discrimination. Section 3.
- **Civil Rights** The right to vote has been extended to almost all Americans more than 18 years old. Section 3.

Critical Thinking Skills

This chapter emphasizes the following critical thinking skills:

- Making Inferences
- Synthesizing Information
- Demonstrating Reasoned Judgment
- Predicting Consequences

Introducing the Chapter

Write the following words on the chalkboard: *vote, election.* Have students suggest what these words mean to them—stress that they need not give definitions. Write suggestions on the chalkboard as they are offered. Point out that as they read this chapter, students will learn that elections and the process of voting are the very basis of our governmental system of representative democracy.

Chapter Project

Have students work cooperatively or individually to put together a time capsule that would give people of the future an idea how American elections operated in the late 1900s. Suggest they include such items as campaign leaflets, buttons, and posters; sample ballots; newspaper stories on candidates; and so on.

Linking Past and Present
Today, most voters expect elected officials to act according to the demands of the people they represent. This belief developed in the 1830s, a decade marked by the growth of popular democracy. The majority of the thousands of new voters brought into the electoral process during this time looked upon casting a ballot as a *quid pro quo* arrangement. Their votes put politicians into office. Therefore, the politicians should respond to their demands.

Setting the Scene Incumbency seems to be the most powerful factor in electoral success. In 1986 and 1988, for example, the reelection rates for incumbents in congressional elections exceeded 95 percent. In 1990, when public opinion polls showed a strong anti-incumbent sentiment among voters, reelection rates were 97 percent for senators and 96 percent for representatives. Money appears to be a major factor in incumbents' success. In 1992, challengers enjoyed a much larger percentage of total campaign spending than usual. The result was the biggest turnover in House and Senate membership in 40 years.

Election Campaigns

Focus

Bell Ringer

While attendance is being taken, ask students to speculate on what connection there might be between Mickey Mouse and presidential elections.

Motivating Activity

Review students' Bell Ringer responses. Then point out that Walt Disney, as well as creating Mickey Mouse and other famous cartoon characters, made presidential campaign commercials during the 1950s. Then show Disney's commercials for Dwight D. Eisenhower included in "Modern Presidential Campaigns," Volume II, *Social Studies Videos*. (You will need to preview the video to locate this material.) Then lead the class in a discussion of the following questions: What movie-making techniques did Disney employ in these commercials? How do these commercials compare to those used by candidates in the last presidential election? How would you rate the effectiveness of these commercials? Why?

Bring the discussion to a close by pointing out that one focus of this section is the use of the electronic media in election campaigns.

Vocabulary Precheck

List the key terms for this section on the chalkboard. Have students develop questions for which each term is an answer.

LEP

Caption Answer
from September to November

Presidential campaigns usually begin in early September, around Labor Day. They end on Election Day—the first Tuesday after the first Monday of November. During the eight weeks of the campaign, each candidate tries to persuade the voters that he or she should be the next President.

It makes sense, therefore, for a presidential candidate to devote most of the campaign effort to the big electoral-vote states. When these largest states appear to be divided between the contenders, however, other states with smaller electoral votes become vital to the candidates.

The Electoral Vote

To be elected President, a candidate must win at least 270 of the 538 electoral votes. To achieve this victory, a candidate must pay special attention throughout the campaign to those states with large numbers of electoral votes. The candidate who wins the greatest number of popular votes in a state receives all of that state's electoral votes.

Electoral Votes and the States The number of a state's electoral votes is based upon the total of its representatives in Congress, House members plus senators. For example, Georgia has 13 electoral votes—11 members of the House of Representatives and 2 senators. California has 54 electoral votes—52 House members and 2 senators.

The larger a state's population, the more electoral votes it has. The 10 biggest states—California (54), New York (33), Texas (32), Florida (25), Pennsylvania (23), Illinois (22), Ohio (21), Michigan (18), New Jersey (15), and North Carolina (14)—have a total of 257 electoral votes. If a candidate can win these states and either Georgia or Virginia—each of which has 13 electoral votes—that candidate would win the presidency with 270 votes.

Campaign Strategy

Planning how to capture key states is only one of the many decisions a presidential candidate must make. For example, should the candidate wage an ag-

Campaign Artifacts
In addition to rallies and parades, campaign banners, hats, buttons, and other campaign materials help attract support for political candidates. **Politics During what time of the year do presidential campaigns generally take place?**

SECTION PREVIEW

Objectives
After studying this section, you should be able to:
- Explain how the electoral system influences presidential campaigns.

- Discuss how modern campaigns are financed.
- Evaluate the impact of the mass media on elections.

Key Terms and Concepts
political action committee, electorate

Themes in Government
- Civic Responsibility
- Political Processes

Critical Thinking Skills
- Making Inferences
- Synthesizing Information

256 UNIT 3: INFLUENCING GOVERNMENT

Classroom Resources for Section 1

- 📁 Guided Reading Activities
- 📁 Reproducible Lesson Plans
- 📁 Section 1 Quiz

- 💾 Testmaker
- 📼 Modern Presidential Campaigns, Volume II
  SAT Practice Tests

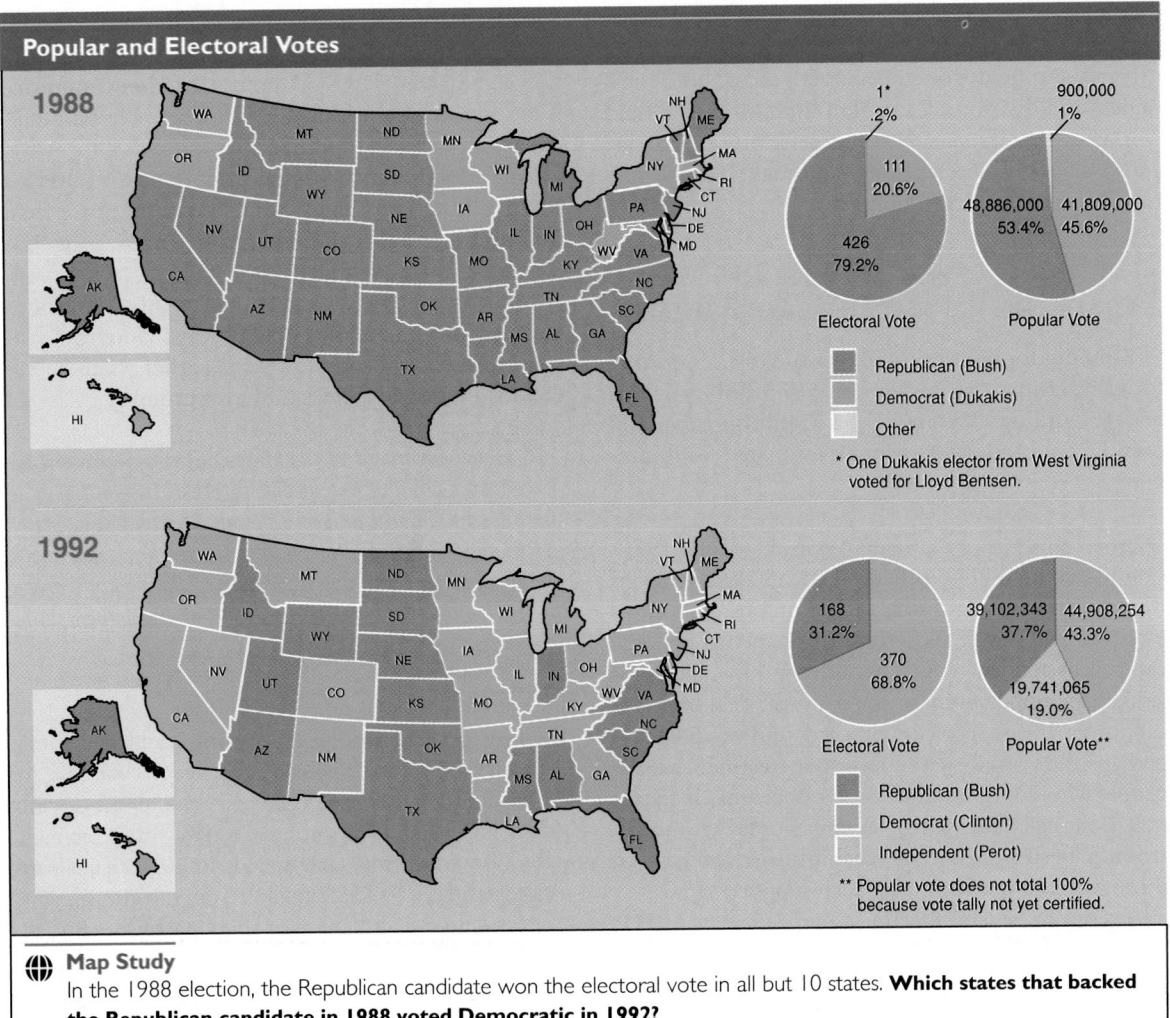

Popular and Electoral Votes

1988

Electoral Vote
- 426 79.2%
- 111 20.6%
- 1* .2%

Popular Vote
- 48,886,000 53.4%
- 41,809,000 45.6%
- 900,000 1%

Republican (Bush)
Democrat (Dukakis)
Other

* One Dukakis elector from West Virginia voted for Lloyd Bentsen.

1992

Electoral Vote
- 370 68.8%
- 168 31.2%

Popular Vote**
- 44,908,254 43.3%
- 39,102,343 37.7%
- 19,741,065 19.0%

Republican (Bush)
Democrat (Clinton)
Independent (Perot)

** Popular vote does not total 100% because vote tally not yet certified.

🌐 **Map Study**
In the 1988 election, the Republican candidate won the electoral vote in all but 10 states. **Which states that backed the Republican candidate in 1988 voted Democratic in 1992?**

gressive, all-out attack on an opponent, or would a more low-key campaign be a better strategy? What should be the theme or slogan of the campaign? What issues should be stressed? How much money should be spent on television commercials, radio advertising, and newspaper ads?

Presidential Campaign Organization The candidate's campaign organization is heavily involved in making key strategic decisions. In addition, it takes care of the enormous number of details that must be dealt with in a campaign. A strong organization is essential to running a presidential campaign.

Heading the organization is a campaign manager, who is responsible for overall strategy and planning. In the national office, individuals handle relations with television, radio, the print media, finances, advertising, opinion polls, and campaign material.

STUDY GUIDE

Themes in Government
Civic Responsibility It is possible for a presidential candidate to win the popular vote but lose the electoral vote, as happened in 1876 and

1888. Why then should people bother to vote?

Critical Thinking Skills
Making Inferences In what way is the national census taken every

10 years an influencing factor on presidental elections?

Background

Studies have found that there is very little bias in what the media say about political candidates and election issues. The media generally give the same amount of coverage and similar numbers of favorable and unfavorable mentions to candidates in an election. However, bias may creep in elsewhere.

For example, if a television newscast leads off with a story about one candidate and covers another candidate's campaign 10 minutes later, it appears that the first candidate is being favored over the second candidate.

Teach

Guided Practice

L1 Politics Write the terms *national, state,* and *local* on the chalkboard. Then ask for volunteers to describe how a presidential campaign is organized at each of these levels. Write the descriptions under the appropriate heading. Have students use the information to construct a diagram showing a presidential campaign organization. **LEP**

L2 Analyzing Ideas Refer students to the maps on page 257. Ask: How might a candidate with less than 50 percent of the popular vote win a comfortable majority in the Electoral College? If such a situation could occur, do you think the Electoral College should be reformed? Why or why not?

📼 **Analyzing Information** Show students the Kennedy-Nixon debates from "Modern Presidential Campaigns," Volume II, *Social Studies Videos.* Then lead students in a discussion of the following: Image is everything in election campaigns.

Map Study Answer
Arkansas, California, Colorado, Connecticut, Delaware, Georgia, Illinois, Kentucky, Louisiana, Maine, Maryland, Michigan, Missouri, Montana, Nevada, New Hampshire, New Jersey, New Mexico, Ohio, Pennsylvania, Tennessee, and Vermont

STUDY GUIDE

Theme Answer
The popular vote determines which candidate wins a state's electoral votes.
Critical Thinking Answer
Census figures determine reapportionment of House seats, which are a factor in determining each state's electoral votes.

Independent Practice

L2 Conducting Interviews Ask students to interview older relatives or other adults about the personal images projected by Presidents Eisenhower, Kennedy, Johnson, Nixon, and Carter. Have students share their findings in class. Then have them discuss the following:

What common images do older voters have of these Presidents?

STUDY GUIDE

Theme Answer
Television is a candidate's most effective means of reaching voters.

Critical Thinking Answer
Both try to "sell" their subjects, show them only in the best light, and are somewhat superficial.

Assess

Check for Understanding

Have students complete Section 1 Review on page 259.

Meeting Objectives

Each section objective is tested by the Section Review questions that follow it in parentheses.
• Explain how the electoral system influences presidential campaigns. (2, 5, 6)
• Discuss how modern campaigns are financed. (3, 4, 5, 8)
• Evaluate the impact of the mass media on elections. (7)

Evaluate

📁 Section 1 Quiz

💻 Testmaker

On the state and local levels, the state party chairperson usually coordinates a campaign. Local party officials and field workers contact voters, hold local rallies, and distribute campaign literature. The field workers, who are usually volunteers, ring doorbells, canvass voters by telephone, and make sure voters turn out to vote on Election Day.

Financing Election Campaigns

Running for political office is expensive. Spending for each House seat cost about $935,000 in 1992. Senate candidates averaged $2.7 million each, and presidential candidates spent an estimated $290 million.

Where the Money Comes From Until the 1970s candidates for public office relied on contributions from business organizations, labor unions, and interested individuals. This system of financing political campaigns tended to give wealthy groups and individuals the opportunity to wield a great deal of political power. It cast suspicion on successful candidates—perhaps they owed special favors or treatment to the people who contributed to their campaigns. It meant that political figures with greater access to money stood a better chance of reaching the voters than those who did not command such support.

A series of Federal Election Campaign Acts (1971, 1974, and 1976) provided for a new system of campaign financing for federal elections based on three principles. These principles were (1) public funding of presidential elections, (2) limitations on the amounts presidential candidates could spend on their campaigns, and (3) public disclosure of how much candidates spend to get elected.

Ceiling on Campaign Contributions Under these laws business organizations and labor unions are now prohibited from making any direct contributions. Individuals, however, may contribute up to $1,000 to any candidate's primary or general election campaign.

Political Action Committees The new election campaign laws encouraged the growth of political action committees (PACs). A **political action committee** is an organization designed to support political candidates with campaign contributions.

An individual may contribute up to $5,000 to a PAC. While a PAC may not contribute more than $5,000 to a single candidate, it may make contributions to as many candidates as it wishes.

Some people believe that special-interest groups have too much influence on elections. Woodrow Wilson expressed this opinion years earlier when he addressed the issue of special-interest groups:

> *The government of the United States at present is a foster-child of the special interest. It is not allowed to have a will of its own. It is told at every move: "Don't do that; you will interfere with our prosperity," and when we ask, "Where is our prosperity lodged?" a certain group of gentlemen say, "With us."*
>
> —WOODROW WILSON

Ceiling on Campaign Spending Presidential candidates have the choice of accepting federal funding for their campaigns. If they do accept—and all major party presidential candidates since 1976 have—they are limited in how much they may spend. In 1992 major party candidates received $55.2 million from the government.

Presidential candidates of third parties qualify for federal funding under certain conditions. They must have received more than 5 percent of the popular vote in the previous presidential election or 5 percent in the current election.

Disclosure Under the federal election laws, candidates, political action committees, and political parties must keep records of contributions and report to the Federal Election Commission (FEC) all contributions over $100. The FEC, an independent agency in the executive branch, administers the federal election laws. The FEC's records are open to public inspection.

STUDY GUIDE

Themes in Government
Political Processes A 30-second television commercial costs $150,000 or more to produce. **Why must presidential candidates be willing to spend this kind of** money for televised political advertising?

Critical Thinking Skills
Synthesizing Information Why do some feel that TV political commercials are not that much different from regular TV product commercials?

Cooperative Learning Activity

Organize students into three groups. Have each group develop a campaign commercial for a candidate from a recent presidential election. One group should design a one-page advertisement for a newspaper, another should script a 30-second to 1-minute radio spot, and the third should script a 30-second to 1-minute television spot. Assign different tasks—researching, writing, designing, and so on—to different group members. Have the first group display its advertisement on the bulletin board and the other two groups perform their scripts for the class.

Presidential Candidates' Images

The image or mental picture that voters have of a candidate is extremely important. The candidate who is perceived as more "presidential" has a decided advantage on Election Day. The mass media is an extremely powerful tool in any campaign because it can create both positive and negative images for the candidates.

The Use of Television The most important communication tool for a presidential candidate is television. A television appearance can reach millions of American homes instantly. Studies have shown that people are more likely to believe what they see and hear on television than what they read in the newspapers or hear on the radio. Television commercials are one way candidates are assured of reaching the voting public. A candidate's organization spends a great deal of time and effort on writing and producing political commercials.

Campaign Coverage on News Programs Just as important as candidates' appearances on television commercials are their appearances on the news programs. Television is now the single most important source of news for most Americans. Television coverage is the only way millions of citizens have of knowing how a campaign is progressing.

Televised Presidential Debates Another way in which candidates use television in presidential campaigns is to participate in debates that millions of viewers watch. Televised debates were held in the 1960, 1976, 1980, 1984, and 1988 campaigns.

Personal Qualities
The personal qualities as well as the political views of a candidate can influence voters. **Psychology What role does the media play in political campaigns?**

Voters' Decisions

Research shows that more than half of the voters in a United States presidential election make their voting decisions before the campaign even begins. If this is the case, why have a campaign at all? Although undecided voters are in the minority, they still represent a significant portion of the **electorate**, or the people entitled to vote. The decisions of these voters will make the difference in election results, and presidential campaigns are usually directed particularly toward them. Campaigns, then, generally do convince some voters to vote one way or another.

---

1 SECTION REVIEW

Section Summary
In a presidential campaign, candidates and their organizations use federal and PAC funding, as well as the media, to their best advantage.

Checking for Understanding
Recalling Facts
1. Define political action committee, electorate.
2. State the number of electoral votes a candidate needs to win the presidential election.
3. Describe the effect the Federal Election Campaign Acts had on campaign financing.
4. Discuss how minor-party candidates can qualify for federal funds for a presidential campaign.

Exploring Themes
5. Civic Responsibility How can an individual get involved in campaigning for a presidential candidate?
6. Political Processes When do small states become key in the race for the presidency?

Critical Thinking Skills
7. Making Inferences Why do you think some people have already made their presidential choices before the campaigning even begins?
8. Synthesizing Information PACs can contribute to as many political candidates as they wish. Why might they contribute to both candidates in a presidential campaign?

Chapter 9, Section 1
Lesson Plan, pages 256–259

Caption Answer
gives voters an impression of the candidate as well as spreading candidate's message

Reteach
Select students to write summaries of how the Electoral College works and read them to the class. Encourage other students to ask questions during the summaries.

Enrich
Ask students to assume the role of a modern media consultant for President Abraham Lincoln's 1864 reelection campaign. Have them research Lincoln and his times and, in that role, write a memorandum to Lincoln's campaign manager setting forth a strategy for improving the President's media image.

Close
Ask students to suggest what controls, if any, they would place on the financing and running of election campaigns. Have them give reasons for their suggestions.

GLENCOE TECHNOLOGY

Focus on Government
Video 19
Lecture Launcher:
The Mass Media
Running Time: 3:13
Videodisc 1, Chap. 19
VHS Tape 1, Begins 54:46

Video 20
Making Connections:
The Media and Politics
Running Time: 1:58
Videodisc 1, Chap. 20
VHS Tape 1, Begins 58:02

Section I Review Answers

1. Definitions of terms appear on pages indicated: **political action committee,** 258; **electorate,** 259
2. 270
3. Candidates may receive federal funds for their campaigns and are limited in how much they may spend. Candidates must publicly disclose the amount spent. The laws limited individual contributions, banned some organizational contributions, and encouraged the growth of political action committees.
4. must have received more than 5 percent of popular vote in previous presidential election or 5 percent in a primary election in present campaign
5. Answers may include distributing campaign literature, canvassing door-to-door or by telephone, driving voters to the polls on election day, and so on.
6. When big electoral-vote states are divided between the contenders, the smaller states become vital to the outcome of the election.
7. Answers may include choice based on past performance of candidate, choice based on candidate's party, or choice based on candidate's image.
8. Typical response: By contributing to both candidates, a PAC will have a friend in office no matter who wins the election.

Focus

Bell Ringer

Write the following on the chalkboard for students to consider while attendance is being taken:

Elections are a crapshoot. There is no logic to the way people make voting decisions. Do you think this statement is true? Why or why not?

Motivating Activity

Discuss students' Bell Ringer responses. Then ask students what factors they think influence the way a person votes. List responses on the chalkboard and then have students write them in their notebooks. Tell students to copy the factor they think is most important first, the next most important second, and so on. Have students keep their lists for use with the Close activity on page 263. Then mention that Section 2 discusses the major factors that influence voting decisions.

Vocabulary Precheck

Ask students to speculate on the meaning of each key term. Have them check their speculations by finding the definitions in the section text. **LEP**

Factors That Influence Voters

During a presidential campaign, candidates want to appeal to the greatest number of voters possible. They try to convince the voters that they have the solution to the nation's many problems. They attempt to create a favorable leadership image. The measure of their success will be evident only on Election Day.

Four major factors influence voter decisions: (1) personal background of the voter; (2) degree of voter loyalty to one of the political parties; (3) issues of the campaign; and (4) voters' image of the candidates.

Personal Background of Voters

The ultimate rulers of our democracy are not a president and senators and congressmen and government officials but the voters of this country.
—FRANKLIN D. ROOSEVELT, 1938

Voters' personal backgrounds affect their decisions. Background includes such things as upbringing, family, age, occupation, income level, and even general outlook on life.

Age Consider, for example, how an individual's age might affect a voting decision. A 68-year-old senior citizen would probably favor a candidate who promised an increase in Social Security payments, provided, of course, that positions the candidate took on other issues did not offend that voter. On the other hand, a young voter of 23 might resent the prospect of having more money deducted from a paycheck to pay for increased Social Security pay-

ments. This young voter might then decide to vote against the candidate.

Other Background Influences Voters' education, religion, and racial or ethnic background also affect their attitudes toward the candidates. For example, an African American might favor a candidate who supports strong anti-discrimination measures in education and employment. A Jewish voter might not vote for a candidate who has expressed strong reservations about American support of Israel.

It is important to understand that people's backgrounds tend to influence them in particular ways. However, individuals do not always vote the way their backgrounds might lead one to believe. Will labor union members always vote for the Democratic presidential candidate, even though they usually do? The large number of union members who voted for Ronald Reagan in 1980 confirms that they do not. Will college-educated voters, most of whom usually vote Republican, always give their votes to the Republican candidate? The landslide vote by which Lyndon Johnson, a Democrat, defeated Republican Barry Goldwater in 1964 indicates that this is not always the case. In short, voters' personal backgrounds are not always sure predictors of actual voting decisions.

The Cross-Pressured Voter One reason why voters' backgrounds do not always forecast how they will vote is that many voters are cross-pressured. A **cross-pressured voter** is one who is caught between conflicting elements in his or her own life. For example, Catholics (religion) are generally more inclined to vote Democratic than Republican. Yet, suppose an individual Catholic voter is also a wealthy business

---

SECTION PREVIEW

Objectives
After studying this section, you should be able to:
- Describe how voters' personal backgrounds influence their votes.
- Explain the impact of issues and image on voters' choices.

Key Terms and Concepts
cross-pressured voter, straight-party ticket

Themes in Government
- Political Processes
- Civic Responsibility

Critical Thinking Skills
- Synthesizing Information
- Demonstrating Reasoned Judgment

260 UNIT 3: INFLUENCING GOVERNMENT

Classroom Resources for Section 2

- Guided Reading Activities
- Reproducible Lesson Plans
- Section 2 Quiz
- Testmaker
- Chapter Transparencies 9
- SAT Practice Tests
- Writer's Guidebook

Trends in Voters' Identification with Parties

Party Identification	1960	1964	1968	1970	1972	1976	1980	1984	1986	1988	1990	1992
Strong Democrat	20%	27%	20%	20%	15%	15%	18%	17%	18%	18%	20%	18%
Weak Democrat	25	25	25	24	26	25	23	20	22	18	19	18
Independent Democrat	6	9	10	10	11	12	11	11	10	12	12	14
Independent	10	8	11	13	13	15	13	11	12	11	11	12
Independent Republican	7	6	9	8	10	10	12	12	11	13	12	12
Weak Republican	14	14	15	15	13	14	14	15	15	14	15	14
Strong Republican	16	11	10	9	10	9	9	12	10	14	9	11
Apolitical	3	1	1	1	1	1	2	2	2	2	2	1

Source: The American National Election Studies, conducted by the Center for Political Studies at the University of Michigan

☑ **Chart Study**
Weak and independent voters are more likely to be influenced by the issues, rather than party loyalty. **During which election did these voters make up more than 75 percent of the voting population?**

executive (income level). Well-to-do business people are usually Republicans. Furthermore, many of this voter's close friends are Democrats (social group). They will no doubt have some influence on this voter's thinking.

How will this person vote? One cannot be sure. Such a voter's personal background, like that of millions of other voters, has conflicting elements. For this voter other areas important to voter decision making—such as campaign issues and the personalities of the candidates—will probably play an equally influential role in determining how he or she will vote.

Loyalty to Political Parties

Another influence on voters' decisions is their loyalty (or lack of it) to one of the political parties. Because the majority of American voters consider

themselves either Republicans or Democrats, most vote for their party's candidates. In 1988, for example, 94 percent of strong Democrats who voted chose the Democratic presidential candidate, Michael Dukakis, and 98 percent of strong Republicans chose George Bush, the Republican.

Strong v. Weak Party Voters Not all voters who consider themselves Republicans or Democrats support their party's candidates with the same degree of consistency. Strong party voters are those who select their party's candidates in election after election. Strong party voters tend not to consider the issues carefully or look critically at the candidates. In the voting booth, they usually vote a **straight-party ticket**—they select the candidates of their party only.

Unlike strong party voters, weak party voters are more likely to switch their votes to the rival party's candidates from time to time. In 1980, as an exam-

Teach

Guided Practice

L1 Making Generalizations
Have students write a generalization about each of the factors that influence the way people vote. Have them read their statements to the class.

🖱 **Interpreting Visuals** Display transparency 9 from the *Chapter Transparencies* in the Teacher's Classroom Resources and use the accompanying teaching strategy and student activity to teach about the United States voting population.

L2 Identifying Issues Have students suggest what issues they think should have been at the center of the most recent presidential campaign. Then have students discuss how well candidates addressed these issues.

L3 Debate Have students debate the following:

Should a candidate's image play a role in voters' electoral decisions? Why or why not?

Chart Study Answer
the 1976 election

STUDY GUIDE

Themes in Government
Political Processes Political parties depend on the support of certain groups at election time. **Identify two groups that tend to support**

Democrats as well as two groups that tend to support Republicans.

Critical Thinking Skills
Synthesizing Information Why do political party candidates count

heavily on the support of strong party voters to offset weak party voters and independent voters?

STUDY GUIDE

Theme Answer
Labor union members and Catholics tend to support Democrats, college-educated voters and well-to-do business people tend to support Republicans.

Critical Thinking Answer
Strong party voters vote based on party loyalty. Weak party voters and independents tend to vote based on issues or candidates' qualities.

CHAPTER 9: ELECTIONS AND VOTING 261

Background

A study conducted by political scientists Raymond E. Wolfinger and Steven J. Rosenstone found that the single most important variable affecting the way people vote and whether they vote is the level of education. The study also found that other variables, such as income, sex, religion, and occupation, have only a marginal impact on voter preference and turnout.

Independent Practice

L2 Opinion Polls Have students ask family members of voting age what factors, in order of importance, have influenced their voting decisions in recent elections. Then have students collate their results to construct a composite list of the most important influences on voting and compare it with the lists they compiled in the Motivating Activity.

GLOBAL CONNECTION

Many political scientists feel that focusing on voter turnout when making political participation comparisons is misleading. In other measures of participation—campaigning for candidates, for example—Americans easily outstrip citizens of other democracies.

Examining the Connection:
Allow students time to present their interview results.

STUDY GUIDE

Theme Answer
They are influenced more by issues and the candidates than by party loyalty.

Critical Thinking Answer
Issues inform voters how candidates will try to solve problems; emphasizing images tells voters little about candidates' ideas.

Assess

Check for Understanding

Have students complete Section 2 Review on page 263.

GLOBAL CONNECTION

Comparing Governments

Voter Participation Only about half those eligible to vote in the United States do so. How does this compare with voter turnout elsewhere? During the 1980s about 94 percent of eligible voters in Australia participated in elections. In Belgium voter turnout was about the same. Australia and Belgium are among the democratic nations that have mandatory voting—laws that require citizens to vote.

Some people argue in favor of mandatory voting in the United States. They feel that citizens should be required to participate in government by exercising their voting rights. They point out that voting is a responsibility. Others argue that mandatory voting interferes with individual freedom of choice.

Examining the Connection
Interview five people to learn their opinion on mandatory voting and report your findings.

ple, 27 percent fewer Democrats voted for Carter than had voted for him in 1976. Weak party voters are more influenced by issues and the candidates than they are by party loyalty.

Independent Voters Another important group of voters is the independent voters, who think of themselves as neither Republicans nor Democrats. Even when independents tend to lean toward one party, their party loyalty is very weak.

The number of independent voters has increased over the years. Because of this increase, they have become a most important element in presidential elections. Along with weak party voters, they hold the key to who wins the right to occupy the White House every four years. In 1992, for example, Bill Clinton won the support of 38 percent of independent voters and 48 percent of self-described moderates, while George Bush won about 33 percent of these groups.

Experts believe that the number of weak party voters and independent voters will increase in the future. Presidential candidates will no longer be able to rely on party loyalty for victory. Analysts predict that the issues of a campaign and the candidates' images will influence more and more voters.

Issues in Election Campaigns

Many voters are not well-informed about all the issues discussed in election campaigns. Still, today's voters are better informed than the voters of earlier years. Several reasons account for this shift.

First, television has brought the issues into almost every home in the country. Second, voters today are better educated than were voters of the past. A third reason is that current problems seem to have a greater impact on the personal lives of many more voters than at any time since the Great Depression of the 1930s. These problems include pollution, the energy crisis, inflation, school busing, gun control, crime, unemployment, and women's rights.

A presidential election that demonstrated the importance of issues was the election of 1980. Many Americans blamed President Carter for the high cost of living, the high rate of inflation, and the high rate of unemployment. In his four years in office the economy had worsened, and Carter seemed unable to turn it around. Carter's opponent, Republican Ronald Reagan, used the economic issue to attack the President's administration.

At the end of the televised debate between the two candidates, Reagan asked the millions of Americans watching, "Are you better off than you were four years ago? Is it easier for you to go and buy things in the stores than it was four years ago?" For most Americans the answer to these questions was "No."

STUDY GUIDE

Themes in Government
Civic Responsibility Voters are classified as Democrats, Republicans, third party, or independent. **How do independent voters generally differ from party voters?**

Critical Thinking Skills
Demonstrating Reasoned Judgment **Why does an election campaign better serve the electorate and the public by focusing more**
on the issues instead of the candidates' images?

262 Unit 3: Influencing Government

Critical Thinking Activity

Synthesizing Information Point out that since the advent of PACs, the number of single-issue election campaigns has increased dramatically. Have students suggest possible connections between these two trends. Also ask them to speculate on what impact this development might have on

the way people make voting decisions. *(Students should link the financial contributions of interest groups with election issues. They should suggest that the trend will increase the number of cross-pressured voters.)*

Reagan's tactic was effective. Because he made such a strong issue of the economy, millions of voters who had voted for Carter four years earlier switched to the Republican challenger.

The Candidate's Image

Just as important as the issues themselves is the way the voters perceive the issues. If, for example, they believe that an administration is dealing effectively with the economy, they may reward the President with their votes. Conversely, if they believe an administration's measures are ineffective, voters may punish the President by voting for the other candidate.

Certainly, most Americans want a President who appears to be someone they can trust as a national leader. All candidates try to convey this image to the public, but not all are successful in doing so. Gerald Ford, running for President in 1976, struck many voters as well-meaning but dull. Adlai Stevenson, who lost to Dwight D. Eisenhower in 1952 and 1956, seemed to many voters too intellectual to be President.

Many voters select candidates on image alone—for the personal qualities they perceive them to have. In 1964 President Lyndon Johnson had the image of a man who wanted peace, while his opponent, Barry Goldwater, was viewed as more willing to lead the nation into war. At the very least, a candidate must be viewed as competent to handle the problems of the day. Many voters rejected Michael Dukakis in 1988 because they believed he was unqualified to deal with the nation's problems. Harry Truman cited the danger of getting this image when he said:

Military Heroes
General Dwight Eisenhower's military career helped him win the presidency. **Politics Why does military service give a candidate a political advantage?**

Being a president is like riding a tiger. A man has to keep riding it or be swallowed. . . . A president is either constantly on top of events or, if he hesitates, events will soon be on top of him.

—HARRY S TRUMAN

A candidate, then, must convey the impression of having the qualities voters expect in a President.

2 SECTION REVIEW

Section Summary
The personal background of voters, loyalty to political parties, campaign issues, and the images of candidates are all factors that influence voters' decisions.

Checking for Understanding
Recalling Facts
1. Define **cross-pressured voter, straight-party ticket.**
2. Identify factors in a voter's personal background that influence that individual's vote.
3. State why the independent voter is so important in an election.
4. List three reasons American voters today are better informed than voters of earlier years.

Exploring Themes
5. Political Processes What are some advantages and disadvantages of voting a straight-party ticket?
6. Civic Responsibility Why do experts predict that campaign issues and the candidates' images may increasingly influence voters?

Critical Thinking Skills
7. Synthesizing Information Which of the four factors do you think is most important in determining how people vote? Why?
8. Demonstrating Reasoned Judgment What qualities of competence and leadership would you look for in a presidential candidate?

Section 2 Review Answers

1. Definitions of terms appear on pages indicated: **cross-pressured voter,** 260; **straight-party ticket,** 261
2. age, occupation, income level, education, religion, ethnic background, outlook on life
3. Their number has increased over the years; therefore, their votes can be decisive in an election.
4. Television brings information on elections to almost every home; American voters are better educated than in

the past; present problems seem to have more impact on voters' personal lives.
5. advantages: the party voter most agrees with will receive full support from that voter; disadvantages: voter may not be addressing important issues and, therefore, may vote for candidate with whom he or she disagrees.
6. Answers may suggest that as voters become better informed on the issues and the candidates, they may make

voting decisions based on those factors rather than on party.
7. Answers will vary. Students should give reasons for their choice.
8. Answers may include candidate's previous experience, responsiveness to public concerns, handling of public trust, actions taken in times of crisis, and image.

Caption Answer
enhances candidate's image as a strong leader

Meeting Objectives
Each section objective is tested by the Section Review questions that follow it in parentheses.
• Describe how voters' personal backgrounds influence their votes. (2, 3, 4, 5, 7)
• Explain the impact of issues and image on voters' choices. (4, 6, 7, 8)

Evaluate
🗀 Section 2 Quiz
▣ Testmaker

Reteach
Have students explain how each of these factors influences voting decisions: personal background, party loyalty, issues, candidate's image.

Enrich
Ask students to review recent election campaigns and report on what "image flaws" may have cost candidates victory at the polls.

Close

Ask students to review and adjust the lists of factors influencing voting that they made for this section's Motivating Activity.

Focus

Bell Ringer

While attendance is being taken, ask students to write a brief answer to the following:

What is entailed in casting a vote?

Motivating Activity

Select students to read their Bell Ringer answers. Then write the following list on the chalkboard:

1. Register
2. Become informed
3. Cast your ballot
4. Monitor results

Explain that to vote, people first must register with their local board of elections. Also, to make sure that their votes are not wasted, people must be well informed about candidates and the issues involved in elections. People also should be aware of how to cast a ballot at the polling place. Finally, people also should check on election results, not only to see *who* won but also to learn *why* those candidates won. Draw the explanation to a close by informing students that the Voter's Handbook discusses in detail the process of voting.

Vocabulary Precheck

Write the key terms and concepts on the chalkboard. Ask students to use those they know in sentences. **LEP**

---

^{Special Report}

VOTER'S HANDBOOK

By Denny Schillings
President-Elect, National Council for the Social Studies

V*oting is a basic political right of all citizens in a democracy who meet certain qualifications set by law. Voting allows citizens to take positive actions to influence or control government.*

Report Preview

Objectives
After studying this report, you should be able to:
- **Describe** the voting process.
- **Describe** the importance of voting in a democracy.

Key Terms and Concepts
canvass, register, polling place, precinct, office-group ballot, ticket-splitting, party-column ballot, Australian ballot, canvassing board, absentee ballot

Themes in Government
This report emphasizes the following government themes:
- **Civic Participation** Citizens in a democracy have a duty to vote.
- **Civil Liberties** Election officials must ensure that all Americans eligible to vote have access to ballots.

Critical Thinking Skills
This report emphasizes the following critical thinking skills:
- **Making Inferences**
- **Evaluating Information**

▲ *Candidates' supporters attempt to influence voters, but must maintain a certain distance from the polling place.*

264

Background

Each precinct in the United States has its own polling place. Polls may be set up in a firehouse, a public school, a private home, a barbershop, the lobby of a hotel, or any place convenient to all voters in the precinct. However, polling places cannot be located where alcoholic beverages are served. Laws in most states prohibit the distribution or display of campaign literature within a certain distance of the polling place, usually 100 feet.

Qualifications to Vote

Today you are qualified to vote if you are not a convicted felon or legally insane and: you are (1) a citizen of the United States and (2) at least 18 years old. Most states also require that you be a resident of the state for a specified period and that you register or enroll with the appropriate local government.

Who Sets the Qualifications to Vote?

Originally, under Article I, Section 2, the Constitution left voting qualifications entirely to the states. The Constitution gave to Congress only the power to pick the day on which presidential electors would gather and to fix "the Times, Places, and Manner of holding elections" of members of Congress.

Since the end of the Civil War, Congress and the federal courts have imposed national standards on state-run elections. A series of constitutional amendments, federal laws, and Supreme Court decisions forced the states to conduct elections without discrimination because of race, creed, color or sex. Even with such federal requirements, however, the registration of voters and regulation of elections are primarily state powers.

Will My Vote Count?

Each person's vote counts. If you doubt it, think about how many elections have been decided by one or just a few votes. In 1976 more than 81 million votes were cast for President. Gerald Ford rather than Jimmy Carter would have won that election if about 9,000 voters in key states had gone for Ford instead of Carter.

When Milton R. Young, a Republican, ran for the Senate in North Dakota, he led his challenger by fewer than 100 votes out of more than 236,000 cast. The offi-

▲ Colorful buttons are a popular way to encourage people to exercise their right to vote.

cial **canvass**, the vote count by the official body that tabulates election returns and certifies the winner, finally confirmed Young's victory. Sometimes victory hinges on a single vote. In a Cincinnati, Ohio, suburb a candidate for the town council was suddenly hospitalized and unable to vote. When the votes were counted, he had lost by one vote.

Registering to Vote

Americans must take the initiative if they want to vote. Unlike in many countries, in the United States you must **register**, or enroll with the appropriate local government.

Why Do You Have to Register to Vote?

Registration became common in the late 1800s as a way to stop voting fraud. In those days the slogan "Vote Early and Often" was not a joke. In Denver in 1900, for example, one man confessed to having voted 125 times on Election Day! Reformers saw registration as a way to stop such abuses and clean up elections by giving officials a list of who could legally vote. In the South, registration laws came to be used to stop African Americans and poor whites from voting.

How Can I Register to Vote?

Registration requirements are set by state law and differ from state to state. Telephone your local board of elections, or county or city government to check on your state's requirements.

Usually, you must register to vote from 15 to 30 days before an election. Only three states (Maine, Minnesota, and Wisconsin) allow you to register on Election Day.

Many states now let voters register by mail. In most of these states you can obtain mail registration forms by contacting the city or county clerk's office, the local board of elections, or the secretary of state's office.

To register in person, go to a local government office, such as the city or county

Teach

Guided Practice

L1 Drawing a Flow Chart To help students better understand registration procedures, you might obtain from your local board of elections informational pamphlets and flyers on how to register to vote. Distribute these materials to the class and discuss their contents. Then have students use the materials to develop a flow chart that illustrates the registration procedure. Suggest that students compare their flow charts by displaying them on the bulletin board. **LEP**

CONNECTIONS

History

Even with registration, ingenious precinct captains have continued to pad the election rolls. A 1970s review of the roll of one ward in a major city gave new meaning to the term "ghost voter." Dozens of voters were registered at addresses that actually were cemeteries. And writers Ernest Hemingway, T.S. Eliot, and James Joyce—long dead and never residents of the ward—were all registered at the same apartment building.

Cooperative Learning Activity

Have students work together to create a four-page informational pamphlet titled "All About the Vote." Have one group of students research such topics as local registration requirements, the kinds of ballots used, the location of polling places, and when elections are held. Another group might design the pamphlet and provide illustrations, while a third group might write the pamphlet. Display the pamphlet on the bulletin board. If you have video facilities, you might have students work at similar tasks to create a short informational film on how to vote. Play the video for other civics and government classes.

◄ Upon entering a polling place voters must identify themselves by signing a form.

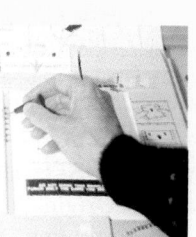

◄ Some polling places use ballots while others have voting machines.▼

L2 Analyzing Ideas If possible, obtain different types of ballots from the board of elections. Display these prominently, or allow students time to review them. Then lead the class in a discussion of the following questions:

1. What is your initial response to seeing the ballots? Explain.
2. Which ballots do you think would encourage straight-party voting? Why?
3. Do you think people would be discouraged from voting by these ballots? Why?
4. What, if any, changes would you make to these ballots to encourage people to vote? Explain.

L3 Panel Discussion Select two teams, each numbering three students, to discuss the following:

National standards should be established for the whole process of voting—from voting qualifications to registration requirements to the type of ballots used.

Encourage the rest of the class to join the discussion by asking questions and challenging team members' arguments.

CONNECTIONS

Political Processes
Most states have some form of permanent registration. Typically, voters remain registered until they move, fail to vote for a certain number of years or elections, are convicted of a serious crime, or are committed to a mental institution.

---

clerk, board of elections, or special registration office. In some states you can also register at such places as libraries, motor vehicle registration centers, post offices or banks, and schools.

Registration forms typically ask for your name, address, place and date of birth, sex, social security number, and date you are registering. You must also sign your name so your signature can be checked at the time you vote.

Voting Procedures

You vote at a **polling place** in your home **precinct**. A precinct is a voting district. Each city or county is usually divided into precincts containing from 200 to 1,000 voters.

What Happens at the Polling Place?

Procedures will vary slightly. Look over the sample ballot posted on a wall near the entryway. Then: (1) Go to the clerk or election judge's table and sign in by writing your name and address on an application form. (2) The clerk will read your name aloud and pass the application to a challenger, a local election official representing a political party. (3) The challenger compares your signature with your voter registration form. If they match, the challenger initials your form and returns it to you. (4) Give your form to a judge and enter the booth to vote.

Can My Right to Vote Be Challenged?

You cannot be stopped from voting because of your race, sex, religion, income, or political beliefs. You can be challenged, however, if there

is any question about your registration or your identification.

What Will the Ballot Look Like?

Two forms of ballots are generally used. An **office-group ballot** lists the candidates of all parties together by the office for which they are running. Their political party affiliation is listed beside their name. Many believe this form of ballot encourages **ticket-splitting**, voting for candidates from different parties for different offices.

The **party-column ballot** lists each party's candidates in a column under the party's name. There is usually a square or circle at the top of each party's column. By putting one mark in the square or circle, you can vote a straight ticket for all the party's candidates. You may also vote for each office individually by marking one box in each column. You may also write in the name of someone not listed on the ballot for any office.

How Do I Use the Voting Machine?

Voting machines are used in many polling places to count votes more quickly and accurately. The two most common types are the punch-card machine and the lever machine.

If you are given a punch-card as your ballot, enter the private booth and insert your card in the voting machine. Your punch-card will then be lined up with the names of the candidates. To vote use the stylus provided to punch holes in the appropriate places on the ballot. Once you punch the card, you cannot change your vote. Put your card in its envelope and give it to the election judge as you leave the booth. The judge will put your card in the ballot box. Your votes will be counted electronically when the polls close.

266 SPECIAL REPORT: VOTER'S HANDBOOK

Special Needs Strategy

Language Disability Students with language processing difficulties might have trouble understanding some of the new terms in this handbook. Select a term, such as *ticket-splitting,* from the key terms list on page 264. Then have students read the definition of ticket-splitting on page 266. (*Ticket-splitting is voting for candidates from different par-* *ties for different offices.*) As a way of helping students remember this new term, compare ticket-splitting to answering a number of multiple-choice questions. Rather than marking A as the answer for all questions, they must examine each question carefully to see which selection—A, B, or C—provides the best answer.

◄Voting machines with levers are designed to make voting fast and easy.

To use the lever machine, enter the booth and pull the large lever to one side to close a curtain around you. The ballot will face you and is part of the machine. To vote pull down the small levers by the names of the candidates you prefer. You can change your vote or correct a mistake by resetting any small lever. Once you have pulled all the small levers you want, pull the large lever again to open the curtain, record your vote, and reset the machine for the next voter.

Will My Vote Be a Secret?

The law entitles you to a secret ballot. Borrowed from a procedure developed in Australia in 1856, the **Australian ballot** was printed at government expense. The ballot listed all candidates, was given out only at the polls on Election Day, was marked in secret, and was counted by government officials. By the late 1800s, all states had adopted this system.

Who Actually Counts the Votes and Certifies a Winner?

A **canvassing board**, or official body that is usually bipartisan, counts votes. As soon as the polls close, the ballots from each precinct are forwarded to city or county canvassing boards. These boards put all the returns together and send them on to the state canvassing authority. Within a few days of the election, the state canvassing authority certifies the election of the winner. Each winner gets a certificate of election from the county or state canvassing board.

Through television and radio, people usually know the winners before canvassing boards certify them. In close elections the result may depend upon the official vote count and certification.

How Can I Prepare to Vote?

The best way to prepare to vote is to stay informed about candidates and public issues. As Election Day nears, newspapers, TV, radio, and news magazines will carry useful information. You might also try the following: (1) The local League of Women Voters may publish a *Voters' Information Bulletin*, a fact-filled, nonpartisan rundown on candidates and issues. (2) Each political party has literature and other information about their candidates and will be eager to share it with you. (3) Many interest groups such as the American Conservative Union, the Sierra Club, or the AFL-CIO Committee on Political Education rate members of Congress on their support for the group's programs. If you agree with the views of an interest group, check their ratings of candidates.

How Can I Choose a Candidate?

Everyone has different reasons for supporting one candidate over another. Asking these questions may help you decide: (1) Does the candidate stand for things I think are important? (2) Is the candidate reliable and honest? (3) Does the candidate have relevant past experience? (4) Will the candidate be effective in office? Look for the resources the person will bring to the job. Does the candidate have good political connections? (5) Does the candidate have a real chance of winning? You have a tough choice to make if it appears that your favorite candidate is a sure loser. You may want to vote for a sure loser to show support for a certain point of view, or as a protest vote. You may also want to vote for someone having the greatest chance of beating the candidate you like the least.

Special Circumstances

With more than 180 million potential voters, special circumstances always affect some voters. Over the years special procedures and protections have been developed to help ensure that despite such circumstances every American has the opportunity to vote.

What Is an Absentee Ballot?

An absentee ballot allows you to vote without going to the polls on Election Day. You must obtain an **absentee ballot** within a specified time

L3 Making Judgments Remind students that they may obtain information on candidates and elections from a variety of sources. These sources include newspapers, television news broadcasts, candidates' commercials and flyers, political party information, the League of Women Voters, and interest groups. Have students draw up annotated lists of sources of election information. Annotations should indicate how reliable and free of bias the sources are. Select students to read their lists to the class.

CONNECTIONS

Political Processes

Absentee voters can and do directly affect election outcomes. In the 1988 Senate race in Florida, two television networks unofficially declared Democrat Buddy McKay the winner on election night. A count of the absentee ballots, however, gave the victory to McKay's Republican opponent, Connie Mack.

Assess

Check for Understanding

Have students complete the Report Review on page 269.

Meeting Objectives

Each objective is tested by the Report Review questions that follow it in parentheses.
• Describe the voting process. (3, 4, 6, 7)
• Describe the importance of voting in a democracy. (5, 8)

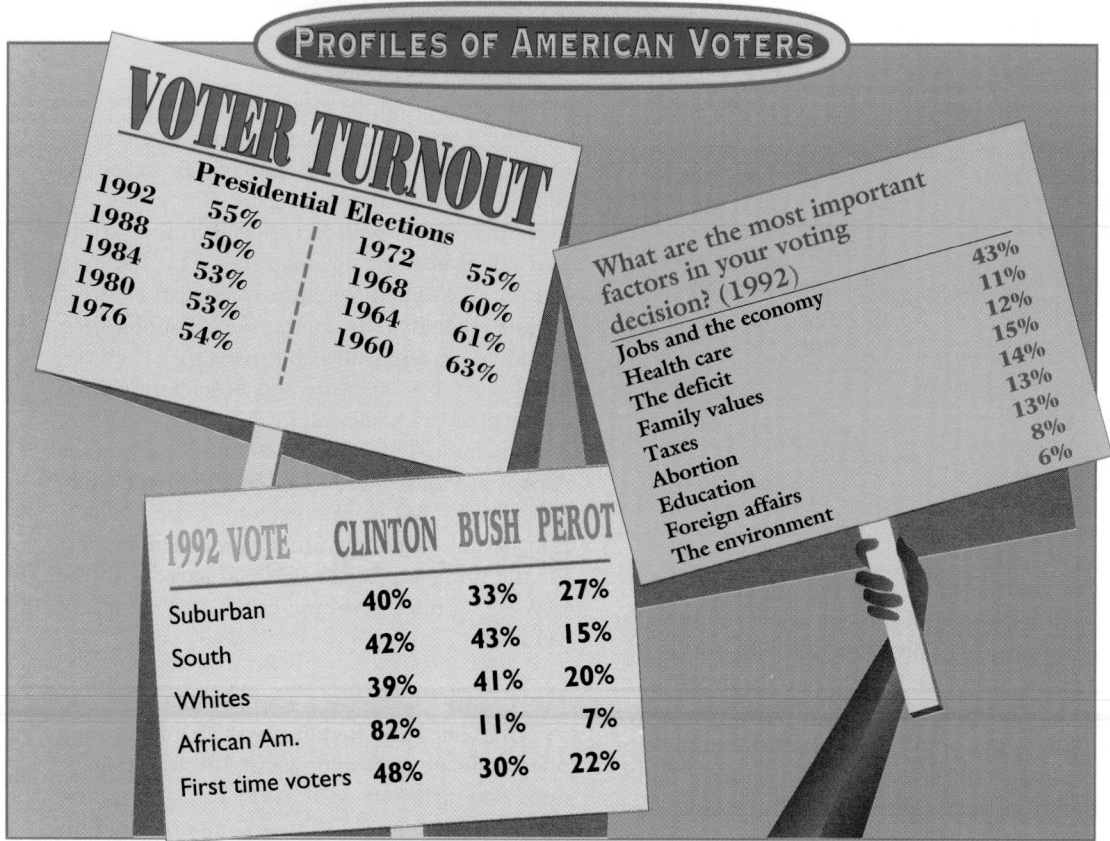

PROFILES OF AMERICAN VOTERS

VOTER TURNOUT

Presidential Elections

1992	55%		
1988	50%	1972	
1984	53%	1968	55%
1980	53%	1964	60%
1976	54%	1960	61%
			63%

What are the most important factors in your voting decision? (1992)

Jobs and the economy	43%
Health care	11%
The deficit	12%
Family values	15%
Taxes	14%
Abortion	13%
Education	13%
Foreign affairs	8%
The environment	6%

1992 VOTE	CLINTON	BUSH	PEROT
Suburban	40%	33%	27%
South	42%	43%	15%
Whites	39%	41%	20%
African Am.	82%	11%	7%
First time voters	48%	30%	22%

The National Voter Registration Law

"Voting is an empty promise unless the people vote. Now there is no longer the excuse of the difficulty of registration." With these words, President Clinton announced his support for the "Motor Voter" bill as he signed it into law on May 20, 1993.

Uphill Road to Passage

For years backers of motor-voter legislation had fought to pass a bill that would boost voter registration. Efforts to promote voter registration had already led to legislation in 27 states by 1992, but state programs varied in their effectiveness.

While nearly all politicians believed in the value of increasing voter participation, partisan politics had prevented a national voter registration law for five years. President Bush vetoed a bill passed by the Democratic Congress in 1992 because he believed it did not contain adequate safeguards against fraud. During the 1992 presidential campaign, Bill Clinton said he would have signed that bill. Legislators heard that very clear signal, and soon after President Clinton took office the House moved to enact a bill

nearly identical to the one Bush had vetoed. With support from a few key Republicans, the House and Senate passed a bill that contained the essential compromise provisions necessary to win support of majorities in both houses.

Key Provisions of the Law

The National Voter Registration law requires states to make registration forms available not only at motor vehicle departments but also at numerous state offices, welfare offices, and agencies that serve the disabled. It also requires states to allow mail-in registration. It permits, but does not require, states to use information from change-of-address forms filed with the Postal Service to update voter lists. Driver's license applicants are required to fill out a separate form for registering to vote. Public agencies must make it clear to beneficiaries that registering to vote is optional and that not registering will not affect the amount of assistance they receive.

Supporters of the bill believed that it would add 50 million citizens to the voting rolls when the changes take effect in 1995.

268

Cooperative Learning Activity

Organize the class into groups of 5. Have groups brainstorm to develop a 10-question fact-check test on information in the handbook. Suggest that groups include at least 2 questions on each of the 4 major sections in the handbook. Remind them to note the answers on a separate sheet. Have groups exchange test sheets. Then, using the round-robin method, have group members write answers to the questions. Have test sheets returned for marking to groups who wrote them.

before an election, fill it out, and return it (usually by mail) to the proper election official. The deadlines to apply for and return absentee ballots vary by state. Check with local election officials for details.

When Can I Use an Absentee Ballot?

Rules vary from state to state. Generally you may vote by absentee ballot if: (1) You will be out of town on Election Day. (2) You will be hospitalized on Election Day. (3) You have a physical disability or special illness that makes it difficult to get to the polling place. In such cases a doctor's certificate may be needed. (4) You cannot vote on Election Day because of religious observances. (5) You will be in jail for a misdemeanor or are awaiting trial.

In an effort to increase voter turnout, some states have relaxed rules on absentee ballots. Texas, for example, allows anyone who wishes to do so to cast an absentee ballot. The voter must simply request one.

How Do I Apply for an Absentee Ballot?

Request an absentee ballot (in person or by mail) from your local board of elections or other appropriate office. In order to receive your ballot, you will need to give your name, voting resi-dence, and reason for being absent from the polls on Election Day.

May Disabled Voters Receive Special Assistance?

Any voter who needs help in voting because of a disability is entitled to receive it. Some states allow you to pick the person to assist you. Other states require that only officials at the polling place can help. To protect disabled voters from pressure, some states require that two election officials from opposite parties be present during voting. Election officials may not disclose any information about how you voted.

Do Non-English-Speaking Voters Receive Special Help?

Under the Voting Rights Act of 1975, ballots and related election materials must be printed in the language of voting minorities as well as in English. This provision applies only in areas where illiteracy in English is high or recent voting turnout was unusually low.

Election materials, for example, are available in Spanish and English in many parts of Florida and in Texas, California, and other southwestern states. In Hawaii, election materials have recently been put into Cantonese, Ilocano, and Japanese as well as English.

REPORT REVIEW

Summary
In the United States, citizens 18 years old and older may exercise their right to vote. On Election Day these voters cast secret ballots in polling places in their precincts. To make informed decisions, voters should prepare for elections by learning about the candidates.

Checking for Understanding
Recalling Facts
1. Define **canvass, register, polling place, precinct, office-group ballot, ticket-splitting, party-column ballot, Australian ballot, canvassing board, absentee ballot.**
2. State the two requirements to vote in the United States.
3. Explain why Americans must register to vote.
4. Discuss the procedures for voting on Election Day.

Exploring Themes
5. Civic Participation How can citizens prepare to vote?
6. Civil Liberties What must election officials do to ensure that everyone who wants to vote is able to do so?

Critical Thinking Skills
7. Making Inferences Why do you think the secret ballot was adopted? What do you think is the most important question that you must ask about potential candidates when deciding how to vote? Why is this question so important?
8. Evaluating Information Many people have criticized early predictions of winners in elections based on exit polls. Do you agree or disagree with these criticisms? Why?

SPECIAL REPORT: VOTER'S HANDBOOK 269

Report Review Answers

1. Definitions of terms appear on pages indicated: **canvass,** 265; **register,** 265; **polling place,** 266; **precinct,** 266; **office-group ballot,** 266; **ticket-split-ting,** 266; **party-column ballot,** 266; **Australian ballot,** 267; **canvassing board,** 267; **absentee ballot,** 267
2. citizens at least 18 years old
3. to stop vote fraud and give election officials a list of who can legally vote

4. Sign an application form at the clerk's or judge's table. The clerk reads the voter's name aloud and passes the form to a challenger. The challenger compares the voter's signature with the signature on the registration form. If they match, the challenger initials the form and returns it to the voter. The voter gives the form to the clerk, enters the booth, and votes.
5. Stay informed about candidates and issues.
6. Be certain that provisions for absentee, disabled, and

non-English-speaking voters are in place.
7. to ensure that voters could not be pressured to vote a certain way; answers will vary: Students might suggest the candidate's honesty is the most important because corrupt officials could destroy the democratic system.
8. Answers will vary. Many students will agree and suggest that early predictions might discourage some people from voting.

Voter's Handbook
Lesson Plan, pages 264–269

Evaluate
Have students research if their local board of elections requires ballots to be printed in languages other than English. Have them write a brief report explaining their findings.

Reteach
For each subsection in the Handbook, have students write a statement summarizing the main idea. Have several students read their statements to the class. Ask the class to select the best summary for each subsection.

Enrich
Ask students to research and write a paper on a local or state election in which the outcome was decided by a few votes. Have students read their papers to the class.

Close
Have students hold a discussion on the importance of voting to the health of a democracy. You might begin the discussion by asking the following questions: Do you consider voting an important part of the democratic form of government? Why or why not? Should Americans be worried that only about 50 percent of those eligible to vote actually cast ballots? Why or why not? What would happen if nobody voted in elections?

Special Report: Voter's Handbook **269**

Focus

Bell Ringer

While attendance is being taken, ask students to react to the statement by John Jay on page 270.

Motivating Activity

To give students an idea of what Jay's statement might mean to them, have them imagine they are 18-year-old citizens. Ask all those who would be eligible to vote in the next presidential election to stand up. *(all should stand)* Then ask all those who would have been eligible to vote in a presidential election in the 1830s to remain standing. *(white males only)* Then point out that earlier in the nineteenth century only white males who owned property could vote. Tell students that this section deals with the various barriers to voting and how they were removed over the years.

Vocabulary Precheck

Write the key terms on the chalkboard. Ask students how each term relates to elections.
LEP

Teach

Guided Practice

L1 **History** Write the following terms on the chalkboard: *grandfather clause, literacy test, poll tax.* Select students to explain how each was used to deprive African Americans of their voting rights.

Caption Answer
African Americans, citizens without property, non-members of dominant churches

---

SECTION 3

The Elimination of Voting Barriers

V oting by United States citizens is absolutely vital to the success of American democracy. After all, democracy means rule by the people. Through their votes, Americans have the power to select more than 500,000 government officials at all levels of government.

The right to vote, or **suffrage**, is the foundation of American democracy. Today all United States citizens 18 years old or older may exercise this right. This situation did not always exist, however. In various periods in the history of the United States, law, custom, and sometimes even violence prevented certain groups from voting.

Early Limitations on Voting

Before the American Revolution, the colonies placed many restrictions upon the right to vote. Women and most blacks were not allowed to vote; neither were white males who did not own property or pay taxes. Also excluded in some colonies were people who were not members of the dominant religious group. As a result, only about 5 or 6 percent of the adult population was eligible to vote.

Why did restrictions exist? Educated men of the time did not believe in mass democracy in which every adult could vote. Even the Founders did not believe in the average person's ability to make wise voting decisions. In their view voting was best left to wealthy, white, property-owning males. As John Jay, first Chief Justice of the United States, put it, "The people who own the country ought to govern it."

During the first half of the nineteenth century, state legislatures gradually abolished property and

religious tests for voting. By the middle of the century the country had achieved universal white adult male suffrage.

Woman's Suffrage

The fight for woman's suffrage dates from the middle of the nineteenth century. Woman's suffrage

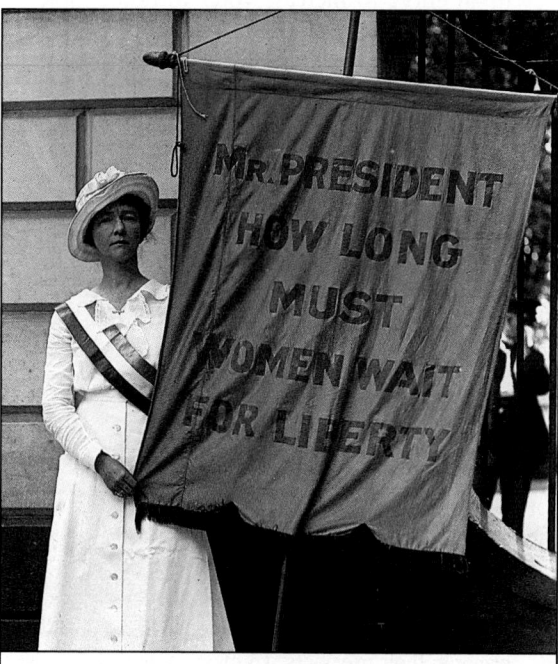

Demonstrating for the Right to Vote
In 1919 Congress approved the Nineteenth Amendment, paving the way for woman's suffrage. History **What other groups were once barred from voting?**

SECTION PREVIEW

Objectives
After studying this section, you should be able to:
■ Cite early restrictions on the right to vote in the United States.

■ Trace the process by which the right to vote was extended to women and to African Americans.

Key Terms and Concepts
suffrage, grandfather clause

Themes in Government
■ Federalism
■ Civil Rights

Critical Thinking Skills
■ Making Inferences
■ Predicting Consequences

270 UNIT 3: INFLUENCING GOVERNMENT

Classroom Resources for Section 3

📁 Guided Reading Activities
📁 Reproducible Lesson Plans
📁 Enrichment Activities 9
📁 Section 3 Quiz

▪ Testmaker
▪ Great Speeches, Volume V
  SAT Practice Tests

groups grew in number and effectiveness in the last half of the century, and by 1914 they had won the right to vote in 11 states, all of them west of the Mississippi. Not until after World War I, when the Nineteenth Amendment was ratified, was woman's suffrage on a nationwide basis put into effect. The Nineteenth Amendment states:

The right of citizens of the United States to vote shall not be denied or abridged by the United States or by any State on account of sex.

—NINETEENTH AMENDMENT, 1920

African American Suffrage

When the Constitution went into effect in 1789, African Americans, both enslaved and free, made up about 10 percent of the population. Yet nowhere were slaves permitted to vote, and free African Americans could vote in only a few states.

The Fifteenth Amendment The first effort to extend suffrage to African Americans on a nationwide basis came shortly after the Civil War when the Fifteenth Amendment was ratified in 1870. The amend-

L2 Making Generalizations
Have students study the graph of African American elected officials on page 272. Then ask students to make a generalization about the progress African Americans have made in being elected to public office. *(major gains at the local level, little progress at state and national level)*

L3 Debating Select six students to form two debate teams. Have the two teams debate the following:

Because young people between 18 and 29 made up less than 15 percent of those who voted in the 1990 elections, the Twenty-sixth Amendment has been a failure.

After the debate, poll the class on whether they agree with the debate proposition.

Focus on Freedom

Point out that the structure and wording of the Seneca Falls Declaration was modeled on the Declaration of Independence. Ask students why they think the members of the Seneca Falls Convention chose to do this. *(to dramatize their argument that they had been denied their "unalienable rights," to declare their "independence" from male oppression, to illustrate the irony of the Declaration of Independence)*

Answers

1. full rights of United States citizenship
2. as having no force or authority over them
3. Because at that time, upon marriage a woman's property rights and wages passed to the control of her husband. She, therefore, had few civil rights.

Focus on Freedom

SENECA FALLS DECLARATION

In the mid-nineteenth century in the United States, the main political issue was the freedom of enslaved African Americans. At the same time, however, many American women felt that they had no more rights than the slaves did. On July 19, 1848, women assembled at the Seneca Falls Convention, in New York, to begin the fight for equal rights. Below are excerpts from their declaration and resolutions.

The history of mankind is a history of repeated injuries and usurpations [seizures] on the part of man toward woman, having in direct object the establishment of an absolute tyranny over her. To prove this, let facts be submitted to a candid world.

He has never permitted her to exercise her inalienable right [to vote].

He has compelled her to submit to laws in the formation of which she had no voice. . . .

He has made her, if married, in the eye of the law, civilly dead.

He has taken from her all right in property, even to the wages she earns. . . .

After depriving her of all rights as a married woman, if single, and the owner of property, he has taxed her to support a government which recognizes her only when her property can be made profitable to it. . . .

He has denied her the facilities for obtaining a thorough education, all colleges being closed against her. . . .

He has endeavored, in every way that he could, to destroy her confidence in her own powers, to lessen her self-respect, and to make her willing to lead a dependent and abject life.

Now, in view of this entire [loss of the right to vote] of one half of the people in this country, their social and religious degradation—in view of

the unjust laws above mentioned, and because women do feel themselves aggrieved, oppressed, and fraudulently deprived of their most sacred rights, we insist that they have immediate admission to all the rights and privileges which belong to them as citizens of the United States. . . .

Resolved, That all laws which prevent woman from occupying such a station in society as her conscience shall dictate, or which place her in a position inferior to that of man, are contrary to the great precept of nature, and, therefore, of no force or authority. . . .

Resolved, That the women of this country ought to be enlightened in regard to the laws under which they live, that they may no longer publish their degradation by declaring themselves satisfied with their present position, nor their ignorance, by asserting that they have all the rights they want.

Examining the Document

Reviewing Facts
1. State the underlying goal the women are seeking.
2. Explain how the women view laws with which they do not agree.

Critical Thinking Skills
3. Making Inferences Why do the women classify themselves, when married, as "civilly dead"?

CHAPTER 9: ELECTIONS AND VOTING 271

Background

The United States' record on voting rights, while not perfect, stands up well in comparisons with other countries. For example, such notable Western democracies as France, Italy, and Belgium, did not give women the vote until the mid-1940s. Further, more than 25 percent of the countries that allow

free elections have a higher age requirement than the United States. Comparisons on minority voting rights, however, are more difficult to make because until recently most other democratic nations did not have such racial diversity.

Independent Practice

 Analyzing Political Speeches Show students President Johnson's speech on signing the 1965 Voting Rights Act from "Great Speeches," Volume V, *Social Studies Videos*. (You will need to preview the video to locate this material.) Have students write a paragraph explaining what Johnson thought was the significance of this legislation.

Graph Study Answer

In some local districts, African Americans are a majority of the voters. Successful state and national candidates need broader support.

Assess

Check for Understanding

Have students complete Section 3 Review on page 273.

GLENCOE
TECHNOLOGY

Focus on Government
Video 12
Making Connections:
Voting Rights
Running Time: 2:30
Videodisc 1, Chap. 12
VHS Tape 1, Begins 32:58

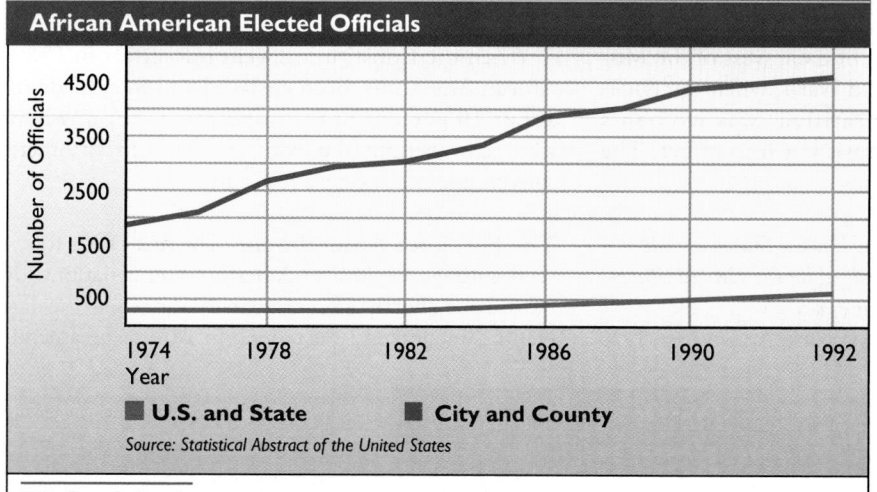

African American Elected Officials

Number of Officials

4500
3500
2500
1500
500

1974   1978   1982   1986   1990   1992
Year

■ **U.S. and State**   ■ **City and County**

Source: Statistical Abstract of the United States

Graph Study
The number of African Americans elected to office is increasing at the local and national levels. **Why do you think African Americans are making larger gains in local than in state and national elections?**

---

ment provided that no state can deprive any citizen of the right to vote "on account of race, color, or previous condition of servitude." In addition to extending suffrage to African Americans, this amendment was important because for the first time the national government set rules for voting, a power that only the states had previously exercised.

Grandfather Clause Although the Fifteenth Amendment was an important milestone on the road to full suffrage, it did not result in complete voting rights for African Americans. Southern states, for example, set up a number of roadblocks designed to limit and discourage the participation of African American voters.

One such roadblock was the so-called **grandfather clause** incorporated in the constitutions of some southern states. The grandfather clause provided that only voters whose grandfathers had voted before 1867 were eligible to vote without paying a poll tax or passing a literacy test. Because the grandfathers of most African American southerners had been enslaved and

had not been permitted to vote, this clause effectively prevented most of them from voting. The Supreme Court declared the grandfather clause unconstitutional in 1915.

Literacy Test Until recent years many states required citizens to pass a literacy test to qualify to vote. Some southern states used the literacy tests to keep African Americans from the polls. While in many cases white voters were judged literate if they could write their names, African American voters were often required to do much more. For example, they were frequently asked to explain a complicated part of the state or national constitution. The Voting Rights Acts of 1965 and 1970 and later additions to these laws outlawed literacy tests.

Poll Tax Another device designed to discourage African American suffrage was the poll tax. A poll tax was an amount of money—usually one or two dollars—that a citizen had to pay before he or she could vote. Because the poll tax had to be paid not only for the current year, but also for previous unpaid years as well, it was a financial burden for poor citizens of all ethnic backgrounds. In addition, the tax had to be paid well in advance of Election Day, and the poll-tax payer had to present a receipt showing payment before being permitted to enter the voting booth. Voters who lost their receipts were barred from voting. Thousands of African Americans in the poll-tax states were excluded from the polls.

Ratified in 1964, the Twenty-fourth Amendment outlawed the poll tax in national elections. The use of

---

STUDY GUIDE

Themes in Government
Federalism The federal government led the effort to end the disfranchisement of African Americans.

Civil Rights Well over 4 million African Americans have registered to vote in the South since 1965.

Critical Thinking Skills
Making Inferences Why did the southern states work so hard to

discourage African Americans from voting after 1870?
Predicting Consequences Identify some consequences resulting from the election of African Americans as big-city mayors.

Cooperative Learning Activity

Have students use *The Statesman's Year-Book, The World Almanac,* and encyclopedias to research information on woman's suffrage in other countries. Some students might like to work together to use this information to construct a chart showing when women won the vote in various countries. Others might like to work together on a report that compares the movement for woman's suffrage in the United States with that in other countries.

the poll tax in state elections, however, was not eliminated until a 1966 Supreme Court decision.

The Voting Rights Acts Despite the elimination of many discriminatory practices by the early 1960s, African American participation in elections, particularly in the South, was still limited. The civil rights movement of the 1960s resulted in national legislation that encouraged African Americans to participate in the electoral process. The first Voting Rights Act, passed in 1965, was one of the most effective suffrage laws ever passed in this country.

The Voting Rights Act of 1965 and later voting rights laws of 1970, 1975, and 1982 brought the federal government directly into the electoral process in the states. It empowered the federal government to register voters in any district where less than 50 percent of African American adults were on the voting lists. The government could also register voters in districts where it appeared that local officials were discriminating against African Americans.

The voting rights laws also forbade the unfair division of election districts in order to diminish the influence of African American voters or of other minority groups. The laws provided for the appointment of poll watchers to ensure that the votes of all qualified voters are properly counted. Literacy tests were abolished. The laws also required that ballots be printed in Spanish for Spanish-speaking communities. Other minority language groups—Native Americans, Asian Americans, Aleuts—were given the same right.

The Voting Rights Acts resulted in a dramatic increase in African American voter registration. In 1960 only 29 percent of all blacks in the South were registered. By the early 1990s, the figure had risen to more than 60 percent.

The opportunity to vote meant that African American southerners became an important factor in political life in the South. More than 1,000 African Americans were elected to political office within a few years of the passage of the Voting Rights Act of 1965. In the North, the election of African American mayors in cities such as Cleveland, Detroit, Chicago, New York, and Newark could be traced to the Voting Rights Acts as well.

The 26th Amendment

For many years 21 was the minimum voting age in most states. In the 1960s, however, a movement to lower the voting age to 18 began throughout the nation. The basic argument for lowering the voting age was that if individuals were old enough to be drafted and fight for their country, they were old enough to vote.

This debate ended with the ratification of the Twenty-sixth Amendment, which states:

> *The right of citizens of the United States, who are eighteen years of age or older, to vote shall not be denied or abridged by the United States or by any State on account of age.*
>
> —TWENTY-SIXTH AMENDMENT, 1971

This amendment gave over 10 million citizens between the ages of 18 and 21 the right to vote.

---

3 SECTION REVIEW

Section Summary
The Fifteenth, Nineteenth, and Twenty-sixth Amendments, as well as the Voting Rights Acts, eliminated legal barriers to voting for women, African Americans and other minorities, and 18-year-olds.

Checking for Understanding
Recalling Facts
1. Define suffrage, grandfather clause.
2. Specify by what means and in what year women were given the right to vote on a nationwide basis.
3. List two important changes in voting the Fifteenth Amendment initiated.
4. Name two results of the Voting Rights Acts.

Exploring Themes
5. Federalism Why were the provisions of the Voting Rights Acts important?
6. Civil Rights What have been the effects of the Voting Rights Acts in relation to African Americans?

Critical Thinking Skills
7. Making Inferences John Jay said, "The people who own the country ought to govern it." What impact did the extension of voting rights have on the meaning of Jay's statement?
8. Predicting Consequences What consequences did the Fifteenth and Twenty-fourth amendments have for African Americans?

CHAPTER 9: ELECTIONS AND VOTING 273

Meeting Objectives
Each section objective is tested by the Section Review questions that follow it in parentheses.
• Cite early restrictions on the right to vote in the United States. (2, 3, 7, 8)
• Trace the process by which the right to vote was extended to women and to African Americans. (2, 3, 4, 6, 8)

Evaluate
📁 Section 3 Quiz
💿 Testmaker

Reteach
Have students write a two-paragraph summary on how the right to vote has been extended in the United States since the country's founding. Select several students to read their summaries to the class.

Enrich
📁 Have students complete activity 9 in *Enrichment Activities* in the Teacher's Classroom Resources.

Close

Ask students: What barriers to voting, if any, still remain? *(Lack of education, disenchantment with the political system, feeling that their vote does not "count" keep some people from voting.)*

Section 3 Review Answers

1. Definitions of terms appear on pages indicated: **suffrage,** 270; **grandfather clause,** 272
2. through the ratification of the Nineteenth Amendment in 1920
3. The federal government for the first time set rules for voting. It also gave the vote to African American men.

4. greatly increased the number of African Americans registered to vote; made African Americans an important factor in political life in the South
5. They empowered the federal government to prevent voting rights discrimination at the state level.
6. enabled African Americans to become a political force, resulted in African Americans being elected to political office

7. Answers may mention that the extension of voting rights to women, African Americans, other minorities, and 18-year-olds considerably broadened membership in the group that "owned" the country.
8. Answers will vary, but most students will note that these amendments helped to lay the foundations of legal protection for African American voting rights.

Focus

Have students locate several maps in this textbook. Tell them to look at the maps and write down the two things every map has. Discuss their responses. *(title and a key)*

Teach

Have a volunteer explain the map key. Ask: What do the colors stand for? Point out that every map contains data that answers questions. Have students generate a list of questions that these maps could answer. *(What political parties were represented in the 1948 presidential election? From what parts of the country did each candidate get the most support? Who got the most votes?)* Write their questions on the chalkboard, and have volunteers use the maps to answer them. Remind students that these election maps do not show results of the popular vote. Ask: Why do election maps focus on electoral votes, not on popular votes? *(Only electoral votes count.)*

Assess

Have students complete the **Practice** exercise.

Close

Ask: What other kinds of political or economic information could be visually presented in map form?

Interpreting an Election Map

Election maps are designed to show information about an election. An election map might show, for example, the results of a presidential election or the outcome of a mayoral election, ward by ward, in a city. Election maps show information at a glance that would be much harder to understand if it were presented in table or paragraph form.

Explanation

To read an election map, follow these steps:
- Examine the map title or caption to determine what election information is being shown.
- Examine the map key to determine how information is being shown.
- Based on this information, decide what kinds of questions the map will answer.

Because we elect Presidents state by state rather than as a nation, an election map most easily shows presidential election results. The title on the map below tells us that it shows information about the distribution of electoral votes in the presidential election of 1948.

The map key tells us that color is used to indicate which candidate received each state's electoral votes. Purple indicates states that voted Republican; green indicates states that voted Democratic. Gold shows the four states that voted for the States' Rights Democratic party candidate, J. Strom Thurmond.

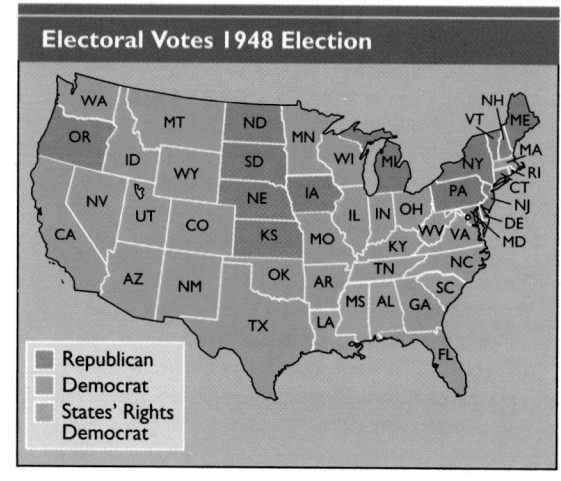

Electoral Votes 1948 Election

This map can answer some questions about the election of 1948 but not others. It does not, for example, answer any questions about the results of the popular vote. It does show the results of the vote in the Electoral College and can be used to calculate the total number of electoral votes each candidate won.

Practice

Examine the map below and use what you have learned to answer the questions that follow.

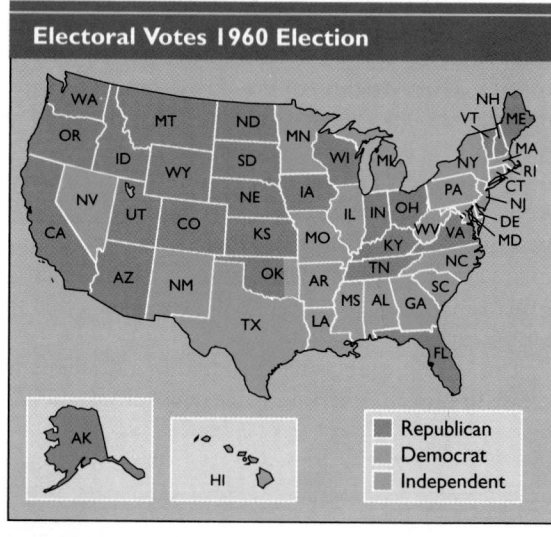

Electoral Votes 1960 Election

Republican
Democrat
Independent

1. What does the color purple indicate on this map?
2. What does the color green indicate on this map?
3. How many states supported the Republican candidate?
4. What states split their electoral vote?
5. Compare the two maps. Which states that voted Republican in 1948 voted Democratic in 1960?

Additional Practice

To practice this skill, see **Reinforcing the Skill** on page 281.

Practice Answers

1. states where the Republican presidential candidate received the electoral votes
2. states where the Democratic presidential candidate received the electoral votes
3. 25
4. Alabama and Oklahoma

5. Pennsylvania, New York, Maryland, Delaware, Michigan, New Jersey, and Connecticut

For additional practice, have students complete activity 9 in *Skill Reinforcement Activities* in the Teacher's Classroom Resources.

SECTION 4

Nonvoters

The historic struggles over the extension of suffrage have resulted in more Americans having the right to vote than ever before. Nevertheless, many Americans who wish to vote cannot do so because they do not meet current voting requirements. At the same time, many Americans do not choose to exercise their right to vote.

Current Voting Requirements

Almost all states have three basic suffrage requirements. These requirements are United States citizenship, residency, and registration. If a voter does not fulfill all of these requirements, then he or she is not permitted to vote.

The Citizenship Requirement All states limit the voting right to American citizens. A citizen is considered part of American political life, while an alien is not. Even people who have lived in this country for many years but who have not formally become United States citizens may not vote in American elections.

The Residency Requirement Most states require voters to be residents of the state for a certain period before they are allowed to vote.

Before 1970 the period of required residence ranged from 3 months to 2 years. The Voting Rights Act of 1970, however, along with two Supreme Court decisions, created a residence period of 30 days in all elections. In a few states, this period may be extended to 50 days. Some states, like New Mexico, have no required residence period at all.

Why is a residency requirement even needed?

When a voter moves to a new state, he or she needs time to become informed about local and state issues and candidates. Suppose a voter moves from Chicago to Atlanta and arrives in Atlanta five days before a city election for mayor. Many people argue that a newcomer cannot become informed about the election in such a short time.

The Registration Requirement All states, with the exception of North Dakota, require voters to register or record their names officially with local election boards. On Election Day, an election official must check voters' names. Voters whose names are on this list sign in by writing their names on a form. Registration is a way to prevent voter fraud or dishonest elections.

In the past some states used a voter registration system that required citizens to reregister every 5 to 10 years. Today all voter registration is permanent. Permanent registration means that a voter, once registered, remains on the list unless he or she dies, moves, or fails to vote within a certain number of years. Alaska, for example, removes the names of those who do not vote for 2 years. Oklahoma, however, waits 8 years before canceling a voter's registration.

Why Citizens Do Not Vote

The percentage of Americans voting in presidential elections has generally declined from about 62 percent in 1960 to 55 percent in 1992. The 1992 figure, however, marked the first increase since 1960, thanks in part to a spirited three-way race. In the presidential election of 1960, about 41 million citizens of voting

---

SECTION PREVIEW

Objectives
After studying this section, you should be able to:
- Outline **current voting requirements.**

- Cite **reasons why many American citizens do not vote.**

Key Terms and Concepts
initiative, proposition, referendum, recall

Themes in Government
- Civic Responsibility
- Political Processes

Critical Thinking Skills
- Making Inferences
- Predicting Consequences

CHAPTER 9: ELECTIONS AND VOTING 275

Classroom Resources for Section 4

- Guided Reading Activities
- Reproducible Lesson Plans
- Participating in Government 9
- Interpreting Political Cartoons 8
- Primary and Secondary Source Readings 9
- Reteaching Activities 9

- Section 4 Quiz
- Chapter 9 Tests
- Testmaker
- Audio Cassettes (English and Spanish)
- Limited English Proficiency Activities 9

Focus

Bell Ringer

While attendance is being taken, ask students to write a response to the following:

Why vote? When millions of votes are cast in an election, one more or less makes no difference.

Motivating Activity

Discuss students' Bell Ringer responses. (*Students should note that by voting, people exercise a hard-won civil right. Also, if people want to influence government, they must take part in the political process.*) Then point out that the polling booth has been described as the world's greatest *civil-righter.* Ask students to speculate on the meaning of this description. (*The voting booth makes people equal because each vote has equal value regardless of who casts it.*) Then ask: Do you think the person who coined this description considered voting important? Why? (*Yes; it suggests that voting gives people equal power.*) Draw this activity to a close by pointing out that only about half of those eligible to vote do so.

Vocabulary Precheck

Call on students to read aloud the definitions of the key terms from the Glossary. Then have volunteers use each term in a sentence. **LEP**

Teach

Guided Practice

L1 Making Inferences Note that more elections are held in the United States than in practically any other democratic country. The only country that holds more—Switzerland—has a slightly lower voter turnout rate than the United States. Ask students to infer what impact, if any, the frequency of elections has on voter turnout. Then have them speculate on other factors that may influence voter turnout.

L2 Analyzing Ideas Have students write a few sentences explaining why the *initiative*, *referendum*, and *recall* are classified as "direct democracy." Ask for volunteers to read their sentences to the class. Discuss how direct democracy differs from representative democracy.

CONNECTIONS

Political Processes
In the 1988 elections, California set something of a record when it placed 29 statewide initiative proposals, or propositions, and referenda on its ballots.

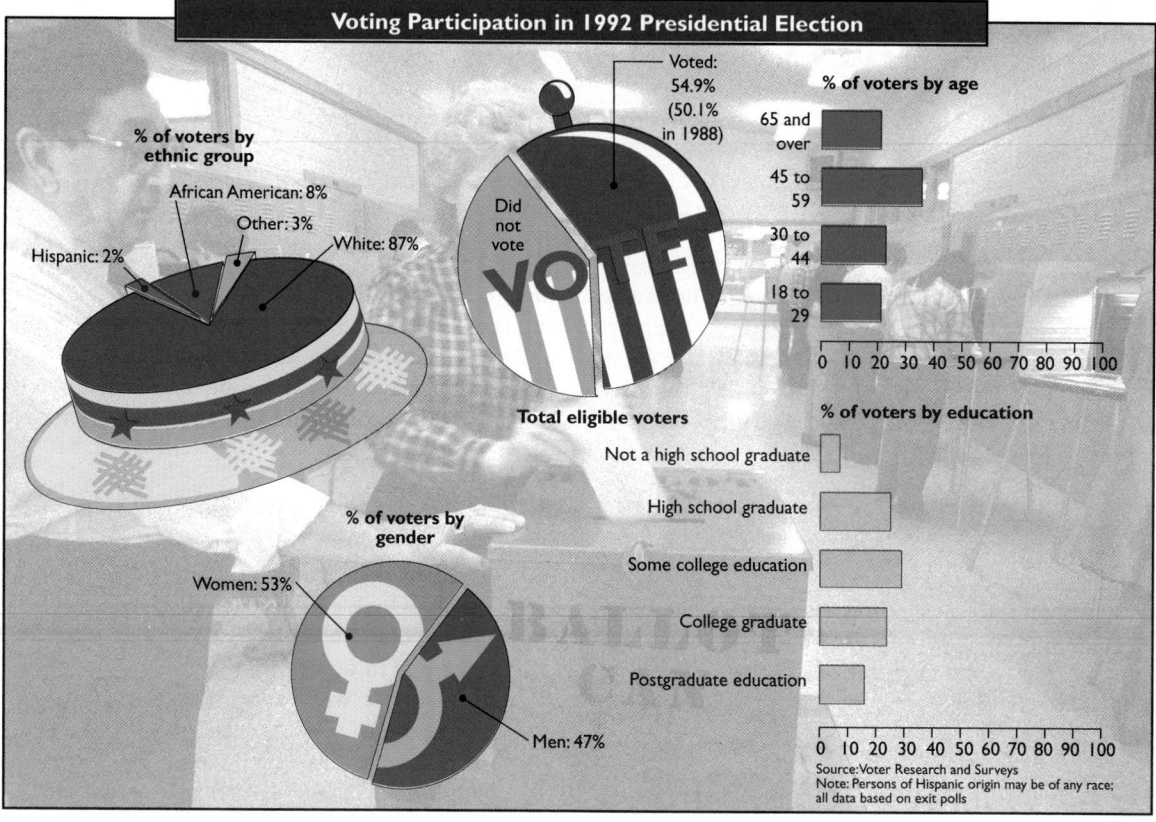

Voting Participation in 1992 Presidential Election

% of voters by ethnic group
- African American: 8%
- Other: 3%
- Hispanic: 2%
- White: 87%

Voted: 54.9% (50.1% in 1988)
Did not vote
Total eligible voters

% of voters by age
- 65 and over
- 45 to 59
- 30 to 44
- 18 to 29

0 10 20 30 40 50 60 70 80 90 100

% of voters by gender
- Women: 53%
- Men: 47%

% of voters by education
- Not a high school graduate
- High school graduate
- Some college education
- College graduate
- Postgraduate education

0 10 20 30 40 50 60 70 80 90 100

Source: Voter Research and Surveys
Note: Persons of Hispanic origin may be of any race; all data based on exit polls

age did not vote. In the 1992 presidential election, the number had grown to about 84 million. Even fewer Americans vote in congressional elections. The voting rate is lower still in state and local elections.

Residency and Registration Requirements
Many Americans do not vote because they do not meet the residency or registration requirements of their states. Surveys reveal that in the 1992 presidential election 59.5 million people were not registered to vote. Millions of other possible voters did not meet the residency requirements.

One problem in meeting residency and registration standards is that American society is highly mobile. Experts estimate that almost one-fifth of Americans move to a new location every five years. A new resident may forget to register. He or she may find that the registration offices are open only a few hours a day, or open at inconvenient times, thus discouraging registration.

Certainly, relatively complicated registration procedures and residency requirements affect voter participation. In recent years, however, these requirements have been made less burdensome, and voter turnout is still low.

A Profile of Regular Voters Citizens who vote regularly have certain positive attitudes toward government and citizenship. They believe that a good citizen has a duty or an obligation to vote. Many regular voters are interested in political events, issues, and candidates. They believe their votes will help select leaders who can deal effectively with the nation's problems. It

276 UNIT 3: INFLUENCING GOVERNMENT

Background

Some recent elections seem to suggest that non-voters will register and turn out if they feel that their vote can make a difference. In the 1983 Chicago mayoral election, African American candidate Harold Washington constantly impressed upon African Americans he could win if they got involved in the electoral process. In response, African Americans registered in droves, and for both the primary and general mayoral elections African American turnout in some neighborhoods was well over 75 percent. This high turnout, coupled with strong support from white liberals, helped Washington to victory.

makes a difference to them which party and which candidates win. These voters feel they have a real say in how the government is run. To put it simply:

Why should anyone vote? There are four reasons: (1) voting is what democracy is all about; (2) the entire system would collapse if no one voted; (3) voting is the only way that you can be sure that your voice will be heard; and (4) voting is simply important in itself.

—ROBERT E. DiCLERICO AND ERIC M. USLANER, *FEW ARE CHOSEN, 1984*

Investigators have found that education, age, and income are important factors in predicting which citizens will vote. The more education a citizen has, the more likely it is that he or she will be a regular voter. Middle-aged citizens have the highest voting turnout of all age groups. Voter regularity also increases with income—the higher a person's income, the more regularly that person votes.

A Profile of Nonvoters Perhaps the most important personal quality of nonvoters is that they are uninterested in politics. They do not seem to care who

wins or loses elections. Their attitude is that "it doesn't make any difference who is elected because things never seem to work out right" and "candidates say one thing before they're elected and do another after they're elected." Robert M. Hutchins describes the effect this attitude has on democracy:

The death of democracy is not as likely to be assassination from ambush. It will be a slow extinction from apathy, indifference, and undernourishment.

—ROBERT M. HUTCHINS

Increases in NonVoting One reason for declining voter turnout is that citizens' views of government have become increasingly negative. Many people believe that government cannot be trusted. Another reason for voter decline is that, as the government faces more serious and more complicated problems, more Americans seem convinced that government can do little to help them.

Ways of Increasing Voter Turnout Political experts who are concerned about the high rate of nonvoting in the United States have suggested a number of ways to get more citizens to the polls on Election

PARTICIPATING IN GOVERNMENT

Exit Polls

Television coverage of presidential campaigns and elections has become big business. On election night networks cover the returns and predict winners in key states. To make these predictions, the networks depend on the results of exit polls.

In an exit poll the networks interview people who have just voted. The questions usually are limited to: (1) Are you a Republican, a Democrat, or an Independent? (2) What candidate did you vote for in the election? The networks then compile the results of the

polls to help them predict a winner, often before the polls have closed in some parts of the country.

Exit polls are often valid projections of election results because the participants are selected at random. Such random selection means that the people questioned will probably represent a cross section of the electorate.

If you are asked to partic-

ipate in an exit poll, you are of course free to refuse to answer questions. If you choose to answer, however, be certain to answer the questions honestly and directly. Then your replies will help make the results of the poll valid.

Investigating Further

Find out the restrictions on political campaigning and exit polls in your community from the League of Women Voters, the election board, or resources in the library and report your findings to the class.

L3 Making Generalizations Have students study the graphs on nonvoters on page 276. Have students write a generalization for each category shown on the graphs. Provide the following example: The rate of voting among voters aged 45 to 64 and those 65 or over is about the same. Have students compare their generalizations by sharing them with the class.

Independent Practice

L2 Making a Poster Have students work cooperatively or individually to create posters encouraging people to vote. Suggest that the focus of their posters should be an attention-grabbing slogan. Have students display their posters on the bulletin board.

Interpreting Political Cartoons Have students complete activity 8 in *Interpreting Political Cartoons* in the Teacher's Classroom Resources.

PARTICIPATING IN GOVERNMENT

Point out that many political scientists feel that broadcasting exit poll results before polling places have closed discourages potential voters. Ask students to discuss how this might affect the outcome of elections.

Allow students time to share the findings of their investigation into exit poll restrictions.

Have students complete activity 9 in *Participating in Government* in the Teacher's Classroom Resources.

Assess

Check for Understanding

Have students complete Section 4 Review on page 278.

Special Needs Strategy

Language Disability Explaining the prefix of each term and then giving related words will help students with language processing problems understand the key terms in this section. For example, *pro* is a prefix meaning "forward." *Propose* and *propo-*

nent are related to *proposal*, all of which carry the sense of putting an idea forward. Have students follow this procedure to explain the meaning of *initiative* and *recall*.

Graph Study Answer
increases number of voters choosing members of Congress

Meeting Objectives

Each section objective is tested by the Section Review questions that follow it in parentheses.

• Outline current voting requirements. (2, 3)
• Cite reasons why many American citizens do not vote. (4, 5, 6, 7, 8)

Evaluate

📁 Section 4 Quiz

💻 Testmaker

Reteach

📁 Have students complete activity 9 of *Reteaching Activities* in the Teacher's Classroom Resources.

Enrich

📁 Have students complete activity 9 in the *Primary and Secondary Source Readings* in the Teacher's Classroom Resources.

Close

Ask students whether they think they will be voters or nonvoters. Have them explain their decisions. Stress their obligation, as good citizens, to exercise their right to vote.

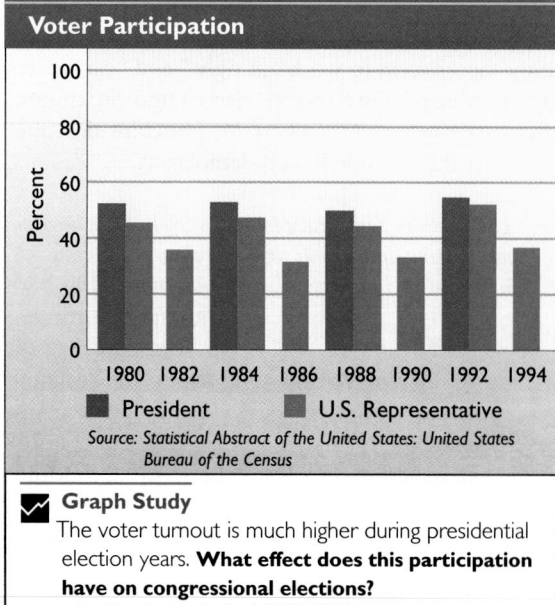

Voter Participation

Source: Statistical Abstract of the United States: United States Bureau of the Census

📈 **Graph Study**
The voter turnout is much higher during presidential election years. **What effect does this participation have on congressional elections?**

Day. For example, shift Election Day from Tuesday to Sunday, so that citizens are free to vote without having to take time off from work. Another idea would be to allow voters to register on Election Day. Some favor a national registration system, so that voters' registration follows them to a new state when they move. Perhaps the most drastic suggestion is to fine citizens who have no valid excuse for not voting.

Studies show that voter turnout increases when voters have an opportunity to participate directly in the legislative process. In many states they may do this through the procedures of the initiative, the referendum, and the recall.

Initiative The **initiative** is a procedure by which voters may propose a law or a state constitutional amendment. The procedure begins when citizens obtain a sufficient number of signatures on a petition calling for a new law or a new amendment. The proposed new law or amendment is called a **proposition**.

In a direct initiative, the proposition is presented directly to the voters in a general election. If the majority of voters approve the proposition, it becomes law. In an indirect initiative, the proposition goes first to the state legislature. If the legislature passes the proposition, it becomes law. If the legislature fails to pass the proposition within a certain time, it goes to the voters for their approval.

Referendum A **referendum** is a procedure by which voters approve or disapprove a measure the state legislature has passed.

An optional referendum allows the legislature voluntarily to provide that a particular bill will not become law until the voters approve it. Some states provide for a mandatory referendum. Under this system certain kinds of bills, such as those dealing with taxes, must be approved by the voters before becoming law.

Recall A **recall** provides a way for voters to remove elected officials who are incompetent or untrustworthy before their terms expire. Officials are recalled at special elections called for that purpose.

---

4 SECTION REVIEW

Section Summary
Many American citizens are nonvoters, due in part to current voting requirements, apathy, and a feeling of powerlessness.

Checking for Understanding
Recalling Facts
1. Define initiative, proposition, referendum, recall.
2. List the three basic suffrage requirements in almost all states.
3. Identify the purpose of voter registration.
4. Explain why the rate of nonvoting has increased recently.

Exploring Themes
5. Civic Responsibility What are some reasons Ameri-

cans give for not exercising their right to vote?
6. Political Processes Many believe that the entire American system of democracy would collapse if no one voted. Do you agree with this view? Support your answer.

Critical Thinking Skills
7. Making Inferences Why do you think middle-aged citizens with more education and higher incomes have the highest voting turnout?
8. Predicting Consequences Fining the nonvoter is a suggestion that has been offered to encourage citizens to vote. How do you think Americans would respond to this?

278 UNIT 3: INFLUENCING GOVERNMENT

Section 4 Review Answers

1. Definitions of terms appear on pages indicated: **initiative,** 278; **proposition,** 278; **referendum,** 278; **recall,** 278
2. United States citizenship, residency, registration
3. to prevent the occurence of fraudulent voting and dishonest elections
4. because citizens' views of government have become increasingly negative and many people feel that govern-

ment officials can do little to solve today's complicated problems
5. Answers may include: failure to meet residency requirements, lack of knowledge about the voting process, apathy, loss of faith in government, disagreement with government policies, or disappointment with candidates
6. Answers should indicate that a democracy would indeed fail if it is not a "government by the people."

7. Answers might suggest that such people may feel they have a greater stake in the outcome of government policies and may be better informed about issues.
8. Answers should address whether or not democracy guarantees the right *not* to vote.

Barbara Jordan on Civic Participation

Barbara Jordan was the first African American woman from a southern state to serve in Congress. A Texas Democrat, Jordan was a member of the House of Representatives from 1973 to 1979. In 1976 she became the first African American keynote speaker at a Democratic Convention. Below are excerpts from that address.

We believe that the people are the source of all governmental power; that the authority of the people is to be extended, not restricted. This can be accomplished only by providing each citizen with every opportunity to participate in the management of the government. . . .

Government which represents the authority of all the people, not just one interest group, but all the people, has an obligation to actively underscore, actively seek to remove those obstacles which would block individual achievement . . . obstacles emanating from race, sex, economic condition. The government must seek to remove them.

We have a positive vision of the future founded on the belief that the gap between the promise and reality of America can one day be finally closed. . . .

These are the foundations upon which a national community can be built.

Let's all understand that these guiding principles cannot be discarded for short-term political gains. They represent what this country is all about. . . . And these are principles which are not negotiable. . . .

A nation is formed by the willingness of each of us to share in the responsibility for upholding the common good.

A government is invigorated when each of us is willing to participate in shaping the future of this nation.

In this election year we must define the common good and begin again to shape a common future. Let each person do his or her part. If one citizen is unwilling to participate, all of us are going to suffer. For the American idea, though it is shared by all of us, is realized in each one of us.

And now, what are those of us who are elected public officials supposed to do? We call ourselves public servants but I'll tell you this: we as public servants must set an example for the rest of the nation. It is hypocritical for the public official to admon-

> *It is hypocritical for the public official to admonish and exhort the people to uphold the common good if we are derelict. . . .*

ish and exhort the people to uphold the common good if we are derelict in upholding the common good. More is required of public officials than slogans and handshakes and press releases. More is required. We must hold ourselves strictly accountable. We must provide the people with a vision of the future. . . .

I am going to close my speech by quoting a Republican President and I ask you that as you listen to these words of Abraham Lincoln, relate them to the concept of a national community . . . "As I would not be a slave, so I would not be a master. This expresses my idea of Democracy. Whatever differs from this, to the extent of the difference is no Democracy."

—BARBARA JORDAN, 1976

Examining the Reading

Reviewing Facts
1. State who the Democratic party considers to be the source of governmental power.
2. Identify the obstacles that Jordan believes block individual achievement.

Critical Thinking Skills
3. Making Inferences How does Jordan differentiate between the civic responsibilities of the average American and those of elected public officials?

Focus

Have students recall a committee on which they served. Discuss the responsibilities that belonged to the committee as a whole and those that belonged to each individual committee member. Ask students to note Jordan's distinctions between governmental and individual responsibility.

Teach

Ask: Whom does Jordan hold responsible for removing obstacles to individual achievement? Why? *(the government; It represents the authority of all the people.)* What people is Jordan censuring in the next to last paragraph? *(self-serving public officials)* What is Jordan's concept of national community?

Assess

Have students complete **Examining the Reading.**

Answers
1. the people
2. obstacles emanating from race, sex, economic conditions
3. The average citizen must participate to reap the rewards of a democracy, while public officials must participate further by setting examples, being accountable, and shaping the future.

Close

Jordan states each American must "share in the responsibility for upholding the common good." What is the "common good"?

More About Personal Perspectives

Inspired by an African American woman lawyer who visited her Houston high school on career day, Barbara Jordan tackled law school and passed both the Massachusetts and Texas bar exams. Unsuccessfully bidding for the Texas State House of Representatives in 1962 and 1964, she won a Texas senate seat in 1966. She successfully ran for the United States House of Representatives in 1972 and with the support of former President Lyndon Johnson, became a member of the House Judiciary Committee. Her participation in the Watergate investigation attracted national attention.

Identifying Terms and Concepts

1. political action committees,
2. suffrage, 3. straight-party
ticket, 4. electorate, 5. proposition, 6. recall

Reviewing Facts and Ideas

1. Since 270 electoral votes are needed to win the presidency, candidates tend to pay special attention to states with large electoral votes. They might make more personal visits to or run special television campaigns in these states.

2. The campaign organization for a presidential campaign operates on the national, state, and local levels. National campaign managers are responsible for the overall strategy and planning of the campaign. The state party chairperson coordinates the state and local levels of the campaign. Local party officials and workers contact voters, hold rallies, and distribute campaign literature.

3. Presidential candidates receive federal funding to conduct their campaigns.

4. Presidential candidates may spend a great deal of time, effort, and money on producing campaign commercials for television. Also, televised debates can make or break presidential candidates.

5. voter's personal background, loyalty to political party, interest in campaign issues, and image of the candidate

6. grandfather clause, literacy test, poll tax

7. It empowered the federal government to register voters in districts in the South where less than 50 percent of eligible African American voters were registered or where it appeared that local electoral officials were discriminating against African Americans.

8. 30 days

9. permanent registration—where voters, once registered, remain on the voting lists until they die,

9 CHAPTER REVIEW

Summary and Significance

Voting is a right and a responsibility of citizens in a democracy. Election campaigns, aimed directly at voters, must be well financed and well organized in order to project a favorable image of the candidate. Personal background, party loyalty, and current issues all influence a voter's choice of candidates. Although most legal barriers to voting have been eliminated, many Americans are nonvoters. Despite efforts to increase voter turnout, many Americans do not believe that their vote can make a difference or that the government is effective in solving the nation's problems, Democracy cannot function effectively without the participation of the citizens it represents.

Identifying Terms and Concepts

Write the key term that best completes each sentence.

proposition   electorate
political action committees   suffrage
straight-party ticket   recall

1. Political candidates often receive campaign contributions and support from _____.
2. Women in the United States gained _____ in 1920.
3. Most independents do not vote a _____.
4. A significant portion of the _____ does not vote.
5. A _____ is a proposed new law or amendment.
6. A procedure known as _____ enables voters to remove elected officials before their terms expire.

Reviewing Facts and Ideas

1. Relate how the number of electoral votes of a state affects presidential campaigning.
2. Describe presidential campaign organizations.
3. Specify what is meant by public funding of presidential elections.
4. Describe what effect television has had on presidential elections.
5. List four factors that influence voters' decisions.
6. Cite the three devices used after 1870 to prevent African Americans from voting.
7. Explain how the Voting Rights Act of 1965 brought the federal government directly into the electoral process of the states.
8. Specify how long a person must reside in a state before he or she is eligible to vote.
9. Describe the voter registration system used today.

Applying Themes

1. Civic Responsibility Franklin D. Roosevelt once said, "A government can be no better than the public opinion that sustains it." Explain why you agree or disagree with this statement.
2. Political Processes Individuals have suggested extending public financing of election campaigns to include congressional campaigns. Explain the advantages and disadvantages of this idea.
3. Federalism Why were the Voting Rights Acts necessary?
4. Civil Rights The right to vote belongs to every United States citizen. In your opinion, what do citizens forfeit if they do not exercise their right to vote?

Critical Thinking Skills

1. Making Inferences The Twenty-sixth Amendment enabled 18-year-olds to vote. In terms of percentage, however, far fewer members of this age bracket actually exercise their right to vote than is the case with any other age group. How might you explain this?
2. Synthesizing Information How do campaign workers try to convince nonvoters that they should vote for a specific candidate?
3. Demonstrating Reasoned Judgment How can voters make informed judgments about candidates?
4. Predicting Consequences Identify at least three consequences that could result from limiting the amount of money an individual could give to a political campaign.

move, or fail to vote for a certain number of years; periodic registration—where voters must re-register every 5, 7, or 10 years, depending on state requirements

Applying Themes

1. Answers should indicate that the quality and responsiveness of a government depends on the knowledge and participation of its citizens.

2. advantages: would enable more people to run for office and would prevent public office from becoming exclusively the realm of the rich; disadvantages: If campaign spending was limited to federal funds, candidates might not be able to stage

Linking Past and Present

I hope you'll look not at who is most handsome, or who has the best rhetoric, the rhetoric that stirs your soul. It does no good to find someone who turns you on if they aren't electable.

—MORRIS UDALL, PRESIDENTIAL CANDIDATE, 1976

What does Morris Udall mean by "electable"? He states that looks or flowery speeches should not be enough to get an individual elected President; yet the physical image a candidate projects seems to increase in importance as the years go by.

Reaction to and discussion of the candidates' looks, however, is nothing new. In the 1860 presidential campaign, southern newspapers made an issue of Abraham Lincoln's physical appearance. The Houston Telegraph stressed Lincoln's bad looks:

Lincoln is the leanest, lankest, most ungainly mass of legs and arms and hatchet face ever strung on a single frame.

—HOUSTON TELEGRAPH, 1860

The New York Tribune, however, defended Lincoln with the following:

Truth constrains us to say that 'Honest Abe' is not a handsome man; but he is not so ill-looking as he has been represented. 'Handsome is as handsome does,' however, is a sensible adage.

—NEW YORK TRIBUNE, 1860

What role should a person's appearance play in their qualifications for public office? Support your opinion.

Writing About Government

Persuasive Writing Write a convincing argument agreeing or disagreeing with the statement below.

My nonvoters, who are called apathetic, really just think unacceptable alternatives are being offered to them. The lesser of two evils is still evil.

—SY LEON, HEAD OF THE UNITED STATES LEAGUE OF NONVOTERS, 1976

Reinforcing the Skill

Interpreting an Election Map Examine the map below and use what you have learned to answer the questions that follow.

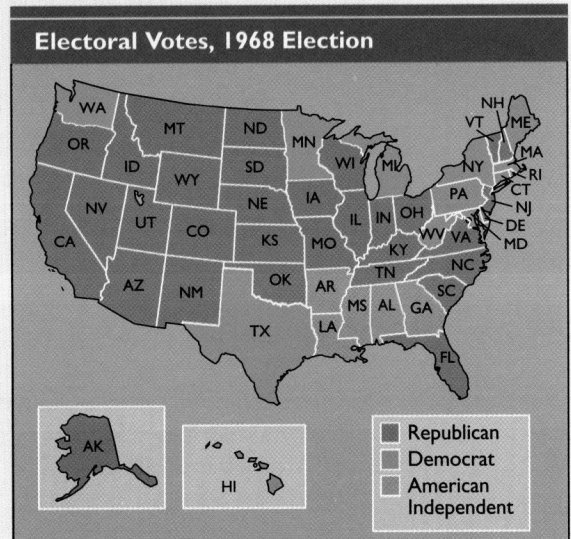

Electoral Votes, 1968 Election

Republican
Democrat
American Independent

1. What does the color green indicate on this map?
2. How does the map show which states voted for Richard Nixon?
3. Where was the American Independent party strong?
4. How would you describe the regional distribution of votes in this election?
5. Compare this map with the map of the 1960 election on page 274. Which states that voted Republican in 1960 voted Democratic in 1968?

Investigating Further

1. **Individual Project** Draw a political cartoon depicting a reason people give for not voting.
2. **Cooperative Learning** Organize into groups of five or six. Each member of the group chooses four qualities a President should have. Agree on eight qualities that you think are important for an officeholder. Arrange the qualities in their order of importance, from most important to least important. How can you find out about the qualifications of those seeking public office? Have a spokesperson share your list with the class.

CHAPTER 9: ELECTIONS AND VOTING **281**

effective campaigns; it would put a great strain on the federal budget.

3. Federal legislation was needed to end discrimination against African Americans.

4. a chance to influence political process, opportunity to elect the kind of official who would represent their interests, and a right to criticize the government

Critical Thinking Skills

1. A typical response might be that they never voted before and that election issues may not seem to apply to their lives.

2. Answers may include showing nonvoters where the candidate stands on issues that will affect their lives or by showing nonvoters that the candidate would represent their interests.

Chapter Organizer

Objectives	Special Feature Pages	Supplemental Materials
Section 1 Organization and Membership *pp. 284–288* **1.** Explain the role of interest groups in the political process. **2.** Distinguish between an interest group and a political party. **3.** Discuss the importance of membership and leadership to the success of an interest group.	Focus on Freedom: *Democracy in America* p. 286	Guided Reading Activities Reproducible Lesson Plans Section 1 Quiz Testmaker Government Themes Transparencies 25 SAT Practice Tests Writer's Guidebook
Section 2 Methods of Interest Groups *pp. 289–294* **1.** Understand the practical value of lobbying and the need for regulation of lobbying activities. **2.** Describe lobbyists and their techniques.	Multicultural Heritage: Minorities and Women in Politics p. 290 Participating in Government: Working Within the System p. 291 Global Connection: Interdependence: International Lobbying p. 293 Critical Thinking Skills: Recognizing Bias p. 294	Guided Reading Activities Reproducible Lesson Plans Participating in Government 10 Enrichment Activities 10 Cooperative Learning Activities 10 Section 2 Quiz Testmaker Chapter Transparencies 10 Skill Reinforcement Activities 10 SAT Practice Tests Writer's Guidebook
Section 3 The Rise of Political Action Committees *pp. 295–299* **1.** Summarize the activities of political action committees. **2.** Describe how political action committees are regulated.	Personal Perspectives: John E. Jacob on the Struggle for Equality p. 299	Guided Reading Activities Reproducible Lesson Plans Interpreting Political Cartoons 10 Primary and Secondary Source Readings 10 Reteaching Activities 10 Section 3 Quiz Chapter 10 Tests Testmaker Audio Cassettes (English and Spanish) Limited English Proficiency Activities 10 SAT Practice Tests

If time does not permit teaching this chapter, assign the Chapter 10 summary in the Unit 3 Digest on pages 355–356.

Key To Ability Levels

Teaching strategies have been coded for varying learning styles and abilities.

L1 Level 1 activities are **basic** activities and should be within the ability range of all students.

L2 Level 2 activities are **average** activities and should be within the ability range of the average to above-average student.

L3 Level 3 activities are **challenging** activities designed for the ability range of above-average students.

LEP These activities should be within the ability range of **Limited English Proficiency** students.

Multicultural Activities

The National Association for the Advancement of Colored People (NAACP) is an interest group pledged to eliminating racial discrimination and segregation, primarily through legal and political action. It is the oldest and largest civil rights group in the United States, founded by African American educator W.E.B. Du Bois and seven others in 1909. Have students research the Niagara Movement which preceded the NAACP's founding, the role of Du Bois in the NAACP, issues the group addresses today, its tactics, or contributions of other NAACP leaders such as Weldon Johnson, Walter White, and Roy Wilkins. Have students explain why the NAACP is considered both a civil rights and interest group and identify other groups that share some of its goals.

The United States has hundreds of groups dedicated to serving the interests of America's ethnic communities. Among them are the League of United Latin American Citizens, Association of Polish Americans, Nigerian American Alliance, and Japanese American Citizens League. Organize students into small groups. Have each use the *Encyclopedia of Associations* available at most public libraries to identify an interest group that represents an ethnic group. A list of ethnic associations appears in the section of the encyclopedia entitled "Fraternal, Foreign Interest, Nationality, and Ethnic Organizations." Have each group write to one such organization to find out about its membership, its political goals or concerns, and the methods it uses to promote the interests of its members.

Chapter Resources

Readings for the Student

Alderson, George and Everett Sentman. *How You Can Influence Congress: The Complete Handbook for the Citizen Lobbyist.* Dutton, 1979.

Berry, Jeffrey M. *Lobbying for the People.* Princeton University Press, 1977.

Drew, Elizabeth. *Politics and Money: The New Road to Corruption.* Macmillan, 1983.

Lipsen, Charles B. *Vested Interest: A Lobbyist's Account of Washington Power and How it Really Works.* Doubleday, 1977.

Wittenberg, Ernest and Elizabeth Wittenberg. *How to Win in Washington: Very Practical Advice About Lobbying, the Grassroots and the Media.* Basil Blackwell, 1989.

Readings for the Teacher

Berry, Jeffrey M. *The Interest Group Society.* Little, Brown, 1984.

Sabato, Larry. *PAC Power.* Norton, 1984.

Stern, Philip M. *The Best Congress Money Can Buy.* Pantheon, 1988.

Wolpe, Bruce C. *Lobbying Congress: How the System Works.* Congressional Quarterly, 1990.

Multimedia

Videocassettes and Films

Lobbying: A Case History. Encyclopedia Britannica Educational Corp. (film, 18 minutes)

Lobbying and Political Action Committees. Close-Up Foundation. (v/c, 60 minutes)

The Unelected. (*The Power Game* series). Philip Burton Productions, Inc. and Maryland Public Television. (v/c, 60 minutes)

Software

MECC Social Studies Vol. 1 (POLICY). Minnesota Educational Computing Consortium (MECC). (Apple, TRS80 disks). POLICY is a complex simulation involving six interest groups in American society that work to achieve their own policy goals. Intergroup cooperation and compromise are needed to achieve most goals.

Interest Groups

Introduce

Chapter Overview

Chapter 10 describes interest groups and their role in American political life.

Section 1 explains what interest groups are and what they do.

Section 2 examines the methods used by interest groups to influence public policy.

Section 3 focuses on the growing role that political action committees play in American political life.

Chapter 10 Themes

Draw students' attention to the Themes in Government in the Chapter Preview. As students read this chapter, have them consider how these themes relate to interest groups. Upon completion of study of the chapter, ask students to write a sentence for each theme explaining the relationship of that theme to the operation of interest groups in the United States. Have students compare their sentences.

Linking Past and Present
Americans long have viewed lobbyists with suspicion. In the mid-1800s, poet Walt Whitman called them the "lousy combings and born freedom sellers of the earth." At the end of that century, President William McKinley denied a cabinet appointment to a highly recommended candidate because that man had been a lobbyist. Today, that continuing suspicion is reflected in laws requiring lobbyists to register with federal and state governments.

CHAPTER 10

People who once had no voice in politics have joined forces to influence government leaders.

About the Chapter Opener

Teaching With Illustrations The Americans with Disabilities Act was signed into law by President Bush in 1990. The legislation provides civil rights protections for people with disabilities equal to those established for women and minorities. The legislation provides civil rights for people with disabilities in areas of employment, public accommodations, state and local government services, and telecommunications. Ask students what issues they feel strongly enough about to join or to create an interest group to deal with the issue.

Chapter Preview

Overview

Interest groups attempt to influence the formation of public policy through access to government officials.

Objectives

After studying this chapter, you should be able to:

1. **Describe** the diverse nature of interest groups.
2. **Identify** the role of interest groups in shaping public opinion and policy.
3. **Explain** the rise of political action committees and their influence in elections.

Themes in Government

This chapter emphasizes the following government themes:

- **Civic Participation** Individuals often participate in interest groups to make government aware of their views. Section 1.
- **Political Processes** Interest groups exert powerful influences on government. Sections 1, 2, and 3
- **Public Policy** Congress has worked to limit the role of lobbyists. Section 2
- **Growth of Democracy** Political Action Committees (PACs) must follow certain rules. Section 3.

Critical Thinking Skills

This chapter emphasizes the following critical thinking skills:

- Understanding Cause and Effect
- Expressing Problems Clearly
- Making Generalizations
- Making Comparisons
- Analyzing Information

CHAPTER 10: INTEREST GROUPS **283**

Introducing the Chapter

To begin study of Chapter 10, ask students to name all the organized groups they can think of. Write group names on the chalkboard as they are volunteered. Next, select various groups from the list and ask students to describe the purpose of each group. Provide guidance by pointing out that the local P.T.A. helps a school to fulfill its educational function, while the purpose of a professional sports team is to provide entertainment.

Bring the discussion to a close by pointing to any interest groups listed on the board. Tell students that, as they read this chapter, they will learn about the specific—and important—function these groups perform in the political process.

Chapter Project

Organize students into four groups. Assign each group one of the following news sources: local newspapers; national newspapers, such as *The New York Times* or the *Washington Post;* local television newscasts; national television newscasts. Have groups monitor their sources for one week to note how often interest groups are mentioned, the names of these groups, and the issues with which the groups are involved. At the end of that time period, have groups compare their lists by answering the following questions: Were the same stories covered by all sources? Were the same interest groups identified? What explanations can you offer for any differences?

Setting the Scene Interest groups can be both persistent and adaptable. The American Medical Association (AMA), for example, consistently opposed the passage of medicare for many years prior to the 1960s. Since the establishment of medicare, however, the AMA has become one of the strongest defenders of the program. As the financing of the American health-care system became more and more chaotic, the AMA considered supporting a national health-insurance plan. When debate over national health care heated up, the AMA was a major participant.

Focus

Bell Ringer

Write the definition of *interest group* on the chalkboard. Then ask students to list the names of interest groups in the United States.

Motivating Activity

Ask students to organize their Bell Ringer lists according to the groups' interests and goals. Offer help by mentioning such categories as business, labor, agriculture, professional associations, public interest, and so on. Have students check their lists against the content of this section.

Vocabulary Precheck

Write the key terms for this section on the chalkboard. Have volunteers skim the section to find each term and read it in context. **LEP**

CONNECTIONS

Economics

Because they do not always share the same economic goals, business interest groups sometimes differ on public policy. For example, department stores want lower tariffs on imported televisions so that they can lower their prices. American manufacturers, however, want high tariffs to make American-made televisions more competitive.

GLENCOE TECHNOLOGY

Focus on Government
Video 17
Lecture Launcher:
Interest Groups
Running Time: 3:45
Videodisc 1, Chap. 17
VHS Tape 1, Begins 47:54

Video 21
Speaking Out:
Political Action Committees
Running Time: 1:47
Videodisc 2, Chap. 21
VHS Tape 2, Begins 0:00

Organization and Membership

The Constitution did not provide for political parties, yet political parties have been a part of United States government for more than 200 years. In addition to parties, Americans have historically formed a wide variety of special-interest groups at every level of government. An **interest group** is a group of people who share common goals and organize to influence government.

Many early leaders in the United States believed that interest groups could be harmful to the function of government. James Madison referred to "factions" as groups of people united to promote some special interests that were "adverse to the rights of other citizens, or to the permanent and aggregate interests of the community." Madison went on to explain that removing the causes of factions was not as acceptable as removing their effects. He believed that the republican form of government under the Constitution would be sufficient safeguard against the potential abuses of these interest groups.

Whether the Constitution has served to eliminate the harmful effects of interest groups is an issue that remains current. Today Americans have organized to pressure all three levels of government through a host of interest groups. These groups supply an increasing share of campaign funds to candidates for local, state, and national office. They spend much time and money in organized efforts to influence officeholders to support laws that they feel will be beneficial. Are the activities of these groups "adverse to the rights of other citizens" as Madison believed they could be? Or do interest groups serve an important role in helping people interact with a government that is often remote and difficult for the individual to influence?

Power of Interest Groups

Historically, Americans have always formed interest groups to influence public policy. Alexis de Tocqueville, a French traveler in the United States in the early 1800s, recognized this tendency toward group membership:

In no country of the world has the principle of association been more successfully used, or applied to a greater multitude of objects, than in America. . . . In the United States associations are established to promote the public safety, commerce, industry, morality, and religion.

—ALEXIS DE TOCQUEVILLE,
DEMOCRACY IN AMERICA, 1835

Defining Interest Groups Although interest groups are concerned about government policies and can play a role in electing candidates to public office, they are different from political parties. Political parties nominate candidates for office and try to win elections to gain control of the government. Interest groups try to influence government officials to support certain policies. Interest groups may support candidates who favor their ideas, but they do not nominate candidates for office.

A second difference between interest groups and political parties is that interest groups usually are concerned with only a few issues or specific problems. They do not try to gain members with different points of view. Political parties, on the other hand, are broad-based organizations. They must attract the support of many opposing groups to win elections. They also must consider conflicting issues and prob-

---

SECTION PREVIEW

Objectives
After studying this section, you should be able to:
■ Explain the role of interest groups in the political process.
■ Distinguish between an interest

group and a political party.
■ Discuss the importance of membership and leadership to the success of an interest group.

Key Terms and Concepts
interest group, tariff

Themes in Government
■ Civic Participation
■ Political Processes

Critical Thinking Skills
■ Understanding Cause and Effect
■ Expressing Problems Clearly

284 UNIT 3: INFLUENCING GOVERNMENT

Classroom Resources for Section I

📁 Guided Reading Activities
📁 Reproducible Lesson Plans
📁 Section 1 Quiz
➕ Testmaker

🎵 Government Themes Transparencies 25
SAT Practice Tests
Writer's Guidebook

---

lems that affect all Americans, not just certain groups.

Finally, interest groups are organized on the basis of common values, rather than on geographic location. Political parties elect officials from geographic areas to represent the interests of people in those areas. National interest groups unite people with common attitudes from every region of the country.

How Interest Groups Function Interest groups help bridge the gap between the citizen and the government. Through interest groups, citizens communicate their "wants," or policy goals, to government leaders—the President, Congress, city council, or state legislators. When lawmakers begin to address the vital concerns of an interest group, its members swing into action.

Political Power How effective is an interest group? By representing more than one individual, an interest group has a stronger bargaining position with leaders in government. Officials in a small community, for example, will listen to a 200-member group of citizens organized into a "Local Association for Street Safety."

On the state and national levels, an interest group draws from the financial resources and expertise of its many members. Organized and equipped with sufficient resources, an interest group can exert influence far beyond the power of its individual members.

Leadership and Membership

Interest group leaders strengthen the political power of the group by unifying its members. They keep members informed of the group's activities through newsletters, mailings, and telephone calls. They act as speakers for their group and try to improve its image in the media. They select qualified people to contact government officials. They plan the group's strategy, and they raise money to run the organization, often by directing their appeals for funds to meet specific objectives. Finally, they oversee all financial decisions of the group.

Power in Numbers
Citizens' group protests school budget cuts. **Civics**
Why do public protests sometimes sway lawmakers' opinions more effectively than does individual, face-to-face persuasion?

Why do people belong to interest groups? First, a group may help promote an individual's economic self-interests. For example, a labor union works to gain higher wages and other benefits for its members. Business groups try to get the government to pass laws and make decisions that will help them increase profits. A senior citizens' group, such as the American Association of Retired Persons (AARP), works for higher social security benefits.

A second reason for joining a group centers around an individual's beliefs, values, or attitudes. Many citizens believe in certain ideas or political principles that they wish to see passed into laws. For example, Sierra Club members work to conserve national resources and protect the environment from pollution. Members want laws passed requiring clean air and water.

Other reasons are nonpolitical. A person who joins a farm organization may simply like the company of other farmers. This social function also helps create group unity, a vital element in attaining the group's political goals.

STUDY GUIDE

Themes in Government
Political Processes In what ways are interest groups different from political parties?

Critical Thinking Skills
Understanding Cause and Effect Why would local elected officials be more likely to respond to the interests of a group of 200 citizens than to the interests of one person, regardless of the issue involved?

Teach

Guided Practice

L1 Designing Posters Organize students into groups of three. Have groups select one of the interest groups mentioned in this section. Ask groups to design and quickly sketch a poster that illustrates one of the issues their interest group represents. Suggest that thinking of a slogan for their interest group might help in designing the poster. As an example, propose that "Protecting the Rights of America's Workers" might be used as a slogan for the AFL-CIO. Lead the class in a discussion of each poster and what it illustrates about the interest group. **LEP**

L2 Making Comparisons Write the following heading on the chalkboard: *Comparing Political Parties and Interest Groups.* Beneath this heading draw two columns, one headed *Similarities,* the other headed *Differences.* Select students to volunteer entries for this table. Write entries in the appropriate columns as they are provided.

Caption Answer
A large vocal group can sometimes command more attention.

STUDY GUIDE

Theme Answer
Interest groups, unlike parties, do not nominate political candidates; they have narrower aims than parties; and they are not organized geographically.

Critical Thinking Answer
A group of 200 has a stronger bargaining position than an individual.

Background

A recent trend in American politics is the tendency of people to identify more with special interests and less with political parties. Direct mailing, public-opinion polls, and television advertising have helped special-interest groups reach a greater audience. As a result, groups representing labor, alternative energy, conservation, peace, pro-choice, prolife, handgun control, right to bear arms, and many other interests have become increasingly powerful and politically influential.

Interpreting Visuals Display transparency 25 from the *Government Themes Transparencies* in the Teacher's Classroom Resources and use the accompanying teaching strategy and student activity to teach how interest groups participate in the political process.

Focus on Freedom

Mention that James Madison, writing in *The Federalist* in the 1780s, warned of the dangers of "factions." However, like de Tocqueville, he recognized the inevitability of factions in a democratic society. "Liberty is to faction what air is to fire," Madison said.

Answers

1. to promote public safety, industry, commerce, morality, and religion
2. They could lead to anarchy; they guarantee against the tyranny of the majority over minorities.
3. Freedom of speech guarantees the right to share ideas; it is often necessary to assemble in order to permit the free exchange of ideas among people.

Independent Practice

L1 Constructing Charts Have students use resources such as the *Encyclopedia of Associations* to find out the membership of the leading interest groups in the United States. Students might like to combine their findings into a chart.

L2 Persuasive Writing Ask students to write a paragraph responding to the following: All interest groups have equal opportunity to influence public policy.

Many people, however, do not belong to any interest group. Studies have shown that people on lower socioeconomic levels are less likely to join such groups. Studies of business organizations and other interest groups also show that membership tends to come from upper income levels. So, while the opportunity to join together to influence government is a right of all, the people who might benefit most do not often exercise that right.

Business and Labor Groups

Almost all Americans have economic interests. They are concerned about taxes, food prices, housing, inflation, unemployment, and so forth. As a result, many interest groups are concerned with economic issues. These business and labor interest groups seek to convince lawmakers of policies that they feel will strengthen the economy.

Focus on Freedom

DEMOCRACY IN AMERICA

Alexis de Tocqueville, a French traveler in the United States in 1831, later wrote an account of his observations that has provided Americans a window on the past for more than 150 years. De Tocqueville observed Americans' penchant for political association, and described its possible causes and results.

In no country in the world has the principle of association been more successfully used. . . than in America. Besides the permanent associations, which are established by law. . . a vast number of others are formed and maintained by the agency of private individuals.

. . . In the United States, associations are established to promote the public safety, commerce, industry, morality, and religion. There is no end which the human will despairs of attaining through the combined power of individuals united into a society. . . .

When an association is allowed to establish centres of action. . . its activity is increased, and its influence extended. . . . Men have the opportunity of seeing each other. . . and opinions are maintained with a warmth and energy which written language can never attain. . . .

The right of association was imported from England, and it has always existed in America; the exercise of this privilege is now incorporated with the manners and customs of the people. . . . The liberty of association has become a necessary guaranty against the tyranny of the majority. . . .

It cannot be denied that the unrestrained liberty of association for political purposes is the privilege which a people is longest in learning how to exercise. If it does not throw the nation into anarchy, it perpetually augments the chances of that calamity. On one point, however, this perilous liberty offers a security against dangers of another kind; in countries where associations are free, secret societies are unknown. In America, there are factions [political associations], but no conspiracies.

The most natural privilege of man, next to the right of acting for himself, is that of combining his exertions with those of his fellow-creatures, and of acting in common with them. The right of association therefore appears to me almost as inalienable in its nature as the right of personal liberty. . . .

In America, the citizens who form the minority associate, in order, first, to show their numerical strength. . . to discover those arguments which are most fitted to act upon the majority: . . . Political associations in the United States are therefore, peaceable in their intentions, and strictly legal in the means which they employ; and they assert with perfect truth, that they aim at success only by lawful expedients.

—ALEXIS DE TOCQUEVILLE, 1835

Examining the Document

Reviewing Facts
1. List five purposes for which associations are formed in America, according to de Tocqueville.
2. Identify one danger and one value of political associations.

Critical Thinking Skills
3. Synthesizing Information De Tocqueville says that the right of association is "almost as inalienable in its nature as the right of personal liberty." The right to peaceably assemble and freedom of speech are included in the First Amendment to the Constitution. How are these two First Amendment rights related?

286   UNIT 3: INFLUENCING GOVERNMENT

Cooperative Learning Activity

Have students work together to write a report on recent actions by an interest group. Organize students into groups of three and ask the groups to assign one of the following tasks to each member: a description of the interest group and the legislation it is attempting to change; a description of the methods the group used to influence legislators; a report of the outcome of the group's actions. Have group members combine their work to create one report. Group representatives should present their reports to the class.

Business-Related Interest Groups Business interest groups are among the oldest and largest in the United States. One of the major business groups today is the National Association of Manufacturers (NAM). The NAM works to lower individual and corporate taxes, limit government regulation of business, and raise **tariffs**, or taxes on imported goods. Another major business group is the United States Chamber of Commerce. Unlike the NAM, which represents large industries, the Chamber of Commerce tends to speak for smaller businesses. A third group is the Business Roundtable, composed of executives from almost 200 of the country's largest and most powerful corporations.

Labor-Related Interest Groups The largest and most powerful labor organization today is the AFL-CIO with about 14.1 million members in 89 separate unions. A separate organization called The Committee on Political Education (COPE) directs the AFL-CIO's political activities. COPE's major goals include fund-raising, voter registration drives, and support for political candidates. Among the many unions in the AFL-CIO are the United Auto Workers (UAW), United Mine Workers (UMW), and the International Brotherhood of Teamsters.

Agricultural Groups

Three major interest groups represent almost 4 million American farmers. The largest of these groups is the American Farm Bureau Federation, which speaks for the larger, more successful farmers and is closely associated with the federal Department of Agriculture.

The National Farmers' Union (NFU) draws its membership from smaller farmers and favors higher price supports for crops and livestock. The group has also supported laws protecting migrant farm workers. The oldest farm group is the Patrons of Husbandry, known as the Grange. Although this group is more of a social organization than an interest group, it has been very outspoken in advocating price supports for crops.

Largest Labor Unions in the United States

	Members
• American Federation of State, County and Municipal Employees of America	1,250,000
• American Federation of Teachers	715,000
• Carpenters and Joiners of America	609,000
• Communications Workers of America	700,000
• International Brotherhood of Electrical Workers	845,000
• International Brotherhood of Teamsters	1,700,000
• Laborer's International Union of North America	570,000
• National Education Association	2,000,000
• Service Employees International Union	925,000
• United Automobile, Aerospace and Agricultural Implement Workers of America	943,582
• United Food and Commercial Workers International Union	1,235,000
• United Steelworkers of America	655,000

Source: 1991 Information Please Almanac/Statistical Abstract of the United States, 1990

 Chart Study
Labor unions represent less than one-fourth of the total workforce. **What interests might the National Education Association represent?**

Other Interest Groups

Besides economic interest groups, there are countless other kinds of interest groups. These range from professional and environmental organizations to governmental and public interest groups.

Professional Associations The American Bar Association (ABA) and the American Medical Association (AMA) are two examples of interest groups that include members of specific professions. Basically,

Special Needs Strategy

Memory Disability Many handicapping conditions—learning disabilities, for example—are associated with memory difficulties. Such difficulties can be overcome by learning memory strategies. Have students list interest-group categories: business, labor, agricultural, professional, environmental, public interest, government, and others. Ask them to note three groups under each category. Next have students repeat the information they have noted and then test themselves on it.

Chart Study Answer
teachers' interests in such areas as wages and benefits, academic freedom, standards, and policy

STUDY GUIDE

Theme Answer
Answers will vary, but may include the cost in money and time, personal beliefs, or apathy.

Critical Thinking Answer
Answers should indicate that those who do not belong still have political power through the vote. They may not, however, have as great an influence as those who belong to an interest group.

Assess

Check for Understanding
Have students complete Section 1 Review on page 288.

Meeting Objectives
Each section objective is tested by the Section Review questions that follow it in parentheses.
- Explain the role of interest groups in the political process. (5, 6, 7, 8)
- Distinguish between an interest group and a political party. (2)
- Discuss the importance of membership and leadership to the success of an interest group. (3, 4)

Evaluate
📁 Section 1 Quiz
💻 Testmaker

Reteach

Have students write a paragraph answering the following question: What is an interest group and how does it compare to a political party?

Enrich

Have students write a brief paper on an interest group of their choice. Suggest that they obtain information by writing to the headquarters of their chosen interest group.

Close

Ask students to imagine they are members of one of the interest groups mentioned in this section. Then have them answer the following questions:

1. What is the name of your interest group?
2. What does this group do for you?
3. What do you do for your group?
4. How effective is your group in political activity?

Powers of the President
Interest Groups
Running Time :31
Side One, Chapter 8

these two groups influence the licensing and training of lawyers and doctors. Both groups, however, are actively involved in political issues. Professional associations also represent bankers, teachers, college professors, police officers, and hundreds of other professions. While these associations are concerned primarily with the standards of their professions, they also seek to influence government policy on issues that are important to them.

Environmental Interest Groups The concern for ecology and the environment has led to the formation of about 3,000 environmental interest groups. Their goals range from conserving natural resources to protecting endangered wildlife. One key environmental organization is the Sierra Club. Other environmental groups include the National Wildlife Federation, Friends of the Earth, and Environmental Action, Inc.

Public Interest Groups Groups concerned about the public interest seek policy goals that they believe will benefit American society. These groups are not concerned with furthering the interest of a narrow group of people. Instead, they claim to work for the interests of all Americans. For example, Ralph Nader's Public Citizen, Inc., devotes itself to consumer and public safety issues affecting the general population. Common Cause, founded in 1970, is a public interest group that has tried to reform various aspects of the American political system.

Interest Groups in Government Organizations and leaders within American government may also act as interest groups. Two powerful organizations today are the National Conference of State Legislators and the National Governors' Association. State and local government officials may seek to influence members of Congress or the executive branch because they want a greater share of federal aid. Interest groups such as the National Association of Counties, the Council of State Governments, or the National League of Cities pressure Congress for policies to benefit cities and states.

Additional Groups Thousands of interest groups have been formed for other reasons. Any list would be inadequate to illustrate the diverse interests. Some are formed to promote a particular cause, such as the Society for the Prevention of Cruelty to Animals, the National Abortion Rights Action League, or the National Right to Life Committee. Church related organizations like the National Council of Churches, B'nai B'rith Anti-Defamation League, the National Catholic Welfare Council, and the National Association of Evangelicals each seek to influence public policy. The American Civil Liberties Union works to protect civil rights. The National Organization for Women (NOW) and the National Association for the Advancement of Colored People (NAACP) support the aims of large segments of the population.

Foreign governments and private interests of foreign nations also seek to influence government in the United States. Foreign interest groups may seek military aid, economic aid, or favorable trade agreements. All foreign agents must register with the United States government.

1 SECTION REVIEW

Section Summary
Interest groups are an important part of politics in the United States, uniting large numbers of people to influence government policy.

Checking for Understanding
Recalling Facts
1. Define interest group, tariff.
2. Explain the difference between an interest group and a political party.
3. List three reasons why citizens join interest groups.
4. Describe the ways that leaders of an interest group unite the membership of the group.
Exploring Themes
5. Civic Participation Why are interest groups more effective in influencing government officials than are individual citizens?
6. Political Processes Why would a professional association such as the American Bar Association, organized to influence the licensing and training of lawyers, become a political interest group?

Critical Thinking Skills
7. Understanding Cause and Effect Why are some of the most powerful interest groups organized around concern over economic issues?
8. Expressing Problems Clearly How do interest groups help make representative government truly government "by the people"?

Section 1 Review Answers

1. Definitions of terms appear on pages indicated: **interest group,** 284; **tariff,** 287
2. political party—tries to control the government by selecting candidates to run for office, usually concerned with broad range of issues; interest group—only supports selected candidates, tries to influence officials on a narrower agenda of issues
3. to promote their economic interests, to communicate their beliefs or values, and to associate with others who have similar interests
4. keep members informed of group's activities, act as speakers for group, and plan group's strategy
5. By representing more than one individual, interest group has stronger bargaining position with government leaders. Organized and equipped with considerable resources, interest group can exert influence on government beyond the power of individual members.
6. A professional association becomes an interest group when it decides to influence public policy in an area that is of concern to its members.
7. Every individual is affected by the economic policies of the government. In order to protect or further their interests, people join together in special-interest groups.
8. After officials are elected to represent the people, they need to be regularly informed of the desires of the people. Interest groups serve to keep government aware of these wants and needs.

Methods of Interest Groups

Most interest groups use a variety of methods to try to influence public policy. Representatives of the group contact government officials directly in Washington, D.C., or a state capital. Interest or pressure groups may also use television, radio, magazine, and newspaper advertising to create public support for their policies. They may even resort to court action to achieve their goals.

The Work of Lobbyists

Most interest groups try to influence government policy by making direct contact with lawmakers or other government leaders. This process of direct contact is called **lobbying** because of the practice of approaching senators and representatives in the outer room or lobby of a capitol. The representatives of interest groups who do this kind of work are called **lobbyists.** Lobbying is one of the most widely used and effective techniques available to interest groups.

Most of the larger and more important interest groups have lobbyists on their payrolls in Washington, D.C. Today more than 6,000 registered lobbyists serve 11,000 clients in the nation's capital. Although lobbyists are usually found trying to persuade members of Congress, at times they also seek to influence the executive branch and even the courts. Lobbyists also work on state and local levels.

Who Are Lobbyists? Essentially, a lobbyist is a "political persuader." To influence the people who control the government, lobbyists must have a good understanding of human nature. They must also know which officials have the most influence.

What kinds of people are lobbyists? Many lobbyists are former government officials. They usually have friends in Congress and the executive branch and know the intricacies of Washington politics. Lobbying has indeed become very attractive to members of Congress:

> *T*empted by the staggering fees that lobbyists can command, lawmakers and their aides are quitting in droves to cash in on their connections. For many, public service has become a mere internship for a lucrative career as a hired gun for special interests.
> —*TIME,* MARCH 3, 1986

Many other lobbyists are lawyers or public relations experts. Understanding the government and how it works is vital to a successful lobbyist. Whatever their backgrounds, however, all lobbyists must know the problems and desires of the groups they represent and be able to communicate them to those in power.

Providing Useful Information One of the most important methods of persuasion is to provide policymakers with useful information that supports an interest group's position. Lobbyists often try to meet personally with members of Congress or other government officials. Meetings may occur in a lawmaker's office or home, or in a more casual location such as at a favorite restaurant or on a golf course.

In order to persuade members of Congress, lobbyists provide legislators with pamphlets, reports, statistics, and other kinds of information. How accurate is this information? How much do members of Congress rely on it? A study of interest groups and public policy revealed:

SECTION PREVIEW

Objectives
After studying this section, you should be able to:
- Understand the practical value of lobbying and the need for regulation of lobbying activities.

- Describe lobbyists and their techniques.

Key Terms and Concepts
lobbying, lobbyist

Themes in Government
- Political Processes
- Public Policy

Critical Thinking Skills
- Making Generalizations
- Making Comparisons

CHAPTER 10: INTEREST GROUPS 289

Classroom Resources for Section 2

- Guided Reading Activities
- Reproducible Lesson Plans
- Participating in Government 10
- Enrichment Activities 10
- Section 2 Quiz

- Cooperative Learning Activities 10
- Testmaker
- Chapter Transparencies 10
- SAT Practice Tests
- Writer's Guidebook

Focus

Poll the class to see what percentage of Americans they think would vote for an African American, woman, and Jewish candidate for President. Compare class data with data in the reading.

Teach

Ask: What evidence supports the change in attitudes of the American people toward minority candidates? *(election of Wilder and Dinkins with substantial white support)* How did these elections change perceptions of African American politicians about their chances of political success? What evidence is there that Hispanics are making political gains in state government? What are two reasons for minorities' gains? *(civil rights movement, litigation)*

Assess

Have students complete **Examining Our Multicultural Heritage.**

Answers

1. Today the American public is much more willing to vote for minority and women candidates.
2. because white voters are providing support for minority candidates
3. Opinions will vary.

Close

Ask the class to speculate about ways greater racial and ethnic diversity might change the nation's domestic agenda.

Multicultural Heritage

Minorities and Women in Politics

Today, women and minorities have more influence on local, state, and national governments than ever before. To a large extent, the situation has changed because attitudes have changed. In 1958, for example, only about 38 percent of those people polled indicated they would be willing to vote for an African American presidential candidate. Fifty-two percent expressed a willingness to vote for a woman and 62 percent for a Jew. Thirty years later the results were quite different as 83 percent said they would vote for an African American, 86 percent for a woman, and 89 percent for a Jew.

The change in attitudes was reflected in the historic 1989 election of L. Douglas Wilder, grandson of a former slave, as governor of Virginia. At the same time, in New York City, African American David Dinkins was elected mayor. Both candidates had considerable support from white voters. As John R. Lewis, representative from Georgia pointed out after the election,

> *I think there was a feeling on the part of many black elected officials that they could have been a congressperson or a mayor only in a district or a city that is majority-black. But the elections of Dinkins and Wilder changed that altogether. Doug Wilder's success sent a strong message to black and Hispanic men and women that you can move up, that you can have a base that is larger than your ethnic group.*
> —REPRESENTATIVE JOHN R. LEWIS, 1989

Achieving that goal, however, has not been easy. Antonia Hernandez, president of the Mexican American Legal Defense and Education Fund, looked back as she described the changes that have taken place in recent years.

> *In this country Hispanics have historically been classified white but treated black. Only through the civil rights movement have we made major strides. Up to 1968 in Texas, most districts operated separate schools for Mexicans and whites. . . . Now that's all changed. In addition, the number of Hispanics in the Texas legislature is getting closer to a level that reflects our share of the population. But*

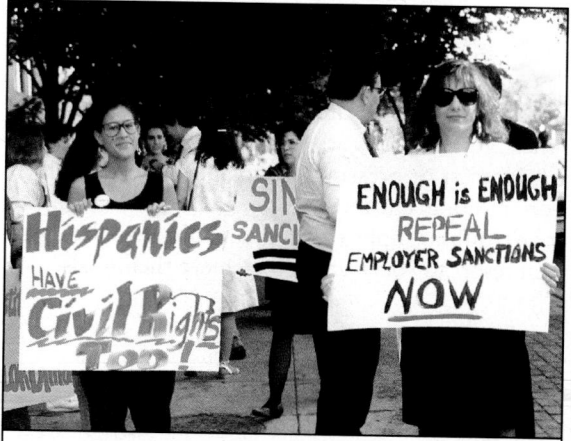

Speaking Out
Minority interest groups are bringing long-ignored issues to public attention. Many of these issues will not be acted upon, however, until minorities achieve greater representation in government.

> *that took 15 years of litigation, a process we're now repeating in California. . . .*
> —ANTONIA HERNANDEZ

Political gains for Asian Americans have not been as dramatic, but that may soon change as well. One writer, Stuart Rothenberg noted, "As younger Americanized (and American-born) Asians enter their adult years, they are likely to become more involved in politics."

Examining Our Multicultural Heritage

Reviewing Facts
1. Describe the change in attitude that has taken place regarding minority and women candidates.
2. Explain why it is no longer necessary for a minority candidate to come only from a minority district or city.

Critical Thinking Skills
3. Making Inferences Do you think there is a relationship between the civil rights movement and the emergence of women and minorities as a political force? Why or why not?

More About Our Multicultural Heritage

Although Congress's heavily white male membership is unlikely to change dramatically in the near future, most political experts believe increased participation by women and minorities will broaden the range of ideas and perspectives debated in Congress to more accurately reflect the concerns of the American people. Minorities are becoming a greater portion of the American population. Both higher immigration and birth rates have led minority groups to increase at a faster rate than the white population. By the year 2030, demographers predict Hispanics and nonwhites will make up one-third of the nation's citizens.

[The lobbyist] wants the facts that will support his case, that will not kick back by exposing him as deceitful. . . . His assumption is that, since he is on the right side, there must be some facts that will help, not hurt. . . . [Members of Congress] frequently said that they would talk to anybody who would bring them really fresh information. Bored to death by hearing the same old stories, they often expressed a real craving for some solid facts that they could believe.

—RAYMOND BAUER, ET AL.,
AMERICAN BUSINESS AND PUBLIC POLICY, 1972

Legislators realize that lobbyists can be biased in presenting their case. A lobbyist who intentionally misrepresents the facts, however, may lose access to the lawmaker permanently, if discovered.

Lobbyists also provide information by testifying before congressional committees. Usually when Congress is considering a bill, lobbyists are invited to testify. For example, lobbyists representing the oil industry may testify before a committee considering legislation to tax oil profits. Finally, when a bill comes to the floor in either house of Congress, lobbyists work hard to influence lawmakers' votes.

Drafting Bills Besides providing information to lawmakers, lobbyists and interest groups may actually help write bills. Many well-organized interest groups have research staffs that help members of Congress draft proposed laws. Studies have shown that interest groups and their lobbyists draft parts of or entire bills for almost 50 percent of all legislation.

Providing Election Support Interest groups can also promise campaign support for legislators who favor their policies, or they can threaten to withhold support. Loss of a sizeable contribution could affect a candidate's chances of winning. Other interest groups with comparable political strength who support opposite goals, however, might back the candidate.

Interest groups raise much of the money used in political campaigns. Interest groups realize that making a campaign contribution does not guarantee that a candidate, if elected, will always vote the way they wish. Such groups, however, know that campaign contributions will at least assure access to the officials they help elect.

Taking Court Action Interest groups may resort to the courts to try to gain their policy goals. For ex-

PARTICIPATING IN GOVERNMENT

Working Within the System

Do we truly have government by the people, for the people? If so, how can citizens make their needs and opinions known? For example, how can you work within the system to change a law that you think is unjust?

There is strength in numbers. Keep this point in mind when you want to make your ideas known to a public official. Your opinion may carry more influence if you join with others.

Choose an appropriate means of expressing your views. If you want to express your concern about a local

Vote No On 13

ordinance, you might attend a city council meeting. If you are objecting to a state law, you might write letters to state legislators. If your target is a federal law, you might write letters to your representatives in Congress. Petitions—formal requests for specific action signed by many people—are also effec-

tive ways to influence government officials.

Other ways of expressing your opinion include writing letters to the editor of a local newspaper or preparing an editorial for a local radio or television broadcast. These activities focus public attention on the issue and may encourage others to contact an official who can do something about it.

Investigating Further

Find out how lobbyists influence lawmakers and other public officials. Report your findings to the class.

CHAPTER 10: INTEREST GROUPS 291

Teach

Guided Practice

L2 Civic Participation List on the chalkboard these tactics used by public interest groups:

1. Go on the attack—make public officials fear you.
2. Concede nothing—compromise only when you have to.
3. Manipulate the media—get them to present your case in a positive way.
4. Kill the opposition with information—seize control of discussion of the issues.

Taking each tactic in turn, discuss: How effective is this approach? Would you be swayed by it? Why or why not?

Interpreting Visuals Display transparency 10 from the *Chapter Transparencies* in the Teacher's Classroom Resources and use the accompanying teaching strategy and student activity to teach how interest groups influence public policy.

PARTICIPATING IN GOVERNMENT

Ask students if they or anyone they know have participated in any kind of political activity designed to influence government policy.

Have students complete activity 10 in *Participating in Government* in the Teacher's Classroom Resources.

CONNECTIONS

Political Processes
An important political trend of the last few years is the rise of grassroots public interest groups. Using aggressive lobbying tactics, these small yet highly organized and dedicated groups have won many politicians to their causes.

Background

The term *lobbying* is an Americanism first used in the 1830s. However, its origin probably lies in another country. Most etymologists suggest that it derives from the name of the entrance hall to the British House of Commons, the Lobby, the place where people traditionally gathered to meet and attempt to influence their members of Parliament. In the early 1800s, it became commonplace for individuals to wait in the public areas of Congress for the chance to have a few words with their legislators. Their actions soon became known as lobbying.

Chapter 10: Interest Groups **291**

Independent Practice

L2 Informative Writing Have students write a report that answers the following: Who lobbies? What is lobbying? Where does lobbying take place? What methods do lobbyists use? Why does lobbying take place?

Caption Answer
more than $1.5 billion

STUDY GUIDE

Theme Answer
Lobbyists can often provide statistics and reports. Many have expertise in specialized fields.

Critical Thinking Answers
They know that their reputation determines whether the public and public officials believe what they say.

Congress and lobbyists represent constituents' interests, but only Congress can pass legislation.

Assess

Check for Understanding

Have students complete Section 2 Review on page 293.

Meeting Objectives

Each section objective is tested by the Section Review questions that follow it in parentheses.
• Understand the practical value of lobbying and the need for regulation of lobbying activities. (2, 4, 6, 7, 8)
• Describe lobbyists and their techniques. (2, 3, 4, 5, 7)

Evaluate

📁 Section 2 Quiz

💻 Testmaker

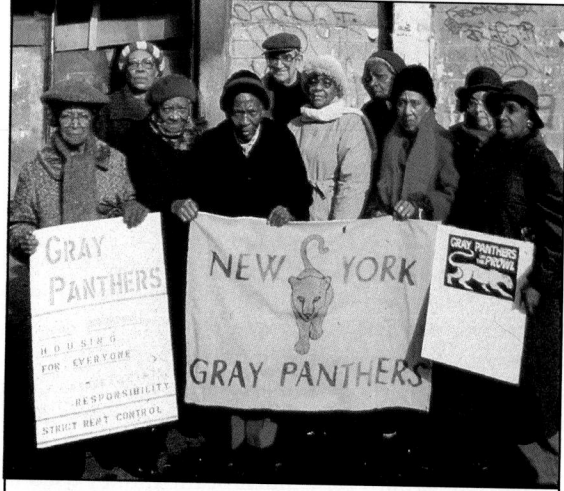

'Gray Panthers' Growl
A lobbying group for the elderly—the Gray Panthers—has grown large and powerful. **Economics How much money do lobbyists spend in a year?**

ample, civil rights groups have asked state and federal courts to protect equality in housing and employment practices. Environmental groups have filed lawsuits against businesses they believe are guilty of pollution. Business groups have often gone to court to protest federal regulations of business.

Winning Public Support

Interest groups run publicity campaigns to win support for their policies. A wide range of techniques is available to interest groups in their effort to influence policymakers.

Media Campaigns Interest or pressure groups use the mass media—television, newspapers, magazines, and radio—to inform the public and create support for their views. For example, the American Petroleum Institute used television advertising to explain the high cost of energy and describe what oil companies were doing to help solve the energy crisis. Environ-

mentalists have run television and magazine ads to dramatize pollution and the hazards it poses.

Letter Writing Many interest groups urge their members to write letters to government officials to demonstrate broad support for or against a public policy. For example, the National Rifle Association can deliver hundreds of thousands of letters from its members. While members of Congress and other public officials understand that these letters may not represent the opinion of the nation, it is one method to make officials aware of an issue that is important to the group.

Regulation of Interest Groups

Are interest groups too powerful in American government? Many Americans believe so. One study found that three-fourths of Americans agreed that "Congress was still too much under the influence of special-interest lobbies." Many feel that interest groups should be closely regulated.

Congress passed the Federal Regulation of Lobbying Act in 1946, requiring all lobbyists to register with the Clerk of the House and the Secretary of the Senate. Lobbyists must identify their employer, report their salaries and expenses, and file quarterly expense reports.

The act is not very far-reaching, and it has many loopholes. First, a lobbyist has to report only money spent on direct contact with legislators. Funds spent on media activities or indirect contacts do not have to be reported. While lobbyists recently reported expenditures of about $50 million per year, the actual figure, including campaign contributions, has been estimated at more than $1.5 billion.

Second, the act requires only that people or organizations whose principal purpose is to influence legislation need register. Thus, any interest group and its lobbyists that claim their principal function is something other than lobbying do not have to register. As a result, only about 6,000 of the more than 13,600

STUDY GUIDE

**Themes in Government
Public Policy** Why do members of Congress rely on lobbyists to provide them information?
Political Processes The American Civil Liberties Union (ACLU) files

lawsuits when it believes that individual rights have been violated.

**Critical Thinking Skills
Making Generalizations** Why do interest groups strive for a good public image?

Making Comparisons How is the work of a member of Congress similar to and different from that of a lobbyist?

292 Unit 3: Influencing Government

Cooperative Learning Activity

Select 10 students and provide each one with a card that describes a lobbying activity. Five of the activities should be ethical, and five should be unethical. Have students role-play their activities for the rest of the class. Then ask class members to identify, with explanations, which activities were ethical and which were unethical. You might use this ex-

ercise as the starting point for a discussion on the ethics of lobbying.

📁 Have students complete activity 10 in *Cooperative Learning Activities* in the Teacher's Classroom Resources.

lobbyists have registered. Moreover, Congress has not established any agency to enforce the lobbying law or to check the reports lobbyists file. Finally, the act does not cover lobbying of executive agencies or testifying before congressional committees.

Other Limitations

The public's perception of interest groups is that they are financially and politically powerful. People believe that these groups exert a strong influence on legislation. How important are these groups in determining public policy?

Interest groups do provide representation for Americans in addition to the representation they have in Congress. They allow Americans to be represented according to their economic, social, or occupational interests. Pressure groups also act as watchdogs and protest government policies that harm their members.

Several factors limit the effectiveness of interest groups. Different interest groups compete for power and influence, keeping any single group from controlling lawmakers and other public officials. Generally, the larger the group the more diverse are the interests of its members. This diversity has meant that nationally organized interest groups have not been able to adopt broad policy goals. As a result, smaller interest groups or those that unite people who have narrower aims have been most effective in shaping policy.

While large interest groups have membership that provides an impressive financial base, most organizations struggle to pay small staffs. Lobbyists do not often approach members of Congress who are fully

committed to the opposite view. Instead, they cultivate working relationships with those who tend to agree with them. Recently the greatest concern about the power of interest groups has focused on their financial contributions to political campaigns.

GLOBAL CONNECTION

Interdependence

International Lobbying Lobbyists use persuasion and expense accounts to influence government officials. However, decisions made by United States government officials may affect many nations. Lobbyists who represent foreign interests therefore try to influence United States government decisions.

Much international lobbying deals with economic matters. The United States is the chief trading partner of Korea and Japan, as well as several other nations. Lobbyists for these nations work to reduce trade barriers, such as tariffs—taxes on imports—or quotas—limits on the quantity of imports. The government regulates the activities of foreign lobbyists to protect the interests of United States manufacturers.

Examining the Connection
Why would members of Congress be willing to listen to lobbyists from other countries?

Mention that international lobbying has come under criticism recently because of such scandals as "Koreagate" of the late 1970s. This involved South Korean lobbyists funneling millions of dollars to members of Congress in return for favorable votes on bills that affected that nation's business.

Examining the Connection Answer: *These lobbyists might represent interests willing to invest in the United States.*

Reteach

Write the term *interest group* on the chalkboard and circle it. Then, on lines radiating from the circle, have students list the major methods used by interest groups to influence public policy.

Enrich

☐ Have students complete activity 10 in *Enrichment Activities* in the Teacher's Classroom Resources.

Close

Lead students in a discussion of how the American political system would be affected if interest groups were illegal.

---

2 SECTION REVIEW

Section Summary
Interest groups hire lobbyists to influence public policy by providing information to lawmakers and helping shape public opinion.

Checking for Understanding
Recalling Facts
1. Define lobbying, lobbyist.
2. Describe three methods lobbyists use to influence lawmakers.
3. Identify the kinds of people who become lobbyists.
4. Explain why Congress asks lobbyists to testify at hearings and to help draft legislation.

Exploring Themes
5. Political Processes How may an interest group use the courts to gain policy goals?
6. Public Policy Why is the Federal Regulation of Lobbying Act ineffective in controlling lobbying at the national level?

Critical Thinking Skills
7. Making Generalizations What qualities of a lobbyist would make that person useful in furthering the goals of democratic government?
8. Making Comparisons Compare the positive values of lobbying with its negative potential.

Section 2 Review Answers

1. Definitions of terms appear on pages indicated: **lobbying,** 289; **lobbyist,** 289
2. provide useful information to policymakers, testify in committee hearings, help to draft bills, provide election support
3. former government officials, lawyers, public relations experts

4. Lobbyists may have research staffs that can provide information, and they may also represent the views of a large number of people.
5. They may file lawsuits in order to gain their policy goals.
6. The act has many loopholes that allow funds to be unreported and many groups to be unregistered. There is no agency to enforce the law or to check reports filed by lobbyists.

7. A lobbyist who was honest, representative of a large number of people, able to gather information quickly and to sort out the useful information would further the goals of democratic government.
8. Lobbying provides representation and access to government for large groups of people with common interests. It may, however, obstruct the interests of the majority by over-representing pressure groups. And it has the potential of corrupting government officials through money and political favors.

CRITICAL THINKING SKILLS

Focus

Have each student prepare to demonstrate without words how he or she feels about their school's football team (or other school activity). Then invite volunteers to do their demonstrations, while the class watches and tries to determine the person's attitudes toward the activity. Help students generalize about the importance of body language in communicating our attitudes.

Teach

Remind students that attitudes are also expressed in words, and that they need to be able to identify bias in a statement. Have students point out language clues in the statements about gun control that show bias. Then ask: In what other ways do people and groups show bias? How could a news broadcast show bias? *(in the choice of news it broadcasts, in how it edits interviews or quotes, or the amount of time given to a news item)* Why can it be difficult to recognize bias? *(It is often hidden; it is subtle.)*

Assess

Have students complete the **Practice** exercise.

Close

Have students summarize ways to identify bias. Emphasize that a person may show bias either for or against a topic.

Recognizing Bias

People often confuse bias with prejudice. Prejudice is a positive or negative opinion based on ignorance. Bias, however, is nothing more than the attitude of a writer or speaker. Learning to recognize bias allows you to distinguish the facts from the opinion of the person presenting them. It will help you to evaluate different points of view on controversial issues.

To check a statement for bias, follow these steps:
- Determine what information is being presented. Ask: What are the basic facts?
- Look for words or phrases that color the facts in a negative or positive light.
- Look for ways in which even neutral-sounding words might influence the reader's response. Ask: Would a supporter and an opponent be equally likely to phrase the statement this way?

Explanation

Consider the following statement about a National Rifle Association (NRA) campaign to vote down a proposed gun control law.

Liberty's watchdog, the NRA, has defeated yet another misguided liberal attempt to reduce crime by making sure that only criminals have access to firearms.

The sentence says that the activities of the NRA helped defeat the gun control law. The difference is in how these facts are presented.

Word choices are a key to detecting bias. In the above quotation the sentence describes the NRA as "liberty's watchdog," the proposed law as a "misguided liberal attempt," and the probable result of its passage as "making sure that only criminals have access to firearms."

Bias is not always so extreme and easy to recognize. Subtle differences in the wording of a newscast or an opinion-poll question can have a powerful effect. For example, consider the difference between the likely answers to the following poll question phrased two different ways:

Do you think interest groups still have too much influence on Congress?

Do you think interest groups have too much influence on Congress?

The first question invites people to say "yes" because the word *still* indicates the pollster's view that interest group influence is a recognized problem. The second form is less biased because it allows the respondent to decide whether a problem exists.

Practice

Read the following statements then answer the three questions that follow.

A. The poor, the uneducated, and the disadvantaged have been left out of the recent growth of PAC influence.

B. Powerful pressure groups like the National Association of Manufacturers and the United States Chamber of Commerce promote the interests of the country club set.

C. Do you think enough has been done to curb the activities of foreign lobbyists in Washington, D.C.?

D. Interest groups are a hallmark of American democracy, bringing millions of Americans into the political process.

E. Americans are three times more likely than Britons to join civic or political organizations.

F. Do you support big labor's efforts to impose higher tariffs on Japanese imports?

1. Which of the statements above is not colored by bias?

2. Rewrite three of the statements or questions above in more objective language.

3. Select three of the biased statements or questions above and rewrite them in words that reflect the bias of an opposing view.

> ### Additional Skills
>
> To practice this skill, see **Reinforcing the Skill** on page 301.

Practice Answers

1. E

2. (A) Members of disadvantaged groups are not as well represented by PACs as other groups in our society. (B) Powerful interest groups like the NAM and USCC lobby to promote business interests. (C) Should the activities of foreign lobbyists be restricted? (D) Interest groups increase political participation. (F) Do you support higher tariff rates on Japanese imports?

3. (A) Poor and uneducated people have not yet learned to take advantage of PACs. (B) The NAM and the USCC guard America's economic future. (C) Do you favor selfish moves to restrict the free speech of international lobbyists? (D) Interest groups threaten democracy. (F) Should we protect our jobs by raising tariff rates?

For additional practice, have students complete activity 10 in *Skill Reinforcement Activities* in the Teacher's Classroom Resources.

SECTION

3

The Rise of Political Action Committees

Lobbying is just one method interest groups use to influence lawmakers. These groups also provide a large percentage of the funds used in candidates' election campaigns. Most of these funds come from **political action committees** (PACs), or organizations specifically designed to collect money and provide financial support for a political candidate. A well-known Washington lobbyist recently said, "I won't even take a client now unless he's willing to set up a political action committee and participate in the [campaign contribution] process."

PACs channel money from interest groups to candidates they support. Money from PACs can be a tool of influence because elections have become very expensive. In 1990 House and Senate candidates spent more than $680 million getting elected.

Origins of and Rules for PACs

Before 1974, wealthy individuals gave large sums to finance political campaigns. Then the federal government passed laws to reform campaign finance. The new laws limited the amounts that individuals could contribute to federal candidates. While federal law prevented corporations and labor unions from making direct contributions to any federal candidate, it permitted their political action committees to do so.

The most dramatic effect of the new laws was to encourage the growth of political action committees. PACs grew from only 600 in 1974 to more than 4,000 today. The government set rules regulating political action committees, including how much money they could give to federal candidates.

Laws Governing PACs The main federal laws governing PACs are the Federal Election Campaign Act (FECA) of 1971; the amendments to it passed in 1974, 1976, and 1979; and the Revenue Act of 1971. Under these laws a PAC must register with the government 6 months before an election. It must raise money from at least 50 contributors and give to at least 5 candidates in a federal election. PACs must also follow strict accounting rules.

PACs can give $5,000 directly to each candidate per election. The government, however, has not limited the total amount a PAC can spend on a candidate's campaign as long as the PAC does not work directly with the candidate. Acting through PACs, interest groups can and do spend large sums of money for or against candidates. These independent expenditures for elections have increased from $2.3 million in 1980 to almost $7 million in recent congressional elections, but these expenditures are just a fraction of what PACs actually spend on elections.

In 1976 the Supreme Court ruled that any independent group may give money to a political candidate as long as the group does not have legal ties to that candidate. From 1974 to 1990 the money all PACs contributed increased from about $12.5 million to more than $159 million per year. PAC money provided about 23 percent of Senate candidates' receipts, and 37 percent of House candidates' receipts.

Federal Election Commission The Federal Election Commission (FEC) issues regulations and advisory opinions that control PAC activities. In 1975, for example, the FEC ruled that corporations could use their own money to administer their PACs and

---

SECTION PREVIEW

Objectives
After studying this section, you should be able to:
- Summarize the activities of political action committees.
- Describe how political action committees are regulated.

Key Terms and Concepts
political action committee, incumbent, grandfather clause

Themes in Government
- Political Processes
- Growth of Democracy

Critical Thinking Skills
- Understanding Cause and Effect
- Analyzing Information

CHAPTER 10: INTEREST GROUPS **295**

Focus

Bell Ringer

Ask students to differentiate between interest groups and political action committees (PACs). *(An interest group attempts to affect public policy by influencing government officials, while a PAC collects money and channels it to political candidates.)*

Motivating Activity

Tell students that a new meal policy, removing all their favorite foods from the menu, has been instituted in the school cafeteria. To deal with the situation, an interest group called Students for Enlightened Nutrition (SEN) is formed, with a fund-raising arm called SENPAC. Ask students to compare the actions that SEN might take to those that SENPAC might take. *(SEN might ask students to write letters to the principal, try to meet with the principal or members of the student council, and attend school board meetings. SENPAC would solicit funds from supporters and use these funds to support the election of candidates for the student council or the board of education.)* Tell students Section 3 provides details about the operation of PACs.

Vocabulary Precheck

Call on volunteers to state what they think each key term means. Have students check the accuracy of these definitions by finding the terms in the Glossary.
LEP

Classroom Resources for Section 3

- Guided Reading Activities
- Reproducible Lesson Plans
- Interpreting Political Cartoons 10
- Primary and Secondary Source Readings 10
- Reteaching Activities 10
- Section 3 Quiz

- Chapter 10 Tests
- Testmaker
- Audio Cassettes (English and Spanish)
- Limited English Proficiency Activities 10
  SAT Practice Tests

Teach

Guided Practice

L1 Understanding Ideas Write the terms *affiliated PACs* and *independent PACs* on the chalkboard. Ask volunteers to define each term. Then ask students to suggest examples of each type of PAC. Enter suggestions under the appropriate heading. **LEP**

Interpreting Political Cartoons Have students complete activity 10 in *Interpreting Political Cartoons* in the Teacher's Classroom Resources.

L3 Making Judgments Rejecting PAC campaign donations and accepting only contributions of less than $500 from individuals, one member of Congress noted that a PAC contribution was an "investment," while an individual donation was a "pledge of support." Ask students to explain what the member of Congress meant. Then have the class discuss whether large-scale acceptance of PAC money is beneficial or harmful to American democracy.

Graph Study Answer

because federal laws limit direct campaign contributions from individuals, corporations, and labor unions, while setting looser regulations on PACs

Growth of PACs and PAC Income

Number of Committees (In Thousands)

1974 1976 1978 1980 1982 1984 1986 1988 1990

In Millions of Dollars

1979-80   1981-82   1983-84   1985-86   1987-88   1989-90

Source: Statistical Abstract of the United States, 1986, 1988, 1990, 1991, 1993

Graph Study
The number of political action committees has increased tremendously since 1974.
What factors could account for such dramatic growth?

may also use payroll deductions to raise money from employees of a PAC.

The FEC's decision stimulated the growth of PACs among business interests. In the decade after the ruling, the number of labor union PACs increased by more than 100 percent, but the number of corporate PACs increased by more than 1,000 percent.

Supreme Court Decisions Several Supreme Court decisions have also affected the growth and operation of PACs. For example, in *Buckley* v. *Valeo* (1976) the Court ruled that different divisions of a corporation or different union locals can set up as many PACs as they wish. This ruling also promoted the growth of PACs.

Affiliated and Independent PACs PACs tied to corporations, labor unions, trade groups, or health organizations are called affiliated PACs. Comprising about 70 percent of all PACs, they raise funds through voluntary contributions from corporate executives, union officials, workers, and stockholders. Examples of affiliated PACs are the Sun Oil Corporation's SunPAC, the Automobile and Truck Dealers Election Action Committee, the Realtors' Political Action Committee, and the Cattlemen's Action Legislative Fund (CALF).

Groups interested in a particular cause, such as abortion, farm subsidies, or the environment set up PACs that are not connected to any existing business or organization. These independent PACs are, in effect, new interest groups, and they make up about 25 percent of all PACs. Examples of independent PACs include Handgun Control, Inc. (favors gun control), Gun Owners of America (against gun control), Council for a Livable World (against nuclear arms), and the American Security Council (favors strong defense).

Independent PACs raise money largely through direct mail appeals to people across the nation. They

Background

Most PACs use political contributions more to gain access than to support a politician committed to their cause. For example, defense-related PACs make donations to influential members of House and Senate defense committees and subcommit-tees, even though such officials may be opposed to defense projects. These officials, regardless of their views, are people defense industry representatives need to talk to on a regular basis.

are very successful and usually raise more money than business or labor PACs. Independent PACs, however, spend less on candidates and elections than do the affiliated PACs because massive direct-mail fund-raising is very costly. Most of the money raised must be used to pay postage and staff workers and to buy mailing lists of potential contributors. Even a well-run independent PAC must spend about 50 cents to raise a dollar. Many spend much more than that.

Strategies for Influence

Political action committees generally follow two strategies to influence public policy. They use their money to gain access to lawmakers and to directly influence election outcomes.

Gaining Access Contributions can make it easier for PAC members to gain access to members of Congress to present their views. Busy lawmakers are more likely to set aside time in their crowded schedules to meet with a group that has given money than to meet with a group that has not. As a result, PACs may give donations to lawmakers who do not always support their views.

PACs generally support **incumbents**, or those government officials already in office. In recent elections 88 percent of corporate and trade PAC donations went to incumbents in House campaigns and more than 65 percent to incumbents in Senate elections.

Influencing Elections The decision to support incumbents has the expected result. Incumbents in both the House and Senate almost always win reelection—about 98 percent of incumbents have been reelected in recent elections. The task of challenging an incumbent for a seat in Congress has become so difficult that many races are no contest. Joan Claybrook, president of Public Citizen, Inc., an interest group Ralph Nader founded, said, "That these PACs feel compelled to contribute to lawmakers who have no opponent shows that what is being sought is ac-

cess and influence." Fred Wertheimer, Common Cause president, complained:

> *When House incumbents can't lose, regardless of performance, and House challengers can't win, regardless of talent, then we don't have representative government.*
>
> —FRED WERTHEIMER, 1988

"THIS HERE COUNTRY AIN'T BIG ENOUGH FOR BOTH OF US"

Problems With PACs
Some PACs wield tremendous power. **Politics Whom do PACs generally support?**

Having a huge campaign fund very early in an election cycle discourages potentially strong challengers from entering either a primary or general election. When there is no real challenge in the election, the incumbent does not need to spend the whole "war chest" of money that has been collected for the campaign. As a result, many members of Congress have accumulated huge amounts of "rainy day" funds. Several House members had accumulated more than $300,000 each by 1990. Congress did pass legislation to prevent misuse of these funds in 1979, as part of the Federal Election Campaign Act. Congress ruled out the use of excess campaign funds for personal

Cooperative Learning Activity

Ask students to prepare a 10-minute television news report on the activities of PACs in the last presidential election. Organize the class into groups and assign one of the following tasks to each: researching the topic; writing the script; serving as re-

porters and news anchors; serving as interview subjects—candidates, PAC representatives, people in the street, and so on. Have students "broadcast" their news report for other government and civics classes.

Independent Practice

L2 **Journalism** Have students research the role of PACs in recent elections and construct a "front page" story detailing the role played by PACs in one particular election.

📁 **Interpreting Source Readings** Have students complete activity 10 in *Primary and Secondary Source Readings* in the Teacher's Classroom Resources.

Caption Answer
incumbents

STUDY GUIDE

Theme Answer
Beliefs will vary.

Critical Thinking Answer
People interested in promoting equal political rights may believe that special interests have too much power and influence.

Assess

Check for Understanding

Have students complete Section 3 Review on page 298.

Meeting Objectives
Each section objective is tested by the Section Review questions that follow it in parentheses.
• Summarize the activities of political action committees. (2, 5, 6, 7, 8)
• Describe how political action committees are regulated. (3, 4, 8)

Evaluate

 Section 3 Quiz

 Testmaker

Reteach

Have each student write a 10-question test on PACs. Have students exchange their tests and complete the one that they receive. Completed tests should be handed back to their authors for grading.

Have students complete activity 10 in *Reteaching Activities* in the Teacher's Classroom Resources.

Enrich

Have students research the affiliated PAC of an interest group of their choice and write reports on their findings.

Close

Have students assess the impact of PACs on the American political system.

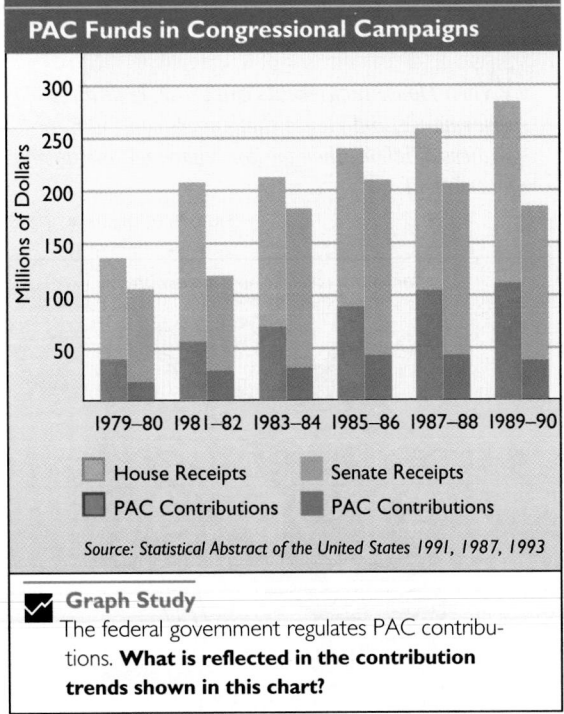

PAC Funds in Congressional Campaigns

Millions of Dollars

1979–80 1981–82 1983–84 1985–86 1987–88 1989–90

☐ House Receipts   ☐ Senate Receipts
☐ PAC Contributions   ☐ PAC Contributions

Source: Statistical Abstract of the United States 1991, 1987, 1993

Graph Study
The federal government regulates PAC contributions. **What is reflected in the contribution trends shown in this chart?**

purposes. The House of Representatives exempted themselves, however, by a **grandfather clause**, a provision that makes an exemption in the law for a certain group based on previous conditions. The grandfather clause allowed all members in office in 1979 to take surplus funds with them upon leaving office. Later, Congress, under public pressure, repealed the grandfather clause, effective in 1992.

How Much Influence Some members of Congress acknowledge the power of the PACs. Representative Barney Frank once said, "We are the only human beings in the world who are expected to take thousands of dollars from perfect strangers and not be affected by it." Other members of Congress disagree. Representative Dan Glickman has claimed, "I do not think any member of Congress votes because of how a PAC gives him money on El Salvador, or the MX missiles, or . . . broader, abstract national issues."

Even the interest groups themselves at times question the value of lobbying, especially the funding of incumbents. Wayne Anderson addressed the National Association of Manufacturers:

> PAC managers will have to account for why they gave an average of over two hundred thousand dollars to incumbents while tossing only a twenty-seven thousand dollars average to challengers. Does a 98 plus percent re-election factor mean that as Public Affairs Professionals you are that overwhelmingly happy with the overall performance of Congress?
> —WAYNE C. ANDERSON, SPEECH TO
> NATIONAL ASSOCIATION OF MANUFACTURERS, 1990

It is perhaps impossible to determine whether the special interest lobbies have an overall positive or negative effect on the government. Public attitudes toward them have turned negative, largely because of their financial impact on political campaigns. The public interest may continue to exert pressure for control over the special interests.

3 SECTION REVIEW

Section Summary
Since the 1970s political action committees (PACs) have become major forces in financing political campaigns. PACs are still powerful, but public attitudes toward them have become negative.

Checking for Understanding
Recalling Facts
1. Define **political action committee, incumbent, grandfather clause.**
2. Explain the basic purpose of a political action committee.
3. List the laws that govern the operations of PACs.
4. Describe three requirements that the laws place on PACs.

Exploring Themes
5. Political Processes Why do PACs sometimes give money to candidates who do not always support their views?
6. Growth of Democracy In what way is campaign financing by independent and affiliated PACs more democratic than funding by wealthy individuals, corporations, and labor unions?

Critical Thinking Skills
7. Understanding Cause and Effect What was the unexpected result of laws passed in the 1970s to reform campaign finance?
8. Analyzing Information Why do you think Congress has been reluctant to limit the financial contributions of PACs in federal elections?

Section 3 Review Answers

1. Definitions of terms appear on pages indicated: **political action committee,** 295; **incumbent,** 297; **grandfather clause,** 298
2. A political action committee is formed by a special interest to raise and direct money to certain political campaigns.
3. Federal Election Campaign Act of 1971; amendments to the act in 1974, 1976, 1979; Revenue Act of 1971

4. They must register with the government six months before an election, raise money from at least 50 contributors, give to at least 5 candidates in a federal election, follow strict accounting rules, and limit gifts to each candidate to $5,000.
5. PACs support candidates who do not share their views because such an action might gain them access to those candidates after the election.

6. PACs generally represent a larger number of people and raise their money through voluntary contributions.
7. increase in political action committees
8. Members of Congress are incumbents in campaigns. As such, they get the major share of PAC funds.

John E. Jacob on the Struggle for Equality

The National Urban League, Inc., is an interest group of about 50,000 members that seeks to further political rights of African Americans. John E. Jacob, the group's President and Chief Executive Officer, delivered the address from which the following excerpt is taken to the Conference on Public Policy and African Americans in October 1989.

There is a school of thought . . . that says there is no racial problem. There is a poverty problem. A housing problem. A health problem. An urban problem. Other problems. But no racial problem. That's been solved.

How wrong can you get?

Those "problems" people talk about without mentioning race are simply euphemisms for race. African Americans are only about twelve percent of the population, but we're a third of the poor. . . .

When today we talk of the problems of the underclass, of the urban poor, of the disadvantaged, we are talking about the same people we talked about 25 years ago when we spoke of racial disadvantage and discrimination.

The vocabulary has changed, but the people remain the same. . . .

Black people today sit in mayors' offices in many of our largest cities. Come November, a black man may be Governor of Virginia, the seat of the Old Confederacy. . . .

We see these people because they are so visible.

But their presence raises important issues related to our topic today.

One issue is the claim that the existence of appreciable numbers of blacks who have made it indicates that racism is no longer a factor.

I strongly disagree with that assumption. The group that has made it in our society is a very small one. It is comprised of individuals whose extraordinary gifts allowed them to take advantage of the breakthroughs of the 1960s. . . .

Their success in no way suggests racism is dead. Rather, it suggests that racism is capable of being suspended temporarily. . . .

Racism pervades our society to such an extent that many people who believe they are free of it actually practice it. They can't escape thinking in stereotypes—thinking that every black male is a potential mugger, that black workers aren't

> *When today we talk of the problems of the underclass . . . we are talking about the same people we talked about 25 years ago.*

as good as whites, that a black family moving next door signals the end of the neighborhood. . . .

Let me be clear, however, that our argument is not with attitudes. It is with behavior. . . .

The Urban League confronts racism through that behavioral side. We have taken as our theme, racial parity by the year 2000. . . .

We need to reach across the divide that separates Americans artificially by race and get to know each other better as people. . . .

And above all we need to make changes in our basic institutions so they become inclusive and reflect a society that is made up of diverse people of all races, backgrounds and beliefs.

—JOHN E. JACOB, 1989

Examining the Reading

Reviewing Facts

1. Identify the terms that Jacob says are euphemisms for racism today.

2. Explain Jacob's argument that those blacks who have made it are not proof that racism is ended.

Critical Thinking Skills

3. Identifying Central Issues
According to Jacob what do Americans need to do in order to ensure that racism in the United States is overcome?

CHAPTER 10: INTEREST GROUPS **299**

More About Personal Perspectives

In the early 1980s, John Jacob became the chief executive officer of the National Urban League at a time when President Ronald Reagan's conservative administration was supporting a backlash against affirmative action and slashing federal social programs. Jacob repeatedly clashed with the administration over civil rights policy, and he denounced the domestic budget as "anti-poor, anti-disadvantaged, and anti-cities." Jacob then pleaded with the private sector to fill the gap by setting up more entry-level job-training programs. Most of the National Urban League's operating funds now come from the business community.

PERSONAL
PERSPECTIVES

Focus

Write the word *euphemism* on the board. Ask students to look up both the meaning and the etymology. Ask students why people might use euphemisms such as *underprivileged* for *poor,* and *untruth* for *lie.* Have students note Jacob's euphemisms.

Teach

Ask: Who is being referred to when people use the terms *underclass, urban poor,* and *disadvantaged? (African Americans)* Why do many Americans feel that racial problems have been solved? What two major reasons do people cite to explain why more African Americans have not been successful? Which explanation does Jacob believe? *(Either they have only themselves to blame, or racism still holds them back. Jacob believes the latter.)*

Assess

Have students complete **Examining the Reading.**

Answers

1. poverty, housing, health, and urban problems
2. The group that made it is a small one and is also the exception.
3. make institutions more inclusive so that they reflect a multi-ethnic society

Close

Ask students the meaning of Jacob's statement—"racism is capable of being suspended temporarily . . . ."

Identifying Terms and Concepts

1. interest group, 2. lobbyist, 3. public interest, 4. political action committee, 5. incumbents

Reviewing Facts and Ideas

1. economic interests, individual social beliefs, function or group unity

2. political parties attempt to gain control of the government, interest groups are concerned with a narrower range of issues

3. newsletters, mailings, and phone calls

4. business interest groups

5. AFL-CIO

6. Farmers from different regions and different economic levels have different policy goals.

7. provides information to lawmakers, testifies at committee hearings, writes drafts of bills, provides election support, and tries to influence government officials

8. They run publicity campaigns using mass media and urge members to write letters to government officials.

9. Most Americans believe that Congress is too much under the influence of these groups and that these groups are too large and powerful.

10. SunPAC, the Automobile and Truck Dealers Election Action Committee, the Realtors' Political Action Committee, and the Cattlemen's Action Legislative Fund

Applying Themes

1. A local interest group can unite large numbers of people to attend a local government meeting and by their numbers force government to respond.

2. A lobbyist who gives false information to a lawmaker may lose access to that lawmaker and perhaps to others as well.

3. by ruling that there is no limit to the number of local PACs that can be set up by different

Summary and Significance

People with similar goals who seek to influence the government often form interest groups. Many of these groups are organized around economic interests. The most powerful groups represent business, labor, and agriculture. Other interest groups represent professions, environmental interests, and the public. Interest groups use lobbyists and help finance campaigns to influence public officials. Lobbyists often provide lawmakers with useful information and sometimes help draft bills in their fields of interest. Federal laws regulate the financial support that political action committees (PACs) give candidates for federal offices. Many Americans believe that interest groups are too powerful and represent only a narrow range of interests. Others feel that interest groups help Americans participate in government and have informed public officials represent their interests.

Identifying Terms and Concepts

Use the following terms to fill in the blanks of the following speech by a leader of a hypothetical pressure group.

public interest, incumbents, lobbyist, political action committee, interest group

Friends and citizens, some people believe that a special (1) may have too much power in Washington. I want to show you how much good we can do. Last year the Friends of Books hired a (2) to provide Congress with information about the need for literacy programs. We believe we are not acting in our own special interest but in the (3) as responsible Americans. Now we are asking for your support as we organize a (4) to raise money to help several legislators who may have real struggles getting reelected. If we give these (5) our support now, we may ask for their help later.

Reviewing Facts and Ideas

1. **Cite** three reasons or concerns that cause people to join interest groups.
2. **Identify** one major difference between an interest group and a political party.
3. **List** three ways that interest group leaders keep their members informed of the group's activities.
4. **Name** one of the oldest and largest categories of interest groups in the United States.
5. **Identify** the largest and most powerful labor union in the United States.

6. **Explain** why most farmers support several different interest groups.
7. **Describe** the work of a lobbyist.
8. **Explain** how interest groups try to influence public opinion to support their policies.
9. **Describe** the beliefs of most Americans regarding interest groups.
10. **Cite** three examples of affiliated PACs.

Applying Themes

1. **Civic Participation** How can an interest group influence local government?
2. **Political Processes** What prevents most lobbyists from giving false information to lawmakers whom they are attempting to influence?
3. **Public Policy** How did the Supreme Court decision in *Buckley* v. *Valeo* encourage the growth of PACs?
4. **Growth of Democracy** Why would it be undemocratic for the federal government to pass a law forbidding interest groups or lobbyists to contact members of Congress?

Critical Thinking Skills

1. **Understanding Cause and Effect** Studies have shown that people on lower socioeconomic levels are less likely to contribute to, lead in, or even join special-interest groups. Why do you think that this is so?

divisions of a corporation or different union locals

4. It would violate the First Amendment. Democracy presumes that people can express their opinions, either individually or as members of a group.

Critical Thinking Skills

1. Answers may include that people on lower socioeconomic levels do not have as much leisure time to devote to such groups, may not have the financial resources necessary to participate, may not believe they can influence government, or may not have an adequate understanding of the political process.

2. Students' opinions will vary.

2. **Expressing Problems Clearly** The reform campaign-finance legislation passed in the 1970s was intended to prevent wealthy interests from controlling elections. The legislation encouraged the growth of PACs. Was the goal of this legislation met? If not, what legislation would you recommend to achieve that goal? Explain your answers.

3. **Making Generalizations** What kinds of interest groups are the largest and most powerful? Why?

4. **Making Comparisons** Interest groups differ in size and composition of their membership and methods that they use to accomplish their goals. Compare an environmental interest group with the AFL-CIO in each of these three areas.

5. **Analyzing Information** Do you believe that interest groups have too much power and influence on public policy? Explain your answer.

Linking Past and Present

The oldest farm group is the Grange. Originally called the National Grange of the Patrons of Husbandry, this farm organization boasted 1.5 million members in 1874. The Grangers' first success was in winning legislation that fixed maximum rates for railroad traffic within certain states in the 1870s. It defended farmers' interests in court, winning the case of *Munn* v. *Illinois* (1877) in the Supreme Court. Why do you think the Grange has become more of a social organization than an interest group today?

Writing About Government

Descriptive Writing Write a paragraph describing an interest group that you would like to see formed to address some interest or concern that you have. Include a description of the concern or interest, goals of the group, the kinds of people who would be likely members of the group, and the methods your group would use to attain its goals.

Reinforcing the Skill

Detecting Bias Read the following paragraph from an essay by the founder of Common Cause, John W.

Gardner. Then use what you have learned about detecting bias to answer the questions that follow.

> *But the deepest problem of citizen participation does not stem from the fact that [government] decisions are made behind closed doors. The most serious obstacle the citizen faces when he sets out to participate is that someone with a lot of money got there first and bought up the public address system. The full-throated voice of money drowns him out. It isn't just that money talks. It talks louder and longer and drowns out the citizen's hoarse whisper. . . . The capacity or willingness of government to find solutions to any of the problems that plague us . . . is complicated by the commanding power of monied interests to define the problem and set limits to public action.*
>
> —JOHN W. GARDNER, IN COMMON CAUSE, 1972

1. What is the author's major topic?
2. What bias does the author show in the second sentence?
3. How might the second sentence be phrased to make it bias-free?
4. What does Gardner believe to be the major obstacle to citizens participating in government?

Investigating Further

1. **Individual Project** On a sheet of paper write the following categories: health and medicine, education, business, labor, professional, public interest. Then, look in the yellow pages of your telephone book under "Associations." Make a list of those that could be placed under each of the categories.

2. **Cooperative Learning** Bring several back issues of national news magazines to class. Organize into groups of four, giving each group member several magazines. Have each group member choose one of the following special interests: business, labor, environment, or education. Then have each member find any articles in which the interest group is mentioned. Have a spokesperson report the news item to the class.

3. Business and labor groups are largest and most powerful because they represent economic concerns—nearly all have economic interests.

4. The Sierra Club and environmental groups are much smaller than the AFL-CIO, although there are many of them. Members, who have this narrow interest, join because of their interest in protecting the environment. They may file lawsuits against polluters.

The AFL-CIO has about 13 million members. Its interests are broader, dealing with the economic interests of workers. It also lobbies state and national governments and buys media ads. Its political action committee (COPE) conducts voter registration drives and supports candidates for office.

Chapter 10 Review Answers (margin column)

5. Answers will vary. Those who believe interest groups have too much influence should cite the fact that lobbyists for these groups write half the national legislation, that their political action committees provide a large percentage of campaign finance, and that it has been necessary to pass several laws to control such groups. Those who believe that they are not too powerful should cite that interest groups compete with one another; members of Congress do not have to listen to them; they do not often approach government officials who are of the opposite opinion.

Linking Past and Present

Other farm organizations today more effectively represent the interests of farmers. The American Farm Bureau Federation represents larger farmers and the National Farmers' Union represents smaller farmers.

Writing About Government

Students' paragraphs will vary.

Reinforcing the Skill

1. the large campaign contributions made by wealthy groups and individuals

2. that people with money have "bought up the public address system" and thus have the ear of government officials

3. Answers will vary but should not include the phrases "someone with money" and "bought up the public address system."

4. overcoming "the commanding power of monied interests"

Investigating Further

1. Students' lists of associations will vary.

2. Articles selected will vary.

Chapter Organizer

Objectives	Special Feature Pages	Supplemental Materials
Section 1 Shaping Public Opinion *pp. 304–308* 1. Identify the factors that shape public opinion. 2. Explain how elected officials shape public opinion. 3. Discuss the relationship between the mass media and public opinion.	Focus on Freedom: The "Four Freedoms" Speech p. 305 Global Connection: Interdependence: Influencing World Opinion p. 306 Social Studies Skills: Understanding a Public Opinion Poll p. 308	Guided Reading Activities Reproducible Lesson Plans Primary and Secondary Source Readings 11 Section 1 Quiz Testmaker Chapter Transparencies 11 Skill Reinforcement Activities 11 SAT Practice Tests Writer's Guidebook
Section 2 Measuring Public Opinion *pp. 309–312* 1. Note the ways by which public opinion is measured. 2. Explain the value of scientific polling.	Participating in Government: Public Opinion Polls p. 310	Guided Reading Activities Reproducible Lesson Plans Participating in Goverment 11 Enrichment Activities 11 Section 2 Quiz Testmaker SAT Practice Tests Writer's Guidebook
Section 3 Public Opinion and Public Policy *pp. 313–317* 1. Examine the influence that public opinion has on the making of government policies. 2. Describe the role that public opinion plays in court decisions that set public policy. 3. Discuss how personal ideologies affect opinions.	Personal Perspectives: Harry P. Pachon on Sampling the Hispanic Universe p. 317	Guided Reading Activities Reproducible Lesson Plans Reteaching Activities 11 Section 3 Quiz Testmaker Chapter 11 Tests Audio Cassettes (English and Spanish) Limited English Proficiency Activities 11 SAT Practice Tests Writer's Guidebook

If time does not permit teaching this chapter, assign the Chapter 11 summary in the Unit 3 Digest on pages 355–356.

Key To Ability Levels

Teaching strategies have been coded for varying learning styles and abilities.

L1 Level 1 activities are **basic** activities and should be within the ability range of all students.

L2 Level 2 activities are **average** activities and should be within the ability range of the average to above-average student.

L3 Level 3 activities are **challenging** activities designed for the ability range of above-average students.

LEP These activities should be within the ability range of **Limited English Proficiency** students.

Multicultural Activities

Every day thousands of Hispanic Americans tune in to Spanish-language television and radio. Los Angeles has a Spanish-language cable television network which reaches 2 million Hispanic households. Nationwide there are about 200 Spanish-language radio stations and 2 major Spanish-language television networks, Univision and Telemundo. Approximately 30 newspapers carry a supplement called "Vista" designed especially for Hispanics. Have students speculate on the kinds of news stories that might be of special interest to the viewers or readers of Hispanic media. How could these media be used to increase civic participation by Hispanic voters? Do these media have a special responsibility to spotlight Hispanic candidates or politicians? Why or why not?

Organize students into groups to analyze the access of racial or ethnic groups to television air time. Have each group pick a different minority for study and identify a variety of television sources such as network news and interview programs, C-SPAN, CNN, and specialized cable networks. Groups can keep logs of the following for a five-day period: appearances of minority public officials, community leaders, or candidates on television and news stories or programs about the group chosen. Logs can indicate how long the minority-group member appeared on the screen and whether news stories were positive, neutral or negative, linked to a problem such as drugs or illegal immigration, or an achievement such as academic success. Have groups' members compare findings and give their minority a media access and image rating.

Chapter Resources

Readings for the Student

Abramson, Paul R. *Political Attitudes in America: Formation and Change.* Freeman, 1983.

Crouse, Timothy. *The Boys on the Bus.* Random House, 1973.

Diamond, Edwin and Stephen Bates. *The Spot: The Rise of Political Advertising on Television.* MIT Press, 1984.

Fanning the Flames: A Look at Propaganda in American History. Perfection Form, 1990.

Halberstam, David. *The Powers That Be.* Dell, 1979.

McGiniss, Joe. *The Selling of the President, 1968.* Pocket Books, 1978.

Rank, Hugh. *The Pitch.* Counter-Propaganda, 1991.

Readings for the Teacher

Asher, Herbert. *Polling and the Public.* Congressional Quarterly, 1991.

Graber, Doris A. *Mass Media and American Politics.* Congressional Quarterly, 1984.

Hess, Stephen. *The Washington Reporters.* Brookings Institution, 1981.

Ranney, Austin. *Channels of Power.* Basic Books, 1985.

Multimedia

Videocassettes

Change, Change. (*A Walk Through the 20th Century with Bill Moyers* series). Corporation for Entertainment and Learning. (v/c, 58 minutes)

Drugs and AIDS: Getting the Message Out. State of the Art, Inc. (v/c, 30 minutes)

Moyers: The Public Mind (4-part series: *Consuming Images, Leading Questions, Illusions of News, The Truth About Lies*). Alvin H. Perlmutter, Inc. and Public Affairs TV, Inc. (4 v/cs, 60 minutes each)

The Psychology of Mass Persuasion. Human Relations Media. (v/c)

The Radio Priest. Irv Drasnin. (v/c, 60 minutes)

The Thirty-Second President. (*A Walk Through the 20th Century with Bill Moyers* series). Corporation for Entertainment and Learning. (v/c, 58 minutes)

Software

The Discussion Generator: AFTERMATH—TV Violence and Special Interest Groups. Tom Snyder Productions. (Apple, IBM disks). A role-playing simulation that encourages students to explore how attitudes develop.

Public Opinion

CHAPTER

11

Introduce

Chapter Overview

Chapter 11 introduces students to the subject of public opinion.

Section 1 discusses the various factors that help to shape public opinion.

Section 2 describes the ways in which public opinion is measured and assessed.

Section 3 analyzes the impact of public opinion on the making of government policies.

Chapter 11 Themes

Have students copy into their notebooks the three government themes in the Chapter Preview. Lead the class in a discussion of how these themes relate to the subject of public opinion. As they read Chapter 11, have students list its major concepts, ideas, issues, and examples under the appropriate theme. At the conclusion of the chapter, ask students to compare their lists.

Linking Past and Present
The first scientific public opinion poll on a presidential election was taken in 1936. Undertaken by one polling firm, the Gallup Organization, it surveyed voter preferences just before the election. In contrast, the three major polling organizations—Gallup, Harris, and Roper—in collaboration with dozens of television stations and newspapers, undertook hundreds of surveys on the 1992 presidential election. The polling began some 18 months before the election and concluded with exit polls on Election Day.

The voting process, as depicted in George Caleb Bingham's *Verdict of the People*, enables citizens to express their preferences on critical issues.

302   UNIT 3: INFLUENCING GOVERNMENT

About the Chapter Opener

Teaching With Illustrations George Caleb Bingham completed *Verdict of the People* in 1855. The painting shows an election-day celebration. Bingham was involved in politics and was elected to the Missouri state legislature in 1848. Bingham's art was known as *genre painting*—a type of art which depicted the lives of people in everyday situations.

Ask students what mood is expressed in the art. Ask how this painting reflects the title of Chapter 11. *(Students might indicate that the voting process is a way of expressing public opinion.)* Then ask: Why do you think there are so few women in the painting?

Chapter Preview

Overview

Almost all public opinion influences government officials, but public opinion does not always cause government to act.

Objectives

After studying this chapter, you should be able to:

1. **Relate** how political opinions are formed.
2. **Describe** the techniques and limitations of scientific polling.
3. **Summarize** the relationship between public opinion and public policy.

Themes in Government

This chapter emphasizes the following government themes:

• **Cultural Pluralism** A person's cultural background is a factor in shaping the opinions that he or she holds. Sections 1 and 2.
• **Political Processes** Public policy helps to shape public opinion. Sections 1 and 3.
• **Public Policy** Public opinion can influence public policy. Sections 2 and 3.

Critical Thinking Skills

This chapter emphasizes the following critical thinking skills:

• Evaluating Information
• Demonstrating Reasoned Judgment
• Synthesizing Information

Introducing the Chapter

Draw on the chalkboard five columns headed *Strongly Support, Support, Don't Know, Oppose,* and *Strongly Oppose.* Then make the following statements:

1. The age at which you may obtain a driver's license should be raised to 25.
2. The Twenty-sixth Amendment should be repealed and the voting age returned to 21.
3. The student council should be given more power in running the school.
4. Teachers' pay raises should be based on evaluations by their students.

For each statement, ask students which heading best represents their feelings. Record the results on the chalkboard.

Inform students that they have just taken part in a *public opinion poll.* Point out that as students read this chapter, they will learn what public opinion is and how it is formed, how it is accurately measured, and what impact it has on government.

Chapter Project

Have students work individually or in groups to construct a collage that illustrates the relationship between public opinion polls and politics. Collages might include charts and graphs showing poll results and newspaper headlines and stories on opinion polls. Suggest that students display their collages on the bulletin board.

Setting the Scene In the first poll, a Pennsylvania newspaper asked in 1824 who should be the next President. It then predicted the election of Andrew Jackson. He did receive the most votes, but the House of Representatives chose John Quincy Adams. The real precursor of today's scientific polling, however, was the market survey. George Gallup and Elmo Roper, pioneers in opinion polling, did their first work for business and advertising organizations. By the mid-1930s, Roper, Gallup, and others had begun polling the American public on a variety of issues.

Shaping Public Opinion

Focus

Bell Ringer

While attendance is being taken, have students write a definition of the term *public opinion*.

Motivating Activity

Review students' Bell Ringer responses. Then ask: What forces and influences shape the opinions you hold? Write responses on the chalkboard. Ask students to study the list and to select and record what they think are the five most important influences in the development of opinions.

Vocabulary Precheck

Write the key terms for this section on the chalkboard. Ask students to use those that they know in sentences. **LEP**

Teach

Guided Practice

L1 **Understanding Ideas** Write on the chalkboard the terms: *diversity, communication, significant numbers*. Ask students to suggest how each is related to public opinion. Write suggestions on the chalkboard and have students use this information to write a definition of *public opinion* that includes the three terms listed above.

Caption Answer
within the family

L2 **Analyzing Ideas** Draw six columns on the chalkboard and label them with the six factors that shape opinion. Ask for examples of how each influences opinion formation. Write responses in the appropriate columns. Then have students discuss how they would rank the factors in importance.

Every elected official wants to know what the public is thinking. "What I want," Abraham Lincoln once declared, "is to get done what the people desire to have done, and the question for me is how to find that out exactly."

The Nature of Public Opinion

Most Americans have opinions or preferences about many matters that affect their lives. These range from opinions about the best baseball players to favorite television programs. Few such opinions, however, have much effect on government. Yet one form of opinion, **public opinion**, has an enormous influence on government. Public opinion includes the

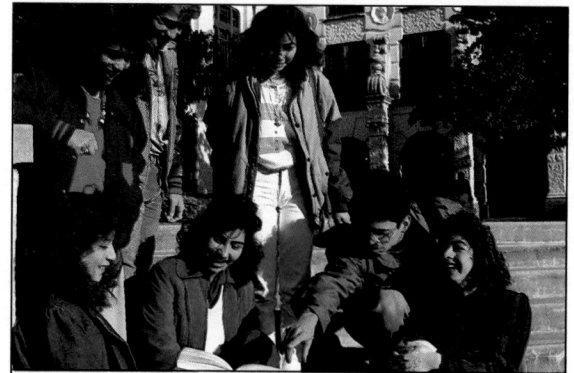

Peer Influence
The opinion of classmates, close friends, or family members can have a powerful influence on your opinion. **Sociology Where are a person's political attitudes first formed?**

ideas and attitudes a significant number of Americans hold about government and political issues. Three factors characterize the nature of public opinion.

Diversity Public opinion is varied. In a nation as vast as the United States, it is unlikely that all citizens will think the same way about any political issue. Because of the diversity of American society, different groups of people hold different opinions on almost every issue.

Communication People's ideas and attitudes must in some way be expressed and communicated to government. Unless Americans make their opinions on important issues clear, public officials will not know what people are thinking. Accordingly, they will not be able to weigh public opinion when making decisions.

Significant Numbers The phrase *a significant number of Americans* in the definition of public opinion means that enough people must hold a particular opinion to make government officials listen to them. For example, perhaps the most important reason why President Lyndon Johnson decided not to run for reelection in 1968 was that so many people opposed his conduct of the Vietnam War.

Political Socialization

Personal background and life experiences exert important influences on opinion formation. Individuals learn their political beliefs and attitudes from their family, school, friends, and coworkers in a process

---

SECTION PREVIEW

Objectives
After studying this section, you should be able to:
■ Identify the factors that shape public opinion.
■ Explain how elected officials shape public opinion.

■ Discuss the relationship between the mass media and public opinion.

Key Terms and Concepts
public opinion, political socialization, peer group, mass media, political culture

Themes in Government
■ Cultural Pluralism
■ Political Processes

Critical Thinking Skills
■ Evaluating Information
■ Demonstrating Reasoned Judgment

304   UNIT 3: INFLUENCING GOVERNMENT

Classroom Resources for Section 1

📁 Guided Reading Activities
📁 Reproducible Lesson Plans
📁 Primary and Secondary Source Readings 11
📁 Section 1 Quiz

💻 Testmaker
📄 Chapter Transparencies 11
SAT Practice Tests
Writer's Guidebook

called **political socialization.** This process begins early in life and continues through adulthood.

Family and Home Influence Political socialization begins within the family. Children learn many of their early political opinions from their parents. In most cases, the political party of the parents becomes the party of their children. A study of high school seniors showed that only a small minority differed in party loyalty from their parents. As adults, more than two-thirds of all voters continue to favor the political party their parents supported.

Chapter 11, Section 1
Lesson Plan, pages 304–308

Interpreting Visuals Display transparency 11 from the *Chapter Transparencies* in the Teacher's Classroom Resources and use the accompanying teaching strategy and student activity to teach about factors that influence public opinion.

Independent Practice

Interpreting Source Readings Have students complete activity 11 in *Primary and Secondary Source Readings* in the Teacher's Classroom Resources.

Focus on Freedom

Mention that the Four Freedoms were an integral part of the United Nations' Universal Declaration of Human Rights.

Answers

1. freedom of expression and religion, freedom from want and fear

2. that people of all nations will not want for economic necessities of life

3. Answers will vary. Students may note that in much of the world the four freedoms have yet to be realized.

Focus on Freedom

THE "FOUR FREEDOMS" SPEECH

On January 6, 1941, Franklin D. Roosevelt delivered his annual State of the Union message to Congress. His message for 1941 was especially important. War had been raging in Europe, Africa, and Asia for 16 months. Although the United States was not yet involved in World War II, the President believed that entry into the conflict could not be avoided. He knew he had to influence public opinion regarding American involvement in the war. In what became known as the Four Freedoms speech, FDR set out to convince Americans that they should be prepared to go to war.

Every realist knows that the democratic way of life is at this moment being directly assailed in every part of the world. . . .

No realistic American can expect from a dictator's peace, international generosity, or return of true independence, or world disarmament, or freedom of expression, or freedom of religion—or even good business.

Such a peace would bring no security for us or for our neighbors. "Those who would give up essential liberty to purchase a little temporary safety deserve neither liberty nor safety."

As a nation, we may take pride in the fact that we are softhearted; but we cannot afford to be softheaded. . . .

In the future days, which we seek to make secure, we look forward to a world founded upon four essential human freedoms.

The first is freedom of speech and expression—everywhere in the world.

The second is freedom of every person to worship God in his own way—everywhere in the world.

The third is freedom from want— . . . economic understandings which will secure to every nation a healthy peacetime life for its inhabitants—everywhere in the world.

The fourth is freedom from fear— . . . a worldwide reduction of armaments to such a point . . . that no nation will be in a position to commit an act of physical aggression against any neighbor—anywhere in the world. . . .

Freedom means the supremacy of human rights everywhere. Our support goes to those who struggle to gain those rights or keep them. . . . To that high concept there can be no end save victory.

Examining the Document

Reviewing Facts
1. List the Four Freedoms of which Roosevelt spoke.
2. Explain the meaning of freedom from want.

Critical Thinking Skills
3. Expressing Problems Clearly Do you think the Four Freedoms have yet been realized? Why or why not?

STUDY GUIDE

Themes in Government
Cultural Pluralism What are the elements of diversity that affect Americans' public opinion on housing subsidies?

Critical Thinking Skills
Evaluating Information During a recession in the United States, why might there be negative

public opinion regarding government food distribution to developing countries?

STUDY GUIDE

Theme Answer
where people live, socioeconomic situation, level of education, political orientation of family and friends, health of family members

Critical Thinking Answer
People who are unemployed or worried about losing their jobs might want surplus food to be available to them.

Background

Social scientists have noted a change in the extent of influence exercised by the various factors that shape public opinion. In the past, income, geographic region, ethnic origin, and religious denomination tended to have the greatest influence on people's opinions and attitudes. Today, however, such factors as race, education, and depth of religious commitment are more likely to cause differences in opinions.

GLOBAL CONNECTION

Point out that American diplomats in many countries work to influence journalists to present a positive image of the United States and its policies.

Examining the Connection: Have students present their findings.

Assess

Check for Understanding

Have students complete Section 1 Review on page 307.

Meeting Objectives

Each section objective is tested by the Section Review questions that follow it in parentheses.

- Identify the factors that shape public opinion. (2, 4, 5, 7)
- Explain how elected officials shape public opinion. (3, 6)
- Discuss the relationship between the mass media and public opinion. (6, 8)

STUDY GUIDE

Theme Answer
provide political information and images that can directly influence political attitudes

Critical Thinking Answer
Answers should reflect understanding of freedom of speech and limits when others are hurt.

GLOBAL CONNECTION

Interdependence

Influencing World Opinion The President, by exercising foreign policy powers, can influence world opinion. For example, by withdrawing diplomats from a nation, the President tells the world that the United States government disapproves of that nation's policies.

World opinion is dramatically influenced when the President sends troops into combat. Such was the case in 1990, when Iraq invaded neighboring Kuwait. President Bush committed American military power to the defense of Kuwait and sent thousands of troops to the area. This action brought condemnation of Iraq's leader, Saddam Hussein, from many nations.

Examining the Connection
Find information detailing in which countries the United States refuses to station diplomats, indicating that the federal government disapproves of those regimes.

Schools School also plays an important part in the political socialization process. In the United States, all students learn about their nation, its history, and its political system. Democratic values are also learned in school clubs and through school rules and regulations.

Peer Groups An individual's close friends, church, synagogue, clubs, and work groups—called **peer groups**—are yet another factor in the political socialization process. A person's peer groups often influence and shape opinions. For example, a member of a labor union whose closest friends belong to the same union is likely to have political opinions similar to theirs.

Social Characteristics Economic and social status is another aspect of political socialization. Whether a person is young or old, rich or poor, rural or urban, easterner or southerner, black or white, male or female may affect his or her opinions.

The Mass Media Television, radio, newspapers, magazines, recordings, movies, and books—the **mass media**—play an important role in political socialization. The media, especially television, provide political information and images that can directly influence political attitudes. For example, broadcasts of a rally against a Supreme Court decision or a riot outside an American embassy can help shape viewers' opinions.

Movies, recordings, novels, and television entertainment can also affect opinions. Showing police as heroes or as criminals, for example, can shape attitudes toward authority. The way the media depict different groups of people such as women, African Americans, Asian Americans, Hispanics, or immigrants can help discredit stereotypes—or create them.

Other Influences Government leaders also play an important role in political socialization. The President, especially, has a tremendous influence on people's opinions. The news media provide almost continuous reports on the President's activities and policy proposals.

Like the President, members of Congress try to influence opinions. They frequently go back to their home states or home districts and talk to their constituents. Many legislators send newsletters or write personal letters to voters. They also appear on television programs and give newspaper interviews on timely issues. Senators and representatives who come across as sincere, personable, and intelligent are particularly effective in influencing opinions on major issues. At state and local levels, lawmakers also use the media to gain public support for their views.

At the same time, interest groups try to shape public opinion. Many interest groups exist solely to influence the opinions of individual citizens about the special issues that concern the group. If an interest

STUDY GUIDE

Themes in Government
Political Processes How do the mass media affect political socialization?

Critical Thinking Skills
Demonstrating Reasoned Judgment Do you think all opinions on a controversial topic, such as school busing to achieve racial

integration, should be permitted to be aired on a radio call-in talk show? Explain.

306   UNIT 3: INFLUENCING GOVERNMENT

Cooperative Learning Activity

Organize students into groups of four or five. Ask each group to create a collage of symbols that are visual representations of the factors that influence opinion formation. Some students might design the symbols or search for suitable pictorial representations of the factors. Other students might write brief captions that explain how the symbols represent the factors. Still others might design and construct the collage. Have groups display their collages on the bulletin board.

group can win enough support among the voters, public opinion may pressure legislators to accept the group's goals.

American Political Culture

Every nation has a **political culture,** a set of basic values and beliefs about a nation and its government that most citizens share. For example, a belief in liberty and freedom is one of the key elements of American political culture. Ralph Waldo Emerson expressed this value when he wrote:

The office of America is to liberate, to abolish kingcraft, priestcraft, castle, monopoly, to pull down the gallows, to burn up the bloody statute-book, to take in the immigrant, to open the doors of the sea and the fields of the earth.

—RALPH WALDO EMERSON

Additional examples of widely shared political values include support for the Constitution and Bill of Rights, commitment to the idea of political equality, belief in the virtue of private property, and an emphasis on individual achievement. The American political culture helps shape public opinion in the United States in two ways.

A Context for Opinion The political culture sets the general boundaries within which citizens develop and express their opinions. Public opinion on any issue or problem almost always fits within the limits

Political Culture
Political culture influences how the public interprets information. **Politics What opinion is the cartoonist expressing about middle-class America?**

the political culture sets. For example, Americans will disagree over just how much the federal government should regulate the airline industry. Very few Americans, however, would urge that government do away with private airlines altogether and take over and run the industry.

Screening Information A nation's political culture also influences how its citizens interpret what they see and hear every day. Put another way, an American and a Russian citizen might interpret the same event quite differently. If shown a photo of people in line outside a grocery store, the Russian might attribute it to a food shortage. The American citizen would likely think there was a sale.

---

1 SECTION REVIEW

Section Summary
Political socialization shapes individual opinions. These opinions and the nation's political culture help mold public opinion.

Checking for Understanding
Recalling Facts
1. Define public opinion, political socialization, peer group, mass media, political culture.
2. Identify five social characteristics that can influence the opinions a person holds.
3. State the methods that elected officials use to shape public opinion.
4. Explain why interest groups want to influence opinions.

Exploring Themes
5. Cultural Pluralism Cite an issue where people's ethnic backgrounds might influence their opinions. Explain how those opinions might be affected.
6. Political Processes How are the mass media and public opinion related?

Critical Thinking Skills
7. Evaluating Information Which of the forces in political socialization do you think is most influential? Explain why.
8. Demonstrating Reasoned Judgment Do you think that the mass media have too much influence on American public opinion? Explain why or why not.

Section 1 Review Answers

1. Definitions of terms appear on pages indicated: **public opinion,** 304; **political socialization,** 305; **peer group,** 306; **mass media,** 306; **political culture,** 307
2. age, sex, race, economic status, and place of residence
3. appear in the media to state opinions, talk to constituents, send newsletters to constituents

4. If an interest group can gain public support for its position, legislators may accept its goals.
5. Answers will vary but should provide examples of the influence a person's race or ethnicity can have on his or her opinions.
6. media afford elected officials opportunities to shape public opinion; media also shape public opinion by the way they present information

7. Answers will vary but should show that students understand the political socialization process.
8. Possible responses: <u>yes</u>—may cite pervasiveness of electronic entertainment, especially television, and its subtle effect on values and attitudes; <u>no</u>—may argue that people recognize that mass media is attempting to influence them.

Caption Answer
Middle-class America is extinct or antiquated, like the dinosaurs or old airplane in the background.

Evaluate

📁 Section 1 Quiz

🔲 Testmaker

Reteach

Have each student write three questions about the formation of public opinion on index cards. Collect and shuffle the cards and go through them, selecting students at random to answer the questions.

Enrich

The movie *To Kill a Mockingbird,* which was based on Harper Lee's novel of the same name, is credited with altering American attitudes on civil rights. Ask students to write a brief report on a movie or book that had a similar impact on American public opinion.

Close

Have students review the lists they made in the Motivating Activity and complete the following sentence:

The greatest influence on opinion formation is . . .

Discuss students' responses.

Focus

Present the following challenge:

Tell students to imagine they are members of Congress, about to introduce a bill to increase funding for vocational education. How would you find out if your constituency supports your idea? *(telephone polls, written surveys, talk shows, asking interest groups, talking to voters)* Ask which method would be the best way to gauge support. Point out that scientific polls are especially useful because properly conducted, they accurately measure public opinion.

Teach

Remind students that because statistical data can be used to support a variety of conclusions, the ability to analyze a poll is important. Review the steps for analyzing a poll. Explain sampling error and why it is important. *(a percentage figure that measures the accuracy of poll results)* Ask why the wording of questions is important? *(Biased questions can lead to unreliable results.)*

Assess

Have students complete the **Practice** exercise.

Close

Ask: Why would the sample be so important in understanding poll results?

Understanding a Public Opinion Poll

Well-designed public opinion polls give us accurate "snapshots" of how Americans are thinking at a given point in time. Knowing how to read data from a public opinion poll will help you to understand what your fellow citizens are thinking.

Explanation

To analyze a public opinion poll, follow these steps:

- Look at the title and the date of the poll to determine a context for what you read.
- Note who was interviewed. Ask: How large was the sample? Sample sizes should be about 1,200 to 1,500 people for high reliability.
- Ask: What was the sampling error? Margins of error are critically important for determining whether differences shown in the poll are significant.
- Note exactly what questions were asked and whether they are phrased in an unbiased way.
- State the results in sentence form.

The heading of the poll data shown below shows that the poll concerns Americans' attitudes about the drug problem. The poll was taken during January 1990.

The sample was 1,200 Americans, with a margin of error of plus or minus 3 percent. We therefore know that the poll is fairly accurate.

It is important that questions be phrased neither to encourage nor discourage a given answer. The first question is not biased. Note that by saying "if any" in the second question the pollsters avoid suggesting that there has necessarily been progress.

The next step is to state the numerical results of the poll in sentence form. For the first question, the results could be stated as "A large majority of Americans approved of the way President Bush was handling the drug problem."

Practice

Use what you have learned about analyzing poll data to examine the following data and answer the questions that follow.

Handgun Laws
In general, do you feel that the laws covering the sale of handguns should be made more strict, less strict, or kept as they are now?

More strict	64%
Less strict	6%
Kept same	27%
No opinion	3%

By Gender

Male		Female	
More strict	55%	More strict	72%
Less strict	8%	Less strict	3%
Kept same	35%	Kept same	20%
No opinion	2%	No opinion	5%

The Drug Problem
Do you approve or disapprove of the way George Bush is handling the drug problem?

Approve	69%
Disapprove	24%
No opinion	7%

How much progress, if any, do you think the Bush administration has made in combating drugs?

A lot	10%
Some	53%
Not too much	26%
None at all	9%
No opinion	2%

1. What is this poll about?
2. Is the question phrased in an unbiased way?
3. Explain in sentence form two differences in the answers given by the subgroups polled.
4. State in sentence form an important similarity between the responses of the two subgroups.

Additional Practice
To practice this skill, see **Reinforcing the Skill** on page 319.

Practice Answers

1. The poll concerns attitudes toward gun control.
2. yes
3. Answers will vary. Almost 20 percent fewer men than women believe that laws governing the sale of firearms should be made more strict. Twice as many men as women think these laws should be less strict.

4. A majority of both men and women feel that laws covering the sale of firearms should be made more strict.

For additional practice, have students complete activity 11 in *Skill Reinforcement Activities* in the Teacher's Classroom Resources.

SECTION 2
Measuring Public Opinion

The people are the source of power in a democracy. Elected officials represent the public, and government policy is to reflect the public's wishes. In a nation of about 250 million people, how can government know what the public wants?

Traditional Methods

In the past, elected officials used a variety of methods to gauge the public mood. They read the newspapers, talked with voters, and met with leaders of interest groups. Politicians still use such techniques even though each can distort public opinion.

Political Party Organizations Through much of American history, local and state political party organizations were a reliable source of information about the public's attitudes. Party leaders were in close touch with voters in their towns, cities, counties, and states. National leaders, in turn, communicated regularly with Republican and Democratic party bosses in such cities as New York, Chicago, Philadelphia, and Detroit. When the two major parties did not respond to issues quickly, support for third parties showed public disapproval. In the early 1900s, however, political reforms designed to curb the abuses of the big city party organizations began to weaken the role of parties in daily political life. Thus their ability to provide reliable information on voters' attitudes declined.

Interest Groups Elected officials have always tried to stay in touch with the leaders of various interest groups. These groups also seek such contact to make sure public officials know the opinions of their members. Interest groups, however, usually represent the attitudes of a vocal minority concerned primarily with specific issues such as gun control, health care, or auto safety. They are not a good measure of broader public opinion.

The Mass Media Television, newspapers, and magazines help officials understand public attitudes about the issues of the day. All politicians keep an eye on the newspaper headlines, magazine cover stories, editorials, letters to the editor, syndicated columns, radio talk shows, and television newscasts.

For several reasons, however, these sources of information may give a distorted view of public opinion. The mass media focus on news that has entertainment value—stories about crime, violence, unusual people, and sensational events. Newspapers may take positions that few people share because their editorials express the opinions of the writers rather than the public. People who write letters to the editor or call radio talk shows often have very strong opinions not found in the general population.

Letter Writing One of the most time-honored forms of expressing opinion in a democracy is to write letters to elected officials. The first major letter-writing campaign convinced George Washington to seek a second term as President in 1792. Letter writing has always increased during times of national crisis such as the Civil War, the Great Depression, and the Watergate scandal. Headline events such as Supreme Court decisions or major presidential speeches also spark letter writing.

SECTION PREVIEW

Objectives
After studying this section, you should be able to:
- Note the ways by which public opinion is measured.
- Explain the value of scientific polling.

Key Terms and Concepts
biased sample, universe, representative sample, random sampling, sampling error, cluster sample

Themes in Government
- Cultural Pluralism
- Public Policy

Critical Thinking Skills
- Evaluating Information
- Demonstrating Reasoned Judgment

CHAPTER 11: PUBLIC OPINION 309

Classroom Resources for Section 2

- Guided Reading Activities
- Reproducible Lesson Plans
- Participating in Government 11
- Enrichment Activities 11

- Section 2 Quiz
- Testmaker
- SAT Practice Tests
- Writer's Guidebook

Teach

Guided Practice

L1 **Mathematics** Tell students to suppose that a scientific poll of 50 residents in a community found that 23 of them favored a law requiring dogs to be leashed in city parks, 20 opposed such a law, and 7 had no opinion. The poll's sampling error was 8 percent. Ask students to interpret and evaluate this poll. *(Of 50 persons, 8 percent is 4 people. The leash law could thus be favored 27 to 16, or opposed 19 to 24—not very accurate results.)* **LEP**

L2 **Organizing Ideas** Draw a table on the chalkboard with vertical column headings of *Personal Interview, Telephone,* and *Mail* and horizontal column headings of *Advantages* and *Disadvantages*. Ask for volunteers to complete the table. Then ask students to discuss which of the three polling methods they think is the best.

GLENCOE TECHNOLOGY

Focus on Government
Video 18
Lecture Launcher:
Public Opinion
Running Time: 3:03
Videodisc 1, Chap. 18
VHS Tape 1, Begins 51:41

Video 54
Speaking Out:
Governing the Schools
Running Time: 1:43
Videodisc 3, Chap. 54
VHS Tape 3, Begins 40:30

PARTICIPATING IN GOVERNMENT

Public Opinion Polls

Public opinion polls provide government leaders with valuable information about people's attitudes on key issues. Politicians pay special attention to the results of these polls because they want to be responsive to the needs of their constituents. How do citizens participate in these polls? How should they answer the questions the pollsters ask?

Most polls today are telephone polls, in part because of the costs and time involved in conducting interviews. If a pollster calls you to participate in one of these polls and you wish to participate, you can do several things to ensure that your answers will be clear and concise. First, answer all questions accurately. For example, if you are asked whether or not you favor a specific piece of legislation that you have not heard of, tell the pollster. If you pretend to have an opinion, the poll results will be inaccurate. Similarly, do not try to give what you think is the "correct" answer. If the pollster asks whether or not you are a registered voter and you are not, answer truthfully.

Sometimes the wording the pollster uses may be confusing. If you do not understand the question, ask the pollster for clarification, or restate the question and ask if that is the intent of the question.

Investigating Further

Design some sample questions to be used in a public opinion poll about a current issue at your school.

The President may even request letters from the public to indicate support for a new policy or to give the White House ammunition for some battle with Congress. Lawmakers, in turn, may urge their constituents to write letters to the President on some key issue. In congressional offices and the White House, full-time staffers read and keep track of the mail to assess the general direction of public opinion.

Today interest groups often stage massive letter and postcard campaigns using computerized mailings to generate thousands of letters on an issue. They may also advertise in newspapers to urge people to write the President or Congress on some issue. Officials often give such letters much less attention than they do more personal letters. Still, letters do remind politicians that the voters care about some issue.

Telephone Calls and Telegrams People register their immediate reactions to speeches, press conferences, and other headline events with telegrams and telephone calls. White House officials often refer to the number of positive telegrams and calls to claim the public supports the President during a crisis.

In 1987, for example, President Reagan was under heavy criticism for allegedly selling arms to Iran to se-

cretly raise money to support guerrilla warfare in Central America. During the Iran-contra affair, as it was called, Reagan talked about the telephone calls he received. "After my speech," Reagan said, "some 84 percent of those people who called in supported me." Telephone calls too can be distorted measurements. The majority who make such calls already are supporters and may not represent general public opinion.

Elections Elections give citizens in a democracy the opportunity to influence government. Voters can "throw the rascals out" and bring in new people with new policies. Election results, however, are an imperfect measure of public opinion on specific issues because people vote for a candidate for many reasons. Some voters may like the candidate's physical appearance or past record in government. Others may support the candidate's position on some issues but not on other issues.

Candidates may take a mix of positions on different issues. In the 1988 presidential election, for example, George Bush took liberal positions on protecting the environment and conservative positions on defense policy. Analysts could not tell which policies voters supported.

Background

Opinion polls have been remarkably successful in predicting the outcome of presidential elections. However, one of the best-known opinion poll blunders came in the 1948 presidential election, which pitted Republican Thomas E. Dewey against the incumbent, Democrat Harry S Truman. Three national polling organizations—Gallup, Roper, and Crossley—all wrongly predicted Dewey as the winner. Their major error was that they had stopped polling several weeks before the election. Truman's last-gasp effort to gain votes, therefore, caught the pollsters by surprise.

Straw Polls Straw polls are unscientific attempts to measure public opinion. Some newspapers, as well as radio and television stations, still use straw polls. Newspapers may print "ballots" in the paper and ask people to "vote" and mail their "ballots" to the editor. Television and radio stations ask questions—"Should the mayor run for reelection?"—and give the audience telephone numbers to call for *yes* or *no*. Members of Congress often send their constituents questionnaires.

Straw polls are not reliable indicators of public opinion because they do not ensure that the group, or sample, of people giving opinions accurately represents the larger population. Straw polls always have a **biased sample**—the people who respond to them are self-selected. They choose to respond.

Scientific Polling

Almost everyone involved in politics today uses scientific polls to measure public opinion. Scientific polling involves three basic steps: (1) selecting a sample of the group to be questioned; (2) presenting carefully worded questions to the individuals in the sample; and (3) interpreting the results.

Sample Populations In polling jargon, the group of people to be studied is called the **universe.** A universe might be all the seniors in a high school, all the people in the state of Texas, or all women in the United States. Since it is not possible to actually interview every person in Texas or every woman in the United States, pollsters question a **representative sample,** a small group of people typical of the universe.

Most pollsters are able to use samples of only 1,200 to 1,500 adults to accurately measure the opinions of all adults in the United States—about 183 million people. Such a small group is a representative sample because pollsters use **random sampling,** a technique in which everyone in the universe has an equal chance of being selected.

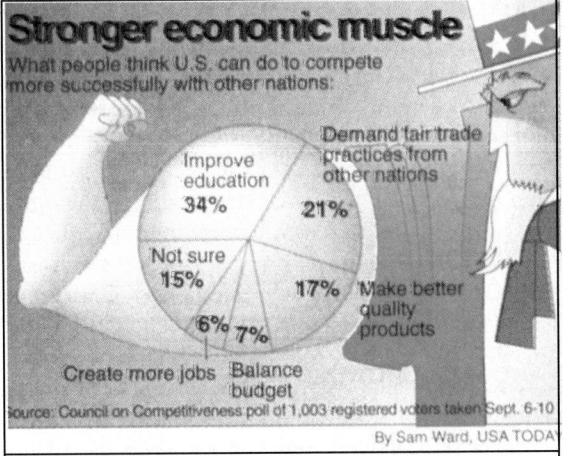

Stronger economic muscle
What people think U.S. can do to compete more successfully with other nations:

Improve education 34%
Demand fair trade practices from other nations 21%
Not sure 15%
Make better quality products 17%
Create more jobs 6%
Balance budget 7%

Source: Council on Competitiveness poll of 1,003 registered voters taken Sept. 6-10
By Sam Ward, USA TODAY

What Does the Average Person Think?
The media frequently use straw polls to gauge opinion. **Politics** Why are straw polls unreliable?

Sampling Error A **sampling error** is a measurement of how much the sample results may differ from the sample universe. Sampling error decreases as the sample size becomes larger. Most national polls use 1,200 to 1,500 people; this number represents the characteristics of any size population, with an error of only plus or minus 3 percent. If a poll says that 65 percent of Americans favor tougher pollution laws, with a 3 percent sampling error, between 62 and 68 percent of the entire population favor such laws.

Sampling error is important when poll data is presented. During the 1976 presidential race, for example, one poll said Jimmy Carter was behind Gerald Ford 48 percent to 49 percent. With a sampling error of 3 percent, Carter could have been ahead. As it turned out, Carter was ahead and won the election.

Sampling Procedures How do pollsters draw random samples of the whole nation? One method, a **cluster sample,** groups, or clusters, people by geographical divisions. The clusters may be counties, congressional districts, or census tracts (regions established by the Census Bureau).

STUDY GUIDE

Themes in Government
Cultural Pluralism What groups should constitute the universe for a scientific poll regarding a new baseball franchise in your city?
Public Policy How reliable are political party organizations in expressing voters' attitudes toward national issues?

Critical Thinking Skills
Evaluating Information Why can a letter-writing campaign to legislators be an effective means to bring about change?

Demonstrating Reasoned Judgment Why do presidential candidates claim that they are not influenced by polls that indicate how people will vote?

CHAPTER 11: PUBLIC OPINION 311

Critical Thinking Activity

Evaluating Information Provide students with the following information about a hypothetical country:
1. about the size of the United States
2. most people live in rural areas
3. transportation systems not well developed
4. illiteracy rates are high

Then ask students to suggest why it might be difficult for the government of this country to learn the opinions of its citizens. *(size of country and poor transportation systems would make administration of public opinion poll difficult; difficulties would be compounded by illiteracy—polls would have to be done face-to-face)*

L3 Analyzing Information
Display the front pages of a number of newspapers on the bulletin board. Have students list the issues covered in the newspaper headlines. Then ask them to speculate—based on information in the newspapers—what public opinion is on these issues.

Independent Practice

L2 Analyzing Opinion Polls
Have students locate a recent opinion poll in a newspaper or magazine and write a brief analysis of it. Their analysis should identify the poll's sponsor and determine why it was taken. Students also should evaluate the polling method, sampling technique, question structure, and accuracy of results.

Caption Answer
The sample of people who volunteer their opinions may not be an accurate representation of the larger population.

STUDY GUIDE

Theme Answers
as ticket buyers: various age, racial, and ethnic groups; also, potential advertisers and vendors

not as reliable as scientific polling because political parties have their own agendas which may be at odds with voters' preferences

Critical Thinking Answers
Elected officials, if they want to be reelected, know that they must be responsive to the concerns of their constituents.

They do not want the polls to predetermine the outcome of the race.

Assess

Check for Understanding

Have students complete Section 2 Review on page 312.

Meeting Objectives

Each section objective is tested by the Section Review questions that follow it in parentheses.
- Note the ways by which public opinion is measured. (2, 3, 4, 6, 8)
- Explain the value of scientific polling. (5, 6, 7, 8)

Evaluate

📁 Section 2 Quiz

💠 Testmaker

Reteach

Ask students to explain how each of this section's key terms is related to public opinion polls.

Enrich

📁 Have students complete activity 11 in *Enrichment Activities* in the Teacher's Classroom Resources.

Close

Have students discuss the following: Should polling organizations question people on the way they intend to vote in elections? Why or why not?

At times pollsters adjust or weight the results of a poll. They do this to overcome defects in sampling and improve accuracy. Pollsters may adjust a poll to take into account variations in such factors as race, sex, age, or education. If pollsters were to find that not enough Americans over the age of 65 had been interviewed, they may give extra weight to the opinions of the senior citizens who were interviewed.

Poll Questions The way a question is phrased can greatly influence people's responses—and poll results. In 1971 the Gallup Poll asked whether people favored a proposal "to bring home all American troops from Vietnam before the end of the year." Two-thirds of those polled answered *yes.* Then the Gallup Poll asked the question differently: "Do you agree or disagree with a proposal to withdraw all U.S. troops by the end of the year regardless of what happens there [in Vietnam] after U.S. troops leave?" When the question was worded this way, less than half agreed to withdrawal. Depending on which of the two poll questions was used, a government official could have argued that public opinion supported or opposed keeping American troops in Vietnam.

Mail and Phone Polls In recent years many public opinion polls have been conducted by mail or by telephone, largely because interviewing people in their homes is expensive. Although the mail questionnaire method is cheaper and more convenient than personal interviews, it has two disadvantages. One is that relatively few questionnaires are returned—usually only

about 10 to 15 percent. Second, pollsters cannot control respondent's careless or confusing replies.

Telephone interviews are now used in many national polls. A telephone poll, like other polls, is based on random sampling. A computer selects numbers from the complete list of telephone numbers in the country. The numbers are chosen so that each region of the nation is represented in proportion to its population. Although telephone polls are more reliable than mail questionnaires, problems do exist. Pollsters may fail to reach the person being called. In addition, some people refuse to answer the questions or are confused by or are inattentive to the interviewer.

Interpreting Results The methods pollsters use have improved markedly since the beginnings of scientific polling in the 1930s. Nevertheless, a number of problems still exist. First, the interviewer's appearance or even the tone of his or her voice can influence answers. Second, individuals sometimes give what they believe is the correct or socially acceptable answer. For example, many people will say they voted in an election when they did not. Third, there is no guarantee that the respondent knows anything about the subject; the person being interviewed may only pretend to have an informed opinion. One poll found that about one-third of its respondents had an opinion about a law that did not exist.

At best, polls only provide a snapshot of public opinion at one point in time, and only on the questions asked. Polling experts themselves urge people to be very careful in interpreting poll results.

---

2 SECTION REVIEW

Section Summary

Although a number of methods are used to determine public opinion, scientific polls are the best way to measure it, but even polls may not always be accurate.

Checking for Understanding
Recalling Facts
1. Define biased sample, universe, representative sample, random sampling, sampling error, cluster sample.
2. Name eight sources that public officials use to determine public opinion.
3. Explain why self-selecting polls may not represent public opinion.
4. List reasons that poll results may not accurately reflect public opinion.

Exploring Themes
5. Cultural Pluralism In conducting a national poll, why is it important to have a variety of racial, ethnic, and religious groups in the sample?
6. Public Policy Why might scientific polls influence the actions of government more than other expressions of public opinion?

Critical Thinking Skills
7. Evaluating Information Why is the phrasing of the questions in an opinion poll so important?
8. Demonstrating Reasoned Judgment Why do politicians pay closer attention to the results of polls conducted through personal interviews rather than through the mail?

Section 2 Review Answers

1. Definitions of terms appear on pages indicated: **biased sample,** 311; **universe,** 311; **representative sample,** 311; **random sampling,** 311; **sampling error,** 311; **cluster sample,** 311
2. state and local party organizations and leaders, contacts with interest groups, media reports, letters received, telephone calls and telegrams received, election results, straw polls, scientific polls

3. because respondents do not represent the population as a whole
4. sample biased or otherwise not representative, wording of questions, method of conducting poll
5. Such groups contain a significant number of people and a national poll that did not adequately represent them could not accurately measure public opinion.

6. Answers should indicate that such polls are usually more accurate than other measures of public opinion.
7. Answers should indicate that the wording of a question may influence a respondent's answer.
8. Very few mail questionnaires are returned so their results are unreliable.

SECTION 3

Public Opinion and Public Policy

Today, public opinion as measured by scientific polls represents one expression of the wishes of the American people. How do these wishes impact public policy—what government chooses to do or not do about some problem in society?

Key Qualities of Public Opinion

Public opinion that displays the qualities of direction, intensity, and stability is much more likely to influence government and public policy than opinion that does not.

Direction Opinions on any issue are likely to vary widely. For example, Americans usually have mixed opinions about the size and role of government. In a recent poll, 62 percent of Americans agreed with the statement, "Government creates more problems than it solves." Only one-third of the public, however, wants to reduce or end government regulations. In effect, **direction** shows whether public opinion is generally positive or negative on a specific issue.

Elected officials tend to pay more attention to issues on which public opinion runs strongly in one direction. They probably will take a strong stand on an issue that 98 percent of Americans favor or oppose. If public opinion is mixed, however, politicians often find it safer to avoid taking clear positions.

Intensity Every person cares more about some issues than others. Certain issues, such as abortion and gun control, provoke powerful feelings. **Intensity**

refers to the strength of people's opinions about a particular issue or topic. Those who feel strongly about an issue are likely to express their opinions in letters to officials or in demonstrations. They are also more likely to vote against officials who do not share their views.

Stability **Stability** refers to the likelihood that public opinion will change in direction or intensity. Research shows that opinions are more likely to change when people lack intensity or information about a subject.

Ideology and Public Policy

An ideology is a set of basic beliefs about life, culture, government, and society. One's political ideology provides the framework for looking at government and public policy. However, Americans tend to determine their positions issue by issue rather than follow a strict ideology. Polls show that many people express inconsistent opinions on issues. For example, most people favor lower taxes, but they also want better schools and increased government services. American political values tend to fall into two broad but distinct patterns of opinions toward government and public policies—liberal and conservative.

Liberal Ideology A **liberal** believes the national government should be very active in helping individuals and communities promote health, education, justice, and equal opportunity. The label *left* often

---

SECTION PREVIEW

Objectives
After studying this section, you should be able to:
- Examine the influence that public opinion has on the making of government policies.
- Describe the role that public opinion plays in court decisions

that set public policy.
- Discuss how personal ideologies affect opinions.

Key Terms and Concepts
direction, intensity, stability, liberal, conservative, moderate

Themes in Government
- Public Policy
- Political Processes

Critical Thinking Skills
- Synthesizing Information
- Demonstrating Reasoned Judgment

CHAPTER 11: PUBLIC OPINION 313

Classroom Resources for Section 3

- Guided Reading Activities
- Reproducible Lesson Plans
- Reteaching Activities 11
- Section 3 Quiz
- Testmaker

- Chapter 11 Tests
- Audio Cassettes (English and Spanish)
- Limited English Proficiency Activities 11
  SAT Practice Tests
  Writer's Guidebook

Focus

Bell Ringer

While attendance is being taken, ask students to consider this question:

How should government respond to public opinion?

Motivating Activity

Select students to give their Bell Ringer responses. *(Typical response: If opinion is shared by large number of people, government should make effort to accommodate it in its policies.)* Then ask for examples of how government has adjusted its policies to reflect public opinion. Next, ask whether government should always be responsive to public opinion. To encourage discussion, present an extreme opinion on some issue, stating that it is held by a large number of people.

Vocabulary Precheck

List this section's key terms on the chalkboard. Have students develop questions for which each term is an answer. **LEP**

Teach

Guided Practice

L1 Recognizing Trends Write the following poll question and results on the chalkboard:

How much of the time can you trust the government to do what's right?

1964: Always or most of the time–76%, Only sometimes– 22%, Never–0

1994: Always or most of the time–19%, Only sometimes–72%, Never–9%

Tell students that more challengers won elections to House and Senate seats in 1992 than in any election since 1942.

Ask students to discuss what trends in political opinion these statistics show. (1964 Poll results from a University of Michigan study. 1994 results from TIME/ CNN telephone poll.) **LEP**

L2 Making Generalizations
Briefly discuss the three key qualities of public opinion—direction, intensity, and stability. Then ask for volunteers to provide generalizations concerning each of the three qualities.

L3 Interpreting Primary Sources Write the following quotation by George Gallup on the chalkboard:

"The people are better fitted to determine ends than to select means. The task of the leader is to decide how best to achieve the goals set by the people."

Begin a discussion of the relationship between public opinion and public policy by asking if Gallup's characterization is appropriate for a democratic system of government. Then ask if it is an accurate description of how government works.

Chart Study Answer
liberal

Theme Answer
If, for example, a person's beliefs include desire for equal opportunities in education and employment, he or she can affiliate with a group that shares such beliefs. There is greater potential to influence public policy by acting as a group.

Critical Thinking Answer
Because liberals want active government involvement and conservatives want very limited government intervention, moderates would want only some government health care programs.

---

identifies liberals. President Harry S Truman, a Democrat, summarized liberal ideology when he said:

We have rejected the discredited theory that the fortunes of the nation should be in the hands of a privileged few. Instead, we believe that our economic system should rest on a democratic foundation and that wealth should be created for the benefit of all.... Every segment of our population and every individual has a right to expect from his government a fair deal.

—PRESIDENT HARRY S TRUMAN

Conservative Ideology A **conservative** believes the role of government in society should be very limited and that individuals should be responsible for their own well-being. Conservatives do not look to the national government to solve social problems. Rather,

they believe that private organizations, local governments, and individuals themselves should promote the common good. The label *right* often identifies conservatives. Former Arizona senator and presidential candidate Barry Goldwater, a Republican, outlined conservative ideology:

Let welfare be a private concern. Let it be promoted by individuals and families, by churches, private hospitals, religious service organizations, community charities and other institutions.... If the objection is raised that private institutions lack sufficient funds, let us remember that every penny the federal government does not appropriate for welfare is potentially available for private use—and without the overhead charge for processing the money through the federal bureaucracy.

—SENATOR BARRY GOLDWATER

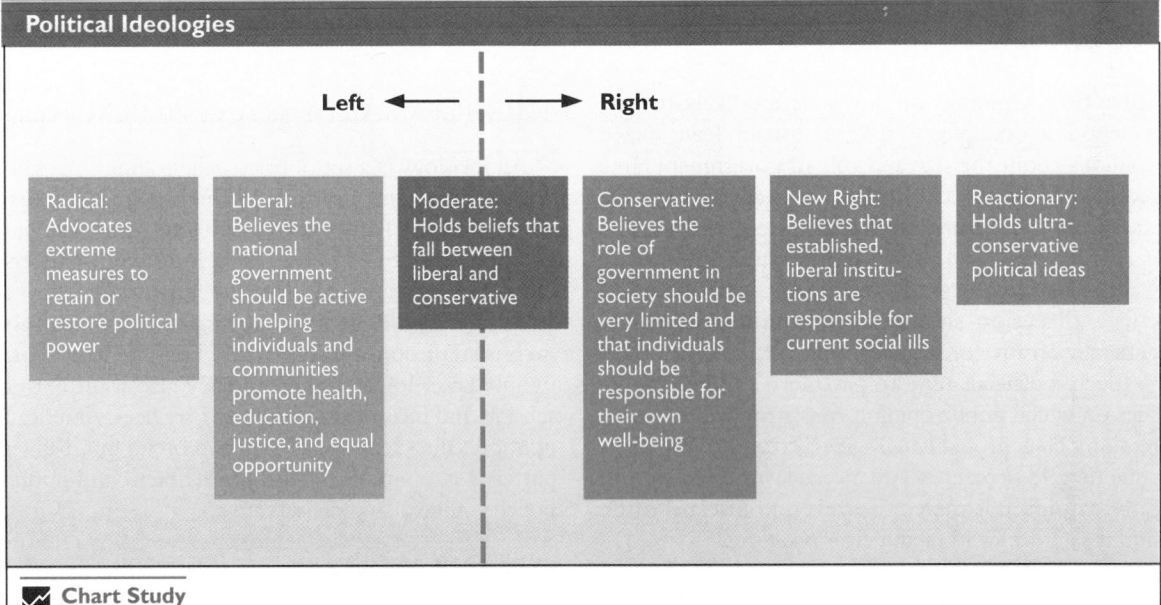

Political Ideologies

Left ← → Right

Radical: Advocates extreme measures to retain or restore political power

Liberal: Believes the national government should be active in helping individuals and communities promote health, education, justice, and equal opportunity

Moderate: Holds beliefs that fall between liberal and conservative

Conservative: Believes the role of government in society should be very limited and that individuals should be responsible for their own well-being

New Right: Believes that established, liberal institutions are responsible for current social ills

Reactionary: Holds ultra-conservative political ideas

Chart Study
People often identify with a different ideological view, depending on the issue at hand. For example, although most conservatives believe government should be very limited and that individuals should be responsible for their own well-being, many conservatives also support social security. **What type of ideological view does someone who believes that the government should take an active role in helping individuals hold?**

Themes in Government
Public Policy How can one's ideology translate to public policy?

Critical Thinking Skills
Synthesizing information From what you know about liberal and conservative ideologies, what is

likely to be the moderate position on government-sponsored health-care programs?

Background

Presidents have adjusted their programs and governing styles according to public opinion poll results since the 1930s. However, Jimmy Carter was the first President to employ a full-time pollster. Under Ronald Reagan, "poll-watching" became an almost daily activity in the White House. In the weeks before the introduction of a new policy or program, Reagan and his aides consulted the polls constantly, adjusting their statements on the issues according to the results.

Moderates Since the 1970s public opinion polls have shown that more Americans identify themselves as moderates than as liberals or conservatives. **Moderates'** opinions and beliefs fall somewhere between liberal and conservative and usually include some of both. Over the last two decades, polls show that about 40 percent of Americans said they were moderates. About 26 percent claimed to be liberal, and 30 percent said they were conservative. Since the 1980s the number of conservatives has grown slightly, and the number of liberals has remained about the same or declined slightly.

The New Right Not all political beliefs fit neatly under the labels *liberal, conservative,* and *moderate.* Throughout American history new ideologies have developed in response to events or new conditions facing society. Sometimes new ideas have become part of everyday political life. One example is the New Right, a political movement that developed in the late 1970s and 1980s.

Generally, the New Right view is that permissive liberal values are responsible for many current social ills. Yet, unlike other conservative ideologies, the New Right does not defend established institutions. Instead, the New Right argues that federal government, big banks, the mass media, large unions, and big corporations have come under the control of liberals, who have made bad decisions and pursued ill-advised policies.

Public Opinion and Policy

Public opinions relate to policy development in a number of ways.

A Source of Public Policy Public opinions can be the direct source of new public policy. Public opinion must have high intensity and stability, and a clear direction. Put another way, people must know what they want and feel strongly about it. Opinions usually deal with issues that directly touch people's daily

lives, such as inflation, unemployment, or the cost of medical care. In addition, people must communicate their opinions, so that policymakers will address the issues.

Government benefits for senior citizens provide a good example of how public opinion helps shape public policy. Pension payments affect senior citizens directly and personally. These citizens are consistent in their attitude that government must provide such support. They are well-informed about policies affecting retirement benefits and are well organized to communicate their opinions directly to policymakers. They vote regularly and feel strongly about such issues. As a result, both liberal and conservative politicians consistently support the social security system.

A Reflection of Public Policy Sometimes policymakers will develop a new policy or pass a law even when the public has not demanded it. The policymakers may do this in response to intense pressure from a small number of activists. When people learn about the policy, they might like it and give it strong support. In such cases, public opinion is reflecting and supporting public policy rather than creating it.

Activists who work for new policies may work inside or outside the government. For example, Ralph Nader, a private attorney, campaigned in the mid-1960s for auto safety laws with his book *Unsafe at Any Speed.* Congress soon established auto safety standards, passed consumer protection laws, and in 1972 created the Consumer Product Safety Commission. Americans now expect the cars they drive and the products they use to be safe and free of defects.

Environmental policy also fits this pattern. *Silent Spring* by scientist Rachel Carson, a 1962 book about the use of pesticides, and efforts of activist groups such as the Sierra Club, helped obtain early environmental protection laws and helped foster the strong public concern for the environment that exists today.

A Limit on Public Policy Public opinion can limit what is politically possible. Foreign aid is a good example of a policy that public opinion may constrain.

Chapter 11, Section 3
Lesson Plan, pages 313–317

Independent Practice

L1 Interpreting Ideas Ask students to write two sentences for each of these issues: unemployment benefits, taxes, defense spending. One of the sentences should represent a typical liberal attitude to the issue, the other should represent a typical conservative attitude.

L2 Research Have students contact an elected official—at the local, state, or national level—to find out how public opinion caused the official to change his or her mind on an issue. Ask students to present their findings to the class.

STUDY GUIDE

Theme Answer
letter writing and telephone calls to legislators; inviting legislators to speak to their groups; joining organizations that lobby government

Critical Thinking Answer
possibly by offering tax incentives to businesses to provide expertise or funds to schools; yes

Assess

Check for Understanding

Have students complete Section 3 Review on page 316.

STUDY GUIDE

Themes in Government
Political Processes How could senior citizens influence government for better health-care benefits?

Critical Thinking Skills
Demonstrating Reasoned Judgment How could government lower tax rates and, at the same time, promote expanded educa-tional opportunities? Is it possible to be in favor of both issues at the same time?

Special Needs Strategy

Learning Strategy Students with learning disabilities often have difficulty remembering main topics. To help students remember how public opinion affects policy development, have them skim the text to locate these headings: "A Source of Public Policy," "A Reflection of Public Policy," "A Limit on Public Policy," "Irrelevant to Public Policy." Then ask students to skim the text for an example that illustrates each of the headings. Have students compare their examples.

Meeting Objectives

Each section objective is tested by the Section Review questions that follow it in parentheses.

- Examine the influence that public opinion has on the making of government policies. (5, 6, 7, 8)
- Describe the role that public opinion plays in court decisions that set public policy. (5)
- Discuss how personal ideologies affect opinions. (2, 3)

Evaluate

📁 Section 3 Quiz

💻 Testmaker

Reteach

Have students write a sentence summarizing the content of each of this section's headings.

📁 Have students complete activity 11 in *Reteaching Activities* in the Teacher's Classroom Resources.

Enrich

Ask students to research the impact of public opinion on candidates' stands on health care.

Close

Have students compare the role of public opinion in a democratic system to its role in an autocratic system.

Presidents often want to provide generous foreign aid because they believe it promotes American foreign policy goals. Polls show lukewarm public opinion on the subject of foreign aid, however. Thus, public opinion limits the amount of foreign aid, but it does not stop such aid altogether.

Irrelevant to Public Policy Sometimes public opinion is simply irrelevant to public policy. Some federal court decisions, in effect, set public policy by doing such things as opening and closing schools, setting routes for highways, or establishing visiting privileges for patients in state mental hospitals. Because federal judges are not elected, however, they do not feel pressured to respond to public opinion. Court decisions on issues such as busing students to integrate schools or protecting the rights of criminals may be controversial or unpopular.

Congress, which is more receptive to public opinion, can try to reverse court actions either by proposing a constitutional amendment or by passing new laws. Of the 26 amendments to the Constitution, 6 were added specifically to negate Supreme Court decisions.

Public Opinion and Democracy

The Framers of the Constitution sought to create a representative democracy that would meet two goals.

The first was to provide for popular rule—to give the people an active voice in government. They did this by allowing voters to elect members of the House of Representatives, a power later expanded to include senators. As such, the people were to have control over the lawmakers who represented them.

The Framers' other goal was to insulate government from the shifting whims of ill-informed public opinion. They recognized that there is nothing sacred about public opinion and that the public can be wrong. Further, they knew large numbers of people could not run the government on a day-to-day basis. They would have understood modern journalist Walter Lippmann who said the people

. . . can elect the government. They can remove it. They can approve or disapprove its performance. But they cannot administer the government. They cannot themselves perform. . . . A mass cannot govern.

—Walter Lippmann

The system the Framers created has worked well. Research shows that the government is responsive to public opinion—to the wishes of the people. At the same time, public opinion is not the only influence on public policy. Interest groups, political parties, the mass media, other institutions of government, and the ideas of activists and public officials themselves also help shape public policy.

---

3 SECTION REVIEW

Section Summary

Depending on its strength, direction, intensity, and stability, public opinion may help shape public policy, limit it, or only reflect it. If policymakers are not elected officials, public opinion may have little influence at all.

Checking for Understanding

Recalling Facts

1. Define direction, intensity, stability, liberal, conservative, moderate.
2. Explain why a person's ideology influences his or her opinions.
3. Distinguish the New Right from other conservative groups.
4. Describe how public opinion can sometimes reflect public policy.

Exploring Themes

5. Public Policy Why is public policy set by federal courts less a product of public opinion than are acts of Congress?
6. Political Processes Describe the characteristics of a group that would be successful in getting government to respond to its interests.

Critical Thinking Skills

7. Synthesizing Information Describe the direction, intensity, and stability of public opinion about an issue on which an elected official would be least willing to act.
8. Demonstrating Reasoned Judgment Voters between the ages of 18 and 21 have the lowest turnout rate at elections. How does this turnout rate affect how much impact this group has on formulating public policy?

Section 3 Review Answers

1. Definitions of terms appear on pages indicated: **direction,** 313; **intensity,** 313; **stability,** 313; **liberal,** 313; **conservative,** 314; **moderate,** 315

2. It is a basic set of beliefs that provides the framework through which a person views politics.

3. Unlike other conservatives, members of the New Right do not defend established institutions, but argue that these institutions have come under liberal control.

4. Sometimes a small group can bring about a change that the general public decides it likes and supports it.

5. It is made by judges who are appointed rather than elected. Thus courts are not as concerned with public opinion as Congress—an elected body.

6. well-informed and organized to communicate its opinion to policymakers, members must feel strongly about the issue and vote regularly

7. direction—opinion divided, no clear majority opinion; intensity—people on each side of the issue are intense about their opinions; stability—unstable, positions on the issue may change

8. Answers should indicate that government is less likely to act in the interests of those who demonstrate little political power.

PERSONAL PERSPECTIVES

Harry P. Pachon on Sampling the Hispanic Universe

Harry P. Pachon is Kenan Professor of Political Studies at Pitzer College in Claremont, California. He also serves as director of the National Association of Latino Elected and Appointed Officials. Pachon addressed the Black and Puerto Rican Legislative Caucus in 1988 on scientific polls and statistics.

All too often we hear populations in need being described in terms of "White" and "nonwhite" categories. In cases like this we assume that White means Anglo and that nonwhite means Black, Hispanics and Asian. It's a wrong assumption since the . . . White . . . category includes Hispanics. Even more frequently, we hear social issues in terms of "White" and "Black" populations. This continuing practice hurts both the Black and Hispanic populations. It obviously affects Hispanics by making them invisible to government policymakers. "If you can't see them, you can't serve them.". . .

The more prevalent area where we do not keep adequate information on Hispanics is in government benefit programs. We still don't fully know how Hispanics underutilize Social Security, Medicare, or participate in other programs. This continuing practice of excluding Hispanics as a separate category when describing social problems in the country also directly affects Black Americans. It hurts the Black community by reducing the difference in the conditions between White and Black America. Thus when we describe the income gap between Blacks and Whites, and we include all the low-income Hispanics among the White population, it obviously makes the differences more narrow. Imagine that the same reporting goes on for describing Black and White children in poverty, for describing health care access, educational achievement and the list goes on. We, as minority communities, need to realize the continuing nature of this problem and attack it head on when anyone, whether from the executive branch, private sector or from a university, adopts it as a means of telling us about our communities.

—HARRY P. PACHON, 1988

The Hispanic community has done much in the political arena. Much more remains to be done. . . . Perhaps it is appropriate to reflect on those issues that will continue to affect the Hispanic community. . . . Rather than reciting the familiar litany of poverty, education, housing, drug abuse, employment and other issues that you know so well, let me address . . . other—and not so frequently discussed—issues where the Hispanic and Black communities face common interests.

The first of these issues is . . . the current practices that government agencies engage in when collecting statistics on minority populations. . . . Let me offer a few examples.

This continuing practice of excluding Hispanics as a separate category when describing social problems in the country also directly affects Black Americans.

Examining the Reading

Reviewing Facts
1. Specify the speaker's complaint about government studies that include Hispanics.
2. Explain how, according to Pachon, the government's treatment of statistics on Hispanics affects African Americans.

Critical Thinking Skills
3. Making Inferences What can you infer from Pachon's statement, "If you can't see them, you can't serve them," about how public policy is made?

CHAPTER 11: PUBLIC OPINION **317**

More About Personal Perspectives

The Hispanic population of the United States has grown considerably over the years and now makes up a significant portion of the population of states such as California, New York, Arizona, Texas, New Mexico, Colorado, and Florida. In 1990 a federal judge ordered the Los Angeles County Board of Supervisors to redraw its districts to allow for more political representation for the county's Hispanic population, then at 35 percent. This is one example of the growing demand by Hispanic people for government recognition of their numbers.

PERSONAL PERSPECTIVES

Focus

Tell students that a vet wants to know how much of her practice is devoted to treating pets vs. wild animals. Her assistant reports back: 70 percent—domestic, 30 percent—wild. The vet asks about animals such as monkeys, rabbits, and snakes that live in the wild but also are kept in homes. "I put them in the wild category," says the assistant. What effect would this have on the way this vet would describe her practice? Ask students to consider the consequences of misleading statistics.

Teach

Ask: How are Hispanics classified in government polls? What is the effect of analyzing social issues in terms of "White" and "Black"? How does this statistical method affect public policy for Hispanics?

Assess

Have students complete **Examining the Reading.**

Answers

1. Hispanics are included with the larger white population.
2. It reduces the difference in conditions between the black and white populations.
3. Government policies address specific problems that are perceived among specific groups.

Close

Ask students what other groups could be hurt by the way statistics are collected.

Identifying Terms and Concepts

1. political culture, 2. political socialization, 3. political culture, 4. political socialization, 5. public opinion, 6. political socialization

Reviewing Facts and Ideas

1. public opinion diverse, communicated to government, held by significant numbers

2. family and home, school, peer groups, social characteristics, mass media, political leaders, interest groups

3. Political culture sets limits on what is acceptable public opinion and influences how individuals interpret the events about which they develop opinions.

4. any four of the following: writing letters to newspapers, writing to elected officials, calling radio talk shows, telephoning offices of elected officials, voting, participating in straw polls

5. Participants are self-selected rather than randomly selected. They do not represent the general public.

6. small number of people selected to represent a larger population; selected in such a way that every member of the population has the same chance of being selected for the sample

7. The sample may not be representative or the questions may be worded in a way that influences responses.

8. a clear direction, high intensity, stability

9. liberal—government should take an active role in solving social problems; conservative—government role in society should be limited, private initiative should solve social problems

10. Public opinion may help shape public policy, it may reflect public policy, it may limit public policy, or it may be irrelevant to public policy.

Summary and Significance

Public opinion is an attitude about a political issue that a significant number of citizens hold. Many factors shape these attitudes. Most important is the political socialization process that results from the influences of family, school, church, friends, co-workers, and the mass media. Public opinion on any issue can be determined in several ways. The most accurate method is the scientific opinion poll. Even polls should be considered carefully, however, because of sampling errors, polling procedures, wording of questions, and misuse of results. Despite the difficulty of accurately measuring public opinion, public officials pay close attention to it, and a close relationship exists between public opinion and the making of public policy.

Identifying Terms and Concepts

Each of the items below is an example of one of the following terms. Label each item with the term that identifies it.
political culture, public opinion, political socialization
1. Personal freedom
2. High school government courses
3. Private property
4. Television programs
5. The right to life movement
6. The Pledge of Allegiance

Reviewing Facts and Ideas

1. **Describe** the three characteristics that distinguish private opinion from public opinion.
2. **Cite** seven forces that influence a person's political socialization.
3. **Explain** the relationship between political culture and public opinion.
4. **Name** four ways people can express opinions.
5. **Explain** why letters and straw polls are not accurate measurements of public opinion.
6. **Discuss** the technique of random sampling.
7. **Cite** two reasons that the results of scientific polls may not be accurate.
8. **Describe** the three qualities that public opinion should have if it is likely to influence government.
9. **Contrast** liberal and conservative ideologies.
10. **Describe** the four ways that public opinion and public policy can be related.

Applying Themes

1. **Cultural Pluralism** Why would people's ethnic or religious backgrounds affect the opinions they form about public policy issues?
2. **Political Processes** Explain the relationship between voting, public opinion, and public policy.
3. **Public Policy** Explain why self-selecting measures of public opinion are not a good way to evaluate public attitudes about a public policy.

Critical Thinking Skills

1. **Evaluating Information** Why is scientific polling a more accurate gauge of public opinion than are the other types of polling?
2. **Synthesizing Information** What conditions should people's opinions satisfy if they are to persuade elected officials to take some action?
3. **Demonstrating Reasoned Judgment** In a democracy, should the making of public policy be insulated from public opinion? List the criteria or reasons you used to make your judgment. Explain why or why not and how you think it might be accomplished.

Linking Past and Present

Serious efforts to scientifically measure public opinion began in the 1930s. In 1936 in the midst of the Great Depression when almost 25 percent of the people in the United States could barely afford to eat,

Applying Themes

1. Ethnicity and religion influence political socialization, a process that plays a major role in the shaping of a person's opinions.

2. People with intense opinions about certain issues are likely to vote for candidates on the basis of those issues. Elected officials are sensitive to this fact when they make policy.

3. The people who respond to such measures are highly motivated to do so. Often they hold opinions on the topic that are stronger than the average person's opinion. Therefore, their opinions do not necessarily represent the majority opinion.

Critical Thinking Skills

1. The three major features of scientific polling—a representative sample, carefully worded questions, and careful interpretation of results—make it much more reliable than other types of polling.

the *Literary Digest* conducted a poll about the upcoming presidential election. The magazine's staff used telephone books and state automobile registration records to compile the names and addresses of more than 10 million Americans. They mailed cards that asked their sample to choose between Democratic President Franklin D. Roosevelt and Republican challenger Alfred M. Landon. When more than 2 million replies indicated a preference for Landon, the *Literary Digest* predicted Roosevelt would be defeated. On Election Day, however, Roosevelt won in one of the biggest landslides in American history. Within months the *Literary Digest* was out of business, branded as inaccurate and dishonest because its poll was so flawed. Using what you have learned about scientific polling techniques, assess what mistakes the *Literary Digest* made in constructing its poll.

Writing About Government

Narrative Writing The National Opinion Research Center conducted a poll exploring how Americans feel about the government's role in solving the nation's problems. Examine the data and write a paragraph that interprets the results of this poll.

What Should the Government's Role Be in Solving the Nation's Problems?			
Respondent's Income	Should Do More	Doing Too Much	Undecided
Less than $10,000	35%	24%	41%
$10,000–14,999	27	31	43
$15,000–19,999	28	33	40
$20,000–24,999	26	37	37
$25,000 and over	18	46	37

Reinforcing the Skill

Understanding a Public Opinion Poll Use what you have learned about analyzing public opinion polls to examine the following poll data and answer these questions:

1. What is this poll about and when was it taken?
2. What specific questions were asked? Can you think of a way that these questions might be phrased that would be less biased?
3. For which subgroups, if any, is poll data given?

4. State the results of the 1990 poll in sentence form.

What Do You Think Is the Most Important Problem Facing this Country Today?* (Gallup Poll Interviewing Dates: 4/5/90–4/8/90)	
Economic Problems	
Economy	7%
Federal budget deficit, failure to balance budget	6
Unemployment	3
Trade deficit, trade relations, balance of trade	2
High cost of living, inflation	1
High cost of borrowing, interest rates	**
Recession, depression	**
Other specific economic problems	3
Other Problems	
Drugs, drug abuse	30%
Poverty, hunger, homelessness	11
Environment, pollution	8
Crime	2
Quality of education	1
Ethics in society, moral decline	1
Fear of war, nuclear war	1
International problems	1
AIDS	1
Dissatisfaction with government	1
Other noneconomic problems	11
No opinion	9

*Totals do not add to 100% due to rounding
**Less than 1%

Investigating Further

1. **Individual Project** Arrange a telephone interview or an in-person interview with a public official in your local or county government. Ask how that official finds out what issues are important to the public, and how he or she measures public opinion on those issues. Compare the results of your interview with other class members.
2. **Cooperative Learning** Identify an issue that concerns your school and then organize the class into four groups. Have each group formulate questions for an opinion poll on that issue. Have the four groups randomly select respondents from the same universe. Representatives of each group should ask its questions to its sample population and record their answers. Compare the results of each poll as a class.

Support for active government generally decreased as income levels rose; support for limited government increased with income. Also, the percentage of respondents who were undecided about this issue declined as income increased. Students may conclude that people with higher incomes tend to be more conservative on social policy and people with lower incomes more liberal.

Reinforcing the Skill

1. The poll is about important national problems. It was taken in April 1990.
2. Only one question: What do you think is the most important problem facing this country today? In this case, the question was phrased in an unbiased manner.
3. none
4. Americans reported that their greatest concern was the drug problem, which they thought was more than twice as important as any other problem.

Investigating Further

1. Results will vary.
2. Polls and questions will vary.

---

2. Public opinion should show a clear direction, be of high intensity so that officials can count on public support for their action, and be stable so that positions are not likely to change.

3. Answers should question whether policies should be based on opinion that is often divided and changeable. They should note that our system of representative government is one way to insulate policy-making from opinion.

Linking Past and Present

A mail poll made their sample self-selecting since not every member of the sample would return the preference card. Also, selecting only those who owned cars or telephones meant that the poll did not reach a representative sample of voters.

Chapter Organizer

Objectives	Special Feature Pages	Supplemental Materials
Section 1 Structure of the Mass Media *pp. 322–327* 1. Describe the framework of the mass media in the United States. 2. Assess American attitudes toward world news.	Global Connection: Issues: Freedom of Expression in the Mass Media p. 325 Social Studies Skills: Interpreting Political Cartoons p. 327	Guided Reading Activities Reproducible Lesson Plans Section 1 Quiz Testmaker Skill Reinforcement Activities 12 SAT Practice Tests Writer's Guidebook
Section 2 The Media and Government *pp. 328–331* 1. Examine the interdependence between the mass media and government. 2. Describe television coverage of Congress. 3. Identify the media's role in government investigations.		Guided Reading Activities Reproducible Lesson Plans Cooperative Learning Activities 12 Section 2 Quiz Testmaker Chapter Transparencies 12 SAT Practice Tests Writer's Guidebook
Special Report: The Press Gallery *pp. 332–337* 1. Trace the development of political reporting throughout United States history. 2. Examine why government leaders want the press to report the news.		
Section 3 Government Regulation of the Media *pp. 338–342* 1. Explain how and why government regulates the media. 2. Trace the media's attempts to win the right of access. 3. Analyze possible conflicts between national security and First Amendment protections.	Focus on Freedom: *New York Times Co.* v. *United States* p. 339	Guided Reading Activities Reproducible Lesson Plans Supreme Court Case Studies 64 Section 3 Quiz Testmaker SAT Practice Tests Writer's Guidebook
Section 4 The Media's Impact on Politics *pp. 343–349* 1. Identify ways that the media affect politics. 2. Assess citizens' responsibilities to weigh media coverage of political candidates.	Participating in Government: Becoming an Informed Voter p. 346 Personal Perspectives: Corazon Aquino on the Power of the Media p. 349 Case Study pp. 352–354 Unit 3 Digest pp. 355–356	Guided Reading Activities Reproducible Lesson Plans Participating in Government 12 Primary and Secondary Source Readings 12 Reteaching Activities 12 Enrichment Activities 12 Section 4 Quiz Chapter 12 Tests Unit Digest Transparencies, Unit 3 Participating in Government, Unit 3

If time does not permit teaching this chapter, assign the Chapter 12 summary in the Unit 3 Digest on pages 355–356.

Key To Ability Levels

Teaching strategies have been coded for varying learning styles and abilities.

L1   Level 1 activities are **basic** activities and should be within the ability range of all students.

L2   Level 2 activities are **average** activities and should be within the ability range of the average to above-average student.

L3   Level 3 activities are **challenging** activities designed for the ability range of above-average students.

LEP   These activities should be within the ability range of **Limited English Proficiency** students.

Multicultural Activities

In 1989 only 7 major newspapers had African American publishers. One Asian American and 3 Latinos published major daily newspapers. In 1989 newsroom supervisors were 95 percent white, 3 percent black, 1 percent each Hispanic and Asian. Native Americans made up less than half of a percent of all supervisors. In the broadcast news media, minorities comprised 11 percent of the work force. There were 2,720 blacks, 1,050 Hispanics, 360 Asians, and 170 Native Americans, according to a study by journalism professor Vernon Stone of the University of Missouri School of Journalism. Ask students whether they think greater ethnic diversity of media owners and journalists would influence political reporting or campaigning. If so, in what ways?

In the summer of 1990, Mohawks in the Canadian province of Quebec began an 11-week protest against government officials over municipal attempts to develop a plot of land the Mohawks claimed as ancestral territory. Media coverage of this event in the United States raised awareness of the land-claim conflicts. Media reports of the violence that occurred during the protest lessened public support for the Mohawks. Have students explore the ways minorities with limited resources can use the media to influence public opinion. What are some ways to get media attention? What do activists hope to gain from this attention? Can protesters control what the public learns about an issue or cause? What are the responsibilities of the media in covering a staged media event by an ethnic group or a politician?

Chapter Resources

Readings for the Student

Berger, Gilda. *Violence and the Media.* Franklin Watts, 1989.

Dahlstrom, Harry S. *Don't Believe Everything You Read.* Dahlstrom, 1986.

Fanning the Flames: A Look at Propaganda in America. Perfection Form, 1990.

Kronenwetter, Michael. *Journalism Ethics.* Franklin Watts, 1988.

Ritchie, Donald A. *Press Gallery: Congress and the Washington Correspondents.* Harvard University Press, 1991.

Seib, Philip. *Who's in Charge: How the Media Shape News and Politicians Win Votes.* Taylor Publishing Co., 1988.

Readings for the Teacher

Dates, Jannette L. and William Barlow, eds. *Split Image: African Americans in the Mass Media.* Howard University Press, 1991.

Graber, Doris A. *Media Power in Politics.* Congressional Quarterly, 1993.

Lee, Martin and Norman Solomon. *Unreliable Sources: A Guide to Detecting Bias in News Media.* Lyle Stuart, 1990.

Sabato, Larry. *Feeding Frenzy: How Attack Journalism Has Transformed American Politics.* Free Press, 1991.

Waldman, Myron S. *Forgive Us Our Press Passes: The Memoirs of a Veteran Washington Reporter.* St. Martin's Press, 1991.

Multimedia

Videocassettes

Literature with a Message: Protest and Propaganda, Satire and Social Comment. Center for Humanities. (v/c, 35 minutes)

The Master Race: History in Action. Films for the Humanities. (v/c, 20 minutes)

A Walk Through the 20th Century with Bill Moyers. (19-part series; recommended: *The Image Makers, The Real World of News, The 30-Second President, World War II: The Propaganda Battle*). Corporation for Entertainment and Learning. (4 v/cs, 58 minutes each)

Software

Television: A Study of Media Ethics. Social Studies School Service. (Apple disk, backup, guide, or IBM PC/PCjr disk, backup, guide). Students learn about media, responsibility, censorship, and so on.

The Mass Media

CHAPTER

12

Introduce

Chapter Overview

Chapter 12 discusses the vital and ever-growing role the mass media play in the political process in the United States.

Section 1 looks at the structure of the mass media in the United States and reviews Americans' attitudes toward world news.

Section 2 discusses the relationship between the media and government.

Section 3 examines how and why the government regulates the media.

Section 4 identifies the impact of the media on the American political system and discusses how citizens might accurately weigh media coverage of politics.

Chapter 12 Themes

Have students read Themes in Government in the Chapter Preview. Then ask them to skim the chapter to find photographs that illustrate the relationship between the mass media and each theme. Select students to explain their choices to the class. If students can find no photographs that illustrate a particular theme, have them suggest an illustration.

Linking Past and Present

The "sound bite" and the quick visual image of the television age had a colonial equivalent in the broadside ballad. Most of these ballads, which were quickly written and often based only loosely on fact, dealt with political issues of the day. Printed on large sheets of paper called "broadsides," they were sold for a penny by hawkers on street corners.

Government officials and the press often have an adversarial relationship, but each group depends on the other.

About the Chapter Opener

Teaching With Illustrations Indicate to students that this photograph shows President Clinton at a White House news conference. Ask students what this photograph suggests about the role of the media in government. *(Answers will vary. Students might indicate that the President depends on the media to explain his policies to the public. The people depend on the media for information about government.)* Ask students what other roles the media play in politics. *(influences or shapes public images of officials or candidates)* Then ask what they think the relationship between the media and government is today. *(Students should give reasons for their opinions.)*

Chapter Preview

Overview

The mass media play a vital and ever-increasing role in the politics and political processes of the United States.

Objectives

After studying this chapter, you should be able to:

1. **Discuss** the structure of the mass media in the United States.
2. **Describe** the interdependence of the mass media and United States government.
3. **Outline** government regulation of the media.
4. **Examine** the media's impact on politics.

Themes in Government

This chapter emphasizes the following government themes:

- **Free Enterprise** Making a profit is a goal of most of the broadcast and print media in the United States. Section 1.
- **Global Perspectives** Media coverage can influence the way international events are perceived and even influence their outcomes. Section 1.
- **Political Processes** The mass media directly influence the political processes of the United States. Sections 2 and 4.
- **Checks and Balances** Government and the mass media have a mutually beneficial but uneasy relationship in which the courts sometimes mediate. Sections 2 and 3.
- **Civic Responsibility** Citizens must evaluate information provided by the media when making decisions. Sections 3 and 4.

Critical Thinking Skills

This chapter emphasizes the following critical thinking skills:

- Synthesizing Information
- Drawing Conclusions

Introducing the Chapter

Write the following statements on the chalkboard:

1. America Held Hostage: Day 350
2. Mayoral Candidate Linked to Mafia Kingpin
3. Olympic Successes Symbolize America's New Spirit
4. Sense of Foreboding Accompanies Statistics on Economy
5. Over the Top! Dow Breaks 2,000 Barrier
6. You've Never Had It So Good!

Inform students that these statements are actual newspaper headlines or lead-in lines on television newscasts during recent election campaigns. Then lead a discussion of the impact these statements might have in an election. Close the discussion by pointing out that this chapter discusses the media's impact on politics and other aspects of life in the United States.

Chapter Project

Have students read a newspaper or magazine or watch television newscasts for several days. Have them select a headline, a photograph, or a television image that had a major impact on them—perhaps moving them to change their position on an issue or a public figure. At the close of the chapter, ask volunteers to present their selections to the class and to explain what caused them to change their minds. Use these explanations to start a discussion on the following: Why are headlines and visual images so powerful?

Powers of the President
The President and the Media
Running Time 1:15
Side Two, Chapter 13

Setting the Scene Early American newspapers—the first was published in 1690—were single folded sheets, making a total of four pages. The bulk of the news was from Britain, usually reprinted from the most recent letters or papers to arrive by ship. Political content began to appear in the years immediately prior to the Revolution. With the development of political parties, newspapers became little more than the sounding horns of the various factions. The politically independent newspapers that we know today did not begin to appear until the 1830s.

Focus

Bell Ringer

Have students complete the following sentence while attendance is being taken:

The news media are . . .

Motivating Activity

Tell students that their completed sentences might read: The news media are newspapers, magazines, television, and radio. Ask students with other responses to share them with the class. Do not discount any responses, especially those that suggest the news media are too powerful, biased, uninformative, dull, and so on. Discuss why many people have such feelings about the media. Draw this activity to a close by noting that this section deals with the nature of the news media and that concerns such as media bias and power are addressed later in the chapter.

Vocabulary Precheck

Write the key terms and concepts for this section on the chalkboard. Ask students to use those that they know in sentences. **LEP**

Caption Answer
3.5 hours

GLENCOE TECHNOLOGY

Focus on Government
Video 14
Electronic Field Trip:
The Today Show
Running Time: 5:51
Videodisc 1, Chap. 14
VHS Tape 1, Begins 37:21

Structure of the Mass Media

Today more homes in the United States have a television than a toilet. The average adult watches 3 hours each day, and the average child watches 4. By the time most American youths graduate from high school, they will have spent more time in front of the television than in class. In addition, Americans average 18 hours per week listening to radio, 3.5 hours per week reading newspapers, and almost 2 hours each week reading magazines. Truly, Americans live in a media age; but what are they learning about their government and politics?

Unless a citizen is actually in the White House, on the floor of a state legislature, or in a foreign capital, he or she cannot experience directly what is happening. Citizens today know the political world largely through the pictures, words, and expressions the mass media communicate to them. In reality, politics and the mass media have become inseparable. Supreme Court Justice Lewis F. Powell explained the importance of the mass media for citizens in a democracy. He stated:

An informed public depends upon accurate and effective reporting by the news media. No individual can obtain for himself the information needed for the intelligent discharge of his political responsibilities. For most citizens the prospect of personal familiarity with newsworthy events is hopelessly unrealistic. In seeking out the news the press therefore acts as an agent of the public at large. It is the means by which the people receive that free flow of information and ideas essential to intelligent self-government. . . .
—LEWIS F. POWELL, dissenting opinion in
SAXBE V. WASHINGTON POST, 1974

The mass media have come to influence American government and politics in ways that politicians from the last century, let alone the Founders, could never have predicted. A CBS producer once asked President Lyndon B. Johnson what was the biggest change in politics during his career—a period that covered 32 years from 1937 to 1969 and included the offices of United States representative, senator, Vice President, and finally, President. Johnson responded:

All you guys in the media. All of politics has changed because of you. You've broken all the [political] machines and the ties between us in Congress and the city [political] machines. You guys have given us a new kind of people. . . . No [political] machine could ever create a Teddy Kennedy. Only you guys. They're all yours. Your product.
—LYNDON B. JOHNSON, 1968

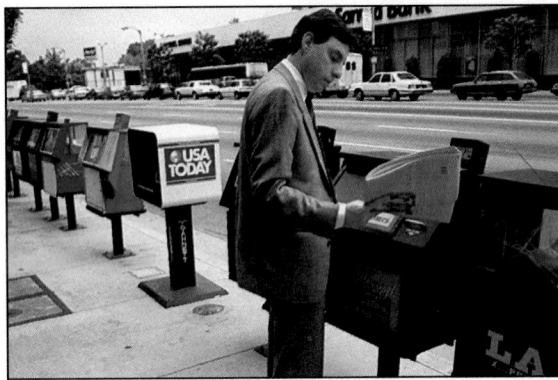

An Information Explosion
News flows to more people more quickly than ever before. **Sociology How many hours per week do people read newpapers?**

SECTION PREVIEW

Objectives
After studying this section, you should be able to:
■ Describe the framework of the mass media in the United States.

■ Assess American attitudes toward world news.

Key Terms and Concepts
wire service, noncommercial

Themes in Government
■ Free Enterprise
■ Global Perspectives

Critical Thinking Skills
■ Synthesizing Information
■ Drawing Conclusions

322 UNIT 3: INFLUENCING GOVERNMENT

Classroom Resources for Section 1

📁 Guided Reading Activities
📁 Reproducible Lesson Plans
📁 Section 1 Quiz

🔲 Testmaker
SAT Practice Tests
Writer's Guidebook

The Media Today

Sometimes called the "fourth branch" of government, the mass media include all the means of communication that bring messages to the public. Equating the mass media with the executive, the legislative, and the judicial branches of the national government indicates the powerful role of mass communications in the United States today.

Broadcast Media Television and radio make up the broadcast media. Today television is the dominant means of mass communication. Ninety-eight percent of American homes have at least one television.

Three national networks—ABC, NBC, and CBS—provide the majority of all commercial programming. Most local commercial stations are tied in with one of these networks. During prime time in the evening about 95 percent of the material on local stations comes from the national networks.

Since a slow start in the 1950s, cable television has become popular. More than one-half of the nation's homes are connected to cable television, and the number is growing. Recently, the Cable News Network (CNN) has come to rival the national networks for news coverage. Many government agencies, foreign embassies, and lobbyists in Washington, D.C., stay tuned to CNN to keep up with the latest news.

Most Americans report that television is their most frequent source of news. In one national survey, 66 percent said they got most of their news from television. Television is also rated by Americans as the most reliable source of news.

Almost all Americans (99.9 percent) have radios in their cars or homes, totaling about 500 million radios. About 5,000 AM radio stations and 4,300 FM stations currently operate. Radio stations specialize in different formats both to compete with other mass media and to attract a specific audience. Radio is widely used to communicate political messages. Political advertisers buy time on certain stations to reach the voting audience they most want to target.

Print Media Newspapers, magazines, and books are included in the category of print media. Almost 11,000 newspapers are printed in the United States. Most of these are published once a week. About

You Are There

Television journalists such as Peter Arnett, reporting from Baghdad during the Gulf War, give viewers a front-row seat on wars and other global crises. **History** How might television news influence government decisions?

1,800 newspapers are published daily, reaching roughly 62.5 million readers a day. These newspapers have the most impact on government and politics.

Newspapers are locally produced and distributed. Thus, most people read their own city-based newspaper such as the *Milwaukee Sentinel*, the *Chicago Tribune*, or the *Miami Herald*. *The New York Times*, the *Washington Post*, and the *Wall Street Journal* also have a national circulation. *USA Today* is the only American newspaper designed specifically for a national mass audience.

More than 10,000 magazines are published every year in the United States. The major weekly national news magazines are *TIME*, *Newsweek*, and *U.S. News & World Report*. Some journals publish essays and stories representing political opinions on current issues. These include the *National Review* that favors conservative points of view and the *New Republic* that presents liberal ideas. Many highly specialized magazines such as *Oil and Gas Weekly* and *Aviation Week and Space Technology* carry news about political issues and government actions of interest to their readers.

Approximately 40,000 books are published every year in the United States. Many have political themes, ranging from memoirs by former Presidents to issues such as foreign policy and acid rain.

Wire Services A **wire service** is an organization that employs reporters throughout the world to col-

Background

In 1920 two radio stations broadcasted Warren G. Harding's victory in the presidential election—to an audience of less than 5,000. In 1940, 2 television stations broadcasted Franklin D. Roosevelt's reelection as President—to an even smaller audience. These inauspicious beginnings belied the great influence both media came to exercise in the American political process.

Teach

Guided Practice

L1 Understanding Ideas Poll the class on the following question: Where do you get most of your news—from television, radio, magazines, or newspapers? Record the results on the chalkboard. Have students skim the section to determine where people get information. Ask students to compare class and public preferences. Then ask: why do you think television is the major source?

L2 Analyzing Ideas Display the front pages of newspapers, such as *The New York Times*, the *Wall Street Journal*, *USA Today*, tabloid dailies, and so on. Taking each front page, ask students: What do you think the major aim of this newspaper is—to entertain or to inform? Why? *(New York Times, Wall Street Journal: inform—few or no illustrations, detailed articles. USA Today: entertain—flashy design and visuals, short articles, little news content. Tabloids: entertain—mostly visuals, sensational stories.)* Ask: Are some media forms more suitable to one function than the other?

Caption Answer

by the pictures, words, and expressions used to convey those decisions

---

CONNECTIONS

Media

The thorough nature of CNN's news coverage was jokingly noted by Secretary of Defense Dick Cheney during the Persian Gulf War. In response to a question on the latest developments in the Gulf he replied, "I only know what I've seen on CNN!"

L3 Debate Briefly discuss the information under the heading "International News Coverage" on page 326. Then have students debate the following question:

Is Americans' lack of knowledge about, and interest in, international events a threat to this nation's security?

Independent Practice

L1 Making Comparisons Have students analyze several network news broadcasts, a newspaper, or newsmagazine to compare coverage of domestic and international news. Have them present their findings in a brief report to the class.

L2 Conducting Polls Ask students to poll family members and friends on the following:

1. How much time each week do you spend watching television? How much of this time is devoted to each of the following: news, entertainment, sports?
2. How much time each week do you spend reading a newspaper? What subjects do you spend most time reading—news, sports, business, or arts and entertainment?

Have students collate their results and create a report that makes several generalizations based on their findings.

STUDY GUIDE

Theme Answer
increased competition for viewers and advertisers

Critical Thinking Answer
Americans get most of their information about government from the mass media. Because the media interpret the news, whoever controls the media influences the way Americans view government.

lect news for subscribers. The two major wire services are Associated Press (AP) and United Press International (UPI). Wire services send the news electronically to subscriber papers and to radio and television stations. Either AP, UPI, or both serve 99 percent of the mass media in the United States. These organizations are not considered mass media in themselves because they do not communicate directly with the public. They are, however, a vital source of news stories.

Media Ownership Who owns the mass media in the United States? Since owners control the messages the media present, the question of ownership is important especially for television, radio, and newspapers.

In many democratic countries such as Britain, France, Israel, and Sweden, newspapers are privately owned; but the government controls the broadcast media. With the exception of Britain, broadcast programming tends to support the policies of the political parties in power.

In the United States, the print and nearly all the broadcast media are privately owned, profit-seeking businesses. Until recently, many different owners have controlled the nation's newspapers and radio and TV stations. Currently, however, media ownership is much more concentrated.

Concentration of Newspaper Ownership Many American cities used to have two or more daily newspapers, providing citizens with a number of viewpoints and features, as well as the benefits of competition for advertisers. Today, however, the newspaper business has become very centralized. As a result of mergers, daily local newspapers have no competitors in 98 percent of American cities. Although New York City still has 3 major newspapers, in 1920 it had 14.

In addition, national chains have bought many independent newspapers. The Gannett newspaper chain, for example, owns more than 100 daily and weekly newspapers across the country, including *USA Today*. Another chain, Park Communications, also owns more than 100 newspapers. Newspaper chains now account for 77 percent of daily newspaper circulation, a large increase since 1960.

Private Broadcasting The Federal Communications Commission (FCC) licenses private owners of broadcast stations in two categories: commercial and noncommercial. Radio licenses are divided between AM and FM bands. Television bands are UHF and VHF. Most commercial TV stations are network affiliated, but more than 400 operate as independents.

FCC rules aim to prevent a few sources from controlling the flow of information. Networks are permitted to own no more than 18 AM and 18 FM stations. They may also own 12 TV stations, as long as they do not reach more than 25 percent of the nation's homes. The three largest networks, ABC, CBS, and NBC, each own broadcast stations that reach just under 25 percent of the homes. To encourage minority ownership, the FCC permits group broadcasters who buy interests in stations more than half owned by minorities to have 21 AM, 21 FM, and 14 TV licenses. Two of these stations in each service must be controlled by minorities.

Public Broadcasting Not all radio and television stations in the United States are commercial—operated for profit. The Public Broadcasting Act of 1967 created the Corporation for Public Broadcasting (CPB) to distribute federal money for **noncommercial**, or nonprofit, radio and television. CPB set up the Public Broadcasting System (PBS) in 1968. PBS schedules, promotes, and distributes programs to television stations that are part of the system. In 1970 CPB set up National Public Radio, the radio counterpart of PBS.

NPR and PBS programs provide alternatives to the commercial networks' programs. Public broadcasts focus on cultural offerings such as classical music, opera, ballet, educational programs, academic lectures, documentaries, and nature shows. These programs generally attract small, but loyal audiences. On an average day or evening, seven percent of the population tunes in to public radio or television.

STUDY GUIDE

Themes in Government
Free Enterprise Television advertising dollars depend on the size of the audience watching a particular program. **What do you think has been the impact of the** growth of the cable television industry on national television networks?

Critical Thinking Skills
Synthesizing Information Why do you think the mass media are referred to as the "fourth branch" of government?

324 UNIT 3: INFLUENCING GOVERNMENT

Cooperative Learning Activity

Students might like to work together to create a museum exhibit on the history of the media in their community. Have one group of students conduct library research on the topic. Ask another group to interview various media personalities—television news reporters, radio announcers, newspaper columnists, and so on. If audiovisual facilities are available, these interviews might be taped. A third group should design the exhibit in which the materials gathered by the other two groups can be displayed.

Public radio and television stations depend on three sources of money: funds from the national government that CPB distributes (from $200 to $300 million per year); grants from private foundations such as the Ford Foundation or the Rockefeller Foundation; and donations from individuals and businesses. The Corporation for Public Broadcasting does not tell stations what programs to broadcast. CPB does influence programming, however, by paying for some programs and not others.

Government Broadcasting The national government owns and directly operates a few radio and television stations for two purposes. First, the government creates and sends radio and television programs to American personnel stationed at military posts throughout the world through the Armed Forces Radio and Television Network. Second, the government sends out general news and information through short wave, medium wave, and FM broadcasts throughout the world. Over the years the Soviet Union, Cuba, and other nations often jammed the signals to prevent these broadcasts from reaching their citizens.

The International Broadcasting Act of 1994 reorganized all U.S. nonmilitary broadcasts, placing the network under the United States Information Agency. The four branches–Voice of America, Radio Martí, Radio Free Europe, and Radio Liberty–are all now operated by the agency's board of governors.

What Makes News?

How do reporters, editors, and television and radio producers decide what to report? News deals with events citizens need or want to learn about. Generally, news events must be current or recently discovered, quickly communicated, and relevant to the audience.

The mass media's need to make a profit is the key reason why news must also be entertaining. The media make money by selling advertising. The larger their audience, the more the media can charge for each commercial advertising spot. Thus, the media want to

GLOBAL CONNECTION

Issues

Freedom of Expression in the Mass Media
Only about one-fifth of the world's people live in countries where the news media are free from government control. These are the English-speaking countries, Western European nations, Israel, and Japan. In most countries the government owns at least one television and radio network, but in free societies, most government-owned stations have complete freedom in presenting news.

Most governments regulate the media. Israel keeps tight control over military news. South Africa restricts coverage of racial conflict. The British press usually restricts news about the private lives of the royal family. The Italian press restricts itself on what it says about the pope.

Examining the Connection
What responsibility do the news media have to the public in a free society?

broadcast news stories that will attract large audiences. To attract these audiences, the media concentrate on stories that include personal drama, conflict and violence, and action.

At the same time, in a democracy the media also have a duty to present news that will inform citizens and promote the public interest. When deciding exactly what to report, the need to entertain and the duty to inform often can conflict. Responsible editors and journalists are aware of this dilemma and usually try to meet both needs. Some argue that by presenting entertaining news they reach large numbers of citizens who might not otherwise pay attention to current events.

GLOBAL CONNECTION

A survey of media freedom in 157 countries conducted in the mid-1980s found the print media was completely free of government control in only 34 percent of the countries, while only 23 percent of the countries had completely free broadcast media.
Examining the Connection Answer: *to present news that will inform citizens and promote the public interest*

STUDY GUIDE

Theme Answer
Major newspapers—staff in major foreign capitals or news hot-spots; may also use wire services and local reporters. *Television networks*—staff in major foreign capitals and news hot-spots. *Radio*—wire services, local reporters, and national radio network coverage.

Critical Thinking Answer
Similarities—All try to provide information and to entertain. *Differences*—private: profit-oriented, attuned to advertisers and audiences, wide program choices; public: must generate funds from sources other than viewers, program choices limited; government: government-funded and has own agenda, generally the only choice for viewers

STUDY GUIDE

Themes in Government
Global Perspectives How does each institution of the mass media cover day-to-day world events?

Critical Thinking Skills
Synthesizing Information How are the goals of private broadcasting, public broadcasting, and

government broadcasting similar? How are they different?

Special Needs Strategy

Learning Strategy Active learning tasks that involve students' own experiences help reinforce concepts for students with learning disabilities. Have students read the paragraphs titled "What Makes News?" on page 325. Then ask them to watch a television newscast and keep a list of the time given to each news story, the weather, sports, and so on. Have them arrange their lists in order from the most time to the least time. Ask students to compare their lists, and then have them discuss why they think certain items were given more time than others.

Assess

Check for Understanding

Have students complete Section 1 Review on page 326.

Meeting Objectives

Each section objective is tested by the Section Review questions that follow it in parentheses.

• Describe the framework of the mass media in the United States. (2, 3, 4, 5, 8)

• Assess American attitudes toward world news. (5, 6, 7)

Evaluate

📁 Section 1 Quiz

⬚ Testmaker

Reteach

Have students write summary statements about the following topics: Media Today, Media Ownership, What Makes News, International News Coverage.

Enrich

Have students write an essay comparing the way news stories are handled by American and foreign print media.

Close

Have students discuss the following:

When it comes to the news, the media's efforts to entertain have damaged their ability to inform.

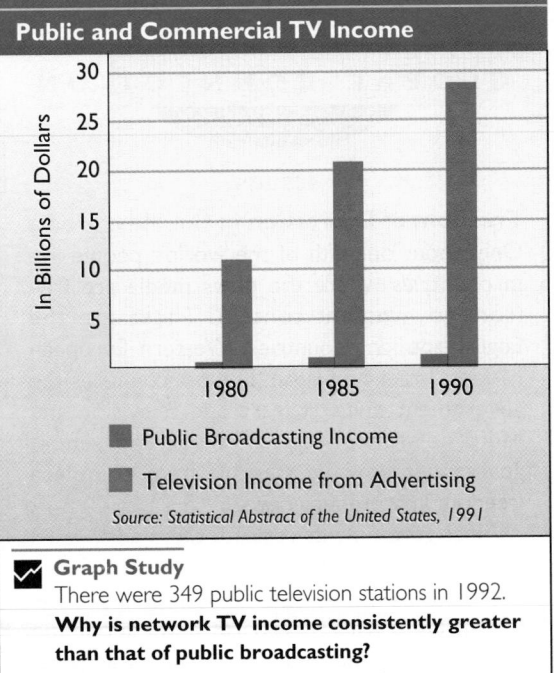

Public and Commercial TV Income

In Billions of Dollars

■ Public Broadcasting Income
■ Television Income from Advertising

Source: *Statistical Abstract of the United States, 1991*

✓ Graph Study
There were 349 public television stations in 1992.
Why is network TV income consistently greater than that of public broadcasting?

International News Coverage

Since only 0.5 percent of United States citizens travel outside the country each year, Americans learn about events in the world primarily from the mass media. Mass media research shows that when given a choice, Americans do not seek out world news. For example, when NBC broadcast a prime-time, one-hour interview with then Soviet leader Mikhail Gorbachev, only 15 percent of the national television audience watched. The rest were watching national network prime-time television comedies or athletic competitions. Public opinion polls show that two-thirds of Americans are usually not aware of foreign news events.

Availability of International News Foreign news usually gets brief space and time compared with major domestic news stories. World affairs stories average 16 percent of all stories on national television newscasts and 11 percent of all stories in newspapers. Foreign affairs must involve more violence and disaster and include more celebrities than domestic events in order to make the news. During a war or other international crisis involving American lives, however, foreign news may replace almost all other news. For example, during the Persian Gulf crisis in 1991 the networks greatly increased international coverage.

A few major newspapers, especially *The New York Times*, the *Washington Post*, the *Christian Science Monitor*, and the *Los Angeles Times*, provide extensive, thorough coverage of world affairs. Top government policymakers and business leaders rely on such papers to keep informed about international events.

Sources of International News Most of the foreign news in American newspapers comes from one of four news gathering organizations: Associated Press (AP), United Press International (UPI), Reuters of Britain, and Agence France-Presse of France. The American mass media employ about 670 full-time overseas correspondents, two-thirds of whom are Americans. About 75 percent of these correspondents are stationed in Western Europe or Asia.

1
SECTION REVIEW

Section Summary
The mass media play a vital role in American political life. Issues facing the media include the concentration of media ownership, determining newsworthy stories, and the indifference of many Americans to the news itself.

Checking for Understanding
Recalling Facts
1. Define **wire service, noncommercial.**
2. Identify the "fourth branch of government."
3. Cite Americans' most common source of news.
4. Name the noncommercial alternatives to commercial broadcasting.

Exploring Themes
5. Free Enterprise How much should making a profit determine the content and selection of news stories?
6. Global Perspectives What are Americans' major sources of world news?

Critical Thinking Skills
7. Drawing Conclusions Why do you think many Americans are generally uninterested in world news?
8. Synthesizing Information What do you think is the most important duty of the media?

---

1. Definitions of terms appear on pages indicated: **wire service,** 323; **noncommercial,** 324
2. the mass media
3. television
4. PBS and NPR

5. Answers may include such issues as the media's public responsibility, the right to free enterprise, the balancing of the two, and so on.
6. Associated Press (AP), United Press International (UPI), Reuters of Great Britain, and Agence France-Presse of France

7. Answers will vary, but may include ethnocentrism and indifference to events seemingly unconnected to themselves.
8. Answers will vary, but should include informing the public, protecting the public interest, influencing public opinion, or entertaining the public. Students should support their answers.

Interpreting Political Cartoons

Political cartoons have a long history in the American mass media. A cartoon expresses the cartoonist's view of a current issue in a humorous form. Knowing how to interpret political cartoons will give you new perspectives on political issues.

Explanation

To interpret a political cartoon, follow these steps:

• Read the caption and any other words printed in the cartoon.
• Analyze each element in the cartoon. Ask: Who or what is represented by each part of the drawing?
• Synthesize these elements to decide the point the cartoonist is making.

Examine the cartoon below that concerns the debate about how the government should deal with Japanese trade barriers.

"HERE'S YER PROBLEM—THIS HERE LITTLE JAPANESE DOO-DAD IS BLOCKING YER TRADE FLOW!"

First, read the cartoon thoroughly. The mechanic is saying, "Here's yer problem—this here little Japanese doo-dad is blocking yer trade flow." Read the labels on the car, as well.

The second step is to analyze each element in the cartoon. The mechanic is labeled "U.S. Government," and the broken-down car is "U.S. Competitiveness." The man in the bow tie does not have a label, but from the context we can guess that he is the owner of the car. Who is the "owner" of "American Competitiveness"? The public.

The final step is to determine what point the cartoonist is making. Here, the mechanic is overlooking all of the obvious reasons that the car will not run, focusing instead on a tiny "doo-dad" under the hood. The cartoonist is likening this incompetent mechanic to government officials who blame America's economic problems on Japanese trade barriers.

Practice

The cartoon below was published during the Persian Gulf War, when thousands of reporters had flocked to Saudi Arabia to cover the fighting. Many objected that they did not have enough freedom to investigate their stories. Use what you have learned about interpreting political cartoons to answer the questions that follow.

1. What is going on in this picture?
2. What words give clues to the cartoon's meaning? What is represented by (a) the military man, (b) the baby, and (c) the baby food?
3. What point is the cartoonist making?

Additional Practice

To practice this skill, see **Reinforcing the Skill** on page 351.

Focus

Have students suggest symbols that could represent the following: the United States, the courts, love, the military, the environment, and world peace. Note that political cartoons use symbols to communicate ideas.

Teach

Have students analyze the car cartoon using the Explanation steps. Ask: How does the relationship between the car and the mechanic symbolize the relationship between the government and American competitiveness? *(Both government and the mechanic are to keep things running smoothly.)* What is the cartoonist's message about the job government is doing in keeping American industry competitive? *(Not good; competitiveness has broken down and government is blaming Japan instead of its own failure.)* What does the cartoon suggest are the real reasons the "car" will not run? *(Costs keep wheels from turning; loaded down by capital gains tax and budget deficit.)*

Assess

Have students complete the **Practice** exercise.

Close

Ask: Can a cartoon adequately tell the story about an issue?

Practice Answers

1. A man dressed in a military uniform is trying to feed a disgruntled baby.
2. The baby carries a tablet labeled "Press" and a pencil. The baby food is labeled "News." The military man is saying "Open wide!" (a) the military; (b) the news media; (c) the version of events that the military wants the media to accept
3. that the military is attempting to feed the media its own version of events in the Gulf War; that the media is not liking this

"news," but that like a baby, the media is helpless to get what it wants

For additional practice, have students complete activity 12 in *Skill Reinforcement Activities* in the Teacher's Classroom Resources.

Focus

Bell Ringer

While attendance is being taken, have students write a sentence explaining what they think is the existing relationship between the media and the government.

Motivating Activity

Read the following statements to the class:

The media are an extension of the government's public relations activities.

Media and government are natural enemies—one will always attack what the other does.

While media and government often are at odds, they help each other to function efficiently.

Poll students to see which statement most closely matches the sentence each wrote for the Bell Ringer activity. Then lead a discussion to see which statement the class thinks best describes media-government relations. Tell students they will be able to check their assessment as they study this section.

Vocabulary Precheck

Write the key terms and concepts for this section on the chalkboard. Ask students how each term and concept relates to media and government. **LEP**

United States government officials and the mass media often have an uneasy relationship. They need to work together, but their jobs often place them in adversarial positions. Politicians want to use the mass media to help them reach their goals, such as convincing the public that their policies are worthwhile and getting reelected. Politicians also want the media to pass on their messages just as they present them.

Journalists in the mass media have their own goals. Journalist H. L. Mencken once said that a reporter's job is to "comfort the afflicted, and afflict the comfortable." Journalists like to play the role of watchdog. They want not only to inform the public about government and current events, but also to analyze events critically and expose wrongdoing.

The watchdog role of the media has a long tradition in American history. In the early 1900s, it was called **muckraking**, or searching out and reporting news stories that exposed major scandals involving prominent people. It included social problems as well, such as inhumane working conditions or unhealthy products. Today this kind of reporting is called investigative journalism. It has become the most popular form of journalism.

In order to deal with reporters, various departments within all branches of the government have public information officers and press secretaries. Their job is to provide reporters with information and ideas for stories. In a recent year, for example, the Department of Defense employed almost 1,500 people to handle relations with the mass media. Journalists sometimes believe that press secretaries withhold damaging information.

The President and the Media

The President and the mass media, especially television, have a mutually beneficial relationship. As a single individual and one of the most powerful government officials in the world, the President is a great source of news. Almost 80 percent of all United States television coverage of government officials focuses on the President. The mass media, in turn, offer Presidents the best way to "sell" their ideas and policies to the public and to other political leaders.

Franklin D. Roosevelt was the first President to master the broadcast media. No television existed at the time, and most newspaper owners did not like FDR. Therefore, he presented his ideas directly to the people with "fireside chats" over the radio. FDR had a great speaking voice. Journalist David Halberstam describes the impact of an FDR fireside chat:

He was the first great American radio voice. For most Americans of this generation, their first memory of politics would be of sitting by a radio and hearing that voice, strong, confident, totally at ease. . . . Most Americans in the previous 160 years had never even seen a President; now almost all of them were hearing him, in their own homes. It was literally and figuratively electrifying.
—DAVID HALBERSTAM, *POWERS THAT BE,* 1980

FDR's successors Harry Truman and Dwight Eisenhower used television to address the nation. Neither one, however, made much use of the new medium. The era of television politics really began with the young, good-looking John F. Kennedy. All

---

SECTION PREVIEW

Objectives
After studying this section, you should be able to:
- Examine the interdependence between the mass media and government.

- Describe television coverage of Congress.
- Identify the media's role in government investigations.

Key Terms and Concepts
muckraking, news release, news briefing, leak, media event

Themes in Government
- Political Processes
- Checks and Balances

Critical Thinking Skills
- Drawing Conclusions
- Synthesizing Information

328 UNIT 3: INFLUENCING GOVERNMENT

Classroom Resources for Section 2

- Guided Reading Activities
- Reproducible Lesson Plans
- Cooperative Learning Activities 12
- Section 2 Quiz

- Testmaker
- Chapter Transparencies 12
- SAT Practice Tests
- Writer's Guidebook

Presidents since have paid great attention to their television image and their use of that medium. In 1970 Senator J. William Fulbright of Arkansas told Congress:

Television has done as much to expand the powers of the President as would a constitutional amendment formally abolishing the co-equality of the three branches of government.

—J. WILLIAM FULBRIGHT, 1970

The White House staff media advisers try to manage relations with the mass media by controlling the daily flow of information about the President. To do so, they use news releases and briefings, press conferences, background stories, leaks, and media events.

News Releases and Briefings A government **news release** is a ready-made story officials prepare for members of the press. The release calls attention to some action or policy and can be printed or broadcast word-for-word. A news release usually has a dateline that states the earliest time it can be published.

During a **news briefing** a government official makes an announcement or explains a policy, decision, or action. Briefings give reporters the chance to ask officials about news releases. The President's press secretary meets daily with the press to answer questions and provide information on the President's activities.

Press Conferences A press conference involves the news media in questioning a high-level government official. Presidents have held press conferences since the days of Theodore Roosevelt. Presidents who relate well with the media are able to use press conferences to build public support for their policies.

Over the years most presidential press conferences have turned into carefully planned events. In preparation for a press conference, the President often studies briefing books that identify potential questions. The White House may limit questions to certain topics. Aides may have friendly reporters ask certain questions they want the President to answer.

Other Means of Sharing Information Sometimes the President or other top official, such as the secretary of state, will give reporters important information called backgrounders. Reporters can use the information in a story, but they cannot reveal their source. Reporters will make this kind of information public by saying, "Government sources said" or "A senior White House official said."

Backgrounders give government officials the opportunity to test new ideas or send unofficial messages to other policymakers, or even foreign governments. The media can, in this manner, make information public without making it official.

When officials give the media information totally off-the-record, reporters cannot print or broadcast the information. Off-the-record meetings can be useful to both government officials and the media. Officials often establish valuable connections with newspapers. Journalists may receive some tips to assist them with their news coverage.

Another way top officials try to influence the flow of information to the press is through a **leak**, or the release of secret information by anonymous government officials. Perhaps they may be seeking public support for a policy that others in the government do not like. Sometimes low-level officials may leak information to expose corruption or to get top officials to pay attention to a problem.

Media Events Modern Presidents often stage a **media event**, a visually interesting event designed to reinforce a politician's position on some issue. A President who takes a strong stand against pollution, for example, makes a stronger statement when he stands in front of a state-of-the-art, administration-supported manufacturing plant rather than in the Oval Office.

President Ronald Reagan was a master of media events. For example, after Reagan cut federal money for student loans and for public schools, public opinion polls showed many voters believed he did not care about education. To change this image, Reagan held televised meetings with students and teachers across the country. These media events were a success. Even though Reagan did not change his position on education, people perceived that he did. The polls showed that regarding the issue of education, President Reagan went from a negative to a positive rating almost overnight.

Today almost everyone involved in politics tries to use media events. Candidates for office promote events to the media that are too "newsworthy" to pass up. In 1978, for example, Robert Graham got a lot of press coverage when he ran successfully for governor of Florida by working at 100 different blue-collar jobs in 100 days.

The widespread use of media events shows just how much politicians and television have come to rely on each other. Television news executives realize politicians are trying to use the media for their own purposes, yet they cannot pass up an interesting story.

Teach

Guided Practice

L1 Understanding Ideas Write the following terms on the chalkboard: *news release, news briefing, press conference, background story, off-the-record story, news leak, media event.* Have students use these terms to write a paragraph on the ways a government administration can control the flow of information to the media. Have students read their paragraphs to the class.

Interpreting Visuals Display transparency 12 from the *Chapter Transparencies* in the Teacher's Classroom Resources and use the accompanying teaching strategy and student activity to teach about media events.

L3 Analyzing Ideas Point out that journalists often complain that the media event is nothing more than manipulation of the media by politicians. Then ask students to discuss the following questions: Do you agree or disagree with this description of the media event? Why? Is staging a media event acceptable behavior for a politician? Why or why not? If the media event does constitute manipulation, who is to blame—the media or politicians? Why?

Independent Practice

L1 Informative Writing Ask students to locate a newspaper or magazine article on a recent act of Congress or Supreme Court decision. Have them write a brief paragraph that summarizes the article.

Background

The term *muckraking* was coined by Theodore Roosevelt in 1906. Roosevelt likened reporters who made sensationalist charges of corruption to the "Man with the Muck-Rake," a character in John Bunyan's *Pilgrim's Progress* who was so involved in raking through the filth that he failed to see the "celestial crown" he was offered. Reporters like Ray Stannard Baker, Lincoln Steffens, and Ida Tarbell soon began to call themselves "muckrakers," even though Roosevelt had used the term as an insult.

L2 Interviewing Ask students to interview reporters who cover the political beat for local newspapers, radio stations, or television stations. Interview questions should elicit answers that will provide a description of the day-to-day life of a political reporter.

Caption Answer
widespread media exposure

STUDY GUIDE

Theme Answers
The event can underscore President's commitment to a particular issue. For example, President can illustrate commitment to giving tax breaks for industries that incorporate pollution controls in new factories by being photographed in front of such a facility.

Television coverage of Congress brings citizens closer to their government at work. Viewers get firsthand information, not media interpretation of the news.

Critical Thinking Answers
President's staff holds daily news briefings; more opportunities for media events. No one in Congress can speak for all 535 members; also, legislative work moves slowly. Supreme Court is not highly visible; Court opinions most often speak for themselves.

Hearings may be the only chance for public to learn the qualifications of nominees.

Assess

Check for Understanding
Have students complete Section 2 Review on page 331.

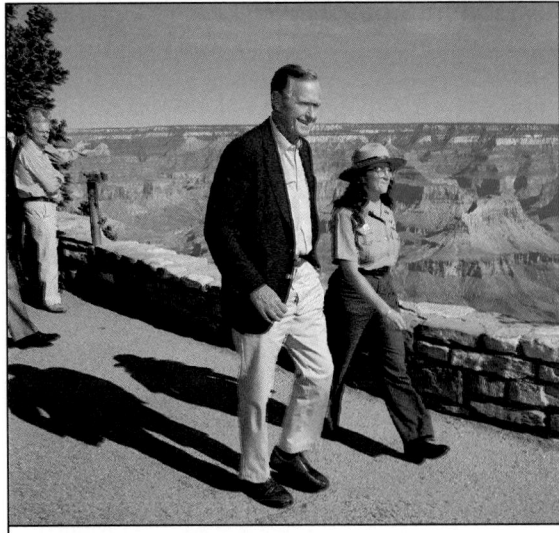

Public Appearances for Political Value
Bush tours the Grand Canyon. **Politics What might the President hope to gain by being seen here?**

George Reedy, press secretary to Lyndon Johnson, observed:

I'd like just once to have the courage to go on the air and say that such and such a candidate went to six cities today to stage six media events, none of which had anything to do with governing America.
—GEORGE REEDY,
TWILIGHT OF THE PRESIDENCY, 1985

Congress and the Media

More than 5,000 reporters have press credentials to cover the House and Senate. About 400 spend all their time on Congress. Most congressional coverage focuses on individual lawmakers and is published mainly in their home states. The news stories usually feature the local angle of the national news stories.

Compared to the President, Congress is difficult for television to cover, because most important congressional work takes place in committees and sub-committees over long periods of time. This slow, complicated work rarely meets television requirements for dramatic, entertaining news.

Additionally, no single congressional leader can speak for all 535 members of Congress. Nationally known lawmakers are seen as spokespersons for their own political parties rather than for Congress. The mass media tend to report on the most controversial aspects of Congress: confirmation hearings, oversight activities, and personal business of members.

Confirmation Hearings The Constitution requires Congress to approve, or confirm, many presidential appointments to high government posts. The Senate usually holds hearings to review such nominations. These hearings can be controversial and therefore attract wide media coverage.

In addition, the media often conduct their own investigations of people nominated for high office. Sometimes the media will uncover damaging information about an appointee. In 1989, for example, President George Bush nominated former Senator John Tower to be his secretary of defense. Media investigations contributed to harsh criticism of Tower's alleged alcoholism and marital problems. Despite a solid legislative record, Tower became the first cabinet nominee the Senate rejected in 30 years. In 1991, President Bush appointed Clarence Thomas to the Supreme Court. The media closely scrutinized Judge Thomas's record and private life. After dramatic televised hearings, the Senate confirmed the appointment.

Oversight Activities Under the process of legislative oversight, Congress has the power to review how the executive branch carries out laws and programs. Oversight is handled through routine hearings. Sometimes, however, lawmakers will uncover and investigate a major scandal. Media coverage of such investigations has created some of the biggest stories in American politics.

In 1987, for example, Congress created a committee to investigate the Iran-contra affair. It involved the secret sale of arms to Iran by Reagan White

STUDY GUIDE

Themes in Government
Political Processes How valuable is a presidential media event?
Checks and Balances In what ways is C-SPAN valuable to Americans?

Critical Thinking Skills
Drawing Conclusions
Why is there more media coverage of the executive branch of the government than of the legislative and judicial branches?

Synthesizing Information
Why are broadcasts of Senate confirmation hearings valuable?

Cooperative Learning Activity

Have students role-play a presidential press conference. One student, acting as President, should prepare and read a brief statement about an important issue or government program selected by the class. Have the rest of the class work in small groups to develop a number of questions on the statement. Have each group select a "reporter" to ask the questions of the President. You might need to moderate the press conference to make certain all reporters get an opportunity to pose questions.

📁 Have students complete activity 12 in *Cooperative Learning Activities* in the Teacher's Classroom Resources.

House aides and the use of money from the arms sale to support a group in Nicaragua called the *contras*. As with the Watergate scandal of 1972, millions of viewers watched the nationally televised hearings.

Personal Business The mass media also try to create big stories by looking for scandal in the personal activities of members of Congress. Until recent decades the media usually overlooked personal problems of lawmakers. Now, however, even powerful lawmakers may not escape media investigation. For example, Speaker of the House Jim Wright was forced to resign in 1989 when the media investigated his personal finances.

C-SPAN Television By the late 1970s, congressional leaders realized that they were losing to Presidents in the never-ending struggle for more media coverage. In 1979 the House allowed closed-circuit television coverage of floor debates. In 1986 the Senate allowed television coverage of Senate debates. The floor proceedings of the House and Senate are now regularly broadcast to lawmakers' offices and to cable television subscribers across the nation via C-SPAN (Cable-Satellite Public Affairs Network).

Congressional Recording Studios Both the House and Senate have extensive recording studios, where lawmakers prepare radio or television messages for the voters in their home districts. Tapes are mailed to hometown stations for use in local news or public affairs programs.

The Court and the Media

Most Americans depend upon the mass media to learn about Supreme Court decisions. Yet the Supreme Court and lower federal courts receive much less media coverage than Congress or the President. During a recent Supreme Court term, for example, *The New York Times* reported on only three-fourths of the Court's decisions. Other newspapers covered less than half of the Court's cases.

Major newspapers and television and radio networks do assign reporters to cover the Supreme Court. However, the judicial branch gets less coverage because of the remoteness of judges and the technical nature of the issues with which the Court deals. Broadcast media are less likely to report court decisions than newspapers, because broadcast news does not allow time to explain issues in depth and television news must be highly visual.

Remoteness of Judges Supreme Court justices and other federal judges are appointed. They almost never seek publicity and generally do not appear on radio or television. Judges fear publicity may interfere with their ability to decide cases fairly.

Technical Issues The Court handles complex issues, many of which interest only a small number of people. In addition, the Supreme Court maintains the tradition that the Court's opinions must speak for themselves. Thus, justices do not hold news conferences to explain major decisions or to answer questions.

SECTION REVIEW 2

Section Summary
Government and the media have an uneasy but interdependent relationship. The mass media cover each of the three branches of the government differently.

Checking for Understanding
Recalling Facts
1. Define muckraking, news release, news briefing, leak, media event.
2. Identify the government officials whose primary job is to deal with the media.
3. Cite the benefits of using backgrounders to communicate information.
4. List the reasons why Congress is a difficult institution for television to cover.

Exploring Themes
5. Political Processes How have government and the media combined to give Americans a better understanding of government investigations?
6. Checks and Balances The media have increasingly scrutinized congressional ethics. Do you think the public should know about the personal lives of government officials? Support your answer.

Critical Thinking Skills
7. Drawing Conclusions Would you agree that a reporter's job is to "comfort the afflicted, and afflict the comfortable"? Support your answer.
8. Synthesizing Information Why do the media and government need each other? Give reasons for your answer.

Meeting Objectives
Each section objective is tested by the Section Review questions that follow it in parentheses.
- Examine the interdependence between the mass media and government. (2, 3, 6, 7, 8)
- Describe television coverage of Congress. (4, 6)
- Identify the media's role in government investigations. (5, 8)

Evaluate
 Section 2 Quiz
 Testmaker

Reteach
Ask students to reread the section and take notes, using words or phrases, on the section's main ideas. Have students use their notes to relate the main ideas to the class.

Enrich
Ask students to write a newspaper article on a recent Senate confirmation hearing or on the activities of a congressional investigative committee.

Close

Have students use information learned in this section to adjust the sentence they wrote in the Bell Ringer activity at the opening of the section. Discuss the adjustments they made.

Section 2 Review Answers

1. Definitions of terms appear on pages indicated: **muckraking,** 328; **news release,** 329; **news briefing,** 329; **leak,** 329; **media event,** 329
2. public information officers, press secretaries, White House media advisers
3. allows officials to send unofficial messages to policymakers or foreign governments
4. The slow, complicated work of Congress rarely meets television requirements for entertaining news, and there is no single congressional leader able to speak for all members of Congress.
5. The process of legislative oversight led Congress to investigate major scandals such as Watergate and Iran-contra. Americans watched the nationally televised hearings as they took place, enabling them to watch government in action.
6. Answers may include that the media and the public should be privy to this information as personal ethics or scruples may be carried over into business. On the other hand, individuals have a right to privacy.
7. Answers will vary, but may include that reporters' roles include acting as the voice of conscience, bringing public attention to those who need help or publicity, and making sure those who have received a public trust deserve to keep it.
8. Students' answers should cite that politicians need the media to present and sell their ideas and policies; and that the government is a great source of news.

Focus

Bell Ringer

While attendance is being taken, ask students to write a response to the following question:

What is *news?*

Motivating Activity

Discuss students' Bell Ringer responses. Then point out that to journalists, news is any important event that happens in a current 24-hour period. Next, have students think of a recent important event that involved the federal government. Ask them to suggest how a journalist might have gathered information to prepare a news story on that event. Provide guidance by mentioning the following: news release, news briefing, press conference, background story, off-the-record story, news leak, media event. End the discussion by pointing out that this special report explains how reporters in Washington, D.C. do their job.

Vocabulary Precheck

Call on students to tell what they think each of the key terms for "The Press Gallery" means. Have students check the accuracy of their definitions in the Glossary. **LEP**

Special Report

The Press Gallery
Reporting the News from Washington

By Donald A. Ritchie
Associate Historian of the United States Senate Historical Office

*H*ow do journalists get the news they report? In Washington, D.C., the center of national news, there are many sources— perhaps too many. The President has a press secretary, as do each of the cabinet members, the various federal agencies, and most of the 535 members of Congress. Television newscaster Ted Koppel has estimated that the federal government employs more than 10,000 press secretaries and public affairs officers.

Report Preview

Objectives
After studying this report, you should be able to:
- **Trace** the development of political reporting throughout United States history.
- **Examine** why government leaders want the press to report the news.

Key Terms and Concepts
correspondent, press gallery

Themes in Government
This report emphasizes the following government themes:
- **Separation of Powers** The press corps gives more coverage to the President than to Congress.
- **Public Policy** Officials often leak information about proposed policies to gauge public opinion.

Critical Thinking Skills
This report emphasizes the following critical thinking skills:
- **Making Inferences**
- **Recognizing Bias**

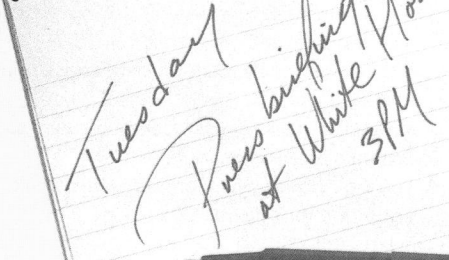

▲ White House press conferences attract a throng of reporters and photographers who strive to keep up with our society's huge appetite for news.

332

Background

The White House press corps has grown considerably over the last 50 years. During President Franklin D. Roosevelt's years in office there were about 550 accredited White House reporters. Today, this number stands at about 1,800. At the same time, however, the number of presidential press conferences has fallen. Roosevelt averaged about 7 press conferences a month during his administration. In contrast, President Bill Clinton held press conferences at a rate of less than 1 every month.

Private organizations and lobbying groups in the capital also seek publicity for their own special issues. Untold numbers of news releases are issued daily, most of which end up in reporters' wastebaskets. When David Stockman was a new member of Congress, he once called a press conference, only to have no reporters attend. The press pays little attention to someone they consider a minor player in government affairs. Later President Reagan appointed Stockman director of the Office of Management and Budget. Then reporters eagerly sought him out because he had risen to become a major source.

Washington reporters need such sources, the more highly placed the better. Otherwise they would be dependent on "handouts"—press releases. They would find it hard to determine how policies are made and what future actions the government is likely to take.

Problems arise when reporters grow too close to their sources. Because press spokespersons do their jobs all too well, Ted Koppel warns, they make the Washington media "too compliant, too trusting, too easily seduced." Politicians are willing to help reporters get the news, but they want favorable treatment in the media in return. Elected officials want their names mentioned in the newspapers or on television news to inform voters back home of what they have been doing. Policymakers want the press to report the news to stimulate public support for their policies. Politicians will also test public opinion by floating "trial balloons," leaking information to the press secretly to judge the response. If the public reacts negatively, the leaker can deny the accuracy of the story or any knowledge of the proposal.

The Evolution of the Washington Press Corps

None of these practices are recent developments. Political attempts to manipulate the news, and close relations between reporters and their sources have a history as old as the federal government itself. In the 1790s cabinet officials such as Treasury Secretary Alexander Hamilton and Secretary of State Thomas Jefferson placed editors on the payrolls of their cabinet offices to write articles promoting their policies. Before the Civil War, each presidential administration had its

"official organ," a newspaper that spoke authoritatively for that administration and whose editors were subsidized by the government. Both the House and the Senate also elected official printers who published newspapers that were sympathetic to the majority party.

▲ In the 1840s correspondents observed the Senate's activities from their new gallery.

National Intelligencer

When the federal government moved from Philadelphia to Washington, D.C., in 1800, the first major newspaper in the new capital was the *National Intelligencer*. Its longest-serving editors, Joseph Gales and William Seaton, received regular financial support from the executive and legislative branches. Acting as stenographers, Gales and Seaton took notes on the speeches in Congress, which they printed in the *Intelligencer*. Then they sent their paper (postage free) to hundreds of newspapers across the country. These newspapers would clip out whatever news of the government they wanted and reprint it for their own readers.

Effects of Sectionalism

By the 1820s sectional issues such as the tariff had deeply divided public opinion in the United States. A single news source like the *Intelligencer* was no longer sufficient. Because northern manufacturers had different interests than southern planters, papers from Boston, Massachusetts, and Charleston, South Carolina, interpreted national news from a regional perspective. Editors across the country began sending their own reporters to Washington to collect news of special interest to their region. These first reporters were known as **correspondents**. The term originated because the telegraph had not yet been invented, and the reporters mailed their stories. Newspapers printed the stories days or even weeks after the events had

Teach

Guided Practice

L1 Reviewing Facts Hold a "Jeopardy"-style quiz by writing on the chalkboard the responses listed below. Have students volunteer an appropriate question for each response.

1. more than 10,000 (*How many press secretaries and public affairs officers does the federal government employ?*)
2. leaking information to the press secretly to judge public reaction (*What is a trial balloon?*)
3. the *National Intelligencer* (*What was the first major newspaper in Washington, D.C.?*)
4. Standing Committee of Correspondents (*Who regulates the congressional press gallery?*)
5. President Grover Cleveland (*Who labeled reporters as "ghouls"?*) **LEP**

L2 Debate Direct students' attention to the quote by President Reagan's press secretary on page 336. Have students debate the following:

Can the news be staged? Is it ethical for the government to stage the news?

CONNECTIONS

Language

The phrase "floating a trial balloon" derives from the meteorological practice of launching pilot, or trial, balloons to determine the speed and direction of the wind.

Cooperative Learning Activity

Have students write and perform a "You Are There" program on the opening of the press gallery in the Senate. One group of students might conduct research on the subject. Another group might write the script for the program. A third group might construct the scenery for the program. The remaining students might take the roles of senators, reporters, and other characters in the script. Have students perform the program for other government and civics classes.

L3 Analyzing Ideas Point out that in his book *Feeding Frenzy: How Attack Journalism Has Transformed American Politics* (1991), political scientist Larry Sabato suggested that modern political journalism in the United States can be divided into three periods. Then write the periods on the chalkboard:

1930s to mid-1960s—lapdog
Mid-1960s to mid-1970s—watchdog
Mid-1970s to the present—junkyard dog

Ask students what Sabato's use of these terms suggests about his assessment of media-government relations during each period. *(lapdog—reporters friendly, uncritical; watchdog—investigative reporting, as in the Watergate affair; junkyard dog—personal attacks, often based on unsubstantiated evidence)* Then lead a discussion of the fairness and accuracy of this classification.

CONNECTIONS

Media

Presidential news conferences usually take place in the East Room of the White House. At these, press corps members are seated according to the size of the organization they represent. For example, reporters from the television networks and national newspapers occupy seats closest to the President's podium.

▼ In the Early 1800s, when newspapers were manually typeset letter by letter, it might take weeks to publish and distribute an edition.

▲ In 1861 the first transcontinental telegraph message was used to convey California's loyalty to the Union.

▼ Coast-to-coast telephone service began in 1915, speeding news transmission.

occurred. Members of Congress did not always appreciate the correspondents' interpretive reporting. One senator denounced them as "miserable scribblers" who earned their living by sending back "vile and dirty misrepresentations of the proceedings here." By 1841, however, the number of correspondents had grown large enough for the Senate to set aside a separate **press gallery**. The gallery was directly over the presiding officer's chair in the chamber so that correspondents could view the proceedings and report the news. The House of Representatives followed a few years later with its own press gallery.

In 1844 Samuel F. B. Morse first tested the telegraph between the Capitol and Baltimore, Maryland. One of the first messages back from Baltimore was: "What is the news in Washington?" Soon news from Congress and the White House could appear in the very next day's newspaper. During the Civil War, readers' eagerness to get news swelled the number of reporters in Washington, D.C., and many stayed to report political news after the war.

Financing

Newspapers depended on political parties and elected officials for financial support until increased subscriptions and advertising revenues enabled them to become politically independent. Even so, nineteenth-century newspapers could only afford to pay their Washington correspondents when Congress was in session—about half the year. To supplement their incomes, some correspondents took part-time positions as clerks to congressional committees or as secretaries to senators and representatives. Naturally, these patronage positions compromised the journalists'

independence, because they could not criticize their employers.

Other reporters used their knowledge and inside positions to lobby for business interests, a practice that further discredited the Washington press corps. In 1879, after several of their colleagues had been involved in public scandals, the Washington correspondents banded together and set rules to govern entry into the congressional press galleries. They convinced the Senate and House to give control of the press galleries to a Standing Committee of Correspondents that the correspondents would elect. To be admitted to the press galleries, reporters needed to file telegraph dispatches for daily newspapers and could never lobby for any legislation. Standing Committees of Correspondents continue to regulate the press galleries today.

By the twentieth century, advertising revenues had risen enough for newspapers to pay their correspondents on an annual basis, ending their need to accept political jobs and outside income. Reporters continue to leave journalism, however, to take jobs as press secretaries or public relations advisers, and many former federal officials write news columns and appear on news programs. This process creates a revolving-door effect that blurs the lines between politicians and the media.

The Twentieth Century

With its public debates, press galleries, and telegraph offices, the Capitol long occupied the center of Washington reporting. Although legislative sessions in both the House and Senate were open to the press, the Senate still debated executive business (nominations and treaties) in closed sessions throughout the nineteenth centu-

---

Special Needs Strategy

Learning Strategy Students with learning problems need concrete examples to understand an abstract concept. Have students turn to page 336 and find the term *symbiotic relationship*. Point out that this derives from a biological term, *symbiosis*, which describes a situation where two very often dissimi-

lar organisms live together in mutual dependence and for mutual benefit. Suggest that a symbiotic relationship might be characterized by the old saying: "One good turn deserves another." Ask students to think of other sayings that might describe this relationship.

▲ TV began to bring images of current events into millions of homes during the 1950s.

▼ The world shrank further in the 1960s as satellites transmitted TV coverage of events—like the Vietnam War—as they occurred.

ry. Although the galleries were emptied and doors barred during executive sessions, reporters had little trouble finding cooperative senators to "leak" stories. Noting that senators received more extensive coverage of the speeches they gave in closed sessions, one correspondent suggested that the Senate conduct all of its business in secrecy! Behind this humor lay the truth that reporters received more notice from their editors and more prominent space in their newspapers when they revealed "secret" information. Secrecy therefore forged another link in the chain of close relationships between reporters and their sources. Not until 1929 did the Senate change its rules to conduct executive sessions in public.

Presidents and Congress

The nineteenth-century Congress offered far more hospitable accommodations to newspaper correspondents than did the executive branch. In contrast to the spacious press galleries and working space above the House and Senate chambers, the White House did not have an inside press room until 1902. Until then reporters stood outside to interview people on their way to

► Theodore Roosevelt broke with tradition by wooing the press.

and from seeing the President. Presidents might talk to reporters, but articles could not quote the chief executive. Presidents addressed the nation through formal speeches and proclamations and did all they could to discourage the press from speculating about their intentions. Perhaps the most extreme case was President Grover Cleveland, who raged against reporters as "ghouls" for invading his privacy and distorting his programs. President Cleveland so hated leaks that a cabinet secretary once asked a reporter not to walk with him near the White House, for fear that the President might spot them together.

Press Conferences

When the young and vigorous Theodore Roosevelt became President, he made himself more available to reporters. His dynamic personality became the focus of press attention. Roosevelt gave regular, informal press conferences, and set aside a room for the press in the new west wing of the White House. With his colorful speech and behavior, Roosevelt personalized the news. Watching him in action, one reporter observed that it was easier for journalists and the public to visualize the President as the government. People could not see Congress "as a thing of flesh and blood, a real living personality." Other strong Presidents followed Roosevelt, and with the coming of radio and television they further shifted press attention to the White House.

A presidential administration spoke with one voice, and the President was easier to spotlight and portray than 535 members of Congress. The closed nature of the White House, however, made the press dependent on White House staff members who

Independent Practice

L1 Summarizing Have students summarize the major events in the development of the Washington press corps. Suggest that students write their summaries in the form of newspaper headlines. For example, one headline might read: PRESS GALLERY GIVES CORRESPONDENTS BIRD'S-EYE VIEW OF SENATE PROCEEDINGS. Encourage students to share their headlines with the rest of the class.

L2 Informative Writing An interesting development in the broadcast media is the celebrity journalist panel program, such as "The McLaughlin Group" on PBS and "Crossfire" and "The Capital Gang" on CNN. Have students write a brief paper on this phenomenon.

CONNECTIONS

Media
The Washington press corps numbers more than 3,500. Most of the television networks and large newspapers have many reporters working in the capital. *The New York Times,* for example, has a Washington staff of more than 35. Some staff members are assigned to the White House, others to Congress, and still others to the various government agencies and departments.

Critical Thinking Activity

Making Inferences Have students reread the quotation from Senate majority leader George Mitchell that closes "The Press Gallery." Then ask: Based on this statement, how do you think Mitchell would characterize the conditions needed for American democracy to work? *(Answers may vary. However, most responses will suggest that openness allows American democracy to work efficiently.)*

L3 Media-Government Relations A group of five students might like to put on a "Nightline" program on the issue of media access to the presidency. Have students work together to research the issue. Then have them select one of the following roles: two reporters who make a two- to three-minute introductory report on the issue; two "experts"—one who thinks access should be restricted, one who wants full access—to debate the issue; and an anchor to introduce the program and moderate the debate. Ask students to put on their program for the class.

Assess

Check for Understanding

Have students complete the Report Review on page 337.

Linking Past and Present
The Reagan administration tightly controlled the media, largely by keeping reporters at arm's length. Franklin Roosevelt used different methods to manage the press. His press conferences were informal affairs, with as many as 200 reporters—all of whom he seemed to know by name—cramming into the Oval Office. With a mixture of charm, openness, and familiarity, Roosevelt built a working relationship with the press unmatched by any other President.

---

sought to present the news in a way most favorable to the President. Correspondents complained about White House management of the news and felt increasingly roped off and confined. One reporter compared his experience to being trapped in the locker room at a football game: "You hear the crowd, you know something is going on. When they let you up to see what is going on, you see a lot of activity, but later you find out that was only the half-time show."

Television Coverage

President Reagan's press secretary once admonished White House reporters: "You don't tell us how to stage the news, and we won't tell you how to cover it." The daily schedule of a modern President almost always includes events that can be broadcast on the evening news. Presidents deliver addresses from dramatic places, using everything from the Berlin Wall to the Grand Canyon as a backdrop. The Capitol dome provides a stirring background for nightly television reports from Capitol Hill. News broadcaster Phil Jones suggested, however, both in jest and frustration, that he could get members of Congress on the air more often if they would ride in a fire truck. Senators and representatives similarly complain of the unfairness of television coverage. Indiana Representative Lee Hamilton said:

A member of Congress will work for months on a complex bill, only to have a television newsman ask him to sum up his case for the bill in 20 seconds or less. . . . Politicians understand that no speech can be carried for more than 30 seconds or so on a thirty-minute evening news program. He must therefore try to coin a catchy phrase. He really cannot expect to get out a whole sentence on television.
—Representative Lee Hamilton

Although the presidency seems better equipped to meet the needs of television broadcasters, Congress continues to provide the most open environment for the print media. In Congress members of two parties compete and offer conflicting opinions and sources of information from which reporters can pick and choose. The largest number of journalists on Capitol Hill are regional reporters who cover national news for groups of papers in a particular state or region, or for a newspaper chain. Regional re-

▲ The faces of some TV newscasters are more familiar to people than those of their elected representatives.

porters tend to gather news from those members who represent districts and states in their region. Critics charge that regional reporters grow so dependent on their congressional sources that they rarely criticize them. This "cozy coverage of Congress" has been described as a symbiotic relationship—one of mutual benefit.

Reporters as Intermediaries

In addition to collecting news, reporters serve as an information-exchange medium between the branches of government. If congressional committees cannot call Presidents of the United States to testify, for example, reporters can question the President at press conferences. If members of Congress suspect some improper behavior in an executive branch agency, they can leak information to the press and use the published stories to call for an investigation. Journalists provide investigating committees with tips and facts they uncover and then report the committee's findings. The press frequently forces Congress into the role of critic by soliciting comments from senators and representatives in response to executive branch activities. Members' answers to these questions quite often receive more publicity than formal speeches and debates do. Sometimes reporters'

Cooperative Learning Activity

Have students imagine that they have to present some of the information in this special report to an audience of average fifth or sixth graders. Some students should organize a planning committee to decide what sections of the special report the class will present and in what form it should be presented. Other students should undertake the writing of the material, while still others might select or design illustrative materials. Students with brothers or sisters in the fifth or sixth grade might present the finished product to their siblings.

sources will ask the reporters questions because journalists often have more current information on an issue than do federal officials.

Officials sometimes resent journalists' roles as intermediaries between the branches of government. A Reagan administration official, Kenneth Adelman, protested that in this intermediary role members of the press too often become participants rather than observers. "The opposition on the Hill feeds material to reporters friendly to them," he noted, "supporters do likewise to try to achieve a semblance of news balance."

Cooperation

Although they are competitors, journalists routinely share news among themselves. One Washington correspondent explained that "an information network of information exchange operates through the press corps: beyond whatever stories are written, there is incessant gossip over who is doing what or who is really saying what." Meeting together in the press galleries or in the corridors outside committee hearings and other events, reporters talk among themselves to verify rumors and fill in missing information. Individual journalists know it can be dangerous to get too far ahead of the pack on a story, particularly if critical information proves to be incomplete or in-

correct. Their editors might be skeptical of news that has not been reported elsewhere. Stories published in smaller newspapers will go unnoticed until they appear in a national paper such as *The New York Times* or on an evening news broadcast.

The multitude of news sources in Washington, D.C., both assists and complicates the correspondents' work. They seek to cultivate sources without being manipulated by those sources. They try not to allow friendships to dull their critical senses. They observe events closely while trying to resist the temptation of becoming participants themselves. These struggles, which have taken place daily over two centuries, have helped Washington reporting move from partisanship to objectivity, independence, and finally increased reliability.

"The Press Galleries are now a permanent fixture," Majority Leader George Mitchell observed on the one hundred fiftieth anniversary of the Senate press gallery in 1991. He continued:

No matter what the hour or the issue, the press is here to monitor and report to the American people our words and deeds. Our form of democracy could not function without a free press to watch over the legislative and other branches of government.

—GEORGE MITCHELL, 1991

REPORT REVIEW

Summary
In the early days of the Republic, reporters who covered the government concentrated on Congress and were often congressional employees. After the Civil War, newspapers began sending correspondents to Washington, D.C., on a permanent basis. By the 1900s the press had become independent of government. In addition, journalists concentrated on reporting on the President rather than on Congress.

Checking for Understanding
Recalling Facts
1. Define correspondent, press gallery.
2. Explain why editors began relying on correspondents in the 1820s.
3. Describe how the telegraph affected reporting news from Congress and the White House.

4. Cite when the first press room was installed in the White House.

Exploring Themes
5. Separation of Powers How does the press, at times, contribute to the division between the President and Congress?
6. Public Policy Why do policymakers and politicians want the press to report the news?

Critical Thinking Skills
7. Making Inferences Why do you think the press has shifted from emphasizing Congress to emphasizing the President?
8. Recognizing Bias In the 1800s the government subsidized reporters. What bias might such subsidies have caused? Why?

Report Review Answers

1. Definitions of terms appear on pages indicated: **correspondent,** 333; **press gallery,** 334
2. Sectional differences made a single news source impractical.
3. made it possible to spread news faster
4. during the presidency of Theodore Roosevelt

5. The press solicits comments from senators and representatives on executive branch decisions.
6. Policymakers want the press to build support for their policies. Politicians want to inform voters of what they are doing. Politicians also use the press to "test the waters" on certain issues.

7. The President is more visible and powerful than Congress.
8. The reporters would have favored government policies because the government paid them.

Meeting Objectives
Each objective is tested by the Report Review questions that follow it in parentheses.
• Trace the development of political reporting throughout United States history. (2, 3, 4, 7, 8)
• Examine why government leaders want the press to report the news. (5, 6, 7)

Evaluate
Hold a "20 Questions" oral quiz on the content of the special report. An element of competition might be added by organizing students into two teams.

Reteach
Have students construct a time line of the major events in the development of the Washington press corps.

Enrich
Have students imagine they are members of the Washington press corps. Have them write a report on how they would research and write a news story on a government-related topic.

Close
Remind students that the relationship between media and government is symbiotic. Then ask students to discuss what benefits media and government receive from their association.

Government Regulation of the Media

Focus

Bell Ringer

Ask students to consider the following question while attendance is being taken:

Is the press in the United States completely free?

Motivating Activity

Discuss students' Bell Ringer responses. Then point out that while the American press is the freest in the world, it is still subject to some government regulation. Ask students the following:

Should government regulate the media? What measures might government take to control the media?

Close by noting that government regulation of the media is discussed in Section 3.

Vocabulary Precheck

List the key terms and concepts for this section on the chalkboard. Have students develop questions for which each term or concept is an answer. **LEP**

Caption Answer

The First Amendment guaranteed to protect the press against government censorship.

The mass media in the United States have more freedom than anywhere else in the world. The First Amendment protects them, and private individuals own them. The mass media, however, are not totally free of government regulation.

Protection for the Print Media

The First Amendment says in part that "Congress shall make no law . . . abridging the freedom . . . of the press." The guarantee of this freedom is fundamental to democracy. Thomas Jefferson described the importance of a free press when he argued:

> *The people are the only censors of their governors.... The only safeguard of the public liberty ... is to give them full information of their affairs through the channel of the public papers & to contrive that those papers should penetrate the whole mass of the people.*
>
> —THOMAS JEFFERSON, 1787

Free Press Guaranteed In the United States, the First Amendment means that print media are free from **prior restraint**, or government censorship of information before it is published. Over the years the Supreme Court has struck down attempts to give government this power. These decisions mean that editors and reporters have freedom to decide what goes in or stays out of their publications.

Libel False written statements intended to damage a person's reputation constitute **libel.** People who be-

lieve a published story has damaged their careers or reputations may sue for libel. However, it is almost impossible for a public official to win a libel suit. The reason is in part that there is no law against criticizing government officials.

Major public figures will sometimes file a libel suit to discourage the press from continuing to do stories about them. If taken to court, publishers must prove that they intended to tell the truth. Defending against a libel suit can be very expensive. In addition, public officials who file libel suits may win sympathy from the public and a jury who resent the way reporters collect and report the news.

The News from Japan
Many foreign news media are government owned.
History Why did the idea of a free press take hold so strongly in the United States?

SECTION PREVIEW

Objectives
After studying this section, you should be able to:
■ Explain how and why government regulates the media.
■ Trace the media's attempts to win the right of access.

■ Analyze possible conflicts between national security and First Amendment protections.

Key Terms and Concepts
prior restraint, libel, shield law, equal time doctrine, fairness doctrine, market

Themes in Government
■ Checks and Balances
■ Civic Responsibility

Critical Thinking Skills
■ Drawing Conclusions
■ Synthesizing Information

338   UNIT 3: INFLUENCING GOVERNMENT

Classroom Resources for Section 3

📁 Guided Reading Activities
📁 Reproducible Lesson Plans
📁 Supreme Court Case Studies 64
📁 Section 3 Quiz

💾 Testmaker
SAT Practice Tests
Writer's Guidebook

The Right to Gather Information Freedom for the media to publish whatever they want means little if they cannot collect information about government actions and decisions. If government officials tell lies, hold secret meetings, or try to limit reporters' access to information in other ways, the media may not be able to provide the information citizens need. Does the First Amendment give the media special rights of access to courtrooms or government offices where they want to collect information? Further, does it give reporters special protection for their news sources— the people they consult to get information?

The Right of Access During the last three decades, the press has gone to court many times to fight for the right of access. The results have been mixed. Generally, the Supreme Court has rejected the idea that the media have special rights of access. In 1965, for example, in *Zemel* v. *Rusk* the Court ruled that "the right to speak and publish does not carry with it the unrestrained right to gather information." A similar ruling came down in 1972 in *Branzburg* v. *Hayes* when the Court decided that "the First Amendment does not guarantee the press a constitutional right of special access to information not available to the public generally."

Teach

Guided Practice

L1 Constructing Tables Write the following title on the chalkboard: *Government Regulation of Media Ownership.* Beneath this title draw a three-column table using these column headings: *One-to-a-Customer Rule, Cross-Ownership Rule, 12-12-12 Rule.* Ask students to complete the table by detailing how these government regulations are applied. Suggest that students retain their completed tables for review purposes. **LEP**

Focus on Freedom

NEW YORK TIMES CO. v. UNITED STATES

On June 13, 1971, The New York Times *published the first of the Pentagon Papers dealing with the history of American involvement in Vietnam. Daniel Ellsberg, a Pentagon employee, had released the classified documents to the press. When the* Times *was about to publish the third part of the secret information, the Justice Department obtained a federal injunction against the newspaper. A similar action was taken against the* Washington Post *for publishing the same material. The Supreme Court rapidly reviewed records of a lower court and ruled against prior restraint of such information.*

The entire thrust of the Government's claim . . . has been that publication of the material sought to be enjoined 'could,' or 'might,' or 'may' prejudice the national interest in various ways. But the First Amendment tolerates absolutely no prior judicial restraints of the press predicated upon surmise or conjecture that untoward consequences may result. . . .

—JUSTICE WILLIAM BRENNAN, 1971

It should be noted at the outset that the First Amendment provides that "Congress shall make no law . . . abridging the freedom of speech or of the press." That leaves, in my view, no room for governmental restraint on the press.

There is, moreover, no statute barring the publication by the press of the material which the *Times* and *Post* seek to use . . . .

The dominant purpose of the First Amendment was to prohibit the widespread practice of governmental suppression of embarrassing information. It is common knowledge that the First Amendment was adopted against the widespread use of the common law of seditious libel to punish dissemination of material that is embarrassing to the powers that be.

—JUSTICE WILLIAM DOUGLAS, 1971

Justice Byron White, who believed that publication of the material might be a criminal offense, stated that prior restraint was nonetheless unacceptable:

Nor, after examining the materials the Government characterizes as the most sensitive and destructive, can I deny that revelation of these documents will do substantial damage to public interests. Indeed, I am confident that their disclosure will have that result. But I nevertheless agree that the United States has not satisfied the very heavy burden which it must meet to warrant an injunction against publication in these cases.

—JUSTICE BYRON WHITE, 1971

Examining the Document

Reviewing Facts

1. Cite the main issue in *New York Times Co.* v. *United States.*
2. Explain what "heavy burden" of proof the government would have to provide to enable it to restrain the publication of sensitive material.

Critical Thinking Skills

3. Drawing Conclusions How might the publication of the Pentagon Papers have affected the national debate on the Vietnam War?

CHAPTER 12: THE MASS MEDIA 339

Focus on Freedom

Some legal scholars have suggested that *New York Times Co.* v. *United States* was not as great a victory for press freedoms as most people believe. There were nine opinions attached to the decision, two of which stated that the First Amendment protected the press against the use of prior restraint. The other seven, in one form or another, stated only that the need for prior restraint had not been proved in this case.

Answers

1. whether it was legal for federal government to enforce prior restraint on a newspaper
2. Answers may include breaching of national security or placing American lives in danger.
3. Answers may include that the material could have increased Americans' knowledge of the war and, therefore, they could have debated it more intelligently and possibly could have come to a different conclusion on United States involvement.

Background

As well as issuing licenses and monitoring program content, the Federal Communications Commission (FCC) regulates media technology. In 1950, for example, the FCC established standards for color television transmission. FCC rules established in the 1960s required that all television sets for sale in interstate commerce have to be equipped to receive VHF channels 2 through 13 and UHF channels 14 through 83.

L2 Panel Discussion Select four or five students to take part in a panel discussion on the fairness doctrine. Begin the discussion by asking the following: Is it necessary for all views on an issue to be represented in the media? Is it possible to represent all views? Should the views of hate-groups and other extremists be given an outlet in the media? Encourage the rest of the class to challenge or question the views of the panel members.

L3 Expressing an Opinion Mention that Ronald Reagan's run for the presidency in 1980 created an interesting problem for the television networks. If they showed any of his movies, would they have to provide equal time for his opponent, Jimmy Carter? Lead students in a discussion of the equal time doctrine. Ask: Should the doctrine apply to non-political as well as political appearances? Why? Since appearances on news shows usually involve discussion of political issues, should not such appearances be subject to the doctrine?

STUDY GUIDE

Theme Answer
The press helps check the power of government and lets citizens know when their freedoms may be abused.

Critical Thinking Answer
Answers will vary. Typical responses: No, if the public does not have access to information, neither should the press. Yes, the press needs to be able to check the power of the government to protect citizens' freedoms.

The lower courts have been more supportive of the right of access. In the last decade the media filed more than 200 right of access lawsuits. They won access in about 60 percent of these cases.

Despite such victories in the lower courts, authorities do not have to give the media special right of access to crime or disaster sites if the general public is excluded, although they usually do. Reporters may be kept out of legislative sessions that are closed to the general public. Neither do they have special access to grand jury proceedings.

Protection of Sources Reporters often need secret informants when investigating government officials, political radicals, or criminals. Success in gathering news may depend on getting information from people who do not want their names made public. If the courts, the police, or legislatures force reporters to name their sources, these sources of information may vanish. On the other hand, criminals may go unpunished if reporters do not give police information about them.

There have been many battles between the press and the government over the media's right to keep sources secret. More than half the states have passed **shield laws** to protect reporters from having to reveal their sources. While no federal shield law exists, the Privacy Protection Act of 1980 prevents all levels of government from conducting surprise searches of newsrooms, except in a few special circumstances.

Regulating Broadcast Media

The federal government has more power to regulate the broadcast media than to regulate the print media, for two reasons. First, a limited number of radio and television airwaves exist. During the 1920s when radio was first popular, stations drowned out each other's signals. As a result, the Radio Act of 1927 created the Federal Radio Commission to divide channels among broadcasters. Then in 1934 Congress created the Federal Communications Commission (FCC) to manage all types of electronic communications.

Second, the airwaves are a public resource and should be regulated like other public utilities such as the electric company or water company. Herbert Hoover helped plan federal regulation of radio when he was secretary of commerce:

> *Radio communication is not to be considered merely a business. . . . It is a public concern impressed with the public trust and to be considered primarily from the standpoint of public interest to the same extent and upon the same general principles as our other public utilities.*
> —HERBERT HOOVER, 1924

The Federal Communications Commission
The FCC is the government agency with authority to regulate over-the-air and cable television, AM and FM radio, telephones, satellites, telegraph, and CB radio. The FCC has five commissioners that the President appoints and the Senate approves. Each commissioner serves a five-year term.

The FCC has broad powers to make rules that require stations to operate in the public interest. The most important power is to grant licenses to all radio and television stations in the country. The FCC's two most important regulatory activities deal with the content of broadcasts and with ownership of the media.

Regulation of Content The FCC cannot censor broadcasts. It can influence the content of broadcasts, however, by fining stations that violate rules and by threatening not to renew a station's license.

One FCC rule is the **equal time doctrine**, which requires stations to give equal airtime to candidates for public office. If one major candidate for office is allowed to buy commercial time, then other candidates must have the same chance to buy an equal amount of time. This rule does not apply to news stories, but it does include "free time" broadcasts on interview shows.

STUDY GUIDE

Themes in Government
Checks and Balances
The FCC cannot censor broadcasts and the government may not exercise prior restraint over print media.

Why is freedom of the press under the First Amendment fundamental to democracy?

Critcal Thinking Skills
Drawing Conclusions
Should the Supreme Court change its position on the press's right of access? Explain your answer.

Cooperative Learning Activity

Have students work together to design, implement, and evaluate a survey on freedom of the press. One group of students might develop suitable questions for the survey. Another group might decide on a survey population—other classes in the school, perhaps—and then implement the survey. A third group might collate and analyze the survey results. Display the results on the bulletin board and use them as the starting point for a discussion on how the class feels about this issue.

The FCC took many steps to deregulate broadcasting during Ronald Reagan's presidency. The most controversial change was removal of the **fairness doctrine**. This doctrine required broadcasters to provide "reasonable opportunities for the expression of opposing views on controversial issues of public importance." The doctrine was supposed to discourage one-sided coverage of issues and encourage stations to present a range of views.

Some broadcasters claimed the fairness doctrine was actually censorship. In addition, they argued it actually caused stations to avoid reporting on any type of controversy. The Supreme Court had upheld the doctrine in 1969 in *Red Lion Broadcasting Co.* v. *FCC*. The Court stated that the doctrine protected "an uninhibited marketplace of ideas in which truth will ultimately prevail." The Court added that a regulation such as the fairness doctrine was justified in the broadcast media because the airwaves are scarce. If print media such as newspapers are presenting one-sided coverage, the Court said anyone could start another paper.

When the FCC wanted to drop the fairness doctrine in 1987, Congress passed a law requiring the FCC to keep it. But President Reagan vetoed the bill, saying:

This type of content-based regulation by the Federal Government is, in my judgement, antagonistic to the freedom of expression guaranteed by the First Amendment.

—RONALD REAGAN

Reagan said the growth of cable television had added so many new outlets for different ideas that the scarcity argument no longer mattered.

Controls on Ownership To ensure the public receives different points of view, the federal government wants to prevent the concentration of media ownership in the hands of a few people. Market size is one factor the FCC takes into account when awarding licenses. A **market** is the area in which a

radio or television station or a newspaper can reach an audience. In large urban areas such as Los Angeles or New York, a market may have a 50-mile (80-kilometer) radius and include millions of people. Markets with the same radius in states such as Nevada or Wyoming might have 200 people.

The FCC limits media ownership in three ways. First is the one-to-a-customer rule. This regulation prohibits any broadcaster from buying more than one AM or FM radio station, or more than one television station in the same market.

Second is the cross-ownership rule that prevents a single person or company from owning different types of media in the same market. Thus, FCC rules prevent a person from buying a radio station and a television station in the same market. These first two rules, however, do not apply to people who owned multiple stations or combinations of stations and newspapers before the 1970s.

High-Flying Programming
New technology such as satellite broadcasting has led to new regulations on the media. **Economics Do you think the airwaves are a public utility? Explain.**

STUDY GUIDE

Themes in Government
Civic Responsibility
Major network stations reach many more people in a television market than do small cable stations.

Do major stations have a responsibility to report various sides of an issue? Why or why not?

Critical Thinking Skills
Synthesizing Information
Why does the federal government have more power to regulate the broadcast media than the print media?

Special Needs Strategy

Learning Strategy Students with attention problems are helped by active learning approaches. Have students work in pairs to locate the boldface terms in this section: *prior restraint, libel, shield laws, equal time doctrine, fairness doctrine,* and *market*. Have pairs write the definition of each

term. Then ask the pairs to check their definitions by reading the terms in the context of this section. Have each pair present their ideas to a second pair to check if they came to the same conclusions about their definitions.

Independent Practice

L1 Media Have students create a cartoon or poster to illustrate an issue of contention in the area of media regulation—media access to information or protection of sources, for example.

Analyzing Supreme Court Cases Assign case 64, *Cohen* v. *Cowles Media, Inc.,* in *Supreme Court Case Studies* in the Teacher's Classroom Resources.

Caption Answer
Yes. They are a limited public resource subject to regulation.

STUDY GUIDE

Theme Answer
<u>Yes</u>: because of their potential influence, major stations should try to be fair to all sides. <u>No</u>: the same rules should apply to all stations, regardless of audience size.

Critical Thinking Answer
Broadcast media uses the airwaves, which are limited in number and are a public resource.

Assess

Check for Understanding

Have students complete Section 3 Review on page 342.

Linking Past and Present
During the Civil War, Union General William T. Sherman said of war correspondents, "They are a pest and shall not approach me and I will treat them as spies which in truth they are."

Caption Answer
because of a free society

Meeting Objectives

Each section objective is tested by the Section Review questions that follow it in parentheses.
• Explain how and why government regulates the media. (2, 5)
• Trace the media's attempts to win the right of access. (3, 4)
• Analyze possible conflicts between national security and First Amendment protections. (6, 7, 8)

Evaluate

📁 Section 3 Quiz

🔒 Testmaker

Reteach

Call on students to name ways in which government regulates the media. Ask others how these methods of regulation are applied.

Enrich

Have students research and write a paper on the legal history of such issues as prior restraint, libel, right of access, or gag rules.

Close

Ask: Which laws regulating media might be relaxed? What, if any, new regulations should be imposed?

THINGS HAVE CHANGED SINCE 'NAM! WE CAN TARGET THESE NEW REPORTERS PRECISELY, WITH VERY LITTLE COLLATERAL DAMAGE!

edSTEIN '91
ROCKY MTN. NEWS · NEA

"Truth is the First Casualty"
The Pentagon limited press coverage of the Gulf War. **History** Why is the tension between the public's right to know and national security inevitable?

Third is the 18-18-12 rule that limits a single company to owning no more than 18 AM and 18 FM radio stations, and 12 television stations in different markets across the country. Thus, 48 is the total number of broadcast media outlets one company may own anywhere in the country.

Media and National Security

Tension between the need for the government to keep secrets to protect national security and the citizens' need for information will always exist in a free society. Tensions are especially evident in foreign affairs where weapons, intelligence information, and military secrets are often involved. Two important ways the government attempts to control information about national security issues are by classifying information as secret and by limiting press coverage of military actions. Reporters and editors usually respect the need for secrecy in national security matters.

The federal government gives a "secret" security classification to much government information—more than 22 million documents in one recent year. Most of these documents came from the Defense Department or the Central Intelligence Agency. During the Vietnam War, *The New York Times* published a secret Defense Department study that described how the United States became involved in the war. The government tried to stop publication. In *New York Times Co.* v. *United States* (1971), however, the Supreme Court ruled that the publication did not harm the nation's security.

When controversy about a military action arises, however, the media may criticize the government and try to dig up secret information. Additional tension between the military and the media was created during the 1991 Persian Gulf War. Throughout the military buildup and the actual war, the Defense Department limited the media to a small group of reporters who were permitted to visit battlefields. These reporters would collect stories to share with all other reporters left behind in press headquarters. Most reporters covering the war had to depend upon official military briefings to gain information about the progress of the war.

3 SECTION REVIEW

Section Summary
While the First Amendment protects the mass media, which are privately owned, the federal government regulates them. This regulation includes the federal government preventing a concentration of media ownership.

Checking for Understanding
Recalling Facts
1. Define prior restraint, libel, shield law, equal time doctrine, fairness doctrine, market.
2. State why broadcast media are more heavily regulated than print media.
3. Cite the advantage of taking the press to court in a libel suit.
4. Identify the types of cases in which the media have been most successful in winning access.

Exploring Themes
5. Checks and Balances What are several reasons the federal government might want to prevent the concentration of media ownership?
6. Civic Responsibility How do you think reporters should balance their roles as citizens and as media workers in relation to national security?

Critical Thinking Skills
7. Drawing Conclusions Should the media have been limited in its coverage in the 1991 Persian Gulf War? Support your answer.
8. Synthesizing Information Why might the need for national security conflict with the First Amendment protections given the media?

Section 3 Review Answers

1. Definitions of terms appear on pages indicated: **prior restraint**, 338; **libel**, 338; **shield law**, 340; **equal time doctrine**, 340; **fairness doctrine**, 341; **market**, 341
2. They use public airwaves.
3. to discourage the press from printing further stories about an individual and to gain potential sympathy from the public and a jury against the methods of reporters

4. decisions involving specific court proceedings that helped the press gain access to the records and activities of the executive branch
5. to make sure citizens receive different points of view, to prevent any organization or group of owners from gaining too much power over American media outlets
6. Answers may include that as well as being the eyes and ears of the American public, reporters are citizens. They must take care not to put their country in jeopardy.

7. Possible responses: Because of the incidence of military personnel deaths from capture, "friendly fire" and the possibility of becoming a POW, the military may have been trying to protect the media. On the other hand, it could be argued that it is within the rights of the media to take risks, barring breaches of national security, to cover the war independently.
8. Answers should reflect the conflict between the media's right of access to information and the government's need to keep sensitive materials secret.

SECTION 4

The Media's Impact on Politics

The mass media have become part of United States daily political life. In reality, how much does the media really influence Americans? This question is not easy to answer. So many different factors influence people's knowledge, attitudes, and behavior toward politics. Experts agree, however, that the mass media have a very great impact on defining the public agenda, and on voting and elections.

Setting the Public Agenda

The public agenda is a list of societal problems that both political leaders and citizens agree need government attention. Aid to the homeless, long-term health care for the elderly, teenage substance abuse, and high crime rates are all problems that are part of the public agenda.

Government cannot and does not pay attention to all problems at once. At one time in the United States, for example, water pollution was not considered part of the public agenda because people did not see government intervention as a solution to the problem. Today, most people expect government to create laws and programs to help solve pollution problems.

The mass media play a very important role in setting the public agenda in the United States. They highlight some issues and ignore others. They define some conditions as problems and let other conditions go unnoticed. They determine which political issues people and their leaders will be discussing. The mass media do this largely by influencing people's awareness of problems and by shaping public opinion as well as people's attitudes and values.

Awareness of Issues The media's greatest power is to define reality for the American people. The media cover some issues more thoroughly than others. Coverage largely determines which issues people think important. A foreign policy expert explains:

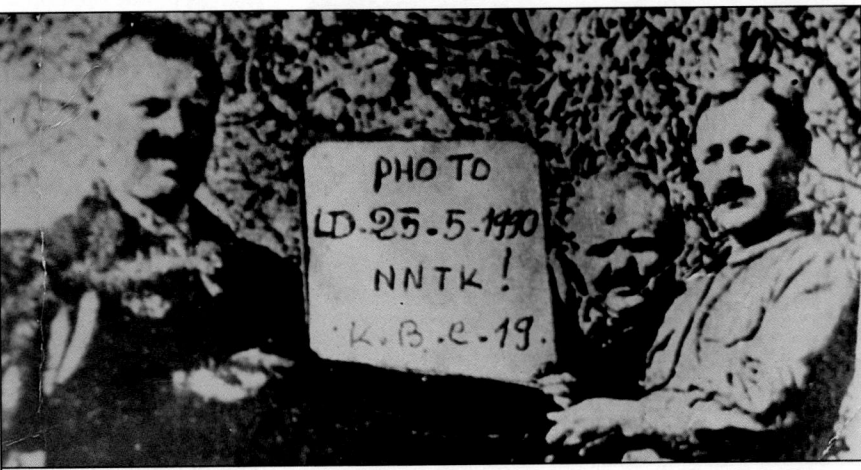

When TV Is Wrong
Networks broadcast this picture of missing United States soldiers still alive in Vietnam; the picture was later found to be a hoax. **Media How does the media influence the public agenda?**

SECTION PREVIEW

Objectives
After studying this section, you should be able to:
- Identify ways that the media affect politics.
- Assess citizens' responsibilities

to weigh media coverage of political candidates.

Key Terms and Concepts
selective perception, horse-race coverage, front-runner, spot advertising

Themes in Government
- Political Processes
- Civic Responsibility

Critical Thinking Skills
- Drawing Conclusions
- Synthesizing Information

CHAPTER 12: THE MASS MEDIA 343

Classroom Resources for Section 4

- 📁 Guided Reading Activities
- 📁 Reproducible Lesson Plans
- 📁 Participating in Government 12
- 📁 Primary and Secondary Source Readings 12
- 📁 Reteaching Activities 12
- 📁 Enrichment Activities 12

- 📁 Section 4 Quiz
- 📁 Chapter 12 Tests
- ➕ Testmaker
- 🎧 Audio Cassettes (English and Spanish)
- 📼 Modern Presidential Campaigns, Volumes II, IV

Focus

Bell Ringer

Ask students to consider the following question while attendance is being taken:

How much impact does television have on you?

Motivating Activity

Write the following on the chalkboard: *A large impact; Some impact; A little impact; No impact.* Poll students as to which of these statements matches their Bell Ringer responses. Enter the results under each heading. Then ask students to discuss the following: Do you believe what you see on television? Have you ever been persuaded by a television advertisement to purchase a particular product? Has a television news program changed your mind on a particular issue? Tell students this section deals with the impact of television on the American political process.

Vocabulary Precheck

Ask students to speculate on the meaning of each of this section's key terms. Then have them check their speculations by finding the correct definition in the section text. **LEP**

Caption Answer
because of its ability to shape opinions, attitudes, and values

Set on Freedom
The Watts Riots, 1965
Running Time :56
Side A, Chapter 27

Teach

Guided Practice

L1 Understanding Ideas Write the following horse-racing terms on the chalkboard: *running mate, front-runner, stalking horse, dark horse,* and *shoo-in.* Point out that reporting of elections uses such terms. Select students to compose sentences that use the terms in an election context. Assist students by providing them with definitions of the terms.

L2 Analyzing Ideas To help students understand the concept of selective perception, read a few paragraphs from a story in a current newspaper or magazine. Then ask students to write their own version of the story you have just read. Select students to read their stories and ask the rest of the class to note differences in the stories. Lead the class in a discussion of how and why these differences might have arisen.

Caption Answer

Influences may include products, programs, personalities, slogans, fashions, information, attitudes.

The mass media may not be successful in telling their audience what to think, but the media are stunningly successful in telling their audience what to think about.

—BERNARD COHEN,
THE PRESS AND FOREIGN POLICY, 1963

During the 1960s, for example, the media helped place discrimination against African Americans and racial equality on the public agenda. The media gave national coverage to the civil rights movement in the South. Dramatic television and newspaper accounts of attacks on civil rights workers trying to register African American voters and on African American children trying to enter white schools captured the nation's attention. Congress, under great pressure to do something about the problem, eventually passed laws promoting racial equality.

TV's Persuasive Power
Television is criticized for its negative influence on children, but TV can be used for beneficial purposes.
Sociology How has television influenced you?

Powerful visual images may affect foreign policy. When American embassy officials were taken hostage in Iran in 1979, television coverage showed angry Iranian mobs demonstrating outside the United States embassy in Tehran. The newscasts aroused the American public to demand that President Carter take action to free the hostages. According to political scientist Murray Edelman:

For most people most of the time politics is a series of pictures in the mind, placed there by television news, newspapers, magazines, and discussions.

—MURRAY EDELMAN,
THE SYMBOLIC USES OF POLITICS, 1967

Thus, issues or problems that get the greatest attention in the media are the ones people think are most important. A study of media coverage of the Vietnam War, for example, found that the content of news stories had less impact on people than the amount of attention given to the war.

Attitudes and Values The media also have an impact on public opinion toward government and issues of the day by influencing people's attitudes and values. The media play an important role in political socialization, the learning process through which children and adults form their basic attitudes and values toward politics. The media, especially television, convey messages to youngsters about war and peace, crime, environmental problems, voting, elections, foreign countries, and so on. Children have extensive contact with the media. In winter, for example, children between the ages of 2 and 11 spend an average of almost 17 hours a week watching television.

As for adults, research shows that the media can more easily create new opinions than they can change attitudes and values people already have. This fact is true because of **selective perception**—mentally screening out ideas and images that do not agree with one's beliefs. Selective perception causes people to get from a news story only information that fits with opinions they already hold. It means that to a large

STUDY GUIDE

Themes in Government
Political Processes During the 1960s several interest groups discovered that one of the best ways to gain television coverage was to stage mass demonstrations. In this way the group's agenda could be placed before the public. **How do the media help set the public agenda?**

Critical Thinking Skills
Drawing Conclusions
The Federal Communications Commission restricts more children's television programming than adult programming. **Why is this so?**

Background

A study of newspaper coverage of crime in large cities found that the media helped put an important issue—combatting crime—on the public agenda and heightened the American people's awareness of the problem. However, the study showed that more coverage was given to violent crime than official figures justified. The study, therefore, concluded that the print media misrepresented the nature of the problem. After the broadcast media joined in focusing public attention on crime as an issue, Congress passed new anti-crime legislation in 1994.

extent most people see and hear only what they want to see and hear. If a person believes that air pollution is not a serious problem, for example, she or he will dismiss information to the contrary.

The media also affect people's general orientation toward politics. Media stories may give people a sense of a world out of control. They may reassure people that all is going well. The media's focus on bad news—scandals, violence, or power struggles between Congress and the President—has led to what some experts call television malaise. This uneasiness is a general feeling of distrust and cynicism toward government and the political system.

On the other hand, it appears that political advertising on television during election campaigns increases support for the political system. According to political scientists Thomas Dye and Harmon Zeigler:

Audiences are not told that they must overthrow the government to bring about change, but rather that they can solve social and economic problems by voting for one candidate or another. Incumbents tell audiences that they are solving problems, and challengers tell audiences that they will solve problems if elected. Both are affirming that electoral politics can solve problems, that voting causes change, that the individual voter can make a difference. Political advertising reinforces our belief in democratic politics.

—THOMAS DYE AND HARMON ZEIGLER, *AMERICAN POLITICS IN A MEDIA AGE*, 1986

Impact on Government Policies By influencing the public agenda and public opinion, the mass media affect government policies. The media's role in the Vietnam War is a classic example. The war in Vietnam was the first "television war." Every night at dinnertime, network news shows reported on the war. Until the late 1960s this media coverage supported the war. The networks had few correspondents in Vietnam. Those that were there based their reports largely on optimistic accounts of events the government provided.

"How Deep You Figure We'll Get Involved, Sir?" Early decisions about the American role in Vietnam were made with little press coverage or public debate. **History** How would media war coverage differ today?

In 1968 the Tet offensive dramatically changed media coverage of the war. On January 30 the North Vietnamese and Vietcong launched a huge attack on many South Vietnamese cities including Saigon, the capital, and United States military headquarters. The attack itself was a military failure. United States-led forces routed the Vietcong, killing almost 33,000 enemy troops in the first two weeks of fighting. The Tet offensive was, however, a great political success for the Communists.

The American mass media interpreted Tet as a major setback for United States forces. Tet undermined the American military's claim that victory was not far away. Instead it showed that no place in South Vietnam was safe from attack. Further, the fighting during Tet was brutal. More than 2,500 American soldiers, 2,500 South Vietnamese troops, and 12,500 civilians were killed. Horrible battle scenes shown

Making Comparisons
Show the sections on the Truman-Dewey campaign of 1948 and the Bush-Dukakis campaign of 1988 from "Modern Presidential Campaigns," Volumes II and IV, *Social Studies Videos*. (You will need to preview the tapes to locate these materials.) Then have students discuss the following questions: How did media coverage of presidential elections change between 1948 and 1988? What developments made these changes possible?

Caption Answer
The media would give more attention.

STUDY GUIDE

Theme Answer
Opposition to the war grew steadily, eventually forcing the American government to withdraw troops.

Critical Thinking Answer
Pro-war Americans would have been influenced more by stories concerning North Vietnamese and Viet Cong atrocities. Anti-war Americans would have been influenced more by scenes of American dead or injured.

STUDY GUIDE

Themes in Government
Civic Responsibility How did American public opinion influence the Vietnam War?

Critical Thinking Skills
Synthesizing Information How could selective perception have affected how Americans felt about the Vietnam War?

CHAPTER 12: THE MASS MEDIA 345

CONNECTIONS

History
While the Tet offensive was primarily a military operation, the North Vietnamese hoped it would also have an impact on people in the United States. They did not anticipate the power of such television images as firefights on the grounds of the American embassy in Saigon. The North Vietnamese, therefore, were surprised at the depth of Tet's psychological impact.

Cooperative Learning Activity

Organize students into groups of five or six and have groups select a former President for whom they would like to organize a media campaign. Suggest they use an American history textbook to find a picture of and personal details about that President and information on major issues of his time.

Then have them work on their media plan. They should note what personal qualities of their candidate they would focus on, which issues they would address, and the kinds of media advertising they would use. Have groups share their plans with the rest of the class.

Independent Practice

L1 Descriptive Writing Have students monitor local television newscasts or local newspapers for a few days. Ask students to note the issues covered in the leading news stories. Then have them write a paragraph answering the following: Based on your findings, what is the community's public agenda? Have students compare their paragraphs.

📁 Interpreting Source Readings Have students complete activity 12 in *Primary and Secondary Source Readings* in the Teacher's Classroom Resources.

PARTICIPATING IN GOVERNMENT

👓 Have examples of printed election materials on hand when students study this feature. Examples of televised debates, speeches, and paid political announcements can be found in "Modern Presidential Campaigns," Volume IV, *Social Studies Videos*.

📁 Have students complete activity 12 in *Participating in Government* in the Teacher's Classroom Resources.

CONNECTIONS

Language

Another horse-racing term used in election coverage is *dark horse*, referring to a candidate about whom little is known or who wins unexpectedly. The first use of this term probably came in the novel *The Young Duke* (1831) by British statesman Benjamin Disraeli. The phrase was in common use in the United States by the end of the 1860s.

---

every night on the evening news shocked American viewers. Walter Cronkite, the highly respected anchor of CBS television news at that time, concluded the war could not be won. He also reasoned that United States military assessments could not be believed. CBS news switched directions in its war coverage. The network's reports on the war became much more critical of United States strategy.

The other major networks soon followed. In addition, many major mass circulation magazines that had strongly supported the war also changed their minds after Tet.

Media's coverage of the war soon had a dramatic effect. Journalist David Halberstam analyzed the impact of Walter Cronkite's decision. He explained:

> *Cronkite's reporting did change the balance; it was the first time in American history a war had been declared over by an anchorman. In Washington, Lyndon Johnson watched and told his press secretary, George Christian, that it was a turning point, that if he had lost Walter Cronkite he had lost Mr. Average Citizen. It solidified his decision not to run again.*
>
> —DAVID HALBERSTAM, *POWERS THAT BE*, 1980

Within six weeks after Tet, people's attitudes toward the war had already begun to change dramatically. The percentage of Americans who approved of President Johnson's handling of the war dropped from 39 to 26. The President's overall approval rating went from 46 to 36 percent. Antiwar protests grew larger. On March 31 President Johnson announced he wanted an end to the war and would not seek another term as President.

Elections and Political Parties

The first televised political advertisements appeared in the 1952 presidential campaign between Dwight Eisenhower and Adlai Stevenson. Since then television has greatly influenced who runs for office, how candidates are nominated, how election campaigns are conducted, and how political parties fit in the election process.

Identifying Candidates Television has influenced the types of candidates who run for office in several ways. First, candidates for major offices must be telegenic—they must project a pleasing appearance and

---

PARTICIPATING IN GOVERNMENT

Becoming an Informed Voter

Your ability to make a wise choice in the voting booth depends on your being well informed about candidates and issues. As an election draws near, the media provide a great deal of information. To prepare yourself to vote, consider the following points:

Laws require television and radio stations to grant equal time to major candidates. Listen to opposing views before deciding who to support. Concentrate on what the candidate says rather than on how the candidate sounds or looks. Keep in mind that paid political announcements are designed to appeal to your emotions. You can understand candidates' views better by watching or listening to interviews and debates.

Newspapers and news magazines often provide more detailed information about a candidate than can broadcast media. Printed materials also allow you to review and compare information by rereading an article about a candidate or an issue.

The League of Women Voters publishes a *Voters' Information Bulletin*. The bulletin provides factual, nonpartisan information about candidates and issues.

Investigating Further

Analyze a recent paid political announcement. What advertising techniques were used? Report your findings to the class.

Special Needs Strategy

Learning Strategy Active learning tasks that involve students' own experience and prior knowledge will help them better understand information. Have students read the information on pages 346–348 concerning the impact of media on elections and political parties. Then ask students to imagine they are managing the election campaign of an unknown candidate. Have them list three characteristics that would make their candidate a winner. Ask them which of these characteristics were exhibited by presidential candidates in elections they remember.

performance on camera. John F. Kennedy and Ronald Reagan were good examples of candidates for the television age. Both were handsome; had good speaking voices; and projected the cool, low-key style that goes over well on television.

Second, television has made it much easier for people who are political unknowns to quickly become serious candidates for major offices. Jimmy Carter had only served one term as governor of Georgia when he ran successfully for the Democratic nomination in 1976. Carter was hardly known outside Georgia; the media kept asking "Jimmy who?" Carter made such skillful use of television, however, that by the time the nominating convention met, he had won enough primary elections to capture the nomination.

Third, television has encouraged celebrities from other fields to enter politics. Actors, astronauts, professional athletes, and television commentators have all run successfully for Congress in recent years. Such people have instant name recognition with voters. They do not have to work their way up through their political party's local and state organizations.

The Presidential Nominating Process The mass media have fundamentally changed nominations for President through **horse-race coverage** of elections. This approach focuses on "winners" and "losers," and "who's ahead," rather than on issues or policy positions. One study of the ABC, CBS, and NBC evening newscasts during the 1988 presidential nominating campaign found that more than one-third of all the stories were horse-race coverage. Only 15 percent of all the stories focused on the issues.

Once the presidential primary elections begin, the media start to narrow the field of candidates. They quickly label candidates "winners" and "losers" and give more coverage to "winners." In the 1976 Democratic race, for example, Jimmy Carter finished second in the Iowa caucuses that were held even before the first primary election. As a result, Carter got 23 times more coverage in *TIME* and *Newsweek*, and 5 times more coverage on network television than his rivals did. When Carter finished first, but only 4 per-

From the Statehouse to the White House
Television helped Bill Clinton, the governor of Arkansas, become identified nationally. **Civics** What other governor used television effectively?

cent ahead of his closest rival in the New Hampshire primary, Carter received 25 times more coverage on network television than his rival did.

In 1980 George Bush also gained credibility with a modest but unexpectedly good showing in the Iowa caucuses as he sought the Republican presidential nomination. Although Bush eventually lost the nomination to Ronald Reagan, Bush's press secretary explained that the media coverage of his good showing gave his campaign an early boost, and "a ride by the press makes a lot of converts."

Early presidential primaries are critically important to a candidate's chances even though the voters in these primaries represent only a small fraction of the national electorate. The media declare a candidate who wins an early primary, even if by a very small margin, a **front-runner**, or early leader. The press largely determines the weight attached to being a front-runner. The label carries great significance, however. It is generally only the front-runners who are able to attract the millions of dollars in loans and campaign contributions as well as the volunteer help needed to succeed in the long, grueling nominating process.

STUDY GUIDE

Themes in Government
Political Processes **How is the presidential nominating process affected by the mass media?**

Critical Thinking Skills
Drawing Conclusions **Why do you think President Reagan**

was such a favorite with the media?

Critical Thinking Activity

Drawing Conclusions Write the following statements on the chalkboard: 1. A majority of Americans say they get most of their news from television. 2. Political candidates make great efforts to get television news coverage of their election cam-

paigns. 3. The use of spot advertising on television by political candidates has increased. Ask students to draw a conclusion from these statements. *(Television plays a major role in political campaigns.)*

L3 **Journalism** Have students work individually or together to create a "magazine supplement" on the role the media played in a recent national, state, or local election. The supplement should consist of at least four pages and include various illustrative materials, such as photographs, maps, charts, and graphs. Have students display their finished magazine supplements on the bulletin board.

Caption Answer
Jimmy Carter

STUDY GUIDE

Theme Answer
Horse-race coverage labels "front-runners," "winners," and "losers," greatly influence the outcome of the nominating process.

Critical Thinking Answer
He was handsome and spoke well. His experience as an actor made him feel comfortable in front of the camera.

Assess

Check for Understanding
Have students complete Section 4 Review on page 348.

Meeting Objectives
Each section objective is tested by the Section Review questions that follow it in parentheses.
• Identify ways that the media affect politics. (2, 3, 4, 5, 7)
• Assess citizens' responsibilities to weigh media coverage of political candidates. (6, 7, 8)

Evaluate

📁 Section 4 Quiz

💡 Testmaker

Reteach

📁 Have students complete activity 12 in *Reteaching Activities* in the Teacher's Classroom Resources.

Enrich

Media specialists called "spin doctors" have become important in political campaigns. Their job is to interpret, or "put a spin on," the news so that it is favorable to the candidate for whom they work. Provide students with headlines on important election issues. Have students put a spin on these headlines favorable to a presidential incumbent or favorable to a presidential challenger.

📁 Have students complete activity 12 in *Enrichment Activities* in the Teacher's Classroom Resources.

Close

Discuss the following: What would election campaigns be like if television had not been developed? What impact would this have on American democracy?

The Portland Genius.

PORTLAND, SEPTEMBER 10, 1856.

E PLURIBUS UNUM.

FOR PRESIDENT,
JOHN C. FREMONT,
of California.

FOR VICE PRESIDENT,
WILLIAM L. DAYTON,
Of New Jersey.

Political Advertising
Throughout United States history, candidates have campaigned using different media. **History What impact has television had on campaigning?**

Campaign Advertising Television has also affected how candidates communicate with the voters. The first candidates in American history did little campaigning; they left such work to political supporters. Andrew Jackson's election started the "torchlight era," in which candidates gave stump speeches, parades, and expensive entertainment for voters and supporters. About 1900, candidates began using advertisements in newspapers and magazines and mass mailings of campaign literature. In 1924 candidates began radio campaigning. Television campaigning began with Eisenhower in 1952.

Candidates today must spend huge sums of money for sophisticated television advertising campaigns. One 30-second commercial in a medium-size market can cost several thousand dollars. Television campaigns use **spot advertising**, the same basic technique that television uses to sell other products. Spot advertisements are brief (30 seconds to 2 minutes), frequent, positive descriptions of the candidate or the candidate's major themes. Advertisements may also present negative images of the opposing candidate.

Political Parties Television has weakened the role of political parties as the key link between politicians and the voters in national politics. It has also made candidates less dependent on their political party organization. Today it is television, rather than the political parties, that provides most of the political news for people interested in politics. Voters can get the information they need to decide how to vote without depending on the party organization. Television also lets candidates appeal directly to the people, bypassing party bosses. Should a candidate do well in the primary elections, the political party has little choice but to nominate him or her even if party leaders do not agree. Finally, television advertising requires so much money that candidates cannot depend solely on their party to provide needed campaign funds. They must approach other donors if they are to run a competitive campaign and win election.

4 SECTION REVIEW

Section Review
The media impact politics by bringing issues to the public and helping to set a public agenda. The media also play an increasingly important role in elections.

Checking for Understanding
Recalling Facts
1. Define selective perception, horse-race coverage, front-runner, spot advertising.
2. Describe how the mass media help set the public agenda in the United States.
3. Specify the media form that is most influential in political socialization.
4. List the ways in which television has influenced the types of candidates who run for office.

Exploring Themes
5. Political Processes Does spot advertising increase support for the United States political system? Support your answer.
6. Civic Responsibility Why does each citizen have a responsibility to look beyond the images of candidates the media present?

Critical Thinking Skills
7. Drawing Conclusions What items do you think should be on the United States public agenda?
8. Synthesizing Information Give three examples to support this statement: "The media's greatest power is in the way they define reality for the American people." Do you agree or disagree with this statement? Explain.

Section 4 Review Answers

1. Definitions of terms appear on pages indicated: **selective perception,** 344; **horse-race coverage,** 347; **front-runner,** 347; **spot advertising,** 348
2. They highlight some issues and ignore others, define some conditions as problems and let other conditions go unnoticed, influence public awareness of problems, and shape public opinion.
3. television

4. Candidates now need to be telegenic. Also, TV has made it easier for political unknowns to quickly become serious contenders for major offices and has encouraged celebrities to enter politics.
5. Answers may include: Yes; spot advertisements do encourage people to believe that change is possible with their vote. No; they only present a slick image of the candidate.

6. Answers may include that citizens need to find out the issues if they are not clearly presented.
7. Answers may include aid to the homeless, health care for the elderly, dealing with the AIDS epidemic, high cost of post-secondary education, the drug problem, and the United States' world role.
8. Answers may include either support or criticism for the media's role, or both.

Corazon Aquino on the Power of the Media

Corazon Aquino became the first woman president of the Philippines in February 1986, succeeding Ferdinand E. Marcos. Marcos, who had governed the Philippines since 1965, won the 1986 election mainly through violence and fraud. Aquino claimed victory through popular vote, and massive public outcry forced Marcos to flee the country.

Aquino had the following to say about the role the media played in the revolution in her country:

Thank you, the media, for the invaluable role you played and continue to play in the transformation of my country. That role was invaluable, for it was the truth that set us free.

The images and events during the elections and the revolution are deeply etched in the memory of our people and give inspiration to the other nations of the world: men and women linked arm to arm guarding the ballot boxes; computer technicians hired by the government to do the official count walking out of the fraudulent tabulation; tens of thousands of men and women, with their children about them, in vigil, half in fear, half in joy, guarding with their bodies the small detachments of rebel soldiers; nuns kneeling in the path of oncoming tanks; a nation rising to a new dignity. These images, and more, chronicled for all the world the courage and pride of a people, their deep faith in the rightness of their cause, the protection of God and the ultimate triumph of democracy.

And so you, the foreign media, have been the companion of my people in its long and painful journey to freedom.

But even as I briefly recount these momentous events, one should recognize an underlying event that they reveal. The reality that you, more than others, should recognize: the liberating virtue of truth and the power of the media to make it happen.

It is a power, it seems, that feeds man's hunger for truth. A hunger that accepts no substitutes, neither promises of material progress nor safe and comforting lies, and will overcome the most intricate and comprehensive web of censorship. Although the Marcos regime effectively controlled the Philippine media, there was never a period when some kind of "alternative press" did not attempt to report the facts and challenge the misinformation published by the government. . . .

Fourteen years of lies in the controlled Philippine press, once the most respected institution in the old Republic, did not dull the appetite for truth or save the dictatorship from it. . . .

We have a long way to go, and it will be a hard climb uphill. I hope that just as you sympathized with us in our hard days of struggle, so you will support us now in our efforts to build a country to match our pride. As you channeled your power to undo a dictatorship, so may you channel it now to help create an enduring democracy. . . .

I ask you to report the truth about the Philippines. . . . Of the truth, which made us free, we obviously have no fear.

—CORAZON AQUINO

> *. . . you, more than others, should recognize: the liberating virtue of truth and the power of the media to make it happen.*

Examining the Reading

Reviewing Facts
1. Cite the role Aquino gives the foreign media in her nation's struggle for independence.
2. State the power that "feeds man's hunger for truth."

Critical Thinking Skills
3. Identifying Central Issues How did the foreign press contribute to the solidarity of the Philippine people?

Focus

Ask students to cite instances in which media coverage of an event has helped shape world opinion.

Teach

Ask: How did Filipinos contribute to the peaceful revolution that brought Aquino to power? *(They protected rebel soldiers, blocked tanks with their bodies, guarded ballot boxes, and so on.)* What role did the world media play in the success of this peaceful revolution? *(Students may suggest that without the focus of world attention, Marcos may have crushed his opposition with force.)*

Assess

Have students complete **Examining the Reading.**

Answers
1. role of companion
2. the power of the media to make things happen
3. by chronicling the solidarity and emotions of the Philippine people

Close

Ask: What evidence is there to suggest that media coverage of this event influenced other people in protests against their governments? *(Students should note that protestors against communist governments in China, Eastern Europe, and the Soviet Union later adopted many of the tactics used in the Philippines.)*

More About Personal Perspectives

The turning point in Corazon Aquino's life came when her husband, an outspoken critic of the Marcos regime, was assassinated in 1983. Her husband's death became the focus of anti-Marcos groups, who, in 1985, began the Cory Aquino for President movement. Aquino agreed to run if one million supporters endorsed her candidacy and Marcos called for an election; her backers collected more than the million signatures. Marcos won the election in 1986, although critics agree it was through intimidation, violence, and fraud; the people swarmed the streets in protest. Less than three weeks after his victory, Marcos fled the Philippines and Aquino became president.

Identifying Terms and Concepts

1. e, 2. c, 3. a, 4. d, 5. b

Reviewing Facts and Ideas

1. executive, legislative, judicial, mass media

2. daily newspaper

3. FCC (Federal Communications Commission)

4. Politicians want the mass media to help them convince the public of their policies; mass media want to critically analyze the decisions and business of the politicians.

5. President

6. Members of Congress are able to stay in touch with their constituents by using the studios to make tapes that are sent to their home states or districts.

7. First Amendment

8. It classifies some information as "secret" and limits press coverage of military actions.

9. political advertising

10. the media

Applying Themes

1. Answers will vary, but may include that the free enterprise system encourages individual media to attract different audiences by offering differing opinions and formats and make their money by doing so.

2. Answers should cite reactions to recent events and include factors such as immediacy, background information gained, and so on.

3. because of their ability to highlight candidates and issues, which in turn influences voter attitudes

4. judicial

5. Answers will vary, but may include that making use of different forms of media can help citizens make well-informed decisions.

12 CHAPTER REVIEW

Summary and Significance

Because the mass media play such a vital role in the daily lives of Americans, it is important to understand the structure of the media and how it influences peoples' thought processes. The media and government have a mutually beneficial relationship that is often antagonistic because of conflicting goals. The courts mediate between the two when necessary. The mass media provide crucial services to the public by providing information and helping to set the public agenda. The duties, responsibilities, and rights of the media will continue to be debated in a democratic society.

Identifying Terms and Concepts

Choose the letter of the correct answer below to complete each sentence.

a. horse-race coverage   d. prior restraint
b. wire service   e. noncommercial
c. equal time doctrine

1. PBS and NPR are examples of _____ television and radio.
2. The _____ requires stations to give the same amount of airtime to major candidates.
3. _____ is based on who is winning a political race rather than the issues.
4. The First Amendment frees the United States media from _____ .
5. A _____ employs reporters internationally to collect news for subscribers.

Reviewing Facts and Ideas

1. List the "four branches" of government.
2. Identify the type of newspaper that has the most impact on government and politics.
3. Name the organization that limits the number of radio and television stations a single company can own.
4. Cite the conflicting goals of politicians and the mass media.
5. State the position of the United States government official who attracts the most media attention.
6. Relate the benefits of congressional recording studios.
7. Identify the amendment that protects the American media.

8. Describe what steps the federal government takes when attempting to control sensitive national security issues.
9. Name the tool used on television during election campaigns that seems to increase support for the American political system.
10. Point out who in recent years has been responsible for picking a front-runner.

Applying Themes

1. Free Enterprise Why is free enterprise a key tool in safeguarding freedom of the press?
2. Global Perspectives How does media coverage shape people's views of world events?
3. Political Processes Why does the media have a major impact on voting and elections in the United States?
4. Checks and Balances What branch of government has the final determination between government officials and mass media?
5. Civic Responsibility Does the media help citizens fulfill their responsibility to be informed about current events? Why or why not?

Critical Thinking Skills

1. Synthesizing Information What two characteristics or features of the mass media have the greatest impact on American government and politics?
2. Drawing Conclusions How could the constant bombardment of media sometimes numb people to actual events and impacts?

Critical Thinking Skills

1. Answers will vary, but may include the variety and availability of mass media, its freedom from government censorship.

2. Answers may include mention of "sensory overload," the media's power to define and interpret reality, overreliance on media as sources of information.

Linking Past and Present

Answers will vary, but students should give examples to support their answers. They may include historical examples or current events.

Linking Past and Present

Americans watch more television today than any other people on earth. Those who lived 100 years ago could not have imagined that such a medium of communication would ever exist. Who could have imagined during the Civil War that the United States would one day fight a war on the other side of the world that Americans at home would watch?

Against the background of technology growing at an amazing rate, is the argument that Americans watch too much television. Many argue that television is responsible for declining IQs as well as a host of other troubles. Should the aim of television be to entertain, to inform, or a combination of both? Explain your answer.

Writing About Government

Descriptive Writing Write an essay in which you describe the role of the mass media in forming your basic ideas about government, politicians, and national and international events. Consider both broadcast and print media.

Reinforcing the Skill

Interpreting Political Cartoons Use what you have learned about interpreting political cartoons to examine the cartoon and answer the questions that follow.

1. What is happening in this picture?
2. What words give clues to the cartoon's meaning?
3. Who are the three figures on the left?
4. Who is the figure on the right?
5. How does his sign differ from those of the other three figures?
6. What attitude do the three figures on the left take toward the figure on the right?
7. What attitude does the figure on the right seem to have toward the figures on the left?
8. What point is the cartoonist making?

Investigating Further

1. **Individual Project** The United States Government Printing Office, or GPO, is the largest multipurpose printing plant in the world. It prints, binds, and distributes publications for the entire federal government. It also sells copies of non-confidential government publications to the general public. The GPO may produce or manage the printing of as many as 2 billion copies of various publications each year, and its sales may be as high as 83 million documents in a single year. A major publication of the GPO is the *Congressional Record*, which is a printed account of the daily events and speeches of members of Congress that is made available to government officials and private citizens alike. Many public libraries act as government depositories and so have copies of several editions of the *Congressional Record* for public use. Call your local public library to find out whether it has any copies of the *Congressional Record*. If it does, visit the library to examine this publication. Try to find a speech by or another reference to your local member of the House of Representatives or a senator from your state.

2. **Cooperative Learning** The mass media have at least some connection to most people's everyday lives. Organize into groups of five or six each. Each group should create a list of the five most important political events they can remember learning about or seeing on television. Compare the lists from each group. Were the listed events national or international? Did the events concern the environment, foreign affairs, local or federal laws or policies, crime, trade, or other topics?

3. environmentalists

4. President Bush

5. While theirs demand bold action to end pollution, his, in small print, says only "seriously consider further study."

6. They do not seem to notice him.

7. He seems to want to fit in.

8. He is saying that President Bush wants to present himself as an environmentalist, but his proposals are too timid.

Investigating Further

1. Examples will vary.

2. Group lists will vary, but students should offer explanations of their choices.

Writing About Government

Answers will vary, but may include exposure to different politicians, presentation of diverse solutions, coverage of events showing how government works, and so on.

Reinforcing the Skill

1. a political demonstration

2. The caption and the messages on the picket signs of the three people on the left tell us that this is an Earth Day demonstration.

CASE STUDY

The Case at a Glance

Who: groups that oppose the government
What: the right to assemble
When: 1917 to the present
Where: United States
Why: fears of subversion

Focus

Have students give examples of times they (or people they know) have exercised their right to freedom of assembly. (*attending a town meeting, marching in support of or against a government policy, and so on*) Ask: Did anyone question your right to assemble?

Tell students that this case study focuses on whether or not an individual has the right to join an organization that the government considers subversive.

Teach

Guided Practice

L1 Making Comparisons Have volunteers summarize each of the Supreme Court cases discussed in the case study. As the cases are summarized, jot down key points on the chalkboard. Then ask: What do the cases have in common? (*Each one advocates the right to assemble even when discussing seditious acts.*) How did the Court rule in each case?

What distinctions did the Court make in the later cases? (*The Court ruled against those individuals who actively advocated violence.*) Why do Americans feel the right of assembly is so important? (*It provides a useful forum for political action.*)

First Amendment: Right To Peaceable Assembly

Powers of Congress

Congress shall make no law . . . abridging the freedom of speech, or of the press, or the right of the people peaceably to assemble, and to petition the Government for a redress of grievances.

—First Amendment, 1791

The Case

" The right of peaceable assembly," Chief Justice Charles Evans Hughes wrote in *De Jonge* v. *Oregon* (1937), "is a right cognate [closely linked] to those of free speech and free press and is equally fundamental." Before that decision, the Supreme Court had ruled that freedom of assembly was designed to enable citizens to petition the government. Therefore, freedom of assembly was tied to the petition process. In the *De Jonge* case, however, the Court extended the right to freely assemble to protect the right of individuals to freedom of association—the right to join political parties, interest groups, clubs, and other organizations.

The question arises, however, does the First Amendment protect an individual's right to join an organization that the government considers subversive? To protect national security, can the government restrict the right of assembly and association?

In *Whitney* v. *California* (1927), the Supreme Court decided that:

The fundamental rights—such as the right of free speech, the right to teach, and the right of assembly may not be abridged or denied. But although the rights of free speech and assembly are fundamental, they are not absolute. Their exercise is subject to their restriction, if the particular restriction proposed is required in order to protect the state from destruction. . . . The necessity which is essential to a valid restriction does not exist unless speech would produce, or is intended to produce, a clear and imminent danger of some substantive evil which the state constitutionally may seek to prevent.

—JUSTICE LOUIS BRANDEIS, 1927

The "clear and present danger" doctrine later became a major issue when the government began to arrest and convict accused subversives, primarily Communist party members.

Background

During World War I, a number of Socialists, Communists, and others who spoke out against the war were convicted under the Espionage Act of 1917 and the Sedition Act of 1918. Then, after the Russian Revolu-

More About the Case

After World War II, many Americans believed that the Soviet Union was trying to spread communism throughout the world. This fear was reinforced when the Canadian government uncovered a Soviet spy ring that had been passing secrets about the development of the atomic bomb to Moscow. Subsequently, the House Un-American Activities Committee disclosed that communist agents had worked in both the Agriculture and Treasury Departments during the 1930s.

In September 1949 Americans learned that the Soviets had detonated their first nuclear device. In February 1950 Klaus Fuchs admitted giving the Soviets information on A-bomb construction while tion in 1917, the federal government restricted the activities of the American Communist party and punished party members as criminals.

Soon state legislatures passed criminal syndicalism laws—laws that made it a crime to call for the violent overthrow of the nation's social, political, and economic systems.

In *Whitney* v. *California* (1927), the Supreme Court reviewed the case of Charlotte Anita Whitney, who in 1919 attended the convention where the Communist Labor party of California was organized. Because the party taught "criminal syndicalism," Whitney was convicted and sentenced for violating California's Syndicalism Act of 1919. The prosecution successfully argued that membership in the party indicated she had committed a crime. The Supreme Court upheld the conviction.

McCarthyism The Soviet Union was the United States' ally against Nazi Germany during World War II. Americans, however, remained deeply suspicious of the Soviet Union's intentions to spread its communist ideology to the United States. After the war, authorities learned that Communists had infiltrated two federal departments during the war. When the Soviets exploded an atomic bomb, the nation learned that a spy ring operating in the United States had provided the Soviet Union with vital atomic secrets. Faced with charges of being soft on Communists, and with a presidential election drawing near, President Harry S Truman ordered a Loyalty Review Board to find and discharge government employees suspected of being security risks.

Many members of Congress, however, believed that the subversives continued to be a threat. In 1950 Congress debated the Internal Security Act, which Truman believed was so broad that it violated individuals' constitutional rights. The President felt compelled to send a message directly to Congress. He told them:

> *L*egislation now pending before Congress is so broad and vague in its terms as to endanger the freedoms of speech, press, and assembly protected by the First Amendment. . . . This kind of legislation is unnecessary, ineffective, and dangerous.
>
> —HARRY S TRUMAN, AUGUST 8, 1950

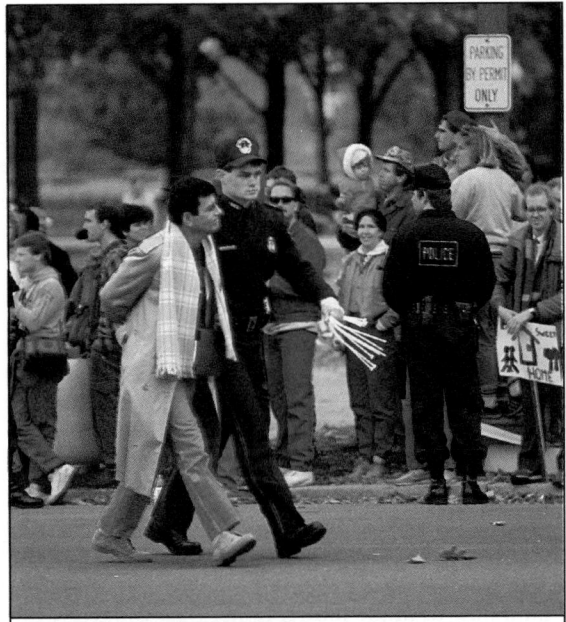

Acting on Personal Beliefs
In Washington, D.C., well-known radio personality Casey Kasem was arrested at a demonstration in support of the homeless.

Anticommunist activities in the United States peaked in the 1950s. A survey taken in the mid-1950s revealed that more than 50 percent of those questioned believed that all known Communists should be imprisoned regardless of their rights.

The Smith Act The Alien Registration Act of 1940, better known as the Smith Act, had called for the registration and fingerprinting of all aliens. More importantly, it was designed as the first peacetime sedition act since 1798. Section 2 of the Smith Act made it:

> *U*nlawful for any person . . . with the intent to cause the overthrow or destruction of any government in the United States, to print, publish, edit, issue, circulate, sell, distribute or publicly display any written or printed matter advocating, advising, or teaching the duty, necessity, desirability, or propriety of overthrowing any government in the United States by force or violence.
>
> —ALIEN REGISTRATION ACT, 1940

L2 History Ask: Why have Americans felt the need to pass legislation to restrict assembly, such as the Espionage Act of 1917, the Sedition Act of 1918, and the Alien Registration Act of 1940? *(They feared that a small group of people could overthrow the government.)* Why do such fears test the right of free assembly? *(Assembly allows people to speak out politically; if we deny those rights to others, we negate our own right to assemble.)*

L3 History Review the events of the Boston Tea Party. Ask how the Court might have looked at the event in light of the Bill of Rights. *(They might have supported the right of assembly but would have condemned the destruction of property.)* Why are certain actions judged subversive in one generation but acceptable in another? Use the events of the civil rights movement and the antiwar protests in the 1960s as examples of such shifts in belief. What accounts for these shifts? *(Fears and anxieties about certain groups change.)*

working on the Manhattan Project. A few months later, Ethel and Julius Rosenberg were charged with passing nuclear secrets to the Soviet Union. They were found guilty and executed in 1953.

In 1948 a former communist, Whittaker Chambers, accused Alger Hiss, a former State Department official, of spying for the Soviet Union during the late 1930s. Because the statute of limitations had run out, Hiss could not be charged with treason. He was convicted of perjury, however, and served more than three years in jail.

CASE STUDY

Independent Practice

L1 Informative Writing Have students research civil rights groups who have used the right to assemble to their political advantage and write a report on what the civil rights movement accomplished using this tactic.

L2 Informative Writing Have students write a report that compares the Alien Registration Act of 1940 with the Espionage Act of 1917 and the Sedition Act of 1918. Have them explain how these acts were related to the right to assemble.

L3 Law Have students investigate local laws that govern assembly. They should find out how to get needed permits, how long it takes for permits to be approved, and what restrictions, if any, are put on groups assembling. Have them speculate why communities pass laws regarding assembly. (*In most cases the laws are intended to control crowds and only rarely do they infringe on people exercising political rights.*)

Assess

Have students complete **Examining the Case.**

Close

Have students review the response of the Court to the cases involving the right to assemble. Ask: What social or political conditions can lead to restrictions on free assembly? (*Students may suggest wars, national security threats, perceived threats of unpopular groups in society, and so on.*)

The government first used the Smith Act in 1943 when the authorities arrested and later convicted the leaders of a socialist group headquartered in Minneapolis. The court of appeals upheld the conviction, ruling that Congress had decided the leaders of the socialist group had posed a "clear and present danger" in advocating the overthrow of the government. The Supreme Court refused to review the case. Five years later the Justice Department arrested and prosecuted 12 leaders of the American Communist party. The Supreme Court in *Dennis* v. *United States* (1951) upheld the convictions.

Later cases, however, modified the findings of *Dennis* v. *United States*. In *Yates* v. *United States* (1957), 14 convictions under the Smith Act were overturned or dismissed. The Court ruled that just advocating a belief in an action was not enough. What had to be shown was "that those to whom the advocacy is addressed must be urged to do something, now or in the future, rather than to merely believe in something."

Two later cases, *Scales* v. *United States* (1961) and *Noto* v. *United States* (1961), specifically dealt with the question of membership in the Communist party. In the *Scales* decision the Supreme Court upheld the constitutionality of the membership clause of the Smith Act. In the *Noto* case, the result was just the opposite. Communist beliefs were present but the actual planning on how to put them into action was never proved. Instead the Court ruled:

> We held in Yates, and we reiterate now, that the mere abstract teaching of Communist theory, including the teaching or moral propriety or even moral necessity for a resort to force and violence is not the same as preparing a group for violent action and steeling it to such action.
>
> —*Noto* v. *United States*, 1961

The Red Scare declined and prosecutions under the Smith Act ended as the nation entered the 1960s. The question of limits on the right of freedom of assembly, however, did not end. During the Vietnam War, the government investigated several groups such as Students for a Democratic Society that openly opposed the war. Although the Supreme Court heard no cases, protesters were jailed on many occasions. The Persian Gulf War brought new groups of protesters. The government closely scrutinized groups such as the National Coalition to Stop U.S. Intervention in the Middle East and the National African American Network Against U.S. Intervention in the Gulf. Because American victory was swift, the protests ended without incident.

Significance

Throughout the 1950s most Americans were convinced that Communists threatened national security. A loyalty oath that was required for labor union officials and many public employees challenged people's right of free assembly and association. The oath required people to deny membership in listed subversive organizations, mainly communist and left-wing organizations.

Cases challenging loyalty oaths failed. Several years later, during the 1960s, however, the Supreme Court reconsidered its earlier decisions. In 1967 the Court ruled in the landmark case of *Keyishian* v. *Board of Regents* that loyalty oaths required for teachers were unconstitutional.

To date, the Communist party and antiwar groups have been the only major organizations singled out for close scrutiny. Whether this will remain the case in the event of a real or a perceived threat to the nation's security in the future remains to be seen.

Examining the Case

Reviewing Facts

1. Explain the reasoning behind the statement that the "rights of free speech and assembly are not absolute."
2. Identify the cases that established or used the doctrine of "clear and present danger."
3. Describe how many Americans viewed the Soviet Union after World War II.

Critical Thinking Skills

4. Understanding Cause and Effect What were the causes of McCarthyism?
5. Drawing Conclusions What do you think might happen to First Amendment rights in a future national emergency? Why?

Examining the Case Answers

1. They may be restricted to protect the government from subversion.
2. *Whitney* v. *California, Dennis* v. *United States*
3. as a threat to the national security of the United States
4. Americans feared that the Soviet Union was trying to spread its ideology and that communists had infiltrated the United States government.
5. Answers may vary, but students might suggest that the government will try to restrict freedoms in order to protect itself from subversion.

Chapter 8
Political Parties

In a democracy the people rule, but the voice and will of the individual citizen can easily be lost in a nation as large and diverse as the United States. One way that citizens ensure that government knows their views is for them to organize into groups that wield political power.

One example of such a group is the political party. A **political party** is a group of people with broad common interests who organize to win elections, control government, and thereby influence government policies. The United States has a two-party system, although minor parties have often formed over a single issue.

In order to succeed, a political party must have a dedicated core of people who are willing to work hard for it. Both the Republicans and the Democrats employ small paid staffs in permanent party offices. Between elections these employees carry out the day-to-day business operations of the party. At campaign time, however, political parties use volunteers to perform a wide range of tasks. To win elections a party must first offer candidates and conduct campaigns. Individuals may seek nomination for public office in one of four ways: (1) caucus; (2) nominating convention; (3) primary election; or (4) petition. A **caucus** is a private meeting of party leaders. A **nominating convention** is an official public meeting of a party to choose candidates. The method most commonly used today to nominate candidates, however, is the **direct primary**, an election in which party members select people to run in the general election. In the **petition** method, a person announces his or her candidacy and files petitions a specified number of voters have signed. These petitions request that the person's name be placed on the ballot.

Chapter 9
Elections and Voting

The most visible election in the United States is the presidential election that is held every four years. A variety of factors, such as strategic planning, careful organization, and sound financing, must be combined to run a presidential campaign.

During a presidential campaign, candidates try to convince the voters that they have the solution to the nation's many problems. Four major factors, however, influence voter decisions: (1) personal background of the voter; (2) degree of voter loyalty to one of the political parties; (3) issues of the campaign; and (4) voters' image of the candidates.

Voting by United States citizens is absolutely vital to the success of American democracy. Through their votes, Americans have the power to select more than 500,000 government officials at all levels of government. Nevertheless, many Americans do not choose to exercise their right to vote and stay away from the polls on Election Day.

Chapter 10
Interest Groups

An **interest group** is a group of people who share common policy interests or goals and organize to influence the government. Most interest groups use a variety of methods to try to influence public policy. These methods include personal contact with lawmakers, letter writing, and advertising. Because personal contact is the best way to influence policy, most interest groups employ people to work in Washington, D.C., and meet with lawmakers or other government leaders. This process of direct contact is called **lobbying** because of the practice of approaching officials in the outer room or lobby of a capitol.

Interest groups also provide a large percentage of the funds used in candidates' election campaigns. Today most of these funds come from **political action committees** (PACs), or organizations specifically designed to collect money and provide financial support for a political candidate. The federal government regulates the activities of PACs through the Federal Election Commission (FEC) and Supreme Court decisions.

Chapter 11
Public Opinion

Most Americans have opinions or preferences about many matters that affect their lives. These range from opinions about the best baseball players

---

Classroom Resources for Unit 3 Digest

 Unit Digest Transparencies, Unit 3   📁 Participating in Government, Unit 3

Use the Unit Digest to introduce, review, reteach, or condense specific chapters or the entire unit. The Unit Digest is enhanced by the corresponding transparencies and activities in the Teacher's Classroom Resources.

Focus

Write the following headings on the chalkboard: *Political Parties, Elections, Interest Groups, Public Opinion, Mass Media.* Ask students to suggest what role each plays in the American political process. Have students review their suggestions as they study Unit 3 Digest.

Teach

L1 Recognizing Trends Mention that when asked to give their political affiliation, most Americans identify themselves as "Democrat," "Republican," or "Independent." Then provide students with the following statistics on political affiliation in the United States.

1972	Rep. 28%	1984	Rep. 31%
	Dem. 43%		Dem. 40%
	Ind. 29%		Ind. 29%
1976	Rep. 23%	1988	Rep. 30%
	Dem. 47%		Dem. 42%
	Ind. 30%		Ind. 28%
1980	Rep. 24%	1992	Rep. 29%
	Dem. 46%		Dem. 38%
	Ind. 30%		Ind. 33%

Source: Gallup Poll

Have students use these statistics to construct a bar or line graph. Then ask students to write a brief description of the trend of party affiliation over the last 20 years. (*The balance of party affiliation has remained relatively stable. However, since 1980 the Democrats have lost followers to the Republicans and Independents.*)

LEP

Interpreting Visuals Display transparency 3 from the *Unit Digest Transparencies* in the Teacher's Classroom Resources and use the accompanying teaching strategy, student activity, and student test to discuss the methods of influencing government.

L3 Making Inferences Ask students to discuss what role a candidate's image plays in the electoral process. Then have them suggest how the development of television campaigning has changed this role. Finally, ask students to write a paragraph on whether or not this change has had a negative impact on the electoral process. Suggest that they illustrate their paragraphs with incidents from recent elections.

Assess

Check for Understanding

Have students complete **Synthesizing the Unit.**

Close

Remind students that the title of this unit is *Influencing Government.* Then ask students to consider the following:

Given the topics explored in this unit, what other titles might you choose? *(Linking People and Government, Connecting People to their Government, The Citizen's Role in Government, and so on)*

to favorite television programs. Few such opinions, however, have much effect on government. Yet one form of opinion, **public opinion**, has an enormous influence on government. Public opinion includes the ideas and attitudes a significant number of Americans hold about government and political issues.

Although public opinion can be measured in many ways, the most accurate is the scientific poll. Scientific polling involves three basic steps: (1) selecting a sample of the group to be questioned; (2) presenting carefully worded questions to the individuals in the sample; and (3) interpreting the results.

Public opinion influences public policy, what government chooses to do or not do about some problem in society. Social scientists use three terms to describe the qualities of public opinion: direction, intensity, and stability. Public opinions that display all three qualities are much more likely to influence government and public policy than opinions that do not. In effect, **direction** shows whether public opinion is generally positive or negative on a specific issue. **Intensity** refers to the strength of people's opinions about a particular issue or topic. **Stability** refers to the likelihood that public opinion will change in direction or intensity.

Chapter 12
The Mass Media

The **mass media**—television, radio, magazines, and newspapers—influence American government and politics, but government officials and the mass media often have an uneasy relationship. Politicians want to use the mass media to help them reach their goals, such as getting reelected and convincing the public that their policies are worthwhile. Politicians also want the media to pass on their messages just as they present them. The mass media want not only to inform the public about government and current events, but also to critically analyze events and expose wrongdoing.

The mass media of many nations are an integral part of the government. Yet American media are probably the freest in the world. The First Amendment protects them, and private individuals own them. The mass media, however, are not totally free of government regulation.

In the United States, the First Amendment means that print media are free from **prior restraint**, or government censorship of information before it is published or broadcast. Over the years the Supreme Court has struck down attempts to give government this power. These decisions mean that editors and reporters have complete freedom to decide what goes in or stays out of their publications. If an individual or the government does not like what is going to be published, the only remedy is to sue the publisher after the story is published.

The federal government has more power to regulate the broadcast media than to regulate the print media, largely because of two reasons. First, broadcasters use a public resource, the airwaves. Second, a limited number of radio and television airwaves exist. As a result, the government argues, broadcasters should be regulated like other public utilities such as the electric company or water company. The Federal Communications Commission is the government agency with authority to regulate broadcasts.

The mass media have become part of United States daily political life. In reality, how much does the media really influence Americans? This question is not easy to answer. Many different factors influence people's knowledge, attitudes, and behavior toward politics. Experts agree, however, that the mass media have a very great impact on defining the public agenda and on voting and elections.

Synthesizing the Unit

Recalling Facts
1. Define political party, caucus, nominating convention, direct primary, petition, interest group, lobbying, political action committee, public opinion, direction, intensity, stability, mass media, prior restraint.
2. List the four factors that influence voter decisions.

Exploring Themes
3. Civic Responsibility Why is it essential in a democracy that citizens exercise their right to vote?
4. Public Policy How does public opinion influence public policy?

Critical Thinking Skills
5. Making Comparisons How are political parties and interest groups different? How are they alike?
6. Drawing Conclusions Which method of choosing candidates is the most democratic? Explain your answer.

Synthesizing the Unit Answers

1. Definitions of terms appear on the pages indicated: **political party,** 355; **caucus,** 355; **nominating convention,** 355; **direct primary,** 355; **petition,** 355; **interest group,** 355; **lobbying,** 355; **political action committee,** 355; **public opinion,** 356; **direction,** 356; **intensity,** 356; **stability,** 356; **mass media,** 356; **prior restraint,** 356

2. personal background of voter; degree of voter loyalty to political party; issues of campaign; voters' image of candidates
3. Through their votes, Americans have the power to select more than 500,000 officials at all levels of government, thus ensuring rule by the people.
4. The direction, intensity, and stability of public opinion

are all factors that determine how much influence it will have on public policy.
5. Unlike political parties, interest groups do not put up candidates to win elections. Both, however, try to influence government policies.
6. Answers will vary, but most students will suggest the direct primary because it involves citizens directly.

The Legislative Branch

UNIT
4

Chapter 13
The Organization of Congress

Chapter 14
The Powers of Congress

Chapter 15
Congress at Work

Introduce

Unit Objectives

After studying this unit, students should be able to:
- Describe the organization, powers, and functions of the legislative branch of the federal government.
- Explain the function of Congress in the system of checks and balances.

Unit Overview

Unit 4 is designed to help students understand the workings of the United States Congress.

Chapter 13 discusses the organizational structure, support systems, and leadership systems of Congress.

Chapter 14 explores the powers of Congress. It also analyzes the relationship between Congress and the executive branch.

Chapter 15 discusses how Congress makes laws and explores the political factors involved in the passage of legislation.

4
UNIT DIGEST

Use the Unit Digest on pages 437–438 to introduce, review, reteach, or condense the information in this unit.

Introducing the Unit

Have students imagine a country the size of the United States that is a direct democracy—all matters are decided by a ballot of all eligible voters. Ask students to discuss the problems involved in getting a piece of legislation enacted. Close the discussion by mentioning that in Unit 4 students will learn that the United States is a representative democracy—representatives elected by voters make legislative decisions.

Unit Project

Have students work cooperatively to create a "Who's Who" handbook of members of Congress from their state. Suggest that for each representative and senator students include some background information, length of service, committee and subcommittee membership, and major accomplishments while in office. Such information may be obtained from *The Almanac of American Politics* by Michael Barone and Grant Ujifusa. Students from states with less than 12 representatives and senators might want to make their handbook a historical Who's Who, focusing on leading members of Congress of the past. Have students display their handbooks for other government classes.

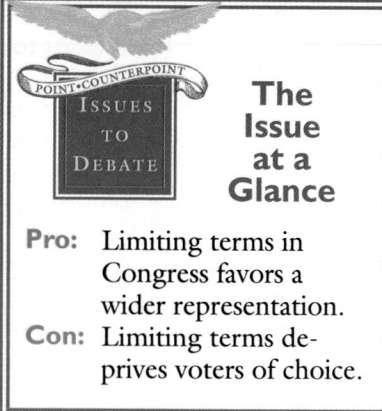

The Issue at a Glance

Pro: Limiting terms in Congress favors a wider representation.

Con: Limiting terms deprives voters of choice.

Focus

Have students state the qualifications for serving in Congress as set forth in the Constitution. Then ask if they can think of any other qualifications that should be applied to holding office in Congress. For example, should lawmakers have certain legal or technical training? Why?

Tell students that this debate focuses on whether the length of time lawmakers serve should be restricted.

Teach

Guided Practice

Point out that the issue of limiting terms of office in Congress has been debated for 200 years. Tell students that limiting the President's term was debated at the Constitutional Convention and was rejected. Not until the passage of the Twenty-second Amendment in 1951 was the President limited to 2 terms.

Have students summarize in their own words arguments for each side. (*pro: The seniority system concentrates power in the hands of a few lawmakers and the districts they represent; democracy requires wider distribution of power; con: Limiting terms reduces lawmakers' incentive to serve those they represent and deprives voters of a choice.*)

ISSUES TO DEBATE

Should We Limit Congressional Terms?

Prior to the 1992 election, incumbent members of Congress were almost certain to win reelection. In a typical election year, such as 1988, the relection rate was 98 percent. Incumbents benefited by name recognition, huge campaign war chests of money donated by special interests, and their ability to deliver on promises to return federal dollars to their home districts. These advantages, however, gave rise to an increasingly powerful movement to limit congressional terms. From national media to local grassrooots organizations, the power of incumbency was challenged. As *TIME* magazine reported:

Voters choices are . . . reduced because so many potential opponents do not see much point in mounting a challenge. The advantages of incumbency [currently holding office] are virtually insurmountable; voluminous free mailings, easy fund raising, large staffs, access to the press. That power creates a vicious circle: incumbents are so entrenched that few challengers of any caliber will run against them.
—NANCY GIBBS, *TIME,* NOVEMBER 19, 1990

What was the solution? Increasingly, the public began to hear about limiting members of Congress to 12 years in office. What are the arguments for and against a constitutional amendment limiting congressional terms in office?

Pro

As early as 1978, Senator Dennis DeConcini of Arizona had proposed such an amendment. In an address to his colleagues in the Senate, Senator DeConcini stated:

The imperative to organize each Chamber in a reasonable and responsible fashion has over the decades evolved into what is now known as the seniority system. Under this rule, responsibilities within the committee structure of the two Houses are allocated on the basis of length of tenure in office. . . .

Each of us, at one time or another, has witnessed or been involved in an election in which [the seniority system] was a central issue. Incumbents have appealed for votes on the grounds that their seniority insured that more of the Federal dollar would be spent in their State or district than would otherwise be true. Or, that seniority would allow the incumbent to pass legislation that a new Member could not conceivably be expected to shepherd through the complex legislative process. And in most instances, these are not vacuous or idle boasts; the nature of the seniority system makes them true. The question at issue is whether it should be thus; whether . . . this is the best democracy can offer. . . .

The theory of democracy demands that as many members of society as possible should be given the opportunity to serve. In some of the early Greek experiments with democracy, community service was demanded; in some cases, public offices were routinely rotated.

Because of the size and complexity of American society, we have moved away from direct democracy to representative democracy. Even though it is impossible for all citizens to participate in public service, we ought to insure that as many individuals as possible have the opportunity for such service. Limiting the number of years any single individual can serve would be an important step in that direction.
—SENATOR DENNIS DECONCINI, 1978

Although Senator DeConcini's amendment failed, the 12-year limitation caught the public's

More About Issues to Debate

During the debates over ratifying the Constitution, many political leaders stated that it needed additional safeguards against excessive national power. To satisfy this outcry, James Madison introduced a series of proposals for amendments to the Constitution during the first session of Congress. Congress chose 12 of these to propose as official

amendments. In addition to the 10 amendments that we now call the Bill of Rights, Madison also called for amendments that would specify the size of the House of Representatives, the compensation for members of Congress, and the length of time they would serve.

After careful consideration, Congress passed 12

attention. One poll indicated that almost 70 percent favored the idea. Supporters called for reform and argued that

A Congress invigorated by frequent infusions of new blood would be a more responsive, more democratic, more varied place. So would a Congress whose majority regularly changed from one party to the other, which a term limit would unquestionably promote....

—Hendrik Hertzberg, "Twelve Is Enough,"
The New Republic, May 14, 1990

Con

Following Senator DeConcini's proposed amendment, sides formed immediately. Political scientist Eric M. Uslaner responded to the term-limit idea:

Telling me how many terms my senator (representative) may serve, in essence, tells me for whom I cannot vote in at least some elections. I can understand why convicted felons, the criminally insane, those under a certain age, or noncitizens might be barred from holding high public office. But it is far more puzzling to me that I might not be able to vote for a person simply because he or she has held that office before....

When Senator DeConcini argues against the evils of the full-time legislature, he cites the many things that incumbents do to keep themselves in office, including pressing for legislation that would directly benefit the districts they represent, working to pass legislation so that they can claim credit for such activity in their next reelection bid, and solving a multitude of personal problems for constituents. Just how devious are these incumbents?

—Eric M. Uslaner, "A Government as Good
as Its People," *Points of View*, 1980

In a similar vein, in 1991 an article in *The Progressive* titled "The Twelve-Year Itch" commented:

What's wrong with the fetching notion of a twelve-year limit? It's the wrong cure for the wrong disease. First of all, entrenched incumbency isn't the real problem. About two-thirds of the U.S. Congress has turned over in the last dozen years, and there's nothing to indicate that the recent arrivals under the Capitol Dome are a significant improvement over their time-worn predecessors....

Second, and more important, to legislate limits on incumbency is to undermine democracy by depriving voters of a choice. It may be a wrong choice, a pernicious or even a catastrophic choice. But in a democracy, voters have a right to be wrong—even to return tired or corrupt

Longest Serving Representative
Democrat Jamie Whitten represented Mississippi in the House for more than 50 years but retired in 1994.

incumbents to office again and again.

—"The Twelve-Year Itch," *The Progressive*,
February, 1991

The Debate Continues

By 1995, 22 states had already set term limits for their representatives. In November 1994, however, the spotlight on this issue shifted to the Supreme Court. Opponents of term limits challenged the state laws on constitutional grounds. Even if the Court struck down the state laws, however, supporters of term limits had hope. A Republican Congress pledged to enact term limits in its first session. "The pressure will be on," said Cleta Mitchell of the Term Limits Legal Institute.

Examining the Issue

Recalling Facts

1. State **DeConcini's** position on limiting congressional terms.
2. Identify **Eric M. Uslaner.**

Critical Thinking Skills

3. Evaluating Information **Contact your senator or representative to learn his or her attitude toward limiting congressional terms. Then write a paragraph evaluating the Congress member's position.**

Ask: What changes do advocates of term limitations want to make in Congress? *(possible responses: to make it more representative, more democratic; to increase the opportunities to serve)* In what ways might limiting terms change the legislative process? *(would change the seniority system, changing leadership of powerful committees; new lawmakers might reflect changes in public demands)* Do students agree with *The Progressive's* view that limiting terms deprives voters of choice? Discuss students' opinions.

Independent Practice

Have each student design and carry out a survey to determine how their classmates and adults they know feel about limiting terms for members of Congress. Have students present their findings in a written report.

Assess

Have students complete **Examining the Issue.**

Answers

1. Terms should be limited in order to allow more members of society to participate in public service.
2. a political scientist who opposes limiting terms
3. Students' paragraphs will vary but should accurately explain the position.

Close

Take an informal survey of class members. Do they support limiting terms for lawmakers? What evidence do they use to support their opinions?

---

of Madison's amendments to the states for approval. State legislatures rejected amendments concerning salaries and term limits for members of Congress. The size of the House and members' pay would better be worked out as laws, they said.

Proposals to limit the terms of lawmakers are supported by groups who wish to unseat powerful members of Congress. Others favor limiting terms so that a wider range of candidates might seek office. New officeholders, they say, will bring fresh insight and expertise to the legislative process.

Chapter Organizer

Objectives	Special Feature Pages	Supplemental Materials
Section 1 Membership of the House and Senate *pp. 362–367* 1. Identify the key differences in membership of the House and Senate. 2. Explain the "one person, one vote" rule. 3. Define gerrymandering and discuss government attempts to limit the practice.	Point/Counterpoint: Should We Limit Congressional Terms? pp. 358–359 Focus on Freedom: *Wesberry* v. *Sanders* (1964) p. 366	Guided Reading Activities Reproducible Lesson Plans Cooperative Learning Activities 13 Interpreting Political Cartoons 37, 39 Supreme Court Case Studies 25, 31 Section 1 Quiz Government Themes Transparencies 41 Testmaker The Living Constitution SAT Practice Tests Writer's Guidebook
Section 2 Organization for Lawmaking *pp. 368–374* 1. Contrast the rules and organization of the House of Representatives with those of the Senate. 2. Analyze the role of filibusters in Senate debates.	Multicultural Heritage: The Concept of Bicameralism p. 369 Global Connection: Comparing Governments: Legislative Powers p. 371	Guided Reading Activities Reproducible Lesson Plans Enrichment Activities 13 Section 2 Quiz Testmaker Chapter Transparencies 13 SAT Practice Tests Writer's Guidebook
Section 3 Congressional Committees *pp. 375–379* 1. Classify the various kinds of committees that help Congress do its work. 2. Analyze the impact of the Legislative Reorganization Act of 1970. 3. Explain how party representation is divided on each congressional committee.	Critical Thinking Skills: Making Generalizations p. 379	Guided Reading Activities Reproducible Lesson Plans Primary and Secondary Source Readings 13 Section 3 Quiz Testmaker Government Themes Transparencies 10 Skill Reinforcement Activities 13 SAT Practice Tests Writer's Guidebook
Section 4 Congressional Staff and Support Agencies *pp. 380–385* 1. Recognize the contributions that congressional staffs and supporting agencies make to members of Congress. 2. Analyze why congressional staff has grown so rapidly. 3. Evaluate the role that congressional staffs take in writing legislation.	Participating in Government: Running for Local Office p. 382 Personal Perspectives: Margaret Chase Smith on Campaigning for the Senate p. 385	Guided Reading Activities Reproducible Lesson Plans Participating in Government 13 Interpreting Political Cartoons 36 Reteaching Activities 13 Section 4 Quiz Chapter 13 Tests Testmaker Audio Cassettes (English and Spanish) Limited English Proficiency Activities 13 SAT Practice Tests Writer's Guidebook

If time does not permit teaching this chapter, assign the Chapter 13 summary in the Unit 4 Digest on pages 437–438.

Key To Ability Levels

Teaching strategies have been coded for varying learning styles and abilities.

L1   Level 1 activities are **basic** activities and should be within the ability range of all students.

L2   Level 2 activities are **average** activities and should be within the ability range of the average to above-average student.

L3   Level 3 activities are **challenging** activities designed for the ability range of above-average students.

LEP   These activities should be within the ability range of **Limited English Proficiency** students.

Multicultural Activities

As soon as the 1990 Census results were tabulated, battles began in state legislatures across the nation to redraw state and congressional districting maps. Hispanic leaders hoped that such states as California, Texas, and Florida, where Latino populations grew greatly in the 1980s, would see large gains in Latino lawmakers. In July 1991 Andy Hernandez, president of the Southwest Voter Registration Education Project, said: "Redistricting is the best chance for Hispanics to protect their rights, participate in government, and make democracy work for them." Have students review recent election results to see what impact redistricting has had on Hispanic political representation.

Have students use the most recent *Almanac of American Politics* to create profiles of minority members of Congress. This resource provides such information as the lawmaker's prior experience, ratings by national liberal and conservative groups, how the lawmaker voted on key bills in the most recent session of Congress, and statistics on the racial and ethnic makeup of the lawmaker's election district. Organize the class into small groups. Have each prepare profiles of three lawmakers. Then as a class decide what generalizations, if any, can be made about minority politicians. Were most minority lawmakers elected from districts with large minority populations? Were most rated liberal or conservative? Were there any bills most supported or opposed? Were there any similarities in prior experiences?

Chapter Resources

Readings for the Student

Bernotas, Bob. *The Federal Government: How It Works.* Chelsea House, 1990.

Bernstein, Richard B., and Jerome Agel. *Into the Third Century.* Walker and Company, 1989.

Cohen, William. *Roll Call: One Year in the United States Senate.* Simon and Schuster, 1981.

Jigsaw Politics: Shaping the House After the 1990 Census. Congressional Quarterly, 1990.

Malbin, Michael. *Unelected Representatives: Congressional Staff and the Future of Representative Government.* Basic Books, 1980.

Power in Congress: Who Has It, How They Got It, How They Use It. Congressional Quarterly, 1987.

Readings for the Teacher

Barone, Michael, and Grant Ujifusa. *The Almanac of American Politics 1992.* National Journal, 1992.

Fox, Harrison W., Jr., and Susan W. Hammond. *Congressional Staffs.* Free Press, 1977.

Jacobson, Gary. *The Politics of Congressional Elections.* Little, Brown, 1983.

Smith, Steven S., and Christopher Deering. *Committees in Congress.* Congressional Quarterly, 1984.

Multimedia

Videocassettes and Films

An Act of Congress. Learning Corporation of America. (film, 58 minutes—in 2 parts)

The Committee: Taxation with Representation. York Associates. (v/c, 58 minutes)

The Congress. (*The Power Game* series). Philip Burton Productions, Inc. and Maryland Public Television. (v/c, 60 minutes)

The House of Representatives. New York Times/Teaching Resources Films. (v/c, 20 minutes)

The Senate. New York Times/Teaching Resources Films. (v/c, 18 minutes)

Software

United States Constitution, Disk 2—*The Preamble and Article I;* Disk 3—*The Legislative Branch.* Tutorsystems (BLS, Inc.). (Apple disks, second and third of a 5-part package). Students complete tutorial programs covering the Preamble, overview of the Legislative Branch, and Article I, Sections 1–6.

United States Constitution Tutor. Micro Learn (division of Micro-Lab). (Apple, IBM, Commodore 64 disks). Students prepare for a test by reviewing United States government as well as facts and concepts about the Constitution.

Introduce

Chapter Overview

Chapter 13, one of three chapters on Congress, discusses the formal organizational structure of Congress, the support system on which it relies, and the leadership system of each house.

Section 1 discusses the structure of the House and Senate and qualifications for membership in each.

Section 2 explains how the organizational structure of the House and Senate differ to enable them to carry out their work of making laws.

Section 3 classifies congressional committees and explains their purpose and makeup.

Section 4 focuses on the contributions of congressional staffs and supporting agencies to Congress.

Chapter 13 Themes

Write the following chapter themes on the chalkboard:

Growth of Democracy
Constitutional Interpretations
Checks and Balances
Political Processes
Federalism

Ask students to use the themes to speculate about topics that will be covered in this chapter. Urge students to look for examples that illustrate each theme as they read the chapter.

Powers of the Congress
Congress Convenes
Running Time :56
Side Two, Chapter 24

The Organization of Congress

CHAPTER

13

Members of Congress, depicted here meeting at the Old House of Representatives in Samuel F.B. Morse's painting, are elected directly by the voters they represent.

About the Chapter Opener

Teaching With Illustrations Samuel F. B. Morse was an inventor who received the patent for the first successful electric telegraph in the United States. He also invented the Morse code. In addition to being an inventor, Morse was a painter. In 1822 he finished the painting that depicted the House of Representatives in session. The painting included recognizable portraits of 80 members. Morse, together with 30 other American artists, founded the National Academy of Design in 1826. Ask students how the House of Representatives today differs from the House of Representatives painted by Morse.

Chapter Preview

Overview

The House of Representatives and the Senate are organized to enable Congress to make laws for the United States.

Objectives

After studying this chapter, you should be able to:

1. **Compare** the qualifications for and membership of the House of Representatives and the Senate.
2. **Describe** ways in which the organization of Congress enables each house to pass laws.
3. **Relate** the roles of committees and committee leadership in moving legislation through Congress.
4. **Explain** the duties of congressional staffs.

Themes in Government

This chapter emphasizes the following government themes:

- **Growth of Democracy** After each census Congress determines how the seats in the House are to be divided among the states. Section 1.
- **Constitutional Interpretations** The Supreme Court has ruled that congressional districts must be equal in population. Section 1.
- **Checks and Balances** The House and Senate committees have differing powers. Sections 2 and 3.
- **Political Processes** The House and Senate have complex rules to guide them. Sections 2, 3, and 4.
- **Federalism** Members of Congress stay in close contact with the voters in their states. Section 4.

Critical Thinking Skills

This chapter emphasizes the following critical thinking skills:

- Making Inferences
- Formulating Questions
- Making Comparisons
- Recognizing Bias
- Demonstrating Reasoned Judgment
- Evaluating Information

Introducing the Chapter

Ask students to name their district's representative and their senators. Ask if the class members have the same representatives or different ones. Why? (*Depending on the boundaries of the school system, students may all reside in the same congressional district, or they may live in a number of different districts.*) Then point out that congressional membership is one aspect of the organization of Congress discussed in this chapter.

Chapter Project

Have students find out what bills are pending in the House and Senate. This information can be found in mailings to students' family homes or in the *Congressional Record* in the library. Have them choose one House bill and one Senate bill to research. They may write to senators and representatives to get information such as the origin of each bill, its purpose, the legislator's stand, and so on. After students complete the chapter, have them present their findings in oral reports and discuss why these bills are important to their state or district.

Linking Past and Present
In the early days of Congress, members from the same geographic region tended to live together in the same boardinghouses, take their meals together, and spend their leisure hours together. Not surprisingly, the political outlook of members of these boardinghouse "fraternities" was quite similar. Studies show that they voted as a bloc more than 70 percent of the time. The boardinghouse fraternity, some political scientists suggest, was the predecessor of the modern congressional caucuses.

Setting the Scene Congress (the House originally) was and still *is* the only branch of federal government directly elected by the people. Not all of the delegates to the Constitutional Convention believed in the ability of average people to govern themselves, however. The structure of the American government was established in spite of delegates such as Elbridge Gerry, who said, "The evils we experience flow from the excess of democracy," and Roger Sherman, who believed that the people "should have as little to do as may be about the Government. They want information and are constantly liable to be misled."

Focus

Bell Ringer

While attendance is being taken, ask students to choose one person they would like to represent them in Congress. Have them list the qualities that would make him or her a good representative.

Motivating Activity

Discuss students' Bell Ringer responses and write them on the chalkboard. When you have listed enough responses to create a "profile," have students copy them into their notebooks. Ask students to compare their lists with the actual qualifications for office noted in this section.

Vocabulary Precheck

Write the vocabulary terms for this section on the chalkboard. Ask students to use those that they know in sentences. **LEP**

Caption Answer
on January 3 of odd-numbered years

Teach

Guided Practice

L1 **Making a Chart** Work with students to create a class chart to compare the membership in both houses of Congress. Use *House* and *Senate* as horizontal heads and *Number of Members, Qualifications, Term of Office,* and *Constituents* as vertical heads. **LEP**

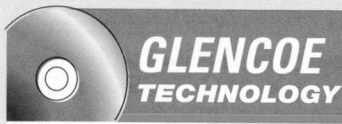
GLENCOE
TECHNOLOGY

Focus on Government
Video 22
Electronic Field Trip:
The Capitol
Running Time: 4:55
Videodisc 2, Chap. 22
VHS Tape 2, Begins 1:49

Video 26
Making Connections:
The 1st and 103rd Congresses
Running Time: 1:42
Videodisc 2, Chap. 26
VHS Tape 2, Begins 16:43

Membership of the House and Senate

The Constitution gave the legislative branch the power to make laws. The Founders indicated the importance of the lawmaking power by describing Congress—the Senate and the House of Representatives—in Article I. They intended Congress to be the central institution of American government and gave it more powers than any other branch of government. As James Madison said, Congress is "the First Branch of the Government."

Today Congress continues to play a central role in formulating policies for the nation. Congress initiates and approves laws dealing with everything from health care to tax changes to energy conservation.

Congressional Sessions

Each term of Congress starts on January 3 of odd-numbered years and lasts for two years. For example, the 103rd Congress began its term in January 1993; the 104th met in January 1995.

Each term of Congress is divided into two **sessions,** or meetings. A session lasts one year and includes breaks for holidays and vacations. Until about 1933 Congress remained in session for only four to six months each year. Because of an ever-increasing workload, today a session of Congress often lasts from January until November or December.

Congress remains in session until its members vote to adjourn. Neither the House nor the Senate may adjourn for more than three days without the approval of the other house. If Congress is adjourned, the President may call it back for a special session.

Membership of the House

With its 435 members, the House of Representatives is the larger body of Congress. The Constitution does not fix the number of representatives in the

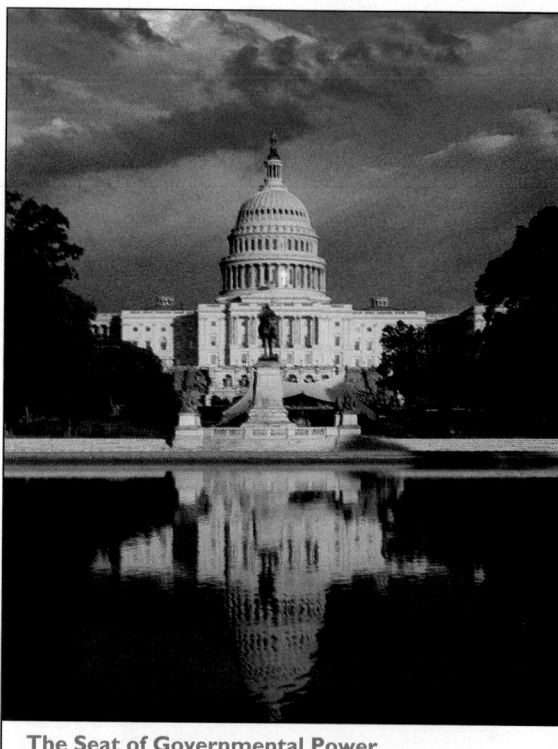

The Seat of Governmental Power
Congress exercises its legislative power at the Capitol. **Civics** **When does a term of Congress begin?**

SECTION PREVIEW

Objectives
After studying this section, you should be able to:
- Identify the key differences in membership of the House and Senate.
- Explain the "one person, one vote" rule.

- Define gerrymandering and discuss government attempts to limit the practice.

Key Terms and Concepts
session, census, apportionment, redistrict, gerrymander, at-large, censure, incumbent

Themes in Government
- Growth of Democracy
- Constitutional Interpretations

Critical Thinking Skills
- Making Inferences
- Formulating Questions

Classroom Resources for Section 1

- Guided Reading Activities
- Reproducible Lesson Plans
- Cooperative Learning Activities 13
- Interpreting Political Cartoons 37, 39
- Supreme Court Case Studies 25, 31
- Section 1 Quiz

- Government Themes Transparencies 41
- Testmaker
- The Living Constitution
- SAT Practice Tests
- Writer's Guidebook

House. It simply states that the number of House seats must be apportioned, or divided, among the states on the basis of population. Each state is entitled to at least one seat in the House, no matter how small its population.

Qualifications The Constitution sets the qualifications for election to the House of Representatives. Representatives must be at least 25 years old, citizens of the United States for at least 7 years, and legal residents of the state that elects them. Traditionally, representatives also live in the district they represent.

Term of Office Members of the House of Representatives are elected for 2-year terms. Elections are held in November of even-numbered years, for example, 1990, 1992, and 1994. Representatives begin their term of office on January 3 following the November election. This means that every two years all 435 members of the House must run for reelection. It also means that the House reorganizes itself every 2 years. Because more than 90 percent of all representatives are reelected, however, there is great continuity in the House. If a representative dies or resigns before the end of the term of office, the governor of the state he or she represented must call a special election to fill the vacancy.

Representation and Apportionment In order to assign representation according to population, the Census Bureau takes a national **census,** or population count, every 10 years. The first census was taken in 1790 and the latest in 1990. The population of each state determines the number of representatives to which each is entitled in a process called **apportionment.** States whose population increases less rapidly than others or whose population decreases may lose representatives, while states whose population grows faster may be entitled to more representatives.

Originally the House had only 64 members. Over the years, as the population of the nation grew, the number of representatives increased. After the 1810 census, the House had 144 members. In the 1912 election, the number of representatives reached 435. Concerned that the increasing size of the House would make it unmanageable, Congress passed a law in 1929 limiting the House to 435 representatives. Now each census determines how those 435 seats will be divided among the 50 states as shown on the map on pages 892-93.

Congressional Redistricting After the states find out their apportioned representation for the 10-year period, each state legislature sets up congressional districts—one for each representative. Representatives are elected from these congressional districts. If a state is entitled to only one representative, it has one congressional district. The state legislature draws the boundary lines for each congressional election district. The process of setting up new district lines after apportionment is **redistricting.**

Over the years some state legislatures have abused the redistricting power. They have done so in 2 ways. First, they created congressional districts of very unequal populations. During the early 1960s, for example, there were 13 states in which the largest district had twice the population of the smallest district. In these states a person's vote in the largest congressional districts had only half the value of a person's vote in the smallest districts.

In a series of decisions during the 1960s, the Supreme Court ended these practices. In the landmark case of *Baker* v. *Carr* (1962), the Court held that federal courts could decide conflicts over drawing district boundaries. Two years later, in *Wesberry* v. *Sanders* (1964), the Court ruled that the Constitution clearly intended that a vote in one congressional district was to be worth as much as a vote in another district. This principle has come to be known as the "one person, one vote" rule. As a result, today each congressional district contains about 575,000 people.

Gerrymandering Legislatures have abused their power to divide the state into congressional districts by gerrymandering. **Gerrymandering** means that the political party that has the majority in a state legislature draws a district's boundaries to gain an advan-

Chapter 13, Section 1
Lesson Plan, pages 362–367

L2 Geography Provide students with a current district apportionment map of your state. Such maps can often be obtained through a representative or the League of Women Voters. Ask students to note the number of districts in their state and differences in those districts. *(size and shape of districts)* Next, have them find their representative's district. Then discuss what should be similar about each district, regardless of geographical size. *(roughly equal populations)*

Interpreting Visuals Display transparency 41 from *Government Themes Transparencies* in the Teacher's Classroom Resources and use the accompanying teaching strategy and student activity to teach congressional redistricting.

STUDY GUIDE

Theme Answer
Number of representatives each state elects to the House is based on population; if census shows population changes, states will gain or lose representatives accordingly. It has no effect on Senate as representation to that body is not based on population.

Critical Thinking Answer
Districts are oddly shaped and not compact and have been gerrymandered to ensure safe districts for a particular party or group of voters.

STUDY GUIDE

Themes in Government
Growth of Democracy **What is the effect of the national census every ten years on the Congress of the United States?**

Critical Thinking Skills
Making Inferences Redistricting allows a state legislature to draw up new congressional district boundaries.

What do you think was the purpose of the unusual boundaries on the map on page 364?

CHAPTER 13: THE ORGANIZATION OF CONGRESS 363

Background

The 1990 census counted 248.7 million Americans, although the Census Bureau admits to missing 5.3 million people, most of them believed to be minorities. The census gave California 7 additional seats in the House of Representatives for an all-time high of 52. Florida gained 4 and Texas 3, while New York lost 3. Several other states gained or lost 1 to 3 seats. Federal funding based on population is also affected by new census totals.

L3 Growth of Democracy
Have students work in small groups to discuss one of the following topics: gerrymandering, increase in congressional salaries, increase of women and minorities in Congress, tendency of incumbents to win reelection. Ask the groups to discuss whether the issues covered by their topics lead to a growth of or a decrease in democracy. Have the groups report their conclusions to the rest of the class.

Independent Practice

L1 Vocabulary Make copies of the following and distribute it to the class:

Write a definition for each term. Then use each term in a sentence that relates to the section content.
  a. census
  b. apportionment
  c. censure
  d. redistricting
  e. incumbent

Have students compare their papers. **LEP**

Map Study Answer
every 10 years, after each census

---

tage in elections. Gerrymandering often results in district boundaries that have very irregular shapes. The term gerrymandering can be traced back to Elbridge Gerry, an early Democratic-Republican governor of Massachusetts. Gerry had signed a redistricting plan that gave his party a big political advantage over the Federalists. To a map of one particularly irregular district, Gilbert Stuart, an artist, added a head, wings, and claws, making it look like a salamander. A newspaper editor published the map as a cartoon and labeled it a "Gerrymander." Federalists popularized the term.

Packing and cracking are ways to gerrymander. Packing a district means drawing the lines so they include as many of the opposing party's voters as possible. Crowding the opposition's voters into one district makes the remaining districts safe for the majority party's candidates. Cracking means dividing an opponent's voters into other districts. This division weakens the opponent's voter base.

The Supreme Court has ruled that congressional districts must be compact and contiguous, or physically adjoining. This requirement, plus the one-person, one-vote ruling, has cut down on some of the worst examples of gerrymandering. Nevertheless, the competitive struggle of the two-party system continues to fuel the practice of gerrymandering.

Membership of the Senate

According to the Constitution, the Senate "shall be composed of two senators from each state." Thus, each state is represented equally. Today's Senate includes 100 members—2 from each of the 50 states.

Qualifications The Constitution provides that senators must be at least 30 years old, citizens of the United States for 9 years before election, and legal residents of the state they represent. All the voters of each state elect senators **at-large,** or statewide.

North Carolina Congressional Districts

Source: North Carolina Assembly

⊕ Map Study
This North Carolina redistricting plan was challenged in the federal courts.
How often do state legislatures redraw congressional districts?

Term of Office Elections for the Senate, like those for the House, are held in November of even-numbered years. Senators also begin their terms on January 3 after the election held the previous November.

The Constitution provided for continuity in the Senate by giving senators six-year terms and by providing that only one-third of the senators would run for reelection every two years. Actually, the Senate has even more continuity than the Framers planned because most senators win reelection.

If a senator dies or resigns before the end of the term, the state legislature may authorize the governor to appoint someone to fill the vacancy until the next election. The governor may also call a special election to fill the seat.

Salary and Benefits The Senate and the House set their own salaries. In 1789 salaries for both houses were $6 per day. Low pay in the early years deterred some people from running for Congress. Congress has voted itself periodic salary increases. In 1991 it voted for a pay hike of $23,000, explaining that the increase would be accompanied by a prohibition on honoraria—money paid for speeches.

Meanwhile, a constitutional amendment affecting legislative salaries was making its way through ratification. Originally proposed by James Madison in 1789, the Twenty-seventh Amendment was finally ratified by the required 38 states when Michigan cast the deciding vote on May 7, 1992. The amendment prohibits a congressional salary increase from taking

364 UNIT 4: THE LEGISLATIVE BRANCH

Cooperative Learning Activity

Organize the class into groups of six, each to represent a group of concerned citizens who wish to redefine the qualifications for congressional membership. Have each group decide which of the current qualifications they wish to retain and/or dispose of and which new ones they wish to add. Have group reporters present their groups' guidelines and the reasons for their decisions. After each group presents, come to a class consensus on qualifications for congressional membership.

☐ Have students complete activity 13 in *Cooperative Learning Activities* in the Teacher's Classroom Resources.

effect until after an intervening election.

Almost immediately a group of plaintiffs, including some legislators, used the new amendment to challenge a congressional pay hike. Congress had voted in favor of a cost-of-living adjustment to raise salaries to $133,600 in January, 1993. A United States District Court Judge ruled that:

Automatic annual adjustments to congressional salaries meet both the language and the spirit of the 27th Amendment…. One way to maintain high-quality government is to provide our elected officials with a living wage that automatically changes to reflect changed economic conditions.
— JUDGE STANLEY SPORKIN, 1992

In addition to their salaries, members of Congress enjoy a number of benefits. These include office space, stationery, postage (called the "franking privilege") for official business, low-cost life insurance, a medical clinic, and a gymnasium.

Members also receive large allowances to pay for their office staff and assistants, trips home, telephones, telegrams, and newsletters. All members are entitled to an income tax deduction to help maintain two residences, one in their home state and one in Washington, D.C. Moreover, when they retire, senators and representatives may be eligible for pensions of up to $50,000 a year for life.

Privileges of Members The Constitution provides members of Congress certain privileges to protect them while carrying out their legislative duties. They are free from arrest "in all cases except treason, felony, and breach of the peace," when they are attending Congress or on their way to or from Congress. In addition, members of Congress cannot be sued for anything they say during congressional sessions. This privilege does not extend to what members may say outside of Congress. In *Hutchinson* v. *Proxmire* (1979), the Supreme Court ruled that members of Congress may be sued for libel for statements they make in any of their news releases or newsletters.

The Senate and the House both may judge members' qualifications and decide whether to seat them. Each house may refuse to seat an elected member by a majority vote. Each house may also "punish its own members for disorderly behavior" by a majority vote and expel a legislator by a two-thirds vote. Only the most serious offenses such as treason or accepting bribes are grounds for expulsion. Members who are guilty of lesser offenses may be censured. **Censure** is a vote of formal disapproval of a member's actions.

The Members of Congress

Congress includes 535 voting members—100 Senators and 435 Representatives. In addition, there are four delegates—one each from the District of Columbia, Guam, American Samoa, and the Virgin Islands—and one resident commissioner from Puerto Rico, all of whom cannot vote but do attend sessions.

Characteristics Nearly half the members of Congress are lawyers. A large number of members also come from business, banking, and education. Why are there so many lawyers? Because lawyers by profession deal with laws, it is logical for them to serve as legislators. Also, members who are lawyers make important contacts in Congress that they can use to help their law careers should they leave their elected office.

Senators and representatives have been typically white, middle-aged males. In 1993 the average age of members of Congress was more than 52. Slowly Congress has begun to reflect the racial, ethnic, and gender diversity of the general population. The 103rd House of Representatives included 38 African Americans, 7 Asian Americans, 47 women, and 17 Hispanics.

Reelection to Congress Membership in Congress has changed very slowly because officeholders seldom lose reelection. One representative put it simply: "All

Special Needs Strategy

Reading Comprehension Students with reading comprehension difficulties can understand new information by relying on a framework of known information. In this section on the organization of Congress, students should call upon their knowledge of Congress, even if it is sketchy. Before they read the section, have students explain what they know about Congress. Ask if they have seen televised sessions of Congress. Prompt them by asking Who? What? Where? When? Why? and How? questions.

📁 **Interpreting Political Cartoons** Have students complete activities 37 and 39 in *Interpreting Political Cartoons* in the Teacher's Classroom Resources.

L2 Political Cartoons Have students skim the text to locate and examine political cartoons. Then have them draw their own editorial cartoons using material from the section. For example: a satire of an incumbent trying to protect a bloated campaign chest, or a white male member of Congress being challenged by African American and Hispanic women running for office. Display selected cartoons on the bulletin board.

STUDY GUIDE

Theme Answer
to provide stability and continuity; staggered elections provide smoother transitions when new senators are elected

Critical Thinking Answer
Possible responses: Why do they need the raise? How will the raise be funded? What perks are they giving up in return for the raise? What other sources of income do they have, and are these going to be controlled?

GLENCOE TECHNOLOGY

Focus on Government
Video 23
Lecture Launcher:
The Organization of Congress
Running Time: 4:26
Videodisc 2, Chap. 23
VHS Tape 2, Begins 6:46

Originally several states elected House members at-large, or to represent the state as a whole. In 1842 Congress passed a law requiring each state to divide into congressional districts. Laws passed in 1872 and 1901 required that these districts have equal populations and be of compact shape. However, these laws were generally ignored until the 1960s.

Answers

1. The Fifth Congressional District had two to three times as many voters as other districts in Georgia.

2. Justice Black said the Constitutional Convention established that the principle of the Great Compromise called for equal representation of people in the House.

3. Incumbents could lose their own districts if these changes were made.

Assess

Check for Understanding

Have students complete Section 1 Review on page 367.

Meeting Objectives

Each section objective is tested by the Section Review questions that follow it in parentheses.

• Identify the key differences in membership of the House and Senate. (2, 7)
• Explain the "one person, one vote" rule. (5)
• Define gerrymandering and discuss government attempts to limit the practice. (6)

members of Congress have one primary interest—in being reelected." There have been a few exceptions. Gordon Humphrey of New Hampshire spent two terms in the Senate, then kept his promise to resign, announcing in 1989, "I do not want to spend 18 years in Congress. It becomes a career at that point and I don't believe people should make a career of Congress." One senator seemed ready to quit near the end of his first term, complaining:

I don't like this town. I don't like the whole atmosphere. There's too much money, too much influence, too much phoniness. And I just don't like it. Period.

—WARREN RUDMAN, 1985

Rudman changed his mind, however. In 1986 after Congress approved a radical new procedure for bal-

WESBERRY v. SANDERS (1964)

Until the 1960s the Supreme Court and Congress had refused to interfere with each state's method of apportioning representation. Then in Baker v. Carr (1962), the Supreme Court ruled that citizens had the right to challenge apportionment of their state legislature. Two years later in Reynolds v. Sims, the Court ruled that the equal protection clause of the Fourteenth Amendment required that the seats in both houses of state legislatures be apportioned on a population basis. In Wesberry v. Sanders in 1964, the Court applied apportionment rulings to congressional districts. Justice Hugo H. Black wrote the majority opinion.

The 1931 Georgia apportionment grossly discriminates against voters in the Fifth Congressional District. A single Congressman represents from two to three times as many Fifth District voters as are represented by each of the congressmen from the other Georgia congressional districts. The apportionment statute thus contracts the value of some votes and expands that of others. If the Federal Constitution intends that when qualified voters elect members of Congress each vote be given as much weight as any other vote, then this statute cannot stand.

We hold that, construed in its historical context, the command of Article I, Section 2, that Representatives be chosen "by the People of the several States" means that as nearly as is practicable one man's vote in a congressional election is to be worth as much as another's.

. . .To say that a vote is worth more in one district than in another would not only run counter to our fundamental ideas of democratic government, it would cast aside the principle of a House of Representatives elected "by the People," a principle tenaciously fought for and established at the Constitutional Convention. . . .

It would defeat the principle solemnly embodied in the Great Compromise—equal

representation in the House of equal numbers of people—for us to hold that, within the States, legislatures may draw the lines of congressional districts in such a way as to give some voters a greater voice in choosing a Congressman than others. . . .

While it may not be possible to draw congressional districts with mathematical precision, there is no excuse for ignoring our Constitution's plain objective of making equal representation for equal numbers of people the fundamental goal for the House of Representatives. That is the high standard of justice and common sense which the Founders set for us.

—JUSTICE HUGO H. BLACK, 1964

Examining the Document

Reviewing Facts

1. Describe the unequal representation that existed under the 1931 Georgia apportionment statute.
2. Demonstrate that Justice Black appealed to constitutional principles in writing the majority opinion in this case.

Critical Thinking Skills

3. Expressing Problems Clearly What considerations might have made state legislators reluctant to enact broad changes in apportionment?

Critical Thinking Activity

Formulating Questions Have students write what questions would have to be answered to determine if state legislatures have abused the redistricting power. *(How many representatives does the state have based on the latest census? Are the districts* *almost equal in population? What do each district's boundaries look like? Are the districts compact and contiguous?)* Have volunteers present their questions to the class.

Profile of the 104th Congress*

		House	Senate
Party	Democrats	203	46
	Republicans	231	54
	Other	1	0
Average Age		51	58
Sex	Men	387	92
	Women	46	8
Race and Ethnic Background	Whites	376	96
	African Americans	38	1
	Hispanics	17	0
	Asian/Pacific Islanders	4	2
	Native Americans	0	1
Education	College degree	90%	93%
	Law degree	35%	57%
Average Length of Service		8 yrs.	11 yrs.

*Source: Congressional
Research Service*
**members' party affiliation as of May 1, 1995*

☑ **Chart Study**
The average length of service in Congress is about 11 years. **What is the total number of Democrats and Republicans in both houses of Congress?**

ancing the federal budget that he helped sponsor, he ran again and won. It is that kind of success and the power of the office that makes most members of Congress want to stay in Washington.

Between 1945 and 1990 about 90 percent of all **incumbents,** or those members already in office, won reelection. In some elections, many seats went un-

challenged because opponents knew that they would have little to no chance of winning.

As one analyst said, winning an election to Congress for most members is like removing olives from a bottle—"after the first one, the rest come easy." Why are incumbents so successful? First, incumbents found it easier to raise campaign funds. Incumbents outspent challengers in one election $390,000 to $100,000 per race. Political Action Committees (PACs), provided substantial campaign funds, usually supporting incumbents. Second, incumbents often represent districts that have been gerrymandered in their party's favor. Third, incumbents are better known to voters, who may have seen them on television, or read about them in newspapers. Finally, incumbents use their position and office staff to help solve problems for voters.

In the 1990s several factors worked together to boost the chances of challengers in congressional races. First came a growing wave of criticism against the entrenched power that seemed to accompany lengthy terms in office. Then the public targeted government as an institution that had to change. In 1992 the voters chose a new Democratic President and 38 new members of Congress. In 1994 the swelling tide against incumbents resulted in the biggest turnabout in Congress in 50 years, placing Republicans in control of both houses for the first time since 1954. Powerful long-term Senators and Representatives lost seats to more than 90 newcomers. Almost half of these freshman members had never held an elected office before.

1 SECTION REVIEW

Section Summary
The 100-member Senate and the 435-member House of Representatives comprise the Congress of the United States.

Checking For Understanding
Recalling Facts
1. Define session, census, apportionment, redistrict, gerrymander, at-large, censure, incumbent.
2. Compare the qualifications for representatives and senators.
3. Explain why the number of representatives has not increased since 1912.
4. Specify the advantages that incumbents have over challengers for election to Congress.

Exploring Themes
5. Growth of Democracy What led to the "one person, one vote" ruling of the Supreme Court?
6. Constitutional Interpretations How has the Supreme Court attempted to limit the effects of gerrymandering?

Critical Thinking Skills
7. Making Inferences Members of Congress spend part of their time working to be reelected. Which house has a greater percentage of time remaining for legislative work? Why?
8. Formulating Questions What questions would have to be answered in order to determine whether congressional salaries today are fair compared to those of the past?

Chart Study Answer
249 Democrats, 285 Republicans

Evaluate

📁 Section 1 Quiz

💻 Testmaker

Reteach

Have students list the characteristics of Congress that have remained constant from the time of the Constitution and those that have changed.

Enrich

Have students create a profile of a House delegation that would match their state's demographics. Have them compare their profiles to the backgrounds of the state's actual delegation. What conclusions can they draw?

📁 Have students complete cases 25 *(Baker v. Carr)* and 31 *(Wesberry v. Sanders)* in *Supreme Court Case Studies* in the Teacher's Classroom Resources.

Close

Have students read the quote by Warren Rudman on page 366. Ask them to speculate on why so many representatives seek reelection, given the negative feelings expressed in this quote.

Section 1 Review Answers

1. Definitions of terms appear on pages indicated: **session,** 362; **census,** 363; **apportionment,** 363; **redistrict,** 363; **gerrymander,** 363; **at-large,** 364; **censure,** 365; **incumbent,** 367

2. House: at least 25 years old, United States citizen for at least 7 years, legal resident of state from which elected. Senate: at least 30 years old, citizen for at least 9 years, legal resident of state he or she represents

3. Concerned that the increasing size of the House would make it unable to carry out its work, Congress passed a law in 1929 stabilizing House membership.

4. often represent districts that have been gerrymandered in their party's favor, have name recognition, use their position and office staff to help solve problems for voters, find it easier to raise campaign funds

5. States had redistricted without trying to make districts equal in population.

6. The Supreme Court has ruled that congressional districts must be compact and contiguous. It also issued the "one-person, one-vote" ruling.

7. The Senate, because senators serve longer terms and do not have to run for reelection as often.

8. How has the cost of living changed? How much longer do members of Congress have to be in session now? What other increased duties and responsibilities do members have? How do members' salaries compare with those of other professions today and in the past?

Focus

Bell Ringer

Write the following question on the chalkboard for students to answer in writing while attendance is being taken:

What is meant by the saying, "The camel is an animal that must have been created by a committee"?

Motivating Activity

Discuss students' Bell Ringer answers. Ask students to think of groups or committees of which they have been members. What general rules are followed in meetings of such groups? How are decisions made? What informal processes play a part in committee decision making? What role do compromise and give-and-take play?

Vocabulary Precheck

Call on students to read aloud the definitions of this section's key terms and concepts from the Glossary. Then have volunteers use each term or concept in a sentence. **LEP**

Linking Past and Present
Organized debate in groups from student councils to the Congress is based on rules centuries old. Called parliamentary procedure, the rules come from the early practices of the British Parliament.

Organization for Lawmaking

The main task of each house of Congress is the same—to make laws. Because the House and Senate differ in many ways, each house has organized itself to carry out its work of making the laws. Complex rules and a structure of leadership enable Congress to carry out its lawmaking duties.

House and Senate Rules

Article I, Section 5, of the Constitution says: "Each House may determine the Rules of its Proceedings." Thomas Jefferson compiled the first parliamentary manual for the Senate when he was Vice President. He emphasized the importance of rules:

> *It is much more material that there be a rule to go by, than what the rule is; that there may be a uniformity of proceeding in business not subject to the caprice [whims] of the Speaker or captiousness [criticisms] of the members.*
>
> —THOMAS JEFFERSON, 1797

Complex Rules The Senate and the House each print their rules every 2 years. House rules for a recent Congress filled more than 650 pages. In contrast, the Senate spelled out its rules in 90 pages. In addition, each chamber has scores of precedents based on past rulings that serve as a guide to conducting business.

House rules are generally aimed at defining the actions an individual representative can take. In the Senate, the rules are more flexible and designed to make certain all senators have maximum freedom to express their ideas. For example, the Senate usually allows unlimited debate on proposed legislation, whereas the House limits representatives to speaking for five minutes or less during a debate.

With fewer rules, the Senate has a more informal atmosphere. Senators may debate a proposal on and off for weeks or even months. In contrast, the complex rules in the House require that legislation move quickly once it reaches the floor. House debates rarely last more than one day. Moreover, leaders of the House of Representatives have more power than leaders in the Senate. For example, the rules of the House allow its leaders to make key decisions about legislative work without consulting other House members.

Differences in Committees Committees do most of the work of Congress. In the House, committee work is more important than in the Senate. Because the House is so large, representatives generally do not make a practice of expressing their positions on the floor, where they have only limited time to speak. In the committees, however, representatives have more influence, and they have the time to study and shape bills.

In addition, representatives tend to specialize in a few issues that are important to the people in the districts they represent. For example, Major R. Owens, a representative from Brooklyn, New York, is the only trained librarian in Congress. He emphasizes the importance of libraries in promoting literacy. As an African American, Owens also supports funding for black colleges and aid for underprivileged students. He explains, "We need more role models who will open new possibilities for those who have been excluded from the dreams that others take for granted."

SECTION PREVIEW

Objectives
After studying this section, you should be able to:
- Contrast the rules and organization of the House of Representatives with those of the Senate.

- Analyze the role of filibusters in Senate debates.

Key Terms and Concepts
constituent, bill, calendar, quorum, filibuster, cloture, majority leader, whip, pro tempore

Themes in Government
- Checks and Balances
- Political Processes

Critical Thinking Skills
- Making Comparisons
- Recognizing Bias

---

368 UNIT 4: THE LEGISLATIVE BRANCH

Classroom Resources for Section 2

📁 Guided Reading Activities
📁 Reproducible Lesson Plans
📁 Enrichment Activities 13
📁 Section 2 Quiz

📇 Testmaker
🖊 Chapter Transparencies 13
SAT Practice Tests
Writer's Guidebook

The Concept of Bicameralism

In the waning years of the nineteenth century, political scientist and future President of the United States, Woodrow Wilson, spoke to an audience and outlined his views of the American government.

Our Government, founded one hundred years ago, was no type of an experiment in advanced democracy, as we allowed Europe and even ourselves to suppose; it was simply an adaption of English constitutional government.

—WOODROW WILSON

One aspect of the United States' English heritage is bicameralism. The concept of bicameralism—a two-house legislature—originated in England and came with the early English colonists to North America.

Bicameralism emerged in England's Parliament. During the 1200s the Great Council that included English nobles and bishops advised the monarch. Knights and elected representatives from towns and regions also met with the Great Council. In the 1300s the elected members and the nobility and bishops began to meet separately, and Parliament became a two-house legislature that included the House of Lords and the House of Commons. Slowly, the Commons gained strength; first by winning the right to discuss tax laws, and later by assuming the power to introduce bills.

After a civil war and the execution of Charles I, Parliament gained control of the government. Then in 1660 Parliament restored the monarchy. By the 1700s nations of the Western world admired and envied Great Britain for its democracy and stability. It was the shining example of the political theory of a balanced government.

"The pure forms of government," noted historian Bernard Bailyn, "were monarchy, the rule of one; aristocracy, the rule of the few; and democracy, the rule of many or of all." He continued,

All three forms in the course of history had degenerated repeatedly into their evil counterparts: tyranny, oligarchy, and . . . mob rule. . . . But some success . . . could be achieved by mixing elements of these pure forms . . .

House of Commons
The British Parliament is divided into two houses, the House of Lords and the more powerful House of Commons, as depicted by Thomas Rowlandson.

The value of such a balance . . . came to characterize the working of the English constitution. English public institutions . . . fitted very well the pattern of mixed government: an element of monarchy in the hereditary crown; an element of aristocracy in the House of Lords; and an element of democracy in the House of Commons.

—BERNARD BAILYN

Following the Declaration of Independence, most states retained their bicameral legislatures. Although abandoned under the Articles of Confederation, bicameralism reemerged in the Constitution with the establishment of Congress.

Examining Our Multicultural Heritage

Reviewing Facts
1. Explain how the theory of a balanced government foresees a government free of tyranny or mob rule.
2. Describe the nature of a bicameral legislature.

Critical Thinking Skills
3. Evaluating Information Do you think a monarchy inevitably leads to tyranny or a democracy to mob rule? Explain the reasons for your answers.

More About Our Multicultural Heritage

Over time the House of Commons became the more powerful of the two houses of Parliament. Its powers came originally from its control of government finances. The powers of the House of Lords have been limited, for the most part, to ceremonial functions since 1911. Membership in the House of Lords is largely an inherited right, although few of the nobility eligible to sit in the House of Lords do so. The House of Commons consists of 651 elected members representing England, Scotland, Wales, and Northern Ireland.

Teach

Guided Practice

L1 Contrasting Ideas To contrast the rule structure of the House and Senate, draw a two-column chart on the chalkboard and label the columns *House* and *Senate*. Complete the chart with the students' answers to the following questions: What is the size of the Senate? the House? Which has more complex rules? which simpler? Which is formal? which informal? Then have students write two main idea sentences, one to describe the rule structure of the House and one of the Senate. **LEP**

L2 Interpreting Primary Sources Have students reread the quotes by former Speaker Jim Wright on page 371 and the former Senate leader on page 372. Hold a class discussion on how these statements illustrate a major difference between the House and Senate.

Caption Answer

by the House Rules Committee

STUDY GUIDE

Theme Answer
Representatives are elected from smaller districts and they must be reelected every two years.

Critical Thinking Answer
Committee work is more important in the House because more work is done by committees; much more specialization by representatives because they focus on specific areas in their committee work. Senators spend more time on debate in full session than on committee work; knowledge more generalized.

Senators, who represent entire states, are expected to know something about and deal with the many issues—from national defense to social issues to farming—that interest the voters in their states. Senators handle issues of special interest to them in the committees they serve on, but they also deal with many other issues on the floor, where there is plenty of time for debate.

Finally, because House members are elected from smaller districts, more of their time is devoted to serving the interests of their **constituents,** or the people that they represent. John J. Duncan, Jr., newly elected to Congress, said:

> *I* have a firm belief we have too many laws on the books now . . . . I've made it pretty clear I believe constituent service is most important and is where a freshman can be most effective.
> —JOHN J. DUNCAN, JR., 1988

Importance of Party Affiliation Many procedures in Congress are organized around the political party affiliation of members. In both the House and Senate, the Republicans sit on the right side of the chamber, the Democrats on the left. Even the Senate's private restaurant has one room for Republicans and another for Democrats. More importantly, in each house the party with the larger number of members, the majority party, selects the leaders of that body and controls the flow of legislative work.

Lawmaking in the House

To a visitor the floor of the House of Representatives may seem totally disorganized. Some representatives talk in small groups or read newspapers. Others constantly walk in and out of the chamber. Most representatives are not even on the floor, because they are in committee meetings, talking with voters, or taking care of other business. Representatives reach the floor quickly, however, when it is time for debate or a vote on proposed bills.

Usually, the House starts its floor sessions at noon. Buzzers ring in members' offices in the House office buildings, committee rooms, and in the Capitol, calling representatives. The House is normally in session from Monday through Friday. Mondays are for routine work. Not much is done on Friday because many representatives leave to go to their home districts over the weekend. Thus, most of the House's important work is done from Tuesday through Thursday.

ONE HUNDRED SECOND CONGRESS

FIRST SESSION | CONVENED JANUARY 3, 1991

CALENDARS

OF THE UNITED STATES
HOUSE OF REPRESENTATIVES
—AND—
HISTORY OF LEGISLATION

LEGISLATIVE DAY 153   CALENDAR DAY 154

Friday, January 3, 1992

HOUSE MEETS AT 11:55 A.M.

From Committee to Calendar
After clearing committee, bills are placed on one of five House calendars for consideration. **Political Processes** How can bills be stalled or speeded up?

How House Bills Are Scheduled All laws start as bills. A proposed law is called a **bill** until both houses of Congress pass it and the President signs it. To introduce a bill in the House, representatives drop it into the hopper, a mahogany box near the front of the chamber.

After a bill is introduced, the speaker of the house sends it to the appropriate committee for study. Of the more than 10,000 bills introduced during each term of Congress, only about 10 percent ever go to the full House for a vote. Bills that survive the com-

---

STUDY GUIDE

Themes in Government
Checks and Balances Why are House members more responsive to their constituents than are senators?

Critical Thinking Skills
Making Comparisons In comparing the legislative process in the House of Representatives with that of the Senate, how does

committee work in the House differ from that in the Senate?

Background

The House Rules Committee sometimes exercises its power by refusing to grant a rule to a bill which has passed the committee. Sometimes this is done when the chairman of the majority of the Rules Committee opposes the bill. Sometimes it is done so that representatives will not have to take a public stand on a controversial bill. There are few limits on the power of the Rules Committee. The only House bills that do not need a rule from the Rules Committee are those reported by the House Appropriations and Ways and Means Committees. Such bills can be considered as privileged motions.

GLOBAL CONNECTION

Comparing Governments

Legislative Powers A bicameral legislature is a common feature of governments. Their powers and organization, however, vary greatly.

Both houses of the United States Congress make laws. The Senate and the House of Representatives have about equal power.

In Japan, the National Diet is the highest organ of power. The Diet is a bicameral legislature consisting of an upper house, called the House of Councilors, and a lower house, called the House of Representatives. The lower house has far more power than the upper house. The House of Representatives elects the prime minister. By a vote of no-confidence, it can force the prime minister to resign or to dissolve the House and call for new elections.

Examining the Connection
In what other countries is the legislature the most powerful branch of government?

mittee process are put on one of the House **calendars.** Calendars are schedules that list the order in which bills will be considered.

The House has five calendars, each scheduling different kinds of bills. The Union Calendar schedules bills dealing with money issues. Major non-money issues are put on the House Calendar. If a bill is considered noncontroversial, it is assigned to the Consent Calendar. The Private Calendar schedules bills dealing with individual or small group legislation. Finally, a Discharge Calendar schedules those bills that the House by majority petition forces out of a committee that is blocking its progress.

The House Rules Committee The Rules Committee serves as the "traffic officer" in the House, helping to direct the flow of major legislation to the floor for discussion and a vote. It is one of the oldest House committees, and the most powerful. After a committee has considered and approved a major bill, it usually goes to the Rules Committee. The Rules Committee can move bills ahead quickly, hold them back, or stop them completely.

Because the Rules Committee is so powerful, it has often been the focus of political battles. From 1858 to 1910, the speaker of the house, as chair of the Rules Committee, dominated the flow of legislation. In 1911 the House revolted against Speaker Joseph G. Cannon's authoritarian leadership and removed him from the Rules Committee.

Recent Democratic majorities in the House have once again placed the Rules Committee under control of the speaker. In 1975 the Democratic Caucus gave the speaker the power to appoint, subject to caucus ratification, all majority-party members of the Rules Committee. A former speaker explained:

> *The Rules Committee is an agent of the leadership. It is what distinguishes us from the Senate, where the rules deliberately favor those who would delay. The rules of the House . . . permit a majority to work its will on legislation rather than allow it to be bottled up and stymied.*
>
> —SPEAKER JIM WRIGHT, 1987

Function of the Rules Committee Major bills that reach the floor of the House for debate and for a vote do so by a "rule"—or special order—from the Rules Committee. As major bills come out of committee, they are entered on either the Union Calendar or the House Calendar in the order received. The calendars have so many bills that if they were taken up in that order, many would never reach the floor before the end of the session. To resolve this problem, the chairperson of the committee that sent the bill to the Rules Committee may ask for it to move ahead of other bills and to be sent to the House floor. If the Rules Committee grants the request, the bill moves ahead. The Rules Committee may also include a time limit for debate on the bill and specify how much the bill may be amended on the floor.

Other Purposes of the Rules Committee The Rules Committee also settles disputes among other House committees. For example, the Armed Services Committee may be considering a bill that involves an area also covered by the Veterans' Affairs Committee. The Rules Committee resolves any dispute between the two committees. In this case the Rules Committee may let the Veterans' Committee offer amendments to the Armed Services Committee's bill.

Finally, the Rules Committee often delays or blocks bills that representatives and House leaders do not want to come to a vote on the floor. In this way the Rules Committee draws criticism away from

CHAPTER 13: THE ORGANIZATION OF CONGRESS 371

GLOBAL CONNECTION

Bicameralism is found in many other countries. For example, Mexico's lower house, called the Chamber of Deputies, has 400 members elected to 3-year terms. Its Senate, the upper chamber, consists of 64 members elected for 6 years. Like Japan, Mexico has a constitution modeled on the United States Constitution. Ask students how a two-chambered legislature illustrates many nations' fear of concentrated power.
Examining the Connection: Have students share their list of countries with the class.

Interpreting Visuals Display transparency 13 from the *Chapter Transparencies* in the Teacher's Classroom Resources and use the accompanying teaching strategy and student activity to teach the responsibilities of the two houses of Congress.

L3 Political Processes Have students make a wall chart to illustrate the powers of the House Rules Committee. After students complete the chart, hold a class discussion of the consequences of the Rules Committee misusing its powers.

Cooperative Learning Activity

Organize the class into groups of five, each to be members of a citizens' group proposing a new bill to their congressional representative. When each group has structured their bill, have them decide on which calendar it should be scheduled (excepting the Discharge Calendar), and why. Have reporters briefly describe their group's bill and identify its appropriate calendar.

Independent Practice

L1 **Federalism** Have students contact members of Congress and ask each about his or her specialized interests and about the bills he or she has sponsored. Once contact has been made, have one student take responsibility for keeping in touch with each representative. **LEP**

L2 **Persuasive Writing** Have students read the quote by Thomas Jefferson on page 368 and write a brief essay that answers the following:

What is his opinion of the desirability of rules and why does he hold that opinion? Do you agree? Why or why not? Can rules become an end in themselves and actually retard the process of the Congress?

STUDY GUIDE

Theme Answer
any member can introduce bill, informal flow to appropriate committee, and then back to floor for vote

Critical Thinking Answer
This Senate leader preferred senators who cooperated with rather than disrupted the process.

CONNECTIONS

Media
Senate committee hearings provided the public's first television coverage of Congress in the 1950s. However, floor proceedings from the House were not broadcast until 1979. The Senate followed suit in 1986. Today, radio and television networks may broadcast floor debates live, or tape excerpts for news programs. Full coverage is relayed over C-SPAN.

members who might have to take an unpopular stand on a bill if it reaches the floor.

A Quorum for Business The House must have a quorum to do its business. A **quorum** is the minimum number of members who must be present to permit a legislative body to take official action. For a regular session, a quorum consists of the majority of the House—218 members. When the House considers bills sent to it by the Rules Committee, however, it may sit as a Committee of the Whole. In that case only 100 members constitute a quorum. This procedure helps speed the consideration of important bills. The Committee of the Whole cannot pass a bill. Instead, it reports the measure back to the full House with whatever changes it has made. The House then may pass or reject the bill.

Lawmaking in the Senate

Visitors going from the House to the Senate are often startled by the difference. The Senate chamber is smaller and quieter than the House chamber. Usually only a few senators attend sessions. The Senate chamber has 100 desks—one for each senator—facing a raised platform where Senate leaders preside over sessions. The party leaders or their assistants stay in the Senate chamber at all times to keep the work moving and to look after their party's interests.

How Senate Bills Are Scheduled As in the House, any member of the Senate may introduce a bill. Procedures for moving bills through the Senate, however, are more informal than in the House. Because it is smaller, the Senate has never felt the need for a committee like the House Rules Committee. Instead, Senate leaders control the flow of bills to committees and to the floor for debate and vote. They do this by consulting closely with one another and with other senators.

Senate leaders also try to schedule sessions to fit the interests and needs of as many senators as possi-

ble. In contrast to the procedure in the House, individual senators have the power to disrupt work on legislation. As one former Senate leader declared, a senator, "if he wants to exercise power, can tie up the Senate for days, and if he allies himself with a few other Senators, he can tie up the Senate for weeks."

The Senate has only two calendars. The Calendar of General Orders lists all the bills the Senate will consider. The Executive Calendar schedules treaties and nominations.

The Senate brings bills to the floor by unanimous consent, a motion by all members present to set aside formal rules and consider a bill from the calendar. The procedure has not changed much through the years. In 1913 Massachusetts Senator Henry Cabot Lodge explained that the Senate conducted most of its business through unanimous-consent agreements:

Not only the important unanimous-consent agreements which are reached often with much difficulty on large and generally contested measures, but constantly on all the small business of the Senate we depend on unanimous consent to enable us to transact the public business.

—HENRY CABOT LODGE, 1913

The Filibuster Because the Senate usually allows unlimited debate on a bill, one way for senators to defeat a bill they oppose is to filibuster against it. To **filibuster** means to keep talking until a majority of the Senate either abandons the bill or agrees to modify its most controversial provisions. Senators who have the floor may continue to stand and talk. After the first three hours, they may talk about any topic they want or even read aloud from a telephone book or a recipe book. Senator Strom Thurmond of South Carolina set the record for a filibuster when he spoke against the Civil Rights Act of 1957 for 24 hours and 18 minutes. A filibuster by a group of senators could go on for weeks or even months.

A filibuster can be stopped when three-fifths of the Senate (60 members) votes for cloture. **Cloture** is a procedure that allows each senator to speak only one

STUDY GUIDE

Themes in Government
Political Processes How are Senate bills scheduled?

Critical Thinking Skills
Recognizing Bias
The statement is made above that a senator, "if he wants to exercise power, can tie up the Senate for days."

What kind of bias was shown by the former Senate leader who made this statement?

Special Needs Strategy

Reading Comprehension Help students who have difficulty understanding our complex governmental system by developing their "schema of knowledge" about government and its processes. Before students read about House and Senate rules, have them develop rules concerning school, such as behavior in study hall or off-campus lunch privileges. Then ask them about other activities that have rules—baseball, football, or driving, for example. Why were these rules developed?

hour on a bill under debate. Obtaining a vote in favor of cloture, however, is usually difficult.

The filibuster is not as strong a weapon as it used to be because the Senate now has a two-track procedural system. If a filibuster starts, the Senate sets aside one time during the day for handling other business. The filibuster then starts up again at the end of such business. With this procedure, filibusters can no longer completely stop the work of the Senate.

Congressional Leadership

Both the House and the Senate have organized leadership to operate efficiently and to coordinate the work of the 535 individual members of Congress. These leaders serve 6 purposes: (1) organizing and unifying party members; (2) scheduling the work of Congress; (3) making certain lawmakers are present for key floor votes; (4) distributing and collecting information; (5) keeping Congress in touch with the President; and (6) influencing lawmakers to support the policies of their political party.

The Constitution provides for the presiding officers of the House and the Senate. Other than that, each house of Congress chooses its leaders.

The Speaker of the House The speaker of the house is the presiding officer of the House and its most powerful leader. The Constitution states that the House "shall choose their Speaker and other officers." A caucus of the majority party chooses the House speaker at the start of each session of Congress.

As both the presiding officer of the House and the leader of the majority party, the speaker has great power. Presiding over the sessions of the House, the speaker can recognize or ignore members who wish to speak. The speaker also appoints the members of some committees, schedules bills for action, and refers bills to the proper House committee. Finally, the speaker of the house follows the Vice President in the line of succession to the presidency.

Today, speakers rely as much on persuasion as on their formal powers to exercise influence. On a typical day, the speaker may talk with dozens of fellow members of Congress. Often the speaker does so just to listen to requests for a favor. As former Speaker Thomas P. "Tip" O'Neill once put it, "The world is full of little things you can do for people." In return, the speaker expects representatives' support on important issues.

Speaker of the House
House Speaker "Tip" O'Neill presided over the House from 1977 to 1987. **History** **Why is the Rules Committee so powerful?**

Other House Leaders The speaker's top assistant is the **majority leader.** The majority leader's job is to help plan the party's legislative program, steer important bills through the House, and make sure the chairpersons of the many committees finish work on bills important to the party. The majority leader is the floor leader of his or her political party in the House and, like the speaker, is elected by the majority party. Thus, the majority leader is not actually a House official but a party official.

The majority leader has help from the majority whip and deputy whips. These **whips** serve as assistant floor leaders in the House. The majority whip's job is to keep a close watch on how majority-party members intend to vote on important bills and to persuade them to vote as the party wishes. The whip also makes certain party members are present to vote.

The minority party in the House also elects its own leaders. These include the minority leader and the minority whips. The responsibilities of these leaders are much the same as those of the majority party's leaders, except they have no power over scheduling work in the House.

Senate Leaders Leadership in the Senate closely parallels leadership in the House, but the Senate has no party official comparable to the speaker of the house. Also, Senate procedures permit individual senators more freedom in their activities. Consequently, party leaders in the Senate do not have as much power and influence over senators as their counterparts in the House.

L3 **Descriptive Writing** Have students watch a session of congressional activity on C-SPAN. Have them write a critical appraisal of the proceedings as if they were television critics, using these questions as guides: Who are the "stars" of the show? What is the plot? *(bills in debate, and so on)* How successful is the session in illustrating the workings of Congress to viewers?

Caption Answer
It determines if and when a bill is sent to the House floor.

CONNECTIONS

Language
The term "whip" comes from the British House of Commons. In the British sport of fox hunting, the "whipper's" job was to keep the running hounds in line—the congressional whip's job today.

Assess

Check for Understanding

Have students complete Section 2 Review on page 374.

Meeting Objectives

Each section objective is tested by the Section Review questions that follow it in parentheses.

• Contrast the rules and organization of the House of Representatives with those of the Senate. (3, 4, 6, 7, 8)
• Analyze the role of filibusters in Senate debates. (5, 7, 8)

Evaluate

 Section 2 Quiz

 Testmaker

Critical Thinking Activity

Recognizing Bias Read aloud the following description of the *Johnson Treatment*—methods of persuasion employed by Lyndon Johnson when he was Senate majority leader:

"Its tone could be supplication, accusation, cajolery, exuberance, scorn, tears, complaint, the hint of threat. . . . Its velocity was breathtaking. . . .

[Johnson] moved in close, his face a scant millimeter from his target . . . [It was] an almost hypnotic experience and rendered the target stunned and helpless."

Ask students to identify and explain the bias in this description.

Caption Answer
Yes, it permits citizens' oversight.

Reteach

Have students write a paragraph describing the rules and leadership of the two houses using the key terms and concepts listed on page 368.

Enrich

Have students research and write a paper on the history of the televising of Congress.

📁 Have students complete activity 13 in *Enrichment Activities* in the Teacher's Classroom Resources.

Close

Refer to the quote by John J. Duncan on page 370. Ask students how making laws might serve constituents' needs and how the legislative process might take away from these needs.

CONNECTIONS

Political Processes

In the past it was not unusual for Senate majority leaders to use "strong-arm" tactics to direct Senate business. Today, however, leaders tend to use friendly persuasion—one recent Senate majority leader called himself the "majority pleader."

Democracy in Action
The cable network C-SPAN provides gavel-to-gavel coverage of debate on the Senate floor. **Politics Is it a good idea to televise congressional debate?**

The Vice President The Constitution names the Vice President as president of the Senate. The Vice President, however, does not have the same role and power as the speaker of the house. The Vice President may recognize members and put questions to a vote. Because the Vice President is not an elected member of the Senate, he or she may not take part in Senate debates. The Vice President may cast a vote in the Senate only in the event of a tie. A Vice President may try to influence the Senate through personal contact with senators, however. Many recent Vice Presidents previously served as senators and thus had close relationships with their former colleagues.

Most Vice Presidents find Senate duties unchallenging and devote much of their time to executive branch activities, leaving little time to preside over the Senate. In the absence of the Vice President, the president pro tempore (or *president pro tem*) presides. **Pro tempore** means for the time being. The Senate elects this leader who is usually a senior member of the majority party.

Senate Majority and Minority Leaders The majority and minority leaders are the most important officers in the Senate. The members of their political parties elect these leaders. The majority leader's main job is to steer the party's bills through the Senate. To do this, the majority leader plans the Senate's work schedule and agenda in consultation with the minority leader. The majority and minority leaders in the Senate are party officials rather than official Senate officers.

The majority leader is responsible for making certain the majority party members attend important Senate sessions and for organizing their support on key bills. The minority leader develops criticisms of the majority party's bills and tries to keep senators in the minority party working together. As in the House, whips and assistant whips assist the majority and minority leaders of the Senate by making sure that legislators are present for key votes.

---

② SECTION REVIEW

Section Summary
The Senate and the House of Representatives have developed elaborate rules and systems of leadership that enable them to handle large volumes of legislation.

Checking for Understanding
Recalling Facts
1. Define constituent, bill, calendar, quorum, filibuster, cloture, majority leader, whip, pro tempore.
2. Name the person who wrote the first manual of rules for the Senate.
3. Specify how a representative introduces a bill in the House.

4. Identify the committee that controls the flow of legislation in the House of Representatives.

Exploring Themes
5. Checks and Balances How does the Senate limit filibusters?
6. Political Processes What specific duties make the speaker the most powerful person in the House?

Critical Thinking Skills
7. Making Comparisons Compare the rules and procedures of the House with those of the Senate.
8. Recognizing Bias Speaker Jim Wright said that "the Rules Committee is an agent of the leadership" unlike the Senate, "where the rules deliberately favor those who would delay." What bias does this statement show?

Section 2 Review Answers

1. Definitions of terms appear on pages indicated: **constituent,** 370; **bill,** 370; **calendar,** 371; **quorum,** 372; **filibuster,** 372; **cloture,** 372; **majority leader,** 373; **whip,** 373; **pro tempore,** 374
2. Thomas Jefferson
3. Representative drops bill into hopper at front of the chamber.
4. Rules Committee

5. A filibuster can be stopped when three-fifths of entire Senate (60 members) votes for cloture. Senate has a two-track procedural system. If filibuster starts, Senate sets aside one time during day for handling other business.
6. The speaker recognizes or ignores members who wish to speak, appoints the members of some committees, schedules bills for action, and refers bills to the proper House committee.
7. House rules aim to define the actions an individual representative can take. In the Senate, rules are more flexible and aim to make sure each senator has maximum freedom to express his or her ideas. Senate has more informal atmosphere, takes its time in considering new laws, permits longer debates. Rules in the House require that legislation move quickly. House debates rarely last more than one day. More of the House's work is done in committees.
8. a bias in favor of the operations of the House leadership, of which Wright was a member for many years

Congressional Committees

Some debates on bills take place on the floors of the House and Senate chambers, and all final votes are taken on their respective floors. The detailed day-to-day work of considering proposed legislation, however, takes place in committees that meet in congressional offices and hearing rooms.

Purposes of Committees

Both the House and Senate depend upon committees to effectively consider the thousands of bills that are proposed each session. Committees help ease the workload and are the key power centers in Congress.

The committee system serves several important purposes. First, it allows members of Congress to divide their work among many smaller groups. Lawmakers can become specialists on the issues their committees consider. This system is the only practical way for Congress to operate because no lawmaker can possibly know the details of each of the more than 10,000 bills introduced in each term of Congress.

Second, from the huge number of bills introduced in each Congress, committees select those few that are to receive further consideration. Committees are where lawmakers listen to supporters and opponents of a bill, work out compromises, and decide which bills will or will not have a chance to become law. Most bills never get beyond the committee stage.

Third, by holding public hearings and investigations, committees help the public learn about key problems facing the nation. Congressional committees have called the public's attention to such issues as

organized crime, the safety of prescription drugs, hunger in America, airline safety, and many others.

Kinds of Committees

Congress has four basic kinds of committees: (1) standing committees; (2) select committees; (3) joint committees; and (4) conference committees. Congress may, however, change the method of committee organization and the number of committees.

Standing Committees Very early in its history Congress set up permanent groups to oversee bills that dealt with certain kinds of issues. These are called **standing committees** because they continue from one Congress to the next. The House and Senate each create their own standing committees and control their areas of jurisdiction, occasionally adding or eliminating a standing committee when necessary. Currently, the House has 22 standing committees, the Senate 16.

In 1988 the House Democratic Caucus revised the classification of standing committees into exclusive, major, nonmajor, and select committees. The Senate revised classifications of its standing committees into major, minor, and select committees.

Because the majority party in each house controls the standing committees, it selects a chairperson for each from among its party members. The majority of the members of each standing committee are also members of the majority party. Party membership on every committee is usually divided in direct propor-

---

SECTION PREVIEW

Objectives
After studying this section, you should be able to:
- Classify the various kinds of committees that help Congress do its work.
- Analyze the impact of the Legislative Reorganization Act of 1970.

Key Terms and Concepts
standing committee, subcommittee, select committee, joint committee, conference committee, seniority system

- Explain how party representation is divided on each congressional committee.

Themes in Government
- Political Processes
- Checks and Balances

Critical Thinking Skills
- Making Comparisons
- Making Inferences

CHAPTER 13: THE ORGANIZATION OF CONGRESS 375

Classroom Resources for Section 3

- 📁 Guided Reading Activities
- 📁 Reproducible Lesson Plans
- 📁 Primary and Secondary Source Readings 13
- 📁 Section 3 Quiz

- Testmaker
- Government Themes Transparencies 10
- SAT Practice Tests
- Writer's Guidebook

Focus

Bell Ringer

While attendance is being taken, have students make a list of the major concerns of running a country. Have them list 10 to 12 areas that they think are important enough to warrant a committee of Congress.

Motivating Activity

Discuss students' Bell Ringer lists. Suggest that they keep their lists and compare them with the list of actual committees they will learn about in this section.

Vocabulary Precheck

Call on volunteers to tell what they think each key term and concept means. Have students check the accuracy of these definitions in the Glossary. **LEP**

Teach

Guided Practice

L1 Understanding Cause and Effect Draw a concept map on the chalkboard using three boxes. Label the first box *Causes*, the second *Event* (fill in this box with: *Congress sets up committees to oversee certain bills.*), and the third *Effects*. Ask students to insert the reasons Congress sets up committees in the *Causes* box. Ask them to insert the benefits of congressional committees in the *Effects* box.

Interpreting Visuals Display transparency 10 from the *Government Themes Transparencies* in the Teacher's Classroom Resources and use the accompanying teaching strategy and student activity to teach the organization of the legislative branch.

L2 Analyzing Ideas Lead a class discussion on why members of Congress seek particular committee assignments. Guide discussion by asking: Why would some members seek assignment to budget or foreign policy committees? Why might a member seek assignment to committees that could benefit his or her constituents? What committees might do this?

Chart Study Answer
Each deals with similar problems and issues.

Independent Practice

L1 Political Processes Have students find out to which committees and subcommittees their own senators and representatives are assigned. Ask them to explain which assignments are most valuable in effectively representing the interests of constituents. **LEP**

Standing Committees of Congress

House Commitees	Senate Committees
Agriculture	Agriculture, Nutrition, and Forestry
Appropriations	Appropriations
Armed Services	Armed Services
Banking, Finance, and Urban Affairs	Banking, Housing, and Urban Affairs
Budget	Budget
District of Columbia	Commerce, Science, and Transportation
Education and Labor	Energy and Natural Resources
Energy and Commerce	Environment and Public Works
Foreign Affairs	Finance
Government Operations	Foreign Relations
House Administration	Government Affairs
Interior and Insular Affairs	Judiciary
Judiciary	Labor and Human Resources
Merchant Marine and Fisheries	Rules and Administration
Post Office and Civil Services	Small Business
Public Works and Transportation	Veterans' Affairs
Rules	
Science and Technology	
Small Business	
Standards of Official Conduct	
Veterans' Affairs	
Ways and Means	

Subcommittees of the Senate Committee on Foreign Relations

Western Hemisphere and Peace Corps Affairs
East Asian and Pacific Affairs
European Affairs
International Economic Policy, Trade, Oceans and Environment
African Affairs
Near Eastern and South Asian Affairs
Terrorism, Narcotics and International Operations

Chart Study
Members of the House may serve on one major committee, while senators may serve on two. **Why do the House and the Senate have similar standing committees?**

tion to each party's strength in each house. For example, if 60 percent of the members of the House are Democrats, then 60 percent of the members of each House standing committee will be Democrats. Thus, a 10-member committee would have 6 Democrats and 4 Republicans.

Subcommittees Most standing committees have from six to eight **subcommittees.** Each subcommittee specializes in a subcategory of its standing committee's responsibility. Subcommittees, like standing committees, usually continue from one Congress to the next.

In recent years the number of subcommittees has grown. One reason for this development is that the workload in Congress has increased, and there is even more need for members to specialize in policy areas than in the past. Another reason is that many members of Congress want to become the chairpersons of subcommittees to accomplish something important, gain prestige, or to improve their image to help win reelection.

Since the early 1970s, House subcommittees have gained power and become more independent of their standing committees. The new rules the Democratic Party Caucus in the House established for subcommittees caused this change. These rules include allowing subcommittee chairpersons to hire their own staffs, requiring all standing committees with more than 20 members to have at least 4 subcommittees, and requiring that all bills received by the standing committee be passed quickly to subcommittees.

Background

Some of the power once held by committee chairpersons now rests with subcommittee chairpersons. A lobbyist once observed that the place to get an unfavorable bill killed was in the subcommittee because when a bill got past the subcommittee and into the full committee, getting it killed would be more difficult. The seniority system is not used to appoint subcommittee chairpersons and, in fact, subcommittees are often chaired by younger members of Congress.

Select Committees From time to time, each house of Congress has created temporary committees. Usually, these committees, called **select committees,** study one specific issue and report their findings to the Senate or the House. These issues can include: (1) matters of great public concern, such as hunger; (2) overlooked problems, such as organized crime; or (3) problems of interest groups, such as senior citizens or Native Americans, who claim that Congress has not met their needs.

Select committees were usually set up to last for no more than one term of Congress, that is, for two years. In practice, however, select committees such as the House Committees on Aging and Hunger have been renewed and continue to meet for several terms of Congress. For this reason both the House and Senate have reclassified several select committees such as the House Permanent Select Committee on Intelligence as standing committees.

Joint Committees Made up of members from both the House and the Senate, **joint committees** may be either temporary or permanent. Like other committees, they have members from both political parties. These committees usually act as study groups with responsibility for reporting their findings back to the House and Senate.

In theory, joint committees coordinate the work of the two houses of Congress. In practice, lawmakers usually limit joint committees to handling routine matters such as government printing or the Library of Congress. Some joint committees, however, have been set up to study matters of greater importance such as atomic energy, defense, and taxation. Joint committees do not have the authority to deal directly with bills or to propose legislation to Congress.

Conference Committees No bill can be sent from Congress to the President until both houses have passed it in identical form. A **conference committee** is a temporary committee set up when the House and Senate have passed different versions of the same bill. Members of the conference committee, called conferees, usually come from the House and Senate standing committees that handled the bill in question. Democrats and Republicans are represented in the same way here as on other committees.

The job of the conference committee is to resolve the differences between the two versions of the bill. Conference committees play a key role in policy-making because they work out a bill that both houses may accept and send to the President. The committee accomplishes this task by bargaining over each section of the bill. A majority of the conferees from each house must accept the final compromise bill—called a conference report—before it can be sent to the floor of the House and Senate. When the conference committee's report—the compromise bill it has finally worked out—reaches the floor of each house, it must be considered as a whole. It may not be amended. It must be accepted or rejected as it comes from the conference committee.

Choosing Committee Members

Assigning members to congressional committees is an extremely important decision in the organization of Congress. Assignment to the right committees can also help strengthen a member's career in several ways. First, membership on some committees can increase a lawmaker's chances for reelection. The best committees are those that deal with bills that will benefit a lawmaker's state or district—for example, an agriculture committee if the member is from a farm area. Second, membership on some committees can mean the lawmaker will be able to influence national policy-making. Committees that often help formulate national policies include those dealing with education, the budget, health, the judiciary, and foreign policy. Third, some committees enable a member to exert influence over other lawmakers because they deal with matters important to everyone in Congress. Some of these committees include the House Rules Committee and taxation and appropriations committees.

STUDY GUIDE

Themes in Government
Checks and Balances **What are the roles of joint committees of Congress?**

Critical Thinking Skills
Making Inferences **Why might some senators prefer to be members of the Foreign Relations**

Committee rather than members of some lesser-known committee?

L2 Persuasive Writing Have students write paragraphs supporting or opposing the seniority method of determining committee leadership. Select students to read their paragraphs to the class.

STUDY GUIDE

Theme Answer
to coordinate the work of the two houses of Congress, to deal with matters of common concern, to investigate or research issues and to report back to House and Senate

Critical Thinking Answer
They may be very knowledgeable about world affairs, desire high visibility, or want to influence government's foreign policy.

Assess

Check for Understanding
Have students complete Section 3 Review on page 378.

Meeting Objectives
Each section objective is tested by the Section Review questions that follow it in parentheses.
• Classify the various kinds of committees that help Congress do its work. (1, 2, 7)
• Analyze the impact of the Legislative Reorganization Act of 1970. (4)
• Explain how party representation is divided on each congressional committee. (5)

Cooperative Learning Activity

Organize the class into groups of three, each to construct a bill to be dealt with by one of the standing committees. Assign a specific standing committee from the chart on page 376 to each group. Each group should identify the bill, its purpose, and its constituents. Suggest that students check recent copies of the *Congressional Record* in the local library to get ideas for the type of bills to be reviewed by their assigned standing committee. Reporters should report to the class on the decisions of their groups.

Evaluate

📁 Section 3 Quiz

🔲 Testmaker

Reteach

Have students outline the material in Section 3 using the following heads:

I. Purposes of Committees
II. Kinds of Committees
III. Committee Membership
IV. Effects of Committee Membership on Representatives

Enrich

📁 Have students complete activity 13 in *Primary and Secondary Source Readings* in the Teacher's Classroom Resources.

Close

Discuss students' opinions on whether or not Senate and House committee sessions should be televised.

Linking Past and Present
One of the most notorious of all special committees was the House Committee on Un-American Activities. Formed in 1938 as a special committee to investigate communist influence in American life, it became a standing committee in 1945. It was finally abolished in 1975.

In the House the key committees are Rules, Ways and Means, and Appropriations. In the Senate the most prestigious committees are Foreign Relations, Finance, and Appropriations. Assignment to the Senate Foreign Relations Committee, for example, will give a lawmaker a chance to directly influence American foreign policy. Senators on this committee usually receive a great deal of publicity.

Assignment to Committees In both the House and Senate, each party has a special committee that assigns party members to the standing committees. These choices are subject to the approval of all party members in each house. Newly elected members of Congress who wish to serve on a particular committee or veteran lawmakers who wish to transfer to another committee may request assignment to the committees on which they want to serve.

The Committee Chairperson's Role Along with party leaders, the chairpersons of standing committees are the most powerful members of Congress. They make the key decisions about the work of their committees—when their committees will meet, which bills they will consider, and for how long. They decide when hearings will be held, whether hearings will be public or private, and which witnesses will be called to testify for or against a bill. In addition, chairpersons may hire and fire most committee staff members and control the committee budget. Finally, they manage the floor debates that take place on the bills that come from their committees.

Since the 1970s the powers of committee chairpersons have been limited somewhat. The Legislative Reorganization Act of 1970 made the committee system more democratic by allowing a majority of committee members to call meetings without the chairperson's approval. It also stated that committee members who disagree with the chairperson must have time to present their views and that reasonable notice must be given for all committee meetings.

The Seniority System The unwritten rule of seniority traditionally has guided the selection of chairpersons. The **seniority system** gave the member of the majority party with the longest uninterrupted service on a particular committee the leadership of that committee. In recent years the system has been criticized. Critics insist that the system ignores ability. They believe that the person most qualified to lead the committee should become the chairperson, not necessarily the person with the longest period of service.

The seniority system is still used today, but it has been modified in several important ways. Since 1971 Republicans in the House have voted by secret ballot to select the highest ranking Republican on each committee. In 1973 the Democrats, who were the majority party in the House, adopted the same procedure. In a historic action in 1975, House Democrats voted to replace three senior committee chairpersons. In the same year, Senate Democrats voted to select chairpersons by a secret ballot whenever 20 percent of the Democrats requested it.

3
SECTION REVIEW

Section Summary
Committees divide the workload of Congress, call attention to key issues, and work out differences between House and Senate versions of bills.

Checking For Understanding
Recalling Facts
1. Define standing committee, subcommittee, select committee, joint committee, conference committee, seniority system.
2. List three important purposes that the committee system serves.
3. Explain how selection to the right committee can strengthen a lawmaker's career.
4. Relate how the Legislative Reorganization Act of 1970 affected the power of committee chairpersons.

Exploring Themes
5. Political Processes How is party membership or representation usually divided on each committee?
6. Checks and Balances Why must a conference committee's report be accepted or rejected as a whole when it reaches the floor of either house?

Critical Thinking Skills
7. Making Comparisons In what ways are joint committees and conference committees similar to and different from each other?
8. Making Inferences Why do you think it is unlikely that Congress will change many of its rules from one term to the next?

Section 3 Review Answers

1. Definitions of terms appear on pages indicated: **standing committee,** 375; **subcommittee,** 376; **select committee,** 377; **joint committee,** 377; **conference committee,** 377; **seniority system,** 378
2. allows Congress to divide up its work among smaller groups, selects those bills that should be considered, and helps the public learn about key issues
3. Membership on some committees can increase a law-

maker's chances for reelection and might enable the lawmaker to influence national policy-making or to exert influence over other lawmakers.
4. It limited the power because it enabled majority of members to call meetings and allowed those who disagreed with the chair to present their views.
5. in direct proportion to each party's strength in each house
6. because it may not be amended and if it is rejected the bill dies

7. Both joint and conference committees are composed of members of the House and Senate. Joint committees act as study groups and report their findings to the House and Senate, while conference committees work out compromise bills that each house acts upon.
8. Answers may include that many members who are in key positions want to keep things as they are; the rules have served Congress well for a long time; adjusting to new rules might be difficult and time-consuming.

Making Generalizations

A generalization is a broad statement based on specific facts. Knowing how to make generalizations will help you see patterns in information.

Explanation

To make a generalization, follow these steps:

- Collect data. Research the topic and gather information that will be useful for analysis.
- Identify relationships among the data. Ask: What features are common to the data?
- Make a general statement from the information.
- Refine your generalization. You may find that you need to qualify the generalization with such words as many, most, as a rule, or often.

Examine the following data about 5 members of the 102nd Congress:

Hispanics in the House of Representatives

Jose E. Serrano

Born	1943	Party		Democrat
Elected	1990	Religion		Roman Catholic
State	NY	Occupation		politician

Solomon P. Ortiz

Born	1937	Party		Democrat
Elected	1982	Religion		Methodist
State	TX	Occupation		police officer

Matthew Martinez

Born	1929	Party		Democrat
Elected	1982	Religion		Roman Catholic
State	CA	Occupation		small business leader

Henry B. Gonzalez

Born	1916	Party		Democrat
Elected	1961	Religion		Roman Catholic
State	TX	Occupation		social service worker

Esteban E. Torres

Born	1930	Party		Democrat
Elected	1982	Religion		none
State	CA	Occupation		int'l trade executive

What similarities do you find among the names on this list? All are males.

Now move to the second category—birth dates. One generalization that you can make is that all of these men were born before 1945.

Next look at the year of election. We find that four of the five were first elected in 1982 or later,

but Henry Gonzalez has served since 1961. Here you must qualify your generalization. You might state: "Most of these members of Congress were elected during the 1980s and 1990s."

The next category is the state each represents. All come from states—New York, California, and Texas—with large Hispanic populations.

Finally, look at party affiliation. That category provides the easiest generalization of all. All of these members of Congress are Democrats.

Practice

Examine the data below and answer the questions that follow.

Senate Leadership—1991

Robert C. Byrd

Born	1917	Party		Democrat
Elected	1958	Religion		Baptist
State	WV	Occupation		small business leader

George J. Mitchell

Born	1933	Party		Democrat
Elected	1980	Religion		Roman Catholic
State	ME	Occupation		attorney

Wendell H. Ford

Born	1924	Party		Democrat
Elected	1974	Religion		Baptist
State	KY	Occupation		insurance executive

Robert Dole

Born	1923	Party		Republican
Elected	1968	Religion		Methodist
State	KS	Occupation		attorney

Alan K. Simpson

Born	1931	Party		Republican
Elected	1978	Religion		Episcopalian
State	WY	Occupation		attorney

1. What is the subject of this data?
2. What generalization can you make about the ages of these leaders?
3. What qualified generalization can you make about the occupations of these senators?

Additional Practice

To practice this skill, see **Reinforcing the Skill** on page 387.

CRITICAL THINKING SKILLS

Focus

Refer students to the photograph on page 380. Ask them what is identical about the three people in the photograph and what is different about them. *(Responses should focus on sex, age, dress, and physical appearance.)* Then ask what similarities *most* of the people in the photograph share. *(possible responses: white, female, well-dressed, wearing glasses)* Tell students that they have made *generalizations* about these people.

Teach

Point out that the ability to make generalizations is useful in seeing patterns in large amounts of information.

Apply the Explanation steps to the first table. Ask: What is the topic of this table? *(Hispanics in the House of Representatives)* What types of data are common to each person in the table? *(birth dates, election dates, states of residence, party affiliations, religions, occupations)*

Assess

Have students complete the **Practice** exercise.

Close

Ask students to characterize Hispanic members of Congress based on data provided in the table. *(male, Roman Catholic, Democrats elected in the 1980s and 1990s from western states)*

Practice Answers

1. It is data about Senate leadership in 1991.
2. They are all 60 or over.
3. More than half are attorneys.

For additional practice, have students complete activity 13 in *Skill Reinforcement Activities* in the Teacher's Classroom Resources.

Congressional Staff and Support Agencies

Focus

Bell Ringer

While attendance is being taken, have students make a short list of problems they believe senators and representatives should be able to help solve for constituents.

Motivating Activity

Using their Bell Ringer lists as a guide, have students as a class make a list of the skills which they believe would be useful to a congressional staffperson.

Vocabulary Precheck

Write the key terms and concepts for this section on the chalkboard. Ask students how each term and concept relates to congressional staff and support agencies. **LEP**

Caption Answer

answer mail and help solve problems

CONNECTIONS

Political Processes

A host of support workers, such as sergeants-at-arms, doorkeepers, and pages, keep order and ensure the smooth running of floor sessions in the House and Senate.

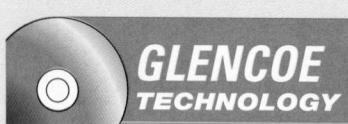

GLENCOE TECHNOLOGY

Focus on Government
Video 25
Lecture Launcher:
Congressional Caseworkers
Running Time: 3:13
Videodisc 2, Chap. 25
VHS Tape 2, Begins 13:28

The work of Congress has become so massive and complicated in recent decades that lawmakers need a trained staff to help them do their work effectively. Staff members also carry out the work of congressional committees. In addition, there are a number of supporting agencies that perform important functions for members.

Congressional Staff Role

When Lowell Weicker of Connecticut was in the Senate, a woman wrote to him complaining about the way an airline had handled her dog. The dog, shipped as animal cargo, had died in flight. One of the senator's secretaries mentioned the letter to the press secretary, who thought that perhaps the incident had news value. He phoned the Federal Aviation Agency and other government offices and found that there had been many similar cases. After informing the senator, the secretary wrote a draft of a bill to authorize the Transportation Department to regulate air transport of animals. Senator Weicker later introduced the legislation on the floor of the Senate. The story became headlines in Weicker's home state, and he received many letters of appreciation.

This story illustrates that congressional staff members do much of the important work on legislation. Lawmakers rely upon their staff to help them handle the growing workload of Congress, communicate with voters, help run committee hearings and floor sessions, draft new bills, write committee reports, and attend committee meetings.

Congressional Staff Growth

Congress has not always relied on staff to accomplish its work. For almost 100 years, senators and representatives had no personal aides. Occasionally they might hire assistants out of personal funds, but Congress provided no paid staff. Inadequate staffing had become an urgent complaint by the time Congress considered the Legislative Reorganization Act in 1946. Since then the number of staff members has increased dramatically. The House and Senate employed 2,000 personal staff members in 1947, but more than 11,500 in 1990. Committee staff increased from 400 to more than 3,000 in that same

Behind Every Great Congresswoman . . .
Behind-the-scenes staff help members of Congress fulfill their duties. **Political Processes** **In what ways do support staff serve the members' constituents?**

SECTION PREVIEW

Objectives
After studying this section, you should be able to:
- Recognize the contributions that congressional staffs and supporting agencies make to members of Congress.
- Analyze why congressional staff has grown so rapidly.

- Evaluate the role that congressional staffs take in writing legislation.

Key Terms and Concepts
personal staff, committee staff, administrative assistant, legislative assistant, caseworker

Themes in Government
- Federalism
- Political Processes

Critical Thinking Skills
- Demonstrating Reasoned Judgment
- Evaluating Information

380 UNIT 4: THE LEGISLATIVE BRANCH

Classroom Resources for Section 4

📁 Guided Reading Activities
📁 Reproducible Lesson Plans
📁 Participating in Government 13
📁 Interpreting Political Cartoons 36
📁 Reteaching Activities 13
📁 Section 4 Quiz

📁 Chapter 13 Tests
➕ Testmaker
🎧 Audio Cassettes (English and Spanish)
📁 Limited English Proficiency Activities 13
SAT Practice Tests
Writer's Guidebook

period. By 1991, each lawmaker spent an average of $5.6 million on employees.

Several reasons explain this growth. First, lawmaking has become more complex as our society has grown and changed since the early 1900s. Lawmakers cannot be experts on all the issues that come before their committees or upon which they must vote in Congress. Having a large staff is one way to get expert help. Second, the demands that constituents place on lawmakers have increased over the years. Members of Congress need a large office staff simply to deal with the many letters from people in their states or congressional districts. Almost all of this mail is answered. In addition to writing to their senators and representatives, voters in increasing numbers have turned to their lawmakers for help in solving problems. One lawmaker explained, "More than half my total staff time is devoted to resolving individual difficulties that have developed between citizens and their government."

Finally, congressional staffs have grown because they are able to do many things to help lawmakers get reelected. Almost all members of Congress use their personal staffs to help them get publicity, keep an eye on political developments back home, and write speeches and newsletters. Staffs also help raise funds for election campaigns, meet with lobbyists and visitors from home, and do many other things that may increase a legislator's chances of reelection.

Personal Staff

Congress includes two types of staffs: **personal staff** and **committee staff.** Personal staff members work directly for individual senators and representatives. Committee staff members work for the many House and Senate committees.

The size of senators' personal staffs varies because allowances to pay for them are based on the population of the senator's state and distance from the capital. Senators each receive from $1.4 million to $2.4 million per year to operate their offices. Most of this amount is to pay staff salaries. About one-third of personal staff members work in the legislators' home states. The rest work in Washington, D.C. Each member of the House is allowed about $550,000 to pay for a personal staff of up to 22 people. The House employs more than 9,000 personal staff aids, the Senate about 4,000. Lawmakers can hire and fire staff members at will.

Administrative Assistants Lawmakers usually have three types of personal staff members in their offices. The **administrative assistant,** called an AA, is a very important legislative aide. The AA runs the lawmaker's office, supervises the lawmaker's sched-

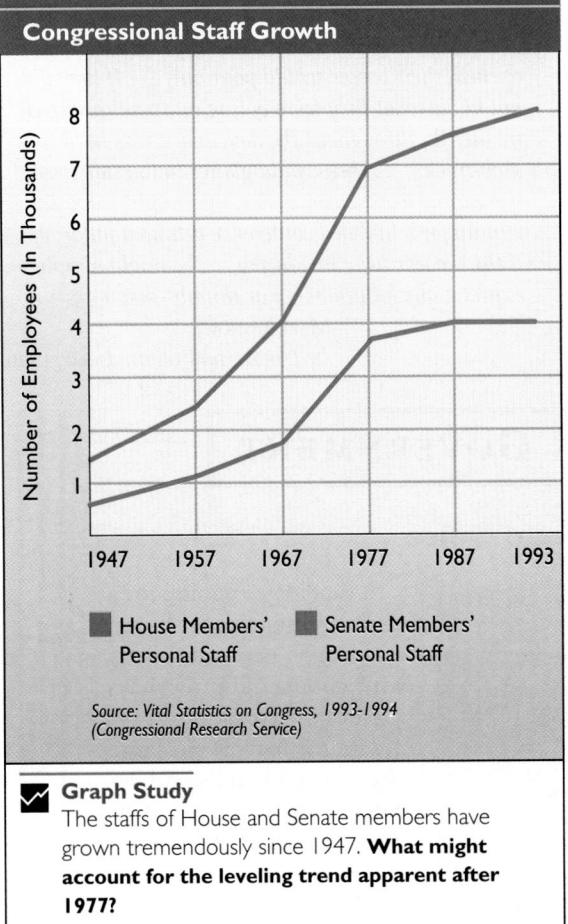

Congressional Staff Growth

Number of Employees (In Thousands)

1947 1957 1967 1977 1987 1993

■ House Members' Personal Staff   ■ Senate Members' Personal Staff

Source: Vital Statistics on Congress, 1993-1994 (Congressional Research Service)

✓ Graph Study
The staffs of House and Senate members have grown tremendously since 1947. **What might account for the leveling trend apparent after 1977?**

Teach

Guided Practice

L1 Classifying Information
Have students tell which of the agencies that support the work of Congress should be consulted for information in the following cases:

a. someone needs to know how much money congressional committees are spending *(Congressional Budget Office)*
b. a member of Congress needs to know whether a bill he or she intends to support is likely to be considered unconstitutional *(General Accounting Office)*
c. a legislative assistant needs to know the crime rate of the three largest United States cities *(Library of Congress)*
d. a representative needs to know how soon she can expect to receive copies of a House floor speech made yesterday *(Government Printing Office)* **LEP**

Graph Study Answer
budget limitations and cuts

STUDY GUIDE

Theme Answer
The administrative assistant runs the office, coordinates the lawmaker's schedule, and might also be in contact with those who may be helpful at election time.

Critical Thinking Answer
No: Allowances are based on size of state population; legislators have offices in their districts as well as in Washington, D.C.; senators may have offices in more than one city. *Yes:* in time of tight budgets, legislators should set example by cutting allowances.

STUDY GUIDE

Themes in Government	Critical Thinking Skills	Based on what you have read, do

Themes in Government
Federalism **Why is the role of the administrative assistant important?**

Critical Thinking Skills
Demonstrating Reasoned Judgment Each legislator receives an allowance for staff workers.

Based on what you have read, do you think the allowances are extravagant? Why or why not?

CHAPTER 13: THE ORGANIZATION OF CONGRESS 381

Background

In *Unelected Representatives,* a study of congressional staffers, political scientist Michael Malbin argues that members of Congress have benefited greatly from staffers' assistance. Staffers, Malbin states, are particularly good at involving lawmakers in new issues that will bolster the lawmakers' reputations with constituents and with other legislators. Also, Malbin suggests, the use of intelligent, driven, and highly efficient staff people has "helped Congress to retain its position as a key initiator of federal policy."

L2 Making Comparisons Work with students to construct a chart on the chalkboard that shows the basic duties of the following: *administrative assistant, legislative assistant, caseworker,* and *committee staff member.* Then discuss what important influences each position could have on the legislative process.

L3 Interpreting Primary Sources Have students read the two quotes on page 383 about the relative power of the legislative staff. Have them write a main idea sentence for each statement. Then ask students for their own opinions on which quote they think is more accurate, and why.

Independent Practice

L1 Research Ask students to research the Government Printing Office to find out the types of material the office makes available to the public. If possible, have them bring in samples of the GPO's catalogs to share with the rest of the class. **LEP**

PARTICIPATING IN GOVERNMENT

Ask students if a local government candidate has ever come to their home to have their parents sign a petition. If so, ask if the candidate explained his/her reasons for wanting to run for office. Ask students how they might participate in the campaign for a candidate in their local government.

📁 Have students complete activity 13 in *Participating in Government* in the Teacher's Classroom Resources.

---

ule, and gives advice on political matters. A good AA also deals with influential people from the lawmaker's congressional district or state, who may influence the lawmaker's reelection.

Legislative Assistants Legislative **assistants,** or LAs, are a second type of personal staff member. An LA makes certain that the lawmaker is well informed about the many bills with which she or he must deal. An LA does research, drafts bills, studies bills currently in Congress, and writes speeches and articles for the lawmaker.

Another important part of the LA's job is to assist the lawmaker in committee meetings and to attend committee meetings when the lawmaker cannot be present. Senators and representatives are members of so many committees and subcommittees that they cannot possibly attend all the committee meetings. When they do attend committee meetings, they often come in at the last minute and briefly talk with their LA to find out what has taken place. The LA, who has followed the meeting and studied the bill in question, may have prepared a short speech for the lawmaker or made up a list of questions for the lawmaker to ask witnesses. Often the senator or representative

has not seen the speech or the questions but relies on the LA's judgment.

LAs also keep track of the work taking place on the floor of Congress, as well as bills that are in committee. While routine legislative business goes on, the lawmaker may be in a committee meeting or talking with voters. When the buzzer rings, signaling time for a vote, lawmakers rush to the floor of the Senate or House from their offices or committee rooms. They may not know what the vote is about unless it involves a major bill that has been scheduled long in advance. As they walk, they look for their LAs. A former LA describes the scene:

As the door of the "Senators Only" elevator opened, their bosses would pour out. . . . If they did not know what they were voting on (votes occurred frequently throughout the day, and it was hard to keep track), . . . they would glance to the side to see if someone were waiting. A staffer might wave and run up for a huddled conference behind a pillar; or if the senator were in a hurry . . . he might simply expect a quick thumbs-up or thumbs-down gesture.
—MARK BISNOW,
IN THE SHADOW OF THE DOME, 1990

PARTICIPATING IN GOVERNMENT

Running for Local Office

Most local officials are elected. What are some local government positions? How does a person become a candidate for local office?

Units of local government include counties, townships, municipalities, and several kinds of special districts. Qualifications for candidates vary according to the office sought. Two common methods of becoming a candidate are the petition method and the caucus.

Under the petition method, the candidate must obtain a petition, an official form requesting permission

from the government, to run for office. The candidate must get a certain number of registered voters to sign the petition, then file the petition with the local board of elections before the deadline. Under the caucus method, party leaders select candidates for local offices.

A candidate running for a position on a school board may rely on personal contact with voters and interviews for local newspapers. A candidate for mayor of a large city may hold rallies and debates, make television commercials and brochures, and use many other forms of publicity to influence voters.

Investigating Further

Interview one of your local government officials. Find out how he or she became a candidate. Ask which campaign strategies were found to be most successful.

Cooperative Learning Activity

Assign students to work in pairs to develop ideas that can make a congressional representative's office run smoothly and keep the representative informed and up-to-date on pending bills. One member of the pair should take on the role of a newsmagazine journalist. The other member of the pair should take on the role of an administrative assistant, a legislative assistant, or a caseworker. Students should write a script for the interview and perform it for the class.

Caseworkers Some personal staff members are called **caseworkers** because they handle the many requests for help from people in a lawmaker's state or congressional district. In addition to their office in Washington, D.C., lawmakers are likely to have offices in key cities in their home state or district. Caseworkers usually staff these offices.

Committee Staff

Every committee and subcommittee in Congress has staff members who work for that committee. The larger and more important a committee is, the more staff people it will have. The committee chairperson and the senior minority party member of the committee are in charge of these staff members. Committee staffers draft bills, study issues, collect information, plan committee hearings, write memos, and prepare committee reports. They are largely responsible for the work involved in making laws.

Some senior committee staff members are very experienced and are experts in the area their committee covers, whether it be tax policy, foreign affairs, or health care. Laurence Woodworth, who spent 32 years on the staff of the Joint Committee on Internal Revenue Taxation, is a good example of such an expert. As the committee's staff director for 14 years, he was largely responsible for all changes in the tax laws. Later, Woodworth left the committee to become assistant secretary of the treasury.

Too Much Power? The people do not elect congressional staffers. Yet they play a key role in lawmaking. Do they have too much influence? Some lawmakers believe they do. For example, Senator Robert Dole has argued, "Professional staffers are assuming too much power and, in some cases, are making policy rather than merely helping with the technical problems as was intended."

Other lawmakers disagree. They say that the staff really collects information and develops alternative courses of action for the lawmakers. Senator Dick

Clark of Iowa explained the staff's role this way: "Dependency on staff is great. Domination, no. There is no question of their influence. In all legislation, they're the ones that lay out the options." Clark and others argue that it is still the lawmakers who make the key decisions on legislation.

Support Agencies

Several agencies that are part of the legislative branch provide services that help Congress carry out its powers. Some of the services these agencies provide are also available to the other branches of government and to private citizens. Congress has created four important support agencies.

The Library of Congress Congress created the Library of Congress in 1800 to "purchase such books as may be necessary for the use of Congress." Today, it is one of the largest libraries in the world. This great center of information contains almost 97 million items, including books, journals, music, films, photographs, and maps. As the administrator of the copyright law, the copyright office in the Library receives two free copies of most published works copyrighted in the United States.

The Library has a Congressional Research Service (CRS) with hundreds of employees. Every year, CRS answers some 450,000 requests for information from lawmakers, congressional staff, and committees. CRS workers will check out anything, from the number of kangaroos in Australia to the crime rate in urban areas. Members of Congress use the CRS to answer requests for information from voters. They also use CRS for research on matters related to bills before Congress.

Congressional Budget Office (CBO) Congress established the CBO in 1974 to coordinate the budget-making work of Congress, study the budget proposals put forward by the President each year, and make cost projections of proposed new programs.

STUDY GUIDE

Themes in Government
Political Processes Why is the role of legislative assistant so important?

Critical Thinking Skills
Evaluating Information Among the three types of personal staff members, what do you think of the scope of the legislative assistant's role? Should it be limited? Why or why not?

Special Needs Strategy

Reading Comprehension One way to help students relate to information they read is to personalize it. This is especially effective for students with reading comprehension problems. Ask students to read about the congressional staff jobs: administrative assistants, legislative assistants, and caseworkers. Ask students which job they think would be most compatible with their own strengths. For example, a person with good interpersonal skills might make a good caseworker.

L2 Expressive Writing Have students write an essay indicating which of the jobs described in this section they would like most and what special talents they would bring to their chosen positions.

STUDY GUIDE

Theme Answer
Because lawmakers are so busy, they cannot stay abreast of every piece of legislation. Legislative assistants follow what is going on and brief lawmakers.

Critical Thinking Answer
Yes: Legislative assistants have too much influence on how lawmakers view legislation. *No:* Legislative assistants' role is to present options so that lawmakers can make informed decisions.

Assess

Check for Understanding
Have students complete Section 4 Review on page 384.

Meeting Objectives
Each section objective is tested by the Section Review questions that follow it in parentheses.
• Recognize the contributions that congressional staffs and supporting agencies make to members of Congress. (3, 4, 5, 7)
• Analyze why congressional staff has grown so rapidly. (2, 6)
• Evaluate the role that congressional staffs take in writing legislation. (8)

Evaluate
 Section 4 Quiz
 Testmaker

Reteach

Have students write sentences that summarize the content of each of the following headings: Congressional Staff Role, Congressional Staff Growth, Personal Staff, Committee Staff, Support Agencies.

📁 Have students complete activity 13 in *Reteaching Activities* in the Teacher's Classroom Resources.

Enrich

📁 Have students complete activity 36 in *Interpreting Political Cartoons* in the Teacher's Classroom Resources.

Close

Remind students that this section states that support agencies allow Congress to be less dependent upon the executive branch for information, helping right the balance of power. Ask students: Do you agree or disagree that Congress should be more independent of the executive branch?

CONNECTIONS

History

The original Library of Congress was burned in August of 1814. When it was rebuilt, the core of the new collection was the more than 6,400 volumes from the library of Thomas Jefferson.

The CBO counterbalances the President's elaborate budget-making organization, the Office of Management and Budget. CBO staff members study economic trends, keep track of how much congressional committees are spending, and prepare a report on the budget each April. They also calculate how Congress's budget decisions might affect the nation's economy.

General Accounting Office (GAO) Established in 1921, this agency is the nation's watchdog over the spending of funds Congress appropriates. A comptroller general appointed to a 15-year term directs the GAO. The agency has a professional staff of about 5,100 people. They review the financial management of government programs that Congress creates, collect government debts, settle claims, and provide legal service.

Many GAO staff members answer requests for information about specific programs from lawmakers and congressional committees. GAO staff members prepare reports on various federal programs for lawmakers, testify before committees, develop questions for committee hearings, and provide legal opinions on bills under consideration. Almost one-third of the GAO's work now comes from congressional requests for information.

Government Printing Office (GPO) The Government Printing Office is the largest multipurpose printing plant in the world. Every day the GPO prints the *Congressional Record*, a daily record of all the bills introduced in both houses and of the speeches and testimony presented in Congress. Members of Congress can make changes in speeches they have made before they are printed in the *Record*. They can even have speeches they never actually made in the House or Senate printed in the *Record*. Congressional staff members spend a good deal of time preparing speeches for lawmakers because those words will be inserted in the *Congressional Record*. Thus, when voters ask about the lawmaker's position on a particular issue, the staff can send a copy of the *Record* containing a speech the lawmaker made on that issue.

Although the GPO is a congressional agency, it also does the printing for the entire federal government. The GPO sold 28.5 million copies of various publications in a recent year—a gross sales value of more than $83 million. Among these publications were 3.7 million copies of the *Congressional Record*.

Another valuable publication of the Government Printing Office is the *Statistical Abstract of the United States,* updated and printed every year since 1878. Published by the Bureau of the Census, this volume provides statistical information about population, government finances, personal income, business, agriculture, education, law enforcement, national defense, elections, and many other topics.

The support agencies provide a vital function for Congress. They have helped the legislative branch become less dependent on the executive branch for information—helping Congress regain some of the power it held in earlier years.

---

4 SECTION REVIEW

Section Summary
People working on personal and committee staffs play a vital role in helping carry out the work of Congress.

Checking For Understanding
Recalling Facts
1. Define personal staff, committee staff, administrative assistant, legislative assistant, caseworker.
2. Describe the dramatic increase in the number of congressional staff members in recent years.
3. List the four important support agencies for Congress.
4. Identify the official daily record of all bills introduced in both houses and all speeches given in Congress.

Exploring Themes
5. Federalism How do members of Congress use caseworkers to keep in touch with people in their home states and districts?
6. Political Processes Why has congressional staff grown so rapidly in the last several years?

Critical Thinking Skills
7. Demonstrating Reasoned Judgment Is it a good idea that the comptroller general of the GAO is appointed to a 15-year term, rather than elected or appointed to a shorter term? Give reasons for your judgment.
8. Evaluating Information Some members of Congress rely heavily on staff, while others try to keep their staffs from having too much power. Do you believe that staff members should write bills and influence policy? Why or why not?

Section 4 Review Answers

1. Definitions of terms appear on pages indicated: **personal staff,** 381; **committee staff,** 381; **administrative assistant,** 381; **legislative assistant,** 382; **caseworker,** 383
2. The House and Senate employed 2,000 personal staff members in 1947 and more than 11,500 in 1990. Committee staff increased from 400 to more than 3,000 in the same period.

3. Library of Congress, Congressional Budget Office, General Accounting Office, Government Printing Office
4. *Congressional Record*
5. Caseworkers often staff offices in key cities in the home states or districts of members of Congress.
6. The congressional staff has grown because of complexity of laws necessary in today's society, an increase in demands that constituents place on lawmakers, and the ability of congressional staffs to do many things to help lawmakers get reelected.

7. Answers will vary, but should note that the position is appointed and the term lengthy to prevent Congress or the people from having political influence over the comptroller general.
8. Answers should include that staff members are not elected representatives of the people and therefore should not have too much power. However, staff members are often people with expertise who can provide sound advice to legislators.

PERSONAL PERSPECTIVES

Margaret Chase Smith on Campaigning for the Senate

The first woman elected to both the Senate and the House of Representatives, Margaret Chase Smith served the people of Maine with intelligence and great personal courage.

I look back on the 80th Congress just adjourned this morning at 6:45 with a great deal of satisfaction for during the past two years I have been able to introduce and cause the enactment of several important bills. I could not have done this without the six years of service in Congress prior to the last two years. Those years gave me the know-how and the contacts and the seniority advantages without which I would not have been able to get my measures through.

I shall never forget my service in the House of Representatives. I can sincerely say that it has been a real pleasure to serve the people of the second district—and I shall not forget my friends in the House who made it possible for me to ac-

complish what I have in the way of legislation because of their personal faith in me and what I proposed. . . .

I believe that the people of Maine have made up their minds as to how they are going to vote tomorrow and that last-minute appeals and charges cannot have any material effect upon them. . . .

I have had several calls today from my supporters throughout the State reporting that desperate last-minute smear sheets have been intensely distributed against me today. This has not given me any concern because these smear sheets merely repeat the misrepresentations which I refuted in detail claim-by-claim weeks ago.

As a matter of fact, the sudden reappearance of these sheets at the last minute has given me even greater confidence that tomorrow will bring victory. . . . These sheets are actually inspiring my thousands of supporters to do even more than they already have—if that is humanly possible. . . .

The candidates for United States Senator are important only for what they symbolize. Each of us symbolizes something to the Maine voters. My supporters say that I am a symbol of a "grass

I shall never forget my service in the House of Representatives. I can sincerely say that it has been a real pleasure to serve the people of the second district. . . .

roots" protest against political machines, money politics, and smears. They say that the issue is simple and clear— that the choice is one way or the other. And with respectful humility, I must say that they are right.

. . . From the bottom of my heart, I say to you that I want to win tomorrow more for the sake of those things which people say that I symbolize—and for the sake of those who have put so much faith in me and have worked so hard for me. . . .

The issue tomorrow is clear. It is the rank-and-file against the paid professionals. What the voters of Maine do tomorrow will do much to either stop or perpetuate machine and money politics in Maine. . . .

—MARGARET CHASE SMITH, 1948

Examining the Reading

Reviewing Facts
1. Discuss the reasons that Smith gave for her success as a member of the House of Representatives.
2. Identify what Smith symbolized, according to her supporters.

Critical Thinking Skills
3. Making Inferences How did Smith keep her campaign focused on her popularity rather than on the smear campaign?

More About Personal Perspectives

Margaret Chase Smith won her first seat in Congress in 1940. In the 1948 Senate race, Smith—without party endorsement and with 3 male opponents—won over 70 percent of the voters, the greatest majority in Maine's history. In 1960 she received the highest percentage totals of all the Republican senatorial candidates. She lost her fifth Senate race in 1972 and although never professing to be a feminist, admitted she hated to leave because there was little chance that a qualified woman would replace her. Membership in the United States Congress still does not begin to represent the total population of women, even 50 years after Margaret Chase Smith entered Congress.

PERSONAL PERSPECTIVES

Focus

Ask students if they or their family has ever received smear campaign literature in the mail or seen smear campaign advertisements on TV. Do they think voters are swayed by these tactics?

Teach

What compliment does Smith pay the people of Maine? *(They are determined enough to not let last-minute smears affect the way they have decided to vote.)* What kinds of Maine people does Smith feel closest to? *(the grass roots, rank-and-file population)* What does Smith define as the enemy of the ordinary Maine voter? *(the paid professional, or money politics)*

Assess

Have students complete **Examining the Reading.**

Answers
1. her know-how, contacts, and seniority
2. "grass roots" protest against political machines, money politics, and smears
3. by focusing on the dedication of her thousands of supporters, by identifying herself with the rank-and-file

Close

Ask students why they think voters sometimes support politicians based on their character, rather than on their position on issues.

13

CHAPTER REVIEW

Identifying Terms and Concepts

<u>House of Representatives:</u> apportionment, gerrymandering, redistricting; <u>Senate:</u> cloture, filibuster, president pro tempore; <u>Both:</u> bill, committee staff, caseworker, censure, constituents, joint committee, majority leader, personal staff, select committee

Reviewing Facts and Ideas

1. Article I

2. January 3 of every odd-numbered year

3. <u>Senate:</u> 30 years old, citizen of United States for 9 years, legal resident of state represented; <u>House:</u> 25 years old, 7 years a citizen, and a legal resident of the state represented

4. The census determines the population of each state so that House representation can be apportioned.

5. office space; stationery; postage; low-cost life insurance; medical clinic; gymnasium; health facilities; allowances for office staff, trips home, telephones, telegrams, newsletters; and an income tax deduction to help maintain two residences

6. Members cannot be sued for anything that they say on the floor of Congress.

7. House Rules Committee

8. Majority party selects chairperson of each committee and the majority of committee members. Committees generally control flow of legislation.

9. *Congressional Record*

Summary and Significance

The House of Representatives and Senate both represent the people. The House with 435 members represents legislative districts; the Senate with 100 members represents entire states. Both houses have established elaborate rules and systems of leadership to enable them to handle the large volume of legislation needed to govern the nation.

Committees do the basic work of Congress, holding hearings, doing research, scheduling legislation, and working out differences when the House and Senate pass different versions of the same bill. Congressional staff and supporting agencies play key roles in assisting members of Congress in their day-to-day duties.

Identifying Terms and Concepts

On a separate sheet of paper write headings for three columns: (1) House of Representatives, (2) Senate, and (3) Both Houses. Choose terms from the list below and place them under the correct headings. **apportionment, bill, committee staff, caseworker, cloture, censure, constituents, gerrymandering, filibuster, joint committee, majority leader, personal staff, president pro tempore, redistricting, select committee**

Reviewing Facts and Ideas

1. **Cite** the article of the Constitution that provides for the legislative branch and describes the duties and powers of Congress.
2. **Identify** when terms of Congress begin.
3. **Enumerate** the qualifications for the Senate and House of Representatives.
4. **Explain** the original purpose of the census taken every 10 years.
5. **List** eight benefits that members of Congress receive in addition to their salaries.
6. **Describe** the provision of the United States Constitution that protects free and unlimited debate in Congress.
7. **Identify** the most powerful committee in the House of Representatives.
8. **Explain** how the majority party in each house determines the flow of legislation.
9. **Cite** the place a constituent could look to find a speech identifying the position of a member of Congress on an important issue.

Applying Themes

1. **Growth of Democracy** Why did Congress decide to stabilize the membership of the House of Representatives at 435?
2. **Constitutional Interpretations** Why is the Vice President, whom the Constitution names as the presiding officer of the Senate, usually absent from the Senate?
3. **Political Processes** What are the purposes of "packing" and "cracking" in drawing congressional districts?
4. **Checks and Balances** How did the Legislative Reorganization Act of 1970 limit committee chairpersons' powers?
5. **Federalism** How do legislative assistants help members of Congress stay informed about conditions in their home districts?

Critical Thinking Skills

1. **Making Inferences** Why are bills that minority party members introduce unlikely to be reported out of committee?
2. **Formulating Questions** What questions or considerations do you think a new member of Congress considers when requesting committee assignments?
3. **Making Comparisons** How do the everyday duties of a congressional administrative assistant differ from those of a legislative assistant?
4. **Recognizing Bias** Senator Robert Dole said, "Professional staffers are assuming too much power." Senator Dick Clark disagreed, claiming,

Applying Themes

1. Congress was concerned that the increasing size of the House would make it difficult for it to carry out its work.

2. Vice Presidents find their Senate duties unchallenging, so they devote their time to executive branch activities.

3. Packing concentrates opposition voters into a few districts so the majority party can control all

the others. Cracking divides opposition voters so they do not have majorities in any district.

4. by allowing a majority of members to call meetings without the approval of the chair, by allowing members who disagree with the chair to present their views, and by requiring reasonable notice to be given for committee meetings

5. They research pending legislation and voters' attitudes toward it.

"Dependency on staff is great. Domination, no." What personal traits of each senator may contribute to these beliefs?

5. **Demonstrating Reasoned Judgment** How does the GAO function as a "watchdog"?

6. **Evaluating Information** Why did the Supreme Court rule that congressional districts must be compact and contiguous?

Linking Past and Present

In some ways the early Senate operated like a private club. It was closed to the public until 1795 and had a quieter, more deliberative atmosphere than the House. Senators were not popularly elected until 1914. What other changes have caused the Senate to become more like the House of Representatives?

Writing About Government

Descriptive Writing People with a variety of talents and traits have been elected to Congress. Write an essay describing the personal talents and character traits that you believe would contribute to the ideal member of Congress.

Reinforcing the Skill

Making Generalizations Use what you have learned about making generalizations to examine the data in the next column and answer the questions.

1. What is the subject of this data?
2. What similarity can you find among the last names of these five people?
3. What similarity can you find among these people on the basis of their birth dates? State this in the form of a generalization.
4. What generalization can you make about the dates when each of these women was elected?
5. What qualified generalization can you make about the religious affiliation of these members of Congress?
6. Would it be reasonable to make the following generalization? More women serve in Congress today than ever before.

Women in the House

Nancy Pelosi

Born	1940	Elected	1987
Religion	Roman Catholic		
Party	Democrat, California		
Occupation	Public Relations Consultant		

Patricia Schroeder

Born	1940	Elected	1972
Religion	United Church of Christ		
Party	Democrat, Colorado		
Occupation	Lawyer		

Nancy L. Johnson

Born	1935	Elected	1982
Religion	Unitarian		
Party	Republican, Connecticut		
Occupation	Civic Volunteer		

Jan Meyers

Born	1928	Elected	1984
Religion	Methodist		
Party	Republican, Kansas		
Occupation	Politician		

Constance Morrella

Born	1931	Elected	1986
Religion	Roman Catholic		
Party	Republican, Maryland		
Occupation	Educator		

Investigating Further

1. **Individual Project** Look at the entries under "United States Government, Congress" in the *Readers' Guide to Periodical Literature*. Identify those articles that deal with a particular current issue or bill that is currently moving through Congress. Check through previous volumes of the *Guide* to determine how long this issue or bill has been under consideration. Write any dates of important events or votes on this legislation and construct a time line showing the history of the issue and congressional concern over it.

2. **Cooperative Learning** As a class, choose four controversial current issues that concern you. Divide the class into four groups. Each group will choose one of the issues and decide what actions Congress should take to deal with the issue. Have each group assign individuals specific aspects of the issue to research. Then bring the group together to compile their research and write a letter urging support for this position to your member of Congress.

Chapter 13 Review Answers

5. It oversees the spending of funds.

6. to avoid the inequities caused by gerrymandering

Linking Past and Present

Today Senate floor proceedings, like House proceedings, are televised on C-SPAN.

Writing About Government

Answers will vary, but students should indicate why the traits and talents are important.

Reinforcing the Skill

1. It is data about five female members of the House of Representatives.

2. all European names

3. Sample generalization: All of these women were born before 1941.

4. Sample: They were all elected in the 1970s and 1980s.

5. Sample: They are mostly Christians.

6. No; there is not enough information

Investigating Further

1. Students' time lines will vary based on bill selected.

2. Groups' letters will vary, but should include pertinent facts from their research.

Critical Thinking Skills

1. Chairperson of a committee is a member of the majority party and majority party controls committee because it has more members.

2. Answers should include: Will the committee be a base for helping my constituents? Will the assignment help me politically? Is the assignment in my field of interest or ability?

3. Administrative assistant runs lawmaker's office and deals with people from legislator's district or state. Legislative assistant keeps lawmaker informed about legislation, does research, drafts bills, and writes speeches and articles for the member of Congress.

4. Answers may indicate that Dole likes to be in control and not rely too much on aides. Clark may feel more comfortable depending on his staff.

Chapter Organizer

Objectives	Special Feature Pages	Supplemental Materials
Section 1 Legislative and Non-Legislative Powers *pp. 390–395* 1. Identify the legislative and non-legislative powers of Congress. 2. Evaluate how executive agreements have affected the role the Senate plays in foreign policy. 3. Detail how Congress may remove an official from office.	Focus on Freedom: Woodrow Wilson's War Message p. 392	Guided Reading Activities Reproducible Lesson Plans Supreme Court Case Studies 3 Primary and Secondary Source Readings 14 Enrichment Activities 14 Section 1 Quiz Testmaker Government Themes Transparencies 14 Chapter Transparencies 14 Great Speeches, Volume III SAT Practice Tests
Section 2 Additional Powers of Congress *pp. 396–400* 1. Identify how Congress oversees the activities of the executive branch. 2. Explain the investigative and oversight powers of Congress.	Global Connection: Interdependence: Congress and Foreign Affairs p. 398 Critical Thinking Skills: Distinguishing Fact From Opinion p. 400	Guided Reading Activities Reproducible Lesson Plans Supreme Court Case Studies 48 Section 2 Quiz Testmaker Skill Reinforcement Activities 14 SAT Practice Tests Writer's Guidebook
Section 3 Shared Powers of Congress *pp. 401–405* 1. Explain the sources of conflict between the President and Congress. 2. Enumerate how Congress may oppose the President's proposals.	Participating in Government: Writing to a Member of Congress p. 403 Personal Perspectives: Senator Daniel Inouye on Congressional Investigations p. 405	Guided Reading Activities Reproducible Lesson Plans Participating in Government 14 Interpreting Political Cartoons 35 Reteaching Activities 14 Section 3 Quiz Chapter 14 Tests Testmaker Audio Cassettes (English and Spanish) Limited English Proficiency Activities 14 SAT Practice Tests Writer's Guidebook

If time does not permit teaching this chapter, assign the Chapter 14 summary in the Unit 4 Digest on pages 437–438.

Key To Ability Levels

Teaching strategies have been coded for varying learning styles and abilities.

L1 Level 1 activities are **basic** activities and should be within the ability range of all students.

L2 Level 2 activities are **average** activities and should be within the ability range of the average to above-average student.

L3 Level 3 activities are **challenging** activities designed for the ability range of above-average students.

LEP These activities should be within the ability range of **Limited English Proficiency** students.

Multicultural Activities

One of the most prized confirmation powers of the Senate is its approval of presidential appointments to the United States Supreme Court. In 1991 Clarence Thomas was nominated by President George Bush to the seat on the Court vacated by Thurgood Marshall. Thomas's confirmation was viewed with special interest by the African American community because both Marshall and Thomas are African Americans. The Senate hearings drew enormous public and media attention after university professor Anita Hill accused Thomas of sexual harassment. Throughout televised Judiciary Committee hearings on these charges, the media polled African Americans for their views. After the hearings, some members of Congress called for changes in the confirmation process. Students might research the confirmation process or the role of African American opinion in Thomas's confirmation by the Senate.

Hawaii's Daniel Inouye began his national career with election to the House of Representatives in 1958. In 1970 voters from New York's South Bronx elected Herman Badillo to the House, making him the first Puerto Rican American to vote in Congress. He remained there until 1978, when he became active in New York City mayoral politics. Henry Gonzalez was first elected to the House in 1961. Barbara Jordan was Texas's first African American state senator since 1883. She went on to win election to the House, where she served from 1973 to 1979. Have students examine the political careers of each lawmaker, focusing particularly on their bases of support, committees of special interest, and legislative initiatives.

Chapter Resources

Readings for the Student

Bernstein, Carl and Bob Woodward. *All the President's Men.* Simon and Schuster, 1974.

Cotton, Norris. *In the Senate.* Dodd, Mead, 1978.

Dodd, Lawrence C. and Richard L. Schott. *Congress Reconsidered.* Congressional Quarterly, 1985.

Hutson, James H. *To Make All Laws: The Congress of the United States, 1789–1989.* Houghton Mifflin, 1990.

Keefe, William J. *Congress and the American People.* Prentice-Hall, 1980.

Weiss, Ann E. *The American Congress.* Messner, 1977.

Readings for the Teacher

Dodd, Lawrence C. *Congress Reconsidered.* Congressional Quarterly, 1993.

King, Anthony, ed. *Both Ends of the Avenue.* American Enterprise Institute, 1983.

Sundquist, James L. *The Decline and Resurgence of Congress.* Brookings Institution, 1981.

Thurber, James A. *Cooperation and Conflict Between the President and Congress.* Congressional Quarterly, 1991.

Multimedia

Videocassettes

All the President's Men. Warners. (v/c, 135 minutes)

Congress: How It Works—and Sometimes Doesn't. Guidance Associates. (v/c, 59 minutes)

Equal Justice Under Law 3: Gibbons v. Ogden. U.S. National Audiovisual Center. (v/c, 30 minutes)

The Impeachment Hearings: Summer of Judgment. WETA. (v/c, 60 minutes)

Mr. Smith Goes to Washington. Columbia. (v/c, 125 minutes)

Point of Order. Social Studies School Service. (v/c, 107 minutes)

Watergate Hearings: Summer of Judgment. WETA. (2 v/cs, 120 minutes)

Software

NewsWorks—Social Studies Data Base Files. (U.S. Government data base). Newsweek. (Apple disk; must be used with Apple-Works data-base program, Apple, Inc.). Students research and analyze data describing the election process, the party system, and the political relationship between Congress and the President, from 1789 to 1984.

United States Constitution Tutor. Micro Learn (division of Micro-Lab). (Apple, IBM, Commodore 64 disks). Students prepare for a test by reviewing United States government as well as facts and concepts about the Constitution.

The Powers of Congress

Introduce

Chapter Overview

Chapter 14 explores the powers of Congress—expressed and implied powers granted by the Constitution, as well as additional non-legislative powers set by tradition. It also considers the relationship between Congress and the executive branch.

Section 1 summarizes the legislative powers of Congress such as the power to tax and spend and to regulate interstate commerce, and non-legislative powers such as treaty ratification and confirmation or removal of federal officials.

Section 2 explains how Congress limits the actions of the executive branch and details the investigative and oversight powers of Congress.

Section 3 describes the powers shared by Congress and the President, and the conflicts that arise in their relationship.

Chapter 14 Themes

Have a volunteer read aloud the government themes in the Chapter Preview. Ask the class to summarize what they already know about separation of powers and checks and balances. Have them speculate why the Constitution grants Congress powers that no other branch of government exercises.

CHAPTER

14

Political progress hinges on cooperation between the President and Congress, but the two often become mired in disputes over budgets and ideology.

388   UNIT 4: THE LEGISLATIVE BRANCH

About the Chapter Opener

Teaching With Illustrations Have students examine the photograph on pages 388 and 389. Ask them if they have ever viewed a television broadcast of the President addressing Congress. *(Students might mention the State of the Union address or the President addressing Congress in 1994 about national health care.)* Ask students how the photograph reflects the government theme of checks and balances. *(Answers will vary. Students might mention the necessity of the President and Congress working together to formulate, enact, and implement policies and programs—and the ability of one branch to block the other when disputes arise.)*

Chapter Preview

Overview

Congress exercises many of its powers without consulting the other branches of government. The Constitution, legislation, and custom, however, require Congress to have a close working relationship with the executive branch, but this relationship is often not a harmonious one.

Objectives

After studying this chapter, you should be able to:

1. **Summarize** the legislative and non-legislative powers of Congress.
2. **Explain** how Congress influences the actions of the executive branch.
3. **Evaluate** how well Congress and the President work together.

Themes in Government

This chapter emphasizes the following government themes:

- **Separation of Powers** The Constitution grants Congress powers that no other branch of government exercises. Section 1.
- **Political Processes** Congress exercises and protects powers in a variety of ways. Sections 1, 2, and 3.
- **Civil Rights** Congressional investigations in some ways are similar to court proceedings. Section 2.
- **Checks and Balances** Congress and the President share some significant powers. Section 3.

Critical Thinking Skills

This chapter emphasizes the following critical thinking skills:

- Making Generalizations
- Drawing Conclusions
- Synthesizing Information

CHAPTER 14: THE POWERS OF CONGRESS 389

Introducing the Chapter

▶▶ Show President Nixon's resignation speech from "Great Speeches," Volume III, *Social Studies Videos*. (You will need to preview the tape to locate this material.) Ask students what they know of this event. Ask what powers of Congress played a role in causing the resignation. *(investigative, impeachment)* Note that in this chapter students will learn about these and other important powers of Congress that affect and shape our nation.

Chapter Project

Have students make a class bulletin board showing the powers of Congress. The major heads on the bulletin board might include the following: *Expressed Powers, Implied Powers, Additional Powers.* As students read the chapter, have them summarize what each set of powers involves. Then ask them to find newspaper and newsmagazine articles that deal with congressional actions. Students should summarize the articles and indicate which type of power Congress exercised. Students should display their articles on the bulletin board under the appropriate head.

Linking Past and Present
One of the first acts of Congress was to pass the Tariff Act on July 4, 1789. The act was intended to raise money for the government's day-to-day operations. Today the primary purpose of tariffs is to protect American industries. Most of the government's revenue comes from income taxes.

Setting the Scene Probably the biggest change in Congress over the years has occurred in regard to policy-making. During the nineteenth century, legislative policies came from Congress as often as from the executive branch. Congressional positions were often comparable to the President's prestige and power. In the twentieth century, however, as the power of the presidency has increased, Congress has relied more on its checks and balances function. Since Franklin Roosevelt, it has been expected that the President will propose legislative programs, and today nearly all aspects of policy-making are initiated by the executive branch.

Focus

Bell Ringer

Have students write a statement explaining the difference between *expressed* and *implied*.

Motivating Activity

Discuss students' Bell Ringer statements. Then ask: If an example of an expressed rule at school is "No fighting," what would be an implied rule that could be derived from the expressed rule? *(Students may suggest that arguments should not get out of control.)*

Point out that just as stated rules imply certain other rules, so too do some powers of government imply other powers. Tell students this section is about the expressed and implied powers of Congress.

Vocabulary Precheck

Write the terms and concepts on the chalkboard. Ask students to use those that they know in sentences. **LEP**

Teach

Guided Practice

L1 Vocabulary Divide the key terms and concepts in the Section Preview into three lists. Then organize the class into three groups and assign each group one of the three lists. Have each group write study questions that use each word on their assigned list. Collect each group's questions and ask them to the rest of the class.

Caption Answer

levying taxes and borrowing money

Legislative and Non-Legislative Powers

The Founders attached great importance to lawmaking and expected Congress to become the most important branch of the national government. Thus, they granted Congress many powers and gave it a vital role in making public policy.

At the same time, however, the Founders feared the abuse of power. Their experience with the British Parliament had shown that legislatures with unchecked powers could pass repressive laws and endanger liberty. Consequently, the powers they gave Congress, unlike those enjoyed by the President and the Supreme Court, are **expressed powers,** powers carefully listed in the Constitution. In the system of checks and balances, many of Congress's powers are shared with the executive and judicial branches. For example, the President can veto acts of Congress, and the Supreme Court has the power to declare them unconstitutional.

Legislative Powers

Most of the expressed powers of Congress are itemized in Article I, Section 8. These powers are also called **enumerated powers.** The expressed powers cover broad themes such as regulating commerce as well as more specific subjects like granting copyrights and patents. Other parts of the Constitution give Congress a few more expressed powers.

Although the powers of Congress seem to be clearly stated, custom has modified many of them. In part, the last clause of Article I, Section 8, the so-called

elastic clause, is responsible for these modifications. This clause gives Congress the right to make all laws "necessary and proper" to carry out the powers expressed in the other clauses of Article I. It is called the elastic clause because over the years it has allowed Congress to stretch its powers to meet new situations the Founders could never have anticipated.

What do the words *necessary and proper* in the elastic clause mean? Almost from the beginning, the meaning of these words was a subject of dispute. The issue turned on the question of whether a "strict" or a "loose" interpretation of the Constitution should be applied. The dispute was addressed in 1819, in the case of *McCulloch* v. *Maryland,* when the Supreme

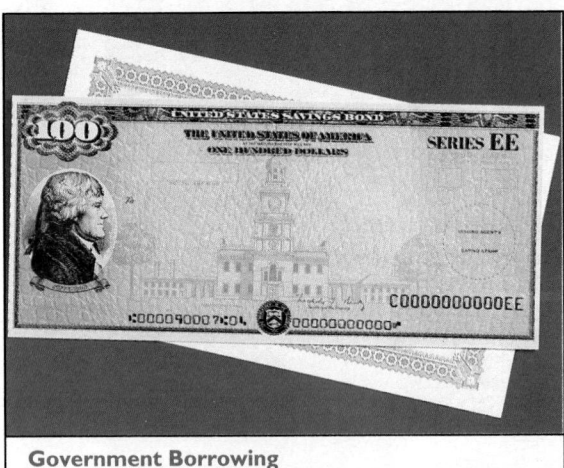

Government Borrowing
Selling bonds is one way the government raises funds.
Economics How else does it collect revenues?

SECTION PREVIEW

Objectives
After studying this section, you should be able to:
- Identify the legislative and non-legislative powers of Congress.
- Evaluate how executive agreements have affected the role the Senate plays in foreign policy.
- Detail how Congress may remove an official from office.

Key Terms and Concepts
expressed powers, enumerated powers, elastic clause, revenue bill, appropriations bill, securities, national debt, bankruptcy, interstate commerce, naturalization, copyright, patent, implied powers, impeachment, writ of habeas corpus, bill of attainder, ex post facto law

Themes in Government
- Separation of Powers
- Political Processes

Critical Thinking Skills
- Making Generalizations
- Drawing Conclusions

Classroom Resources for Section 1

- Guided Reading Activities
- Reproducible Lesson Plans
- Supreme Court Case Studies 3
- Primary and Secondary Source Readings 14
- Enrichment Activities 14

- Section 1 Quiz
- Testmaker
- Government Themes Transparencies 14
- Chapter Transparencies 14
- Great Speeches, Volume III
- SAT Practice Tests

Court ruled in favor of a loose interpretation. The Court supported the idea that the elastic clause gave Congress the right to make any laws necessary to carry out its other powers.

The Taxing and Spending Power Sometimes called "the power of the purse," the power to levy taxes and provide for the general welfare of the United States is among the most important powers of Congress. It allows Congress to influence national policy in many areas because no government agency can spend money without congressional authorization.

Article I, Section 7, requires that all **revenue bills,** laws proposed to raise money, must start in the House of Representatives. The more populous states such as Virginia and Pennsylvania insisted on having a greater voice in tax policy than the smaller states. Because representation in the House was to be based on population, the Founders agreed that revenue bills would originate there. As with all legislation, the Senate must also pass a revenue bill for it to become law.

The legislative process for **appropriations bills**—proposed laws to authorize spending money—is not spelled out in the Constitution. It has developed through usage. Article I, Section 9, merely requires that "No Money shall be drawn from the Treasury, but in Consequence of Appropriations made by Law." Spending requests generally come from the executive branch. Today, most are presented to Congress in the President's annual budget proposal.

Over the years Congress has used its taxing and spending authority to expand its regulatory powers. For example, when Congress authorizes money for state or local governments, it frequently requires that local officials follow specific federal regulations as a condition of the grant. Moreover, by levying heavy taxes on products such as tobacco that it considers undesirable, Congress may restrict their use.

Congress also uses its money powers to regulate the economy. For example, cutting individual income taxes to stimulate the economy gives taxpayers more money to spend. Conversely, Congress may try to slow economic growth by increasing taxes, leaving taxpayers with smaller paychecks.

Other Money Powers In addition to levying taxes and authorizing that money be spent, Article I allows Congress to borrow to help pay for the cost of government. Congress does this in various ways. The most common method is by authorizing the sale of government **securities**—bonds or notes. When people buy savings bonds, Treasury bills, or Treasury notes, they are lending the government money. In return the government promises to repay buyers with interest at the end of a specified period of time—3 months to 30 years, depending on the type of security.

Because it must borrow money to meet its operating expenses, the government has a **national debt**—the total amount of money the government owes at any given time. By the mid-1990s, the national debt was almost $5 trillion. Although the Constitution does not restrict government borrowing, since 1917 Congress has attempted to set an annual limit on the national debt. In recent years, however, it has raised the ceiling time after time so that the government could borrow more money to pay its bills.

As part of Congress's money powers, the Constitution gives the legislative branch the power to coin money and to regulate its value. All currency the federal government issues is legal tender, meaning that it must be accepted as payment. In addition, Congress has the power to punish counterfeiters—people who print postage stamps, paper money, or government securities illegally—and to establish a system of standard weights and measures.

The money powers of Congress also include the authority to make laws concerning **bankruptcy**—legal proceedings to administer the assets of a person or business that cannot pay its debts. Despite this authority, for more than a century Congress generally left bankruptcy matters to the states. Finally, in 1898, it passed a federal bankruptcy law. Today, the states have little power in this area, and almost all bankruptcy cases are heard in federal courts.

Chapter 14, Section 1
Lesson Plan, pages 390–395

Interpreting Visuals Display transparency 14 from the *Chapter Transparencies* in the Teacher's Classroom Resources. Use the accompanying teaching strategy and student activity to teach expressed and implied powers.

L2 Interpreting Primary Sources Have students read Representative Rodino's statement on page 394. What does he say the Founders meant by impeachable offenses? What did they *not* mean? *(Students should suggest that a President should be impeached only for illegal acts, not for decisions that turn out to be wrong.)* Ask students if they agree. Ask: Should repeated bad judgment or incompetence be impeachable offenses?

STUDY GUIDE

Theme Answer
sale of government securities—bonds or notes

Critical Thinking Answer
After enumerating 17 clauses of specific powers, the 18th clause's "necessary and proper" language gives Congress implied powers.

CONNECTIONS

History
The colonies had laws against counterfeiters even before the Constitution provided for this power. Offenders could be sentenced to death. Engraver James Mar, facing the hangman's noose, was granted clemency by the governor of New York after the women of the surrounding community presented him with a petition.

STUDY GUIDE

Themes in Government
Separation of Powers Article I, Section 8, of the Constitution has 18 clauses giving powers to Congress. The second clause allows Congress to "borrow money on the credit of the United States." **How does Congress do this?**

Critical Thinking Skills
Making Generalizations **How does the elastic clause support a "loose" interpretation of the powers of Congress?**

Background

A survey conducted by the House of Representatives discovered how the average member spends his or her day. The usual working day lasts 11 hours and 26 minutes, about 39 percent—or 4 hours 25 minutes—of which is spent on the House floor or in committee and subcommittee meetings. Of 3 hours and 19 minutes of office time, nearly 2 hours is spent meeting constituents, answering letters, and making phone calls. Another hour is taken up with personal and committee staff meetings. The balance of the time goes for reading and writing speeches and legislation. A further 3 hours and 42 minutes is spent around Washington, D.C., at various meetings and special events.

Focus on Freedom

There was strong resistance in Congress to Wilson's request. Four days later, after bitter debate, it voted (Senate 82–6, House 373–50) to declare war. Have students identify the emotional language in Wilson's address. What effect is such language intended to have on listeners?

Answers

1. because world peace and freedom is threatened
2. democracy; people's right to have a voice in their governments; the rights and liberties of small nations; safety and freedom of all nations
3. when peace, democracy, and security are threatened

Interpreting Visuals Display transparency 14 from *Government Themes Transparencies* in the Teacher's Classroom Resources and use the accompanying teaching strategy and student activity to teach congressional checks and balances.

Independent Practice

L1 Making a Chart Have students chart the expressed powers of Congress under these heads: *Taxing and Spending, Foreign Policy, Commerce, Other Powers.* **LEP**

Powers of the Congress
Declaring War
Running Time :32
Side One, Chapter 17

Foreign Policy Powers Congress has important powers in the areas of foreign policy and national defense. Chief among these are the power to declare war, to create and maintain an army and navy, to make rules governing land and naval forces, and to regulate foreign commerce.

Congress shares foreign policy and national defense responsibilities with the President. Throughout American history, however, it generally has submitted to presidential leadership in this area. Although Congress has declared war only 5 times, the President, as commander in chief, has used military force in other nations on more than 160 occasions. Most significant of these were the Korean War, 1950 to 1953, and the Vietnam War, 1965 to 1973. Both conflicts were fought without declarations of war.

After the Vietnam War, Congress acted to reassert its foreign policy powers. Congress held that the Constitution never intended the President to have the power to involve the nation in undeclared wars. Therefore in 1973, over President Nixon's veto, Congress passed the War Powers Act. This law forbids the President to commit American forces to combat for more than 60 days without congressional notification within 48 hours. Almost every President since the act's passage has protested its constitutionality. During this period Presidents used military force in Cambodia (1975), Iran (1980), Grenada (1983), Lebanon (1983), Libya (1986), the Persian Gulf (1987), Panama (1989), Iraq (1991), and Haiti (1994). Most of these were quick strikes. Nevertheless, in most cases the President notified Congress of the action.

Focus on Freedom

WOODROW WILSON'S WAR MESSAGE

When World War I broke out in Europe in August 1914, President Woodrow Wilson asked Americans to remain neutral. Yet events over the next 31 months drew the nation ever closer to conflict. Finally, on April 2, 1917, Wilson asked Congress to declare war.

I have called Congress into extraordinary session because there are serious, very serious choices of policy to be made, and made immediately, which it was neither right nor constitutionally permissible that I should assume the responsibility of making. . . .

With a profound sense of the solemn and even tragical character of the step I am taking and of the grave consequences which it involves, but in unhesitating obedience to what I deem my constitutional duty, I advise that the Congress declare the recent course of the Imperial German Government to be in fact nothing less than war against the Government and people of the United States. . . .

Neutrality is no longer feasible or desirable where the peace of the world is involved and the freedom of its peoples, and the menace to that peace and freedom lies in the existence of autocratic Governments, backed by organized force which is controlled wholly by their will. . . . We have seen the last of neutrality in such circumstances. . . .

It is a fearful thing to lead this great, peaceful people into war, into the most terrible and disastrous of all wars, civilization itself seeming to be in the balance. . . .

We shall fight for the things which we have always carried nearest our hearts—for democracy, for the right of those who submit to authority to have a voice in their own Governments, for the rights and liberties of small nations, for a universal dominion of right by such a concert of free peoples as shall bring peace and safety to all nations and make the world itself at last free.

To such a task we can dedicate our lives and our fortunes, everything that we are and everything that we have, with the pride of those who know that the day has come when America is privileged to spend her blood and her might for the principles that gave her birth and happiness, and the peace that she has treasured.

God helping her, she can do no other.
—WOODROW WILSON, 1917

Examining the Document

Reviewing Facts
1. Explain why Wilson rejects continued neutrality.
2. Cite the principles for which Wilson states the American people will fight.

Critical Thinking Skills
3. Expressing Problems Clearly What issue does Wilson believe justifies war?

392 UNIT 4: THE LEGISLATIVE BRANCH

Cooperative Learning Activity

Organize the class into groups of five, each group to consider one of the expressed powers of Congress (taxing and spending, regulating commerce, foreign policy and national defense, providing for nation's growth, other powers). Have each group discuss why its power was delegated to Congress rather than to the executive branch. Have a reporter from each group summarize its conclusions for the class.

The Commerce Clause Article I, Section 8, Clause 3, the so-called commerce clause of the Constitution, authorizes Congress to regulate **interstate commerce,** or commerce among the states. In this clause the Founders provided what has become one of the most sweeping powers of government. The Supreme Court has promoted the expansion of this power by consistently ruling that the meaning of *commerce* far exceeds the mere buying and selling of goods and services.

The landmark decision on this subject came in *Gibbons* v. *Ogden* (1824). The case centered on whether a state or the federal government would regulate boats transporting passengers across the Hudson River between New York and New Jersey. The argument for state control was that commerce involved only products. The Court rejected this narrow view, however, and ruled that all forms of business across state lines come under federal authority.

Over the years, the Court has expanded its definition of commerce to give Congress even greater power. Any widespread activity that can possibly be considered interstate commerce is subject to federal control. The long list includes broadcasting, banking and finance, and air and water pollution.

Congress has used its power over interstate commerce to set policy in many other areas, too. For example, Congress requires that businesses engaged in interstate commerce pay their employees a minimum wage. Almost all businesses deal in some way with someone in another state. This power enables Congress to regulate working conditions across the nation.

One of the most significant applications of the commerce clause has been in the area of civil rights. In 1964 Congress used its power to regulate interstate commerce to pass the landmark Civil Rights Act. This law prohibited discrimination in places of public accommodation such as restaurants, hotels, and motels. It also prohibited job discrimination.

A Georgia motel owner immediately attacked the law, claiming that the motel was a local business. It was therefore not part of interstate commerce, and the law should not apply. On appeal to the Supreme Court, the justices disagreed. In *Heart of Atlanta Motel* v. *United States* (1964), the Court noted that public places of accommodation served interstate travelers and sold food that had crossed state lines.

> *We, therefore, conclude that the action of Congress in the adoption of the Act as applied here to a motel which concededly serves interstate travelers is within the power granted it by the Commerce Clause of the Constitution, as interpreted by this Court for 140 years.*
>
> —JUSTICE TOM C. CLARK, 1964

Providing for the Nation's Growth The Constitution also grants Congress power over **naturalization,** the process by which immigrants to the United States may become citizens. In addition, Article IV, Section 3, authorizes Congress to admit new states and pass laws needed to govern any territories. Today, United States territories such as Guam, the Virgin Islands, and Wake Island fall under this provision. Finally, both Article I and Article IV empower Congress to pass laws to govern federal property. The Founders envisioned such property as military bases and government buildings. Today, however, these provisions establish federal authority over national parks, historic sites, and hundreds of millions of acres designated as public lands.

Other Legislative Powers Article I, Section 8, gives Congress the power to grant copyrights and patents. A **copyright** is the exclusive right to publish and sell a literary, musical, or artistic work for a specified period of time. Under the present law, this period is the lifetime of the creator plus 50 years. A **patent** is the exclusive right of an inventor to manufacture, use, and sell his or her invention for a specific period, currently 17 years, and may be renewed.

Article I, Section 8, also grants Congress the power to establish a post office and federal courts. Congress also has used its postal power to combat criminal activity. For example, using the mail for any illegal act is a federal crime.

Interpreting Source Readings **Interpreting Source Readings** Have students complete activity 14 in *Primary and Secondary Source Readings* in the Teacher's Classroom Resources.

Analyzing Supreme Court Cases Assign case 3 in *Supreme Court Case Studies* in the Teacher's Classroom Resources.

STUDY GUIDE

Theme Answer
The act limited the power of the President to commit troops to combat for more than 60 days without congressional approval.

Critical Thinking Answer
Yes; when the Court decided that people were interstate commerce in the *Gibbons* case, it established a basis for ruling that a hotel serving interstate travelers was engaging in interstate commerce.

CONNECTIONS

Law
George Washington signed the first United States copyright act into law May 31, 1790. It protected plays, books, and maps for 14 years. It also allowed for renewal for another 14 years.

STUDY GUIDE

Themes in Government
Political Processes What was the impact of the War Powers Act of 1973?

Critical Thinking Skills
Drawing Conclusions Do you think *Gibbons* v. *Ogden* (1824) provided a basis for the Court's position in *Heart of Atlanta Motel* v. *United States* (1964) that a hotel is a part of interstate commerce? Give reasons for your answer.

Special Needs Strategy

Study Strategy All students, but especially those with learning problems, need a strategy that will structure their approach to studying a textbook. One such approach is SQ3R, which stands for Survey, Question, Read, Recite, Review. Survey techniques help students with reading comprehension difficulties understand material more quickly and easily because it focuses attention on essential information. In this section, have students read the headings and subheadings and then write as many as they remember. Then have them repeat the task. How good were they at remembering the headings?

L2 Informative Writing Have students explain in an essay why the commerce clause is considered to be "one of the most sweeping powers of the government."

L3 Persuasive Writing Have students write newspaper editorials expressing either approval or disapproval of the "implied powers" clause.

Caption Answer
veto power

CONNECTIONS

Political Processes

Convicted impeached officials may be punished by more than removal from office. The Senate may prohibit them from ever holding government office, and the official may be tried in a regular court of law.

Assess

Check for Understanding

Have students complete Section 1 Review on page 395.

Meeting Objectives

Each section objective is tested by the Section Review questions that follow it in parentheses.
• Identify the legislative and non-legislative powers of Congress. (2, 3, 4, 7, 8)
• Evaluate how executive agreements have affected the role the Senate plays in foreign policy. (3, 5)
• Detail how Congress may remove an official from office. (6)

Implied Powers The powers given to Congress in the elastic clause are called **implied powers.** The Constitution does not directly grant these to Congress, but they are presumed "necessary and proper" for Congress to exercise its expressed powers. For example, the Constitution does not give Congress the power to create an air force, as it did in 1947. The implied power to create the United States Air Force is based in Congress's expressly stated war powers. Similarly, federal authority to improve rivers and harbors can be implied from the expressed power of Congress to regulate commerce and to maintain a navy.

Non-Legislative Powers

In carrying out their legislative powers, both the House and the Senate perform the same basic tasks—considering, amending, and voting on bills. While most of their non-legislative functions also require their joint efforts, usually each house has a different role in exercising these powers.

The Power to Choose a President The Constitution requires a joint session of Congress to count the Electoral College votes. In modern times this has become a largely ceremonial function.

If no candidate for President has a majority of the electoral votes, the House of Representatives chooses the President from the three candidates with the most votes. Each state's House delegation has one vote. The Senate chooses the Vice President from the two candidates with the most votes. Only two times in American history has no presidential candidate captured a majority of the electoral votes. In 1800 the House elected

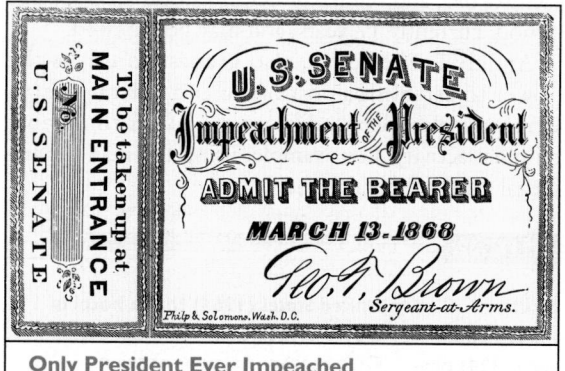

Only President Ever Impeached
Andrew Johnson narrowly avoided being ousted by the Senate in 1868. **Politics What power does the President hold to balance that of Congress?**

Thomas Jefferson over Aaron Burr, and in 1824 it chose John Quincy Adams over Andrew Jackson.

The Twentieth and Twenty-fifth Amendments give Congress the power to settle problems arising from the death of candidates and from presidential incapacity or resignation. The Twenty-fifth Amendment provides that when the office of Vice President becomes vacant, the President appoints a replacement. Both houses of Congress must confirm the appointment. During the 1970s, two Vice Presidents—Gerald Ford and Nelson Rockefeller—gained office under this amendment.

The Removal Power Article I, Section 2, of the Constitution grants Congress the power to remove any member of the executive or judicial branches of government from office. The House of Representatives has exclusive power over **impeachment**, a formal accusation of misconduct in office against a public official. Impeachment is only a charge of wrongdoing; it is not a determination of guilt.

If a majority of the House votes to impeach an official, the case goes to the Senate for trial. A two-thirds vote of those present is required for conviction. When the impeachment proceeding involves a President, the Chief Justice of the United States presides.

Since 1789 the Senate has tried 15 people on impeachment charges—a President, a Supreme Court justice, a senator, a cabinet secretary, and 11 federal judges. Seven of these cases ended in conviction. The most dramatic case was the impeachment of President Andrew Johnson in 1868. The Senate acquitted him by only 1 vote. In 1974 the House Judiciary Committee recommended impeachment of President Nixon for his role in the Watergate scandal. Nixon resigned, however, before the House could vote on it.

House Judiciary Committee chairperson, Peter Rodino, opened the impeachment proceedings against President Nixon. He summarized the meaning of impeachment power:

> *The Founding Fathers clearly did not mean that a President might be impeached for mistakes, even serious mistakes, which he might commit in the faithful execution of his office. By "high crimes and misdemeanors" they meant offenses more definitely incompatible with our Constitution.*
>
> —PETER RODINO, 1974

The Confirmation Power The Senate has the power to approve presidential appointments of federal officials. Because most of these appointments involve

---

Critical Thinking Activity

Drawing Conclusions By the mid-1990s, the national debt of the United States was almost $5 trillion. Two possible solutions to this economic problem are to increase taxes or decrease spending. What are the arguments, pro and con, for each solution? What opposition would each solution likely face in Congress? *(Answers should note the dilemma caused when citizens oppose more taxes but also oppose reducing the benefits that government provides them—entitlements that must be paid for with tax revenues and borrowed money.)*

the promotions of military officers, Senate action is usually only a formality. Each year, however, the Senate looks more closely at several hundred nominations to cabinet and subcabinet positions, regulatory agencies, major diplomatic and military posts, and the federal judiciary. Nominees to the Supreme Court receive the most scrutiny. The Senate has rejected about 20 percent of Court nominations.

The Ratification Power Article II, Section 2, of the Constitution gives the Senate the exclusive power to ratify treaties between the United States and other nations. To ratify a treaty, two-thirds of the senators present must vote for it. This power is one of the key ways in which Congress helps shape foreign policy.

In 1980 many senators opposed the second Strategic Arms Limitation Treaty (SALT II) between the United States and the Soviet Union. This opposition prevented a vote, and the treaty was not ratified. With a few exceptions Senate action on treaties has not been a major factor in American foreign policy. Nevertheless, in recent years Presidents have often bypassed the treaty ratification process by negotiating executive agreements with other heads of state. These agreements do not require Senate approval.

The Amendment Power Congress shares with state legislatures the power to propose amendments. Amendments may be proposed by a two-thirds vote of both houses or by a convention called by the legislatures of two-thirds of the states. Congress also has the power to determine whether state conventions or state legislatures will ratify a proposed amendment.

To date, all of the constitutional amendments have started in Congress. The states have approved 27 proposed amendments and have failed to ratify only 6. Congress has required all amendments, except the Twenty-first Amendment (1933), to be ratified by state legislatures.

Powers Denied to Congress

The powers of Congress, like those of the other branches of the national government, are limited. One important constitutional limit on congressional power is the Bill of Rights. In addition, Article I, Section 9, denies other powers to Congress. Congress may not suspend the **writ of habeas corpus,** a court order to release a person accused of a crime to court to determine whether he or she has been legally detained. Another important limitation denies Congress the authority to pass **bills of attainder,** laws that establish guilt and punish people without a trial. Congress is also prohibited from passing **ex post facto laws,** laws that make crimes of acts that were legal when they were committed. Article I, Section 9, also denies several other powers to Congress, among them the power to tax exports.

Evaluate
- Section 1 Quiz
- Testmaker

Reteach
Have students outline the material in Section 1, using the following framework:

Powers of Congress
I. Legislative Powers
II. Non-legislative Powers
III. Denied Powers

Enrich
Have students complete activity 14 in *Enrichment Activities* in the Teacher's Classroom Resources.

Close

Have students discuss whether the commerce power of Congress or its power to tax has had the more sweeping impact on American life and society.

CONNECTIONS

History
The most bitter battle on treaty ratification in American history took place in 1919 when, despite the urging of President Woodrow Wilson, the Senate refused to ratify the Treaty of Versailles to end World War I.

---

1 SECTION REVIEW

Section Summary
Among the major legislative powers of Congress are the power to tax and spend and to regulate interstate commerce. Prominent among its non-legislative powers are treaty ratification and the power to confirm or remove federal officials.

Checking for Understanding
Recalling Facts
1. Define **expressed powers, enumerated powers, elastic clause, revenue bill, appropriations bill, securities, national debt, bankruptcy, interstate commerce, naturalization, copyright, patent, implied powers, impeachment, writ of habeas corpus, bill of attainder, ex post facto law.**
2. Cite five expressed powers of Congress that help it control the nation's finances.
3. State the foreign policy powers of Congress.
4. List four powers that Article I, Section 9, of the Constitution denies to Congress.

Exploring Themes
5. Separation of Powers How has the President's use of executive agreements affected the constitutional role of the Senate in foreign affairs? Explain why Presidents use this power.
6. Political Processes Describe the process by which Congress may remove a member of the executive or judicial branch from office.

Critical Thinking Skills
7. Making Generalizations How did giving Congress the power to coin money and establish standard weights and measures help accomplish the Preamble to the Constitution's stated goal of forming "a more perfect Union"?
8. Drawing Conclusions Why, do you think, the Founders gave the power to borrow money to Congress alone rather than giving all or part of this power to the executive branch?

Section 1 Review Answers

1. Definitions of terms appear on pages indicated: **expressed powers,** 390; **enumerated powers,** 390; **elastic clause,** 390; **revenue bill,** 391; **appropriations bill,** 391; **securities,** 391; **national debt,** 391; **bankruptcy,** 391; **interstate commerce,** 393; **naturalization,** 393; **copyright,** 393; **patent,** 393; **implied powers,** 394; **impeachment,** 394; **writ of habeas corpus,** 395; **bill of attainder,** 395; **ex post facto law,** 395

2. levying taxes, authorizing spending, borrowing money, coining money, punishing counterfeiters
3. declaring war, maintaining an army and navy, regulating foreign commerce, ratifying treaties, confirming diplomatic appointments
4. may not suspend the writ of habeas corpus, pass bills of attainder, pass ex post facto laws, or tax exports
5. Its role has weakened because, unlike treaties, executive agreements do not require Senate approval.
6. House Judiciary Committee investigates charges and, if

a majority of entire House votes for impeachment, case is tried in Senate, where a two-thirds majority is needed to convict.
7. Answers should include that standard systems of money and weights and measures facilitate economic activity among the states.
8. Answers should suggest that only Congress has the means (through taxation) to pay debts incurred by government.

Focus

Bell Ringer

Write the following on the chalkboard for students to answer:

If you were a member of Congress, how would you know what laws to pass?

Motivating Activity

List students' Bell Ringer responses on the chalkboard. *(executive initiatives, constituent suggestions, perceived problems, investigations)* Tell students this section describes Congress's powers to oversee government programs and to investigate the need for change.

Vocabulary Precheck

List the terms and concepts on the chalkboard. Have volunteers skim the section to find each term and read it in context. **LEP**

Teach

Guided Practice

L1 Distinguishing Fact From Opinion Organize the class into two groups, half to review the power of Congress to conduct investigations, the other half to review the power of Congress to conduct legislative oversight. Have each student write four statements, two of fact and two of opinion, about their assigned power. Have volunteers read their statements, while listeners determine if they are fact or opinion. **LEP**

Additional Powers of Congress

Most congressional powers fall into two of four categories. They are either legislative or non-legislative powers, and they are either expressed powers or implied powers. Over the years, however, Congress has developed additional powers not expressly mentioned in the Constitution. These powers are the power to investigate and the power of legislative oversight.

The Power to Investigate

The Founders neither granted nor denied Congress the power to conduct investigations. Nevertheless, in 1792, after Native Americans soundly defeated the United States Army, Congress launched an investigation of the military. This power has played an important role in American politics ever since.

The Investigation Process A standing committee or a select committee may conduct investigations. Investigations may last for several days or go on for months. The committee's staff members may travel around the country collecting evidence and scheduling witnesses. Dozens of witnesses may be called to testify, sometimes under oath, at committee hearings.

Congressional investigations occur for many reasons. Most get little notice, but a few have become media events. House investigations of communism in the United States attracted widespread attention in the 1940s and 1950s. In 1954 Senator Joseph McCarthy headed a nationally televised investigation that charged that Communists had infiltrated the government. In the late 1950s, during a Senate committee investigation of possible links between labor unions

and organized crime, the committee's attorney, Robert Kennedy, caught the public eye.

Investigations also may have a variety of consequences. Most commonly they lead to new legislation to deal with a problem or changes in a government program. Sometimes, however, congressional investigations result in indictments of individuals or in the loss of government contracts for businesses. In 1973 and 1974, the Senate investigated a break-in at the Democratic party's national headquarters in the Washington, D.C., Watergate building complex. The investigation uncovered that President Nixon's top aides and key members of his reelection committee were involved. This evidence eventually brought criminal convictions and prison terms for these officials.

Investigations can sometimes damage innocent people, however. Baseless accusations by Senator McCarthy in the 1950s, for example, destroyed many careers. A senator from Maine noted:

The danger inherent in such a congressional-committee investigation is that the person under scrutiny will not survive with his reputation intact or unstained. . . . Acts of innocence or error when magnified under the microscope of the committee and the kleig lights of the national television networks will emerge as calculated wrongdoing.
—WILLIAM S. COHEN, 1981

Congressional Powers and Witness Rights Although congressional investigations are not trials, Congress has several powers that help committees collect evidence. Like courts, congressional committees have the power to subpoena witnesses. A **subpoena** is a legal order that a person appear or produce request-

---

SECTION PREVIEW

Objectives
After studying this section, you should be able to:
■ Identify how Congress oversees the activities of the executive branch.

■ Explain the investigative and oversight powers of Congress.

Key Terms and Concepts
subpoena, perjury, contempt, immunity, legislative veto

Themes in Government
■ Civil Rights
■ Political Processes

Critical Thinking Skills
■ Making Generalizations
■ Synthesizing Information

396 UNIT 4: THE LEGISLATIVE BRANCH

Classroom Resources for Section 2

📁 Guided Reading Activities
📁 Reproducible Lesson Plans
📁 Supreme Court Case Studies 48
📁 Section 2 Quiz

💻 Testmaker
SAT Practice Tests
Writer's Guidebook

ed documents. Congress makes great use of this power. The Senate Watergate Committee, for example, issued hundreds of subpoenas during its 18-month investigation.

Also like courts, congressional committees can require witnesses to testify under oath. Witnesses who do not tell the truth can be criminally prosecuted for **perjury,** or lying under oath. In addition, committees may punish those who refuse to testify or otherwise cooperate by holding them in **contempt,** or willful obstruction, of Congress. Persons found in contempt of Congress may be arrested and jailed. While the Constitution does not grant Congress this power, court decisions have generally upheld it. Since 1789 Congress has voted about 400 contempt citations.

Until recent years witnesses called before a congressional committee had few rights. In 1948, for example, the chairperson of a House committee told one hapless witness: "The rights you have are the rights given you by this committee. We will determine what rights you have and what rights you do not have before the committee."

Today this situation has changed, and witnesses have important rights when appearing before a congressional committee. In *Watkins* v. *United States* (1957), the Supreme Court ruled that Congress must respect witnesses' constitutional rights just as a court does. The Court stated:

W*itnesses cannot be compelled to give evidence against themselves. They cannot be subjected to unreasonable search and seizure. Nor can the 1st Amendment freedoms of speech, press, religion, or political belief and association be abridged.*
—Chief Justice Earl Warren, 1957

One way that congressional committees have sidestepped this requirement is by granting immunity to witnesses. **Immunity** is freedom from prosecution for witnesses whose testimony ties them to illegal acts. Of course, the Fifth Amendment states that people cannot be forced to testify against themselves. Witnesses who are granted immunity, however, can be required

to testify about illegal activities in which they are involved. Those who refuse may be held in contempt and jailed. The Watergate Committee, for example, gave immunity to 27 witnesses.

In 1987 a committee chaired by Senator Daniel Inouye investigated charges against officials in the Reagan administration. They were charged with selling arms to Iran and using the money to finance a guerrilla war in Nicaragua. Faced with contradictory testimony about who was involved, the committee granted immunity to Colonel Oliver North, an employee of the President's National Security Council.

Compelled to testify, North implicated the President's National Security Adviser, Admiral John Poindexter, and others in the scheme. Poindexter was

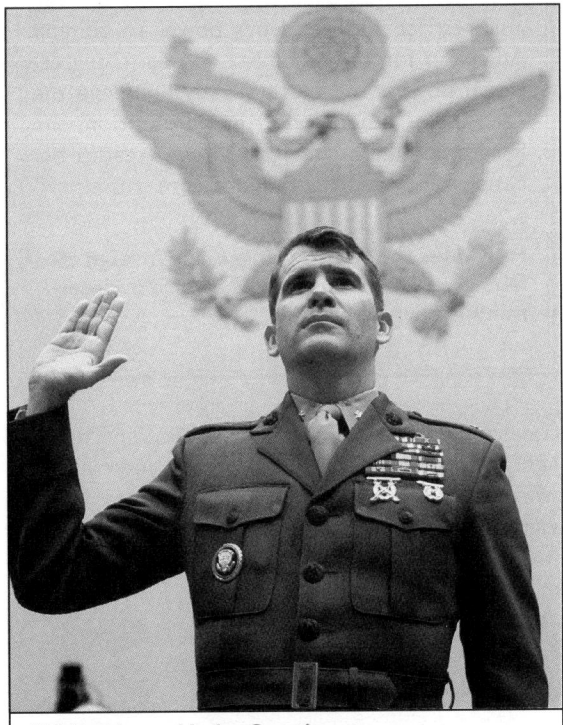

White House Under Scrutiny
Some senators favored immunity for Oliver North, expecting him to implicate the President. **History What happened as a result of his testimony?**

CHAPTER 14: THE POWERS OF CONGRESS 397

Themes in Government
Civil Rights **What was the impact of *Watkins* v. *United States*?**

Critical Thinking Skills
Making Generalizations Do you think that citizens required to testify in the McCarthy com-

munism hearings and found innocent were able to maintain their prior good reputations? Why or why not?

📁 **Demonstrating Reasoned Judgment** Have students read case 48 in *Supreme Court Case Studies* in the Teacher's Classroom Resources. After students complete the written activity, ask their opinions on the legislative veto. Do they believe it violates separation of powers, or is it an important part of checks and balances?

L2 Analyzing Ideas Have students read the 1948 comment by the chairperson of a House committee about witness rights on page 397. Have them consider whether a committee of Congress should be able to conduct investigative proceedings without observing the legal safeguards of the Bill of Rights. *(Some students may argue that since such investigations lead to no legal criminal or civil finding, the safeguards need not apply.)*

Caption Answer
He implicated the national security adviser.

Theme Answer
Congress must respect witnesses' constitutional rights as do the courts.

Critical Thinking Answer
No; reputations were tarnished by all the attention by the government and the media.

Independent Practice

L1 Drawing a Political Cartoon Have students draw a political cartoon that focuses on ways that lawmakers exercise the power of legislative oversight. **LEP**

Background

A number of investigative committees of Congress have been well received. However, in the years after World War II, some committees—organized to investigate crime, labor racketeering, and communism—were widely criticized. Critics claimed that such investigations were "fishing expeditions" with no special legislative purpose, that they accused witnesses on hearsay evidence and denied the accused legal safeguards, and that they investigated issues only to provoke publicity. One frequent target of criticism was the House Un-American Activities Committee.

Tell students that the labels *hawk* and *dove* first gained widespread use during the Vietnam War. Ask what they think these descriptions mean when applied to Congress. Ask: Is it important to know whether your representative is a hawk or a dove?
Examining the Connection Answer: *Voters can vote for members of Congress who share their foreign policy views.*

STUDY GUIDE

Theme Answer
size and complexity of federal programs; little public interest in oversight—so political value limited; many laws lack clear objectives; legislators work closely with agencies they oversee, relationships make oversight awkward

Critical Thinking Answer
They help ensure that needed evidence will be available to legislators during congressional investigative committees.

Assess

Check for Understanding

Have students complete Section 2 Review on page 399.

Focus on Government
Video 24
Lecture Launcher:
The Powers of Congress
Running Time: 2:11
Videodisc 2, Chap. 24
VHS Tape 2, Begins 11:15

GLOBAL CONNECTION

Interdependence

Congress and Foreign Affairs The President is primarily responsible for United States relations with other countries. Congress, however, shares this responsibility.

The Constitution grants only to Congress powers to declare war. It can also raise and support armies, maintain a navy, and make rules governing land and naval forces. According to the War Powers Act of 1973, Congress can also restrict the President's power to commit American forces to combat abroad. Congressional powers therefore greatly influence the security of other countries. In addition, the Senate has the power to approve treaties between the United States and foreign nations.

Examining the Connection
How does the role of Congress in foreign affairs give American citizens a voice in determining foreign policy?

---

convicted on criminal charges, but his conviction was later overturned. North also was tried and convicted. Although his sentence was later commuted, his conviction was overturned on appeal because evidence used against him was uncovered as a result of his protected congressional testimony.

Legislative Oversight

Many, if not most, congressional investigations are related to another power that Congress has developed. The power of legislative oversight involves a continuing review of how effectively the executive

---

branch carries out the laws Congress passes. In exercising this power, congressional committees keep watch over the agencies of the executive branch.

The Practice of Legislative Oversight Legislative oversight is a way for Congress to determine if laws are being carried out as intended. It is a good example of the constitutional principle of checks and balances at work. As the legislative branch, Congress makes the laws. The job of the executive branch is to carry them out. In doing so, the executive branch has the power to decide what legislation means and how it should be put into effect. Through its power of legislative oversight, Congress can check on how the executive branch is administering the law.

Congress has defined its oversight functions in several laws. The Legislative Reorganization Act of 1946 calls for Congress to exercise "continuous watchfulness" over executive agencies. In the Reorganization Act of 1970, Congress went even further. That law states, "Each standing committee shall review and study, on a continuing basis, the application, administration, and execution" of laws in areas for which it is responsible.

Limits on Legislative Oversight In practice, however, lawmakers exercise the power of legislative oversight in an inconsistent way. Vice President Hubert Humphrey once said that Congress "sometimes gets in the habit of 'pass it and forget it' lawmaking." Very few congressional committees review the actions of the executive branch on a regular basis. Instead, legislative oversight usually occurs in bits and pieces as lawmakers, congressional staffs, and committees go about their other business.

Several reasons explain why legislative oversight is not carried out more systematically. First, the huge size and complexity of federal government programs make oversight difficult. For example, the Department of Veterans Affairs alone has about 250,000 employees. Lawmakers do not have enough staff, time, or money to keep track of everything going on—even in this one agency in the executive branch. It simply is not possi-

STUDY GUIDE

Themes in Government
Political Processes Laws that define legislative oversight seem to direct Congress to a thorough and continuing process. **Why is legislative oversight an inconsistent process?**

Critical Thinking Skills
Synthesizing Information How do the use of the subpoena and perjury and contempt charges assist legislators in the hearing process?

Cooperative Learning Activity

Have students prepare an in-depth news report on Congress's power to investigate and its power of legislative oversight. Organize students into groups—those who will gather information about the powers, those who will prepare written copy for the telecast, and those who will serve as reporters and anchors for the show. Students' reports should include descriptions of the two powers, as well as examples of each.

ble for Congress to effectively monitor the routine activities of the many executive agencies.

Second, lawmakers know there are not many votes to be gained from most oversight activities. Voters and the news media seldom are interested in oversight activities unless an investigation turns up a scandal or an unusual problem. For example, when Congress found that some defense contractors were grossly overcharging the military for common items available in most hardware stores, the discovery attracted widespread media attention. Both the voters and the press, however, generally ignore a billion-dollar program that is working fairly well. As a result, many oversight activities focus on specific problems or situations that are likely to receive public attention. As one lawmaker aptly put it, "Where there is publicity to be gained, there is oversight to be had."

Third, the unclear objectives of many laws can make it hard for Congress to oversee them. The language of some laws is so vague that it is very difficult to judge exactly what they mean. Without clear objectives, lawmakers have little basis for judging whether or not the executive branch is carrying out the law's intent.

Finally, committees sometimes come to favor and support the federal agencies they are supposed to oversee. Lawmakers on a committee and the officials who work for a federal agency often become well acquainted. They spend long hours working together on common problems, and they both get to know the people the agency serves. In such cases a committee is not likely to engage in careful, critical oversight of an agency.

Congressional Limits on Executive Activities
Congress exercises its oversight power in several ways. One way is for Congress to require executive agencies to submit reports to Congress on their activities. The 1946 Employment Act, for example, requires the President to send Congress an annual report on the nation's economy. During a recent term of Congress, federal agencies submitted more than 1,000 such reports to Capitol Hill.

A second oversight technique is for lawmakers to ask one of the congressional support agencies, such as the General Accounting Office (GAO), to study an executive agency's work. The GAO, for example, monitors the finances of federal agencies to make sure public money has been spent according to law.

The power of Congress to appropriate money provides yet another means of oversight. Each year, as part of the federal budget process, the House and Senate review the budgets of all agencies in the executive branch. This review gives Congress the opportunity to shape public policy by expanding, cutting back, or even eliminating certain programs.

For years Congress used the **legislative veto.** In a legislative veto, Congress wrote certain provisions into some laws. These provisions allowed it to review and cancel actions of the executive agencies that carried out those laws. This device gave Congress authority over officials who are subordinates of the President. In 1983 the Supreme Court ruled in *Immigration and Naturalization Service* v. *Chadha* that the veto was unconstitutional because it violated the principle of separation of powers.

2 SECTION REVIEW

Section Summary
Congressional committees investigate problems to assess the need for new legislation. They also review how well the executive branch carries out existing law.

Checking for Understanding
Recalling Facts
1. Define subpoena, perjury, contempt, immunity, legislative veto.
2. Explain how the investigative and oversight powers of Congress differ from the rest of its powers.
3. Identify three congressional investigations that attracted wide media attention.
4. Cite three reasons Congress does not carry out legislative oversight on a regular basis.

Exploring Themes
5. Civil Rights What steps can Congress take if a witness at a congressional investigation cites Fifth Amendment protections and refuses to testify?
6. Political Processes What arguments might be advanced to support a legislative veto power for Congress?

Critical Thinking Skills
7. Making Generalizations Why might, as Senator Cohen suggests, a witness's reputation be in danger if he or she testifies at a televised congressional hearing?
8. Synthesizing Information What relationship, if any, exists between the oversight power of Congress and its investigative power?

Meeting Objectives
Each section objective is tested by the Section Review questions that follow it in parentheses.
• Identify how Congress oversees the activities of the executive branch. (3, 4, 6)
• Explain the investigative and oversight powers of Congress. (2, 3, 5, 7, 8)

Evaluate
Section 2 Quiz

 Testmaker

Reteach
Have students write a paragraph that connects the investigative powers of Congress with its power of legislative oversight.

Enrich
Have students research one of the congressional investigations discussed in this section. What were the political issues? Who were the major players? Who, if anyone, was prosecuted? Did any laws change as a result of the investigation?

Close

Have students discuss the pros and cons of the use of immunity during investigations. Does it advance or retard justice? How and why?

Section 2 Review Answers

1. Definitions of terms appear on pages indicated: **subpoena,** 396; **perjury,** 397; **contempt,** 397; **immunity,** 397; **legislative veto,** 399
2. They are neither expressed nor implied in the Constitution but have simply been assumed by Congress.
3. Accept any three: House investigations of communists in government, McCarthy investigation of communists in government, Senate investigation of possible links between labor unions and organized crime, Watergate investigation, Iran-contra investigation.
4. Accept any three: Government is too large and complex; there are not many votes to be gained in oversight activities; many laws lack clear objectives against which to judge performance; congressional committees become too close to the agencies they are supposed to oversee.
5. It can grant the witness immunity from prosecution for his or her testimony. If the witness still refuses, Congress may hold the witness in contempt.
6. Answers should center on right of Congress to assure that intent of laws it passes is carried out.
7. Answers should suggest that lawmakers could use hearings to make themselves look good to voters at witness's expense. Also, networks may be more interested in exciting news than in total accuracy.
8. Answers should recognize that investigations can be part of a larger oversight power.

CRITICAL THINKING SKILLS

Focus

Organize the class into groups and give each group one or two pages from the newspaper. Tell them to choose an article and circle the statements in the article that could be proven. Invite each group to then read their list and tell how each statement they circled could be proven. Do the articles contain many statements that could be proven? by what methods?

Teach

Review the statements concerning the NEH and the NEA. Ask: What are some ways to prove factual statements? *(Verify data from records, talk to original sources, and so on.)* Have students examine the NEH statement. Ask what language clues indicate that it is a statement of opinion rather than of fact. *(worthy guardian)* Ask: Can opinions be proven? *(Sample: Yes, an opinion may be a prediction that is borne out in time.)* Why is it difficult to separate facts from opinions? *(People often mix opinions with facts or use facts to support faulty opinions.)*

Assess

Have students complete the **Practice** exercise.

Close

Have students return to their newspaper articles and reread the statements they circled. Have their ideas changed as to which could be proven or not?

Distinguishing Fact From Opinion

Knowing how to distinguish between *facts*, which can be proven or disproven, and *opinions*, which are based on people's differing values and beliefs, is an important skill. If you can distinguish fact from opinion, you will be better able to make judgments based on a combination of factual information and your own personal values and beliefs.

Explanation

To distinguish between fact and opinion, follow these steps:

• Read the statement carefully.
• Ask: What evidence supports this statement? What makes me confident that this statement is valid?
• If the statement can be proven, it is factual. For example, it is a fact that *Thomas Jefferson served as the third President*. Historical evidence supports the statement.
• If the statement refers to situations that are desirable or undesirable, important or unimportant, or likely or unlikely, then the statement is an opinion. For example, it is an opinion that *Thomas Jefferson was the greatest President*. This assertion is based on someone's preferences or ideas.

The statement below is taken from debate over whether Congress should continue to spend tax money to support the arts through the National Endowment for the Humanities (NEH) and the National Endowment for the Arts (NEA).

The NEH has proved a worthy guardian and sponsor of our nation's cultural history.
— REP. E. THOMAS COLEMAN

Can this statement be proven? It might seem that data about the number of projects the NEH has aided would help prove this statement, but that would not really be evidence that the NEH has been "a worthy guardian." A critic might agree that the NEH has backed many projects but claim they were not worthy projects. The worthiness of a project is based on values and beliefs. This statement is an opinion.

In the 25-year history of the NEA, fewer than 25 grants out of some 85,000 have even caused a stir.
— REP. CLAUDINE SCHNEIDER

This is a statement of fact. By examining NEA records, one could determine how many of its grants have been controversial. The controversy may have been over questions of opinion, such as whether the projects were ugly or offensive or a waste of money, but whether or not there was a controversy is a fact.

Practice

Use what you have learned about distinguishing fact from opinion to examine the statements below that are taken from a 1991 congressional debate over the use of force against Iraq. Decide whether each is a statement of fact or opinion and explain what evidence would be needed to support it.

1. It is equally clear that [Iraq] has spent billions . . . to acquire a . . . nuclear weapons production capability, is actively producing biological weapons, and has stockpiled thousands of tons of chemical weapons.
— SENATOR JOHN McCAIN, R-ARIZONA

2. We as a people have to be bold enough and mature enough to move beyond the cave man mentality that says we must fight and maim as a way of solving human problems.
— REP. RONALD DELLUMS, D-CALIFORNIA

3. If [Iraq's president Saddam] Hussein succeeds in facing down the United States, he will feel free to start hitting U.S. targets with his terrorism.
— SENATOR ORRIN HATCH, R-UTAH

Additional Practice

To practice this skill, see **Reinforcing the Skill** on page 407.

Practice Answers

1. Fact; intelligence reports and photographs, statements by the Iraqi government, and records of arms merchants are hard evidence that could prove or disprove this statement.
2. Opinion; it states a value judgment, that war is an outmoded and immature response to problems. The evidence to persuade others would be based on arguments about what is moral and right.
3. Opinion; no factual evidence could prove or disprove it. The best evidence the speaker could produce would be actions of past leaders after they "faced down" the United States. The audience would have to use its own judgments and beliefs about what was likely in this case.

For additional practice, have students complete activity 14 in *Skill Reinforcement Activities* in the Teacher's Classroom Resources.

Shared Powers of Congress

Former Senate majority leader Mike Mansfield once observed, "We want [the President] to exercise the leadership . . . but we would appreciate closer cooperation." Mansfield's comment illustrates the close but often competitive relationship between the legislative and executive branches.

When the Founders established the principle of separation of powers, they did not make the three branches completely independent. Although each branch has its own functions, they are related in a system of checks and balances. As a result, Congress and the President share certain powers. Thus, many of the President's most important executive responsibilities—such as making treaties, appointing federal officials and judges, and paying the expenses of the executive branch—require congressional cooperation.

On the other hand, all bills Congress passes require the President's signature before they become law. Overriding a presidential veto requires a two-thirds majority in each house of Congress, which usually is difficult to obtain. Consequently, a veto or even the threat of one is an important legislative power the President exercises. In addition, modern Presidents are expected to develop a legislative program and secure its adoption by Congress.

Congress and the President

The level of cooperation between Congress and the President has varied throughout history. Usually, the best relations exist between the two branches when the President makes few demands on Congress. Less active Presidents—such as Dwight D. Eisenhower during the 1950s—who do not take an aggressive

role in shaping legislation may get along well with Congress. Those who propose major new programs will almost surely come into conflict with the legislative branch. Recent Presidents have frequently found it hard to work with Congress for several reasons.

Constituents and Conflict A large national electorate chooses Presidents who promote policies they feel are in the best interests of the entire nation. Individual states and congressional districts, however, elect members of Congress. Because they represent much narrower interests, members of Congress often have ideas very different from the President about what constitutes desirable public policy.

Checks and Balances and Conflict The system of checks and balances gives Congress and the President the power to counteract each other. For example, the President may threaten a veto, arguing that a particular bill spends too much money and would spur inflation harmful to the nation. Some members of Congress may cooperate in attempting to amend the bill or override a veto because their states or districts would benefit from the bill.

Thus, while members of Congress expect the President to propose new legislation, they often seek to modify his or her initiatives to suit the interests of the people in their states or districts. In the struggle over the shaping of public policy, each branch uses the powers it enjoys under the system of checks and balances to influence the other branch. Political historian James MacGregor Burns contends that the system is "designed for deadlock and inaction." He argues that these checks and balances result in the "President versus Congress."

SECTION PREVIEW

Objectives
After studying this section, you should be able to:
- Explain the sources of conflict between the President and Congress.

- Enumerate how Congress may oppose the President's proposals.

Key Terms and Concepts
national budget, impoundment

Themes in Government
- Checks and Balances
- Political Processes

Critical Thinking Skills
- Synthesizing Information
- Drawing Conclusions

CHAPTER 14: THE POWERS OF CONGRESS   401

Classroom Resources for Section 3

- Guided Reading Activities
- Reproducible Lesson Plans
- Participating in Government 14
- Interpreting Political Cartoons 35
- Reteaching Activities 14
- Section 3 Quiz

- Chapter 14 Tests
- Testmaker
- Audio Cassettes (English and Spanish)
- Limited English Proficiency Activities 14
- SAT Practice Tests
- Writer's Guidebook

Focus

Bell Ringer

List these words on the chalkboard: *compromise, divergence, deadlock, debate, conflict* and ask students which carry a positive connotation and which carry a negative connotation.

Motivating Activity

Discuss students' Bell Ringer responses. Then organize students into groups of four and provide each group with a different copy of a daily newspaper. Ask each group to identify and summarize an article that involves compromise or conflict between the President and Congress.

Vocabulary Precheck

Call on students to read aloud the definitions of *national budget* and *impoundment* from the Glossary. Then have them restate each definition in their own words.
LEP

Teach

Guided Practice

L1 Creating a Table Create a table on the chalkboard showing the factors that contribute to conflict between the President and Congress. Use the horizontal headings *President* and *Congress* and vertical headings *Constituents, Checks and Balances, Organization, Party Politics,* and *Timetables.* Have students suggest entries for the chart. **LEP**

L2 **Analyzing Ideas** Present the following case:

Congress appropriates money to provide special housing for the homeless. The President opposes the program because it will cost too much money and vetoes the law. Congress overrides the veto. The President refuses to spend the money.

Discuss what Congress could do to get the program started, what further actions the President could take to oppose it, and which branch of government should be blamed by the public if the policy is ineffective.

L3 **Interpreting Primary Sources** Have students read the quote by former President Lyndon Johnson on page 402. Have them paraphrase the paragraph to clarify its meaning. Ask volunteers to put their paragraphs on the chalkboard for discussion by the class.

Caption Answer
President promotes national policies; Congress represents more local, narrower interests

STUDY GUIDE

Theme Answer
When an election is approaching, both parties act largely in their political self-interest to assure reelection. When a President is concluding a second term, he or she is a lame duck and has little influence over Congress.

Critical Thinking Answer
They often blame each other for failures.

Organization as a Cause of Conflict The organization of Congress provides many weapons to those who want to resist a legislative proposal of the President. Rules of procedure, such as the Senate's unlimited debate rule, can be used to block action on legislation. Even when congressional leaders support the President, they may struggle to push presidential initiatives through Congress.

Because the basic shape of legislation is set in committees and subcommittees, the committee system also may be a weapon against the President. Committee chairpersons are powerful members of Congress, and they use their positions to influence bills. Some of the greatest conflicts in government occur when a President wants a major proposal approved and a committee tries to delay, revise, or defeat it.

Party Politics Partisan political differences can affect the relationship between the President and Congress. Lawmakers generally find it easier to support a President of their party than they would one from another party. Because in recent decades the President's party rarely has controlled either house of Congress, conflict between the branches has increased. One lawmaker noted:

Deflecting the Political Heat
The President and Congress often blame each other for failures. **Politics** **How do their goals differ?**

During this whole process, political considerations have an importance not always discussed. While they may be outweighed by other concerns, they are nevertheless always present. If the congressman is a member of the political party which occupies the White House, he has some responsibility for helping to pass the President's programs.

—Representative Bill Frenzel, 1985

Differing Political Timetables Conflicts may also occur because the President and Congress have different political timetables. Presidents have only four years to develop, present, and move their programs through Congress before they have to busy themselves running for reelection. At best, they have only eight years to accomplish their agenda.

Members of Congress have political timetables quite different from the President. Representatives, who serve only two-year terms, are always running for reelection. Senators, whose terms are six years, can be more patient in handling controversial legislative proposals. Thus, lawmakers in both houses, each for their own reasons, may not be eager to act on legislation that does not directly benefit their states or districts.

Members of Congress are not limited to two terms in office as is the President. Most can look forward to being reelected for many terms, no matter how well or how poorly any President's legislative program does in Congress.

Lyndon Johnson served as Senate majority leader and later became President. He once described the timetable a President must have when dealing with Congress:

You've got to give it all you can that first year. . . . You've got just one year when they treat you right, and before they start worrying about themselves. The third year, you lose votes. . . . The fourth year's all politics. You can't put anything through when half the Congress is thinking how to beat you.

—Lyndon Johnson

STUDY GUIDE

Themes in Government
Checks and Balances Because most members of Congress can be fairly confident of reelection, their timetable for legislation may not match the President's.

Why is it difficult for the President to accomplish his or her legislative agenda in the third or fourth year of office?

Critical Thinking Skills
Synthesizing Information What does the political cartoon above indicate about the conflict between Congress and the President?

Cooperative Learning Activity

Organize students into five groups and assign each group one of the reasons for conflict between Congress and the President—constituents, checks and balances, organization of Congress, party politics, political timetables. Each group should develop a teaching tool that explains the conflict, gives a specific example of the conflict, and any suggestions the group has for ways the conflict might be alleviated. Ask each group to present their teaching tool to the class.

PARTICIPATING IN GOVERNMENT

Writing to a Member of Congress

Do you have strong views about a bill that is pending before Congress? One effective means of expressing your views is to write a letter to your legislator.

Use the following guidelines when writing to a member of Congress.

Make sure you have the correct spelling of your senator's or representative's name. Consult your local library or political party headquarters if you are not sure. Send your letter to:

Senator _____
United States Senate
Washington, DC 20510

or to:

Representative _____
House of Representatives
Washington, DC 20515

If your letter concerns pending legislation, identify the bill by its number or name such as H.R. 377 or the Farm Aid Bill. Send your letter before the bill is out of committee or has passed the Senate or the House.

Give specific reasons for your point of view. Be brief.

Keep in mind that legislators receive hundreds of letters each week. Do not be surprised if you receive a personalized computer form letter in reply to your letter. This does not mean that your opinion has been ignored. Members of Congress welcome your views.

Investigating Further

Contact the local office of your senator or representative. Find out other ways that you can make your views known to your legislators.

The Struggle for Power

Throughout American history the balance of power between Congress and the President has shifted back and forth. For most of the first 150 years of the Republic, Congress dominated policy-making. At times, however, strong Presidents such as Andrew Jackson and Abraham Lincoln challenged congressional supremacy. They increased presidential powers as they dealt with changing social and economic conditions.

The system of checks and balances makes it likely that the President and Congress will always compete for power. Which branch will dominate in any specific period depends on many factors, including the political issues of the time and the leaders in Congress and the executive branch. Since the 1930s many political observers have noted a steady growth in the powers of the presidency at the expense of Congress. Aggressive Presidents from both political parties have acted in ways that expand their authority.

During the mid-1970s, however, this trend toward presidential dominance began to stimulate a reaction from Congress. Congressional efforts to reassert lost authority and to gain new influence in public policy dealt with the President's emergency powers, the federal budget, and the legislative veto.

Curbing the President's Emergency Powers In times of crisis, Congress has delegated additional powers to the President. Presidents have declared martial law, seized property, controlled transportation and communication, and sent armed forces overseas.

STUDY GUIDE

Themes in Government
Political Processes How do the political timetables of Presidents, representatives, and senators contribute to political conflict?

Critical Thinking Skills
Drawing Conclusions Presidents represent all the people; senators represent the people of their states; representatives serve smaller legislative districts.

Do you think the fact of these different constituencies helps to slow the political process? Explain your answer.

PARTICIPATING IN GOVERNMENT

The volume of mail delivered to members of Congress each year is staggering, but most of it is answered. Have each student choose an area of personal interest and write a letter to his or her senators or representative, asking his or her position on the issue.

📁 Have students complete activity 14 in *Participating in Government* in the Teacher's Classroom Resources.

Independent Practice

📁 **Interpreting Political Cartoons** Have students complete activity 35 in *Interpreting Political Cartoons* in the Teacher's Classroom Resources.

L2 Checks and Balances Have students review a recent month's issues of a weekly newsmagazine received by the library. Have them list subjects of presidential-congressional conflict chronicled during that period.

STUDY GUIDE

Theme Answer
President runs every four years, with the goal of being elected for two terms, or eight years. Two terms give ample time to accomplish a President's agenda. Senators run every six years and are most often reelected, so they feel they may move slowly. However, since representatives must run for reelection every two years, they have very little time to accomplish their goals.

Critical Thinking Answer
Yes; each of these constituencies is likely to have different concerns.

Critical Thinking Activity

Synthesizing Information Remind students that one expert has described the system of checks and balances as one of "deadlock and inaction" that results in the "President versus Congress." Ask students if they agree or disagree with this point of view and to give reasons for their opinion. (*Answers will vary, but students might include the idea that competition between the branches is inherent because of the system of checks and balances.*)

Assess

Check for Understanding

Have students complete Section 3 Review on page 404.

Meeting Objectives

Each section objective is tested by the Section Review questions that follow it in parentheses.
- Explain the sources of conflict between the President and Congress. (2, 4, 6, 7, 8)
- Enumerate how Congress may oppose the President's proposals. (3, 5, 7)

Evaluate

📁 Section 3 Quiz

💻 Testmaker

Reteach

📁 Have students complete activity 14 in *Reteaching Activities* in the Teacher's Classroom Resources.

Enrich

Have students investigate the positions of their congressional representatives on the President's current policy initiatives.

Close

Have students consider the quote by Bill Frenzel on page 402 and explain why they agree or disagree with it.

President Franklin D. Roosevelt gained vast authority during the Great Depression and World War II. In 1933, Congress empowered the President to close the nation's banks. Legislation during World War II gave Roosevelt even broader control over the nation's economy, including industries, wages and prices, and the rationing of consumer goods. Later Presidents continued the emergency powers initially granted to Roosevelt, and technically the United States remained in a state of emergency. In 1971, for example, President Nixon froze wages and prices to combat economic problems stemming from the Vietnam War.

In 1976 Congress passed the National Emergencies Act that ended the 35-year state of emergency as of September 30, 1978. Since that date Presidents no longer possess automatic emergency powers. Presidents must notify Congress when they intend to declare a national emergency. A state of emergency now cannot last more than 1 year unless the President repeats the process. In addition, Congress can end a state of emergency at any time by a majority vote in both houses.

The Budget Impoundment and Control Act

Over the years Presidents have assumed more responsibility for planning the **national budget,** the yearly financial plan for the national government. By the early 1970s, Congress had slipped into the role of merely reacting to budget proposals.

In 1974 Congress passed the Congressional Budget and Impoundment Control Act in an effort to increase its role in planning the budget. The act established a permanent budget committee for each house and created a Congressional Budget Office (CBO) to provide financial experts to help Congress. In addition, the act limited the President's ability to impound funds. **Impoundment** is the President's refusal to spend money Congress has voted to fund a program. The law requires that appropriated funds be spent unless the President requests and both houses of Congress agree that they not be spent.

Use of the Legislative Veto

Since 1932 more than 200 laws have contained some form of legislative veto. The veto was not widely used, however, until Congress reasserted its authority in the 1970s. Many members of Congress argued that the device was an effective way to ensure that the executive branch listened to congressional intentions.

Presidents have opposed the legislative veto and regarded it as a challenge to their authority. President Carter complained that its use was "excessive." Others argued that it violated separation of powers. Because the Supreme Court agreed with that position, Congress has searched for a constitutional alternative to the legislative veto.

Congressional actions continue to illustrate the struggle for power between the branches of government. This competition may make the process of government seem tortuous, but it is a natural part of the system, helping ensure that neither branch can assume total control of the national government.

---

3 SECTION REVIEW

Section Summary
Although the President and Congress share important powers, conflict often characterizes their relationship.

Checking for Understanding
Recalling Facts
1. Define national budget, impoundment.
2. Describe how the political-party system contributes to conflict between the President and Congress.
3. State how the organization of Congress allows its members to oppose the President's proposals.
4. Explain how emergency powers have strengthened the presidency.

Exploring Themes
5. Checks and Balances How can a small group in the House or Senate block a President's request for legislation?

6. Political Processes Why do the different constituencies of the President and Congress contribute to the conflict between the executive and legislative branches?

Critical Thinking Skills
7. Synthesizing Information One analyst described the constitutional arrangements between Congress and the President as "an invitation to struggle." How does the information in this section support this description?
8. Drawing Conclusions When Senator Adlai Stevenson stated, "The way to move Congress is by moving people. . . . Only the President can lead," what judgment was he making about the relationship between the two branches?

Section 3 Review Answers

1. Definitions of terms appear on pages indicated: **national budget,** 404; **impoundment,** 404
2. When different parties control Congress and the White House, party politics adds to congressional opposition to President's proposals.
3. Rules on debate and committee system allow members of Congress to obstruct legislation requested by the President.

4. In times of national crisis, Congress has granted vast powers to the President, which the office did not relinquish when the emergency ended.
5. They could alter shape of legislation in committees and subcommittees, or could delay it. On the floor they could further delay it through debate.
6. Senators and representatives speak for a narrower group of people than does the President, who represents all the people. A program in the national interest may hurt the people of a state or congressional district.

7. Because the Constitution requires that Congress share powers with the executive branch and because Congress has developed the power to investigate and to oversee the executive branch, the relationship between these branches is marked by conflict.
8. Members of Congress are sensitive to the needs of their constituents. The President's constituency is broader and more diverse. Hence Congress is less likely to have cohesive opinions on most issues, allowing the President to exercise more leadership than Congress.

Senator Daniel Inouye on Congressional Investigations

Hawaii's senior senator, Daniel K. Inouye, served on the 1973 Senate committee that investigated Watergate. In 1987 he chaired an investigation of the Iran-contra scandal. In May 1987 Senator Inouye addressed the George Washington University law school, where he commented on the conduct of congressional investigations.

The sights and sounds are familiar: the Senate Caucus Room overflowing with people and overheating with television floodlights; the questions about what the President knew and when he knew it; what the President's men did and why they did it; what laws were bent, broken, or ignored by zealots for whom the end was more important than the means.

On Tuesday, May 5, 1987, almost 14 years to the day since the Watergate hearings began in the same room, two select committees of Congress begin public hearings into the Iran-contra affair. There was a sense of deja vu.

But the Iran-contra affair is not Watergate. . . . Watergate was . . . a domestic political scandal. . . .

[The Iran-contra affair] involves the constitutional relationship between the executive and legislative branches in the shaping of foreign policy. . . .

A political operation that spins out of control may lead to electoral abuses. A runaway foreign policy may lead to international mistrust, broken relations and heightened tensions. Because of the profound issues in question, we in Congress are compelled to investigate the episode. And for precisely the same reason, we are compelled to insure that the investigation is conducted in an atmosphere free of partisanship and theatrics. . . .

We are obligated to investigate the conduct of the highest Government officers, and we are determined to let the facts lead us where they will. . . .

The Senate committee that investigated Watergate, on which I served, had the same mandate as do today's select committees: to seek the facts about the events in question and propose legislation to prevent a repetition.

But the structure of our Watergate committee staff encouraged partisanship. There were majority (Democratic) and minority (Republican) lawyers, there were majority

We are obligated to investigate the conduct of the highest Government officers, and we are determined to let the facts lead us where they will.

and minority investigators, majority and minority secretaries. Even the committee's budget was divided into Democratic and Republican portions. . . .

My one condition for assuming the role as chairman of the Senate [Iran-contra] committee was that there would be no majority and minority staffs, but a unified staff whose members report to the committee as a whole and not to the Democrats or the Republicans. . . .

The structure of the staff would be meaningless if the members of the committee . . . [made] this investigation a partisan matter. . . .

At the opening of the Watergate hearings, chairman Sam Ervin reminded his audience that "the purpose of these hearings is not prosecutorial or judicial, but rather investigative and informative." Our purpose is the same.

—SENATOR DANIEL K. INOUYE, 1987

Examining the Reading

Reviewing Facts

1. Summarize Senator Inouye's description of the Iran-contra affair.
2. Compare the way the Watergate and Iran-contra investigating committees were structured.

Critical Thinking Skills

3. Understanding Cause and Effect How might the structure of a congressional investigating committee affect its investigation?

Focus

Ask students if they have ever watched a congressional hearing on television. What were their reactions? What are their opinions on how the hearing was conducted?

Teach

Ask: How was the background of the Iran-contra and Watergate investigations similar? *(Both involved high government officials and lawbreaking by people who thought their goals were more important than the law.)* What is the purpose of select investigative committees, according to Inouye? *(to seek the facts, to propose legislation to prevent repetition of wrongdoing)*

Assess

Have students complete **Examining the Reading.**

Answers

1. a runaway foreign policy operation
2. *Watergate:* partisan staffs and budgets; *Iran-contra:* a unified staff reporting to the entire committee
3. Such formal partisanship might hamper the investigation or even lead to further attempts to cover up the truth.

Close

Inouye differentiates between Watergate and the Iran-contra scandal. Do students agree?

CHAPTER 14: THE POWERS OF CONGRESS 405

More About Personal Perspectives

Senator Daniel Inouye began his career as a young lawyer. He was severely wounded during World War II while serving in the 442nd Regimental Combat Team, the Japanese-American unit that became the most decorated Army unit in American history. He is the only politician in Hawaii to hold a major political office in every year since it achieved statehood in 1959. Generally low-key, he earned national attention and high praise in the televised Watergate hearings for his tough but fair questioning of Nixon aides. His appointment to chair the Iran-contra hearings symbolized the high regard in which he was held by his Senate colleagues.

Chapter 14 Review Answers

Identifying Terms and Concepts

1. implied power, 2. appropriations bill, 3. subpoena, 4. impoundment, 5. naturalization

Reviewing Facts and Ideas

1. Implied powers are those necessary to carry out the expressed powers.

2. The definition of interstate commerce has expanded over the years to give Congress authority over virtually everything that crosses state lines.

3. admits states, legislates to govern territories, and has power over naturalization of new citizens

4. chooses the President and Vice President if no candidate has a majority in the Electoral College, charges federal officials suspected of misconduct in office and removes them if guilty, proposes amendments to Constitution, Senate confirms presidential appointments of federal officials, Senate ratifies treaties

5. to investigate charges of wrongdoing and problems that may require new legislation

6. subpoena witnesses, require that witnesses testify under oath, grant immunity to witnesses, hold those who refuse to cooperate in contempt

7. requires that executive agencies report on their activities, asks the GAO to study an agency's work, reviews the budget of each agency

8. enacting laws, appointing federal officials, and making treaties

9. different constituencies, system of checks and balances, congressional organization, party politics, as well as differing political timetables

10. Accept any three: increased its role in planning the national budget (Congressional Budget and Impoundment Control Act, 1974), reestablished control over the use of military force (War Powers Act, 1973), reduced the President's emergency powers

---

Summary and Significance

Congress has both legislative and non-legislative powers. These powers are either expressly stated in the Constitution or are implied as necessary to carry out the expressed powers. The Constitution also requires that Congress share powers with the executive branch. In addition, Congress has developed the power to investigate and the power to oversee the executive branch. For these and other reasons, the relationship between the two branches is marked by conflict.

Identifying Terms and Concepts

Match each of the descriptions below with the term it describes. Not every term will have a description.

appropriations bill   implied power
impoundment   legislative veto
naturalization   subpoena

1. Power not specified in the Constitution
2. Grants money to carry out programs
3. Compels a witness to appear
4. Refusing to spend funds
5. Allows immigrants to become citizens

Reviewing Facts and Ideas

1. Explain how expressed powers and implied powers are related.
2. Discuss why the power to regulate interstate commerce has become such an important power of Congress.
3. Identify three ways that Congress is empowered to regulate the nation's growth.
4. Cite five non-legislative powers of Congress.
5. Describe why Congress conducts investigations.
6. List the powers that Congress has in conducting investigations.
7. Name three methods that Congress uses to oversee the activities of the executive branch.
8. Identify three powers that Congress and the President share.
9. State the main causes of conflict between the President and Congress.
10. Cite three ways that Congress has tried to recover power lost to the executive branch.
11. Discuss why Presidents oppose the legislative veto.

Applying Themes

1. Separation of Powers Why are the powers to tax and spend among the most important powers of Congress?
2. Civil Rights Explain how the Constitution's commerce clause, authorizing Congress to regulate interstate commerce, has helped African Americans obtain equal rights.
3. Checks and Balances What role does the system of checks and balances play in the continuing conflict between the executive and legislative branches?
4. Political Processes In considering legislation, the Senate has the reputation of being slower and more deliberative than the House. What explanations can you offer for this difference between the two houses of Congress?

Critical Thinking Skills

1. Drawing Conclusions Do you think the continued struggle for power between the President and Congress has the effect of strengthening or weakening the national government? Explain your answer.
2. Making Generalizations On what basis might the Founders, who wrote the Constitution, have decided which powers should go only to Congress and which powers Congress should share with the President?
3. Synthesizing Information Congress and the President frequently disagree over issues of foreign policy. How successfully can Congress use its powers to influence the President's actions in this area?

(National Emergencies Act, 1976), increased use of legislative veto.

11. They claim it is an unconstitutional violation of the separation of powers principle.

Applying Themes

1. Through the power to tax, Congress raises the money to finance government programs. The power to spend gives Congress control over what programs will be funded and at what levels. Through the budget process Congress has a measure of control over executive agencies.

2. Congress has used this power to outlaw racial discrimination by businesses that are in any way part of interstate commerce. This use of the commerce clause has ranged from serving travelers who cross state lines to businesses that get supplies or products from other states.

Linking Past and Present

At his inauguration in March 1933, President Franklin D. Roosevelt addressed the American people about what was needed to combat the Great Depression. He said:

> *I am prepared under my constitutional duty to recommend the measures that a stricken Nation in the midst of a stricken world may require....*
>
> *In the event that the national emergency is still critical . . . I shall ask the Congress for. . . broad Executive power to wage a war against the emergency, as great as the power that would have been given to me if we were in fact invaded by a foreign foe.*
>
> —FRANKLIN D. ROOSEVELT, MARCH 1933

Congress responded with legislation that gave Roosevelt indirect but sweeping powers over agricultural and industrial production and prices, wages and hours of employment, and banks and other financial institutions.

Would Congress be likely to grant such broad powers to the President today? Under what circumstances, if any, might today's Congress permit the President broad emergency powers similar to those that were granted to Roosevelt?

Writing About Government

Persuasive Writing Consider the following statement: *Conflict between the President and Congress leads to good government.*

Do you agree or disagree with the statement? Review what you have learned about Congress and its relations with the President. Then write a persuasive essay that sets forth your position on the statement and that attempts to persuade others to agree with that opinion.

Reinforcing the Skill

Distinguishing Fact From Opinion Examine the statements below. Tell whether each is a statement of fact or opinion.

> 1. *Today . . . voter participation is lower in our country than in any Western democracy.*
> —REPRESENTATIVE WILLIAM H. GRAY III

> 2. *The National Voter Registration Act is a bipartisan bill which assures citizens a wider and more convenient registration while still maintaining the integrity of our electoral process.*
> —REPRESENTATIVE WILLIAM H. GRAY III

> 3. *[A] recent poll of nonvoters showed 97 percent of nonvoters gave reasons other than problems with the registration process. Further, 56 percent of those polled could not give a specific reason for not being registered or simply had no interest in the election.*
> —REPRESENTATIVE BARBARA VUCANOVICH

> 4. *If we want more people to vote, then we should run more stimulating and competitive campaigns.*
> —REPRESENTATIVE BOB MICHEL

Investigating Further

1. **Individual Project** Use the *Readers' Guide to Periodical Literature* and other research guides to learn about an incident in which the President has used military force since Congress passed the War Powers Act. Write a summary of this event.
2. **Cooperative Learning** With the class divided into three groups, organize each group to research the relationships that the last five Presidents have had with Congress. Each group should rank the Presidents according to how well they got along with Congress. Compare the rankings of the three groups.

2. Answers should suggest that the Founders divided powers they thought were basic to the process of government and which would influence the exercise of other powers.

3. Answers will vary. Students who argue that Congress can be a major influence may point to the confirmation of diplomats, appropriations for foreign aid, and treaty ratification. Others may note that the President sidesteps congressional authority in this area through executive agreements and by deploying American military forces without a declaration of war.

Linking Past and Present

Answers should include that increased political partisanship between modern Presidents and Congress and efforts of Congress to regain powers lost over the years make similar grants less likely. Students' assessments of the circumstances under which such a grant would be made will vary.

Writing About Government

Students' essays will vary.

Reinforcing the Skill

1. Fact; proven or disproved by voter turnout figures

2. A mixed statement; whether or not the Act is a bipartisan bill is a fact proven by who supported it. Whether it would assure citizens "wider and more convenient registration . . ." is opinion.

3. Fact; either there was or was not a poll that showed these results.

4. Opinion; the speaker thinks that more stimulating campaigns would increase voter turnout, but cannot prove this with hard evidence.

Investigating Further

1. Summaries will vary.

2. Students' rankings will vary.

3. Students should recognize that requiring the cooperation of both branches to accomplish key functions and responsibilities has built conflict between the President and Congress into the constitutional structure of government.

4. Answers should note the two-year terms for House members gives them less time than senators to please constituents before they must stand for

reelection. Senators, who serve six-year terms, feel less public pressure and have more patience.

Critical Thinking Skills

1. Those who say "strengthens" may note that it keeps either from becoming too powerful and assures general agreement before actions are taken. Those who say "weakens" may point to the prolonged inertia it often creates.

Chapter Organizer

Objectives	Special Feature Pages	Supplemental Materials
Section 1 How a Bill Becomes a Law *pp. 410–416* 1. Examine how a bill becomes a law. 2. Evaluate the advantages of holding hearings on bills.	Images of Government: A Capitol Idea pp. 412–413	Guided Reading Activities Reproducible Lesson Plans Enrichment Activities 15 Section 1 Quiz Testmaker Chapter Transparencies 15 SAT Practice Tests Writer's Guidebook
Section 2 Influences on Lawmakers' Decisions *pp. 417–422* 1. Specify factors that influence members of Congress. 2. Explain the types of issues on which lawmakers pay little attention to voter opinion.	Focus on Freedom: Gulf of Tonkin Resolution p. 419 Critical Thinking Skills: Making Comparisons p. 422	Guided Reading Activities Reproducible Lesson Plans Cooperative Learning Activities 15 Interpreting Political Cartoons 38 Section 2 Quiz Testmaker Skill Reinforcement Activities 15 SAT Practice Tests Writer's Guidebook
Section 3 Taxing and Spending *pp. 423–426* 1. Describe Congress's role in taxing and spending. 2. Compare authorization bills with appropriations bills. 3. Analyze the duties of the House Ways and Means Committee.	Global Connection: Issues: Congressional Junkets p. 425	Guided Reading Activities Reproducible Lesson Plans Section 3 Quiz Testmaker SAT Practice Tests Writer's Guidebook
Section 4 Helping Constituents *pp. 427–431* 1. Examine how lawmakers help their constituents. 2. Compare the methods of obtaining pork-barrel legislation with those of obtaining federal grants and contracts.	Participating in Government: Applying to be a Congressional Page p. 428 Personal Perspectives: Representative Patsy Mink on Education p. 431 Case Study: The Decision to Go to War in the Persian Gulf pp. 434–436 Unit 4 Digest pp. 437–438	Guided Reading Activities Reproducible Lesson Plans Participating in Government 15 Primary and Secondary Source Readings 15 Reteaching Activities 15 Section 4 Quiz Chapter 15 Tests Testmaker Audio Cassettes (English and Spanish) SAT Practice Tests Writer's Guidebook Unit Digest Transparencies, Unit 4 Participating in Government, Unit 4

If time does not permit teaching this chapter, assign the Chapter 15 summary in the Unit 4 Digest on pages 437–438.

Key To Ability Levels

Teaching strategies have been coded for varying learning styles and abilities.

L1   Level 1 activities are **basic** activities and should be within the ability range of all students.

L2   Level 2 activities are **average** activities and should be within the ability range of the average to above-average student.

L3   Level 3 activities are **challenging** activities designed for the ability range of above-average students.

LEP   These activities should be within the ability range of **Limited English Proficiency** students.

Multicultural Activities

In October 1986 Congress passed the Immigration Reform and Control Act. The bill, sponsored in the Senate by Alan Simpson of Wyoming and in the House by Peter Rodino of New Jersey and Romana Mazzoli of Kentucky, prohibited employers from hiring illegal aliens but gave the aliens secure legal status if they had entered the United States before January 1, 1982. The passage of this law came after five years of sometimes bitter fighting in Congress. Representatives of various ethnic groups lobbied for and against this bill. Have students use the *Congressional Quarterly Almanac* for 1986, *Readers' Guide to Periodical Literature,* or newspapers to trace the steps in the passage of this law.

In October 1983 the Senate voted 78 to 22 to make the third Monday in January a federal holiday honoring Reverend Martin Luther King, Jr. The House had approved similar legislation in August. President Reagan signed the bill into law 1 month after the Senate's action. The designation of this day as a national holiday did not come easily. Republican Senator Jesse Helms of North Carolina led a determined fight against the bill beginning with a 1-day filibuster. The Senate battle over the measure provides interesting insight into the power politics of the Senate. Students might use the *Readers' Guide to Periodical Literature* or *Congress and the Nation,* published every 4 years by Congressional Quarterly, to learn more about how the legislative process produced a new national holiday.

Chapter Resources

Readings for the Student

Drew, Elizabeth. *Senator.* Simon and Schuster, 1978.
Oleszek, Walter. *Congressional Procedures and the Policy Process.* Congressional Quarterly, 1984.
Redman, Eric. *The Dance of Legislation.* Simon and Schuster, 1974.
Switzer, Ellen. *There Ought to Be a Law! How Laws Are Made and Work.* Atheneum, 1972.

Readings for the Teacher

Cooper, Joseph and G. Calvin Mackenzie, eds. *The House at Work.* University of Texas Press, 1981.
Draper, Theodore. *A Very Thin Line: The Iran-contra Affair.* Hill and Wang, 1991.
Green, Mark. *Who Runs Congress?* Viking, 1979.
Hamilton, Charles V. *Adam Clayton Powell, Jr.: The Political Biography of an American Dilemma.* Atheneum, 1991.
Light, Paul. *Artful Work: The Politics of Social Security Reform.* Random House, 1985.
Stanley, Harold W. and Richard G. Niemi. *Vital Statistics on American Politics.* Congressional Quarterly, 1993.

Multimedia

Videocassettes and Films
An Act of Congress. Learning Corporation of America. (film, 58 minutes—in 2 parts)
The Committee: Taxation with Representation. York Associates. (v/c, 58 minutes)
Congress: Reflecting the Public Will. Close-Up Foundation. (v/c, 30 minutes)
Lobbying: A Case History. Encyclopedia Britannica Educational Corp. (film, 18 minutes)
Other People's Money. (*Frontline* series). The Documentary Consortium. (v/c, 60 minutes)

Software
The Congressional Bill Simulator. Focus Media. (Apple, TRS80, Commodore, IBM disks). Students participate in moving a bill through Congress.
The Discussion Generator: Lobbying. Tom Snyder Productions. (Apple, IBM disks). Students are placed within the environment of lobbyists, faced with often conflicting (though realistic) information and confronted with action choices that change according to previous decisions. Disk-based management included.
How a Bill Becomes Law. Intellectual Software. (Apple, IBM, Macintosh disks). Students, as members of Congress, try to get a bill passed through both the House and Senate.

Introduce

Chapter Overview

Chapter 15 discusses how Congress makes laws and also emphasizes the political factors involved in passing legislation. Students will learn about obstacles to passage of bills, factors that influence legislators' decisions, the special responsibilities of Congress related to taxes and spending, and the responses Congress has to its constituents.

Section 1 describes the role of committees and subcommittees in reviewing bills and the formal process by which a bill becomes a law.

Section 2 explains those factors that influence members of Congress—nature of issues, voters, political parties, the President, special-interest groups—and those that do not.

Section 3 discusses Congress's role in taxing and spending, explains the function of the House Ways and Means Committee, and compares authorization and appropriations bills.

Section 4 describes how members of Congress help their constituents through casework, pork-barrel legislation, and federal grants and contracts.

Chapter 15 Themes

Ask students to read Themes in Government on this page and to write one question about each theme. Ask volunteers to read their questions and write them on the chalkboard. Tell students to look for answers to their questions as they read the chapter.

Congress at Work

CHAPTER

15

In May 1991, Queen Elizabeth II addressed a rare joint session of Congress. Congress meets jointly to hear from the President, to honor visiting dignitaries, and to commemorate key events.

408 Unit 4: The Legislative Branch

About the Chapter Opener

Teaching With Illustrations Have students read the caption and examine the photograph on pages 408 and 409. Point out to students that since little real work can be accomplished at a joint session of Congress, its value is largely ceremonial. Ask students what Queen Elizabeth II's address to a joint session of Congress indicates about her country's relationship with the United States. What is the major work of Congress? To whom is Congress ultimately responsible?

Introducing the Chapter

Discuss what students already know about how a bill becomes a law. Write students' responses on the chalkboard and keep them there for the class to compare with the information in the chapter.

Chapter Project

Have students collect newspaper or magazine articles on the legislative process. One day's paper may contain news of hearings on a current bill; another day may bring news of the introduction, passage, or defeat of one or more bills. Have students select one article, summarize it, and indicate how its content relates to the chapter theme(s).

> **Linking Past and Present**
> Legislators today have much more to do than their predecessors. In the first Congress (1789), only a few hundred bills were introduced and just 118 were enacted into law. Each term of Congress during the 1980s averaged more than 10,000 bills, most of which died. In the 101st Congress (1992-1993) 6,775 bills were introduced, of which 609 were enacted into law.

Chapter Preview

Overview

Lawmakers are subject to many influences that they must consider when performing their duties.

Objectives

After studying this chapter, you should be able to:

1. **Explain** how a bill becomes a law.
2. **List** factors that influence members of Congress.
3. **Discuss** the role of Congress in both taxing and spending.
4. **Describe** various ways in which lawmakers help their constituents.

Themes in Government

This chapter emphasizes the following government themes:

- **Political Processes** The legislative branch must go through a series of complex steps to pass laws and do its other jobs. Sections 1, 2, 3, and 4.
- **Checks and Balances** To ensure a just use of powers, checks and balances are built into the legislative process. Sections 1, 2, and 3.
- **Public Policy** Members of Congress have certain responsibilities to their constituents. Section 4.

Critical Thinking Skills

This chapter emphasizes the following critical thinking skills:

- Synthesizing Information
- Drawing Conclusions
- Making Inferences

CHAPTER 15: CONGRESS AT WORK **409**

Setting the Scene In a national survey, the four most important jobs of a lawmaker, as seen by the public, are directly related to how well the lawmaker serves his or her constituents. When lawmakers can clearly identify what the majority of voters of their party want, they will vote in agreement with them about 49 percent of the time. Members of Congress are constantly working to secure benefits for their constituents, district, and state. Through the give-and-take of this process, the federal government distributes its resources and services to various groups around the country.

Focus

Bell Ringer

As you take attendance, have students list three topic areas on which they would like to see Congress legislate.

Motivating Activity

Write students' Bell Ringer responses on the chalkboard. When you have enough responses to see a pattern, say; "Several of you want a bill passed to [clean up pollution of the nation's rivers and streams]. Who are some individuals and groups that might support such a bill? Who might work for its defeat?" Have students discuss why they think various people and groups might be for and against legislation in areas they have suggested.

Vocabulary Precheck

Write the vocabulary terms for this section on the chalkboard. Ask students to use those that they know in sentences. **LEP**

Caption Answer
They face a lengthy and complicated process.

CONNECTIONS

History

The bill which eventually led to the Federal Criminal Code Reform Act was extremely complex and more than 600 pages long!

How a Bill Becomes a Law

During each 2-year term of Congress, thousands of bills are introduced—numbering well above 10,000 each term. Why are so many introduced? Congress, as the national legislature, is open to all Americans who want things from the government. The President, federal agencies, labor unions, business groups, and individual citizens all look to Congress to pass laws favorable to their varied interests.

Congress spends much of its time listening to and trying to meet the demands of many groups. One of the most important ways for Congress to respond to such demands is to pass new laws or change existing ones.

They may be debated for weeks or even months before they become law. If a bill is not passed before the end of a congressional term, it must be reintroduced in the next Congress to be given further consideration.

Congress may also pass several types of resolutions to deal with unusual or temporary matters. A **resolution** covers matters affecting only one house of Congress and is passed by that house alone. **Joint resolutions** require passage by both houses. If the President signs a joint resolution, it becomes law. Joint resolutions may correct an error in an earlier law, for example, or appropriate money for a special purpose. Congress also uses joint resolutions to propose constitutional amendments.

Types of Bills and Resolutions

Two types of bills are introduced in Congress. **Private bills** deal with individual people or places. They often involve people's claims against the government or their immigration problems. Private bills long accounted for a large number of the bills introduced in Congress. Lately, however, their numbers have declined. In a recent Congress, only about 230 of the 11,824 bills introduced were private bills, and they accounted for only 16 of the 666 bills passed.

On the other hand, **public bills** deal with general matters and apply to the entire nation. They are often controversial. Major public bills usually receive significant media coverage. They may involve such issues as raising or lowering taxes, national health insurance, gun control, civil rights, or abortion.

Major public bills account for about 30 percent of the bills passed in each term of Congress.

Farmers Demand Help
Farm aid bills are often hotly contested in Congress.
Politics **Why might such bills be defeated?**

SECTION PREVIEW

Objectives
After studying this section, you should be able to:
- Examine how a bill becomes a law.
- Evaluate the advantages of holding hearings on bills.

Key Terms and Concepts
private bill, public bill, resolution, joint resolution, concurrent resolution, rider, hearing, conference report, veto, pocket veto

Themes in Government
- Political Processes
- Checks and Balances

Critical Thinking Skills
- Synthesizing Information
- Drawing Conclusions

Classroom Resources for Section 1

- 📁 Guided Reading Activities
- 📁 Reproducible Lesson Plans
- 📁 Enrichment Activities 15
- 📁 Section 1 Quiz

- 🖥 Testmaker
- 💠 Chapter Transparencies 15
- SAT Practice Tests
- Writer's Guidebook

Concurrent resolutions cover matters requiring the action of the House and Senate, but on which a law is not needed. A **concurrent resolution**, for example, may set the date for the adjournment of Congress. Both houses of Congress must pass concurrent resolutions. They do not require the President's signature, and they do not have the force of law.

Bills and resolutions usually deal with only one subject, such as civil rights or veterans' benefits. Sometimes, however, a rider is included in a bill. A **rider** is a provision on a subject other than the one covered in the bill. The rider is attached to a bill that is likely to pass. Riders often deal with very controversial matters that are not likely to become law on their own merit.

Why So Few Bills Become Laws

Less than 10 percent of all bills introduced in Congress become public laws. Why so few?

The lawmaking process itself is very long and complicated. A congressional study found that more than 100 specific steps may be involved in passing a law. Thus, at many points in the lawmaking process a bill can be delayed, killed, or changed. This process has two important results. First, it means that groups who oppose a bill have an advantage over those who support it. Opponents can amend the bill or kill it at many steps along the way. If they fail to stop a bill at one point, they always have another chance at the next step.

Second, because the lawmaking process has so many steps, sponsors of a bill must be willing to bargain and compromise with lawmakers and interest groups. Compromise is the only way to get support to move a bill from one step to the next. Without strong support, most major bills have little chance of becoming law. Moreover, bills that important interest groups oppose are not likely to be passed.

Another reason so few bills become law is that lawmakers sometimes introduce bills they know have no chance of ever becoming law. Members of Congress may introduce such bills to go on record in support of an idea or policy. Members may also want to satisfy an important group from their state or district. Still another reason is to call attention to the need for new legislation in an area such as health care or highway safety.

Finally, introducing a bill can help lawmakers avoid criticism at reelection time. By introducing a bill, lawmakers can report they have taken action on a particular problem. When the bill does not move forward, they can blame a committee or other lawmakers.

Introducing a Bill

The Constitution sets forth only a few of the many steps a bill must go through to become law. The remaining steps have developed as Congress has grown in size and complexity and as the number of bills has increased.

How Bills are Introduced The first step in the legislative process is proposing and introducing a new bill. The ideas for new bills come from private citizens, interest groups, the President, or officials in the executive branch. Various people may write new bills, such as lawmakers or their staffs, lawyers from a Senate or House committee, a White House staff member, or even an interest group itself. Only a member of Congress, however, can introduce a bill in either house of Congress. Lawmakers who sponsor a major public bill usually try to find co-sponsors to show that the bill has wide support.

To introduce a bill in the House, a representative simply drops the bill into the hopper, a box near the clerk's desk. To introduce a bill in the Senate, the presiding officer of the Senate must first recognize the senator who then formally presents the bill.

Bills introduced in the House and Senate are printed and distributed to lawmakers. Each bill is given a title and a number. The first bill introduced during a session of Congress in the Senate is designated as S.1, the second bill as S.2, and so forth. In the House, the first bill is H.R. 1, the second bill, H.R. 2, and so on. This process is the first reading of the bill.

STUDY GUIDE

Themes in Government
Political Processes A situation arises whereby Congress passes a bill that waives immigration requirements so that an American woman

can marry a Greek man. **Explain what type of bill this is.**

Critical Thinking Skills
Synthesizing Information Why would someone who insists on

always having things their own way have difficulty trying to help a proposed bill become law as a member of Congress?

Teach

Guided Practice

L1 **Classifying** Read the following hypothetical actions to students and have them identify if each action exemplifies a *private bill, public bill, resolution, joint resolution,* or *concurrent resolution.* Ask students to explain the reasons for their choices.

1. an action by the House and Senate to congratulate the United States Olympic winners *(concurrent resolution)*
2. an action to change the vacation schedule of the House *(resolution)*
3. an action to reintroduce the Equal Rights Amendment *(joint resolution)*
4. an action to speed overdue social security payments to a needy recipient *(private bill)*
5. an action to raise taxes on luxury items *(public bill)* **LEP**

STUDY GUIDE

Theme Answer
private bill because it deals with an individual case

Critical Thinking Answer
Members of Congress must be able and willing to compromise in order to gain support to keep bills they favor moving along.

CONNECTIONS

Language
The origin of "pigeonholing" is related to early American furniture. Old-fashioned desks had small compartments, or "pigeonholes," into which minor or unimportant papers could be stuffed, often to be lost or forgotten.

Background

A study of the lawmaking process does not always pay sufficient attention to the markup sessions conducted by subcommittees and full committees. The markup sessions take place after the public hearings are over and before a bill is sent to the floor. Many congressional observers maintain that the markup of a bill is not merely a step in the legislative process but for most bills, it *is* the legislative process. Later approval by the full committee and on the floor is, for many bills, a formality. There may be debate and opposition, but the outcome of a bill on the floor is usually predictable.

👆 **Interpreting Visuals** Display transparency 15 from the *Chapter Transparencies* in the Teacher's Classroom Resources and use the accompanying teaching strategy and student activity to teach how few bills become law.

L2 **Interpreting Primary Sources** Have a student read aloud the quote by Szulc on page 412. Discuss with students the difference between a committee and a subcommittee. Ask how a subcommittee system, in theory, would be expected to expedite legislation. *(increased specialization, increased maximum workload)* Ask why Szulc believes it has not. *(The average representative spends too much time on subcommittees.)* Can students suggest any other reasons that the subcommittee system may actually slow the work of Congress? *(creates another level bills must pass through, with all the political and procedural pitfalls)*

Images of Government

Point out that work on the Capitol was not interrupted by the outbreak of the Civil War. President Lincoln saw the symbolic value of completing the project. "I take it as a sign that the Union will continue," he said.

Answers

1. Ancient Greece was the birthplace of democracy and the source of many of the fundamental principles of United States government.
2. It was cast by slave laborers.

Committee Action In each house of Congress, new bills are sent to the committees that deal with their subject matter. Committee chairpersons may, in turn, send the bill to a subcommittee. Under the chairperson's leadership, the committee can ignore the bill and simply let it die. This procedure is called "pigeonholing." The committee can kill the bill by a majority vote or recommend that the bill be adopted as it was introduced with certain changes. It can also make major changes or completely rewrite the bill before sending it back to the House or Senate for further action.

The House and Senate almost always agree with a committee's decision on a bill. Committee members and staff are considered experts on the subject of the bill. If they do not think a bill should move ahead, other lawmakers are usually reluctant to disagree with them. Besides, all members of Congress are also members of various committees. They do not want the decisions of their own committees overturned or questioned, so they usually go along with the decisions other committees make. Time is also a serious factor. Lawmakers have heavy workloads and must depend on the judgment of their peers. A political commentator addressed this issue and his perceived inadequacy of the system several years ago when he stated:

The subcommittee system . . . has smothered or splintered legislation more often than it has expedited it. The 96th Congress has inherited 29 standing committees and 151 subcommittees in the House, 21 committees and 112 subcommittees in the Senate. . . . The average representative sits on three subcommittees, the average senator, five. . . .

—Tad Szulc, *Saturday Review*, March 3, 1979

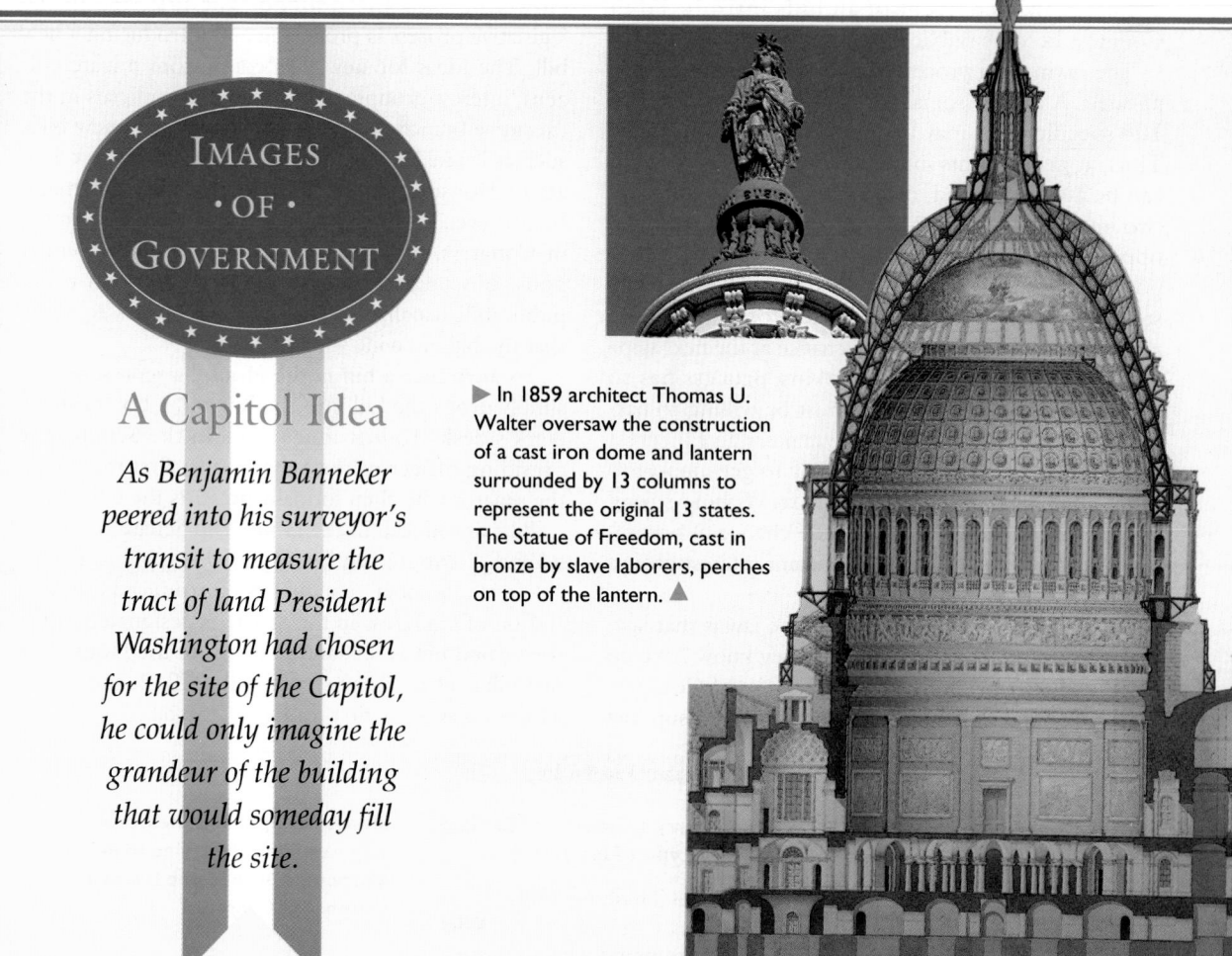

IMAGES OF GOVERNMENT

A Capitol Idea

As Benjamin Banneker peered into his surveyor's transit to measure the tract of land President Washington had chosen for the site of the Capitol, he could only imagine the grandeur of the building that would someday fill the site.

▶ In 1859 architect Thomas U. Walter oversaw the construction of a cast iron dome and lantern surrounded by 13 columns to represent the original 13 states. The Statue of Freedom, cast in bronze by slave laborers, perches on top of the lantern. ▲

SECTION through DOME of U.S. CAPITOL

412 Unit 4: The Legislative Branch

Cooperative Learning Activity

Form groups of four to research a current bill in Congress. Assign each group a different bill. Within each group, one student should call a representative's office to obtain up-to-date information on the bill, another should research background on this kind of bill, a third should record its legislative history, and a fourth should be prepared to summarize the group's findings to the class.

When a committee decides to act on a bill, the committee (or subcommittee) will hold hearings on the bill. **Hearings** are sessions at which a committee listens to testimony from people interested in the bill. Witnesses who appear at the hearings may include experts on the subject of the bill, government officials, and representatives of interest groups concerned with the bill.

The hearings on a bill may last for as little as an hour or go on for many months. Hearings are supposed to be an opportunity for Congress to gather information on the bill. Most detailed information about the bill comes from research done by the committee staff.

Hearings can be very important in their own right, though. Skillful chairpersons may use hearings to influence public opinion for or against a bill or to test the political acceptability of a bill. Hearings can also help focus public attention on a problem or give interest groups a chance to present their opinions. In addition,

hearings are often the best point in the lawmaking process to influence a bill. It is during hearings that letters and telegrams from interested citizens can have their greatest impact on the bill.

After the hearings are completed, the committee meets in a markup session to decide what changes, if any, to make in the bill. In this session committee members go through the bill section by section penciling in changes they wish to make. If the members cannot agree on a certain change, a vote is taken. A majority vote determines the decision.

When all the changes have been made, the committee votes either to kill the bill or to report it. To report the bill means to send it to the House or Senate for action with the committee's recommendation for passage.

Along with the revised bill, the committee will send to the House or Senate a written report the committee staff has prepared. This report is important. It explains

◄ Constantino Brumidi, an Italian artist, painted the fresco that decorates the dome of the Capitol. His allegorical figure of Armed Freedom stands victorious over Tyranny and kingly Power.

◄ Benjamin Latrobe supervised the construction of the Capitol. His corn and tobacco columns, representing the indigenous plants of the United States, won overwhelming support from Congress.

Questions for Discussion

1. **The design of the Capitol is based on Greek architecture. Why do you think the Capitol designers looked to the works of ancient Greece for their inspiration?**

2. **What is ironic about the construction of the Statue of Freedom?**

CHAPTER 15: CONGRESS AT WORK   413

L3 Synthesizing Information
Have students work in three groups, each to plan a congressional hearing. Assign each group one of these policy topics: aid to the homeless, funding for victims of child abuse, funding for drug education in the schools. Then have groups meet to decide what experts might testify at the hearings and what questions the committee members might ask these experts. Have a spokesperson for each group present the group's findings to the rest of the class.

Independent Practice

L1 Political Processes Have students identify and write descriptions of two groups who might appear at hearings to support the following proposals, and two groups who would appear to testify against these proposals: a bill to fund research into solar heating, a bill to raise the income tax rate of corporations and lower that of individuals, a bill to allow businesses to pay lower wages to workers who do not speak English. Have students present their descriptions to the class.

CONNECTIONS

Political Processes
If a legislator must be absent during a vote, he or she will sometimes try to "pair off" with an opposition colleague who will also be absent. The two absent votes thus cancel each other out and do not affect the result.

Powers of the Congress
Congressional Committees
Running Time 1:07
Side Two, Chapter 28

Special Needs Strategy

Reading Comprehension Surveying reading material helps students with reading comprehension problems recognize the structure and flow of material. Sometimes the author gives clues to the organization, but the clues are not always at the beginning of the paragraph. Have students scan the subsection "Why So Few Bills Become Laws" on page 411 for the words *First, Second, Another,* and *Finally.* Have students write one important piece of information that corresponds to these marker words.

L2 Media Have students choose a contemporary bill and write broadcast copy to be aired on the six o'clock news. The story may cover any part of the process that the student chooses—hearings, floor action, presidential veto, congressional override attempts, and so on.

L2 Informative Writing Have students research recent legislation that has been rejected by the President. Have them summarize the bill's topic, the method the President used to reject it, and the reasons given for rejection.

L3 Persuasive Writing Have students consider the following statements from the section: "Groups who oppose a bill have an advantage over those who support it." "Bills that important interest groups oppose are not likely to be passed." "Compromise is the only way to get support to move a bill from one step to the next." Have them write a newspaper editorial on one or more of these, taking the position that the situation enhances or hinders the democratic process.

CONNECTIONS

Political Processes

According to *Civitas: A Framework for Civic Education*, the single most important influence on congressional voting is political party affiliation—7 of every 10 members of Congress regularly vote with a majority of their party on votes that divide a majority of one party against the majority of another.

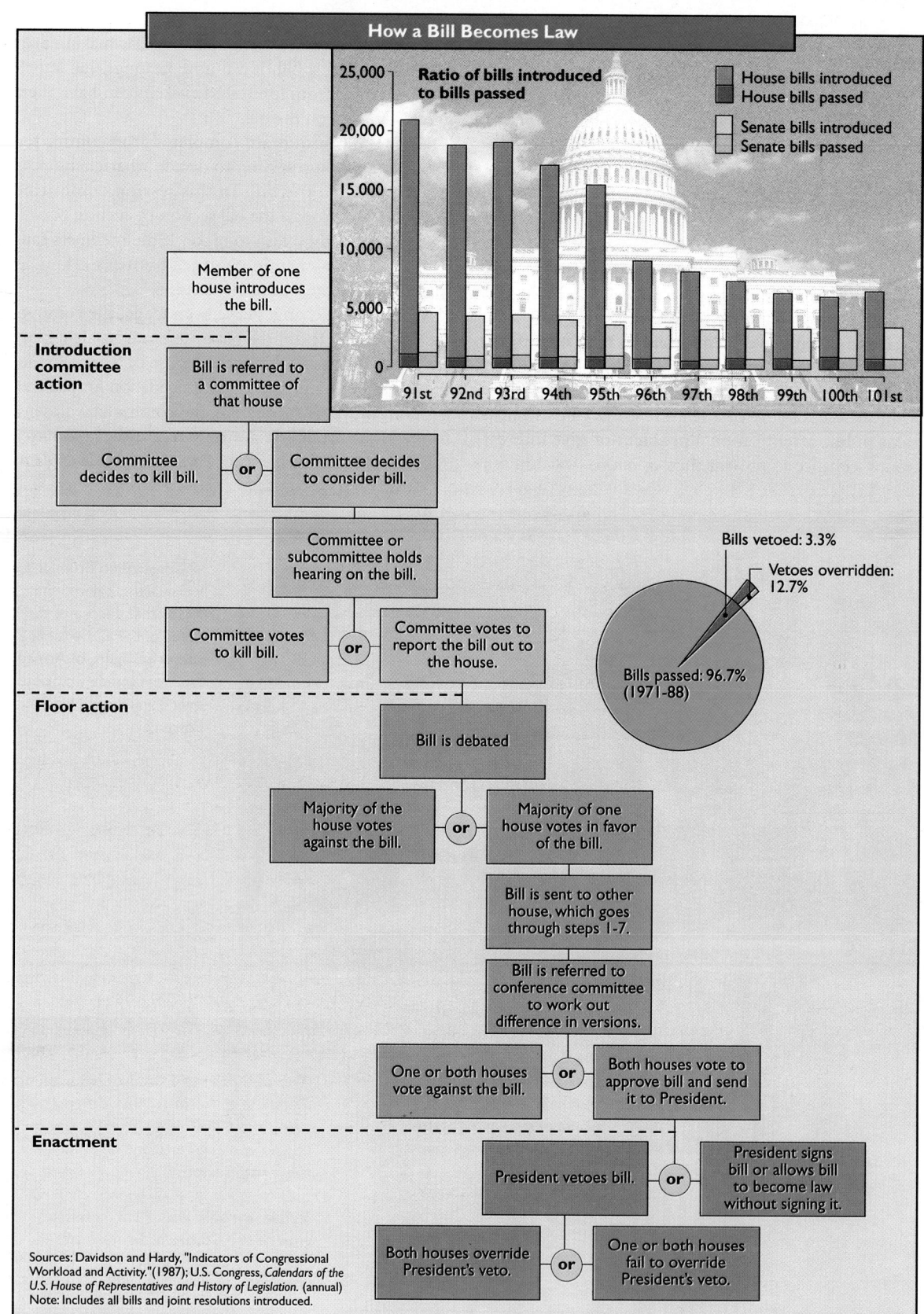

How a Bill Becomes Law

Sources: Davidson and Hardy, "Indicators of Congressional Workload and Activity." (1987); U.S. Congress, *Calendars of the U.S. House of Representatives and History of Legislation.* (annual)
Note: Includes all bills and joint resolutions introduced.

414   UNIT 4: THE LEGISLATIVE BRANCH

Critical Thinking Activity

Drawing Conclusions Have students answer the following: Does a session of Congress that passes many laws do a better job for the nation than a session that passes few laws? What other criteria could you use to evaluate a session of Congress? *(Answers will vary. Students may suggest that specific issues ad-* *dressed or ignored are a better measure than volume of legislation. Others may argue that few laws mean a divided and ineffective Congress. Students may suggest a survey or election results to evaluate how citizens view their Congress.)*

the committee's actions, describes the bill, lists the major changes the committee has made, and gives opinions on the bill. The report is often the only document many lawmakers read before deciding how to vote on a bill.

Floor Action

The next important step in the lawmaking process is the debate on the bill on the floor of the House and Senate. Voting on the bill follows the debate.

Amending Bills Usually, only a few lawmakers take part in floor debates. The pros and cons of the bill have been argued in the committee hearings and are already well known to those with a real interest in the bill. The floor debate over a bill, however, is the point where amendments can be added to a bill. During the floor debate, the bill receives its second reading. A clerk reads the bill paragraph by paragraph. After each paragraph is read, amendments may be offered. Any lawmaker can propose an amendment to a bill during the floor debate.

Amendments range from the introduction of major changes in a bill to the correction of typographical errors. Opponents of the bill sometimes propose amendments to slow its progress through Congress or even to kill it. One strategy opponents use is to load it down with so many objectionable amendments that it loses support and dies. In both houses amendments are added to a bill only if a majority of the members present approves them.

Voting on Bills After the floor debate, the bill, including any proposed changes, is printed in its new form and is ready for a vote. A quorum, or a majority, of the members must be present. The House or Senate now receives the third reading of the bill. A vote on the bill is then taken. Passage of a bill requires a majority vote of the members present.

House members vote on a bill in one of four ways. The first is a voice vote, in which members call out

"Aye" or "No." The speaker determines which side has the most voice votes. The second way of voting is by a standing vote, in which those in favor of the bill stand and are counted, then those opposed stand and are counted. The third method is a teller vote, in which representatives in favor of a bill walk down the aisle and are counted. Then those opposed walk down the aisle and are counted. The last type is a record vote, in which members' votes are recorded electronically. Their votes are flashed on large display panels in the House chamber.

The Senate has three methods of voting. These methods include a voice vote, a standing vote, and a roll call. The voice vote and the standing vote are the same as in the House. In a roll-call vote, senators respond "Aye" or "No" as their names are called in alphabetical order. Roll-call votes are recorded and over the years have become increasingly common.

Final Steps in Passing Bills

To become law both houses of Congress must pass a bill in identical form. Bills passed in one house often differ somewhat from a bill on the same subject that the other house has passed.

Conference Committee Action Often, one house will accept the version of a bill the other house has passed. At times, however, the bill must go to a conference committee made up of senators and representatives to work out the differences. The members of the conference committee are called conferees or managers. They usually come from the House and Senate committees that handled the bill originally.

The conferees work out the differences between the two bills by bargaining and arranging compromises. Conference committees rarely kill a bill. The conference committee is supposed to consider only the parts of a bill on which there is disagreement. In actual practice, however, the members of the committee sometimes make important changes in the bill or add provisions neither the House nor Senate previously

Background

The general use of riders is to get an unpopular proposal enacted by attaching it to a bill likely to pass. A bill's opponents, however, if they cannot muster the votes to defeat it, may attach a rider in order to make the bill undesirable to some of its supporters.

In 1964 Senate opponents of the Civil Rights Act tried to kill it by adding a rider to prohibit sex discrimination in the workplace. To their surprise both bill and rider passed, giving the nation a law against both race and sex discrimination.

═══ STUDY GUIDE ═══

Theme Answer
The committee chairperson can ignore the bill and simply let it die.

Critical Thinking Answer
A roll-call vote would be taken so each senator's vote on the bill is noted and recorded.

Assess

Check for Understanding
Have students complete Section 1 Review on page 416.

Meeting Objectives
Each section objective is tested by the Section Review questions that follow it in parentheses.
• Examine how a bill becomes a law. (2, 3, 4, 5, 6, 7, 8)
• Evaluate the advantages of holding hearings on bills. (3, 5, 7)

Evaluate
📁 Section 1 Quiz
⊞ Testmaker

Reteach
Have students use the chart on page 414 to orally elaborate on each step in the process of how a bill becomes a law.

═══ CONNECTIONS ═══

Political Processes
To record their votes electronically, legislators insert a plastic card in 1 of more than 40 voting stations located on the House floor.

Caption Answer
President may sign bill, and it becomes law; may keep bill for 10 days without signing, and if Congress is in session, bill becomes law without President's signature; may use veto or pocket veto.

Enrich

Have students write a letter to their senators or representative that supports or opposes a bill currently before Congress. Have the class keep track of congressional responses to their letters in a folder.

Have students complete activity 15 in *Enrichment Activities* in the Teacher's Classroom Resources.

Close

Have students list the various ways a bill can be blocked or hindered in its progress through the legislative system. Ask students if they think it would be more or less democratic if it were easier to pass laws.

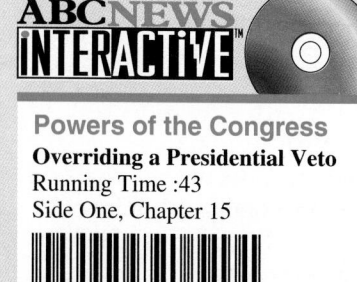

Powers of the Congress
Overriding a Presidential Veto
Running Time :43
Side One, Chapter 15

Law At Last
Most bills die before reaching the signing stage. **Political Processes How may a President act on a bill?**

considered. A majority of the members of the conference committee from each house must accept the final compromise bill, called a **conference report**. Once it is accepted, the bill can be submitted to each house of Congress for final action.

Presidential Action on Bills   Article I of the Constitution states that:

Every Bill which shall have passed the House of Representatives and the Senate, shall, before it becomes a Law, be presented to the President of the United States. . . .

—Article I, Section 7

After both houses of Congress have approved a bill in identical form, it is sent to the President. The President may take any one of several actions. First, the President may sign the bill, and it will become law. Second, the President may keep the bill for 10 days without signing it. If Congress is in session, the bill will become law without the President's signature. This happens very rarely. Presidents may use this procedure if they approve of most of the provisions of a bill but object to others. By letting the bill become law without a signature, the President indicates dissatisfaction with these provisions. Most of the time, however, Presidents sign the bills that Congress sends them.

The President can also reject a bill in two ways. First, the President may veto a bill. In a **veto** the President refuses to sign the bill and returns it to the house of Congress in which it originated. The President also includes reasons for the veto. Second, the President may kill a bill passed during the last 10 days Congress is in session simply by refusing to act on it. This veto is called a **pocket veto.** Because Congress is no longer in session, it cannot override the veto.

Congressional Override of a Veto Congress can override a President's veto with a two-thirds vote in both houses. If Congress overrides the veto, the bill becomes law. Congress does not override vetoes very often because it is usually difficult to get the necessary two-thirds vote in each house of Congress. Opponents of a bill, on the other hand, need to have only one-third of the members present and voting plus one additional vote in either the Senate or the House to uphold a veto.

1 SECTION REVIEW

Section Summary
Before a bill can become a law, it must go through a series of steps. If both houses pass the bill, it then goes to the President. The President may sign it, let it become law without a signature, or veto it.

Checking For Understanding
Recalling Facts
1. Define private bill, public bill, resolution, joint resolution, concurrent resolution, rider, hearing, conference report, veto, pocket veto.
2. List the four courses of action a committee may take on a bill.
3. State the advantages of having a hearing on a bill.

4. Describe the purposes of amending bills.
Exploring Themes
5. Political Processes Why do so few bills actually become laws?
6. Checks and Balances How can Congress override a President's veto?

Critical Thinking Skills
7. Synthesizing Information Why is it easier to defeat proposed laws than to get them passed?
8. Drawing Conclusions Is it possible for all members of Congress to keep abreast of bills under consideration? Support your answer.

Section 1 Review Answers

1. Definitions of terms appear on pages indicated: **private bill,** 410; **public bill,** 410; **resolution,** 410: **joint resolution,** 410; **concurrent resolution,** 411; **rider,** 411; **hearing,** 413; **conference report,** 416; **veto,** 416; **pocket veto,** 416
2. ignore the bill and let it die, kill the bill by a majority vote, recommend that the bill be adopted as it was introduced

with certain changes, make major changes or completely rewrite the bill
3. Public opinion can be stirred up for or against a bill; political acceptability can be tested; public attention can be focused on the problem; interest groups may be given a chance to present their opinions.
4. to introduce major changes, to correct typos, to slow down a bill or even kill it
5. The process is long and complicated, providing ample opportunity to change, delay, or kill a bill.

6. by two-thirds vote in both houses
7. The lengthy and complicated process enables a bill's opponents to challenge it repeatedly, at every step. It is much more difficult for a bill's supporters to resurrect it once it has been killed.
8. Answers should include that it is not, and that is why Congress has the subcommittee system and why members of Congress have aides, party leaders, and so on.

SECTION 2

Influences on Lawmakers' Decisions

I n their role as lawmakers, members of Congress must constantly make decisions. They decide which policies they want to support and when to yield or not to yield to political pressures. They must also decide how to vote on controversial issues and when to make speeches explaining their views. Each of these decisions gives lawmakers a chance to influence government policies. A lawmaker's speech, for example, can help shape the public's views about a particular bill that is before Congress.

Lawmakers face important decisions each time they vote for or against a bill or a resolution. In a single session, members of Congress may have to cast more than 1,200 votes on bills. These bills may range from regulating atomic power plants to appropriating money to remodel the zoo in the nation's capital.

Influences on Lawmakers

A great many factors influence a lawmaker's decisions. Sometimes the very nature of the issue determines the factors that will influence lawmakers most. For example, concerning a controversial issue such as gun control, a lawmaker may pay close attention to the voters back home, no matter what his or her own beliefs may be. On issues that have little direct effect on their home states or districts, most lawmakers are likely to rely on their own beliefs or on the advice and opinions of other lawmakers.

Congressional staff members can also influence lawmakers' decisions—sometimes by screening the information they give their employers. The staff also sets agendas for individual lawmakers and for congressional committees.

Friendly Persuasion
Lobbying today is a sophisticated profession. **Politics**
Who else influences lawmakers?

Thus, many factors affect a lawmaker's decision on any given issue. Most lawmakers agree that the most important influences on their decision making are the voters back home, their own political parties, the President, and special-interest groups.

The Influence of Voters

The political careers of all lawmakers depend upon how the voters feel about their job performance. Only very unusual lawmakers would regularly vote against the wishes of the people in their home states or districts. Thus, a major influence on the decisions of members of Congress is what they believe the voters want.

SECTION PREVIEW

Objectives
After studying this section, you should be able to:
■ Specify factors that influence members of Congress.

■ Explain the types of issues on which lawmakers pay little attention to voter opinion.

Key Terms and Concepts
lobbyist, lobbying

Themes in Government
■ Political Processes
■ Checks and Balances

Critical Thinking Skills
■ Drawing Conclusions
■ Making Inferences

CHAPTER 15: CONGRESS AT WORK   417

Classroom Resources for Section 2

▫ Guided Reading Activities
▫ Reproducible Lesson Plans
▫ Cooperative Learning Activities 15
▫ Interpreting Political Cartoons 38

▫ Section 2 Quiz
▪ Testmaker
SAT Practice Tests
Writer's Guidebook

Focus

Bell Ringer

As you take attendance, have students list three needs of the community or state that they think could be addressed by congressional legislation.

Motivating Activity

Discuss students' Bell Ringer lists and write several responses on the chalkboard. Ask the class how they think their representatives would likely vote on bills on these needs, and why they would vote that way. (*Students may recognize the many pressures that influence a lawmaker's vote.*)

Vocabulary Precheck

Call on students to read aloud the definitions of the terms and concepts from the Glossary. Then have volunteers use each term in a sentence. **LEP**

L1 Constructing a Chart Have students list the major factors that influence a legislator's decisions and write them on the chalkboard. (*personal beliefs, constituents' wishes, other lawmakers' opinions, staff input, political parties, the President, special-interest groups*) Have students give examples of how each factor influences lawmakers. **LEP**

Caption Answer
voters, staff members, party members, the President

Teach

Guided Practice

▫ **Group Discussion** Organize groups to complete activity 15 on the various responsibilities of lawmakers in the *Cooperative Learning Activities* in the Teacher's Classroom Resources.

L3 Political Processes Have a team of students choose a bill they have researched and role-play influences on lawmakers. One student should play the legislator, another a constituent, and others interest group lobbyists, PAC representatives, the President, a party official, and so on. As they portray the meetings, have the class list the arguments made by each influence. At the conclusion of the role play, ask the class to characterize the process.

Caption Answer
issues that affect their district, state, and daily lives

GLENCOE TECHNOLOGY

Focus on Government
Video 27
Speaking Out:
Congressional Decision Making
Running Time: 1:45
Videodisc 2, Chap. 27
VHS Tape 2, Begins 18:26

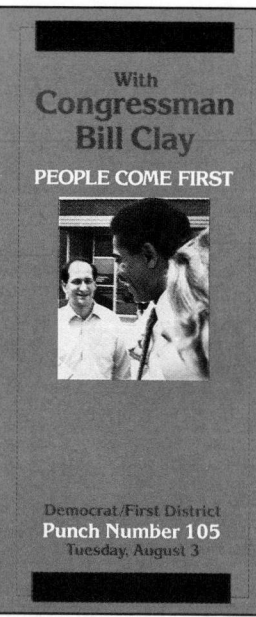

With
Congressman
Bill Clay

PEOPLE COME FIRST

Democrat/First District
Punch Number 105
Tuesday, August 3

While many politicians are deliberately ignoring the problems facing a lot of us today, Congressman Bill Clay has never forgotten why he went to Washington.

During his years in Congress, Clay has fought for the things that mean the most to all of us: more jobs; lower interest rates; lower utility rates; improved Social Security, Medicare and Medicaid; better educational opportunities; and preservation of wilderness areas.

Bill Clay delivers jobs

A good Congressman should help return to his district those federal tax dollars paid by the people who elect him.

In the past four years, Congressman Clay has helped win more than $80 million in federal construction contracts for our area. And those tax dollars helped provide 5,000 new jobs. These projects include:

■ $11.5 million for Lambert International Airport

■ $46.5 million for Bi-State Transit Authority facilities

■ $8 million for St. Louis Job Corps Center

In addition, Clay has helped obtain federal grants for a job referral center, a business resource center and $13 million for area schools.

Right now Congressman Clay is:

■ Working hard to obtain $20 million to rehabilitate our Union Station, providing 600 new construction jobs and 2,000 more permanent jobs; and

"What Have You Done For Me Lately?"
That's what many voters ask their representatives. This campaign flyer is one Congressman's response.
Politics What issues concern voters most?

What Voters Expect Experienced lawmakers know that their constituents expect them to pay a great deal of attention to their state or district. Most people expect their representatives to put the needs of their district ahead of the needs of the nation. What if a conflict arises between what the lawmaker believes should be done and what the people in the district want? In a national opinion survey, most people said their lawmaker should "follow what people in the district want."

The voting behavior of most members of Congress reflects the results of this survey. On issues that affect their constituents' daily lives, such as civil rights and social welfare, lawmakers generally go along with the voters' preferences. In contrast, on issues where constituents have less information or interest, such as foreign affairs, lawmakers often make up their own minds.

Voters say they want their lawmakers to follow their wishes on the issues and enact laws that reflect their needs and opinions. Most voters, however, do not take the trouble to find out how their senators and representatives cast their votes in Congress. Sometimes voters are not even aware of all the issues lawmakers must decide and vote on. Why, then, is the way lawmakers vote so important to their chance of reelection?

In an election campaign, the candidate from the other party and opposing interest groups will bring up the lawmaker's voting record. They may demand that the lawmaker explain votes that turned out to be unpopular back home. The opposite is also true. A legislator running for reelection may call attention to his or her votes on certain measures in order to attract constituents' support. As a result, voters who might otherwise not know how the lawmaker voted are told how well he or she "paid attention to the folks back home." Historically, the margin between a candidate's victory and defeat often has been only a small number of votes. Consequently, a small group of voters on either side—those who were unhappy with a lawmaker's voting record and those who strongly supported that record—meant the difference between the candidate's victory and defeat.

Learning What Voters Want Most lawmakers use several methods to try to keep track of their constituents' opinions. One method is to make frequent trips home to learn the local voters' concerns. Members of the House of Representatives make an average of more than 35 trips to their home districts each year. During these trips they will try to speak with as many voters about the issues concerning them as possible.

In addition, staff members usually screen the lawmaker's mail to learn what issues concern voters the most. Many lawmakers also send questionnaires to their constituents asking for their opinions on various issues. Near election time lawmakers often hire professional pollsters to conduct opinion surveys among the voters of their districts.

STUDY GUIDE

Themes in Government
Political Processes Some argue for imposing term limitations on how long lawmakers can serve. How could this affect the way that lawmakers now vote?

Critical Thinking Skills
Drawing Conclusions Why do you think a lawmaker stays in better touch with constituents and has a better sense of their

concerns by visiting constituents in the home district rather than by reading the mail they send to Washington?

Background

Although lobbying has long been practiced in government and is legal in the United States, some attitudes toward it have changed. A lobbyist for the fur trade was censured by the House in 1796. He was found in contempt for trying to influence lawmakers on behalf of his business instead of the good of the community. No one today disputes that lobbyists are protecting their clients' interests, but they are still expected to obey the law. In 1987, former Reagan aide Michael Deaver was convicted of perjury for lying about his lobbying efforts after leaving the Reagan administration. Deaver was charged under a 1978 Ethics in Government Act, which limits lobbying by former government officials.

The Influence of Parties

Almost every member of Congress is either a Republican or a Democrat. Both political parties generally take stands on major issues and come out for or against specific legislation. Political party identification is one of the most important influences on a lawmaker's voting behavior. In most cases knowing which political party members of Congress belong to will help predict how they will vote on major issues. Political party membership often will indicate how a lawmaker votes better than knowing almost anything else about the lawmaker.

Party Voting On major bills most Democrats tend to vote together, as do most Republicans. In the House of Representatives, members vote with their party about two-thirds of the time. Senators, who are generally more independent than House members, are less likely to follow their party's position.

Party voting is much stronger on some issues than on others. On issues relating to government intervention in the economy, party members tend to vote the same way. Party voting is also strong on farm issues and fairly strong on social-welfare issues. Party voting is much weaker on foreign-policy issues because the two parties often do not have very fixed positions on international questions. On certain other issues, such as civil rights, party position is often less influential than local or regional voter preferences in determining how a legislator votes.

Focus on Freedom

GULF OF TONKIN RESOLUTION

On August 4, 1964, President Lyndon B. Johnson announced that two United States destroyers had been attacked in the Gulf of Tonkin—although this attack has never been confirmed. Nonetheless, Johnson ordered air strikes against North Vietnam and asked Congress for powers to take any necessary measures to repel attacks against the United States and to stop further aggression. On August 7 Congress approved these powers in the Gulf of Tonkin Resolution. Although Congress never officially declared war on North Vietnam, Johnson based increased United States' involvement on the broad powers the resolution gave him. The United States' role in the Vietnam War remains one of the most debated issues in American history.

Resolved by the Senate and House of Representatives of the United States of America in Congress assembled, That the Congress approves and supports the determination of the President, as Commander in Chief, to take all necessary measures to repel any armed attack against the forces of the United States and to prevent further aggression.

Sec. 2. The United States regards as vital to its national interest and to world peace the maintenance of international peace and security in southeast Asia. Consonant with the Constitution of the United States and the Charter of the United Nations and in accordance with its obligations under the Southeast Asia Collective Defense Treaty, the United States is, therefore, prepared, as the President determines, to take all necessary steps, including the use of armed force, to assist any member or protocol state of the Southeast Asia Collective Defense Treaty requesting assistance in defense of its freedom.

Sec. 3. This resolution shall expire when the President shall determine that the peace and security of the area is reasonably assured by international conditions created by action of the United States or otherwise, except that it may be terminated earlier by concurrent resolution of the Congress.

—Joint Resolution of Congress,
H.J. Res. 1145, August 7, 1964

Examining the Document

Reviewing Facts
1. Name the President of the United States who ordered air strikes against North Vietnam.
2. Explain why Congress issued the Gulf of Tonkin Resolution.

Critical Thinking Skills
3. Making Inferences Why do you think Congress was so eager to support the President in the Gulf of Tonkin Resolution?

CHAPTER 15: CONGRESS AT WORK 419

When Lyndon Johnson ordered "retaliation" against North Vietnam, he was involved in a presidential campaign against conservative Barry Goldwater, who had accused him of being "soft on communism," a common slur during the cold war. Johnson's concern about the veracity of the reported attack on the destroyers was minimal. As he said to an aide, "For all I know, those sailors were just shooting at flying fish." Only two senators voted against the Gulf of Tonkin Resolution. Both went on to become highly vocal critics of the war in Vietnam. Ask students what influences might have prompted lawmakers to vote as they did.

Answers

1. Lyndon B. Johnson
2. because of reports that North Vietnam had attacked American warships
3. Answers might include patriotism, public pressure, need to resist aggression and communism, belief that response would be limited, desire to support President.

Independent Practice

L1 Political Processes Have students decide which of the following would more likely influence a lawmaker's vote on a bill and why:

a. an employer from another state who owns a factory in the district or an employee in that factory
b. 1,000 people who send form letters or 100 people who send original letters
c. a PAC contributor or a voter from the legislator's political party

---

Cooperative Learning Activity

Organize students into six groups. Assign each group one of these roles: representative's constituents, his or her staff, congressional colleagues, a special-interest group, the President and advisers, the legislator. Assign a current or hypothetical bill to the groups. Each group should develop ways they would attempt to influence their legislator either to vote for or against. Have each group present their case to the legislator group. Have the legislator group keep track of the major arguments made by each group and then tell how they have decided to vote and why.

L2 Conducting a Poll Have students poll five people about the influences on their representatives—constituents, interest groups, the President, other legislators, the lawmaker's party. Students should have each respondent rank these influences from the one he or she thinks should be most influential to the least influential. Have students put their findings into a graph.

Interpreting Political Cartoons Have students complete activity 38 in *Interpreting Political Cartoons* in the Teacher's Classroom Resources.

STUDY GUIDE

Theme Answer
use television to influence public and pressure Congress; give to or withhold from lawmakers favors and support

Critical Thinking Answer
PACs are often better organized and better funded than lobbyists.

Assess

Check for Understanding

Have students complete Section 2 Review on page 421.

Meeting Objectives

Each section objective is tested by the Section Review questions that follow it in parentheses.
• Specify factors that influence members of Congress. (2, 3, 5, 6, 7, 8)
• Explain the types of issues on which lawmakers pay little attention to voter opinion. (4, 7)

The Importance of Parties One reason Republicans or Democrats vote together is that members of each party are likely to share the same general beliefs about public policy. As a group, Democratic lawmakers are more likely than Republicans to favor social-welfare programs, job programs through public works, tax laws that help lower-income people, and government regulation of business. Taken as a group, Republican members of Congress are likely to support less spending for government programs, local and state solutions to problems rather than solutions by the national government, and policies that favor business and higher-income groups.

Another reason for party voting is that most lawmakers simply do not have strong opinions about every issue on which they vote. They do not know enough about every issue to decide how to vote. They cannot possibly know the details of all the bills on which they must vote. Consequently, they often seek advice on how to vote from other lawmakers who know more about the issue. According to one senator:

> *When it comes to voting, an individual will rely heavily not only on the judgment of staff members, but also on a select number of senators whose knowledge he has come to respect and whose general perspectives [views] he shares.*
>
> —SENATOR WENDELL FORD

Lawmakers generally go to members of their own political parties who share the same basic ideas and sources of support for advice. Lawmakers agree that their most important source of help on how to vote is other lawmakers in their parties.

On some issues party leaders pressure members to vote for the party's position. Often, party leaders support the President's program if the President is a member of the same party. On the other hand, leaders of the opposing party may vote against the President's program and seek to turn such opposition into a political issue. Very few issues are unaffected by political party affiliation.

Other Influences on Lawmakers

Although voter preferences and political parties strongly influence the decisions of lawmakers, two other influences are often equally strong. These influences are the President and interest groups.

The Influence of the President All Presidents try to influence Congress to pass the laws they want. Some Presidents work harder at gaining support in Congress than others. Some Presidents are more successful in getting Congress to pass their programs than others.

Members of Congress have always complained that Presidents have more ways to influence legislation and policy than do lawmakers. Presidents can appear on television to try to influence public opinion and put pressure on Congress.

In late 1990 and early 1991, President Bush deployed United States troops to Saudi Arabia. Twenty-four weeks of military build-up followed, in which the United States government attempted to force Iraq out of Kuwait. Congress let the President take the lead in responding to Iraq. President Bush took every opportunity to express his views. With growing public support for military action behind the President, Congress was forced to vote on whether or not to approve military action in the Persian Gulf. Presidential influence, in this instance of policy-making, had tremendous influence.

Presidents may also use their powers to influence members of Congress. They can give or withhold favors and support that are important to lawmakers. In the mid-1960s, for example, Senator Frank Church of Idaho criticized President Lyndon Johnson's conduct of the Vietnam War. To support his viewpoint, Church once showed President Johnson a newspaper column written by journalist Walter Lippmann criticizing the war. "All right," Johnson said, "the next time you need a dam for Idaho, you go ask Walter Lippmann."

Since the early 1900s, many Presidents have sought to increase their influence over Congress and

STUDY GUIDE

Themes in Government
Checks and Balances Congress has taken steps in recent years to limit the President's influence over Congress. **Name two ways in** which a President can influence Congress.

Critical Thinking Skills
Making Inferences Why do some think that political action committees (PACs) now have more influence over members of Congress and the process of congressional legislation than do individual lobbyists?

Special Needs Strategy

Reading Comprehension Students with problems in reading comprehension can become overwhelmed by the reading task itself and miss main points. Surveying "topic" sentences can help students select essential or main ideas. Have students write the topic sentences of the first two paragraphs in the subsection "Influences on Lawmakers." Have students read the sentences aloud and explain why they are topic sentences.

the lawmaking process. They have succeeded in doing so. In more recent years, however, Congress has taken a number of steps that will limit the President's influence, letting Congress remain a more autonomous legislative body.

The Influence of Interest Groups Another very important influence on members of Congress is the representatives of interest groups who are called **lobbyists**. Lobbyists try to get Congress and government officials to support the policies that the interest group they represent favors. The work they do to persuade officials to support their point of view is called **lobbying**. More than 6,000 lobbyists representing 11,000 clients are registered in Washington. The largest and most powerful of these lobbies have their own buildings and full-time professional staffs in the nation's capital.

Lobbyists represent a wide variety of interests such as business organizations, labor unions, doctors, lawyers, education groups, minority groups, and environmental organizations. In addition, lobbyists work for groups that sometimes form to support or to oppose a specific issue.

Lawmakers in particular are under pressure from lobbyists to support their group's point of view. Lobbyists use various methods to influence members of Congress. They provide lawmakers with information about policies they support or oppose. They visit lawmakers in their offices or in the lobbies of the Capitol (hence the name "lobbyists") and try to persuade them to support their position. They encourage citizens to write to members of Congress on the issues they favor or oppose.

Power in Numbers
Powerful interest groups can bring thousands of people to the nation's capital. **Politics How may this help a lobbyist?**

Interest groups and their lobbyists also focus much of their attention on congressional committees. For example, farm groups will concentrate a great deal of their attention on influencing the committees responsible for laws on agriculture. Labor unions will likewise focus much of their effort on committees dealing with labor laws and the economy. Some believe that during recent years the importance of the individual lobbyist has declined as political action committees, known as PACs, have gained more influence with the lawmakers.

Caption Answer
provides lobbyists backing in their attempt to get Congress and government officials to support their programs and policies

Evaluate

📁 Section 2 Quiz

💾 Testmaker

Reteach
Have students identify and write a brief explanation of each factor that influences a legislator's voting decisions.

Enrich
Have students imagine they are a representative deciding how to vote on a bill that would establish a toxic waste dump in her district. The lawmaker knows that the health of people living near the dump will be affected. But the lawmaker's constituents are desperate for jobs and want the bill passed. Have students write a newsletter from the legislator to her constituents that explains her vote on this legislation.

Close

Have students reread the passage that describes the confrontation between Senator Frank Church and President Lyndon Johnson (page 420). What does Johnson's reply indicate about the nature of the legislative process?

---

2 SECTION REVIEW

Section Summary
The decisions of lawmakers are subject to many influences—chief among them are the nature of the issues, voters, political parties, the President, and special-interest groups.

Checking For Understanding
Recalling Facts
1. Define lobbyist, lobbying.
2. List six factors that influence the decisions of members of Congress.
3. Describe two ways lawmakers keep in touch with voters' opinions.
4. Specify on which type of issues lawmakers tend to pay less attention to voter opinion.

Exploring Themes
5. Political Processes Why are political parties an important influence on lawmakers' decisions?
6. Checks and Balances What is the relationship between Congress and the President regarding legislation?

Critical Thinking Skills
7. Drawing Conclusions How closely do you think the votes of members of Congress should reflect the opinions of their voters? Explain.
8. Making Inferences Close elections decide fewer and fewer House seats. Why might this be so?

Section 2 Review Answers

1. Definitions of terms appear on pages indicated: **lobbyist,** 421; **lobbying,** 421
2. the nature of the issues, Congressional staff members, voters, political party, the President, and special-interest groups
3. frequent trips back home, screening mail to learn voters' concerns, questionnaires, opinion surveys

4. on issues where voters have less information or interest, such as foreign affairs
5. Members of a party are likely to share the same general beliefs about public policy. Most lawmakers simply do not have strong opinions on every issue so they seek advice from other lawmakers in their political party.
6. Presidents try to influence members of Congress to pass the laws they want, and members of Congress complain that Presidents have more ways to influence legislation.

In addition, Presidents can also give or withhold favors from lawmakers.
7. Answers should include that on regional issues, Congress should vote to reflect their voters' opinions, but on other matters they are at liberty to vote as they wish; or Congress should always reflect the clear-cut opinions of voters.
8. Answers should include that single-issue voters may be a factor, as well as the fact that incumbents are difficult to unseat.

Focus

Write the following on the chalkboard: *football, basketball.* Ask students what elements they could consider in comparing these sports. List responses on the chalkboard. (*examples: number of players, scoring system, size of playing area*) Have students make some sample comparisons of the elements they listed. Tell them that people make comparisons often, and that there are strategies for making valid comparisons.

Teach

Review the Explanation steps and their application to the two passages in the skill. Then, to illustrate the skill, draw two overlapping circles on the chalkboard. Label them *House* and *Senate.* Ask students for common characteristics of these bodies. Write them in the overlapping area. Write unique characteristics in each circle outside the overlapping area. Ask: How does this diagram help in making comparisons?

Assess

Have students complete the **Practice** exercise.

Close

Have students compare local governing bodies such as the school board and city council.

Making Comparisons

When you make comparisons, you determine how two items are alike and how they are different. Knowing how to make comparisons will help you organize information. Making comparisons is also an important citizenship skill because it helps you choose between alternative candidates or policies.

Explanation

To compare two items, follow these steps:
- Decide on two items you want to compare.
- Find a common area or areas in which you can make comparisons.
- Look for similarities and differences in these areas. Look at the two statements below. Each is a reaction to a pay raise for Congress.

The manner in which the recent congressional pay hike was accomplished tells the story. Working furtively, in the dead of night, the leadership rushed through this outrageous increase, leaving the citizenry to discover their loss in the morning, like the victims of a burglary.
—LETTER TO THE EDITOR, *WATERVILLE TIMES-HERALD*

Though we do not approve of the manner in which the pay increase was handled, we support the modest increases Congress has awarded itself. It is high time that hardworking members of Congress got a raise. In order to attract good people to government, the public must be willing to pay them a decent salary. Any member of Congress—and there are a few—who doesn't deserve this increase wasn't earning the old salary either.
—EDITORIAL, *TOPSFORD DAILY LEDGER*

Areas in which these two statements might be compared include their subject matter (a congressional pay increase), the source of each statement (one is a letter to the editor, the other an editorial), whether the authors support the pay increase (the first does not, the second does), and whether they support the manner in which it was done (neither does).

Practice

Study the two cartoons below, then answer the questions that follow.

1. What is the subject of both of these cartoons?
2. What is an area in which the cartoons can be compared?
3. What are two things that the two cartoons have in common?
4. What are two things that are different about the two cartoons?

Additional Practice

To practice this skill, see **Reinforcing the Skill** on page 433.

Practice Answers

1. Congress
2. how Congress is handling its job
3. Both show an individual member of Congress to represent Congress as a whole, mention challenges facing Congress, make their point by drawing the members of Congress sitting in an unusual position.
4. One presents Congress as inept, the other as overwhelmed by conflicting demands. One is sympathetic toward Congress; the other is critical. One shows an unpleasant caricature of a member of Congress; the other shows a member of Congress looking like "everyman."

For additional practice, have students complete activity 15 in *Skill Reinforcement Activities* in the Teacher's Classroom Resources.

SECTION 3

Taxing and Spending

I n 1971 Wilbur Mills, a long-time member of the House of Representatives from Arkansas, was thinking about running for the presidency. This puzzled many of his colleagues. One representative asked, "Wilbur, why do you want to run for President and give up your grip on the country?"

The question was a good one. For 17 years, Mills had chaired the House Ways and Means Committee. This committee is responsible for starting and reviewing all tax laws in the United States. As head of this committee, Mills was already one of the most powerful people in Washington, D.C.

Meeting the Nation's Needs
President Franklin D. Roosevelt signs tax legislation.
Political Processes Which house of Congress must initiate all tax bills?

Passing laws to raise and spend money for the national government is one of the most important jobs of Congress. The government could not operate without money to carry out its many programs and services. Today, running the national government costs about $1.5 trillion a year. The Constitution gives Congress the authority to decide where this money will come from and where it will go.

Making Decisions About Taxes

The national government gets most of the money it needs from taxes. **Taxes** are money that people and businesses pay to support the government. The Constitution states:

*T*he Congress shall have the power to lay and collect taxes, duties, imposts and excises, to pay the debts and provide for the common defense and general welfare of the United States. . . .
—ARTICLE I, SECTION 8

The House's Power Over Revenue Bills The Constitution gives the House of Representatives the exclusive power to start all revenue measures. Almost all important work on tax laws occurs in the House Ways and Means Committee. The Ways and Means Committee decides whether to go along with presidential requests for tax cuts or increases. It also proposes the numerous rules that determine who will pay how much tax. This committee influences, for example, how much of a tax deduction parents are allowed on their income tax for each child living at

---

SECTION PREVIEW

Objectives
After studying this section, you should be able to:
- Describe Congress's role in taxing and spending.
- Compare authorization bills with appropriations bills.

- Analyze the duties of the House Ways and Means Committee.

Key Terms and Concepts
tax, closed rule, authorization bill, appropriations bill, entitlement

Themes in Government
- Checks and Balances
- Political Processes

Critical Thinking Skills
- Synthesizing Information
- Drawing Conclusions

CHAPTER 15: CONGRESS AT WORK **423**

Classroom Resources for Section 3

- Guided Reading Activities
- Reproducible Lesson Plans
- Section 3 Quiz

- Testmaker
  SAT Practice Tests
  Writer's Guidebook

Focus

Bell Ringer
As you take attendance, ask students to make a list of three important areas in which Congress makes laws.

Motivating Activity
Discuss students' Bell Ringer lists. If raising and spending money is volunteered by a student, point out that this is one of Congress's most important duties. Next, ask students to list all the taxes that Americans pay. *(sales tax, gas, luxury, income, property, corporate, and so on)* Explain to students that government at all levels collects tax money to pay for its activities.

Vocabulary Precheck
Ask students to speculate on the meaning of each term and concept. Then have them check their guesses by finding the definition in the section text. **LEP**

Caption Answer
House of Representatives

Powers of the Congress
Revenue Bills
Running Time :30
Side One, Chapter 40

Teach

Guided Practice

L1 Constructing a Chart Write *House, Senate,* and *House Ways and Means Committee* on the chalkboard. Ask students to explain the roles each plays in tax legislation. As students volunteer answers, insert them on the chart.
LEP

L2 Debate Have students debate the following:

In raising and spending money, Congress should be more responsive to the will of the people.

Keep track of students' major pro and con arguments on the chalkboard.

L3 Political Processes Have students propose solutions to the problems that entitlement programs pose for the federal budget. Have them assess the likelihood that their proposals would pass.

Caption Answer
House of Representatives

home. It decides what kind of tax benefit businesses can claim for building new factories.

Representative Dan Rostenkowski, as Chairman of the House Ways and Means Committee, received a good deal of negative feedback from special-interest groups. These groups were unhappy with tax legislation. In one instance:

> *The final indignity came during the August recess, when he [Rostenkowski] was chased down a Chicago street by placard-waving senior citizens protesting a new catastrophic-insurance tax his panel authored. . . . Now, a spreading seniors' revolt makes repeal of the measure increasingly likely.*
> —Douglas A. Harbrecht, *Business Week,* September 18, 1989

For many years the committee's tax bills were debated on the House floor under a closed rule. A **closed rule** forbids members to offer any amendments to a bill from the floor. This rule meant that

New Revenue Sources
Congress, in its "power to lay and collect taxes, duties, imposts, and excises," continually seeks new means to help pay for federal programs.
Economics Where do all revenue measures start?

only members of the Ways and Means Committee itself could have a direct hand in amending a tax bill.

Other House members accepted this closed-rule procedure on tax bills for several reasons. House leaders claimed that tax bills were too complicated to be easily understood outside the committee. Leaders also warned that representatives would come under great pressure from special interests if tax bills could be revised from the floor. Floor amendments, they argued, might upset the fair and balanced legislation recommended by the committee.

In the 1970s House members revolted against the Ways and Means Committee. In 1973 the House allowed people to amend a tax bill on the floor. In 1974 it forced powerful Chairman Mills to resign following a personal scandal, and in 1975 it ended the privileged status of tax bills. Critics charged that tax bills soon became a collection of amendments written to please special interests.

In the Senate, where no closed rule exists, tax bills often do become collections of amendments. Many tax bills are amended so often on the Senate floor they are known as "Christmas tree bills." Like a Christmas tree full of ornaments, a tax bill in the Senate soon fills up with special tax provisions.

The Senate's Role in Tax Legislation All tax bills start in the House. Article I, Section 7, of the Constitution, however, says, "The Senate may propose . . . amendments. . . ." Because of this provision, the Senate often tries to change tax bills the House has passed. As a result, many people view the Senate as the place where interest groups can get House tax provisions they do not like changed or eliminated.

The Senate Committee on Finance has primary responsibility for dealing with tax matters. Like the House Ways and Means Committee, the Senate Finance Committee is powerful. Although the Senate Finance Committee has subcommittees, the full committee does most of the work on tax bills. As a result, the chairperson of the Finance Committee is an extremely important figure not only in the Senate but also in Washington, D.C., in general.

STUDY GUIDE

Themes in Government
Checks and Balances All House members face reelection every two years. **How does this fact relate to the fact that all revenue bills begin in the House of Representatives?**

Critical Thinking Skills
Synthesizing Information In light of the usual means of advancing bills through Congress, what sets the House Ways and Means Committee apart from other law-

making committees found in the House of Representatives?

Background

Of all the taxes paid by Americans, the income tax is the heaviest. Early attempts to tax incomes failed. An income tax law passed in 1894 was found unconstitutional by the Supreme Court a year later. In the early 1900s, calls for a progressive income tax (the more you earned, the more you paid) continued. Lawmakers, however, feared another clash with the Supreme Court. The answer—the Sixteenth Amendment to the Constitution, which, when ratified in 1913, gave Congress the power to levy an individual income tax. The first permanent tax on incomes was soon passed, levying a 1- to 6-percent tax on individual incomes above $3,000 and incomes of married couples above $4,000.

Appropriating Money

In addition to passing tax laws to raise money, Congress has another important power over government spending. The power of appropriation, or approval of government spending, is a congressional responsibility. In Article I, Section 9, the Constitution states, "No money shall be drawn from the Treasury, but in consequence of [except by] appropriations made by law." Thus, Congress must pass laws to appropriate money for the federal government. Congress's approval is needed before departments and agencies of the executive branch such as the Department of Defense or the Federal Communications Commission can actually spend money.

How Congress Appropriates Money Congress follows a two-step procedure in appropriating money. Suppose the President has just signed a bill to help control rats in the inner cities. One provision of the law limits the amount of money that can be spent on the program to $10 million a year. This kind of law is an authorization bill. An **authorization bill** sets up a federal program and specifies how much money may be appropriated for that program. It is the first step Congress uses in appropriating money. The rat-control law also specifies that the Department of Housing and Urban Development (HUD) will administer the program. HUD, however, does not yet actually have any money to carry out the program.

The second step in the appropriations procedure comes when HUD requests that Congress provide the $10 million. This kind of bill is an **appropriations bill** and provides the money needed to carry out laws Congress has passed. HUD's request for the $10 million for the rat-control program will be only one small item in the multi-billion-dollar budget HUD will send to Congress for that year. HUD's budget, in turn, will be part of the President's total annual budget for the executive branch. Each year the President's budget comes to Congress as a series of appropriations bills.

It is unusual for Congress to appropriate the full

amount of money each executive department and agency requests. Consequently, Congress might decide to grant HUD only $5 million to carry out the rat-control program. HUD then would have only this amount of money to spend for the program for that year. Next year, HUD would have to ask for another appropriation to continue the program.

The Appropriations Committees The House and Senate appropriations committees and their subcommittees handle appropriations bills. Both the House and Senate appropriations committees have 13 subcommittees that deal with the same policy areas in each house. Thus, the same appropriations

GLOBAL CONNECTION

Issues

Congressional Junkets Many lawmakers make junkets—trips financed by the government or private interest groups—to gather information related to their duties. Such fact-finding missions are legal, but congressional junkets have become controversial.

Many members of Congress argue that trips abroad help spread goodwill and promote better understanding among nations. Critics say that lawmakers spend more time vacationing than tending to government business.

House and Senate rules limit the congressional travel allowance. They also prohibit private sources from paying a lawmaker's travel expenses for more than a certain number of days.

Examining the Connection
Do you think members of Congress should be allowed to travel at taxpayers' expense? Why or why not?

Cooperative Learning Activity

Divide the class into pairs of interviewers and citizens. Each interviewer and citizen are to construct a question-and-answer format to address the following subjects: income taxes, sales taxes, and luxury taxes. Citizens may express any opinion they feel or believe that large numbers of Americans may have. Each pair should be prepared to present their interview to the rest of the class.

GLOBAL CONNECTION

Point out that senators' and representatives' trips to their home states or districts are not classified as junkets. The costs of these trips may be paid for out of each congressperson's official expense account. These accounts are used to pay for all office expenses. In the past Congress limited the number of government–paid trips home. From 3 trips per year in the early 1960s, the number rose to 33 for representatives and about 40 for senators. In 1980 the limits were abolished. **Examining the Connection Answer:** *Students' opinions will vary but should be supported with reasons.*

Independent Practice

L2 Creating a Chart Have students create flow charts to illustrate the process by which Congress passes tax laws.

STUDY GUIDE

Theme Answer
Congress funds its programs with tax money and controls how much can be spent on each program.

Critical Thinking Answer
Congress may want an agency to avoid wasteful spending or force an agency to concentrate its allotted spending on the most effective measures.

Assess

Check for Understanding
Have students complete Section 3 Review on page 426.

Caption Answer
to answer questions and explain
their budget requests

Meeting Objectives

Each section objective is
tested by the Section Review
questions that follow it in
parentheses.
- Describe Congress's role in
  taxing and spending. (2, 3,
  4, 5, 6, 7, 8)
- Compare authorization bills
  with appropriations bills. (3)
- Analyze the duties of the
  House Ways and Means
  Committee. (5)

Evaluate

 Section 3 Quiz

 Testmaker

Reteach

Have students create a flow
chart explaining the two-step
procedure that Congress follows
in appropriating money.

Enrich

Have students research and
write a paper about the history of
social security legislation.

Close

Have students consider the
question posed to Representative
Wilbur Mills on page 423. Should
one person in government have
so much power?

Money for Defense
Congress appropriates military funds. **Economics**
Why do agencies testify before subcommittees?

appropriations subcommittees about their budgets.
During the budget hearings, these officials answer
questions from lawmakers about their programs and
explain why they need the money they have requested.
These hearings are an important way for Congress to
oversee the work of the executive branch. Each year
agency officials must return to Congress to request
the money they need to operate in the coming year. In
this way lawmakers have a chance to become familiar
with the federal agencies and their programs.

As the appropriations subcommittees in Congress
go through this same process year after year, they
often develop close relationships with certain agencies
and projects that they tend to favor in appropriating
funds. In addition, some federal agencies deal with
powerful interest groups in the course of their work.
Many of these same interest groups try hard to influence Congress and the appropriations subcommittees
to give these agencies all the money they request.

subcommittees in the House and the Senate would
review the HUD budget, including its rat-control
program.

Unlike other committees the appropriations committees do not have the power to kill bills. They must
report out all the bills that are sent to them. This requirement is necessary so that the federal government
has money to continue operating. The appropriations
committees have the job of carefully reviewing all appropriations bills. After this review they often make
changes by cutting agency budgets, or, occasionally,
increasing them.

Every year heads of departments and agencies and
program directors testify before the House and Senate

Uncontrollable Expenditures The House and
Senate appropriations committees, however, do not
have a voice in all the spending of the federal government. About 70 percent of the money the federal
government spends each year is beyond their control.
Past government actions require that most of this
money be spent for certain purposes. Such required
spending includes social security payments, interest
on the national debt, and federal contracts that already are in force. Some of these expenditures are
known as **entitlements** because they are social programs that continue from one year to the next. The
government has given up control over how these
funds are to be spent.

SECTION 3 REVIEW

Section Summary
Congress is charged with passing laws to raise and
spend money for the United States government.

Checking For Understanding
Recalling Facts
1. Define **tax, closed rule, authorization bill, appropriations bill, entitlement.**
2. Name the House and Senate committees responsible for tax laws.
3. Explain the difference between an authorization bill
   and an appropriations bill.
4. Relate what a "Christmas tree bill" is.

Exploring Themes
5. Checks and Balances What control does the House
   Ways and Means Committee exert over presidential requests for changes in tax laws?
6. Political Processes Why did the House use a closed
   rule to debate most tax laws?

Critical Thinking Skills
7. Synthesizing Information Do you think Congress
   should have both the power to raise and to spend
   money? Support your answer.
8. Drawing Conclusions Why do you think the House
   was given the power to originate all revenue bills?

426 UNIT 4: THE LEGISLATIVE BRANCH

Section 3 Review Answers

1. Definitions of terms appear on pages indicated: **tax,** 423;
closed rule, 424; **authorization bill,** 425; **appropriations bill,** 425; **entitlement,** 426
2. House Ways and Means Committee and Senate Committee on Finance
3. An authorization bill sets up a federal program and specifies how much money may be appropriated for that pro-

gram. An appropriations bill provides the money needed to
carry out the laws passed by Congress.
4. a tax bill that becomes a collection of amendments and
is filled with special tax provisions
5. decides whether to go along with presidential requests
for tax cuts or increases
6. Because tax laws are complicated, many lawmakers felt
they did not understand tax legislation well enough to offer
amendments. Also, it prevented tax bills from being a collection of amendments to please special interests.

7. Answers should include that the checks and balances
provided between the two houses of Congress and between
the houses and the President are sufficient, and that
Congress has a better handle on this information than does
any other branch.
8. Answers should include that the House is more representative of the people.

Helping Constituents

Experienced lawmakers have learned they are expected to do more in Washington, D.C., for their constituents than debate great issues. To be reelected, they must spend much of their time on two other important tasks. First, they must act as problem solvers for voters who have difficulties with departments or agencies of the federal government. Second, they must make sure that their district or state gets its share of federal money and projects such as new post offices, military bases, and contracts.

These two duties are not new to members of Congress, but in recent years they have become increasingly important. As the national government has grown, they have become an extremely time-consuming part of the lawmaker's job.

Handling Problems

All lawmakers today are involved with **casework**—helping constituents with problems. One House member put it this way:

Rightly or wrongly, we have become the link between the frustrated citizen and the very involved federal government in citizens' lives. . . . We continually use more and more of our staff time to handle citizens' complaints.

—REPRESENTATIVE DAN ROSTENKOWSKI

Many Different Requests Every year senators and representatives respond to thousands of requests from voters for help in dealing with agencies in the executive branch. Typical requests include: (1) A soldier

would like the Army to move him to a base close to home because his parents are seriously ill. (2) A local businessperson claims the Federal Trade Commission (FTC) is treating her business unfairly. She wants to meet with top FTC officials. (3) An agency has canceled a veteran's GI life insurance policy. The agency says the veteran failed to fill out and return a certain form. The veteran says he never got the form, but he wants the life insurance.

Sometimes voters make foolish requests or ask for help that a lawmaker is unwilling to deliver. A representative from New York, for example, was asked to fix a speeding ticket. Another House member got a call during a blizzard in his state. The caller wanted to know what the lawmaker was going to do about the lack of snow shovels at a local hardware store.

Who Handles Casework All lawmakers have staff members called caseworkers to handle the problems of their constituents. In most instances the caseworkers are able to handle the requests for help themselves. Sometimes the problem can be solved with a simple question from a caseworker to the agency involved. At other times, however, the senator or representative may have to get directly involved.

Many lawmakers complain that voters say they want less government but at the same time demand more services from their members of Congress. The volume of requests for help is already great and keeps increasing. In 1991, for example, the House received almost 176 million pieces of mail. That was 15 million more than in 1981, only 10 years earlier. Most of this mail came from people asking for help or who were angered by some problem with an agency of the federal government.

SECTION PREVIEW

Objectives
After studying this section, you should be able to:
- Examine how lawmakers help their constituents.
- Compare the methods of

obtaining pork-barrel legislation with those of obtaining federal grants and contracts.

Key Terms and Concepts
casework, pork-barrel legislation, logrolling

Themes in Government
- Political Processes
- Public Policy

Critical Thinking Skills
- Drawing Conclusions
- Synthesizing Information

CHAPTER 15: CONGRESS AT WORK 427

Classroom Resources for Section 4

Focus

Bell Ringer
Have students write a situation for which they think it is appropriate for a constituent to ask a senator or representative for help.

Motivating Activity
Have volunteers read their Bell Ringer responses and write them on the chalkboard. Have students decide which ones should be addressed and which should not. What criteria would they establish for making such a determination?

Vocabulary Precheck
Write the terms and concepts on the chalkboard. Ask students to tell how each relates to legislation by Congress. **LEP**

Teach

Guided Practice
L1 Classifying Write these headlines on the chalkboard:

NEW FIGHTER PLANE TO BE BUILT BY LOCAL COMPANY: 500 NEW JOBS CREATED
(winning grants and contracts)

TRAFFIC BY PLANE FACTORY TO BE EASED BY WIDENING OF INTERSTATE HIGHWAY
(pork-barrel legislation)

SENATOR BLOCKS CANCELLATION OF NEW FIGHTER PLANE IN DEFENSE CONTRACT
(keeping federal projects)

SENATOR GETS SOCIAL SECURITY ADMINISTRATION TO REVIEW DENIAL OF BENEFITS TO WORKER INJURED AT PLANE FACTORY
(casework)

Have students match each headline to one of these categories and explain their selection: *casework, pork-barrel legislation, winning grants and contracts, keeping federal projects.* **LEP**

L2 **Expressing Opinions** Ask students if they think casework, securing pork-barrel projects, or voting on legislation is the most important part of a representative's job, and why.

L3 **Synthesizing Information** Write the following statements on the chalkboard:

Casework is campaigning.
Casework is democracy in action.
Casework is representative government.

Have students explain why they agree or disagree with each of these characterizations.

PARTICIPATING IN GOVERNMENT

Discuss the skills students might have that qualify them to be a congressional page. Urge interested students to contact their representatives' offices to obtain the necessary paperwork. Assist students writing the required essay.

📁 Have students complete activity 15 in *Participating in Government* in the Teacher's Classroom Resources.

CONNECTIONS

Language
In the days before refrigeration, pork was salted and stored in barrels to prevent spoilage. The pork barrel thus sustained a family in much the same way that pork-barrel legislation provides for a lawmaker's constituents with federally funded projects.

Purposes of Casework Why do lawmakers spend so much of their time on casework? Lawmakers are involved in casework because it serves three important purposes. First, casework helps lawmakers get reelected. Lawmakers know that helping voters with problems is part of what they can do for the people in their states or districts. "I learned soon after coming to Washington," a Missouri lawmaker once said, "that it was just as important to get a certain document for somebody back home as for some European diplomat—really, more important, because that little guy back home votes."

As a result, many lawmakers actually look for casework. One lawmaker, for example, regularly sends invitations to almost 7,000 voters in his district asking them to bring their problems to a town meeting his staff runs. Another encourages voters to call collect with their problems on a special "hot line." Many representatives have vans that drive through their districts as mobile offices to keep watch on problems back home.

Second, casework is one way in which Congress oversees the executive branch. Casework brings problems with federal programs to the attention of members of Congress. It provides opportunities for lawmakers and their staffs to get a closer look at how well the executive branch is handling such federal programs as social security, veterans' benefits, or worker's compensation.

Third, casework provides a way for the average citizen to cope with the huge national government. In the years before the national government grew so large, most citizens with a problem turned to their local politicians—called ward heelers—for help. One member of Congress explained that:

In the old days, you had the ward heeler who cemented himself in the community by taking care of everyone. Now the Congressman plays the role of ward heeler—wending his way through bureaucracy, helping to cut through red tape and confusion.

—SAM RAYBURN

Helping the District or State

Besides providing services for their constituents, members of Congress also try to bring federal government projects and money to their districts and states. Lawmakers do this in three ways: (1) through

---

PARTICIPATING IN GOVERNMENT

Applying To Be a Congressional Page

Working in Congress is not just for legislators and their staff members. Many teenagers work on Capitol Hill in the congressional page program.

Pages generally work from 10:00 a.m. to 5:00 p.m. or later, if necessary. They carry messages from one office to another or run errands for members of Congress. They also make sure that legislators have all paperwork dealing with pending bills or resolutions. Other pages work in a senator's or representative's office. They may do general office work, such as typing or filing. They may research newspapers from a legislator's home state or district to find information of interest to the senator or representative. Pages receive a monthly salary.

To be eligible for the congressional page program, you must be at least 16 years old and be entering your junior year of high school. You must have a cumulative grade point average of "B" or better in all major subjects and agree to serve for at least one semester.

Members of Congress sponsor a limited number of teens from their home districts to work as pages in Washington, D.C. To obtain an application, contact your senator or representative.

Investigating Further

Members of Congress also employ teens part-time in their district offices. Find out more about opportunities to work for a lawmaker close to home.

Background

Legislators' constituencies are often divided into four groups: *geographic, reelection, primary,* and *personal.* Geographic constituents are those who have economic interests in the legislators' work based on the problems in their district. Reelection constituents are those who supported the legislators in the last election. Primary constituents are those who have shown consistent and continued support through a number of the legislators' election campaigns. Personal constituents are those political or personal friends whom the legislators trust and with whom they may discuss political strategy and may count on for emotional support.

pork-barrel legislation; (2) through federal grants and contracts; and (3) through keeping federal projects.

Pork-Barrel Legislation Every year, through public-works bills, Congress appropriates billions of dollars for local projects. These projects may include such things as post offices, dams, military bases, harbor and river improvements, federally funded highways, veterans' hospitals, pollution-treatment centers, and mass-transit projects.

Such projects can bring jobs and money into a state or district. Texas lawmakers, for example, helped the city of Houston's future growth by getting NASA's Manned Space Center located there. Lawmakers from different parts of the country often want different types of projects for their areas. Those from dry western states may want federal water and river projects to bring badly needed water to their states. Lawmakers from coastal towns may want a new harbor or a seawall built to protect against high tides.

When Congress appropriates money for such local federal projects, it is often called **pork-barrel legislation.** The idea of pork-barrel legislation is that any part of the country sooner or later gets to dip into the "pork barrel" (the federal treasury) and pull out a fat piece of "pork" (a local project).

Economic growth in their home districts has always been a major concern of members of Congress. Recently members have found a whole new area of the pork barrel to tap.

For years the National Park Service designated special wilderness areas and historic sites that should be preserved. Federal money paid for the restoration or preservation projects. Until lately, nominations for these sites were reviewed by a Park Service panel that included historians, scientists, and specialists. Then President Reagan, who opposed spending money to open new sites, disbanded the panel. This left to Congress the responsibility of choosing sites.

Considerations of the historic or wilderness significance of the site had always been important when selecting where the money would be spent. That changed. Members of Congress discovered that Park

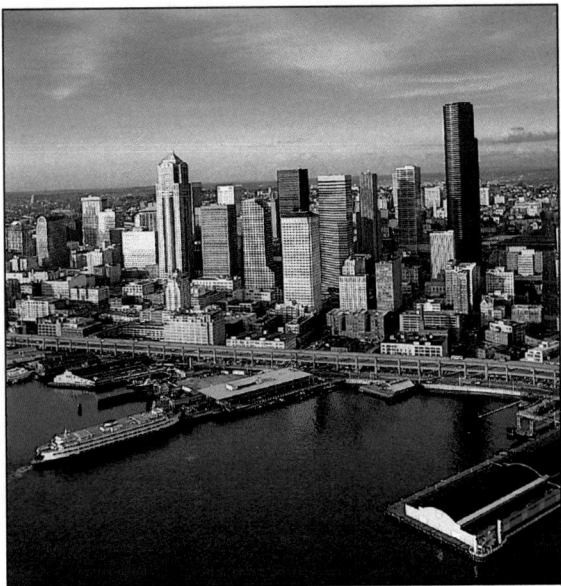

Federally Funded Port
Seattle won funding to rejuvenate its seaport. Economics **What other projects does Congress fund?**

Service money can promote economic growth in their home districts. Within a short time 20 new sites obtained millions of dollars of federal project money.

Lawmakers believe that getting federal projects for their state or district is a key part of their job. They usually help each other do this through **logrolling,** an agreement by two or more lawmakers to support each other's bills. The idea is: "You scratch my back and I'll scratch yours."

Thus, lawmakers do not fight one another for federal projects. Instead, they try to help one another to gain "pork" projects. Consequently, lawmakers from Ohio will vote for a dam project in Colorado even though that project will not help Ohio voters. They know that soon they may want the Colorado lawmakers to vote for a mass-transit project in Ohio. Of course, the government never has enough money for all lawmakers to get all the federal projects they want. Lawmakers know, however, that in time they are bound to get some projects.

Independent Practice

L1 Classificatory Writing Have students write a paragraph differentiating logrolling, pork-barrel legislation, and federal grants and contracts.

📁 **Interpreting Source Readings** Have students complete activity 15 in *Primary and Secondary Source Readings* in the Teacher's Classroom Resources.

Caption Answer
post offices, dams, military bases, highways, hospitals, mass transit, and other local projects

STUDY GUIDE

Critical Thinking Answers
Voters have grown more angry, frustrated, and demanding.

Cooperating is necessary for winning pork-barrel measures; competing is necessary for winning grants and contracts.

Assess

Check for Understanding

Have students complete Section 4 Review on page 430.

Focus on Government
Video 23
Lecture Launcher:
The Organization of Congress
Running Time: 4:26
Videodisc 2, Chap. 23
VHS Tape 2, Begins 6:46

Video 25
Lecture Launcher:
Congressional Caseworkers
Running Time: 3:13
Videodisc 2, Chap. 25
VHS Tape 2, Begins 13:28

STUDY GUIDE

Themes in Government
Political Processes Many House members mail newsletters to people in the home districts.
Public Policy Voters everywhere are demanding that lawmakers address national health care.

Critical Thinking Skills
Drawing Conclusions What does the huge increase in mail sent to the House say about voter attitudes?
Synthesizing Information Why must lawmakers be able to both cooperate and compete?

Critical Thinking Activity

Making Inferences Have students reread the quote by the Missouri lawmaker on page 428. What does the lawmaker suggest is the most important factor that determines who is helped by a legislator and who is not? *(Is the person a voter?)*

What does this suggest about the needs and wishes of people who do not vote, such as children and minors, the mentally ill, certain criminals, and aliens? How are these people represented?

Meeting Objectives

Each section objective is tested by the Section Review questions that follow it in parentheses.
• Examine how lawmakers help their constituents. (2, 3, 4, 6, 7)
• Compare the methods of obtaining pork-barrel legislation with those of obtaining federal grants and contracts. (2, 3, 5, 8)

Evaluate

📁 Section 4 Quiz

💠 Testmaker

Reteach

📁 Have students complete activity 15 in *Reteaching Activities* in the Teacher's Classroom Resources.

Enrich

Have students research a recent pork-barrel project or federal grant awarded to their state or district by contacting their senators' or representatives' offices.

Close

Discuss why casework and pork-barrel legislation unfairly favor the incumbent at election time. Ask students whether this solution benefits or harms our system of government.

Winning Grants and Contracts Lawmakers also try to make sure their districts or states get their fair share of the available federal grants and contracts. A senator from Colorado put it this way, "If a program is to be established, the state of Colorado should get its fair share."

Federal grants and contracts are very important to lawmakers and their districts or states. They are an important source of money and jobs. Every year federal agencies such as the Department of Defense spend billions of dollars to carry out hundreds of government projects and programs. For example, when the Air Force decided to locate a new project at one of its bases in Utah, almost 1,000 jobs and millions of dollars came into the state.

Unlike pork-barrel projects, however, lawmakers often compete for such grants or contracts. For example, several other states wanted the Air Force project, but Utah's lawmakers won the prize for their state. In another case, Virginia and Pennsylvania lawmakers recently battled over a $2.5 billion contract to repair four aircraft carriers for the Navy. Navy officials could not agree on where the work should be done. Virginia's senators claimed the project could be done more cheaply in Virginia. Pennsylvania's lawmakers, however, finally got the contract and the money for their home state.

Lawmakers do not have the direct control over grants and contracts they do over pork-barrel legislation. Instead, agencies of the executive branch such as the Department of Defense or the Department of Labor award federal grants and contracts. Lawmakers, however, may try to influence those decisions in several ways. They may pressure agency officials to give a favorable hearing to their state. They also may try to put people from their state in touch with agency officials. If problems come up when someone from their state is arranging a grant or contract, they may step in to help.

Many lawmakers assign one or more of their staff members to act as specialists in contracts and grants. These staff members become experts on how individuals, businesses, and local governments can qualify for federal money. They will help constituents apply for contracts and grants. Their job is to make sure federal grants and contracts keep coming into their state or district.

Keeping Federal Projects Finally, lawmakers try to prevent federal projects from leaving their district. Recently, for example, the Department of Defense wanted to move the production of Navy A-6E attack planes from Long Island in the state of New York. This move would have caused the loss of 1,000 jobs in Representative Thomas Downey's district.

As a result, Representative Downey began working on the problem right away. He was a member of the House Armed Services Committee, which has great influence on the Navy's budget. With the help of other lawmakers on the committee, Downey was able to get the Navy to change its decision, keeping the project and the jobs in his district.

Members of Congress constantly work to get benefits from the government for their constituents, district, and state. Through the give-and-take of this process, the federal government distributes its resources and services to various groups and regions around the country.

---

4 SECTION REVIEW

Section summary
Lawmakers work to help their constituents by using caseworkers, obtaining federal projects, and winning grants and contracts for their states and districts.

Checking For Understanding
Recalling Facts
1. Define casework, pork-barrel legislation, logrolling.
2. List the ways lawmakers bring federal projects and money to their districts and states.
3. State the branch of government that awards federal contracts.
4. Identify the legislative staff members who handle the problems of constituents.

Exploring Themes
5. Political Processes How are the methods for obtaining pork-barrel legislation different from the methods for obtaining federal grants and contracts?
6. Public Policy Why do lawmakers spend much of their time on casework?

Critical Thinking Skills
7. Drawing Conclusions Why do you think legislative casework has grown considerably in recent years?
8. Synthesizing Information Which legislative task is more important—casework or winning federal projects and money? Support your opinion.

Section 4 Review Answers

1. Definitions of terms appear on pages indicated: **casework,** 427; **pork-barrel legislation,** 429; **logrolling,** 429
2. through pork-barrel legislation, federal grants and contracts, and keeping federal projects
3. executive branch
4. caseworkers

5. Congress appropriates the money for pork-barrel legislation, but lawmakers must appeal to the agencies of the executive branch in order for their home states to be awarded federal grants and projects.
6. Casework helps lawmakers get reelected, allows Congress to oversee the executive branch, and provides a way for the average citizen to cope with the huge national government.

7. Answers should include to keep up with growing federal agencies, a complicated bureaucracy, and so on.
8. Answers should include a combination of both to cover more personal issues affecting voters and also issues that affect their pocketbooks, employment, and so on.

Representative Patsy Mink on Education

Patsy Mink is a Democratic representative from Hawaii who sits on the Education and Labor Committee. In 1991 the Budget Committee added an amendment to the proposed budget allowing $2 billion for education.

Representative Mink had the following remarks in urging the House to adopt the amendment:

Mr. Chairman, I rise in very vigorous and strenuous support of the recommendation of our committee Chair here for additional funds in the educational function.

It is a question of determining where your priorities are. This is an investment in our future. It is not a funding for today or a look back to yesterday. This is an effort of this Congress to look to the future of this country. There is no better way to spend an additional $400 million than on the future of our country and our children. This investment will pay enormous dividends.

If we are concerned about crime, about drugs, and about all these other things that plague our Nation, it is an investment in our children, in education, to give them an opportunity to see that there is a chance for them in the future to make a difference.

I admit that we should stand here and congratulate the Budget Committee for coming up with $2 billion additional money for education beyond the budget, but this is only a paltry beginning. Think of it. We have over 12 million children in our country who come from poverty levels, and yet we are only able to accommodate a little over a third in a Head Start Program that everybody says is the most excellent program that ever has been put in place by Congress in years past.

We can only fund it at 35 or 36 percent. This is really tragic. We have to only talk about full funding in the next 7 or 8 years. I would like to see full funding right now, but I am content to say that we must make progress in small steps, and I cannot describe this amendment that our chairman has offered as anything but a small step toward a future that is so essential.

—REPRESENTATIVE PATSY MINK,
APRIL 17, 1991

There is no better way to spend an additional $400 million than on the future of our country and our children.

Representative Mink later noted that education has helped Asian Americans make many contributions to American life:

Americans of Asian and Pacific Island ancestry have gained national and international prominence in the fields of science, business, and the arts, leaving a distinctive mark in virtually every aspect of American life.

Let us recognize these successes of Asians and Pacific Islanders in the past and look forward to even greater achievements from these Americans as they contribute to the improvement of our world community.

—REPRESENTATIVE PATSY MINK,
APRIL 24, 1991

Examining the Reading

Reviewing Facts
1. Relate the values Mink puts forth in her remarks.
2. Describe Representative Mink's reaction to the amount of money the Budget Committee allocated to education.

Critical Thinking Skills
3. Demonstrating Reasoned Judgment In your opinion, how persuasive is Representative Mink in her argument?

CHAPTER 15: CONGRESS AT WORK   431

More About Personal Perspectives

An early opponent of the Vietnam War and supporter of feminist and environmental movements, Patsy Mink served in the United States House of Representatives from 1965 to 1976. She began her political career in the Hawaii Territorial House of Representatives, lost the 1976 Senate primary, the 1986 gubernatorial primary, and the 1988 primary for Honolulu mayor. She sprang back in 1990 to regain her seat in the United States House—winning 66 percent of the vote.

Focus

Have students imagine they have been given several million dollars to improve their community's schools. How would they spend it?

Teach

Ask: What connection does Mink make between education and the problems of crime and drugs? *(Educational opportunities allow people to see there is a chance for them in the future.)* What point in a student's education does Mink identify as being most able to make a real difference? *(when children are young)*

Assess

Have students complete **Examining the Reading.**

Answers

1. Spending on education is investing in the future.
2. She is glad to have it but thinks it is not nearly enough.
3. Students should support their responses, which may include that she is persuasive but that there are also other factors for the Budget Committee and House to consider.

Close

Ask why educational funding is so difficult to obtain compared to spending for defense or agribusiness. Encourage students to consider the respective constituent groups when forming a response.

Identifying Terms and Concepts

1. a, **2.** i, **3.** b, **4.** h, **5.** e, **6.** c, **7.** f, **8.** j, **9.** d, **10.** g

Reviewing Facts and Ideas

1. Private bills deal with individual persons or places. Public bills deal with matters that apply to the nation as a whole. A resolution deals with matters affecting only one house of Congress. Joint resolutions deal with unusual or temporary matters. Concurrent resolutions deal with matters requiring the action of both houses.

2. to be on record in support of an idea or policy, to satisfy an interest group or group of voters, or to call the public's attention to the need for legislation

3. Anyone may write new bills.

4. members of Congress

5. sign the bill into law, veto the bill, pocket veto the bill, or leave the bill unsigned and allow it to become law after 10 days if Congress is still in session

6. Answers should include the nature of the issue, voters at home, other lawmakers, staff members, political parties, the President, special-interest groups, and his/her own beliefs.

7. on major issues, including government intervention in the economy, farm issues, and social welfare issues

8. They provide lawmakers with information about policies they support or oppose. They visit lawmakers in their offices to get their support. They encourage citizens to write members of Congress on the issues they favor or oppose.

9. initiates and reviews all the tax laws

10. through pork-barrel legislation, federal grants and contracts, and keeping federal projects

Summary and Significance

A key task of Congress is passing bills, many of which deal with raising and spending money. The series of steps through which a bill passes before becoming law incorporates checks and balances between the houses of Congress, and Congress and the President. Lawmakers' decisions are subject to many influences, chief among them are the nature of the issues, voter opinion, political-party affiliation, the President, special-interest groups, and the beliefs and staff of the lawmakers themselves. Lawmakers help their constituents with problems with the federal government and try to bring jobs, money, and projects into their states and districts. The more voters understand the legislative process and responsibilities of lawmakers, the better they are able to affect this process and use the services of lawmakers when they find it beneficial.

Identifying Terms and Concepts

Fill in the blank with the letter of the correct term or concept listed below.

a. joint resolution
b. rider
c. hearing
d. pocket veto
e. lobbyist
f. closed rule
g. authorization bills
h. entitlements
i. casework
j. pork-barrel legislation

1. Congress uses a _____ to propose a constitutional amendment.
2. _____ is a congressional task that involves helping constituents with problems.
3. A _____ is an often controversial provision tacked on to a bill pertaining to a different subject.
4. Interest on the national debt and social security payments are examples of _____ .
5. A person who represents a special-interest group to Congress and other government officials is known as a _____ .
6. Witnesses usually offer testimony in a committee _____ regarding a specific bill.
7. Under a _____ , House members were forbidden to offer amendments to tax bills from the floor.
8. _____ is when Congress passes laws to appropriate money for local federal projects.
9. The President gives a _____ by not signing a bill during the last 10 days Congress is in session.
10. _____ set up federal programs and specify how much money may be appropriated for those programs.

Reviewing Facts and Ideas

1. Describe the two types of bills that may be introduced and three types of resolutions that may be passed in Congress.
2. Explain why lawmakers sometimes introduce bills that they know have no chance of being passed.
3. Identify who may write bills.
4. Specify who may introduce bills in Congress.
5. List the four actions a President may take on a bill.
6. Cite four factors that influence lawmakers when they consider legislation.
7. Point out when members of Congress are most likely to vote with their political party.
8. Describe how lobbyists influence lawmakers.
9. Explain the role that the House Ways and Means Committee plays in tax legislation.
10. Discuss the means lawmakers use to bring federal projects or money to their states or districts.
11. Specify federal funding in which congressional appropriations committees have no say.
12. Cite a key tool lawmakers use to secure the passage of pork-barrel legislation.

Applying Themes

1. **Political Processes** What are the key points in the legislative process when lawmakers can influence the fate of a bill?
2. **Checks and Balances** Why is the process by which a bill becomes a law a good example of checks and balances at work?

11. entitlements, such as social security payments, interest on the national debt, and federal contracts that already are in force

12. logrolling

Applying Themes

1. during committee meetings, the markup session, and debate when amendments may be offered

2. Answers should include that before a bill can become a law, it must be presented to the President, who uses this opportunity to sign a bill into law or reject it. Congress can override a President's veto with a two-thirds vote in both houses.

3. Answers should cite helping lawmakers get re-elected, as a means for Congress to oversee the executive branch, and to help citizens cope with the federal government.

3. **Public Policy** In your opinion, what is the most important purpose of casework?

Critical Thinking Skills

1. **Synthesizing Information** Sessions of Congress are currently televised. What impact might this have on how Congress conducts its business?
2. **Drawing Conclusions** The American lawmaking process has often been criticized as being too slow to be truly responsive to public needs. Other people believe that a slow, deliberate process helps protect the nation against unwise legislation. With which opinion do you agree? Support your answer.
3. **Making Inferences** Given the long, complex procedures for passing a law, make a list of the characteristics a bill should display in order to have a good chance of making it through the process to become a law.

Linking Past and Present

For much of its history, Congress met for only a few months each year. Today, however, lawmakers meet for most of the year. What factors do you think account for these extended sessions?

Writing About Government

Persuasive Writing Thomas Jefferson once said, "When a man assumes a public trust, he should consider himself a public property." Do you agree or disagree with this statement? Which reasons best express why you do or do not agree? Write a paragraph persuading someone to share your point of view.

Reinforcing the Skill

Making Comparisons Examine and compare the two images below, then answer the questions that follow.

1. **Name** two areas in which these images can be compared.

2. **What** two things do these images have in common?
3. **What** are three things that are different about these two pictures?

Investigating Further

1. **Individual Project** Write a letter to your senator or representative stating and supporting your opinion about an issue or current event that interests you. When you receive a reply to your letter, share it with the class.
2. **Cooperative Learning** Organize into groups of five. As a group, devise a case presenting opposing viewpoints on a hypothetical bill to present to Congress. Trade cases with other groups and determine which viewpoint is most likely to receive a lawmaker's vote.

CHAPTER 15: CONGRESS AT WORK **433**

CASE STUDY

The Case at a Glance

Who: Congress and the President
What: free Kuwait
When: 1990–1991
Where: Washington, D.C.
Why: who has authority to commit troops

Focus

Ask students to discuss what would happen if the United States experienced a surprise attack. What would the President do? *(send reinforcements to protect American troops under attack, deploy support forces, plan retaliation strikes)* What would Congress likely do? *(provide financial backing for support of the troops in the field, perhaps declare war)* Point out that control of the military is a shared responsibility, one that has created both conflict and harmony.

Teach

Guided Practice

L1 Drawing Conclusions Ask: Why did the Framers of the Constitution divide the authority to commit American troops to combat between the President and the Congress? *(to prevent one branch of government from controlling the military)* Point out that the President as commander in chief has to set policy but cannot carry out policy without Congress's approval. Also, the Framers feared that some leaders might overstep their power.

Powers of the President

The President shall be Commander in Chief of the Army and Navy of the United States.

—Article II, Section 2

Powers of Congress

The Congress shall have power. . . to declare war.

—Article I, Section 8

The Decision to Go to War in the Persian Gulf

The Case

When the newly elected 102nd Congress convened on January 3, 1991, congressional leaders faced a unique dilemma. In the searing desert on the shores of the Persian Gulf nearly 430,000 United States troops faced an equally large Iraqi army. President George Bush had sent the American troops to the Gulf area after Saddam Hussein, the dictator of Iraq, launched a brutal invasion of Kuwait on August 2, 1990.

The President had also organized a 30-nation coalition to stand with the Americans against Iraq. Further, the United Nations had placed economic sanctions on Iraq and had authorized the use of military force unless Hussein withdrew from Kuwait by January 15, 1991.

Congress, however, the only branch of the American government with the formal power to declare war, still had not acted. As the January 15 deadline approached, President Bush asserted that as commander in chief he did not need congressional approval to go to war. Senate Majority Leader George Mitchell disagreed. "Under the Constitution," Mitchell warned, "the President has no legal authority to commit the U.S. to war. Only Congress can do that." With the world watching, Congress and the executive branch debated a key constitutional question: Could President Bush send troops into combat without congressional approval?

The Background

The showdown between Bush and Congress stemmed directly from the separation of powers built into the Constitution more than 200 years ago. The Framers of the Constitution feared that putting military power and executive power together in one branch of government would lead to tyranny. Thus, they divided things up.

The Framers gave Congress the power to declare war. James Madison, a key Framer who went on to become President himself, explained why:

The Constitution supposes what the history of all governments demonstrates, that the Executive is the branch of power most interested in war and most prone to it. It has accordingly with studied care vested the question of war in the Legislature.

—JAMES MADISON, 1798

More About the Case

Before 1700 there were few settlements in Kuwait. In 1710 an Arabian people, the Arab Anaiza, migrated into the Kuwait Bay area to escape massive drought in Arabia. Here they built a port that later became the city of Kuwait. As trade increased, the group elected Sabah I as their ruler. The Al-Sabah family has ruled Kuwait since 1756. A few years later Britain used Kuwait as a point from which to ship mail to Syria. British interest in the area grew because of Kuwait's strategic location. By 1899 Britain concluded a treaty with the Al-Sabah ruler to provide for the defense of the area.

At the same time, the Framers wanted the new nation to be able to defend itself, especially against surprise attacks. They believed command of military forces required the unified leadership that only a single person, the President, could give. Thus, the Constitution gave the President power as commander in chief.

The constitutional debate between President Bush and congressional power unfolded gradually in the autumn of 1990. Following the Iraqi invasion in August, Bush had used his authority as commander in chief to build up American forces in the Persian Gulf without asking for congressional approval.

Initially, Congress offered little resistance to Bush's actions. Congress was not in session in August when Bush sent the first troops to the Persian Gulf. When lawmakers were busy running for reelection in September and October, they had little to say.

Many members of Congress feared that challenging the President's actions would make Saddam Hussein think that Americans were divided. "It's awfully difficult for us to do anything of substance without creating the impression of . . . divisiveness," said Representative Lee Hamilton.

Further, there were real political risks. If Bush chose war and was successful, lawmakers who opposed the President could become unpopular.

After Bush ordered more troops to the Persian Gulf in November, however, the political pressure for Congress to use its constitutional war powers grew dramatically. Lawmakers could no longer remain silent with two huge armies, bristling with modern weapons, squared off against each other in the Persian Gulf region.

By mid-December a full-scale debate on the President's war powers was underway in the Washington courtroom of Federal Judge Harold Greene. Led by Representative Donald Dellums, 54 lawmakers asked the court for an injunction to stop President Bush from attacking Iraq without the consent of Congress.

Congressional Argument In court, advocates of congressional authority focused on Article I, Section 8, of the Constitution. Representative Dellums argued: "The Constitution clearly gives Congress the right to declare war. This situation is too grave for one person to take us into it alone." Eleven constitutional experts, including liberals and conservatives, prepared a brief supporting the Dellums lawsuit.

Going to War
Congress, in this cartoon's view, slept as Bush sailed to war. When Congress awoke, debate focused on executive versus congressional war-making powers.

Backers of congressional power pointed to the records of the debates at the Constitutional Convention to support their position. Duke law professor Walter Dellinger argued, "The discussions at the constitutional convention clearly suggest that the framers intended to give Congress the exclusive authority to determine the policy question of whether or not to go to war."

Lawmakers also contended that even though past Presidents had sent troops into combat without a congressional declaration of war, Congress had not lost the war power. Many such cases, lawmakers pointed out, were very limited, short-term events rather than major wars.

The President's Response Defenders of President Bush countered with their own interpretation of the Constitution. Secretary of State James Baker claimed that because the President had consulted regularly with congressional leaders, there was no need for a declaration of war.

Stuart Gerson from the Justice Department represented the President's position in court. Gerson argued that history provided many examples of Presidents using their power as commander in chief without waiting for a declaration of war. Thomas Jefferson, for example, sent the navy to attack the Barbary pirates without congressional approval. In addition, Gerson argued that nothing in the Constitution says Congress has to declare war before fighting begins.

Ask students to name conflicts in the 1950s and 1960s in which the President committed troops to prolonged combat without a congressional declaration of war. *(Korea and Vietnam)* What would James Madison have said about such actions? *(Madison likely would have said both actions illustrated excessive use of presidential power.)* Point out that even though Presidents might have overstepped their constitutional powers in Korea or Vietnam, each had the support of Congress.

L2 Summarizing Have students summarize the actions of President Bush and Congress during the Persian Gulf crisis. Ask: How did the actions of each illustrate the struggle for power over control of the military? Does the separation of powers lead to cooperation or competition between the President and Congress? Have students support their opinions with evidence from the case.

L3 History Have students contrast the attitudes of Madison and Hamilton toward giving Congress the power to declare war. *(Madison believed the executive branch is more interested in war and most prone to it and therefore Congress should have the power to declare war; Hamilton believed a unified leadership was necessary in times of crisis.)* Are the ideas of Hamilton and Madison toward this issue still current? Will the conflict ever be resolved?

During the 1930s oil was discovered in Kuwait. Drilling began in 1936 and by 1945 it became a major oil-exporting nation. With the influx of wealth came economic security, and political independence in 1961. Kuwait joined the Arab League that year and the United Nations in 1963.

Iraq's Saddam Hussein contended that Kuwait was actually a province of Iraq and should not be independent. Hussein used this argument to justify his 1990 invasion of the desert emirate.

L1 History Have students research how Congress and the President resolved the conflict over peace terms with the South after the Civil War. Have students explain how the resolution represented the separation of powers over control of the military.

L2 Research Have students research the War Powers Act and why Congress passed it.

L3 Expressive Writing Have students write an essay on the effect the availability of nuclear weapons has on the formality of declaring war. Students should know that even though the President has control of the "button," he or she would most probably consult with members of Congress before pushing it. Do students think the short time a President would have to respond to a nuclear attack signals a need to rethink the separation of war powers?

Assess

Have students complete **Examining the Case.**

Close

Ask if students can think of circumstances that would justify giving the President exclusive power to declare war.

Greene dismissed the lawsuit. In his ruling, the judge stated that the issue of who could send American troops into war was a political question that Congress and the President must settle on their own.

The Vote for War The issue came to a head when the newly elected 102nd Congress convened on January 3. Moments after the opening session came to order, Senator Tom Harkin leapt to his feet, declaring that Congress could wait no longer to decide on peace or war. Harkin said war is "being talked about in coffee shops, in the work place, and in the homes. Now is the time and here is the place to debate."

After months of avoiding asking for congressional approval, President Bush changed tactics. On January 8, he formally asked Congress for its support, and the White House circulated a draft resolution calling for congressional approval for the use of military force.

The mood was somber on January 9 when the formal debates began. Congressional aides and lawmakers' families filled most seats in the House and Senate galleries. The general public had to wait three hours for seats. Long lines twisted through the Capitol hallways. "It's history in the making" explained one visitor standing in line. Longtime observers of Congress called the speeches serious and often eloquent as the lawmakers rose to state their positions.

Senator Robert Dole said the time to approve the use of force had come. "Let's not pull the rug out from under the President when the pressure is building on Saddam Hussein by the minute," Dole urged. "Let's don't give him any relief."

Representative Robert H. Michel said: "President Bush has openly and forthrightly asked for our help. How can we turn our backs on him?"

Representative David E. Bonior urged House members to "ask the same question that thousands of Americans are asking their families today. Is this cause for which you would ask your son or daughter to risk their life?"

Senator Sam Nunn wanted to let the economic sanctions weaken Iraq before authorizing war. "We are playing a winning hand. I see no compelling reason to rush to military action."

After three days of debate, the Senate approved the use of military force by a vote of 52 to 47. In the House the vote was 250 to 183.

At a news conference moments after the votes,

President Bush said the action by Congress "unmistakably demonstrates the United States commitment to enforce a complete Iraqi withdrawal from Kuwait."

The Significance

On January 16, President Bush ordered American forces and their allies to drive Iraq out of Kuwait. Operation Desert Storm had begun. Massive air and ground attacks and American-led forces smashed the Iraqi forces in an amazingly short 42 days with minimal American casualties. On February 27, a triumphant George Bush announced a cease-fire, declaring "Kuwait is liberated, Iraq's army is defeated."

Would President Bush have attacked without congressional approval? No one can say for sure. History, however, clearly indicates that Presidents from Harry S Truman on have often chosen to send American forces into combat. At the same time, Presidents have almost always felt the need to consult with or involve Congress in such decisions.

The decision to go to war in the Persian Gulf shows how the constitutional principle of separation of powers shapes American government and politics today. One scholar calls separation of powers "an invitation to struggle"; it creates tension between the executive and legislative branches and brings the judgement of one branch to bear on the judgment of the other.

Examining the Case

Reviewing Facts

1. Summarize why Congress delayed in reacting to President Bush's buildup of American troops.
2. Explain why the Framers of the Constitution divided the war power.

Critical Thinking Skills

3. Evaluating Information Is it a good idea to require the President to get congressional approval before sending American forces into battle? Give reasons to support your answer.
4. Synthesizing Information Does the evidence in this case study support this hypothesis: separation of powers requires the President and Congress to cooperate. Explain your answer.

Examining the Case Answers

1. Congress was not in session when the buildup began: lawmakers were busy running for reelection.
2. They feared that combining military and executive power would lead to tyranny.
3. Answers will vary, but may include that requiring congressional approval ties the President's hands; on the other hand, congressional approval is desirable to ensure the support of the American people and to prevent tyranny.
4. Answers may include that yes, they are required to cooperate; a divided home front could prove beneficial to the enemy nation's cause.

Chapter 13
The Organization of Congress

With its 435 members, the House of Representatives is the larger body of Congress. Representatives must be at least 25 years old, citizens of the United States for at least 7 years, and legal residents of the state that elects them. Members of the House of Representatives are elected for 2-year terms.

According to the Constitution, the Senate "shall be composed of two senators from each state." Thus, each state, no matter what its size or population, is represented equally in the Senate. Today's Senate includes 100 members—2 from each of the 50 states. Senators must be at least 30 years old, citizens of the United States for 9 years before election, and legal residents of the state they represent. All the voters of each state elect senators **at-large**, or statewide, for terms of 6 years.

The main task of each house of Congress is the same—to make laws. Because the House and Senate differ in many ways, each house has organized itself differently to carry out its work of making laws.

Some debates on bills take place on the floor of Congress, and all final votes are taken on the floor. The detailed day-to-day work of considering proposed legislation, however, takes place in committees that meet in congressional offices and hearing rooms.

Congress has four basic kinds of committees: (1) standing committees; (2) select committees; (3) joint committees; and (4) conference committees. **Standing committees** are permanent groups that oversee bills. Most standing committees have from six to eight **subcommittees**. Each subcommittee specializes in a subcategory of its standing committee's responsibility.

From time to time, each house of Congress has created temporary committees, called **select committees**. Select committees study one specific issue and report their findings to the Senate or the House.

Made up of members from both the House and the Senate, **joint committees** may be either temporary or permanent. These committees usually act as study groups with responsibility for reporting their findings back to the House and Senate. A **conference committee** is a temporary joint committee set up when the House and Senate have passed different versions of the same bill.

The work of Congress has become so massive and complicated in recent decades that lawmakers need a trained staff to help them do their work effectively. Staff members also carry out the work of congressional committees. In addition, Congress has established a number of supporting agencies that perform important functions for members.

Chapter 14
The Powers of Congress

Most of the powers of Congress, unlike those enjoyed by the President and the Supreme Court, are **expressed powers**, powers carefully listed in the Constitution. Most of these powers are itemized in Article I, Section 8. The expressed powers cover broad themes such as regulating commerce as well as more specific subjects like granting copyrights and patents.

Although the powers of Congress seem to be clearly stated, custom has modified many of them. In part, the last clause of Article I, Section 8, the so-called **elastic clause**, is responsible for these modifications. This clause gives Congress the right to make all laws "necessary and proper" to carry out the powers expressed in the other clauses of Article I. It is called the elastic clause because over the years it has allowed Congress to stretch its powers to meet new situations the Founders could never have anticipated.

The powers given to Congress in the elastic clause are called **implied powers.** The Constitution does not directly grant Congress these powers, but they are presumed "necessary and proper" for Congress to exercise its expressed powers.

In carrying out their legislative powers, both the House and the Senate perform the same basic tasks—considering, amending, and voting on bills. While most of their non-legislative functions also require their joint efforts, each house usually has a different role in exercising these powers. For example, the House of Representatives has exclusive power over **impeachment,** a formal accusation of misconduct in office against a public official. The Senate has the power to approve presidential appointments of federal officials and to ratify treaties.

The Constitution denies Congress certain powers. For example, Congress may not suspend the **writ of**

Using the Unit 4 Digest

Use the Unit Digest to introduce, review, reteach, or condense specific chapters or the entire unit. The Unit Digest is enhanced by the corresponding transparencies and activities in the Teacher's Classroom Resources.

Focus

Write the following statements on the chalkboard:

1. Members of Congress negotiate an arms-reduction treaty with a foreign country.
2. Congress impeaches a federal judge.
3. Congress passes a bill raising income tax rates.
4. Congress passes a law making the sale of certain franchises illegal. Sales made in the two years prior to the passage of the law will be considered illegal.

For each statement, ask: Does Congress have the right to do this? Why or why not? If students have difficulty answering, suggest that they look at Article 1 of the Constitution on pages 99–105.

Teach

L1 Constructing a Table Draw on the chalkboard a table, titled *Powers of Congress,* with the following four column headings: *Expressed Powers, Implied Powers, Powers Shared with Other Branches, Limits to Power.* Have students work in small groups to complete the table. Have groups present and discuss their completed tables.

Classroom Resources for Unit 4 Digest

Unit Digest Transparencies, Unit 4   Participating in Government, Unit 4

Interpreting Visuals Display transparency 4 from the *Unit Digest Transparencies* in the Teacher's Classroom Resources and use the accompanying teaching strategy, student activity, and student test to teach how the legislative branch of American government operates.

L3 Political Processes Ask students to select a piece of legislation recently signed into law by the President. Have students use newspapers, newsmagazines, and such sources as the *Congressional Quarterly* and *Congressional Quarterly Weekly Review* to track how that legislation moved through Congress. Have them present their findings in an annotated time line or a concept map.

Assess

Check for Understanding

Have students complete **Synthesizing the Unit.**

Close

Point out that many of the founders of our nation assumed that the legislature would be the preeminent branch of government because it was the only branch directly elected by the people. Ask students if they think Congress is the preeminent branch of government. Have them explain their responses.

---

habeas corpus, a court order to release a person accused of a crime to court to determine whether he or she has been legally detained. Another important limitation denies Congress the authority to pass **bills of attainder**, laws that establish guilt and punish people without a trial. Congress is also prohibited from passing **ex post facto laws**, laws that make crimes of acts that were legal when they were committed. Article I, Section 9, also denies several other powers to Congress, among them the power to tax exports.

Over the years Congress has developed additional powers not expressly mentioned in the Constitution. These powers are the power to investigate and the power of legislative oversight. Legislative oversight involves a continuing review of how effectively the executive branch carries out the laws Congress passes.

The three branches of the federal government are not completely independent. Although each branch has its own functions, they are related in a system of checks and balances. As a result, Congress and the President share certain powers. Thus, many of the President's most important executive responsibilities—such as making treaties, appointing federal officials and judges, and paying the expenses of the executive branch—require congressional cooperation.

On the other hand, all bills Congress passes require the President's signature before they become law. Overriding a presidential veto requires a two-thirds majority in each house of Congress, which usually is difficult to obtain. Consequently, a veto is an important legislative power the President exercises.

Chapter 15

Congress at Work

Two types of bills are introduced in Congress. **Private bills** deal with individual people or places. They often involve claims against the government or immigration concerns. **Public bills** deal with general matters and apply to the entire nation. Major public bills account for about 30 percent of the bills passed in each term of Congress. They may be debated for weeks or even months before they become law.

Congress may also pass several types of resolutions. A **resolution** covers matters affecting only one house of Congress and is passed by that house alone. **Joint resolutions**, which both houses of Congress must

pass, may correct an error in an earlier law or appropriate money for a special purpose. **Concurrent resolutions** cover matters requiring the action of the House and Senate, but on which a law is not needed.

The Constitution sets forth only a few of the many steps a bill must go through to become law. The remaining steps have developed over time. The first step is proposing and introducing a new bill. The bill is then sent to a committee. The committee may kill the bill or return it to the House or the Senate for debate and a vote. If the Senate and House pass the bill, it is sent to the President. The President may sign the bill into law, veto it and return it to Congress, or ignore it. If the President ignores the bill, it becomes law after 10 days if Congress is still in session. If Congress has adjourned, however, the bill dies.

The national government gets most of the money it needs from taxes that Congress passes. The power of appropriation, or approval of government spending, is another congressional responsibility.

Another duty of members of Congress is to help the people in their home districts. First, they act as problem solvers for voters who have difficulties with departments or agencies of the federal government. Second, they make sure that their district or state gets its share of federal money and projects such as new post offices, military bases, and contracts.

Synthesizing the Unit

Recalling Facts

1. Define at-large, standing committee, subcommittee, select committee, joint committee, conference committee, expressed powers, elastic clause, implied powers, impeachment, writ of habeas corpus, bill of attainder, ex post facto law, private bill, public bill, resolution, joint resolution, concurrent resolution.
2. List the four types of congressional committees.

Exploring Themes

3. Checks and Balances What role does the President play in lawmaking?
4. Constitutional Interpretations How has the elastic clause expanded the powers of Congress?

Critical Thinking Skills

5. Making Comparisons How do resolutions differ from bills?
6. Drawing Conclusions Why does it take so long for a bill to become a law?

Synthesizing the Unit Answers

1. Definitions of terms appear on the pages indicated: **at-large,** 437; **standing committee,** 437; **subcommittee,** 437; **select committee,** 437; **joint committee,** 437; **conference committee,** 437; **expressed powers,** 437; **elastic clause,** 437; **implied powers,** 437; **impeachment,** 437; **writ of habeas corpus,** 437; **bill of attainder,** 438; **ex post facto law,** 438; **private bill,** 438; **public bill,** 438; **resolution,** 438; **joint resolution,** 438; **concurrent resolution,** 438

2. standing, select, joint, conference

3. The President may sign a bill into law, may veto the bill, or may do nothing.

4. It has allowed Congress to stretch its powers to meet new situations the writers of the Constitution could never have envisioned.

5. Resolutions do not require presidential action.

6. because the bill has to pass through many stages

The Executive Branch

UNIT

5

Chapter 16:
The Presidency

Chapter 17:
Presidential
Leadership

Chapter 18:
The Federal
Bureaucracy

Introduce

Unit Objectives

After studying this unit, students should be able to:
- Summarize the qualifications, duties, and powers of the President.
- Explain the system of checks and balances among the three branches of government.
- Describe the structure and functions of the federal bureaucracy.

Unit Overview

Unit 5 focuses on the office of President and the executive branch of the national government.

Chapter 16 examines the formal and structural dimensions of the national executive and provides insight into the political aspects of the presidency.

Chapter 17 describes the various departments and agencies that make up the executive branch.

Chapter 18 details the organization of the federal bureaucracy and the role this "fourth branch" of government plays in the making of public policy.

5
UNIT DIGEST

Use the Unit Digest on pages 535–536 to introduce, review, reteach, or condense the information in this unit.

Introducing the Unit

Have students study the unit-opening illustration and name the four Presidents pictured. *(George Washington, Thomas Jefferson, Theodore Roosevelt, Abraham Lincoln)* Then have students discuss what they believe were the greatest contributions of these four men to the office of President.

Unit Project

Have students work cooperatively or individually to write a proposal for a museum exhibit on the history of the United States presidency. The proposal should include brief background information on the origins of the office; biographical sketches of the greatest Presidents; information on major events and historical turning points that changed the nature of the presidency; and illustrations or descriptions of buildings, artifacts, and images that are linked with the office. Students also should include in the proposal selections of artwork and other visual materials and sketches, as well as a design prototype for the exhibit. Have students display their proposals on the bulletin board.

ISSUES
TO
DEBATE

The Issue at a Glance

Pro: Presidents must adhere to powers named in the Constitution.

Con: Presidents can expand powers of the executive office if necessary.

Focus

Have students suppose that some of their classmates are failing a course required for graduation. The principal is requiring these students to attend after-school study sessions until their grades improve. Ask: Should the principal have the power to unilaterally impose this requirement? Who else, if anyone, should be involved? *(Students may suggest parents, district administrators, and/or the school board.)*

Tell students that the reading debates the limits of executive power as it applies to the President of the United States.

Teach

Guided Practice

Point out that, in addition to the powers granted in the Constitution, a President's actions and personality can expand or limit the authority of the office. Remind students that several Presidents have faced serious national crises. Ask: What crisis did Franklin Roosevelt face? *(the Great Depression)* What crisis did Lincoln and Buchanan each face? *(secession)*

How did each interpret his authority as President in this crisis? *(Buchanan felt he had no authority to get involved, so he did nothing; Lincoln felt it his duty to preserve the nation.)*

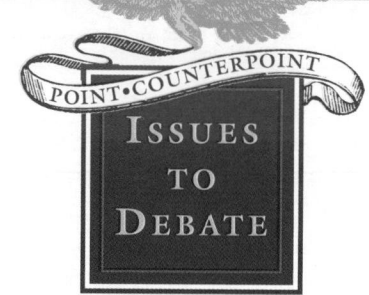

POINT·COUNTERPOINT
ISSUES
TO
DEBATE

Does the Constitution Limit Presidential Powers?

The debate over the role of the President of the United States emerged almost as one with the debate over the Constitution. "This Constitution," proclaimed Patrick Henry in his speech in 1788, "is said to have beautiful features; but when I come to examine these features . . . they appear to be horribly frightful." He went on to explain: "Among other deformities . . . it squints toward monarchy. . . . Your President may easily become king."

Although no monarchy arose in the United States, scholars do agree that today's modern presidency is far stronger than it was years ago. Americans continue to debate exactly how powerful the President should be.

Pro

Scholars often categorize past Presidents according to their views of the constitutional powers of their office. Those categorized as literalist Presidents believe in strict adherence to the Constitution and its concept of separation of powers. One of these Presidents was James Buchanan. Faced with the possible secession of the southern states before President-elect Abraham Lincoln could take office, President Buchanan stated:

Apart from the execution of the laws, so far as this may be practicable, the Executive [the President] has no authority to decide what shall be the relations between the federal government and South Carolina. He has been invested with no such discretion. He possesses no power to change the relations existing between them, much less to acknowledge the independence of that State. This would be to invest a mere executive officer

with the power of recognizing of the confederacy [the Union] among our thirty-three sovereign states. . . .
—JAMES BUCHANAN, MARCH 3, 1860

More than 50 years later, President William Howard Taft took a similar position regarding the constitutional limits on the powers of the President.

The true view of the Executive function is, as I conceive it, that the President can exercise no power which cannot be fairly and reasonably traced to some specific grant of power or justly implied and included with such express grant as proper and necessary to its exercise. Such specific grant must be either in the federal Constitution or in an act of Congress in pursuance thereof.
—WILLIAM HOWARD TAFT, 1916

Dale Vinyard, in his book *The Presidency*, sums up the literalist point of view as a "view of presidential power . . . generally held by presidents who have little taste for policy innovation or change." Few recent Presidents would accept the literalist point of view.

Con

The opposite point of view is the position often referred to as that of the strong President. "The days of a passive Presidency," future President Richard Nixon said in 1968, "belong to a simpler past. . . . The President today cannot stand aside from crisis; he cannot ignore division; he cannot simply paper over disunity. He must lead."

It is this concept of the presidency that Abraham Lincoln brought to the White House when he succeeded James Buchanan in 1861. By that time seven

More About Issues to Debate

Abraham Lincoln took office during one of the nation's greatest crises. Several Southern states had left the union and seized federal land and property within their borders. When federal troops refused to vacate Fort Sumter in the harbor of Charleston, South Carolina, Southern forces fired on the fort and ignited the Civil War. Lincoln then instituted several measures to preserve the nation. He put some areas under martial law and suspended or restricted civil rights. He imposed a blockade on Southern ports, raised an army, and waged a four-year war without formal congressional approval.

southern states had seceded. President Lincoln proclaimed his response to the nation's crisis:

If the United States be not a government proper, but an association of States in the nature of contract merely, can it, as a contract, be peaceably unmade by less than all the parties who made it? One party to a contract may violate it—break it, so to speak—but does it not require all to lawfully rescind it?...

I therefore consider that in view of the Constitution and the laws, the Union is unbroken; and to the extent of my ability I shall take care, as the Constitution itself expressly enjoins upon me, that the laws of the Union be faithfully executed in all the States.

—Abraham Lincoln, March 4, 1861

Throughout the Civil War, President Lincoln used his power to raise an army and to suppress criticism of his sometimes harsh steps.

During the Great Depression, President Franklin D. Roosevelt echoed Lincoln's concept of the need for strong presidential action:

I am prepared under my constitutional duty to recommend the measures that a stricken nation in the midst of a stricken world may require. These measures, or such other measures as the Congress may build . . . I shall seek, within my constitutional authority, to bring to speedy adoption.

But in the event that the Congress shall fail to take one of these two courses, and in the event that the national emergency is still critical, I shall not evade the clear course of duty that will then confront me. I shall ask the Congress for the one remaining instrument to meet the crisis—broad executive power to wage a war against the emergency as great as the power that would be given me if we in fact were invaded by a foreign foe.

—Franklin D. Roosevelt, March 4, 1933

No one questioned that President Roosevelt intended to exercise the full powers of his office.

The Debate Continues

After the experience of the long war in Vietnam, more political scientists began to question the growth of the President's power. As one observer, Arthur M. Schlesinger, Jr., noted, "The Vietnam experience thus provided an unexpected demonstration that a strong Presidency might have its drawbacks."

While some literalist Presidents believed in strict adherence to the constitutional concept of separation of powers, strong Presidents like Lincoln believed the presidency is capable of innovation and change.

Within recent years there have been a number of suggestions for presidential reforms that range from a parliamentary system to a single six-year term for President. What the outcome will be in the future remains uncertain.

Examining the Issue

Recalling Facts
1. State the major point of the literalist point of view.
2. Explain Franklin D. Roosevelt's view of presidential power.

Critical Thinking Skills
3. Recognizing Bias How does the statement that the literalist viewpoint is "generally held by presidents who have little taste for policy innovation or change" reflect the writer's feelings about the presidency?
4. Demonstrating Reasoned Judgment Do you agree that the "days of a passive Presidency belong to a simpler past?" Why or why not?

Investigating Further
Use your textbook and other sources to compile two lists: the powers of Congress and the powers of the President. Compare the lists and identify the powers shared by the two branches.

The Great Depression was a national crisis of another kind. Two days after taking office in March 1933, President Franklin D. Roosevelt suspended all banking activity in order to save the nation's financial system. During his first 100 days as President, he worked closely with Congress to enact and implement 15 major laws that attacked the nation's worst economic crisis in history. Most were proposed by the President and were passed by Congress with little or no debate. Seldom before, or since, has a President enjoyed such overwhelming support and power.

Had Patrick Henry been alive in 1860, whose position would he likely have supported? Why? *(Buchanan's because he believed presidential power should be limited)*

Write the following from Shakespeare's *Twelfth Night* on the chalkboard:

Some are born great, some achieve greatness, and some have greatness thrust upon them.

Ask students how this quote can be applied to what they have learned in the reading about the exercise of presidential power.

Independent Practice

Ask each student to develop a list of characteristics and behaviors that describes active (strong) Presidents and another list that describes passive (weak) Presidents.

Assess

Have students complete **Examining the Issue.**

Answers

1. Separation of powers limits the President to only those powers traceable to the United States Constitution.
2. In a crisis, a President should exercise broad powers.
3. He believes literalist Presidents are weak and prefers a strong President.
4. Students' answers should recognize the changing nation and world.

Close

Discuss with students whether the current President is an active or a passive President.

Chapter Organizer

Objectives	Special Feature Pages	Supplemental Materials
Section 1 Requirements of the Office of President *pp. 444–449* 1. Examine the constitutional and personal qualifications for the office of President. 2. Describe the duties of the Vice President. 3. Discuss the order of presidential succession.	Point/Counterpoint: Does the Constitution Limit Presidential Powers? pp. 440–441 Study and Writing Skills: Writing an Essay p. 449	Guided Reading Activities Reproducible Lesson Plans Section 1 Quiz Testmaker Skill Reinforcement Activities 16 The Living Constitution SAT Practice Tests Writer's Guidebook
Section 2 The Electoral College *pp. 450–455* 1. Evaluate the Electoral College method of choosing the President. 2. Describe the ways that some people want to change the way the President is elected.	Focus on Freedom: John F. Kennedy's Inaugural p. 453	Guided Reading Activities Reproducible Lesson Plans Cooperative Learning Activities 16 Section 2 Quiz Testmaker Government Themes Transparencies 42 Great Speeches, Volumes I, V The Living Constitution SAT Practice Tests Writer's Guidebook
Section 3 Sources and Limitations of Presidential Power *pp. 456–460* 1. Describe the sources of the growing power of the President since the time of the writing of the Constitution. 2. Analyze the checks that Congress can exercise to control presidential power.	Participating in Government: Writing a Letter to the Editor p. 459	Guided Reading Activities Reproducible Lesson Plans Participating in Government 16 Interpreting Political Cartoons 12 Enrichment Activities 16 Section 3 Quiz Testmaker Chapter Transparencies 16 Great Speeches, Volume II The Living Constitution SAT Practice Tests Writer's Guidebook
Section 4 Presidential Leadership *pp. 461–469* 1. Describe the President's foreign-policy duties. 2. Explain the President's role in shaping domestic policy.	Global Connection: Interdependence: Presidential Influence p. 466 Personal Perspectives: The Clintons on Balancing Work and Family Life p. 469	Guided Reading Activities Reproducible Lesson Plans Primary and Secondary Source Readings 16 Interpreting Political Cartoons 11 Reteaching Activities 16 Section 4 Quiz Chapter 16 Tests Testmaker Audio Cassettes (English and Spanish) Limited English Proficiency Activities 16 SAT Practice Tests Writer's Guidebook

If time does not permit teaching this chapter, assign the Chapter 16 summary in the Unit 5 Digest on pages 535–536.

Key To Ability Levels

Teaching strategies have been coded for varying learning styles and abilities.

L1   Level 1 activities are **basic** activities and should be within the ability range of all students.

L2   Level 2 activities are **average** activities and should be within the ability range of the average to above-average student.

L3   Level 3 activities are **challenging** activities designed for the ability range of above-average students.

LEP   These activities should be within the ability range of **Limited English Proficiency** students.

Multicultural Activities

Throughout United States history, Presidents have reacted differently to challenges to the rights of minorities. In 1832 the case of *Worcester* v. *Georgia* considered the right of Georgia officials to ignore a federal treaty made with the Cherokee and subject their land to state control. Chief Justice John Marshall ruled that Georgia had no authority over Cherokee land and could not force them to give it up. Georgia ignored the Court's decision and began forcible removal of the Cherokee. President Andrew Jackson refused to intervene. In 1957 Arkansas officials resisted integration of a Little Rock high school despite the Supreme Court's decision in *Brown* v. *Board of Education of Topeka*. Have students find out how President Eisenhower reacted and compare the responses of the two Presidents.

Most United States Presidents have come from northern European family backgrounds. In 1988 Michael Dukakis became the first American of Greek descent to become a major party's candidate for President. However, to date no ethnic or racial minorities have won the race for the White House. Have students suggest factors that have limited access by minorities to the presidency. *(Students may suggest limited resources, narrow base of support or constituency, public opinion, lack of support from political parties.)* Ask students to agree or disagree with the prediction that future presidential candidates will be chosen from a broader spectrum of Americans. Have students give reasons for their optimism or pessimism.

Chapter Resources

Readings for the Student

Beard, Charles A. and Detlev Vogts. *The Presidents in American History.* Messner, 1989.

Hodgson, Godfrey. *All Things to All Men: The False Promise of the American Presidency.* Simon and Schuster, 1980.

Lindop, Edmund. *Presidents by Accident.* Franklin Watts, 1991.

Wayne, Stephen J. *The Road to the White House.* St. Martin's Press, 1980.

White, Theodore. *The Making of the President, 1976.* Atheneum, 1977.

Readings for the Teacher

Cannon, Lou. *President Reagan: The Role of a Lifetime.* Simon and Schuster, 1991.

Edwards, George. *The Public Presidency.* St. Martin's Press, 1983.

Fisher, Louis. *The Politics of Shared Power, Congress and the Executive.* Congressional Quarterly, 1992.

Goldstein, Joel K. *The Modern American Vice-Presidency.* Princeton University Press, 1982.

Jones, Charles O. *The Presidency in a Separated System.* The Brookings Institution, 1994.

Schlesinger, Arthur M., Jr. *The Imperial Presidency.* Houghton Mifflin, 1973.

Multimedia

Videocassettes and Films

The Presidency. (*The Power Game* series). Philip Burton Productions, Inc. and Maryland Public Television. (v/c, 60 minutes)

The Presidency, The Press, and the People. KPBS. (v/c, 120 minutes)

President of the United States: Too Much Power? Encyclopedia Britannica Educational Corp. (film, 25 minutes)

Television and the Presidency. On the Air. (v/c, 98 minutes)

Software

The Presidency Series, Disk 2—*Presidential Roles and Uses of Power.* Focus Media. (Apple, TRS80, Commodore, IBM disks; second of a 3-part series). A tutorial program on the executive branch of government.

United States Constitution, Disk 4—*Articles II–VII.* Tutorsystems (BLS, Inc.). (Apple disk, fourth of a 5-part package). A tutorial program covering Articles II–VII of the Constitution.

United States Constitution Tutor. Micro Learn (division of Micro-Lab). (Apple, IBM, Commodore 64 disks). A test-preparation program for reviewing United States government.

The Presidency

Introduce

Chapter Overview

Chapter 16 focuses on the formal and structural dimensions of the office of the President and provides insight into the political aspects of the presidency.

Section 1 provides an overview of the qualifications and characteristics of the presidency.

Section 2 discusses the Electoral College system and the alternative suggestions of its critics.

Section 3 explains the sources of the President's power and the causes and effects of this growing power.

Section 4 describes the responsibilities of the President in foreign and domestic affairs.

Chapter 16 Themes

Write the chapter themes on the chalkboard. Ask students why they think each theme is included in a chapter called "The Presidency." For example, for the theme *Constitutional Interpretations,* students might answer that the Constitution was written broadly, allowing for flexibility of interpretation on the limits of the President's powers.

Linking Past and Present
On September 24, 1789, the first Congress fixed the salary of the President of the United States at $25,000 a year, to be paid quarterly, in full consideration for his service. Have students compare this salary to the current compensation listed on page 445.

CHAPTER

16

On Inauguration Day, the President solemnly swears to preserve, protect, and defend the Constitution of the United States.

About the Chapter Opener

Teaching With Illustrations Point out to students that the President's oath of office is stated in Article II, Section I, Clause 8, of the United States Constitution. The oath states: "I do solemnly swear (or affirm) that I will faithfully execute the Office of President of the United States, and will to the best of my Ability, preserve, protect and defend the Constitution of the United States." The oath of office is generally administered by the Chief Justice of the United States. Ask students in what ways they think the President preserves, protects, and defends the Constitution.

Chapter Preview

Overview

The Constitution provides the President broad powers, balanced by the powers of Congress and the courts.

Objectives

After studying this chapter, you should be able to:

1. Summarize the formal and informal qualifications for the presidency.
2. Discuss the Electoral College and the alternative suggestions of its critics.
3. Explain the causes and effects of the growing power of the presidency.
4. Describe the far-reaching responsibilities of a President in foreign and domestic affairs.

Themes in Government

This chapter emphasizes the following government themes:

- **Checks and Balances** The Constitution gives each branch of the government powers to check and balance the other branches. Sections 1, 3, and 4.
- **Federalism** The federal system gives the states influence in electing the President. Section 2.
- **Civil Rights** The right to vote includes the right of each vote to be of equal value. Section 2.
- **Constitutional Interpretations** The broad statements of the Constitution leave room for interpretation. Sections 1 and 4.
- **Separation of Powers** The Constitution distributes power among the branches. Section 3.

Critical Thinking Skills

This chapter emphasizes the following critical thinking skills:

- Drawing Conclusions
- Identifying Alternatives
- Determining Relevance
- Understanding Cause and Effect
- Distinguishing Fact From Opinion

CHAPTER 16: THE PRESIDENCY **443**

Powers of the President
Constitution and the President
Running Time 1:14
Side One, Chapter 2

Introducing the Chapter

Ask students to name some Presidents who are historically considered weak and some who are considered strong and to discuss possible reasons for these weaknesses or strengths. Discuss several of the powers the President has and ask students if they think all Presidents have the same amount of power. Point out that Chapter 16 discusses factors that shape the powers and responsibilities of the President.

Chapter Project

Organize the class into seven groups. Assign each group one of the following presidential roles: head of state, chief executive, chief legislator, economic planner, party leader, chief diplomat, commander in chief. As students study the chapter, have them read and cut out newspaper articles that deal with the role assigned to their group. Prepare a bulletin-board display of each group's articles. Upon completion of the chapter, have group members present an analysis of their articles to the class.

CD Rom
The Presidents: A Picture History of Our Nation
Use this interactive encyclopedia to view clips of presidential events, hear great speeches, research election facts, and more.

Setting the Scene The executive branch would have been headed by three people, not one President, if Edmund Randolph and George Mason had persuaded other members of the Constitutional Convention to accept this idea. Randolph suggested that the dangers of monarchy could be averted by a plural executive. Moreover, people from different sections of the country could be appointed to give all regions representation in the executive branch. Eventually, this proposal was defeated.

Focus

Bell Ringer

Write the following on the chalkboard for students to answer:

Complete the following statement: "All American Presidents have been . . ."

Motivating Activity

Discuss students' Bell Ringer answers. Then ask them to suggest who they think were the three best American Presidents. After students have explained their choices, lead a discussion that focuses on the criteria they used to make their selections. Tell students that in this section they will study the presidency from the point of view of the constitutional provisions for the office.

Vocabulary Precheck

Call on volunteers to tell what they think each key term and concept means. Have students check the accuracy of the definitions in the Glossary. **LEP**

Caption Answer
George Washington

CONNECTIONS

Biography

According to genealogists, President Franklin Delano Roosevelt was distantly related to 11 former Presidents—5 by blood and 6 by marriage.

GLENCOE TECHNOLOGY

Focus on Government
Video 33
Speaking Out:
The Character of the Presidency
Running Time: 1:38
Videodisc 2, Chap. 33
VHS Tape 2, Begins 35:25

Video 48
Making Connections:
From Governor to President
Running Time: 1:50
Videodisc 3, Chap. 48
VHS Tape 3, Begins 24:28

Requirements of the Office of President

When the Framers of the Constitution created the presidency in 1787, no one was certain what a President should do or accomplish. People were not even sure how to address the first President. One suggestion was "His Excellency." Another was "His Mightiness." As it turned out, George Washington wanted to be called simply "Mr. President." Washington himself was unsure of what would be considered proper conduct in the office. However, Washington's careful approach to the presidency established lasting precedents that helped to define the office.

As heads of the executive branch, Presidents have developed enormous power and responsibility over the years. The President acts as commander in chief of the armed forces in peace and war. The President symbolizes what the nation stands for to the world and to the American people. Congress expects the President to propose legislation intended to build the nation's strength and prosperity. Because of the powers of the presidency, the American system of government is often called presidential government.

President Coolidge and His Cabinet
The secretaries, or heads, of executive departments form the presidential cabinet. **History Which President established many of the precedents still followed?**

President's Term and Salary

Originally, the Constitution did not specify how many four-year terms a President may serve. George Washington set a long-held precedent when he served for eight years and refused to run for a third term. In 1940 and 1944, Franklin D. Roosevelt broke this tradition when he ran for a third and a fourth term.

The Twenty-second Amendment To secure the traditional presidential limitation of two terms, Congress and the states adopted the Twenty-second Amendment in 1951. In addition, the amendment allows a Vice President who takes over the presidency and serves two years or less of the former President's term to serve two additional terms. Thus, it is possible for a President to serve up to 10 years.

Salary and Benefits It was decided at the Constitutional Convention that Presidents should receive compensation. The Constitution did not specify the amount of **compensation**, or salary, but left the matter for Congress to determine.

SECTION PREVIEW

Objectives
After studying this section, you should be able to:
■ Examine the constitutional and personal qualifications for the office of President.

■ Describe the duties of the Vice President.
■ Discuss the order of presidential succession.

Key Terms and Concepts
compensation, presidential succession

Themes in Government
■ Constitutional Interpretations
■ Checks and Balances

Critical Thinking Skills
■ Drawing Conclusions
■ Identifying Alternatives

---

444 Unit 5: The Executive Branch

Classroom Resources for Section 1

📁 Guided Reading Activities
📁 Reproducible Lesson Plans
📁 Section 1 Quiz
📄 Testmaker

The Living Constitution
SAT Practice Tests
Writer's Guidebook

Today the President receives $200,000 a year in taxable salary and $50,000 a year for expenses connected with official duties. The Executive Office of the President also provides up to $120,000 for travel and entertainment. Congress cannot increase or decrease the salary during a President's term.

Presidents have the use of *Air Force One*, a specially equipped jet, as well as other planes, helicopters, and limousines. They receive free medical, dental, and health care. They live in the White House, a 132-room mansion with a swimming pool, bowling alley, private movie theater, and tennis courts. The White House domestic staff of more than 80 people does the cooking, shopping, cleaning, and other chores for the President's family.

When Presidents retire, they receive a lifetime pension of $99,500 a year. They also have free office space, free mailing services, and up to $96,000 a year for office help. When Presidents die, their spouses are eligible for a pension of $20,000 a year.

While these benefits are equal to a gross taxable annual income of almost $20 million, money is not the reason that people seek the presidency. The expenses of the office are about equal to the compensation.

Presidential Qualifications

The Constitution sets some of the qualifications for President. Other qualifications reflect personal qualities Americans expect in their Presidents.

State Dinners
To some people the President's salary is modest, considering his status and duties as a world leader. **Political Processes** What are some of the benefits that go with the office of President of the United States?

Constitutional Requirements In Article II, Section 1, the Constitution defines the formal requirements for the office of President. The President must be: (1) a natural-born citizen of the United States; (2) at least 35 years old; and (3) a resident of the United States for at least 14 years before taking office. The same requirements apply to the Vice President.

Government Experience Many other qualities are necessary for a person to have a real chance of becoming President. Experience in government is an unwritten but important qualification. Since 1868, for example, only five major-party candidates for the presidency had no previous government experience, with Dwight D. Eisenhower as the most recent example. In this century candidates who have served as United States senators or as state governors have most often won the presidential nomination. A political career provides the opportunity to form political alliances necessary to obtain a party's nomination as well as the name recognition necessary to win votes.

STUDY GUIDE

Themes in Government
Constitutional Interpretations
The youngest elected President was John Kennedy at 43. **Why do you think the Framers of the**

Constitution in 1787 set the minimum age for President at 35?

Critical Thinking Skills
Drawing Conclusions Why do you think President Washington

felt that eight years was a long enough term of office for anyone to serve as President?

CHAPTER 16: THE PRESIDENCY **445**

Teach

Guided Practice

L1 Cooperative Learning Show students several help-wanted ads in the newspaper. Then have them work in small groups to construct a help-wanted ad for the positions of President and Vice President. After a 15-minute time period, have the groups use their suggestions to construct a combined class ad on the chalkboard.

L2 Synthesizing Information Have students consider each of the following hypothetical situations and determine what should happen in each case, according to the Twenty-fifth Amendment.

1. The President needs open-heart surgery and will be unable to discharge duties for at least one month. *(inform Congress of an inability to perform in office; Vice President becomes acting President; President must inform Congress that disability no longer exists)*
2. The President and Vice President are both killed in plane crashes. *(The speaker of the house becomes President and nominates someone for Vice President; Congress must approve the nomination.)*

Caption Answer
special aircraft, free health care, the White House, pension

STUDY GUIDE

Theme Answer
The Framers believed that someone 35 would be mature enough to handle the responsibilities of the office.

Critical Thinking Answer
Anything longer would have begun to resemble a monarch's reign.

Background

The decision by the Constitutional Convention to have a strong executive branch was surprising considering that only 11 years before, the colonists had rejected a monarchical system. However, the government under the Articles of Confederation had suffered from a lack of leadership, and the delegates knew the nation required a strong leader. Furthermore, the delegates realized with relief that the head of the executive branch would almost certainly be George Washington. Also, they knew that they had empowered the legislative branch to remove a President who acted contrary to the Constitution.

L3 Identifying Alternatives
Organize the class into small groups and have them draw up a list of weaknesses in the office of Vice President. Have the class review the groups' lists and rewrite the items on the lists as criteria for improving the position. Use the criteria to propose changes in the Vice President's responsibilities.

Independent Practice

L1 Language Arts Have students summarize the main ideas in Section 1 by writing a sentence that expresses the main idea of each subhead. Have them share their summaries with the class.
LEP

L2 Mathematics Have students use *The World Almanac* and other reference books to obtain information about salaries of professional athletes, business leaders, college presidents, governors, and the President of the United States. Students might present the information in the form of a bar graph. Students should write a paragraph indicating whether they think the President should earn more or less money than others on the graph and give reasons why.

L3 Expressive Writing Have students write an editorial responding to the following: If so many people are eligible to become President, why has every President so far been a white male?

Importance of Money A serious candidate for the presidency must have access to large amounts of money. Even though the federal government provides funds for some aspects of presidential campaigns, running for the presidency means raising money from supporters and using one's own personal finances. Campaigning in the primaries, paying for television time, hiring campaign staff and consultants, and sending out mailings adds up to tens of millions of dollars. Congress has set an upper limit on such spending. In 1992 the law allowed candidates to spend up to $27.6 million before the national nominating convention and an additional $55.2 million between the convention and the election. If candidates spend more than the limit, they lose millions of dollars of public funds that the Federal Election Commission distributes to eligible candidates.

Political Beliefs Because extremely liberal or conservative candidates have little chance of being elected, the major parties usually choose candidates who hold moderate positions on most issues. Exceptions do, however, sometimes occur. In 1964 Barry Goldwater, a very conservative Republican, became his party's presidential candidate. In 1972 a very liberal Democrat, George McGovern, won the nomination. Both of these candidates lost the general election.

Personal Characteristics What personal qualities does a person need to become President? Most Presidents have come from northern European family backgrounds. A few have been from poor families (Abraham Lincoln and Harry S Truman, for example) and a few from rich ones (both Theodore and Franklin Roosevelt and John F. Kennedy). Most Presidents, however, have come from middle-class backgrounds.

Presidents generally have been white, married, Protestant, financially successful men. No woman, African American, or Hispanic American has been President or Vice President. In 1960 John F. Kennedy became the first Roman Catholic to win the office. Margaret Chase Smith, a Republican senator, sought her party's presidential nomination in 1964. Geraldine Ferraro, Democratic candidate for Vice President in 1984, was the first woman that a major party nominated for high office. Jesse Jackson, an African American, won the support of many delegates in the 1988 Democratic convention.

Personal Growth Holding presidential office tends to underscore a person's inner personal strengths and weaknesses. Succeeding to the presidency on the death of Franklin Roosevelt, President Harry S Truman said at the time that he felt "like the moon, the stars, and all the planets had fallen on me." Later Truman explained the loneliness of the office:

The presidency of the United States carries with it a responsibility so personal as to be without parallel. . . . . No one can make decisions for him. . . . Even those closest to him . . . never know all the reasons why he does certain things and why he comes to certain conclusions. To be President of the United States is to be lonely, very lonely at times of great decisions.

—HARRY S TRUMAN, *MEMOIRS*, 1986

Presidential Succession

Eight Presidents have died in office—bullets struck down four; four died of natural causes. After John Kennedy was killed in 1963, the country realized that the rules for **presidential succession** the Constitution established were inadequate. The nation needed a new set of rules to determine who would fill the President's office in case of a vacancy.

Order of Succession Ratified in 1967, the Twenty-fifth Amendment established the order of succession to the presidency and spelled out what happens when the vice presidency becomes vacant:

Section 1. In case of the removal of the President from office or of his death or resignation, the Vice President shall become President.

Section 2. Whenever there is a vacancy in the office of the Vice President, the President shall nominate a Vice President who shall take office upon confirmation by a majority vote of both Houses of Congress.

—TWENTY-FIFTH AMENDMENT, 1967

The amendment was first applied in 1973 after Spiro Agnew resigned as Richard Nixon's Vice President. President Nixon then nominated Gerald Ford as Vice President, and Congress approved the nomination. A year later, when President Nixon resigned from office, Vice President Ford became President. Ford then nominated Nelson Rockefeller, former governor of New York, to be Vice President, and Congress again approved the nomination. This pro-

446 UNIT 5: THE EXECUTIVE BRANCH

Cooperative Learning Activity

Point out to students that the President of the United States depends on public support to push his programs through Congress. Organize the class into small groups. Ask each group to select and discuss an issue of concern to them. Have each group write a letter to the President expressing their concern. Each member of the group should contribute to the development of the letter. Have students note how long it takes to receive a response and who signed the response. Have them share their responses with the class.

cess marked the only time in United States history that both the President and Vice President were not elected officials.

What would happen if the offices of President and Vice President both became vacant at the same time? The Presidential Succession Act of 1947 established the order of succession. According to this law, the next in line for the presidency is the speaker of the house. The president *pro tempore* of the Senate follows the speaker. Next in line are the cabinet officers, starting with the secretary of state. The other 13 department heads follow in the order in which Congress created the departments.

Presidential Disability What happens if a President becomes seriously disabled while in office? Several Presidents were not able to fulfill their responsibilities. President James Garfield lingered between life and death for 80 days after he was shot in 1881. During that period, no one was officially designated to take on the duties of the President. A stroke disabled President Woodrow Wilson in October 1919. During his recovery, Mrs. Wilson often performed his duties. In 1955 President Dwight D. Eisenhower's heart attack completely disabled him for four days. For 20 weeks after that, he could do only a limited amount of work. During his illness Eisenhower's assistants ran the executive branch while Vice President Nixon stood in for him on ceremonial occasions.

The Twenty-fifth Amendment sets forth a series of rules to be followed when a President becomes disabled. The amendment provides that the Vice President becomes acting President under one of two conditions. First, the Vice President assumes the President's duties if the President informs Congress of an inability to perform in office. Second, the amendment says that the Vice President will take over for the President if the Vice President and a majority of the cabinet or another body authorized by law informs Congress that the President is disabled. This second provision would take effect if a disabled President was unwilling or unable to inform Congress that he or she could not continue to carry out presidential duties.

Under the terms of the Twenty-fifth Amendment, the President can resume the powers and duties of office at any time simply by informing Congress that a disability no longer exists. If, however, the Vice President and a majority of the cabinet or other body authorized by law contends that the President has not sufficiently recovered to perform properly, Congress must settle the dispute within 21 days. Unless Congress decides in the Vice President's favor by a two-thirds vote in each house, the President may resume office.

Assassination of Presidents
Lincoln, Garfield, and McKinley were assassinated while in office. **Political Processes** How does the order of succession preserve the presidency?

The Vice President's Role

The Constitution gives the Vice President only two duties. First, the Vice President presides over the Senate and votes in that body in case of a tie. Most

Caption Answer
by determining who automatically becomes President in case of a vacancy

STUDY GUIDE

Theme Answer
Gerald Ford became President without having been elected as either President or Vice President.

Critical Thinking Answer
The Vice President and an authorized group could inform Congress that the President is disabled.

Assess

Check for Understanding
Have students complete Section 1 Review on page 448.

Meeting Objectives
Each section objective is tested by the Section Review questions that follow it in parentheses.
- Examine the constitutional and personal qualifications for the office of President. (2, 5, 7)
- Describe the duties of the Vice President. (3, 4, 8)
- Discuss the order of presidential succession. (3, 4, 6, 8)

Evaluate
Section 1 Quiz
Testmaker

Critical Thinking Activity

Drawing Conclusions Pose the following question to students: Should a President be allowed to serve more than two terms? Why or why not? (*Answers will vary. Some students might indicate that a President should be allowed to remain in office for as long as people are willing to elect him or her. Consecutive terms allow for a continuity of policy. Other students might indicate that a President could become too powerful and endanger our democracy. Limiting the number of terms brings new people and new ideas into the office.*)

Reteach

Have students write a paragraph summarizing the requirements for and the limits on the office of President, set forth in Article II, the Twenty-second Amendment, and the Twenty-fifth Amendment of the Constitution, as well as the method for presidential succession.

Enrich

Have students research Vice Presidents in history to find out which became President by election and which by the death or disability of the President. Ask students to determine how successful Vice Presidents who succeeded to the presidency were in later being elected President in their own right.

Close

Remind students that the presidential candidates run in primaries but handpick their running mates. Ask students whether Presidents and Vice Presidents should run as a team or if voters should have a greater voice in selecting a Vice President.

Presidential Recovery
Illnesses briefly encumbered President Reagan. **Political Processes** What duties might the Vice President assume if the President becomes seriously ill?

stances. Harry S Truman became President in 1945, near the end of World War II, when Franklin D. Roosevelt died in office. Although Roosevelt had not kept his Vice President informed on matters of foreign policy or military strategy, Truman immediately had to make key decisions in both these vital areas.

Increased Responsibilities The Presidents before Eisenhower (1953-1961) usually ignored their Vice Presidents. Since Eisenhower, however, Presidents have tried to give their Vice Presidents more responsibility. Vice Presidents today often represent the President overseas, attending state funerals and other ceremonial functions, serving in a diplomatic role, and visiting with heads of state. In addition, they may make speeches around the country defending the President's policies and decisions. Today Vice Presidents are members of the National Security Council, the President's staff of foreign and military policy advisers. When President Jimmy Carter took office in 1977, he made his Vice President, Walter Mondale, an active member of several groups that advised the President. To help carry out his expanded responsibilities, Mondale was given an office near Carter in the White House. Similarly, Vice President Al Gore serves as a close adviser to President Bill Clinton and oversees areas such as the organization of government and environmental issues.

Vice Presidents spend very little time in this job. Second, under the Twenty-fifth Amendment, the Vice President helps decide whether the President is disabled and acts as President should that happen.

Standby Work A Vice President's work and power depend upon what responsibilities, if any, the President assigns. Hubert Humphrey, Lyndon Johnson's Vice President, once said, "The only authority he [the Vice President] has is what the President gives him. He who giveth can taketh away."

Nine Vice Presidents have taken over the office of President. Some have done so under difficult circum-

Vice Presidents have generally been experienced politicians. It is only fair to them and the Presidents they serve that their abilities be utilized.

1 SECTION REVIEW

Section Summary
The office of President has both formal or constitutional qualifications and informal requirements.

Checking for Understanding
Recalling Facts
1. Define compensation, presidential succession.
2. List three constitutional qualifications for the office of President.
3. Enumerate the first four officers in the line of succession to the presidency.
4. Explain why having a Vice President who is well-informed about national and international policies of the United States is important.

Exploring Themes
5. Constitutional Interpretations How have the powers of the President increased over time?

6. Checks and Balances How would the government settle a dispute between the President and Vice President over whether the President is disabled?

Critical Thinking Skills
7. Drawing Conclusions Why do presidential candidates who represent moderate views usually win elections?
8. Identifying Alternatives The speaker of the house may be from a different political party than the President. What alternative to the current presidential succession could you suggest to keep the President's party in office if both the President and Vice President were unable to serve? Explain why you would favor or oppose such a succession.

Section 1 Review Answers

1. Definitions of terms appear on pages indicated: **compensation,** 444; **presidential succession,** 446
2. a natural-born citizen of the United States, at least 35 years old, and a resident of the United States for at least 14 years
3. Vice President, speaker of the house, president *pro tempore* of the Senate, secretary of state

4. A Vice President may become President during a national crisis.
5. The President acts as commander in chief of the armed forces, symbolizes what the nation stands for, and proposes legislation intended to build the nation's strength and prosperity.
6. Congress has 21 days to settle the dispute. The Presi-

dent resumes office unless Congress decides in favor of the Vice President by a two-thirds vote in each house.
7. Candidates with moderate views are more acceptable to voters because most voters hold moderate views.
8. Answers will vary. Cabinet members, appointed by the President, could directly succeed, or the minority leader of the House or Senate could be next in line.

Writing an Essay

To write an essay choose a topic, find information about that topic, organize your ideas, and write them in paragraph form. Being able to write a good essay is a valuable skill that you can use throughout life, whether you are writing a term paper, a business report, or a letter to the editor.

Explanation

To write an essay, follow these steps:

- Choose a topic. Then limit the topic so that you will be able to provide details in your essay.
- Note your data and ideas about this topic and arrange them in outline form.
- Organize your outline into paragraphs.
- Write an introduction that sparks the reader's interest and a conclusion that sums up the major points you have made.

Suppose that you have been asked to write a five-paragraph essay about President Lincoln. The first step is to decide that an essay about his whole life will not permit you to tell much about any one thing. In this case, let us say next that you decide to write about Lincoln's election to the presidency. You find a number of facts about it. Once you have jotted them down, make an outline:

I. Republicans had advantage in 1860
  A. Democrats split between a northern wing and a southern wing
  B. A new Constitutional Union party
  C. Lincoln concentrated on party unity
    1. Strongly endorsed the party platform
    2. Avoided saying anything about which Republicans might disagree
II. 1860 election a turning point
  A. Won 40 percent of the popular vote, majority in the Electoral College
  B. Did not carry a single southern state
  C. Southerners saw Lincoln as an abolitionist who did not represent their interests

Once you have an outline, put it into full paragraphs, connecting the various points. For example, the material under II might be written into the following paragraph:

The 1860 election was a turning point in United States history. Although Lincoln won only 40 percent of the popular vote, he won a decisive majority in the Electoral College. He did so without winning a single state in the South where people viewed him as a dangerous abolitionist. By the time Lincoln took office in March 1861, seven slave states had seceded from the Union.

The final step is to write an introduction and conclusion. An introduction should spark readers' interest—make them want to find out more. A good way to introduce this essay would be to set the scene of the 1860 election, recalling the high tensions over slavery that had marked the 1850s.

You also need a conclusion that sums up your main point in this way: "By the time of his inauguration the Republican President would face a divided country."

Practice

Use what you have learned to turn the following outline into an essay on the first months of Franklin D. Roosevelt's presidency. Do not forget to include an introduction and a conclusion.

I. Roosevelt worked to restore confidence in banking system
  A. Called a "bank holiday" to stop people from withdrawing their money
  B. Created Federal Deposit Insurance Corporation
II. Created programs that would give immediate help to unemployed Americans
  A. Civilian Conservation Corps—jobs on environmental projects
  B. Works Progress Administration—jobs on construction projects—roads, bridges, sewers, etc.

Additional Practice

To practice this skill, see **Reinforcing the Skill** on page 471.

Focus

Ask students what they think are the steps in writing a thoughtful essay. Have them compare their list with the Explanation steps.

Teach

Review the Explanation steps with students. Ask: Why is limiting one's topic so important? *(Limiting the topic helps you decide what to research.)* Point out the value of making an outline, and tell students that an outline can be manipulated at the writing stage if a different order seems more appropriate. Point out that some common ways of ordering information in an essay are chronological order, by order of importance, or by parallel concepts. Ask: Why is a detailed outline easier to write from than a partial outline? *(With a complete outline, a writer can simply turn phrases into sentences and add transitions and effective language.)*

Assess

Have students complete the **Practice** exercise.

Close

Ask: Why does the skill recommend writing the introduction and conclusion last? What is the value of this advice?

Practice Answers

Essays should include all the ideas on the outline and contain an introduction and conclusion.

For additional practice, have students complete activity 16 in *Skill Reinforcement Activities* in the Teacher's Classroom Resources.

Focus

Bell Ringer

Write the following on the chalkboard for students to answer in writing:

If a candidate for President received less than half of the popular vote, how could he or she win the election?

Motivating Activity

Discuss students' Bell Ringer answers. Have students suppose that the candidate who wins the most popular votes for student council president does not win the election. What kind of election procedure would make this possible? What would happen if the school voted by classrooms and each room had only one vote? *(The candidate who received the most votes in the room would receive its vote and the candidate with the most rooms would win.)* Point out that a candidate could lose most rooms by very small margins, and win a few by huge margins, and lose the student council election despite having the majority of individual student votes. Tell students that this system is similar to the one used to elect the President of the United States.

Vocabulary Precheck

Call on students to read aloud the definitions for each term and concept from the Glossary. Then have them restate each definition in their own words. **LEP**

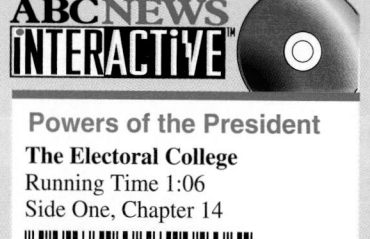

Powers of the President
The Electoral College
Running Time 1:06
Side One, Chapter 14

The Electoral College

The writers of the Constitution argued long and hard about how to choose a President. At first most of the Founders wanted Congress to select the President. They gave up this idea because it violated the principle of separation of powers and might have made it possible for Congress to dominate the presidency.

Popular vote was another possible method for electing the President. Many of the Founders, however, feared that citizens could not make a wise choice because they knew little about potential leaders. In addition, some believed that the most popular candidates might not be the best Presidents.

After many weeks of debate, the Founders finally settled on a compromise that Alexander Hamilton introduced. This compromise set up an indirect method of election called the Electoral College. With a few changes, that system is still in use today.

The Original System

Article II, Section 1, established the Electoral College. It provided that each state would choose electors according to a method the state legislatures set up. At election time, the electors would meet in their own states and cast votes for two presidential candidates. This vote is the **electoral vote.**

Electoral votes from all the states would be counted before a joint session of Congress. The candidate receiving a majority of the electoral votes would become President. The candidate receiving the second highest number of votes, who also had a majority, would become Vice President. In case of a tie, or if no one received a majority, the House of Representa-

tives would choose the President, with each state having one vote.

As expected, the Electoral College unanimously chose George Washington as the nation's first President in 1789 and 1792. After President Washington retired, however, the problems inherent in this system surfaced.

The Impact of Political Parties

By 1800 two national political parties—the Federalists and the Democratic-Republicans—had formed. Each party nominated its own candidate for President and Vice President. Each party also nominated candidates for electors in every state. It was understood that if they were chosen, these electors would vote for their party's candidates.

In the election of 1800, the Democratic-Republicans won a majority of electoral votes. As agreed, each Democratic-Republican elector cast one vote for each of the party's candidates—Thomas Jefferson and Aaron Burr. While most electors wanted Jefferson as President, both Jefferson and Burr wound up with 73 votes. Because of the tie, the election went to the House of Representatives.

The opposing party, the Federalists, controlled the House of Representatives. Popular opinion in the nation supported Jefferson, but many Federalists in the House favored Burr. The House debated day and night for six days. Thirty-six ballots were taken before Jefferson was finally elected President and Burr Vice President. The 1800 election clearly demonstrated the need for a change in the rules before the next election.

SECTION PREVIEW

Objectives
After studying this section, you should be able to:
- Evaluate the Electoral College method of choosing the President.

- Describe the ways that some people want to change the way the President is elected.

Key Terms and Concepts
electoral vote, elector

Themes in Government
- Federalism
- Civil Rights

Critical Thinking Skills
- Identifying Alternatives
- Determining Relevance

Classroom Resources for Section 2

- Guided Reading Activities
- Reproducible Lesson Plans
- Cooperative Learning Activities 16
- Section 2 Quiz
- Testmaker
- Government Themes Transparencies 42

- Great Speeches, Volumes I, V
- The Living Constitution
- SAT Practice Tests
- Writer's Guidebook

The Twelfth Amendment was added to the Constitution in 1804 to solve the problem. It requires that the electors cast separate ballots for President and Vice President. The amendment also provides that if no candidate receives a majority of the electoral votes, the House chooses from the three candidates who have the largest number of electoral votes. If no candidate for Vice President gets a majority of electoral votes, the Senate chooses from the top two candidates for Vice President.

The System Today

The Electoral College is still the method of choosing the President and Vice President. Over the years, however, the system has been modified.

Voters cast their ballots for President every four years (1992, 1996, 2000, etc.) on the Tuesday after the first Monday in November. While the candidates' names are printed on the ballot, the voters are not actually voting directly for President and Vice President. Rather, they are voting for all of their party's **electors** in their state. These electors will later cast the official vote for President and Vice President. Thus, a vote for the Democratic candidate is actually a vote for the Democratic electors, and a vote for the Republican candidate is a vote for the Republican electors.

The Electoral College includes 538 electors—a number determined by the total of House and Senate members plus 3 for the District of Columbia. Each state has as many electors as it has senators and representatives in Congress. California with 52 representatives and 2 senators has 54 electoral votes. Wyoming with 1 representative and 2 senators has 3 electoral votes. To be elected President or Vice President, a candidate must win at least 270 of the 538 votes.

The Electoral College is a winner-take-all system. The party whose candidate receives the largest popular vote in a state wins all the electoral votes of that state even if the margin of victory is only one popular vote.

The winning presidential candidate is usually announced on the same day as the popular election because popular-vote counts indicate who won each state. The formal election, however, begins on the Monday following the second Wednesday in December when the electors meet in each state capital and cast their ballots. The electoral ballots from each state are sealed and mailed to the president of the Senate for a formal count. On January 6 both houses of Congress meet in the House of Representatives to

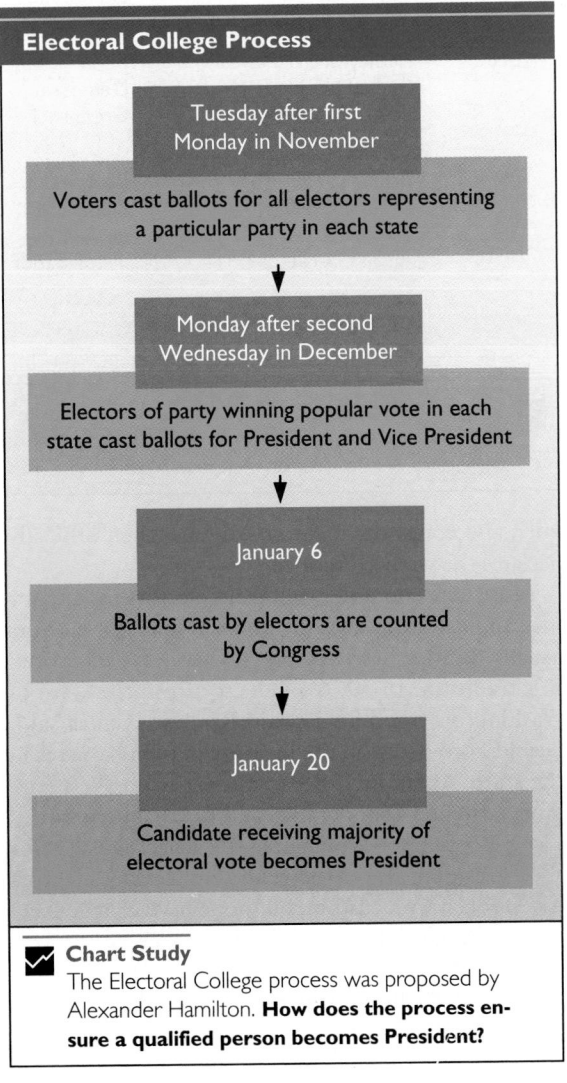

Electoral College Process

Tuesday after first Monday in November

Voters cast ballots for all electors representing a particular party in each state

↓

Monday after second Wednesday in December

Electors of party winning popular vote in each state cast ballots for President and Vice President

↓

January 6

Ballots cast by electors are counted by Congress

↓

January 20

Candidate receiving majority of electoral vote becomes President

✓ **Chart Study**
The Electoral College process was proposed by Alexander Hamilton. **How does the process ensure a qualified person becomes President?**

Chapter 16, Section 2
Lesson Plan, pages 450–455

Teach

Guided Practice

📹 **Media** Have students view the inaugural addresses by various Presidents from "Great Speeches" (Volume V: "Franklin D. Roosevelt, First Inaugural"; Volume I: "John F. Kennedy, Inaugural Address") of the *Social Studies Videos*. Discuss how the speeches reflected each President's ideas about leadership and the needs of the country. **LEP**

L2 Law Have students read the material on the Electoral College in the Constitution (Article II and Twelfth Amendment). Then ask them to compare the Electoral College systems established by each. *(The Twelfth Amendment provides for electors in each state to vote separately for the President and Vice President. The candidates who receive the majority of electoral votes are elected. If no presidential candidate receives a majority, the House chooses from the three leading candidates. If no vice-presidential candidate receives a majority of the electoral votes, the Senate chooses from the two leading candidates.)*

Chart Study Answer
President is elected by electors who are elected by popular vote.

STUDY GUIDE

Themes in Government
Federalism By the election of 1800, the United States had grown to 16 states. **Both then and now, how was each state represented in the Electoral College?**

Critical Thinking Skills
Identifying Alternatives
What factor explains why some states have many electoral votes while other states have fewer electoral votes in the Electoral College?

STUDY GUIDE

Theme Answer
Each state's electors equal its number of senators and representatives in Congress.

Critical Thinking Answer
Each state's number of representatives is determined by population, meaning that the more populous states have more electoral votes.

Background

Despite the problems of the Electoral College system, defenders of the system point out that it almost always selects the candidate with the popular vote plurality. Only twice—in 1801 and 1825—has the House had to elect the President. The Electoral College system maintains the stability of the two-party system. Defenders of the system point out that reforming or abolishing the Electoral College system would be time-consuming because a constitutional amendment would be required.

Interpreting Visuals Display transparency 42 from *Government Themes Transparencies* in the Teacher's Classroom Resources and use the accompanying teaching strategy and student activity to teach about the Electoral College.

Group Discussion Have students complete activity 16 on the fairness of the Electoral College system in *Cooperative Learning Activities* in the Teacher's Classroom Resources.

Independent Practice

L1 Informative Writing Have students write a newspaper article describing the ideas for reform of the Electoral College system and the criticism of each.

Chart Study Answer
chosen by the House

STUDY GUIDE

Theme Answer
They could have provided a candidate with more popular votes, which could have affected electoral votes and resulted in a different outcome.

Critical Thinking Answer
Democracy generally refers to majority rule. However, in these elections candidates who received less than a majority of the popular vote were elected.

Presidents Elected While Losing the Popular Vote

Date	Candidates	Party	Total Electoral Vote	Total Popular Vote
1824	John Quincy Adams*	Democratic-Republican	84	108,740
	Andrew Jackson	Democratic-Republican	99	153,544
	William H. Crawford	Democratic-Republican	41	46,618
	Henry Clay	Democratic-Republican	37	47,136
1876	Rutherford B. Hayes*	Republican	185	4,033,768
	Samuel J. Tilden	Democrat	184	4,285,992
	Peter Cooper	Greenback	0	81,737
1888	Benjamin Harrison*	Republican	233	5,440,216
	Grover Cleveland	Democrat	168	5,538,233
	Clinton B. Fisk	Prohibition	0	249,506
	Alson J. Streeter	Union Labor	0	146,935

* Winners of Presidential Elections

Sources: *1991 Information Please Almanac, Hammond United States History Atlas*

✔ **Chart Study**
Three Presidents won election despite popular vote losses. Eleven others—Polk, Taylor, Buchanan, Lincoln, Garfield, Cleveland, Wilson, Truman, Kennedy, Nixon, and Clinton—won with a plurality of popular votes. **How did Adams win?**

---

open and count the ballots. Congress then officially declares the winner President.

Most states do not legally bind electors to vote for the candidate who wins the popular vote, but electors usually do so. A few electors, however, have ignored this tradition. In 1976 an elector from the state of Washington voted for Ronald Reagan, even though Gerald Ford had won the majority of popular votes in the state. Again in 1988 an elector from West Virginia switched Democratic candidates and voted for Lloyd Bentsen for President and Michael Dukakis for Vice President. Over the years, eight other electors have broken with custom, but none have changed any final election results.

Electoral College Issues Because the Electoral College is a winner-take-all system, critics argue that votes cast for a losing candidate in a state count for nothing. For example, in the 1992 election, more than 2 million Texans voted for Bill Clinton, but Clinton did not receive any of Texas's electoral votes.

Three times in American history—in the elections of John Quincy Adams in 1824, Rutherford B. Hayes in 1876, and Benjamin Harrison in 1888—the candidate who lost the popular vote won the election. In the 1888 election, Democrat Grover Cleveland won 95,000 more popular votes than Republican Benjamin Harrison. Because Harrison won in more states with large electoral votes, however, he received 233 electoral votes to 168 for Cleveland.

The 1960 election almost became another example. Democrat John Kennedy defeated Republican Richard Nixon in a very close popular vote. Kennedy won Illinois and Texas by a narrow margin of about 1 percent of the popular vote. If Nixon had won these states, he would have won the election by win-

STUDY GUIDE

Themes in Government
Civil Rights Presidential elections after the Civil War showed close popular votes. **If millions of African Americans had been** allowed to vote freely, what effect could they have had on the outcome of presidential elections?

Critical Thinking Skills
Determining Relevance **Explain why the election results of 1824, 1876, and 1888 are good arguments that the Electoral College system is undemocratic.**

Cooperative Learning Activity

Organize the class into two groups. Ask one group to determine the advantages and the other group the disadvantages of the current Electoral College system. After each member of the group has contributed to a group list, have each group discuss how to either reform or abolish the present system. Then have each group share their conclusions with the other group. Take a class vote on whether the Electoral College system should be retained, abolished, or reformed.

ning the electoral vote while narrowly losing the popular vote.

Critics also argue that a third-party candidate can win enough electoral votes to prevent either major party candidate from receiving a majority of the votes. The third-party candidate could then bargain to release electoral votes to one of the two major party candidates, thus influencing the outcome of the election. The election could also be forced into the House of Representatives.

Some people say Governor George Wallace of Alabama wanted to use this tactic in the 1968 election.

JOHN F. KENNEDY'S INAUGURAL

On January 20, 1961, the youngest man ever elected President of the United States took the oath of office. Robert Frost, a friend of the Kennedy family, read a poem into the icy sunlight. Then as Kennedy spoke to the nation, he also addressed the world. Speaking to a world divided into two camps—communist and free— Kennedy asked for a new spirit of cooperation.

We observe today not a victory of party but a celebration of freedom—symbolizing an end as well as a beginning—signifying renewal as well as change. For I have sworn before Almighty God the same solemn oath our forbears prescribed nearly a century and three-quarters ago.

The world is different now. For man holds in his mortal hands the power to abolish all forms of human poverty and all forms of human life. And yet the same revolutionary beliefs for which our forebears fought are still at issue around the globe—the belief that the rights of man come not from the generosity of the state but from the hand of God.

We dare not forget today that we are the heirs of that first revolution. Let the word go forth from this time and place, to friend and foe alike, that the torch has been passed to a new generation of Americans—born in this century, tempered by war, disciplined by a hard and bitter peace, proud of our ancient heritage—and unwilling to witness or permit the slow undoing of those human rights to which this nation has always been committed. . . .

Let every nation know, whether it wishes us well or ill, that we shall pay any price, bear any burden, meet any hardship, support any friend, oppose any foe to assure the survival and the success of liberty. . . .

So let us begin anew—remembering on both sides that civility is not a sign of weakness, and sincerity is always subject to proof. Let us never negotiate out of fear. But let us never fear to negotiate. . . .

And if a beachhead of cooperation may push back the jungle of suspicion, let both sides join in creating a new endeavor—not a new balance of power but a world of law, where the strong are just and the weak secure and the peace preserved. . . .

In the long history of the world, only a few generations have been granted the role of defending freedom in its hour of maximum danger. I do not shrink from this responsibility—I welcome it. I do not believe that any of us would exchange places with any other people or any other generation. The energy, the faith, the devotion which we bring to this endeavor will light our country and all who serve it—and the glow from that fire can truly light the world.

And so, my fellow Americans: Ask not what your country can do for you—ask what you can do for your country.

My fellow citizens of the world: Ask not what America can do for you but what together we can do for the freedom of man.

—John F. Kennedy, January 20, 1961

Examining the Document

Reviewing Facts

1. Discuss what Kennedy says has changed about the world and what remains the same.
2. Identify what Kennedy believes is worth any price or hardship to defend.

Critical Thinking Skills

3. Making Inferences What approach toward relations with communist nations did Kennedy signal in this address?

CHAPTER 16: THE PRESIDENCY   453

Robert Frost's reading of his poem "The Gift Outright" at Kennedy's inauguration reflected Kennedy's interest in the arts. Kennedy stressed his hope of leading the country into a new era dedicated to the ideals of the country's founders. Ask students to point out the parallels Kennedy draws in his speech to "that first revolution."

Answers

1. The world is now capable of abolishing poverty or abolishing life itself. The belief in human rights has not changed.

2. the survival and the success of liberty

3. He is willing to negotiate and discontinue the suspicions of the past, but remembering that "sincerity is subject to proof."

L2 Geography Provide each student with an outline map of the United States. Have students use reference materials to determine the distribution of electoral votes in the latest presidential election. Instruct students to indicate the distribution on the maps and to use color to easily see the outcome of the election. Finally, have students determine the smallest number of states needed to win a presidential election and which states they are.

CONNECTIONS

Political Processes
Electors are customarily nominated by their political parties at their parties' respective state conventions. An elector cannot be a member of Congress or hold a federal office.

Special Needs Strategy

Study Strategy Students with language expression difficulties may need help developing appropriate questions. Organize the class into two teams, assigning one team to develop questions for the subheading "The Original System," and the other team for the subheading, "The System Today." Alternate between the two teams as you write the questions on the board. Encourage the use of the usual questioning words (*who, what, where, why, when, how*), and focus special attention on other more complex question markers such as *In what way?* and *How many?*

Caption Answer
It sets out the new President's ideas.

Assess

Check for Understanding

Have students complete Section 2 Review on page 455.

Meeting Objectives

Each section objective is tested by the Section Review questions that follow it in parentheses.
• Evaluate the Electoral College method of choosing the President. (2, 3, 4, 5, 6, 7)
• Describe the ways that some people want to change the way the President is elected. (6, 7, 8)

Linking Past and Present

Not only has the Electoral College chosen Presidents who did not carry the popular vote, but the system also tends to exaggerate popular results. In 1936, for example, Roosevelt received 98.5 percent of the electoral vote to 1.5 percent for Landon. But the popular totals were 60.8 percent to 36.5 percent respectively. In 1960 Kennedy gained 56.3 percent of the electoral vote to Nixon's 40.7 percent. But he won at the polls by 49.7 percent to 49.5 percent, a much narrower margin.

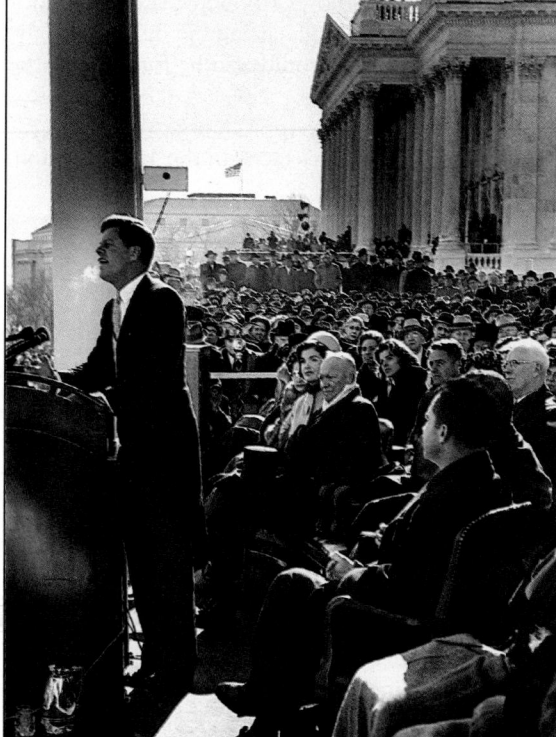

Kennedy's Inaugural Address
A President speaks to the nation and the world during his Inaugural Address. **History Why would people of other nations want to hear this speech?**

Wallace ran as the American Independent party's candidate and won 5 states and 46 electoral votes. The election between Richard Nixon and Hubert Humphrey was very close, with Nixon winning by only about 500,000 popular votes. If Humphrey had beaten Nixon in a few more states, Nixon would not have won a majority of the electoral votes. The election would have then gone to the House of Representatives.

Election by the House When the House of Representatives must decide a presidential election, each of the 50 states casts one vote. The candidate who receives the majority, or 26, of the votes is elected President.

Election by the House involves three problems: (1) States with small populations such as Alaska or Nevada have as much weight as states with large populations such as New York or California. (2) Under the rules, if a majority of representatives from a state cannot agree on a candidate, the state loses its vote. (3) If some members of the House favor a strong third-party candidate, it could make it very hard for any candidate to get the 26 votes needed to win.

Ideas for Reform Many changes to the system have been proposed. One idea is to choose electors from congressional districts. Each state would have two electoral votes, plus one vote for each congressional district in the state. The candidate winning the most votes in a congressional district would win the electoral vote in that district. The candidate winning the most districts in a state would, in addition, receive the two statewide electoral votes. The district plan would eliminate the problems of the winner-take-all system. Both Presidents Johnson and Nixon favored this plan. This plan, however, would still make it possible for a candidate who lost the popular vote to win the Electoral College vote.

Another plan proposes that the presidential candidates would win the same share of a state's electoral vote as they received of the state's popular vote. If a candidate captured 60 percent of the popular vote, for example, the candidate would earn 60 percent of the state's electoral vote.

This plan too would cure the winner-take-all problem. Moreover, it would remove the possibility of electors voting for someone that they are not pledged to support. Critics of the plan point out that it could possibly enlarge the role of third parties and complicate the election process. Because third-party candidates could get at least some share of the electoral vote in each election, they might also have a greater chance to force a presidential election into the House of Representatives.

Another plan is to do away with the Electoral College entirely. Instead, the people would directly elect the President and Vice President. While this alternative may seem obvious, some have criticized it on the grounds that it would greatly change the structure of the federal system. It would undermine federalism because the states would lose their role in the choice of a President. It would also mean that candidates would concentrate their efforts in densely populated areas. Large cities would control the election.

How the President Takes Office

The new President, called the President-elect until the inauguration, takes office at noon on January 20 in the year following the presidential election. The Constitution requires the President to take this simple oath:

Critical Thinking Activity

Identifying Alternatives Pose the following questions to students: Should the United States adopt a system of direct popular vote for President? What would be the advantages and the disadvantages of such a system? *(Students' answers will vary.*

Possible advantage may be that every person's vote would count toward election. Possible disadvantage may be that such a system would eliminate the role of states and make elections more costly.)

I do solemnly swear (or affirm), that I will faithfully execute the office of President of the United States, and will, to the best of my ability, preserve, protect, and defend the Constitution of the United States.

—ARTICLE II, SECTION 8

By custom, an inaugural ceremony is held outside the Capitol in Washington, D.C.—weather permitting. The new President rides with the outgoing President from the White House to the Capitol for the inauguration ceremonies. With the outgoing President, family members, government officials, and citizens looking on, the oath of office is administered by the Chief Justice. The new President then gives an Inaugural Address that sets out ideas about government and the needs of the country. Certain phrases or sentences within the speech may set a tone or capture the spirit of what the new President hopes to accomplish. Several Presidents have made notable inaugural speeches that have become part of the nation's heritage. Abraham Lincoln spoke to a divided nation in 1861:

In your hands, my dissatisfied fellow countrymen, and not in mine is the momentous issue of civil war. . . . You have no oath registered in heaven to destroy the government, while I shall have the most solemn one to "preserve, protect, and defend" it.

—ABRAHAM LINCOLN,
FIRST INAUGURAL ADDRESS, 1861

At his inauguration in the depths of the Great Depression, Franklin D. Roosevelt lifted the spirits of his fellow Americans with the words, "The only thing we have to fear is fear itself." In 1961 John F. Kennedy called on all Americans to "ask not what your country can do for you—ask what you can do for your country." In 1989 George Bush told Americans:

I come before you and assume the Presidency at a moment rich with promise. We live in a peaceful, prosperous time but we can make it better. For a new breeze is blowing and a world refreshed by freedom seems reborn; for in man's heart, if not in fact, the day of the dictator is over. The totalitarian era is passing, its old ideas blown away like leaves from an ancient, lifeless tree.

—GEORGE BUSH, JANUARY 20, 1989

Inaugural Addresses have varied enormously in length. George Washington's second inaugural speech was the shortest —135 words. William Henry Harrison spoke the longest —8,500 words. Harrison, who had attempted to prove his stamina in the cold weather, caught pneumonia and died within a month of the inauguration.

Members of Congress, foreign diplomats, other officials, and thousands of citizens attend the inaugural ceremony. Millions watch on television. After the speech, a parade goes from the Capitol to the White House. That evening official parties celebrate the inauguration and thank people who supported the President's election campaign.

2 SECTION REVIEW

Section Summary
Under the Electoral College, the states choose electors who represent the winning party in each state and cast the final vote for the President and Vice President.

Checking for Understanding
Recalling Facts
1. Define electoral vote, elector.
2. Explain why California has 54 electoral votes.
3. Identify what the term *winner-take-all* means in presidential elections.
4. Describe the events that occur when a new President takes office.

Exploring Themes
5. Federalism How does the Electoral College help maintain the principle of federalism?
6. Civil Rights On what grounds could a person from a state with a large population argue that his or her vote is not equal to that of a person from a state with a smaller population?

Critical Thinking Skills
7. Identifying Alternatives What proposal, if any, do you support for changing the Electoral College? Explain your answer.
8. Determining Relevance In judging the Electoral College, how important is it to know that on several occasions an elector broke with custom and voted independently?

CHAPTER 16: THE PRESIDENCY 455

Evaluate

📁 Section 2 Quiz

💽 Testmaker

Reteach

Ask students to work in pairs to prepare a chart that shows the ways elections have changed since the Electoral College was designed. Chart headings should be *The Original System, The Twelfth Amendment Changes,* and *The System Today.*

Enrich

Have students investigate the effects of the 1990 census on the number of each state's electoral votes and indicate *changes* on an outline map of the United States.

Close

Discuss with students how the number of electoral votes in each state might affect the campaign plans of presidential candidates.

CONNECTIONS

History
George Washington was inaugurated as the first President of the United States on April 30, 1789. John Adams was sworn in as Vice President nine days earlier. There was no set procedure for either event. On June 1, 1789, the first law enacted by Congress established the procedure for administering oaths of office.

Section 2 Review Answers

1. Definitions of terms appear on pages indicated: **electoral vote,** 450; **elector,** 451
2. California has 52 representatives and 2 senators for a total of 54 electoral votes.
3. The party whose candidate has the most popular votes in a state wins all of that state's electoral votes.

4. The President takes an oath and gives an Inaugural Address. A parade goes from Capitol to White House. Evening parties celebrate the inauguration.
5. The Electoral College system gives the states a direct role in selecting the President.
6. They could argue that their vote is worth less because the smallest states have three electoral votes. Based on

population, this is proportionally more than that of larger states.
7. Answers will vary, but have students justify reasons for their choices.
8. An elector voting independently has never affected the outcome of an election. However, the potential of an independent elector affecting an election still remains.

Focus

Bell Ringer

Write the following quotation and question on the chalkboard for students to answer in writing:

"There are so many things I would like to do instantly. The difficult thing is to recognize the limitations of a President's power."

Jimmy Carter

What does this quote indicate President Carter felt about presidential power?

Motivating Activity

Discuss students' Bell Ringer answers. Then conduct a poll to determine whether they believe the President has too much power, not enough power, or the right amount of power. Direct a follow-up discussion about the poll results, asking several students to explain their opinions. Tell students that in this section they will learn about the sources of presidential power and about limitations on this power.

Vocabulary Precheck

Call on students to read aloud the definitions of the terms and concepts from the Glossary. Then have volunteers use each term in a sentence. **LEP**

Caption Answer
commander in chief

GLENCOE TECHNOLOGY

Focus on Government
Video 29
**Lecture Launcher:
The Presidency**
Running Time: 2:12
Videodisc 2, Chap. 29
VHS Tape 2, Begins 25:02

---

3 Sources and Limitations of Presidential Power

Presidential responsibilities and powers have grown enormously since George Washington assumed office in 1789. Washington had so little to do on some days that he advertised in the newspaper the times when he would entertain visitors.

In contrast, modern Presidents' schedules are timed minute by minute. They preside over a White House staff of almost 400, a military force of several million, and a vast **federal bureaucracy** made up of all government employees.

Constitutional Powers

The Founders created the office of President. They made the President the head of the executive branch of the new national government. Having revolted against the hated king of England, the Founders certainly did not want to create their own king. At the same time, they did want a national government with a strong executive. They had two major reasons for this.

Need for a Strong Executive First, the Founders knew that one of the main weaknesses of the Articles of Confederation was its lack of an independent executive. Without an executive the government had no one to carry out the acts of Congress. Moreover, this lack made it difficult for the government to respond quickly to problems and to enforce laws.

Second, many of the Founders distrusted direct participation by the people in decision making. The Founders feared that mass democratic movements might try to redistribute personal wealth and threaten

private property. Consequently, they wanted a strong executive branch that would protect liberty, private property, and businesses and hold the legislative branch, which the people could influence, in check.

Presidential Powers in Article II Article II of the Constitution granted the President broad but vaguely described powers. As a result, the exact meaning of the President's power in specific situations was left open to interpretation.

Article II begins simply by stating: "The Executive Power shall be vested in a President of the United States of America." Some scholars call this sentence the "wild card" in the deck of presidential powers. What they mean is that this particular sentence may be "played," or interpreted, in different ways, like the wild card in a card game. The sentence gives the Pres-

Clinton and Cabinet
President Washington appointed a secretary of war.
Political Processes What is the President's military title?

SECTION PREVIEW

Objectives
After studying this section, you should be able to:
- Describe the sources of the growing power of the President since the time of the writing of the Constitution.

- Analyze the checks that Congress can exercise to control presidential power.

Key Terms and Concepts
federal bureaucracy, mass media

Themes in Government
- Checks and Balances
- Separation of Powers

Critical Thinking Skills
- Understanding Cause and Effect
- Distinguishing Fact From Opinion

456   UNIT 5: THE EXECUTIVE BRANCH

Classroom Resources for Section 3

📁 Guided Reading Activities
📁 Reproducible Lesson Plans
📁 Participating in Government 16
📁 Interpreting Political Cartoons 12
📁 Enrichment Activities 16
📁 Section 3 Quiz

🖥 Testmaker
🕯 Chapter Transparencies 16
📀 Great Speeches, Volume II
   The Living Constitution
   SAT Practice Tests
   Writer's Guidebook

ident a broad and general executive power, that can be used in many different situations. For example, under the executive power, the President can fire officials in the executive branch, make agreements with foreign nations, or take emergency actions to save the nation, even though none of these powers is specifically mentioned in the Constitution.

Sections 2 and 3 of Article II do define some presidential powers. (1) The President is commander in chief of the armed forces (now the army, navy, and air force) and the state militia (National Guard) when they are called into federal service. (2) The President appoints—with Senate consent—heads of executive departments (such as the Department of Labor). (3) The chief executive may pardon people convicted of federal crimes, except in cases of impeachment, or reduce a person's jail sentence or fine. (4) The President makes treaties with the advice and consent of the Senate. (5) The President appoints ambassadors, federal court judges, justices of the Supreme Court, and other top officials, with Senate consent. (6) The chief executive delivers an annual State of the Union message to Congress and sends other special messages to Congress from time to time. (7) The President calls Congress into special session when necessary. (8) The President meets with heads of state, ambassadors, and other public officials of foreign countries. (9) The President commissions all military officers of the United States. (10) The President ensures that the laws Congress passes are "faithfully executed."

Informal Sources of Power

The Constitution's list of presidential powers is brief and simple. Yet, since Washington's time, the President's powers have greatly expanded. Today the President's powers come from several sources in addition to the Constitution.

Ideas and Actions of Past Presidents Over the years several Presidents have added to the power of the presidency simply by the way they handled the

job. Among the Presidents most responsible for enlarging the powers of the presidency were George Washington, Thomas Jefferson, Andrew Jackson, Abraham Lincoln, Theodore Roosevelt, Woodrow Wilson, Franklin D. Roosevelt, Harry S Truman, and Lyndon B. Johnson. These men set examples that later Presidents followed.

In 1803 Thomas Jefferson made the decision to purchase the Louisiana Territory from France. Nothing in the Constitution, however, stated that a President had the power to acquire territory. Jefferson decided that the presidency had inherent powers, powers attached to the office itself. These were powers the Constitution did not specifically define but that Article II implied. The Senate agreed with Jefferson and ratified the Louisiana Purchase treaty.

Abraham Lincoln took action during the Civil War that caused people to call him a dictator. He suspended the writ of habeas corpus and jailed opponents of the Union without a trial or legal authority to do so. He raised an army before getting Congress's approval. He took illegal action against the South by blockading its ports. Lincoln claimed the Constitution gave him the authority to do what was necessary to preserve the Union. In the end, the nation agreed.

Theodore Roosevelt expressed the broad view of presidential power, explaining that it was both the President's right and duty to "do anything that the needs of the Nation demanded, unless such action was forbidden by the Constitution or by the laws." In a letter to a contemporary historian Roosevelt explained:

> *I have used every ounce of power there was in the office and I have not cared a rap for the criticisms of those who spoke of my "usurpation of power; . . . I believe that the efficiency of this Government depends upon its possessing a strong central executive. . . .*
>
> —THEODORE ROOSEVELT, 1908

Franklin D. Roosevelt used the power of the presidency to expand the role of the federal government in

Teach

Guided Practice

L1 Biography Have students tell which President established each of the following examples in the use of presidential power:

1. expanding the nation's territory *(Jefferson)*
2. taking strong action to preserve national unity *(Lincoln)*
3. taking any needed action not specifically prohibited by the Constitution or laws *(T. Roosevelt)*
4. expanding the role of the federal government in the nation's economy *(F.D. Roosevelt)*
5. obtaining from Congress special emergency war-making powers *(Johnson)* **LEP**

Media Have students view Barbara Jordan's "Statement on Impeachment" from "Great Speeches," Volume II, *Social Studies Videos*. Discuss with students Jordan's views on presidential power.

Interpreting Visuals Display transparency 16 from the *Chapter Transparencies* in the Teacher's Classroom Resources and use the accompanying teaching strategy and student activity to teach about the boundaries of presidential power.

STUDY GUIDE

Themes in Government	How did the Constitution	Critical Thinking Skills
Checks and Balances During the 1794 Whiskey Rebellion in western Pennsylvania, President Washington sent troops to collect a tax which Congress had imposed on liquor.	**strengthen executive power?**	**Understanding Cause and Effect** **Explain how Jefferson's view of presidential power led to the expansion of United States territory in the early 1800s.**

CHAPTER 16: THE PRESIDENCY   **457**

STUDY GUIDE

Theme Answer
The Constitution provided for an executive power that had the authority to enforce the acts of Congress.

Critical Thinking Answer
Jefferson's view of inherent and implied powers in the presidency led him to purchase the Louisiana Territory.

Background

One of the sources of presidential power is the fact that the President is the leader of his or her political party. The Constitution did not foresee the development of political parties or the power that political parties would add to the presidency. As head of one of the two major political parties, the President can exert pressure for legislation and can give or withhold support for a senator's or a representative's reelection.

Independent Practice

L1 Informative Writing Have students illustrate their understanding of the words *mass media* and *bureaucracy* by writing a paragraph about each.

L2 Media Have students survey newspapers and television broadcasts for examples of how the President uses the media. Ask them to write a report describing the example and evaluating the President's reason for such use—to inform the public, to propose solutions, or to gain public support.

L3 Informative Writing Have students write an essay explaining how the system of checks and balances has placed limitations on presidential power.

Caption Answer
talked about the nation's problems and his proposed solutions for them

=== STUDY GUIDE ===

Theme Answer
Congress passed a resolution that authorized the President to use armed force in Vietnam, which gradually expanded into an undeclared war.

Critical Thinking Answer
The reporter would emphasize factual information; the commentator would provide personal opinions.

CONNECTIONS

Technology
To reach the same amount of people the President does in a prime-time television speech, the President would have to appear before capacity crowds 50 times in each of the 27 pro football stadiums.

---

the nation's economy. At a time of severe economic depression, Roosevelt persuaded Congress to create many new social and economic programs and set up new federal agencies to run them. When Roosevelt became President, about 600,000 people worked in the federal government. By the time he died in 1945, more than 3 million workers were serving in the federal government.

After Roosevelt's administration Americans came to expect the President to take a firm hand in directing the nation's economic as well as political life. Today people often measure a President's use of executive power against Roosevelt's. Most modern Presidents have tried to act as strong leaders and have taken a broad view of presidential power.

Congress As a Source of Presidential Power
Members of Congress sometimes complain about Presidents having too much power. Yet Congress has often granted a President special powers, especially during emergencies. In 1964, for example, President

Informal Radio Broadcasts
President Roosevelt created an informal rapport with the nation through his "fireside chats." **History
What did Roosevelt talk about in these broadcasts?**

Lyndon Johnson reported that two American destroyers had been attacked in the Gulf of Tonkin. To enable the President to cope with the situation in Vietnam, Congress passed the Gulf of Tonkin Resolution. This resolution gave the President authority to "take all necessary steps, including the use of armed force" to protect Americans in Southeast Asia. Johnson used the powers this resolution granted to enlarge the war in Vietnam.

While presidential leadership in military and foreign affairs is clearly outlined in the Constitution, Congress has also asked for presidential leadership in economic matters. Franklin Roosevelt set the precedent by taking control of the economy during the Depression. Such leadership continues today. President Bush addressing the Economic Club of New York said:

Our administration's economic policies are designed to strengthen the foundation of solid recovery and guarantee the highest possible rate of sustained economic growth. . . .

Later this month, the administration will release our National Energy Strategy. The strategy will propose federal, state, and private sector initiatives. . . .
—George Bush, February 6, 1991

Use of the Mass Media Presidents use all forms of **mass media**—radio, television, magazines and newspapers—to communicate their ideas to the public. Franklin D. Roosevelt was the first President to realize that radio had great potential for political use. Roosevelt broadcast "fireside chats" on the radio to the American people. He talked informally about the nation's problems and his proposed solutions for them.

Today, television gives Presidents even greater power to convey their ideas and personality directly to the American people. The media called President Ronald Reagan the "Great Communicator" partly because of his ability to deliver his message directly to the people through television. People often judge a President's ideas according to the personal appeal of

=== STUDY GUIDE ===

Themes in Government
Separation of Powers According to the Constitution, only Congress has the power to declare war. **How did Congress relinquish some of its power in this regard in 1964?**

Critical Thinking Skills
Distinguishing Fact From Opinion How would you expect a White House reporter's story about a presidential activity to dif- fer from that of a television network commentator speaking about the same presidential activity?

Cooperative Learning Activity

Organize the class into groups of three. Have groups select one of the following Presidents: George Washington, Andrew Jackson, Abraham Lincoln, Franklin D. Roosevelt, Harry Truman, John Kennedy, Lyndon Johnson, or Richard Nixon. Help each group choose three areas in which that President impacted presidential powers, and have each student research one of the areas. When students are finished, have them combine their research into a bulletin-board display.

PARTICIPATING IN GOVERNMENT

Writing a Letter to the Editor

Suppose you disagree with a government policy, a recent law, a Supreme Court decision, or a popular opinion. How might you express your concerns in an effective way?

Writing a letter to the editor of a newspaper or magazine is one way. Newspapers and magazines can publish only a few of the many letters they receive. The following guidelines will help improve the chances of your letter appearing in print:

- Choose a timely topic that has widespread interest.
- Catch the editor's (and the readers') attention

with your opening sentence.
- Stick to the topic, and express your views in clear, concise paragraphs.
- Present reasonable, constructive arguments. Balance negative comments with positive suggestions.
- Rely on facts or personal experience to support

your opinions.
- Type your letter or write legibly in ink. Try not to exceed the usual length of letters in the newspaper or magazine you are writing.
- Include your name and address. You can ask that your name not be printed, but the editor must know the source of the letter.

Investigating Further

Apply the guidelines above and write a letter to the editor of your local newspaper.

---

the President on television, a fact Presidents know very well and try to use to their advantage.

When a President wants to talk to the nation, the networks usually make available free time on television. A prime-time television speech or press conference can reach 80 million or more Americans.

Major newspapers and magazines also provide a forum for presidential messages. These media, in addition to television and radio networks, assign reporters to cover the President full time. White House staff members make sure the reporters receive a steady flow of information about the President's activities and ideas. One of the staff's objectives is to create the image of a President as an active, personable servant of the people.

Limits on Presidential Power

The Founders built significant safeguards against the abuse of presidential power into the Constitution. Both Congress and the courts have powers that limit the President's authority. Other factors, not mentioned in the Constitution, also affect the President's actions.

Congressional Limitations The Constitution gives Congress the power to pass legislation over a President's veto. A congressional override may limit a President's effectiveness in carrying out a legislative program or in using executive powers. In 1973 Congress overrode President Nixon's veto of the War Powers Act that prevented Presidents from committing troops to combat for more than 60 days without congressional approval. Congress felt that Nixon and previous Presidents had abused their power as commander in chief. They had done so by involving American soldiers for prolonged periods in an undeclared war in Vietnam. Congress's view was that the presidency needed to be checked, which was the intention of the War Powers Act.

Congress also has the power to impeach a President. Impeachment is a drastic measure that has been used very infrequently in United States history. The House of Representatives impeached Andrew Johnson in 1868, but the Senate acquitted him by a margin of one vote. In 1974 a House committee voted to recommend impeachment of President Nixon over his role in the Watergate scandal, but he resigned the presidency before the matter could be brought to the full House.

Special Needs Strategy

Study Strategy As students with reading comprehension difficulties become used to employing questioning techniques, they will find that their reading is more efficient. Subheadings help them direct their reading energy toward the essential information in the passages. Ask students to turn to the subsection "Presidential Powers in Article II" on page 456. Have each student write questions about the subsection only. Then have them read the text under the heading to answer their questions.

Interpreting Political Cartoons Have students complete activity 12 in *Interpreting Political Cartoons* in the Teacher's Classroom Resources.

PARTICIPATING IN GOVERNMENT

Provide students with a few letters to the editor from your local newspaper, or ask students to bring such letters to class. Choose a few letters and ask why they think these particular letters were chosen to be published. Ask if the topics of the letters concerned something they have read about or have seen on television. Ask how well the letters follow the guidelines for writing a letter to the editor.

Have students complete activity 16 in *Participating in Government* in the Teacher's Classroom Resources.

Assess

Check for Understanding

Have students complete Section 3 Review on page 460.

Meeting Objectives

Each section objective is tested by the Section Review questions that follow it in parentheses.
- Describe the sources of the growing power of the President since the time of the writing of the Constitution. (2, 3, 4, 6, 7, 8)
- Analyze the checks that Congress can exercise to control presidential power. (5, 6, 7)

Evaluate

Section 3 Quiz

Testmaker

Caption Answer

created public dissatisfaction with the President and forced him to not run for reelection

Reteach

Have students write a paragraph listing three of the President's constitutional powers, three other sources of presidential power, and present-day examples of each.

Enrich

Have students use the library to research the campaign of 1960, the first in which television played a key role in shaping voter opinions. Then have them present an oral report to the class, discussing the campaign and the ways in which it was influenced by television.

Have students complete activity 16 in *Enrichment Activities* in the Teacher's Classroom Resources.

Close

President John Kennedy described the presidency as "the vital center of action in our whole scheme of government." Ask students if they agree or disagree with Kennedy and explain why.

Greeting the Troops
President Johnson believed South Vietnam had to be defended against communism. **Politics How did the Vietnam War affect the President's powers?**

Limitation by the Federal Courts The federal courts have a constitutional power to limit a President. The case of *Marbury* v. *Madison* (1803) established the Supreme Court's right to review legislative actions. During the Great Depression, the Supreme Court ruled some of President Franklin D. Roosevelt's New Deal legislation unconstitutional.

Supreme Court justices, like members of Congress, are inclined to respect Presidents' views and authority. During World War II, President Franklin D. Roosevelt ordered thousands of American citizens of Japanese descent to relocation camps. Such an order clearly violated the civil rights and liberties of loyal citizens. At the time, however, the Supreme Court upheld President Roosevelt's action.

Limitation by the Bureaucracy The federal bureaucracy sometimes limits presidential powers. Bureaucrats can obstruct Presidents' programs unintentionally by failing to provide needed information, by misinterpreting instructions, and by neglecting to complete a task properly. Powerful bureaucrats with connections to committee and subcommittee chairpersons in Congress may intentionally obstruct presidential leadership. Congress and the bureaucracy may work together to carry out their own programs rather than those of the President.

Public Opinion Public opinion can also limit a President. In 1968 public dissatisfaction with President Lyndon Johnson's conduct of the Vietnam War forced him to not run for reelection. Without favorable public opinion, a President cannot succeed in carrying out a political program. One reason President Carter lost the 1980 election was that the public doubted his ability to carry out his policies.

The American people expect their Presidents to be symbolic leaders of the nation and moral leaders as well. They expect Presidents to always act with courage and dignity. If they fail to live up to these standards, the nation usually condemns their actions.

The Founders could not build into the Constitution provisions for regulating the moral character of a President. As the American people found in the case of President Nixon in 1974, the checks and balances provisions of the Constitution do continue to work, if at times slowly. Mass media and public opinion support the checks and balances that serve to limit the powers of a President.

3 SECTION REVIEW

Section Summary
Presidential powers derive from the Constitution, actions of past Presidents, congressional decisions, and the use of mass media.

Checking For Understanding
Recalling Facts
1. Define federal bureaucracy, mass media.
2. List five constitutional powers of the President.
3. Discuss ways in which two former Presidents have expanded the power of their office.
4. Name the President who used "fireside chats" over radio to influence public opinion.

Exploring Themes
5. Checks and Balances What two constitutional provisions allow Congress to balance the power of the President?
6. Separation of Powers Why did President Johnson ask Congress for authority to use armed force in Vietnam?

Critical Thinking Skills
7. Understanding Cause and Effect Why do presidential powers tend to grow during national emergencies?
8. Distinguishing Fact from Opinion President Wilson said the President "is at liberty, both in law and conscience, . . . to be as big a man as he can." Is this a statement of fact or opinion? Support your answer.

Section 3 Review Answers

1. Definitions of terms appear on pages indicated: **federal bureaucracy,** 456; **mass media,** 458
2. commander in chief, appoints heads of executive departments, pardons people convicted of federal crimes, makes treaties, appoints ambassadors and other officials, delivers State of Union address, calls Congress into special session, meets heads of state and foreign officials, commissions military officers, executes laws

3. Jefferson purchased the Louisiana Territory, suggesting President had inherent powers. Lincoln raised an army without Congress's approval; F.D. Roosevelt expanded the role of government in the economy.
4. Franklin D. Roosevelt
5. power to pass laws over the President's veto and power to impeach a President
6. While the Constitution names the President as commander in chief of the armed forces, it reserves to Congress the power to declare war.

7. At these times, people expect the government to respond quickly. The President is able to respond more effectively than Congress because Congress is decentralized and divided between parties, while the executive is centralized.

8. Some students may say it is opinion because other Presidents believed that the Constitution limits the President's power. Others may say fact because Presidents have historically molded the office to their own interpretations of the Constitution.

SECTION 4

Presidential Leadership

Presidents have seven major duties. Five of these are based on the Constitution: serving as head of state, chief executive, chief legislator, chief diplomat, and commander in chief. Two other roles not mentioned in the Constitution have developed over the years. These are economic planner and political party leader.

Head of State

As head of state, the President represents the nation and performs many ceremonial duties. Serving as host to visiting kings, queens, and heads of governments, the President is the nation's chief diplomat. Other ceremonial duties are less vital, but receive much attention. Lighting the national Christmas tree, giving awards and medals, making public service statements on important issues, meeting public figures from musicians to business leaders are all considered a part of the role of President.

The President is both head of state and chief executive. In most countries these two duties are distinct. One person—sometimes a king or queen, sometimes a president without real power—is the ceremonial head of state. Another person—a prime minister or premier—directs the government.

This difference is important. Much of the awe, mystery, and excitement of the presidency exists because Presidents are more than politicians. To millions around the world and to millions at home, the President *is* the United States. As a living symbol of the nation, the President is not just a single individual, but the collective image of the United States.

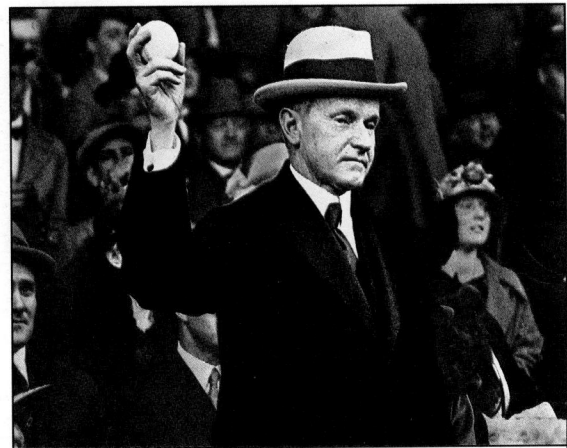

Ceremonial Duties
Like Calvin Coolidge, Presidents often throw out the first ball to begin a baseball game. **History How is the President a living symbol of the nation?**

Chief Executive

As the nation's chief executive, the President sees that the laws of Congress are carried out. These laws range over a great many areas of public concern from social security, taxes, housing, flood control, and energy to civil rights, health care, education, and environmental protection.

The executive branch employs more than 2 million people to enforce the many laws and programs Congress establishes. The President is in charge of these employees and the federal departments and agencies for which they work. Of course, no President could directly supervise the daily activities of all

---

SECTION PREVIEW

Objectives
After studying this section, you should be able to:
■ Describe the President's foreign-policy duties.
■ Explain the President's role in

shaping domestic policy.

Key Terms and Concepts
executive order, impoundment, reprieve, pardon, amnesty, item veto, patronage, treaty, executive agreement

Themes in Government
■ Checks and Balances
■ Constitutional Interpretations

Critical Thinking Skills
■ Drawing Conclusions
■ Understanding Cause and Effect

CHAPTER 16: THE PRESIDENCY 461

Classroom Resources for Section 4

📁 Guided Reading Activities
📁 Reproducible Lesson Plans
📁 Primary and Secondary Source Readings 16
📁 Interpreting Political Cartoons 11
📁 Reteaching Activities 16
📁 Section 4 Quiz

📁 Chapter 16 Tests
➕ Testmaker
🎧 Audio Cassettes (English and Spanish)
🎧 Limited English Proficiency Activities 16
  SAT Practice Tests
  Writer's Guidebook

Focus

Bell Ringer

Write the following on the chalkboard for students to answer in writing:

What is the title of the person who holds each of the following jobs in the federal government: chief executive, chief diplomat, commander in chief? *(President of the United States)*

Motivating Activity

Write the three jobs of the President as given in the Bell Ringer activity in a horizontal line on the chalkboard. Then ask students to brainstorm ideas about the duties of the President of the United States that would fall under each heading. List their responses under the suggested heading. Keep the list on the chalkboard and use it for the Close activity on page 468.

Vocabulary Precheck

Call on students to read aloud the definitions of the terms and concepts from the Glossary. Then have volunteers use each term in a sentence. **LEP**

Caption Answer
The President is the collective image of the United States

Teach

Guided Practice

L1 **Concept Mapping** Make a concept map on the chalkboard that shows the seven duties of the President. Write the word *President* and circle it. Extend seven lines from the circle, and ask students to name the President's duties. Then ask students to give an example of each duty shown on the map. **LEP**

L2 Synthesizing Information
For each item below, have students tell which of the seven presidential roles the President is carrying out. Students should also indicate whether the role is based on a constitutional power or on an informal source of power.

1. tosses out the first baseball of the season (*head of state; constitutional*)
2. makes a speech endorsing a Senate candidate (*political party leader, informal*)
3. issues an executive order authorizing the sale of thousands of acres of federal land to private buyers (*chief executive, constitutional*)
4. threatens to veto a bill unless it contains a certain provision (*chief legislator, constitutional*)
5. negotiates an international agreement to limit the spread of nuclear weapons technology (*chief diplomat, constitutional*)

Caption Answer
An executive order has the force of law.

STUDY GUIDE

Theme Answer
The Senate must approve all presidential appointments to the bench.

Critical Thinking Answer
A government worker's beliefs have little impact on setting policy, but an agency head's beliefs must generally mirror those of the President who appointed him or her to the position.

Powers of the President
State of the Union
Running Time 1:15
Side One, Chapter 23

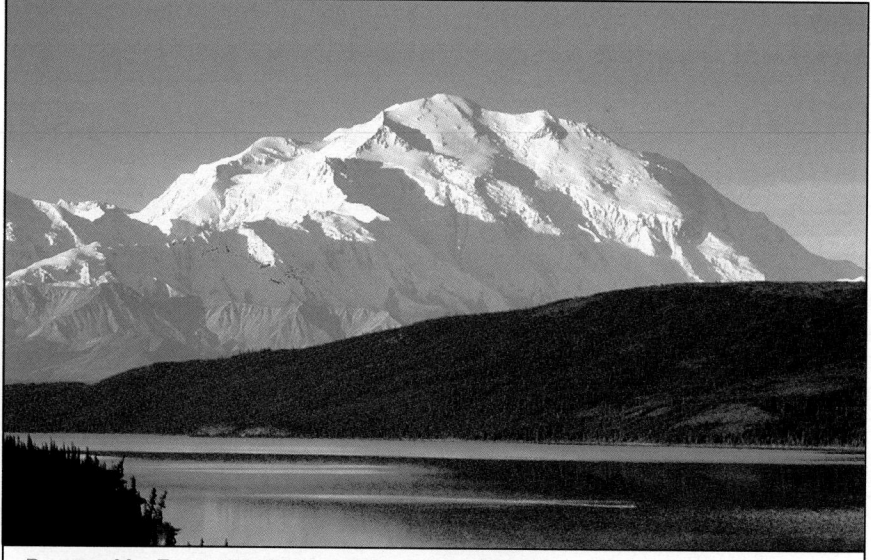

Reserved by Executive Order
President Carter used an executive order to place these Alaskan lands within the control of the National Park Service. **Political Processes How is an executive order a tool for the President?**

these people. Presidents can hope only to influence the way laws are implemented so that they follow the President's philosophy of government.

Tools of Influence Presidents have several tools to influence how laws are carried out. One is **executive orders,** or rules that have the force of law. Presidents issue executive orders to spell out many of the details of policies and programs Congress enacts. For example, President Carter used an executive order to put thousands of acres of land in Alaska under the control of the National Park Service. Carter was exercising power under a law permitting the President to keep certain lands free of commercial development.

Besides appointing cabinet members, Presidents appoint "with the advice and consent of the Senate" about 2,200 top-level federal officials. These officials include agency directors, deputy directors, and their assistants. Presidents try to appoint officials who share their political beliefs because they want these

officials to carry out their policies.

A third tool that Presidents may use is the right to remove officials they have appointed. President Nixon, for example, fired his secretary of the interior for opposing his conduct of the war in Vietnam. It is not always easy, however, to remove a popular official, who may have congressional and public support. The former director of the FBI, J. Edgar Hoover, was such a person. He headed the FBI for 48 years. Evidence indicates that several Presidents had doubts about his capacities and conduct near the end of his career, but Hoover was too popular to fire. Hoover held the office of director of the FBI until his death on May 1, 1972.

Fourth, for a variety of reasons, a President may refuse to permit a federal department or agency to spend the money Congress has appropriated for it. This process is known as impoundment of funds. **Impoundment** means that the President puts aside, or refuses to spend, the money Congress has appropriated for a certain purpose. Presidents have practiced impoundment for years. In 1803, for example, President Jefferson did not spend money Congress set aside for new gunboats until less costly designs were found. Most impoundments have been for routine matters. Money is appropriated; the need for spending changes; the President impounds the money; Congress agrees.

President Nixon tried to impound funds in the early 1970s to eliminate a number of social programs

---
STUDY GUIDE

Themes in Government
Checks and Balances Between 1981 and 1991, Presidents Ronald Reagan and George Bush appointed six Supreme Court justices. **What is necessary for presidential**

appointments of judges to take effect?

Critical Thinking Skills
Drawing Conclusions Why are a government worker's political

beliefs and opinions not as important as those of the agency or department head under whom he or she works?

Background

President Clinton vetoed no bills during his first year in office. All former Presidents have vetoed bills, but the use of the veto power has varied widely, from 1 veto (President Monroe) to 635 (Franklin Roosevelt). On very few occasions has

Congress been able to override a presidential veto—only about 4 percent of all vetoes. In fact, Presidents Kennedy and Johnson had no vetoes overridden, and President Bush had only one.

he did not favor. He impounded huge sums of money—as much as $13 billion in a single year. Groups who stood to benefit from the impounded programs took President Nixon to court in an effort to release the money they had expected to receive. The court ordered the President to spend the appropriated money. To prevent such wholesale impounding, Congress passed a law forbidding impoundments without congressional approval.

As chief executive the President appoints, with Senate approval, all federal judges, including the justices of the Supreme Court. Presidents can use this power to influence the course of government. For example, Republican Presidents who served between 1969 and 1993 appointed justices such as Clarence Thomas who generally had more conservative views than their predecessors.

Reprieves and Pardons As chief executive the President can grant "reprieves and pardons for offenses against the United States." A **reprieve** grants a *postponement* of legal punishment. A **pardon** is a *release* from legal punishment. Presidents usually grant pardons to people after they have been convicted of federal crimes. In 1974, however, President Gerald Ford granted "a full, free and absolute pardon unto Richard Nixon" for any crimes the former President might have committed in connection with the Watergate scandal. Nixon had not been indicted or convicted of any crimes at that time.

Amnesty Finally, the President may also grant amnesty. **Amnesty** is a group pardon to individuals for an offense against the government. Amnesty usually applies to military personnel. For example, Presidents Ford and Carter granted amnesty to men who fled the draft during the Vietnam War. Civilians also can be granted amnesty. In the 1890s President Benjamin Harrison granted amnesty to those Mormons who had been accused of practicing polygamy (the practice of having more than one wife at a time) in violation of federal law.

Chief Legislator

Congress expects the executive branch to propose legislation it wishes to see enacted. President Eisenhower once wanted Congress to act on a particular problem he was concerned about. The White House, however, neglected to draft a bill to deal with the situation. A member of Congress scolded the President's staff: "Don't expect us to start from scratch on what you people want," he said. "That's not the way we do things here. You draft the bills, and we work them over."

The President's Legislative Program Usually the President describes a legislative program in the annual State of the Union message to Congress. It calls attention to the President's ideas about how to solve key problems facing the country. A detailed legislative program presented to Congress during the year reflects the President's values and political beliefs.

The President has a large staff to help write legislation. This legislation determines much of what Congress will do each year. The President's office also

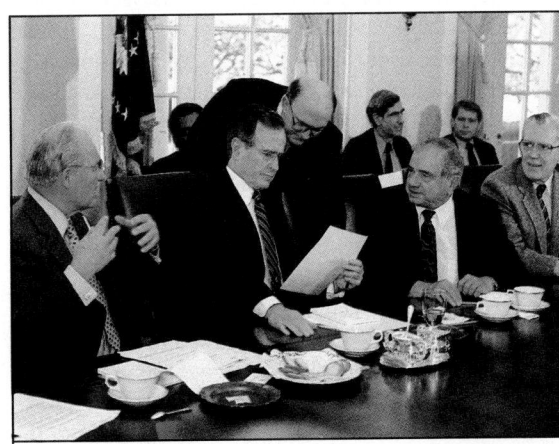

Power Breakfast
The President and members of Congress meet to discuss new legislation. **Politics** When do Presidents usually describe their legislative programs?

STUDY GUIDE

Themes in Government
Constitutional Interpretations
Presidents often grant pardons on the eve of leaving office. How does a presidential pardon differ from a presidential reprieve?

Critical Thinking Skills
Understanding Cause and Effect
Why do you think people with liberal beliefs would object to the string of conservative judges whom Presidents have appointed to the Supreme Court in recent years?

Cooperative Learning Activity

Organize the class into four groups. Assign 10 or 11 Presidents to each group. Have members of each group divide responsibilities in creating a time line of American Presidents. Have students in each group label sections of the time line with each President's name and term of office. Then have them find examples of each President in the role of chief executive, chief diplomat, and commander in chief, and add these items to the time line in the appropriate time period. Have all groups combine their information into one time line, illustrating the chief roles of the presidency throughout United States history.

L3 Creating Political Cartoons
Ask the class to think of symbols that might be used to characterize the current President's leadership in carrying out the seven major duties. Have each student use the symbols to create a political cartoon about the President. Have them share their cartoons and discuss the way the symbols were used to create a positive or a negative image of the President.

Caption Answer
in the State of the Union message

STUDY GUIDE

Theme Answer
A pardon releases from legal punishment; a reprieve postpones legal punishment.

Critical Thinking Answer
Liberals fear that conservative justices will judge issues before the Court from a conservative viewpoint or overturn previous liberal rulings.

CONNECTIONS

Biography
Jimmy Carter has remained an active ex-President by involving himself in domestic and international social and political issues. For example, he served as an impartial observer in elections in Nicaragua and Panama and helped negotiate the return of Haiti's elected president to power in 1994. At home he has participated in the rehabilitation and construction of housing for the poor throughout the country.

L1 Geography Remind students that as commander in chief, the President of the United States has historically used his powers to send troops to countries throughout the world. On an outline map of the world, have students locate areas to which Presidents have sent troops. **LEP**

L2 Persuasive Writing Ask students if they think the office of President is too much for one person to handle. Have them write an essay explaining their answer and suggesting possible alternatives.

📁 Interpreting Political Cartoons Have students complete activity 11 in *Interpreting Political Cartoons* in the Teacher's Classroom Resources.

STUDY GUIDE

Theme Answer
Congress finds it hard to gather enough votes to override a presidential veto.

Critical Thinking Answer
The President will probably be given credit for the positive state of the economy, which will be of benefit at election time.

---

presents Congress a suggested budget and an annual economic report.

Taking office after the assassination of President Kennedy, Lyndon B. Johnson called upon Congress to enact Kennedy's programs:

> *I believe in the ability of Congress, despite the divisions of opinions which characterize our nation, to act—to act wisely, to act vigorously, to act speedily when the need arises. The need is here. The need is now.*
>
> —LYNDON B. JOHNSON, 1963

Congress responded by passing a host of new domestic legislation the administration proposed.

When the President and the majority of Congress are from different political parties, however, the President must work harder to influence members of Congress to support a particular program. Presidents often meet with senators and representatives to share their views with them, and they appoint several staff members to work closely with Congress on new laws.

Presidents may hand out political favors to get congressional support. They may visit the home state of a member of Congress to support his or her reelection. Or a President may start a new federal project that will bring money and jobs to a member of Congress's home state or district. Presidents may also invite members of Congress to important White House social events.

An important presidential tool in lawmaking is the veto power. Each bill Congress passes is sent to the President for approval. The President may sign the bill, veto the bill, or lay it aside. Presidents sometimes use the threat of a veto to force Congress to stop a bill or change it to fit their wishes. The threats succeed because Congress finds it very difficult to gather enough votes to override a veto.

One power that most state governors have, and the President does not have, is an **item veto.** Many state governors may veto only the parts of a bill that they disapprove of while letting other parts pass into law. Presidents must accept or reject the entire bill.

Economic Planner

The President's role as chief economic planner has grown rapidly since Franklin D. Roosevelt's New Deal. The Employment Act of 1946 gave new duties to the President. This law directed the President to submit an annual economic report to Congress. The law also created a Council of Economic Advisers to study the economy and help prepare the report for the President. In addition, the law declared for the first time that the federal government had the responsibility to promote high employment, production, and purchasing power.

Since 1946 Congress has continued to pass laws giving Presidents more power to deal with economic problems. In 1970, for example, Congress gave President Nixon power to control prices and wages. One year later, the President used this power to put a 90-day freeze on all prices, rents, wages, and salaries. The law then expired and was not renewed.

The President also has the duty to prepare the federal budget every year. The President supervises this work and spends many months with budget officials deciding what government programs to support and what programs to cut back. The size of the budget, decisions about the budget deficit, and choices concerning where monies will be allocated all affect the national economy.

Party Leader

The President's political party expects the chief executive to be a party leader. The President may give speeches to help party members running for office. The President may attend fund-raising activities to help raise money for the party. The President selects the party's national chairperson. Often, the President helps plan the party's future election strategies.

Presidents are expected to appoint members of their party to available government jobs. These appointments ensure that supporters will remain committed to a President's programs. Political **patronage,**

STUDY GUIDE

Themes in Government
Checks and Balances In 1991 President Bush threatened to veto a civil rights bill unless certain changes and deletions were made so that the final bill would meet his approval. **Why does Congress try to pass bills that the President will not veto?**

Critical Thinking Skills
Understanding Cause and Effect
Why does a President consider it to be in his or her best political interests to preside over a healthy, booming economy?

Special Needs Strategy

Study Strategy By now students will have had ample opportunity to practice developing relevant questions about the material covered in the text. Organize students into small cooperative groups, and ask each group to write five questions based on the material in Section 4 that they could ask on a test. Be sure that students with reading problems are evenly dispersed among these groups. Have each group present their questions to the class and discuss them.

or appointment to political office, rewards those persons who support the President and the party during an election.

Being a political party leader can be a difficult role for a President. People expect a President, as head of the government, to represent all Americans. Political parties, however, expect Presidents to provide leadership for their own political party. Sometimes these conflicting roles cause problems. When Presidents take steps that clearly are in their party's interest, the media and the public often criticize them. On the other hand, party leaders may complain that Presidents do not take the party's needs sufficiently into account.

Chief Diplomat

The President directs the foreign policy of the United States, making the key decisions about United States relations with other countries in the world. In this role the President is the nation's chief diplomat.

Because Congress also has powers related to foreign policy, there has been a continuing struggle between the President and Congress over who will exercise control of the country's foreign policy. Presidents usually have an advantage in this struggle. One reason is that a President has access to more information about foreign affairs than do most members of Congress. The administration sometimes classifies this information as secret. The Central Intelligence Agency (CIA), the State Department, the Defense Department, and the National Security Council constantly give the President the latest information needed to make key foreign-policy decisions. Skillful Presidents use this information to plan and justify actions they want to take. Members of Congress, who lack access to this kind of information, often find it difficult to challenge the President's decisions.

In addition, the ability to take quick decisive action has greatly added to the power of the presidency in foreign affairs. Unlike Congress, where the individual opinions of 435 representatives and 100 senators

Chief of Exports and Imports
President Clinton negotiated to encourage fair trade between the United States and Japan. **Economics What does the cartoonist indicate about the President's attitude toward this subject in the past?**

must be coordinated, the executive branch is headed by a single person. In a national emergency involving foreign affairs, the responsibility for action rests with the President.

Unless Presidents have had experience with foreign affairs as lawmakers or government officials, they often need some time to master this complicated aspect of the presidency. Former Secretary of State Dean Acheson, who served under President Truman from 1949 to 1953, offered this evaluation:

It takes all of our Presidents a good deal of time to learn about foreign affairs. Roosevelt took many years and never got a real grasp. Mr. Truman caught hold pretty quickly, perhaps 18 months. Ike [President Eisenhower] never learned much of anything [about it]. Jack Kennedy was just catching on in 1963. L.B.J. [President Johnson] tends to concentrate where the most noise is coming from. The way our system works, instruction in foreign affairs does not play much of a part in the education of prospective Presidents.

—DEAN ACHESON

STUDY GUIDE

Themes in Government
Constitutional Interpretations
Article II spells out the powers of the President in relation to foreign governments. **How does this put** lawmakers opposed to the President at a disadvantage?

Critical Thinking Skills
Drawing Conclusions
Why do state governors, such as Franklin Roosevelt before he was President, have little experience with foreign affairs?

Critical Thinking Activity

Drawing Conclusions Remind students that the President shares with Congress the power to make war. Ask the following question: Why is the President often given power in times of war that would be unthinkable in peacetime? Discuss students' answers. *(Answers will vary, but should include that the President is given extra power to make it possible to direct and coordinate an effective war effort. In times of war, action needs to be taken quickly.)*

L3 Expressive Writing Ask students to write an article indicating if they think a presidential candidate's influence as party leader decreases after he or she becomes President. Students' articles should include reasons for their opinions.

Caption Answer
It was not as firm and perhaps not very convincing.

STUDY GUIDE

Theme Answer
gives President access to more information about foreign affairs than most members of Congress

Critical Thinking Answer
A state governor's concerns are mainly on domestic matters.

CONNECTIONS

Biography
One of the major duties of the President is to execute the laws of the land. Appropriately, most of the Presidents were lawyers—25 out of 41. The occupations of the remaining Presidents include farmer, businessman, soldier, tailor, author, educator, editor, engineer, and actor.

GLOBAL CONNECTION

Explain to the students how in 1991 and 1992 President Bush initially withheld recognition of the independent republics of the former Soviet Union, fearing that to do so might be perceived as meddling in that nation's internal affairs. As the disintegration of the Soviet Union accelerated, however, Bush found himself reacting to events more than influencing them—an unusual position for him. After decades of policies aimed at achieving change in the Soviet Union, an American President was wanting to slow the pace of change in order to preserve stability in a critical area of the world.
Examining the Connection Answer: *powers to make treaties and executive agreements, power to recognize foreign governments*

STUDY GUIDE

Theme Answer
The Senate must approve all treaties by a two-thirds vote.

Critical Thinking Answer
Presidents hoped that the lack of goods would create internal popular unrest with Cuba's communist government.

GLOBAL CONNECTION

Interdependence

Presidential Influence As head of the United States government, the President is one of the most influential world leaders. Other heads of state pay close attention to the President's stand on international issues.

As chief diplomat the President directs foreign relations. By quickly recognizing the existence of a new government, the President influences other nations to do so. By withholding or withdrawing recognition, the President may influence the policies of a foreign government. The President can also initiate programs to aid other countries. President Kennedy established the Peace Corps to help improve living conditions in developing countries.

Examining the Connection
Which executive powers give the President the most influence over foreign governments? Explain your answer.

The Power to Make Treaties As chief diplomat the President has sole power to negotiate and sign **treaties**—formal agreements between the governments of two or more countries. As part of the constitutional system of checks and balances, however, two-thirds of the Senate must approve all treaties before they can go into effect.

The Senate takes its constitutional responsibility about treaties very seriously. Sometimes, the Senate will refuse to approve a treaty. After World War I, the Senate rejected the Treaty of Versailles, the agreement to end the war and to make the United States a member of the League of Nations. More recently, in 1978, only after lengthy debates and strong opposi-

tion did the Senate approve two treaties giving eventual control of the Panama Canal to the government of Panama.

The Power to Make Executive Agreements The President also has the authority to make executive agreements with other countries. **Executive agreements** are pacts between the President and the head of a foreign government. These agreements have the same legal status as treaties, but they do not require Senate consent.

Most executive agreements involve routine matters. Presidents, however, have used executive agreements to conclude more serious arrangements with other countries. Because these agreements do not require Senate approval, most Presidents prefer them to treaties. For example, Franklin D. Roosevelt lent American ships to the British in exchange for leases on British military bases. At the time, the British were fighting Nazi Germany, but the United States had not yet entered the war. Roosevelt knew that the strongly isolationist Senate would not ratify a treaty. He therefore negotiated an executive agreement.

Some Presidents have kept certain executive agreements secret. To prevent this, Congress passed a law in 1950 requiring the President to make all executive agreements signed each year public. Presidents have sometimes ignored this law, however, and kept those agreements they considered important to national security secret. For example, in 1969, Congress discovered that several Presidents had never made public many executive agreements that involved giving American military support to South Vietnam, Laos, Thailand, and the Philippines.

Recognition of Foreign Governments As chief diplomat the President decides whether the United States will recognize governments of other countries. This power means the President determines whether the government will acknowledge the legal existence of another government and have dealings with that government. Presidents sometimes use recognition as a foreign-policy tool. For example, since 1959 Presi-

---

STUDY GUIDE

Themes in Government
Checks and Balances Concluding treaties are part of a President's foreign-policy-making powers.

What government control is exercised over the President's authority to make treaties?

Critical Thinking Skills
Understanding Cause and Effect
Besides withholding diplomatic recognition, why have Presidents since the 1960s also forbidden trade with Fidel Castro's Cuba?

Background

One of the most powerful people in the country, the chairman of the Federal Reserve Board, is appointed by the President. The Federal Reserve has the power to control the country's money supply and consequently the health of the economy. Increasing the amount of money available to banks

for loans is one way that the "Fed" expands the economy, creates jobs, and stimulates prosperity. Although this prosperity is artificially created, the Fed has been known to use this technique effectively prior to presidential elections.

dents have refused to recognize the communist government of Cuba. By withholding diplomatic recognition, the United States is indicating its displeasure with the policies of the Cuban government.

Commander in Chief

Presidents can back up their foreign-policy decisions with military force when necessary. The Constitution makes the President commander in chief of the armed forces of the United States.

Power to Make War The President shares with Congress the power to make war. President Bush asked for and received congressional approval to make war on Iraq before he ordered a massive air strike in January 1991. This approval prevented a serious constitutional question that could have divided the nation if the President had sent American troops into combat without congressional approval.

Several Presidents have sent American forces into action without a formal declaration of war. For example, Thomas Jefferson used force against the Barbary Pirates of North Africa, and several Presidents sent forces into Latin America in the early 1900s. Since 1973, however, no President has officially challenged the constitutionality of the War Powers Act. When President Bush ordered an invasion of Panama to overthrow the dictator Manuel Noriega, he did not seek congressional approval. A constitutional challenge to the War

Powers Act did not arise, however, because the operation ended quickly. The issue could become critical in the future if Congress demands withdrawal of troops from an area of actual or threatened combat and the President refuses to do so.

Military Operations and Strategy Generals, admirals, and other military leaders run the armed forces on a day-to-day basis. The President, however, is responsible for key military decisions. Perhaps no President has been as well prepared to exercise the powers of commander in chief as was George Washington. Taking office just six years after leading the American military forces to victory over the British, Washington had firsthand knowledge of military strategy. He exercised his constitutional authority over the military in 1794 when defiant whiskey distillers in western Pennsylvania refused to pay the federal tax on their product.

Alexander Hamilton urged the President to take action against the rebels by ordering mobilization of

Foreign Policy
President Nixon reopened trade between China and the United States. Trade relations had ended during the Korean War. **Diplomacy** **Why did President Nixon and recent Presidents refuse to recognize Cuba's government?**

CHAPTER 16: THE PRESIDENCY   467

STUDY GUIDE

Themes in Government
Constitutional Interpretations
The United States has been involved in eight foreign wars between 1812 and 1991. **Who gives final approval to go to war?**

Critical Thinking Skills
Drawing Conclusions **Why do you think it best that the United States Constitution stipulates that** a civilian President rather than a general is commander in chief of the armed forces of the country?

Cooperative Learning Activity

Organize students into groups and assign a general topic to each group, such as the environment, the economy, or health care. Then subdivide each group into three groups. One subgroup should propose legislation on its assigned topic from an apolitical viewpoint, possibly using public opinion polls as its guide. The other two subgroups should research the viewpoints of the Democratic and Republican parties on their assigned issues and then propose appropriate legislation from those viewpoints. Have subgroups compare their results in class and explain how a President's role as chief legislator can be affected by party affiliation.

Caption Answer
to indicate displeasure with policies of the Cuban government

STUDY GUIDE

Theme Answer
Congress gives final approval to go to war.

Critical Thinking Answer
It lessens the chances of a military takeover.

Assess

Check for Understanding
Have students complete Section 4 Review on page 468.

Meeting Objectives
Each section objective is tested by the Section Review questions that follow it in parentheses.
• Describe the President's foreign-policy duties. (2, 3, 4, 5, 6, 8)
• Explain the President's role in shaping domestic policy. (2, 3, 7, 8)

Evaluate
Section 4 Quiz
Testmaker

Powers of the President
Declaring War
Running Time 1:19
Side One, Chapter 32

Reteach

Have students imagine they are the President and write a journal entry describing one day's activities.

📁 Have students complete activity 16 in *Reteaching Activities* in the Teacher's Classroom Resources.

Enrich

📁 Have students complete activity 16 in *Primary and Secondary Source Readings* in the Teacher's Classroom Resources.

Close

Refer to the list of presidential duties that students brainstormed for the Motivating Activity. Ask what additional duties they can now add to the list. Discuss which of the seven roles they think is the most important and why.

CONNECTIONS

Biography

Most ex-Presidents retire from government. Two, however, continued their public service. John Quincy Adams was elected to Congress and William Howard Taft became Chief Justice of the United States.

War Powers
Military force can add might to foreign policy. **Political Processes** **When has a President sent forces into action without congressional approval?**

15,000 state militia. Hamilton himself rode west with the troops; Washington journeyed out to Carlisle, Pennsylvania, to inspect them. When troops arrived in Pittsburgh, there was little opposition to the demonstration of executive strength.

Perhaps it is not unusual that several Presidents have come from a military background. Besides Washington, others have included Andrew Jackson, William H. Harrison, Zachary Taylor, Ulysses S. Grant, and Dwight D. Eisenhower.

Many Presidents have become directly involved in military operations. Presidents Johnson and Nixon made the key military decisions—sometimes daily—in the Vietnam War. President Carter sent a special military force into Iran in 1980 in an effort to free American diplomats who were being held hostage there. In 1991 President Bush decided to give the military more freedom to make strategy decisions when the United States went to war against Iraq. Still, the responsibility for directing overall military strategies remained with the President.

As commander in chief, the President has the authority to order the use of atomic weapons, an awesome responsibility. President Nixon once said, "I can walk into my office, pick up the telephone, and in twenty minutes 70 million people will be dead."

The President has other duties as commander in chief. During a war the President takes actions at home that will support the war effort. Congress usually grants the President special powers to do this. During World War II, Franklin D. Roosevelt demanded and received from Congress power over price controls, gas and food rationing, and government control of industries needed to produce goods to conduct the war.

The President may also use the military to control serious disorders in the nation. Presidents have used federal troops to put down rioting in American cities. In case of a natural disaster, such as a flood, the President may send needed supplies or troops to help keep order.

The role as head of state, chief legislator, economic planner, chief diplomat, and commander in chief gives the President broad powers. Today, the President of the United States is the most powerful single individual in the world.

---

4 SECTION REVIEW

Section Summary
The President's role includes a wide variety of domestic and foreign responsibilities.

Checking for Understanding
Recalling Facts
1. Define executive order, impoundment, reprieve, pardon, amnesty, item veto, patronage, treaty, executive agreement.
2. Describe three of the President's major duties that are based upon the Constitution.
3. Enumerate the officials the President may appoint.
4. Explain why the President has the advantage over Congress in the struggle over control of the nation's foreign policy.

Exploring Themes
5. Checks and Balances How did Congress attempt to control the President's use of secret executive agreements in 1950?
6. Constitutional Interpretations Under what circumstances could the War Powers Act become a constitutional issue?

Critical Thinking Skills
7. Drawing Conclusions Why has Congress refused to give the President the power of the item veto?
8. Understanding Cause and Effect Why does Congress usually adjust its view of presidential power in times of national emergency?

Section 4 Review Answers

1. Definitions of terms appear on pages indicated: **executive order,** 462; **impoundment,** 462; **reprieve,** 463; **pardon,** 463; **amnesty,** 463; **item veto,** 464; **patronage,** 464; **treaty,** 466; **executive agreement,** 466
2. as head of state performs ceremonial duties, as chief executive carries out the laws, as chief legislator develops a legislative program, as chief diplomat directs United States foreign policy, as commander in chief directs the armed forces
3. cabinet members, agency directors, deputy directors and their assistants, federal judges, and justices of the Supreme Court
4. The President has access to more information through the CIA, the State Department, the Defense Department, and the National Security Council. Members of Congress do not have ready access to this information, and so find it difficult to challenge the President's decisions.
5. It passed a law requiring all executive agreements signed each year to be made public.
6. if the President refused Congress's demand to withdraw troops from combat
7. Power to veto items within legislation would enable the President to have more influence over the work of Congress, thus diminishing the power of Congress to control legislation.
8. Congress usually gives the President more power in order to respond to the emergency.

The Clintons on Balancing Work and Family Life

With the inauguration of Bill Clinton, a working couple with one child took up residence in the White House. The President gave the First Lady key responsibilities and relied on her for advice. Four months into the first term, Bill and Hillary Rodham Clinton talked with U.S. News and World Report correspondents Kenneth T. Walsh and Matthew Cooper about how they balance their work and family life.

Dividing responsibility for Chelsea.

Mrs. Clinton: Well, she comes over to see us and, on a few occasions, brings her homework. . . .
The president: I do the math.
Mrs. Clinton: Yes, he does the math. That's his domain. And then, depending upon what's going on, we'll check in to see what she needs. . . .We've had girls over for meals and for overnights, and we both try to be there when that happens so that we can meet the parents as they pick them up and drop them off.

On Chelsea's 13th-birthday weekend.

The president: I really liked when she had all those girls over. That was great.
Mrs. Clinton: Of course, they stayed

up all night long. It was wonderful, except we're too old for that anymore.

Advice for working people.

The president: All I can say is that we have really struggled with it, and we've worked at it for 20 years . . . . I think about how hard it is for us just to take time out for each other or take time out for our daughter. And then I think about all these people out there where it's not even an option. Just to stay alive, they have to give up everything that's personal to them. . . .
Mrs. Clinton: I always feel kind of presumptuous to give advice. We lead a life that in many ways is like the lives of other people who are working and raising families, but it obviously is very different. And I think the real heroes of America are those people who struggle against a lot of odds to keep their families together and to support their children in school, send that child out of that door every morning knowing that there's violence in the streets— all kinds of dangers—and try to provide a safe haven for their child even though they have to work. . . .

The White House mailbag.

The president: I'll tell you what I do. I get a representative sample of mail every week, and I sign a fair number of letters that go out every week, real citizens talking about

their problems of what they think. And that's important. I must say one of the most rewarding but frustrating aspects of this—we're getting more mail than any family ever has. We just can't keep up with it. . . .
Mrs. Clinton: It's really distressing, though, because we always answered every letter, felt a real obligation to people who reached out to do that. And it is very distressing to us personally that we have just been deluged. I mean, the good news is that people want to share their thoughts, and there are a lot of very not only heartfelt letters but good ideas coming in from people. The bad news is that we're just incapable right now of getting all that answered.

—FROM "DON'T SACRIFICE YOUR BASIC RELATIONSHIPS," COPYRIGHT © MAY 10, 1993, *U.S. NEWS AND WORLD REPORT*

Examining the Reading

Reviewing Facts
1. Name the person who helps Chelsea with her math homework.
2. Identify the main reason that the White House mailbag is a problem.

Critical Thinking Skills
3. Making Inferences Mrs. Clinton says that her family's life is different from that of other people who are working and raising families. What are some specific differences?

Focus

Ask students to imagine what life would be like if they were either the President or the President's spouse. What things would they like or dislike about the public acclaim and scrutiny? What could one accomplish as the President's spouse?

Teach

How were the Clintons' decisions about Chelsea's education different from those of most parents? *(They had several options of where she would go to school, but had to announce the decision publicly.)* Why might living in the White House be difficult for a young person? *(not having as much privacy, having to consider what other people think of everything you do, having to plan ahead for time together with parents)*

Assess

Have students complete **Examining the Reading.**

Answers
1. President Clinton
2. There is so much mail that Bill and Hillary Clinton cannot answer it all.
3. Answers will vary, but may include that their lives are not as private as other people's, they have more social events, and they spend more money.

Close

Some people resented the position of influence the First Lady had in the White House. Do you believe the President was right in assigning her significant tasks.

More About Personal Perspectives

Hillary Rodham met Bill Clinton at Yale Law School. From the beginning of their marriage she was his most important adviser. Sensitive questions about their marriage that surfaced during the presidential campaign seemed to draw the couple closer together. Because of her education and successful law practice, Hillary brought unusual cre-

dentials to the office of First Lady. Many people had questions or were nervous about Hillary's role, but the President did not hesitate to assign Hillary significant duties. Even before the election she was one of only five people among Bill Clinton's inner circle that reviewed names of candidates for top jobs in the administration.

Identifying Terms and Concepts

1. h, 2. a, 3. f, 4. j, 5. b, 6. d, 7. c, 8. e

Reviewing Facts and Ideas

1. use of *Air Force One* and other transportation, free medical and dental care, use of the White House with a large staff; after retirement: lifetime pension, office space, mailing service, money for office staff, and pension for spouse

2. Parties select moderate candidates because they usually win. Their views are more like those of the majority of people.

3. Any candidate who wins more popular votes in a state than other candidates wins all that state's electoral votes.

4. appointment: appoints heads of executive departments, ambassadors, federal judges and Supreme Court justices; military: commander in chief of armed forces and state militia when they are in federal service, commissions all military officers; legislative: State of the Union message and other messages to Congress, calls Congress into session, ensures that laws are executed; foreign relations: makes treaties, meets with heads of state, ambassadors, and other foreign officials; judicial: may pardon people or reduce a sentence or fine (Some students may include appoints judges.)

5. President prepares an annual budget and an annual economic report to Congress.

6. President helps party members who are running for office, helps to raise funds for the party, selects the national chairperson, and helps plan election strategies.

16
CHAPTER REVIEW

Summary and Significance

The President serves a four-year term and may be elected twice. In addition to constitutional qualifications, a person's experience in government, access to campaign finances, political beliefs, and personal qualities are also important requirements for election. The Founders established the Electoral College as an indirect method of electing the President. Because of dissatisfaction with this method, several reform proposals have been suggested. Although the Constitution grants specific powers to the President, other sources of presidential power include the actions of past Presidents, grants of power from Congress, and the President's use of the mass media. Over the years the trend has been toward increased power in the office of the President. The powers of Congress, the courts, the federal bureaucracy, and public opinion balance presidential powers.

Identifying Terms and Concepts

On a separate sheet of paper choose the letter of the term identified in each statement below.

a. presidential succession   b. electoral vote
c. executive order   d. elector
e. reprieve   f. pardon
g. amnesty   h. item veto
i. treaty   j. executive agreement

1. The power to accept or reject only parts of a congressional bill
2. Specific circumstances under which the Vice President becomes President
3. A release from legal punishment
4. A pact between the President and the head of a foreign government
5. Takes place in December following a presidential election
6. One of the 538 people who meet to cast votes for President and Vice President
7. Presidential decree that has the force of law
8. Postponement of a person's legal punishment

Reviewing Facts and Ideas

1. List four special benefits that the President receives while in office.
2. Discuss reasons that candidates who win the presidency are usually moderate in their political views.
3. Describe how the winner-take-all system of the Electoral College operates.

4. Classify the presidential powers listed in the Constitution as either appointment, military, legislative, foreign relations, or judicial powers.
5. Identify two duties of the President that affect the economy of the nation.
6. Explain the President's role as party leader.

Applying Themes

1. **Civil Rights** How did President Lincoln's actions during the Civil War violate some people's civil rights?
2. **Separation of Powers** Congress has fought for its share of military powers but has surrendered some of its economic powers. What economic events have caused Congress to turn to the President for leadership?
3. **Checks and Balances** How could Congress have prevented President Jefferson from purchasing the Louisiana Territory?
4. **Federalism** Why do some who support federalism criticize plans for the direct popular election of the President?
5. **Constitutional Interpretations** How could an acting President become President?

Critical Thinking Skills

1. **Drawing Conclusions** Candidates for the office of President are not much interested in the salary. Why do you think these people run for the office?

Applying Themes

1. Some people were denied a fair trial or due process of law before they were jailed.

2. During the Depression, Congress expected the President to propose economic solutions. In other times of economic distress, Congress has looked to the President for answers. Today it is usual for the President to present economic programs.

3. Congress could have refused to ratify the treaty or refused to raise the money for the purchase of the Louisiana Territory.

4. Some people believe that direct popular election would eliminate the role of states in electing the President, thus diminishing federalism.

2. **Identifying Alternatives** Rank the proposals for reforming the Electoral College system from most to least desirable. Give reasons for your ranking. Can you think of another alternative?

3. **Determining Relevance** Several Presidents may have wanted to remove J. Edgar Hoover, director of the FBI, but he was too popular to fire. Should the President carefully consider public opinion in making all key decisions? Explain your answer.

4. **Understanding Cause and Effect** Why did President Johnson decide not to run for reelection in 1968?

5. **Distinguishing Fact From Opinion** Dean Acheson, former secretary of state, said that it "takes all of our Presidents a good deal of time to learn about foreign affairs." Is this fact or opinion? What gave Acheson credibility in making such a statement?

Linking Past and Present

Early Presidents were able to oversee all the daily activities of the executive office and still have time for leisurely conversation. Today the President's schedule is packed with meetings, reports, decisions, and ceremonial duties. With all this activity, a President may not have time to keep abreast of the everyday decisions of hundreds of executive agencies and offices. What part, if any, of the President's responsibilities should be delegated to another person or agency?

Writing About Government

Narrative Writing Imagine that you are President. One of your habits is to write a paragraph in your personal diary at the end of the day, summarizing the most important events and decisions. Write the narrative of one such entry and include at least three kinds of activities from among the seven major duties of the President listed at the beginning of Section 4.

Reinforcing the Skill

Writing an Essay Use what you have learned to put the following outline in essay form. The outline

shows how George Washington set the tone of the presidency. Include an introduction and a conclusion in your essay.

I. Washington a lofty and formal, but democratic President
  A. Greatly respected and admired as war hero
    1. Gave Americans confidence in the new government
    2. Encouraged other high-calibre people to accept government positions
  B. Aristocratic background and personal reserve kept people at a distance—never shook hands
  C. Refused to become king
II. Set many precedents that strengthened the presidency
  A. Appointed the first cabinet—group of advisers
  B. Took primary responsibility for foreign policy
  C. Did not leave lawmaking to Congress—proposed his own legislative program

Investigating Further

1. **Individual Project** Make a list of the last six Presidents. Ask 10 different people who are approximately 40 years old or older to rank these Presidents in order of their most to least favorite. Record their rankings, then average your findings to determine the overall first through sixth ranked President.

2. **Cooperative Learning** Organize into four nearly equal groups of students. Each group should choose one of the following time periods:

  a. 1789-1840   b. 1841-1880
  c. 1881-1944   d. 1945-present

The groups should then list the names of the Presidents who served in their time period. Each group member may choose one of the names and research notable quotations and anecdotes about the President. When the group meets again, each member should report his or her findings. The group should then prepare a poster that includes at least 10 of the best quotations. Have group spokespersons share the best anecdotes with the class.

2. Answers will vary, but students should explain reasons for their answers.

3. Answers will vary. Those who support considering public opinion should also emphasize the democratic nature of our government. Those who oppose considering public opinion in key decisions should point out that only the President has enough information in some cases to make a wise judgment.

4. Johnson realized that public opinion had turned against him, and he would not be able to run a strong campaign.

5. opinion; Acheson served in the top office that deals with foreign affairs.

Linking Past and Present

Answers will vary, but may include that the Vice President or First Lady could do most of the ceremonial duties; an appointed official could manage the huge bureaucracy; cabinet officials could be given more decision-making powers.

Writing About Government

Students' paragraphs will vary.

Reinforcing the Skill

Students' essays will vary, but should include an introduction and conclusion.

Investigating Further

1. Students' lists will vary.
2. Groups' posters will vary.

5. Answers will vary, but should include that a President would have to be permanently unable to carry out the duties of the office before Congress would recognize the acting President as the President.

Critical Thinking Skills

1. Answers should consider the power of the office, the sense of duty to serve the nation, the opportunity to affect the course of events, or the mark of success in political life that it represents.

Chapter Organizer

Objectives	Special Feature Pages	Supplemental Materials
Section 1 The Cabinet's Limited Role *pp. 474–479* 1. Explain how the cabinet is selected. 2. Evaluate the role the cabinet plays in advising the President.	Focus on Freedom: Jefferson's Inaugural Address p. 475 Participating in Government: Protecting Our Environment p. 478	Guided Reading Activities Reproducible Lesson Plans Participating in Government 17 Section 1 Quiz Testmaker Government Themes Transparencies 15 SAT Practice Tests Writer's Guidebook
Section 2 The Executive Office of the President *pp. 480–486* 1. Describe the components of the Executive Office of the President. 2. Analyze the duties of the Office of Management and Budget.	Global Connection: Comparing Governments: Presidential Power p. 484 Critical Thinking Skills: Formulating Questions p. 486	Guided Reading Activities Reproducible Lesson Plans Supreme Court Case Studies 42 Cooperative Learning Activities 17 Section 2 Quiz Testmaker Skill Reinforcement Activities 17 SAT Practice Tests Writer's Guidebook
Section 3 Styles of Presidential Leadership *pp. 487–493* 1. Relate the leadership styles of modern Presidents to the qualities of successful leaders. 2. Explain how a President's interactions with close aides, openness to new ideas, and presidential isolation are related.	Images of Government: Busy Days pp. 490–491 Personal Perspectives: Presidents on the Presidency p. 493	Guided Reading Activities Reproducible Lesson Plans Primary and Secondary Source Readings 17 Reteaching Activities 17 Enrichment Activities 17 Section 3 Quiz Chapter 17 Tests Testmaker Chapter Transparencies 17 Audio Cassettes (English and Spanish) Limited English Proficiency Activities 17

If time does not permit teaching this chapter, assign the Chapter 17 summary in the Unit 5 Digest on pages 535–536.

Key To Ability Levels

Teaching strategies have been coded for varying learning styles and abilities.

L1   Level 1 activities are **basic** activities and should be within the ability range of all students.

L2   Level 2 activities are **average** activities and should be within the ability range of the average to above-average student.

L3   Level 3 activities are **challenging** activities designed for the ability range of above-average students.

LEP   These activities should be within the ability range of **Limited English Proficiency** students.

Multicultural Activities

"We have talked long in this country about equal rights . . . . It is time now to write the next chapter—and to write it in the books of law." President Lyndon Johnson made these remarks to Congress in November 1963 as he urged passage of civil rights legislation following the assassination of President John Kennedy. Johnson is given much of the credit for getting such legislation as the Civil Rights Act of 1964 through Congress and into law. With his urging, bills long buried in committee sailed through Congress. His lobbying technique, known as the Johnson Treatment, "rendered the target stunned and helpless" said journalists Evans and Novak. Have students research this period and identify the leadership qualities and skills Johnson used in the fight for civil rights.

Among the minority group members who have served in a President's cabinet in recent years are Ron Brown, Manuel Lujan, Jr., Henry Cisneros, Hazel O'Leary, Samuel Pierce, Jr., and Louis Sullivan. Have students research the constituencies each represented, qualifications each had for the job, party affiliation, department, and administration in which each served. Then ask: Have any served in the departments that make up the inner cabinet? Does a minority cabinet member necessarily represent or share concerns of minorities? What are other avenues of access to the President for minority constituencies? *(interest groups, public opinion, minority congressional representatives)* Should a President's cabinet have a racial or ethnic balance? Why or why not?

Chapter Resources

Readings for the Student

Burns, James MacGregor. *Roosevelt: The Lion and the Fox.* Harcourt, Brace, Jovanovich, 1956.
Larsen, Rebecca. *Richard Nixon: The Rise and Fall of a President.* Franklin Watts, 1991.
Meltzer, Milton. *George Washington and the Birth of Our Nation.* Franklin Watts, 1986.
The Presidency. Jackdaw, 1991.

Readings for the Teacher

Colodny, Len and Robert Gettlin. *Silent Coup: The Removal of a President.* St. Martin's Press, 1991.
Neustadt, Richard E. *Presidential Power and the Modern Presidents: Roosevelt to Reagan.* Free Press, 1990.
Nossiter, Bernard D. *Fat Years and Lean: The American Economy Since Roosevelt.* Harper & Row, 1990.
Phillips, Kevin. *The Politics of Rich and Poor: Wealth and the American Electorate in the Reagan Aftermath.* Random House, 1990.
Shogan, Robert. *The Riddle of Power: Presidential Leadership from Truman to Bush.* Dutton, 1991.
Wicker, Tom. *One of Us: Richard Nixon and the American Dream.* Random House, 1991.

Multimedia

Videocassettes and Films

The Election Held Hostage. (*Frontline* series). Robert Ross. (v/c, 60 minutes)
LBJ: A Remembrance. Charles Guggenheim and WETA. (v/c, 60 minutes)
Nixon. (*The American Experience* series). Elizabeth Dean. (3 v/cs, 180 minutes)
The Real Life of Ronald Reagan. (*Frontline* series). Martin Smith Productions. (v/c, 90 minutes)
Truman and the Uses of Power. Learning Corporation of America. (film, 18 minutes)

Software

Evaluating Presidential Leadership. Focus Media. (Apple disk). Students research the successes and failures of presidential administrations.
The Presidency Series, Disk 2—*Presidential Roles and Uses of Power;* Disk 3—*Organization of the Presidency.* Focus Media. (Apple, TRS80, Commodore, IBM disks—second and third of a 3-part series). Tutorial programs on the executive branch of government.

Presidential Leadership

Introduce

Chapter Overview

Chapter 17 focuses on the departments and agencies created to assist Presidents in carrying out their duties as head of the executive branch.

Section 1 describes how the cabinet is selected and explains the role it plays in advising the President.

Section 2 details the resources that modern Presidents depend on for information and advice.

Section 3 relates the leadership styles of modern Presidents to the qualities of successful leaders.

Chapter 17 Themes

Display transparency 15 from the *Government Themes Transparencies* in the Teacher's Classroom Resources and use the accompanying teaching strategy to discuss how the system of checks and balances both limits and extends the powers of the presidency. Point out that this transparency is one way to illustrate how the theme of *checks and balances* relates to presidential leadership. Then ask students to skim the text to find illustrations that show the relationship between presidential leadership and the other chapter themes: *political processes* and *public policy*.

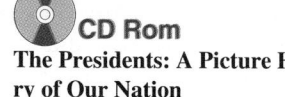

CD Rom

The Presidents: A Picture History of Our Nation
Use this interactive encyclopedia to view clips of presidential events, hear great speeches, research election facts, and more.

CHAPTER
17

President Clinton met with the leaders of seven major industrial nations to discuss aid to Ukraine and global trade agreements in July 1993.

472   Unit 5: The Executive Branch

About the Chapter Opener

Teaching With Illustrations In July 1994 President Clinton toured Europe, attending a weekend summit meeting with the Group of Seven major industrial powers in Naples, Italy. The seven countries agreed to a multibillion-dollar aid package for Ukraine. However, President Clinton was forced to withdraw an initiative aimed at attacking trade barriers not covered under a recently completed global trade agreement (GATT). Ask students how the photograph on pages 472 and 473 reflects the title of this chapter. (*Students might indicate that the President is exercising leadership in foreign affairs.*)

Chapter Preview

Overview

Although the heads of the executive departments traditionally assist the President in making public policy, this function has gradually shifted to the White House staff.

Objectives

After studying this chapter, you should be able to:

1. **Explain** the factors that limit the cabinet's role in presidential decision making.
2. **Describe** the resources for information and advice the President has.
3. **Discuss** the personal characteristics that can influence the decisions a President makes.

Themes in Government

This chapter emphasizes the following government themes:

- **Checks and Balances** Most executive agencies have ties to Congress, but White House advisers are relatively free from congressional control. Sections 1 and 2.
- **Political Processes** Presidential advisers often are motivated by other considerations as well as loyalty to the President. Sections 1 and 3.
- **Public Policy** Policy decisions in the executive branch are increasingly made directly in the White House. Sections 2 and 3.

Critical Thinking Skills

This chapter emphasizes the following critical thinking skills:

- Identifying Alternatives
- Synthesizing Information
- Drawing Conclusions

Setting the Scene In the early days of the United States, several former cabinet members were elected President. In the twentieth century, however, only two Presidents served as cabinet secretaries—William H. Taft, Secretary of War (1904) and Herbert Hoover, Secretary of Commerce (1921). One reason for the decline seems to be that the duties of cabinet secretaries have become increasingly more numerous, complex, and specialized. Cabinet members tend to be seen as specialists rather than as generalists. Further, the increased emphasis on the EOP and the declining importance of the cabinet has made the cabinet a less valuable training ground for future political leaders.

Introducing the Chapter

Tell students that the Constitution makes no provision for a staff for the President. Ask students what kind of help they think they would need if they were elected President and how many people they think they would need to hire. Have students discuss their ideas. You might mention to students that since the 1970s the staff of the White House Office—the President's personal advisers and their assistants—has numbered anywhere from 300 to 600 people. Point out that Chapter 17 discusses the offices and agencies that assist the President in making public policy.

Chapter Project

As students study Chapter 17, have them listen to and/or watch daily news broadcasts and read newspapers and magazines and take notes on the activities of the following: the President's cabinet, the Executive Office of the President, and the White House staff. For each broadcast or article, students should note the name and the office of the person involved, as well as the issue. Students might combine their information in a bulletin-board display to be referred to during chapter study.

Linking Past and Present
The number of cabinet posts in existence today provides an illustration of the expanding leadership role of the President. George Washington had 3 cabinet heads to advise him—Thomas Jefferson (Department of State), Alexander Hamilton (Department of the Treasury), and Henry Knox (Department of War). Edmund Randolph, the Attorney General, did not head a department, though he met with the cabinet. Today, there are 14 executive departments.

Focus

Bell Ringer

While attendance is being taken, ask students to list as many of the 14 positions in the President's cabinet as they can.

Motivating Activity

List students' Bell Ringer responses on the chalkboard. Discuss missing cabinet positions and finalize the list of cabinet posts.

Ask students what they think the job descriptions of the various cabinet positions are.

Vocabulary Precheck

Write the vocabulary terms for this section on the chalkboard. Ask students to use those that they know in sentences. **LEP**

Chart Study Answer
experience in land policy and conservation issues

CONNECTIONS

Political Processes

Eisenhower expressed the politics of filling cabinet posts in describing his search for an interior secretary. It seemed logical to name a westerner, he said, but "the matter was made more complex by differences among several Western states over the amount of water each could take out of a river which flowed across state lines . . . . Any appointee from a state involved in those conflicts . . . would be suspect. Nebraska and Oregon, and possibly Washington and the Dakotas, seemed to be more nearly neutral than others, and it was in them that we looked for a satisfactory individual."

SECTION

1

The Cabinet's Limited Role

The executive branch consists of numerous agencies and commissions and 14 major executive departments. A secretary appointed by the President and approved by the Senate heads each department. These 14 secretaries, the Vice President, and several other top officials make up the **cabinet.** This advisory group helps the President make decisions and set government policy.

Soon after President Washington's election, Congress created a Department of State, a Department of War, a Department of the Treasury, and the Attorney General's office. The President met regularly with his department heads and sought their advice on policy matters. The newspapers of the time called this group Washington's *cabinet,* the general term for the advisers around any head of state. The name stuck.

The Selection of the Cabinet

In selecting their department heads, Presidents must balance a great many political, social, and management considerations. Secretaries should have some credible expertise in the policy areas their departments will manage. Appointees must be acceptable to all groups with political power. They should provide geographic and racial balance. Women should be represented. Patronage and party loyalty also are usually important.

Major Factors in Making Appointments The selection of a President's cabinet is largely a political process. Of course, one consideration is that an appointee have a background that is compatible to the department he or she will head. This qualification

---

14 Presidential Cabinet Positions

- Secretary of State
- Secretary of the Treasury
- Secretary of Defense
- Attorney General
- Secretary of the Interior
- Secretary of Agriculture
- Secretary of Commerce
- Secretary of Labor
- Secretary of Health and Human Services
- Secretary of Housing and Urban Development
- Secretary of Transportation
- Secretary of Energy
- Secretary of Education
- Secretary of Veterans Affairs

 Chart Study
The secretary of the interior controls 34% of all land in the United States. **What kind of experience does a secretary of the interior need?**

---

also can bring some geographic balance to the cabinet. The secretary of the interior, for example, typically is someone from a western state who has experience in land policy and conservation issues. The secretary of housing and urban development (HUD) generally has a big city background. The secretary of agriculture usually is from a farm state.

Equally important is the President's need to satisfy powerful interest groups that have a stake in a depart-

---

SECTION PREVIEW

Objectives
After studying this section, you should be able to:
- Explain how the cabinet is selected.

- Evaluate the role the cabinet plays in advising the President.

Key Terms and Concepts
cabinet, leak, inner cabinet, outer cabinet

Themes in Government
- Checks and Balances
- Political Processes

Critical Thinking Skills
- Identifying Alternatives
- Drawing Conclusions

474 Unit 5: The Executive Branch

Classroom Resources for Section 1

- Guided Reading Activities
- Reproducible Lesson Plans
- Participating in Government 17
- Section 1 Quiz

- Testmaker
- Government Themes Transparencies 15
- SAT Practice Tests
- Writer's Guidebook

ment's policies. The secretary of labor, therefore, generally must be someone acceptable to labor unions. The secretary of commerce is expected to have a good reputation with business and industry. The secretary of the treasury is often a banker or someone with close ties to the financial community.

In addition, it is important that appointees have high-level administrative skills and experience. Cabinet officers are responsible for huge departments that employ thousands of people and spend billions of dollars each year. If inefficiency or scandal should result, blame will fall on the secretary—and on the President.

As women and minority groups have gained political power, Presidents have considered the race, sex, and ethnic background of candidates when making their appointments. In 1966 Lyndon Johnson named the first African American department secretary,

Robert Weaver, to lead HUD. Franklin D. Roosevelt appointed the first woman to the cabinet, Secretary of Labor Frances Perkins, in 1933. Women in the cabinet remained rare until 1975, when President Ford appointed Carla Hills as HUD secretary. Since then, every President's cabinet has included women and African Americans. President Reagan named the first Hispanic, Lauro F. Cavazos, as secretary of education, in 1988. Hispanics have continued to hold cabinet posts in the Bush and Clinton administrations.

Even after people who satisfy all the requirements are selected, obstacles still exist. It is not always easy to convince them to take the positions. Faced with giving up a secure career for a possible short-term appointment, many qualified candidates find the pay, the work, or life in Washington politics to be unattractive. Almost all modern Presidents have been turned down by people they have invited to join their cabinets.

Teach

Guided Practice

L1 Informative Writing Referring to the list of cabinet positions students made for the Bell Ringer activity, organize students into pairs and assign each pair a cabinet position. Have each pair write an imaginary help-wanted ad for its assigned post and a brief résumé for the person hired. Have the pairs present their ads and résumés to the class. Ask the class if important qualifications for any of these posts were overlooked in the ads and résumés.

Focus on Freedom

JEFFERSON'S INAUGURAL ADDRESS

When Thomas Jefferson became the third President of the United States, the nation was divided. The two political factions, as many feared, had become full-blown political parties. Facing his inaugural audience, Jefferson sought to reassure them that good intentions would underlie his policies and actions as President.

Though the will of the majority is in all cases to prevail . . . the minority possess their equal rights, which equal law must protect, and to violate would be oppression. . . . Let us then, fellow citizens, unite with one heart and one mind. . . . Having banished from our land that religious intolerance under which mankind so long bled and suffered, we have yet gained little if we countenance [allow] a political intolerance as despotic, as wicked, and capable of as bitter and bloody persecutions. . . . Every difference of opinion is not a difference of principle. We have called by different names brethren of the same principle. We are all Republicans; we are all Federalists. . . . Sometimes it is said that man cannot be trusted with the government of himself. Can he, then, be trusted with the government of others? Or have we found angels in the forms of kings to govern him? Let history answer this question. . . .

I ask so much confidence only as may give firmness and effect to the legal administration of your affairs. I shall often go wrong through defect of judgment. When right, I shall often be thought wrong by those whose positions will not

command a view of the whole ground. I ask your indulgence for my own errors, which will never be intentional, and your support against the errors of others, who may condemn what they would not if seen in all its parts. . . . My future solicitude [attention] will be to retain the good opinion of those who have bestowed it in advance, to conciliate that of others by doing them all the good in my power, and to be instrumental to the happiness and freedom of all.

—THOMAS JEFFERSON, 1801

Examining the Document

Reviewing Facts
1. Cite the type of intolerance Jefferson fears.
2. Explain what Jefferson means by the questions he asks in his speech.

Critical Thinking Skills
3. Making Inferences What inference can be drawn from Jefferson's statement, "We are all Republicans; we are all Federalists"?

CHAPTER 17: PRESIDENTIAL LEADERSHIP   475

The election of 1800 marked a turning point for the United States. For the first time, the Federalist party was not in power. The growing democratic spirit of the country was reflected in the election of Jefferson, the Democratic-Republican candidate.

Answers

1. intolerance of political differences of opinion
2. He is asking whether humankind is capable of self-rule or if monarchy is the natural form of government.
3. Americans are more united by their commitment to democracy than they are divided by political party differences.

Background

The first cabinet had three departments (state, war, treasury) and an Attorney General and postmaster general. In 1798 the position of secretary of the navy was created, lasting until 1947, when the Department of Defense was formed from the departments of war and navy. The Home Department, formed in 1849, later became the Department of the Interior. The Department of Commerce and Labor, established in 1903, was divided into 2 departments 10 years later. The Department of Health, Education, and Welfare, created in 1953, was divided into Health and Human Services and Education in 1979. The postmaster general was eliminated as a cabinet position in 1971.

L2 **Formulating Questions** Tell students that the President is replacing the secretary of state, secretary of the treasury, secretary of defense, and Attorney General and names of replacements have been leaked. Have students imagine they are reporters. Ask: What *one* question would you ask the candidate for each post to establish his or her competency for the position?

L3 **Role-playing** Discuss the qualities a President should look for in selecting people for cabinet positions. Pair students to role-play the President and a reporter conducting a five-minute interview on the difficulties faced in appointing cabinet members. Interviewers should focus on the variety of factors a President must consider in making such appointments.

Caption Answer
Department of Labor

STUDY GUIDE

Theme Answer
Nominee must appear before Senate committee that oversees the cabinet department.

Critical Thinking Answer
higher salary and assurances that they will play a role in policy-making

CONNECTIONS

Political Processes
In 1989 the Senate rejected John Tower, former chairman of the Senate Armed Services Committee, as Bush's secretary of defense. Although well qualified, Tower's work as a consultant to defense contractors after leaving the Senate raised conflict of interest issues.

Woman's Place Is in the Cabinet
Frances Perkins was the first woman to serve in a President's cabinet. **History** **Which cabinet department was she appointed to head?**

Background of Cabinet Members What kind of person does accept appointment to the cabinet, and why? Almost without exception, cabinet members are college graduates. Many have advanced degrees. Most are leaders in the fields of business, industry, law, science, and education.

Because cabinet secretaries earn $143,800 per year, many cabinet members assume government jobs at a financial sacrifice. Some take their posts out of a deep sense of public service. Typically they move easily in and out of government posts from their positions in private industry or the legal, financial, or educational world.

Nominations and Confirmation The selection process for a new President's cabinet begins long before Inauguration Day. The President-elect draws up a list of candidates after consulting with campaign advisers, congressional leaders, and representatives of interest groups. Key campaign staffers meet with potential candidates to discuss the issues facing the department they may be asked to head. Before making final decisions, members of the President-elect's team may **leak,** or deliberately disclose, some candidates' names to the news media. They do this to test the reaction of Congress, interest groups, and the public.

The Senate holds confirmation hearings on the President's nominees for cabinet posts. The nominee to head each department appears before the Senate committee that oversees the department to answer questions about his or her background and views.

The cabinet is viewed as part of the President's official family. The Senate, therefore, usually cooperates in the appointment process, and most confirmation hearings are routine. Of more than 500 cabinet appointments since George Washington, the Senate has rejected only 9.

The Role of the Cabinet

As individuals, cabinet members are responsible for the executive departments they head. As a group, the cabinet is intended to serve as an advisory body to the President. The extent to which it fulfills this role depends on the use each President makes of the cabinet. For many reasons, most Presidents have been reluctant to give the cabinet a major advisory role.

The cabinet meets when the President calls it together. Meetings may be once a week but usually are much less frequent, depending on how a President uses the cabinet. Meetings take place in the cabinet room of the White House and are usually closed to the public and the press.

The Cabinet in History From the beginning the President in office has defined the cabinet's role in government. Stronger Presidents in particular have paid it little attention. Andrew Jackson depended on a small group of friends for advice. Since they often

STUDY GUIDE

Themes in Government
Checks and Balances President Bush's choice for secretary of defense in 1989 was rejected by the Senate. **What procedure allows for a cabinet nominee to be approved or rejected?**

Critical Thinking Skills
Identifying Alternatives **What steps could be taken to attract reluctant candidates to accept cabinet posts?**

Cooperative Learning Activity

Organize the class into 14 groups. Assign each group a cabinet position. Have group members brainstorm to create several examples of advice or policy recommendations that their cabinet member might make to the President. *(For example: Roadways and railroads need extensive repair to create an efficient system for getting farm products to market.—Transportation)* Students should write their examples on 3″ x 5″ cards along with the name of their cabinet post. Collect each group's cards, shuffle them, and then read the examples aloud and have the class indicate which cabinet member gave the advice.

met in the White House kitchen, the group became known as the "kitchen cabinet."

Some members of Lincoln's cabinet thought he was weak and that they would run the government. They soon learned otherwise. Secretary of State William Seward acknowledged, "The President is the best of us. There is only one vote in the Cabinet, and it belongs to him." Lincoln's treatment of his cabinet illustrates the role it has played through much of American history. Before issuing the Emancipation Proclamation, he called his cabinet together to inform them of his intention to end slavery. He told them:

I have gathered you together to hear what I have written down. I do not wish your advice about the main matter. That I have determined for myself.
—ABRAHAM LINCOLN, 1862

Woodrow Wilson did not involve his cabinet in any major decisions during World War I, nor did Franklin D. Roosevelt during World War II. During the Great Depression, Roosevelt relied on a group of university professors called the "brain trust" and his wife Eleanor.

The Modern Cabinet Several postwar Presidents have attempted to increase the role of the cabinet in decision making. In the end, however, most have given up and turned elsewhere for advice. President Eisenhower drew upon his military experience as commander of Allied forces in World War II and tried to use his cabinet as a general would use his staff officers for briefing and information. He appointed a person to take notes and to circulate an agenda of items to be discussed before each meeting. Yet neither Eisenhower nor his cabinet felt the system worked well. Cabinet officers often were unprepared and discussions drifted. Fewer and fewer meetings were held.

After President Kennedy was assassinated, Lyndon Johnson was anxious to get along with his predecessor's cabinet. He felt he needed them for a smooth transition of power and wanted them to brief him on what was going on in their departments. Soon Johnson, too, was calling on the cabinet less and less. When a meeting occurred, it was generally to give department heads what one presidential assistant called their "marching orders." Johnson's cabinet fared better than Richard Nixon's, however. Some of Nixon's cabinet members did not get to see him for months at a time.

Jimmy Carter began his presidency by announcing that after years of neglect, the cabinet in his administration would have more authority. Yet after two years in office, things had not gone the way Carter planned. In a major shakeup, he fired or accepted the resignations of five cabinet members in one week. At the same time, Carter expanded the authority of his White House staff.

At the start of his presidency, Ronald Reagan also pledged to make greater use of the cabinet. He stated that his department heads would be his "inner circle of advisors." In an attempt to improve its usefulness,

Wielding Influence in the President's Cabinet
In each administration, the power of departments has varied. **Politics** What does the cartoonist imply about Bush's attitude toward the proposed cabinet department?

Independent Practice

L1 Political Processes Assign students various executive departments. Have them research the following information about their assigned department: the name of the department secretary, when the department was established, number of employees, divisions within the department, and its functions. **LEP**

L3 Persuasive Writing Ask students to write an essay in which they discuss the factors that limit the role of the cabinet. Their essays should indicate the factor that they feel is the most crucial in limiting the cabinet's role and include suggestions for changes to make the cabinet a more effective advisory board.

Caption Answer
that environmental policy was not a high priority for Bush

STUDY GUIDE

Theme Answer
The cabinet serves as an advisory body to the President.

Critical Thinking Answer
Modern Presidents have relied more on personal assistants than on their cabinets as advisory bodies.

CONNECTIONS

History
President Lyndon Johnson appointed fellow Texan Ramsey Clark as Attorney General in 1967. Clark's father, Texan Tom Campbell Clark, had served as Attorney General under President Truman 20 years earlier. The Clarks are the only father and son to have held the Attorney General's office.

STUDY GUIDE

Themes in Government
Political Processes Modern Presidents often include the Vice President in cabinet meetings. **What is the main role of the cabinet?**

Critical Thinking Skills
Drawing Conclusions Modern Presidents, without much success, have tried to increase the role of their cabinets in decision making.

Why have modern Presidents failed to use their cabinets effectively?

CHAPTER 17: PRESIDENTIAL LEADERSHIP 477

Special Needs Strategy

Modeling One of the most effective instructional practices for teaching students with reading comprehension problems is *modeling*—having a teacher make the activity of reading explicit. In order to do this, the modeler must read aloud from a section of text and tell the listener exactly what his or her thinking/analysis processes are. Read each sentence aloud in the subsection "Major Factors in Making Appointments," noting that you are reading to find out what Presidents must consider when they make appointments. After each sentence ask aloud, "What did that sentence tell me about how Presidents make appointments?"

L3 Classificatory Writing Ask students to research the role of the cabinet in history and to write an essay that compares it with the role of the modern cabinet. Tell students to illustrate their essays with examples other than those already in the text.

PARTICIPATING IN GOVERNMENT

Share with students an Illinois school's attempt to protect the environment. Concerned parents created the "Environmental Handbook for Parents and Kids" in 1989. The 14-page guide offers tips on what students, parents, and schools can do to protect the environment. Over 10,000 copies have been distributed at $1 a copy. Ask students what ideas they have for protecting the environment at home and at school.

 Have students complete activity 17 in *Participating in Government* in the Teacher's Classroom Resources.

Assess

Check for Understanding

Have students complete Section 1 Review on page 479.

Meeting Objectives

Each section objective is tested by the Section Review questions that follow it in parentheses.
- Explain how the cabinet is selected. (2, 3, 7)
- Evaluate the role the cabinet plays in advising the President. (4, 5, 6, 7, 8)

Evaluate

📁 Section 1 Quiz

🖥 Testmaker

Reagan divided his cabinet into smaller groups. Each group was responsible for a broad policy area such as natural resources or food and agriculture. After only a year in office, however, Reagan began to rely mainly on his White House aides for advice. Once again, the White House formulated policy. Like his predecessors, President Bush attempted to reverse this pattern. Most modern cabinets, however, have been more a sounding board for the President's ideas than the advisory body President Washington envisioned.

The Influence of Cabinet Members Although the advisory role of the cabinet has diminished, during each presidential administration a few cabinet members do influence the President. Sometimes they do so because the President knows and trusts them and values their judgment. President Kennedy depended heavily on his brother, Attorney General Robert Kennedy, for advice not only on Justice Department matters but on other issues as well.

More frequently, however, cabinet members who work closely with the President wield influence because they head departments that are concerned with truly national issues. The secretaries of state, defense, treasury, and the Attorney General fill this role in most administrations. These officials are sometimes called the **inner cabinet.** Other secretaries who head departments that represent narrower interests such as agriculture or veterans affairs form the **outer cabinet.** Generally, they are less influential and have less direct access to the President.

Limiting the Cabinet's Role

Presidents frequently experience difficulty in controlling the executive branch. The reasons for such problems help explain why appointment to the cabinet may be unattractive to many people and why secretaries are replaced during a President's administration. They also help explain why the cabinet no longer plays as important a role in presidential decision making.

Conflicting Loyalties No President commands the complete loyalty of cabinet members. Even though the President appoints them, cabinet officials have three other constituencies that require loyalty: career officials in their own department, members of Congress, and special interest-groups. Each of these

---

PARTICIPATING IN GOVERNMENT

Protecting our Environment

Have you heard the slogan, "Give a hoot, don't pollute?" Perhaps you have seen a bumper sticker warning, "Don't Mess With Texas." Does your state or local government sponsor an "Adopt a Highway" program? These efforts are part of a growing movement to promote awareness of Americans' responsibility to protect the environment. How can you participate in this movement?

Solid waste makes up the most visible form of environmental pollution. The materials people throw away litter roadsides, parks, waterways, and city sidewalks. Efforts to control waste and litter depend on the cooperation of many citizens.

Groups of citizens throughout the country have formed private organizations whose goal is to protect the environment. Such organizations call public attention to pollution problems. They also put pressure on government and industry to act on these problems. Find out about citizens' groups in your community, and volunteer your services.

Investigating Further

Join with other students to initiate an anti-litter campaign in your school. Establish goals and create a program to promote awareness and cooperation. After a specified time period, evaluate the results of your campaign.

Critical Thinking Activity

Drawing Conclusions Have students review the current role of the cabinet. Ask the following questions: What limits the cabinet's effectiveness as an advisory body? What can be done to improve the cabinet's effectiveness in this area? Should the President continue to call upon personal assistants for advice? Why or why not? *(Answers will vary, but should at least point out how the bureaucracy of the cabinet department is a limiting factor.)*

groups has its own stake in the department's programs. Each may push the secretary in directions that are not always in accord with the President's plans and policies.

Internal Disputes Disagreements among secretaries may result from loyalty to their department's programs or to its constituent groups. In addition, competition between secretaries for control of a program may cause conflict in the cabinet. President Reagan's secretary of state, George Shultz, and Secretary of Defense Caspar Weinberger battled to influence the President on arms control and foreign policy for almost two years before Weinberger finally resigned in 1987.

Conflict may also result when a secretary strongly disagrees with a President's action. In 1980 Secretary of State Cyrus Vance resigned in protest when Carter decided upon a military rescue of American hostages held in Iran.

Secrecy and Trust The cabinet's apparent inability to maintain secrecy after discussion of sensitive topics further diminishes its usefulness for most Presidents. Many Presidents have discovered cabinet debates reported in the press.

Presidents, like anyone else, would prefer to discuss tough problems with people they know and trust. Yet, because of all the factors that must be considered when choosing department heads, Presidents generally appoint relative strangers to their cabinets. President Kennedy, for example, had never met his

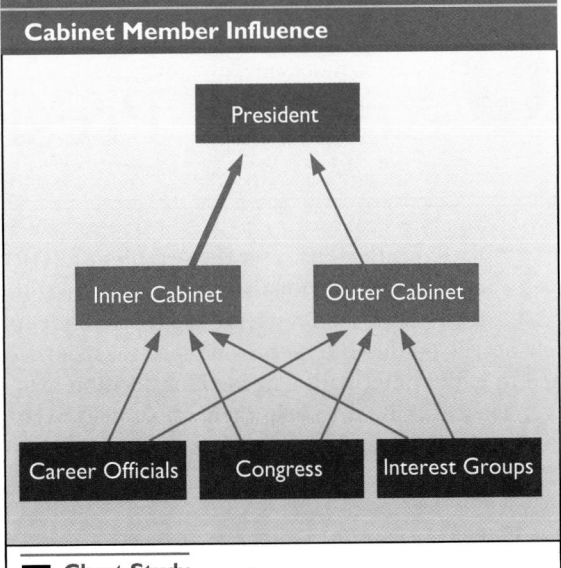

Cabinet Member Influence

President

Inner Cabinet — Outer Cabinet

Career Officials — Congress — Interest Groups

✔ **Chart Study**
Inner and outer cabinet members are influenced by three common factors. **Which cabinet group has a stronger influence on the President?**

secretary of defense and secretary of the treasury before he appointed them.

Thus, most Presidents have discovered that complex problems are best discussed in secret with a few trusted advisers. For these reasons and others they generally have turned away from their cabinets for advice. Instead they have increasingly turned to the Executive Office of the President and to their own personal White House staffs for help.

1
SECTION REVIEW

Section Summary
Although the President's cabinet has grown from 4 to more than 14 members, its role in advising the President has diminished. The multiple loyalties of cabinet members, conflict in the cabinet, and the lack of secrecy have contributed to its decline.

Checking for Understanding
Recalling Facts
1. Define cabinet, leak, inner cabinet, outer cabinet.
2. Cite five factors that Presidents consider when choosing cabinet officers.
3. Explain why prospective cabinet members might not want the job but accept it anyway.
4. List three groups to which a cabinet member must be responsive.

Exploring Themes
5. Checks and Balances Explain how the decline of the cabinet as an advisory body to the President weakens the system of checks and balances.
6. Political Processes Why is it difficult for a President to rely on the cabinet in making key decisions?

Critical Thinking Skills
7. Identifying Alternatives What could a President do when choosing cabinet members to increase their value as advisers?
8. Drawing Conclusions Does conflict in a President's cabinet make it more useful or less useful as an advisory body? Explain.

Section I Review Answers

1. Definitions of terms appear on pages indicated: **cabinet,** 474; **leak,** 476; **inner cabinet,** 478; **outer cabinet,** 478
2. Any five of the following: compatible background; geographic balance; acceptable to interest groups; high-level administrative skills and experience; race, ethnic, and sex balance; party loyalty

3. Appointees may have to make financial sacrifice, may not want to be in political spotlight; but they may accept out of a sense of public service.
4. career officials in their own departments, interest groups, Congress
5. Congress has indirect control over cabinet through its oversight, appropriations, and confirmation powers. Cabinet's decline reduces Congress's ability to influence presidential policy-making.
6. Secretaries have loyalties to many different groups of

people besides the President. Cabinet members find it difficult to maintain secrecy after discussion of sensitive topics. Presidents often appoint people they do not know very well and therefore lack trust in them.
7. Answers should include the politics in the selection process and suggest that personal ties and loyalty be a bigger factor.
8. Answers will vary. Conflict due to personal clashes or departmental jealousies reduces a cabinet's usefulness.

Chart Study Answer
the inner cabinet

Reteach

Ask students to write a newspaper article explaining why the cabinet plays a limited role in assisting the President.

Enrich

Have students write a biographical sketch of one current cabinet member. Have students share their sketches with the class.

Close

Ask students what they consider to be the most serious problem in the United States today. Have them suggest a new cabinet post that should be created to deal with this problem and what qualifications its secretary should have.

CONNECTIONS

Political Processes
Career officials may have worked on department programs for years, so their interests may not match a new President's goals. Yet a cabinet secretary must rely on them for the operation of the department.

Focus

Bell Ringer

While attendance is being taken, ask students to define *executive privilege* and explain why it is used.

Motivating Activity

Discuss students' Bell Ringer answers. Then ask students whether they think a President should be able to use executive privilege when asked to provide Congress with information. How far should executive privilege extend to presidential advisers?

Vocabulary Precheck

Call on a student to read aloud the definitions of the key terms from the Glossary. Then have volunteers use each term in a sentence.
LEP

Teach

Guided Practice

L1 Completing Charts Draw a three-column chart on the chalkboard with the following headings: *Agency, Purpose,* and *Relationship to Cabinet Departments.* Have students complete the chart by providing this information for the three main agencies of the Executive Office of the President—OMB, NSC, and the Council of Economic Advisers. **LEP**

Caption Answer
the Great Depression

Focus on Government
Video 28
**Electronic Field Trip:
The White House**
Running Time: 4:46
Videodisc 2, Chap. 28
VHS Tape 2, Begins 20:14

Video 32
**Making Connections:
The White House Communications Office**
Running Time: 2:53
Videodisc 2, Chap. 32
VHS Tape 2, Begins 32:30

SECTION

2

The Executive Office of the President

The Executive Office of the President (EOP) consists of individuals and agencies that directly assist the President. Modern Presidents rely heavily on the EOP to provide specialized advice and to gather information needed for decision making. They also use it to help them implement presidential decisions and to gain more control over the executive branch.

Executive Office Agencies

Created by President Franklin D. Roosevelt in 1939, the Executive Office of the President is a relatively new body. When Roosevelt took office in 1933 during the Great Depression, he immediately proposed a vast number of federal programs to deal with the country's serious economic problems. As Congress passed one special program after another, the size of the national government began to grow rapidly.

By the mid-1930s, Roosevelt and his few White House assistants felt overwhelmed because they could not coordinate all the new programs and gather all the information the President needed. Consequently, in 1935 Roosevelt appointed the President's Committee on Administrative Management to study the problem. In its report the Committee recommended that a personal staff be "installed in the White House itself, directly accessible to the President." This staff was to assist the President in:

Obtaining quickly and without delay all pertinent information . . . so as to guide him in making responsible decisions, and then when decisions have been made, to assist him in seeing to it that every administrative department and agency affected is promptly informed.

—THE PRESIDENT'S COMMITTEE ON
ADMINISTRATIVE MANAGEMENT, 1937

In response Congress passed the Reorganization Act of 1939 that created the Executive Office of the President. At the same time, Roosevelt moved the Bureau of the Budget out of the Treasury Department into the EOP, where it would be more responsive to his wishes. As another part of the EOP, he established the White House Office which he intended to be a small group of advisers working directly with the President.

Bigger Problems, Bigger Staff
President Kennedy meets with the staff of the National Security Council, October 1962. **History**
What event first created a need for a new EOP?

SECTION PREVIEW

Objectives
After studying this section, you should be able to:
■ Describe the components of the Executive Office of the President.

■ Analyze the duties of the Office of Management and Budget.

Key Terms and Concepts
central clearance, executive privilege

Themes in Government
■ Public Policy
■ Checks and Balances

Critical Thinking Skills
■ Synthesizing Information
■ Identifying Alternatives

480 UNIT 5: THE EXECUTIVE BRANCH

Classroom Resources for Section 2

📁 Guided Reading Activities
📁 Reproducible Lesson Plans
📁 Supreme Court Case Studies 42
📁 Cooperative Learning Activities 17

📁 Section 2 Quiz
💻 Testmaker
SAT Practice Tests
Writer's Guidebook

Organization and Growth Today the EOP consists of the White House Office and several specialized agencies that all report directly to the President. Agency staffs include attorneys, scientists, social scientists, and other highly technical or professional personnel. The EOP currently has more than 1,500 full-time employees, most of whom work in the west wing of the White House or next door in the old Executive Office Building.

The Executive Office of the President has grown rapidly for three reasons. First, every President has reorganized it, adding new agencies or expanding existing ones in response to the problems of the day. For example, after an American-sponsored invasion of Cuba failed in 1961, President Kennedy enlarged the National Security Council staff.

Second, because some problems facing the nation's industrial society are so complex, Presidents have wanted experts readily available to advise them about issues related to those problems. The Council of Economic Advisers was created for this reason.

Third, many of today's huge federal programs require several executive departments and agencies to work together. EOP staff members have been added to help coordinate these efforts and settle disputes. For example, President Bush created the Office of National Drug Control Policy in 1989. This department coordinates the activities of more than 50 federal agencies involved in the war on drugs.

The three oldest agencies in the EOP have played the greatest role in presidential decision making. They are the Office of Management and Budget, the National Security Council, and the Council of Economic Advisers.

The Office of Management and Budget Before 1970 the Office of Management and Budget (OMB) was called the Bureau of the Budget. It is the largest agency in the EOP. Its director, usually a trusted supporter of the President, has become as important as the cabinet secretaries. The OMB prepares the national budget that the President proposes to Congress each year.

The Executive Office of the President

1939	White House Office
	Bureau of the Budget
1991	Office of Management and Budget
	National Security Council
	Council of Economic Advisers
	White House Office
	National Economic Council
	National Science and Technology Council
	Office of United States Trade Representative
	Office of Administration
	Domestic Policy Council
	Office of Environmental Policy
	Council on Environmental Quality
	Office of Science and Technology Policy
	Office of National Drug Control Policy
	Office of the Vice President

Source: Congressional Quarterly's
Washington Information Directory, 1994-1995

✓ **Chart Study**
The number of presidential advisers has grown over the years. **Which agency would advise the President on pollution control?**

Budgets reflect priorities—what is important and what is not. The OMB's budget indicates what programs the federal government will pay for and how much it will spend on them. Thus, the budget is a key way for a President to influence the government's direction and policies. In 1980 Ronald Reagan campaigned on a pledge to reduce the federal government's role in society and trim federal spending. Immediately after taking office, Reagan ordered David Stockman, his budget director, to prepare detailed plans to cut billions of dollars from government programs. Since the Reagan administration, the budget director has taken an active role in shaping national policy.

L2 Political Processes List on the chalkboard the major duties of the White House staff, and have students give specific examples of how the staff carries out these duties:

1. gather information and provide advice to the President about key issues (*Policy specialists provide advice in such areas as foreign affairs, energy problems; political strategists analyze political impact of President's policy decisions; counsel advises on legal issues.*)
2. act as enforcers (*ensure that executive agencies and departments carry out President's directives*)
3. present the President's views to outside world (*hold press conferences, make public statements for the President, advise President on Congress's reaction to White House decisions, lobby lawmakers to support President's programs*)
4. screen information and people that reach President (*read reports and memos from executive departments and agencies, decide who will see the President*)

Then ask students to discuss why the President relies more on the White House staff than on the cabinet.

Chart Study Answer
Council on Environmental Quality

STUDY GUIDE

Themes in Government
Public Policy A recession made President Ford set up a Council on Wage Price Stability. **Besides dealing with problems, what two other reasons have accounted for the rapid growth of the EOP?**

Critical Thinking Skills
Synthesizing Information Why is it important that Presidents rely on experts instead of themselves to solve complex problems?

STUDY GUIDE

Theme Answer
the need for experts and the need for coordination among executive departments and agencies

Critical Thinking Answer
Presidents do not have the time nor the expertise to deal effectively with all complex problems.

Background

At first, both the director and the deputy director of the OMB were appointed by the President without Senate confirmation. A law passed in March 1973 required that future directors and deputy directors of the OMB receive Senate confirmation. One reason for this change was the belief of many members of Congress that administration officials confirmed by the Senate are less protected by executive privilege than officials appointed by the President. For although the case of *United States* v. *Nixon* settled the question of the legality of executive privilege under certain circumstances, suggesting it might well be absolute for national security issues, it left other questions unanswered.

L3 Expressing Opinions Have students discuss the following:

Do you agree or disagree that the Supreme Court by defending the constitutional basis of executive privilege has opened the way for even more secrecy in the White House? Give reasons for your answer.

Independent Practice

L1 Careers Have students use the library's reference department to research some of the careers that are available in the Executive Office of the President and in the White House. Students might choose an area of the administration that interests them and research job opportunities and requirements. For example, students who enjoy math or economics might research the Office of Management and Budget; those who are interested in political science might research the White House Office.

Caption Answer
to reduce the role of government in people's lives

CONNECTIONS

Political Processes
Executive agencies develop strategies for avoiding central clearance. For example, the Department of Agriculture may ask a constituent group, such as a farm organization, to develop and propose legislation, and a senator or representative from a farm state to sponsor it in Congress. Still, central clearance provides a way for the President to maintain some control over the legislative agenda of the executive branch.

Tightening the Financial Belt
David Stockman, President Reagan's budget director, plans to cut government expenditures. **Politics Why did Reagan want to cut federal spending?**

Each year all executive agencies submit their budgets to the OMB for review before they go into the President's budget. OMB officials then recommend to the President where to make cuts in each agency budget. To challenge an OMB recommendation, an agency director must appeal directly to the President or a top adviser. This system gives OMB real and continuing influence over executive agencies.

The OMB also reviews all legislative proposals executive agencies prepare. This review is called **central clearance.** If, for example, the Department of Agriculture drafts a bill on farm price supports, OMB officials will review the bill before it goes to Congress. They make sure it agrees with the President's policy objectives.

The National Security Council Congress created the National Security Council (NSC) in 1947 to advise the President and help coordinate American military and foreign policy. Headed by the President, the council also includes the Vice President, secretary of state, and secretary of defense. Occasionally the President may ask other advisers, such as the CIA director or the chairman of the Joint Chiefs of Staff, to participate in NSC meetings.

A special assistant for national security affairs, commonly called the national security adviser, directs the NSC staff. Perhaps more than most other advisory groups, the importance of the NSC has varied with the President's use of it. Truman did little with the NSC. Eisenhower held frequent NSC meetings, but he relied more on the advice of his

secretary of state, John Foster Dulles, when making key foreign-policy decisions. Under Kennedy the NSC assumed more importance in presidential decision making. Although he did not call many formal NSC meetings, he relied heavily on his national security adviser.

During President Nixon's first term from 1969 to 1973, national security adviser Henry Kissinger and his staff had a great deal of authority. Working closely with Nixon, Kissinger developed the NSC into a kind of alternate State Department in the White House. In 1973 he negotiated the end of the Vietnam War. He negotiated the opening of diplomatic relations with China, an event that then Secretary of State William Rogers did not learn of until he saw the news on television. Kissinger also coordinated arms-control talks with the Soviet Union. Rogers finally resigned.

President Carter experienced similar overlap in the activities of his national security adviser and his secretary of state. The governments of other nations complained about the confusion this situation created and asked whether the NSC or the State Department spoke for the United States in foreign-policy matters.

The NSC traditionally has been free of legislative oversight that Congress gives to the State Department. During the Reagan administration, this independence allowed NSC staff to conduct a secret operation to sell arms to Iran in exchange for the release of United States hostages held in Lebanon. Profits from the arms sales were diverted to Nicaragua to support rebels, called *contras,* who were fighting a socialist government there. The resulting congressional investigation into the Iran-contra affair has decreased the power of the NSC to conduct foreign policy.

The National Economic Council Since the Great Depression, the President has been the nation's chief economic planner. Created in 1946, the Council of Economic Advisers (now the National Economic Council) helps the President formulate the nation's economic policy. It consists of 3 top economists and a staff of about 60 other economists, attorneys, and political scientists. The council assesses the nation's economic health, predicts future economic conditions, and aids other executive agencies involved with economic planning. The council also proposes solutions to specific problems, such as unemployment or inflation. To carry out these functions, it has access to information any federal department gathers having to do with American economic activity.

Cooperative Learning Activity

Have students work in small groups to research the duties of the following positions on the White House staff—the President's chief of staff, deputy chief of staff, White House counsel, and the press secretary. After research has been completed, ask group members to role-play before the class how

each position might have been involved in a critical policy decision.

Have students complete activity 17 in *Cooperative Learning Activities* in the Teacher's Classroom Resources.

Other EOP Agencies The number and size of EOP agencies can vary from administration to administration, according to the policies each President thinks are important. For example, President Johnson set up an Office of Economic Opportunity to help implement his domestic programs. President Nixon, however, opposed some of Johnson's social policies and eliminated the agency.

Recently the EOP consisted of the following executive agencies in addition to the four agencies already noted. The Domestic Policy Council helps the President plan and carry out long-range policies in domestic areas such as farming and energy. The Office of Environmental Policy advises the President on environmental issues and policies. It works closely with the Environmental Protection Agency and the departments of Interior, Agriculture, and Energy. The Office of Science and Technology Policy advises the President on all scientific and technological matters that affect national policies and programs. The National Science and Technology Council advises the President about research and development, including the Space Program. The Office of the United States Trade Representative helps establish United States trade policy and helps negotiate trade agreements with other nations. The Office of Administration provides support services such as data processing and clerical help for the other EOP agencies.

The White House Office

The nation's first Presidents had no personal staff. George Washington hired his nephew at his own expense to be his personal secretary. When James Polk was President from 1845 to 1849, his wife Sarah served as his secretary. During the 1890s both Presidents Cleveland and McKinley personally answered the White House telephone. As late as the 1920s, Herbert Hoover's personal staff consisted of a few secretaries, several administrative assistants, and a cook.

In its 1937 study of the executive branch, the President's Committee on Administrative Management concluded that:

> *The President needs help. His immediate staff assistance is entirely inadequate. He should be given a small number of executive assistants who would be his direct aides in dealing with the managerial agencies and administrative departments.*
> —THE PRESIDENT'S COMMITTEE ON
> ADMINISTRATIVE MANAGEMENT, 1937

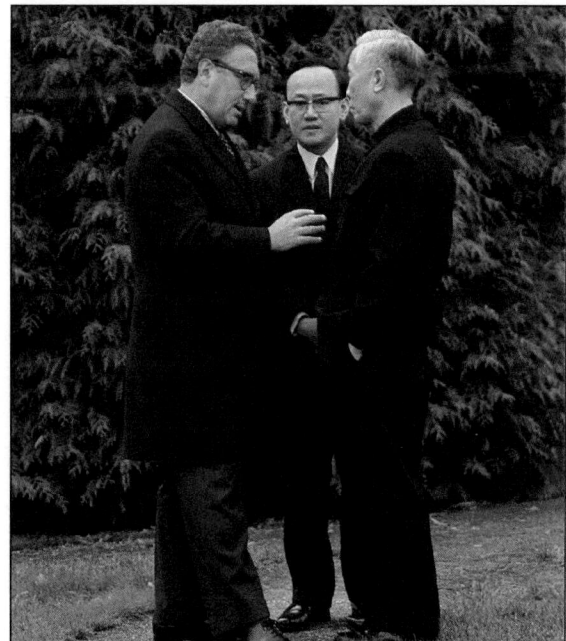

Foreign Relations Expert
Henry Kissinger strongly influenced international affairs during Nixon's first term. **Politics Why were some cabinet members resentful of Kissinger?**

Organization and Growth The President appoints White House staff without Senate confirmation. Key aides usually are longtime personal supporters of the President. Many are newcomers to Washington. They do not usually have large constituencies, as do some cabinet officers.

The White House Office has become the most important part of the Executive Office of the President. From about 50 people under Roosevelt, the White House staff grew to almost 600 under Nixon. Bush's White House Office consisted of about 370 people, a small number of whom reported directly to the President. These top assistants have become an inner circle around the President. Chief among them are the President's chief of staff, deputy chief of staff, White House counsel, and press secretary.

Duties of the White House Staff White House aides perform whatever duties the President assigns them. Some aides become very influential. One former presidential adviser confided to an interviewer, "I had more power over national affairs in a few years in the White House than I could if I spent the rest of my life in the Senate."

One task of the White House Office is to gather information and provide advice about key issues facing

📁 **Analyzing Supreme Court Cases** Assign case 42, *United States* v. *Nixon,* from the *Supreme Court Case Studies* in the Teacher's Classroom Resources.

L2 Informative Writing Have students write an essay discussing how the nation's budget reflects the President's priorities and why the budget is an important way for the President to influence the federal government. Select students to read their essays to the class.

L3 Research Have students research some of the major issues that have been faced by the Office of Management and Budget, the National Security Council, or the Council of Economic Advisers in recent years. Students might present their research in the form of an oral or written report.

Caption Answer
They felt that Kissinger was usurping duties that belonged to them.

CONNECTIONS

Political Processes
During his first two years as President, Jimmy Carter worked without a chief of staff. Instead, Carter had several different aides report to him. This approach, however, proved chaotic and, in part, contributed to his indecisive image and his difficulties with Congress. For the final two years of his administration, Carter returned to the traditional organizational system.

Special Needs Strategy

Reading and Language Disabilities Section 2 requires readers to recognize the resources that modern Presidents have come to depend on for information and advice. Students with reading and language problems may need this task more explicitly defined. Write the word *resources* on the chalkboard, and ask students to look in the section for the agencies and organizations that could be included under this heading. *(Office of Management and Budget, National Security Council, and so on)* Then have students find specific ways in which each group serves as a resource for the President.

GLOBAL CONNECTION

Great Britain is a typical example of the parliamentary system. The monarch is the symbolic head of state, and the prime minister heads the government. A major difference between the American and British systems is that in the United States, the executive can belong to one party and the majority of the legislature can belong to the other. In Britain, the prime minister and his or her government are always chosen from the majority party in Parliament. **Examining the Connection:** Have students share their reports on parliamentary systems.

STUDY GUIDE

Theme Answer
Congress has claimed that its oversight powers give it the right to obtain information from executive branch. Supreme Court rejected Nixon's claim of executive privilege in Watergate cover-up.

Critical Thinking Answer
Answers will vary, but should note that staff members are not liable to congressional oversight, as are federal agencies.

Assess

Check for Understanding

Have students complete Section 2 Review on page 485.

GLOBAL CONNECTION

Comparing Governments

Presidential Power In most presidential systems, the president is both the head of government and the head of state.

In many parliamentary systems, a prime minister is the head of government, and a monarch is the head of state. The prime minister is a member of parliament, functions under its control and is responsible to it.

France combines elements of both systems. The French president is the nation's chief executive, chosen in a nationwide election. The president appoints a prime minister, who directs the administration of government. The prime minister is directly responsible to parliament but is not a member.

Examining the Connection
Find other examples of parliamentary systems and write a brief report on one of the systems.

---

the President. Some staffers are policy specialists in specific areas such as foreign affairs or energy problems. Others are political strategists, mainly concerned with the political impact of policy decisions the President makes. The White House counsel advises the President on the legal consequences of those decisions.

Top staff members also act as enforcers, trying to make sure the executive agencies and departments carry out key directives from the President. Bill Moyers, press secretary to President Johnson, explained, "The job of the White House assistant is to help the President impress his priorities on the Administration."

Key White House staffers present the President's views to the outside world. A press staff headed by the press secretary handles the President's relations

with the White House press corps, sets up press conferences, and issues public statements in the President's name. Other staff people work directly with members of Congress. The chief assistant for legislative affairs, for example, advises the President about possible reactions in Congress to White House decisions. These staff members also lobby the lawmakers to gain support for presidential programs.

The executive departments and agencies write the President thousands of reports and memos. In addition, a steady stream of people from inside and outside the government want to see the President. Key aides decide who and what gets through to the President.

Recent Presidents have given their top White House staff increased authority over actual policy-making. As a result, more and more policy decisions are being made in the White House rather than in federal agencies.

The Use of Executive Privilege

Presidents do not want the information they receive from their advisers to become public knowledge. In order to keep White House discussions and policy-making confidential, modern Presidents have sometimes used executive privilege. **Executive privilege** is the right of the President to refuse to testify before, or provide information to, Congress or a court.

Although the Constitution does not mention executive privilege, the concept rests on the principle of separation of powers. Presidents since George Washington have claimed that executive privilege is implied in the powers granted in Article II. Congress has disputed executive privilege, claiming that its oversight powers give it the right to obtain all necessary information from the executive branch.

Limits of Executive Privilege Presidents have long claimed that executive privilege also protects their communication with other members of the executive branch. They argue that executive privilege is

STUDY GUIDE

Themes in Government
Checks and Balances Executive privilege rests on the principle of separation of powers. **How have**

Congress and the Supreme Court attempted to limit this presidential power?

Critical Thinking Skills
Identifying Alternatives Which should be allowed to make more policy decisions: the White House staff or federal agencies? Explain your answer.

Critical Thinking Activity

Synthesizing Information Review the reasons for the establishment of the Executive Office of the President and the White House Office. Ask how the President is both helped and hindered by their activities, how they derive their powers, and what limits they have. (*Answers will vary, but make sure*

students realize the control the President exercises and the way the President can be controlled by staff members and advisers. The Nixon administration provides a pertinent example of the relationship between the President and staff advisers.)

necessary if they are to get frank opinions and advice from their assistants.

Until recently, neither Congress nor the courts had much need to question members of the White House staff. These presidential aides traditionally had little to do with making policy. The various cabinet departments made key policy decisions, and Congress could call department heads to testify as part of its oversight function. Because more policy-making has been taking place in the Executive Office of the President, however, the constitutionality and limits of executive privilege have become an important question.

Supreme Court Orders Surrender of Tapes
Nixon gave up the Watergate tapes. **Political Processes What was the ruling on executive privilege?**

A Major Court Test In 1974 the Supreme Court issued a major decision on executive privilege. President Nixon had secretly tape-recorded his conversations with key aides about the Watergate cover-up. In *United States* v. *Nixon,* the Court unanimously ruled that the President had to surrender the tapes to the special prosecutor investigating the scandal.

Although the Court rejected Nixon's claim of executive privilege in this case, it ruled that because executive privilege "relates to the effective discharge of a President's powers, it is constitutionally based." The Court held that:

> *A President and those who assist him must be free to explore alternatives in the process of shaping policies and making decisions; and to do so in a way many would be unwilling to express except privately.*
>
> —CHIEF JUSTICE WARREN BURGER, 1974

Reactions to the controversy over executive privilege have been mixed. Some people fear that the Court's decision has made it more difficult for Presidents to get advice. Others argue that by defending the constitutional basis of executive privilege the Court has opened the way for even more secrecy in the White House. They fear that Presidents have a legal basis for hiding misdeeds from Congress. As yet, this fear has not been realized. Although the President's right of executive privilege is legally recognized, the question of how far it extends to presidential advisers remains unanswered.

2 SECTION REVIEW

Section Summary
Congress responded to the growth of federal government programs and responsibilities by creating the Executive Office of the President. This office provides specialized information, advice, and assistance in carrying out programs. The White House Office is closest to and most influential with the President.

Checking for Understanding
Recalling Facts
1. Define central clearance, executive privilege.
2. Explain why Congress created the Executive Office of the President.
3. Summarize the duties of the three most important agencies in the Executive Office of the President.
4. Identify the major tasks the White House Office staff performs.

Exploring Themes
5. Public Policy Explain how the Office of Management and Budget can influence the direction and policies of the entire national government.
6. Checks and Balances How does the appointment process for White House Office staff differ from appointment to other key executive branch positions? Why is this difference important?

Critical Thinking Skills
7. Synthesizing Information How does the influence of key presidential aides affect the checks and balances established by the Constitution?
8. Identifying Alternatives Is it better that the secretary of state or the national security adviser manages sensitive foreign-policy issues? Explain your choice.

Caption Answer
It is constitutionally based.

Meeting Objectives
Each section objective is tested by the Section Review questions that follow it in parentheses.
- Describe the components of the Executive Office of the President. (2, 3, 4, 5, 6, 7, 8)
- Analyze the duties of the Office of Management and Budget. (3, 5)

Evaluate
📁 Section 2 Quiz

⬛ Testmaker

Reteach
Have students make a poster identifying and describing the role of three agencies in the EOP that assist the President.

Enrich
Have students research and write a report about well-known White House staff members such as Bill Moyers, John Ehrlichman, H.R. Haldeman, Donald Regan, and John Sununu.

Close
Have students discuss the pros and cons of subjecting top White House staff members to Senate confirmation.

Section 2 Review Answers

1. Definitions of terms appear on pages indicated: **central clearance,** 482; **executive privilege,** 484
2. Executive's tasks had become too large and complex to be coordinated by President's small staff.
3. OMB—reviews executive agencies' budget proposals, prepares national budget; NSC—coordinates military and foreign policy; Council of Economic Advisers—assesses current and future economic conditions, advises President on economic policies
4. provides advice about key issues facing President, assures that presidential directives are carried out by executive agencies, presents President's views to public, lobbies lawmakers for presidential programs, screens information and people that reach President
5. Through central clearance, OMB can influence agency programs and legislative proposals; budget power gives it influence on programs and policy priorities.
6. White House staff appointments do not need Senate confirmation; President has complete freedom in appointing these closest advisers.
7. Growing power of appointees who lack Senate confirmation reduces Congress's influence over presidential decision making and weakens checks and balances.
8. Answers will vary. Secretary of state is legally charged with that responsibility, but national security adviser can also coordinate with military. Also, national security adviser is privileged and cannot be called to testify before Congress.

Chapter 17: Presidential Leadership **485**

CRITICAL THINKING SKILLS

Focus

Present the following challenge to students: The President of the United States is coming to your school to announce a new education policy aimed at high schools. Write several questions you would ask the President to clarify the policy and its effects. *(Samples: What is the new policy? How does it affect us? When will the new policy take effect?)*

Teach

Have students judge the questions they wrote in the Focus activity against the criteria listed in the Explanation steps. Point out that the importance of the "W" questions change with the topic. Ask: Which questions are important concerning the new candidate? Why? Why are some less important? *(Which are more and less important will vary with the specific situation.)* Discuss the importance of asking specific questions. *(The more direct a question, the more specific the answer.)* Point out that the second level of questions frequently may arise from answers received with the first line of questions.

Assess

Have students complete the **Practice** exercise.

Close

Have students analyze a news article and formulate a list of questions they think the reporter asked prior to writing.

Formulating Questions

Asking questions requires that you first determine the information you need and then compose questions designed to produce this information. The ability to formulate effective questions will save you a lot of effort on research—whether you are shopping for a stereo system or reporting on why the Environmental Protection Agency was formed.

Explanation

To formulate questions, follow these steps:
- Determine what information you need to know.
- Break each type of information into its component parts. Ask: who, what, when, where, and why?
- Compose a question about each particular fact you want to know.
- Keep revising your list as new information becomes available.

News reporters, who are old hands at asking effective questions, follow a simple formula. With every breaking story, they find out the five *Ws*—who, what, where, when, and why? These are not questions, of course, but aids to forming questions.

Suppose that you are a reporter covering the national convention of a major political party. Balloting has been going on for days, because the delegates cannot agree on a presidential candidate. Suddenly a name that you have never heard is placed in nomination and wins a majority vote. The candidate calls a news conference. Reporters are asking one another, what is going on here? Of course, this question is too vague to get the information you need to write your story on this development. You need to find out specific facts about the situation. Using the five *Ws*, you compose a quick list of questions:
- Who is this candidate?
- What are the candidate's political views?
- Where is the candidate from?
- When did the candidate decide to run?
- Why did the party reach this decision?

Remember that the five *Ws* are only aids. All five may not be needed. In this case, for example, who, what, and why are clearly more important to the story than when and where.

Next, break each general question down into more specific questions that will get the information you need. For example, "Who is this candidate?" is still too vague. You want to know specifics: What political experience has the candidate had? What is the candidate's professional background?

"What are the candidate's political views?" also needs to be broken down into questions about the candidate's positions on controversial issues. "Where is the candidate from?" also can be broken down into specific questions: Where was the candidate born? Where does the candidate live now?

Go through this process for each of your five-*W* questions. Then go over your list to make sure that it will obtain all of the facts you want. Add any questions that are needed.

Finally, remember that this is only a preliminary list. Once the news conference begins, the answers you get will suggest new questions. Effective questioning depends on a constant interplay between what you already know and what more you need to know.

Practice

Suppose you have been given an assignment to write a report on the resignation of President Nixon in August 1974. Your five-*W* questions may read as follows:
- Who helped President Nixon make this decision?
- What was the public's reaction to the resignation?
- When did President Nixon reach the decision?
- Where was the Vice President when the decision was announced?
- Why did Nixon decide to resign when he did?

Use what you have learned about formulating effective questions to make a list of more specific questions that you could ask to guide your library research.

Additional Practice

To practice this skill, see **Reinforcing the Skill** on page 495.

Practice Answers

Students' questions will vary, but should emphasize the *who, what,* and *why* aspects of the Critical Thinking Skill.

For additional practice, have students complete activity 17 in *Skill Reinforcement Activities* in the Teacher's Classroom Resources.

Styles of Presidential Leadership

In summer 1981 President Ronald Reagan and his assistants had prepared complex legislation to cut federal taxes. One day the President's secretary of the treasury, Donald Regan, was working out details of the tax bill with key congressional leaders at a White House meeting. At one point the President stopped by to see how things were going. "Would you like to join us?" the secretary asked with a smile. "Heck, no," the President replied, "I'm going to leave this to you experts. I'm not going to get involved in details."

Reagan's response illustrated one aspect of his leadership style. He focused on what his aides called the "big picture." He let others in the cabinet, the EOP, and the White House Office work out the details of the policies he favored. President Carter, Reagan's predecessor, took a very different approach. He spent many hours studying the complex details of policies and often became directly involved with his assistants in handling those details. Both Presidents had the same tools of power available to them. Each chose to use those tools differently in exercising their leadership responsibilities.

When they wrote the Constitution, the Founders anticipated that Congress, not the President, would lead the nation. At best the President was to be the nation's chief administrator and, in time of war, its commander in chief. Instead, over the years the powers and duties of the President have grown steadily. Today the President has the main responsibility for national leadership. Public opinion surveys clearly show that Americans look to the President to exercise strong leadership, to keep the peace, to solve economic and social problems, and generally to get things done.

Sometimes Presidents demonstrate leadership by introducing bold new ideas. President Truman did this in 1948 when he announced strong measures to end discrimination against African Americans. More often, however, Presidents demonstrate leadership by responding to crises, problems, or opportunities as they occur. President Nixon took advantage of tensions between the Soviet Union and China to open diplomatic relations between the People's Republic of China and the United States. President Bush silenced those who questioned his leadership abilities with his handling of the crisis when Iraq invaded Kuwait.

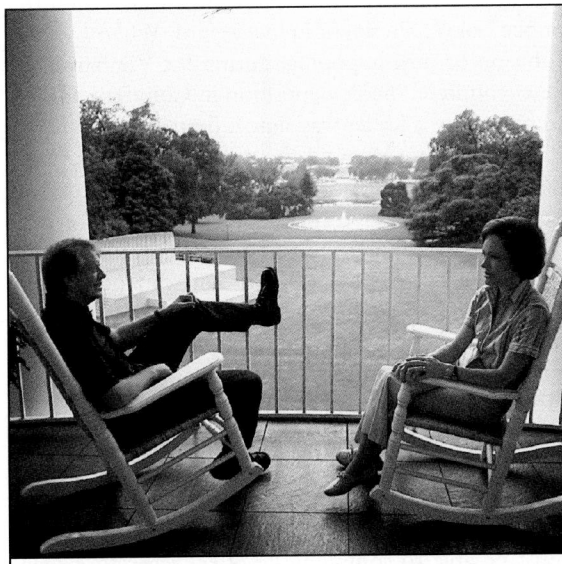

One President's Style
The Carters relax "at home" in the White House.
Politics What style of leadership did President Carter exercise in the area of policy-making?

SECTION PREVIEW

Objectives
After studying this section, you should be able to:
- Relate the leadership styles of modern Presidents to the qualities of successful leaders.

- Explain how a President's interactions with close aides, openness to new ideas, and presidential isolation are related.

Key Terms and Concepts
de facto, covert

Themes in Government
- Political Processes
- Public Policy

Critical Thinking Skills
- Synthesizing Information
- Drawing Conclusions

CHAPTER 17: PRESIDENTIAL LEADERSHIP   **487**

Classroom Resources for Section 3

- 📁 Guided Reading Activities
- 📁 Reproducible Lesson Plans
- 📁 Primary and Secondary Source Readings 17
- 📁 Reteaching Activities 17
- 📁 Enrichment Activities 17
- 📁 Section 3 Quiz

- 📁 Chapter 17 Tests
- 🖥 Testmaker
- 🔧 Chapter Transparencies 17
- 🎧 Audio Cassettes (English and Spanish)
- 📁 Limited English Proficiency Activities 17

Focus

Bell Ringer
Write the following on the chalkboard for students to work on while attendance is being taken:

Name some people you consider leaders and give reasons why you consider them so.

Motivating Activity
Discuss students' Bell Ringer answers. As students give reasons for selecting certain leaders, list their reasons on the chalkboard. Then ask students to determine which qualities are important to a successful President and to explain why. Place a check after the qualities students choose.

Vocabulary Precheck
Ask students to speculate on the meaning of each term and concept. Then have them check their guesses by finding the definitions in the section text. **LEP**

Teach

Guided Practice
L1 Summarizing Using the list developed in the Motivating Activity, work with students to prepare a list that summarizes the most important qualities and skills that are necessary for a President to exercise leadership. Then lead students in a discussion of specific examples from the text that illustrate how former Presidents have demonstrated these qualities.

Caption Answer
Carter spent time studying details and became directly involved in handling policy details.

L2 Synthesizing Information
Discuss with students the ways that people who are elected to leadership positions might become isolated from the ideas of their supporters. Ask how they think it happens in the case of a President.

Caption Answer
He announced measures to end discrimination against African Americans.

STUDY GUIDE

Theme Answer
Franklin D. Roosevelt and Ronald Reagan

Critical Thinking Answer
Such argument allows the President to see all points of view, which can then be addressed when the President's side of the issue is presented to the public.

CONNECTIONS

Media
President Carter's leadership and communications problems were demonstrated in 1977, when he gave four nationally televised speeches intended to build support for his energy conservation program. After these speeches a Gallup Poll found that only 33 percent of Americans believed the energy shortage was an important national problem.

GLENCOE TECHNOLOGY

Focus on Government
Video 30
**Lecture Launcher:
Presidential Leadership**
Running Time: 2:31
Videodisc 2, Chap. 30
VHS Tape 2, Begins 27:16

Video 33
**Speaking Out:
The Character of the Presidency**
Running Time: 1:38
Videodisc 2, Chap. 33
VHS Tape 2, Begins 35:25

Leadership Qualities and Skills

What kinds of qualities and skills do Presidents need to exercise leadership? Although they are inter-related, several specific leadership qualities can be identified. Presidents who display these qualities are likely to make better use of the power available to them than Presidents who do not.

Understanding the Public A President must know and understand the American people. The most successful Presidents have had a genuine feel for the hopes, fears, and moods of the nation they seek to lead. Understanding the people is necessary to gain and hold their support.

Public support, in turn, can give a President real leverage in influencing lawmakers. As a representative body, Congress is very sensitive to the amount of public support a President can generate. When a President is popular, presidential proposals and policies are better received by Congress than when the public holds a President in low regard. When Lyndon Johnson became unpopular during the Vietnam War, he encountered fierce opposition in Congress. His effectiveness as a leader was almost destroyed.

Failure to understand the public mood can bring disaster to a President. In 1932 when the nation was mired in the Great Depression, President Herbert Hoover believed that the public did not want government to take an active role in confronting the nation's economic problems. Actually, with millions out of work, Americans wanted their problems solved by any means, including federal intervention if necessary. Hoover's failure to understand the mood and fears of the people cost him the 1932 election. He lost to Franklin D. Roosevelt in a landslide.

Ability to Communicate Successful Presidents must be able to communicate effectively—to explain their policies clearly and to present their ideas in a way that inspires public support. President Herbert Hoover met infrequently with the press and only answered questions that had been written in advance.

No Buck Passing
President Truman's sign reminded him that all decisions were his responsibility. **History What bold decision did Truman make during his presidency?**

In contrast, Franklin D. Roosevelt was a master at communicating. He held weekly press conferences during which he answered all questions. After one of his "fireside chats" on the radio, he sometimes received as many as 50,000 letters of support a day.

A President who cannot communicate effectively may have difficulty exercising leadership. President Carter, for example, had problems in winning public support for his policies. President Reagan, on the other hand, was a very effective communicator. The press dubbed the former movie actor "the Great Communicator" because of his ability to sell his ideas to the public.

Sense of Timing A successful President must know when the time is right to introduce a new policy or to make a key decision as well as when to delay doing so. During the crisis in the former Soviet Union in the early 1990s, President Bush agreed that American economic aid would help encourage democratic reforms there. He decided to delay acting on this policy, however, until the Soviet political situation was clearer and more stable. On the other hand, when some

STUDY GUIDE

Themes in Government
Political Processes President Carter had difficulty convincing people that the energy shortage

was serious. **Which two Presidents in the twentieth century were recognized as skilled communicators?**

Critical Thinking Skills
Synthesizing Information How can a President's willingness to let a staff argue both sides of an issue help the President to communicate better?

Background

Few Presidents have readily accepted criticism—or even bad news—from their aides. An adviser to Franklin D. Roosevelt, for example, noted that the aides who lasted longest were those who did not challenge the President's thinking. When asked how long someone critical of his ideas would last on

his staff, President Truman snapped, "I would not have him around six minutes." Presidents Nixon, Carter, and Reagan routinely fired advisers who opposed their policies. And President Johnson had an especially bad reputation for bullying his assistants and for only wanting good news from them.

Soviet republics declared independence, Bush was quick to recognize their sovereignty.

Skillful Presidents often use their assistants or cabinet secretaries to test a position on a controversial issue. One way is to deliberately leak information to the press. Another device is to have a cabinet secretary or an aide make a statement about the issue or give a speech about it. If public and congressional responses are favorable, the President then supports the position and may implement the policy. If reaction is unfavorable, the idea may be quietly dropped, or the President may begin a campaign to shape public opinion on the issue.

Openness to New Ideas Good leadership also requires the capacity to be flexible and open to new ideas. As events in Eastern Europe and the Soviet Union demonstrated in the early 1990s, situations can change rapidly in the modern world. Consequently, an effective President must be receptive to new solutions to problems.

Presidents who are flexible are willing to engage in informal give-and-take sessions with their advisers. Presidents Roosevelt and Kennedy liked to hear their staffs argue differing positions on an issue. In contrast, President Reagan did not tolerate serious dissension among his staff.

Ability to Compromise A successful President must be able to compromise. The nature of politics is such that even the President must often be willing to give up something in order to get something in return. Presidents who are successful leaders are able to recognize that sometimes they may have to settle for legislation by Congress, for example, that provides only part of what they want. Presidents who will not compromise risk accomplishing nothing at all.

Perhaps the most tragic example of a President's unwillingness to compromise is the experience of Woodrow Wilson after World War I. President Wilson favored a League of Nations. The League was to be a global organization that would help prevent future wars. Wilson personally attended the peace conference outside Paris to help draft a peace treaty that included the League.

When the treaty came before the Senate for ratification, several senators raised objections to parts of the plan for the League. President Wilson, however, would not even consider compromise. He refused to make any changes in the plan for the League to satisfy the senators' objections. Instead, he began a speaking tour to build public support for his version of the League plan.

The speaking tour ended suddenly and in disaster. The exhausted Wilson suffered a stroke and was paralyzed. By insisting on everything he wanted, Wilson lost everything. The Senate rejected the treaty and the United States never joined the League.

Political Courage A successful leader must have political courage. Sometimes Presidents must go against public opinion in taking actions they believe are vital to the nation's well-being. To be great leaders, Presidents must at times have the courage to make decisions they know will be unpopular with the voters.

President Lincoln made the greatest of such decisions during the Civil War. The early years of the war went very badly for the North. Despite some Union victories, the casualty list was horrendous, and the war's end seemed nowhere in sight. As time passed the war became increasingly unpopular, and the President came under intense public and political pressure to negotiate a peace with the South. Despite his belief that his decision would cause him to be defeated for reelection in 1864, Lincoln decided to continue the war and to preserve the nation.

Presidential Isolation

Information and realistic advice are key ingredients for successful decision making. As Presidents have become more dependent on the White House staff, however, the danger they may become isolated from the information and advice they need has increased.

STUDY GUIDE

Themes in Government
Public Policy Following World War I President Wilson dashed United States involvement in the League of Nations when he refused to let the Senate change any parts of the plan for the League. **Why must a President be willing to compromise?**

Critical Thinking Skills
Drawing Conclusions **Why is political courage often hard for an incumbent President to exercise?**

Cooperative Learning Activity

Organize the class into small groups. Have students in each group "huddle up" and discuss answers to the following questions: What recent acts of the current President are an indication of leadership? Has the President introduced important new ideas? Has the President taken advantage of crises, problems, or opportunities to respond in new ways? After students complete their discussion, have each group make a generalization about the leadership ability of the President. Randomly call on students to report their group's progress.

L3 Debate Have students debate the following point:

A high approval rating by the public indicates that a President is demonstrating good leadership.

(*pro: When a President has a high approval rating, presidential proposals and policies are better received by Congress, therefore enabling the President to exert greater influence on lawmakers; con: Sometimes going against public opinion may be necessary to ensure nation's well-being. Being popular does not necessarily indicate good leadership.*)

Interpreting Visuals Display transparency 17 from the *Chapter Transparencies* in the Teacher's Classroom Resources and use the accompanying teaching strategy and student activity to teach about the power and limits of presidential leadership.

STUDY GUIDE

Theme Answer
Presidents must be willing to give up something to get something in return, even if what they get is only part of what they want.

Critical Thinking Answer
An incumbent President is concerned with reelection; taking politically risky actions might cost votes.

CONNECTIONS

Political Processes
President Nixon often asked his Vice President, Spiro Agnew, to speak on controversial topics. This allowed Nixon to test the reaction without risking the prestige of the presidency.

Independent Practice

L1 Persuasive Writing Have students write newspaper editorials in which they suggest ways that Presidents might avoid becoming isolated from the information and advice they need to become effective leaders. Students should use the information in the section to develop their editorials.

L2 Conducting Opinion Polls Have students refer to newspapers and current-affairs magazines to obtain several samples of polls that rate the President's popularity. Then ask students to design their own poll, using questions about the President's recent actions and decisions. Have students interview classmates, friends, parents, and neighbors to find out the President's current popularity. Students might carry out the interviews over a period of several months. Then have students create a line graph based on the results of the polls, and have them indicate possible reasons for fluctuations in the President's popularity.

Images of Government

To illustrate the President's busy schedule, ask students to list recent meetings, conferences, or events involving the President that they have read about in newspapers or magazines or seen on television.

Answers

1. The chief of staff is principally in charge of managing the President's daily affairs. Other staff members who provide advice include the President's counsel and press secretary.

2. The chief of staff, by and large, controls who gets to meet with the President.

Interaction Between Presidents and Their Staff

Modern Presidents get very special treatment. George Reedy, an adviser to President Johnson, noted:

> The life of the White House is the life of a court. It is a structure designed for one purpose and one purpose only—to serve the material needs and desires of a single man. . . . He is treated with all the reverence due a monarch. . . . No one ever invites him to 'go soak your head' when his demands become petulant and unreasonable.
>
> —GEORGE REEDY, 1967

In such an atmosphere, it is easy for Presidents to see themselves as deserving only praise and to consider their ideas as above criticism.

Presidents may discourage staff members from disagreeing with them or giving them unpleasant advice.

Lincoln once asked his cabinet for advice on a proposal he favored. Every member of the cabinet opposed it—to which Lincoln responded, "Seven nays, one aye; the ayes have it."

No matter how well they know the President as a person, the *office* of President awes almost all staff advisers. A close adviser and friend of President Kennedy put the feeling this way: "I saw no halo, I observed no mystery. And yet I found that my own personal, highly informal relationship with him changed as soon as he entered the Oval Office." An assistant to President Nixon had similar feelings. He explained that even after working closely with Nixon, "I never lost my reverent awe of the President, or the presidency, which for me were synonymous." Such feelings can make it difficult for staff to present unpleasant news or voice criticism, which may mean that the President sometimes receives one-sided views of an issue.

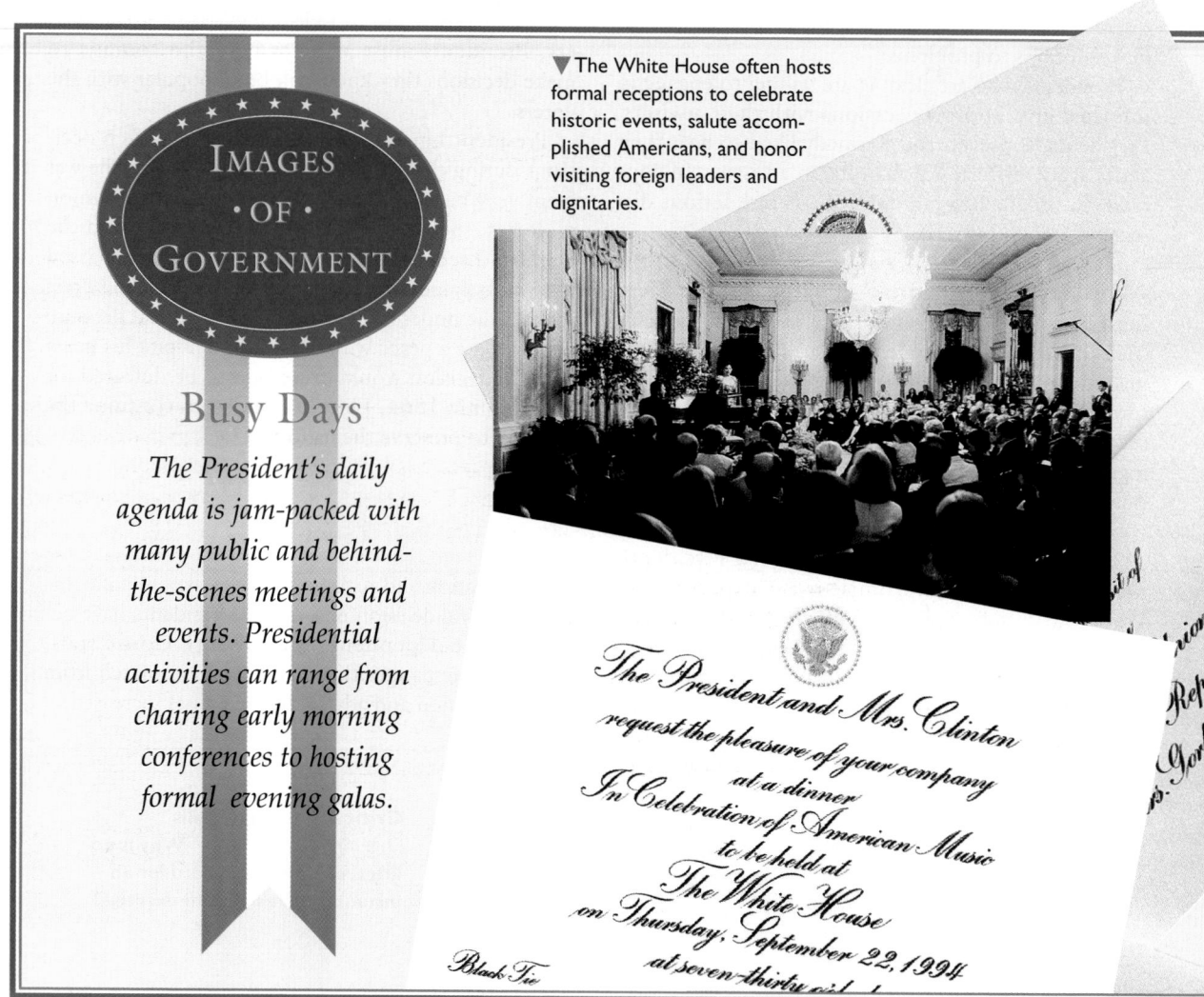

▼The White House often hosts formal receptions to celebrate historic events, salute accomplished Americans, and honor visiting foreign leaders and dignitaries.

IMAGES ·OF· GOVERNMENT

Busy Days

The President's daily agenda is jam-packed with many public and behind-the-scenes meetings and events. Presidential activities can range from chairing early morning conferences to hosting formal evening galas.

The President and Mrs. Clinton request the pleasure of your company at a dinner In Celebration of American Music to be held at The White House on Thursday, September 22, 1994 at seven-thirty o'clock

Black Tie

490 UNIT 5: THE EXECUTIVE BRANCH

Critical Thinking Activity

Synthesizing Information Review with students the qualities needed for effective presidential leadership. Focus on the need for understanding the public and the ability to communicate. Then ask students the following: If you were President, what are some things you could do to keep in touch with the people of the nation? What could you do to build public support for your policies? Discuss students' responses.

Access to the President A veteran political observer once noted that "power in Washington is measured in access to the President." Top members of the White House staff are closer to the President than any other government officials. The surest way not to lose access is to agree with the President, bring the President only good news, or flatter the President.

William Safire, one of the speechwriters for President Nixon, tells a story that shows what can happen to the careless staffer who happens to disagree with the President. Safire once challenged the accuracy of a statement that Nixon had made. When Nixon insisted that he was correct, Safire produced evidence to show that the President was wrong. As a result, Safire recalls, "For three solid months I did not receive a speech assignment from the President, or a phone call, or a memo, or a nod in the hall as he was passing by."

Woodrow Wilson's closest adviser, Colonel Edward House, admitted that he constantly praised his boss. Most aides treat their Presidents in much the same way. As for bad news, one presidential adviser explained that the strategy everyone followed was "to be present either personally or by a proxy piece of paper when 'good news' arrives and to be certain that someone else is present when the news is bad."

The Dangers of Isolation Not only do top staffers have easy access to the President, they also use their closeness to control others' access. Sherman Adams, Eisenhower's chief of staff, had great authority because no messages of any kind would go to Eisenhower without Adams first seeing them. H. R. Haldeman played a similar role for President Nixon. Few people, including most other White House staff members, got to see Nixon without Haldeman's approval.

Interpreting Source Readings Have students complete activity 17 in the *Primary and Secondary Source Readings* in the Teacher's Classroom Resources.

CONNECTIONS

History

After a disagreement over strategy during the Korean War, President Harry S Truman fired the immensely popular General Douglas MacArthur from his position as commander of American troops in Korea. Americans immediately expressed outrage. Truman was booed at public appearances and some members of Congress threatened him with impeachment. Today, however, Truman is applauded for having the political courage to do what he believed was right.

THE WHITE HOUSE
Office of the Press Secretary

▼ The President's schedule frequently includes staff meetings in the Oval Office of the White House and domestic and foreign flights in *Marine One.* ▶

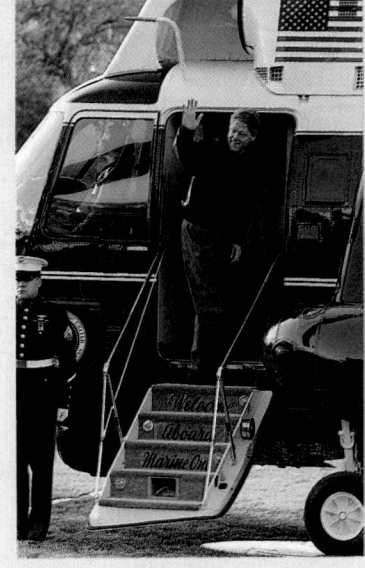

Wednesday, December 7

8:00 am	National Security briefing, Oval Office
8:15 am	Meeting with the Chief of Staff, Oval Office
8:45 am	Meeting with the Vice President, Oval Office
12:45 pm	Address National Policy Conference, Willard Hotel
2:00 pm	Meet with World War II veterans, Blue Room
4:00 pm	Meeting with Secretary of Defense, Oval Office

Questions for Discussion

1. Which presidential staff members help the President manage his daily affairs?

2. How can the White House chief of staff exercise control over an administration?

CHAPTER 17: PRESIDENTIAL LEADERSHIP **491**

Assess

Check for Understanding

Have students complete Section 3 Review on page 492.

Meeting Objectives

Each section objective is tested by the Section Review questions that follow it in parentheses.
- Relate the leadership styles of modern Presidents to the qualities of successful leaders. (2, 3, 6, 8)
- Explain how a President's interactions with close aides, openness to new ideas, and presidential isolation are related. (3, 4, 5, 7)

Special Needs Strategy

Reading Disability Students with reading problems will not always profit from the modeling approach to learning critical thinking skills, which are called for in this and other sections. In the Section Review, students are asked which leadership quality is most important to the success of the presidency. Discuss this in class by having students give a quality and tell its importance. Be sure that all students have a chance to participate. If a student does not participate, try to evoke a response by offering a choice of characteristics and asking which one that student thinks is most important.

Caption Answer

can isolate the President from
needed information and advice

Evaluate

📁 Section 3 Quiz

💾 Testmaker

Reteach

Write the following items on
the chalkboard: *understanding the
public, sources of power, ability to
compromise, cooperating with
White House staff, ability to communicate, courage, secrecy, openness to new ideas, multiple loyalties,
sense of timing.* Have students
summarize how each of these factors affects presidential leadership.

📁 Have students complete
activity 17 in *Reteaching Activities* in the Teacher's Classroom
Resources.

Enrich

📁 Have students complete
activity 17 in *Enrichment Activities* in the Teacher's Classroom
Resources.

Close

Refer students to the quote by
George Reedy on page 490.
Based on this quotation, ask stu-
dents to discuss the ways a mem-
ber of the President's White
House staff might prevent the
President from effectively carry-
ing out his job.

President Nixon Confers with Haldeman
Chief of Staff H. R. Haldeman determined who could
have access to the President. **Politics What are the
disadvantages of such an arrangement?**

President Reagan at first depended heavily on several top advisers. During his second term, however,
his new chief of staff, Donald Regan, severely restricted access to the President. One Reagan staffer called
Regan the **de facto** President, meaning that although
he did not legally hold the office, he exercised power
as though he was President. Like Nixon before
Watergate, President Reagan became increasingly isolated. This isolation may explain why the President
apparently was unaware of the **covert,** or secret,
activities his National Security Council staff in the
Iran-contra affair were conducting.

Perhaps in response to the events of the Nixon and
Reagan presidencies, President Bush reversed the
trend toward consolidating power in the White
House Office. Although most Presidents appoint
their close friends to the White House staff, Bush appointed them to the cabinet instead. As one presidential aide explained, "The cabinet has played a very
important role in all major decisions. [The President]
wants them to be running things—not the White
House staff."

Many observers believed that the leadership
changes that Bush made were positive moves. Close
advisers often tell a President what they think he
wants to hear. Relying more on advice from officials
who were not so close to White House operations
gave the President access to a greater variety of views.

Most political observers caution, however, that despite a President's best intentions, power will inevitably
drift toward the White House. Keeping in direct touch
with the public can be very difficult, if not impossible,
for a modern President. The need for cabinet members
to protect the interests of their departments and the
constituent groups they serve always influences the advice they give.

President Clinton brought plans for major domestic
legislation to Washington in 1993. Dealing with White
House staff problems became a major distraction,
however. The President relied on key staffers for input
in frequent brainstorming sessions that often lasted for
hours. Many sessions were inconclusive, and the President's agenda lost momentum. To increase efficiency
the President found it necessary to reorganize the staff.

3 SECTION REVIEW

Section Summary
Presidents must guard against becoming too isolated.
To use powers effectively, a President must understand the public mood, communicate well, have a
sense of timing, be open to new ideas, be able to compromise, and show political courage.

Checking for Understanding
Recalling Facts
1. Define de facto, covert.
2. List six qualities of presidential leadership.
3. Cite two ways that Presidents test public opinion
   before announcing new policies.
4. Identify the source of power of top White House staff.

Exploring Themes
5. Political Processes Explain how and why close aides
   may isolate a President.
6. Public Policy Why is political courage an important
   part of presidential decision making?

Critical Thinking Skills
7. Synthesizing Information How are a President's interactions with close aides, openness to new ideas,
   and presidential isolation related?
8. Drawing Conclusions Which leadership quality do
   you think is most important to the success of a
   President? Explain why.

Section 3 Review Answers

1. Definitions of terms appear on pages indicated:
de facto, 492; **covert,** 492
2. understanding the public, ability to communicate, sense
of timing, openness to new ideas, ability to compromise,
political courage
3. A presidential aide deliberately leaks information to the
press or makes a statement or gives a speech about an
issue so the President can observe public reaction before
actually announcing the policy.
4. their ready access to the President
5. They can prevent information, ideas, and people from
reaching the President. They may do this to guard or protect
the President. They may do it to make sure that the President does not get news, fearing that they might otherwise
lose access to the President and, hence, the source of their
power.

6. As the nation's leader, the President must be able to go
against public or congressional opinion to take actions that
are in the best interests of the United States.
7. Answers should indicate that Presidents who are feared
by their staffs are inflexible, and those who discourage debate or dissent are likely to become separated from truth
and reality.
8. Answers will vary, but students should defend their
choices.

Presidents on the Presidency

The Presidents of the United States come from a variety of backgrounds. Their ranks include businesspeople, farmers, lawyers, generals, a history professor, and a tailor. Many were wealthy, but some were of modest means. Despite their diversity, they all respected the awesome responsibilities of their office. Some reflected on the burdens of such power.

The presidency of the United States carries with it a responsibility so personal as to be without parallel. . . . No one can make decisions for him. No one can know . . . all the reasons why he does certain things and why he comes to certain conclusions. To be President of the United States is to be lonely, very lonely at times of great decisions.

—HARRY S TRUMAN, 1955

To be President of the United States is to be lonely, very lonely at times of great decisions.

Every problem that you take up has inevitably a terrific meaning for millions of people, so there is no problem that comes up in the Presidency—even some that appear trivial—that is handled as easily as you would handle your own daily living.

—DWIGHT D. EISENHOWER, 1956

Every day, almost every hour, I have to decide very big as well as very lit-tle questions. . . . It has been very wearing, but I have thoroughly enjoyed it, for it is fine to feel one's hand guiding great machinery . . . for the best interests of the nation as a whole.

—THEODORE ROOSEVELT, 1902

I can with truth say that mine is a situation of dignified slavery.

—ANDREW JACKSON, 1829

In addition to reflecting on their duties, Presidents frequently have lamented the isolation "at the top."
One of the things about the presidency is that you're always somewhat apart. You spend a lot of time going by too fast in a car someone else is driving, and seeing people through tinted glass. . . . And so many times [I've] wanted to . . . reach out . . . and connect.

—RONALD REAGAN, 1989

So much is expected . . . that I feel an insuperable [overwhelming] diffidence [insecurity] in my own abilities. I feel, in the execution of the duties of my arduous Office, how much I shall stand in the need of the countenance and aid of every friend to myself . . . and of every lover of good Government.

—GEORGE WASHINGTON, 1789

There's such a difference between those who advise or speak or legis-late, and between the man who must make . . . the policy of the United States. It's much easier to make the speeches than it is to finally make the judgments. . . . If you take the wrong course, and on occasion I have, the President bears the burden. . . . The advisers may move on to new advice.

—JOHN F. KENNEDY, 1962

I am tired of an office where I can do no more good than many others, who would be glad to be employed in it. To myself, personally, it brings nothing but unceasing drudgery and daily loss of friends. . . . My only consolation is in the belief that my fellow citizens at large will give me credit for good intentions.

—THOMAS JEFFERSON, 1807

Examining the Reading

Reviewing Facts
1. Describe **President Theodore Roosevelt's attitude about the presidency.**
2. Compare **the viewpoints of Presidents Jefferson and Kennedy about presidential critics.**
Critical Thinking Skills
3. Making Inferences **Why might a President characterize the presidency as "a situation of dignified slavery"?**

Focus

Have students think of a time in which they had to make an important decision that would affect not only themselves but others. How did they feel?

Teach

Ask: What words suggest Washington was weighted down by the presidency? How does Theodore Roosevelt indicate he enjoys the presidency? Both Truman and Kennedy speak of being alone at the time of great decisions. To what might each of them be referring? In what ways did Washington and Jefferson enlist the help of their fellow citizens?

Assess

Have students complete **Examining the Reading.**
Answers
1. excited about doing great things for the nation
2. Both feel it is easy to criticize the President.
3. The President needs to serve the nation's best interests, but disputes over just what are those best interests severely limit a President's freedom.

Close

Ronald Reagan uses the image of going by too fast in a tinted glass car to suggest the isolation of the President. In what other ways might a President feel, or be, isolated?

CHAPTER 17: PRESIDENTIAL LEADERSHIP **493**

More About Personal Perspectives

Some Presidents have acted in what many observers considered to be an arrogant manner while they served in office. It is therefore surprising to find that not all of them thought they were worthy of the presidency. Warren G. Harding said, "I am a man of limited talents from a small town." Dwight Eisenhower, when criticized for not being a more forceful leader, snapped, "Now look, this idea that all wisdom is in the President, in me, that's baloney . . . no one has a monopoly on the truth."

Identifying Terms and Concepts

Students' sentences will vary.

Reviewing Facts and Ideas

1. Treasury, State, War

2. Key presidential aides screen candidates and make recommendations to the President. The President selects a nominee and sends his or her name to the Senate, which holds hearings during which the nominee, supporters, and opponents testify. After the hearings, the Senate usually confirms the nominee.

3. Many have attempted to increase its role but most ended up depending on it less and less for advice.

4. conflicting loyalties, internal disputes, lack of secrecy and trust

5. The interests of two or more departments' constituent groups may clash in the cabinet. Secretaries may battle for influence with the President. A secretary may strongly oppose an action taken by the President.

6. inner cabinet—heads of departments with truly national scope, such as defense, treasury, state, and justice; outer cabinet—the heads of departments that represent narrower interests, such as labor or commerce.

7. Every President has reorganized it, adding agencies or expanding existing ones as complex new problems arise.

8. OMB, NSC, Council of Economic Advisers, Office of National Drug Control Policy, Office of Policy Development, Council on Environmental Quality, Office of Science and Technology Policy, National Space Council, Office of the United States Trade Representative, Office of Administration, White House Office, Office of the Vice President, National Critical Materials Council

9. prepares President's budget proposals, reviews legislation proposed by executive departments and agencies for compliance with President's policies

---

Summary and Significance

The President's cabinet traditionally consists of the heads of the departments of the executive branch. Although membership in the cabinet has grown over the years, its influence on presidential decision making has declined. Some individual cabinet secretaries are influential, but the Executive Office of the President has assumed the cabinet's role of informing and advising the President. The EOP consists of the White House Office and several other agencies such as the National Security Council and the Office of Management and Budget. The White House Office in particular has become very powerful because its key staff have direct access to the President. Certain leadership qualities, however, can help overcome that obstacle and make a President's administration successful.

Identifying Terms and Concepts

Define each of the following terms and use it in a sentence that is appropriate to its meaning.

central clearance
covert
executive privilege
de facto

Reviewing Facts and Ideas

1. **Name** the three departments in the first cabinet.
2. **Outline** the process by which cabinet members are selected and appointed.
3. **Summarize** how twentieth-century Presidents have treated the cabinet.
4. **Identify** three reasons the cabinet has not functioned well in advising the President.
5. **Cite** reasons for conflict in a President's cabinet.
6. **Differentiate** between the inner cabinet and the outer cabinet.
7. **Explain** why the Executive Office of the President has grown.
8. **List** the agencies of the Executive Office of the President.
9. **Discuss** the two major functions of the Office of Management and Budget.
10. **Describe** the functions of the Council of Economic Advisers.
11. **Trace** changes in the way the National Security Council has been used since its creation.
12. **Name** the four key positions on the White House Office staff.

13. **Describe** how the President uses top White House staff in dealing with other offices in the executive branch.
14. **Explain** why the ability to communicate is important to a President's success.
15. **Analyze** why failing to understand the public's mood can weaken a President's power.
16. **Summarize** how presidential aides usually treat the President.
17. **Generalize** about the way that Presidents treat their staffs.
18. **Describe** how most presidential aides view the office of President.
19. **Identify** reasons a top presidential aide might misuse his or her position.
20. **Explain** how Presidents may become isolated.

Applying Themes

1. **Public Policy** What factors might influence the opinions a cabinet officer holds about policies that affect his or her department?
2. **Checks and Balances** Why has the controversy over the limits of executive privilege become such an important constitutional question?
3. **Political Processes** Why is compromise such a vital ingredient for a successful presidency?

Critical Thinking Skills

1. **Identifying Alternatives** What actions could Congress take to enhance the influence and pres-

---

10. assesses the nation's economic health, predicts future economic conditions, aids agencies involved in economic planning, advises President on economic policy

11. Truman and Eisenhower relied more on their secretaries of state. Its power grew under Kennedy, Nixon, and Carter as they relied heavily on their national security advisers. Under Reagan its staff conducted the Iran-contra operation. As a result, its influence was reduced under Bush and Clinton.

12. chief of staff, deputy chief of staff, White House counsel, press secretary

13. The staff makes sure that the President's directives and priorities are carried out by the executive departments and agencies and screens memos and reports from those offices to the President.

14. A President must be able to present policies

tige of the cabinet as an advisory body to the President?

2. **Synthesizing Information** Will a President who relies on the cabinet for advice be more or less informed than one who depends on close White House advisers? Explain your answer.

3. **Drawing Conclusions** What are the dangers in depending only on the cabinet for advice? Only on presidential aides?

Linking Past and Present

In 1787 some opponents of the Constitution argued that Congress and not the President should fill important positions in the executive branch. Alexander Hamilton defended this presidential power.

> *One man of discernment is better fitted to analyze and estimate the peculiar qualities adapted to particular offices, than a body of men of equal or perhaps even of superior discernment. . . . He will have fewer personal attachments to gratify, than a body of men who may each be supposed to have an equal number; and will so much the less liable to be misled by the sentiments of friendship and of affection. A single well-directed man, by a single understanding, cannot be distracted and warped by that diversity of views, feelings, and interests, which frequently distract and warp the resolutions of a collective body.*
>
> —ALEXANDER HAMILTON,
> THE FEDERALIST, No. 76, 1788

How accurately did Hamilton predict the process by which Presidents choose the key people to help them administer the government?

Writing About Government

Persuasive Writing Suppose that you are the President's chief assistant for legislative affairs. The new President has asked you to write a memo advising whether or not public opinion should be an important factor in making policy decisions on major issues. Compose a memo stating and supporting your position.

Reinforcing the Skill

Formulating Questions Suppose that you are a reporter in the White House press corps. You have just been handed a brief announcement stating that the President has "accepted the resignation of the secretary of state." You know that this could mean that the secretary either was fired or voluntarily resigned for personal or political reasons. Your list of five-*W* questions looks like this:

- Who will be the new secretary of state?
- What did the letter say about the reasons the current secretary is resigning?
- When is the secretary leaving office?
- Where will the secretary be working after leaving office?
- Why did the secretary (really) resign?

Use what you have learned about asking effective questions to break down these general questions into a list of more specific questions that will help you find out what you need to know.

Investigating Further

1. **Individual Project** Much has been written about Watergate and the Nixon presidency and about the Iran-contra affair and the Reagan presidency. In both cases the President's style of leadership became an important issue. Choose one of these scandals and investigate it using materials in your school or local library. Make sure to read both reports published during the events and articles published afterward. Then prepare a report showing how the President's leadership style might have been a factor in the scandal.

2. **Cooperative Learning** Organize into groups of six. Each group should choose a different former President in order to research how well he fulfilled the six qualities of an effective leader. The entire group should then evaluate its President in each area. A spokesperson for the group should summarize its findings for the class. After all summaries are completed, poll the class on which Presidents were least effective and most effective in using presidential power.

CHAPTER 17: PRESIDENTIAL LEADERSHIP **495**

Applying Themes

1. whether the policy will benefit or hurt the department, the effect of the policy on department programs, how the policy will affect the department's constituent groups, the attitude of those groups toward the policy, how the department's career officials feel about the policy

2. because more policy-making has been taking place in the Executive Office of the President

3. To get something from Congress, a President must be ready to give up something in return.

Critical Thinking Skills

1. Answers may suggest ways to weaken the power of the White House staff to make it equal with the cabinet.

2. Answers should suggest that such a President would be exposed to ideas and influences from departments' constituencies, debate among cabinet members, and so on.

3. Answers may suggest that depending only on the cabinet exposes a President to the influence of interest groups and the self-interest of departments. Relying only on aides risks isolation and little open exchange of ideas.

Linking Past and Present

The concerns Hamilton had about Congress appointing department heads have been realized in the highly politicized process by which the President makes selections.

Writing About Government

Student memos will vary.

Reinforcing the Skill

Students' questions will vary.

Investigating Further

1. Reports will vary.

2. Students' summaries should include examples.

clearly and in a way that inspires public support.

15. Such a President may lose public support. Without the leverage of public support, relations with Congress will be difficult and the President's effectiveness diminished.

16. They generally praise the President, refrain from criticism, withhold bad news, and do not voice disagreement.

17. They generally discourage disagreement or criticism.

18. They generally are awed by it.

19. to increase his or her power or to keep from losing it

20. Most information comes through close aides who screen out what they do not want the President to see. Thus the flow of information and ideas to the President is severely limited.

Chapter Organizer

Objectives	Special Feature Pages	Supplemental Materials
Section 1 A Large and Complex Bureaucracy *pp. 498–502* 1. Describe how the federal bureaucracy is organized. 2. Characterize recent trends in government regulations.	Focus on Freedom: Ronald Reagan's First Inaugural p. 499	Guided Reading Activities Reproducible Lesson Plans Interpreting Political Cartoons 16, 17 Primary and Secondary Source Readings 18 Section 1 Quiz Testmaker Chapter Transparencies 18
Special Report: The President's Cabinet *pp. 503–512* 1. List the 14 executive departments of the federal government. 2. Describe the major duties of each of the executive departments.		
Section 2 The Civil Service System *pp. 513–518* 1. Discuss why the civil service system was created. 2. Compare the civil service system and the spoils system.	Multicultural Heritage: Origins of the Civil Service System p. 515 Global Connection: Comparing Governments: Filling Government Jobs p. 517	Guided Reading Activities Reproducible Lesson Plans Section 2 Quiz Testmaker SAT Practice Tests Writer's Guidebook
Section 3 The Bureaucracy and Public-Policy Decisions *pp. 519–524* 1. Describe how the federal bureaucracy influences public policy. 2. Explain why the federal bureaucracy's role in public policy has grown.	Participating in Government: Petitioning to Put an Issue on the Ballot p. 521 Critical Thinking Skills: Identifying Assumptions p. 524	Guided Reading Activities Reproducible Lesson Plans Participating in Government 18 Enrichment Activities 18 Section 3 Quiz Testmaker Government Themes Transparencies 47 Skill Reinforcement Activities 18 SAT Practice Tests Writer's Guidebook
Section 4 Influences on Bureaucratic Decision Making *pp. 525–529* 1. Describe how Congress influences the decisions of federal agencies. 2. Discuss the impact of the federal courts on agency decision making. 3. Explain how client groups influence public policy.	Personal Perspectives: Loret Miller Ruppe on a Successful Government Agency p. 529 Case Study: Expanding Presidential Powers pp. 532–534 Unit 5 Digest pp. 535–536	Guided Reading Activities Reproducible Lesson Plans Reteaching Activities 18 Section 4 Quiz Chapter 18 Tests Testmaker Audio Cassettes (English and Spanish) Limited English Proficiency Activities 18 Unit Digest Transparencies, Unit 5 Participating in Government, Unit 5 SAT Practice Tests Writer's Guidebook

If time does not permit teaching this chapter, assign the Chapter 18 summary in the Unit 5 Digest on pages 535–536.

Key To Ability Levels

Teaching strategies have been coded for varying learning styles and abilities.

L1   Level 1 activities are **basic** activities and should be within the ability range of all students.

L2   Level 2 activities are **average** activities and should be within the ability range of the average to above-average student.

L3   Level 3 activities are **challenging** activities designed for the ability range of above-average students.

LEP   These activities should be within the ability range of **Limited English Proficiency** students.

Multicultural Activities

Several agencies within the federal bureaucracy are concerned specifically with minority rights. The Equal Employment Opportunity Commission (EEOC) investigates workers' charges of discrimination by private companies or federal agencies because of race, color, religion, national origin, age, or sex. The Civil Rights Commission examines a broad range of minority rights issues such as voting rights, housing, employment, and administration of justice. Have students investigate and write a report on the organization, aims, and activities of each agency.

The financial and human resources of federal regulatory agencies depend on the federal budget. When federal revenues increase, most agencies add staff and expand their services. When budgets are tight, the agencies often face cutbacks. During the last part of the Reagan administration, the President and Congress wrestled with budget deficits. As a result, some agencies lost revenue and personnel. Among these were several agencies that are charged with investigating discrimination. The EEOC's budget was cut by 7 to 8 percent in 1988 and 1989. The Office of Federal Contract Compliance Programs lost nearly one-third of its employees, and the Civil Rights Division of the Justice Department suffered severe staff cuts. Have students speculate on the effect these cutbacks may have had on the ability of agencies charged with investigating discrimination to perform their regulatory duties. What more far-reaching effects could such cutbacks have?

Chapter Resources

Readings for the Student

Koop, C. Everett. *Koop: The Memoirs of America's Family Doctor.* Random House, 1991.

Lucas, Scott. *The FDA.* Celestial Arts, 1978.

Peters, Charles. *How Washington Really Works.* Addison-Wesley, 1980.

Williams, J.D. *Public Administration: The People's Business.* Little, Brown, 1980.

Readings for the Teacher

Crenson, Matthew A. *The Federal Machine: Beginnings of Bureaucracy in Jacksonian America.* Johns Hopkins, 1975.

Kerwin, Cornelius M. *Rulemaking, How Government Agencies Write Law and Make Policy.* Congressional Quarterly, 1994.

Nachmias, David and David H. Rosenbloom. *Bureaucratic Government, USA.* St. Martin's Press, 1980.

Rourke, Francis E. *Bureaucratic Power in National Politics.* Little, Brown, 1978.

Seidman, Harold. *Politics, Positions, and Power: The Dynamics of Federal Organization.* Oxford University Press, 1980.

Multimedia

Videocassettes and Films

From Where I Sit. United States National Audio-Visual Center. (film, 27 minutes)

The Regulators: Our Invisible Government. Learning Corporation of America. (film, 50 minutes)

The Regulatory Agencies. New York Times/Teaching Resources Film. (v/c, 15 minutes)

Software

The Presidency Series, Disk 3—*Organization of the Presidency.* Focus Media. (Apple, TRS80, Commodore, IBM disks—third of a 3-part series). Tutorial programs on the executive branch of government. Disk 3 examines the development of the cabinet and the executive office over time.

Decisions, Decisions: The Environment, simulation, 512E, 1MB, 3.5" disk drive, printer, Education Products Information Exchange Institute, Hampton Bays, New York, 11946.

The Federal Bureaucracy

Introduce

Chapter Overview

Chapter 18 deals with the organization of the federal bureaucracy and the role of this "fourth branch" of government in the making of public policy.

Section 1 focuses on the characteristics of the federal bureaucracy and explains the organization of cabinet departments, executive agencies, and regulatory commissions.

Section 2 discusses the development of the civil service system and describes civil service today.

Section 3 describes the role of the federal bureaucracy in lawmaking, settling disputes, providing advice to decision makers, responding to international crises, attacking economic problems, and responding to citizen's demands.

Section 4 explains how the President, Congress, courts, client groups, and the interaction of executive agencies influence bureaucratic decision making.

Chapter 18 Themes

Write the chapter themes on the chalkboard for students as a preview of the chapter content. Ask students to hypothesize about what topics may be covered in the chapter, based on the themes. Write their ideas on the chalkboard under each theme. Keep the list for the Section 4 Close activity.

CHAPTER 18

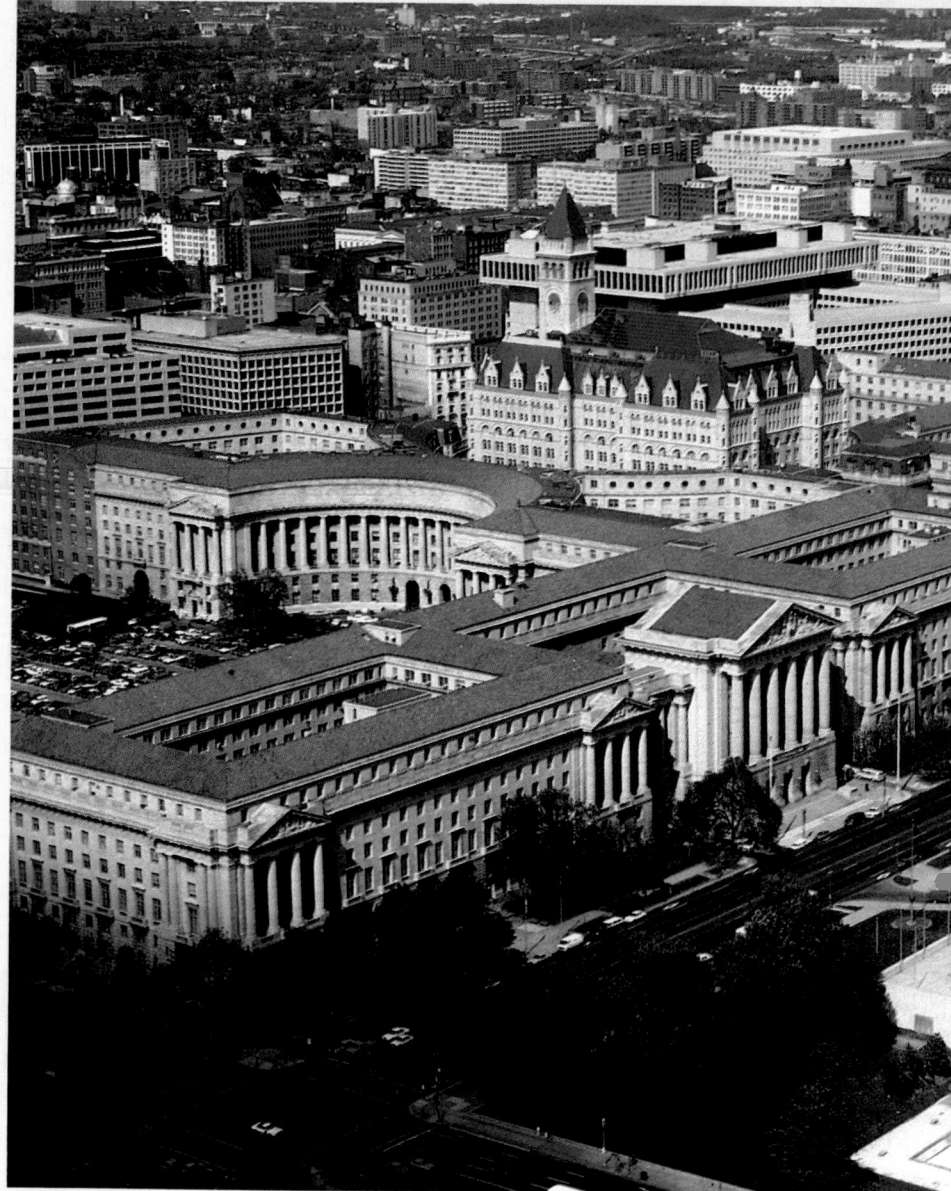

Washington, D.C., is the headquarters of hundreds of agencies and millions of employees that make up the federal bureaucracy.

About the Chapter Opener

Teaching With Illustrations Have students read the caption and examine the photograph on pages 496 and 497. Refer students to the title of Chapter 18 and to the Overview on page 497. Ask students how the photograph reflects the information in the Overview. *(Answers will vary. However, students might mention that the vast size of the headquarters of the federal agencies shown in the photograph is an indication that the federal bureaucracy is large and complex.)*

Chapter Preview

Overview

The federal bureaucracy is large, complex, and key in making major decisions about public policy.

Objectives

After studying this chapter, you should be able to:

1. **Understand** the characteristics and organization of the federal bureaucracy.
2. **Explain** how and why the civil service system was created.
3. **Describe** the role of the federal bureaucracy in making public policy.
4. **Discuss** the influences on bureaucratic decision making.

Themes in Government

This chapter emphasizes the following government themes:

- **Political Processes** A large bureaucracy has many rules, regulations, and processes that must be followed. Sections 1, 2, 3, and 4.
- **Checks and Balances** A sharing and monitoring of power is necessary in a large bureaucracy. Sections 1, 2, and 4.
- **Public Policy** A bureaucracy is heavily involved in making policy in a democratic society. Section 3.

Critical Thinking Skills

This chapter emphasizes the following critical thinking skills:

- Making Inferences
- Drawing Conclusions
- Synthesizing Information

CHAPTER 18: THE FEDERAL BUREAUCRACY **497**

Introducing the Chapter

Ask students how many people they think work for the federal government. *(Students who guessed around 3 million would be correct.)* Ask students to speculate what functions employees of the executive branch might perform. Point out that the employees of the departments, agencies, and commissions of the executive branch are part of the federal bureaucracy. Tell students that Chapter 18 discusses the organization of the federal bureaucracy and how it impacts the making of public policy.

Chapter Project

As students study Chapter 18, have them obtain articles from newspapers and newsmagazines about the departments, independent agencies, and regulatory commissions in the federal bureaucracy. For each article they find, have them highlight with a felt-tip marker the information that relates to a public policy. Then have them summarize the relationship in a paragraph.

Linking Past and Present

The Postal Service is one of the largest government corporations. The first postal service job in the colonies was held jointly by Benjamin Franklin and William Hunter. They had been appointed in 1753 by the British Crown to serve as Deputy Postmasters General of the colonies. Although the king fired Franklin for his political activities, Franklin got the job back after the Revolution and became the first U.S. Postmaster General. Today, the U.S. Postal Service employs approximately 740,000 people to handle over 150 billion pieces of mail every year.

Setting the Scene The federal bureaucracy contains over 60 independent agencies that are not part of any executive department. These independent agencies were established for a number of reasons. For some, their roles simply do not fit into existing departments. Others, such as the General Services Administration, perform services for the entire government. Some agencies were made independent so that Congress could exercise greater control over them. A few, like the Nuclear Regulatory Commission, for example, were organized in this manner to protect them from partisan politics.

A Large and Complex Bureaucracy

Focus

Bell Ringer

Write the following on the chalkboard for students to complete:

Identify someone you know who works for the government, indicate the level of government at which the person works, and describe what he or she does.

Motivating Activity

Discuss students' Bell Ringer answers, list them on the chalkboard, and categorize them by level of government. Ask whether all the people who work in these positions are *bureaucrats.* Discuss the negative images this term evokes and why. Then have a volunteer define the term *bureaucracy.* Tell students that this section explains the organization of the federal bureaucracy.

Vocabulary Precheck

Call on volunteers to tell what each key term and concept means. Have students check the accuracy of their definitions in the Glossary. **LEP**

Caption Answer

It occupied more buildings in Washington, D.C., and the tasks it performed became more varied.

Teach

Guided Practice

L1 Classifying Information
Write the following three headings on the chalkboard: *Cabinet Departments, Independent Executive Agencies, Regulatory Commissions.* For each heading, have students give three examples and a brief description of their functions. **LEP**

The federal bureaucracy is made up of departments and agencies that do the work of the federal government. Most of these departments and agencies are part of the executive branch. The people who work for these organizations are **civil servants** or **bureaucrats.**

The federal bureaucracy is organized into departments, agencies, boards, commissions, corporations, and advisory committees. Most of these organizations are responsible to the President, although some of them report to Congress. Acts of Congress created almost all of them.

Bureaucracy Abroad
Embassies are part of the bureaucracy. **History As the bureaucracy grew, how did it change?**

The Constitution provides indirectly for the bureaucracy. Article II states that:

He [the President] may require the Opinion, in writing, of the principal Officer in each of the executive Departments, upon any subject relating to the Duties of their respective Offices, . . .
—ARTICLE II, SECTION 2

Article II also gives the President the power to appoint the heads of those departments.

Thus, the Founders anticipated the need for creating federal agencies that would carry on the day-to-day business of government. However, they would probably be shocked by the size the federal bureaucracy has grown to today.

In the early years of the Republic, the federal bureaucracy was quite small. When Jefferson became President in 1801, the federal government employed only 2,120 people. These employees were mainly Indian commissioners, postmasters, customs collectors, tax collectors, marshalls, and clerks.

Today, more than 3 million civilians work for the federal government. In contrast, General Motors, the largest corporation in the United States recently had about 400,000 employees.

In President Jackson's time in 1832, federal workers were based in 4 buildings near the White House. Today, federal agencies are located in about 442,000 buildings scattered across the nation and the world. The forms and paperwork these agencies generate each year would fill 11 buildings as tall as the Washington Monument. Federal workers administer more than 1,000 different aid programs. In a recent year, these workers issued almost 772 million checks.

SECTION PREVIEW

Objectives
After studying this section, you should be able to:
- Describe how the federal bureaucracy is organized.
- Characterize recent trends in government regulations.

Key Terms and Concepts
civil servant, bureaucrat, government corporation, deregulate

Themes in Government
- Political Processes
- Checks and Balances

Critical Thinking Skills
- Making Inferences
- Drawing Conclusions

Classroom Resources for Section 1

- Guided Reading Activities
- Reproducible Lesson Plans
- Interpreting Political Cartoons 16, 17
- Primary and Secondary Source Readings 18
- Section 1 Quiz

- Testmaker
- Chapter Transparencies 18
- SAT Practice Tests
- Writer's Guidebook

The Cabinet Departments

The 14 cabinet departments are a major part of the federal bureaucracy. One of President Washington's first acts in 1789 was to ask Congress to create the Departments of Treasury, State, and War, and the office of Attorney General. The Department of State was to handle foreign relations. The Department of the Treasury was to take care of money matters. The Department of War was to oversee military affairs. Today the Attorney General is the head of the Department of Justice. The Attorney General handles legal matters. Since 1789, 10 additional departments have been created. These departments include the Department of Energy and the Department of Education among others.

A secretary who is a member of the President's cabinet heads each of the departments in the executive branch. Departments usually have a second in command called the deputy secretary or under secretary. In addition, departments have assistant secretaries. The President appoints all these officials.

The next level under these top officials includes the directors of the major units that make up the cabinet department, along with their assistants. These units have various names including bureau, agency,

---

Focus on Freedom

RONALD REAGAN'S FIRST INAUGURAL

Ronald Reagan became the fortieth President of the United States on January 20, 1981. In his inaugural address, Reagan reiterated certain points that he had made throughout his campaign—such as the dangerous economic condition of the country and the need to reduce the federal bureaucracy.

In this present crisis, government is not the solution to our problem; government is the problem. From time to time we've been tempted to believe that society has become too complex to be managed by self-rule, that government by an elite group is superior to government for, by, and of the people. Well, if no one among us is capable of governing himself, then who among us has the capacity to govern someone else? All of us together, in and out of government, must bear the burden. . . .

So, as we begin, let us take inventory. We are a nation that has a government—not the other way around. And this makes us special among the nations of the Earth. Our government has no power except that granted it by the people. It is time to check and reverse the growth of government, which shows signs of having grown beyond the consent of the governed.

It is my intention to curb the size and influence of the Federal establishment and to demand recognition of the distinction between the powers granted to the Federal Government and those reserved to the States or to the people. All of us need to be reminded that the Federal Government did not create the States; the States created the Federal Government.

Now, so there will be no misunderstanding, it's not my intention to do away with government. It is rather to make it work—work with us, not over us; to stand by our side, not ride on our back. Government can and must provide opportunity, not smother it; foster productivity, not stifle it.

In the days ahead . . . steps will be taken aimed at restoring the balance between the various levels of government. Progress may be slow, measured in inches and feet, not miles, but we will progress. It is time to reawaken this industrial giant, to get government back within its means, and to lighten our punitive tax burden. And these will be our first priorities, and on these principles there will be no compromise.

—RONALD REAGAN, JANUARY 20, 1981

Examining the Document

Reviewing Facts
1. Point out how Reagan believes the United States is different from other nations.
2. Describe the role Reagan believes government should have.

Critical Thinking Skills
3. Identifying Central Issues What do you think the proper role of the federal government should be?

CHAPTER 18: THE FEDERAL BUREAUCRACY **499**

Focus on Freedom

Point out to students that Americans most attracted to Reagan's approach were those who believed that government should withdraw from most areas of American life. They believed that business should be freed from government restraint so it could become more profitable and thus strengthen the country. Because this philosophy was similar to the conservative government philosophy in the 1920s, it was called *neoconservatism*, or "new" conservatism.

Answers

1. The people rule the government, not the other way around.
2. Government should work with the people, not rule over them.
3. Answers may include that government should be a tool and not a ruler, or that deregulation may not always bring positive results.

L2 Formulating Questions
Have each student write five questions about cabinet departments, independent agencies, and regulatory commissions on one side of half sheets of paper and answers on the other side. Then play a "Jeopardy"-style game with the class in which you present the answers and students provide the questions.

Linking Past and Present
The Internal Revenue Service is part of the Department of the Treasury. It was created in 1862 to collect the country's first income tax to provide the money needed for the Civil War effort.

Background

The power of the executive branch is far-reaching, affecting various aspects of the lives of Americans. The quality of food is controlled by the Department of Agriculture. Air and water purity is monitored by the Environmental Protection Agency. Money is printed by the Bureau of Engraving and Printing, part of the Treasury Department. The Federal Communications Commission regulates the television, radio, and telephone industries. For example, it sets aside certain radio frequencies for special uses, such as police communications. The FCC also enforces laws such as the one passed by Congress banning cigarette commercials on television broadcasts.

Chart Study Answer
serves as a second in command

Interpreting Visuals Display transparency 18 from the *Chapter Transparencies* in the Teacher's Classroom Resources and use the accompanying teaching strategy and student activity to teach the federal bureaucracy.

Independent Practice

L1 Constructing a Graph Have students develop line graphs to show the increase in the number of employees in the executive branch of government from 1900 to the present. Students might consult *Statistical Abstracts of the United States* and *Historical Statistics of the United States.* **LEP**

STUDY GUIDE

Theme Answer
Because it is a unit of the Department of Transportation, a cabinet department in the executive branch, the FAA reports to the President.

Critical Thinking Answers
that cabinet departments are large, specialized, and complex

No, many have gone out of business. Yes, remaining airlines can compete for routes and set their own fares.

CONNECTIONS

Language
The last paragraph of the CIA Credo reads: "We get our inspiration and commitment to excellence from the inscription in our foyer: 'And Ye shall know the truth and the truth shall make you free.'"

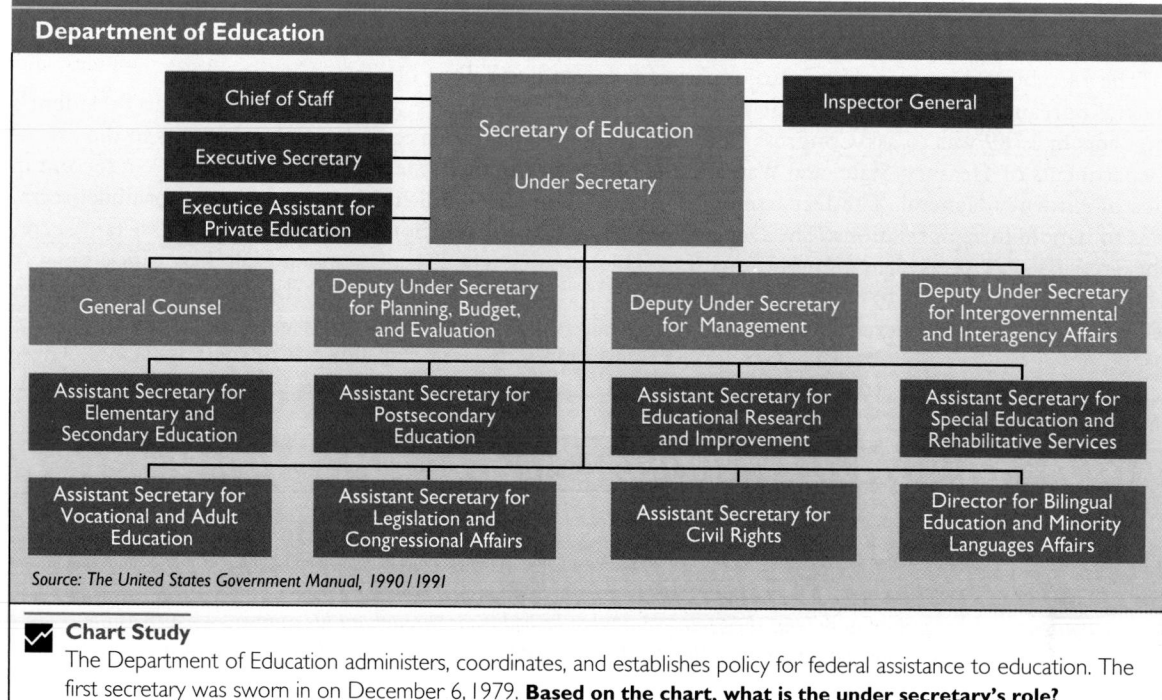

Department of Education

Source: The United States Government Manual, 1990/1991

✓ **Chart Study**
The Department of Education administers, coordinates, and establishes policy for federal assistance to education. The first secretary was sworn in on December 6, 1979. **Based on the chart, what is the under secretary's role?**

office, administration, or division. In the Department of Transportation, for example, one of the major units is the Federal Aviation Administration (FAA). The FAA promotes air traffic safety. Almost 50,000 people work for the FAA. One of the FAA's major jobs is training and supervising the thousands of air-traffic controllers who direct takeoffs and landings at airports across the country.

The top officials in each department—the secretaries, agency directors, deputy directors, and their assistants—set overall department policy. They make the key political decisions that interest Congress, the President, the mass media, and major interest groups. The secretary of transportation, for example, may make decisions about auto safety requirements such as air bags. The secretary of defense may make decisions about building new weapons systems. The di-

rector of the FAA may decide how strict the rules limiting aircraft noise should be.

These top leaders rely on ideas and information from career officials who are specialists and business managers in the department. These officials are responsible for the day-to-day operation of the department's many programs. Often, these career workers are the people who do the research to provide the alternatives from which the top leaders choose.

Independent Agencies

The federal bureaucracy also contains more than 100 independent agencies, boards, and commissions that are not part of any cabinet department. The President appoints the heads of these organizations.

STUDY GUIDE

Themes in Government
Political Processes The cabinet departments are: State, Treasury, Defense, Justice, Interior, Agriculture, Commerce, Labor, Health and Human Services, Housing and Urban Development, Transportation, Energy, Education, Veterans Affairs.

Checks and Balances Why does the Federal Aviation Administration (FAA) report to the President?

Critical Thinking Skills
Making Inferences What do you infer about the size and scope of

the cabinet department detailed on the chart above?
Drawing Conclusions Based on what you read on page 502 and what you know about airline deregulation, do you think airlines have benefited from the government changes?

Cooperative Learning Activity

Organize the class into small groups and assign each a federal agency. Have the group list 10 effects if their agency lost its funding and was dissolved. Have a recorder in each group compile a list of student responses and have each group decide which effects would have the greatest impact upon the lives of Americans. Ask each group to decide whether each effect they have selected is primarily positive or negative and indicate with a + or – sign. Have a reporter from each group report the group's findings to the rest of the class. Then ask the class how perceptions of the bureaucracy have changed after hearing the lists.

The Space Agency
Established in 1958, the National Aeronautics and Space Administration conducts space exploration.
History To whom do federal agency heads report?

A few of these agencies are almost as large and well known as cabinet departments. Two examples are the Environmental Protection Agency (EPA) and the National Aeronautics and Space Administration (NASA). Other agencies such as the Civil Rights Commission and the Small Business Administration are much smaller. Most independent agencies have few employees, small budgets, and attract little public attention. Some examples of these include the American Battle Monuments Commission and the Migratory Bird Conservation Commission.

Assisting the Executive Branch Some independent agencies perform services for the executive branch. The General Services Administration (GSA) and the Central Intelligence Agency (CIA) are two examples. The General Services Administration is responsible for constructing and maintaining all government buildings. It also supplies equipment for federal offices. The National Archives and Record Administration maintains government records and publishes all rules applying to various federal agencies.

The Central Intelligence Agency provides a very different kind of service. The CIA gathers information about what is going on in other countries, evalu-ates it, and passes it on to the President and other foreign-policy decision makers. The CIA uses its own secret agents, paid informers, foreign news sources, and friendly governments to collect such information.

Government Corporations Some independent agencies, such as the Small Business Administration, directly serve the public. Many of the most important of these agencies are **government corporations**, or businesses the federal government runs.

Today, the executive branch has at least 60 government corporations. The Postal Service is one of the largest, employing more than 830,000 people. The Tennessee Valley Authority (TVA) is another. The TVA has built dams and supplies electric power for an 8-state area in the South.

The Federal Deposit Insurance Corporation (FDIC) is also a government corporation. It insures bank accounts up to a certain amount. If a bank fails, the FDIC takes it over and pays the depositors. Recently there have been a number of bank failures.

Government corporations are organized somewhat like private businesses. Each has a board of directors and a general manager who directs the day-to-day operations. Most of the corporations earn money that is put back into the "business." Unlike private businesses, however, money from Congress, not funds from private investors, supports government corporations.

Regulatory Commissions

Regulatory commissions occupy a special place in the federal bureaucracy. They are independent of all three branches of the national government. Each commission has from 5 to 11 commissioners whom the President appoints with Senate consent. Unlike other bureaucrats, these commissioners do not report to the President, nor can the President fire them.

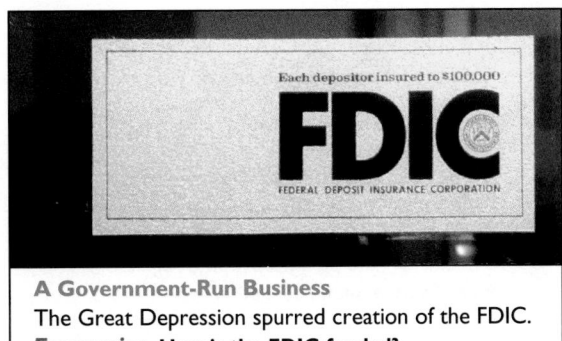

A Government-Run Business
The Great Depression spurred creation of the FDIC.
Economics How is the FDIC funded?

Chapter 18, Section 1
Lesson Plan, pages 498–502

Caption Answers
to the President
with money from Congress

📁 **Interpreting Political Cartoons** Have students complete activities 16 and 17 in *Interpreting Political Cartoons* in the Teacher's Classroom Resources.

📁 **Interpreting Source Readings** Have students complete activity 18 in *Primary and Secondary Source Readings* in the Teacher's Classroom Resources.

L3 Classifying Have students use phone books and directories to list what federal agencies have offices in the community or county. Ask them to classify each according to its type (bureau, agency, government corporation, and so on) and to determine the *local* function each performs. *(for example, FAA at local airport, Department of Agriculture to administer food stamps, United States Postal Service to deliver mail, and so on)*

Assess

Check for Understanding
Have students complete Section 1 Review on page 502.

Special Needs Strategy

Study Strategy Metacognitive strategies refer to those self-regulatory processes that are often missing or underdeveloped in students with learning disabilities and attention problems. The first thing students need to do is to make predictions concerning various aspects of their learning. For instance, in this section have students read the Section Preview and Study Guide features and ask them to develop their own Section Review using the headings: Recalling Facts, Exploring Themes, and Critical Thinking. Then have them look at the Section Review. Were any of the questions and answers they wrote the same as those in the Section Review? How did they differ?

Meeting Objectives

Each section objective is tested by the Section Review questions that follow it in parentheses.
- Describe how the federal bureaucracy is organized. (2, 4, 5, 6, 7)
- Characterize recent trends in government regulations. (3, 6, 7, 8)

Evaluate

📁 Section 1 Quiz

💾 Testmaker

Reteach

Have students construct an organizational chart to classify and differentiate the elements of the federal bureaucracy. Have them list functions and examples for each classification and subdivision.

Enrich

Ask students to find out more about an executive agency, regulatory commission, or government corporation that interests them. Ask them to prepare a brief report to present to the class.

Close

Have students suggest executive agencies they believe should be expanded and agencies they believe should be cut back or eliminated. Discuss students' reasons for their opinions.

Purpose of the Commissions The independent regulatory commissions were created to make rules for large industries and businesses that affect the interests of the public. Commissions also regulate the conduct of these businesses and industries. The regulatory agencies decide such questions as who will receive a license to operate a radio station or build a natural gas pipeline to serve a large city. The commissions may also act like courts. They may investigate a business for breaking one of the commission's rules. The commission may hold hearings, collect evidence, and set penalties for any business that violates the rules.

Some Problems Decisions of regulatory commissions can involve millions of dollars and greatly affect businesses. As a result, these agencies are often under intense pressure from lobbyists. Lawyers for industries that the commissions regulate have sometimes tried to go in the "back door" to argue their clients' cases in private with agency officials.

Critics of the commissions also charge that the commissions and the industries they are supposed to regulate sometimes have a revolving door relationship. Commissioners often are former executives in a regulated industry and sometimes leave the commission for high-paying jobs in the same industry. As a result, critics charge, some commissioners have seemed more interested in protecting regulated industries than in making sure that they serve the public interest.

Others point out that most agencies have had a good record of protecting the public interest. The Securities and Exchange Commission, for example, has protected investors in the stock market from fraud.

Deregulation Two recent Presidents, Carter and Reagan, have called for less government regulation. In a 1976 campaign speech, Jimmy Carter called for a reduction in the number of federal agencies. He cited the increasing difficulty of tracking the effectiveness of existing programs in an overregulated society. According to Carter:

> *W*e need increased program evaluation. Many programs fail to define with any specificity what they intend to accomplish. Without that specification, evaluation by objective is impossible. . . .
> —JIMMY CARTER, 1976

In recent years Congress has responded to complaints of overregulation by taking steps to **deregulate**, or reduce, the powers of regulatory agencies. In 1978, for example, Congress ordered the Civil Aeronautics Board (CAB) to simplify its procedures and cut back on regulation of the airlines. Congress also specified that the CAB was to go out of business in 1985.

Deregulation of the airlines had both expected and unexpected results. As predicted, airline competition increased, and air fares were reduced. A few low-cost carriers entered the market. Then the major airlines fought back by providing special package rates and service. Soon they were able to buy out the upstarts. Dozens of mergers and nearly 150 bankruptcies in the first 10 years of deregulation reshaped the airline industry. Some fliers wondered whether airline cost-cutting measures threatened passengers' safety. Congress opened hearings on competitiveness in the airline industry.

1
SECTION REVIEW

Section Summary
The departments and agencies making up the large federal bureaucracy were established to carry on the work of the federal government.

Checking for Understanding
Recalling Facts
1. Define civil servant, bureaucrat, government corporation, deregulate.
2. Name three independent executive agencies.
3. Discuss why the powers of some regulatory agencies have been reduced in recent years.
4. Specify the document that provides for the federal bureaucracy.

Exploring Themes
5. Political Processes How are cabinet departments organized?
6. Checks and Balances Why were the independent regulatory commissions created?

Critical Thinking Skills
7. Making Inferences Why is it important that regulatory commissions be free from political pressures?
8. Drawing Conclusions Do you agree with Jimmy Carter that evaluating existing programs is important in a society with a large bureaucracy? Support your opinion.

Section 1 Review Answers

1. Definitions of terms appear on pages indicated: **civil servant** and **bureaucrat,** 498; **government corporation,** 501; **deregulate,** 502
2. Answers may include EPA, NASA, GSA, or CIA.
3. Many businesses have complained of the expenses of overregulation, and some agencies have seemed more interested in protecting the industries than with making sure they serve the public interest.

4. the Constitution
5. There is a secretary who heads the department, a deputy or under secretary, and assistant secretaries appointed by the President. Under these top officials are the directors of the department's major units and their assistants.
6. to make rules for, and regulate conduct of, large industries and businesses that affect public interest

7. Answers may include so that they can be fair about their policies and subject to fewer influences.
8. Answers may include that they should be evaluated to avoid duplication, waste, and obsolescence.

THE PRESIDENT'S CABINET

By John Wolfe
American Historical Association

*T*he 14 executive departments do much of the work of the federal government. A secretary, appointed by the President and confirmed by the Senate, heads each of the departments except the Department of Justice, which the Attorney General heads. All department heads advise the President and are members of the cabinet.

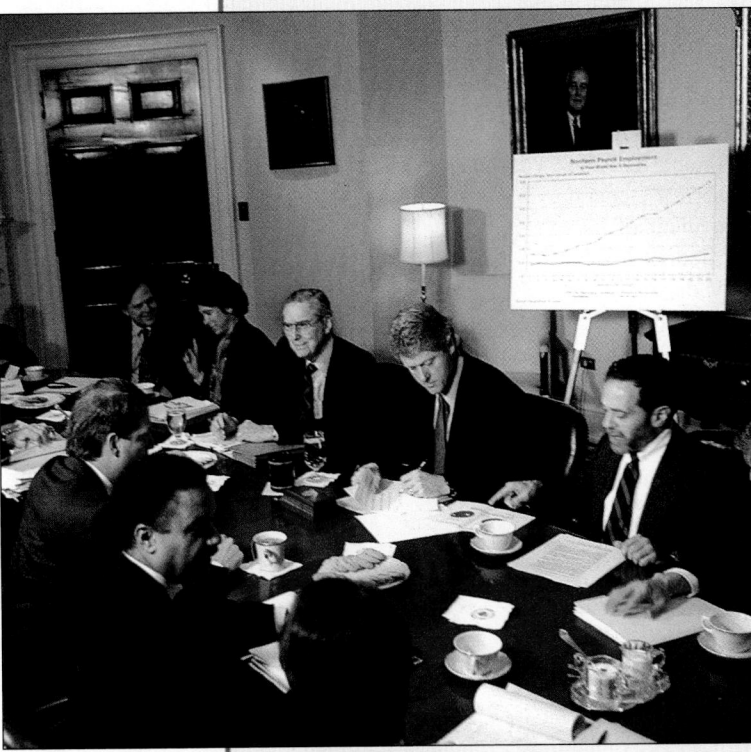

▲ President Bill Clinton meeting with members of his cabinet. The practice of holding cabinet meetings is adapted by each President to suit his or her own needs.

Report Preview

Objectives
After studying this report, you should be able to:
- **List** the 14 executive departments of the federal government.
- **Describe** the major duties of each of the executive departments.

Key Terms and Concepts
kitchen cabinet, counterfeit currency

Themes in Government
This report emphasizes the following government themes:
- **Checks and Balances** The Senate approves cabinet appointments.
- **Public Policy** The cabinet advises the President on major policy decisions.

Critical Thinking Skills
This report emphasizes the following critical thinking skills:
- **Making Inferences**
- **Making Comparisons**

503

Focus

Bell Ringer
Write the following on the chalkboard for students to complete while attendance is being taken:

List the departments whose heads make up the President's cabinet.

Motivating Activity
Discuss students' Bell Ringer lists. Ask students which department they think is most important in advising the President and to explain why they think so. Students might first discuss what issues are of top priority in the nation today. With that in mind, they might attempt to determine which department(s) would most likely address these issues. Tell students that this Special Report will describe the major duties of the executive departments.

Vocabulary Precheck
Ask students to speculate on the meaning of each term and concept. Then have them check their guesses by finding the definition in the section text. **LEP**

> **Linking Past and Present**
> Today the heads of the 14 executive departments are commonly referred to as the *cabinet*. Although popular use of this label dates back to the administration of George Washington, not until 1907 did the term gain official recognition in a federal statute.

Background

In seventeenth-century France, the term *cabinet* referred to a small room in which the king met privately with his advisers. Although the term still signifies such a meeting in the United States, a cabinet's role is dependent on a nation's political structure and processes. Unlike Britain, whose cabinet government has both executive and legislative power, the United States cabinet derives its power from the President. William S. Livingston of the University of Texas describes the United States cabinet as "a body of administrators rather than an advisory council. It is quite consistent with the pluralist character of American democracy, . . ."

Teach

Guided Practice

L1 **Summarizing** Have students write a one-sentence summary of the main function of each of the executive departments. Collect their sentences, read selected ones aloud, and have the class determine to which department each sentence refers. Write the sentences on the chalkboard. *(Department of State—responsible for the overall foreign policy of the United States; Department of the Treasury—serves as the financial division of the government; Department of the Interior—protects public lands and natural resources of the United States; Department of Agriculture—helps farmers improve their incomes and expand their worldwide markets; Department of Justice—oversees the nation's legal affairs; Department of Commerce—promotes and protects the industrial and commercial segments of the American economy; Department of Labor—protects American workers; Department of Defense—protects the security of the United States; Department of Health and Human Services—directs programs concerned with the health and social services needs of the American people; Department of Housing and Urban Development—works to preserve the nation's communities; Department of Transportation—regulates all aspects of American transportation needs; Department of Energy—plans energy policy and develops energy technology; Department of Education—coordinates federal assistance programs for schools; Department of Veterans Affairs—administers programs designed to benefit veterans and their families.)* **LEP**

As close advisers to the President, the members of the Cabinet yield considerable power and influence. They are, however, appointees of the President, and the President may choose to ignore them, even to dismiss them if the chief executive believes that they are disloyal to the administration's policies.

Beginnings

The cabinet is not a formal organization mandated by law. Rather, the cabinet has developed as an informal group of advisers throughout the history of the Republic. Today Presidents often invite the Vice President, the ambassador to the United Nations, and selected top officials to attend cabinet meetings.

In the meetings the President listens to how the various department heads view challenges facing the nation. Afterwards the department heads suggest policy goals. It is the President, however, who makes the final decisions. Presidents can and often do disagree with the cabinet's viewpoints and ignore its advice.

The First Congress of the United States created the first three executive departments: State, Treasury, and War. Congress also established the office of Attorney General. The Attorney General then became the head of the Department of Justice when it was created in 1870. George Washington consulted with the heads of departments on a regular basis, thus beginning a tradition that all other Presidents have followed.

Not all Presidents, however, have used the cabinet in the same way. President Andrew Jackson, for example, usually ignored the members of his cabinet. He chose to rely on a group of informal advisers, known as the **kitchen cabinet,** who had no official role in the government. Because the members of the kitchen cabinet were his close and trusted friends, Jackson weighed their advice carefully. At the other extreme, President Jimmy Carter depended on his cabinet's advice at the beginning of his administration in an attempt to give department secretaries more authority. When Carter discovered that cabinet members openly disagreed with some of his policies, however, he began to rely more on the advice of the White House staff than on the cabinet.

Every President, beginning with George Washington, has formed a relationship with the cabinet based on his own personal style.

GEORGE WASHINGTON
established the practice of cabinet meetings which has been followed ever since, despite the fact that it is not stated in the Constitution.

Cooperative Learning Activity

Organize the class into small groups. Assign an executive department to each group. Have students find out about the budget, work force, divisions, and activities of its assigned department. Within each group students should discuss how to research the information, how to organize the information, and, finally, how to present the information to the class. Then each group should assign individuals to work on these tasks. When the groups complete their research, have each group present its findings to the class. Then open the findings for class discussion.

ANDREW JACKSON
Some Presidents, notably Andrew Jackson, have preferred to consult advisers outside of the cabinet. Jackson's informal advisers became known as the kitchen cabinet.

ABRAHAM LINCOLN
A President may disregard his cabinet's opinion. President Lincoln took a vote among his cabinet members in which they unanimously opposed him. Said Lincoln, "Seven nays, one aye: the ayes have it."

JOHN F. KENNEDY
During his presidency John F. Kennedy set a fairly low priority on formal cabinet meetings, though he consulted the Attorney General—his brother, Robert Kennedy—and others frequently.

RONALD REAGAN
Ronald Reagan depended on his cabinet to keep him informed; he held cabinet meetings an average of twice per week.

L2 Public Policy Discuss with students the ways that Presidents in the past have used the cabinet. *(Students should indicate that some Presidents have consulted with the cabinet on a regular basis while others did not rely on the cabinet's advice.)* Then have students note the use of the cabinet by Presidents Washington, Jackson, and Carter. Ask students to speculate about what the way a President uses the cabinet might suggest about presidential personality or leadership style. For what other reasons might a President be reluctant to use the cabinet? Where else might the President obtain information and advice?

CONNECTIONS

Biography

Henry Kissinger served as secretary of state under President Nixon. In 1973 Kissinger shared the Nobel Peace Prize with Le Duc Tho of North Vietnam for negotiating a cease-fire in the Vietnam War. In 1983 President Reagan named Kissinger head of a federal commission set up to develop United States policy on Central America.

Special Needs Strategy

Visual Learners Charts, concept maps, and photographs with accompanying captions are especially useful tools to help visual learners remember relationships. To aid these learners, draw a concept map of the President's cabinet. Write the words *The President's Cabinet* on the chalkboard, box them, and draw 14 lines extending downward from this box. Then at the end of each line, add one of the 14 cabinet positions. Then as you point to each department, have students describe the specific duties of each department.

L2 Formulating Questions Pair students and assign each pair one of the cabinet positions. Have students imagine that they will be interviewing the present-day secretary. Have them develop a list of questions they would ask. Have pairs present their questions to the class and discuss. Assign students to research any unanswered questions.

CONNECTIONS

Language

In the 1960s members of the Washington press corps named the State Department "Foggy Bottom" because of its location in an area long known as Foggy Bottom. The area is land reclaimed from a swamp near the Potomac River. Some reporters have suggested that the name is apt because of the confusing, obscure, jargon-filled press releases that the department's public relations division issues.

Today

Today the 14 executive departments include the three established by the First Congress—State, Treasury, and Defense (formerly called the Department of War), and the Department of Justice, as well as 10 other departments that Congress created as the need arose. Each department has specific duties as it helps carry out the policies of the chief executive.

▼ *The State Department's head-quarters are in Washington, D.C. Candidates for the Foreign Service undergo a rigorous screening process, beginning with the Foreign Service exam.*

Department of State

The most visible department, the Department of State, is responsible for the overall foreign policy of the United States. It staffs embassies in foreign countries, analyzes data about American economic and security interests in other countries, and speaks for the United States in the United Nations. The secretary of state is often among the President's most trusted advisers.

Why is the Department of State so important today? First, the department oversees embassies and consulates throughout the world. Members of the United States Foreign Service staff these facilities and act as representatives of the United States in the host country. Often the only contact that citizens of these countries have with Americans is through these embassy staffs. Second, as the leading world power, the United States maintains a high profile in international affairs. As the overseer of foreign policy, the Department of State is often in the limelight.

Critical Thinking Activity

Making Inferences Discuss with students the recent changes in world affairs. Specifically, discuss the end of the cold war. Point out that the Department of Defense is the largest executive department. Then ask students: In view of the changes in world affairs, what inferences can you make about the future role of the Department of Defense?

(Some students might indicate that a large defense department is not necessary. The funds and personnel allocated for this department might better be used to improve the domestic situation. Other students might indicate that to maintain its strength, the United States needs to be prepared for any possibility of conflict or war.)

Department of the Treasury

The Department of the Treasury serves as the financial division of the government. It manages the public debt, collects taxes through the Internal Revenue Service, and manufactures coins and currency. In addition, the department administers explosive and firearm laws and regulates the production and distribution of alcohol and tobacco through the Bureau of Alcohol, Tobacco, and Firearms.

The United States Secret Service is also a part of the Department of the Treasury. This agency provides highly trained bodyguards to protect the President, Vice President, former Presidents, major presidential and vice-presidential candidates, visiting heads of foreign governments, and their families. Before the Secret Service, Presidents had no official bodyguards, although soldiers sometimes guarded the chief executive during times of national crisis. The Secret Service also investigates the production of **counterfeit currency,** or illegally manufactured money, and forged federal securities.

Department of the Interior

By the mid-1800s the United States had acquired vast new lands with a large Native American population. By 1848 the Louisiana Purchase, Florida, the Mexican Cession, the Oregon Territory, and Texas were part of the United States. To protect public lands and natural resources throughout the United States and to oversee relations with Native Americans, Congress established the Department of the Interior in 1849.

As part of the Department of the Interior, the Bureau of Indian Affairs develops educational and other opportunities for Native Americans. The Bureau also works with local, state, and federal agencies to develop opportunities for the economic advancement of Native Americans.

The Interior Department also includes the Bureau of Mines and the Office of Surface Mining Reclamation and Enforcement to oversee the mining of natural resources. At the same time, the National Park Service manages national monuments, historic sites, recreational areas, and national parks. The United States Fish and Wildlife Service protects and conserves endangered species. The Service also protects migratory birds, fish, and marine mammals.

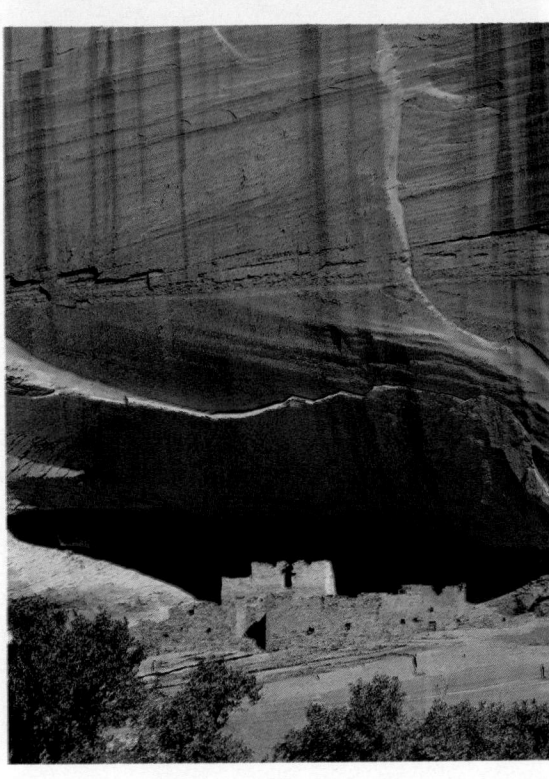

► *The National Park Service oversees national parks such as Yosemite (above), and national monuments such as Canyon de Chelly National Monument in Arizona.*

The President's Cabinet Lesson Plan, pages 503–512

L3 Art Have students work in small groups to create posters symbolizing each of the 14 executive departments. Assign a different department to each group. Discuss with students the use of symbolism in literature and art. Point out the impact that symbols can have on viewers. Suggest to students that they first review the functions of each of the 14 executive departments and study the photographs in this Special Report. Then have them focus on what they believe is the major purpose of each department. With this in mind, have each group decide on an appropriate symbol for each department. When students complete their posters, lead a class discussion to evaluate the effectiveness of the symbols that were used.

Linking Past and Present
In his last cabinet meeting, President Abraham Lincoln approved the establishment of the Secret Service, whose function was to find and punish counterfeiters. In 1901, after President William McKinley was assassinated, the Secret Service assumed the role as presidential protector. However, not until 1906 did Congress appropriate funds for this function. The agency had six successful decades until the assassination of President John F. Kennedy in 1963. The Warren Commission in its investigation of the assassination concluded that the Secret Service had insufficient staff to carry out its ever more complex role of protecting the President. By 1992 agents increased from 361 to more than 2,000 and the agency's budget jumped from more than $7 million to more than $475 million.

Background

Cabinet secretaries often earn more than their $148,400-per-year salaries when they work in private industry. For example, members of President Carter's cabinet served on boards of directors of 30 major corporations and had average annual incomes of $211,000. Also, cabinet secretaries often move in and out of government service. Harold Brown, President Carter's secretary of defense, for example, was secretary of the air force for President Johnson and a special diplomatic representative under President Nixon. Between his government posts, he served as a university president and on the board of directors of IBM and the Times-Mirror Corporation.

Independent Practice

L1 Chronology Have students create a time line showing the development of the 14 executive departments. The time line should show the year that each of the departments was established, the basic responsibility of each department, and the current head of each department.

▼ *Conducting soil tests is one way that the Department of Agriculture assists farmers.*

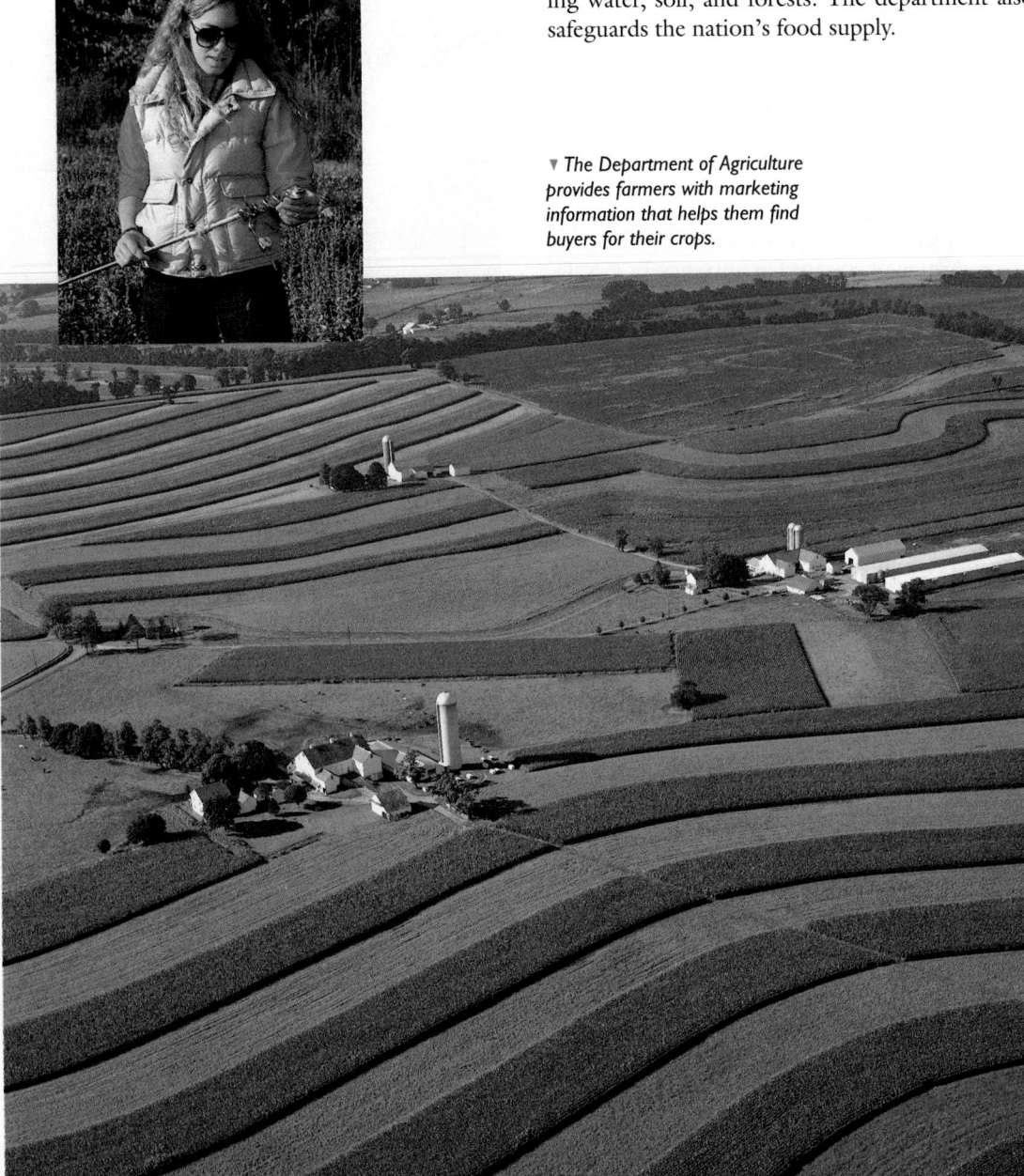

▼ *The Department of Agriculture provides farmers with marketing information that helps them find buyers for their crops.*

Department of Agriculture

Although fewer than 2 percent of the American people engage in farming, American farmers produce enough food for the United States as well as enough to export throughout the world. The Department of Agriculture was created to help these farmers improve their incomes and expand their worldwide markets. The department develops conservation programs, provides financial credit, and assists property owners in protecting water, soil, and forests. The department also safeguards the nation's food supply.

508 SPECIAL REPORT: THE PRESIDENT'S CABINET

Cooperative Learning Activity

Organize the class into 14 groups and assign each group one of the executive departments. Ask each group to brainstorm and list concerns or questions which directly relate to the functions and expenditures of their assigned department. For example, students assigned to the Department of Education might list a concern such as, "What percentage of federal assistance goes to public schools versus private schools?" Those analyzing the role of the Department of Agriculture might list, "How is the department helping farmers expand their worldwide markets?" Allow groups 15 minutes to write their lists. Then have a spokesperson for each group present his or her group's list.

HURRICANE
6 PM EDT
21 SEPTEMBER 1989
135 MPH 941 MB

▲ Maps produced by the National Oceanic and Atmospheric Administration are available to all citizens.

L2 Informative Writing Have students write newspaper articles that list the purpose of the agencies that are part of one of the following departments: Department of the Treasury, Department of the Interior, Department of Agriculture, Department of Justice, Department of Commerce, Department of Labor, and the Department of Defense. Assign specific departments to students to ensure coverage of each one. Discuss and display students' articles.

L2 Research Have students use library resources to research the Food for Peace program. This program, administered in part by the Department of Agriculture, is designed to provide farm products to less developed nations and to the needy. Students might also contact the department to find the most current information on this program. Students might present their findings in a written or an oral report.

Department of Justice

Although Congress established the office of Attorney General in 1789 to oversee the nation's legal affairs, it did not create the Department of Justice until 1870. Today, the most visible agencies in this department are the Federal Bureau of Investigation (FBI), the Immigration and Naturalization Service (INS), and the Drug Enforcement Administration (DEA). The FBI acts as the nation's police force, investigating violations of federal law. INS supervises the entry of aliens into the United States, encourages citizenship, and deports illegal aliens. The DEA administers federal narcotic and controlled substance abuse laws. During the Bush administration, the DEA played a pivotal role in the attempts to control drug trafficking and dealing throughout the nation.

The Department of Justice includes other agencies as well. The Antitrust Division, for example, enforces antitrust laws and conducts grand jury inquiries into practices that restrain trade or reduce competition. The department also includes the Bureau of Prisons, the Civil Rights Division, and the Criminal Division.

Department of Commerce

Founded in 1903, the Department of Commerce promotes and protects the industrial and commercial segments of the American economy. Its agencies include the Economic Development Administration, the International Trade Administration, the United States Travel and Tourism Administration, and the National Telecommunications and Information Administration.

The Department of Commerce is charged with carrying out certain governmental functions mandated in the Constitution. The Bureau of the Census, for example, counts the people of the United States every 10 years. Census results are then used to redraw congressional district boundaries so that each district is relatively equal in population. The Patent and Trademarks Office examines and issues patents for new inventions and registers trademarks. The National Institute of Standards and Technology provides uniform standards for weights and measurements as well as technical services and data.

The Department of Commerce also provides valuable services to American citizens. The Minority Business Development Agency helps minority-owned businesses become successes. The National Oceanic and Atmospheric Administration maps the global oceans, predicts conditions in space, and provides weather information.

GLENCOE TECHNOLOGY

Focus on Government
Video 39
**Electronic Field Trip:
The FBI Training Academy**
Running Time: 5:37
Videodisc 2, Chap. 39
VHS Tape 2, Begins 52:28

SPECIAL REPORT: THE PRESIDENT'S CABINET   509

Critical Thinking Activity

Making Comparisons Review with students the purpose of the Department of State and the Department of Defense. Then ask the following: How might the responsibilities of the Departments of State and Defense overlap and how do the decisions of one department affect those of the other? *(Answers will vary. Students might indicate that both de-* *partments deal with the nation's foreign policy. The foreign policy developed by the Department of State is carried out by the Department of Defense. On the other hand, the stability or military strength of the Defense Department also provides the conditions that make certain foreign policies possible.)*

L3 Mathematics Have students create a graph in which they illustrate the most recent federal budget outlays for each of the executive departments. Students might consult *Statistical Abstract of the United States.* Students might extend the activity by also creating a line graph for each department in which they illustrate the change in the federal budget outlay for the particular department since 1980. Then ask students to use the information from their graphs to write several generalizations about the changes in federal budget outlays for the executive departments.

CONNECTIONS

History

Cabinet secretaries sometimes clash because their departments have opposing interests in the same area of public policy. For example, during former President Carter's administration, the secretary of health, education, and welfare (HEW) opposed Agriculture Secretary Robert Bergland's program to subsidize tobacco growers because of HEW's anti-smoking campaign. After several months of controversy, Carter asked HEW Secretary Joseph Califano to resign.

Department of Labor

Responding to the call to protect American workers, Congress created the Department of Labor in 1913. Today the department ensures safe working conditions, safeguards a minimum wage, and protects pension rights. Through the Bureau of Labor Statistics, the department collects and analyzes data on employment, unemployment, wages, and compensation. The Employment and Training Administration handles job training, apprenticeship standards, and unemployment insurance. Another branch of the department, the Employment Standards Administration, regulates wage rates paid on federal contracts, monitors nondiscrimination and affirmative action on federal contracts, and oversees the minimum wage. Finally, the Office of Labor-Management Standards regulates labor union procedures and protects the rights of union members.

Department of Defense

First called the Department of War and then the United States Military Establishment until 1949, the Department of Defense protects the security of the United States. It oversees the armed forces through the Joint Chiefs of Staff, which includes the leaders of the Army, Navy, Marines, and Air Force. The largest of the cabinet departments, the Department of Defense played a key role during the cold war between the United States and the Soviet Union after World War II. With the end of the cold war during the Bush administration, the government began to drastically cut back on the number of employees in this vital department.

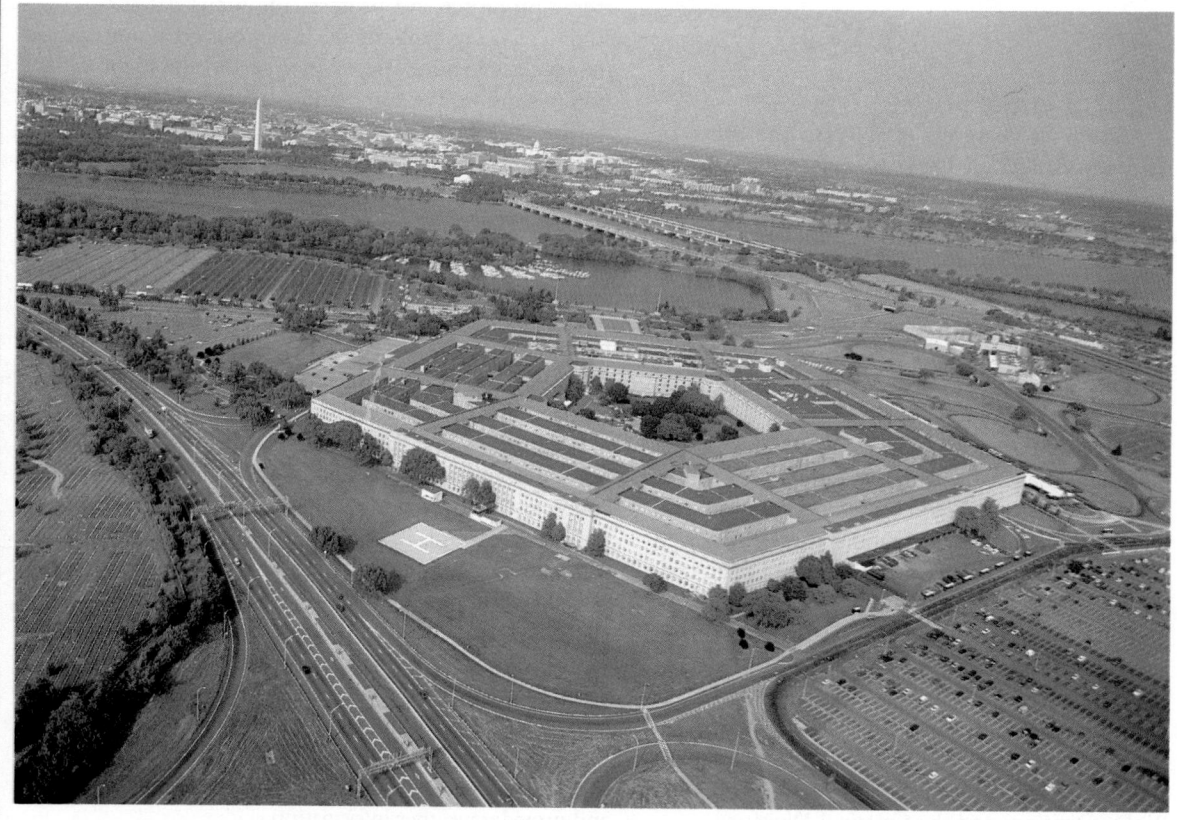

◀ *The Amalgamated Clothing and Textile Workers Union logo (left). The Department of Defense has its headquarters in the Pentagon (below), a building that covers 26 acres.*▼

Background

The history of the Department of Education began in 1867, with the establishment of a non-cabinet agency called the Department of Education. This agency eventually became known as the Office of Education. The agency was part of the Department of the Interior until 1939 when it became a part of the Federal Security Agency. The Department became part of the Department of Health, Education, and Welfare (HEW) in 1953, and in 1972 Congress made it the Educational Division within HEW. Congress created the Department of Education in 1979, and at that time the new department absorbed the Education Division of HEW. HEW became the Department of Health and Human Services.

Department of Health and Human Services

The Department of Health and Human Services directs programs concerned with the health and social services needs of the American people. The department's Office of Human Development Services, for example, coordinates federal, state, local, and private human service programs. The department also manages the federal medicare and medicaid programs that provide medical assistance to the elderly and the needy. The department further aids senior citizens and less fortunate Americans through the Social Security Administration, which directs a program of contributory social insurance into which employees and employers pay contributions.

Perhaps the most visible part of the Department of Health and Human Services—particularly since the outbreak of the AIDS epidemic in the early 1980s—has been the Public Health Service. This important government agency helps implement a national health policy, conducts medical research, and ensures the safety of food and drugs. The Food and Drug Administration inspects food and drug proccesing plants and approves new drugs for treating various diseases.

▼ *AIDS research is funded by the Public Health Service. Private foundations, such as AMFAR (American Foundation for AIDS Research), also fund studies.*

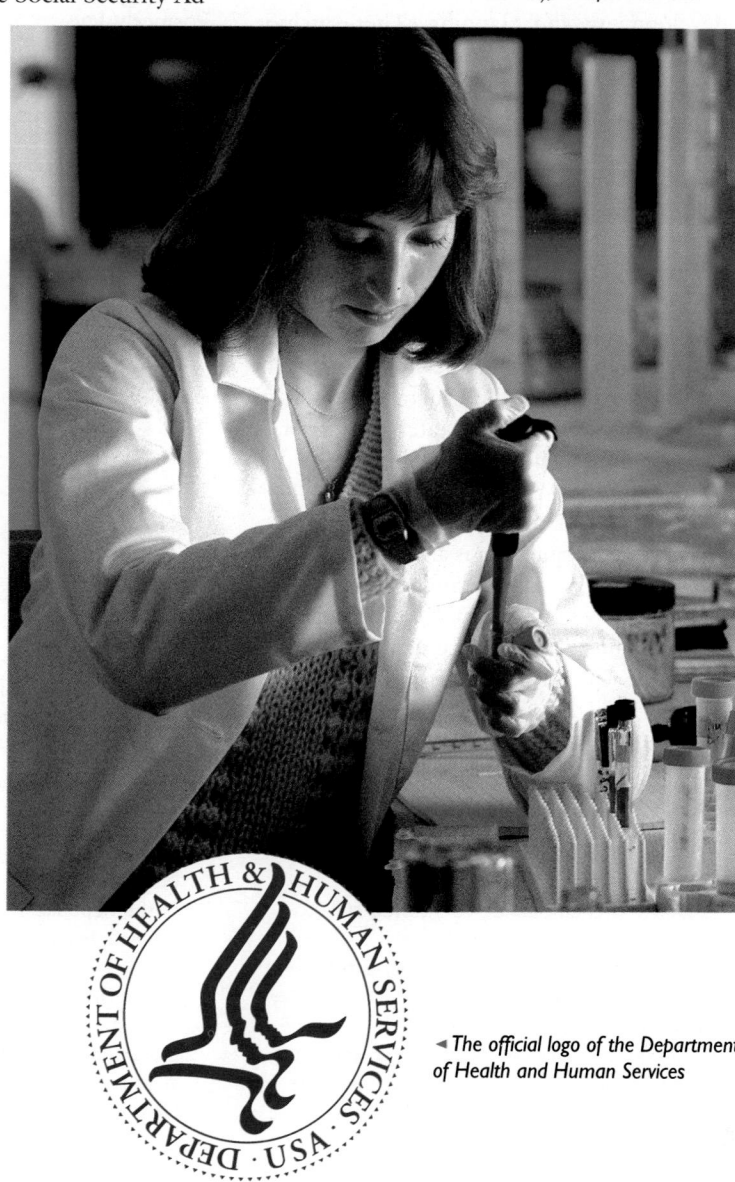

◄ *The official logo of the Department of Health and Human Services*

Cooperative Learning Activity

Have students prepare an imaginary meeting between the President and the cabinet about a topic of current national or international concern. Organize students into groups and assign each group a particular topic. Allow the groups time to gather information about their assigned topic. Have group members decide among themselves who will research the topic and who will play the roles of President and cabinet members. Tell them to determine the policy position their department would likely have on the issue. Then have the groups role-play a meeting in which they advise the President on the particular issue.

Assess

Check for Understanding

Have students complete the Report Review on page 512.

Meeting Objectives

Each Report objective is tested by the Report Review questions that follow it in parentheses.
- List the 14 executive departments of the federal government. (1, 2)
- Describe the major duties of each of the executive departments. (3, 4, 5, 6)

Evaluate

Remind students that the Departments of State, Treasury, and Defense have existed since George Washington's time. Ask students to write a paragraph which explains why they think these departments have endured.

Reteach

Have students play the following matching game. Write the 14 cabinet departments on the chalkboard. Then, item by item, present the following and have students tell to which department it relates.

a. conservation
b. rebuilding neighborhoods
c. airline safety
d. fuel
e. vocational training
f. oversees armed forces
g. farmers
h. business
i. occupational safety
j. law enforcement
k. poverty
l. veterans' benefits
m. census
n. FBI
o. mining
p. bodyguards

Enrich

Have students research the backgrounds of each of the current cabinet members. Then have students compare the backgrounds with the knowledge and skills demanded by their respective departments. Have students evaluate the cabinet members to determine if each is qualified to head his or her department. Have students present their findings to the class.

Close

Point out to students that 6 of the 14 executive departments were created since 1950. Discuss with students how these departments reflect some of the modern concerns of government. *(Students might point out that the needs of United States society have changed drastically and that new executive departments have been created by the government to address these needs.)*

Linking Past and Present

The first cabinet post held by a woman was that of secretary of labor. This post was held by Frances Perkins, who was appointed in 1933 by President Franklin D. Roosevelt. Since that time women have served as attorney general and as secretaries of health, education, and welfare; housing and urban development; commerce; health and human services; education; and transportation.

Department of Housing and Urban Development

Created in 1965, the Department of Housing and Urban Development works to preserve the nation's communities and ensure that all Americans have equal housing opportunities. The Government National Mortgage Association, for example, helps make mortgage money available for people to buy homes.

Department of Transportation

The Department of Transportation regulates all aspects of American transportation needs, policy development, and planning. These include aviation, railroads, highways, and mass transit. The department also includes the United States Coast Guard, which assists with search and rescue operations, enforces maritime laws against smuggling, and ensures safety standards on commercial sea-going vessels.

Department of Energy

Created in 1977, the Department of Energy plans energy policy and researches and develops energy technology. One of the most important parts of the department, the Federal Energy Regulatory Commission, sets the rates for interstate transmission of natural gas and electricity.

Department of Education

An educated population is an essential feature of a democratic form of government. Without informed citizens who are capable of participating in government, a democracy cannot survive. Although the United States has a long tradition of public education, it was not until recently that the federal government began to play a more active role in educating American youth. In 1979 Congress created the Department of Education to coordinate federal assistance programs for public and private schools. Today the department oversees programs to help students with limited English proficiency as well as programs for physically challenged students.

Department of Veterans Affairs

The newest cabinet department, the Department of Veterans Affairs, was founded in 1989. Formerly known as the Veterans Administration, this department administers several hospitals as well as educational and other programs designed to benefit veterans and their families.

▲ *The Department of Transportation (logo, right) was created in 1966 to regulate transportation.*

REPORT REVIEW

Checking for Understanding

Reviewing Facts

1. Define **kitchen cabinet, counterfeit currency.**
2. List the first executive departments that Congress created.

Exploring Themes

3. **Checks and Balances** What power does the Senate have over the selection of members of the President's cabinet?
4. **Public Policy** In what ways do the members of the cabinet help shape public policy?

Critical Thinking Skills

5. **Making Inferences** Throughout the history of the Republic, Presidents have used their cabinets in different ways. Why might strong Presidents rely less on their cabinets' advice than weak Presidents?
6. **Making Comparisons** How do the roles of the Department of Health and Human Services and the Department of Housing and Urban Development compare?

Report Review Answers

1. Definitions of terms appear on pages indicated: **kitchen cabinet,** 504; **counterfeit currency,** 507
2. State, Treasury, and War
3. confirms appointments

4. They advise the President, carry out the President's directives, as well as carry out congressionally mandated actions.
5. Strong Presidents would probably have already decided which policies they want to follow.

6. Both departments are concerned with the well-being of the American people.

Many people think of a federal bureaucrat as a pencil pusher shuffling papers in Washington, D.C. This image, however, is not accurate. First of all, only 11 percent of all federal government employees work in Washington, D.C. Most of them work in regional and local offices scattered across the United States and the world. Second, FBI agents, forest rangers, and air-traffic controllers are as much part of the federal bureaucracy as are secretaries and file clerks. Their activities have little to do with bureaucratic paperwork.

Federal government employees play a vital role in assuring the smooth functioning of the United States government. President Eisenhower addressed this role when he said:

The government of the United States has become too big, too complex, and too pervasive in its influence on all our lives for one individual to pretend to direct the details of its important and critical programming. Competent assistants are mandatory.

—DWIGHT D. EISENHOWER

Just who are the people who work for the many departments and agencies that make up the federal bureaucracy? The typical man or woman in the federal service is about 43 years old and has worked for the government for a total of about 15 years. He or she earns an annual salary between $25,000 and $35,000.

About 27 percent of federal workers are minority group members, compared with about 14 percent in the private work force. Women make up about 48 percent of federal workers, roughly the same percentage of women as in the total labor force.

Federal workers are better educated than workers in the general population. About 55 percent have some college training, while 15 percent have done graduate work at universities.

Federal workers hold a great variety of jobs. About half of the federal employees are administrative and clerical workers. The government also employs doctors, veterinarians, lawyers, cartographers, scientists, engineers, accountants, and many other professionals.

Origins

Today almost all federal jobs are filled through the competitive civil service system. To understand this system, it helps to see how and why it got started.

The Spoils System George Washington declared that he appointed government officials according to "fitness of character." At the same time, however, he did favor members of the Federalist party.

When Thomas Jefferson entered the White House, he found most federal workers opposed him and his political ideas. Consequently, Jefferson fired hundreds of workers who were Federalists. He replaced these workers with people from his own political party, the Democratic-Republican party.

By the time Andrew Jackson became President in 1829, the federal government had begun to grow. Jackson fired about 1,000 federal workers and gave their jobs to his own political supporters. Jackson defended his actions by arguing that it was more democratic to have rotation in office. Long service in the same jobs by any group of workers, he claimed, would only promote tyranny.

Objectives
After studying this section, you should be able to:
■ Discuss why the civil service system was created.

■ Compare the civil service system and the spoils system.

Key Terms and Concepts
spoils system, civil service system

Themes in Government
■ Checks and Balances
■ Political Processes

Critical Thinking Skills
■ Making Inferences
■ Synthesizing Information

CHAPTER 18: THE FEDERAL BUREAUCRACY   513

Classroom Resources for Section 2

📁 Guided Reading Activities
📁 Reproducible Lesson Plans
📁 Section 2 Quiz

▪ Testmaker
SAT Practice Tests
Writer's Guidebook

Bell Ringer

Write the following on the chalkboard for students to complete while attendance is being taken:

Define *civil service*.

Motivating Activity

Discuss students' Bell Ringer responses. Describe the following situation to the class:

A presidential candidate promises to make the federal bureaucracy more productive and more responsive to people's needs. Once elected, the President discovers that the workers are generally competent and cannot easily be fired. The President wishes, however, to replace them with persons who support the administration. Ask whether the current employees or new ones would be better for the nation.

Vocabulary Precheck

Write the vocabulary terms for this section on the chalkboard. Ask students to use those that they know in sentences. **LEP**

Teach

Guided Practice

L1 **Chronology** Have each student write a sentence on a half sheet of paper that summarizes a step in the development of the civil service system from the time of George Washington to the present time. Then work with them to construct a civil service time line on the chalkboard. After all student steps are on the time line, ask if any steps have been overlooked. **LEP**

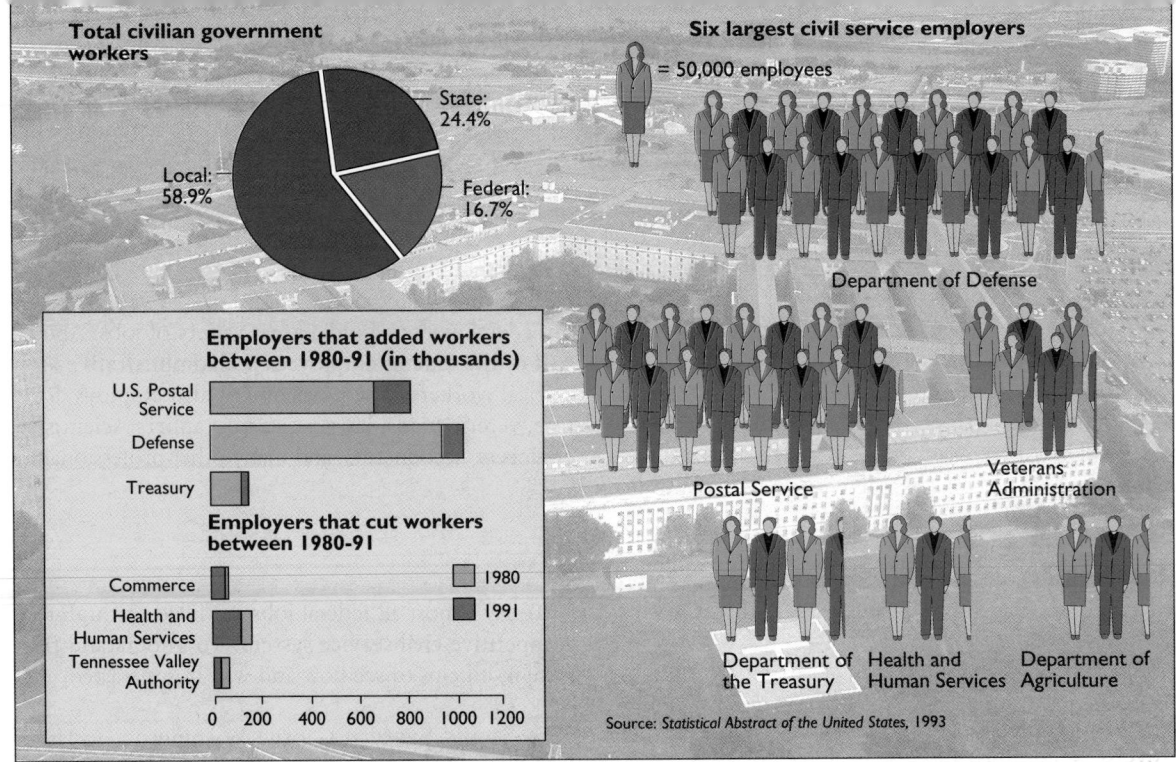

Total civilian government workers

State: 24.4%
Local: 58.9%
Federal: 16.7%

Employers that added workers between 1980-91 (in thousands)

U.S. Postal Service
Defense
Treasury

Employers that cut workers between 1980-91

Commerce
Health and Human Services
Tennessee Valley Authority

☐ 1980
☐ 1991

0 200 400 600 800 1000 1200

Six largest civil service employers

= 50,000 employees

Department of Defense
Postal Service
Veterans Administration
Department of the Treasury
Health and Human Services
Department of Agriculture

Source: *Statistical Abstract of the United States, 1993*

A New York senator at this time put it another way. He defended Jackson's actions by stating, "To the victor belong the spoils." The spoils system came to be the phrase that was used for Jackson's method of appointing federal workers. Today, the term ***spoils system*** describes the practice of victorious politicians rewarding their followers with government jobs.

For the next 50 years, national, state, and local politicians used the spoils system. Political supporters of candidates expected to be rewarded with jobs if their candidate won. As the federal government grew larger, so did the spoils system.

Calls for Reform Along with the growth of the spoils system came inefficiency and corruption.

Inefficiency grew because, as government became more complex, many jobs required experts to handle them. Yet most federal workers were not experts in their jobs. Their specialty was working in election campaigns to secure victory for their candidates.

Corruption developed as people used their jobs for personal gain. Government employees did special favors for interest groups that would support their candidates. Jobs were often bought and sold. Some people made large profits from government contracts. Instead of giving jobs to the lowest bidder, bureaucrats gave them to their friends.

In the 1850s groups of citizens began to call for reforms. Influential newspapers and magazines pointed out the problems with the spoils system.

STUDY GUIDE

Themes in Government
Checks and Balances List briefly the steps that led to the Pendleton Act and our current civil service system in 1883.

Critical Thinking Skills
Making Inferences The spoils of war were all the goods that a victorious army captured from its enemy. **What do you think the statement,**

"To the victor belong the spoils," means in the political sense?

Origins of the Civil Service System

When the United States began to establish its civil service system in the nineteenth century, it had a long history upon which to draw. Historians believe that public government officials—civil servants—date back to the early civilizations of the Middle East. The longest stable civil service in history, however, first developed in China.

China's civil service "established and elaborated the world's greatest system of competitive examination," according to Professor Karl A. Wittfogel, author of *Oriental Despotism*. The idea of merit rating for promotions, which is a characteristic of modern civil service systems, also originated within the Chinese system.

Although the Chinese system originated much earlier, the empire centralized the system about 200 B.C. With some improvements, the system continued to govern China until 1912 when a revolution created the Republic of China.

The basic characteristic of China's civil service system was an educated and honest bureaucracy. Candidates were tested not only on their grasp of specific topics of government but also on their knowledge of history, literature, poetry, and art. Frequently, only 1 out of every 100 candidates passed the examinations and won a position. Every several years thereafter, officeholders were tested again. The results, along with periodic merit ratings based on job performance, determined whether they received a promotion, retained their present level, or were dismissed. Although existing officials could, and did, nominate relatives for public offices, the examinations theoretically were open to all males. Historian E. A. Kracke, Jr., noted:

A considerable accession to the civil service of men without official background was made possible by the examination.

—E. A. Kracke, Jr.

Some type of civil service examinations became an accepted practice in many later civil systems, both in Europe and the United States.

Today, the civil service in the United States shares some of the characteristics common to the systems of

Building an Honest, Educated Bureaucracy
The Chinese for centuries relied upon the civil service exam (depicted above) to test the prospective public official's knowledge and skills in several fields.

China, Great Britain, and other European nations. In particular they share the concepts of examinations for appointment and promotions based on merit. At the same time, the United States civil service also maintains individual characteristics based on the American system of government and values. The belief in the right of every citizen to hold a public office or to work as a government employee, however, is particularly American.

Examining Our Multicultural Heritage

Reviewing Facts
1. Identify **two basic characteristics of the Chinese civil service that exist today in many modern systems.**
2. Explain **why examinations for civil service positions may be considered to be more democratic.**

Critical Thinking Skills
3. Making Comparisons **How does a civil service system differ from a spoils system?**

More About Our Multicultural Heritage

While the Chinese civil service exam was open to men of all classes, only rarely could anyone other than the sons of nobles, government officials, or wealthy merchants afford the years of study needed to pass the test. Although almost no peasants entered the ranks of the civil servants, sons of moderately wealthy families were able to move up in the world through the civil service. To pass the tests, candidates required a thorough knowledge of Confucian thought and writings. Those who passed joined the privileged class of scholar-officials who did not have to pay taxes or serve in the army.

Focus

Ask students to explain how they think most people obtain government jobs.

Teach

Ask: What was the goal of China's civil service system? *(to create an educated and honest group of government workers)* How did the examination system reflect this goal? Once hired what two factors determined whether workers were promoted or fired? *(job performance and performance on exams)* How does this system compare to the current American system? *(much less democratic, closed to women)*

Assess

Have students complete **Examining Our Multicultural Heritage.**
Answers
1. appointment and promotion based on merit
2. All citizens have a right to take the examination.
3. In spoils system victorious politicians reward their followers with government jobs. In civil service system government jobs are obtained on the basis of competitive examinations and merit.

Close

Ask students to explain what was undemocratic about the Chinese civil service system. *(only males could apply)*

Independent Practice

L1 **Summarizing** Have students summarize the main ideas in Section 2 by writing a newspaper headline for each subhead in the section. For example, a headline for the first subhead might read "Spoils System Major Method of Employment for Government Jobs". **LEP**

L2 **Persuasive Writing** Have students write an editorial addressing the problems associated with the spoils system. Have students share their editorials with one another.

L3 **Community Resources** Have students research the different types of federal government jobs in their community. Have them find out how people apply for these jobs and what are the qualifications and salaries.

Caption Answer
open, competitive examinations and merit

President Grant, whose own administration was filled with corruption, persuaded Congress in 1871 to set up the first Civil Service Commission. By 1875, however, reform efforts faltered as Congress failed to appropriate money for the new commission.

It took a tragedy to restart the reform effort. In 1881 President James A. Garfield ignored Charles Guiteau's requests for a job in the diplomatic service. Infuriated at not being appointed, Guiteau shot President Garfield in the back at a Washington railway station on July 2, 1881. Garfield died 80 days later.

The Pendleton Act The public was outraged. Chester A. Arthur, the new President, pushed hard for reform. In 1883 Congress passed the Pendleton Act creating the present federal civil service system. The **civil service system** is the principle and practice of government employment on the basis of open, competitive examinations and merit. The law set up the Civil Service Commission to administer examinations and supervise the operation of the new system.

The Civil Service Commission operated for 95 years. In 1979, two new agencies replaced it. The Office of Personnel Management handles recruitment, pay, retirement policy, and examinations for federal workers. The Merit System Protection Board settles job disputes and investigates complaints from federal workers.

Assassination Leads to Civil Service System
After a disgruntled lawyer assassinated President Garfield, Congress created the civil service system.
Politics Which principle and practice serve as the basis for the civil service system?

The Civil Service System Today

Has the present civil service system created new problems while solving those problems linked with the spoils system?

Getting a Job Competition for federal jobs today is stiff. In recent years every job opening had about 76 applications. This competition will probably continue. While the federal bureaucracy is huge, the number of federal jobs has not increased much since 1950. Yet the number of people wanting federal jobs keeps on increasing.

The Office of Personnel Management, along with individual agencies, is responsible for filling federal jobs. Job notices are usually posted in post offices, newspapers, and Federal Job Information Centers located in many communities.

Most secretarial and clerical jobs require the applicant to take a written examination. For other jobs such as accountants, social workers, managers, and so on, applicants are evaluated on the basis of training and experience. Veterans are given special preference.

Benefits and Problems Government jobs are attractive because of the many benefits they offer. Salaries are competitive with those in private industry. Federal workers get from 13 to 26 days of paid vacation every year, depending on the length of their service. They have extensive health insurance plans and 13 days of sick leave every year. They may retire at age 55. Government workers who retire after 30 years of service on the job get half pay for the rest of their lives.

Each government job is assigned a certain grade ranging from GS-l, the lowest level, to GS-18, the highest. Civil service workers have job security. They may be fired, but only for specific reasons and only after a very long, complex series of hearings. A federal worker threatened with firing may drag out a hearing about his or her job performance for months or even years. As one federal worker put it, "We're all like headless nails down here—once you get us in, you can't get us out."

Many supervisors and top officials find it is easier to put up with an incompetent worker than fire one. As a result, the government's rate of discharge for inefficiency is less than 1 percent. For a small business with 10 employees that would be the same as firing one person every 10 years.

Thus, an ironic situation has developed. On the one hand, the civil service was designed to hire

Cooperative Learning Activity

Organize the class into three groups. Pose the following questions, one to each group: Ask the first group to list the advantages and disadvantages of the Hatch Act. Ask the second group to list the advantages and disadvantages that would result from repeal of the Hatch Act. Have students take turns contributing to their group by writing a response on a piece of paper and passing the paper to the left. Have reporters from each group report their group's findings. Then have students in the third group use these findings to predict three changes that would likely take place if the law were repealed.

federal workers on merit and protect them from being fired for political reasons. In achieving this goal, however, the system also helps protect a small number of incompetent and inefficient employees.

The Hatch Act The Hatch Act limits how involved federal government employees can become in elections. Congress passed this law—named after its chief sponsor, Senator Carl Hatch—to prevent a political party from using federal workers in election campaigns. If that happened, it would raise the dangerous possibility that workers' promotions and job security could depend on their support of candidates from the party in power.

The Hatch Act has led to more than 3,000 rules and regulations concerning elections for federal employees. The Hatch Act specifies what federal workers may not do in elections. They may not campaign for or against a party, serve as an officer of a political party, serve as a delegate to party conventions, raise funds for a party, or run for political office. The Hatch Act also states what federal employees may do in elections. They may vote, join a political party, attend political rallies, and express their opinions on political issues.

Many federal workers dislike the Hatch Act. They argue that the law violates freedom of speech. They also claim the act discourages political participation by people who may be well-informed about political issues.

Supporters of the Hatch Act state it is needed to keep the federal civil service politically neutral. They claim the act protects workers from political pressure from superiors. In 1973 the Supreme Court ruled that the act was constitutional.

Political Appointees in Government

In each presidential election year, the House or Senate publishes a book known by Washington insiders as the *plum book*. The word *plum* stands for *politi-*

GLOBAL CONNECTION

Comparing Governments

Filling Government Jobs Systems to put the most qualified people into government jobs did not begin in the United States.

In the second century B.C., China required job applicants to pass tests on job skills and Chinese classics. In the 1700s Great Britain developed a civil service system to bring effective government to its colony in India. The Indian system later formed the basis for civil service in Great Britain.

The British system and a German system that developed about the same time provided models for American civil service reform in 1883. Today, some developing nations in Asia, Latin America, and Africa use similar programs to fill government jobs.

Examining the Connection
What are some arguments for and against a civil service system?

cal plum—a job the new President may fill. The plum book lists all such jobs.

Upon taking office every President has the chance to fill about 2,200 top-level jobs in the federal bureaucracy. These jobs are outside the civil service system. They are sometimes called unclassified employees, as opposed to the classified employees hired by the civil service system. About 10 percent of executive branch jobs are appointed by the President. They include 14 cabinet secretaries, about 300 top-level bureau and agency heads, about 150 ambassadorships, and about 1,700 aide and assistant positions.

Filling these jobs gives Presidents an opportunity to place loyal supporters in key positions. These polit-

---

GLOBAL CONNECTION

Point out that Japan's large civil service carries out many of the administrative and technical duties of the government. Civil servants in Japan enjoy a great deal of power and esteem.
Examining the Connection: Allow students time to present their arguments.

STUDY GUIDE

Theme Answer
They are forced to remain politically "neutral," which protects them from pressure from superiors, but also minimizes their role in the political process.

Critical Thinking Answer
They seek the challenge of such jobs and may wish to be close to the centers of power and to meet influential people.

Assess

Check for Understanding
Have students complete Section 2 Review on page 518.

Meeting Objectives
Each section objective is tested by the Section Review questions that follow it in parentheses.
- Discuss why the civil service system was created. (3, 5, 6, 7)
- Compare the civil service system and the spoils system. (2, 4, 5, 6, 7, 8)

CHAPTER 18: THE FEDERAL BUREAUCRACY   517

Special Needs Strategy

Study Strategy Although it is often helpful for students with reading comprehension difficulties to *think* about reading, a more precise measure of understanding is whether they can write a summary of what has just been read. In Section 2, have each student read a subsection. Tell students they must summarize the information by writing only two or three sentences. Allow students to work with a partner to go over their summaries. Did they both write similar information? If not, how were they different? Which one made the better choice? Why did it seem so?

Caption Answer
for the challenge and a chance to wield power and influence; short tenure, salaries less than could be made in industry or business

Evaluate

 Section 2 Quiz

Testmaker

Reteach

Have students work in pairs to develop a chart that shows the disadvantages and advantages of the spoils system and civil service system.

Enrich

Have students compare the requirements of the Hatch Act to restrictions on civil service employees in their state government and to determine the limits on the personal freedoms and activities of state civil service workers.

Close

Ask students whether they think either the spoils system or the civil service system should be expanded at the expense of the other. For example, should cabinet secretaries be put under civil service? Should postal workers' jobs be part of the spoils system? Should either system be eliminated? Have students support their views.

JOHN BRANCH
Courtesy Chapel Hill News

Presidential Puzzle
One cartoonist satirizes the task that President Carter confronted when building his administration. **Politics** **Why would someone want a plum job? Why not?**

ical appointees head agencies, offices, and bureaus and make key political decisions. They are expected to try to implement the President's decisions. Unlike career civil service workers, their employment usually ends when a new President is elected. Who are the people with these plum political jobs?

People at the Top The people appointed to the non-civil service positions are first and foremost the President's political supporters. Many of them actively supported the President's election campaign. Most are well-educated. More than 96 percent are college graduates. About 77 percent have advanced degrees, mostly as lawyers. Others are successful

leaders from businesses or professions.

These people are usually not experts in the work of the agency they head, though they may have served in government before. When the President leaves office, most of them return to other jobs outside the government.

A Short Tenure Top political appointees hold their positions for only a few years. Because federal agencies are so large and complex, the short tenure makes it difficult for them to learn about their jobs. It can take the head of a large agency a year or more to learn all the issues, programs, procedures, and personalities involved in running the agency. One new political appointee discovered, "I was like a sea captain who finds himself on the deck of a ship that he has never seen before. I did not know the mechanism of my ship, I did not know my officers—and I had no acquaintance with the crew."

Short tenures of presidential appointees mean that much of the real power over daily operations remains with the career civil service officials. Many of their day-to-day decisions do not make headlines, but they do shape the policy of the national government on key problems.

2 SECTION REVIEW

Section Summary
The civil service system developed because of inefficiency and corruption in filling federal jobs.

Checking for Understanding
Recalling Facts
1. Define spoils system, civil service system.
2. Describe how to find out what federal jobs are available.
3. List the two agencies that now make up the former Civil Service Commission.
4. State the purpose of the Hatch Act.

Exploring Themes
5. Checks and Balances What are the advantages and disadvantages of the spoils system?
6. Political Processes What are the advantages and disadvantages of the civil service system?

Critical Thinking Skills
7. Making Inferences What would be the effect on the federal bureaucracy if all government employees were replaced each time a new President was elected?
8. Synthesizing Information Do you agree with the Supreme Court decision regarding the Hatch Act? Support your opinion.

Section 2 Review Answers

1. Definitions of terms appear on pages indicated: **spoils system,** 514; **civil service system,** 516
2. Notices for federal jobs are usually listed in post offices, newspapers, and Federal Job Information Centers.
3. the Office of Personnel Management and the Merit System Protection Board
4. to prevent a political party from using federal workers in election campaigns

5. It allows the victorious politician to reward his or her followers, but it can also result in inefficiency and corruption.
6. advantages: competitive salaries, early retirement, job security; disadvantages: it is difficult to get rid of incompetent workers

7. Answers may include that the experienced workers would be gone and the government might not run smoothly for quite some time.
8. Answers may include that yes, it limits the freedoms of workers, or no, it protects the workers' jobs from political backlash, or a combination of the two where the decision should be left up to the individual.

The Bureaucracy and Public-Policy Decisions

Simply defined, public policy is whatever action the government chooses to take or not to take. The decision of Congress, for example, to provide federal funds for businesses run by handicapped persons is a public-policy decision. The decision of the President to refuse to send military aid to a Latin American country is also public policy.

In theory, federal bureaucrats only carry out the policy decisions the President and Congress make. In practice, however, federal bureaucrats today also help make public policy. They often play key roles both in choosing goals the government will try to meet and in selecting programs to achieve those goals. By choosing what or what not to do in various situations, federal bureaucrats are setting policy. Should people who were not elected make policy? Administering federal programs seems to require that they do.

In recent years federal agencies have made key decisions about many policy issues. These include establishing safety requirements for nuclear power plants and deciding the extent to which the nation will depend on oil for energy. Federal agencies are also responsible for setting the eligibility requirements for federal health and welfare programs.

Influencing Policy

Federal bureaucrats help make policy in several ways. The most important of these involves administering the hundreds of programs that have an impact on almost every aspect of national life. Administering these programs requires federal bureaucrats to write rules and regulations and set standards to implement laws Congress passes.

Making Rules When Congress passes a law, it cannot possibly spell out exactly what needs to be done to enforce it. It is the bureaucracy that determines what the law actually means. The chief way federal agencies do this is by issuing rules and regulations designed to translate the law into action. One study has shown that, on an average, the bureaucracy formulates 20 rules or regulations to carry out each law.

In 1935, for example, Congress passed the Social Security Act establishing the Social Security system. The law makes it possible for disabled workers to receive payments from the government. What does the word *disabled* mean? Are workers disabled if they can work only part-time? Are they disabled if they can work, but not at the same job they once had?

The Social Security Administration in the Department of Health and Human Services has developed 14 pages of rules and regulations describing disability. These regulations even state what blindness means and specifically how it is to be measured. Without such rules, people who are not blind might receive benefits they do not deserve. At the same time, the rules help ensure that anyone who meets the established standard cannot unfairly be denied benefits. It is through thousands of decisions such as this that bureaucrats make federal government policy affecting disabled people.

Often, rule-making by federal agencies is the same as lawmaking. For example, the Department of Housing and Urban Development (HUD) has created guidelines for building contractors to follow when hiring minority employees. These guidelines are used to decide whether contractors can work on federally funded construction projects. The HUD guidelines have the force of law. In order to work on the projects, contractors must follow them.

SECTION PREVIEW

Objectives
After studying this section, you should be able to:
■ Describe how the federal bureaucracy influences public policy.

■ Explain why the federal bureaucracy's role in public policy has grown.

Key Terms and Concepts
allegation, client group

Themes in Government
■ Public Policy
■ Political Processes

Critical Thinking Skills
■ Drawing Conclusions
■ Making Inferences

CHAPTER 18: THE FEDERAL BUREAUCRACY 519

Classroom Resources for Section 3

📁 Guided Reading Activities
📁 Reproducible Lesson Plans
📁 Participating in Government 18
📁 Enrichment Activities 18
📁 Section 3 Quiz

🖥 Testmaker
💾 Government Themes Transparencies 47
SAT Practice Tests
Writer's Guidebook

Focus

Bell Ringer
Write the following on the chalkboard for students to complete while attendance is being taken:

What is "red tape"?

Motivating Activity
Discuss students' Bell Ringer responses. Ask if the school demonstrates characteristics of a bureaucracy. Ask students to answer the following questions and to provide examples for each: Does the school operate under standard and established routines? Are workers' jobs specialized? Do school officials administer policies made by someone else? Do they make policy? Are there rules and regulations to carry out policies? Is there red tape? Tell students that in this section they will learn the extent to which each of these characteristics is typical of a bureaucracy.

Vocabulary Precheck
Call on students to read aloud the definitions for each term and concept from the Glossary. Then have them restate each definition in their own words. **LEP**

Teach

Guided Practice
L1 Political Processes Write the term *Public Policy* on the chalkboard and circle it. Then ask students to name the ways that federal bureaucrats help make public policy—and add these to lines extending from the circle. (*making rules, drafting bills, settling disputes, providing advice*)

L2 **Public Policy** Have students write scenarios that illustrate a way bureaucrats influence public policy. Have each student read his or her scenario aloud and ask the class to identify by which means —rule-making, dispute resolution, legislative process, or expert advice—public policy has been influenced.

Interpreting Visuals Display transparency 47 from the *Government Themes Transparencies* in the Teacher's Classroom Resources and use the accompanying teaching strategy and student activity to teach how federal agencies are involved in making public policy.

Caption Answer
when an agency creates regulations that have the force of law

---

STUDY GUIDE

Theme Answer
Many agencies can make rules and settle disputes related to rules or laws they are empowered to enforce.

Critical Thinking Answer
to achieve equal protection of law, so that all persons claiming a disability are judged by the same criteria no matter when or where the claim is reviewed

---

CONNECTIONS

Language
The term *red tape* describes bureaucratic tie-ups because in the past red was the color of the tape used to tie official documents.

Hiring Guidelines Set by HUD
Building contractors who work on HUD projects must hire minority workers. **Economics How does agency rule-making become lawmaking?**

The number of rules and regulations federal agencies issue has been growing. Agency regulations now run more than 50,000 printed pages a year. Along with more regulations has come more paperwork. More than 2 billion forms must be filled out and submitted to the federal government each year.

Involvement in Lawmaking The bureaucracy also shapes public policy by helping draft new bills for Congress, testifying about legislation, and providing lawmakers with technical information. In addition, lawmakers know that it can be difficult to pass major bills without the advice of the federal agencies most concerned with the bills' contents.

Often, the ideas for new laws come from within the bureaucracy itself. Lawyers within the Justice Department, for example, drafted the Safe Streets Act of 1968 that created a new division within the Justice Department called the Law Enforcement Assistance Administration that existed into the 1980s. In the same way, bureaucrats in what is now the Department of Health and Human Services, along with some hospital administrators and labor unions, worked hard for the law that set up the medicare program.

Settling Disputes Some federal agencies shape public policy by deciding disputes over the application of a law or set of rules. When agencies do this, they act almost like courts. The regulatory commissions in particular make government policy in this way. They have the authority to hear and resolve disputes among parties that come under their regulatory power. The rulings of these agencies have the same legal status as that of courts.

The Interstate Commerce Commission (ICC), for example, has the power to settle disputes between trucking companies over the rates they charge. If one company thinks a competitor is charging a rate that is too low, it may file an **allegation**, or formal complaint, with the ICC. The ICC has the power to investigate, call witnesses to testify, and reach a decision settling the dispute.

Providing Advice Bureaucrats also help shape public policy by providing top political decision makers with information and advice. Many career bureaucrats are experts in their areas. In addition, federal agencies collect information and research on a variety of subjects.

Federal agencies may use their information to support or oppose a particular public policy. Several years ago, for example, studies by the Public Health Service on the effects of smoking led to new laws and regulations designed to cut down on the use of cigarettes.

Thus, the federal bureaucracy does more today than simply fill in the details of laws. The bureaucracy plays a role in determining what those policies will be.

STUDY GUIDE

Themes in Government
Public Policy What are the two main regulatory roles of federal agencies in public policy?

Critical Thinking Skills
Drawing Conclusions Why do you think that the Department of Health and Human Services

(HHS) has 14 pages of rules and regulations describing *disability*?

Background

The arsenic pollution standard set by the EPA primarily affected Tacoma, Washington, residents because the Tacoma plant was the only copper smelter in the United States using arsenic-rich ore imported from the Philippines. The proposed standard would have required the smelter to reduce its level of arsenic emissions from 310 tons per year to 189 tons. This was a pollution level that the EPA argued would still be toxic. The company, however, maintained that its arsenic emissions could not be directly linked to health problems, especially cancer. Although Ruckelshaus encouraged public discussion, he had the responsibility for making the final decision on the arsenic standards.

Why Bureaucracy Makes Policy

The federal bureaucracy has grown and assumed an important role in making public policy for five reasons: (1) growth of the nation, (2) international crises, (3) economic problems at home, (4) citizens' demands, and (5) the nature of bureaucracy itself.

National Growth and Technology The growth of the federal bureaucracy mirrors the growth of the United States. For almost 60 years, the 3 original cabinet departments and the Attorney General's office handled the work of the executive branch. As the population grew, so did the government. The same number of officials who ran a country of 50 million people cannot govern a country of more than 250 million.

In addition, rapid advances in technology have made life much more complex. Today, a single President and 535 lawmakers in Congress cannot possibly have all the knowledge and time needed to deal with the many complicated issues that face the nation. These issues include nuclear power, education reform, space exploration, environmental protection, cancer research, health care, and many other aspects of life.

In 1983, for example, Environmental Protection Agency (EPA) Director William D. Ruckelshaus announced new standards for arsenic pollution. A copper-smelting plant pumped $35 million per year into the Tacoma area economy, while it was emitting cancer-causing arsenic. Ruckelshaus

> . . . left open a tough choice between a reduced but still clear risk of cancer for Tacoma residents and the loss of hundreds of jobs if the plant shuts down. Ruckelshaus' solution was a radically new departure in environmental policy: ask the community to help make the decision.
>
> —"Tough Decision for Tacoma," *TIME*, July 25, 1983

Many other tasks such as regulating atomic energy or launching communications satellites also require some government involvement. The President and Congress establish bureaucracies and give them the money and authority to carry out their tasks.

International Crisis Competition with the Soviet Union and international crises since World War II furthered the growth of the federal bureaucracy. During the cold war from the mid-1940s to the 1980s,

---

PARTICIPATING IN GOVERNMENT

Petitioning to Put an Issue on the Ballot

What can be done if legislators fail to take action on a law that the people want passed? Twenty-one states allow proposed laws to be placed on the ballot by the initiative. Seventeen states allow proposed constitutional amendments to be introduced by the initiative. Several other states allow the use of the initiative only at the local—county or city—level.

To initiate a law, a voter must obtain a petition from the appropriate governing body. Then he or she must have the required number of voters sign the petition. The

number of signatures needed to initiate a law varies from place to place. In some states it must be a certain percentage of the population or of registered voters. In others the requirement is a percentage of the number of votes cast for governor in the last election.

In states that use the direct initiative, a signed petition puts the proposition on the ballot at the next general election. The voters decide whether or not the proposition becomes law. In the indirect initiative, the proposition goes to the state legislature first. If the proposed law does not pass the legislature, it goes to the voters. The governor cannot veto a law passed in this way.

Investigating Further

Find out whether your state allows the use of the initiative. What are some arguments against the use of the initiative?

CHAPTER 18: THE FEDERAL BUREAUCRACY **521**

Chapter 18, Section 3
Lesson Plan, pages 519–524

Independent Practice

L1 Informative Writing Ask students to write a paragraph listing and explaining the five reasons that the federal bureaucracy has assumed an important role in making public policy.

L2 Using Reference Sources Have students use the public library to obtain rules a federal agency has created to carry out a specific law. (The *Federal Register* or the *Code of Federal Regulations* provide such rules.)

L3 Creating a Flow Chart Have each student create a chart that diagrams the stages at which, and the methods by which, bureaucrats influence policy-making—from involvement in the legislative process to rule-writing to settling enforcement disputes. The influences of client groups at appropriate stages should also be charted.

PARTICIPATING IN GOVERNMENT

Like the initiative, the referendum is a way for voters to participate more directly in the lawmaking process. A referendum is a method by which voters can approve or reject a measure already passed by the state legislature or by the local government.

📁 Have students complete activity 18 in *Participating in Government* in the Teacher's Classroom Resources.

Cooperative Learning Activity

Organize the class into groups of four called "Home Teams." Assign each team member the number 1, 2, 3, or 4. Have the same-numbered students from each Home Team form an Expert Team. Assign each of the four Expert Teams one of the four ways in which federal bureaucrats influence public policy. Have the Expert Teams develop a teaching tool, such as a chart, that pertains to their topic. Then have "experts" return to their Home Teams to share their teaching tools.

STUDY GUIDE

Theme Answer
Their economy and health
would be affected greatly by either choice Ruckelshaus made.

Critical Thinking Answer
Happy, nobody wants war;
peace is in everyone's best interest. Uneasy, the department's budget may be cut, and
jobs lost.

Assess

Check Understanding

Have students complete Section 3 Review on page 523.

Meeting Objectives

Each section objective is
tested by the Section Review
questions that follow it in
parentheses.
• Describe how the federal
bureaucracy influences public policy. (2, 5, 6, 7)
• Explain why the federal bureaucracy's role in public
policy has grown. (2, 3, 4, 5,
6, 7)

Evaluate

📁 Section 3 Quiz

🔲 Testmaker

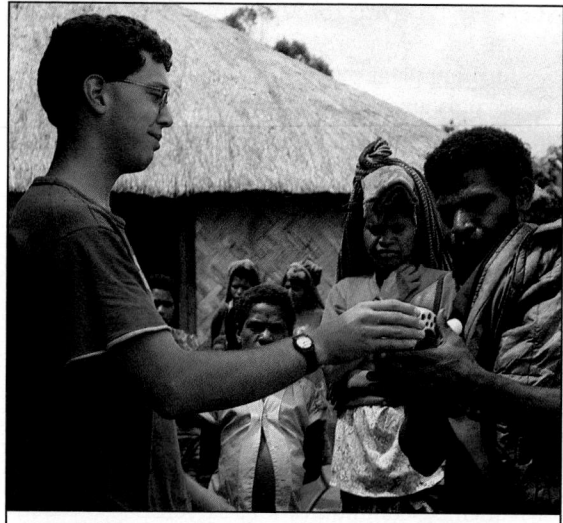

Peace Corps, a Helping Hand to Poor Nations
During the cold war the United States created programs to influence developing countries to turn to
democracy. **Economics How might the Peace
Corps help people in developing countries?**

States Information Agency, and the Peace Corps.

The Korean War from 1950 to 1953 and the Vietnam War from 1964 to 1973 involved millions of
American soldiers. Both wars led to the continued
need for the Veterans Administration, which was elevated to the cabinet level in 1989, and renamed the Department of Veterans Affairs. It is one of the largest
federal agencies.

Economic Problems President Franklin D. Roosevelt greatly expanded the size of the federal bureaucracy as he attempted to combat the Depression during the 1930s. By 1940 the number of federal
workers had almost doubled. Many people accepted
the idea that the federal government had a duty to
assist the ill, the disabled, the retired, and the neglected. As a result, the federal government now
spends billions of dollars each year on hundreds of assistance programs.

The Depression years also led to the idea that the
federal government has a special responsibility both
to stimulate the nation's economy and to regulate
unfair business practices. Thus, agencies that help
business, such as the Department of Commerce, have
grown along with agencies that regulate businesses,
such as the Federal Trade Commission.

Citizen Demands The bureaucracy has also grown
in response to demands from various interest groups
within the country. This is not a new phenomenon.
Congress, for example, created the Departments of
Agriculture (1862), Commerce (1903), and Labor
(1913) in part to meet the demands of farmers, business people, and workers.

Once it is established, each agency has client
groups that it serves. **Client groups** are the individuals and groups who work with the agency and are
most affected by its decisions. The client groups of
the Department of Defense, for example, include the
defense contractors who make weapons and supplies
for the armed forces. The client groups of the Department of Agriculture are largely the farmers and
others in the business of agriculture.

the United States and the Soviet Union never fought
each other directly. Each country did, however, develop new weapons to defend itself, and both countries
gave aid to other countries they wanted as allies. In
order to accomplish defense goals, the United States
in 1949 created the Department of Defense from
the United States Military Establishment. The Defense Department soon grew to be the largest single
department in the federal government. With the end
of the cold war, the department began to be reduced.

After the Soviet Union launched *Sputnik I,* the
first space satellite in 1957, the federal government
started a large-scale program to improve science and
mathematics instruction. The government established
NASA in 1958 to direct the nation's space exploration program. As a further result of the cold war,
the government created several other new agencies.
These included the Central Intelligence Agency, the
Arms Control and Disarmament Agency, the United

STUDY GUIDE

Themes in Government
Political Processes
**Why did Environmental Protec-
tion Agency (EPA) Director**

**William Ruckelshaus ask the
Tacoma residents to help him
make his decision in 1983?**

Critical Thinking Skills
Making Inferences
**Do you think the end of the cold
war makes the Defense Department uneasy or happy? Explain
your answer.**

522 UNIT 5: THE EXECUTIVE BRANCH

Critical Thinking Activity

Drawing Conclusions Remind students that in
theory bureaucrats merely carry out the policies established by elected officials, but in practice bureaucrats help determine public policies. Ask
students if they think bureaucrats should be allowed to help make public policy or if they think
there is a danger in this situation. Students should
provide reasons for their thinking.

Client groups often lobby both Congress and the agency itself for more programs and services. Sometimes competition develops. If business leaders can have "their" people in the Commerce Department, labor leaders want "their" people in the Labor Department to make sure they get their "fair share."

The Nature of Bureaucracy Another reason for the growth of federal agencies is that the country's needs may change. Once created, however, federal agencies almost never die. They seem to exist for their own sake. Several years ago Congress created the Federal Metal and Non-Metallic Safety Board of Review. A bureaucrat named Jubal Hale was appointed as its director. The board, however, never received any cases to review. As a result, Hale had no work to do. He spent the next four years reading and listening to phonograph records in his office. Finally, he suggested the agency be abolished, and it was.

Former President Ford put it this way:

One of the enduring truths of the nation's capital is that bureaucrats survive. Agencies don't fold their tents and quietly fade away after their work is done. They find something new to do.

—GERALD FORD

'OK, FILL OUT THESE FORMS AND SUBMIT YOUR PROPOSAL FOR REORGANIZING FEDERAL BUREAUCRACY IN TRIPLICATE. WE'LL CONTACT YOU IN DUE COURSE.'

Creating a Monster?
Presidents promise to trim the bureaucracy; few succeed. **Politics Why are cuts so difficult to achieve?**

Statistics supported Ford's observation. One study found that in a recent 50-year period, 246 new federal departments, agencies, and bureaus had been created, while only 27 had been abolished. The same study found that 148 of the 175 agencies at work in 1923 still exist.

Agencies survive for several reasons. First, when a new problem arises, Congress and the President usually set up a new agency to deal with it rather than assign it to an existing agency. Second, client groups of an agency, along with the bureaucrats themselves and some key supporters in Congress, usually have enough influence to prevent abolishing an agency even if it is no longer needed. Sometimes an agency simply gets overlooked.

SECTION 3 REVIEW

Section Summary
The bureaucracy influences and makes major public policy decisions.

Checking for Understanding
Recalling Facts
1. Define allegation, client group.
2. List the four ways in which federal bureaucrats influence public policy.
3. Cite the five reasons the federal bureaucracy has assumed an important role in making public policy.
4. Explain why so few federal departments and agencies have been abolished.

Exploring Themes
5. Public Policy To what extent is the bureaucracy involved in lawmaking? Explain.
6. Political Processes Why has the bureaucracy's role in making public policy grown?

Critical Thinking
7. Drawing Conclusions Do you see any advantages in bureaucrats taking a greater role in policy-making? Support your answer.
8. Making Inferences Why, do you think, do people sometimes get frustrated with the "red tape" of government?

Caption Answer
When new problems arise, new agencies often are set up to deal with them. Client groups, bureaucrats, and supporters in Congress may work to prevent the abolition of agencies.

Reteach
Have students write nine newspaper headlines which illustrate the four ways that the bureaucracy influences public policy and the five reasons the bureaucracy becomes involved in policy decisions.

Enrich
Have students research what client groups in their state have lobbied government agencies concerning programs and services for the state.

📁 Have students complete activity 18 in *Enrichment Activities* in the Teacher's Classroom Resources.

Close

Ask students to suppose that drastic budget cuts have forced the federal bureaucracy to be reduced substantially. Review with students the reasons why the bureaucracy has grown and have students use them to develop criteria for making the cuts.

Section 3 Review Answers

1. Definitions of terms appear on pages indicated: **allegation,** 520; **client group,** 522
2. make rules, are involved in lawmaking, settle disputes, provide advice
3. national growth and technology, international crises, economic problems, citizen demands, the nature of bureaucracy
4. Client groups of an agency, along with the bureaucrats themselves and supporters in Congress, have enough influence to prevent the abolishing of an agency that is no longer needed. Sometimes agencies are overlooked.
5. Bureaucrats are very involved because today they help make public policy by choosing what course of action to follow or not follow.
6. Answers may include the growth of the United States, international crises, economic problems at home, citizens' demands, and the nature of the bureaucracy itself.
7. Answers may include that bureaucrats have good advice to offer and may be very well-versed in their area. This could be a strength in making public policy.
8. Answers may include that red tape grows with additional regulations, and sometimes regulations may overlap or be too numerous or complicated to understand.

CRITICAL THINKING SKILLS

Focus

Tell students that assumptions are beliefs that people take for granted. Ask them to suggest assumptions about government. *(Examples: Government collects taxes and uses them for our benefit; federal programs waste money.)* Explain that the world runs on assumptions, and that informed citizens need to be able to judge the validity of assumptions.

Teach

Organize the class into three groups and ask each group to analyze one of the three statements regarding the Immigration Reform and Control Act of 1985. Using the Explanation steps, each group should break down the assumptions and analyze them. When they have completed the task, ask each group if the assumptions satisfy the premise of the statement. Why or why not? *(Opinions will vary.)* What assumptions could you add to each statement?

Assess

Have students complete the **Practice** exercise.

Close

Have students suggest assumptions the Framers of the Constitution made. How are their assumptions expressed in the Constitution?

Identifying Assumptions

Identifying assumptions involves paying attention to the ideas that an author takes for granted. Assumptions are the building blocks of every policy or opinion. If these assumptions are invalid, the policy or opinion may also be invalid. Being able to recognize and assess assumptions allows you to make a more informed decision about whether you agree or disagree with a given statement.

Explanation

To identify the assumptions behind a given statement or policy, follow these steps:
- Read the statement carefully.
- Determine what "missing links" are in the argument. Ask: What is being taken for granted here?
- Break down the assumptions on which the statement is based into their component parts and examine them critically.

Most statements and policies are based on a number of assumptions. These assumptions may or may not be correct. Recognizing that they exist is an important step toward deciding what you think about the statement or policy.

The following are statements about the Immigration Reform and Control Act of 1985. Each is followed by some of the unstated assumptions on which it is based.

The law tries to limit immigration by imposing penalties on employers who knowingly hire illegal aliens.

Assumptions: Illegal aliens are attracted by the availability of jobs. If penalties for hiring illegal aliens exist, fewer jobs will be available. If fewer jobs are available, fewer illegal aliens will enter the country.

The law tries to limit immigration by making it a crime to counterfeit or alter entry documents for sale to illegal aliens.

Assumptions: The availability of false entry papers makes it easier for illegal aliens to remain in the country. If penalties are set for altering or counterfeiting documents, fewer people will engage in these activities. If fewer people are engaged in these activities, fewer false documents will be available. If fewer false documents are available, fewer illegal aliens will be able to remain in the United States.

The law authorizes the Attorney General of the United States to admit specified numbers of foreign guest workers at harvest time if not enough United States workers to fill jobs are available.

Assumptions: American workers should be given priority in getting available jobs. At harvest time there may be more jobs than American workers can fill. It is important to ensure that enough workers are available to fill harvest-time jobs.

Practice

Now find at least one assumption behind each of the following statements about the establishment of a national speed limit.
1. In order to conserve gasoline in response to the 1973 oil embargo, Congress passed a national speed limit of 55 miles per hour that was well below existing state speed limits.
2. After the oil embargo ended, Congress extended the 55-mile-per-hour speed limit, citing reductions in highway fatalities.
3. Federal law mandates periodic checks on actual speeds driven in each state; states with non-compliance rates of more than 50 percent risk losing federal financial aid for highway programs.
4. In 1986 Congress lifted the 55-mile-per-hour limit on rural interstates but not on other roads.

> **Additional Practice**
>
> To practice this skill, see **Reinforcing the Skill** on page 531.

Practice Answers

1. If the speed limit is lowered, people will drive more slowly. If people drive more slowly, they will use less gasoline. It is important to conserve gasoline.
2. The lower speed limit was a factor in reducing highway fatalities. Reducing highway fatalities is an important goal.
3. State governments have influence over whether or not the speed limit is obeyed. State governments may choose not to enforce the speed limit. The threat of losing federal highway funds will cause state governments to enforce the speed limit.
4. Rural interstates are in some way different from other types of roads.

For additional practice, have students complete activity 18 in *Skill Reinforcement Activities* in the Teacher's Classroom Resources.

SECTION 4
Influences on Bureaucratic Decision Making

The function of bureaucracy is to make decisions about public policy that implement the aims of government. As Abraham Lincoln noted:

The legitimate object of government is to do for a community of people whatever they need to have done, but cannot do for themselves in their separate and individual capacities.

—ABRAHAM LINCOLN

While the federal bureaucracy attempts to serve the people by doing what they "cannot do for themselves," it does not make public policy in isolation. The President, Congress, the courts, and client groups influence federal agencies as they conduct business and shape policy.

The Influence of Congress

Lawmakers and bureaucrats interact with each other frequently. Bureaucrats are careful to build support with congressional committees that have authority over their agencies. The Department of Defense, for example, seeks to maintain good relations with lawmakers serving on the Armed Services committees of the House and the Senate.

Each cabinet department has employees who are called **liaison officers**. They help promote good relations with Congress. They keep track of bills moving through Congress that might affect the agency, as well as responding to requests for information from lawmakers.

Laws in the Skies
Congress has responded to concern about flight safety. **Law How does Congress influence agencies?**

For its part, Congress has two major tools it may use to influence decision making in federal agencies. These tools are new legislation and the budget.

New Legislation Lawmakers can pass laws to change the rules or regulations a federal agency establishes or to limit an agency in some way. Sometimes Congress is successful in these attempts. In 1979, for example, the Internal Revenue Service ruled that donations to private schools were not tax deductible unless the schools enrolled a certain number of minority students. The ruling caused a great deal of controversy, and Congress overturned it with new legislation.

SECTION PREVIEW

Objectives
After studying this section, you should be able to:
- Describe how Congress influences the decisions of federal agencies.
- Discuss the impact of the federal courts on agency decision making.

- Explain how client groups influence public policy.

Key Terms and Concepts
liaison officer, injunction, iron triangle

Themes in Government
- Checks and Balances
- Political Processes

Critical Thinking Skills
- Drawing Conclusions
- Making Inferences

CHAPTER 18: THE FEDERAL BUREAUCRACY   525

Classroom Resources for Section 4

- Guided Reading Activities
- Reproducible Lesson Plans
- Reteaching Activities 18
- Section 4 Quiz
- Chapter 18 Tests

- Testmaker
- Audio Cassettes (English and Spanish)
- Limited English Proficiency Activities 18
  SAT Practice Tests
  Writer's Guidebook

Focus

Bell Ringer
Ask students to make a list of factors they think influence public policy decisions made by federal agencies.

Motivating Activity
Discuss students' Bell Ringer lists. Place a composite list of factors on the chalkboard in what students judge to be their order of importance as influences. Keep the list on the chalkboard and use it for the Close activity in this section.

Vocabulary Precheck
Call on volunteers to tell what they think each key term and concept means. Have students check the accuracy of their definitions in the Glossary. **LEP**

Teach

Guided Practice
L1 Checks and Balances Create a table on the chalkboard headed *Influences on the Bureaucracy*. Write the following headings at the top of the table: *Congressional Influences, Judicial Influences, Client Group Influences,* and *Other Agency Influences*. Have students complete the table by providing examples of the influences each group has on agency decision making.

Caption Answer
by passing new legislation and controlling their budgets

L2 Identifying Alternatives Ask why federal agencies are so resistant to budget cuts. Ask students to suggest how agencies such as the Department of Defense or EPA might apply a strategy similar to Amtrak's to restore funding. (*selective base closings, shut down air quality monitoring*) Discuss what other strategies an agency can adopt to maintain or restore funding levels.

L3 Government Have students suppose that the Department of Education has written regulations to implement a law to fund vocational education. The regulations favor awards to private companies. Congress prefers awards to school districts. Discuss how Congress can get the kind of regulations it wants.

Independent Practice

L1 Illustrating Ideas Have students diagram an iron triangle by using the example of the Department of Veterans Affairs discussed in this section. Then have them diagram any other iron triangles they can think of. **LEP**

L2 Journalism Have students use newspapers and magazines to research current situations in which decision making in a federal agency has been influenced by Congress, the federal courts, client groups, or other federal agencies.

STUDY GUIDE

Theme Answer
Agencies have developed ways of getting around budget cuts, such as cutting key programs to stimulate client groups.

Critical Thinking Answer
Through inefficient administration of policies, the public might suffer.

Given its workload and the difficulty in passing new laws, Congress does not use this method of influence too often. Moreover, lawmakers opposed to an agency action often cannot find enough votes to overturn that action. When the Federal Trade Commission ordered an end to all cigarette advertising on television, some lawmakers from tobacco-growing states tried but failed to overturn the ruling.

The Power of the Budget Congress's major power over the bureaucracy is the power of the purse. The nation's lawmakers control each agency's budget. They can add to or cut an agency's budget and, in theory at least, refuse to appropriate money for the agency. What happens more often, however, is that Congress can threaten to eliminate programs that are important to the agency.

Even the power of appropriation has limits as a way for Congress to influence agency decisions. Much of an agency's budget may be used for entitlement expenditures. These expenditures are for basic services already required by law, such as social security or pensions for retired government employees. Such services are almost impossible for Congress to cut.

Second, agencies have developed strategies for getting around possible budget cuts. Suppose, for example, that Congress says an agency will receive only $8 billion for the next year instead of the $9 billion the agency wanted. When the agency sends in its budget, it will underestimate the amount it needs for its entitlement expenditures. At the same time, it will ask for full funding for other parts of its program it does not want to cut. If the agency runs short of money for entitlements midway through the year, Congress must pass a supplemental appropriation to cover the shortage. If it does not, Congress will face many angry constituents who are suddenly being denied benefits.

Another strategy agencies use is that when threatened with budget cuts, they reduce essential services first rather than last. The idea is that voters will quickly miss those services. The voters will then pressure Congress to restore the agencies' programs.

As part of this strategy, agencies may sometimes target their cuts in the districts or states of key members of Congress who have the power to get budget cuts restored. In 1975, for example, Congress said it wanted to reduce the budget for Amtrak, the federal agency that operates passenger trains in the United States. Amtrak almost immediately announced plans to comply with the reduced budget by cutting vital passenger service in the districts of key congressional leaders. The announcements had their desired effect: these leaders succeeded in restoring most of the Amtrak funds.

Even though Congress can influence agency decisions, it cannot totally control them. Harvard professor Graham T. Allison commented on this relationship:

> *To be responsive to a wide spectrum of problems, governments consist of large organizations, among which primary responsibility for particular tasks is divided. Each organization attends to a special set of problems and acts in quasi-independence on these problems. . . . Government leaders can substantially disturb, but not substantially control, the behavior of these organizations.*
>
> —GRAHAM T. ALLISON

The Influence of the Courts

Federal courts do not actively seek to influence the federal bureaucracy. The courts, however, can have an important impact on policymaking, hence on the everyday lives of citizens because agency decisions can often be appealed to the courts. The Administrative Procedures Act of 1946 allows citizens directly affected by the actions of federal agencies to challenge those agencies' actions in court. A federal court may issue an **injunction**—an order that will stop a particular action or enforce a rule or regulation.

Challenging Agency Procedures Most court challenges to federal agencies focus on the proce-

STUDY GUIDE

Themes in Government
Checks and Balances Why is the "power of the purse" not always effective as a means for Congress to control the bureaucracy?

Critical Thinking Skills
Drawing Conclusions What problems could result if Congress and a number of important federal agencies were to engage in

political warfare over a long period of time?

Background

As federal agencies conduct business and carry out public policy, they are often scrutinized by the President, the courts, Congress, and client groups. For example, the Compensation and Liability Act of 1980 (also called "Superfund") provided the Environmental Protection Agency (EPA) with $1.6 billion to clean up hazardous toxic waste. In 1983 public interest groups criticized the agency's handling of the Superfund and accused the agency of delays in cleaning up the environment, leading to a congressional investigation. The agency's problems resulted in the resignation of the EPA administrator. In 1986, however, legislation reauthorized Superfund and provided an additional $9 billion.

dures an agency uses, such as promoting job safety or protecting the environment rather than its overall goals. The Environmental Protection Agency (EPA) once sent a team of investigators to a chemical plant in Michigan. The EPA did not have a specific complaint against the plant. Rather, the EPA officials wanted to look around the plant to see if the plant might be violating any federal regulation.

The chemical plant refused to admit the EPA investigators without a search warrant. Getting a warrant would have required the EPA to specify the purpose of the search. Instead, the EPA hired an airplane and flew over the plant, taking detailed pictures.

The plant owners then went to court. They claimed that the EPA's action violated their constitutional protection against unreasonable search and seizure, their privacy, and their right to legal due process. The plant owners claimed the EPA was conducting a "fishing expedition." The court issued an injunction against the EPA and impounded the photos. A number of other companies have taken similar actions against government agencies.

Success in Court Cases While the courts can have a real impact on the bureaucracy, citizens have not had much success in court cases against the bureaucracy. One study shows that the courts do not usually revise the decisions of federal regulatory commissions. For example, the Federal Power Commission and the Federal Trade Commission have won 91 percent of the cases they have argued before the Supreme Court. The National Labor Relations Board and the Internal Revenue Service have won 75 percent of their cases.

The Influence of Client Groups

As stated earlier, each agency has client groups. The Department of Education spends much of its time dealing with state and local school administrators. The Food and Drug Administration works closely with major drug companies. The Commerce Department identifies with and promotes business interests. The Department of Labor has a similar relationship with labor unions.

Client groups often attempt to influence agency decisions. Most groups have lobbyists in Washington, D.C. These lobbyists work to get their groups' ideas across to agency officials. Lobbyists may testify at agency hearings, write letters, keep track of agency decisions, and take other steps to support their groups' interests.

Congressional committees, client groups, and a federal department or agency often cooperate closely to make public policy. When agencies, congressional committees, and client groups continually work together, such cooperation is called an **iron triangle**, or a subgovernment.

Such a relationship is called a triangle because together congressional committees, client groups, and agencies all have the necessary resources to satisfy each other's needs. The adjective *iron* is used because the relationship is so strong that it is often difficult

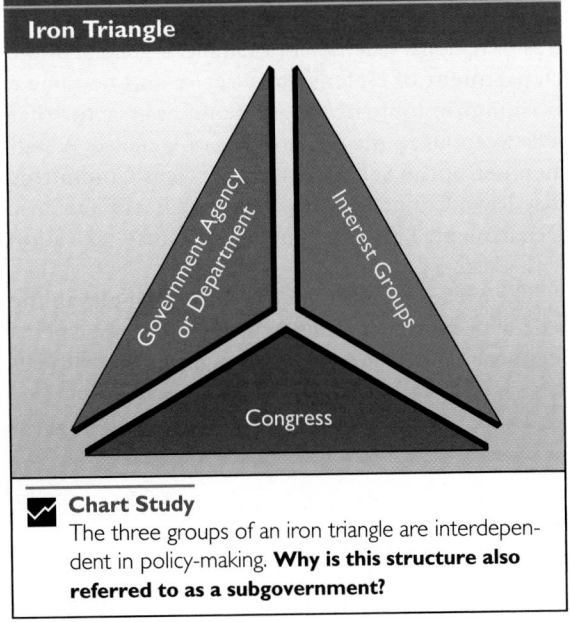

Iron Triangle

Government Agency or Department

Interest Groups

Congress

☑ **Chart Study**
The three groups of an iron triangle are interdependent in policy-making. **Why is this structure also referred to as a subgovernment?**

CHAPTER 18: THE FEDERAL BUREAUCRACY 527

STUDY GUIDE

Themes in Government
Political Processes Client groups are those persons or groups most directly affected by the policies of government agencies.

What client groups are likely to be associated with the Department of Justice?

Critical Thinking Skills
Making Inferences Do you think that iron triangles undermine or serve the public interest? Explain your answer.

Cooperative Learning Activity

Organize the class into several groups. Have students in each group suggest ways that a law of their choosing may be affected by an "iron triangle." Have each group assign its members specific tasks such as library research work, note-taking, or presenting. Have a spokesperson from each group present an oral report. Then open each group's topic for class discussion.

L3 Persuasive Writing Have students write essays in which they indicate whether they think client groups are a positive or a negative force in influencing bureaucratic decision making.

Chart Study Answer
It represents interest groups' close association with agencies, departments, and congressional committees of the government.

STUDY GUIDE

Theme Answer
civil rights groups, bar associations, law enforcement groups

Critical Thinking Answer
Answers will vary depending on how the student views government regulation and interest group policies.

CONNECTIONS

Political Processes
In the 1980s President Reagan's policy of deregulation ran against the environmental movement. Reagan often sided with business. He suggested that some damage to the environment was the price the country had to pay if it wanted companies to provide jobs and strengthen the economy. As a result, during Reagan's administration, the budget for the EPA dropped sharply.

Assess

Check for Understanding
Have students complete Section 4 Review on page 528.

Meeting Objectives

Each section objective is tested by the Section Review questions that follow it in parentheses.

• Describe how Congress influences the decisions of federal agencies. (3, 4, 6, 7)
• Discuss the impact of the federal courts on agency decision making. (5, 7, 8)
• Explain how client groups influence public policy. (3, 5, 6, 7)

Evaluate

📁 Section 4 Quiz

💻 Testmaker

Reteach

📁 Have students complete activity 18 in *Reteaching Activities* in the Teacher's Classroom Resources.

Enrich

Have students write an essay which answers this question:

Is the process of democratic government corrupted more by cooperative and friendly interactions or by adversarial and competitive relationships among the bureaucracy, Congress, and client groups?

Close

Review students' Bell Ringer list and ask how they would change it.

for other individuals and groups outside the triangle to influence policy in the area.

Public policy toward veterans' affairs is an example of the iron triangle. The Department of Veterans Affairs (VA) provides important services such as hospital care, but the VA needs resources to continue offering such services to veterans. Lawmakers on congressional committees responsible for veterans' affairs supply the VA with money but need electoral support to remain in office. Congressional committees also need political support to win internal struggles for power in Congress. Client groups, such as the American Legion, provide the political support that the lawmakers need to remain in office. They in turn, however, need the VA's goods and services to satisfy the demands of their members.

Thus, it is the working combination of these three groups concerned with veterans' affairs that basically determines what the policy of the national government toward veterans will be. Similar iron triangles operate in many policy areas such as agriculture, business, labor, and national defense.

People often move from one side of the triangle to another almost as in a game of musical chairs. In the area of national defense, for example, a general in the Department of Defense may retire and become a Washington lobbyist for a defense contractor that sells weapons to the Department of Defense. A staff member of the Senate Armed Services Committee may leave Congress and go to work in the Defense Department. Later, the same person may take a job with a defense contractor.

The existence of hundreds of iron triangles in the federal government tends to give such arrangements legitimacy. There are, however, many critics who believe that iron triangles allow interest groups undue influence in public policy. Critics say that because these subgovernments operate outside the control of the executive branch, Congress should pass laws to regulate their supporting interest groups.

Agency Influence

Bureaucrats in different federal agencies interact with each other. These interactions may occur for several reasons. One is that programs or regulations in different agencies sometimes conflict with each other. For example, rules the Occupational Safety and Health Administration makes about noise standards in factories may contradict regulations the Environmental Protection Agency establishes. Decision makers in each agency may try to influence the others to accept their program or rules. Often, interagency task forces or committees settle such disputes.

Bureaucrats from different agencies may also compete because many problems do not fit exactly under the jurisdiction of one agency. During the 1960s the federal government increased its efforts to deal with the problems of housing, unemployment, and law enforcement in large American cities. In 1965 President Johnson established a new Department of Housing and Urban Development. Creating the new agency was an effort to reduce duplication and competition between different agencies dealing with similar problems.

All in all, many factors influence the decisions federal agencies must make about public policy. The most important of these influences are the President, Congress, the courts, client groups, and other agencies themselves.

4
SECTION REVIEW

Section Summary
Many groups such as Congress, the courts, and government agencies influence bureaucratic decision making.

Checking for Understanding
Recalling Facts
1. Define liaison officer, injunction, iron triangle.
2. List two tools Congress may use to influence federal agencies.
3. Discuss why federal agencies might conflict with one another.
4. Cite how agencies can bypass budget cuts.

Exploring Themes
5. Checks and Balances How do the courts influence the bureaucracy?
6. Political Processes Give an example of how the iron triangle works.

Critical Thinking
7. Drawing Conclusions Why is cutting essential services the best strategy for agencies to use when threatened with budget cuts?
8. Making Inferences Why is it important that most court challenges to federal agencies focus on procedures rather than goals?

Section 4 Review Answers

1. Definitions of terms appear on pages indicated: **liaison officer**, 525; **injunction**, 526; **iron triangle**, 527
2. new legislation and the budget
3. Programs or regulations in different agencies sometimes conflict. Many problems do not exactly fit under the jurisdiction of one agency.
4. They reduce essential services first. They ask for less money for entitlement than is needed and full funding for

the rest of the budget. Since entitlement expenditures are mandated by law, Congress must later restore them to the budget.
5. An agency's decision can often be appealed to the courts.
6. Examples should include the interaction of a department or agency, Congress, and a client group.

7. because lawmakers hear quickly and strongly from voters—they do not want to risk losing votes
8. Answers should indicate that procedural problems can involve constitutional questions and are appropriate for the court, but it is an executive or legislative task to deal with agency goals.

Loret Miller Ruppe on a Successful Government Agency

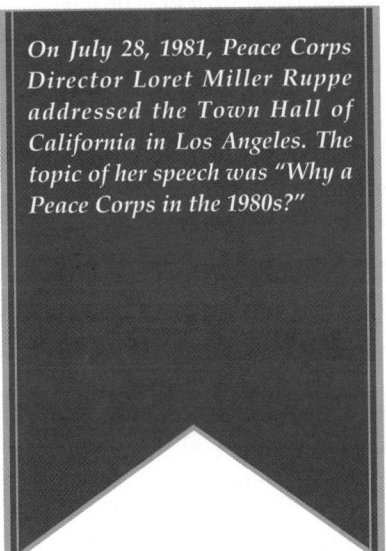

On July 28, 1981, Peace Corps Director Loret Miller Ruppe addressed the Town Hall of California in Los Angeles. The topic of her speech was "Why a Peace Corps in the 1980s?"

I represent a government agency that has great credibility, . . . but whose fine work for the past ten years or so, . . . has been submerged within the mainstream of American life. There are too many people across the United States who, when Peace Corps is mentioned, say, "Oh, is that still around? I haven't heard of it in years." To say that this is a matter of concern for us would be to characterize it too lightly. It is of grave concern. . . .

What are they [volunteers] doing? Well, first of all, they are living up to the true and basic mandate of the Peace Corps Act —promoting world peace and friendship by sharing America's talents and skills, its trained manpower, with countries who more and

more are asking America for those volunteers, and who need them more now in 1981 than in 1961 when the Peace Corps was born. They need them more because economic conditions, due to inflation, due to the energy crisis, due to growing populations and shrinking food supply, are putting world peace and survival on the line. . . .

If you were to ask, "Why a Peace Corps in the 80's?" . . . who would you go to to get a valid report? Wouldn't it be logical to ask Americans who have been overseas, of their impressions? In Washington, all the newly appointed ambassadors make courtesy calls on the heads of whatever agencies have input into the countries they represent. I want to report to you that I have now had meetings with approximately twenty ambassadors, who represent extensive overseas experience. Each one has told me that they consider our Peace Corps volunteers and their work to be one of the most positive and appreciated American presences in the countries they have served in . . . and they ask me to keep the same number of volunteers, or better yet, send more.

Where else would you go for a

. . . sharing America's talents and skills, its trained manpower, with countries who more and more are asking America for those volunteers . . .

valid report on this success story? I have met with each assistant secretary at the State Department—They represent each region of the world—and they tell me the same thing. The realization that the work of volunteers is truly helping developing countries, even if an inch at a time, is happening. Twenty years of inches have produced a yardstick of positive results, and have made permanent bonds of friendship, in many cases kinship between thousands of American volunteers and individual villagers, farmers, educators, businessmen, and government officials in those 90 countries where Peace Corps has had programs.

—LORET MILLER RUPPE,
JULY 28, 1981

Examining the Reading

Reviewing Facts
1. Explain **the basic mandate of the Peace Corps act.**
2. Relate **who Ruppe considers experts to evaluate the Peace Corps program.**

Critical Thinking Skills
3. Making Inferences **Although Peace Corps volunteers receive benefits and an allowance from the government, do you see their jobs as similar to or different from most federal jobs? Give reasons for your answer.**

Focus

Discuss what students know about the Peace Corps.

Teach

Ask: Why does Ruppe say that Peace Corps volunteers were needed more in the 1980s than they were in the 1960s? *(Economic conditions had put world peace and survival on the line.)* What benefits for American foreign policy does Ruppe feel the Peace Corps provides? *(The Peace Corps is one of the most positive American presences in these countries; it fosters kinship between Americans and their host peoples.)*

Assess

Have students complete **Examining the Reading.**
Answers

1. to promote world peace and friendship by sharing America's talents, skills, and trained workers with other countries
2. individuals representing government agencies that work overseas, ambassadors, members of the State Department
3. Answers may include that bureaucrats influence and make policy but volunteers carry it out at a more personal and all-encompassing level than most federal employees.

Close

Have students discuss why the Peace Corps appeals to some Americans even though they are paid a very small stipend.

More About Personal Perspectives

The idea of a group of people to "fight" for peace was originated in 1904 by William James, an American philosopher. The American Friends Service Committee, a Quaker organization, began sending its members to work on socially useful projects in overseas countries, particularly among the poor, in 1917. Other groups followed suit after World War

II. In 1960 Senator Hubert Humphrey proposed a "peace corps" and John F. Kennedy used the idea as a campaign issue when he ran for President in 1960. Founded in 1961, the Peace Corps has utilized the skills of over 80,000 Americans in more than 90 countries.

Identifying Terms and Concepts

1. b, g; **2.** d, h; **3.** c; **4.** i; **5.** j;
6. e; **7.** a; **8.** f

Reviewing Facts and Ideas

1. cabinet departments, independent executive agencies, and regulatory commissions

2. Government corporations are supported directly by money from Congress, not by funds from private investors.

3. Independent of all three branches of the national government, they regulate business.

4. because of the widespread inefficiency and corruption of the spoils system

5. The Civil Service Commission was replaced in 1979 by the Office of Personnel Management, which now handles the recruitment, pay, retirement policy, and examinations for all federal workers.

6. 2 to 5 weeks paid vacation, extensive health insurance plans and generous sick leave, retirement at age 55 with half-pay for the rest of their lives if they have worked for 30 years

7. Supporters feel that it keeps the federal civil service politically neutral and protects workers from threats by superiors for political reasons. On the other hand, federal workers consider the law a violation of the constitutional guarantee of freedom of speech and claim that the act discourages political participation by people who are well informed about political issues.

8. The President appoints people to about 2,200 positions outside the civil service system. These top political appointees hold their positions for only a few years, and their employment usually is terminated when a new President is elected.

9. the Depression

10. Most client groups are represented by lobbyists who work to get their ideas across to agency officials.

Summary and Significance

The federal bureaucracy consists of cabinet departments, independent executive agencies, and regulatory commissions. These departments and agencies carry on the work of the federal government. Most federal jobs are filled through the civil service system, with the exception of top-level employees. The bureaucracy both influences and sets public policy. The government creates new agencies and departments to deal with new problems and demands as they arise. Congress, the courts, and client groups work with the federal agencies to influence decisions and set policy in particular areas. It is important to understand how the federal bureaucracy works and cooperates with other agencies and branches of government in order to effect change and comprehend public policy.

Identifying Terms and Concepts

Choose the letter of the correct term or concept below to complete the sentence.

a. injunction   f. iron triangle
b. civil servant   g. bureaucrat
c. government   h. spoils system
   corporation
d. civil service system   i. deregulate
e. client group   j. allegation

1. An individual who works for the federal government is a _____ or a _____.
2. Before the _____, many people got government jobs through the _____.
3. Some people work for a _____, such as the Postal Service.
4. Some people lost their jobs when Congress began to _____ the Civil Aeronautics Board and cut down on its procedures.
5. A complaint is also called an _____.
6. A _____, such as a special-interest group, is a key factor in influencing public policy.
7. In some cases, a court will issue an _____ to stop a particular action.
8. A cooperative effort on the parts of congressional committees, a federal agency, and client groups is called an _____.

Reviewing Facts and Ideas

1. Describe the three types of agencies that make up the federal bureaucracy.

2. Explain the major difference between a government corporation and a private business.
3. Examine the special role of independent regulatory commissions in the federal bureaucracy.
4. State why the United States created the civil service system.
5. Discuss the connection between the Civil Service Commission and the Office of Personnel and Management.
6. Name three job benefits to which federal workers are entitled.
7. State the arguments for and against the Hatch Act.
8. Explain why not all employees of the United States government come under the civil service system.
9. Cite the event that led to the practice of government assisting the ill and the neglected.
10. Describe how client groups attempt to influence the decisions that agencies of the United States government make.

Applying Themes

1. **Political Processes** Officials appointed by the President hold top management and executive positions within the federal bureaucracy. Thus, with every new administration, new people are named to these positions. Explain the advantages and disadvantages of this system.
2. **Checks and Balances** In what ways can Congress attempt to change or limit a federal agency in some way?

Applying Themes

1. <u>advantages:</u> new people with new ideas come into government; they are supportive of the new administration and can urge the bureaucracy to implement new programs; <u>disadvantages:</u> people are inexperienced and it takes them a long time to learn their jobs and get the bureaucracy to do what they want

2. by passing legislation that affects the operation of that agency or by adjusting that agency's budget

3. Answers will vary. Those who agree will probably base their argument on the fact that bureaucrats are the most informed in the policy area. Those who disagree will probably use the argument that only elected officials should make policy since they were chosen by voters.

3. **Public Policy** In theory bureaucrats merely carry out the policies of elected officials. In practice bureaucrats help make public policy. Should bureaucrats be allowed to actually help determine public policy? Support your answer.

Critical Thinking Skills

1. **Making Inferences** Why do you think people often view and refer to the federal bureaucracy in a negative way? Cite examples to support your point of view.
2. **Drawing Conclusions** Although many Presidents have attempted to reduce the size and complexity of the federal bureaucracy, few have succeeded. Why do you think their efforts have generally failed?
3. **Synthesizing Information** President Andrew Jackson argued that rotation in office of federal employees was a democratic procedure. The civil service system, on the other hand, rewards government employees with job security. Which system do you support? Give reasons for your answer.

Linking Past and Present

The growth of the federal bureaucracy can be gauged by the increase in the number of civilian employees. In 1792 approximately 780 people worked for the national government, while the figure had risen to almost 7,000 by 1821. Today, more than 3 million civilians work for the federal government. Many of these positions were created during the Great Depression. Most Americans claim to be against "big government," yet they expect the government to be responsive to their needs. State the name of the department, agency, or commission that you believe currently serves the greatest public interest. Support your answer.

Writing About Government

Expressive Writing Write an essay about why you would or would not choose to work for the federal government as a bureaucrat. In your essay be certain

to evaluate both the positive and negative aspects of pursuing a career as a civil servant.

Reinforcing the Skill

Identifying Assumptions The following statements concern the National and Community Service Act of 1990. This bill, which failed to pass, would have used federal money to encourage and reward people who perform a variety of types of service to their communities, such as tutoring, environmental clean-up, or helping the elderly. Use what you have learned about identifying assumptions to examine each statement. Give at least one assumption on which it rests.

---

1. *If the compensation offered for non-military service is equal to that offered for military service, it will be difficult to recruit soldiers.*

2. *Financial reward should not be made an incentive for community service.*

3. *Not offering to pay for community service means that many who want to and should be allowed to serve will not be able to do so.*

Investigating Further

1. **Individual Project** Create a political cartoon depicting a problem that has given bureaucracy a negative image. Problems may include rigidity of the procedures, confusing language used in regulations, "red tape," and intradepartmental divisions within the bureaucracy. You may find it necessary to include a caption beneath your cartoon.
2. **Cooperative Learning** Organize into groups of five or six students each. Make a list of the ways in which the federal departments or agencies or commissions of the federal bureaucracy may affect your life on a daily basis. Use this list to rank each of the influences in order of their importance. Rejoin the class and compare lists.

3. Answers should include the following: the spoils system gives many people a chance to hold office and makes the bureaucracy responsive to the President in power, although it often results in corruption and inefficiency. The civil service system gives workers job security and assures the nation of an experienced trained bureaucracy. It is difficult, however, to get rid of incompetent workers, and the bureaucracy is often not responsive to the President in power.

Linking Past and Present

Students should cite a current department, agency, or commission of the federal bureaucracy and support their answer.

Writing About Government

Essays will vary, but students should support their choices.

Reinforcing the Skill

1. Most people, when given the choice, will prefer non-military to military service.
2. The spirit in which community services are performed is an important aspect of the program. If people expect financial reward for the services they perform, they will not be doing the work in the right spirit.
3. Many poor people will want to perform community service. Poor people may not be able to participate unless they receive pay. It is important that everyone who wants to serve should be able to do so.

Investigating Further

1. Cartoons should reflect problems of bureaucracy.
2. Answers may include food being inspected by the Department of Agriculture, the Department of Education setting standards for education, the Department of Labor regulating work standards and hours, and so on. Answers should indicate that bureaucracy is involved in most aspects of students' lives.

Critical Thinking Skills

1. Answers may include that because it is so large and complex, it is sometimes difficult to understand how it works and how all the pieces are connected. People also get tired of the red tape and runaround associated with bureaucracy and the fact that so many different elements are tied together.

2. Answers may include the nature of the bureaucracy itself. Once created, federal agencies never seem to die. As new problems arise, more agencies are created. These agencies are then kept by the support of client groups, supporters in Congress, and the bureaucrats themselves.

CASE STUDY

The Case at a Glance

Who: Lyndon Johnson
What: President's relationship with Congress
When: 1963–1968
Where: Washington, D.C.
Why: expansion of presidential powers

Focus

Ask students what an executive of a large corporation has in common with the President of the United States. *(Both have power over great numbers of people; both have great responsibilities; both are leaders of people.)* How does the President lead the nation? *(by persuading the public and Congress to accept his or her policies)* What may happen if a President cannot provide effective leadership? *(may lose support of people and Congress)* Tell students that the importance of presidential leadership is the focus of this case study.

Teach

Guided Practice

L1 Making a Time Line Skim the case study with students to locate the years of the Johnson presidency. Draw a time line on the chalkboard using the dates 1963 and 1968 as the beginning and end points. Have students fill in the key events of the Johnson presidency on the time line.

Powers of Congress

He [the President] shall from time to time give to the Congress Information of the state of the Union, and recommend to their Consideration such Measures as he shall judge necessary and expedient. . . .

—Article II, Section 3

Powers of the President

The principal power that the President has is to bring them in and try to persuade them to do what they ought to do without persuasion. That's what I spend most of my time doing. That's what the powers of the President amount to.

—President Harry S Truman, May 1948

Expanding Presidential Powers

The Case

The Constitution of the United States grants the President a number of formal powers. At first glance it appears that the President has considerable leverage. The annual State of the Union address, the submission of bills for consideration, the veto power, the power of appointment, and patronage seem to provide tremendous power. It is becoming apparent today, however, that one of the most important resources at the President's disposal is the ability to persuade. Although the President can propose legislation and veto bills, the President can do little to ensure that his or her proposed measures will be enacted.

President Lyndon B. Johnson observed that:

In some ways . . . Congress is like a dangerous animal that you're trying to make work for you. You push him a little bit and he may go just as you want but you push him too much and he may balk and turn on you. You've got to sense just how much he'll take and what kind of mood he's in every day. For if you don't have a feel for him, he's liable to turn around and go wild. And it all depends on your sense of timing.

—LYNDON B. JOHNSON, 1964

During most of his time in office, President Johnson was one of the two Presidents most skilled in getting his legislation adopted. The other was Franklin D. Roosevelt during the first year of his New Deal that was designed to curb the nation's Great Depression. Of the modern Presidents, only Lyndon Johnson through his Great Society programs has matched the successful legislative record of the New Deal. Political scientists, writers, and politicians all have speculated about what made Lyndon Johnson so successful at first. Was it the time, the program, or the man? Perhaps it was all three.

Background

Most observers agree that Lyndon B. Johnson, who became the youngest Senate majority leader in 1955, was an astute student of Congress and a master of persuasion. Washington correspondent Jack Bell described the way it worked:

More About the Case

If Abraham Lincoln could be called a lawyer's lawyer, then Lyndon Johnson was a politician's politician. Johnson's first experiences with the legislative process came as a young boy when he escorted his father to the Texas house of representatives, where his father represented the Hill Country of central Texas. After college, Johnson taught for a year and then became secretary to United States Representative Richard M. Kleberg in 1931.

In 1937 Johnson ran for a vacant congressional seat in central Texas. He won the election by pushing himself to give 7 to 10 speeches a day during

While he served as the Senate's Democratic leader, the Texan . . . maintained a furious pace. Operating from his frontrow desk he was always prodding everyone in sight to get along with the business in hand. . . . He busied himself collaring colleagues, thrusting his face within inches of his victim's as he argued and cajoled. . . .

There was no gainsaying the record. Johnson was effective in the Senate. What Lyndon wanted, Lyndon nearly always got. . . .

—JACK BELL, *THE JOHNSON TREATMENT*, 1965

By the late 1950s, Lyndon Johnson had set his sights on the 1960 Democratic presidential nomination. At the national convention, however, John F. Kennedy won the nomination. Kennedy then offered Johnson the vice presidential nomination. In an extremely close election, the Democratic ticket won and President John F. Kennedy and Vice President Lyndon B. Johnson took office in January 1961.

The Great Society Following the tragic assassination of President Kennedy on November 22, 1963, Lyndon B. Johnson became the thirty-sixth President of the United States. In keeping with his senatorial experience, the new President set about to create support for his presidency and for Kennedy's legislative programs that were stalled in Congress. On November 27, five days after the assassination, President Johnson went to address Congress, "prepared for a dramatic and emotional effort to unify Congress and the American people behind him. . . ."

He began his speech with the statement, "All I have I would gladly have given not to be standing here today." Johnson continued:

No memorial oration or eulogy could more eloquently honor President Kennedy's memory than the earliest possible passage of the civil rights bill for which he fought so long. We have talked long enough in this country about equal rights. We have talked for one hundred years or more. It is time now to write the next chapter—and to write it in the books of law.

—LYNDON B. JOHNSON, 1963

The new President went on to confirm commitments to foreign countries and to call upon Congress to

"Anything you say, Lyndon . . ."

Presidential Influence
Presidents with strong connections to Congress, like LBJ, fare better in getting their legislation passed than do "outsiders" such as Jimmy Carter.

enact the tax cut President Kennedy had proposed as well. Most members of Congress warmly received the call for action.

President Johnson's relationship with Congress played a major role in the success of his first years in office. Under his leadership Congress eagerly passed the stalled legislation of Kennedy's New Frontier, including the Civil Rights Act of 1964 and a cut in taxes. It was that year that Lyndon Johnson also announced his program of reform—the Great Society:

The Great Society rests on abundance and liberty for all. It demands an end to poverty and racial injustice, to which we are totally committed in our time. But that is just the beginning.

The Great Society is a place where every child can find knowledge to enrich his mind and to enlarge his talents. It is a place where leisure is a welcome chance to build and reflect, not a feared cause of boredom and restlessness. It is a place where the city of man serves not only the needs of the body and the demands of commerce, but the desire for beauty and the hunger for community.

—LYNDON B. JOHNSON, 1964

UNIT 5: THE EXECUTIVE BRANCH **533**

(Kennedy assassination; passage of civil rights legislation; passage of Great Society legislation for social security, medicaid, and medicare; war on poverty; 1964 election; unraveling of the consensus in 1966)

Have students use the time line to provide examples of Johnson's success and failure as a leader.

L2 Making Generalizations
Discuss Johnson's leadership in the Senate. Ask: What was Johnson's leadership style? Why was he unpopular with the public toward the end of his administration? *(The Vietnam War eroded his public support.)* What generalization can you make about presidential leadership, using Johnson as an example? *(An effective leader needs to have a close working relationship with Congress.)*

L3 Analyzing Ideas List on the chalkboard the techniques Johnson used to pass legislation through Congress. Ask: How did Johnson bring about consensus? *(by unifying both Congress and the American people after the Kennedy assassination)* What destroyed the consensus? *(rising inflation, inner-city riots, draft riots, the Vietnam War)*

the campaign and by strongly aligning himself with President Franklin D. Roosevelt. Once in Congress, Johnson used his office to fund rural electrification for central Texas, thereby increasing his popularity among farmers and construction companies.

In 1948 Johnson was elected to the United States Senate, becoming minority leader in five years. Johnson acted on legislation only if he knew he had enough votes to win. If he did not have the required votes, he would begin a campaign of persuasion. Hubert Humphrey called Johnson a "genius in the art of the legislative process."

Independent Practice

L1 Persuasive Writing Have students write a paragraph that answers the following: Was Johnson an effective President? Why or why not?

L2 Research Have students research how Theodore Roosevelt and Franklin Roosevelt shaped a consensus, not only in the nation but with Congress. Have students focus on how each created a supportive public image. How did each use the media to his best advantage?

L3 Informative Writing Have students write a report on the Great Society. Whom did it benefit? What parts are still funded by Congress today?

Assess

Have students complete **Examining the Case**.

Close

Have students cite recent events involving Congress and the President. What is the current President's relationship with Congress? What parallels, if any, can students see in the current relationship to the relationship described in the case study?

In fall 1964 the nation rallied behind its new President, giving him a landslide victory for another term. At the same time, successful Democratic congressional candidates swept into office in such large numbers that the previous coalition of Southern Democrats and conservative Republicans were easily outnumbered in both houses of Congress. Johnson was assured of the consensus he needed in the legislature to put the Great Society into action.

When the Eighty-ninth Congress met in 1965, the President outlined the legislation he deemed necessary. The result was astonishing. Congress passed 84 of the 87 bills requested. Included were bills covering medicare and medicaid, another civil rights act, War on Poverty legislation, aid to elementary and secondary education, and several conservation measures.

Many observers credit the amazing first year of the administration to the President's uncanny understanding of Congress. Johnson counseled his staff:

> *You've got to give it all you can that first year. Doesn't matter what kind of a majority you come in with. You've got just one year when they treat you right and before they start worrying about themselves. The third year, you lose votes . . . the fourth year's all politics. You can't put anything through when half of Congress is thinking about how to beat you. So you've got one year.*
>
> —LYNDON B. JOHNSON, 1965

These were prophetic words because in 1966, rising inflation, inner-city riots, draft riots, and the war in Vietnam spelled the end to Johnson's run of successes. Congress had grown weary of the President's endless calls for more legislation. At the same time, the President turned his attention to the war in Southeast Asia and spent less time cultivating Congress. Congress quickly assumed a new attitude of independence.

Significance

What was it exactly that enabled Lyndon Johnson to accomplish with Congress what so many other Presidents were unable to do? Was it because of his style, or was Johnson a beneficiary of his time? In the President's opinion:

> *If I were to name the one factor above all others that helped me in dealing with the Congress, I would say it was the genuine friendship and rapport I had with most Congressmen and Senators.*
>
> —LYNDON B. JOHNSON

Was this the answer, or was it as Doris Kearns concluded:

> *He succeeded, and for many reasons: one, the circumstances of his assumption of office, creating a mood of strong national unity; two, the fortuitous state of Kennedy's administration at the time he was killed—the legislative programs had been articulated but not passed; and three (the most important reason, but dependent on the first and second), his transformation of the conduct of the Presidency in such a way that he could utilize those techniques that had served him so well in the Senate: one-to-one relations, bargaining, consensus, and insulation from choice.*
>
> —DORIS KEARNS, 1976

Whatever the reason, the results can still be seen today. Many Great Society programs fell disappointingly short of success, but others remain to the benefit of people in the 1990s. One can only guess what might have happened if the war in Vietnam had not divided the nation and led to the end of the Johnson presidency.

Examining the Case

Reviewing Facts
1. Explain why President Truman felt that the ability to persuade was so important for a President.
2. Describe how Johnson won support for the Great Society.
3. Identify three reasons President Johnson was so successful in 1965.

Critical Thinking Skills
4. Making Comparisons How did President Kennedy and President Johnson differ in their relations with Congress?
5. Predicting Consequences Would the Great Society have succeeded if the United States had not been involved in Vietnam? Explain your answer.

Examining the Case Answers

1. He believed that the only major power available to a President was the power to persuade.
2. He capitalized on his strong connections to, and understanding of, Congress.
3. The people supported his programs; he had a Democratic Congress; he understood Congress.

4. Johnson had a better understanding of Congress than did Kennedy.
5. Answers may vary, but students might suggest that it might have succeeded if the Vietnam War had not divided the nation.

Chapter 16
The Presidency

As head of the executive branch, Presidents have developed enormous power and responsibility over the years. The President acts as commander in chief of the armed forces in peace and war. The President symbolizes what the nation stands for to the world and to the American people. Congress expects the President to propose legislation intended to build the nation's strength and prosperity. Because of the powers of the presidency, the American system of government is often called presidential government.

People who wish to become President must meet certain qualifications. The Constitution sets some of these qualifications. A President must be (1) a natural-born citizen of the United States, (2) at least 35 years old, and (3) a resident of the United States for at least 14 years before taking office. Other qualifications are personal qualities that Americans expect their Presidents to have. Experience in government is an unwritten but important qualification. A serious candidate for the presidency must also have access to large amounts of money to fund a campaign.

Voters cast their ballots for President every four years (1992, 1996, 2000, etc.) on the Tuesday after the first Monday in November. While the candidates' names are printed on the ballot, the voters are not actually voting directly for President and Vice President. Rather, they are voting for all of their party's **electors** in their state. These electors will later cast the official vote for President and Vice President.

The Electoral College includes 538 electors—a number determined by the total of House and Senate members plus 3 for the District of Columbia. Each state has as many electors as it has senators and representatives in Congress. To be elected President or Vice President, a candidate must win at least 270 of the 538 votes. The new President, called the President-elect until the inauguration, takes office at noon on January 20 in the year following the presidential election.

In addition to their many powers, Presidents have seven major duties. Five of these are based on the Constitution: serving as head of state, chief executive, chief legislator, chief diplomat, and commander in chief. Two other roles not mentioned in the Constitution have developed over the years. These are economic planner and political party leader.

Chapter 17
Presidential Leadership

The executive branch consists of numerous agencies and commissions and 14 major executive departments. A secretary appointed by the President and approved by the Senate heads each department. These 14 secretaries, the Vice President, and several other top officials make up the **cabinet.** This advisory group helps the President make decisions and set government policy.

Another part of the executive branch—the Executive Office of the President (EOP)—consists of individuals and agencies that directly assist the President. Modern Presidents rely heavily on the EOP to provide specialized advice and to gather information needed for decision making. They also use it to help them implement presidential decisions and to gain more control over the executive branch.

Today the EOP consists of the White House Office and several specialized agencies that all report directly to the President. Agency staffs include attorneys, scientists, social scientists, and other highly technical or professional personnel. The EOP currently has more than 1,500 full-time employees, most of whom work in the west wing of the White House or next door in the old Executive Office Building.

Presidents do not want the information they receive from their advisers to become public knowledge. In order to keep White House discussions and policy-making confidential, modern Presidents have sometimes used **executive privilege**. Executive privilege is the right of the President to refuse to testify before, or provide information to, Congress or a court.

With the help of their advisers, Presidents have the main responsibility for national leadership. Public opinion surveys clearly show that Americans look to the President to exercise strong leadership, to keep the peace, to solve economic and social problems, and generally to get things done.

Chapter 18
The Federal Bureaucracy

The **federal bureaucracy** is made up of departments and agencies that do the work of the govern-

---

Using the Unit 5 Digest

Use the Unit Digest to introduce, review, reteach, or condense specific chapters or the entire unit. The Unit Digest is enhanced by the corresponding transparencies and activities in the Teacher's Classroom Resources.

Focus

Select about a dozen headlines from recent newspaper and magazine articles on a variety of activities performed by the President. Display the headlines prominently in the classroom. Then ask students to discuss the following: Based on these headlines, what do you think is the major function of the President? Why? What powers does the President need to perform this function? Why?

Bring the discussion to a close by mentioning that presidential duties and powers are discussed in this Unit Digest.

Teach

L1 Constructing a Diagram Have students construct a diagram that shows the three-part structure of the executive branch of the United States government—the Executive Office of the President, the President's Cabinet, and independent offices and agencies. A useful source of information for this activity is the *United States Government Manual.* Display a number of diagrams on the bulletin board and use them as the basis for a discussion on the different roles these three sections play in the running of the government. **LEP**

Classroom Resources for Unit 5 Digest

Unit Digest Transparencies, Unit 5

Participating in Government, Unit 5

Interpreting Visuals Dis-
play transparency 5 from the
Unit Digest Transparencies in the
Teacher's Classroom Resources
and use the accompanying teaching strategy, student activity, and
student test to teach about the
executive branch.

L3 History Have students review American history texts to
select 10 presidential decisions
that resulted in a major change in
the course of national affairs. Suggest John Adams's appointment
of John Marshall as Chief Justice
of the United States, Thomas
Jefferson's purchase of the
Louisiana Territory, Abraham
Lincoln's refusal to recognize
secession, and Franklin
Roosevelt's New Deal legislation
as examples. Have students use
their selections to construct an
annotated time line titled *Presidential Decisions that Changed the
United States.* Select time lines to
display on the bulletin board.

Assess

Check for Understanding

Have students complete
Synthesizing the Unit.

Close

Have students express their
reactions to the following:

It is not only the President's
duty but his right to do anything
that the well-being of the nation
demands.

---

ment. Most of these departments and agencies are in
the executive branch. The people who work for these
organizations are **civil servants** or **bureaucrats**.

The federal bureaucracy is organized into offices,
boards, commissions, corporations, and advisory
committees. Most of these organizations are responsible to the President, although some of them report to
Congress.

The 100 boards and commissions are not part of
any cabinet department. The President appoints the
heads of these organizations. Most independent
agencies have few employees, small budgets, and attract little public attention.

The regulatory commissions are independent of all
3 branches of the national government. Each commission has from 5 to 11 commissioners whom the
President appoints with Senate consent. Unlike other
bureaucrats, these commissioners do not report to
the President, nor can the President fire them.

Today almost all federal jobs are filled through the
competitive civil service system. Under this system
applicants must pass rigorous examinations before receiving jobs.

Every President has the chance to fill about 2,200
jobs in the federal bureaucracy. They include 14 cabinet secretaries, about 300 top-level bureau and agency heads, about 150 ambassadorships, and about
1,700 aide and assistant positions.

Filling these jobs allows Presidents to place loyal
supporters in key positions. They are expected to try
to implement the President's decisions. Unlike career
civil service workers, their employment usually ends
when a new President is elected.

Federal bureaucrats help make policy in several
ways. The most important of these involves administering hundreds of programs that have an impact on
almost every aspect of national life. Administering
these programs requires federal bureaucrats to write
rules and regulations and set standards to implement
laws Congress passes.

When Congress passes a law, it cannot possibly
spell out exactly what needs to be done to enforce it.
It is the bureaucracy that determines what the law actually means. The chief way federal agencies do this is
by issuing rules and regulations designed to translate
the law into action.

The bureaucracy also shapes public policy by helping draft new bills for Congress, testifying about leg-

islation, and providing lawmakers with technical information. Lawmakers also know that it can be difficult
to pass major bills without the advice of the federal
agencies most concerned with the bills' contents.

Some federal agencies shape public policy by deciding disputes over the application of a law or set of rules.
When agencies do this, they act almost like courts. The
regulatory commissions in particular have the authority
to resolve disputes among parties that come under
their regulatory power. The rulings of these agencies
have the same legal status as that of courts.

Bureaucrats also help shape public policy by providing top political decision makers with information
and advice. Many career bureaucrats are experts in
their areas. In addition, federal agencies collect information and research on a variety of subjects.

The federal bureaucracy has grown and assumed
an important role in making public policy for five reasons. These reasons are (1) the growth of the nation,
(2) international crises, (3) economic problems at
home, (4) citizens' demands, and (5) the nature of
bureaucracy itself.

Before making decisions about public policy, the
American bureaucracy consults other branches and
organizations of government. The President,
Congress, the courts, client groups, and other agencies all influence federal agencies. The bureaucracy
does not make public policy in isolation.

Synthesizing the Unit

Recalling Facts
1. Define elector, cabinet, executive privilege, federal bureaucracy, civil servant, bureaucrat.
2. List the qualifications for President.

Exploring Themes
3. Checks and Balances How might the use of executive
privilege interfere with the principle of checks and
balances?
4. Public Policy What role do federal bureaucrats play in
making public policy?

Critical Thinking Skills
5. Checking Consistency Federal bureaucrats make rules
to enforce laws, yet Congress has no control over
these rules. Is this consistent with the concept of
representative democracy? Why or why not?
6. Synthesizing Information Modern Presidents wield
more power than Congress does. Why is this so?

Synthesizing the Unit Answers

1. Definitions of terms appear on pages indicated: **elector,**
535; **cabinet,** 535; **executive privilege,** 535; **federal bureaucracy,** 535; **civil servant,** 536; **bureaucrat,** 536
2. a natural-born citizen of the United States, at least 35
years old, must reside in United States at least 14 years
prior to taking office
3. enables President to withhold information from
Congress

4. help draft new bills, testify before congressional committees, write rules and regulations to carry out laws, decide disputes over the application of laws and rules, provide
information and advice to top decision makers
5. no: As appointed officials, bureaucrats are not directly
responsible to the people as are elected lawmakers; yes:
Congress does exercise some control over rule-making
through its legislative oversight powers.

6. For most of this century, Congress has deferred power
to the President. In addition, presidential power is vested in
a single executive while legislative power is split among
535 senators and representatives.

The Judicial Branch

Chapter 19
The Federal Court System

Chapter 20
Supreme Court Decision Making

Unit Project

Organize students into five groups and assign one of the following topics to each: religion, free speech, civil rights, free enterprise, due process. Have groups construct an annotated time line of the major Supreme Court decisions concerning their assigned topic. Group members should work together to select decisions to be included, and then each member should research an equal number of those cases selected. Time line entries should include the case title, the issue involved, and a brief description of the decision. Have groups display their time lines on the bulletin board.

Introduce

Unit Objectives

After studying this unit, students should be able to:
- Describe the organization and structure of the judicial branch of the national government.
- Analyze the impact of federal court decisions on public policy.
- Discuss the role of the federal judiciary in the American governmental system.

Unit Overview

Unit 6 introduces students to the judicial branch of the national government.

Chapter 19 describes the federal court system, which applies and interprets federal law and the Constitution.

Chapter 20 focuses on the day-to-day operation of the Supreme Court, examining how the Court influences public policy and how the Court itself is influenced by outside forces.

6 UNIT DIGEST

Use the Unit Digest on pages 587–588 to introduce, review, reteach, or condense the information in this unit.

Introducing the Unit

Write the following on the chalkboard: *equal justice under the law, due process of law, adversary system of justice,* and *presumption of innocence.* Ask for volunteers to explain each one. Then have students discuss what relevance these concepts have for government in the United States. Close by noting that as they read Unit 6, students will discover these are the four basic principles that drive the American system of justice.

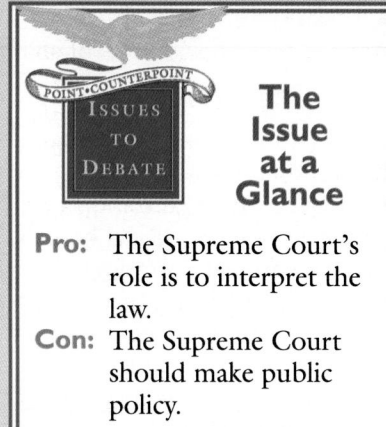

Focus

Before assigning the reading, poll the class to determine if students believe there is a difference between judges and policymakers. Ask students on each side to explain their opinions. Then ask if judges *should* make public policy.

Tell students that the debate they will read centers on this very issue.

Teach

Guided Practice

Point out that the Supreme Court's power and role in society has long been debated. Ask students to define judicial restraint and judicial activism. *(judicial restraint—justices consider only legal issues in interpreting Constitution; judicial activism—justices consider broader social needs and policies in interpreting Constitution)* Does Sobran support judicial activism or judicial restraint? *(restraint)* What criticism does he have of the Court's behavior? *(that it has made social policy in the name of preserving constitutional rights)* How, according to Sobran, has the Court failed in its constitutional duty? *(Instead of checking federal expansion, it is an instrument of that expansion.)*

Does the Supreme Court Abuse Its Power?

The debate over the Supreme Court's role and its power within the national government began in the early 1800s. Chief Justice John Marshall's landmark decision in *Marbury* v. *Madison* in 1803 established the Court's right of judicial review. In Marshall's view "it is emphatically the province and duty [of the Court] to say what the law is."

Today, people's views of the Supreme Court usually fall into one of two philosophical camps. The two camps generally reflect either a conservative ideology—which favors judicial restraint—or a liberal ideology—favoring judicial activism. Normally, these views are defended on a constitutional basis or on an ideological one.

Pro

Former United States Senator Sam J. Ervin, Jr., raised the constitutional issue when he wrote about whether the Supreme Court should be a policymaker or an adjudicator, or judge:

The Constitution answers this question with unmistakable clarity. There is not a syllable in it which gives the Supreme Court any discretionary power to fashion policies. . . . On the contrary, the Constitution provides in plain and positive terms that the role of the Supreme Court is that of an adjudicator.

—SAM J. ERVIN, JR., *ROLE OF THE SUPREME COURT: POLICYMAKER OR ADJUDICATOR*, 1970

On the ideological front, journalist Joseph Sobran, writing in *National Review* took a strong stand against the activist tradition in the Supreme Court. In his view:

For a generation the Court implemented the liberal agenda on social policy in the name of preserving (or somehow "expanding") constitutional rights. It struck down legislation or simply dictated policy in the areas of public-school prayer, aid to private schools, racial segregation, police arrest procedures, legislative redistricting, pornography, birth control, and abortion. . . .

What has made this mess possible? One factor is that the liberal community, so powerful in the academy and mass communications, has run interference for the Court as long as the Court has promoted the liberal agenda. . . .

Since 1925, the Court has used a dubious interpretation of the Fourteenth Amendment to "incorporate" the Bill of Rights into state constitutions. In a progressive and piecemeal way, it has held that the states are bound as much as Congress to observe the separation of church and state, . . . the free exercise of religion, the freedom of speech and of the press, the privilege against self-incrimination, and so forth. . . .

And so the Supreme Court, conceived originally as a check on federal expansion, has turned judicial review into an instrument of federal expansion.

—JOSEPH SOBRAN, "MINORITY RULE," *NATIONAL REVIEW*, 1985

Opponents of the Supreme Court's former judicial activism note with satisfaction that recent appointments to the Court by Presidents Reagan, Bush, and even Clinton reflect a far more conservative viewpoint. These opponents support the Court's move toward judicial restraint, returning many matters to state control. At the same time, however, other people remain firm advocates of an active Court, one willing to meet the challenges of a changing world.

More About Issues to Debate

In reaction to the liberal rulings of the Supreme Court in the 1960s and 1970s, many conservatives wanted to change the composition of the Court. As a result, both Ronald Reagan and George Bush nominated conservatives to be justices.

Perhaps the most famous attempt to change the Court's composition occurred during Franklin Roosevelt's administration. The United States was in the depth of the Great Depression. Roosevelt tried diligently to correct this condition through a series of laws collectively known as the New Deal. In 1935 the Supreme Court declared one of these laws, the National Recovery Act, unconstitutional. In the following years, the Agricultural Adjustment

BREAKING AND ENTERING

Lock Up or Open Up the Bill of Rights?
Some people feel the Supreme Court should focus on the "original intent" of the Constitution, while others favor a "current" approach.

Con

On the other side of the question, Justice William J. Brennan, Jr., favors judicial activism and rejects strict adherence to the intentions of the Founders:

When Justices interpret the Constitution they speak for their community, not for themselves alone. The act of interpretation must be undertaken with full consciousness that it is, in a very real sense, the community's interpretation that is sought. . . .

We current Justices read the Constitution in the only way that we can: as twentieth century Americans. We look to the history of the time of framing and to the intervening history of interpretation. But the ultimate question must be, what do the words of the text mean in our time. For the genius of the Constitution rests not in any static meaning it might have had in a world that is dead and gone, but in the adaptability of its great principles to cope with current problems and current needs. What the constitutional fundamentals meant to

the wisdom of other times cannot be their measure to the vision of our time. . . .
—JUSTICE WILLIAM BRENNAN, JR., OCTOBER 12, 1985

The Debate Continues

President Clinton's two appointees, Ruth Bader Ginsburg and Stephen Breyer, may hold the key to whether the Supreme Court returns to an activist role. Both new justices defy easy predictions, however. Each seems to hold centrist views, and little evidence of their ideological positions surfaced during confirmation hearings. Perhaps some insight into Stephen Breyer's influence on the Court was offered by Stuart Pollack, a municipal judge in San Francisco and one of Breyer's longtime friends:

Ours was the age of Kennedy. That was when we were coming out of law school. Government was there as a tool to bring about change. It could be done, absolutely. I don't think that Steve ever had his faith in public institutions shaken. I think he has retained his faith in the ability to deal with our problems.
—Stuart Pollack, THE WASHINGTON POST NATIONAL WEEKLY EDITION, JULY 4-10, 1994

Whether the Supreme Court returns to a policy of activism or continues to follow a policy of restraint, the debate about the Court's role will continue.

Examining the Issue

Recalling Facts
1. List the two views of the Supreme Court.
2. Describe Justice Brennan's attitude toward the role of the Supreme Court.

Critical Thinking Skills
3. Recognizing Ideologies Do you think that Joseph Sobran might accept judicial activism on the part of a conservative Supreme Court? Why or why not?
4. Recognizing Bias Do you think that Sam Ervin's former duties as a senator affected his view of the Supreme Court as a policymaker? Explain your answer.

Investigating Further
Use your text and other sources to identify the Supreme Court justices appointed during the Reagan, Bush, and Clinton administrations. Then use the *Readers' Guide* to locate current articles on Supreme Court decisions and try to determine whether or not the recent appointees are liberal or conservative in their decisions.

Act and the Railroad Retirement Act were also declared unconstitutional.

Roosevelt was furious. In 1937 he proposed changes: force justices to retire at age 70; increase the total number of justices to 15. Roosevelt believed he would then have the opportunity to name justices more sympathetic to his policies. The pro-

posals created a political storm. Even many of Roosevelt's loyal allies abandoned him on this issue. However, the Court quickly changed its attitude about the New Deal. From that point, most New Deal programs were upheld and many of its policies remain in force to this day.

Unit 6 Issues to Debate Lesson Plan, pages 538–539

How does Justice Brennan defend the appropriateness of an activist Court? *(In interpreting the Constitution, the Court speaks not for the justices, but for the community.)* Ask: What areas of Court action might illustrate an activist point of view? *(Students might mention discrimination, affirmative action, abortion.)* Ask: Do you think that minority groups would generally prefer judicial activism or judicial restraint on the Supreme Court? Why? *(activism, because they may lack the political power to change public policy through the legislative process)*

Independent Practice

Have students explain in a one-page essay whether they support the philosophy of judicial restraint or judicial activism and why.

Assess

Have students complete **Examining the Issue.**

Answers

1. judicial restraint, judicial activism
2. Brennan supported judicial activism.
3. Yes, Sobran's attack focuses on the Court's "liberal agenda" and its expansion of federal power. *Not* acting in the areas he criticizes would also set public policy.
4. Students may recognize that an activist Court seizes legislative initiative from Congress.

Close

Ask: Is the Supreme Court currently an activist Court? What predictions can you make about the Court's future behavior in this area?

Chapter Organizer

Objectives	Special Feature Pages	Supplemental Materials
Section 1 Authority of the Federal Courts *pp. 542–545* 1. Define the jurisdiction of the federal courts. 2. Explain differing court procedures under civil, criminal, and constitutional law. 3. Summarize the guiding principles of the American legal system.	Point/Counterpoint: Does the Supreme Court Abuse Its Power? p. 538–539 Global Connection: Issues: Rights of the Accused p. 544	Guided Reading Activities Reproducible Lesson Plans Section 1 Quiz Testmaker The Living Constitution SAT Practice Tests Writer's Guidebook
Section 2 Lower Federal Courts *pp. 546–552* 1. Discuss the duties of constitutional courts. 2. Identify federal legislative courts. 3. Evaluate the method of selecting federal judges.	Multicultural Heritage: The Legal Heritage of Greece and Rome p. 547 Participating in Government: Serving on a Jury p. 550 Critical Thinking Skills: Making Inferences p. 552	Guided Reading Activities Reproducible Lesson Plans Participating in Government 19 Government Themes Transparencies 12 Section 2 Quiz Testmaker Chapter Transparencies 19 Skill Reinforcement Activities 19 SAT Practice Tests Writer's Guidebook
Section 3 The Supreme Court *pp. 553–559* 1. Define the jurisdiction of the Supreme Court. 2. Describe the duties of Supreme Court justices. 3. Examine the method of selecting and appointing Supreme Court justices.	Focus on Freedom: *Gideon* v. *Wainwright* p. 557 Personal Perspectives: Sandra Day O'Connor on Appointment to the Supreme Court p. 559	Guided Reading Activities Reproducible Lesson Plans Interpreting Political Cartoons 19 Primary and Secondary Source Readings 19 Reteaching Activities 19 Enrichment Activities 19 Section 3 Quiz Chapter 19 Tests Testmaker Audio Cassettes (English and Spanish) Limited English Proficiency Activities 19 SAT Practice Tests

If time does not permit teaching this chapter, assign the Chapter 19 summary in the Unit 6 Digest on pages 587–588.

Key To Ability Levels

Teaching strategies have been coded for varying learning styles and abilities.

L1 Level 1 activities are **basic** activities and should be within the ability range of all students.

L2 Level 2 activities are **average** activities and should be within the ability range of the average to above-average student.

L3 Level 3 activities are **challenging** activities designed for the ability range of above-average students.

LEP These activities should be within the ability range of **Limited English Proficiency** students.

Multicultural Activities

Have students read and paraphrase Section 1 of the Fourteenth Amendment which guarantees all citizens equal protection under the law. The equal protection standard has been used by the federal courts to examine a variety of issues related to minority rights. It has been applied in cases related to jury selection, voting, use of public facilities, transportation, housing, and education. Among the landmark Supreme Court cases in this area are *Brown* v. *Board of Education, Swann* v. *Charlotte-Mecklenburg Board of Education, Shelley* v. *Kraemer,* and *Regents of University of California* v. *Bakke.* Organize students into groups. Have each use a reference, such as *American Constitutional Law* by Robert Steamer and Richard Maiman, to identify the equal protection issues raised by each case. Groups can also decide whether they agree with the majority opinion in each case.

From 1789 to 1991, only 29 Supreme Court nominees have not been confirmed by the Senate. Some of the most vigorous lobbying in recent years surrounded the 1987 nomination of Robert Bork and the 1991 nomination of Clarence Thomas. A variety of civil rights interest groups including the NAACP and the Urban League, as well as the Congressional Black Caucus, took positions on the Thomas appointment. Have students use the *Readers' Guide to Periodical Literature* to find out why civil rights groups took an active part in each confirmation hearing, how they attempted to influence the nomination and confirmation process, and what the outcome of their lobbying efforts were.

Chapter Resources

Readings for the Student

Abraham, Henry J. *The Judicial Process.* Oxford University Press, 1980.
Ball, Howard. *Courts and Politics.* Prentice-Hall, 1980.
Brill, Steven, et al. *Trial By Jury.* Simon and Schuster, 1989.
Friedman, Jane M. *America's First Woman Lawyer: The Biography of Myra Bradwell.* Prometheus Books, 1994.
The Judiciary: Perspectives on Our Judicial System. Close-Up Foundation, 1987.
Kratoville, Betty Lou. *Great Trials in History.* Academic Therapy Publications, 1990.

Readings for the Teacher

Abraham, Henry J. *Justices and Presidents.* Penguin, 1974.
Elder, W. H. *Congressional Quarterly's Guide to the U.S. Supreme Court.* Congressional Quarterly, 1990.
Goldman, Sheldon and Thomas P. Jahnige. *The Federal Courts as a Political System.* Harper & Row, 1985.
Jacob, Herbert. *Justice in America: Courts, Lawyers, and the Judicial Process.* Little, Brown, 1978.
Witt, Elder. *Guide to the U.S. Supreme Court.* Congressional Quarterly, 1989.

Multimedia

Videocassettes

A History of the Court. WETA. (v/c, 60 minutes)
The Insanity Plea: Legal Loophole or Legitimate Defense? Social Studies School Service. (v/c, 60 minutes)
Inside the Supreme Court. WETA. (v/c, 60 minutes)

Software

United States Constitution, Disk 4—*Articles II-VII.* Tutorsystems (BLS, Inc.). (Apple disk, fourth of a 5-part package)
Jury Trial II. Navic. (Apple diskette and guide or IBM PC diskette and guide). Students role-play simulation of courtroom drama.

The Federal Court System

Introduce

Chapter Overview

Chapter 19 introduces the federal court system, which applies and interprets federal law and the Constitution.

Section 1 explains the functions of the federal courts.

Section 2 outlines the structure of federal courts and describes the selection of federal judges.

Section 3 describes the jurisdiction of the Supreme Court, the selection of Supreme Court justices, and the duties the justices fulfill.

Chapter 19 Themes

Have students read Themes in Government in the Chapter Preview. Then ask: Based on this information, which topics do you think might be covered in Chapter 19? Write responses on the chalkboard. Then have students discuss why they think each topic noted might be included in the chapter. Bring the discussion to a close by pointing out that the details of these topics will help students understand the structure and functions of the federal judicial system.

CHAPTER 19

The Court has given jobs to women and rights to criminals, desegregated schools, and permitted flag burning. Some critics see it as too intrusive, others say it's too passive.

540 UNIT 6: THE JUDICIAL BRANCH

About the Chapter Opener

Teaching With Illustrations Have students examine the photograph on pages 540 and 541. Tell students that the words *Equal Justice Under Law* are inscribed over the entrance to the Supreme Court building. These words describe the goal of the justice system. Point out that the Supreme Court building has a white marble exterior and resembles a Greek temple. Ask them how the building is a reflection of the work that is carried out inside. *(Answers will vary. Students might mention the contribution of the Greeks to democracy.)*

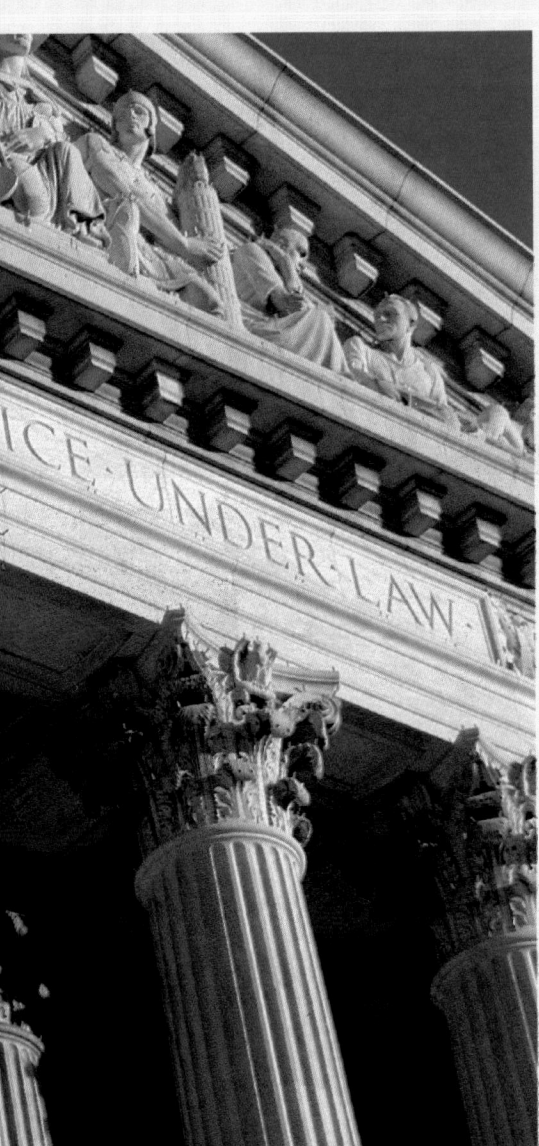

Chapter Preview

Overview

Federal courts have been established to apply and interpret federal laws and the Constitution.

Objectives

After studying this chapter, you should be able to:

1. **Classify** the kinds of cases in which federal courts have jurisdiction.
2. **Outline** the system of lower federal courts.
3. **Describe** the jurisdiction of the Supreme Court and the duties of its justices.

Themes in Government

This chapter emphasizes the following government themes:

- **Federalism** A dual court system divides jurisdiction between federal and state courts. Sections 1 and 2.
- **Civil Rights** The Constitution provides for equal justice under the law and due process of law. Sections 1 and 3.
- **Cultural Pluralism** Recent Presidents have appointed more women and minorities to positions in the federal judicial system. Section 2.
- **Checks and Balances** The President, with the consent of the Senate, appoints Supreme Court justices and federal court judges. Section 3.

Critical Thinking Skills

This chapter emphasizes the following critical thinking skills:

- Predicting Consequences
- Identifying Alternatives
- Demonstrating Reasoned Judgment
- Understanding Cause and Effect

CHAPTER 19: THE FEDERAL COURT SYSTEM 541

Introducing the Chapter

Though students may already have some knowledge of courts and trials, they may not know much about the differences between state and federal courts. Moreover, they may not know about the many different types of federal courts. Some students may already know something about the Supreme Court, but the relationship of the highest court to state courts and the many federal courts may be a more difficult area.

Point out the chapter title to students. To ascertain students' prior knowledge ask: What kinds of courts do you know about? What document allows Congress to establish courts? If Congress repealed all legislation establishing courts, what courts would be left? Then read aloud the Linking Past and Present on page 541 to give students an idea of how the federal court system has changed over the years.

Chapter Project

Have students make a citizen handbook called "How the Federal Judiciary Works." To do this students should create fact sheets, charts, and a glossary about the judiciary. This handbook can also serve as a study tool for students.

> **Linking Past and Present**
> Before 1891, when Congress created circuit courts of appeals, each Supreme Court justice traveled to a specific region of the nation to hear appeals from the federal district courts. Officially renamed "courts of appeals" in 1948, these appellate courts are often still called "circuit courts." Although they have their own federal judges, a Supreme Court justice remains assigned to each court of appeals.

Setting the Scene The power of the courts to declare laws or government actions null and void because they conflict with the Constitution is called *judicial review.* From 1790 to 1890, the Supreme Court found various federal laws or provisions of federal laws to be unconstitutional on only 17 occasions. All but 2 of these decisions were made between 1860 and 1890. In the next 100 years, the Supreme Court found 109 federal laws unconstitutional, a 6-fold increase.

Focus

Bell Ringer

Ask students to answer the following question while attendance is being taken:

What happens in a court of law?

Motivating Activity

Discuss students' Bell Ringer answers. Ask students if they know what the term *jurisdiction* means. If they do not, have them look up the term in the Glossary. Tell students this section explains the jurisdiction of federal and state courts.

Vocabulary Precheck

Write the key terms for this section on the chalkboard. Ask students to use those that they know in sentences. **LEP**

Teach

Guided Practice

L1 Summarizing Organize students into three groups and assign each group one of the three types of law in federal court jurisdiction. For each type of law, students should define it and provide an example of a case that would fall under it. Have group representatives present their summaries to the class.

Caption Answer
34 years

Authority of the Federal Courts

The Constitution provided for a Supreme Court of the United States as part of a court system that would balance the powers of the other two branches of government. Unlike the President and Congress, however, the Supreme Court played a very minor role until Chief Justice John Marshall, who was appointed in 1801 and served until 1835, helped increase the power of the Court.

Over the years the Court's growing role in American government met serious challenges:

Nothing in the Court's history is more striking than the fact that, while its significant and necessary place in the Federal form of Government has always been recognized by thoughtful and patriotic men, nevertheless, no branch of the Government and no institution under the Constitution has sustained more continuous attack or reached its present position after more vigorous opposition.
—CHARLES WARREN, *THE SUPREME COURT IN UNITED STATES HISTORY*, VOL. 1, 1924

Today the judicial branch of government is well established as an equal with the legislative and executive branches.

Emerging From the Political Shadows
Chief Justice John Marshall made the Court a coequal branch of government. **History How long did John Marshall serve as Chief Justice?**

Jurisdiction of the Courts

The judiciary of the United States has two different levels of courts. On one level are the federal courts whose powers derive from the Constitution and federal laws. On the other are the courts of each of the 50 states whose powers derive from state constitutions and laws. Some have described the two court systems existing side by side as a dual court system.

SECTION PREVIEW

Objectives
After studying this section, you should be able to:
- Define the jurisdiction of the federal courts.
- Explain differing court procedures under civil, criminal, and constitutional law.
- Summarize the guiding principles of the American legal system.

Key Terms and Concepts
jurisdiction, concurrent jurisdiction, trial court, original jurisdiction, appellate jurisdiction, civil law, plaintiff, defendant, equity law, injunction, writ of mandamus, criminal law, prosecution, constitutional law, due process of law, substantive due process, procedural due process, adversary system

Themes in Government
- Federalism
- Civil Rights

Critical Thinking Skills
- Predicting Consequences
- Identifying Alternatives

Classroom Resources for Section 1

- Guided Reading Activities
- Reproducible Lesson Plans
- Section 1 Quiz
- Testmaker

The Living Constitution
SAT Practice Tests
Writer's Guidebook

Federal Court Jurisdiction Every court, whether it is a federal court or a state court, has the authority to hear certain kinds of cases. This authority is called the **jurisdiction** of the court. In the dual court system, state courts have jurisdiction over cases involving state laws, while federal courts have jurisdiction over cases involving federal laws. Sometimes the jurisdiction of the state courts and the jurisdiction of the federal courts overlap.

Two factors determine the jurisdiction of federal courts—the subject matter of a case and the parties in a case. Federal courts try cases that involve United States laws, treaties with foreign nations, or interpretations of the Constitution. Cases involving admiralty or maritime law—the law of the sea, including ships, their crews, and disputes over actions and rights at sea—also come under federal court jurisdiction. Federal courts also try cases involving bankruptcy.

Federal courts hear cases if certain parties or persons are involved. These include: (1) ambassadors and other representatives of foreign governments; (2) two or more state governments; (3) the United States government or one of its offices and agencies; (4) citizens of different states; (5) a state and a citizen of a different state; (6) citizens of the same state claiming lands under grants of different states; and (7) a state or its citizens and a foreign country or its citizens.

Concurrent Jurisdiction In most cases the difference between federal and state court jurisdiction is clear. In some instances, however, both federal and state courts have jurisdiction, a situation known as **concurrent jurisdiction.** Concurrent jurisdiction exists, for example, in a case involving citizens of different states in a dispute concerning at least $10,000. In such a case, a person may sue in either a federal or a state court. If the person being sued insists, however, the case must be tried in a federal court.

Original and Appellate Jurisdiction The court in which a case is originally tried is known as a **trial court.** A trial court has original jurisdiction. In the federal court system, the district courts as well as several other lower courts have only **original jurisdiction.**

If a person who loses a case in a trial court wishes to appeal a decision, he or she may take the case to a court with appellate jurisdiction. The federal court system provides courts of appeals that have only **appellate jurisdiction.** Thus, a party may appeal a case from a district court to a court of appeals. If that party loses in the court of appeals, he or she may appeal the case to the Supreme Court, which has both original and appellate jurisdiction.

When Juries Make Mistakes
The right of appeal is a key protection for the accused. **Law** **Describe the appeals process.**

The Federal Court Jurisdiction

The federal courts deal with three types of law. These three types include civil law, criminal law, and constitutional law.

Civil Law Most of the cases tried in the federal courts involve civil law. **Civil law** concerns disputes between two or more individuals or between individuals and the government. The **plaintiff** is the person who brings charges in a civil suit. The person against whom the suit is brought is the **defendant.** The plaintiff in a civil suit usually seeks damages—an award of money—from the defendant. If the court decides in favor of the plaintiff, the defendant must pay the damages to the plaintiff. Usually the defendant is also required to pay court costs. If the court decides in favor of the defendant, the plaintiff must pay the court costs.

In another type of civil case, the plaintiff sues to prevent a harmful action from taking place. Such a case is called a case in equity law. **Equity law** is a system of rules by which disputes are resolved on the grounds of fairness. In an equity case, a plaintiff may ask the court to issue an **injunction,** a court order

L2 **Interpreting Visuals** Draw the following diagram on the chalkboard:

National	State
U.S. Supreme ← Supreme	
Court	Court
↑	↑
U.S. Courts	Appellate
of Appeals	Courts
↑	↑
U.S. District	Trial
Courts	Courts

Select volunteers to tell what type of law each court handles and the jurisdiction it has. Have them enter the information in the appropriate place on the diagram. Then ask students why the American legal system is described as a "hierarchy."

L3 **Panel Discussion** Call on four students to act as a panel of experts who will explain the four guiding principles of the American legal system. Act as moderator of the panel to clarify any points about which students may be confused.

Independent Practice

L1 **Law** Ask students to determine whether the following cases are under state or federal jurisdiction and to indicate the type of law—criminal or civil—each deals with: immigration *(federal, civil)*, counterfeiting *(federal, criminal)*, divorce *(state, civil)*, mail fraud *(federal, criminal)*, store robbery *(state, criminal)*

L2 **Classificatory Writing** Have students research the legal system in another country and write a paper that compares its system with the principles of the United States legal system.

Caption Answer
A case from district court may be appealed to a court of appeals; it may then be appealed to the Supreme Court.

Background

Begun in 1983, the Computer Integrated Courtroom (CIC) was designed to enable court officials to quickly retrieve and display on screen pertinent legal information. Dallas' 116th District Court, for example, is entirely computer integrated. On their computer terminals lawyers can see trial transcripts during testimony and retrieve all transcript material relating to persons or places in a case. The CIC allows both judges and lawyers to research in the courtroom by accessing databases.

GLOBAL CONNECTION

Have students research the countries where the accused is presumed guilty until proven innocent. A useful source of information is the *United Nations Human Development Report,* which ranks countries according to the freedoms they allow their citizens.
Examining the Connection Answer: *It balances the rights of the accused and the accuser.*

STUDY GUIDE

Critical Thinking Answers
Anything that the arrested person says cannot be used as evidence in court.

As an unreasonable regulation, it would violate substantive due process.

Assess

Check for Understanding

Have students complete Section 1 Review on page 545.

Meeting Objectives

Each section objective is tested by the Section Review questions that follow it in parentheses.
• Define the jurisdiction of the federal courts. (5, 8)
• Explain differing court procedures under civil, criminal, and constitutional law. (3, 4, 7)
• Summarize the guiding principles of the American legal system. (2, 6)

GLOBAL CONNECTION

Issues

Rights of the Accused The Fifth, Sixth, and Eighth Amendments protect the rights of people accused of committing a crime. All legal systems, however, are not the same.

In the United States and other countries whose legal systems are based on English common law, an accused person is presumed innocent. In countries whose legal systems are based on Roman law, an accused person is presumed guilty.

The principle of presumed innocence balances the rights of the accused and the accuser. On the accuser's side stand law enforcement officials, the court system, and law-abiding citizens. The accused stands alone, but, if presumed innocent, has equal rights under the law.

Examining the Connection
How does presumption of innocence protect individual liberty?

that forbids a defendant to take or continue a certain action. For example, suppose a company plans to build a factory next to a residential area. Citizens believe that the factory would pollute the air. They take the factory owner to court and argue that residents would suffer serious health problems if the factory is constructed. If the citizens win this suit in equity, the judge issues an injunction ordering the company not to build its factory.

In another equity case, the plaintiff may ask the court to order a person or persons to *do* something. A court order requiring a specific action is called a **writ of mandamus** (man•DAY•muhs). Suppose someone has a new stereo receiver that stops working, but the

manufacturer refuses to repair it. Because the stereo is guaranteed, he or she takes the company to court. If the court decides for the plaintiff, it issues a writ of mandamus ordering the company to repair the stereo.

Criminal Law In a federal **criminal law** case, the United States government charges someone with breaking a federal law. In criminal cases the government is always the **prosecution,** bringing charges against the defendant. A federal criminal case might involve such crimes as tax fraud, counterfeiting, selling narcotics, mail fraud, kidnapping, and driving a stolen car across state lines. If the court finds a person guilty, the judge may order the defendant to serve a term in prison, to pay a fine, or both.

By far, most crimes committed in the United States break state laws and are tried in state courts. The number of criminal law cases that come before federal judges, however, has been increasing markedly in recent years as the crime rate has risen.

Constitutional Law The third category of cases heard in federal courts involves constitutional law. **Constitutional law** relates to the meaning and application of the United States Constitution. For the most part, cases involving constitutional law decide the limits of the government's power and the rights of the individual. Cases may deal with either civil or criminal law.

Only federal courts try cases involving constitutional law—they decide whether a law or action conflicts with the Constitution. If a lower court decision is appealed, the Supreme Court makes the final ruling.

Legal System Principles

Four basic principles underlie the operation of both federal and state courts and the actions of the thousands of men and women who serve in the American legal system. These principles include equal justice under the law, due process of law, the adversary system of justice, and the presumption of innocence.

STUDY GUIDE

Themes in Government
Federalism The Supreme Court did not rule on a single case during its first three years.
Civil Rights The Fourteenth Amendment defines due process as

every citizen's privilege.

Critical Thinking Skills
Predicting Consequences What happens if the police forget to tell an arrested person his or her rights?

Identifying Alternatives **Allowing** rental agencies not to rent apartments to families with children would violate what kind of due process?

Cooperative Learning Activity

Organize students into groups and present the following case: The creators of *Monty Python's Flying Circus,* a British television show, leased the American rights for their show to ABC. In the contract, however, they did not sign a clause that allowed ABC to edit the program. When they learned that ABC planned to broadcast an edited version, they

took the network to court. Have students determine a) what type of court would hear this case (*federal district court*), b) what type of law it involves (*civil, or constitutional if free speech is raised*), and c) what actions could be taken by the court (*award damages, issue court order*). Have each group relate how it reached its conclusions.

Equal Justice Under the Law The phrase *equal justice under the law* refers to the goal of the American court system to treat all persons alike. It means that every person, regardless of wealth, social status, ethnic group, gender, or age is entitled to the full protection of the law. The equal justice principle grants all Americans rights, such as the right to a trial by a jury of one's peers. The Fifth through the Eighth Amendments to the Constitution spell out these specific guarantees.

Due Process of Law Closely related to the principle of equal justice is the principle of **due process of law.** Due process is difficult to define precisely, but in general it means that a law must be applied in a fair manner. The Fifth and Fourteenth Amendments contain the due process principle.

If a court decides a law is unreasonable, it rules that the law violates **substantive due process.** Examples of laws that the Supreme Court has found to violate substantive due process include: (1) a law that limits dwellings to single families, thus preventing grandparents from living with their grandchildren; (2) a school board regulation that prevents a female teacher from returning to work sooner than three months after the birth of her child; and (3) a law that requires all children to attend public schools and does not permit them to attend private schools.

Cases about the way a law is administered involve **procedural due process.** Procedural due process requires the authorities to avoid violating an individual's basic freedoms when enforcing laws. For example, the police must warn an individual who is arrested that anything he or she says may be used as evidence.

The Adversary System American courts operate according to the adversary system of justice. Under the **adversary system,** the courtroom is a kind of arena in which lawyers for the opposing sides try to present their strongest cases. The lawyer for each side feels compelled to do all that is legally permissible to advance the cause of his or her client. The judge in the court has an impartial role and should be as fair to both sides as possible.

Some observers of the judicial system have attacked the adversary system. They have claimed that it encourages lawyers to ignore evidence not favorable to their side and to be more concerned about victory than justice. Supporters of the adversary system, on the other hand, maintain that it is the best way to bring out the facts of a case.

Presumption of Innocence In the United States system of justice, the government's police power is balanced against the presumption that a person is innocent until proven guilty. The notion of presumed innocence is not mentioned in the Constitution, but it is deeply rooted in the English legal heritage. The burden of proving an accusation against a defendant falls on the prosecution. Unless the prosecution succeeds in proving the accusation, the court must declare the defendant not guilty.

Evaluate

📁 Section 1 Quiz

🔲 Testmaker

Reteach

Ask students to create a dictionary with the key terms and concepts. Students should write a sentence about each of the terms and alphabetize them. This assignment may be added to the chapter handbook project.

Enrich

Take students to visit a local court. Contact a local judge's office and make the necessary arrangements or invite a lawyer to talk to the class to discuss his or her work.

Close

Refer students to the section themes: *federalism* and *civil rights.* Ask: In what way is the concept of federalism reflected in our court system? How are civil rights protected by our court system?

CONNECTIONS

Law
More than 90 percent of court cases begin and end in the court of original jurisdiction.

1
SECTION REVIEW

Section Summary
The federal courts have jurisdiction in cases arising under United States civil and criminal law and cases that involve the Constitution.

Checking for Understanding
Recalling Facts
1. Define jurisdiction, concurrent jurisdiction, trial court, original jurisdiction, appellate jurisdiction, civil law, plaintiff, defendant, equity law, injunction, writ of mandamus, criminal law, prosecution, constitutional law, due process of law, substantive due process, procedural due process, adversary system.
2. Name four guiding principles of the American legal system.
3. Identify the prosecution in all criminal cases.

4. Enumerate the types of law that apply in cases that come before federal courts.

Exploring Themes
5. Federalism What factors determine whether a case will be tried in a state court or a federal court?
6. Civil Rights What is the difference between procedural due process and substantive due process?

Critical Thinking Skills
7. Predicting Consequences What action would a court take if a state won a civil case against another state that had permitted industries to dump pollutants into a river that flowed through both states?
8. Identifying Alternatives What choice of jurisdiction would be available to a person who was being sued by a citizen of another state for damages amounting to $20,000?

Section 1 Review Answers

1. Definitions of terms appear on pages indicated: **jurisdiction,** 543; **concurrent jurisdiction,** 543; **trial court,** 543; **original jurisdiction,** 543; **appellate jurisdiction,** 543; **civil law,** 543; **plaintiff,** 543; **defendant,** 543; **equity law,** 543; **injunction,** 543; **writ of mandamus,** 544; **criminal law,** 544; **prosecution,** 544; **constitutional law,** 544; **due process of law,** 545; **substantive due process,** 545; **procedural due process,** 545; **adversary system,** 545

2. equal justice under the law, due process of law, adversary system, presumption of innocence
3. the government
4. civil law, criminal law, constitutional law
5. subject matter of a case and the parties involved; examples might include: <u>subject</u>—interpretation of Constitution, federal law, treaty with a foreign nation; <u>parties</u>—foreign ambassadors, two or more state governments, citizens of different states

6. Procedural due process deals with the way in which a law is carried out; substantive due process deals with the content of the law.
7. Court issues an injunction ordering state that lost case to stop polluting the river.
8. Person being sued could choose to have the case tried in the state court or in a federal court.

Focus

Bell Ringer

While attendance is being taken, ask students to consider the following question:

What qualifications should a person have to be a federal judge?

Motivating Activity

Discuss students' Bell Ringer answers. Write the answers on the chalkboard and retain them for the section Close activity. Then extend the discussion by asking students to debate how judges should be selected and how long they should serve. Ask: Should judges be appointed or elected? Should they stay on the bench for life?

Vocabulary Precheck

Write the key terms for this section on the chalkboard. Ask students how each term relates to the structure and functions of lower federal courts. **LEP**

Linking Past and Present

Petit juries, or trial juries, were first used in Europe more than 1,000 years ago. The first juries consisted of neighbors of the accused who gave evidence on what they thought had happened. The jury did not take on its present-day role of reviewer of evidence for another 700 years.

Lower Federal Courts

The Constitution names only one federal court—the Supreme Court. Congress used its constitutional authority to establish a network of other federal courts beginning with the Judiciary Act of 1789. Over the years Congress has established a variety of lower trial and appellate courts to handle a growing number of federal cases. These courts are of two basic types—constitutional federal courts and legislative federal courts.

Constitutional Courts

Courts Congress established under the provisions of Article III of the Constitution are **constitutional courts.** These courts include the federal district courts, the courts of appeals, and the United States Court of International Trade.

District Courts Congress created **district courts** in 1789 to be trial courts. These districts followed state boundary lines. As the population grew and cases multiplied, Congress divided some states into more than 1 district. Today the United States has 91 districts, each state having at least 1 district court. Large states—California, New York, and Texas—each have 4 district courts. Washington, D.C., and Puerto Rico also have 1 district court each. More than 550 judges preside over the district courts.

United States district courts are the trial courts for both criminal and civil federal cases. They use 2 types of juries in criminal cases. A **grand jury,** which usually includes 16 to 23 people, hears charges against a person suspected of having committed a crime. If the grand jury believes there is sufficient evidence to bring the person to trial, it issues an indictment. An **indictment** is a formal accusation charging a person with a crime. If the jury believes there is not sufficient evidence, the court sets the person free.

A **petit jury,** which usually consists of 6 or 12 people, is a trial jury. Its function is to weigh the evidence presented at a trial in a criminal or civil case. In a criminal case, a petit jury renders a verdict of guilty or not guilty. In a civil case, the jury finds for either the plaintiff or the defendant. Sometimes the parties in a civil case do not wish to have a jury trial. In that case a judge or a panel of three judges weighs the evidence.

District courts are the workhorses of the federal judiciary, hearing about 270,000 cases each year. This caseload represents more than 80 percent of all federal cases. District courts have original jurisdiction but may also receive appeals from state courts if constitutional questions are involved. In the vast majority of their cases, district courts render the final decision. Few are appealed to or changed by a higher court. One scholar explained the significance of district judges' decisions:

Trial judges, because of the multitude of cases they hear which remain unheard or unchanged by appellate courts, as well as because of their fact- and issue-shaping powers, appear to play an independent and formidable part in the policy impact of the federal court system upon the larger political system.

—Kenneth M. Dolbeare, 1969

SECTION PREVIEW

Objectives
After studying this section, you should be able to:
- Discuss the duties of constitutional courts.
- Identify federal legislative courts.
- Evaluate the method of selecting federal judges.

Key Terms and Concepts
constitutional court, district court, grand jury, indictment, petit jury, judicial circuit, legislative court, senatorial courtesy

Themes in Government
- Cultural Pluralism
- Federalism

Critical Thinking Skills
- Identifying Alternatives
- Demonstrating Reasoned Judgment

Classroom Resources for Section 2

- 📁 Guided Reading Activities
- 📁 Reproducible Lesson Plans
- 📁 Participating in Government 19
- 📁 Section 2 Quiz
- 📇 Government Themes Transparencies 12
- 🖥 Testmaker
- 📇 Chapter Transparencies 19
- SAT Practice Tests
- Writer's Guidebook

Multicultural Heritage

The Legal Heritage of Greece and Rome

The United States is often described as a nation of laws, not of people. No person, regardless of position in government or society is above the law. American law, however, has its roots in the classical civilizations of Greece and Rome.

The ancient Greeks were among the first to develop a concept of law that separated everyday law from religious beliefs. Before the Greeks most civilizations attributed their laws to their gods or goddesses. Instead, the Greeks believed that laws were made by the people for the people.

In the seventh century B.C., Draco drew up Greece's first written code of laws. Under Draco's code death was the punishment for most offenses. Thus, the term *draconian* usually applies to unusually harsh measures. Several decades passed before Solon—poet, military hero, and ultimately, Athens' lawgiver—devised a new code of laws. Trial by jury, an ancient Greek tradition was retained, but enslaving debtors was prohibited as were most of the harsh punishments of Draco's code. Typical of the principle of justice designed by Solon is the penalty for theft:

If a man has recovered the article which he has lost, the thief shall be condemned to pay the double value; if not to pay tenfold . . . and he shall be kept in the stocks five days and as many nights as the jury-tribunal shall have imposed.

—SOLON'S CODE, 500S B.C.

Under Solon's law citizens of Athens were eligible to serve in the assembly and courts were established in which they could appeal government decisions.

What the Greeks may have contributed to the Romans was the concept of "natural law." In essence, natural law was based on the belief that certain basic principles are above the laws of a nation. These principles arise from the nature of people, of nature, or of a higher religious entity. In the Preamble of the United States Declaration of Independence they are referred to as laws of nature.

The concept of natural law and the development of the first true legal system had a profound effect on the modern world. As professor Alan Watson has said:

Rome's greatest legacy to the modern world is undoubtedly its private law. Roman law forms the basis of all the legal systems of Western Europe with the exception of England (but not Scotland) and Scandinavia. Outside Europe, the law of places so diverse as Louisiana and Ceylon [Sri Lanka], Quebec and Japan, Abyssinia [Ethiopia] and South Africa is based firmly on Roman law. Even in England and the countries of Anglo-American law in general, the influence of Roman law is considerable and is much greater than is often admitted.

—ALAN WATSON,
THE LAW OF THE ANCIENT ROMANS, 1970

In ancient Greece, plaintiffs and defendants in trials had to speak for themselves. Demosthenes (384–322 B.C.) began as a speechwriter for such occasions and went on to become a great orator and defender of democracy.

Examining Our Multicultural Heritage

Reviewing Facts
1. Identify the legal contributions of the ancient Greeks.
2. Explain the bases for the principle of natural law.
3. List the references to natural law in the Declaration of Independence.

Critical Thinking Skills
4. Understanding Cause and Effect How did the Romans' conquest of the Greeks contribute to the spread of the concept of natural law? Give evidence that this concept influenced the United States.

CHAPTER 19: THE FEDERAL COURT SYSTEM · 547

Multicultural Heritage

Focus

Ask students where we get our laws. *(Some may respond that government is the source; others may cite the religious, democratic, and historic origins of law.)*

Teach

Point out the early connection between law and religion and ask if religion continues to influence law. *(example: Islamic law)* Besides Draco's, can students think of earlier written laws? *(the biblical Commandments)* What similarities exist between United States laws and the Greek codes? *(trial by jury, written laws)* What element of these ancient laws might not be acceptable in a modern democracy? *(harshness, written by one person)*

Assess

Have students complete **Examining Our Multicultural Heritage.**

Answers

1. separated law from religious beliefs, written laws, trial by jury
2. basic human rights higher than nations' laws
3. equality; right to life, liberty, happiness
4. The Romans adopted and spread the Greek concept of natural law; the Declaration of Independence refers to the laws of nature.

Close

Ask why laws that recognize basic human rights are critical to the success of a multicultural society.

More About Our Multicultural Heritage

Roman law differed from United States law in important ways. Under Roman law all people were not equal before the law. A person's rights depended on his or her status: free or slave, citizen or alien, man or woman. Roman law did establish the idea, however, that all people of equal status deserve equal treatment under the law. The Romans' achievement was the development of laws that addressed the problems of settling disputes between people in a large and complex society—an area we call civil law. Civil law governs such activities as borrowing money, buying a home, or signing a job contract.

Teach

Guided Practice

L1 Classifying Information
Have volunteers read aloud Article III of the Constitution. Then ask the class to determine what terminology gave Congress the right to set up the lower federal courts. Make a chart on the chalkboard of the two types of courts established by Congress—constitutional and legislative. Have students list examples and explain the purpose of each. **LEP**

Interpreting Visuals Display transparency 19 from the *Chapter Transparencies* in the Teacher's Classroom Resources and use the accompanying teaching strategy and student activity to teach about the federal judiciary.

Caption Answer
make arrests, secure jurors, keep order in courtroom

STUDY GUIDE

Theme Answer
13 federal courts of appeals and 179 federal appeals judges

Critical Thinking Answer
Appeals court will tend to uphold most decisions as too many reversals would disrupt the authority of the district courts.

Interpreting Visuals Display transparency 12 from *Government Themes Transparencies* in the Teacher's Classroom Resources and use the accompanying teaching strategy and student activity to teach about types of federal courts.

In Custody of a United States Marshal
Federal offenses include mail fraud and kidnapping.
Law What are the duties of a marshal?

Officers of the Court Many appointed officials provide support services for district courts. Each district has a United States attorney to represent the United States in all civil suits brought against the government and to prosecute people charged with federal crimes. Each district court appoints a United States magistrate who issues arrest warrants and helps decide whether the arrested person should be held for a grand jury hearing. A bankruptcy judge handles bankruptcy cases for each district. A United States marshal carries out such duties as making arrests, securing jurors, and keeping order in the courtroom. With the help of deputy clerks, bailiffs, and a stenographer, a clerk keeps records of court proceedings.

Federal Courts of Appeals Good records are important because a person or group that loses a case in a district court may appeal to a federal court of appeals or, in some instances, directly to the Supreme Court. Congress created the United States courts of appeals in 1891 to ease the appeals work load of the Supreme Court. The caseload of appellate courts has almost doubled every 10 years since 1970, to almost 41,000 annual cases in recent years.

The appellate level includes 13 United States courts of appeals and 179 judges. The United States is divided into 12 **judicial circuits,** or regions, with one appellate court in each circuit. The thirteenth is a special appeals court with national jurisdiction. Usually, a panel of three judges sits on each appeal. In a very important case, all of the circuit judges may hear the case.

As their name implies, the courts of appeals have only appellate jurisdiction. Most appeals arise from decisions of district courts, the United States Tax Court, and various territorial courts. These courts also hear appeals concerning the rulings of various regulatory agencies such as the Federal Trade Commission and the Federal Communications Commission.

The courts of appeals may decide an appeal in one of three ways: uphold the original decision, reverse that decision, or send the case back to the lower court to be tried again. Unless appealed to the Supreme Court, decisions of the courts of appeals are final.

In 1982 Congress set up a special court of appeals called the United States Circuit Court of Appeals for the Federal Circuit. This appellate court hears cases brought to it from a federal claims court, the Court of International Trade, the United States Patent Office, and several other executive agencies. The court's headquarters are in Washington, D.C., but it sits in other parts of the country as necessary.

The Court of International Trade Formerly known as the United States Customs Court, this court has jurisdiction over cases dealing with tariffs. Citizens who believe that tariffs are too high bring most of the cases heard in this court.

The Court of International Trade is based in New York City, but it is a national court. The judges also hear cases in other major port cities around the country such as New Orleans and San Francisco. The Circuit Court of Appeals for the Federal Circuit hears decisions appealed from this court.

STUDY GUIDE

Themes in Government
Cultural Pluralism Supreme Court Justice Clarence Thomas had previously served as a federal appeals judge. **How many federal courts of appeals and judges are there?**

Critical Thinking Skills
Identifying Alternatives Do you think a federal court of appeals tends to uphold or reverse most decisions that come before it? Why or why not?

Background

Some political scientists have suggested that the selection process for federal judgeships is quite democratic. The American Bar Association (ABA), the largest lawyers' organization in the United States, rates appointees according to their abilities and judicial temperament. The Senate reviews appointments, and in doing so listens to depositions from concerned interest groups and individuals. And the press, through editorials supporting or opposing appointments, can also play a role in the selection process.

Legislative Courts

Along with the constitutional federal courts, Congress has created a series of courts referred to as legislative courts. The **legislative courts** help Congress exercise its powers, as spelled out in Article I of the Constitution. Thus, it was the power of Congress to tax that led to the creation of the United States Tax Court. The congressional power of regulating the armed forces led to the formation of the Court of Military Appeals. The duty of Congress to govern overseas territories such as Guam and the Virgin Islands led to the creation of territorial courts. Similarly, congressional supervision of the District of Columbia led to the establishment of a court system for the nation's capital.

United States Claims Court Congress established the present Claims Court in 1982. It is a court of original jurisdiction that handles claims against the United States for money damages. A person who believes that the government has not paid a bill for goods or services may sue in this court. The Claims Court's headquarters are in Washington, D.C., but it hears cases throughout the country as necessary. The Circuit Court of Appeals for the Federal Circuit hears any appeals from the Claims Court.

United States Tax Court Acting under its power to tax, Congress provided for the present Tax Court in 1969. As a trial court, it hears cases relating to federal taxes. Cases come to the Tax Court from citizens who disagree with Internal Revenue Service and other Treasury Department agency rulings about the federal taxes they must pay. The Tax Court is based in Washington, D.C., but it hears cases throughout the United States. A federal court of appeals handles cases appealed from the Tax Court.

The Court of Military Appeals Congress established the Court of Military Appeals in 1950. It is the armed forces' highest appeals court. This court hears cases involving members of the armed forces convicted of breaking military law. As its name implies, it has appellate jurisdiction. This court is sometimes called the "GI Supreme Court." The United States Supreme Court has jurisdiction to review this court's decisions.

Territorial Courts Congress has created a court system in the territories of the Virgin Islands, Guam, the Northern Mariana Islands, and Puerto Rico. These territorial courts are roughly similar to district courts in function, operation, and jurisdiction. They handle civil and criminal cases, along with constitutional cases. The appellate courts for this system are the United States courts of appeals.

Courts of the District of Columbia Because the District of Columbia is a federal district, Congress has developed a judicial system for the nation's capital. Along with a federal district court and a court of appeals, various local courts handle both civil and criminal cases.

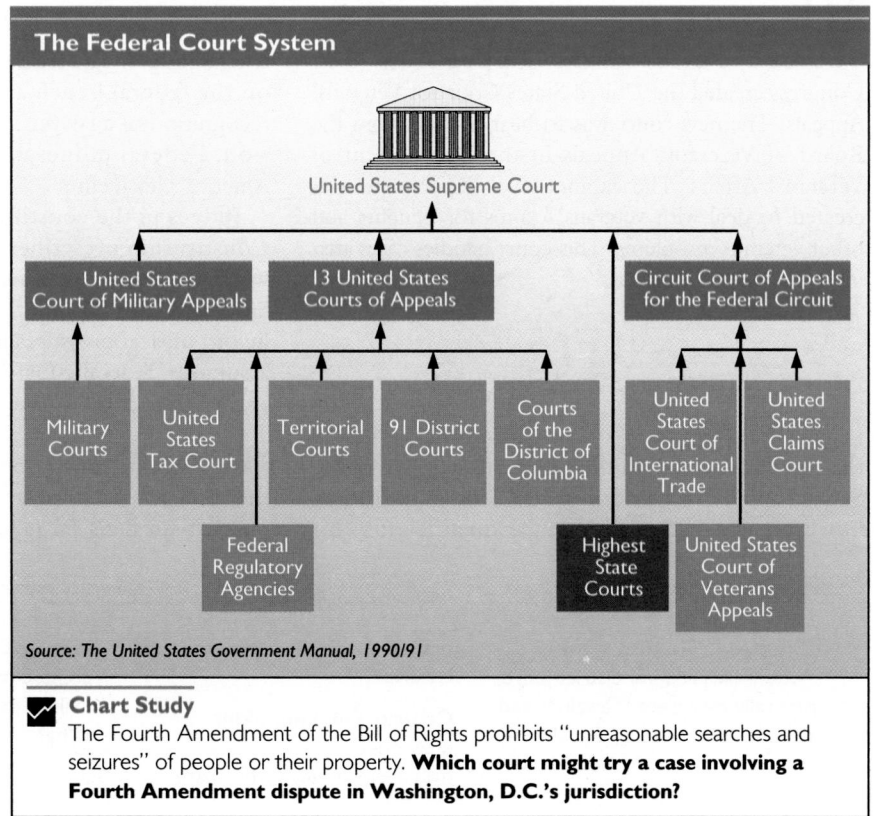

The Federal Court System

Source: The United States Government Manual, 1990/91

📈 **Chart Study**
The Fourth Amendment of the Bill of Rights prohibits "unreasonable searches and seizures" of people or their property. **Which court might try a case involving a Fourth Amendment dispute in Washington, D.C.'s jurisdiction?**

Chapter 19, Section 2
Lesson Plan, pages 546–552

L2 Synthesizing Information
Ask students to differentiate between constitutional and legislative courts. Then ask which court would handle each of the following cases. Have students explain their answers.

a. A man challenges an IRS ruling to disallow a deduction on his income tax return. *(Tax Court)*
b. The man above loses his case and appeals. *(court of appeals)*
c. A woman is arrested in Washington, D.C., for robbery. *(District of Columbia courts)*
d. The woman above loses her case and appeals. *(district court)*
e. A man challenges denial of a patent on an invention. *(court of appeals)*
f. A woman wants payment for damages done to her barn during army war games. *(Court of Claims)*

Independent Practice

L1 Political Cartoons Have students create a political cartoon on one aspect of the criteria for selecting federal judges. Students should write a caption for their cartoons. **LEP**

L2 Informative Writing Have students write essays in which they explain how the existence of legislative courts helps assure "equal justice under the law."

L3 Classificatory Writing Contact your federal district court to obtain biographical information about its judges. Share this data with students and ask them to write an essay showing how the judges' backgrounds reflect criteria Presidents use in making such appointments.

Chart Study Answer
the district court for Washington, D.C., or a court of the District of Columbia

Cooperative Learning Activity

Have students review the criteria usually considered by Presidents in making appointments to the federal bench. Then organize students into groups of six. Tell groups that they are presidential commissions charged with designing a system for improving the method of appointing federal judges. Have groups brainstorm to devise a set of criteria for nominating federal judges and a procedure for Presidents to follow to identify possible appointees. Have group representatives present their ideas to the class.

Ask what other questions lawyers might have in screening prospective jurors. *(those designed to uncover biases)* Point out that in major trials juries may be sequestered. Ask what precautions other juries should take to avoid outside influences. *(avoid news reports about the crime or trial; do not discuss case with friends)* Have students find out how jury lists are developed in their state.

📁 Have students complete activity 19 in *Participating in Government* in the Teacher's Classroom Resources.

STUDY GUIDE

Theme Answer
The President first submits the candidate's name to the senators from the candidate's state.

Critical Thinking Answer
Because of their lifetime tenure, judges enjoy independence from political pressures.

Assess

Check for Understanding

Have students complete Section 2 Review on page 551.

Meeting Objectives

Each section objective is tested by the Section Review questions that follow it in parentheses.
• Discuss the duties of constitutional courts. (2, 3)
• Identify federal legislative courts. (2)
• Evaluate the method of selecting federal judges. (4, 5, 6, 7, 8)

PARTICIPATING IN GOVERNMENT

Serving on a Jury

How are members of a jury chosen? What should you do if you are called for jury duty?

State and federal courts usually select names for jury duty from lists of registered voters, property-tax payers, or licensed drivers. If your name is selected, you will receive a summons requiring you to appear in court at a certain time and place.

When you report to the courthouse, you will probably have to wait in a room with other prospective jurors until your name is called. Then you will be escorted into a courtroom where the attorneys for both sides will question you. Questions about your family, your work, and your interests help the lawyers determine whether you can make a fair judgment in the case. A lawyer can disqualify you if he or she thinks your judgment may be biased.

If you are chosen to serve on a jury, you must take an oath to consider only the testimony of the witnesses. As the trial proceeds, you hear the opening arguments, the evidence introduced, and the questioning and cross-examining of witnesses. Jurors usually are not permitted to take notes, so you must try to remember the details of the case.

Investigating Further

Interview two or more people who have served on a jury. Compare their views of the system.

The Court of Veterans' Appeals In 1988 Congress created the United States Court of Veterans' Appeals. The new court was to hear appeals from the Board of Veterans' Appeals in the Department of Veterans' Affairs. The cabinet-level department was created to deal with veterans' claims for benefits and other veterans' problems. This court handles cases arising from unsettled claims.

Selection of Federal Judges

Article II, Section 2, of the Constitution provides that the President, with the advice and consent of the Senate, appoints all federal judges. The Constitution, however, sets forth no particular qualifications for federal judges. The legal profession regards a position on the federal bench as a highly desirable post, a recognition of a lawyer's high standing in the profession. Federal judges are sometimes described as America's legal elite.

Judges in the constitutional courts serve, as the Constitution prescribes, "during good behavior," which, in practice, means for life. The reason for the life term is that it permits judges to be free from public or political pressures in deciding cases. With this assurance, federal court judges know that their jobs are safe even if they make unpopular decisions.

Party Affiliation Although Presidents often state that they intend to make judicial appointments on a nonpartisan basis, in practice they favor judges who

STUDY GUIDE

Themes in Government
Federalism Federal district judges generally represent the values and attitudes of the states that they serve. **How can a President assure** that an appointee meets this criterion?

Critical Thinking Skills
Demonstrating Reasoned Judgment A judge who shares a President's views when first appointed may change views when making decisions on the bench. **Why?**

Special Needs Strategy

Sequencing Problems Students with problems organizing ideas and information into categories can improve their skills by making charts and lists into which they can arrange this information. For Section 2, have students write the headings "Constitutional Courts" and "Legislative Courts" and list the courts which fall into each category. Then have them rearrange their lists so that the list demonstrates the order in which an appeal would be made from the lowest court to the highest court. Discuss with them how all the courts feed cases up to the Supreme Court.

belong to their own political party. In recent years the percentage of appointed federal judges who belong to the President's party has ranged from 81 percent in the case of President Gerald Ford's appointments to a high of 99 percent in President Ronald Reagan's case.

Another significant factor that emphasizes the political nature of court appointments is the power of Congress to increase the number of judgeships. Studies have shown that when one party controls both the presidency and Congress, it is more likely to dramatically increase the number of judicial posts. When President Kennedy was elected in 1960, the Democratic Congress immediately passed a new omnibus judgeship bill creating 71 new positions for the President to fill.

Judicial Philosophy Presidents often try to appoint judges who share their own point of view. Abraham Lincoln expressed this position when he appointed Salmon P. Chase as Chief Justice of the United States in 1864. "We wish for a Chief Justice who will sustain what has been done in regard to emancipation [of the slaves] and the legal tenders [money policies]." Studies have shown that Presidents have appointed judges who share their judicial philosophy in about 75 percent of the cases.

Presidents follow this practice because they wish to have their own point of view put into effect in the courts. Because judges are appointed for life, Presidents view judicial appointments as an opportunity to perpetuate their political ideologies after leaving the White House.

Senatorial Courtesy In naming judges to trial courts, Presidents customarily follow the practice of senatorial courtesy. Under the **senatorial courtesy** system, a President submits the name of a candidate for judicial appointment to the senators from the candidate's state before formally submitting it for full Senate approval. If either or both senators oppose the President's choice, the President usually withdraws the name and nominates an acceptable candidate.

The practice of senatorial courtesy is limited to the selection of judges to the district courts and other trial courts. It is not followed in the case of nominations to the courts of appeals and the Supreme Court. Courts of appeals' circuits cover more than one state, so that an appointment to this court is regional in nature. A position on the Supreme Court is a national selection rather than a statewide or a regional one.

The Background of Federal Judges Almost all federal judges have had legal training and have held a variety of positions in law or government. This includes service as law school professors, members of Congress, leading attorneys, and federal district attorneys. About one-third of district court judges have served as state court judges.

Until very recently few women, African Americans, or Hispanics were appointed as judges in the lower federal courts. President Carter did much to change this situation in his appointments to the federal bench. President Reagan appointed the first woman to the Supreme Court. Earlier, President Johnson appointed the first African American justice of the Supreme Court.

---

2 SECTION REVIEW

Section Summary
Congress established a network of lower federal courts. The President appoints all federal judges.

Checking for Understanding
Recalling Facts
1. Define constitutional court, district court, grand jury, indictment, petit jury, judicial circuit, legislative court, senatorial courtesy.
2. Classify the two major divisions of federal courts that Congress has created.
3. Identify the courts that handle most federal cases.
4. Demonstrate two ways that political parties influence the federal court system.

Exploring Themes
5. Cultural Pluralism Why do you think President Carter appointed more women, African Americans, and Hispanics as judges in the lower federal courts?
6. Federalism How do district court boundaries and senatorial courtesy support the concept of federalism?

Critical Thinking Skills
7. Identifying Alternatives Should legislation be adopted to ensure that federal court appointments are less political? Why or why not?
8. Demonstrating Reasoned Judgment What are the advantages and disadvantages of the practice of senatorial courtesy in selecting judges?

Evaluate
📁 Section 2 Quiz
 Testmaker

Reteach
Refer students to the key terms and concepts on page 546. Have students write ten questions that can be answered with these terms. Have students exchange questions and answer them.

Enrich
Have students conduct an interview with a federal court official or employee about how the court operates. Have them share their findings with the class.

Close

Refer to the list of federal judges' qualifications that students listed for the Bell Ringer. Ask students what they would add to the list.

Linking Past and Present
Impeachment procedures involving federal judges came in 1989, when district judges Alcee L. Hastings of Florida and Walter L. Nixon of Mississippi were removed from office. John Pickering, a United States district court judge from New Hampshire, was the first federal judge to be impeached. He was removed from office in 1804.

Section 2 Review Answers

1. Definitions of terms appear on pages indicated: **constitutional court,** 546; **district court,** 546; **grand jury,** 546; **indictment,** 546; **petit jury,** 546; **judicial circuit,** 548; **legislative court,** 549; **senatorial courtesy,** 551
2. constitutional courts: Supreme Court, federal district courts, Court of International Trade, and courts of appeals; legislative courts: United States Tax Court, Court of Military Appeals, Territorial Courts, Washington, D.C. courts
3. federal district courts
4. Presidents choose mainly members of their own party for judges; Congress often increases number of judgeships
5. Carter wanted to change the balance of judges to increase the number of minorities and women.
6. Each state has at least one federal district court. Presidents submit names of candidates for federal judgeships to senators of each candidate's state for their approval.
7. Some students may say that legislation should be passed to make selections less political so that judges could be selected only on qualifications. Others may say that the current system works well because judges reflect the views of the electorate.
8. advantage: screens candidates and promotes the federal relationship between the states and national government; disadvantage: takes some of the constitutional power of appointment out of the hands of the President

Making Inferences

Focus

Have students suppose that the following quote appeared in the school paper: "The coach said, 'It looks like I'll finally have a winning team.'" Ask what conclusions they might draw from the coach's statement if they knew nothing about the team. *(The coach has coached the team in the past; the team has not been a winning team in the past; the season is not over.)* Tell students that such conclusions are inferences and that *making inferences* is a key skill of critical thinkers.

Teach

Discuss the Explanation steps with students. Then ask a volunteer to read the *Newsweek* passage aloud. After they review the four possible inferences, have students search the passage for evidence to support each one. Then ask: What additional information would be needed to help determine the validity of the other inferences?

Assess

Have students complete the **Practice** exercise.

Close

Ask how the ability to make inferences is important to making informed decisions about political candidates.

When you use the facts an author presents to draw a conclusion that is not explicitly stated, you are making an inference. Knowing how to make valid inferences will help you to understand and learn from everything you read.

Explanation

To make an inference, follow these steps:
- Read or listen carefully, making sure that you understand the information that is presented.
- Decide what conclusions might be drawn beyond what the author has said directly.
- Examine each inference critically to make sure that it is based on careful analysis of the information you have. Ask: On what evidence do I base this inference?

Application

Consider the following passage from a magazine article that discusses the successful campaign by liberal groups to block confirmation of Robert H. Bork to the Supreme Court:

After Bork was defeated and Douglas H. Ginsburg's nomination went up in . . . smoke, Anthony M. Kennedy breezed through confirmation by being cheerfully evasive. Yet Kennedy went on to vote with Justice Antonin Scalia, the court's archetype conservative, 88 percent of the time from 1987 to 1990. Kennedy's basically all Bork with no bite.
—NEWSWEEK, AUGUST 12, 1991

Based on this passage, which of the following inferences might be made about the author's views?
1. The author thinks that Bork, Ginsburg, and Kennedy were all equally conservative.
2. The author thinks that it is wrong to oppose Supreme Court nominees on ideological grounds.
3. The author thinks that liberals did not gain much by defeating the nomination of Robert Bork.
4. The author thinks it is important that both liberal and conservative opinion be represented on the Court.

The only valid inference to be drawn from this passage is item 3. From the statement that Kennedy votes 88 percent of the time with the "archetype conservative" Justice Scalia, you can infer that the author thinks that Bork's rejection did liberals little good.

Practice

Examine the following table that shows the characteristics of federal district judges Presidents Carter and Reagan appointed. Then use what you have learned about making inferences to decide which of the inferences listed below is valid. Explain your answers.

Appointments of District Judges

		Carter	Reagan
Sex	Male	86 %*	91 %
	Female	14	9
Race	Black	14	1
	White	78	93
	Hispanic	7	5
College	Public	57	34
	Private	33	50
	Ivy League	10	16
Party	Democrat	94	3
	Republican	5	97
	Independent	2	0

* Percentages may not add up to 100 because of rounding.

1. More men than women serve as federal district court judges.
2. Few African Americans are Republicans.
3. More women are Democrats than Republicans.
4. Party affiliation plays an important role in appointments to the district court.
5. Carter preferred to appoint judges who had attended public universities.

Additional Practice

To practice this skill, see **Reinforcing the Skill** on page 561.

Practice Answers

1. Valid. Both appointed far more men than women.
2. Invalid. Reagan did not appoint many African Americans, but perhaps for reasons other than that he could not find enough African American Republicans.
3. Invalid. Carter appointed more women, but not necessarily because more women are Democrats.
4. Valid. Both Carter and Reagan overwhelmingly appointed members of their own party.

5. Invalid. Carter appointed more judges who had attended public universities, but not necessarily because they had attended public universities.

For additional practice, have students complete activity 19 in *Skill Reinforcement Activities* in the Teacher's Classroom Resources.

SECTION 3

The Supreme Court

The Supreme Court stands at the top of the American legal system. Article III of the Constitution created the Supreme Court as part of a coequal branch of the national government, along with Congress and the President.

The Supreme Court is the court of last resort in all questions of federal law. It has final authority in any case involving the Constitution, acts of Congress, and treaties with other nations. Most of the cases the Supreme Court hears are appeals from lower courts. The decisions of the Supreme Court are binding on all lower courts.

Nomination to the Supreme Court today is a very high honor. It was not always so. Several of George Washington's nominees turned down the job. Until 1891 justices earned much of their pay while **riding the circuit** or traveling to hold court in their assigned regions of the country. One justice, after a painful stagecoach ride in 1840, wrote to his wife:

> *I think I never again, at this season of the year, will attempt this mode of journeying. . . . I have been elbowed by old women—jammed by young ones—suffocated by cigar smoke—sickened by the vapours of bitters and w[h]iskey—my head knocked through the carriage top by careless drivers and my toes trodden to a jelly by unheeding passengers.*
> —Justice Levi Woodbury, 1840

Today the Court hears all its cases in the Supreme Court building in Washington, D.C., in a large first-floor courtroom that is open to the public. Nearby is a conference room where the justices meet privately to decide cases. The first floor also contains the offices of the justices, their law clerks, and secretaries.

Supreme Court Jurisdiction

The Supreme Court has both original and appellate jurisdiction. Article III, Section 2, of the Constitution sets the Court's original jurisdiction. It covers two types of cases: (1) cases involving representatives of foreign governments and (2) certain cases in which a state is a party. Congress may not expand or curtail the Court's original jurisdiction.

Many cases have involved two states or a state and the federal government. When Maryland and Virginia argued over oyster fishing rights, and when a dispute broke out between California and Arizona over the control of water from the Colorado River, the Supreme Court had original jurisdiction.

The Supreme Court's original jurisdiction cases form a very small part of its yearly work load—an average of fewer than five such cases a year. Most of the cases the Court decides fall under the Court's appellate jurisdiction.

Under the Supreme Court's appellate jurisdiction, the Court hears cases that are appealed from lower courts of appeals, or it may hear cases from federal district courts in certain instances where an act of Congress was held unconstitutional.

The Supreme Court may also hear cases that are appealed from the highest court of a state, if claims under federal law or the Constitution are involved. In such cases, however, the Supreme Court has the au-

---

SECTION PREVIEW

Objectives
After studying this section, you should be able to:
- Define the jurisdiction of the Supreme Court.
- Describe the duties of Supreme Court justices.

- Examine the method of selecting and appointing Supreme Court justices.

Key Terms and Concepts
riding the circuit, opinion

Themes in Government
- Checks and Balances
- Civil Rights

Critical Thinking Skills
- Understanding Cause and Effect
- Predicting Consequences

CHAPTER 19: THE FEDERAL COURT SYSTEM   553

Classroom Resources for Section 3

- Guided Reading Activities
- Reproducible Lesson Plans
- Interpreting Political Cartoons 19
- Primary and Secondary Source Readings 19
- Reteaching Activities 19
- Enrichment Activities 19

- Section 3 Quiz
- Chapter 19 Tests
- Testmaker
- Audio Cassettes (English and Spanish)
- Limited English Proficiency Activities 19
  SAT Practice Tests

Focus

Bell Ringer

While attendance is being taken, ask students to write a response to the following:

Write one fact about the United States Supreme Court.

Motivating Activity

Discuss students' Bell Ringer answers. Then write on the chalkboard a number of "headlines" that provide further information about the Court. You might include such headlines as:

'NINE OLD MEN' CHALLENGED BY ROOSEVELT

SENATE COMMITTEE GRILLS SUPREME COURT NOMINEE

O'CONNOR BECOMES FIRST WOMAN SUPREME COURT JUSTICE

SUPREME COURT THROWS OUT NEW DEAL LEGISLATION

Have students use their facts and the headlines as a starting point for a discussion on what the Supreme Court is and what it does. Point out that the structure and functions of the Supreme Court are detailed in this section.

Vocabulary Precheck

Write the key terms for this section on the chalkboard. Have students skim the section to find each term and read it in context.
LEP

Focus on Government
Video 34
**Electronic Field Trip:
The Supreme Court**
Running Time: 5:07
Videodisc 2, Chap. 34
VHS Tape 2, Begins 37:05

Teach

Guided Practice

L1 Synthesizing Information
Write *original jurisdiction* and *appellate jurisdiction* on the chalkboard. Then have students give examples of the types of cases the Supreme Court would decide under each type of jurisdiction. (*original: cases involving representatives of foreign governments, cases involving two states or a state and the federal government; appellate: cases appealed from lower appellate courts, cases from federal district courts where an act of Congress was held unconstitutional, cases appealed from states' highest courts if claims involve federal law or the Constitution*)

📁 **Interpreting Source Readings** Have students complete activity 19 in the *Primary and Secondary Source Readings* in the Teacher's Classroom Resources. Then lead them in a discussion of the following statements: The process of selecting Supreme Court justices is fatally flawed. Presidents select their appointees according to factors other than legal qualifications.

Caption Answer
most are appeals from lower courts

thority to rule only on the federal issue involved, not on any issues of state law. A state court, for example, tries a person charged with violating a state law. During the trial, however, the accused claims that the police violated Fourteenth Amendment rights with an illegal search at the time of the arrest. The defendant may appeal to the Supreme Court on the constitutional issue only. The Supreme Court has no jurisdiction to rule on the state issue (whether the accused actually violated state law). The Court will decide only whether Fourteenth Amendment rights were violated.

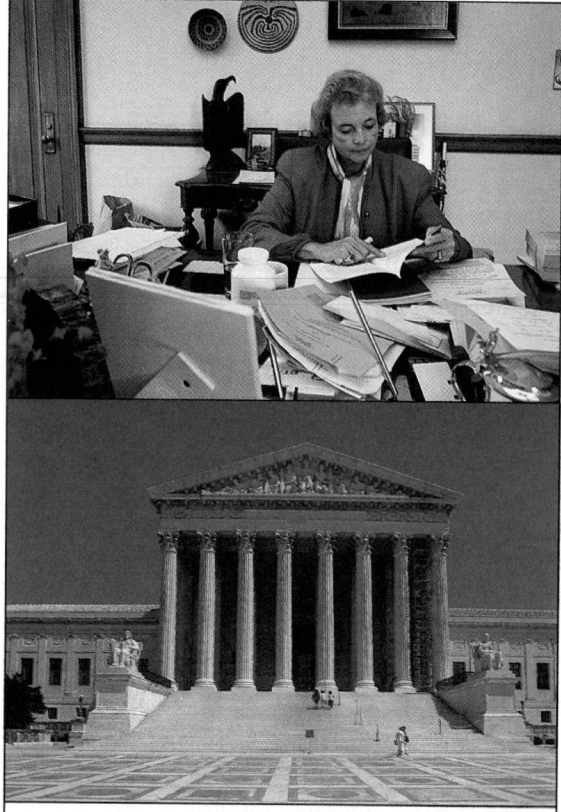

Inside and Outside the "Marble Palace"
An aura of wisdom and impartiality surrounds the Court, but some of its rulings have been bitterly disputed, even reversed. **Political Processes Where do most cases heard by the Supreme Court come from?**

Supreme Court Justices

The Supreme Court is composed of 9 justices: the Chief Justice of the United States and 8 associate justices. Congress sets this number and has the power to change it. Over the years it has varied from 5 to 10, but has been 9 since 1869. In 1937 President Franklin D. Roosevelt attempted to gain greater control of the Court by asking Congress to increase the number of justices. Congress refused, in part because the number 9 was well established.

The eight associate justices receive salaries of $159,000 per year. The Chief Justice receives a salary of $166,200. Congress sets the justices' salaries and may not reduce them.

Under the Constitution Congress may remove Supreme Court justices, like other federal officials, through impeachment for and conviction of "treason, bribery, or other high crimes and misdemeanors." No Supreme Court justice has ever been removed from office through impeachment, however. The House of Representatives impeached Justice Samuel Chase in 1804 because of his participation in partisan political activities, but the Senate found him not guilty.

Duties of the Justices The Constitution does not describe the duties of the justices. Instead, the duties have developed from laws and through tradition. The main duty of the justices is to hear and rule on cases. This involves them in three decision-making tasks: deciding which cases to hear from among the thousands appealed to the Court each year; deciding the case itself; and determining an explanation for the decision, called the Court's **opinion**.

The Chief Justice has several additional duties such as presiding over sessions and conferences at which the cases are discussed. The Chief Justice also exercises leadership in the Court's judicial work and helps administer the federal court system.

Background

Since appointments to the Supreme Court are for life, Presidents can have an impact on American politics long after they have left office. The justices appointed by Ronald Reagan—Sandra Day O'Connor, Antonin Scalia, and Anthony Kennedy—by George Bush—David Souter and Clarence Thomas—and by Bill Clinton—Ruth Bader Ginsburg and Stephen Breyer—all were in their 40s or 50s when appointed. They may serve on the Supreme Court well into the twenty-first century.

Judicial Branch

Protestant 60%
Jewish 12%
Catholic 28%

Independent 4%
Other .4%
Democrat 27%
Republican 69%

Hispanic 5%
Asian .6%
African American 6%
White 89%

Female 12%
Male 88%

Annual salary of federal judges

$171,500	Chief Justice of the United States
$164,100	Associate justice of the Supreme Court
$141,700	U.S. circuit judges
$133,600	U.S. district judges
$133,600	Judges, U.S. Court of International Trade
$133,600	Judges, U.S. claims court
$133,600	Judges, U.S. Tax Court

Source: *Sourcebook of Criminal Justice Statistics–1992* (Washington DC: U.S. Government Printing Office, 1992) Note: Data for gender, religion and political party are based on U.S. court of appeals and U.S. district court judgeship appointments 1976-1992. Totals may not add to 100% because of rounding.

Powers of the Supreme Court
Senate Judiciary Committee
Running Time 1:45
Side Two, Chapter 11

L2 Debate Organize the class into two groups to debate the following:

Resolved, that the composition of the Supreme Court should represent the racial, geographic, and sexual composition of the United States.

Before the debate begins, have each student prepare at least three arguments with supporting statements for his or her side. After the debate, have the class list the arguments presented and decide which arguments and supporting statements are the strongest.

Independent Practice

L1 Biographical Sketches Have students consult the *Congressional Directory*, almanacs, or other library references to compile a list of the current justices on the Supreme Court. For each justice, have students list place of birth, educational background, professional experience, race or ethnic origin, age, and party affiliation.

L2 Informative Writing Have students write a research paper on one of the historical giants of the Supreme Court. Students might choose Benjamin Cardozo, former Senator Hugo Black, New Deal reformer William O. Douglas, or Governor Earl Warren. Have them focus on the criteria the Presidents used to select these men and special merits in the justices' careers.

All the justices also have limited duties related to the 12 federal judicial circuits. One Supreme Court justice is assigned to each of these federal circuits. Three of the justices handle 2 circuits each. The justices are responsible for dealing with requests for special legal actions that come from their circuit. In 1980, for example, a lower federal court ruled against the federal government's program of draft registration. Lawyers for the federal government then requested the Supreme Court to temporarily set aside the lower court's decision. The Supreme Court justice who was responsible for the federal judicial circuit in which the issue arose heard this request.

Infrequently, justices take on additional duties. In 1945 Justice Robert Jackson served as chief prosecutor at the Nuremberg trials of Nazi war criminals. In 1963 Chief Justice Earl Warren headed a special commission that investigated the assassination of President Kennedy. Justices limit such external activities because of the Court's heavy work load.

To maintain their objectivity on the bench, justices are careful not to become involved in outside activities that might prevent them from dealing fairly with one side or the other on a case. If justices have any personal or business connection with either of the parties in a case, they usually disqualify themselves from participating in that case.

Law Clerks In 1882 Justice Horace Gray hired the first law clerk—mainly to be his servant and barber. Today the Court's law clerks assist the justices with many tasks, enabling the justices to concentrate on their pressing duties. Law clerks read all the appeals filed with the Court and write memos summarizing the key issues in each case. When cases are decided, the clerks help prepare the Court's opinions by doing research and sometimes writing first drafts of the opinions.

The justices each hire a few law clerks from among the top graduates of the nation's best law schools. These young men and women usually work for a justice for one or two years. After leaving the Court, many clerks go on to distinguished careers as judges, law professors, and even Supreme Court justices themselves.

Background of the Justices Throughout the Court's history more than 100 men and one woman have served as justices. What type of people become the top judges in the land? Although not a formal re-

Cooperative Learning Activity

Organize students into four groups to research the Supreme Court justices of today and 50, 100, and 150 years ago. Assign each group one of these time periods. Have groups focus on the changes in the composition of the Supreme Court by addressing questions such as: How does the age composition of the Court today compare with that of Courts of the past? How has the regional and religious balance of the Court changed over time? Have groups compare their findings and determine how much the Supreme Court has changed over the past 150 years.

Set on Freedom
Thurgood Marshall, First African American named to Supreme Court
Running Time :31
Side A, Chapter 35

📁 **Interpreting Political Cartoons** Have students complete activity 19 in *Interpreting Political Cartoons* in the Teacher's Classroom Resources.

L3 Classificatory Writing In the confirmation process, the Senate Judiciary Committee reviews the ABA ratings, interviews the appointee, and hears from groups and individuals supporting and opposing the nomination. Have students write a brief essay that assesses the validity of the information the committee uses in making its decision.

Caption Answer
the Attorney General, Justice Department officials

STUDY GUIDE

Theme Answer
two African Americans, two women

Critical Thinking Answer
Concern over the philosophies of the justices will continue to arouse objection from groups that hold differing views.

CONNECTIONS

Biography
The first Catholic justice, Roger B. Taney, was nominated by Andrew Jackson in 1835. Woodrow Wilson nominated the first Jewish justice, Louis Brandeis, in 1916. Thurgood Marshall, the first African American on the Supreme Court, was appointed by Lyndon Johnson in 1967; and Ronald Reagan selected the first woman justice, Sandra Day O'Connor, in 1981.

The Supreme Court, 1995
Justice Stephen Breyer replaced retiring Justice Harry Blackmun in 1994. **Political Processes Who helps the President find candidates for the Supreme Court?**

quirement, a justice usually has a law degree and considerable legal experience. A majority of all justices have been state or federal court judges or have held other court-related positions such as attorney general. One former President, William Howard Taft, served as Chief Justice. Younger people are not typically appointed to the Court. Most of the justices selected in the twentieth century were in their fifties when they were appointed to the Court. Nine were younger than 50 and the remainder were more than 60 years old.

Justices have not been representative of the general population in social class, background, and race. Most justices have come from upper socioeconomic levels. Through 1994 only two African American justices, Thurgood Marshall and Clarence Thomas, and only two women, Sandra Day O'Connor and Ruth Bader Ginsburg, have been appointed.

Appointing Justices

Justices reach the Court through appointment by the President with Senate approval. The Senate usually grants such approval, but it is not automatic. A re-

spected President is less likely to have a candidate rejected, but the Senate did reject one of President Washington's nominees. During the nineteenth century, more than 25 percent of the nominees failed to win Senate approval. By contrast, during the early part of the twentieth century, the Senate was much more supportive of presidential choices. More recently, the Senate rejected two of President Nixon's nominees and Reagan's nomination of Robert Bork in 1988. The Senate closely scrutinized Justice Clarence Thomas's nomination in 1991 but accepted the nomination by a vote of 52 to 48.

As is the case with lower court judges, political considerations often affect a President's choice of a nominee to the Court. Usually Presidents will choose someone from their own party, sometimes as a reward for faithful service to the party.

Presidents prefer to nominate candidates they believe sympathize with their political beliefs. Several Presidents have discovered, however, that it is very difficult to predict how an individual will rule on sensitive issues once he or she becomes a member of the Court. After securing the nomination of Tom Clark, President Truman expressed his displeasure:

> *Tom Clark was my biggest mistake. No question about it. . . . I don't know what got into me. He was no . . . good as Attorney General, and on the Supreme Court . . . he's been even worse. He hasn't made one right decision I can think of.*
> —HARRY S TRUMAN

When President Eisenhower named Earl Warren as Chief Justice in 1953, he expected Warren to continue to support the rather conservative positions he had taken as governor of California. The Warren Court, however, turned out to be the most liberal, activist Court in the country's history.

In identifying and selecting candidates for nomination to the Court, the President receives help from the Attorney General and other Justice Department officials. The Attorney General usually consults with the legal community and proposes a list of possible candi-

---

STUDY GUIDE

Themes in Government
Civil Rights Some feel that a Hispanic judge should be selected by the President to fill a vacancy on the Supreme

Court. **What record does the Supreme Court show as regards minority and female judges?**

Critical Thinking Skills
Predicting Consequences
Why will selecting future Supreme Court justices continue to be an intense political issue and a matter of concern for interested citizens?

Special Needs Strategy

Sequencing Problems Students who experience problems understanding the relationship of events to each other will be helped by making a diagram of the relationship or process. After students have read about the way a Supreme Court justice is chosen, have them make a flow chart showing the order of the nomination and selection process. Section 3 mentions the role of the President, the Senate, the American Bar Association, interest groups, and Supreme Court justices. Have students indicate in the flow chart where each of these individuals or groups influences the selection of a Supreme Court justice.

dates for the President to consider. In making the final selection, the President and the Attorney General may also check with leading members of Congress. In addition, they hear from several different groups that have a special interest in the selection of a justice.

The Role of the American Bar Association The American Bar Association (ABA) at times has played an important role in the selection of justices. The ABA is a national organization of attorneys and the major voice of the legal profession in the United States. The ABA's Committee on the Federal Judiciary rates the qualifications of Supreme Court nominees from "exceptionally well-qualified" to "not qualified." While the President does not have to pay attention to the ABA's ratings, an ABA rejection of a nominee may lead the Senate to disapprove the nominee. When he first assumed office, President Nixon indicated that he would not appoint any judge who did not have the approval of the ABA. After the Senate turned down two Nixon candidates who had ABA approval, Nixon's confidence in the ABA eroded. At the same time, the ABA began to scrutinize candidates more closely. While the ABA still rates candidates, recent Presidents have not as faithfully consulted the ABA about appointments.

Focus on Freedom

GIDEON v. WAINWRIGHT

Clarence Gideon was arrested and charged with breaking and entering a pool hall—a felony under Florida law. Too poor to afford a lawyer, he requested that the trial judge appoint one. When the judge refused, Gideon conducted his own defense. Found guilty, he appealed to the United States Supreme Court, arguing that his rights under the Sixth and Fourteenth Amendments had been violated.

Since 1942, when *Betts* v. *Brady* . . . was decided by a divided Court, the problem of a defendant's federal constitutional right to counsel in a state court has been a continuing source of controversy and litigation in both state and federal courts. . . .

The facts upon which Betts claimed that he had been unconstitutionally denied the right to have counsel appointed to assist him are strikingly like the facts upon which Gideon here bases his federal constitutional claim. . . . Upon full reconsideration we conclude that *Betts* v. *Brady* should be overruled. . . .

The fact is that in deciding as it did—that "appointment of counsel is not a fundamental right, essential to a fair trial"—the Court in *Betts* v. *Brady* made an abrupt break with its own well-considered precedents. In returning to these old precedents . . . we but restore constitutional principles established to achieve a fair system of justice. Not only these precedents but also reason and reflection require us to recognize that in our adversary system of criminal justice, any person haled into court, who is too poor to hire a lawyer, cannot be assured a fair trial unless counsel is provided for him. This seems to be an obvious truth. Governments, both state and federal, quite properly spend vast sums of money to establish machinery to try defendants accused of crime. Lawyers to prosecute are everywhere deemed essential to protect the public's interest in an orderly society. Similarly, there are few defendants . . . who fail to hire the best lawyers they can get to prepare and present their defenses. That government hires lawyers to prosecute and defendants who have the money hire lawyers to defend are the strongest indications of the widespread belief that lawyers in criminal courts are necessities, not luxuries. The right of one charged with crime to counsel may not be deemed fundamental and essential in some countries, but it is in ours.

— JUSTICE HUGO BLACK

Examining the Document

Reviewing the Facts
1. Explain what the Court decided to do about the *Betts* v. *Brady* decision.
2. Describe what proof Justice Black offered that lawyers are necessities, not luxuries, in court.

Critical Thinking Skills
3. Making Inferences Why does our "adversary system of criminal justice" require counsel?

CHAPTER 19: THE FEDERAL COURT SYSTEM   557

Critical Thinking Activity

Predicting Consequences Remind students that in the 1930s President Franklin D. Roosevelt attempted to increase the number of justices on the Supreme Court to 15. Have students predict what might happen if the Supreme Court was enlarged to 12 or 15 justices. Ask: How might this affect the racial, social, and gender makeup of the Court? What impact would it have on the Court's workload? How might the Court's decisions on controversial issues be affected?

Focus on Freedom

Remind students that the Supreme Court accepts only cases that involve a "substantial federal question." Ask: What substantial federal question was involved here? What were the Sixth Amendment and Fourteenth Amendment issues? *(Sixth—right to an attorney; Fourteenth—due process, equal protection issues)* What kind of jurisdiction was the court exercising here? *(appellate)*

Answers

1. to overturn the decision

2. The state and those who can afford them always hire lawyers.

3. The prosecution's case always will be presented by an attorney.

Assess

Check for Understanding

Have students complete Section 3 Review on page 558.

Meeting Objectives

Each section objective is tested by the Section Review questions that follow it in parentheses.
- Define the jurisdiction of the Supreme Court. (2, 3)
- Describe the duties of Supreme Court justices. (2, 3)
- Examine the method of selecting and appointing Supreme Court justices. (4, 5, 6, 7, 8)

Evaluate

📁 Section 3 Quiz

💻 Testmaker

Caption Answer
Nominees may have opinions that run counter to those of a particular organization.

Reteach

Have students close their textbooks. Then ask them to write 5 to 10 questions based on the information they learned in Section 3. Have them select 3 or 4 of their questions to ask the class.

📁 Have students complete activity 19 in *Reteaching Activities* in the Teacher's Classroom Resources.

Enrich

Ask students to research recent controversies surrounding Supreme Court nominations. Ask students to assess the impact these controversies had on the selection and confirmation process.

📁 Have students complete activity 19 in *Enrichment Activities* in the Teacher's Classroom Resources.

Close

Discuss the important issues raised about the compatibility of appointed justices with a democracy. Ask: Why do you think the Framers of the Constitution chose to make it almost impossible to remove a judge?

Choosing an Acceptable Nominee
Justice Breyer's moderate views assured his confirmation.
Politics Why do groups oppose some nominees?

The Role of Other Interest Groups Interest groups that have a stake in Supreme Court decisions may attempt to influence the selection process. Generally these groups make their positions on nominees known through their lobbyists and the media. Strong opposition to a nominee by one or more major interest groups may influence the senators who vote on the nominee.

Labor unions, for example, may oppose a nominee if they believe the nominee is antilabor, based upon his or her previous court decisions, speeches, or writings. Similarly, the National Organization for Women (NOW) may oppose a nominee who is considered to be against women's rights. This was the case with President Ford's selection of John Paul Stevens in 1975. Despite NOW's criticism, however, the Senate approved Stevens. More recently, NOW expressed its opposition to the nominations of David Souter in 1990 and Clarence Thomas in 1991. In both instances NOW was concerned that both candidates might cast a deciding vote against *Roe* v. *Wade*.

Civil rights groups are also usually active during the selection process. Groups such as the National Association for the Advancement of Colored People (NAACP) carefully examine nominees' views on racial integration and minority rights.

The Role of the Justices Members of the Supreme Court have a big stake in the selection of new justices. As leaders of the Court, chief justices have often been very active in the selection process. Justices who must work with the newcomers often participate in the selection process. They may write letters of recommendation supporting candidates who have been nominated, or they may lobby the President for a certain candidate.

Chief Justice Howard Taft intervened frequently in the nominating process. He personally led a campaign for the nomination of Pierce Butler, who was named to the Court in 1922. Chief Justice Warren Burger suggested the name of Harry Blackmun, who was also confirmed. Knowing a member of the Court personally helped Sandra Day O'Connor. She received a strong endorsement from former law school classmate Justice William Rehnquist in 1981.

3 SECTION REVIEW

Section Summary
The Supreme Court is the highest court in the land and has both original and appellate jurisdiction. The President appoints Supreme Court justices, and the Senate approves them.

Checking for Understanding
Recalling Facts
1. Define riding the circuit, opinion.
2. Identify the two kinds of cases in which the Supreme Court has original jurisdiction.
3. Specify the conditions under which a case may be appealed from a state court to the Supreme Court.
4. Describe the constitutional grounds for impeachment of a Supreme Court justice.

Exploring Themes
5. Checks and Balances How has the Senate historically used its power to approve or disapprove presidential nominees to the Supreme Court?
6. Civil Rights What role do interest groups play in assessing the civil rights record of Supreme Court nominees?

Critical Thinking Skills
7. Understanding Cause and Effect Why do Presidents generally choose Supreme Court justices who are members of their own party and who share their own political beliefs?
8. Predicting Consequences How are the President's intentions to influence policy by appointing Supreme Court justices sometimes frustrated?

Section 3 Review Answers

1. Definitions of terms appear on pages indicated: **riding the circuit,** 553; **opinion,** 554
2. cases involving the representatives of foreign governments, cases in which a state is a party
3. if claims involve federal law or the Constitution
4. treason, bribery, or other high crimes or misdemeanors

5. During the nineteenth century, the Senate rejected about 25 percent of Supreme Court nominees. During the twentieth century the Senate has been much more supportive of presidential choices. Even so, a close vote on a nominee is an indication of the Senate's power.
6. Groups such as the NAACP examine candidates' views and make their positions known through the media and during hearings on nominations.

7. Presidents hope to have a Court sympathetic to their policies.
8. Sometimes a President chooses a nominee who later makes decisions against that President's views.

PERSONAL PERSPECTIVES

Sandra Day O'Connor on Appointment to the Supreme Court

On May 19, 1983, Justice Sandra Day O'Connor, the newest justice on the Supreme Court addressed the annual dinner of the American Law Institute. As the first woman appointed to the Court, she spoke about the process of becoming a justice.

President John Adams once said, "My gift of Chief Justice John Marshall to the people of the United States was the proudest act of my life." Another, less satisfied President referred to one of his appointments as "my biggest mistake." Among the reasons Presidents care about the quality of their appointments on the Court is the fact that the Justices not only are not obligated to reflect the views of the President who appointed them, but they usually are in power many, many years after the person who appointed them has left office. Under our system the President makes the proposal, but the marriage for better or for worse, for richer or for poorer, till death do

> *... the marriage for better or for worse, for richer or for poorer, till death do they part, is between the Court and the Justice, not between the President and the Justice....*

they part, is between the Court and the Justice, not between the President and the Justice....

The language of the Constitution concerning appointments with the advice and consent of the Senate was inserted during the closing days of the Constitutional Convention, to replace the original language which had been "reject and approve." In the intervening years, the practice has almost always been that the President selects the nominee for the Court without any advice from the Senate, and merely forwards the nomination for the confirmation process....

Certainly a President contemplating an appointment to the Court also considers the likelihood of Senate confirmation, geographical and religious balance, the person's reputation and ability, and the person's ideological beliefs and positions....

As of 1981, it appears that another factor to be considered in the selection process is the gender of the nominee, at least that is a rumor I once heard.

It is crystal clear, as far as our Founding Fathers were concerned, that representativeness on the Court was not even considered, let alone advocated. Merit was the criterion in the minds of the delegates and representativeness was reserved for the legislative bodies....

The practice of asking a nominee to personally appear and orally respond to questions by members of the Senate Committee is of relatively recent origin. In earlier times it was thought improper for a nominee to respond to direct questions. Justice Brandeis, for example, expressed the view that he should decline to answer questions by members of the Senate Committee. More recently, nominees have responded to numerous questions on a wide range of issues.

—SANDRA DAY O'CONNOR, 1983

Examining the Reading

Reviewing Facts
1. State the Senate's traditional role in the appointment of a Supreme Court justice.
2. List the four factors that Presidents usually consider in selecting a nominee.

Critical Thinking Skills
3. Evaluating Information What did Justice O'Connor mean when she said that the marriage is "between the Court and the Justice, not between the President and the Justice"?

PERSONAL PERSPECTIVES

Focus

Have students consider the qualifications needed to become a United States Supreme Court justice.

Teach

Ask: Why is the appointment of a justice one of the most crucial decisions a President makes? *(Justices remain for years after Presidents leave office.)* What changes does O'Connor note in the appointment process since the Constitution was written? *(Nominees were only recently asked to appear for confirmation; balance and representativeness are considerations in addition to merit.)*

Assess

Have students complete **Examining the Reading.**

Answers

1. The Senate confirms or rejects nominees.
2. likelihood of confirmation, geographical and religious balance, reputation and ability, ideological beliefs and positions
3. After appointment and confirmation, the justice has no obligation to the President, but only to serve the Court to the best of his or her ability.

Close

Justice O'Connor says that in earlier times it was thought improper for a nominee to respond to direct questions. Why has the process changed?

More About Personal Perspectives

Sandra Day O'Connor was named associate justice of the United States Supreme Court by President Reagan in 1981; until the appointment of Ruth Bader Ginsburg in 1993 she was the only woman to serve on the Court. O'Connor was a lawyer, an assistant attorney general, a state senator, and a Court of Appeals judge, all in Arizona, before being named to the high court. Although she is not a feminist, she occasionally dealt with her isolation on the bench with humor. In 1991 during a prison-rights case hearing, a lawyer representing Louisiana said to the justices, "I would like to remind you gentlemen of an important legal point." Leaning forward, O'Connor responded, "Would you like to remind me, too?"

19
CHAPTER REVIEW

Summary and Significance

Federal courts have jurisdiction in all cases involving the United States Constitution, federal laws, differences between states, and between citizens of different states. Trial courts have original jurisdiction, while appellate courts hear cases that come from lower courts. Federal courts deal with civil law, criminal law, and constitutional law. Congress has established constitutional courts and legislative courts. District courts are trial courts that hear both civil and criminal cases. Courts of appeals help relieve the Supreme Court of its heavy caseload. The Supreme Court is the final authority.

Identifying Terms and Concepts

Insert the terms below into the following paragraph to describe the federal court system. Use no term more than once.

concurrent jurisdiction, indictment, original jurisdiction, defendant, prosecution, district courts, grand jury

Federal (1) handle the largest caseload of the federal system. These courts have (2) in cases that involve the Constitution or federal laws. In a criminal case, the government is the (3), bringing charges against the (4). The (5) issues the formal charge, which is also called the (6).

Reviewing Facts and Ideas

1. **Explain** the difference between a civil case and a criminal case.
2. **Compare** "equal justice under law" with "due process of law."
3. **Trace** the origin of the notion of presumed innocence in the United States system of justice.
4. **Summarize** the duties of a grand jury in a criminal case.
5. **Relate** the main duties pertaining to a United States marshal.
6. **Justify** the claim that the caseload of appellate courts is growing rapidly.
7. **Discuss** the main reason that federal judges serve for life.
8. **Describe** the three decision-making tasks of a Supreme Court justice.
9. **Identify** three duties of the Chief Justice of the United States.

10. **Name** three persons or organizations that provide input in the selection process for Supreme Court justices.

Applying Themes

1. **Federalism** When the Supreme Court justices rule in a case that they agreed to hear on appeal from a state court, what restriction applies to the Court's ruling?
2. **Civil Rights** If the issue is whether a person's civil rights had been violated in a court decision, through what levels of courts might that person appeal?
3. **Cultural Pluralism** How may the principle of "equal justice under law" applied in federal court cases benefit minorities, poor people, or young people?
4. **Checks and Balances** Early in United States history the Supreme Court was viewed as an inferior branch of the federal government. How did the Supreme Court win its respected role as an equal with the other branches?

Critical Thinking Skills

1. **Predicting Consequences** Why is the Supreme Court often not a reflection of former Presidents' political ideologies, even though Presidents appoint party members and those who tend to agree with them politically?
2. **Identifying Alternatives** Do you think Supreme Court justices should hire more law clerks to organize the work of the Court and write opinions,

or should the Court limit the number of cases it hears? Explain your answer.

3. **Demonstrating Reasoned Judgment** Why do Supreme Court justices avoid outside interests such as owning stock in major corporations, serving on boards of large businesses, or participating in political rallies?

4. **Understanding Cause and Effect** If a President ignored senatorial courtesy in appointing people to serve on district courts and attempted to appoint justices and judges purely on the basis of political favors, what would happen to frustrate the President's goals?

Linking Past and Present

United States district courts have a long and colorful history, gilded by the legend of the federal marshals of the old West. Federal marshals appointed to district courts in the West became national heroes. James Butler "Wild Bill" Hickok lasted less than two months as marshal of Abilene, Kansas, in 1871, but that did not prevent moviemakers from creating a legend of the frontier character. Wyatt Earp served under the assistant marshal in Wichita for only one year and had an undistinguished career as assistant marshal in Dodge City. Earp was, nonetheless, immortalized by Ned Buntline's dime novels. Today federal marshals also serve district courts. What kinds of problems do federal marshals encounter in the major cities of the United States? How is federal law enforcement today different from law enforcement in the old West?

Writing About Government

Persuasive Writing When a President has the opportunity to fill a vacancy on the Supreme Court, interest groups attempt to influence the decision. Assume that you are the president of a national interest group who wants to prevent an appointment of an individual who is known to oppose your interests. Write a letter to the President expressing your concern and suggesting a candidate whom you prefer—a person who would likely be confirmed by the Senate. Explain the advantages to the President of supporting

your candidate and the disadvantages of supporting the person whom you oppose.

Reinforcing the Skill

Making Inferences Read the following excerpt from a news article about legal reforms Vice President Dan Quayle proposed. Then decide which of the statements listed below are valid inferences.

---

*C*ap punitive damages. Juries can [currently] award plaintiffs compensation for their injuries and larger punitive damages to punish defendants. The proposal would limit punitive damages to the amount of compensatory awards and permit only judges to levy them.

Attorney's fees. Quayle's proposal would include experiments with having the losers pay the winner's legal fees. Sometimes called the English Rule, this is more accurately referred to as the rest-of-the-world rule. Proponents believe this proposal will discourage frivolous suits.

—*NEWSWEEK, AUGUST 26, 1991*

---

1. In most countries the party that loses a lawsuit has to pay the expenses of the winning side.
2. Quayle believes that if the losers of lawsuits had to pay the winner's legal fees, fewer people would file unnecessary lawsuits.

Investigating Further

1. **Individual Project** Write a brief biographical sketch of one of the Supreme Court justices appointed since 1981.
2. **Cooperative Learning** Organize the class into nine, seven, or five groups. List current issues that might someday come before the Court. Present each issue to each group as a position statement. Have members of each group vote individually on paper to support or oppose the statement (*yes* or *no*). Have the entire class discuss the results.

CHAPTER 19: THE FEDERAL COURT SYSTEM **561**

Linking Past and Present

Today, federal marshals have to deal with such problems as organized crime and drug trafficking. Few are as flamboyant as the legendary marshals of the old West.

Writing About Government

Students' letters will vary but should include an explanation of advantages and disadvantages involved.

Reinforcing the Skill

1. Valid. The excerpt says this "is more accurately referred to as the rest-of-the-world rule," implying that most other countries use this system.
2. Valid. The excerpt says that proponents of this reform believe it "will discourage frivolous suits." Quayle is clearly a proponent.

Investigating Further

1. Students' biographical sketches will vary.
2. Students' votes on issues will vary, but should show an understanding of the types of cases on which the Supreme Court rules.

Critical Thinking Skills

1. The person chosen may not reflect the President's ideas because people change over time and justices serve long terms. Also, the President may not know enough about the candidate to predict how he or she will think about cases before the Supreme Court.

2. Answers will vary, but those who favor more clerks may note that justices should assign the ev-

eryday tasks to clerks and retain the important decisions for themselves. Those who oppose more clerks may argue that the justices should be deciding only the most important cases.

3. These interests might conflict with court decisions that they would have to make.

4. The Senate would refuse to confirm appointments.

Chapter Organizer

Objectives	Special Feature Pages	Supplemental Materials
Section 1 Supreme Court Decisions and Public Policy *pp. 564–568* 1. Identify ways the Supreme Court shapes public policy. 2. Characterize the cases that come before the Supreme Court. 3. Describe the factors that limit the Supreme Court's power.	Global Connection: Comparing Governments: Legal Systems p. 566 Focus on Freedom: *Miranda* v. *Arizona* p. 567	Guided Reading Activities Reproducible Lesson Plans Supreme Court Case Studies 1, 41 Section 1 Quiz Testmaker Government Themes Transparencies 37 The Living Constitution SAT Practice Tests
Section 2 The Supreme Court at Work *pp. 569–574* 1. Specify how cases reach the Supreme Court. 2. Describe how the Supreme Court selects, hears, and decides cases. 3. Explain the importance of Supreme Court opinions.	Images of Government: Justice for All pp. 570–571 Critical Thinking Skills: Interpreting a Primary Source p. 574	Guided Reading Activities Reproducible Lesson Plans Primary and Secondary Source Readings 20 Enrichment Activities 20 Section 2 Quiz Testmaker Skill Reinforcement Activities 20 The Living Constitution SAT Practice Tests Writer's Guidebook
Section 3 Factors Influencing the Court's Decisions *pp. 575–581* 1. Explain how social forces influence Supreme Court decisions. 2. Describe how individual justices shape Supreme Court decisions.	Participating in Government: Serving as an Election Judge p. 579 Personal Perspectives: John M. Harlan on the Role of Oral Argument p. 581 Case Study: The Supreme Court Changes Its Mind pp. 584–586 Unit 6 Digest pp. 587–588	Guided Reading Activities Reproducible Lesson Plans Participating in Government 20 Supreme Court Case Studies 52 Reteaching Activities 20 Section 3 Quiz Chapter 20 Tests Testmaker Government Themes Transparencies 16, 26 Audio Cassettes (English and Spanish) Limited English Proficiency Activities 20 Unit Digest Transparencies, Unit 6 Participating in Government, Unit 6 SAT Practice Tests

If time does not permit teaching this chapter, assign the Chapter 20 summary in the Unit 6 Digest on pages 587–588.

Key To Ability Levels

Teaching strategies have been coded for varying learning styles and abilities.

L1   Level 1 activities are **basic** activities and should be within the ability range of all students.

L2   Level 2 activities are **average** activities and should be within the ability range of the average to above-average student.

L3   Level 3 activities are **challenging** activities designed for the ability range of above-average students.

LEP   These activities should be within the ability range of **Limited English Proficiency** students.

Multicultural Activities

Among the Supreme Court decisions civil rights groups have watched most closely are those involving affirmative action issues. In speaking for the majority in the 1978 *Bakke* case, Justice Lewis Powell said: "The guarantee of equal protection cannot mean one thing when applied to one individual and something else when applied to a person of another color." Many minority groups sided with dissenting Justice Harry Blackmun who said: "In order to get beyond racism, we must first take account of race . . . . And in order to treat some persons equally, we must treat them differently." A review of *Martin* v. *Wilks* (1989), *City of Richmond* v. *Croson Company* (1989) and *Firefighters* v. *Stotts* (1984) will show students how the conservative Supreme Court of the 1980s shaped public policy on this issue.

A good example of how the system of checks and balances influences the work of the Supreme Court concerns the 1984 *Grove City College* v. *Bell* decision. In this case the Court ruled on a law barring sex discrimination in schools receiving federal aid. The decision had the effect of narrowing or weakening four federal civil rights laws that barred discrimination based on race, sex, and national origin. The Department of Education's Office of Civil Rights soon dropped dozens of anti-discrimination lawsuits. Civil rights groups and members of Congress began a four-year battle to enact a law to reverse the Court's ruling, and a new law was passed in 1988 over President Reagan's veto. Have students research this decision, reaction to it, and the legislative battle to reverse it.

Chapter Resources

Readings for the Student

Baum, Lawrence. *The Supreme Court*. Congressional Quarterly, 1989.

Irons, Peter. *The Courage of Their Convictions*. Penguin, 1990.

Lawson, Don. *Landmark Supreme Court Cases*. Enslow, 1987.

Rodell, Fred. *Nine Men: A Political History of the Supreme Court from 1790 to 1955*. Random House, 1955.

The Supreme Court at Work. Congressional Quarterly, 1990.

The Supreme Court: Justice and the Law. Congressional Quarterly, 1983.

Woodward, Bob, and Scott Armstrong. *The Brethren*. Simon and Schuster, 1979.

Readings for the Teacher

Bartholomew, Paul C., and Joseph F. Menez. *Summaries of Leading Cases on the Constitution*. Helix Books, 1990.

Berger, Raoul. *Death Penalties: The Supreme Court's Obstacle Course*. Harvard University Press, 1982.

Douglas, William O. *The Court Years, 1939–1975: The Autobiography of William O. Douglas*. Random House, 1980.

Schwartz, Herman, ed. *The Burger Years: Rights and Wrongs in the Supreme Court*. Viking, 1987.

Multimedia

Videocassettes and Films

Gideon's Trumpet. Social Studies School Service. (v/c, 104 minutes)

John Marshall. (*Profiles in Courage* series.) Zenger Films. (v/c, 50 minutes)

Marbury v. Madison. Judicial Conference of the U.S. (v/c, 36 minutes)

The Road to Brown. California Newsreel. (v/c, 50 minutes)

Thurgood Marshall: Portrait of an American Hero. Columbia Video Productions. (v/c, 30 minutes)

The United States Supreme Court: Guardian of the Constitution. Concept Films. (film, 24 minutes)

Software

Supreme Court Decisions. Intellectual Software. (Apple, IBM disks; TRS80 version available from Social Studies School Service.). Students take on the role of attorneys preparing and arguing a civil or criminal case.

United States Constitution Tutor. Micro Learn (division of Micro-Lab). (Apple, IBM, Commodore 64 disks). A test-preparation program for reviewing United States government, including facts and concepts about the Constitution.

Supreme Court Decision Making

Introduce

Chapter Overview

Chapter 20 focuses on the day-to-day operation of the Supreme Court. It considers how the Court influences public policy and how the Court itself is influenced by outside forces and by limits on its powers.

Section 1 explains how Supreme Court decisions shape public policy and focuses on factors that limit the Court's power.

Section 2 elaborates the steps that the Supreme Court follows to choose, hear, and decide cases.

Section 3 discusses factors that influence the Supreme Court's decisions.

Chapter 20 Themes

Write the chapter themes on the chalkboard. Call on students to give examples of how the chapter might address each of the themes. Have them scan the chapter to locate photographs that illustrate the themes.

Linking Past and Present

The United States Supreme Court is unique in the history of the great tribunals of the world. Unlike the common-law courts of western Europe that developed slowly over centuries, the Supreme Court was created by Article III of the Constitution. However, it was 14 years after the Court was established before it truly assumed its role as an equal government branch. Under the leadership of John Marshall, who was appointed Chief Justice in 1801, the Court began to maneuver to maximize the power and prestige it continues to enjoy today.

CHAPTER 20

Within the courtroom of the Supreme Court building in Washington, D.C., the justices hear the cases they consider to be the most important and announce their sometimes historic rulings.

About the Chapter Opener

Teaching With Illustrations Ask students to describe the photograph on pages 562 and 563. *(Students might mention that the courtroom is empty.)* Point out to students that although spectators can observe sessions of the Court, photographers are not allowed in the courtroom when the Court is in session. Ask students how they feel about this policy and to give reasons for their opinions. *(Answers will vary. Some students might indicate that photographers should be allowed because that would help inform the public about the cases being heard. Other students might indicate that having photographers at the sessions might reduce the sessions to a media event and hamper the work of the justices.)*

Chapter Preview

Overview

The Supreme Court's judicial functions give it an important share of the policy-making power the executive and legislative branches also exercise.

Objectives

After studying this chapter, you should be able to:

1. **Explain** how the Supreme Court affects public policy.
2. **Describe** the process by which the Supreme Court chooses, hears, and decides cases.
3. **Discuss** the factors that influence the Supreme Court.

Themes in Government

This chapter emphasizes the following government themes:

- **Constitutional Interpretations** The Supreme Court hears cases involving constitutional questions the justices believe have national importance. Sections 1 and 2.
- **Public Policy** The Court shapes society and is influenced by it. Sections 1 and 3.
- **Political Processes** The Court's composition and its handling of cases make the justices political as well as judicial officials. Sections 2 and 3.

Critical Thinking Skills

This chapter emphasizes the following critical thinking skills:

- Demonstrating Reasoned Judgment
- Making Inferences
- Drawing Conclusions

CHAPTER 20: SUPREME COURT DECISION MAKING 563

Introducing the Chapter

Students may already be familiar with many of the kinds of issues handled by the Supreme Court. However, they probably cannot give reasons why the Court does not handle other issues. Students may be surprised by the fact that the Supreme Court helps to make government policy and that factors other than law influence decisions of the Court.

Review with students the functions of the Supreme Court. Ask: What role did the Framers assume the Supreme Court would have? Has it fulfilled the role that the Framers intended?

Ask students to express what they know about how the Supreme Court selects and decides cases. Discuss students' responses and tell them to save them. At the end of the chapter have students compare them with the ideas in Chapter 20.

Chapter Project

Organize students into three groups to identify and investigate important cases that have come before the Supreme Court this decade. Have students select cases of particular interest to them. Group 1 should establish criteria for determining the importance of a case and identify several cases that meet its criteria. Group 2 should gather information on each case and summaries of the issues and decision. Group 3 should determine and execute a method for presenting this information to the class.

Powers of the Supreme Court

A Typical Day
Running Time 1:08
Side Two, Chapter 3

Setting the Scene The Supreme Court exercises its powers within the American system of government so that rights guaranteed to the people by the Constitution are not abridged. Evidence of its importance exists in the right of African Americans to vote, in freedom of speech and of the press, in the rights of people accused of crimes, and in many other areas of society. French philosopher Alexis de Tocqueville recognized its importance to constitutional government from the very beginnings of the republic when he observed, "courts of justice are called upon to try only the controversies of private individuals, but the Supreme Court of the United States summons sovereign powers."

Focus

Bell Ringer

While attendance is being taken, ask students to consult Article III of the Constitution to list the authority it grants to the Supreme Court.

Motivating Activity

List students' Bell Ringer responses on the chalkboard. Ask students what major power of the Court today is missing from the list. *(judicial review)* Note that the Court took this power in 1803 in *Marbury* v. *Madison.* Tell them that Section 1 relates how the Court uses this power to shape public policy.

Vocabulary Precheck

Call on students to read aloud the definitions for each term and concept from the Glossary. Then have them restate each definition in their own words. **LEP**

Teach

Guided Practice

L1 Constructing a Chart Construct a three-column chart on the chalkboard. Ask students to name three ways the Court shapes government policy and write these as column heads. *(Judicial Review, Interpreting Laws, Overturning Earlier Decisions)* Then call on students to provide examples of each for the chart.

Powers of the Supreme Court

In Conference
Running Time 1:20
Side Two, Chapter 16

Precedent
Running Time 1:47
Side Two, Chapter 18

SECTION

1 Supreme Court Decisions and Public Policy

The Supreme Court is both a political and a legal institution. It is a legal institution because it is ultimately responsible for settling disputes and interpreting the meaning of laws. The Court is a political institution because when it applies the law to specific disputes it often determines what national policy will be. For example, when the Court rules that certain provisions of the Social Security Act must apply to men and women equally, it is determining government policy.

Tools for Shaping Policy

Congress makes policy by passing laws. The President shapes policy by carrying out laws and by drawing up the national budget. As the Supreme Court decides cases, it determines policy in three ways. These include: (1) using judicial review, (2) interpreting the meaning of laws, and (3) overruling or reversing its previous decisions. Justice William Brennan once described the policy-making role of the Court:

Our framework is the activist philosophy of government that . . . has been called a Positive State. The positive state conceives of government as having an affirmative role—a positive duty to make provisions for jobs, social security, medical care, housing, and thereby give real substance to our established values of liberty, equality, and dignity.
—JUSTICE WILLIAM BRENNAN, 1969

Judicial Review The Supreme Court's power to examine the laws and actions of local, state, and national governments and to cancel them if they violate the Constitution is called **judicial review.** The Supreme Court first assumed the power of judical review and ruled an act of Congress unconstitutional in the case of *Marbury* v. *Madison* in 1803. Since then, the Court has invalidated more than 100 provisions of federal law. This number may seem insignificant when compared to the thousands of laws Congress has passed, but when the Court declares a law unconstitutional, it often discourages the passage of similar legislation for years. In addition, some of these rulings have had a direct impact on the nation's direction. In the *Dred Scott* case (1857), the Court's ruling that the Missouri Compromise, which banned slavery in some territories, was unconstitutional added to the tensions leading to the Civil War.

The Supreme Court may also review presidential policies. In the classic case of *Ex parte Milligan* (1866), the Court ruled President Lincoln's suspension of certain civil rights during the Civil War unconstitutional. More recently, in *Train* v. *City of New York* (1975), the Court limited the President's power to **impound**, or refuse to spend, money Congress has appropriated.

The Supreme Court exercises judicial review most frequently at the state and local levels. Since 1789 the Court has overturned more than 1,000 state and local laws. In recent years the Court has used judicial review to significantly influence public policy at the state level in the areas of racial desegregation, reapportionment of state legislatures, and police procedures.

Judicial review of state laws and actions may have as much significance as the Court's activities at the

---

SECTION PREVIEW

Objectives
After studying this section, you should be able to:
- Identify ways the Supreme Court shapes public policy.
- Characterize the cases that come before the Supreme Court.

- Describe the factors that limit the Supreme Court's power.

Key Terms and Concepts
judicial review, impound, stare decisis, precedent, advisory opinion

Themes in Government
- Constitutional Interpretations
- Public Policy

Critical Thinking Skills
- Demonstrating Reasoned Judgment
- Making Inferences

564 UNIT 6: THE JUDICIAL BRANCH

Classroom Resources for Section 1

- Guided Reading Activities
- Reproducible Lesson Plans
- Supreme Court Case Studies 1, 41
- Section 1 Quiz

- Testmaker
- Government Themes Transparencies 37
- The Living Constitution
- SAT Practice Tests

federal level. In *Brown* v. *Board of Education* (1954), the Court held that laws requiring or permitting racially segregated schools in four states were unconstitutional. The *Brown* decision cleared the way for the end of segregated schools throughout the nation. In *Miranda* v. *Arizona* (1966), the Court ruled that police had acted unconstitutionally and violated a suspect's rights. The *Miranda* decision brought major changes in law enforcement policies and procedures across the nation.

Interpretation of Laws One expert has said that judicial review is "like a boxer's big knockout punch." An equally important but less dramatic way for the Court to shape public policy is by interpreting the meaning of existing federal laws.

Congress often uses very general language in framing its laws, leaving it to others to interpret how the law applies to a specific situation. For example, the Americans with Disabilities Act of 1990 requires that businesses provide "reasonable" accommodations for disabled customers and employees. Disputes over the meaning of such language may wind up in federal court. The Civil Rights Act of 1964 prohibits discrimination on the grounds of "race, color, or national origin" in any program receiving federal aid. In the case of *Lau* v. *Nichols* (1974), the Court interpreted the law to require schools to provide special instruction in English to immigrant students. Equality is not achieved by merely providing the same opportunities for all, the Court said. Poor English skills prevented these students from fully participating in school.

Because a Supreme Court decision is the law of the land, this ruling's impact was not limited to San Francisco. Local courts and legislatures across the nation, for example, took the Court's decision to mean that classes must be taught in Spanish for Hispanic students who did not speak English well. It is not important whether Congress even considered that teaching Hispanic students in English was a form of discrimination when it wrote the Civil Rights Act in 1964. The Supreme Court nevertheless decided what Congress meant.

Many of the major acts of Congress have come before the Court repeatedly for interpretation in settling disputes. These include the Interstate Commerce Act, the Sherman Antitrust Act, and the National Labor Relations Act. Justice Tom Clark once summarized the Supreme Court's constitutional role as:

Somewhat of an umpire. It considers what the Congress proposes, or what the executive proposes, or what some individual claims, and rules upon these laws, proposals, and claims by comparing them with the law as laid down by the Constitution . . . and then calls the strikes and the balls.

—JUSTICE TOM CLARK

Overturning Earlier Decisions One of the basic principles of law in making judicial decisions is *stare decisis* (STAH•ray dih•SY•suhs)—a Latin term that means "let the decision stand." Under this principle, once the Court rules on a case, its decision serves as a

Chief Justices of the United States

Name	Appointed by	Years
John Jay	Washington	1789-1795
John Rutledge[a,b]	Washington	1795
Oliver Ellsworth	Washington	1796-1800
John Marshall	J. Adams	1801-1835
Roger B. Taney	Jackson	1836-1864
Salmon P. Chase	Lincoln	1864-1873
Morrison R. Waite	Grant	1874-1888
Melville W. Fuller	Cleveland	1888-1910
Edward D. White[b]	Taft	1910-1921
William Howard Taft	Harding	1921-1930
Charles Evans Hughes[b]	Hoover	1930-1941
Harlan F. Stone[b]	F. D. Roosevelt	1941-1946
Fred M. Vinson	Truman	1946-1953
Earl Warren	Eisenhower	1953-1969
Warren E. Burger	Nixon	1969-1986
William H. Rehnquist[b]	Reagan	1986-

[a]Appointed by Washington, but not confirmed by Senate
[b]Served as associate justice before being appointed chief justice

✔ **Chart Study**
Oliver Ellsworth was Chief Justice for only 4 years.
Which Chief Justice served the longest?

Background

Although relatively insulated from politics through appointment rather than election, Supreme Court justices have always confronted the difficult political issues of their time. Until the Civil War, the Court's cases focused on the nature and powers of the federal government. From the war's end until World War II, the Court was frequently asked to determine the proper role of government regulating the growth of a diverse agricultural and industrial economy. Since World War II, the most important issues the Court has agreed to hear have involved personal freedom and social and political equality.

Chapter 20, Section I
Lesson Plan, pages 564–568

📖 **Interpreting Visuals** Display transparency 37 from the *Government Themes Transparencies* in the Teacher's Classroom Resources and use the accompanying teaching strategy and student activity to teach about the ways the Supreme Court shapes policy.

L2 Class Discussion Discuss with students the limits on the powers of the Supreme Court. As students note each limit, list it on the chalkboard. Ask volunteers to suggest scenarios that illustrate each limit.

Chart Study Answer
John Marshall

═══════ STUDY GUIDE ═══════

Theme Answer
Through the process of judicial review, the Court decides whether or not a federal law violates the Constitution.

Critical Thinking Answer
Students might note that this power is balanced by executive and legislative powers over the Court.

═══════ CONNECTIONS ═══════

Law
Because of its French heritage, the state of Louisiana is the only state in the United States not based on a common-law system. The Supreme Court has struck down more Louisiana laws than those of any other state.

Powers of the Supreme Court

Judicial Review
Running Time 1:19
Side Two, Chapter 20

Point out to students that some scholars feel common-law and civil-law systems are beginning to converge. For example, jury trials in civil cases are rarely used in Britain today, although they remain a constitutional right in the United States. Significant inroads in codifying federal and state law in the United States are taking place. Have students research additional information on differences between common-law and civil-law systems.

Examining the Connection:
Have students share their lists of countries with the class.

Independent Practice

📁 **Analyzing Supreme Court Cases** Assign case 1, *Marbury* v. *Madison,* from the *Supreme Court Case Studies* in the Teacher's Classroom Resources.

STUDY GUIDE

Theme Answer
In a democracy all the people have equal protection under the law. To achieve this the law must be consistent and predictable.

Critical Thinking Skill
because many more cases involving the rights of Americans arise than do cases involving foreign nations that fall under Supreme Court jurisdiction

---

GLOBAL CONNECTION

Comparing Governments

Legal Systems A country's legal system is based on its heritage and traditions. Countries have either a common-law system or a civil-law system.

The common-law system developed in early England. After many judges ruled the same way in similar cases, the ruling became common law. The United States, Canada, and most other nations colonized by England have legal systems based on legal precedents that became common law.

In a civil-law system, judges base their decisions on codes—sets of rules. Among the earliest examples of this system are the Napoleonic Codes that took effect in France in 1804. Most European countries, Mexico, some South American countries, and the state of Louisiana have civil-law systems.

Examining the Connection
What other countries have common-law systems?

---

precedent, or model, on which to base other decisions in similar cases. This principle is important because it makes the law predictable. If judges' decisions were unpredictable from one case to another, what was legal one day could be illegal the next.

On the other hand, the law needs to be flexible and adaptable to changing times, social values and attitudes, and circumstances. Flexibility exists partially because justices sometimes change their minds. As one noted justice said, "Wisdom too often never comes, and so one ought not to reject it merely because it comes late."

More often, the law is flexible because of changes in the Court's composition. Justices may be appoint-

---

ed for life, but they do not serve forever. As justices die or retire, the President appoints replacements. New justices may bring different legal views to the Court and, over time shift its position on some issues.

In 1928, for example, the Court ruled in *Olmstead* v. *United States* that wiretaps on telephone conversations were legal because they did not require police to enter private property. Almost 40 years later, however, the Court's membership and society's values had changed. In *Katz* v. *United States* (1967), the Court overturned the *Olmstead* decision, ruling that a wiretap was a search and seizure under the Fourth Amendment and required a court order.

Limits on the Supreme Court

Despite its importance the Court does not have unlimited powers. Restrictions on the types of issues the Court will hear, limits on the kinds of cases it will hear, limited control over its own agenda, lack of enforcement power, and the system of checks and balances curtail the Court's activities.

Limits on Types of Issues Despite the broad range of its work, the Court does not give equal attention to all areas of national policy. For example, the Court has played only a minor role in making foreign policy. Over the years most Supreme Court decisions have dealt with civil liberties, economic issues, federal legislation and regulations, due process of law, and suits against government officials.

Civil liberties cases, which tend to involve constitutional questions, comprise the largest block of the Court's cases. Appeals from prisoners to challenge their convictions account for another 26 percent of the Court's decisions. Most of these cases concern such constitutional issues as the right to a fair trial and the proper use of evidence. Many of the Court's other cases deal with economic issues such as government regulation of business, labor-management relations, antitrust laws, and environmental protection.

STUDY GUIDE

Themes in Government
Public Policy Sometimes the Supreme Court will overturn an earlier decision. Generally, however, the Court's use of precedent

makes their decisions, and therefore public policy, predictable. **Why is this predictability important to democratic government?**

Critical Thinking Skills
Making Inferences
Why does the Supreme Court handle many civil liberties cases but very few foreign-policy cases?

Cooperative Learning Activity

Organize "Home Teams" of five. Have each team rank the following limits on Supreme Court power in order of importance: 1.) types of issues, 2.) types of cases, 3.) control over agenda, 4.) enforcement powers, 5.) checks and balances. Next have members of each team count off from 1 to 5. Have like-numbered persons from each team take its ranking and form an "Expert Team" to discuss the like-numbered limit above. Then reassemble Home Teams so that members can share the information from their Expert Teams. Have a spokesperson from each Home Team explain any changes in its ranking that resulted from the Expert Teams.

Many of these cases involve the interpretation of laws and regulations rather than constitutional questions.

Finally, the Court also spends some time resolving issues that arise in the federal structure. Cases of this kind involve disputes between the national government and the states and disagreements that arise among the states themselves.

Limits on Types of Cases The Supreme Court has developed many rules and customs over the years. As a result, the Court will hear only cases that meet certain criteria.

First, the Court will consider only cases where its decision will make a difference. It will not hear a case merely to decide a point of law. Thus, the Court refused to decide whether the state of Idaho could retract its ratification of the Equal Rights Amendment. Not enough states had ratified the amendment, and

the deadline had already expired. Whether or not Idaho could change its vote on ERA made no difference. Further, unlike courts in some countries, the Supreme Court will not give **advisory opinions**—rule on a law or action that has not been challenged.

Second, the person or group bringing the case must have suffered real harm, such as denial of civil liberties or economic loss. The Court generally will not hear a case in which no harm to an individual or a specific class of people has occurred. It is not enough for someone merely to object to some law or an action because they think it is unfair. Plaintiffs must show that the law or action being challenged has harmed them.

Third, the Court accepts only cases that involve a substantial federal question. The legal issues in dispute must affect many people or the operation of the political system itself. The Court is not interested in

---

Focus on Freedom

MIRANDA v. ARIZONA

In 1963 Ernesto Miranda was arrested in Arizona and charged with several felonies. After two hours of police questioning, Miranda confessed to the crimes. In Miranda v. Arizona *(1966), the Court reversed his conviction and established the procedures that police now follow in questioning suspects.*

We deal with the admissibility of statements obtained from an individual who is subjected to custodial police interrogation and the necessity for procedures which assure that the individual is accorded his privilege under the Fifth Amendment to the Constitution not to be compelled to incriminate himself. . . .

Our holding will be spelled out with some specificity in the pages which follow but briefly stated it is this. . . . Prior to any questioning, the person must be warned that he has a right to remain silent, that any statement he does make may be used as evidence against him, and that he has the right to the presence of an attorney. . . . The defendant may waive . . . these rights, provided that the waiver is made voluntarily, knowingly, and intelligently. If, however, he indicates in any manner and at any stage of the process that he wishes to consult with an attorney before speaking, there can be no questioning. . . .

The principles announced today deal with the protection which must be given to the privilege against self-incrimination when the individual is first subjected to police interrogation while in

custody . . . or otherwise deprived of his freedom of action in any significant way. . . .

There is no requirement that police stop a person who enters a police station and states that he wishes to confess to a crime, or a person who calls the police to offer a confession or any other statement he desires to make. Voluntary statements of any kind are not barred by the Fifth Amendment and their admissibility is not affected by our holding today.

—CHIEF JUSTICE EARL WARREN, 1966

Examining the Document

Reviewing Facts
1. State which constitutional right police violated when they questioned Miranda.
2. Specify the procedure police must follow before questioning a suspect whom they have detained.

Critical Thinking Skills
3. Demonstrating Reasoned Judgment Why would the Court allow a confession to be phoned in to police but not one made by a person in custody?

Chapter 20, Section 1
Lesson Plan, pages 564–568

Focus on Freedom

Have students explain in what ways the *Miranda* case has extended the rights of those people accused of crimes.

Answers
1. the Fifth Amendment protection against self-incrimination
2. Police must tell suspects they have right to remain silent, right to an attorney, and any statement they make may be used as evidence against them.
3. Students should note the voluntary nature of a phone conversation versus the coercive nature of being in custody.

CONNECTIONS

History
Since 1953 the Court has overruled its previous decisions more than 100 times.

Assess

Check for Understanding

Have students complete Section 1 Review on page 568.

Meeting Objectives

Each section objective is tested by the Section Review questions that follow it in parentheses.
- Identify ways the Supreme Court shapes public policy. (2, 4, 5, 6, 7, 8)
- Characterize the cases that come before the Supreme Court. (3, 7)
- Describe the factors that limit the Supreme Court's power. (4)

Powers of the Supreme Court
Miranda v. Arizona
Running Time 4:00
Side Two, Chapter 23

Special Needs Strategy

Learning Disability Students with difficulties synthesizing information will need help meeting the Section Preview objective which requires them to "Characterize the cases that come before the Supreme Court." Have students turn to the subheadings, "Judicial Review," "Interpretation of Laws," "Overturning Earlier Decisions." Ask students to search for words within each section that explain the meaning of these subheadings. Match the words or phrases "examine," "interpreting the meaning," and "let the decision stand" with each type of case heard by the Supreme Court.

Evaluate

📁 Section 1 Quiz

🖥 Testmaker

Reteach

Review pages 566–568 on the limitations on the Supreme Court's powers. Then ask students to give an example of an issue which describes one of the limitations on one side of a 3″ x 5″ notecard. Have them furnish which limitation the case illustrates on the reverse side. Then quiz the class using the cards.

Enrich

To find out more about decisions overturned by the Court, students may be interested in reading one of the following books: *Gideon's Trumpet* by Anthony Lewis, *Simple Justice* by Richard Kluger, or *Landm..rk Supreme Court Cases* by Don Lawson.

📁 Assign case 41, *Lau* v. *Nichols*, in *Supreme Court Case Studies* in the Teacher's Classroom Resources.

Close

Tell students that although any single branch of government can shape public policy, generally all three branches are involved. Offer the example of civil rights. Ask students to suggest how all three branches of government shape public policy in this area.

cases that affect only the parties in the case and do not have broader significance.

Finally, the Court has traditionally refused to deal with political questions—issues the Court believes the executive or legislative branches should resolve. No clear line, however, separates political questions from the legal issues the Court will hear. In the 1840s two groups each claimed to be the legal government of Rhode Island. The Supreme Court decided the dispute was political rather than legal and that Congress should settle it. In the end, the difference between a political question and a legal question is whatever the Court determines it to be.

Limited Control Over Agenda A third limit on the Supreme Court's power to shape public policy is that with few exceptions it can decide only cases that come to it from elsewhere in the legal system. As a result, events beyond the Court's control shape its agenda. When Congress abolished the draft in the mid-1970s, for example, it ended the Court's ability to decide religious freedom cases involving refusal to serve in the military. On the other hand, passage of the 1964 Civil Rights Act and similar laws created a large volume of civil liberties cases for the Court to decide.

Of course, the Court can and does signal its interest in a subject by deliberately taking on a specific case. In 1962, for example, the Court entered the area of legislative apportionment by agreeing to hear *Baker* v. *Carr*. In that Tennessee case, the Court reversed its 1946 position that drawing state legislative districts was a political question. As a result of the *Baker* decision, many cases

challenging the makeup of legislative districts were brought to the Court. Still, even when the Court wishes to rule in an area, it may have to wait years for the right case in the proper context to come along.

Lack of Enforcement Power A fourth factor limiting the Court's power to shape public policy is the Court's limited ability to enforce its rulings. President Andrew Jackson recognized this limitation when he refused to carry out a Court ruling he disliked, saying "[Chief Justice] John Marshall has made his decision, now let him enforce it."

Noncompliance may occur in several ways. Lower court judges may simply ignore a Supreme Court decision. During the 1960s many state court judges did not strictly enforce the Court's decisions banning school prayer. During the same period, some officials, ranging from school principals to judges to governors, sought ways to avoid Court rulings on integrating schools. Moreover, the Supreme Court simply is not able to closely monitor the millions of trial decisions throughout the United States to make sure its rulings are followed. Nevertheless, most Court decisions are accepted and generally enforced.

Checks and Balances The Constitution provides the other two branches of the national government several ways to try to influence or check the Court's power. These checks include the President's power to appoint justices and Congress's power to impeach and remove them.

---

① SECTION REVIEW

Section Summary
The authority to review laws and interpret their meanings, though limited, gives the Supreme Court of the United States power to shape national policy and influence daily life.

Checking For Understanding
Recalling Facts
1. Define judicial review, impound, stare decisis, precedent, advisory opinion.
2. Describe three ways that the Supreme Court shapes public policy.
3. Identify three issues on which the Supreme Court spends the most time hearing cases.
4. Cite four reasons that the Supreme Court's power to shape public policy is limited.

Exploring Themes
5. Constitutional Interpretations Chief Justice Charles Evans Hughes once said, "The Constitution is what the judges say it is." Explain the meaning of this statement.
6. Public Policy Explain Justice Brennan's view of the policy-making role of the courts.

Critical Thinking Skills
7. Demonstrating Reasoned Judgment Do you think the Supreme Court's power would be enhanced or diminished if it would give advisory opinions? Explain your answer.
8. Making Inferences Why did Justice Clark describe the Supreme Court as an umpire that calls balls and strikes?

Section I Review Answers

1. Definitions of terms appear on pages indicated: **judicial review,** 564; **impound,** 564; **stare decisis,** 565; **precedent,** 566; **advisory opinion,** 567
2. judicial review, interpreting meaning of laws, reversing its own decisions
3. civil liberties (equal treatment, freedom of speech and religion); criminal appeals (fair trials, use of evidence);

economic issues (antitrust, environment, labor-management relations)
4. restrictions on kinds of cases it can or will hear, limited control over its agenda, lack of enforcement powers, checks and balances
5. Judges' interpretation of what the Constitution's words mean is law.
6. In Brennan's view the Court should be active in looking out for the public's welfare by ensuring that people have jobs, medical care, housing, and the like.

7. Answers will vary. If they influenced executive or legislative actions, its power would grow. If its advice was ignored, its power would diminish.
8. Answers will vary, but should suggest that the Court determines whether laws or actions fall within the limits of the Constitution (strikes) and when they fall outside those limits (balls).

SECTION 2 — The Supreme Court at Work

The Supreme Court meets for about nine months each year. Each term begins the first Monday in October and runs as long as the business before the Court requires, usually into July. A term is named after the year in which it begins. Thus, the 1992 term began in October 1992 and ended in July 1993. Between terms the justices study prospective new cases and catch up on other Court work.

During the term the Court sits for two consecutive weeks each month. At these sittings the justices listen to oral arguments by lawyers on each side of the cases before them. Later they announce their opinions on cases they have heard. The Court hears oral arguments from Monday through Wednesday, and the public is permitted to be present. On Wednesdays and Fridays the justices meet in secret conferences to decide cases.

After a two-week sitting, the Court recesses and the justices work privately on paperwork. They consider arguments in cases they have heard and study petitions from plaintiffs who want the Court to hear their cases. They also work on opinions—written statements on cases they have already decided.

More than 5,000 cases are appealed to the Supreme Court each year. The Court usually decides from 400 to 450, but of these not more than about 150 cases receive full hearings and written opinions. In the opinions that accompany this small number of cases, the Court sets out general principles that apply to the nation as well as to the specific parties in the case. It is mainly through these cases that the Court interprets the law and shapes public policy.

How Cases Reach the Court

Historically, Congress has set complex and changing requirements for appealing a case to the Supreme Court. A few cases start at the Court because they fall under its original jurisdiction. The vast majority of cases reach the Court only as appeals from lower court decisions. These cases come to the Supreme Court in one of two ways—on appeal or by writ of *certiorari*.

On Appeal Certain types of cases are said to go to the Court on appeal. Most are cases in which a lower

Preparing to Appeal
In certain cases, an inmate, working with a lawyer, can help prepare an appeal of a conviction. **Judicial Processes How does the decision of the Supreme Court affect a lower court ruling?**

SECTION PREVIEW

Objectives
After studying this section, you should be able to:
- Specify how cases reach the Supreme Court.
- Describe how the Supreme Court selects, hears, and decides cases.

- Explain the importance of Supreme Court opinions.

Key Terms and Concepts
writ of certiorari, per curiam opinion, brief, amicus curiae, lobbying, unanimous opinion, majority opinion, concurring opinion, dissenting opinion

Themes in Government
- Constitutional Interpretations
- Political Processes

Critical Thinking Skills
- Drawing Conclusions
- Demonstrating Reasoned Judgment

CHAPTER 20: SUPREME COURT DECISION MAKING 569

Classroom Resources for Section 2

- 📁 Guided Reading Activities
- 📁 Reproducible Lesson Plans
- 📁 Primary and Secondary Source Readings 20
- 📁 Enrichment Activities 20
- 📁 Section 2 Quiz

- 🖥 Testmaker
- The Living Constitution
- SAT Practice Tests
- Writer's Guidebook

Focus

Bell Ringer
While attendance is being taken, ask students to answer the following question in writing:
What would happen if the Supreme Court reversed lower court decisions in most of the cases appealed to it?

Motivating Activity
Discuss students' Bell Ringer answers. Point out that over 5,000 cases are appealed to the Supreme Court each year. Its refusal to review about 90 percent of these cases means that most lower court decisions remain unchanged. Suggest that if a higher percentage of lower court decisions were overturned, more appeals would be encouraged, the law would become unpredictable, and it would indicate problems in the justice system.

Vocabulary Precheck
List the terms and concepts on the chalkboard. Have volunteers skim the section to find each term and read it in context. **LEP**

Caption Answer
Supreme Court decisions are binding upon lower courts.

CONNECTIONS

Law
On the first day of the fall 1991 term, the United States Supreme Court added 69 cases to its docket. The Court declined to hear more than 1,300 other cases.

GLENCOE TECHNOLOGY

Focus on Government
Video 35
**Lecture Launcher:
How a Case Reaches the Supreme Court**
Running Time: 2:54
Videodisc 2, Chap. 35
VHS Tape 2, Begins 42:15

Video 36
**Lecture Launcher:
Supreme Court Decision Making**
Running Time: 3:15
Videodisc 2, Chap. 36
VHS Tape 2, Begins 45:11

Teach

Guided Practice

L1 **Interpreting a Graph** Refer students to the graph on page 573 and ask: What has the general trend been in the Court's caseload since 1950? What is the trend in the number of opinions it has issued over that time? How would you describe the relationship between cases appealed and cases heard? How do you account for these trends? **LEP**

Images of Government

Have students study the picture of Justice. Point out the caption indicates what the blindfold and the scales symbolize. What do you think the sword symbolizes? *(that justice can be backed up by force; that those who break the law may be punished)*

Answers

1. Justices must remain impartial as they consider the arguments in a case in order to preserve the integrity of our system of justice.
2. Respect for different viewpoints is a basic tenet of United States government.

GLENCOE
TECHNOLOGY

Focus on Government
Video 37
Making Connections:
The Rules of the Supreme
Court
Running Time: 2:04
Videodisc 2, Chap. 37
VHS Tape 2, Begins 48:28

---

federal court or the highest state court has ruled a law unconstitutional. Some are cases in which the highest court of a state upholds a state law against the claim that it violates federal law or the Constitution. The Court is required to at least consider all cases involving the constitutionality of a law.

Only about 10 percent of the Court's cases arrive on appeal, and most are dismissed because they do not raise an important constitutional issue. When a case is dismissed, the decision of the lower court becomes final. Dismissal also has other legal consequences. Lower court judges are supposed to note that the Court believes similar types of cases do not involve a basic conflict with federal laws or the Constitution.

Writ of Certiorari The main route to the Supreme Court is by a **writ of** *certiorari* (suhr•shee•uh•

RAR•ee)—an order from the Court to a lower court to send up the records on a case for review. Either side in a case may petition the Court for certiorari, or "cert," as lawyers call it. Such petitions must argue that the lower court made a legal error in handling the case, or they must raise some serious constitutional issue.

Because these appeals do not involve the constitutionality of a law, the Court is free to choose which cases it will consider. More than 90 percent of the requests for certiorari are rejected. Denial of certiorari does not necessarily mean that the justices agree with a lower court's decision. They may see the case as not involving a significant public issue. It may involve a question the Court does not want to address, or it may not be the best case for ruling on a specific issue. Regardless of the reason, when the Court denies certiorari, the lower court's decision stands.

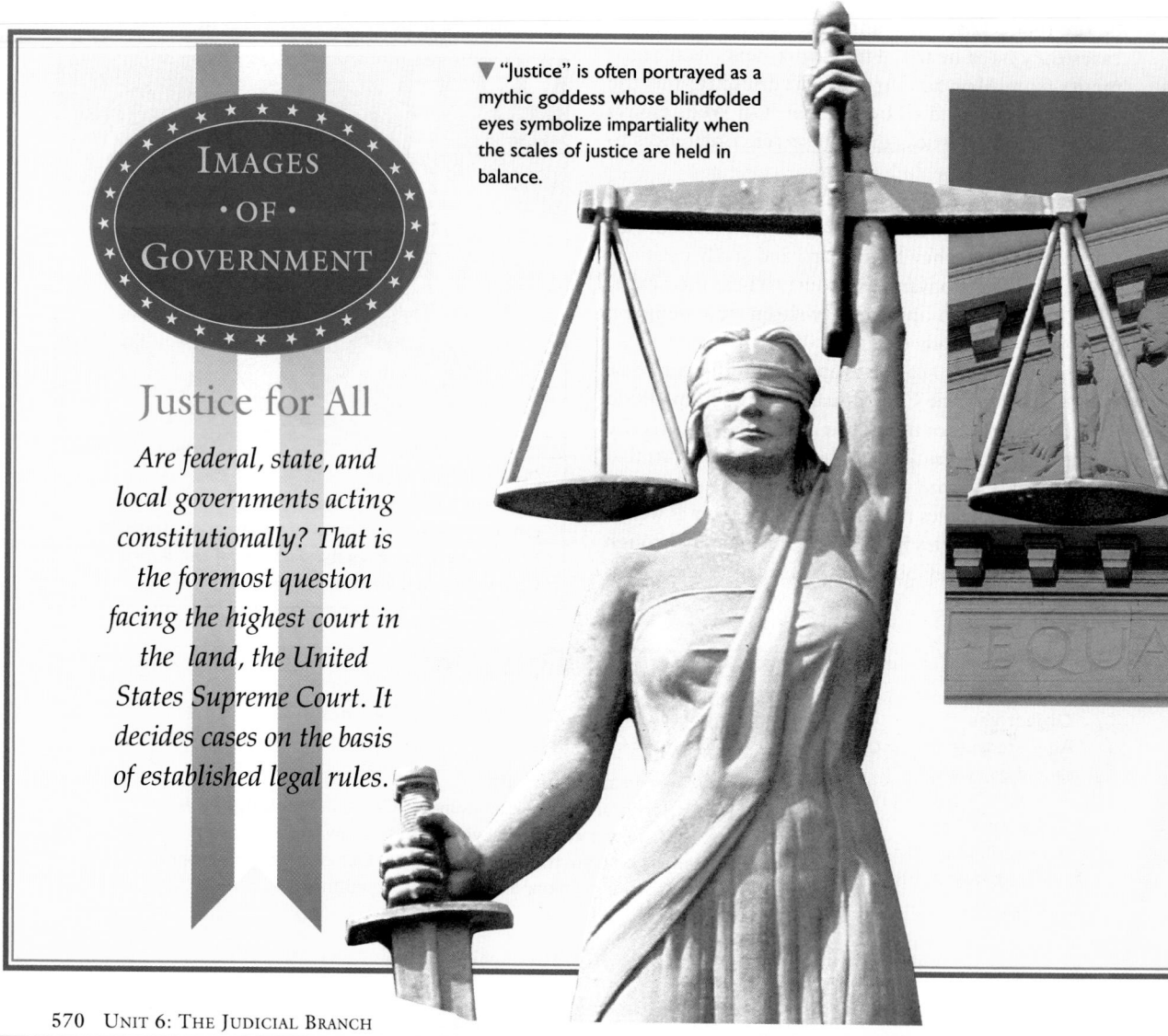

IMAGES
· OF ·
GOVERNMENT

Justice for All

Are federal, state, and local governments acting constitutionally? That is the foremost question facing the highest court in the land, the United States Supreme Court. It decides cases on the basis of established legal rules.

▼ "Justice" is often portrayed as a mythic goddess whose blindfolded eyes symbolize impartiality when the scales of justice are held in balance.

570   UNIT 6: THE JUDICIAL BRANCH

Background

The Supreme Court's heavy caseload is a serious problem. Many of the justices complain of "cert fatigue" due to the number of *certiorari* petitions that come before them. The Court's workload grew from 3,893 cases to 5,268 a decade later. Some 70 to 80 petitions are filed weekly during the

year and diplomatic pouches of certs follow the justices as they leave Washington, D.C., in the summer months. To alleviate this situation, a congressional commission has recommended a new National Court of Appeals to screen all cases appealed to the Supreme Court.

Selecting Cases Justice William O. Douglas once called the selection of cases "in many respects the most important and interesting of all our functions." When petitions for certiorari come to the Court, the justices or their clerks identify cases worthy of serious consideration and the Chief Justice puts them on a "discuss list" for all the justices to consider. All other cases are automatically denied a writ unless a justice asks that a specific case be added to the list.

Almost two-thirds of all petitions for certiorari never make the discuss list. At the Court's Friday conferences, the Chief Justice reviews the cases on the discuss list. Then the justices—armed with memos from their clerks, other information on the case, and various law books—give their views. In deciding to accept a case, the Court operates by the rule of four. If four of the nine justices approve, the Court will accept the case for decision.

When the justices accept a case, they also decide either to ask for more information from the opposing lawyers or to rule quickly on the basis of written materials already available. Cases decided without further information are either returned to the lower court for a new decision or announced with a *per curiam* (puhr KYUR•ee•ahm) **opinion**—a brief unsigned statement of the Court's decision. More than half the cases the Court accepts are handled this way. The remaining cases go on for full consideration by the Court.

Steps in Deciding Major Cases

The Supreme Court follows a set procedure in hearing important cases. Much of this activity goes on behind the scenes, with only a small part taking place in an open courtroom.

▲ Thurgood Marshall, who as an attorney successfully argued before the Supreme Court the historic case of *Brown v. Board of Education of Topeka*, served as the first African American member of the Supreme Court from 1967 to 1991.

▲ The frieze above the entrance to the Supreme Court building in Washington, D.C., reminds all who enter that the Court's primary goal is the safeguarding of justice and equality as guaranteed in the United States Constitution.

Questions for Discussion

1. Why must a judge or Supreme Court Justice "weigh" all arguments equally?

2. Why is it important that people with unpopular views receive the same treatment under the law?

CHAPTER 20: SUPREME COURT DECISION MAKING 571

L2 Debate Call on students to contrast *majority opinion, concurring opinion,* and *dissenting opinion.* Then have them debate the following:

Does the practice of publishing dissenting opinions demonstrate a weakness or a strength in our judicial system?

L3 Class Discussion Ask students how interested parties who are not directly involved in a case can influence the Supreme Court. *(submission of written briefs as* amicus curiae*)* Should those who are not party to a case be permitted to express their opinion to the Court? Why or why not?

Independent Practice

L1 Creating a Flow Chart Have students make flow charts to illustrate the steps by which successful appeals reach the Supreme Court. *(Case sent to Court on appeal or by* certiorari; *accepted for discuss list; case accepted; briefs filed; oral arguments presented; case discussed; the opinion of the Court written; decision of the Court announced)* **LEP**

L2 Informative Writing Have students write an essay on the topic: In what way does the functioning of the Supreme Court provide "equal justice under the law"?

CONNECTIONS

Law
In a 1963 ruling, *Gideon* v. *Wainwright,* the Court held that persons accused of felonies have a right to an attorney, and that a state must provide one free if the accused cannot afford one. Gideon, convicted after being denied counsel, printed his own "cert" petition in pencil and sent it to the Court from his cell in a Florida penitentiary.

Cooperative Learning Activity

Organize the class to conduct a mock Supreme Court appeal. Select one of the cases in *Supreme Court Case Studies* in the Teacher's Classroom Resources to provide the background material for the appeal. Have 9 students serve as justices and others assist them as their law clerks. Organize the remainder of the class into plaintiff and defense teams to prepare written briefs for the Court. On hearing day give a spokesperson for each team 15 minutes to present its case. Allow the justices to interrupt with questions. Have the justices rule, but first have all students write opinions.

📁 **Interpreting Source Readings** Have students complete activity 20 in *Primary and Secondary Source Readings* in the Teacher's Classroom Resources.

STUDY GUIDE

Theme Answers
They do not raise an important constitutional issue.

To allow this would subject individual justices to lobbying.

Critical Thinking Answers
Opinions must give adequate reasons for decisions because they establish public policy.

to help assure that each case will be considered equally, and to speed the work of the Court

---

Assess

Check for Understanding
Have students complete Section 2 Review on page 573.

Meeting Objectives
Each section objective is tested by the Section Review questions that follow it in parentheses.
• Specify how cases reach the Supreme Court. (2)
• Describe how the Supreme Court selects, hears, and decides cases. (3, 5, 6, 7, 8)
• Explain the importance of Supreme Court opinions. (4, 6)

Evaluate
📁 Section 2 Quiz
⬛ Testmaker

Submitting Briefs After the Court accepts a case, the lawyers on each side submit a **brief**. A brief is a written statement setting forth the legal arguments, relevant facts, and precedents supporting their side of the case.

Parties not directly involved in the case, but who have an interest in its outcome, may also submit written briefs. Called *amicus curiae* (uh•mee•kuhs KYUR•ee•ay)—or "friend of the court"—briefs, they come from individuals, interest groups, or government agencies claiming to have information useful to the Court's consideration of the case. In a recent major civil rights case, 53 amicus curiae briefs were filed—37 for one side and 16 for the other.

Amicus curiae briefs are a gentle way of **lobbying**, or trying to influence, the Court. Sometimes the briefs present new ideas or information. More often, however, they are most useful for indicating which interest groups are on either side of an issue.

Oral Arguments After briefs are filed, a lawyer for each side is asked to present an oral argument before the Court. Each side is allowed 30 minutes to summarize the key points of its case. Justices often interrupt the lawyer during his or her oral presentation, sometimes challenging a statement or asking for further information. The lawyer speaks from a lectern that has a red light and a white light. The white light flashes five minutes before the lawyer's time is up. When the red light comes on, the lawyer must stop instantly, even in the middle of a sentence.

The Conference On Fridays the justices meet in conference to discuss the cases they have heard. The nine justices come into the conference room and, by tradition, each shakes hands with the other eight. Everyone else leaves. Then one of the most secret meetings in Washington, D.C., begins.

For the next six to eight hours, the justices debate the cases. No meeting minutes are kept. The Chief Justice presides over the discussion of each case and usually begins by summarizing the facts of the case and offering recommendations for handling it.

In the past the justices discussed cases in detail. Today the Court's heavy caseload allows little time for such debates. Instead, each decision gets about 30 minutes of discussion. Cases being considered for future review each get about 5 minutes. The Chief Justice merely asks each associate justice, in order of seniority, to give his or her views and conclusions. Then the justices vote. Each justice's vote carries the same weight.

A majority of justices must be in agreement to decide a case, and at least six justices must be present for a decision. If a tie occurs, the lower court decision is left standing. The Court's vote at this stage, however, is not necessarily final.

Writing the Opinion For major cases the Court issues at least one written opinion. The opinion states the facts of the case, announces the Court's ruling, and explains its reasoning in reaching the decision. These opinions are as important as the decision itself. Not only do they set precedent for lower courts in future cases, they also are the Court's way to communicate with Congress, the President, interest groups, and the public.

The New York Times Supreme Court reporter Linda Greenhouse recognized the importance of the Court's opinions and the challenge of reporting them. According to Greenhouse:

*H*ere . . . the Court tries to explain itself—often at great length. The challenge is to distill the central ideas from thirty or more pages of prose, often convoluted and jargon-filled. . . .

But simply translating the Court's jargon into English is only the beginning. To be helpful to the reader, the story must indicate how this particular decision fits in with the others, how it changes the law, how it affects the parties who brought the case, and what it portends for the future. . . .

The opinion itself may provide only a hint of the long-range implications, so the reporter must probe the Court's language for any hidden messages.

—LINDA GREENHOUSE, 1985

STUDY GUIDE

Themes in Government
Constitutional Interpretations
Why does the Court dismiss most appeals cases?
Political Processes Supreme Court justices generally avoid personal contact with people interested in the outcomes of cases. **Why?**

Critical Thinking Skills
Drawing Conclusions Supreme Court opinions are often very lengthy. **Is this necessary? Explain.**

Demonstrating Reasoned Judgment Why are Supreme Court procedures so rigid?

Special Needs Strategy

Learning Disability Learning-disabled students may not be able to reason while they work on more routine tasks like writing. It often helps to provide outlines that show a flow of ideas. Before discussing how Supreme Court cases are selected, give each student a copy of the flow chart at the right which shows the two kinds of cases that can arrive at the Supreme Court. As you discuss the Supreme Court's selection process, have students write key words in the spaces provided.

APPEAL ➔ SUPREME COURT ◄ WRIT OF CERTIORARI

1. _____   1. _____
2. _____   2. _____
3. _____   3. _____

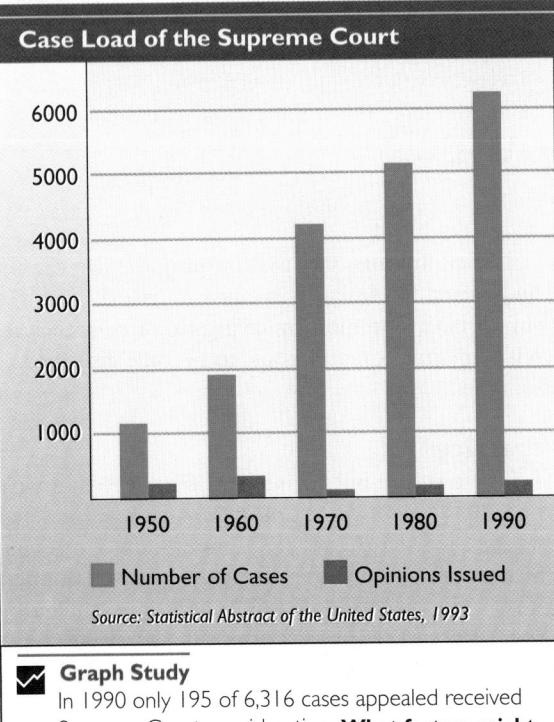

Case Load of the Supreme Court

	1950	1960	1970	1980	1990

■ Number of Cases ■ Opinions Issued

Source: Statistical Abstract of the United States, 1993

✓ Graph Study
In 1990 only 195 of 6,316 cases appealed received Supreme Court consideration. **What factors might account for the disparity in numbers?**

The Court issues four kinds of opinions. In a **unanimous opinion**, all justices vote the same way. About one-third of the Court's decisions are unanimous. A **majority opinion** expresses the views of the majority on a case. One or more justices who agree with the majority's conclusions about a case but do so

for different reasons write a **concurring opinion**. A **dissenting opinion** is the opinion of justices on the losing side in a case. Because the Court does change its mind on issues, a dissenting opinion may even become the majority opinion on a similar issue many years later.

If the Chief Justice has voted with the majority on a case, he or she assigns someone in the majority to write the opinion. When the Chief Justice is in the minority, the most senior associate justice among the majority assigns one of the justices on that side of the case to write the majority opinion. Public policy established from a case may depend in large part on who writes the opinion. For this reason Chief Justices often assign opinions in very important cases to themselves or to a justice whose views on the case are similar to their own.

Usually with the help of his or her law clerks, a justice prepares a first draft of an opinion and circulates it among the other justices for their comments. They may accept the draft with minor alterations, or they may find fault with the draft. In that case the writer must make major changes to keep their support.

When the other justices do not accept the initial draft of a majority opinion, a bargaining process often begins. Memos and new versions of the opinion may be written as the justices try to influence or satisfy one another.

Weeks or even months may go by as the justices bargain and rewrite their opinions. Finally, however, the case is settled and the decision is announced during a sitting. All the while, the Court is selecting and hearing new cases.

Chart Study Answer
The Court selects only a few cases based on their significance.

Reteach
Have students write five questions on "How the Supreme Court Decides Cases." Then divide them into two groups. Have members from each group take turns quizzing the other group.

Enrich
📁 Have students complete activity 20 in *Enrichment Activities* in the Teacher's Classroom Resources.

Close

Ask: What roles do negotiating, bargaining, and compromise play on the Court?

CONNECTIONS

Law
One way a justice can influence a decision is the threat to write a dissenting opinion. Also justices can switch sides before a decision is announced. A justice may demand a point be added to or deleted from an opinion as the price for his or her support.

---

2 SECTION REVIEW

Section Summary
The Court accepts relatively few cases for decision, and fewer yet receive full consideration. For those that do, the Court provides at least one written opinion to explain the decision.

Checking for Understanding
Recalling Facts
1. Define writ of certiorari, per curiam opinion, brief, amicus curiae, lobbying, unanimous opinion, majority opinion, concurring opinion, dissenting opinion.
2. Identify the three ways by which cases reach the Supreme Court.
3. List the steps the Supreme Court takes in selecting, hearing, and deciding cases.

4. Explain why the Supreme Court's opinions in cases are as important as its decisions in those cases.
Exploring Themes
5. Constitutional Interpretations Why does the Supreme Court refuse to hear so many cases?
6. Political Processes Why can writing a majority opinion be such a difficult task?

Critical Thinking Skills
7. Drawing Conclusions Do you think the Supreme Court's system for selecting cases is a problem in the American judicial system? Explain.
8. Demonstrating Reasoned Judgment Do you believe that it is proper that the Supreme Court's deliberations are secret and that no minutes are kept? Explain.

Section 2 Review Answers

1. Definitions of terms appear on pages indicated: **writ of *certiorari,*** 570; **per curiam opinion,** 571; **brief,** 572; ***amicus curiae,*** 572; **lobbying,** 572; **unanimous opinion,** 573; **majority opinion,** 573; **concurring opinion,** 573; **dissenting opinion,** 573
2. original jurisdiction, on appeal, by writ of *certiorari*

3. Justices discuss cases and by the "rule of four" accept those involving important constitutional questions; lawyers for each side file briefs and then present oral argument; after voting, the Court issues a written opinion explaining its decision.
4. They explain the Court's reasoning, help guide lower courts, and communicate its position.
5. They may not involve an important constitutional question or be the best case for deciding an issue; also the Court may not want to confront the issue.

6. The reasons the writer presents for the decision must satisfy enough justices to maintain the majority.
7. Yes—the Court may let rights' violations stand if the case does not have broad constitutional significance; politics should not be a factor in choosing cases. No—the volume of appeals would otherwise overwhelm the Court and create an unmanageable and hopeless backlog.
8. Answers should cite relationship between secrecy, judicial independence, and political or public pressure.

CRITICAL THINKING SKILLS

Focus

Ask students to imagine that a classmate has gone to another country as part of an exchange program. Ask which of the following would be a firsthand account of her experiences: a poster announcing the exchange program, a local television report, her letter to the class, an interview in the school paper.

Teach

Have the class apply the Explanation steps to the passage about flag burning. Ask: Why is this passage a primary source. (*It is an actual record of a Court ruling.*) Would a newspaper article reporting this decision be a primary source? (*No, because it is not a firsthand account.*) Why would this passage not be a primary source for the event that led to the case? What kinds of sources would be primary sources for the event? (*examples: eyewitness accounts, police records of the arrest, statement of the accused*)

Assess

Have students complete the **Practice** exercise.

Close

Ask students if firsthand accounts are likely to be more accurate or less accurate accounts than those that are not primary sources. (*Answers should consider issues of bias.*)

Interpreting a Primary Source

A primary source is a firsthand account—original information such as a letter, a diary, or an eyewitness account. Knowing how to interpret a primary source will enable you to make your own judgments instead of relying on second-hand interpretations.

Explanation

To interpret a primary source, follow these steps:
- Determine the origins of the document. In what way is it a primary source?
- Read the document once. Concentrate on its main ideas. Summarize it in your own words to make sure that you understand it clearly.
- Read the document a second time. This time pay attention to details and note how they support the author's main points.

The following passage is from the Supreme Court's majority opinion in *Texas* v. *Johnson*, a 1989 case about a person who had burned the American flag in a political protest.

The state's position . . . amounts to a claim that an audience that takes serious offense at particular expression is necessarily likely to disturb the peace and that the expression may be prohibited on this basis. Our precedents do not countenance such a presumption. On the contrary, they recognize that a principal "function of free speech under our system of government is to invite dispute. . . ."

Thus, we have not permitted the Government to assume that every expression of a provocative idea will incite a riot, but have instead required careful consideration of the actual circumstances surrounding such expression. . . .

We are fortified in today's conclusion by our conviction that forbidding criminal punishment for conduct such as Johnson's will not endanger the special role played by our flag. . . .

—JUSTICE WILLIAM BRENNAN, 1989

This passage is Justice Brennan's firsthand account of the views of the majority of the justices. In this sense, it is a primary source.

Justice Brennan says that burning the flag cannot be banned for fear it will cause a disturbance. He supports this opinion by saying that free speech itself sometimes causes people to become disturbed.

Practice

The passage below is taken from the majority opinion in *Reynolds* v. *Sims*. Alabama had modeled its state legislature on the United States Congress. Seats in the lower house were assigned by population, while one state senator came from each county regardless of its population. Use what you have learned about interpreting primary sources to answer the questions that follow.

Legislatures represent people, not trees or acres. Legislators are elected by voters, not farms or cities or economic interests. As long as ours is a representative form of government, and our legislatures are those instruments of government elected directly by and directly representative of the people, the right to elect legislators in a free and unimpaired fashion is a bedrock of our political system. . . .

The seats in both houses of a bicameral legislature must be apportioned on a population basis. . . . An individual's right to vote for state legislators is unconstitutionally impaired when its weight is in a substantial fashion diluted when compared with votes of citizens living in other parts of the State. . . .

—CHIEF JUSTICE EARL WARREN, 1964

1. Is this document a primary source in the sense that it gives a firsthand account of (a) the view of the United States Congress? (b) the Alabama state legislature? (c) the Supreme Court's view?
2. Briefly state the main idea of the passage.
3 How does Warren support the argument?

Additional Practice

To practice this skill, refer to **Reinforcing the Skill** on page 583.

Practice Answers

1. (a) no (b) no (c) yes
2. Truly representative democracy depends on legislative districts of equal population.
3. He supports the idea of electing the state legislature on the basis of population rather than on unequal geographical considerations.

For additional practice, have students complete activity 20 in *Skill Reinforcement Activities* in the Teacher's Classroom Resources.

Factors Influencing the Court's Decisions

Why do justices decide cases as they do? What factors influence how each votes on a case? Five forces shape the decisions the Court makes. They are (1) existing laws, (2) the personal views of the justices, (3) the justices' interactions with one another, (4) social forces and public attitudes, and (5) Congress and the President.

Basing Decisions on the Law

Law is the foundation for deciding cases that come before the Supreme Court. Justices, like other people, often hold strong opinions on issues that come before them. In the end, however, they must base their decisions on principles of law, and not simply on their personal opinions.

Laws and the Constitution, however, are not always clear in their meaning. If they were, a Supreme Court would not be needed. The First Amendment, for example, prohibits any law "abridging freedom of speech," but does this right provide absolute freedom or do limits exist? Does freedom of speech mean that a person has the right to falsely cry "Fire" in a crowded theater? The Fourth Amendment prohibits unreasonable searches and seizures, but what is unreasonable? Can tapping a person's telephone be considered an unreasonable search?

Most of the cases the Supreme Court is asked to rule on involve difficult questions like these. Where the meaning of a statute or a provision of the Constitution is not clear, the justices of the Court must interpret the language, determine what it means, and apply it to the circumstances of the case.

In interpreting the law, however, justices are not free to give it any meaning they wish. They must relate their interpretations logically to the Constitution itself, to statutes they believe are relevant to the case at hand, and to legal precedents established in similar cases. The Court goes to great lengths to explain the legal principles behind their new interpretation of the law.

Views of the Justices

Supreme Court justices, like other political figures, are people with active interests in important issues. Some justices, for example, may believe that individual rights must be protected at almost all costs, even if that means a few criminals may go unpunished. Other justices may be more concerned about rising crime rates. They may feel that a little loss of freedom from wiretaps or stop-and-frisk laws is acceptable if it helps curb crime.

Over the years some justices become identified with specific views on certain issues. Justice William O. Douglas, for example, was known as a consistent supporter of the rights of the underprivileged during his 36 years on the Court. Because, like Douglas, most justices take consistent positions in areas of personal concern, voting **blocs**, or coalitions of justices, exist on the Court on certain kinds of issues. In recent years one group of justices has consistently tended toward liberal positions on civil rights and economic issues. A different bloc has consistently tended to take more conservative positions on the same issues.

SECTION PREVIEW

Objectives
After studying this section, you should be able to:
■ Explain how social forces influence Supreme Court decisions.

■ Describe how individual justices shape Supreme Court decisions.

Key Terms and Concepts
bloc, swing vote

Themes in Government
■ Political Processes
■ Public Policy

Critical Thinking Skills
■ Demonstrating Reasoned Judgment
■ Making Inferences

CHAPTER 20: SUPREME COURT DECISION MAKING 575

Focus

Bell Ringer

While attendance is being taken, ask students to provide the following:

List the factors you believe influence Supreme Court decisions.

Motivating Activity

Discuss students' Bell Ringer answers and list them on the chalkboard. Tell students that they can check the accuracy of their answers as they read this section, which focuses on forces that shape the Supreme Court's decisions. Keep the list on the chalkboard for use with the Close activity on page 580.

Vocabulary Precheck

Call on students to read aloud the definitions for each term and concept from the Glossary. Then have them restate each definition in their own words. (LEP)

CONNECTIONS

Sociology
Although all Supreme Court justices have had legal backgrounds, only about half have had judicial experience. For example, Chief Justice Earl Warren, former California governor and attorney general, had never served as a judge.

Focus on Government
Video 11
Lecture Launcher:
Assuring Equal Justice for All
Running Time: 2:27
Videodisc 1, Chap. 11
VHS Tape 1, Begins 30:29

Classroom Resources for Section 3

📁 Guided Reading Activities
📁 Reproducible Lesson Plans
📁 Participating in Government 20
📁 Supreme Court Case Studies 52
📁 Reteaching Activities 20
📁 Section 3 Quiz

📁 Chapter 20 Tests
💾 Testmaker
🔦 Government Themes Transparencies 16, 26
🎧 Audio Cassettes (English and Spanish)
📁 Limited English Proficiency Activities 20
   SAT Practice Tests

Teach

Guided Practice

L1 Checks and Balances Call on students to cite the ways Congress and the President check the Supreme Court's actions. Then ask: Why is the Supreme Court often open to criticism? Are they valid criticisms? Should the Court be watched by the other two branches? As an unelected branch, should it be accountable to the other branches or the public? Discuss students' answers.

Interpreting Visuals Display transparency 16 from *Government Themes Transparencies* in the Teacher's Classroom Resources and use the accompanying teaching strategy and student activity to teach the relationship between the Court and society.

Caption Answer

because the Court's authority and power depend in part on public acceptance of and support for its decisions

---

CONNECTIONS

Law

Some analysts believe party, age, and issue may be the important factors in determining how a justice will vote. On issues such as labor, criminal procedures, and regulation of business, party affiliation seems to be important. On these issues Democrats tend to be more liberal than Republicans. Age, on the other hand, seems to be more important in civil liberties cases. Older judges have tended to be more conservative than younger judges on such issues.

Supreme Court Justices
William H. Rehnquist, right, became Chief Justice of the United States in 1986. **Political Processes Why are the justices concerned with public opinion?**

When justices retire and new appointments take their place, the size and power of each bloc may change. A majority bloc on certain issues may gradually become the minority bloc. If the Court is badly split over an issue, a justice whose views are not consistent with either bloc may represent a **swing vote**, or the deciding vote. When new justices are appointed, the Court sometimes overturns precedents and changes direction in its interpretations.

Relations Among the Justices

In the early years of the Supreme Court, the justices lived and ate together in a Washington boardinghouse during the Court's term. Because the term was fairly short, they did not move their families to Washington, D.C. Justice Joseph Story described life at the boardinghouse:

> *Judges here live with perfect harmony, and as agreeably as absence from friends and families could make our residence.... Our social hours, when undisturbed with the labors of the law, are passed in gay and frank conversation.*
>
> —JUSTICE JOSEPH STORY, 1812

Today the justices work almost the entire year and live with their families in or near Washington, D.C. In 1976 Justice Lewis F. Powell said, "As much as 90 percent of the time we function as nine small, independent law firms," meeting as a group only for the oral argument sessions and conferences. The justices, he added, communicate with one another mostly in writing. "Indeed, a justice may go through an entire term without being once in the chambers of all the other eight members of the Court."

Harmony or Conflict Despite the lack of frequent interaction, the quality of personal relations among the justices influences the Court's decision making. A Court marked by harmony is more likely to agree on decisions than one marked by personal antagonisms. Justices who can work easily with one another will be more likely to find common solutions to problems.

Even when justices are at odds with one another, they will try to avoid open conflict. A news reporter once asked a justice why he did not complain about certain actions of the Chief Justice, whom he disliked. The justice replied, "YOU don't have to live here for the rest of your life."

Relatively good personal relations among justices who disagreed strongly on legal issues marked some modern Courts. At other times severe personal conflicts have seriously divided the Court.

Influence of the Chief Justice The Chief Justice has several powers that can be used to influence the Court's decisions. In presiding over the Court during oral arguments and in conference, the Chief Justice can direct discussion and frame alternatives. In addition, the Chief Justice makes up the first version of the discuss list and assigns the writing of opinions to the justices.

These advantages do not necessarily guarantee leadership by a Chief Justice. Like other leaders, Chief Justices must make skillful use of the tools of influence available to them if they are to be effective leaders and shape the Court's decisions. How the Chief Justice uses these tools can influence the amount of personal conflict that exists on the Court.

The Court and Society

Harold Burton was appointed to the Supreme Court in 1945, after having served in Congress. When asked what the switch was like, he replied, "Have you ever gone from a circus to a monastery?"

Background

Practical application of the Constitution sometimes results in clashes between its rights and protections that make the Court's decisions even more difficult. The First Amendment, for example, forbids Congress to abridge the freedom of the press, while the Sixth Amendment guarantees a defendant in a criminal case a trial by "an impartial jury." Today, however, television and other media sometimes may generate such widespread and prejudicial publicity that a defendant cannot be tried by a truly impartial jury. Justice John Marshall Harlan once claimed that in such cases the courts must balance the interests involved.

Major Decisions of the Supreme Court

Marbury v. Madison (1803)
Established the power of the Supreme Court to declare an act of Congress or of the executive branch unconstitutional

McCulloch v. Maryland (1819)
Ruled that a state government cannot tax the property of the federal government. Broadened the power of Congress to use its "implied" powers

Cohens v. Virginia (1821)
Declared that a decision of a state court is subject to review by United States Supreme Court

Gibbons v. Ogden (1824)
Ruled that a state cannot interfere with the right of Congress to regulate interstate commerce

Dred Scott v. Sandford (1857)
Declared that African Americans cannot be citizens of the United States and that Congress has no power to forbid slavery in United States territories

Plessy v. Ferguson (1896)
Held that separate but equal facilities for African Americans are not a violation of the Constitution

Schenck v. United States (1919)
Established the clear-and-present-danger principle as the test of whether the government may limit free speech

Brown v. Board of Education of Topeka (1954)
Reversed *Plessy v. Ferguson* and ruled that separation of the races in public schools violates the constitutional guarantee of equal rights

Gideon v. Wainwright (1963)
Ruled that defendants have the right to be represented by counsel in state trials and that the state must provide a lawyer if defendant cannot afford to pay for one

Miranda v. Arizona (1966)
Ruled that statements made by accused persons who have not been informed of their right to remain silent may not be used as evidence against them

Roe v. Wade (1973)
Legalized a woman's right to an abortion under certain circumstances

Regents of the University of California v. Allan Bakke (1978)
Ruled that race may be used as one factor, but not the only one, in making affirmative action decisions

Cruzan v. Director, Missouri Department of Health (1990)
Upheld Missouri's requirement for "clear and convincing" proof of a patient's desire that life-sustaining treatment be withdrawn

CHAPTER 20: SUPREME COURT DECISION MAKING 577

L3 Political Processes Ask students if the Court more often shapes public attitudes or responds to them. Ask the class to discuss and evaluate the following methods some have suggested to make the Court more "democratic": televising Court proceedings, putting a set length on justices' terms, establishing a mandatory retirement age, specifying Republican and Democratic seats on the Court, televising all confirmation hearings for Court nominees.

Linking Past and Present
The office of Chief Justice is not mentioned in Article III, which created the Court. But it is assumed to exist in Article I, Section 3, which provides that the Chief Justice shall preside over impeachment proceedings in the Senate if the President is on trial. For 50 years after its creation, the office was called the Chief Justice of the Supreme Court. During the Civil War, Salmon P. Chase claimed the grandiose title of Chief Justice of the United States.

Cooperative Learning Activity

Organize the class into groups and assign each group to present a 10-minute "television documentary" on one of the following topics: freedom of speech, due process of law, equality before the law, and freedom of religion. In its documentary each group should cover the history and controversies behind the topic, the court cases involved, and landmark Supreme Court decisions. Suggest that each group divide its tasks into research, script, and presenting teams. Conclude the activity by having each group present its documentary. One person in the group should be the television commentator, perhaps interviewing interested parties on the issue.

Independent Practice

L1 Making Comparisons Have students research their state supreme court to determine how its powers, structure, and selection process for justices compare with the United States Supreme Court. Ask them to construct a chart to present their comparisons. **LEP**

L2 Informative Writing Have students consult American history books to identify the conflict between President Andrew Jackson and the Supreme Court. Ask them to summarize the events in a short essay and explain how it illustrates the constitutional principle of checks and balances.

📁 Analyzing Supreme Court Cases Assign case 52, *South Dakota v. Dole,* in *Supreme Court Case Studies* in the Teacher's Classroom Resources. After students read the case, have them suggest in an essay how the factors that influence Court decisions may have applied in this case.

STUDY GUIDE

Theme Answer
Answers will vary. Students should note that justices are not elected and that the Court shies away from highly political issues.

Critical Thinking Answer
Answers will vary, but should weigh the importance of objectivity against the judiciary's need for public support.

Justice Burton's remark illustrates that, unlike Congress, the Court is fairly well insulated from public opinion and daily political pressures. The insulation results from the lifetime tenure of the justices and from rules that limit the way interest groups may try to influence the Court.

Still, the Supreme Court does not exist in a vacuum. The justices are interested in the Court's prestige and in maintaining as much public support as possible. In addition, the justices are part of society and are affected by the same social forces that shape public attitudes.

Concern for Public Support As already noted, the Court relies on the cooperation and goodwill of others to enforce its decisions. The justices recognize that the Court's authority and power depend in part on public acceptance of and support for its decisions. They know that when the Court moves too far ahead or lags too far behind public opinion, it risks losing valuable public support and may weaken its own authority. For example, in one ruling against voter discrimination in the South, Justice Felix Frankfurter, a northerner, was assigned to write the Court's opinion. After thinking it over, the Court reassigned the opinion to Justice Stanley Reed, a southerner. The justices hoped this change would ease the resentment that they believed was almost inevitable in the South.

Influence of Social Forces The values and beliefs of society influence Supreme Court justices. As society changes, attitudes and practices that were acceptable in one era may become unacceptable in another. In time the Court's decisions will usually reflect changes in American society, providing another reason why the Court sometimes reverses its earlier decisions.

Two major decisions on racial segregation provide an example of how the Court changes with the times. In the 1890s many restaurants, schools, and trains were segregated. In Louisiana, Homer Plessy had attempted to sit in a section of a train marked "For Whites Only." When he refused to move, Plessy was arrested and convicted of violating Louisiana's segregation law. Plessy appealed his conviction to the Supreme Court, which in 1896 upheld the Louisiana law as constitutional in the case of *Plessy* v. *Ferguson.*

The Court ruled that the equal protection clause of the Fourteenth Amendment permitted a state to require separate facilities for African Americans as long as those facilities were equal to the facilities available to whites. Of course, the facilities for African Americans were not truly equal, but few whites at the time were concerned about the needs of African Americans. The *Plessy* decision served as a legal justification for racial segregation for the next half-century.

By the 1950s society's attitudes toward race relations were beginning to change. World War II made it harder to support segregation openly because so many African Americans had fought and died for American ideals. In addition, social science research began to document the damaging effects segregation had on African American children. Civil rights groups were demanding an end to racial discrimination.

These social forces helped persuade the Supreme Court to overturn the precedent established in *Plessy.* During its 1952 term, in *Brown* v. *Board of Education of Topeka, Kansas,* the Court heard a challenge to its 56-year-old interpretation of the Fourteenth Amendment. In 1954 the Court ruled unanimously that separate-but-equal educational facilities were unconstitutional.

In writing the Court's opinion, Chief Justice Earl Warren clearly recognized how important changes in society were to deciding the case. He reviewed the history of education in the late 1800s. He then added:

> *Today, education is perhaps the most important function of state and local governments. . . . In these days, it is doubtful that any child may reasonably be expected to succeed in life if he is denied the opportunity of an education. Such an opportunity . . . is a right which must be made available to all on equal terms.*
>
> —CHIEF JUSTICE EARL WARREN, 1954

STUDY GUIDE

Themes in Government	**Supreme Court** is as political as	**Critical Thinking Skills**
Political Processes Supreme Court justices have personal political opinions. **Do you think the**	the other branches? Why or why not?	**Demonstrating Reasoned Judgment Do you think that the Supreme Court should consider public opinion in deciding cases? Explain.**

Special Needs Strategy

Learning Disability In this section students are asked to consider the influences on the Supreme Court. Students will need to understand how law and opinion come together in the most influential court in the land. Ask students to categorize these important words and phrases under the categories of law or opinion: *interpretation, precedent, active interests, views, personal concern, principles, statute.*

PARTICIPATING IN GOVERNMENT

Serving as an Election Judge

ELECTION JUDGE

The success of our democratic system rests on free and open elections. At the polls, election judges ensure the integrity of the election. Who are the election judges? What are their duties?

Election judges generally are appointed through a political party's committee person for each precinct, or voting district. If you are a registered voter and are interested in serving as an election judge, you should contact the Democratic or Republican committee person in your precinct. Before an election these people sub-

mit a list of names to the county clerk or board of elections. The clerk or election commissioners appoint election judges from each political party for each precinct.

If you are chosen, you may be asked to attend a training session. Some counties increase the pay you receive for being an election judge if you attend.

On Election Day, you and the other election judges must see that ballots, ballot boxes, or voting machines are available at the polls. You make sure that only qualified voters cast ballots in your precinct. After the polls close, the election judges must count the votes. You certify the results and turn in the ballots to the county clerk or board of elections.

Investigating Further

Talk to someone who has served as an election judge. Report to the class about his or her experiences.

Chief Justice Warren declared that separate was inherently unequal, and violated the equal protection clause of the Fourteenth Amendment. Times had changed, and so did the Court's position.

Balancing the Court's Power

The Supreme Court, like the two other branches of the national government, operates within the system of separation of powers and checks and balances. Thus, the powers of Congress and the President affect the Court's decisions.

The President's Influence A President's most important influence over the Court is the power to ap-

point justices, with Senate consent. Presidents generally use this appointment power to choose justices who seem likely to bring the Court closer to their own philosophy.

Every full-term President except Jimmy Carter has made at least one Court appointment. President Nixon appointed four justices, including a Chief Justice, and President Reagan appointed three—all sharing the conservative philosophies of these Presidents. The importance of being able to make even a single Court appointment can be decisive when the votes of only one or two justices can swing the direction of Court decisions.

Presidents may also exercise influence with the Court in less formal ways. As head of the executive branch, the President plays a role in enforcing Court

---

STUDY GUIDE

Themes in Government
Public Policy Court decisions shape public policy just as laws of Congress do. Because decisions set precedents, people are governed by what the Court says.

Critical Thinking Skills
Making Inferences
What would happen in the federal government if the Supreme

Court, the Congress, and the President determined to oppose one another on every issue?

Display transparency 26 from the *Government Themes Transparencies* in the Teacher's Classroom Resources and use the accompanying teaching strategy and student activity to teach the ways citizens can participate in an election other than by voting.

Tell students that in some areas citizens' groups station observers called *poll watchers* to ensure that election judges perform their tasks honestly and accurately.

Have students complete activity 20 in *Participating in Government* in the Teacher's Classroom Resources.

STUDY GUIDE

Critical Thinking Answer
Government would come to a standstill, because each branch has the power to stall the efforts of the other branches.

Assess

Check for Understanding

Have students complete Section 3 Review on page 580.

Meeting Objectives

Each section objective is tested by the Section Review questions that follow it in parentheses.
- Explain how social forces influence Supreme Court decisions. (2, 3, 5, 8)
- Describe how individual justices shape Supreme Court decisions. (3, 4, 6, 7)

Critical Thinking Activity

Demonstrating Reasoned Judgment Political considerations have great influence on the nomination and appointment of justices. Indeed, nominees usually reflect the President's political party and its views. However, predicting how a nominee will vote once on the Court is not always reliable. President Eisenhower's supposedly conservative appointment, Chief Justice Earl Warren, turned out to be a liberal supporter of civil rights. Ask: How well does the nomination and appointment process serve to indicate how a potential justice will decide cases? How important should this factor be in selecting or confirming a nominee?

Evaluate

📁 Section 3 Quiz

💿 Testmaker

Reteach

Have students write a short summary paragraph for each of the factors that influences Court decisions. Have them order their paragraphs as they would rank the importance of these factors.

📁 Have students complete activity 20 in *Reaching Activities* in the Teacher's Classroom Resources.

Enrich

Ask students to use library resources to identify trends in Supreme Court rulings on civil rights issues (such as school desegregation, equal employment opportunity, police procedures, and abortion) since the 1970s and to suggest reasons for changes in these areas.

Close

Refer students to the Motivating Activity list on the chalkboard. Are there any factors they would remove from the list, modify, or add to it? Poll the class on which factor they think is most important. Have advocates for each factor explain why they chose it as most important.

decisions. Executive departments and agencies must enforce Court decisions in such areas as integration and equal employment opportunity if they are to have any impact. An administration may enforce such Court decisions vigorously or with little enthusiasm, depending on its views on these issues.

The Influence of Congress The system of checks and balances also can be used to try to shape the Court's decisions. Congress controls the Court's appellate jurisdiction by limiting the Court's ability to hear certain cases. In the late 1950s, for example, members of Congress, angry over Court decisions regarding subversive activities, unsuccessfully attempted to end the Court's authority to hear such cases. Congress also can pass laws that limit the Court's options in ordering remedies. By the early 1980s, some members of Congress became frustrated by liberal Court rulings on issues ranging from school busing to abortion. They introduced hundreds of bills to limit the Court's remedies in such cases.

After the Court has rejected a law, Congress may reenact it in a different form, hoping that the justices will change their minds. In the 1930s Congress tried to help the nation recover from the Depression by regulating industry. After the Court rejected the National Industrial Recovery Act in 1935, Congress reenacted essentially the same law but limited it to the coal industry. The Court upheld this law in 1937.

Congress also may propose a constitutional amendment to overturn a Court ruling. This strategy has been used successfully several times. For example, in 1793 the Court ruled in *Chisholm* v. *Georgia* that a citizen of another state could sue a state in federal court. To counter this decision, Congress passed and the states approved the Eleventh Amendment that prohibited such action. In an 1895 case, the Court ruled that a tax on incomes was unconstitutional. The Sixteenth Amendment, ratified in 1913, allowed Congress to levy an income tax.

Another way Congress exercises power over the Court is through its right to set the justices' salaries. Although Congress cannot reduce the justices' salaries, at times it has shown its anger toward the Court by refusing the justices raises.

Congress also sets the number of justices on the Court. In 1937 when President Franklin D. Roosevelt wanted to add six justices to the Court to change its direction and prevent it from declaring New Deal legislation unconstitutional, even lawmakers from the President's own party rejected the proposal.

Finally, in recent years the Senate has used its confirmation power to shape the Court's position. When the President nominates someone to the Court, the Senate scrutinizes the nominee's attitudes about sensitive social issues. Two of President Bush's appointees, David Souter and Clarence Thomas, were questioned intensely in Senate confirmation hearings about their views on abortion. To avoid this kind of questioning, President Clinton chose nominees who had centrist views on sensitive issues. Judging the nominee's stand on selected issues has given Congress increased power to influence the direction the Court will take in shaping public policy.

---

3 SECTION REVIEW

Section Summary

Although the justices must base their opinions about a case on points of law, their personal views, relations with one another, and social and political positions also influence the Court's decisions.

Checking for Understanding

Recalling Facts

1. Define bloc, swing vote.
2. Identify the basis for Supreme Court decisions.
3. List five forces that shape Supreme Court decisions.
4. Explain how a Chief Justice can influence the Supreme Court's decisions.

Exploring Themes

5. Political Processes How can Congress and the President influence the decisions of the Supreme Court?
6. Public Policy How do the personal opinions of Supreme Court justices affect public policy?

Critical Thinking Skills

7. Demonstrating Reasoned Judgment How important should a Supreme Court nominee's political and social views be in determining whether he or she will sit on the Court? Explain your answer.
8. Making Inferences Why did the Supreme Court refuse to "turn back the clock" in deciding the *Brown* case?

Section 3 Review Answers

1. Definitions of terms appear on pages indicated: **bloc,** 575; **swing vote,** 576

2. Justices must base their decisions on relevant laws and precedents and on the Constitution.

3. existing law, justices' personal views, interactions of the justices, social forces and public attitudes, the other two branches

4. The Chief Justice initiates the discuss list, directs conferences, and writes the majority opinion or assigns it to another justice with similar views.

5. A President can enforce a Court decision vigorously or choose not to. As vacancies occur, presidential appointments influence the Court's future directions. Congress can change the Court's appellate jurisdiction, and the Senate can refuse to confirm certain nominees.

6. All justices have their personal legal views, areas of interest, and opinions on social issues that affect the way each votes in certain cases.

7. Answers will vary. Some will contend that the Court should mirror society. Others may cite the importance of judicial independence.

8. The environment of *Brown* was so far removed from precedents that they had little relevance to modern society's needs and conditions.

John Marshall Harlan on the Role of Oral Argument

John Marshall Harlan served as associate justice of the United States Supreme Court from 1955 until 1971. Justice Harlan was known for his clear, well-reasoned opinions. In this passage, he reflects on the value of the oral arguments presented in cases to which the Court grants a full hearing.

I think that there is some tendency . . . to regard the oral argument as little more than a traditionally tolerated part of the appellate process. The view is widespread that when a court comes to the hard business of decision, it is the briefs, and not the oral argument, which count. I think that view is a greatly mistaken one. . . .

First of all, judges have different work habits. There are judges who listen better than they read and who are more receptive to the spoken word than the written word.

Secondly, the first impressions that a judge gets of a case are very tenacious [firm]. They frequently persist into the conference room. And those impressions are usually

The first impressions that a judge gets of a case are very tenacious. . . . And those impressions are usually gained from the oral argument. . . .

gained from the oral argument, if it is an effective job. While I was on the court of appeals, I kept a sort of informal scorecard of the cases in which I sat, so as to match up the initial reactions which I had to the cases after the close of the oral argument with the final conclusions that I had reached when it came time to vote at the conferences on the decision of those cases. I was astonished to find that during the year I sat on that court how frequently—in fact, more times than not—the views which I had at the end of the day's session jibed with the final view that I formed after the more careful study of the briefs. . . .

Thirdly, the decisional process in many courts places a special burden on the oral argument. . . . In one of the courts of appeals where I was assigned to sit temporarily the voting on the cases took place each day following the close of the arguments. In the Supreme Court, our practice, as is well known, has been to hold our conferences at the end of each week of arguments. . . . Under either of these systems you can see the importance which the oral argument assumes.

Fourth, and to me this is one of

the most important things, the job of courts is not merely one of an umpire in disputes between litigants. Their job is to search out the truth, both as to the facts and the law, and that is ultimately the job of the lawyers, too. And in that joint effort, the oral argument gives an opportunity for interchange between court and counsel which the briefs do not give. For my part, there is no substitute, even within the time limits afforded by the busy calendars of modern appellate courts, for the Socratic method [question and answer] of procedure in getting at the real heart of an issue and in finding out where the truth lies.

—Justice John Marshall Harlan

Examining the Reading

Reviewing Facts
1. Describe how Justice Harlan believes the public and attorneys view oral argument.
2. List the reasons why Justice Harlan believes oral argument is important.

Critical Thinking Skills
3. Demonstrating Reasoned Judgment How would the length of time that passes before a case is decided affect the importance of briefs and oral arguments?

CHAPTER 20: SUPREME COURT DECISION MAKING **581**

Focus

Hand out a brief letter to the editor from the local newspaper and have students read it. Then read the letter aloud. Ask students which form, oral or written, was more persuasive. Why?

Teach

Ask: What personal experience does Harlan cite to point to the efficiency of oral arguments? What process occurs during oral arguments that cannot occur during the study of briefs? Why do you think that tradition grants more importance to written than to oral arguments?

Assess

Have students complete **Examining the Reading.**
Answers
1. It is a tradition and not otherwise important.
2. Some judges listen better than they read; oral argument persists better in conference; the need to dispose of cases quickly; questioning can occur.
3. As delays between argument and decision lengthen, spoken words are forgotten and briefs assume more importance. When decisions are reached quickly, there is less study of briefs and oral arguments assume more importance.

Close

Ask: Would you prefer that justices base their decisions on oral arguments or written ones? Why?

More About Personal Perspectives

John Marshall Harlan was named for one Supreme Court justice and was the grandson of another (John Marshall Harlan—1833-1911). Although a Wall Street lawyer most of his career, he was an assistant United States Attorney from 1925 to 1927 and chief counsel to the New York State Crime Commission from 1951 to 1953.

Socrates (469–399 B.C.) was a logical choice for reference by a Supreme Court justice. A Greek teacher and philosopher, he taught his students by questioning them and then analyzing their answers. He defined the process of inductive reasoning—working from specific facts to reach general principles.

20 CHAPTER REVIEW

Identifying Terms and Concepts

1. writ of *certiorari*, 2. *stare decisis*, 3. precedent, 4. *per curiam*, 5. *amicus curiae*, 6. brief, 7. majority opinion, 8. concurring opinion, 9. dissenting opinion

Reviewing Facts and Ideas

1. settles disputes between national government and states and disputes among the states

2. The Court must wait until an issue is brought to it in a case, usually through the appeals process.

3. The decision of the lower court stands.

4. The justices meet in conference to discuss the case. They vote on the decision and an opinion is written to explain the majority position.

5. It instructs lower courts on how to act in the future and communicates the Court's thinking to government, interest groups, and the public.

6. The dissenting opinion may become the basis for a majority opinion if the Court changes its mind in the future.

7. Supreme Court's prestige and authority depend on public acceptance of and support for its decisions.

8. Justices are members of society and share many of the same social attitudes, which influences their votes on related issues.

9. Reversals often reflect changes in society over time.

Summary and Significance

By ruling on the constitutionality of local, state, and federal laws, and by interpreting their meaning, the Supreme Court has great influence on government operations and policies. Limits exist on this power. For example, the Court cannot rule until a case is brought to it. The Court accepts few of the cases that come to it, however, and even fewer are granted full hearings before the justices. The opinions the justices write in deciding these cases set precedent and determine future policy. The law that applies to a case, the justices' legal views, public attitudes and social forces, and the actions of the President and Congress influence Court decisions.

Identifying Terms and Concepts

Match each of the following terms with the statement below that correctly identifies the term.
amicus curiae, precedent, stare decisis, dissenting opinion, brief, concurring opinion, majority opinion, per curiam, writ of certiorari
1. Order to lower court for records on a case to be handed up for review
2. Lets a decision stand
3. Earlier decision on similar cases
4. Short unsigned statement of Supreme Court's decision
5. An interested party not directly involved in a case
6. Sets forth facts and legal arguments to support one side of a case
7. Sets forth reasons for a Supreme Court decision
8. Sets forth reasons for agreeing with a Supreme Court decision
9. Sets forth reasons for disagreeing with a Supreme Court decision

Reviewing Facts and Ideas

1. Describe how the Supreme Court protects the federal system.
2. Explain why the Supreme Court must sometimes wait for years before it can rule in an area.
3. State what happens when the Supreme Court refuses to hear a case.
4. Describe the procedure the justices follow in reaching a decision in a case.
5. Explain the importance of a Supreme Court majority opinion.

6. Examine the importance of a dissenting opinion.
7. Summarize the role of public opinion in Supreme Court decisions.
8. Discuss the influence of the justices' personal opinions on Supreme Court decisions.
9. Explain why the Supreme Court sometimes reverses its earlier decisions.

Applying Themes

1. **Constitutional Interpretations** The Constitution is a written document. Explain why the Supreme Court may interpret the same words differently over the years.
2. **Political Processes** Describe the ways in which the Supreme Court is a "political" institution.
3. **Public Policy** Cite changes in society that Supreme Court decisions have caused.

Critical Thinking Skills

1. **Drawing Conclusions** Some people claim that the Supreme Court actually makes laws. Explain whether you agree or disagree with this assessment of the Court.
2. **Demonstrating Reasoned Judgment** Can the principles of judicial review and majority rule successfully coexist in a democracy? Explain why or why not.
3. **Making Inferences** Why do you think President Woodrow Wilson once described the Supreme Court as "a constitutional convention in continuous session"?

Applying Themes

1. The circumstances of each case might be slightly different, public attitudes and social values may have changed, new people on the Court may bring different legal viewpoints and social attitudes.

2. Politics is a factor in the appointment and confirmation of justices. Court decisions reflect the individual political philosophies of the justices.

Much of the Court's power depends on public acceptance of its decisions, on the willingness of Congress to abide by its decisions, and on the power of the executive branch to enforce its decisions. Justices weigh such factors when making decisions.

3. Answers will vary, but should include references to civil rights, school desegregation, equal employment opportunity, school prayer, and so on.

Linking Past and Present

In *The Federalist*, No. 78, published in 1788, Alexander Hamilton assessed the judicial branch:

> *Whoever attentively considers the different [branches of government] must perceive that . . . the judiciary, from the nature of its functions, will always be the least dangerous to the political rights of the Constitution; because it will be least in a capacity to annoy or injure them. The Executive . . . holds the sword of the community. The legislature not only commands the purse, but prescribes the rules by which the duties and rights of every citizen are to be regulated. The judiciary, on the contrary, has no influence over either the sword or the purse. . . .*
>
> *This simple view of the matter suggests several important consequences. It proves incontestably, that the judiciary is beyond comparison the weakest of the three [branches]. . . .*
>
> —ALEXANDER HAMILTON,
> THE FEDERALIST, No. 78, 1788

In your opinion, does Hamilton's assessment of the Supreme Court apply today? Explain your answer.

Writing About Government

Informative Writing Write a biographical essay about a prominent current or past Supreme Court justice. Include information about the justice's education, career, important opinions, and influence.

Reinforcing the Skill

Interpreting a Primary Source The following is an excerpt from the majority decision in *Engel* v. *Vitale* (1962). In that case a group of parents challenged a New York law requiring a specific prayer at the beginning of each school day. Use what you have learned about interpreting a primary source to answer the questions that follow the passage.

> *There can be no doubt that New York's state prayer program officially establishes the religious beliefs embodied in the [state's] prayer. . . . That the [state's] prayer is "nondenominational" and the fact that the program . . . permits those who wish to do so to remain silent or be excused from the room, ignores the essential nature of the program's constitutional defects. Neither the fact that the prayer may be denominationally neutral nor the fact that its observance on the part of the students is voluntary can serve to free it from the limitations of the . . . First Amendment. . . . [It] is violated by the enactment of laws which establish an official religion whether those laws operate directly to coerce nonobserving individuals or not. . . . When the power, prestige, and financial support of government is placed behind a particular religious belief, the indirect coercive pressure upon religious minorities to conform to the prevailing officially approved religion is plain. . . . A union of government and religion tends to destroy government and to degrade religion.*
>
> —JUSTICE HUGO BLACK, 1962

1. Briefly state the main idea of this passage.
2. What details support the main idea?

Investigating Further

1. **Individual Project** Select one of the cases discussed in this chapter or another famous case of your choosing and prepare a report presenting the arguments on both sides of the case.
2. **Cooperative Learning** Organize 10 to 14 people into a group and then divide it into two subgroups of equal size. Have one subgroup study the Warren Court and the other subgroup the Burger Court. Each subgroup should research its Court, paying particular attention to the Court's decisions on minority rights and criminal justice. Have the entire group compare each subgroup's findings. Ask each group to summarize its court's position on these issues and to propose possible explanations for any differences it discovered.

CHAPTER 20: SUPREME COURT DECISION MAKING 583

CASE STUDY

The Case at a Glance

Who: Supreme Court
What: judicial review
When: 1878 to the present
Where: United States
Why: to adjust to changing society

Focus

Have students think about the following: Why are people willing to waive their constitutional rights to privacy during a routine security check at an airport? *(Most people waive this right to guarantee a safe flight.)* Tell students that the issue of search and seizure is one that the Supreme Court has dealt with on many occasions. It illustrates the Court's ability to overturn precedent and gives meaning to the term *living Constitution.*

Teach

Guided Practice

L1 Analyzing Ideas Discuss the evolution of the Supreme Court's decisions regarding the Fourth Amendment. Ask: What is meant by *living Constitution?* *(the ability to interpret the Constitution to meet changing times)* How has the principle of *stare decisis* made judicial review controversial? *(Even though the Court has the right to change decisions, the Court usually stands on its past decisions.)* Ask how the Court has defined *unreasonable* in various circumstances. Have students provide examples.

Powers of the People

The right of the people to be secure in their persons, houses, papers, and effects against unreasonable searches and seizures, shall not be violated, and no Warrants shall issue, but upon probable cause, supported by Oath or affirmation, and particularly describing the place to be searched, and the persons or things to be seized.

—Fourth Amendment, 1791

The Supreme Court Changes Its Mind

The Case

Undoubtedly, one of the strengths of the Constitution is its flexibility to meet changing times. Basic to this characteristic is the Supreme Court which, through interpretation and by overruling precedent, provides the nation with a "living constitution."

The nation's courts long have adhered to the principle of *stare decisis*— "let the decision stand." This doctrine binds courts to follow their own past decisions and the decisions of higher courts. In most instances, the Supreme Court has applied the principle when deciding constitutional questions. As Justice Harry Blackmun noted recently, however:

Although . . . the doctrine of stare decisis serves profoundly important purposes in our legal system, this Court has overruled a prior case on the comparatively rare occasion when it has bred confusion or been a derelict or led to anomalous [abnormal] results.

—JUSTICE HARRY BLACKMUN

Justice Blackmun's comment came in a majority opinion about a case involving search and seizure. The Court's interpretation of the Fourth Amendment is a good example of precedent and, ultimately, of change in the justice system.

Clearly, the Fourth Amendment does not forbid searches, nor does it specify that a search warrant is always required. What it does specifically forbid is "unreasonable searches and seizures." The question of what constitutes an unreasonable search has become a major legal issue in the twentieth century.

Background

One of the earliest cases involving unreasonable search came before the Supreme Court in 1878. In that case the Court decided a warrant was necessary to open and examine first-class mail. Not until 1914, however, did it offer a major interpretation of the Fourth Amendment. In *Weeks* v. *United States,* the Court formulated the "exclusionary rule"—a precedent that barred federal courts from allowing illegally seized material to be used as evidence.

More About the Case

Two of the most common types of judicial warrants are the *arrest warrant* and the *search warrant.* The perceived abuse of these documents inflamed American colonists, who, after establishing their freedom from Britain, included protection against unreasonable searches in the Fourth Amendment.

Another judicial warrant is the *escape warrant* that permits the recapture of prisoners. Judges can also issue warrants to bring a bankrupt person before the court when there is reasonable doubt that the person will appear in court.

The presentation and content of a warrant is

The case arose when local authorities searched Weeks's home without a search warrant. They turned over seized documents to federal officials because some of the material indicated that Weeks intended to conduct illegal activities through the mails. When Weeks's lawyer protested, some of the documents were returned. The rest were used as evidence to convict Weeks. The constitutional issue of unreasonable search and seizure brought the case to the Supreme Court, which reversed the conviction.

By ruling that evidence seized in unreasonable searches could not be used in court, the Supreme Court established a precedent for federal courts to follow in future federal cases.

In 1961, in *Mapp* v. *Ohio,* the Court ruled that the Fourth Amendment was binding on the states as well as on the federal government. As a result, unless a suspect agrees to a search, local authorities generally must obtain a search warrant from a court. To obtain a warrant, police must establish that there is probable cause for the search. In addition, the warrant must specify what place or places will be searched and what is being sought.

A number of exceptions to these requirements, however, do exist. One involves the search of vehicles. On May 31, 1991 a headline in *The New York Times* announced "High Court Eases Car Search Rules." The Supreme Court had overruled a previous decision and established a new precedent for itself and other courts to follow regarding searches and seizures.

Automobile Searches Over the years the Supreme Court has considered a series of cases directly bearing on the right of police to search an automobile and to seize evidence without a warrant. The first important case, *Carroll* v. *United States,* reached the Supreme Court in 1925 after federal agents stopped a car driven by George Carroll. The car, they believed, contained liquor that the Volstead Act and the Eighteenth Amendment prohibited. They searched the car without a warrant and, cutting open the car's door linings and seats, found the liquor. Based on evidence seized in the warrantless search, Carroll was tried and convicted of illegally transporting liquor for sale. When Carroll appealed, contending his constitutional rights had been violated by an unreasonable search and seizure, the Supreme Court ruled against him.

CAUTION: Detach Instructions and Affidavit before writing on this form

TRIAL COURT OF THE COMMONWEALTH

AFFIDAVIT, APPLICATION AND SEARCH WARRANT

Under General Laws chapter 276, §§ 1-7

INSTRUCTIONS FOR PREPARING "AFFIDAVIT IN SUPPORT OF APPLICATION FOR SEARCH WARRANT"

Is a Search Warrant Necessary?
When determining what constitutes "unreasonable searches and seizures," the Supreme Court has often considered the public's attitude toward crime.

After *Mapp* v. *Ohio* applied the Fourth Amendment to the states, warrantless searches of vehicles by state and local police became subject to review by federal courts. Many questions now arose. For example, did police need a search warrant after the driver was in custody, the vehicle seized and not likely to move? The Court answered that question in 1970. In *Chambers* v. *Maroney* it upheld a conviction based on evidence obtained in a warrantless search of a car at the police station after its driver was arrested for armed robbery. Extending the Carroll precedent, the Court ruled that police can search later what they could have searched earlier.

The Court further extended the warrantless search of automobiles in *South Dakota* v. *Opperman* in 1976. It upheld the conviction of a defendant when police discovered marijuana in the glove compartment of his car after towing it away for parking violations. Because listing the contents of an impounded car was standard police procedure, the Court ruled that the search was not unreasonable under the Fourth Amendment.

Inevitably the need for guidance in searching a vehicle's contents arose. The *Carroll* precedent and the

L2 Making a Time Line Work with students to make a time line on the chalkboard of the Court's decisions regarding the Fourth Amendment as described in the case study. Include the first-class mail decision in 1878, *Weeks* v. *United States* in 1914, *Carroll* v. *United States* in 1925, *Mapp* v. *Ohio* in 1961, *Chambers* v. *Maroney* in 1970, *South Dakota* v. *Opperman* in 1975, *United States* v. *Chadwick* in 1977, *Arkansas* v. *Sanders* in 1979, and *California* v. *Acevedo* in 1991. Then have students discuss the social and political reasons for the decisions in each case.

L3 Class Discussion Discuss the case study as one example of how the Court responds to societal changes. Ask: How and why has the Court changed its position on search and seizure? *(The technology for transporting illegal goods has changed, making it necessary for the courts to change their interpretation.)* On what other issues has the Court adjusted or changed its decisions? *(segregation, civil rights, rights of the accused)*

---

strictly regulated. A search warrant, for example, must provide a description of the property to be seized or the place to be searched. The officer executing the warrant has no discretion in the identification of items. Even a valid warrant may become void if its execution is delayed. The search must be conducted before 8:00 P.M., unless the person or property to be seized is only in that location at night. Finally, an officer executing the warrant can use force only to overcome resistance to the search. An invalid search may mean the officer conducting the search can be charged with trespassing.

L1 **Interviewing** Have a representative from the local police department discuss the legal definition of search and seizure. Have students prepare a list of questions beforehand.

📁 **Analyzing Supreme Court Cases** Assign case 58, *California v. Acevedo,* from the *Supreme Court Case Studies* in the Teacher's Classroom Resources.

L3 **Research** Have students research the provisions their state's constitution includes about search and seizure. Has the policy changed over the years? Why or why not?

Assess

Have students complete **Examining the Case.**

Close

Ask students whether they think the Court will change its mind on other issues in the future. What decision might they consider overturning? Why might they consider changing the decision?

---

later cases clearly established that a warrantless search of all parts of a car was constitutional. What remained unclear was whether police could also search containers and packages within the car.

In *United States* v. *Chadwick* (1977), the Court established that a warrant was needed to search a foot locker being loaded into the trunk of a car. Confusion persisted, however, and in *Arkansas* v. *Sanders* (1979), the Court decided to rule again on this issue.

Acting on a tip, Little Rock police had watched Lonnie James Sanders claim a suitcase from airline baggage, hail a cab, place the suitcase in the trunk, and leave the airport. They pursued and stopped the taxi, seized the suitcase, searched it without a warrant, and discovered drugs. Upon appeal, the Court struck down Sanders's conviction for drug possession. It reasoned that

> *Luggage is a common repository for one's personal effects, and therefore is inevitably associated with the expectation of privacy. Once police have seized a suitcase from an automobile, the extent of its mobility is in no way affected by the place from which it was taken.*

California v. Acevedo (1991) In October 1987, police officers observed Charles Steven Acevedo leaving a suspected drug house. He carried a paper bag the size of a package of drugs they knew had been mailed from Hawaii. When Acevedo drove off, the police stopped his car, opened the trunk, searched the bag, and found a pound of marijuana. When the defense moved to suppress the evidence police found in the car, the trial court denied the motion. Acevedo then pleaded guilty but appealed the court's refusal to exclude the marijuana as evidence.

On May 30, 1991, the Supreme Court finally ended a situation that, in its own words, "not only has failed to protect privacy but . . . has also confused courts and police officers and impeded effective law enforcement." In *California* v. *Acevedo,* the Court overruled its *Sanders* decision and established a new precedent to be used in automobile searches. The police are free to "search an automobile and the containers within it where they have probable cause to believe contraband or evidence is contained." As *The New York Times* observed, "Overturning a 12-year-old precedent, the Supreme Court today broadened the ability of police officers who have no court warrant to search bags, suitcases and other containers they find in automobiles."

Significance

When *Mapp* v. *Ohio* was decided, critics accused the Court of deliberately finding a reason to apply the Fourth Amendment to the states, even though the appeal in the case was based on First Amendment issues. Today most political scientists accept the charge that the Supreme Court sets national policy. Is it wrong for the Court to shape society? For example, Justice Thurgood Marshall wrote, "For many years, no institution of American government has been as close a friend to civil rights as the United States Supreme Court." Was it wrong for the Court to take such a position?

Defenders of the Court argue that in the absence of strong leadership in certain areas by the President or Congress, the Court has stepped in to meet the nation's needs. Whatever position one takes on the proper role of the Supreme Court, almost all agree with Chief Justice Charles Evans Hughes, who once said: "We are under the Constitution, but the Constitution is what the judges say it is." On issues of search and seizure, it may be that today the Court is responding to a public that demands a strong "war on drugs."

Examining the Case

Reviewing Facts
1. Define the doctrine of *stare decisis.*
2. Identify the case in which the Supreme Court found it constitutional to search a package during a warrantless search of a car.
3. Explain why a warrant is not necessary to search packages in a vehicle stopped for probable cause.

Critical Thinking Skills
4. Determining Relevance What relationship exists between the Supreme Court's position on search and seizure and the public's attitude about drugs?
5. Distinguishing Fact From Opinion Do you agree or disagree with the statement "Supreme Court decisions follow election returns"?

Examining the Case Answers

1. binds courts to follow their own past decisions and the decisions of higher courts
2. *California* v. *Acevedo*
3. Police might think the automobile is carrying contraband or evidence.
4. The public favors the war on drugs and allows the authorities more leeway in searching suspects if such leeway helps win the war.
5. Answers may vary, but many students might suggest that the Court is not subject to political pressures because justices are appointed for life.

Chapter 19
The Federal Court System

The Constitution provided for a Supreme Court of the United States as part of a court system that would balance the powers of the other two branches of government. In the early years of the Republic, the Court played a relatively minor role. A series of strong justices, however, gradually increased the Court's role. Today the judicial branch of government is well established as an equal with the legislative and executive branches.

The judiciary of the United States has two different levels of courts. On the first level are the federal courts. On the other are the courts of each of the 50 states. Every court, whether it is a federal court or a state court, has the authority to hear certain kinds of cases. This authority is called the **jurisdiction** of the court. State courts have jurisdiction over cases involving state laws, while federal courts have jurisdiction over cases involving federal laws. Sometimes the jurisdiction of the state courts and the jurisdiction of the federal courts overlap.

In most cases the difference between federal and state court jurisdiction is clear. In some instances, however, both federal and state courts have jurisdiction, a situation known as **concurrent jurisdiction.** Concurrent jurisdiction exists, for example, in a case involving citizens of different states in a dispute concerning at least $10,000. In such a case, a person may sue in either a federal or a state court. If the person being sued insists, however, the case must be tried in a federal court.

The federal courts deal with three types of law. These three types include civil law, criminal law, and constitutional law. **Civil law** concerns disputes between two or more individuals or between individuals and the government. In **criminal law** cases, the government charges someone with breaking a law. **Constitutional law** deals with interpretations of the Constitution.

Four basic principles underlie the operation of both federal and state courts and the actions of the thousands of men and women who serve in the American legal system. These basic principles include equal justice under the law, due process of law, the adversary system of justice, and the presumption of innocence.

The Constitution names only one federal court—the Supreme Court. Over the years, however, Congress has established a variety of lower trial and appellate courts to handle a growing number of federal cases. These courts are of two basic types—constitutional federal courts and legislative federal courts. Constitutional courts include the federal district courts, the courts of appeals, and the United States Court of International Trade.

The legislative courts help Congress exercise its powers, as spelled out in Article I of the Constitution. Thus, it was the power of Congress to tax that led to the creation of the United States Tax Court. The congressional power of regulating the armed forces led to the formation of the Court of Military Appeals. The duty of Congress to govern overseas territories such as Guam and the Virgin Islands led to the creation of Territorial Courts. Similarly, congressional supervision of the District of Columbia led to the establishment of a court system for the nation's capital.

At all levels of federal courts, the President, with the advice and consent of the Senate, appoints judges. The Constitution, however, sets forth no specific qualifications for federal judges.

Judges in the constitutional courts serve for a life term. This makes judges free from public or political pressures in deciding cases. Federal court judges' jobs are safe even if they make unpopular decisions.

In the federal judiciary, the Supreme Court is the court of last resort in all questions of federal law. It has final authority in any case involving the Constitution, acts of Congress, and treaties with other nations. Most of the cases the Supreme Court hears are appeals from lower courts. The decisions of the Supreme Court are binding on all lower courts.

The Supreme Court is composed of 9 justices: the Chief Justice of the United States and 8 associate justices. Congress sets this number and has the power to change it. Over the years it has varied from 5 to 10, but has been 9 since 1869. In 1937 President Franklin D. Roosevelt attempted to gain greater control of the Court by asking Congress to increase the number of justices. Congress refused, in part because the number 9 was well established.

The eight associate justices receive salaries of $159,000 per year. The Chief Justice receives a salary of $166,200. Congress sets the justices' salaries and may not reduce them.

Classroom Resources for Unit 6 Digest

 Unit Digest Transparencies, Unit 6   📁 Participating in Government, Unit 6

Using the Unit 6 Digest

Use the Unit Digest to introduce, review, reteach, or condense specific chapters or the entire unit. The Unit Digest is enhanced by the corresponding transparencies and activities in the Teacher's Classroom Resources.

Focus

Point out to students that above the east portico of the Supreme Court Building in Washington, D.C., the words *JUSTICE THE GUARDIAN OF LIBERTY* are inscribed. Have students discuss whether they think this is an appropriate description of the role of the judiciary in American government. End the discussion by mentioning that the structure and functions of the judicial branch of government are the subject of this Unit Digest.

Teach

L1 Law Provide copies of the following cases to students. For each case, have students indicate whether the federal or state courts have jurisdiction or whether there is concurrent jurisdiction.

1. A Texas farmer sues a New Mexico farmer for building fences and pasturing cows on his land. He asks for damages of $200,000. *(concurrent)*
2. An Illinois company is charged with a violation of the Clean Air Act. *(federal)*
3. A German visitor is charged with driving without a license in Pennsylvania. *(state)*
4. A California company is charged with employing a number of illegal aliens. *(federal)*

Interpreting Visuals Display transparency 6 from the *Unit Digest Transparencies* in the Teacher's Classroom Resources and use the accompanying teaching strategy, student activity, and student test to teach about the judicial branch of the American government.

L3 Informative Writing Point out that the Supreme Court under Chief Justice Earl Warren was described as a liberal activist court. Conversely, the Supreme Court under Chief Justice William Rehnquist has been described as a conservative activist court. Have students research and write a report on three decisions by each court that support these descriptions. Reports should include a brief outline of each decision and why it represents liberal or conservative activism. Have students read their reports to the class.

Assess

Check for Understanding

Have students complete **Synthesizing the Unit.**

Close

Have students debate the following questions:

Should judges be elected or appointed? Why?

Should judges serve life terms, or should their terms in office be limited? Why?

Chapter 20

Supreme Court Decision Making

The Supreme Court is both a political and a legal institution. It is a legal institution because it is ultimately responsible for settling disputes and interpreting the meaning of laws. The Court is a political institution because when it applies the law to specific disputes, it often determines what national policy will be. For example, when the Court rules that certain provisions of the Social Security Act must apply to men and women equally, it is determining government policy. Thus, as it decides cases, the Supreme Court joins the President and Congress in making national policy.

Congress makes policy by passing laws. The President shapes policy by proposing and carrying out laws and by drawing up the national budget. As the Supreme Court decides cases, it determines policy in three ways. These include: (1) using judicial review, (2) interpreting the meaning of laws, and (3) overruling or reversing its previous decisions.

The Supreme Court's power to examine the laws and actions of local, state, and national governments and to cancel them if they violate the Constitution is called judicial review. In recent years the Court has used judicial review to significantly influence public policy at the state level in the areas of racial desegregation, reapportionment of state legislatures, and police procedures.

Despite its importance the Court does not have unlimited powers. Restrictions on the types of issues the Court hears, the kinds of cases the Court can or will hear, limited control over its own agenda, lack of enforcement power, and checks and balances curtail the Court's activities.

The Court does not give equal attention to all areas of national policy. For example, the Court has played only a minor role in making foreign policy. Over the years most Supreme Court decisions have dealt with civil liberties, economic issues, federal legislation and regulations, due process of law, and suits against government officials.

The Supreme Court meets for about nine months each year. Each term begins the first Monday in October and runs as long as the business before the Court requires, usually into July. During the term the Court sits for two consecutive weeks each month. At these sittings the justices listen to oral arguments by lawyers on each side of the cases before them. Later they announce their opinions on cases they have heard. The Court hears oral arguments from Mondays through Wednesdays, and the public is permitted to be present. On Wednesdays and Fridays the justices meet in secret conferences to decide cases. Between the sittings the justices work privately.

More than 5,000 cases are appealed to the Supreme Court each year. The court usually decides from 400 to 450, but of these not more than about 150 cases receive full hearings and written opinions. In the opinions that accompany this small number of cases, the Court sets out general principles that apply to the nation as well as to the specific parties in the case. It is mainly through these cases that the Court interprets the law and shapes public policy.

The Supreme Court follows a set procedure in hearing important cases. Much of this activity goes on behind the scenes, with only a small part taking place in an open courtroom.

For major cases the Court issues at least one written opinion. The opinion states the facts of the case, announces the Court's ruling, and explains its reasoning in reaching the decision. These opinions are as important as the decision itself. Not only do they set precedent for lower courts in future cases, they also are the Court's way to communicate with Congress, the President, interest groups, and the public.

Five forces shape the decisions the Court makes during its proceedings. They are (1) existing laws, (2) the personal views of the justices, (3) the justices' interactions with one another, (4) social forces and public attitudes, and (5) Congress and the President.

Synthesizing the Unit

Recalling Facts
1. Define jurisdiction, concurrent jurisdiction, civil law, criminal law, constitutional law.
2. List the four principles that underlie the operation of courts.
3. Compare constitutional courts and legislative courts.

Critical Thinking Skills
4. Analyzing Information How have strong justices expanded the powers of the Supreme Court?

Synthesizing the Unit Answers

1. Definitions of terms appear on the pages indicated: **jurisdiction,** 587; **concurrent jurisdiction,** 587; **civil law,** 587; **criminal law,** 587; **constitutional law,** 587
2. equal justice under the law, due process of law, adversary system of justice, presumption of innocence
3. Constitutional courts interpret the Constitution and include the federal district courts, the courts of appeals, and the United States Court of International Trade. Legislative courts help Congress exercise its powers, such as the powers to tax, to regulate the armed forces, to govern overseas territories, and to supervise the District of Columbia. Separate courts handle cases involving each of these powers.

4. The Supreme Court often determines what national policy will be when it applies a law to specific disputes. Strong justices might select and rule on cases in such a way that they shape an entire body of laws or reinterpret some of the nation's most fundamental laws.

Public Policies and Services

UNIT
7

Chapter 21
Taxing and Spending

Chapter 22
Foreign Policy and National Defense

Chapter 23
Social and Domestic Policy

Introduce

Unit Objectives

After studying this unit, students should be able to:

- Compare the taxing and spending functions of the national government.
- Analyze the role of government in shaping social and economic policy.
- Explain the system of checks and balances in the making of foreign policy.

Unit Overview

Unit 7 focuses on how the national government makes public policy.

Chapter 21 provides an overview of the federal budget process, the sources of federal revenue, and the effects of government spending on the national economy.

Chapter 22 deals with the conduct of American foreign policy.

Chapter 23 examines how the federal government both regulates and assists the nation's economy and provides for the welfare of its citizens.

7
UNIT DIGEST

Use the Unit Digest on pages 677–678 to introduce, review, reteach, or condense the information in this unit.

Introducing the Unit

Ask students to volunteer answers to the following questions: What does the national government do? Why does it do these things? How does it raise funds to cover the costs of undertaking these actions? Note responses on the chalkboard and have students copy them into their notebooks. Have students check the accuracy of these responses as they study Unit 7.

Unit Project

Have students work cooperatively to trace how national budget priorities have changed since the 1960s. Organize students into six groups and assign one of the following time periods to each: 1965 to 1969, 1970 to 1974, 1975 to 1979, 1980 to 1984, 1985 to 1989, and 1990 to the present. Each group should develop an illustrated report on government spending during its assigned time period. Useful sources of information include *Economic Report of the President* and *Statistical Abstract of the United States*. Suggest that group members share among themselves such tasks as researching, developing charts and graphs, and writing. Have groups display finished reports on the bulletin board.

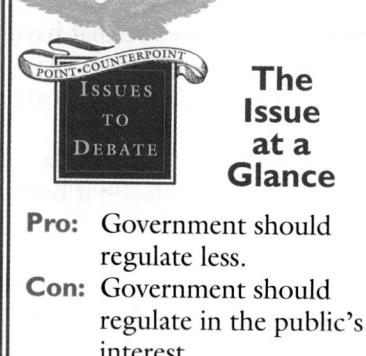

ISSUES TO DEBATE

The Issue at a Glance

Pro: Government should regulate less.
Con: Government should regulate in the public's interest.

Focus

Have students list aspects of their lives that are controlled by government regulations—for example, age restrictions on driving, traffic regulations, work permits, contents of food and cosmetics. Do students feel regulation is necessary in each instance they list?

Point out that government's proper regulatory role in industry is the subject of this debate. Have them keep in mind some of the areas of regulation in their lives as they read.

Teach

Guided Practice

Have students summarize the debate over government regulation using the example of the automotive industry. What do critics cite as negative effects of government regulation? *(higher production costs, decreased ability to compete and to meet demands of the marketplace)* What do proponents of regulation use as ammunition in their fight to regulate the auto industry? *(Consumer health and safety must be protected, oil consumption must be reduced, the public's needs must be met.)*

POINT·COUNTERPOINT
ISSUES TO DEBATE

Should the Government Regulate Less Than It Does?

The government's regulation of business and industry dates back to the nineteenth century and the establishment of the Interstate Commerce Commission in 1887. Since that time the government has been praised for its efforts to protect consumers and workers from dangerous drugs, contaminated food, and unsafe products and places of work. Critics, on the other hand, charged that government regulations often discourage innovations, raise costs, limit competition, and reduce employment opportunities. Throughout the 1980s and into the 1990s the debate about the government's regulatory role continued. Today, the question remains: Are government regulations excessive, and do they harm the nation's businesses and economy?

Pro

The election of President Ronald Reagan in November 1980 encouraged those who believed government regulations were excessive. Reagan campaigned on the program of "getting the government off people's backs." Upon taking office, President Reagan led the fight to deregulate the nation's economy. For some observers the 1980s were a dramatic decade.

In Washington we have a rather awesome regulatory system. . . . Every year they churn out thousands of regulations designed to make life safer or fairer. . . . Sometimes they succeed, but often they create tangled webs of laws that stop progress. Looking back on the Eighties I was struck by how many good things happened only because government . . . let go a little.
—JOHN STOSSEL, *ABC 20/20*, DECEMBER 1989

Other critics analyzed the effects regulations have on certain industries, such as the automotive industry. One economist reported:

With all the American automobile manufacturers operating deep in the red—running up losses totaling $4.7 billion in just six months—it is hard to remember that the automobile industry was once the showcase of American capitalism. . . . How did the automobile industry go from being a showcase to being a basket case?

No doubt many factors have been involved, but it is no coincidence that the era of its decline has been the era of its politicization. Those who have politicized the automobile have ranged from Ralph Nader to Lee Iacocca, and have included protectionists, environmental extremists and those who simply believe that the government is best that governs most. . . .

A major contribution to the politicization of the automobile came in the early 1970s when the OPEC cartel drove up the price of petroleum. From this crisis came congressional legislation mandating that cars achieve more miles per gallon. Again, there has been no looking back at what the marketplace had achieved before political intervention complicated the situation.

The continuing politicization of the automobile led to continuing design changes to meet congressional demands for higher gasoline mileage and/or "safety" features—even though the two demands are in conflict. The principal means of getting more miles per gallon has been to reduce the weight of the automobile, and the principal effect of building lighter cars has been to increase the risk of injury and death in the event of an accident. A 1989 study by scholars . . . showed . . . that this translated into upwards of 2,000 additional deaths in auto accidents over the lifetime of each model year's fleet of automobiles. That's really trading blood for oil. . . .

590 UNIT 7: PUBLIC POLICIES AND SERVICES

More About Issues to Debate

One of the best examples of government involvement with business is the breakup of American Telephone and Telegraph Company (AT&T) in 1982. AT&T was incorporated in 1885 for the purpose of providing telephone communication throughout the United States. By 1974 it controlled 80 percent of all telephones in the United States and all long distance and overseas services. Its research division, Bell Labs, was credited with the development of the transistor and the Telstar satellite system. In addition, AT&T built large manufacturing plants to supply the system with telephone parts. This giant even controlled the printing of telephone directories.

[T]here will be no end in sight to the troubles of the American automobile industry until the politicians and the public begin to understand that you cannot just continue to load even more requirements on any product without regard to the costs.

—THOMAS SOWELL, *FORBES*, JUNE 10, 1991

Con

Opponents of deregulation argue that regulations protect the public and the nation. Representative Dan Glickman commented that:

Legislation to increase the Corporate Average Fuel Economy (CAFE) standards is imperative to ensure a safe environment and national security.

We must address . . . this country's failure to respond to our growing dependence on foreign oil.

New CAFE legislation if implemented will build on improvements in fuel efficiency and will further our goal of U.S. energy security. My legislation, H.R. 612, requires each automobile manufacturer to increase CAFE standards by 25 percent by 1996 and by 50 percent in 2001. If implemented, the United States would save about 3 million barrels of oil a day by 2005 and American drivers would save close to $40 million dollars per day in gasoline costs. . . .

The savings of nearly 3 million barrels of oil per day by increasing the CAFE standards would more than offset the amount of oil imported into the United States each day from the Persian Gulf. According to a recent poll . . . 84 percent of the respondents support increasing federal fuel economy standards to 40 mpg by 2000.

—DAN GLICKMAN, THE AMERICAN LEGION, MAY 1991.

Susan and Martin Tolchin, a professor of public administration and a correspondent for *The New York Times* respectively, oppose efforts to deregulate or reduce the federal government's regulations in a somewhat broader context. For them,

The most serious consequence of the trend to deregulate is the dismantling of the social regulation, which provide a connective tissue between the needs of the public and private sectors. Private industry is entitled to make a profit, but its employees are entitled to their health and safety, their consumers are entitled to safe and well-made products, and the public is entitled to have its air, water, and quality of life safeguarded.

—SUSAN AND MARTIN TOLCHIN, *DISMANTLING AMERICA*, 1983

Cleaning Up Somebody Else's Mess
When it comes to regulating hazardous chemicals, some people proclaim "protect the environment," while others scream "restraint of trade."

The Debate Continues

Some critics accused President George Bush of failing to build upon the Reagan legacy of deregulation. Others accused Bush of not fulfilling his pledge to be an environmental President. With Bill Clinton's election, advocates of government regulation anticipated a new round of rule making. The 103rd Congress responded by considering new regulations on banking, credit reporting, the government bond market, insurance, limited partnerships, the political activities of government employees, labels on toys, the sale and use of pesticides, and telemarketing. The debate about government regulations continues.

Examining the Issue

Critical Thinking Skills
1. Recognizing Ideologies Do you think the statement "Many good things happened only because government . . . let go a little" reflects a particular political ideology? Why or why not?
2. Understanding Cause and Effect How have international events played a role in the field of government regulations?
3. Identifying Alternatives What is another method, other than government regulations, that might be used to reduce the use of gasoline and to avoid pollution from car emissions?

Investigating Further
Research whether government regulation of a major industry has increased or decreased in the last decade. Report your findings to the class.

**Unit 7 Issues to Debate
Lesson Plan, pages 590–591**

Discuss with students other sectors of the economy that have been deregulated in recent years, such as the airlines or savings and loans. Ask what happened in those industries. Did deregulation benefit the industry? Did it benefit the public?

Independent Practice

Ask students to write an essay indicating whether they favor more, less, or the same level of government regulation of American business, and to explain why they hold this view.

Assess

Have students complete **Examining the Issue.**

Answers

1. It reflects a conservative ideology of the benefits of limited government.
2. Answers should consider relationships between regulation and topics such as oil imports, foreign competition for American industries and markets, and international environmental issues.
3. Students may suggest alternative energy sources, alternative transportation programs, higher gas prices to discourage consumption.

Close

Ask students if there is any business area they believe should be deregulated or that should be regulated more. Ask respondents to explain their views.

In 1974 the federal government undertook an eight-year legal battle to break up the giant communications company. The government charged that the company did not allow competition. AT&T gave up control of regional telephone systems, which subsequently formed independent companies. In exchange, AT&T was allowed to stay in the long distance communications market, as well as to enter computer services and information processing business, which had been previously denied to it. As of 1993, AT&T remains not only the largest communications company in the world, it also is the sixth largest United States corporation, with stocks valued at about $67 billion.

Chapter Organizer

Objectives	Special Feature Pages	Supplemental Materials
Section 1 How the Government Raises Money *pp. 594–598* 1. Identify the main taxes that provide federal revenue. 2. Explain how taxes affect the national economy. 3. Discuss methods of federal borrowing.	Point/Counterpoint: Should the Government Regulate Less Than It Does? pp. 590–591 Participating in Government: Understanding Why We Pay Taxes p. 595 Global Connection: Comparing Governments: Taxation p. 596	Guided Reading Activities Reproducible Lesson Plans Participating in Government 21 Primary and Secondary Source Readings 21 Section 1 Quiz Testmaker Chapter Transparencies 21 SAT Practice Tests Writer's Guidebook
Section 2 Preparing the Federal Budget *pp. 599–604* 1. Relate the roles of executive offices in the preparation of the federal budget. 2. Evaluate the difficulties in balancing the budget. 3. Summarize the steps in congressional budget making.	Focus on Freedom: Articles of Confederation p. 602 Critical Thinking Skills: Analyzing Editorials p. 604	Guided Reading Activities Reproducible Lesson Plans Section 2 Quiz Testmaker Skill Reinforcement Activities 21 SAT Practice Tests Writer's Guidebook
Section 3 Government Spending and the Economy *pp. 605–609* 1. List the main categories of federal spending. 2. Examine the influence of fiscal policy on the economy. 3. Discuss the influence of monetary policy on the economy.	Personal Perspectives: Phil Gramm on Balancing the Budget p. 609	Guided Reading Activities Reproducible Lesson Plans Cooperative Learning Activities 21 Reteaching Activities 21 Enrichment Activities 21 Section 3 Quiz Chapter 21 Tests Testmaker Audio Cassettes (English and Spanish) Limited English Proficiency Activities 21 SAT Practice Tests

If time does not permit teaching this chapter, assign the Chapter 21 summary in the Unit 7 Digest on pages 677–678.

Key To Ability Levels

Teaching strategies have been coded for varying learning styles and abilities.

L1   Level 1 activities are **basic** activities and should be within the ability range of all students.

L2   Level 2 activities are **average** activities and should be within the ability range of the average to above-average student.

L3   Level 3 activities are **challenging** activities designed for the ability range of above-average students.

LEP   These activities should be within the ability range of **Limited English Proficiency** students.

Multicultural Activities

Note that presidential budgets reflect a President's policy priorities. In the 1960s President Johnson, with broad support from minority groups, began a War on Poverty with legal-aid, job-training, and education programs. To pay for these programs, Johnson greatly increased the social welfare budget. The number of people living in poverty dropped from 39.9 million in 1960 to 24.1 million in 1969. In the 1980s President Reagan, who believed in limiting government's role, had different priorities. Although overall spending rose, budgets for such social programs did not. Head Start, however, is one Johnson antipoverty program that remains today. Have students research presidential requests for funding for this program in the 1990s and speculate on the domestic policy priorities funding levels reflect.

According to the *American Political Dictionary* by Jack Plano and Milton Greenberg, entitlements are government benefits to which recipients have legally enforceable rights. Such expenditures make up about 60 percent of government spending. Among the recipients of mandated benefits are 307 Native American groups in the continental United States. Along with some 200 Alaskan village communities, the federally recognized groups are guaranteed federal funds for such services as health, education, and welfare. Many of the payments represent compensation to the Native Americans for treaty violations or past takeovers of Native American land. Others were mandated by the Indian Self-Determination Act of 1975. Have students research the specific federal benefits this statute provides.

Chapter Resources

Readings for the Student

Budgeting for America. Congressional Quarterly, 1982.
Ippolito, Dennis S. *The Budget and National Politics*. Freeman, 1978.
Lubov, Andrea. *Taxes and Government Spending*. Lerner, 1990.
Proxmire, William. *The Fleecing of America*. Houghton Mifflin, 1980.
Watkins, Alfred J. *Red Ink II: A Guide to Understanding the Continuing Deficit Dilemma*. Hamilton Press, 1988.
Wildavsky, Aaron. *The Politics of the Budgetary Process*. Little, Brown, 1980.

Readings for the Teacher

Anderson, Rolf R. *Atlas of the American Economy*. Congressional Quarterly, 1994.
Edsall, Thomas Byrne and Mary D. Edsall. *Chain Reaction: The Impact of Race, Rights, and Taxes on American Politics*. Norton, 1991.
Fallows, James. *National Defense*. Vintage, 1981.
Wildavsky, Aaron. *The Politics of the Budgetary Process*. Little, Brown, 1980.
Woolley, John. *Monetary Politics*. Cambridge University Press, 1984.

Multimedia

Videocassettes
The Power of the Purse: Confrontation in Government. Random House Media/CNN. (v/c, 20 minutes)
Who Pays for AIDS? (*Frontline* series). Martin Smith. (v/c, 60 minutes)

Software
Budget Process: A Question of Balance. Social Studies School Service. (Apple disk, backup, guide, or IBM PC/PCjr disk, backup, guide). Students work through congressional budget process.
NewsWorks—Social Studies Data Base Files. (United States Economy data base). Newsweek. (Apple disk—must be used with AppleWorks data-base program. Apple, Inc.). Students research and analyze data on economy.
PFS: File—United States Government. (Federal Spending data base). Scholastic Publishing Company. (Apple IIe or IIc, at least 64K & 1 disk drive—must be used with *PFS: File, PFS: Report*; 2nd disk drive and printer recommended). Students research, build, and analyze their own data bases.

Taxing and Spending

Introduce

Chapter Overview

Chapter 21 provides an overview of the federal budget process, the sources of federal revenue, and the effects of government spending on the nation's economy. The chapter details how the government tries to influence the nation's economy with its policies.

Section 1 identifies the various taxes that the federal government collects to raise revenue, describes how it borrows to raise revenue, and explains how borrowing is related to the national debt.

Section 2 describes the major steps in the process of making the federal budget.

Section 3 describes the three main spending items of the federal government and explains how the federal government uses fiscal policy and monetary policy to influence the economy.

Chapter 21 Themes

Write the chapter themes and section titles on the chalkboard as a preview of the chapter content. Ask students to hypothesize how these themes may be related to the topic of this chapter.

Each year the United States government must raise large sums of money through taxation to support its activities.

592 UNIT 7: PUBLIC POLICIES AND SERVICES

About the Chapter Opener

Teaching With Illustrations Point out to students that the architecture of the United States Treasury building shown on pages 592–593 reflects the Greek Revival style. Point out that the Department of Treasury is part of the executive branch. Its main function is to manage and oversee the nation's finances. Ask students how the photograph reflects the title of the chapter. *(Students might indicate that the United States Treasury is the building in which many of these decisions are made.)*

Chapter Preview

Overview

The federal government uses fiscal and monetary policies to influence the economy of the United States.

Objectives

After studying this chapter, you should be able to:

1. Identify the federal government's sources of tax revenue.
2. Discuss the role of the federal budget in carrying out the policies of the executive and legislative branches.
3. Evaluate the economic policies of the federal government.

Themes in Government

This chapter emphasizes the following government themes:

- **Civic Responsibility** The federal government depends on taxpayers to finance its many services. Section 1.
- **Public Policy** The federal government uses taxes, the budget, and monetary policy to influence the economy. Sections 1, 2, and 3.
- **Political Processes** The political goals of Congress and the President often affect economic decisions. Section 2.
- **Federalism** The federal government provides revenue to states and localities. Section 3.

Critical Thinking Skills

This chapter emphasizes the following critical thinking skills:

- Making Generalizations
- Identifying Alternatives
- Analyzing Information
- Expressing Problems Clearly

CHAPTER 21: TAXING AND SPENDING   593

Introducing the Chapter

To help students understand why governments need money, ask them to imagine that they have just been appointed to the budget committee of their student government, which is responsible for supporting all extracurricular activities at the school. Ask the students to suggest expenses they might incur. Discuss where the money to pay these expenses might come from. Point out that rising costs must be considered in projecting a budget. Tell students that this chapter explains how the federal government conducts the budgeting process.

Chapter Project

Throughout their study of this chapter, ask students to clip articles pertaining to the federal budget from newspapers and magazines. Have them make a list of the current issues concerning the budget.

> **Linking Past and Present**
> When taxes were first collected by the federal government, there was debate about where federal funds should be held. At the suggestion of Treasury secretary Alexander Hamilton, Congress voted to charter a Bank of the United States. Today, the Federal Reserve System carries out many of the functions of Hamilton's national bank.

Setting the Scene Although the Articles of Confederation gave Congress spending power, the power to tax did not come until the Constitution was ratified. The federal government moved quickly to exercise its new authority. In 1789 Congress levied a tariff, and in 1791 a domestic tax, an excise tax on whiskey. When some people resisted this tax, President Washington ordered 12,900 troops to crush the Whiskey Rebellion, showing that government would not tolerate behavior of the kind that preceded the Revolution. But this display of federal power also increased support for a group led by Thomas Jefferson, who called for a limited government.

Focus

Bell Ringer

Write the following on the chalkboard for students to answer:

List some of the different kinds of taxes people pay.

Motivating Activity

List students' Bell Ringer responses on the chalkboard. Then discuss with students the kinds of benefits that are provided by the federal government. *(Students might indicate social security, welfare programs, national parks, and the armed forces.)* Ask how the federal government is able to provide these benefits. Tell students that this section describes the government's revenue sources.

Vocabulary Precheck

Write the terms and concepts on the chalkboard. Ask students to use those that they know in sentences. **LEP**

Caption Answer

income minus deductions and personal exemptions

CONNECTIONS

Economics
The federal government's annual expenses have exceeded $1 trillion for the last few years. If you were able to spend $1 million every day, you would need nearly 3,000 years to spend $1 trillion.

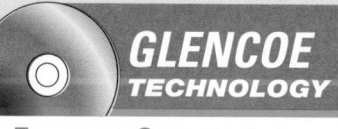

GLENCOE TECHNOLOGY

Focus on Government
Video 40
Lecture Launcher:
Taxing and Spending
Running Time: 3:44
Videodisc 3, Chap. 40
VHS Tape 3, Begins 0:00

SECTION

1

How the Government Raises Money

The federal government plays a major role in the United States economy. The amount of money the government collects in revenues and the government's budget are calculated in figures too large for most people to comprehend. In a recent year the national government took in almost $1.5 trillion in revenues. That figure represents an average of almost $6,000 for each person in the nation. What are the sources of all this money? Two major ones are taxes and borrowing.

Taxes as a Source of Revenue

Benjamin Franklin once said, "In this world, nothing is certain but death and taxes." **Taxes** are payments by individuals and businesses to support the activities of government. The Constitution states that Congress

Shall have power to lay and collect taxes, duties, imposts, and excises, and to pay the debts and provide for the common defence [sic] and general welfare of the United States. . . .

—Article I, Section 8

Today, taxes are the chief way the federal government raises money.

Individual Income Tax The individual income tax is the federal government's biggest single source of revenue. About 45 cents of every dollar the government collects comes from this source. In a recent year, the individual income tax produced more than $450 billion.

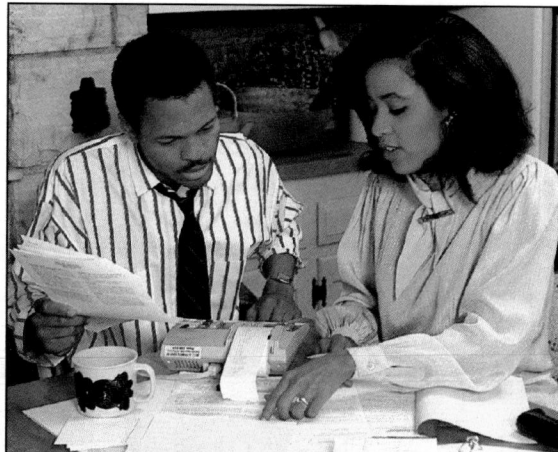

A Long, Sometimes Painful, Chore
Many taxpayers need help filling out their forms.
Math How is taxable income computed?

The income tax is levied on a person's **taxable income**, or the total income of an individual minus certain deductions and personal exemptions. People may take deductions for contributions made to charity, state and local income taxes paid, home mortgage interest, and other expenses. The government also permits deductions for personal exemptions based on the number of people who are dependent on the wage earner who pays the income tax. A **dependent** is one who depends primarily on another person for such things as food, clothing, and shelter.

The income tax is a progressive tax, one based on a taxpayer's ability to pay—the higher a person's income, the higher the tax rate. People with higher incomes,

SECTION PREVIEW

Objectives
After studying this section, you should be able to:
■ Identify the main taxes that provide federal revenue.
■ Explain how taxes affect the national economy.

■ Discuss methods of federal borrowing.

Key Terms and Concepts
taxes, taxable income, dependent, withholding, social insurance taxes, excise taxes, customs duties, estate tax, tax credits, securities, national debt

Themes in Government
■ Civic Responsibility
■ Public Policy

Critical Thinking Skills
■ Making Generalizations
■ Identifying Alternatives

594 Unit 7: Public Policies and Services

Classroom Resources for Section 1

however, can often take advantage of certain deductions not available to those in lower tax brackets.

The deadline for filing income tax returns each year is April 15. Nearly everyone with taxable income in the preceding calendar year must file income tax returns by that date. During the year employers withhold a certain amount of money from the wages of people who earn salaries. This **withholding** pays the anticipated taxes ahead of the April 15 filing date. Self-employed people—business owners and professionals—who do not receive regular salaries are expected to file estimates of their income four times a year and make payments with each estimate. In this way those taxpayers who owe large amounts in taxes avoid having to make one large annual payment on April 15. At the same time, the government receives a steady flow of income taxes throughout the year.

Taxpayers send income tax returns to one of 10 regional Internal Revenue Service (IRS) centers. The IRS, a bureau of the United States Treasury Department, collects these taxes. The IRS receives and processes about 200 million returns and supplemental documents each year. IRS staff members and computers quickly check each return. They audit, or check more closely, a small percentage of returns each year.

The IRS also investigates many suspected criminal violations of the tax laws each year.

Corporate Income Tax Corporations, as well as individuals, must pay income taxes. The federal government taxes all earned income of a corporation beyond its expenses and deductions. Corporate income taxes represent about 10 percent of federal government revenues. Churches, colleges, labor unions, and other nonprofit organizations are exempt from this tax.

Social Insurance Taxes The federal government collects huge sums of money each year to pay for social security, medicare, and unemployment compensation programs. The taxes collected to pay for these major social programs are called **social insurance taxes**. Employees and employers share equally in paying the tax for social security and medicare. Employers deduct it directly from each worker's paycheck, add an equal amount, and send the total to the federal government. The unemployment compensation program is a combined federal-state operation financed largely by a federal tax on the payroll of businesses. All these social insurance taxes are often called payroll taxes.

PARTICIPATING IN GOVERNMENT

Understanding Why We Pay Taxes

Did you buy your lunch in the school cafeteria today? Have you visited a national park or historical monument? Does a grandparent receive benefits from social security or medicare? These programs and facilities are examples of federal government expenditures.

Elderly people, disabled people, widows, orphans, college students, veterans, retired workers, and victims of natural disasters all look to the government for financial aid. All citizens depend on the government to protect our country by main-

taining armed forces and military weapons. In addition to these expenses, the government constructs and maintains the highways and transportation systems. It provides money for space exploration and medical research. It maintains recreational areas and provides funds to cities and states to improve and restore run-down neighborhoods.

Tariffs and excise taxes were the early sources of federal revenue. As the role of the federal government grew, so did the need for additional taxes. Today, individual income taxes provide almost half the money the federal government takes in. We all participate in government by paying a share of its expenses.

Investigating Further

Three general principles of taxation are productivity, equity, and elasticity. Find out what these terms mean. Does our federal tax system satisfy these principles? Explain.

CHAPTER 21: TAXING AND SPENDING **595**

Background

Income tax laws have been reformed and changed many times since their adoption in 1913. One of the most drastic changes was the pay-as-you-go system that began in 1943. Before this change taxpayers filed once a year, at which time they paid the income tax owed for the previous year. But people often found it difficult to come up with the lump sum of money, making it a long process for the federal government to collect the taxes owed. The pay-as-you-go system collected the taxes at the source—from the individual's paycheck.

Teach

Guided Practice

L1 Economics Create a chart on the chalkboard to describe the taxes the federal government collects. Headings for the columns should be *type, description,* and *source.* Ask students to name and give a short description of each tax. Ask how social insurance taxes differ from the others they noted. *(not for general fund, returned as direct benefits)* **LEP**

L2 Civic Responsibility Obtain copies of income tax materials from the local post office or the IRS. Have students study and discuss them. Show students how to use the tax tables. Show how tax rates become higher as incomes increase. Note the kinds of deductions taxpayers can take.

PARTICIPATING IN GOVERNMENT

Some economists believe that taxation should satisfy the principle of *neutrality*—that the taxes people pay should not affect how much they spend or save. Ask how important this principle should be when government sets tax rates. What other factors must government consider?

Allow time for students to present their **Investigating Further** answers.

Have students complete activity 21 in *Participating in Government* in the Teacher's Classroom Resources.

GLOBAL CONNECTION

Point out that the governments of Great Britain and Sweden provide many benefits to their people. For example, both countries provide free medical care, and Sweden also guarantees a four-week paid vacation for all workers. Ask students how such benefits might explain the amount of taxes paid by citizens in these countries.

Examining the Connection:
Allow time for students to explain their answers.

Interpreting Visuals Display transparency 21 from the *Chapter Transparencies* in the Teacher's Classroom Resources and use the accompanying teaching strategy and student activity to teach federal taxing and spending policies.

Independent Practice

L1 Mathematics Have students create a bar graph showing the amount of net receipts of the federal government from the various types of taxes discussed in this section. (Students might refer to the most recent copy of *The World Almanac and Book of Facts*.) **LEP**

STUDY GUIDE

Theme Answer
These are deducted from workers' pay and not adjusted by annual tax returns.

Critical Thinking Answer
More revenue comes from income tax than from any other tax.

GLOBAL CONNECTION

Comparing Governments

Taxation Income taxes have long been a major source of government revenue in industrial nations. Although tax laws vary greatly from country to country, among the major Western industrial nations only Britons pay higher national income taxes than Americans—based on comparable taxable salaries. Swedes traditionally have paid among the highest income taxes in the world, but in 1991 Sweden changed its laws to rely more heavily on indirect taxes.

Americans also pay indirect taxes—sales and excise taxes, for example. Most other industrial nations use a value-added tax, however, levied at each stage in the production of an item or service. In Sweden the value-added tax generates the largest share of that nation's revenue.

Examining the Connection
Would you be willing to sacrifice some government services to reduce the level of taxation? Explain your answer.

Social insurance taxes have become the fastest growing source of federal income. In 1950 they amounted to only $4 billion. In fiscal year 1991, these taxes brought in about $421 billion. Social insurance taxes are the second largest source of federal tax income, contributing about 36 cents of every dollar collected.

Unlike other taxes, social insurance taxes do not go into the government's general money fund. Instead, they go to Treasury Department special trust accounts. Congress then appropriates money from these accounts to pay out benefits. Social insurance taxes are regressive taxes because lower-income people usually pay a larger portion of their income for these taxes than do higher-income people.

Excise Taxes Taxes on the manufacture, transportation, sale, or consumption of goods and the performance of services are called **excise taxes**. The Constitution permits levying excise taxes, and since 1789 Congress has placed taxes on a variety of goods. Some early targets for excise taxes were carriages, snuff, and liquor. Today the government imposes excise taxes on gasoline, oil, tires, cigars, cigarettes, liquor, airline tickets, long-distance telephone service, and many other things. Some excise taxes are called luxury taxes because they are levied on goods such as cigarettes and liquor, not considered necessities. Excise taxes contribute less than $40 billion a year to the federal government, with taxes on liquor and tobacco bringing in the most income.

Customs Duties Taxes levied on goods imported into the United States are called **customs duties**, tariffs, or import duties. The federal government imposes customs duties to raise revenue or to help protect the nation's industry, business, and agriculture from foreign competition.

The Constitution gives Congress the authority to levy customs duties. Congress can decide which foreign imports will be taxed and at what rate. Congress, in turn, has given the President authority by executive order to raise or lower the existing tariff rates by as much as 50 percent. Today, the government levies customs duties on thousands of imported items, ranging from diamonds and cameras to wool and shoes.

Before the income tax, customs duties were a major source of federal income. Now they produce about $17 billion a year, or less than 2 cents of every tax dollar collected.

Some customs duties are important, however, because they protect American industry from foreign competition. The government can discourage imports of foreign goods by setting a high customs duty on them. Such a duty is called a protective tariff. Many business, labor, and farm groups strongly support the idea of protective tariffs, especially during business downturns or recessions.

STUDY GUIDE

Themes in Government
Civic Responsibility The IRS investigates many cases where it believes people are cheating on or not paying income taxes. **Why is it** harder to avoid paying social insurance taxes?

Critical Thinking Skills
Making Generalizations What general statement can you make as a result of comparing the revenue from income taxes and other tax sources?

Cooperative Learning Activity

Organize the class into four groups to analyze the two ways to reduce the federal deficit. Assign two groups to research and present arguments for and against raising taxes. Assign two groups to research and present arguments for and against reduced government spending. Allow each group time to prepare their arguments. Then have a representative of each group report their arguments to the class. Have the class evaluate the arguments and decide which method would be best for reducing the deficit.

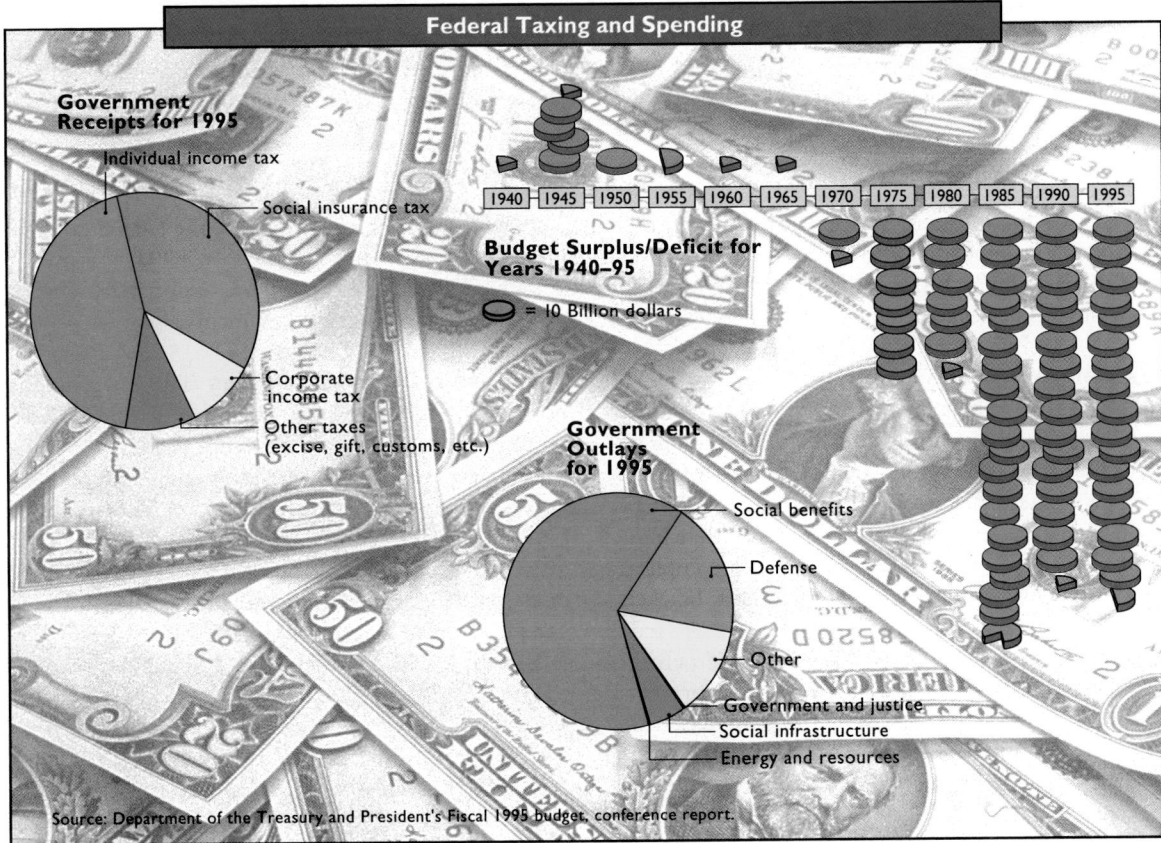

Federal Taxing and Spending

Government Receipts for 1995
- Individual income tax
- Social insurance tax
- Corporate income tax
- Other taxes (excise, gift, customs, etc.)

Budget Surplus/Deficit for Years 1940–95
⬤ = 10 Billion dollars

1940 | 1945 | 1950 | 1955 | 1960 | 1965 | 1970 | 1975 | 1980 | 1985 | 1990 | 1995

Government Outlays for 1995
- Social benefits
- Defense
- Other
- Government and justice
- Social infrastructure
- Energy and resources

Source: Department of the Treasury and President's Fiscal 1995 budget, conference report.

L2 Persuasive Writing Have students write letters to the editor of the local newspaper explaining why federal taxes do (or do not) contribute to the redistribution of wealth in the United States. Discuss students' letters in class.

📁 **Interpreting Source Readings** Have students complete activity 21 in the *Primary and Secondary Source Readings* in the Teacher's Classroom Resources.

STUDY GUIDE

Theme Answer
gasoline, oil, tires, tobacco, liquor, airline tickets, long-distance phone service

Critical Thinking Answer
Although taxes are unpopular, borrowing adds to the national debt and threatens the nation's economic security.

Assess

Check for Understanding
Have students complete Section 1 Review on page 598.

CONNECTIONS

Sociology
The use of the gift tax exclusion to avoid estate taxes is not fully utilized by wealthy people. Studies conducted by the U.S. Treasury show that as few as 60 percent of millionaires make such gifts during their lifetime. Reasons range from fearing loss of control over their assets, to reluctance to plan for their death, to simple ignorance of tax laws.

Estate and Gift Taxes The federal government collects an **estate tax** on the assets (property and money) of a person who dies and a gift tax on gifts of money from a living person. Levied in 1916, the estate tax today is assessed on amounts over $600,000. An individual may give up to $10,000 in any year to another person without paying the gift tax. These taxes redistribute the wealth of families and individuals as well as raise revenue. The gift tax prevents people from avoiding an estate tax by giving money to relatives and friends before death—money given to a spouse is exempt.

The estate tax and the gift tax are progressive taxes—the larger the gift or estate, the higher the tax rate. They bring in about $10 billion a year to the federal treasury.

Taxes and the Economy

The tax laws in the United States are very complex. The federal government sometimes uses taxes to influence economic decisions. For example, individual income tax deductions for home mortgage interest provide an incentive for home ownership and aid the construction industry.

Groups affected by tax increases have sometimes influenced Congress to pass special exemptions in order to reduce the taxes they have to pay. The result is that the tax system contains many special provisions designed to affect certain groups.

Tax Loopholes People who believe that provisions favoring certain groups are unfair often call these ex-

STUDY GUIDE

Themes in Government
Public Policy The federal government first levied many excise taxes that are still in effect as a means of raising emergency income during

World War II. **What items have excise taxes on them?**

Critical Thinking Skills
Identifying Alternatives Why does the government raise most

of its revenues through taxing rather than borrowing?

Critical Thinking Activity

Identifying Alternatives Remind students that the individual income tax is a progressive tax. Ask them if they favor or oppose the principle of a higher tax rate for people who make more money and to give reasons for their opinion. (*Some students might indicate that it would be fairer to tax every-one at the same rate. Other students might indicate that people with higher incomes can more easily afford a higher tax rate.*) Then ask students to develop and evaluate an alternative way of taxing individual incomes.

Meeting Objectives

Each section objective is tested by the Section Review questions that follow it in parentheses.

- Identify the main taxes that provide federal revenue. (2, 3, 4, 5)
- Explain how taxes affect the national economy. (6, 7)
- Discuss methods of federal borrowing. (8)

Evaluate

 Section 1 Quiz

 Testmaker

Reteach

Have students explain how the federal government raises money by writing a summary paragraph for each of the following: *Taxes as a Source of Revenue* and *Borrowing For Revenue*

Enrich

Ask students to research reasons for the large increase in the federal deficit since 1980. Have volunteers present their findings in oral reports to the class.

Close

Have students list the three major sources of federal revenue. Then ask what they think the three most important sources *should* be. Students should provide reasons for their answers.

---

emptions tax loopholes. Some people can afford to hire attorneys and tax specialists who can find loopholes in the complex tax laws. People in high-income brackets have used strategies, such as declaring business losses or investing in tax shelters that enable them to avoid high taxes.

Other exemptions represent government efforts to encourage or support an activity. A tax exemption on oil exploration encourages people to invest their money in businesses searching for new energy sources.

Tax Reforms In 1985 President Reagan proposed tax changes to eliminate what he termed "an endless source of confusion and resentment." After much debate, Congress passed the Tax Reform Act of 1986. The act reduced or ended a confusing variety of tax deductions, tax credits, and tax shelters that many claimed made the old system unfair or too complicated. The act also reduced the number of tax brackets. Depending on their income, individuals were taxed a bottom rate of 15 percent or a top rate of 28 percent.

Since 1986 Congress has added two new brackets. President Clinton's proposal in 1993 increased the top marginal rate to 36 percent. A new 10 percent surtax on higher incomes made the effective top rate 39.6 percent.

Tax Credits The federal government today provides tax credits generally to people in lower income brackets. **Tax credits** allow taxpayers to reduce their income tax liability. Each dollar of tax credit offsets a dollar of tax liability. The earned income credit enables many low-income families to receive refunds. A credit for child and dependent care expenses benefits taxpayers who have daycare for their children

while they work. Certain elderly and retired people may be entitled to a tax credit, depending on the amount of their income.

Borrowing for Revenue

In addition to collecting taxes, the federal government borrows to raise money. In 1991 borrowing amounted to about $276 billion, or about 20 cents of every dollar the federal government raised.

Bonds and Other Securities The government borrows by selling federal securities to individuals, corporations, and other institutions. Government **securities** are financial instruments that include bonds, notes, and certificates. The most popular bonds for small investors are savings bonds. In return for lending the government money, investors earn interest on their bonds. Thus, borrowing costs the federal government a huge amount of interest.

Federal government securities are popular with investors because they are safe. Many people feel that if the national government cannot pay its debts, then the whole national economy will collapse and no company or organization would be able to pay its debts. Investors benefit because interest on some federal government investments is not taxable.

The National Debt When the government's spending is greater than its income, it must borrow and thus go into debt. The total accumulated amount the federal government owes as a result of borrowing is the **national debt**. Government borrowing and the size of the national debt have important effects on the federal budget and the economy.

---

1 SECTION REVIEW

Section Summary
The federal government collects revenue, primarily through taxes, to provide services to the nation.

Checking for Understanding
Recalling Facts
1. Define taxes, taxable income, dependent, withholding, social insurance taxes, excise taxes, customs duties, estate tax, tax credits, securities, national debt.
2. Name the federal government's biggest single source of revenue.
3. Identify who must file an income tax return.
4. List six items that have an excise tax.

Exploring Themes
5. Civic Responsibility By what process is the federal income tax collected?
6. Public Policy How is it possible for the federal government to use the income tax to influence economic decisions?

Critical Thinking Skills
7. Making Generalizations What were the government's primary aims in the Tax Reform Act of 1986?
8. Identifying Alternatives What two measures could the federal government take if the national debt seemed to be growing too fast?

Section 1 Review Answers

1. Definitions of terms appear on pages indicated: **taxes,** 594; **taxable income,** 594; **dependent,** 594; **withholding,** 595; **social insurance taxes,** 595; **excise taxes,** 596; **customs duties,** 596; **estate tax,** 597; **tax credits,** 598; **securities,** 598; **national debt,** 598
2. individual income tax
3. everyone who received taxable income in the preceding calendar year

4. gasoline, oil, tires, cigars, cigarettes, liquor, airline tickets, long-distance telephone service, and many other items
5. Employers withhold estimated taxes from wage earner's pay during the year and send these to the IRS. By April 15 of the following year, each taxpayer must file a return, calculating the exact tax owed.

6. The government may give tax deductions for certain expenses. For example, deductions for home mortgage interest provides an incentive for home ownership and aids the construction industry.
7. to reduce complexities in the tax laws and loopholes that made the old system unfair or too complicated
8. It could increase taxes and/or reduce spending.

Preparing the Federal Budget

In order to predict and control revenue and spending for each year, the federal government uses a budget. The federal budget operates in a **fiscal year**—a 12-month accounting period that extends from October 1 of one year to September 30 of the next.

The budget is also an important policy document. It reflects the federal government's view of the nation's needs and priorities. By showing how much will be spent on various national concerns such as defense and social welfare, it serves as a blueprint for the federal government's spending.

George Washington was able to put all the figures for the national government's first budget on one large sheet of paper. Today the federal budget consists of more than 1,000 pages of small type.

Preparation of the budget involves thousands of people and goes on continuously. Work on a budget starts a full 19 months before a fiscal year begins. Thus, before one year's budget is completed, work on the next year's budget is already under way.

The executive and legislative branches share in the preparation of the budget—an example of checks and balances at work. Under the President's leadership, the executive branch draws up a proposed budget. Congress examines, revises, and finally approves the President's budget proposals.

Making the President's Budget

During much of American history, Presidents have traditionally played a limited role in researching and drawing up the budget. Various federal agencies usu-ally sent their budget requests directly to the secretary of the treasury, who passed them on to Congress.

The Budget and Accounting Act of 1921 changed this procedure. As a result of this law, today the President is responsible for directing the preparation of the budget and making the major decisions about national budget priorities. The law requires the President to propose to Congress the budget for the entire federal government each fiscal year. This budget must be delivered within 15 days after Congress convenes each January.

The actual day-to-day preparation of the budget is the responsibility of the Office of Management and Budget (OMB). The OMB, along with the President's Council of Economic Advisers (CEA), confers with the President on budgetary matters.

Now that Interest Payments are the largest item in the National Budget:

The Pentagon

IOU

The Debtagon

Defensible?
Defense costs often contribute to the national debt.
Economics What causes an unbalanced budget?

SECTION PREVIEW

Objectives
After studying this section, you should be able to:
- Relate the roles of executive offices in the preparation of the federal budget.

- Evaluate the difficulties in balancing the budget.
- Summarize the steps in congressional budget making.

Key Terms and Concepts
fiscal year, uncontrollable, entitlement, incrementalism

Themes in Government
- Political Processes
- Public Policy

Critical Thinking Skills
- Analyzing Information
- Expressing Problems Clearly

CHAPTER 21: TAXING AND SPENDING 599

Bell Ringer

Write the following on the chalkboard for students to answer:

What does it mean to "live within one's means"?

Motivating Activity

Discuss students' Bell Ringer answers. Students may note the importance of having a budget to monitor spending and conflicting demands on limited resources. Ask why it is important for the federal government to have a budget. Then ask students if they think the federal government lives within its means. Tell them that Section 2 will answer this question.

Vocabulary Precheck

List the terms and concepts on the chalkboard. Have students develop questions for which each term or concept is an answer.
`LEP`

Caption Answer
when expenditures exceed income

CONNECTIONS

Language
The word *budget* comes from an ancient French word for a kind of leather bag. The word *fiscal* derives from a Latin word for basket or purse.

Teach

Guided Practice

L1 Political Processes Draw a two-part flow chart to illustrate the budget-making process. Label one part *executive branch* and the other *legislative branch.* Provide four steps inside each part. Between the parts write *January—President submits budget to Congress* and after them *October—budget takes effect.* Have the class complete the chart by listing each branch's steps in creating the federal budget. *(executive—agency requests, OMB review, agency review, presidential review; Congress—committees review, reconciliation, appropriations, GRH cuts)* Have the class assign time frames to the chart. Ask volunteers to detail each step.

STUDY GUIDE

Theme Answer
OMB, Council of Economic Advisers

Critical Thinking Answer
An increasing debt means an increased interest payment, which must be figured into the budget.

Start of the Process Budget making begins in early spring for the budget that is to go into effect a year from the following October. Each federal agency draws up a list of its own spending plans and sends these requests to the OMB. How do the agencies decide how much they need? Aaron Wildavsky, a political scientist, studied the process and concluded:

> *M*ost agencies cannot simply ask for everything they would like to have. . . . They risk a loss of confidence by the Budget Bureau. . . . The result is that . . . [they] seek signals from the environment—supporting interests, their own personnel, current events, last year's actions, attitudes of Congressmen, and so on. . . .
>
> —Aaron Wildavsky, *Political Implications of Budgetary Reform,* 1961

The Director of OMB takes the first set of figures to the President, along with OMB's analysis of the nation's economic situation. At this point the President, assisted by the secretary of the treasury and the CEA, makes key decisions about the impact of the preliminary budget on the administration's general economic policy and goals. They discuss such questions as: Will the budget increase or reduce federal spending? Which federal programs will be cut back and which will be expanded? Will the federal government need to borrow more money? Should taxes be raised or lowered?

Agencies Review Their Budgets The White House returns its decisions on the budget to the agencies and departments with guidelines to help them prepare their final budgets. The Department of Defense, for example, may be told to cut its budget $5 billion, and the Transportation Department may be told it can increase its budget by $1 billion.

Over the next few months, the executive departments and agencies work on detailed budget plans fitting the President's guidelines. During this time OMB officials and agency heads negotiate cuts and additions in each agency's budget.

Final Presidential Review During the fall, the OMB submits a complete budget document to the President for final review and approval. Some last-minute juggling always takes place. Agency heads may make last-ditch efforts to convince the President to overrule an OMB decision and save a particular program. The President may order changes in parts of the budget in response to pressure from interest groups or political party members.

Finally, the administration rushes the President's budget to the printer—often only days or perhaps hours before the January deadline. The President formally sends the budget to Congress along with an annual budget message. Congress then takes the next steps in working out the federal budget.

Uncontrollables Despite having a key role in the process, the President does not have complete freedom in making budgetary decisions. About 70 percent of the federal budget consists of what are called **uncontrollables.** **Uncontrollables** are expenditures required by law or resulting from previous budgetary commitments.

A large portion of the uncontrollables are called **entitlements,** or benefits that Congress has provided by law to individuals, and which they have an established legal right to receive. Entitlements include social security, pensions for retired government employees, medicare, medicaid, and veterans' benefits.

Another item in the budget largely beyond control is the interest that must be paid on the national debt. As yearly budgets have forced the federal government to borrow more and more money, the interest on the debt has grown. In 1991 a national newspaper reported:

> *T*his year it appears interest on the federal debt will be Uncle Sam's single largest expenditure—exceeding even military spending. Interest expense came close to that in fiscal '91. Last year's Defense Department budget: $298.3 billion. Interest on the debt: $288.7 billion.
>
> —Mark Memmott, *USA Today,* October 1, 1991

STUDY GUIDE

Themes in Government
Political Processes During the budget-making process, each agency will try to increase its budget for the upcoming year. **Which two groups work closely with the President on budget matters?**

Critical Thinking Skills
Analyzing Information What is the significance of the newspaper excerpt above in light of a national debt growing larger every year?

Background

Besides social welfare expenditures, the single largest outlay in the federal budget is military spending. The amount of the defense component of the federal budget has, of course, an important impact on inflationary or deflationary trends. But it also often creates a significant regional effect in those areas where employment depends on industries that rely upon defense contracts. The funding of a new weapons system or the continued production of an already deployed system can mean the difference between economic health or economic disaster for a metropolitan area or an entire region.

Congressional Budget Action

Article I, Section 9, of the Constitution requires that Congress approve all federal spending. Thus, the President draws up budget proposals, but only Congress has the power to raise revenue and pass appropriations. No money can be spent and no taxes are collected until Congress approves.

Congress can revise the President's budget proposals as it sees fit. Conflict between Congress and the President over the budget is inevitable. If the opposing party controls either house of Congress, that house will loudly criticize the President's budget. Even if the President's own party controls Congress, lawmakers may have different ideas than the President as to how money should be allocated. Key lawmakers and the President often must negotiate over different parts of the budget. Compromises are usually necessary on both sides before a budget is passed.

Congressional Budget Act of 1974 For years separate subcommittees of the Senate and House handled each agency's requested expenditures. This separation made it difficult for Congress to keep track of the total annual budget. To remedy this situation, Congress passed the Congressional Budget Act in 1974. This law set up House and Senate Budget Committees and a Congressional Budget Office (CBO).

The CBO's job is to carefully evaluate the overall federal budget for Congress. The CBO has its own professional staff of experts. It acts as a counterbalance to the OMB in the executive branch.

Gramm-Rudman-Hollings Act By the mid-1980s the size and growth of the national debt worried economists. In 1985 Congress enacted the Balanced Budget and Emergency Deficit Control Act, known as Gramm-Rudman-Hollings (GRH) after the senators who designed it. This law was aimed at forcing the President and Congress to work together to reduce huge federal budget deficits that had developed by the mid-1980s.

Steps in the Budget-Making Process

18 Months Before Start of Fiscal Year

May	**Preliminary Requests**
June	Agencies submit spending needs and plans to the Office of Management
July	and Budget (OMB).
Aug	**Reappraisal of Preliminary Requests**
Sept	Agencies revise their requests, based on presidential directives.
Oct	
Nov	**Final Presidential Review**
	OMB submits budget to the President
Dec	for final review and approval.

10 Months Before Start of Fiscal Year

Jan	**President's Budget Message**
Feb	President sends proposed budget to Congress for approval.
Mar	**Reappraisal of Preliminary Requests**
Apr	House and Senate Budget Committees review and make adjustments in the
May	President's budget for full congressional approval.
June	**Reconciliation**
July	Spending plans fit with existing programs
Aug	**Gramm-Rudman-Hollings**
Sept	Procedure to fit budget to deficit reduction targets
	Fiscal Year Begins
Oct	**Budget In Effect**
	The agencies may start spending for the next fiscal year, which extends from October 1 of one year to September 30 of the next year.

☑ **Chart Study**
Budget making is governed by the system of checks and balances. **How does the executive branch check the legislative branch?**

L2 **Checks and Balances** Discuss with students how the budget process demonstrates the constitutional principle of checks and balances. Ask how it reflects public policy, one of the government themes for this chapter.

L3 **Public Policy** Ask students to form small groups and discuss the pros and cons of *incrementalism* as a principle in budget making. Have each group develop a position and present a short report to the class that summarizes its discussion.

Independent Practice

L1 **Making a Chart** Ask each student to develop a chart illustrating the roles of the following in the federal budget process: Office of Management and Budget, House Budget Committee, Senate Budget Committee, House of Representatives, Congressional Budget Office. **LEP**

Chart Study Answer
executive prepares budget and makes major decisions on national budget priorities

STUDY GUIDE

Theme Answer
passed the Gramm-Rudman-Hollings Act

Critical Thinking Answer
A budget gives both the opportunity to figure how much income each will have and how much each can allocate to various expenditures.

Cooperative Learning Activity

Organize the class into four groups. Have two groups evaluate the role of the executive branch in the preparation of the federal budget. Have the other groups assess the role of the legislative branch. Have one person in each group take notes on the discussion and report the group's conclusions to the class. Have the class compare each group's findings. Did both groups considering the executive branch reach the same conclusions? the legislative branch groups? Encourage members of each group to challenge the judgments of the other groups.

L2 **Classificatory Writing** Ask students to research and write a report on the federal budget for the current year. Their reports should indicate the agencies to be cut, those with increases, and generalizations about the spending philosophy reflected in the budget.

L3 **Economics** Have students research *zero-base budgeting* and explain why it is an alternative to *incrementalism* in budgeting. Ask students to explain the advantages and disadvantages of incrementalism and zero-base budgeting.

Focus on Freedom

Point out to students that in 1783 a few hundred unpaid soldiers caused Congress to flee the capital at Philadelphia, bringing the national government to a temporary halt. Ask how the lack of a taxing power inhibited the powers given the national government by the Articles.

Answers

1. It gave more power to the states than to the central government.

2. It could not always implement its decisions or priorities.

3. Answers will vary, but may include that in order to receive benefits of living in a society, people pay a portion of their resources to assure services such as transportation, education, and protection.

Assess

Check for Understanding

Have students complete Section 2 Review on page 603.

GRH and later amendments required OMB and CBO to issue a joint report each year estimating how much the proposed budget would exceed income and how much it should be cut to meet deficit reduction targets. The OMB then had authority to make automatic cuts in the final budget if the President and Congress could not agree to do so. As each budget failed to meet its goals, the federal government revised the 1985 GRH deficit-cutting targets. Still under pressure to reduce deficits, in 1990 the White House and Congress agreed on a five-year package of tax hikes and spending cuts. A recession in 1991-1992 slowed federal revenues, again derailing the deficit-cutting plan. The 1993 budget aimed to cut the deficit by $504.8 billion in fiscal 1994-1998. About half the reduction would come from new tax revenue and half from spending cuts.

Key Steps in Congressional Budget Making
The budget-making process is complex but generally follows three steps. First, House and Senate Budget Committees review the major features of the President's budget proposals. On April 15 these committees prepare a concurrent resolution. With the President's proposals as a starting point, this resolution sets forth the total federal spending and tax plan for the coming fiscal year.

The next step, called reconciliation, occurs between April 15 and June 15. During reconciliation various House and Senate committees reconcile, or fit, the spending and taxing plans set out in the concurrent resolution with existing programs. The committees put the changes made during this process in a reconciliation bill that both the House and Senate must approve. The House then passes an appropriations bill,

Focus on Freedom

ARTICLES OF CONFEDERATION

The Articles of Confederation, drafted in 1777 by the Second Continental Congress, was the first document that bound the states together. Most members of the Continental Congress were wary of a strong central government, and the Articles of Confederation reflected this concern. It guaranteed the independence and sovereignty of each state and gave the states all powers not specifically granted to Congress.

Article 8. All charges of war, and all other expenses that shall be incurred for the common defense of general welfare and allowed by the United States in Congress assembled shall be defrayed out of a common treasury, which shall be supplied by the several states, in proportion to the value of all land within each state, granted to or surveyed for any person, as such land and the buildings and improvements thereon shall be estimated according to such mode as the United States in Congress assembled shall from time to time direct and appoint. The taxes for paying that proportion shall be laid and levied by the authority and direction of the legislatures of the several states within the time agreed upon by the United States in Congress assembled.

Congress, then, could not levy taxes but depended upon the states themselves to raise income. During the period between 1781 and 1789, the states supplied Congress with only one-sixth of the funds it requested. This played havoc with foreign trade and even prevented soldiers from

receiving their pay at times. The Articles did give Congress the authority

To ascertain the necessary sums of money to be raised for the service of the United States, and to appropriate and apply the same for defraying the public expenses; to borrow money or emit [print and circulate] bills on the credit of the United States, transmitting every half year to the respective states an account . . .

Examining the Document

Reviewing Facts
1. Explain how the Articles of Confederation reflected the writers' dislike of a strong central government.
2. State a result of the weak central government under the Articles of Confederation.

Critical Thinking Skills
3. Demonstrating Reasoned Judgment Congress can levy taxes. Many people complain about taxes. What value do you see in them?

602   UNIT 7: PUBLIC POLICIES AND SERVICES

Special Needs Strategy

Study Strategy Practice in note-taking helps students with organizational and reasoning problems develop abilities to make judgments about what is important and what is unimportant in their reading. Ask students to choose five words or phrases from this section which represent important ideas on the preparation of the budget, such as *fiscal year,*

agencies review their budgets, presidential review, compromise, reconciliation. Discuss students' choices and ask them what ideas or processes they had to leave out. Then have each student write three or four sentences about the budget-making process using their own choices.

officially setting aside money for all expenditures approved through the reconciliation process. Congress is supposed to complete this bill by June 30, but it is often delayed.

The final step in the budget process involves the procedures spelled out in the GRH Act. The fiscal year begins on October 1. On October 15 the OMB issues a final report and may make cuts in the budget if needed to fit deficit reduction targets.

Incremental Budget Making

Some political scientists use the term *incrementalism* to explain the budget-making process. **Incrementalism** means that generally the total budget changes only a little (an increment) from one year to the next. Thus, the best forecaster of this year's budget is last year's budget, plus a little more.

Incrementalism means that most of the time federal agencies can assume they will get at least the same amount they received in the previous year. Incrementalism also means that most budget debates focus on a proposed increment or reduction for an agency. For example, budget battles rarely center on whether the FBI should continue to exist, but rather on how much of an increase or decrease the FBI should get for the particular year.

Of course, some exceptions do occur. In the 1960s, for example, President John F. Kennedy gave the space program high priority. He set the goal of landing astronauts on the moon before the end of the 1960s. Congress accepted the idea and appropriated huge amounts of money for a new space program and

On Guard
The 1980s saw a rise in military spending.
Economics **What factors have affected the military budget?**

agencies such as the National Aeronautics and Space Administration (NASA).

A budget may reflect a President's specific policy. President Reagan's budget proposals in 1981 and 1982 called for slower growth in spending for some social programs and increases in the rate of defense spending. Congress approved the first of these budgets but passed the second with significant modifications. After relations with the Soviet Union improved, the federal government began to reduce defense spending.

2 SECTION REVIEW

Section Summary
The federal budget spells out tax and spending plans for the fiscal year.

Checking for Understanding
Recalling Facts
1. Define fiscal year, uncontrollable, entitlement, incrementalism.
2. Summarize the importance of the budget as a guide to government policies each year.
3. List four entitlements that are a part of the federal budget.
4. Identify the office that counterbalances the Office of Management and Budget.

Exploring Themes
5. Political Processes How is the budget process affected if Congress and the President are from different political parties?
6. Public Policy Why does the budget change little from one year to the next?

Critical Thinking Skills
7. Analyzing Information What budgetary decisions would the federal government face if an international development threatened world peace?
8. Expressing Problems Clearly Why is it so difficult for the federal government to reduce spending or raise taxes in order to balance the budget?

Section 2 Review Answers

1. Definitions of terms appear on pages indicated: **fiscal year,** 599; **uncontrollable,** 600; **entitlement,** 600; **incrementalism,** 603
2. The budget determines all federal spending for the coming year. The President makes the major decisions about national budget priorities. Congress examines, revises, and approves the President's budget proposals.
3. social security, veterans' benefits, pensions for federal employees, medicare, medicaid.
4. the Congressional Budget Office (CBO)
5. The process is slower and more difficult because both must agree on a budget and each may have different priorities.
6. Incrementalism means that each agency receives an amount based on the previous year's spending. Some changes occur, but few agencies are either discontinued or greatly enlarged.
7. The government would have to decide whether to in-
crease defense spending. If it did so, the government would have to decide whether to raise taxes, borrow more money, or reduce spending in other programs to pay for the defense increase.
8. Elected officials are unwilling to take the political risks. Slowing the growth of entitlements or cutting the favorite programs of special interests would mean a loss of campaign support. Raising taxes could mean defeat for a President or members of Congress.

Meeting Objectives
Each section objective is tested by the Section Review questions that follow it in parentheses.
• Relate the roles of executive offices in the preparation of the federal budget. (2, 4, 6)
• Evaluate the difficulties in balancing the budget. (3, 6, 7, 8)
• Summarize the steps in congressional budget making. (4, 5, 6)

Evaluate
📁 Section 2 Quiz
🔒 Testmaker

Reteach
Have students chart the steps in the budget-making process.

Enrich
Have students write a book report on *The Education of David Stockman and Other Americans* by William Greider.

Close

Discuss why it is important for citizens to be informed about the government's budget activities.

SOCIAL STUDIES SKILLS

Focus

Have each student take a stance on the following issue, writing their opinions in a paragraph:

Students should pay for participation in varsity sports.

Gather the paragraphs and read several aloud. What positions do students take? Do students with experiences in school sports programs tend to have similar opinions? Discuss how a person's experiences may affect the opinions they hold.

Teach

Ask a volunteer to explain the difference between a news story and an editorial. Point out that learning to analyze editorials is an important skill for an informed citizen. Discuss the Explanation steps. Then ask: After determining the topic of an editorial, what should a reader look for? *(loaded words and other devices that try to persuade the reader)* Does an editorial give a balanced view? Why or why not? *(No; the purpose is to persuade.)*

Assess

Have students complete the **Practice** exercise.

Close

Discuss why newspapers include editorials, pointing out that news organizations may have financial or political interests they wish to protect.

Analyzing Editorials

American newspapers have a long tradition of taking stands on important issues. Editors make a sharp distinction between news stories, which make up most of the contents of the daily paper, and editorials, which are placed in a special section. Unlike a news story, whose purpose is to inform, the purpose of an editorial is to persuade the reader to accept a certain point of view.

Explanation

To analyze an editorial, follow these steps:
* Determine what topic is being discussed.
* Read the editorial carefully to find out what opinion the editors are expressing on that topic.
* Note the arguments and evidence they present to back up their opinion.
* Decide whether you think the editorial is persuasive. Ask: Do I have enough information to form an opinion on this issue?

Consider the following editorial, which appeared in the *Buffalo News*, April 13, 1991.

You could almost hear the wails from coast to coast, . . . of all those members of Congress protesting Defense Secretary Richard Cheney's proposal that 43 military installations . . . be closed . . . over the next five years or six years. . . .

The Soviet collapse has changed our defense needs and created an opportunity for savings in a time of huge deficits. . . .

Decisions on base closings should turn solely on their usefulness—or lack of it—to national defense.

The topic under discussion in this editorial is presented in the first paragraph: Defense Secretary Richard Cheney had proposed that dozens of military bases be shut down or scaled back in order to cut government costs. The purpose of the editorial is to express the editors' support for Cheney's proposal. The arguments they present to back up their opinion are (1) that changes in the Soviet Union

have made it possible for the United States to cut its military spending and that such cuts are necessary to reduce the budget deficit; (2) that if a base is not necessary to the national defense, it should be closed down without regard to other considerations.

The final step is to decide whether or not you agree with the opinion expressed. You may decide that you need more information in order to make a decision. For example, you might want to know more about how decisions were made to close these particular bases.

Practice

Read the following editorial, which appeared in the *Boston Herald* on February 6, 1991. Then answer the questions that follow.

We've all gotten used to the weary rhythm of federal budget-making. . . .

It's a sloppy, overlong, and inefficient procedure. If a corporation allowed its finances to be cobbled together in such a . . . manner, you'd expect it to end up deeply in debt. . . .

The plan he [President Bush] proposed Monday calls for . . . a deficit of $318 billion. . . . This is the result of last year's "budget reduction" package. . . . It was a pipe dream. As we and others warned, whenever the government's revenues are increased, it spends more than the increase.

1. What topic is being discussed?
2. What opinion do the editors express?
3. What evidence and arguments do they present to back up their opinion?
4. Do you have enough information to make a decision about whether you agree with the editors' point of view? If not, what more information would you like?

Additional Practice

To practice this skill, see **Reinforcing the Skill** on page 611.

Practice Answers

1. the federal budget proposed by President Bush
2. Sloppy and inefficient budgeting procedures are responsible for the debt.
3. Raising taxes has not decreased but increased the budget deficit because the more revenue the government has, the more it spends.

4. Students might say they would like to know more of the particulars of the proposed budget.

For additional practice, have students complete activity 21 in *Skill Reinforcement Activities* in the Teacher's Classroom Resources.

SECTION 3
Government Spending and the Economy

The way the federal government spends hundreds of billions of dollars each year has a significant bearing on the economy. Federal officials know that when serious economic troubles disrupt people's lives, they generally vote against those who are in office. The legislature and the executive branch make difficult decisions to try to promote a healthy economy.

Where the Money Goes

The federal government was spending about $3 billion a year before Franklin D. Roosevelt became President in 1933. Today, that amount would pay for about one day of the federal government budget. The government currently spends more than $1 trillion a year.

How can a person imagine such a large amount of money? Perhaps it is more meaningful to break the total amount down into its four major components. Besides interest on the national debt, the main spending items are direct benefit payments to individuals, national defense, and grants to state and local communities.

Direct Benefit Payments Spending for social security, social-welfare, and health-care programs has become one of the biggest items in the federal budget. Almost half of every dollar spent goes for such items. In a recent budget, the federal government allocated about $600 billion for direct benefit payments of one kind or another.

Uncontrollable expenditures make up a large amount of this budget item. The biggest entitlement program is social security. In a recent year social security benefits totaled $230 billion.

National Defense Spending for national defense has been one of the biggest items in the budget since the beginning of World War II. About 19 cents of every dollar spent goes for national defense. Limiting defense spending is difficult for the President and Congress. One reason is that modern weapons systems are very costly. In addition, events around the world beyond the United States' control often influence defense spending.

When Ronald Reagan became President in 1981, he made a bigger Defense Department budget a major objective of his administration. He felt that the world situation called for further increases in spending for military equipment, training, and weapons.

When sweeping changes in the Soviet Union and Eastern Europe signaled an end to the cold war, President Bush announced major changes in United States defense. He said he would eliminate some nuclear weapons and end the round-the-clock alert posture of strategic bombers. In a nationally broadcast address the President said:

We can now take steps to make the world a less dangerous place than ever before in the nuclear age. I have asked the Soviets to go down this road with us—to destroy their entire inventory of ground-launched theater nuclear weapons.
—PRESIDENT GEORGE BUSH, SEPTEMBER 27, 1991

SECTION PREVIEW

Objectives
After studying this section, you should be able to:
- List the main categories of federal spending.
- Examine the influence of fiscal policy on the economy.

- Discuss the influence of monetary policy on the economy.

Key Terms and Concepts
fiscal policy, monetary policy, gross national product (GNP), discount rate, reserve requirement, open-market operations

Themes in Government
- Federalism
- Public Policy

Critical Thinking Skills
- Identifying Alternatives
- Analyzing Information

CHAPTER 21: TAXING AND SPENDING **605**

Classroom Resources for Section 3

- Guided Reading Activities
- Reproducible Lesson Plans
- Cooperative Learning Activities 21
- Reteaching Activities 21
- Enrichment Activities 21
- Section 3 Quiz

- Chapter 21 Tests
- Testmaker
- Audio Cassettes (English and Spanish)
- Limited English Proficiency Activities 21
  SAT Practice Tests

Chapter 21, Section 3
Lesson Plan, pages 605–609

Focus

Bell Ringer

Have students rank what they think should be the federal government's top five spending priorities.

Motivating Activity

Discuss students' Bell Ringer responses. Then choose one of the federal government's major expenses—direct benefit payments, national defense, or grants to states and local governments. Ask students to predict the domestic consequences if severe spending cuts were made in that area. Tell students that Section 3 explains how government spending affects the nation's economy.

Vocabulary Precheck

Ask students to speculate on the meaning of each term and concept. Then have them check their guesses by finding the definition in the section text. **LEP**

Teach

Guided Practice

L1 Concept Mapping Help students make a concept map of the three major categories of federal government spending. Write *Where the Money Goes* on the chalkboard and draw a circle around it. Then, as students give the major categories, draw lines from the circle and add these categories at the ends. Ask students to provide specific examples for each category. **LEP**

GLENCOE TECHNOLOGY

Focus on Government
Video 43
Making Connections: Changes in Government Spending
Running Time: 2:16
Videodisc 3, Chap. 43
VHS Tape 3, Begins 10:41

Chapter 21: Taxing and Spending **605**

📁 **Group Debate** Organize groups to complete activity 21 on reducing the deficit in *Cooperative Learning Activities* in the Teacher's Classroom Resources.

L3 Economics Present the economic problems below. Ask how the Federal Reserve might react to each problem and why it would take that action.

a. prices rising rapidly *(raise reserve requirement/discount rate, sell securities—cut money supply and inflation)*
b. unemployment rising *(lower reserve requirement/discount rate, buy securities—increase money supply and borrowing for expansion and jobs)*
c. automobiles, houses, and other "big ticket" items not selling *(lower reserve requirement/discount rate—reduce interest rates and encourage borrowing)*

STUDY GUIDE

Critical Thinking Answers
Answers may include: reduce size of military, cut back overseas commitment, slow development of new weapons systems.

so that it may consider the nation's economic interests free of political pressure

---

Grants to States and Localities The federal government sends a sizable portion of its tax revenues back to state and local governments. These governments use federal money for a great variety of purposes such as road repair, public housing, police equipment and training, school lunch programs, flood insurance, mental health services, and so on.

States and communities have come to rely on this intergovernmental revenue for an increasing share of their total revenue. Between 1980 and 1989, however, the percentage of federal funds granted to state and local governments declined. More recent federal budgets have increased federal aid to states while shifting federal grants away from infrastructure investments and toward public-welfare programs.

Managing the Economy

Beginning with the Great Depression of the 1930s, the federal government has taken an increasing role in managing the nation's economy. Arguments continue over just how much of a part the government should play in the economy. Debates arise because in the modified free enterprise system control over the economy is divided between government and the private sector—individuals and business. Yet most Americans expect the federal government to play a significant role in moderating the economy's ups and downs, while promoting steady economic growth.

The government uses two primary devices to influence the direction of the economy: (1) fiscal policy and (2) monetary policy. **Fiscal policy** involves using government spending and taxation to influence the economy. **Monetary policy** involves controlling the supply of money and credit to influence the economy. This control is exercised through the Federal Reserve System.

Fiscal Policy The federal budget is a major tool of fiscal policy because it shapes how much money the government will spend and how much the government will collect through taxes and borrowing. The President and Congress can use the budget to pump money into the economy in order to stimulate it or to take money out of the economy in order to slow it down.

To stimulate the economy, the government may spend more money than it takes in. Through increased spending the government aims to put more people back to work and increase economic activity.

Another way that the government could stimulate the economy is through reducing taxes. Lower taxes give consumers and investors more purchasing power.

When the government increases spending or reduces taxes, it is likely to run a deficit because it must spend money that it does not have. Since the 1930s the United States has had deficit, or unbalanced, federal budgets most of the time. One reason for these deficits is that for many years these unbalanced budgets were thought to benefit the economy. In addition, this policy was very popular politically because it allowed the government to spend heavily on social programs that many Americans were demanding.

This policy of deficit spending led to increasingly large budget deficits and a growing national debt. During the 1970s and early 1980s, economists began to worry about the effects this would have on the nation's future.

Demands for cutting the deficit and even balancing the budget grew. Many economists, however, criticized this idea. They argued that a balanced budget would mean the federal government could not use fiscal policy to shape the economy. Some said that the deficit as a percentage of the **gross national product (GNP)** was more important than the deficit alone. The GNP is the sum of all goods and services produced by American companies in a year. They pointed out that the deficit still represented only 5 to 6 percent of the GNP.

Other economists disagreed. They pointed to the rapid growth of the deficit and of the national debt itself. When Congress promised to balance the budget in 1981, the deficit was $79 billion. By 1991 it had reached $269 billion.

Deficits swelled the national debt. The United States entered World War II with a national debt of about $40 billion. The government emerged from

STUDY GUIDE

Themes in Government
Federalism A 1946 law spelled out the federal government's responsibility to promote national economic health.
Public Policy Some feel that reduced defense spending should result in a "peace dividend."

Critical Thinking Skills
Identifying Alternatives What actions could further reduce defense spending?

Analyzing Information Why must the Fed operate free of pressures from the President or Congress?

Background

Economists often disagree over the extent to which government spending causes inflation in any particular period of time. There is general agreement, however, that the level of federal expenditures and indebtedness is an extremely important factor in the stability of prices. One of the most important governmental tools available to fight inflation is the monetary policies set by the Federal Reserve Board, which administers the Federal Reserve System.

the war owing about $260 billion. By 1994 the national debt of nearly $5 trillion demanded interest payments of more than $300 billion each year, making the job of budgeting even more difficult.

Monetary Policy The United States economy is a money economy. Americans exchange goods and services through a vast system of money and credit. The Constitution gives the national government authority to "coin money [and] regulate the value thereof." Today, the federal government tries to regulate the economy through its monetary policy.

Monetary policy involves controlling the supply of money and the cost of borrowing money—credit—according to the needs of the economy. The government does this through the Federal Reserve System.

The Federal Reserve System

The Federal Reserve System, known as the Fed, is the central banking system of the United States. When people or corporations need money they may borrow from a bank. When banks need money they may go to the Fed. The Federal Reserve System is a banker's bank.

Organization of the Fed The United States is divided into 12 Federal Reserve Districts. Each district has one main Federal Reserve Bank. Most Federal Reserve Banks also have branches in their districts.

About 5,000 of the approximately 12,000 banks in the United States are members of the Federal Reserve System. These include all the large, important banks

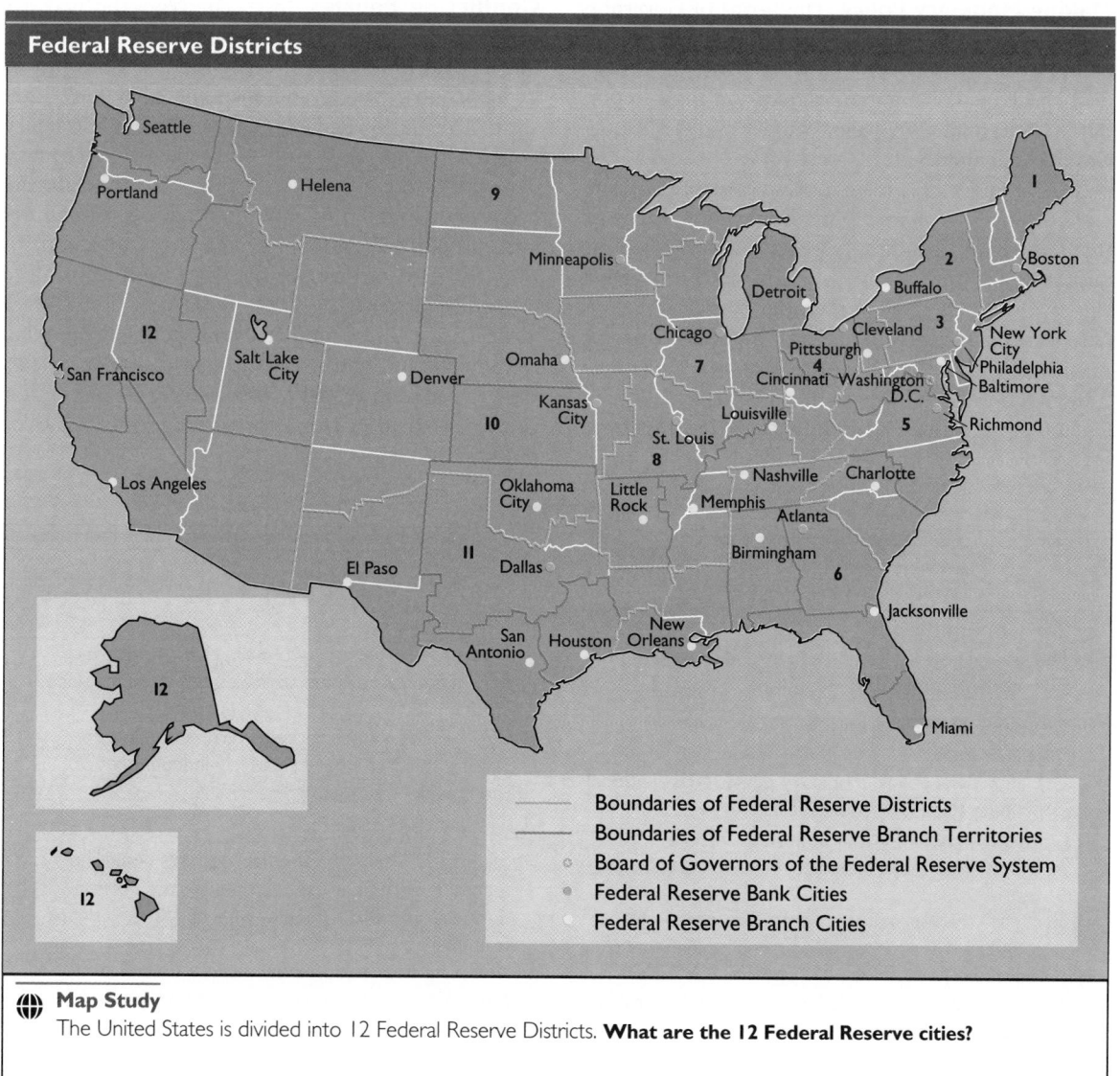

Federal Reserve Districts

- —— Boundaries of Federal Reserve Districts
- —— Boundaries of Federal Reserve Branch Territories
- ○ Board of Governors of the Federal Reserve System
- ● Federal Reserve Bank Cities
- ● Federal Reserve Branch Cities

Map Study
The United States is divided into 12 Federal Reserve Districts. **What are the 12 Federal Reserve cities?**

Cooperative Learning Activity

Organize the class into four groups and ask each group to assume one of the following roles: small business owners, persons living on fixed incomes, persons with investment incomes, workers in a large factory. Have each group determine how the Federal Reserve Board should respond to these economic conditions: prosperity with high interest rates and high prices; recession with low interest rates and falling prices. Have a member of each group report its conclusions to the class. *(Some groups may have difficulty reaching consensus, demonstrating economic cross-pressures and the mixed consequences of changing monetary policy.)*

Independent Practice

L1 Informative Writing Ask students to provide a newspaper or magazine illustration of a federal government activity that affects the nation's economy. Have them write a paragraph that identifies the activity and explains its economic impact. **LEP**

L2 Mathematics Have students use library resources, such as the most recent copy of the *Statistical Abstract of the United States*, to make a graph showing the percentage of total federal expenditures for national defense since 1970. Have students write several generalizations about government spending on national defense based on their graph.

L3 Informative Writing Have students gather information from library sources and government publications to write a report concerning the organization and responsibilities of the Federal Reserve Board and its impact on economic and monetary policies.

CONNECTIONS

History
President Woodrow Wilson pressured Congress to pass the Federal Reserve Act of 1913, which overhauled the nation's banking and currency system.

Caption Answer
San Francisco, Minneapolis, Kansas City, Dallas, St. Louis, Chicago, Atlanta, Cleveland, Philadelphia, New York City, Boston, Richmond

Assess

Check for Understanding

Have students complete Section 3 Review on page 608.

Meeting Objectives

Each section objective is tested by the Section Review questions that follow it in parentheses.

- List the main categories of federal spending. (2, 3, 5)
- Examine the influence of fiscal policy on the economy. (4, 6, 7, 8)
- Discuss the influence of monetary policy on the economy. (6, 7, 8)

Evaluate

📁 Section 3 Quiz

💻 Testmaker

Reteach

Ask students to explain how policymakers use fiscal and monetary policies to manage the economy.

📁 Have students complete activity 21 in *Reteaching Activities* in the Teacher's Classroom Resources.

Enrich

📁 Have students complete activity 21 in *Enrichment Activities* in the Teacher's Classroom Resources.

Close

Ask: When the federal government increases spending to stimulate the economy, on what categories should it spend? Why?

---

in the country. These member banks control the largest share of total bank deposits in the United States.

Board of Governors A seven-member Board of Governors in Washington, D.C., supervises the entire Federal Reserve System. The President appoints these members with Senate consent. The President selects one of the board members to chair the Board of Governors for a four-year term.

Once appointed, board members and the chairperson are independent of the President. Even Congress exercises little control or influence over the board, since the board does not depend on Congress for an annual appropriation for operating expenses.

Making Monetary Policy The Board of Governors has two major responsibilities. First, it supervises the operations of the Federal Reserve Banks in the 12 districts across the country. Second, and most important, it determines the general money and credit policies of the United States.

The Fed uses three main tools to control the financial activities of the nation's banks and, through them, the nation's monetary policy. First, the Fed can raise or lower the discount rate. The **discount rate** is the rate the Fed charges member banks for loans. Low discount rates encourage banks to borrow money from the Fed to make loans to their customers. High discount rates mean banks will borrow less money from the Fed and thus have less money to loan.

Second, the Fed may raise or lower the **reserve requirement** for member banks. Member banks must keep a certain percentage of their money in Federal Reserve Banks as a reserve against their deposits. If the Fed raises the reserve requirement, banks must leave more money with the Fed. Thus, they have less money to lend. When the Fed lowers the reserve requirement, member banks have more money to lend.

Third, and most important, the Fed can put money into the economy by buying government bonds and other securities on the open market. These actions are known as **open-market operations.** The Fed may also sell government securities. As investors spend their money on these securities, money is taken out of the economy.

Conflicting Policies In recent years the Fed has become an important and independent policy-making institution. While the President and Congress largely control taxing and spending, they have little control over the Fed, which determines monetary policy. Thus, the Fed's policy may aid or hinder presidential and congressional attempts to stimulate the economy. Conflicting economic policies sometimes arise, causing Presidents or Congress to complain that the Fed is interfering with their economic programs.

Because of such conflicts, some people would like to limit the Fed's role and make it less independent. Others maintain that the nation needs an institution removed from political pressures to watch over monetary policy.

---

3 SECTION REVIEW

Section Summary
The federal government uses fiscal and monetary policy to control the national economy.

Checking for Understanding
Recalling Facts
1. Define fiscal policy, monetary policy, gross national product (GNP), discount rate, reserve requirement, open-market operations.
2. List the four main federal government spending categories.
3. Specify the approximate percentage of federal spending that goes for direct benefit payments to individuals.
4. Identify two ways the federal government uses fiscal policy to stimulate the economy.

Exploring Themes
5. Federalism What are two changes in the distribution of federal revenue to states and localities since 1980?
6. Public Policy Why has the government made the Federal Reserve Board relatively independent of the President and Congress?

Critical Thinking Skills
7. Identifying Alternatives What methods could the federal government use to stimulate the economy during a time when people were opposed to deficit spending?
8. Analyzing Information Why might it be difficult for the average voter to determine who to blame for bad economic conditions?

Section 3 Review Answers

1. Definitions of terms appear on pages indicated: **fiscal policy,** 606; **monetary policy,** 606; **gross national product (GNP),** 606; **discount rate,** 608; **reserve requirement,** 608; **open-market operations,** 608
2. interest on the national debt, defense, direct benefit payments to individuals, aid to state and local governments
3. 50 percent

4. increase spending, lower taxes
5. The total amount has declined and grants have shifted from infrastructure to payments, such as medicare, to individuals.
6. so that its decisions are not influenced by political considerations
7. The government would have to rely on monetary rather than fiscal policy. The Fed could lower the discount rate,

lower the banks' reserve requirement, or expand credit through open-market operations.
8. Many sources influence the economy. Government and the private sector share influence. In the government the President, Congress, and the Federal Reserve Board each have influence.

PERSONAL PERSPECTIVES

Phil Gramm on Balancing the Budget

Republican Senator Phil Gramm of Texas is one of the engineers of the Balanced Budget and Emergency Deficit Control Act, also known as Gramm-Rudman-Hollings. Before the enactment of the bill in 1985, Senator Gramm stated his position in an interview.

On a mandatory procedure to balance the budget:
We are about to raise the debt ceiling to 2 trillion dollars—an admission that Congress and the budget process have failed. This plan sets in place a concrete program to force Congress and the President to make hard choices necessary to wipe out budget deficits by 1990.

On how his proposal would actually work:
It requires the President to submit and Congress to pass budgets that reduce the deficit by 36 billion dollars annually for the next five years. Each October 1 at the end of the budget process, the Congressional Budget Office and the Office of Management and Budget would project the deficit for the coming year. If it exceeds the target signifi-

It has teeth. It is binding on Congress and sets out to achieve what the American people want.

cantly, the President would have to make across-the-board cuts of equal proportion in a wide array of programs so as to eliminate the overage. The President and Congress would have a short time to come up with an alternative plan to get the budget on target and avoid the automatic cuts.

On Presidential and constitutional authority:
A President would have no discretionary power to make those [national] cuts, which would occur only if Congress fails to act. What it [the bill] does do is reduce the power of the President and Congress to *fail* to make decisions.

On mandatory cuts unfairly hitting programs for the poor:
Across-the-board cuts would occur only if we refuse to do our job. Those who think certain programs shouldn't be cut can prevent that by enacting a budget.

On why tax hikes should be avoided:
Anyone may propose a tax increase. But I'm not willing to write into the bill a provision that simply says, "If we don't do our job, taxes automatically go up."

On why Congress won't be forced to raise taxes:
Not at all. Revenues are growing by 70 billion dollars a year because of economic growth. We're talking about cutting the deficit by 36 billion a year. That means half of new revenues from economic growth would be applied to reduce the deficit. As it is now, we're spending all of it.

On why Americans should expect this plan to work when others haven't:
Because it's different from anything we've ever done before. It is patterned on a procedure used successfully in 43 states. It has teeth. It is binding on Congress and sets out to achieve what the American people want.

Examining the Reading

Reviewing Facts
1. State why Gramm believes there is a need for a mandatory balanced budget procedure.
2. Discuss whether you think Gramm-Rudman-Hollings changes constitutional authority for the executive and legislative branches in budget-making.

Critical Thinking Skills
3. Making Inferences What does Senator Gramm perceive to be the job of government in regard to the budget?

CHAPTER 21: TAXING AND SPENDING 609

Focus

Ask: What happens if you spend more money than you have? What are the repercussions? What are the consequences if the government spends more money than it has?

Teach

Ask: Why does Gramm oppose a tax hike to balance the budget? *(Raising taxes does not encourage Congress to do its job of cutting spending.)* How does he propose to wipe out the budget deficit? *(Apply half the annual $70 billion revenue increase to the deficit instead of spending it.)* Why does Gramm think this proposal will be successful? *(patterned on a successful procedure used in 43 states)*

Assess

Have students complete **Examining the Reading.**

Answers

1. It offers a concrete program to follow.
2. No, but it forces the President and Congress to make tough decisions.
3. to balance it and to achieve what the American people want

Close

Ask: What programs would you cut the most to balance the budget? How do you think those who depend on those programs for jobs, business profits, or other needs would react to your plan?

More About Personal Perspectives

Texas Senator Phil Gramm is considered to be efficient but unpopular. This does not seem to bother him. In his zeal to limit federal spending, he has cheerfully stepped on the toes of those with seniority. As a Democratic congressman he co-sponsored the Gramm-Latta budget resolution of 1981. Discovered leaking Democratic strategy to the Republicans, he was thrown off the Budget Committee by House Speaker Tip O'Neill. Gramm resigned, changed parties, and won reelection in a 1983 special election. He then captured John Tower's Senate seat when the latter retired. Gramm said to voters, "I had to choose between Tip O'Neill and y'all, and I decided to stand with y'all."

Identifying Terms and Concepts

1. taxes, 2. withholding, 3. taxable income, 4. fiscal year, 5. incrementalism or entitlements, 6. incrementalism or entitlements, 7. national debt, 8. GNP, 9. fiscal policy, 10. monetary policy

Reviewing Facts and Ideas

1. Office of Management and Budget

2. to collect taxes, to check tax returns, to investigate suspected criminal tax violations

3. individual and corporate income taxes, social insurance taxes, excise tax, customs duties, estate and gift taxes

4. They are safe and some are tax-exempt.

5. Much of the budget consists of uncontrollables, agencies expect to grow incrementally, special interests promote spending for favorite programs.

6. to force the President and Congress to reduce federal deficits

7. reduced the number of tax brackets and reduced or ended a number of complicated deductions, credits, and shelters

8. At the beginning of World War II the national debt was about $40 billion. By 1995 the national debt reached $5 trillion.

9. road repair, public housing, police equipment, school lunches, flood insurance, mental health, and payments to individuals for services such as medicare

10. April 15 of each year

11. churches, colleges, labor unions, other non-profit organizations

---

21 CHAPTER REVIEW

Summary and Significance

The federal government raises revenue through taxing and borrowing. The individual income tax is the largest single source of federal revenue. Social insurance taxes and many other taxes combined raise more than $1 trillion each year. Recent changes in the federal income tax laws have eliminated some tax loopholes and made the rules less complex.

Preparing the federal budget is a long, often difficult process. The President receives help from the Office of Management and Budget and works together with departments and agencies of the executive branch to prepare a budget that is submitted to Congress. The Congressional Budget Office reviews the budget and recommends changes. The final budget represents compromises between the two branches.

Since the 1930s the federal government has played an active role in regulating the nation's economy. Through its fiscal and monetary policies the federal government tries to maintain healthy economic growth. Taxing, spending, and borrowing comprise fiscal policy. The Federal Reserve Board has power to control the nation's money supply through Federal Reserve Banks located in districts throughout the nation.

Identifying Terms and Concepts

Insert the terms below into the following paragraph to describe how the federal government regulates the economy. Do not use a term more than once.

withholding, securities, national debt, taxes, taxable income, incrementalism, fiscal policy, GNP, monetary policy, fiscal year, entitlements

The federal government collects more than $1 trillion in (1) each year. Through a system of (2) wage earners pay taxes on their (3) during the year. The government's (4) begins on October 1. Because of (5) and (6) in the budget, government spending often exceeds revenue, a factor that enlarges the (7). Some economists are not alarmed because deficits are only about five percent of the (8). Others would like to see changes in (9) to control spending or raise taxes. By its (10) the Fed may stimulate economic growth to relieve some of these concerns.

Reviewing Facts and Ideas

1. Identify the executive agency that is charged with preparing the federal budget.
2. List three responsibilities of the Internal Revenue Service.
3. Name four types of taxes that the federal government collects.

4. Explain why federal securities such as bonds are popular with investors.
5. Describe the factors that make it difficult for Congress to cut spending.
6. Summarize the goal of the Gramm-Rudman-Hollings Act.
7. Describe the changes the Tax Reform Act of 1986 introduced.
8. Compare the size of the national debt at the beginning of World War II in the 1940s to the national debt in the 1990s.
9. Identify state and local uses of intergovernmental revenues.
10. Cite the deadline for filing individual income tax returns.
11. Name three institutions that are exempt from the federal income tax.

Applying Themes

1. **Civic Responsibility** How do self-employed people provide withholding of their income taxes?
2. **Public Policy** For what two reasons has the United States been unable to balance the national budget most of the time beginning in the 1930s?
3. **Political Processes** What are the likely sources of conflict between the President and Congress over the federal budget?

Applying Themes

1. Self-employed people are expected to file estimates of their income four times a year and make payments with each estimate.

2. People thought that deficits benefited the economy, and the policy was politically popular because it supported people's favorite social programs.

3. If the President and Congress are from different political parties, they will have different priorities. Also, even congressional members of the President's party may have different goals than the President.

4. all the large, important banks in the nation

4. **Federalism** What kinds of banks are members of the Federal Reserve System?

Critical Thinking Skills

1. **Making Generalizations** How does the government try to influence the economy through fiscal policy?
2. **Identifying Alternatives** Some people favor an amendment to the Constitution requiring Congress to pass a balanced budget each year. What is your opinion on such a proposal? Explain your answer.
3. **Analyzing Information** How did the Budget and Accounting Act of 1921 formalize the budget process?
4. **Expressing Problems Clearly** Many people believe that politics interferes with government budgeting. What role does politics play in the inability of the federal government to control deficit spending?

Linking Past and Present

The federal government first used the income tax to help finance the Civil War. Congress levied a tax of 5 to 10 percent on yearly incomes above $600. In those years, when the average worker earned less than $2 per day, the majority did not pay the tax. The Supreme Court declared the income tax unconstitutional in 1895, thus requiring the Sixteenth Amendment to restore the tax in 1913. For many years only wealthy people paid the income tax, but it now touches nearly every wage earner. Why do you think the income tax has become the main source of federal revenue?

Writing About Government

Persuasive Writing Two of the most regularly discussed methods of reducing federal budget deficits are raising taxes and cutting federal spending. Write a paragraph supporting one or both of these measures. Be sure to emphasize the seriousness of the deficit problem.

Reinforcing the Skill

Analyzing Editorials Read the editorial from the *St. Louis Post-Dispatch* on the Gulf War below. Then answer the questions that follow.

> *The Persian Gulf war is draining billions of dollars from the federal treasury. . . .*
> *Even those who agree with President Bush that the United States must drive Iraq out of Kuwait must be struck by the sense of priorities revealed in the administration's response to Saddam Hussein's aggression. Why is it that this nation can afford to do battle with a despot who does not threaten its vital interests but cannot afford to guarantee a job for all who want one or provide affordable housing, repair its transportation system or safeguard the welfare of its children? In short, how large a deterioration in the quality of life and the standard of living are the Bush administration and Congress willing to accept in the name of the New World Order?*

1. What is the topic under discussion?
2. What do the editors think the government needs to do instead of launching the war? What arguments do they present to back up their position? What do they fear will happen instead?
3. Do the editors agree or disagree with the President's policy in the Persian Gulf? Explain.
4. Do you find this editorial persuasive? Explain.

Investigating Further

1. **Individual Project** Locate a pay stub—your own, a family member's, or friend's. Notice the categories and amounts of money deducted for city income tax, state income tax, FICA, Social Security, etc. Divide the amount in each category by the gross pay to determine what percentage of the earned wages were deducted in each category.
2. **Cooperative Learning** Divide the class into five equal groups. Each group should make a poster to illustrate the national debt—about $5 trillion. For example, the debt represents 100 million sports cars valued at $50,000 each.

CHAPTER 21: TAXING AND SPENDING   611

Linking Past and Present

Incomes tend to remain stable from year to year, thereby providing a reliable source of taxation. Taxing incomes also allows for spreading the tax burden somewhat equitably.

Writing About Government

Students' paragraphs will vary, but should include supporting arguments.

Reinforcing the Skill

1. the Gulf War and budget priorities
2. They believe the government should fund social and domestic programs, which they say already are underfunded. They fear further deterioration of these programs because of the war.
3. They are opposed to the Gulf War because they think there are many more important domestic problems that require money and attention. They do not think that Saddam Hussein is a threat to the vital interests of the United States.
4. Students' responses will vary.

Investigating Further

1. Percentages will vary.
2. Students' posters will vary.

Critical Thinking Skills

1. Through its taxing and spending policies the government tries to keep a healthy economy. If the economy is sluggish, the government may cut taxes or increase spending.
2. Those supporting the amendment should cite the difficulty that the government has had in trying to balance the budget in the past. Those opposed should question the advisability of eliminating one of the government's main ways of regulating the economy.
3. By requiring the President to submit a budget for the whole federal government to Congress, it paved the way for the OMB and CBO.
4. Partisan differences may cause disputes over taxing and spending policies and priorities. Also, individual lawmakers may have home district programs they want to fund or protect.

Chapter Organizer

Objectives	Special Feature Pages	Supplemental Materials
Section 1 United States Foreign Policy *pp. 614–617* 1. Identify the major objectives of American foreign policy. 2. Describe major developments in American foreign policy through history.		Guided Reading Activities Reproducible Lesson Plans Section 1 Quiz Testmaker SAT Practice Tests Writer's Guidebook
Section 2 The Role of the President in Foreign Policy *pp. 618–622* 1. Describe the powers and responsibilities of the President in foreign policy. 2. Identify the President's foreign-policy advisers.	Focus on Freedom: Wilson's Fourteen Points p. 619 Social Studies Skills: Reading a Cartogram p. 622	Guided Reading Activities Reproducible Lesson Plans Section 2 Quiz Testmaker Skill Reinforcement Activities 22 Great Speeches, Volume VI SAT Practice Tests Writer's Guidebook
Section 3 Congress and Foreign Policy *pp. 623–626* 1. Relate the foreign-policy powers granted to Congress by the Constitution. 2. Describe the checks and balances of the President and Congress in terms of foreign affairs.	Participating in Government: Conducting Interviews p. 625	Guided Reading Activities Reproducible Lesson Plans Participating in Government 22 Primary and Secondary Source Readings 22 Section 3 Quiz Testmaker SAT Practice Tests Writer's Guidebook
Section 4 The Departments of State and of Defense *pp. 627–630* 1. Outline the structure and functions of the Departments of State and Defense. 2. Discuss the importance of civilian control of the military in American government.	Global Connection: Comparing Governments: Control of the Military p. 629	Guided Reading Activities Reproducible Lesson Plans Interpreting Political Cartoons 47, 48 Section 4 Quiz Testmaker Government Themes Transparencies 33 Great Speeches, Volume III Writer's Guidebook
Section 5 Achieving Foreign-Policy Goals *pp. 631–637* 1. Discuss the tools the United States uses to achieve foreign-policy goals. 2. Describe the role of the United Nations as a peacekeeping force.	Personal Perspectives: Angela Dickey on Life in the Foreign Service p. 637	Guided Reading Activities Reproducible Lesson Plans Reteaching Activities 22 Enrichment Activities 22 Chapter Transparencies 22 Section 5 Quiz Chapter 22 Tests Testmaker Government Themes Transparencies 34 Audio Cassettes (English and Spanish) Limited English Proficiency Activities 22

If time does not permit teaching this chapter, assign the Chapter 22 summary in the Unit 7 Digest on pages 677–678.

Key To Ability Levels

Teaching strategies have been coded for varying learning styles and abilities.

L1   Level 1 activities are **basic** activities and should be within the ability range of all students.

L2   Level 2 activities are **average** activities and should be within the ability range of the average to above-average student.

L3   Level 3 activities are **challenging** activities designed for the ability range of above-average students.

LEP   These activities should be within the ability range of **Limited English Proficiency** students.

Multicultural Activities

In the early 1980s, African American leaders made a concerted effort to influence United States policy toward South Africa. In November 1984 Eleanor Holmes Norton, Walter Fauntroy, and other prominent African American leaders launched a sit-in campaign at the South African Embassy to protest the minority white South African government's policy of apartheid and its imprisonment of black South African labor leaders. The sit-in and similar protests on college campuses contributed to Congress's decision in 1986 to pass economic sanctions against South Africa. Ask students why African Americans had a particular interest in United States policy toward South Africa. Have students identify other foreign policy issues of special interest to various ethnic groups. Discuss various ways such groups try to influence presidential or congressional foreign policy-making.

Since 1948, when President Truman desegregated the armed forces, chances for minority advancement have become better in the military than in civilian jobs, says David C. Ruffin of the Joint Center for Political Studies. "You could make general. . ., whereas you couldn't rise to become CEO of a corporation." The number of African American officers in the armed services grew from 2.5 percent in 1973 to 8 percent in 1993. The Army leads all services in minority promotion. The number of African American generals tripled between 1973 and 1993. Army General Colin Powell, son of Jamaican immigrants, heads the Joint Chiefs of Staff. Ask students: Is job discrimination less likely in a federal agency like the Department of Defense than in a private corporation? Why or why not?

Chapter Resources

Readings for the Student

Cooney, James R. *Think About Foreign Policy: The U.S. and the World.* Walker, 1991.

Dolan, Edward F. *America After Vietnam: Legacies of a Hated War.* Franklin Watts, 1989.

Salzman, Marian and Ann O'Reilly. *War and Peace in the Persian Gulf: What Teenagers Want to Know.* Peterson's, 1991.

Spanier, John. *Games Nations Play.* Congressional Quarterly, 1992.

Readings for the Teacher

Beschloss, Michael R. *The Crisis Years: Kennedy and Khrushchev, 1960–1963.* Harper/Collins, 1991.

Howard, Michael. *The Lessons of History.* Yale University Press, 1991.

Kennan, George F. *Sketches from a Life.* Pantheon, 1989.

Prados, John. *Keepers of the Keys: A History of the National Security Council from Truman to Bush.* Morrow, 1991.

Toland, John. *In Mortal Combat: Korea, 1950–1953.* Morrow, 1991.

Weintraub, Stanley. *Long Day's Journey into War: December 7, 1941.* Dutton, 1991.

Multimedia

Videocassettes

A Line in the Sand. Social Studies School Service. (v/c, 50 minutes)

The Missiles of October. Social Studies School Service. (v/c, 150 minutes)

The Pentagon. (*The Power Game* series). The Documentary Consortium. (v/c, 60 minutes)

Secret Intelligence (4-part series: *The Only Rule Is Win, Intervention, Learning to Say No, The Enterprise*). KCET. (4 v/c, 60 minutes each)

The Spy Who Broke the Code. (*Frontline* series). William Cran, Stephanie Tepper, Scott Malone. (v/c, 60 minutes)

Software

Foreign Governments and the United Nations. Sliwa Software. (Apple, IBM disks). A drill program covering the organization of the United Nations, seven United Nations member nations, and comparative governments (monarchy, fascism, and socialism).

Interactive Communication Simulation, Arab-Israeli Conflict Exercise. The University of Michigan, School of Education. (requires communications software). Students participate "long-distance" in a simulation on Arab-Israeli conflict.

Introduce

Chapter Overview

Chapter 22 deals with the conduct of America's foreign policy.

Section 1 explains the aims of American foreign policy and provides a historical perspective of this policy.

Section 2 describes the role of the President in developing and carrying out the nation's foreign policy.

Section 3 describes the role of Congress in developing and carrying out the nation's foreign policy.

Section 4 explains the roles of the Departments of State and Defense in shaping and implementing the nation's foreign policy.

Section 5 classifies the methods used to achieve the nation's foreign-policy goals.

Chapter 22 Themes

Have students read the Themes in Government for Chapter 22. Then have them write a specific example of each theme. Have volunteers share their examples. Write the themes on the chalkboard and list student examples under the correct theme.

Foreign Policy and National Defense

CHAPTER

22

Our government sometimes hosts talks between foreign leaders. In 1994 President Clinton invited Israel's Prime Minister Yitzhak Rabin and PLO leader Yasir Arafat to the White House for peace negotiations.

612   UNIT 7: PUBLIC POLICIES AND SERVICES

About the Chapter Opener

Teaching With Illustrations Have students read the caption and examine the photograph on pages 612 and 613. Point out that the President often welcomes foreign dignitaries, such as Yitzhak Rabin of Israel and Yasser Arafat of the PLO pictured here. Ask students which of the Themes in Government on page 613 the photograph reflects and how it does so. (*Public policy—photograph shows public policy on an international level; growth of democracy— by receiving dignitaries from other nations, the United States is encouraging the growth of democracy there; political processes—a formal welcoming of dignitaries contributes to the achievement of foreign-policy goals.*)

Chapter Preview

Overview

The President and Congress have active but separate roles in creating and enforcing American foreign policy.

Objectives

After studying this chapter, you should be able to:

1. Identify the major objectives of American foreign policy.
2. Describe the powers and responsibilities of the President in foreign policy.
3. Relate the foreign-policy powers of Congress.
4. Outline the structure and functions of the Departments of State and Defense.
5. Discuss the tools the United States uses to achieve foreign-policy goals.

Themes in Government

This chapter emphasizes the following government themes:

- **Public Policy** The foreign policy of the United States is public policy on an international level. Sections 1, 2, 3, and 5.
- **Growth of Democracy** Helping other nations move toward democracy is a key element of American foreign policy. Sections 1 and 5.
- **Political Processes** The President and Congress strive toward foreign-policy goals. Sections 2 and 4.
- **Checks and Balances** The Constitution gives the President and Congress specific powers regarding foreign policy. Sections 3 and 4.

Critical Thinking Skills

This chapter emphasizes the following critical thinking skills:

- Drawing Conclusions
- Demonstrating Reasoned Judgment
- Making Inferences
- Analyzing Information

CHAPTER 22: FOREIGN POLICY AND NATIONAL DEFENSE **613**

Introducing the Chapter

Before students begin to read the chapter, conduct a preview to help them clarify what they already know about the topics to be covered. As part of the preview, ask students the following: If you were visiting another country and people there asked your opinion about American foreign policy toward their area of the world, what would you be able to say with confidence? Discuss students' answers and list them on the chalkboard. Tell students that Chapter 22 discusses the foreign policy of the United States and ways that it is implemented.

Chapter Project

As students read this chapter have them collect newspaper and magazine articles dealing with United States foreign policy. Have students display the articles and short summaries of them on a class bulletin board. Divide the bulletin board by continent and have students post their articles in the appropriate category.

Linking Past and Present
Woodrow Wilson was the first President to travel to Europe while in office. In 1918, Wilson landed in France to head the American delegation to the Versailles Peace Conference near Paris. Many Americans objected to his trip and questioned whether a President could leave the continent and legally remain in office. Today, Presidents' travels to foreign countries are an accepted part of a President's duties in implementing the nation's foreign policy.

Setting the Scene During much of its early history, the United States was able to remain isolated from the upheavals of other nations. Bordered by two major oceans, the United States was distant from conflicts in Europe, Africa, and Asia. French historian Alexis de Tocqueville toured the United States in the early 1830s. He observed that the United States followed a "fundamental doctrine that the true interests of . . . Americans was never to take part in the internal quarrels of Europe." The invention of modern transportation and communications systems, however, brought the rest of the world much closer to American shores.

Focus

Bell Ringer

Write the following on the chalkboard for students to complete while attendance is being taken:

What does *international relations* mean?

Motivating Activity

Discuss students' Bell Ringer answers. Ask: How might the following headline affect your lives? "Foreign Auto Imports Hit Record High" *(declining domestic car sales, job loss, ripple effect through economy)* Point out that foreign policy involves economic as well as political issues, and that both impact directly on this nation's well-being and security.

Vocabulary Precheck

Call on students to read aloud the definition for each term and concept from the Glossary. Then have them restate each definition in their own words. **LEP**

Teach

Guided Practice

L1 Concept Mapping Write *American Foreign Policy* on the chalkboard and circle it. Then on five lines extending from the circle, ask students to add the objectives of American foreign policy. *(national security, world peace, democratic governments, free and open trade, concern for humanity)* Have volunteers describe each objective and provide examples. **LEP**

Caption Answer
isolationism and internationalism

United States Foreign Policy

In the early 1990s, newspapers across the United States heralded the demise of the Soviet Union. What had begun several years earlier when Soviet President Mikhail Gorbachev began political and economic reforms ended with the disintegration of the Soviet Union.

The collapse came after a handful of communist hard-liners tried to seize control of the Soviet Union in August 1991. When the coup failed and Gorbachev returned to power, one Soviet republic after another declared its independence. In the minds of many experts, the 46-year-old cold war between the United States and the Soviet Union had ended. In many respects the events in the Soviet Union were the products of the United States' post-World War II foreign policy. Secretary of State James A. Baker clearly outlined this policy:

> *The strategy and policies we have pursued* vis-à-vis *the Soviet Union in the postwar years have been successful. Containment, which focused on holding in check the military and ideological threat of Soviet communism, has met its major objectives. As a result of reform in the Soviet Union, signs of new international behavior by Moscow and the vitality of the Western democracies, we are in a strong position to push for change that will advance long-term U.S. interests.*
>
> —JAMES A. BAKER,
> *AMERICAN LEGION MAGAZINE,* FEBRUARY 1990

The long-term interests Secretary Baker referred to included the basic aims of United States' foreign policy.

Aims of Foreign Policy

American **foreign policy** consists of the strategies and principles that guide the national government's relations with other countries and groups in the world. Although the details of American foreign policy may change from one administration to another, objectives of United States foreign policy remain constant.

National Security The principal goal of American foreign policy is to preserve the security of the United States. **National security** refers to a nation's deter-

Baker at 1991 Middle East Peace Conference
Secretary of State James A. Baker speaks to members of the Israeli delegation. **Public Policy** **What two directions has United States foreign policy followed?**

SECTION PREVIEW

Objectives
After studying this section, you should be able to:
- Identify the major objectives of American foreign policy.
- Describe major developments in American foreign policy through history.

Key Terms and Concepts
foreign policy, national security, isolationism, internationalism, containment, détente

Themes in Government
- Public Policy
- Growth of Democracy

Critical Thinking Skills
- Drawing Conclusions
- Demonstrating Reasoned Judgment

Classroom Resources for Section 1

📁 Guided Reading Activities
📁 Reproducible Lesson Plans
📁 Section 1 Quiz

🔲 Testmaker
SAT Practice Tests
Writer's Guidebook

---

mination to remain free and independent and to be secure from foreign influence or invasion.

The goal of national security helps determine how the United States deals with other nations. Every part of American foreign policy—from maintaining an ambassador in a small Latin American country to signing a mutual assistance treaty with allies in Europe—is related to the nation's security.

World Peace American foreign policy has other goals as well. One of these goals has been to promote world peace. American leaders have worked for world peace because they believe it is another way to guarantee national security. They believe that if other nations are at peace, the United States runs little risk of being drawn into a conflict. To achieve this vital goal, the United States government has cooperated with other governments to settle disputes. The United States has also supplied economic aid to other countries, in part to prevent uprisings and revolutions. The desire for world peace was the main reason the United States helped organize the United Nations after World War II.

Democratic Governments Throughout its history the United States has been an example of democracy. In addition, the United States aids democratic nations and helps others create democratic political systems. With the help of the United States, many of the formerly communist nations in Europe are forming democratic political systems.

Free and Open Trade Maintaining trade with other nations and preserving access to necessary natural resources has been another basic goal of American foreign policy. Trade is an absolute necessity for the United States. American factories and farms need foreign markets in which to sell their products. The United States also needs a number of natural resources, including oil.

Concern for Humanity Even though self-interest guides each nation's foreign policy, concern for the well-being of others may play a role in a nation's actions. The United States, for one, has often demonstrated its concern for others. Victims of natural disasters or starvation have looked to the United States for help. In such times of crisis, the United States has responded by providing food, medical supplies, and technical assistance for humanitarian reasons. At the same time, this aid helps maintain political stability in the world.

Development of Foreign Policy

Until the late 1800s, American foreign policy was based on **isolationism**—avoiding involvement in world affairs, especially in the affairs of Europe. During the twentieth century, Presidents and their foreign-policy advisers followed a policy of **internationalism.** Internationalists believed that involvement in world affairs was necessary for national security. A look at the history of American foreign policy since 1789 will reveal how these approaches to foreign policy developed.

Isolationism When George Washington became President in 1789, the United States was a small nation, deeply in debt and struggling to build a new government. For this reason American leaders believed that the United States should not become involved in the politics and wars of Europe. Before leaving office President Washington urged Americans to follow a path of isolationism.

President Thomas Jefferson also warned against forming "entangling alliances" with foreign nations. He stated that "Americans should never ask for privileges from foreign nations, in order not to be obliged to grant any in return."

The Monroe Doctrine In 1823 President James Monroe announced a new foreign-policy doctrine that extended the meaning of isolationism. Known as the Monroe Doctrine, it stated:

> *The American continents, by the free and independent condition which they have assumed and maintain, are henceforth not to be considered as subjects for future colonization by any European powers. . . . We owe it . . . to candor, and to the amicable relations between the United States and those powers to declare that we should consider any attempt on their part to extend their system to any portion of this hemisphere as dangerous to our peace and safety. . . .*
> —JAMES MONROE, MONROE DOCTRINE, 1823

The United States as a World Power By the 1890s the United States was rapidly becoming one of the great industrial nations of the world. Accordingly, the United States began to look for world markets for its products and for new sources of raw materials. For some government leaders, isolationism no longer fit the United States' role as an economic power. These leaders believed the United States should play a more active role in world affairs. In their minds the nation needed to expand and acquire a colonial empire.

CHAPTER 22: FOREIGN POLICY AND NATIONAL DEFENSE **615**

L2 Synthesizing Information Explore with students the relationship between tariff or trade policy and foreign policy. Ask if any connection exists between a nation's tariffs and its international relations. (*Students should suggest that protective tariffs are isolationist and that free trade is internationalist.*)

L3 Demonstrating Reasoned Judgment Remind students that cold war tension between the United States and the Soviet Union increased with escalations in the arms race. Ask: How might the United States have countered the Soviet aggression in some other way? What are the pros and cons of this method and of alternative methods? (*Students might note economic policy alternatives, such as foreign aid and the Marshall Plan.*)

Independent Practice

L1 Chronology Have students make time lines and place on them significant foreign-policy events since 1789. Have them use brackets to show periods of isolation and internationalism. Have students compare their time lines. **LEP**

L2 Persuasive Writing Have students write a letter to George Washington or Thomas Jefferson explaining why the policy of avoiding "entangling alliances" is not possible today.

GLENCOE TECHNOLOGY

Focus on Government
Video 41
Lecture Launcher:
Foreign Policy and National Defense
Running Time: 3:08
Videodisc 3, Chap. 41
VHS Tape 3, Begins 3:46

Background

The Monroe Doctrine has been a cornerstone of American foreign policy from very early in our nation's history. This policy came as a response to revolutions in the Spanish colonies of Latin America. American officials feared that Europe's powers would try to help Spain recapture its former colonies and that a successful campaign could threaten national security. The United States, however, was not really capable of enforcing the doctrine or of defending the Western Hemisphere. Only the backing of Great Britain's naval fleet stood between Spain and reconquest of its colonies in America.

L3 Informative Writing Ask students to write an essay to explain the relationship between the American economy, world trade, and American foreign policy.

Caption Answer
détente and nuclear arms agreements

Critical Thinking Answers
Answers may indicate that small nations may no longer feel intimidated, which could allow their conflicts to grow more serious.

Presidents play the leading role in foreign relations because they can speak for the United States with one voice. Congress concentrates more on domestic policy where most issues call for debate and compromise.

Assess

Check for Understanding

Have students complete Section 1 Review on page 617.

Meeting Objectives
Each section objective is tested by the Section Review questions that follow it in parentheses.
• Identify the major objectives of American foreign policy. (2, 5, 7, 8)
• Describe major developments in American foreign policy through history. (3, 4, 6)

Evaluate

📁 Section 1 Quiz
🔒 Testmaker

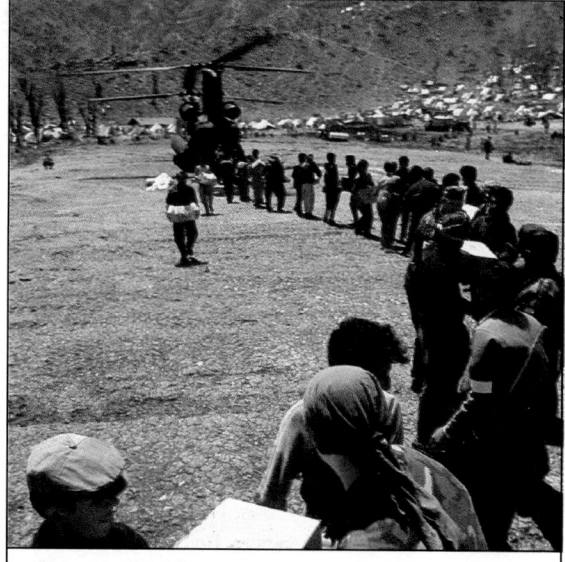

Concern for Humanity
The United States Army delivers food to a refugee camp in Turkey. **Politics What actions did United States foreign policy take to ease cold war tensions?**

In 1898 the United States fought the Spanish-American War, in part to free Cuba from Spanish rule. As one result of that war, the United States acquired the Philippine Islands, Guam, and Puerto Rico. Hawaii was then annexed in 1898 and Samoa in 1900. Although isolationist sentiments survived, the United States now had a colonial empire and was a major power in the Pacific and Eastern Asia.

Involvement in Two World Wars When World War I broke out in Europe in 1914, isolationist sentiment in the United States was still strong. After Germany used unrestricted submarine warfare against neutral ships—including those of the United States—President Wilson asked Congress to declare war against Germany in 1917. For the first time in United States history, American troops went overseas to fight in a European war.

Disillusioned by the terrible cost in human lives, Americans eagerly returned to isolationism after the war. Throughout the 1920s and 1930s, most Americans wanted to avoid again becoming involved in European political affairs. During these years, however, ruthless dictators came to power—Mussolini in Italy, Hitler in Germany, and military leaders in Japan. By the 1930s, these nations were using military force to overtake other nations.

When World War II broke out in 1939, the United States officially remained neutral. The Japanese attack on Pearl Harbor in 1941, however, brought the United States into the war. Since then, the United States has based its foreign policy on internationalism.

The Cold War The United States emerged from World War II as the leader of the free nations of the world. The United States' new role soon brought it into conflict with the Soviet Union, which had also emerged from the war as a world power. American government leaders viewed the power and ambitions of the Soviet Union as a threat to national security. Between 1945 and 1949, the countries of Eastern Europe fell under Soviet domination. In 1949 the Chinese Communists seized control of China. The communist takeovers in these nations convinced American leaders that they must do something to halt communist aggression.

As the rivalry between the United States and the Soviet Union intensified, it became clear that a cold war had begun. The cold war was a war of words and ideologies rather than a shooting war.

Containment and the Truman Doctrine Faced with the threat of expanding communism, the United States responded with a policy known as containment. The idea of **containment** was to keep the Soviet Union from expanding its power beyond Eastern Europe.

American leaders wanted to halt the spread of communism by giving economic aid to nations they said were threatened by totalitarian regimes. In keeping with the containment policy, President Harry S Truman announced what later became known as the Truman Doctrine in a speech in 1947.

Themes in Government
Public Policy The United States must now deal directly with many republics in what was the USSR. **Growth of Democracy** Secretary of State Baker said, "Once people have tasted the fruits of freedom and democracy, it is impossible to turn back the forces of history."

Critical Thinking Skills
Drawing Conclusions Without two superpowers, will local conflicts erupt into war? Explain.
Demonstrating Reasoned Judgment Why do many feel that Presidents concentrate on foreign policy and not on domestic issues?

Cooperative Learning Activity

Organize the class into groups and assign one of the five foreign policy objectives to each. Tell each it is a State Department policy group formed to study American foreign policy alternatives. Have the group list ways to achieve its goal, discuss and evaluate each, and decide whether to recommend it to the President. A spokesperson for each group should report its findings to the class. Ask: Are there any similarities in each group's recommendations? What similarities are there in the rejected strategies? What differences? *(similarities and differences may include military solutions, cooperative approaches, and collective actions)*

I believe that we must assist free peoples to work out their own destinies in their own way. I believe that our help should be primarily through economic and financial aid which is essential to economic stability and orderly political processes. . .

The free peoples of the world look to us for support in maintaining their freedoms. If we falter in our leadership, we may endanger the peace of the world—and we shall surely endanger the welfare of this nation.

—HARRY S TRUMAN, TRUMAN DOCTRINE, 1947

Three months later the Marshall Plan provided badly needed economic aid for war-torn Europe. Within four years the United States gave nations of Western Europe more than $13 billion.

The Arms Race and Arms Control Cold war tensions also led the Soviet Union and the United States to try to gain a military advantage over each other. As a result, for years the two nations engaged in a costly arms race to create more weapons of increasingly greater destructive power. At the same time, the two nations signed a series of arms-control agreements to limit and regulate the competition. Between 1963 and 1991, the United States and the Soviet Union completed more than 10 arms-control agreements.

The Policy of Détente Because of their hopes for peace and their fears of nuclear war, United States leaders began to explore possibilities for easing the tensions of the cold war. Over the years Americans began to understand that there were differences among the communist nations, just as there were differences among the democracies. Consequently, American leaders began to look for new ways to improve relations between communist nations and free nations. President Nixon and his secretary of state, Henry Kissinger, spoke of a diplomatic concept called **détente**, or a relaxation of tensions.

Although some foreign-policy experts had recommended a policy of détente for some time, the Nixon administration put the policy into effect. President Nixon announced his intention in 1971 to go to the People's Republic of China to meet with Chinese leaders. The following year the President held his first summit meeting with Soviet leader Leonid Brezhnev. At the time both nations were almost equal in the nuclear arms race, and both nations felt the pinch of increasing defense costs. The result was SALT I—the first Strategic Arms Limitations Talks. Many other agreements followed. Despite the treaties, the arms race continued as the Vietnam War dragged on and fighting broke out in the Middle East.

A Harder Line In 1979 Soviet troops invaded Afghanistan, and tensions between the Soviet Union and the United States mounted. Then, in November of 1980, a strongly anticommunist Ronald Reagan was elected President. Reagan adopted a harder line with the Soviet Union. By the late 1980s, however, changes within the Soviet Union under the leadership of Mikhail Gorbachev led to new diplomatic efforts. Soviet troops withdrew from Afghanistan in 1989. By the early 1990s, relations between the United States and the Soviet Union had become more cordial.

Reteach

Ask students to write a paragraph on foreign policy that uses all the Key Terms and Concepts listed in the Section Preview on page 614.

Enrich

Have students choose a recent President and write a report evaluating how well that President's foreign policy met the five goals of American foreign policy outlined in this section.

Close

Ask the class to rank the major objectives of the United States' foreign policy in what they consider to be their order of importance. Discuss the extent of agreement or disagreement among individual student rankings.

CONNECTIONS

History
At the time of the Soviet Union's collapse in 1991, more than 80 treaties were in force between the United States and the Soviet Union.

**1
SECTION REVIEW**

Section Summary
American leaders follow certain guiding principles in making foreign-policy decisions.

Checking For Understanding
Recalling Facts
1. Define foreign policy, national security, isolationism, internationalism, containment, détente.
2. List the most important objective of American foreign policy.
3. Name the policy that extended the meaning of isolationism.
4. Cite the event that caused the United States to base its foreign policy on internationalism.

Exploring Themes
5. Public Policy What are the basic aims of American foreign policy?
6. Growth of Democracy How did the United States carry out its policy of containment?

Critical Thinking Skills
7. Drawing Conclusions Do you believe the United States could follow a policy of isolationism at this time? Support your answer.
8. Demonstrating Reasoned Judgment Do you think world peace is ever possible? Support your answer.

CHAPTER 22: FOREIGN POLICY AND NATIONAL DEFENSE 617

Section 1 Review Answers

1. Definitions of terms appear on pages indicated: **foreign policy,** 614; **national security,** 614; **isolationism,** 615; **internationalism,** 615; **containment,** 616; **détente,** 617
2. national security
3. the Monroe Doctrine
4. World War II

5. national security, world peace, spreading democracy, free and open trade, concern for humanity
6. through economic and military aid to nations that would resist communism
7. Answers will vary, but may indicate that because of fast-changing world events the United States could not follow a policy of isolationism now.

8. Answers will vary, but may indicate students are encouraged by recent events to say yes; or that no, someone somewhere will always be fighting.

Focus

Bell Ringer

Ask students to complete the following task while attendance is being taken:

Find photos in the textbook that illustrate the President's roles in foreign policy.

Motivating Activity

Discuss students' Bell Ringer responses. Ask what role each photo illustrates and list the roles on the chalkboard. Tell students to refer to the list as they study Section 2, to determine if they have included all the foreign-policy powers of the President.

Vocabulary Precheck

List the terms and concepts on the chalkboard. Have students develop questions for which each term or concept is an answer.
LEP

Caption Answer
as commander in chief and head of state; by appointing ambassadors and key foreign-policy advisers; by making treaties with other countries

---

Teach

Guided Practice

L1 Classifying Information
Have students brainstorm the foreign-policy activities of the President. List their responses on the chalkboard. Then draw a three-column chart and label the columns *commander in chief,* *chief diplomat,* and *head of state.* Ask them to assign each activity on the list to the appropriate column in the chart. **LEP**

The Role of The President in Foreign Policy

The Framers of the Constitution attempted to divide the responsibility for foreign affairs between the President and the Congress. They did not, however, clearly outline the boundaries of power of each branch. As a result, on many occasions the President and Congress have vied for power.

Over the years events have enabled the President to assume more responsibility in foreign policy. Today, according to one political scientist, "Any discussion of the making of United States foreign policy must begin with the President. He is the ultimate decider." Although Congress plays an important role in foreign policy, the major responsibility in this area rests with the President.

Powers and Responsibilities

The President derives power to formulate foreign policy from two sources. First, the Constitution lists certain presidential powers related to foreign policy. Second, as the head of the world's superpower, the President functions as an important world leader.

Constitutional Powers of the President President Bill Clinton spoke to the American people on September 15, 1994:

*M*y fellow Americans, tonight I want to speak to you about why the United States is leading an international effort to restore democratic government in Haiti. Haiti's dictators, led by [Lt.] General Raoul Cedras, control the most violent regime in our hemisphere . . . . In the face of this continued defiance

Supporting Democracy in Russia
President Clinton meets with Boris Yeltsin. **Politics**
How does a President influence foreign policy?

and with atrocities rising, the United States has agreed to lead a multinational force to carry out the will of the United Nations. . . . No president makes decisions like this without deep thought and prayer.
—BILL CLINTON, 1994

President Clinton's speech illustrates the President's ability to commit the nation in foreign affairs.

The Constitution grants the President specific powers in foreign affairs. The most important is the power to be the commander in chief of the nation's military forces. As commander in chief, the President

---

SECTION PREVIEW

Objectives
After studying this section, you should be able to:
■ Describe the powers and responsibilities of the President in foreign policy.

■ Identify the President's foreign-policy advisers.

Key Terms and Concepts
ambassador, treaty

Themes in Government
■ Political Processes
■ Public Policy

Critical Thinking Skills
■ Making Inferences
■ Demonstrating Reasoned Judgment

618   UNIT 7: PUBLIC POLICIES AND SERVICES

Classroom Resources for Section 2

📁 Guided Reading Activities
📁 Reproducible Lesson Plans
📁 Section 2 Quiz
➕ Testmaker

📼 Great Speeches, Volume VI
SAT Practice Tests
Writer's Guidebook

may send troops, ships, planes, or even use nuclear weapons anywhere in the world, without congressional approval. For example, President Bush decided to send military forces to Saudi Arabia soon after Iraq had invaded Kuwait.

In addition to powers as commander in chief, Article II, Section 2, gives the President certain diplomatic powers. The President appoints **ambassadors,** officials of the United States government who represent the nation in diplomatic matters. The President also receives ambassadors from foreign governments. By receiving an ambassador or other diplomat from a certain country, the President gives formal recognition to that government. President Bush did this in September 1991 when he established diplomatic relations with Latvia, Estonia, and Lithuania. Formal recognition of a government is vital because it qualifies that government to receive economic and other forms of aid. Conversely, by refusing to receive an ambassador, the President can withhold diplomatic recognition of a foreign government.

Article II, Section 2, also gives the President power to make treaties. A **treaty** is a formal agreement between the governments of two or more nations.

The President as Head of State The President's position as head of state plays an important part in controlling foreign policy. As head of state, the President represents the United States and symbolizes the leadership and policies of the nation to the world. In an international crisis, Americans also look to their President for leadership.

Foreign-Policy Advisers

The President has the final responsibility for making American foreign policy and protecting national security. Before making foreign-policy decisions, however, Presidents usually consult advisers. Generally, chief executives rely upon the information and advice of the cabinet members, the White House staff, and officials in specialized agencies dealing with foreign policy. At times Presidents also go outside the government and seek advice from private individuals who have specialized knowledge in foreign affairs.

The Secretaries of State and Defense All members of the President's cabinet must concern them-

---

Focus on Freedom

WILSON'S FOURTEEN POINTS

In 1917 President Wilson stated that the United States would fight to make the world "safe for democracy." On January 8, 1918, he presented his goals for the war to Congress.

XIV. A general association of nations must be formed . . . for the purpose of affording mutual guarantees of political independence and territorial integrity to great and small states alike.

In regard to these essential rectifications of wrong and assertions of right we feel ourselves to be intimate partners of all the governments . . . against the Imperialists. We cannot be separated in interest or divided in purpose. . . .

We have spoken now, surely, in terms too concrete to admit . . . any further doubt or question. An evident principle runs through the whole program I have outlined. It is the principle of justice to all peoples and nationalities, and their right to live on equal terms of liberty and safety with one another, whether they be strong or weak. Unless this principle be made its foundation, no part of the structure of international justice can stand. The people of the United States could act upon

no other principle; and to the vindication of this principle they are ready to devote their lives, their honor, and everything that they possess. The moral climax of this, the culminating and final war for human liberty, has come, and they are ready to put their own . . . integrity and devotion to the test.

—WOODROW WILSON, 1918

Examining the Document

Reviewing Facts

1. Explain the purpose of Wilson's general association of nations.
2. Describe the principle upon which Wilson based his program.

Critical Thinking Skills

3. Making Inferences How would the general association of nations promote peace?

CHAPTER 22: FOREIGN POLICY AND NATIONAL DEFENSE 619

Background

The National Security Council (NSC) serves as an advisory board on defense, foreign policy, and intelligence matters. It advises the President on security problems, and it supervises the Central Intelligence Agency (CIA). In 1986 the NSC was criticized for exceeding its role as an advisory board

when it was revealed that the NSC staff was involved in secret arms sales to Iran, the proceeds of which were used to support the *contras* in Nicaragua. As a result of the criticism, in 1987 President Reagan added a legal adviser to the staff of the NSC.

Caption Answer
Iraq's invasion of Kuwait, collapse of USSR and the end of the cold war

STUDY GUIDE

Theme Answers
as commander in chief

It gathers and analyzes information about other nations.

Critical Thinking Answers
by exchange of ambassadors

Answers should address concerns about family members' expertise.

Assess

Check for Understanding

Have students complete Section 2 Review on page 621.

Meeting Objectives

Each section objective is tested by the Section Review questions that follow it in parentheses.
• Describe the powers and responsibilities of the President in foreign policy. (2, 7, 8)
• Identify the President's foreign-policy advisers. (3, 4, 5, 6)

selves with international problems. In their specialized fields, cabinet members bring international problems to the President's attention and recommend how to deal with them. For two cabinet departments, however—the Department of State and the Department of Defense—foreign affairs are a full-time concern.

The secretary of state supervises all the diplomatic activities of the American government. In the past most Presidents have relied heavily on their secretaries of state. In the early years of the Republic, four secretaries of state—Thomas Jefferson, James Madison, James Monroe, and John Quincy Adams—went on to become President.

Normally, the secretary of state carries on diplomacy at the highest level. The secretary frequently travels to foreign capitals for important negotiations with heads of state and represents the United States at major international conferences.

The secretary of defense supervises the military activities of the United States government. The President receives information and advice from the secretary of defense on the nation's military forces, weapons, and bases.

CIA—Downsizing in the 1990s
Congress pressed CIA Director R. James Woolsey to cut spending. **History What series of events led some critics to declare the CIA no longer necessary?**

Former national security adviser and professor of government Zbigniew Brzezinski described how the influence of the secretaries of state and defense varies from one presidential administration to another. He wrote:

*B*roadly speaking, John Kennedy, Richard Nixon, and Jimmy Carter embraced the presidential system. They did not permit any member of their cabinets, including the secretary of state or secretary of defense, to play a central role in shaping and managing U.S. foreign policy. Presidents Harry Truman, Dwight Eisenhower, Lyndon Johnson, and Gerald Ford . . . [allowed] the secretary of state . . . to be the preeminent player in influencing foreign-policy decisions.

—ZBIGNIEW BRZEZINSKI,
IN QUEST OF NATIONAL SECURITY, 1988

The National Security Adviser Professor Brzezinski also points out that in recent administrations the national security adviser—who is also the director of the National Security Council (NSC)—has played a major role in foreign affairs. Under President Nixon, for example, the national security adviser, Henry Kissinger, not only presented options but also recommended policies. He was the President's closest adviser. Yet in the Bush administration, the national security adviser, Brent Scowcroft, played an important but far less public role than did Secretary of State James Baker.

The Central Intelligence Agency In order to make foreign-policy decisions, the President and his advisers need information about the governments, economies, and armed forces of other nations. The task of gathering and coordinating this information is primarily the responsibility of the Central Intelligence Agency (CIA).

The National Security Act established the CIA and defined its duties in 1947. Today the CIA coordinates the intelligence activities of other agencies. The organization also safeguards top-secret information and

STUDY GUIDE

Themes in Government
Political Processes On what authority did President Reagan send troops to Grenada to protect American citizens in 1983?
Public Policy A Senate committee

questioned Robert Gates before he became CIA director. **Why is the CIA important in foreign policy?**

Critical Thinking
Making Inferences How is an

emerging nation granted recognition by the world community?
Demonstrating Reasoned Judgment Should a President's family members offer foreign-policy advice to the President?

620 UNIT 7: PUBLIC POLICIES AND SERVICES

Cooperative Learning Activity

Form several groups for students to research ways recent Presidents have used the advice available to them to formulate foreign policy. The following topics may be used: the Cuban missile crisis, the Soviet invasion of Afghanistan, the decision by President Johnson to send combat troops to Vietnam, the invasion of Grenada, the invasion of Kuwait by Iraq, and the return of Haiti's elected President to office. Have a member in each group take on a specific task such as identifying resources, researching and note-taking, report-writing, and presenting the findings.

conducts intelligence operations that the National Security Council authorizes.

Although it does use foreign agents, or spies, to obtain information, such undercover operations are only a small part of the CIA's function. Most of the agency's employees simply gather and evaluate information, much of it available from foreign officials in the news media, and official publications in foreign countries.

Recently critics of the CIA have questioned the agency's efficiency. Inefficiency was most evident after the CIA failed to predict Iraq's invasion of Kuwait in 1990. In addition, the surge of events in the Soviet Union during 1991 caught the CIA by surprise. With the end of the cold war, one prominent news magazine carried a lead article titled "Is the CIA Obsolete?"

Making Foreign Policy The government employs hundreds of foreign-policy experts whom the President may consult before making a decision. In some cases family members and trusted political friends have had more influence on a President than the secretary of state. A mild-mannered Texan named Colonel Edward House was President Woodrow Wilson's most trusted adviser, especially during World War I, even though he held no cabinet post.

In recent years, however, each President has taken a different approach to foreign policy. President Eisenhower relied heavily on Secretary of State John Foster Dulles for foreign-policy advice. President Kennedy, on the other hand, put together a team of foreign-affairs experts who worked together in the basement

Johnson's Tuesday Meeting
President Johnson's "Tuesday Cabinet" discussed international affairs over lunch. **Politics** **What are the advantages and disadvantages of such meetings?**

of the White House. A group of advisers who lunched with the President in the White House every Tuesday often influenced President Johnson's decisions on the Vietnam War. Included in this "Tuesday Cabinet" were the director of the CIA and the White House press secretary. In contrast, the opinions of National Security Adviser Henry Kissinger were the major influence on President Nixon. Presidents Carter and Reagan sought advice equally from their national security adviser and the secretary of state.

In the final analysis, however, it is the President who determines what policies are to be followed. As President Ronald Reagan wrote, only the President can "respond quickly in a crisis or formulate a coherent and consistent policy in any region of the world."

Caption Answer
advantages: President receives advice from people with varied backgrounds; disadvantages: Advisers may not have foreign-policy background.

Evaluate

📁 Section 2 Quiz

💻 Testmaker

Reteach

Have students write a one-paragraph summary of the information under "Powers and Responsibilities" in this section, and a one-sentence summary for each minor heading under "Foreign-Policy Advisers."

Enrich

Have students select a post-World War II President and report on foreign-policy problems experienced during his term.

Close

Refer students to the Brzezinksi quote on page 620. Ask students which system for making foreign-policy decisions they believe is best and why.

---

② SECTION REVIEW

Section Summary
The President plays a key role in making American foreign policy and consults a variety of advisers.

Checking For Understanding
Recalling Facts
1. Define **ambassador, treaty.**
2. List two of the President's foreign-policy powers.
3. Identify which cabinet members generally work most closely with the President on foreign policy.
4. Name the agency responsible for providing information about foreign governments.

Exploring Themes
5. Political Processes Why does the President rely on advisers when formulating foreign policy?
6. Public Policy Why do the roles of foreign-policy advisers differ from President to President?

Critical Thinking Skills
7. Making Inferences In recent years the President has assumed more responsibility in foreign policy. What inference about the balance of power among the branches of government can you make from this information?
8. Demonstrating Reasoned Judgment Do you think the President has too much power in making foreign policy? Explain your answer.

Section 2 Review Answers

1. Definitions of terms appear on pages indicated: **ambassador,** 619; **treaty,** 619
2. Answers should include: is commander in chief of the nation's military forces, appoints ambassadors and receives ambassadors from foreign governments, makes treaties.
3. the secretaries of state and of defense

4. the Central Intelligence Agency
5. Answers will vary, but should include that the President's advisers usually have specialized knowledge in foreign affairs.
6. Answers will vary, but may indicate that Presidents may have different priorities and may place more weight on the opinions and information of some advisers than on those of others.

7. Answers may include that congressional authority in this area is weaker due to the need for rapid response to changing world events.
8. Answers will vary, but students may believe that some situations call for immediate action and cannot wait for Congress, others may believe the President is overstepping this power. Examples for both answers include the Vietnam War and the Persian Gulf War.

Focus

Write the following population figures on the chalkboard and challenge students to think of creative methods to show comparisons:

California—29,760,021
Iowa—2,776,755
New Jersey—7,730,188
Ohio—10,847,115
New York—17,990,455

Point out that large numbers become hard to visualize after a point, and that different graphics are used to compare statistics for different purposes.

Teach

Discuss the steps for reading a cartogram. Ask: What is the topic of the cartogram on this page? *(population)* How does the cartogram show variations in population? *(The size of the countries shown is determined by their population, not by their area.)* How does your knowledge of geography help you read a cartogram? *(Knowledge of a country's actual land area enables you to make relative comparisons.)*

Assess

Have students complete the **Practice** exercise.

Close

What other types of data, besides that noted in the skill, might be shown on a cartogram? *(agricultural or industrial production, GNP, election results, and so on)*

Reading a Cartogram

A cartogram is a stylized map that presents statistical information. The most common type of cartogram includes states or countries drawn in proportion to their relative size on a single statistical measure. On a cartogram that showed birthrate, for example, the United States, which has a low birthrate, would be shown as much smaller than India, which has a high birthrate. Cartograms present complex information in graphic form.

smaller than Saudi Arabia adds to your understanding of the information presented in the cartogram.

More insight may be gained from studying two cartograms that present different information. For example, a cartogram that shows each nation's consumption of energy or resources placed beside one that illustrates population can help a student understand the vast differences that exist between the industrial nations and the developing ones.

Population of the Near East and Middle East

Explanation

To read a cartogram, follow these steps:

- Determine what type of statistical information is being presented.
- Determine what political units are being shown on the cartogram.
- Compare the sizes of the political units on the cartogram.
- Use your knowledge of geography and relative sizes of nations to draw further conclusions about the data.

The more you know about geography, the easier it will be for you to learn from a cartogram. For one thing, if you know where to look for a particular country, you will be able to find it faster. In addition, knowledge of geography will help you make more complex comparisons than those shown. For example, knowing that Egypt is geographically much

Practice

Examine the cartogram above and answer the questions that follow. You may refer, if necessary, to the world map in the Atlas.

1. What statistic is shown on this cartogram?
2. What political units does the cartogram present?
3. Which country has the largest population?
4. Which country has a larger population, Turkey or Iraq?
5. Which country has more people, Pakistan or Egypt? Compare the cartogram to a world map. Does Pakistan or Egypt have greater population density? How can you tell?

Additional Practice

To practice this skill, see **Reinforcing the Skill** on page 639.

Practice Answers

1. population
2. nations
3. Pakistan
4. Turkey; about three times larger
5. Pakistan; Pakistan, because it is geographically smaller than Egypt but is shown larger on the cartogram.

For additional practice, have students complete activity 22 in *Skill Reinforcement Activities* in the Teacher's Classroom Resources.

SECTION 3

Congress and Foreign Policy

Although the President directs United States foreign policy, Congress plays an important role. The basis for this role lies in the Constitution. Most Presidents have looked upon foreign affairs as their responsibility, however, and have often carried out policies without consulting Congress. President Reagan expressed the view held by many others when he stated:

Congress, of course, has a legitimate role in the foreign policy process, but only the President can act. . . . Efforts to weaken the Presidency only weaken the country.

—RONALD REAGAN,
THINKING ABOUT AMERICA, 1988

Constitutional Powers

The Constitution gives Congress some important foreign-policy powers, including the power to declare war and appropriate money. The Senate must ratify treaties and confirm diplomatic appointments. Even though Congress has these powers, some people believe it has seldom used them effectively. Instead, Congress has, in the words of former Senator Barry Goldwater, revealed its "inability to act decisively in time of need."

Power to Declare War The Constitution balances the President's powers as commander in chief by granting Congress the power to declare war. Although the President may send troops anywhere in the world, only Congress may declare war. Yet Congress has exercised its power to declare war only

five times in our nation's history. It declared war in 1812 against Britain, in 1846 against Mexico, in 1898 against Spain, in 1917 against Germany, and in 1941 against Japan, Germany, and Italy. Only in these five cases was the United States officially at war with a foreign government. In each instance the President asked Congress for a declaration of war. Then, in accordance with the Constitution, both houses of Congress adopted the war resolution by a majority vote.

In other instances, instead of requesting a formal declaration of war, Presidents have asked Congress to pass a joint resolution concerning the use of American troops. In 1964, for example, President Lyndon Johnson asked Congress for authority to use troops in Vietnam. In response to an alleged North Viet-

Fighting the British
The battleship *Constitution* saw action in the officially declared War of 1812. **History** **What other times has Congress declared war?**

Objectives
After studying this section, you should be able to:
- Relate the foreign-policy powers granted to Congress by the Constitution.

- Describe the checks and balances of the President and Congress in terms of foreign affairs.

Key Terms and Concepts
executive agreement, bipartisan

Themes in Government
- Public Policy
- Checks and Balances

Critical Thinking Skills
- Analyzing Information
- Drawing Conclusions

CHAPTER 22: FOREIGN POLICY AND NATIONAL DEFENSE 623

Focus

Bell Ringer
Ask students to list the foreign-policy powers of Congress while attendance is being taken.

Motivating Activity
Place students' Bell Ringer responses on the chalkboard. Then refer students to the United States Constitution and have volunteers read Article I, Section 8. Compare the powers granted to powers in the Bell Ringer list. Ask students how these powers demonstrate the principle of checks and balances. Tell students that in Section 3 they will learn how Congress exercises its foreign-policy powers.

Vocabulary Precheck
List the terms and concepts on the chalkboard. Have volunteers skim the section to find each term and read it in context. **LEP**

Caption Answer
1846—Mexico; 1898—Spain; 1917—Germany; 1941—Japan, Germany, and Italy

Teach

Guided Practice
L1 **Summarizing** Have students summarize the foreign-policy powers of Congress by writing newspaper headlines. *(example: Senate Rejects Arms Treaty)* Ask students to read their headlines and have the class determine which power is illustrated. **LEP**

Classroom Resources for Section 3

- 📁 Guided Reading Activities
- 📁 Reproducible Lesson Plans
- 📁 Participating in Government 22
- 📁 Primary and Secondary Source Readings 22

- 📁 Section 3 Quiz
- 🖥 Testmaker
  SAT Practice Tests
  Writer's Guidebook

L2 Checks and Balances Ask students what, if anything, Congress could do to block the President in each of the following actions.

a. The President sends money to support the rebels in a civil war in another country.
b. The President signs a treaty to aid a nation if it is attacked.
c. The President recognizes the government of a new nation.
d. The President signs an executive agreement to send surplus weapons to another country.

Ask students if they can cite real examples of these scenarios.

L3 Panel Discussion Have students hold a panel discussion on the question of whether Congress should assume greater leadership and power in foreign policy. Students should develop arguments for and against greater foreign-policy power for Congress.

STUDY GUIDE

Critical Thinking Answers
War requires unity among government officials and citizens to be successful.

Modern warfare has such destructive potential that the President's actions should not go unquestioned or unchallenged.

namese attack on United States ships that occurred in the Tonkin Gulf off Vietnam's coast, Congress passed the Gulf of Tonkin Resolution. The resolution authorized the President "to take all necessary measures to repel any armed attack against the forces of the United States."

Dismayed by the results of the Gulf of Tonkin Resolution, Congress tried to check the President's power to send troops into combat by passing the War Powers Act in 1973. The act declared that the President could not send troops into combat for more than 60 days without the consent of Congress. Seventeen years later, after the 1990 Iraqi invasion of Kuwait, some members of Congress questioned President Bush's commitment of troops in the Middle East. The War Powers Act was not invoked, however. Instead, Congress authorized the use of force against Iraq, and Operation Desert Storm defeated the Iraqi forces.

Former Senator Jacob Javits explained the dilemma facing members of Congress who support the War Powers Act. He stated:

> *The reluctance to challenge the president is founded in an awareness that he holds, in large degree, the fate of the nation in his hands. We all wish to assist and sustain the presidency. But I have come to the conclusion that the awesome nature of the power over war in our time should require us to withhold, in relevant cases, that unquestioning support of the presidency.*
>
> —JACOB JAVITS,
> "WAR POWERS RECONSIDERED," 1985

Power to Appropriate Money By far the greatest source of congressional power in foreign policy derives from its control over government spending. Only Congress can appropriate the funds to equip American armed forces and to build new weapons. Congress must authorize funds for defense and foreign aid each year. If Congress disapproves of a President's action, such as committing troops to a limited war, it can refuse to provide the funds to maintain the force.

In a similar fashion, Congress may refuse to provide funds for aid to other nations. Congress also may decide not only the sum to be granted but also the conditions that a foreign country must meet to be eligible for aid.

Power in Treaty Making The Constitution also gives the Senate the power of "advice and consent" on all treaties. The President may make treaties with foreign governments, but a two-thirds vote of the Senate must ratify them. In reality, then, Congress is called upon for its consent, not its advice—a practice that actually began with President Washington.

The Senate's power in treaty making is, however, real. Several times in American history, Presidents have had trouble obtaining the necessary two-thirds vote. In 1899, for example, President William McKinley encountered fierce opposition over a proposed treaty with Spain providing for the American takeover of the Philippines. Only after months of debate did the Senate approve it, and then by a margin of only two votes. Similarly, in 1978 President Jimmy Carter faced strong opposition from conservatives in the Senate regarding his proposed Panama treaties. The Senate did eventually ratify both treaties.

On occasion Presidents will bypass Congress by making executive agreements with other nations. **Executive agreements** are pacts between the President and the head of a foreign government that have the same legal status as treaties but do not require Senate approval. In 1940, for example, when many isolationists in Congress opposed involvement in the war in Europe, President Roosevelt entered into an executive agreement to supply 50 old destroyers to Great Britain to help in its fight against Nazi Germany.

Power to Confirm Appointments The Senate must also confirm presidential appointments to diplomatic posts. This power was intended to give the Senate an opportunity to screen applicants for foreign-policy positions and thus help determine foreign policy. Usually the Senate is willing to accept the persons the President appoints to diplomatic posts.

STUDY GUIDE

Themes in Government
Public Policy United States forces have been involved in more than 20 military actions other than declared wars.
Checks and Balances The Senate,

52-47, and the House 250-183, authorized the President to use military force against Iraq.

Critical Thinking Skills
Analyzing Information Why is bipartisan support essential for

something as serious as a war?
Drawing Conclusions In what way do you find Senator Javits' conclusion to be forceful?

Background

The disadvantages of executive agreements include the need for congressional statutes and appropriations to implement them. When secrecy is a factor, public and congressional suspicion can be an issue. This situation occurred in the Yalta Conference near the end of World War II, as public decisions over the future of Europe were accompanied by se-

cret understandings not revealed until years later, and became an issue in subsequent elections. Many executive agreements in recent years, however, have involved trade questions, and their number has steadily increased. When strong public support is desired, Presidents still tend to rely on treaties as a way of achieving and implementing a policy.

The President and Congress Congress's powers could enable the legislature to block some of a President's foreign policies and even initiate policies of its own. Congress, however, waits for the President to set a direction in foreign policy. On most issues Congress passes the foreign-policy bills and treaties the President and his advisers propose.

Over the past several decades, especially in times of war and severe crisis, the President's foreign policies have enjoyed **bipartisan,** or two-party, congressional support. For example, Republican and Democratic members of Congress readily supported President Wilson in World War I and President Roosevelt in World War II. During the Persian Gulf War in 1991, President Bush also received bipartisan support from Congress. Bipartisan support began to unravel, however, during the Vietnam War when Congress and the public were deeply divided about the nation's role in the long and costly war.

Presidential Advantages The President has several advantages over Congress in conducting foreign policy. One is the President's position as the leader of the entire nation. Only the President—or a chosen spokesperson such as the secretary of state—can speak for the nation in its dealings with other governments. It is the President to whom Americans look for leadership in foreign affairs.

A second advantage is that the President controls those agencies, such as the Department of State and the National Security Council, that help formulate and carry out foreign policy on a day-to-day basis. Consequently, the President has greater access to vital secret information about foreign affairs. Such information often is not available to members of Congress.

A third advantage is that the President is able to take quick decisive action. Today it is often necessary to respond to events rapidly, and at times extreme secrecy is essential. The House and Senate must discuss, vote, and take into consideration the opinions of many members. Congress simply cannot act as quickly as the President or maintain secrecy with so many people involved.

Finally, by using executive agreements, the President can bypass the Senate when making agreements with other nations. The result of these advantages has been the steady increase in the President's control over foreign-policy matters.

PARTICIPATING IN GOVERNMENT

Conducting Interviews

The Senate must decide whether to approve the nomination of a Supreme Court justice. Local residents want to choose the best candidate for a school board position. How can these people get the information they need in order to make a decision? People frequently rely on interviews for information about candidates.

A successful interview requires effective questions.

Effective questions are relevant—related to what you want to know. Asking about a candidate's hobbies may provide interesting informa-

tion, but it will not clarify his or her views on an issue.

Effective questions are significant—meaningful. Time for interviews generally is limited. Ask for information that is important.

Effective questions are specific—precise and easy to understand. Specific questions require clear-cut an-swers that provide the information you are seeking.

A good interview requires careful planning and research. Learn as much as you can about the interviewee. Then determine a purpose for the interview. Prepare effective questions that will help you achieve the purpose.

Investigating Further

Plan an interview with a local government official or a candidate for local office. Using the guidelines above, formulate a list of questions for the interview.

CHAPTER 22: FOREIGN POLICY AND NATIONAL DEFENSE 625

Independent Practice

L1 Expressive Writing Remind students that the United States Senate has a strong influence over foreign policy. Have students write a letter to one of their senators expressing their opinions on a current foreign-policy matter. Have students read their letters to the class before mailing them.

📁 **Interpreting Source Readings** Have students complete activity 22 in the *Primary and Secondary Source Readings* in the Teacher's Classroom Resources.

L3 Persuasive Writing Have students write a one-page essay in which they take a position on the constitutionality and wisdom of the War Powers Act of 1973. Ask volunteers to share their essays with the class.

PARTICIPATING IN GOVERNMENT

Ask students to watch a television interview by their favorite reporter or talk-show host. Have students evaluate the interview, using the guidelines mentioned in the feature.

Have students discuss their **Investigating Further** questions.

📁 Have students complete activity 22 in *Participating in Government* in the Teacher's Classroom Resources.

Assess

Check for Understanding

Have students complete Section 3 Review on page 626.

Cooperative Learning Activity

Organize the class into three groups. Assign one of the following topics to each group: foreign-policy powers granted to Congress by the Constitution, constitutional checks and balances in foreign affairs, and public opinion and foreign policy. Students should use textbooks and reference materials to gather information on their topic. Have students in each group take on specific tasks such as identifying resources, researching, organizing information, or presenting. Have the spokesperson for each group present a short report on its topic to the class. Then open the topic for class reaction.

Caption Answer
Antiwar sentiment influenced
President Nixon to begin pulling
American troops out of Vietnam.

Meeting Objectives

Each section objective is
tested by the Section Review
questions that follow it in
parentheses.
• Relate the foreign-policy
  powers granted to Congress
  by the Constitution. (2, 3,
  5, 6, 8)
• Describe the checks and
  balances of the President
  and Congress in terms of
  foreign affairs. (4, 5, 6, 7, 8)

Evaluate

📁 Section 3 Quiz

⊡ Testmaker

Reteach

Have students list the checks
and balances that exist in conducting American foreign policy.

Enrich

Ask students to write a report
on the conflict between Woodrow
Wilson and the Senate over the
Treaty of Versailles.

Close

Ask students why the President
has become the dominant figure
in shaping foreign policy.

Influences of Public Opinion

Though the President and Congress have the
major responsibility for making foreign policy, public
opinion often influences their decisions. Public opinion, for example, directly influenced two wars. One
war began because of the public's continued calls for
involvement, and another war ended when public
opinion opposed continued fighting.

The Spanish-American War The first instance
occurred in the late 1890s when newspapers featured
sensational stories about Spanish mistreatment of
people in Cuba, a colony of Spain. In 1895 the
Cubans had revolted against Spain. Americans found
out about the revolt in Cuba through newspapers
whose reports aroused American sympathy for the
Cuban rebels and fanned American public opinion
against Spain. The stories outraged the American
public. Then a mysterious explosion sank an American battleship, the *Maine,* anchored in Havana harbor. The cry "Remember the *Maine*" swept across
the nation. Eventually, public opinion forced President McKinley to ask Congress for a declaration of
war against Spain.

The Vietnam War In a somewhat similar view,
mass protests and demonstrations in the 1960s and
the early 1970s had a direct impact on foreign policy.
Early on, most Americans supported the fighting in
Vietnam. But as the number of Americans wounded
and killed in Vietnam grew, public opinion slowly
began to turn against the war. The protests began as
student groups staged antiwar demonstrations
throughout the country and called for an end to the

Remember the *Maine*
Press and public furor over the mysterious sinking of
the *Maine* led to the Spanish-American War. **History**
How did public opinion affect the Vietnam War?

Vietnam War. As the war dragged on, other groups
joined the protests. The growing discontent contributed heavily to Lyndon Johnson's decision not to
seek reelection in 1968 and later influenced President
Nixon's decision to begin pulling American troops
out of Vietnam.

3
SECTION REVIEW

Section Summary
Congress's chief source of power in foreign-policy is
based on its control over government spending.

Checking For Understanding
Recalling Facts
1. Define executive agreement, bipartisan.
2. Name the foreign-policy powers of Congress.
3. List the two foreign-policy powers of the Senate.
4. Differentiate between an executive agreement and
   a treaty.

Exploring Themes
5. Public Policy How do forces outside the government influence foreign policy?
6. Checks and Balances How does the Constitution
   provide for checks and balances in foreign affairs?

Critical Thinking Skills
7. Analyzing Information Do you think the President
   should be able to begin military action without a
   declaration of war by Congress? Why or why not?
8. Drawing Conclusions In what ways are congressional appropriations for foreign policy a powerful
   tool?

Section 3 Review Answers

1. Definitions of terms appear on pages indicated:
executive agreement, 624; **bipartisan,** 625
2. the power to declare war and appropriate money for
foreign affairs
3. the power to ratify treaties and confirm diplomatic
appointments
4. A treaty requires approval of the Senate, an executive
agreement does not.

5. It is influenced by public opinion and also by organized
pressure groups that lobby in Congress.
6. Answers should indicate that while constitutional powers enable Congress to block some presidential policy decisions and create its own policies, Congress is willing, in
general, to follow the President's lead in foreign policy. The
President can bypass Congress in not calling a conflict a
war and by taking military action himself, and Congress can
refuse to fund a war.

7. Answers will vary. Students may cite the need for a
speedy response to events and the greater information
available to the President. Others may believe this is an example of too much presidential power.
8. This gives Congress its main opportunity to influence
foreign policy by supporting the President's policy financially or severely crippling it. Congress also decides the relationship the United States may have with other nations
through the control of aid.

The Departments of State and of Defense

It is the duty of the President and Congress to make American foreign policy. Appointed officials in the executive branch, however, carry out foreign policy on a day-to-day basis.

Two departments in the executive branch are primarily responsible for foreign policy and for national security. The Department of State, one of the smallest cabinet-level departments in terms of employees, carries out foreign policy. The Department of Defense is the largest of all the executive departments both in terms of money spent and people employed. It looks after the national security of the United States.

The Department of State

In 1789 the State Department was the first executive department Congress created. At that time it was known as the Department of Foreign Affairs but was soon renamed the Department of State. The secretary of state, head of the State Department, is generally considered to be the most important member of the cabinet, ranking just below the President and Vice President.

The State Department advises the President and formulates and carries out policy. Officially, the Department of State's "primary objective in the conduct of foreign relations is to promote the long-range security and well-being of the United States." The Department of State carries out four other important functions: (1) to keep the President informed about international issues, (2) to maintain diplomatic relations with foreign governments, (3) to negotiate treaties with foreign governments, and (4) to protect the interests of Americans who are traveling or conducting business abroad.

Organizational Structure Five assistant secretaries direct the five geographic bureaus of the State Department. These supervise American policies in different regions of the world. The bureaus are the Bureaus of African Affairs, European and Canadian Affairs, East Asian and Pacific Affairs, Inter-American Affairs, and Near Eastern and South Asian Affairs. Other bureaus analyze information about specific foreign-policy topics. One such bureau deals with educational and cultural affairs, another with political-military problems, and another with intelligence and research. The work of the State Department, therefore, is organized by both topics and regions.

The Foreign Service Of the slightly more than 25,000 employees of the State Department, about 16,000 serve in other countries. The officials who are assigned to serve abroad in foreign countries belong to the Foreign Service.

College graduates who seek a career in the Foreign Service must pass an extremely demanding civil service exam. Successful applicants then receive training in special schools. Foreign Service Officers (FSOs) usually spend several years abroad in a diplomatic post. Then they may be recalled to Washington, D.C., to participate in foreign-policy discussions at the State Department.

For many FSOs, an overseas assignment is valued, but for others it may be a life of hardship. As one observer of the State Department noted:

Working at State demands far more than the usual 40-hour week. . . . Officers stationed overseas are almost never off duty. Not only may they be called on

---

SECTION PREVIEW

Objectives
After studying this section, you should be able to:
- Outline the structure and functions of the Departments of State and Defense.

- Discuss the importance of civilian control of the military in American government.

Key Terms and Concepts
embassy, consulate, consul, passport, visa, conscription

Themes in Government
- Political Processes
- Checks and Balances

Critical Thinking Skills
- Making Inferences
- Demonstrating Reasoned Judgment

CHAPTER 22: FOREIGN POLICY AND NATIONAL DEFENSE 627

Classroom Resources for Section 4

- Guided Reading Activities
- Reproducible Lesson Plans
- Interpreting Political Cartoons 47, 48
- Section 4 Quiz
- Testmaker

- Government Themes Transparencies 33
- Great Speeches, Volume III
- SAT Practice Tests
- Writer's Guidebook

Chapter 22, Section 4
Lesson Plan, pages 627–630

Focus

Bell Ringer

Write the following on the chalkboard for students to complete while attendance is being taken:

What cabinet departments are responsible for foreign policy and for national security?

Motivating Activity

Discuss students' responses to the Bell Ringer activity. *(the Department of State and the Department of Defense)* Ask students to suggest what some functions of these departments might be. Tell them that Section 4 describes the structure of these two departments and their function in implementing American foreign policy.

Vocabulary Precheck

Call on volunteers to tell what they think each key term and concept means. Have students check the accuracy of their definitions in the Glossary. **LEP**

Teach

Guided Practice

L1 Making Comparisons Have students compare and contrast the roles of the Departments of Defense and State in international affairs. *(State: suggests, formulates, and carries out foreign policy; Defense: protects national security and carries out military aspects of foreign policy)*

Analyzing Information Have students view President Eisenhower's "Atoms for Peace" speech from "Great Speeches," Volume III, *Social Studies Videos.* Ask volunteers to summarize the foreign-policy ideals the President expressed. Ask if students agree with his proposals.

👆 **Interpreting Visuals** Display transparency 33 from the *Government Themes Transparencies* in the Teacher's Classroom Resources and use the accompanying teaching strategy and student activity to teach about diplomacy.

L2 Debate Have students debate the following issue:

The United States should have compulsory military service for all American citizens.

Independent Practice

L1 Informative Writing Have students locate the nearest foreign consulate. Have them write a short paragraph explaining why that country has a consulate in the area and what services it provides.

📁 **Interpreting Political Cartoons** Have students complete activity 48 in *Interpreting Political Cartoons* in the Teacher's Classroom Resources.

Caption Answer
The President appoints and the Senate confirms ambassadors.

STUDY GUIDE

Theme Answer
Some bureaus are organized by world regions; others by specialties or topics.

Critical Thinking Answer
as a reward

---

at any hour of the day or night, they also represent the government in every aspect of their lives and personal encounters. Even socializing is work. Attending parties, seemingly an attractive way of making a living, pales after weeks of mandatory and boring appearances following an intensive workday.
—BARRY RUBIN, *SECRETS OF STATE,* 1985

In their service abroad, Foreign Service Officers are normally assigned either to an American embassy or to an American consulate.

Embassies The United States maintains **embassies** in the capital cities of foreign countries — such as Tokyo, Paris, and Nairobi. An embassy includes the official residence and offices of the ambassador and his or her staff. The primary function of an embassy is to make diplomatic communication between governments easier. Currently, the State Department directs the work of about 150 American embassies.

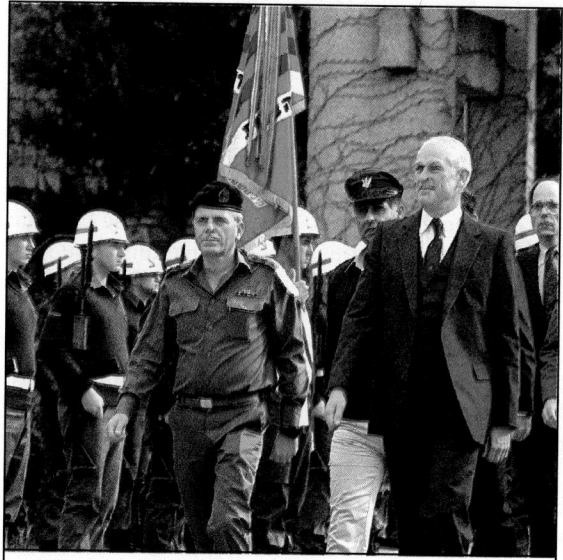

Representing the United States
United States ambassador to Israel William Brown reviews Israeli troops in 1988. **Politics** Who appoints and who confirms ambassadors?

Embassy officials keep the State Department informed about the politics and foreign policies of the host government. They also keep the host government informed about American policies.

An ambassador heads each American embassy. Most ambassadors today come from the ranks of the Foreign Service as experienced and highly qualified professional diplomats. Some ambassadors, however, may be political appointees, selected for reasons other than their diplomatic knowledge or experience. In every case, however, an ambassador is appointed by the President and must be confirmed by the Senate.

Each embassy includes specialists who deal with political and military matters, trade, travel, and currency. The specialists help resolve disputes that arise between the host country and the United States. Most disputes are minor enough to be settled by the embassy staff. In the case of major disagreements, governments may break off diplomatic relations by closing their embassies. Such action represents the strongest sign of displeasure that one government can show toward another.

Consulates The United States also maintains offices known as **consulates** in major cities of foreign nations. Consulates are not normally involved in diplomatic negotiations with foreign governments. They function primarily to promote American business interests in foreign countries and to serve and safeguard American travelers in the country.

Heading each consulate is a Foreign Service Officer called a **consul.** In the course of a routine day, the consul and staff handle individual problems and inquiries about such matters as shipping schedules, business opportunities, and travel needs.

Passports and Visas For Americans traveling abroad, the State Department issues a document called a **passport.** The traveler whose photograph and signature appear on the passport is entitled to certain privileges and protection established by an international treaty. With a passport, an American citizen can expect to be granted entry into many countries.

STUDY GUIDE

Themes in Government
Political Processes People who work for the State Department complain that it has too many bureaus, too many committees, and too much paperwork. **How** are the bureaus of the State Department organized?

Critical Thinking Skills
Making Inferences In making political appointees of ambassadors, why would the President appoint as ambassador a party member who made large financial contributions?

Background

Defense spending declined by about $20 billion between 1990 and 1994. Largely, the cuts in military personnel and materials reflected the national perception of a decreased threat from former communist nations. At the same time, several isolated threats to national security seemed to call for an American response, and some people wondered whether it was wise to make major cuts in military spending in a world that has so many potential trouble spots. While defense cuts do not have any substantial effect on the national economy, closing of bases and the decline in government purchases for defense have affected the economies of many localities.

In some cases, however, it is necessary to obtain another document called a visa. A **visa** is a special document issued by the government of the country that a person wishes to enter. If a citizen of Kenya wishes to visit the United States, for example, he or she must apply for a visa at an American embassy or consulate in one of the major Kenyan cities.

American immigration laws require almost all foreign visitors to obtain a visa. The countries of Western Europe, however, do not require American travelers to carry visas, only passports.

The Department of Defense

To protect national security, the Department of Defense (DOD) supervises the armed forces of the United States and makes sure these forces are strong enough to defend American interests. The Department of Defense assists the President in carrying out the duties of commander in chief.

Establishing the Department of Defense Before 1947 the Departments of War and the Navy were responsible for the nation's defense. The country's experiences in coordinating military forces in World War II, however, prompted a military reorganization. The result was the National Security Establishment that two years later became the Department of Defense. From the outset, the secretary of defense was a member of the President's cabinet.

Civilian Control of the Military Civilian control of the military is one of the most important principles of American government. The Founders made sure that the military would always be subordinate to the civilian leaders of the government. Thus, the ultimate authority for commanding the armed forces rests with the civilian commander in chief, the President.

Congress also exercises considerable authority over military matters. Because of its constitutional power over appropriations, Congress determines how much money the Department of Defense will spend each year.

GLOBAL CONNECTION

Comparing Governments

Control of the Military Revolutions and military coups in many Latin American countries show that a strong military can pose a threat to a free government. Uncontrolled military power also triggered the Persian Gulf crisis in 1990 when Iraq's Saddam Hussein seized control of Kuwait.

Armed forces are vital to the United States' defense, but the Constitution restricts the power of the military by placing it under civilian control. Ultimate military control rests with a civilian, the President, who is elected by the people. Congress, made up of elected representatives, exercises control by determining how much money is available for the military. In addition, the Defense Department is staffed by civilians.

Examining the Connection
What role do United States citizens play in civilian control of the military?

Congress also has the power to determine how each branch of the armed forces shall be organized and governed. In order to maintain civilian control of the military, the top leaders of the Department of Defense all are required to be civilians.

Size of the Department of Defense With more than 1 million civilian employees and about 2 million military personnel on active duty, the Defense Department is the largest executive department. It is headquartered in the Pentagon in Washington, D.C.

Army, Navy, and Air Force Among the major divisions within the Department of Defense are the De-

GLOBAL CONNECTION

Review with students the reason for civilian control of the military in the United States. Ask students to find out in what countries the military is very powerful and to explain why this is so.

Examining the Connection Answer: *President is commander in chief. Congress determines how much money Department of Defense can spend and determines organization of armed forces. Citizens elect President and members of Congress.*

📁 **Interpreting Political Cartoons** Have students complete activity 47 in *Interpreting Political Cartoons* in the Teacher's Classroom Resources.

STUDY GUIDE

Theme Answer
Congress, annually

Critical Thinking Answer
Answers will vary, but may include that some volunteers may join for other than patriotic reasons.

Assess

Check for Understanding

Have students complete Section 4 Review on page 630.

STUDY GUIDE

Themes in Government
Checks and Balances Past Defense Department spending ranged from 25 to 30 percent of the nation's total budget. **To whom and how often does the Defense Department answer for its money?**

Critical Thinking Skills
Demonstrating Reasoned Judgment **Do you think an armed forces made up of volunteers will perform better or worse than draftees? Explain your answer.**

Cooperative Learning Activity

Group students into "Home Teams" and then have them number off 1–10 to form "Expert Teams." Expert Teams consist of one member from each Home Team. Assign each Expert Team one of the subheads under the main headings "The Department of State" and "The Department of Defense". Students in the Expert Teams should discuss the material pertaining to their assigned subheading and create a teaching tool that will help in sharing the material with their Home Team.

Meeting Objectives

Each section objective is tested by the Section Review questions that follow it in parentheses.
- Outline the structure and functions of the Departments of State and Defense. (2, 3, 4, 5, 7, 8)
- Discuss the importance of civilian control of the military in American government. (6)

Evaluate

 Section 4 Quiz

Testmaker

Reteach

Have students list the ways that the State Department and the Defense Department influence American foreign policy and the factors that limit their influence.

Enrich

Ask students to research and write a report on methods used by other countries to recruit soldiers.

Close

Ask students: Is there any need for the military to be subordinate to civilian leaders?

Uncle Sam Wants Volunteers
A young man enlists in the Navy. **History What events sparked the use of conscription?**

partment of the Army, the Department of the Navy, and the Department of the Air Force. A civilian secretary, assisted by senior military officers, heads each of these branches. The United States Marine Corps, which is under the jurisdiction of the Navy, maintains its own leadership, identity, and traditions.

The Joint Chiefs of Staff The President, the National Security Council, and the secretary of defense rely on the Joint Chiefs of Staff (JCS) for military advice. This group is made up of the top-ranking officers of the armed forces. Included are the Chief of Staff of the Army, Chief of Staff of the Air Force, and the Chief of Naval Operations. The Commandant of the Marine Corps also attends meetings of the Joint Chiefs of Staff. The fifth member is the Chairman of the Joint Chiefs of Staff, who is appointed for a two-year term by the President.

A Volunteer Military The United States first used compulsory military service, or **conscription,** during the Civil War. It was again initiated in World War I. Since that time the armed services have used two methods to recruit soldiers. One method was conscription, or the draft, that was reinstituted in 1940 and lasted into the 1970s. The second method has been to enlist volunteers in the all-volunteer armed forces Congress established in the mid-1970s.

By executive order, President Richard Nixon suspended the draft in 1973. The law that originally created the Selective Service System was not repealed, however, merely suspended. This suspension means that males between the ages of 18 and 25 could be drafted if conscription is reinstituted.

Since 1980 all males of eligible age have been required to register their names and addresses with local draft boards. The requirement applies to all young men residing in the United States who have passed their eighteenth birthdays.

Though women are not eligible to be drafted, they may volunteer to serve in any branch of the armed services. All military services are now committed to the goal of increasing the number of female recruits.

4 SECTION REVIEW

Section Summary
The two departments responsible for carrying out American foreign policy on a day-to-day basis and protecting national security are the Departments of State and Defense.

Checking For Understanding
Recalling Facts
1. Define embassy, consulate, consul, passport, visa, conscription.
2. Identify four functions of the State Department.
3. Name the two executive departments that are responsible for foreign policy and national security.
4. List the people who make up the Joint Chiefs of Staff.

Exploring Themes
5. Political Processes To whom do the Joint Chiefs of Staff serve as advisers?
6. Checks and Balances While the ultimate authority for commanding the armed forces rests with the President, Congress also has authority to affect military matters. Describe these powers of Congress.

Critical Thinking Skills
7. Making Inferences Why do you think embassies have been a target for political protests and terrorist activities in recent years?
8. Demonstrating Reasoned Judgment American servicewomen fought in the Persian Gulf War of 1991. This role of women in battle created a controversy at home. Do you support women being on the battlefield? Explain your answer.

630 UNIT 7: PUBLIC POLICIES AND SERVICES

Section 4 Review Answers

1. Definitions of terms appear on pages indicated: **embassy,** 628; **consulate,** 628; **consul,** 628; **passport,** 628; **visa,** 629; **conscription,** 630
2. to keep the President informed about international issues, to maintain diplomatic relations with foreign governments, to negotiate treaties with foreign governments, to protect the interests of Americans who are traveling or conducting business abroad

3. Department of State, Department of Defense
4. Chief of Staff of the Army, Chief of Staff of the Air Force, Chief of Naval Operations, Commandant of the Marine Corps, Chairman of the Joint Chiefs of Staff
5. to the President, the National Security Council, and the secretary of defense
6. determines how much money the Department of Defense will spend each year and how each branch of the armed forces shall be organized

7. Answers may vary, but should indicate that embassies are the nerve centers of the countries they represent on foreign soil. They are the diplomatic and communications link to the home country. So statements or actions made at embassies have the most profound effect.
8. Answers will vary, but students should agree or disagree with women's efforts and demands for more inclusive and equal treatment.

Achieving Foreign-Policy Goals

SECTION 5

The desire to preserve national security and economic well-being often can lead to conflicts between nations. To minimize the danger to national security, the United States tries to settle such conflicts peacefully and to negotiate agreements with foreign governments. The tools that are available include alliances, programs of foreign aid, economic sanctions, and, in extreme circumstances, military action. Speaking to the American people, President Clinton affirmed, "When national security interests are threatened we will use diplomacy when possible and force when necessary."

Alliances and Pacts

Throughout history when nations felt a common threat to their security, they negotiated **mutual defense alliances.** Nations that became allies under such alliances usually agreed to support each other in case of an attack.

Through such alliances, the United States has committed itself to defending three regions of the world. These regions are Western Europe and the North Atlantic, Central and South America, and the island nations of the South Pacific. The United States has signed mutual defense treaties with nations in these three regions. The treaties that protect these areas are referred to as **regional security pacts.**

The North Atlantic Treaty Organization After World War II, the United States and several nations in Western Europe wanted to defend themselves against the Soviet Union. The Truman Doctrine and the

Marshall Plan were part of the resulting policy of containment. The leaders of the free world also developed a regional security pact to guarantee the security of Western Europe and other nations. This treaty created the North Atlantic Treaty Organization (NATO). Under this mutual defense treaty it was stated that "The parties agree that an armed attack against one or more of them in Europe or North America shall be considered an attack against them all."

Under NATO, hundreds of thousands of troops were stationed on military bases in Western Europe. Troops from the United States, West Germany, Great Britain, and other NATO nations served under a common command: the Supreme Allied Command Europe (SACEUR). France, though still a member of NATO, withdrew its armed forces from the NATO command.

While military in nature, NATO's goals, in the words of Paul Henri Spaak, a secretary general of NATO, are:

> *To maintain the security of the North Atlantic area, and to guarantee the principles on which Western civilization rested—respect for individual rights and human dignity and the exercise of government through the consent of the governed.*
> —PAUL HENRI SPAAK,
> "NATO: ALLIANCE FOR PEACE," 1981

For more than 40 years, NATO countered the Soviet-led Warsaw Pact nations' military might. As the Soviet Union crumbled and the cold war ended, however, the rivalry lost momentum. In November 1990, the *International Herald Tribune* reported:

SECTION PREVIEW

Objectives
After studying this section, you should be able to:
- Discuss the tools the United States uses to achieve foreign-policy goals.

- Describe the role of the United Nations as a peacekeeping force.

Key Terms and Concepts
mutual defense alliance, regional security pact, multilateral treaty, bilateral treaty, collective security, sanction, domino theory

Themes in Government
- Growth of Democracy
- Public Policy

Critical Thinking Skills
- Demonstrating Reasoned Judgment
- Drawing Conclusions

CHAPTER 22: FOREIGN POLICY AND NATIONAL DEFENSE   631

Classroom Resources for Section 5

- Guided Reading Activities
- Reproducible Lesson Plans
- Reteaching Activities 22
- Enrichment Activities 22
- Section 5 Quiz
- Chapter 22 Tests

- Testmaker
- Chapter Transparencies 22
- Government Themes Transparencies 34
- Audio Cassettes (English and Spanish)
- Limited English Proficiency Activities 22
  SAT Practice Tests

Chapter 22, Section 5
Lesson Plan, pages 631–637

Focus

Bell Ringer

Write the following on the chalkboard for students to complete while attendance is being taken:

Identify the following abbreviations: UNICEF, WHO, FAO.

Motivating Activity

Discuss students' Bell Ringer responses. (*UNICEF—United Nations Children's Fund, WHO—World Health Organization, FAO—Food and Agriculture Organization*) Tell students that these are the more familiar of the United Nations' specialized agencies. Determine what students know about the purpose of the United Nations. Tell them Section 5 discusses the functions of the United Nations and the various tools the United States uses to achieve foreign-policy goals.

Vocabulary Precheck

Write the terms and concepts on the chalkboard. Ask students to use those that they know in sentences. **LEP**

CONNECTIONS

Global Perspectives
At the NATO summit meeting held in November of 1991, members decided to formalize links with Czechoslovakia, Hungary, and Poland. The commitment of NATO to these Eastern European nations was not concrete, however. Many members of NATO did not want to guarantee military aid to these former members of the Warsaw Pact. NATO also agreed to cut nuclear weapons in Europe by 90 percent by 1995 and to reduce "central region" forces by 50 percent.

Teach

Guided Practice

L1 Geography Call on volunteers to find on a world map the areas of the world involved in the alliances promoted in these treaties and pacts: NATO, the Warsaw Pact, the Rio Pact, OAS, the ANZUS Pact. **LEP**

Interpreting Visuals Display transparency 34 from the *Government Themes Transparencies* in the Teacher's Classroom Resources and use the accompanying teaching strategy and student activity to teach about the Peace Corps.

Map Study Answer

Foreign military presence in the Western Hemisphere will not be tolerated.

STUDY GUIDE

Theme Answer
NATO

Critical Thinking Answer
A nation would not depend on itself alone for security.

Linking Past and Present

In 1991 Belize and Guyana became the thirty-fourth and thirty-fifth members of the OAS. The OAS finally included all Latin American and Caribbean nations, except Cuba. Also, for the first time since the formation of the OAS in 1948, all member nations were led by democratically elected governments.

---

*L*eaders of the 22 members of the North Atlantic Treaty Organization and the Warsaw Pact abandoned more than four decades of military confrontation on Monday by signing an arms treaty that will dramatically reduce non-nuclear arsenals in Europe.

In a companion pledge disavowing any future aggression against each other, the leaders declared that the end of the Cold War era meant that they are no longer adversaries, will build new partnerships and extend to each other the hand of friendship.

—WILLIAM DROZDIAK,
INTERNATIONAL HERALD TRIBUNE, 1990

Latin America and the Pacific In 1947 the United States and its Latin American neighbors signed the Rio Pact. Among its provisions is this statement:

*A*n armed attack by any State against an American State shall be considered as an attack against all the American States, and, consequently, each one of the . . . contracting parties undertakes to assist in meeting the attack. . . .

—RIO PACT, 1947

Since 1947, most Latin American nations and the United States have participated in the Rio Pact. Following its revolution, Cuba withdrew from the pact in 1960.

In 1948 the United States signed a related treaty, establishing the Organization of American States (OAS). Unlike the Rio Pact, the OAS is primarily concerned with promoting economic development. A second goal of the OAS nations is "to help each other settle international disputes by peaceful means."

The United States also has a regional security pact with Australia and New Zealand. The ANZUS Pact, signed in September, 1951, obliged Australia, New Zealand, and the United States to come to one another's aid in case of attack. In 1984 the government of New Zealand adopted a policy that excluded nuclear weapons and nuclear-powered ships from the nation's ports and waters. In response to this policy, the United States announced in 1986 that it would no longer guarantee New Zealand's security under the ANZUS treaty.

Bilateral Treaties of Alliance NATO, the Rio Pact, OAS, and ANZUS are all examples of multilateral treaties. **Multilateral treaties** are international agreements signed by several nations. The United States has also signed bilateral treaties of alliance. A **bilateral treaty** involves only two nations.

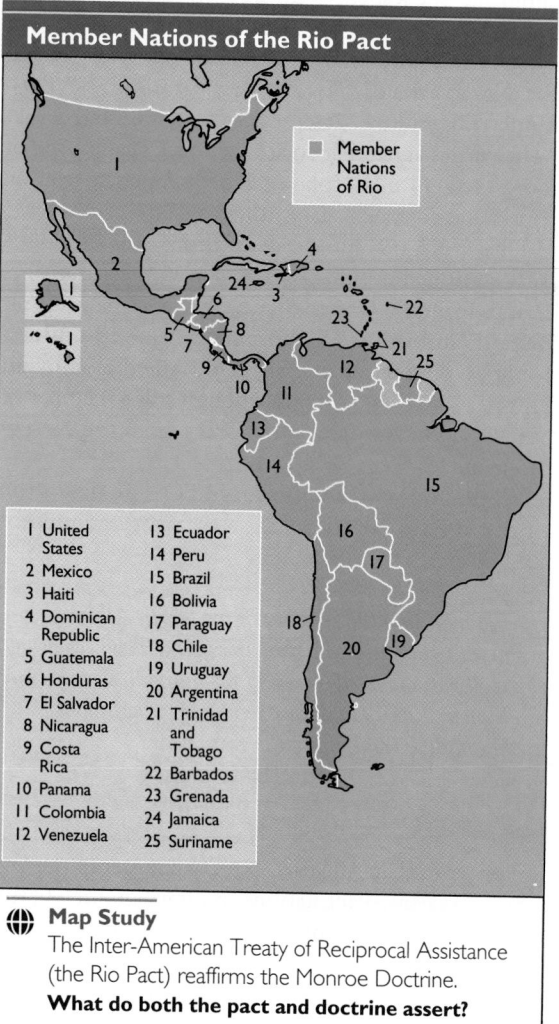

Member Nations of the Rio Pact

■ Member Nations of Rio

1 United States	13 Ecuador
2 Mexico	14 Peru
3 Haiti	15 Brazil
4 Dominican Republic	16 Bolivia
5 Guatemala	17 Paraguay
6 Honduras	18 Chile
7 El Salvador	19 Uruguay
8 Nicaragua	20 Argentina
9 Costa Rica	21 Trinidad and Tobago
10 Panama	22 Barbados
11 Colombia	23 Grenada
12 Venezuela	24 Jamaica
	25 Suriname

⊕ Map Study
The Inter-American Treaty of Reciprocal Assistance (the Rio Pact) reaffirms the Monroe Doctrine.
What do both the pact and doctrine assert?

STUDY GUIDE

Themes in Government
Growth of Democracy Warsaw Pact countries, once dominated by the Soviet Union, have adopted democratic governments. **Which** alliance stood guard against the former Warsaw Pact?

Critical Thinking Skills
Demonstrating Reasoned Judgment Why would the stipulation of "an attack against one shall be considered as an attack against all" create a sense of security?

Background

The biggest obstacle to passing foreign aid legislation is the public sentiment that more United States money should be spent on domestic and less on foreign problems. Congress is, therefore, reluctant to increase or even to vote on foreign aid legislation. When a foreign aid bill does reach the floor, it is usually attacked in all the particulars. For example, in 1993 one lawmaker tried to reduce economic development assistance to India unless that government repealed laws to punish dissidents in Punjab and Kashmir. Another tried to cut funds for the Agency for International Development because of allegations of corruption and mismanagement at the agency. Sometimes Congress attaches foreign aid appropriations as amendments to other legislation, just to get something passed.

One bilateral treaty, signed in 1951, makes the United States an ally of Japan. A similar treaty, also signed in 1951, pledges the United States to the defense of the Philippines. A third bilateral treaty, signed in 1953, makes the United States an ally of South Korea.

The United States has alliances with almost 50 nations. These nations can count on the military support of the United States in case of an attack. The objective of these treaties is to provide collective security for the United States and its allies. **Collective security** is a system by which the participating nations agree to take joint action against a nation that attacks any one of them.

Foreign Aid Programs

Military alliances are one benefit that the United States may offer to friendly nations. American leaders can also offer military support in the form of grants or loans to purchase American armaments. Economic aid is another benefit American leaders can offer. Economic aid has long been used to forge closer ties between the United States and the world's developing nations. Since the end of World War II, this aid has had two purposes. One purpose has been to establish friendly relations with these nations. The second purpose has been to help these nations emerge as eventual economic partners.

Many developing nations have problems satisfying even the minimum needs of their people for food, housing, and education. They urgently need loans and technical assistance. Since 1946 the United States has provided more than $220 billion in economic aid worldwide and about $140 billion in military aid. Today, the Agency for International Development (AID), an agency of the State Department, administers American programs of economic aid. AID has considerable independence, however, and its officials dispense loans and technical assistance with very little direction from the secretary of state.

Economic Sanctions

Alliances and economic benefits are two methods of influencing the policies of other nations. The withdrawal or denial of benefits is a third diplomatic strategy. American policymakers sometimes use this strategy when they deal with governments that follow policies the United States dislikes.

One way of withdrawing benefits is by applying sanctions. **Sanctions** are measures such as withholding loans, arms, or economic aid to force a foreign government to cease certain activities. During this century, the United States has employed sanctions more than 75 times. Sanctions were directed against Iraq, beginning in 1990.

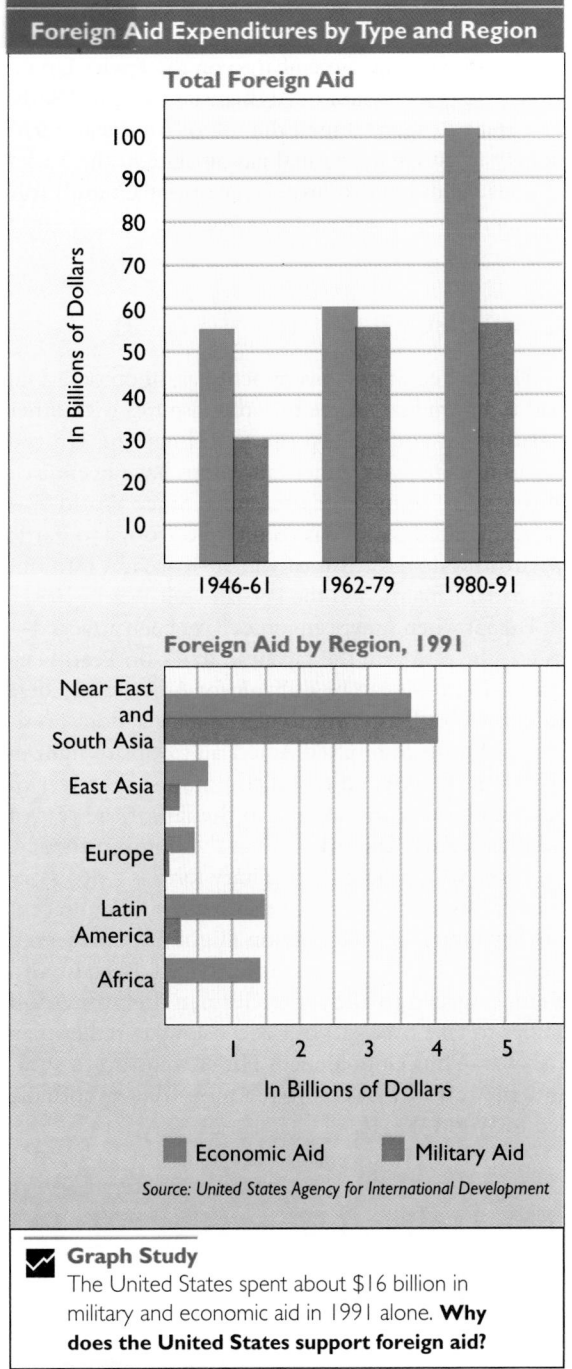

Foreign Aid Expenditures by Type and Region

Total Foreign Aid

In Billions of Dollars

1946-61   1962-79   1980-91

Foreign Aid by Region, 1991

Near East and South Asia
East Asia
Europe
Latin America
Africa

In Billions of Dollars

■ Economic Aid   ■ Military Aid

Source: United States Agency for International Development

Graph Study
The United States spent about $16 billion in military and economic aid in 1991 alone. **Why does the United States support foreign aid?**

L2 Synthesizing Information Present students with the following examples and have them identify the foreign-policy tool that is illustrated.

a. Three countries agree to aid one another if one of them is attacked. (*multilateral treaty*)
b. One country agrees to give farm equipment if another's government will agree to resist communism. (*foreign aid*)
c. One country stops giving assistance to another because its human rights record is poor. (*economic sanctions*)
d. One country sends helicopters and pilots to help another country combat rebels who are fighting the current government. (*military force*)

L3 Public Policy Discuss with students the various factors that influence foreign-policy formation. Stage a class debate on the following topic:

The most important influences on American foreign policy are the condition and goals of the nation's economy.

Graph Study Answer
to forge friendly relations with nations receiving aid, and to help developing nations emerge as eventual economic partners

CONNECTIONS

History
In 1946 John D. Rockefeller, Jr., donated $8.5 million to the United Nations to build a headquarters along the East River in New York City. Today, the UN Headquarters is considered international territory.

Cooperative Learning Activity

Organize the class into seven groups. Assign one of the following areas to each group: South Africa, China, Japan, Western Europe, Eastern Europe, Latin America, the Middle East. Have each group present a report on American policy today toward their assigned area. Have each student from each group take on a specific task such as obtaining resources, researching, writing, or presenting. Have the spokesperson for each group present a five-minute report, then open the topic for class discussion.

Interpreting Visuals Display transparency 22 from the *Chapter Transparencies* in the Teacher's Classroom Resources and use the accompanying teaching strategy and student activity to teach about alliances.

Independent Practice

L1 Art Have students research to find out about the special agencies of the United Nations, such as UNESCO, WHO, and WMO. Have them make posters illustrating the work of the agencies. **LEP**

STUDY GUIDE

Theme Answer
Sanctions withhold items or goods that are needed by a country.

Critical Thinking Answer
The UN includes most of the world's nations.

CONNECTIONS

Political Processes
In 1976 Congress determined that the government of Uruguay was guilty of grossly violating the human rights of its citizens. Therefore, it attached to its Foreign Assistance Act the provision that Uruguay receive no military aid.

GLENCOE
TECHNOLOGY

Focus on Government
Video 55
Electronic Field Trip: The United Nations
Running Time: 4:16
Videodisc 3, Chap. 55
VHS Tape 3, Begins 42:15

The United States may also restrict trade with another nation as an economic sanction. President Carter imposed a grain embargo on the Soviet Union after its 1979 invasion of Afghanistan. In the 1980s, President Reagan banned the use of American technology in building a natural gas pipeline in the Soviet Union. He did this to protest the Soviet Union's role in suppressing a trade union in Poland.

The Use of Military Force

The United States government has, upon occasion, had to use military force to settle disputes with other nations. In addition to the five times the United States declared war, American troops have been used abroad on a number of occasions. Since World War II, the United States has committed troops to battle without a declaration of war in Korea, Vietnam, Grenada, Panama, and the Persian Gulf War in 1991.

Except when American forces have been attacked—as was the case with the Japanese attack on Pearl Harbor in 1941—it can be difficult for American leaders to know whether or not to use military action. President Johnson committed American troops to fight in Vietnam. He argued that a communist takeover of South Vietnam would lead to the fall of the rest of Southeast Asia. This is known as the **domino theory**.

Those who believe that military force is a necessary tool of foreign policy argue that many times in recent history limited military action might have preserved peace. In 1938, for example, Great Britain and France agreed to allow the German dictator Adolf Hitler to take over part of Czechoslovakia rather than risk war. Thus emboldened, Hitler went on to swallow the rest of that country, a move that eventually led to World War II.

The United Nations

In 1945 the United States and other nations helped establish the United Nations (UN) to provide a forum for nations to settle their disputes by peaceful means. The resulting rivalry between the communist bloc nations and the nations of the free world, however, severely limited the UN's capacity to maintain peace. Yet, as President Bush noted after the 1991 Persian Gulf War:

Now, we can see a new world order coming into view. . . . A world where the United Nations, freed from cold war stalemate, is poised to fulfill the historic vision of its founders. A world in which freedom and respect for human rights find a home among all nations. . . .
—GEORGE BUSH, "THE WAR IS OVER," 1991

The Charter of the United Nations identifies the organization's three major goals. One is to preserve world peace and security. The second is to encourage nations to be just in their actions toward one another. The third is to help nations cooperate in trying to solve their problems.

UN membership is open to all "peace-loving states." More than 165 nations of the world are now members.

Three bodies in the UN help fulfill the organization's goals. They include the General Assembly, the Security Council, and the International Court of Justice. UN headquarters are in New York City, where the General Assembly and the Security Council are based. The International Court of Justice holds its sessions in The Hague, Netherlands.

The General Assembly The largest of the UN's peacekeeping bodies is the General Assembly. It discusses, debates, and recommends solutions for problems presented to the UN. Each member may send a delegation of five representatives to the General Assembly, but each nation has only one vote. Most questions in the General Assembly are decided by a majority vote.

The UN Charter gives the General Assembly the authority to make recommendations to the UN's smaller peacekeeping body, the Security Council.

STUDY GUIDE

Themes in Government
Public Policy Some argued that President Bush did not allow enough time for economic sanctions to take effect against Iraq.

Why are sanctions at times an effective policy against nations that become aggressive?

Critical Thinking Skills
Drawing Conclusions Why do you think the United Nations may be instrumental in building a new world order?

Special Needs Strategy

Attention Problems Attention problems are often characterized by high levels of distractibility. Students may be surprised at the noise level in even the quietest settings and how this background noise can affect reading comprehension. Demonstrate this by having students read "Foreign Aid Programs" on page 633, and, while doing so, jot down every background noise they hear. Have them compare their lists with others in the class. What is most distracting? Were distractions the same for everyone? How can they protect themselves from distractions?

The United Nations

Economic and
Social Council

Trusteeship
Council

Security
Council

Conference
Building

Secretariat
Building

General Assembly Building

Dag
Hammarskjöld
Library

General Assembly
All UN members belong to the General Assembly. It discusses matters of world peace and security and recommends actions to the Security Council.

Security Council
Its 15 members have the authority to make peacekeeping decisions for the UN.

International Court of Justice
This court hears disputes over international law brought to it by UN members. It is located in The Hague, Netherlands.

Trusteeship Council
Its five members supervise territories that were formerly colonies of other nations.

Secretariat
Headed by the UN Secretary General, this organization carries out the daily activities of the UN.

Economic and Social Council
With 54 members, this body works to advance human rights and improve worldwide standards of living.

Specialized Agencies
Twenty-two independent agencies work to improve social and economic conditions on a global scale, operating in special fields such as Food and Agricultural Organization, International Labor Organization, Universal Postal Union, World Health Organization.

CHAPTER 22: FOREIGN POLICY AND NATIONAL DEFENSE **635**

L2 **Journalism** Have students examine newspaper and magazine articles to find examples of the tools of foreign policy in use. Students should give a brief summary of the article and indicate the tool used.

L3 **Mathematics** Have students construct bar or line graphs to illustrate trends in federal money allocated for foreign aid in recent years. Students might refer to the *Statistical Abstract of the United States*. Have students use the graphs to write generalizations about United States foreign aid.

CONNECTIONS

Biography
One of the first delegates to the new United Nations was Eleanor Roosevelt, appointed by President Truman. In 1946 she was named chairperson of the UN Commission on Human Rights.

Assess

Check for Understanding

Have students complete Section 5 Review on page 636.

Meeting Objectives

Each section objective is tested by the Section Review questions that follow it in parentheses.
• Discuss the tools the United States uses to achieve foreign-policy goals. (2, 3, 5, 6)
• Describe the role of the United Nations as a peace-keeping force. (4, 6, 7, 8)

Evaluate

📁 Section 5 Quiz

 Testmaker

Critical Thinking Activity

Drawing Conclusions Point out to students that although member nations contribute to the operations of the United Nations, the United States pays a larger percentage of the cost than any other nation. Ask the following: Considering recent changes in the world, do you think that United States support for the UN should continue unchanged? Why or why not? Then have the class react to each respondent's position.

Caption Answer
to preserve world peace and security, to encourage nations to be just in their actions, to encourage nations to solve problems together

Reteach

📁 Have students complete activity 22 in *Reteaching Activities* in the Teacher's Classroom Resources.

Enrich

📁 Have students complete activity 22 in *Enrichment Activities* in the Teacher's Classroom Resources.

Close

Have students explain whether or not they think the United Nations would be more effective as a peacekeeping force if it had a standing army.

CONNECTIONS

Global Perspectives
Some observers suggest that the election of Boutros Boutros-Ghali of Egypt to the position of UN Secretary General in 1992 was an acknowledgment of the importance of the Middle East in world affairs.

New Secretary General of the United Nations
Boutros Boutros-Ghali (left) greets predecessor Perez De Cuellar. **History** Name the major UN goals.

Important issues must be adopted by a two-thirds vote in the Assembly. Other issues are decided by a simple majority.

The Security Council The Security Council is the UN's principal agency for maintaining peace. It is composed of 15 nations. Five of these nations are permanent members of the Security Council. They are the United States, Russia, the People's Republic of China, France, and Great Britain. The General Assembly elects the other 10 members for 2-year terms.

The Security Council has the authority to make peacekeeping decisions for the United Nations. The Council may call for breaking off relations with a nation, ending trade with a nation, or using military force. Because of its rules of procedure, however, the Security Council rarely makes such decisions.

According to the UN Charter, 9 of the Council's 15 members must vote in favor of any course of action. On important matters, however, the 9 members must include the votes of all permanent members. Thus, if only 1 permanent member vetoes a measure, the Security Council is unable to act.

International Court of Justice and Special Agencies The third peacekeeping body of the UN is the International Court of Justice. Member nations may voluntarily submit disputes over international law to this court for settlement. The General Assembly and the Security Council select the 15 judges that sit on the International Court of Justice.

The UN has been especially effective in using its special agencies to advance peace and aid the social and economic progress of developing nations. The World Food Council coordinates the delivery of millions of tons of food to developing countries every year. Meanwhile, the World Health Organization (WHO) has helped raise health levels in many nations. Among its many other accomplishments, WHO successfully fought a cholera epidemic in Egypt and conducts drives against malaria and other diseases.

The relaxation of tensions between the world's superpowers promises to produce a new world order. If so, the United Nations may emerge as a true peacekeeping force in the years to come.

---

5 SECTION REVIEW

Section Summary
The United States uses alliances, treaties, aid programs, economic sanctions, and military force to achieve foreign-policy goals.

Checking For Understanding
Recalling Facts
1. Define mutual defense alliance, regional security pact, multilateral treaty, bilateral treaty, collective security, sanction, domino theory.
2. List two mutual defense alliances, besides NATO, in which the United States is a partner.
3. Describe the purpose of NATO.
4. Name the three bodies of the United Nations.

Exploring Themes
5. Growth of Democracy What two purposes are served by foreign aid?
6. Public Policy How does the United States achieve foreign-policy goals?

Critical Thinking Skills
7. Demonstrating Reasoned Judgment Do you think the United States could depend on agreements made through the United Nations and stop making treaties of alliance? Support your answer.
8. Drawing Conclusions The United Nations has often been criticized for its ineffectiveness in maintaining peace. In what areas do you think the United Nations has been particularly successful?

Section 5 Review Answers

1. Definitions of terms appear on pages indicated: **mutual defense alliance,** 631; **regional security pact,** 631; **multilateral treaty,** 632; **bilateral treaty,** 632; **collective security,** 633; **sanction,** 633, **domino theory,** 634
2. the Rio Pact and the ANZUS Pact
3. It is a mutual defense alliance between the United States and several nations in Western Europe. It was

formed because these nations felt they had to defend themselves against the ambitions of the Soviet Union.
4. the General Assembly, the Security Council, the International Court of Justice
5. It establishes friendly relationships with developing nations and helps these nations emerge as eventual economic partners.

6. alliances, programs of foreign aid, economic sanctions, military action
7. Answers will vary, but students may cite the historical inability of the UN to enforce all its agreements.
8. Answers should reflect humanitarian concerns.

Angela Dickey on Life in the Foreign Service

Angela Dickey, a member of the United States Foreign Service, recalled her entry into Mauritania on the west coast of Africa. Working for the American ambassador, her job was to represent the United States and gather information about Mauritania.

The night flight from Paris to Nouakchott has lasted more than five hours. I am disoriented from a lack of sleep and from the foreign chatter of my fellow passengers; though I catch a few words of French here, a phrase or two of Arabic there, I am for the most part lost in a sea of African languages.

It is 5 A.M. Nouakchott time. As our plane hovers over the city, I see nothing but swirling sand below. There are no lights to guide our way, yet the pilot miraculously brings us safely down onto a thin strip of pavement. Someone props a ladder against the shell of the plane so that we can climb down. For a moment, just before I step onto

the ladder, I think of home, of America, where the crisp cool days of fall have just begun.

Suddenly, a hot blast of wind roars at me from out of nowhere. I have the impression of falling into a furnace. Then I remember: This is my home now. The Sahara.

It has been three years since I joined the Foreign Service, and during that time I have not been bored one single day. I have been challenged, thrilled, exhausted, and overwhelmed—but never bored.

My first tour took me to Montreal, Canada, where I worked as a visa and citizenship officer in the United States consulate. Montreal is the second-largest French-speaking city in the world (after Paris), and there I had the opportunity to practice the language that I had studied for so many years in school. In Montreal my main job was to interview people—Canadians, Europeans, Africans, South Americans—who wanted to travel to the United States, either for a visit or to live permanently. I was responsible for deciding which of these persons would be given a permit, or visa, to enter our country. . . .

. . . since I joined the Foreign Service, . . . I have not been bored one single day. I have been challenged, thrilled, exhausted, and overwhelmed—but never bored.

Today I find myself in the country of Mauritania, on the northwest coast of Africa. I must adapt quickly, because again, I will be here for only two years.

What have I learned thus far? For starters, Mauritania is a fascinating and complicated place, primarily because of its geographical location. To the north is the Arab world; to the south, black Africa. . . . As the political officer at the United States embassy, I work for the American ambassador. . . . I am still speaking French (Mauritania was once a French colony), and I am still interviewing people (government officials, businesspeople, farmers, even desert nomads), but this time my purpose is not to give visas but to gather information about the country.

—ANGELA DICKEY, 1992

Examining the Reading

Reviewing Facts
1. Explain why the language she practiced in Montreal will help Angela Dickey in Mauritania.
2. Identify the officer for which Dickey will work in Mauritania.

Critical Thinking Skills
3. Making Inferences What educational background do you think a person needs to pursue a career in the Foreign Service?

Focus

Ask students what agencies of the United States government offer jobs that involve travel to foreign countries.

Teach

Ask: What emotion does Dickey say she never feels in her work? *(boredom)* From Dickey's descriptions, what kinds of skills are required by someone who joins the Foreign Service? What are some duties a Foreign Service employee performs? How, according to Dickey, do Foreign Service employees feel about home? *(They learn to think of whatever country they serve in as their home.)*

Assess

Have students complete **Examining the Reading.**

Answers
1. Mauritania was once a French colony.
2. the American ambassador
3. Answers will vary, but might include language training, communications, and social studies.

Close

Have students consider which countries they would like to serve in as an employee of the Foreign Service.

More About Personal Perspectives

The United States Foreign Service is part of the Department of State. It carries out American foreign policy through the assignment of staff to embassies and consulates in foreign countries. Any United States citizen who is 21 years or older (or 20, if they have completed a junior year at college) may apply for the Foreign Service. Competition is stiff: it includes a written examination; an assessment of candidates' skills in many areas, including communication; and a medical exam. Although there was no formal foreign service in the early days of the nation, many famous Americans were diplomats—Benjamin Franklin, Thomas Jefferson, John Quincy Adams, and James Monroe, for example.

Identifying Terms and Concepts

1. h, **2.** j, **3.** e, **4.** a, **5.** f, **6.** c, **7.** i, **8.** b, **9.** g, **10.** d

Reviewing Facts and Ideas

1. Since World War II the foreign policy of the United States has been based on active participation in world affairs and resistance to communism. Recently the United States and communist nations achieved détente.

2. executive and legislative branches

3. the White House staff, the National Security Council, the Central Intelligence Agency, and private individuals who have specialized knowledge in foreign affairs

4. to equip the armed forces and build new weapons and for foreign aid

5. The President is the leader of the entire nation, controls those agencies that help to formulate and carry out foreign policy, can take quick and decisive action, and can use executive agreements to bypass Congress.

6. The work of the State Department is organized by topics and regions.

7. to protect national security by overseeing the military and providing information and advice to the President

Applying Themes

1. Answers will vary, but may indicate that Presidents have more freedom of action in foreign policy and are not as closely checked by Congress.

2. Answers may vary, but should include: by providing economic assistance, by diplomatically recognizing new governments, and by creating new alliances.

Summary and Significance

The fundamental objectives upon which American foreign policy is based include preserving national security, encouraging democracy in other nations, maintaining free and open trade, and providing humanitarian aid to other nations. The Constitution gives certain powers to the President and to Congress relating to foreign policy. At times the President and Congress have vied for power in foreign policy. The Departments of State and Defense are responsible for carrying out American foreign policy on a day-to-day basis. Civilian control of the military is a fundamental principle of American government.

In order to reach its foreign policy goals, the United States uses alliances, aid programs, economic sanctions, and military force as a last resort. A working knowledge of the history and priorities of American foreign policy help promote understanding of the role of the United States in the world order.

Identifying Terms and Concepts

Choose the letter of the correct term or concept below to complete the sentence.

a. executive agreement
b. internationalism
c. foreign policy
d. bipartisan
e. sanction
f. consulate
g. domino theory
h. isolationism
i. multilateral treaty
j. ambassador

1. In the 1800s, the United States avoided involvement in world affairs, a policy known as ＿＿＿.
2. The highest ranking diplomat one nation sends to represent it in another nation is an ＿＿＿.
3. When the United States imposes an economic ＿＿＿ on another nation, it restricts trade with that nation.
4. A pact between the President and the head of a foreign government, called an ＿＿＿, does not require the Senate's approval.
5. Located in major cities of foreign nations, a ＿＿＿ promotes American business interests and safeguards American travelers.
6. A nation's ＿＿＿ guides its relations with other countries and groups in the world.
7. An international agreement signed by a group of several nations is called a ＿＿＿.
8. The United States now follows a policy of ＿＿＿ regarding world affairs.
9. The United States became involved in Vietnam mainly because it adhered to the ＿＿＿.
10. The President's foreign policies often have enjoyed ＿＿＿ congressional support.

Reviewing Facts and Ideas

1. **Discuss** the major goals of American foreign policy since 1945.
2. **List** the branches of the federal government that have foreign-policy responsibilities outlined in the Constitution.
3. **Identify** who, in addition to the cabinet, advises the President on foreign policy.
4. **Describe** the foreign-policy purposes for which Congress appropriates money.
5. **Explain** the three advantages that the President has over Congress in conducting foreign policy.
6. **Describe** the organization of the State Department.
7. **Examine** the responsibility of the Department of Defense in foreign policy.

Applying Themes

1. **Public Policy** In many cases throughout American history, Presidents have found it easier to achieve success in foreign policy than in domestic affairs. Explain why this might be so.
2. **Growth of Democracy** Some former communist nations are rejecting communism and embracing democracy. How do you think the United States can help them in their goal?
3. **Political Processes** Should Congress play a greater role in the formation of American foreign policy? Why or why not?

---

3. Answers will vary, but may indicate that those who think Congress should play a greater role probably believe the President needs to be checked and that an open forum in discussing foreign policy would be in the nation's best interest. Those who disagree will hold that foreign-policy decisions should be made quickly and in secret.

4. Answers will vary, but may include that the advisers will have different slants on information, and differing views and priorities may enable the President to be more objective.

4. Checks and Balances How might the President's cabinet provide a system of checks and balances in their priorities and in the information they give to the President?

Critical Thinking Skills

1. **Drawing Conclusions** With the changes in the world order, do you believe the role of the CIA will change? Give reasons for your answers.
2. **Demonstrating Reasoned Judgment** In late 1991, President Bush announced his intention to drastically cut back on American weapons in Western Europe. What is your opinion on this? Support your answer.
3. **Making Inferences** Many recent Presidents have relied on executive agreements rather than treaties when dealing with foreign countries. What inference can you make about the power of the President in relation to the power of Congress in foreign affairs?
4. **Analyzing Information** What are the advantages and disadvantages of an all-volunteer military?

Linking Past and Present

The most serious challenges to the Monroe Doctrine in recent years have been the establishment of a communist government in Cuba and pro-communist insurgents in Central American countries such as Guatemala and El Salvador. The politics of these countries are a sensitive issue insofar as the Monroe Doctrine guarantees that each Latin American nation may choose its own government, while at the same time warning against foreign intervention. In light of these provisions, do you think the United States has a right to interfere in the politics of Central American nations? Give reasons for your answer.

Writing About Government

Persuasive Writing Write a letter to one of your state's senators persuading him or her to support or oppose a treaty reducing the number of nuclear weapons.

Reinforcing the Skill

Examine the cartogram below and answer the questions that follow. You may refer, if necessary, to the atlas at the end of this textbook.

Gross National Products of South America

1. What statistical information is shown in this cartogram?
2. What political units does this cartogram use?
3. Which country has a larger gross national product, Colombia or Brazil?
4. Which country has a larger gross national product, Chile or Bolivia?
5. Which two countries have the largest gross national products in South America?

Investigating Further

1. **Individual Project** American leaders and the public are trying to decide how to spend all the extra money that will be available after the United States cuts down on its defense budget. Create a political cartoon on this topic.
2. **Cooperative Learning** Organize into groups of five or six students and consider the following issue. American attitudes concerning foreign aid are much more negative today than they were years ago. As a group, make a list of criteria that you would impose upon a nation being considered for aid. Why, for example, would you choose some countries and not others? When finished, meet as a class and discuss the group lists.

Chapter Organizer

Objectives	Special Feature Pages	Supplemental Materials
Section 1 Government and Commerce *pp. 642–647* 1. Explain the constitutional basis for federal government regulation of the economy. 2. Summarize the causes and effects of anti-trust legislation. 3. Describe how the law protects consumers.	Multicultural Heritage: Cultural Pluralism p. 644 Global Connection: Issues: FDA Drug Testing p. 647	Guided Reading Activities Reproducible Lesson Plans Interpreting Political Cartoons 33 Chapter Transparencies 23 Section 1 Quiz Testmaker The Living Constitution SAT Practice Tests Writer's Guidebook
Section 2 Business and Labor Policy *pp. 648–653* 1. Identify ways in which the federal government aids business. 2. Explain the need for laws regulating working conditions. 3. Describe laws that regulate labor unions.	Critical Thinking Skills: Drawing Conclusions p. 653	Guided Reading Activities Reproducible Lesson Plans Section 2 Quiz Testmaker Skill Reinforcement Activities 23 SAT Practice Tests Writer's Guidebook
Section 3 Agriculture and the Environment *pp. 654–658* 1. Summarize ways the federal government historically has helped the farmer. 2. Describe current federal farm policy. 3. Evaluate national energy and environmental policies.	Participating in Government: Improving Your Neighborhood p. 656	Guided Reading Activities Reproducible Lesson Plans Participating in Government 23 Primary and Secondary Source Readings 23 Enrichment Activities 23 Section 3 Quiz Testmaker Government Themes Transparencies 27
Section 4 Health and Public Assistance *pp. 659–664* 1. Identify social insurance and public assistance developments in the 1930s. 2. Describe social insurance, public assistance, and health programs today. 3. Discuss concerns about public assistance that Congress addressed in welfare reform legislation.	Images of Government: At Your Service pp. 662–663	Guided Reading Activities Reproducible Lesson Plans Section 4 Quiz Testmaker SAT Practice Tests Writer's Guidebook
Section 5 Education, Housing, and Transportation *pp. 665–671* 1. Discuss federal interest in education. 2. Evaluate urban renewal and federal housing policies. 3. Describe the federal government's role in transportation.	Focus on Freedom: I Have a Dream p. 667 Personal Perspectives: Whitney M. Young, Jr., Asks, "Can the City Survive?" p. 671 Case Study pp. 674–676 Unit 7 Digest pp. 677–678	Guided Reading Activities Reproducible Lesson Plans Reteaching Activities 23 Section 5 Quiz Chapter 23 Tests Testmaker Audio Cassettes (English and Spanish) Limited English Proficiency Activities 23 Unit Digest Transparencies, Unit 7 Participating in Government, Unit 7 Writer's Guidebook

If time does not permit teaching this chapter, assign the Chapter 23 summary in the Unit 7 Digest on pages 677–678.

Key To Ability Levels

Teaching strategies have been coded for varying learning styles and abilities.

L1   Level 1 activities are **basic** activities and should be within the ability range of all students.

L2   Level 2 activities are **average** activities and should be within the ability range of the average to above-average student.

L3   Level 3 activities are **challenging** activities designed for the ability range of above-average students.

LEP   These activities should be within the ability range of **Limited English Proficiency** students.

Multicultural Activities

Italians, Poles, Russian Jews, and other ethnics made up the work force in the factories in the nation's largest cities in the early 1900s. Many were recent immigrants. Russian Jews, such as Rose Schneiderman, led the fight in the garment industry to organize unions and protect workers. Schneiderman organized the hat and cap makers union, helped build the International Ladies Garment Workers Union, and was president of the Women's Trade Union League (WTUL), which sought better working conditions for women through such laws as a minimum wage and a 48-hour work week. Students can research Schneiderman's later political career and the role of the WTUL in the fight for federal legislation to protect workers.

America's immigration policy has at times been linked to its agricultural policy. During World War II, farmers in the Southwest experienced a shortage of agricultural workers. To fill this need, the United States and Mexico negotiated an agreement under which the Mexican government supplied United States farmers with contract workers known as *braceros*. Thousands of Mexicans came to the United States on temporary visas. In 1944 over 62,000 *braceros* entered the United States; most were poorly paid and lived in substandard housing. Although the labor shortage ended at war's end, the program continued until 1965. The program was opposed by many Mexican Americans living in the Southwest, and it increased the number of undocumented aliens in the United States. Have students speculate on why the Mexican government agreed to this program and why it continued after the war.

Chapter Resources

Readings for the Student

Consumer Adviser: An Action Guide to Your Rights. Reader's Digest, 1989.

Fanning, Beverly. *Workfare vs. Welfare.* GEM, 1989.

Hyde, Margaret O. *The Homeless: Profiling the Problem.* Enslow, 1989.

Pertschuk, Michael. *Revolt Against Regulation: The Rise and Fall of the Consumer Movement.* University of California Press, 1982.

Trager, Oliver, ed. *America's Health Care Crisis.* Facts on File, Inc., 1993.

Readings for the Teacher

Fritschler, A. Lee and Bernard H. Ross. *Business Regulation and Government Decision-making.* Little, Brown, 1982.

Kotlowitz, Alex. *There Are No Children Here: The Story of Two Boys Growing up in the Other America.* Doubleday, 1991.

Lemann, Nicholas. *The Promised Land: The Great Black Migration and How It Changed America.* Knopf, 1991.

Light, Paul. *Artful Work: The Politics of Social Security Reform.* Random House, 1985.

Trattner, Walter I. *From Poor Law to Welfare State: A History of Welfare in America.* Princeton University Press, 1994.

Multimedia

Videocassettes

Buyer Be Aware: Avoiding Rip-Offs. Learning Seed. (v/c, 24 minutes)

Little Injustices: Laura Nader Looks at the Law. (*Odyssey* series). Public Broadcasting Associates. (v/c, 60 minutes)

Matewan. Cinecom. (v/c, 100 minutes)

Norma Rae. 20th Century Fox. (v/c, 113 minutes)

Software

Cartels and Cutthroats. Strategic Simulations. (Apple, IBM, Commodore 64 disks). Students explore the rigors of managing a large American corporation, including government intervention.

Simpolicon. Cross Educational Software. (Apple with 2 disk drives). A complex simulation on national economic development, and the stresses (both internal and international) generated by government economic decisions.

Social and Domestic Policies

Introduce

Chapter Overview

Chapter 23 focuses on how the federal government both regulates and assists the nation's economy and provides for the welfare of its citizens.

Section 1 deals with the laws Congress has passed to regulate business and protect the public.

Section 2 discusses how government aids business and protects workers.

Section 3 outlines federal policies to support agriculture and to protect the environment.

Section 4 discusses ways the federal government addresses the social welfare and health of its citizens.

Section 5 describes federal programs to support education, housing, and transportation.

Chapter 23 Themes

Write the chapter themes on the chalkboard. Explain how each theme relates to a topic in this chapter. For example, the theme of *federalism* can be observed in federal programs to assist states in education or to provide matching funds for highway construction.

CHAPTER

23

A national park ranger leads a group of tourists through one of the many parks protected and administered by the United States government.

About the Chapter Opener

Teaching With Illustrations The National Park Service, a branch of the Department of the Interior, oversees the nearly 80 million acres of national parks across the United States. Ask students to read the caption and examine the photograph on pages 640 and 641. Have them relate any experiences they may have had with national parks. Ask how the National Park Service makes and carries out domestic policy. Then ask what problems the National Park Service has encountered in recent years. *(crime, overcrowding, pollution)* Ask what they know about how the government is dealing with these problems.

Chapter Preview

Overview

The federal government regulates the economy and promotes the well-being of United States citizens.

Objectives

After studying this chapter, you should be able to:

1. **Discuss** the relationship between the federal government and the United States economy.
2. **Summarize** federal regulation of business and labor.
3. **Evaluate** national agricultural, energy, and environmental policies.
4. **Describe** federal social programs.
5. **Identify** the role of the national government in education, housing, and transportation.

Themes in Government

This chapter emphasizes the following government themes:

- **Free Enterprise** Federal laws promote the growth of United States business. Sections 1 and 2.
- **Constitutional Interpretations** The commerce clause of the Constitution underlies federal regulation of the economy. Sections 1 and 4.
- **Federalism** The federal government cooperates with the states in many ways. Sections 2, 3, 4, and 5.
- **Civic Participation** Citizens help carry out government policy. Section 3.
- **Public Policy** Federal expenditures in education, housing, and transportation support national policies. Section 5.

Critical Thinking Skills

This chapter emphasizes the following critical thinking skills:

- Identifying Assumptions
- Identifying Central Issues
- Demonstrating Reasoned Judgment
- Predicting Consequences

CHAPTER 23: SOCIAL AND DOMESTIC POLICIES   641

Introducing the Chapter

Ask students to imagine that the following situations have occurred in their community:

Three different grocery store chains have always competed for customers. Now one of the chains has bought out the other two.

There have been many accidents at a local factory. Workers who complain about the hazardous conditions are fired.

Ask students if they would have any concerns about each situation. Should government take action in these situations and, if so, what should these actions be? Tell students that Chapter 23 discusses how the federal government promotes the general welfare of the nation.

Chapter Project

As students study Chapter 23, have them collect visual evidence of government regulation in our society. *(product content labels, warning statements in advertisements, and so on)* Have students make a bulletin-board display with their findings.

> **Linking Past and Present**
> In the late 1800s, many people called the impure meat they ate "embalmed beef." In 1906 the government required inspection of meat in interstate commerce. Then poultry inspection was mandated. Recent moves to inspect fish show that government involvement in this area continues to expand.

Focus on Government
Video 7
Speaking Out:
Social and Domestic Policy
Running Time: 1:41
Videodisc 1, Chap. 7
VHS Tape 1, Begins 18:17

Setting the Scene In the years following the Civil War, large corporations grew rapidly and eventually came to dominate the American economy. As this happened, the United States government began to intervene in the marketplace and to regulate certain business practices such as monopolization, interlocking directorates, and price-fixing because of lack of local competition. Regulation was a public response to the actions of a small but influential class of business entrepreneurs such as John D. Rockefeller, Jay Gould, J. Pierpont Morgan, Andrew Carnegie, and Cornelius Vanderbilt.

Focus

Bell Ringer

While attendance is being taken, ask students to describe in writing a situation of monopoly that they encounter in everyday life.

Motivating Activity

Discuss students' Bell Ringer responses. *(Examples might be a family member monopolizing a car or television, a friend monopolizing conversation, a basketball player monopolizing the ball, and so on.)* Ask students to explain why monopolizing a conversation is undemocratic. *(Students may indicate that it is because others are not able to make their ideas known.)* Tell students that Section 1 describes how government has acted against business monopolies to preserve economic democracy as expressed in the free enterprise system.

Vocabulary Precheck

Call on students to read aloud the definitions for each term and concept from the Glossary. Then have them restate each definition in their own words. **LEP**

CONNECTIONS

Economics

President Reagan believed that government regulation of business retarded economic growth. Financial institutions were major beneficiaries of his deregulation policies, as they moved into previously forbidden business activities. In less than a decade many of these institutions collapsed, costing taxpayers billions of dollars to protect savings accounts.

SECTION

Government and Commerce

Free enterprise, based upon private ownership of property and individual economic decisions, is the foundation of the American economic system. The government, however, plays a major role in the economy, and a more accurate description of the American system is that of a mixed economy. A **mixed economy** is one in which the government both supports and regulates private enterprise. During the twentieth century, regulating and supporting business and labor have become major functions of the federal government.

Some Americans believe that government regulation of the economy is at best a mixed blessing. These people usually agree with the sentiments expressed by economist Arthur B. Laffer:

> *Those who advocate, in their desperation, more government to solve the problems of our society are demonstrably wrong. . . . The solution rests in less—not more—government!*
> —ARTHUR B. LAFFER, *THE SOLUTION TO TODAY'S PROBLEMS: LESS GOVERNMENT*

Writer Victor Kamber expressed the opposite point of view. In Kamber's opinion:

> *Many Americans have forgotten that we set up regulatory agencies in the first place to protect the public interest. Industries considered vital to the public—such as transportation, food, finance, communications, and nuclear power—were regulated in order to provide the public a steady flow of safe products in a stable environment.*
> —VICTOR KAMBER, *USA TODAY*, JULY 1984

Whether a person agrees with one or the other point of view sometimes depends upon whether the person is being regulated or is benefiting from the regulation. Nevertheless, federal regulation of economic activity springs from a constitutional provision.

The Constitutional Basis

The Constitution grants Congress the power to "lay and collect taxes" for the general welfare and to "regulate commerce . . . among the several states." Most regulatory laws enacted in the twentieth century are based upon these two powers.

The Commerce Power The commerce clause in Article I, Section 8, provides the primary constitutional basis for government regulation of the economy. The Founders designed this clause to allow the federal government to control interstate commerce, eliminating one major deficiency of the Articles of Confederation. Over the years the Supreme Court has broadened the interpretation of interstate commerce to include a wide variety of economic activities. For example, interstate commerce today covers the production and transportation of goods, communications, mining, and the sale of stocks and bonds. Citing the commerce clause, Congress has passed many laws regulating these activities. Moreover, the meaning of regulation has changed over the years. Besides restricting certain activities, regulation now includes prohibiting, promoting, protecting, assisting, and establishing standards for many aspects of interstate commerce.

SECTION PREVIEW

Objectives
After studying this section, you should be able to:
■ Explain the constitutional basis for federal government regulation of the economy.
■ Summarize the causes and effects of antitrust legislation.

■ Describe ways in which the law protects consumers.

Key Terms and Concepts
mixed economy, laissez-faire, trust, monopoly, interlocking directorate, oligopoly, securities

Themes in Government
■ Free Enterprise
■ Constitutional Interpretations

Critical Thinking Skills
■ Identifying Assumptions
■ Identifying Central Issues

642   UNIT 7: PUBLIC POLICIES AND SERVICES

Classroom Resources for Section 1

📁 Guided Reading Activities
📁 Reproducible Lesson Plans
📁 Interpreting Political Cartoons 33
📁 Section 1 Quiz
▪ Testmaker

Chapter Transparencies 23
The Living Constitution
SAT Practice Tests
Writer's Guidebook

The Purpose of Regulation Today more than 100 federal agencies and commissions regulate American businesses. Federal regulations for American industry would fill an estimated 60 volumes of 1,000 pages each.

Those who favor government regulation of business say that it is necessary for the protection and welfare of the general public. In the past, they say, too many businesses engaged in unfair competitive practices, ignored the health and safety of workers, polluted the environment, and sold worthless and even harmful goods. To prevent such abuses, Congress has passed regulatory laws to control the size of businesses and to protect the public. Governments at various levels also regulate natural monopolies, such as electric and gas companies.

Antitrust Legislation

Until the late 1800s, the federal government played a limited role in the economy and for the most part took a hands-off, or *laissez-faire*, approach. The states passed the few regulations that limited business activities. Businesses were generally small, locally owned, and primarily served local markets.

History of Business Regulations By the late 1800s, the American economy had changed. Rapid industrialization led to many abuses. Huge corporations dominated American industry. Business combinations consolidated control of an industry in the hands of one or a few giant corporations that squeezed smaller companies out of business. Without competition, the combinations could charge whatever they wanted for their services. Railroads, for example, charged high rates and took advantage of farmers who depended on them to bring their crops to market. Because of these abuses, Americans began to demand government regulation of business.

Congress responded by passing the Interstate Commerce Act in 1887. This act established the first federal regulatory agency, the Interstate Commerce

Stock Exchange
Stock traders buy and sell stocks at the New York Stock Exchange. **Law Besides the sale of stocks, what else does interstate commerce include?**

Commission (ICC), and placed certain limits on the freight rates railroad companies charged. Congress later passed two measures to control corporations that threatened to destroy competition.

The Sherman and Clayton Antitrust Acts In the late 1800s, the trust became a popular form of business consolidation. In a **trust** several corporations combined their stock and allowed a board of trustees to run the corporations as one giant enterprise. The trustees could set production quotas, fix prices, and control the market, thereby creating a **monopoly**. A monopoly is a business that controls so much of a product, service, or industry that no competition exists.

The Standard Oil Trust organized by John D. Rockefeller was an example of such a trust. In 1879 it controlled the production and sale of 90 percent of the oil refined in the United States. The Standard Oil Trust consisted of several oil companies whose stock was held by a single board of trustees. The chief stockholder and trustee was Rockefeller himself. At the time monopolistic trusts like Rockefeller's dominated many industries.

STUDY GUIDE

Themes in Government
Free Enterprise The constitutional power of Congress to regulate commerce provides the primary basis for government regulation of

the economy. What events in the late 1800s led to government regulation of business?

Critical Thinking Skills
Identifying Assumptions Why would some businesspeople be in favor of a laissez-faire economy, while others would be opposed?

Teach

Guided Practice

L1 Constitutional Interpretations Ask students to name the two constitutional bases for the federal government's regulation of the nation's economic activity. *(taxation and commerce powers)* Ask them to find and read aloud the passages in the Constitution that grant these powers. *(Article I, Section 8, clauses 1 and 3)* Then ask for examples of how these powers can be used to regulate economic activity.

Interpreting Visuals Display transparency 23 from the *Chapter Transparencies* in the Teacher's Classroom Resources and use the accompanying teaching strategy and student activity to teach about consumer protection.

Caption Answer
production and transportation of goods, communications, mining

STUDY GUIDE

Theme Answer
consolidation eliminated competition; high railroad charges

Critical Thinking Answer
Answers should indicate that uncontrolled competition benefits strong businesses and hurts weak ones.

Background

After the Civil War, economists agreed unanimously that expanding production was beneficial. To that end, *laissez-faire* was encouraged. The government promoted expanding productivity in a variety of ways. It made the country's resources available through land laws, internal improvements, and federal rail subsidies. In addition, immigration was unrestricted. The massive land grants made to railroads along their right-of-way was a giant windfall, which benefits them even today. As rail business declined, land holdings became the railroad's biggest assets, which they either sold or developed. Few railroads today survive only on their rail business.

Multicultural Heritage

Focus

Have students suggest definitions of the term *cultural pluralism* and give examples of cultural
diversity in their own community.

Teach

Ask students to explain how
Carl Degler's quote supports the
assertion that cultural pluralism is
not a new concept in American
history. How does Henry Cisneros counter the argument that
cultural pluralism is a danger to
national unity? What reasons does
Cisneros give for believing new
immigrant groups will willingly
adopt the "American way of life"?

Assess

Have students complete **Examining Our Multicultural
Heritage.**

Answers

1. a culture of many diverse ethnic and racial groups
2. because of the variety of
groups in the colonies
3. Answers will vary, but students
should present sound reasons to
support their opinions.

Close

Explain that at one time the
term "melting pot" was used to
describe the multicultural makeup
of American society. Many people
today reject this term because it
suggests that all groups give up
their own culture as they become
Americanized. Have students
make up phrases to describe the
cultural pluralism of American
society.

Multicultural Heritage

Cultural Pluralism

Today, cultural pluralism, or multiculturalism, is viewed as a new concept in American history. The idea, however, is neither particularly new nor novel. As noted historian and writer Carl N. Degler observed:

> *Multiculturalism may be a fashionable neologism [new word or expression] of our times, but as a cultural fact of American life it is considerably older than the Constitution. Even worries about its danger to national unity are hardly new. As early as the 1750s Benjamin Franklin complained about the Germans flooding into Pennsylvania: "Why should the Palatine boors be suffered to swarm into our settlements, and, by herding together, establish their language and manners to the exclusion of ours?" he asked in 1751. Their large number caused Franklin to wonder why "Pennsylvania founded by the English" should "become a colony of aliens who will shortly be so numerous as to germanize us, instead of our anglifying them?"*
> —CARL N. DEGLER, 1991

Since its founding, the United States has been the destination for people in search of opportunity and a new way of life. Each group inevitably has contributed ideas and cultural traits to its new home. Religious groups such as the Shakers and the Amish pursued a way of life based on distinct beliefs and ideas. Throughout the nation racial and ethnic enclaves, particularly in major cities, came to be known as "Little Italy," "Polonia," and "Chinatown." Within these neighborhoods racial and ethnic minorities maintained many of the customs and practices of their native culture. For example, in Polonia—the Polish neighborhood in Chicago that had the largest concentration of Poles outside of Poland—an old shopkeeper remembered when "you couldn't tell whether you were in Chicago or Poland" when you were in Polonia.

What cultural pluralism has meant for the United States is the creation of an American culture that many diverse ethnic and racial cultures enliven. Continued immigration and the natural growth of the nation's minorities will continue the existing cultural

Melting Pot or Salad Bowl?
Many ethnic groups have contributed their diverse, rich styles and ideas to the culture of the United States.

pluralism. Many people agree with Hispanic leader and former mayor of San Antonio, Texas, Henry Cisneros, who believes that minorities and future immigrants will strengthen the nation. He wrote:

> *Many people fail to see that immigrants who come to America today, whether Asian or Hispanic, are predisposed to the American way of life. . . . Those coming from Mexico, for example, have no inclination to go back because they have seen the fallacies and failures of other systems—economically, politically, and in terms of personal freedom and upward mobility. Therefore, the commitment they are making to the United States is total.*
> —HENRY CISNEROS, 1988

Examining Our Multicultural Heritage

Reviewing Facts
1. Define cultural pluralism.
2. Explain why cultural pluralism is said to be older than the Constitution.

Critical Thinking Skills
3. Drawing Conclusions Do you think that cultural pluralism poses a threat to the future unity of the United States? Why or why not?

More About Our Multicultural Heritage

Henry Cisneros's own success story gives him reason to believe that minorities and future immigrants have a role to play in American political life. Cisneros, born in San Antonio, Texas, was the first person of Mexican descent elected mayor of a major United States city. He served as San Antonio's mayor from 1981 to 1989. His popularity with the voters led to four terms as mayor. Cisneros attended Texas A&M University and earned graduate degrees from Harvard University and George Washington University. Before winning election as mayor, he served on San Antonio's city council where he became a spokesperson for the city's large Hispanic community.

Congress's first attempt to halt monopolies came in 1890 with the passage of the Sherman Antitrust Act. The first two sections of the act stated that:

Every contract, combination in the form of trust or otherwise, or conspiracy, in restraint of trade or commerce among the several states, or with foreign nations is hereby declared illegal.

Every person who shall monopolize, or attempt to monopolize, or combine or conspire with any other person or persons to monopolize any part of the trade or commerce among the several states . . . shall be guilty of a misdemeanor.

—SHERMAN ANTITRUST ACT, 1890

Today, violating the second section is a felony.

The language of the act did not specify what restraint of trade meant. The Sherman Antitrust Act, therefore, proved difficult to enforce. It was, however, successfully enforced in one notable case. In 1906 the federal government charged the Standard Oil Company with violating the first two sections of the act. Convicted, the company ultimately appealed to the Supreme Court, which upheld the conviction and ordered the company to be split into a number of smaller companies. For the first time in the nation's history, the government declared a major trust illegal.

Despite the conviction, the trend toward larger and larger business combinations continued. Then in 1914 Congress passed the Clayton Antitrust Act to clarify the Sherman Act. The Clayton Act prohibited certain business practices. It prohibited charging high prices in an area where little competition existed, while at the same time charging lower prices in an area with strong competition. Businesses could not buy stock in other corporations in order to reduce competition. Finally, the act outlawed **interlocking directorates**—where the same people served on the boards of directors of competing companies.

Enforcing the Antitrust Laws The same year that Congress passed the Clayton Act, it established the Federal Trade Commission (FTC). The government charged this independent regulatory agency with carrying out the provisions of the Clayton Act. The commission may define unfair competitive practices, issue orders to halt these practices, examine corporate purchases of stock, and investigate trade practices. Since its creation the FTC's duties have expanded. Today the FTC has many responsibilities in addition to enforcing the Clayton Act. These include enforc-

ing laws that prohibit false advertising and requiring truthful labels on textiles and furs. The FTC also regulates the packaging and labeling of certain consumer goods, requires full disclosure of the lending practices of finance companies and retailers who use installment plans, and checks consumer credit agencies.

Despite additional antitrust legislation passed since the Clayton Act, a few large corporations dominate several industries. Today, instead of trusts and monopolies, economic power belongs to **oligopolies**. Oligopolies exist when a few firms dominate a particular industry. By the 1990s about 50 multibillion-dollar companies controlled approximately one-third of the manufacturing capacity in the United States.

Enforcing the country's antitrust laws is the responsibility of the Antitrust Division of the Department of Justice. Working with the Federal Trade Commission, it brings suits against suspected violators of antitrust laws.

Consumer Protection

Besides antitrust laws, Congress has passed other regulatory laws protecting consumers and ensuring fair product standards. Congress has also established independent regulatory agencies that protect con-

Monster of Monopoly
By 1881 the Standard Oil Trust controlled almost all production of oil in the United States. **Economics**
How is a trust a threat to competition?

L2 Demonstrating Reasoned Judgment Have students discuss whether government regulation helps or hinders economic activity and the public welfare. Have them consider events in the banking and airline industries in recent years in making this judgment.

Independent Practice

L1 Summarizing Have students use the subheads of Section 1 as the main ideas of the section. Then ask them to summarize the section by writing supporting details for each main idea.

L2 Civics Ask students to choose an area of government regulation that interests them. Have them write a letter to one of their United States senators or their representative, in which they ask about his or her stance toward government regulation in that area. Ask students to share the lawmaker's response with the class.

Interpreting Political Cartoons Have students complete activity 33 in *Interpreting Political Cartoons* in the Teacher's Classroom Resources.

Caption Answer
A trust can fix prices and control the market, thereby creating a monopoly.

Cooperative Learning Activity

Organize the class into three groups to investigate the ways in which community groups and their local government agencies protect the rights of consumers. Assign each group one of the following questions to investigate: What local ordinances protect consumers? What local government agencies handle consumer complaints? What local private organizations help consumers? Have each student in the groups take on a specific task such as research, report-writing, or presenting. Have the presenter for each group present a 10-minute report. Then open the topic for class discussion.

Theme Answer
Both advertising and the products represented are part of interstate commerce.

Critical Thinking Answer
practices including mislabeling, false advertising, and selling faulty products

Assess

Check for Understanding

Have students complete Section 1 Review on page 647.

Meeting Objectives

Each section objective is tested by the Section Review questions that follow it in parentheses.

- Explain the constitutional basis for federal government regulation of the economy. (2, 3, 6, 7)
- Summarize the causes and effects of antitrust legislation. (4, 5)
- Describe ways in which the law protects consumers. (6, 8)

Evaluate

 Section 1 Quiz

Testmaker

---

sumers or regulate certain economic activities. These regulatory agencies are independent in the sense that they are to a large extent beyond the control of the executive branch.

To maintain this independence, Congress decided that each agency would have from 5 to 11 members, each appointed by the President and confirmed by the Senate. Normally the term of each of the commissioners is long enough to prevent a President from appointing enough new members to control the agency. The President may remove a member only for certain reasons specified by Congress.

The types of independent regulatory agencies vary widely. They range from the Interstate Commerce Commission, established in 1887, to the Consumer Product Safety Commission, established in 1972.

Consumer Protection Laws Before 1900 many corporations were not overly concerned about whether their products were healthful or safe. Some truly deplorable practices were common in the food processing and drug industries. Some companies mislabeled foods and sold foods contaminated by additives. Other foods such as meat were tainted because of the unsanitary conditions in processing plants. Consumers were duped into buying medicines that were often worthless and sometimes dangerous.

Shortly after the turn of the century, Upton Sinclair, in his book, *The Jungle,* described conditions in a meat-packing house. He wrote:

> *There would be meat stored in great piles in rooms; and the water from leaky roofs would drip over it, and thousands of rats would race about it. . . . These rats were nuisances, and the packers would put poisoned bread out for them; they would die, and then rats, bread, and meat would go into the hoppers together.*
>
> —UPTON SINCLAIR, 1906

In addition to Sinclair's stinging condemnation, magazine articles about similar conditions aroused public indignation. As a result, Congress passed the

Pure Food and Drug Act in 1906 to make it illegal for a company engaged in interstate commerce to sell contaminated, unhealthful, or falsely labeled foods or drugs. The Meat Inspection Act, also passed in 1906, provided for federal inspection of all meat-packing companies that sold meats across state lines.

The Food and Drug Administration (FDA) is responsible for protecting the public from poorly processed and improperly labeled foods and drugs. Scientists at FDA laboratories inspect and test prepared food, cosmetics, drugs, and thousands of other products every year. Agents from the FDA inspect factories, food processing plants, and drug laboratories. They also check labels for accuracy. If a product fails to meet FDA standards, the FDA may force it off the market.

Protection Against False Advertising The Federal Trade Commission (FTC) protects consumers from misleading and fraudulent advertising. The FTC has the power to review the advertising claims made about all products sold in interstate commerce. It may determine whether an advertisement for a product is false or unfair. If it is, the FTC can order a company to change the ad to comply with FTC standards. As a result of one FTC ruling, cigarette manufacturers must place a health warning on cigarette packages. According to another FTC regulation, all manufacturers must clearly list the contents of packaged products on the label.

Consumers and Product Safety Books and articles about the ways in which consumers are cheated and deceived in the marketplace have always been popular. One such book accelerated consumerism in the 1960s. In 1965 Ralph Nader warned about poorly designed automobiles that were "unsafe at any speed." Nader became a leader in the consumer movement.

As result of this movement, Congress created the Consumer Product Safety Commission (CPSC) in 1972. Its purpose was to protect consumers against "unreasonable risk of injury from hazardous prod-

Themes in Government
Constitutional Interpretations
Why is the Federal Trade Commission authorized to enforce laws that prohibit false advertising?

Critical Thinking Skills
Identifying Central Issues The Food and Drug Administration, the Federal Trade Commission, and the Consumer Product Safety Commission were created by Congress to

protect consumers. **What business practices make these agencies necessary?**

Critical Thinking Activity

Identifying Central Issues Review with students the ways that the federal government protects the rights of consumers. Then ask the following question: Are there sufficient government regulations to protect consumers? Should there be more consumer-protection regulations? Are there too many such regulations already? Ask students to support their opinions. *(Answers should consider product safety, labeling issues, and advertising.)*

ucts." The risk of product-related injuries was real and widespread. According to one government study, about 20 million people every year suffer at least minor injuries from the products they purchase. More than 100,000 of these injuries are serious enough to cause permanent disabilities.

To reduce consumer risks, the CPSC investigates injuries caused by merchandise, such as lawnmowers, kitchen appliances, toys, and sports equipment. It then establishes standards of safety for each type of consumer product. If any product fails to meet these standards, the CPSC can order it off the market.

Regulating the Sale of Stocks Another form of government regulation protects small investors from being cheated and misled about the value of stocks and bonds. Since 1934 the Securities and Exchange Commission (SEC), has regulated the trading of **securities**, or stocks and bonds.

The origins of the SEC go back to the stock market crash of October 1929. After the crash a congressional investigation uncovered many examples of fraud and unsound financing schemes in the nation's stock markets and brokerage houses. As a result, Congress created the SEC.

Today the SEC licenses people who sell securities in the national market, investigates cases of suspected fraud in the sale of securities, and regulates the nation's stock markets. It also regulates the securities issued by public utility companies and requires all corporations that issue public stock to file regular reports on their assets, profits, sales, and other financial data. These reports must be made available to investors so that they may judge the true value of a company's stock offerings.

GLOBAL CONNECTION

Issues

FDA Drug Testing American hospitals are considered the safest in the world. Even so, Americans suffering from serious illness often leave the United States because the Food and Drug Administration (FDA) has not yet approved some drugs already available in other countries.

FDA testing of a drug can take up to 10 years. First, a drug is tested on animals. Then drug companies must pay for three phases of clinical tests on humans. In Phase I healthy volunteers take increasing doses of the drug to judge its safety. In Phase II the drug is tested on sick people who take the drug to check its side effects. In Phase III sick people take the drug for three or four years to judge its long-term effects.

Examining the Connection
Critics argue that lives are lost while patients wait for FDA testing. How would you respond to this point of view?

GLOBAL CONNECTION

Ask students their thoughts about using experimental treatments on patients who fail to respond to approved treatments for cancer or AIDS.
Examining the Connection Answer: *Speeding the process would increase the risk involved and could cost more lives in the long run.*

Reteach

Ask students to describe government regulation of the American economy in a brief paragraph using the following terms: *mixed economy, commerce power, antitrust legislation, consumer protection,* and *regulatory agencies.*

Enrich

Have students research the two kinds of warranties—written warranties and implied warranties—that come with the purchase of certain products and the recourse consumers have if manufacturers fail to honor their warranties.

Close

Refer students to the two quotations on page 642. Ask students which point of view they agree with and why.

---

1 SECTION REVIEW

Section Summary
Based on its commerce power, Congress has passed laws regulating business and protecting the public.

Checking For Understanding
Recalling Facts
1. Define mixed economy, laissez-faire, trust, monopoly, interlocking directorate, oligopoly, securities.
2. Identify the constitutional basis for regulatory laws that Congress has passed to control the economy.
3. Describe the federal government's broad interpretation of interstate commerce today.
4. Name the first federal regulatory agency.

Exploring Themes
5. Free Enterprise How did the Sherman and Clayton Antitrust acts attempt to restore competition in industry?
6. Constitutional Interpretations How is the Consumer Product Safety Commission related to the power of Congress to regulate commerce?

Critical Thinking Skills
7. Identifying Assumptions Why would Congress not want one President to appoint the majority of the members of an independent regulatory agency?
8. Identifying Central Issues What general problem do the Federal Trade Commission, the Securities and Exchange Commission, and the Consumer Product Safety Commission address?

Section 1 Review Answers

1. Definitions of terms appear on pages indicated: **mixed economy,** 642; *laissez-faire,* 643; **trust,** 643; **monopoly,** 643; **interlocking directorate,** 645; **oligopoly,** 645; **securities,** 647
2. The Constitution grants Congress power to "lay and collect taxes" and to "regulate commerce . . . among the several states."

3. Interstate commerce covers the production of goods; transportation by water, land, and air; communications by telephone, television, and radio; mining of resources; and the sale of stocks and bonds.
4. Interstate Commerce Commission
5. by making combinations in restraint of trade, such as monopolies, illegal and by outlawing unfair competitive practices

6. Most products are considered to be part of interstate commerce.
7. One President's political ideas might unduly influence the decisions of the agency.
8. protecting the public from deceit or physical harm

SECTION

2

Business and Labor Policy

Focus

Bell Ringer

Write the following on the chalkboard for students to complete:

What does the statement "In union there is strength" mean?

Motivating Activity

Students' responses to the Bell Ringer activity should indicate that people united have the strength to achieve things that are beyond the power of an individual. Ask students for examples of groups that demonstrate this principle. *(labor unions, interest groups, trade associations, and so on)* Ask how it might apply to workers. Tell students that Section 2 discusses the relationship between the federal government, business, and labor unions.

Vocabulary Precheck

List the terms and concepts on the chalkboard. Have students develop questions for which each term or concept is an answer.

LEP

Caption Answer
Consumers benefit from the lower cost of imported goods.

Regulating business is a relatively recent function of the federal government, dating back slightly more than 100 years. The active promotion and protection of business has been a major activity of United States government since George Washington was President. Washington's secretary of the treasury, Alexander Hamilton, claimed that emerging American manufacturers needed protection from foreign competition. He first proposed a protective tariff in 1791, but Congress shelved the report. After the War of 1812, British goods flooded American markets, threatening to destroy newly planted industries. A member of Parliament in 1816 explained Britain's advantage:

It was well worth while to incur a loss upon the first exportation, in order, by the glut, to stifle in the cradle, those rising manufactures in the United States, which the war has forced into existence, contrary to the natural course of things.
—HENRY BROUGHAM, ESQ., 1816

The United States responded with higher tariffs.

Government and Business

More recently the federal government has emphasized lower tariffs and promoted free trade for many items. Consumers have benefited from the lower cost of many imported goods. Although current rates are at an all-time low, tariffs are still used to protect American industries from foreign competition. The government also restricts some imports through **quotas**—

setting a limit on the number of imports. In 1981 the federal government asked Japan to reduce the number of cars it was sending to the United States. Fearing that the United States might set a quota, Japan voluntarily reduced its exports of cars to the United States.

Types of Federal Subsidies Today the federal government provides four types of **subsidies**, or aids to business. One is tax incentives that allow businesses to deduct certain expenses from their annual tax returns. A second is government loans, or credit subsidies, that

ARCADIO
LA NACION
San Jose
COSTA RICA

arcadio

Cartoonists & Writers Syndicate

Can NAFTA Fulfill Big Promises?
The North American Free Trade Agreement lowers trade barriers among the three partners.
Economics What are the advantages of free trade between countries?

SECTION PREVIEW

Objectives
After studying this section, you should be able to:
- Identify ways in which the federal government aids business.
- Explain the need for laws regulating working conditions.

- Describe laws that regulate labor unions.

Key Terms and Concepts
quota, subsidy, collective bargaining, yellow-dog contract, closed shop, union shop, right-to-work law

Themes in Government
- Federalism
- Free Enterprise

Critical Thinking Skills
- Identifying Central Issues
- Demonstrating Reasoned Judgment

---

648   UNIT 7: PUBLIC POLICIES AND SERVICES

Classroom Resources for Section 2

📁 Guided Reading Activities
📁 Reproducible Lesson Plans
📁 Section 2 Quiz

▪ Testmaker
SAT Practice Tests
Writer's Guidebook

Car Quotas
Since 1981, Japan has voluntarily restricted the number of cars it exports to the United States. **Economics** Why did Japan enact these restrictions?

provide funds for businesses at low interest rates. A third type of subsidy is free services, such as weather information, census reports, and other information valuable to businesses across the nation. Finally, the government provides direct cash payments to businesses whose products or services are considered vital to the general public. Businesses in the field of transportation often receive this type of subsidy.

Commerce Department Aid to Business A separate department of the executive branch, the Department of Commerce, was formed in 1913 for the sole purpose of promoting business interests. Congress mandated that the department "foster, promote, and develop the foreign and domestic commerce of the United States."

The main functions of the Commerce Department are to provide information services, financial assistance, and research and development services. Several agencies within the Commerce Department supply businesses with valuable information and subsidies, particularly the Bureau of the Census, which provides businesses important economic data.

Help for Small Businesses Because competition is important to the free-enterprise system, the federal government tries to help small businesses. An important independent executive agency outside the Commerce Department that aids businesses is the Small Business Administration (SBA). In addition to offering credit subsidies, the SBA gives free advice and information to small business firms.

Regional offices of the SBA offer government-sponsored classes on sound management practices for owners of small businesses. Businesses may also seek advice from the SBA on how to overcome their problems. The SBA also conducts programs to help women and minorities in business.

Government and Labor

Federal law also regulates the relationship between employers and employees. As large corporations multiplied in the late 1800s, the relationship between employer and employee first became impersonal, then deteriorated even more. Some businesses failed to provide a safe, clean work environment and fair wages. Employers used several methods to break up labor unions and fired workers who joined.

Protecting Unions and Workers Labor unions in the United States date back to the early 1800s. It was not until the 1850s, however, that the first nationwide union was organized. Under pressure from employers, and without support from the government, early unions failed to survive for long. The first successful national union, the American Federation of Labor, was founded in the 1880s.

Workers organized unions to obtain higher wages and better working conditions. They elected leaders to represent them in negotiations with employers for labor contracts that specified wages, hours, and working conditions. This practice of negotiating labor contracts is known as **collective bargaining**.

Employers generally refused to negotiate with unions. As a result, unions often resorted to strikes to

Teach

Guided Practice

L1 Making a Chart Work with students to create a chart on the chalkboard that summarizes the following labor laws: the Norris-LaGuardia Act, the Wagner Act, the Taft-Hartley Act, the Landrum-Griffin Act. Ask students if they can see any trends in government policy toward unions from the chart. (*Students may see a shift from a strong prolabor stance in the 1930s to a more moderate position.*)

Caption Answer
because it feared the United States would set a quota

Background

The strongest unions in the United States have 20 percent to 40 percent of workers in a particular industry in their membership. The most powerful unions include teamsters, automobile workers, steel workers, machinists, electrical workers, and retail clerks. Generally the weakest unions have been those for service industries, especially those made up largely of minority groups and women—domestic workers, farm laborers, clerks. However, almost all unions have lost power due to increased global competition. Businesses have the option to move to areas that provide cheaper non-union labor either here or, especially, abroad.

L2 Federalism Discuss with students the ways the federal government aids business. *(tariffs; subsidies that include tax incentives, government loans, free services, cash benefits; services through the Department of Commerce; the Small Business Administration)* Then ask students which government aid to business they consider most important and to give reasons for their opinion.

L3 Panel Discussion Hold a panel discussion in which students discuss whether workers need government protection today, or whether American industry needs government protection from workers.

Graph Study Answer
favorable labor laws in the 1930s; shift from manufacturing to service industries in the 1990s

---

STUDY GUIDE

Theme Answer
Strikes disrupted the nation's economy.

Critical Thinking Answer
Both sides are heard and compromise is possible.

CONNECTIONS

History
The American Federation of Labor (AFL) was a federation of craft unions in which all members had the same skill. The Congress of Industrial Organizations (CIO) was a group of industrial unions to which all workers in a single industry belonged, regardless of the job they performed. In 1955 the two organizations merged, forming the AFL-CIO, thereby increasing the strength of organized labor.

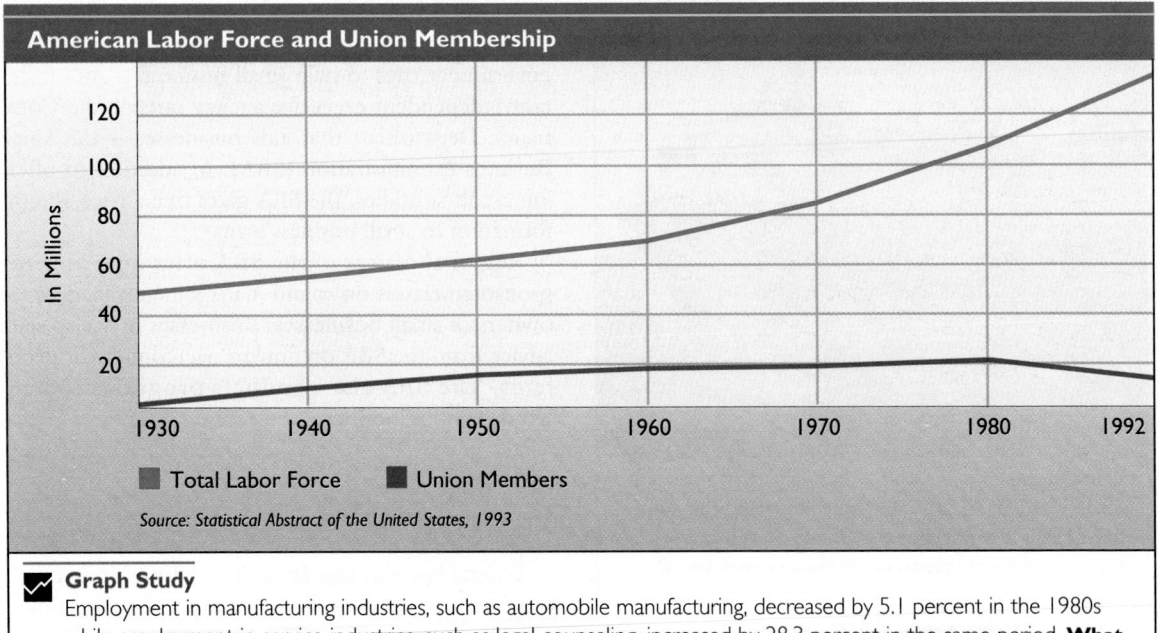

American Labor Force and Union Membership

In Millions

Source: Statistical Abstract of the United States, 1993

■ Total Labor Force ■ Union Members

Graph Study
Employment in manufacturing industries, such as automobile manufacturing, decreased by 5.1 percent in the 1980s while employment in service industries, such as legal counseling, increased by 28.3 percent in the same period. **What might account for the contrasting trends apparent in union membership of the 1930s and the 1980s?**

---

try to obtain concessions. Between 1881 and 1905, American unions called about 37,000 strikes.

For many years, the government favored business at the expense of labor unions. Federal troops and state militia broke up some strikes. The courts even used the Sherman Antitrust Act, originally intended to regulate business, to prohibit union activities as being in "restraint of trade."

The government's attitude toward labor began to change in the early 1900s. Some leaders felt that federal laws were needed to protect labor unions and to prevent strikes from constantly disrupting the economy. The Clayton Antitrust Act, passed in 1914, included a provision that labor unions were not to be treated as "conspiracies in restraint of trade."

Before the 1930s employers were often successful in challenging laws that regulated wages and working conditions. In 1937, however, the Supreme Court upheld a minimum wage set by the Industrial Welfare Committee of the state of Washington, saying:

> *The exploitation of a class of workers who are in an unequal position with respect to bargaining power and are thus relatively defenseless against the denial of a living wage is not only detrimental to their health and well being, but casts a direct burden for their support upon the community. . . . The community may direct its lawmaking power to correct the abuse.*
>
> —CHIEF JUSTICE CHARLES EVANS HUGHES, *WEST COAST HOTEL* V. *PARRISH,* 1937

Today, laws set minimum wages and maximum working hours and prohibit child labor. In addition, the Department of Labor, established in 1913, provides employment offices and job-training programs for people in search of a job, collects helpful data, and offers unemployment insurance.

STUDY GUIDE

Themes in Government
Federalism Generally, state laws, rather than national laws, governed the relationships between business and labor before 1900.

What conditions caused the federal government to pass legislation in this area?

Critical Thinking Skills
Demonstrating Reasoned Judgment Why is collective bargaining important?

Cooperative Learning Activity

Organize students into four groups. Assign each group one of the following roles: small business owners, non-union workers in high-paying professions, non-union workers in low-paying professions, industrialists. Ask students in each group to discuss the pros and cons of unions for their particular group. Students might research information to support their positions. One person from each group should report the group's ideas to the class and have the class react to each group's presentations.

Labor Laws of the 1930s The greatest gains of organized labor occurred during the Great Depression of the 1930s. Under President Roosevelt's New Deal, Congress passed a series of favorable labor laws in this period. These laws are often called "labor's bill of rights." They guaranteed labor's right to bargain collectively and strike, and generally strengthened labor unions.

In 1932 Congress passed the Norris-LaGuardia Act that gave workers the right to join unions and to strike. It outlawed **yellow-dog contracts**, under which workers were forced to sign contracts agreeing not to join a union. The act also restricted the use of federal court injunctions against labor unions. Frequently courts had issued injunctions that required striking unions to end their strikes.

In 1935 Congress passed the Wagner Act, guaranteeing the right of all workers to organize and bargain collectively. To achieve this goal, the law prohibited employers from engaging in certain "unfair labor practices." According to the Wagner Act, employers could not refuse to bargain collectively with recognized unions nor interfere in union organization. Finally, employers could not discharge or otherwise punish a worker because of union activities.

To enforce these prohibitions, the Wagner Act created the National Labor Relations Board (NLRB). The board had power to supervise elections to determine which union a group of workers wanted to represent it. The NLRB could also hear labors' complaints and issue "cease and desist" orders to end unfair labor practices.

Under the Wagner Act, unions gained tremendously in membership and strength. In 1935 when the act was passed, about 4.2 million workers belonged to unions. By 1939 union membership had risen to nearly 9 million.

Regulating Unions Soon after the passage of the Wagner Act, business leaders began to protest that labor unions were growing too powerful. Critics of the Wagner Act claimed that it was one-sided and too favorable to labor. They complained that many work-

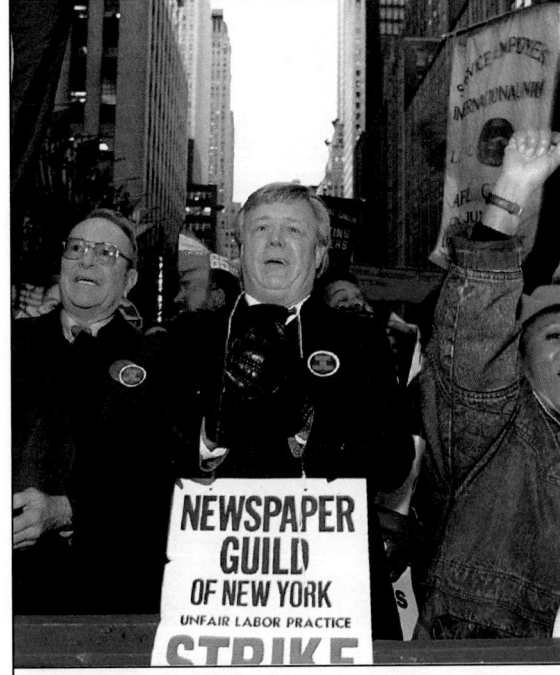

New York Daily News on Strike
Workers have a legal right to organize and bargain collectively. **Law Which act guaranteed this right?**

ers were being forced to join unions against their will. Also, employers were being forced to hire only those workers who belonged to a union. To avoid strikes employers had to agree to establish a closed shop. In a **closed shop**, only members of a union may be hired.

Responding to criticisms of the Wagner Act, Congress passed the Taft-Hartley Act in 1947. Its purpose was to restore the balance between labor and management. It was the federal government's first attempt to regulate certain practices of large unions.

The Taft-Hartley Act required unions to give 60 days notice before calling a strike. This "cooling-off period" was intended to provide additional time for labor and management to settle their differences. The act also restored limited use of the injunction.

STUDY GUIDE

Themes in Government
Free Enterprise During the 1930s Congress passed a series of laws that attempted to establish a balance between the power of business and labor. **Why was the National Labor Relations Board formed?**

Critical Thinking Skills
Identifying Central Issues Why has the relationship between labor and business frequently been confrontational?

Critical Thinking Activity

Demonstrating Reasoned Judgment Ask students to imagine they are workers in an industrial plant. Ask them whether they think it would be better to work under a closed-shop or a union-shop arrangement and whether they would call for right-to-work laws in their state. *(Students should explore the advantages and disadvantages of the closed shop, union shop, and right-to-work laws before making a decision.)*

Independent Practice

L1 Making Generalizations Refer students to the graph on page 650. Ask them to write three generalizations based on the information in the graph.

L2 Technology Have students look up expenditures on research and development by Japanese, German, and American businesses in *The World Almanac*. Ask them to compare the figures and draw some conclusions.

L3 Classificatory Writing Have students research the role of labor unions in Germany and Japan, and write a summary of the similarities and differences with American unions.

Caption Answer
the Wagner Act

STUDY GUIDE

Theme Answer
to enforce the Wagner Act

Critical Thinking Answer
Workers and employers often have different goals, and unions have allowed workers power to confront their employers.

CONNECTIONS

Music
Woody Guthrie was a songwriter and performer during the 1930s, who wrote songs about the everyday lives of working people, including the struggle to organize unions.

Assess

Check for Understanding
Have students complete Section 2 Review on page 652.

Caption Answer
Norris-LaGuardia Act, Wagner Act

Meeting Objectives

Each section objective is tested by the Section Review questions that follow it in parentheses.

- Identify ways in which the federal government aids business. (2, 3, 6)
- Explain the need for laws regulating working conditions. (4)
- Describe laws that regulate labor unions. (5, 7, 8)

Evaluate

 Section 2 Quiz

Testmaker

Reteach

Ask students to identify two ways the federal government supports business and three ways it aids workers.

Enrich

Have students contact the SBA to obtain information about the services it provides and to prepare a report on these services.

Close

Ask students what they think the future direction of government aid to business and labor unions will be. Have them provide reasons for their predictions.

Singer of the People
Folk singer Woody Guthrie wrote many pro-union songs during the Great Depression. **Law What two pro-union laws did Congress pass in the 1930s?**

An important provision of the act prohibited the closed shop. The act did, however, permit the union shop. In a **union shop**, workers are required to join a union soon after they have been hired (but not before). Under the law, union shops can be formed if a majority of workers vote for them. They cannot be formed, however, in any state that has passed a "right-to-work" law. **Right-to-work laws** are state labor laws that prohibit both closed shops and union shops. They provide that all work places be open shops where workers may freely decide whether or not to join a union.

Protecting Union Members Labor unions have not always acted in the best interests of their members. In 1957, for example, a Senate investigating committee found that some leaders of the powerful Teamsters Union had misused and, in some cases, stolen funds. The same leaders were accused of associating with gangsters and racketeers and of having used bribery, threats, and violence against those who tried to challenge them.

These widely publicized labor scandals led to the passage of the Landrum-Griffin Act of 1959. This law made misusing union funds a federal crime. The Landrum-Griffin Act also protected union members from being intimidated by their leaders. It was also helpful in eliminating fraud in union elections. The act included a "bill of rights" for union members. This guaranteed the right of members to nominate and vote by secret ballot in union elections, to participate and speak freely at union meetings, to sue their union for unfair practices, and to examine union records and finances.

In strikes that endanger the nation, the President could obtain an injunction to stop the strike for 80 days. According to the Taft-Hartley Act, employers may sue unions for damages inflicted during a strike.

SECTION 2 REVIEW

Section Summary
Federal laws promote business, control working conditions, and regulate labor unions.

Checking For Understanding
Recalling Facts
1. Define quota, subsidy, collective bargaining, yellow-dog contract, closed shop, union shop, right-to-work law.
2. Identify the first federal proposal designed to promote American business.
3. List four types of subsidies that benefit business.
4. Describe "unfair labor practices" that some businesses used before the government passed laws to empower labor unions.

Exploring Themes
5. Federalism What state legislation regarding unions in the workplace does the federal government honor?
6. Free Enterprise What are the aims of the Small Business Administration?

Critical Thinking Skills
7. Identifying Central Issues What different opinions of labor did the Wagner Act in 1935 and the Taft-Hartley Act in 1947 reflect?
8. Demonstrating Reasoned Judgment Do you think that the Landrum-Griffin Act of 1959 served to strengthen or to weaken unions? Explain your answer.

Section 2 Review Answers

1. Definitions of terms appear on pages indicated: **quota,** 648; **subsidy,** 648; **collective bargaining,** 649; **yellow-dog contract,** 651; **closed shop,** 651; **union shop,** 652; **right-to-work law,** 652
2. protective tariff in 1791
3. tax incentives, credit subsidies, free services, cash benefits

4. refused to negotiate with unions, forced workers to sign yellow-dog contracts, fired strikers and those who joined unions
5. right-to-work laws
6. The SBA aids small businesses by offering credit subsidies, giving advice and information, and helping women and minorities.

7. Wagner Act supporters saw unions as weak and unable to defend workers against unfair practices by business; Taft-Hartley supporters believed that large unions had upset the balance between labor and management.
8. While it may have weakened some union leaders, it generally strengthened unions by giving power to rank-and-file members.

Drawing Conclusions

During the afternoon before a history exam, your teacher tells you to "concentrate on understanding the big ideas, not memorizing names and dates." You probably draw the conclusion that the exam will not be made up of questions about details. To draw conclusions, you need to examine the evidence you have about a topic and use your reasoning to gain further insight.

Explanation

To draw conclusions, follow these steps:
• Closely examine the data you have.
• State two or three things that seem important about the information.
• Decide what inferences you can reasonably make from the data you have to draw a conclusion that goes beyond the facts.

Consider the following graph, which shows data about immigration to the United States between 1931 and 1990.

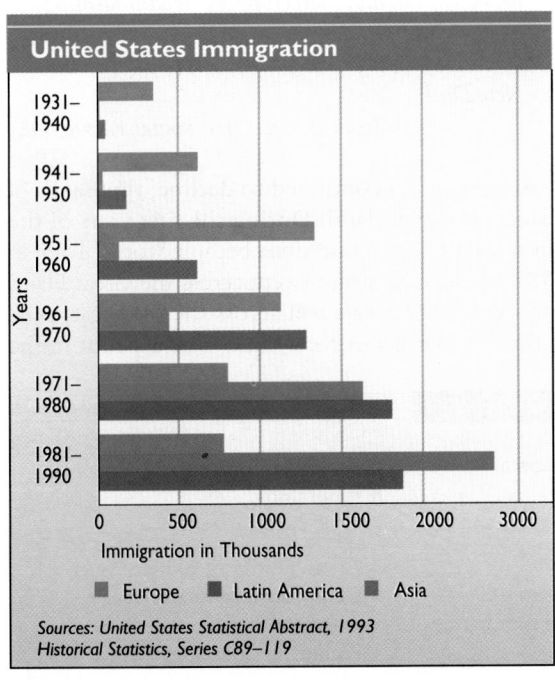

United States Immigration

Years: 1931–1940, 1941–1950, 1951–1960, 1961–1970, 1971–1980, 1981–1990

Immigration in Thousands: 0, 500, 1000, 1500, 2000, 3000

■ Europe   ■ Latin America   ■ Asia

Sources: United States Statistical Abstract, 1993
Historical Statistics, Series C89–119

On this graph immigration data is broken down by region of origin. Which region provided the greatest number of immigrants to the United States during the 1930s? (Europe) About how many immigrants entered the United States from Latin America during the 1980s? (1,500,000)

The next step is to analyze the information and formulate some statements about it. This data shows that the number of immigrants entering the United States has increased sharply since 1931. Another is that immigration from Asia rose dramatically and steadily throughout this period.

The last step is to draw reasonable conclusions based on the information you have. You might, for example, conclude that the United States was considered a desirable place to live.

Practice

Consider the following table, which shows population broken down into age groups from 1960 to 1990. Then answer the questions that follow.

Population by Age Groups

	1960	1970	1980	1990*
65 and over	9.2%	9.8%	11.3%	12.4%
50–64	14.0	14.5	14.7	13.3
35–49	19.4	17.1	16.3	19.7
20–34	18.9	20.8	26.0	25.7
5–19	27.2	29.3	24.6	21.4
under 5	11.3	8.4	7.2	7.5

* Estimated   Source: Statistical Abstract of the United States, 1991

1. Which age group increased steadily as a percentage of the population between 1960 and 1990?
2. In what year did all people under the age of 20 first make up less than 30 percent of the population?
3. Based on the table, what conclusions can you draw about the population of the United States?

Additional Practice

To practice this skill, see **Reinforcing the Skill** on page 673.

CHAPTER 23: SOCIAL AND DOMESTIC POLICY 653

Focus

Direct students' attention to the graph on immigration and have each student jot down one fact they learned from it. Invite volunteers to present their facts; then discuss what general information about immigration these facts could be used to present.

Teach

Remind students of the need to be able to grasp "big ideas," rather than memorize statistics. Then, using the Explanation steps, draw some conclusions from the graph. Ask: What information do you use to draw conclusions? *(data, plus prior knowledge of people, places, and history)* What knowledge of history and/or geography, for example, could help you draw conclusions about immigration trends? *(samples: distances people would need to travel to get to the United States; political events that might cause people to want to move; immigration regulations in the United States)* Discuss ways students can judge the reasonableness of their conclusions.

Assess

Have students complete the **Practice** exercise.

Close

Ask students to bring a graph or chart from the business section of the newspaper and be prepared to draw one or two conclusions from it.

Practice Answers

1. 65 and older
2. 1990
3. Students may suggest that the American population is aging, that people are living longer due to improved health care and/or that the birth rate is declining.

📁 For additional practice, have students complete activity 23 in *Skill Reinforcement Activities* in the Teacher's Classroom Resources.

Focus

Bell Ringer

Write the following on the chalkboard for students to complete:

List several current environmental problems in the United States.

Motivating Activity

Write students' Bell Ringer responses on the chalkboard. Ask students who they think should be responsible for solving the environmental problems of the nation. Tell students that Section 3 discusses the agricultural, energy, and environmental policies of the federal government.

Vocabulary Precheck

Call on volunteers to tell what they think each key term and concept means. Have students check the accuracy of their definitions in the Glossary. **LEP**

Teach

L1 Chronology Work with students to make a time line on the chalkboard of agricultural legislation that the federal government has enacted over the years to support farmers. **LEP**

CONNECTIONS

Literature

In his novel *The Grapes of Wrath*, John Steinbeck chronicles the experiences of a farm family forced to leave its home in Oklahoma as a result of the terrible dust storm that swept the Great Plains during the 1930s.

SECTION 3
Agriculture and the Environment

In 1790 about 95 percent of the American people lived in rural areas, and most Americans were farmers. Farming remained the major occupation until after the early 1900s. Today, however, less than 5 percent of the American people are farmers. The United States is an urban nation with more than 75 percent of the people residing in towns and cities.

American Farms From 1935 to the present, the number of farms in the United States has declined from 6.8 million to slightly more than 2 million because small family farms are disappearing. Even though median farm income is not as high as median nonfarm family income, the average farm in the United States is worth about $400,000. The average farm today is almost twice as large as the average farm of 30 years ago. Large corporate farms are making agriculture big business.

While the total number of farms has decreased, farm output per work hour has increased almost every year. In 1900 one farmer could feed about seven people. Now the average farmer can feed approximately 80 people.

Federal Farm Policy

Despite the transition from a rural to urban nation, the federal government has always encouraged American agriculture. Because farming is so vital to the nation, governments at the federal, state, and local levels provide support and assistance to farmers.

Early Agricultural Legislation Congress passed three acts that were important to farmers in 1862.

One law created the Department of Agriculture. In the beginning the chief purpose of this department was to show farmers how to improve and modernize their agricultural methods. In 1889 the Department of Agriculture was elevated to cabinet-level status.

A second law, the Morrill Act, aided states in establishing colleges of agriculture. The government granted millions of acres of federal land to northern states to establish state-operated colleges. The third law, the Homestead Act, gave land to those willing to farm it.

Farm Problems In the 1920s the nation's farms faced serious problems. A historian's view creates a dismal picture:

The high tariff enacted by the Republicans after World War I helped destroy the farmer's European market; the changing diet of the American family and immigration restriction curtailed the farmer's market at home. Low crop prices, threats of foreclosures, an inadequate credit supply, soil erosion, locusts, droughts, sharecropping, tenant farming, and migrant farming complete the dismal picture of farm conditions in the United States prior to the New Deal.

—JOHN H. CARY, *THE SOCIAL FABRIC*, 1981

As farm prices continued to decline, thousands of farmers lost their land. During the first years of the Great Depression, conditions became worse. Then in 1933 a huge dust storm swept across the Great Plains and carried the area's soil across the Midwest, even darkening the sky in New York. One account in the

---

SECTION PREVIEW

Objectives
After studying this section, you should be able to:
- Summarize the ways that the federal government has helped the farmer throughout United States history.
- Describe current federal agricultural policy.
- Evaluate national energy and environmental policies.

Key Terms and Concepts
price-support, acreage allotment, target price

Themes in Government
- Federalism
- Civic Participation

Critical Thinking Skills
- Demonstrating Reasoned Judgment
- Predicting Consequences

654 UNIT 7: PUBLIC POLICIES AND SERVICES

Classroom Resources for Section 3

- Guided Reading Activities
- Reproducible Lesson Plans
- Participating in Government 23
- Primary and Secondary Source Readings 23
- Enrichment Activities 23

- Section 3 Quiz
- Testmaker
- Government Themes Transparencies 27
- SAT Practice Tests
- Writer's Guidebook

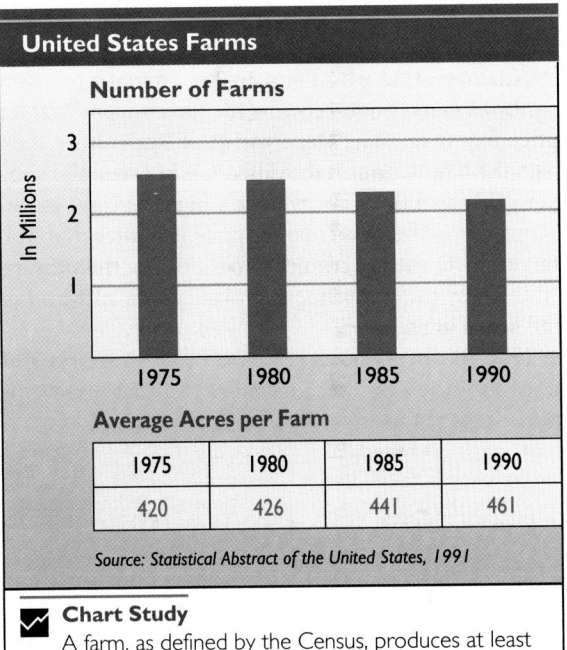

United States Farms

Number of Farms

In Millions

	1975	1980	1985	1990

Average Acres per Farm

1975	1980	1985	1990
420	426	441	461

Source: Statistical Abstract of the United States, 1991

✓ **Chart Study**
A farm, as defined by the Census, produces at least $1,000 worth of agricultural products. **What do the above trends reveal about the small farmer?**

Saturday Evening Post described the scene in South Dakota:

> *When the wind died and the sun shone forth again, it was a different world. There were no fields, only sand drifting into mounds. . . . In the farmyard, fences, machinery, and trees were gone, buried. The roofs of sheds stuck out through drifts deeper than a man is tall.*

—R.D. Lusk, November 1933

Responding to the disastrous situation on the farms, President Roosevelt's New Deal enacted laws to help the farmers. The legislation limited the production of certain crops that were in oversupply in order to raise the price of farm products. Under the Agricultural Adjustment Act (AAA), the government paid farmers for not producing their usual amount of corn, wheat, hogs, and other commodities. It also provided loans to help farmers keep their land. Although the Supreme Court declared the AAA unconstitutional in 1936, Congress quickly passed a similar act that overcame the Court's objections.

Aid for Farmers Today

The Department of Agriculture provides services essential to farmers. The chief functions are to help farmers market their produce, stabilize farm prices, conserve land and develop rural areas, and promote research in agricultural science.

The Department of Agriculture has also helped develop rural areas and improve life for farmers. Rural Electrification Administration loans have brought electricity and telephone service to many rural areas. The Farmers Home Administration was established to provide loans for farmers to buy land, livestock, seeds, equipment, and fertilizer, to build homes, to dig wells, and to obtain disaster relief.

Marketing Services Several agencies of the Department of Agriculture are principally concerned with helping farmers find buyers for their crops. The Agricultural Marketing Service advises farmers on the demand for crops, current prices, and transportation methods. It also performs market research to help farmers know when and where to sell their products. The Foreign Agricultural Service promotes the sale of American farm goods in foreign markets.

Programs for Stabilizing Prices The federal government has tried several methods for preventing farm prices from falling below a certain level. The current approach involves the coordination of three programs—price supports, acreage allotments, and marketing quotas. The Commodity Credit Corporation (CCC) administers these programs.

Under the **price-support** program, Congress establishes a support price for a particular crop. The CCC then lends the farmer money equal to the support price for the crop. If the actual market price falls

Guided Practice

✦ **Interpreting Visuals** Display transparency 27 from the *Government Themes Transparencies* in the Teacher's Classroom Resources and use the accompanying teaching strategy and student activity to teach about environmental issues.

Chart Study Answer
decreasing

STUDY GUIDE

Theme Answer
created Department of Agriculture and passed laws to help states found colleges of agriculture and to give land to farmers

Critical Thinking Answer
As farms have grown fewer in number, they have grown larger in average size and can produce more crops.

L2 Interviewing Invite a spokesperson for the local chapter of an environmental organization, such as the Audubon Society or the Sierra Club, to speak to the class about its political activities. Have students prepare questions about the group's position on the environmental policies discussed in this section.

Background

According to the National Wildlife Federation's Environmental Quality Index, the United States is facing a serious soil erosion threat. Millions of acres of farmland and wildlife habitat are literally being blown away. The Federation's report warns that if the federal government does not take action, the nation could face a situation worse than the Dust Bowl catastrophe of the Great Depression era. The culprit now, however, is not the weather but the failure of American farmers to follow effective erosion prevention measures.

L3 Synthesizing Information
Explore with the class the links between agricultural and environmental policy. Ask how fertilizers and pesticides might impact water quality policies. Ask what agreements and disagreements farmers might have with conservation policies.

PARTICIPATING IN GOVERNMENT

Point out to students that a community's geography, services and facilities, organizations, recreation, and its society are factors that help to make a community unique. Ask students how these factors apply to their community.

Have students present their **Investigating Further** projects.

📁 Have students complete activity 23 in *Participating in Government* in the Teacher's Classroom Resources.

Independent Practice

L1 Art Have students create posters that illustrate federal air, water, conservation, or energy policies. **LEP**

L2 Identifying Trends Have students use *Statistical Abstracts* to research changes in the number and size of farms in their state in the past two decades. Tell them to choose a table, graph, or summary paragraph as the method to present their findings.

---

below the support price, the farmer repays the loan with the crop.

The Commodity Credit Corporation holds the surplus crops in government storage facilities until the market price goes up and the crop can be sold. It also uses surplus crops in welfare programs, for school lunches, and for famine relief overseas. Even so, from time to time, huge surpluses of some products have accumulated when market prices stay at a low level.

In order to avoid large surpluses every year, the government has adopted the idea of acreage restriction or **acreage allotment**. In this program officials in the Department of Agriculture estimate the probable demand for a crop in world and national markets. Then they estimate the number of acres that will produce that amount. Based on these estimates, the government assigns farmers acreage allotments and pays support prices for only the crops grown on the assigned number of acres.

When a crop has been overproduced and large surpluses threaten to lower prices, the government turns to marketing quotas. Aided by Department of Agriculture officials, farmers set up marketing quotas among themselves and agree to market only an assigned portion of their overproduced crop.

In the 1970s the government tried the **target price** method to avoid storing overproduced grain. Suppose, for example, that wheat farmers are offered a price on the open market that is below the government's target price for wheat. The Department of Agriculture then pays the wheat farmers the difference between the market price and the government's higher target price. However, if the open market price is higher than the target price, the government does not pay the subsidy. In this way the government avoids buying and storing the actual grain.

Not all observers agree with price supports and farm subsidies. Some economists feel that price supports benefit the large, not the small, farmer.

Protecting the Environment

The federal government protects not only the farmer but also the land, air, and water. This headline appeared in a 1990 article in *Business Week:* "A Clean-Air Bill is Easy. Clean Air is Hard. Now a weakened EPA [Environmental Protection Agency] must try to enforce the law in a flat economy." The article dealt with amendments to the nation's Clean Air Act, first

---

PARTICIPATING IN GOVERNMENT

Improving Your Neighborhood

Residents can be the most effective force in solving neighborhood problems. What issues and problems does your neighborhood face? What can you do to help? Each neighborhood is unique, but the following guidelines apply to many different situations:

Crime prevention and neighborhood beautification are common needs. Talk to your neighbors. Is burglary or street crime a problem? Is there a vacant lot or existing park that needs improvement?

Neighborhood improvement requires cooperation. Enlist the help of your

neighbors. Determine what strengths and talents your group members can share.

Your local police department can provide suggestions for reducing crime in your neighborhood. You can form a Neighborhood Watch —a program in which neighbors monitor the area and report any suspicious activity to

the police. You can request additional police patrols and perhaps street lighting.

Organize a fund-raiser, such as a car wash or a bake sale, to earn money for your projects. Ask your local newspaper or radio station to promote your effort. The publicity may bring additional donations.

Investigating Further

Identify one problem or issue in the neighborhood where your school is located. Formulate a plan for improvement. Work with others to carry out the plan.

Special Needs Strategy

Teaching Strategy Students with learning problems have often had few opportunities to experience success in the learning environment. Successful learning experiences can be provided if students can relate textbook content to their everyday lives. Section 3 discusses agriculture, energy, and environmental policies. Ask students which has had the most impact on their lives. Have students find articles from a local newspaper and magazines that highlight a problem in one of these areas. Have students explain to the class how the articles relate to the information in Section 3.

passed in 1963. John D. Dingell, head of the House Energy and Commerce Committee, noted, "It is the most complex, comprehensive, and far reaching environmental law any Congress has ever considered."

Air Pollution Policies Congress first expressed concern about air pollution as early as 1955 when it passed the Air Pollution Act. This act, however, was limited to promoting research on air quality and providing technical assistance to states and communities.

In the 1960s Congress passed two stronger laws, the Clean Air Act of 1963 and the Air Quality Control Act of 1967. The 1967 law required states to set clean air standards and to prepare acceptable plans for their enforcement. These laws and subsequent efforts to assess air quality helped call public attention to air pollution.

The basic air pollution legislation in effect today includes the 1990 amendments to the Clean Air Act of 1970. Under the new rules, the government requires automobile-emission reductions beginning with the 1994 models. Industries must reduce by 90 percent the emission of 189 toxic chemicals, and power companies must reduce emissions of carbon dioxide. More than 110 power companies must cut their emissions by one-half by the year 2000. Strictly enforced, the act is designed to dramatically reduce both air and water pollution.

Water Pollution Policies While the strengthened Clean Air Act will reduce water pollution caused by acid rain, the government has targeted pollution from other sources as well. The Water Pollution Control Act of 1948 first provided for federal technical assistance to the states but, as with the early pollution laws, the act was weak. More recent legislation has been stronger. The Water Quality Improvement Act of 1970 prohibited the discharge of harmful amounts of oil and other dangerous materials into navigable waters. The law concerned such sources as ships, onshore refineries, and offshore oil drilling platforms. It also provided for extensive control over pesticide drainage into the Great Lakes.

Protecting Salmon Runs
Recently federal agencies have moved to protect natural resources and wildlife. **Economics Why is it difficult to formulate a national environmental policy?**

The major legislation to end water pollution was the Water Pollution Control Act of 1972. In this law Congress set the goal of completely eliminating the discharge of pollutants into the nation's waterways. Under the act all polluters dumping waste into waterways—cities, industries, or farmers—must have a permit. The EPA's responsibility is to study each dumping location to judge how much discharge is necessary and monitor the dumper's compliance with regulations. Many lawsuits have resulted that involve the EPA. On the one hand, environmentalists have often sued because they thought the EPA was too permissive about dumping. On the other hand, industries have sued the EPA, arguing that the agency was unreasonable in its standards.

Promoting Conservation Conserving the nation's land and forests is a vital responsibility of agencies in the Department of Agriculture. The Forest Service has restored millions of acres of forests used for outdoor recreation, grazing, timber, and for fish

---

L2 Informative Writing Have students write a report on the problems of toxic waste. Students' reports should address the problem of who is responsible for paying for the clean-ups.

Interpreting Source Readings Have students complete activity 23 in *Primary and Secondary Source Readings* in the Teacher's Classroom Resources.

Caption Answer
Each state has its own environmental standards and laws.

STUDY GUIDE

Theme Answer
clean up neighborhoods, recycle, use public transportation

Critical Thinking Answer
another shortage created by suppliers who oppose American foreign policy

---

Assess

Check for Understanding
Have students complete Section 3 Review on page 658.

Meeting Objectives
Each section objective is tested by the Section Review questions that follow it in parentheses.
- Summarize the ways that the federal government has helped the farmer throughout United States history. (2, 4)
- Describe current federal agricultural policy. (4)
- Evaluate national energy and environmental policies. (3, 5, 6, 7, 8)

STUDY GUIDE

Themes in Government
Civic Participation Generally, federal legislation to protect the environment has been aimed at pollution caused by industry.

What can students do to help protect the environment?

Critical Thinking Skills
Predicting Consequences **What could result if the United States continues its dependence on foreign oil as a major source of its energy?**

Critical Thinking Activity

Demonstrating Reasoned Judgment Review with students the ways the Department of Agriculture aids farmers. Then ask the following question: Is it proper for the government to subsidize businesses, such as farming, when such subsidies are provided through taxes on all Americans? Why or why not? *(Those who agree might argue that the subsidies serve to aid the economy and, therefore, the country as a whole. Those opposed might argue that taxes should not be used to promote such businesses because they involve only a small segment of the population.)*

Evaluate

📁 Section 3 Quiz

🖥 Testmaker

Reteach

Have students turn each of the section's main heads into a statement that reflects its main idea, and each subhead into a statement that provides evidence to support the main head.

Enrich

Have students research and give oral reports on the types of energy resources used in the state.

📁 Have students complete activity 23 in *Enrichment Activities* in the Teacher's Classroom Resources.

Close

Have students use the information in Section 3 to evaluate the belief some people hold that some risk or damage to the environment is the price the nation has to pay in order to have jobs, profits, and a strong economy.

and wildlife. The Soil Conservation Service works through 3,000 soil conservation districts and with farmers to manage conservation problems.

Energy and the Environment

In the 1950s most Americans were not familiar with terms like *energy crisis, environmental pollution,* and *ecology.* Today, however, the declining quality of the environment and the diminishing supply of cheap energy have forced the national government to place these important matters high on its policy agenda.

The Native Americans who first settled this land and the settlers who came later found great natural resources—unending forests; clear lakes and rivers; rich deposits of coal, iron ore, oil, and copper, silver, and other metals. For hundreds of years, Americans used increasingly sophisticated technology to use these resources to build a strong industrial nation. During most of this time, they gave little thought to the possibility that these resources might be depleted or that the careless exploitation of resources could have a serious impact on the environment.

By the early 1960s, however, the costs became obvious. Many rivers and lakes were dirty, fouled by sewage and chemical wastes. Smog engulfed major cities, oil spills polluted the beaches, and the heavy use of pesticides endangered wildlife.

During the winter of 1973-1974, Americans suddenly found themselves in an energy crisis. Arab countries cut off shipments of oil to the United States because the United States had supported Israel dur-

ing an Arab-Israeli war. Industries dependent on oil laid off workers. Many gas stations closed, and long lines formed at the ones that were open. States lowered speed limits, and people set thermostats lower to save energy.

The federal government responded with emergency legislation, but many people called for a long-term energy policy. As the national government began to fashion a new energy policy in the mid-1970s to meet future energy crises, people began to realize that there are often built-in costs and conflicts. These included the costs of a cleaner environment and conflicts among interest groups with different goals. Americans discovered that preserving clean air might require them to drive cars with pollution-control devices. These devices not only raised the cost of the cars but also lowered their gas mileage. Oil companies wanted to drill for more offshore oil, while environmentalists believed that it posed too great a risk.

As the federal government studied the nation's energy needs, competing interest groups such as energy companies, conservation organizations, and consumer advocates struggled to shape new policies and programs that reflected their concerns. The resulting Energy Policy Act of 1992, signed into law by President Bush, was a major attempt to curb United States oil dependence. The huge document represented months of energy policy debates. It touched on nearly every sector of the energy industry—utilities, alternative-fuel vehicles, nuclear power plants, coal production, and energy research. Senator Tim Worth of Colorado called the act "the beginning of a balance between environmental and energy policy."

3 SECTION REVIEW

Section Summary
The federal government has passed legislation to support farm prices, protect the environment, and meet energy crises.

Checking For Understanding
Recalling Facts
1. Define price-support, acreage allotment, target price.
2. List three acts that Congress passed in 1862 to aid farmers.
3. Compare federal clean air legislation of the 1950s and 1960s with legislation in 1990.
4. Describe the ways the federal government currently aids agriculture.

Exploring Themes
5. Federalism How did the federal government involve the states in addressing the air pollution problem?
6. Civic Participation What three interest groups have sought to influence national energy policies?

Critical Thinking Skills
7. Demonstrating Reasoned Judgment What goals should a national energy policy for the United States have?
8. Predicting Consequences In your opinion, what will be the economic and environmental effects of recent air and water pollution legislation?

Section 3 Review Answers

1. Definitions of terms appear on pages indicated: **price-support,** 655; **acreage allotment,** 656; **target price,** 656
2. act creating the Department of Agriculture, Morrill Act, Homestead Act
3. Legislation in the 1950s was limited to promoting research on air quality and providing technical assistance to states and communities. In the 1960s stronger laws re-quired states to set clean air standards and to prepare acceptable enforcement plans. The 1990 requirements are more specific—drastic reductions in automobile emissions, emission of toxic chemicals by industry, and emissions of carbon dioxide by power companies.
4. help to market produce, stabilize farm prices, conserve land, develop rural areas, as well as promote agricultural research
5. The Air Quality Control Act of 1967 required states to set clean air standards and to prepare acceptable plans for their

enforcement.
6. energy companies, conservation organizations, consumer advocates
7. The United States needs to reduce vulnerability to energy disruption, improve the environment, and increase energy efficiency.
8. Answers will vary, but may predict improvement in the quality of air and water, and that the costs of this improvement will be paid by consumers and taxpayers.

SECTION 4
Health and Public Assistance

For many years the hardships of ill health, old age, poverty, blindness, and disability were private matters. Local and state governments provided very limited help for needy Americans in the form of orphanages, alms houses, and poor farms. Most people in need depended on themselves and on churches and private charitable organizations.

The Great Depression of the 1930s changed the public attitude toward assistance or welfare. During that decade the national government started two types of programs: social insurance and public assistance.

The Impact of the Depression

Thousands of individuals, banks, and companies lost money in the stock market crash of 1929. Stock values and the American economy continued to slump badly month after month for the next several years. Unemployment increased from about 3 percent of the nation's work force in 1929 to almost 25 percent in 1933. Millions of Americans were poor and hungry. The song, "Brother, Can You Spare a Dime?" expressed the mood of the early 1930s. Almost overnight, unemployment, hunger, and poverty became massive national problems.

New Deal Programs As the Depression deepened, private charities and local and state governments could not cope with the problems of the poor. To ease the nation's suffering, President Franklin D. Roosevelt proposed and Congress passed the Social Security Act in 1935. This act was the first of many

government-supported social insurance, public assistance, and health-care programs. The government envisioned these programs as long-term ways to provide some economic security for all citizens.

Today the United States has two kinds of social programs. **Social insurance programs** are designed to help elderly, ill, and unemployed citizens. **Public assistance programs** distribute public money to poor people. The government uses general tax revenues to pay for these programs. Unlike social insurance, public assistance does not require recipients to contribute to the cost of the programs.

Social Insurance Programs

The Social Security Act and its later amendments created a social insurance system with three main components. The first component is social security, or Old Age, Survivors, and Disability Insurance (OASDI). The second component is a health-insurance program called medicare, and the third is unemployment insurance.

The Social Security Administration administers OASDI from its huge headquarters in Baltimore and from 1,300 local offices around the country. The Health Care Financing Administration manages the medicare program. Both of these agencies are important units within the Department of Health and Human Services. The Department of Labor runs the unemployment insurance program.

Financing Social Security An equal tax on employers and employees finances the social security sys-

---

SECTION PREVIEW

Objectives
After studying this section, you should be able to:
- Identify the historic developments in social insurance and public assistance in the 1930s.
- Describe the main federal social insurance, public assistance, and health programs in effect today.

- Discuss concerns about public assistance that Congress addressed in welfare reform legislation.

Key Terms and Concepts
social insurance programs, public assistance programs, unemployment insurance

Themes in Government
- Federalism
- Constitutional Interpretations

Critical Thinking Skills
- Identifying Assumptions
- Predicting Consequences

CHAPTER 23: SOCIAL AND DOMESTIC POLICY 659

Classroom Resources for Section 4

- Guided Reading Activities
- Reproducible Lesson Plans
- Section 4 Quiz

- Testmaker
- SAT Practice Tests
- Writer's Guidebook

Teach

Guided Practice

L1 Comparing and Contrasting Ask students to compare the purposes of social insurance programs and public assistance programs and to contrast the source of their funding. List the programs on the chalkboard and discuss the comparisons.

L2 Federalism Review with students the ways the federal government promotes public health. Ask students how they feel about national health insurance. Students should provide reasons for their opinions.

tem. Self-employed persons also must pay a social security tax. A major portion of the medicare program, a health-insurance plan for persons 65 or older, is paid for in the same way. More than 90 percent of those employed in the United States participate and are covered by the social security system.

In 1981 the social security system faced a severe cash shortage as outgoing payments rose faster than incoming payroll taxes. The original idea was to build a large self-sustaining trust fund from which benefits would be paid. The government, however, was quickly using up the system's reserve funds. In one month of 1982, for example, the system had to borrow about $2 billion to meet its payments.

The social security system's financial crisis became so acute that President Reagan appointed a bipartisan commission to recommend ways of rescuing the system from bankruptcy. The commission made a number of proposals that became the basis for the first major changes in the social security system. In 1983 Congress passed a law that included a gradual rise in the retirement age from 65 to 67 by the year 2027. It also required that social security benefits of some higher-income retired people be subject to federal income tax. The law required federal workers to join social security, increased the social security payroll tax, and deferred cost-of-living increases to retirees.

By the end of the 1980s, social security revenue increased. The government estimated that the fund's surplus would grow past the year 2000. Some experts, however, believe that without additional changes, OASDI funds could be used up midway through the next century.

Medicare Health Insurance In 1965 Congress added medicare to the social security program. More than 30 million senior citizens participate in medicare. The basic plan pays a major share of a person's hospital bills.

A second portion of the medicare program is voluntary. For those who choose to pay an extra amount, medicare helps pay doctors' bills and costs of Xrays, surgical dressings, and so on. Almost all the people covered by the basic plan are enrolled in the voluntary portion of the medicare plan.

Unemployment Insurance The 1935 Social Security Act also set up **unemployment insurance** programs for people who are out of work. Under these programs, federal and state governments cooperate to provide the needed help.

Workers in every state are eligible to receive unemployment payments if their employers dismiss them from their jobs. To fund the program, employers pay a tax to the federal government. Then, when workers are involuntarily laid off, they may apply for weekly benefits from a state, not a federal, employment office.

Public Assistance Programs

The federal government has added public assistance programs in recent years. Although the federal government provides most of the money for these programs from general tax revenues, state and local welfare agencies actually run the programs. The four major public assistance programs are: Aid to Families with Dependent Children (AFDC), Supplemental Security Income (SSI), food stamps, and medicaid.

Aid to Families with Dependent Children Aid to Families with Dependent Children is designed to help families in which the main wage earner has died, been disabled, or left the family. In its early years, about 75 percent of those receiving aid were children of fathers who had died or been disabled. Today more than 80 percent of the children receiving aid have fathers who have either deserted their families or who have never married the mothers of the children.

A family with dependent children is eligible for AFDC assistance if its income is too low according to criteria set by the state. A dependent child is generally defined as a person under 18 years of age who is deprived of normal parental support and is living with a parent or specified relative. In 1991 the Census Bureau issued its report on poverty. It showed that more

Background

Since the end of World War II, the United States has greatly increased its funding for social insurance and public assistance. In 1950, for instance, the federal government spent $2.1 billion on social insurance. In 1992, authorities reported that 1989 federal expenditures had reached $387 billion. A similar trend can also be seen in federal expenditures on public assistance. In 1950, the United States provided public aid worth $1.1 billion. By 1989, federal expenditures reached $80 billion.

Social Welfare Expenditures

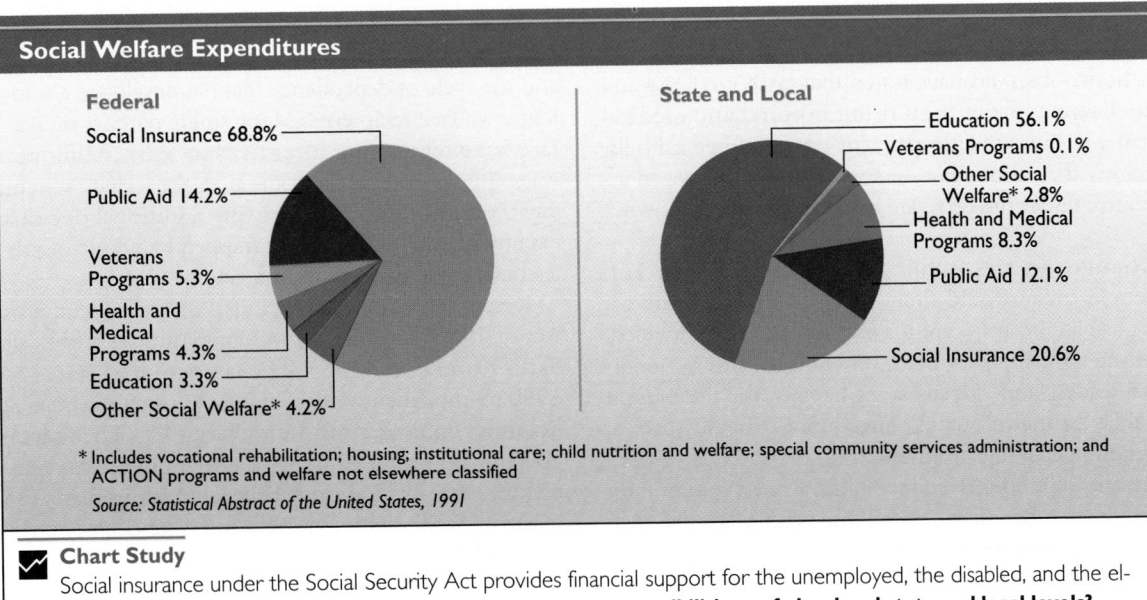

Federal

Social Insurance 68.8%

Public Aid 14.2%

Veterans Programs 5.3%

Health and Medical Programs 4.3%

Education 3.3%

Other Social Welfare* 4.2%

State and Local

Education 56.1%

Veterans Programs 0.1%

Other Social Welfare* 2.8%

Health and Medical Programs 8.3%

Public Aid 12.1%

Social Insurance 20.6%

* Includes vocational rehabilitation; housing; institutional care; child nutrition and welfare; special community services administration; and ACTION programs and welfare not elsewhere classified

Source: Statistical Abstract of the United States, 1991

Chart Study
Social insurance under the Social Security Act provides financial support for the unemployed, the disabled, and the elderly. **What does this chart reveal about social welfare responsibilities at federal and state and local levels?**

than 21 percent of the nation's children under the age of 15 were living in poverty despite the government's efforts under AFDC.

The AFDC program is often criticized. Some critics argue that the program promotes illegitimacy. They also claim that it promotes fatherless families by encouraging men to leave their families in order to make their children eligible for aid. Critics on the opposite side charge that AFDC is more concerned with rules and enforcement procedures than with the living conditions and well-being of children. Over the years Congress has attempted to modify the program, but it remains controversial.

Supplemental Security Income (SSI) Set up by Congress in 1974, SSI brought together under federal control all state programs for the aged, the blind, and the disabled. Under the original Social Security Act, the states had administered these programs, and benefits and procedures varied greatly from state to state. SSI sought to simplify these programs and streamline the administration of benefits.

The Social Security Administration runs the program. The federal government makes a monthly payment to anyone who is 65 or older, who is blind or disabled, and who has little or no regular income.

Food Stamps President Kennedy started the food stamp program by executive order in 1961. Congress created a food stamp system by law in 1964. The purpose of the food stamp program was to increase the food-buying power of low-income families and help dispose of America's surplus agricultural production. When the program started, approximately 367,000 people received food stamps. In 1991 more than 23 million Americans received food stamps at a cost to the government of more than $14 billion each year.

Medicaid Congress established the medicaid program in 1965 as part of the social security system. Medicaid is designed to help pay hospital, doctor, and other medical bills for persons with low incomes. General federal, state, and local taxes fund this pro-

STUDY GUIDE

Themes in Government
Constitutional Interpretations
In the 1930s when Congress began to pass social legislation, the Supreme Court ruled that the Constitution did not give the fed-

eral government the authority to set up public assistance programs.

Critical Thinking Skills
Predicting Consequences With the steady increase of the aged population in the United States,

what do you think might happen if social security funds run out early in the twenty-first century?

Chart Study Answer
The chart reveals that social insurance programs in the United States, such as social security and medicare, are more of a federal responsibility, while education is primarily a state and local responsibility.

STUDY GUIDE

Critical Thinking Answer
Some people that want or need to retire may not be able to; taxes may go up to fund anticipated larger numbers of retirees; benefits may be reduced; cost-of-living raises may be eliminated.

CONNECTIONS

Economics
In 1992 numerous changes took effect in the federal government's nationwide fee schedule for medicare payments to family doctors and general practitioners. According to the Health Care Financing Administration, the average medicare physician rate for a routine office visit in 1992 was $66—up from $57 in 1991.

Cooperative Learning Activity

The text identifies Aid to Families with Dependent Children as one of the most controversial public assistance programs. Divide the class into small groups and have group members work together to write an answer to the following question: How can the United States establish programs to provide for dependent children that do not encourage a parent to desert his or her children? Answers should be developed in three stages—brainstorming, first draft, and final draft. Call on groups randomly to report their progress.

Independent Practice

L1 Language Arts Have students summarize in the form of newspaper headlines the ways that the federal government addresses the concerns of social insurance, public assistance, and public health. For example, one headline might read MEDICARE PROVIDES HEALTH INSURANCE FOR THE ELDERLY.

Images of Government

Ask students to identify the people, events, or movements commemorated by the stamps shown in the feature. Then have students discuss the following: Are there any people, events, or movements that should not have been commemorated with stamps? Why? What limits should there be on who or what is commemorated by stamps? Why?

Answers

1. Printing and distributing money and stamps is crucial to business.
2. The Department of the Treasury collects federal taxes and customs duties.

CONNECTIONS

History

By the time President Reagan took office, perceived inadequacies in public assistance programs were being attacked on a bipartisan front. In 1986 Reagan put "welfare reform" on the congressional agenda. In the following years, the National Association of Governors worked closely with Congress to help draft reform legislation, which included mandatory work and training programs for recipients of public assistance.

---

gram that aids more than 24 million people at a cost of about $54 billion each year.

Some observers have noted that both medicaid and medicare contribute to rising hospital and medical costs. Because the government pays the medical bills, neither the patients nor doctors or hospitals have an incentive under this program to try to keep costs down.

Changes in the Public Assistance System Few people today would deny that society has some responsibility to help care for its poor, sick, and disabled. At the same time, for many different reasons few political leaders and citizens seem happy with the present public assistance system. After more than 30 years of rapidly increasing program costs, the level of poverty remains high in the United States. Recent figures indicate that more than 33 million people are living in poverty in this country today.

There has been great public frustration over the welfare system, stemming from reports of welfare fraud and the cycle of dependence that has developed among many welfare recipients. Many single parents on welfare have few strong incentives to work. Minimum wage jobs provide less income than the welfare system, and working often means paying additional day-care expenses. Poor people seem trapped in a cycle of joblessness, inadequate education, and welfare.

Recent legislation has included the Family Support Act of 1988, creating a Job Opportunities and Basic Skills program (JOBS). The law required states by 1990 to implement welfare-to-work programs aimed at helping people get off the welfare rolls. The federal government promised to pay a share of the costs of education and job training. Federal funding for JOBS began at $600 million in 1989 and is scheduled to rise to $1.3 billion in 1995.

▼ The United States Postal Service, established in 1971, provides mail services and sells stamps. Stamps, printed by the Department of the Treasury, often commemorate noteworthy people, events, and movements in United States history.

IMAGES ·OF· GOVERNMENT

At Your Service

From enacting laws to levying taxes, the federal government performs many functions affecting people's lives. To facilitate communication and commerce, the United States prints and distributes money and stamps.

A Nation of Readers USA 20c

Special Needs Strategy

Teaching Strategy Section 4 provides detailed information about programs that are used by our society to provide for what is considered by many to be a more "equitable" distribution of benefits. Many students with learning problems will not understand the differences among these programs. As an aid to comprehension, have each student make a list of the programs mentioned in this section, such as medicare, unemployment insurance, AFDC, and SSI, and detail the benefits of each. Tell them that because of lack of funds, the government must eliminate one of the programs. Have each student choose which program should be eliminated and defend the choice.

The new jobs program included a provision that welfare recipients who took jobs and got off the welfare rolls would continue to be eligible for subsidized child care and health benefits for one year. In addition, it provided that no parent would be required to accept a job that would result in a reduction in the family's net cash income.

Two unusual aspects of the new welfare reform legislation were that it was patterned after successful state welfare reforms and it developed from close cooperation between Democrats and Republicans and between Congress and the governors.

Promoting Public Health

In 1792 Secretary of the Treasury Alexander Hamilton urged Congress to provide hospital care for "sick and disabled seamen." Congress responded by establishing the United States Public Health Service in 1798. Ever since that time, the federal government has been concerned with public health.

Health Programs Today the largest percentage of federal government spending on health goes for the medicare and medicaid programs. In addition to these, however, the government operates several programs designed to promote and protect public health. The Department of Defense, for example, provides hospital and other medical care for active and retired American military personnel and their families. In addition, the Veterans Administration (VA) operates medical, dental, and hospital care programs for needy veterans.

The Department of Defense and VA programs are for citizens connected with the military. The Public

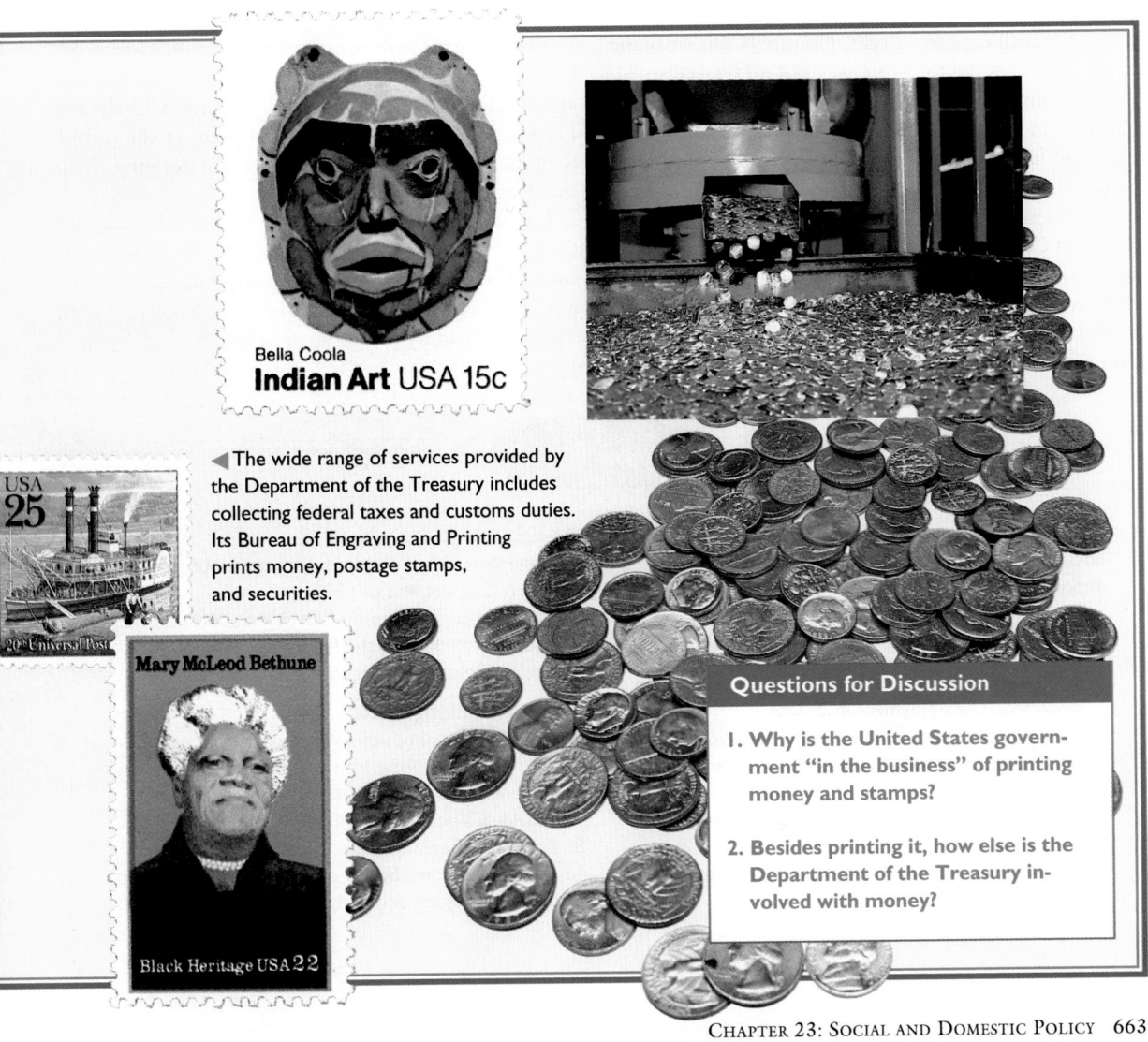

Bella Coola
Indian Art USA 15c

USA 25
20th Universal Post

Mary McLeod Bethune

Black Heritage USA 22

◀ The wide range of services provided by the Department of the Treasury includes collecting federal taxes and customs duties. Its Bureau of Engraving and Printing prints money, postage stamps, and securities.

Questions for Discussion

1. Why is the United States government "in the business" of printing money and stamps?

2. Besides printing it, how else is the Department of the Treasury involved with money?

CHAPTER 23: SOCIAL AND DOMESTIC POLICY   663

Critical Thinking Activity

History

Pharmacology is the study of the effect of drugs on living things. Although people had used various remedies to treat diseases for centuries, pharmacology began in the 1900s with the rise of chemistry. The listing of tables of drugs and their properties in the United States was standardized by the Federal Food and Drug Act in 1906.

Evaluate

📁 Section 4 Quiz

🖥 Testmaker

Reteach

Ask students to write a newspaper article explaining the two kinds of social welfare programs in the United States today and list two activities of each.

Enrich

Have students contact their state legislators or state human services department to inquire about recent social welfare reform in their state. Ask volunteers to report their findings to the class.

Close

Ask students if they feel that the federal government will need to increase its involvement in social welfare and health programs. Ask students to support their predictions by using what they have learned about public policy and political processes.

Health Service, on the other hand, which is now a part of the Department of Health and Human Services, operates research, grant, and action programs designed to promote the health of all citizens.

National Health Care Debate Candidate Bill Clinton raised the health-care issue during the 1992 campaign. Nearly 38 million Americans had no health insurance, while rising health costs and an economic recession had caused many others to fear losing their insurance along with their jobs. Five days after his inauguration, the President announced that his wife, Hillary Rodham Clinton, would oversee a health-care task force to study the issue and make recommendations. After 500 different interest groups had met with the task force and numerous trial balloons had been floated in major media, the President finally announced his comprehensive health-care plan in September.

By the time the President's proposal reached Capitol Hill, the media had speculated on nearly every aspect of health care for a year. Congress was near its year-end recess, so the issue was not addressed until 1994. Committee work on the health-care bill got a late start in 1994, pushing back floor action until August and leaving little time for resolving House and Senate differences.

Several alternative health-care proposals were introduced in Congress. Negative advertising by the insurance industry and other special interests raised fears that the President's proposal would lead to rationing of medical care. Public confusion grew. Opinion polls found that a slight majority thought the health-care issue should wait for a new Congress in 1995. Even the White House pollster acknowledged, "The country is scared of [health-care reform] and right now they are kind of skeptical of anything." At the same time polls showed there was still support for health-care reform, even though the improving economy had erased the urgency of a national health-care system.

Food and Drug Protection The Food and Drug Administration (FDA) tests samples of food and drug products in its laboratories. The agency has the power to ban or withdraw from distribution drugs it finds unsafe or ineffective. As a result, the FDA often finds itself involved in controversy. Some doctors, for example, claim FDA policies make it almost impossible for the public to receive the benefits of certain drugs. Sometimes people suffering from a particular disease, such as cancer or AIDS, will travel outside the United States to obtain drugs permitted elsewhere.

In contrast, some consumer protection groups believe the FDA is not tough enough in banning drugs and food additives that may be harmful. Clearly, the FDA has a difficult job. It must protect the public from dangerous substances while not denying them the drugs they need.

Federal agencies, such as the Centers for Disease Control and Prevention, work to control diseases such as AIDS, diphtheria, measles, and many different strains of flu. The CDC is also concerned with diseases spread by insects such as malaria and typhus.

---

4 SECTION REVIEW

Section Summary
Social insurance, public assistance, and health are important concerns of the federal government.

Checking For Understanding
Recalling Facts
1. Define social insurance programs, public assistance programs, unemployment insurance.
2. Describe the events that led many Americans to change their attitudes about public assistance in the 1930s.
3. List the four main public assistance programs in effect today.
4. Identify the people who are eligible for Supplemental Security Income (SSI).

Exploring Themes
5. Federalism What did the states contribute to the Family Support Act of 1988?
6. Constitutional Interpretations What constitutional issue surfaced when the federal government first began to pass social legislation in the 1930s?

Critical Thinking Skills
7. Identifying Assumptions What assumption about the rights of an American citizen does government make when it passes legislation to ensure the individual's health and welfare?
8. Predicting Consequences What would happen in the congressional health-care debates if a recession or rapid inflation seriously affected the economy?

Section 4 Review Answers

1. Definitions of terms appear on pages indicated: **social insurance programs,** 659; **public assistance programs,** 659; **unemployment insurance,** 660
2. The stock market crash signaled the beginning of the Great Depression. Within a few years, 25 percent of workers were unemployed. Many were hungry. Private charities and state and local governments could not handle the large task of assisting all these people. Many decided that the federal government should step in.
3. Aid to Families with Dependent Children, Supplemental Security Income, food stamps, and medicaid
4. anyone who is 65 or older, who is blind or disabled, and who has little or no regular cash income
5. The act was patterned after state programs; and governors helped Congress to work on the legislation.

6. whether the Constitution gave Congress specific authority to pass such legislation
7. The assumption is that as an American a person is entitled to certain minimum necessities for living.
8. Answers will vary, but should include that certain helpful drugs that have not yet been approved would come on the market, other harmful or untested drugs would also become available. The consumer would not feel safe.

SECTION 5

Education, Housing, and Transportation

President Thomas Jefferson was convinced that democracy could not survive without educated citizens. He concluded, "Any nation that expects to be ignorant and free . . . expects what never was and never will be."

Providing for public education is one of the main powers the Constitution reserves for the states. For many years the states left the primary responsibility for education with local governments. Connecticut created the first school fund in 1795 with money from the sale of public lands. Indiana set up the first modern public school system in 1816.

Education Programs

Today public education in the United States is a huge enterprise. In most states elementary and high school education remains a local responsibility under state guidelines. The basic administrative unit for public schools throughout the nation is the local school district.

Federal Aid to Education Public elementary and secondary education remains largely under local control. The federal government, however, plays an ever-increasing role in education and provides aid to local schools in several forms. In a recent year, the federal government contributed more than $1 billion in direct aid to local public schools and about $10 billion of additional funds to be distributed through the states. The federal government provides even more support for higher education—about $17 billion to institutions of higher learning in a recent year.

Federal Support of Colleges
The Ohio State University is a land-grant college.
History What are two laws passed by Congress that gave federal support to public schools?

Aid to Public Schools Congress began to provide aid for specific educational activities in the schools with the Smith-Hughes Act of 1917. This act set up matching grants to the states for teaching courses in agriculture and home economics. Since then Congress has passed several laws directed toward other aspects of elementary and secondary education.

During the mid-1960s, President Lyndon Johnson made improved education a major goal of his Great Society program. In 1965, during the height of public support for Johnson's ideas, Congress passed the first general-aid-to-education law—the Elementary and Secondary Education Act. This act and later amendments provided federal aid to most of the nation's school districts.

SECTION PREVIEW

Objectives
After studying this section, you should be able to:
- Discuss the increasing federal interest in education.
- Evaluate urban renewal and federal housing policies.

- Describe the federal government's role in transportation.

Key Terms and Concepts
urban renewal, public housing, mass transit

Themes in Government
- Public Policy
- Federalism

Critical Thinking Skills
- Demonstrating Reasoned Judgment
- Identifying Central Issues

CHAPTER 23: SOCIAL AND DOMESTIC POLICY 665

Classroom Resources for Section 5

- 📁 Guided Reading Activities
- 📁 Reproducible Lesson Plans
- 📁 Reteaching Activities 23
- 📁 Section 5 Quiz
- 📁 Chapter 23 Tests

- ➕ Testmaker
- 🎧 Audio Cassettes (English and Spanish)
- 📁 Limited English Proficiency Activities 23
- SAT Practice Tests
- Writer's Guidebook

Focus

Bell Ringer

Put the following questions on the chalkboard and while attendance is being taken, ask students to consider them:

Should the federal government:

set national graduation requirements?
regulate the content of courses?
test and license all teachers?
provide all funds for education?
operate all public schools?

Motivating Activity

Discuss students' Bell Ringer answers. Poll the class to see how many agree and disagree with each proposal. Ask students to explain their positions.

Vocabulary Precheck

List the terms and concepts on the chalkboard. Have volunteers skim the section to find each term and read it in context. **LEP**

Caption Answer
Smith-Hughes Act of 1917 and the Elementary and Secondary Education Act of 1965

Linking Past and Present
Thomas Jefferson campaigned for a four-point educational proposal: **1.** free elementary school education for all citizens at a local school; **2.** a more advanced education would be offered at county grammar schools free to those who could not afford it; **3.** a free university education to those select students who were deemed exceptional and in financial need; **4.** establishment of a state university. Although these were radical ideas in Jefferson's time, our modern educational system bears an amazing resemblance to his innovations.

Teach

Guided Practice

L1 Group Discussion Ask students how an uneducated public can weaken a democracy. Ask what government can do to ensure an educated citizenry. Should government deny uneducated people the right to vote? *(Students should recognize the antidemocratic nature of such a proposal.)*

L2 Public Policy Have students suppose that a new President proposes to respond to the need to cut federal spending by combining the Departments of Transportation and Housing and Urban Development and cutting the programs each administers. Have students propose which programs should be kept and which should be dropped and provide a rationale for each decision.

Caption Answer
Housing Act of 1949

STUDY GUIDE

Theme Answer
local government

Critical Thinking Answer
It is in the entire nation's best interest to have educated citizens as an investment in the future of the United States.

CONNECTIONS

History
The first community to establish a property tax to support public schools was Dorchester, Massachusetts, in 1639.

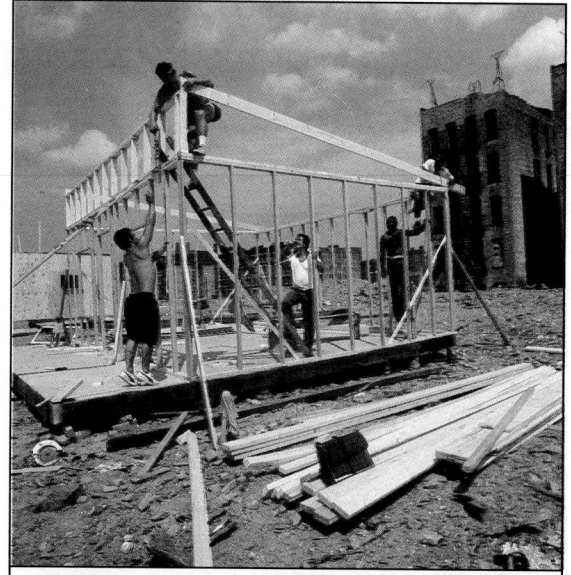

"Suitable Living Environment"
Urban renewal projects receive federal funding.
History Which act assured federal housing policy?

cern. They say federal aid leads to federal control of the curriculum and school systems. The president of a major university put it this way: "Federal spending power is used indirectly to control colleges in ways the government could not use directly."

In 1983 the National Commission on Excellence in Education, appointed by President Reagan, issued its report. On a series of international tests, United States students generally ranked below their European and Asian peers. The commission called for many reforms. The excellence movement that sprang from the report had mixed results. Barbara Lerner was one of the first to explain the gap in test scores:

> *Data from good domestic tests . . . show that in an absolute sense we did not really get worse in the 1980's as we had done in the 1960's and 70's, but neither did we get much better. For the most part we stood still. . . . Our foreign competitors, however, did not stand still; they surged ahead. . . .*
> —BARBARA LERNER, 1991

Aid to Higher Education Until 1862 higher education was a private undertaking. In that year Congress passed the Morrill Act, giving a boost to higher education in America. This law granted the states about 11.3 million acres (4.6 million hectares) of public land for the endowment of colleges to teach "agriculture and the mechanical arts." States established 69 so-called land-grant colleges under the Morrill Act and a second similar law.

In recent years Congress has provided a number of specific programs to aid higher education. The best known are the various G.I. Bills of Rights. These programs enabled veterans of World War II, the Korean War, and the Vietnam War to gain a college education financed by federal funds.

Education Issues The government's policy of providing general federal aid to public schools and colleges has been controversial. Opponents of such aid argue that education should be a state and local con-

Some educators suggested that the United States needed a national education program to raise achievement. In the 1988 campaign George Bush promised to be the education President. In 1991 the Bush administration proposed an "America 2000" plan that included voluntary testing, merit pay for teachers, and a school choice proposal. Partisan differences in Congress, however, blocked reform.

President Clinton resurrected the education reform issue. Clinton's "Goals 2000: Education America Act" included six national education goals including raising high school graduation rates, making schools safer, and raising competency in math, science, and English. The bill that Congress passed in 1994 included voluntary opportunity-to-learn standards and language that sought to assure states and local schools that the federal government was not interfering in their right to control public education. Schools were allowed to either adopt the national guidelines voluntarily or use them as a guide to develop their own standards. The law set aside $400 million in federal grant money for public education.

STUDY GUIDE

Themes in Government
Public Policy Which area of government is most often responsible for public primary and secondary education?

Critical Thinking Skills
Demonstrating Reasoned Judgment Why has the federal government involved itself in the area of public education formerly

reserved to state and local governments?

Background

After a very slow start, federal involvement with public education accelerated during the 1950s and 1960s. The initial impetus came from the Soviet launching of *Sputnik I.* Reacting to an apparent challenge to United States technological supremacy, Congress passed the National Defense Education Act in 1958. The rise of social consciousness during the 1960s brought the Economic Opportunity Act of 1964 and the Elementary and Secondary Education Act of 1965, which funded some innovative programs such as Head Start and provided support for disadvantaged children. This flurry of legislative activity marked the true beginning of the federal government's current broad involvement in education.

Housing and Urban Programs

Adequate housing and transportation are an important part of the general welfare of any society. The federal government has developed several programs to ensure adequate housing and transportation for all citizens.

Housing Policy The government first became involved in housing policy during the Great Depression. Millions of Americans were losing their homes or farms because they could not meet their mortgage payments. Housing construction came almost to a halt. The government responded to this catastrophe with a series of federally funded loan and housing support programs.

After World War II, Congress assured the government's continuing role in housing policy by passing the Housing Act of 1949. In this law Congress declared its goal to be "a decent home and a suitable living environment for every American family."

Promoting Home Buying and Building The government has developed several programs to promote building and purchasing houses. The best known is the program the Federal Housing Adminis-

L3 Federalism Have students identify and discuss the issues involved in the controversy over federal aid to education. Then have them decide if education is a legitimate area of involvement for the federal government or if it should be left to the states.

Focus on Freedom

I HAVE A DREAM

Delivered at the Lincoln Memorial in Washington, D.C., in 1963, the "I Have a Dream" speech reached an immediate audience of 250,000. Most of the listeners had just participated in the March on Washington for Jobs and Freedom. Dr. Martin Luther King, Jr., who delivered the address, had spent several years promoting nonviolent demonstrations against racial discrimination. In this excerpt the most noted civil rights leader of his time articulated the hopes of African Americans during a time of tension and change.

I am happy to join with you today in what will go down in history as the greatest demonstration for freedom in the history of our nation.

Five score years ago, a great American, in whose symbolic shadow we stand today, signed the Emancipation Proclamation. . . .

But one hundred years later, the Negro is still not free. One hundred years later, the life of the Negro is still sadly crippled by the manacles of segregation and the chains of discrimination. One hundred years later, the Negro lives on a lonely island of poverty in the midst of a vast ocean of material prosperity. . . .

In a sense we've come to our nation's Capitol to cash a check. When the architects of our republic wrote the magnificent words of the Constitution and the Declaration of Independence, they were signing a promissory note to which every American was to fall heir. This note was a promise that all men—yes, black men as well as white men—would be guaranteed . . . life, liberty, and the pursuit of happiness. . . .

As we walk we must make the pledge that we shall always march ahead. We cannot turn back. There are those who ask the devotees of civil rights, "When will you be satisfied?" We can never be satisfied as long as the Negro is the victim of the unspeakable horrors of police brutality. . . . We can never be satisfied as long as our children are . . . robbed of their dignity by signs saying "For Whites Only." . . .

I say to you today, my friends, so even though we face the difficulties of today and tomorrow, I still have a dream. It is a dream deeply rooted in the American dream.

I have a dream that one day this nation will rise up and live out the true meaning of its creed: "We hold these truths to be self-evident; that all men are created equal."

—Dr. Martin Luther King, Jr., 1963

Examining the Document

Reviewing Facts
1. **Cite** how long it had been from the Emancipation Proclamation to the March on Washington.
2. **Discuss** the basic freedoms that King says have been denied to African Americans.

Critical Thinking Skills
3. **Making Inferences** Why did Dr. King call the Constitution and the Declaration of Independence "a promissory note"?

CHAPTER 23: SOCIAL AND DOMESTIC POLICY **667**

Focus on Freedom

Civil rights leaders in 1963 were looking for ways to gain support for the civil rights bill that President Kennedy had recently sent to Congress. They decided that a march on the capital was the best way to get the support. As a result, people of all races from all parts of the nation gathered in Washington to show their support for equal rights for all.

Answers

1. 100 years
2. equality, life, liberty, the pursuit of happiness
3. because at the time these documents were signed the freedoms they mentioned were not enjoyed by all Americans, but they held the promise of wider application in the future

L1 Journalism Have students examine newspapers and magazines to find articles on housing and transportation programs. Students should choose one article and write a summary of the problems and issues it addresses.

GLENCOE TECHNOLOGY

Focus on Government
Video 50
Electronic Field Trip: Urban Renewal in Atlanta
Running Time: 5:34
Videodisc 3, Chap. 50
VHS Tape 3, Begins 28:07

Cooperative Learning Activity

Organize the class into groups of three called "Home Teams." Assign each Home Team member the number 1, 2, or 3. Have all the same-numbered students from each Home Team form an "Expert Team." Assign each of the three Expert Teams one of the three main topics in Section 5—education, housing, and transportation. Have Expert Teams create a teaching tool (chart, outline, concept map, poster) that pertains to their topic. Then have "experts" return to their Home Teams to share their teaching tools.

Independent Practice

L2 Expressive Writing Have students interview a grandparent or other older adult about that person's educational experience and opportunities. Based on information they obtain, have students write reports comparing education then and now. Reports should explain how federal programs and policies have helped bring about any changes they noted.

L3 Informative Writing Have students obtain information about Habitat for Humanity—an organization that builds or remodels homes for low-income families. Have students research and write a report on the history and operation of this organization.

STUDY GUIDE

Theme Answer
provided funding and incentives to developers to clean up slum areas and rebuild

Critical Thinking Answer
They may think that poor people will be pushed out if new buildings are constructed.

GLENCOE
TECHNOLOGY

Set on Freedom
The Fair Housing Bill is Passed, 1968
Running Time :38
Side A: Chapter 41

---

tration (FHA) administers. The FHA, a part of the Department of Housing and Urban Development (HUD), guarantees banks and other private lenders against losses on loans they make to those who wish to build, buy, or rent homes. By acting as an insurer for these mortgages, the FHA has allowed many low- and middle-income families who might not have qualified for private loans to purchase their own homes.

The FHA program almost completely supports itself and costs the taxpayers very little. The FHA charges an extra ½ percent interest on loans in order to pay for its services. The money gained from this charge, along with income from investments and other fees, provides funds to run the program.

The majority of the federal housing programs HUD administers are targeted on cities. The federal government has addressed urban problems with two types of programs: urban renewal and public housing.

Urban Renewal To arrest the decline and deterioration of central cities, the federal government supports **urban renewal** programs. Under these programs cities can apply for federal aid to clear deteriorating or slum areas and to rebuild. Most urban renewal projects begin by removing run-down properties. Private developers may then buy the land at a reduced price and rebuild the area according to plans approved by the city and HUD. As part of urban renewal, federal mortgage insurance is available to the private developers.

The goal of urban renewal policies for more than 40 years has been to restore slum areas and make cities more attractive places in which to live. These policies, however, have had some negative effects. Critics charge that urban renewal neglects new housing for the poor. Instead, urban renewal has forced poor people from their homes to make way for middle- or upper-income housing and commercial centers. As one leader of the poor said of urban renewal, "We're already living nowhere, and now they're going to move us out of that." In addition, urban renewal has destroyed some of the social fabric of the city by dispersing residents of ethnic neighborhoods and uprooting local businesses.

Supporters of urban renewal argue that the policy has represented a useful effort on the part of the national government to get local governments and private investors to work together to save the cities. They also point to the Housing and Community Development Act of 1974, which requires cities to demonstrate that they are actually serving the needs of the poor when redeveloping slum areas.

Public Housing Programs Since 1937 and especially after the 1949 Housing Act, the federal government has given aid to local governments to construct and operate **public housing** for low-income families. To implement the program, a city first sets up a "public housing authority" to which the federal government can make low-interest loans that may cover up to 90 percent of the housing construction costs. The government also grants subsidies to these agencies to allow them to operate by charging very low rents. Income from the rents is used to repay the federal loan. About 4 million households live in public housing, largely concentrated in the major cities.

Over the years public housing projects have faced serious problems and opposition from many groups. Local authorities have mismanaged some public housing projects. Many such projects have turned into high-rise slums and centers of crime. The situation had grown so grave by 1973 that President Nixon halted federal aid for public housing projects. In doing so, Nixon stated, "All across America, the federal government has become the biggest slumlord in history."

The government has yet to find a truly effective public housing policy. In 1976 Congress resumed federal aid for public housing projects on a limited scale. At the same time HUD has experimented with rent subsidies as one alternative to public housing. Under this plan poor families pay a percentage of the rent—normally 30 percent—for private housing, and the government pays the rest of the rent directly to the landlord.

STUDY GUIDE

Themes in Government
Federalism **How has the federal government supported urban renewal programs?**

Critical Thinking Skills
Identifying Central Issues **Despite the efforts of the federal government to clear slum areas and make cities more attractive** places in which to live, why do some people resent urban renewal programs?

Special Needs Strategy

Teaching Strategy Students with difficulties abstracting information will need help summarizing "the role of the FHA in helping individual families afford housing," as called for in item 4 in the Section 5 Review. Explain the purpose of a summary, and have students read the Chapter 23 summary on page 672. Point out that summaries usually capture the main ideas of paragraphs on a particular topic. Ask students to reread the two paragraphs about the FHA on pages 667 and 668 and to answer the question, "How does the FHA help individuals afford housing?" in their own words. Some students who have difficulty summarizing in writing may be quite successful doing this aloud.

President Bush's Secretary of Housing and Urban Development, Jack Kemp, observed that "Public Housing is our own Eastern Europe. It's our socialism for the poor." One columnist explained:

In public housing, the state decides almost everything, the tenants nearly nothing. . . . [Jack Kemp] already has demonstration projects in major cities across the country, in which units are being turned over to tenant ownership and/or management.

—MICHAEL NOVAK, *FORBES*, 1991

In 1995 Congress considered bills that would give localities more flexibility in using federal housing funds and would relax rent requirements for working families.

Transportation Programs

In 1632 the Virginia legislature proclaimed, "Highways shall be layed out in such convenient places . . . as the parishioners of every parish shall agree." Governments at all levels in the United States have been concerned about improving transportation ever since.

The national government's first direct entry into the field of transportation began in 1806 when Congress voted funds to build the National Road from Cumberland, Maryland, to the Ohio River. The federal government continued to contribute, usually through some form of subsidy, to the building of channels, locks, dams, canals, ports, highways, railroads, and airports.

In 1966 Congress created the Department of Transportation (DOT) to coordinate national transportation policies and programs. This department brought together more than 30 agencies dealing with transportation that had been scattered throughout the government. Today the DOT employs more than 60,000 people and operates through seven major agencies that reflect the various forms of transportation.

Other Agencies Numerous agencies within the Department of Transportation provide important services. The Federal Aviation Administration (FAA)

Moving the Masses
The federal government grants funds to cities seeking to improve their mass transit systems. **Economics Which agency administers the grant program?**

works to ensure safety in aviation. It licenses pilots and enforces safety rules for air traffic. The Federal Highway Administration (FHWA) oversees the vast network of federal roads. The Federal Railroad Administration promotes and regulates the nation's railroad transportation. The National Highway Traffic Safety Administration is responsible for enforcing laws to protect drivers and promote highway safety.

The Interstate Commerce Commission remains the chief independent regulatory agency in the field of transportation. It has the authority to regulate railroads, trucks, buses, and pipelines, setting minimum and maximum rates and safety standards.

Building and Maintaining Highways The Federal Road Act of 1916 set the pattern for the development of federal highway programs. Under this law the federal government provided yearly grants for

STUDY GUIDE

Theme Answer
to coordinate national transportation policies and programs, including air, train, auto routes, and safety issues

Critical Thinking Answer
Public housing for low-income families was not always as good in reality as in theory.

Assess

Check for Understanding
Have students complete Section 5 Review on page 670.

Meeting Objectives
Each section objective is tested by the Section Review questions that follow it in parentheses.
- Discuss the increasing federal interest in education. (2, 3, 7)
- Evaluate urban renewal and federal housing policies. (4, 6)
- Describe the federal government's role in transportation. (5, 8)

STUDY GUIDE

Themes in Government
Public Policy What is the role of the Department of Transportation in managing the nation's transportation network?

Critical Thinking Skills
Identifying Central Issues What was President Nixon referring to when he said in regard to the

federal government and public housing programs, "All across America, the federal government has become the biggest slumlord in history"?

Critical Thinking Activity

Demonstrating Reasoned Judgment Remind students that federal funds have covered 90 percent of the cost of the Interstate Highway System. Point out to students that the construction of interstate highways was done, in part, as a national defense measure. Ask students the following question: Could an interstate highway system help promote our national security needs? How? (*Yes, it could facilitate the movement of troops, weapons, and supplies.*)

Evaluate

📁 Section 5 Quiz

⬛ Testmaker

Reteach

📁 Have students complete activity 23 in *Reteaching Activities* in the Teacher's Classroom Resources.

Enrich

Have students contact local city, highway, mass transit, and airport officials, and real estate companies and mortgage holders to determine the impact of the programs administered by HUD and the Department of Transportation on their own community. Students should prepare a report of their findings.

Close

Hold a class discussion on the following statement:

Every American citizen has the right to adequate education, housing, and health care.

Ask students if they agree with this statement. Then ask them if they feel that involvement by the federal government is necessary to guarantee the rights mentioned in the statement. Students should support their opinions with reasons.

road-building to the states and required each state to match this aid on a dollar-for-dollar basis. These grants-in-aid, administered by the FHWA, form the basis of today's federal highway programs.

Under the Federal Aid Highway Act of 1944 and subsequent amendments, states now receive billions of dollars every year to build and improve the Interstate Highway System that crisscrosses the nation. This system, begun in 1956, consists of more than 45,000 miles of 4-to-8-lane superhighways connecting almost all of the nation's major cities. Federal funds cover 90 percent of the cost of the Interstate Highway System. The money for federal highway grants comes from the Highway Trust Fund. This fund is a special account that receives federal excise taxes on gasoline, tires, truck parts, and related items.

While the federal government provides the financial aid, the states do the work of constructing and improving the interstate highways. Once the work has been completed, the interstate roads belong to the state or local governments, which have the responsibility of maintaining them.

Today the Federal Highway Administration oversees federal highways. The FHWA also applies federal safety standards to trucks and buses and does planning and research on highway construction and maintenance. The FHWA's main job, however, is to administer the massive federal-aid highway program that supports the construction and upkeep of about 25 percent of the nation's roads.

Mass Transit The traffic helicopter seldom broadcasts good news for city dwellers. The streets and highways of large and small cities are clogged daily with automobile traffic, and urban planners warn of additional gridlock, where traffic hardly moves. Still, many people prefer to drive their own vehicles when traveling in and around cities.

Could the urban transportation problem be solved with better **mass transit** systems such as subways, commuter railroads, and bus lines? When properly operated, such facilities can transport more people than individual automobiles and help to reduce congestion and air pollution. The Urban Mass Transit Administration (UMTA) administers federal grant programs aimed at improving such transit systems in urban areas. These programs date from the 1970s when the federal government began to help cities cope with the growing need for better mass transit systems as a substitute for the automobile.

The cost of building new mass transit systems is more than most cities can afford. However, communities are trying to improve their present transportation systems. Efforts are underway to upgrade existing bus service, promote car and van pooling, and think of ways to make use of existing rail systems in and around cities.

Congress generally considers mass transit as part of general transportation legislation. Appropriations bills for mass transit also include funds for Coast Guard, aviation, and highway construction. Beginning in 1991 Congress concentrated on providing federal dollars to implement a National Highway System. In 1992 the Federal Aviation Administration was the only transportation agency to receive a large spending increase. Since then Congress has not significantly increased funds for mass transit.

5 SECTION REVIEW

Section Summary
The federal government provides state and local governments major funding for education, housing, and transportation.

Checking For Understanding
Recalling Facts
1. Define urban renewal, public housing, mass transit.
2. Identify the federal legislation that provided the first general aid to most of the nation's public schools.
3. Relate the method and the results of the Morrill Act supporting higher education.
4. Summarize the role of the FHA in helping individual families afford housing.

Exploring Themes
5. Public Policy How did the federal government attempt to coordinate national transportation policy in 1966?
6. Federalism How does the federal government cooperate with cities to restore urban areas?

Critical Thinking Skills
7. Demonstrating Reasoned Judgment Why do governments at all levels spend so much money to support education?
8. Identifying Central Issues What issues have slowed the development of urban mass transit systems as an answer to traffic congestion?

Section 5 Review Answers

1. Definitions of terms appear on pages indicated: **urban renewal,** 668; **public housing,** 668; **mass transit,** 670
2. Elementary and Secondary Education Act of 1965
3. The act granted the states more than 13 million acres of public land for the endowment of colleges to teach "agriculture and the mechanical arts." States established 69 so-called land-grant colleges.

4. The FHA guarantees banks and other private lenders against losses on loans they make to those who wish to build, buy, or rent homes. By insuring mortgages, the FHA has allowed many low- and middle-income families who might not have qualified for private loans to purchase their own homes.
5. Congress created the Department of Transportation to bring together more than 30 transportation agencies that had been scattered throughout the government.

6. Cities apply for federal aid to clear slum areas and to rebuild. Private developers may then buy the land at a reduced price and rebuild the area according to plans approved by the city and HUD. Federal mortgage insurance is available to the private developers.
7. An educated public is a means to ensure democratic government; educated people are able to earn better incomes and thus help the economy and pay more taxes.
8. individuals' preference to drive their own cars and the high initial cost of mass transit

Whitney M. Young, Jr., Asks, "Can the City Survive?"

In 1961 Whitney M. Young became the Director of the National Urban League. He addressed the issue of inequities in employment in a speech to a conference of the National Association of Bank Loan and Credit Officers in 1968.

Only the most hopeless optimist would fail to acknowledge that our country is in deep crisis. The issues before us are several. We face a depolarization, a division between the young and the unyoung, between black and white, and between urban and rural populations. This is not a crisis that one can easily dismiss. . . .

I can remember in the early 1930's when there was about to be a major, a true revolution in this country when white people were all out of work. Overnight this country passed massive measures to put people to work—NYA, FERA, WPA, CCC, Social Security, and all kinds of welfare programs. . . .

Our response has also been to echo that familiar phrase, "We made it, why can't they." And there's no statement I know that's more hypocritical. The reason white people and earlier immigrants made it and black people have not made it is so simple and so clear. . . . The reason black people haven't made it is because we were the first and only involuntary immigrants to the country. . . .

The others made it because there was a period when immigrants were given land. . . . They had freedom of choice. They could move where they want to. . . .

The Federal Government built the suburbs with your help. The Federal Government put public housing all in the central city which led to the kind of immigration, containment, and segregation that has increased in our society. And this situation is not going to change unless, hopefully, we have developed a new generation of people who have as much creativity, imagination, and commitment to inclusion and to decency as your forefathers had to exclusion and to cruelty, and to segregation in this society. . . .

Please do something about the attitudes, do something about housing, do something about education. You see, in the same breath that you tell me that you can't find any qualified people, you are also telling me how dumb you are because you are taxed twice. You pay the big taxes to maintain a public school system. And then you have to train people again for your companies. Why don't you get involved and see to it that these schools turn out people who can go to work for you right away? You need to disperse the housing and you play a crucial role in dispersal. . . . You are the one that suffers if this community becomes blacker and poorer. If people become tax eaters rather than tax producers, if people produce crime and welfare costs instead of producing goods and services, you pay the costs. And those are the sheer alternatives. . . .

—WHITNEY M. YOUNG, 1968

> *Please do something about the attitudes, do something about housing, do something about education.*

Examining the Reading

Reviewing Facts
1. Point out reasons that Young gives to explain why white immigrants were more successful than blacks in America.
2. Demonstrate how the federal government contributed to segregation in the cities.

Critical Thinking Skills
3. Identifying Alternatives What are the "sheer alternatives" Young believes the bankers face?

CHAPTER 23: SOCIAL AND DOMESTIC POLICY 671

PERSONAL PERSPECTIVES

Focus

Ask students to what era the following refer—Vietnam War protests, urban riots, Robert Kennedy, Dr. Martin Luther King, Jr., black power.

Teach

Ask: To what three factors does Young attribute the division of Americans? *(job opportunity, housing, education)* How are these factors related? *(Answers will vary.)*

Assess

Have students complete **Examining the Reading.**
Answers
1. Unlike African Americans whites immigrated voluntarily, were offered land, could move freely.
2. It put public housing in the central city, leading to containment and segregation.
3. If the banks do not help people become productive, costs for welfare and crime will rise.

Close

Ask students if they think the conditions Young identified have changed. Why or why not?

Set on Freedom
Martin Luther King, Jr.
Running Time 3:40
Side B, Chapter 4

More About Personal Perspectives

Whitney Moore Young, Jr., was born in 1921 in rural Kentucky. He graduated from Kentucky State College and earned a master's degree at the University of Minnesota. He worked for the Urban League in St. Paul, Minnesota, and Omaha, Nebraska, before leaving in 1953 to become dean of the Atlanta University School of Social Work. He returned to the Urban League as its national director in 1961 and served in that position until his death 10 years later. Perhaps his major accomplishment was the founding of the Head Start program. Young also started job training and tutoring programs and helped thousands of African Americans find jobs.

Identifying Terms and Concepts

1. e, **2.** f, **3.** h, **4.** i, **5.** j, **6.** d, **7.** a, **8.** b, **9.** c, **10.** g

Reviewing Facts and Ideas

1. Industrialization led to abuses. Large corporations abused workers, squeezed smaller companies out of business, fixed prices, and created monopolies.

2. The government charged the FTC with carrying out the provisions of the Clayton Antitrust Act.

3. to inspect food, cosmetics, drugs, and other products; to inspect factories, plants, and labs where foods and drugs are made; to check labels for accuracy; to force off the market products that fail to meet standards

4. the Consumer Product Safety Commission

5. Taft-Hartley Act

6. In 1790 about 95 percent of Americans lived in rural areas where farming was the main occupation. Farming remained the occupation of the majority until 1900. Today less than 5 percent of the people are in farming, and only 25 percent live in rural areas.

7. price supports, acreage allotments, marketing quotas

8. The Act was the first social insurance program to come out of the Depression, designed as a long-term solution to the problem of providing economic security for American citizens.

9. a family with dependent children whose income is too low to meet its needs according to criteria set by the state

10. AFDC, Supplemental Security Income, food stamps, medicaid

---

Summary and Significance

During the twentieth century, regulation and support of business and labor became a major function of the federal government. Some Americans believed government regulation to be a mixed blessing; but under the commerce clause of the Constitution, the federal government has played an ever-increasing role in the economy. Besides antitrust laws, Congress has passed other regulatory laws to protect consumers and to ensure fair product standards. Congress has also established a number of independent regulatory agencies to protect consumers or to regulate certain types of economic activities. The federal government also assists businesses and regulates labor unions.

Governments at the federal, state, and local levels provide support and assistance to farmers. The federal government has developed conservation and energy policies and has established two types of social programs—social insurance and public assistance. Federal support for education, housing, and transportation has become a vital part of state and local revenues.

Identifying Terms and Concepts

Choose the letter of the correct term or concept below to complete the sentence.

a. collective bargaining   f. quota
b. public assistance   g. securities
c. social insurance   h. oligopoly
d. right-to-work laws   i. subsidy
e. urban renewal   j. price support

1. The federal government supports _____ in cities to help replace old buildings.
2. The government may use a _____ to place a limit on certain imported goods.
3. A small number of powerful companies controlling a market is called an _____.
4. The government provides a rent _____ to certain low-income families.
5. The federal government has provided farmers a _____ for crops that may be overproduced.
6. Some states have _____ that limit the power of unions.
7. Unions negotiate with employers through their _____ powers.
8. A federal program of _____ provides a certain minimum standard of living to those who do not earn enough income.
9. Federal _____ programs are designed to provide insurance against such social problems as old age, illness, and unemployment.
10. Stocks and bonds are forms of _____.

Reviewing Facts and Ideas

1. Describe the business environment that led to the Sherman and Clayton Antitrust Acts.
2. Explain the purpose behind the establishment of the Federal Trade Commission.
3. List the duties of the FDA.
4. Name the Commission created in 1972 to protect consumers against hazardous products.
5. Name the 1947 act that was intended to restore the balance between labor and management.
6. Relate changes in the farm population from 1790 to the present.
7. Identify three programs that the federal government uses to prevent low farm prices.
8. Explain why the government enacted the Social Security Act of 1935.
9. Point Out who is eligible for AFDC.
10. List the four major public assistance programs of the federal government.

Applying Themes

1. **Free Enterprise** How does the federal government attempt to preserve competition among business enterprises today?
2. **Constitutional Interpretations** What two clauses of the Constitution underlie federal regulation of the economy and federal government support for social programs?

Applying Themes

1. The federal government aids small businesses and monitors large business for violations of antitrust laws.

2. The Constitution grants Congress the power to "lay and collect taxes" for the general welfare and to "regulate commerce . . . among the several states."

3. It was patterned after successful state welfare reforms, and it developed from close cooperation—between Democrats and Republicans and between Congress and the governors.

4. They fear losing more direct local control over education.

5. conflicts between saving jobs and money, and saving the environment; and conflicts among different interest groups

3. **Federalism** What unusual applications of federalism benefited welfare reform legislation in 1988?

4. **Civic Participation** Why do some people object to the federal government's involvement in public education?

5. **Public Policy** What conflicts have prevented the United States from having a clear and consistent energy policy?

Critical Thinking Skills

1. **Identifying Assumptions** What underlying assumptions about social problems can you identify in Arthur B. Laffer's assertion that "The solution rests in less—not more—government," and in Victor Kamber's view that "we set up regulatory agencies in the first place to protect the public interest"?

2. **Identifying Central Issues** Why do some people oppose federal aid to education?

3. **Demonstrating Reasoned Judgment** Is it proper for government to subsidize certain interests such as farming and small business through taxes on all Americans? Explain your answer.

4. **Predicting Consequences** If population trends indicate a rapid rise in the elderly population and slower growth for the population under age 30, what will be the eventual effect on the social security trust funds?

Linking Past and Present

Many early roads in the United States were toll roads. Owners of these roads charged a small fee for each vehicle to travel on the road. There are a few toll roads operated by the states today. Do you think that tolls are a more fair or less fair way to support roads? Why?

Writing About Government

Expressive Writing Write an essay in which you describe an environmental or conservation problem that exists in your local area. You may wish to gather information by reading local newspaper articles or interviewing local officials.

Reinforcing the Skill

Drawing Conclusions Study the chart below, then answer the questions that follow:

Drug Use By College Students			
	1980	1985	1990
Marijuana	51.2	41.7	29.4
Cocaine	16.8	17.3	5.6
Crack[1]	NA	NA	0.6
Heroin	0.4	0.2	0.1
Stimulants[2]	NA	11.9	4.5
Alcohol	90.5	92.0	89.0
Cigarettes	36.2	35.0	35.5

Percent Who Used in Last Twelve Months

[1] This drug was asked about in one of the five questionnaire forms in 1986, and in two of the five questionnaire forms thereafter.

[2] Adjusted. Based on data from a revised question attempting to exclude inappropriate reporting of non-prescription stimulants.

NA= Data not available.

Source: *Information Please Almanac, 1992*

1. In 1980 about what percentage of college students said they had used marijuana?

2. In 1985 about what percentage of college students said they had smoked cigarettes?

3. Which drug was used more than any other?

4. Use of which drug fell off by about 50 percent between 1985 and 1990?

5. What two conclusions can you draw about drug use among college students from the data?

Investigating Further

1. **Individual Project** Interview three or four elderly people who have used medicare. Ask them the following questions: (1) In what way is the medicare system helpful to you? (2) What, if any, problems have you had with the system? (3) What could be improved in the way medicare operates? Record and compare your answers.

2. **Cooperative Learning** Divide the class into six groups. Have each group choose two topics from the following list: Medicare, Public Housing, Transportation, Education, Energy, Social Security, Public Assistance, Business Regulations, Conservation. Have each group collect articles related to their topics for two weeks, then report to the class on significant developments.

CHAPTER 23: SOCIAL AND DOMESTIC POLICY   673

---

4. Because workers fund the system and retirees benefit, the reserve funds would be depleted from paying benefits out of less income.

Linking Past and Present

Students' opinions will vary, but should be supported with reasons.

Writing About Government

Students' essays will vary.

Reinforcing the Skill

1. 51

2. 35

3. alcohol

4. cocaine

5. Answers will vary, but may include: The majority of college students are not frequent users of any drug other than alcohol. All types of drugs were less frequently used by college students in 1989 than in 1980.

Investigating Further

1. Students' results will vary based on interviewees.

2. Students' reports will vary based on topic selected.

Critical Thinking Skills

1. Laffer assumes that people could resolve many of these issues without the help of government. Kamber assumes that the public interest cannot be protected without government help.

2. Some believe that it is unconstitutional. Others believe that it gives the federal government too much control over local educational decisions.

3. Answers will vary. Those supporting government subsidies should point out that the public interest is served. For example, it is in the interest of the public that competition be preserved; supporting small business encourages competition. Those who oppose subsidies should point out that free enterprise means that each individual or business is free to succeed or fail based on its own decisions, not government aid.

CASE STUDY

CASE STUDY

The Case at a Glance

Who: welfare recipients
What: government role in providing welfare
When: 1920s to the present
Where: United States
Why: who should provide the general welfare

Focus

Ask students what government agencies are responsible for helping people who are suffering economically? *(Suggest that all levels of government help fund and administer antipoverty programs, including unemployment insurance, medicare, medicaid, AFDC, food stamps, subsidized housing.)* Tell students that the government's role in providing for people's general welfare is the focus of this case study.

Teach

Guided Practice

L1 Making Comparisons Create a chart on the chalkboard with the headings: *1920s, 1930s, 1960s, 1980s,* and *1990s.* Have students provide a brief description of the kind of social services the government has provided during each decade and write their answers in the appropriate column. Ask: How have social services programs changed over time? What factors played a role in the change? *(Students should notice that during hard economic times, the government often increases funds for social services.)*

Promote the General Welfare

We the people of the United States in Order to form a more perfect Union, establish Justice, Insure domestic Tranquility, Provide for the common defence, promote the general welfare, and secure the Blessings of Liberty to ourselves and our Posterity, do ordain and establish this Constitution for the United States of America.

—Preamble

National Outlook

Our National outlook, once that of the individualistic pioneer, has become a social outlook.

—Historian Allan Nevins

How Should the Government Provide for the General Welfare?

The Case

Almost a year to the day before the 1992 presidential election, a newspaper headline forecast: "History lesson: Economy imperils Bush presidency." The article related that:

If history is any guide, weak economic conditions do more to bring about a change in White House leadership than almost any other factor. Recessions and slow or declining growth in purchasing power played major roles in undermining support for the presidency in 1952, 1960, 1968, 1976, and 1980.

—CHICAGO TRIBUNE, NOVEMBER 5, 1991

During the 1990–1991 recession, President Bush's approval rating among Americans had fallen considerably. The drop, in large measure, was a result of a declining economy and the realization that 33.6 million Americans were living in poverty.

During 1991 an average of 2,200 American workers lost their jobs each day. The year set a record for the number of workers permanently laid off. When the President vetoed an extension of unemployment benefits, cries for aid for the jobless rose.

More Americans turned to such government programs as food stamps to survive the nation's economic doldrums. Once again the question of what role the federal government should play in providing social services arose. Federal funding of payments for the poor, the homeless, and the needy continued to be a topic of debate.

Background

Before the Great Depression of the 1930s, state and local agencies and private charities made relief, or welfare, payments. When the Great Depression struck, American cities tried to respond to the growing needs of

674 UNIT 7: PUBLIC POLICIES AND SERVICES

More About the Case

The debate over volunteerism as an answer to public welfare is not new. Perhaps the best example of this kind of program occurred during Herbert Hoover's presidency.

Hoover never lost faith in the American economic system, even though it was crumbling around him. He relied on voluntary efforts to relieve the suffering brought on by massive unemployment. He asked private charities and local governments to provide relief. As the tax base and profit margins dwindled, however, these efforts provided little relief. People became more cynical, especially when Hoover claimed that prosperity was just around the corner.

the unemployed. The cities' lack of revenue, however, meant they could do little. In New York City, for example, only about 25 percent of the unemployed received relief payments, and those payments averaged out to less than $3.00 a week. When the cities appealed for help from the states, the lack of funds at the state level further stymied efforts to aid unemployed and needy Americans. At the same time, contributions to private charities shrank, meaning those organizations had to decrease payments to the needy.

At the beginning of the Great Depression, however, the federal government's welfare role remained limited, and President Herbert Hoover announced that people and local agencies should provide help for those in need. He stated,

This is not an issue as to whether people shall go hungry or cold in the United States. It is solely a question of the best method by which hunger and cold shall be prevented. . . . The basis of successful relief in national distress is to mobilize and organize the infinite number of agencies of self-help in the community. That has been the American way of relieving distress among our own people and the country is successfully meeting its problem in the American way today.

—HERBERT HOOVER, C. 1931

In 1932 the American public, no longer convinced that voluntary efforts could end the suffering, elected a new President, Franklin D. Roosevelt. Basing its efforts on the constitutional phrase, "promote the general welfare," the federal government instituted relief programs—called the New Deal. Among the first efforts was the Federal Emergency Relief Administration (FERA). By 1933 the FERA had provided more than $324 million to the states and territories. By 1934 about 4.5 million people were receiving welfare payments, usually through local and state agencies using funds the federal government provided.

What effect did the New Deal programs ultimately have upon the nation's political structure? Professor Michael B. Katz in his study of welfare programs in the United States described the changes:

The New Deal had expanded vastly the role of the federal government and altered its relation to the states. . . . Still, the new structure had been erected

Giving Children a Head Start
President Johnson's Operation Headstart helped disadvantaged children receive preschool educations.

partly on an old foundation. . . . It modified but did not erase archaic distinctions between the worthy and unworthy or the ablebodied and impotent [powerless] poor; it created walls between social insurance and public assistance that preserved class distinctions and reinforced the stigma attached to relief or welfare. . . .

—MICHAEL B. KATZ, 1986

The War on Poverty In the 1960s and 1970s, the nation's social welfare programs underwent a massive expansion. Various programs emerged from the combined efforts of the civil rights movement and antipoverty groups, efforts that changed the country's welfare system.

Among the new programs enacted during the presidencies of Kennedy, Johnson, and Nixon were medicare and medicaid that provided health services. Another program, Aid to Families with Dependent Children (AFDC), was first developed during the New Deal and then greatly expanded in the 1960s and early 1970s. New rules for AFDC allowed the number of families eligible for aid to grow significantly. In addition, federally funded food stamps were available through state agencies for those in need.

Aid to education increased during the same years. Operation Headstart provided preschool education for disadvantaged children. Upward Bound prepared disadvantaged children for success in college. Programs that subsidized school breakfasts and lunches for poor children received more funding. In addi-

L2 Analyzing Ideas Point out to students that in his 1992 State of the Union Address, President Bush stated: "Americans are the most generous people on earth. But we have to go back to the insight of Franklin Roosevelt who, when he spoke of what became the welfare program, warned that it must not become a narcotic and a subtle destroyer of the spirit."

Have students hold a panel discussion to discuss ways that public welfare may destroy the human spirit and what could be done to prevent this destruction.

L3 Synthesizing Information Remind students that workers pay social security taxes and in so doing, give up some of their wealth to ensure their well-being when they are older. Ask: How does this system illustrate government's involvement in providing for the general welfare? Discuss how the system might fail. *(If the size of the work force decreases, fewer people will be contributing to the plan; money available to pay recipients will decrease.)* Discuss with students what they think the government might do in such a situation. *(Leaders might increase social security taxes or reduce benefits.)* What, do you think, would workers do?

He called industry leaders to the White House and recommended that they maintain prices and wages at high levels. His recommendations fell on deaf ears; companies cut their prices and wages to survive, and Hoover's program failed.

As the crisis deepened, Hoover shifted his stance and requested tax cuts in Congress, instituted several federal public works projects such as Boulder Dam, and proposed the Reconstruction Finance Corporation that loaned money to corporations to keep them from bankruptcy. Hoover, however, never proposed massive public works or direct relief to the unemployed.

Independent Practice

L1 Research Have students research how Congress solved unemployment and welfare problems during and after the Civil War. Have students focus on the policy of providing free land for colleges and what it suggests about Congress's approach to solving the problem of poverty.

L2 Informative Writing Have students research and write a report on ways in which Congress has stimulated the economy to increase output of new products. Students might research topics such as NASA, use of tariffs, or research grants.

L3 Comparing Governments Have students compare the United States government approach to providing for the general welfare with a socialist system such as Sweden. Tell students to focus on Sweden's approach to this problem from the 1920s to the present.

Assess

Have students complete **Examining the Case.**

Close

Ask students why education is one of the best ways to improve the nation's general welfare. Do they think government can help improve the level of people's education? In what ways? Have students provide support for their opinions.

---

tion, the federal government established job-training programs to reduce unemployment among the young.

Results of the War on Poverty Many observers believe that some of the programs designed to reduce joblessness and poverty have failed, although not all can agree why. Certainly economic factors played a role. Automotive and steel industries suffering from declining sales and foreign competition responded by permanently reducing their work forces.

Some blamed the educational system for not producing qualified workers. Others thought that increasing the level of the federal minimum wage would provide more incentive for people to work.

Believing that more government spending would not solve the problem of poverty, President Reagan reduced the rate of increase in federal social programs. He said he favored more private efforts:

We passed our reforms in Washington but change must begin at the grass roots, on the streets where you live. And that's why on September 24, I announced that we were launching a nationwide effort to encourage citizens to join with us in finding where need exists and then to organize volunteer programs to meet those needs. . . .

A recent Roper poll found a large majority believe that Government does not spend tax money for human services as effectively as a leading private organization like the United Way.
—RONALD REAGAN, JANUARY 15, 1983

One outspoken critic of the existing system was Charles Murray, who proposed a program that

Consists of scrapping the entire federal welfare and income-support structure of working-aged persons, including AFDC, Medicaid, Food Stamps, Unemployment Insurance, Workers' Compensation, subsidized housing, disability insurance, and the rest. I would leave the working-aged person with no recourse whatsoever except the job market, family members, friends, and public or private locally funded services. It is the Alexandrian solution; cut the knot, for there is no way to untie it.
—CHARLES MURRAY, 1984

Economics professor Richard Coe working with Greg Duncan responded to Mr. Murray in the *Wall Street Journal*. They found that most of those on government assistance programs "mix work and welfare" and "welfare dependency" is not "typically transmitted from one generation to the next." In their view,

Charles Murray sees welfare as a sinister, debilitating force, creating more poverty than it alleviates. But he and other neoconservative writers have simply failed to digest the emerging facts about the dynamic nature of welfare use. We see the system as an indispensable safety net in a dynamic society, serving largely as insurance against temporary misfortune and providing some small measure of equal opportunity in the home environments of children who, after all, constitute the majority of recipients.
—RICHARD D. COE AND GREG J. DUNCAN, MAY 15, 1985

Significance

President Clinton promised to "end welfare as we know it" during the 1992 campaign. Once in office, however, the President gave welfare reform a back seat as he concentrated on health care, crime, and trade. By 1994 Congress focused on a modest reform proposal to gradually limit the amount of time welfare recipients could get benefits. It would also require certain AFDC recipients to find work or accept a federally subsidized job within two years of accepting aid.

Examining the Case

Reviewing Facts
1. Explain why the federal government's role in the nation's welfare system increased during the Great Depression.
2. Describe how the FERA provided government relief.
3. Identify three current welfare programs.

Critical Thinking Skills
4. Determining Relevance How are the economy and the nation's welfare system related?
5. Recognizing Ideologies What two ideologies are represented by Charles Murray on one hand and Richard Coe and Greg Duncan on the other?

Examining the Case Answers

1. because local and state agencies did not have the necessary funds

2. provided more than $324 million to states and territories, and welfare payments to 4.5 million people

3. AFDC, medicare, medicaid, unemployment insurance, food stamps, Operation Headstart

4. Welfare payments tend to increase during hard economic times.

5. Murray: conservative; Coe and Duncan: liberal

Chapter 21
Taxing and Spending

The federal government plays a major role in the United States economy. The amount of money the government collects in revenues and the government's budget are calculated in figures too large for most people to comprehend. In a recent year, the national government took in almost $1.5 trillion in revenues. That figure represents an average of almost $6,000 for each person in the nation. What are the sources of all this money? Two major ones are taxes and borrowing.

The individual income tax is the federal government's biggest single source of revenue, accounting for 45 cents of every dollar the government collects. The income tax is levied on a person's **taxable income**, or the total income of an individual minus certain deductions and personal exemptions. The federal government also levies income taxes on corporations; social insurance taxes on employees and employers; and excise taxes on the manufacture, transportation, sale, or consumption of goods and the performance of services. In addition, taxes on imports and estates of deceased persons increase government revenues.

The second major source of government funds includes borrowing. The government borrows by selling federal securities to individuals, corporations, and other institutions.

In order to predict and control revenue and spending for each year, the federal government uses a budget. The federal budget operates in a **fiscal year**—a 12-month accounting period that extends from October 1 through September 30 of the next year.

The budget is also an important policy document. It reflects the federal government's view of the nation's needs and priorities. By showing how much will be spent on various national concerns such as defense and social welfare, it serves as a blueprint for the federal government's spending.

Beginning with the Great Depression of the 1930s, the federal government has taken an increasing role in managing the nation's economy. Debates arise because in the American free enterprise system, control over the economy is divided between government and the private sector—individuals and business. Yet most Americans expect the federal government to play a significant role in moderating the nation's ups and downs, while promoting steady economic growth.

The government uses two primary devices to influence the direction of the economy: (1) fiscal policy and (2) monetary policy. **Fiscal policy** involves using government spending and taxation to influence the economy. The President and Congress can use the budget to pump money into the economy in order to stimulate it, or take money out of the economy in order to slow it down. **Monetary policy** involves controlling the supply of money and credit to influence the economy. This control is exercised through the Federal Reserve System. The Federal Reserve System, known as the Fed, is the central banking system of the United States. The Fed uses three main tools to control the nation's monetary policy. These tools include the discount rate, the reserve requirement, and open-market operations.

Chapter 22
Foreign Policy and National Defense

American **foreign policy** consists of the strategies and principles that guide the national government's relations with other countries and groups in the world. Although the specific details of American foreign policy may change from one administration to another, objectives of United States foreign policy remain constant.

The principal goal of American foreign policy is to preserve the security of the United States. **National security** refers to a nation's determination to remain free and independent and to be secure from foreign influence or invasion. Throughout American history the government has placed this goal above all other foreign-policy goals.

American foreign policy has other goals as well. One of these goals has been to promote world peace. American leaders have worked for world peace because they believe it is another way to guarantee national security. They believe that if other nations are at peace, the United States runs little risk of being drawn into a conflict. To achieve this vital goal, the United States government has cooperated with other governments to settle disputes. Other goals of American foreign policy include encouraging democratic governments, promoting free trade, and working to protect human rights.

Although the Framers of the Constitution attempted to divide the responsibility for foreign affairs

Classroom Resources for Unit 7 Digest

Unit Digest Transparencies, Unit 7

Participating in Government, Unit 7

Use the Unit Digest to introduce, review, reteach, or condense specific chapters or the entire unit. The Unit Digest is enhanced by the corresponding transparencies and activities in the Teacher's Classroom Resources.

Focus

Ask students to name as many federal government programs and services as they can. List responses on the chalkboard. Then ask students how the government might raise money to pay for all these programs. (*taxes, charging user fees, selling certain government services, borrowing*) Point out that the methods of raising money, and the amount of money that can be raised, are limited. But the list of government programs and services on which money must be spent, potentially, is unlimited. Close by mentioning that how the government balances raising funds with spending is discussed in this Unit Digest.

Teach

L1 Seeing Relationships Point out that the government pours money into the economy by adopting an *expansionary fiscal policy,* which involves cutting taxes and increasing government spending. The government can take money out of the economy with a *restrictive fiscal policy* of increasing taxes and reducing government spending. Ask students to suggest what policies the Federal Reserve System might adopt to parallel these two fiscal policies. (*expansionary—increase money supply, make credit easier to get; restrictive—decrease money supply, make credit harder to get*)

Interpreting Visuals Display transparency 7 from the *Unit Digest Transparencies* in the Teacher's Classroom Resources and use the accompanying teaching strategy, student activity, and student test to teach about public policies and services.

L3 Informative Writing Write the following American foreign-policy goals on the chalkboard:

preserving national security, promoting world peace, encouraging the development of democratic governments, promoting free trade, protecting human rights

Ask students to use this textbook and history texts to find examples of foreign-policy actions that were taken by the United States government to fulfill these goals. For each example, have students write a paragraph explaining how the action relates to the goal. Have students read their paragraphs to the class.

Assess

Check for Understanding

Have students complete **Synthesizing the Unit.**

Close

Have students discuss the following question:

Which should be the major focus of American government spending, domestic policy or foreign policy? Why?

---

between the President and Congress, the President has assumed most of the responsibility in foreign policy. The President derives this authority to control foreign policy from the constitutional powers as commander in chief, the right to appoint ambassadors, and the role of head of state.

Presidents, however, do not act alone when they formulate foreign policy. Almost all Presidents rely heavily on the secretaries of state and of defense, the national security adviser, and the Central Intelligence Agency.

Congress also plays an important role in foreign policy. Only Congress can declare war, approve treaties, and confirm ambassadorial appointments.

Chapter 23
Social and Domestic Policy

Free enterprise, based on private ownership of property and individual economic decisions, is the foundation of the American economic system. The government, however, plays a major role in the economy, and a more accurate description of the American system is a mixed economy. A **mixed economy** is one in which the government both supports and regulates private enterprise. During the 1900s, regulating and supporting business and labor have become major functions of the federal government.

Today the federal government provides four types of subsidies, or aids to business. One is tax incentives that allow businesses to deduct certain expenses from their annual tax returns. A second is government loans, or credit subsidies, that provide funds for businesses at low interest rates. A third type of subsidy is free services, such as weather information and other information valuable to businesses. Finally the government provides direct cash payments to businesses whose products or services are considered vital to the general public.

Federal law also regulates the relationship between employers and employees. As large corporations multiplied in the late 1800s, some businesses failed to provide a safe, clean work environment and fair wages. Employers used several methods to break up labor unions and fired workers who joined. The government responded with laws to protect factory workers, miners, and other workers.

The government also heads programs to help American citizens in need. The government provides subsidies to help farmers. Because farming is so vital to the nation, governments at the federal, state, and local levels provide support and assistance to farmers.

The federal government is not only interested in the welfare of those who farm the land. Federal laws today protect the land, air, and water—the environment. Federal laws also provide assistance to poor people, the elderly, and the unemployed.

The government provides programs to aid the nation's infrastructure as well. In 1966 Congress created the Department of Transportation (DOT) to coordinate national transportation policies and programs. This department brought together more than 30 agencies dealing with transportation that had been scattered throughout the government. Today the DOT employs more than 60,000 people and operates through 7 major agencies that reflect the various forms of transportation.

The Federal Road Act of 1916 set the pattern for the development of federal highway programs. Under this law the federal government provided yearly road-building grants to the states and required each state to match this aid on a dollar-for-dollar basis. These grants-in-aid, administered by the FHWA, form the basis of today's federal highway programs.

Under the Federal Aid Highway Act of 1944 and subsequent amendments, states now receive billions of dollars every year to build and improve the Interstate Highway System that crisscrosses the nation. This system, begun in 1956, consists of more than 45,000 miles of 4-to-8-lane superhighways connecting almost all the nation's major cities. Federal funds have covered 90 percent of the cost of the Interstate Highway System.

Synthesizing the Unit

Recalling Facts
1. Define **taxable income, fiscal year, fiscal policy, monetary policy, foreign policy, national security, mixed economy.**
2. List the two major sources of federal government revenue.
3. State the principal goal of American foreign policy.

Critical Thinking Skills
4. Evaluating Information What responsibilities does government have to provide programs to help the needy? Support your answer.

Synthesizing the Unit Answers

1. Definitions of terms appear on the pages indicated: **taxable income,** 677; **fiscal year,** 677; **fiscal policy,** 677; **monetary policy,** 677; **foreign policy,** 677; **national security,** 677; **mixed economy,** 678
2. The two major sources of government revenue are individual income tax and borrowing.

3. The principal goal of American foreign policy is to preserve the security of the United States.
4. Answers will vary. Students who think the government has a responsibility to offer programs for the needy may say that one purpose of government is to provide for the general welfare. They may also point out that the government

cannot ignore the poor, the unemployed, and the elderly because to operate effectively it needs the support and confidence of all citizens. Those students who disagree with this view may point out that self-help and using one's freedom to make one's way are strong traditions in the United States.

State Government

UNIT
8

Chapter 24
Organization of State Government

Chapter 25
State Government in Action

Introduce

Unit Objectives

After studying this unit, students should be able to:
- Generalize about the executive, legislative, and judicial structures and functions of state government.
- Analyze the division of powers between national and state governments.

Unit Overview

Unit 8 introduces students to the structure, functions, and operations of state governments.

Chapter 24 focuses on the structure of government, with emphasis on the variety of state constitutions and the organization of the states' executive, legislative, and judicial branches.

Chapter 25 focuses on the programs and services state governments provide and explores the sources of revenue used to fund them.

8
UNIT DIGEST

Use the Unit Digest on pages 745–746 to introduce, review, reteach, or condense the information in this unit.

Introducing the Unit

Write the following national government offices and institutions on the chalkboard: President, Vice President, Attorney General, secretary of the treasury, Congress, House of Representatives, Senate. Ask students to name the equivalent offices and institutions in their state. Then have students discuss the similarities and differences between these national and state offices and institutions. Close the discussion by mentioning that parallels between national and state governments are a focus of this unit.

Unit Project

Have students write a report on some aspect of their state government. Topics might include recent amendments to the state constitution, the use of the item veto by the governor, relations between the governor and the legislature, recent budgetary problems, or party politics in state government. Another possible topic is a unique feature of the state government, such as Nebraska's unicameral legislature or Texas's two supreme courts. Suggest that students illustrate their reports with quotations from leading state politicians and, where appropriate, charts, graphs, and diagrams. After study of the unit is completed, select a number of students to read their reports to the class.

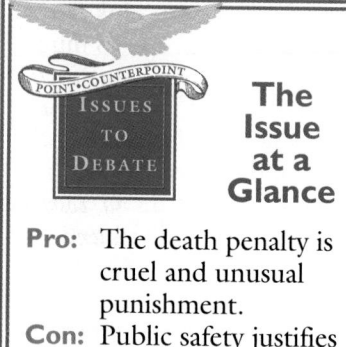

Pro: The death penalty is cruel and unusual punishment.

Con: Public safety justifies the death penalty.

Focus

Ask students which they think is a greater deterrent to breaking school rules, the severity of punishment or the certainty of it. Ask which they think is a greater deterrent to people who commit crimes.

Point out that society has had difficulty fitting punishment to crime, especially when the penalty is a life. Explain that the moral and practical elements of capital punishment are at the heart of this debate.

Teach

Guided Practice

Discuss with students the difference between abolishing capital punishment and finding the way that it is applied to be unconstitutional. Point out that in *Furman* the Court ruled punishment by death was not unconstitutional in itself, but cruel and unusual in the inconsistent way it was applied.

Ask: What common thread runs through the arguments of Justices Marshall and Brennan in opposing the death penalty? *(Both stress the intrinsic worth of the individual and that capital punishment dehumanizes society.)* Ask how Justices White and Stewart rebut this argument. *(Both argue that the protection of society is more important than the individual.)*

Note the poll results that show 75 percent of Americans favoring the death penalty.

Does the Death Penalty Constitute Cruel and Unusual Punishment?

In 1972 three cases that involved the death penalty reached the Supreme Court. In each case the Court found the death sentence unconstitutional. At the time many Americans believed that the Supreme Court had abolished the death penalty as "cruel and unusual punishment" prohibited by the Eighth Amendment. The Court did not, however, rule the death penalty unconstitutional. Instead, in the 1972 cases the Court overturned the verdicts based on the way the death penalty was administered in the state courts. Once the states changed the way they imposed the death penalty, the Supreme Court approved the penalty in a series of cases. As a result, the death penalty remains a hotly debated topic.

Pro

Most people who object to the death penalty view it as cruel and unusual punishment and immoral. These issues were foremost in the mind of Justice Thurgood Marshall in 1972. He wrote,

In striking down capital punishment, this Court does not malign our system of government. On the contrary, it pays homage to it. Only in a free society could right triumph in difficult times, and could civilization record its magnificent advancement. In recognizing the humanity of our fellow beings, we pay ourselves the highest tribute. We achieve "a major milestone in the long road from barbarism" and join the approximately 70 other jurisdictions in the world which celebrate their regard for civilization and humanity by shunning capital punishment.

—Justice Thurgood Marshall, *Furman* v. *Georgia,* 1972

Four years later, another case that dealt with capital punishment reached the Supreme Court. In *Gregg* v. *Georgia,* the death sentence was upheld. Justice William J. Brennan, who along with Justice Marshall argued that the death penalty was "cruel and unusual punishment," dissented. He wrote,

My opinion in Furman v. Georgia concluded that our civilization and the law had progressed to the point that therefore the punishment of death, for whatever crime and under all circumstances is "cruel and unusual" in violation of the Eighth and Fourteenth Amendments of the Constitution.... I emphasize ... that foremost among the "moral concepts" recognized in our cases ... is the primary moral principle that the State, even as it punishes, must treat its citizens in a manner consistent with their intrinsic worth as human beings.... The fatal constitutional infirmity in the punishment of death is that it treats "members of the human race as nonhuman, as objects to be toyed with and discarded." ... I therefore would hold, on that ground alone, that death is today a cruel and unusual punishment prohibited by the [Constitution].

—Justice William J. Brennan, 1976

One of the people who opposes capital punishment on moral grounds is Donal E. J. MacNamara who argues, "The law of God is 'Thou shall not kill,' and every system of ethics and code of morals echoes this injunction. . . ." He continues,

Individuals in groups or societies are subject to the same moral and ethical codes which govern their conduct as individuals. The state, through its police agents, may take human life when such ultimate measure of force is necessary to protect its citizenry from the immi-

More About Issues to Debate

The Supreme Court's 5 to 4 decision in *Furman* v. *Georgia* (1972), striking down Georgia's death penalty, found the justices deeply divided on this issue. Of the majority, all holdovers from the liberal Warren Court, only Brennan and Marshall found the death penalty to be unconstitutional under all circumstances. Justice William O. Douglas believed that because the death penalty was not applied uniformly—affecting mostly African Americans and poor people—it denied equal protection of the law. Stewart and White emphasized the cruelty of the rare and unpredictable circumstances in which it *nent danger of criminal action. . . . Once, however, the prisoner has been apprehended and either voluntarily submits to custody, or is effectively safeguarded against escape . . . the right of the state to take his life . . . does not exist in moral law.*

—Donal E. J. MacNamara, 1961

Con

Those who favor the death penalty often cite the need for the states to protect their citizens and to punish criminals for serious crimes. Justice Byron R. White's decision concurs.

Petitioner [defendant] has argued in effect that no matter how effective the death penalty may be as a punishment, government, created and run as it must be by humans, is inevitably incompetent to administer it. This cannot be accepted as a proposition of constitutional law. Imposition of the death penalty is surely an awesome responsibility for any system of justice and those who participate in it. Mistakes will be made and discriminations will occur which will be difficult to explain. However, one of society's most basic tasks is that of protecting the lives of its citizens and one of the most basic ways in which it achieves the task is through criminal laws against murder. I decline to interfere with the manner in which Georgia has chosen to enforce such laws. . . . Neither can I agree with the petitioner's other basic argument that the death penalty, however imposed and for whatever crime, is cruel and unusual punishment.

—Justice Byron R. White, *Gregg v. Georgia*, 1976

In a somewhat different vein, Justice Potter Stewart replied to those critics who condemned capital punishment on moral grounds. He wrote:

In part, capital punishment is an expression of society's moral outrage at particularly offensive conduct. . . . Indeed, the decision that capital punishment may be the appropriate sanction in extreme cases is an expression of the community's belief that certain crimes are themselves so grievous an affront to humanity that the only adequate response may be the penalty of death. . . .

[T]he moral consensus concerning the death penalty and its social utility as a sanction, require us to conclude, in the absence of more convincing evidence, that the infliction of death as punishment for murder is not without justification and thus is not unconstitutionally severe.

—Justice Potter Stewart, *Gregg v. Georgia*, 1976

Professor Walter Berns supports the death penalty, also.

The abolitionists condemn it [the death penalty] because it springs from revenge, they say, and revenge is the ugliest passion in the human soul. They condemn it because it . . . serves no purpose beyond inflicting pain on its victims. Strictly speaking, they are opposed to punishment. . . . But, contrary to abolitionist hopes and expectations, the Court did not invalidate the death penalty. It upheld it. It upheld it on retributive grounds. In doing so, it recognized, at least implicitly, that the American people are entitled as a people to demand that criminals be paid back, and that the worst of them be made to pay back with their lives. In doing this, it gave them the means by which they might strengthen the law that makes them a people, and not a mere aggregation of selfish individuals.

—Walter Berns, *Capital Punishment*, 1979

The Debate Continues

The topic of capital punishment continues to draw attention. Although opponents campaign for its abolition, they also admit their chances are not good. As one official of the American Civil Liberties Union (ACLU) admitted: "We have exhausted the major constitutional issues. We don't have any more in the oven." Further complicating the issue for the opponents of the death penalty is the fact that in a recent poll, approximately 75 percent of the people polled supported capital punishment. Whether this attitude will change in the future remains to be seen.

Examining the Issue

Recalling Facts
1. Describe why Donal E. J. MacNamara opposes the death penalty.

Critical Thinking Skills
2. Analyzing Information Why do you think the Supreme Court has been called on to rule on capital punishment?
3. Predicting Consequences What do you think would be the effect on the nation's crime rate if the Supreme Court abolished capital punishment?

Investigating Further
Research recent articles in periodicals regarding the death penalty. Try to determine if the attitude toward capital punishment in any way reflects a political ideology. Write a brief paragraph detailing your conclusion.

was inflicted—like being struck by lightning, Stewart said. The 4 Nixon appointees stood together in voting to uphold Georgia's law.

More than 30 states responded to the Court's ruling by passing new laws that automatically imposed the death penalty for certain crimes. In 1976, however, the Court returned to this issue. While again upholding the principle of capital punishment, it struck down the principle of mandatory sentences. Instead, in *Gregg v. Georgia* the Court upheld procedures to consider circumstances of the crime and the criminal's past before passing sentence. Such procedures remain in use today in states that impose the death penalty.

Ask: Why do you think that capital punishment has so much support? (*Speculation may include rising crime rates, repeat offenders, increased criminal violence, societal revenge and protection motives, prison overcrowding, costs of keeping prisoners for life, and so on.*)

Independent Practice

Ask students to identify and copy the sentence in each justice's argument that best summarizes his point of view on capital punishment in a free society. Then have them restate each sentence in their own words.

Assign case 43, *Gregg* v. *Georgia*, in *Supreme Court Case Studies* in the Teacher's Classroom Resources.

Assess

Have students complete **Examining the Issue.**
Answers
1. He opposes it on moral and ethical grounds.
2. Answers may vary, but should cite the constitutional question raised by the Eighth Amendment.
3. Answers will vary depending on attitudes toward capital punishment as a deterrent. Some may predict a rise in crime; others will foresee no change.

Close

Tell students that some reformers suggest that life sentences without a chance for parole will accomplish the same goal of protecting society as will the death penalty. Ask: Do you think this alternative would be acceptable to death penalty advocates? to opponents of the death penalty?

Chapter Organizer

Objectives	Special Feature Pages	Supplemental Materials
Section 1 State Constitutions *pp. 684–690* 1. Describe four important functions of state constitutions in state government. 2. Summarize the common characteristics of state constitutions. 3. Discuss the various methods states use to amend their state constitutions.	Point/Counterpoint: Does the Death Penalty Constitute Cruel and Unusual Punishment? pp. 680–681 Focus on Freedom: Fundamental Orders of Connecticut p. 685 Critical Thinking Skills: Expressing Problems Clearly p. 690	Guided Reading Activities Reproducible Lesson Plans Section 1 Quiz Testmaker Skill Reinforcement Activities 24 The Living Constitution SAT Practice Tests Writer's Guidebook
Section 2 The Legislature: The Lawmaking Branch *pp. 691–696* 1. Describe the trend toward professional state legislatures. 2. Compare the structure and organization of state legislatures to the national Congress. 3. Identify the roles of interest groups, legislators, and governors in state legislation.		Guided Reading Activities Reproducible Lesson Plans Supreme Court Case Studies 30 Primary and Secondary Source Readings 24 Section 2 Quiz Testmaker SAT Practice Tests Writer's Guidebook
Section 3 The Governor: The Executive Branch *pp. 697–704* 1. Define five roles of governors. 2. Discuss the development of the power of the governor's office. 3. Compare the state executive branch with the national executive branch.	Images of Government: State Invitations pp. 698–699 Global Connection: Comparing Governments: Powers of States and Provinces p. 703	Guided Reading Activities Reproducible Lesson Plans Section 3 Quiz Testmaker Chapter Transparencies 24 SAT Practice Tests Writer's Guidebook
Section 4 State Courts: The Judicial Branch *pp. 705–711* 1. Classify civil and criminal cases. 2. Outline the structure of the state court system. 3. Evaluate various methods for selecting state judges.	Participating in Government: Choosing a Lawyer p. 707 Personal Perspectives: Lawrence H. Cooke on the American Court System p. 711	Guided Reading Activities Reproducible Lesson Plans Participating in Government 24 Cooperative Learning Activities 24 Reteaching Activities 24 Enrichment Activities 24 Section 4 Quiz Chapter 24 Tests Testmaker Audio Cassettes (English and Spanish) Limited English Proficiency Activities 24 SAT Practice Tests

If time does not permit teaching this chapter, assign the Chapter 24 summary in the Unit 8 Digest on pages 745–746.

Key To Ability Levels

Teaching strategies have been coded for varying learning styles and abilities.

L1 Level 1 activities are **basic** activities and should be within the ability range of all students.

L2 Level 2 activities are **average** activities and should be within the ability range of the average to above-average student.

L3 Level 3 activities are **challenging** activities designed for the ability range of above-average students.

LEP These activities should be within the ability range of **Limited English Proficiency** students.

Multicultural Activities

One reason many people turn to state courts rather than federal courts is that they expect a more favorable hearing in state courts because many state constitutions specifically spell out more rights than does the United States Constitution. According to Ronald K.L. Collins, a scholar on state constitutional law, from 1986 to 1990, state courts handed down 600 opinions that went beyond the minimum constitutional protections established by the United States Supreme Court in such areas as speech, press, and search and seizure. Have students speculate on how such factors as the selection process for state court judges might influence decision making in state courts.

Redistricting at the state level has been greatly affected by the Voting Rights Act of 1965. The act has been used to attack redistricting plans that may discriminate against African Americans or Hispanics or abridge their voting rights by diluting voting strength of minority populations in the state. Through court rulings and congressional amendments, the Voting Rights Act has been used to help elect African American and Hispanic candidates by drawing district boundaries with large African American and Hispanic majorities. Students might research the redistricting issues that arose in their state in 1991-92 following the most recent census or find out how the Supreme Court case *Thornburg* v. *Gingles* (1986) affected minority representation in state redistricting plans.

Chapter Resources

Readings for the Student

Beyle, Thad L., ed. *State Government: CQ's Guide to Current Issues and Activities, 1991–1992.* Congressional Quarterly, 1992.

Jigsaw Politics: Shaping the House After the 1990 Census. Congressional Quarterly, 1990.

Sabato, Larry. *Goodbye to Good-time Charlie: The American Governorship Transformed.* Congressional Quarterly, 1983.

State and Local Government 1991–1992: Annual Editions Series. Dushkin, 1992.

Readings for the Teacher

Adams, Willi P. *The First American Constitutions: Republican Ideology and the Making of the State Constitutions in the Revolutionary Era.* University of North Carolina Press, 1980.

Beyle, Thad L., and Lynn Muchmore, eds. *Being Governor: The View From the Office.* Duke University Press, 1983.

Bingham, Richard D., and David Hedge. *State and Local Government in a Changing Society,* 2nd ed. McGraw-Hill, 1991.

———.*Governors and Legislatures: Contending Powers.* Congressional Quarterly, 1990.

Houseman, Gerald L. *State And Local Government: The New Battleground.* Prentice-Hall, 1986.

Rosenthal, Alan. *Legislative Life: People, Process, and Performance in the States.* Harper & Row, 1981.

Multimedia

Videocassettes

Betting on the Lottery. (*Frontline* series). Marian Marzynski. (v/c, 60 minutes)

Software

PFS: File—United States Government. Scholastic Publishing Company. (Apple IIe or IIc, at least 64K & 1 disk drive—must be used with *PFS: File, PFS: Report;* 2nd disk drive and printer recommended). Students research and analyze data bases relating to state government.

Organization Of State Government

Introduce

Chapter Overview

Chapter 24 focuses on the structure of state government, with emphasis on the variety of state constitutions and the organization of the states' executive, legislative, and judicial branches.

Section 1 explains the function of state constitutions as frameworks for state government.

Section 2 discusses the organization of state legislatures and describes the state legislative process.

Section 3 summarizes the election, roles, and powers of state governors.

Section 4 describes the structure, operation, and jurisdiction of state courts.

Chapter 24 Themes

Write the chapter themes on the chalkboard. Ask students to write these themes in their notebooks and as they read the chapter to list each major topic discussed under the appropriate theme.

CHAPTER

24

A state capitol, like this one in Denver, Colorado, is the building in which the state legislature assembles to make laws.

About the Chapter Opener

Teaching With Illustrations   Have students study the photograph of the Colorado state capitol on pages 682 and 683. Then ask them the following questions: On what government building in Washington, D.C., is this building modeled? *(United States Capitol)* What similarities are there between the two buildings? *(classic-style architecture, huge dome topped by a statue)* Since these buildings are similar, is the work that goes on inside the same? *(Yes; both buildings house legislatures; lawmaking is the major activity that goes on inside them.)*

Chapter Preview

Overview

State governments, under their individual constitutions, parallel the structure of the national government.

Objectives

After studying this chapter, you should be able to:

1. Recognize how a state constitution serves as a framework for state government.
2. Relate recent trends in the powers and organization of state legislatures and the political process of passing legislation.
3. Evaluate the factors affecting the power of state governors.
4. Classify state courts by their jurisdiction.

Themes in Government

This chapter emphasizes the following government themes:

- **Federalism** State governments exercise sovereignty that is limited by the federal Constitution. Sections 1 and 4.
- **Political Processes** Democratic principles govern political processes in state government. Sections 1, 2, 3, and 4.
- **Public Policy** Legislatures systematically create public policy. Section 2.
- **Constitutional Interpretations** The amount of detail in a constitution helps determine the extent of its potential interpretation. Section 3.

Critical Thinking Skills

This chapter emphasizes the following critical thinking skills:

- Identifying Central Issues
- Making Generalizations
- Making Comparisons
- Drawing Conclusions
- Formulating Questions

CHAPTER 24: ORGANIZATION OF STATE GOVERNMENT **683**

Introducing the Chapter

Have students discuss their perceptions of how state government compares with federal government. For instance, do they see a governor as simply a less powerful President? Does a state legislature differ from the Congress? Tell students to check the accuracy of their perceptions against the information in the chapter.

Chapter Project

Obtain copies of the state constitution from the secretary of state's office (one copy for each five or six students). Have students compare it with what they learn about other state constitutions in the chapter. Also, have students find examples in the document of each element discussed in the chapter.

Linking Past and Present
In *Democracy In America*, Alexis de Tocqueville says, "To study the Union before studying the state is to follow a path strewn with obstacles. The federal government was the last to take shape in the United States; . . . The great political principles which now rule American society were born and grew up in the state; there is no room for doubt about that. So one must understand the state to gain the key to the rest." Ask students if they feel that the state continues to be an important aspect of American government.

Setting the Scene The Constitutional Convention of 1787 was originally called to improve the Articles of Confederation, which had proven an unsatisfactory framework for resolving the many problems among the states. Only after the convention began did its tasks evolve into creation of a strong national government. The concern of the states about the national government's impact on their sovereignty is reflected in the debates and compromises over slavery and the legislative branch. Yet the Founders' commitment to federalism is easily seen in the final document: the states are referred to more than 50 times in the 7,300-word document.

Focus

Bell Ringer

Ask students to write an answer to the following question while attendance is being taken:

Since the Constitution protects individual rights, why must each state also have a constitution?

Motivating Activity

Discuss students' Bell Ringer answers. *(Answers should recognize the broader reasons for constitutions.)* Tell students that Section 1 explains why state constitutions are necessary.

Vocabulary Precheck

Call on volunteers to tell what they think each key term and concept means. Have students check the accuracy of their definitions in the Glossary. **LEP**

Caption Answer

to create the structure of state government and establish the powers of each element

---

Linking Past and Present
The first state constitutions reflected a distrust of executive power and a belief in legislative power. In the 1800s, however, rewritten constitutions placed increasing limits on legislative powers, particularly in the areas of taxation, spending, and borrowing. Many of these constitutions are still in effect today.

GLENCOE
TECHNOLOGY

Focus on Government
Video 46
Lecture Launcher:
Organization of State Government
Running Time: 1:56
Videodisc 3, Chap. 46
VHS Tape 3, Begins 19:13

State Constitutions

Constitutional government in America began with colonial charters, long before the United States Constitution. When the colonies declared their independence in 1776, some states kept their old colonial charters as their state constitutions. Other states, like Virginia and Pennsylvania, drew up new constitutions. Since 1776 the 50 states have had a total of 146 constitutions. Only 19 states have kept their original documents, and all the states have added many amendments. Louisiana has had 11 constitutions since it became a state in 1812.

Colonial Charter
In America old colonial charters like this one from Rhode Island were the beginning of constitutional government. **History What is the purpose of a state constitution?**

Importance of Constitutions

State constitutions are important for a number of reasons. First, constitutions create the structure of state government itself. Like the federal Constitution, every state constitution provides for separation of powers among three branches of government—legislative, executive, and judicial. State constitutions outline the organization of each branch, the powers and terms of various offices, and the method of election for state officials. For example, a typical state constitution describes the powers of the state legislature, as well as the legislators' terms of office and qualifications. Similarly, a state constitution specifies the powers and duties of the governor—including such provisions as the governor's power to veto legislation. Most state constitutions also set up a court system, with a state supreme court and lower courts.

Second, state constitutions are important because they establish the different types of local government, such as counties, townships, municipalities, special

districts, parishes, and boroughs. State constitutions usually define the powers and duties as well as the organization of these local governments.

Third, state constitutions regulate the ways state and local governments can raise and spend money. In many states, for example, the state constitution limits the taxing power of local governments. It usually specifies the kinds of taxes that state and local governments may impose. These may include property taxes, sales taxes, and income taxes. The state constitution

---

SECTION PREVIEW

Objectives
After studying this section, you should be able to:
■ Describe four important functions of state constitutions in state government.
■ Summarize the common characteristics of state constitutions.

■ Discuss the various methods states use to amend their constitutions.

Key Terms and Concepts
initiative, constitutional convention, constitutional commission

Themes in Government
■ Federalism
■ Political Processes

Critical Thinking Skills
■ Identifying Central Issues
■ Making Generalizations

---

684 Unit 8: State Government

Classroom Resources for Section 1

📁 Guided Reading Activities
📁 Reproducible Lesson Plans
📁 Section 1 Quiz
⊞ Testmaker

The Living Constitution
SAT Practice Tests
Writer's Guidebook

may also specify how certain revenues must be used. In some states, for example, the constitution requires that money taken in through a state lottery must be earmarked for education or for aid to senior citizens.

Fourth, state constitutions establish independent state agencies, boards, and commissions that have power in areas that affect citizens' lives directly. These include, for example, public utility commissions that regulate gas and electric rates, and state boards of education that help administer public schools throughout the state.

As the basic law of the state, the state constitution is supreme above all other laws made within the state.

Laws the state legislature or local governments pass must be consistent with the provisions of the state constitution. At the same time, the state constitution cannot contain provisions that clash with the United States Constitution. Article VI makes the national Constitution "the supreme law of the land."

Characteristics

Throughout the 50 states, constitutions vary widely. At the same time, most state constitutions share some basic characteristics.

Teach

Guided Practice

L1 Concept Mapping Write *State Constitutions* on the chalkboard, circle it, and draw four lines radiating from the circle. Then ask students to give the four reasons for having state constitutions and write each at the end of one of the four lines. *(create structure of state government, establish types of local government, regulate state and local taxing and spending, establish state agencies, boards, and commissions)* Ask students for an example of each reason. **LEP**

Focus on Freedom

FUNDAMENTAL ORDERS OF CONNECTICUT

Reverend Thomas Hooker and his congregation established the Connecticut settlement at Hartford in 1636. Together with others who had settled at Windsor and Wethersfield, the free citizens of Hartford assembled and drew up the document that has been called the first American state constitution.

Forasmuch as it has pleased Almighty God by the wise disposition of His Divine Providence so to order and dispose of things that we, the inhabitants and residents of Windsor, Hartford, and Wethersfield are now . . . dwelling in and upon the river Conectecotte [Connecticut] and the lands thereunto adjoining; and well knowing where a people are gathered together the Word of God requires that, to maintain a peace and union of such a people, there should be an orderly and decent government established according to God, to order and dispose of the affairs of the people at all seasons as occasion shall require; do therefore associate and conjoin ourselves to be as one public state or commonwealth, and do, for ourselves and our successors and such as shall be adjoined to us at any time hereafter, enter into combination and confederation together, to maintain and preserve liberty and purity of the Gospel of our Lord Jesus which we now profess, as also the discipline of the churches, which, according to the truth of the said Gospel, is now practised among us. As also in our civil affairs to be guided and governed according to such laws, rules, orders, and decrees as shall be made, ordered, and decreed, as follows:

1. It is ordered, sentenced, and decreed that there shall be yearly two general assemblies or courts; . . . The first shall be called the Court of Election, wherein shall be yearly chosen . . . so many magistrates and other public officers as shall be found requisite. Whereof one to be chosen governor for the year ensuing and until another be chosen, and no other magistrate to be chosen for more than one year; provided always there be six chosen besides the governor. . . .

5. It is ordered . . . that to the aforesaid Court of Election the several towns shall send their deputies, and, when the elections are ended, they may proceed in any public service as at other courts. Also, the General Court in September shall be for making of laws, and any other public occasion which concerns the good of the Commonwealth.

—FUNDAMENTAL ORDERS OF CONNECTICUT, 1639

Examining the Document

Reviewing Facts
1. Describe the function of the Court of Election.
2. Identify the main role of the General Court.

Critical Thinking Skills
3. Identifying Assumptions Why did the people of Connecticut believe that it was necessary to organize a government?

CHAPTER 24: ORGANIZATION OF STATE GOVERNMENT **685**

Focus on Freedom

Connecticut colonists formed a government that gave their legislators a great deal of control. In 1662, Charles II granted Connecticut a royal charter similar to the one he granted Rhode Island in 1663. It preserved the rights in Connecticut's constitution and forbade royal governors to interfere in colonists' legislative actions. Both colonies kept the power to choose their own royal governors. With very few alterations, both colonies' charters became the new states' post-Revolution constitutions.

Answers

1. to elect the governor and other officials
2. to pass laws
3. They believed God required it to preserve peace, unity, liberty, and the purity of their beliefs.

Background

When the colonies became states in 1776, they wrote new constitutions to establish government legally independent of British authority. Most of these early constitutions contained bills of rights. These documents became the basis of the Bill of Rights in the United States Constitution, as the states sought to protect individual liberties from the new national government. Thus, the principle of individual liberty was and is paramount; many of today's state constitutions position their bill of rights first, not as amendments, as does the United States Constitution.

L2 Political Processes Write *Methods of Proposal* and *Methods of Ratification* on the chalkboard. Have students list and explain the methods used to propose and ratify amendments to state constitutions. Then ask students to look in their state constitution to identify how amendments are proposed and ratified.

L3 Debate Have students debate whether lengthy, specific, and detailed constitutions with frequent amendments create governments that are more democratic than those operating under the short "outlines" favored by Chief Justice Marshall.

Chart Study Answer
Massachusetts (1780)

The State Constitutions

	First Constitution Adopted	Total Number of Constitutions	Present Constitution Adopted		First Constitution Adopted	Total Number of Constitutions	Present Constitution Adopted		First Constitution Adopted	Total Number of Constitutions	Present Constitution Adopted
Alabama	1819	6	1901	Maine	1819	1	1819	Ohio	1802	2	1851
Alaska	1956	1	1956	Maryland	1776	4	1867	Oklahoma	1907	1	1907
Arizona	1911	1	1911	Massachusetts	1780	1	1780	Oregon	1857	1	1857
Arkansas	1836	5	1874	Michigan	1835	4	1963	Pennsylvania	1776	5	1968
California	1849	2	1879	Minnesota	1857	1	1857	Rhode Island	1663	2	1842
Colorado	1876	1	1876	Mississippi	1817	4	1890	South Carolina	1776	7	1895
Connecticut	1638	4	1965	Missouri	1820	4	1945				
Delaware	1776	4	1897	Montana	1889	2	1972	South Dakota	1889	1	1889
Florida	1839	6	1968	Nebraska	1866	2	1875	Tennessee	1796	3	1870
Georgia	1777	10	1982	Nevada	1864	1	1864	Texas	1827	7	1876
Hawaii	1840*	6**	1950	New Hampshire	1776	2	1784	Utah	1895	1	1895
Idaho	1889	1	1889					Vermont	1777	3	1793
Illinois	1818	4	1970	New Jersey	1776	3	1947	Virginia	1776	6	1970
Indiana	1816	2	1851	New Mexico	1911	1	1911	Washington	1889	1	1889
Iowa	1846	2	1857	New York	1777	4	1894	West Virginia	1863	2	1872
Kansas	1859	1	1859	North Carolina	1776	3	1970				
Kentucky	1792	4	1891					Wisconsin	1848	1	1848
Louisiana	1812	11	1974	North Dakota	1889	1	1889	Wyoming	1889	1	1889

*(as a kingdom)   **(as a kingdom and then a republic)

Chart Study
Only 18 state constitutions have gone unrevised. The newest unrevised state constitution in use is Alaska's, which was adopted in 1956. **Which state has the oldest unrevised constitution in use today?**

Bill of Rights Besides a provision for separation of powers among the three branches of state government, all state constitutions contain a Bill of Rights. This section includes all or most of the protections of the Bill of Rights in the Constitution of the United States. In addition, many state constitutions contain protections not provided for in the national Constitution. These protections include the workers' right to join unions, a ban on discrimination based on sex or race, and certain protections for the physically challenged, among others.

Length Originally, state constitutions were about the same length as the United States Constitution. Over the years additions to state constitutions in many states have resulted in very long documents. While the national Constitution has about 7,000 words, the average state constitution today has more than 28,000 words. Very long constitutions are found in such states as Texas, with 62,000 words, and Alabama, with about 174,000 words—equal to about 200 pages of this textbook.

Detail Long state constitutions are filled with details, often covering many varied and unusual aspects of life in a state. Such constitutions might include any of the following: a special tax to help veterans of the Civil War; a requirement that public schools teach agricultural subjects; fixed salaries for certain state and local officials; or a declaration of state holidays.

686   Unit 8: State Government

Cooperative Learning Activity

Organize the class into five or six groups to formulate a proposed amendment to their state constitution. Provide copies of amendments already made to the state constitution as examples for students. Have each group focus on a different area, such as taxes, the structure of government, the power of corporations, education, and so on. One person from each group should report to the class on the group's amendment and the reasons behind it. Encourage students from other groups to ask questions after each presentation. Have the class vote on ratification of each proposal.

One state constitution even has a provision authorizing a twine and rope plant at the state penitentiary. In 1796 the Tennessee Constitution barred clergy from public office. The provision claimed:

Ministers of the gospel are, by their professions, dedicated to God and the care of souls, and ought not to be diverted from the great duties of their functions.

—TENNESSEE CONSTITUTION, 1796

Critics of state constitutions claim that such detailed, specific provisions are not needed in a constitution, but rather should be handled in state laws. Chief Justice John Marshall once wrote that a constitution "requires only that its great outlines should be marked, its important objects designated." The federal Constitution, for example, is very general, including only the basic goals of government, its structure, and basic rights.

A major reason for the development of lengthy and detailed state constitutions has to do with politics. State constitutions are sometimes very detailed because certain groups and individuals have succeeded in including provisions that are to their advantage. These special interests know that including such provisions in the state constitution protects them against being changed by a simple vote of the legislature.

Amendments and Changes

Changing a constitution may be necessary because society itself changes, and new conditions require new actions or policies from government. In recent years, for example, some state constitutions have been amended to provide greater powers for the governor. Many people believe that modern conditions require stronger executive leadership than most early state constitutions allowed. In recent years constitutional changes have given the governor of Ohio power to fill a vacancy in the office of lieutenant governor. On the other hand, the governor of New Mexico received expanded powers over the removal of certain officials. The governor of Oregon was granted more time to veto bills after a legislative adjournment. The governor of California received power to deny parole to convicted murderers.

Some amendments to state constitutions provide for very specific policies. As a result, some state constitutions have an enormous number of amendments. These usually only add to the length and detail of the

Process of Constitutional Amendment

Proposal (Four Methods)

State Legislature

Popular Initiative

Constitutional Convention

Constitutional Commission

↓

Ratification

By Popular Vote*

Except Delaware, where two consecutive sessions of the state legislature vote to ratify.

☑ **Chart Study**
One power of a state constitutional convention is to propose amendments. **What is another power?**

constitution. Alabama's constitution has 513 amendments, California's has 471, and Texas's has 339.

The amendment process has two steps: proposal and ratification. To propose an amendment is to legally present it for consideration. To ratify an amendment is to legally approve it, usually after considerable discussion and debate.

Methods of Proposal Constitutions of the 50 states provide 4 different methods of proposing amendments. These include methods by state legislatures, by popular initiative, by a constitutional convention, or by a constitutional commission.

In every state the state legislature has the power to propose an amendment to the state constitution. This method is the most commonly used, accounting for about 92 percent of proposed amendments in a recent year. The actual practice of legislative amendment proposals varies somewhat from state to state. In 17 states a majority vote of the members of each house of the legislature must propose an amendment to the state constitution. In 18 states a two-thirds vote of all members of each house is required. In 9 states a three-fifths majority vote of the legislature is required. Finally, a few states require the legislature to vote for an amendment in 2 different sessions before the proposal is official.

CHAPTER 24: ORGANIZATION OF STATE GOVERNMENT 687

Independent Practice

L1 Federalism Have students examine their state's bill of rights. Have them list protections that are also present in the United States Constitution. Have them make separate lists of any rights in the national Bill of Rights that are not in their state bill of rights and vice versa.

L2 Classificatory Writing Have students examine the amendments to their state constitutions. Have them make two lists—one of amendments no longer relevant to government and society today, and another of amendments that remain important. Ask them to briefly explain each amendment's classification.

CONNECTIONS

History
Although the slavery issue was compromised in the Constitution, many state officials believed its presence to be immoral in a democratic republic. By 1804 every state north of Maryland had by law, constitution, or court action required emancipation. Several southern states encouraged voluntary emancipation or prohibited importation of enslaved persons.

Special Needs Strategy

Learning Problems Students with learning problems may have trouble discriminating among sounds and so have difficulty processing and producing meaningful language at grade level. Words that are difficult for students to pronounce are easily forgotten or not used. Write the following words from Section 1 on an overhead or on the chalkboard and pronounce each word for students: *initiative, municipalities, adjournment, lieutenant, petition.* Ask students to write these words, pronounce them, and circle any part of a word they had difficulty pronouncing.

L3 Informative Writing Have students choose one of the more recent amendments to their state constitution and write a short essay that explains the amendment and speculates about the political issues or concerns that may have motivated it.

Caption Answer
to propose amendments to the state constitution, or to replace it

STUDY GUIDE

Theme Answer
Obtaining the necessary number of petition signatures requires a huge, expensive organizational effort.

Critical Thinking Answer
because special interests have succeeded in including provisions that are to their advantage; because society itself changes, and new conditions require new actions or policies from government

Assess

Check for Understanding

Have students complete Section 1 Review on page 689.

Seventeen states also allow the people to propose amendments by popular initiative. An **initiative** is a method by which citizens propose a constitutional amendment or a law. The initiative process begins when an individual or group writes a proposed amendment. People in favor of the amendment then circulate it as part of a petition to obtain the signatures of a required number of eligible voters. The number of signatures required varies from state to state. Massachusetts requires only 3 percent of the total votes cast for governor in the preceding election. Arizona requires 15 percent of the total votes cast for governor at the last election. Constitutional

Time for a New State Constitution
The 1970 Virginia Constitutional Convention met at the College of William and Mary. **Politics** What is the purpose of a state constitutional convention?

initiatives account for only about 5 percent of the proposed amendments to state constitutions.

The third method of proposing amendments to a state constitution is by convening a state constitutional convention. A **constitutional convention** is a gathering of citizens, usually elected by popular vote, who meet to consider changing or replacing a constitution. In most cases these representatives to a state conven-

tion will propose major changes in the state constitution. Usually these changes take the form of a series of amendments to the existing constitution.

Finally, many states have used a fourth method, the constitutional commission, to propose constitutional amendments. A **constitutional commission** is a group of experts appointed to study the state constitution and recommend changes. Eight states established constitutional commissions in the 1980s, but few of their recommendations resulted in amendments. Kentucky's commission recommendations in 1987 serve as a typical example:

> *A*mong the 77 recommendations were the merit selection of judges, tort caps [limits on awards in civil suits], electing the governor and lieutenant governor on a joint ticket, allowing the governor to serve while out of the state, a privacy right, and a new equal rights amendment. . . . In 1988, only one of the 77 recommendations was referred by the Legislature to the voters as a constitutional amendment. . . The referendum was approved by the voters at the general election.
> —JANICE C. MAY, THE BOOK OF THE STATES, 1990

Methods of Ratification The method of ratification, or approval, of an amendment to the state constitution is relatively simple. All states except Delaware require ratification by popular vote. The kind of majority necessary to approve an amendment varies throughout the states. Forty-four states require a simple majority of those who vote on the proposed amendment. Three other states require a majority of all voters who cast ballots in the election. Illinois requires either a majority of all voters who cast ballots in the election or three-fifths of those voting on the amendment. New Hampshire requires a two-thirds majority. In Delaware two consecutive sessions of the state legislature must vote to ratify an amendment to the constitution.

Studies show that once an amendment is placed on the ballot, it has a good chance of being ratified. Between 1980 and 1990, for example, voters approved

STUDY GUIDE

Themes in Government
Political Processes
The initiative attempts to place power in the hands of ordinary citizens. **Why do you think the** initiative method for proposing amendments to state constitutions accounts for so few proposals?

Critical Thinking Skills
Identifying Central Issues States amend their constitutions much more frequently than the national government. **Why is this so?**

Critical Thinking Activity

Identifying Central Issues Have students consider the following: About 92 percent of recent proposed constitutional amendments came from state legislatures. Special-interest groups have great power, and sometimes can persuade a legislator to propose an amendment. What effect does this process have on democracy? *(Students may suggest that the power of special-interest groups retards the democratic process. Others may note that in almost every state even amendments sought by special interests must be ratified by the voters.)*

more than 70 percent of all amendments to state constitutions submitted to them.

Criticisms and Reforms

Over the years many criticisms have been leveled at state constitutions. People have criticized them for being too long and too full of needless detail. Some people contend that state constitutions contain too many provisions that should exist as state law. Others have suggested that the states should adopt brief, general, and flexible constitutions. One frequent suggestion is that state constitutions should be more like the national Constitution. Can old constitutions be replaced? What are the procedures by which new state constitutions might be enacted?

Constitutional Convention In order to replace existing state constitutions, most states require a constitutional convention. In a few states, a special commission may also draft a new constitution that must be reviewed by the state legislature, followed by ratification by the people.

In every state the process of calling a constitutional convention begins when the state legislature proposes the convention, which is usually put to the voters for approval. If the people agree, the state holds an election to choose delegates. The delegates may write a new constitution or suggest changes in the existing document. The proposed changes or the new consti-

tution is submitted to the voters for ratification. Between 1776 and 1990, various states held more than 230 such conventions.

Although 14 states require that a popular vote be held periodically on the question of calling a convention, the voters more recently have opposed the idea. Only five were held in the 1980s.

Although many people have called for reform, most states have kept their existing constitutions. Twenty-eight states have constitutions that are more than 100 years old. Many, including Massachusetts (1780), Wisconsin (1848), and Oregon (1857), still have their original constitutions. Recently, however, some states have adopted new constitutions: Virginia and Illinois (1970), North Carolina (1971), Montana (1972), Louisiana (1974), and Georgia (1982).

Judicial Interpretation In the 1980s the number of formal amendments and revisions to state constitutions declined. More and more state judges, however, began to interpret state constitutions independently of the United States Constitution. State judicial review was not new to the 1980s, but the increase of constitutional interpretations by state judges was a notable change. Added to the formal amendment process, judicial review has become an important means of constitutional change in the states as well as the national government. As the number of formal amendments continues to decline, judicial review affects state constitutions in the same manner it does the national Constitution.

---

1 SECTION REVIEW

Section Summary
State constitutions are the foundations of state government.

Checking For Understanding
Recalling Facts
1. Define initiative, constitutional convention, constitutional commission.
2. Compare the structure of government in state constitutions with the structure of government in the federal Constitution.
3. Explain why state constitutions are much longer than the federal Constitution.
4. List four methods of proposing state constitutional amendments.

Exploring Themes
5. Federalism What is the relationship of local governments to the state constitution?
6. Political Processes Why are state constitutions amended more frequently than the federal Constitution?

Critical Thinking Skills
7. Identifying Central Issues While states have been willing to adopt frequent amendments to their constitutions, the people have been reluctant to approve of constitutional conventions for reform. Why do you think this is so?
8. Making Generalizations Summarize the chances of a proposed amendment to a state constitution being recommended by the legislature and then ratified by popular vote.

CHAPTER 24: ORGANIZATION OF STATE GOVERNMENT 689

Meeting Objectives

Each section objective is tested by the Section Review questions that follow it in parentheses.
- Describe four important functions of state constitutions in state government. (2, 5)
- Summarize the common characteristics of state constitutions. (2, 3, 5, 6)
- Discuss the various methods states use to amend their constitutions. (4, 6, 7, 8)

Evaluate

📁 Section 1 Quiz

⬛ Testmaker

Reteach

Have students summarize the section with a State Constitution outline, using these main heads: I. What They Do, II. Characteristics, III. Methods of Amending, IV. Ratification.

Enrich

Have students research any current proposals for amending their state constitution or proposed amendments recently rejected.

Close

Ask students whether it should be easier or harder to amend state constitutions. Have them give reasons for their opinions.

Section 1 Review Answers

1. Definitions of terms appear on pages indicated: **initiative,** 688; **constitutional convention,** 688; **constitutional commission,** 688
2. They are much the same with descriptions of three branches–legislative, executive, and judicial; and with a bill of rights.

3. State constitutions contain more detail about government because political groups have used them to include provisions that favor their interests.
4. legislative proposals, initiative, constitutional convention, constitutional commission
5. State constitutions establish the types of local governments and regulate their activities.
6. State constitutions are more detailed and deal with

more immediate concerns, which means that they go out of date more easily.
7. Answers may include that people may fear major changes that would come with a new constitution, preferring to fix the old one.
8. In most cases, voters approve amendments submitted to them by state legislatures.

Focus

Choose a newspaper article that depicts a policy problem that your state or local government has faced and write the article's headline on the chalkboard. Have students restate the problem in their own words. Tell students that the first step in solving a problem is to state the problem clearly.

Teach

Have students read the Explanation steps and the example that follows it. Ask: Why is there usually more than one solution to problems facing governments? (*Problems are complex; groups offer solutions that fit their political or economic interests.*) Why do new problems emerge in the problem-solving process? (*Solutions often create another set of circumstances with problems of their own.*)

Assess

Have students complete the **Practice** exercise.

Close

Use the stated problem on the chalkboard, and as a class work to identify the solutions to the problem and determine what additional problems might result if each solution was implemented.

Expressing Problems Clearly

All government policies are designed to prevent potential problems or solve existing ones. Whenever you read about a specific government action, it is helpful to ask yourself, "What problem is being addressed?" Understanding the problem that underlies a policy will help you to understand why the policy is being proposed and assess the effects it is likely to have.

Explanation

To express a problem clearly, follow these steps:
- Collect available information about the policy.
- Decide what problem the policy is designed to alleviate. Ask: What problem do proponents think will be solved if this policy is adopted?
- Pinpoint exactly how the proposed policy is expected to alleviate the problem. Ask: How might this policy help?
- Determine what additional problems might be caused if this policy is implemented.

Consider, for example, the following newspaper headline:

Governor OKs Tax Hike for Highway Repairs

The problem being addressed by the government policy described in this headline is the deterioration of state highways. Further reading reveals that the state has not had enough funds for repairs during the last 10 years. The policy being proposed is a tax increase. Proponents of the increase want to use the money from the tax increase to pay for repairs to older highways. The new law places an additional tax of 5 cents per gallon on gasoline. All revenue from the tax is to be designated for repair of state highways. How might this policy help? The governor's office estimates that within 3 years the state will be able to eliminate 80 percent of the serious potholes and other deterioration to state highways and bridges. The first repairs will be made on highways that serve major metropolitan areas. As you have learned in earlier chapters of this text, there are few proposed solutions to problems that do not

arouse controversy. A good way to imagine what problems might be caused by a given solution is to think about its indirect, or "ripple" effects. Ask yourself what the likely effects of a policy will be and who may be adversely affected.

For example, with this policy it is unlikely that there will be enough money to make every needed repair. Government officials will have to make difficult choices about which highways are most in need of repair and, in each case, whether it is best to patch up existing roads or replace them. These decisions are, in part, political, and will raise controversies. Each community is likely to demand that its highways get top priority. Another consideration is that if taxes are raised to get money for highway repairs, taxpayers will have less money to spend for individual needs, so people—especially those who will not benefit from the repairs—may object to the tax increase. In addition, highway repairs usually involve disruptions in the flow of traffic. Citizens may be angry about having to spend even more time commuting to work because of lowered speed limits, fewer lanes, and time-consuming detours.

Practice

Read the headlines listed below. For each, tell what problem is being addressed, how proponents may think this policy will solve the problem, and what potential additional problems may arise if the policy is implemented.

1. *Law Requires Mental-Health and Criminal Record Checks for Gun Buyers*
2. *Governor Bans Prosecution of Native Americans Using Narcotics [Peyote] in Traditional Religious Ceremonies*
3. *Court Holds Gang Members' Families Responsible for Payment of Unpaid Fines*

Additional Practice

To practice this skill, see **Reinforcing the Skill** on page 713.

Practice Answers

1. <u>problem</u>: irresponsible/criminal use of guns; <u>solution</u>: sellers required to do background checks on purchasers; <u>potential problems</u>: constitutional challenges, delays for purchasers, bureaucratic headaches

2. <u>problem</u>: use of narcotics by Native Americans during traditional religious ceremonies; <u>solution</u>: governor prohibits prosecution of such persons; <u>potential problems</u>: Persons charged with peyote possession may claim participation in religious ceremonies.

3. <u>problem</u>: gang members fail to pay fines; <u>solution</u>: court orders families to pay fines out of their own pockets; <u>potential problems</u>: Fines may be an undue burden on poor families of gang members.

For additional practice, have students complete activity 24 in *Skill Reinforcement Activities* in the Teacher's Classroom Resources.

The Legislature: The Lawmaking Branch

Each state capital contains the offices of state government—the governor's office, the state court buildings, and many state agencies, bureaus, and commissions. Here, too, is a state capitol, housing the state legislature.

The state legislature passes laws that deal with a variety of matters, including health, crime, labor, education, and transportation. The state legislature has the power to tax and the power to spend and borrow money. Finally, the state legislature acts as a check on the power of the governor and the bureaucracy.

State legislatures are known by various names. In 19 states, the state legislature is called the general assembly. In New Hampshire and Massachusetts, the legislature is known as the general court. In North Dakota and Oregon, it is called the legislative assembly.

Almost every state has a **bicameral** state legislature: one with two houses, like the United States Congress. The upper house is always called the senate, and the lower house is usually called the house of representatives. In some states, the lower house is called the general assembly, the legislative assembly, or the general court. Nebraska has the only **unicameral**, or one-chambered, state legislature in the country.

The Road to the Legislature

The state legislature is made up of elected representatives. Members of each house are elected from legislative districts of relatively equal population.

Elections Until 1964 many state voting districts were based on area rather than population. In most

The Minnesota House of Representatives
A state legislature assembles in the capitol to deal with many issues affecting the state. **Politics** **How do a bicameral and unicameral legislature differ?**

states, for example, the state constitution made the county the basic voting district for the state senate. Because of differing rates of population growth, this system often resulted in striking differences in representation. A county with a population of 1,500 was entitled to elect one senator, as was a county with a population of 800,000.

In 1964 the Supreme Court ruled that voting districts for both houses of state legislatures had to be based on roughly equal populations. Chief Justice Earl Warren stated the Supreme Court's position in

---

SECTION PREVIEW

Objectives
After studying this section, you should be able to:
- Describe the trend toward professional state legislatures.
- Compare the structure and organization of the state

legislatures to the national Congress.
- Identify the roles of interest groups, legislators, and governors in state legislation.

Key Terms and Concepts
bicameral, unicameral

Themes in Government
- Public Policy
- Political Processes

Critical Thinking Skills
- Making Comparisons
- Drawing Conclusions

CHAPTER 24: ORGANIZATION OF STATE GOVERNMENT   691

Focus

Bell Ringer
As you take attendance, have students complete the following:
List one difference between our state legislature and the national Congress.

Motivating Activity
Discuss students' Bell Ringer statements and list them on the chalkboard. (*Differences could include its structure, name of houses, representation differences, length of terms.*) Tell students they can check the accuracy of this list as they study Section 2, which compares state legislatures and the national Congress.

Vocabulary Precheck
Call on students to read aloud the definitions of the terms and concepts from the Glossary. Then have volunteers use each term in a sentence. **LEP**

Caption Answer
bicameral—two houses, *unicameral*—one house

CONNECTIONS

History
Legislative sessions in the early years of the nation were determined by the growing season. Since many legislators were also farmers, they could not meet during peak growing months. So they met from January to March, after harvesting and before planting.

Classroom Resources for Section 2

- Guided Reading Activities
- Reproducible Lesson Plans
- Supreme Court Case Studies 30
- Primary and Secondary Source Readings 24
- Section 2 Quiz
- Testmaker
- SAT Practice Tests
- Writer's Guidebook

Teach

Guided Practice

L1 **Making Comparisons** Organize the class into two groups, one to represent Congress, the other, state legislatures. Have a volunteer from one group make a statement, such as "Our upper house is called the senate." Then have a student from the other group make a statement to show either a similarity or a difference; for example, "Our upper house is also called the senate." Have the groups alternate in presenting initial and responding statements. Statements should consider issues such as structure, pay, session length, leadership, committees, and so on. Allow students from either group to challenge the other's statements if they believe them to be in error. **LEP**

the case of *Reynolds* v. *Sims* (1964): "Legislators are elected by voters, not farms or cities or economic interests."

Leaders in urban and suburban areas strongly welcomed the Supreme Court's decision. In most states voting districts were redrawn to comply with the Court's "one person, one vote" ruling. While cities gained from voting districts based on equal population, in most states suburbs made bigger gains than cities. In highly populated states like Illinois, Michigan, New York, and New Jersey, the suburbs, which had grown rapidly in population, gained many seats in the state legislatures. In a few southern states, like Georgia and Alabama, where there had been faster urban growth and increased urban populations, cities gained more seats in the state legislatures.

Qualifications The state constitutions define the legal qualifications for state legislators. In most states a person must be a resident of the district he or she wishes to represent. To serve as a senator, a person usually must be at least 25 years old and a resident of the state for some specified time. To serve in the lower house, a person usually must be at least 21 years old and meet residency requirements.

Legal qualifications aside, the office of state legislator seems to attract certain kinds of people. Many state legislators—about 20 percent, according to one survey—are lawyers. A sizable number of state legislators also come from professions that state laws directly affect, like the real estate and insurance professions. Unlike members of the United States Congress, the great majority of state legislators work part-time and are not well paid. Therefore, they must have another job or a profession that gives them the time and the financial security to serve as legislators.

In about two-thirds of the states, legislators are paid a yearly salary of less than $20,000. California, Michigan, New York, Ohio, and Pennsylvania are the few states that pay more than $40,000 a year. In 11 states legislators are paid only when the legislature is in session. Payment ranges from $5 a day (Rhode Island) to $119 a day (Kansas).

Term of Office In most states members of the senate serve four-year terms, while members of the lower house serve two-year terms. In Alabama, Maryland, Louisiana, and Mississippi, members of both houses serve four-year terms of office.

Legislative Sessions In the past, sessions of the state legislatures were surprisingly brief. A typical state legislature might meet for one or perhaps two months and then not meet for the rest of the year. Some state legislatures met as infrequently as every other year.

Times have changed, and today the length and frequency of legislative sessions have increased. In more than three-fourths of the states, the state legislature now holds regular sessions every year. Texas is the largest of the seven states where the legislature still meets every other year. Nevertheless, most state legislatures are not full-time bodies. Unlike the United States Congress, which now meets throughout the year, about half the state legislatures meet no more than a few months of the year.

Trend Toward Professional Legislators The amount of time a legislature is in session and the salaries of the legislators affect the type of people who seek office. Traditionally, some people have argued that legislatures benefit from having a variety of people with diverse interests serving short terms in the legislature and then going back to their vocations. More recently, the complexity of issues and the increased demands for legislation have strengthened the argument for full-time or professional legislators. Just as a trend toward stronger governors has developed, a trend toward professional legislators has also developed.

The number of members who consider themselves to be full-time legislators is increasing. In a 1986 study conducted by NCSL [National Conference of State Legislatures], 11 percent of all legislators designate the legislature as their sole profession.
—RICH JONES, THE BOOK OF THE STATES, 1990-91

═══ STUDY GUIDE ═══

Themes in Government
Public Policy After 1964 states redrew voting districts according to the "one person, one vote"

ruling. **Why did urban leaders welcome the Supreme Court's decision in *Reynolds* v. *Sims* ?**

Critical Thinking Skills
Making Comparisons Compare a state legislature with the United States Congress on the basis of salaries, terms of office, and length of sessions.

Background

The humor to be found in watching a state legislature in action has been the subject of several writers. Molly Ivins, Texas political commentator, wrote, "The Texas Legislature consists of 181 people who meet for 140 days once every two years. This catastrophe has now occurred sixty-three times [as of 1975]." Former Governor Thomas Kean of New Jersey, who served in the state legislature, concurs, "The lower body of the state legislature in New Jersey is the people's house—democratic government at its coarsest and most unrestrained, unruly, unkempt, and raucous. It is sometimes chaotic but never boring."

Some states moved toward professional legislatures by making the job of legislator full-time and adequately paid. In addition, many states increased funds for staff to assist legislators. Since 1901, when Wisconsin created the first state legislative staff, the number of people working for legislators has grown significantly. In the 1980s total state legislative staff members grew from 27,000 to 33,000—a 24 percent increase across the nation. Most state governments today provide legislators with research assistance and help in drafting bills.

How efficient have professional legislatures been? People expected that legislators who served full-time, were well paid, and had large well-trained staffs would become efficient at passing good laws. California became the model for the nation after the state decided in the 1960s to encourage a professional legislature with high pay and large, full-time staffs. While California's legislature responded with intense year-round activity, recent results have not been as positive as people expected. One result was a change in the motivations of people who ran for office. Dan Walters of the *Sacramento Bee* explained:

> *The new people ran for office on the assumption it was a career. It changed the psychological focus, from practicing politics to the end of making policy, to using policy as the end for politics.*
> —DAN WALTERS, 1991

Analysts of the legislature found that the lawmakers' concern for protecting their political careers

State Legislatures

State	Limitations on Length of Sessions[*]	Upper House Members	Upper House Term	Lower House Members	Lower House Term
Alabama	30 L days	35	4	105	4
Alaska	120 C days	20	4	40	2
Arizona	None	30	2	60	2
Arkansas	60 C days	35	4	100	2
California	None	40	4	80	2
Colorado	140 C days	35	4	65	2
Connecticut	5 months[c]	36	2	151	2
Delaware	June 30	21	4	41	2
Florida	60 C days	40	4	120	2
Georgia	40 L days	56	2	180	2
Hawaii	60 L days	25	4	51	2
Idaho	None	35	2	84	2
Illinois	None	59	4	118	2
Indiana	61 L days, 30 L days	50	4	100	2
Iowa	None	50	4	100	2
Kansas	None, 90 C days	40	4	125	2
Kentucky	60 L days	38	4	100	2
Louisiana	60 L days	39	4	105	4
Maine	100 L	35	2	151	2
Maryland	90 C days	47	4	141	4
Massachusetts	None	40	2	160	2
Michigan	None	38	4	110	2
Minnesota	120 L days	67	4	134	2
Mississippi	90 C days[d]	52	4	122	4
Missouri	6 months[c]	34	4	163	2
Montana	90 L days	50	4	100	2
Nebraska	90 L days, 60 L days	49	4	—	—
Nevada	60 C days[a]	21	4	42	2
New Hampshire	45 L days	24	2	400	2
New Jersey	None	40	4	80	2
New Mexico	60 C days, 30 C days[b]	42	4	70	2
New York	None	61	2	150	2
North Carolina	None	50	2	120	2
North Dakota	80 L days	49	4	98	2
Ohio	None	33	4	99	2
Oklahoma	90 L days	48	4	101	2
Oregon	None	30	4	60	2
Pennsylvania	None	50	4	203	2
Rhode Island	60 L days[a]	50	2	100	2
South Carolina	5 months[c]	46	4	124	2
South Dakota	40L days, 35 L days	35	2	70	2
Tennessee	90 L days[a]	33	4	99	2
Texas	140 C days	31	4	150	2
Utah	45 C days	29	4	75	2
Vermont	None	30	2	150	2
Virginia	30 C days, 60 C days	40	4	100	2
Washington	105 C days, 60 C days	49	4	98	2
West Virginia	60 C days	34	4	100	2
Wisconsin	None	33	4	99	2
Wyoming	40 L days, 20 L days[b]	30	4	60	2

*L=legislative (in-session) days; C=calendar days
[a]Indirect limit; legislators' pay and/or expenses cease, but session may continue.
[b]Annual session every other year is budget session, held in even-numbered years.
[c]Approximate length. In Connecticut, session must adjourn by the Wednesday after first Monday in June (odd years) and May (even years); in Missouri, session must adjourn by June 30 in odd-numbered years and by May 15 in even-numbered years; in South Carolina, first Thursday in June.
[d]Except 125 days every fourth year (the first year of a new gubernatorial term).

Sources: State constitutions and statutes, and information furnished by appropriate State officials and Council of State Governments.

✔ **Chart Study**
Each state varies widely in the length of session and number of house members. **Which states, those with longer or shorter legislative sessions, have more efficient legislatures?**

L2 Political Processes Work with students to develop a concept map on the chalkboard of the process of a bill becoming a law through a state legislature. The map should include the ways a bill may be written and introduced, the path the bill takes through the legislature after introduction, and the governor's role in the process.

After the map is completed, have volunteers explain in detail what happens at each step.

L3 Debate Have students debate the following:

The people of a state would benefit if they had full-time legislators.

Chart Study Answer
There generally seems to be little difference. Though the trend is toward longer sessions and full-time legislators, results have been disappointing.

Independent Practice

L1 Informative Writing Have students obtain and report the following information about their state: number of legislators in each house, major committees in each house, names of legislators from students' districts and their committee assignments. **LEP**

Cooperative Learning Activity

Organize students into groups of three or four. Assign each group the task of investigating the activities of one of the committees in the state legislature. Encourage students to pick areas that are important to them personally or to the area in which they live. Have a student from each group take on one specific task, such as researching, talking with legislators, report-writing, or presenting. Have a spokesperson for each group present a five-minute report. After each group's presentation allow time for class discussion.

L2 Persuasive Writing Tell students that supporters of the one-house system of the state of Nebraska say it is a much more efficient form of government than the bicameral system, and saves money, too. Do students agree or disagree? Have them write a brief letter to the editor either for or against the unicameral legislative system in state government.

Analyzing Supreme Court Cases Assign case 30, *Reynolds* v. *Sims*, (1964), in *Supreme Court Case Studies* in the Teacher's Classroom Resources.

STUDY GUIDE

Theme Answer
Lawmakers avoided difficult issues because they were concerned about reelection and about protecting their political careers.

Critical Thinking Answer
Lobbyists might develop stronger influence through lasting personal contacts with more permanent legislators. Part-time legislators might be more independent.

---

caused them to avoid the more difficult issues that California needed to resolve. In addition, special interests began to deadlock legislative procedures with heavy lobbying. California's disappointed voters passed Proposition 140 in 1990, cutting lawmakers pensions and staffs—the first setback for the national trend toward professional state legislatures.

Organization of Legislatures

Most state legislatures are organized like the United States Congress, with various kinds of leaders and regular procedures for handling legislation.

Size One might expect that the size and population of a state would determine the size of its legislature. Generally, however, such is not the case. A large and populous state like California has 80 members in its lower house, while much smaller Vermont has 150. New Hampshire, another relatively small state, has 400 members in its lower house.

On the average, membership in the lower house of a state legislature is about 100. State senates, on the other hand, average only about 40 members.

Leadership All state legislatures have presiding officers. In the lower house, the presiding officer is called the speaker of the house. This position is very similar to that of the speaker of the national House of Representatives. House members elect the speaker. In practice, the political party with the majority in the lower house usually chooses the speaker.

The speaker can influence and sometimes control many of the activities of the lower house. The speaker can select who may speak during house debates and interpret house rules. Most important, the speaker has a power that the speaker of the House of Representatives no longer has. In almost all state legislatures, the speaker can appoint the chairpersons along with all other members of house committees. In Alaska, Hawaii, and Kentucky, however, the speaker is denied this power.

In 27 states the presiding officer of the upper house is the lieutenant governor. He or she serves very much like the Vice President of the United States, who presides over the Senate of the United States Congress. In those states that do not have a lieutenant governor, senators usually elect the presiding officer of the senate.

Where the lieutenant governor serves as presiding officer of the senate, the position usually has limited power. The lieutenant governor, like the Vice President, is not really part of the legislative branch. Therefore, the lieutenant governor does not take part in legislative debates and votes only in case of a tie. He or she can recognize who may speak and in some states has limited power over senate rules and committee appointments. In those states without a lieutenant governor, the senate president usually has considerable power.

The Committee System Just as in Congress, committees conduct much of the work of the state legislature. Because most state legislatures have fairly large memberships, full participation by the members on every issue would be inefficient, if not impossible. Also, the full legislature simply cannot handle all the legislative work. In most state legislatures, more than 1,000 bills are introduced each session.

A typical state legislature has more than 30 standing, or permanent, committees. A typical state legislator may serve on three or four standing committees. Normally, a legislative committee for each of the following legislative areas exists: labor, education, highways, appropriations, and welfare. Although state legislative committees are not as powerful as committees in Congress, they still play an important role in processing legislation.

The Course of Legislation

State legislatures are very similar to Congress with respect to the lawmaking process. Bills must go through a number of steps before they become state law.

STUDY GUIDE

**Themes in Government
Political Processes** What were some of the negative effects of higher pay and full-time staffs for legislators on the legislative process in California?

**Critical Thinking Skills
Drawing Conclusions**
One effect of the development of professional legislatures was the increased power of lobbyists. **Why** might lobbyists have more influence with professional legislators than with part-time legislators?

Special Needs Strategy

Learning Problems Metalinguistic awareness is the ability to make conscious judgments about language. Many students need help recognizing when they are apt to have difficulties with the language of their textbooks. Ask them to read aloud the subsection, "Trend Toward Professional Legislators" and list those words they did not know and those they knew but had trouble pronouncing. Discuss students' lists and explain how the text's Glossary and a dictionary can help students.

Writing a Bill A member of the state legislature introduces each bill. The legislator who introduces a bill, however, often is not the person who actually wrote the bill. Many legislative bills actually originate in the departments and agencies within the executive branch of state government. For example, someone in the state's department of insurance may write a bill dealing with changes in car insurance rates. Many bills also come out of the governor's office. These bills may be included in messages that the governor sends the legislature.

Interest groups such as labor unions, business organizations, or even an association of bird-watchers may propose a bill. Such groups spend much time, effort, and money lobbying lawmakers to legislate in their favor. An interest group may write a bill and submit it to a sympathetic state legislator, who then introduces the bill to the state legislature. Interest groups are a major source of bills submitted in each session. These groups may also provide experts to testify for the bill in committee hearings.

Many bills are products of the legislators' own ideas and experience, but legislators get assistance in the writing and research that goes into preparing a bill. Most state governments now have a legislative reference service, an agency that provides assistance in drafting bills to members of the legislature.

Other important sources of proposed legislation also exist. Units of local government, like a county or a special district, may submit a bill to the state legislature. Any citizen can send a bill to a state legislator in hopes that it will receive consideration.

The Path of a Bill

Lower House

Introducing Member	Chief Clerk	Speaker of the House	House Standing Committee	Committee on Rules & Order
① Read first time by title	② For filing	③ Referred to Standing Committee	④ Considered by appropriate Standing Committee	
⑤ Reading and record of committee report				⑥ Considered by appropriate Standing Committee
⑦ Read second time section by section				⑧ To be placed on calendar for third reading
⑨ Third reading and final passage	⑩ Certification			
	⑰ Enrolled		⑱ Enrolling Committee	
		⑲ Signed in open session		

Upper House

Secretary of Senate	President of Senate	Senate Standing Committee	Rules and Joint Rules Committees
⑪ Read first and second times	⑫ Referred to Senate Standing Committe	⑬ Reading and record of committee report	⑭ To be placed on the calendar for third reading
⑮ Third reading section by section and final passage	⑯ Certification		
⑳ Signed in open session			

Executive

Governor	Secretary of State
㉑ Original signed if approved.	㉒ Gives bill chapter number in session laws, bill permanently filed.

✓ Chart Study
In most states, the third reading, step nine, is the point at which a bill's fate is sealed by a vote of the chamber. **At which step along the path of a bill does the system of checks and balances come into play?**

Critical Thinking Activity

Drawing Conclusions Have students consider the ethical issues involved in having legislators who are also full-time professionals in areas such as insurance or real estate. What conflicts of interest might develop? What policies might students institute to prevent corruption in lawmaking based on this situation? *(Suggested answer: Legislators involved in areas being considered for legislation would not be permitted to take part, either as advisers or as voters.)*

📁 **Interpreting Source Readings** Have students complete activity 24 in *Primary and Secondary Source Readings* in the Teacher's Classroom Resources.

L3 Political Processes Have students contact their state legislature for information about its pay scale, session frequency and length, tenure of members, and members' occupations and staff size. Have them use this data to evaluate if the legislature is a professional legislature.

Chart Study Answer
at step 21, when it goes to the governor for signing

Assess

Check for Understanding

Have students complete Section 2 Review on page 696.

Meeting Objectives

Each section objective is tested by the Section Review questions that follow it in parentheses.
• Describe the trend toward professional state legislatures. (6, 8)
• Compare the structure and organization of state legislatures to the national Congress. (3, 4, 7)
• Identify the roles of interest groups, legislators, and governors in state legislation. (4, 5, 7)

Evaluate

📁 Section 2 Quiz

⊡ Testmaker

Reteach

Have students work in pairs to make a chart that compares their state legislature with the national Congress.

Enrich

Have students research the changes made in their state legislature as a result of the *Reynolds* v. *Sims* decision in 1964. Have them note whether changes were made primarily in the upper house, lower house, in both houses, or if little change was needed at all. Maps could be prepared to show the differences.

Close

Ask students whether they agree with the concept of professional legislators and to explain why or why not.

Have students check the accuracy of the statements they made for the Bell Ringer. What statements would they change?

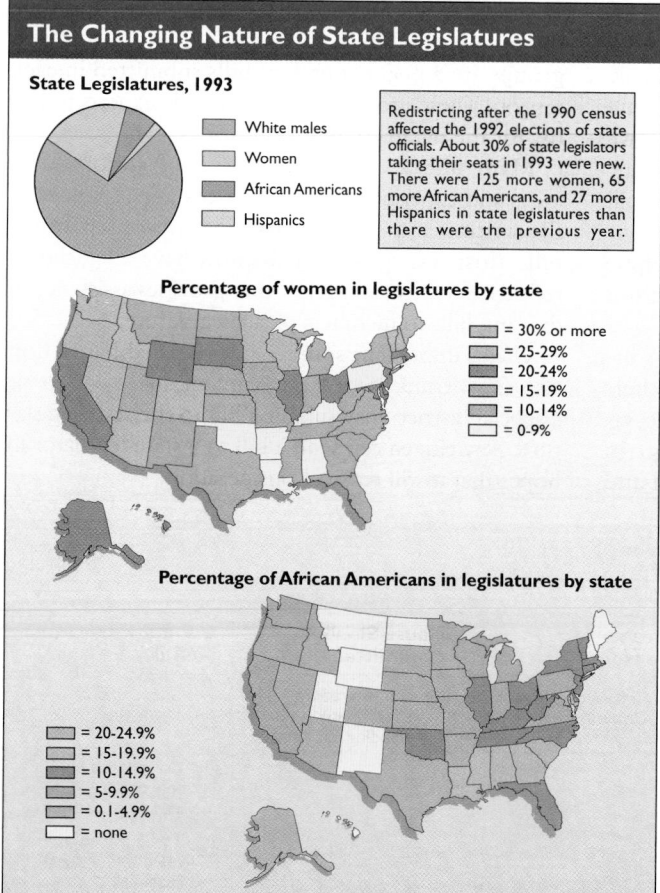

The Changing Nature of State Legislatures

State Legislatures, 1993

- White males
- Women
- African Americans
- Hispanics

Redistricting after the 1990 census affected the 1992 elections of state officials. About 30% of state legislators taking their seats in 1993 were new. There were 125 more women, 65 more African Americans, and 27 more Hispanics in state legislatures than there were the previous year.

Percentage of women in legislatures by state

- = 30% or more
- = 25-29%
- = 20-24%
- = 15-19%
- = 10-14%
- = 0-9%

Percentage of African Americans in legislatures by state

- = 20-24.9%
- = 15-19.9%
- = 10-14.9%
- = 5-9.9%
- = 0.1-4.9%
- = none

The Path of a Bill A legislator or a group of legislators may introduce a bill in either house of the state

legislature. The bill may then follow a rapid and direct path toward a final vote, or a path that is full of obstacles. The speaker of the house and the presiding officer of the senate have considerable power over the progress of a bill. The support of the legislative leadership can usually ensure a bill's passage.

The presiding officer of the state legislature sends the bill to a committee that specializes in the subject matter of the bill. The committee discusses the bill and may hold public hearings. It may rewrite the bill or modify it. Following this review, the committee will send the bill back to the full house along with its recommendation that the bill be passed or not passed.

Once a bill is on the agenda of the full house, it is ready for discussion and vote. If one house passes a bill, it must go through a similar process in the other house. Sometimes, the second house changes a bill it has received from the other house. In this case the legislature creates a conference committee from both houses to resolve the differences. Both houses then must vote on the bill the conference committee produces.

Because the path is long and treacherous, many bills never reach a final vote. If passed, bills go to the governor for signature or veto. Of the bills that are introduced, less than one-fourth become laws.

---

2 SECTION REVIEW

Section Summary
The state legislature, with the help of the executive branch and other groups, passes laws for the state.

Checking For Understanding
Recalling Facts
1. Define bicameral, unicameral.
2. Identify the groups within states that benefited from the Supreme Court's decision in *Reynolds* v. *Sims*.
3. Discuss trends in the length of legislative sessions and in the use of legislative staff.
4. Summarize the similarities in leadership between the state legislatures and the Congress of the United States.

Exploring Themes
5. Public Policy Why do you think members of the executive branch agencies often write bills that are introduced in the state legislature?
6. Political Processes What changes in state laws led to professional legislatures in some states?

Critical Thinking Skills
7. Making Comparisons How is the path a bill takes to become a law similar in a state legislature and the national Congress?
8. Drawing Conclusions Do the advantages of a professional legislature outweigh its disadvantages? Explain your answer.

Section 2 Review Answers

1. Definitions of terms appear on pages indicated: **bicameral,** 691; **unicameral,** 691

2. urban and suburban people

3. Sessions are becoming longer and are held every year. Many states have added to legislative staffs as the work of the legislatures has grown.

4. In both lower houses the presiding officer is called the speaker of the house. The duties of the lieutenant governor in the upper house are much like those of the Vice President in the Senate.

5. Answers should include that members of executive agencies are often close to problems that call for legislation.

6. making the job full-time, well-paid, and providing legislators large staffs

7. In both cases the bill is introduced by legislators, sent to a committee, reported back to the house, passed by both houses, and signed by the chief executive. Also, a conference committee may resolve differences between the two houses, if necessary, and the legislature may pass a bill over an executive veto by two-thirds majority vote in both houses.

8. Professional legislatures have more experienced members with better staffs, enabling them to deal with a greater volume of work. On the other hand, professional legislators may become too closely tied to special-interest groups in an attempt to win reelection.

The Governor: The Executive Branch

Every state has an executive branch of government headed by a governor. The governor is usually the most visible and well-known person in state government.

Like the office of President, the office of governor has generally become more powerful in recent years. The roles of governors are almost the same in every state. Because of the great differences in the area and population of states, however, a vast difference in the power and influence of the 50 governors exists.

Becoming a Governor

As the best-known person in state government, the governor is often visible throughout the nation as well as the state. Some governors have used their office as a stepping-stone to the presidency. Seven Presidents in the twentieth century were once governors: William McKinley, Theodore Roosevelt, Woodrow Wilson, Calvin Coolidge, Franklin D. Roosevelt, Jimmy Carter, and Ronald Reagan. The position of state governor is an attractive one, and competition for the office is usually heavy. The road to the governor's office, however, is not easy.

Qualifications State constitutions spell out the few legal or formal qualifications for becoming governor. In most states a governor must be at least 30 years old, an American citizen, and a state resident for 5 or more years. Citizenship and residency requirements vary widely. Mississippi and New Jersey require that a governor be a United States citizen for 20 years. Missouri requires that its governor be a state resident for 10 years. In addition to these legal qualifications,

however, a person must meet certain political qualifications to attain the governor's office. Experience in government is important. Most governors, for example, have served in state and local government before running for governor. Many have served as state lieutenant governor or state attorney general. One-half of the governors elected in recent years were lawyers. In addition, most successful candidates for governor have a broad political base. A candidate's **political base** is the popularity and support he or she has among certain groups and sections of the state. For example, in an agricultural state, support from farmers

Stepping-stone
Calvin Coolidge was a state governor before he became President. **Political Process** How can the state governorship be a stepping-stone to the presidency?

Focus

Bell Ringer
As you take attendance, have students list duties of a governor that are similar to those of the President of the United States.

Motivating Activity
List students' Bell Ringer responses on the chalkboard and discuss. Ask what similar activities of the governor and President students have seen on television. Tell students that Section 3 compares the state executive branch with the national executive branch.

Vocabulary Precheck
List the terms and concepts on the chalkboard. Have students develop questions for which each term or concept is an answer.
`LEP`

Caption Answer
Governors have national visibility.

CONNECTIONS

Biography
The first woman governor was Nellie Tayloe Ross of Wyoming, elected in 1924 to fill her husband's unexpired term. The first woman to hold a state governorship without being preceded by her husband was Ella Grasso, who served as governor of Connecticut from 1975 to 1981. Virginia's Douglas Wilder, elected in 1989, was the nation's first African American elected governor.

SECTION PREVIEW

Objectives
After studying this section, you should be able to:
■ Define five roles of governors.
■ Discuss the development of the power of the governor's office.

■ Compare the state executive branch with the national executive branch.

Key Terms and Concepts
political base, party primary, plurality, item veto

Themes in Government
■ Public Policy
■ Constitutional Interpretations

Critical Thinking Skills
■ Formulating Questions
■ Making Comparisons

CHAPTER 24: ORGANIZATION OF STATE GOVERNMENT 697

Classroom Resources for Section 3

📁 Guided Reading Activities
📁 Reproducible Lesson Plans
📁 Section 3 Quiz
💠 Testmaker

⛳ Chapter Transparencies 24
SAT Practice Tests
Writer's Guidebook

GLENCOE TECHNOLOGY

Focus on Government
Video 48
**Making Connections:
From Governor to President**
Running Time: 1:50
Videodisc 3, Chap. 48
VHS Tape 3, Begins 24:28

Teach

Guided Practice

L1 **Political Processes** Write the governor's roles on the chalkboard: *Chief Executive, Chief Legislator, Party Leader, State Spokesperson, Public Relations Figure.* Then have volunteers stand and identify an activity the governor performs in each role. For instance, a student representing the governor's role as party leader might say, "I support and campaign for candidates of my party at public functions." **LEP**

Images of Government

Ask students to list the special features of their state—places of natural beauty or historic interest, museums, sports teams, and so on—that might attract tourists. Have students write advertising slogans that include these features.

Answers

1. Tourist dollars and taxes levied on tourism bring revenue to the state. Investment in the state can also create jobs for state residents.
2. The governor of the state often serves as a spokesperson for the state in efforts to attract investment. Television commercials and professional sports teams are two things that attract tourists to a state.

---

is a vital part of a candidate's political base. Finally, successful candidates for governor usually have influence in a major political party.

Election In most states the process for electing a governor has two steps. First, an individual must gain the nomination of a major political party, usually by winning a nominating election, called a **party primary**. In a party primary, which is usually held several months before the general election, voters choose from among several candidates who are seeking their party's nomination. Only three states—Connecticut, Utah, and Virginia—still use the older convention method to nominate candidates for governor. Once chosen, the party nominee then moves on to the second step, the general election.

In most states the candidate who wins a plurality vote is elected governor. A **plurality** is the largest number of votes in an election. In five states, however, a majority is required for election. In Arizona, Georgia, and Louisiana, if no one receives a majority, a run-off election is held between the two candidates who receive the most votes in the general election. In Mississippi the lower house of the state legislature chooses the governor if no candidate obtains a majority in the general election. In Vermont the house and senate choose.

Term of Office Most governors serve for a four-year term. In three states—Rhode Island, Vermont, and New Hampshire—the term of office is only two years.

Many states also limit the number of terms a governor may serve in office. Twenty-four states have a two-term limit. Kentucky, Mississippi, and Virginia forbid their governors successive terms in office.

IMAGES OF GOVERNMENT

▼ States often produce and distribute attractive, informative guides and other printed materials that sing the praises of each state's history, economy, landscape, and culture.

State Invitations

All fifty states spend a great deal of money and energy to entice visitors and investors to come to their state. Dollars from tourism and new business investment translate into jobs and increased revenues for the state.

698 Unit 8: State Government

Background

A present-day governor would find little to recognize in comparing his or her duties and powers with those of a counterpart 200 years ago. Early governors were defined more by what they could not do than by what they could. A figurehead at best, an early state governor had little if any executive, political, or veto power. Legislatures elected the chief executive, made important political appointments, and generally passed on everything the governor did.

Salary The average salary of the 50 state governors is about $80,000 a year. Salaries range from $130,000 in New York to $53,000 in Montana. Most states also pay a governor's official expenses and provide state vehicles for transportation. In addition, 45 states provide an official residence for the governor.

The Roles of the Governor

Like the President of the United States, the governor of a state performs several important functions. The governor's activities range from proposing and signing legislation to visiting foreign countries to seek business for the state.

Chief Executive The executive branch of state government carries out laws the state legislature passes.

The governor's responsibilities may include budgeting, appointing officials, planning for economic growth, and coordinating the work of executive departments. The amount of control that a governor has over the executive branch varies widely from state to state.

The governor is responsible for the executive branch. He or she must try to coordinate state policies and work out disputes between different agencies and departments. Because citizens view the governor as the head of the executive branch, they may blame the governor for any scandal or inefficiency that occurs within the administration.

Chief Legislator People in most states look to the governor for leadership. Therefore, the governor is expected to play an important legislative role. Theodore Roosevelt, who served as governor of New

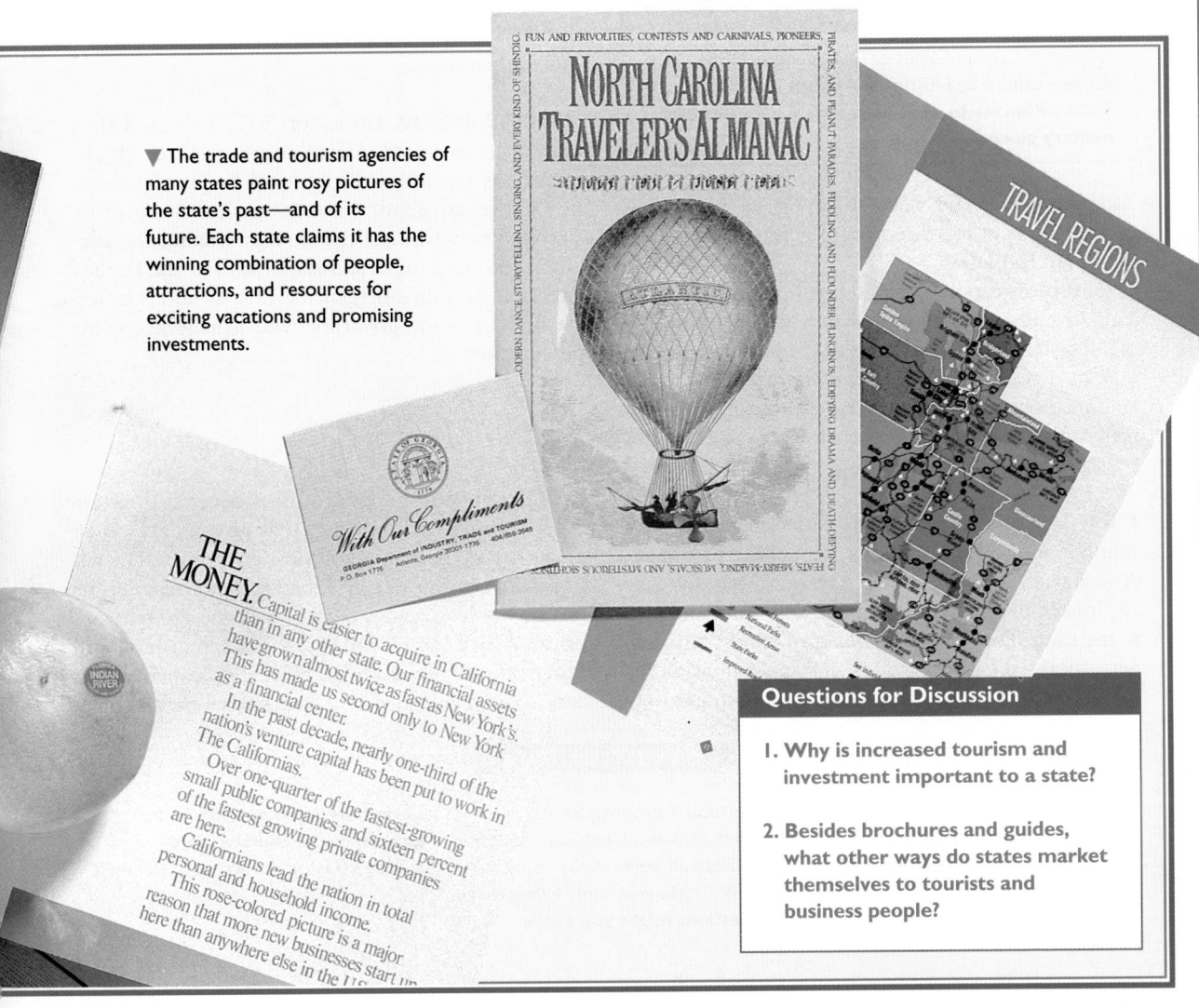

▼ The trade and tourism agencies of many states paint rosy pictures of the state's past—and of its future. Each state claims it has the winning combination of people, attractions, and resources for exciting vacations and promising investments.

NORTH CAROLINA TRAVELER'S ALMANAC

TRAVEL REGIONS

THE MONEY. Capital is easier to acquire in California than in any other state. Our financial assets have grown almost twice as fast as New York's. This has made us second only to New York as a financial center.

In the past decade, nearly one-third of the nation's venture capital has been put to work in The Californias.

Over one-quarter of the fastest-growing small public companies and sixteen percent of the fastest growing private companies are here.

Californians lead the nation in total personal and household income. This rose-colored picture is a major reason that more new businesses start up here than anywhere else in the U.S.

Questions for Discussion

1. Why is increased tourism and investment important to a state?

2. Besides brochures and guides, what other ways do states market themselves to tourists and business people?

CHAPTER 24: ORGANIZATION OF STATE GOVERNMENT **699**

Cooperative Learning Activity

Organize the class into groups of six to discuss how to improve the quality of life for people in their state. Assign students in each group the following roles: governor, lieutenant governor, secretary of state, attorney general, state treasurer, and a reporter. Each of the "officials" is to identify their goals for the state and tell how they, in their official position, could help realize these goals. The reporter should take notes on the discussion and report the group's ideas to the class.

CONNECTIONS

Political Processes
In a recent year, there were more than 200 separately elected state administrative officials other than the governor in the 50 states. More than 10 state officials are separately elected in Georgia, Kentucky, North Carolina, South Carolina, and North Dakota. However, in Maine, New Hampshire, and New Jersey only the governor is elected statewide.

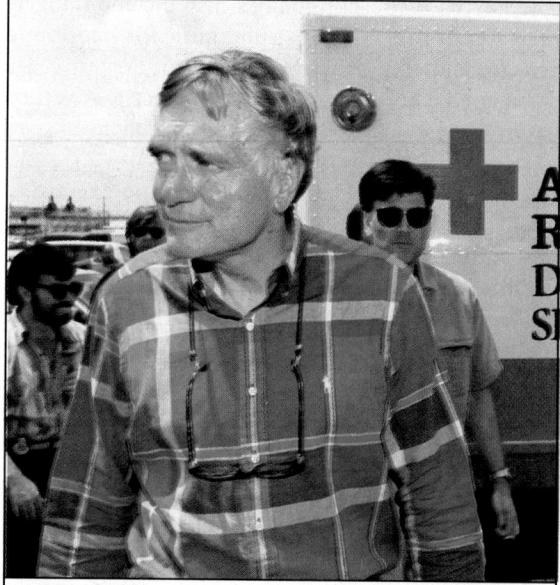

Prepared for Emergencies
Governor Lawton Chiles of Florida inspects the damage caused by Hurricane Andrew in 1992.
Public Policies In what ways may a governor use military power?

York State, once said, "More than half of my work as governor was in the direction of getting needed and important legislation."

Governors can have significant influence over the legislative process, although they have only a few formal legislative powers. The governor has an advantage over state legislators, who are often underpaid and inexperienced. The governor also can appeal directly to the people of the state to support a piece of legislation.

Party Leader Almost all governors gain office after running on the Democratic or Republican party ticket in a state. After becoming governor, they are usually looked upon as the leader and voice of their party in the state. The governor attends political-party dinners, speaks at party functions, and may campaign for party candidates in local elections. In addition, gover-

nors participate in events like the Democratic or Republican Governors' Conference, which is an annual meeting of governors from the same party.

In practice, however, the governor's power over his or her political party may not always be strong. The governor, for example, may not have much influence over party nominations to other state and local offices. Also, when a governor loses popularity, he or she usually loses influence within the political party.

Spokesperson for the State The governor may speak for the state in a number of situations. Frequently governors attempt to negotiate grants from the national government in such areas as aid to schools, urban aid, or highway construction. Governors may also represent their states in seeking cooperation from other states in such areas as transportation and pollution control. More recently, governors have even represented their states internationally as they have tried to encourage foreign businesses to locate in their states.

Public Relations Governors have increased their efforts to promote their programs through the media. As the state official most frequently in the news, the governor influences public opinion. Through newspapers, television, and radio, the governor can bring important state issues to the public's attention. During emergencies, such as floods or forest fires, it is the governor who usually keeps the public informed.

The Powers of the Governor

Is the governor a kind of President on the state level? Actually, the President's powers are much greater than the powers of most governors. The national Constitution makes the President responsible for the whole executive branch, with the ability to appoint White House aides, cabinet members, and other officials. In contrast, most state constitutions have created a divided executive branch that is some-

Special Needs Strategy

Learning Problems Students with learning problems often have more trouble than their peers in areas of morphology, such as the proper use of plurals, possessives, and tenses. They are less able to manipulate the structures of language. In order to give them practice in morphology, ask them to rewrite the first paragraph in "Becoming a Gover-

nor" in the past tense. Were they able to keep all the tenses in the paragraph in the same relationship, that is, "is" to "was," "have used" to "had used," and so on? After their individual attempts, put the paragraph on an overhead or on the chalkboard with blanks for the verbs and ask them to fill in the blanks as a group.

Powers and Duties of the Governor

Carries out state laws and supervises the executive branch	Reports to the legislature on the state of the state	Approves or vetoes all bills or parts of bills passed by the legislature
May pardon persons found guilty of state crimes	Proposes new laws and programs to the legislature	May call special sessions of the legislature
Appoints and may remove some state officials	Prepares the state budget for the approval of the legislature	Represents the state at ceremonies and public functions

Chart Study
A governor is the chief executive of a state. **How do the duties of a governor include executive, legislative, and judicial powers?**

Chart Study Answer
executive by virtue of the office; legislative in proposing and signing legislation; judicial because of the pardon power

Independent Practice

L1 **Media** Have students keep track of their governor's activities as reported in the media by clipping newspaper articles or watching local television news and making notes of items which concern the governor or the state executive branch. When students have collected enough items, have them classify them according to the governor's roles and powers identified in the text. **LEP**

L2 **Persuasive Writing** Have students write a paragraph that supports or disputes the following statement:

I would be more confident with a governor who is obviously interested in the presidency than one who is only interested in governing the state.

times difficult for a governor to administer. The national Constitution is also very general and has placed few specific restrictions on presidential power. Most state constitutions, on the other hand, have been very specific about what a governor may and may not do.

Limitations on governors' powers have historic origins. The office of governor, in a sense, was born weak. Because of their bad experience as colonies with royal governors, the early states limited the powers of their governors. This practice continued through the nation's history, as most state constitutions severely restricted the governor's powers. Until 1965 most governors had short terms of office, a one-term limit on their service, and weak executive powers. During his term as governor of Pennsylvania, William W. Scranton stated:

Hardly a day has passed when the attorney-general or someone else has not told me of some constitutional restriction on proposed or needed action.

—WILLIAM W. SCRANTON

Managing the Executive Branch The governor's executive powers include two basic components: the power to carry out the law and the power to supervise the executive branch of state government. The governor's ability to carry out the law depends on cooperation from the rest of the executive branch. In

seeking cooperation governors sometimes run into roadblocks.

The constitutions of many states have created a divided executive branch, making many executive officials politically and legally independent of each other. In more than half the states, for example, the people elect the governor, the lieutenant governor, the attorney general, and the secretary of state. In addition, they often serve for different terms of office and have specific and separate responsibilities that the state constitution defines.

Thus, state executive branches are often made up of officials from different political parties who have different ideas and conflicting political ambitions. Cooperation is often difficult, leaving the governor limited control over the executive branch.

Some states, like Tennessee and New Jersey, give the governor considerable control over the executive branch. The constitutions of these states have created an executive branch with only one elected official or only a few such officials. The governor in these states has the power to appoint many department and agency heads, giving him or her more control over the executive branch. This concentration of power enables the governor to coordinate policies and execute the law more effectively than those without such powers.

Even with this power, however, governors may run into problems. Some states have hundreds of state agencies. Even with strong appointive powers, some

CHAPTER 24: ORGANIZATION OF STATE GOVERNMENT 701

CONNECTIONS

History
A governor's record can be a great help to candidates considering a move from statehouse to White House–but it also can be a hindrance. In 1976, for example, Georgia governor Jimmy Carter parlayed his state's economic renaissance into a successful bid for the presidency. But in 1988 George Bush blamed his opponent, Massachusetts governor Michael Dukakis, for the state's high taxes and environmental problems. This tactic helped Bush defeat Dukakis in the election.

Critical Thinking Activity

Formulating Questions Have students imagine they are news reporters who are interviewing a candidate for governor or any other state executive position. What kinds of questions might they ask to find out the person's qualifications for the office? What areas should the questions address? What

areas should reporters avoid? *(Suggested answer: Questions should focus on political principles, relevant experience, goals for the state and office, and so on. Questions of a personal nature, for the most part, should be avoided.)*

L3 Political Cartoons Have students create political cartoons of a governor engaging in an activity that illustrates his or her roles or powers. For example, they might create a cartoon that shows the governor's "editing" a piece of legislation with his or her veto power.

Chart Study Answer
It gives the governor more control over them than if they were elected.

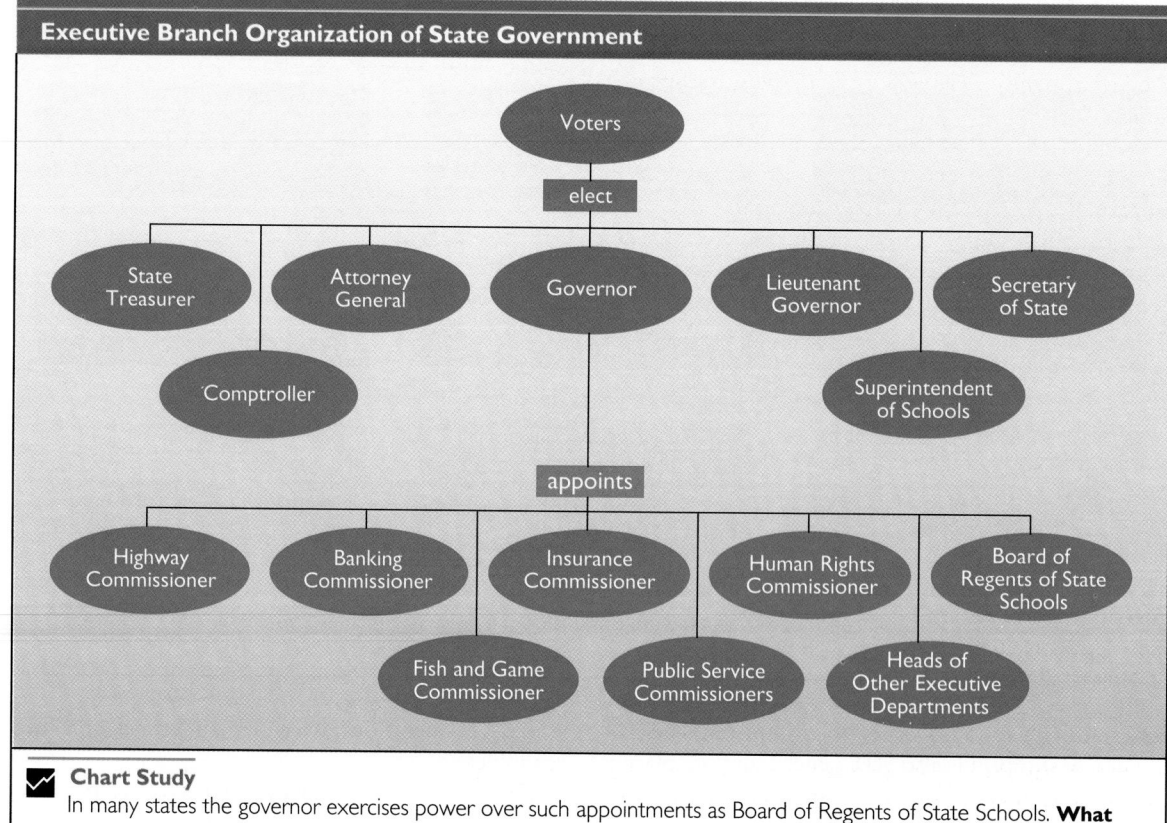

Executive Branch Organization of State Government

Voters → elect → State Treasurer, Attorney General, Governor, Lieutenant Governor, Secretary of State; Comptroller; Superintendent of Schools

Governor → appoints → Highway Commissioner, Banking Commissioner, Insurance Commissioner, Human Rights Commissioner, Board of Regents of State Schools, Fish and Game Commissioner, Public Service Commissioners, Heads of Other Executive Departments

✓ **Chart Study**
In many states the governor exercises power over such appointments as Board of Regents of State Schools. **What kind of political impact does this have on how these and other appointed officials make decisions?**

governors find it impossible to administer so many agencies.

Most governors also have significant budgetary powers. In all but eight states, the governor has full responsibility for preparing the state budget. Once prepared, this budget will be submitted to the state legislature for approval. The power to make up the budget allows a governor to push certain programs and policies. For example, a governor who wants more prisons built in a state will probably propose a very substantial budget for the state department of corrections.

All governors can exercise military powers through their role as commander in chief of the state National Guard. The National Guard can be used in a national emergency, such as a war, if the President calls it into action. Normally, however, the National Guard serves as a state militia, under the governor's control. State constitutions allow the governor to use the National Guard to maintain law and order in case of floods, riots, dangers to public health, and other state emergencies.

Executive Reform Since 1965 more than half the states have reformed their constitutions to give the governor greater executive power. In addition to lengthening the governor's term of office, many states have provided that the lieutenant governor

━━━━━ STUDY GUIDE ━━━━━

Themes in Government
Constitutional Interpretations
Why did many state constitutions provide for a divided executive branch? How did they do this?

Public Policy Because the governor is a full-time official with control over many state agencies, preparation of the state budget naturally falls to the governor's

office. **How does influence over the budget extend the governor's power over other legislation?**

Background

Taxpayers understandably want to get as much as they can for their money. A 1990 survey of governors' salaries showed that California taxpayers receive the most service for their money. For every dollar of the governor's $85,000 salary, 341 Californians are governed. Texas is next, with 181 taxpayers for each governor's salary dollar. Ohio (167), Pennsylvania (141), and New York (138) follow. Constituents in Alaska and Wyoming probably love their wide open spaces, but they get considerably less for their governors' salaries—only 6½ people are governed per dollar in Alaska and 6¾ in Wyoming.

must run on a joint ticket with the governor. This procedure helps assure that the second highest executive department official will support the governor on issues.

Other changes that have strengthened the governor's executive powers include giving the governor more control over appointments to departments and agencies. In some states the executive branch has been reorganized by combining and eliminating a number of state agencies. In Georgia more than 253 state agencies were combined to create 22 major agencies.

Legislative Powers As does the President, a governor has legislative power without being part of the legislative branch. A governor can propose legislation to the state legislature. He or she can send legislative messages to the state legislature and can present new programs as part of the state budget. In addition, a governor can try to arouse public opinion to support these legislative proposals.

Almost all governors have a veto power over legislation the state legislature passes. Only in North Carolina does the governor lack this power. In all but a few states the governor possesses an item veto. An **item veto** is the power to turn down a particular section or item in a piece of legislation without vetoing the entire law. A state legislature can override a governor's veto under certain conditions. Usually a two-thirds vote of all the legislators in each house is required to override a veto.

The governor's power of the item veto may generate controversy and sometimes cause battles with the state legislature. In Wisconsin, for example, governors have interpreted their partial veto authority very broadly. They do this

> *By vetoing whole sections of spending plans as well as individual sentences, words, parts of words, single letters, digits, spaces and even the drafting symbols that appear in enrolled bills.*
>
> —MICHAEL H. MCCABE,
> *STATE GOVERNMENT NEWS*, AUGUST 1991

GLOBAL CONNECTION

Comparing Governments

Powers of States and Provinces Canada is made up of 10 provinces and 2 territories. The central government in Ottawa represents all the people of Canada. Each province has its own government that functions somewhat like a state government in the United States.

Like states, provinces are responsible for such matters as education and administration of justice. Each province has an elected one-house legislature. Unlike states, however, provinces have a lieutenant governor who is appointed by the governor general. The head of government in nine of the provinces is a premier. The province of Quebec has a prime minister. The premier or prime minister leads the majority party in a provincial legislature.

Examining the Connection
How is the concept of federalism similar in the United States and Canada?

Lawmakers in Wisconsin challenged, without success, the governor's creative use of the partial veto. State courts sided with the governor. Failing there, some lawmakers took the case to the federal courts, losing again. If the courts continue to uphold the broad interpretation of the partial veto, only an amendment to the state constitution can reduce the governor's power.

A third legislative power of the governor is the ability to call a special session of the state legislature. Legislatures meet at regularly scheduled times, but the governor can call a special session to deal with legislation he or she feels is vital to the state's best interests and well-being.

GLOBAL CONNECTION

The original Canadian confederation in 1867 gave enormous power to the national government—the Canadians had perceived weaknesses in the United States system during the Civil War. Gradually, provincial governments increased their powers and today the governor general has little personal authority and is guided by the Canadian cabinet.
Examining the Connection Answer: *Provinces, like states, have some sovereignty. For example, they are responsible for education and administration of justice.*

STUDY GUIDE

Critical Thinking Answer
The item veto gives governors of 43 states a type of power over legislation that the President does not have.

Assess

Check for Understanding
Have students complete Section 3 Review on page 704.

Meeting Objectives
Each section objective is tested by the Section Review questions that follow it in parentheses.
• Define five roles of governors. (5, 7)
• Discuss the development of the power of the governor's office. (3, 5)
• Compare the state executive branch with the national executive branch. (2, 4, 6, 8)

STUDY GUIDE

Themes in Government
Constitutional Interpretations
Many times state constitutions are criticized for being too specific. In the case of the governor's item

veto power, Wisconsin lawmakers found that their state constitution may not have been specific enough.

Critical Thinking Skills
Making Comparisons How does the veto power of most governors compare with that of the President of the United States?

CHAPTER 24: ORGANIZATION OF STATE GOVERNMENT 703

Cooperative Learning Activity

Organize the class into seven groups to research the history of governors in the state. Have each group pick two or three governors to research (oversee the selection process to prevent duplications). Then have group members divide the following tasks: identifying resources, researching, collecting graphics and photographs, and keeping a general outline. Have each group report on the governors they have chosen and then open the discussion to the class, with the reporter in charge.

Evaluate

📁 Section 3 Quiz

⬚ Testmaker

Reteach

Have students summarize the section by preparing a chart which compares and contrasts the roles and powers of a governor and the President.

Enrich

Have students choose a recent state governor and do research on his or her administration(s). With which major legislation was the governor involved? What kind of public roles did he or she play? Was he or she a popular or unpopular party leader?

Close

Discuss why the power of the governorship has increased over time. What attitudes have allowed for this change?

CONNECTIONS

Media

Media coverage of governors' races is apparently important no matter who wins. In 1991 David Duke, a former Nazi party member and Ku Klux Klan leader, ran for governor of Louisiana. Although Duke forced a run-off election with the other top contender, intense national media attention contributed to his defeat.

Judicial Powers A governor normally has some limited powers over the state court system and the administration of justice. Governors appoint almost one-fourth of all state judges throughout the country. Also, a governor may have one or more of the following powers over people convicted of crimes: the right to grant pardons, shorten sentences, forgive fines, and release prisoners on parole.

Other Executive Officers

In all but three states—Maine, New Hampshire, and New Jersey—other elected officials are part of the executive branch. Less visible than the governor, these executives often hold important positions.

The Lieutenant Governor Forty-three states have a lieutenant governor, a position similar to that of the Vice President of the United States. In 42 states, the people elect the lieutenant governor. In Tennessee the speaker of the senate also serves as the lieutenant governor.

The lieutenant governor becomes governor in case the governor leaves office. Also, the lieutenant governor usually presides over the state senate.

The Attorney General In all but seven states the people elect the top legal officer in the state government, the attorney general. In the remaining states, the governor usually appoints the attorney general. The attorney general supervises the legal activities of all state agencies, gives legal advice to the governor, and acts as a lawyer for the state in cases in which it is involved. In some states the attorney general also administers the state police.

Probably the most significant power of the attorney general is the power to issue opinions, or written interpretations of the state constitution or laws. If governors, agency heads, or legislators have any doubt about the legality of their actions, they can ask the attorney general for an opinion. These opinions carry legal authority unless a court overturns them.

The Secretary of State In the federal government, the secretary of state deals with foreign relations. At the state level, the position of secretary of state is very much what its name describes—the chief secretary or clerk of state government. The secretary of state is in charge of all state records and official state documents including all the official acts of the governor and the legislature.

The State Treasurer The state treasurer manages the money that a state government collects and pays out. He or she pays the bills of state government and often serves as the state tax collector. In most states the state treasurer also has the power to invest state funds in stocks, bonds, and securities.

Other Officers Many other executive officers work in state governments. Most states have a state comptroller or auditor, a superintendent of public instruction, and other agencies, boards, and commissions.

---

3 SECTION REVIEW

Section Summary
The state governor and the executive branch administer the laws and manage the agencies of the state.

Checking For Understanding
Recalling Facts
1. Define political base, party primary, plurality, item veto.
2. Cite the length of a term in office for most governors.
3. Discuss the historic reason for limiting state governors' powers.
4. Name four executive officers other than the governor who are elected in most states.

Exploring Themes
5. Public Policy How does granting the governor more appointive powers over executive offices affect the governor's ability to coordinate policies?
6. Constitutional Interpretations Of what importance are the written opinions of an attorney general regarding state constitutional issues?

Critical Thinking Skills
7. Formulating Questions Prepare four questions that might be asked of a state governor to determine whether the office is relatively powerful compared to other states.
8. Making Comparisons How is the state office of lieutenant governor similar to and different from the national office of Vice President?

Section 3 Review Answers

1. Definitions of terms appear on pages indicated: **political base,** 697; **party primary,** 698; **plurality,** 698; **item veto,** 703
2. four years
3. The colonies had a bad experience with royal governors before independence, so states attempted to limit governors' power. These limitations continued until 1965 when states began to give governors more power.

4. lieutenant governor, treasurer, secretary of state, attorney general
5. When the governor has power to appoint the main executive officers, he or she is better able to coordinate policy and administer the law.
6. The opinions carry legal authority unless they are overturned by a court.
7. Questions may include: How long is the governor's term? How many terms may the governor serve? Does the governor have item veto power? How many top-level executive

officers does the governor appoint? What percentage of state judges does the governor appoint? Who prepares the state budget?
8. The Vice President and lieutenant governor are both first in line to assume the chief executive office, each presides over the upper house. Unlike the Vice President, a lieutenant governor in some states may be from a different political party than the chief executive.

SECTION 4

State Courts: The Judicial Branch

The court system of the states or nation is called the **judiciary**. Vital to the operation of state governments, the judiciary interprets and applies state laws. In doing so state courts help resolve conflicts like business disagreements and grievances that citizens may have against each other. State courts also punish crimes that violate state laws.

The Importance of State Courts

Because the national courts apply federal law and interpret the Constitution, some people think of the national judiciary as a "higher" court system. The system of appealing some cases from a state to a federal court may seem to diminish the importance of state courts. State courts are important, however, because state laws are important. Most laws that affect the ordinary citizen in an average day are state laws and local laws. State and local governments make housing codes and zoning laws, traffic laws, and health laws. Most crimes are violations of state laws.

State courts interpret and apply state and local laws. State courts decide most cases of murder, assault, and reckless driving, which are usually violations of state laws. State courts also decide

cases that involve local laws, like littering or illegal parking. All local courts are part of a state court system. The local municipal court in which a person challenges a traffic ticket is also part of a state court system. To get an idea of the importance of state courts, consider that more than 25 million cases were introduced in state courts in a recent year. This figure compares to about 300,000 cases introduced into federal courts.

Civil and Criminal Cases

State courts deal with two general types of legal disputes: civil and criminal cases. A **civil case** usually involves a dispute between two or more private individuals or organizations. The dispute may have to do with property rights such as a conflict between a

Civil and Criminal Cases

Civil Cases	Criminal Cases
Usually involve a dispute between two or more individuals or private organizations. Dispute may be over property rights, violation of a contract, etc. Include suits for damages. The state is usually not involved in these cases.	State brings charges against citizens for violation of law. Involve misdemeanors, which are minor crimes such as littering, or felonies, which are major crimes such as murder or arson. The state is the prosecution in these cases.

 Chart Study
Growing concern for drunk driving has resulted in new state laws. **Would a dispute involving a drunk driving incident be considered a civil or a criminal case?**

SECTION PREVIEW

Objectives
After studying this section, you should be able to:
- Classify civil and criminal cases.
- Outline the structure of the state court system.

- Evaluate various methods for selecting state judges.

Key Terms and Concepts
judiciary, civil case, criminal case, misdemeanor, felony, partisan election, nonpartisan election, court observer

Themes in Government
- Federalism
- Political Processes

Critical Thinking Skills
- Making Comparisons
- Drawing Conclusions

CHAPTER 24: ORGANIZATION OF STATE GOVERNMENT 705

Classroom Resources for Section 4

- 📁 Guided Reading Activities
- 📁 Reproducible Lesson Plans
- 📁 Participating in Government 24
- 📁 Cooperative Learning Activities 24
- 📁 Reteaching Activities 24
- 📁 Enrichment Activities 24
- 📁 Section 4 Quiz
- 📁 Chapter 24 Tests
- 💾 Testmaker
- 🎧 Audio Cassettes (English and Spanish)
- 📁 Limited English Proficiency Activities 24
  SAT Practice Tests

Focus

Bell Ringer

As you take attendance, have students list five situations that they think would likely end up in state courts.

Motivating Activity

Discuss students' Bell Ringer responses and write a selection on the chalkboard in two lists, those that are civil cases and those that are criminal. Then point out that some violations of the law are more serious than others. Depending upon each violation, each case would be heard in a different kind of court. Ask students if they know the names of any of the state courts. (*Students may know small claims court, traffic court, and what they might call criminal court.*) Tell students that Section 4 explains the structure of state courts and how judges are selected.

Vocabulary Precheck

List the terms and concepts on the chalkboard. Have volunteers skim the section to find each term and read it in context. **LEP**

Chart Study Answer
a criminal case

Teach

Guided Practice

L1 Journalism Have students create headlines to illustrate an element of each section subheading. For example, a headline for the subheading "The Importance of State Courts" might read OFFICIALS CONCERNED ABOUT STATE COURT CASE OVERLOAD. Write volunteers' headlines on the chalkboard and have the class give details to support each headline.

📁 **Group Discussion** Organize groups to complete activity 24 on selecting state judges in *Cooperative Learning Activities* in the Teacher's Classroom Resources.

STUDY GUIDE

Theme Answer
Generally, state courts have jurisdiction over cases involving state and local laws, and federal courts over federal laws and constitutional issues.

Critical Thinking Answer
Because state courts deal with almost 75 times as many cases, there must be many more state courts.

CONNECTIONS

Federalism

In recent years some states have begun to extend their state constitution's bill of rights beyond those set by the United States Constitution. For example, the California supreme court has extended the right of free speech to shopping malls, whereas the United States Supreme Court holds that free speech is not protected in malls because they are private property.

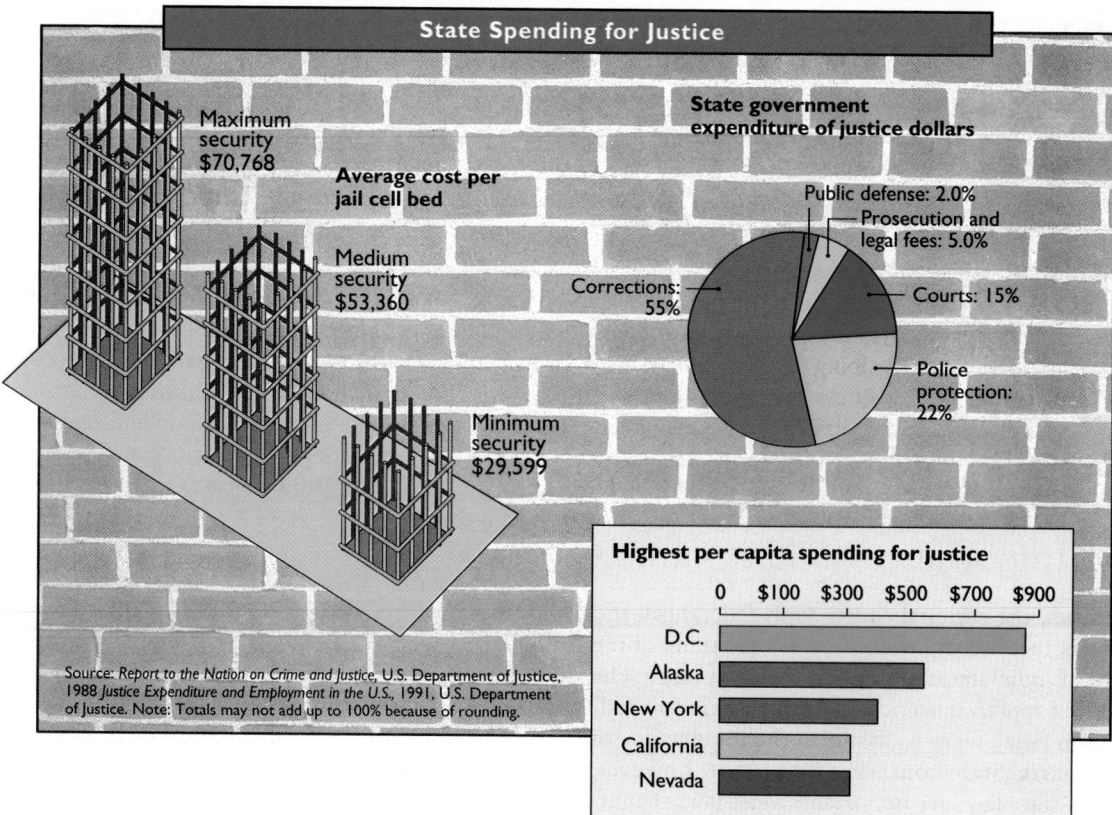

State Spending for Justice

Average cost per jail cell bed

Maximum security $70,768

Medium security $53,360

Minimum security $29,599

State government expenditure of justice dollars

Public defense: 2.0%
Prosecution and legal fees: 5.0%
Corrections: 55%
Courts: 15%
Police protection: 22%

Source: *Report to the Nation on Crime and Justice*, U.S. Department of Justice, 1988 *Justice Expenditure and Employment in the U.S.*, 1991, U.S. Department of Justice. Note: Totals may not add up to 100% because of rounding.

Highest per capita spending for justice

	0	$100	$300	$500	$700	$900
D.C.						
Alaska						
New York						
California						
Nevada						

landlord and a tenant. It may have to do with a business arrangement, like the violation of a contract to install plumbing. Civil cases may also include suits for damages resulting from traffic accidents and family disputes. More than 90 percent of civil cases are settled before or during trial without a jury decision.

In a **criminal case**, the state brings charges against a citizen for violating the law. Criminal cases involve either a misdemeanor or a felony. A **misdemeanor** is a minor or less serious crime such as littering, which usually involves a minor punishment. A **felony**, however, is a major crime such as murder, arson, or assault. The state is always the prosecution in criminal cases, while it is usually not involved in civil cases.

State Court Systems

State court systems vary in their structure. They also vary in the names the states give the courts. In general, state court systems include three types of courts: minor courts, general trial courts, and appeals courts.

Minor Courts Many legal matters are part of the natural course of life. Collecting wages due from an employer or compensation for limited damage to property may require legal action. Minor courts deal with these kinds of matters. These courts are also known as minor courts of limited jurisdiction, local trial courts, and inferior trial courts. Their jurisdiction is usually limited to civil cases dealing with

STUDY GUIDE

Themes in Government
Federalism How is jurisdiction generally divided between federal and state courts?

Critical Thinking Skills
Making Comparisons Judging only by the number of cases that each system handles each year,

how would you compare the number of federal courts to the number of state courts?

Background

To deal with the problem of congested courts and backlogged cases, the specialty of court management has developed. The application of modern business management techniques to the functioning of courts has improved courtroom efficiency. Techniques now employed include requiring pre-hearing settlement conferences, diverting certain kinds of cases to arbitration or mediation, being more flexible in handling increased workloads, instituting procedural reforms for stricter control of case flow, reducing time limits for filing briefs, reducing formal written briefs only to certain kinds of cases, and using videotape to take testimony.

money matters involving less than $1,000. Minor courts also try criminal cases in which the jail sentence involved is less than one year.

The best known minor court, especially in small towns and rural areas, is the justice court, presided over by a justice of the peace. The justice of the peace performs marriages, handles minor civil and criminal cases, and legalizes documents. Many justices of the peace have been average citizens with no legal background or education. In recent years, however, justice courts have become less important as special courts and trained officials have taken over some of their activities. In many cities and suburbs, police courts, municipal courts, or magistrate courts handle minor legal matters. Sometimes these minor courts deal with specific kinds of matters, like petty crimes or property disputes.

States include a whole range of minor courts. Small claims courts hear civil arguments that involve small amounts of money. Juvenile courts hear cases involving people under the age of 18. Domestic relations courts handle disputes between husbands and wives and other family members. Traffic courts hear cases dealing with traffic and parking violations. Probate courts handle cases involving the inheritance of property.

General Trial Courts The courts that stand above minor courts in the state court system are the general trial courts. These courts may hear any type of case, civil or criminal. Cases involving serious crimes like murder, arson, and robbery are heard in these courts.

General trial courts are known by different names, depending on the state. These names include county courts, circuit courts, and district courts. In some states general trial courts are known as superior courts or courts of common pleas. In New York State, general trial courts are known as supreme courts, although they are not the highest courts in the state.

Appeals Courts Appeals courts, also called appellate courts, are above general trial courts. These courts review cases that a lower court has already decided.

Not all cases can reach an appeals court. An appeals court will review a case if any one of these three conditions is met: if new evidence has been found; if the original trial was unfair; or if the state law applied in the case is unconstitutional.

The highest state court is usually called the supreme court. The supreme court is the state court

PARTICIPATING IN GOVERNMENT

Choosing a Lawyer

As you know, a person accused of a crime is entitled to legal representation. Many other situations, however, require the services of an attorney. Among them are buying or selling property, personal injury, job-related complaints, tenant issues, civil rights violations, and will preparation. Many lawyers practice general law, while others specialize in a certain area of the law, such as real estate or divorce.

You might choose a lawyer's name out of the yellow pages. Choosing any professional in this way, however, is somewhat risky.

The telephone company is not responsible for checking the credentials of anyone who advertises in its directory. You might ask people you know for recommendations of lawyers whose services they have used. You might also contact your state or county bar association. These organizations have listings of licensed lawyers in

your area. They can provide you with the names of attorneys who handle a particular branch of the law.

If you cannot afford a private attorney, your community may have a legal clinic where you can obtain routine legal services at reduced rates.

Investigating Further

The American Civil Liberties Union (ACLU) provides lawyers and legal advice for individuals or groups in certain cases. Find out more about the purpose and accomplishments of this organization.

Cooperative Learning Activity

Organize the class into groups of six. Assign the following roles: plaintiff, defendant, the lawyers of each, a judge, and a news reporter. Have each group create a small claims case and write out brief presentations for the opposing parties, their lawyers, and the judge. Have the reporter take notes on the group's presentation. Then have volunteer groups present their mock court cases to the class and, afterward, allow each reporter to answer questions from the rest of the class.

Independent Practice

L1 Law Have students identify court cases reported in the newspaper for a week and classify each as a civil case or a criminal case. Have them summarize briefly which characteristics of each case make it civil or criminal.

L2 Persuasive Writing Have students choose a specific method of judge selection and write an editorial to persuade local residents of the method's merit. Editorials should also state why the other methods are inferior.

STUDY GUIDE

Theme Answer
They want to remove judges from political influences as much as possible.

Critical Thinking Answer
supreme court and appeals courts

Traffic Violations May Lead to Court Trials
When motorists receive traffic citations, they often choose to have their case heard in court. **Law What state court official assigns punishments?**

Selecting State Court Judges

The judge is the most important official in a state court. The judge conducts the trial, interprets the law, hands down decisions, and assigns punishments. The judge is the authority in the courtroom and sets the tone for all court activities. Judges generally take this responsibility very seriously, partly because their reputation is at stake in every decision. Judge Robert Satter explained that it is embarrassing for a higher court to reverse a judge's decision:

Always a bit of my pride is bruised. Every Tuesday I run down the index of appellate and supreme court cases in the Connecticut Law Journal. . . . *If one of my decisions has been ruled upon, I anxiously leaf through the pages to it. If it has been upheld, I sigh with satisfaction. If it has been overturned, I just sigh.*

—JUDGE ROBERT SATTER, *DOING JUSTICE,* 1990

State judges are selected in four different ways. Some are elected in a popular election; others in an election by the legislature. Some judges receive gubernatorial appointment. Still others are selected through a method called the Missouri Plan that combines appointment by the governor and popular election.

Election by the People Many people have disagreed about the wisdom of electing judges. Those who favor popular election believe that if government is "of the people, by the people, and for the people," then the people must choose their judges. Critics argue that popular election may make state judges too concerned about the effect of their decisions on the public. They fear that judges who are thinking about reelection might be tempted to please the voters more than administer the law impartially. Further, voters often know little or nothing about the candidates for judicial posts and have no way of discriminating among candidates.

Despite these concerns, popular election is still a common method of selecting judges in 21 states.

of final appeal. In Maryland and New York this court is called the court of appeals. A state's supreme court, whatever its name, may review cases lower courts have already decided. The state's supreme court performs another significant function. It interprets the state's constitution and laws.

Three-fourths of the states have additional appeals courts, called intermediate appellate courts. These courts operate between the general trial courts and the state supreme court. Like any appeals court, the intermediate courts review lower court decisions. These courts were created to relieve the state supreme court of the large number of cases that were being appealed. The intermediate appellate courts are similar in purpose to the federal courts of appeals.

STUDY GUIDE

Themes in Government
Political Processes
States select their state court judges in a variety of ways. **Why** do you think most states that elect judges to state courts do so in nonpartisan elections?

Critical Thinking Skills
Drawing Conclusions **Which levels of state courts generally have the most highly trained, qualified judges?**

Special Needs Strategy

Learning Problems Students with learning problems often know fewer words than their classmates and have a limited understanding of multiple meanings of words. Such semantic disorders make it difficult for them to make comparisons or draw conclusions, the two critical thinking skills emphasized in this section. Ask students to find at least two meanings for the following words in the dictionary: *violate, diminish, private, minor, petty.* Then have them scan for these words in Section 4 and tell which meaning is most appropriate in context.

Judges may be elected in one of two ways: partisan elections and nonpartisan elections. In **partisan elections**, individual political parties nominate judges. People who want to serve as a state judge must win a party primary to gain the party's nomination. After gaining the nomination, they must also win a general election against a candidate of another party. Only a few states use partisan elections for most of their judges.

In **nonpartisan elections**, judges are chosen in elections in which political parties may not participate. In such elections, however, a political leader like a governor or a popular mayor can influence the outcome by endorsing a particular candidate.

Election by the State Legislature In only four states—Connecticut, Rhode Island, South Carolina, and Virginia—does the state legislature elect judges. In these states the state legislature elects Supreme Court justices and some other judges. Election of judges by the state legislature has sometimes been criticized for being based more on candidates' political connections than on their merits as jurists.

Appointment by the Governor In eight states, the governor appoints all or almost all state judges. Gubernatorial appointment has been criticized on the same grounds as election by the state legislature. Although governors have often chosen excellent and highly qualified judges, campaign supporters and defeated candidates of the governor's political party sometimes are given a judgeship as a reward for their political services. In some cases governors have allowed local party leaders to select judges in their own areas. Critics believe that these practices can result in the selection of unqualified judges.

The Missouri Plan It is clear that a major problem in the selection of judges is the possibility that unqualified people will be chosen because of politics. Still, the people in a democracy should have the right to determine whether their officials have served them well. To address these concerns many states have turned to the Missouri Plan. In the remaining states, the governor appoints most or all state judges, with final approval depending on popular election. This form of selection was first used in California in 1934 but gained national attention when Missouri adopted it in 1940. Very popular with judicial reformers, the Missouri Plan has spread to a number of states in recent years.

Under the Missouri Plan, the governor receives a list of nominees for judgeships from a judicial nominating commission. This commission is usually made up of people who are experts on the judicial process—practicing attorneys, former judges, and citizens who know a great deal about courts and the law. The governor then appoints judges from the names on the list.

The appointed judges usually serve at least one year. Then they run in a general election, but not against another candidate. The judges run without opposition, the people voting either yes to approve, or no to disapprove. If the voters approve, the elected judge usually serves a term of 6 or 12 years, depending on the state. If the voters disapprove—and this very rarely happens—the whole process begins again.

People have praised the Missouri Plan for a number of reasons. First, through the judicial nominating commission, it involves highly qualified people in the selection process. Second, the plan is democratic because it allows voters to accept or reject an appointed judge. Third, judges can maintain their independence because they do not have to run in frequent elections against opposing candidates. This allows them to avoid becoming obligated to a political party.

Judicial Compensation Recently some analysts of the courts have expressed concern that judges are not receiving adequate compensation in salaries or fringe benefits. While the average salary of judges is about $80,000, some believe that the figure is not high enough to retain the best judges. Edward B. McConnell explained that keeping good judges is as difficult as finding them. He claims:

L3 **Expressive Writing** Ask students to interview a local judge. Among the questions they should ask are how long the judge has sat on that bench, how he or she first came to that bench, if he or she has any lower court judicial experience, and what other legal background he or she has. Have students summarize their interview in a report.

STUDY GUIDE

Theme Answer
A disciplinary board or commission investigates complaints and makes a recommendation to the state supreme court, which may remove the judge.

Critical Thinking Answer
It provides highly qualified candidates for appointment but they must have voter approval to stay in office.

Assess

Check for Understanding
Have students complete Section 4 Review on page 710.

Meeting Objectives
Each section objective is tested by the Section Review questions that follow it in parentheses.
- Classify civil and criminal cases. (2, 3)
- Outline the structure of the state court system. (2, 3, 5, 8)
- Evaluate various methods for selecting state judges. (4, 6, 7)

STUDY GUIDE

Themes in Government
Political Processes What is the process for removing unqualified judges in most states?

Critical Thinking Skills
Making Comparisons
The Missouri Plan represents a compromise between appointment and election of judges. **How does** the Missouri Plan combine the best aspects of popular election and appointment of judges?

CHAPTER 24: ORGANIZATION OF STATE GOVERNMENT 709

Drawing Conclusions Remind students that when people propose making the salaries of judges and legislators competitive with what these people could earn in private practice, they are drawing conclusions about what is important to professional people. What are these conclusions, and do students agree with them? *(Students may suggest professionals will only do good work when they receive very high salaries. This assumes that no one is motivated by public service. Students may either agree or disagree with this perception of professionals. They may question why society does not worry about the low salaries of teachers or people who work with disturbed children, or any other public service job.)*

Caption Answer
judges might make popular, rather than fair, decisions to gain favor with voters; voters often know very little about judicial candidates

Reteach

Have students work in pairs to outline Section 4 by using the following main heads:

I.   Role of State Courts
II. Types of Cases
III. Structure of State Courts
IV. Selection of Judges
V.   Removal of Judges

After pairs complete their outlines, have them choose one main topic head and give an oral report to the class on the details they listed under the head .

Have students complete activity 24 in *Reteaching Activities* in the Teacher's Classroom Resources.

Enrich

Have students complete activity 24 in *Enrichment Activities* in the Teacher's Classroom Resources.

Close

Have students read the quote by Judge Robert Satter on page 708. Have them speculate on the reasons a lower court judge's ruling might be overturned.

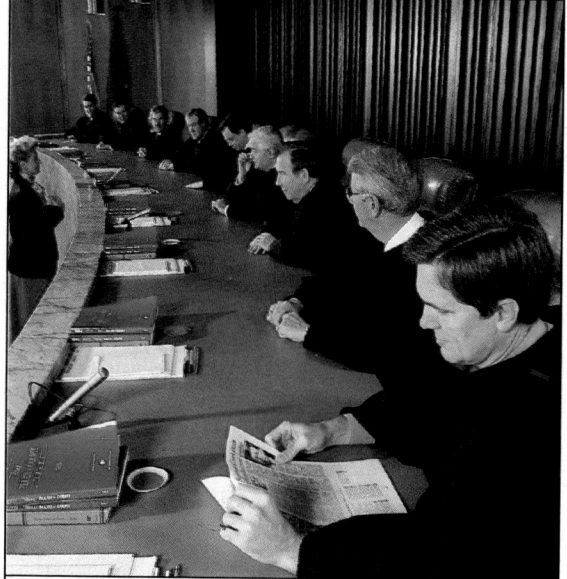

State Judges
State judges may be selected by popular election, the state legislature, the governor, or the Missouri Plan.
Politics Why do some people oppose selection of judges by popular election?

A state must be able to . . . keep good judges from leaving the bench to return to the practice of law. . . . Because of this correlation between quality and compensation, a state cannot expect to attract and retain good judges and thereby maintain a top-quality court system at compensation levels that are comparable to those of the less experienced or less competent lawyers.

—EDWARD B. MCCONNELL, PRESIDENT, NATIONAL CENTER FOR STATE COURTS

Removal of Judges The quality of judicial performance largely determines the quality of justice. A judge must demonstrate a minimum level of competence, skill, and knowledge. The judge often makes the final ruling in a case and has the last word about very critical decisions in people's lives. If judges are so important, it should be possible to evaluate their performance and remove those who are unqualified. How is this done?

One method of removing judges is through impeachment. Impeachment is a procedure through which charges are brought against a judge, or any public official, accused of misconduct. Impeachment of judges, however, has proved to be inefficient and time-consuming.

Instead, in recent years, most states have created disciplinary boards or commissions to investigate complaints about judges. These judicial conduct organizations, established to strengthen the integrity of the judicial process, now exist in almost every state, as well as the District of Columbia and Puerto Rico.

They are usually made up of both lawyers and nonlawyers. If a disciplinary board finds that a judge has acted improperly or unethically, it makes a recommendation to the state's supreme court. The court then may suspend or remove the judge.

A number of states have also begun to use court observers. **Court observers** are citizen volunteers who observe the daily activities in a courtroom. Often they will concentrate on a particular aspect of courtroom activities, such as the behavior of a judge or the type of evidence the judge allows in a trial. Although court observers have no official power, their presence has often been found useful in keeping a check on courtroom proceedings.

4 SECTION REVIEW

Section Summary
The state courts are important because most crimes are violations of state law.

Checking For Understanding
Reviewing Facts
1. Define judiciary, civil case, criminal case, misdemeanor, felony, partisan election, nonpartisan election, court observer.
2. List five kinds of minor courts.
3. Identify the state courts that deal with most serious crimes and civil cases.
4. Discuss two methods of removing judges in state courts.

Exploring Themes
5. Federalism What is the jurisdiction of state courts in the federal system?
6. Political Processes Why do some people favor the election of judges while others oppose it?

Critical Thinking Skills
7. Making Comparisons Compare the methods of selecting state judges. What method do you believe is the best? Why?
8. Drawing Conclusions Why do all state court systems have the same three types of courts—minor courts, general trial courts, and appeals courts?

Section 4 Review Answers

1. Definitions of terms appear on pages indicated: **judiciary,** 705; **civil case,** 705; **criminal case,** 706; **misdemeanor,** 706; **felony,** 706; **partisan election,** 709; **nonpartisan election,** 709; **court observer,** 710
2. justice court, police court, municipal court, small claims court, juvenile court, domestic relations court, traffic court, probate court
3. general trial courts

4. Impeachment is a method in which charges are brought against a judge for misconduct, but is inefficient and time-consuming. Disciplinary boards or commissions investigate complaints about judges. They may recommend that the state supreme court remove or suspend a judge.
5. State courts try cases involving state law.
6. Some believe it is more democratic for the judges to represent the people and to be elected by them. Others fear that popular election makes judges too concerned with pleasing voters to always decide objectively.

7. Some are elected in a popular election; some in an election by the legislature; some by gubernatorial appointment; some by the Missouri Plan. Students' opinions on the best method will vary.
8. All states need minor courts to handle everyday affairs, general trial courts to handle more serious cases, and appeals courts to review cases that have already been decided.

Lawrence H. Cooke on the American Court System

Lawrence H. Cooke, a retired chief judge of New York State, believes in courtrooms with "open doors." In an address to the Pre-Law Association at Rochester Institute of Technology, he explained that the courts belong to the people.

Justice is the most profound aspiration of men and women on earth; it is the allotment to each person of that to which he or she is entitled; it exists only when there has been adherence to principles of rectitude and fairness and disregard of other considerations. . . .

In every layer of history, in every society, disputes arise between people. The word "court" originally meant the enclosed space in a courtyard where the ruler sat to decide the controversies of his subjects. Down through the centuries, the character of a particular government or civilization could be measured best by the sort of justice meted out to its citizens. One barometer has been a good indicator. In the more advanced and more humane governances, trials have taken place in courtrooms to which the public has been admitted. On the other hand, secret trials have almost invariably been the telltale sign of oppressive and autocratic regimes. Indeed, the grant of a fair trial is the greatest contribution of any jurisprudence.

The difference in openness is not without significance. It is not a matter of mere entertainment. It is far more serious than that. First and foremost, accessible and unobstructed courtrooms are a guarantee of fairness and justice. When the people have the right to examine their courtrooms and the proceedings within them, there is also a likelihood that the physical facilities of the locations will be kept up-to-date and in a dignified manner and that the litigation being conducted therein will move in an efficient manner. The need for change will be apparent and necessary funds to effect them more easily obtained. Furthermore, the public officials functioning therein can be observed so that those performing well may be retained and those not may be replaced. . . .

The law must be adaptable to changing times and conditions. We live in a television and press age and we should take advantage of means to familiarize the masses with their courts. There were fears of histrionics and excessive rhetoric but there are methods to reduce these risks and the fears have proven to be unfounded. . . .

I am worried about what seems to be an increasing antipathy toward the media and concurrent attempts to narrow the doors leading into courtrooms by distinguishing ancillary or supplemental proceedings from trials themselves. Freedom of the press and open courtrooms go together. . . .

The law has its rewards but none exceed in glory and satisfaction the betterment of the human justice condition.

—LAWRENCE H. COOKE,
FEBRUARY 10, 1988

> *Indeed, the grant of a fair trial is the greatest contribution of any jurisprudence.*

Examining the Reading

Reviewing Facts
1. Point out one way that the character of a government or civilization may be measured.
2. Identify the means that Judge Cooke would use to make trials more public.

Critical Thinking Skills
3. Identifying Assumptions Why does Judge Cooke believe that open courtrooms will solve many problems of the justice system?

Focus

Ask students to imagine they are on trial for a serious crime. Would they want the procedure to take place in a closed or public session? Why?

Teach

Ask: What is Cooke's definition of justice? *("the allotment to each person of that to which he or she is entitled")* What relationship does Cooke draw among justice, openness, and fairness? *(that justice is not possible without fairness, and that neither are possible without openness)* How do you think Cooke would likely feel about live television inside courtrooms?

Assess

Have students complete **Examining the Reading.**

Answers

1. by studying the sort of justice meted out to its citizens
2. by admitting the press and television
3. Cooke believes that when courts are observed, they try to perform more efficiently, more fairly, and in a dignified manner.

Close

Note that Cooke implies that some people consider televised court proceedings as "entertainment." Ask students if the development, seen in this light, would strengthen or weaken the judicial system.

More About Personal Perspectives

Lawrence H. Cooke was the chief justice of the New York State Court of Appeals from 1979–1984. He returned to private practice in 1985. A colorful judge, he took on the New York District Attorney Robert Morgenthau over the issue of court efficiency. Cooke's reforms included the shortening of judges' vacation times, the abolishment of the Sheriff's Jury, a system by which privileged avoided jury duty, and other policies geared to speeding efficiency. Cooke has been the recipient of several media and legal awards related to his work with the First Amendment.

Identifying Terms and Concepts

1. unicameral, 2. initiative, 3. criminal case, 4. partisan election, 5. plurality, 6. item veto, 7. party primary, 8. civil case, 9. felony, 10. misdemeanor

Reviewing Facts and Ideas

1. by state legislatures, by popular initiative, by constitutional convention, and by a constitutional commission

2. popular vote

3. Most states have kept their constitutions because voters oppose the idea of holding constitutional conventions to change them.

4. Voting districts were based on areas such as counties and had not changed for years.

5. urban areas and suburban areas

6. Length and frequency of sessions will likely increase to several months each year.

7. by increasing salaries, making the job full-time, and increasing funds for staffs

8. power to appoint the chairpersons and other members of house committees

9. A candidate should have experience serving in state and local government, possess a knowledge of law, build a strong political base of support, and have influence in a major party.

10. Colonists greatly disliked the royal governors appointed by Britain and, therefore, early states limited the powers of their governors.

11. popular election, election by state legislatures, appointment by the governor, and the Missouri Plan

Applying Themes

1. State laws must be consistent with the state constitution, just as federal laws must agree with the United States Constitution. A state constitution cannot contain provisions that clash with the Constitution of the United States, nor can a state law.

Summary and Significance

State constitutions are the foundation of state governments. Many state constitutions are longer and much more detailed than the Constitution of the United States. They also place more limitations on the three branches of state government. The state legislature makes the laws of the state. Most state legislatures meet for only part of a year and some meet only every other year. Traditionally legislators have been part-time and not well-paid. Recently states have provided for more professional legislators. State legislatures are organized much like Congress in the way they handle legislation. The governor heads the executive branch. In some ways the position of governor is similar to that of the President of the United States. The governor carries out state laws, proposes legislation, is the leader of his or her political party, and appoints people to state office. Every state has a system of trial courts and appellate courts to interpret and apply state laws. Judges are elected, appointed, or selected by a combination of appointment and election called the Missouri Plan.

Identifying Terms and Concepts

On a separate sheet of paper numbered 1 to 10, write the term from the list below that best completes each sentence.

initiative, bicameral, unicameral, political base, party primary, plurality, item veto, judiciary, civil case, criminal case, misdemeanor, felony, partisan election

1. Nebraska has the only _____ legislature.
2. Some constitutional amendments are proposed by the people through the use of the _____.
3. In a _____ the government is the prosecution.
4. Some state judges are chosen in a _____.
5. In some states a governor may win election with a _____ of the votes.
6. In most states the governor has an _____ over legislation.
7. The _____ is held before the general election.
8. In a _____, the court may award damages to the plaintiff.
9. A serious crime is a _____.
10. A less serious crime is a _____.

Reviewing Facts and Ideas

1. **List** four methods of proposing amendments to state constitutions.
2. **Identify** the method that almost all states use to ratify an amendment to the state constitution.

3. **Summarize** the attitude most people have toward replacing their state's constitution.
4. **Explain** why in many states voting districts before 1964 were unequal in population.
5. **Identify** the two areas that gained most from the Supreme Court's decision that voting districts had to be based on roughly equal populations.
6. **Predict** the likely changes in the length and frequency of state legislative sessions, based on recent trends.
7. **Point out** three ways that states have promoted the development of professional legislatures.
8. **State** a power that the speaker of the lower house of a state legislature has but that the speaker of the United States House of Representatives does not have.
9. **Discuss** the political qualifications that a person must meet to become governor.
10. **Relate** the historic reason for limiting the powers of state governors.
11. **List** four methods states use to appoint state judges.

Applying Themes

1. **Federalism** In the federal system how is sovereign power divided among state and federal laws and constitutions?
2. **Constitutional Interpretations** Why have governors, unlike the President, been unable to ex-

2. State constitutions are much more specific than the national Constitution regarding the powers of the executive branch.

3. After serving one year, judges must run unopposed in a general election. At that time voters may vote to approve or disapprove of them.

4. longer terms, joint tickets, more control over executive appointments, consolidation of executive branch

Critical Thinking Skills

1. State constitutions are generally longer and contain much more specific detail than the United States Constitution.

2. Answers may include that bills are probably more singular in purpose and avoid including provisions that legislators know the governor will almost certainly disapprove.

pand their powers through constitutional interpretations?

3. **Political Processes** Under the Missouri Plan, how are voters involved in evaluating judges?

4. **Public Policy** What recent changes have increased some governors' executive powers?

Critical Thinking Skills

1. **Making Comparisons** How do state constitutions compare in length and detail to the United States Constitution?

2. **Making Generalizations** How does the governor's power of the item veto affect the substance of bills that legislatures pass?

3. **Identifying Central Issues** Why are some people concerned that judges may not be receiving adequate compensation?

4. **Formulating Questions** What are three questions that must be answered in order to determine whether a minor court, a general trial court, or an appeals court should hear a civil case?

5. **Drawing Conclusions** Why is there often conflict in the state executive branch?

Linking Past and Present

Many state constitutions contain historic provisions that are no longer applicable, such as a tax to help veterans of the Civil War. These provisions add to the length of the constitutions but have no effect on government today. People have been reluctant to approve constitutional conventions to replace or update state constitutions. Do you think that states should take the time to find a way to eliminate these outdated provisions? Why or why not?

Writing About Government

Descriptive Writing Imagine that you are corresponding with a person from another country. Write a letter describing a geographic area of your state. Choose a location that has a particularly interesting historical background, unique culture, or unusual physical characteristics.

Reinforcing the Skill

Expressing Problems Clearly Read the headlines listed below. For each, tell what problem is being addressed, how proponents think this policy will solve the problem, and what potential problems may arise if the policy is implemented by a state government.

---

1. *Legislature OKs Automatic Driver's License Suspensions in DUI Arrests*

2. *State Police Hope Anonymous Hotline Will Boost Effectiveness of Statewide "War" on Drug Dealers*

3. *Legislator Proposes Law to Prosecute Pregnant Smokers, Drinkers, Illegal Drug Users*

Investigating Further

1. **Individual Project** Almost all adults in a state know the name of the governor. How well do people know the other executive officers? Make a list of the top 3 or 4 state executive offices in your state (lieutenant governor, secretary of state, attorney general, treasurer, etc.). Ask 10 or more adults whether they can name any of these officials. Record the results of your survey. Draw a conclusion about the name recognition of state officials.

2. **Cooperative Learning** Secure several highway maps of your state. Organize the class into three groups. Using the maps, have members of the first group prepare short-answer questions about the locations of major cities, rivers, and geographic features in the state. (What city is the capital of Washington County? What river flows through Harrisburg?) Have the remaining two groups study the maps of the state while the first group prepares questions. Determine rules for a contest between groups two and three using the prepared questions. Then have a spokesperson for group one read the questions to the other two groups.

CHAPTER 24: ORGANIZATION OF STATE GOVERNMENT   713

---

3. They believe that salaries may not be high enough to retain the best judges, causing some to return to the practice of law.

4. How much money is being sought by the plaintiff? Does the case belong under the jurisdiction of a special court—juvenile, domestic, or probate? Has the case already been tried in a lower court?

5. When executive officials are elected, they feel less loyalty to the governor than do appointed officials. In addition, they may be from the opposition party.

Chapter Organizer

Objectives	Special Feature Pages	Supplemental Materials
Section 1 Safeguarding the Economy and the Environment *pp. 716–721* 1. Describe the many ways that state governments affect daily life. 2. Explain states' roles in granting corporate charters.	Focus on Freedom: *McCulloch* v. *Maryland* p. 718 Multicultural Heritage: Spanish Legal Contributions p. 721	Guided Reading Activities Reproducible Lesson Plans Section 1 Quiz Testmaker SAT Practice Tests Writer's Guidebook
Section 2 Protecting Life and Property *pp. 722–727* 1. Evaluate the problems that states face in protecting life and property. 2. Analyze the advantages and disadvantages of a decentralized criminal justice system.		Guided Reading Activities Reproducible Lesson Plans Interpreting Political Cartoons 20, 51 Section 2 Quiz Testmaker Chapter Transparencies 25 SAT Practice Tests Writer's Guidebook
Section 3 Providing for Public Health, Education, and Welfare *pp. 728–733* 1. Examine the increasing role of the states in providing public health, education, and welfare services. 2. Describe recent changes in school funding programs.	Participating in Government: Displaying the American Flag p. 729 Critical Thinking Skills: Checking Consistency p. 733	Guided Reading Activities Reproducible Lesson Plans Participating in Government 25 Primary and Secondary Source Readings 25 Enrichment Activities 25 Section 3 Quiz Testmaker Skill Reinforcement Activities 25 SAT Practice Tests Writer's Guidebook
Section 4 Sources of State Revenue *pp. 734–739* 1. Recognize the many and varied sources of state revenue. 2. Analyze the limitations on states' taxing powers.	Global Connection: Interdependence: Tax Incentives p. 736 Personal Perspectives: Linda Winikow on Managing Diversity p. 739 Case Study: Mandatory Sentences: Overcrowded Prisons pp. 742–744 Unit 8 Digest pp. 745–746	Guided Reading Activities Reproducible Lesson Plans Interpreting Political Cartoons 50 Reteaching Activities 25 Section 4 Quiz Chapter 25 Tests Testmaker Audio Cassettes (English and Spanish) Limited English Proficiency Activities 25 SAT Practice Tests Writer's Guidebook Unit Digest Transparencies, Unit 8 Participating in Government, Unit 8

If time does not permit teaching this chapter, assign the Chapter 25 summary in the Unit 8 Digest on pages 745–746.

Key To Ability Levels

Teaching strategies have been coded for varying learning styles and abilities.

L1 Level 1 activities are **basic** activities and should be within the ability range of all students.

L2 Level 2 activities are **average** activities and should be within the ability range of the average to above-average student.

L3 Level 3 activities are **challenging** activities designed for the ability range of above-average students.

LEP These activities should be within the ability range of **Limited English Proficiency** students.

Multicultural Activities

In 1989 L. Douglas Wilder joined a growing number of minority candidates who have won election by attracting broad-based support. Wilder became the nation's first African American to be elected governor—in Virginia, a state where almost 80 percent of the population is white. Many northern Virginia white voters liked his fiscal conservatism, while some African American voters appreciated his fight for a state holiday honoring Martin Luther King, Jr., and for fair housing legislation. Minority candidates hoped this victory signaled a political trend among white voters to greater acceptance of minority candidates. Have students contrast the challenges for minority candidates of running for state legislative offices and for governor.

"Most people like to deal with us," said Wilma Mankiller, "as though we were in a museum or a history book." Mankiller, principal chief of the Cherokee nation of Oklahoma, is the first woman to head a major Native American nation in North America. As chief, Mankiller heads a governing body that has a unique relationship to Oklahoma state government. The legal status of a Native American nation is that of a trust territory. Most Native American lands are excluded from state jurisdictions and only federal laws apply. Despite their official status as independent, such groups and state governments often find themselves cooperating or facing conflict particularly on issues related to land use. Interested students might research the "intergovernmental" relationship between Native American groups and state governments in Alaska, Arizona, New Mexico, Minnesota, and South Dakota.

Chapter Resources

Readings for the Student

Civil Justice: Living Law. Scholastic/The Constitutional Rights Foundation, 1988.

Criminal Justice: Living Law. Scholastic/The Constitutional Rights Foundation, 1988.

Davis, Bertha. *Instead of Prison.* Franklin Watts, 1986.

Harnett, Bertram. *Law, Lawyers, and Laymen.* Harcourt, Brace, Jovanovich, 1984.

State and Local Government. Scholastic, 1989.

Weiss, Ann E. *Lotteries: Who Wins, Who Loses?* Enslow, 1991.

Readings for the Teacher

Dilger, Robert Jay. *The Sunbelt/Snowbelt Controversy: The War over Federal Funds.* NYU Press, 1982.

Elazar, Daniel J. *American Federalism: A View from the States.* Harper & Row, 1984.

Kozol, Jonathan. *Savage Inequalities: Children in America's Schools.* Crown, 1991.

Zimmerman, Joseph F. *State-Local Relations: A Partnership Approach.* Praeger, 1983.

Multimedia

Videocassettes and Films

AIDS—Changing the Rules. AIDSFILMS. (2 v/cs, 1 English, 1 Spanish, 30 minutes each)

The Bill of Rights in America—The Story of a Trial. BFA Educational Media. (film, 21 minutes)

Handguns: An American Tragedy. New York Times. (v/c, 17 minutes)

Inside the Jury Room. (*Frontline* series). Al Levin and Stephen Herzberg. (v/c, 58 minutes)

Monuments of Failure: America's Prison Crisis. KNME. (v/c, 60 minutes)

Who Profits from Drugs? (*Frontline* series). Charles Stuart. (v/c, 60 minutes)

Software

Criminal Law. Intellectual Software. (2 Apple disks). A detailed tutorial on criminal law, including the elements of crimes, categories of crimes, and legal defenses.

Criminal Procedure. Intellectual Software. (Apple, IBM disks). A tutorial on the various criminal procedures.

Jury Trial II. Navic. (Apple, IBM disks). A simulation requiring the prosecution to prove the guilt of the defendant, based on evidence gained through the "interrogation" of witnesses and the application of legal strategies used by prosecutors and defense attorneys.

State Government in Action

Introduce

Chapter Overview

Chapter 25 focuses on the services state governments provide and the revenue sources used to fund them. The chapter discusses the programs and services in health, education, welfare, economic development, environmental protection, and criminal justice provided by the state.

Section 1 lists the ways in which state governments help determine their state's economic growth and help protect their state's environment.

Section 2 discusses the public safety services that states provide.

Section 3 summarizes the state's role in public health, education, and welfare, and how state programs in these areas are funded.

Section 4 identifies sources of state revenue, such as taxes, bonds, lotteries, and grants.

Chapter 25 Themes

Write the chapter themes on the chalkboard. Ask students to write these themes in their notebooks and as they study the chapter to list each section's subheadings under the appropriate theme.

CHAPTER 25

A network of state and federally supported highways, which are vital to commerce and tourism, crisscrosses the United States countryside.

About the Chapter Opener

Teaching With Illustrations Point out that paved, durable highways like the one pictured above were practically unknown in the United States before the automobile. Automobiles did not last long on rutted, dirt roads, so drivers soon began to demand that governments build decent roads. Officials complied, and in the first half of the twentieth century the total mileage of paved roads increased tenfold to more than 1.5 million miles. The passage of the Federal Aid Highway Act in 1956 led to the construction of another 45,000 miles of high-quality roads. Ask how governments' providing roads illustrates the concept of federalism.

Chapter Preview

Overview

State government actions and services affect the lives of citizens every day.

Objectives

After studying this chapter, you should be able to:

1. **Enumerate** the many ways in which state government helps determine each state's economic environment.
2. **Evaluate** state criminal justice systems.
3. **Discuss** the state's role in public health, education, and welfare.
4. **Describe** the various sources of state revenue.

Themes in Government

This chapter emphasizes the following government themes:

- **Free Enterprise** States support free enterprise by granting corporate charters. Section 1.
- **Public Policy** State policy creates each state's economic environment. Sections 1 and 4.
- **Federalism** States cooperate with the federal government in providing services. Sections 2, 3, and 4.
- **Civil Rights** State courts apply constitutional protections. Section 2.
- **Constitutional Interpretations** State courts apply constitutional interpretations to state government policies. Section 3.

Critical Thinking Skills

This chapter emphasizes the following critical thinking skills:

- Expressing Problems Clearly
- Drawing Conclusions
- Distinguishing Fact from Opinion
- Understanding Cause and Effect

CHAPTER 25: STATE GOVERNMENT IN ACTION 715

Introducing the Chapter

Before students study Chapter 25, review federal government programs in the areas of economic growth, environmental protection, health, education, welfare, and justice. Ask students: What do you know about state responsibilities in these areas? In what ways would you expect the programs carried out by the state to be different from the programs carried out by the federal government? What do you know about the similarities and differences in sources of revenue for state governments and the federal government? What kinds of taxes do people in your state pay to the state government? Discuss students' answers.

Chapter Project

As they read the chapter, have students keep and update a class chart on how the state collects and spends money. Have volunteers contact state agencies and other official sources to collect information on how much money the state allots each year for education, unemployment, roads, environmental protection, and so on. Also have them find out how much money in taxes, licenses, and other revenue is collected each year. At the end of the chapter, review the students' chart and analyze where the state's money comes from and where it goes. (See Section 4 Close activity.)

Linking Past and Present

A Connecticut trading company, organized in 1723, became the first commercial corporation in the colonies. However, British and colonial laws hampered the movement of currency and products and provided a poor climate for businesses to thrive. Today the federal government promotes interstate commerce, and state governments compete to attract companies from other states and from overseas.

Setting the Scene The federal government long has been a major source of financial aid to the states. But with pressure on to reduce the federal deficit, some analysts believe states must stop counting on Washington. Concerns remain, however. Recent studies show the gap between wealthier and poorer jurisdictions widening. Also, increasing federal regulation coupled with decreasing aid has strained relations between state and national governments. Finally, in a period of regional or national economic distress, states' abilities to continue essential services without increased aid could be seriously diminished.

Focus

Bell Ringer

As you take attendance, have students think about the activities they complete in the course of a full day. Have them list several activities they think might be regulated or funded by the state.

Motivating Activity

Write students' Bell Ringer responses on the chalkboard. Suggest some of the following if they do not: funding school buses, planning traffic light sequences, building roads, regulating work and safety standards at students' after-school jobs, and so on. As students study the chapter, tell them to look for examples of state government activities that affect their lives.

Vocabulary Precheck

Call on students to read aloud the definitions of the terms and concepts from the Glossary. Then have volunteers use each term in a sentence. **LEP**

CONNECTIONS

Economics

Initiated by federal funding, a new four-lane highway will connect the cities of St. Paul, Minnesota, and St. Louis, Missouri. Officials of both states, as well as Iowa, which the highway will cross, hope the project will bring increased business. Called the Avenue of the States, the project is to be completed by the year 2000.

Caption Answer
business, labor, professions, insurance and banking, public utilities

Safeguarding the Economy and the Environment

Many people are not aware of the extent to which state laws govern daily life. A resident of Ohio saw an automobile strike a deer on the road near his house. He assisted the motorist and then kept the dead deer. Later, the local sheriff found out about the incident and turned the matter over to the state game protector. Because the resident had no proof of how the deer was killed, the state arrested him for possession of the animal—a violation of Ohio law.

The great expansion of the federal government in economic affairs in the twentieth century often obscures the reality of state power. The Constitution, however, reserved most economic powers to the states. As one political scientist noted:

The states continue to have the last word in . . . the law of ordinary commerce, tort law, property law; the law of marriage and divorce. States and cities make up and enforce many ordinary rules that govern the average man in his daily life. They draft building codes, plumbing codes, and electrical codes for cities and towns. . . . They regulate dry cleaners, license plumbers, and dictate the open season on pheasants and deer. They control the right to marry, to own a dog, to sell vegetables, to open a saloon.
—LAWRENCE M. FRIEDMAN,
A HISTORY OF AMERICAN LAW, 1973

State governments have historically retained the power to regulate business, labor, and the professions. They also establish laws dealing with property ownership, contracts, corporations, and torts. A **tort** is any wrongful act that could result in a lawsuit.

States closely regulate insurance and banking, set the rules governing public utilities, and encourage business development. States administer and control natural resources such as land, water, and animal life. Through their police powers, state governments protect consumers from unfair economic practices. In addition, state governments control certain benefit programs.

In some cases states share authority with the federal government over important aspects of economic life. Workers' safety, employment policy, and consumer protection are just some of the areas in which both state and federal governments have significant influence.

State Game Warden on the Scene
States administer and control wild-game hunting.
Economics What other areas do states regulate?

SECTION PREVIEW

Objectives
After studying this section, you should be able to:
■ Describe the many ways state governments affect daily life.
■ Explain states' roles in granting corporate charters.

Key Terms and Concepts
tort, corporate charter, public utility, monopoly, workers' compensation, unemployment compensation, tax credit

Themes in Government
■ Free Enterprise
■ Public Policy

Critical Thinking Skills
■ Expressing Problems Clearly
■ Drawing Conclusions

716 UNIT 8: STATE GOVERNMENT

Classroom Resources for Section 1

📁 Guided Reading Activities
📁 Reproducible Lesson Plans
📁 Section 1 Quiz

✚ Testmaker
SAT Practice Tests
Writer's Guidebook

State Regulation of Business

In the United States, every business corporation must have a charter issued by a state government. A **corporate charter** is a document that grants certain rights, powers, and privileges to a corporation. A charter is important because it gives a corporation legal status.

Corporation Law The corporate form of business developed because it had advantages over businesses owned by one or two individuals. It helped businesses expand to serve the needs of a growing nation. Corporation law evolved with the rise of giant businesses in the nineteenth century. Every state constitutional convention between 1860 and 1900 wrestled with problems of corporation law.

Before 1860 state charters greatly restricted the powers of corporations. By the 1890s, however, courts and legislatures, influenced by business interests and aware that giant corporations were becoming indispensable, had relaxed controls over business. States that continued to restrict corporations found their major businesses moving to other states where the laws were more lenient.

In the twentieth century, consumer groups demanded regulation of giant corporations. In response, federal and state governments passed stronger regulations. Legislation regulated all kinds of corporations, but laws regulating banks, insurance companies, and public utilities were especially rigorous. State laws regulated interest rates that banks could charge. States helped set insurance companies' rates, administered licensing exams, and generally protected consumer interests.

Public Utilities All states regulate the rates that public utility companies may charge. A **public utility** is an organization, either privately or publicly owned, that supplies such necessities as electricity, gas, telephone service, or transportation service to the public. In the United States, private stockholders own most public utility companies. States give public utility companies the exclusive right to supply service in the state or part of the state. In return for granting the right to operate as a **monopoly**, or a business that has no competition, the state assumes the right to regulate rates.

Consumer Protection Since the 1950s consumer protection has been an increasingly important activity of state governments. States have acted to protect consumers from unfair and deceptive trade practices such as false advertising. Three-fourths of the states have laws regulating landlord-tenant relations. Most states also regulate health-care industries.

State governments have enacted legislation dealing with consumer sales and service—everything from regulating interest charges on credit cards to setting procedures for estimating the cost of automobile repairs. Most states also try to protect consumers in a number of housing-related areas, such as home repair costs and home mortgages. Several states also require consumer education in the schools.

As part of their consumer-protection activities, all states issue occupational and professional licenses. Even before 1900 most states granted licenses to lawyers, physicians, dentists, pharmacists, and teachers. Today state governments license many more workers, including accountants, psychologists, architects, nurses, veterinarians, engineers, barbers, and funeral directors. One of the purposes of state licensing is to protect the consumer by making sure that qualified people work in these professions. Most states require continuing education as well.

Labor Regulations and Benefits The states have pioneered the enactment of legislation related to working conditions. Almost all states have laws that regulate the safety and sanitary conditions of factories. Federal child-labor rules limit the number of hours that 14- and 15-year-olds may work and place other restrictions on work for those under age 18. In addition to the federal rules, many states regulate the hours that 16- and 17-year-olds may work. Most states require minors to have work permits.

Teach

Guided Practice

L1 Guest Speaker Invite a banker, public utility executive, or a licensed professional (barbers, pharmacists, cosmetologists, or funeral directors may be best) to speak to the class about state regulation of their businesses.

L2 Panel Discussion Have students hold a panel discussion to illustrate the conflict between the states' duty to encourage business and corporate interests and their duty to protect consumers and the environment. Have students discuss examples of conflicts they have read or heard about.

STUDY GUIDE

Theme Answer
because charters give corporations legal status

Critical Thinking Answer
because they operate as monopolies and could charge very high rates if not regulated

CONNECTIONS

Biography
Ralph Nader is an American lawyer famous for his work for consumer-protection laws. As a result of Nader's efforts, California voters passed Proposition 103 in 1988. This law provided for lowering some auto insurance costs to consumers.

STUDY GUIDE

Themes in Government
Free Enterprise Why would it be impossible for business corporations to operate without a charter from state government?

Critical Thinking Skills
Expressing Problems Clearly Why do states regulate the rates that public utility companies charge for supplying elec- tricity, gas, phone service, and transportation service to the public?

CHAPTER 25: STATE GOVERNMENT IN ACTION **717**

Background

Foreign companies, many of them Japanese, look at more than cost when they consider an industry site. They also consider the community's utility and road systems, the training level of the workforce, and the educational system. Though the industries are ultimately dependent upon the local systems, state funds are often used to make potential industry sites more attractive. Among the states with the most money invested in United States affiliates of foreign companies are California, Texas, New York, Alaska, Illinois, Ohio, Louisiana, New Jersey, Pennsylvania, and North Carolina.

The issues in this case were implied powers and national supremacy. The power to tax implied that Congress had other powers, Marshall said, such as creating a national bank in which to deposit federal funds. Also, to tax an agent of the federal government gave a state power over that agent, a federal-state relationship that Marshall could not let stand. This decision explains why federal property is exempt from state and local taxes today.

Answers

1. The Constitution was ratified by the states, making federal actions subject to state approval.

2. The American people ratified the Constitution, making federal law supreme over state law.

3. They would have been subject to a variety of state laws and could have been weakened or destroyed by state regulation.

L3 Classifying Provide examples of several businesses such as the ones below and have students tell what levels of regulation (local, state, or federal) they think the business would receive in their state and why: bars and liquor stores, pharmacies, city buses, electric-power companies, banks, restaurants, coal mines.

The state governments also provide **workers' compensation**—payment to people unable to work as a result of job-related injury or ill health. Workers who lose their jobs may receive **unemployment compensation** under programs that state governments set up and regulate.

Workers in all states have the right to belong to labor unions, but some states protect workers from being forced to join unions. More than one-third of the states have passed laws, often called "right-to-work" laws, that prohibit the union shop. The union shop is an agreement between a union and an employer that all workers must join a union—usually within 30 days of being hired.

Business Development State governments have been very active in trying to attract new business and industry. Governors often travel throughout the country or even to foreign countries to bring new business to their states. Television advertising, billboards, brochures, and newspaper advertisements promote travel or business opportunities.

States use two methods to lure new development—industrial development bonds and tax credits. Beginning in the 1930s, state governments sold industrial development bonds to people or institutions and used the money to help finance industries that relocated or expanded within the state. The state paid off the bond within a specified time period from money

---

Focus on Freedom

McCULLOCH v. MARYLAND

In 1818 the state of Maryland passed a statute taxing all banks operating in Maryland not chartered by the state. When James McCulloch, a cashier of the Bank of the United States in Baltimore, refused to pay the tax, Maryland prosecuted. The United States Supreme Court reversed the Maryland Court of Appeals in 1819.

The first question made in the cause is—has congress power to incorporate a bank? . . .

The bill for incorporating the Bank of the United States did not steal upon an unsuspecting legislature, and pass unobserved. Its principle was completely understood. . . .

The counsel for the state of Maryland have deemed it of some importance . . . to consider that instrument [the constitution], not as emanating from the people, but as the act of sovereign and independent states. The powers of the general government, it has been said, are delegated by the states, who alone are truly sovereign. . . . It would be difficult to sustain this proposition. The convention which framed the constitution was indeed elected by the state legislatures. But the instrument [constitution], when it came from their hands, was a mere proposal, without obligation, or pretentions to it. . . . The instrument was submitted to the people. They acted upon it . . . by assembling in convention. . . . From these conventions, the constitution derives its whole authority. . . .

After the most deliberate consideration, it is the unanimous and decided opinion of this court, that the act to incorporate the Bank of the United States is a law made in pursuance of the constitution, and is part of the supreme law of the land. . . .

If the States may tax one instrument, employed by the government in the execution of its powers, they may tax any and every other instrument. They may tax the mail; they may tax the mint; they may tax patent rights. . . . This was not intended by the American people. . . .

We are unanimously of opinion, that the law passed by the legislature of Maryland, imposing a tax on the Bank of the United States, is unconstitutional and void. . . .

—CHIEF JUSTICE JOHN MARSHALL

Examining the Document

Reviewing Facts
1. Explain on what basis Maryland argued against the Bank of the United States.
2. Describe how Marshall proved that national law was sovereign over state law.

Critical Thinking Skills
3. Predicting Consequences What could have happened to national institutions if Marshall had ruled in favor of Maryland?

Cooperative Learning Activity

Organize the class into groups to consider the following: Since, increasingly, states are paying for programs that used to be financed by the federal government, should state taxes rise when federal aid falls? Should federal funds be used to pay for some programs wholly, and state funds used for other programs completely? Each group should assign members to talk with state legislators and the offices of their national legislators. Others should take discussion notes, prepare the report, or present it to the class.

that the industry paid back to the state in the form of taxes. The advantage of the state loan to the new business or industry was lower interest than a bank loan would have been able to offer.

A state may offer a **tax credit**, or a reduction in taxes, in return for the creation of new jobs or new business investment. Generally, business and industry are attracted to states with low corporate income taxes and low labor costs. For these and other reasons, many industries in the last few decades have relocated to states in the South and West.

States and the Environment

State governments are concerned about two goals that sometimes clash: economic growth and environmental protection. A thriving economy brings money, jobs, and business to a state. Economic growth can, however, cause environmental problems. Factories provide jobs, but they can also produce air and water pollution. Building new homes and office buildings creates many benefits—better housing, more jobs, and increased business activity. On the other hand, new construction can create sewage problems, place greater demand on water, energy, and educational facilities, and may damage the environment.

Environmental Concerns In recent years the quality of the physical environment has become a major concern of the general public. Medical scientists have warned that air and water pollution endanger public health. Parents have worried about the effects that nuclear power plants and wastes, coal-burning power plants, and the unregulated dumping of chemical wastes have on their children.

The states' reaction to environmental issues has been mixed. In conservation and land use, the states took a leading role. In the 1940s California was the first state to pass an anti-pollution law. Most state governments acted to combat pollution, however, only after the federal government had passed stringent environmental laws.

Not until the 1980s, when the federal government took less regulatory action, did the states reclaim many regulatory powers from Washington, D.C. States passed new laws regulating everything from roadside billboard advertising to the labeling of food products, assuming some of the functions of the Federal Trade Commission.

Business seemed threatened from a new direction. Once fearful of federal regulation, it now turned to the national government for protection from the states' new restrictions. One observer of this turnaround noted:

> *California, for example, passed a law in 1986 requiring food processors to warn consumers about any food containing carcinogenic chemicals. Processors and grocers are not asking the state to change its mind; they are trying to get Congress to pass legislation preempting all such state laws.*
>
> —DAVID RAPP, *GOVERNING*, OCTOBER 1990

Influenced by a giant oil spill off the coast of Alaska in 1989, however, Congress actually strengthened state power with a law that allows states to impose any liability standards on business that they choose.

Pollution Control Pollution is one of the painful by-products of modern life. The technology that brought automobiles also brought air pollution. The growth of cities and suburbs led to the massive dumping of wastes, both human and industrial, that caused water pollution.

Before 1964 only nine states had enacted regulations to control air pollution. Beginning in 1963, however, the federal government passed a number of laws aimed at curbing pollution. Included were the Clean Air Act (1963), the Water Quality Act (1965), the Flood Control, River, and Harbor Acts (1966), the Air Quality Control Act (1967), and the National Environmental Policy Act (1969). These laws set up federal standards for air and water quality. The laws also provided federal money to states and localities to improve the quality of the air and water.

Independent Practice

L1 Public Policy Have students make charts that list the areas in which the state has regulatory powers. (*Heads: Business, Consumer Protection, Labor, Public Utilities*) Have them fill in their charts with examples for each category. **LEP**

L2 Persuasive Writing Have students identify an environmental problem in their state or county and then write to their state legislator about whether or not solving this problem should take precedence over any business considerations that might be involved.

STUDY GUIDE

Theme Answer
to protect the health, social, and educational needs of young people

Critical Thinking Answer
to require minimum levels of expertise in essential public services

Assess

Check for Understanding

Have students complete Section 1 Review on page 720.

Meeting Objectives

Each section objective is tested by the Section Review questions that follow it in parentheses.
- Describe the many ways that state governments affect daily life. (2, 3, 4, 6, 8)
- Explain states' roles in granting corporate charters. (5, 7)

STUDY GUIDE

Themes in Government
Public Policy Why do states regulate the working hours and conditions of those under age 18?

Critical Thinking Skills
Drawing Conclusions Why do states require licenses for physicians, teachers, and accountants

but not for musicians, farmers, and artists?

CHAPTER 25: STATE GOVERNMENT IN ACTION 719

Special Needs Strategy

Writing Disability Some students with learning problems have trouble with written expression. On examinations they write less than their classmates, write simpler sentences, and use limited vocabulary. Often they rely on their oral speech patterns for written expression. Ask students to verbally summarize the subsection, "States and the Environment," as you tape-record their summaries. Then ask them to transcribe their summaries and evaluate with them the differences between oral and written expression, noting false starts, incomplete sentences, and repetitious vocabulary.

Evaluate

📁 Section 1 Quiz

▪ Testmaker

Reteach

Have students summarize the
section by writing a sentence that
states the main idea for each subhead.

Enrich

Have students determine
which state agency regulates an
occupation or a business in which
they may be interested. Have
them contact that agency for information about requirements
and regulations and report their
findings to the class.

Close

Have students read the quote
on page 719. Ask: What do you
think will happen if the federal
government does not preempt
such state laws? *(Varying regulations will raise cost of doing business in more than one state;
companies may seek out states with
lax regulations.)*

The states have more recently taken steps to control pollution. Most states now require environmental
impact statements for major governmental or private
projects, describing how the project is likely to affect
the environment.

Many states require industries to secure permits if
their wastes pollute the air or water. Often, such permits are so costly that the industry finds it cheaper to
install anti-pollution devices. Most states have developed waste-management programs. Most states also
regulate the disposal of radioactive wastes.

Costs of Pollution Control Federal and state interest in pollution control remains strong. Recent
trends, however, indicate that local governments will
bear the major burden of financing programs to control pollution. Federal Environmental Protection
Agency expenditures have fallen sharply from 1981
levels. State governments are also spending a smaller
share. Experts predict that municipal spending in this
area will have to double by the year 2000.

Conservation Conservation is the care and protection of natural resources including the land, lakes,
rivers, and forests; oil, natural gas, and other energy
sources; and wildlife. In recent years state governments have increased their efforts to conserve these
resources.

A number of states have passed laws that allow the
state government to plan and regulate how land will
be used. Through a land-use law, for example, a state
government can preserve certain land from industrial
development and set aside other land for parks.

Preserving the Land
Many states have enacted laws that set aside land for
public parks. **Environment Why is this a good idea?**

Hawaii was the first state to enact a land-use law.
Wyoming, Idaho, and Florida soon followed.

Other states have taken action to protect land and
water resources. Oregon has taken major steps in protecting 500 miles of rivers and in banning billboards
and disposable bottles. Nearly half of the states have
passed laws to control strip mining, a form of mining
that removes the topsoil and vegetation.

These actions only touch the surface of what states
have done in the area of conservation. More action is
likely to follow as the environment remains an important public issue.

1
SECTION REVIEW

Section Summary
States have broad powers to regulate economic life
and protect the environment.

Checking for Understanding
Recalling Facts
1. Define tort, corporate charter, public utility,
   monopoly, workers' compensation, unemployment
   compensation, tax credit.
2. Name the three industries over which states
   passed the most rigorous regulations.
3. List eight professions and occupations that require
   state licenses.
4. Demonstrate one way in which economic growth
   may conflict with environmental protection.

Exploring Themes
5. Free Enterprise Why did states relax restrictions
   on corporate charters after 1860?
6. Public Policy How did states respond to the change
   in federal government regulatory policy in the
   1980s?

Critical Thinking Skills
7. Expressing Problems Clearly What factors must a
   state legislature weigh carefully when considering
   taxing or regulating large business corporations?
8. Drawing Conclusions Why have states enacted so
   much legislation to protect the environment?

Section 1 Review Answers

1. Definitions of terms appear on pages indicated: **tort,**
716; **corporate charter,** 717; **public utility,** 717;
monopoly, 717; **workers' compensation,** 718; **unemployment compensation,** 718; **tax credit,** 719
2. banks, insurance, public utilities
3. lawyers, physicians, dentists, pharmacists, teachers, accountants, psychologists, architects, nurses, veterinarians,
engineers, barbers, and funeral directors

4. Answers will vary, but should indicate the impact of
industrial, business, or population growth on the environment.
5. As corporations became larger and more powerful, they
pressured state legislatures. States realized the economic
value of corporate businesses and did not want to lose them
to other states.
6. As the federal government relaxed its regulatory function, the states reclaimed many regulatory powers over
businesses.

7. They must consider the effect on business and the
possibility that the state may not be attractive to business
if it taxes too heavily.
8. In recent years medical scientists have warned that air
and water pollution endanger public health. Since the federal government began to take less regulatory action, states
enacted their own legislation to protect the environment.

Spanish Legal Contributions

By the mid-1600s, Spain controlled Central America, part of South America, Mexico, and the southwestern region of what today is the United States. From this empire came a rich heritage that influenced many aspects of life in the United States. In much of the southwestern United States, cultural and legal traditions reflect the traditions of the Spaniards who settled and controlled the region long before the United States expanded westward.

The Spaniards also contributed to the legal system in the United States. In many respects, Spanish law contained legal concepts not found in English common law at the time. Under Spanish law, for example, women had distinct rights such as the right to enter into contracts and to manage their own property, rights not found in English common law. In addition, under English common law, property a woman owned before marriage became the property of her husband, as did all of the married couple's earnings. Also under English common law, the wife retained only a small portion of the couple's wealth. Spanish law, on the other hand, included the concept of community property that is common in most states today. Under Spanish law a wife retained the right to one-half of all earnings acquired during the marriage. The wife also had to approve any sale of the couple's lands. This concept of community property was first adopted in the southwestern states that formerly had been part of Spain's empire in North America—Texas, Arizona, and California. Later, the entire United States was affected. As historian Donald E. Worcester noted:

> *Probably the most significant extension of the Spanish doctrine of community property is the joint income tax return, which appeared first in the borderland states. In 1948, because of its obvious advantages, this benefit was extended to all married couples in the United States for income tax purposes.*
>
> —DONALD E. WORCESTER, 1976

Each year joint income tax returns enable many married couples to enjoy tax savings not always available to single taxpayers.

Early California Settlers
The Lugos, a large ranching family of Spanish descent, were among the Mexicans who settled in California, a state whose culture reflects a rich Mexican heritage.

Other Spanish legal contributions included a protection for debtors that prevented creditors from seizing their property. This protection attracted settlers from the United States who migrated and settled in Spanish Texas. Spanish law also provided free or inexpensive land for settlers long before the United States followed suit with its Homestead Act in the 1860s. Later, Spanish and Mexican laws provided the basis for settling disputes over water and mineral rights.

Today the United States with its growing Hispanic population continues to reflect the rich cultural and legal heritage of the Spaniards in North America. This heritage has enriched this nation's language, art, and architecture, as well as its legal system.

Examining Our Multicultural Heritage

Reviewing Facts
1. Identify the rights of women under the Spanish legal system.
2. Explain the concept of community property.

Critical Thinking Skills
3. Determining Relevance How does the joint income tax return reflect the concept of community property?

Focus

Have students identify the part of the United States where the Spanish heritage is strongest today. Discuss what aspects of Spanish culture are associated with the American Southwest.

Teach

Have students give examples of the property rights of women under Spanish law. Contrast these rights with the way women's property rights were treated under English common law. Ask students why they think the concept of community property was first adopted in the southwestern states. *(because of Spanish legal traditions)*

Assess

Have students complete **Examining Our Multicultural Heritage.**

Answers

1. right to own property, enter into contracts, and the right of community property
2. Earnings acquired during a marriage are equally the property of the wife and the husband.
3. Filing a joint return accurately reflects the shared earnings of a husband and wife, even though only one is employed.

Close

Have students think of other examples of ways in which cultural diversity has influenced state laws or government.

More About Our Multicultural Heritage

The borderland states of Texas, New Mexico, Arizona, and California were part of the Spanish empire for over 300 years. Spain laid claim to the Southwest through explorations in the early 1500s. Conflicts between the Spanish and Native American groups discouraged settlement as did the absence of gold and other treasure. However by the 1700s, some settlers from Mexico and Spain had taken up ranching throughout the borderlands. Texas, New Mexico, and Arizona came under Mexican control following the Mexican War of Independence from Spain. These states became United States territories through the Treaty of Guadalupe Hidalgo and the Gadsden Purchase.

Focus

Bell Ringer

As you take attendance, have students make a list of as many different kinds of crimes they can think of.

Motivating Activity

List students' Bell Ringer responses on the chalkboard. Then ask students how the list can be divided into two groups. In this way lead students to appreciate that crimes are committed either against people or against property.

Vocabulary Precheck

List the terms and concepts on the chalkboard. Have students develop questions for which each term or concept is an answer.

LEP

CONNECTIONS

Economics

In many states when people are convicted of certain crimes, any property tied to the crime is forfeited. Cash, cars, boats, planes, and even houses are seized in this way. Funds raised from such seizures are often used to finance law enforcement activities.

GLENCOE TECHNOLOGY

Focus on Government
Video 47
Lecture Launcher:
State Government in Action
Running Time: 3:14
Videodisc 3, Chap. 47
VHS Tape 3, Begins 21:12

SECTION

② Protecting Life and Property

In 1990 a serious crime such as murder, assault, or burglary occurred every two seconds in the United States. Even more alarming, violent crimes are occurring five times more frequently today than in the 1960s. Crimes against property such as robbery and automobile theft have also been increasing.

What are the reasons for the increase in crime against people and property? Many causes have been suggested. Possible causes include the effects of poverty and urban decline; a decreasing respect for law and authority; understaffed and overworked police forces; and a slow and inefficient court system.

State criminal justice resources are not keeping pace with crime. In 1990 the executive director of the Illinois Criminal Justice Information Authority stated:

S tate and local administrators are desperately trying to match up limited resources with seemingly unlimited demands, but the system continues to lose ground. And we're losing ground not just in our day-to-day workload. We're also losing ground in our investments in technology, training, and other efficiency measures that could relieve some of the pressure down the road.

—J. David Coldren, 1990

Criminal Justice Systems

For the most part, protecting life and property is the responsibility of state and local governments. These governments provide more than 90 percent of all employees in the criminal justice system. Laws dealing with most common crimes come directly from state government. The federal government has only limited jurisdiction over most crimes. Local governments usually do not make criminal laws, but they have the primary responsibility for enforcing state laws that protect life and property.

State Criminal Laws Laws regulating such crimes as murder, rape, assault, burglary, and the sale and use of dangerous drugs are all part of the state criminal code. Local governments can only enact laws dealing with crime that their state governments allow them to pass.

The federal system allows for great variety in the ways states deal with crime, permitting the states to experiment with new programs and techniques. In addition, while some states impose the death penalty for certain types of homicide, other states impose prison sentences.

Each state sets its own system of punishment. Several states have introduced mandatory sentencing for drug-related crimes. **Mandatory sentencing** is a system of fixed, required terms of imprisonment for certain types of crimes. In most other states, a judge has greater flexibility in imposing sentences on drug offenders.

To take another example, about 4 out of 5 states have passed victim compensation laws, whereby state government provides financial aid to victims of certain crimes. In Utah and Mississippi, a different technique has been used. In these states a state court judge may order a criminal to compensate victims.

SECTION PREVIEW

Objectives
After studying this section, you should be able to:
■ Evaluate the problems states face in protecting life and property.
■ Analyze the advantages and disadvantages of a decentralized criminal justice system.

Key Terms and Concepts
mandatory sentencing, extradition, public defender, bail, indictment, information, arraignment, bench trial, hung jury, plea bargaining, probation, parole, shock probation, shock incarceration, house arrest

Themes in Government
■ Federalism
■ Civil Rights

Critical Thinking Skills
■ Understanding Cause and Effect
■ Expressing Problems Clearly

722   Unit 8: State Government

Classroom Resources for Section 2

📁 Guided Reading Activities
📁 Reproducible Lesson Plans
📁 Interpreting Political Cartoons 20, 51
📁 Section 2 Quiz

✚ Testmaker
🔖 Chapter Transparencies 25
SAT Practice Tests
Writer's Guidebook

Problems of Decentralized Justice Because criminal justice is usually a state responsibility, the justice system has often been described as decentralized, or even fragmented. Generally, however, decentralization has been regarded as an advantage. Urbanized states like New York and California tend to have higher crime rates than mostly rural states like West Virginia and North Dakota. Different crime rates, along with different living conditions, may call for criminal laws specifically geared to a particular state.

Decentralized justice does create some problems, however. Generally these problems occur when local communities in the same state or in different states fail to cooperate with each other in prosecuting a crime. This problem often occurs when a state seeks extradition. **Extradition** is a legal procedure through which a person accused of a crime who has fled to another state is returned to the state where the crime took place. Article IV of the United States Constitution specifically requires extradition.

Most states honor requests for extradition. Sometimes, however, people accused of crimes flee to another state and live model lives. Some governors have been reluctant to agree to extradite such people. Extradition controversies also may result from separation and divorce. If a parent leaves a state and refuses to provide financial support for a dependent child, the state to which the parent has moved may be unwilling to return that person for prosecution.

Another issue that decentralized justice makes difficult is gun control. A strong gun-control bill in one state can be rendered ineffective if a neighboring state has few controls. Also, in the case of organized crime, cooperation between the states is required to provide effective prosecution. Sometimes this cooperation is hard to achieve.

State Police Forces

Most law enforcement officers serve local governments. Although the state police are now a common sight on major highways, no state police force existed until the twentieth century. The well-known Texas Rangers were formed in 1835 as a border patrol force. The first actual state police force, however, was the Pennsylvania State Constabulary, organized in 1905.

As the automobile became more widely used, states needed statewide, mobile police forces. Today all states except Hawaii have a state police force. State police forces are normally limited in the functions they perform—most are basically highway patrol units. The state police have investigative powers in many states, and in only a few states do they possess broad police responsibilities. The more than 50,000 state police officers in this country today represent only 10 percent of the total number of police officers nationwide.

Many state police forces do perform special services for local police departments. Frequently they provide services that localities may not be able to afford, such as crime laboratories, information-gathering facilities, and lie-detector tests. In a number of states, the state police also operate training academies for recruits to local police departments.

Crossing the Border
States must extradite criminals and fugitives from justice. **Law** Which article of the Constitution requires extradition?

<table>
<tr><td colspan="3">STUDY GUIDE</td></tr>
</table>

Themes in Government
Federalism **Why does the federal government have limited jurisdiction over most crimes?**

Critical Thinking Skills
Understanding Cause and Effect **What do you think is the purpose of allowing state court judges to** order criminals to compensate the victims of crimes?

Teach

Guided Practice

L1 Constitutional Interpretations Write the following on the chalkboard: *Article IV, Fifth Amendment, Sixth Amendment, Eighth Amendment.* Have volunteers explain how these parts of the Constitution affect the procedures in the criminal justice system. **LEP**

Interpreting Visuals
Display transparency 25 from the *Chapter Transparencies* in the Teacher's Classroom Resources and use the accompanying teaching strategy and student activity to teach about state judiciary spending.

Caption Answer
Article IV

=== STUDY GUIDE ===

Theme Answer
Laws dealing with most crimes are state laws.

Critical Thinking Answer
Answers may include that criminals realize the damage they do or that victims are paid for their loss or suffering.

CONNECTIONS

Law
Thirty-seven states have capital punishment laws that impose the death penalty for certain types of homicide.

Background

Public dissatisfaction with state criminal justice systems is at an all-time high. Even though states are spending massive amounts on new prisons, ironically, some cannot open their newly completed buildings because their operating budgets have been cut. Public confidence is certainly linked to the perception that despite the increasing number of people who are behind bars, crime also continues to increase. One estimate indicates that state courts are processing about 600,000 serious criminal cases each year, an increase that overloads state court resources.

L2 Creating a Flow Chart
Have students create a flow chart on the chalkboard to show a defendant going through the criminal justice system. *(arrest, preliminary hearing and bail, indictment, arraignment, trial, and sentencing and correction)* Have students explain what happens at each stage. Ask where they would place plea bargaining on the chart.

L3 Debate Have students debate the following:

Does bail promote or hinder justice? *(Setting a defendant free gives the person opportunity to commit other crimes. Keeping the accused in jail violates the presumption of innocence.)*

CONNECTIONS

Economics
In 1990 the New York City Criminal Court disposed of 230,000 cases; of these cases, there were only 973 trials, a rate of 0.4 percent. To hold trials in only 10 percent of the court's cases—instead of 0.4 percent—would require 5 times as many judges, prosecutors, and defense attorneys!

Procedures in Criminal Cases

State courts handle the great majority of all criminal cases in the United States. One estimate indicates that state courts hear more than 600,000 serious criminal cases each year. Each year state and local courts also handle millions of minor charges such as traffic violations.

Arrest Criminal cases start with the arrest of a suspect. When the crime is a minor one—a misdemeanor—the defendant is usually brought before a judge. The judge reviews the available evidence, decides guilt or innocence, and hands out a penalty. In the case of a felony, or serious crime, court procedure is more involved.

The Prosecution In a felony case, the prosecutor represents the state and brings charges against the defendant. The prosecutor is usually elected at the local level, and in many states is known as the district attorney, the state's attorney, or the public prosecutor. Localities in the United States have more than 2,500 district attorneys, each one usually serving one county. In areas with many criminal cases, the prosecutor has a staff of attorneys to assist the state in conducting cases.

The prosecutor is one of the most powerful government officials. Robert Jackson, a former justice of the United States Supreme Court, once wrote that the prosecutor has "more control over life, liberty, and reputation than any other person in America."

The Defense Attorney The Sixth Amendment states that a person accused of a crime has the right to counsel. The defense attorney acts to protect the rights of the defendant and to present the best case possible. If an individual cannot afford a lawyer, the courts must provide free legal help.

The Supreme Court established the requirement of free legal counsel in the case of *Gideon* v. *Wainwright*, (1963). As a result of this decision, state and local governments have employed two methods of providing free legal counsel—assigned counsel and the public defender system.

Under the assigned counsel method, the judge chooses a lawyer for the defendant. Often the judge will assign the case to a young lawyer who may not yet have an established law practice. In some cities, such as Detroit and Houston, experienced lawyers set aside some of their time for assigned counsel cases. The lawyers' fees are paid out of public funds.

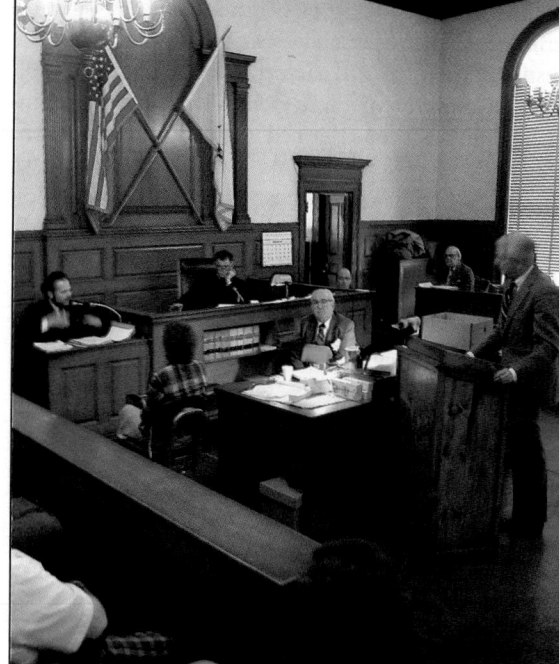

Handling Criminal Cases
From misdemeanors to felonies, state courts hear the bulk of the country's criminal cases. **Law What happens if a jury can not agree on a verdict?**

The public defender system, on the other hand, provides lawyers whose full-time job is to defend poor clients. **Public defenders** are state or local government employees, or they work for so-called legal aid societies that the state or local government finances. As a regular part of the criminal justice system, public defenders come to know the ins and outs of local courts, as well as the personal characteristics of judges and prosecutors. For these reasons many people believe that the public defender system provides better legal aid than the assigned counsel system. Twenty-nine states have public defender offices. In many of these states, however, the program is available only in major cities.

Preliminary Hearing and Bail After they make a felony arrest, the police file evidence against the suspect with the prosecutor's office. The prosecutor then decides whether or not to charge the person with the crime. If evidence is lacking, the case will be dropped. If the prosecutor has enough evidence, he or she brings the suspect before a judge for a preliminary hearing. At this hearing the state files charges against the suspect, and the judge decides whether the person should be held in jail or released on bail.

Cooperative Learning Activity

Organize the class into groups of seven. In each group, one person should assume each of these roles: defendant, police officer, prosecutor, grand jury, trial jury, judge, and reporter. The defendant should suggest a crime he or she has committed. Then each member of the criminal justice system should use the discretionary power of his or her role, giving one reason for stopping the process and one for continuing. For example, the police officer should give a reason for not making an arrest, then for making an arrest, moving the process on to the prosecutor, and so on. The reporter takes notes and presents a brief summary of the process to the class.

Bail is a pledge of money or property used as a guarantee that the accused will return to court for trial.

The Eighth Amendment provides that "excessive bail shall not be required." Courts have interpreted this amendment to mean that the amount of bail should be related to the seriousness of the charge. Prosecutors often ask the judge to set a high bail, while defense attorneys naturally ask for the lowest possible bail. Defendants who cannot supply the bail may have to stay in jail until their case comes to trial—often weeks or even months. Many courts now release defendants on their "own recognizance," without bail, if the defendants seem likely to appear for trial.

Indictment by Grand Jury After a preliminary hearing, the prosecutor must arrange for an indictment against the accused. An **indictment** is a charge by a grand jury that the person committed a particular crime. The Fifth Amendment states that "no person shall be held to answer for a capital, or otherwise infamous crime, unless on a presentment or indictment of a grand jury."

A grand jury of 16 to 23 citizens hears evidence intended to show that the defendant committed the crime in question. The grand jury weighs the evidence. If a majority of the jurors believe the evidence is sufficient to hold the person for trial, the indictment is issued. If a majority of the grand jurors believe there is insufficient evidence, the person is freed.

State judicial systems established the grand jury to check the power of the prosecutor. In reality, this rarely occurs. In practice, the grand jury almost always follows the prosecutor's recommendation. One study of grand juries found that they went along with the prosecutor in 98 percent of the cases.

Because growing crime rates have made the grand jury process time-consuming and expensive, in most states prosecutors charge people with minor crimes by filing a formal accusation, called an **information**, with a judge. More than half the states use this procedure for some serious crimes as well.

Arraignment After the indictment process comes the **arraignment**—a procedure during which the defendant comes into court before a judge who reads the formal charges in the indictment. The defendant then pleads guilty or not guilty. At this point most defendants plead not guilty in the hope of being acquitted or getting a reduced charge in the next steps of the criminal procedure.

Trial The Sixth Amendment guarantees an accused person "a speedy and public trial, by an impartial jury of the state and district wherein the crime shall have been committed." If the accused wishes, he or she can decide not to have a jury trial. Instead, the court may order a bench trial. In a **bench trial**, the case is presented before a judge alone. The judge hears the evidence the prosecution and the defense present and decides the case.

Major criminal cases involving, for example, armed robbery or murder use a jury. The trial jury is more formally known as a petit jury, as opposed to a grand jury. In most states a petit jury has 12 members, but some states permit juries of as few as 6 people.

Because of a jury's serious responsibilities, most states require that a jury's verdict be unanimous in all criminal cases. Some states make an exception for minor criminal cases in which only a majority vote is required. A jury that cannot agree on a verdict is commonly called a **hung jury**. In this event the court declares a mistrial and holds a new trial with a new jury, or the prosecutor may drop the charges against the defendant.

Plea Bargaining Most criminal cases never come to trial. About 90 percent of such cases are settled before trial through plea bargaining. **Plea bargaining** is a process by which an accused person agrees to plead guilty in exchange for a promise from the prosecutor to reduce the charges. In some courts the judge is part of this process.

Suppose the state charges John Jones with murder in the first degree. If convicted, Jones could go to jail for life. The prosecutor believes there is ample evi-

Independent Practice

L1 Making Comparisons Have students work in pairs to list the advantages and disadvantages of a decentralized criminal justice system.

📁 **Interpreting Political Cartoons** Have students complete activities 20 and 51 in *Interpreting Political Cartoons* in the Teacher's Classroom Resources.

L2 Persuasive Writing Have students research one of the present-day methods for dealing with overcrowded prisons and use their research to write an editorial in which they defend or oppose their selected method.

STUDY GUIDE

Critical Thinking Answer
A younger, less experienced attorney may be assigned the case.

CONNECTIONS

Law
Persons convicted of multiple crimes may be required to serve the sentence for each crime consecutively, or the judge may allow them to serve their sentence concurrently—at the same time. One exception is when a gun is used in a crime. Many states require a mandatory additional sentence in such cases, to be added to the end of the sentence for the crime.

STUDY GUIDE

Themes in Government	Critical Thinking Skills	represented by counsel under the assigned counsel method?
Civil Rights Bail allows defendants freedom to continue their normal work and family lives and prepare their cases before trial.	**Expressing Problems Clearly** **Why is it possible that a poorer defendant may not be as well**	

Special Needs Strategy

Writing Disability Students who have trouble pronouncing and spelling words are not as able to remember new vocabulary or use a wide range of vocabulary in their writing. Make sure students can both pronounce and spell the key terms and concepts in this section correctly. With a word like *indictment,* point out that the pronunciation "hides" the silent letter "c." Then have students write sentences using each of the terms and have them read their sentences aloud to check their understanding.

Graph Study Answer
rise in crime rates and repeat offenders

L3 Civil Rights Have each student write a brief scenario of the arrest, conviction, and sentencing of a fictional person. The account should contain three procedural errors, which students should identify on a separate sheet of paper. Then have students exchange papers and identify the three errors.

Assess

Check for Understanding

Have students complete Section 2 Review on page 727.

Meeting Objectives

Each section objective is tested by the Section Review questions that follow it in parentheses.
- Evaluate the problems that states face in protecting life and property. (3, 4, 7, 8)
- Analyze the advantages and disadvantages of a decentralized criminal justice system. (5, 6, 8)

CONNECTIONS

Law
Polls showing that the public wanted to lock up offenders for longer periods of time and to be tougher on repeat offenders influenced Congress to pass Clinton's new anti-crime legislation in 1994. The bill proposed to add many more law enforcement officers on the streets. If they were effective, already overcrowded prisons could face a major crisis.

dence against Jones but is not sure that a jury will convict him of first-degree murder. Besides, the courts are crowded, and the Jones case may not come up for months, by which time the witnesses may have forgotten the details of the case. The prosecutor offers to reduce the charges against Jones to manslaughter in exchange for a plea of guilty. Because manslaughter carries a lighter sentence, Jones, who knows he cannot present a strong defense, accepts the offer. The judge then sentences Jones to jail on the manslaughter charge.

Plea bargaining has been controversial for a number of reasons. Critics contend that it is unjust to reduce a charge if a person really has committed a crime that fits the charge. Plea bargaining, they claim, makes a mockery of the law by allowing a defendant to bargain for leniency. Critics also condemn plea bargaining because it increases the already powerful role of the prosecutor.

Those who favor plea bargaining argue that it actually increases the power of defendants in the legal process. The basic argument in favor of plea bargaining stresses convenience and efficiency. The courts' calendars are very crowded, and prosecutors and judges are often overworked. Plea bargaining helps reduce the pressure on judges and courts.

Sentencing and Correction

A sentence is the penalty that a court imposes on a person convicted of a crime. A sentence normally involves a specific term in prison, sometimes with time off for good behavior. It may also require the convicted person to pay a fine.

In some cases a judge may decide that a more suitable sentence than either a prison term or a fine is to place the criminal on probation. The court grants a person **probation**—liberty subject to good behavior under the supervision of a probation officer.

Another possible choice for a judge is to sentence the criminal and then suspend the sentence. In a suspended sentence, the court postpones or even cancels the punishment, provided the guilty person avoids further trouble with the law. Judges often give suspended sentences to first-time offenders.

Differences in Sentencing Because each state has its own criminal laws, dramatic differences exist among states when it comes to sentencing. Sharp differences in sentencing within the same state also exist because judges have considerable latitude in sentenc-

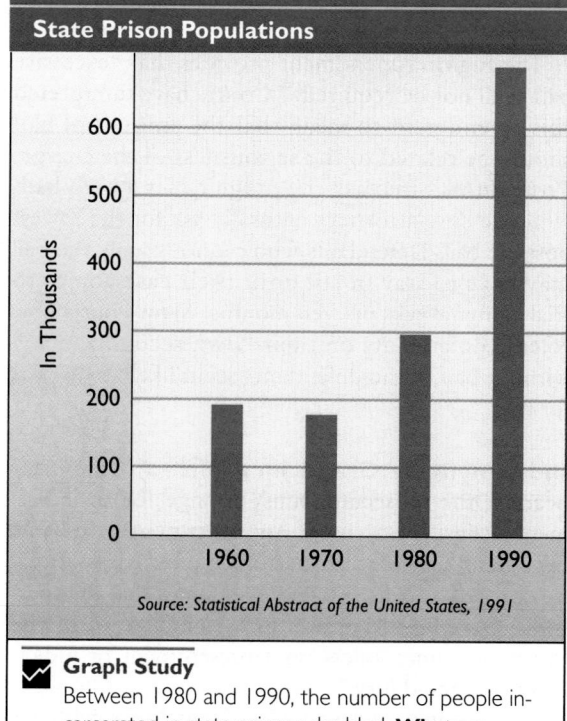

State Prison Populations

In Thousands

600
500
400
300
200
100
0

1960 1970 1980 1990

Source: *Statistical Abstract of the United States, 1991*

Graph Study
Between 1980 and 1990, the number of people incarcerated in state prisons doubled. **What are some reasons for the enormous growth in the prison population?**

ing. One study found that the typical criminal convicted of armed robbery in northern Wyoming received a 10- to 12-year sentence. In southern Wyoming, a person convicted of armed robbery normally received a 2- to 3-year sentence. Similar differences exist in other states.

The Correction System State prisons, county and municipal jails, and other houses of detention throughout a state make up a state's correction system. State spending for corrections is growing faster than for education, public welfare, hospitals, or highways. A California criminal justice official explained the trend:

As crime continued to grow, as violence continued to grow, and there was an incarcerative response, then there was a necessity to build. Of course, building prisons is extremely expensive. And when you build them, you must staff them, and that's extremely expensive.

—G. ALBERT HOWENSTEIN, 1990

The need for more prisons resulted from the growth of correctional populations—more than

Critical Thinking Activity

Expressing Problems Clearly Have students work in pairs to consider several of the areas discussed in the section, for example, plea bargaining, extradition, public defender system, high bail, low bail, and so on. Have each pair conclude their work by stating two problems connected with each area

or process. For example, two problems related to the public defender system might be: 1) A public defender often is put in a position of having to defend an obviously guilty person, or 2) If public defenders are more competent than assigned counsel, they should be available in all states.

750,000 people were in state prisons by 1991. Overcrowding in state prisons affects daily life in prison, state budgets, and the operation of the court system. As states rushed to build additional prisons to house an increasing number of people convicted of crimes, the United States Congress passed an omnibus crime bill. The new legislation aimed to put an additional 100,000 police officers on the streets. More officers would likely mean more arrests and more convictions. This could only increase the pressure on an already crowded prison system.

Judges, aware of the strains on the system, are likely to choose probation as a sentence. Today almost 2.4 million people are on probation. The parole population has swelled to more than 400,000. **Parole** means that a prisoner serves the rest of the sentence in the community under the supervision of a parole officer. Because of probation and parole, three out of every four offenders who might otherwise be in prison are in the community.

Many states are giving judges more sentencing options. Some of these are shock probation, shock incarceration, intensive supervision probation or parole, and house arrest.

Several states introduced **shock probation** in the 1960s. It was designed to show young offenders how terrible prison life could be through a brief prison incarceration followed by supervised release. **Shock incarceration**, a relatively new program, involves shorter sentences spent in a highly structured, military-style environment where offenders participate in work, community service, education, and counseling.

Constant Surveillance
Criminals on strictly supervised probation are often monitored electronically. **Law** Why have states been forced to use probation frequently?

Intensive supervision probation or parole keeps high-risk offenders in the community, but under close supervision that involves frequent home visits or even nightly curfew checks. The court usually requires that offenders also pay restitution, participate in community service programs, remain employed, and submit to drug testing. Electronic monitoring often accompanies this process. The offender wears an electronic device that continually signals his or her location.

A related alternative sentence is **house arrest**, which requires an offender to stay at home except for certain functions the court permits. Several states are using this approach to incarceration.

---

2 SECTION REVIEW

Section Summary
State laws define crimes, and the state justice system focuses on arrests, convictions, and corrections.

Checking for Understanding
Recalling Facts
1. Define mandatory sentencing, extradition, public defender, bail, indictment, information, arraignment, bench trial, hung jury, plea bargaining, probation, parole, shock probation, shock incarceration, house arrest.
2. Name the titles of the attorney for the state and for the accused in a criminal case.
3. Explain the function of bail in supporting the presumption that the accused is innocent until proven guilty.

4. Describe how state correctional systems are strained to meet the demands placed upon them.
Exploring Themes
5. Federalism What is the main advantage and disadvantage of a decentralized criminal justice system?
6. Civil Rights Why has the Supreme Court decided that it is everyone's right to have an attorney when accused of a crime?

Critical Thinking Skills
7. Understanding Cause and Effect Choose two of the causes of increasing crime listed in the introduction to Section 2. Write a paragraph showing how these causes are related to the growth of crime.
8. Expressing Problems Clearly Why have states been unable to slow increasing crime rates?

Evaluate

📁 Section 2 Quiz

🔲 Testmaker

Reteach

Have students write a section summary in which they use all the key terms and concepts.

Enrich

Have students research ways in which their state has experimented with innovative programs to reduce crime and increase respect for the law.

Close

Have students read the statements by J. David Coldren on page 722 and by G. Albert Howenstein on page 726. What problems do these writers indicate face the criminal justice system today? What solutions can students suggest?

CONNECTIONS

Economics
Florida's Community Control Program keeps about 5,000 criminals in their homes daily, reducing the expense of confinement to about 10 percent of the costs of traditional imprisonment.

Section 2 Review Answers

1. Definitions of terms appear on pages indicated: **mandatory sentencing,** 722; **extradition,** 723; **public defender,** 724; **bail,** 725; **indictment,** 725; **information,** 725; **arraignment,** 725; **bench trial,** 725; **hung jury,** 725; **plea bargaining,** 725; **probation,** 726; **parole,** 727; **shock probation,** 727; **shock incarceration,** 727; **house arrest,** 727

2. the prosecutor, the defense attorney
3. Bail allows the person who will be tried to remain free until the day of the trial, while assuring the court that the person will appear at the trial.
4. More than 15,000 people who should be in state prisons are held in local jails, because state prisons are overcrowded.
5. Decentralization allows the system to adapt to regional needs. It creates problems when authorities in the same

state or in different states fail to cooperate in prosecuting crimes or in making activities universally illegal.
6. Defense counsel was not a universal right; it is fair to the defendant to provide an equal representation.
7. Suggested causes: effects of poverty and urban decline, decreasing respect for law, understaffed and overworked police forces, slow and inefficient court system.
8. Answers should include that much money goes to corrections, rather than to prevention.

Providing for Public Health, Education, and Welfare

Focus

Bell Ringer

Write the words *Health, Education,* and *Welfare* on the chalkboard. As you take attendance, have students write a definition and example of each.

Motivating Activity

Take several volunteers' Bell Ringer responses and write them on the chalkboard. Ask students which level of government (local, state, or federal) they think is responsible for the regulation and funding of programs in each of these areas. Ask students to give reasons for their responses. Point out to students that in Section 3 they will learn about the regulatory powers and the funding responsibilities of local, state, and federal governments in the areas of health, education, and welfare.

Vocabulary Precheck

List the terms and concepts on the chalkboard. Have volunteers skim the section to find each term and read it in context. **LEP**

Linking Past and Present
The philosophical basis for state-supported education comes from the Northwest Ordinance (1787), which called for land in each new state to be set aside for public schools. "Religion, morality and knowledge being necessary to good government and the happiness of mankind, schools as the means for education shall be forever encouraged," the Ordinance said.

State health, education, and welfare services touch the lives of many citizens. Health, education, and welfare programs combined make up the largest part of state spending. In a recent year, for example, 64 percent of all state expenditures were in these three areas. Education accounted for about 37 percent of state spending, welfare for 19 percent, and health for 8 percent.

Public Health

All state governments possess **police power**—the power to promote and protect public health, safety, morals, and welfare. In the area of health, the police power allows the state to license doctors and dentists, regulate the sale of drugs, and require vaccination for schoolchildren. State governments also provide a wide range of health services, from hospitals to pollution control.

Health Expenditures State governments spend more than $42 billion on health services each year. States support hospitals, mental health clinics, and institutions for the disabled. Many state health agencies also administer medicaid, a program for needy people who cannot afford health care.

Health expenditures are divided among the three levels of government. State governments raise about half of the total money spent on public health, while the federal government contributes nearly half. Local governments provide slightly less than 2 percent of the total, and some is contributed from fees for services paid by patients.

State health agencies serve five broad areas. These areas include personal health, health resources, environmental health, laboratories, and aid to local health departments.

Personal Health State health agencies give direct personal health services to almost one out of every four citizens. These services include the care of mothers and their newborn children, treatment of contagious diseases and chronic illnesses, mental health care, operation of public dental clinics, provisions for health checkups, and immunization against communicable and other diseases. State-supported hospitals and other institutions provide many of these services. Personal health expenditures make up more than two-thirds of all state public health costs.

Health Resources For budgeting purposes the people and equipment that are necessary to provide quality health care are called health resources. Health resources include doctors, nurses, and medical technicians; medical apparatus such as X-ray machines, magnetic resonance imaging machines, and electrocardiogram machines; and even the buses and vans that transport people to public health care facilities. State governments spent more than $1 billion in a recent year on health resources.

Environmental Health State governments are now involved in a number of environmental health activities, including air and water quality control, radiation control, and hazardous waste management. State spending for environmental health is about $500 million each year.

SECTION PREVIEW

Objectives
After studying this section, you should be able to:
- Examine the increasing role of the states in providing public health, education, and welfare services.
- Describe recent changes in school funding programs.

Key Terms and Concepts
police power, public welfare, human services, relief, general assistance.

Themes in Government
- Federalism
- Constitutional Interpretations

Critical Thinking Skills
- Drawing Conclusions
- Understanding Cause and Effect

Classroom Resources for Section 3

- Guided Reading Activities
- Reproducible Lesson Plans
- Participating in Government 25
- Primary and Secondary Source Readings 25
- Enrichment Activities 25
- Section 3 Quiz
- Testmaker
- SAT Practice Tests
- Writer's Guidebook

Laboratories All state health agencies provide laboratory services. Medical personnel may investigate a mysterious disease or identify a chemical pollutant in the air. These laboratory services are also available to local health departments that often cannot afford to maintain their own facilities.

Local Health Departments State governments often pay the bill for public health services that local authorities deliver and administer. Much of the money that state governments allot for personal health services really goes to the 3,000 local health departments in the United States.

Increasing Role in Education

The United States has a long tradition of local control over public schools. For many years the control and financing of public schools was almost entirely in local hands.

The states also played an early role in public education. As early as 1795, Connecticut established a state fund to provide money for local schools. In 1812 New York became the first state to establish the position of state superintendent of schools. All early state constitutions recognized the state's responsibility to encourage education. In terms of money spent, authority over education, and the growth of higher education, state government plays an expanding role in American public education.

Expenditures for Education The growth in state expenditures for education is certainly impressive. In 1900 state governments contributed 17 percent of all the costs of public education. Today states contribute about 45 percent of public school revenues.

Differences among the states in terms of public school financing exist. Hawaii has no local school districts, and the state government administers all the public schools, contributing about 90 percent of all public school funds. In New Hampshire, Nebraska, Oregon, and South Dakota, the state contributes less than 30 percent of public school funds. Local funds in these states account for the largest share of school revenues.

There are also differences in the total amount of spending per pupil among the states and among localities within each state. In a recent year, for example, while the national average per pupil spending for

---

PARTICIPATING IN GOVERNMENT

Displaying the American Flag

Do you know the proper way to display the American flag in a parade? Where should the flag be placed when it is displayed in an auditorium? When can a flag be flown at half-mast?

The United States flag code establishes rules for displaying and honoring the flag. Federal and state laws provide penalties for using the flag improperly or disrespectfully. Guidelines for displaying the flag include:

Hanging the Flag
• On buildings and flag-poles outdoors, the flag generally should be displayed

only in good weather from sunrise to sunset.
• When the flag is displayed vertically or horizontally against a wall, the blue field must be in the upper left corner.

Carrying the Flag
• In a parade with one other flag, the American flag should be carried on the marching right.
• In a line of flags, the

American flag should be carried in front of the center of the line.

Flying the Flag
• The American flag should be hoisted briskly and lowered slowly. When displayed with other flags, it should be raised first and lowered last.
• The flag is flown at half-mast only as a sign of national mourning.

Investigating Further

Find out the proper dimensions of the American flag. Make an accurate scale drawing of the flag.

CHAPTER 25: STATE GOVERNMENT IN ACTION   729

Background

As the economy declined in the early 1990s, people suffered along with it. Welfare payments were cut off or reduced, sending general assistance clients from one state to another seeking to improve their situation. In a pattern that was repeated elsewhere, Michigan cut 82,000 people from its welfare rolls in October 1991. Ohio officials, just across the state line, geared up for an increase in welfare applications, which require no minimum residency. California and Wisconsin also experienced increased applications from new residents during this period.

Teach

Guided Practice

L1 Public Health Have students work in pairs to illustrate each subhead in the "Public Health" section. Have one person choose a section head and make up an example to present to his or her partner. The partner should then identify the area of public health being described. Example: Student A says she runs a clinic that offers free blood pressure evaluations to citizens. Student B identifies this example as *Personal Health*. **LEP**

PARTICIPATING IN GOVERNMENT

The improper use of the flag is no longer certain, since the Supreme Court ruled in 1989 that flag burning is protected by the First Amendment. However, the United States government rules on use of the flag forbid the following, among other uses: to carry, hold, or deliver anything; as bedding, drapery, or clothing (as a costume); as a logo on paper napkins or other disposable items; and for advertising purposes. Ask: Why do you think the use of the flag in materials publicizing the armed forces is not forbidden? Is this not an example of advertising?

Have students complete activity 25 in *Participating in Government* in the Teacher's Classroom Resources.

Focus on Government
Video 45
Electronic Field Trip:
California Emergency Services
Running Time: 4:59
Videodisc 3, Chap. 45
VHS Tape 3, Begins 14:12

Video 49
Speaking Out:
States' Rights
Running Time: 1:45
Videodisc 3, Chap. 49
VHS Tape 3, Begins 26:20

L2 Interpreting Visuals Have students study the chart on page 730 and write three generalizations based on the chart. Have volunteers present their generalizations and have the class tell if they agree or disagree with them and explain why.

L3 Debate Have students debate the following: Is equality of educational opportunity guaranteed by the Constitution as is equality under the law? If not, should it be? List students' major arguments on the chalkboard.

Independent Practice

L1 Public Policy Have students find out and list the variety of state regulations that their school system must comply with and administer.

Chart Study Answer
state government

CONNECTIONS

Economics

Experts suggest one way for states to handle rising higher education costs is to raise tuition at their state universities to the level of those for private institutions. For example, in 1991 student charges at Berkeley's University of California were about $9,000 annually, compared to Stanford's $22,000.

Government Expenditures for Education in 1990: Grades K-12

	Students (in thousands)	Expenditures (in millions)				Students (in thousands)	Expenditures (in millions)		
		Federal	State	Local			Federal	State	Local
Alabama	722	308	1,532	442	Montana	151	59	306	294
Alaska	112	67	412	202	Nebraska	271	51	259	752
Arizona	615	125	1,202	1,340	Nevada	188	36	334	472
Arkansas	434	140	859	445	New Hampshire	178	28	82	858
California	4,890	1,880	15,617	5,868	New Jersey	1,096	331	3,628	4,779
Colorado	573	133	977	1,363	New Mexico	308	139	889	135
Connecticut	476	134	1,637	1,884	New York	2,571	920	7,900	10,080
Delaware	99	45	379	144	North Carolina	1,084	318	3,254	1,346
District of Columbia	84	56	–	497	North Dakota	118	31	219	191
Florida	1,817	572	5,120	3,868	Ohio	1,765	415	3,650	3,679
Georgia	1,146	322	3,011	1,612	Oklahoma	575	179	1,211	660
Hawaii	175	63	728	1	Oregon	464	147	621	1,551
Idaho	215	49	409	225	Pennsylvania	1,654	310	3,447	4,895
Illinois	1,800	704	3,484	5,000	Rhode Island	136	36	363	429
Indiana	955	182	2,381	1,456	South Carolina	620	211	1,327	1,003
Iowa	467	110	1,068	916	South Dakota	129	43	127	295
Kansas	432	104	870	1,035	Tennessee	818	260	1,336	1,173
Kentucky	623	209	1,588	480	Texas	3,315	1,105	6,095	6,992
Louisiana	791	303	1,464	1,237	Utah	441	80	721	471
Maine	214	76	601	453	Vermont	94	31	213	340
Maryland	717	207	1,618	2,354	Virginia	1,005	236	1,718	3,010
Massachusetts	829	270	1,802	2,962	Washington	812	235	2,979	844
Michigan	1,572	370	2,849	4,629	West Virginia	318	109	850	364
Minnesota	742	173	2,071	1,767	Wisconsin	782	166	1,648	2,403
Mississippi	496	245	880	450	Wyoming	96	23	275	227
Missouri	816	197	1,340	1,991					

Source: Statistical Abstract of the United States, 1991

✓ Chart Study
Each level of government contributes to funding public schools around the country. **Which level of government has an increasing role in public education policy?**

public schools was $5,245, nine states spent less than $4,000 per pupil, and five states spent more than $7,000.

The differences between rich and poor school districts within some states are so great that recently state courts have struck down several funding systems as unconstitutional.

> *In the most sweeping decision of them all, the Kentucky Supreme Court struck down not only the state's school finance system but all of its education statutes and regulations. The legislature responded by revamping the entire school system, scaling down the state Education Department and giving more control to the schools themselves. . . .*
>
> —JEFFREY L. KATZ, *GOVERNING*, AUGUST 1991

Courts also struck down school financing systems in Montana, Texas, and New Jersey. The New Jersey Supreme Court ruled that children in poor districts were entitled to per pupil expenditures "substantially equal" to those in wealthier districts. The states have

begun to address the difficult problem of assuring equal educational opportunities through more equal funding.

State Educational Authority Money provides only one view of the state's role in public education. Just as important is state governments' authority over the way public education is carried on. They have been using this authority more in recent years.

State governments establish local school districts and give these districts the power to administer public schools. State governments regulate the taxes that school districts may levy and the amount of money they may borrow. They set forth many of the policies that school districts must administer. For example, nearly half of the states require a minimum competency test for graduation. In addition, states normally regulate other aspects of public education. States stipulate the number of days schools must stay open, the number of years a student must go to school, the number of grades that must be taught, the types of courses a school must offer, the number of course credits required for grad-

Cooperative Learning Activity

Organize students into three groups and assign each group one of the section's major topics—public health, education, and welfare. Have each group create a presentation about their assigned topic that outlines the services the states provide and depicts innovative programs. Group members should divide the tasks—researching, preparing visuals, writing, and presenting. Have students give their presentation to other classes, at a teachers' meeting, or PTA meeting.

uation, the minimum salaries of teachers, and general teacher qualifications. Some state governments also establish detailed course content, approve textbooks, and create statewide examinations that all students must take.

Higher Education While state expenditures have increased for education in general, they have skyrocketed in the area of higher education. During the 1980s state spending for higher education almost doubled, outpacing federal and local support for colleges and universities by a wide margin. In a recent year, state governments spent more than $35 billion on higher education.

State governments have long been involved in higher education, dating back to the creation of the first state university, the University of Georgia, founded in 1785. Several factors are responsible for the recent spurt in state expenditures. First, a higher percentage of high school graduates go on to college. Second, college costs for such items as new classroom buildings, laboratories, dormitories, and faculty salaries have rapidly increased. State governments have also increased financial aid to students.

Public Welfare

Government efforts to maintain basic health and living conditions for those people who have insufficient resources of their own are called **public welfare** or **human services**. In earlier times welfare assistance was referred to as **relief**.

Public welfare programs have grown at every level of government in the twentieth century. The greatest growth, however, has been at the federal and state levels. In 1900 welfare functions were few; local governments and private charitable organizations provided those that did exist. By 1934 more than half the states had public welfare programs, although these programs were not able to meet the needs the Great Depression caused. By the 1990s all three levels of government were spending billions of dollars on wel-

fare programs. These federal, state, and local programs covered a wide range of benefits, from food stamps to cash payments.

Federal-State Programs The federal government's major involvement in public welfare began in 1935, with the passage of the Social Security Act. Under this act the federal government created three areas of public assistance to provide financial help to state governments. These were Aid to Families with Dependent Children, Aid to the Blind, and Old Age Assistance. Congress added Aid to the Permanently and Totally Disabled in 1950.

These programs receive about half their funding from the federal government, while the other half comes primarily from state governments. The federal government establishes minimum standards for the programs and requires that state governments apply these standards fairly throughout the state.

State governments have considerable influence over how these programs operate. For example, in the Aid to Families with Dependent Children program, state governments can set standards of eligibility, residence requirements, and the amount of cash assistance provided to recipients. The federal government requires only minimum standards. State governments can go beyond these standards if they choose. Thus, large differences among state welfare payments exist. In a recent year, California allowed a family of four more than five times the monthly public assistance that Alabama provided. Differences in state programs reflect differences in the cost of living, the ability of the state to fund the program, and the number of recipients eligible for funds.

The federal government created medicaid, another federal-state welfare program, in 1965. Medicaid provides money to the states to help people who cannot afford necessary medical services. The program covers elderly people with insufficient funds, the blind and disabled, and low-income families with dependent children. State governments administer medicaid, set certain conditions for eligibility, and provide almost 45 percent of the total cost.

Interpreting Source Readings Have students complete activity 25 in the *Primary and Secondary Source Readings* in the Teacher's Classroom Resources.

L2 Research Have students determine how much their state spends for health, education, and welfare programs annually, and how these expenditures rank with other states' funding levels.

L2 Interviewing Have students interview a local or county public health official about public health services the state provides or a school district financial officer about sources that fund their school system. Students should develop a list of questions before conducting their interview.

STUDY GUIDE

Theme Answer
In 1900 local government and charities were the main providers. By 1990 all three levels of government provided billions of dollars.

Critical Thinking Answer
By increasing funding, states established an interest in education and assumed more power to regulate local schools.

Differences in the cost of living, the ability of states to fund the programs, and the number of recipients account for most of the differences in welfare payments.

STUDY GUIDE

Themes in Government
Federalism How did public welfare administration change between 1900 and 1990?
Constitutional Interpretations The movement toward equal funding for schools is based on interpretation of the Fourteenth Amendment.

Critical Thinking Skills
Drawing Conclusions Relate the states' increasing share of education costs with increasing state regulation of schools.
Understanding Cause and Effect Why are there big differences among state welfare programs?

Assess

Check for Understanding
Have students complete Section 3 Review on page 732.

Special Needs Strategy

Writing Disability Students with learning problems often include irrelevant information in their written responses to assignments. Showing them the process of how to structure their responses is more helpful than just showing them a correct sample. One of the objectives in Section 3 is for stu-

dents to be able to describe recent changes in school funding programs. After students read the section on education, model the process of describing by writing a paragraph on an overhead or on the chalkboard, showing them where in the text you found the information.

Caption Answer
It provides education and training to people on welfare.

Meeting Objectives

Each section objective is tested by the Section Review questions that follow it in parentheses.
- Examine the increasing role of the states in providing public health, education, and welfare services. (2, 3, 4, 5, 7, 8)
- Describe recent changes in school funding programs. (4, 6)

Evaluate

📁 Section 3 Quiz

💾 Testmaker

Reteach

Have students formulate main idea statements for each subhead in Section 3.

Enrich

📁 Have students complete activity 25 in *Enrichment Activities* in the Teacher's Classroom Resources.

Close

Have students point out connections among the three service areas provided by states.

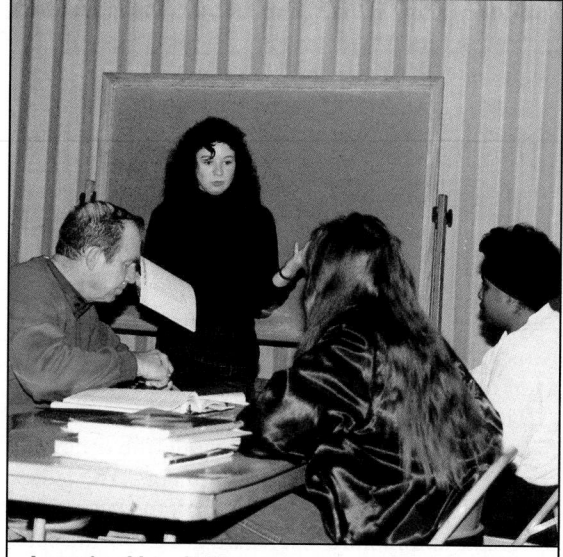

Learning New Skills
The JOBS program aims to stimulate financial independence. **Law How does it work?**

pand welfare-to-work programs. The aim of welfare reform is to move people from dependence on welfare to financial independence through training and education. The reform represents a major breakthrough. It accepts the liberal view that it is cost-effective to provide education and training along with social services and the conservative view that healthy adults on welfare should have to work. The law created a program called JOBS—Job Opportunities and Basic Skills.

While the states agreed with the goal, coming up with the revenue was a major problem. With rising welfare caseloads, the states could not match the federal government's funding.

In fiscal 1990, for example, states were able to come up with enough to claim only an estimated 67 percent of the $800 million in federal funds Congress appropriated for the program that year, and are projected to be able to match only 56 percent of the $1 billion available in fiscal 1991.
—JULIE ROVENER, *GOVERNING*, JANUARY 1991

In recent years state costs for medicaid have risen sharply, partly because Congress has mandated that states expand health-care coverage for the poor. State costs began to increase by several billion dollars a year beginning in 1990, after Congress mandated that states add pregnant women, infants, and the elderly to medicaid coverage.

Welfare Reform In 1988 Congress passed the Family Support Act, requiring states to create or ex-

State Welfare Programs For people who do not fall into any of the federal mandated categories, most states have programs of **general assistance**. States administer and finance general assistance programs, with some help from local governments. Their benefits vary from state to state. Urbanized states like New York, California, Michigan, and Massachusetts tend to have more generous programs than do less urbanized states.

---

3 SECTION REVIEW

Section Summary
In the federal system the states share most of the cost of public health, education, and welfare.

Checking for Understanding
Recalling Facts
1. Define police power, public welfare, human services, relief, general assistance.
2. List the percentage of total spending that states contribute in each of the following: public health, public education, welfare.
3. Cite the approximate percentage of citizens receiving personal health services from state health agencies.
4. Specify three examples of state regulation of public elementary and secondary education.

Exploring Themes
5. Federalism How does the federal government ensure that states will provide welfare assistance such as medical services to the poor?
6. Constitutional Interpretations Why have several states been forced in recent years to revise their school funding programs?

Critical Thinking Skills
7. Drawing Conclusions Which area of state spending—health, education, or welfare—do you think should increase most in the coming years? Why?
8. Understanding Cause and Effect Why is there a great difference in the amount of welfare payments from one state to another?

Section 3 Review Answers

1. Definitions of terms appear on pages indicated: **police power,** 728; **public welfare,** 731; **human services,** 731; **relief,** 731; **general assistance,** 732
2. health: 55 percent, education: 45 percent, welfare: 50 percent
3. about 25 percent
4. States regulate the number of days schools must stay open, the number of years a student must go to school, the number of grades which must be taught, the types of courses a school must offer, the number of course credits required for graduation, the minimum salaries paid to teachers, and general teacher qualifications.
5. The federal government mandates certain programs and matches funds for some.
6. State courts have ruled some funding unconstitutional because it provides very unequal local educational opportunities.
7. Answers will vary, but students should provide reasons for their choices.
8. The cost of living varies from state to state, some states are more able to pay than others, and some states have more people receiving payments.

Checking Consistency

Checking consistency includes analyzing two or more sets of data to see whether they follow the same principles. Checking consistency is an important citizenship skill.

Explanation

To check consistency, follow these steps:
- Examine each set of data carefully.
- Do the sets deal with the same subject?
- If one set of data expresses an idea not contained in the other set, it does not necessarily mean they are inconsistent. If, however, one statement contradicts the other, then the two statements are inconsistent.

Consider the following statements.

Although it is the duty of all men frequently to assemble together for the public worship of Almighty God; and piety and morality, on which the prosperity of communities depends, are thereby promoted; yet no man shall or ought to be compelled to attend any religious worship, to contribute to the erection or support of any place of worship, or to the maintenance of any ministry, against his own free will and consent.
—DELAWARE BILL OF RIGHTS

All men have a natural and indefeasible right to worship Almighty God according to the dictates of their own consciences; no man can of right be compelled to attend, erect, or support any place of worship, or to maintain any ministry against his consent. No human authority can, in any case or manner whatsoever, control or interfere with the right of conscience; and no preference shall ever be given by law to any religious establishment, denomination, or mode of worship above any other.
—ARKANSAS BILL OF RIGHTS

The two statements are comparable because they deal with religious liberty. Both say that no citizen can be forced to support a particular religion.

The two are also somewhat different. The Delaware constitution asserts that all people should worship regularly so they can contribute to their communities. If the Arkansas constitution stated that religious worship had no effect or had a negative effect on community life, the two statements would be inconsistent. Instead, the Arkansas constitution says nothing either to agree or disagree. Therefore, the two statements remain consistent.

Practice

Read the following clauses from state constitutions. Then answer the questions below.

The right of trial by jury shall be secured to all, and remain inviolate; but in civil actions three fourths of the jury may render a verdict. A trial by jury may be waived in all criminal cases, not amounting to felony, by the consent of both parties, expressed in open Court, and in civil actions by the consent of the parties, signified in such manner as may be prescribed by law.
—CALIFORNIA CONSTITUTION

In all criminal prosecutions, the accused shall enjoy the right to a speedy and public trial, by an impartial jury of the county in which the crime shall have been committed: Provided, That the venue may be changed to any other county of the judicial district in which the indictment is found, upon the application of the accused, in such manner as now is, or may be prescribed by law.
—ARKANSAS CONSTITUTION

1. What is the general subject of both excerpts?
2. On what point or points do the two clauses agree?
3. What are the key differences in the statements?
4. On what points, if any, are the two clauses inconsistent? Explain.

Additional Practice

To practice the skill, see **Reinforcing the Skill** on page 741.

CHAPTER 25: STATE GOVERNMENT IN ACTION 733

Focus

Have students suggest a movie or actual courtroom drama they know of. Ask: Who or what is on trial? What is the prosecution's case? What is the defense's case? What "holes" are there in either case, for example, lack of an alibi or lack of truly incriminating evidence?

Explain that informed citizens must match facts and locate inconsistencies in evaluating government and society, just as judges and juries do in courtrooms.

Teach

Discuss the Explanation steps. Then ask students to evaluate the first two statements by putting the concepts in their own words. Students also might construct simple charts to compare their ideas. Suggest that students construct comparison charts to evaluate the statements in the Practice exercise.

Assess

Have students complete the **Practice** exercise.

Close

Review the steps for checking consistency of data. Ask: What do you think is the most important step? Why? *(determining whether the two sets deal with the same topic, so you have a valid base for comparison)*

Practice Answers

1. Both are about the right to a jury trial.
2. Both guarantee the right of a jury trial.
3. In civil cases, the jury can decide a case by a three-fourths vote. In criminal cases that are not felonies and in civil cases, a jury trial may be waived if both parties consent.
4. None. Although each contains guarantees not mentioned by the other, neither contains statements that contradict anything in the other. Therefore, they are consistent.

For additional practice, have students complete activity 25 in *Skill Reinforcement Activities* in the Teacher's Classroom Resources.

Focus

Bell Ringer

As you take attendance, have students list the items they can think of that are exempt from sales tax.

Motivating Activity

Discuss students' Bell Ringer responses. *(Students likely will not list many items.)* Note that states have different laws regarding sales taxes, but that they are a major source of state revenue. Point out that Section 4 explains the limits of the states' taxing powers and why states tax in varying ways.

Vocabulary Precheck

List the terms and concepts on the chalkboard. Have students develop questions for which each term or concept is the answer. **LEP**

Teach

Guided Practice

L1 Expressing Ideas Call on a student to come to the front of the room and describe a form of state financing without giving away the answer; for example, "a tax on the rent your tenant pays" *(income tax)*, or "a tax on your property when you die" *(inheritance tax)*, and so forth. When a student called on answers correctly, he or she becomes the next "describer." If a student answers incorrectly, the describer calls on another student and continues the process. **LEP**

SECTION 4

Sources of State Revenue

Since the early 1930s, state government expenditures have increased dramatically. Between 1932 and 1990, state government expenditures rose from $2.8 billion to about $570 billion. Federal spending, although higher than the state total, increased at a slower rate during this same period. The rapid increase in state expenditures is largely because of expansion in public health, education, welfare, and environmental protection spending.

Tax Revenue

State taxes raise nearly half of the general revenue of state governments. States levy taxes on income, on property, or on the goods and services that people buy. For most state governments, the sales tax and the income tax are the major sources of revenue.

Limitations on State Taxation Individual state constitutions limit state taxing powers. In addition, the federal Constitution limits a state's taxing powers in three ways. (1) A state cannot tax goods or products that move in or out of the state or the country. These imports and exports make up interstate and foreign commerce that only Congress can tax or regulate. (2) A state cannot tax federal property, nor can its taxing power interfere in any way with federal activities. (3) A state cannot use its taxing power to deprive people of "equal protection of the law." A state also cannot use its taxing power to deprive people of life, liberty, or property without "due process of the law." These Fourteenth Amendment protections aim

to prevent states from taxing people unfairly. For example, a state cannot tax people of one race or religion differently from other people.

State constitutions also impose limits on state taxing powers. Most state constitutions prevent states from taxing property used for educational, charitable, or religious purposes. Some state constitutions specifically prohibit or limit certain taxes such as the sales tax and the income tax. In other states voters have approved constitutional amendments limiting property taxes.

The Sales Tax As state expenditures have increased, most state governments have had to search for new sources of revenue. Because people generally object to higher taxes, the states have limited choices when it comes to tax sources. Most states rely on the sales tax as the major source of tax revenue.

State governments began using the sales tax during the Great Depression in the 1930s. Today almost all states have some type of sales tax, which accounts for about half the total tax revenue of state governments. Two types of sales tax exist. The **general sales tax** is a tax imposed on a broad range of items people buy—cars, clothing, household products, and many other types of merchandise. In some states, food and drugs are not subject to this tax. The **selective sales tax** is a tax imposed on certain items such as gasoline, liquor, or cigarettes. The selective sales tax is also called an **excise tax**.

Sales taxes have certain distinct advantages over other taxes. They are generally easy to administer, and—compared to other taxes—relatively painless to

---

SECTION PREVIEW

Objectives
After studying this section, you should be able to:
- Recognize the many and varied sources of state revenue.
- Analyze the limitations on states' taxing powers.

Key Terms and Concepts
general sales tax, selective sales tax, excise tax, regressive tax, progressive tax, proportional tax, severance tax, estate tax, bond, intergovernmental revenue, grant-in-aid, categorical-formula grant, project grant, block grant, mandate

Themes in Government
- Federalism
- Public Policy

Critical Thinking Skills
- Understanding Cause and Effect
- Distinguishing Fact From Opinion

Classroom Resources for Section 4

- Guided Reading Activities
- Reproducible Lesson Plans
- Interpreting Political Cartoons 50
- Reteaching Activities 25
- Section 4 Quiz
- Chapter 25 Tests

- Testmaker
- Audio Cassettes (English and Spanish)
- Limited English Proficiency Activities 25
- SAT Practice Tests
- Writer's Guidebook

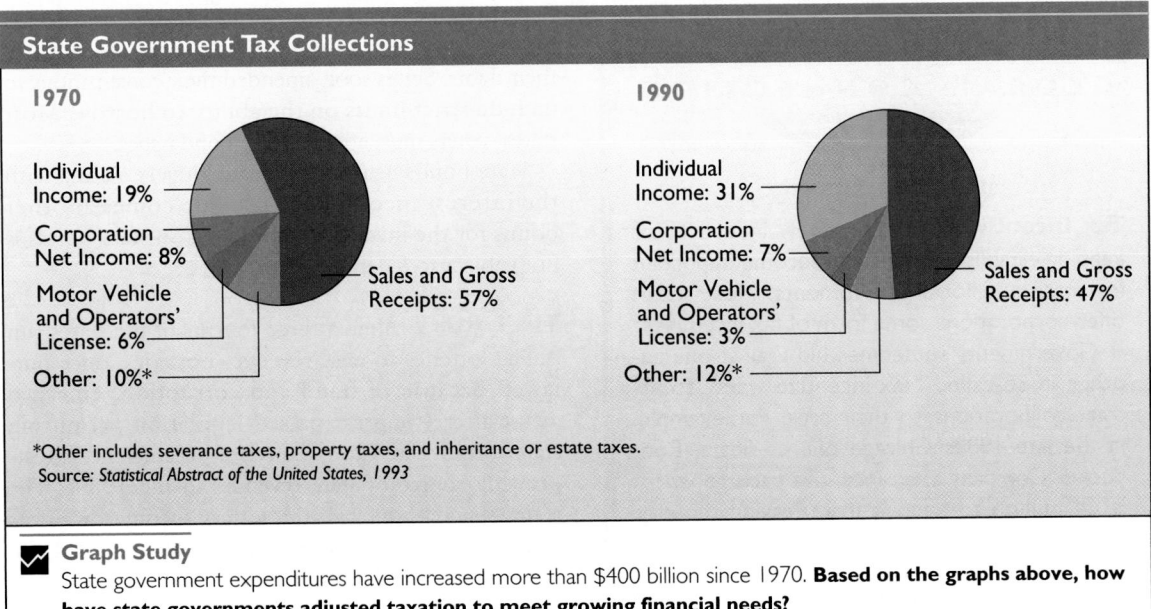

State Government Tax Collections

1970

Individual Income: 19%
Corporation Net Income: 8%
Motor Vehicle and Operators' License: 6%
Other: 10%*
Sales and Gross Receipts: 57%

1990

Individual Income: 31%
Corporation Net Income: 7%
Motor Vehicle and Operators' License: 3%
Other: 12%*
Sales and Gross Receipts: 47%

*Other includes severance taxes, property taxes, and inheritance or estate taxes.
Source: *Statistical Abstract of the United States, 1993*

✓ **Graph Study**
State government expenditures have increased more than $400 billion since 1970. **Based on the graphs above, how have state governments adjusted taxation to meet growing financial needs?**

📁 **Interpreting Political Cartoons** Have students complete activity 50 in *Interpreting Political Cartoons* in the Teacher's Classroom Resources. Then use the activity to launch a discussion of the relationship among federal grants, state taxes, and state services. Ask: What happens to the states when the federal government cuts taxes to stimulate economic growth or cuts spending to reduce the federal deficit? *(Federal aid to states is reduced, state taxes go up, and/or state services are reduced.)*

L3 Debate Have students debate the sales tax vs. the income tax issue. Call on students to make a statement which compares the two and finds one preferable—or simply to make a statement, supported by reasons, for or against each type of tax. Keep track of arguments on the chalkboard and at the end of a certain time period, tally up the pros and cons to see which tax the class prefers.

Graph Study Answer
by greatly increasing the collection of individual income taxes

---

CONNECTIONS

Economics
Who says tax collectors have no fun? The West Virginia state tax department announced in late 1991 that it was commencing "Operation Season's Greetings" to collect unpaid business taxes. Its plan—to show up at delinquent businesses in malls and shopping centers all over the state during the height of the Christmas shopping rush.

---

the taxpayer. The sales tax is easy to administer because the person who sells an item, the grocery store clerk or restaurant cashier, collects the tax. It is a less painful type of tax because the taxpayer pays it a little at a time.

People have strongly criticized the sales tax, however, as a regressive tax. A **regressive tax** is a tax that affects people with low incomes more than those with higher incomes. Because everyone buys necessary items such as clothing, the sales tax represents a higher percentage of the poorer person's income.

The State Income Tax Today 43 states have individual income taxes, and 46 states have corporate income taxes. Despite much opposition, the state income tax now accounts for more than 30 percent of all state tax revenues, compared to 10 percent in 1956. The state imposes the income tax on the earnings of individuals and corporations. These earnings, or income, can take the form of wages, profits, rents, or interest on investments.

State income tax rates usually correlate to a person's income. For example, on an income of less than $10,000 a year, a person might pay a tax rate of 2 percent. On an income of $30,000, the rate could be 7 or 8 percent. This kind of tax is called a **progressive tax** because it directly varies with a person's ability to pay. Some states assess income taxes at the same rate for every wage earner. For example, each income might be taxed 10 percent. In this case it is called a **proportional tax**.

License Taxes States require license fees for a wide variety of businesses and professions—doctors, realtors, lawyers, electricians, and others. Likewise, many states issue licenses for bus lines, bars, amusement parks, and other businesses. Fees for motor vehicle registration and driver's licenses bring in the most license tax revenue that states collect.

Severance Taxes States impose **severance taxes** on the removal of natural resources such as oil, gas, coal, uranium, and fish from state land or water. Severance taxes are especially good sources of revenue in oil- and gas-producing states such as Oklahoma and Texas. Kentucky brings in considerable revenue from a severance tax on coal.

Other Taxes Most states have numerous taxes that are less well known. Many still use the state property tax, which is a tax on certain kinds of property such as jewelry and furniture. Every state except Nevada has inheritance or **estate taxes**. These are taxes that states collect on the money and property inherited when a person dies.

Other Revenue Sources

Because states differ so widely, the sources of revenue they use also vary. In addition to the sources mentioned above, some states use special business taxes. Some states levy amusement taxes and taxes on

Background

The economic policies of the Reagan era caused state and local governments to complain of "the three Rs—*recession, (tax) revolts,* and *reductions* in federal aid," according to political scientists David Hedge and Richard Bingham. States had to both raise more money and cut spending. While some risked tax increases, others looked to lotteries, user fees—such as those for automobiles, parks, and other services—and impact charges. User fees not only raise revenues for the state, but by requiring those who benefit from a service to pay for it, the state also encourages civic responsibility. For example, higher water fees pay for cleaner water but also encourage users to conserve water.

Independent Practice

L1 Constructing a Chart Have students construct a chart that identifies the various kinds of taxes collected by states. Have students list on their charts examples of each tax where appropriate.

STUDY GUIDE

Theme Answer
Answers may include that sales tax is taken in smaller bites or that people have some choice on whether to buy certain taxed items.

Critical Thinking Answer
It would give them opportunity to frustrate programs of the federal government.

admission to sporting events. Like individuals who struggle to keep their checkbooks balanced, state political leaders have difficulty finding the necessary revenue to pay for state programs.

State taxes pay only a part of state government expenses. To finance the rest, states turn to borrowing, lotteries, and the federal government.

State Borrowing States usually borrow money to pay for large, long-term expenditures such as highway construction or other building projects. State governments borrow by selling bonds. **A bond** is a contractual promise on the part of the borrower to repay a certain sum plus interest by a specified date.

In the nineteenth century, many state governments borrowed so much money that they could not pay their debts. States soon amended their constitutions to include strict limits on the ability to borrow. Most states' voters must approve new bond issues.

State bonds usually find ready buyers. Along with the interest income they provide comes another bonus for the investor: the interest on state bonds is not subject to federal income tax.

The Lottery Almost three-fourths of the states run public lotteries to raise revenue. Lotteries, once outlawed because of fraud and corruption, emerged again after Congress passed legislation permitting state lotteries in 1963. Lotteries became the fastest-growing source of state revenues in the 1980s. The states spend about half the lottery income on prizes and 6 percent on administration. They pocket the rest—about $9 billion in 1990.

Some criticize state lotteries, saying that they encourage abusive gambling or give false hopes by downplaying the incredible odds. H. Roy Kaplan of the Florida Institute of Technology found no hard evidence that the games are harmful. He claims:

> *Y*ou don't find too many people abusing lotteries—not like with the more insidious gambling: sports betting, casinos, and race tracks. . . . All us losers can't seem to bear the idea that the winners are happy.
>
> —H. Roy Kaplan, 1989

Studies show that people with lower incomes are more likely to play the lottery. While some supporters defend the lottery as a voluntary tax, others point out that it is a regressive tax, taking more money from poorer people.

Intergovernmental Revenue

State governments do not raise enough revenue from sources within their own states to balance their

STUDY GUIDE

Themes in Government
Public Policy Why do you think most people prefer a state sales tax to a state income tax?

Critical Thinking Skills
Understanding Cause and Effect
In the case of *McCulloch* v. *Maryland* in 1819, the Supreme Court ruled that the state of Maryland could not tax the Bank of the United

States. **What would be the effect if states were permitted to tax federal property?**

Cooperative Learning Activity

Assign students to work in pairs to discuss the allotment of tax dollars in their state. In each pair one student is to represent a director of an agency in the area of health, education, or welfare, and the other student a reporter. The reporter should ask questions of the director about his or her work and why he or she thinks it needs more state funding. Encourage interviewers to play devil's advocate in their interviews.

budgets. Some states that have weak economies may have rapidly rising costs. These states may have just as much or more public pressure to provide a wide range of government services. **Intergovernmental revenue**, or revenue distributed by one level of government to another, helps to fill some of this need. The federal government, with its vast revenue and taxing power, provides about 20 percent of all state revenues.

Federal Grants Programs One way the federal government provides funds to states is through federal grants. These grants, also called **grants-in-aid**, are sums of money given to the states for a variety of specific purposes. Federal grants cover a wide range, from child health care to aid to the handicapped, from sewage control to women's sports.

Federal grants not only supply funds, but, by stipulating how the grants are to be used, also influence the states in a number of ways. (1) Grants supply funds for programs that states may not otherwise be able to afford. (2) Grants also stimulate programs and goals that the federal government believes are necessary. For example, President Bush called for states to enact mandatory sentences for serious drug crimes and Congress added more money to the war on drugs. (3) Finally, grants set certain minimum standards in the states. For example, the federal government provides grants to make sure that all states provide a minimum public welfare program.

Under **categorical-formula grants**, federal funds go to all the states on the basis of a formula. Different amounts go to different states, often depending on the state's wealth. These grants usually require states to provide matching funds. Under **project grants** state or local agencies, or even individuals, may apply for funds for a variety of specific purposes: to fight crime, to improve a city's subway system, to control air and water pollution, among other things.

Revenue Sharing The federal government designed revenue sharing to give states greater freedom in using federal funds. Beginning in 1972 under the

Living off the Lottery
Since 1964 lotteries have become a revenue source for states across the country. **Economics Why do some critics of lotteries call them a regressive tax?**

Nixon administration, the federal government gave back to states and localities some of the revenue that had been collected through the federal income tax. The most important limit on the use of the funds was that no revenue-sharing funds could be used in programs that practiced racial or ethnic discrimination. The revenue-sharing program provided more than $6 billion annually to states and localities between the years 1972 and 1980. Revenue sharing ended for state governments in 1980 and for local governments in 1986.

Block Grants State governments usually prefer block grants over categorical grants as a form of federal aid. A **block grant** is a large grant of money to a state or local government to be used for a general purpose, such as public health or crime control. Block grants have fewer guidelines, and state officials have considerably more choice over how the money will be spent.

STUDY GUIDE

Themes in Government
Federalism How does the national government use grants to influence state policy?

Critical Thinking Skills
Distinguishing Fact From Opinion List one fact and one opinion from Norman Beckman's

statement about the intrusion of the federal government on state sovereignty on page 738.

Critical Thinking Activity

Distinguishing Fact From Opinion Distribute several local newspapers to students and have them find articles on issues of local concern, including those about state revenues, budgets, and so on. Have each student find an example of a sentence

that states a fact and a sentence that states an opinion. Encourage students to find their examples in news stories rather than editorials, as the latter are likely to be mostly opinion. In each case, have students explain their choices.

L2 Political Cartoons Have students draw cartoons that express a taxpayer's response to the taxes he or she must pay. Display cartoons in the classroom. **LEP**

L3 Law Have students draw up a tax reform bill for their state. The bill should include items or activities to be exempted from tax or the kind of income to be taxed and who is exempt. Have volunteers present their bills to the class and explain the reasons for their proposed reforms.

Caption Answer
because they take more money from poorer people

STUDY GUIDE

Theme Answer
They stimulate state programs that the federal government believes necessary; they also set minimum standards for state programs.

Critical Thinking Answer
fact: A CSG review showed at least 10 examples of intrusive preemptions; opinion: Congress has shown little interest in correcting the imbalance developing in the federal system.

Assess

Check for Understanding

Have students complete Section 4 Review on page 738.

Meeting Objectives
Each section objective is tested by the Section Review questions that follow it in parentheses.
• Recognize the many and varied sources of state revenue. (3, 4, 5, 6, 7, 8)
• Analyze the limitations on states' taxing powers. (2)

Chart Study Answer

Federal priorities seem to lie most in transportation, education, health, and income security.

Evaluate

📁 Section 4 Quiz

💾 Testmaker

Reteach

📁 Have students complete activity 25 in *Reteaching Activities* in the Teacher's Classroom Resources.

Enrich

Have students consult *Statistical Abstract* for data about their state's revenue and spending policies. Have them report their findings in graphic or written form. Topics for their reports might include how state revenue sources or spending priorities compare to other states and/or how those sources or priorities have changed over time.

Close

Have students read the quote by H. Roy Kaplan on page 736. Do they agree or disagree?

Allow time to review students' chapter project chart on state taxing and spending. Ask students how the information on the chart compares to the general information about state taxing and spending contained in the chapter.

Federal Aid to State and Local Governments

	In Millions of Dollars		
	1970	1980	1992
National Defense	$37	$93	$318
Natural Resources and Environment	411	5,363	3,947
Energy	25	499	448
Agriculture	604	569	1,142
Transportation	4,599	13,087	20,616
Community and Regional Development	1,780	6,486	4,437
Education, Employment, Training, Social Services	6,417	21,862	29,060
Health	3,849	15,758	71,416
Income Security	5,795	18,495	43,504
Veterans Benefits and Services	18	90	164
Administration of Justice	42	529	987
General Government	479	8,616	2,272

Source: US Office of Management and Budget

Chart Study
The chart shows an increase of federal aid to state and local governments from 1970 to 1993, but some programs show decreases in federal aid. **How does the chart reflect trends in federal priorities?**

Federal Regulations Increasingly today, guidelines accompany federal grants. These guidelines are really requirements or conditions that states must meet if they accept the grants. Guidelines are most often at-tached to categorical-formula grants and project grants.

In recent years the federal government's share of state and local government revenue has declined, but federal regulatory **mandates** have increased. A mandate is a formal order given by a higher authority, in this case by the federal government. Between 1980 and 1990, federal assistance as a percentage of state-local government spending declined from 25.8 percent to about 20 percent. Meanwhile, the federal government increased the number of mandated programs for which state and local governments had to raise their own revenue. State and local officials began to complain about the increasing number of unfunded and underfunded federal mandates in areas such as health and the environment. Some people believed that the federal government had intruded on areas of state sovereignty. Norman Beckman, former director of The Council of State Governments' Washington Office, reported that:

Recent years have seen an increase in federal preemption of state and local authority.... A CSG [Council of State Governments] review of current and federal pending legislation showed at least 10 examples of intrusive preemptions.... Congress, which has caused most of the mandate and preemption frictions, has shown little interest in correcting the imbalance developing in the federal system.

—NORMAN BECKMAN, 1990

---

4 SECTION REVIEW

Section Summary
States raise revenue through taxes, through issuing bonds, and through federally sponsored programs.

Checking for Understanding
Recalling Facts
1. Define general sales tax, selective sales tax, excise tax, regressive tax, progressive tax, proportional tax, severance tax, estate tax, bond, intergovernmental revenue, grant-in-aid, categorical-formula grant, project grant, block grant, mandate.
2. Describe two limitations on a state's taxing power.
3. Name three sources of state revenue in addition to state taxes.
4. Specify the two main categories of state tax revenue.

Exploring Themes
5. Federalism Why do state officials prefer block grants as a form of federal aid?
6. Public Policy Why do taxpayers prefer the state sales tax to the state income tax?

Critical Thinking Skills
7. Understanding Cause and Effect How does Congress influence state policies through its distribution of federal grants?
8. Distinguishing Fact From Opinion "States should abandon lotteries as a source of revenue, because they are regressive forms of taxation. Poorer people, who are more likely to play the lottery, are also more likely to become addicted to gambling." What parts of these statements are fact and what parts are opinion?

Section 4 Review Answers

1. Definitions of terms appear on pages indicated: **general sales tax,** 734; **selective sales tax,** 734; **excise tax,** 734; **regressive tax,** 735; **progressive tax,** 735; **proportional tax,** 735; **severance tax,** 735; **estate tax,** 735; **bond,** 736; **intergovernmental revenue,** 737; **grant-in-aid,** 737; **categorical-formula grant,** 737; **project grant,** 737; **block grant,** 737; **mandate,** 738
2. A state cannot tax goods or products which move in or out of the state or the country, cannot tax federal property, and cannot use its taxing power to deprive people of equal protection of the law. Nor can a state use its taxing power to deprive people of life, liberty, or property without due process of the law.
3. intergovernmental revenue, bonds or borrowing, lotteries, licenses
4. sales tax and income tax
5. State officials have more control over these funds because they come without guidelines.

6. because it is paid in smaller doses and the person who sells an item collects the taxes on it
7. by stimulating programs and goals which the federal government believes are necessary and by setting certain minimum standards in the states
8. fact: Lotteries are regressive taxation; poorer people are more likely to play. opinion: States should abandon lotteries; poorer people are more likely to become addicted to gambling.

Linda Winikow on Managing Diversity

Linda Winikow moved from politics to corporate executive. A proponent of the kind of changes that are taking place in corporate business, she spoke of the need for diversity. The following excerpts are from her address to the Women's Bureau Conference, Washington, D.C., October 1990.

There's no question in my mind—none whatsoever—that we have an opportunity today to tap a huge reservoir—the pool of cultural diversity. Our challenge is not only to *accommodate* diversity, but to actually *use* it to bring new and richer perspectives to our jobs, to our customers and to our whole social climate. . . .

The fundamental question we have to ask ourselves, of course, is "How much has changed in the last eighty or ninety years?" The answer is mixed.

On the one hand, civil rights legislation and labor laws have done an enormous amount to wipe out the legal impediments [obstacles] to equality. And the Department of Labor has played a key role. . . .

But while the *laws* to combat discrimination have changed, all-too-many of the *attitudes* that prevented the flowering of diversity still exist. . . .

Just as the United States was made great—not by making everyone the same but rather by respecting their differences—so, too, can corporations achieve new levels of greatness. Cultural, religious and ethnic diversity in both the corporate boardroom and in the corporate trenches make that company better understand and more in tune with its customers. . . .

When I first became involved in politics, back in the early 1970s, men found it difficult to swallow that I could be a member of the Zoning Board of Appeals and be pregnant simultaneously!

. . . while the laws to combat discrimination have changed, all-too-many of the attitudes that prevented the flowering of diversity still exist. . . .

. . . There are lessons both for the managers and the managed. First, most traditional managers are afraid of change. Recognize that fear as something natural, and work with them to overcome it. . . .

As we progress as a society, that ladder becomes increasingly crowded. But it certainly comes as no surprise to learn that women are still being excluded from the top, any more than it's a surprise to learn that women and minorities hold a disproportionate share of the menial or lesser-paying jobs. . . .

Today I'm talking as a businessperson. But this wasn't always the case. For 10 years, as a New York State Senator, the struggle for women and minority rights was always at the top of my agenda.

What I did in the Senate was respond to constituents' needs by changing laws, creating programs and shaping attitudes. Legislation which protected working women and minorities were among my proudest achievements. . . .

Now, I'm with Orange and Rockland, and I recognize that it's not just government that has a role in righting the wrongs.

—LINDA WINIKOW, 1990

Examining the Reading

Reviewing Facts
1. Explain what Linda Winikow believes is the challenge facing corporate business today.
2. Identify the issues that the speaker addressed when she served in the New York Senate.

Critical Thinking Skills
3. Making Inferences What does Winikow believe to be government's and the manager's roles in achieving diversity in the workplace?

CHAPTER 25: STATE GOVERNMENT IN ACTION   739

More About Personal Perspectives

Linda Winikow was involved in politics for over a decade before she was named the first woman vice president of Orange and Rockland Utilities in 1984. In the same speech excerpted here, Winikow cites these figures: African Americans make up only 10 percent of the utility work force in the United States and Hispanics 5 percent. Only 4 percent of utility managers are African Americans; only 2 percent Hispanic. Asians and other minorities make up even smaller percentages. In the Fortune 500, only 6 chief executive officers are women, and only 5 percent of all corporate board members are women.

Focus

Take a classroom poll to see how many ethnic groups are represented. If the class is largely homogenous, ask students to speculate on what it would be like to have classmates from varying cultures. If the class is heterogenous, have them speculate on what it would be like to attend school with only those from the same culture.

Teach

Ask: How does Winikow believe the work situation for women and minorities has changed in the past 80 or 90 years? How does she believe it has not changed? What does Winikow believe women have to realize about managers in order to be effective in the workplace?

Assess

Have students complete **Examining the Reading.**

Answers

1. using cultural diversity to improve jobs, business, and society
2. protection for working women and minorities
3. Government deals with the legal obstacles to equality, while managers must change attitudes toward diversity.

Close

Ask: Which is more important in achieving equality: legal changes or attitude changes?

Identifying Terms and Concepts

1. tort, 2. monopoly, 3. extradition, 4. arraignment, 5. probation

Reviewing Facts and Ideas

1. A corporation charter is a document by which the state grants rights, powers, and privileges to a corporation. A charter gives a corporation legal status.

2. All states regulate the rates that public utility companies may charge.

3. Workers' compensation helps employees who are unable to work as a result of job-related injury or ill health. Unemployment compensation provides money for workers who lose their jobs.

4. Congress passed a bill allowing states to impose any liability standards on business that they choose.

5. Under the assigned counsel method the judge chooses a lawyer, often a young attorney who may not have an established practice, for the defendant. In some cities experienced lawyers set aside some of their time for assigned counsel cases. The public defender system provides lawyers whose full-time job is the defense of poor clients. Public defenders are state or local government employees, or they work for organizations that are financed by the state or local government. They know the ins and outs of local courts, as well as the personal characteristics of judges and prosecutors.

6. They include care of mothers and their newborn children, treatment of contagious disease and chronic illness, mental health care, operation of public dental clinics, provisions for health check-ups, and immunization against communicable and other diseases.

7. Most states amended their constitutions to include strict limits on the ability to borrow and provided that the voters must approve new bond issues.

Summary and Significance

State governments affect the lives of citizens every day. States promote the economy and protect the environment. They try to attract new business and industry by offering inducements such as low-interest loans and tax credits. States also regulate businesses and encourage conservation.

Protecting life and property is also a duty of state government. States enact laws dealing with most crimes and provide criminal justice systems that include courts and prisons. Most criminal cases are settled through a process known as plea bargaining. If tried and found guilty, a criminal may be sentenced to prison. Overcrowded prisons have forced courts to look for alternative forms of sentencing.

States provide for public health, education, and welfare. Expenditures for these three services account for more than half of all state spending. Most state revenues come from sales taxes and income taxes. The federal government also provides funds for various programs, and states often borrow money by issuing bonds.

Identifying Terms and Concepts

Write the term that best completes each sentence.
arraignment, tort, extradition, excise tax, plea bargaining, monopoly, probation, house arrest

1. A _____ is any wrongful act that could result in a lawsuit.
2. A business that has no competition is known as a _____.
3. Through the legal procedure of _____ a person accused of a crime is returned to the state where the crime supposedly took place.
4. The _____ is a procedure in which the defendant comes before a judge who reads the formal charges in the indictment.
5. _____ is liberty granted to a convicted person, conditioned on good behavior, under the supervision of a court official.

Reviewing Facts and Ideas

1. Explain the function of a corporation charter.
2. Describe a way in which states regulate public utilities.
3. Compare the goal of workers' compensation with that of unemployment compensation.
4. Summarize changes in state environmental powers that resulted from a large oil spill off the coast of Alaska in 1989.
5. Compare the public defender system with the assigned counsel system of legal representation.

6. List five functions of state-supported personal health services.
7. Identify two methods states use to limit borrowing by state governments.

Applying Themes

1. **Free Enterprise** What relationships developed between corporations and state governments between 1860 and 1890?
2. **Public Policy** What have states done to attract businesses and to keep others from leaving?
3. **Federalism** How does the federal government use shared revenues to influence state policies?
4. **Civil Rights** How was the right of free legal counsel for a person who is accused of a crime established?
5. **Constitutional Interpretations** Why are most criminal cases heard in state courts rather than in federal courts?

Critical Thinking Skills

1. **Expressing Problems Clearly** In recent years state officials have complained that federal mandated programs have made financial demands on state budgets without providing sufficient federal funding. Do you believe the federal government should abandon programs for which it is unable to provide total funding? Give reasons for your answer.

Applying Themes

1. State constitutional conventions wrestled with problems of corporation law. Corporations effectively lobbied state legislatures to relax laws regulating business.

2. States have provided businesses money for growth through sales of bonds and have sought to attract business by offering tax credits.

3. The federal government stipulates what grant monies are to be used for, supplies funds for programs which states may not otherwise be able to afford, stimulates programs and goals which the federal government believes are necessary, and sets certain minimum standards which states must apply.

4. The Sixth Amendment to the Constitution says that a person accused of a crime has the right to the assistance of counsel. The Supreme Court estab-

2. **Drawing Conclusions** What are the likely long-term results of a criminal justice system that includes overworked courts, overcrowded prisons, and an emphasis on corrections rather than prevention of crime?

3. **Understanding Cause and Effect** Why is there a great difference in the level of spending for education among local districts?

4. **Distinguishing Fact from Opinion** Read the following quotation and explain which statements are fact and which are opinion.

> *Recent years have seen an increase in federal preemption of state and local authority. . . . A CSG review of current and federal pending legislation showed at least 10 examples of intrusive preemptions. . . . Congress, which has caused most of the mandate and preemption frictions, has shown little interest in correcting the imbalance developing in the federal system.*
> —NORMAN BECKMAN, *THE BOOK OF THE STATES*, 1990

Linking Past and Present

When your grandparents went to high school, most students concentrated on basics—math, science, social studies, and English. Today high schools offer many more courses ranging from psychology to ceramics. Have these changes produced graduates who are better prepared to participate in their communities? Are you receiving a better education than your grandparents? Should more emphasis be placed on the basic courses? Explain your opinions.

Writing About Government

Informative Writing State government touches the life of every citizen. In business regulations, consumer affairs, the justice system, health, education, welfare, and taxation state policies affect the way we live, work, and play. Write a descriptive paragraph about the ways in which state government has affected your life this week.

Reinforcing the Skill

Checking Consistency Read the clauses from state constitutions, then answer the questions that follow.

> *That every citizen has a right to bear arms in defense of himself and the State. That no standing army shall be kept up without the consent of the Legislature, . . . and the military shall . . . be in strict subordination to the civil power.*
> *That no soldier shall, in time of peace, be quartered in any house without the consent of the owner. . . .*
> —ALABAMA CONSTITUTION

> *That the right of no person to keep and bear arms in defence of his home, person, and property . . . shall be called in question; but nothing herein contained shall be construed to justify the practice of carrying concealed weapons. . . .*
> *That the military shall always be in strict subordination to the civil power; that no soldier shall . . . be quartered in any house without the consent of the owner . . . except in the manner prescribed by law.*
> —COLORADO CONSTITUTION

1. What is the general subject of both excerpts?
2. On what points do the two clauses agree?
3. On what points, if any, are the two clauses inconsistent? Explain.

Investigating Further

1. **Individual Project** Skim through several editions of a local newspaper. Identify several issues facing your state, then rank these issues in what you believe to be their order of importance.

2. **Cooperative Learning** Organize the class into two groups. Pairs from one group should conduct a public opinion poll on crime in their community. Pairs from the other group should research the changing crime rate in the state or community over several years. Compare the findings of the groups.

lished the requirement of free legal counsel in the case of *Gideon* v. *Wainwright* (1963).

5. The federal government does not have jurisdiction because most criminal laws are state laws rather than federal laws.

Critical Thinking Skills

1. Answers will vary depending on whether the student believes that the programs are necessary or optional and whether the federal government should take the lead in initiating, as well as funding, such programs.

2. Answers will vary, but should include that rates of crime are likely to increase.

3. Each local district has a different tax base that determines its ability to support education. Also community attitudes toward education affect funding support for various programs.

4. *Facts:* Recent years have seen an increase in federal preemption of state and local authority. A CSG review of current and federal pending legislation showed at least 10 examples of intrusive preemptions. *Opinion:* Congress, which has caused most of the mandate and preemption frictions, has shown little interest in correcting the imbalance developing in the federal system.

Linking Past and Present

Answers will vary, but students should give reasons for their opinions.

Writing About Government

Paragraphs will vary, but should give specific examples from student's life.

Reinforcing the Skill

1. The right of citizens to bear arms guarantees against abuses by the military.

2. Both state that citizens have the right to keep and bear arms for self-defense, that no soldiers can be quartered in private houses in peacetime, that in wartime quartering in private houses must be done according to law, and that the military should be in strict subordination to the civil government.

3. Students may see the Colorado clause forbidding concealed weapons as inconsistent with the Alabama clause that states that every citizen has the right to bear arms in defense of himself and the state.

Investigating Further

1. Issues will vary.
2. Findings will vary.

The Case at a Glance

Who: judges, legislatures, criminals

What: inconsistent sentencing, mandatory sentencing, overcrowded prisons

When: 1960s to the present

Where: courts

Why: ensure equal protection

Focus

Ask students how society has tried to fight the increase in the crime rate. *(more arrests, longer prison terms)* Ask: How could such get-tough measures upset the constitutional guarantees of equal protection under the law? *(Judges could be more interested in keeping criminals off the streets than providing fair and impartial jail terms.)* Point out that as society tries to cope with new problems, the courts and the legislatures attempt to respond. Their response, however, must ensure that constitutional rights are not abused.

Teach

Guided Practice

L1 Understanding Cause and Effect Have students identify the three key forces that have an impact on the criminal justice system today. *(increased crime, increased demand by the public to imprison criminals, protecting the rights of the prisoner once incarcerated)* Then have students summarize the effects these forces have had on the prison population. *(The*

Criminal Prosecutions

In all prosecutions the accused shall enjoy the right to a speedy and public trial . . . and to be informed of the nature and cause of the accusation; to be confronted with the witnesses against him . . . and to have assistance of counsel for his defense.

—Eighth Amendment

. . . nor shall any state . . . deny to any person within its jurisdiction the equal protection of the laws.

—Fourteenth Amendment

Mandatory Sentences: Overcrowded Prisons

The Case

Although the Constitution protects the rights of the accused in court, what happens to the accused upon conviction can be uncertain. In 1972, for example, Judge Marvin E. Frankel concluded that:

A defendant who comes up for sentencing has no way of knowing or reliably predicting whether he will walk out of the courtroom on probation, or be locked up for a term of years that may consume the rest of his life, or something in between.

—JUDGE MARVIN E. FRANKEL, *CRIMINAL SENTENCES*, 1972

Judge Frankel was referring to indeterminate sentencing. This system of sentencing left to "the sentencing judge a range of choice [of a sentence] that should be unthinkable in a 'government of laws, not of men.'"

The public called for stricter law enforcement, tougher sentences, and less judicial leniency; the states and the federal government made changes. Determinate sentences imposing mandatory minimum and maximum sentences for certain crimes began to replace indeterminate sentences. Trial judges still had some leeway to fit the punishment to the circumstances of the crime, but the call for certain sentences remained constant.

Background

In the 1960s and early 1970s, studies showed that sentences for similar crimes differed from judge to judge, city to city, state to state, and from one federal district court to another. A Federal Sentencing Institute study recounted a possibly amusing but certainly dismaying story:

A visitor to a [state] court . . . was amazed to hear the judge impose a suspended sentence where a man had pleaded guilty to manslaughter. A few minutes later the same judge sentenced a man who pleaded guilty to stealing a horse and gave him life imprisonment. When the judge was asked by the visitor about the disparity of the two sentences, he replied, "Well, down here there is some men that need killin', but there ain't no horses that need stealin'."

—JUDGE EDWARD LOMBARD, 1965

More About the Case

In the federal courts and the court systems of 33 states, natural life—life imprisonment without hope of parole—is a determinate sentence option for such crimes as murder, kidnapping, armed robbery, and drug trafficking. Many law enforcement officials favor this sentence, because of its value as a deterrent. It also is popular with the many Americans who have expressed shock and outrage at the increase in violent crime. Many government officials, however, have begun to express concern about the impact such sentences will have on state penal systems.

Between 1986 and 1991, the number of prisoners in federal and state penitentiaries serving natu-

The effect of the judge's attitude toward the defendant also was a factor in deciding sentences. In one case the judge had decided upon a four-year sentence and then asked the defendant if he had anything to say before the judge announced his sentence. After the defendant criticized the judge and the court in relatively strong terms, the judge decided that a five-year sentence was more appropriate. In essence, the defendant received a one-year sentence for speaking his mind.

Inconsistencies in sentencing also existed in federal courts. A former Director of the Federal Bureau of Prisons spoke of the various inmates then in federal prisons.

> *That some judges are arbitrary and even sadistic in their sentencing practices is notoriously a matter of record. . . .*
>
> *In one of our institutions a middle-aged . . . treasurer is serving 117 days for embezzling $24,000 in order to cover his gambling debts. On the other hand, another middle-aged embezzler with a fine past record and a fine family is serving 20 years, with 5 years probation to follow. At the same institution is a war veteran, a 39-year-old attorney who has never been in trouble before, serving 11 years for illegally importing parrots into this country.*
>
> —JAMES V. BENNETT, 1964

In the mid-1970s, states began to turn to determinate sentences, coupled with severe limits on the right of parole boards to release prisoners. The number of repeat offenders convinced many people that many convicted felons could not be rehabilitated. Instead, the idea of rehabilitation was replaced with the idea of taking offenders off the street and keeping them in prison, thus limiting the number of crimes they might commit. At the same time, other critics of indeterminate sentencing pointed out that equal justice was seldom served when studies showed that such things as racial prejudice and even geography influenced sentences. In Pittsburgh, for example, a first-time convicted felon was far more likely to be placed on probation than was one in Minneapolis.

These views, combined with the rising crime rate led to a strong movement for tougher laws and sterner determinate sentences. State legislatures responded with tough anti-crime bills and Congress followed

Overcrowded Prisons Declared Unconstitutional
Tougher law enforcement and sentencing has lead to overburdened prisons, a problem that states with insufficient funds have been unable to remedy fully.

suit. In 1984 Congress created the United States Sentencing Commission. After review of about 50,000 sentences, the Commission issued a determinate system of sentencing for federal judges. The system, to be used for all crimes committed after November 1, 1987, set up stringent sentencing guidelines for more than 40 types of federal crimes. At the same time, the Commission abolished federal paroles and limited reductions in sentences for good behavior. The use of probation also was restricted.

The new federal guidelines quickly created confusion. Nearly 160 judges declared the guidelines unconstitutional; another 116 judges ruled them constitutional. Faced with this widespread confusion, the Supreme Court reacted swiftly. In January 1989, by an 8 to 1 vote, the Court ruled the Sentencing Commission's actions and the guidelines constitutional. The chairman of the American Bar Association immediately predicted, "We're going to see dramatic increases in prison terms and prison overcrowding."

The Results In 1991 *TIME* magazine asked the question, "What nation locks up the highest percentage of its population?" The answer was that the Unit-

United States has the largest percentage of its population imprisoned; prisons overcrowded; prisoners complain about poor treatment.) Ask: Has justice been served by imprisoning criminals? In what other ways could society respond to rising crime rates? (*improving education, providing jobs, and controlling the availability of drugs*)

L2 Class Discussion Review prison policy since the 1970s. (*Prison terms have increased; parole use has been limited; there has been less emphasis on rehabilitation.*) Whose needs have these policies served? Have the policies provided fair and equal treatment under the law? (*Students should state that although the immediate needs of the public have been served, the needs of criminals have not been met. Society has not put a premium on rehabilitation, education of criminals, and the like.*)

L3 Making Comparisons Discuss determinate sentencing and indeterminate sentencing. Ask: What are some drawbacks of having state legislatures set guidelines for sentencing? (*Guidelines preclude extenuating circumstances; they treat all offenders in the same way.*) What are the drawbacks of allowing judges a full range of punishment? (*Every judge sentences differently; judges may be responding to public pressure.*) How do these policies affect the equal protection under the law set forth in the Fourteenth Amendment?

ral life sentences increased some 70 percent to 12,000. As these prisoners grow older, the cost of keeping them behind bars will rise. For example, medical-care costs for inmates more than 55 years old are as much as 3 times those for inmates under age 30. Most experts believe that in the future state judicial systems will balance their budgets by sentencing young violent offenders to shorter prison terms. Such offenders, statistics show, are much more likely than older prisoners to commit crimes after their release. Mandatory sentences like natural life, then, may create as many problems as they were designed to solve.

CASE STUDY

Independent Practice

L1 Informative Writing Have students research the crime rates and resultant prosecution and incarceration data in their state during the last 10 years. Ask them to summarize this information in a brief report.

L2 Global Perspectives Ask students to research crime rates and incarceration data from another industrialized country, such as Japan or Sweden. Have students compare the information they locate with that in the case study. How do the attitudes toward incarceration in other countries compare with the attitudes suggested in the case study?

L3 Economics Have students research prison construction in the United States between 1950 and the present. How much money was spent on new construction on a decade-by-decade basis? Have students determine the percentage of increase over each decade.

Assess

Have students complete **Examining the Case.**

Close

Ask if students can think of any ways mandatory sentencing restricts the court's ability to make punishment fit the crime. Do students think it is vital to protect the rights of the convicted? Why or why not?

---

ed States was sending 426 per 100,000 people to jail, the highest rate in the world. Most observers concluded that the high rate was a result of the mandatory sentencing and stronger antidrug enforcement. As a result, by 1989 approximately 771,000 inmates in state prisons, an increase of 59,000 in just 1 year, crowded into American jails. To keep pace with this increase analysts estimated that a 1,000-bed prison would have to be built every 6 days.

Federal courts have declared more than 60 percent of the state prisons unconstitutionally overcrowded. With the demand for other state services and the nation's economic downturn that began in 1989, state revenues proved insufficient to meet the growing needs. A newspaper column reported,

The latest state expenditure report . . . showed double-digit spending increases in three-fourths of the states for corrections and Medicaid—keeping prisoners out of the way and paying medical bills for the poor.
Those fastest-growing elements of state spending are squeezing out programs the middle class really values. . . . The share of state spending going to elementary and secondary schools has sunk to its lowest level in five years.
—DAVID BRODER,
WASHINGTON POST WRITERS GROUP, 1991

Analysts estimate that governments spend about $10 million a day to build prisons, but even this expenditure is too little to end prison overcrowding. As a result, states have been forced to adopt early release programs.

Significance

The realities of mandatory, and in some cases harsher, sentences have alerted all levels of government to the problems facing the nation's criminal-justice system. With the public calling for authorities to get tough on crime, financing the country's penal system has become a major issue.

Among the proposed remedies is for states to adopt a system similar to that now being used in Minnesota. In that state, sentencing guidelines are based on the state's existing or planned prison resources.

The Washington bureau chief of the National Law Journal summed up the difficulty of adopting this type of guideline:

A sentencing system driven largely by prison capacity may seem radical in the moral laden arena of crime and punishment, and it may well be less than ideal. But it is like any other mechanism . . . that governments use to impose self-discipline and to de-politicize tough and controversial decisions.
—FRED STRASSER, JANUARY 1989

Other recommendations to alleviate overcrowding in the prison system include residential confinement, fines, restitution to victims, community service, and work-release programs. Other critics are calling for more far-reaching solutions. The Milton S. Eisenhower Foundation called for the "reconstruction of urban life." They estimated the cost would run about $10 billion a year for 10 years. It would include funds for preschool children, job-training programs, and drug counseling. The Foundation added that additional funds also would be needed for better housing and for improving schools, all of which it said would improve society and reduce crime.

Currently, lawyers, judges, political scientists, and legislators are continuing to study and debate the sentencing issue. At the same time, additional anti-crime bills continue to be introduced to appease a public that demands curbs on violent crimes.

Examining the Case

Reviewing Facts
1. Explain the difference between indeterminate and determinate sentences.
2. Identify the effects the system of determinate sentences has had on the nation's prison system.

Critical Thinking Skills
3. Predicting Consequences What do you think will happen if the nation continues to follow a get-tough-on-crime policy and determinate sentencing?
4. Recognizing Ideologies Do you think societal reform rather than severe punishments for crimes will be supported by conservatives or liberals? Explain your answer.

Examining the Case Answers

1. Indeterminate sentencing leaves the decision up to the court. Determinate sentencing sets minimum and maximum sentences for specific crimes.
2. More prisoners have been incarcerated for longer terms.

3. Answers may vary, but many students will point out that prison overcrowding will continue to be a problem.
4. Answers may vary, but many students will suggest that liberals would be more likely to favor societal reform while conservatives would favor more severe punishments.

Chapter 24

Organization of State Government

Constitutional government in America began with colonial charters, long before the United States Constitution. When the colonies declared their independence in 1776, some states kept their old colonial charters as their state constitutions. Other states, like Virginia and Pennsylvania, drew up new constitutions. Since 1776 the 50 states have had a total of 146 constitutions. Only 19 states have kept their original documents, and all the states have added many amendments. Louisiana has had 11 constitutions since it became a state in 1812.

State constitutions are important for a number of reasons. First, constitutions create the structure of state government itself. Second, state constitutions are important because they establish the different types of local government, such as counties, townships, municipalities, special districts, parishes, and boroughs. Third, state constitutions regulate the ways state and local governments can raise and spend money. Fourth, state constitutions establish independent state agencies, boards, and commissions that have power in areas that affect citizens' lives directly.

All state constitutions provide for a state legislature to pass laws that deal with a variety of matters, including health, crime, labor, education, and transportation. Each state legislature has the power to tax and the power to spend and borrow money. Finally, each state legislature acts as a check on the power of the governor and the state bureaucracy.

In every state except Nebraska, the state legislature has a **bicameral** structure—two houses, like the United States Congress. The upper house is always called the senate, and the lower house is usually called the house of representatives. In some states, the lower house is called the general assembly, the legislative assembly, or the general court. Nebraska has the only **unicameral**, or one-chambered, state legislature in the country.

In addition to the legislative branch, every state has an executive branch headed by a governor. The governor is usually the most visible and well-known person in state government. Like the office of President, the office of governor has generally become more powerful in recent years. The roles of governors are almost the same in every state. Because of the great differences in the area and population of states, however, a vast difference in the power and influence of the 50 governors exists.

In all but three states—Maine, New Hampshire, and New Jersey—other elected officials are part of the executive branch. Although they are less visible than the governor, these executives often hold important positions. They include the lieutenant governor, the attorney general, the secretary of state, the state treasurer, and other executive officers.

Each state also includes a judicial branch. Vital to the operation of state governments, the judiciary interprets and applies state laws. In doing so, state courts help resolve conflicts like business disagreements and grievances that citizens may have against each other. State courts also punish crimes that violate state laws.

State courts deal with two general types of legal disputes: civil and criminal cases. A **civil case** usually involves a dispute between two or more private individuals or organizations. The dispute may have to do with property rights such as a conflict between a landlord and a tenant. It may have to do with a business arrangement, like the violation of a contract to install plumbing. Civil cases may also include suits for damages resulting from traffic accidents and family disputes. More than 90 percent of civil cases are settled before or during trial without a jury decision.

In a **criminal case**, the state brings charges against a citizen who is accused of violating the law. Criminal cases involve either a misdemeanor or a felony. A **misdemeanor** is a minor or less serious crime such as littering, which usually involves a minor punishment. A **felony**, however, is a major crime such as murder, arson, or assault. The state is always the prosecution in criminal cases, while it is usually not involved in civil cases.

Chapter 25

State Government in Action

The great expansion of the federal government in economic affairs in the twentieth century often obscures the reality of state power. The Constitution reserved most economic powers to the states, and the states still provide the basic laws governing the everyday economic decisions of their citizens.

Using the Unit 8 Digest

Use the Unit Digest to introduce, review, reteach, or condense specific chapters or the entire unit. The Unit Digest is enhanced by the corresponding transparencies and activities in the Teacher's Classroom Resources.

Focus

List the following policy areas on the chalkboard in a vertical column: *education, highway construction and public transportation, prison administration, welfare and other aid programs, public housing construction and administration, health insurance, pollution control, drug reform, medical research, national defense.* Then write *federal, state, local* as horizontal heads. Ask students at which level of government basic decisions on each policy area should be made. Tabulate responses on the chalkboard. Ask students to discuss why they look upon certain policy areas as being within the realm of state government. End the discussion by pointing out that this Unit Digest focuses on the structure and functions of state government.

Teach

L1 Understanding Ideas Point out that the powers of state governments discussed in this Unit Digest were reserved to the states by the United States Constitution. The Constitution also denied the states a number of powers. Have students turn to the Constitution on pages 99–122 and ask them to review Article I and the amendments to locate and list the powers denied to the states. Have students read their lists to the class. Use the lists to begin a discussion on why the Constitution denied the states these powers.

Classroom Resources for Unit 8 Digest

📖 Unit Digest Transparencies, Unit 8

📁 Participating in Government, Unit 8

Interpreting Visuals Display transparency 8 from the *Unit Digest Transparencies* in the Teacher's Classroom Resources and use the accompanying teaching strategy, student activity, and student test to teach the structure and functions of state government.

L3 Informative Writing Ask students to write a letter to someone in another country describing their state government. Letters should include information on the state constitution, the structure of the three branches of government, and the American system of federalism. In writing their letters, students should assume that their correspondent has little knowledge of the American governmental system. Select students to read their letters to the class.

Assess

Check for Understanding

Have students complete **Synthesizing the Unit.**

Close

Ask students to discuss what they think are the major problems facing state governments today. If they were state officials, what actions would they take to solve these problems?

State governments have historically retained the power to regulate business, labor, and the professions. They also establish laws dealing with property ownership, contracts, corporations, and torts. A **tort** is any wrongful act that could result in a lawsuit.

States closely regulate insurance and banking, set the rules governing public utilities, and encourage business development. States administer and control natural resources such as land, water, and animal life. Through their police powers, state governments protect consumers from unfair economic practices. In addition, state governments control certain benefit programs, such as unemployment compensation, that affect many workers.

For the most part, protecting life and property is the responsibility of state and local governments. These governments provide almost 90 percent of all employees in the criminal justice system. Laws dealing with most common crimes come directly from state government. The federal government has only limited jurisdiction over most crimes. Local governments usually do not make criminal laws, but they have the primary responsibility for enforcing state laws that protect life and property.

Laws regulating such crimes as murder, rape, assault, burglary, and the sale and use of dangerous drugs are all part of the state criminal code. Local governments can only enact laws dealing with crime that their state governments allow them to pass.

Each state sets its own system of punishment for crimes, permitting the states to experiment with new programs and techniques. Six states, for example, have introduced mandatory sentencing for drug-related crimes. **Mandatory sentencing** is a system of fixed, required terms of imprisonment for certain types of crimes. In most other states, a judge has greater flexibility in imposing sentences on drug offenders. To take another example, at least four of every five states have passed victim compensation laws, whereby state government provides financial aid to the victims of certain crimes. In Utah and Mississippi, a different technique has been used. In these states a state court judge may order a convicted criminal to compensate crime victims.

All state governments possess **police power**—the power to promote and protect public health, safety, morals, and welfare. In the area of health, the police power allows the state to license doctors and dentists, regulate the sale of drugs, and require vaccination for schoolchildren. State governments also provide a wide range of health services, from hospitals to pollution control.

The states have become increasingly involved in public education in recent years. In terms of money spent, authority over education, and support for higher education, state governments have become an important force in American public education.

The states need massive funds to pay for the programs they sponsor. Since the early 1930s, state government expenditures have increased dramatically. Between 1932 and 1990, state government expenditures rose from $2.8 billion to about $570 billion. Federal spending, although higher than the state total, increased at a slower rate during this same period. The rapid increase in state expenditures is largely because of expansion in public health, education, welfare, and environmental protection spending.

State taxes raise nearly half of the general revenue of state governments. States levy taxes on income, property, or on the goods and services that people buy. For most state governments, the sales tax and the income tax are the major sources of revenue.

These sources, however, do not raise enough revenue to balance many states' budgets. Some states that have weak economies may have rapidly rising costs. These states may have just as much or more public pressure to provide a wide range of government services. **Intergovernmental revenue**, or revenue distributed by one level of government to another, fills some of this need. The federal government, with its vast revenue and taxing power, provides about 20 percent of all state revenues.

Synthesizing the Unit

Recalling Facts
1. Define **bicameral, unicameral, civil case, criminal case, misdemeanor, felony, tort, mandatory sentencing, police power, intergovernmental revenue.**
2. List the four reasons state constitutions are important.
3. Name the offices that are usually part of the executive branch.

Critical Thinking Skills
4. Making Comparisons Compare the powers of state governments with those of the federal government.

Synthesizing the Unit Answers

1. Definitions of terms appear on the pages indicated: **bicameral,** 745; **unicameral,** 745; **civil case,** 745; **criminal case,** 745; **misdemeanor,** 745; **felony,** 745; **tort,** 746; **mandatory sentencing,** 746; **police power,** 746; **intergovernmental revenue,** 746
2. State constitutions create a structure for state government; establish different types of local government; regulate ways state and local governments can raise and spend money; and establish independent state agencies, boards, and commissions.
3. governor, lieutenant governor, attorney general, secretary of state, state treasurer
4. Most students will note that state governments may exercise power nearly as considerable as that of the federal government. The Constitution reserves most economic powers to the states, and the states still provide the basic laws governing the everyday economic decisions of their citizens. Also, the criminal justice system is administered primarily at the state level.

Local Government

UNIT 9

Chapter 26
Organization of Local Government

Chapter 27
Governing Metropolitan Areas

Introduce

Unit Objectives

After studying this unit, students should be able to:
- Analyze the executive, legislative, and judicial structures and functions of local government.
- Examine the taxing and spending functions of local government.

Unit Overview

Unit 9 develops students' understanding of the nature of local government in the United States.

Chapter 26 examines the forms and functions of local governments.

Chapter 27 focuses on government in our country's metropolitan areas.

9 UNIT DIGEST

Use the Unit Digest on pages 799–800 to introduce, review, reteach, or condense the information in this unit.

Introducing the Unit

Ask students the following questions about their local governments: What form of county government do we have? What form of municipal government? What are the powers of each? What are the major offices of our county and municipal governments? Are they filled by election or appointment? What special district governing bodies, such as park districts or utilities boards, operate in our community?

When students have answered these questions, which they probably will find quite difficult, have them discuss why local government is sometimes called "the forgotten government."

Unit Project

Arrange for students to attend local government meetings, such as a session of the county board, city council, or town or village board. Students who have cable television may want to check the schedules of local access channels, as these often carry local government meetings. Have students write a report on the meetings they attended or viewed on television. Reports should include such information as which officials attended, who presided over the meetings, what issues were discussed, and what resolutions were reached. Upon completion of study of this unit, have students compare their reports by reading them to the class.

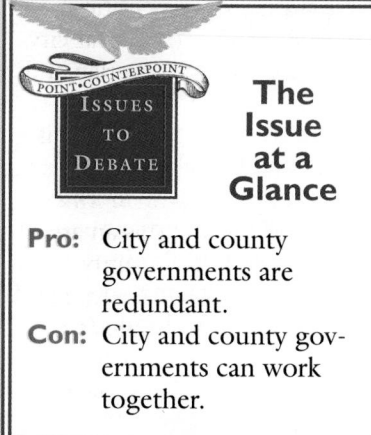

The Issue at a Glance

Pro: City and county governments are redundant.

Con: City and county governments can work together.

Focus

Ask students to identify the major offices of their municipal government. *(mayor, council, and so on)* Write their lists on the chalkboard and ask them to name the people who fill these positions. Then ask them to do the same for their county government. *(Typically, students will be much less knowledgeable about county offices or leaders.)* Ask if this means that county government is less important than city government. Tell students that this reading focuses on this question.

Teach

Guided Practice

Ask: Why do county governments exist? *(Constitutions in many states require them.)* What reasons do the critics of county government offer to explain its ineffectiveness? *(Counties have numerous elected officials and their powers are limited by state laws.)* Ask how supporters of county government respond to these arguments. *(County government is strong and active, provides vital services, and its officials are important decision makers and political party leaders.)*

Point out that some critics say state officials deliberately made county government weak by creating so many elected offices. Ask them to explain this relationship. *(Answers should focus on division of executive power.)*

748 Unit 9: Local Government

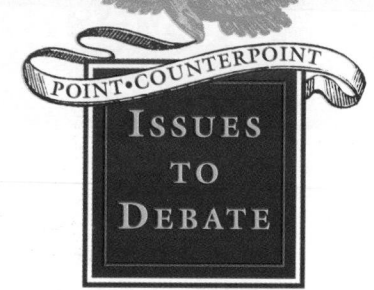

Are County Governments Obsolete?

Among the first books about county government in the United States, one was titled *The County, The "Dark Continent" of American Politics*. Although author H.S. Gilbertson criticized the nation's county governments, he wanted to reform rather than abolish these governments. He did acknowledge, however, that "without a doubt, the urban, and particularly the metropolitan county, is the county at its worst."

Since that time, reformers have attacked county governments, particularly in counties undergoing urbanization. Many reformers feel that county governments in metropolitan areas have failed to deliver needed services. Some also believe that county governments are obsolete and in need of reorganization.

Pro

Critics who believe that existing county governments are obsolete reject the idea of merging city and county governments. They base their rejection on the nature of county government.

Another serious obstacle to city-county consolidation is that the typical county government organization is still unused to administering urban functions. Often the county has limited powers under state law (even more limited than cities), it may have numerous elected officials and a cumbersome and antiquated organization, and it may be unaccustomed to effective and efficient performance of the heavy responsibilities of metropolitan government. Before counties can be granted authority to provide urban services, they will probably have to be reorganized.

—THOMAS R. DYE, 1969

Why are county governments in metropolitan areas considered to be incapable of providing needed services such as water, sewage, waste disposal, and traffic control? One authority traces the background and the causes of the "Impotence of County Government."

Many state constitutions prescribe the structure of local governments, create particular local officers, and provide for their functions. This is especially true of counties. The functional shortcomings of counties are inherent in their organizational structure. Because of the history of English counties and the American experience with royal governors, the framers of state constitutions made sure that counties did not have strong executive or administrative powers. The limitation on executive power was achieved by providing for a long list of separately elected county officers. Most states mention at least some of the following in their constitution: county attorney, auditor, bailiff, clerk, constable, coroner, sheriff, marshal, registrar of wills, recorder of deeds, revenue commissioner, road commissioner, assessor, surveyor, tax collector, and treasurer. These officers are to serve in addition to elected county commissioners who are empowered to handle whatever functions are not performed by the independently elected officials.

Therefore, both legislators and citizens, in considering problems arising from the unrestrained incorporation of new municipalities in the suburbs or in trying to meet new service needs in unincorporated areas, were denied one logical alternative—namely, dependence upon county government to provide local government services outside the boundaries of major cities. Occasional attempts . . . to modernize county government nearly always have been met by staunch opposition from independently elected officials. Furthermore, in

More About Issues to Debate

Most counties receive funds from both state and federal governments. These monies come in the form of grants or shared revenues. According to 1990 data, 36.4 percent of all county revenues come from intergovernmental accounts. The second-largest source of income is property taxes, constituting 28 percent of the total. Sales taxes add about 10 percent, while special taxes on utilities and insurance trusts account for nearly 4 percent of the total.

Nearly 90 percent of all intergovernmental aid to counties comes from state governments. Since 1986 when the Federal Revenue Sharing program ended, most counties have asked state legislatures several states, county commissioners have seemed to be content with their limited role and have been most reluctant to become involved in providing urban services.

Consequently, citizens in outlying areas have found it necessary either to incorporate or to form special districts in order to provide needed services. . . .

—WILLIAM G. COLMAN, 1975

Con

Not all political scientists dismiss county governments as obsolete or ineffective. Professors Thomas Murphy and John Rehfuss point out:

A county is the basic geographic subdivision of a state, and county government significantly affects most Americans. . . . Counties occupy a key position in the U.S. political party system. Not only do they act as the primary organizational unit of political party systems, but county leaders play an important role in government decisionmaking at the metropolitan level. Increased urbanization has given suburban counties greater influence in metropolitan areas. . . .

—THOMAS P. MURPHY AND JOHN REHFUSS, 1976

The former executive director of National Association of Counties also responded to the critics of county government's efforts to provide needed services. He wrote:

Counties have met metropolitan problems through the use of multi-county arrangements. . . . If the county is proving that it can be placed in combination like building blocks, it is also showing that it is divisible too! Counties everywhere are reporting great success in creating special districts to provide special services to selected parts of the county. All residents of the county pay a basic tax for county-wide service such as welfare, education, and the administration of justice. In addition any area that wants water and sewerage, for example, can have it provided by the county and pay separately for the service. Thus the special service district under the control of the county governing body can provide municipal services to those that need them and who will pay for them without interfering with the farm resident who does not need them. Thus we have the farmer and the city dweller living happily side by side and serviced by the same county, and once again the county has shown its adaptability to the needs of its residents and their circumstances. . . . County government is not dead. Instead, it has just begun to live.

—BERNARD F. HILLENBRAND, May 1960

Policing the County
The debate surrounding the efficiency of county governments centers on their ability to deliver such vital services as sanitation and police protection.

The Debate Continues

No one has conclusively resolved the debate about whether or not county governments can adequately supply the services needed in a modern metropolitan area. Many county governments are trying to provide these services. Cooperation between municipalities and counties is producing results through the sharing of equipment, resources, and services. How well these "intergovernmental marriages" will succeed in the future is still not clear, but some observers are optimistic.

Examining the Issue

Recalling Facts
1. Explain why most state constitutions tend to limit the executive power of the counties.
2. Identify five independently elected county officials.

Critical Thinking Skills
3. Identifying Central Issues Why do you think the existence of independently elected county officials can impede county government?
4. Drawing Conclusions What do you think will be the future of county governments in urban areas in the years to come?

Investigating Further
Write or visit one of your county commissioners. Request the commission's view about the positive or negative effects of independently elected county officials. Report the results to your class.

to find new sources of funding. In response, states granted counties more authority to raise taxes. The increased financial demand has outraged many citizens, particularly some property owners who have seen their property taxes double in the early 1990s.

County governments spend their money on public welfare, health, transportation, and education. Specifically, their responsibilities include jails, elections, judicial administration, licensing, public record-keeping, upkeep of roads, tax assessment, and community colleges.

Note that another criticism of the county structure is that city and county services overlap and duplicate each other. Can students think of examples of this in their locale? *(Examples likely will focus on law enforcement and education.)* Ask: Is this an argument for or against county government? *(Actually, "against," because consolidation would eliminate overlap and duplication of services and thus eliminate waste.)*

Independent Practice

Have students write a sentence that summarizes the *Pro* argument and another that summarizes the *Con* argument in this reading.

Assess

Have students complete **Examining the Issue.**

Answers

1. historic distrust of centralized executive power
2. county attorney, auditor, bailiff, clerk constable, coroner, sheriff, marshall, registrar of wills, recorder of deeds, revenue commissioner, road commissioner, assessor, surveyor, tax collector, treasurer
3. As independently elected, the large number of officials are not answerable to a central authority, thus limiting the government's ability to act cohesively.
4. Students' conclusions should draw on information presented in the reading.

Close

Ask students which side they support in the debate. Can they name services that would change if county governments were abolished?

Chapter Organizer

Objectives	Special Feature Pages	Supplemental Materials
Section 1 Local Government Services *pp. 752–758* 1. Explain how local governments serve the people. 2. Describe zoning laws.	Point/Counterpoint: Are County Governments Obsolete? pp. 748–749 Focus on Freedom: Charter of Government for Providence p. 753 Images of Government: Local Scene pp. 754–755 Global Connection: Comparing Governments: Education Systems p. 756 Critical Thinking Skills: Determining Relevance p. 758	Guided Reading Activities Reproducible Lesson Plans Enrichment Activities 26 Section 1 Quiz Testmaker Audio Cassettes (English and Spanish) Skill Reinforcement Activities 26 SAT Practice Tests Writer's Guidebook
Section 2 Counties, Townships, and Special Districts *pp. 759–764* 1. Explain local governments' responses to the changing needs of their constituents. 2. Discuss local government in New England.	Multicultural Heritage: The Legal Heritage of France p. 762	Guided Reading Activities Reproducible Lesson Plans Primary and Secondary Source Readings 26 Section 2 Quiz Testmaker Chapter Transparencies 26 SAT Practice Tests
Section 3 Local Government Revenue Sources *pp. 765–769* 1. Determine local governments' need for reliable sources of revenue. 2. Explain block grants and revenue sharing.	Participating in Government: Volunteering for the Armed Forces p. 766 Personal Perspectives: Sharon Mayell on a Computer Network in City Government p. 769	Guided Reading Activities Reproducible Lesson Plans Participating in Government 26 Cooperative Learning Activities 26 Reteaching Activities 26 Section 3 Quiz Chapter 26 Tests Testmaker Limited English Proficiency Activities 26 SAT Practice Tests

If time does not permit teaching this chapter, assign the Chapter 26 summary in the Unit 9 Digest on pages 799–800.

Key To Ability Levels

Teaching strategies have been coded for varying learning styles and abilities.

L1   Level 1 activities are **basic** activities and should be within the ability range of all students.

L2   Level 2 activities are **average** activities and should be within the ability range of the average to above-average student.

L3   Level 3 activities are **challenging** activities designed for the ability range of above-average students.

LEP   These activities should be within the ability range of **Limited English Proficiency** students.

Multicultural Activities

At the local government level, redistricting can have an impact on minority electoral success. Although more than 3 million of Los Angeles County's 8.8 million people are Hispanic, voters there did not elect a Hispanic member, Gloria Molina, to the Los Angeles County Board of Supervisors until 1991. The position is one of the most powerful in local government because the 5-member board controls the county's annual multimillion dollar budget. Molina's election came after a federal judge ruled that a 1981 redistricting plan had diluted the county's Hispanic vote. The judge ruled that one district had to be drawn so that at least 50 percent of its eligible voters were Hispanic. Students might research the controversy that preceded Gloria Molina's election.

For an in-depth look at local government politics, have students read about Carl Stokes in *Voices of Freedom* by Henry Hampton and Steven Fayer. An anthology of primary sources on the civil rights movement from the 1950s through the 1980s, one chapter profiles Stokes's bid to become the nation's first African American mayor of a major city. It tracks his efforts from his unsuccessful 1965 campaign, when he lost by less than 1 percent of the vote, to his victory in 1967. Said Stokes of his victory: "My election . . . had a great deal of meaning . . . . It illustrated the ability of white people to vote for a black candidate. . . . To black people, it introduced a whole new echelon of political power." Have students choose a local election where a minority candidate was successful and research it.

Chapter Resources

Readings for the Student

Arneson, D. J. *Toxic Cops.* Franklin Watts, 1991.

Lingeman, Richard. *Small Town America.* Putnam's, 1980.

State and Local Government 1991–1992: Annual Editions Series. Dushkin, 1992.

Torrence, Susan Walker. *Grass Roots Government: The County in American Politics.* Robert B. Luce, 1974.

Zipco, Stephen J. *Toxic Threat: How Hazardous Substances Poison Our Lives.* Messner, 1990.

Readings for the Teacher

Elazar, Daniel. *Building Cities in America: Urbanization and Suburbanization in a Frontier Society.* Hamilton Press, 1987.

Zimmerman, Joseph F. *State-Local Relations: A Partnership Approach.* Praeger, 1983.

Multimedia

Videocassettes

Other Faces of AIDS. Maryland Public Television. (2 v/cs, 1 English, 1 Spanish, 60 minutes each)

Software

Hometown: A Local Area Study. Active Learning Systems. (2 disks. Apple IIe, IBM, Commodore 64, BBC Acorn, printer recommended). Students analyze data and generate requested statistical demographic reports.

Our Town Meeting: A Lesson in Civic Responsibility. Tom Snyder Productions. (Apple disk, backup, or IBM PC diskette, backup). Students role-play city planners and evaluate project proposals.

Introduce

Chapter Overview

Chapter 26 focuses on the forms and functions of local government in the United States.

Section 1 discusses the many services provided by local government.

Section 2 describes four forms of local government—counties, townships, municipalities, and special districts.

Section 3 examines the sources of revenue for local government.

Chapter 26 Themes

Write the phrases *civic responsibility* and *growth of democracy* on the chalkboard. Have volunteers define each. Then ask students to suggest ways in which the two themes might be related. Focus discussion by having students speculate about how civic responsibility might be expressed in the local community and how civic responsibility supports the growth of democracy.

CONNECTIONS

Language

The word *county* had its origins in the medieval period. It referred originally to a territory ruled by a count.

CHAPTER
26

Organization of Local Government

Small-town celebrations of Independence Day, such as this one in Vermont, embody a grassroots commitment to participatory democracy.

About the Chapter Opener

Teaching With Illustrations Have students study the photograph of the Independence Day parade on pages 750 and 751. Ask them to suggest how such celebrations embody a grassroots commitment to participatory democracy. *(Such celebrations provide citizens with an opportunity to express support for political ideas and government institutions, to display symbols of the government and country, and to take part in political activities.)* Then lead a discussion of other ways citizens can show a commitment to grassroots democracy. *(attending local government meetings, getting involved in political campaigns, writing to elected officials, and so on)*

Chapter Preview

Overview

Local governments, established by the states, provide essential public services.

Objectives

After studying this chapter, you should be able to:

1. Describe the various services that local governments provide.
2. Discuss the changing roles of counties, townships, and special districts.
3. Evaluate the issues that affect sources of local government revenue.

Themes in Government

This chapter emphasizes the following government themes:

* **Federalism** Local, state, and national governments share responsibilities and intergovernmental revenues. Sections 1 and 3.
* **Civic Responsibility** Local government depends on citizen participation. Sections 1 and 2.
* **Growth of Democracy** Representative government maintains democracy when direct participation is impractical. Section 2.
* **Public Policy** States permit local governments to develop individual responses to issues. Section 3.

Critical Thinking Skills

This chapter emphasizes the following critical thinking skills:

* Analyzing Information
* Making Inferences
* Identifying Alternatives
* Making Comparisons

CHAPTER 26: ORGANIZATION OF LOCAL GOVERNMENT 751

Setting the Scene Although services provided by local government and actions taken by local lawmakers have a more direct impact on the lives of students than many decisions made by state and federal governments, most students do not know or appreciate the role local governments play in their lives. Local elections that do not coincide with national or state votes rarely draw even half of the eligible voters in most communities. Yet this level of government offers citizens the greatest chance for personal involvement in the political process and the greatest chance of influencing policy.

Introducing the Chapter

Poll the class to see how many students think they can correctly name the United States President and their state's governor. Then ask how many can name the mayor or city manager of their community, the sheriff, and the chief of police. Typically people of all ages know more about the operation of state and federal government than they do about government in their own community. Have students suggest possible reasons for this. *(less media attention, taken for granted, appears less glamorous)* Tell the class that in this chapter they will learn the part local government plays in people's daily lives.

Chapter Project

Have students create a series of radio or television public service announcements to inform new residents about the local community. Groups might prepare an announcement on community services provided by different local agencies or on how the services that citizens receive are funded.

Linking Past and Present
In the late 1800s and early 1900s, residents of New York City dumped food, toilet waste, and coal or wood ash into sidewalk gutters. Trash was towed out to sea in barges and shoveled into the ocean to later wash ashore on New Jersey beaches. Today most people take for granted a service such as garbage collection. However, for local officials this service continues to pose a serious problem. "Everyone wants you to pick up their garbage," said a local government official, "but no one wants you to put it down." Especially in their backyard, he might have added. For many local governments, providing a basic service like garbage removal is a critical and controversial issue.

Focus

Local Government Services

Bell Ringer

As you take attendance, ask students to think about what this text statement means:

"Local government is the level of government closest to the people."

Motivating Activity

Discuss students' Bell Ringer responses. Ask students how often they think they benefit from local government services—frequently, occasionally, rarely? Then ask for a show of hands as you read each part of this question to the class: Have you ever played on a city or county sports team, been to a public swimming pool, attended a program at a local stadium or convention center, or used a public library, health clinic, or park? Ask the class what these activities have in common. *(They are services provided by local government.)* Tell the class that in this chapter they will examine the many ways local government affects their lives.

Vocabulary Precheck

Call on students to read aloud the definitions of the terms and concepts from the Glossary. Then have volunteers use each term in a sentence. **LEP**

L ocal government is the level of government closest to the people. It is the government of the county and the city, town, village, or suburb. Each person in the United States lives under one national government and one state government, but most people live under three or more local governments. The United States has about 85,000 local governments. In a recent year, state governments employed 173 full-time and part-time workers per 10,000 population, while local governments employed 417. Local governments provide basic services that everyone takes for granted—until problems arise.

The Role of the State

Although the United States has a strong tradition of local self-government, local governments have no legal independence. Established by the state, they are entirely dependent on the state governments under which they exist. The state may even abolish them.

State constitutions usually set forth the powers and duties of local governments. A state constitution may also describe the form of government a locality may adopt, depending on its size and population. State laws may regulate even the kinds of taxes that local communities may levy. Nevertheless, states give most local governments considerable power to manage their own affairs. Many state governments grant their larger cities home rule. **Home rule** means that the cities have the power to govern themselves without the approval of the state legislature. Home rule allows the city greater freedom to choose the form and functions of its government. Moreover, in some states traditions of local self-government are very strong.

Types of Local Government

The United States has four basic types of local government—the county, the township, the municipality, and the special district. All four do not exist in every state, and their powers vary from state to state.

The County The **county** is normally the largest territorial and political subdivision of the state. County governments supervise elections, issue certain licenses, keep records of vital statistics, and administer many services, including hospitals, sports facilities, and public welfare programs.

The Township **Townships** exist as units of local government in fewer than half the states. The size and powers of townships vary from region to region. In New England the township is another name for the town, a fairly small community with a population usually less than 5,000. In states such as New Jersey and Pennsylvania and throughout the Midwest, a township is a large subdivision of the county. In rural areas townships have been losing power, but some urban townships have recently increased power.

The Municipality A **municipality** is an urban unit of government—a town, borough, city, or urban district that has legal rights granted by the state through its charter. The first charters were much like charters for private corporations, except that towns and cities were much more narrowly controlled. Each municipality had an individual special charter until state legislatures began to pass general laws after 1850. These early charters and statutes contained curious powers.

SECTION PREVIEW

Objectives
After studying this section, you should be able to:
■ Explain how local governments serve the people.
■ Describe zoning laws.

Key Terms and Concepts
home rule, county, township, municipality, special district, zoning

Themes in Government
■ Federalism
■ Civic Responsibility

Critical Thinking Skills
■ Analyzing Information
■ Making Inferences

752 UNIT 9: LOCAL GOVERNMENT

Classroom Resources for Section 1

📁 Guided Reading Activities
📁 Reproducible Lesson Plans
📁 Enrichment Activities 26
📁 Section 1 Quiz

💾 Testmaker
🎧 Audio Cassettes (English and Spanish)
SAT Practice Tests
Writer's Guidebook

For example, Ohio gave its cities power to regulate the transportation of gunpowder; to prevent the immoderate riding of horses; to provide for measuring hay, wood, coal, or other articles for sale; and to suppress riots, gambling, bowling, and billiards. Also in the Midwest:

Wisconsin cities . . . were given the right to control the "assize of bread" [from the medieval practice of controlling the price of bread]. This meant something to the 15th-century borough, but was Greek to midwestern America. The "assize of bread" even cropped up in some charters as the "size of bread"; no one seemed to notice the mistake.

—LAWRENCE M. FRIEDMAN,
A HISTORY OF AMERICAN LAW, 1973

By the twentieth century, most states divided municipalities into classes depending on their population. In this way they could provide each class a more standard type of charter.

The Special District The **special district** is a unit of local government that deals with a specific func-

Teach

Guided Practice

L1 **Analyzing Ideas** Have each student take a sheet of paper and fold it in half lengthwise. On one side have them list activities in a typical school day, such as brush teeth, ride school bus, eat lunch. On the other side have students link each activity to local services. For example, the water used to brush teeth comes from public utilities; stoplights on the way to school are locally maintained. Ask volunteers to read their lists aloud. Use student lists to illustrate the types of local government. For example, in coming to school, students may have traveled on city, township, and county roads. **LEP**

Focus on Freedom

CHARTER OF GOVERNMENT FOR PROVIDENCE

Roger Williams, whom the colony called a "godly minister" in 1631, was banished from Massachusetts in 1635. Williams had criticized the civil authorities in the Puritan colony, claiming they had no authority to enforce church law. He and his followers determined to provide a more tolerant atmosphere in Providence, Rhode Island, where they drew up the following plan of government in 1640.

We, Robert Coles, Chad Browne, William Harris, and John Warner, being freely chosen by the consent of our loving friends and neighbors, the inhabitants of this town of Providence, having many differences among us, they being freely willing and also bound themselves to stand to our arbitration in all differences among us, to rest contented in our determination being so betrusted, we have seriously and carefully endeavored to weigh and consider all those differences being desirous to bring unity and peace . . . have gone the fairest and the equalest way to produce our peace.

I. Agreed. We have with one consent agreed that in the parting those particular properties which some of our friends and neighbors have in Pawtuxet, from the general common of our town of Providence to run upon a straight line from a fresh spring being in the gulley, at the head of that cove running by that point of land called Saxafras unto the town of Mashipawog to an oak tree standing near unto the cornfield, being at this time the nearest cornfield unto Pawtuxet, the oak tree having four marks with an axe, till some other landmark be set for a certain bound. . . .

II. Agreed. We have with one consent agreed that for the disposing of those lands . . . belong-

ing to the town of Providence to be in the whole inhabitants by the choice of five men for general disposal to be betrusted with disposal of lands and also of the town's stock. . . .

VII. Agreed. That the town, by the five men, shall give every man a deed of all his lands lying within the bounds of the plantation, to hold it by for after ages . . . .

IX. Agreed. That the clerk shall call the five disposers together at the month-day and the general town together every quarter, to meet upon general occasions from the date hereof.

—ROGER WILLIAMS, 1640

Examining the Document

Reviewing Facts

1. Describe the kinds of boundaries that the town of Providence had.
2. Specify how often the town meeting would be held.

Critical Thinking Skills

3. Demonstrating Reasoned Judgment Why is it necessary for a community to have a written charter?

CHAPTER 26: ORGANIZATION OF LOCAL GOVERNMENT 753

Focus on Freedom

Williams's other unusual views also got him into trouble with the colony's leaders. For example, he insisted that the king had no authority to give the English colonists land belonging to Native Americans. Instead, Williams wanted the colonists to buy the land. When he was banished from Massachusetts, he bought land from the Narragansetts and founded the town of Providence. Judging by this document, what was one responsibility of Rhode Island colonial government?

Answers

1. Boundaries followed common landmarks such as trees and cornfields.
2. every quarter
3. It gives authority to those who govern, by showing that the governed have consented to the decisions of the government.

Background

Special districts are geographical areas established to provide a single service. Such districts play a vital role in providing services to citizens. They include: flood control, animal control, forestry, fire, water, sewage, hospital, transportation, soil conservation, irrigation, mosquito control, and noise abatement. Apart from school districts, which are found throughout the country, special districts vary widely by region of the country. In the dry Southwest, where water is scarce and widely used for farming, irrigation and water districts abound. Flood control districts can be found along the Mississippi River and in some coastal areas.

L2 Geography Distribute maps of students' community and have them make inferences about the zoning in various parts of the community, based on their own knowledge of where stores and houses are found. Point out areas zoned for commercial, industrial, and residential use. Then choose a residential area with which most students are familiar. Tell them to suppose that a developer has petitioned local government to allow a shopping center in this area. Ask students what factors they should consider in deciding if zoning should be changed.

L3 Ranking Organize students into small groups, and have each list local public services that it considers most important to the functioning of the community as a whole. Have groups rank these essential services in order from most to least important, giving reasons for their rankings. Place the groups' lists on the chalkboard. Then note that in economic hard times local governments are often forced to cut back on services. Have the class pick services to reduce or eliminate from among those considered most essential, explaining and justifying their choices.

Images of Government

Display a replica of your community's seal. Ask students to identify what the symbols on the seal represent.

Answers

1. They are an example of "pure" or direct democracy, in which citizens—not elected representatives—speak and vote on issues.
2. to honor visiting dignitaries or to recognize the generosity of a city benefactor

---

tion, such as education, water supply, or transportation. Special districts are the most common type of local government, and they deal with a wide variety of special services. The local school district is the most common example of a special district.

Local Government Services

Local governments provide many services. These services include education, fire and police protection, water, sewage and sanitation, trash collection, libraries, and recreation.

Education Judged by its cost and its effect on the community, education is one of the most important functions of government. Because most school districts raise revenues through local taxes, people have at least some interest in the local education system.

In many states a large share of local tax revenues goes to pay for public schools. Some states pay a large percentage of local public school costs, but local school districts generally provide most of the money and make the key decisions regarding the operation of the public schools.

Zoning Local governments use **zoning** to regulate the way land and buildings may be used. Through zoning, a local government can shape the way in which a community develops. It can plan for regulated growth, preserve the character of neighborhoods, and prevent the decline of land values. A zoning board may rule that certain districts (zones) can be used only for homes, others only for businesses, and others only for parks. In this way zoning laws control how different parts of a community are used.

Some people criticize zoning. They claim that zoning is an excessive use of government power because it

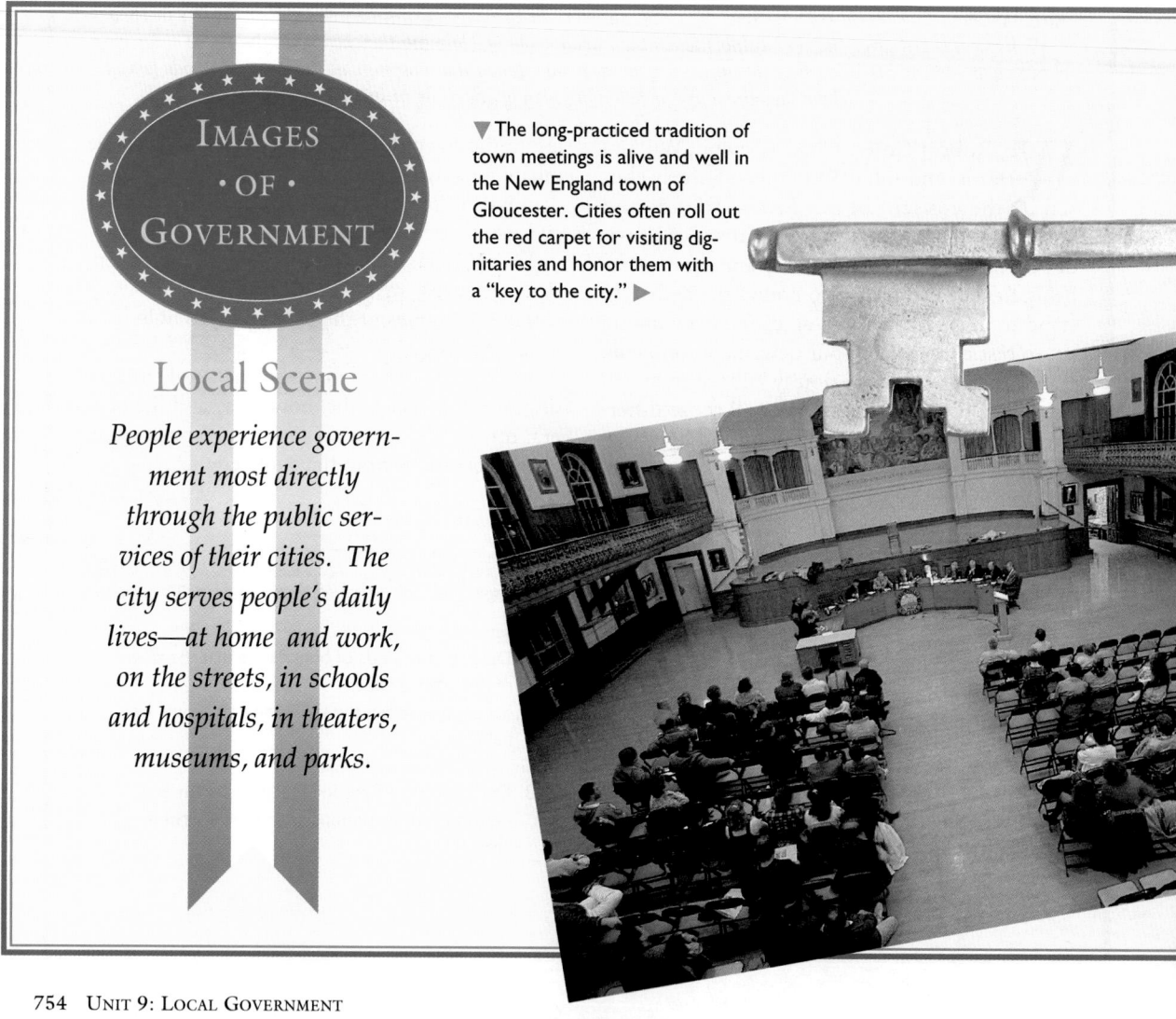

IMAGES
· OF ·
GOVERNMENT

Local Scene

People experience government most directly through the public services of their cities. The city serves people's daily lives—at home and work, on the streets, in schools and hospitals, in theaters, museums, and parks.

▼ The long-practiced tradition of town meetings is alive and well in the New England town of Gloucester. Cities often roll out the red carpet for visiting dignitaries and honor them with a "key to the city." ▶

754 UNIT 9: LOCAL GOVERNMENT

Cooperative Learning Activity

Organize students into groups of six. Have each choose a debater, recorder, and researchers. Write the following topic on the chalkboard: "*Resolved:* Zoning laws violate the rights of private citizens and should be abolished." The debater in each group will join a debating team to argue the topic. To prepare, have each group review the section in the text on zoning. The recorder can list arguments favoring zoning and reasons for opposing it. For each argument listed, have group members suggest counterarguments. When research has been shared with the group, assign all debaters to a debating team and hold a class debate.

limits how people can use their property. Some criticize zoning laws that make it difficult for certain people, often minorities or families with children, to move into a particular neighborhood. Critics call this restrictive zoning. For example, a zoning law could require that all houses built in a neighborhood have at least 2,000 square feet of floor space, on lots of at least three acres. This law would be restrictive because only people with very high incomes could move into such an area. In some states restrictive zoning has been declared unconstitutional. Advocates of zoning claim that without zoning, a community might develop in ways that would lower property values and make it an unpleasant place to live.

Police and Fire Protection No community could exist without police or fire protection. Local government administers these important services. Police and fire services are expensive and make up a large part of the local budget. Police protection, for example, is the second largest expense of many American cities, after public education.

Fire protection is a local function that varies with the size of the community. In small towns and villages, volunteers usually staff the fire department. In large cities professional, full-time fire departments provide the necessary protection. Professional fire departments also serve some small towns that have many factories and businesses.

Water Supply Local governments make the vital decisions regarding water service. In smaller communities they may contract with privately owned companies to supply water. The threat of water pollution and water shortages has prompted some local governments to create special water district arrangements. In case of a water shortage, such districts or local governments may attempt to limit the amount

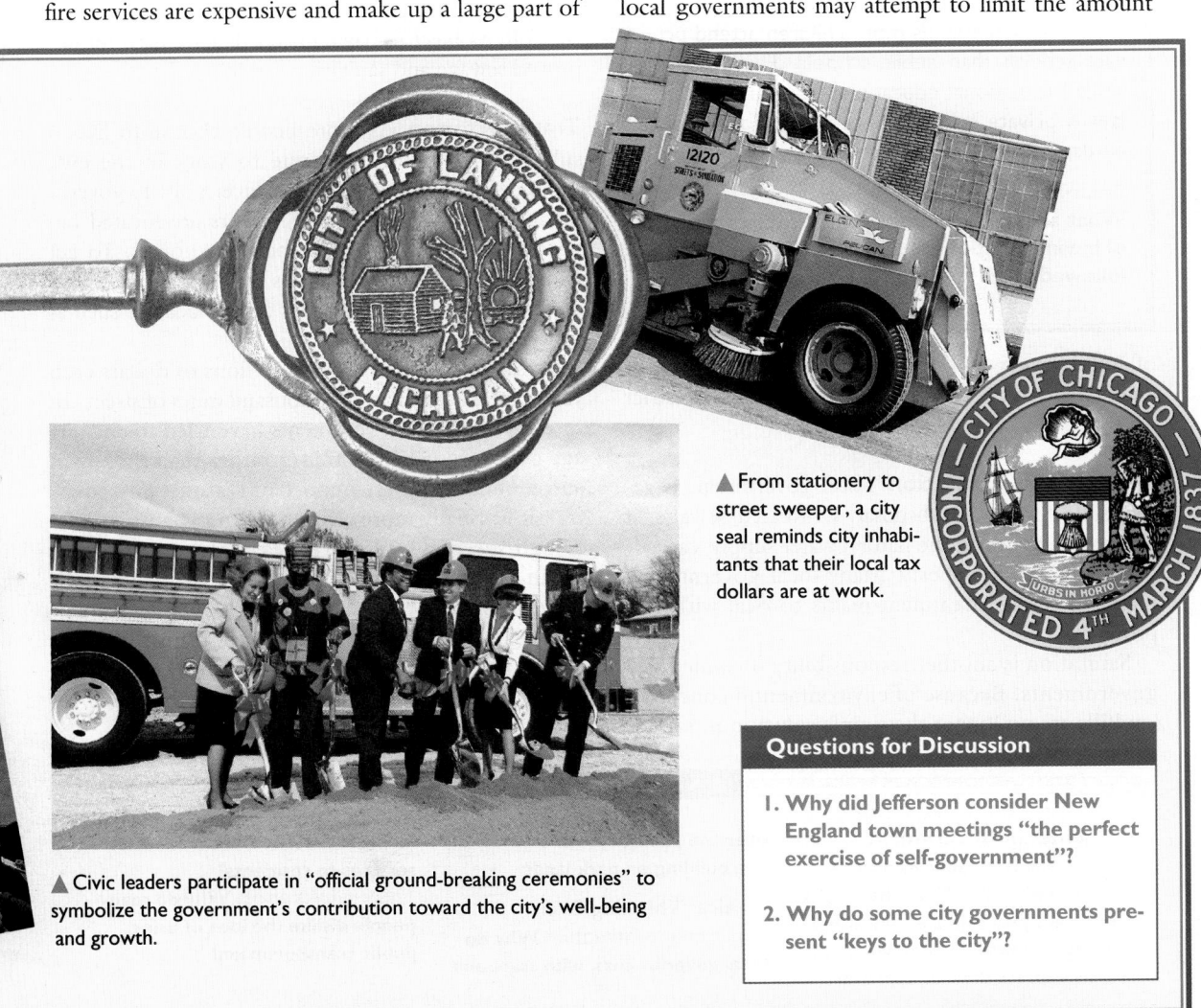

▲ From stationery to street sweeper, a city seal reminds city inhabitants that their local tax dollars are at work.

▲ Civic leaders participate in "official ground-breaking ceremonies" to symbolize the government's contribution toward the city's well-being and growth.

Questions for Discussion

1. Why did Jefferson consider New England town meetings "the perfect exercise of self-government"?

2. Why do some city governments present "keys to the city"?

Independent Practice

L1 Politics Duplicate the pages of the local telephone book that list local government agencies. Have pairs of students each contact one agency to find out who it serves and what services it provides. Ask pairs to report their findings to the class. **LEP**

L2 Informative Writing Have students find newspaper articles that give examples of local government services. Have students summarize their articles, identifying the service, agency, or unit of government providing the service, recipients of the service, and any controversy about the service.

L3 Science In recent years solid and toxic waste disposal have become major problems for both state and local governments. Have students research and report to the class why neither incinerators nor older landfills are considered suitable sites for toxic waste disposal.

CONNECTIONS

Law

There are no statewide zoning laws in any state. But each state has the authority to permit local government to regulate zoning. Local governments also can penalize violators for not complying with zoning laws—often by fines or injunctions. Most cities in the United States have zoning laws.

Special Needs Strategy

Auditory Processing Disability Students with auditory processing problems often have difficulty understanding lectures. They will be more successful when they know what to listen for from the start. Before you introduce information from Section 1, write the words *education, zoning, police and fire protection, water supply, sewage and sani-* *tation, transportation,* and *recreation* on the chalkboard. Have students read the section and note one fact or issue to discuss under each topic.

🎧 Have students listen to the chapter summary on the *Audio Cassettes* in the Teacher's Classroom Resources.

STUDY GUIDE

Theme Answers
local: sets most policy, responsible for most funding; *state:* sets guidelines for local districts, provides much funding; *national:* funds certain specialized programs

check zoning laws to see if commercial development is permitted; if so, they can try to change zoning law

Critical Thinking Answers
People without jobs, without proper health care, or who cannot afford food, clothing, or shelter need assistance.

They dislike crowded public transportation and like convenience of cars.

Assess

Check for Understanding

Have students complete Section 1 Review on page 757.

GLOBAL CONNECTION

Comparing Governments

Education Systems In the United States, state and local governments control and support public school systems. In most other countries, however, the central government has complete or partial control over education.

The central government of Great Britain, for example, shares control of education with local authorities. The national ministry (department) of education in France determines educational policy and manages all public schools. Private schools may also obtain public money if they permit some government control.

In the Netherlands more children attend private schools than public schools. The Netherlands has national educational standards set by law. If private schools meet the national standards, they receive government funds.

Examining the Connection
What are the advantages and disadvantages of having a national curriculum that must be followed by all students in a country?

of water homes and businesses use. In a drought emergency, the mayor or other officials may restrict water use and set fines for violators.

Sewage and Sanitation Local government is responsible for sewage disposal. Untreated sewage, if allowed to return to the natural water supply, can endanger life and property. Many local governments maintain sewage treatment plants to deal with this problem.

Sanitation is another responsibility of some local governments. Because of environmental concerns, landfills are no longer the simple solution to sanita-

tion that they once were. Some local governments use garbage-processing plants to dispose of the community's solid wastes.

Sewage and sanitation disposal are very expensive local services. For cities with populations of less than 50,000, sewage and sanitation combined comprise the second highest local governmental expenditure after police and fire protection. Effective sewage and sanitation programs require large investments in complex facilities. These costs have forced some smaller communities to contract with private companies to provide their sewage and sanitation services.

Sewage and sanitation also often require that officials make difficult political decisions. For example, where should sewage treatment plants be located? Although such plants are necessary, people often oppose having them near their homes. Another difficult decision involves how to pay for these services. Although people want a clean and healthy community, they often object to paying taxes that are used for improved sewage and sanitation services.

Transportation As more people choose to live in suburban areas but continue to work in the city, transportation becomes a real concern of city government. In addition, shopping centers are located beyond walking distance from people's homes. To get to work and to shop, millions of Americans rely on either the automobile or mass transit facilities such as subways, trains, and buses.

Local governments spend millions of dollars each year to maintain their 650 thousand miles of streets. In recent years local governments have tried to encourage people to use mass transit rather than their own automobiles for three important reasons. First, mass transit is usually more efficient than the automobile. A high-speed rail system, for example, can transport about 10 times more people each hour than a modern expressway. Second, mass transit causes less pollution than automobiles. Third, mass transit uses less energy per person than automobiles. Still, many people prefer the independence of driving their own vehicles, despite the traffic congestion.

STUDY GUIDE

Themes in Government
Federalism What roles do local, state, and national branches of government play in public education?
Civic Responsibility How can citizens express their disapproval

over the planned location of an office building on park land?

Critical Thinking Skills
Analyzing Information Why do local governments, with state and

federal assistance, provide social services to residents?
Making Inferences Why do many people dislike the idea of using public transportation?

Critical Thinking Activity

Drawing Inferences Have students answer the following: What change in residential patterns has made transportation a concern of local government? *(more people living in suburbs and working in cities)* How has this affected cities? *(Suburban cars going into and out of cities on workdays create traffic congestion, increase noise and air pollution.)*

How have local governments responded to this problem? *(by building and encouraging use of mass transit systems)* Why aren't mass transit systems more widely used? *(convenience of driving own car, crowded buses, lack of comfort or safety)* How might such attitudes be changed?

Social Services Many local governments offer important services to citizens who cannot afford them. Normally, local governments provide services to people who have special needs that may result from unemployment, low income, ill health, or from a permanent handicap.

Several different types of social services programs exist. One type provides aid to people who are temporarily unemployed. This aid consists of cash payments and help in finding new jobs. A second program is hospital care for people who need medical attention and cannot afford the expense. The third is direct assistance to needy people in the form of cash payments. This third type of social service has come to be what many people refer to when they use the term "welfare."

Local governments, especially cities, have a huge fiscal responsibility for social services. Paying for these programs is one of the biggest single expenditures for many large cities in the United States today. Although the federal and state governments pay part of the cost, the share that local governments pay toward these programs continues to rise. Because of this, the mayors of many large cities have suggested that the federal government assume all of the costs. They maintain that funding social services is really a national rather than a local problem. Their proposal has not been accepted, however.

Recreation and Cultural Activities As the leisure time of Americans has increased, local governments have responded with recreation and cultural programs. Many local communities offer programs in swimming, dancing, puppetry, and arts and crafts. In addition, many localities provide programs in baseball, football, and other sports. The maintenance of parks, zoos, and museums is also a function of local government. Many cities and counties have helped build stadiums, arenas, and convention centers that are used for sports and entertainment.

Changing Economic Conditions

During times of economic prosperity, people generally take local government services for granted. In times of recession, local government budget cuts make headlines.

In the 1980s state aid to local governments increased, and states gave localities options to enact income and sales taxes. Local governments took on major projects in transportation and sanitation, and they increased their education, welfare, and recreation budgets. Then recession slowed tax revenues, and the states began to cut aid. Local governments were hit hard. Bridgeport, Connecticut, unable to cope, declared bankruptcy. It had already cut services. Even before that decision was made, it had stopped cleaning its streets, eliminated its programs, and cut by 50 percent its funds for libraries and services for the elderly.

Some argue that recessions have some positive value. They force localities and businesses to study their priorities and become more efficient. Generally governments survive downturns by cutting less essential services and emerge healthier.

1
SECTION REVIEW

Section Summary
Local governments provide vital services to their people.

Checking for Understanding
Recalling Facts
1. Define home rule, county, township, municipality, special district, zoning.
2. Describe three goals of zoning.
3. List five services that local governments provide.
4. Explain why cities have encouraged people to use mass transit.

Exploring Themes
5. Federalism What is the relationship between a state and a municipality within that state?
6. Civic Responsibility Most states give local governments a great amount of sovereignty. What assumption do these states make about local participation in government?

Critical Thinking Skills
7. Analyzing Information In what way do early municipal charters reveal that states had not developed standard forms of municipal government?
8. Making Inferences How do cycles of prosperity and recession influence decisions that local officials make about government services?

Meeting Objectives

Each section objective is tested by the Section Review questions that follow it in parentheses.
• Explain how local governments serve the people. (3, 4, 5, 6, 7, 8)
• Describe zoning laws. (2)

Evaluate

📁 Section 1 Quiz

💻 Testmaker

Reteach

Ask students to complete the following: "If the local government were to shut down tomorrow, the effects on me and this community would be . . ."

Enrich

📁 Have students complete activity 26 in *Enrichment Activities* in the Teacher's Classroom Resources.

Close

Have students predict what impact these changes would have on the need for and cost of community services: increase in the number of retired people, the closing of a major manufacturing plant, growth of the town as a tourist attraction, an increase in non-English-speaking immigrants. Students should identify types of services that would need to be increased in each instance.

Section 1 Review Answers

1. Definitions of terms appear on pages indicated: **home rule,** 752; **county,** 752; **township,** 752; **municipality,** 752; **special district,** 753; **zoning,** 754
2. to plan for regulated growth, preserve the character of neighborhoods, prevent the decline of land values
3. education, police and fire protection, water, sewage and sanitation, transportation, social services, recreation and cultural activities

4. Compared to automobiles, mass transit is usually more efficient, causes less pollution, and uses less energy per person.
5. The state creates the municipality by granting it a charter to govern.
6. Traditions of local self-government are very strong in some states. State government assumes that local people will govern themselves through responsible democratic participation.

7. Each municipality had an individual special charter that contained curious powers.
8. During prosperous times, people generally take local government services for granted. Officials may expand services. In a recession local government must make budget cuts.

Focus

Have students create a web on taxes. Tell them to write *taxes* in a circle and then write around the circle as much information about taxes as they can think of. Have a volunteer copy his or her web on the chalkboard. Discuss the information in the web. Is it all related to taxes? Are some items more relevant than others? How did you decide?

Teach

Have students read the article up through the statements concerning what kind of automobile the police department should purchase. Ask: Which statements do you think are relevant? Which are not? Then compare their responses with the ones in the lesson. Ask: What makes a statement relevant? *(one that illuminates or helps solve a problem)* Does irrelevancy mean the statement is wrong? *(No, it could be factual; it just does not provide useful information.)*

Assess

Have students complete the **Practice** exercise.

Close

Have students suggest several relevant and irrelevant statements for the following car buyers: a teenager, a family, a person who sells on the road.

Determining Relevance

As a student and as a citizen, you are constantly confronted with problems or issues that you need to understand and make decisions about. As you research an issue, you must be able to sift through the many sources of information available to you, deciding what information will be relevant, or useful, and what will not.

Explanation

To determine the relevance of a statement, follow these steps:

- Identify the main idea or topic under discussion.
- Examine the statement and decide whether it is directly related to the main topic. Ask: Does this statement define, explain, or illustrate the topic? Does it show a cause or effect of the topic?
- If the answer to each of the above is "No," the statement is irrelevant.

Suppose some members of your town council have proposed that the next fleet of police patrol cars the town buys should be compact cars with four-cylinder engines. You want to make a decision about this issue, so you read several newspaper accounts of the debate. The following is a list of statements from these newspaper articles: (1) The purchase price of smaller cars would be lower. (2) Smaller cars would be cheaper to run because of greater fuel economy. (3) It is a waste of money to buy new cars when the ones currently in use are still reliable. (4) Four-cylinder engines are not powerful enough for high-speed chases, which may be necessary at any time. (5) The cost of replacing the fleet with the same (large, eight-cylinder) cars now in use would be beyond the city's budget, so a tax increase would be necessary. (6) A majority on the town council has voted to buy only American-made cars.

We will examine the relevance of each statement. Item 1 is relevant because cost is an important consideration when tax dollars are being spent. Item 2 is relevant for the same reason. Item 3 is not relevant, or irrelevant, to the question at hand, which is not whether new cars should be bought now, but what kind of cars to buy the next time a purchase is neces-

sary. Item 4 is relevant because police sometimes have to chase suspects. Item 5 is relevant for the same reason as 1 and 2. Item 6 is irrelevant because there are plenty of American-made cars of all sizes.

Practice

Suppose that your town council is debating the issue of a curfew for minors. The proposed ordinance would impose a curfew of 11:00 P.M. on weeknights and midnight on weekends for all persons under the age of 18. The curfew would be enforced by the police and fines of $100 would be issued to persons found guilty of violations. Here are some of the statements made by citizens speaking for and against the curfew at a town meeting. Read them carefully, then explain whether each is relevant or irrelevant to deciding whether the ordinance should be passed in its present form.

1. Some minors have evening jobs that require them to be out past the curfew.
2. Five years ago a a similar curfew was proposed, but did not win passage.
3. Parents, not governments, should be in charge of setting curfews for minor children.
4. The fine of $100 is too high to impose on minors and would be especially burdensome to minors from poorer families.
5. Two years ago a neighboring town passed a similar curfew, with the result that juvenile crime rates dropped by 20 percent.
6. Businesses that cater to teenagers will be hurt by earlier closing times.
7. The school board supports the curfew because it says too many students are coming to school without sufficient sleep.
8. Vandalism has become an increasing problem in recent years.

Additional Practice

To practice this skill, refer to **Reinforcing the Skill** on page 771.

Practice Answers

1. Relevant; shows curfew would interfere with people's earning a livelihood.
2. Irrelevant; has nothing to do with this vote.
3. Relevant; as an opinion about legitimacy of government-imposed curfews.
4. Relevant; perhaps the fine should be lowered.
5. Relevant; perhaps drop in crime rate related to curfew.
6. Relevant; need to consider law's indirect effects.
7. Relevant; if one accepts a connection between having to be home earlier and getting more sleep.
8. Irrelevant; no clear connection between the rise in vandalism, teenagers, or late hours.

For additional practice, have students complete activity 26 in *Skill Reinforcement Activities* in the Teacher's Classroom Resources.

Counties, Townships, and Special Districts

Local government in the United States assumes many forms. Counties, townships, and special districts are the three most common forms of local government. Together, they make up about 65 percent of the approximately 86,000 units of local government in the United States.

County Government

State governments have created counties to assist in administering state laws. The county form of government is found in every state except Connecticut and Rhode Island. In Louisiana counties are called **parishes**, and in Alaska they are called **boroughs**.

Counties of the United States display tremendous variety. First, the number of counties within a state varies from state to state. Texas has 254 counties, while Delaware has only 3 counties. Second, counties also differ in size and population. Los Angeles County in California covers an area of more than 4,000 square miles (10,360 square kilometers) with a population exceeding 7 million people. In contrast, Howard County in Arkansas has an area of only 574 square miles (1,477 square kilometers) and a population of about 13,500.

Further, county governments vary considerably in influence. In rural areas and in the South, county government has been vital. In these places early settlements were spread out over large areas, with few towns and villages. One town in each county became the seat of county government. The county courthouse became a popular political gathering place.

On the other hand, county government has never been very important in New England. In this region

people settled in towns, and each township—rather than the county—became the significant unit of local government.

Recently in some metropolitan areas, county governments have grown in importance as they have taken over some of the functions that municipalities once handled. For example, the government of Dade County, Florida, now administers transportation, water supply, and other services for the Miami area. In many other places, however, county governments have declined in importance but continue to exist in spite of attempts to change or even abolish them.

The Functions of County Government As administrative subdivisions of the state, county governments enforce and administer state laws. In so doing, they perform many of the "housekeeping" functions of government. Perhaps because of this, the public seldom thinks about county activities. County officials rarely make dramatic decisions that attract public attention.

State constitutions specify many functions for county governments, however. Counties administer a variety of public facilities such as airports and hospitals. They maintain roads, register voters, supervise elections, and keep voting records. Most county governments maintain records of births, deaths, and property ownership. County governments also are usually responsible for assessing and collecting taxes; for issuing hunting, fishing, and marriage licenses; and for administering justice and corrections through the courts and jails.

A county may include a number of cities, towns, and villages. County governments deal with area-wide problems such as crime and transportation that

---

SECTION PREVIEW

Objectives
After studying this section, you should be able to:
- Explain local governments' responses to the changing needs of their constituents.

- Discuss local government in New England.

Key Terms and Concepts
parish, borough, county board, town meeting, selectmen, school board

Themes in Government
- Growth of Democracy
- Civic Responsibility

Critical Thinking Skills
- Making Inferences
- Identifying Alternatives

CHAPTER 26: ORGANIZATION OF LOCAL GOVERNMENT 759

Focus

Bell Ringer

Ask students to respond in writing to the following while attendance is being taken:

Most local government in the United States today is an example of direct democracy. True or false?

Motivating Activity

Discuss students' Bell Ringer answers. *(false, mostly representative)* Explain that an exception is the township form of government in New England with its town meeting.

Have students name their township and/or county and think of public buildings such as hospitals, jails, libraries, courthouses, and parks that have the county or township name. Judging by the activities carried on in each building, have students speculate about what services the county or township government provides. Tell students that they will learn more about these services as they read this section.

Vocabulary Precheck

Ask students to speculate on the meaning of each term and concept. Then have them check their guesses by finding the definition in the section text. **LEP**

CONNECTIONS

Language
The word *parish* reflects Louisiana's period of Spanish rule, when the area was organized into religious divisions called parishes.

Classroom Resources for Section 2

- 📁 Guided Reading Activities
- 📁 Reproducible Lesson Plans
- 📁 Primary and Secondary Source Readings 26
- 📁 Section 2 Quiz

- 🖥 Testmaker
- 📊 Chapter Transparencies 26
- SAT Practice Tests

Teach

Guided Practice

L1 Interpreting a Primary Source Ask students why Jefferson called politics in New England towns "the perfect exercise of self-government." *(At town meetings all citizens can take part in decision making.)* How and why has township government changed? Is this trend likely to continue? Why?

Interpreting Visuals Display transparency 26 from the *Chapter Transparencies* in the Teacher's Classroom Resources and use the accompanying teaching strategy and student activity to teach the organization of local government.

L2 Constructing a Chart Make a three-column chart on the chalkboard, labeled *Problem, Causes, Possible Solutions.* Organize students into three groups, and assign each group one of the problems facing county governments: *lack of effective leadership, limited powers, inefficiency.* Have each group identify causes of its problem, suggest possible solutions, and report its findings on the class chart.

Caption Answer
rural areas and the South

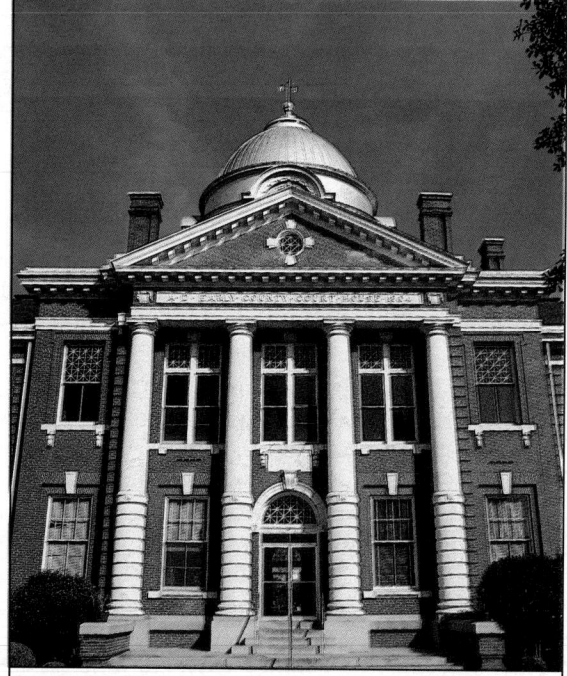

Local Justice
State laws are often administered at county courthouses. **History In which region of the country are these courts vital?**

an individual city or town may not have authority to oversee. County government is often better able to respond to such problems than local governments. In some places, such as Nashville, Tennessee, county governments have been given the power to deal with many regional matters.

The Structure of County Government States provide county governments with a variety of organizational structures. A **county board** has the authority to govern most counties. The name of this board varies from state to state. It may be called the county board of supervisors, the board of county commissioners, or the board of freeholders, among other names. Board members are almost always popularly elected officials.

State law strictly limits the legislative powers of county boards. For the most part, county boards decide on the county budget, taxes, and zoning codes.

In many counties the county board has both executive and legislative powers. Board members often divide executive power, with each member responsible for a different county department, such as public welfare, roads, or recreation. In many counties the county board shares executive power with other officers who are usually elected. These officials may include the county sheriff, attorney, clerk, coroner, recorder of deeds, treasurer, auditor, assessor, surveyor, and superintendent of schools.

County Government Problems

Some people believe that county government may have served well in older, rural America but cannot cope with the complex problems of local government today. Those who point out the need for change focus on three major problems of county government: lack of effective leadership, limited powers, and inefficiency.

Lack of Effective Leadership In most county governments, power is divided among county board members and other officers, sometimes resulting in waste and inaction. When power is divided among so many people, the average citizen often finds it impossible to learn which official is responsible for what.

In an effort to provide more effective leadership, many larger counties have turned to a county executive or county administrator. This official is responsible for administering county services. About one-third of the counties have either an appointed or elected administrator.

Changing the historic structure of county government to include an administrator can create new problems. County boards, with deep political ties to local interest groups, have long-established methods for dealing with issues. The county board may not readily surrender its authority to the new administra-

Background

There are 16,666 townships and towns in the United States, most located in the northeast and north central states. Connecticut and Rhode Island, the two states that do not have any form of county government, are organized along the lines of townships. After the state abolished county government in 1959, local government in Connecticut centered in 169 towns. The towns may include several communities and rural areas under one government. Rhode Island towns also operate much like townships. In both states local town governments hold town meetings.

tor. If authority is divided, the county staff may have to choose between supporting the board or the administrator. In such cases, policymaking and execution come to a standstill. One Florida county that created the position of administrator in 1973 was still wrestling with the issue of what the role of administrator and board should be 16 years later. The assistant county administrator offered some advice:

Things work best when elected officials concentrate on policy, to make sure it is current and is really accomplishing the objectives they believe people want for their county or city. They should rely on the professionals to carry out that policy, according to the judgment of the professionals as to what will work best.
—LARRY BLICK, ASSISTANT ADMINISTRATOR, HILLSBOROUGH COUNTY, FLORIDA, 1989

Limited Powers Most state constitutions severely restrict the powers of county boards. Some people believe that these boards cannot respond effectively to modern problems because they have only limited ability to tax, spend, and legislate.

Most county officials strongly support home rule for counties. They believe that home rule would make it easier to take the action necessary to solve pressing county problems. Twenty-eight state constitutions now provide some form of home rule for counties, permitting them to draw up their own county charters or constitutions. Only 100 of the 1,500 eligible counties, however, have taken advantage of this opportunity.

Inefficiency The United States has more than 3,000 counties, many with very small populations. The multitude of counties contributes to inefficiency in local government. Some people have suggested consolidation of small counties into larger units, with the aim of cutting waste and duplication of services. Others have proposed a county civil service to make it possible to choose the best-qualified people for county jobs. Because these proposals are controversial, few counties have put them into effect.

Vital Services
Local governments provide fire protection. **Political Processes** Name two forms of local government.

Townships and Towns

The early settlers in New England in the 1600s established the first townships in America. Today, 20 states—mostly in New England and the Midwest—have townships.

Variations in Townships In many states, counties are subdivided into townships. The size and jurisdiction of townships vary greatly from one state to another. As mentioned earlier, township government in New England refers to municipal governments that began with the small, struggling communities of the early Puritan settlers. In New Jersey, however, the township covers a large area that may include several municipalities.

The activities that township governments undertake vary from state to state as well. In states such as Nebraska and Missouri, the primary function of

STUDY GUIDE

Themes in Government
Civic Responsibility States that provide county governments more power through home rule may assume that local citizens will participate to make government effective.

Citizen involvement in government generally remains low, however, unless major problems develop.

Identifying Alternatives What can citizens do to influence the policies of town or county governments?

L3 Geography Bring to class a state map that shows counties. Have students characterize the state according to the number, size, and shape of counties in the state. Have students consider possible geographic reasons for these differences. *(landforms, population densities, state or international boundaries)* Have students also identify county seats. Do these cities or towns tend to have the highest populations in their counties? What might be reasons for this? *(established early, grew because of their role as government centers)*

Independent Practice

L1 Language Arts Have students obtain information about the structure of their own county government. Students should find out what name their county board uses, what its powers are, and where the county seat is located. Have students use the information to create a chart for newcomers which explains the county government organization. **LEP**

Caption Answer
counties and townships

STUDY GUIDE

Critical Thinking Answer vote for elected officials, run for public office, get involved in the school system, lobby town or county officials, attend meetings, or write letters to the editor

Cooperative Learning Activity

Organize students into groups and have each select a special district in the state for an in-depth study. Within each group, students can assume the roles of writers, editors, interviewer, researchers. Researchers can use newspaper and public library sources to identify the purpose of the district, how it is financed, how officials are chosen, and how citizens can oversee its work and influence its decisions. The interviewer's job is to contact an official of the special district to find out how closely the researchers' findings match the actual work of the district. Writers and editors are responsible for creating a written report, using the group members' information.

Focus

Review briefly the reasons for the strong French influence in Louisiana. *(part of France's North American empire prior to Louisiana Purchase)*

Teach

Have students explain why some scholars believe the Civil Code may need revision. *(no longer responsive to needs of society)* Why might a legal system based on civil law need revision over time more than one based on common law? *(Common law is constantly revised through court decisions.)*

Assess

Have students complete **Examining Our Multicultural Heritage.**

Answers

1. Louisiana civil law is written, while common law is unwritten and is based on previous court decisions.
2. the Napoleonic Code
3. With a written civil code the same law is applied to each case and interpreted in light of the facts, while in English common law a decision will be based on prior court decisions and may be more open to interpretation.

Close

Ask: What are advantages of a civil law system? Why might the people of Louisiana resist revision of their law code today?

Multicultural Heritage

The Legal Heritage of France

Every society has a working system of laws to govern itself and settle disputes among people. Laws gradually change over time to reflect the continual changes in society. Rooted in English law from the time of the colonies, the American legal system also contains elements of Dutch, Spanish, and French law. The office of district attorney may be of Dutch origin. Spanish or Mexican law influenced the legal system in much of the West. French law established a lasting influence in Louisiana.

Louisiana is the only state with a civil law code based on the French Napoleonic Code. All other states use the English common law. The Louisiana Legislative Council best described the difference: "Briefly stated, civil law is code or written law, and common law is unwritten or case law." The Council added:

> *Civil law is drafted by authorities in the various fields of law—judges, teachers, practicing attorneys—but always must be adopted by the legislative body. . . . The common law, on the other hand, is unwritten law; that is, much of it has never been adopted by a legislative body in statutory form. Instead it has grown and developed as a result of consistent court decisions on the same or similar questions.*
>
> —LOUISIANA LEGISLATIVE COUNCIL, 1975

Originally French, the Louisiana Territory was ceded to Spain and then returned to France in 1800. Three years later the Louisiana Purchase brought the Territory into the United States. President Jefferson sought to establish English common law in place of the French and Spanish laws then in effect in Louisiana. The inhabitants of the territory resisted the efforts, and in 1808 the local legislature passed the Digest of Civil Laws that was closely modeled after the Napoleonic Code then in force in France. About 85 percent of the written articles of the Code of 1808 were based on French laws, the other 15 percent reflected the territory's Spanish heritage. Revised in 1825 and then again during Reconstruction, the Civil Codes of Louisiana remain largely intact today.

Although one legal scholar in Louisiana described the codes as "The most precious heritage we have re-

President Jefferson's Triumph
The Louisiana Purchase Treaty, accompanied by the French seal, was signed by Napoleon Bonaparte and his foreign minister, Talleyrand, on April 30, 1803.

ceived from our ancestors," some people believe the Civil Code should be revised and updated. As professor A.N. Yiannopoulos of Tulane University in New Orleans commented: "In countries sharing our legal heritage . . . there has been an awareness of the need for revision for quite a while because civil codes in force there are no longer responsive to the needs of society. The Louisiana Civil Code belongs to the same category." Although this call for revision may ultimately be met, the long traditional heritage of French law in Louisiana will continue in whatever new civil codes that are adopted.

Examining Our Multicultural Heritage

Reviewing the Facts
1. Explain the difference between common law and the type of civil law in effect in Louisiana.
2. Identify the French legal code that was the basis for much of the 1808 Civil Code in Louisiana.

Critical Thinking Skills
3. Drawing Conclusions Why do you think some people might prefer written civil codes rather than English common law?

More About Our Multicultural Heritage

Under civil-law systems judges are not bound by judicial precedent. Rather than reviewing prior court decisions, they rely on the writings of academic lawyers interpreting the codes. Louisiana based its civil code on France's Napoleonic Code of 1804. The Napoleonic Code influenced the laws of Germany, Italy, Spain, Portugal, the Netherlands, and Belgium. The French carried their legal system to their colonies in Africa and to Canada where it can be seen in the laws of the French province of Quebec. As colonizers, the Spanish and Portuguese took the civil-law tradition to Latin America. In the twentieth century Japan and Turkey adopted legal systems based on civil law.

township government is road-building and road maintenance. In Pennsylvania, townships provide a wide array of government services, including police and fire protection.

In many rural areas, townships have lost population and power in the last few decades. For example, many townships in Kansas have lost power to county governments. In some other areas of the Midwest, such as Indiana, control over education has passed from the township to either the county or the local school district.

In some urban areas, however, township government has taken on increased importance. In areas of rapid metropolitan growth, townships have assumed some functions of city government including water supply, sewage disposal, and police protection. Urban townships in states such as Michigan and New Jersey have become increasingly important in recent years.

The New England Town Township or town government has long been a part of New England tradition. Beginning in earliest colonial times, the area of a town encompassed a village and the surrounding forests and farms. Thomas Jefferson once described politics in the typical New England town as "the perfect exercise of self-government." With the strong community spirit fostered by their founders, these towns became models of citizen participation in local government.

The **town meeting** served as the centerpiece of town government in New England. In the past, town meetings had been open to all voters. Those who attended could express their opinions or just mingle and socialize with their neighbors. At the town meeting, citizens participated in the lawmaking process, decided on taxes, and appropriated money for any public projects they thought necessary. They elected town officials, called **selectmen**. Selectmen were responsible for administering the local government between town meetings.

Over the years, as New England towns grew and their governments became more complex, the town meeting form of direct democracy became impractical. Today, in some very small towns, the town meeting still operates much as it used to. In larger towns and cities, however, the voters elect representatives to attend the meeting in their stead. In addition, selectmen now make some of the decisions that citizens once made. Finally, some towns have hired town managers to perform duties similar to those of county administrators.

Special Districts in Government

Local governments often face such problems as providing a safe water supply and adequate transportation. From time to time, to solve these problems, local governments establish special units of government. The local school district is such a special unit. The water commission and the port authority are two of the thousands of special districts in the United States. Special districts also are responsible for airports, sewage disposal, and roads.

As the most common unit of local government, the special district is found in every state except Alaska. Counting school districts, more than 47,000 special districts, comprising more than half of all the local governmental units in the country, exist. In some places special districts are also called commissions or authorities.

Reasons for Special Districts Special districts are better able to respond to specific problems than other units of local government. Modern problems, such as water supply and sewage treatment, often affect large areas in which many local governments are located. A special district can handle a problem that may involve a wider area than that of a single local government. For example, a local reservoir might supply 20 or 30 towns in a region, each with its own government. Instead of each local government trying to control the flow of water, a regional water commission might provide better service and planning for the entire area. Some special districts have jurisdiction over a region that includes parts of more than one state. The Port Authority of New York and New Jersey is an example of such a regional district.

The second reason for special districts is the financial limitations states impose on other units of local government. Most state governments limit the taxing and borrowing powers of local governments. Some states also have laws that limit how much local governments may spend. Creating a new special district not subject to such limitations becomes a practical solution for local leaders whose budgets are strained to meet local needs. Most special districts may make their own policies, levy taxes, and borrow money.

Disadvantages of Special Districts Although they provide needed services, special districts have certain disadvantages. They contribute to the fragmentation and disorganization of local government across the United States. In some areas independent special districts administer education, sewage and

CHAPTER 26: ORGANIZATION OF LOCAL GOVERNMENT **763**

Interpreting Source Readings Have students complete activity 26 in *Primary and Secondary Source Readings* in the Teacher's Classroom Resources.

L2 Public Policy Have students make a list of various local county officials. Organize students into pairs and have each pair contact and interview a county official about his or her responsibilities and problems related to county government. Have each pair report their findings to the class.

L3 Research Organize a research scavenger hunt. Have students identify places in the community where citizens can: get a copy of a birth certificate, get a marriage license, register to vote, get a hunting or fishing license, report a hole in a street, find out the election returns for the most recent local election. Have students identify the unit of government that provides each service.

Assess

Check for Understanding

Have students complete Section 2 Review on page 764.

Meeting Objectives

Each section objective is tested by the Section Review questions that follow it in parentheses.
- Explain local governments' responses to the changing needs of their constituents. (2, 3, 6, 7, 8)
- Discuss local government in New England. (4, 5)

Focus on Government
Video 53
**Making Connections:
Town Hall Meeting**
Running Time: 2:02
Videodisc 3, Chap. 53
VHS Tape 3, Begins 38:26

Video 54
**Speaking Out:
Governing the Schools**
Running Time: 1:43
Videodisc 3, Chap. 54
VHS Tape 3, Begins 40:30

Critical Thinking Activity

Identifying Alternatives List the advantages of special districts. *(can respond to specific problems better than other units of local government, handle problems that cut across large areas, levy taxes and borrow money)* Then list the disadvantages. *(source of fragmentation of local government, reduce understanding and citizen participation in local government)*

For each disadvantage suggest ways to overcome it. Then review the concept of regionalization, looking at the examples of the Port Authority of New York and New Jersey and Portland's Metro. Decide what problems might stand in the way of creating regional governing bodies in your state.

Evaluate

📁 Section 2 Quiz

🖱 Testmaker

Reteach

On a map of the United States have students locate the areas where county and township forms of government are strongest and describe the differences between the two forms of local government. Then have students name the most common form of special district. *(school)*

Enrich

Have students obtain data from the local board of elections on the percentage of eligible voters taking part in the local school board election over the past 10 years. Ask students to display their findings in a graph and decide whether their data supports the assertion that most voters do little to influence school policy in their community.

Close

Write the section summary statement on the board: *Units of local government have gradually changed to meet the needs of communities.* Have students cite specific examples from the text to support this statement. *(Students might cite changes in townships and regional arrangements in New York, New Jersey, and Oregon.)*

---

water supply, parks and recreation, and even police and fire protection. With so many separate units of government, planning is difficult, and coordination among governments is often impossible.

In addition, the existence of so many independent units of government makes it difficult for people to understand government and to participate in it. For example, Chicago has more than 1,200 units of local government, and Philadelphia has more than 860 units.

The School District In recent decades the number of school districts has declined. Better transportation has allowed many school districts to consolidate, thus saving money. Today the United States has about 14,550 school districts, a sharp drop from the 108,579 districts that existed in 1942. Texas, California, and Illinois have the largest number of school districts, each with more than 1,000.

The **school board** is usually an elected local body that governs the school district. The school board is responsible for setting school policies, hiring a superintendent of schools, and running the schools on a daily basis. It also makes up the school budget, decides on new school programs and facilities, and often has the final decision about hiring teachers and supervisory staff. In some places the school board may also decide on the amount of school taxes to be levied.

Citizens often have strong feelings about how their schools should be run. In many communities, however, less than one-third of the eligible voters actually vote in school board elections. Turnout is usually higher when citizens vote on issues dealing with

money, such as school bond referendums and school tax levies.

Regional Arrangements

In the 1990s local governments are joining to develop creative approaches to regional issues. Cooperative efforts are dealing with everything from waste management to law enforcement. Although voters resist attempts at outright consolidation, they have generally supported joint efforts.

Recently five rural counties in Alabama formed a waste management authority. Officials realized that they would have more bargaining power with the company that operates the landfills they use if they joined together. City police departments and county sheriffs' offices in some areas share crime laboratories, keep joint records, operate joint radio bands, and share the cost of training personnel. Fire departments have made agreements that require the fire station closest to answer the first alarm, ignoring political boundaries. Perhaps the most venturesome regional arrangement is Portland, Oregon's, Metropolitan Service District (Metro). Metro may become a national model for regional government. As the nation's only regional authority with multiple responsibilities run by elected officials, Metro covers three counties. Its main task is controlling growth under Oregon's land-use laws. It also does all the transportation and water-quality planning for the area, runs the zoo, manages the convention center and coliseum, and deals with solid waste and recycling.

2
SECTION REVIEW

Section Summary
Units of local government have gradually changed to meet the needs of communities.

Checking for Understanding
Recalling Facts
1. Define parish, borough, county board, town meeting, selectmen, school board.
2. Identify two areas of the country in which counties have been important units of local government.
3. List seven administrative functions of county government.
4. Explain why the town meeting has become impractical in some New England towns.

Exploring Themes
5. Growth of Democracy How did populous New England towns preserve democratic control over their local governments when they discontinued town meetings?
6. Civic Responsibility Find evidence in the section to support this statement: "Local government gives citizens many opportunities to participate in politics."

Critical Thinking Skills
7. Making Inferences Do you think voters share county officials' enthusiasm for home rule? Why?
8. Identifying Alternatives What changes in the size and structure of county government might make it more efficient?

Section 2 Review Answers

1. Definitions of terms appear on pages indicated: **parish,** 759; **borough,** 759; **county board,** 760; **town meeting,** 763; **selectmen,** 763; **school board,** 764
2. rural areas and the South
3. Counties administer airports and hospitals, maintain roads, register voters, supervise elections, and keep voting records; maintain records of births, deaths, and property ownership; assess and collect taxes; issue hunting, fishing,

and marriage licenses; and administer justice and corrections through courts and jails.
4. The growth of population and complexity of government have made it impractical to have all the voters assemble in one location to conduct business.
5. They elected representatives to attend the town meeting.
6. attend town meetings, run for office, vote for school board and county board

7. No, because only a small percentage of the counties eligible for home rule have taken advantage of the opportunity.
8. adding a county civil service, combining some administrative tasks under one executive, enlarging county government's powers, and consolidating smaller counties into larger units

Local Government Revenue Sources

L ike individuals, governments make decisions about how to raise money and where to spend it. The economic decisions that governments make are more complicated.

Government must weigh the requirements of the general welfare against the available revenue. They must also consider the wants of individuals and interest groups. Sharp disagreements over which services or programs government should finance often arise. Should a local government spend money on a recreation program for its young people or repave a road that might bring more business to local merchants? Should it try to support both programs by borrowing the money or seeking state or federal aid?

Revenue From the Property Tax

One of the oldest taxes, property taxes, once provided revenue for all levels of government. Today property taxes are the most important source of revenue for local governments, accounting for more than two-thirds of all their tax revenues.

Property taxes are collected on real and personal property. **Real property** includes land and buildings. **Personal property** consists of such things as stocks and bonds, jewelry, furniture, automobiles, and works of art. Most local governments now tax only real property. Personal property taxes are not a major source of revenue, and if personal property is taxed at all, the rate is usually very low.

Calculating the Property Tax How do local governments determine what the real property tax will be? The process involved in calculating the value of

the property to be taxed is called **assessment**. The **tax assessor** is the official responsible for determining the value of real property each resident owns.

The process of calculating the property tax is complicated. It begins when the tax assessor examines the homes and other types of real property in the community and then appraises the market value of each property. The **market value** of a house or a factory is the amount of money the owner may expect to receive if the property is sold. The tax assessor may reappraise property periodically as market values change.

The government normally does not tax real property at its appraised worth or market value, however. Instead, it taxes property based on its assessed value, which is usually only a percentage of its appraised worth. The local government establishes the percentage that will be used. For example, a house that has an appraised worth of $80,000 may have an assessed value of 30 percent of that figure, or $24,000.

The local legislative body determines how much money is needed from the property tax to pay for government services. After this, it establishes the property tax rate. For example, a city council might decide that it needs to collect $800,000 from the property tax. Suppose the total assessed value of real property in the community is $40,000,000. The city government computes the tax rate by dividing the desired tax revenue, $800,000, by the total assessed value, $40,000,000. The tax rate is then 2 percent. The city then computes an individual homeowner's tax bill by multiplying the assessed value of the property by the tax rate. For example, a homeowner with a house having an assessed value of $18,000 would pay a property tax of 2 percent. The total tax would be $360 ($18,000 x .02 = $360).

SECTION PREVIEW

Objectives
After studying this section, you should be able to:
- Determine local governments' need for reliable sources of revenue.

- Explain block grants and revenue sharing.

Key Terms and Concepts
real property, personal property, assessment, tax assessor, market value

Themes in Government
- Federalism
- Public Policy

Critical Thinking Skills
- Making Comparisons
- Identifying Alternatives

Classroom Resources for Section 3

- Guided Reading Activities
- Reproducible Lesson Plans
- Participating in Government 26
- Cooperative Learning Activities 26
- Reteaching Activities 26

- Section 3 Quiz
- Chapter 26 Tests
- Testmaker
- Limited English Proficiency Activities 26
  SAT Practice Tests

Bell Ringer

While attendance is being taken, have students answer the following:

What might be the major expenses of local governments?

Motivating Activity

Discuss students' Bell Ringer responses. (*public services*) Pose this question from the introductory paragraph of the lesson: Should a local government spend money on a recreation program for teenagers or use it to repave a road that might bring more business to local merchants? Have students make a list of questions they would want answered before making a decision.

Vocabulary Precheck

Call on students to read aloud the definitions for each term and concept from the Glossary. Then have them restate each definition in their own words. **LEP**

Teach

Guided Practice

L1 Mathematics Use these math problems to check students' understanding of property tax calculation: The city council needs to collect $360,000 from the property tax. The total assessed value of real property in the community is $9 million. What should the tax rate be? (*4 percent*) How much property tax will be paid each year on a house with an assessed value of $27,000, if the property tax is 3 percent? (*$810*)

📁 **Group Discussion** Have students complete activity 26 in *Cooperative Learning Activities* in the Teacher's Classroom Resources.

L2 Economics Discuss the reasons for opposition to property taxes. Why are they called regressive? *(heaviest burden on poor and people with fixed incomes)* Why are property values hard to assess fairly? *(Assessors may be poorly trained or open to influence in their appraisals.)* Why do wealthy communities have more money to spend on public services than poor communities? *(Real property in a wealthy community brings in more revenue through property taxes.)* What is the effect of exempting nonprofit institutions? *(Homeowners and businesses bear a heavier share of the tax burden.)*

PARTICIPATING IN GOVERNMENT

The GI Bill of Rights, known officially as the Servicemen's Readjustment Act, offers a wide variety of services for armed forces veterans. Passed in 1944, the GI Bill makes many veterans eligible for vocational training as well as for dental and medical care at veterans' hospitals. It provides loans to buy or build a home. Today educational benefits vary according to date and length of service. Subsequent acts have extended the benefits of the GI Bill to all who serve in the armed forces whether during wartime or peacetime. Ask students if they know why joining the armed forces is considered participating in government.

📁 Have students complete activity 26 in *Participating in Government* in the Teacher's Classroom Resources.

The Debate Over the Property Tax In recent years many Americans have become increasingly critical of the property tax. Across the country antitax groups have formed. Public opinion surveys indicate that most Americans view the property tax as unfair. Why do so many people criticize the property tax?

The major charge against the property tax is that it is regressive—placing a heavier burden on people with lower incomes than on those with higher incomes. The property tax also weighs heavily on retired homeowners with fixed incomes.

The second criticism of the property tax is that it is often very difficult to determine property values on a fair and equal basis. Standards may vary with each tax assessor. Tax assessors are elected officials, often underpaid and inadequately trained. People have accused some assessors of underappraising certain homes for political reasons or being easily influenced by public pressure or individuals in the community.

A third criticism is that reliance on the property tax results in unequal public services. A wealthy community with a large tax base can afford better public services than a less wealthy community with a small tax base. Based on this criticism, in 1971 the California Supreme Court ruled against using the property tax to pay for local schools. It stated that using property taxes to support schools was a violation of the Fourteenth Amendment's guarantee of equal protection of the law. The court argued that this method of financing schools discriminated against students in poor communities.

Finally, property that certain institutions own is exempt from the property tax. Property used for nonprofit, educational, religious, or charitable purposes and government property is usually not taxed. Some areas give tax exemptions to new businesses and industries to encourage them to relocate in the local community. As a result, the nonexempt property owners must bear a heavier share of the tax burden.

Property Tax Revolt In a recent three-year period, 87 percent of local communities increased taxes on real property by an average of 24 percent. Homeowners, especially those on fixed incomes, responded with a movement to oppose the property tax. As a result of public pressure, several states passed legislation limiting taxes on residential property.

The successful revolt against property tax increases spelled trouble for local government budgets. A national news magazine predicted:

PARTICIPATING IN GOVERNMENT

Volunteering for the Armed Forces

Do you know someone who has a military career? What opportunities do the armed forces offer you?

The military services differ in their requirements, tours of duty, training, and occupational opportunities. In general, men and women who volunteer for the armed forces must be between the ages of 17 and 35. Applicants must be citizens of the United States or registered aliens. They must have a high school diploma, be physically fit, and may not have a criminal record. All applicants must pass a physi-

cal examination, which includes drug testing.

The Armed Services Vocational Aptitude Battery (ASVAB) is a basic enlistment qualification test which is administered to all applicants. The scores on this multiple-choice test help to identify your academic and vocational strengths. The results are used to qualify you

for certain military training programs.

The goal of the armed services is to build a well-trained, highly skilled military force. To accomplish this goal, the services offer technical training in hundreds of military occupations. Most of the skills and experience can be transferred to civilian careers.

Investigating Further

Visit your local recruiting station to find out more about opportunities in the armed forces.

Background

During the 1980s the percentage of the average local government budget provided by federal funds was cut in half from about 9 percent to less than 4 percent. While federal funding has declined, localities have been increasingly affected by federal mandates in such areas as education, environmental protection, and transportation. Such mandates have added to the cost of local government. States, on the other hand, have taken some of the financial burden from local governments in such areas as education, solid-waste disposal, and land-use planning.

The dark side of their revolt may ultimately catch up with the nation. Residential property tax revenue traditionally has represented the majority of income for most U.S. cities and counties. . . . This is very bad news for America's already battered states, cities, and towns, which currently are running a collective budget deficit of $50 billion a year.

—U.S. News & World Report, August 6, 1990

As the tax revolt has cut funds, local governments have begun to look for new sources of revenue. Some have turned to impact fees, charged to builders on all new construction because of the impact that it would have on community services. These fees have helped pay for new roads, schools, water, and sewers in developing communities. They also raised the cost of new housing. Other local governments have cut park, library, and school budgets to save money.

The property tax remains the basic income for local government. Local governments, whose tax sources are limited by the states, have no other source of revenue that yields as much.

Other Local Revenue Sources

Local governments must have other revenue sources. These include local income taxes, sales taxes, fines and fees, and government-owned businesses.

The local income tax is a tax on personal income. Several states, primarily in the East, make this source of revenue available to local governments. In some cities such as New York, it is an important source of revenue. If the state and the local community both have an income tax, the taxpayer pays three income taxes: federal, state, and local.

The sales tax is a tax on most items sold in stores. Many states allow their local governments to use this tax. In some places it is a selective sales tax in that it is applied to only a few items.

Fines paid for traffic, sanitary, and other violations, and fees for special services provide part of the in-

come for local governments. Special assessments are fees that property owners must pay for local services that benefit them. For example, a city may impose a special assessment when it improves a sidewalk or installs sewers that benefit homeowners or shopkeepers. Some cities also earn revenue through housing projects, markets, and parking garages.

States permit local governments to borrow money in the form of bonds—certificates that promise to repay the borrowed money with interest by a certain date. Investors consider local government bonds good investments because their earned interest is not subject to federal income taxes. Municipal bonds raise money for large, expensive projects such as a sports stadium, school buildings, or government office buildings.

Intergovernmental Revenue

In addition to local sources of revenue, most local governments receive economic aid from state and federal governments, often in the form of grants.

State Grants State governments provide several types of aid to local governments. When local governments carry out state laws or administer state programs such as constructing highways or matching welfare payments, they receive state aid. State governments also grant funds for specific purposes such as recreation and education. Today states provide more than 33 percent of the general revenue of local governments. This revenue can be broken down into two types—general government support, or revenue sharing, and support for specific programs, called categorical grants. Most state aid consists of categorical grants that are used for education, highways, public welfare, and health and hospitals.

Federal Grants Federal financial aid has come in two forms: grants-in-aid and revenue sharing. Local governments often receive grants-in-aid directly from a particular department of the federal government.

STUDY GUIDE

Themes in Government
Federalism Why are property taxes vital to local governments?
Public Policy Why are certain not-for-profit groups exempt from property taxes?

Critical Thinking Skills
Making Comparisons How are state grants to local governments similar to federal grants?

Identifying Alternatives If a community votes to reduce property taxes, what choices does local government have?

CHAPTER 26: ORGANIZATION OF LOCAL GOVERNMENT   767

Cooperative Learning Activity

Organize students into groups of six. Have each select an issue related to budget decisions in the local community. Newspapers and local TV newscasts are sources for this information. Then have each group prepare a position paper on the selected issue. Within each group, two students can identify the choices available to decision makers on this issue, another pair can identify costs and benefits of all choices, while the third pair can describe the choice the group favors and explain why. As a follow-up activity, each group can write a letter to the appropriate local officials recommending the action favored by the group.

L3 Understanding Cause and Effect Point out that for several decades wealthier residents and many businesses have been moving from cities to suburbs. Ask: What effects has this demographic change had on local government funding sources? What might be the effects on local governments of designating a large part of a county as parkland?

Independent Practice

L1 Classifying Have students write L for local, S for state, and F for federal next to each of these sources of revenue for local governments. Note that one source of revenue can come from more than one level of government: **1.** grants-in-aid *(F);* **2.** property tax *(L);* **3.** categorical grants *(S);* **4.** revenue sharing *(S, F);* **5.** traffic fines *(L);* **6.** sales tax *(L).*

STUDY GUIDE

Theme Answers
Property taxes account for two-thirds of all local government revenues.

Their goal is to provide services for citizens, not to make money.

Critical Thinking Answers
State grants may be general support for ongoing programs or categorical grants for specific projects. Federal government also funds special projects with grants-in-aid.

It can introduce or increase fees in other areas, such as sales tax, income tax, use of special services; or it can cut back on expenses by reducing services.

Assess

Check for Understanding

Have students complete Section 3 Review on page 768.

Meeting Objectives

Each section objective is tested by the Section Review questions that follow it in parentheses.

- Determine local governments' need for reliable sources of revenue. (2, 4, 6, 8)
- Explain block grants and revenue sharing. (3, 5, 7)

Evaluate

 Section 3

 Testmaker

Reteach

Have students complete activity 26 in *Reteaching Activities* in the Teacher's Classroom Resources.

Enrich

Have students research the state and federal grants that their local governments have received and how they have been used.

Close

Have students explain and defend this statement: "The economic decisions that governments make are more complicated than those the average citizen makes." Then ask students what they think would be the most difficult aspect of economic decision making as a local government leader.

For example, a city might receive a grant from the Department of Transportation to help pay for a new highway. Other grants-in-aid may be funneled to local governments through the state government.

Today hundreds of federal grant programs exist. They range from police training programs to aid for sewage control. Approximately two-thirds of federal grant money goes for welfare and highway costs.

Many federal grants are categorical grants, for example, for education, mass transit, or flood control. Usually Congress includes guidelines with the grants. These guidelines are standards that local governments must follow.

While local officials usually welcome federal aid, they sometimes object that the guidelines limit their freedom of choice. Also, some people do not want federal interference in local government.

Criticism of categorical grants led Congress to establish revenue sharing in 1972. This program represented a major change in relations between the national government and local governments. Revenue sharing was to return a portion of the taxes the federal government collected to the state and local governments. Between 1972 and 1987, local governments received more than $80 billion in revenue-sharing funds from the federal government. Congress voted to end revenue sharing in 1986.

Block grants replaced revenue sharing as a major means for the national government to give almost unrestricted aid to local governments. Block grants transfer cash from the federal government to community development or social services.

Problems of Interdependence State and federal aid illustrate the interdependence of local, state, and federal governments. In this type of financing, the local government provides valuable services with funds from the other two levels of government.

Depending on state or federal funds can create problems for local governments, however. When state or federal budgets are tight, the state and federal governments cut intergovernmental spending programs. Some local officials believe that state governments have been willing to balance their budgets at local expense. States may mandate programs but provide no funds for them; they may charge local governments fees for services; or they may simply cut aid to local governments. A member of the League of Minnesota Cities recently worried that the era of state and local partnership was ending:

> *T*he situation is deteriorating. The recession confirms the separation. . . . Whenever a state agency can pass a fee on to localities, they do it. They're not ashamed to dun [demand payment from] us.
> —Don Slater,
> League of Minnesota Cities, 1991

Local governments, facing increasing financial burdens from state-mandated programs, joined a movement to amend state constitutions. By 1990 more than one-fourth of the states had constitutional restrictions that limited the authority of the state government to issue mandates or required the state to pay for the costs of these programs.

---

3 SECTION REVIEW

Section Summary

Local governments receive revenue from taxes, fees, assessments, and state and federal aid.

Checking for Understanding

Recalling Facts

1. Define **real property, personal property, assessment, tax assessor, market value.**
2. Explain **four charges against the property tax as an unfair tax.**
3. List **four local services that depend on state categorical grants.**
4. Summarize **the objections of local government officials to state-mandated programs.**

Exploring Themes

5. Federalism **How are local, state, and federal government expenditures tied together financially?**
6. Public Policy **For what kinds of spending do states permit local governments to borrow money through issuing bonds?**

Critical Thinking Skills

7. Making Comparisons **Why do local officials prefer block grants to categorical grants?**
8. Identifying Alternatives **What methods other than election might be used to fill the office of local tax assessor?**

Section 3 Review Answers

1. Definitions of terms appear on pages indicated: **real property,** 765; **personal property,** 765; **assessment,** 765; **tax assessor,** 765; **market value,** 765

2. It is regressive and results in unequal public services. Also it is difficult to determine property values on a fair and equal basis. Property that some institutions own is exempt from property tax, so non-exempt property owners pay a larger share of the tax burden.

3. education, highways, social services, and health programs and hospitals

4. Federal guidelines limit local government's freedom of choice. When state or federal budgets are tight, the state and federal governments cut intergovernmental spending programs. States may charge local governments fees for their services or may cut aid to local governments.

5. Federal and state governments provide aid to local government through grants. Local governments collect some taxes for state governments.

6. for large projects such as public buildings

7. Categorical grants do not permit local officials freedom of choice about where to spend the money.

8. The tax assessor might be appointed by the local government or hired as a civil servant on the basis of merit.

PERSONAL
PERSPECTIVES

Sharon Mayell on a Computer Network in City Government

Sharon Mayell is project manager for the Santa Monica, California Public Electronic Network. Begun with city funding in 1989, the network, called PEN, has made access to city officials much easier. Sharon Mayell wrote about "New Channels to City Hall."

Frank Mullin . . . sends a message to City Hall via the free Public Electronic Network:

"I was awakened at 7 a.m. to the sound of jackhammers and electric saws. What time are construction crews allowed to begin work in residential neighborhoods anyway?"

. . . At 8:45 A.M. Wednesday, the Police Department turns on the computer and responds: "Construction hours are 7 A.M. - 5 P.M. Monday to Friday, 9 A.M. - 5 P.M. Saturdays."

. . . That afternoon, Mayor Pro Tempore Ken Genser checks into the computer network from his home and adds: "Coincidentally, at last night's City Council meeting we requested that the ordinance be amended to move the hour to 8 A.M. We have had a lot of complaints about construction noise."

Santa Monica's Public Electronic Network, known as PEN, connects residents to city departments and officials around-the-clock from home and office computers, and from public terminals in city libraries and recreation centers. More than 3,500 residents have registered to use PEN. In its first two years, the network has garnered several awards and drawn media attention and academic scrutiny as the first government-sponsored experiment in "electronic democracy." . . .

The public uses PEN to write an average of 215 electronic mail messages a month to city departments. Staff check the messages daily and respond within 24 hours, when possible. Electronic mail messages run the gamut from comments on upcoming City Council agenda items to complaints about traffic signals to notes of thanks for recycling buckets.

The computer conferences are electronic town hall meetings, where residents and city leaders are not required to be at the same place at the same time to participate. . . .

Many residents have used PEN

Electronic mail messages run the gamut from comments on upcoming City Council agenda items to complaints about traffic signals to notes of thanks for recycling buckets.

as their entryway into city affairs, since using PEN is more convenient than writing a letter or attending time-consuming city meetings.

The network also has spawned a citizens' group, dubbed the PEN Action Committee. After months of PEN discussion on the plight of the homeless, residents developed a plan to provide showers, washers and lockers to homeless persons, preparing them to find a job.

The project . . . is developing a job bank for the homeless. A number of homeless persons participating on PEN from public computers were instrumental in bringing practical focus to the group.

—SHARON MAYELL, 1989

Examining the Reading

Reviewing Facts

1. Identify the places where citizens have access to computer terminals in the Public Electronic Network.

2. Describe how PEN is used to conduct town hall meetings.

Critical Thinking Skills

3. Predicting Consequences A municipal judge in Santa Monica said that PEN has the potential to help return government to the citizenry. What are some potential developments that could come from this experiment?

PERSONAL
PERSPECTIVES

Focus

Ask students whom they can contact with home or school computers. If they were able to access community officials and departments, how would they use such a link?

Teach

Ask: Why does Mayell call PEN an experiment in "electronic democracy"? Do students agree that PEN is "more convenient than writing a letter or attending time-consuming city meetings"? Is it a better method of exchanging information?

Assess

Have students complete **Examining the Reading.**

Answers

1. home, office, city library, recreation centers

2. Residents and city leaders can participate in computer conferences without being in the same location.

3. Answers will vary, but may include that citizens could express their opinions or even vote on issues or candidates in the future; government could take surveys; people could file tax reports.

Close

Ask: Is the computer system a better method of communicating than the telephone? Why or why not?

More About Personal Perspectives

Sharon Mayell's responsibilities for PEN include planning, supplementing, and overseeing the daily operations of the network. She earned her MA degree in Communications Management from the Annenberg School of Communication at the University of Southern California. She hopes that the PEN system will draw in noncomputer users. Community outreach has sought to make the system accessible to specific organizations as well as the public at large.

Identifying Terms and Concepts

1. town meeting, 2. real property, 3. township, 4. county, 5. municipality, 6. special district, 7. zoning, 8. home rule

Reviewing Facts and Ideas

1. the state constitution

2. county, township, municipality, special district

3. education

4. The laws might require that houses be built to a certain size or that they have a certain size lot, thus making them unaffordable to people with lower incomes.

5. sewage and sanitation

6. social services

7. People settled in towns, and townships became the significant units of local government.

8. Counties administer airports, hospitals, maintain roads, register voters, supervise elections, keep voting records; they keep records of births, deaths, and property ownership; assess and collect taxes; issue licenses; and administer justice and corrections through courts and jails.

9. County government lacks effective leadership, has limited powers, and is inefficient.

10. The town consisted of a village and the surrounding forests and farms.

11. Counties are joining together to deal with waste management; police and fire departments are cooperating; cities and counties are creating regional authorities to handle joint concerns.

12. Increases in the property tax affected homeowners, especially those on fixed incomes. Public pressure forced several states to limit property taxes.

13. Its earned interest is not subject to federal income tax.

Summary and Significance

The authority of local governments comes from the states. Counties, townships, municipalities, and special districts are the four types of local government. Local governments provide a wide range of services including education, police and fire protection, water supply, sewage disposal, sanitation, transportation, public welfare, and recreational and cultural activities.

Counties, the largest subdivisions of the states, vary greatly in size, population, and authority. Township government has remained important in some states and diminished in importance in others. Local governments create special districts to deal with specific responsibilities such as education, transportation, and water supplies.

The main source of revenue for local government is the property tax. Federal and state aid are also important sources of revenue. Local officials have learned, however, that intergovernmental revenue comes with restrictions and may not be reliable when federal and state budgets are strained.

Identifying Terms and Concepts

From the list below, write the term that best completes each sentence.

county, home rule, market value, municipality, real property, special district, town meeting, township, zoning

1. The New England _____ has become impractical in heavily populated areas.
2. Local governments rely on _____ taxes as a main source of revenue.
3. In New England and the Midwest _____ government remains strong.
4. In the South and in rural areas _____ government is important.
5. Originally, a charter for a _____ was much like one that states granted to corporations.
6. A public school is a _____ established by local government.
7. Local governments may use _____ to control growth.
8. While county officials prefer _____, few counties have taken advantage of state provisions for it.

Reviewing Facts and Ideas

1. Identify the document that specifies the powers and duties of local government.
2. List the four basic types of local government in the United States.

3. Identify the single largest public service provided by local tax revenues.
4. Explain how zoning laws may make it difficult for minorities or families with children to move into a certain area.
5. Name two services that small communities have contracted with private companies to provide.
6. Specify the biggest single government expenditure for large American cities.
7. Explain why county government was never important in New England.
8. Demonstrate ways in which county governments handle administrative rather than legislative responsibilities.
9. Identify three major problems associated with county government.
10. Describe the area of a New England town in colonial times.
11. Summarize the ways that local governments are cooperating in regional arrangements.
12. Discuss the reason for the success of the recent property tax revolt.
13. Identify an advantage of a municipal bond to an investor.

Applying Themes

1. Public Policy Why did the California Supreme Court rule against using the property tax to pay for local schools?

Applying Themes

1. Using property tax to support schools was a violation of the Fourteenth Amendment's guarantee of equal protection of the law. The court held that it discriminated against students in poor communities.

2. Answers will vary, but should include the national government, state government, county or township government, and school district.

3. In a democracy, people should vote for candidates who hold the same views on taxes as they do. They should also write their legislators, petition the government, as well as promote their ideas in the media.

4. Home rule allows the cities power to govern themselves and to choose the form and functions of their governments.

2. **Federalism** How many governments do you live under? Name them.

3. **Civic Responsibility** How should people living in a democracy express their objection to unfair or high taxes?

4. **Growth of Democracy** What advantage does home rule give to large cities?

Critical Thinking Skills

1. **Making Comparisons** How is a local government's charter similar to and different from a state's constitution?

2. **Identifying Alternatives** What two options do local governments have when states or the federal government cut aid?

3. **Analyzing Information** How have local governments adapted to population growth, improved transportation, and increasing regional needs?

4. **Making Inferences** Why may local governments develop more creative innovations to solve problems than state and federal governments?

Linking Past and Present

Until the 1950s most school districts were small, serving the needs of communities and neighborhoods. Consolidation created large districts that had economic and educational advantages but sometimes became impersonal and lost the feeling of community spirit. How well does your community support your school?

Writing About Government

Expressive Writing Many open areas of land are being replaced by apartments, condominiums, and shopping malls. Citizens agree and disagree with the decisions made by zoning boards. However, a reluctance to zone land for development may discourage new residents and businesses, which provide an expanded tax base for local government. Write a paragraph in which you express your opinions about the decisions concerning development and zoning in your area.

Reinforcing the Skill

Determining Relevance Suppose you are a member of the town council, which is about to vote on a recycling program. Determine whether each item is relevant or irrelevant to your decision about how to vote on the issue.

1. Most plastics are not recyclable.
2. The recycling program will cost more initially than current methods of disposing of solid waste.
3. Citizens are about evenly divided on the issue of recycling.
4. Newspaper subscriptions have dropped 20 percent over the past 10 years.
5. The high school environmental club has agreed to provide volunteers to deliver recycling bins to individual households.
6. Some of the costs can be defrayed by income from companies that buy recycled materials.
7. The state is considering passage of a law that will require deposits on aluminum cans and certain types of glass bottles for purposes of recycling.
8. Experts estimate that the program will cut annual landfill use by 30 percent. The town has limited room in its current landfill dump site, and additional sites are expensive.

Investigating Further

1. **Individual Project** Study a road map of your state. Rank the top 10 municipalities by population. Select the 10 most unusual names of towns or villages. Identify and list the names of the counties that surround the one in which you live.

2. **Cooperative Learning** How much do you know about the cost of your education? Organize the class into three equal groups. The first group will research local taxes to find out how much local revenue goes to education and how much to other services. The second group will research the sources of revenue for education. How much does the state provide? How much does the local government provide? The third group will research educational spending by the local district, including per pupil expenditures and total spending. What percentage goes to salaries, to plant costs, to classroom supplies, and so on?

CHAPTER 26: ORGANIZATION OF LOCAL GOVERNMENT 771

Linking Past and Present
Students' answers will vary.

Writing About Government
Paragraphs will vary, but should recognize the conflicting issues and interesting zoning disputes.

Reinforcing the Skill

1. irrelevant because the issue is whether to recycle those plastics that are recyclable

2. relevant because costs are always an important consideration (though a responsible decision should be based not only on short-term, but also long-term costs)

3. relevant because as an elected official you must be responsive to public opinion

4. irrelevant because the issue is recycling whatever newspapers are bought

5. relevant because it is related to the costs of the program and shows citizen support

6. relevant because it is related to the costs of the program

7. relevant because it is related to what kind of recycling program should be implemented on a local level

8. relevant because it is related to the long-term benefits of a recycling program

Investigating Further

1. Lists will vary.
2. Findings will vary.

Critical Thinking Skills

1. A charter provides the structure and rules for local government, just as a constitution provides the structure and rules for state government. States write their own constitutions, but local governments receive their charters from the state.

2. They may seek new sources of revenue or cut services to save money.

3. Local governments have developed special districts, consolidated school districts, and joined in regional cooperative efforts.

4. Answers will vary, but may include: Local governments are closer to the problems; they are smaller and can be more flexible; they have less financial resources, so they must be creative.

Chapter Organizer

Objectives	Special Feature Pages	Supplemental Materials
Section 1 Governing Cities, Towns, and Villages *pp. 774–779* 1. Identify the types of communities found in metropolitan areas. 2. Explain the process of municipal incorporation. 3. Describe the three forms of municipal government.	Focus on Freedom: The Housing Crisis p. 776	Guided Reading Activities Reproducible Lesson Plans Section 1 Quiz Testmaker Chapter Transparencies 27 Audio Cassettes (English and Spanish) SAT Practice Tests Writer's Guidebook
Section 2 Challenges of Urban Growth *pp. 780–787* 1. Summarize the great challenges facing large municipalities and their governments. 2. Evaluate policies addressing housing and drug abuse problems. 3. Discuss big city financial problems.	Participating in Government: Serving on a School Board p. 783 Critical Thinking Skills: Demonstrating Reasoned Judgment p. 787	Guided Reading Activities Reproducible Lesson Plans Participating in Government 27 Interpreting Political Cartoons 26, 28 Primary and Secondary Source Readings 27 Cooperative Learning Activities 27 Enrichment Activities 27 Section 2 Quiz Testmaker Government Themes Transparencies 28 Skill Reinforcement Activities 27 SAT Practice Tests Writer's Guidebook
Section 3 New Approaches to Problems *pp. 788–793* 1. Identify reasons for cities' loss of political influence with state and federal governments. 2. Discuss arguments for and against consolidation of metropolitan government. 3. List three creative approaches to government that cities have taken.	Global Connection: Interdependence: Sister Cities p. 790 Personal Perspectives: C. Kenneth Orski on the Problem of Traffic Congestion p. 793 Case Study: Zoning: Controversy Over Regulation of Land Use pp. 796–798 Unit 9 Digest pp. 799–800	Guided Reading Activities Reproducible Lesson Plans Reteaching Activities 27 Section 3 Quiz Chapter 27 Tests Testmaker Limited English Proficiency Activities 27 SAT Practice Tests Writer's Guidebook Unit Digest Transparencies, Unit 9 Participating in Government, Unit 9

If time does not permit teaching this chapter, assign the Chapter 27 summary in the Unit 9 Digest on pages 799–800.

Key To Ability Levels

Teaching strategies have been coded for varying learning styles and abilities.

L1   Level 1 activities are **basic** activities and should be within the ability range of all students.

L2   Level 2 activities are **average** activities and should be within the ability range of the average to above-average student.

L3   Level 3 activities are **challenging** activities designed for the ability range of above-average students.

LEP   These activities should be within the ability range of **Limited English Proficiency** students.

Multicultural Activities

Since 1967 African Americans have been elected to the office of mayor in Cleveland, Gary, Newark, Atlanta, Los Angeles, Washington, D.C., Detroit, New Orleans, Philadelphia, Chicago, Baltimore, Minneapolis, Seattle, and New York City. Analysts expect the pattern of African American or Hispanic leadership of big city governments to continue because of changing demographics. Have students describe the population changes that have helped minorities win control of city halls. *(concentration of minorities in cities, white flight to suburbs creating cities with ethnic group majorities)* How is the population shift to the suburbs likely to affect the impact big-city mayors have on national policy and politics? *(reduce it, especially as redistricting occurs)*

In 1990 census analysts identified the nation's most racially diverse counties. Two-thirds of these counties are in metropolitan areas. Counties in New York boroughs, San Francisco, Oakland, San Diego, and Dallas are on the list. Fifteenth on the list is Dade County where Miami is located. In 1989 Miami's population was about 42 percent Hispanic, 40 percent non-Hispanic white, and 18 percent African American. Managing a multiethnic city can be challenging as Cuban American Xavier Suarez has learned during his years as the city's mayor. First elected in 1985, Suarez built support among a diverse Hispanic community from Puerto Rico, Mexico, the Dominican Republic, and Cuba. Have students suggest special challenges and opportunities involved in governing a multiethnic city such as Miami.

Chapter Resources

Readings for the Student

Conot, Robert. *An American Odyssey*. Morrow, 1974.
Dolan, Edward F. and Margaret M. Scariano. *The Police in American Society*. Franklin Watts, 1988.
McCullough, David. *The Great Bridge*. Simon & Schuster, 1972.
State and Local Government. Scholastic, 1989.

Readings for the Teacher

Bernard, Richard M., ed. *Snowbelt Cities: Metropolitan Politics in the Northeast and Midwest since World War II*. Indiana University Press, 1990.
Bollens, John C. and Henry J. Schmandt. *The Metropolis*. Harper & Row, 1970.
Judd, Dennis R. *The Politics of American Cities*. Little, Brown, 1979.
Peterson, Paul E. *City Limits*. University of Chicago, 1981.
Smerk, George M. *The Federal Role in Urban Mass Transportation*. Indiana University Press, 1991.

Multimedia

Videocassettes and Films
A Neighborhood Redeemed. WTVS-Detroit. (v/c, 60 minutes)
A Concern for Community with Ernie Cortes, Parts I & II. (*A World of Ideas with Bill Moyers—Season II* series). Public Affairs Television. (2 v/c, 30 minutes each)
Seven Days in Bensonhurst. Thomas Lennon. (v/c, 60 minutes)
Urban Teens in Crisis. WETA. (v/c, 30 minutes)
The World that Moses Built. (*The American Experience* series). Mark Obenhaus and Edward Gray. (v/c, 60 minutes)
City Government: Closest to the People. Encyclopaedia Britannica Educational Corporation. (film, 20 minutes)

Software
Block Grant: A Simulation of Lobbying and Decision Making. DAC Publications. Students role-play local officials and lobbyists to allocate federal funds.
PFS: File—United State History. (20th Century data base), Scholastic Publishing Company. (IBM [MS/DOS] with 128K; Apple IIe or IIc, at least 64K & 1 disk drive; must be used with *PFS:File; PFS:Report*, 2nd disk drive and printer recommended.)

Governing Metropolitan Areas

Introduce

Chapter Overview

Chapter 27 focuses on America's metropolitan areas.

Section 1 examines the types of communities in metropolitan areas and describes the strengths and weaknesses of the three forms of municipal government.

Section 2 focuses on the problems and challenges facing metropolitan areas—housing, drugs, deteriorating infrastructure, transportation, finance, and economic development.

Section 3 describes why cities have lost political influence with state and federal authorities and highlights creative approaches cities have taken toward establishing efficient and economical government.

Chapter 27 Themes

Write the terms *separation of powers* and *federalism* on the chalkboard. Remind students that they have discussed both these terms as they apply to national and state government. Then have students speculate how each might apply to municipal governments.

CHAPTER

27

Cities are densely populated areas of complex social and administrative activities. Common events like a victory parade tend to occur on a large scale in a city.

772 UNIT 9: LOCAL GOVERNMENT

About the Chapter Opener

Teaching With Illustrations Point out that many different kinds of parades, such as those celebrating a championship team or a group's ethnic heritage—Saint Patrick's Day and Cinco de Mayo parades, for example—or about some group or policy take place in cities and small towns. Ask students to discuss what challenges a victory parade like the one pictured above might present a local government. *(cost of organizing the parade, policing the parade, controlling the impact of the parade on traffic and business, and free speech questions—how to handle demonstrators and protestors)*

Chapter Preview

Overview

Metropolitan governments face the challenges of urban living, growth, and development.

Objectives

After studying this chapter, you should be able to:

1. Describe three forms of municipal government.
2. Evaluate the many challenges facing metropolitan areas.
3. Discuss municipal governments' changing approaches to solving urban problems.

Themes in Government

This chapter emphasizes the following government themes:

- **Separation of Powers** Local governments often follow the constitutional pattern of separating legislative and executive powers. Sections 1 and 3.
- **Comparative Government** Municipal governments draw from federal and county government structures. Sections 1 and 3.
- **Federalism** Local governments depend on federal and state government funding. Section 2.
- **Free Enterprise** Municipalities attract business and investment through incentives. Section 2.

Critical Thinking Skills

This chapter emphasizes the following critical thinking skills:

- Predicting Consequences
- Drawing Conclusions
- Analyzing Information
- Identifying Central Issues

Introducing the Chapter

Ask the class what they think of when they hear the phrase *big city*. What images does this phrase suggest? Write all responses on the chalkboard. Are responses largely negative or positive? Ask: What are some advantages of city life? disadvantages? What might be the biggest challenges of governing a city? the biggest rewards? Repeat this process using the term *suburb*. Note differences in responses.

Chapter Project

Have students develop a questionnaire they can use to poll local officials on the most pressing urban problems in the local community today and on the challenges for the year 2020. Students should select officials performing a wide variety of functions to interview for the poll. Then students can compile results, compare present and future challenges, and identify any problems that might best be solved through consolidation or cooperation among several local governments.

Linking Past and Present
In 1950 suburbanization was just beginning and the nation had 14 metropolitan areas of 1 million people or more. The combined population of these 14 areas accounted for less than 30 percent of the country's total population. In 1990, census-takers found the nation had 39 metropolitan areas of at least 1 million people. About half of all Americans lived in these 39 areas.

Setting the Scene In the half century following 1870, the United States urbanized rapidly. In 1830 only 1 of every 10 Americans lived in an urban area. By 1870 1 out of 4 did. That number increased to 1 in 3 by 1890, to almost 1 out of 2 in 1910. Since the 1970s, 3 out of 4 Americans have lived in an urban area. Although Americans increasingly live in urban areas, their place of residence within these areas has shifted. Today more Americans live in suburbs than in cities. As wealthier residents have moved from city to suburb, city governments have seen property values decline and the tax base and services supported by taxes diminish.

Focus

Bell Ringer

While attendance is being taken, have students write answers to the following questions:

What is a metropolitan area? Do you live in a metropolitan area?

Motivating Activity

Discuss students' Bell Ringer answers. Then draw three interlocking circles on the board. Label one *city,* the second *town,* the third *suburb.* Have volunteers name communities in their state that fit each designation, giving reasons for their choices. Write place-names in appropriate circles. Note areas where circles overlap and ask students what they think these areas have in common. *(similar needs such as police and fire protection, electricity, road repair)* How are their needs different? *(greater complexity and scale of services needed in cities, harder to govern, lifestyle differences)*

Vocabulary Precheck

Write the terms and concepts on the chalkboard. Have students speculate about how each term and concept relates to the section's title. **LEP**

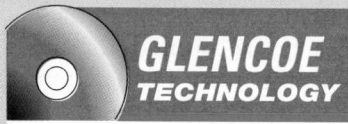

Focus on Government
Video 50
Electronic Field Trip: Urban Renewal in Atlanta
Running Time: 5:34
Videodisc 3, Chap. 50
VHS Tape 3, Begins 28:07

Video 52
Lecture Launcher: Governing Metropolitan Areas
Running Time: 2:25
Videodisc 3, Chap. 52
VHS Tape 3, Begins 36:00

774 Unit 9: Local Government

SECTION

Governing Cities, Towns, and Villages

Today three of every four people in the United States live in an urban area, either in a central city or a surrounding suburb. Nearly half of the population lives in metropolitan areas of a million or more people. These are areas of rapid change, complex governmental issues, and difficult societal problems.

Metropolitan Communities

Metropolitan communities are known as cities, towns, and villages. These urban communities differ greatly in size, ranging from a few thousand to millions of people.

The Census Bureau classifies any community with 2,500 people or more as an urban community. Whether an urban community is called a city, a town, or a village depends on local preference or sometimes on state charter classifications. What is called a city in one state may be called a town or a village in another.

The Metropolitan Area The Office of Management and Budget has classified large urban areas as Metropolitan Statistical Areas. More than half of the American population is clustered in these urban communities. A **metropolitan area** or metropolis is a large city and its surrounding suburbs. This area may also include small towns that lie beyond the suburbs.

Cities Cities are densely populated areas with commercial, industrial, and residential sections. They are chartered by the state as municipal corporations.

The changing city has played an important role in United States history. Change may be an essential factor for cities, as a television commentator noted:

Cities change or they stagnate. But how they change—how the rights of property are made to balance with the less tangible public interest—is one mark of civilization.

—BILL MOYERS, 1987

Most cities in the United States became major urban centers during the Industrial Revolution of the 1800s. They attracted African Americans, Americans from rural areas, and immigrants who sought jobs and better living conditions. After World War I, many more African American families migrated to large cities throughout the country in search of better opportunities. Since 1945 newcomers from Puerto Rico, Mexico, Cuba, and other Spanish-speaking regions, as well as immigrants from Asia, have contributed to rapid urban growth in the United States.

During the 1970s and 1980s, cities in the South and West became the growth leaders. Recent census statistics show a shift in urban population away from the Northeast and Midwest to cities in the region known as the Sunbelt. New industries attracted people to Sunbelt cities such as Houston, Texas; Phoenix, Arizona; and San Diego, California. Between 1970 and 1990, for example, Houston's population rose by 88 percent. Most of the fastest growing metropolitan areas were in Florida, Texas, and California.

SECTION PREVIEW

Objectives
After studying this section, you should be able to:
■ Identify the types of communities found in metropolitan areas.
■ Explain the process of municipal incorporation.
■ Describe the three forms of municipal government.

Key Terms and Concepts
metropolitan area, suburb, municipal government, incorporation, home rule, mayor-council form, strong-mayor system, weak-mayor system, commission form, council-manager form

Themes in Government
■ Separation of Powers
■ Comparative Government

Critical Thinking Skills
■ Predicting Consequences
■ Drawing Conclusions

774 UNIT 9: LOCAL GOVERNMENT

Classroom Resources for Section 1

📁 Guided Reading Activities
📁 Reproducible Lesson Plans
📁 Section 1 Quiz
➕ Testmaker

🖌 Chapter Transparencies 27
🎧 Audio Cassettes (English and Spanish)
SAT Practice Tests
Writer's Guidebook

Meanwhile, the 10 largest cities in the Northeast and Midwest all lost population. In many of these older cities, job opportunities and financial resources dried up. Many people were forced to leave these troubled urban areas. Detroit's population was 1.67 million in the 1960 census; by 1990 it was 1.03 million. Chicago lost 7.4 percent of its population in the 1980s alone.

Towns Early in United States history, most Americans lived in small towns and villages. After the 1860s large cities grew faster than towns and villages. Between 1970 and 1990, as cities faced problems, several factors made rural areas and small towns once again attractive to Americans. Many towns and villages experienced growth, but the fastest expanding areas were the suburbs.

Suburbs After the 1990 census, the Census Bureau classified 396 areas of the United States as urbanized areas. Each of these concentrations of people contains 50,000 or more residents. These areas are made up of one or more central cities plus the adjacent densely settled territory—the **suburbs**. Today more Americans live in suburbs than in cities or rural areas. A suburb may be called a village, a town, or a city, and it usually has its own government.

Many people began to move to the suburbs after World War II. Between 1950 and 1990, middle-class families seeking to buy homes flocked to new residential suburbs. By 1970 an important population shift had occurred—most people living in urban areas resided in the suburbs. Even in the South, cities lost population to suburban areas. Atlanta, Georgia, experienced a 20.7 percent decline while the surrounding metropolitan area increased 173.1 percent.

The first rapid suburban growth took place close to the edge of cities in the 1950s and 1960s. Federal money for highways and home loans induced families to move to the suburbs while the federal Urban Renewal Program demolished hundreds of thousands of low- and middle-income urban units in

Metropolitan Chicago

WISCONSIN

McHenry County

Lake County

Lake Michigan

Cook County

Kane County

DuPage County

Chicago

Kendall County

Will County

Lake County

ILLINOIS

INDIANA

Map Study
Metropolitan areas include the densely populated areas surrounding major cities. **Why do you think Lake County, Indiana, is designated as part of metropolitan Chicago, Illinois?**

the cities. Federal Housing Administration and Veterans Administration programs subsidized homes for almost 14 million families—the majority built in the suburbs.

By the 1980s older suburbs close to cities' edges began to take on the character of the city. Once again people moved, this time to an outer suburban ring. These new suburban communities, 15 to 50 miles from the city center, attracted middle-class workers and professional people.

The growth of suburbia signaled political change. In an article "The Empowering of the Suburbs," Rob Gurwitt predicted:

STUDY GUIDE

Themes in Government
Separation of Powers **What was the legislative impact of population shifts to the Sunbelt?**

Critical Thinking Skills
Predicting Consequences **What is likely to happen to inner cities if people, instead of living and**

working in the city, decide to live in the suburbs and work close to home?

Teach

Guided Practice

Interpreting Visuals Display transparency 27 from the *Chapter Transparencies* in the Teacher's Classroom Resources and use the accompanying teaching strategy and student activity to teach about urban population shifts.

Map Study Answer
Cities affect surrounding areas, regardless of state borders.

STUDY GUIDE

Theme Answer
States in the South and West gained increased representation in Congress.

Critical Thinking Answer
loss of business, jobs, and tax base

CONNECTIONS

History
Today, the United States is one of the most urbanized countries in the world, but in 1790 when the first census was taken America had only 24 urban places. Only two, Philadelphia and New York, had more than 25,000 residents. Not until 1920 did the census show that the old rural majority, living on farms or in small towns and villages, had become a minority.

Background

Suburban growth has been a fairly recent development. In 1910 only about 12 percent of Americans lived in suburbs, while 26 percent lived in cities. By 1960, the percentage of suburban and urban dwellers was almost equal with 31 percent living in suburbs and 32 percent in cities. By the late 1960s, however, the percentage of suburban residents exceeded city dwellers. If the present trend continues, by the end of the century, most Americans will live in suburbia. Many will also work and shop in suburbia, going to cities only to visit an art museum or attend a concert or sports event.

L2 **Making Comparisons** Make a four-column chart on the chalkboard with the headings *Form of Government, Where and How Used, Separation of Powers, Advantages/Disadvantages.* In the first column list *mayor-council, commission,* and *council-manager.* Have students volunteer answers to complete the chart. Then ask students which form of government would be best for their community and why.

Focus on Freedom

City housing authorities, made up of commissioners appointed by the mayor or local governing body, coordinate housing for low-income families. They plan, develop, and manage public housing projects. Some also run programs that place families into affordable private rental homes.

Answers

1. to produce housing outside the central city
2. tightening credit, slowing down the economy
3. While the national government told cities to tear down substandard buildings and to provide relocation housing, it did not provide funds for such programs.

Linking Past and Present

In the late 1800s, the development of railroads influenced suburban growth. People could live outside the city and ride the railroad to work. Today, about 75 percent of all United States rail passengers ride commuter trains. This, however, is less than 1 percent of all intercity commuter traffic. Most city workers who live in the suburbs depend on cars to get to work.

Politics in the outer reaches of suburbia—the land of mega-malls and endless commuting—will soon attract the attention of a lot of people who never really had to think about it before. . . . In several legislatures, the suburbs as a whole will be the new heavyweights, outnumbering the urban or rural delegations that once held unquestioned sovereignty.
—ROB GURWITT, *GOVERNING THE STATES AND LOCALITIES,* FEBRUARY 1991

States provide for city, town, and village governments in the United States. Such governments are called either **municipal governments** or city governments. Although urban communities differ greatly in size and in other ways, they are all municipalities and use some form of municipal government.

Municipal Incorporation A municipal government may be formed when a group of people ask the state legislature to permit their community to incorporate, or set up a legal community. This process, called **incorporation**, varies from state to state. Generally, a community must meet certain requirements for incorporation. These requirements usually include having a population of a certain minimum size and petitions signed by a specified number of residents requesting incorporation. At times, a referendum may be held to determine whether the people want incorporation.

Focus on Freedom

THE HOUSING CRISIS

During the 1960s and 1970s, cities began to experience severe shortages of adequate housing. Richard J. Daley, mayor of Chicago, testified before the House Banking and Currency Committee on urban housing needs in 1970.

Unfortunately, in the past, the thrust of private enterprise and for that matter, the policy of the national government, has served to produce housing outside of the central city. This has been recognized by the Congress which has sought to fill the gap by the passage of many measures directed to the housing needs of low and moderate income families in the cities. . . .

Despite all these efforts, we have not been able to meet the needs of low and moderate [income] families in the cities and today we find that even middle income families have been priced out of the market throughout the Nation. . . .

All the recent actions of these agencies in tightening credit and slowing down the economy to halt inflation is rapidly creating a crisis condition in the housing market.

Oddly enough, our efforts to improve housing conditions—with the active support of the National Government—have only served to worsen the situation. All of us are agreed that in our affluent society there is no justification for slums or substandard housing. The city of Chicago, like other cities, has many programs underway to reduce and eliminate these substandard conditions. . . .

The housing programs arise directly from the insistent demands by our citizens and the Department of Housing and Urban Development that slums be eliminated and housing standards be strictly enforced. But, as essential as these programs are—and they must be carried on—they, nevertheless, contribute directly to a reduction in the housing supply.

Frankly, the cities are caught in a dilemma. Our citizens and the Federal Agencies rightly demand we tear down every substandard home. At the same time, the same Federal Agencies say we cannot tear down bad buildings until we relocate the tenants in standard housing. Meanwhile, they say they cannot provide the resources to build relocation housing or new housing.
—MAYOR RICHARD J. DALEY, 1970

Examining the Document

Reviewing Facts
1. Describe what Mayor Daley believes to have been the effect of government policy and private enterprise on housing in the past.
2. Identify the policy of the federal government that was slowing down the private housing industry.

Critical Thinking Skills
3. Expressing Problems Clearly How were government policies for urban housing contradictory?

Cooperative Learning Activity

Organize students into groups of three. Have each prepare an organizational chart showing the form of municipal government in a different city or town within the metropolitan area closest to their community. Encourage some to report on suburban government and others on city or small-town government. Within each group, one member can collect the information for the chart, another can draw the chart, and another can summarize and describe the information on the chart to the class. As groups give their reports, encourage students to look for similarities and differences among forms of municipal government within metropolitan areas.

Once a community is incorporated, the state issues it a charter. The charter allows the community to have its own government and gives the municipal corporation legal status. The municipality now has the right to enter into contracts, to sue and be sued in court, and to purchase, own, and sell property. The state legislature can change the powers granted to a municipal government at any time.

Home Rule In an attempt to provide more self-government for municipalities, many states now provide for home rule. **Home rule** is the system by which the state legislature grants local government the power to manage its own affairs. Home rule gives a municipality power to choose its type of government, to change its charter, and to create new policies. About two-thirds of cities with populations above 100,000 now have some measure of home rule. Having home rule, however, does not give the city total independence. The state maintains some control over the city. Moreover, the city is still subject to the state constitution and cannot enact ordinances that contradict state law.

Municipal Governments

Every municipal charter provides for the type of government the community is to have. The charter also describes the powers of the different parts of the government. Today urban areas in the United States use one of three basic forms of municipal government: the mayor-council form, the commission form, or the council-manager form.

The Mayor-Council Form The most widely used form of municipal government is the **mayor-council form**. It is also the oldest type of municipal government in the United States. Until the 1900s it was used in most American cities, regardless of their size. Today about half the cities in the United States use this form. It is the form of government preferred by the largest cities.

The mayor-council form follows the traditional concept of separation of powers. Executive power belongs to an elected mayor and legislative power to an elected council. All cities except one have unicameral, or one-house, councils.

Most city councils have fewer than 10 members, who usually serve 4-year terms. Some larger cities, however, have larger councils. For example, Chicago has a 50-member council, the largest in the nation. In most cities, council members are elected from the city at-large. In some cities, however, citizens of individual wards or districts of the city elect council members.

Two main types of mayor-council government exist, depending upon the power given the mayor. These two types are the strong-mayor system and weak-mayor system. In the **strong-mayor system**, the municipal charter grants the mayor strong executive powers. A strong mayor usually has the power to veto measures the city council passes, and many of his or her actions may not require council approval. The mayor can appoint and fire department heads and high-ranking members of the municipal bureaucracy. In addition, a strong mayor can prepare the municipal budget, subject to council approval, and propose legislation to the city council. The mayor usually serves a four-year term. The strong-mayor system is most often found in large cities.

Many small cities, especially in New England, use the **weak-mayor system** of municipal government. In this form the mayor has only limited powers. The mayor has little control over the budget or the hiring and firing of municipal personnel. The city council makes most policy decisions, and the mayor's veto power is limited. The mayor usually serves only a two-year term. In some small municipalities, the office of the mayor is only a part-time position.

The success of the mayor-council form of government depends to a large extent on the individual who serves as mayor. In the strong-mayor system, a politically skillful mayor can provide effective leadership. Under the weak-mayor plan, because official responsibility is in many hands, success depends upon the cooperation of the mayor and the council.

L3 Drawing Conclusions The text points out that a disadvantage of the council-manager plan may be its lack of strong political leadership. Have students explain why it lacks a strong leader. *(No one person has leadership role; mayor has limited powers, short term; city manager not elected and reports to council.)* Why might an ethnically and economically diverse city need strong leadership? *(to encourage cooperation and reduce conflict among city residents and special-interest groups)*

Independent Practice

L1 Interviewing Have students ask a council member or an elected or appointed executive official his or her opinion of the effectiveness of the community's current form of government. Have them ask their interviewee how appropriate each of the other forms might be for their community.

=== STUDY GUIDE ===

Theme Answer
have more control over budget and hiring and firing key personnel

Critical Thinking Answer
It gives communities more power to manage their own affairs.

=== STUDY GUIDE ===

Themes in Government
Comparative Government What can a mayor do in a strong-mayor system of municipal government that he or she cannot do in a weak-mayor system?

Critical Thinking Skills
Drawing Conclusions
Why would home rule be an important issue that municipal leaders would favor and seek to gain for their communities?

CHAPTER 27: GOVERNING METROPOLITAN AREAS 777

Special Needs Strategy

Learning Styles Auditory learners do best when information is presented so they can hear it; visual learners, of course, learn best by seeing information. Students who are primarily visual learners can explain the information presented through diagrams and pictures. Have students draw a diagram of the different-sized metropolitan communities, their sizes, and their features. Is it easier for them to understand the diagram or easier when they read the text and discuss it in class?

🎧 Have students listen to the chapter summary on the *Audio Cassettes* in the Teacher's Classroom Resources.

L2 Informative Writing Have pairs of students pick a large United States city that has lost or gained population in the last 10 years and write reports identifying reasons for the population changes and describing the impact of these changes on city life. The *Readers' Guide to Periodical Literature* and magazines such as *Nation's Cities* are resources for this activity.

Chart Study Answer
the mayor-council form because voters directly elect the mayor

STUDY GUIDE

Theme Answer
Council is the legislative body; city manager assumes executive responsibilities.

Critical Thinking Answer
The growth of the system means that managers have become more visible and often more powerful.

Assess

Check for Understanding
Have students complete Section 1 Review on page 779.

Meeting Objectives
Each section objective is tested by the Section Review questions that follow it in parentheses.
• Identify the types of communities found in metropolitan areas. (3, 4, 7)
• Explain the process of municipal incorporation. (2)
• Describe the three forms of municipal government. (5, 6, 8)

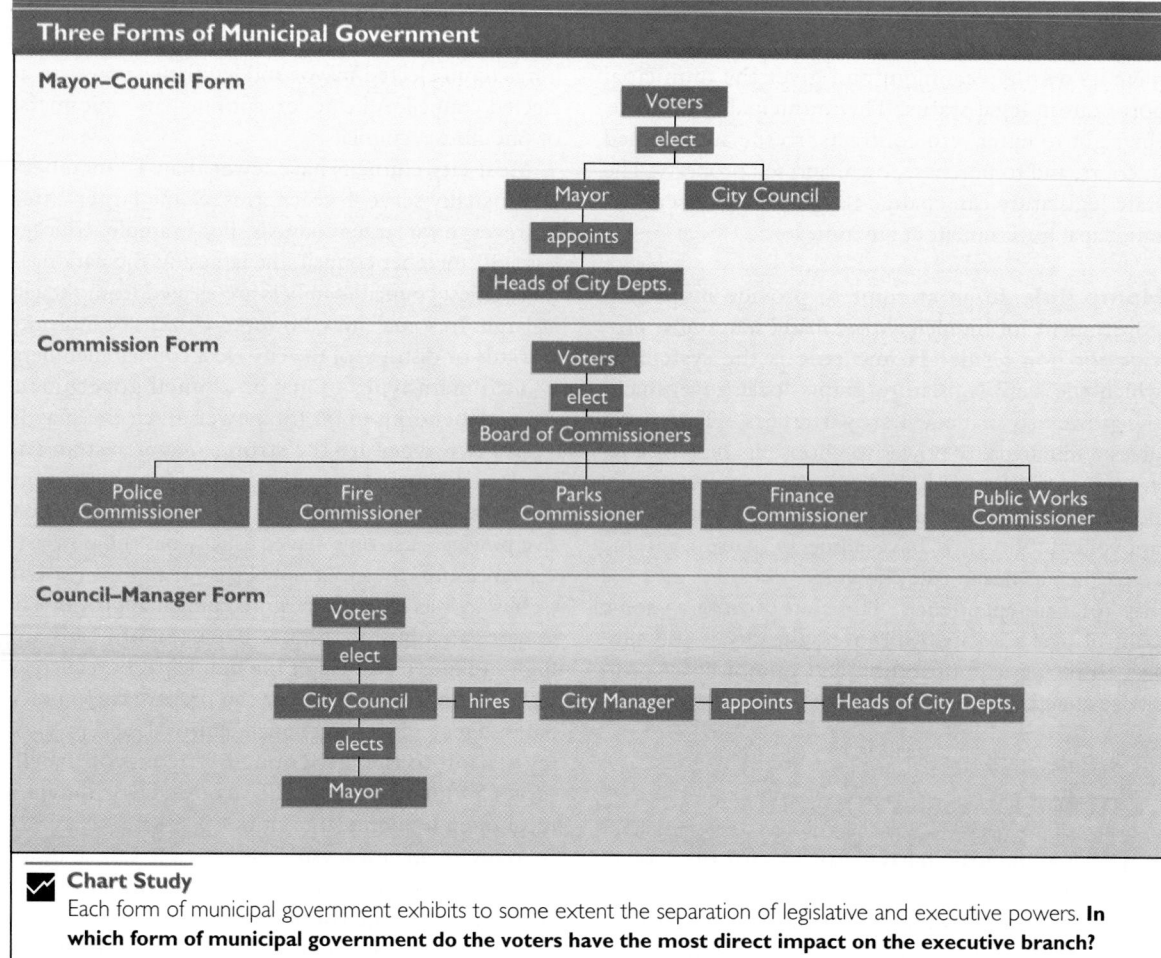

Three Forms of Municipal Government

Mayor–Council Form

Voters → elect → Mayor / City Council

Mayor → appoints → Heads of City Depts.

Commission Form

Voters → elect → Board of Commissioners

Police Commissioner / Fire Commissioner / Parks Commissioner / Finance Commissioner / Public Works Commissioner

Council–Manager Form

Voters → elect → City Council — hires → City Manager — appoints → Heads of City Depts.

City Council → elects → Mayor

Chart Study
Each form of municipal government exhibits to some extent the separation of legislative and executive powers. **In which form of municipal government do the voters have the most direct impact on the executive branch?**

The Commission Form The **commission form** of municipal government combines executive and legislative power in an elected commission, usually composed of five to seven members. Each commissioner heads a specific department and performs executive duties related to that department. The most common departments are police, fire, public works, finance, and parks. The commissioners also meet as a legislative body to pass laws and make policy decisions. One of the commissioners usually has the title of mayor. The mayor has no additional powers, however, and usually carries out only such ceremonial functions as greeting important visitors and officiating at the dedication or opening of hospitals and other institutions.

The commission form of municipal government grew out of a devastating tidal wave that struck Galveston, Texas, in 1900. As the citizens of Galveston tried to rebuild their city, they found their mayor-council government unable to handle the many urgent problems stemming from the disaster. Consequently, the Texas state legislature permitted

STUDY GUIDE

Themes in Government
Separation of Powers In the council-manager form of municipal government, how are the legislative and executive powers distributed?

Critical Thinking Skills
Drawing Conclusions As the council-manager form of municipal government has become more common, why has the role of city manager become more important in recent years?

Critical Thinking Activity

Drawing Conclusions Review the quote by Bill Moyers on page 774. Ask: In what ways has the community you live in changed? How might this city be different today if these changes had not taken place? Would it have grown more or less rapidly? Do you agree with Moyers' assertion that cities must change or stagnate? In what ways can cities balance property rights of individuals against public interest? *(where to build a shopping center, where to put a waste dump, where to build a new highway)* Why does Moyers say the way cities balance conflicting needs is one mark of civilization? *(Such decisions raise issues of fairness, equity, and civic responsibility.)*

Galveston to elect five leading citizens to oversee the city's reconstruction. The commission form proved so successful in Galveston that it became very popular with municipal leaders in their communities. By 1920 more than 500 cities had adopted the commission form of government.

Despite its early success, only 3 percent of American cities use the commission form. Over the years municipal leaders discovered that this form of government had serious defects. First, in the absence of a powerful leader, the commission form can lead to a lack of cooperation and planning in government. No strong executive can persuade or force the commissioners to act as an effective group. When commissioners disagree, it may be very difficult to make decisions or establish policies. Second, when commissioners do agree, it may be simply to support one another's budget requests. As a result, the municipal budget may be far more generous than it should be.

The Council-Manager Form Under a **council-manager form** of government, legislative and executive powers are separated. The council of between five and nine members acts as a legislative body and makes policy for the municipality. A manager carries out the council's policies and serves as chief administrator. First used in 1908, the council-manager form is now one of the most common forms of municipal government in the United States. More than 40 percent of cities, mostly in the West and the South, use

this form. Two large cities that have council-manager governments are Dallas, Texas, and Cincinnati, Ohio.

The office of city manager is the special feature of the council-manager plan. Appointed by the council, the city manager is the chief executive. He or she carries out policy, appoints and fires municipal workers, prepares the budget, and runs the day-to-day affairs of the city. The city manager may also make policy recommendations to the council. Most city managers are professionals trained in public administration. They must answer to the council and are subject to dismissal by the council.

The council-manager form usually includes a mayor with limited powers. In most cases the mayor is a council member whom the council elects for a two-year term.

Political experts believe the council-manager form brings better management and business techniques into government. For many cities it has provided effective and responsible government. Executive and legislative powers are clearly separated, and it is easy for the voters to assign praise or blame for what the government has done.

Some critics, however, point out disadvantages associated with council-manager government. Citizens do not elect the city manager. Many managers are not even residents of the city at the time of their appointment. Also, the council-manager plan may not provide the strong political leadership that is necessary, especially in large cities with ethnically and economically diverse populations.

1 SECTION REVIEW

Section Summary
Most Americans today live in urban areas served by municipal governments.

Checking for Understanding
Recalling Facts
1. Define metropolitan area, suburb, municipal government, incorporation, home rule, mayor-council form, strong-mayor system, weak-mayor system, commission form, council-manager form.
2. Specify what determines whether a municipality is called a city, a town, or a village.
3. Identify four large categories of people who migrated to United States cities between the 1860s and 1990s.
4. Describe recent population shifts that resulted in rapid suburban growth.

Exploring Themes
5. Separation of Powers How is separation of powers in the mayor-council form of municipal government similar to that of the federal government?
6. Comparative Government Which two forms of municipal government are similar to forms of government used in counties?

Critical Thinking Skills
7. Predicting Consequences If suburban population continues to grow rapidly, what will happen in state legislatures and Congress to increase suburban influence in government?
8. Drawing Conclusions Why do many large cities prefer the council-manager form of municipal government?

CHAPTER 27: GOVERNING METROPOLITAN AREAS 779

Evaluate

📁 Section 1 Quiz

🔒 Testmaker

Reteach

Have each student write a paragraph describing the type of community in which he or she lives—city, suburb, or town—and the type of government in the community.

Enrich

Have students research one of the political "bosses" of American urban history—such as James Curley (Boston), Richard J. Daley (Chicago), Thomas Pendergast (Kansas City), or William Tweed (New York)—and write a report on how the boss impacted city government.

Close

Ask students whether they expect the population trends outlined in this section to continue. If so, which of the three forms of municipal government do students think would be best suited to the cities and suburbs of the future? Have students give reasons for their opinions.

Section 1 Review Answers

1. Definitions of terms appear on pages indicated: **metropolitan area,** 774; **suburb,** 775; **municipal government,** 776; **incorporation,** 776; **home rule,** 777; **mayor-council form,** 777; **strong-mayor system,** 777; **weak-mayor system,** 777; **commission form,** 778; **council-manager form,** 779
2. local preference or state charters

3. rural people, European immigrants, African Americans, Spanish-speaking people, Asian immigrants
4. By 1970 a majority of people previously living in urban areas resided in the suburbs. In the 1980s people moved to an outer ring of suburbs 15 to 50 miles from the city.
5. The mayor has executive powers similar to the President; the council has legislative powers similar to Congress.

6. commission form, council-manager form
7. These areas will gain representation by reapportionment.
8. It has provided effective and responsible government because executive and legislative powers are clearly separated, making it easy for the voters to assign praise or blame. Also, the administrator is a trained professional.

Focus

Bell Ringer

While attendance is being taken, have students list what they consider to be the most serious problems facing cities today.

Motivating Activity

Discuss students' Bell Ringer lists and write their responses on the chalkboard. Point out that differences in size, cultural diversity, and region of the country may affect the types of problems cities have. Then ask: Does the federal, state, or local government have a responsibility to help solve these problems? Why or why not? Tell students this section examines the problems confronted by urban dwellers.

Vocabulary Precheck

Call on volunteers to tell what they think each key term and concept means. Have students check the accuracy of their definitions in the Glossary. **LEP**

CONNECTIONS

Technology

Telecommuting allows people to use workstations far from their inner city offices. With federal government support, Southern Maryland offers modular work areas in the suburbs, to help ease traffic congestion and environmental problems. The project is studying ways to make telecommuting more attractive to workers.

GLENCOE TECHNOLOGY

Focus on Government
Video 44
Speaking Out:
Housing the Homeless
Running Time: 1:10
Videodisc 3, Chap. 44
VHS Tape 3, Begins 13:00

---

2 Challenges of Urban Growth

By the 1990s more than three-fourths of the American population lived in or near an urban area. What has this growth of urban areas meant for the people and their local governments?

Concentrating many people in limited space creates problems. Today many urban areas in the United States confront housing shortages, inadequate transportation, pollution, poverty, and crime. Although these problems are most acutely experienced in big cities, they also exist in the surrounding suburbs and small towns.

Population and Housing

Recall the four kinds of population shifts that have taken place in recent years. First, cities and suburbs in the South and West grew rapidly. Second, cities in the Northeast and Midwest lost population. Third, the population of small towns and rural areas increased. Finally, many people moved from cities to nearby suburban areas.

What are the causes and results of these changes? What challenges have these changing growth patterns presented for local communities? Studying the changes in housing is a key to understanding many urban problems.

Housing and Urban Development As the population in an area increases, available land becomes more scarce and, hence, more costly. Local governments often have to decide whether available land should be used for new housing, industry, stores, or office buildings.

Municipal governments attempt to manage land use to provide an environment for orderly growth. What action should be taken when an area begins to deteriorate?

In the 1950s some areas of inner cities showed signs of decline. Those who could afford new housing left the inner cities and moved to the suburbs; poorer people remained. Jobs became scarce as industries moved out—either to attractive suburban areas or to new locations in the South and West. Inner-city housing deteriorated, slums multiplied. Residents had to endure inadequate heating, leaky pipes, and poor sanitary conditions. Crimes ranging from theft to arson became a constant threat to life and property.

Local government officials became increasingly aware of changes in their communities caused by the population shifting from the cities to the suburbs. Mayors of large cities appealed to the federal government for help. As a solution the federal government supported the urban renewal program. With hundreds of millions of federal dollars for new construction in the 1950s and 1960s, cities attempted to address their housing problems. Generally the approach was to tear down existing housing and build giant new apartment complexes. Cities uprooted millions of people in an effort to renew blighted areas. In some cases urban renewal forced residents out of their old neighborhoods and replaced older buildings with new luxury apartment houses that the original residents could not afford.

After years of massive spending, the results were not encouraging. Fewer affordable new housing units were created than were needed. Unemployment remained a problem. New Haven, Connecticut, was typical:

SECTION PREVIEW

Objectives
After studying this section, you should be able to:
- Summarize the great challenges facing large municipalities and their governments.
- Evaluate policies addressing housing and drug abuse problems.

- Discuss big city financial problems.

Key Terms and Concepts
renovation, public housing program, infrastructure, mass transit, revitalization, gentrification

Themes in Government
- Federalism
- Free Enterprise

Critical Thinking Skills
- Analyzing Information
- Predicting Consequences

Classroom Resources for Section 2

- Guided Reading Activities
- Reproducible Lesson Plans
- Participating in Government 27
- Interpreting Political Cartoons 26, 28
- Primary and Secondary Source Readings 27
- Cooperative Learning Activities 27

- Enrichment Activities 27
- Section 2 Quiz
- Testmaker
- Government Themes Transparencies 28
- SAT Practice Tests
- Writer's Guidebook

Urban Renewal
Federal support helped revive cities such as Pittsburgh. **Urban Planning** How may urban renewal damage the social network city officials hoped to preserve?

Teach

Guided Practice

L1 Sociology Point out that many policy decisions have both intended and unintended consequences. Such was the case with urban renewal. Have students identify its intended and unintended consequences. (*intended—to provide more and better inner-city housing; unintended—many low-income people displaced, fewer housing units created than needed*) Have students give reasons for these unintended consequences and suggest possible unintended consequences of other efforts to solve city problems. **LEP**

📁 **Group Discussion** Organize groups to complete activity 27 on ways to combat drug problems in *Cooperative Learning Activities* in the Teacher's Classroom Resources.

Caption Answer
To renew blighted areas, cities often uprooted low-income residents without rebuilding enough affordable new homes.

*T*he most important effect of the first core area projects and then those in the next ring was to produce a continuous flow of displaced persons, as much as one-fifth of the entire population of the city was uprooted between 1956 and 1974. Community social networks were in part destroyed by the very officials who sought to stop decay and make New Haven slumless.

—SUSAN F. FAINSTEIN AND NORMAN L. FAINSTEIN, *RESTRUCTURING THE CITY: THE POLITICAL ECONOMY OF URBAN REDEVELOPMENT*, 1986

One part of the problem was that fewer homes were built. Low-rent public housing units under construction increased from 14,000 units in 1956 to 126,800 units in 1970. Meanwhile, privately owned new housing unit construction that peaked at 1.6 million in 1955 leveled off to about 1.4 million by 1970. Low-rent or subsidized government housing in cities discouraged private investment in apartment units.

In the 1970s inflation and high interest rates again slowed construction of new houses. The number of houses constructed in the United States actually decreased from 2 million in 1978 to 1.1 million in 1982. The construction of new rental units declined from about 750,000 in 1972 to 297,000 in 1980.

Housing Discrimination To make matters worse, some Americans suffered the effects of discrimination in housing. For many years smaller communities and suburban areas excluded African Americans and other minorities. Meanwhile, inner-city living developed a cycle of few job opportunities, low pay, poor housing, inadequate education, and unemployment.

Suburbs have also at times kept out the poor, the elderly, and people with children. Some apartment owners are unwilling to rent to people with children. A 1981 study in Los Angeles found that owners excluded families with children from 71 percent of the apartments surveyed.

The courts have consistently ruled against discrimination in housing. Moreover, in 1968 Congress passed a federal Open Housing Act that bars discrimination in the sale and rental of housing. Nevertheless, housing discrimination is sometimes difficult to prove, and the government has not always enforced laws against it.

Coping with Housing Shortages Cities have more recently responded to the housing shortage by renovating older housing units. **Renovation** projects have rewired homes, installed new plumbing, and rebuilt floors and walls. Many major cities, including Atlanta, New Orleans, and Philadelphia, have established reno-

---

STUDY GUIDE

Themes in Government
Federalism Why would federal, state, and local governments all be involved in planning urban renewal programs?

Critical Thinking Skills
Analyzing Information
The number of low-rent public housing units under construction has increased. Why would

low-rent or subsidized government housing discourage private investment in urban apartment units?

STUDY GUIDE

Theme Answer
to arrange funding and subsidies

Critical Thinking Answer
difficult to compete with the federal government in building or in managing low-rent housing

CHAPTER 27: GOVERNING METROPOLITAN AREAS 781

Background

Some experts contend that housing shortages in major cities have largely been caused by the massive cuts in federal funds to cities over the 1980s by the Reagan and Bush administrations. Lacking federal support or direction, the amount of low-cost housing built in the 1980s dropped sharply. Critics of

enterprise zones in declining neighborhoods point out that taxes paid to local and state governments represent such a small share of the costs of doing business that the tax breaks have not offered much incentive for businesses to move to these areas.

L2 Identifying Impacts Have students give specific examples of the infrastructure in their own community. *(bridges, roads, sewers, tunnels, public buildings)* List responses on the chalkboard. Have students speculate on the economic and social consequences for the community if each item listed was allowed to go unrepaired. Why is infrastructure a concern of local government? *(Such duties as city street and public building repair and sanitation are local government functions.)* Why should community residents be concerned about upkeep of infrastructure? *(Answers can note economic, safety, and transportation effects.)*

Caption Answer
joblessness, alcoholism, drug addiction, criminal record, mental illness

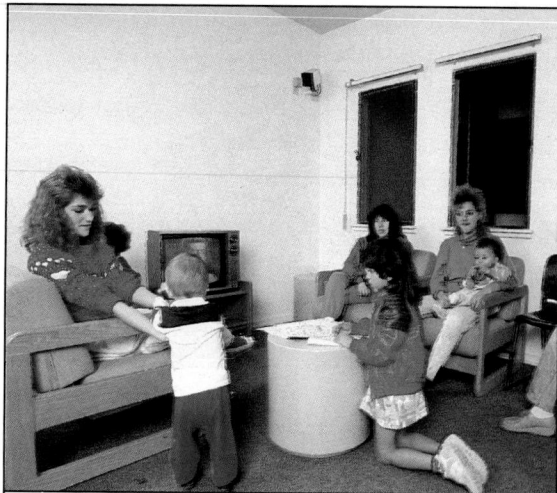

Relief for the Homeless
Shelters alone cannot solve homelessness. **Sociology What personal problems can contribute to homelessness?**

CONNECTIONS

Sociology
In 1991 sociologists said that about a third of the 600,000 to 3 million homeless in the United States were families. The experts believe that about a third of the homeless are working poor who cannot afford rent. Lack of resources has caused many cities to take "quick fix" approaches to the homeless, such as passing laws that forbid panhandling and outdoor sleeping. In many large cities problems of homelessness have been intensified by cost-cutting programs that have taken the mentally ill from mental institutions and put them on the streets.

vation programs. In cities such as Baltimore and Des Moines, funds from the city government along with federal, state, and private funds have made some highly successful renovation programs possible.

The federal government also provides low-interest loans to local housing authorities through **public housing programs.** These loans are used to build housing projects for low-income residents. Local housing authorities receive federal aid to help maintain rents at affordable levels.

Social Problems

Large cities face serious social problems. The concentration of poverty, homelessness, crime, and drug and alcohol abuse is easily identified in large cities. The local and national media often report on these problems, raising the national awareness of their seriousness. City governments, however, must be more than aware of these social conditions. They must try to alleviate them.

Homelessness Housing shortages are only one side of the housing problem in major cities. The other side is the human issue—homelessness. The media have estimated the number of homeless in the United States as high as 3 million people. Surveys show that about 600,000 people spend their nights in shelters or on the streets. Certainly unemployment and the housing shortage contribute to this problem.

In addition, two-thirds of the homeless have a serious personal problem that contributes to their plight—alcoholism, drug addiction, or a criminal record. About one-third are mentally ill. The average homeless adult has been out of work for four years. Housing alone will not solve this problem. Rehabilitation programs are needed to address the personal problems that caused people to be homeless.

Private and religious charitable organizations contribute the most to relieve homelessness. The federal government provides a very small portion of assistance. In a recent year, the federal government provided about the same amount of assistance for the whole nation that the city of New York spent for its own homeless people.

Drug Abuse Closely associated with homelessness in many cities is drug abuse and addiction. A news magazine reported:

In Philadelphia over the last two decades, the Diagnostic and Rehabilitation Center (DRC) detoxified tens of thousands of homeless adults, the vast majority of whom, up until 1987, were alcoholics. Now, however, more than half of the DRC's homeless clients have a primary diagnosis of crack addiction, and some 90 percent of the crack addicts are problem drinkers, too.

—U.S. NEWS & WORLD REPORT,
JANUARY 15, 1990

Crack, a supercharged cocaine, became the scourge of the cities in the 1980s. "Rock houses," or residences used for dealing crack, first surfaced as a problem in Miami in 1982. Crack showed up in Los Angeles in 1983, and by late that same year dealers were selling it in New York City. Street gangs built a network for selling the drug in most of the nation's cities before the federal Drug Enforcement Administration realized the extent of the problem.

Inner-city teenagers, unable to find low-skill jobs, rationalized crack selling as a gateway to prosperity. Many worked long, hard hours in the drug trade and hoped to escape the poverty cycle. While a few successful operators could make $100,000 in a year of drug dealing, for the majority the rewards did not match the danger. Studies done in two major cities showed that many crack dealers earned no more than the minimum wage. For many the earnings were quickly consumed in drug use.

By 1986 the national media had focused on drugs as a major problem in the United States. Some called

---

Cooperative Learning Activity

Organize students into groups and ask each to pick a group leader. Assign each group an urban problem discussed in this lesson. Have the group as a whole agree on a statement of the problem, identifying the issue. Next all group members can do some preliminary research to create a list of possible solutions to the problem, sharing their lists with the group. Then the group leader can assign each group member one of the solutions for further study. After researching proposed solutions, each person can summarize strengths and weaknesses of his or her solution. Then the group as a whole can pick the most promising solutions and present them to the class.

it a $25 billion drain on the national wealth. Most noted that drugs were implicated in the renewed rising crime rates in the cities. One national magazine that made a commitment to cover drug abuse said:

We plan accordingly to cover it as a crisis, reporting it as aggressively and returning to it as regularly as we did the struggle for civil rights, the war in Vietnam, and the fall of the Nixon presidency.
—*NEWSWEEK*, JUNE 16, 1986

In November 1988, Congress responded to President Reagan's request for new antidrug legislation. The new law created an office of federal drug "czar" and increased spending for drug treatment and law enforcement. The war on drugs had three aims: to stop the drug trade at its source, to launch a drug prevention campaign, and to fund treatment programs. It also provided tougher penalties for violations of drug laws.

By 1991 the Justice Department's budget reached $10 billion, much of it targeted for fighting drug trafficking. There was some evidence that federal intervention was having an effect. A survey released in January 1990 reported a decline in the number of high school seniors who said they had tried illegal drugs. Use of crack showed the sharpest decline—a 50 percent drop from the 1985 figure. Surveys of college students in the 1990s also showed a decline in drug use.

Infrastructure and Transit

People who live in cities take for granted such facilities as paved streets and sidewalks, pipes that bring water to their homes, and sewers that dispose of liquid wastes. These basic facilities make up what is known as the **infrastructure** of a city. Also included in the infrastructure are bridges, tunnels, and public buildings.

A Deteriorating Infrastructure In America's older cities, the infrastructure shows severe signs of wear. Much of it is in dire need of repair or replacement. An economist who is an expert on the subject has warned, "Much of our infrastructure is on the verge of collapse."

Of the more than 577,000 bridges that federal officials inventoried in a recent year, 41 percent needed

---

PARTICIPATING IN GOVERNMENT

Serving on a School Board

Who are the members of your local school board? How did they get their jobs?

In every state except Hawaii local school districts are responsible for operating public schools. Each district has a school board that sets general policies regarding such matters as planning curriculum, hiring teachers, and maintaining buildings and grounds. Most districts have a superintendent of schools who is appointed by the board to carry out its policies.

School board members generally are elected by the voters in a school district.

Candidates who wish to run for office obtain applications from the local board of elections. To get on the ballot, they must file the application with the required number of signatures. Sometimes a nominating committee of people in the school district interviews candidates and endorses those who are best qualified for the board. Voters then choose from the candidates the committee has endorsed. The number of board members and terms of office vary among school districts.

School boards hold regular meetings, generally open to the public. Board members prepare for these meetings by studying the issues to be discussed. Serving on a school board demands a major commitment of time. People who participate in government at this level place a high value on education.

> **Investigating Further**
>
> Interview a member of your district's board of education. Find out why he or she chose to serve on the school board.

CHAPTER 27: GOVERNING METROPOLITAN AREAS **783**

Interpreting Visuals Display transparency 28 from the *Government Themes Transparencies* in the Teacher's Classroom Resources and use the accompanying teaching strategy and student activity to teach about community service programs.

L3 History Explain to students that the Marshall Plan encouraged European nations to work together to rebuild war-torn Europe after World War II. The United States agreed to aid Europe if the countries would meet to decide what they needed. Next, read aloud this quote from Ray Jenkins of the *Baltimore Evening Sun*: "What . . . must be done if this country is to be livable for any of us, is the kind of massive attack on the social pathology of the inner cities that was mounted in the Marshall Plan. . . ." Discuss if and how the United States could launch a domestic Marshall Plan.

PARTICIPATING IN GOVERNMENT

Discuss school boards' decisions that directly affect the lives of students, such as setting age limits for school bus drivers and approving rules of conduct for students. Point out school boards also decide how many schools a district will have and set policy in areas such as religious holiday or multicultural observances in the district. Ask: What qualifications do you think a person serving on the school board should have?

Have students complete activity 27 in *Participating in Government* in the Teacher's Classroom Resources.

Independent Practice

L1 Art Provide students with a variety of big city newspapers. Ask students to skim newspapers for headlines indicating social and financial problems facing cities. Have students group headlines by categories indicating various types of urban social and economic problems and create a collage or bulletin board entitled *Challenges of Urban Growth.* **LEP**

L2 Understanding Cause and Effect Ask students to write a short paragraph explaining the connection between each pair of city problems: (a) unemployment and homelessness, (b) homelessness and drug abuse, (c) decaying infrastructure and transportation, (d) crime and unemployment in big cities, rising costs for city government, (e) declining resources for city governments, suburban growth.

📁 Interpreting Source Readings Have students complete activity 27 in *Primary and Secondary Source Readings* in the Teacher's Classroom Resources.

Caption Answer
bridges, tunnels, streets, sidewalks, water pipes and sewers, public buildings

STUDY GUIDE

Theme Answer
Answers will vary, but may include: cooperating in urban renewal, reducing industrial pollution, creating partnership with education.

Critical Thinking Answer
If the system were clean, economical, efficient, and fast, people might be willing to change their commuting habits.

The Aging Infrastructure
The infrastructure of a city requires ongoing care and expenditure. **Economics What are some major facilities of urban infrastructure?**

million potholes. In Albuquerque, New Mexico, motorists suffered through frequent traffic jams caused by repairs to crumbling sewer lines under the city streets.

Cities face mounting costs for cleanup of polluted water, sewer system replacement, and waste treatment plants. Infrastructure costs are so enormous that local governments cannot do the job alone. State and federal aid is available for road-building, water and sewage systems, bridge construction, and many other public works. The federal government's role has become especially important in recent years. In 1982 Congress placed a 5-cent-a-gallon tax on gasoline, with the proceeds to be used to repair the nation's highways.

repair or replacement. Federal officials estimate that the cost would be more than $50 billion. Even worse, bridges are deteriorating at a faster rate than they are being repaired. A report by the secretary of transportation said the current backlog and new bridge construction would require an investment of $93 billion through the year 2005.

Repairing the infrastructure means huge expenditures for local governments. It cost all levels of government about $10 billion in 1960 for airports, highways, railroads, and transit. By 1990 government spending for these forms of transportation reached $100 billion a year. The crisis in transportation is primarily an urban one. While 85 percent of rural highway capacity is unused, highways in metropolitan areas are clogged.

For Americans living in cities, the problems of infrastructure became particularly acute in the 1980s. In the summer of 1982, residents of Jersey City, New Jersey, had no tap water for four days because of ruptured water pipes. In Houston, Texas, a local magazine estimated that the city's streets had about 1.5

Mass Transit Maintaining a sound transportation network is a serious challenge that local governments face. In city after city, chronic traffic jams and air pollution have resulted from the millions of Americans using their automobiles to commute to work. An alternative to automobile use in urban areas is **mass transit**—buses, subways, and rail lines. Mass transit moves large numbers of people, produces less pollution, and consumes much less fuel than automobiles. Despite these advantages of mass transit, however, most Americans prefer to drive to work alone in their automobiles. A Census Bureau study of transportation patterns in 20 metropolitan areas during the energy shortages between 1970 and 1977 found that, despite rising gasoline prices, the use of mass transit declined in all but 3 of the metropolitan regions.

Many local leaders believe that more people would use mass transit facilities if they were cleaner, faster, and more efficient. Making significant improvements in bus, subway, and rail lines, however, requires a vast expenditure of money. Some major cities have invested heavily in mass transit. Elaborate mass transit systems have been built in Washington, D.C., Atlanta, and in the San Francisco-Oakland area. San Francisco's Bay Area Rapid Transit system cost twice its original estimate to build. High costs discourage planners in other cities from taking on such projects.

STUDY GUIDE

Themes in Government
Free Enterprise What roles could American businesses have in renewing inner cities?

Critical Thinking Skills
Predicting Consequences How do you think people might react to the development of a new or

vastly improved mass transit system in the urban area closest to where you live?

Critical Thinking Activity

Predicting Consequences Organize students into groups. Have each group create a best-case and worst-case scenario for life in America's big cities in the year 2020. A best-case scenario might include successful revitalization programs or a national war on urban decay with financial help from the federal government. A worst-case scenario might describe the impact on city life of intensifying social and economic problems. Have students present their scenarios to the rest of the class.

In order to pay the operating costs of mass transit systems, local governments often increase fares. As fares go up, however, the number of riders who use mass transit usually goes down. Consequently, local governments have turned increasingly to the state and federal governments for mass transit aid. In states such as Pennsylvania, Michigan, California, and Colorado, the state government provides major assistance for local mass transit. The federal government, under the Urban Mass Transportation Act of 1964, provided more than $18 billion for local use between 1965 and 1981. About $13 billion of this sum was spent for the purchase of 25,000 buses and rail cars. By the late 1980s, however, the federal administration called for large budget reductions in mass transit programs.

Economic Challenges

Meeting the challenges facing municipal governments now and in the years ahead demands imagination, citizen involvement, and good leadership. In most cases it also demands large investments of money. Municipalities will continue to depend on help from state and federal governments. The level of aid may not satisfy big cities, however. The federal government is not as free with urban aid as it was in the 1960s and 1970s. For example, Boston received only $10,000 from the federal government in 1960. By 1980 that amount had snowballed to $90 million. In 1988 it was cut to $36 million.

Big City Financial Problems Although all communities will have to meet these challenges, large cities have special problems which add to their financial burdens. Big cities usually have higher rates of poverty, crime, and unemployment than smaller localities. In 1979, for example, about one-third of all people living below the federally defined level of poverty resided in large cities.

For these reasons, large cities find it difficult to pay the costs of necessary social services, police and fire protection, and housing rehabilitation. Programs such as public welfare, aid to the elderly, and public health are necessary but very expensive. Moreover, while costs have been rising, the cities' sources of revenue have been decreasing. Many cities have been losing sources of tax revenues as middle-class families and businesses move to the suburbs. Recently, more than 70 cities have instituted payroll or commuter taxes. These are taxes on the income earned by people who work in the city but live in the suburbs.

Moving People
Maintaining a clean and reliable mass transit system is a challenge for most large cities. Economics **What are some benefits of mass transit?**

Cities in Crisis In the 1970s the cycle of rising costs and declining resources combined to push many cities into deep and unprecedented financial crises. In 1975 New York City could not even pay the interest on its outstanding loans. Only financial help from the state and federal governments, large banks, and municipal unions prevented the country's largest city from being forced to declare bankruptcy. Similar problems occurred in cities such as Cleveland, Detroit, and Baltimore. A 1980 congressional study reported that 70 percent of all large cities spent more money than they took in.

In the early 1990s several cities again faced severe economic crises. New York City faced a budget shortfall of $800 million in 1991. Washington, D.C., Philadelphia, Chicago, Detroit, San Francisco, Boston, and Los Angeles also faced budget problems. The mayor of the nation's largest city blamed New York City's plight on recession and cutbacks in federal aid. Critics believed that the city could be more efficient, because its spending had doubled in 10 years as it added 71,000 employees to the payroll.

The Need for Economic Development Cities have struggled with different solutions to their financial problems. These solutions have included state and federal aid, loans, budget cuts, and layoffs of city workers. Many cities have also tried to deal with their financial woes by stimulating greater economic development. Economic development is especially critical for cities that have lost jobs to both the suburbs and the Sunbelt over the past 30 years.

Caption Answer
moves large numbers of people with less pollution and less energy consumption than automobiles

Interpreting Political Cartoons Have students complete activities 26 and 28 in *Interpreting Political Cartoons* in the Teacher's Classroom Resources.

L3 Economics Have students pick one of these cities and research the financial problems the city faced in the early 1990s: New York, Boston, Miami, Washington, Philadelphia, Chicago, Detroit, Dallas, Los Angeles.

Assess

Check for Understanding
Have students complete Section 2 Review on page 786.

Meeting Objectives
Each section objective is tested by the Section Review questions that follow it in parentheses.
- Summarize the great challenges facing large municipalities and their governments. (2, 3, 4, 5, 6, 7, 8)
- Evaluate policies addressing housing and drug abuse problems. (3, 4, 7)
- Discuss big city financial problems. (2, 4, 6, 8)

Evaluate
Section 2 Quiz
Testmaker

Reteach
Have students explain why many cities are searching for new ways to raise funds. Then have them describe three strategies for stimulating growth.

Background

A new and growing problem for the nation's cities is the thousands of children born in the mid-1980s to crack-cocaine addicts. In 1991 many hospitals in New York, Los Angeles, Detroit, and Washington reported 20 percent or more of newborns showing effects of drugs. In California drug-exposed babies stay in the hospital almost 5 times as long as normal ones. Many crack infants must later be placed in foster care. In New York City the cost of providing such care has risen sharply from $320 million in 1985 to $795 million in 1991. As crack-cocaine children reach school age, they will put new strains on city school systems.

Caption Answer
to revitalize the local economy, to provide jobs and growth

Enrich

If the community has a homeless shelter or substance abuse clinic, students can interview shelter or clinic administrators to find out how it meets community needs and to what extent local, state, or federal governments support its efforts.

Have students complete activity 27 in *Enrichment Activities* in the Teacher's Classroom Resources.

Close

Have students discuss the following statement: The way we treat our cities tells us a great deal about our values and about our society as a whole.

CONNECTIONS

Sociology

Successful projects to revitalize inner cities include the restoration of rundown or abandoned market buildings or docks instead of replacing them with new buildings. Successfully recycled cityscapes include San Francisco's Ghirardelli Square, Sacramento's Skid Row, Baltimore's Harborplace, Manhattan's South Street Seaport, and Boston's Quincy Market.

Economic Development
Many cities have made large investments in new facilities like this one in Baltimore, Md. **Economics Why have city officials spent millions on urban facilities?**

How can municipal governments stimulate economic development? One approach is revitalization. **Revitalization** means that local governments make large investments in new facilities in an effort to promote economic growth. In recent years, a number of major cities have attempted to revitalize their downtown areas. Baltimore built a $170-million office and residential complex. Detroit invested more than $200 million in a regional shopping mall and two giant office buildings. Funds usually come from both local government and private investors. State and federal aid may also be available for revitalization projects.

The second major approach to economic development is tax incentives to industries that relocate in a community. Tax incentives may take a number of forms. Local governments, especially in suburban areas, often try to attract new business by offering lower property tax rates. Some states, such as Connecticut and Indiana, offer tax reductions to businesses that relocate in areas of high unemployment. Similarly, the federal government also offers tax reductions, or credits, to businesses that move into areas of poverty and unemployment.

Gentrification One of the most debated issues of the revitalization movement concerns **gentrification**. Sometimes called "displacement," gentrification is the phenomenon of new people moving into a neighborhood, not only forcing out those who live there, but also changing the area's essential character.

By the 1980s some middle-income suburbanites and recent immigrants began to move into the cities, often into areas where they could restore old houses and other buildings and take advantage of the lower housing costs while enjoying the benefits of city life.

The positive side of gentrification is that it restores vitality to the city by reclaiming deteriorating property and bringing new business to decayed areas. It also has a negative effect, however. It accelerates property sales, inflating property values and increasing taxes. Property becomes too expensive for poorer residents who live in these neighborhoods to stay. If the displaced residents are largely from a minority group, the issue may become a heated one. Some cities have defused this issue by passing legislation that slows or prevents displacement. For example, Savannah, Georgia, preserved much of its social diversity by providing its limited-income residents help in restoring their properties.

2 SECTION REVIEW

Section Summary
Large cities cope with problems that include housing shortages, drug trafficking, crime, decaying infrastructures, and financial troubles.

Checking for Understanding
Recalling Facts
1. Define renovation, public housing program, infrastructure, mass transit, revitalization, gentrification.
2. Explain why jobs became scarce in the inner cities.
3. Identify the drug that created major problems for cities in the 1980s.
4. List five major problems facing city governments today.

Exploring Themes
5. Federalism How did the federal government influence the development of mass transit in urban areas?
6. Free Enterprise What have cities, states, and the federal government done to attract business to areas of high unemployment?

Critical Thinking Skills
7. Analyzing Information What were the main causes of urban housing shortages beginning in the 1950s?
8. Predicting Consequences What additional problems will cities face if governments cannot sufficiently fund replacement of urban infrastructures?

Section 2 Review Answers

1. Definitions of terms appear on pages indicated: **renovation,** 781; **public housing program,** 782; **infrastructure,** 783; **mass transit,** 784; **revitalization,** 786; **gentrification,** 786
2. Businesses moved out of the cities to suburbs and to new locations in the South and West.
3. crack cocaine

4. housing shortages and homelessness, traffic congestion, pollution, poverty, drug trafficking, crime, decaying infrastructure, financial problems
5. Under the Urban Mass Transportation Act of 1964, the federal government provided over $18 billion for local use between 1965 and 1981. By the late 1980s, the federal government cut funds for mass transit programs.

6. revitalization; tax incentives or credits
7. Inner-city housing deteriorated; urban renewal replaced fewer units than it tore down; private housing construction declined because it could not compete with government-subsidized housing; and inflation brought high interest rates for construction loans.
8. more traffic congestion, problems with services such as water, sewage disposal, and sanitation

Demonstrating Reasoned Judgment

Demonstrating reasoned judgment involves using your own knowledge and experience to evaluate policies or decisions. You may have to evaluate a variety of proposed solutions to a given problem and decide which you think should be implemented.

Explanation

To make a reasoned judgment, follow these steps:
- Examine all of the proposed solutions to a particular problem.
- Pinpoint how each proposal is expected to work and decide whether it is likely to be effective.
- Taking into account all that you know about the problem, decide which approaches you favor.

Suppose that you are the mayor of a large city in which traffic congestion is a major problem. The city council suggests the following proposals:
1. Tax all-day parking lots to raise rates and discourage use.
2. Narrow sidewalks in order to build new traffic lanes on major thoroughfares.
3. Lower fares on buses and trains.
4. Initiate ad campaign to encourage carpooling and use of mass transit.
5. Encourage businesses to adopt flexible work schedules, easing traffic congestion at peak times.

First write how each of the proposals is expected to alleviate the problem.

Next decide whether you favor one of the general approaches proposed or whether you think it is best to combine two or more approaches to the problem. In making decisions, you should take into account as many factors as possible. For example, you may consider such issues as air pollution, economic growth, and finances.

Finally, write a paragraph or two explaining why you favor or reject each proposal. Here is a sample:

To alleviate traffic congestion, I favor policies aimed at reducing the number of cars in use and streamlining traffic flow. Encouraging public transportation through an ad campaign will also reduce air pollution. Our ad campaign must also encourage commuters to carpool and businesses to adopt flexi-

ble work schedules so that every employee in the city is not trying to get to work at the same time.

I oppose lowering fares on city trains and buses because the city cannot afford to subsidize public transportation. I also oppose increasing the tax on all-day parking lots because higher rates would cause downtown stores to lose valuable business. Finally, I oppose widening streets because it would be costly and would eat up the limited pedestrian space.

Practice

Suppose that you are the mayor of a major city in which illegal drug use and trafficking are problems. Most of the illegal activity is centered in three neighborhoods that also have high unemployment rates. Read the following proposals for dealing with the problem, then answer the questions that follow.
1. Drug education programs should be created for grades 1-12.
2. Police should walk rather than drive around the areas they patrol.
3. Judges should be encouraged to give stiffer penalties for possession or sale of illegal drugs.
4. Job training programs for unemployed young people should be started in these neighborhoods.
5. Neighborhood Crime Watch programs should be organized.
6. The city should enlist the help of churches and community groups to provide recreational activities and counseling services for teenagers.
7. Drug rehabilitation centers should be established.

A. Write a sentence explaining how each proposal might alleviate the problem of illegal drug use.
B. On a scale of 1 (low) to 10 (high), indicate how effective each proposal would be if used alone.
C. Write a paragraph explaining which proposals you support and how they would work together.

Additional Practice
To practice this skill, see **Reinforcing the Skill** on page 795.

Focus
Present students with the following:

You are at a party. At the party you find out that the person who was to take you home has already left. What are your options? Take a ride with anyone going your way? Call a friend? Call a family member? Take the bus? Remind students that solving problems often involves making judgments, and that making judgments often involves considering options.

Teach
Have students read the Explanation steps, the problem, and the proposed solutions. Ask: Will any one of the solutions solve the parking problem? *(Probably any of them could help, but not be a total solution.)* Why would a city council suggest multiple solutions? *(One solution might not solve all the factors behind the problem.)* Which approaches do students think would be the most workable? Why?

Assess
Have students complete the **Practice** exercise.

Close
Have students work in groups to list multiple solutions to a local problem, such as refuse disposal, economic decline, crowded classrooms. Have groups share their solutions with the class.

Practice Answers

A. 1. If students are educated about the dangers of illegal drug use, fewer will use drugs. **2.** If police walk their beats, they will relate better to people in the neighborhood, and their presence will discourage street crime. **3.** Stiff penalties will deter people from using and selling drugs. **4.** Young people are less likely to turn to drugs if they have the opportunity to earn a living. **5.** Drug traffic will be discouraged if concerned citizens report illegal activity to the police. **6.** Teenagers who have support systems are less likely to use drugs. **7.** Many people may want to be rehabilitated but cannot afford it.
B. Assessments of effectiveness will vary.
C. Proposals will vary.

For additional practice, have students complete activity 27 in *Skill Reinforcement Activities* in the Teacher's Classroom Resources.

Focus

Bell Ringer

Tell the class a major airport has a chance to buy a radar device that will make landings and take-offs much safer. Ask who should be taxed to pay for this equipment—only airport users, residents of the city where the airport is located, suburbanites who use the airport in largest numbers, or rural residents. Have students write and support their opinions while attendance is being taken.

Motivating Activity

Discuss students' Bell Ringer responses. Explain that when issues such as airport safety are discussed, cities and their suburbs may agree on the benefits of co-operation. But on issues like mass transit, pollution cleanup, crime, drug trafficking, and homelessness, suburban voters often resist becoming involved with cities. Ask students why they think this is. What might be the benefits of cooperating for cities? for suburbs? What might be the costs? Tell students they will look more closely at these questions in this lesson.

Vocabulary Precheck

List the terms and concepts on the chalkboard. Have volunteers skim the section to find each term and read it in context. **LEP**

New Approaches to Problems

People easily identify issues such as crime, decaying infrastructure, and traffic congestion as urban problems. Cities today, however, face an additional problem—one of their identity.

A New Federal and State Focus

In the 1960s the nation presumed that something had to be done to address cities' problems. The United States Senate held hearings on the crisis of the cities and the role of the federal government in meeting it. While cities today still have the same problems, the federal and state governments are not as likely to grant cities huge amounts of money to address them. The mayor of Boston explained his frustration:

> *B*oston had one-third of all drug arrests in the Commonwealth of Massachusetts last year (1990). Yet we got only 7 percent of the federal drug money sent to the state (by the federal government).
> —RAYMOND L. FLYNN, 1991

City mayors and lobbyists worked unsuccessfully to get Congress to renew revenue sharing in the 1980s. Meanwhile, the federal government eliminated programs such as Urban Development Action Grants, and the Comprehensive Employment Training Act. The League of Cities tracked the decline of federal grants to local governments from $50 billion to about $19 billion from 1981 to 1991.

Why were federal and state governments less responsive to city problems? Perhaps these governments had changed their priorities. A federal commission on Urban America in the Eighties suggested that social and economic migration to the suburbs was a natural, even an advantageous, development that should not be discouraged. It added that federal aid to the cities should not try to stop this trend.

Clearly, the suburbs were becoming powerful economic and political entities. The growth of the suburbs signaled this change in political power. After the census of 1990, new district lines gave suburbs more seats in Congress and state legislatures than they ever had. The nation's focus seemed to be shifting from city problems to suburban opportunities. If cities were to survive as healthy communities, perhaps they would have to solve their own problems.

Michael White, mayor of Cleveland, suggested a cause of the city's loss of political clout:

> *B*ig cities are becoming a code name for a lot of things; for minorities, for crumbling neighborhoods, for crime, for everything that America has moved away from.
> —MICHAEL WHITE, 1991

Search for Solutions

Metropolitan areas need creative solutions to urban problems. Some people believe that consolidating the overlapping units of government provides a better way to handle urban problems. **Consolidation** provides a single government for an entire metropolitan area.

SECTION PREVIEW

Objectives
After studying this section, you should be able to:
■ Identify **reasons for cities' loss of political influence with state and federal governments.**
■ Discuss **arguments for and against consolidation of metropolitan government.**

■ List **three creative approaches to government that cities have taken.**

Key Terms
consolidation, metropolitan federation, annexation, council of government

Themes in Government
■ Comparative Government
■ Separation of Powers

Critical Thinking Skills
■ Identifying Central Issues
■ Drawing Conclusions

---

788 UNIT 9: LOCAL GOVERNMENT

Classroom Resources for Section 3

📁 Guided Reading Activities
📁 Reproducible Lesson Plans
📁 Reteaching Activities 27
📁 Section 3 Quiz
📁 Chapter 27 Tests

➕ Testmaker
📁 Limited English Proficiency Activities 27
    SAT Practice Tests
    Writer's Guidebook

Arguments for Metropolitan Government

Those who favor metropolitan government make a number of persuasive points. They emphasize that most problems do not affect just one city or local community. Instead, they are problems of an entire region. Air pollution created in a city spreads to nearby suburbs and rural towns. Similarly, suburban residents use city services, but they do not help to pay for these services in the form of taxes. Because a metropolitan area is an interdependent region, those who favor metropolitan government feel that one government for an entire metropolitan area would be better equipped to handle regional problems.

The existence of many independent governments makes it extremely difficult to respond to area-wide problems. For example, creating a new mass transit system might require cooperation between a major city and perhaps 30 surrounding communities.

Many people feel that a metropolitan government would reduce government waste and duplication of services. For example, one metropolitan sewage treatment plant might just as easily serve many communities. This would save each local government the cost of creating its own sewage treatment facility. Other services, such as water supply and transportation, might also be provided more economically on an area-wide basis.

Finally, those who favor metropolitan government believe that it can unite cities and suburbs in a common effort to deal with their problems. As one local official from Minneapolis has said, "You can pour all kinds of federal aid into cities, but it will be wasted if you don't stop this city-suburb rivalry."

Arguments Against Metropolitan Government

Those who oppose metropolitan government fear a loss of local power and independence. They believe metropolitan government would turn into a giant bureaucracy unable to respond to the needs of a particular community.

The strongest opposition has come from suburban residents who want to remain apart from problems they associate with the city. Some African American urban leaders also have opposed metropolitan government because they do not want to give up control over inner-city politics. They also worry that their cities would wield less influence under a metropolitan arrangement. Others have opposed metropolitan government because higher taxes might result.

Major Metropolitan Areas in 1990

City	1980 Population	1990 Population	Percent Growth
New York[1]			3.1
Los Angeles[2]			26.4
Chicago[3]			1.6
San Francisco[4]			16.5
Philadelphia[5]			3.9

Population in Millions: 0, 5, 10, 15, 20

[1] New York–Northern New Jersey–Long Island, NY–NJ–CT CMSA. [2] Los Angeles–Anaheim–Riverside CA CMSA. [3] Chicago–Gary–Lake County, IL–IN–WI CMSA. [4] San Francisco–Oakland–San Jose, CA CMSA. [5] Philadelphia–Wilmington–Trenton, PA–NJ–DE–MD CMSA. Source: Statistical Abstract of the United States, 1991

Graph Study
Above are the top five Consolidated Metropolitan Statistical Areas (CMSA) listed according to population percentage gain. **How can the metropolitan New York area have the highest population and one of the lowest percentage growth rates?**

STUDY GUIDE

Themes in Government
Comparative Government How can a metropolitan government be more beneficial to citizens than several smaller local governments?

Critical Thinking Skills
Identifying Central Issues Why might some citizens oppose consolidating city and county governments?

Background

Slightly over half of Minnesota's 4.4 million people live in the metropolitan area around Minneapolis-St. Paul. During the 1950s and early 1960s, this area faced contamination problems from inadequate sewage facilities and air and water pollution, and controversy over airport location and mass transit. Local leaders responded by forming a metropolitan federation. To gain support for consolidation, the council agreed to deal only with regional problems, such as sewage, water supply, mass transit and airport location. Each municipality kept most of its previous functions. Thus few local officials and employees lost their jobs or power bases.

Teach

Guided Practice

L1 Politics Provide students with a definition of *political clout*. *(influence)* Then review the quote from Michael White on page 788. Ask: What gives a group political clout? *(size or large numbers of voting members, such resources as money, time, and commitment)* Why did Cleveland's mayor lose clout? *(Population shift to suburbs led to fewer city voters and less representation in Congress and state legislatures.)*

Graph Study Answer
Percentage growth rate accounts for the number of new residents in relation to the number of previous residents.

STUDY GUIDE

Theme Answer
Consolidation of services may be more economical; funding and solution of region-wide problems is more likely to be resolved by larger population area.

Critical Thinking Answer
They may want to maintain their own power base and independence, may be wary of larger bureaucracy.

CONNECTIONS

Geography
Through consolidation and annexation, New York City became a metropolis of five boroughs: Manhattan, Queens, Brooklyn, Bronx, and Staten Island. In the 1980s Staten Island began a campaign to secede. Many residents felt their borough had more in common with suburban communities on nearby Long Island.

L2 Constructing a Chart Construct on the chalkboard a two-column chart labeled *Advantages* and *Disadvantages*. Have students complete the chart by summarizing arguments favoring and opposing metropolitan government. Then ask students why they think that despite the longer list of advantages, voters have approved few metropolitan government plans. *(resistance to power-sharing and fear of increased tax burden by suburban voters)*

L3 Debate Have students debate the following topics:

Is opposition to consolidation selfishness or enlightened self-interest?

Political boundaries between cities and suburbs are outdated and should be abolished.

GLOBAL CONNECTION

In 1989, Fort Worth, Texas, sent almost 250 people to tour its sister cities in Europe and Asia. Fort Worth also welcomed almost 700 visitors from these cities. Information sessions and sports events broadened understandings and promoted friendships between visitors and hosts. As a result, Fort Worth expanded its Sister Cities affiliations to include Bandung, Indonesia, and Budapest, Hungary.
Examining the Connection Answer: *political and economic stability and cultural diversity*

Not many proposals for metropolitan government have been approved by the voters. Generally, it is the opposition of suburban voters that defeats proposals for metropolitan government.

Two Kinds of Government

There are two different plans of metropolitan government currently being used. One form involves the consolidation of city and county governments. The other is a metropolitan federation in which there is a central government with local governments below it.

City-County Consolidation Under this plan, both the city and county governments consolidate into an entirely new form of metropolitan government. An elected executive and an elected legislature share power. The metropolitan area is divided into separate tax districts, with tax rates geared to the amount of services each district receives. Supporters claim that this plan has led to tax cuts and greater economy in government.

Jacksonville, Florida, and Nashville, Tennessee, are good examples of city-county consolidation. In 1962 voters approved the merger of the city of Nashville with Davidson County. The merger created a new metropolitan government with authority over a wide range of services. It has a mayor-council form of government and one school system and police department for the entire area. The metropolitan government also provides fire protection, water and sewage services, and public works.

In addition to Jacksonville and Nashville, city-county consolidations have been created in Baton Rouge, Louisiana; Carson City, Nevada; and Lexington, Kentucky. Voters in other areas, however, have rejected most proposals to merge city and county governments.

In some places, city-county consolidation has been partial, with local governments keeping control over some services. UNIGOV, formed in 1969 by the consolidation of Indianapolis and Marion County, Indiana, is an example of partial consolidation. Citizens in the Indianapolis metropolitan area receive most of their basic services from UNIGOV. Education, however, remains the responsibility of independent school districts. Moreover, a number of small cities and townships within Marion County remain independent and provide many of their own services.

Metropolitan Federation Another kind of metropolitan government is called the metropolitan

GLOBAL CONNECTION

Interdependence

Sister Cities The Sister Cities program promotes cultural and economic exchanges through agreements between participating cities. Sister Cities International now consists of more than 1,300 cities in 91 countries.

In 1990 Fort Worth, Texas, won the Best Overall Program award based on its Sister-City links with Reggio Emilia, Italy; Trier, West Germany; and Nagoya, Japan.

Successful economic exchanges include trade agreements between Portland, Oregon, and Sapporo, Japan; a joint manufacturing and selling venture between Baltimore, Maryland, and Hsiamen, China; and import-export agreements between Louisville, Kentucky, and Montpellier, France.

Examining the Connection
What factors would a city consider in deciding which foreign cities it should contact for cultural and economic exchanges?

federation. This is a two-tier approach that is similar to the plan in the federal Constitution, where powers are divided between the federal government and state governments.

In a **metropolitan federation**, a higher level of government makes overall policy for the entire metropolitan region and carries out certain broad functions. Under this government, local governments administer policy and maintain some of their own independent functions, such as education and police protection. Like the states in the federal system, local governments maintain their identity and keep some of their independent powers.

An example of metropolitan federation is the Twin Cities Metropolitan Council. The Minnesota state legislature set up this federation in the Minneapolis-St. Paul area in 1967. The Metropolitan Council, made up of 17 members appointed by the governor, represents 139 municipalities and 50 townships. It has the power to make decisions on sewage and water systems, mass-transit highway routes, airports, parks, land use, and public housing. The Metropolitan Council also has the power to tax, to charge local

Cooperative Learning Activity

Organize students into groups. Tell students that a proposal on the ballot in upcoming local elections calls for consolidating county and city governments in the nearest urban area. All groups have been hired by supporters of this plan to prepare two-minute television ads explaining and urging voters to support the proposal. The job of each group is to create an ad. Within groups have students pick a director, several scriptwriters, a sound person and/or props person, and actors. Encourage students to be creative, using visuals, music, celebrity endorsements, and person-on-the-street interviews to make their ads appealing to voters.

790 Unit 9: Local Government

Population Fluctuation and Urban Growth

Regional shift in population

Northeast −

West +   Midwest −

South +

Population in the Northeast and Midwest decreased while population in the South and West increased.

23.3%
32.8%
30.6%
32.3%
37.2%
31.4%
43.3%
43.9%
37.0%
31.4%
24.2%
32.0%

1950
1960
1970
1980

Urban
Suburban
Rural

Source: Bureau of the Census

Independent Practice

L1 Geography Have students research the areas of their city (or a nearby one) that have been added through annexation in the last 10 years and use this data to shade in parts of a county or city map to show approximate areas of annexation. This information can be obtained from the city or town public information officer. **LEP**

L2 Making Comparisons Have students write papers comparing city-county and metropolitan federation consolidation plans. Suggest that they cover the following topics in their papers: how each is organized, the powers given to each government unit, and the advantages and disadvantages of each.

governments for services, and to seek federal and state grants.

In 1957 Miami and Dade County, Florida, also adopted a metropolitan federation type of government. Under this plan, Miami and surrounding suburban cities control local functions, but the metropolitan government handles area functions such as fire and police protection and transportation.

One of the newest metropolitan federations is Portland, Oregon, which adopted this form of government in 1979. In the Portland area, the Metropolitan Service District now has authority over many basic municipal functions, including pollution control and transportation.

Some foreign cities use this form of government as well. Toronto is one example.

Other Regional Arrangements

Some areas have created special districts to handle specific functions for an entire region. Other cooperative efforts include regional planning agencies, consolidated school and library systems, and compacts between states. Many local governments are cooperating to solve problems, especially regional problems such as pollution control and transportation. Suburbs and cities are finding ways to work together on problems of mutual concern.

Annexation Annexation is an old method that cities have used in the past to extend their authority into the larger metropolitan region. **Annexation** is a process by which a local government absorbs new

STUDY GUIDE

Theme Answer
because local governments administer policies and can maintain some independent functions, while a higher level of government is responsible for making broad policy

Critical Thinking Answer
They are searching for creative solutions to urban problems.

STUDY GUIDE

Themes in Government
Separation of Powers Why might the metropolitan federation, in which there is a central government with local govern-

ments below it, be a good choice for metropolitan government?

Critical Thinking Skills
Drawing Conclusions Why are urban areas adopting new and different systems of government?

Assess

Check for Understanding
Have students complete Section 3 Review on page 792.

CHAPTER 27: GOVERNING METROPOLITAN AREAS   791

Critical Thinking Activity

Drawing Conclusions Have students draw conclusions about each of these questions: Based on current trends, over the next 20 years is there likely to be an increase or decrease in the a) tax base of big cities? b) level of federal involvement in and support for solving urban problems? c) number of

urban areas forming consolidated or federated metropolitan governments? Then ask: What might reverse trends toward declining tax base and reduced federal involvement in urban affairs? Have students give reasons for their opinions.

Meeting Objectives

Each section objective is tested by the Section Review questions that follow it in parentheses.

- Identify reasons for cities' loss of political influence with state and federal governments. (8)
- Discuss arguments for and against consolidation of metropolitan government. (2, 3)
- List three creative approaches to government that cities have taken. (2, 4, 5, 6, 7)

Evaluate

📁 Section 3

💽 Testmaker

Reteach

📁 Have students complete activity 27 in *Reteaching Activities* in the Teacher's Classroom Resources.

Enrich

Have students choose one of the regional arrangements discussed in the section and write a paper describing how it might work in their area.

Close

Have students explain why big cities have had to seek new solutions to urban problems and why such changes have been difficult to implement.

---

territory. Generally, cities have used annexation to take in unincorporated areas—areas which do not have their own local governments. As a result, annexation has been the most common means whereby cities have grown in size and population.

Because state law regulates annexation, it varies from state to state. Usually states require approval by a majority of voters in both the city and the area proposed for annexation. In seven states—Arizona, Missouri, North Carolina, Oklahoma, Texas, Tennessee, and Virginia—land can be annexed by a city itself or through a court order. These states do not require voter approval by the annexed area. Likewise, in some cities in Texas, the city council can approve of annexation without voter consent.

Since 1960 almost 75 percent of the nation's large cities have annexed some surrounding territory. Most of these annexations have occurred in the South and West, where there is still much unincorporated territory surrounding a city. Older cities in the Northeast and Midwest have run into opposition from suburbs, which block any attempts at annexation.

Councils of Government Every metropolitan area also has a council of government. A **council of government** is a voluntary regional organization that attempts to plan and coordinate policies for a metropolitan area. The council of government may also be known as a regional planning agency or a regional council.

Each council of government is made up of local elected officials, such as mayors and county supervisors. These local officials meet to discuss common problems, share information, and develop master plans for an entire metropolitan area. A council of government also tries to coordinate the policies of different local governments. Thus, for example, it will try to make sure that a community's new sewage plant does not interfere with an existing system in another community.

In addition to planning and coordination, councils of government also review applications for federal grants which have been submitted by local governments. Since 1966 the federal government has tried to foster regional cooperation by requiring that urban development grants be reviewed by councils of government.

Despite these various functions, some people have described councils of government as "toothless tigers" because they lack real powers. Moreover, councils of government are voluntary. Local governments do not have to participate, although many choose to do so. Still, many planners believe that councils of government do promote some metropolitan cooperation. Also, they hope that some day these councils will develop into genuine metropolitan governments.

Service Contracts Most American cities buy some services from their county government. The best-known example is the Lakewood Plan in Los Angeles County. Under this plan, the county sells a variety of services, including police protection and water supply, to many small cities in the county.

3 SECTION REVIEW

Section Summary
Faced with difficult problems, cities are trying creative approaches to government including city-county consolidation, metropolitan federation, and regional arrangements.

Checking for Understanding
Recalling Facts
1. Define consolidation, metropolitan federation, annexation, council of government.
2. Describe three advantages of a metropolitan government.
3. Identify the voters who usually defeat proposals for metropolitan government.
4. Explain why annexation has been more frequent in the South and West than in other parts of the nation.

Exploring Themes
5. Comparative Government How is a metropolitan federation like the constitutional relationship between federal and state government?
6. Separation of Powers How are executive and legislative authority divided in city-county consolidations?

Critical Thinking Skills
7. Identifying Central Issues What financial advantages do city governments seek when they promote consolidation and annexation?
8. Drawing Conclusions Why will suburbs likely wield greater influence in national and state government in coming years?

Section 3 Review Answers

1. Definitions of terms appear on pages indicated: **consolidation,** 788; **metropolitan federation,** 790; **annexation,** 791; **council of government,** 792
2. It is better able to handle regional problems, reduces waste and duplication of services, produces cooperation and unites cities and suburbs in a common effort.
3. suburban voters

4. In the South and West more unincorporated territory is close to cities. Suburbs in the Northeast and Midwest often oppose annexation to large cities.
5. In a metropolitan federation, a higher level of government makes overall policy. Local governments administer policy and maintain some of their own independent functions, such as education and police protection. Like the states in the federal system, local governments do not lose their identity and keep some of their independent powers.

6. An elected executive and an elected legislature share the power of the new government.
7. Cities seek the tax base of surrounding areas to provide revenue for services and economy in government by eliminating duplication of services.
8. Suburbs will gain representation in state and national legislatures.

C. Kenneth Orski on the Problem of Traffic Congestion

Introduced as the "Dean of Suburban Mobility," C. Kenneth Orski, President of Urban Mobility Corporation, delivered an address to the Traffic Improvement Association of Oakland County, Bloomfield Hills, California.

Commuters on Route 28 in Fairfax County in Northern Virginia, find themselves faced with the disorienting experience of being locked in stop-and-go bumper to bumper traffic while surrounded by pastoral vistas of cornfields, farmhouses, and grazing cattle. . . .

And on the LBJ Freeway in Dallas, they say, the only way to change lanes is to trade cars. . . .

What these anecdotes suggest is that the very nature of traffic congestion has changed. Once a phenomenon confined in space and time, traffic congestion has become endemic and pervasive, affecting suburbs and central cities alike, and intruding on the lives of an ever expanding universe of people.

On the traffic congestion front I can report some good news and some bad news. The good news is that we are beginning to learn how to manage congestion. . . .

The bad news is that it does not seem likely we can build our way out of the problem permanently. . . . New roads will not eliminate traffic congestion. They fill up with cars almost as soon as the ribbon is cut. . . .

How about transit? Can rail transit offer lasting relief from traffic congestion? This was our rhetoric back in the 70's, when I . . . appeared before Congressional committees to plead for multi-million dollar authorizations for new rail systems. . . . Today, you will find few DOT [Department of Transportation] officials asserting that rail systems reduce traffic congestion. . . . By stimulating high density office developments that continue to rely heavily on the automobile, our Metrorail system has actually exacerbated congestion in some places. . . .

Managing congestion means doing whatever is necessary to contain traffic within the limits of public tolerability. . . .

People drive to work not just because they like the comfort and

. . . more than 70 percent of suburban office workers use their cars on a regular basis to make intermediate stops on their way to or from work. . . .

privacy of their cars, or because of some irrational "love affair" with the automobile. No, people drive because they need their car before, during or after work—whether to drop off or pick up a child at a day-care center, shop on the way home, or simply escape the company cafeteria during the lunchbreak. Our surveys indicate that more than 70 percent of suburban office workers use their cars on a regular basis to make intermediate stops on their way to or from work. . . .

Traffic congestion is an extraordinarily complex problem that defies simple, quick fix solutions. . . . We strongly prefer to live and work in widely scattered locations, leaving us little choice but to rely on personal means of transportation.

—C. KENNETH ORSKI, 1989

Examining the Reading

Reviewing Facts
1. Describe how the nature of traffic congestion has changed.
2. Identify one reason that Orski believes rail transit will not solve the problem.

Critical Thinking Skills
3. Evaluating Information Why does Orski believe that people will have to learn to live with traffic congestion?

Focus

Ask students what forms of transportation they and their families use and to indicate problems connected with each.

Teach

Ask: Why, according to Orski, is building new roads not an answer to traffic congestion? *(They fill up with more cars the minute they open.)* What faults does he find with mass transit? *(It does not truly relieve congestion; many people cannot give up their cars.)* What answers does he provide? *(that congestion cannot be solved until people make basic changes in lifestyle)*

Assess

Have students complete **Examining the Reading.**

Answers

1. It has become endemic and pervasive.
2. People continue to need cars for errands before, during, or after work.
3. It is a complex problem that defies simple solutions so long as Americans live and work in scattered locations.

Close

Ask students if they think Orski's perception of why people drive to work is accurate. Do students ride mass transit? Would they if it was available?

More About Personal Perspectives

C. Kenneth Orski founded Urban Mobility Corporation, a transportation consulting firm, in 1981. The firm specializes in the design of traffic congestion management plans and the formation of methods to improve traffic mobility in suburban areas. Mr. Orski has advised more than 30 state bodies on problems related to increasing traffic congestion. In the 1970s he served in both the Nixon and Ford administrations as Associate Administrator of the Urban Mass Transportation Administration.

27 CHAPTER REVIEW

Identifying Terms and Concepts

1. b, **2.** g, **3.** h, **4.** e, **5.** j, **6.** a, **7.** d, **8.** c, **9.** i, **10.** f

Reviewing Facts and Ideas

1. Spanish-speaking peoples and immigrants from Asia

2. Federal Housing Administration and Veterans Administration

3. A municipal charter gives the municipal government legal status and allows the community to have its own government.

4. mayor-council, commission, council-manager

5. Cities and suburbs in the South and West grew rapidly, cities in the Northeast and Midwest lost population, population of small towns and rural areas increased, people moved from inner cities to suburbs.

6. urban renewal program

7. Unemployment and a shortage of inexpensive housing are factors. In addition, many homeless people have personal problems such as alcoholism, drug addiction, a criminal record, and mental illness.

8. The cost is too high.

Applying Themes

1. In the strong-mayor system the mayor has power equal to that of council; in the weak-mayor system the council has most of the power.

2. The commission form combines executive and legislative power in one commission. Each commissioner heads a department.

3. Today, power is shifting to the suburbs as suburban population growth outpaces city population growth.

4. Answers will vary, but may include paying lower wages, tax and other incentives, lower land and construction costs, closer to growing markets.

Summary and Significance

Three out of four Americans live in metropolitan areas that include a large city and surrounding suburbs. Urban areas have adjusted to great shifts of population over the years. Today suburbs are growing faster than either cities or rural areas. Municipal charters provide three forms of government for urban communities—mayor-council, commission, and council-manager. Cities face serious problems in housing, transportation, drugs, crime, and decaying infrastructures. Beginning in the 1960s with help from the federal government, cities tried urban renewal programs, renovation, revitalization, and mass transit to address these issues. As federal and state funding decreased beginning in the 1980s, cities sought new approaches to their problems. More cities turned to consolidation of metropolitan governments, regional arrangements, annexation, and contracting for services.

Identifying Key Terms and Concepts

Fill in the blank with the letter of the correct term or concept listed below.

a. **consolidation**　　b. **suburbs**
c. **annexation**　　d. **metropolitan federation**
e. **infrastructure**　　f. **mass transit**
g. **incorporation**　　h. **renovation**
i. **revitalization**　　j. **gentrification**

1. Today more Americans live in _____ than in cities or rural areas.
2. Requirements for _____ usually include having a population of a certain minimum size and petitions signed by a specified number of residents.
3. Many cities have rewired old homes, installed new plumbing and rebuilt floors in various _____ projects.
4. Basic facilities such as streets, water lines, and public buildings make up what is known as the _____ of a city.
5. Sometimes called "displacement," _____ has often changed the essential character of an urban area.
6. By _____ urban communities may provide a single government for an entire metropolitan area.
7. A _____ is a form of government similar to the plan in the federal Constitution.
8. Through _____ a local government absorbs new territory in surrounding areas.
9. To promote economic growth local governments have tried _____ through large investments in new facilities.
10. Several financial setbacks have prevented cities from using _____ to solve their traffic problems.

Reviewing Facts and Ideas

1. **Identify** two main groups of people who migrated to United States cities beginning in 1945.
2. **Name** two federal programs that subsidized housing for families, primarily in the suburbs.
3. **Discuss** the main functions of a municipal charter.
4. **List** the three main forms of municipal government.
5. **Describe** four kinds of population shifts in metropolitan areas since 1950.
6. **Name** the federal government program that helped cities tear down deteriorating urban housing and build new apartment complexes.
7. **Discuss** the major causes of homelessness in the nation's cities.
8. **Identify** the main reason that many cities have not built mass transit systems.

Applying Themes

1. **Separation of Powers** Why is the separation of powers better illustrated by the strong-mayor system than by the weak-mayor system of municipal government?
2. **Comparative Government** How is the distribution of executive and legislative authority different

Critical Thinking Skills

1. Answers should include candidates will focus attention on the needs of these areas. If one candidate identifies more with the cities' needs, the other will probably address the needs of the suburbs.

2. State legislatures that redraw district lines are dominated by rural and city interests.

3. Local governments are responsible for much of these facilities. Citizens expect local governments to make the repairs. Federal and state governments will take a supporting role.

4. Answers will vary. Some will support prevention, some treatment, others controlling the supply.

in the commission form of municipal government than the other forms?

3. **Federalism** What factors contributed to the cities' declining influence in the federal government?

4. **Free Enterprise** What economic factors, do you think, attracted business into the South and West?

Critical Thinking Skills

1. **Predicting Consequences** Given the voting power of cities and suburban areas, what campaign strategies will presidential candidates likely adopt in coming elections?

2. **Drawing Conclusions** What political reality will prevent suburban areas from making very rapid gains in representation in state legislatures and in Congress in the next few years?

3. **Analyzing Information** Why will local governments probably pay the biggest share of the costs of repairing the nation's decaying infrastructure?

4. **Identifying Central Issues** In your view, which of the federal government's goals in dealing with the illegal drug problem is the most important? Why?

Linking Past and Present

Before 1950 few four-lane roads existed in the nation. In the 1950s the federal government began a massive interstate highway construction program. Huge cloverleaf interchanges connected these multi-lane systems. Then governments built giant bypasses to encircle the major cities. Today most of these highways are overflowing with traffic. Where is the worst interstate highway congestion in your area? What caused it?

Writing About Government

Persuasive Writing Mayors of large cities have not been as successful as they once were in getting federal funds to address city problems. What could a mayor say to the President to support the cities' cause? Write a short letter to the President explaining the need for federal money to support a particular project for your city.

Reinforcing the Skill

Demonstrating Reasoned Judgment Suppose that you are the mayor of a city that has a large and growing population of homeless people. Existing shelters for the homeless are crime-ridden and do not have enough space to shelter everyone who needs space. Most of the homeless people have no access to health care, and many of their children cannot attend school. Many are hungry. The following measures have been proposed. Read them, then answer the questions that follow.

1. The city should buy abandoned warehouses, renovate them, and turn them into temporary shelters.

2. The city should assign police officers to keep order in existing homeless shelters.

3. Church and community leaders should be consulted to see what services they might provide for homeless persons.

4. The city should provide transportation to take homeless children to school.

5. The city should open a free clinic to provide medical care for homeless persons.

6. The city should build low-rent permanent housing.

7. The city should operate soup kitchens.

8. The city should freeze rents at existing prices.

A. Write a sentence telling how each of the measures above might alleviate the problems of the homeless. Include at least one drawback to each.

B. If you had to choose only two of the proposals, which would you choose and why?

Investigating Further

1. **Individual Project** Investigate the government of your city or a nearby city by reading the newspaper. Answer the following questions: What kind of government does the city have? Who seem to be the key people involved in the issues? Is there general cooperation or strong rivalry among leaders?

2. **Cooperative Learning** Organize the class into several groups representing various interests that want to influence municipal government. For example, one group could call for more regular garbage collection. After research, the class should hold hearings to determine which need should be addressed first.

Reinforcing the Skill

A. 1. Additional shelters would provide more beds for the homeless, but buying and renovating buildings would be expensive. **2.** Police patrols would make existing shelters safer, but this would either cost money because more police would have to be hired or take police away from work they are currently doing. **3.** Private charities can provide some aid to the homeless, but their efforts cannot be closely controlled by the government and may not be reliable. **4.** Transportation to school would help to prevent homeless children from falling behind in school, thus dooming them to future problems, but would be expensive. **5.** A free clinic would ensure medical care for the homeless, but would be expensive to run. **6.** Building low-rent permanent housing would provide homes for some of the homeless, but such a project would take a long time and would be expensive. **7.** Government-run soup kitchens would ensure a steady supply of food for the homeless, but might duplicate private efforts. **8.** A freeze on rents might prevent more people from becoming homeless, but it would do nothing to help those who have already lost their housing and would be protested by landlords.

B. Answers will vary, but students should support their choices.

Investigating Further

1. Students' selections will vary.

2. Allow time for groups to make presentations to the panel.

Linking Past and Present
Students' choices will vary.

Writing About Government
Students' letters will vary, but they should use facts to support their requests.

Focus

Ask students what they think are the purposes of zoning regulations. *(control population density, separate manufacturing and residential areas)* Ask: Should government control how people use their private property? Tell students that the constitutional protection of private property is the subject of this case study.

Teach

Guided Practice

L1 Making Comparisons Have students compare the New York City zoning laws with those in Euclid, Ohio. Ask: How did each community solve the problem of public welfare versus the right of property owners to determine use of their own property? *(Both communities tried to develop zoning regulations that were oriented toward safety and protection of property value.)* Was the full use of the land denied property owners? What compromises must property owners make?

CASE STUDY

No person shall . . . be deprived of life, liberty, or property without due process of law; nor shall private property be taken for public use without just compensation.

—Fifth Amendment

No state shall . . . deprive any person of life, liberty, or property, without due process of law . . . .

—Fourteenth Amendment

Zoning: Controversy Over Regulation of Land Use

The Case

In the fall of 1990 the trustees of a prestigious village in New York State upheld an old zoning law that prohibited building accessory structures on the front half of housing lots. The question first arose when some village residents criticized freestanding basketball backboards. The old village ordinance dated back to the turn of the century and had been drawn up to prohibit placing horse hitching posts in front of houses. Following the residents' complaints, the ordinance was applied to the basketball backboards. Although the backboard owners protested, the restriction was enforced and the hoops became things of the past.

Since their inception in the early 1900s, zoning laws have stirred up controversy. They continue to do so today. In late 1991, for example, the New Hampshire Supreme Court found "snob zoning" illegal. It ruled that suburbs could not use zoning laws to prohibit low-income housing within their boundaries. Some wealthy residential districts had used this practice by requiring large-sized lots of one acre or more and certain types of home construction that put houses beyond the reach of all but the most wealthy. In New Hampshire the supreme court ruled that towns "may not refuse to confront the future by building a moat around themselves and pulling up the drawbridge." As yet, the United States Supreme Court has not ruled on this type of zoning legislation, but it has dealt with the question of whether or not zoning laws violate the Fifth or Fourteenth Amendments and the protection of private property.

Background

Comprehensive urban zoning traces its roots to New York City. As one zoning expert observes,

The birth of the zoning institution was in a year and in a city stirring with climactic events, New York was the city, 1913 the year.
Between 1913 and 1916, New York took the turbulence of more than a half-century of American and European experience and harnessed it with the nation's first comprehensive zoning law. More than a half-century later, most Americans were urban and most of their cities were zoned.
—SEYMOUR I. TOLL, 1969

More About the Case

Since colonial times, land use in the United States has been regulated according to a principle of English common law—"use your property so as not to injure another's." Such an approach, however, proved inadequate to the task of controlling the rapid urban growth of the late 1800s. Quickly, American cities began to pass ordinances that limited land use within their boundaries. In 1883, San Francisco restricted the location of certain industries. Then, during the 1890s, a number of cities, including Baltimore, Boston, and Indianapolis, limited the heights of new buildings. New York City's 1916 ordinance, however, was the first comprehensive zoning plan. Other cities soon adopted

What happened in New York began in 1913 with the establishment of the Heights of Building Commission. Its mission was to regulate skyscrapers and other buildings, particularly those near an exclusive neighborhood along New York's Fifth Avenue. At issue was the

> Seriously increasing evil of the shutting off of light and air [by the skyscrapers] from other buildings and from the public streets, to prevent unwholesome and dangerous congestion, both in living conditions and in street and transit traffic and to reduce the hazards of fire and peril to life. . . .
>
> —RESOLUTION, 1913

At the time the skyscrapers were considered to contribute to eye strain by shutting out sunlight available to office workers and to contribute to the spread of tuberculosis through overcrowding. Zoning also could be employed to maintain the exclusive nature of the Fifth Avenue residential area.

New York City's comprehensive zoning regulations sparked similar zoning ordinances in major cities across the United States in the 1920s. As a result, zoning ordinances were challenged in state and federal courts on the basis that building restrictions reduced the "normal value of . . . property" and deprived individuals of "life, liberty, and property without due process of law." The first zoning case reached the United States Supreme Court in 1926 in *Village of Euclid* v. *Amber Realty Co.*

Deciding the Constitutional Question The *Euclid* case reached the Supreme Court on appeal from a federal district court that had halted the enforcement of Euclid's zoning ordinance. As is true in most zoning cases, property values were a major issue. Land value issues frequently arose because early zoning ordinances usually were designed to maintain property values in residential areas at the expense of nearby land that was planned for commercial development.

During the early 1920s, Amber Realty had acquired land adjoining the wealthy and attractive residential area along Euclid Avenue in Euclid, Ohio. The company planned to hold the land for a time and then sell it at a profit as factory sites. The village, anxious to prevent undesirable changes, established districts zoned for certain types of use, from single

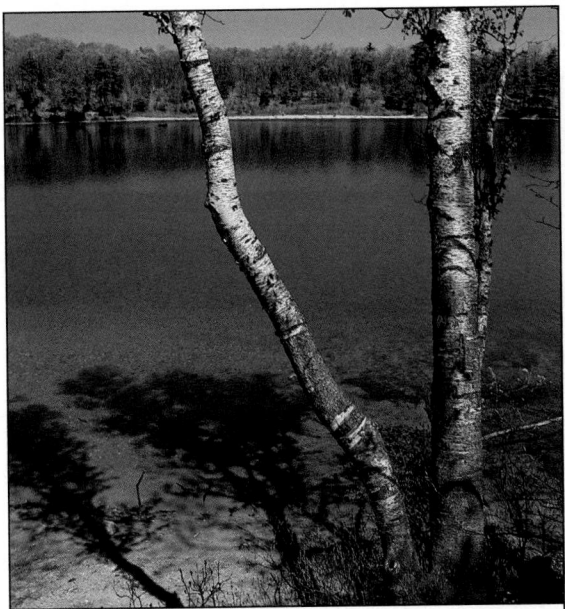

To Develop or to Preserve?
Immortalized in Henry David Thoreau's writings, scenic Walden Pond in Concord, Massachusetts, has been the focus of a long-standing zoning battle.

family to industrial. Amber's land along Euclid Avenue was zoned single- and two-family dwellings. Farther away from Euclid Avenue, apartment buildings were permitted. Farthest from the avenue, the zoning law permitted factories. Amber Realty immediately sued, arguing that the land's value had fallen from $10,000 an acre to no more than $2,500 an acre. Amber also claimed the new zoning ordinance violated the provisions of the Fourteenth Amendment.

Although the Ohio federal district court agreed with Amber Realty's argument, the Supreme Court did not. It overturned the lower court's decision and upheld Euclid's right to enforce its zoning regulations. The Court ruled "The ordinance under review, and all similar laws and regulation, must find their justification in some aspect of the police power, asserted for the public welfare." The Court went on to state that "it is enough for us to determine, as we do, that the ordinance in its general scope and dominant features . . . is a valid exercise of authority. . . ."

Although the ruling seemed to leave the door open for future cases, city leaders across the nation breathed sighs of relief as Euclid's zoning laws were upheld.

New York's system, and by the mid-1920s more than 30 million Americans—fully one-third of the country's urban population—lived in areas with some form of zoning controls.

Few of these areas linked their zoning to any kind of long-range land-use plans. Over time, however, most communities saw and corrected this problem. Even so, many of these communities continued to enforce outdated and irrelevant zoning requirements. Such requirements, some observers suggest, create much of the negative feeling about zoning.

L2 Summarizing Write *positive* and *negative* on the chalkboard. Then ask students to provide examples from the case study that indicate the positive and negative effects of zoning laws. (*positive: protects people's health, maintains property values, controls land use, prevents overdevelopment; negative: violates constitutional rights, segregates socio-economic classes, prevents many people from owning homes.*)

L3 Synthesizing Information Explain that in recent years environmental factors have become important in determining zoning laws. Some communities have been built over toxic waste sites. Ask: Do laws to prevent construction on these sites deprive property owners of their rights? (*The laws are intended to protect people's lives, which government is pledged to protect.*) Point out that the most famous example is the Love Canal community of Niagara Falls, New York. After evidence of the contamination became apparent, New York State bought the property and cleaned up the site. Ask: In such a case, what legal issues might arise? (*possibilities: determining worth of property no one wants, determining ultimate responsibility for the disaster, and so on*) Do students think the state was justified in its action? Have students support their opinions with evidence from the case study.

CASE STUDY

Independent Practice

L1 Research Have students research the zoning laws in their own community. Have them find out if their community maintains strict compliance of these codes or if individuals can appeal and ask for a variance or a change in the code to meet individual needs. Ask students to explain if a variance protects public safety and allows property owners freedom to use their property as they wish.

L2 Persuasive Writing Have students write an editorial in response to the following: Property owners should be able to build any structure they wish on their private property.

L3 Informative Writing Have students research the effects of various types of pollution on property values. Students can start by reviewing how New York State is trying to resell areas of the Love Canal community. Have students write a brief report on how zoning laws protect the environment.

Assess

Have students complete **Examining the Case.**

Close

Ask students what changes they foresee in their community's zoning laws. What might cause a community to change its zoning laws?

The Critics of Zoning Among the most outspoken critics of zoning laws is law professor Bernard H. Siegan, who argues that:

Many people appear to take it for granted that persons who own land have no inherent rights to do anything with it except what the government will allow. That notion, however, is totally inconsistent with the ideals of a free society in which people should be able to do as they please unless their acts clearly harm or interfere with the liberties of others. This is the nature of freedom. The exercise of freedom is meaningful only when it involves unpopular actions or expressions. Obviously there is never a problem in engaging in conduct everyone approves. But this infrequently occurs inasmuch as people differ greatly in interests and desires. In a free society, consequently, freedom should only be limited when its exercise actually diminishes someone else's freedom; surely not when it is merely contrary to the will of the majority. By that standard, freedom in the use of property has vanished in most of this country since those who control zoning do not have to justify it on any such grounds.

—BERNARD H. SIEGAN, 1976

Still other critics strongly oppose certain types of zoning restrictions that appear to be designed to protect communities from an "invasion" of different ethnic groups or socio-economic classes. This segregation is accomplished through zoning restrictions on land use. How is it done? In an article titled "The Battle of the Suburbs," *Newsweek* magazine explains:

Besides raising the prices of developing land, many suburbs impose so-called "Cadillac requirements." For example, building codes may call for relatively expensive materials, thus barring cheaper, factory-produced units; or they may require the construction of costly sidewalks, water lines and sewers before a house or apartment can be built. But the ultimate weapon of the exclusionists is what the open-door forces call "snob zoning." These are ordinances that permit only single-family homes to be built—and then only on relatively large 1- or 2- acre plots.

—NEWSWEEK, NOVEMBER 15, 1971

Today exclusionary zoning laws affect many Americans. A presidential zoning commission, for example, recently decided that exclusionary zoning laws are a factor putting many houses beyond the reach of many potential home buyers. How will New Hampshire's ruling against such zoning ordinances affect similar regulations in other states? The issue remains to be decided.

Significance

Zoning regulations and other land-use regulations seemingly affect a large number of Americans. As more people espouse NIMBY (Not In My Backyard) and demand stricter zoning laws, housing opportunities for minorities and low-income groups continue to shrink. In a somewhat similar fashion, environmental regulations restricting land use may deny certain property owners the full use of their land. For example, consider the 1991 case of a South Carolina resident. The resident was denied the right to build two homes on his oceanfront land by a state law designed to control beach erosion. The angry landowner argued that the government has made his land worthless and should pay him for his loss. A lower South Carolina court agreed and awarded the landowner $1.2 million. The state's supreme court, however, reversed the lower court's decision. The United States Supreme Court ruled that property owners may be entitled to compensation when government regulation deprives their property of all economic value.

Examining the Case

Reviewing Facts
1. Identify the grounds on which the Supreme Court upheld Euclid's zoning ordinance.
2. Explain the purpose of exclusionary zoning laws.

Critical Thinking Skills
3. Determining Relevance What was the relationship between skyscrapers and the development of comprehensive zoning ordinances in New York City?
4. Demonstrating Reasoned Judgment Do you think that zoning ordinances are justified? Why or why not?

Examining the Case Answers

1. Communities have a right to enforce zoning ordinances based upon their power to safeguard public welfare.
2. to limit access for certain ethnic or socio-economic groups
3. Laws were passed to prevent overcrowding and to protect exclusive neighborhoods.
4. Answers may vary, but many students might suggest that they are justified to protect property values and the public welfare.

Chapter 26
Organization of Local Government

Local government is the level of government closest to the people. It is the government of the county and the city, town, village, or suburb. Each person in the United States lives under one national government and one state government, but most people live under three or more local governments.

Although a strong tradition of local government exists in the United States, local governments have no legal independence. Established by the state, they are entirely dependent on the state governments under which they exist. The state may even abolish them if they so choose.

The United States has four basic types of local government—county, township, municipality, and special district. The **county** is normally the largest territorial and political subdivision of the state. **Townships** exist as units of local government in about half the states. A **municipality** is an urban unit of government—a town, borough, city, or urban district that has legal rights granted by the state through its charter. The **special district** is a unit of local government that deals with a specific function, such as education, water supply, or transportation.

Local governments provide their communities many services. One of the most important of these is education. Through taxes, the local school district generally provides most of the money for public schools. Zoning is a method through which local governments regulate the use of land and buildings. While zoning may provide for orderly growth, some critics believe that its restrictions adversely affect minorities or families with children.

Police and fire protection make up a large portion of local budgets. Water service, and sewage and sanitation are also the responsibility of local governments. These services are becoming very expensive because of the increasing cost of waste disposal. Often the question of who should pay for these services becomes a major issue in local politics. Maintaining streets and providing adequate transportation systems, administering social services, and providing recreation and cultural activities are also a part of local government functions.

Like individuals, governments make decisions about how to raise money and where to spend it. The economic decisions that governments make are more complicated than the average citizen's decision, however.

Government must weigh the requirements of general welfare against the available revenue. It must also consider the wants of individuals and interest groups. Sharp disagreements over which services or programs government should finance often arise. Should a local government spend money on a recreation program, or should it use this money to repave a road that might bring more business to local merchants? Should it try to support both programs by borrowing the money or seeking state or federal aid?

One of the oldest taxes, property taxes, once provided revenue for all levels of government. Today property taxes are the most important source of revenue for local governments, accounting for more than two-thirds of all their revenues.

Local governments must have sources of revenue other than property taxes. These include local income taxes, sales taxes, fines and fees, government-owned businesses, and intergovernmental revenue. The local income tax is a tax on a personal income. The sales tax is a tax on most items sold in stores. Fines paid for traffic, sanitary, and other violations, and fees for special services provide part of the income for local governments. States also permit local governments to borrow money in the form of bonds—certificates that promise to repay the borrowed money with interest by a certain date. Investors consider local government bonds good investments because their earned interest is not subject to federal income taxes. In addition to local sources of revenue, most local governments receive economic aid from state and federal governments.

Chapter 27
Governing Metropolitan Areas

Today three of every four people in the United States live in an urban area, either in a central city or a surrounding suburb. Nearly half the population lives in metropolitan areas of a million or more people. These are areas of rapid change, complex governmental issues, and sometimes huge societal problems.

The Office of Management and Budget has classified large urban areas as Metropolitan Statistical

Classroom Resources for Unit 9 Digest

Unit Digest Transparencies, Unit 9

Participating in Government, Unit 9

Use the Unit Digest to introduce, review, reteach, or condense specific chapters or the entire unit. The Unit Digest is enhanced by the corresponding transparencies and activities in the Teacher's Classroom Resources.

Focus

Provide students with copies of the telephone directory for the local government offices in your community. Select a number of offices at random and ask students what services they think these offices provide. Then have students discuss the following questions: Do these services duplicate those offered by state or federal government? Why or why not? What purpose, do you think, does local government play in the American political system? Close the discussion by mentioning that the role of local governments in the United States is the focus of this Unit Digest.

Teach

L1 Analyzing Ideas Draw a table on the chalkboard with *Mayor-council Form, Council-manager Form,* and *Commission Form* as horizontal headings and *Advantages* and *Disadvantages* as vertical headings. Ask students to name the advantages and disadvantages of these three forms of local government. Enter responses in the appropriate columns. Then have students discuss the following: Given the kinds of problems facing local governments today, what is the most efficient governmental form? Why?

Interpreting Visuals
Display transparency 9 from the *Unit Digest Transparencies* in the Teacher's Classroom Resources and use the accompanying teaching strategy, student activity, and student test to teach about local government.

L3 **Persuasive Writing** Point out that two diametrically opposed approaches have been suggested to improve local government. Citing unnecessary and costly duplication of services, some officials have suggested consolidating cities or townships with counties to form one "super" local government. Others, stressing the need for greater citizen involvement at the local level, have called for the creation of neighborhood or district councils. Have students write a newspaper editorial supporting or opposing one of these approaches. Have students read their editorials to the class.

Assess

Check for Understanding
Have students complete **Synthesizing the Unit.**

Close

Have students discuss the following questions:

What changes will take place in local government over the next 10 years? What changes *should* take place?

Areas. More than half the American population is clustered in these urban communities. A **metropolitan area** or metropolis is a large city and its surrounding suburbs. Such an area may also include small towns that lie beyond the suburbs.

Many United States cities became major urban centers during the Industrial Revolution. Immigration was responsible for much of their growth. During the 1970s and 1980s, population growth shifted to the South and West, while the 10 largest cities in the Northeast and Midwest lost population. The other area of rapid growth was in the suburbs. Between 1950 and 1990, middle-class families flocked to residential suburbs. Federal money for highways and home loans induced this movement. These shifts in population affected a change in the centers of political power.

States provide for city, town, and village governments in the United States. Such governments are called either **municipal governments** or city governments. Although urban communities differ greatly in size and other ways, they are all municipalities and use some form of municipal government.

Today urban areas in the United States use one of the three basic forms of municipal government: the mayor-council form, the commission form, or the council-manager form.

The **mayor-council form** follows the traditional concept of the separation of powers. Executive power belongs to an elected mayor and legislative power to an elected council. All cities except one have unicameral, or one-house, councils.

The **commission form** combines executive and legislative power in an elected commission, usually of five to seven members. Each commissioner heads a specific department and performs executive duties related to that department.

Under a **council-manager form**, legislative and executive powers are separated. The council of between five and nine members acts as a legislative body and makes policy for the municipality. A manager carries out the council's policies and serves as chief administrator.

Whatever their form of government, many urban areas in the United States today confront the problems of housing shortages, inadequate transportation, pollution, poverty, and crime. Although these problems are most acute in big cities, they can also be

---

found in the surrounding suburbs and outlying small towns.

Many of America's older cities also have a declining **infrastructure**—basic facilities. Much of it is in dire need of repair or replacement. An economist who is an expert on the subject has warned, "Much of our infrastructure is on the verge of collapse."

People easily identify issues such as crime, decaying infrastructure, and traffic congestion as urban problems. Cities today, however, face a more vital problem—one that has to do with their identity.

In the 1960s the nation presumed that something had to be done to address cities' problems. The United States Senate held hearings on the "crisis" of the cities and the government's role in meeting it. While today people still identify cities with these problems, the federal and state governments are not as likely to grant cities huge amounts of money to address them.

Why are federal and state governments less responsive to city problems? Perhaps these governments have changed their priorities. A federal commission on Urban America in the Eighties suggested that social and economic migration to the suburbs was a natural, even an advantageous, development that should not be discouraged. It added that federal aid to the cities should not try to stop this trend.

Clearly, the suburbs were becoming powerful economic and political entities. The growth of the suburbs signalled this change in political power. After the census of 1990, new district lines gave suburbs more seats in Congress and state legislatures than they ever had. The nation's focus seemed to be shifting from city problems to suburban opportunities. If cities were to survive as healthy communities, they would have to solve their own problems.

Synthesizing the Unit

Recalling Facts
1. Define county, township, municipality, special district, metropolitan area, municipal government, mayor-council form, commission form, council-manager form, infrastructure.
2. Demonstrate that all United States citizens live under several governments.

Critical Thinking
3. Making Comparisons How do the various levels of government differ?

Synthesizing the Unit Answers

1. Definitions of terms appear on the pages indicated: **county,** 799; **township,** 799; **municipality,** 799; **special district,** 799; **metropolitan area,** 800; **municipal government,** 800; **mayor-council form,** 800; **commission form,** 800; **council-manager form,** 800; **infrastructure,** 800

2. In any location in the United States, a citizen's life is affected by the federal government, a state government, and one or more local governments, such as county, township, municipal, or special district governments.

3. Answers will vary, but most will mention the following differences: size—in terms of numbers of employees, jurisdictions, and budgets; services provided; types of authority exercised; and governmental structure.

Comparative Government and Economic Systems

UNIT 10

Chapter 28
Comparing Systems of Government

Chapter 29
Comparing Economic Systems

Chapter 30
An Interdependent World

Introduce

Unit Objectives

After studying this unit, students should be able to:
- Compare political institutions, processes, and civic values of the United States with those of other nations.
- Compare the relationship of government and economic systems in the United States with this relationship in other nations.

Unit Overview

Unit 10 introduces students to the governmental and economic systems of other nations. It also focuses on the challenges facing the world's nations as the twenty-first century approaches.

Chapter 28 outlines the structure and functions of the governments of Great Britain, France, Japan, China, and Mexico.

Chapter 29 describes the three types of economic systems in the world today—capitalism, socialism, and communism.

Chapter 30 introduces students to the challenges they face as citizens of the modern world— global economic stability, international security, and environmental protection.

**10
UNIT DIGEST**

Use the Unit Digest on pages 883–884 to introduce, review, reteach, or condense the information in this unit.

Unit Project

Have students work cooperatively to develop a questionnaire on the greatest challenges facing the world as the twenty-first century begins. Then organize students into three teams and assign each the task of administering the questionnaire to one of the following groups: students in other classes, school faculty, adults in the community. Suggest that teams review the information in Chapter 11 before designing a group sample. Teams should then collate results and present them to the class. Representatives from each team should then combine results into a report on the five greatest challenges facing the world today. Display the report on the bulletin board.

Introducing the Unit

In this unit students will learn that even though nations share political and economic ideologies, their systems of government might differ. Then mention that political and economic systems differing greatly from those of the United States will also be discussed in this unit.

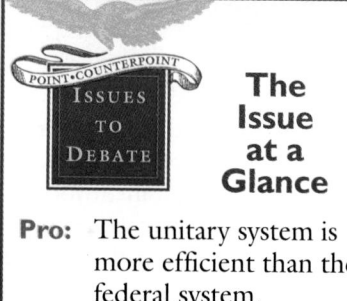

The Issue at a Glance

Pro: The unitary system is more efficient than the federal system.

Con: The federal system satisfies American political needs.

Focus

Remind students that the Framers of the Constitution were wary of authoritarian government. Ask: How did they guard against this in the Constitution they created? *(a federal system in which national and state governments share power, and that further divides power into legislative, judicial, and executive authority)*

Point out that the strengths and weaknesses of that federal system are debated in this reading.

Teach

Guided Practice

Ask: What do critics of a federal system cite as its basic weaknesses? *(It lacks centralized authority to deal with problems that are national in scope.)* Ask students to cite examples of national problems. Do they think the current system is dealing with them effectively? Why or why not? *("Yes" answers should cite growth of national government's power and authority; "no" answers may cite the reading's criticisms of federalism.)* Ask students to identify the two principles of American government that Pfaff attacks in the selection from his newspaper column. *(checks and balances, separation of powers)* Remind students that these were the very safeguards the Framers created to combat abuse of power.

Is the Unitary System Better Than Our Federal System?

In 1831 and 1832, French aristocrat Alexis de Tocqueville studied social and political life in the United States. When he returned to France he published his observations. Among these observations was an analysis of the nation's system of federalism. "One can hardly imagine," he wrote, "how much this division of sovereignty contributes to the well-being of each of the states which compose the Union."

De Tocqueville, however, was not completely captivated by the system. He was equally capable of noting a possible flaw or weakness in the system as well as its virtues, for as he observed:

The federal system not only has no centralized administration, and nothing that resembles one, but the central government is imperfectly organized, which is always a great cause of weakness when the nation is opposed to other countries which are themselves governed by a single authority.

—ALEXIS DE TOCQUEVILLE, 1840

Today, social scientists are still divided in their opinions of this nation's federal system of government.

Pro

In the minds of some observers, federalism lacks the centralized authority needed to deal with conditions that are now national in scope; conditions, that if left to state governments will not be solved. One commentator noted:

The states have been unable to follow a single course even in such comparatively noncontroversial areas as

are covered by the so-called uniform state laws. If minimum standards are desired for the nation as a whole in a particular policy area such as health or welfare, it is the central government that must act to assure these ends. To leave the matter exclusively to the states means that there will be a variation in standards from very low to quite high.

—EDWIN W. WEIDNER

Not all of those who support a strong centralized government see the nation's problems resting only with the states. In their view, the Constitution should be amended to allow for more cooperation among the various branches of the federal government. Many people also favor establishing a system of government similar to Great Britain's parliamentary system. During the Bicentennial celebration of the Constitution, a column in the *Los Angeles Times* echoed that sentiment.

In other democracies the executive is formed by men and women drawn from the parliament and responsible to it. The American system was created to be different. The branches of government deliberately were set against one another in order to check abusive power. It is an extremely wasteful and inefficient system. . . .

The United States is and will remain, in this respect, a flawed great power. The flaw does not lie in the national character, but in the nation's Constitution, 200 years old this year and likely to be around for a long time to come.

—WILLIAM PFAFF, MAY 14, 1987

In the same year the Committee on the Constitutional System, a non-partisan group, reported some of its conclusions.

More About Issues to Debate

One of the best ways to illustrate the complex way services are funded and provided in a federal system is to look at social security programs. For example, about 100 million workers are covered by unemployment insurance laws. To provide these benefits, employers are taxed at a uniform rate in each state based on their payrolls. This money is collected and deposited in the unemployment trust fund of the United States Treasury, where it is credited to the state from which it came. States can withdraw money from their accounts only to pay benefits. Yet within this centralized system, it is the states that each have the responsibility for developing their own unemployment compensation policies. Thus

The Constitution now bars members of Congress from serving as heads of administrative departments or agencies or holding any other executive-branch position. . . . If the barrier were removed from the Constitution, Presidents would have the option of appointing leading legislators to cabinet positions, and legislators would have the option of accepting such offers, without being required to give up their seats in Congress. Such ties might encourage closer collaboration and help prevent stalemates.

—COMMITTEE ON THE CONSTITUTIONAL SYSTEM, 1987

Power Flows from the Center
France's unitary government features a strong executive with a bicameral legislature, the Parliament, consisting of the National Assembly and the Senate.

Con

Opposition to a stronger, perhaps unitary government is not uncommon. Many of those opposed see a new type of federalism emerging that can meet the challenges that face the nation. Federalism, in their view, is hardly static and has changed over the years, particularly since the New Deal.

What emerged from this change is best described by political scientist Daniel J. Elazar as "that complex mechanism of intergovernmental relations, characteristic of the American federal-state-local partnership known today as cooperative federalism." Elazar went on to comment:

Within the large area of concurrent powers provided, explicitly or implicitly, by the federal constitution, the federal and state governments have been able to divide responsibility among their separate jurisdiction . . . or to divide the works of government cooperatively, sharing responsibility in specific programs, with all units directed toward common goals that extend along the entire chain of concurrent powers ("cooperative federalism").

—DANIEL J. ELAZAR, 1964

Many who support the federal system believe cooperative federalism will answer the nation's problems.

At the same time, opposition to a parliamentary system of government has grown. Historian Arthur Schlesinger, Jr., stated:

The argument for the parliamentary system is that the fusion of powers will assure cooperation and partnership between the executive and legislative branches. In fact, fusion of powers assures the almost unassailable dominance of the executive over the legislative.

—ARTHUR SCHLESINGER, JR., 1982

Many Americans fear that changes in the federal system "would leave Americans with an overly powerful central government that could all too easily disregard public opinion in pursuit of its own agenda."

The Debate Continues

Both sides in the controversy are at a standoff. As one observer noted: "Outside of Washington when you talk about federalism you are likely to make people's eyes glaze over." If the federal system is flawed, it seems reasonable to assume that it will remain so in the future unless the debate is resolved.

Examining the Issues

Recalling Facts
1. Explain why de Tocqueville felt the United States might be at risk in a great war.
2. Identify the benefits the Committee on the Constitutional System felt would be gained by allowing members of Congress to serve in the cabinet.
3. Describe what Arthur Schlesinger, Jr. believes is wrong with a parliamentary system.

Critical Thinking Skills
4. Identifying Central Issues Why do you think some people are opposed to the federal system of government?
5. Drawing Conclusions Do you agree with the statement that "a unitary system of government is more beneficial for a nation's people"? Why or why not?

---

weekly benefits vary widely from state to state.

The Social Security Act also began a federal program known as Aid to Families with Dependent Children to help needy families. Like unemployment, the administration of this program is also complex. The cost of the program is shared by local, state, and federal authorities. The federal government sets basic guidelines, but implementation is left to the states, which determine minimum standards for clothing, food, and shelter. As a result, the state with the highest benefits provides five times the monthly amount provided by the state with the lowest benefits.

Ask for students' opinions about whether the Framers were successful in achieving their goal. Do they think that increased central authority, as in the British system, would be an improvement?

Discuss the possibility of adapting a unitary system of government. What would be some advantages and disadvantages? *(Obviously fewer people involved in implementing policy would make government more efficient, and yet eliminating layers makes government less responsive. New rivalries and conflicts could emerge.)*

Independent Practice

Have students write a paragraph to summarize each side's argument in this debate.

Assess

Have students complete **Examining the Issue.**

Answers

1. Its federal system might weaken its unity.
2. might encourage cooperation between executive and legislative branches
3. executive dominance over legislative branch
4. Answers may cite poor cooperation and competition among levels of authority, weakness and division.
5. Students should support their conclusions with information from the reading.

Close

Ask students if they would be willing to give up some of their freedom in exchange for a perfect system of government that is able to take care of every problem they—and all society—have.

Chapter Organizer

Objectives	Special Feature Pages	Supplemental Materials
Section 1 Great Britain *pp. 806–810* **1.** Outline the structure of the British government. **2.** Compare parliamentary government to presidential government. **3.** Identify the role of political parties in a parliamentary system.	Point/Counterpoint: Is the Unitary System Better Than Our Federal System? pp. 802–803 Global Connection: Comparing Governments: Forms of Democracy p. 808	Guided Reading Activities Reproducible Lesson Plans Enrichment Activities 28 Section 1 Quiz Testmaker Chapter Transparencies 28 SAT Practice Test Writer's Guidebook
Section 2 France *pp. 811–815* **1.** Relate the powers of France's president. **2.** Describe the relationship between the branches of French government. **3.** Discuss the role of political parties in the government of France.	Focus on Freedom: Declaration of the Rights of Man p. 814	Guided Reading Activities Reproducible Lesson Plans Section 2 Quiz Testmaker Government Themes Transparencies 29 SAT Practice Tests Writer's Guidebook
Section 3 Japan *pp. 816–819* **1.** Discuss the origin and purpose of Japan's constitution. **2.** Describe the Diet and its relation to Japanese bureaucracy. **3.** Explain the effect of having one majority party on the Japanese government.		Guided Reading Activities Reproducible Lesson Plans Section 3 Quiz Government Themes Transparencies 30 SAT Practice Tests Writer's Guidebook
Section 4 The People's Republic of China *pp. 820–824* **1.** Relate how China's political background led to communist rule. **2.** Outline the Chinese Communist party organization. **3.** Explain the relationship between the Communist party and the government.	Critical Thinking Skills: Identifying Alternatives p. 824	Guided Reading Activities Reproducible Lesson Plans Section 4 Quiz Government Themes Transparencies 31 Skill Reinforcement Activities 28 SAT Practice Tests Writer's Guidebook
Section 5 The United States of Mexico *pp. 825–829* **1.** Summarize Mexico's federal system. **2.** List the powers of Mexico's president. **3.** Discuss the political influence of the Institutional Revolutionary party.	Participating in Government: Serving in the Peace Corps p. 826 Personal Perspectives: Lech Walesa on the Polish Economy p. 829	Guided Reading Activities Reproducible Lesson Plans Participating in Government 28 Primary and Secondary Source Readings 28 Reteaching Activities 28 Section 5 Quiz; Chapter 28 Tests Testmaker Limited English Proficiency Activities 28 Government Themes Transparencies 32 Audio Cassettes (English and Spanish)

If time does not permit teaching this chapter, assign the Chapter 28 summary in the Unit 10 Digest on pages 883–884.

Key To Ability Levels

Teaching strategies have been coded for varying learning styles and abilities.

L1 Level 1 activities are **basic** activities and should be within the ability range of all students.

L2 Level 2 activities are **average** activities and should be within the ability range of the average to above-average student.

L3 Level 3 activities are **challenging** activities designed for the ability range of above-average students.

LEP These activities should be within the ability range of **Limited English Proficiency** students.

Multicultural Activities

Attitudes of ethnic Americans toward the government in their countries of origin can influence both their political party affiliation and United States policymaking. Since 1959, when Fidel Castro took power in Cuba, south Florida—especially Dade County where Miami is located—has had a large Cuban community. Many are exiles who left Cuba following Castro's takeover. Believing the Republican party was most strongly anti-Castro and anticommunist, many have joined it. In 1991 the Republican party of Dade County included 85 percent of the area's Cuban Americans. Cuban Americans have also formed lobbying groups to work for a return to democracy in Cuba. Have students research the ways Cuban American citizens and interest groups have worked to end communism in Cuba.

Many of the nation's newest ethnic groups came to this country as a result of political upheaval in their homelands. Southern California has over 40,000 Cambodians. Orange County, California, is home to more than 80,000 Vietnamese Americans. Over 12,000 Hmong people of Laos live in St. Paul, Minnesota. Many Southeast Asians first entered the United States as refugees. From 1952 to 1980, United States law defined a refugee as "a person fleeing from a Communist-dominated country . . . or from any country within the Middle East." The Refugee Act of 1980 broadened the definition to include immigrants who could not return to their own country because of persecution due to "race, religion, nationality, membership in a particular social group, or public opinion." Have students research the process for obtaining refugee status.

Chapter Resources

Readings for the Student

Barber, Benjamin, and Patrick Watson. *The Struggle for Democracy.* Little, Brown, 1988.
Comparative Politics 90/91: Annual Editions Series. Dushkin, 1990.
Curtis, Michael, ed. *The Great Political Theories.* Avon, 1981.
Rourke, John T. *Taking Sides: Clashing Views on Controversial Issues in World Politics.* Dushkin, 1991.
Smith, Geoffrey, and Nelson W. Polsby. *British Government and Its Discontents.* Basic Books, 1981.
Ward, Harriet. *World Powers in the Twentieth Century.* Heinemann, 1985.

Readings for the Teacher

Hourani, Albert. *A History of the Arab Peoples.* Belknap/Harvard, 1991.
Mufson, Steven. *Fighting Years: Black Resistance and the Struggle for a New South Africa.* Beacon Press, 1990.
Richardson, Bradley M., and Scott C. Flanagan. *Politics in Japan.* Little, Brown, 1984.
Rose, Richard. *Politics in England.* Little, Brown, 1980.

Multimedia

Videocassettes
Capitalism and Communism: Comparison and Contrasts. Associated Press. (v/c, 48 minutes)
Poland—The Morning After. (*Frontline* series). Ofra Bikel. (v/c, 60 minutes)

Software
Election Simulation. Intellectual Software. (Apple disk). A simulation of a British election, allowing students to predict and test election outcomes.
Foreign Governments and United Nations. SEI. (Apple disk and guide or IBM disk and guide). Students test knowledge of world affairs and systems of monarchy, fascism, and socialism.
Revolutions: Past, Present, Future. Focus Media. (5 Apple disks, 4 TRS80 disks). Students compare American, French, and Russian Revolutions and explore key factors that lead to revolution.

Comparing Systems of Government

Introduce

Chapter Overview

Chapter 28 introduces students to the governments of five countries—Great Britain, France, Japan, China, and Mexico. For each country, the chapter examines the structure of the government, the role of key government officials, and the way in which government officials carry out the business of government. Comparisons among the governments of these five countries—and with American government—are highlighted throughout the chapter.

Section 1 discusses the limited constitutional monarchy of Great Britain.

Section 2 describes the strong presidential system of France.

Section 3 examines the relationship between parliamentary government and bureaucracy in Japan.

Section 4 assesses the communist system of government in China.

Section 5 reviews the dominance of the executive branch in Mexican government.

Chapter 28 Themes

Note this chapter's themes on the chalkboard. Have students copy the themes into their notebooks, one theme to a page. As they read this chapter, have students construct a "theme map" for each theme. They should draw lines from each theme and, at the end of these lines, note the main ideas related to that theme. At the end of the chapter, have students compare their maps.

CHAPTER 28

In ceremonies marking his ascension to the throne in 1990, Emperor Akihito pledged to observe the constitution of Japan, which echoes the United States Constitution.

804 UNIT 10: COMPARATIVE GOVERNMENT AND ECONOMIC SYSTEMS

About the Chapter Opener

Teaching With Illustrations Mention that Japan's standing among the world's nations is seen in the fact that Emperor Akihito's coronation was attended by heads of state, royalty, and other dignitaries from about 150 countries. Then point out that the ceremonies included certain rites of the Shinto religion that are centuries old. Ask students to note traditional features shown in the picture on pages 804 and 805. *(Akihito's robes, the setting, and so on)* Also during the ceremony, the emperor pledges to observe the constitution of Japan. Ask students how this pledge parallels the oath of office the United States President makes on Inauguration Day.

Chapter Preview

Overview

Each nation's system of government is unique to its historical development and its culture.

Objectives

After studying this chapter, you should be able to:

1. **Summarize** the governmental structure of a constitutional monarchy in a parliamentary system.
2. **Discuss** the power and influence of the president in the French system of government.
3. **Compare** parliamentary and presidential systems that have one, two, or more major parties.
4. **Evaluate** the methods that the Communist party has employed to govern the People's Republic of China.
5. **Examine** the roles of the president and of the majority party in governing Mexico.

Themes in Government

This chapter emphasizes the following government themes:

- **Comparative Government** Governments exercise varying degrees of power in democratic and authoritarian systems. Sections 1, 2, 3, and 5.
- **Growth of Democracy** Monarchy loses power to the representatives of the people. Section 1.
- **Political Processes** The number of parties in a political system and their relationship to government influence lawmaking. Sections 2, 3, 4, and 5.
- **Civil Liberties** People risk their lives for basic freedoms. Section 4.

Critical Thinking Skills

This chapter emphasizes the following critical thinking skills:

- Identifying Assumptions
- Demonstrating Reasoned Judgment
- Recognizing Ideologies
- Synthesizing Information

CHAPTER 28: COMPARING SYSTEMS OF GOVERNMENT   805

Introducing the Chapter

Introduce the topic of comparative government by asking students to suggest why countries have different forms of government. Then ask them to volunteer any information they have on the five governments discussed in the chapter. Note responses on the chalkboard. Then point out that analyzing different forms of government will help students develop a better understanding of political processes. Further comparing these governments with the American system will enable students to evaluate the strengths and weaknesses of their own government.

Chapter Project

Have students work together to construct a large wall chart that compares the five governments discussed in this chapter. You might organize students into five groups and make each group responsible for entering information about one government on the wall chart. Topics groups should focus on include *type of government, constitution, branches of government,* and *political parties.*

> **Linking Past and Present**
> From earliest times, the Chinese believed that their emperors ruled by divine right, that they had the Mandate of Heaven. Peace and prosperity was an indication that the Mandate of Heaven had been bestowed upon a ruler. Conversely, famine, defeat in war, or internal unrest signified that a ruler had lost the Mandate of Heaven. Some banners paraded by students in Tiananmen Square in 1989 said that the old Communist party leaders had lost the Mandate of Heaven and ought to be replaced.

Setting the Scene Comparative government is the branch of political science concerned with the analysis and interpretation of government structures and functions in different countries. While some general studies have been undertaken, most political scientists make comparisons of two or three governments. These comparisons often emphasize the differences as much as the parallels among governments. While some general principles have been drawn from these studies, most throw light on a particular subject, such as the nature of constitutional monarchy.

Focus

Bell Ringer

While attendance is being taken, have students complete the following two sentences:

A monarchy is . . .
A republic is . . .

Motivating Activity

Discuss students' Bell Ringer responses. *(A monarchy is a form of government headed by a king or queen who attains office through heredity. A republic is a form of government in which power rests with the people and is exercised by their elected representatives.)* Point out Great Britain is a monarchy, while the United States is a republic. Even so, the governments of these two countries share many common features. Ask students to suggest what these common features are. Then ask them to suggest how the governments of Great Britain and the United States are different. Tell students to assess the accuracy of their suggestions after they complete this lesson.

Vocabulary Precheck

Write the key terms and concepts for this section on the chalkboard. Ask students to use those that they know in sentences. **LEP**

Caption Answer
Over the centuries the monarch's powers were stripped away and Parliament's powers increased.

CONNECTIONS

History
The actual title of leader of the government was "First Lord of the Treasury." *Prime minister* was not officially recognized as a title until 1937.

---

1 Great Britain

Historically the United States derived much from Great Britain's system of government. Britain's political system embraces many of the ideals held by Americans today. Political scientist S.E. Finer wrote:

Britain provides an outstanding example of the liberal-democratic type of government. The regime is stable and has been so for generations, and so are the individual governments generated . . . by it. The executive enjoys wide authority and extensive administrative capabilities, and yet, as a whole, government is both representative of public opinion, and liberal in its concern for minorities.
—S.E. FINER, *COMPARATIVE GOVERNMENT,* 1970

Although the United States and Great Britain share many basic principles of government, there are many differences in the structure of their political systems. Both are democracies, but the United States is also a republic. Great Britain, in contrast, is a constitutional monarchy, with a king or queen as the head of state. Although Great Britain has a constitutional government as does the United States, its government is based on an unwritten constitution that has developed over hundreds of years.

The British Constitution

Unlike the United States Constitution that sets forth the structure of the government, the British constitution does not consist of a single document.

Only parts of the British constitution are in written form. The written parts consist of centuries-old court decisions, charters such as the Magna Carta and the English Bill of Rights, and laws passed by Parliament—the British legislature. Important parts of the British constitution, however, are unwritten and consist of customs and traditions of government generally accepted by the British people. For example, no written document spells out that a **prime minister** elected by Parliament is to head the British government. Rather, this method of electing a prime minister has come about over the years as a result of tradition.

Long Lived the Queen
The 63-year reign of Queen Victoria, portrayed by Sir Francis Grant, is the longest in British history.
History Why is the monarch's power ceremonial?

SECTION PREVIEW

Objectives
After studying this section, you should be able to:
- Outline the structure of the British government.
- Compare parliamentary government to presidential government.
- Identify the role of political parties in a parliamentary system.

Key Terms and Concepts
prime minister, ministers, parliamentary government, unitary government

Themes in Government
- Comparative Government
- Growth of Democracy

Critical Thinking Skills
- Identifying Assumptions
- Demonstrating Reasoned Judgment

---

806 UNIT 10: COMPARATIVE GOVERNMENT AND ECONOMIC SYSTEMS

Classroom Resources for Section 1

- 📁 Guided Reading Activities
- 📁 Reproducible Lesson Plans
- 📁 Enrichment Activities 28
- 📁 Section 1 Quiz

- 🔲 Testmaker
- Chapter Transparencies 28
- SAT Practice Tests
- Writer's Guidebook

Because there is no one written document setting forth the form and operation of the government, the British constitution needs no complicated amendment procedure. Parliament may change the constitution by passing a law that overturns precedent. Such flexibility has permitted the British constitution to grow and change with the times. One change is the role of the monarch. At one time strong monarchs tightly controlled Great Britain. Today, however, the British monarchy is a ceremonial position with little real power. This constitutional change in Britain's system of government took place gradually over time as the power of the Parliament increased.

Not all Britons, however, are content with the way the constitution has developed. A writer in the London-based *The Economist* criticized the nation's constitution as

A constitution which evolved for an imperial nation-state and stopped evolving shortly afterwards. It ain't broke, but . . . its proper place is in a museum. It does not need to be fixed. It needs to be replaced.

—*THE ECONOMIST, MAY 11, 1991*

The vast majority of the British people, however, support the country's political system with its constitutional monarchy.

The British Monarchy

A century ago a British writer noted with some alarm that the monarch, Queen Victoria, still held the same powers as earlier monarchs. In theory, at least, she could declare war and refuse to accept acts of Parliament. Actually, the people did not expect that the monarch would exercise these powers, because it would be considered unconstitutional. Today the monarch's few governmental responsibilities are mere formalities. The king or queen, for example, appoints the prime minister and the cabinet that make up the British government. The monarch's appointment power, however, is only ceremonial. The majority party of the House of Commons selects the prime minister and cabinet. In short, it is said, "the British monarch reigns but does not rule." The monarchy, however, is above party politics and stands as a symbol of the unity of the nation.

Parliament

Parliament, the national legislature, holds almost all governmental authority in Great Britain. Parliament is a bicameral (two-house) legislature, consisting of the House of Commons and the House of Lords. Both have a role in enacting legislation, but

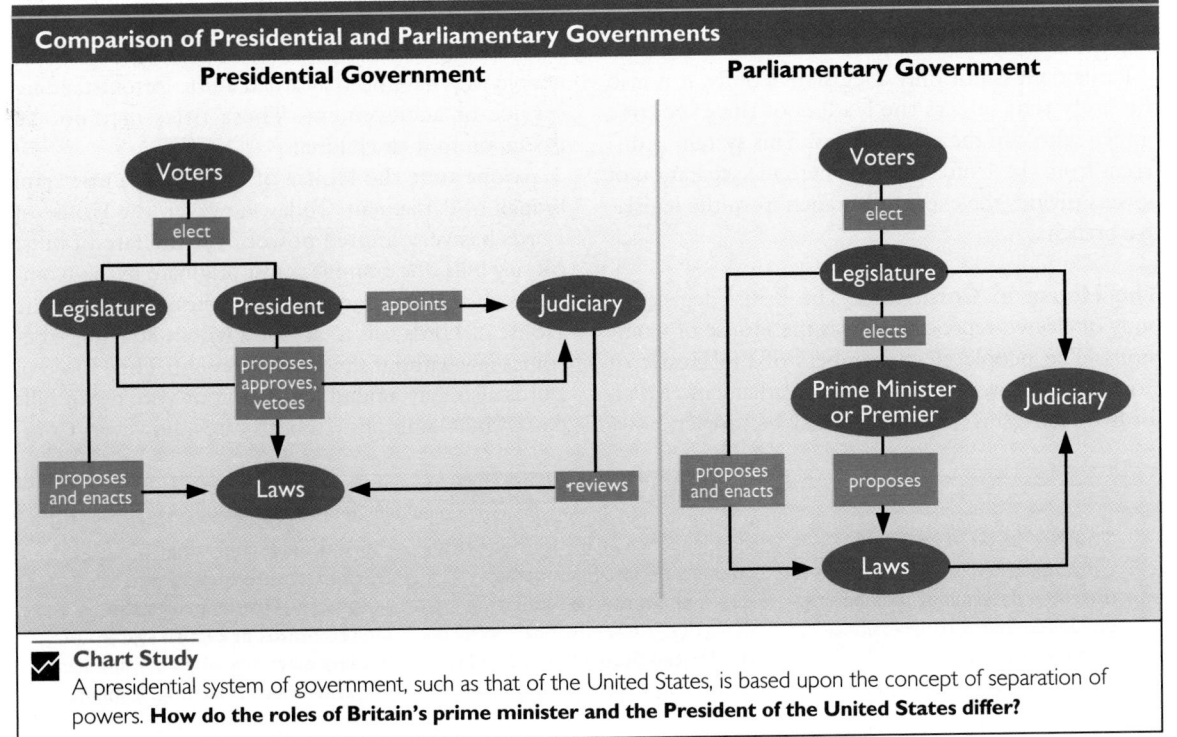

Comparison of Presidential and Parliamentary Governments

Presidential Government

Parliamentary Government

✓ Chart Study
A presidential system of government, such as that of the United States, is based upon the concept of separation of powers. **How do the roles of Britain's prime minister and the President of the United States differ?**

CHAPTER 28: COMPARING SYSTEMS OF GOVERNMENT   807

Background

Parliament won ascendancy over the monarchy in 1688, when it deposed James II and invited his daughter, Mary, and her husband, William of Orange, to assume the throne. The crown officially recognized parliamentary supremacy the following year, when William and Mary signed the English Bill of Rights. This document stated that the monarch could not levy taxes, change laws, or maintain an army during peacetime without consent of Parliament. It also guaranteed free elections, frequent meetings of Parliament, and freedom of speech for MPs. While England remained a monarchy, the power to rule now rested with Parliament.

Teach

Guided Practice

Interpreting Visuals Display transparency 28 from the *Chapter Transparencies* in the Teacher's Classroom Resources and use the accompanying teaching strategy and student activity to teach how American government and British government compare.

L2 Analyzing Ideas Draw a table on the chalkboard using *Executive Branch* and *Legislative Branch* to head horizontal rows and *United States* and *Great Britain* for vertical columns. Ask volunteers for information to complete the chart. Then ask students to compare the executive and legislative branches of each nation. Next ask them to discuss the relationship between the executive and legislature in the two countries. Finally, have them discuss the strengths and weaknesses of each system.

L3 Debate Select a number of students to debate the following statement:

Times change, and governments must adjust to these changes. Unwritten constitutions provide the best means for such adjustments.

Chart Study Answer
The prime minister is a member of Parliament. The President and Congress are separate.

Independent Practice

L1 Constructing a Flow Chart Refer students to the flow chart on page 414 that shows how a bill becomes a law in Congress. Then have students construct a similar flow chart showing the process of lawmaking in the British Parliament. **LEP**

GLOBAL CONNECTION

Point out that of all the world's democracies, Switzerland holds the most elections. At the same time, however, it has one of the lowest voter turnout rates.
Examining the Connection Answer: *Most democracies have large voting populations, but direct democracy functions well only when a relatively small number of voters are involved.*

STUDY GUIDE

Critical Thinking Answers
Because senators serve relatively long terms and lords do not have to stand for election, they can largely ignore politics and deliberate more fully and objectively than representatives and MPs.

Answers will vary. Britain has the advantage of not having to wait for a designated election time, but such systems can be less stable.

Focus on Government
Video 59
Making Connections: Parliamentary vs. Presidential Systems
Running Time: 1:47
Videodisc 3, Chap. 59
VHS Tape 3, Begins 54:12

GLOBAL CONNECTION

Comparing Governments

Forms of Democracy The government of Switzerland is one of the world's most democratic. The Swiss Constitution of 1848 established a federal republic with political powers divided between the central government and the cantons (states).

Some Swiss cantons are direct democracies. People vote by a show of hands at an open-air meeting.

Swiss citizens control laws through the referendum and the initiative. The referendum allows voters to accept or veto a law. A popular vote must be held if 50,000 people request it. The initiative allows citizens to change government policy or amend the constitution. A vote on specific issues requires a petition signed by 100,000 people.

Examining the Connection
Why do you think so few examples of direct democracies exist in the world today?

---

the House of Commons has much greater power than the House of Lords.

Parliament is not only a legislative body, it is also the body that selects the leaders of the executive branch who run the government. This system is different from the United States where the separation of powers divides the executive branch from the legislative branch.

The House of Commons The British legislative body of elected representatives is the House of Commons. The people elect members of the House of Commons, known as Members of Parliament (MPs), for five-year terms. Their terms may be shorter, how-

ever, if Parliament is dissolved for new elections before the end of the five-year period.

The House of Commons, which consists of 651 Members of Parliament, meets in a rather small chamber in Westminster. This ancient, majestic Parliament building is located on the Thames River in London. Five rows of benches line each side of the chamber. The front row on each side is reserved for the leading members of each major party. Behind them sit the rank-and-file MPs, who are called backbenchers. The members of the party in power sit on one side of the chamber. The opposition party members sit on the other side.

The House of Commons determines Great Britain's legislative and financial policies. While any MP may introduce legislation, most bills are introduced by the government, the majority party. After the government introduces a bill, members debate it on the floor of the Commons and then send it to one of eight standing committees. These committees are not highly specialized as are the committees in the United States Congress. Instead, each committee considers bills dealing with a wide range of subjects. Committees work out final details of all bills and then must report out every bill to the House of Commons for a vote. A majority vote is needed for passage.

The House of Lords The House of Lords, as its name implies, is primarily an aristocratic body. About 800 of its approximately 1,200 members have inherited titles. In addition, there are about 350 life peers, people who have been awarded a title for outstanding service or achievement. These titles may not be passed on to their children.

At one time the House of Lords was a powerful branch of Parliament. Today, however, the House of Lords has very limited power over the fate of bills. Money bills, for example, must originate in the Commons. If the Commons passes a money bill and the House of Lords fails to act on it within 30 days, it becomes law without the Lords' consent. The House of Lords also may amend legislation or vote down bills passed by Commons. In both cases, however, Com-

---

STUDY GUIDE

Themes in Government
Comparative Government Expertise often determines membership on United States congressional committees.
Growth of Democracy After

independence, many former British colonies retained democracy.
Critical Thinking Skills
Identifying Assumptions Why do the United States Senate and the British House of Lords spend

more time deliberating?
Demonstrating Reasoned Judgment Do you prefer the United States or British system of holding elections when confidence in government is lacking? Explain.

Cooperative Learning Activity

Organize students into groups of six and tell the groups their task is to create a museum exhibit that illustrates important developments in British parliamentary democracy. Suggest that they divide their exhibit into three sections: an important person, a major event, and an influential idea. Have groups brainstorm to make their selections. Then

have group members take on particular tasks—some might undertake research, others might design the exhibit, still others might construct exhibit items or write an exhibit catalog. Have groups display their finished exhibits for other government and civics classes.

---

mons may overrule the upper chamber and make their own bill a law.

Because the House of Lords has so little real authority over legislation, some critics argue that it is not needed. As one critic put it:

The system is as flawed as a tone-deaf orchestra. It is absurd to retain a second chamber which depends so heavily on the medieval hereditary system abandoned by every other modern country. It is inefficient to run a parliament which has so little . . . ability to scrutinize, question and challenge the executive—and where so much debate takes place in a two-thirds empty chamber, late at night.
—THE ECONOMIST, MAY 11, 1991

The House of Lords does serve an important function. Because its members do not have to stand for election, they can ignore politics and deliberate more calmly and objectively than MPs. As a result, when the House of Lords reviews legislation passed by the Commons, it may suggest improvements acceptable to the lower chamber. Also, the Lords' ability to delay legislation may keep the legislature from acting rashly in certain situations.

The National Government

One of the most striking differences between the United States and British governments is that Great Britain has no separation of powers or balance of powers between the executive and legislative branches. In Great Britain the leaders of the executive branch are members of Parliament. The leader of the party that has a majority in the House of Commons becomes the prime minister and picks the other **ministers**, appointing each to head an executive department and serve in the cabinet. For this reason the British system is often called a **parliamentary government**. Most of the ministers are members of the majority party in the House of Commons, while a few may be drawn from the House of Lords.

Since 1979, when Margaret Thatcher became Great Britain's first female prime minister, the Conservative party has maintained a majority control of the House of Commons. Later, Thatcher became the first prime minister to be elected to three consecutive terms in this century. Losing the support of her own majority party, she resigned in November 1990. At that time Conservative party leader John Major became prime minister.

Major Succeeds Thatcher
Following Margaret Thatcher's resignation in 1990, John Major became the British prime minister. **Political Processes How is the prime minister selected?**

In Great Britain the prime minister and the cabinet together are referred to as the *Government*, a word equivalent to the American use of the word *administration*. Thus, while Americans refer to the Bush administration, the British speak of the Major Government.

The Government is responsible to Parliament. It must always have the support of a majority of the House of Commons. If the Government should lose a vote on an important issue, it is said to have "lost the confidence of the House" and must resign. Parliament is then dissolved, and new general elections are held. Even though MPs are elected to five-year terms, when Parliament is dissolved, they must run for re-election.

Sometimes the Government dissolves Parliament even while it still has a majority in the House of Commons. This dissolution may happen if a Government senses that public support for it is so strong that it will elect more members of its party than it currently has. Then, at the prime minister's request, Parliament is dissolved and a general election is held to select members of the Commons.

CHAPTER 28: COMPARING SYSTEMS OF GOVERNMENT   809

L2 Chronology Have students research the development of the British Parliament. Have them use their findings to construct an illustrated time line showing the major events in this development from the signing of the Magna Carta to the present day. Have students display their time lines on the bulletin board.

L3 Media Have students watch a session of Prime Minister's Question Time on C-SPAN. (Program schedules may be obtained from C-SPAN, 400 North Capitol Street, NW, Washington, DC 20001.) Then ask them to write a brief essay answering the following:

Prime Minister's Question Time has been called "democracy in action." Do you agree or disagree with this characterization? Give reasons for your answer.

Caption Answer
by the majority party in the House of Commons

Assess

Check for Understanding
Have students complete Section 1 Review on page 810.

Meeting Objectives
Each section objective is tested by the Section Review questions that follow it in parentheses.
• Outline the structure of the British government. (2, 3, 4, 6, 7)
• Compare parliamentary government to presidential government. (5)
• Identify the role of political parties in a parliamentary system. (4, 8)

Special Needs Strategy

Language Disability Students with expressive language difficulties may have problems performing many different classroom activities. For example, they may not easily be able to ask questions in class. Such students are often aided in this task if they have time to prepare in advance. Assign small groups of students to be "questioners of the day." Ask them to prepare some simple questions about the content of this section, such as, "What is the Magna Carta?" or "What is a unitary government?"

Evaluate

📁 Section 1 Quiz

💿 Testmaker

Reteach

Have students summarize in a paragraph the structure of the British system of government. Select students to read their paragraphs to the class.

Enrich

📁 Have students complete activity 28 in *Enrichment Activities* in the Teacher's Classroom Resources.

Close

Remind students of the comparison of the governments of the United States and Great Britain that they made in the Motivating Activity. Ask them to use information learned in this lesson to modify their comparison.

CONNECTIONS

History

The first British political parties—the Tories and the Whigs—developed during the 1670s over who should succeed the childless Charles II. The Tories favored a strong hereditary monarch, and were willing to accept Charles' brother James, even though he was a Catholic. The Whigs, however, would accept only a Protestant monarch.

Political Parties

Since the end of World War I, two major parties, the Labour party and the Conservative party, have dominated British political life. The Labour party relies on the support of working people, especially those in the country's strong labor unions. The Conservative party receives its support mainly from middle-class and upper-class Britons, although many workers not in unions also vote Conservative. Each party has controlled the Government several times since 1940.

The Liberal party is now a small third party, although until the 1920s it was one of the major parties. The newer Social-Democratic party broke away from the Labour party in 1981, won seats in Parliament, then merged with the Liberal party.

Because the Government depends on maintaining its majority in the Commons, party discipline is much stricter than in the United States Congress. MPs are expected to support the Government on all major votes. In general elections the parties decide which candidates will run in which districts, and voters tend to choose candidates on the basis of party rather than personal appeal. This practice is in sharp contrast to decentralized politics in the United States where members of Congress must live in their districts or states.

In the House of Commons, the minority party is officially called the opposition. Its purpose is to watch the Government's actions with a critical eye. The leaders of the minority party are organized into a shadow cabinet, a group that would form the Government when and if its party assumed power.

Four times each week, the opposition makes use of a "question time" to quiz the prime minister or cabinet members about government policies, plans, and actions. Often the questions focus on a certain Government program or on a cabinet minister who is the subject of criticism in the press. Most of the time, the prime minister and the cabinet can answer to the satisfaction of the members of their own party. Sometimes, however, the criticism causes the Government to lose support of some party members, who then "bolt" to the opposition. If the Government loses enough support, it may lose a vote of confidence and be forced to resign.

Local Government

Great Britain has a **unitary government,** one in which governmental power is centralized in the national government. This contrasts with the federal government of the United States, where governmental power is shared between the national government and the governments of the 50 states.

The central government controls local governments in Great Britain. The main units of local government are county boroughs and administrative councils. Members of local governmental units are elected, but far fewer people vote in local elections than in general elections for Parliament. Local government is responsible for police and fire services, public education, health services, housing, streets, roads, and transportation.

---

1 SECTION REVIEW

Section Summary
Great Britain is a constitutional monarchy with a democratically elected parliamentary government.

Checking for Understanding
Recalling Facts
1. Define prime minister, ministers, parliamentary government, unitary government.
2. Identify three written components of the British constitution.
3. Describe the current role of the British monarch.
4. Explain what happens when the Government in Britain loses a vote in Parliament.

Exploring Themes
5. Comparative Government How does government in the United States compare to government in Great Britain?
6. Growth of Democracy What changes in the power of the British monarch indicated a growth of democracy in Great Britain?

Critical Thinking Skills
7. Identifying Assumptions What do the changing roles of the House of Lords and the House of Commons show about the British attitude toward democracy?
8. Demonstrating Reasoned Judgment When would it be wise for the prime minister to dissolve Parliament and order new elections?

Section 1 Review Answers

1. Definitions of terms appear on pages indicated: **prime minister,** 806; **ministers,** 809; **parliamentary government,** 809; **unitary government,** 810
2. centuries-old court decisions, charters such as the Magna Carta and the English Bill of Rights, and laws passed by Parliament
3. The monarch's responsibilities are mere formalities—nominally appointing the prime minister and the cabinet, for

example. The British monarch, however, does serve a useful function as a symbol of the unity of the nation.
4. It is said to have "lost the confidence of the House" and must resign. Parliament is then dissolved and new general elections are held.
5. *Great Britain:* constitutional monarchy, no separation of powers between executive and legislative branches, unitary government, parliamentary system, autocratic remnants; *United States:* federal republic, separation of

legislative and executive branches, leaders of both democratically elected
6. The monarch lost powers such as control over the military and retained only a ceremonial role. Parliament, representatives of the people, assumed authority.
7. It indicates that the British believe democratically elected representatives should have more power.
8. when the prime minister's policies are popular and could strengthen the majority party in Parliament

France has a democratic government that is in some ways similar to Great Britain's government. Both nations are unitary states. In other ways the French government resembles the United States government. For example, France is a republic and has a written constitution. Still, in many ways the French government has its own unique features.

The government of France under its present constitution, adopted in 1958, is known as the Fifth Republic. Beginning in 1791, France has had four other republics, and 16 separate constitutions, 2 of which were never applied at all. In particular the Third and Fourth Republics proved to have serious shortcomings in their ability to govern the country. An important reason for their failures was that the chief executive had only very limited power. The more powerful legislature was divided among a fairly large number of competing political parties.

Before 1958 France had a number of large parties and dozens of smaller ones. Political divisions ran so deep that party members found compromise on any issue difficult. Under those circumstances it was difficult for any political party or group of parties to form a stable government, receive majority support, and stay in power. Between 1946 and 1958, for example, France had 27 different governments under 17 premiers. The average life span of a government during the Fourth Republic was less than 6 months. As one professor noted, "France was not ruled; she was administered." Fortunately, the nation's desperate situation changed with the adoption of the 1958 constitution that provided for a very strong president and a relatively weak legislature.

The Last Ruling Bonaparte
The president of France's Second Republic, Napoleon III, proclaimed himself emperor in 1852. **History**
How many republics have there been in France?

The President's Powers

Until the Fifth Republic, the office of the president of France was similar in function to that of the British monarch. During the Fourth Republic, for example,

---

SECTION PREVIEW

Objectives
After studying this section, you should be able to:
■ Relate the powers of the president of France.
■ Describe the relationship between the executive and legislative branches of the French government.

■ Discuss the role of political parties in the government of France.

Key Terms and Concepts
premier, left wing, right wing, department

Themes in Government
■ Comparative Government
■ Political Processes

Critical Thinking Skills
■ Recognizing Ideologies
■ Demonstrating Reasoned Judgment

Focus

Bell Ringer

While attendance is being taken, have students write what they think is the significance of the words *Liberty, Equality, Fraternity.*

Motivating Activity

Discuss students' Bell Ringer responses. Mention that while "Liberty, Equality, Fraternity" is the motto of the Fifth Republic of France—the present-day French government—it originally was the slogan of the French Revolution of 1789. Ask students what important American document these words suggest. *(the Declaration of Independence, which states that "all men are created equal" and that liberty is an "unalienable right")* Point out that similar ideas fired the revolutions that led to the creation of the American and French republics.

Vocabulary Precheck

Call on students to read aloud the definitions of this section's key terms and concepts from the Glossary. Then have volunteers use each term or concept in a sentence. **LEP**

Caption Answer
five

Classroom Resources for Section 2

📁 Guided Reading Activities
📁 Reproducible Lesson Plans
📁 Section 2 Quiz
⊞ Testmaker

📔 Government Themes Transparencies 29
  SAT Practice Tests
  Writer's Guidebook

Teach

Guided Practice

L1 Explaining Ideas Write on index cards various terms, titles, and names that appear in this section—Fifth Republic, President, François Mitterrand, Edith Cresson, for example. Put the cards in a large box or bowl and have students pick one. Ask students to explain the role in French government of the items on their cards.

Interpreting Visuals Display transparency 29 from the *Government Themes Transparencies* in the Teacher's Classroom Resources and use the accompanying teaching strategy and student activity to teach the structure of the French government.

Caption Answer
The French president is elected by popular vote, not by an electoral vote.

─────────── CONNECTIONS ───────────

Political Processes
The president, Charles de Gaulle said, is "responsible for the fate of the nation." The premier's function, in contrast, "is to run the executive, to direct current policy and to deal with day-to-day contingencies."

---

the president performed as a figurehead who represented the nation on ceremonial occasions such as the opening of hospitals and the launching of ships.

The 1958 constitution helped transform the office of president into the most powerful position in the government. Today the president of France, who serves a seven-year term, is the only member of the government directly elected by voters of the nation at-large.

During a presidential election, all political parties may put forward candidates. With multiple candidates it is common that none receives a majority of the votes. When this occurs, a second election is held. This runoff election is between the two candidates who received the most votes in the first election.

As the only nationally elected official, the French president often claims to speak for the entire nation. The first president of the Fifth Republic, for example, was the national World War II hero General Charles de Gaulle. He summed up the position and power of the presidency in 1964, explaining that "the indivisible authority of the state is completely delegated to the president by the people who elected him."

Much like chief executives in other democracies, the president of France is responsible for negotiating treaties, appointing high officials, and acting as chair of the high councils of the armed forces. In addition, the French president has two special powers—the right to appeal directly to the people by means of a referendum and dictatorial powers in times of national emergency. In 1962 President Charles de Gaulle ordered a referendum to approve a constitutional amendment providing for the direct election of the president, rather than by an electoral college. Voters approved the referendum with a 62 percent majority.

The president maintains contact with the legislative branch of the French government through a **premier**, whom the president appoints. (*Premier* is the French word for "first" and is the name given to the French equivalent of prime minister.) The premier, in turn,

Leader by Compromise
In 1988 Socialist leader François Mitterrand was re-elected president of France. **Comparative Government How does the election of the president in France differ from that in the United States?**

names ministers, who form the cabinet. Together they conduct the day-to-day affairs of the government. Theoretically, the premier and the cabinet are responsible to the National Assembly—the lower house of the French Parliament. Unlike in the parliamentary system in Great Britain, however, the premier and the ministers are not members of the Assembly. They may, however, sit in the Assembly and defend their programs.

In practice, the premier and the cabinet answer to the president rather than the National Assembly. In regular meetings with the premier and the cabinet, the president makes sure that they continue to guide the president's program.

Under the constitution the president also has the authority to dissolve the National Assembly and call for new elections. This power may be used if the president loses the support of a majority of the Assembly. With this power even the threat of dissolving the Assembly may be enough to force the deputies to accept the president's leadership.

─────────── STUDY GUIDE ───────────

Themes in Government
Comparative Government A weak executive led to new constitutions in both France (1958) and the United States (1789).
Political Processes A referendum

defeat in 1969 forced de Gaulle to step down from office.

Critical Thinking Skills
Recognizing Ideologies How do left-wing and right-wing parties

differ on making changes?
Demonstrating Reasoned Judgment Why does the lower house of Parliament in France have more power than the upper house?

Background

The 1958 French constitution created the dominant executive office of president. However, the constitution was quite vague in defining exactly what were the powers of the president. As a result, the actions of Charles de Gaulle and his successors established the limits of presidential power. For example, the constitution did not assign responsibility for foreign policy to any particular branch of government. De Gaulle simply declared that it was within the presidential realm. Since that time, conducting foreign policy has been one of the president's duties.

The Role of the Cabinet

Before the 1958 constitution, cabinet ministers were chosen from the legislature, as in Great Britain. At that time, when they left the cabinet, they returned to their seats in the legislature. Today legislators who become cabinet members must resign their seats. Later, when they leave the cabinet, they may not return to their former seats until they are reelected. This requirement prevents former cabinet members from returning to the legislature as part of the opposition that tries to bring down the government.

The cabinet maintains strict control of the legislative process. First, the cabinet sets the agenda for the legislature, and all bills introduced by cabinet ministers take priority over other matters. Such bills can be modified in only minor ways, and debate over some matters, such as the budget, is limited. Members of the National Assembly, for example, may not introduce bills that would increase spending or reduce taxes. If the budget is not acted on within a set period of time, it goes into effect without the legislature's approval.

The government can also declare a vote on an important bill to be a "matter of confidence." The bill then automatically becomes law unless the National Assembly passes a motion of censure against the government. Such a motion, if passed, forces the government to resign.

The French Legislature

The French legislature is called Parliament. A bicameral body, it consists of the National Assembly and the Senate. The National Assembly is the lower house, the Senate is the upper house.

The French Parliament meets for two sessions a year. The first, which begins in October, lasts for 80 days. The second session starts in April and cannot last for more than 90 days. As a result, the Parliament meets for less than 6 months each year, a situation that limits its legislative role.

The Legislators The National Assembly's 577 members are elected for 5-year terms. Members may, however, face reelection if the National Assembly dissolves before their terms expire.

Electoral colleges in local and regional districts select the 321 senators for 9-year terms. Their role in the legislative process is largely limited to delaying legislation. Actual legislative power rests with the National Assembly.

Powers of Parliament France's current constitution was designed to limit the powers of the legislative branch. The Parliament, for example, may pass legislation only on matters specified in the constitution such as civil rights, election procedures, criminal procedure,

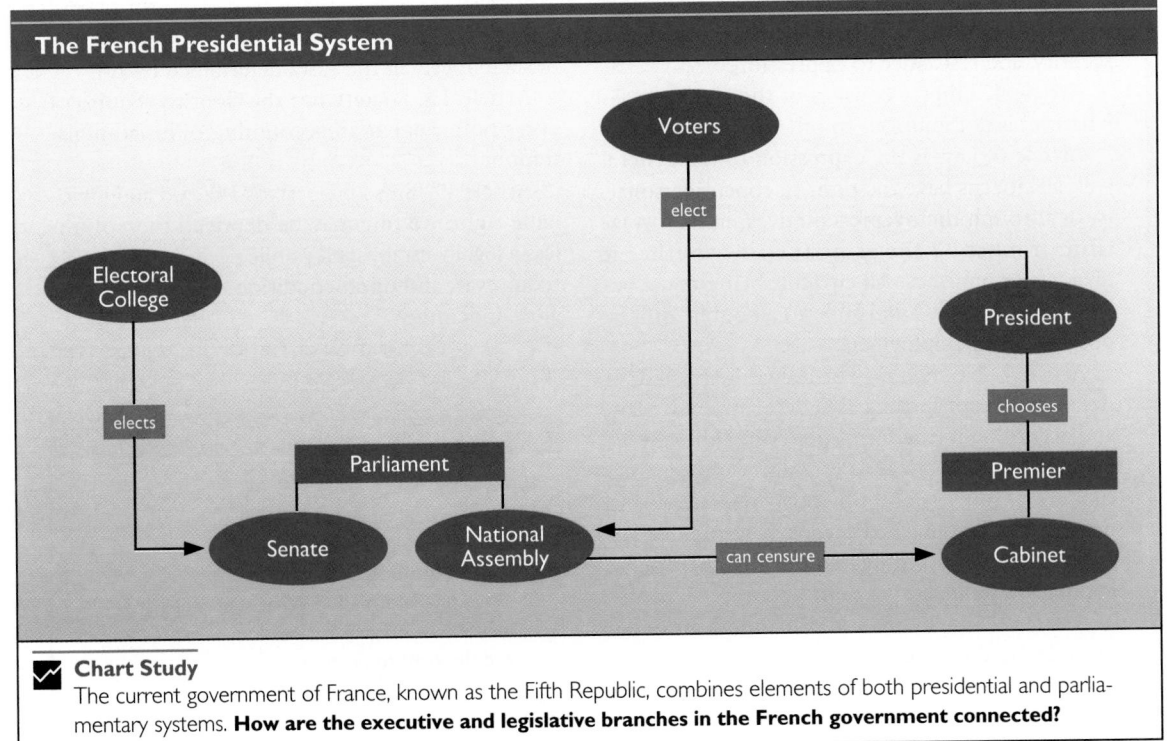

The French Presidential System

✔ **Chart Study**
The current government of France, known as the Fifth Republic, combines elements of both presidential and parliamentary systems. **How are the executive and legislative branches in the French government connected?**

Cooperative Learning Activity

Organize students into groups of five and tell groups that their task is to create some form of game that tests knowledge of the French governmental system. As examples of games suggest a form of "Scrabble" that involves only terms related to French government and politics, a board game similar to "Chutes and Ladders" where players advance only after correctly answering question cards, or a jigsaw puzzle of a diagram such as that on page 813. Once groups have decided on the games they will create, group members should divide tasks, such as obtaining materials, designing the game, writing instructions, and so on, among themselves. Have groups exchange completed games.

L3 Analyzing Ideas Quiz the class on the presidential form of government by asking: Which powers do the French president and the United States President have in common? Which powers does the French president possess that the United States President does not? Which powers does the United States President possess that the French president does not?

Then have students discuss the following: Which leads to greater political stability—the French presidential system or the United States presidential system? Why?

Independent Practice

L1 Geography Provide students with outline maps of France. Ask them to use atlases in the library to draw in the boundaries and names of the departments. Have students title their maps and add a brief explanation of the origin of the department system. (*In 1789 the National Assembly, in an effort to nationalize the administration of local government, created the department system.*) **LEP**

L2 Making Comparisons Have students create a table on French political parties using such headings as *Major Parties* and *Source of Support*. Have them extend the table by adding information on political parties in Great Britain and the United States. Then have them write a paragraph answering the following questions: Which parties in the three countries correspond to each other? How do their sources of support compare?

Chart Study Answer
The president is connected to the legislature through the premier and cabinet; the National Assembly may remove the premier, but the president may dissolve the National Assembly.

The first Declaration of Rights was presented to the National Assembly by the Marquis de Lafayette on July 11. In writing the draft, Lafayette had sought the help of the American ambassador to France, Thomas Jefferson.

Answers

1. They have rights to liberty, property, security, resistance to oppression, free speech, and a free press; are equal before the law; and are equally eligible for public office.

2. No one can be accused, arrested, or detained except in cases determined by law. Everyone is presumed innocent until proven guilty.

3. Answers will vary, but may include: Freedom of expression is necessary in order for people to seek truth. Property rights are important because all people deserve to be rewarded for their work.

Assess

Check for Understanding

Have students complete Section 2 Review on page 815.

Meeting Objectives

Each section objective is tested by the Section Review questions that follow it in parentheses.

• Relate the powers of the president of France. (2, 5, 8)
• Describe the relationship between the executive and legislative branches of the French government. (3)
• Discuss the role of political parties in the government of France. (4, 6, 7)

---

and national defense. On matters not specified in the constitution, the executive is able to enact laws by decree without the approval of Parliament.

For a bill to become law in France, it must be passed by both houses of Parliament and signed by the president. When the two houses pass different versions of the same bill, the premier appoints a committee to work out a compromise. If no compromise can be reached, the government has the right to ask the National Assembly to make the final decision. In such a case, the bill becomes law without the Senate's approval.

The National Assembly also has a degree of control over the executive branch. While the president has the power to name the premier, only the Assembly has the power to remove the premier. It exercises this power either through a censure motion or a vote of no confidence.

Political Parties While France still has many small political parties, the 1958 constitution encouraged small parties to combine into larger parties. The national election for the presidency helped bring this about.

Still, France has several major parties and a number of smaller ones. Generally speaking, the major parties can be grouped according to whether they are **left wing** or **right wing**. To the left of center, for example, are the Socialists and Communists. At the right of center are the Gaullists and the Union for French Democracy (UDF) of Valéry Giscard d'Estaing. Recent developments have brought most of the major parties close to the center of the political spectrum, and

---

DECLARATION OF THE RIGHTS OF MAN

In one night the National Assembly of France accomplished what it would take some nations 100 more years to achieve. It destroyed the old feudal order. In the Declaration of the Rights of Man, in August of 1789, the National Assembly announced the principles of the modern state, based on unity and law.

Article 1. Men are born and remain free and equal in rights. . . .

Article 2. The aim of every political association is the preservation of the natural and inalienable rights of man; these rights are liberty, property, security, and resistance to oppression.

Article 4. Liberty consists of the power to do whatever is not injurious to others. . . .

Article 6. Law is the expression of the general will; all citizens have the right to concur personally, or through their representatives, in its formation; it must be the same for all, whether it protects or punishes. All citizens, being equal before it, are equally admissible to all public offices, positions, and employments. . . .

Article 7. No man may be accused, arrested, or detained except in the cases determined by law, and according to the forms prescribed thereby.

Article 8. The law is to establish only penalties that are absolutely and obviously necessary; and no one may be punished except by virtue of a law established and promulgated prior to the offense and legally applied.

Article 9. Every man is presumed innocent until declared (proven) guilty. . . .

Article 10. No one is to be disquieted because

of his opinions, even religious, provided their manifestation does not disturb the public order established by law.

Article 11. Every citizen may speak, write, and print freely, subject to responsibility for the abuse of such liberty in the cases determined by law.

Article 15. Society has the right to require of every public agent an accounting of his administration.

Article 17. Since property is a sacred and inviolable right, no one may be deprived thereof unless a legally established public necessity obviously requires it, and upon condition of a just and previous indemnity.

—DECLARATION OF THE RIGHTS OF MAN, 1789

Examining the Document

Reviewing Facts
1. State how all citizens are equal.
2. Explain the rights of an accused person.

Critical Thinking Skills
3. Evaluating Information What supporting arguments can you give for freedom of expression and the right to property?

Critical Thinking Activity

Recognizing Ideologies Write the following on the chalkboard and have students identify each as relating to ideologies of the left, right, or center.

making wholesale changes in society *(left)*
providing a "safety-net" of basic welfare programs *(center)*

allowing businesses to operate without government interference *(right)*
requiring some government regulation of business *(center)*
reducing the size of government *(right)*
providing a comprehensive welfare system *(left)*

they are commonly referred to as left-centrist and right-centrist parties.

All of France's major political parties are represented in the National Assembly. Unlike Great Britain, however, the French people do not tend to identify exclusively with any party, except, perhaps, the supporters of the Communist party. The Communist party, which once was a major political force, today is only one of a number of small parties. One Paris-based correspondent speculated on the decline of the Communist party:

The problem with the French Communist party is less that people do not know what it stands for than that they know all too well. Elsewhere in Europe, communists are rushing to reform or abolish themselves. In France the party under Mr. Georges Marchais seems determined to learn and forget nothing. Mr. Marchais diagnoses his critics as suffering from anti-communist fever, as if it were winter flu. He is a survivor, but time is against his style of communism.
—THE ECONOMIST, FEBRUARY 11, 1990.

Just as French voters shift parties from election to election, politicians may switch from one party to another. President François Mitterrand, elected president in 1981, and his predecessor, President Valéry Giscard d'Estaing, switched parties during their political careers. Even so, some generalizations about France's political parties are possible. Today, for example, the strong Socialist party draws much of its support from teachers, civil service workers, skilled workers, and middle-class people. Meanwhile, the nation's farmers and business leaders tend to favor the right-of-center political parties, such as the Union for French Democracy.

In recent parliamentary elections, French political parties have formed coalitions when no single party has controlled a majority of the seats in the National Assembly. Although Socialist party leader François Mitterrand won reelection as president in 1988, the Socialists failed to gain a majority in the Assembly. Later, Premier Edith Cresson had to gain help from other parties to get the government's program through Parliament. To gain support, Premier Cresson had to make certain compromises. She observed, "One always needs to govern more in the centre than one wants. Compromises are sometimes necessary."

French Local Government

The unitary French government does not share its power with local governments. France has one of the most highly centralized governments of all the democracies in Europe.

France is divided into 96 **departments**, or territories. The national government in Paris appoints a commissioner to administer each department. When President Mitterrand assumed office in 1981, he resolved to give the individual departments more say in their own affairs. So ingrained was the practice of central control that he met considerable resistance to his proposed changes from local officials and even from the people. Nevertheless, the central government gave more authority to local officials in 1982.

---

2 SECTION REVIEW

Section Summary
The French constitution of 1958 provided a strong president and parliamentary democracy.

Checking for Understanding
Recalling Facts
1. Define premier, left wing, right wing, department.
2. Discuss the difference between the French offices of president and premier.
3. Compare the powers of the French Parliament to the powers of the United States Congress.
4. Identify four French political parties.

Exploring Themes
5. Comparative Government What powers does the President of France have that the President of the United States does not have?
6. Political Processes What effect does the large number of political parties in France have on the election of that nation's president?

Critical Thinking Skills
7. Recognizing Ideologies What evidence suggests that French politics has become more moderate and centrist in recent years?
8. Demonstrating Reasoned Judgment What evidence suggests that the expansion of presidential powers has brought political stability to France?

CHAPTER 28: COMPARING SYSTEMS OF GOVERNMENT 815

Evaluate

📁 Section 2 Quiz

🖥 Testmaker

Reteach

Have students write a brief paragraph that provides supporting details for the following:

The office of president is supreme over all other branches of the French government.

Enrich

Ask students to write biographical sketches of one of the presidents of the French Fifth Republic—Charles de Gaulle, Georges Pompidou, Valéry Giscard d'Estaing, or François Mitterrand. Have students read their sketches to the class.

Close

Conduct a class debate on the advantages and disadvantages of unitary government and federal government.

CONNECTIONS

Language
The terms used to describe the spectrum of political opinion—*right wing, center,* and *left wing*—date from the French Revolution. In the legislature of the 1790s, conservatives tended to sit on the right of the room, while moderates sat in the center, and radicals sat on the left.

Section 2 Review Answers

1. Definitions of terms appear on pages indicated: **premier,** 812; **left wing,** 814; **right wing,** 814; **department,** 815
2. The president is the chief executive officer with strong powers. The premier serves the president by running the executive office and keeping contact with the legislative branch.
3. The French Parliament has far less power than Congress.

Bills of cabinet members take priority in the National Assembly. The National Assembly's influence over financial matters is very limited, and the French Senate's role is limited to delaying legislation.
4. Gaullists, National Front, Communist, Socialist, or Union for French Democracy
5. may appeal directly to the people through referenda, may dissolve National Assembly and call for elections, and has dictatorial powers in national emergencies
6. It is difficult for a candidate to win a majority in the first

election, so a runoff election is held between the top two candidates.
7. The Communist party has declined; the major parties have moved closer to the center of the political spectrum; and many French people do not identify exclusively with one party.
8. Between 1946 and 1958 France had 27 different governments. The situation changed after 1958. Since then, governments have survived longer; people have moved toward centrist politics.

Japan

Focus

Bell Ringer

While attendance is being taken, ask students to list as many facts as they can about Japan's political system.

Motivating Activity

Review students' Bell Ringer lists. Have students combine information on their lists to create a "political profile" of Japan. Then ask such questions as: What kind of political system does Japan have? Does Japan have a unitary or federal government?

Tell students that this section answers such questions. Suggest that they add to their political profile of Japan as they read the section.

Vocabulary Precheck

Call on volunteers to tell what they think each key term or concept means. Have students check the accuracy of their definitions in the Glossary. **LEP**

Caption Answer
lost his divine status; his office became largely symbolic

In many respects the Japanese government resembles the government of Great Britain. It is a constitutional monarchy with a parliamentary government, a prime minister, a cabinet, and a bicameral legislature. Like the governments of Great Britain and France, the Japanese government is a centralized, unitary government that allows only limited local autonomy or self-rule. The nation's hereditary emperor has very little actual authority, even less than the British monarch, serving simply as a symbol of the nation.

The Japanese Constitution

In 1945, following Japan's surrender in World War II, American forces under General Douglas MacArthur occupied the country and set up an Occupation Government. One of the major tasks of this government was to prepare a new constitution for Japan. Under General MacArthur's supervision, the new constitution was written in 1946 and went into effect in 1947.

Before this constitution was adopted, the Japanese people regarded the emperor as a god. For many years Japan had been an authoritarian oligarchy that was led by powerful military and industrial leaders. One main goal of the new constitution was to make Japan a more democratic nation.

Popular Sovereignty The 1947 constitution states that political power rests with the people. Echoing the words of the preamble to the American Constitution, it begins:

We, the Japanese people, acting through our duly elected representatives in the National Diet [legislature] . . . do proclaim that sovereign power resides with the individual people and do firmly establish this Constitution.

—JAPANESE CONSTITUTION, 1947

This simple statement represented a revolutionary change for Japan, from an absolute monarchy to a con-

---

SECTION PREVIEW

Objectives
After studying this section, you should be able to:
■ Discuss the origin and purpose of Japan's constitution.
■ Describe the Diet and its relation to Japanese bureaucracy.

■ Explain the effect of having one large majority party on the Japanese government.

Key Terms and Concepts
no confidence, faction

Themes in Government
■ Comparative Government
■ Political Processes

Critical Thinking Skills
■ Identifying Assumptions
■ Synthesizing Information

---

816   UNIT 10: COMPARATIVE GOVERNMENT AND ECONOMIC SYSTEMS

Classroom Resources for Section 3

📁 Guided Reading Activities
📁 Reproducible Lesson Plans
📁 Section 3 Quiz

🎵 Government Themes Transparencies 30
SAT Practice Tests
Writer's Guidebook

stitutional monarchy with political power vested in the people. An earlier constitution had established the emperor as "sacred and inviolable," and assigned all powers of government to the emperor. Those powers were never meant to be exercised by the emperor. Instead, the legislature and government ministers, who were dominated by military and business leaders, made political decisions. The new constitution ended this system, stating that the emperor "shall not have powers related to government."

War Renounced To ensure that the government of Japan would not again be in a position to wage war, the constitution also provided that

> *The Japanese people forever renounce war as a sovereign right of the nation and the threat or use of force as a means of settling international disputes. Land, sea, and air forces . . . will never be maintained.*
> —JAPANESE CONSTITUTION, 1947

When the constitution went into effect, the Japanese people welcomed this provision. Many Japanese felt that World War II had been a tragic mistake. In more recent times, however, some Japanese have expressed dissatisfaction with this clause. Many Japanese feel it is an unfair limitation on the sovereignty of the nation or its ability to defend itself. Today Japan maintains a self-defense force that numbers about 250,000.

The Structure of Government The writers of the Japanese constitution did not provide for an American type of presidential system. The people felt that a parliamentary system of government similar to Great Britain's would be more in keeping with the traditions of Japan. Accordingly, the constitution established a parliament of two houses called the National Diet. The upper house is the House of Councilors, and the lower house, the House of Representatives. The lower chamber has far more power than the House of Councilors, which has only a limited power to delay legislation.

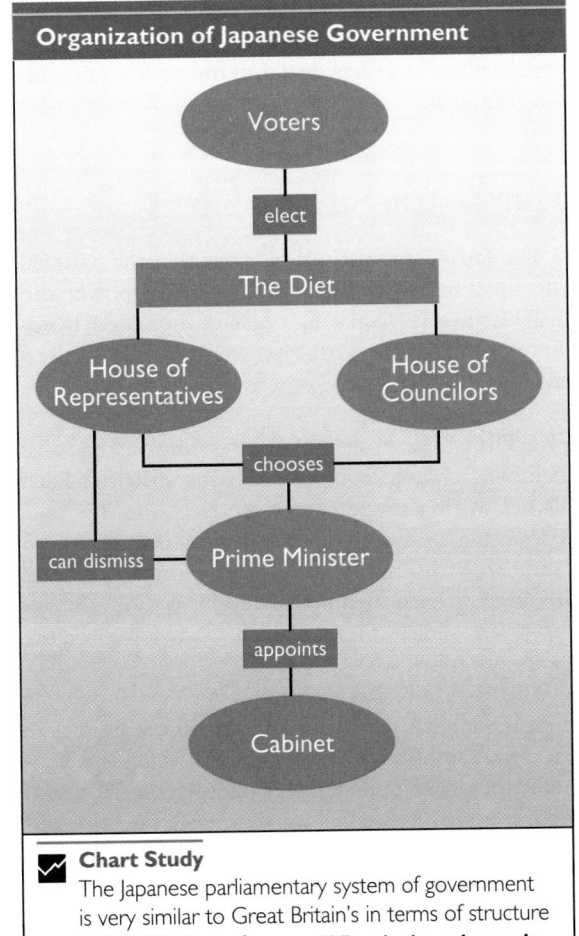

Organization of Japanese Government

Voters
↓ elect
The Diet
→ House of Representatives
→ House of Councilors
↓ chooses
Prime Minister
← can dismiss
↓ appoints
Cabinet

☑ **Chart Study**
The Japanese parliamentary system of government is very similar to Great Britain's in terms of structure and distribution of power. **What is the prime minister's role in the Diet?**

A cabinet led by a prime minister exercises the executive power in the central government. The prime minister, who is the leader of the majority party in the House of Representatives, appoints the cabinet ministers, more than half of whom must be members of the Diet.

One uniquely American feature of the Japanese government is the constitutional provision for an independent Supreme Court that has the power of judicial review. Because the Japanese people traditionally

---

STUDY GUIDE

Themes in Government
Comparative Government
Japan's 1947 constitution, like the United States Constitution, can be amended. **Which clause do some Japanese want to see amended?**

Political Processes
As it does in Great Britain, the parliamentary system allows the executive and legislative functions of Japanese government to work closely together.

Critical Thinking Skills
Identifying Assumptions Why, do you think, the new constitution of 1947 did not do away completely with the position of emperor?

CHAPTER 28: COMPARING SYSTEMS OF GOVERNMENT   817

Background

The Japanese bureaucracy attempts to involve those who are affected by its decisions in the decision-making process. This technique is known as *nemawashi*, or "root-binding." A gardening term, *nemawashi* is the process of carefully untangling and binding the roots of a tree before replanting it. Similarly, the Japanese bureaucracy insures that all concerned parties are untangled and then bound together in an understanding of the problems involved in, and ramifications of, a decision.

Teach

Guided Practice

L1 Making Comparisons Draw a chart on the chalkboard with *Lower House* and *Upper House* as horizontal headings and *Similarities* and *Differences* as vertical headings. Title it: *Comparing the United States and Japanese Legislatures.* Have students complete the chart by offering similarities and differences between the two legislatures. **LEP**

⚑ **Interpreting Visuals** Display transparency 30 from the *Government Themes Transparencies* in the Teacher's Classroom Resources and use the accompanying teaching strategy and student activity to teach about the Japanese Diet.

L3 Analyzing Ideas Note that government bureaucracy in the United States has a poor reputation among Americans, while the Japanese bureaucracy is highly regarded by the Japanese people. Lead students in a discussion on why this situation exists. *(Some students may suggest Japanese bureaucrats have more power. Others may cite differences in attitudes about authority and power.)*

Chart Study Answer
leads the cabinet, leads majority party, and appoints cabinet members

STUDY GUIDE

Theme Answer
the clause renouncing war and maintaining military forces

Critical Thinking Answer
to maintain a link with Japanese tradition

Chapter 28: Comparing Systems of Government   **817**

Independent Practice

L2 Persuasive Writing Have students review current newspapers and magazines to locate articles on United States-Japanese relations. Then ask students to write an editorial supporting or opposing the Japanese stance on the issue covered in their selected articles. Have students read their editorials to the class.

STUDY GUIDE

Theme Answer
Members of the majority party are expected to vote with the government.

Critical Thinking Answer
Americans imposed a feature of government with which the Japanese were unfamiliar and uncomfortable

Assess

Check for Understanding

Have students complete Section 3 Review on page 819.

Meeting Objectives

Each section objective is tested by the Section Review questions that follow it in parentheses.
- Discuss the origin and purpose of Japan's constitution. (2, 3, 4)
- Describe the Diet and its relation to Japanese bureaucracy. (5, 7, 8)
- Explain the effect of having one large majority party on the Japanese government. (6)

Evaluate

📁 Section 3 Quiz

💾 Testmaker

---

have been suspicious of courts and formal legal processes, however, the Supreme Court has not played a significant role. It has declared only a few laws unconstitutional.

The Legislature of Japan

The Japanese constitution states that the national Diet shall be the "highest organ of state power and shall be the sole lawmaking organ of the state." In addition, the Diet has authority over the nation's fiscal policies.

The Diet The House of Representatives has 512 members, chosen from 130 election districts. Each district, with a single exception, elects from 3 to 5 representatives. Each voter has 1 vote, but the 3 to 5 candidates who receive the largest number of votes are elected. Each member of the lower house serves for 4 years unless the parliament is dissolved before the term expires.

The House of Representatives elects the prime minister and has the power to vote **no confidence** in the prime minister and the cabinet. When this happens, the prime minister may dissolve the House of Representatives and call for new elections. In addition, the House of Representatives is the chamber that first considers budgetary matters and treaties. They become effective in 30 days even if the upper house does not agree but remains in session.

Although both houses consider legislative measures, the House of Representatives may override a negative vote in the House of Councilors by passing the bill a second time by a two-thirds majority.

The House of Councilors consists of 252 members who are chosen for 6-year terms. Because the House of Councilors may not be dissolved, its members usually serve their full terms of office. The majority of the members of the upper house have belonged to the Liberal Democratic party.

Similar to the upper houses of other governments, the House of Councilors provides a calmer, more detached form of deliberation than the House of Representatives. In this way, it helps moderate any hasty actions the lower house takes.

The Diet at Work Committees carry on much of the work of both houses of the Diet. Cabinet ministers often testify before committees where they face penetrating questions from members of the opposition party. Committee proceedings tend to be very lively, and they are often televised. In contrast, the proceedings of the full Diet tend to be dull. Unlike the American Congress or the British Parliament, no colorful politicians play to the gallery or the press corps.

When voting on legislation, members of the majority party are expected to vote with the government. If they do not agree with the legislation, they simply abstain. Because the opposition parties are rarely strong enough to do more than delay legislation, most legislation is passed.

The Cabinet

Twelve members of the cabinet preside over departments or ministries of the government. These include the ministries of justice, foreign affairs, finance, education, health and welfare, agriculture and forestry, and labor. The remaining cabinet members are so-called "ministers of state." They include the deputy prime minister and heads of various agencies such as the Economic Planning Agency and the Science and Technology Agency.

The cabinet normally operates on the principle of collective responsibility. This principle means that all members of the cabinet share responsibility for cabinet decisions. If a cabinet member disagrees with a decision, that member is expected to resign or be dismissed by the prime minister.

The existence of **factions** or interest groups within the country's political parties also causes a high rate of turnover in the cabinet. Members of these factions often receive cabinet posts to gain political experience or as a reward for their support and service to the fac-

STUDY GUIDE

| **Themes in Government** **Political Processes** The prime minister's cabinet drafts most bills and presents them to the Diet. | **Why does the Diet pass most legislation that comes before it?** | **Critical Thinking Skills** **Synthesizing Information Why was the constitutional provision for a Supreme Court an example of what some Japanese might call "cultural arrogance"?** |

Cooperative Learning Activity

Organize students into groups of six to eight. Tell them their task is to act as the Japanese cabinet and come to some agreement on a number of issues—lowering import barriers on rice from the United States, limiting automobile exports to the United States, or providing generous government pensions to all senior citizens. Have groups select and debate two issues, limiting debate time to five minutes per issue. Remind students that the Japanese cabinet operates under the principle of collective responsibility, and consensus rather than conflict rules its meetings. After debate has been completed, ask each group to select a prime minister to report its decisions.

tions. The various powerful factions within the majority party also serve as a check against the cabinet or the prime minister assuming too much power.

The Bureaucracy

With the high turnover in the cabinet—often a minister remains in the cabinet only for a year—Japan needs a permanent bureaucracy of capable and experienced high-level civil servants. Today these bureaucrats, as one political scientist stated, "represent the major ruling force in Japanese politics."

The government of Japan emphasizes long-term planning. Bureaucrats provide the Diet with the expert knowledge required for such planning. In addition, the government usually phrases its policies in very general terms, assuming that the bureaucrats in each department will know best how to implement them. A former ambassador to Japan says bureaucrats actually originate most legislation:

Most laws, including all important bills, are drafted not by the Diet but by the bureaucracy in behalf of the cabinet. They are presented . . . to the Diet and are then passed by the same Diet majority that has chosen the prime minister in the first place.
—EDWIN O. REISCHAUER, *THE JAPANESE TODAY*, 1988

Japanese society regards membership in the upper ranks of the bureaucracy as a high honor. Leading graduates of the major universities receive jobs in the ministries and government agencies. Although socially esteemed, high-ranking Japanese civil ser-

vants normally work long hours and their pay is lower than it would be in industry.

While the officials in the bureaucracy operate with great independence, they are accountable for their actions. Many have meetings almost every day with reporters, political figures, business leaders, and citizens' groups. These groups expect bureaucrats to be able to explain and justify the decisions of their offices.

Political Parties

Japan has a multiparty system in which one party, the Liberal Democratic party (LDP), has been dominant since it was founded in 1955. Large business interests, farmers, members of the middle class, and bureaucrats usually support the LDP, whose outlook favors free enterprise, cooperation with the United States, and the growth of Japanese interests in Asia.

Japan also has two leftist opposition parties. The leading opposition party is the Japanese Socialist party that has consistently held more than 100 seats in the Diet. Its support comes mainly from members of the large trade unions. The second opposition group on the left is the Japanese Communist party, a legal party that has held less than 10 percent of the seats in the Diet. A third opposition party is the Komei, or "Clean Government party." Its objective is to purify Japanese politics and improve the quality of life in Japan.

Unlike politics in Western democracies, Japanese politics takes place largely within the majority party rather than between opposing parties. In addition, politics in Japan results less from philosophical differences than from practical problems of the bureaucracy.

Chapter 28, Section 3
Lesson Plan, pages 816–819

Reteach

Have students describe the ways in which Japan's constitution reflects the United States Constitution. Have them write several sentences explaining the reasons for these similarities.

Enrich

After the death of Emperor Hirohito in 1989, many conservative Japanese called for a reassessment of the emperor's role in government. Have students research and write a paper on the governmental role played by the present emperor, Akihito.

Close

Select five or six students to take part in a panel discussion of the following question:

How does the structure and function of the Japanese government reflect Japanese character?

Encourage other students to challenge panel members' arguments.

CONNECTIONS

Political Processes
In 1986 Takako Doi became the first woman to head a major political party in Japan. Under her leadership, the Socialist party began to threaten the dominance of the Liberal Democrats.

---

3 SECTION REVIEW

Section Summary
Japan's parliamentary government depends on a highly trained bureaucracy to implement national policy.

Checking for Understanding
Recalling Facts
1. Define no confidence, faction.
2. Cite the circumstances that gave rise to the new Japanese constitution in 1947.
3. Discuss the constitutional limitation on Japan's military.
4. List three ways in which Japan's government is similar to that of Great Britain.

Exploring Themes
5. Comparative Government How is the lower house of the Japanese Diet similar to and different from the United States House of Representatives?
6. Political Processes How does Japan's one large majority party influence the political processes in its government?

Critical Thinking Skills
7. Identifying Assumptions Why does the Japanese government allow bureaucrats rather than elected officials to develop plans for implementing policies?
8. Synthesizing Information What evidence shows the significance of democracy in Japan's political system?

CHAPTER 28: COMPARING SYSTEMS OF GOVERNMENT 819

Section 3 Review Answers

1. Definitions of terms appear on pages indicated: **no confidence,** 818; **faction,** 818
2. After World War II, General Douglas MacArthur remained in Japan to oversee the reorganization of the Japanese government. The new constitution was written under direction of MacArthur's occupation government.
3. The constitution says that land, sea, and air forces will never be maintained.

4. It is a constitutional monarchy with parliamentary and centralized government.
5. similarities: members are elected from districts, acts first on budgetary matters, has lawmaking powers; differences: members serve four years, elects the executive, considers treaties, may override a negative vote of the upper house
6. Matters are debated within the party and are over practical policy rather than philosophical differences.

7. The government assumes that bureaucrats are well-qualified to carry out policies. A lack of philosophical differences among bureaucrats and elected officials means that most decisions involve practical matters rather than political ones.
8. The people elect the legislature; there are political parties and factions within the parties that influence government; and several groups and special commissions keep a check on the work of the bureaucracy.

The People's Republic of China

Focus

Bell Ringer

Have students make a list of the words and phrases they associate with China.

Motivating Activity

Review students' Bell Ringer lists. Write the most frequently noted items on the chalkboard. Have students discuss why they associate these words and phrases with China. Ask students to keep their lists and, as they read this section, have them add or delete words and phrases as appropriate.

Vocabulary Precheck

Write the key terms and concepts for this section on the chalkboard. Ask students how each term or concept relates to Chinese politics and government.
LEP

Teach

Guided Practice

L1 Making Comparisons On the chalkboard draw a table with *United States Congress* and *National People's Congress* as horizontal headings, and *Similarities* and *Differences* as vertical headings. Have students suggest how these two legislative bodies are alike and how they are different.
LEP

Caption Answer

because of disputes over whether it was the legitimate government of China

---

In 1949 communist revolutionaries seized power in the world's most heavily populated nation. Led by Mao Zedong, communist forces defeated the Nationalists who fled to safety on the offshore island of Taiwan, where they remain today.

As a guide to establishing a communist economy and government, the People's Republic of China turned to the Soviet Union:

> *We must learn . . . from the advanced experience of the Soviet Union. The Soviet Union has been building socialism for forty years, and its experience is very valuable to us. . . . Now there are two different attitudes towards learning from others. One is the dogmatic attitude of transplanting everything, whether or not it is suited to our conditions. . . . The other attitude is to use our heads and learn those things which suit our conditions, that is to absorb whatever experience is useful to us. That is the attitude we should adopt.*
>
> —MAO ZEDONG, 1957

Following the Soviet Union's example, the Chinese leaders proceeded to establish a totalitarian government strictly controlled by the Chinese Communist party (CCP), in much the same way that the Soviet Communist party once controlled the Soviet Union.

China's Political Background

Following its establishment as a republic in 1912, rival factions divided China. Not until 1929 did China achieve some measure of political unity. Then the Nationalist party, under the leadership of Chiang Kai-shek, defeated its rivals and gained at least partial control of the nation. Still, rival regimes existed, particularly in the north where the Communists had taken refuge. Actual unity came when Japan invaded China in the 1930s. The invasion brought the rival factions together to defend their country.

After Japan's defeat in World War II, a civil war broke out between the Nationalists and the Communists in China. After intense fighting Communists drove the Nationalists out of mainland China and established their dictatorship, the People's Republic of China (PRC). The Nationalists, then firmly in power

China's Revolutionary Leader
Mao Zedong led the People's Republic of China from 1949 to 1976. **Politics Why did the United States not recognize the People's Republic until 1979?**

SECTION PREVIEW

Objectives
After studying this section, you should be able to:
- Relate how China's political background led to communist rule.
- Outline the Chinese Communist party organization.

- Explain the relationship between the Communist party and the Chinese government.

Key Terms and Concepts
cadre, martial law

Themes in Government
- Political Processes
- Civil Liberties

Critical Thinking Skills
- Recognizing Ideologies
- Identifying Assumptions

---

820   UNIT 10: COMPARATIVE GOVERNMENT AND ECONOMIC SYSTEMS

Classroom Resources for Section 4

- Guided Reading Activities
- Reproducible Lesson Plans
- Section 4 Quiz

- Government Themes Transparencies 31
- SAT Practice Tests
- Writer's Guidebook

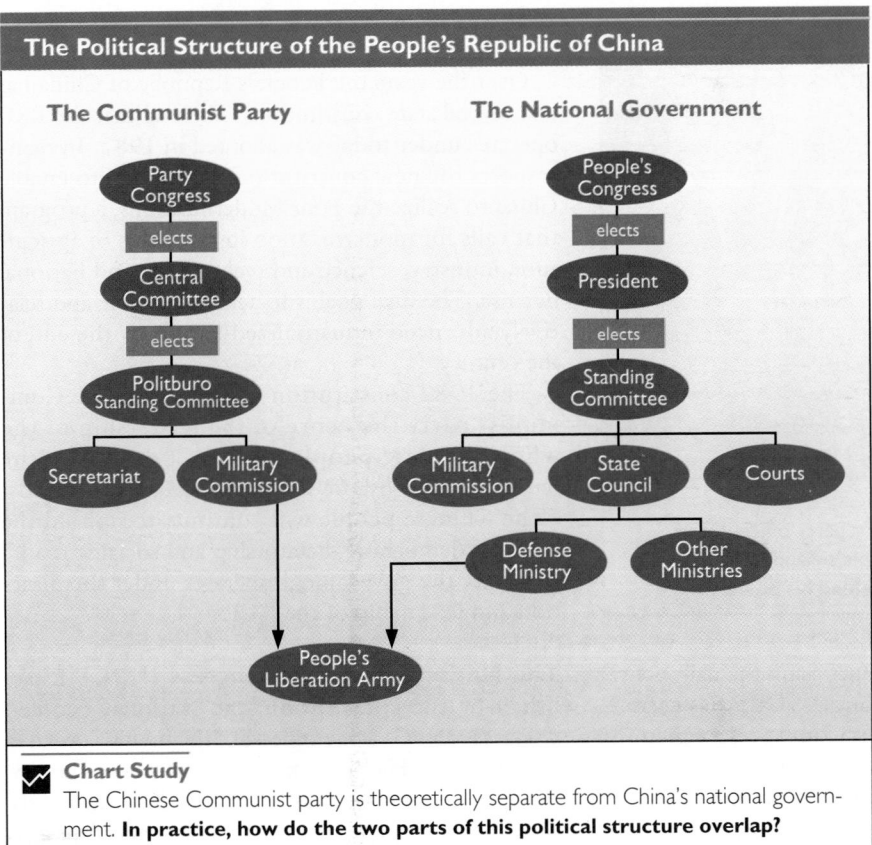

The Political Structure of the People's Republic of China

The Communist Party

Party Congress
elects
Central Committee
elects
Politburo Standing Committee
Secretariat — Military Commission

The National Government

People's Congress
elects
President
elects
Standing Committee
Military Commission — State Council — Courts
Defense Ministry — Other Ministries

People's Liberation Army

☑ **Chart Study**
The Chinese Communist party is theoretically separate from China's national government. **In practice, how do the two parts of this political structure overlap?**

governmental policies and ensures that the government carries out the party's policies and decisions. At every level, officials referred to as **cadre,** hold key posts. Most of these are party members, even though only about 4 percent of the Chinese people belong to the Communist party.

At one time the CCP attempted to follow the Soviet Union's pattern of party and government organization but abandoned this policy in part in 1958. From that time on, the CCP and the government have moved to create a truly Chinese political system while retaining a devotion to communism under the slogan "socialism with Chinese characteristics."

in Taiwan and supported by the United States, continued their claim to be the only legitimate Chinese government. Finally, in 1971 the United Nations dismissed this claim, and the General Assembly agreed that the members of the delegation from the PRC were "the only legitimate representatives of China." The United States agreed with that position after President Nixon's visit to the People's Republic of China in 1972. Almost seven years passed, however, before the United States formally recognized the PRC in January 1979.

The Chinese Communist Party

The Communist party in China controls the policies and the operation of the government. Despite recent upheavals in Eastern Europe and the former Soviet Union, in the PRC the Chinese Communist party (CCP) and its leaders remain firmly in control.

The Party's Role in China Although the CCP is not an official organ of the government, it determines

Party Organization In 1982 China adopted 2 new constitutions, 1 for the party and another for the national government. Under its new constitution, theoretically at least, the Communist party's highest governing body is the National Party Congress, composed of between 1,500 and 2,000 delegates. Members of party organizations across the nation select these delegates. In practice, however, the National Party Congress merely serves as a rubber stamp for policies of the party's leaders.

The National Party Congress does, however, elect the party's Central Committee that serves in place of the Congress when it is not in session. The number of members of the Central Committee runs between 200 and 300 full and alternate members. Its major responsibility is to elect the members of the party's Political Bureau—the Politburo. The Politburo usually is composed of about 20 top party leaders.

The Politburo's Standing Committee, which functions when the full Politburo is not meeting, is even more elitist and is composed of the top six CCP leaders. The Politburo's Standing Committee appoints members of the Secretariat. The Secretariat then im-

---

📖 **Interpreting Visuals** Display transparency 31 from the *Government Themes Transparencies* in the Teacher's Classroom Resources and use the accompanying teaching strategy and student activity to teach the organization of the Chinese political system.

L3 Political Processes Lead a class discussion comparing political parties in China and in the United States. Students should note similarities in structure between the CCP and major United States parties. Ask what differences exist in the relationship between chief executive and party in the two political systems. *(In China, the government leader is not always the party's leader.)* Ask about other differences. *(Students should note that China is a one-party system, and that this party dominates all aspects of political life.)*

Independent Practice

L1 Summarizing Ideas Have students select a newspaper or magazine article about Chinese government and politics and summarize it in a written paragraph.

Chart Study Answer
Both the CCP and the Defense Ministry organize the army, control of which effectively gives the party complete power.

CONNECTIONS

History
With the words "let a hundred flowers bloom and a thousand schools of thought contend," Mao Zedong launched a program of liberalization in 1956. When his leadership was criticized, however, Mao brought the program to an end.

Background

The communist revolution in China did not fit the model of revolution described by Karl Marx. For example, Marx predicted that the industrialized nations would experience revolution first. China, however, was mostly rural and had little industry. Marx also argued that the workers, tiring of oppression, would lead the revolution. While the Chinese Communist party was characterized as an organization of the oppressed classes, its leadership included few workers or peasants. Mao Zedong and Zhou Enlai, for example, were both students from well-to-do backgrounds.

L2 Descriptive Writing Have students assume the role of a Chinese student in Tiananmen Square in the spring of 1989. Have them write to a friend in the United States explaining why they joined the protest, and recounting what happened.

Caption Answer
his experience and his age

Assess

Check for Understanding

Have students complete Section 4 Review on page 823.

Meeting Objectives

Each section objective is tested by the Section Review questions that follow it in parentheses.
• Relate how China's political background led to communist rule. (2, 7)
• Outline the Chinese Communist party organization. (3, 4)
• Explain the relationship between the Communist party and the Chinese government. (5, 6, 8)

Evaluate

📁 Section 4 Quiz

⬛ Testmaker

Chinese Strongman
Though he holds no official or party office, Deng Xiaoping dominates the People's Republic of China.
Politics What factors lie behind his power?

China's National Government

Over the years the People's Republic of China has had several state constitutions. The one that the PRC operates under today was adopted in 1982. In many respects the new constitution is designed to enable China to realize the Four Modernizations, a program that calls for modernization in the fields of agriculture, industry, science and technology, and national defense. The final goal is to achieve a stable and relatively advanced industrialized nation by the end of the century.

The 1982 constitution calls the Chinese Communist party the "core of the leadership of the whole Chinese people," while it describes the nation as "led by the Communist Party." It adds, "The Chinese people will continue to uphold the people's democratic dictatorship and socialist road." In reality the government operates under the direction and leadership of the CCP.

plements party policies by supervising the daily activities of the party. In addition, the CCP has various other organizations that carry out special functions under the direction of the Secretariat.

At the top of the CCP, and presumably the most powerful party leader, is the General Secretary who may or may not be a prominent government official as well. Many members of the Politburo hold top government posts. Politburo member Li Peng, for example, also serves as China's premier. From the late 1970s to the 1990s, however, the unquestioned leader of China was Deng Xiaoping, who held no official government or party position. It is important to understand that leadership in China often may rest upon background rather than upon position.

China's preeminent leader, Deng Xiaoping, embraced communism while studying in France during the early 1920s and later served in the battles against the Nationalists in the 1930s. Among the less than 12 other older but still important revolutionary veterans, Deng Xiaoping, in his late eighties, seemed reluctant to pass on his power to younger leaders.

The National People's Congress (NPC) Established by the constitution, the National People's Congress (NPC) is identified as "the highest organ of state power." The NPC has little real power, however, and often functions as little more than the legislative branch of government. It sends official policies down to the lower branches of government at the province, county, or municipal levels, which are expected to implement the policies.

Supposedly, the nation's legislative power rests with the National People's Congress and its Standing Committee that serves when the NPC is not in session. The NPC and its Standing Committee, however, have little independent legislative power. Many of the leaders of the Standing Committee do hold important leadership posts in the Communist party that actually decides on the government's actions and policies. In reality, the NPC serves as a symbol of citizen participation in the nation's government when it selects the country's ceremonial president and vice president and the premier who presides over the State Council.

822 UNIT 10: COMPARATIVE GOVERNMENT AND ECONOMIC SYSTEMS

Special Needs Strategy

Language Disability Participating in classroom discussion and other oral language activities is often unnerving for students with expressive language problems. They are not as fast or as efficient as their peers at finding words and formulating sentences. Conduct a class discussion of the information on the Chinese government in this section. After a volunteer has made a point, encourage students to agree with, add to, or modify the point. You might ask such questions as: "How many students knew that answer?" or "How many students agree with that point?"

The State Council In China the State Council carries out the same functions that a cabinet or council of ministers carries out in other nations. Although the State Council is supposedly responsible to the National People's Congress and its Standing Committee, it answers to the CCP's Politburo. Most of the leaders in the State Council also hold high posts in the CCP.

The State Council, which meets about once a month, operates as the executive branch of the government. It makes decisions, prepares legislation for the National People's Congress, determines the nation's budget, and ensures the Communist party's policies are followed. The State Council's Standing Committee headed by the premier carries out most of these functions, however. The Standing Committee meets several times each week and carries out the day-by-day decision-making process for the government.

Political Parties

Although the Chinese Communist party dominates the government in China, it permits eight minority parties to exist. These are largely made up of people from China's middle-class or of intellectuals—a term that often also includes students. These parties are expected to work under the leadership of the Communist party. An opposition party, the Federation for a Democratic China (FDC) was formed in Paris following the Chinese government's massacre of protesters in Tiananmen Square in the heart of Beijing, China's capital city, in 1989.

Tiananmen Square

Historically, the Chinese Communist party has tolerated little opposition. In April 1989, resentment against low pay for professional workers, restrictions on students studying abroad, and growing inflation brought thousands of demonstrators to Tiananmen Square. One student said the demonstrations were "for democracy, for freedom." Soon, protesters began a hunger strike in the square. Coming at the time of Soviet leader Mikhail Gorbachev's visit to China, it embarrassed China's leaders.

On May 20 Premier Li Peng declared parts of Beijing under **martial law**—military control. He sent unarmed troops to clear the square. When that failed, armed troops moved in. On June 3, 1989, they began firing on demonstrators who were determined to block their way. The next day the Tiananmen Square massacre shocked the world. Government and civilian estimates of deaths differ. An eyewitness, upon visiting one hospital, described the tragedy:

> *The doctors were crying, and took me to the morgue. They didn't have enough drawers for the bodies, so they had to stack them. All of the victims were young men, all of them were bare-chested, and none of them had any shoes. Many had writing on their chests and were wearing headbands. They were just piled up in there, half-way to the ceiling.*
> —MARGARET HERBST, 1989

Since the massacre at Tiananmen Square, the Chinese government has imposed strict controls on the nation's younger generation.

Reteach

Have students write a paragraph explaining the relationship between the Chinese government and the Chinese Communist party.

Enrich

Have students research and write a report on how either the Great Proletarian Cultural Revolution of the 1960s or the Four Modernizations program of the 1970s and 1980s has affected life in China today.

Close

Have students discuss the following: Could the changes that took place in Eastern Europe and the former Soviet Union also take place in China?

CONNECTIONS

Political Processes
Activities in Tiananmen Square showed a strong American influence. Students erected a 30-foot plaster figure called the "Goddess of Democracy" that looked remarkably like the Statue of Liberty. And in the impromptu seminars that sprang up all over the square, Thomas Jefferson's ideas on liberty and democracy were often mentioned.

4
SECTION REVIEW

Section Summary
The Chinese Communist party controls the government of China, limiting all important positions to party members.

Checking for Understanding
Recalling Facts
1. Define cadre, martial law.
2. Describe events that led to the communist control of China.
3. Name the most powerful position in the Chinese Communist party.
4. List five governing bodies of the Chinese Communist party.

Exploring Themes
5. Political Processes How does the Chinese Communist party ensure that it will control the government?
6. Civil Liberties Why did young Chinese demonstrate in Tiananmen Square in 1989?

Critical Thinking Skills
7. Recognizing Ideologies Why did Mao Zedong believe China should study the Soviet Union's experience?
8. Identifying Assumptions What assumptions about popular protest did the Chinese government make in 1989? In your opinion, are these assumptions correct? Explain your answer.

Section 4 Review Answers

1. Definitions of terms appear on the pages indicated: **cadre,** 821; **martial law,** 823
2. During World War II Communists and Nationalists cooperated to defend China. After Japan's defeat, civil war broke out between the Nationalists and Communists. The Communists drove the Nationalists from the mainland and established a Soviet-style government.
3. General Secretary

4. National Party Congress, Central Committee, Politburo, Standing Committee, Secretariat
5. Party members can hold the key posts in government. The 1982 constitution calls the party the "core of the leadership of the whole Chinese people."
6. They opposed some government policies, low pay for professional workers, restrictions on studying abroad, and were worried about rampant inflation.
7. The Soviet Union had been building socialism for 40

years. Mao believed that some Soviet ideas could be adapted to China's conditions.
8. Answers will vary, but may include: The government assumed that the protests would stir public pressure for change, perhaps even cause a revolt. It also assumed that the protesters would disband when faced by the military. Finally it assumed that having broken up the protest by force, the movement would die out. The first assumption was true. The rest were not.

Identifying Alternatives

Focus

Ask students to define *alternatives*. Ask: Why is the ability to identify alternatives a valuable life skill? (*Answers should recognize that freedom of choice expands as alternatives are identified.*)

Teach

Ask students if they think incumbents or challengers would be more responsive to public opinion. (*Answers should recognize other pressures on sitting lawmakers.*)

Tell students that as citizens and voters they may be asked in the future to decide on some basic reform in the structure and operation of Congress. Ask them to identify the three alternatives proposed to reform Congress. (*limit candidate spending, eliminate the seniority system, more balanced media coverage of congressional races*) Have them evaluate possible positive and negative consequences of each proposal.

Assess

Have students complete the **Practice** exercise.

Close

Ask students why being able to evaluate alternatives, as well as to identify them, is valuable.

When you identify alternatives, you search for solutions to a well-defined problem, then evaluate each solution in terms of its costs and benefits. If you can identify alternatives, you will be better able to solve problems and anticipate future challenges.

Explanation

To identify alternatives, follow these steps:
- Define the problem in a concise statement or paragraph.
- Determine what particular conditions, attitudes, laws, or institutions create this problem.
- Imagine various reforms or solutions that might alleviate the problem.
- Evaluate what positive and negative effects each solution would be likely to have.
- Decide whether any of the proposed solutions seems superior to the status quo.

Consider, for example, that in recent decades more than 90 percent of incumbents in the House of Representatives have won reelection. Many observers regard this as a problem because they believe that incumbents, knowing they are very likely to win reelection, are less responsive to public opinion than they should be.

There are a number of reasons that incumbents have a strong advantage over challengers in congressional elections. Three reasons are:

1. Incumbents receive much more campaign support than challengers. Political action committees and individuals contribute more to incumbents because they want to support the likely winner.
2. Senior members of the House have more power than new members, so voters benefit from reelecting their representatives.
3. Incumbents are better known to voters because the media has been identifying them throughout their terms.

A reform that would address the first cause would be to limit the amount of money that a candidate could spend. Because candidates for Congress receive no federal funds, however, the Supreme Court has ruled these spending limits unconstitutional.

A reform that would do away with the second cause would be to throw out the seniority system in Congress. This reform would not involve a major change in other laws, attitudes, or institutions. The benefits might be that incumbents would have less advantage over challengers, and younger (or at least newer) chairpersons might add vigor to committees. Its costs would be that chairpersons would be less powerful and less experienced.

The third cause is a difficult one to overcome. People who are already members of Congress naturally get more coverage in the press and have greater name recognition. One alternative would be to make sure voters are informed about the issues and both the incumbent and the challenger. This would not necessarily require major changes in laws or institutions but would require an important change in attitude on the part of some voters. How could voters be better informed? Providing more thorough campaign coverage in House races could produce a better-informed electorate. Because most people watch television, stations could make more airtime for debates and in-depth coverage of candidates available.

Deciding whether any of these alternatives is superior to the system now in place is a matter of personal judgment. Remember that even if you decide against all of these reforms, infinite possibilities for change in politics exist.

Practice

In the United States the President is often a member of one party while the other party dominates Congress. The contrast between the programs of the two parties can create legislative deadlock. The President vetoes legislation and Congress rejects the President's proposals. Meanwhile, important problems go unattended. Use the steps outlined above to identify and assess some possible reforms.

> **Additional Practice**
>
> To practice this skill, see **Reinforcing the Skill** on page 831.

Practice Answers

problem: When the President is a member of one party and Congress is dominated by the other party, a legislative deadlock can occur; *what creates the problem:* incumbency advantages; President can veto legislation; many voters prefer to maintain system of checks and balances; *possible reforms:* adopt parliamentary system of government, require voters to vote a straight ticket, propose a constitutional amendment to remove President's veto power; *effects:* Students should indicate the drastic change each

reform would require; students should identify advantages and disadvantages of each proposal. *decide:* Students should decide if each proposed reform is superior to the present system.

For additional practice, have students complete activity 28 in *Skill Reinforcement Activities* in the Teacher's Classroom Resources.

The United States of Mexico

Like the United States, Mexico is a federal republic. The United States of Mexico is made up of 31 states and a single federal district, Mexico City. Each of the states exercises political power through a state governor and a state legislature. The constitution of 1917 divides the national government into three branches: executive, legislative, and judicial.

Federal Government

After Mexicans rose up to depose the dictator Pofirio Diaz in 1910, various factions warred with each other to determine the direction of the country and who would govern. When civil war ended, the constitution of 1917 established a national government that provided a variety of individual, social, and economic rights for citizens.

The Constitutional Framework The constitution spells out the structure of the federal system of 31 states and the federal district as well as the organization and powers of the three branches of the national government. In many respects it is a complex document. A recent United States government publication reported:

The constitution that was promulgated on February 5, 1917 . . . represents a political bargain struck by contending armies and as such includes various contradictory provisions representative of the heterogeneity [variety] of the groups that wrote it. It supports socialism, capitalism, political democ-

Salinas Pursues Reform
In 1990, President George Bush visited Mexico's President Carlos Salinas de Gortari. History **How is the Mexican president's power limited?**

racy, authoritarianism, corporatism, interest group liberalism, and a host of unimplemented provisions for specific social reforms.
—MEXICO: A COUNTRY STUDY, 1985

Unlike the Constitution of the United States that tends to be brief and general, the Mexican constitution is very specific about certain matters. For example, it says that religious groups cannot take part in any type of political activity and clerical garb may not be worn in public. It forbids churches and foreigners from owning property, but it empowers the government to seize private property, particularly land, and

---

SECTION PREVIEW

Objectives
After studying this section, you should be able to:
- Summarize the Mexican federal system.
- List the powers of Mexico's president.

- Discuss the political influence of the Institutional Revolutionary party.

Key Terms and Concepts
patronage, deputy

Themes in Government
- Comparative Government
- Political Processes

Critical Thinking Skills
- Demonstrating Reasoned Judgment
- Identifying Assumptions

CHAPTER 28: COMPARING SYSTEMS OF GOVERNMENT 825

Focus

Bell Ringer
Write the following statements on the chalkboard:

equal in area to the southwestern United States
population about one-third of that of the United States
shares a 2,000-mile border with the United States

While attendance is being taken, ask students to identify the country described by these statements.

Motivating Activity
Check students' Bell Ringer responses. *(Mexico)* Then query students on their knowledge of Mexico's government and political system. Write responses on the chalkboard and have students copy them into their notebooks. Suggest that they check the accuracy of the responses as they study this section.

Vocabulary Precheck
Ask students to speculate on the meaning of each of this section's key terms and concepts. Then have them check their speculations by finding the definitions in the section text. **LEP**

Caption Answer
cannot be reelected to a second term

Classroom Resources for Section 5

- 📁 Guided Reading Activities
- 📁 Reproducible Lesson Plans
- 📁 Participating in Government 28
- 📁 Primary and Secondary Source Readings 28
- 📁 Reteaching Activities 28
- 📁 Section 5 Quiz

- 📁 Chapter 28 Tests
- 📁 Testmaker
- 📁 Government Themes Transparencies 32
- 🎧 Audio Cassettes (English and Spanish)
- 📁 Limited English Proficiency Activities 28

Teach

Guided Practice

L1 **Making Generalizations** To focus students' attention on the Mexican constitution, write the following partial sentences on the chalkboard:

The Mexican and United States constitutions are alike because . . .

The Mexican and United States constitutions are not alike because . . .

Have students suggest generalizations that complete the sentences. Note responses on the chalkboard.

Interpreting Visuals Display transparency 32 from the *Government Themes Transparencies* in the Teacher's Classroom Resources and use the accompanying teaching strategy and student activity to teach the organization of the Mexican government.

L3 **Demonstrating Reasoned Judgment** Ask how the United States, Mexico, and Canada each can benefit from a free trade agreement that, from trade and industry respects, eliminates these countries' borders. Ask what drawbacks might result from such an arrangement.

PARTICIPATING IN GOVERNMENT

Mention that in his message to Congress recommending the creation of the Peace Corps, President John F. Kennedy suggested that the agency's benefits "will not be limited to the countries in which it serves." Have students discuss what Kennedy meant by this.

Have students complete activity 28 in *Participating in Government* in the Teacher's Classroom Resources.

---

to redistribute it. The government exercised this provision after the revolution when it seized large landholdings and redistributed the land among farmers and peasants.

The constitution of Mexico also protects the rights of workers and peasants to strike and provides for a minimum wage, equal pay for equal work, and an eight-hour workday. One political scientist described the provisions of the constitution as the "most advanced labor code in the world at its time."

The Executive Branch The president, who exercises strong control over the government, heads the executive branch. Porfirio Muñoz Ledo, a former party president, once supported this power:

The Mexican Constitution excluded religious groups from any kind of political activity . . . to strengthen civil authority. Moreover it set up a strong executive power. The presidential system, which is a common feature of the democracies in this hemisphere, took on sharper contours . . . due to our historical tradition and the need to harmonize political stability with social change. But the dangers of a concentration of power were checked by the principle of nonreelection, which favors a turnover in political leadership.

—PORFIRIO MUÑOZ LEDO, 1982

Ledo, now a critic of the dominant party, no longer holds this position. The president's power and the control of the government by 1 political party for more than 60 years have led political opponents to describe the Mexican government as authoritarian rather than democratic.

Directly elected for one six-year term, the president derives power from several sources. One source is the 1917 constitution that allows the president to appoint cabinet ministers, supreme court justices, ambassadors, and high military officers. The constitution also names the president as the commander in chief of the armed forces. In addition, the president, through the cabinet, has the power to recommend legislation that takes precedence over all other legislation when it reaches the bicameral Congress.

Another source of presidential power is as leader of the dominant political party. Presidential power also stems from the vast array of **patronage** positions, or government jobs that may be awarded to loyal supporters.

PARTICIPATING IN GOVERNMENT

Serving in the Peace Corps

Do you know someone who has served in the Peace Corps? Have you ever considered working as a volunteer in a developing nation?

For more than 30 years, American volunteers have served in Africa, Asia, and Latin America. Peace Corps volunteers live and work with the people of a host country—a nation that has requested their help.

The corps cooperates with the government of a host country to determine what projects to undertake. Peace Corps volunteers train the people of the host country to carry on the projects they have started. In other words, the Peace Corps helps people help themselves.

Peace Corps volunteers must be at least 18 years old. The corps seeks willing workers who can adapt to cultures and living conditions that are quite different from their own.

Peace Corps volunteers receive several weeks of training, generally in the host country. They study the language, culture, and history of the country. During their two years of service, volunteers are provided with housing, medical care, and transportation. They receive an allowance for living costs while they are in the host country.

Investigating Further

Find out more about serving in the Peace Corps by writing to Peace Corps, Washington, DC 20525.

826 UNIT 10: COMPARATIVE GOVERNMENT AND ECONOMIC SYSTEMS

Background

The Mexican Constitution of 1917 was a bundle of compromises that left some of the revolutionary leaders dissatisfied. Rebel leaders Emiliano Zapata and Pancho Villa had hoped the constitution would create a completely new social order and, as a result, they were constantly at odds with the national government. Both were killed in clashes with government forces. Venustiano Carranza, the first president under the new constitution, hoped to overcome the "no reelection" clause by naming a successor whom he could control. However, he was overthrown by one of his generals, Álvaro Obregón, who succeeded to the presidency. Under Obregón, the country achieved a degree of stability.

The Legislative Branch Mexico's legislative branch, or Congress, is composed of 2 houses, the Senate and the Chamber of Deputies. The people elect 64 senators for 6-year terms that coincide with the 6-year term of the president. Each state, including the federal district, elects two senators. The lower house, the Chamber of Deputies, in contrast, is made up of 500 deputies. The people elect 300 of the deputies. The remaining 200 are drawn from the competing political parties based on the proportion of the popular vote each party receives in the election. **Deputies** serve for 3 years and, like the senators, they may not immediately run for reelection.

Both the Senate and the Chamber of Deputies begin their sessions on September 1 of each year and adjourn on December 31. During the period when Congress is not in session, a permanent committee of 15 deputies and 14 senators handles the nation's legislative duties.

Although the constitution provides for a separation of powers between the executive and legislative branches, in reality the president dominates Congress. As leader of the dominant political party, the Partido Revolucionario Institucional (the Institutional Revolutionary Party or PRI), the president traditionally selects senatorial candidates and helps select the candidates for the Chamber of Deputies. The power of the PRI was clearly evident in 1990, when it controlled 60 of the 64 Senate seats and held a strong majority of the seats in the Chamber of Deputies. This situation remained much the same in the 1991 elections, when the PRI won more than 60 percent of the nation's vote.

The Judicial Branch Consistent with Mexico's federal system of government, the nation's judicial system is composed of federal and state courts. At the highest federal level is the Supreme Court with 26 justices divided into 6 divisions to handle criminal, civil, labor, and administrative cases. The president selects the justices, who have all been members of the PRI. Below the Supreme Court are circuit courts and district courts.

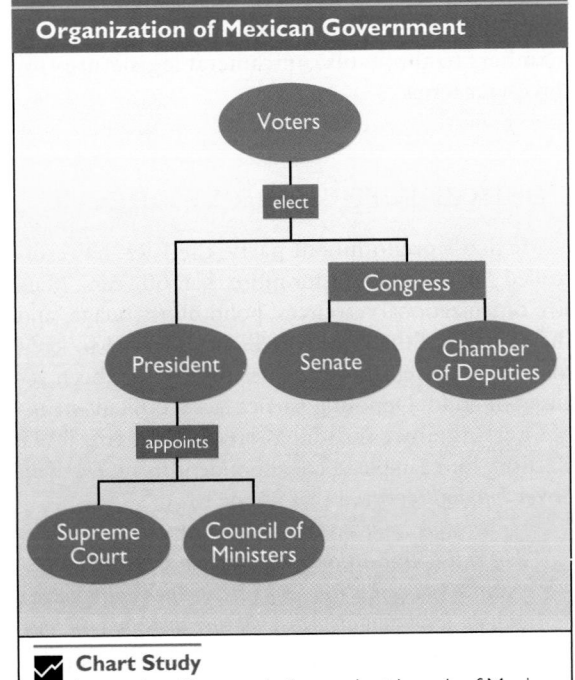

Organization of Mexican Government

Voters → elect → Congress → President, Senate, Chamber of Deputies

President → appoints → Supreme Court, Council of Ministers

☑ **Chart Study**
In practice, Congress is the weakest branch of Mexico's government. **How does this organization compare to that of the United States government?**

Each state also has a Supreme Court of Justice whose members are appointed by the state governor. In general, state courts handle less important matters, although they do handle trials for homicide.

State and Local Governments

The constitution of 1917 established Mexico as a "representative, democratic, and federal republic formed by free and sovereign states in all matters which concern their internal government, but united in a stabilized federation." At the same time, the constitution also limited the powers of the federal government to only those powers specifically granted to it by the constitution. It reserved all other powers to the states.

STUDY GUIDE

Themes in Government
Comparative Government The Tenth Amendment to the United States Constitution limits federal powers and reserves powers to the states.

Political Processes The voting age in Mexico is 18.

Critical Thinking Skills
Demonstrating Reasoned Judgment State why you like or dislike the nonreelective feature of the Mexican presidency.

Identifying Assumptions Why do you think the 1917 constitution strongly restricted religion?

CHAPTER 28: COMPARING SYSTEMS OF GOVERNMENT   827

Independent Practice

📁 **Interpreting Source Readings** Have students complete activity 28 in *Primary and Secondary Source Readings* in the Teacher's Classroom Resources.

Chart Study Answer
Mexico's structure is similar to that of the United States in that legislative and executive branches are separate, and the president appoints supreme court justices.

STUDY GUIDE

Critical Thinking Answers typical responses: *like*—president not hampered by politics; *dislike*—president can too easily dismiss public opinion

to offset the sometimes too prominent role church played in Mexican life in the past

Assess

Check for Understanding
Have students complete Section 5 Review on page 828.

Meeting Objectives
Each section objective is tested by the Section Review questions that follow it in parentheses.
• Summarize the Mexican federal system. (2, 4, 5, 8)
• List the powers of Mexico's president. (6)
• Discuss the political influence of the Institutional Revolutionary party. (3, 7)

Critical Thinking Activity

Identifying Assumptions Write on the chalkboard: *Assumption:* The PRI assumed it would face little opposition in the 1988 presidential elections.
Then have students discuss the following questions:
1. On what did the PRI base this assumption?

2. Based on this assumption, what kind of election campaign do you think the PRI might have conducted?
3. What kind of election campaign do you think the PRI would have conducted if it had not made this assumption?

Evaluate

📁 Section 5 Quiz

▣ Testmaker

Reteach

Select three students to work together to write "Jeopardy"-style answers on the content of this section. Then have them quiz other members of the class with their answers.

📁 Have students complete activity 28 in *Reteaching Activities* in the Teacher's Classroom Resources.

Enrich

Have students research and write a report on a political problem facing the Mexican government today.

Close

Allow students time to display the wall chart they constructed for the Chapter Project. Then have them suggest what features, if any, of the five governments they have studied in this chapter the United States should adopt. Ask them to give reasons for their choices.

Each state elects its governor to a single six-year term. Reelection is not permitted. The people elect members to the states' unicameral legislatures for three-year terms.

Political Parties and Change

Mexico's predominant party, the PRI, has controlled the government for more than 60 years. Massive organizational resources, political patronage, and the support of the major media have served to keep the PRI in power. In some cases the PRI has been accused of fraud. Opposing parties face a difficult struggle getting any candidates elected. In the 1991 election, for example, a correspondent from *The Wall Street Journal* reported that in one town:

> *T*he ruling Instutitional Revolutionary Party (PRI) organized a big musical festival . . . which culminated with the local candidate distributing thousands of toys to the children of those attending. Meanwhile parents were reminded to vote for the PRI.
> —SERVIO SARMIENTO, *THE WALL STREET JOURNAL*, AUGUST 23, 1991

As the 1994 election approached, improving economic conditions and the new North American Free Trade Agreement with the United States and Canada promised a brighter future. Mexico's President Carlos Salinas de Gortari handpicked his successor, Luis Donaldo Colosio, to complete the nation's transition to a market-oriented democracy. During the campaign, however, Colosio was assassinated. Speculation about a conspiracy filled the press. One leader spoke for many when he said:

> *T*he assassination looks like a plot. It could be the work of drug traffickers or of unhappy and resentful politicians who wanted to finish off the president, Carlos Salinas Gortari. And we can't rule out the possibility that some international forces were looking to destabilize the country.
> —JESÚS GONZALEZ, 1994
> DIRECTOR OF THE NATIONAL
> CONFEDERATION OF RURAL LANDOWNERS

The assassination was the second major violent activity during the campaign. In January an uprising of peasants in the state of Chiapas had called attention to poverty in southern Mexico. Opposition parties warned of further revolts if they found evidence of fraud in the election.

The PRI replaced Colosio with Ernesto Zedillo Ponce de Leon as its presidential candidate. In August, Zedillo won with about 50 percent of the votes. The National Action Party was second with less than 30 percent. Seven other parties divided the remaining votes. The election once again gave the PRI large majorities in the Senate and Chamber of Deputies.

Domestic and foreign observers considered the level of election irregularities to be far lower than in previous elections. President-elect Zedillo promised to invite opposition politicians to join in a broad dialogue on government policies.

---

5 SECTION REVIEW

Section Summary
The executive branch dominates Mexico's constitutional government.

Checking for Understanding
Recalling Facts
1. Define patronage, deputy.
2. Contrast Mexico's constitution with the United States Constitution.
3. Identify three sources of presidential power in Mexico.
4. Demonstrate that the government of Mexico is a federal system.

Exploring Themes
5. Comparative Government What are the similarities and differences between the United States' and Mexico's judicial systems?
6. Political Processes How does the power of the presidential office in Mexico serve to prevent a second party from gaining national strength?

Critical Thinking Skills
7. Demonstrating Reasoned Judgment If political or economic reform comes to Mexico, is it likely to come from competing political parties or through the PRI?
8. Identifying Assumptions Why do you think Mexico limits the terms of the president, the Congress, and state governors?

828 UNIT 10: COMPARATIVE GOVERNMENT AND ECONOMIC SYSTEMS

Section 5 Review Answers

1. Definitions of terms appear on the pages indicated: **patronage,** 826; **deputy,** 827
2. The constitution of Mexico is much more specific than that of the United States.
3. the constitution, the president's role as leader of the dominant political party, and the president's command of patronage positions
4. constitution divides power between the national and state governments, states choose their own governors and legislatures, each state has its own court system
5. similarities: composed of federal and state courts, state courts handle cases of limited importance, president chooses the justices in both nations; differences: Mexico's Supreme Court has 26 justices, divided into criminal, civil, labor, and administrative divisions; United States Supreme Court, with 9 justices, has jurisdiction over cases involving federal-state relations, interstate relations, and the Constitution

6. Because the president controls patronage, helps select candidates for Congress, and initiates most legislation, the president's party dominates elections.
7. Any political reform is likely to come through the leading political party. No other group has shown it has the power to carry out reform.
8. Term limitation assumes that if a person can win reelection, that person might become too powerful.

Lech Walesa on the Polish Economy

Lech Walesa, the leader of the Solidarity party in Poland, emerged as the champion of the reform to open political and economic opportunities for his people. In an address before a joint session of the United States Congress in November 1989, Walesa urged cooperation between the United States and Poland.

Ladies and Gentlemen, it was 10 years ago, in August 1980, that there began in Gdansk shipyard the famous strike which led to the emergence of the first independent trade union in Communist countries, which soon became a vast social movement supported by the Polish Nation. I was 10 years younger then, unknown to anybody but my friends in the shipyard, and somewhat slimmer. And I must frankly say, it was important. An unemployed man at that time, fired from my job for earlier attempts to organize workers in the fight for their rights, I jumped over the shipyard wall and rejoined my colleagues who promptly appointed me the leader of the strike. . . .

For the first time in half a century Poland has a non-Communist and independent government, supported by the nation.

Peacefully and prudently, with their eyes open to dangers, but not giving up what is right and necessary, the Poles gradually paved the way for historic transformations. . . .

For the first time in half a century Poland has a non-Communist and independent government, supported by the nation.

But on our path there looms a serious obstacle, a grave danger. Our long subjection to a political system incompatible with national traditions, to a system of economy incompatible with rationality and common sense, coupled with the stifling of independent thought and disregard for national interests—all this has led the Polish economy to ruin, to the verge of utter catastrophe. The first government in 50 years elected by the people and serving the people has inherited from the previous rulers of the country a burden of an economy organized in a manner preventing it from satisfying even the basic needs of the people. . . .

I know that America has her own problems and difficulties, some of them very serious. We are not asking for charity, we are not expecting philanthropy. But we would like to see our country treated as a partner and a friend. We would like cooperation under decent and favorable conditions. We would like Americans to come to us with proposals of cooperation bringing benefits to both sides.

We believe that assistance extended to democracy and freedom in Poland and all of Eastern Europe is the best investment in the future and in peace, better than tanks, warships, and war planes. . . .I wish all of you to know and to keep in mind that the ideals which underlie this glorious American Republic and which are still alive here, are also living in faraway Poland. And although for many long years efforts were made to cut Poland off from these ideals, Poland held her ground and is now reaching for the freedom to which she is justly entitled. . . .

—LECH WALESA,
ADDRESS TO CONGRESS, 1989

Examining the Reading

Reviewing Facts
1. Name the action that led to the first independent trade union in a communist country.
2. State how long Poland was under communist rule.

Critical Thinking Skills
3. Analyzing Information How does Walesa believe each side will benefit from cooperation?

CHAPTER 28: COMPARING SYSTEMS OF GOVERNMENT   829

More About Personal Perspectives

After 13 years as an electrician in the Lenin Shipyard in Gdansk, Walesa came to world attention as a leader of the famous 1980 strike, which gained for Poles the right to organize unions independent of their government. A new union, Solidarity, was born. Within months, however, the government declared martial law, outlawed the union, and arrested its leaders. In 1983, free again, Walesa received the Nobel Peace Prize for his efforts to prevent violence in the confrontation between workers and Poland's communist government. In 1990 Walesa became Poland's first truly democratically elected president in more than 60 years.

PERSONAL
PERSPECTIVES

Focus

Ask students to name people who have been political prisoners. *(King, Mandela, Solzhenitsyn)* Point out that Lech Walesa was a political prisoner who became the president of Poland.

Teach

Ask: What problems does Walesa cite that face independent Poland? *(a long totalitarian tradition, an irrational economy, controlled behavior, and so on)* Why would these factors, which are now past history, be problems for Poland today? *(Living Poles have no democratic or free enterprise experience to guide them.)* When Walesa says "the wall that was separating people from freedom has collapsed," what do you think he means? *(Some may cite the Berlin Wall; others may suggest metaphorical references to totalitarianism.)*

Assess

Have students complete **Examining the Reading.**

Answers

1. a strike by shipyard workers in Gdansk
2. for 50 years
3. Poland would improve its economic conditions, thus stabilizing Eastern Europe and promoting world peace.

Close

Ask: Is it in the best interests of the United States to provide financial aid to struggling new democracies?

Identifying Terms and Concepts

1. unitary government; 2. premier; 3. no confidence; 4. faction; 5. cadre; 6. patronage; 7. department; 8. deputy; 9. prime minister; 10. right-wing

Reviewing Facts and Ideas

1. The government, or majority party, introduces most bills. Members debate the bill on the floor of the Commons and then send it to one of eight standing committees. Committees work out final details of all bills and then report out every bill to the House of Commons for a vote. A majority vote is needed for passage.

2. Conservative, Labour

3. negotiates treaties, appoints high officials, and acts as commander in chief of the military; in addition, the French president has two special powers—the right to appeal directly to the people by means of a referendum and dictatorial powers in times of national emergency

4. business interests, farmers, members of the middle class, and bureaucrats

5. the Politburo's Standing Committee

6. the State Council

7. Mexico's president alone selects and appoints various government officials. Most of the United States President's appointments must be confirmed by the Senate. Both presidents are the commanders in chief of the nation's armed forces. Mexico's president has the additional power to recommend legislation that takes precedence over all other legislation in Congress.

8. The constitution of 1917 established Mexico as a "representative, democratic, and federal republic formed by free and sovereign states . . . united in a stabilized federation." At the same time the constitution also limited the powers of the federal government to only those powers specifically granted to it by the constitution.

Summary and Significance

Great Britain is a constitutional monarchy with a parliamentary system. The nation's constitution is not a single document but consists of court decisions, charters, laws, and unwritten traditions. Almost all governmental authority rests in Parliament, a bicameral legislature.

France has a strong presidential government under a written constitution adopted in 1958. The president keeps in contact with the Parliament through an appointed premier who chooses ministers to head various departments. Because France has several political parties, most governments rule by forming coalitions.

Japan has a parliamentary government based on a constitution that was adopted after World War

II. The Liberal Democratic Party has dominated Japan's government for many years, and factions within that party debate most political issues.

The Communist party dominates the government of the People's Republic of China providing the great majority of local and national leaders. While the government permits some opposition parties to exist, it discourages criticism of, or protests against, state policy.

Mexico's constitution divides power among the legislative, executive, and judicial branches. It also specifies protections for workers and limits the influence of religious groups. The president has broad powers of appointment, and one political party dominates Mexican politics.

Identifying Terms and Concepts

Insert the correct terms from the following list into the sentences below.

faction, prime minister, unitary government, premier, patronage, left wing, right wing, department, no confidence, cadre, deputy, martial law

1. Great Britain has a centralized or _____ dominated by Parliament.
2. In France the president appoints a _____ to keep contact with the legislature.
3. In parliamentary government, a vote of _____ means that there will be new elections.
4. Japan has a large majority political party in which a _____ may influence policy.
5. A Chinese government official, usually a member of the Communist party, is called a _____.
6. The president of Mexico may use _____ as a means to enhance political power.
7. A unit called a state in the United States is called a _____ in France.
8. A member of Mexico's legislature is a _____.
9. The _____ is the leader of the majority party in Parliament.
10. The Gaullists are a _____ party in France.

Reviewing Facts and Ideas

1. **Summarize** how a bill becomes a law in the British Parliament.
2. **Name** the two political parties that have dominated British government since World War II.
3. **Discuss** the broad powers of the president of France.
4. **List** four groups that support the Liberal Democratic party in Japan.
5. **Identify** the elitist group that is composed of the top six Chinese Communist party leaders.
6. **Name** the governing body that operates as the executive branch of the Chinese government.
7. **Compare** the powers of the president of Mexico with those of the President of the United States.
8. **Cite** the constitutional provisions for a federal government in Mexico.

Applying Themes

1. **Comparative Government** How do the sources of power of the presidents of Mexico and of France differ?

Applying Themes

1. The president of Mexico derives power from the constitution and the fact that the president's party has dominated the government for many years. France provides most of its president's power through the constitution.

2. The House of Lords reviews legislation, and may suggest improvements. Although it has no power to prevent laws from being passed by the House of Commons, it may delay legislation.

3. Term limitation can make it possible for a larger number of people to serve in government.

4. Authoritarian governments fear the power certain freedoms give to the people.

2. **Political Processes** What is the role of the House of Lords in British lawmaking?

3. **Growth of Democracy** How does term limitation such as is found in Mexico support broader participation in government?

4. **Civil Liberties** Why do democracies generally provide more civil liberties than authoritarian governments?

Critical Thinking Skills

1. **Identifying Assumptions** Why do you think the French constitution of 1958 encouraged smaller parties to combine into larger parties?

2. **Demonstrating Reasoned Judgment** In your opinion, in which of the following countries—Mexico, France, or Japan—would constitutional reform be less likely to occur? Why?

3. **Recognizing Ideologies** Rank these countries from most socialistic to least socialistic and give reasons for your ranking: Great Britain, France, Japan, China, Mexico.

4. **Synthesizing Information** What are the advantages and disadvantages of a parliamentary system? a presidential system?

Linking Past and Present

In the 1930s, as Western democracies suffered through depressions, many people looked to the Soviet economic system as a model for progress. By 1989 severe economic trouble in the Soviet Union weakened support for centrally planned economies in many countries. From Hungary to Mexico, from Cuba to Nigeria, leaders talked of moving toward free market economies. Do you think that free markets will become widespread in the future, or will many governments shift back to central planning? Support your answer.

Writing About Government

Persuasive Writing Imagine that you are a citizen of one of the five countries studied in Chapter 28. Write a persuasive paragraph supporting your system

of government. Explain the advantages to you, as a citizen, of the government under which you live. Also point out the benefits that all citizens of the nation share. Mention some of the disadvantages of your system of government and explain why they are not very significant.

Reinforcing the Skill

Identifying Alternatives In recent decades American voter turnout has been lower than that of any other Western democracy. Many people see this as a problem. What are the roots of voter apathy and how can it be overcome? Use the following steps to identify and assess some possible reforms that would increase voter turnout.

1. Define the problem.
2. Determine the causes of the problem.
3. List possible solutions.
4. Evaluate the effects of the solutions.
5. Decide whether any one solution is superior to the status quo.

Investigating Further

1. **Individual Project** Choose a nation whose government was not described in Chapter 28. Do library research to find out about that nation's government. Is it authoritarian or democratic? presidential or parliamentary? federal or unitary? Does it have representatives? How are they chosen? Do political parties compete for offices? What rights are guaranteed by the constitution or the government? Present your findings to the class.

2. **Cooperative Learning** The Soviet Union, now known as the Commonwealth of Independent States, and several Eastern European nations began reforms in the 1980s. Several important changes, including free elections, more free market economic decisions, and the rise of political parties have already occurred. Divide the class into several groups. Have each group select one nation formerly controlled by a Communist party and gather the most current information on the reforms that are taking place. Compile the information and compare their progress.

Critical Thinking Skills

1. The writers of the constitution assumed that fewer parties would make it easier for coalitions to form and stabilize the French government.

2. Answers may include: *Mexico*—the ruling party that controls the state would probably resist changes that might threaten its power; *Japan*—the Japanese government relies more on bureaucratic policy than on legislative change; *France*—the con-

stitution adopted in 1958 has served to stabilize politics. The great number of competing party interests would make constitutional change difficult.

3. Answers may include: *China*—Communist party in control of industry, science, technology through government; *Mexico*—constitutional power of government to seize property, especially land; *France*—a strong Socialist party, but Communist party

weakening; *Japan*—Liberal Democratic party is conservative in outlook, but Socialist party has 100 seats in Diet; *Great Britain*—many socialist policies enacted in the post-war years have been overturned by the Conservative party.

4. Answers may include: A parliamentary system allows for more coordination between the legislative and executive functions of government. A parliamentary system may be less stable, because the policies of the majority may at any time lead to a vote of no confidence in government. A presidential system prevents the abuse of power by one branch by dividing the executive and legislative authority. It may become inefficient when the president and the legislature do not cooperate.

Linking Past and Present
Answers will vary.

Writing About Government
Paragraphs will vary.

Reinforcing the Skill

Sample answer: **1.** low voter turnout in the United States; **2.** stringent requirements for voter registration, other obligations on Election Day prevent voting, lack of interest in politics; **3.** (a) allow mail-in registration, (b) make Election Day a national holiday, (c) make voting a legal requirement for all citizens, (d) educate citizens about importance of voting; **4.** (a) positive: more people might register, negative: possible voting fraud; (b) positive: more people might vote, negative: loss of economic productivity; (c) positive: huge increase in voter turnout, negative: violation of people's liberties, (d) positive: more people might vote, negative: could be very expensive and not guaranteed to be effective; **5.** Decisions will vary.

Investigating Further

1. Findings will vary.
2. Information will vary.

Chapter Organizer

Objectives	Special Feature Pages	Supplemental Materials
Section 1 The Capitalist Economic System *pp. 834–840* 1. Describe how the factors of production are controlled in a capitalist economic system. 2. Explain the laws of supply and demand. 3. Summarize government regulations in the United States economic system.	Images of Government: Making Peace pp. 836–837 Study and Writing Skills: Writing a Term Paper p. 840	Guided Reading Activities Reproducible Lesson Plans Interpreting Political Cartoons 34 Primary and Secondary Source Readings 29 Section 1 Quiz Testmaker Chapter 29 Transparencies Government Themes Transparencies 49, 50 Skill Reinforcement Activities 29 SAT Practice Tests Writer's Guidebook
Section 2 The Socialist Economic System *pp. 841–844* 1. Explain the historic origins of socialism. 2. Discuss the role of central planning in a socialist economic system. 3. Summarize the effect of socialism in developing nations.	Focus on Freedom: *The Wealth of Nations* p. 842	Guided Reading Activities Reproducible Lesson Plans Cooperative Learning Activities 29 Section 2 Quiz Testmaker SAT Practice Tests Writer's Guidebook
Special Report: The European Union *pp. 845–848* 1. Trace the development of the European Union. 2. Evaluate the goals and results of Project 1992.		
Section 3 The Communist Economic System *pp. 849–853* 1. Describe the early goals and methods of Soviet central planning. 2. Evaluate the problems that plagued the Soviet economy. 3. Discuss economic decisions facing the new Commonwealth of Independent States.	Participating in Government: Understanding Foreign Exchange Rates p. 851 Global Connection: Interdependence: The Global Economy p. 852 Personal Perspectives: Boris Yeltsin on The Economic Policy of Russia p. 853	Guided Reading Activities Reproducible Lesson Plans Participating in Government 29 Interpreting Political Cartoons 41, 43 Reteaching Activities 29 Enrichment Activities 29 Section 3 Quiz Chapter 29 Tests Testmaker Government Themes Transparencies 51 Audio Cassettes (English and Spanish) Limited English Proficiency Activities 29

If time does not permit teaching this chapter, assign the Chapter 29 summary in the Unit 10 Digest on pages 883–884.

Key To Ability Levels

Teaching strategies have been coded for varying learning styles and abilities.

L1 Level 1 activities are **basic** activities and should be within the ability range of all students.

L2 Level 2 activities are **average** activities and should be within the ability range of the average to above-average student.

L3 Level 3 activities are **challenging** activities designed for the ability range of above-average students.

LEP These activities should be within the ability range of **Limited English Proficiency** students.

Multicultural Activities

In 1993 the United States approved an agreement creating a North American free trade zone. Within this area tariffs and other barriers to trade will be gradually eliminated. Debate over the impact of this arrangement, known as the North American Free Trade Agreement, on minorities was heated. Critics viewed the treaty as a threat to job security of minority workers. California representative Maxine Waters asserted that "For every industry that goes [to Mexico] and opens a plant, there's a loss of jobs in our community . . . jobs that average people can get to earn a living." John Robinson of the National Minority Business Council disagreed, saying free trade would create more jobs in the minority community. Have students research the agreement, identifying its costs and benefits, and its possible impact on minority workers.

Beginning in 1989, the sweeping economic and political changes taking place in Eastern Europe led over 500,000 people to apply for asylum in Western European nations such as Germany, France, Switzerland, and Belgium. Hundreds of thousands more entered illegally. In some Western European countries political groups formed to oppose entry of new immigrants, spurred in part by rising unemployment at home. Ask students: What difficulties might immigrants have going from a command to a socialist or capitalist economic system? What strains does mass immigration put on a nation's economic system? Is one kind of economic system better able than others to help immigrants become productive citizens?

Chapter Resources

Readings for the Student

Davis, Bertha. *Crisis in Industry: Can America Compete?* Franklin Watts, 1989.

Feinberg, Barbara Silberdick. *Marx and Marxism.* Franklin Watts, 1985.

Heilbroner, Robert and Lester Thurow. *Economics Explained.* Simon & Schuster, 1987.

Orwell, George. *1984.* Signet, 1984.

O'Toole, Thomas. *Global Economics: Economics for Today.* Lerner, 1991.

World Economic Data: A Compendium of Current Economic Information for All Countries of the World. ABC-CLIO, 1989.

Readings for the Teacher

Krugman, Paul. *The Age of Diminished Expectations: U.S. Economic Policy in the 1990s.* MIT Press, 1990.

Kuttner, Robert. *The End of Laissez-Faire: National Purpose and the Global Economy After the Cold War.* Knopf, 1991.

Nau, Henry R. *The Myth of America's Decline: Leading the World Economy into the 1990s.* Oxford University Press, 1990.

Porter, Michael E. *The Competitive Advantage of Nations.* Free Press, 1990.

Multimedia

Videocassettes

American Game, Japanese Rules. (*Frontline* series). Ofra Bikel. (v/c, 60 minutes)

Capitalism and Communism: Comparisons and Contrasts. Associated Press. (v/c, 48 minutes)

Fred Smith: Corporate Creativity: The Story of Federal Express. (*Creativity with Bill Moyers* series). CEL Communications. (v/c, 29 minutes)

Imperialism. EAV. (v/c, 44 minutes)

Software

Cartels and Cutthroats. Strategic Simulations. (Apple, IBM, Commodore 64 disks). Students explore the rigors of managing a large American corporation.

Economic Indicators. Focus Media. (2 Apple disks). Students analyze data explaining major economic indicators.

Comparing Economic Systems

Introduce

Chapter Overview

Chapter 29 details the three types of economic systems in the world today—capitalism, socialism, and communism. It discusses each system individually, explaining how each works. The chapter also explores the benefits of, and challenges faced by, each system.

Section 1 illustrates that in a capitalist, or free enterprise, economy, answers to the basic economic questions are determined by buyers and sellers.

Section 2 outlines the development and characteristics of socialism, an economic system in which the government owns or controls the major industries and provides many social welfare benefits.

Section 3 shows how failings of the government-controlled communist economy of the Soviet Union led to major economic restructuring.

Chapter 29 Themes

Display transparency 29 from the *Chapter Transparencies* in the Teacher's Classroom Resources and use the accompanying teaching strategy and student activity to compare the three major economic systems. Then ask students to suggest how the information shown illustrates the government themes for this chapter.

Communism and the Cold War

Growing Up Communist
Running Time 1:19
Side One, Chapter 9

A New Soviet Union
Running Time 3:15
Side One, Chapter 21

CHAPTER

29

The hustle and bustle of the Tokyo Stock Exchange, a major seat of the international capitalist system, reflects the hopes and frustrations of investors worldwide.

832 Unit 10: Comparative Government and Economic Systems

About the Chapter Opener

Teaching With Illustrations Point out that since Tokyo is 13 hours ahead of New York, the Tokyo exchange's business day is over before the New York Stock Exchange begins trading. Activity on the Tokyo Stock Exchange, then, may signal or influence a rise or fall in stock prices in New York. Draw students' attention to the caption. Ask them what about the picture suggests economic activity. *(large crowds, picture gives a sense of movement, and so on)*

Chapter Preview

Overview

Each nation's economic system determines how the factors of production will provide for the wants of the people.

Objectives

After studying this chapter, you should be able to:

1. **Explain** the roles of free enterprise and government regulation in the United States economic system.
2. **Summarize** the main elements of the socialist economic system.
3. **Evaluate** the communist economic system and its effects in the former Soviet Union.

Themes in Government

This chapter emphasizes the following government themes:

- **Free Enterprise** The market economy allows individuals to answer basic economic questions by their independent decisions. Sections 1, 2, and 3.
- **Public Policy** The United States has adopted a policy of regulatory legislation. Section 1.
- **Comparative Government** Economic and political systems have differences and similarities. Sections 2 and 3.

Critical Thinking Skills

This chapter emphasizes the following critical thinking skills:

- Making Comparisons
- Understanding Cause and Effect
- Analyzing Information
- Distinguishing Fact From Opinion

CHAPTER 29: COMPARING ECONOMIC SYSTEMS 833

Introducing the Chapter

Note that while Chapter 28 compared forms of government, this chapter looks at the similarities and differences among economic systems. Write *Free Enterprise, Socialism,* and *Communism* on the chalkboard and tell students that these are the major types of systems recognized by economists. Ask students to indicate what they know about these systems. List each response under the appropriate heading on the chalkboard. Suggest that they review this list for accuracy as they study Chapter 29.

Chapter Project

Have students work together or individually to create a three-part bulletin-board display that illustrates the three major economic systems. Suggest that they use the following titles for the three parts: *Free Enterprise at Work, Socialism at Work,* and *Communism at Work.* The display should include photographs, sketches, tables, charts, and graphs—accompanied by captions—that illustrate the three titles.

> **Linking Past and Present**
> In April 1945, Red Army soldiers raised the Soviet flag over the Reichstag in Berlin, Germany, signaling the emergence of the Soviet Union as a great world power. A little more than 46 years later, on December 25, 1991, officials of the Russian Republic lowered the Soviet flag from the Kremlin in Moscow, signaling the end of the Soviet empire and nation.

Setting the Scene All economic systems, regardless of the way they are structured or how they function, must face the problem of scarcity. The economic resources available to a country are scarce, or in limited supply. At the same time, however, that country's economic wants are unlimited. Decisions have to be made on which resources will be used and which wants will be met. How different economic systems make these decisions is the major focus of Chapter 29.

The Capitalist Economic System

Focus

Bell Ringer

While attendance is being taken, ask students to list the words or phrases that come to mind when they hear the term *free enterprise*.

Motivating Activity

List Bell Ringer responses on the chalkboard. Ask if any free enterprise system is truly and completely free. Ask if it should be. Tell students that free enterprise is also called *capitalism,* and that in this lesson they will learn about the characteristics of this system.

Vocabulary Precheck

Write this section's key terms and concepts on the chalkboard. Ask students to use those that they know in sentences. **LEP**

Teach

Guided Practice

L1 Classifying Ask students to identify the four factors of production in an economic system. *(land, labor, capital, management)* Ask them how each resource is important to a fast-food restaurant. *(land: roads for customers, land for building; labor: cooks, counter help, dish washers; capital: food preparation equipment, money to pay employees and suppliers, restaurant building; management: shift supervisors, general manager, district manager)* Ask: In what kind of business could labor and management be the same? *(in a small business)* **LEP**

Caption Answer
Managers combine land and labor to create it.

Every nation has its own economic system. An **economic system** is an organized method of satisfying the various wants of people from the means of production that are available. The laws, customs, and traditions of the people define this system as people work with their resources to produce goods and services.

All economic systems must provide answers to three questions: *What* should be produced with available resources? *How* should goods and services be produced? *Who* gets the goods and services that are produced? Different economic systems around the world answer these questions in different ways.

In the United States, for example, private owners make decisions about what to produce, how to organize production, and how to market what is produced. The government regulates these decisions, but does not dominate them. In some other countries, such as Cuba and North Korea, the government makes many of these decisions. The authority to make decisions about the use of available resources determines the various kinds of economic systems.

A Means of Production
Factories are one example of capital, one of the four factors necesssary to produce goods and services.
Economics How is capital created?

Factors of Production

The resources of an economic system are called **factors of production** because they are what any economy needs to produce goods and services. They may be grouped into four categories: land, labor, capital, and management.

Land The **land** includes all natural resources such as soil, water, and air. Minerals such as copper or iron ore are land resources. Rich soil for farming is a land resource, as are forests that yield timber. Some countries such as the United States, Canada, and the Commonwealth of Independent States are blessed with many land resources. Still, in the modern world no country has all the land resources it needs.

SECTION PREVIEW

Objectives
After studying this section, you should be able to:
■ Describe how the factors of production are controlled in a capitalist economic system.
■ Explain the laws of supply and demand.
■ Summarize government

regulations in the United States economic system.

Key Terms and Concepts
economic system, factors of production, land, labor, capital, management, capitalism, free enterprise system, entrepreneur, monopoly, profit, market system, law of supply, law of demand, sole

proprietorship, partnership, corporation, dividends

Themes in Government
■ Free Enterprise
■ Public Policy

Critical Thinking Skills
■ Making Comparisons
■ Understanding Cause and Effect

834 UNIT 10: COMPARATIVE GOVERNMENT AND ECONOMIC SYSTEMS

Classroom Resources for Section 1

📁 Guided Reading Activities
📁 Reproducible Lesson Plans
📁 Interpreting Political Cartoons 34
📁 Primary and Secondary Source Readings 29
📁 Section 1 Quiz

🔲 Testmaker
📎 Chapter 29 Transparencies
📎 Government Themes Transparencies 49, 50
SAT Practice Tests
Writer's Guidebook

Labor Labor is human resources—people who produce goods and services. Factory workers, farmers, doctors, plumbers, teachers, and everyone else who is employed are part of an economy's labor force. Some countries have a large skilled labor force, others do not.

Capital Capital is the means of production—money, factories, heavy machinery—used to produce other products and goods. The furnaces in a steel mill that convert iron ore to steel are capital. A printing press in a newspaper plant is capital. A truck that a builder uses to deliver a water heater to a home site is capital. Capital is not to be consumed. The steel mill will sell its steel but will keep its furnaces to produce more steel. The newspaper will sell its papers but keep its presses to print more papers. The builder will sell the home but keep the truck to use in building more homes.

Management Management includes the people who organize and direct the other three factors of production. Capital tends to be the most scarce factor of production because it requires the other three factors to create it. Thus, good managers are skilled at combining the other factors to create capital.

Characteristics of Capitalism

In modern times three types of economic systems have emerged in various countries around the world:

Forms of Business Compared

	Ownership	Control and Management	Profits and Losses
Sole Proprietorship	Individual	By owner or persons employed by owner	Owner receives profits but is personally liable for losses
Partnership	Jointly by one or more investors	By partners or persons employed by partners	Shared according to partnership agreement
Corporation	Shareholders according to the number of shares they own	Board of directors elected by the shareholders, who often hire professional managers to handle the day-to-day running of the corporation	Profits distributed to shareholders on a per share basis. Shareholders' liability limited to the price they paid for their shares in the corporation.

✓ Chart Study
In a capitalist economy the factors of production are privately controlled. **In each form of business, who decides what is to be produced and how?**

capitalism, socialism, and communism. Each of the three systems has provided its own set of very different answers to the three basic economic problems stated at the beginning of this chapter. In doing so, each system deals with the factors of production in different ways.

People have strong opinions about the strengths and weaknesses of the three principal economic systems. The authors of a book on comparative economic systems said:

In evaluating the strengths and weaknesses of capitalism, one is confronted with the possibility that the capitalist system may best sustain the fundamental human values of liberty and freedom of the individual. Indeed, it may even be the only context within which Western democratic political institutions can flourish.

—WILLIAM LOUCKS AND WILLIAM WHITNEY, *COMPARATIVE ECONOMIC SYSTEMS*, 1969

STUDY GUIDE

Themes in Government
Free Enterprise In a recent year, the American economy produced more than $5 trillion worth of goods and services.

Public Policy In the free enterprise system, capitalists, not a central authority, make the decisions affecting production.

Critical Thinking Skills
Making Comparisons Why is competition better than monopoly?
Understanding Cause and Effect How does competition force some companies out of business?

Background

The right to own and use private property in a capitalistic system is not absolute. In the United States, for example, taxes collected by all levels of government—from property taxes, to sales taxes, to income taxes—limit private property rights. Zoning restrictions, health and building codes, and environmental regulations also place limits on how people may use their private property. Further, federal laws prevent people from using their property to make certain products, such as illegal drugs or alcohol. No matter how much the citizens of the United States cherish individual freedom, public welfare will require some regulation of private property.

Interpreting Visuals Display transparency 49 from the *Government Themes Transparencies* in the Teacher's Classroom Resources and use the accompanying teaching strategy and student activity to teach about free enterprise.

L2 Economics Draw a supply curve and a demand curve on the chalkboard. Refer to the diagrams as you guide students through the following questions:
1. Tensions in the Middle East interrupt the flow of oil exports. What happens to the price of oil in the United States? Why?
2. What happens to the price of summer clothes in fall? Why?
3. New silicon-chip technology cuts the cost of producing compact-disc players. What happens to the price of CD players? Why?
4. Frost destroys about 25 percent of Florida's citrus crop. What happens to the price of orange juice? Why?

Chart Study Answer
proprietorship: sole owner; partnership: partners; corporation: depending on size, major stockholders, hired managers, or board of directors

---

STUDY GUIDE

Critical Thinking Answers
Competition offers consumers greater choices. Competition also results in lower prices.

Competitors may sell products at a price that another company cannot match. As a result, that company loses business and profits and eventually fails.

GLENCOE TECHNOLOGY

Focus on Government
Video 57
Lecture Launcher:
Comparing Economic Systems
Running Time: 2:15
Videodisc 3, Chap. 57
VHS Tape 3, Begins 49:34

Interpreting Visuals Display transparency 50 from the *Government Themes Transparencies* in the Teacher's Classroom Resources and use the accompanying teaching strategy and student activity to review the role of government in a free enterprise system.

L3 Analyzing Ideas Point out that in a typical year about 60,000 businesses fail in the United States. Ask students to suggest reasons for this large figure. Then ask whether being an entrepreneur involves too many risks. How might those who want to start a business reduce their personal risk? *(incorporate)*

Images of Government

Ask for volunteers to describe recent diplomatic events that involved the United States. Have the class discuss how these events benefitted the United States.

Answers

1. for international stability, to increase trade, to attract investment from another country

2. should be knowledgeable about and sensitive to cultural differences; should also possess strong communication and mediation skills

---

CONNECTIONS

Language

The term *entrepreneur* derives from the French word *entreprendre,* which means "to undertake," "to attempt," or "to try."

Free Enterprise In the United States, capitalism is the basic economic system. **Capitalism** is based on private ownership of the means of production and on individual economic freedom. A capitalist economic system is often called a **free enterprise system**.

In the free enterprise system, people who own the means of production are called capitalists. The owner of a small corner grocery store, the person who owns a few shares of stock in a huge corporation, industrialists who own large factories or coal mines, and those who own financial institutions are all capitalists.

Most capitalist economies today have five main characteristics. These include private ownership, individual initiative, competition, freedom of choice, and profit (or loss).

Private Ownership Capitalist economies depend on the right of private ownership of property and control of economic resources. In the United States and other capitalist countries, individuals, not the state, own most of the means of production. Governments at local, state, and national levels provide some public services such as road building, water and sewers, parks, and libraries. In addition, the government may own land, as in the case of national parks. In a capitalist system, such cases are the exception rather than the rule, however.

Capitalism also emphasizes respect for personal property not used in production. This concept means people have the right to own many kinds of goods. In the United States, the Fourth Amendment guarantees a person's property against "unreasonable search and seizure." The Fifth Amendment states that the government shall not deprive people of their property "without due process of law; nor shall private property be taken for public use, without just compensa-

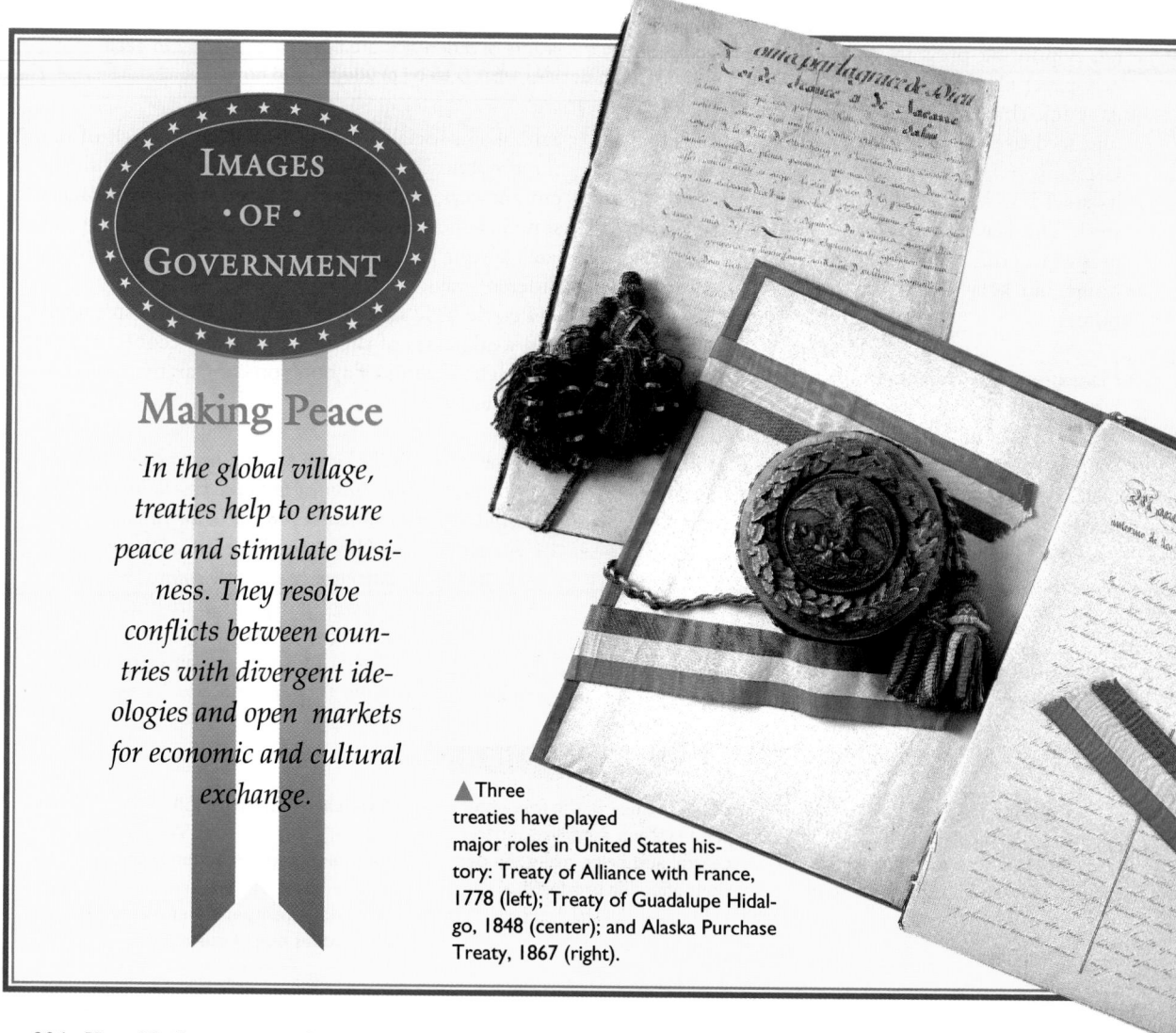

IMAGES OF GOVERNMENT

Making Peace

In the global village, treaties help to ensure peace and stimulate business. They resolve conflicts between countries with divergent ideologies and open markets for economic and cultural exchange.

▲ Three treaties have played major roles in United States history: Treaty of Alliance with France, 1778 (left); Treaty of Guadalupe Hidalgo, 1848 (center); and Alaska Purchase Treaty, 1867 (right).

836 Unit 10: Comparative Government and Economic Systems

Cooperative Learning Activity

Organize students into three groups and assign one of the following to each: the role of government, the role of consumers, the role of business. Tell groups that their task is to produce some form of illustration—a billboard design, for example—that illustrates their assigned role as it relates to the American automobile industry. Have group members brainstorm for five minutes to come up with an illustration idea. Then have group members share tasks in producing the illustration—some might make preliminary designs, others might write captions and similar explanatory materials, and still others might construct the illustration. Display illustrations on the bulletin board.

tion." The right to inherit property is another feature of private ownership in a capitalist system. In the United States, people may arrange to pass on their property to whomever they choose after they die. In a pure capitalist system there would be no limit on this right. In the United States, inheritance taxes limit this feature.

Individual Initiative In a capitalist system, the law does not prevent anyone from trying to be an entrepreneur. An **entrepreneur** is a person who takes a risk making a new product or selling a service in the hope of making a profit. Each year thousands of Americans go into business for themselves. In a recent year, for example, Americans started more than 230,000 new businesses. Many of these start-ups were in such fast-growing fields as microcomputers, bioengineering, robotics, electronic communication,

and energy. The risk stems from the fact that a new business may succeed or fail.

Starting a business sometimes involves finding a new way to put together existing products and methods. Ray Kroc founded the McDonald's food chain, but he did not invent the hamburger or the drive-in restaurant. He figured out how to provide appealing food quickly and at a low price.

Competition Another essential aspect of capitalism is competition. Competition exists when there are a number of sellers of a product or service, and no one seller can exercise control over the market price. For example, competition exists when a neighborhood or town has several different supermarkets that compete with one another for business. The supermarket that offers the best combination of price, quality, and service is likely to get the largest share of the business.

Independent Practice

L1 Free Enterprise Point out that some economists see a relationship between the development of capitalism and the development of democracy. Then have students write an answer to the following:

What aspects of democracy might encourage the growth of capitalism? Explain.

Interpreting Source Readings Have students complete activity 29 in *Primary and Secondary Source Readings* in the Teacher's Classroom Resources.

L2 Interviewing Have students talk with a local entrepreneur about the health of the free enterprise system. Interviewers should ask their subjects about the current business climate, the state of the economy, and government policies that impact their businesses. Select students to present their reports to the class.

In the 1800s, letters of credence were the credentials diplomats presented to the host countries. This one was given by Chang Yen Hoon, Chinese minister to the United States, to President Grover Cleveland on April 29, 1886.

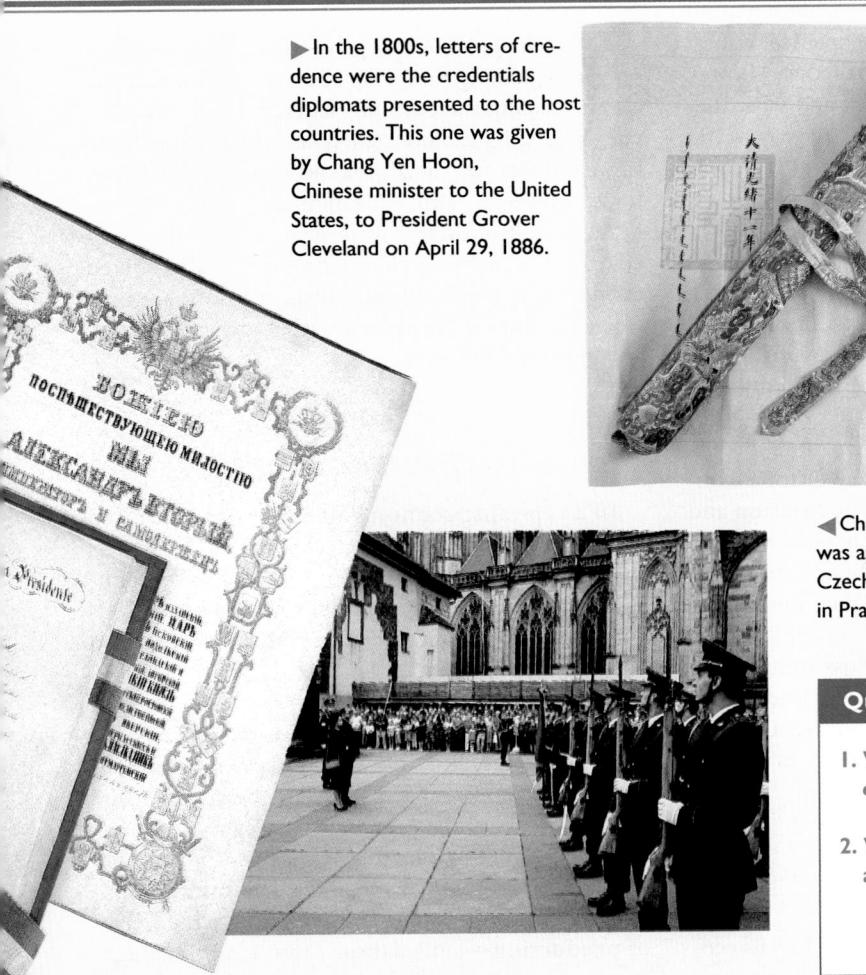

Child movie star Shirley Temple Black, who was appointed United States Ambassador to Czechoslovakia in 1989, reviews Czech troops in Prague.

Questions for Discussion

1. What are some of the reasons that countries would enter into treaties?

2. What are the important qualities an ambassador should possess?

CONNECTIONS

Economics
Businesses compete in areas other than prices. A major form of *nonprice* competition is advertising, which is designed to persuade consumers to buy certain products. Advertisers use many different approaches to convey their messages. Some focus on the qualities of the product, while others suggest an image that is created when an individual uses the product.

CHAPTER 29: COMPARING ECONOMIC SYSTEMS 837

Special Needs Strategy

Memory Impairment Traumatic brain injury (TBI) is a "new" category of disability in the special education field. There are many subtle manifestations of traumatic brain injury, the most common of which are attention and memory problems. Instructional interventions are needed to remediate and provide students with ample op-

portunities to exercise these functions. Refer students to the list of key terms and concepts in the Section Preview. Discuss techniques students can use to remember the terms—flashcards, recitation, mnemonic devices, and categorizing, for example—and demonstrate each one in class.

📁 **Interpreting Political Cartoons** Have students complete activity 34 in *Interpreting Political Cartoons* in the Teacher's Classroom Resources.

L3 Classificatory Writing Have students select a newspaper or magazine article and write an economic analysis of it. The analysis should include: a brief summary of the event discussed in the article, its economic or business impact, its impact on consumers, and the role played by government in the event.

Assess

Check for Understanding

Have students complete Section 1 Review on page 839.

Meeting Objectives

Each section objective is tested by the Section Review questions that follow it in parentheses.
- Describe how the factors of production are controlled in a capitalist economic system. (2, 4)
- Explain the laws of supply and demand. (4, 7)
- Summarize government regulations in the United States economic system. (5, 6)

Competition helps assure that the consumer will get good quality products at low prices. It also weeds out some less efficient producers, leaving those that can efficiently offer better service and products at lower prices.

Monopoly A **monopoly** is the opposite of competition. Monopoly exists when an industry includes only one seller or very few sellers, resulting in a lack of competition.

When businesses merge or when they agree to divide a market and not compete with each other, businesses limit competition. To ensure competition in free enterprise economies, governments pass laws against monopolies that try to control their markets.

Freedom of Choice Buyers, sellers, and workers all have freedom of choice in a capitalist system. Consumers can buy the products they can afford from whatever companies are selling those products. At the same time, businesses are free to provide whatever legal goods and services they think people will want.

Workers, too, are free to make their own choices. They can decide where they will work and what they will do. When new jobs open up at better pay, workers may move from one job to another. If people want to change careers, they are free to do so.

Profit (and Loss) The capitalist system is based on the profit motive. **Profit** is the difference between the amount of money used to operate a business and the amount of money the business takes in. Profits are the fuel that keep a free enterprise economy running along.

To stay alive a business must have profits. Profits are part of the reward to the entrepreneur for assuming the risk. They also pay for future expansion and provide for unexpected events. Business owners use some profits for their own income. In addition, they may reinvest some of these profits in their business or in some other company.

In a capitalist economy, the risk of loss accompanies the potential for profits. Many companies lose money or go out of business in the United States each year. Entrepreneurs must be willing to take chances and risk losses to be successful in a capitalist system.

The Role of Government

Each nation's government closely relates to its economic system. No country has ever had a pure capitalist economy, one without some government intervention. In the United States, government has played a growing role in the economy.

For the first 100 years, the United States government played a limited role in the national economy, and business was free to do largely as it wished.

By the late 1800s, a number of business practices aroused public concern. Powerful land owners, railroad barons, and industrialists squeezed out competitors and began creating monopolies. Farmers and other shippers complained that the railroads were charging discriminatory freight rates. Because immigration brought an abundance of laborers, wages fell. Families with low incomes were forced to allow their children to work. Some industries used children to work long hours in terrible conditions.

As a result of these conditions, public attitudes toward business changed. Both the states and the national government began to adopt regulatory legislation to ensure competition and promote public safety.

Today the government plays an important role not only in regulating business, labor, and agriculture but also in shaping the economy through fiscal and monetary policy. In addition, government has assumed responsibilities for social policies involving housing, transportation, health, education, and welfare.

As a result of these government policies, the United States today has what economists call a mixed economy or modified capitalism. In this economy free enterprise is combined with and supported by government regulation.

Free Enterprise at Work

In a capitalist economy like that of the United States, the market directs the economy. In its simplest form, the **market system** consists of buyers (consumers) and sellers (businesses that produce goods and services) linked together through the operation of supply and demand.

The Role of Consumers In a market system, the consumer is the boss. It is the pocketbook decisions of individual consumers that dictate the direction and level of activity of the economy.

Almost every product or service is produced because business thinks consumers will want it. Consumer demand motivates producers to use the factors of production—land, labor, capital, and management—to create goods and services in hope of mak-

838 UNIT 10: COMPARATIVE GOVERNMENT AND ECONOMIC SYSTEMS

Critical Thinking Activity

Making Comparisons Write the headings *Characteristics of Capitalism* and *Characteristics of the American Economy* on the chalkboard. Ask students to volunteer information on the above subjects. Enter students' responses under the appropriate heading. Then have students compare the "model" capitalist economy shown on the chart with the American economy. Ask: How does the American economic system comply with the model of capitalism? What aspects of the American economic system are not capitalistic? Close the activity by leading a discussion on why the United States does not have a perfectly capitalistic economy.

ing a profit. The individual decisions of more than 250 million American consumers about what and how much to buy and how much to save or invest are at the very heart of the free enterprise system. Businesses spend money and time trying to predict just how consumers are likely to spend their money.

Supply and Demand Prices are the key guideposts in a free enterprise economy. The market system matches consumer wants and needs with the goods and services businesses offer at a price considered fair by both parties. How are prices set?

In a free enterprise economy, the laws of supply and demand set prices. The **law of supply** says that prices depend on the supply of goods. The greater the supply, the lower the price; the smaller the supply, the higher the price. The **law of demand** says that prices also depend on the demand for goods. The greater the demand, the higher the price; the less the demand, the lower the price.

Businesses try to maximize their profits by making or selling goods that are most in demand. The more consumers want an item, the higher the price they are likely to pay for it. Most consumers, on the other hand, usually try to find the goods and services they want at the lowest prices available. Prices are a mechanism that helps determine what goods and services will be produced.

Forms of Business Organization The modern free enterprise economy has three forms of business: sole proprietorship, partnership, and corporation.

Most businesses in the United States are sole proprietorships. A **sole proprietorship** is a business that is owned by an individual. Most sole proprietorships are small businesses such as neighborhood retail stores, restaurants, farms, and medical practices.

A **partnership** is a business owned by two or more individuals. In a partnership, each partner shares in the profits, but, as in a sole proprietorship, each is personally responsible for the debts of the business. Most partnerships, like sole proprietorships, are small businesses.

The **corporation** has become the dominant form of business in the United States in the past 100 years. Individuals who purchase shares of stock are the actual owners of the corporation. Each share represents a very small part of ownership, however. If a corporation has 100,000 shares, for example, a person who holds 1,000 shares owns one one-hundredth of the company. One advantage of a corporation is that the shareowners' liability is limited to what they invested in the corporation, which is normally what they paid for their shares. They receive a share of the profits as **dividends** that are allocated at a certain amount per share.

Another advantage of the corporation is that because it can have many shareholders, it has access to a larger amount of capital than either the sole proprietorship or the partnership. Many businesses, such as manufacturers of automobiles, computers, or steel, that require a great deal of capital are corporations. Corporations produce more than half the total output of goods and services in the United States.

---

1 SECTION REVIEW

Section Summary
In a free enterprise economy, the decisions of buyers and sellers determine what will be produced, how much will be produced, and how it will be distributed.

Checking for Understanding
Recalling Facts
1. Define economic system, factors of production, land, labor, capital, management, capitalism, free enterprise system, entrepreneur, monopoly, profit, market system, law of supply, law of demand, sole proprietorship, partnership, corporation, dividends.
2. List the three questions that all economic systems must answer.
3. Name three economic systems that have emerged in the world.

Exploring Themes
4. Free Enterprise How are the three basic economic questions answered in the free enterprise system?
5. Public Policy What were two objectives of government regulatory legislation that began near the end of the 1800s?

Critical Thinking Skills
6. Making Comparisons How does the role of the United States government in the economy today compare to its role in the early 1800s?
7. Understanding Cause and Effect How do supply and demand interact to determine price in a market economy?

Evaluate

📁 Section 1 Quiz

💾 Testmaker

Reteach

Have students use the following main headings to outline the content of Section 1: Factors of Production, Characteristics of Capitalism, The Role of Government, Free Enterprise at Work.

Enrich

Have students contact a local business and report the following information: its form, type (wholesale, retail, service, and so on), size (work force and business volume), and history; its products or services, market (area served and type of customers), and competitors. Allow students to present their reports in tabular, written, or oral form.

Close

Lead a class discussion on the following question:

What do you think is the most important aspect of capitalism? Why?

Section 1 Review Answers

1. Definitions of terms appear on pages indicated: **economic system**, 834; **factors of production**, 834; **land**, 834; **labor**, 835; **capital**, 835; **management**, 835; **capitalism**, 836; **free enterprise system**, 836; **entrepreneur**, 837; **monopoly**, 838; **profit**, 838; **market system**, 838; **law of supply**, 839; **law of demand**, 839; **sole proprietorship**, 839; **partnership**, 839; **corporation**, 839; **dividends**, 839

2. *What* should be produced? *How* should it be produced? *Who* gets what is produced?
3. capitalism, socialism, communism
4. decisions of buyers and sellers determine answers to What? How? and Who?
5. ensure competition, promote public safety
6. In the 1800s government played a limited role. Today, government plays a greater role, regulating business and labor, shaping the economy through fiscal and monetary policy, and taking on responsibility for social policies on housing, transportation, health, and welfare.
7. The law of supply says that prices depend on the supply of goods and services. The law of demand says that prices also depend on the demand for goods and services. The interaction of supply and demand, therefore, determines prices.

Focus

Ask students to recall term papers they have written. What steps did they follow to plan, research, and write the paper? Write students' responses on the chalkboard.

Teach

Ask students to compare their responses with the Explanation steps. What steps listed on the chalkboard match those in the Explanation? Are any steps in the Explanation missing on the class list? Ask: What should you consider when choosing a topic? *(amount of information available on the topic, length the paper is to be, the amount of detail you want to include)* Why may outlines need revision? What are some ways to organize information in a term paper? *(chronologically, by order of importance, comparing or contrasting advantages or disadvantages, and so on)* Is there a place for your personal opinion in a term paper? Explain. *(Students may say yes, as long as it is clear it is their opinion.)*

Assess

Have students complete the **Practice** exercise.

Close

Challenge students to list three or four topics from this chapter that would be good ideas for term papers.

Writing a Term Paper

Researching and writing a term paper allows you to organize your ideas in a logical manner. It also allows you to study a particular topic that interests you in depth.

Explanation

To write a term paper, follow these steps:

- Choose the topic that you wish to study. As you identify topics, focus on the resources that would be available. Your topic should be broad enough to have adequate information available, yet narrow enough to focus easily on the topic.
- Make a tentative outline for your report.
- Use library resources such as the *Readers' Guide to Periodical Literature* and the card catalog to find information on your topic.
- Use note cards to record your research. These note cards will make it easier for you to organize your term paper.
- Revise your outline based on your research.
- Write a rough draft.
- Revise your draft.

Suppose you want to research recent events in Eastern Europe. If you wrote about all the countries in the region, you could not go into depth on any events. If, however, you chose one country, you could examine it in depth. You might also decide to further limit your topic to "Changes in the Communist party in Poland."

Would you find enough information to write a report? To decide you should consult the *Readers' Guide* in the library. You will find more than enough material for the term paper.

Next, write an outline for your paper. You might write:

Changes in the Communist Party in Poland
I. Rise of Solidarity
  A. 1980 Strike in Gdansk
    1. Role of Lech Walesa
    2. Official Recognition of Solidarity
  B. Suppression of Solidarity and Martial Law
    1. Underground Activities
    2. Nobel Peace Prize
II. Return of Solidarity
  A. End of Martial Law
    1. Role of General Wojciech Jaruzelski
    2. Release of Walesa
  B. Rise of Democratic Movement
    1. Demonstrations for Solidarity
    2. 1988
III. Free Elections
  A. New Leaders
  B. Democracy Triumphant
IV. Noncommunist Poland

Using your outline, the *Readers' Guide*, and the card catalog, research your topic. Be certain to take notes on note cards so that you can organize your information according to subtopic.

Use your notes to write a rough draft. After you have completed the draft, revise it. Be certain that your information is correct. Is the information presented in complete sentences? Does each paragraph have a topic sentence? Does your paper have an introduction? Does your paper include a conclusion? The final step in your revision should be to check for punctuation and spelling.

Practice

Use what you have learned about writing a term paper to answer the following questions.

1. Would the topic "The Legislative Branch" be appropriate for a four-page term paper? Why or why not?
2. Would the topic "The Reunification of Germany" be appropriate for a six-page term paper? Why or why not?
3. If you chose to write a term paper on "Lech Walesa's Role in Solidarity," what would be your first step?

Additional Practice

To practice this skill, see **Reinforcing the Skill** on page 855.

Practice Answers

1. No; topic is too broad.
2. Yes; topic has narrow enough focus.
3. Make a tentative outline.

For additional practice, have students complete activity 29 in *Skill Reinforcement Activities* in the Teacher's Classroom Resources.

The Socialist Economic System

Socialism is primarily an economic system, but it is also a political philosophy. It calls for putting the major means of production in the hands of society, either directly or through government. Thus, socialism calls for public ownership of most land, factories, and other means of production. Socialists believe in shifting economic power from individuals to society, as well as distributing wealth and income more equally among people.

Various forms of socialist economic systems exist in many countries today. Great Britain, the Scandinavian countries, and much of Western Europe are democratic countries with economic systems that are largely socialist.

Socialist political parties promote socialism in many democratic countries. These parties believe that socialist economic ideas can be put into operation through the normal procedures of democracy. Their candidates compete with other parties for office in free elections. In Sweden, Denmark, and France, social-democratic candidates have often been elected.

The Development of Socialism

The idea of collective ownership of property goes back at least to the ancient Greeks. The word *socialism*, however, was first used in the early 1800s. Socialist writers reacted to shortcomings of the Industrial Revolution to provide for the needs of large numbers of people.

During the 1800s the industrialization of Western Europe brought on many serious social problems.

Large factories began to replace small shops and home industries. Factory wages were low. It was not unusual for women and children, along with men, to work 14 to 16 hours a day for 6 days a week. Many were disabled or killed working at machines that were often unsafe. Housing in fast-growing industrial cities was typically overcrowded and unhealthful.

Early Socialists The early socialists criticized the developing capitalist economies for causing great hardships among working people they employed. In

Born of the Industrial Revolution
Karl Marx advocated socialism as a means of alleviating the plight of workers. **Economics** **What social problems did the Industrial Revolution create?**

SECTION PREVIEW

Objectives
After studying this section, you should be able to:
- Explain the historic origins of socialism.
- Discuss the role of central planning in a socialist economic system.

- Summarize the effect of socialism in developing nations.

Key Terms and Concepts
socialism, nationalization, command economy, developed nations, developing nations

Themes in Government
- Comparative Government
- Free Enterprise

Critical Thinking Skills
- Analyzing Information
- Distinguishing Fact from Opinion

Classroom Resources for Section 2

- 📁 Guided Reading Activities
- 📁 Reproducible Lesson Plans
- 📁 Cooperative Learning Activities 29
- 📁 Section 2 Quiz

- ▪ Testmaker
  SAT Practice Tests
  Writer's Guidebook

Focus

Bell Ringer

While attendance is being taken, have students explain the following statement by Karl Marx:

"From each according to his ability, to each according to his needs!"

Motivating Activity

Review students' Bell Ringer explanations. Note that Marx's statement represents the ultimate aim of socialism. Have students describe a socialist economy based on Marx's statement. Guide them by asking: Who would own the factors of production? How would wealth be distributed? Write and edit the description on the chalkboard as students develop it. Ask students to review the accuracy of their description as they study the section.

Vocabulary Precheck

List the key terms and concepts on the chalkboard. Have volunteers skim the section to find each term and concept and read it in context. **LEP**

Caption Answer
unsafe factories, low pay, long hours, child labor, crowded and unhealthful housing

---

CONNECTIONS

Economics
Why did socialism not develop a strong following in the United States? In 1906 German historian Werner Sombart pointed out that the success of capitalism had given Americans the highest standard of living in the world. "All socialist utopias come to nothing on roast beef and apple pie!" he concluded.

Teach

Guided Practice

L1 Illustrating Ideas Write the following headings on the chalkboard: *Public Ownership of Property, A Command Economy,* and *Distribution of Wealth and Income.* Ask students to give examples from specific countries of how each of these principles of socialism works. Enter responses under the appropriate heading.

📁 **Group Debate** Organize groups to complete activity 29 on the socialist system in *Cooperative Learning Activities* in the Teacher's Classroom Resources.

Focus on Freedom

Smith opposed retaliatory measures against foreign nations who set high tariffs on imports because he felt they further injured the economy. Ask students to discuss how Smith might react to calls to "buy American" and to impose high tariffs on Japanese imports.

Answers

1. the domestic producers who are protected from foreign competition
2. It will cost him more time and money to make them than to buy them.
3. It directs the people and their capital into industries in which they are less efficient.

Communism and the
Cold War
Perspective on Capitalism
Running Time :26
Side One, Chapter 7

Great Britain around 1830, Robert Owen was one of the first to use the term *socialism* to refer to plans for a better society that would more equally distribute wealth among all citizens. In 1867 Karl Marx set out the basic socialist criticisms of the capitalist system in his book *Das Kapital:*

> *The essential difference between the various economic forms of society, between, for instance, a society based on slave labor, and one based on wage labor, lies only in the mode in which this surplus labor is in each case exacted from the actual producer, the laborer.*
>
> —KARL MARX, *DAS KAPITAL,* 1867

Many socialists accepted Marx's criticisms of capitalism. They were divided, however, over his belief that history was destined to lead to a violent class struggle between the workers and the capitalists.

By the late 1800s, socialists in Europe and the United States had formed political parties. Soon these parties were united in an international socialist movement based on the ideas of Marx and other socialist thinkers.

Modern Socialists Socialists today compete for political power and influence within the framework of their countries' own political systems. In Great Britain, for example, the Labour party represents so-

---

Focus on Freedom

THE WEALTH OF NATIONS

Adam Smith published a 900-page study of economics in 1776. Primarily interested in promoting the prosperity of his nation, Smith influenced the whole course of economic ideas and development in the West, including the United States. His work became the classic statement of the doctrine of laissez-faire capitalism and signaled the end of mercantilism. In this excerpt Smith demonstrates the folly of regulation and the wisdom of free trade among nations.

By restraining, either by high duties, or by absolute prohibitions, the importations of such goods from foreign countries as can be produced at home, the monopoly of the home market is more or less secured to the domestic industry employed in producing them. . . .

That this monopoly of the home market frequently gives great encouragement to that particular species of industry which employs it, and frequently turns towards that employment a greater share of both the labour and stock of the society than would otherwise have gone to it, cannot be doubted. But whether it tends either to increase the general industry or the society, or to give it the most advantageous direction, is not, perhaps altogether so evident. . . .

To give the monopoly of the home market to the produce of domestic industry, in any particular art or manufacture, is in some measure to direct private people in what manner they ought to employ their capitals, and must in almost all cases be either a useless or a hurtful regulation. If the produce . . . can be bought there as cheap as that of foreign industry, the regulation is evidently useless. If it cannot, it must generally be hurtful.

It is the maxim of every prudent master of a family, never to attempt to make at home what it will cost him more to make than to buy. The tailor does not attempt to make his own shoes, but buys them of the shoemaker. . . .

What is prudence in the conduct of every private family, can scarcely be folly in that of a great kingdom. If a foreign country can supply us with a commodity cheaper than we ourselves can make it, better buy it of them with some part of the produce of our own industry.

—ADAM SMITH, 1776

Examining the Document

Reviewing Facts
1. Explain **who benefits from restrictions on foreign trade.**
2. Describe **why the tailor does not make his own shoes.**

Critical Thinking Skills
3. Demonstrating Reasoned Judgment **In what way is the regulation or restriction of free trade hurtful to the nation that attempts it?**

Background

Modern socialist theory was first advanced by a number of French utopian philosophers in the early 1800s. The most influential of these was Comte Henri de Saint-Simon. People from many fields and very different political persuasions—utopian socialist Robert Owen, anarchist Pierre Joseph Proudhon, Italian nationalist Giuseppe Garibaldi, economist John Stuart Mill, and sociologist Auguste Comte, for example—acknowledged a debt to him. Karl Marx, too, was influenced by Saint-Simon's writings. As he developed his own philosophy, however, Marx became disenchanted with Saint-Simon's utopianism, calling it "silly, stale, and reactionary from the roots up."

cialist ideas. From 1945 to 1951, the Labour party controlled the government. During this period it instituted many socialist programs. These programs included putting about one-fifth of the country's industry under government control and passing the National Health Service Act. That law established government-sponsored free medical and dental care for the entire population.

Main Principles of Socialism

How do socialist economic systems work? As with capitalism, socialism does not exist in pure form. No socialist government owns all property or all business. Great Britain and Sweden, for example, have mixed economies.

Public Ownership of Production A major principle of socialism is that the means of production should be publicly owned. Socialists believe government ownership will help replace the drive for profits with cooperation and social responsibility. Government ownership, Socialists argue, requires industry to take the needs of society into account rather than to be concerned primarily with making a profit.

Socialist governments often take control of industry through a process called nationalization. When **nationalization** occurs in democratic countries, the government pays private owners of the businesses that they take over. In less democratic countries, socialist governments have taken over private property with little or no compensation to the owners.

Socialist governments in different countries do not always nationalize the same industries. In Denmark, Sweden, and Norway, socialist governments nationalized only those industries considered vital to the economy and industries such as gas and electric power that are often publicly owned in some capitalist systems. Great Britain, under socialist governments, had nationalized coal mining, airlines, railways, electric power, gas, inland canal transportation, the steel industry, and the Bank of England.

A Command Economy In a capitalist system, the free market determines what goods and services are produced and at what prices. This system is called a market economy.

In socialist economies public ownership of industries affects the operation of the market. The result is what economists often call a command economy. In a **command economy**, the government makes many major economic decisions. Both socialist and communist economies are command economies. Important differences, however, distinguish the command systems in democratic socialist economies and communist economies.

One difference is that in a democratic country like Great Britain the voters can replace those in command of the economy and the government. In a communist country, there is only one party, and the people have no control over those who lead the economy.

A second difference is that most socialist countries use the command system to control only parts of their economy. Great Britain, France, Sweden, and Denmark fall into this group. The governments in these countries operate such important industries as mining and transportation. They may not operate industries that produce food, clothing, or household items like furniture or television sets. In contrast, in communist economies, government planners control every part of the economy.

Distribution of Wealth and Income Socialists believe that wealth should be distributed as equally as possible. Practically, they have tried to achieve this goal by making basic goods and social services equally available to everyone.

Modern socialist governments provide a wide array of so-called "cradle-to-grave" benefits for their citizens. Usually these benefits include free hospital, medical, and dental care; tuition-free education through college; generous retirement benefits; and low-rent public housing. Other government-provided services may include maternity allowances, free treatment for alcohol and drug abuse, and generous unemployment payments.

L3 Making Comparisons Lead students in a discussion of the socialist and capitalist economic systems. Ask: What are the strengths and weaknesses of each? What aspect of each do you think is most beneficial to society? Why?

Independent Practice

L2 Making Comparisons Ask students to research the tax rates and the methods of raising taxes in some of the democratic socialist countries mentioned in this section. Have them present their findings in the form of a chart.

STUDY GUIDE

Critical Thinking Answers Public ownership recognizes the needs of the many rather than the profits of the few.

conditions and problems related to industrialization in Western Europe

Assess

Check for Understanding

Have students complete Section 2 Review on page 844.

Meeting Objectives

Each section objective is tested by the Section Review questions that follow it in parentheses.
- Explain the historic origins of socialism. (2, 8)
- Discuss the role of central planning in a socialist economic system. (3, 4, 5, 7)
- Summarize the effect of socialism in developing nations. (6)

STUDY GUIDE

Themes in Government
Comparative Government
Active socialist parties exist in Europe, India, and Australia.
Free Enterprise Between 1953 and 1956, the Conservative party returned the nationalized British steel industry to private ownership.

Critical Thinking Skills
Analyzing Information Why do some think public ownership is more humanitarian than private ownership?
Distinguishing Fact from Opinion On what facts did early Socialists base their opinions?

CHAPTER 29: COMPARING ECONOMIC SYSTEMS   843

Special Needs Strategy

Memory Impairment Students with traumatic brain injuries often are impulsive in their responses. Establish ways to monitor their performance, with ample checkpoints to evaluate their levels of understanding. For example, have some students read this section and take notes that are to be given to you for review, or have some students read the paragraphs under the heading "Main Principles of Socialism" and write three main-idea sentences for your review. Provide students with immediate feedback on their assignments.

Evaluate

📁 Section 2 Quiz

💾 Testmaker

Reteach

Have students compare a command economy to a market economy. Ask them to describe the differences in the way the two systems answer the basic economic questions.

Enrich

Have students research and write a report on the role of socialism in the economy of a developing country in Africa, Asia, or Latin America.

Close

Have students discuss the meaning of the following statement by Peruvian novelist Mario Vargas Llosa:

"You cannot be a modern man and a Marxist."

CONNECTIONS

Language
The sweeping changes in Eastern Europe and the collapse of the Soviet Union have tainted words like *socialist* and *communist*. Political parties with such words in their names have made changes to avoid any negative reactions. Many now call themselves Social Democrats or Democratic Left or the like.

Critics of socialism claim such policies create a welfare state and make people overly dependent on government. Socialists answer that every person should be able to receive such basic necessities as food, shelter, clothing, and medical care.

Cradle-to-grave services do not come free, however. Socialist governments require citizens to pay very high taxes to pay for social services. Businesses in socialist economies are also heavily taxed.

When socialist governments in socialist democracies are voted out of office, the governments that replace them may change their programs. In most countries socialist welfare measures have been popular with voters and have been retained. Sometimes, however, nationalized industries have been returned to private ownership.

Socialism in Developing Areas

Socialism has different characteristics in developing nations from those in developed nations. **Developed nations** are countries that have successfully used natural resources to develop a way of life based on business and industry. Most of these countries enjoy a high standard of living.

Developing nations are countries that are still trying to develop industrial economies. They do not yet have large, complex industries to produce goods and services in great quantities. Some, like Zaire, have many valuable natural resources but are just beginning to create the facilities to take advantage of them.

Other developing countries, such as Ethiopia and Burkina Faso, are very poor and have few resources.

Many developing nations believe that they can make economic progress only by adopting socialist programs. Socialism in developing nations aims to raise the standard of living of the large masses of poor people. Socialist governments in these countries often use centralized planning to an even greater extent than developed socialist nations do. They believe only central planning can achieve rapid industrial growth. In many of these nations, authoritarian governments take over economic planning. Many of these governments focus on welfare and education programs for the poor.

In many developing nations, socialism has had disappointing results. Despite attempts to raise the standard of living of their people, not much progress has been made. As a result, in many cases socialist governments have been overthrown. Totalitarian or authoritarian regimes have replaced some. In others, people have elected leaders who promise free-enterprise solutions. A recent news item from Uruguay is a typical example:

Montevideo—Opposition candidate Luis Alberto Lacalle . . . was elected president November 26 in Uruguay's first free elections since 1971. . . . A rancher and lawyer, Lacalle has promised to solve economic stagnation and rising inflation by privatizing state companies, cutting government spending, encouraging a free economy. . . .
—THE WORLD & I, FEBRUARY 1990

---

2 SECTION REVIEW

Section Summary
In a socialist economy the government owns or controls the major industries and provides many social welfare benefits.

Checking for Understanding
Recalling Facts
1. Define socialism, nationalization, command economy, developed nations, developing nations.
2. Summarize the origins of socialism.
3. List the wide array of cradle-to-grave benefits socialist governments provide their citizens.
4. Compare a socialist command economy in a democratic country with a command economy in a communist country.

Exploring Themes
5. Comparative Government What difference exists between the role of a Socialist party in a democratic nation and the Communist party in a communist state?
6. Free Enterprise Why have some leaders in developing nations promised to encourage a free-market economy?

Critical Thinking Skills
7. Analyzing Information How have developments in Eastern Europe and the former Soviet Union affected the debate over Marxism and capitalism?
8. Distinguishing Fact from Opinion Why have people often confused facts and opinions when discussing capitalism, socialism, and communism?

Section 2 Review Answers

1. Definitions of terms appear on pages indicated: **socialism,** 841; **nationalization,** 843; **command economy,** 843; **developed nations,** 844; **developing nations,** 844
2. The Industrial Revolution brought on serious social problems. The early socialists criticized the developing capitalist economies for causing great hardships among working people and called for a society that would more equally dis-

tribute wealth.
3. free medical care, free education, generous unemployment and retirement benefits, low-rent public housing, maternity allowances
4. democratic country—government controls only parts of economy, voters can replace government, and those controlling economy, through elections; communist country—government commands all of economy, only one party and voters have no control over those who are in command of the economy

5. The Socialist party in a democratic state competes with other parties to run the government. In a communist state, the Communist party has no competition.
6. because socialism has had disappointing results
7. When these nations abandoned communism in favor of democratic socialism or moving toward more free market economies, many people challenged Marxism.
8. Answers may include: these are highly-charged emotional issues; people have such strong opinions that they may believe that these opinions are facts.

THE EUROPEAN UNION

By Nigel Armstrong
United States Foreign Service, Retired

*T*he leaders of the major nations of Europe created Project 1992 in the mid-1980s. Designed to eliminate internal trade barriers and make Europe competitive with the United States, Project 1992 had its origins in trade pacts signed in the 1950s.

Report Preview

Objectives
After studying this report, you should be able to:
- **Trace** the development of the European Union.
- **Evaluate** the goals and results of Project 1992.

Key Terms and Concepts
nationalism, sovereignty

Themes in Government
This report emphasizes the following government themes:
- **Global Perspectives**
  Twelve nations of Western Europe united to form the European Community (now the European Union) and reduce trade restrictions.
- **Comparative Government**
  Project 1992 was designed to create a unified Europe.

Critical Thinking Skills
This report emphasizes the following critical thinking skills:
- **Analyzing Information**
- **Understanding Cause and Effect**

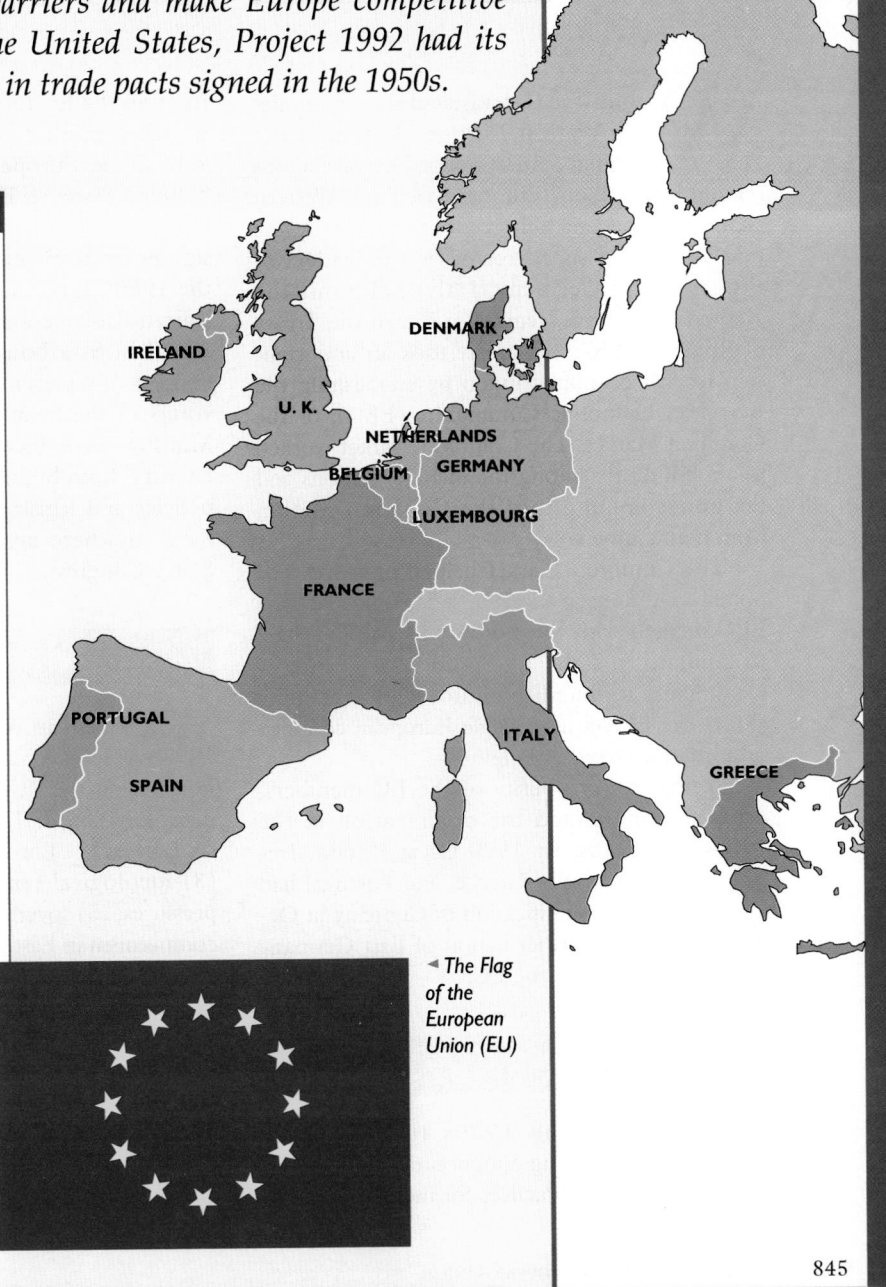

◄ The Flag of the European Union (EU)

Focus

Bell Ringer
While attendance is being taken, have students write a definition of the word *community*.

Motivating Activity
Ask for volunteers to give their Bell Ringer definitions. Focus on such words and phrases as *geographic area, groups of nations, association, common interests, mutual advantage,* writing them on the chalkboard. Then point out that the community discussed in this special report is the European Union, formerly the European Community, an association of nations that have common political, economic, and trade interests.

Vocabulary Precheck
Call on students to read aloud the definitions for each key term and concept from the Glossary. Then have them restate each definition in their own words. **LEP**

CONNECTIONS

Geography
The EU promotes a common European identity and awareness through the use of a community flag and anthem and the issue of such documents as European passports and driver's licenses. At the same time, the EU encourages national and regional cultural identities by conducting business in nine official languages and supporting a number of minority languages.

845

Background

In 1950 French diplomat Jean Monnet and French foreign minister Robert Schuman took the first steps toward European economic unity when they put forward the Schuman Plan, a program to establish a tariff-free market in coal and steel. The following year France, West Germany, Italy, Belgium, Luxembourg, and the Netherlands signed the Treaty of Paris, creating the European Coal and Steel Community (ECSC). At the 1957 meeting in Rome, as well as creating the European Economic Community (EEC), these six nations also established the European Atomic Energy Community (EAEC).

Teach

Guided Practice

L1 Making Comparisons On the chalkboard draw a table with *United States* and *European Union* as vertical headings and *Similarities* and *Differences* as horizontal headings. Ask students to make suggestions on entries for the table. Write responses in the appropriate columns. **LEP**

L2 Debate Organize students into two groups. Have the groups debate the following statement:

The collapse of the Soviet Union and the violent breakup of countries such as Yugoslavia indicate that the European Union has little chance of achieving real unity among its members.

Independent Practice

L1 Geography Provide students with the following information on EU membership:

France, West Germany, Italy, Belgium, Luxembourg, and the Netherlands—original members; Great Britain, Ireland, and Denmark admitted in 1973; Greece admitted in 1981; Spain and Portugal admitted in 1986; East Germany automatically admitted after German reunification in 1990; Austria, Sweden, Finland, and Norway to be admitted in 1995. As the Soviet Union collapsed in late 1991, the EC considered offering associate status to eastern European nations. An EC foreign commissioner said, "It is possible we will end up with a community of 24 or more."

Give students outline maps of Europe. Ask them to use information in the text and in news magazines to construct a map showing when countries became EU members or will be considered for membership. Remind them that their maps must be accompanied by a key. **LEP**

► London was bombed heavily by German planes during the London Blitz of 1940-1941. Many buildings were destroyed and about 30,000 residents were killed.

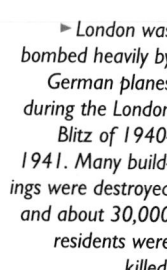

World War II devastated the economies of Western Europe. Although the United States provided massive aid to rebuild bombed-out European facilities, Western economies had not fully recovered—even by the mid-1950s. To speed recovery, the leaders of France, West Germany, Italy, Belgium, the Netherlands, and Luxembourg signed the Treaty of Rome in 1957. The treaty took an important step toward economic union by establishing the European Economic Community (EEC), or the Common Market. The Common Market worked to abolish tariffs among the member nations and tax goods coming into the Common Market from nonmembers.

The Common Market helped improve economic conditions in the 1960s. Then in 1967 the EEC merged with the European Coal and Steel Community and the European Atomic Energy Community to found the European Community (EC). The EC set up a single European commission headquartered in Belgium.

Seeing the prosperity of the EC members, other nations joined the organization in the 1970s and 1980s. By 1990 Great Britain, Ireland, Denmark, Spain, Greece, and Portugal had joined. With the reunification of Germany in October 1990, the former nation of East Germany also became a part of the EC.

Project 1992

Throughout the 1980s the EC made progress toward setting common taxation, credit, and worker benefit practices for member nations.

In 1986 the EC formally launched Project 1992 to achieve full economic integration by that year. Some Europeans even hoped to create a "United States of Europe." Although European unity remained an elusive goal, the EC made significant gains even before Project 1992. In the 1960s, for example, the EC created the European Parliament and the Council of Ministers. Based in Strasbourg, France, the Parliament consists of representatives elected directly by the voters of the member nations. The Council of Ministers includes major leaders from each EC country. Both bodies play significant roles in EC policies and legislation. They do not, however, have anywhere near the power of the United States Congress.

Mixed Results

Although no one can dispute that Project 1992 has toppled almost all trade barriers, it has not created the "United States of Europe" that many envisioned. The mixed results were due to six factors: (1) Europe's history; (2) nationalism; (3) ideological tensions; (4) internal political pressures; (5) sovereignty; and (6) the collapse of communism in Eastern Europe.

History Although many Europeans desire political and economic unity, individual nations have long histories of quarrels. For example, Britain and France have long suspected each other's goals. Spain and France have quarrelled over boundaries, as well. France and Germany have fought three major wars since 1871. The histo-

846 SPECIAL REPORT: THE EUROPEAN UNION

Cooperative Learning Activity

Organize students into teams of seven to take part in a "speed round" activity. Write a seven-question review of the content of the Special Report or, to save time, use the Report Review on page 848. Give teams a few minutes to decide which member will answer which question. Then have teams race each other to finish the review as quickly and as accurately as possible. While speed is important, the team that finishes the review with the fewest or no mistakes is the winner. Work through the review and have teams adjust incorrect answers.

◄ *Present-day London is one of the vibrant cultural and political capitals of Europe.*

L2 Comparative Government
Refer students to the diagram on page 78 that shows the structure of the national government. Have students construct a similar diagram to show the organization and structure of the government of the EU. Select students to display their diagrams on the bulletin board.

ries of such disputes are not easy to put aside. As one political scientist noted:

Having been neighbors for so long, the Europeans have come to view each other as neighbors so often do: with friendly disdain. Like the members of a close family, they know each other too well for idealism to be the basis of a lasting relationship.
—TERRY CLARK, BUSINESS HORIZONS, 1991

Nationalism European countries also have a long tradition of **nationalism,** or intense pride in and loyalty to one's native country. Most Americans tend to think of themselves as Americans first and Floridians, New Yorkers, or Texans second. In contrast many Europeans feel just the opposite—as German, British, or Spaniard first and as European second. In addition, each nation has a distinct culture that few if any citizens want to abandon. As yet, a separate and united European culture does not exist.

Ideological Tensions Europeans have not yet agreed on the form or even the purpose of a united Europe. Some, such as former British prime minister Margaret

Thatcher, want it to be strictly economic, designed to make Europe competitive with the United States. Others, such as French president François Mitterrand, want the union to provide social services and protect European workers from outside competition.

Internal Pressures European nations have traditionally restricted immigration, in part to protect jobs. With no national boundaries, workers from all over Europe would move to find the best jobs. A glut of foreign laborers settling in Spain, for example, would lead to local resentment and perhaps even to labor unrest.

▲ *The European Union has headquarters in Brussels, Belgium.*

SPECIAL REPORT: THE EUROPEAN UNION **847**

Assess

Check for Understanding
Have students complete the Report Review on page 848.

Meeting Objectives
Each report objective is tested by the Report Review questions that follow it in parentheses.
• Trace the development of the European Union. (2, 3, 4)
• Evaluate the goals and results of Project 1992. (4, 5, 6, 7)

CONNECTIONS

History
At a historic meeting in Maastricht, the Netherlands, in December 1991, leaders of the EC's member states committed to establishing a single internal market by January 1993; a common European currency by 1999; and a common European defense force, the Western European Union (WEU), immediately.

Evaluate
Have students write brief explanations of the six factors that might keep the European Union from complete unity. Call on several students to read their explanations to the class.

Critical Thinking Activity

Understanding Cause and Effect Have students complete the following cause/effect relationships:
1. Cause: Western European economies had not recovered from World War II. Effect: (*Leaders of France, West Germany, Italy, Belgium, Luxembourg, the Netherlands signed Treaty of Rome in 1957.*)
2. Cause: (*EU members prospered.*) Effect: Other nations sought to join the EU.
3. Cause: EU members disagree over the purpose of a united Europe. Effect: (*Complete European unity is threatened.*)
4. Cause: (*Communism collapsed in Eastern Europe and the Soviet Union.*) Effect: A real political threat to Western Europe was removed.

Reteach

Have students research and write a report on the progress of the European Union toward political and economic unity. Suggest that they use the *Readers' Guide to Periodical Literature* to locate useful articles.

Enrich

Have students research the operations of the EU by seeking information from the EU Information Service, 2100 M Street NW, Suite 707, Washington, DC 20037. Have students share the information they receive.

Close

Have students imagine they are American political and business leaders. Ask them to explain how they feel about the creation of a single market in Europe.

CONNECTIONS
Economics
In 1973, when Great Britain joined the EC, only 30 percent of its trade was with EC members. Today, more than 50 percent of Britain's trade is with its European partners.

A meeting of the European Community, Paris, 1989

Sovereignty A key characteristic of a nation-state is its **sovereignty**—that the nation retains all power within its borders. A unified Europe calls for nations to voluntarily give up this sovereignty—in effect to renounce their status as independent nations. Seldom have nations done so.

Fall of Communism Communist nations of Eastern Europe posed a very real political threat to Western Europe during the cold war. With that threat removed, vast markets opened in Eastern Europe. European leaders knew that in time the European Union would encompass both east and west.

Progress

Project 1992 helped bring a degree of political unity to the European Community. The economic success of the European Union, however, is largely responsible for its attractiveness to potential members. Austria, Finland, Sweden, and Norway were on track to join the EU in January 1995. Austria's voters overwhelmingly supported the idea. The addition of the three Nordic nations would greatly expand the EU's borders and its economic power. The EU's population would be about 370 million and its total GDP would reach $6.3 trillion. For the first time, the European Union would share a border with Russia. How far would the EU eventually extend? Norway's Prime Minister speculated a union of all Europe "maybe in the future."

REPORT REVIEW

Summary
Rising from the ashes of World War II, six nations of Western Europe formed the Common Market, or European Economic Community, in 1957. By 1991 six other nations had joined what became known as the European Community (EC). One of the goals of the EC was to promote a unified Europe to compete in international trade with Japan and the United States. Although unity remained elusive, the EC, now called the European Union, continued to gain members.

Checking for Understanding
Recalling Facts
1. Define nationalism, sovereignty.
2. List the three organizations that joined to form the European Community.
3. Name the 12 members of the EU.

Exploring Themes
4. Global Perspectives **What was the major goal of Project 1992?**
5. Comparative Government **How do Britain and France view the role of a unified Europe differently?**

Critical Thinking Skills
6. Analyzing Information **Why might nations be reluctant to surrender their sovereignty to a unified Europe?**
7. Understanding Cause and Effect **What effect might a unified Europe have on the American economy?**

Report Review Answers

1. Definitions of terms appear on pages indicated: **nationalism,** 847; **sovereignty,** 848
2. European Economic Community, European Coal and Steel Community, and European Atomic Energy Community
3. France, Germany, Italy, Belgium, the Netherlands, Luxembourg, Great Britain, Ireland, Denmark, Greece, Spain, and Portugal

4. full economic integration of Europe by 1992
5. Britain wants an economic union, while France wants the union to provide social services throughout the community and to protect European workers from outside competition.
6. because, in effect, this would entail renouncing their status as independent states
7. Answers will vary. negative effects: Since there will be

no tariffs, EU members will prefer trade among themselves instead of with countries outside EU—this will have harmful impact on American exports; new environmental and quality standards for goods established by EU might require American manufacturers to retool factories; positive effects: One market and common standards could cut administrative and production costs for American companies that trade with EU members.

The Communist Economic System

Communism is both a political and an economic system. Socialism and communism have many ideas in common. Both economic systems stem from the ideas of Karl Marx, a German thinker who first called his ideas scientific socialism.

Communists believe force and revolution must overthrow capitalism. Unlike democratic countries with a socialist economic system, communist states operate their economies on the basis of a dictatorship. In theory this dictatorship will exist until pure communism is achieved. Under pure communism, no private property exists, and each person works for the good of all.

Soviet Economic Overview

Beginning in 1917 the Soviet Union built the world's leading communist economic system. The Soviet Union officially called itself a socialist economy, but the Soviet Union used the term *socialism* in a different sense from the democratic socialist countries. The Soviet Union regarded its socialism as an intermediate stage in the transformation of Soviet society from capitalism to pure communism.

A major difference between noncommunist socialist systems and the Soviet economy was that an authoritarian political party—the Communist party—closely controlled every part of the Soviet economy. In the Soviet Union, the government, meaning in actual practice, the Communist party, made nearly all economic decisions. Almost all enterprises were state owned and operated. The government also controlled labor unions, wages, and prices.

Soviet Economic Problems

The Soviet Union built one of the world's largest economies and came to rival the United States as a superpower. Its defense industries almost matched anything the United States made. Yet the rest of the Soviet economy faced very serious problems.

Beginning in the mid-1980s, the Soviet gross national product (GNP) grew by only 2 or 3 percent a year. Development of heavy industry, once a bright spot for the Soviets, slowed. Soviet products could not compete in world markets. The huge, oppressive state bureaucracy that managed every detail of Soviet production bred economic stagnation.

Mikhail Gorbachev, Soviet leader at the time, described the situation this way:

> *A*t some point the country began to lose momentum. Economic failures became more frequent. Difficulties began to accumulate . . . . Elements of stagnation began to appear in the life of society.
> —MIKHAIL GORBACHEV

Soviet central planning created four main problems. First, it encouraged producers to meet targets with goods that were easy to produce rather than with goods that were the most needed. Second, the system failed to produce badly needed consumer goods and services. Third, the quality of goods suffered. Finally, the system discouraged new ideas.

The Easy Way Out Factory managers, anxious to meet their production targets, often turned out those goods that were easiest to produce. For example, a

---

SECTION PREVIEW

Objectives
After studying this section, you should be able to:
- Describe early goals and methods of Soviet central planning.
- Evaluate the problems that plagued the Soviet economy.

- Discuss economic decisions facing the new Commonwealth of Independent States.

Key Terms and Concepts
communism, state farm, collective farm, coup

Themes in Government
- Free Enterprise
- Comparative Government

Critical Thinking Skills
- Analyzing Information
- Understanding Cause and Effect

CHAPTER 29: COMPARING ECONOMIC SYSTEMS   849

Classroom Resources for Section 3

- 📁 Guided Reading Activities
- 📁 Reproducible Lesson Plans
- 📁 Participating in Government 29
- 📁 Interpreting Political Cartoons 41, 43
- 📁 Reteaching Activities 29
- 📁 Enrichment Activities 29

- 📁 Section 3 Quiz
- 📁 Chapter 29 Tests
- 📇 Testmaker
- 🔊 Government Themes Transparencies 51
- 🎧 Audio Cassettes (English and Spanish)
- 📁 Limited English Proficiency Activities 29

Focus

Bell Ringer

While attendance is being taken, ask students to write what they think is meant by the term *central planning*.

Motivating Activity

Review students' Bell Ringer responses. Focus on answers that mention that decision making is limited to a small number of people or institutions. Then point out that in an economic context, central planning means that all economic decisions are made by a small group of government officials. Ask students to relate this approach to the decision-making process in the American economy.

Vocabulary Precheck

List the key terms and concepts on the chalkboard. Have students develop questions for which each term or concept is an answer. **LEP**

Teach

Guided Practice

L1 **Understanding Ideas** Point out that during the 1980s, prior to the introduction of *perestroika*, the Soviet Union produced about 1.2 million automobiles each year. Ask students to describe how Soviet central planners arrived at this decision. As a guide, remind students of the three basic economic questions: *What* should be produced? *How* should it be produced? *For whom* should it be produced? **LEP**

Focus on Government
Video 56
Lecture Launcher:
Comparing Systems of Government
Running Time: 2:59
Videodisc 3, Chap. 56
VHS Tape 3, Begins 46:32

Video 57
Lecture Launcher:
Comparing Economic Systems
Running Time: 2:15
Videodisc 3, Chap. 57
VHS Tape 3, Begins 49:34

Interpreting Visuals Display transparency 51 from the *Government Themes Transparencies* in the Teacher's Classroom Resources and use the accompanying teaching strategy and student activity to teach the development of free enterprise in the former Soviet Union.

L3 Panel Discussion Select four or five students to take part in a panel discussion on the following statement:

It is in the best interests of the United States and other Western nations to provide economic aid to the former Soviet republics.

Encourage other students to challenge panel members' arguments.

Independent Practice

L1 Mathematics Have students collect 5 to 10 pieces of statistical information that illustrate the economic problems facing the Commonwealth of Independent States. Have students share their findings with other members of the class. **LEP**

Caption Answer
Because all economic decisions were made by government, initiative was unnecessary and unrewarded.

STUDY GUIDE

Critical Thinking Answers
Perestroika allowed for the establishment of private enterprises in certain industries and the decentralization of decision making in many state-owned businesses.

Shortages of food and consumer goods caused the Soviet people to become dissatisfied with the Soviet government and the communist system.

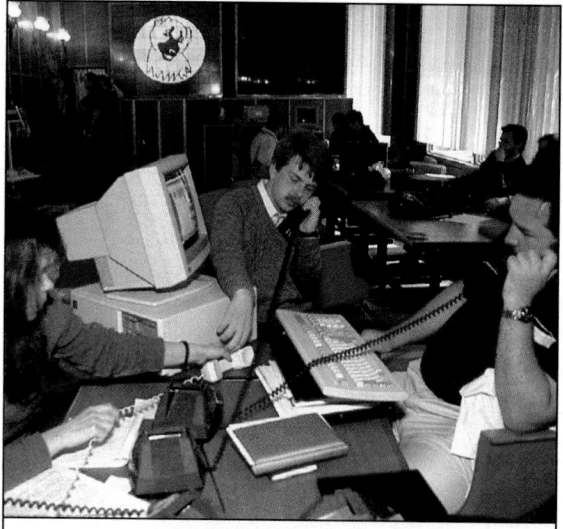

Brand New: A Russian Commodities Exchange
With the demise of Soviet communism, many private businesses sprang up throughout Russia. **Economics Why didn't communism foster initiative?**

factory that made nails was told to produce 100 tons of nails. The factory manager produced large nails because fewer such nails were needed to reach the 100-ton target. Builders and carpenters in another part of the economy, however, really needed small nails. Situations like this created shortages of needed items in various parts of the Soviet economy.

Few Consumer Goods and Services Central planning directed most Soviet resources into heavy industry and military hardware. In an era that stressed consumer goods, the Soviet economy was not able to deliver the goods and services consumers needed. Items such as potatoes, onions, toothpaste, well-made clothing, coffee, and sugar were hard to find in state stores. People had money but there was little or nothing to buy.

Little Concern for Quality Economic planners made few provisions for quality. Instead, they focused on quantity. As a result, the quality of goods pro-

duced suffered because the Soviets had, in effect, created a system that valued the production of 100 clunking, low-quality tractors more highly than the creation of 10 smoothly running ones.

Consumer goods in the Soviet Union acquired a reputation for shoddiness. Soviet economists reported that only 10 percent of their finished products could compete with those made in the West.

Resistance to New Ideas Hard-pressed Soviet plant managers trying to meet production targets often resisted efforts to install new machines or new methods. The managers believed interruption would slow down production and cause them to miss their production quotas. Everyone wanted to stick with traditional ways of doing things. This attitude led to an inefficient economic system.

Agriculture in the Soviet Union

About 98 percent of all Soviet farmland was under government control. As a result, farming, like industry, had to follow government production plans. About two-thirds of Soviet farmland consisted of state farms. **State farms** were owned by the government and run like factories, with the farm workers being paid wages.

The remaining one-third of Soviet farmland consisted of collective farms. On a **collective farm,** a large number of farm families were grouped into a collective to work the land together. The government owned the land but rented it to the collective.

Causes of Problems Many of the Soviet Union's problems with agriculture came not so much from natural causes like droughts but from government mismanagement of production. Farm workers had little incentive to work hard on vast state-run farms. Inefficiency was widespread. For example, 20 percent of the grain and fruit harvest and 50 percent of the potato crop were wasted each year because of either late harvesting or inadequate storage facilities.

STUDY GUIDE

Themes in Government
Free Enterprise Capitalism rewards taking risks, the Soviet economy rewarded caution.
Comparative Government The Commonwealth of Independent

States resembled the American states after the Revolutionary War.

Critical Thinking
Analyzing Information How did *perestroika* **help reshape the economy?**

Understanding Cause and Effect How did economic problems affect the morale of the Soviet people?

Background

The blueprint for the Soviet economy was a national plan. Soviet strategy developed a new plan every 5 years. *Gosplan,* the powerful state planning committee, created the plan, and set most prices and production goals for heavy industry. This, obviously, was an enormous task. One Soviet expert estimated that *Gosplan* handled 7 million documents and made 83 million calculations each year! Traditionally, the key measure for success in the Soviet economy was the extent to which the plan's quotas were met, rather than the amount of profit or loss—the standard in capitalist economies.

Beginnings of Perestroika

Mikhail Gorbachev, who came to power in 1985, began a major campaign to reform and improve the Soviet economy. This effort was called *perestroika*, or full-scale economic restructuring.

Examples of Reconstruction Under Gorbachev's leadership Soviet officials sought immediate results. They put in place hundreds of new economic decrees and laws.

An individual labor law legalized small-scale service businesses in such areas as plumbing, auto repair, and dressmaking. The law gave Soviets a chance to legally start and run their own businesses by registering their activities with the government.

Another law put more than 76,000 factories and farms on a self-financing basis. These units would now depend on their own earnings rather than government money to operate. The aim was to increase production by punishing inefficient units and rewarding high achievers.

Agricultural Reform As part of perestroika, planners made a number of changes in Soviet agriculture.

They merged five different farm ministries, gave greater freedom to state-run farms, and permitted an increasing number of crops to be sold at uncontrolled prices.

Farm work was reorganized. Small teams of workers contracted to run the farms. They used the land, as well as equipment, for the period of the contract. Team members were totally responsible for managing their own work. Each team's income at the end of the contract depended on how hard they worked and how much they produced.

Results of Perestroika

After 6 years of attempts at economic reform, the Soviet economy suffered severe setbacks. The Soviet gross national product fell 10 percent in the first half of 1991, and prices rose 48 percent. Experts expected inflation to reach 250 percent. Soviet citizens called for Gorbachev's resignation.

Soviet Troubles Several republics threatened to secede from the Soviet Union. Then, in August 1991 a group of Communist hard-liners attempted to seize

---

PARTICIPATING IN GOVERNMENT

Understanding Foreign Exchange Rates

If you travel to Mexico, you will have to exchange your dollars for pesos. If you go to France, you will need francs. In Britain, you will need pounds. What determines the rate of exchange?

An exchange rate is the price of one country's currency expressed in terms of another country's currency. Rates vary from day to day in relation to worldwide demand for each nation's currency. If Americans buy increasing amounts of Japanese goods, for example, the Japanese hold more American dollars. The value

of the dollar decreases in relation to the yen (Japanese currency). Each country keeps a reserve of foreign currency. A government will use some of its foreign currency to buy back enough of its own currency to stabilize the exchange rate.

If you travel to Britain when the exchange rate is $1.40 per pound, each of your dollars will buy about

.71 of a pound. In other words, you would get about 71 pounds in exchange for 100 dollars. The exchange rate also affects the price of imported goods. Using the exchange rate from the example above, you would pay $14 for an imported scarf that cost 10 pounds in Britain.

Investigating Further

Many newspapers publish daily reports on the exchange rates of major currencies. Check the current rates. Find out where you could get the best exchange rate for the dollar.

CHAPTER 29: COMPARING ECONOMIC SYSTEMS 851

Cooperative Learning Activity

Organize students into groups of three and tell them their task is to create a time capsule that will tell people of the future what a communist economic system was like. Suggest that students search for photographs or other forms of illustrations; written materials such as books, pamphlets, or slo-

gans; or artifacts that illustrate some aspect of communism. Have students display the materials that they locate. Then have the class as a whole select the best materials for inclusion in the time capsule. You might display the time capsule contents for other civics and government classes.

L2 Informative Writing Have students write a biographical sketch of Mikhail Gorbachev or Boris Yeltsin.

Interpreting Political Cartoons Have students complete activities 41 and 43 in *Interpreting Political Cartoons* in the Teacher's Classroom Resources.

PARTICIPATING IN GOVERNMENT

When the dollar strengthens against other currencies, American consumers are happy because imported goods are cheaper. American exporters, however, are unhappy because the prices of American goods increase in foreign countries.

Have students complete activity 29 in *Participating in Government* in the Teacher's Classroom Resources.

Assess

Check for Understanding
Have students complete Section 3 Review on page 852.

Meeting Objectives
Each section objective is tested by the Section Review questions that follow it in parentheses.
- Describe the early goals and methods of Soviet central planning. (2)
- Evaluate the problems that plagued the Soviet economy. (3, 4, 6)
- Discuss economic decisions facing the new Commonwealth of Independent States. (7)

Evaluate
Section 3 Quiz

Testmaker

GLOBAL CONNECTION

Point out that location is a major factor in encouraging business. Liechtenstein in the Alps, Monaco on the Mediterranean coast, and San Marino near the Adriatic coast all offer attractions for foreigners.
Examining the Connection Answer: *Students will suggest that it would suffer shortages of goods it could not produce and would have no international market for those it could, causing the economy to collapse.*

Reteach

📁 Have students complete activity 29 in *Reteaching Activities* in the Teacher's Classroom Resources.

Enrich

📁 Have students complete activity 29 in *Enrichment Activities* in the Teacher's Classroom Resources.

Close

Have students discuss the following:

Was Mikhail Gorbachev a success or a failure? Why? How do you think he will be viewed by historians of the future? Why?

GLOBAL CONNECTION

Interdependence

The Global Economy The size of a country does not always reflect its ties to the global economy. Liechtenstein, for example, collects money by taxing more than 5,000 foreign businesses that have headquarters there because of its low tax rate. In addition, collectors throughout the world purchase Liechtenstein's postage stamps.

Monaco, like Liechtenstein, collects money from foreign-owned businesses and from the sale of postage stamps. This small country also attracts more than 600,000 tourists each year.

Tourism provides San Marino's chief source of income. More than 2.5 million tourists visit this little country each year. San Marino's postage stamps also have a worldwide market.

Examining the Connection
What disadvantages would face a nation that severed its ties to the global economy?

power. Soviet citizens responded to the **coup**, a planned but sudden grab for power. They built barricades in the streets of Moscow and confronted the army. Russian President Boris Yeltsin, leader of the largest Soviet republic, called for nationwide resis-

tance. Across the Soviet Union people gathered in support of Yeltsin and Gorbachev. Within three days the coup failed.

The pace of events quickened. Soviet citizens staged anticommunist demonstrations and toppled statues of communist leaders, including even those of Lenin himself. Gorbachev resigned as Communist party leader but remained Soviet president. Several Soviet republics declared their independence.

In the wake of these changes, the Soviet economy remained lifeless. Gorbachev appeared unwilling to replace central planning with a market economy. Overall production of goods fell. Inflation ran at an annual rate of 200 percent. Facing severe shortages, Gorbachev sought help from the West. Western countries criticized Gorbachev for retreating from plans to develop a market economy. They claimed he had destroyed the old command system but offered nothing in its place.

A New President Several independent Soviet republics formed a confederation called the Commonwealth of Independent States. The new government effectively put an end to the Soviet Union. When Boris Yeltsin, president of Russia, emerged as a popular leader, Mikhail Gorbachev resigned his office as president. Yeltsin faced the same difficult problems that Gorbachev had faced. The old bureaucracy refused to crumble, crime became a major concern, and as the economy continued to stagger along, the people became impatient. Sharp political confrontations in 1993 threatened to lead to civil war. Boris Yeltsin survived as President of the Russian Federation and continued to seek the support of Western democracies.

3 SECTION REVIEW

Section Summary
In the communist economy of the former Soviet Union, shortages of consumer goods and other problems led to restructuring of the system.

Checking for Understanding
Recalling Facts
1. Define communism, state farm, collective farm, coup.
2. Identify four problems that Soviet central planning created.
3. Describe three kinds of reform laws that Gorbachev instituted under perestroika.

Exploring Themes
4. Free Enterprise What part of Soviet agricultural reform was similar to free enterprise?
5. Comparative Government How was the Soviet Union's relationship to its member states similar to the United States federal system?

Critical Thinking Skills
6. Analyzing Information Why would some Soviet bureaucrats and managers have resisted the changes that leaders like Mikhail Gorbachev and Boris Yeltsin were initiating?
7. Understanding Cause and Effect How might Soviet reforms shape the future of the Commonwealth?

852 UNIT 10: COMPARATIVE GOVERNMENT AND ECONOMIC SYSTEMS

Section 3 Review Answers

1. Definitions of terms appear on pages indicated: **communism,** 849; **state farm,** 850; **collective farm,** 850; **coup,** 852
2. encouraged producers to meet targets with goods easy to produce; failed to produce badly needed consumer goods and services; goods produced of poor quality; discouraged new ideas
3. legalized small-scale service businesses in such areas as

plumbing, auto repair, and dressmaking; placed more than 76,000 factories and farms on self-financing basis; reduced power of central planning agencies
4. Work was contracted to small teams. Team members were totally responsible for managing their own work. Each team's income at the end of the contract depended on how hard they worked and how much they produced.
5. The United States is made up of states that have some

political sovereignty, as did the individual republics of the Soviet Union.
6. Those in positions of authority would not want to lose their power, influence, and privileges.
7. Answers may suggest that the failure of Soviet reforms to improve economic conditions may make people increasingly impatient. Pressure on the republics to move rapidly toward market economies may become intense.

Boris Yeltsin on the Economic Policy of Russia

After surviving a strong political challenge in 1993, Boris Yeltsin, president of the Russian Federation, delivered this address to the Federal Assembly in Moscow on February 24, 1994. In this address he spells out his plan for additional economic reforms.

The reform efforts have brought us both to success and sometimes to bitter disappointment. If you ask me today whether I was prepared to start these difficult transformations all over again, I would say a firm yes. I have always been convinced that we didn't have another option. . . .

We are bitterly learning that the state-ruled self-consuming economy, in which ten people are busy with the work that can be reasonably done by one person, has no future.

We don't have a normal market economy so far. On the other hand, swindlers and rippers are feeling nice and easy. Honest and industrious people, who don't fear to be self-employed have enormous difficulties getting on.

We are bitterly learning that the state-ruled self-consuming economy . . . has no future.

My heart is breaking to say this, but it is true. We have greater freedom in this country, yes. But this is not enough. Our strategic goal is to develop justice, security and confidence in Russia. . . .

In its current shape, the state fails to perform its major functions, which includes in the first place the ensurance of public order, human rights and safety. The country is flooded by crime. Institutional structures are permeated by irresponsibility and arbitrariness.

Human life in our country is more and more ensnared by countless petty orders and limitations. The work of federal and local state authorities has been marked by muddle and great confusion. The army of bureaucrats has rapidly expanded. . . .

We need a general programme of state reforms in the Russian Federation. Here are its goals:

One. The state authorities should not work for themselves, but rather for Russia's interests and those of its citizens. . . .

Two. Power must be efficient. This implies a striving and ability to finish off what has been started and assess in the strictest possible manner the potential costs of deci-

sions, which are to be [made]. . . .

Three. We must bring an end to the bureaucracy's boundless nature, when any sensible decisions and initiatives are strangled by the deadly embrace of the bureaucracy. . . .

Four. Power must become open and understandable to the people. That means we must develop a dialogue, contribute to the formation of a civic society. Power should not be screened off from the mass media. . . . However, this must be done in fair measure. The television channel . . . should be state owned.

A strong state is required above all to curb crime. This is the most important problem of the year.

FROM "THE ECONOMIC POLICY OF RUSSIA" BY BORIS YELTSIN. *VITAL SPEECHES OF THE DAY*, APRIL 1, 1994

Examining the Reading

Reviewing Facts
1. List the major functions of a state, according to Boris Yeltsin.
2. Explain what Yeltsin meant when he said that freedom is not enough.

Critical Thinking Skills
3. Predicting Consequences Can the mass media be free to contribute to a civic society if the only television channel is state owned? Explain your answer.

CHAPTER 29: COMPARING ECONOMIC SYSTEMS   853

More About Personal Perspectives

When President Yeltsin addressed the Federal Assembly in Moscow, he said Russia was living through the most difficult period in its history. This was a remarkable statement, given the epic struggles Russians had endured in the twentieth century–World War I, the October 1917 revolution, and World War II. Although the people had voted for a new constitution in a democratic election, Russia faced major problems. The weakened state could not provide even elementary order. Organized crime strangled the productive energies of the nation. Ordinary citizens despaired of making any personal economic progress. Foreign investors were hesitant to risk large amounts of capital in Russia because of unstable conditions.

Identifying Terms and Concepts

1. A, **2.** C, **3.** B, **4.** A, **5.** A, **6.** C, **7.** B or C, **8.** A

Reviewing Facts and Ideas

1. land, labor, capital, management

2. Fifth Amendment

3. helps to assure that the consumer will get good quality products at low prices; it also means that some less efficient producers will go out of business

4. Consumer choices determine what will be produced, because producers must satisfy consumer demand. These choices affect prices because as demand increases, producers can charge higher prices.

5. Karl Marx

6. Socialists established political parties and worked within the democratic process to gain power; communists promoted revolutions.

7. Socialists say that everyone should receive basic necessities such as food, clothing, shelter, and medical care. Critics of socialism say that the "welfare state" makes people overly dependent on government.

8. *both:* inefficiency, poor planning and coordination, mismanagement; *industry:* low quality, few consumer goods, lack of innovation; *agriculture:* lack of incentive, waste, shortages

9. *Perestroika* meant full-scale economic restructuring entailing the decentralization of economic decision making and the introduction of elements of free enterprise.

10. Boris Yeltsin

Summary and Significance

Capitalism, also called the free enterprise system, is based on private ownership of property. It emphasizes individual initiative, competition, and freedom of choice. In the United States, the government regulates the free enterprise economy, but the free choices of buyers and sellers in the market determine prices.

Socialism and communism stem from the ideas of Karl Marx, a critic of capitalism. Socialists organized political parties and worked within democratic governments to bring about public ownership of production and command economies. They emphasized welfare programs and a more equal distribution of wealth. Several European nations later adopted socialist economic policies.

Communists believed that capitalist governments should be overthrown by force if necessary. The Soviet Union became the leading communist state following a revolution in 1917. The government under the Communist party controlled the economy. After initial growth, the Soviet economy experienced several problems. Few consumer goods, low quality, and slow growth led to a major campaign for reform. Perestroika, or restructuring, began in 1985 under Mikhail Gorbachev. His economic reforms failed to revive the Soviet economy. A failed coup against the government in 1991 eventually led to the end of the Soviet Union and its command economy. These were replaced by a new confederation government and the beginnings of a market economy.

Identifying Terms and Concepts

Match each of the following terms with one of the three economic systems below.

A. capitalism B. socialism C. communism
1. free enterprise system
2. state farm
3. nationalization
4. law of supply
5. entrepreneur
6. collective
7. command economy
8. corporation

Reviewing Facts and Ideas

1. List the four factors of production.
2. Identify the amendment to the Constitution that protects citizens' rights to property.
3. Explain the role of competition in the free enterprise system.
4. Relate how consumer choices and the law of demand affect production and prices in a capitalist economy.

5. Identify the leading critic of capitalism whose ideas formed the basis of socialist and communist economic systems.
6. Compare the socialist and communist methods of gaining political power in capitalist countries of the world.
7. Summarize the debate over the benefits that socialist governments provide their citizens.
8. Describe industrial and agricultural problems that were associated with the Soviet economy.
9. Explain the meaning of *perestroika* in Soviet economic reform.
10. Name the president of Russia, the leader of the largest Soviet republic who denounced the coup in 1991.

Applying Themes

1. **Free Enterprise** How does the free market system promote freedom of the press in the United States?
2. **Public Policy** Which of the economic systems discussed in the chapter needs the most government bureaucrats? Why?

Applying Themes

1. Business advertising provides the financial support for the media, thus allowing the media to criticize the government.

2. The communist system needs the most bureaucrats because government bureaucrats must make all the economic decisions regarding production and distribution.

3. Under communism the government has complete control of the factors of production. Political opposition to government policies would frustrate the economic planning and therefore, would not be tolerated.

3. **Comparative Government** Why does a communist economic system prevent the development of political parties?

Critical Thinking Skills

1. **Making Comparisons** How does the ownership of land as a factor of production in a capitalist system differ from land ownership in a planned economy?
2. **Understanding Cause and Effect** What is the relationship between price and supply in a capitalist system?
3. **Analyzing Information** What is the role of federal regulation in the free enterprise system in the United States?
4. **Distinguishing Fact From Opinion** Write three statements of fact and three statements of opinion about communism.

Linking Past and Present

A Socialist-Labor party entered the presidential race in the United States in 1892. A faction of that party founded the Socialist party in 1899. Perhaps the most popular of the Socialist candidates was Eugene V. Debs who was the Socialist party's candidate for President five times between 1900 and 1920. Debs, however, never captured much of the popular vote. His highest popular vote (about 6 percent) was cast in 1912. Other Socialist candidates fared no better at the polls. Even during the dark days of the Depression, Socialists failed to persuade many Americans to support their cause. In 1932 the Socialists polled only 900,000 votes—about 2 percent of the total. Why do you think Americans were not attracted to socialism?

Writing About Government

Narrative Writing Using the following terms, write a narrative paragraph about Soviet reforms initiated under Mikhail Gorbachev.

perestroika	**individual labor law**
central planning	**collective contracts**

Reinforcing the Skill

Writing a Term Paper The 1990s have been a time of tumultuous change in world events. Germany became reunified. Europe sought to establish economic unity. A loose confederation of independent states replaced the Soviet Union.

Use what you have learned about writing a term paper to answer the following questions.
1. Would the topic "The Fall of the Berlin Wall" be appropriate for a six-page term paper? Why or why not?
2. Would the topic "The European Union" be appropriate for a four-page term paper? Why or why not?
3. If you choose to write a term paper on "Boris Yeltsin's Role in Suppressing the 1991 Coup," what would be your first step?

Investigating Further

1. **Individual Project** Economic conditions in the Commonwealth of Independent States are of particular importance to the United States. Watch the newspaper for articles about the Commonwealth's economy. Collect articles and try to determine whether the Commonwealth's prospects for the future are promising or dismal. Write a short paragraph describing your projections of the Commonwealth's economy for the following year.
2. **Cooperative Learning** Some economists believe that the new global order will be based on three central economic players—the United States, the European Union (EU), and Japan. In addition, the developing nations will enter the global market. Divide the class into four groups, each representing one of these economic players. Have each group research the strength of their economic player by measuring the total GNPs, the number of people represented, the average per capita income, and the total imports and exports. After collecting the information, have the groups work together to prepare four large graphs showing the relative strength of each player in each of the economic measurements.

4. Answers may include: <u>fact</u>—Communism called for the overthrow of capitalism by force. Under pure communism, there is no private property. The Soviet Union built the world's leading communist economic system; <u>opinion</u>—Communism was a major political threat to the United States. Karl Marx's ideas of communism will die out in a few years. Communism is more concerned with the welfare of the people than socialism or capitalism.

Linking Past and Present

Answers will vary, but may include that Americans are deeply rooted in the dream of free enterprise—becoming financially successful. Americans view socialism as a radical system that is foreign to their ideals. Also, the United States government has taken steps to address major social problems before they resulted in extreme dissatisfaction with the system.

Writing About Government

Narrative paragraphs will vary, but should include all the terms indicated.

Reinforcing the Skill

1. yes, not too broad for a six-page paper
2. no, topic is too broad for paper's length; should be narrowed
3. focus on available resources

Investigating Further

1. Students' projections will vary, based on newspaper articles they collect.
2. Have students present and explain their completed graphs.

Critical Thinking Skills

1. In a capitalist system land, which means all the natural resources, belongs to private individuals. They make the decisions regarding its use. In a command economy, the government decides how natural resources will be used.

2. The supply of goods or services helps determine the price. If the supply is greater than demand, prices come down. (Some students may perceive that prices influence supply. If high prices create large profit margins, more producers will enter the market.)

3. Federal regulation is intended to ensure fair competition and to protect consumers, workers, and the environment.

Chapter Organizer

Objectives	Special Feature Pages	Supplemental Materials
Section 1 Global Issues in Today's World pp. 858–861 1. Discuss the characteristics of global issues. 2. Describe the factors that influence how a country responds to global issues.	Participating in Government: Hosting a Foreign Exchange Student p. 860	Guided Reading Activities Reproducible Lesson Plans Participating in Government 30 Cooperative Learning Activities 30 Section 1 Quiz Testmaker Chapter Transparencies 30 SAT Practice Tests Writer's Guidebook
Section 2 Global Economic Security pp. 862–866 1. Explain the advantages of trade among nations. 2. Describe three major emerging trading blocs. 3. Evaluate the economic problems of developing nations.	Multicultural Heritage: Immigration in an Interdependent World p. 864	Guided Reading Activities Reproducible Lesson Plans Section 2 Quiz Testmaker SAT Practice Tests Writer's Guidebook
Section 3 International Security and Conflict pp. 867–872 1. Discuss the need for national, international, and global security. 2. Describe the five types of conflict that threaten the security of states. 3. Evaluate the problem of proliferating nuclear and conventional weapons.	Focus on Freedom: United Nations Charter p. 868 Critical Thinking Skills: Predicting Consequences p. 872	Guided Reading Activities Reproducible Lesson Plans Interpreting Political Cartoons 49 Section 3 Quiz Testmaker Government Themes Transparencies 35 Skill Reinforcement Activities 30 SAT Practice Tests Writer's Guidebook
Section 4 The Environment and Scarce Resources pp. 873–877 1. Identify the pollution threatening the global environment. 2. Discuss the effects of population growth in developing nations. 3. Explain the need to conserve and manage limited resources.	Global Connection: Interdependence: Protecting the Environment p. 875 Personal Perspectives: Joseph Nanven Garba on Hope, Resolve, and Change p. 877 Case Study: Foreign Aid: The Role of the United States pp. 880–882 Unit 10 Digest pp. 883–884	Guided Reading Activities Reproducible Lesson Plans Interpreting Political Cartoons 55 Primary and Secondary Source Readings 30 Reteaching Activities 30 Enrichment Activities 30 Section 4 Quiz Chapter 30 Tests Testmaker Great Speeches, Volume VII Audio Cassettes (English and Spanish) Limited English Proficiency Activities 30 Unit Digest Transparencies, Unit 10 Participating in Government, Unit 10

If time does not permit teaching this chapter, assign the Chapter 30 summary in the Unit 10 Digest on pages 883–884.

Key To Ability Levels

Teaching strategies have been coded for varying learning styles and abilities.

L1   Level 1 activities are **basic** activities and should be within the ability range of all students.

L2   Level 2 activities are **average** activities and should be within the ability range of the average to above-average student.

L3   Level 3 activities are **challenging** activities designed for the ability range of above-average students.

LEP   These activities should be within the ability range of **Limited English Proficiency** students.

Multicultural Activities

The United States-Japan trade imbalance and the success of Japanese products in American markets has led to "Japan-bashing" among some Americans but more positive attitudes toward the Japanese among others. In the Pacific Northwest, where trade with such Pacific Rim entities as South Korea, Taiwan, Singapore, Hong Kong, and Japan is brisk, Asian Americans have strengthened trade links with Asia and brought new sources of investment capital into the United States, particularly in such areas as real estate, banking, and commerce. In cities and towns across the United States where Japanese automakers are major employers, attitudes also vary. To what extent do students think ethnic and race relations among Americans is likely to be affected by global economic competition?

In an interdependent world, political conflict in one country has effects far beyond its borders. Unrest in Central America offers one example. Until the 1970s immigration from Central America to the United States was quite small. In the 1970s and 1980s, it soared as a result of war and political unrest in El Salvador, Guatemala, and Nicaragua. In the 1980s over 130,000 Salvadorans officially entered the United States. An even larger number came illegally. Today Los Angeles is the second largest Salvadoran city in the world. Have students identify current areas of political or economic unrest around the globe. Then ask: What impact might these changes have on future United States immigration policy? As the global village grows smaller, is the ethnic and cultural diversity of the United States likely to increase or decrease?

Chapter Resources

Readings for the Student

Aaseng, Nathan. *Overpopulation: Crisis or Challenge?* Franklin Watts, 1991.

Dolan, Edward F., and Margaret M. Scariano. *Nuclear Waste: The 10,000 Year Challenge.* Franklin Watts, 1990.

Durrell, Lee. *State of the Ark: An Atlas of Conservation in Action.* Doubleday, 1986.

MacEachern, Diane. *Save Our Planet: 750 Everyday Ways You Can Help Clean up the Earth.* Dell, 1990.

Rohr, Janelle. *The Third World: Opposing Viewpoints.* Greenhaven Press, 1989.

Seager, Joni, ed. *The State of the Earth Atlas.* Touchstone, 1990.

Readings for the Teacher

Brown, Lester R. *State of the World 1992: A Worldwatch Institute Report on Progress Toward a Sustainable Society.* Norton, 1992.

Lappe, Frances Moore, and Joseph Collins. *World Hunger: Twelve Myths.* Grove Press, 1986.

Reich, Robert B. *The Work of Nations: Preparing Ourselves for 21st-Century Capitalism.* Knopf, 1991.

Shevardnadze, Edward. *The Future Belongs to Freedom.* The Free Press, 1991.

Multimedia

Videocassettes

AIDS 202. [AIDS crisis in Poland] (*AIDS Quarterly* series). WGBH Boston. (v/c, 60 minutes)

Born in Africa. [AIDS in Africa] (*Frontline* series). John Zaritsky. (v/c, 90 minutes)

Inside the Cartel. (*Frontline* series). Leslie and Andrew Cockburn. (v/c, 60 minutes)

Mandela: The Man and His Country. ABC News. (v/c, 50 minutes)

Moyers/The Arab World. (5-part series). Public Affairs Television. (30 minutes each)

Oil. (8-part series). Grampian Television, Norwegian National Radio and Television Corporation. (8 v/cs, 60 minutes each)

Spaceship Earth: Our Global Environment. Worldlink. (v/c, 25 minutes)

The State of the World with Lester Brown. Public Affairs Television. (v/c, 30 minutes)

Software

Balance of the Planet. Chris Crawford. (IBM requires 512K and CGA, EGA, or VGA graphics; Macintosh requires 800K disk drive, hard disk with 1 MB of memory). Students make policy decisions affecting the global environment from 1990–2035, using information from 150 screens.

Our Interdependent World

Introduce

Chapter Overview

Chapter 30 introduces students to the challenges they face as citizens of the modern world—global economic stability, international security, and environmental protection.

Section 1 describes the nature of global challenges and discusses how nations respond to them.

Section 2 examines two major factors that affect global economic stability—the free flow of international trade and the continued economic growth of the world's poor nations.

Section 3 considers such threats to international security as nuclear proliferation, the spread of conventional weapons, and terrorism.

Section 4 investigates the need for protecting the environment and for the wise use of the world's scarce resources.

Chapter 30 Themes

Write on the chalkboard this chapter's Themes in Government. Ask students how each theme might relate to the chapter title. Then ask them to write one question for each theme that they think will be answered in the chapter. After study of the chapter has been completed, select students to read their questions to the class. Have other class members answer the questions based on their study of the chapter.

Communism and the Cold War

Challenge of Reform
Running Time 2:34
Side Two, Chapter 17

Disarmament
Running Time :34
Side Two, Chapter 20

CHAPTER 30

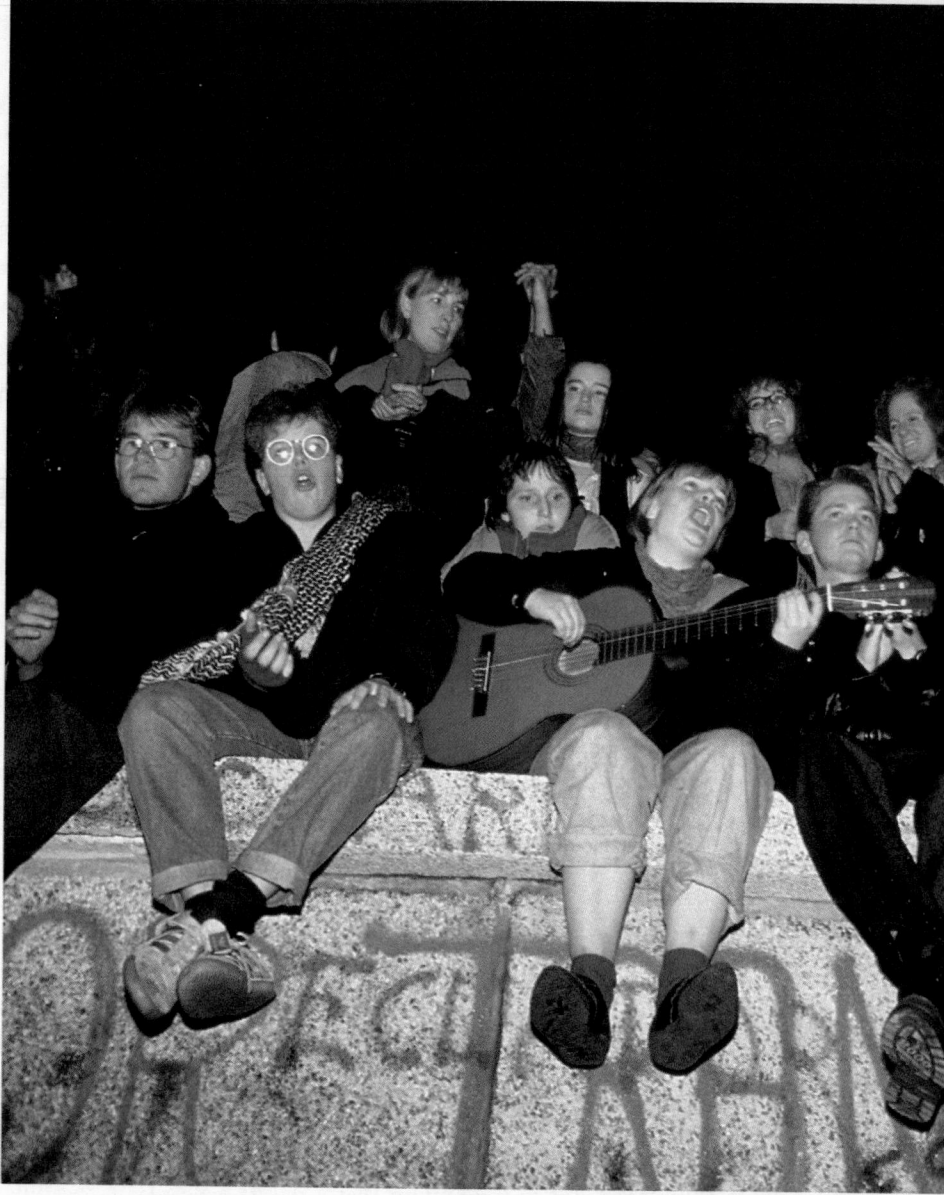

Through the wonder of instantaneous global communications, people around the world experienced the joy and drama of the fall of the Berlin Wall in fall 1989.

856 UNIT 10: COMPARATIVE GOVERNMENT AND ECONOMIC SYSTEMS

About the Chapter Opener

Teaching With Illustrations Mention that at the stroke of midnight on November 9, 1989—the time appointed by the East German government for the opening of the Berlin Wall—people gathered to sing "Such a Beautiful Day Should Last Forever," an old folk song sung at birthdays and other cele-brations. Ask students why many people in the West considered the fall of the Berlin Wall the most mo-mentous of the events in Eastern Europe during 1989 and 1990. (*They looked on the Berlin Wall as the physical embodiment of the Iron Curtain and the cold war.*)

Chapter Preview

Overview
Increasing interdependence and shared concerns over the economy, security, and the environment contribute to a sense that the world is a global village.

Objectives
After studying this chapter, you should be able to:
1. **Discuss** trends that create increasing interdependence among nations.
2. **Explain** major recent international economic developments.
3. **Identify** the major problems of global security.
4. **Evaluate** key environmental concerns.

Themes in Government
This chapter emphasizes the following government themes:
- **Global Perspectives** Growing interdependence means that events in one part of the world have an impact on other parts of the world. Sections 1, 2, 3, and 4.
- **Free Enterprise** The nations of the world are working together to lower trade barriers and promote the efficient use of scarce resources. Sections 2 and 4.
- **Public Policy** Governments of the world must deal with global issues and promote international security. Sections 1 and 3.

Critical Thinking Skills
This chapter emphasizes the following critical thinking skills:
- Making Inferences
- Predicting Consequences
- Drawing Conclusions
- Expressing Problems Clearly

CHAPTER 30: OUR INTERDEPENDENT WORLD 857

Introducing the Chapter
Prominently display a large wall map of the world. Then read the following statements:

1. grain harvest fails in Ukraine
2. volcanic eruption at Mount Pinatubo in the Philippines
3. Berlin Wall falls
4. toxic wastes dumped in Pacific Ocean
5. regional war in the Middle East

After each statement, point out on the map the geographic location mentioned. Then point to the continental United States. Ask: Do these distant events have any influence on the United States? Why or why not? End the discussion by pointing out that Chapter 30 will illustrate that such events do have a global impact.

Chapter Project
Have students work individually or cooperatively to design a logo for an organization involved in finding solutions for one of the problems discussed in the chapter. As an example, you might mention the guitar shaped like the African continent used for the Live Aid Concert. After study of the chapter has been completed, have students display their logos on the bulletin board.

Linking Past and Present
Communications in the early 1800s were relatively slow—for example, the fastest ship might take three weeks or more to cross the Atlantic. As a result, the most famous American victory of the War of 1812—the Battle of New Orleans—came two weeks after the treaty ending hostilities was signed in Europe. In contrast, satellite communications systems brought the news of President Clinton's 1994 trip to Europe at the very moment it took place.

Setting the Scene In a 1988 article on citizenship in the twenty-first century, Canadian educator Moyra Tooke noted that the first photographs of Earth from space vividly illustrated the concept of interdependence. Perhaps for the first time, people saw that the planet they shared with one another was really rather small. They also saw, Tooke suggested, the reality of interdependence—not only do people "share one Earth; they also share the effects of one another's actions and concerns for one another's development." This reality is the focus of Chapter 30.

Focus

Bell Ringer

While attendance is being taken, ask students to write a few lines on why incidents on another continent—the 1986 accident at the Chernobyl nuclear power plant in Ukraine, for example—should concern them.

Motivating Activity

Select students to read their Bell Ringer responses to the class. Briefly note on the chalkboard the major points of these presentations.

Display transparency 30 from the *Chapter Transparencies* in the Teacher's Classroom Resources and use the accompanying teaching strategy and student activity to show how a problem in one nation can have global ramifications.

Point out that the nature of global challenges is the subject of this section.

Caption Answer

fosters economic cooperation and cultural exchange

CONNECTIONS

Science

Some scientists estimate the greenhouse effect will cause a gradual rise in average temperatures over the next 75 years—a development beyond the range of normal temperature change. Such a warming process could devastate some of the world's most productive agricultural areas.

GLENCOE TECHNOLOGY

Focus on Government
Video 60
Speaking Out:
Moving Toward Democracy
Running Time: 2:49
Videodisc 3, Chap. 60
VHS Tape 3, Begins 56:01

Global Issues in Today's World

In the world today, events in one nation often affect events throughout the world. A bad harvest in Russia, for example, affects grain prices in Iowa. A new invention in Tokyo makes life easier for American homemakers. High interest rates in the United States influence the value of money in Germany. As Ernest Boyer, a leading educator, explains:

> *The world may not yet be a global village, but . . . what happens in the farthest corner of the world now touches us almost instantly. . . . The world has become a more crowded, more interconnected, more volatile and unstable place.*
> —ERNEST BOYER, "THE GLOBE, THE NATION, AND OUR SCHOOLS," *KETTERING REVIEW*, 1984

In today's world, every nation must face the challenges **global issues** pose. These issues are major problems that cross national boundaries, affect most of the world's people, and cannot be solved by any nation acting alone. Global issues include instability in the world economy, pollution, overpopulation, loss of natural resources such as croplands and forests, hunger, international conflict, and climatic changes such as global warming and depletion of the ozone layer.

Characteristics of Global Issues

Some global issues such as war have been part of the world scene for a long time; others are new and stem from technological developments. Global issues share four characteristics.

Will the Russian Harvest Be Sufficient?
Whether in Russia or Ethiopia, the success or failure of harvests reverberates globally. Economics **What are the positive aspects of global interdependence?**

Cross National Boundaries Global issues such as environmental pollution show no respect for national borders. Acid rain caused by sulfur dioxide emissions from factories and power plants, for example, blows freely across borders and endangers not only lakes and forests but peoples' health. The World Health Organization (WHO) estimates that acid rain threatens the well-being of half a billion people worldwide.

Global issues cross national borders in another way. Some have become global because the world community has placed them on the global agenda. In 1974, for example, a World Food Conference first

SECTION PREVIEW

Objectives
After studying this section, you should be able to:
■ Discuss the characteristics of global issues.
■ Describe the factors that influence how a country responds to global issues.

Key Terms and Concepts
global issue, deforestation, global warming, sovereign, developed nation, newly developed nation, developing nation

Themes in Government
■ Global Perspectives
■ Public Policy

Critical Thinking Skills
■ Making Inferences
■ Predicting Consequences

Classroom Resources for Section 1

📁 Guided Reading Activities
📁 Reproducible Lesson Plans
📁 Participating in Government 30
📁 Cooperative Learning Activities 30
📁 Section 1 Quiz

🔲 Testmaker
Chapter Transparencies 30
SAT Practice Tests
Writer's Guidebook

brought the world's attention to major problems in the way food is distributed in the world. The conference adopted resolutions aimed at dealing with food problems and created the World Food Council to work on solving such problems.

No Unilateral Solutions The resolution of most global issues requires the cooperation of many different kinds of international actors, especially nation-states. The spread of nuclear weapons is an example.

No single nation has the ability or authority to prevent other countries from developing their own nuclear weapons. Hence, in 1968 the United States, the Soviet Union, and Great Britain sponsored the Nuclear Nonproliferation Treaty (NPT). By 1971, more than 100 nations had signed the treaty. The treaty is not perfect because several key nations, such as France and India, have not signed and others, such as Iraq, have cheated. The collapse of the Soviet Union presented a new nuclear proliferation problem. Individuals, for profit, began selling nuclear materials out of the Soviet arsenal on the black market.

Linked Together Global issues are linked to each other in complex ways. First, it can be very difficult to solve one problem without dealing with others at the same time. For example, **deforestation**, the widespread destruction of trees and other vegetation, is a major environmental problem. Almost 1.5 acres of forest are being destroyed every second, or about 50 million acres a year. Much of this destruction is occurring in the earth's tropical forests.

Deforestation contributes to soil erosion. More than 26 billion tons of topsoil are blown away every year. This erosion results in the loss of farmland, which in turn contributes to lowering agricultural productivity and increasing the world food problem. At the same time, deforestation contributes to air pollution. Tropical forests in Brazil help to clear a huge amount of carbon dioxide from the air.

Conflicting Expert Opinion Decision making about many global issues involves a great deal of un-

certainty about the causes and best solutions to such problems. Uncertainty arises because current scientific knowledge about complex problems like depletion of the earth's ozone layer is very incomplete and constantly changing as new scientific discoveries are made.

The controversy over global warming provides a good example. **Global warming** is the prediction that increasing amounts of gases released into the atmosphere from industrial activity will trap heat in the earth's surface just as glass traps heat in a greenhouse. This warming could create a "greenhouse effect," raising the earth's temperature and thereby changing rainfall patterns, climate zones, and agricultural production.

Scientists do not fully understand global warming. As a result, disagreement about the causes of and the dangers posed by global warming has arisen. Some researchers argue that solar flares and volcanic eruptions are the cause. Other scientists predict global warming might actually increase agricultural production in such places as Russia and China. Still others believe that acid rain and smog could actually prevent global warming by acting like a shade against harmful rays from the sun. In the face of such uncertainty, national governments are unsure how to respond to the problem.

Responding to Global Issues

All nations and other international organizations must respond in some way to pressing global issues. They must find ways to work cooperatively to develop global policies such as the Nuclear Nonproliferation Treaty that individual nations are willing to follow. Because nations are **sovereign** with supreme power within their territorial boundaries, however, such policies cannot be forced on them. A country's place in the international system influences how it responds to global issues.

Place in the System The most traditional means of determining a nation's place in the international sys-

---

STUDY GUIDE

Themes in Government
Global Perspectives Because nations are sovereign, the international community must address global issues through cooperation.

Public Policy Today, a nation's public policy may be influenced by world opinion.

Critical Thinking Skills
Making Inferences Why has the international community not

moved swiftly against global warming?
Predicting Consequences What will eventually happen if deforestation continues to increase?

Vocabulary Precheck

Write this section's key terms and concepts on the chalkboard. Ask students to use those that they know in sentences. **LEP**

Teach

Guided Practice

📁 **Group Discussion** Organize groups to complete activity 30 on global problems in *Cooperative Learning Activities* in the Teacher's Classroom Resources.

L2 Applying Ideas Draw a table on the chalkboard with the following horizontal headings: *Cross National Boundaries*, *No Unilateral Solutions*, *Linked Together*, and *Conflicting Expert Opinions*. Ask students to suggest some global issues. Use responses as vertical headings. Have students explain the four dimensions of each of these issues. Enter their responses in the appropriate columns.

L3 Analyzing Ideas Refer students to the statement by Greek philosopher Thucydides on page 860:

"The strong do what they have the power to do and the weak accept what they must."

Have students discuss how this statement applies to international politics. Suggest that they back their arguments with examples.

STUDY GUIDE

Critical Thinking Answers because there is disagreement about the causes of and the dangers posed by it

Loss of farmland and increased air pollution will add to world's hunger and health problems.

Background

The United States itself provides a powerful illustration of global interconnectedness. The American population is made up of peoples from practically every nation in the world. During the 1980s, for example, the state of New York alone registered new immigrants from close to 150 different nations. The United States' trade relationships with

other nations are as extensive. Also, some nations have looked to the United States for assistance or leadership when international security has been threatened. Many more have looked to the United States as a model on which to base their governmental and economic systems.

Independent Practice

L1 Creating a Poster Have students design and construct a poster that illustrates one of the global issues mentioned in this section. Suggest that students make the focus of the poster why young Americans should be concerned about the issue. Have students display their posters on the bulletin board. **LEP**

L2 Expressive Writing Ask students to choose which of the global issues discussed in this section in their opinion presents the most serious challenge for the world. Which is most critical for the people of the United States? Have them explain their choices in an essay.

PARTICIPATING IN GOVERNMENT

Tell students that they may obtain more information about student exchange programs from the Council on International Educational Exchange, 205 East 42nd Street, New York, NY 10017.

📁 Have students complete activity 30 in *Participating in Government* in the Teacher's Classroom Resources.

Assess

Check for Understanding

Have students complete Section 1 Review on page 861.

---

tem is in terms of power. Thus scholars talk about "great powers" and "small powers." A nation's power is usually measured in terms of size, population, wealth, industrial development, military forces, and geographic location.

Powerful nations such as the United States, Germany, or Japan usually have more influence in developing global policies than do smaller powers such as Argentina or Kenya. In world politics the 2,000-year-old saying of the Greek philosopher Thucydides often applies today, "the strong do what they have the power to do and the weak accept what they must."

A second way of looking at how the more than 170 nations of the world line up on global issues is in terms of their wealth and economic development. Scholars and policymakers have classified countries in terms of developed, newly developed, and developing nations. **Developed nations** are the rich, strong, industrialized states. The key developed nations are the United States, the Western European nations, Japan, and Australia.

Newly developed nations are middle-income states with some industrial base. These include countries of Eastern Europe, several Middle Eastern states, and countries like South Korea, Mexico, and Argentina.

Developing nations are states with little or no industry. The great majority of these countries, like Haiti or Ethiopia, are very poor. A few, such as Saudi Arabia and Kuwait, are rich, usually because of oil. Most were former colonies of Western European nations and gained their independence after World War II. More than 75 percent of the earth's 5.3 billion people live in developing nations.

Developing nations have tried to present a common front on global issues, especially on international economic issues. On such issues developing nations often demand policies they believe would correct injustices they suffered when they were colonies of the European nations. On other issues, such as the environment, they may resist policies the developed nations advocate. For example, developing nations might argue that pollution regulations would limit their ability to open new factories and promote economic growth.

Interdependence and Dependence A second factor affecting how states respond to global issues is growing interdependence in today's world. International relations scholar Marvin Soroos states that, "At the international level, interdependence implies

PARTICIPATING IN GOVERNMENT

Hosting a Foreign Exchange Student

Does your school participate in a student exchange program? Has your family or anyone whom you know ever hosted a high school student from another part of the world?

Families who support or participate in intercultural exchange programs believe that the experience promotes understanding and respect among the world's people. Hosting an exchange student provides your family with a chance to learn firsthand about another country or culture. It also allows you to share your way of life with the visiting student.

Intercultural programs vary; families may host a student for a summer, a semester, or a year. Visiting students generally are members of the junior or senior class in high school. Some communities, however, participate in exchange programs for college students, teachers, or elementary

school students. Host families may have members who are the same age as the visiting student. Families with young children, couples with no children, and single people, however, also host exchange students.

Organizations that sponsor exchange programs provide orientation meetings as well as professional staff to help make the experience valuable for everyone.

Investigating Further
Interview a host family or an exchange student to find out about their experience.

Cooperative Learning Activity

Organize students into 5 or 6 teams to take part in a "scavenger hunt." Provide each team with a copy of a previously prepared 10-question test related to the content of this section. Each question should be accompanied with a clue indicating where the answer might be found. Sources of information might include this textbook; books, magazines, and other materials in the class; or materials in the school library. Suggest that each team member should be assigned one or more questions. The team that finishes the test fastest with the fewest errors is the winner.

Talking Trade
President Bush shakes hands with South Korean president Roh Tae-Woo at the 1992 trade summit. **Economics How does foreign trade affect employment in the United States?**

States, for example, about 4 out of 5 new jobs result from foreign trade, one-third of American corporate profits come from international activities, and more than 6,000 American companies have some operations abroad.

The economic relationship between Japan and the United States provides an example of interdependence. President Carter's former national security adviser Zbigniew Brzezinski explains that:

> *America needs Japanese capital to finance its industrial renovation and technological innovation; it needs Japanese cooperation in protecting its still significant lead in creative R&D [research and development] and in opening up new scientific frontiers for both peaceful and military uses. . . . Japan needs American security protection for its homeland; it needs open access to the American market for its continued well-being and, through cooperation with America, secure access to. . . . a world market.*
> —Zbigniew Brzezinski

that nations are sensitive or vulnerable in significant ways to developments taking place beyond their borders." Foreign policy expert John Spanier adds, "Two or more countries are interdependent when none of them can withdraw from a relationship without being hurt by doing so."

Interdependence has been present for a long time in military issues. When one important country has developed new weapons, for example, other countries have often countered with new weapons of their own. In recent decades global interdependence has grown dramatically in economic matters. In the United

Interdependence has encouraged developed nations to support economic cooperation. Many developing nations, however, have become more dependent on developed nations, instead of interdependent. Developing nations rely on the developed nations for their well-being. As sources of raw materials and agricultural products for developed nations, they depend on the developed nations for manufactured goods and even for loans to pay their foreign debts.

SECTION REVIEW 1

Section Summary
Global issues are major problems that cross national boundaries. These issues challenge the cooperative efforts of the world's nations.

Checking for Understanding
Recalling Facts
1. Define global issue, deforestation, global warming, sovereign, developed nation, newly developed nation, developing nation.
2. Cite evidence that deforestation is a major environmental problem.
3. Relate the problem with controlling nuclear proliferation.
4. Describe the uncertainty over global warming.

Exploring Themes
5. Global Perspectives Why should a global perspective be important to the average citizen?
6. Public Policy Why does the United States government promote foreign trade?

Critical Thinking Skills
7. Making Inferences Why might developing nations be skeptical of the global initiatives of developed nations?
8. Predicting Consequences How might the international community react if a developed nation refused to accept any responsibility for air pollution?

Caption Answer
Four out of five new jobs result from foreign trade.

Meeting Objectives
Each section objective is tested by the Section Review questions that follow it in parentheses.
- Discuss the characteristics of global issues. (2, 3, 4, 5)
- Describe the factors that influence how a country responds to global issues. (6, 7, 8)

Evaluate
📁 Section 1 Quiz
🔲 Testmaker

Reteach
Have students differentiate between developed, newly developed, and developing nations and outline how each approaches global challenges.

Enrich
Have students research and write a report on a global issue that has an impact on their community.

Close

Ask students how the seventeenth-century English poet John Donne's statement "no man is an island, entire of itself . . . .." might be applied to global issues.

Section 1 Review Answers

1. Definitions of terms appear on pages indicated: **global issue**, 858; **deforestation**, 859; **global warming**, 859; **sovereign**, 859; **developed nation**, 860; **newly developed nation**, 860; **developing nation**, 860
2. About 50 million acres of forest are being destroyed each year. Deforestation leads to soil erosion and the loss of farmland and contributes to air pollution.

3. Several key nations have not signed the nonproliferation treaty and others have cheated.
4. Scientists are not sure of the causes or the full impact of global warming.
5. because global issues affect every person's daily life

6. because it benefits from foreign trade through new jobs, corporate profits, and new technology
7. Developing nations suffered under the policies of developed nations in the past.
8. Negative world opinion would put pressure on that nation to change its policy.

Focus

Bell Ringer

While attendance is being taken, ask students to write what they think the term *global economy* means.

Motivating Activity

Discuss students' responses to the Bell Ringer activity. *(typical response: the relationship among nations in the international exchange and production of goods and services)* You might illustrate the concept of the global economy with the following example: A pair of shoes bought in Houston could have been made from Australian leather with German machinery in a factory in South Korea and transported to the United States by a Greek ocean freight line.

Vocabulary Precheck

Call on students to read aloud the definitions of the key terms and concepts from the Glossary. Then have volunteers use each term or concept in a sentence.
LEP

Caption Answer
It finances social and industrial progress.

CONNECTIONS

Economics

Since 1947 GATT has been renegotiated seven times. As a result of the latest round of negotiations, held in Uruguay (1993), tariffs were reduced on a broad range of products and nations agreed to cut agricultural and aerospace subsidies that had hurt United States exports.

---

② Global Economic Security

All nations of the world have a stake in the stability of the global economy. Whether rich or poor, large or small, every nation must find some way to compete in an interconnected system of markets throughout the world. Two of the most important factors affecting stability in the global economy are the free flow of international trade and the continued economic development of the poor nations of the world.

International Trade

Trade among nations is a major aspect of global interdependence. International trade allows consumers to buy imported goods at lower prices than similar products on the national market. These lower prices are possible because some nations produce certain goods more efficiently or have cost advantages in raw materials or labor. The principle of **comparative advantage** says that each country should produce those goods that it can make more efficiently and purchase those that other nations produce more efficiently.

Industrialized countries lead in trade because they have the most-specialized industries. The United States, Germany, Japan, Great Britain, and France are the world's leading trading nations. The United States imports many raw materials, foods, and manufactured products. United States exports include agricultural products, high technology products, and a wide variety of manufactured goods.

To promote international trade, 90 countries subscribed to a General Agreement on Tariffs and Trade (GATT) in 1947. Under the provisions of this agreement, member nations continue to meet to remove

A Lending Hand
The World Bank is committed to financing economic and educational development in developing countries.
Economics Why is this aid important?

or reduce trade barriers such as tariffs. In addition, three emerging regional **trading blocs** are removing barriers to trade among participating nations. Groups of nations in Europe, Asia, and North America are developing regional economic cooperation.

The European Economic Community In 1957 several Western European nations agreed to move toward a common trading market called the European Economic Community (EEC). In 1967 the EEC merged with two other organizations to become the European Community (EC).

The goal was to remove all economic restrictions, permitting workers, capital, goods, and services to move freely throughout the member nations. In 1985 the EC set 1992 as the target date for comple-

---

SECTION PREVIEW

Objectives
After studying this section, you should be able to:
- Explain the advantages of trade among nations.
- Describe three major emerging trading blocs.

- Evaluate the economic problems of developing nations.

Key Terms and Concepts
comparative advantage, trading bloc

Themes in Government
- Global Perspectives
- Free Enterprise

Critical Thinking Skills
- Predicting Consequences
- Drawing Conclusions

862 UNIT 10: COMPARATIVE GOVERNMENT AND ECONOMIC SYSTEMS

Classroom Resources for Section 2

📁 Guided Reading Activities
📁 Reproducible Lesson Plans
📁 Section 2 Quiz

🔲 Testmaker
SAT Practice Tests
Writer's Guidebook

---

tion of the union and began the EC 92 program. Its principal aim was to sharpen Europe's economic competitiveness. It would also prepare the way for the complete monetary and political union of Europe.

When Eastern European nations began to break free of communist governments, their new leaders recognized the value of belonging to a unified European market. Almost immediately they began negotiations to join their emerging free economies with Western Europe.

Development and Cooperation in Asia After World War II, with aid from the United States and the World Bank, Japan emerged as the dominant economy of Asia. From 1953 to 1966, Japan was an active borrower from the World Bank. By 1970 Japan reversed roles and became a major lender. According to a World Bank vice president:

> *Japan is thus a success story of development cooperation. It has now emerged as the number one aid donor in the world and will continue as a dominant contributor . . . during the 1990s and beyond. . . . I am convinced that we can build an even more productive collaboration between the World Bank and Japan for Asia's development in the 1990s.*
> —ATTILA KARAOSMANOGLU, 1991

During the 1980s and 1990s, several other Asian countries with free market economies rapidly industrialized. South Korea, Thailand, Malaysia, and Indonesia each experienced significant economic growth. The two giants, India and China, also made progress. Other nations such as Laos, Nepal, the Philippines, and Vietnam made few if any gains. The future of economic development in Asia depends in part on aid from the World Bank and other nations. Because of its large population, Asia represents both a great challenge and an opportunity.

North American Trade Agreements The third large emerging trading bloc is North America. Long an advocate of free trade, the United States has negotiated with Canada and Mexico to take steps toward greater economic cooperation. The United States and Canada completed an agreement to reduce tariffs, which went into effect in 1989. Over 10 years, this pact would eliminate most trade restrictions between the 2 nations.

In 1991 Mexican President Carlos Salinas de Gortari, seeking to improve his nation's finances, suggested talks to establish a free-trade agreement with the United States. President Bush opened negotiations in 1991, and President Clinton concluded the North American Free Trade Agreement, effective January 1, 1994. Some economists and many American workers worried that such an agreement could cause job losses in the United States. Mexican trade with the United States, however, would create new markets for United States exports—an incentive that supported a North American trading bloc.

Developing Nations

While the industrial nations negotiated favorable economic agreements, many other nations concentrated on feeding their people and reducing debt. The difference between rich and poor in the world is truly enormous. About 97 percent of people in the developed nations can read, versus 42 percent in the developing nations. The wealthy countries spend $432 per person for health care each year, compared to $2 in the poorest.

Economist Michael Todaro is a leading authority on development. He describes life for a typical family in a developing country in Asia:

> *The Asian household is likely to comprise ten or more people. . . . They have a combined annual income . . . of from $150 to $200. . . . None of the adults can read or write; of the five school age children only one attends school regularly. . . . There is only one meal a day. . . .*
> —MICHAEL P. TODARO, *ECONOMIC DEVELOPMENT IN THE THIRD WORLD,* 1989

STUDY GUIDE

Themes in Government
Global Perspectives Asian nations that have spent the most on education are developing fastest.
Free Enterprise How did the EC support free enterprise?

Critical Thinking Skills
Predicting Consequences What are the potential benefits of investment in developing nations?

Drawing Conclusions Which obstacle to development do you believe to be the most significant? Why?

CHAPTER 30: OUR INTERDEPENDENT WORLD 863

Teach

Guided Practice

L1 Analyzing Ideas Lead students in discussion of the following question:

How does international trade affect your everyday life?

Guide the discussion by reminding students of the origin of many everyday items they use—athletic shoes made in South Korea, electrical appliances made in Japan, and so on.

L2 Applying Ideas Have students review the information on the laws of supply and demand on page 839. Then have them discuss how barriers to trade, such as tariffs and import quotas, affect the workings of the forces of supply and demand. *(Tariffs, essentially a surcharge on imported goods, lessen the role of supply and demand in setting prices. Quotas create an artificially low level of supply, forcing up prices of imported goods.)*

STUDY GUIDE

Theme Answer
The EC wants to remove economic restrictions to permit workers, capital, goods, and services to move freely among its members.

Critical Thinking Answers
Developing nations could become vast markets for goods and services. Investment also might help to ease social turmoil in developing nations.

Students should provide supporting reasons for the obstacles they cite.

Background

Trade between different societies probably began sometime between 8000 and 5000 B.C. Archaeologists base this assumption on flint tools and ornaments made of obsidian and such semi-precious stones as turquoise found in graves located great distances from the point of origin of these materials. Such trade, however, did not become widespread until the Bronze Age (3500 to 1000 B.C.). Bronze weapons and tools, because they were far superior to those made of stone or copper, were in great demand by peoples who did not have either the technology or the raw materials to make them.

Multicultural Heritage

Focus

Poll the class to see whether they agree or disagree with the text statement in the last sentence of the first paragraph. Have volunteers explain why they responded as they did.

Teach

Discuss how attitudes toward American life might differ among immigrants who plan to return to their native lands and those who expect to become American citizens. Have students identify ways the United States benefits from immigration and the possible benefits to the countries of origin of new immigrants.

Assess

Have students complete **Examining Our Multicultural Heritage.**

Answers

1. Latin America and Asia

2. when a family sponsors the migration of relatives to their new homeland

3. <u>yes</u>: They may be accused of taking jobs from other Americans. <u>no</u>: They usually take undesirable jobs scorned by other Americans.

4. Answers will vary; the United States could encourage larger families or turn to increased automation.

Close

Identify the costs to foreign countries of losing their highly trained professionals and the benefits for the United States.

Immigration in an Interdependent World

Latest census figures place the nation's population at more than 250 million and growing. An important source of this growth is increased immigration, largely from Latin America and Asia. More often than not, Americans welcome the newcomers. In a recent poll reported in *U.S. News & World Report*, for example, 83 percent responded that immigrants "who have just come to this country [can] be every bit as much an American as someone whose ancestors fought in the American Revolution."

Modern-day immigrants often are fleeing impossible situations in their homelands. Few have any intention of returning. Many earlier immigrants did have this intention. The London-based *The Economist* reported that:

> *Few of the Poles who came to America during the two biggest waves of Polish emigration . . . intended to stay for long. Between 1906 and 1914, three out of every ten who arrived went home again. But many who intended to leave did not. Instead they were caught up in communities that were, even by early immigrant standards, remarkably proud and self-sufficient.*
>
> —THE ECONOMIST, OCTOBER 5, 1991

Statistics indicate that many of the current immigrants come from countries that have close economic ties with or are dependent on the United States for economic support. In many instances these immigrants send part of their earnings to families or relatives back home. In "Little Saigon" just south of Los Angeles, the average family sends $100 a month to relatives in Vietnam. In an interdependent world this type of immigration and exchange of monies benefits both nations. The United States benefits from a growing source of needed labor in a highly competitive world, while the homelands of the immigrants benefit from an influx of currency. In addition, for the United States, immigrants are:

> *One of the great sources of strength in this country. Over a fifth of our engineers are foreign-born engineers. Look at the enormous positive role Asians have played—the 1989 class at Harvard is 14%*

"Little Saigon"
The Vietnamese neighborhood of Los Angeles blends Vietnamese and American cultures.

> *Asian-American. These are the sources of strength which make us so very different from both the Soviet Union and the Japanese—the sources that will keep us on top.*
>
> —JOSEPH NYE, NEW PERSPECTIVES QUARTERLY, SUMMER, 1988

Although many groups retain their distinctive cultures and close ties to their homelands, their loyalty is to their new nation. Examples of "chain migration" abound as one family prospers and sponsors other family members' journeys to the United States.

Examining Our Multicultural Heritage

Reviewing Facts

1. Identify the two major sources of immigration to the United States today.
2. Define chain migration.

Critical Thinking Skills

3. Understanding Cause and Effect Do you think there might be a growth of a resentment against immigrants during a time of economic hard times? Why or why not?
4. Identifying Alternatives In the face of recent studies that indicate the United States will face a labor shortage in the next century, what other alternatives are there besides encouraging immigration?

More About Our Multicultural Heritage

The Immigration Act of 1990 raised the number of immigrants that can be admitted to the United States to 700,000 excluding refugees. Under this law, immigration totals drop to 675,000 in 1995. First preference goes to relatives of people already living in the United States. Workers most likely to gain entry are people of "extraordinary ability . . . in the sciences, arts, education, business, and athletics." Second highest priority goes to professionals with advanced degrees in these fields. The 1990 law also created a "millionaire's visa" for 7,000 foreign-born investors who agree to put $1 million into projects in urban areas.

Reasons for Improvement A world divided between rich and poor states is dangerous. Political instability in developing nations has led to many wars. Also, developing nations are becoming more important markets in the world economy. More than 36 percent of United States exports go to these countries.

Traditional Economic Goals Economic development is a process that involves the reorganization of a social and economic system to improve the quality of peoples' lives. From the 1950s through the mid-1970s, however, leaders saw development strictly in economic terms. Traditionally, the goal was to increase the gross national product (GNP) of developing nations by 5 to 7 percent each year. The idea was that big gains in GNP would "trickle down" to the poorest people in the form of jobs and other opportunities.

By the mid-1970s many developing nations had achieved regular increases in their GNP. Living conditions for the poor in most countries, however, did not improve. Simply raising GNP was not good enough. United Nations agencies, other international organizations, and developing nations had to rethink the goals of international development policy.

New Economic Goals In 1976 a World Employment Conference resolved that along with economic growth and industrialization, basic human needs should become a focus of development policies. Those needs include food, shelter, health, protection, the chance to develop self-esteem, and the freedom to make basic choices about one's life. According to a leading economist, since then:

*E*conomic development came to be redefined in terms of the reduction or elimination of poverty, inequality, and unemployment within the context of a growing economy.

—MICHAEL P. TODARO

Obstacles to Development

Why is it so difficult to achieve the goals of development? Major obstacles to development include lack of national unity, military rule, overpopulation, hunger, and lack of capital.

Lack of National Unity Leaders of many developing nations have had to be nation builders. Until the end of World War II, their countries were colonies of one of the great industrial powers. When the colonial rulers left, old fears and hatreds suppressed during colonial years surfaced. Peoples' lives and loyalties in these new nations were tied to their ethnic groups, regions, or religious, racial, or language groups rather than to the new country. For example, in Nigeria, a former British colony, differences between Muslim Hausas and Christian Ibos led to modern Africa's bloodiest civil war, killing more than 1 million people.

Military Rule Military control of national governments has slowed development. During the 1970s and 1980s, military governments controlled more than half the nations of Africa. More than two-thirds of the nations of Asia, the Middle East, and Latin America have had military governments at some time since 1945.

While the people accepted military leaders as reformers who helped end colonial rule, military rule has not usually promoted development. Under military rule the portion of the national budget going to the military often increases at least 50 to 75 percent, using up money that might have gone to economic development.

Population Growth A third obstacle to development is population growth in developing nations. More than 75 percent of the world's people live in the poorest countries, and the number is growing rapidly. For example, in 1950 Kenya had 6 million people; now it has about 24 million. China's population has increased by nearly 500 million people since 1950.

Poor Health In the least developed nations, life expectancy averages only 49 years compared to 75 years in many developed countries. Three sources of poor health in developing nations are hunger, poor water, and lack of medical care.

In the 1980s Africa faced terrible famine. About 30 million people in some 20 African nations were starving. A member of the United States Congress, Mickey Leland, helped sponsor a $1 billion relief package in 1985. Leland, who realized the need to extend such aid beyond the immediate crisis, died in a plane crash in Ethiopia in 1989.

Unclean drinking water is another major source of poor health. Diseases carried in water are responsible for 35 percent of the deaths of young children in Latin America, Africa, and Asia.

Finally, developing nations lack adequate medical care. The poorest nations have only 9 doctors per 100,000 people. These countries do not have enough

CHAPTER 30: OUR INTERDEPENDENT WORLD **865**

L3 Panel Discussion Select five or six students to serve on a panel discussing the best policy to encourage economic growth in developing nations. To launch the discussion offer the following slogan:

TRADE, NOT AID

Invite students on the panel to challenge, support, or modify the slogan.

Independent Practice

L1 Geography Point out that economists have suggested that three major trading blocs are developing—the European Community, the Pacific Rim, and the Western Hemisphere. Have students mark on outline maps of the world the boundaries of these three blocs. Then have them write a few sentences suggesting which of the blocs other nations might join. **LEP**

L2 Informative Writing Have students write an essay discussing the obstacles to development facing the developing nations. Suggest that they provide examples of obstacles different from those used in the text.

Assess

Check for Understanding

Have students complete Section 2 Review on page 866.

Meeting Objectives

Each section objective is tested by the Section Review questions that follow it in parentheses.
- Explain the advantages of trade among nations. (2)
- Describe three major emerging trading blocs. (8)
- Evaluate the economic problems of developing nations. (3, 4, 5, 6, 7)

Special Needs Strategy

Test Taking Higher level activities, such as the critical thinking questions in the Section Review, will present a challenge for students with learning problems. While many such students may not attempt these higher level questions alone, they can handle them successfully in a group situation. Select question 7 or 8 in the Section Review and have students work together to prepare a group response according to certain criteria: paraphrasing the question, discussing related information in the chapter, and so on.

Evaluate

📁 Section 2 Quiz

⬛ Testmaker

Reteach

Have students write a main-idea sentence for each of the following major headings in the section: "International Trade," "Developing Nations," "Obstacles to Development," and "Policies Toward Development."

Enrich

Have students write a report on the "Enterprise for the Americas Initiative" (EAI), the plan to establish a Western Hemisphere trading bloc.

Close

Have students discuss the following:

How would life in the United States be affected if all international trade were suspended?

Expanding the Goals of Development
Increasing the gross national product is the traditional goal of economic development. **Economics What other needs must be met for meaningful growth?**

hospitals or clinics, and such facilities are often in the cities rather than in the countryside where most people live.

Accumulating Capital Developing nations must accumulate capital if they wish to build industrial economies. Capital refers to the money, factories, tools, and machinery needed to produce goods. The problem for developing nations is that they depend on selling raw materials to other countries to get the capital they need. More than 90 developing nations rely on exporting natural resources other than oil for more than 50 percent of their export earnings.

Policies Toward Development

Most developing nations want the world community to develop policies that will ensure a more fair distribution of the world's resources and encourage development. National governments and international organizations such as the United Nations, however, have no general agreement on development policy. Since 1974 many international conferences have discussed several plans. Little has been accomplished, however. Recent changes in the international economic system such as the growing United States budget deficit and huge banking failures have hindered progress.

The United States, most of the other industrialized nations, and the World Bank generally believe that developing nations have capital resources in land and people that their governments must use to promote growth. In this view the best way to make good use of existing capital resources is to rely on what President Ronald Reagan called the "magic of the marketplace." In short, these governments should adopt free market economies and concentrate on solving internal problems such as illiteracy and poor health rather than depending on aid from the highly industrized nations.

Advocates of the free market approach point to the success of South Korea, Taiwan, Singapore, Malaysia, and Thailand in developing their economies. When these once poor states with government-directed economies turned to free market models, they experienced economic growth, improved health care, lowered infant death rates, extended life expectancy, and improved literacy.

2 SECTION REVIEW

Section Summary
Two conditions characterize the global economy—the move toward major trading blocs and efforts to close the gap between the rich and poor nations.

Checking for Understanding
Recalling Facts
1. Define comparative advantage, trading bloc.
2. Discuss the primary reasons nations trade with one another.
3. Identify the six basic human needs that the World Employment Conference said should become a focus of development policies.
4. List four obstacles to development in poor nations.

Themes in Government
5. Global Perspectives What potential benefits could developed nations receive by giving aid to developing nations?
6. Free Enterprise What examples support the use of free markets to encourage economic development in poor nations?

Critical Thinking Skills
7. Predicting Consequences What problems could Asia experience if population growth outpaces educational and economic improvement?
8. Drawing Conclusions Why are major trading blocs arising in Europe, Asia, and North America?

Section 2 Review Answers

1. Definitions of terms appear on pages indicated: **comparative advantage,** 862; **trading bloc,** 862
2. Nations trade to exercise their comparative advantage in products and services. This brings in goods and services at lower cost to their consumers than those produced at home. It also provides markets for goods that they produce more efficiently.

3. food, shelter, health, protection, the chance to develop self-esteem, and the freedom to make basic choices about one's life
4. lack of national unity, military rule, poor health, overpopulation, lack of capital
5. Such aid would relax tensions in the world by bringing about political stability in the developing nations. It would promote better relations, and developing nations may become important markets.

6. Japan rose from World War II to become a leading industrial nation. Other Asian nations that have developed through free markets include South Korea, Taiwan, Malaysia, and Thailand.
7. Hunger and poor living conditions could become worse, leading to starvation; local wars could break out and erupt into wider conflicts.
8. Nations in these regions are realizing the advantages of cooperative trade and economic ventures. One regional cooperative venture has led to others.

International Security and Conflict

The Framers of the Constitution understood the need for security. In 1787 they worried about how to defend the new nation against European powers that held territory in the Western Hemisphere. The Preamble to the Constitution charged the new national government "to provide for the common defense."After the War of 1812, the United States experienced no serious external threat to national security for more than a century. In today's world with more than 170 nations, threats to security include not only wars between nations but also civil wars, terrorist activities, and stockpiling of more and more dangerous weapons.

The Need for Security

International relations take place today in the context of the experience of two world wars and the fighting that punctuated the cold war. The need for security preoccupies leaders because many unresolved issues could ignite a war. Even though the United Nations is committed to preserving peace, every nation is generally responsible for its own safety.

Nations may try to enhance their security by increasing their military forces. As each country tries to increase its power to ensure its security, other countries are likely to see such behavior as threatening and feel more insecure. When these nations respond by trying to increase their own power, the result is a "security dilemma."

Meaning of Security Basically **national security** means protection of a nation's borders and territories against invasion or control by foreign powers. This goal is basic because no nation can achieve other values such as improving its educational system, or providing better health care or economic development if it is under attack.

In today's global economy, however, national security means more than military defense. A nation's vital international economic interests must also be protected. Harold Brown, secretary of defense under President Jimmy Carter, described both aspects of national security when he defined the term as meaning:

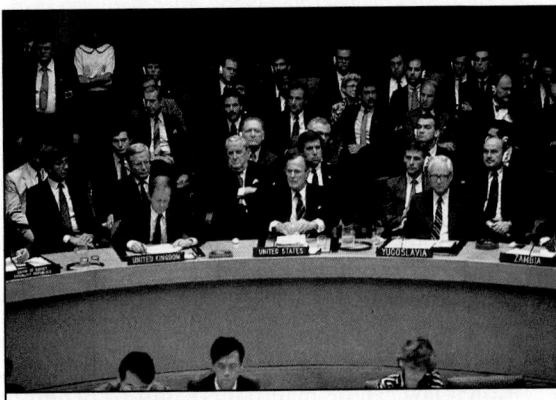

United We Stand
The United Nations works for world peace and security. **Political Processes** In contrast, how do nations acting individually try to ensure security?

SECTION PREVIEW

Objectives
After studying this section, you should be able to:
- Discuss the need for national, international, and global security.
- Describe five types of conflict that threaten the security of states.

- Evaluate the problem of proliferating nuclear and conventional weapons.

Key Terms and Concepts
national security, international security, global security, first-strike capability, second-strike capability, mutually assured destruction, limited war, nuclear proliferation

Themes in Government
- Global Perspectives
- Public Policy

Critical Thinking Skills
- Making Inferences
- Predicting Consequences

CHAPTER 30: OUR INTERDEPENDENT WORLD   867

Classroom Resources for Section 3

- Guided Reading Activities
- Reproducible Lesson Plans
- Interpreting Political Cartoons 49
- Section 3 Quiz

- Testmaker
- Government Themes Transparencies 35
- SAT Practice Tests
- Writer's Guidebook

Focus

Bell Ringer
While attendance is being taken, ask students to write a definition of the term *security*.

Motivating Activity
Review students' responses to the Bell Ringer activity. (*Most responses will use such phrases as "free from fear," "feeling of well-being," and "being protected from danger."*) Then ask students how the concept of security might be applied to the field of international relations. (*nations or the world as a whole should be protected from danger*) Point out that the subject of international security is discussed in this section.

Vocabulary Precheck
Call on volunteers to tell what they think each key term and concept means. Have students check the accuracy of their definitions in the Glossary. LEP

Teach

Guided Practice
L1 **Applying Ideas** Write the following headings on the chalkboard: *National Security, International Security,* and *Global Security.* Ask students to suggest an event, action, or policy that might threaten each form of security and an event, action, or policy that might enhance each form of security. Write responses under the appropriate heading. Use the entries as a starting point for a discussion on the importance of security. LEP

Caption Answer
by increasing their military forces, negotiating with other nations, and signing mutual defense pacts

🎈 **Interpreting Visuals** Display transparency 35 from the *Government Themes Transparencies* in the Teacher's Classroom Resources and use the accompanying teaching strategy and student activity to discuss the problem of nuclear proliferation.

Focus on Freedom

Other articles in the charter detailed qualifications for membership, the rights and obligations of members, the structure and functions of the various constituent bodies of the UN, and measures the UN would take to settle disputes and deal with threats to the peace.

Answers

1. will take collective measures to prevent such threats, suppress acts of aggression, and try to settle disputes
2. to promote the economic and social advancement of all peoples; to solve international problems of an economic, social, cultural, or humanitarian character; and to promote human rights
3. By solving economic, social, and cultural problems, the UN may remove many causes of war.

CONNECTIONS

History

The first international organization dedicated to world peace, the League of Nations, was a failure. Its charter and pronouncements largely went ignored. The League's ineffectiveness in international relations allowed the conflicts that gave rise to World War II to develop.

The ability to preserve the nation's physical integrity and territory; to maintain its economic relations with the rest of the world on reasonable terms; to protect its nature, institutions, and governance from disruption from outside; and to control its borders.
—HAROLD BROWN, *ESSENTIALS OF NATIONAL SECURITY: A CONCEPTUAL GUIDEBOOK FOR EDUCATORS*, 1989

Many policymakers and scholars today also talk about **international security**. By this they mean the creation of world stability as a result of the interaction of many nations' policies. They argue that today no nation can ensure its own security in isolation.

Finally, some observers have begun to talk about **global security**. They believe that the key issue today is the safety of the entire world, not simply agreements that preserve the security of several nations. Political scientist B. Thomas Trout explains that to those calling for global security such dangers as nuclear war or depletion of the ozone layer are not national or even international problems. They are "global" because their effects could bring disaster to the entire planet.

Types of International Conflict

What types of conflict have threatened the security of the nations of the world? They include several different types—nuclear war, limited war, regional war, civil wars, and nonmilitary conflicts.

Focus on Freedom

UNITED NATIONS CHARTER

Delegates from 50 nations met in San Francisco on April 25, 1945, to create a world organization dedicated to preserving peace. After many weeks of debate, they drafted the United Nations Charter and sent it to the nations for ratification. On October 24, the United Nations was born.

We the peoples of the United Nations, determined to save succeeding generations from the scourge of war, which twice in our lifetime has brought untold sorrow to mankind, and to reaffirm faith in fundamental human rights, in the dignity and worth of the human person, in the equal rights of men and women and of nations large and small, and to establish conditions under which justice and respect for the obligations arising from treaties and other sources of international law can be maintained, and to promote social progress and better standards of life in larger freedom, and for these ends to practice tolerance and live together in peace with one another as good neighbors, and to unite our strength to maintain international peace and security, and to ensure, by the acceptance of principles and the institution of methods, that armed force shall not be used, save in the common interest, and to employ international machinery for the promotion of the economic and social advancement of all peoples have resolved to combine our efforts to accomplish these aims.

Accordingly, our respective governments . . . do hereby establish an international organization to be known as the United Nations.

Article 1
The Purposes of the United Nations are
1. To maintain international peace and security, and to that end: to take effective collective measures for the prevention and removal of threats to the peace, and for the suppression of acts of aggression or other breaches of the peace, and to bring about . . . adjustment or settlement of international disputes. . . .
2. To develop friendly relations among nations based on respect for the principle of equal rights and self-determination of peoples. . . .
3. To achieve international co-operation in solving international problems of economic, social, cultural, or humanitarian character. . . .

Examining the Document

Reviewing Facts
1. List the specific methods the United Nations uses to remove immediate threats to the peace.
2. Describe the aims of the United Nations.
Critical Thinking Skills
3. Predicting Consequences How may solving international economic or social problems help to preserve the peace?

Background

Recently, efforts have been made to control a major threat to global security—the spread of all kinds of weapons. In October 1991 the permanent members of the United Nations Security Council, which together are responsible for 85 percent of the world's arms exports, established unofficial guidelines for the sale of conventional weapons. They agreed that sales that prolonged an existing war, increased regional tensions, supported terrorism, undermined the buyer's economy, or went beyond the buyer's security needs would not be made. UN officials hoped that the guidelines eventually would be extended to include nuclear weapons and technology.

Nuclear War Fortunately a nuclear war has never erupted, although the possibility remains. For years the United States and the Soviet Union alone possessed enough nuclear weapons to destroy the world many times over. In addition, Great Britain, France, India, China, and a growing number of countries have nuclear weapons.

A country with nuclear weapons has a **first-strike capability** when it can launch its weapons against an opponent. It has a **second-strike capability** when it can still launch a devastating nuclear attack after getting hit by one itself. Every nation with nuclear weapons wants to convince real or potential enemies that it will use its nuclear weapons for self-defense. At the same time, it wants to reduce the danger that either side will ever use its weapons. To do this it must have a second-strike capability. Pursuing these goals led to a situation called **mutually assured destruction (MAD)**, between the United States and the former Soviet Union. MAD simply meant that if either side attacked the other first, it would itself be destroyed by a second strike.

Many scholars and policymakers believed that MAD actually reduced the danger of nuclear war. Further, they argued that the very existence of nuclear weapons has limited other conflicts between the major powers because they feared starting a nuclear holocaust. Nevertheless, the potential for nuclear holocaust has led the major powers to reduce their nuclear weapons arsenals.

Limited War The first limited war of the post-World War II era took place in Korea. **Limited war** refers to a war in which the more powerful nation or nations will not go beyond certain limits. In June 1950, North Korea invaded South Korea with the permission and military support of the Soviet Union. The United States came to the aid of South Korea, and about 50,000 American soldiers were killed in the conflict. Even though American leaders held the Soviet Union responsible, however, the United States limited fighting to the Korean Peninsula and did not use nuclear weapons.

Hostage Terry Waite Released
Middle East terrorists took hostages in order to draw attention to their cause. **History** **What other types of international conflict have occurred in the Middle East?**

Regional Wars Regional wars are conflicts in a particular area or region of the world that do not involve the major powers. The Arab-Israeli Wars in 1948-49, 1956, 1967, and 1973 are examples, as are the India-Pakistan Wars of 1965 and 1971, and the Iran-Iraq War of the 1980s.

Regional wars usually occur near or along the borders of the nations involved. Third parties may sometimes get involved in the fighting, and they often aid the combatants.

Civil Wars Civil wars result from struggles for power within a nation. Since 1945 civil wars have killed almost 4 million people on the battlefield and numberless additional civilians. Civil wars are a matter of great international concern because they often draw in other nations and could escalate into even greater violence. For example, China, Syria, Cuba, South Africa, Turkey, and Vietnam have all intervened in recent civil wars.

L3 Identifying Alternatives
Have students select a number of conflicts examined in this section. Then have them discuss what means, other than the use of military force, might have been used to settle these conflicts. Suggest that they predict what the outcomes of these conflicts would have been if they had been settled through non-military means.

Independent Practice

L1 Understanding Ideas Ask students to write two or three headlines for each of the types of international conflict discussed in this section. The headlines, while not including a definition, should illustrate each type of conflict. Suggest the following as an example:

NUCLEAR WAR ASSURES DESTRUCTION OF ALL THOSE INVOLVED!

Have students compare their headlines by reading them to the class. **LEP**

Caption Answer
regional wars and civil wars

STUDY GUIDE

Theme Answer
The action might lead other nuclear powers to intervene and plunge the world into nuclear holocaust.

Critical Thinking Answers
No nation would want to bring destruction upon itself.

Terrorists might threaten to use such weapons to achieve their goals.

STUDY GUIDE

Themes in Government
Global Perspectives
When the Soviet Union dissolved, the former Soviet republics each received a seat in the United Nations.

Public Policy Why might the more powerful nation in a limited war hesitate to use nuclear weapons?

Critical Thinking Skills
Making Inferences Why did many scholars and policymakers believe that MAD reduced the danger of nuclear war?

Predicting Consequences What might happen if terrorists possess nuclear weapons?

CHAPTER 30: OUR INTERDEPENDENT WORLD 869

Cooperative Learning Activity

Organize students into groups of five and tell them their task is to construct an illustrated chart showing the major events in the effort to control the spread of nuclear weapons. Suggest that all group members conduct research and then hold a meeting to present their findings and decide on the events they wish to include in the chart. Group members should then share among themselves the work of designing, constructing, illustrating, and annotating the chart. Have groups display completed charts on the bulletin board.

📁 **Interpreting Political Cartoons** Have students complete activity 49 in *Interpreting Political Cartoons* in the Teacher's Classroom Resources.

L3 Analyzing Ideas Have students write an essay supporting or opposing the following statement:

Terrorist acts in the cause of freedom are a case of the end justifying the means.

Chart Study Answer
limit the export of plutonium-processing technologies, use diplomacy to eliminate underlying causes for acquiring them

Assess

Check for Understanding

Have students complete Section 3 Review on page 871.

Meeting Objectives

Each section objective is tested by the Section Review questions that follow it in parentheses.
- Discuss the need for national, international, and global security. (5, 6, 8)
- Describe five types of conflict that threaten the security of states. (2)
- Evaluate the problem of proliferating nuclear and conventional weapons. (3, 4, 5, 7, 8)

Nonmilitary Conflict Nations frequently engage in international conflict without using military force. They may employ psychological warfare by using propaganda. For example, the Soviet Union's Radio Moscow broadcast propaganda about the glories of communism. The United States countered by establishing the Voice of America radio network and the United States Information Agency (USIA).

Nations may also impose economic sanctions against another country. When the Soviet Union invaded Afghanistan in 1979, for example, President Carter imposed a grain embargo, stopping sales of grain to the Soviets. Carter's goal was to pressure the Soviets to withdraw from Afghanistan.

Nations sometimes use secret operations or covert actions to protect themselves or deal with enemies. In 1981, for example, the Bulgarian government was implicated in the attempted assassination of Pope John Paul II. In the same year, the Israelis destroyed a nuclear weapons facility being built by Iraq.

Finally, terrorism has become another form of international violence in the last several decades. Nongovernmental groups such as the Palestine Liberation Organization (PLO), the Red Brigades in Italy, or the Basque separatist organization in Spain have used bombings, hijackings, hostage taking, and murder to try to influence the actions of nations. In addition, countries such as Syria and Libya sponsored terrorism in the 1980s.

The Spread of Nuclear Weapons

In the beginning of the 1990s the world faced a major security problem because of the spread of nuclear weapons. Six nations—the United States, the Soviet Union, Great Britain, France, China, and India—admitted to having nuclear weapons. In addition, Israel, South Africa, Argentina, Taiwan, and Pakistan were believed to possess nuclear weapons or to be able to assemble them very quickly. Iraq has been trying to develop such weapons since at least 1980. World leaders became concerned about Soviet nuclear weapons when the Soviet Union dissolved. Former Soviet republics argued over who would control the nuclear weapons in their territories.

Why Nuclear Weapons Have Spread In addition to being highly destructive, nuclear weapons are very expensive. Why would nations want to develop such weapons? One reason is national security. Countries such as Israel and Taiwan, for example, have powerful, hostile neighbors. Both feel increasingly isolated because they are under great political pressure from the international community to settle longstanding conflicts. Both countries also depend on the United States to guarantee their security, and their governments worry about whether or not the United States would honor its defense commitments.

A second reason is prestige. Defeated early in World War II, France suffered one international humiliation after another, including the loss of a long, bitter war in Indochina in 1954. Nuclear weapons returned some respect for French military power.

Finally, building nuclear weapons may divert attention from pressing domestic problems. A successful drive to develop these weapons can mobilize support for the government and promote patriotic feelings.

Limiting the Spread The international community uses three strategies to contain the spread of nuclear weapons, sometimes called **nuclear proliferation**. The first is to strictly limit the export of plutonium-processing technologies needed to build weapons. The major powers have agreed to a set of guidelines for regulating their nuclear exports. Countries buying

Multilateral Arms Control Agreements

Year	Agreement
1959	Antarctic Treaty
1963	Nuclear Test Ban Treaty
1967	Outer Space Treaty
1967	Treaty of Tlatelolco (Latin America Nuclear Free Zone)
1968	Nuclear Nonproliferation Treaty
1971	Seabed Treaty
1972	Biological Weapons Convention
1978	Environment Modification Agreement
1986	Conference on Disarmament in Europe (CDE) (accord on confidence- and security-building measures)
1992	Strategic Arms Reduction Treaty (START) and "Open Skies" Treaty

✔️ **Chart Study**
Multilateral arms control agreements, the last of which was signed in 1992, have been an important means of limiting nuclear weapons. **By what other methods have arms been limited?**

Critical Thinking Activity

Predicting Consequences Point out that the breakup of the Soviet Union left the control of thousands of nuclear weapons in question. Further, some 2,000 Soviet scientists were experienced in building nuclear bombs. As many as 5,000 others knew how to produce the fuel for nuclear bombs. Many people feared that these scientists might sell their knowledge to the highest bidder. Western Europe tightened security when customs agents found nuclear materials crossing their borders. Ask students what steps might be taken by the United States and other countries to prevent the spread of nuclear devices and materials.

such exports must agree they will not use them to make weapons and must follow safeguards set up by the International Atomic Energy Agency (IAEA). Unfortunately, the IAEA has few legal powers and only a small staff. Without the permission of countries that purchase nuclear technologies, it cannot carry out inspections.

A second strategy has been the Nuclear Nonproliferation Treaty (NPT). Countries with nuclear weapons that signed the treaty agreed not to provide nuclear weapons to other countries. Non-nuclear powers that signed agreed not to develop such weapons. The success of the treaty, however, depends on countries not cheating.

A third strategy is for the nuclear powers to use diplomacy to try to eliminate the underlying causes that drive smaller countries to acquire nuclear weapons. Some diplomats argue that major nuclear powers could pressure smaller countries to limit weapons spread. In 1988 the United States successfully pressured Saudi Arabia to sign the NPT.

The Conventional Arms Trade

The world is arming itself with conventional weapons at a rapid rate. In a recent year, global arms sales totalled $41.3 billion. More than 75 percent of the worldwide arms sales went to developing nations.

Buyers and Sellers The United States has been a large supplier of arms to developing nations. Many other countries, including some developing nations, have started exporting conventional arms. China, for example, sold nearly $5.2 billion of weapons to developing nations in a recent year.

During the early 1970s, East Asian nations were major buyers of conventional arms. By the mid-1970s, Southwest Asia had become the major arms-importing region, in large part because of the continuing Arab-Israeli conflict, the civil war in Lebanon, and the Iran-Iraq war of 1980-1988. Other developing nations in Africa and Latin America greatly increased their arms purchases during the same period. For example, Ethiopia, a very poor nation, bought more than $1 billion in arms from the Soviet Union in the mid-1980s.

Many developing nations buy simple weapons such as rifles, grenades, or helicopters that can be used in civil wars or counter-insurgency operations. In the last decade, however, more countries have purchased sophisticated, high-technology weapons such as fighter jets, tanks, and precision-guided missiles.

Arms Control Possibilities The leading military powers have taken some steps to limit sales. In 1987, for example, the United States, Canada, Britain, France, Italy, Germany, and Japan adopted a common policy to limit the export of technology that could help other countries build missiles. At the same time, however, these same nations increased other weapons sales. Despite the risks to international security, controlling trade in conventional weapons remains a low priority for nearly all governments.

---

3 SECTION REVIEW

Section Summary
Because of the spread of nuclear and conventional weapons, the threat of terrorism, and unresolved issues that could ignite a war, security is a major concern for every nation.

Checking for Understanding
Recalling Facts
1. Define national security, international security, global security, first-strike capability, second-strike capability, mutually assured destruction, limited war, nuclear proliferation.
2. List five types of international conflict.
3. Identify three reasons for nuclear proliferation.
4. Demonstrate the large amount of conventional arms being sold to developing nations.

Exploring Themes
5. Global Perspectives How do problems such as nuclear weapons, environmental pollution, and depletion of the ozone layer relate to global security?
6. Public Policy In addition to defending its borders and citizens from attack, what other security goals become part of a nation's public policy?

Critical Thinking Skills
7. Making Inferences Why do leading military powers continue to sell arms to developing nations, despite the risks to peace?
8. Predicting Consequences What could result if the major powers totally abolished their nuclear weapons?

Evaluate
📁 Section 3 Quiz
💾 Testmaker

Reteach
Ask students to write a brief explanation of why maintaining national, international, and global security is important. Then have them outline the major challenges to security.

Enrich
Have students construct a graph, chart, or map showing the countries that possess, or are suspected of possessing, nuclear weapons. Information on this subject may be found in almanacs, encyclopedias, and such sources as *The State of the World Atlas*. Have students display their graphs, charts, and maps on the bulletin board.

Close
Have students discuss the impact of the end of the cold war on global security.

CONNECTIONS

Technology
The Persian Gulf War of 1991 was labeled as the first "high-tech" war. The weapons used included Stealth jets designed to evade radar, laser-guided bombs, missiles with computerized guidance systems, and rifles with infrared night-sights.

Section 3 Review Answers

1. Definitions of terms appear on pages indicated: **national security,** 867; **international security,** 868; **global security,** 868; **first-strike capability,** 869; **second-strike capability,** 869; **mutually assured destruction,** 869; **limited war,** 869; **nuclear proliferation,** 870
2. nuclear war, limited war, regional war, civil war, non-military conflict
3. Some nations are threatened by hostile neighbors and want nuclear weapons to assure their security. Other nations find that nuclear weapons provide a certain amount of prestige. Also, building a nuclear arsenal diverts attention from domestic problems.
4. In a recent year global arms sales totalled some $41.3 billion.
5. have the potential for destroying the security of the world, not just of individual nations
6. Nations try to protect their vital economic interests, safeguarding the free flow of energy supplies and raw materials. They seek to protect government and other institutions from disruption from outside.
7. Controlling trade in conventional weapons remains a low priority because such arms support major powers' allies, thereby defending their own interests. Arms sales also provide money for defense industries.
8. Answers may include that other nations with nuclear weapons could become more aggressive or that other nations would agree to abolish their own nuclear weapons because of the pressure of world opinion.

Focus

Have students list possible consequences if they drove a car while their license was under suspension. Ask: Which consequences would be positive and which would be negative? After making this assessment, are you more likely or less likely to drive under such circumstances?

Teach

Read to students the proposal in the Explanation (*the first paragraph under the steps*). Then read the next paragraph, which defines the issue. Ask students how they would vote on this bill if they were senators. Then have them brainstorm possible consequences of the bill. List their responses on the chalkboard and have them identify which are intended consequences and which may be unintended. Then have them decide if each consequences is positive or negative.

Assess

Have students complete the **Practice** exercise.

Close

Have students compare their list of consequences to the list in the Explanation. Then ask if knowledge of these possible consequences would affect their vote on this bill.

Predicting Consequences

Decisions that we make every day have consequences. Each time a person or group makes a choice among alternatives there are consequences because these choices set up a chain of results. Consequences may be seen as negative or positive depending upon one's goals and values. Predicting consequences is valuable because it helps to prevent negative results.

Explanation

To predict the consequences of a policy, follow these steps:
- Define the issue that the policy will address.
- Gather facts and evidence that are directly related to the issue.
- Determine the potential positive and negative effects of the policy.

Imagine that a Senate committee is studying an energy bill. The bill proposes a 50-cent-a-gallon tax on gasoline to cut consumption. The revenue from the proposed tax would be used to fund research into alternative sources of energy. As a member of the committee, you must decide whether or not to support the bill. You need to predict the consequences of the bill.

Define the issue that the bill will address. Gasoline consumption depletes oil reserves. The United States is heavily dependent on foreign oil and may be drawn into international competition or conflict over supplies. Development of alternative energy sources could improve the nation's competitive economic position and strengthen its world leadership.

Gather facts that are directly related to the issue. Committee hearings reveal the relationship between increased cost of gasoline and consumption. An oil industry leader relates the relationship between the cost of energy and production in other industries. The director of the Office of Management and Budget testifies concerning the relationship between increased taxes and the national economy.

The hearings and your own staff's research indicate the following potential effects of the policy:
Positive: (1) decrease in the amount of gasoline consumed because of carpooling and less leisure driving; (2) decrease in the amount of imported oil; (3) increase in research on alternative fuel sources; (4) increase in federal tax revenue; (5) decrease in air pollution.
Negative: (1) decrease in consumer spending for other goods and services; (2) increase in prices of other energy sources; (3) decrease in industrial production because of energy cost increases; (4) rise in unemployment; (5) negative public reaction to those who support the bill.

By being able to predict the consequences, you can now vote intelligently on the bill.

Practice

The collapse of communism and the end of the Soviet Union called for new analyses of many issues. One concern was about arms proliferation. What arrangements would prevent nuclear or conventional military actions? How could the Commonwealth of Independent States control arms that were scattered among a number of republics? What dangers do terrorists or small states with arms represent?

Consider the consequences of the following policy proposal:

The United States and other developed nations would give specified amounts of foreign aid to any nation or group that agreed to destroy nuclear or conventional weapons. For each weapon destroyed the developed nations would also destroy an equal weapon. A United Nations task force would assess compliance.

1. What issue would this policy address?
2. What additional facts are related to this issue?
3. List two potential positive and two negative effects of this policy.

Additional Practice

To practice this skill, see **Reinforcing the Skill** on page 879.

Practice Answers

1. controlling the spread and use of conventional and nuclear weapons as central authority in the former Soviet Union disappeared
2. The additional facts students cite will vary, but they should recognize the interplay of such issues as world stability, arms proliferation, and the aims of small militant states and terrorist groups.

3. Potential positive and negative effects will vary, but should be related to the facts presented.

For additional practice, have students complete activity 30 in *Skill Reinforcement Activities* in the Teacher's Classroom Resources.

SECTION

4

The Environment and Scarce Resources

With almost 6 billion people in the world and the number growing daily, human activity has begun to threaten the very systems that support all life on the planet. These systems include the oceans, lakes and rivers, the soil, the forests, and the very air people breathe. People have become aware that more care must be taken of the environment because environmental damage such as the extinction of a species cannot be reversed.

Further, government leaders are discovering that environmental problems and scarce natural resources may lead to international conflict. Some scholars predict that environment and resource issues may replace the cold war as one of the greatest threats to stability in the international system.

Environmental Issues

Modern industrial society is placing ever greater demands upon world resources. Issues arising from problems such as land erosion, water pollution, or deforestation have several unique characteristics.

Local-Global Link Environmental issues always appear first within a local community. Large and small businesses located in villages, towns, and cities across the world create air or water pollution. Before distant national governments become involved, villagers living along a stream notice that all the fish in the stream are dying.

Eventually local environmental problems spill over and become national, regional, and often global problems. When local power plants in southern Ohio burn high sulfur coal, acid rain kills trees and fish in New England and Canada. Rapid population growth in one region may cause millions of people to migrate across national borders in search of food and other necessities.

Renewable Resources Environmental issues involve one of two types of resources, renewable and nonrenewable. **Renewable resources** can regenerate after becoming overused or exhausted. Vegetables, cotton, wood, coffee, fish and the like are examples of renewable resources. With proper management renewable resources such as forests can continue to produce trees indefinitely.

Problems arise, however, when nations begin to overharvest or exceed the limits of a renewable resource ecosystem. Overharvesting exists when a resource is depleted faster than it can regenerate. For example, if fishers from several countries using high technology take too many fish too quickly from North Atlantic fisheries, they will overharvest the fisheries. When that happens, the fish may not be able to reproduce fast enough to meet the fishers' needs or even to survive as a species. In a similar manner, loggers often overharvest forests, leading to the depletion of valuable timber resources. Wise use of renewable resources such as fishing grounds and forests helps prevent this overharvesting.

Nonrenewable Resources Industrial nations depend heavily upon **nonrenewable resources**. These resources are all mineral-based, such as metals and ceramics. The earth has a fixed, finite quantity of such resources. Scientists may continue to discover new copper deposits, but the planet has only so much copper. When all the economically minable copper has

---

SECTION PREVIEW

Objectives
After studying this section, you should be able to:
- Identify the pollution threatening the global environment.
- Discuss the effects of population growth in developing nations.

- Explain the need to conserve and manage limited resources.

Key Terms and Concepts
renewable resources, nonrenewable resources, strategic minerals

Themes in Government
- Global Perspectives
- Free Enterprise

Critical Thinking Skills
- Expressing Problems Clearly
- Drawing Conclusions

CHAPTER 30: OUR INTERDEPENDENT WORLD **873**

Classroom Resources for Section 4

- Guided Reading Activities
- Reproducible Lesson Plans
- Interpreting Political Cartoons 55
- Primary and Secondary Source Readings 30
- Reteaching Activities 30
- Enrichment Activities 30

- Section 4 Quiz
- Chapter 30 Tests
- Testmaker
- Great Speeches, Volume VII
- Audio Cassettes (English and Spanish)

Focus

Bell Ringer

While attendance is being taken, ask students to consider what energy problems, if any, we face in the United States today.

Motivating Activity

 Review students' responses. Then show students President Jimmy Carter's speech on the energy crisis from "Great Speeches," Volume VII, of the *Social Studies Videos.* (You will need to preview the video to locate this material.) Then ask students to discuss whether they agree with Carter's description of the energy problem as the "moral equivalent of war." Close the discussion by pointing out that how to meet energy wants with limited resources is one subject covered in this section.

Vocabulary Precheck

Write the key terms and concepts on the chalkboard. Ask students how each term and concept relates to the environment. **LEP**

Teach

Guided Practice

L1 Summarizing Ideas Organize students into groups of three. Assign each group one of this section's major heads. Have members work together to skim the material under their assigned head and write a summary of its content. Have group representatives read their summaries.

GLENCOE
TECHNOLOGY

Focus on Government
Video 58
Lecture Launcher:
Our Interdependent World
Running Time: 2:19
Videodisc 3, Chap. 58
VHS Tape 3, Begins 51:51

L2 **Analyzing Ideas** Select three environmental challenges mentioned in this section and write them on the chalkboard. For each, have students discuss the following questions: Why is this a challenge for the United States? What can the American government do about this challenge? What *ought* the American government do about this challenge?

Ask students to write a 25-word telegram to the President or a member of Congress summarizing the discussion on one of the challenges. Have students read their telegrams to the class.

L3 **Interpreting Ideas** Write the following quote by Ralph Waldo Emerson on the chalkboard:

"We do not inherit the Earth from our ancestors, we borrow it from our children."

Have students discuss what this statement means in terms of environmental protection and the use of scarce resources.

Independent Practice

L1 **Understanding Ideas** Have students review local media for a story on an environmental concern in their community. Have students share their news stories with the class.

Chart Study Answer
It contributes to air pollution and global warming.

Linking Past and Present
In the late 1800s a major source of pollution in American cities was manure left by the principal means of transportation—the horse. When the automobile was introduced in the early 1900s, most Americans considered it as an improvement in terms of pollution.

Worst Cases of Deforestation in the 1980s			
Regions and Countries	Forest Area	Annual Deforestation	Percent Per Year
	(in thousand hectares)		
Cote d'Ivoire	9,834	510	5.2
Nigeria	14,750	400	2.7
Zaire	177,590	347	0.2
Mexico	48,350	615	1.3
Argentina	44,500	1,550	3.5
Brazil	514,480	2,323	0.5
Colombia	51,700	890	1.7
Ecuador	14,730	340	2.3
Indonesia	116,895	620	0.5
Thailand	15,675	379	2.4

Source: World Resources Institute, World Resources 1988–89 (New York: Basic Books, 1988), 286-87.

Chart Study
Brazilian rain forest fires can be seen from the outer atmosphere. **Why is deforestation a global issue?**

been located, mined, and used, future supplies will depend on recycling.

International Organizations International organizations now play an important role in the politics of environmental issues. These issues often reach the agenda of international governmental organizations (IGOs) such as the World Health Organization (WHO) that have been created to deal with transnational issues. For example Vice President Al Gore attended an environmental summit in Brazil in 1994. In addition, international nongovernmental organizations such as the Nature Conservancy have played a role in identifying environmental problems.

Air and Water Pollution

Pollution must be dealt with internationally because air currents and rivers flow freely across international borders. Pollutants may wind up in the atmosphere, oceans, or in the very ground itself.

Air Pollution At present, three types of air pollution are of special concern to policymakers. Coal-fired power plants, smelting operations, and automobile exhaust create acid rain. It has been linked to the destruction of forests and lakes and has damaged historic buildings such as the Taj Mahal in India. Global warming, or the so-called "greenhouse effect," appears to be resulting from the buildup of carbon dioxide in the atmosphere. Finally, the release of chlorofluo-

rocarbons into the air from sources like refrigerators is thinning out the ozone layer in the stratosphere.

Water Pollution Unfortunately, the world's oceans have been used for decades as the dumping grounds for everything from raw sewage to radioactive wastes. Cities and industries dump many pollutants into rivers that flow into the seas. An additional threat has come from oil spills from gigantic supertankers or blowouts from offshore oil drilling.

Conflicting Policies Developed and developing nations have conflicting views on the international policies needed to control air and water pollution. While developed nations are beginning to urge pollution controls, developing nations have argued that industrialized economies created the pollution problem. It is unfair, they claim, to place restrictions on poorer nations that are now trying to catch up in economic development. Their money could be better spent on pressing economic and social needs.

Population Growth

The world's population increases by nearly 95 million people every year. This annual increase is about the same number of people as are currently living in Eastern Europe. It took 105 years, from 1825 to 1930, to add 1 billion people to the world. The latest billion was added in less than 15 years.

Population in Developing Nations Nine out of every 10 children being born today are born in developing nations. Between 1980 and 2000, the number of people 20 to 40 years of age will increase by 630 million in the developing states, compared to about 20 million in the industrial countries.

Robert McNamara, former World Bank president, described the impact on developing nations:

Rapid population growth, in sum, translates into rising numbers of labor force entrants, faster-expanding urban populations, pressure on food supplies, ecological degradation, and increasing numbers of "absolute poor." All are rightly viewed by governments as threats to social stability and orderly change.

—ROBERT MCNAMARA

If present trends continue, experts warn that developed nations will have to absorb excess population

874 UNIT 10: COMPARATIVE GOVERNMENT AND ECONOMIC SYSTEMS

Background

A 1991 report issued by the UN underscored the magnitude of the problem of rapid population growth. The report estimated that world population will double to about 10 billion by 2050. Some 95 percent of this growth will come in the poorer, developing regions of the world. Over the last decade of this century alone, Africa's population will increase by 39 percent to about 900 million. During the same time period, the population of Latin America and the Caribbean will grow by 23 percent to 540 million, and 300 million more people will live in South Asia. This incredible rate of growth will place a heavy burden on the world's already scarce resources.

from the poorer nations of the globe as they flee political turmoil and terrible living conditions.

Growth of Cities More than half of the world's people will live in overcrowded cities by the year 2000. Four of the six largest cities will be in the developing nations. Mexico City is predicted to go from today's 21 million to 27 million people. In India, Calcutta and Bombay will each have about 15 million people. City planners worry that such huge numbers of people could strain already weak transportation, housing, sanitation, and education services beyond the breaking point.

Differing Views Experts disagree on just how serious these population trends are. Paul R. Ehrlich wrote *The Population Bomb* (1968) and *The Population Explosion* (1990). He argued that overpopulation threatens the existence of civilization by contributing to a host of global problems from starvation to the spread of AIDS. Other experts argue that new technologies have already introduced improved grain and farming methods that can feed many millions more. Still other experts blame poverty on mismanagement and the lack of free and productive economic systems.

Food and Hunger

International relations scholar Barry Hughes asks a simple question: "Which has been growing faster in the last forty years, world population or world food supply?" The answer is food. The world food situation today is marked by terrible paradox: by 1980 world food production reached record high levels and yet 40 percent of the world population suffers from malnutrition. People are going hungry for several reasons: an inability to produce or buy food, inadequate distribution systems, and government indifference.

Food Production and Marketing As a result of using high technology, developed nations can pro-

GLOBAL CONNECTION

Interdependence

Protecting the Environment Destruction of the ozone layer is a global issue. Ozone—a gas that forms a layer about 30 miles (48.4 kilometers) above the earth's surface—shields living things from the sun's ultraviolet rays. Harmful doses of ultraviolet light increase the danger of skin cancer.

Since the 1970s world governments have negotiated to control the use of chlorofluorocarbons (CFCs)—chemicals that destroy ozone. CFCs are found in coolants used in air conditioners and refrigerators. In 1987, 43 nations signed the Montreal Protocol—an agreement to cut back consumption and production of CFCs. In 1989 the leaders of 100 nations, including the United States, announced a plan to eliminate the use of CFCs by the end of the century.

Examining the Connection
Why does protection of the ozone layer require worldwide cooperation?

duce more food than ever before. American farmers, for example, can grow 5 times more crops on the same land than they could 50 years ago.

A few developing nations, such as China and India, have dramatically increased food production in recent decades. Most developing nations and some industrialized countries, however, must still import food. Many do not have enough money to buy food on the world market.

Inadequate Distribution When starvation threatens, governments of developing nations call upon the rich nations for emergency food aid. These nations

Interpreting Source Readings Have students complete activity 30 in *Primary and Secondary Source Readings* in the Teacher's Classroom Resources.

Interpreting Political Cartoons Have students complete activity 55 in *Interpreting Political Cartoons* in the Teacher's Classroom Resources.

STUDY GUIDE

Theme Answer
Answers may include the Indian government, the international community through charitable contributions, or industries that cause pollution.

Critical Thinking Answers
Since pollution is a global problem, attempts at controlling it that do not include all nations will achieve only limited success.

It is unlikely because so much of the hunger problem is tied to politics.

GLOBAL CONNECTION

In 1993 researchers disclosed that the 1992 average concentration of ozone in the upper atmosphere was 2 to 3 percent lower than any previous reading. **Examining the Connection Answer:** *The ozone layer surrounds the earth. If all nations do not take protective measures, ozone depletion will continue.*

STUDY GUIDE

Themes in Government
Global Perspectives Boutros Boutros-Ghali, former foreign minister of Egypt, stated: "The next war in our region will be over the waters of the Nile, not over politics."

Free Enterprise Who should pay for repairs if acid rain damages the Taj Mahal?

Critical Thinking Skills
Expressing Problems Clearly How could conflicting policies

among developed and developing nations slow progress on pollution control?

Drawing Conclusions Can the world eliminate hunger by A.D. 2000? Explain your answer.

CHAPTER 30: OUR INTERDEPENDENT WORLD 875

Assess

Check for Understanding
Have students complete Section 4 Review on page 876.

Special Needs Strategy

Test Taking Because of repeated failure, frustration, or low self-esteem, students with learning problems often stop trying to master new information. One way to instigate learning is to show students that the information has special relevance for them. Section 4 deals with powerful topics that are

relatively easy to personalize. As an evaluation of understanding of the topics presented, have students clip a related magazine article to add to a "Critical Issues" poster or discover three facts about a related local issue.

Meeting Objectives

Each section objective is tested by the Section Review questions that follow it in parentheses.
- Identify the pollution threatening the global environment. (3, 4, 5)
- Discuss the effects of population growth in developing nations. (6, 7)
- Explain the need to conserve and manage limited resources. (2, 8)

Evaluate

📁 Section 4 Quiz

💻 Testmaker

Reteach

Have students outline the content of Section 4.

📁 Have students complete activity 30 in *Reteaching Activities* in the Teacher's Classroom Resources.

Enrich

📁 Have students complete activity 30 in *Enrichment Activities* in the Teacher's Classroom Resources.

Close

Ask students to discuss what they think is the most important global environmental challenge. Have them give reasons for their answers.

---

and many international organizations always respond by making food available. Food distribution facilities in many developing nations, however, are totally inadequate. Donated food often rots on piers of port cities or is eaten by pests as it awaits distribution.

Government Indifference Sadly, some governments do not want the world to know their agricultural policies are a failure, so they will not ask for help. This happened, for example, in China from 1959 to 1962 when the communist government followed Soviet examples and collectivized agriculture. Millions of people are believed to have starved as a result of the so-called "Great Leap Forward."

Perhaps one of the cruelest examples of both government indifference and the use of food as a weapon was in Marxist Ethiopia during the 1980s. By 1985 millions were starving or already dead from starvation in Ethiopia. The government tried to hide the starvation from the Western news media. When the story got out, relief agencies began providing food and even trucks to move the food. The Ethiopian government would not allow food to be distributed to rebellious areas.

Depletion of Natural Resources

Industrial nations that make up about 25 percent of the world's population consume 75 percent of the world's energy, 85 percent of its forest products, and 71 percent of its steel. For example, the United States has about 5 percent of the world's population. Americans, however, use 60 percent of the world's natural

gas, 40 percent of the world's coal and aluminum, and 30 percent of minerals such as nickel and copper.

Energy—Master Resource In approximately the last 120 years, there has been a 75-fold increase in energy use by the United States. Developing nations also need large amounts of energy to increase food production and achieve economic development. Still, as these nations begin to achieve economic development, their energy needs increase even more.

Mineral Resources Minerals are important nonrenewable resources. Coal generates electricity. Potash is a fertilizer. In addition, some **strategic minerals** are used for military purposes. For example, cobalt, chromium, and nickel are used in the engines of some fighter aircraft. The United States depends upon imports for 86 percent of its cobalt, 77 percent of its chromium, and 68 percent of its nickel.

Many parts of the world are not yet fully explored and may contain important supplies of minerals. In addition, new technologies for extracting minerals from the earth are constantly developing. Finally, if prices go up high enough, it is sometimes possible to use known deposits of minerals that were too costly to mine when prices were low.

Resource Policies All nations are concerned about the overall drain of natural resources, especially as more nations create industrial economies that require more natural resources. Scientists point out that industrial nations simply must begin to find ways to conserve natural resources while the search for new resources and substitutes for old resources continues.

---

4 SECTION REVIEW

Section Summary
Environmental and resource issues are potential threats to global security.

Checking for Understanding
Recalling Facts
1. Define renewable resources, nonrenewable resources, strategic minerals.
2. Name three international organizations handling transnational environmental and resource issues.
3. List three kinds of air pollution that are of concern to policymakers.
4. Discuss why developing nations oppose environmental regulations.

Exploring Themes
5. Global Perspectives How are many leaders' views concerning the global environment changing?
6. Free Enterprise What is the free-enterprise based solution to the problem of feeding a growing population?

Critical Thinking Skills
7. Expressing Problems Clearly Why are so many people in the world starving or hungry?
8. Drawing Conclusions The depletion of which category of resources could pose the most serious threat to human life in the future?

Section 4 Review Answers

1. Definitions of terms appear on pages indicated: **renewable resources,** 873; **nonrenewable resources,** 873; **strategic minerals,** 876
2. World Health Organization (WHO), Nature Conservancy, and Sierra Club
3. acid rain, carbon dioxide in the atmosphere, and the release of chlorofluorocarbons into the atmosphere

4. Developing nations say that developed nations created the pollution problem. Also, they claim that it is unfair for them to be regulated while trying to catch up in economic development. Further, it would be very costly for developing nations to equip all their factories to meet international pollution standards.
5. Government leaders are finding that environmental problems and scarce natural resources may lead to international conflict. They therefore have become more concerned with environmental issues.

6. introduction of new technologies that improve farming methods and create productive economic systems
7. Some of the world's most populated regions are underdeveloped and not able to provide adequate food. When food aid is sent to these regions, inadequate transportation systems, government policies, poor organization, and outright theft prevent supplies from reaching the starving people.
8. Answers should consider which resources are more vital for sustaining life.

Major-General Joseph Nanven Garba on Hope, Resolve and Change

Joseph Nanven Garba, CFR, Major-General of Nigeria spoke to the board of African Profiles The Magazine in New York City on March 12, 1994. The former president of the 44th UN General Assembly stressed that hope, resolve, and change are necessary to overcome Africa's problems.

A frica is today a continent bedeviled and wracked by economic and political upheavals. One needs only to look at what is going on in Angola, Liberia, Burundi, Rwanda, Sudan and Somalia, to name just a few. Our continent has become a basket case; but unfortunately, one that many people care little about. Among those who do profess to care, the situation is not well understood, and therefore they are unable to come to grips with it. . . .

In assessing Africa's problems, I see two critical factors responsible: *unfulfilled aspirations and unkept promises.*

The first problem arises from failed leadership in Africa. The second, from the extraneous factors of unkept promises from our Western Friends. . . . In the first instance, those lucky or calculating enough to acquire political power, soon

shut out public opinion and excluded meaningful discourse and advice. Experience has taught us that in most instances these people are the least qualified to govern.

In the second instance, our Western interlocutors [go-betweens in a dialogue] and erstwhile colonial masters, in their enlightened self-interest have made promises that they never intended to keep. . . . The end result is that Africa cannot make any meaningful progress away from its problems; rather it is constantly kept tethered on the precipice of disaster, allowed only enough rope not to go over the edge. . . .

I have heard it said . . . that Africa is worse off now than it was at the beginning of the 1980s. Certainly there are more African conflicts now than there were then. Africa's per capita income has dropped drastically as its indebtedness grows. . . .

We know all too well what has been the fate of Liberia and Somalia. . . . Somalia especially, typifies yet another promise unkept, as the United States, after a brief sojourn there, has all but withdrawn, taking along with it its allies. They have left behind a dangerous political vacuum. . . .

The dismal instances of policy failure that abound in Africa are also grave indictments of the international community, and of its

watchdog, the United Nations. . . .

While indicting the West, I must on balance point to the follies of Africa's leadership that are the bane of our continent. In the true African sense and tradition, something must be gravely amiss when a conflict between cousins of different clans . . . require extra-African intervention to resolve. . . . Africans must now assume a lead role in finding solutions to Africa's problems. . . .

If it ever was in doubt, it is now abundantly clear that in the evolving post-Cold War era, Africa, having lost its strategic significance founded on superpower rivalry, must now confront its own limitations and realities. From here on, there must be hope, political resolve and an unquenchable desire for positive change.

—JOSEPH NANVEN GARBA, 1994

Examining the Reading

Reviewing Facts
1. Identify **two critical factors responsible for Africa's problems.**
2. List **three measurements that indicate Africa is worse off today than before the 1980s.**

Critical Thinking Skills
3. **Drawing Conclusions** Why does Garba believe Africa's problems must be resolved by Africans?

Focus

Ask students to identify some current problems in Africa.

Teach

Ask: Why do so few people seem to understand the problems of Africa? *(Foreigners have not taken time to study these problems, and African leaders have not consulted public opinion.)*

Assess

Have students complete **Examining the Reading.**

Answers

1. unfulfilled aspirations because of poor leadership and unkept promises made by the West and the United Nations
2. There are more conflicts, per capita income is down, and debt is higher.
3. The West and the UN have not shown enough interest, nor do they understand the problems. Also, with the end of the cold war, Africa is less significant to the superpowers.

Close

Discuss reasons for and against Western interest in and aid to resolve Africa's problems.

More About Personal Perspectives

On May 5, 1990 Major General Joseph Nanven Garba delivered a major speech at Harvard University. Speaking as president of the 44th UN General Assembly, Garba said, "The Cold War is over, and Africa lost." In 1994 Dr. Chudi Uwazurike, of *African Profiles International,* invited Major-General Garba to deliver the keynote address at the second anniversary of the founding of the magazine. By that time it was already evident that Garba's concerns over the fate of Africa were becoming a reality.

Identifying Terms and Concepts

1. global issues, 2. nonrenewable resources, 3. strategic minerals, 4. national security, 5. developed nation, 6. developing nation, 7. global security

Reviewing Facts and Ideas

1. acid rain, global warming

2. areas with a high concentration of developing nations

3. the United States, Germany, Japan, Great Britain, France

4. General Agreement on Tariffs and Trade, a 1947 agreement among 90 nations

5. The EC wants to remove all economic restrictions on workers, capital, goods, and services so that they can move freely throughout member nations. This will establish a common trading market and lead to a united Europe.

6. South Korea, Thailand, Malaysia, and Indonesia

7. Simple justice and compassion are good reasons. The division of the rich and poor nations is dangerous because political instability could lead to wars. Also developing nations represent potential markets for industrial nations' products.

8. Some developing nations were once colonies of other countries. After colonial rule ended, people returned to loyalty to their regional, religious, racial, or language groups.

9. hunger, poor water, lack of medical care

10. the Korean War

11. Several key nations, such as France and India, have not signed the treaty, and others, such as Iraq, have cheated.

12. cobalt, chromium, and nickel

13. Mexico City, Calcutta, Bombay

Applying Themes

1. From the 1950s to the 1970s, leaders saw development strictly in economic terms. They wanted to increase GNP by 5 to 7 percent per year, hoping that the benefits would "trickle down." Since the 1970s leaders have concentrated on basic human needs such as food, shelter, health, protection, the chance to develop self-esteem, and the freedom to make basic choices about one's life.

Summary and Significance

Global issues are major problems that affect people around the world. Nations and international organizations must find ways to respond to these issues and work cooperatively to develop global policies.

The international community has several concerns. First, the global economy that connects the individual economies of nations has weaknesses. While emerging trading blocs among developed nations will increase competition and production, many developing nations face serious shortages of basic necessities. Unless developing nations with rapidly expanding populations improve their educational and economic systems, famine and social disruptions could lead to violence. The international community is responding with aid to developing nations.

While the major powers are reducing their stockpiles of nuclear weapons, many nations continue to increase their military capabilities. Even developing nations are major consumers of conventional weapons. World leaders are also concerned about the environment and natural resources. Air and water pollution problems cross national boundaries. Population growth in developing nations increases the strains on already scarce resources. Developed nations must take the lead in finding new technologies to solve these problems.

Identifying Terms and Concepts

Use the following terms to fill in the blanks in the paragraph below.

strategic minerals, developed nation, developing nation, national security, global security, renewable resources, nonrenewable resources, global issues

In today's world, every nation must face (1), challenges or problems that cross national boundaries. The global village has a limited amount of (2) such as iron, copper, and other metals. Some of these are (3), vital to the (4) of many countries. The United States, a (5), is concerned about its educational systems. A (6), however, may be more concerned about basic needs such as providing enough food. Because of these economic problems potential social disruptions could threaten (7).

Reviewing Facts and Ideas

1. Cite evidence that global issues are problems that cross international boundaries.
2. Identify areas of the world that have high rates of population growth.
3. Name the world's five leading trading nations.
4. Identify GATT.

5. Explain the short- and long-term goals of the European Union.
6. List four Asian nations that experienced significant economic growth in the 1980s.
7. Discuss reasons why developed nations should give financial aid to developing nations.
8. Summarize the causes of a lack of national unity in some developing nations.
9. Identify three causes of poor health in developing nations.
10. Cite the first limited war in the post-World War II era.
11. Discuss the imperfections of the Nuclear Nonproliferation Treaty.
12. Specify three minerals that the United States must import for defense purposes.
13. Identify three international cities that will probably experience great population growth in the next few years.

Applying Themes

1. **Public Policy** What are the differences between the traditional and the new economic goals to promote development in developing nations?
2. **Free Enterprise** What did President Bush mean when he said, "Economic growth and environ-

2. Economic development need not be sacrificed for pollution control; economic competition brings innovations that satisfy both needs.

3. Developed nations may have to absorb people fleeing from political turmoil and terrible living conditions. Famine relief and other aid would cost more.

mental integrity need not be contradictory priorities. One reinforces the other"?

3. **Global Perspectives** In what ways could the growth of population in the poorest nations affect developed nations?

Critical Thinking Skills

1. **Predicting Consequences** What potential benefits might result if developed nations redirected more of their foreign aid toward education in developing nations with large populations?

2. **Making Inferences** What changes in the direction of education in the United States could result from increased technology and foreign competition?

3. **Expressing Problems Clearly** How could the world's pollution problem become more serious, even if industrialized nations find ways to reduce their pollutants?

4. **Drawing Conclusions** Are economic problems, security problems, or environmental problems the most critical issues facing the world today? Support your answer.

Linking Past and Present

In the days before telecommunications, newspapers covered fewer stories, but in greater depth. As radio and television news developed, news organizations attached greater importance to getting the news first. Because of limited time for the newscast, however, the coverage may leave many unanswered questions. How do you think this change in news reporting affects the perceptions of the viewer concerning national and international events?

Writing About Government

Narrative Writing If you have traveled anywhere outside your home community, you probably have noticed that people have different customs, traditions, and ways of living. Write a paragraph about the most interesting or striking differences that you observed while traveling or living in another community, state, or nation.

Reinforcing the Skill

Predicting Consequences As you have read, the world is becoming "smaller" and more interdependent because of technological advances that have made international trade and travel easy. Because of the importance of international trade, nations watch one another's trade policies closely. As American industry has faced increasing competition from abroad, some leaders have urged citizens to "buy American" and have advocated policies that would give American companies the advantage in domestic markets. One policy that has been advocated is to limit the number of foreign cars that can be sold in the United States. Suppose that Congress has passed such a law. To promote sales of American-made cars, the law limits the number of imports to three-quarters of the number that were imported during the previous year.

1. What would be the intended consequences of this bill?

2. What might be an unintended consequence of this bill as it relates to the American automobile industry?

3. What might be an unintended consequence in the area of foreign relations?

4. What might be an unintended consequence in the area of American politics?

Investigating Further

1. **Individual Project** Determine the global perspective of adults and students. Prepare a set of 10 simple questions to use as a survey. Ask 10 adults and 10 students to try to answer questions such as "What nation has the largest population?"

2. **Cooperative Learning** Organize the class into three groups. Have each group track a type of global issue in the print or broadcast media—economic, security, or environmental. After collecting information, determine those instances in which groups have selected the same news articles because these issues overlap.

CHAPTER 30: OUR INTERDEPENDENT WORLD **879**

Critical Thinking Skills

1. Answers may include: As education improved, emerging student leaders in developing countries would become more able to offer solutions to problems. Many more people would be prepared to work in higher-paying jobs, which might attract major industries from developed nations. Educated people would demand more freedoms, bringing about more democratic government.

2. Answers should suggest that education will change in ways that confront and attempt to overcome the challenges these developments pose.

3. Developing nations continue to produce more pollutants as they move toward industrialization. They may resist international controls, because they believe them to be unfair.

4. Students should consider the size of the problems, the potential for crisis, and the difficulties in solving these problems as they support their answers.

Linking Past and Present

Answers may include: Viewers know a little about many unrelated events, but they may not perceive the relative importance of interrelationships of these events.

Writing About Government

Answers will vary. Make certain students provide reasons for their choices.

Reinforcing the Skill

1. to protect domestic jobs and industries by encouraging American consumers to buy more American cars

2. Answers may include: It might feel less pressure to produce cars that would compete well with foreign imports, or it might raise prices on its cars because of increased demand.

3. Answers may include: There might be increased tension between the United States and Japan or other automobile-exporting countries, or other automobile-exporting countries might impose similar restrictions on imports of American cars and other products.

4. Answers may include: Other industries might demand similar protection from Congress, or American consumers might be angered by limits placed on their ability to choose which car to buy.

Investigating Further

1. Students' findings will vary.

2. Results will vary.

The Case at a Glance

Who: federal government, American public
What: foreign-aid programs
When: 1947 to the present
Where: United States
Why: evaluate the purpose of foreign aid

Focus

Ask students what responsibilities the United States has toward other nations in the world. *(promote democracy, maintain international harmony)* Ask: What part can foreign aid play in achieving these goals? *(Aid can help create economic stability and pro-American attitudes.)* Why might the American people wish to discontinue foreign aid? Tell students that this case study focuses on the United States' foreign-aid policies.

Teach

Guided Practice

L1 Constructing a Chart Draw a two-column chart on the chalkboard with the headings *For* and *Against*. Have students summarize the *for* and *against* opinions in the case as you write them in the appropriate column. Then have students use the chart data to answer the following: Why does foreign aid have more support from leaders than from citizens? *(Leaders see benefits that the general population does not; citizens are more concerned about their own economic status.)* What could change the attitudes of the

Foreign Aid: The Role of the United States

Foreign Assistance [foreign aid] is a prudent investment abroad. It assists us in the effective implementation of our foreign policy objectives, promotes global economic and political freedom, and reflects the humanitarian concerns of the American people.

—William Schneider, Jr., United States State Department, 1985

The United States is in no position to underwrite a new Marshall Plan for the world's budding democracies. We simply cannot afford it anymore, and our highest priority must be the renewal of our own nation.

—David Gergen, *U.S. News & World Report,* September 9, 1991

The Case

Many Americans have strong opinions regarding this nation's foreign-aid programs. At the same time, many Americans know very little about the issue. A poll taken in the 1980s indicated that about 61 percent of the public believed that the United States was spending far too much in aid for other nations. As one letter writer to the State Department complained, "We have to work 5 months out of every year just to pay our taxes. Are we going to bankrupt the United States so we can support the world?" A poll taken at about the same time the letter was written showed that many Americans believe that foreign aid accounts for about 40 percent of the federal budget. In reality, foreign aid takes up less than 1 percent of the federal budget.

Nevertheless, many question whether the United States should offer foreign aid when the country is in an economic recession.

Background

The United States foreign-aid policies began in 1947 with the implementation of the Marshall Plan. It was then that Secretary George C. Marshall announced the nation's policy in helping other nations of the world. He stated:

> *It is logical that the United States should do whatever it is able to do to assist in the return of normal economic health in the world, without which there can be no political stability and no assured peace. Our policy is not directed against any country or doctrine but against hunger, poverty, desperation, and chaos. Its purpose should be the revival of a working economy in the world so as to permit the emergence of political and social conditions in which institutions can be free.*
>
> —GEORGE C. MARSHALL, 1947

The more than $13 billion in aid that the United States provided to Western Europe enabled that part of the world to undergo a remarkable and sustained economic recovery that continues today. The Marshall Plan also benefited the United States. As Secretary of State George Shultz observed many years later:

More About the Case

Western Europe recovered very slowly from the devastation of World War II. A harsh winter in 1947 and reduced crop yields forced millions of people to the brink of starvation. Discontented workers started voting for communists, especially in Italy and France.

Secretary of State George Marshall had his staff develop a plan for massive economic recovery in Europe. He proposed economic aid to all nations of Europe if they developed free social and political institutions. Communist-bloc nations were invited to join. The Soviets rejected the proposal, claiming that the United States was only interested in undermining control of their satellite nations. The

*T*he success of the Marshall Plan . . . demonstrates that foreign affairs is not always a "zero sum game." We do not necessarily advance our own vital interests at another nation's cost. On the contrary, more often than not, the most effective way of promoting our basic goals is by working with others to achieve their basic goals. That is what a Democratic President and a Republican Congress understood in 1947 when they allocated 11 cents out of every Federal dollar to fund the Marshall Plan.

—GEORGE SHULTZ, 1987

Since 1945 the United States has spent more than $200 billion in economic aid. Today the annual foreign-aid budget exceeds $15 billion. Nations receiving most of the aid are Israel, Egypt, Pakistan, El Salvador, and the Philippines. With the breakup of the Soviet Union, the nations of Eastern Europe began to receive aid.

Over the years Presidents have requested money from Congress for economic and military aid. Although no strong public support existed, foreign aid bills have passed. In some instances, however, Congress has tried to restrict the aid. The Foreign Assistance Act of 1973, for example, stated that "the President should deny any economic assistance to the government of any country which practices internment or imprisonment of that country's citizens for political purposes." The attempts to tie foreign aid to human rights have typically failed, though.

Public Opinion and Foreign Aid The Chicago Council on Foreign Relations recently conducted a survey to determine if gaps existed between the foreign-policy preferences of leaders and the public.

The differences in opinion often varied widely. When asked, for example, if the nation should be involved in world affairs, 69 percent of the public said *yes.* Leaders responded *yes* 98 percent of the time, a difference of 29 percent. Larger gaps appeared when the subject was foreign economic aid. As the Chicago Council on Foreign Affairs reported:

*L*eaders are much more favorable to economic aid in general [Leaders 91 percent, Public 50 percent], and especially more favorable to increasing aid to Eastern Europe and underdeveloped countries of

Feeding the World
United States farmers provide food for many countries. Twenty percent of American farmland, for example, produces food for foreign aid export.

Africa and Asia [75 percent to 27 percent of the public]. Leaders are also somewhat more in favor of increasing aid to South American countries combatting the drug problem, more opposed to decreasing aid to Egypt, and more favorable to increasing aid to Arab countries suffering from the Iraqi invasion of Kuwait.

—CHICAGO COUNCIL ON FOREIGN RELATIONS, 1990

The media's coverage of foreign aid also helps shape public opinion. A recent article titled "Foreign-Aid Follies" stated that Ireland would receive $20 million in economic aid awarded to that nation as a "goodbye present for [former House speaker] Tip O'Neill" whose ancestors were Irish. Such disclosures have eroded some support assistance.

Support for Foreign Aid Defenders of the nation's foreign-aid policies try to refute certain misconceptions. One misconception is that foreign aid "represents a massive outflow of dollars from the United States." The undersecretary of state for political affairs refutes this argument:

*T*he truth is that 70% of the money appropriated for bilateral foreign assistance is spent in the United

other nations of Europe, however, requested the aid.

Congress was slow to approve Marshall's package. Only after extensive lobbying and a successful coup that established communism in Czechoslovakia did Congress agree to the program. The Economic Cooperation Administration

(ECA) administered the Marshall Plan. The nations receiving aid established the Organization for European Economic Cooperation (OEEC) to develop cooperative programs between members. Congress provided the ECA $13 billion over a four-year period. By the 1950s recovery in Europe became self-sustaining.

general population? *(possible responses: increased wealth in the United States, more poverty in the world)*

L2 **Economics** Have students compare the percentage of foreign aid under the Marshall Plan with foreign-aid figures today. *(Americans gave up 11 cents out of every dollar in taxes to support the Marshall Plan; today foreign aid is only 1 percent of the total federal budget.)* Ask: What accounts for the drop in aid? *(The United States felt threatened by the Soviet Union in 1949. However, recent events have removed this threat. The United States economy is not as strong as it was in the 1940s; people are more concerned about their own economic stability.)*

Point out that World War II created a surplus of savings. This money could be lent to foreign countries. With money in hand, foreigners could buy manufactured goods from the United States. How did such policies help create the image of the United States as a superpower?

L3 **Analyzing a Point of View** Discuss the Department of State's position on foreign aid. Ask: Why is foreign aid seen as a vital part of diplomacy? *(Aid helps maintain American influence in the world.)* How does the administration encourage Congress to fund foreign aid even though the public opposes it? *(They claim that 70 percent of all foreign-aid dollars are spent on American goods; they believe that it is the responsibility of a superpower to aid other countries.)*

Independent Practice

L1 Conducting a Poll Have students poll their peers on the following: Americans should continue to provide foreign aid at its present level. Why or why not? Have students collect their data and compare it with the data in the case study.

L2 Geography Have students locate major recipients of American foreign aid on a map. Have them find out the total dollars each country receives. Have students write a report that explains why the United States supports the countries it does.

L3 Research Have students research the economic and political agreements that were made between the United States and its allies during the Persian Gulf crisis of 1990–1991. Have students consider whether the agreements resulted in shifts in United States foreign aid.

Assess

Have students complete **Examining the Case.**

Close

Discuss ways the United States could aid countries in ways other than providing financial assistance.

States, not abroad. American firms supply commodities, equipment, consulting services, and other expertise to foreign assistance projects, which are then exported.

—MICHAEL H. ARMACOST, 1985

Foreign aid is often a large federal subsidy for the nation's agriculture and industries. At one point, for example, analysts estimated that 20 percent of American farmland was producing food for export around the world.

Supporters of foreign aid also point out that aid programs contribute to the stability of developing nations, prevent political unrest, and protect the national security of the United States. As President Ronald Reagan said in a State of the Union address:

We cannot play innocents abroad. . . . nor can we be passive when freedom is under siege. Without resources, diplomacy cannot succeed. Our security assistance programs help friendly governments defend themselves and give them confidence to work for peace. . . . [d]ollar for dollar, security assistance contributes as much to global security as our own defense budget.

—RONALD REAGAN, FEBRUARY 6, 1985

Critics of Foreign Aid Many Americans oppose foreign-aid policies. Normally criticisms fall into three categories. One is that the aid often fails to reach the people who need it. James Bovard, who writes for *Human Events,* observed:

America's foreign aid programs are still some of the biggest fiascos around. Most American aid still goes to foreign governments, instead of to the private sector. Most American aid still goes to countries where governments so mismanage the economy that an infusion of dollars only hides some of the damage. . . . A few countries have changed a few policies, but our foreign aid programs continue to provide little relief for the Third World poor.

—JAMES BOVARD, 1985

A second criticism is that aid may hinder economic development of a developing nation's economy. As New York University economics professor Melvyn B.

Krauss notes, "food aid, by increasing food supply, depresses the price of agricultural products in the recipient countries. . . . The influx of free foreign food into the domestic market can ruin local producers."

A third criticism is that the United States is no longer an economic giant. Many of the nation's industries have fallen on hard times and real income has declined in the last two decades. "The Patriot missile" one observer noted, "is cheered around the world at the very same time that American manufacturers' share of the consumer electronics market has shrunk from 70 percent to 10 percent." Representative David R. Obey summed up the problem recently:

The U.S. government must . . . focus as much attention on the problems of American families as it does on the problems of Kuwaitis. If we do not, we will define ourselves as a warrior nation without peer and an economic competitor nation without a prayer.

—DAVID R. OBEY, FEBRUARY 5, 1991

Significance

Political instability is a real and worldwide threat. Former communist nations now face the dual threats of shortages and inflation. The possibility remains that new totalitarian regimes will take control. The question confronting the United States is what its proper role should be in helping the nations of Eastern Europe and developing nations, particularly in the realm of foreign aid.

Examining the Case

Reviewing Facts

1. Explain what Secretary of State George Shultz meant when he said that "foreign affairs is not necessarily a zero sum game."
2. Identify which of the two groups, leaders or the public, showed greater support for foreign aid.

Critical Thinking Skills

3. Analyzing Information Why do you think the general public does not strongly support foreign aid?
4. Drawing Conclusions Do you think the United States will furnish greater amounts of foreign aid to Eastern Europe in the future? Why or why not?

882 UNIT 10: COMPARATIVE GOVERNMENT AND ECONOMIC SYSTEMS

Examining the Case Answers

1. He meant that when one nation advances, it is not always at the expense of other nations.
2. the leaders
3. A typical answer probably will include the view that many Americans are more concerned with their own domestic problems than with those of people in other nations.

4. A positive response might be based on the conclusion that the United States will provide more aid to promote stability and the future of the present governments as long as there is a possibility that a new totalitarian government will be established. A negative response may be based on the conclusion that less money can be spent on foreign aid because of continuing domestic economic problems.

Chapter 28
Comparing Systems of Government

Both the United States and Great Britain are democracies, but the United States is also a republic. Great Britain, in contrast, is a constitutional monarchy, with a king or queen as the head of state.

The British constitution does not consist of a single document like the United States Constitution. Only parts of the British constitution are written. The written parts consist of centuries-old court decisions, charters such as the Magna Carta and the English Bill of Rights, and laws passed by Parliament—the British legislature. Important parts of the British constitution are unwritten and consist of customs and traditions of government generally accepted by the British people.

Almost all governmental authority in Great Britain stems from Parliament. The British Parliament is a bicameral (two-house) legislature, consisting of the House of Commons and the House of Lords.

Parliament is not only a legislative body, it is also the body that selects the leaders of the executive branch who run the government. This system is different from the United States where the separation of powers divides the executive branch from the legislative branch.

France has a democratic government that is in some ways similar to Great Britain's government. Both nations are unitary states. In other ways the French government resembles the United States government. For example, France is a republic and has a written constitution. The French constitution provides for a very strong president and a relatively weak legislature.

France's current constitution was designed to limit the powers of the legislative branch. The Parliament, for example, may pass legislation only on matters specified in the constitution such as civil rights, election procedures, and declarations of war. On matters not specified in the constitution, the executive may enact laws without the approval of Parliament.

In many respects the Japanese government resembles the government of Great Britain. It is a constitutional monarchy with a parliamentary government, a prime minister, a cabinet, and a bicameral legislature. Like the governments of Great Britain and France, the Japanese government is a centralized, unitary government that allows only limited local autonomy.

The 1947 constitution that guides Japan today established a parliament of two houses called the National Diet. The upper house is the House of Councilors, and the lower house, the House of Representatives. The lower chamber has far more power than the House of Councilors, which has only limited power to delay legislation.

A cabinet led by a prime minister exercises the executive power in the central government. The prime minister, who is the leader of the majority party in the House of Representatives, appoints the cabinet.

Following the example of the Soviet Union, the leaders of the People's Republic of China (PRC) established a totalitarian government. The Chinese government is strictly controlled by the Chinese Communist party (CCP), in much the same way that the Soviet Communist party once controlled the Soviet Union. Although the CCP is not an official organ of the government, it determines governmental policies and ensures that the government carries out the party's policies and decisions.

Like the United States, Mexico is a democratic, federal republic. The United States of Mexico is made of 31 states and a single federal district, Mexico City. Each of the states exercises political power through a state governor and a state legislature. The constitution of 1917 divides the national government into three branches—executive, legislative, and judicial.

At the head of the executive branch of government is the president. The Mexican president exercises strong control over the national government. Mexico's legislative branch, or Congress, is composed of two houses—the Senate and the Chamber of Deputies.

Consistent with Mexico's federal system of government, the nation's judicial system is composed of federal and state courts. At the highest federal level is the Supreme Court. Twenty-six justices are divided into four divisions to handle criminal, civil, labor, and administrative cases.

Chapter 29
Comparing Economic Systems

An **economic system** is an organized method of satisfying the various wants of people from the means of production that are available. The laws, customs, and traditions of a nation define its economic system.

UNIT 10: COMPARATIVE GOVERNMENT AND ECONOMIC SYSTEMS **883**

Using the Unit 10 Digest

Use the Unit Digest to introduce, review, reteach, or condense specific chapters or the entire unit. The Unit Digest is enhanced by the corresponding transparencies and activities in the Teacher's Classroom Resources.

Focus

Write the following types of economic system on the chalkboard: *capitalism, communism, socialism.* Have students skim the textbook to locate visual materials that illustrate these three systems. Ask for five volunteers to share their selections with the rest of the class. For each selection, have students discuss how the illustration represents the system. Then have students select the visual that best illustrates each system. Close by mentioning that these three forms of economic system are discussed and compared in the Unit 10 Digest.

Teach

L1 Making Comparisons Have students draw a table in their notebooks using *United States, Great Britain, France, Japan, China,* and *Mexico* as horizontal headings. Have them complete the table by making a comparison of these countries' economic, political, and governmental systems. Suggest that they use such vertical headings as *Type of Economic System, Major Features of Economy, Type of Political System,* and *Major Features of Government.* Have students compare their tables by displaying them on the bulletin board.

Classroom Resources for Unit 10 Digest

Unit Digest Transparencies, Unit 10   Participating in Government, Unit 10

L3 Descriptive Writing Have students work in groups to develop a script for a "You Are There" program on a topic related to the content of this Unit Digest. Possible topics include a session of the British Parliament, a Japanese cabinet meeting, the massacre in Tiananmen Square, or the global challenge of pollution. If video equipment is available, have students make recordings of their programs. If not, have them perform their scripts for other government and civics classes.

Assess

Check for Understanding
Have students complete **Synthesizing the Unit.**

Close

Remind students of the foundations of United States government that they studied in Unit 1. Have students consider how these foundations have prepared the United States to meet the challenges of the 1990s and beyond.

All economic systems must provide answers to three questions: What should be produced with available resources? How should goods and services be produced? Who gets the goods and services that are produced? Different economic systems around the world answer these questions in different ways.

In modern times three types of economic systems have emerged in various countries around the world— capitalism, socialism, and communism. Each system has provided its own set of answers to the three basic economic questions.

In the United States, capitalism is the basic economic system. **Capitalism** is based on private ownership of the means of production and on individual economic freedom. A capitalist economic system is often called a **free enterprise system.**

Socialism is primarily an economic system, but it is also a political philosophy. It calls for putting the major means of production in the hands of society, either directly or through government. Thus, socialism calls for public ownership of most land, factories, and other means of production. Socialists believe in shifting economic power from individuals to society, as well as distributing wealth and income equally among people.

Communism is both a political and an economic system. The People's Republic of China, Cuba, and some nations in Southeast Asia and Africa have communist systems. Socialism and communism have many ideas in common. Both economic systems stem from the ideas of Karl Marx, a German thinker who first called his ideas "scientific socialism." Yet Socialists in democratic countries are often enemies of Communists. Why?

Communists believe capitalism must be overthrown by force and revolution. Unlike democratic countries with a socialist economic system, communist states operate their economies on the basis of a dictatorship.

Chapter 30
Our Interdependent World

In today's highly interdependent world, every nation must face the challenges of issues that cross national boundaries. Global issues are major problems that affect most of the world's people and cannot be solved by any nation acting alone. Such issues include air and water pollution, the loss of natural resources such as croplands and forests, and widespread hunger and poverty.

Interdependence has also changed the way Americans view the world. In the past United States producers saw the world only as an array of market opportunities. Such is no longer the case. American manufacturers must now compete in an interconnected system of markets throughout the world—part of the global economy.

The potential for nuclear catastrophe today makes international security a vital issue. The need for security preoccupies leaders because many unresolved issues could ignite a war. Even though the United Nations is committed to preserving peace, every nation is generally responsible for its own safety.

In addition to the threat of war, human activity has begun to endanger the very systems that support all life on the planet. These systems include the oceans, lakes and rivers, the soil, the forests, and the very air people breathe. In the past the leaders of national governments have often sacrificed the environment to promote national security and economic development. In the wake of irreversible environmental damage, such as the continual extinction of numerous plant and animal species, many people today have become aware that more care must be taken to safeguard the environment.

Further, government leaders are discovering that environmental problems and scarce natural resources may lead to international conflict. Some scholars predict that environment and resource issues may replace the cold war as one of the greatest threats to stability in the international system.

Synthesizing the Unit

Recalling Facts
1. Define **economic system, capitalism, free enterprise system, socialism, communism.**
2. State **why international security is such a vital issue today.**
3. Describe **how interdependence has changed the way American manufacturers view world markets.**

Critical Thinking Skills
4. Making Comparisons **Compare the governments of Great Britain, France, and Mexico.**

Synthesizing the Unit Answers

1. Definitions of terms appear on the pages indicated: **economic system,** 883; **capitalism,** 884; **free enterprise system,** 884; **socialism,** 884; **communism,** 884
2. It is a vital issue because of the proliferation of nuclear weapons. If nuclear weapons were used in a war in one region, the consequences would be felt by nations completely uninvolved in the conflict. Such an action could threaten the safety of the entire globe.

3. In the past American manufacturers viewed the world as one huge market for their goods. Today, American goods must compete with goods from other countries in an interconnected system of markets.
4. Great Britain, France, and Mexico all have democratic governments. France and Mexico are republics, while Britain is a constitutional monarchy. Britain, unlike France and Mexico, does not have a written constitution. Of the three countries, only Mexico has a federal system of government. In France and Mexico, the president wields considerable power. In Britain, however, the legislature selects the executive branch.

Reference Section

ATLAS KEY

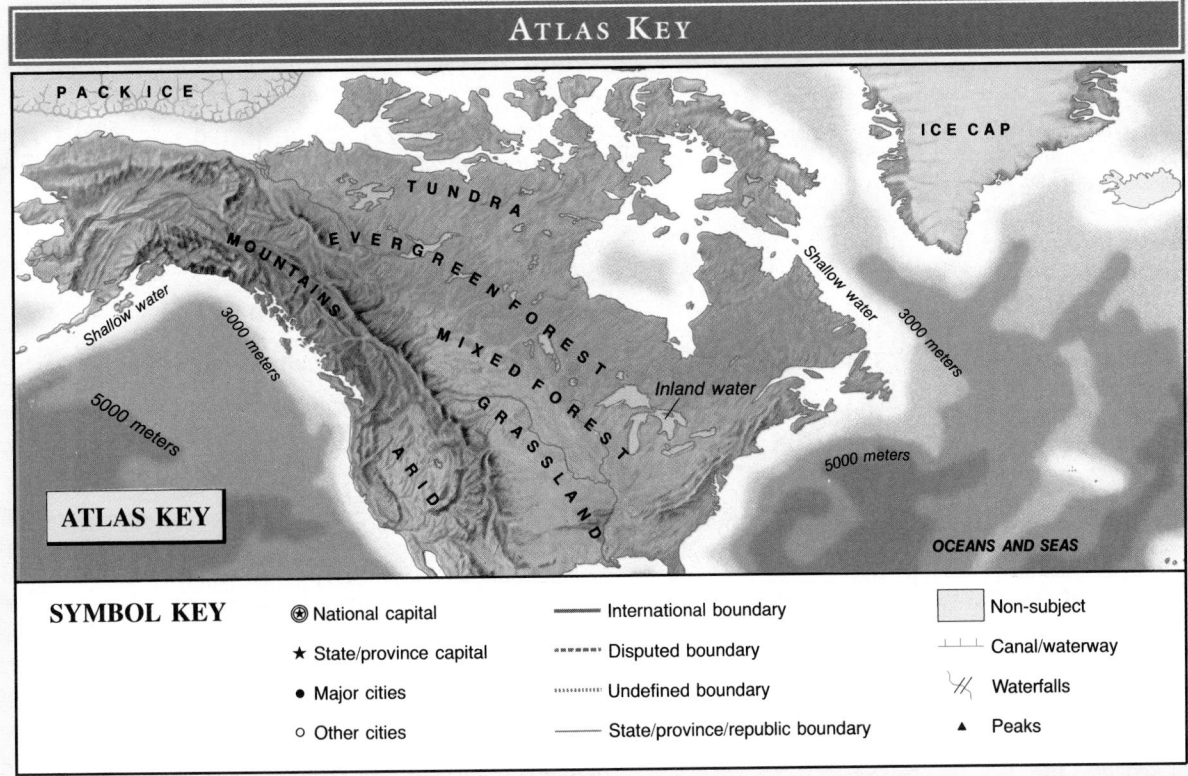

PACK ICE

ICE CAP

TUNDRA

EVERGREEN FOREST

MOUNTAINS

MIXED FOREST

Shallow water

Inland water

GRASSLAND

ARID

Shallow water

3000 meters

3000 meters

5000 meters

5000 meters

ATLAS KEY

OCEANS AND SEAS

SYMBOL KEY

⊛ National capital

★ State/province capital

● Major cities

○ Other cities

—— International boundary

------- Disputed boundary

·········· Undefined boundary

—— State/province/republic boundary

Non-subject

⊢⊢⊢ Canal/waterway

✕ Waterfalls

▲ Peaks

⚖ SUPREME COURT CASE INDEX

The following Supreme Court cases are arranged chronologocally and by category. A description of each case may be found on the text pages indicated.

The Federal System

Marbury v. Madison (1803)	p. 79, 460, 538
McCulloch v. Maryland (1819)	p. 129,130, 132, 390-91
Cohens v. Virginia (1821)	p. 577
Gibbons v. Ogden (1824)	p. 393
Barron v. Baltimore (1833)	p. 170
Ex parte Milligan (1866)	p. 564
Watkins v. United States (1957)	p. 397
Baker v. Carr (1962)	p. 363, 568

Wesberry v. Sanders (1964)	p. 363
Reynolds v. Sims (1964)	p. 692
United States v. Nixon (1974)	p. 485
Train v. City of New York (1975)	p. 564
Buckley v. Valeo (1976)	p. 296
Hutchinson v. Proxmire (1979)	p. 365
Immigration and Naturalization	
Service v. Chadha (1983)	p. 399

Freedom of the Press

Near v. Minnesota (1931)	p. 193
Burstyn v. Wilson (1952)	p. 196
New York Times v. Sullivan (1964)	p. 187
Zemel v. Rusk (1965)	p. 339
Sheppard v. Maxwell (1966)	p. 194
Red Lion Broadcasting Co. v. FCC (1969)	p. 341
New York Times Company v. United States (1971)	p. 193, 339, 342
Branzburg v. Hayes (1972)	P. 339
Miller v. California (1973)	p. 196
Bigelow v. Virginia (1975)	p. 196

Nebraska Press Association v. Stuart (1976)	p. 194
Gannett Co., Inc. v. De Pasquale (1979)	p. 194
Richmond Newspapers, Inc. v. Virginia (1980)	p. 195
Wilkinson v. Jones (1987)	p. 196
Hazelwood School District v. Kuhlmeier (1988)	p. 194
Hustler Magazine v. Falwell (1988)	p. 187

Freedom of Assembly

Whitney v. California (1927)	p. 352-353
De Jonge v. Oregon (1937)	p. 189,352
Thornhill v. Alabama (1940)	p. 192
Cox v. New Hampshire (1941)	p. 190
Hughes v. Superior Court (1950)	p. 192
International Brotherhood of Teamsters, Local 695 v. Vogt (1950)	p. 192
Feiner v. New York (1951)	p. 191
Scales v. United States (1961)	p. 354
Noto v. United States (1961)	p. 354
Cox v. Louisiana (1965)	p. 190
Adderly v. Florida (1966)	p. 190
Gregory v. Chicago (1969)	p. 191

Grayned v. City of Rockford (1972)	p. 190
Police Department of Chicago v. Mosley (1972)	p. 190
Lloyd Corporation v. Tanner (1972)	p. 190
Skokie v.The National Socialist Party of America (1977)	p. 191
Terry v. New York National Organization for Women (1990)	p. 190
Hirsch v. Atlanta (1990)	p. 190
National Organization for Women, Inc., et al. v. Scheidler, et al. (1994)	p. 190

Freedom of Speech

Schenck v. United States (1919)	p. 185
Gitlow v. New York (1925)	p. 170-71,185
Chaplinsky v. New Hampshire (1942)	p. 187
Dennis v. United States (1951)	p. 187, 354
Yates v. United States (1957)	p. 187, 354
Keyishian v. Board of Regents (1967)	p. 354
United States v. O' Brien (1968)	p. 185
Tinker v. Des Moines School District (1969)	p. 185

Brandenburg v. Ohio (1969)	p. 187
Sutherland v. Illinois (1976)	p. 185
Bethel School District v. Fraser (1986)	p. 188
Hazelwood School District v. Kuhlmeier (1988)	p. 188
Texas v. Johnson (1989)	p. 185
United States v. Eichman (1990)	p. 185

886

Freedom of Religion

Rights of the Accused

Equal Protection and Citizenship

THE WORLD

- • World's most populous cities
- —— International boundary
- —— Republic boundary
- — — Disputed boundary
- ········ Undefined boundary

0 1000 2000 Miles
0 1000 2000 Kilometers

Projection: Robinson

CENTRAL AMERICA AND WEST INDIES

Projection: Bipolar Oblique Conic Conformal

0 250 500 Miles
0 250 500 Kilometers

UNITED STATES

- ⊛ National capital
- ★ State capital
- ● Major city
- ○ Other city
- ▬▬ International boundary
- ▬▬ State boundary

```
0        100        200 Miles
0   100   200 Kilometers
```

Projection: Albers Equal Area

WASHINGTON
9
(+1)

Seattle
Olympia★

Portland· Columbia River
★Salem

OREGON
5

IDAHO
2
★Boise

MONTANA
1
(-1)
Helena★

NORTH DAKOTA
1 ★Bismarck

SOUTH DAKOTA
1 ★Pierre

WYOMING
1

Great
Salt
Lake

Salt Lake ★
City

Cheyenne★

NEBRASKA
3

Lincoln
Platte River

North Platte River
South Platte River

★Carson City
★Sacramento
San
Francisco·
·Oakland
·San
Jose

NEVADA
2

UTAH
3

Denver★

COLORADO
6

Arkansas

KANSAS
4
(-1)

River

CALIFORNIA
52
(+7)

Las Vegas·

·Los Angeles
·San Bernardino
Long·
Beach
·San Diego

Colorado River

ARIZONA
6
(+1)

·Phoenix

·Tucson

NEW
MEXICO
3

Rio Grande

★Santa Fe

OKLAHOMA
6

Oklahoma City★

Red River

Dallas·
Fort Worth·

TEXAS
30
(+3)

Austin★

PACIFIC

OCEAN

GULF OF
CALIFORNIA

120°   115°
160°   155°

Honolulu
★

HAWAII
2
PACIFIC
OCEAN

20°   20°

0   100 Miles
0   100 Kilometers
160°   155°
170°

180°   170°   160°   140°
Arctic Circle
70°

Bering Strait

Yukon   River

ALASKA
1

130°

San Antonio·

Rio

MEXICO

Grande

60°

BERING SEA

0   250   500 Miles
0   250   500 Kilometers

GULF OF
ALASKA

CANADA

Juneau★

60°

100°

CANADA

MAINE
2
★ Augusta

MINNESOTA
8

MICHIGAN
16 (-2)

NEW YORK
31 (-3)

Montpelier ★
VT.
1

N.H.
2
Concord ★

MASS.
10 (-1)

Minneapolis • St. Paul ★

WISCONSIN
9

Grand Rapids •
Lansing ★
Detroit •

Lake Ontario
Albany ★
Rochester •
Syracuse

Boston •

Providence ★

R.I.
2

Madison ★
Milwaukee •

Lake Erie

Buffalo •

Hartford ★
Bridgeport •

CONN.
6

IOWA
5 (-1)

Chicago •
Gary •
Hammond

Toledo •

Cleveland •
Akron •
Canton

PENNSYLVANIA
21 (-2)

Youngstown •

Newark •
New York

N.J.
13 (-1)

Des Moines ★

ILLINOIS
20 (-2)

OHIO
19 (-2)

Pittsburgh •

Harrisburg ★

Philadelphia •

Trenton ★
Camden •

Omaha •

Springfield ★

Indianapolis ★

Dayton •
Columbus ★

Baltimore •

MD.
8

Dover ★
DEL. 1

INDIANA
10

Cincinnati •

WEST VIRGINIA
3

D.C.

Annapolis ★
Washington, D.C.

Topeka ★

Kansas City •

St. Louis •
East St. Louis

Ohio River

Frankfort ★
Louisville •

Charleston ★

VIRGINIA
11 (+1)

Richmond ★

ATLANTIC OCEAN

Newport News •
Norfolk •

Kansas City
Jefferson City ★

MISSOURI
9

KENTUCKY
6 (-1)

Tulsa •

Nashville ★

Raleigh ★

NORTH CAROLINA
12 (+1)

ARKANSAS
4

Memphis •

TENNESSEE
9

Tennessee R.

Columbia ★

SOUTH CAROLINA
6

Little Rock ★

Atlanta ★

Birmingham •

ALABAMA
7

GEORGIA
11 (+1)

LOUISIANA
7 (-1)

Jackson ★

Montgomery ★

Jacksonville •

MISSISSIPPI
5

Tallahassee ★

Houston •

Baton Rouge ★

New Orleans •

FLORIDA
23 (+4)

Orlando •

UNITED STATES
(Showing 1990 Reapportionment)

	Gained seats
	Lost seats
	No change
(+1)	Number of seats lost or gained
⊛	National capital
★	State capital
•	Major city
——	International boundary
——	State boundary

0   100   200 Miles
0   100   200 Kilometers

Projection: Albers Equal Area

Tampa •
St. Petersburg •

Miami •

GULF OF MEXICO

N

THE BAHAMAS

CUBA

State*	Year Admitted	Population 1990	Area Sq. Mile	Capital	Largest City	House Rep. 1990**
1. Delaware	1787	666,168	2,057	Dover	Wilmington	1
2. Pennsylvania	1787	11,881,643	45,333	Harrisburg	Philadelphia	21
3. New Jersey	1787	7,730,188	7,836	Trenton	Newark	13
4. Georgia	1788	6,478,216	58,876	Atlanta	Atlanta	11
5. Connecticut	1788	3,287,116	5,609	Hartford	Bridgeport	6
6. Massachusetts	1788	6,016,425	8,257	Boston	Boston	10
7. Maryland	1788	4,781,468	10,577	Annapolis	Baltimore	8
8. South Carolina	1788	3,486,703	31,055	Columbia	Columbia	6
9. New Hampshire	1788	1,109,252	9,304	Concord	Manchester	2
10. Virginia	1788	6,187,358	40,817	Richmond	Norfolk	11
11. New York	1788	17,990,445	49,576	Albany	New York	31
12. North Carolina	1789	6,628,637	52,586	Raleigh	Charlotte	12
13. Rhode Island	1790	1,003,464	1,214	Providence	Providence	2
14. Vermont	1791	562,758	9,609	Montpelier	Burlington	1
15. Kentucky	1792	3,685,296	40,395	Frankfort	Louisville	6
16. Tennessee	1796	4,877,185	42,244	Nashville	Memphis	9
17. Ohio	1803	10,847,115	41,222	Columbus	Cleveland	19
18. Louisiana	1812	4,219,973	48,523	Baton Rouge	New Orleans	7
19. Indiana	1816	5,544,159	36,291	Indianapolis	Indianapolis	10
20. Mississippi	1817	2,573,216	47,716	Jackson	Jackson	5
21. Illinois	1818	11,430,602	56,400	Springfield	Chicago	20
22. Alabama	1819	4,040,587	51,609	Montgomery	Birmingham	7
23. Maine	1820	1,227,928	33,215	Augusta	Portland	2
24. Missouri	1821	5,117,073	69,686	Jefferson City	St. Louis	9
25. Arkansas	1836	2,350,725	53,104	Little Rock	Little Rock	4
26. Michigan	1837	9,295,297	58,216	Lansing	Detroit	16
27. Florida	1845	12,937,926	58,560	Tallahassee	Jacksonville	23
28. Texas	1845	16,986,510	267,339	Austin	Houston	30
29. Iowa	1846	2,776,755	56,290	Des Moines	Des Moines	5
30. Wisconsin	1848	4,891,769	56,154	Madison	Milwaukee	9
31. California	1850	29,760,021	158,693	Sacramento	Los Angeles	52
32. Minnesota	1858	4,375,099	84,068	St. Paul	Minneapolis	8
33. Oregon	1859	2,853,733	96,981	Salem	Portland	5
34. Kansas	1861	2,477,574	82,264	Topeka	Wichita	4
35. West Virginia	1863	1,793,477	24,181	Charleston	Huntington	3
36. Nevada	1864	1,201,833	110,540	Carson City	Las Vegas	2
37. Nebraska	1867	1,578,385	77,227	Lincoln	Omaha	3
38. Colorado	1876	3,294,394	104,247	Denver	Denver	6
39. North Dakota	1889	638,800	70,665	Bismarck	Fargo	1
40. South Dakota	1889	696,004	77,047	Pierre	Sioux Falls	1
41. Montana	1889	799,065	147,138	Helena	Billings	1
42. Washington	1889	4,887,941	68,192	Olympia	Seattle	9
43. Idaho	1890	1,006,749	83,557	Boise	Boise	2
44. Wyoming	1890	455,975	97,914	Cheyenne	Cheyenne	1
45. Utah	1896	1,727,784	84,916	Salt Lake City	Salt Lake City	3
46. Oklahoma	1907	3,145,585	69,919	Oklahoma City	Oklahoma City	6
47. New Mexico	1912	1,515,069	121,666	Santa Fe	Albuquerque	3
48. Arizona	1912	3,665,228	113,909	Phoenix	Phoenix	6
49. Alaska	1959	550,043	586,412	Juneau	Anchorage	1
50. Hawaii	1959	1,108,229	6,450	Honolulu	Honolulu	2
District of Columbia (Washington, D.C.)	—	606,900	68	—	—	—
United States of America	—	248,709,873	3,615,124	Washington, D.C.	New York	435

* Numbers denote the order in which states were admitted.

** Number of members in House of Representatives

1

George Washington
1789-1797

Born: 1732
Died: 1799
Born in: Virginia
Elected from: Virginia
Age when became President: 57
Occupations: Planter, Soldier
Party: None
Vice President: John Adams

2

John Adams
1797-1801

Born: 1735
Died: 1826
Born in: Massachusetts
Elected from: Massachusetts
Age when became President: 61
Occupation: Lawyer
Party: Federalist
Vice President: Thomas Jefferson

3

Thomas Jefferson
1801-1809

Born: 1743
Died: 1826
Born in: Virginia
Elected from: Virginia
Age when became President: 57
Occupations: Planter, Lawyer
Party: Republican**
Vice Presidents: Aaron Burr,
    George Clinton

4

James Madison
1809-1817

Most of the
Presidents are
portrayed in this
section by their
official White
House portrait.

**The Republican
party during this
period developed
into today's
Democratic party.
Today's Republi-
can party originat-
ed in 1854.

Born: 1751
Died: 1836
Born in: Virginia
Elected from: Virginia
Age when became President: 57
Occupation: Politician
Party: Republican**
Vice Presidents: George Clinton,
    Elbridge Gerry

5

James Monroe
1817-1825

Born: 1758
Died: 1831
Born in: Virginia
Elected from: Virginia
Age when became President: 58
Occupations: Politician, Lawyer
Party: Republican**
Vice President: Daniel D.
    Tompkins

6

John Quincy Adams
1825-1829

Born: 1767
Died: 1848
Born in: Massachusetts
Elected from: Massachusetts
Age when became President: 57
Occupation: Lawyer
Party: Republican**
Vice President: John C. Calhoun

7

Andrew Jackson
1829-1837

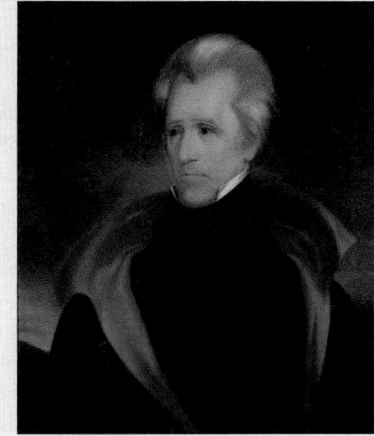

Born: 1767
Died: 1845
Born in: South Carolina
Elected from: Tennessee
Age when became President: 61
Occupation: Lawyer
Party: Democratic
Vice Presidents: John C. Calhoun,
Martin Van Buren

8

Martin Van Buren
1837-1841

Born: 1782
Died: 1862
Born in: New York
Elected from: New York
Age when became President: 54
Occupation: Lawyer
Party: Democratic
Vice President: Richard M.
Johnson

9

William H. Harrison
1841

Born: 1773
Died: 1841
Born in: Virginia
Elected from: Ohio
Age when became President: 68
Occupation: Soldier
Party: Whig
Vice President: John Tyler

10

John Tyler
1841-1845

Born: 1790
Died: 1862
Born in: Virginia
Elected as V.P. from: Virginia
Assumed presidency upon
Harrison's death
Age when became President: 51
Occupation: Lawyer
Party: Whig
Vice President: None

11

James K. Polk
1845-1849

Born: 1795
Died: 1849
Born in: North Carolina
Elected from: Tennessee
Age when became President: 49
Occupation: Lawyer
Party: Democratic
Vice President: George M. Dallas

12

Zachary Taylor
1849-1850

Born: 1784
Died: 1850
Born in: Virginia
Elected from: Louisiana
Age when became President: 64
Occupation: Soldier
Party: Whig
Vice President: Millard Fillmore

13

Millard Fillmore
1850-1853

Born: 1800
Died: 1874
Born in: New York
Elected as V.P. from: New York
Assumed presidency upon Taylor's death
Age when became President: 50
Occupation: Lawyer
Party: Whig
Vice President: None

14

Franklin Pierce
1853-1857

Born: 1804
Died: 1869
Born in: New Hampshire
Elected from: New Hampshire
Age when became President: 48
Occupation: Lawyer
Party: Democratic
Vice President: William R. King

15

James Buchanan
1857-1861

Born: 1791
Died: 1868
Born in: Pennsylvania
Elected from: Pennsylvania
Age when became President: 65
Occupation: Lawyer
Party: Democratic
Vice President: John C. Breckinridge

16

Abraham Lincoln
1861-1865

Born: 1809
Died: 1865
Born in: Kentucky
Elected from: Illinois
Age when became President: 52
Occupation: Lawyer
Party: Republican
Vice Presidents: Hannibal Hamlin,
  Andrew Johnson

17

Andrew Johnson
1865-1869

Born: 1808
Died: 1875
Born in: North Carolina
Elected as V.P. from: Tennessee
Assumed presidency upon Lincoln's death
Age when became President: 56
Occupations: Tailor, Politician
Party: Republican
Vice President: None

18

Ulysses S. Grant
1869–1877

Born: 1822
Died: 1885
Born in: Ohio
Elected from: Illinois
Age when became President: 46
Occupations: Farmer, Soldier
Party: Republican
Vice Presidents: Schuyler Colfax,
  Henry Wilson

19

Rutherford B. Hayes
1877-1881

Born: 1822
Died: 1893
Born in: Ohio
Elected from: Ohio
Age when became President: 54
Occupation: Lawyer
Party: Republican
Vice President: William A. Wheeler

20

James A. Garfield
1881

Born: 1831
Died: 1881
Born in: Ohio
Elected from: Ohio
Age when became President: 49
Occupations: Lawyer, Politician
Party: Republican
Vice President: Chester A. Arthur

21
Chester A. Arthur
1881-1885

Born: 1830
Died: 1886
Born in: Vermont
Elected as V.P. from: New York
Assumed presidency upon Garfield's death
Age when became President: 50
Occupation: Lawyer
Party: Republican
Vice President: None

22, 24
Grover Cleveland
1885-1889 1893-1897

Born: 1837
Died: 1908
Born in: New Jersey
Elected from: New York
Age when became President: 47; 55
Occupation: Lawyer
Party: Democratic
Vice Presidents: Thomas A. Hendricks, Adlai E. Stevenson

23
Benjamin Harrison
1889-1893

Born: 1833
Died: 1901
Born in: Ohio
Elected from: Indiana
Age when became President: 55
Occupation: Lawyer
Party: Republican
Vice President: Levi P. Morton

25
William McKinley
1897-1901

Born: 1843
Died: 1901
Born in: Ohio
Elected from: Ohio
Age when became President: 54
Occupation: Lawyer
Party: Republican
Vice Presidents: Garret Hobart, Theodore Roosevelt

26
Theodore Roosevelt
1901-1909

Born: 1858
Died: 1919
Born in: New York
Elected as V.P. from: New York
Assumed presidency upon McKinley's death
Age when became President: 42
Occupations: Author, Politician
Party: Republican
Vice President: Charles W. Fairbanks

27

William H. Taft
1909-1913

Born: 1857
Died: 1930
Born in: Ohio
Elected from: Ohio
Age when became President: 51
Occupation: Lawyer
Party: Republican
Vice President: James S. Sherman

28

Woodrow Wilson
1913-1921

Born: 1856
Died: 1924
Born in: Virginia
Elected from: New Jersey
Age when became President: 56
Occupation: College Professor
Party: Democratic
Vice President: Thomas R. Marshall

29

Warren G. Harding
1921-1923

Born: 1865
Died: 1923
Born in: Ohio
Elected from: Ohio
Age when became President: 55
Occupations: Newspaper Editor,
  Publisher
Party: Republican
Vice President: Calvin Coolidge

30

Calvin Coolidge
1923-1929

Born: 1872
Died: 1933
Born in: Vermont
Elected as V.P. from: Massachusetts
Assumed presidency upon Harding's death
Age when became President: 51
Occupation: Lawyer
Party: Republican
Vice President: Charles G. Dawes

31

Herbert C. Hoover
1929-1933

Born: 1874
Died: 1964
Born in: Iowa
Elected from: California
Age when became President: 54
Occupation: Geologist
Party: Republican
Vice President: Charles Curtis

32
Franklin D. Roosevelt
1933-1945

Born: 1882
Died: 1945
Born in: New York
Elected from: New York
Age when became President: 51
Occupation: Lawyer
Party: Democratic
Vice Presidents: John N. Garner,
   Henry A. Wallace, Harry S Truman

33
Harry S Truman
1945-1953

Born: 1884
Died: 1972
Born in: Missouri
Elected as V.P. from: Missouri
Assumed presidency upon Roosevelt's death
Age when became President: 60
Occupation: Businessman
Party: Democratic
Vice President: Alben W. Barkley

34
Dwight D. Eisenhower
1953-1961

Born: 1890
Died: 1969
Born in: Texas
Elected from: New York
Age when became President: 62
Occupation: Soldier
Party: Republican
Vice President: Richard M. Nixon

35
John F. Kennedy
1961-1963

Born: 1917
Died: 1963
Born in: Massachusetts
Elected from: Massachusetts
Age when became President: 43
Occupations: Author, Politician
Party: Democratic
Vice President: Lyndon B. Johnson

36
Lyndon B. Johnson
1963-1969

Born: 1908
Died: 1973
Born in: Texas
Elected as V.P. from: Texas
Assumed presidency upon Kennedy's death
Age when became President: 55
Occupations: Teacher, Politician
Party: Democratic
Vice President: Hubert H. Humphrey

37

Richard M. Nixon
1969-1974

Born: 1913
Died: 1994
Born in: California
Elected from: New York
Age when became President: 56
Occupations: Lawyer, Politician
Party: Republican
Vice Presidents: Spiro T. Agnew,
   Gerald R. Ford

38

Gerald R. Ford
1974-1977

Born: 1913
Born in: Nebraska
Appointed by Nixon as V.P. upon
   Agnew's resignation; assumed
   presidency upon Nixon's resignation
Age when became President: 61
Occupations: Lawyer, Politician
Party: Republican
Vice President: Nelson A. Rockefeller

39

Jimmy Carter
1977-1981

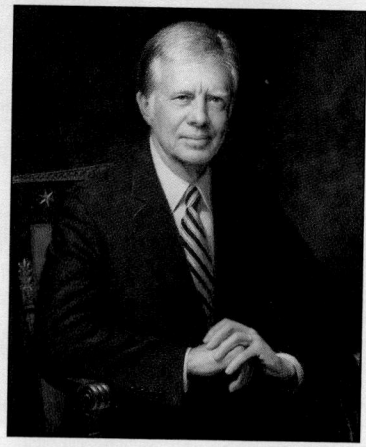

Born: 1924
Born in: Georgia
Elected from: Georgia
Age when became President: 52
Occupations: Businessman,
   Politician
Party: Democratic
Vice President: Walter F. Mondale

40

Ronald Reagan
1981-1989

Born: 1911
Born in: Illinois
Elected from: California
Age when became President: 69
Occupations: Actor, Politician
Party: Republican
Vice President: George H.W. Bush

41

George H.W. Bush
1989-1993

Born: 1924
Born in: Massachusetts
Elected from: Texas
Age when became President: 64
Occupations: Businessman, Politician
Party: Republican
Vice President: J. Danforth Quayle

42

William J. Clinton
1993-

Born: 1946
Born in: Arkansas
Elected from: Arkansas
Age when became President: 46
Occupations: University Professor,
Lawyer, Politician
Party: Democratic
Vice President: Albert Gore, Jr.

abridge limit (p. 181)

absentee ballot one that allows a person to vote without going to the polls on Election Day (p. 267)

absolute monarch one who has complete and unlimited power to rule his or her people (p. 30)

acreage allotment the program under which the government pays support prices for farmers' crops grown on an assigned number of acres (p. 656)

administrative assistant a lawmaker's chief aide (p. 381)

adversary system a judicial system in which lawyers for the opposing sides present their cases in court (p. 545)

advisory opinion ruling on a law or action that has not been challenged (p. 567)

affirmative action requirement that employers and other institutions must take positive steps to remedy the effects of past discrimination against minorities and women (pp. 214, 226)

alien a person who lives in a country where he or she is not a citizen (p. 162)

allegation formal complaint (p. 520)

ambassador government official who represents his or her nation in diplomatic matters (p. 619)

amendment change to the Constitution (p. 77)

amicus curiae (uh•MEE•kuhs KYUR•ee•ay) a Latin term meaning "friend of the court"; a brief from an individual, interest group, or government agency claiming to have information useful to a court's consideration of a case (p. 572)

amnesty a group pardon to individuals for an offense against the government (pp. 168, 463)

anarchy political disorder (p. 69)

annexation the process by which a local government absorbs new territory (p. 791)

appellate jurisdiction authority to hear a case that is appealed from lower court (p. 543)

apportionment the process of determining the number of representatives to which each state is entitled (p. 363)

appropriations bill a proposed law to authorize spending money (pp. 391, 425)

arraignment the procedure during which the defendant comes before a judge to hear formal charges in the indictment and to plead guilty or not guilty (p. 725)

arrest warrant an order signed by a judge naming an individual to be arrested for a specific crime (p. 88)

article one of seven main divisions of the body of the Constitution (p. 76)

assessment the process involved in calculating the value of property to be taxed (p. 765)

at-large as a whole; for example, statewide (pp. 364, 437)

Australian ballot one that is printed at government expense, lists all candidates, and is given out only at the polls on Election Day, marked in secret, and counted by government officials (p. 267)

authorization bill one that sets up a federal program and specifies how much money may be appropriated for that program (p. 425)

autocracy rule by one person (p. 30)

bail money or property the accused deposits with the court to gain release from jail until the trial (p. 725)

balanced budget a financial plan requiring that federal government spending does not exceed its income (p. 80)

bankruptcy the legal proceedings to administer the assets of a person or business that cannot pay its debts (p. 391)

bench trial a case presented before a judge alone (p. 725)

biased sample in polling, a group that does not represent the larger population (p. 311)

bicameral two-house legislative body (pp. 691, 745)

bilateral treaty an agreement signed by two nations (p. 632)

bill a proposed law (p. 370)

bill of attainder a law that establishes guilt and punishes people without a trial (pp. 395, 438)

bipartisan consisting of members of both major political parties (p. 625)

bloc a group united to promote a common interest (p. 575)

block grant a large grant of federal funds to a state or local government to be used for a general purpose (p. 737)

bond a contractual promise on the part of a borrower to repay a certain sum plus interest by a specified date (p. 736)

borough political division in Alaska, similar to a county in other states (p. 759)

boss powerful party leader (p. 243)

bourgeoisie (BOOR•zhwah•ZEE) capitalists who own the means of production (p. 39)

brief a written statement setting forth the legal arguments, relevant facts, and precedents supporting one side of a case (p. 572)

bureaucracy the organization of government administrators (p. 142)

bureaucrat one who works for one of the departments or agencies of the federal government (pp. 498, 536)

cabinet an advisory group that helps the President make decisions and set government policy (pp. 474, 535)

cadre government officials in China (p. 821)

calendar a schedule that lists the order in which bills will be considered in Congress (p. 371)

canvass to call on people in a district or group to determine political support or opinions (p. 265)

canvassing board the official body that tabulates election returns and certifies the winner (p. 267)

capital the means of production—money, factories, heavy machinery—used to produce goods (p. 835)

capitalism an economic system based on private ownership of the means of production and on individual economic freedom (pp. 36, 836, 884)

casework the work that a lawmaker does to help constituents with problems (p. 427)

caseworker a member of a lawmaker's personal staff who handles requests for help from constituents (p. 383)

categorical-formula grant the means by which federal funds are distributed to states on the basis of a state's wealth (p. 737)

caucus a private meeting of party leaders to choose candidates for office (pp. 243, 355)

cede yield (p. 63)

censure a vote of formal disapproval of a member's actions by other members of a legislative body (p. 365)

census population count (p. 363)

central clearance Office of Management and Budget's review of all legislative proposals executive agencies prepare (p. 482)

change of venue new trial location (p. 88)

checks and balances the system whereby each branch of government exercises some control on the others (p. 79)

civil case a dispute between two or more individuals or organizations (pp. 705, 745)

civil law one relating to disputes between two or more individuals or between individuals and the government (pp. 134, 543, 587)

civil rights movement the efforts to end segregation (pp. 213, 226)

civil servant a person who works for the government (pp. 498, 536)

civil service system the principle and practice of government employment on the basis of open, competitive examinations and merit (p. 516)

client group individuals and groups who work with a government agency and are most affected by its decisions (p. 522)

closed primary an election in which only members of a political party can vote (p. 244)

closed rule one that forbids members of Congress to offer any amendments to a bill from the floor (p. 424)

closed shop a place of employment where only union members may be hired (p. 651)

cloture the procedure that allows each senator to speak for only one hour on a bill under debate (p. 372)

cluster sample a polling method that groups people by geographical divisions (p. 311)

coalition government one formed by several parties who combine forces to obtain a majority (p. 233)

collective bargaining the practice of negotiating labor contracts (p. 649)

collective farm government-owned land worked by a large number of farm families who receive a share of earnings from the sale of the farm's output (p. 850)

collective naturalization the process by which a whole group of people living in the same geographic area become citizens of a country (p. 160)

collective security a system by which participating nations agree to take joint action against a nation that attacks any one of them (p. 633)

command economy the system in which the government makes economic decisions (pp. 39, 843)

commission form municipal government that combines executive and legislative power in an elected commission (pp. 778, 800)

committee staff the people who work for House and Senate committees (p. 381)

communism the economic and political system in which property and goods are owned by the government and products are shared by all (pp. 39, 849, 884)

comparative advantage the economic principle that each country should produce those goods that it can make most efficiently and purchase those that other nations produce more efficiently (p. 862)

compensation salary (p. 444)

concurrent jurisdiction authority shared by federal and state courts (pp. 543, 587)

concurrent powers those powers that both the national government and the states have (p. 127)

concurrent resolution a statement that covers matters requiring the action of the House and Senate but on which a law is not needed (pp. 411, 438)

concurring opinion a Court decision expressing the views of one or more justices who agree with the majority's conclusions about a case but do so for different reasons (p. 573)

conference committee temporary joint committee set up when the House and Senate have passed different versions of the same bill (pp. 377, 437)

conference report the final compromise bill worked out by a committee of senators and representatives (p. 416)

conscription compulsory military service; also called a draft (p. 630)

consensus agreement (p. 19)

conservative someone who believes that the role of government in society should be very limited and that individuals should be responsible for their own well-being (p. 314)

consolidation combining municipal governments to form a single government for an entire metropolitan area (p. 788)

constituent a person a member of Congress represents (p. 370)

constitution a plan that provides the rules for government (p. 27)

constitutional commission a group of experts appointed to study a state constitution and recommend changes (p. 688)

constitutional convention a gathering of citizens, usually elected by popular vote, who meet to consider changing or replacing a constitution (p. 688)

constitutional court one Congress established under the provisions of Article III of the Constitution (p. 546)

constitutional law one relating to interpretation and application of the Constitution (pp. 29, 544, 587)

constitutional monarch one who shares governmental powers with elected legislatures or serves mainly as the ceremonial leader of the government (p. 31)

consul a government official who represents his or her country's commercial interests in a foreign city (p. 628)

consulate the office that promotes a nation's business interests in a foreign country and safeguards its nation's travelers in that country (p. 628)

containment the policy designed to keep the Soviet Union from expanding its power beyond Eastern Europe (p. 616)

contempt willful obstruction of justice, such as refusal to testify or cooperate (p. 397)

copyright the exclusive right to publish and sell a literary, musical, or artistic work for a specified period of time (p. 393)

corporate charter a document that grants certain rights, powers, and privileges to a corporation and gives it legal status (p. 717)

corporation a business owned by individuals who purchase shares of its stock (p. 839)

correspondent reporter who is sent on assignment and sends stories to the home newspaper (p. 333)

council-manager form a type of municipal government in which legislative and executive powers are separated (pp. 779, 800)

council of government a voluntary regional organization that attempts to plan and coordinate policies for a metropolitan area (p. 792)

counsel an attorney (pp. 204, 226)

counterfeit currency illegally manufactured money (p. 507)

county the largest territorial and political subdivision of a state (pp. 752, 799)

county board the governing body of a county (p. 760)

coup a planned but sudden attempt to seize power (p. 852)

court observer a citizen volunteer who observes the daily activities in a courtroom (p. 710)

covert secret (p. 492)

criminal case one involving violation of the law (pp. 706, 745)

criminal law one that defines crimes and provides for their punishment (pp. 544, 587)

cross-pressured voter one who is caught between conflicting elements in his or her own life (p. 260)

customs duties the taxes levied on goods imported into the United States; also called tariffs or import duties (p. 596)

de facto existing "in fact" rather than officially or legally (p. 492)

defamatory speech false speech that damages a person's good name, character, or reputation (p. 187)

defendant a person against whom a civil or criminal suit is brought in court (p. 543)

deforestation the widespread destruction of trees and other vegetation (p. 859)

delegated powers those powers the Constitution grants to the national government (p. 126)

democracy rule by many persons (p. 30)

democratic socialism an economic system in which people have basic human rights and some control over government officials through free elections and multiparty systems, but the government owns the basic means of production and makes most economic decisions (p. 38)

denaturalization the loss of citizenship through fraud or deception during the naturalization process (pp. 160, 225)

department a political division of France (p. 815)

dependent one who depends primarily on another person for such things as food, clothing, and shelter (p. 594)

deputy a member of the lower house of Mexico's legislature (p. 827)

deregulate to reduce the powers of regulatory agencies (p. 502)

détente the relaxation of tensions between nations (p. 617)

developed nation one that has successfully used natural resources to develop a way of life based on business and industry (pp. 21, 844, 860)

developing nation one that is only beginning to develop industrially (pp. 21, 844, 860)

direct democracy a government in which people rule themselves by voting on issues individually as citizens (p. 32)

direction an indication of whether public opinion is generally positive or negative on a specific issue (p. 313)

direct primary an election in which party members select people to run in the general election (pp. 244, 355)

discrimination unfair treatment of individuals on the basis of race, sex, ethnic group, age, or religion (p. 211)

discount rate the interest rate the Federal Reserve System charges member banks for loans (p. 608)

dissenting opinion the views of one or more justices opposing the majority opinion (p. 573)

district court trial court created by Congress for both criminal and civil federal cases (p. 546)

dividends a share of the profits of a corporation that are paid to shareholders (p. 839)

divine right the view that God granted those of royal birth the right to rule their people (p. 30)

domino theory the belief that a communist takeover of one country would lead to the fall of the rest of the area (p. 634)

double jeopardy retrial of a person found not guilty in a previous trial for the same crime (pp. 207, 226)

due process of law the principle requiring that a law must be applied in a fair manner (pp. 88, 545)

economics the study of human efforts to satisfy seemingly unlimited wants through the use of limited resources (p. 36)

economic system the organized method of satisfying the various wants of people from the means of production that are available (pp. 834, 883)

elastic clause Article I, Section 8, of the Constitution, which gives Congress the right to make all laws "necessary and proper" to carry out the powers granted to the federal government (pp. 126, 390, 437)

elector a member of a political party chosen by popular vote in each state to formally elect the President and Vice President (pp. 451, 535)

electoral vote the official vote for President and Vice President by electors in each state (p. 450)

electorate the people who are entitled to vote during an election (p. 259)

embargo an agreement prohibiting trade (p. 54)

embassy an ambassador's official residence and offices in a foreign country (p. 628)

eminent domain the power of government to take private property for public use (p. 88)

enabling act the first step in the admission procedure which, when passed by Congress and signed by the President, enables the people of a territory to prepare a constitution (p. 137)

enemy alien a citizen of a nation with which the United States is at war (p. 163)

entitlement a required government expenditure, such as social security payments (pp. 426, 600)

entrepreneur a person who takes a risk making a new product or selling a service in the hope of making a profit (p. 837)

enumerated powers those government powers itemized in the Constitution; also called expressed powers (pp. 126, 390)

equal time doctrine a rule that requires stations to provide equal airtime to all candidates for a public office (pp. 195, 340)

equity law the system of rules by which disputes are resolved on the grounds of fairness (p. 543)

establishment clause the First Amendment guarantee that Congress shall make no law respecting the establishment of religion (pp. 178, 225)

estate tax the money the federal government collects on the assets of a person who dies (pp. 597, 735)

excise tax one levied on the manufacture, transportation, sale, or consumption of goods and the performance of services (pp. 596, 734)

exclusionary rule a law prohibiting the use of illegally obtained evidence in a federal court (p. 203)

executive agreement one made directly between the President and another head of state (pp. 93, 466, 624)

executive order a rule issued by the President that has the force of law (p. 462)

executive privilege the President's right to refuse to testify before, or provide information to, Congress or a court (pp. 484, 535)

expatriation giving up one's citizenship by leaving one's native country to live in a foreign country (pp. 160, 225)

ex post facto law one that makes crimes of acts that were legal when they were committed (pp. 395, 438)

expressed powers those powers that are directly stated in the Constitution (pp. 126, 390, 437)

extradite to deliver a criminal to the jurisdiction of another authority (p. 134)

extradition the legal procedure through which a person accused of a crime who has fled to another state is returned to the state where the crime took place (p. 723)

extralegal not sanctioned by law (p. 69)

faction an interest group within a country's political parties (p. 818)

factors of production resources that an economy needs to produce goods and services (p. 834)

fairness doctrine a rule requiring broadcasters to provide reasonable opportunities for the expression of opposing views on controversial issues of public importance (p. 341)

federal bureaucracy departments and agencies that do the work of the federal government (pp. 456, 535)

federalism a system under which power is divided between national and state governments (p. 77)

federal system one that divides the powers of government between the national government and state or provincial governments (p. 20)

felony a major crime (pp. 706, 745)

filibuster a method of defeating a bill in the legislature by the use of lengthy speeches (p. 372)

first-strike capability the ability of a country with nuclear weapons to launch its weapons against an opponent before the opponent launches its weapons (p. 869)

fiscal policy a government's use of spending and taxation to influence the economy (pp. 606, 677)

fiscal year the twelve-month accounting period (pp. 599, 677)

foreign policy the strategies and principles that guide the national government's relations with other countries and groups in the world (pp. 614, 677)

free enterprise the opportunity to make economic gains and to control one's economic decisions (p. 34)

free enterprise system one in which buyers and sellers make economic decisions in the marketplace with minimal government control (pp. 836, 884)

free exercise clause First Amendment guarantee that Congress will not prohibit the free exercise of religion (pp. 178, 225)

free market the economic system in which buyers and sellers are free to make unlimited economic decisions in the marketplace (p. 36)

front-runner the early leader in an election (p. 347)

fundamental right one that the Constitution explicitly guarantees (p. 211)

gag order one by which a judge bars the press from publishing certain types of information about a pending court case (p. 194)

general assistance state welfare programs (p. 732)

general sales tax one imposed on a broad range of items people buy (p. 734)

gentrification the movement of new people into a neighborhood, forcing out those who live there and changing the area's essential character (p. 786)

gerrymander drawing a district's boundaries to gain an advantage in elections (p. 363)

global issue a major problem that crosses national boundaries and that cannot be solved by any nation acting alone (p. 858)

global security the safety of the entire world (p. 868)

global warming the prediction that increasing amounts of gases released into the atmosphere from industrial activity will trap heat in the earth's surface (p. 859)

government the institution through which the state maintains social order, provides public services, and enforces decisions that are binding on all people living in the state (p. 20)

government corporation a business the federal government runs (p. 501)

grandfather clause a provision that makes an exemption in the law for a certain group based on previous conditions (pp. 272, 298)

grand jury the group that hears charges against a person suspected of having committed a crime and decides whether there is sufficient evidence to bring the person to trial (p. 546)

grant-in-aid a sum of money given by the federal government to the states for a specific purpose (p. 737)

gross national product (GNP) the sum of all goods and services produced by a nation's industries in a year (p. 606)

hearing a session at which a committee listens to testimony from people interested in a bill (p. 413)

heckler's veto public interference with the free speech and assembly rights of unpopular groups by claiming that demonstrations will result in violence (p. 191)

Holocaust the mass extermination of Jews and other groups by the Nazis during World War II (p. 191)

home rule the power of cities or local governments to govern themselves (pp. 752, 777)

horse-race coverage a method of reporting elections that focuses on "winners," "losers," and "who's ahead," rather than on issues or policy positions (p. 347)

house arrest a sentence that requires an offender to stay at home except for certain functions the court permits (p. 727)

human rights fundamental freedoms (p. 169)

human services government efforts to maintain basic health and living conditions for those people who have insufficient resources of their own; also called public welfare (p. 731)

hung jury one that cannot agree on a verdict (p. 725)

ideological party a political party that focuses on overall change in society rather than on some specific issue (p. 235)

ideology basic belief (p. 233)

illegal alien a person who comes to the United States without a legal permit (p. 163)

immunity freedom from prosecution for witnesses whose testimony ties them to illegal acts (p. 397)

impeach to accuse a public official of misconduct in office (p. 92)

impeachment the formal accusation of misconduct in office against a public official (pp. 394, 437)

implied powers powers not specifically listed in the Constitution, which the national government requires to carry out expressed powers (pp. 126, 394, 437)

impound refuse to spend (p. 564)

impoundment the President's refusal to spend money Congress has voted to fund a program (pp. 404, 462)

income tax one levied on individual and corporate income (p. 132)

incorporation the process of setting up a legal community (p. 776)

incrementalism the term political scientists use to explain that the total federal budget changes only a little from one year to the next (p. 603)

incumbent a government official already in office (pp. 297, 367)

independent a voter who does not support any one party (p. 237)

indictment a charge by a grand jury that a person committed a particular crime (pp. 546, 725)

information a formal accusation of a crime made by a prosecuting attorney (p. 725)

infrastructure the basic facilities of a city, such as paved streets and sidewalks, water pipes, sewers, bridges, and public buildings (pp. 783, 800)

inherent powers those powers that the national government may exercise simply because it is a government (p. 127)

initiative the procedure by which voters may propose a law or a state constitutional amendment (pp. 278, 688)

injunction an order that will stop a particular action or enforce a rule or regulation (pp. 526, 543)

inner cabinet the advisory group consisting of the secretaries of state, defense, treasury, and the Attorney General (p. 478)

intensity an indication of the strength of people's opinions about a particular issue or topic (p. 313)

interest group people who share common policy interests or goals and organize to influence the government (pp. 284, 355)

intergovernmental revenue the income distributed by one level of government to another (pp. 737, 746)

interlocking directorate arrangement whereby the same people serve on the boards of directors of several companies (p. 645)

internationalism involvement in world affairs (p. 615)

international security the creation of world stability as a result of the interaction of many nations' policies (p. 868)

interstate commerce trade among the states (pp. 68, 393)

interstate compact a written agreement between two or more states (p. 136)

iron triangle a relationship formed among government agencies, congressional committees, and client groups who work together (p. 527)

isolationism the avoidance of involvement in world affairs (p. 615)

item veto the power to reject a particular section or item in a piece of legislation without vetoing the entire law (pp. 464, 703)

Jim Crow law one requiring racial segregation in such places as schools, neighborhoods, public transportation, restaurants, and hotels (p. 211)

joint committee one made up of members from both the House and the Senate that acts as a study group with responsibility for reporting its findings back to the House and Senate (pp. 377, 437)

joint resolution a statement passed by both houses of Congress that deals with unusual or temporary matters, such as proposed constitutional amendments (pp. 410, 438)

judicial activism the belief that the Supreme Court should play an active role in shaping national policies (p. 94)

judicial circuit a region with an appellate court (p. 548)

judicial restraint the belief that the Supreme Court should avoid taking the initiative on social and political questions (p. 94)

judicial review the power of the Supreme Court to declare laws and actions of local, state, or national governments invalid if they violate the Constitution (pp. 79, 564)

judiciary the court system (p. 705)

jurisdiction the authority of a court to hear certain kinds of cases (pp. 77, 543, 587)

jus sanguinis (YOOS SAHN•gwuh•nuhs) the principle that grants citizenship on the basis of the citizenship of one's parents (p. 157)

jus soli (YOOS SOH•lee) the principle that grants citizenship to people born in a country (p. 157)

kitchen cabinet a group of informal advisers in Andrew Jackson's administration (p. 504)

labor people who produce goods and services (p. 835)

laissez-faire the theory that government should keep its hands off the economy (pp. 36, 643)

lame duck official serving out a term after defeat for reelection (p. 90)

land natural resources such as soil, water, air, and minerals (p. 834)

law of demand the economic principle that prices rise as demand increases and prices fall as demand decreases (p. 839)

law of supply the economic principle that prices fall as supply increases and prices rise as supply decreases (p. 839)

leak to deliberately disclose information (pp. 329, 476)

left wing liberal (p. 814)

legislative assistant a member of a lawmaker's personal staff (p. 382)

legislative court one created to help Congress exercise its powers (p. 549)

legislative veto the provisions Congress wrote into some laws that allowed it to review and cancel actions of the executive agencies that carried out those laws (p. 399)

liaison officer a cabinet department employee who helps promote good relations with Congress (p. 525)

libel written or published statements intended to damage a person's reputation (pp. 86, 187, 338)

liberal someone who believes the national government should be very active in helping individuals and communities promote health, education, justice, and equal opportunity (p. 313)

limited government one in which the power of the monarch, or government, is limited, not absolute (p. 46)

limited war one in which the more powerful nation or nations will not go beyond certain limits (p. 869)

lobbying making direct contact with lawmakers or other government leaders to try to influence government policy (pp. 289, 421, 572)

lobbyist representative of an interest group (pp. 289, 421)

logrolling the agreement by two or more lawmakers to support each other's bills (p. 429)

majority leader the member of the political party that holds the majority of seats in a legislative body who helps plan the party's legislative program (p. 373)

majority opinion the Court's decision expressing the views of the majority of justices (p. 573)

management the people who organize and direct land, labor, and capital (p. 835)

mandate a formal order given by a higher authority (p. 738)

mandatory sentencing the system of fixed, required terms of imprisonment for certain types of crimes (pp. 722, 746)

market the area in which a radio or television station or a newspaper can reach an audience (p. 341)

market system one in which buyers and sellers are linked together through the operation of supply and demand (p. 838)

market value the amount of money an owner may expect to receive if property is sold (p. 765)

martial law military control (p. 823)

mass media means of communication, such as television, radio, and newspapers, that influence large audiences (pp. 306, 356, 458)

mass transit the facilities such as subways, commuter railroads, and bus lines that are used to transport large numbers of people (pp. 670, 784)

mayor-council form a type of municipal government in which executive power belongs to an elected mayor and legislative power to an elected council (pp. 777, 800)

media event a visually interesting event designed to reinforce a politician's position on some issue (p. 329)

metropolitan area a large city and its surrounding suburbs (pp. 774, 800)

metropolitan federation the type of municipal government in which a higher level of government makes overall policy for an entire metropolitan area (p. 790)

militia an armed force of citizens (p. 87)

ministers the heads of executive departments in British government (p. 809)

misdemeanor a minor or less serious crime (pp. 706, 745)

mixed economy one in which the government both supports and regulates free enterprise (pp. 642, 678)

moderate a person whose opinions and beliefs fall somewhere between liberal and conservative and usually include some of both (p. 315)

monarchy a government in which a king, queen, or emperor exercises supreme powers (p. 30)

monetary policy control of the supply of money and credit to influence the economy (pp. 606, 677)

monopoly a business that has no competition (pp. 643, 717, 838)

muckraking searching out and reporting news stories that expose major scandals involving prominent people (p. 328)

multilateral treaty an international agreement signed by several nations (p. 632)

municipal government a city government (pp. 776, 800)

municipality an urban unit of government (pp. 752, 799)

mutual defense alliance an agreement between nations to support each other in case of an attack (p. 631)

mutually assured destruction (MAD) the situation that exists between two nations with second-strike capability (p. 869)

nation any sizeable group of people who are united by common bonds of race, language, custom, tradition, and sometimes, religion (p. 18)

national budget a yearly financial plan for the national government (p. 404)

national committee a large group, composed of representatives from the 50 state party organizations, which runs a political party (p. 238)

national convention the gathering of party members and local and state party officials every four years to nominate the party's presidential and vice-presidential candidates (p. 238)

national debt the total amount of money the government owes as a result of borrowing (pp. 391, 598)

nationalism intense pride in and loyalty to one's native country (p. 847)

nationalist position one that favors national action in dealing with social and economic problems (p. 130)

nationalization the process by which a government takes control of industry (pp. 170, 843)

national origins system one which established quotas for immigrants from each foreign country (p. 167)

national security a nation's determination to remain free and independent and to be secure from foreign influence or invasion (pp. 614, 677, 867)

nation-state a country in which the territory of both the nation and the state coincide (p. 18)

naturalization the legal process by which a person is granted the rights and privileges of a citizen (pp. 156, 393)

necessary and proper clause Article I, Section 8, of the Constitution, which gives Congress power to make all laws that are necessary and proper for carrying out its duties; also called elastic clause (p. 126)

newly developed nation one that is a middle-income state with some industrial base (p. 860)

news briefing a meeting during which a government official announces or explains a policy, decision, or action to reporters (p. 329)

news release a ready-made story government officials prepare for reporters (p. 329)

no confidence a vote that forces a prime minister to dissolve the government and call for new elections (p. 818)

nominating convention the official public meeting of a political party to choose candidates (pp. 243, 355)

noncommercial nonprofit (p. 324)

nonpartisan election one in which candidates do not run as nominees of political parties (p. 709)

nonrenewable resources those that are mineral-based and exist in a fixed, finite quantity (p. 873)

non-resident alien a person from a foreign country who expects to stay in the United States for a short, specified period of time (p. 163)

nuclear proliferation the spread of nuclear weapons (p. 870)

office-group ballot one that lists the candidates of all parties together by the office for which they are running (p. 266)

oligarchy rule by a few persons (p. 30)

oligopoly the domination of an industry by a few firms (p. 645)

open-market operations the means the Federal Reserve System uses to influence the economy by buying or selling securities on the open market (p. 608)

open primary an election in which all voters may participate (p. 244)

opinion a Supreme Court decision (p. 554)

ordinance law (p. 63)

original jurisdiction the authority of a trial court to be first to hear a case (p. 543)

outer cabinet an advisory group consisting of secretaries who head departments that represent narrow interests (p. 478)

pardon release from legal punishment (p. 463)

parish a political division in Louisiana, similar to a county in other states (p. 759)

parliamentary government the system that gives governmental authority to a legislature, which selects the executive from its own members (p. 809)

parochial school one operated by a church or religious group (p. 178)

parole means by which a prisoner is permitted to serve the rest of a sentence in the community under the supervision of a parole officer (p. 727)

partisan election one in which political parties nominate candidates (p. 709)

partnership a business owned by two or more individuals (p. 839)

party-column ballot one that lists each party's candidates in a column under the party's name (p. 266)

party primary the nominating election for choosing a political party's candidate for a general election (p. 698)

passport a document entitling a traveler to certain privileges and protection established by international treaty (p. 628)

patent exclusive right of an inventor to manufacture, use, and sell an invention for a specified period of time (p. 393)

patronage the practice of granting favors to reward party loyalty (pp. 241, 464, 826)

peer group an individual's close friends, church, clubs, or work groups (p. 306)

per curiam opinion (puhr KYUR•ee•AHM) a brief unsigned statement of the Court's decision (p. 571)

perjury lying under oath (p. 397)

personal property belongings such as stocks and bonds, jewelry, furniture, automobiles, and works of art (p. 765)

personal staff the people who work directly for individual senators and representatives (p. 381)

petition a written request (p. 80)

petit jury a trial jury of 12 people that weighs the evidence presented in court and renders a verdict (p. 546)

picket to patrol an establishment to convince workers and the public not to enter it (p. 190)

plaintiff the person who brings charges in a court of law (p. 543)

plank an individual section of a political party platform (p. 248)

platform the statement of a political party's principles, beliefs, and positions on vital issues (p. 248)

plea bargaining the process under criminal law by which an accused person agrees to plead guilty in exchange for a promise from the prosecutor to reduce the charges (p. 725)

plurality the largest number of votes in an election (pp. 244, 698)

pocket veto means by which the President may kill a bill passed during the last 10 days Congress is in session by simply refusing to act on it (p. 416)

police power government power to exercise reasonable control over persons and property to protect public health, safety, morals, and welfare (pp. 728, 746)

political action committee an organization specifically designed to collect money and provide financial support for political candidates (pp. 258, 295, 355)

political base the popularity and influence a candidate has among certain groups or sections (p. 697)

political culture a set of basic values and beliefs about a nation and its government that most citizens share (p. 307)

political party a group of people with broad common interests who organize to win elections, control government, and influence government policies (pp. 33, 232, 355)

political socialization the process by which individuals learn their political beliefs and attitudes through life experiences (p. 305)

politics efforts to control or influence the conduct and policies of government (p. 26)

polling place the location in a precinct where people vote (p. 266)

poll tax money paid in order to vote (p. 90)

polygamy the practice of having more than one spouse (p. 181)

popular sovereignty rule by the people (p. 77)

pork-barrel legislation the money that Congress appropriates for local federal projects (p. 429)

precedent the model on which to base later decisions or actions (pp. 182, 566)

precinct a voting district (pp. 237, 266)

precinct captain a volunteer who organizes party workers to distribute information about the party and its candidates and to get voters to the polls (p. 237)

premier the government official in France who forms a cabinet and carries out the day-to-day business of government (p. 812)

presidential succession the order in which officials fill the office of President in case of a vacancy (p. 446)

press gallery a place reserved in the Senate or House for correspondents (p. 334)

price support the program under which Congress establishes a support price for a crop and buys farmers' crops if the market price falls below that price (p. 655)

prime minister highest ranking member of the executive branch of a parliamentary government (p. 806)

prior restraint government censorship of information before it is published or broadcast (pp. 86, 193, 338, 356)

private bill proposed legislation dealing with individual people or places (pp. 410, 438)

private law legislation that applies to a particular person (p. 168)

probable cause a reasonable basis for believing that a person or premise is linked to a crime (p. 88)

probation suspending the sentence of a criminal offender subject to good behavior under the supervision of a probation officer (p. 726)

procedural due process the principle that requires authorities to avoid violating an individual's basic freedoms when enforcing laws (p. 545)

profit the difference between the amount of money a business takes in and the amount of money used to operate the business (p. 838)

progressive tax one that varies with a person's ability to pay (p. 735)

project grant the means by which individuals and state or local agencies may apply for federal funds for a specific purpose (p. 737)

proletariat workers who produce the goods (p. 39)

proportional representation a system in which several officials are elected to represent voters in an area (p. 236)

proportional tax one that is assessed at the same rate for everyone (p. 735)

proposition a new law or amendment proposed through an initiative (p. 278)

prosecution the party who brings charges against the defendant in a criminal case (p. 544)

pro tempore a Latin term meaning "for the time being" (p. 374)

public assistance programs those by which the government distributes public money to poor people (p. 659)

public bill one dealing with general matters that apply to the entire nation (pp. 410, 438)

public defender a lawyer employed by a state or local government to defend poor clients (p. 724)

public housing government-subsidized housing for low-income families (p. 668)

public housing program federal loans to local housing authorities to build housing projects (p. 782)

public opinion the ideas and attitudes a significant number of Americans hold about such things as government and political issues (pp. 304, 356)

public utility an organization that supplies such necessities as electricity, gas, telephone service, or transportation service to the public (p. 717)

public welfare government efforts to maintain basic health and living conditions for people who have insufficient resources of their own (p. 731)

pure speech the verbal expression of thought and opinion before an audience that has chosen to listen (pp. 184, 225)

quorum the minimum number of members who must be present to permit a legislative body to take official action (p. 372)

quota proportional part of a fixed quantity (p. 648)

random sampling a polling technique in which everyone in the universe has an equal chance of being selected (p. 311)

ratify approve (pp. 61, 80)

rational basis test means the Court uses to determine whether a state law is reasonably related to an acceptable goal of government (p. 209)

real property land and buildings (p. 765)

recall the procedure by which voters may remove elected officials before their terms expire (p. 278)

redistrict to set up new district lines after a census (p. 363)

referendum the procedure by which voters approve or disapprove a measure the state legislature has passed (p. 278)

regional security pact a mutual defense treaty among nations of a region (p. 631)

register to record one's name officially with a local election board (p. 265)

regressive tax one that affects people with low incomes more than those with large incomes (p. 735)

relief welfare assistance provided by the government (p. 731)

renewable resources those that come from living organisms that can grow and reproduce themselves (p. 873)

renovation restoration to a good condition (p. 781)

representative democracy a government in which the people elect representatives to make laws and conduct government (p. 32)

representative government one in which people elect delegates to make laws and conduct government (p. 47)

representative sample a small group of people, typical of the universe, that a pollster questions (p. 311)

reprieve the postponement of legal punishment (p. 463)

republic a government in which voters hold sovereign power; elected representatives who are responsible to the people exercise that power (p. 32)

reserved powers those powers that belong strictly to the states (p. 127)

reserve requirement the percentage of money member banks must keep in Federal Reserve Banks as a reserve against their deposits (p. 608)

resident alien a person from a foreign nation who has established permanent residence in the United States (p. 162)

resolution a statement that covers matters affecting only one house of Congress and is passed by that house alone (pp. 410, 438)

revenue bill a law proposed to raise money (p. 391)

revenue the money the government collects from taxes or other sources (p. 54)

revitalization investments in new facilities in an effort to promote economic growth (p. 786)

rider a provision included in a bill on a subject other than the one covered in the bill (p. 411)

riding the circuit traveling to hold court in a justice's assigned region of the country (p. 553)

right-to-work law a state labor law that prohibits both closed shops and union shops (p. 652)

right wing conservative (p. 814)

runoff primary a second primary election between the two candidates who received the most votes in the first primary (p. 244)

sampling error the measurement of how much the sample results may differ from the universe being sampled (p. 311)

sanction a measure such as withholding loans, arms, or economic aid to force a foreign government to cease certain activities (p. 633)

school board an elected or appointed local body that governs a school district (p. 764)

search warrant an order signed by a judge describing a specific place to be searched for specific items (p. 88)

second-strike capability the ability of a country with nuclear weapons to launch a devastating nuclear attack after getting hit by one itself (p. 869)

secular nonreligious (p. 181)

securities bonds or notes sold as a means of borrowing money with a promise of repaying the buyer with interest at the end of a specified period of time (pp. 391, 598, 647)

security classification system the provision that information on government activities related to national security and foreign policy may be kept secret (p. 217)

seditious speech speech urging resistance to lawful authority or advocating the overthrow of the government (p. 185)

select committee a temporary committee that studies one specific issue and reports its findings to the Senate or the House (pp. 377, 437)

selective perception mentally screening out ideas and images that do not agree with one's beliefs (p. 344)

selective sales tax one imposed on certain items; also called excise tax (p. 734)

selectmen the town officials elected to administer local government (p. 763)

self-incrimination testifying against oneself (pp. 205, 226)

senatorial courtesy the practice under which a President submits the name of a candidate for appointment to the senators from the candidate's state before formally submitting it for full Senate approval (p. 551)

seniority system one that gives leadership of a committee to the member with the longest service (p. 378)

separate but equal doctrine the policy allowing separate facilities for different races as long as those facilities were equal (p. 212)

separation of powers the division of power among the legislative, executive, and judicial branches of government (pp. 50, 78)

sequester hold apart or segregate (p. 194)

session a regular period of time during which a legislative body conducts business (p. 362)

severance tax one imposed by a state on the removal of natural resources intended for use in other states (p. 735)

shield law one that gives reporters some protection against disclosing confidential information or sources in state courts (pp. 195, 340)

shock incarceration a prison sentence emphasizing a highly structured, military environment where offenders participate in work, community service, education, and counseling (p. 727)

shock probation a program designed to show young offenders how terrible prison life could be through a brief prison incarceration followed by supervised release (p. 727)

single-issue party a political party that focuses on one major social, economic, or moral issue (p. 234)

single-member district an electoral district in which only one candidate can be elected to each office (p. 236)

slander false speech intended to damage a person's reputation (pp. 86, 187)

social insurance programs those designed to help elderly, ill, and unemployed citizens (p. 659)

social insurance taxes the money the federal government collects to pay for major social programs, such as social security, medicare, and unemployment compensation (p. 595)

socialism an economic system in which the government owns the basic means of production, determines the use of resources, distributes products and wages, and provides social services such as education, health care, and welfare (pp. 38, 841, 884)

sole proprietorship a business owned by an individual (p. 839)

sovereign having supreme power within territorial boundaries (p. 859)

sovereignty the supreme and absolute authority within territorial boundaries (pp. 20, 848)

special district a unit of local government that deals with a specific function (pp. 753, 799)

speech plus actions such as marching or demonstrating (pp. 184, 225)

splinter party a political party that has split away from one of the major parties because of some serious disagreement (p. 235)

spoils system the practice of victorious politicians rewarding their followers with government jobs (p. 514)

spot advertising the brief, very frequent, positive descriptions of a candidate or a candidate's major themes broadcast on television or radio (p. 348)

stability an indication of the likelihood that public opinion will change in direction or intensity (p. 313)

standing committee a permanent group in Congress that oversees bills (pp. 375, 437)

stare decisis (STAH•ray dih•SY•suhs) a Latin term meaning "let the decision stand"; once the Court rules on a case, its decision stands as a precedent for other cases (p. 565)

state a political community that occupies a definite territory and has an organized government with power to make and enforce laws without approval from any higher authority (p. 18)

state central committee a group composed of representatives from a political party's county organizations which chooses the party's state chairperson (p. 238)

state farm one owned by the government (p. 850)

states' rights position one that favors state and local action in dealing with social and economic problems (p. 130)

straight-party ticket the candidates of one party only (p. 261)

strategic minerals those used for military purposes (p. 876)

strong-mayor system the type of mayor-council government in which the mayor has strong executive powers (p. 777)

subcommittee one of six or eight groups within a standing committee that specializes in a subcategory of that committee's responsibility (pp. 376, 437)

subpoena a legal order that a person appear or produce requested documents (p. 396)

subsidy the aid the government provides to business (p. 648)

substantive due process the constitutional requirement that a law be reasonable (p. 545)

suburb a densely settled territory adjacent to a city (p. 775)

suffrage the right to vote (p. 270)

sunset law one that requires periodic checks of government agencies to see if they are still needed (p. 139)

sunshine law one that prohibits public officials from holding meetings not open to the public (p. 140)

supremacy clause a statement in Article VI of the Constitution, establishing that the Constitution, laws passed by Congress, and treaties of the United States are superior to state laws and local ordinances (p. 77)

suspect classification one that is subject to strict judicial scrutiny (p. 211)

swing vote the deciding vote (p. 576)

symbolic speech the use of actions and symbols, instead of words, to express opinions (pp. 184, 225)

target price government-established price for a particular crop (p. 656)

tariff a tax on imported goods (p. 287)

tax the money that people and businesses pay to support the government (pp. 423, 594)

taxable income the total income of an individual minus certain deductions and personal exemptions (pp. 594, 677)

tax assessor the official responsible for determining the value of real property each resident owns (p. 765)

tax credit a reduction in taxes (pp. 598, 719)

theocracy a government controlled by religious leaders (p. 232) third party any political party other than one of the two major parties (p. 234)

ticket the candidates for President and Vice President (p. 245)

ticket-splitting voting for candidates from different parties for different offices (p. 266)

tort wrongful act that could result in a lawsuit (pp. 716, 746)

totalitarian dictatorship one in which the ideas of a single leader or group of leaders are glorified (p. 30)

town meeting a gathering of all the voters of a town to express their opinions and decide on matters of local jurisdiction (p. 763)

township a subdivision of a county (pp. 752, 799)

trading bloc a group of nations that trade without economic barriers such as tariffs (p. 862)

transcript a summary record (p. 217)

treaty a formal agreement between the governments of two or more nations (pp. 93, 466, 619)

trial court one in which a case is originally tried (p. 543)

trust a form of business consolidation in which several corporations combine their stock and allow a board of trustees to run the corporations as one enterprise (p. 643)

unanimous opinion a Court decision in which all justices vote the same way (p. 573)

uncontrollable government expenditure required by law or previous commitments (p. 600)

unemployment compensation the payment to workers who lose their jobs (p. 718)

unemployment insurance programs in which federal and state governments cooperate to provide help for people who are out of work (p. 660)

unicameral a single-chamber legislature (pp. 61, 691, 745)

union shop a place of employment where workers are required to join a union soon after they have been hired (p. 652)

unitary government one in which governmental power is centralized in a national government (p. 810)

unitary system one that gives all key powers to the national or central government (p. 20)

universe a group of people from which samples are taken for polls or statistical measurement (p. 311)

urban renewal programs under which cities can apply for federal aid to clear deteriorating or slum areas and to rebuild (p. 668)

veto rejection of a bill (pp. 79, 416)

visa a document foreign visitors are required to obtain to enter certain countries (p. 629)

ward a large district comprised of several adjoining precincts (p. 238)

weak-mayor system a type of mayor-council government in which the mayor has only limited powers (p. 777)

whip an assistant to the party floor leader in the legislature (p. 373)

wire service an organization that employs reporters throughout the world to collect news for subscribers who pay for this service (p. 323)

withholding an amount of money an employer deducts from wages as payment of an employee's anticipated income tax (p. 595)

workers' compensation a payment to employees unable to work as a result of job-related injury or ill health (p. 718)

writ of certiorari (SUHR•shee•uh•RAR•ee) an order from the Court to a lower court to send up the records on a case for review (p. 570)

writ of habeas corpus a court order to release a person accused of a crime to court to determine whether he or she has been legally detained (pp. 395, 437)

writ of mandamus (man•DAY•muhs) a court order requiring a specific action (p. 544)

yellow dog contract a system that forced workers to promise not to join a union after employment (p. 651)

zoning means a local government uses to regulate the way property may be used (p. 754)

914 GLOSSARY

Brown, Harold, q868
Brown, Ronald, q251
Brown, William, 148, p628
Brown v. *Board of Education,* 212, 565, c577, 578-79
Brussels, Belgium, p847
Brutus, 14, q15
Brzezinski, Zbigniew, q620, q861
Buchanan, James, q440, 897
Buckley v. *Valeo,* 296
Buddhism, p181
budget, 423; Bureau of, 480; Congressional action on, 601-03, c601; control of, 404, 526; preparation of, 599-603; unbalanced, 606
Budget and Accounting Act of 1921, 599
Budget Committee (House), 601, 602
Budget Committee (Senate), 601, 602
Bui Van Binh, 173
Bull Moose party, 235
Bunn v. *North Carolina,* 181
Bureau of _____ , *see* _____ , Bureau of
bureaucracy, 142; as check on presidential power, 460; Congress and, 525-26; Constitutional provision for, 498; interagency influences, 528; Japanese, 819; nature of, 523; policymaking by, 519-23; relations with courts, 526-27; size of, 498, ctn523; *see also* civil service
bureaucrats, 498
Burger, Warren, q196, q215, q485, 558, c565
Burkina Faso; government of, 30
Burns, James MacGregor, 401
Burr, Aaron, 394, 450
Burstyn v. *Wilson,* 196
Burton, Harold, 576, 578
Bush, George, 133, 233, 250, 261, 262, 306, 310, 330, 347, ctn402, 420, 434-36, ctn435, q455, q458, 467, 481, 487, 488-89, ctn558, q605, 624, 625, q634, 669, 737, p825, p861, 863, 902; budget under, 602, 605; cabinet of, 478, 492, p503; and education, 666; election of, m257; and energy, 658; environmental policy of, 148; popularity of, 674; state power, 150; White House staff of, 483
business; government and, 648-49; regulation of, 642-47; organization of, 839; state encouragement of, 718-19; state regulation of, 717-18; types of, c835, 839
business interest groups, 286-87
Butler, Pierce, 558
Byrd, Robert, c379
Byron, Beverly, c387

C

CAB, *see* Civil Aeronautics Board
cabinet, c474, 498; defined, 474; departments of, 499-500; described, 504-12; French, 813; history of, 504-05; influences on, c479; Japanese, 818-19; limitations of, 478-79; role of, 476-78; selection of, 474-76; women and minorities in, 474, 475, p476
Cable News Network, 323
Cable-Satellite Public Affairs Network, 331, p374
cable television, 323, 324; regulation of, 196
cadre; defined, 821
Calcutta; population of, 875
calendars; House, 370-71; Senate, 372
California; constitution of, 687, 733; electoral votes of, 256; environmental laws of, 719; governor's powers in, 687; judicial selection in, 709; legislature of, 692, 693, 694; public education in, 766; public welfare in, 732
California v. *Acevedo,* 586
California v. *Greenwood,* 202
Cambodia; military action in, 392; refugees from, 173
campaign; financing of, 258, 297-98; issues in, 262-63; of 1992, 886-87; strategy for, 256-58; working in, 239, 240
Canada; French culture in, 18; government of, 20, 703; multinational corporations in, 23; taxation in, 596; trade with United States, 21, c21, 863
candidate; image of, 259, 263; nomination of, 245-50, 347; selection of, 382
Cannon, Joseph, 371
Cantons (Switzerland), 32
canvass, 265
canvassing board, 267
capital; as factor of production, 835; and growth, 866
capitalism; characteristics of, 835-38; Communist criticism of, 39; described, 36-38; government and, 838; practice of, 838-39; theory of, 36-37
capital punishment, m206, 207, 722
Carpenters and Joiners of America, c287
Carroll v. *United States,* 585
Carson, Rachel, 315
Carson City, NV; city government in, 790
Carter, Jimmy, 80, 247-48, 262, 311, 448, 460, 463, 468, 482, ctn518, 902; on bureaucracy, q502; cabinet of, 477, 479, 504; election of, m257, 265; and

foreign policy, 620, 621, 624; judicial appointments by, 551, c552; style of, 487, p487, 488
cartograms, 622
Cary, John, q654
casework, 427; purposes of, 428
caseworkers; defined, 383
categorical-formula grants, 737, 768
Cattlemen's Action Legislative Fund, 296
caucus, 245, 246, 382; defined, 243, 355
Cavazos, Lauro, 475
CBO, *see* Congressional Budget Office
CCC, *see* Commodity Credit Corporation
censorship, 152-53, 196, ctn327, ctn342
censure; defined, 365
census, 363
Census Bureau, 217, 363, 509
Centers for Disease Control, 664
central clearance, 482
Central Intelligence Agency, 465, 501, 522, 620-21
certiorari, 569, 570
Chadwick, United States v., 586
Chamber of Deputies (Mexico), 827
Chambers v. *Maroney,* 585
Chamorro, Violeta Barrios de, 41
change of venue, 88
Chaplinsky v. *New Hampshire,* 187-88
charity; contributions to, 217
charter; colonial, p684; corporate, 717
Chase, Salmon, 551, c565
Chase, Samuel, 554
checks and balances, 9, 67, c78, 78, 401, 403, 568; *see also* separation of powers
Cheney, Richard, 604
Chiang Kai-shek, 820
Chicago, 736, m775; city council of, 777; financial problems of, 785; local government in, 764, m775; population of, 775, c789
Chicago Council on Foreign Relations, q881
chief executive; President as, 461-63
Chief Justice of the United States, 554, c565; duties of, 572, 573; influence of, 576
child labor, 650, 717
Chile; revolution in, 23, 32
China; civil service in, 515, 517; civil war in, 820; communism in, 40, 616, 821-22; demography of, 18; food production in, 875, 876; government of, 28-29, 39, 232, 822-23; Nationalist, 820; nuclear capability of, 870; political background of, 820-21; political parties

in, 823; political structure of, c821; political unrest in, 823; population growth in, 865; recognition of, 482, 487, 617; Republic of, *see* Taiwan; trade with, p467

Chinese Exclusion Act of 1882, 165-66

Chisholm, Shirley, q43, q82

Chisholm v. Georgia, 89, 580

chlorofluorocarbons, 875

Church, Frank, 420

CIA, *see* Central Intelligence Agency

Cincinnati, OH; government of, 779

circuit courts, 548; "riding the circuit," 553; state, 707

Cisneros, Henry, q644

cities; defined, 774; financial problems of, 785-86; government of, 769, 776; growth of, 875; problems of, 671, 788-90; revitalization of, 786

citizenship; by birth, 157-58; defined, 156-57; dual, 158; loss of, 160; by naturalization, 158-60; participation, 31, 32-34, 63, 93, 140, 166, 195, 217, 239, 264-69, 277, 291, 310, 346, 382, 403, 428, 459, 478, 521, 550, 579, 595, 625, 656, 707, 729, 766, 783, 826, 851, 860; rights of, 89-90, 169-71, 275; responsibilities of, 9, 172, 309-10, 316; state, 157

city-county consolidation, 790

city manager, 779

Civil Aeronautics Board, 502

civil case; defined, 705-06; vs. criminal case, c705

civil law, 134, 543-44

civil-law system, 566

civil liberties, 9, 24, 47-48, 566, 814; freedom of assembly, 87, 189-92; freedom of religion, 86, 178-82, 191; freedom of press, 86, 193-96, 338-40; freedom of speech, 86-87, 170, 184-88, 575

civil rights, 186, 204, 210; equal protection, 210-13, 214-18; rights of the accused, 202-07, 557, 567

Civil Rights Act of 1957, 372

Civil Rights Act of 1964, 132, 213, 214, 216, 393, 565, 568

Civil Rights Commission, 501

civil rights movement, 9, 192, p200-01, 213; federal assistance to, 129; media on, 344; Supreme Court and, 578-79

civil servants, 498; *see also* bureaucracy

civil service; benefits and problems of, 516-17; employees of, 513, c514; jobs in, 516; origins of, 513-16

Civil Service Commission, 516

Civil War Amendments, 89-90

civil wars, 820, 865, 869, 871

Claims Court, 548, 549

Clark, Dick, 383

Clark, Terry, q847

Clark, Tom, q224, q393, 556, q565

Clay, Bill, p418

Claybrook, Joan, 297

Clayton Antitrust Act, 645, 650

Clean Air Act of 1963, 656-57, 719

Clean Air Act of 1970, 147

clear and present danger test, 185

Cleveland, Grover, 128, 335, 452, 483, 899

Cleveland, OH; financial problems of, 785

client groups, 522; influence of, 527-28

Clinton, Bill, q21, 22, 150, m257, 262, p442, 448, 452, 591, 598, q618, q631, 664, 666, 676, 863, 886

Clinton, Hillary Rodham, 664

closed primary, 244

closed shop; defined, 651

cloture; defined, 372-73

cluster sample, 311-12

CNN, *see* Cable News Network

coalition government, 233

Coast Guard, 512, 670

Coe, Richard, q676

COGs, *see* councils of government

Cohen, Bernard, q344

Cohen, William, q396

Cohens v. Virginia, c577

cold war, c26, 510, 521-22, 616-17

Coldren, J. David, q722

Coleman, E. Thomas, q400

collective bargaining, 649

collective farms, 850

collective naturalization, 160

collective security, 633

colonies, m49; government of, 49-50; relations with Britain, 51, 53-55; unification of, 51, 52-56

Colorado; constitution of, 741; sunset laws in, 139

Colosio, Luis Donaldo, 828

Commager, Henry Steele, q223

command economy, 39-40, 843

commander in chief; President as, 467-68

commerce; judicial definition of, 132

commerce clause, 393, 642

Commerce Department, 509, 522, 523; functions of, 649; secretary of, 475

commission form of government, c778, 779

Commission on Wartime Relocation, 224

Committee for Public Education v. Regan, 179

Committee of the Whole, 372

Committee on Political Education, 287

committees, c376, 412, 413, 415; appropriations, 425-26; of British parliament, 808; chair of, 375, 378; House vs. Senate, 368, 370; membership of, 377-78; party, 238-39; party membership on, 375-76; purposes of, 375; staff of, 381, 383; in state legislatures, 694; types of, 375-77

Commodity Credit Corporation, 655-56

Common Cause, 288, 297

common-law system, 566

Common Market, *see* European Community

Common Sense, 55

Commonwealth of Independent States, 852

Communications Workers of America, c287

communism, 38-40, ctn40; in China, 616, 821-22; collapse of, 848; freedom of religion vs., 191; House investigations of, 396; in U.S., 352-54

Communist Manifesto, 39

Communist party, 158, 189; American, 235; Chinese, 40, 821-23; French, 815; in one-party system, 232; Soviet, 39-40

community property, 721

comparative advantage, 862

compensation; defined, 444

competition; in free enterprise system, 37, 837-38

Comprehensive Employment Training Act, 788

compromise; at Constitutional Convention, 67-69; importance of, 489

computers; in government, 769

concurrent jurisdiction, 543

concurrent powers, 127

concurrent resolution, 411

concurring opinion, 573

Confederation; achievements under, 63-64; difficulties of, 64; government of, 61; weaknesses of, 61-62

Confederation, Iroquois, 52

conference committees, 377, 415-16

Conference on Disarmament in Europe, c870

confidentiality of sources, 340

confirmation hearings, cabinet, 476; Congress, 330, 394-95

Congo, People's Republic of, 32

Congress; appropriations by, 425-26, 624; and budget, 601-03; checks on executive power, 330, 401, 403-04, 459, 625; committees of, 412, 413, 415; compensation of members, 364-

65; constituency of, 401, 427-30; and Constitution, 91-92, 395; floor action in, 415; in foreign affairs, 392, 398, 623-26; influence on Supreme Court, 580; investigations by, 396-98, 405; leadership roles in, 373-74; legislative oversight by, 398-99; legislative procedures of, 410-16; membership of, 362-67, c367; override of veto by, 416; oversight function of, 330-31; pages in, 428; powers denied to, 395; powers of, 390-404; in presidential election, 394; privileges of members, 365; public opinion and, 306, 316; recording studios used by, 331; relations with bureaucracy, 525-26; relations with media, 330-31, 335-36; relations with President, 401-04, 420-21, 463-64; seniority system in, 378; sessions of, 362; television coverage of, 331; terms of, 362; war powers of, 132, 392, 468, 623-24; women in, 385; writing to, 403

Congressional Budget Impoundment and Control Act of 1974, 404, 601

Congressional Budget Office, 383-84, 404, 601

Congressional Record, 384

Congressional Research Service, 383

congressional staff; growth of, 380-81, c381; role of, 380; types of, 381-83

Connecticut; charter of, 50; Fundamental Orders of, 685; governor's election in, 698; public education in, 665, 729

Connecticut Compromise, 68

conscription; 216, 630

consensus; democracy and, 34

consequences; predicting, 872

conservation, 720

conservative; defined, 314

Conservative party (Britain), 810, 843

consistency, 733

consolidation, 788

constituents; defined, 370; interests of, 401, 427

constitution; British, 806-07; Colonial, 49-50; defined, 27-29; Filipino, 70; French, 29; importance of, 684-85; Indian, 29, 70; Japanese, 816-18; Mexican, 825-26; state, 56, c686, 733; Swiss, 808

Constitution (United States), 9, 24, 26, 98-123; articles of, 76-77; citizen rights guaranteed by, 169-71; commerce clause of, 393, 642-43; Congress and, 91-92; court decisions and, 94; criticisms of, 14-15; custom and usage related to, 94; drafting of, 28, 66-69; executive powers granted by, 440-41, 456-57; form of, 29; legal

issues involving, 543; necessary and proper clause, 126, 131, 390-91, 394; powers defined by, 126-29; Preamble to, 29, 76; President and, 92-93, 456-57; 618-19; principles of, 77-79, c77; ratification of, 69-70, c69; separation of powers in, 50, 78, 684; supremacy of, 77, 127, 129, 685; *see also* amendments

constitutional commission; state, 688

Constitutional Convention, ptg44-45, 66-69

constitutional conventions (state), c687, 688, 689

constitutional courts, 546

constitutional government, 28

constitutional law, 29, 543-44

constitutional monarchy, 31

constitutional republic; defined, 32

constitutions, state; Alabama, 686, 687, 741; amendments to, 687-89; California, 687, 733; characteristics of, 685-87; Colorado, 741; Georgia, 689; Illinois, 689; judicial interpretation of, 689; Louisiana, 684, 689; Massachusetts, 689; Montana, 689; North Carolina, 689; Oregon, 689; Pennsylvania, 684; reform of, 689; Tennessee, 687; Texas, 686, 687; Virginia, 684, 689; Wisconsin, 689

consulates, 628

consuls, 628

Consumer Product Safety Commission, 315, 646-47

consumer protection, 645-47; by states, 717

consumers; in market economy, 838-39

containment doctrine, 616, 631

contempt of Congress, 397

Continental Congresses, 54-55, 61, 71

convention, p230, 243; mechanics of, 246-49; and nominating process, 249-50

Cooke, Lawrence, q711

Coolidge, Calvin, p461, 697, p697, 900

COPE, *see* Committee on Political Education

copyright, 393

corporate charter, 717

corporate income tax, 595

corporation, c835; defined, 839

Corporation for Public Broadcasting, 324

corporation law, 717

correspondent; defined, 333; *see also* press

corruption, 514

Council for a Livable World, 296

council-manager government, c778,

779

Council of Economic Advisers, 482, 599

Council of State Governments, 288

councils of government, 792

counsel; right to, 204-05, 724

counterfeit currency; defined, 507

counties; consolidation with urban area, 790; defined, 752; functions of, 759-60; problems of, 760-71

county board, 760

county courts, 707

coup; defined, 852; in Soviet Union, 853

court observers, 710

courts; of appeals, 548, 569-70; and bureaucracy, 526-27; as check on executive power, 460, 526-27; of common pleas, 707; constitutional, 546; county, 707; district, 546, 548; establishment of, 393; importance of, 711; jurisdiction of, 542-44; legislative, 549-50; in Mexico, 827; officers of, 548; organization of, c549; state, 684, 689, 704, 705-10; system of, 91, 94

covert; defined, 492

Cox v. *Louisiana,* 190

Cox v. *New Hampshire,* 190

Coyle v. *Smith,* 137

CPB, *see* Corporation for Public Broadcasting

CPSC, *see* Consumer Product Safety Commission

"cradle-to-grave" services, 843-44

Creation Science, 180-81

credentials committee; at convention, 248

credit; equal opportunity for, 216; regulation of, 607-08; reporting of, 218

Cresson, Edith, 815

crime, 722; federal legislation on, 727; federal vs. state prosecution for, 207; loss of citizenship for, 160; prevention of, 656; rates, g726; and search and seizure, 202-04; white collar, 206

criminal case; defined, 706; vs. civil case, c705

criminal justice; costs of, c706; decentralized, 723; laws, 722

criminal law, 544

Cronkite, Walter, q153, 346

cross-pressured voter, 260-61

Cruzan v. *Director, Missouri Department of Health,* c577

C-SPAN, *see* Cable-Satellite Public Affairs Network

Cuba; government of, 232, 466-67; refugees from, 163; relations with U.S., 632; in Spanish-American War, 626

Cuban Americans, p159

cultural pluralism, 10, 52, 159, 173, 210, 219, 251, 279, 290, 299, 305, 317, 365, 369, 379, c379, 387, c387, 431, 475, 515, 547, 644, 671, 721, 762, 864

culture; local government and, 757

Customs Court, 548

customs duties, 596

Czechoslovakia; German invasion of, 634

D

Dade County, FL, 759

Daley, Richard, 248, 776

Dallas, TX; government of, 779

Davie, William, q62

DEA, *see* Drug Enforcement Administration

death penalty, m206, 207, 722

debate; congressional, 368, 372-73, 402; preprimary, p246; presidential, 259

Declaration and Resolves, 55

Declaration of Independence, 55-56, ptg57, 57-60, 156, 169

Declaration of the Rights of Man, 814

DeConcini, Dennis, q358, 359

defamatory speech, 187

defendant; defined, 543, 544

defense; budget for, 26, c26, 603, 605; contractors, 430

defense attorney, 724

Defense, Department of, 510; as adviser to President, 465; budget of, 600; client groups of, 522, 528; described, 629-30; employees of, c514; economic impact of, 430; formation of, 522; health programs of, 663-64; influence on media, 342; secretary of, 619-20

deficit spending, 606

deforestation, 859, c874

De Gaulle, Charles, 812

Degler, Carl, q644

De Jonge v. Oregon, 189, 352

Dekanawida, 52

Delaware; amendments to constitution, 688; bill of rights of, 733

delegated powers, 126

delegates, 245

Dellinger, Walter, 435

Dellums, Ronald, q400, 435

demand; law of, 839

democracy; characteristics of, 32-33; colonial, 49-50; growth of, 9, 14-15, 28, 34, 41, 169-72, 232, 233, 234, 235, 237-41, 270-73, 286, 290, 305, 310, 316, 349; in France, 811-15; in Great Britain, 806-10; in India, 29, 70; in Japan, 816-19; in Mexico, 825-28;

in Switzerland, 808; origins of, 46-48; promotion of, 615; requirements for, 34; types of, 31-32

Democratic party, 141, c261; origin of, 233; modern, 233, 234; post–Civil War decline of, 140

democratic socialism, 38

Democratic-Republican party, 233, 450

demonstrations; limits on, 190

denaturalization, 160

Deng Xiaoping (Teng Hsiao-p'ing), 822, p822

denied powers, 127-28

Denmark; economy of, 843

Dennis v. United States, 187, 354

Department of _____ , *see* _____ , Department of

departments (French), 815

dependent; defined, 594

deregulation, 502, 590-91

Desert Storm, Operation, 152, 436, 624; *see also* Persian Gulf War

Des Moines; renovation projects in, 782

détente, 617

Detroit; financial problems of, 785; population loss in, 775

developed nations, 21, 844, 860

developing nations, 21, 844, 860, 861, 863, 865-66; population growth in, 874-75

DeWitt, John, 223

Dickey, Angela, q637

DiClerico, Robert, q277

dictatorship, 30

Diet (legislature of Japan), 817, 818

Dingell, John, 657

Dinkins, David, 290

diplomacy; President and, 465-67

direct democracy, 32

direction; defined, 313, 356

direct primary, 244, 355

disability; defined, 519

disclosure; campaign spending, 258

discount rate, 608

discrimination; defined, 211; in employment, 214-15, c215; in housing, 781; intent as factor in, 211; racial, 94, 132; immigration, 165-66, 211-13, 299, 487, 578; sex, 215-16, c215; by states against nonresidents, 135

dissenting opinion, 573

district courts, 546, 548; state, 707

District of Columbia; courts of, 549

diversity, 304; immigration and, 864; managing, 739

diversity visa, 167

dividends; defined, 839

divine right of monarch, 30

Dolbeare, Kenneth, q546

Dole, Robert, c379, 383, 436

domestic disorders; federal intervention in, 128-29

domino theory, 634

DOT, *see* Transportation, Department of

double jeopardy; protection against, 88, 206-07

Douglas, William O., 194, q339, 571; philosophy of, 575

Douglass, Frederick, p115

Downey, Thomas, 430

Draco, 547

draft; 216, 555, 630; abolition of, 568

Dred Scott v. Sandford, 156-57, 564, c577

Drozdiak, William, q632

Drug Enforcement Administration, 509, 782

drugs; abuse of, c308, c673, 782-83; evaluation of, 647

due process, 88, 89-90; procedural, 545; substantive, 545

due process clause, 170

Dukakis, Michael, m257, 261, 452; image of, 263

Dulles, John Foster, 482, 621

Duncan, Greg, q676

Duncan, John, q370

Dye, Thomas, q345

E

East Asian and Pacific Affairs, Bureau of, 627

East Germany, 40

eavesdropping, 203

EC, *see* European Community

Economic Advisers, Council of, 482, 599

economic sanctions, 633-34

economic status; influence on public opinion, 306

economic systems; defined, 834; democracy and, 34; types of, 36-40

economics; defined, 36; government role in, 26; as political issue, 262-63; President and, 464, ctn465; Supreme Court and, 566

economy; command, 39, 843; government regulation of, 37-38, 606-08; government spending and, 605-07; and local conditions, 757, 785-86; market, 37, 838-39; mixed, 642, 838

Edelman, Murray, q344

education, 729-31; bilingual, 565; "choice" in, 666; church-sponsored, 179; democracy and, 34; discrimination in, 212-13, 565, 568; expenditures for, 431, 729-30, c730; government involvement in, 665-66; higher,

340-41

Federal Criminal Code Reform Act of 1978, 410

Federal Deposit Insurance Corporation, 501

Federal Election Campaign Acts, 258, 295

Federal Election Commission, 258, 446; regulation of PACs by, 295-96

Federal Emergency Relief Administration, 675

Federal Energy Regulatory Commission, 512

federal government, 20, 63, 77; in Mexico, 825; see also government (U.S.)

federal grants, 737-38, c738, 767-68

Federal Highway Administration, 669, 670

Federal Housing Administration, 667-68, 775

Federal Job Information Centers, 516

Federal Metal and Non-Metallic Safety Board of Review, 523

Federal Power Commission, 527

Federal Radio Commission, 340

Federal Railroad Administration, 669

Federal Regulation of Lobbying Act of 1946, 292-93

Federal Reserve System, 607-08, m607

Federal Road Aid Act of 1916, 669

federal system of government, 20, 63, 77

Federal Trade Commission, 522; antitrust activities of, 645; on cigarette advertising, 526, 646; in court, 527

federalism, 69, 77, 126, 130-33, 542, 737, 738, 768, 802-03; and federal funding, 780-86; political importance of, 9, 139-42; progressive, 143

Federalist, The, q14, p15, 70, 131

Federalist party, 14, 233, 450

Feiner, Irving, 191

Feiner v. *New York,* 191, 192

felony; defined, 706

Ferraro, Geraldine, 250

FHA, *see* Federal Housing Administration

Fifteenth Amendment, 90, 117, 123, 271-72

Fifth Amendment, 88, 113, 123, 171, 205-07, 397, 544, 725

"fighting words," 187-88

filibuster, 372-73

Fillmore, Millard, 897

Finance Committee (Senate), 378

Finer, S. E., q806

fines; as revenue source, 767

fire protection, 755

"fireside chats," 458, 488

First Amendment, 86-87, 113, 123, 170; and assembly, 189-92, 352-54; and the press, 193-96; and religion, 178-82; and speech, 184-88, 575

First Lady, 469

first-strike capability, 869

fiscal policy, 606-07

fiscal year, 599

Fish and Wildlife Service, 507

flag, 197; burning, 184, 185, 574; displaying, 729; salute of, 182

Flag Protection Act of 1989, 185

Flood Control, River, and Harbor Acts of 1966, 719

floor debate, 415

Florida; citizenship of residents of, 160; electoral votes of, 256; land-use laws in, 720; sunshine law in, 140

Flynn, Raymond, q788

Foley, Thomas, p373

Food and Drug Administration, 511, 527, 646; drug evaluation by, 647, 664

food; distribution of, 875-76; production of, 875

food stamp program, 661

Ford, Gerald, q79, m257, 265, 311, 446, 452, 463, 475, 620, 902; on bureaucracy, q523; image of, 263; judicial appointments by, 551, 558; as Vice President, 394

Ford, Wendell, c379, q420

Foreign Agricultural Service, 655

foreign aid, 633, c633, 880-82

Foreign Assistance Act of 1973, 881

foreign exchange, 851

foreign exchange students, 860

Foreign Intelligence Surveillance Act of 1978, 204

foreign policy, 306; advisers for, 619-21; agencies of, 627-30; aims of, 614-15, 631-36; Congress and, 392, 398, 623-26; development of, 615-17; President and, 465-67, 618-21; recognition of foreign governments, 466-67

Foreign Relations Committee (Senate), 378

Foreign Service, 627-29, 637

Forest Service, 657-58

Fort Worth, TX; Sister Cities program in, 790

foundations; funding of public broadcasting by, 325

"Four Freedoms" speech, 305

Fourteen Points, 619

Fourteenth Amendment, 89, 116-17, 123, 157, 170-71, 209, 211, 218, 554, 578-79, 766

Fourth Amendment, 88, 113, 123, 202-03, 566, 575, 584-86

France; as nation-state, 18; cabinet in, 813; constitution of, 29, 82; economy of, 843; education in, 756; government of, 20, 484, c813; legal system of, 566, 762; legislature of, 813-14; life expectancy in, 21; NATO membership of, 631; nuclear capability of, 870; premier of, 812; President of, 811-12; relations to neighbor nations, 846; taxation in, 596; in World War II, 634

Frank, Barney, 298

Frankfurter, Felix, q192

Franklin, Benjamin, 32, 47, 54, 66, 69, 594

freedom of assembly, 87, 189-92

freedom of choice, 838

freedom of expression; in mass media, 325

freedom of information, 216-17, 339

Freedom of Information Act of 1966, 217

freedom of press, 86, 193-96, 338-40

freedom of religion, 86, 178-82, 191

freedom of speech, 86-87, 170, 184-88, 575

free enterprise, 10, 36, 37-38, 606, 836, 841; capitalism and, 36-37, 838-39; democracy and, 32, 34, 649; media ownership and, 324; productivity and, 499; profit and, 36, 838

free exercise clause, 178, 181-82

free market, 36, p37; successes of, 866

Free Soil party, 234

French and Indian War, 53

Frenzel, Bill, q402

Friedman, Lawrence, q716, q753

Friends of the Earth, 288

front-runner; for nomination, 347

Fulbright, J. William, q329

Fuller, Melville, c565

full faith and credit rule, 134

Fundamental Orders of Connecticut, 685

fundamental rights test, 211

Furman v. *Georgia,* 207

G

gag order, 194

Gales, Joseph, 333

Gallup Poll, 312

Galveston, TX, 778

Gandhi, Mohandas, 210

Gannett Co. v. *De Pasquale,* 194

Gannett newspapers, 324

GAO, *see* General Accounting Office

Garba, Joseph Nanven, q877

Gardner, John W., q301

Garfield, James, 447, 516, 898

GATT, *see* General Agreement on Tariffs and Trade

General Accounting Office, 384, 399
General Agreement on Tariffs and Trade, 862
General Assembly, 634, 636
general assistance, 732
General Motors, 23; number of employees, 498
general sales tax, 734
General Services Administration, 501
generalizations; making, 379
gentrification; defined, 786
George III, king of England, 53, 54, 55
Georgia; constitution of, 689; electoral votes of, 256; executive reorganization in, 703; governor's election in, 698; University of, 731
Gergen, David, q880
Germany; citizens residing in U.S., 163; civil service in, 517; NATO membership of, 631; relations with France, 846; reunification of, 846; taxation in, 596; U.S. declaration of war on, 623; in World Wars, 616
Gerry, Elbridge, 364
gerrymandering, 363-64, m364
Gerson, Stuart, 435
Ghali, Boutros, see Boutros-Ghali
Gibbons v. Ogden, 393, c577
Gibbs, Nancy, q358
G.I. Bills of Rights, 666
Gideon, Clarence, 204
Gideon v. Wainwright, 204-05, 557, 724
gift tax, 597
Ginsburg, Douglas, 552
Ginsburg, Ruth Bader, 539, 556
Giscard d'Estaing, Valéry, 814, 815
Gitlow v. New York, 170, 185
Glickman, Dan, q298, q591
Glickman, James, q298
global issues; 9, 82, 158, 204, 325, 425, 544, 647; characteristics of, 858-59; defined, 858; interdependence, 22, 293, 306, 398, 466, 736, 790, 862, 875; responses to, 859-61
global warming, 859, 874
glossary, 903-914
GNP, see Gross National Product
"Goals 2000: Education America Act", 666
Goldwater, Barry, 260, q314, 446, 623; image of, 263
Gonzalez, Henry, c379
Gonzalez, Jésus, q828
Gorbachev, Mikhail, 326, 614, 617, 823, q849, 851, 852, q853
Gore, Al, 448
government; city, 769, 776; coalition, 233; communist, 38-39; comparative, 9, 70, 128, 191, 247, 262, 371, 484, 517, 566, 596, 629, 703, 756, 806-853; confederal, see confederation; democratic, 615; federal, 20, 77; limited, 28, 46-47, 79; local, see county, local government, township; metropolitan, 789-90; municipal, 776, 777-79, c778; parliamentary, 484, 809; parliamentary vs. presidential, 128, c807; processes of, 9; purposes of, 24-26; representative, 32, 47; socialist, 38; stability of, 82; state, see state government; student, 31; types of, 20, 30-32; unitary, 20, 802-03, 810
government corporations, 501
Government National Mortgage Association, 512
Government Printing Office, 384
government (U.S.); and agriculture, 654-56; aid to states, 132-33; and business, 648-49; bureaucracy in, 498-502; colonial, 49-50; constitutional powers of, 126-29; economic regulation by, 37, 590-91; employees of, c127; entitlements by, 426, 600, 605; and environment, 656-58; expansion of, 716; expenditures of, 425-26, c597, 605-07; and free enterprise system, 838; grants to states and communities, 606, 737-38, c737, 767-68, 785; growth of, 132; interest groups within, 288; and labor, 649-52; levels of, c24; mandates by, 738; obligations to states, 128; political appointees in, 517-18; political parties and, 240; politics and, 26-27; regulations, 590-91; relations with states, 127
governor; election of, 698; emergency powers of, 700, p700, 702; functions of, 699-700; powers of, 684, 687, 700-04, c701, 709; qualifications for, 697-98; roles of, 699-700; salary of, 699; term of office of, 698
GPO, see Government Printing Office
Graham, Robert, 329
Gramm, Phil, 609
Gramm-Rudman-Hollings Act, 601-02, 603, 609
grand jury, 171, 546, 725
grandfather clause, 272, 298
Grange, 287
Grant, Francis, ptg806
Grant, Ulysses, 468, 516, 898
grants-in-aid, 737, 767-68
Gray, Horace, 555
Grayned v. City of Rockford, 190
Gray Panthers, p292
Gray, William III, q407
Great Britain, see Britain
Great Depression, 37, 480, 488; and bureaucracy, 522; impact of, 659, 667; labor laws passed during, 651; and political parties, 233; and presidential power, 404; social programs during, 674-75
Great Lakes; pollution of, 657
Great Society, 665
Greece; legal heritage of, 547
Greene, Harold, 435
Greenhouse, Linda, q572
greenhouse effect, 859, 874
Gregg v. Georgia, 207
Gregory, Dick, 191-92
Gregory v. Chicago, 191-92
Grenada; military action in, 152, ctn342, 392, 634
GRH, see Gramm-Rudman-Hollings Act
Grodzins, Martin, q141
Gross National Product, 606
Guam; acquisition of, 616
Guiteau, Charles, 516
Gulf of Tonkin Resolution, 419, 458, 624
gun control, c308, 723
Gun Owners of America, 296
Gurwitt, Rob, q775-76
Guthrie, Woody, p652

H

habeas corpus, 395
Haiti, 392; military rule, 241; refugees from, 163, 164
Halberstam, David, q328, q346
Haldeman, H. R., 491, p492
Hale, Jubal, 523
Halper, United States v., 207
Hamilton, Alexander, 70, q130, 333, 450, c451, 467-68, q495, q583, 663
Hamilton, Lee, q336, 435
Hand, Learned, q169
Handgun Control, Inc., 296
handicapped; accommodations for, 565; equal protection for, p209; voting by, 269
Harbrecht, Douglas, q424
Harding, Warren, 900
Harkin, Tom, 436
Harlan, John Marshall, q212, q581
Harrison, Benjamin, 452, 463, 899
Harrison, William Henry, 92, 468, 896; inauguration of, 455
Hatch, Carl, 517
Hatch, Orrin, q400
Hatch Act, 517
Hawaii, 20; annexation of, 616; citizenship of residents of, 160; land-use laws in, 720
Hayes, Rutherford, 452, 898
Hazelwood School District v. Kuhl-

meier, 188, 194

head of state; President as, 461, 619

Headstart, 675

Health and Human Services Department, 511, 659, 664; employees of, c514

health care, 605, 664; in developing nations, 865-66; public, 663-64, 728-29

Health Care Financing Administration, 659

hearing; congressional, 413

Heart of Atlanta Motel v. *United States,* 393

heckler's veto, 191

Henry, Patrick, 54, q69, q131, q440

Herbst, Margaret, q823

Hernandez, Antonia, q290

Hertzberg, Hendrik, q359

Hiawatha, 52

Highway Trust Fund, 670

highways, 669-70; congestion on, 793; financing of, 775

Hills, Carla, 475

Hirabayashi v. *United States,* 223

Hirohito, emperor of Japan, p816

Hirsch v. *Atlanta,* 190

Hispanics; in cabinet, 475; in Congress, 365, c379; education of, 565; migration to cities by, 774; political participation by, 317

Hitler, Adolf, 30, 634

Hobbes, Thomas, 24

Hoffman Estates, IL, 736

Holder, Richard, q22

Holmes, Oliver Wendell, q185, 187

Holocaust, 191

homelessness, 782

home loans, 775

Homer, Winslow, ptg33

home rule, 752, 777

Homestead Act, 654, 721

Hooker, Thomas, 685

Hoover, Herbert, q340, 483, 488, q675, 900

Hoover, J. Edgar, 462

House, Edward, 491, 621

house arrest, 727

House of Commons (Britain), 47, 369, 807-808

House of Deputies (Mexico), 827

House of Lords (Britain), 47, 369, 807, 808-809

House (U.S.), ptg360; bills in, 370-71; electoral function of, 450, 454; impeachment role, 394, 554; leaders of, 373; membership of, 362-64, c367; and presidential elections, 394; procedures of, 370-72; qualifications for, 363; representation by state, c894; rules of, 368, 370; salary and benefits

of, 364-65; speaker of, 370, 371, p373, 447; term of office in, 358-59, 363, 402; women in, c367; *see also* names of specific committees

housing; discrimination in, 781; shortages in, 776, 781-82

Housing Act of 1949, 667

Housing and Community Development Act of 1974, 668

Housing and Urban Development, Department of, 512, 528, 776; functions of, 668-69; rules for minority hiring, 519; secretary of, c474, 475

Howard County, AR, 759

Howenstein, G. Albert, q726

HUD, *see* Housing and Urban Development, Department of

Hughes, Barry, 875

Hughes, Charles Evans, 189, q190, 352, c565, 586, q650

Hughes v. *Superior Court,* 192

humanitarianism, 615, p616

human rights, 169

Humphrey, Hubert, 235, 398, 448, 454

Hunger, Committee on (House), 377

hung jury, 725

Hussein, Saddam, 306, 434, 629

Hustler Magazine v. *Falwell,* 187

Hutchins, Robert, q277

Hutchinson v. *Proxmire,* 365

I

ICC, *see* Interstate Commerce Commission

Idaho; land-use laws in, 720; retraction of ERA ratification, 567

ideological party, 235

ideologies; recognizing, 242; spectrum of, 313-15, c314

illegal aliens, 163

illegal immigration, 168

Illinois; constitution of, 689; electoral votes of, 256

immigration, 156, c159, 162-63, c653; and diversity, 864; illegal, 168; policy towards, 164-68; special, 168

Immigration Act of 1924, 166-67

Immigration Act of 1990, 167-68

Immigration and Naturalization Service, 158, 163, 509

Immigration and Naturalization Service v. *Chadha,* 399

Immigration Reform Act of 1965, 167

Immigration Reform and Control Act of 1985, 524

Immigration Reform and Control Act of 1986, 168

immunity from prosecution, 397

impeachment, 91-92, 394, 459, 554; of state judges, 710

implied powers, 126, 394

imports; restrictions on, 648

impoundment of funds, 404, 462, 564

income taxation, 90, 132, c133, 580, 594-95, 721; local, 767; state, 735

incorporation; defined, 776

incrementalism, 603

incumbent; defined, 297; reelection rate of, 297-98

independent agencies, 498, 500-01

independent PACs, 296-97

independent voter; defined, 237; importance of, 262

India; constitution of, 29, 70; food production in, 875; government of, 20; nuclear capability of, 870

Indian Affairs, Bureau of, 507

Indianapolis; city government in, 790

Indians, *see* Native Americans; *see also* individual Native American nations

India-Pakistan Wars, 869

indictment, 546; grand jury, 725

indirect democracy, 32

industrial development bonds, 718-19

inequality; among nations, p20, 21; *see also* developing nations; economic, 21; racial; *see* civil rights movement, discrimination

information; analyzing, 65; freedom of, 216-17, 339; synthesizing, 183

information explosion, p322

infrastructure; repair of, 783-84

inherent powers, 127

initiative; individual, 837; petition, 278, 688, 808

injunction, 526, 543-44

inner cabinet, 478

innocence; presumption of, 544, 545

Inouye, Daniel, 397, q405

INS, *see* Immigration and Naturalization Service

integration, *see* African Americans; civil rights movement; racial discrimination

Intelligence, Permanent Select Committee on (House), 377

intensity; defined, 313, 356

Inter-American Affairs, Bureau of, 627

Inter-American Treaty of Reciprocal Assistance, 632, m632

interdependence; among jurisdictions, 768; among nations, 21-22, 860-61

interest groups, p27, 141, p189, 258, 306-07, 309, 421, 424; and cabinet, 474-75, 522; defined, 284, 355; function of, 285; leadership of, 285-86; government employment and, 514; limitations on, 292-93; methods of,

289-92; minority, p290; power of, 285; and Supreme Court nominations, 558; and tax loopholes, 597-98; types of, 286-88
intergovernmental revenue, 736-38
Interior Department, 483, 507; secretary of, 474
interlocking directorates, 645
Internal Revenue Service, 217, 525; court cases involving, 527, 549; function of, 595
Internal Revenue Taxation, Joint Committee on, 383
International Atomic Energy Agency, 871
International Broadcasting Act of 1994, 325
International Brotherhood of Electrical Workers, c287
International Court of Justice, 634, 636
international organizations, 23
International Telephone and Telegraph, 23
International Trade, Court of, 548
internationalism, 615
internment; of Japanese Americans, 33, 163, p163, 222-24
interstate commerce; regulation of, 68, 393, 642-43
Interstate Commerce Act of 1887, 565, 643
Interstate Commerce Commission, 520, 669
interstate compacts, 135-36
Interstate Highway System, 670
interview; conducting, 625
Intolerable Acts, 54
investigation; Congressional, 396-98
investment; government regulation of, 37; and free enterprise, 839
Iran; government of, 232; hostage crisis in, 344, 468, 479; military action in, 392; war with Iraq, 869
Iran-contra affair, 310, 330-31, 482, 492; Senate investigation of, 397, 405
Iraq; invasion of Kuwait, 21, 306, 392, 420, 434-35, 467, 487, 621, 624, 629; sanctions against, 633; war with Iran, 869; weapons capabilities of, 870
Irons, Peter, 224
iron triangle, 527-28
Iroquois Confederation, 52
Ishigo, Estelle, p163
Islam, 191; political power of, 232
isolationism, 615
Israel, 260; as foreign aid recipient, 881; nuclear capability of, 870
issues; in election campaigns, 262-63
Italy; government of, 20; in World War II, 616; taxation in, 596; U.S. declaration of war on, 623
item veto, 703
ITT, *see* International Telephone and Telegraph

J

Jackson, Andrew, 233, 245, 348, 394, 457, 468, 476; cabinet of, 504, 505, 896; expansion of presidential powers, 403; government under, 498, 513-14; on presidency, q493; view of Supreme Court, 568
Jackson, Jesse, q219, 446
Jackson, Robert, q182, 555
Jacksonville, FL; city government in, 790
Jacob, John, q299
Jacobson v. *Massachusetts,* 181
jails, 726
James II, king of England, 28
Jamestown, 46, p46, 53
Japan; bureaucracy in, 819; cabinet of, 818-19; constitution of, 816-18; Diet of, 818; government of, 31, 371, 816-19, c817; growth of, 863; media in, p338; political parties in, 819; relations with U.S., 633; U.S. trade with, 293, ctn327, 648, p649, 861; U.S. declaration of war on, 623; in World War II, 616
Japanese Americans; internment of, 33, 163, p163, 222-24
Javits, Jacob, q624
Jay, John, 70, 130, q270, c565
Jefferson, Thomas, 47, q56, q368, 620, 763, 895; on democracy, q34; on education, 665; election of, 233, 394, 450; expansion of presidential powers, 457, 462; government under, 498, 513; inauguration of, q475; and international affairs, 615; on the presidency, q493; and the press, 333, q338; war powers used by, 435, 467
Jehovah's Witnesses, 182, 190
Jews; Holocaust, 191; religious symbols of, 181; Soviet, 164; support for Israel, 260
Jim Crow laws, 211-12
Job Opportunity and Basic Skills program (JOBS), 662, p732
jobs; seeking, 166
John, king of England, 46, 171
John Paul II, pope, 870
Johnson, Andrew, 92, 394, 459, 898
Johnson, Lyndon, 128, 250, 260, 304, q322, 330, q402, 419, 420, 448, 454, 457, 460, q464, 468, 475, 484, 488, 528, 620, 621, 623-24, 626, 675, 901; cabinet of, 477; on civil rights, 213; and education, 665; image of, 263; judicial appointments by, 551
Johnson, Nancy, c387
Johnson Act, 166-67
Johnson v. *Transportation Agency, Santa Clara County,* 214
Joint Chiefs of Staff, 510, 630
joint committees, 377
joint resolution; defined, 410
Jones, Phil, 336
Jones, Rich, q692
Jordan, Barbara, q279
journalism, *see* media
judges; appointment of Federal, 550-51, appointment of state, 704, 709; compensation of, c555, 709; demography of, c552, c555; election, 579; removal of, 710; state, 708-10
judgment; exercising, 787
judicial activism, 94
judicial branch; establishment of, 77; state, 706-10
judicial circuits, 548
judicial philosophy, 551
judicial proceedings; defined, 134
judicial restraint, 94
judicial review, 79, 94, 564-65
Judiciary Act of 1789, 91
Judiciary Committee (House), 394
junkets, 425
jurisdiction, 543; of federal courts, 543-44; of Supreme Court, 553-54
jury; grand, 171, 546, 725; hung, 725; petit, 546, 725; right to, 89, 171; service on, 170, 550
jus sanguinis, 157-58
jus soli, 157
Justice Department, 499, 509, 520; Antitrust Division of, 645; budget of, 783; divisions of, 509
justice of the peace, 707

K

Kamber, Victor, q642
Kansas; legislature of, 692
Kapital, Das, 39
Kaplan, H. Roy, q736
Karaosmanoglu, Attila, q863
Kasem, Casey, p353
Katz, Jeffrey, q730
Katz, Michael, q675
Katz v. *United States,* 203, 566
Kayden, Xandra, q238
Kemp, Jack, 669
Kennedy, Anthony, 552
Kennedy, Edward, 247-48, 322
Kennedy, John, 129, 250, 328, 347, 445, 446, 452, 464, 466, p480, 490,

555, 675, 901; cabinet of, 478, 479, 489, 505; and foreign policy, 620, 621; inauguration of, q453, p454, 455; judicial appointments by, 551; on the presidency, q493; space program of, 603

Kennedy, Robert, 396, 478

Kentucky; constitutional commission in, 688; governor's term of office, 698; industry in, 735

Kentucky Fried Chicken restaurants, 22

Kenya; population growth in, 865

Kerrey, Bob, 676

Key, Francis Scott, 197

Keyishian v. *Board of Regents,* 354

KGB, 39

King, Martin Luther, Jr., q210, 213, q667

Kissinger, Henry, 482, p483, 617, 620, 621

"kitchen cabinet," 477, 504, 505

Knox, Henry, q64

Koppel, Ted, 333

Korea; economy of, 866; relations with U.S., 633; taxation in, 596; trade with, 293, p861

Korean War, 392, 522, 634, 869

Korematsu v. *United States,* 33, 223-24

Kracke, E. A., q515

Kristol, Irving, q253

Kroc, Ray, 837

Ku Klux Klan, 187

Kuwait; invasion of, 21, 306, 420

L

labor, 527; as factor of production, 835; government relations with, 649-52; interest groups related to, 287; state oversight of, 717; *see also* unions

Labor Department, 510, 522, 523, 527; economic impact of, 430; secretary of, 475; and unemployment insurance, 659

Laborers' International Union, c287

labor-management relations; government regulation of, 37

Labor Statistics, Bureau of, 510

Labour party (Britain), 810, 842-43

Lacalle, Luis Alberto, 844

Laffer, Arthur, q642

laissez-faire economics, 36-37, 643

Lakewood Plan, 792

lame duck; defined, 90

land; as factor of production, 834

land-grant colleges, 654, 666

landlord-tenant relations, 717

Landrum-Griffin Act of 1959, 652

land use, 754-55, 796-98

Latin America; relations with U.S., 632

Latin Americans, *see* Hispanics; Mexican Americans

Latin America Nuclear Free Zone Treaty, c870

Lau v. *Nichols,* 565

law; admiralty, 543; bureaucracy and, 520; civil, 134, 543-44; constitutional, 544; corporate, 717; criminal, 544; enactment of federal, 410-16; enactment of state, 694-96, c695; ex post facto, 395; equity, 543-44; interpretation of, 565; martial, 823; private, 168; Roman, 544

law clerks, 555

Law Enforcement Assistance Administration, 520

lawmakers, *see* Congress; legislators

law of the soil, 157

lawsuits; between states, 136

lawyer, *see* attorney

Lazarus, Emma, q164

leadership; qualities of, 488-89

League of Nations, 466, 489

League of Women Voters, 267

leak; news, 329, 476

Lebanon; civil war in, 871; U.S. military action in, 392

Lee, Richard Henry, 54, 55, 61

left wing, 814

legal system; principles of, 544-45; types of law, 543-44

legislation, *see* bill; law

legislative assistant, 382

legislative branch; establishment of, 76; state, 691-96

legislative courts, 549-50

legislative oversight, 398-99

Legislative Reorganization Act of 1946, 380, 398

legislative veto; 404, unconstitutionality of, 399

legislators; influences on, 417-21; President as chief of, 463-64; responsibility to constituency, 427-28; responsibility to district, 428-29; state, 692-94; travel by, 425

legislatures; colonial, 50; French, 813-14; Japanese, 817, 818; organization of, 694; staff of, 693; state, 691-96, c693; *see also* Congress

Leland, Mickey, 865

Leon, United States v., 203

Lerner, Barbara, q666

letter writing, 309-10; to the editor, 291, 459; to legislators, 291, 292, 403

Levitt v. *Committee for Public Education,* 179

Lewis, John R., q290

Lexington, KY; city government in, 790

Li Peng, 822, 823

liaison officers, 525

libel, 86, 187, 338

liberal; defined, 313-14

Liberal party (Britain), 810

Libertarian party, 235

liberty; individual, 32

Liberty party, 234

Library of Congress, 383

Libya; military action in, 392

licensing; occupational and professional, 717, 735

Liechtenstein, 852

lieutenant governor, 701, 702, 704

limited government, 28, 46-47, 79

Limited Test Ban Treaty, c870

limited war, 869

Lincoln, Abraham, q25, 32, q186, 440, q441, 446, p447, q455, q477, 490, 898; cabinet of, 505; courage of, 489; expansion of presidential powers, 403, 457; judicial appointments by, 551

Lippmann, Walter, q316, 420

literacy tests; for voting, 272

Lloyd Corporation v. *Tanner,* 190

lobbying and lobbyists, p417, 421, 527; defined, 289, 355; function of, 289, 291-92

lobbyists; defined, 289; international, 293; regulation of, 292-93; of Supreme Court, 572; work of, 289, 291-92

local government; regional arrangements among, 764, 790-92; revenues of, 765-67; services of, 754-57; types of, 752-54

Locke, John, q24, 47-48, q48

Lodge, Henry Cabot, 372, q372

logrolling; defined, 429

London, England, p846, p847

loopholes, 597-98

Los Angeles, 759; financial problems of, 785; population of, c789; services provided by county, 792; urban problems in, 782

lottery; state, 736

Loucks, William, q835

Louisiana; constitutions of, 684, 689; governor's election in, 698; legal system of, 566, 762; legislature of, 692; local government in, 759

Louisiana Purchase, 457, p762; citizenship of residents of, 160

Louisville; Sister Cities program in, 790

Loyalty Review Board, 353

Lurton, Horace, q137

Lusk, R. D., q655

Lutheran Church, 191

Lynch v. *Donnelly,* 181

M

MacArthur, Douglas, 816
MAD, *see* mutually assured destruction
Madison, James, q27, 47, 66, 67, 70, 130, q131, 170, 364, q434, 620, 895; on Constitution, q14; on political parties and factions, q233, 284
magistrate, 548
Magna Carta, 46-47, p47, q171
Mahe, Eddie, Jr., q238
Maine, battleship, 626
Major, John, p809
major committees, 375
majority leader; of the House, 373; of the Senate, 374
majority opinion, 573
majority rule, 32-33
Malaysia; economy of, 866
management; as factor of production, 835
mandamus, 544
mandate; defined, 737-38
mandatory sentencing, 722
Mansfield, Mike, 401
Mao Zedong (Mao Tse-tung), q820, p820
Mapp v. *Ohio*, 203, 585, 586
Marbury v. *Madison*, 79, 92, 460, 564, c577
Marcos, Ferdinand, 70
Marine Corps, 630
maritime law, 543
market; defined, 341
market economy, 37, 838-39
market value; defined, 765
Marsh v. *Chambers*, 181
Marshal, U.S., 548
Marshall, George, q880
Marshall, John, c77, q80, q92, 130, 170, 542, c565, 568, q687, q718
Marshall, Thurgood, 556, 586
Marshall Plan, 617, 631, 880
martial law, 823
Martinez, Matthew, c379
Marx, Karl, 38-39, q39, p841, q842, 842, 849
Maryland; legislature of, 692
mass media, *see* media
mass transit, p669, 670, 756, 784-85
Massachusetts Bay Colony, 50
Massachusetts; constitution of, 689; initiative petition in, 688; legislature of, 691
May, Janice, q688
Mayell, Sharon, q769
Mayflower Compact, 48, 49
mayor-council government, 777, c778
mayors, 142
McCabe, Michael, q703

McCain, John, q400
McCarthy, Joseph, 396
McCarthyism, 353
McCollum v. *Board of Education*, 179-80
McConnell, Edward, q710
McCulloch v. *Maryland*, 129, 130, 132, 390-91, c577, 718
McDonald's restaurants, 22, 837
McGovern, George, 446
McKinley, William, p447, 483, 624, 697, 899
McNamara, Robert, q874
Meat Inspection Act of 1906, 37, 646
media; broadcast, 195-96, 323, p323, 324-25; coverage of Supreme Court, 331; defined, 356; executive branch and, 328-29, 458-59; foreign, p338; freedom of expression in, 325; impact on elections, 346-48; impact on public agenda, 343-46; importance of, 322; interest groups and, 292; legislative branch and, 330-31; national security and, 193-94, 342; ownership of, 324; and public opinion, 306, 309, 349; print, 323, 338-40; protection of sources by, 195; regulation of, 340-42
media event, 329
medicaid, 511, 600, 661-62, 663, 675, 731
medicare, 511, 520, 595, 600, 660, 663, 675
Meek v. *Pittinger*, 179
Memmott, Mark, q600
Mencken, H. L., q328
Merit System Protection Board, 516
metropolitan area; defined, 774; government of, 774-777, 789-90
metropolitan federation, 790
Metropolitan Service District, 764, 791
Mexico; branches of government of, 826-27; constitution of, 825-26; government of, 20, 232, c827; Institutional Revolutionary Party (PRI), 828; National Action Party, 828; political parties in, 828; state and local government in, 827-28; trade with United States, 21, c21, 863, 877; U.S. declaration of war on, 623
Mexico City; population of, 875
Meyers, Jan, c387
Miami, FL, 759; city government in, 791; urban problems in, 782
Michel, Robert, q407, 436
Michigan; electoral votes of, 256; legislature of, 692
middle class, crt307
Middle East; tensions in, 617
Migratory Bird Conservation Com-

mission, 501
Military Appeals, Court of, 549
military; actions of, 634; censorship by, 152-53, ctn327, ctn342; control of, 629; rule of nations by, 865
military strategy, 467-68
militia, 87
Miller v. *California*, 196
Milligan, Ex parte, 564
Mills, Wilbur, 423
mineral resources, 876
Minersville School District v. *Gobitis*, 182
Mines, Bureau of, 507
minimum wage, 650
ministers; British cabinet, 809
Mink, Patsy, q431
Minneapolis; city government in, 790
Minnesota; legislature of, p691
minor committees, *see* nonmajor committees
Minority Business Development Agency, 509
minorities, hiring of, 519; *see also* specific groups by name
minority leader; of the House, 373; of the Senate, 374
minority-owned broadcast stations, 324
minority rights, 32-33; interest groups protecting, 290
Miranda v. *Arizona*, 205, 206, 565, 567, c577
misdemeanor; defined, 706
Mississippi; governor's election in, 698; governor's term of office, 698; legislature of, 692; qualifications for governor, 697; victim compensation laws in, 722
Missouri Compromise, 564
Missouri Plan, 709
Missouri; judicial selection in, 709; qualifications for governor, 697
mistrial, 725
Mitchell, George, q337, c379, 434
Mitterrand, François, p812, 815, 847
mixed economy, 38, 642, 838
moderate; defined, 315
Monaco, 852
monarchy; absolute, 30; constitutional, 31; British, 807
Mondale, Walter, 250, 448
monetary policy, 606, 607, 608
money; regulation of, 391
monopoly; defined, 643, 717; free enterprise vs., 838
Monroe, James, 615, 620, 895
Monroe Doctrine, 615; reaffirmation of, 632
Montana; constitution of, 689; gover-

patronage, 241, 464-65, 826
Patrons of Husbandry, 287
payroll taxes, 595
Payton v. *New York*, 202
PBS, *see* Public Broadcasting System
peace; as foreign policy goal, 615
Peace Corps, 522, p522, 826
Pearl Harbor, 616
peer groups; influence on public opinion, p304, 306
penal system, *see* prisons
Pendleton Act, 516
Pennsylvania; defense projects in, 430; electoral votes of, 256; legislature of, 692
pensions, 600
Pentagon, p510
Pentagon Papers, 193-94, 339, 342
per curiam opinion, 571
perestroika, 851-52
Perez de Cuellar, Javier, p636
Pericles, 32
perjury; defined, 397
Perkins, Frances, 475, p476
Perot, Ross, 236, 240
Persian Gulf; 1987 military action in, 392
Persian Gulf War, 21, c26, 163, 342, 354, 420, 434-36, 467, 487, 624, 625, 629, 634
personal property, 765
personal staff; congressional, 381-83
Peru; constitution of, 82
petit jury, 546, 725
petition; for action, 291; for ballot inclusion of candidate, 244, 355, 382; for ballot inclusion of issue, 521; initiative, 688
Pfaff, William, q802
Philadelphia; financial problems of, 785; local government in, 764; population of, c789; renovation projects in, 781; urban problems in, 782
Philippines; acquisition of, 616, 624; constitution of, 70; as foreign aid recipient, 881
picketing, 190, 192
Pierce, Franklin, 897
Pierce v. *Society of Sisters*, 218
pigeonholing, 412
Pilgrims, 48, 49
Pinochet, Augusto, 32
Pittsburgh v. *ACLU*, 181
plaintiff; defined, 543
planks; defined, 248
platform, party; defined, 248
Platt, Henry, 224
plea bargaining, 725-26
Pledge of Allegiance, 178
Plessy v. *Ferguson*, 212, c577, 578
PLO, *see* Palestine Liberation Organiza-

tion
plum book, 517
pluralism, cultural; *see* cultural pluralism
plurality; defined, 244, 698
pocket veto, 416
Poindexter, John, 397-98
Poland; communism and free elections in, 40; economy of, 829; trade unions in, 634
police; local, 755; state, 723
Police Department of Chicago v. *Mosley*, 190
police power, 728
policy; bureaucracy and, 519-23; federalism and, 139-40; Federal Reserve and, 608; fiscal, 606-07; foreign, 614-36, *see also* foreign policy; monetary, 606, 607, 608; public opinion and, 313-16; Supreme Court and, 564-68
Politburo; Chinese, 821
political action committees, 258, 295-98, 355, 367, 421; affiliated vs. independent, 296-97; expenditures of, c298; growth and income of, c296; origin of and rules for, 295-97; problems with, ctn297; strategies of, 297-98
political base; defined, 697
political cartoons, 327
political culture, 307, crt307
political participation, 9, 141-42, p141, 172, 262, c276, c278, 279; by minorities, 248, 260, 317
political parties, 33, 309; in Britain, 810; in Congress, 370, 373, 374, 375-78, 402; convention of, p230, 246-50; defined, 232, 355; federalism and, 140-41; in France, 814-15; functions of, 239-41; governor's role in, 700; growth of, 233-34; importance of, 420; influence on legislators, 419; in Japan, 819; judgeships and, 550-51; media effect on, 348; membership in, 237; in Mexico, 828; nominating process, 243-50, 347; organization of, 237-39, c238; platform of, 248; President and, 464-65; and public opinion, 239-40; systems of, 232-33; third, 234-36; voter identification with, c261
political patronage, 464-65
political socialization, 304-05
politics; defined, 26; importance of, 27
Polk, James, 483, 897
Polk, Sarah, 483
Pollack, Stuart, 539
poll taxes, 90, 272-73
polling place, 266
polls; exit, 277; public opinion, 308, 310, 418; questions for, 312; scientific, 311-12; straw, 311, p311

pollution; combating, 478, 719-20, 874; interregional, 873; laws against, 139, 657, 719; water, 755-56
polygamy; defined, 181
Ponce de Leon, Ernesto Zedillo, 828
popular sovereignty, 77
population, 19; growth of, 865, 874-875; by state, c894; of U.S., c653, c791
pork-barrel legislation, 429
Port Authority of New York and New Jersey, 763
Portland, OR; city government in, 791; regional government in, 764; Sister Cities program in, 790
Post Office, 393
Postal Service, 501; employees of, c514
Powell, Lewis, q322, 576
Powell v. *Alabama*, 204
powers, constitutional; 126-29, 132
prayer; school, 180, 568
Preamble to the Constitution, 29, 76
precedent; defined, 182; defined, 566
precinct, 266; defined, 237
precinct captain; defined, 237
preferred position doctrine, 186-87
preliminary hearing, 724
premier; of France, 812
President, 895-902; appointments by, 463; and budget, 599-600; cabinet of, *see* cabinet; campaigning for, 257-58, 259; checks on, 459-60, 625; Congress's role in choosing, 394; Constitutional role of, 92-93, 440-41, 456-57, 618-19; direct election of, 454; election by electoral college, 89, 394; emergency powers of, 403-04; Executive Office of the, 480-85; and foreign policy, 465-67, 618-21; of France, 811-12; ideology of, 446; inauguration of, 454-55; influence on Congress, 420-21, 484; influence on public opinion, 306; influence on Supreme Court, 579-80; informal powers of, 457-59; international influence of, 466; isolation of, 489-92; leadership of, 487-92; leadership roles of, 461-68; nomination of candidates for, 245-50, 347; relations with Congress, 401-04, 420-21, 463-64; relations with media, 328-30, 335-36, 458-59; requirements for office, 158, 444, 445-46; signing of bill by, 416; term and salary, 444-45; veto by, 416
presidential government, 128, c807
presidential succession, 90, 92-93, 446-47; Congress's role in, 394
Presidential Succession Act of 1947, 447
president pro tempore of the Senate;

representative sample; defined, 311
reprieve; defined, 463
republic; defined, 32
Republican party, 141, c261; modern, 233-234; origin of, 233
reserve requirement, 608
reserved powers, 127
residency requirement; for voting, 275, 276
resident aliens, 162
resolution; congressional, 410
resources; depletion of, 876; renewable vs. nonrenewable, 873-74
Reuters, 326
revenue; borrowing for, 598; collection of, p390, 391; *see also* taxation
Revenue Act of 1971, 295
revenue sharing, 737, 767
revitalization; defined, 786
Reynolds v. *Sims,* 366, 574, 692
Reynolds v. *United States,* 181
Rhode Island; charter of, 50; governor's term of office, 698; legislature of, 692
Rhodes v. *Chapman,* 207
Richmond Newspapers, Inc. v. *Virginia,* 195
rider; defined, 411
right to know, 216-17
right-to-life protests, 190
right-to-work laws, 652
right wing, 814
Rio Pact, 632, m632
Rockefeller, John D., 643
Rockefeller, Nelson, q95, 394, 446
Rodino, Peter, q394
Roe v. *Wade,* 218, 558, c577
Rogers, William, 482
Roh Tae-Woo, p861
Rome; legal heritage of, 544, 547; Treaty of, 846
Roosevelt, Eleanor, 477
Roosevelt, Franklin, 233, q305, p423, q441, 446, 448, 468, 475, 483, 488, 697, 901; advisers and cabinet of, 477, 480, 489; budget under, 605; bureaucracy of, 522; on Constitution, q91; court-packing plan of, 554, 580; diplomacy of, 466; expansion of presidential powers, 404, 457-58; inaugurations of, q407, 455; and internment policy, 223; New Deal of, 132, 651, 659, 675; terms of office of, 29, 90, 120; use of media by, 328, 458; and World War II, 624, 625
Roosevelt, Theodore, 329, 446, 697, 699-700, 899; and Bull Moose party, 235; expansion of presidential powers, q457; on presidency, q493; use of media by, 335
Rossiter, Thomas, ptg98

Rostenkowski, Dan, 424, q427
Rothenberg, Stuart, q290
Rousseau, Jean Jacques, 24
Rovener, Julie, q732
Rowlandson, Thomas, ptg369
Rubin, Barry, q627-28
Ruckelshaus, William, 521
Rudman, Warren, q366
rules committee; of House, 371-72, p373, 378; of party convention, 247-48
running for office, 245-50, 347, 382
runoff primary; defined, 244
Ruppe, Loret Miller, q529
Rural Electrification Administration, 655
Russian Federation, 852-53
Russian Revolution, 352-53
Rutledge, John, c565

S

SACEUR, *see* Supreme Allied Command Europe
Safire, William, 491
Saint Paul, MN; city government in, 790
sales tax, 734-35, 767
Salinas de Gortari, Carlos, p825, 828, 863, q877
SALT I, *see* Strategic Arms Limitation Talks
SALT II, *see* Strategic Arms Limitation Treaty
Samoa; annexation of, 616
sample; biased, defined, 311; cluster, defined, 311-12; random, defined, 311; representative, defined, 311
sampling error; defined, 311
sanctions; defined, 633-34
San Francisco; financial problems of, 785; mass transit in, 784; population of, c789
sanitation, 756
San Marino, 852
Sarmiento, Sergio, q828
Satter, Robert, q708
Saudi Arabia; government of, 30
Savannah, GA; urban programs in, 786
savings bonds, 598
Saxbe v. *Washington Post,* 322
SBA, *see* Small Business Administration
Scales v. *United States,* 354
Schenck v. *United States,* 185, c577
Schlafly, Phyllis, q228
Schlesinger, Arthur, q441, q803
Schneider, Claudine, q400
Schneider, William, q880
school boards, 764, 783
school districts, 764

schools; aid to, 665; influence on public opinion, 306; prayer in, 180; records of, 218; search and seizure in, 203; single-sex, 216
science policy, 483
Scowcroft, Brent, 620
Scranton, William, q701
Seabed Treaty, c870
search and seizure; protection against illegal, 202-04; warrant for, 88, 202, 566, 584-85; warrantless, 202-03, 585-86
search warrant, 88, 202, 584-86
Sears, Roebuck, and Co., 736
Seaton, William, 333
Seattle, WA, p429
Second Amendment, 87, 113, 123, 171
second-strike capability, 869
Secret Service, 507
secretary of state; state, c702, 704; U.S., 619-20, 627; *see also* State Department
securities; defined, 647; government, p390, 391, 598; regulation of, 647
Securities and Exchange Commission, 502, 647
security; collective, 633; global, 868; international, 868; national, 25-26, 342, 352-54, 614-15, 867
Security Council, 634, 636
sedition; laws against, 187
Sedition Act of 1918, 352
seditious speech, 185
segregation, *see* African Americans; civil rights movement; discrimination
select committees, 375, 377
selective perception; defined, 344-45
selective sales tax, 734, 767
Selective Service System, 630
selectmen, 763
self-incrimination; right to avoid, 88, 205-06
Senate (France), 813
Senate (Mexico), 827
Senate (U.S.); bills in, 372; confirmation hearings by, 330, 394-95; leaders of, 373-74, c379; membership of, 364-65, c367; popular election of, 90; President pro tem of, 447; procedures of, 372-73; qualifications for, 364; ratification of treaties by, 395, 466; rules of, 368, 370, 402; salary and benefits of, 364-65; ctn696; term of office in, 358-59, 364, 402
Senate Finance Committee, 424
senatorial courtesy, 551
Seneca Falls Convention, 271
senior citizens; as special-interest group, 285, p292, q424; government benefits for, 315; voting by, 260

seniority system, 378

sentencing, 726

separate but equal doctrine, 212

separation of church and state, 178-82

separation of powers, 9, 50, 67, 77, 78, c78, 399

sequestered; defined, 194

Serrano, Jose, c379

service contracts, 792

Service Employees International Union, c287

Seventeenth Amendment, 90, 117, 123

Seventh Amendment, 89, 114, 123, 171

severance taxes, 735

sewage disposal, 756

Seward, William, q477

shared powers, 401-04; *see also* checks and balances

Shays's Rebellion, 64

Sheppard, Samuel H., 194

Sheppard v. *Maxwell,* 194

Sherman, Roger, 68

Sherman Antitrust Act, 565, 643, 645, 650

shield laws; defined, 195, 340

shock incarceration, 727

shock probation, 727

Shultz, George, 479, q881

Siegan, Bernard, q798

Sierra Club, 285, 288, 315, 874

significant number; defined, 304

Silent Spring, 315

Simpson, Alan, c379

Sinclair, Upton, q646

Singapore; economy of, 866

single-issue party; defined, 234

single-member district; defined, 236

Sister Cities program, 790

Sixteenth Amendment, 90, 117, 123, 580

Sixth Amendment, 88-89, 113-114, 123, 204-05, 544, 725

Skokie, IL; demonstration in, 191

slander, 86, 187

Slater, Don, q768

slavery; abolition of, 186, 477; Constitution and, 69; *Dred Scott* case and, 156-57; Fourteenth Amendment and, 89, 157; Republican party formed in opposition to, 233; Three-Fifths Compromise and, 68; trade in, 68

Small Business Administration, 501, 649

Smith, Adam, 36-37, q842

Smith, Margaret Chase, q385, 446

Smith Act, 354

Smith-Hughes Act of 1917, 665

social contract, 24-25

social insurance; local government and, 757; programs, 659-60; taxes for, 595-

96

socialism, 38, p38; in developing areas, 844; development of, 841-43; principles of, 843-44

Socialist Labor party, 235

social order, 24

social security, 37, 260, 511, 519, 600, 605; taxes to pay for, 595

Social Security Act of 1935, 519, 659, 731

Social Security Administration, 659

social status; influence on public opinion, 306

social welfare, *see* welfare

Society for the Prevention of Cruelty to Animals, 288

Soil Conservation Service, 658

sole proprietorship, c835; defined, 839

Solon, 547

Somalia, 877

Soroos, Marvin, q860-61

sources; protection of, 340

Souter, David, 558, 580

South Africa; nuclear capability of, 870

South Dakota; public education in, 729

South Dakota v. *Opperman,* 585

South Korea, *see* Korea

sovereignty; defined, 20, 848, 859

Soviet Union, 26, 39, 40, 603; agriculture in, 850; breakup of, 488-89, 614, 621, 631, 851-52; and cold war, 521-22, 616-17; competition with U.S., 521-22; coup in, 853; economic problems in, 849-50; economic sanctions against, 634; nuclear capability of, 870; reform in, 851-52; refugees from, 164; *see also* Commonwealth of Independent States

Sowell, Thomas, q590-91

Spaak, Paul Henri, q631

Spain; legal system of, 721; relations with France, 846; U.S. declaration of war on, 623

Spanier, John, q861

Spanish-American War, 616, 626

speaker of the house, 370, 371, 373, 447

special assessments, 767

special district; defined, 753-54; disadvantages of, 763-64; functions of, 763

special immigration, 168

special-interest groups, *see* interest groups

speech; freedom of, 86-87, 170, 184-88; regulation of, 185-87; student, 188; types of, 184-85, c184; unprotected, 187-88

speech plus; defined, 184

splinter party; defined, 235

spoils system; defined, 513-14

Sporkin, Stanley, q365

spot advertising, 348

Sputnik, 522

SSI, *see* Supplemental Security Income

stability; defined, 313, 356

Stalin, Josef, 30

Stamp Act Congress, 54

Stamp Act of 1765, 53

Standard Oil, 643, 645, ctn645

standing committees, 375-76, c376

stare decisis, 565, 584

state; defined, 18; features of, 18-20; government's relation to, 24-29; modern, 20-22

state central committee; of party, 238

State Council (China), 822

State Department, 465, 506; establishment of, 474, 499; secretary of, 619-20, 627; structure and function of, 627-29

state farms (Soviet), 850

state government; criminal justice systems, 722-27; executive branch of, 697-704, c702; functions of, 717-20, 722-32; judicial branch of, 705-10; legislative branch of, 691-96; in Mexico, 827-28; power of, 716; revenues of, 734-38, c735

state grants, 767

state of emergency, 404

states; admission of, 136-37; agreements between, 135-36; borrowing by, 736; citizenship of, 157; differences among, 142; electoral votes of, 256; environmental policy of, 719-20; facts about, c894; federal aid to, 132-33; government obligations to, 128-29; lawsuits between, 136; lotteries in, 736; obligations to federal government, 129; relations among, 134-36; relations with federal government, 127; role in amendment process, 129; role of, 752

states' rights position, 130

Statue of Liberty, 164

Stearns, Junius, ptg44-45

Stevens, John Paul, 558

Stevens, Thaddeus, q34

Stevenson, Adlai, 346; image of, 263

Stewart, Potter, 180

Stockman, David, 333, 481, ctn482

stocks; regulation of, 647

Stone, Harlan Fiske, q223, c565

STOP ERA, 83

Story, Joseph, q576

Stossel, John, q590

straight-party ticket; defined, 261

Strategic Arms Limitation Talks, 617

Strategic Arms Limitation Treaty, 395

strategic minerals, 876

straw polls, 311, p311

strikes, 649-50, p651; federal intervention in, 128, 650
strong-mayor government, 777
Stuart, Gilbert, ptg51, 364
student government, 31
students; freedom of speech of, 188; property rights of, 218
subcommittees, 376; c376
subpoena; defined, 396-97
subsidies, 648-49
substantive due process, 545
suburb; defined, 775
succession, presidential, 90, 92-93; Congress's role in, 394; order of, 446-47
suffrage; defined, 270; *see also* voters; voting
Sullivan, John, 52
Sunbelt, 774
SunPAC, 296
sunset laws, 139
Sunshine Act of 1976, 217
sunshine laws, 140
Sununu, John, ctn477
"Super Tuesday," 246
superior courts, 707
Supplemental Security Income, 661
supply; law of, 839
supremacy clause, 77, 127, 129, 685
Supreme Allied Command Europe, 631
Supreme Court, 546; as arbiter between state and federal governments, 129; authority of, 92, 94; case load of, c573; Congress and, 580; enforcement of decisions of, 568, 579-80; forces acting on, 578-79; functioning of, 569-73; ideology of, 338-39; influences on, 575-80; on interstate commerce, 642; judicial review by, 564-65; jurisdiction of, 553-54, 566-67; justices of, 554-59; legal interpretation by, 565; limitations on, 566-68; major decisions of, c577; media coverage of, 331; nomination to, 395; overturning earlier decisions, 565-66; President and, 579-80; on property rights, 798; public opinion and, 578; society and, 578-79
supreme courts; Japanese, 817-18; New York, 707; other state, 707-708
suspect classification, 211
suspended sentence, 726
Sutherland v. *Illinois,* 185
Sweden; economy of, 843; government of, 30, 31; state religion of, 191; taxation in, 596
swing vote, 576
Switzerland; government of, 20, 808; local government in, 32
symbolic speech, 184-85

Szulc, Tad, q412

T

Tacoma, WA, 521
Taft, William Howard; as President, 137, 235, q440, 900; on Supreme Court, 556, 558, c565
Taft-Hartley Act, 651-52
Taiwan; and Chinese civil war, 820; economy of, 866; nuclear capability of, 870
Talleyrand, 762
Taney, Roger, 130, 157, c565
Tanzania; government of, 38
target price method, 656
tariffs, 287, 293, 595
Tarr-Whelan, Linda, q143
taxable income, 594
tax assessor, 765
taxation, 62, 423; Congress and, 423-24; benefits derived from, 595; constitutional authority for, 91, 132, 391, 423; estate and gift, 597, 735; excise and customs, 596, 597, 734; importance of, 595; income, 90, 132, c133, 580, 721, 735, 767; license, 734; local, 765-67; loopholes in, 597-98; poll, 90; progressive, 735; property, 765-66; proportional, 735; reforms of, 598; regressive, 596, 735, 766; sales, 734-35, 767; severance, 735; social insurance, 595-96; state, 684, 734-36, c734; withholding system, 595
Tax Court, 548, 549
tax credits, 598, 719, 786
taxes; defined, 594; *see also* taxation
tax incentives, 736
tax increases, 602
Tax Reform Act of 1986, 598
Taylor, Zachary, 468, 897
Teamsters, 287, 652
Teamsters Local 695 v. *Vogt,* 192
technocracy, 142
technology; and policymaking, 521
Teitel Film Corp. v. *Cusack,* 196
telegrams; public opinion and, 310
telephone calls; public opinion and, 310
television, 306, p343; cable, 196, 323, 324; election coverage by, 259, 277, 346-48; freedom of press and, 195-96; importance of, 262, 323, p344; income from, c326; prevalence of, 322, 344; war coverage by, 345-46
Tennessee Valley Authority, 37, 501
Tennessee; constitution of, 686; governor of, 701
Tenth Amendment, 89, 114, 123, 130, 171
term paper; writing, 840

territorial courts, 549
territory; defined, 20; government of, 393
terrorism, 22
Terry v. *New York National Organization for Women,* 190
Texas; citizenship of residents of, 160; Constitution of 1876, 686, 687; electoral votes of, 256; pork-barrel projects in, 429; public education in, 730
Texas Rangers, 723
Texas v. *Johnson,* 185, 574
Thailand; economy of, 866
Thatcher, Margaret, 809, 847
theocracy; defined, 232
Third Amendment, 88, 113, 123, 171
third parties, 234-36
Thirteenth Amendment, 89, 115, 123
Thomas, Clarence, 330, 463, 556, 558, 580
Thompson, Alfred, ptg54
Thornhill v. *Alabama,* 192
Three-Fifths Compromise, 68
Thucydides, q35, 860
Thurmond, Strom, 372
Tiananmen Square, 40, 823
ticket; presidential, defined, 245; straight-party, 261
ticket-splitting, 266
Tinker v. *Des Moines School District,* 185, 188
Tlatelolco, Treaty of, c870
Tocqueville, Alexis de, q284, q286, 802, q802
Todaro, Michael, q863, q865
Tolchin, Martin, q591
Tolchin, Susan, q591
Toledano, Ralph de, q152
Toll, Seymour, q796
Toronto, Ontario; city government in, 791
Torres, Esteban, c379
tort; defined, 716
torture; outlawing of, 204
totalitarian dictatorship, 30
Tower, John, 330
town; defined, 775
town meeting, 32, 763
township, 761, 763; defined, 752
Toyota, 736
trade; international, 21, c21, 293, 467, 483, 615, 860, 861, 862-63; quotas and, 648; slave, 68
trading bloc; defined, 862
traffic congestion, 793
Train v. *City of New York,* 564
transcript; defined, 217
"Transition Diversity Program," 167
transportation; local government and, 756; *see also* highways

Transportation, Department of, 380, 500, 512, 669

treasurer; state, 704

Treasury Department, 507, 549; employees of, c514; establishment of, 474, 499; secretary of, 475; see also Internal Revenue Service

treaty; bilateral, 632; court cases involving, 543; examples of, 633; executive agreement vs., 93; multilateral, 632; negotiation and ratification of, 395, 466, 624

trial, 725; free press and, 194-95; right to fair, 88

"trial balloon"; defined, 333

trial court, 543

Trout, B. Thomas, 868

Truman, Harry, 191, q263, q314, 328, q353, 436, q446, 448, 457, 487, 620, 901; judicial appointments of, q556; style of, p488; on presidency, q493

Truman Doctrine, 616, q617, 631

Trumbull, John, ptg57

trust; defined, 643

"Tuesday Cabinet," 621

Turkey, p616; as foreign aid recipient, 881

TVA, see Tennessee Valley Authority

Twelfth Amendment, 89, 114-15, 123, 451

Twentieth Amendment, 90, 118-19, 123, 394

Twenty-fifth Amendment, 90, 121-22, 123, 394, 446, 447

Twenty-first Amendment, 90, 119, 123, 395

Twenty-fourth Amendment, 90, 121, 123

Twenty-second Amendment, 29, 90, 120, 123, 444

Twenty-seventh Amendment, 364-65

Twenty-sixth Amendment, 90, 122, 123, 273

Twenty-third Amendment, 90, 120, 123

Twin Cities Metropolitan Council, 790

two-party system, 140-41, 233

Two Treatises on Government, 47

Tyler, John, 92-93, 896

U

UAW, see United Auto Workers

UMW, see United Mine Workers

unanimous opinion, 573

uncontrollables; defined, 600

unemployment insurance, 659, 660, 718; local government and, 757

unicameral; defined, 61, 691

UNIGOV, 790

unions, c287; freedom of assembly of, 190, 192; government relations with, 510, 649-52; as interest group, 287

union shop, 652, 718

unitary system of government, 20, 802-03, 810

United Auto Workers, 287

United Automobile, Aerospace, and Agricultural Implement Workers, c287

United Food and Commercial Workers International Union, c287

United Mine Workers, 287

United Nations, 615, 634, 636, p867, 877; charter of, 868; organization of, c635

United Press International, 324, 326

United States; facts about, 894; foreign aid of, 633; government units in, c24; NATO membership of, 631; nuclear capability of, 870; origin of term, 18; physical geography of, 890-91; political geography of, 892-93; relations with Latin America, 632; territory of, m19, 20; trade of, 21, c21, 293, p467, 483, 615; as world power, 615-17; see also government (U.S.)

United States attorney, 548

United States Conference of Mayors, 142

United States Information Agency, 325, 522, 870

United States Trade Representative, 483

United Steelworkers of America, c287

universe; defined, 311

unlimited debate rule, see filibuster

Unsafe at Any Speed, 315

UPI, see United Press International

Upward Bound, 675

urban communities, 774

Urban Development Action Grants, 788

urban growth, c791

Urban Mass Transit Administration, 670

Urban Mass Transportation Act of 1964, 785

urban renewal, 668, 775

Uruguay, 844

Uslaner, Eric, q277, q359

Utah; defense projects in, 430; governor's election in, 698; victim compensation laws in, 722

V

value-added tax, 596

values; media impact on, 344

Van Buren, Martin, 896

Vance, Cyrus, 479

Vermont; governor's election in, 698; governor's term of office, 698; legislature of, 694

Versailles, Treaty of, 466

veterans; benefits for, 600

Veterans Administration, 522, 663, 775; employees of, c514

Veterans Affairs, Department of, 398, 512, 522; client groups of, 528; court cases involving, 550

Veterans Affairs Committee (House), 371

Veterans Appeals, Court of, 550

veto, 401, 416; item, 703; legislative, defined, 399, 404; override of, 416; pocket, 416

Vice President, 90, 92-93; appointment of, 394; nomination of candidate for, 250; in presidential succession, 446, 447; role of, 447-48; in Senate, 374

victim compensation laws, 722

Victoria, queen of England, ptg806, 807

Vietnam; aggression by, 623-24; government of, 232; refugees from, 173, 864

Vietnam War, c26, 184, 185, 190, 193-94, 248, 304, 312, 345-46, ctn345, 354, 392, 419, 420, 459, 460, 462, 463, 522, 617, 621, 623-24, 625, 634; economic effects of, 404; end of, 482; operations of, 468; public opinion of, 626

Vinson, Fred, q191, c565

Vinyard, Dale, 440

Virginia, 669; constitutional convention in, p688; governor's election in, 698; governor's term of office, 698; House of Burgesses of, 50

Virginia Plan, 67

visa, 629; applying for, 93; diversity, 167; for "extraordinary abilities," 168

Voice of America, 325, 870

volunteering, 195, 217; for the armed forces, 766

voters; apathy of, 275-77; background of, 260-61, 276-77; effect of campaigning on, 259; handbook for, 264-69; participation of, 172, 262, c278; political parties and, 261-62

voting; age for, 90, 273; in Congress, 415; early restrictions on, 270; Fifteenth Amendment and, 90, 271-72; information gathering for, 346; machines for, 266; party, 419; poll tax and, 90, 272-73; procedures for, 266-67, 269; qualifications for, 265; registration for, 265-66, c268, 275, 276;

requirements for, 275; responsibility for, 172, 262; right of, p139, 316; Twenty-third Amendment and, 90; women suffrage, 90, 215, 271

Voting Rights Acts; of 1965, p139, 273; of 1970, 273, 275; of 1975, 269; of 1982, 273

Vucanovich, Barbara, q407

W

wage-price controls, 404, 464
Wagner Act, 651
Waite, Morrison, c565
Waite, Terry, p869
Walesa, Lech, q829
Wallace, George, 453-54
Walters, Dan, q693
war; declaration of, 458, 623, 634; draft for, 216, 630
War Department; establishment of, 474, 499; superseded, 510, 522, 629
War on Poverty, 675-76
war powers, 132, 392, 467-68, 623-24
War Powers Act of 1973, 392, 398, 459, 467, 624
ward; defined, 238
ward heelers, 428
warrant; arrest, 88; search, 88, 527, 584-86
Warren, Charles, q542
Warren, Earl, 94, 205, q206, q212, q397, 555, 556, c565, q567, q574, q578, 579, 691
Warsaw Pact, 631, 632
Washington, DC; financial problems of, 785; mass transit in, 784
Washington, George, ptg44-45, 54, 55, 66, 70, 93, 309, 450, 457, 483, 895; appointments of, 513; budget under, 599; cabinet of, 474, 478, 504; farewell address of, q233, q249-50; as general, 467-68; inauguration of, 455; judicial appointments of, 553; on presidency, q493
Washington State, Industrial Welfare Committee of, 650
Washington v. *Davis*, 211
Watergate scandal, 331, 405, 459, p485; Senate investigation of, 396, 397
Water Pollution Control Act of 1948, 657
Water Pollution Control Act of 1972, 657
Water Quality Act of 1965, 719
Water Quality Improvement Act of 1970, 657
water supply, 755-56; pollution of, 865, 874
Watkins v. *United States*, 397

Watson, Alan, q547
Wattenburg, Martin, q240
Ways and Means Committee (House), 378, 423, 424
weak-mayor government, 777
wealth; distribution of, 843-44
Wealth of Nations, 36, 842
Weaver, Robert, 475
Weeks v. *United States*, 203, 584-85
Weicker, Lowell, 380
Weidner, Edwin, q802
Weinberger, Caspar, 479
welfare programs, 605, 606, 674-76; changes to, 662-63; described, 660-62; expenditures on, c661; federal-state, 731; local, 757; reform of, 732; state, 732
Wertheimer, Fred, q297
Wesberry v. *Sanders*, 363, 366
West Virginia; admission to statehood, 129
West Virginia State Board of Education v. *Barnette*, 182
Westside Community Schools v. *Mergens*, 180
Whigs, 233
whip; defined, 373
Whiskey Rebellion, 457, 467-68
White, Byron, 188, q339
White, Edward, c565
White, Michael, q788
White, Theodore, q244
White House Office, 483-84
Whitney, William, q835
Whitney v. *California*, 352, 353
Whitten, Jamie, p359
WHO, *see* World Health Organization
widows; preferential tax treatment of, 216
Wildavsky, Aaron, q600
Wilder, L. Douglas, 290
wildlife; protection of, 657-58
Wilkinson v. *Jones*, 196
Williams, Pete, q153
Williams, Roger, 753
Wilson, James, 66
Wilson, Woodrow, q369, 447, 457, 489, 491, 697, 900; cabinet of, 477; election of, 235; foreign policy of, 621; on interest groups, q258; on war, q392; and World War I, 616, q619, 625
Winikow, Linda, q739
wire services, 323-24
wiretapping, 203-04, 566
Wisconsin; constitution of, 689; governor's veto in, 703; legislature of, 693; local government in, 753
Wisconsin v. *Yoder*, 182
withholding, 595

witness; rights of, 397
Wittfogel, Karl, 515
Wolman v. *Walter*, 179
women; Abigail Adams on rights of, 71; in armed forces, 630; in cabinet, 475; in Congress, 365, c367; discrimination against, 215-16; employment of, c215, 216; in politics, 290; property rights of, 721; voting rights of, 90, 215, 270-71, p270
Woodbury, Levi, q553
Woodson v. *North Carolina*, 207
Woodworth, Laurence, 383
Worcester, Donald, q721
workers' compensation, 718
World Bank, p862, 863
World Food Conference, 858-59
World Food Council, 636, 859
World Health Organization, 636, 858, 874
World Meteorological Organization, 23
world opinion, 306
World War I, 392, 616
World War II, 404, 605, 616; effects on Europe, 846; and national debt, 606-07
Wright, Jim, 331, q371
writ; of *certiorari*, 569, 570; of habeas corpus, defined, 395; of mandamus, 544
Wyoming; land-use laws in, 720; sentencing in, 726

Y

Yasui v. *United States*, 223
Yates, Robert, 14
Yates v. *United States*, 187, 354
yellow-dog contracts, 651
Yeltsin, Boris, 852, 853
Yeutter, Clayton, q251
Yiannopoulos, A. N., q762
Young, Milton, 265
Young, Whitney, q671

Z

Zaire, 844
Zeigler, Harmon, q345
Zemel v. *Rusk*, 339
zoning, 754-55, 796-98

Front Cover Robert Llewellyn; **VII** American Numismatic Assoc.; **VIII** Wally McNamee/Woodfin Camp; **X** The Office of the Architect of the Capitol of the United States; **XI** The Office of the Architect of the Capitol of the United States; **XII** Robert Llewellyn; **XIV–XV** Office of the Mayor of Lansing, Michigan; **XV** Bureau of Printing & Engraving; **XVI** City of Chicago, Department of Streets and Sanitation; **XVII** Schlowsky Photography; **XVIII** Photograph courtesy of the New York State Museum; **8** UPI Bettmann/Newsphotos; **9** Amy Wrynn/Ligature; **11** Dennis Brack/Black Star; **12** ©Lou Jones; **13** Robert Llewellyn; **15** American Antiquarian Society; **16** Uniphoto/Pictor; **20** Andy Hernandez/SYGMA; **23** Karen Schulenburg/Gamma-Liaison; **25** The Food and Drug Administration, Washington, D.C.; **27** David Cross/TIME Magazine; **33** ©Addison Gallery of American Art, Phillips Academy, Andover, MA; **35** SCALA/Art Resource, NY; **37** Spencer Jones/Bruce Coleman, Inc.; **38** Mary Evans Picture Library/Photo Researchers; **40** Brookins/Richmond Times-Dispatch; **41** B. Gentile/Sipa; **44** Virginia Museum of Fine Arts, Richmond. Gift of Colonel and Mrs. Edgar W. Garbisch; **46** Jamestown-Yorktown Foundation; **47** Dept. of the Environment, London/The Bridgeman Art Library; **51** New York State Historical Association, Cooperstown; **52** Photograph courtesy of the New York State Museum; **53** Library of Congress; **54** The Connecticut Historical Society, Hartford; **55** National Portrait Gallery, Smithsonian Institution; **57** Yale University Art Gallery; **66** North Wind Picture Archives; **71** New York State Historical Association, Cooperstown; **74** Cynthia Johnson/Gamma-Liaison; **81** Cynthia Johnson/Gamma Liaison; **83** Schlowsky Photography; **86** Courtesy of The New-York Historical Society, N.Y.C.(l); **86–87** Schlowsky Photography; **87** Schlowsky Photography(c); Camerique/H. Armstrong Roberts(l); Jonathan Wallen(r); **102** UPI/Bettmann; **106** White House Historical Assoc.; **112** White House Historical Assoc.(t); Donaldson, Lufkin & Jenrette Collection of Americana(b); **115** The Bettmann Archive; **118** Nebraska State Historical Society; **120** PG (both); **122** Bob Daemmrich; **123** Independence National Historical Park; **124** Robert Frerck/Odyssey; **135** Univ. of Texas, Austin; **136** Courtesy of the Salem Evening News; **139** AP/Wide World; **141** Amy Wrynn/Ligature; **143** Center for Policy Alternatives; **147** Grant Heilman; **151** Kathleen Campbell/Gamma-Liaison; **154** UPI/Bettmann Newsphotos; **156** Bob Daemmrich/Uniphoto; **159** Richard Vogel/Gamma-Liaison; Rafael Macia/Photo Researchers; **162** The Bettmann Archive; **163** Harry N. Abrams, Inc.; **163–164** Schlowsky Photography; **164** Walter Frerck/Odyssey(b); Photo Researchers(t); **165** Mark Sherman/Bruce Coleman, Inc.; **169** Cynthia Johnson/Gamma Liaison; **170** COMSTOCK; **173** Reuters/Bettmann; **176** Judith Aronson; **179** C. Simonpietri/SYGMA; **181** Eve Arnold/Magnum; **182** J. Irwin/H. Armstrong Roberts; **187** The Bettmann Archive; **188** Bob Daemmrich; **189** Globe Photos; **193** AP/Wide World; **196** CNN, Inc.; **197** Stan Barouk/Uniphoto; **200** UPI/Bettmann; **202** Rick Friedman/Black Star; **203** Schlowsky Photography; **209** Johnson/Gamma-Liaison; **210** R. Bedi/Camera Press/Globe Photos; **216** Tim Davis/Photo Researchers; **218** Schlowsky Photography; **219** Rick Friedman/Black Star; **223** UPI/Bettmann; **227** Gilles Peress/Magnum; **229** Mike Keefe/The Denver Post; **230** Dennis Brack/Black Star; **232** PG; **234–235** PG(all); **236** Rueters/Bettmann; **240** Amy Wrynn/Ligature; **241** Sandra Rues/Liaison International; **243** Culver Pictures; **244** Bob Daemmrich; **245** University of Hartford, J. Doyle Dewitt Collection; **246** Carol Bernson/Black Star; **248** AP/Wide World; **250** Rick Friedman/Black Star; **251** R. Maiman/SYGMA(t); Republican National Committee(b); **254** Roark Johnson/Liaison International; **256** PG; **259** Ira Wyman/SYGMA; **263** AP/Wide World; **264** Amy Wrynn/Ligature; **265** Schlowsky Photography; **266** Markel/Gamma-Liaison(l); Amy Wrynn/Ligature(c, r); **267** Camerique/H. Armstrong Roberts; **270** UPI/Bettmann; **276** Shelly Katz/Black Star; **279** Bob Daemmrich/Uniphoto; **282** Terry Ashe/Gamma-Liaison; **285** Adam Scull/Globe Photos; **290** National Council of La Raza; **292** Mario Ruiz/TIME Magazine; **297** from *Herblock On All Fronts* (New American Library, 1980); **299** National Urban League, Inc.; **302** From the Art Collection of The Boatmen's National Bank of St. Louis; **304** Robert Frerck/Odyssey; **307** Dick Locher/Chicago Tribune; **311** © Sam Ward/USA TODAY; **317** NALEO; **320** ©Jeffrey Markowitz/Sygma; **322** Michael Grecco/Picture Group; **323** CNN, Inc.; **327** Walt Handelsman/The Times-Picayune/Tribune Media Services(r); H. Payne/Scripps-Howard/United Feature Syndicate(l); **330** Larry Downing/Woodfin Camp; **332** AP/Wide World(c); Schlowsky Photography(b, t); **333** Historical Society of Washington, D.C., Machen Collection; **334** The Bettmann Archive(c); Schlowsky Photography(l); New England Telephone, Telephone Pioneer Museum of Boston(r); **335** NMAH, Smithsonian Institution(l); Michael G. O'Conner/The Image Bank(r); The Bettmann Archive(b); **336** NBC Photo by Al Levine; **338** Jim Anderson/Woodfin Camp; **341** NASA; **342** Ed Stein/Rocky Mtn. News; **343** Trippett/Sipa; **344** Courtesy of MTV; **345** Bill Canfield, Courtesy of the Newark Star Ledger; **347** Rueters/Bettmann; **348** University of Hartford, J. Doyle Dewitt Collection; **349** Andy Hernandez/SYGMA; **351** Rogers/The Pittsburgh Press/United Feature Syndicate; **353** Mark Reinstein/Uniphoto; **357** Stuart Conen/COMSTOCK; **359** Courtesy the House of Representatives; **360** Corcoran Gallery of Art; **362** Hiroyuki Matsumoto/Black Star; **369** British Library, London/The Bridgeman Art Library; **370** House of Representatives; **373** J.L. Atlan/Sygma; **374** C-Span; **380** Robert Houser/COMSTOCK; **385** AP/Wide World; **388–389** Rueters/Bettmann; **390** Schlowsky Photography; **394** Library of Congress; **397** Wally McNamee/Woodfin Camp; **402** Kevin Siers, The Charlotte Observer; **405** Terry Ashe/Gamma-Liaison; **408** Mark Reinstein/Photoreporters; **410** Wally McNamee/Woodfin Camp; **412** Office of the Architect of the Capitol of the U.S.(r); Ken Ross/Viesti Assoc.(l); **413** Office of the Architect of the Capitol of the United States(both); **414** Dennis Brack/Black Star; **416** Ron Sachs/SYGMA; **417** David Burnett/Contact Stock Images/Woodfin Camp; **418** Courtesy of Bill Clay; **421** Dennis Brack/Black Star; **422** Ed LeCocq/Rothco(t); Taylor/Albuquerque Tribune(b); **423** UPI/Bettmann; **424** Kirk Walters/Toledo Blade; **426** Andy Hernandez/SYGMA; **429** Kuhn, Inc./The Image Bank; **431** House of Representatives, Hawaii; **433** The Granger Collection, New York(t); Michael J. Pettypool/Uniphoto(b); **435** Ed Stein/Rocky Mtn. News; **439** Uniphoto/Pictor; **441** Chicago Historical Society/Photo Researchers; **442** Dennis Brack/Black Star; **444** Stan Sherer/Forbes Library, Calvin Coolidge Collection, Northampton, MA; **445** Laski/Sipa; **447** Courtesy of The New-York Historical Society, NYC; **448** J.L. Atlan/SYGMA; **454** UPI/Bettmann; **456** © Jeffrey Markowitz/Sygma; **458** UPI/Bettmann; **460** Fred Ward/Black Star; **461** The Bettmann Archive; **462** E. Spiegelhalter/Focus/Woodfin Camp; **463** Diane Walker/Gamma-Liaison; **465** Reprinted with permission: Tribune Media Services; **467** Magnum Photos; **468** Steve Liss/TIME Magazine; **469** © Dennis

Brack/Black Star; **472** Cynthia Johnson/Liaison International; **476** AP/Wide World; **477** Mike Keefe/The Denver Post; **480** UPI/Bettmann; **482** Frank Evers/New York Daily News; **483** SYGMA; **485** Schlowsky Photography; **487** Dennis Brack/Black Star; **488** Harry S Truman Library; **490** © Joe McNally/Sygma (l); White House Photo (r); **491** White House Photo (l); Robert Llewellyn (c); Reuters/Bettmann (r); **492** Bettmann Newsphotos; **493** Brad Markel/Globe Photos; **496** Bill Weems/Woodfin Camp; **498** Antonello Nusca/Gamma-Liaison; **501** Amy Wrynn/Ligature(br); NASA(tl); **503** © Dennis Brack/Black Star; **504–505** White House Historical Assoc.(all); **506** Robert Llewellyn; **507** Alan Pitcairn/Grant Heilman(t); David L. Brown/Nawrocki Stock Photo; **508** Larry Lefever/Grant Heilman(b); U.S. Department of Agriculture Soil Conservation Service(t); **509** National Oceanic and Atmospheric Administration; **510** Robert Llewellyn; **511** Sepp Seitz/Woodfin Camp; **512** Amtrak; **514** Robert Llewellyn; **515** Bibliotheque Nationale, Paris; **516** The Bettmann Archive; **518** John Branch/Courtesy Chapel Hill News; **520** Alfred Gescheidt/The Image Bank; **522** Carolyn Watson/Peace Corps Photo; **523** Oliphant, ©1972 Universal Press Syndicate, reprinted with permission. All rights reserved.; **525** Courtesy of Continental Airlines, Inc.; **529** Dennis Brack/Black Star; **533** Roy Paul/The Eugene Register-Guard; **537** Bill Weems/Woodfin Camp; **539** ©1979 Herblock, from *Herblock on All Fronts* (New American Library, 1980); **540** ©Lou Jones; **542** Architect of the Capitol of the United States; **543** R. Michael Stuckey/COMSTOCK; **547** Robert Frerck/Odyssey; **548** Bill Foley/TIME Magazine; **554** Lynn Johnson/Black Star(t); Russ Kinne/COMSTOCK(b); **555** Robert Llewellyn; **556** © The National Geographic Society, courtesy of the Supreme Court Historical Society, (inset) © Rick Friedman/Black Star; **558** Reprinted with permission: Tribune Media Services; **559** Cynthia Johnson/Gamma-Liaison; **562** Collection of the Supreme Court of the United States; **569** Bob Daemmrich; **570** Wally McNamee/Woodfin Camp(l); **570–571** Collection of the Supreme Court of the United States; **571** Arthur Grace/SYGMA; **576** J.L. Atlan/SYGMA; **581** Collection of the Supreme Court of the United States; **585** Schlowsky Photography; **589** ©Lou Jones; **591** Jeffrey D. Smith/Woodfin Camp; **592** Schlowsky Photography; **594** Elyse Lewin/The Image Bank; **597** Murray Alcosser/The Image Bank; **599** McNelly/Chicago Tribune; **603** Co Rentmeester/The Image Bank; **609** David Burnett/Contact Stock Images/Woodfin Camp; **612** Larry Downing/Sygma; **614** Peter Turnley/Black Star; **616** Marc Deville/Gamma-Liaison; **618** (c) Ira Wyman/Sygma; **620** (c) Jeffrey Markowitz/Sygma; **621** Y.R. Okamoto/LBJ Library; **623** U.S. Naval Academy Museum; **626** Culver Pictures; **628** Feinblatt/Sipa; **630** Charles Fiel/Uniphoto; **636** Nina Berman/Sipa; **637** Courtesy of A. Dickey; **640** Jonathan Blair/Woodfin Camp; **643** Nubar Alexanian/Woodfin Camp; **644** Carl Schroeder/Globe Photos; **645** Culver Pictures; **648** ARCADIO/Costa Rica/Cartoonist & Writers Syndicate; **649** Alain Evrard/Photo Researchers; **651** Charlyn Zlotnik/Woodfin Camp; **652** AP/Wide World; **657** Alan Pitcairn/Grant Heilman; **662** Bureau of Printing & Engraving(all); **663** Schlowsky Photography(br); Bureau of Printing & Engraving(tr); **665** Ohio State University; **666** Andy Levin/Photo Researchers; **669** Jose Fernandez/Woodfin Camp; **671** AP/Wide World; **675** Jacques Chenet/Woodfin Camp; **679** Carol Lee/Uniphoto; **682** James Steinberg/Photo Researchers; **684** The R.I. Dept. of Economic Development/C. Browning; **688** Gleason/Viscom/Williamsburg; **691** Tom Olmscheid/MN House of Rep.; **696** Gary Brookins/Richmond Times-Dispatch; **697** Stan Sherer/Forbes Library, Calvin Coolidge Collection,

Northampton, MA; **698** Schlowsky Photgraphy; **700** The Miami Herald/Angel Valentin; **706** Amy Wrynn/Ligature; **708** Cary Wolinsky/Stock Boston; **710** Bob Daemmrich/Uniphoto; **711** State of New York, Court of Appeals; **714** George Hall/Woodfin Camp; **716** Pennsylvania Game Commission; **720** Washington State Parks & Recreation Commission; **721** Seaver Center for Western History Research; **723** Tom McHugh/Photo Researchers; **724** Charles Steiner/SYGMA; **727** F. Paolini/SYGMA; **732** Courtesy, Kentucky Cabinet for Human Resources; **736** Schlowsky Photography; **739** Courtesy L. Winikow, Orange and Rockland Utilities, Inc.; **743** David Woo/Stock Boston; **747** Rob Crandall/Picture Group; **749** Bob Daemmrich/Uniphoto; **750** Susan Lapides/Woodfin Camp; **754** Nubar Alexanian/Woodfin Camp(l); **754–755** Courtesy of the City of Lansing, Michigan; **755** Miguel A. Casanova/City of Dallas, Public Works Department(l); City of Chicago, Department of Streets and Sanitation(r, tc); **760** Tommy Thompson/Black Star; **761** Mike Yamashita/Woodfin Camp; **762** Jonathan Wallen; **769** Courtesy, Sharon Mayell; **772** A. Tannenbaum/SYGMA; **781** Michael Melford/The Image Bank; **782** James Aronovsky/Picture Group; **784** R. Maiman/SYGMA; **785** Adam Woolfitt/Woodfin Camp; **786** Pamela Zilly/The Image Bank; **791** Van Bucher/Photo Researchers; **793** Urban Mobility Corp.; **797** Bonnie McGrath; **801** Jay Freis/The Image Bank; **803** Alain Nogues/SYGMA; **804** WOC/Sipa; **806** By Courtesy of Crown Estate Commisioners, London/The Bridgeman Art Library; **809** Stewart Mark/Camera Press/Globe Photos; **811** Giraudon/Art Resource, NY; **812** Villard/Sipa; **816** AP/Wide World; **820** Audrey Topping/Photo Researchers; **822** Reuters/Bettmann; **825** Diana Walker/Gamma-Liaison; **829** J.L. Atlan/SYGMA; **832** Rene Burri/Magnum; **834** Tom Sobolik/Black Star; **836** Jonathan Wallen; **837** Eric Pasquier/SYGMA(bl); Jonathan Wallen(tr); **841** UPP/Photoreporters; **846** UPI/Bettmann Newsphotos; **847** Anthony Howarth/Woodfin Camp(t); Color Day Productions/The Image Bank(b); **848** P. Robert/SYGMA; **850** Laski/Sipa; **853** Hashimoto/Sygma; **856** Alexandra Avakian/Woodfin Camp; **858** AP/Wide World; **861** AP/Wide World; **862** UPI/Bettmann; **864** UPI/Bettmann; **866** Leong Katai/Woodfin Camp; **867** Trippett/Sipa; **869** UPP/Photoreporters; **877** UN photo #174334 by John Isaac; **881** Kevin Horan/Picture Group; **895–902** White House Historical Association(all except 902lr); **902** courtesy Arkansas Governor's Office (lr)

Maps and Charts
By Ligature, Inc.

Special Report '96 Election

▲ President Clinton, winner of the 1996 presidential election, asked Americans to help him "build a bridge to the 21st century."

Election Preview

Objectives
• Examine the issues that were the focus of the campaign.
• Analyze campaign strategies and election results.

Key terms and concepts
partisanship, "gridlock," warchests, "coattail effect," soft money, "spin doctors," exit polls

This report emphasizes the following government themes:
• **Political Processes**   The 1996 campaigners sought the middle ground.
• **Civic Participation**   Despite the large amount of money that was spent to influence opinion, voter apathy was evidenced by a low turnout at the polls.

Critical Thinking Skills
• **Understanding Cause and Effect**
• **Drawing Conclusions**

Introduce

Report Overview

Congress Sets the Campaign Agenda Individual items on the congressional agenda, listed in the Republicans' Contract with America, were important in the 1996 election. The Contract itself became the focus of much of the campaign.

Fighting for Control of Congress Control of Congress seemed just as important in this campaign as winning the White House. Both parties fought fiercely to gain a majority in the House and Senate.

Running to the Middle Never was the effort to identify with moderates more evident than in 1996.

Powers of the President
The Election Campaign
The traditions of American presidential campaigns
Side One, Chapter 11

About the Report Opener

Setting the Scene During the campaign the President wanted to "build a bridge to the 21st century." Parts of that bridge were already under construction. Congress and the President had agreed on some key legislation before the nominating conventions. Issues that arose out of communism's collapse had challenged Bill Clinton in his first term. Bridges to eastern Europe, Russia, and other emerging economies were not yet completed.

Focus

Bell Ringer

Write the following on the chalkboard for students to complete while attendance is being taken. Name each of these federal government elected officials:
President:
Vice President:
Your State's Senators:
Your Representative:

Motivating Activity

Discuss the students' Bell Ringer lists. Who, if any, of these people were first elected in 1996? What message did the voters in the election of 1996 send to Washington, D.C.? Tell students that this Special Report will describe the campaign and election, helping them to understand political trends in the United States.

Vocabulary Precheck

Ask students to speculate on the meanings of **partisanship, gridlock,** and **warchests.** Have them check their guesses by finding the definitions in the section text.

Caption Answer
They did not have enough votes to override presidential vetoes.

Powers of the Congress
Congressional Leadership
The roles played by various leaders of Congress, focusing on the majority and minority leaders
Side Two, Chapter 25

Congress Sets the Campaign Agenda

For the first time in nearly a half century the legislative agenda played the major role in determining the issues of the presidential campaign. Ann F. Lewis, President Clinton's deputy campaign manager, observed that the election was "almost like a parliamentary election." Two unique circumstances supported her observation. Never before had a Senate majority leader led his party's national ticket, and not since 1948 had a presidential election focused so much attention on the work of Congress.

Newt and the Newcomers

The battle lines for the 1996 presidential election were drawn in 1994 when Republicans won majorities in both the Senate and House. The GOP added 52 House seats and 8 Senate seats—their most impressive election victory in 48 years.

Difficult Times for Democrats Thomas Foley, Democratic speaker of the House, and other promi-

nent Democrats lost their bids for reelection in 1994. Meanwhile, not one Republican incumbent lost a congressional race. Even after the election, Democrats continued to lose representation, as some Southern members switched parties. Like former Democratic President Harry Truman, Bill Clinton had to work with a Republican Congress.

Contract with America House Republicans, led by their new speaker, Newt Gingrich, and encouraged by 74 freshmen representatives, signed a Contract with America. In it they pledged sweeping reforms. They said they would pass a balanced budget amendment, limit congressional terms, cut taxes, reform welfare and health care, build more prisons, and raise defense spending.

The Senate also had new leadership. Majority Leader Bob Dole was in a position to shepherd bills through the Senate. Bob Dole knew that success in passing legislation would enhance his prospects as the Republican candidate for the White House in 1996.

Democrats Respond

The Democrats, who were outnumbered in Congress, had a friend in the White House. They went on the defensive. When key legislation was presented, Congressional Democrats allied with President Clinton to thwart the Republican majority. **Partisanship,** or strong party loyalty, divided the 104th Congress, reaching its highest level in 40 years. The result was what the media termed **"gridlock."**

Contract with America
Newt Gingrich and Republicans, elated by their victory in the 1994 election, announce a revolution. **Politics Why did the Republican agenda stall in Congress?**

Background

Prior to 1996, fourteen incumbent American Presidents had run successfully for reelection. Twenty-one incumbent Presidents either chose not to run or lost their reelection bids. Counted in these statistics are eight incumbent Presidents who had succeeded to the office rather than winning their own election. Of these eight incumbents, Theodore Roosevelt, Harry Truman, and Lyndon Johnson won election to the office after serving out the previous term.

Senate Leaders Clash
When Bob Dole resigned to run for President, new Senate Majority Leader Trent Lott (left) faced filibuster threats from Democrats led by Tom Daschle (right). **Political Process How did the public react to Congress when the government shut down some operations beginning in late 1995?**

Gridlock Fatality One major fatality of the divided government was campaign finance reform. President Clinton had pledged in 1992 to free the political system from the hold of big-money interests. Many Republicans elected in 1994 made similar promises. Each side charged the other with breaking campaign finance rules. However, emotional debates in Congress about the direction of reform served only to prevent compromise. In 1996 the House soundly rejected a final effort to change campaign finance rules.

Other Stalled Legislation Without enough votes to override presidential vetoes, Republicans lost key votes on amendments to balance the budget and to limit the terms of members of Congress. They also found little agreement with the White House on the budget itself. When the White House and Congress failed to reach agreement on the budget, the government had to shut down many of its operations for lack of funds during the winter of 1995-1996. Public reaction to the government shutdown would become a serious problem for congressional Republicans in the upcoming election.

Republicans were able to find common ground with Democrats on only a few minor issues. Legisla-

tion on nuclear waste, health care, drinking water, and antiterrorism stalled in Congress. Would gridlock become a liability to Republicans in the 1996 election?

Public Disapproval of Congress

Republican legislators, who had been elated over their 1994 congressional campaign victories, soon felt the sting of public reaction. The tide of opinion began to turn against Congress in late 1995. By May 1996, one poll showed that 65 percent of the respondents disapproved of the way the legislature was handling its job. Another poll revealed that Americans who said the economy had gotten better tended to credit the President, while those who believed the economy was worse blamed Congress. Democrats, reading the polls, were elated by the possibility of winning back one or both houses in the 1996 election.

Welfare Reform Stalls

By the summer of 1996 welfare reform seemed destined to be another big fatality of partisan politics. During his presidential campaign in 1992, Bill Clinton had promised to "end welfare as we know it."

SPECIAL REPORT: '96 ELECTION **E3**

L3 **Setting the Agenda** Before its recess in August 1996, Congress rushed to pass a number of bills that had been tied up in political debates for months. Part of the task of Congress is to set priorities for legislation, to determine what is more important and what is less. If you were a member of Congress, what priority would you have given to the following list of legislation that Congress faced? Be prepared to discuss the reasons for your choices.

- *Revise the welfare system*
- *Health insurance for workers who leave their jobs*
- *Safe drinking water*
- *Raise the minimum wage*
- *Authorize money for defense*
- *Provide for disposal of nuclear waste*
- *Antiterrorism—airport security*

CONNECTIONS

Social Welfare

The 104th Congress passed major welfare legislation that President Clinton signed in the summer of 1996. One aim of this legislation was to require able welfare recipients to go to work. When liberals in his own party complained about the new welfare legislation, President Clinton proposed a program to create jobs for people on welfare. At the heart of his program was a series of tax breaks aimed at encouraging businesses to hire welfare recipients.

Caption Answer
welfare, health insurance, and minimum wage bills

Focusing on health care, however, the President never seriously pushed his plan for welfare reform, and Congress did not act on it. As the 1996 presidential primaries neared, Republicans passed their own welfare overhaul through the House. The Senate passed a more moderate bill that drew President Clinton's praise. However, the President vetoed two compromise welfare proposals within the next four months.

Republicans prepared another welfare bill that would also overhaul Medicaid. President Clinton called the Medicaid provisions unacceptable. Congress then dropped the Medicaid provisions and prepared a bill that would force the President to either sign it or face charges that he never seriously intended to reform welfare. If they could not get their key issues passed, Republicans hoped to use Bill Clinton's vetoes against him in the upcoming election.

Conflict and Compromise

As the national political conventions neared, fresh winds of compromise blew into Washington. Both the President and Congress seemed ready to respond to the public frustration over gridlock. Contention gave way to cooperation.

Welfare Bill Signed The President's desire to fulfill his campaign pledge on welfare reform prevailed over his misgivings about the proposed legislation. Despite outcries from liberals in his own party, he announced that he would sign the welfare bill.

Bipartisan Legislation Just before the August recess, lawmakers began bipartisan efforts to reach agreement on several other bills. Senate and House versions of a health insurance bill were reconciled when Senator Edward M. Kennedy and Representative Bill Archer agreed to compromise. When Kennedy agreed to stop blocking the health insurance bill, the Republicans withdrew their threat to block a bill on minimum wages. The Democrat's bill, raising the minimum wage by 90 cents in two steps to $5.15, included a Republican package of tax breaks for small businesses. The President signed the welfare, health insurance, and minimum wage bills, ending the stalemate.

Avoiding a Shutdown Congress passed other measures, such as the Safe Drinking Water Act, that had been held up for

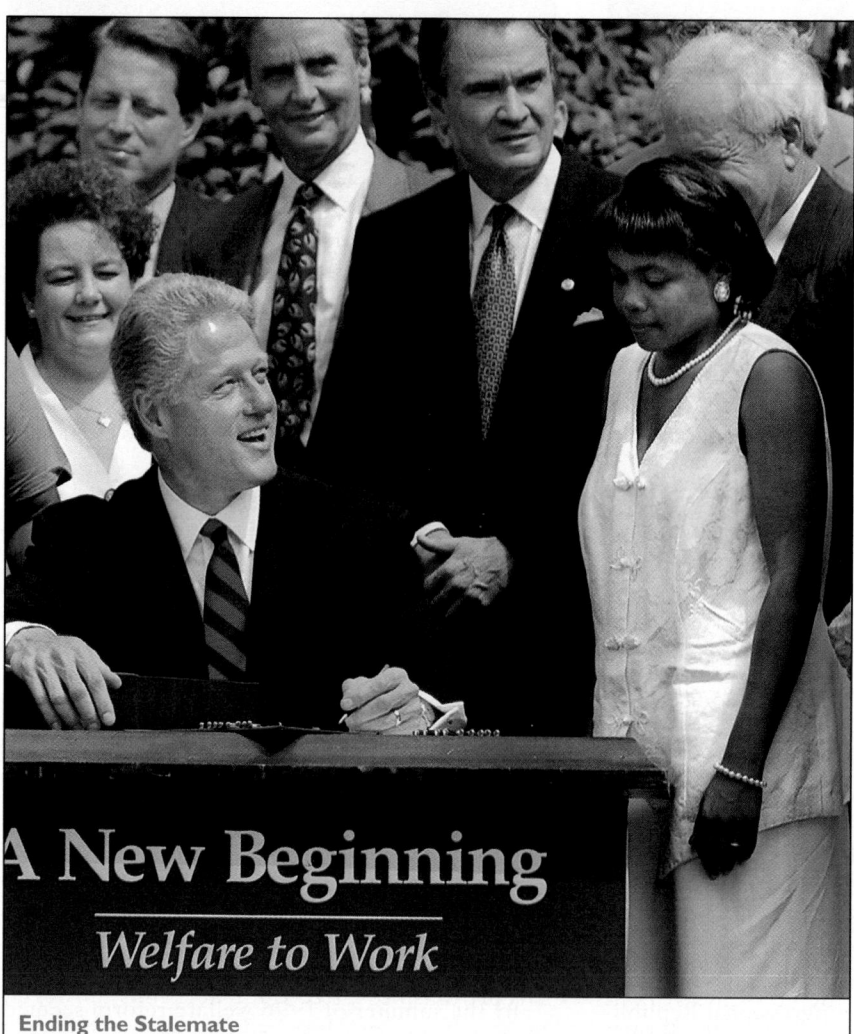

A New Beginning
Welfare to Work

Ending the Stalemate
Compromise resulted in several key bills being passed in 1996. **Political Process** **What three important pieces of bipartisan legislation did President Clinton sign?**

Special Needs Strategy

Visual Learning Photographs are especially useful to help visual learners remember political figures. Collect photographs from newspapers or have students bring in old news magazines with photographs of presidential candidates, members of Congress, and leading state and local officials. Create a collage of photographs and have students write captions for each.

months. In October, just before the fiscal year ended, Congress presented the President with a $389 billion spending bill that would avoid another government shutdown. The legislation restored spending that Congress had tried to cut earlier, but it prevented Democrats from using the issue of gridlock that had affected the public perception of Republican leadership early in 1996. Despite its tighter control on immigration, President Clinton signed the bill. Facing a government shutdown if the bill was not approved, Senate Minority Leader Tom Daschle spoke for Democrats when he said, "we ought to quit while we are ahead." Would these accomplishments be enough to boost incumbent legislators to victory in November? How would they affect voters' opinions of the incumbent President?

The Primaries

The presidential primaries had begun against a backdrop of partisan stalemate. President Clinton, however, enjoyed popular support, while Republican presidential hopefuls waged war against each other in primaries across the nation.

Republican Contenders The Republicans' wide-open campaign included senators Phil Gramm of Texas and Bob Dole of Kansas. Pat Buchanan, a conservative columnist and commentator, depended on grassroots contributions. Steve Forbes, a publisher, spent much of his own money. Lamar Alexander, Alan Keyes, Bob Dornan, and others had small **warchests,** or earmarked funds, to support their campaigns. They needed early victories to bring in additional funds.

Narrowing the Field When Phil Gramm narrowly lost the Louisiana caucus, his hopes for victory in other states faded. Many Iowa voters, who had indicated that they would support Gramm, swung their votes to Buchanan. Pat Buchanan surprised the field by attracting large numbers of supporters who were worried about their jobs and the government's failure to control illegal immigration. Buchanan, however, was unable to win the support of more moderate Republicans. Too many of them had negative feelings about his approach to the issues.

Steve Forbes won early support by advocating a flat tax that would do away with the complexities of the income tax. The idea made headlines at first. Then, as Forbes support waned, Jack Kemp, former Housing and Urban Development secretary, endorsed Forbes in a last-ditch effort to save his cam-

Front-runner
Bob Dole kicks off the presidential primary season in New Hampshire. **Politics Why is a victory in such a small state important?**

paign. Even after he lost the New York primary to Bob Dole, however, Forbes pledged to keep up the pressure for his ideas.

Decisions That Win Votes

As the primaries heated up, campaign organizations used more and more negative advertising, especially on television. Despite strong public reaction against these messages, polling showed that the negative ads were often effective.

Dole Wins Primaries Some Republican contenders faded in the early going. By March of 1996, front-runner Bob Dole faced challenges from Buchanan, Alexander, and Forbes on two critical Tuesdays. Dole won impressive victories in several Southern states, assuring him enough delegates to win the nomination at the upcoming convention.

Clinton Courts Moderates Enjoying a wide lead in the polls, President Clinton was careful to express moderate views on nearly every issue. Some people said he sounded almost like a Republican. The President said that a tax cut could provide a quick shot of consumer confidence. He talked about reducing the size of government and lowering the budget deficit. His pro-business, free-trade decisions, however, upset some White House advisers and members of Congress who wanted the President to remember that Democratic support came from workers.

SPECIAL REPORT: '96 ELECTION **E5**

CONNECTIONS

Federalism
The welfare legislation passed by the 104th Congress gave states broad authority over their own welfare programs. Federal funding would be sent to states in predetermined lump-sum payments called block grants. The federal government had never before transformed a major individual entitlement program into a block grant to the states.

Caption Answer
Because it is the first primary, it influences the perceptions of future primary voters.

Powers of the President
Nominating a Candidate
The role of political conventions in the process of selecting a candidate to run for President
Side One, Chapter 10

Critical Thinking Activity

Identifying Alternatives Financing national campaigns means raising millions of dollars. In the primaries, the candidate who has the best financial support has an advantage. Candidates Ross Perot and Steve Forbes were willing to spend much of their own money in 1996. Others depended on their campaign organizations to raise funds. Have students consider alternative ways to finance campaigns. What are the advantages and disadvantages of each?

Fighting for Control of Congress

Opinion poll results in April 1996 showed that more people were likely to vote for a Democrat than a Republican in congressional races. Clearly, Republicans had lost the momentum of the 1994 elections. Democrats predicted that growing public dissatisfaction with the Republicans would help them regain control of Congress. Republicans responded that the election was a long way off and that poll results change frequently.

Campaign Strategies

Some Republicans were worried about the possible effect of a landslide victory by President Clinton. For months the President was running 15 to 20 points ahead of Bob Dole in national polls. Republicans were concerned about the **"coattail effect."** Historically a President who wins by a large majority can influence the vote for his party's legislative candidates across the country—carrying them along "on his coattails." Many analysts, however, believed that the presidential race would not have much influence on congressional races. Democratic Senator Bob Kerry, chairman of the Senatorial Campaign Committee agreed. "The coattails are small, if any," he said. The President, however, continued to hold a lead in national polls. The question of whether the "coattail effect" would influence the election remained a significant one as the campaigns rolled on.

Republican Advantages Each party, intent on winning control of Congress, developed its campaign strategy around certain advantages. Republicans believed that they had an edge because there were more Democrats than Republicans retiring from the legislature. In the Senate, 8 Democrats and 5 Republicans announced that they were retiring. In the House, 21 Democrats and 12 Republicans said they would not run in 1996.

Democratic Strategy In this campaign both parties' strategies called for seizing the middle ground. Sometimes that meant depicting the opposition as extremist. The President's strategists believed they could capitalize on the public's perception of House Speaker Newt Gingrich as too conservative. "The American public has rejected the Gingrich brand of revolution," reported Mark Mellman, a Democratic strategist. Democratic party advertising referred to the Republican ticket as "Dole/Gingrich" rather than "Dole/Kemp."

Marketing the Candidate
Republicans hoped that candidates like Robert Aderholt (right) in Alabama, seeking to win an open seat, would help the GOP retain control of the House. **Election In what section of the country did the GOP target the most open seats?**

Background

The 1994 election did not end in November. Nor was it entirely over on January 4, 1995, when House and Senate members were sworn in. Four House winners and one Senate winner faced formal challenges that were investigated by the House and Senate committees. In the end, none of the challenges succeeded. The majority party added some members after the election. Between March and December, 1995, one Senator and five House members switched from the Democratic to the Republican side of the aisle.

GOP Targets the South Republicans targeted several open seats in the South, a growing base of party strength. Retiring Democrats in Arkansas gave the GOP a chance to win a Senate seat and two open House seats. In Texas six of the seven House seats being vacated were held by Democrats. Republicans believed they could win four of those six. Republicans also targeted open House seats in Florida, Georgia, and Alabama.

Poll Favors Democrats Democrats believed that they could defeat many of the 74 Republican freshmen who had won their 1994 campaigns by slim margins. While recapturing both the Senate and House would be an uphill battle, they were encouraged by early polling. A "generic ballot" poll taken in April gave Democrats a six-point lead over Republicans. Democrats hoped that this lead would boost fund-raising efforts, thus helping to support their candidates in many crucial races.

Democrats expected a better voter turnout than they had in 1994. One political scientist said, "This year, Republicans seem demoralized and Democrats are energized." Another political forecaster, however, predicted a low turnout among all voters.

Campaign Finance

Federal laws passed in the 1970s attempted to control campaign spending by limiting the amounts that individuals could contribute to federal candidates. The laws also regulated the contributions of political action committees (PACs). However, the limits did not apply if the PAC did not work directly with a candidate. This exception permitted unregulated spending that gave rise to thousands of new PACs. It also opened the door to the influence of **soft money,** or funds which can be raised in unlimited amounts and used for general advertisements that benefit all candidates of a given party.

Soft Money Warchests In the 1996 campaign the Federal Election Commission (FEC) reported that $170 million in soft money had been collected by Democrats and Republicans. Early in the campaign, however, the Democratic National Committee had committed only half as much aid for House campaigns in 1996 as it had handed out in 1994. Republicans, on the other hand, had spent some $7 million in 30 tight races—mostly for GOP freshmen—in one month. As the campaign heated up, labor unions countered Republican spending with soft money

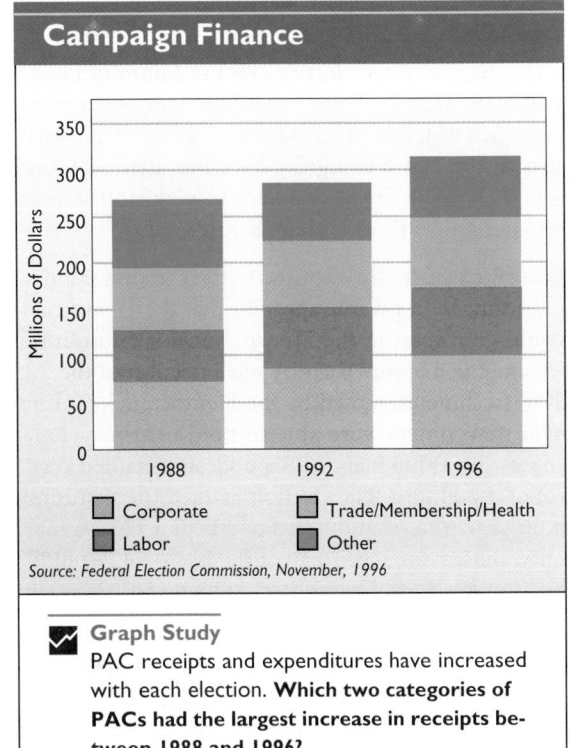

Campaign Finance

Millions of Dollars

1988   1992   1996

☐ Corporate   ☐ Trade/Membership/Health
☐ Labor   ☐ Other

Source: Federal Election Commission, November, 1996

☑ Graph Study
PAC receipts and expenditures have increased with each election. **Which two categories of PACs had the largest increase in receipts between 1988 and 1996?**

contributions to support Democrats. Republicans reacted by accusing "big labor bosses" of trying to buy Democratic candidates.

Pledges to Reform What do campaign contributors get for their money? Most analysts stop short of saying that votes on specific legislation can be bought. The contributors, however, have much easier access to government officials. The amount of soft money is a growing concern of election analysts.

Ross Perot financed his own campaign in 1992, while criticizing the influence of special interests. Candidate Clinton vowed to work for reform in 1992. House Speaker Newt Gingrich later made a similar pledge. Such pledges were not carried out, because politicians worried about how the changes would affect their own parties. Any revision could put one party at a disadvantage. In 1996 candidate Dole promised another commission to study the issue and a ban on foreign contributions if he was elected. Despite all the talk, the major parties spent more money than ever in 1996. Special interests added tens of millions in soft money. Charges of illegal contributions increased as Election Day neared.

Guided Practice

L1 Understanding Cause and Effect Explain how political polls are taken and why they have become a significant part of the news in campaigns. Ask students whether they think their voting decision could be affected by the results of a poll. Could the votes of other people be affected by a poll? Of these two—poll results and voters opinions—which is cause and which is effect?

L2 Making Inferences When running for the House or Senate, history shows that incumbents usually have an advantage. Brainstorm and write on the chalkboard the advantages and disadvantages of incumbency in a campaign. Students may offer: *Advantages:* name recognition, knowing how to win in their district or state, easier to raise funds, longer service means better committee appointments and more influence for their constituency. *Disadvantages:* having to defend their record, general public attitude against incumbent politicians.

Graph Study Answer
Corporate and Labor

Background

The Federal Election Commission has the duty of overseeing campaign finance laws enacted to regulate campaign spending. Loopholes, however, have allowed the major parties to circumvent the intent of the legislation. In addition, the Supreme Court ruled that spending limits were an unconstitutional violation of free speech. The Supreme Court also threw out federal restrictions on what state political parties could spend on congressional elections as long as the money was not used to back a specific candidate. Thus, millions of dollars of so-called "soft money" are raised and spent outside the limits of the election laws.

L1 Slogans Campaigns frequently attempt to express the main ideas of their candidate in short slogans. People who identify with a slogan may vote for the candidate without ever taking the time to read or listen to the candidate's ideas. Have the class divide into groups to brainstorm ideas for a political campaign and then come up with slogans that capture the essential points.

L2 Research Have several students conduct research to find out what issues and events were important in determining the winner of their congressional district in the 1996 election. Ask the group to present their findings to the class.

Chart Study Answer
218

A Narrow Margin of Victory

On the eve of the election, House Minority Leader Richard Gephardt and House Speaker Newt Gingrich each watched to see who would be the majority party in the 105th Congress. Vice President Al Gore hoped that the Democrats could pick up the few seats needed to tie or win the Senate.

Republicans Retain House As the evening tabulations came in, it became apparent that the Democrats would gain seats in the House, but not enough to become the majority party. A small fraction of the 73 GOP freshmen targeted by the Democrats lost, but most newcomers were able to hold off their challengers. By a thin margin, Republicans retained control of the House. The election marked the first time in 66 years that Republicans had kept a House majority. Bill Paxton, chairman of the National Republican Congressional Committee, announced, "We will control the legislative process."

Southern Strategy Pays Off One key to GOP congressional power was the continued shift toward Republican candidates in the South. As Southern Democrats retire from Congress, seats traditionally held by Democrats become fair game for Republican candidates. For example, Tom Bevill, a Democrat, served the 4th congressional district of Alabama for 15 terms. After Bevill's retirement in 1996, Robert Aderholt, a Republican, won a close race for the open seat. In all, Democrats lost 7 of 19 open seats in the South. Republican losses in other regions were nearly offset by this continuing shift.

Analysts speculated that Republicans lost six seats in California, Oregon, and Washington because of reduced voter turnout when the media projected Clinton's victory before polls on the West coast closed. Recounts determined the winners in several close elections. The political division of the House was not final until December, when three runoff elections were held in Texas.

Redrawn Districts In the past few years there have been court challenges against gerrymandered districts in some Southern states. Several congressional districts had been drawn to separate voting majorities into African American and white constituencies. One effect was that some African American candidates won a few congressional elections, while white candidates made gains in other districts. The more recent challenges resulted in redrawn districts that included more white voters where there had been African American majorities. Despite their altered constituencies, in the 1996 election African American incumbents prevailed in the South.

GOP Adds to Senate Majority In 1994 Republicans had won control of the Senate by a margin of 53 to 47 seats. With 8 Democrats and only 5 Republicans retiring in 1996, the GOP had a better chance of strengthening its lead. Several races were decided by only a few

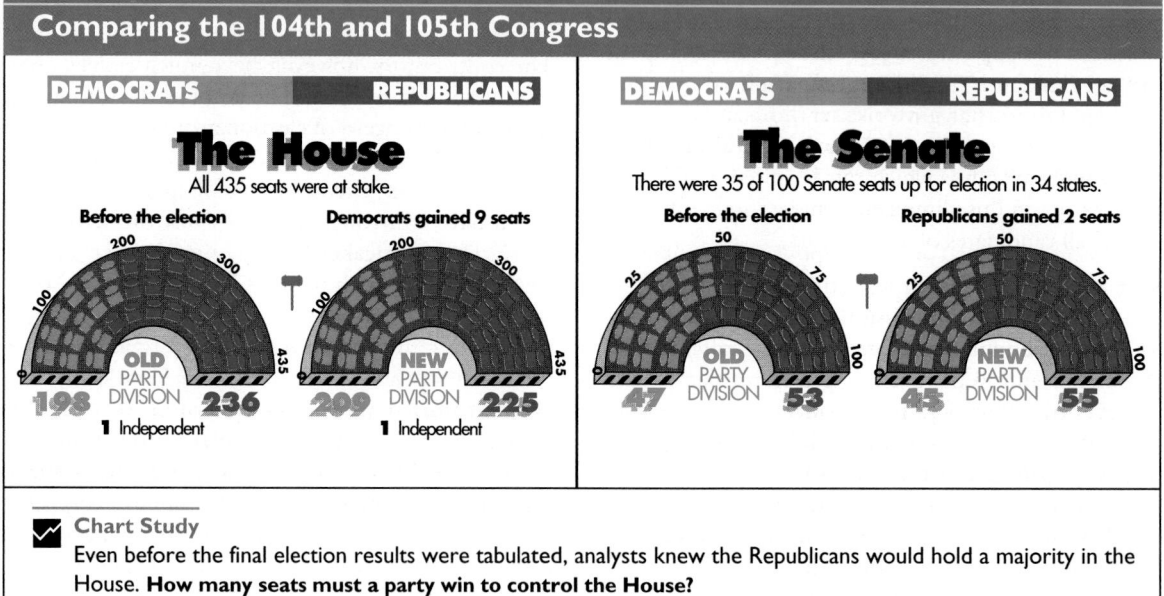

Comparing the 104th and 105th Congress

Chart Study
Even before the final election results were tabulated, analysts knew the Republicans would hold a majority in the House. **How many seats must a party win to control the House?**

E8 SPECIAL REPORT: '96 ELECTION

Students might like to work together to create a bulletin board display that identifies members of Congress who were elected in their state. They may obtain photographs and background information from their representatives by writing or calling the members' local or Washington offices. To find the names and addresses of members of Congress, students should use a congressional directory at the school or city library or find available resources on the Internet.

thousand votes. When the polling was completed, the net change in the Senate was just 2 seats. In Oregon—the closest race—a Republican held on to a slight lead, giving the Republicans a new majority of 55 to 45 seats.

The 105th Congress

"They did win the election, but they didn't win it by much," was the assessment of Martin Frost, head of the Democratic Congressional Committee. Most analysts believed that the election strengthened the positions of moderate Democrats and moderate Republicans in Congress. Public reaction against "gridlock" between the 104th Congress and the President had affected legislation early in 1996. Would the new Congress be more likely to compromise with President Clinton? Would the President, not having to worry about running for election again, be inclined to work with Congress beginning in 1997?

Issues Facing Congress Only a few items in the 10 major categories of the Republicans' Contract with America were enacted by the end of the 104th Congress. These included a presidential line-item veto, changes to the welfare program, benefits for families and children, reduction of unfunded state mandates, and reduction of federal paperwork. Surveying the future, Newt Gingrich told reporters that in an afternoon telephone conversation he and President Clinton had pledged to work together. He believed that the two parties had common ground on issues such as balancing the budget, downsizing government, reforming welfare, and stopping the sale of illegal drugs. Speaker Gingrich said the President would find he is working with a kinder, gentler House. President Clinton later suggested that he would be more willing to work with Congress if Congress was not so aggressive in investigating allegations against his administration.

Focus on Cooperation The Speaker's conciliatory words contrasted with the talk of revolution and government restructuring that had characterized the 1994 Republican congressional takeover. Newt Gingrich offered a more moderate approach to investigations of alleged ethical and financial charges against the President and his administration. Eight House committees were currently involved with investigating improprieties, but Gingrich said, "I don't want so many people focusing on investigations that they can't also focus on legislation." Democrats wondered whether the softer approach

was meant to affect their ongoing pressure for investigations of the Speaker.

Even before the 104th Congress adjourned, however, many members had been talking about the need for cooperation in the future and a different approach from the partisanship that had characterized both sessions. Retiring Democratic Senator David Pryor announced, "Whether we win or lose in the House or win or lose in the Senate, the message has been sent that the great majority of Americans don't want extremism in politics." A freshman Republican reflected, "You have to work hard for a more sustained period of time and appreciate that you're making progress rather than immediately reaching a goal."

The voters had earlier turned thumbs down on a stalemate between President Clinton and the Republican Congress. In the 1996 election, they rewarded both sides for the deals that brought welfare, immigration, and health-care legislation in the final days of the 104th Congress. The era of big government ideas was apparently over, but Americans seemed to want carefully crafted legislation and evolutionary, rather than revolutionary, change. The key lesson of early 1996 politics—that the people wanted moderation and compromise—was not only important to congressional campaigns, it influenced the presidential race as well.

Congressional Profile, 1997

CONGRESS

	104th Congress Senate	104th Congress House	105th Congress Senate	105th Congress House
Democrats	47	197	45	209
Republicans	53	235	55	225
Independents/others	0	3	0	1
Women	8	49	9	51
Men	92	386	91	384
Whites	96	377	95	378
African Americans	1	38	1	39
Hispanics*	0	18	0	18
Asian/Pacific Islander	2	6	2	5
Native American	1	0	1	0

* Hispanics can be of any race.
Source: Congressional Quarterly

✓ Chart Study
Incumbents did well in the 1996 congressional elections. **How did this affect the percentage of women and minorities in each chamber?**

CONNECTIONS

Political Processes
Campaign finance reform bills presented to the 104th Congress proposed a ban on "soft money," suggested a ban on incumbents sending franked mail (free mailing for members) during an election, and required candidates to raise 60 percent of their funds in-state. The bills died despite support from outside interest groups.

L3 Gerrymandering Find a copy of the most recent legislative districts of your state in the library or on the Internet. Ask students to determine whether they believe that the districts are apportioned fairly or gerrymandered. What factors might have contributed to drawing district lines that appear irregular?

Chart Study Answer
Women and minorities remained a small percentage of the total in each chamber.

Background

One of the main issues that faced the federal government in 1997 was funding entitlement programs. In particular, Social Security and Medicare were in trouble. If no changes were made, the widening gap between a smaller workforce and a growing retiree population threatened to swamp the entitlement system. The Congressional Budget Office warned that if the nation did not come to grips with this problem, the national debt could explode or the nation could face a severe recession.

Focus

Bell Ringer

Write the following terms across the top of the chalkboard: *Liberal, Conservative, Moderate*

Have students write their own definitions of these terms while you are taking role.

Motivating Activity

Write the following subjects of government policy in a column along the left side of the chalkboard:

> *education*
> *health care*
> *social welfare*

Ask students to identify a conservative position, a moderate position, and a liberal position on one of these subjects.

Vocabulary Precheck

Ask students to speculate on the meanings of **"spin doctors"** and **exit polls.** Have them check their guesses by finding the definitions in the section text.

Chart Study Answer
35 percent

Powers of the President

Primaries and Caucuses
The role of primaries and caucuses in the process of selecting a candidate to run for President

Side One, Chapter 9

Running to the Middle

Independent voters have played a large and increasing role in electing a President. In 1992 Ross Perot captured many independent votes, although he did not win any electoral votes. Early preference polls, however, showed that Perot had less support in 1996. Both Bill Clinton and Bob Dole targeted independent voters, realizing their importance in the November election. Both also believed that most independent voters were moderates. Running to the middle of the political spectrum seemed to be sound strategy.

The Changing Role of Conventions

The nominating process in presidential elections is changing. National conventions used to be meetings at which presidential candidates and their running mates were selected by the delegates. Party divisions broke out and tough battles among differing factions made conventions interesting live political events. This has not been so in recent years.

The Primaries The last time a party gathered without knowing its nominee for certain was in 1976, when Gerald Ford narrowly won a first-ballot nomination over Ronald Reagan. In 1996 both parties not only knew their nominee well in advance, they also had resolved differences and prepared the party platforms ahead of time. With these essentials completed, convention managers had time to turn the conventions into weeklong television infomercials.

What factors have contributed to the changing role of the national convention? Earlier, more

conclusive presidential primaries are partly responsible. Some states have moved their primaries to earlier dates, in order to have a greater influence on the outcome. Television also helps to narrow the field of candidates. Those candidates who gather few votes in early primaries find they cannot raise enough money for expensive television advertising later. Parties benefit from having an earlier winner, because it allows more time to organize the convention. By the latter part of the primary season there may be only two or three viable candidates left. In a narrow field of contenders it is more likely that one will emerge with enough pledged delegates to assure victory on the first convention ballot.

Unifying the Party Bob Dole's victories in the 1996 Republican primaries eliminated the possibility that the Republican convention would choose the presidential candidate. The party then settled important platform issues. Dole removed one last bit of suspense by naming Jack Kemp as his running mate before the convention began. What task was left for the conven-

Party Identification

Party Identification	1984	1986	1988	1990	1992	1994
Strong Democrat	17%	18%	18%	20%	18%	15%
Weak Democrat	20	22	18	19	18	19
Independent Democrat	11	10	12	12	14	13
Independent	11	12	11	11	12	10
Independent Republican	12	11	13	12	12	12
Weak Republican	15	15	14	15	14	15
Strong Republican	12	10	14	9	11	16
Apolitical	2	2	2	2	1	1

Source: The American National Election Studies, conducted by the Center for Political Studies at the University of Michigan

Chart Study
Candidates needed votes from three categories of independent voters to win in 1996. **What percentage of all voters identified with the three independent categories in 1994?**

Cooperative Learning Activity

Who watches televised national nominating conventions? Have students conduct a survey among friends, neighbors, and relatives who are old enough to vote. They should record the age of each respondent. The only questions should be: *Did you watch the Democratic National Convention in* *1996? Did you watch the Republican National Convention in 1996? About how many total hours did you watch?* Have groups of five or more students combine their survey results—perhaps on a computer spreadsheet—and report their findings to the class.

Televising the Convention
Despite the carefully-scripted convention programs, television audiences for the national conventions are shrinking.
Media Why were fewer people interested in the conventions in 1996?

tion? Republicans used their national convention in San Diego to deliver the message of party unity to the American people. Speakers were carefully chosen to represent a consensus. Key state-level political leaders, who the party believed could be national leaders in the future, were given an opportunity to address the television audience. The choices included two moderate women—New Jersey Governor Christie Whitman, chosen to help open the convention, and Congresswoman Susan Molinari, who gave the keynote speech.

The Media's Impact Planners designed the convention hall for television coverage. Giant screens behind the speakers were set up to show video features, even breaking into the middle of speeches at key moments. Network television commentators, having little drama to report, felt they were mere tools of the convention planners. The three major networks had reduced their coverage to a few hours of prime time. One network cut away from its coverage for commercials during an entire video tribute to Ronald Reagan, explaining that the taped segment was not news.

Political parties realized the growing impact of the Internet. Their national organizations took advantage of the Internet to keep their message to voters current throughout the 1996 campaign.

According to the Script The Democrats also opened their convention as a scripted television event. Laser lights, music, and colorful video presentations were designed to attract and hold the television audience. The President was beamed into the

convention hall via satellite. Some speakers were not politicians at all, but were chosen because they could relate dramatic stories or had strong emotional appeal. George McGovern, the 1972 Democratic presidential nominee, with the perspective of four decades of convention attendance, said, "You could see it coming: TV, marketing, computerizing—all the things that go with modern salesmanship."

Reform Party Convention Ross Perot called the Reform party's meeting the "unconventional convention." This was not because of its television programming, although cable TV did carry it. The convention was different in that party members chose Ross Perot over Richard Lamm voting by mail, telephone, and electronic mail.

Being Presidential

In a presidential election year an incumbent President must divide his time between campaigning and governing. This disadvantage can be offset by the positive image the incumbent generates by doing official business—being presidential. For example, one month before the election President Clinton intervened in a dispute between Israel and the Palestinians. The trouble had begun when Palestinians reacted to Israel's opening of a walled passageway near Muslim and Jewish holy sites in East Jerusalem. Riots near the ancient tunnel left more than 70 dead. The Clinton administration arranged a summit

SPECIAL REPORT: '96 ELECTION E11

Understanding Cause and Effect Presidential campaigns have changed greatly over the years. In the early years of our nation, the United States had no political parties. Research the effects that one of the following changes have had on the presidential election process: (1) the development of political parties, (2) nominating conventions, or (3) primary elections. Students should write a short summary of their research.

Independent Practice

L1 **Persuasive Writing** Ross Perot believed that he should have been allowed to participate in the televised presidential debates in 1996, as he had in 1992. He was not permitted because an independent panel said that he did not have sufficient support and a chance to be elected President. Have students write paragraphs supporting or opposing Perot's view.

CONNECTIONS

Media

The second presidential debate in 1996 was the least watched in the history of televised debates. This was also true of the 1996 Democratic and Republican conventions.

Caption Answer

People see the President in leadership roles.

Powers of the President

Presidential Debates
The effect that televised debates have had on the process of electing a President
Side One, Chapter 12

Presidential Leadership
Attending to business while the campaign is going on divides the President's attention.
Politics Why can this be an advantage for the incumbent President?

Debating the Debate
Lawyers for Perot and another candidate, John Hagelin of the Natural Law party, appealed the commission's decision to a federal court. The court ruled that the complaint should be "with Congress and the federal regulatory framework it established." This meant that the Federal Election Commission should decide. Unfortunately for the minority party candidates, a FEC spokeswoman said the agency's complaint process would not be completed before Election Day. Perot's running mate, Pat Choate, said the issue was an example of "how closed the political system has become."

meeting between Israeli Prime Minister Benjamin Netanyahu and Palestinian Authority Chairman Yasser Arafat. The two-day summit at the White House emphasized the President's role as peacemaker. National media carried video, photos, and reports of President Clinton with the two leaders. Republican candidate Bob Dole could only complain that the event was primarily a photo opportunity for the President.

Televised Debates

Nationally televised debates play an important role in presidential elections. In 1992, the debates included a third-party candidate, Ross Perot. Although Perot won 19 percent of the popular vote in that election, he won no electoral votes. In 1996, Ross Perot was once again a presidential candidate. Opinion polls, however, showed that he was likely to win fewer votes than he had in 1992. An independent Commission on Presidential Debates ruled that Ross Perot could not participate this time. It said that Perot did not have a reasonable chance to win the election. Candidate Perot pointed out that the commission was made up of Democrats and Republicans.

Debating the Issues Televised debates between presidential candidates have become theatrical events. To prepare for their debates both Clinton and Dole rehearsed for hours, learning to walk the fine line between cheerfulness and political aggressiveness. Advisers coached the candidates on details such as how to respond to difficult questions and when to smile. Each candidate memorized long lists of statistics that would support his arguments.

The debates helped to define the candidates' positions on the issues. Senator Dole talked about his plans to cut taxes and to get tough on crime. He also challenged the President's record on anti-drug enforcement. The President stressed favorable economic news and spoke to voters' concerns about education, drugs, and health.

Many media political analysts said that Bob Dole would need a dramatic win in the debates to turn the presidential race around. The President, however, was known to be the better speaker. Both candidates were congenial in the first debate. Bob Dole was more aggressive in the second. Most analysts, however, concluded that the debates did not change many people's minds.

E12 SPECIAL REPORT: '96 ELECTION

Background

H. Ross Perot grew up in Texarkana, a city that straddles the border of Texas and Arkansas. The Perots lived on the Texas side, just thirty miles away from where Bill Clinton was born, in Hope, Arkansas. Perot likes to say he had a Norman Rockwell childhood. By the 1980s, as head of Electronic Data Services, a major computer firm, Perot had made his fortune. A billionaire who often contributed to charities, he once gave $10 million to the symphony and declined to have the concert hall named after him.

Courting Middle America

The election did not give voters a clear choice between big-government liberals and budget-cutting conservatives. Instead, it became a contest for the middle ground. "We're at a period in time where the changes in our society and in our world are so profound that old liberal and old conservative descriptions don't work," was how President Clinton summed it up. Bob Dole told his party that it was time to "reach out and attract more people, blacks, Hispanics, Asians, women, men, working people."

"Spinning" the Campaigns Each party presented itself as the real moderate party that spoke for the majority of Americans. Ross Perot, meanwhile, claimed to be the only candidate who would address the issues that affected people the most. Each party had its own **"spin doctors,"** people who interpreted events, polls, and speeches in the most favorable way for its candidates.

Promises, Promises Bob Dole sought to attract the mass of working people by promises of a 15 percent tax cut. Not to be outdone by this strategy, Vice President Al Gore promised "targeted tax cuts for middle-income families" and a "$10,000 deduction for college tuition." When Dole chose Jack Kemp as his running mate, it was obvious that he wanted a moderate who was known for his work in addressing inner-city social problems. President Clinton promised to balance the budget. Each candidate said that his election would ensure a brighter future for the country.

Labels While each candidate tried to claim the middle ground, each also tried to label the other as an extremist. Bob Dole often referred to Clinton as a liberal. The President's campaign warned people that Dole's cuts would hurt Medicare and that Dole's tax cut would "blow a hole in the budget." While Clinton refrained from saying that Dole was too old to be President, he implied as much by saying that Dole's ideas were too old. Republicans raised the issue of trust, pointing to the President's "failed promises." In the second debate, Dole alluded to ethics problems in the Clinton administration, including a number of Clinton's appointees who had been indicted.

Negative Ads in Congressional Races Senator Bob Kerry of Nebraska chaired the Democratic Senatorial Campaign Committee. He was determined to run a campaign of principle. He said it would be counterproductive to use the label extremist against Republicans and wrong to employ scare tactics on the issue of Medicare. Despite Kerry's objections, strong negative advertising characterized both Democratic and Republican congressional campaigns. Ads for Democrats repeatedly declared, "Republicans tried to cut Medicare by $270 billion." Republicans charged that big labor was trying to buy the election for the Democrats. While surveys tended to show that the people were not favorably impressed with these ads, the failure of a candidate to respond immediately to such charges was known to have affected the outcome of races in prior elections.

Polls and More Polls Opinion polls have been around a long time, but the debate about their effect on campaigns and voters has not been settled. The pervasive polls in the 1996 election convinced some analysts that polls were the "driving force of this campaign." Weekly and daily polls were supplemented with devices that tracked minute-by-minute voter reactions during the presidential debates. Most polls showed President Clinton with a significant lead. Candidates who lead in the polls usually have more faith in them than those who are behind. Bob Dole discounted the polls and told supporters that the only polls that count are held on Election Day.

On the Campaign Trail
Candidates traditionally travel across the country, speaking to large audiences. **Politics Why does this method provide more exposure for the money than buying television time?**

Politics

A $25 million campaign industry has developed to dig up negative information about opposition candidates. It is called opposition research, or "oppo" for short. Working in small offices, courthouses, and libraries, teams of researchers pour through old newspaper files, tax records, and databases to find out any negative facts about opponents. These facts can be used in political ads. Oppo specialists say they are not sleazy, "All we do is give information to the voters. . . . We don't do garbage cans."

Caption Answer
Television covers the event as news, so the cost is only for the event, not the television time.

Cooperative Learning Activity

A poll taken on Election Day in 1992 found that many people wait until the last few days to decide whom to vote for in the presidential election. The poll found that 25 percent of people made their choice in the last week. Another 18 percent decided in the final two weeks. About 24 percent decided in early fall, and only 33 percent had made a decision before the conventions. Organize teams to conduct a similar poll among those who voted in the previous election.

Map Study Answer
Eleven (CA, NY, TX, FL, PA, IL, OH, MI, NJ, NC, and VA or GA= 270).

Many people have questions about the polls. Could distortions in the polls mislead the public? What is a poll's real margin of error? Many polls use a method of random sampling by computerized telephone banks. One problem with this is the non-response rate. Americans, subjected to daily telemarketing, often slam down the phone before they know who is calling. Others may not want to reveal their vote, even to a pollster. How does this affect poll results? Whether the polls were right or wrong, the public seemed to want to know daily shifts in opinion.

Racing to Victory

As Election Day neared, the candidates increased their efforts in the states where the race was closest. Each made several visits to states like Ohio, Florida, and California where many electoral votes depended on just a small percentage of undecided voters. Bob Dole, knowing he needed a strong finish, campaigned day and night, sleeping only a few hours on the plane between stops. Ross Perot bought blocks of time on network television to appeal directly to voters across the nation. President Clinton tried to boost congressional candidates by appearances in states where close races could determine the majority party in Congress.

Voter Drives Despite the candidates' best efforts, opinion polls showed voter interest to be low in 1996. Motor-voter registrations had been designed to make it easy to register to vote. Voters, however, were more apathetic than they had been in 1992. When asked whether they had thought much about the campaign, most said they had not. Candidates were not the only ones trying to get people to the polls. Up to the final minutes, interest groups such as the AFL-CIO union ran phone operations to encourage their voters to show up.

Clinton Wins Second Term Early election returns showed that President Clinton would win the Northeast. His margin of victory nationally was not as large as expected, but it was consistent across this region. The President also carried every state in the Great Lakes region except Indiana. This gave Clinton all the electoral votes in a broad sweep from Maine through the Midwest. Before the polls closed in California, analysts projected Clinton's electoral majority. When the final votes were counted, the President had less than half the popular vote. He had won 31 states and the District of Columbia, however, giving him 379 electoral votes. Bob Dole had captured 159 electoral votes in the remaining 19 states.

In 1992 people's worries about the economy helped elect Bill Clinton. In 1996 confidence in the economy helped him win reelection. Most of those who supported the President believed that the economy was improving. Issues that Bob Dole had tried to raise in the campaign were not received as vital. Some analysts believed that Dole, the candidate, had

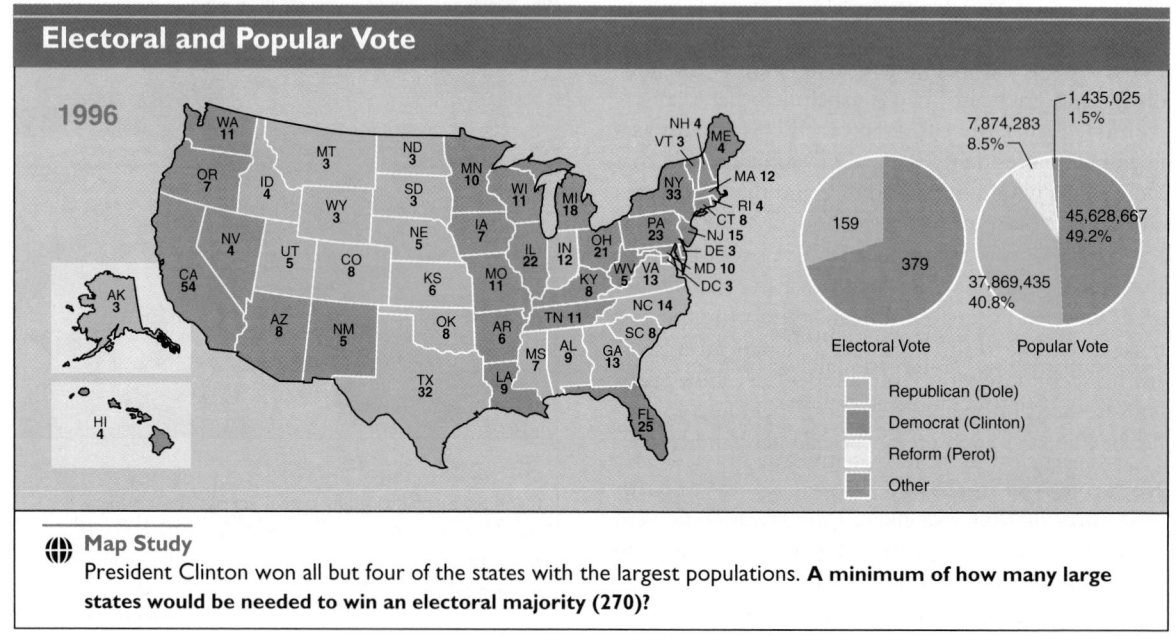

Electoral and Popular Vote

1996

Republican (Dole)
Democrat (Clinton)
Reform (Perot)
Other

Electoral Vote: 159, 379
Popular Vote: 7,874,283 — 8.5%; 1,435,025 — 1.5%; 45,628,667 — 49.2%; 37,869,435 — 40.8%

Map Study
President Clinton won all but four of the states with the largest populations. **A minimum of how many large states would be needed to win an electoral majority (270)?**

Cooperative Learning Activity

Certain states are known as "swing states" because they usually vote for the winner of the presidential election, whether the winner is a Republican or Democrat. Divide the class into four groups. Have each group find an electoral map of one of the last four elections. Bring these maps together to determine which states consistently chose the winning candidate.

not been effective because he had not focused on one issue and had no central campaign theme. In fact, Dole had, for several months, attempted to find something that people really cared about. A 15 percent tax cut, stronger drug enforcement, moral issues, and anticrime messages were all received with an equal lack of enthusiasm. When asked in September 1996 what the main problem facing the country was, voters divided nearly evenly among 10 choices. By comparison, when asked the same question in 1992, more than half of the respondents had identified jobs and the economy as the main problem.

Analyzing the Voters Compared to 1994, the overwhelming impression of the 1996 campaign was that people wanted things to remain pretty much as they were. The angry voters of 1994 had tasted revolution and seemed tired of it. Incumbents were, once again, favored over challengers. To the average voter no issue of the campaign seemed critical. **Exit polls** taken after people voted revealed that most voters who supported Clinton believed that he had "a vision for the future," but few could say what that vision was.

Low Voter Turnout Fewer than half of the eligible voters went to the polls in 1996, continuing a general trend that began in 1960. The 49 percent turnout was a 172-year low for presidential elections. Some election analysts suggested that voter turnout goes down when people think they know the outcome. That was true for this presidential race, but it did not account for the many close congressional elections across the country. The low voter turnout also reflected some people's dissatisfaction with the choices of candidates available, their distaste for negative advertising, and a feeling that little would change regardless of who won. Beyond that, the election reflected Americans' general lack of interest in government when times are relatively prosperous. Political issues are generally considered more lively in times of real or perceived crises.

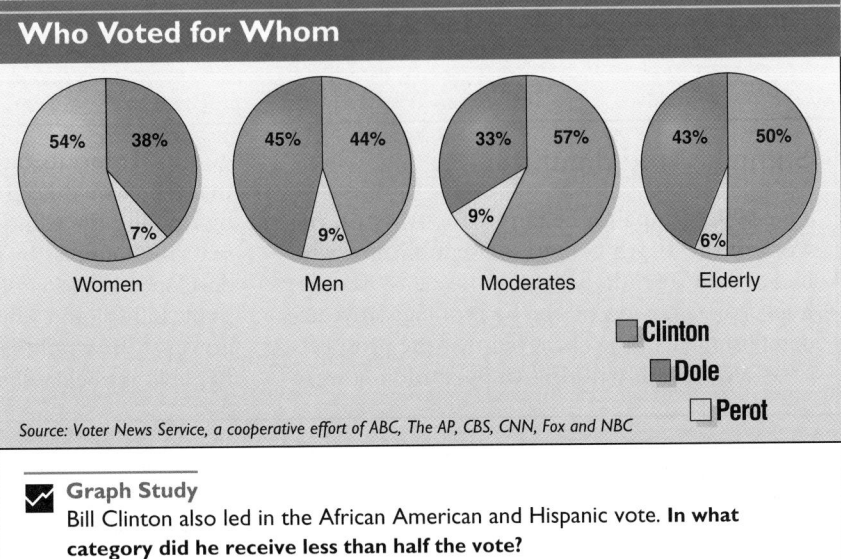

Who Voted for Whom

Women: 54% 38% 7%
Men: 45% 44% 9%
Moderates: 33% 57% 9%
Elderly: 43% 50% 6%

■ Clinton
■ Dole
□ Perot

Source: Voter News Service, a cooperative effort of ABC, The AP, CBS, CNN, Fox and NBC

Graph Study
Bill Clinton also led in the African American and Hispanic vote. **In what category did he receive less than half the vote?**

Who Voted for Whom The President had solid support from women, the elderly, and youth. He held his expected support among African Americans. Bob Dole's support was stronger among men, college graduates, people in upper-income brackets, and Asian Americans. While there was some ticket splitting, most people chose a presidential candidate and congressional candidates from the same party. This allowed the Democrats to pick up 11 House seats. Ticket splitting in some states, however, accounted for the Democrats' loss of two Senate seats. Ross Perot, the Reform party candidate, saw his support drop to less than half of its 1992 level. His biggest decline was among women. This switch accounted for most of President Clinton's margin of victory in 1996.

Governing to 2000 The President and Congress faced a wide array of problems after the election. One immediate concern was campaign finance reform. Among other budget and taxation issues, the long-term problem of financing Medicare and Social Security had to be addressed. Illegal immigrants arriving at a rate of 300,000 a year presented difficulties for several states. Juvenile crime and the drug problem demanded attention. Waste management and other environmental questions divided legislators. Congress also faced issues that determined its future relations with the states in education, health, and safety. The ability or inability of the President and Congress to reach agreement on a significant number of these questions could determine the political environment of the 1998 and 2000 elections.

SPECIAL REPORT: '96 ELECTION E15

Linking Past and Present
The federal government provided Bill Clinton and Bob Dole grants of $61.8 million each to use for the general election. Ross Perot received 19 percent of the vote in 1992, qualifying him for a grant of $29 million. No other candidate received the necessary 5 percent of the vote to qualify for federal funds.

CONNECTIONS

History
With President Clinton holding a strong lead in the polls, Democrats began to forecast a landslide. Since 1824, when reliable voting results became available, only four Presidents have won more than 60% of the popular vote. They were: Warren G. Harding (60.3%), Franklin D. Roosevelt (60.8%), Lyndon B. Johnson (61.1%), and Richard M. Nixon (60.7%).

Graph Study Answer
men

Special Needs Strategy

Reading Comprehension Students with learning problems need concrete examples to understand abstract concepts. Have students read Governing to 2000 on this page. Ask students what they think are the most important issues facing the President and Congress today. For any of the issues they identify ask why it is difficult for Congress and the President to reach agreement on how to handle it.

Identifying
Terms and Concepts

1. partisanship **2.** "gridlock"
3. warchests **4.** soft money
5. "spin doctors" **6.** "coattail effect" **7.** exit polls

Reviewing Facts and Ideas

1. Democrat: Bill Clinton, Al Gore; Republican: Bob Dole, Jack Kemp; Reform: Ross Perot, Pat Choate

2. welfare, health insurance, and minimum wage bills

3. President Clinton won most of the states with large populations. This gave him 379 electoral votes to Bob Dole's 159, even though the President won less than half of the popular vote.

Applying Themes

1. National nominating conventions have become media events. The drama of selecting candidates has been replaced with scripted productions intended to show party unity.

2. Opinion polls showed President Clinton with a large lead, some people did not think their vote would mean much, some were turned off by negative advertising, and others were not happy with the candidate selection.

Critical Thinking Skills

1. First, Republicans had fewer vacant seats to defend than Democrats in the House and in the Senate. Second, Republican victories in the South helped offset losses in other regions. Finally, Clinton's margin of victory was not as large as had been predicted.

2. Answers will vary. Those who believe the 105th Congress will be more effective should refer to the promises of cooperation made by members of both parties after the election. Those who do not believe it will be more effective should cite the fact that each party held nearly the same position it had before the election.

Report Review

Summary and Significance

The 1996 campaign began by focusing on the work of the 104th Congress. Republicans, who had set the agenda for the House and Senate, hoped to gain votes on the basis of legislative accomplishments. They believed that the prospects of a Republican winning the presidency were good. Democrats, meanwhile, were encouraged that they would keep control of the White House by running the Clinton/Gore team and also gain seats in Congress by pointing to "gridlock" that developed in the legislature. Both sides were partly right. Bill Clinton won a second term. Once again, however, he would face a Congress in which the Republicans held a slim majority.

Identifying Terms and Concepts

Insert the terms below into the following paragraph to explain the 1996 election.

soft money   partisanship   "gridlock"
exit polls   warchests   "coattail effect"
"spin doctors"

Congress and the President could not agree on legislation as _____ divided the government. The media called the stalemate _____. As the 1996 primaries neared, the parties built their _____ from campaign contributions. Some of the funds were _____ that is not regulated by federal election laws. During the campaign each party had its _____ who interpreted events favorably for its own candidates. One concern among Republicans was the possible _____ President Clinton might have in influencing votes for Congress. After the voting, _____ revealed that voters believed the President had a vision for the future, but Republicans would control Congress.

Reviewing Facts and Ideas

1. Name the 1996 presidential and vice presidential candidates of the Democratic, Republican, and Reform parties.

2. Identify three major pieces of legislation that were passed in 1996.

3. Summarize the electoral college results in the 1996 election.

Applying Themes

1. Political Processes How have national nominating conventions changed in the past 20 years?

2. Civic Participation Why was voter turnout lower in 1996 than in earlier elections?

Critical Thinking Skills

1. Understanding Cause and Effect What were the major reasons that Republicans were able to maintain majorities in the House and Senate despite President Clinton's victory?

2. Drawing Conclusions Do you think the 105th Congress will be more effective in passing legislation than the 104th Congress was? Why or Why not?

Linking Past and Present

How often are the polls an accurate reflection of the way people eventually vote? Visit a library that keeps newspapers on microfilm. Search through the front pages of a major city newspaper printed in October of 1980, 1984, 1988, and 1992. Which candidates were ahead in the polls? By how many percentage points? How did that compare with the actual vote (see *Statistical Abstract of the United States*)?

Linking Past and Present

In the 1996 election opinion polls varied considerably, but most gave President Clinton a larger lead than his actual election margin. Taken together, the four elections in the student assignment represent a normal margin of error in recent elections.